HANDBOOK

OF

INFORMATION SECURITY

Information Warfare; Social, Legal, and International Issues; and Security Foundations

Volume 2

Hossein Bidgoli
Editor-in-Chief
California State University
Bakersfield, California

WILEY

John Wiley & Sons, Inc.

This book is printed on acid-free paper. ⊗

Copyright © 2006 by John Wiley & Sons, Inc. All rights reserved.

Published by John Wiley & Sons, Inc., Hoboken, New Jersey.
Published simultaneously in Canada.

For general information on our other products and services please contact our Customer Care Department within the U.S. at (800) 762-2974, outside the United States at (317) 572-3993 or fax (317) 572-4002.

Wiley also publishes its books in a variety of electronic formats. Some content that appears in print may not be available in electronic books. For more information about Wiley products, visit our web site at www.Wiley.com.

Library of Congress Cataloging-in-Publication Data:

The handbook of information security / edited by Hossein Bidgoli.
    p. cm.
  Includes bibliographical references and index.
    ISBN-13: 978-0-471-64830-7, ISBN-10: 0-471-64830-2 (CLOTH VOL 1 : alk. paper)
    ISBN-13: 978-0-471-64831-4, ISBN-10: 0-471-64831-0 (CLOTH VOL 2 : alk. paper)
    ISBN-13: 978-0-471-64832-1, ISBN-10: 0-471-64832-9 (CLOTH VOL 3 : alk. paper)
    ISBN-13: 978-0-471-22201-9, ISBN-10: 0-471-22201-1 (CLOTH SET : alk. paper)
    1. Internet–Encyclopedias.   I. Bidgoli, Hossein.
TK5105.875.I57I5466   2003
004.67′8′03–dc21

                  2002155552

Printed in the United States of America

10 9 8 7 6 5 4 3 2 1

To so many fine memories of my mother, Ashraf, my father, Mohammad, and my brother, Mohsen, for their uncompromising belief in the power of education.

About the Editor-in-Chief

Hossein Bidgoli, Ph.D., is professor of Management Information Systems at California State University. Dr. Bidgoli helped set up the first PC lab in the United States. He is the author of 43 textbooks, 27 manuals and over five dozen technical articles and papers on various aspects of computer applications, information systems and network security, e-commerce and decision support systems published and presented throughout the world. Dr. Bidgoli also serves as the editor-in-chief of *The Internet Encyclopedia* and the *Encyclopedia of Information Systems*.

The *Encyclopedia of Information Systems* was the recipient of one of the *Library Journal's* Best Reference Sources for 2002 and *The Internet Encyclopedia* was recipient of one of the PSP Awards (Professional and Scholarly Publishing), 2004. Dr. Bidgoli was selected as the California State University, Bakersfield's 2001–2002 Professor of the Year.

Editorial Board

Contents

Volume I: Key Concepts, Infrastructure, Standards, and Protocols

Part 1: Key Concepts and Applications Related to Information Security

Part 2: Infrastructure for the Internet, Computer Networks, and Secure Information Transfer

Volume II: Information Warfare; Social, Legal, and International Issues; and Security Foundations

Part 1: Information Warfare

Volume III: Threats, Vulnerabilities, Prevention, Detection, and Management

Part 1: Threats and Vulnerabilities to Information and Computing Infrastructures

Part 2: Prevention: Keeping the Hackers and Crackers at Bay

Part 3: Detection, Recovery, Management, and Policy Considerations

Contributors

Tarek F. Abdelzhaer
University of Virginia
Security and Web Quality of Service

Dawn Alexander
University of Maryland
Protecting Web Sites

Edward Amoroso
AT&T Laboratories
Network Attacks

Michael R. Anderson
SCERC
*Computer Forensics—Computer Media Reviews
in Classified Government Agencies*

Nadeem Ansari
Wayne State University
Home Area Networking

Amy W. Apon
University of Arkansas
Public Network Technologies and Security

Onur Ihsan Arsun
Isik University, Turkey
Security Insurance and Best Practices

Vijay Atluri
Rutgers University
Mobile Commerce

Pierre Balthazard
Arizona State University
*Groupware: Risks, Threats, and Vulnerabilities
in the Internet Age*

William Bard
The University of Texas, Austin
Digital Communication

William C. Barker
National Institute of Standards and Technology
E-Government Security Issues and Measures

Kent Belasco
First Midwest Bank
*Online Retail Banking: Security Concerns, Breaches,
and Controls*

István Zsolt Berta
Budapest University of Technology and Economics,
Hungary
Standards for Product Security Assessment

Bhagyavati
Columbus State University
E-Mail and Instant Messaging

Hossein Bidgoli
California State University, Bakersfield
*Guidelines for a Comprehensive Security System
Internet Basics*

Gerald Bluhm
Tyco Fire & Security
Patent Law

Andrew Blyth
University of Glamorgan, Pontypridd, UK
Computer Network Operations (CNO)

Robert J. Boncella
Washburn University
*Secure Sockets Layer (SSL)
Wireless Threats and Attacks*

Charles Border
Rochester Institute of Technology
Client-Side Security

Nikita Borisov
University of California, Berkeley
WEP Security

Noureddine Boudriga
National Digital Certification Agency and University
of Carthage, Tunisia
*Forensic Computing
IPsec: AH and ESP
Security Policy Guidelines
Server-Side Security*

Sviatoslav Braynov
University of Illinois, Springfield
E-Commerce Vulnerabilities

Susan W. Brenner
University of Dayton School of Law
Cybercrime and the U.S. Criminal Justice System

Roderic Broadhurst
Queensland University of Technology
*Combating the Cybercrime Threat: Developments
in Global Law Enforcement*

Christopher L. T. Brown
Technology Pathways
Evidence Collection and Analysis Tools

Duncan A. Buell
University of South Carolina
*Number Theory for Information Security
The Advanced Encryption Standard*

Levente Buttyán
Budapest University of Technology and Economics,
Hungary
Standards for Product Security Assessment

Jon Callas
PGP Corporation
E-Mail Security

L. Jean Camp
Harvard University
Peer-to-Peer Security

Randy Canis
Greensfelder, Hemker & Gale, P.C.
Copyright Law

Lillian N. Cassel
Villanova University
Security and the Wireless Application Protocol

Tom S. Chan
Southern New Hampshire University
Spyware

Steve J. Chapin
Syracuse University
Forensic Analysis of Windows Systems

Thomas M. Chen
Southern Methodist University
Electronic Attacks

Hamid Choukri
Gemplus & University of Bordeaux, France
Fault Attacks

Chao-Hsien Chu
Pennsylvania State University
Hacking Techniques in Wired Networks

Fred Cohen
University of New Haven
*The Use of Deception Techniques: Honeypots
and Decoys*

J. Philip Craiger
University of Central Florida
*Computer Forensics Procedures
and Methods*
Law Enforcement and Digital Evidence

Lorrie Faith Cranor
Carnegie Mellon University
*P3P (Platform for Privacy Preferences
Project)*

Marco Cremonini
University of Milan, Italy
Contingency Planning Management
Network-Based Intrusion Detection Systems

Dipankar Dasgupta
University of Memphis
*The Use of Agent Technology for Intrusion
Detection*

Magnus Daum
Ruhr University Bochum, Germany
Hashes and Message Digests

Jaime J. Davila
Hampshire College
Digital Divide

S. De Capitani di Vimercati
Università di Milano, Italy
Access Control: Principles And Solutions

Mathieu Deflem
University of South Carolina
*Law Enforcement and Computer Security
Threats and Measures*

Lynn A. DeNoia
Rensselaer Polytechnic Institute
Wide Area and Metropolitan Area Networks

David Dittrich
University of Washington
Active Response to Computer Intrusions
Hackers, Crackers, and Computer Criminals

Hans Dobbertin
Ruhr University Bochum, Germany
Hashes and Message Digests

Hans-Peter Dommel
Santa Clara University
Routers and Switches

Matthew C. Elder
Symantec Corporation
Electronic Attacks

Mohamed Eltoweissy
Virginia Tech
Security in Wireless Sensor Networks

David Evans
University of Virginia
Hostile Java Applets

G. E. Evans
Queen Mary Intellectual Property
Research Institute, UK
Online Contracts

Ray Everett-Church
PrivacyClue LLC
Privacy Law and the Internet
Trademark Law and the Internet

Seth Finkelstein
SethF.com
Electronic Speech
The Digital Millennium Copyright Act

Susanna Frederick Fischer
Columbus School of Law, The Catholic University
of America
Internet Gambling

Dario V. Forte
University of Milan, Crema, Italy
Forensic Analysis of UNIX Systems

Allan Friedman
Harvard University
Peer-to-Peer Security

Song Fu
Wayne State University
Mobile Code and Security

G. David Garson
North Carolina State University
E-Government

Karin Geiselhart
University of Canberra and Australian National
University, Canberra, Australia
*International Security Issues of
E-Government*

Craig Gentry
DoCoMo USA Labs
IBE (Identity-Based Encryption)

Michael Gertz
University of California, Davis
Database Security

Robert Gezelter
Software Consultant
Internet E-Mail Architecture
OpenVMS Security

April Giles
Johns Hopkins University
Protecting Web Sites

Julia Alpert Gladstone
Bryant University
Global Aspects of Cyberlaw

James E. Goldman
Purdue University
Firewall Architectures
Firewall Basics

Nicole Graf
University of Cooperative Education,
Germany
Security Architectures

Sven Graupner
Hewlett-Packard Laboratories
Web Services

Robert H. Greenfield
Computer Consulting
Security in Circuit, Message, and Packet Switching

Steven J. Greenwald
Independent Information Security Consultant
S/MIME (Secure MIME)

Qijun Gu
Pennsylvania State University
Hacking Techniques in Wired Networks

Mohsen Guizani
Western Michigan University
TCP over Wireless Links

Harald Haas
International University Bremen (IUB),
Germany
*Air Interface Requirements for Mobile Data
Services*

Mohamed Hamdi
National Digital Certification Agency, Tunisia
Forensic Computing
Security Policy Guidelines

David Harley
NHS Connecting for Health, UK
E-Mail Threats and Vulnerabilities

Jan Ll. Harris
University of Salford, UK
Hacktivism

Robert W. Heath Jr.
The University of Texas, Austin
Digital Communication

Peter L. Heinzmann
University of Applied Sciences, Eastern Switzerland
Security of Broadband Access Networks

Kenneth Einar Himma
Seattle Pacific University
Active Response to Computer Intrusions
Legal, Social, and Ethical Issues of the Internet
Hackers, Crackers, and Computer Criminals

Chengdu Huang
University of Virginia
Security and Web Quality of Service

Ali Hushyar
San Jose State University
Multilevel Security Models

Renato Iannella
National ICT, Australia (NICTA)
Digital Rights Management

Cynthia E. Irvine
Naval Postgraduate School
Quality of Security Service: Adaptive Security
Security Policy Enforcement

Gene Itkis
Boston University
*Forward Security Adaptive Cryptography: Time
Evolution*

William K. Jackson
Southern Oregon University
E-Education and Information Privacy and Security

Charles Jaeger
Southern Oregon University
Cyberterrorism and Information Security
Spam and the Legal Counter Attacks

Sushil Jajodia
George Mason University
Intrusion Detection Systems Basics

Markus Jakobsson
Indiana University, Bloomington
Cryptographic Privacy Protection Techniques
Cryptographic Protocols

Abbas Jamalipour
University of Sydney, Australia
Wireless Internet: A Cellular Perspective

Jiwu Jing
Chinese Academy of Sciences, Beijing, China
Information Assurance

Ari Juels
RSA Laboratories
Encryption Basics

Jonathan Katz
University of Maryland
Symmetric Key Encryption

Charlie Kaufman
Microsoft Corporation
IPsec: IKE (Internet Key Exchange)

Doug Kaye
IT Conversations
Web Hosting

Rick Kazman
University of Hawaii, Manoa
Risk Management for IT Security

Wooyoung Kim
University of Illinois, Urbana-Champaign
Web Services

Nancy J. King
Oregon State University
E-Mail and Internet Use Policies

Jerry Kindall
Epok, Inc.
Digital Identity

Dominic Kneeshaw
Independent Consultant, Germany
Security Architectures

David Klappholz
Stevens Institute of Technology
Risk Management for IT Security

Graham Knight
University College, London, UK
Internet Architecture

Prashant Krishnamurthy
University of Pittsburgh
Wireless Network Standards and Protocol (802.11)

Christopher Kruegel
Technical University, Vienna, Austria
Host-Based Intrusion Detection

Priya Kubher
Wayne State University
Home Area Networking

Stan Kurkovsky
Central Connecticut State University
VPN Architecture

Selahattin Kuru
Isik University, Turkey
Security Insurance and Best Practices

Zenith Y. W. Law
JustSolve Consulting, Hong Kong
Fixed-Line Telephone System Vulnerabilities

Margarita Maria Lenk
Colorado State University
Asset–Security Goals Continuum: A Process for Security

Arjen K. Lenstra
Lucent Technologies Bell Laboratories
and Technische Universiteit Eindhoven
Key Lengths

Albert Levi
Sabanci University, Turkey
Digital Certificates

Timothy E. Levin
Naval Postgraduate School
Quality of Security Service: Adaptive Security

John Linn
RSA Laboratories
Identity Management

Helger Lipmaa
Cybernetica AS and University of Tartu, Estonia
Secure Electronic Voting Protocols

Peng Liu
Pennsylvania State University
Hacking Techniques in Wired Networks
Information Assurance

David J. Loundy
Devon Bank University College of Commerce
Online Stalking

Michele Luglio
University of Rome Tor Vergata, Italy
Security of Satellite Networks

Chester J. Maciag
Air Force Research Laboratory
Forensic Analysis of Windows Systems

Normand M. Martel
Medical Technology Research Corp.
Medical Records Security

Prabhaker Mateti
Wright State University
Hacking Techniques in Wireless Networks
TCP/IP Suite

Cavan McCarthy
Louisiana State University
Digital Libraries: Security and Preservation
Considerations

Patrick McDaniel
Pennsylvania State University
Computer and Network Authentication

J. McDermott
Center for High Assurance Computer System, Naval
Research Laboratory
The Common Criteria

David E. McDysan
MCI Corporation
IP-Based VPN

Daniel J. McFarland
Rowan University
Client/Server Computing: Principles and Security
Considerations

Matthew K. McGowan
Bradley University
EDI Security

John D. McLaren
Murray State University
Proxy Firewalls

A. Meddeb
National Digital Certification Agency and University
of Carthage, Tunisia
IPsec: AH and ESP

Mark S. Merkow
University of Phoenix Online
E-Commerce Safeguards

M. Farooque Mesiya
Rensselaer Polytechnic Institute
Mobile IP

Pascal Meunier
Purdue University
Cracking WEP
Software Development and Quality Assurance

Mark Michael
Research in Motion Ltd., Canada
Physical Security Measures
Physical Security Threats

Pietro Michiardi
Institut Eurecom, France
Ad Hoc Network Security

Brent A. Miller
IBM Corporation
Bluetooth Technology

Refik Molva
Institut Eurecom, France
Ad Hoc Network Security

Robert K. Moniot
Fordham University
Software Piracy

Roy Morris
Capitol College
Voice-over Internet Protocol (VoIP)

Scott Nathan
Independent Consultant
Corporate Spying: The Legal Aspects

Randall K. Nichols
The George Washington University & University of
Maryland University College
Wireless Information Warfare

Daryle P. Niedermayer
CGI Group Inc.
Security in Circuit, Message, and Packet Switching

Peng Ning
North Carolina State University
Intrusion Detection Systems Basics

M. S. Obaidat
Monmouth University
Digital Watermarking and Steganography
Forensic Computing
IPsec: AH and ESP
Security Policy Guidelines

Server-Side Security
Wireless Local Area Networks
VPN Basics
S. Obeidat
Arizona State University
Wireless Local Area Networks
Stephan Olariu
Old Dominion University
Security in Wireless Sensor Networks
G. Massimo Palma
Università degli Studi di Milano, Italy
Quantum Cryptography
Cynthia Pandolfo
Villanova University
Security and the Wireless Application Protocol
Raymond R. Panko
University of Hawaii, Manoa
Computer Security Incident Response
  Teams (CSIRTs)
Digital Signatures and Electronic Signatures
Internet Security Standards
G. I. Papadimitriou
Aristotle University, Greece
VPN Basics
Wireless Local Area Networks
C. Papazoglou
Aristotle University, Greece
VPN Basics
S. Paraboschi
Università di Bergamo, Italy
Access Control: Principles and Solutions
Radia Perlman
Sun Microsystems Laboratories
PKI (Public Key Infrastructure)
Sebastien Petit
Gemplus, France
Smart Card Security
Thomas L. Pigg
Jackson State Community College
Conducted Communications Media
Mark Pollitt
DigitalEvidencePro
Law Enforcement and Digital Evidence
A. S. Pomportsis
Aristotle University, Greece
VPN Basics
Daniel N. Port
University of Hawaii, Manoa
Risk Management for IT Security
Stephanie Porte
Gemplus, France
Smart Card Security
Dennis M. Powers
Southern Oregon University
Cyberlaw: The Major Areas, Development,
  and Information Security Aspects
Anupama Raju
Western Michigan University
TCP over Wireless Links
Jeremy L. Rasmussen
Sypris Electronics, LLC
Password Authentication

Indrajit Ray
Colorado State Univesity
Electronic Payment Systems
Julian J. Ray
University of Redlands
Business-to-Business Electronic
  Commerce
Drummond Reed
OneName Corporation
Digital Identity
Slim Rekhis
National Digital Certification Agency and University
  of Carthage, Tunisia
Server-Side Security
Jian Ren
Michigan State University, East Lansing
Managing A Network Environment
Vladimir V. Riabov
Rivier College
SMTP (Simple Mail Transfer Protocol)
Marcus K. Rogers
Purdue University
Internal Security Threats
Pankaj Rohatgi
IBM T. J Watson Research Center
Side-Channel Attacks
Arnon Rosenthal
The MITRE Corporation
Database Security
Emilia Rosti
Università degli Studi di Milano, Italy
IP Multicast and Its Security
Neil C. Rowe
U.S. Naval Postgraduate School
Electronic Protection
Bradley S. Rubin
University of St. Thomas
Public Key Algorithms
K. Rudolph
Native Intelligence, Inc.
Implementing a Security Awareness
  Program
B. Sadoun
Al-Balqa' Applied University, Jordan
Digital Watermarking and Steganography
Akhil Sahai
Hewlett-Packard Laboratories
Web Services
Antonio Saitto
Telespazio, Italy
Security of Satellite Networks
Atul A. Salvekar
Intel Corporation
Digital Communication
Pierangela Samarati
Università di Milano, Italy
Access Control: Principles and Solutions
Contingency Planning Management
Shannon Schelin
The University of North Carolina, Chapel
  Hill
E-Government

William T. Schiano
Bentley College
Intranets: Principals, Privacy, and Security
  Considerations
Matthew Schmid
Cigital, Inc.
Antivirus Technology
E. Eugene Schultz
University of California–Berkeley Lab
Windows 2000 Security
Denial of Service Attacks
Mark Shacklette
The University of Chicago
UNIX Security
P. M. Shankar
Drexel University
Wireless Channels
J. Eagle Shutt
University of South Carolina
Law Enforcement and Computer Security
  Threats and Measures
Nirvikar Singh
University of California, Santa Cruz
Digital Economy
Robert Slade
Vancouver Institute for Research into User
  Security, Canada
Computer Viruses and Worms
Digital Courts, the Law and Evidence
Hoax Viruses and Virus Alerts
Nigel Smart
University of Bristol, UK
Elliptic Curve Cryptography
Richard E. Smith
University of St. Thomas
Multilevel Security
Min Song
Old Dominion University
Mobile Devices and Protocols
Mike Speciner
Independent Consultant
Data Encryption Standard (DES)
Richard A. Spinello
Boston College
Internet Censorship
Lee Sproull
New York University
Online Communities
Evdoxia Spyropoulou
Technical Vocational Educational School of Computer
  Science of Halandri, Greece
Quality of Security Service: Adaptive Security
William Stallings
Independent Consultant
Kerberos
Operating System Security
Mark Stamp
San Jose State University
Multilevel Security Models
Philip Statham
CESG, Cheltenham, Gloucestershire, UK
Issues and Concerns in Biometric IT Security

Charles Steinfield
Michigan State University
Click-and-Brick Electronic Commerce
Electronic Commerce
Ivan Stojmenovic
University of Ottawa, Cananda
Cellular Networks
Robin C. Stuart
Digital Investigations Consultant
Digital Evidence
M. A. Suhail
University of Bradford, UK
Digital Watermarking and Steganography
Wayne C. Summers
Columbus State University
Local Area Networks
Jeff Swauger
University of Central Florida
Law Enforcement and Digital Evidence
Mak Ming Tak
Hong Kong University of Science and
  Technology, Hong Kong
Fixed-Line Telephone System Vulnerabilities
Thomas D. Tarman
Sandia National Laboratories
Security for ATM Networks
Paul A. Taylor
University of Leeds, UK
Hacktivism
Dale R. Thompson
University of Arkansas
Public Network Technologies and Security
Jimi Thompson
Southern Methodist University
Electronic Attacks
Stephen W. Thorpe
Neumann College
Extranets: Applications, Development, Security,
  and Privacy
Amandeep Thukral
Purdue University
Key Management
Michael Tunstall
Gemplus & Royal Holloway University,
  France
Fault Attacks
Smart Card Security
Okechukwu Ugweje
The University of Akron
Radio Frequency and Wireless Communications
  Security
István Vajda
Budapest University of Technology and
  Economics, Hungary
Standards for Product Security Assessment
S. Rao Vallabhaneni
SRV Professional Publications
Auditing Information Systems Security
Nicko van Someren
nCipher Plc., UK
Cryptographic Hardware Security
  Modules

Phil Venables
Institute of Electrical and Electronics Engineers
Information Leakage: Detection and Countermeasures

Giovanni Vigna
Reliable Software Group
Host-Based Intrusion Detection Systems

Linda Volonino
Canisius College
Security Middleware

Richard P. Volonino
Canisius College
Security Middleware

Ashraf Wadaa
Old Dominion University
Security in Wireless Sensor Networks

Blaze D. Waleski
Fulbright & Jaworski LLP
The Legal Implications of Information Security: Regulatory Compliance and Liability

Jonathan Wallace
DeCoMo USA Labs
Anonymity and Identity on the Internet

Siaw-Peng Wan
Elmhurst College
Online Retail Banking: Security Concerns, Breaches, and Controls

Yongge Wang
University of North Carolina, Charlotte
PKCS (Public-Key Cryptography Standards)

John Warren
University of Texas, San Antonio
Groupware: Risks, Threats, and Vulnerabilities in the Internet Age

James L. Wayman
San Jose State University
Biometric Basics and Biometric Authentication

Edgar R. Weippl
Vienna University of Technology, Austria
Security in E-Learning

Stephen A. Weis
MIT Computer Science and Artificial Intelligence Laboratory
PGP (Pretty Good Privacy)
RFID and Security

Susanne Wetzel
Stevens Institute of Technology
Bluetooth Security

A. Justin Wilder
Telos Corporation
Linux Security

Raymond Wisman
Indiana University Southeast
Search Engines: Security, Privacy, and Ethical Issues

Paul L. Witt
Texas Christian University
Internet Relay Chat

Avishai Wool
Tel Aviv University, Israel
Packet Filtering and Stateful Firewalls

Cheng-Zhong Xu
Wayne State University
Mobile Code and Security

Xu Yan
Hong Kong University of Science and Technology, Hong Kong
Fixed-Line Telephone System Vulnerabilities

Mustafa Yildiz
Isik University, Turkey
Security Insurance and Best Practices

Adam L. Young
Cigital, Inc.
Trojan Horse Programs

Meng Yu
Monmouth University
Information Assurance

Sherali Zeadally
Wayne State University
Home Area Networking

Jingyuan Zhang
University of Alabama
Cellular Networks

Xukai Zou
Purdue University
Key Management
Public Key Standards: Secure Shell

William A. Zucker
Gadsby Hannah LLP
Corporate Spying: The Legal Aspects

Preface

The Handbook of Information Security is the first comprehensive examination of the core topics in the security field. *The Handbook of Information Security*, a 3-volume reference work with 207 chapters and 3300+ pages, is a comprehensive coverage of information, computer, and network security.

The primary audience is the libraries of 2-year and 4-year colleges and universities with computer science, MIS, CIS, IT, IS, data processing, and business departments; public, private, and corporate libraries throughout the world; and reference material for educators and practitioners in the information and computer security fields.

The secondary audience is a variety of professionals and a diverse group of academic and professional course instructors.

Among the industries expected to become increasingly dependent upon information and computer security and active in understanding the many issues surrounding this important and fast-growing field are: government, military, education, library, health, medical, law enforcement, accounting, legal, justice, manufacturing, financial services, insurance, communications, transportation, aerospace, energy, biotechnology, retail, and utility.

Each volume incorporates state-of-the-art, core information, on computer security topics, practical applications and coverage of the emerging issues in the information security field.

This definitive 3-volume handbook offers coverage of both established and cutting-edge theories and developments in information, computer, and network security.

This handbook contains chapters by global academic and industry experts. This handbook offers the following features:

1) Each chapter follows a format including title and author, outline, introduction, body, conclusion, glossary, cross-references, and references. This format allows the reader to pick and choose various sections of a chapter. It also creates consistency throughout the entire series.

2) The handbook has been written by more than 240 experts and reviewed by more than 1,000 academics and practitioners from around the world. These experts have created a definitive compendium of both established and cutting-edge theories and applications.

3) Each chapter has been rigorously peer-reviewed. This review process assures accuracy and completeness.

4) Each chapter provides extensive online and off-line references for additional readings, which will enable the reader to learn more on topics of special interest.

5) The handbook contains more than 1,000 illustrations and tables that highlight complex topics for further understanding.

6) Each chapter provides extensive cross-references, leading the reader to other chapters related to a particular topic.

7) The handbook contains more than 2,700 glossary items. Many new terms and buzzwords are included to provide a better understanding of concepts and applications.

8) The handbook contains a complete and comprehensive table of contents and index.

9) The series emphasizes both technical as well as managerial, social, legal, and international issues in the field. This approach provides researchers, educators, students, and practitioners with a balanced perspective and background information that will be helpful when dealing with problems related to security issues and measures and the design of a sound security system.

10) The series has been developed based on the current core course materials in several leading universities around the world and current practices in leading computer, security, and networking corporations.

We chose to concentrate on fields and supporting technologies that have widespread applications in the academic and business worlds. To develop this handbook, we carefully reviewed current academic research in the security field from leading universities and research institutions around the world.

Computer and network security, information security and privacy, management information systems, network design and management, computer information systems (CIS), decision support systems (DSS), and electronic commence curriculums, recommended by the Association of Information Technology Professionals (AITP) and the Association for Computing Machinery (ACM) were carefully investigated. We also researched the current practices in the security field carried out by leading security and IT corporations. Our research helped us define the boundaries and contents of this project.

TOPIC CATEGORIES

Based on our research, we identified nine major topic categories for the handbook.

- Key Concepts and Applications Related to Information Security
- Infrastructure for the Internet, Computer Networks, and Secure Information Transfer
- Standards and Protocols for Secure Information Transfer
- Information Warfare
- Social, Legal, and International Issues

- Foundations of Information, Computer, and Network Security
- Threats and Vulnerabilities to Information and Computing Infrastructures
- Prevention: Keeping the Hackers and Crackers at Bay
- Detection, Recovery, Management, and Policy Considerations

Although these topics are related, each addresses a specific concern within information security. The chapters in each category are also interrelated and complementary, enabling readers to compare, contrast, and draw conclusions that might not otherwise be possible.

Though the entries have been arranged logically, the light they shed knows no bounds. The handbook provides unmatched coverage of fundamental topics and issues for successful design and implementation of a sound security program. Its chapters can serve as material for a wide spectrum of courses such as:

Information and Network Security
Information Privacy
Social Engineering
Secure Financial Transactions
Information Warfare
Infrastructure for Secure Information Transfer
Standards and Protocols for Secure Information Transfer
Network Design and Management
Client/Server Computing
E-commerce

Successful design and implementation of a sound security program requires a thorough knowledge of several technologies, theories, and supporting disciplines. Security researchers and practitioners have had to consult many resources to find answers. Some of these resources concentrate on technologies and infrastructures, some on social and legal issues, and some on managerial concerns. This handbook provides all of this information in a comprehensive, three-volume set with a lively format.

Key Concepts and Applications Related to Information Security

Chapters in this group examine a broad range of topics. Theories, concepts, technologies, and applications that expose either a user, manager, or an organization to security and privacy issues and/or create such security and privacy concerns are discussed. Careful attention is given to those concepts and technologies that have widespread applications in business and academic environments. These areas include e-banking, e-communities, e-commerce, e-education, and e-government.

Infrastructure for the Internet, Computer Networks, and Secure Information Transfer

Chapters in this group concentrate on the infrastructure, popular network types, key technologies, and principles

for secure information transfer. Different types of communications media are discussed followed by a review of a variety of networks including LANs, MANs, WANs, mobile, and cellular networks. This group of chapters also discusses important architectures for secure information transfers including TCP/IP, the Internet, peer-to-peer, and client/server computing.

Standards and Protocols for Secure Information Transfer

Chapters in this group discuss major protocols and standards in the security field. This topic includes important protocols for online transactions, e-mail protocols, Internet protocols, IPsec, and standards and protocols for wireless networks emphasizing 802.11.

Information Warfare

This group of chapters examines the growing field of information warfare. Important laws within the United States criminal justice system, as they relate to cybercrime and cyberterrorism, are discussed. Other chapters in this group discuss cybercrime, cyberfraud, cyber stalking, wireless information warfare, electronic attacks and protection, and the fundamentals of information assurance.

Social, Legal, and International Issues

Chapters in this group explore social, legal, and international issues relating to information privacy and computer security. Digital identity, identity theft, censorship, and different types of computer criminals are also explored. The chapters in this group also explain patent, trademark, and copyright issues and offer guidelines for protecting intellectual properties.

Foundations of Information, Computer, and Network Security

These chapters cover four different but complementary areas including encryption, forensic computing, operating systems and the common criteria and the principles for improving the security assurance.

Threats and Vulnerabilities to Information and Computing Infrastructures

The chapters in this group investigate major threats to, and vulnerabilities of, information and computing infrastructures in wired and wireless environments. The chapters specifically discuss intentional, unintentional, controllable, partially controllable, uncontrollable, physical, software and hardware threats and vulnerabilities.

Prevention: Keeping the Hackers and Crackers at Bay

The chapters in this group present several concepts, tools, techniques, and technologies that help to protect information, keep networks secure, and keep the hackers and computer criminals at bay. Some of the topics discussed include physical security measures; measures for protecting client-side, server-side, database, and medical records; different types of authentication techniques; and preventing security threats to e-commerce and e-mail transactions.

Detection, Recovery, Management, and Policy Considerations

Chapters in this group discuss concepts, tools, and techniques for detection of security breaches, offer techniques and guidelines for recovery, and explain principles for managing a network environment. Some of the topics highlighted in this group include intrusion detection, contingency planning, risk management, auditing, and guidelines for effective security management and policy implementation.

Acknowledgments

Many specialists have helped to make the handbook a resource for experienced and not-so-experienced readers. It is to these contributors that I am especially grateful. This remarkable collection of scholars and practitioners has distilled their knowledge into a fascinating and enlightening one-stop knowledge base in information, computer, and network security that "talks" to readers. This has been a massive effort, as well as a most rewarding experience. So many people have played a role, it is difficult to know where to begin.

I would like to thank the members of the editorial board for participating in the project and for their expert advice on selection of topics, recommendations of authors, and review of the materials. Many thanks to the more than 1,000 reviewers who provided their advice on improving the coverage, accuracy, and comprehensiveness of these materials.

I thank my senior editor, Matt Holt, who initiated the idea of the handbook. Through a dozen drafts and many reviews, the project got off the ground and then was managed flawlessly by Matt and his professional team. Many thanks to Matt and his team for keeping the project focused and maintaining its lively coverage.

Tamara Hummel, editorial coordinator, assisted the contributing authors and me during the initial phases of development. I am grateful for all her support. When it came time for the production phase, the superb Wiley production team took over. Particularly, I want to thank Deborah Schindlar, senior production editor. I am grateful for all her hard work. I thank Michelle Patterson, our marketing manager, for her impressive marketing campaign launched on behalf of the handbook.

Last, but not least, I want to thank my wonderful wife, Nooshin, and my two children, Mohsen and Morvareed, for being so patient during this venture. They provided a pleasant environment that expedited the completion of this project. Mohsen and Morvareed assisted me in sending out thousands of e-mail messages to authors and reviewers. Nooshin was a great help in designing and maintaining the authors' and reviewers' databases. Their efforts are greatly appreciated. Also, my two sisters, Azam and Akram, provided moral support throughout my life. To this family, any expression of thanks is insufficient.

Hossein Bidgoli
California State University, Bakersfield

Guide to The Handbook of Information Security

The Handbook of Information Security is a comprehensive coverage of the relatively new and very important field of information, computer, and network security. This reference work consists of three separate volumes and 207 different chapters on various aspects of this field. Each chapter in the handbook provides a comprehensive overview of the selected topic, intended to inform a broad spectrum of readers, ranging from computer and security professionals and academicians to students to the general business community.

This guide is provided to help the reader easily locate information throughout *The Handbook of Information Security*. It explains how the information within it can be located.

Organization

This is organized for maximum ease of use, with the chapters arranged logically in three volumes. While one can read individual volumes (or articles) one will get the most out of the handbook by becoming conversant with all three volumes.

Table of Contents

A complete table of contents of the entire handbook appears in the front of each volume. This list of chapter titles represents topics that have been carefully selected by the editor-in-chief, Dr. Hossein Bidgoli, and his colleagues on the editorial board.

Index

A subject index for each individual volume is located at the end of each volume.

Chapters

The author's name and affiliation are displayed at the beginning of the chapter.

All chapters in the handbook are organized in the same format:

Title and author
Outline
Introduction
Body
Conclusion
Glossary
Cross-References
References

Outline

Each chapter begins with an outline that provides a brief overview of the chapter, as well as highlighting important subtopics. For example, the chapter "Internet Basics" includes sections for Information Superhighway and the World Wide Web, Domain Name Systems, Navigational Tools, Search Engines, and Directories. In addition, second-level and third-level headings will be found within the chapter.

Introduction

Each chapter begins with an introduction that defines the topic under discussion and summarized the chapter, in order to give the reader a general idea of what is to come.

Body

The body of the chapter fills out and expands upon items covered in the outline.

Conclusion

The conclusion provides a summary of the chapter, highlighting issues and concepts that are important for the reader to remember.

Glossary

The glossary contains terms that are important to an understanding of the chapter and that may be unfamiliar to the reader. Each term is defined in the context of the particular chapter in which it is used. Thus the same term may be defined in two or more chapters with the detail of the definition varying slightly from one chapter to another. The handbook includes approximately 2,700 glossary terms. For example, the chapter "Internet Basics" includes the following glossary entries:

Extranet A secure network that uses the Internet and Web technology to connect two or more intranets of trusted business partners, enabling business-to-business, business-to-consumer, consumer-to-consumer, and consumer-to-business communications.
Intranet A network within the organization that uses Web technologies (TCP/IP, HTTP, FTP, SMTP, HTML, XML, and its variations) for collecting, storing, and disseminating useful information throughout the organization.

Cross-References

All chapters have cross-references to other chapters that contain further information on the same topic. They appear at the end of the chapter, preceding the references. The cross-references indicate related chapters that can be consulted for further information on the same topic. The handbook contains more than 1,400 cross-references in all. For example, the chapter "Computer Viruses and Worms" has the following cross references:

Hackers, Crackers and Computer Criminals, Hoax Viruses and Virus Alerts, Hostile Java Applets, Spyware, Trojan Horse Programs.

References

The references in this handbook are for the benefit of the reader, to provide references for further research on the given topic. Review articles and research papers that are important to an understanding of the topic are also listed. The references typically consist of a dozen to two dozen entries, and do not include all material consulted by the author in preparing the chapter.

PART 1

Information Warfare

Cybercrime and the U.S. Criminal Justice System

Susan W. Brenner, *University of Dayton School of Law*

INTRODUCTION

Cybercrime, which is essentially the use of computer technology in the commission of criminal activity, presents many challenges for the U.S. legal system. On the one hand, state and federal law adequately criminalizes most of the basic cybercrime offenses; on the other hand, there is substantial disagreement as to the penalties that are appropriate for those who commit these offenses. The disagreement over penalties is exacerbated by the fact that many offenders are juveniles; the federal system, especially, is not equipped to deal with juveniles. Charging decisions can be difficult because it is not easy to parse cybercrime into offenses: Is the dissemination of a virus that damages a million computers one crime or a million crimes? As is explained below, these are only a few of the ways in which cybercrime challenges the basic assumptions that structured traditional criminal law.

DIFFERENCES FROM CIVIL JUSTICE SYSTEM

The criminal justice system in the United States—as elsewhere—differs from the civil justice system in several important ways. One difference is substantive: the goal of the civil justice system is to provide redress for accidental or conventional injuries or losses one "person," which can be an individual or a corporate entity, has suffered as the result of another's actions or failure to act (LaFave, 2003). The goal of the criminal justice system, on the other hand, is to allow the state—acting on behalf of the people in a specific society—to inflict punishment on those who inflict deliberate, serious injuries upon others. Technically, therefore, in the criminal justice system, the state is the injured party, and criminal proceedings are brought in the name of the appropriate government, which will be federal, state, or local (LaFave, 2003).

Another difference is procedural: the U.S. Constitution sets limits on what law enforcement officers can do when investigating crimes such as hacking or cyberfraud. State and federal officers must tender the *Miranda* warnings to anyone whom they take into custody for the purposes of interrogation (LaFave, Israel, & King, 1999). The Fourth Amendment requires that they either obtain a search warrant or invoke a valid exception to the warrant requirement to search for and seize evidence of a cybercrime; so, if officers believe child pornography is located in a suspect's computer in his or her bedroom, they must persuade a magistrate to issue a warrant allowing them to search the computer or convince the suspect to consent to such a search (consent being an exception to the warrant requirement) (LaFave et al., 1999).

There are other procedural differences that distinguish criminal trials from civil trials: In a criminal trial, the prosecution must prove its case "beyond a reasonable doubt," which is a far more demanding standard than the "preponderance of the evidence" standard used in civil trials (LaFave et al., 1999). If the civil standard were used in a hacking prosecution, the government would only have to prove it was "more likely than not" that the defendant engaged in hacking; under the criminal standard, the government must prove beyond a reasonable doubt that the crime of hacking was committed and that it was committed by the defendant (LaFave et al., 1999). This higher standard protects those who are accused of crimes and thereby helps to avoid wrongful convictions; other rules that work to the same end are the presumption that a defendant is innocent and an indigent defendant's right to appointed counsel (LaFave et al., 1999). The size of criminal juries also contributes to this goal; in the federal system and in most states, 12 jurors are required in criminal trials (LaFave et al., 1999). Civil trials often involve fewer jurors, frequently as few as six (LaFave et al., 1999). The size of the jury is important because studies have shown larger juries are more likely to result in fair deliberations (LaFave et al., 1999).

BASIC INSTITUTIONAL STRUCTURE

Law enforcement in the United States takes place at three distinct levels: federal, state, and local government (LaFave et al., 1999). At the federal level, the Federal Bureau of Investigation and the Secret Service actively pursue cybercrime investigations, but their efforts account for only a fraction of the total number of investigations; in the United States, state and federal law enforcement have traditionally been primarily responsible for pursuing criminal cases (LaFave et al., 1999). As a result, U.S. cybercrime laws can overlap: The federal system and all of the states have laws that criminalize hacking, cyberfraud, and other common cybercrimes (Ditzion, Geddes, & Rhodes, 2003). The default assumptions are that (a) state and local authorities have jurisdiction to prosecute and (b) federal authorities must be able to bring a hacking or other cybercrime case within a federal jurisdictional predicate to be able to prosecute (LaFave, 2003). The most common federal jurisdictional predicate used in cybercrime cases is an effect on interstate or foreign commerce; this is the predicate used in the general federal cybercrime statute, 18 U.S. Code §1030 (Ditzion, Geddes, & Rhodes, 2003). So, to prosecute someone for hacking in violation of §1030, federal prosecutors have to show that the hacking had an impact on interstate or foreign commerce, which is usually not difficult to do (American Bar Association Task Force, 1998).

When a cybercrime occurs, the investigation is undertaken by local, state, or federal law enforcement officers who may work in conjunction with a prosecutor and who often work in conjunction with computer forensic and other experts, such as forensic psychologists (LaFave et al., 1999). Given the complexity of cybercrime cases, these investigations are increasingly undertaken by task forces in which local, state, and federal officers collaborate with private investigators to pursue a cybercriminal (Miami Electronic Crimes Task Force, 2003). Indeed, one of the distinguishing aspects of cybercrime cases is the essential involvement of the private sector: cybercrimes are often committed against businesses, which must decide if they want to report the matter to the authorities or handle it in-house. There are disincentives for reporting a cyberattack; aside from anything else, news that a company has been victimized by a cyberattacker can undermine confidence in the business and in its ability to protect client or customer information (Brenner & Schwerha, 2002). If a business is attacked and decides to report the matter to the authorities, it will have to decide if it wants to contact federal, state, or local authorities (Brenner & Schwerha, 2002). There are certain advantages to seeking federal prosecution; federal agencies often have more resources and expertise in dealing with computer crime, and they are not hampered by the jurisdictional impediments that confront state authorities. A federal search warrant, for example, is enforceable anywhere in the United States; a state search warrant, a New York warrant, say, is enforceable only within the state of New York.

Because cybercrime cases can be difficult to investigate and prosecute, there is an emerging emphasis on avoiding the need for both by preventing cybercrime. Prevention is a major focus of the Secret Service's Electronic Crime Task Forces and the Federal Bureau of Investigation's Infragard program. Both initiatives bring together representatives from law enforcement, the private sector, and academia to share information and resources, thereby facilitating the prevention of cybercrime and the investigation of completed cybercrimes.

Prosecutor

The central figure in any cybercrime case is the prosecutor. In the U.S. justice system, prosecutors occupy a unique role; they serve as advocates for the state and in that sense play a role analogous to that of the defense lawyer. As advocates, defense lawyers are obliged to use every tactical advantage permitted under the law to obtain their client's acquittal, even if doing so keeps the jury from the truth (LaFave et al., 1999). Prosecutors are held to a higher standard; their duty is to ensure justice is done, not merely to win a criminal case (LaFave et al., 1999). But when a state or federal prosecutor does take a case to trial, his or her goals will generally be to obtain a conviction (LaFave et al., 1999).

Because crimes are considered a wrong against the government, prosecutions are undertaken in the name of the government, whether federal, state, or local, and victims consequently play a minor role (LaFave et al., 1999). Victims typically have little say in the charging or plea bargaining processes; their role is usually limited to that of witness (LaFave et al., 1999). Prosecutors control charging and plea bargaining; they have wide discretion in deciding (a) whether someone will be prosecuted and (b) if someone is to be prosecuted, what charges they will face (LaFave et al., 1999). In a hacking case, for instance, the prosecutor might decide not to prosecute the offender because he is a juvenile. This is particularly likely to occur in the federal system, which is not set up to deal with juvenile offenders (Esbenshade, 2002–2003). As a result, federal prosecutors tend to concentrate on adult offenders and turn juveniles over to the juvenile court of the appropriate state, pursuant to the Federal Juvenile Delinquency Act (Esbenshade, 2002–2003).

Another large class of cybercrime cases in the United States involves intellectual property (U.S. Department of Justice Computer Crime and Intellectual Property Section, 2001): "Legal regimes have created enforceable rights in certain intangibles that have become familiar as intellectual property, including copyrights, trademarks, patents, and trade secrets" (U.S. Department of Justice Computer Crime and Intellectual Property Section, 2001). At the federal level, various statutes are used to prosecute the unlawful appropriation of intellectual property: 18 U.S. Code §2320 makes it a crime to counterfeit trademarks. 18 U.S. Code §§1831 and §§1832 make the theft of trade secrets a federal crime. And copyright infringement is criminalized by 17 U.S. Code §506(a) and 18 U.S. Code §2319. Patent infringement "is not generally a criminal violation" (U.S. Department of Justice Computer Crime and Intellectual Property Section, 2001). Federal law preempts state law governing copyright violations, so prosecutions can be brought only at the federal level (Nicholson et al., 2000). Federal law does not preempt state law governing trademark violations, except insofar as the state and federal statutory provisions conflict (Kahn, 2004).

In deciding whether to prosecute intellectual property crimes, such as criminal copyright infringement, federal prosecutors must consider the strength of their case, the person's culpability in connection with the crime(s), the person's history (if any) of prior criminal activity, current federal law enforcement priorities, and the extent to which such a prosecution would deter others from engaging in similar conduct (U.S. Department of Justice Computer Crime and Intellectual Property Section, 2001). These factors, and perhaps most notably the federal interest in protecting U.S.-based intellectual property rights, have prompted federal prosecutions of those who use the Internet to supply "warez," that is, pirated copies of software (U.S. Department of Justice Computer Crime and Intellectual Property Section, 2001). A study of federal cybercrime prosecutions found that in 2001 the Department of Justice declined to prosecute in 496 of 631 referred cases; 135 cases were prosecuted, resulting in 107 convictions and 28 dismissals or acquittals on all charges (National Association of Criminal Defense Lawyers, Electronic Frontier Foundation & Sentencing Project, 2003). The primary reason given for declining prosecution was lack of evidence or inadmissible evidence (National Association of Criminal Defense Lawyers, Electronic Frontier Foundation & Sentencing Project, 2003). The next most commonly cited reasons were (a) that the person would be prosecuted at the state level and (b) the lack of a federal interest in prosecuting (National Association of Criminal Defense Lawyers, Electronic Frontier Foundation & Sentencing Project, 2003).

Even when prosecutors decide to charge someone, the defense attorney may be able to arrange a plea bargain: in 1995, hacker Kevin Mitnick pled guilty to 1 of 23 counts brought against him in a North Carolina federal prosecution (Goldman, 1995). By pleading guilty, he was guaranteed a sentence of no more than 8 months and avoided prosecution on the remaining 22 counts (Goldman, 1995). Plea bargains offer defendants the opportunity to accept a lesser penalty in return for avoiding at least the possibility of a greater penalty, but they also offer certain advantages for prosecutors. Plea bargains let prosecutors resolve cases without having to go to trial, which alleviates the burden on a criminal justice system that is swamped with cybercrime and real-world crime cases; plea bargains also let prosecutors trade lesser sentences for a defendant's cooperation in prosecuting other, presumably more culpable, offenders. The potential for cooperation is one of the factors federal prosecutors consider in deciding whether to bring charges and whether to plea bargain charges that have already been brought (U.S. Department of Justice Computer Crime and Intellectual Property Section, 2001).

As noted, law enforcement in the United States operates on three levels: local, state, and federal. This is also true for prosecutors. Local prosecutors generally operate at the county or parish level; there is typically an elected prosecutor who is usually known either as the county prosecutor or the district attorney (LaFave et al., 1999). He or she functions with the aid of a number of assistants, who are known as assistant district attorneys, deputy county prosecutors, or similar titles (LaFave et al., 1999). Moving up a tier, each state has an attorney general whose jurisdiction varies from state to state: in some states, attorney generals are authorized only to prosecute certain, specialized crimes such as antitrust or organized crime cases; in other states, attorney generals have much

more limited jurisdiction to prosecute and may be limited to substituting when a local prosecutor is disqualified (LaFave et al., 1999). Like local prosecutors, attorney generals function with the aid of assistants, who are usually known as deputy attorney generals or assistant attorney generals. Many state attorney general's offices have established cybercrime units and the National Association of Attorneys General has its own cybercrime initiative (National Association of Attorneys General—Computer Crime, 2003). Moving up to the third tier, the federal justice system is headed by an attorney general, who also functions with the aid of assistants and deputies (LaFave et al., 1999). The attorney general also heads up a nationwide organization of United States attorneys; a United States attorney is appointed for every federal judicial district in the United States; they function in a fashion analogous to county prosecutors; that is, they deal with federal crimes committed in a specified geographical area (LaFave et al., 1999). The Department of Justice, headed by the attorney general, also deals with federal crime on a more global level; the department has a specialized unit—the Computer Crime and Intellectual Property Section—which deals with cybercrime as a general phenomenon (Ditzion, Geddes, & Rhodes, 2003).

After a prosecutor has taken a case to trial and obtained a conviction or entered into a plea bargain with a defendant, the next step in the process is sentencing (LaFave et al., 1999). In all but a few U.S. jurisdictions, which allow for jury sentencing even in noncapital cases, the determination and imposition of an appropriate sentence are a matter for the court (LaFave et al., 1999). The U.S. system uses four types of sanctions: financial (fines, restitution), community release (probation, unsupervised release, house arrest), incarceration in a jail (for shorter sentences) or a prison (for longer sentences), and capital punishment (for murder) (LaFave et al., 1999). Courts can combine these sanctions; in one cybercrime case, for example, the court sentenced the defendant to 3 years' probation, a $40,000 fine, and the payment of $20,000 in restitution (U.S. v. Hicks, 1995). In the federal system and a number of states, sentences are determinate; that is, the offender serves the entire sentence imposed by the court (except for "good time" credit) (LaFave et al., 1999). The other states use indeterminate sentencing, in which the court sets a maximum period and a minimum period of incarceration and the state parole board decides how much time the offender will exactly serve (LaFave et al., 1999). Both systems are increasingly using sentencing guidelines, which are standards that limit the judge's discretion in imposing sentence (LaFave et al., 1999). Until recently, cybercrime offenders often received sentences of probation only, or, at most, a short period of incarceration (Beauprez, 2003). In November 2003, new sentencing guidelines went into effect in the federal system that will increase punishments in at least some cybercrime cases (Beauprez, 2003).

Defense Attorney

The defense attorney's role is to ensure that no conviction is obtained unless (a) the prosecution proves its case beyond a reasonable doubt or (b) the defendant accepts a plea bargain that is advantageous for him or her (LaFave et al., 1999). As noted, when charges have been brought, it is defense counsel's task to utilize every tactical advantage at his or her disposal to obtain the best outcome for the client (LaFave et al., 1999). Unlike the prosecutor, the defense attorney's advocacy is not constrained by external principles; in our adversarial system of justice, defense counsel is charged with pursuing the client's best interests without regard to other concerns (LaFave et al., 1999). That includes ensuring that the trial or the plea bargaining process is conducted in accordance with constitutional and other legal requirements; for that reason, ineffective assistance of defense counsel is a basis for setting aside a conviction (LaFave et al., 1999). But although defense counsel must represent his or her client zealously and loyally, defense attorneys, like prosecutors, are ethically obligated not to misrepresent matters of fact or law to the court, not to suborn perjury by one's client, and not to destroy, alter, or conceal evidence (American Bar Association, 2003).

The Sixth Amendment creates a right to counsel for those charged with the commission of crimes; the Supreme Court has held that this right attaches to all "critical" stages of a prosecution, such as the arraignment, plea negotiations, and trial (LaFave et al., 1999). In both the state and federal systems, defendants are represented either by privately retained attorneys or by attorneys provided by the government (LaFave et al., 1999). If a defendant cannot afford to retain private counsel, the court will arrange for appointed counsel to represent him or her (LaFave et al., 1999). States use three systems to accomplish this: in most counties, indigents are represented by public defenders—attorneys whom the county employs to represent those who cannot afford private counsel (LaFave et al., 1999). The second most commonly used system relies on private attorneys whom judges appoint to represent indigents; these private attorneys are paid at a rate determined by the local government (LaFave et al., 1999). Finally, a few counties use a system in which a private law firm or a bar association contracts with the county to provide representation for indigents (LaFave et al., 1999). In the federal system, federal public defenders represent indigents in a number of judicial districts, whereas the others rely on court-appointed private counsel (LaFave et al., 1999).

The defense of a cybercrime case is a difficult matter, because it requires special expertise as to substantive law [i.e., the offense(s) charged], procedural law (i.e., the legality of the tactics employed in the investigation), and the intricacies of computer technology. So far, there appears to be a serious scarcity of attorneys who specialize in cybercrime cases, no doubt because such cases are still relatively rare, considered in relation to the other types of criminal cases being brought. To date, many of those charged with cybercrime have relied on privately retained counsel, perhaps because hackers and others involved with computer technology are less likely to be indigent than, say, those charged with drug offenses. There have, however, been exceptions: Adrian Lamo, who became famous as the "homeless hacker," relied on a public defender when he was prosecuted federally for hacking into systems, including the *New York Times'* computer system (Reuters Wired News, 2003).

Adjudication

Perhaps the most critical decision the defense has to make, especially in a computer crime trial, is whether to have the case tried by a jury ("jury trial") or a judge ("bench trial"). The Sixth Amendment guarantees criminal defendants the right to trial by an impartial jury drawn from the state and district in which the crime(s) allegedly occurred (Right to Jury Trial, 2003). The right attaches when one has been charged with an offense which is punishable by a prison sentence of 6 months or more; as to crimes for which one can serve less than 6 months in prison, the right to jury trial does not attach unless the presence of additional statutory or regulatory penalties indicates that the legislature considered the offense a "serious" crime (Right to Jury Trial, 2003).

Usually, the jury in a criminal trial consists of 12 jurors, but the Supreme Court has held that 6 jurors are enough to satisfy the Sixth Amendment (Right to Jury Trial, 2003). Court rules, such as Rule 23 of the Federal Rules of Criminal Procedure, require the impaneling of 12 jurors in federal criminal trials, absent a written waiver executed by the parties and approved by the court (Right to Jury Trial, 2003). The Supreme Court has consistently held that jurors in federal criminal trials must return a unanimous verdict (Right to Jury Trial, 2003). As for state criminal trials, the jury must be unanimous if it consists of only 6 jurors; if the jury consists of 12 jurors, they can return a nonunanimous verdict (Right to Jury Trial, 2003). Traditionally, jurors were required to be purely passive spectators at a trial; they were not allowed to ask questions or otherwise participate in the proceedings (Hans, 2002). More and more, however, jurors are being allowed to ask questions, take notes, and discuss the case with each other during the trial (Hans, 2002).

A jury trial is a defendant's constitutional right, but it may or may not be the best choice, depending on the nature of the case. If the defense attorney believes the case is likely to inflame the passions of the jury against his or her client, the best course may be to ask for a bench trial. This can, for example, be an advisable tactic in a child pornography case: even though there may be valid evidentiary and/or legal reasons to acquit the accused, the jurors may be so disturbed by the images the prosecution presents that they will ignore those reasons and convict, leaving the matter to be appealed. In such an instance, the wiser course may well be for the defendant to waive his right to a jury trial and have the case tried by the court. The same can be true for crimes involving difficult legal and technical issues, such as actions under the Digital Millennium Copyright Act (*Universal City Studios, Inc. v. Corley*, 2001).

A defendant can waive his or her right to a jury trial by (a) obtaining the court's approval and the government's consent and (b) executing a written waiver that is knowing, voluntary, and intelligent (Right to Jury Trial, 2003). The government's consent is required because the Supreme Court has held that there is no constitutional right to a bench trial (Right to Jury Trial, 2003). Because there is no constitutional right to a nonjury trial, the prosecution can, in effect, veto a defendant's wish to have his or her case heard by the court instead of a jury; all that is required is for the prosecution to refuse to consent to a bench trial (Right to Jury Trial, 2003).

Once a criminal case has been tried to its conclusion, the defendant cannot be tried again for the crimes at issue in that proceeding, as the Fifth Amendment declares that one cannot be twice "put in jeopardy" for the "same offence" (LaFave et al., 1999). The double jeopardy clause not only prevents the retrial of cases that have produced a conviction or acquittal; it can also prevent retrials after a case has been begun and is then terminated before the matter goes to the jury (LaFave et al., 1999). The basic rule is that "jeopardy" attaches (a) after the first witness has been sworn in a bench trial and (b) after the jurors have been sworn in for a jury trial (LaFave et al., 1999).

The protections of the double jeopardy clause are subject to certain exceptions: for one thing, the government may be able to reprosecute a defendant even when a trial has been dismissed after jeopardy has attached; in certain circumstances, a retrial can occur after a mistrial has been declared (LaFave et al., 1999). For another, the protection only applies to a second prosecution by the same government; consequently, it is not a violation of double jeopardy for a state to prosecute someone for crimes that were at issue in a preceding federal prosecution that produced a judgment of conviction or acquittal (LaFave et al., 1999). Perhaps the most famous instance of this, in recent years, is the state prosecution Oklahoma has brought against Terry Nichols for his role in the bombing of the Oklahoma City Federal Building; Nichols, of course, has already been prosecuted and convicted in a federal proceeding arising out of the same event (Romano, 2004).

Another important constitutional protection is the Sixth Amendment right to speedy trial. The Supreme Court has explained that this right is essential to protect at least three basic demands of justice: "(1) to prevent undue and oppressive incarceration prior to trial, (2) to minimize anxiety and concern accompanying public accusation and (3) to limit the possibilities that long delay will impair the ability of an accused to defend himself" (*Smith v. Hooey*, 1969). Indeed, this right is considered so important that the Sixth Amendment guarantee has been supplemented by statutory and rule-based protections in both the state and federal systems (LaFave et al., 1999).

Basic Defenses

As to defending himself or herself, the substantive criminal law provides an array of theories defendants can use to argue that they should be acquitted of the charges brought against them. Analytically, these defenses fall into two categories: (1) failure of proof defenses and (2) affirmative defenses (LaFave, 2003).

Failure of proof defenses are not "true" defenses; they are merely a way of attacking the prosecution's case. As one scholar explains, a "failure of proof defense is one in which the defendant has introduced evidence at his criminal trial showing that some essential element of the crime charged has not been proved beyond a reasonable doubt" (LaFave, 2003). Because criminal liability requires a voluntary act (*actus reus*) done with the appropriate mental state (*mens rea*), defendants often argue that they cannot be held guilty because they either were not acting voluntarily or, if they were acting voluntarily, did not possess the mental state required for the offense (LaFave, 2003). Assume, for example, that an employee of a company is charged with hacking (i.e., with unauthorized intrusion into an area of the company's computer system); the premise of the charges is that although the employee had authorized access to part of the company's computer system, he exceeded the scope of that authorized access and explored parts of the system that he was not legitimately entitled to access (*United States v. Czubinski*, 1997). Assume, further, that the charge against the employee is that he "knowingly" gained "unauthorized access" to parts of his employer's computer system. The defendant can mount a failure of proof defense by claiming that, although he did exceed the scope of his authorized access to the computer system, he did not do so "knowingly"; he could argue, for example, that he believed he had full access to the entire system because no security measures prevented his exploring parts of the system beyond those he used in the course of his everyday tasks. If the employer did not have policies that made it clear that employees were not to exceed a specifically defined scope of access to the computer system, this failure of proof defense might well work. Predicating a failure of proof defense on the theory that one was not acting voluntarily at the time the offense was committed is much more difficult when computer crimes are involved: generally speaking, claims that one was not acting voluntarily require the defendant to show that he or she was in a state of unconsciousness at the time the offense was committed; such claims rest, for example, on assertions that the defendant was sleepwalking, suffering from an epileptic seizure, or in a fugue state induced, say, by brain trauma or a reaction to medication (LaFave, 2003). Claims such as these can be credible when the offense involves simple acts, such as driving a car; they are hardly likely to be credible when the offense involves complex activity requiring the application of specialized technical knowledge and skills.

Unlike failure of proof defenses, affirmative defenses do not involve attacking the prosecution's ability to prove the elements of its case (LaFave, 2003). One who asserts an affirmative defense is, in effect, saying "yes, but...."; that is, the defendant is saying, in effect, "Yes, I committed the crime but there are valid reasons why I should not be held liable for doing so." The basic affirmative defenses are (a) insanity, (b) self-defense, (c) defense of others, (d) defense of property, (e) duress, and (f) choice of evils (LaFave, 2003). Insanity and duress are "excuse" defenses; one who asserts these affirmative defenses is, in essence, saying "Yes, I committed the crime but I should not be held liable" because (a) I was insane and therefore did not know right from wrong or (b) I was forced to commit the crime by threats or violence from another person (LaFave, 2003). The other four are "justification" defenses; one who asserts these affirmative defenses is, in essence, saying "Yes, I committed the crime but I did the right thing in doing so" because I acted to protect myself, to protect someone else, to protect property or to avoid some harm greater than that resulting from the commission of this crime (LaFave, 2003). Although the prosecution bears the burden of proving every element of the crime beyond a reasonable doubt, the defendant bears the burden of producing evidence that is sufficient to raise a cognizable claim that the affirmative defense applies; a defendant must, for example, produce evidence that supports his or her claim of having acted in self-defense (LaFave, 2003).

Generally speaking, these traditional affirmative defenses tend to have little applicability in cybercrime prosecutions. One who seeks to raise an insanity defense will encounter some of the same logical obstacles as a defendant who tries to argue that he or she was not acting voluntarily at the time the crime was committed; although it might be possible to show, say, that the defendant was acting under the influence of command hallucinations when he or she hacked into NASA, both juries and judges are likely to be skeptical of such claims when the charges involve crimes the commission of which necessarily entails a course of structured, sequenced conduct. The same is true of duress: to qualify for the duress defense, a defendant must show that he or she committed the crime(s) at issue because he was forced to do so by another person, who threatened him with death or serious bodily injury if he did not comply with that person's demands (LaFave, 2003). It is, of course, quite possible that someone could use force or the threat of force to coerce a person with computer skills into hacking into a system, releasing a virus or otherwise violating state or federal cybercrime laws. The likelihood of this happening seems, however, rather remote; the duress defense is often raised when one participant in criminal activity (A) is coerced by another participant in that activity (B) to "go further" than A had intended or desires (LaFave, 2003). It is exceedingly rare for the defense to be raised in an instance of "stranger danger" (i.e., when a stranger forces an otherwise law-abiding citizen to commit a crime by using or threatening force). Because computer crimes tend, so far, to be committed by those who have no history of violent criminal activity, it is unlikely that the duress defense will be successfully asserted in cybercrime prosecutions for the foreseeable future.

It may be somewhat easier to raise a justification defense. Self-defense requires a use of "force" that the defending party deemed was necessary to protect himself or herself from another's use of force, either deadly or nondeadly (LaFave, 2003). Historically, "force" has meant physical force, but there is no reason why we could not expand the concept to encompass "virtual force" (i.e., an assault using computer technology). Even if we did so, however, the assault would have to threaten a human being with death or serious physical injury for the defending party to be able to utilize self-defense as the justification for retaliative actions; an attack focusing solely on a computer system would not suffice as the basis for invoking this defense (LaFave, 2003). In 2001, a Chinese man claimed to have hacked into a computer system in self-defense: he said he hacked into the other system because he thought the operators of that system had attacked his computer (Ying-Cheng, 2001). Even if this gentleman had been correct in that belief, he would not, under U.S. law, have been able to claim self-defense because the attack

was not a personal attack (i.e., was not directed at causing physical harm to him) (LaFave, 2003).

The same would be true if this gentleman had tried to assert the related affirmative defense of defense of others; defense of others requires that one has acted because such action was necessary to prevent another person or other persons from death or physical injury (LaFave, 2003). It is of course conceivable that such a defense could be asserted successfully in the context of a cyberassault: assume, for instance, that during the dead of winter a cyberterrorist is in the process of attacking a computer system that controls electrical power to a midwestern city; if the cyberterrorist succeeds in taking over the system and shutting down power to the city, people will be without light, heat, and other services. Many will die from exposure; others will die from panic, from their inability to gain assistance, from emergency services, and for other reasons. A computer technician discovers that the attack is in progress and knows it will succeed before he would have time to contact the authorities and secure official intervention; if this technician hacks into the cyberterrorist's computer or otherwise takes defensive measures to prevent the attack, he should be able to assert a claim of self-defense in the improbable instance he is charged with hacking into the computer which is the cyberterrorist's target. In this example, the computer technician is using a type of "force," virtual force, to prevent injury to other persons and is, therefore, justified in attacking the cyberterrorist's computer.

This brings us to defense of property; like self-defense and defense of others, defense of property has traditionally required that one use physical force. In this instance, the force is used to preserve one's possession of, or the integrity of, real or personal property (LaFave, 2003). The Chinese gentleman discussed above, who hacked into a computer system because he believed the operators of that system had attacked his system, was really asserting a defense of property theory (Ying-Cheng, 2001). He claimed he had to take affirmative action against those whom he believed were attempting to harm his computer system (Ying-Cheng, 2001). Because he believed he was acting to protect his property from unlawful conduct, he could, subject to the qualifications discussed below, assert a defense of property claim when he was charged with unlawful hacking.

The final justification defense is choice of evils. Choice of evils justifies the commission of a crime when one commits that crime to avoid a harm or evil greater than the harm or evil resulting from the commission of this offense (LaFave, 2003). The choice of evils defense would, for example, be available to one who cut a hole in a dam that was about to burst to prevent the dam from collapsing and flooding a town; the defense is available even if, by cutting the hole in the dam, the actor caused a nearby farm to flood, killing livestock or even a person (LaFave, 2003). As long as the harm sought to be avoided (i.e., flooding the town, which would cause great loss of life and property) is greater than the harm inflicted (i.e., damage to the dam plus the loss of a single life and property damage at the farm), the actor is entitled to the choice of evils defense (LaFave, 2003). This defense could therefore serve as an alternative basis for justifying the actions of the computer technician discussed earlier: the one who frustrated the efforts of the cyberterrorist. His actions could be characterized either as defense of others (if we focus on the threat coming from another person) or as choice of evils (if we focus on the harm to be avoided versus the harm resulting from his hacking into the computer system).

As this discussion of justification defenses should demonstrate, they raise difficult issues of law and policy. When we allow someone to assert a justification defense, we are, in effect, saying that they did the right thing by taking the law into their own hands; because the legal system cannot tolerate people's taking the law into their own hands as a matter of general practice, the law imposes restrictions on the assertion of the justification defenses to ensure that they can be successfully asserted only in truly compelling cases (LaFave, 2003). The restriction that is common to all of the justification defenses is that the actor believed it was "necessary" to, in effect, take the law into his or her own hands (LaFave, 2003). "Necessary" in this context means that there were no viable, lawful alternatives (LaFave, 2003). To use the examples given above, the computer technician who hacked into a computer system to prevent the cyberterrorist's attack from succeeding would no doubt qualify for a justification defense (defense of others or choice of evils) because it seems he had no lawful alternatives; if he had contacted the authorities and asked for their assistance, the attack would have succeeded (LaFave, 2003). Conversely, the Chinese gentleman who hacked a computer system he thought was being used to attack his own system would not qualify for a justification defense because it was not "necessary" for him to take the law into his own hands; he could have gone to the authorities, reported the attacks on his system, and given them the information that led him to believe a particular computer system was being used in the attacks. The authorities could have handled matters from there.

Hack Back Defense

The above discussion of justification defenses logically leads to the issue of vigilante action—what the law calls "self-help"—as a response to cybercrime. Some argue that because the law enforcement response to cybercrime is likely to be ineffective given the limited resources law enforcement has for this purpose plus the fact that many cybercrimes are transnational in nature, it is only reasonable to allow victims of hacking and other computer crimes to "strike back" at the offenders (Loomis, 2001). Those who advocate this approach claim that "you can't reason with attackers and you can't coddle them—the only language they understand is force" (Loomis, 2001). Those who take this position believe that if a victim strikes back at his/her attacker with sufficient force, this will deter that attacker and similarly situated attackers from launching future assaults on the victim's system (Loomis, 2001). This argument has an undeniable visceral appeal, because of the apparent impunity with which many cybercriminals operate. Indeed, it has even led to the introduction of proposed federal legislation that would legitimize self-help against those who engage in criminal copyright violations (H.R. 5211, 2002).

Society, however, cannot tolerate vigilante behavior. This was true in the 19th century, when vigilantes were active in the American West, and it is still true today (Hine, 1998). The drift toward vigilantism as a response to cybercrime is not surprising; vigilantism tends to appear in "frontier" situations (i.e., when law enforcement is ineffective or absent; Hine, 1998). This is, of course, true of cyberspace, which is often analogized to the Wild West. The problem is that although self-help can be a viscerally satisfying approach to one's victimization, it creates more problems than it solves: for one thing, vigilantes commit crimes. In the examples given in the previous section, both the computer technician who is responding to the cyberterrorist's activities and the Chinese gentleman who is responding to the attacks on his system are violating the law by hacking. It is a fundamental premise of every legal system that citizens are not privileged to commit crimes (LaFave et al., 1999). It is true that, as the previous section explained, the law does absolve citizens who take the law into their own hands under certain, very limited, situations; however, this is very different from a blanket authorization for online retaliative behavior. Aside from anything else, such behavior is objectionable because of the risks that innocent parties will be targeted for retaliation; the consequences of this risk are particularly intolerable in cyberspace, where it can be impossible to know precisely from which system an attack was launched (Loomis, 2001). It is to avoid the possibility of harm to an innocent actor that the legal system has developed a complex structure of rules and processes governing the imposition of sanctions upon those who are believed to have committed crimes (LaFave et al., 1999).

Evidentiary Issues

Cybercrime cases present a variety of evidentiary issues, which can be broken down into two categories: (1) the process of gathering evidence and (2) the process of introducing evidence at trial.

The process of gathering evidence differs depending on whether the evidence is located in a stand-alone computer (desktop or laptop) or is on a network. If the evidence is located on a stand-alone computer, the basic principle governing law enforcement's gaining access to the evidence is the Fourth Amendment, which protects citizens from "unreasonable" searches and seizures (LaFave, Israel, & King, 1999). If a seizure is "reasonable," it does not violate the Fourth Amendment (LaFave, Israel, & King, 1999). To be "reasonable," a search or seizure conducted by law enforcement agents must be carried out either under the authority of a search warrant or under one of the exceptions to the warrant requirement, such as consent (LaFave, Israel, & King, 1999). So, assume federal agents are investigating allegations that John Doe has child pornography on his home computer. In scenario 1, they have gathered enough information to establish probable cause to believe there is child pornography on his computer. They take that information to a magistrate—in the form of an application for a search warrant and a sworn affidavit attesting to their probable cause—and obtain a warrant to search for and seize child pornography (LaFave, Israel, & King 1999). They take the warrant to John Doe's house and conduct the search either onsite, at his home, or seize his computer and take it away for an offsite search. In scenario 2, the agents either do not have enough information to establish the probable cause they need to get a warrant or prefer to proceed without a warrant. They approach John Doe and ask him if they can search his computer; if he consents, he waives his Fourth Amendment rights and surrenders his ability to object to the search at a later date (LaFave, Israel, & King, 1999).

The process of gathering evidence is far more complex when the evidence is located on a network or on several networks (Dean, 2003). Continuing the example used above, assume the agents have received information that John Doe is corresponding online with minors whom he sends child pornography and whom he arranges to meet for the purposes of having sexual relations. The agents could proceed as outlined above with regard to evidence located on John Doe's computer, but they also need information about his e-mail contacts with the minors. To learn about that, they need information from Doe's Internet service provider (ISP). Because the Supreme Court has held that the Fourth Amendment does not apply to records held by a third party, the agents are not constitutionally required to get a warrant to obtain the information they need from the Internet service provider (LaFave, Israel, & King, 1999). But because Congress was concerned about unrestricted law enforcement access to records, it adopted a series of statutes—the Electronic Communications Privacy Act of 1986 (ECPA)—which require law enforcement to go through certain procedures to get evidence from an Internet service provider and others who provide electronic communications services (Electronic Communications Privacy Act). Under ECPA, the agents will have to use a search warrant, a subpoena, or a court order to obtain the information they need from the Internet service provider (Dean, 2003). ECPA sets up different requirements for different types of information, but the critical difference between it and the Fourth Amendment is that agents can often use either a subpoena or a court order, neither of which requires probable cause, to get the information they require (Electronic Communications Privacy Act).

The process of introducing electronic evidence, such as that described above, at trial is a very complex one which is quite beyond the scope of this chapter. Generally, for evidence to be admissible at trial it must be (a) relevant, (b) authentic, and (c) reliable (*Daubert v. Merrell Dow Pharmaceuticals, Inc.*, 1993). The issue of relevance is seldom problematic; evidence is "relevant" when it tends to prove the fact for which it is offered (i.e., child pornography was found on John Doe's computer) and when that fact is material to an element in the case (i.e., John Doe is being prosecuted for possessing child pornography; Mueller & Kilpatrick, 2003). Authenticity can be problematic, because digital evidence can be altered easily, the party offering digital evidence must be able to establish that it is what it is claimed to be (U.S. Department of Justice Computer Crime and Intellectual Property Section, 2002). To establish this and rebut defense claims that evidence has been altered, the prosecution will typically establish a chain of custody for the evidence; that is, the prosecution will typically trace the processes that were used to find the evidence and retrieve it from a computer or from a network (U.S. Department of Justice Computer Crime and Intellectual Property Section, 2002). Establishing a chain of custody authenticates digital evidence by showing that it was never left unsecured in conditions that would have permitted its alteration (U.S. Department of Justice Computer Crime and Intellectual Property Section, 2002) Reliability raises similar concerns; the defense may, for example, claim that a computer-generated record that the prosecution is offering as evidence is not reliable because the program used to create it contained serious programming errors (U.S. Department of Justice Computer Crime and Intellectual Property Section, 2002). For the prosecution to overcome such a challenge and establish the reliability of the record in question, it will have to establish that the computer program did, in fact, meet the requisite standard of reliability (U.S. Department of Justice Computer Crime and Intellectual Property Section, 2002).

Sentencing

As explained, sentencing is done by a judge; in imposing sentence, a judge is guided by a set of rules that define either the required sentence or an allowable range of sentences (LaFave et al., 1999). There are four basic rationales for inflicting punishment on offenders: incapacitation (to physically prevent this person from reoffending), deterrence (to discourage this person and others from committing similar crimes), rehabilitation (to educate the person so that he/she no longer desires to commit crimes), and retribution (to retaliate for the harm the offender has caused) (LaFave, 2003). Since the 1980s, sentencing in the federal and state systems has been based on deterrence, retribution, and incapacitation, a reaction against rehabilitation, which had been the primary rationale for sentencing since the 19th century. A new approach began in the 1970s and culminated in the adoption of new sentencing provisions that emphasize the need to deter and incapacitate offenders and society's need for retribution (Vitiello, 1991).

Victims and their families have increasingly been given input into the sentencing process; the federal system and most states either permit or require the use of victim impact statements, which assess a crime's impact on the victim and the victim's family at sentencing (LaFave et al., 1999). This practice extends to cybercrime cases; in the federal system, for example, victims of criminal copyright infringement are statutorily guaranteed the right to submit a victim impact statement documenting their losses prior to sentencing (U.S. Department of Justice Computer Crime and Intellectual Property Section, 2001).

In 2003, three groups submitted a statement to the U.S. Sentencing Commission arguing that those convicted of computer crimes are already being punished more severely than those convicted of similar crimes that do not involve the use of computer technology (National Association of Criminal Defense Lawyers, Electronic Frontier Foundation & Sentencing Project 2003). The statement argued against increasing penalties for federal computer crimes (a) because the incidence of computer crime is low, (b) because loss calculations currently in use lead to disproportionate sentences that do not accurately reflect the offender's culpability, and (c) because harsh penalties can "chill legitimate computer research, business development, and reporting on security vulnerabilities" (National Association of Criminal Defense Lawyers, Electronic Frontier Foundation & Sentencing Project, 2003). The Sentencing Commission ultimately responded by increasing the penalties for certain of the cybercrime offenses defined by federal law (U.S. Sentencing Commission, 2003). The Commission found that the amendments reflected the "serious and risky nature of many computer offenses" (U.S. Sentencing Commission, 2003).

RELATIONSHIP BETWEEN STATE AND FEDERAL CRIMINAL JUSTICE SYSTEMS

The United States has over 50 legal systems, each with its own definitions of "crimes." The federal system traditionally dealt with a limited set of "crimes" that protected special federal interests, such as the integrity of the currency (counterfeiting), the safety of federal officials (assassination), the viability of the taxing scheme (tax fraud), and the nation's security from its enemies (treason and espionage) (American Bar Association, 1998). There has been a tremendous expansion in federal crimes over the past century. The primary basis for this expansion has been the commerce clause of the Constitution, which lets the federal government regulate matters that can negatively affect the country's ability to sustain and engage in interstate or foreign commerce (American Bar Association, 1998). Using this power, the federal system has criminalized hacking and related crimes and has used more generic offenses (such as wire fraud and the interstate transportation of stolen property) to pursue cybercriminals (American Bar Association, 1998).

The federal government's exclusive power to criminalize conduct is limited to a few areas, including those noted above; except for these areas, both the federal and state governments can outlaw certain types of activity (American Bar Association, 1998). The drafters of the Constitution intended that criminal activity be prosecuted primarily at the state level; they saw federal criminal jurisdiction as an exception to this principle that should be carefully restricted in scope (American Bar Association, 1998). Consequently, notwithstanding the expansion in substantive federal criminal law, states still retain primary responsibility for defining and prosecuting criminal activity (American Bar Association, 1998).

Because both the federal and state governments can outlaw certain types of activity, including cybercrime, a defendant can be prosecuted by the federal government and a state government for offenses rising out of the same course of conduct; as noted, prosecutions by separate governments do not violate the prohibition on double jeopardy (LaFave et al., 1999). To prevent unfairness, the Department of Justice has adopted a policy—known as the *Petite* policy—which bars federal prosecution after a state prosecution unless certain conditions are met (LaFave et al., 1999). Basically, a subsequent federal prosecution will be barred unless the case involves a substantial federal interest that was not vindicated in the prior prosecution and unless an assistant attorney general approves the prosecution (LaFave et al., 1999).

CRIMINAL JUSTICE SYSTEM AND CYBERCRIME
Federal Cybercrime Law

The basic federal cybercrime statute is 18 U.S. Code §1030. Section 1030(a) makes it a federal offense to (1) knowingly access a computer without authorization and obtain information that can be used to the disadvantage of the United States and deliver it to someone not entitled to it; (2) intentionally access a computer without authorization and obtain information contained in a financial record; (3) intentionally and without authorization access a computer used exclusively by a federal agency; (4) knowingly with the intent to defraud access a computer without authorization and obtain anything of value unless the thing obtained is only the use of the computer and does not exceed $5,000 in any 1-year period; (5) *either* (a) knowingly cause a program, information, or code to be transmitted and intentionally damage a computer, intentionally access a computer without authorization and recklessly cause damage, *or* intentionally access a computer without authorization and cause damage *and* (b) cause or attempt to cause physical injury, modification of a medical diagnosis, loss aggregating $5,000 in 1 year, a threat to public health or safety or damage to a computer used in furtherance of the administration of justice, national security, or national defense; (6) knowingly and with intent to defraud traffic in a password if the trafficking affects interstate commerce or the password can be used to access a federal government computer; and (7) transmit a threat to damage a computer with the intent to extort any thing of value.

Another important area is copyright law; copyright gives the author of a creative work the exclusive right to control its use for a fixed period of time (U.S. Department of Justice Computer Crime and Intellectual Property Section, 2001). Copyright derives from the Constitution and is therefore exclusively federal (U.S. Department of Justice Computer Crime and Intellectual Property Section, 2001). It is a crime for someone willfully to infringe a copyright for purposes of commercial advantage or private financial gain or by reproducing or distributing one or more copies of one or more copyrighted works having a total retail value in excess of $1,000 during any 180-day period (U.S. Department of Justice Computer Crime and Intellectual Property Section, 2001).

Child pornography is another priority: federal law has long criminalized obscenity, which is considered to be outside the First Amendment's protection of free speech; in 1982, the Supreme Court held that pornography portraying minors engaging in sexually explicit activity can be criminalized even though it is not obscene (*New York v. Ferber*, 1982). The *Ferber* Court held that child pornography can be criminalized because its production inflicts physical and emotional abuse on the children involved. In 2002, the Supreme Court struck down a federal statute—18 U.S. Code §2252A—that criminalized the possession and distribution of "virtual" child pornography (i.e., pornography created using morphed or other artificial images of children) (*Ashcroft v. Free Speech Coalition*, 2002). The Court found that the statute violated the First Amendment because (a) the material was not obscene and (b) no real children were harmed in its creation (*Ashcroft v. Free Speech Coalition*, 2002). Congress has since adopted legislation reinstituting the ban on virtual child pornography; its constitutionality is uncertain (Feldmeier, 2003).

State Cybercrime Law

Every state prohibits hacking (unauthorized access to a computer system) and cracking (unauthorized access to commit theft, damage, or other offenses) (Brenner, 2001). States tend to distinguish between basic unauthorized access (simple hacking) and unauthorized access that results in the commission of some further criminal activity, such as copying or destroying data (aggravated hacking), defining the two as distinct crimes (Brenner, 2001). They generally make simple hacking a misdemeanor and aggravated hacking a felony (Brenner, 2001).

A number of states outlaw the dissemination of viruses, worms, and other types of malware (Brenner, 2001). Many lump varieties of malware into one category: "computer contaminant" (Brenner, 2001). California, for example, defines it as "any set of computer instructions that are designed to modify, damage, destroy, record, or transmit information within a computer, computer system, or computer network without the intent or permission of the owner of the information" (California Penal Code, 2003).

States vary widely in how they criminalize the use of computers to commit traditional crimes, such as theft and forgery (Brenner, 2001). Some states outlaw computer forgery as a distinct offense. New Jersey makes it a crime to possess "forgery devices," which include computers, computer equipment, and computer software "specifically designed or adapted to such use" (Brenner, 2001). A substantial number outlaw using computers to commit fraud. Instead of making computer fraud a separate crime, a few states increase the penalties for aggravated hacking if the offense was committed for the purpose of devising or executing a scheme to defraud (Brenner, 2001). Many states outlaw "computer theft," which encompasses several different crimes, including information theft, software theft, computer hardware theft, and theft of computer services (Brenner, 2001). A number of states have "identity theft" or "identity fraud" statutes and some make it a crime to traffic in stolen identities (Brenner, 2001).

Cyberstalking is using computer technology to stalk or harass someone. A number of states outlaw cyberstalking (Brenner, 2001). Some criminalize "computer invasion of privacy," which typically consists of using a computer to examine "employment, salary, credit or any other financial or personal information" pertaining to another person (Brenner, 2001). A few make it a crime to introduce false information into a computer for the purpose of "damaging or enhancing" someone's "financial reputation" (Brenner, 2001). Some states have a "misuse of computer information" offense that prohibits copying, receiving, or using information that was obtained by violating a hacking or cracking statute (Brenner, 2001).

A surprising number of states have an "offense against computer equipment or supplies," which consists of modifying or destroying "equipment or supplies that are ... intended to be used in a computer" (Brenner, 2001). A number make it a crime to deny or disrupt computer services or access to a computer and a few make it a crime to destroy computer equipment (Brenner, 2001).

Defenses

As explained, defendants in cybercrime cases can avail themselves of traditional "failure of proof" and "affirmative defenses" to the extent the facts of the case support the assertion of such a claim. This means, for example, that one who has been charged with hacking can defend on the basis that (a) his access to the computer in question was authorized, (b) he did not know his access to the computer in question was not authorized, or (c) he knew his access to the computer in question was not authorized but believed his hacking was justified.

Cybercrime defendants also raise less traditional defenses, two of which merit discussion here. One involves the nature of theft: in an Oregon case, a defendant was charged with computer theft for copying a password file belonging to Intel, his employer; he challenged the legal sufficiency of the charge, claiming that *copying* the file did not constitute *stealing* the file (*State v. Schwartz*, 2001). He pointed out that the essence of "theft" is depriving the rightful owner of property of its possession and use and argued that because Intel still had the file he had not deprived Intel of its property (*State v. Schwartz*, 2001). The court disagreed, holding that he did commit theft, albeit theft of intangible property (*State v. Schwartz*, 2001). This argument illustrates how computer technology can challenge the assumptions that have historically animated criminal law; with intangible property, theft ceases to be a zero-sum event. Therefore, instead of drafting theft statutes to reach a deprivation of tangible property, it becomes necessary to utilize a diminution theory (i.e., that the defendant deprived the rightful owner of some quantum of the value of his property, such as the right to its exclusive use).

Another approach is the Trojan horse defense, which as been notably successful in the United Kingdom. In 2003, Aaron Caffrey, a 19-year-old British hacker, was prosecuted for launching a denial of service attack that shut down computer systems at the Port of Houston (Questions cloud cybercrime cases, 2003). His defense was that a hacker had used a Trojan horse program to take over his computer and launch the attack. Even though experts found no trace of a Trojan on the computer, a jury acquitted Caffrey of the charges against him (Questions cloud cybercrime cases, 2003). The same theory was used successfully in several child pornography prosecutions in the United Kingdom (Bean, 2003). An American accountant was acquitted of charges of filing false tax returns because he convinced the jury that a computer virus was responsible for the errors on the returns (Auditor acquitted, 2003). These cases raise a difficult issue for prosecutors: how is it possible to prove beyond a reasonable doubt that no Trojan horse or virus was responsible for the crime charged? Some argue that the solution lies in scanning the computer to determine if it contains a Trojan horse or other type of malware; if it does, then it would be necessary to determine if the malware could do what it is claimed to have done (The Trojan horse defense in child pornography, 2003). If the computer does not contain malware capable of having committed the crime, so the argument goes, then the jury should convict (The Trojan horse defense in child pornography, 2003). Of course, Aaron Caffrey was acquitted even though experts found no trace of a Trojan on his computer. The Trojan horse and related defenses illustrate the difficulties that can be involved in presenting highly technical evidence to a lay jury; some have suggested that the solution lies in bench trials, but because of the Sixth Amendment, that option remains solely with the defendant ("Trust me, I'm an IT expert," 2003).

Other Problematic Areas

Clearly, the most challenging aspect of cybercrime as far as law enforcement is concerned is its pronounced tendency to cross borders, especially national borders (Brenner & Schwerha, 2002). Law is territorially based, whether it is national or the law adopted by a component state in a federal system like the United States (Brenner & Schwerha, 2002). Cybercrime's ability to transcend national borders created problems for cybercrime investigators and prosecutors.

There are two ways to obtain evidence from another country. One is informal cooperation; the other is relying on the formal mechanisms that have traditionally been used to gather evidence (Brenner & Schwerha, 2002). A 1994 case illustrates informal cooperation: in 1994, system administrators at the Rome Air Development Center in New York found hackers had installed password sniffers on the Rome Labs networks (Brenner & Schwerha, 2002). The Air Force's Office of Special Investigations (AFOSI) used informants to identify one of the hackers, a 16-year-old from the United Kingdom (Brenner & Schwerha, 2002). Having established a relationship with New Scotland Yard, AFOSI agents contacted them (Brenner & Schwerha, 2002). Working together, AFOSI and New Scotland Yard developed probable cause to believe evidence of the intrusions would be found at the juvenile's home; New Scotland Yard used this information to get a warrant to search his residence (Brenner & Schwerha, 2002). They executed the warrant and seized incriminating evidence; Pryce was prosecuted and eventually pled guilty to 12 counts of hacking (Brenner & Schwerha, 2002).

Traditionally, informal cooperation depended on networking; few local police officers had the opportunity to network with officers from abroad (Brenner & Schwerha, 2002). In cybercrime cases, officers who have never had the opportunity to network with officers from other countries may find they need assistance from abroad. To meet this need, two entities—Interpol and the G8—have established 24 networks officers can use to obtain assistance from officers in other countries (Brenner & Schwerha, 2002). These networks qualify as informal cooperation because they bypass the processes discussed below (Brenner & Schwerha, 2002). As is explained below, informal cooperation is usually the most expeditious way to proceed.

The basic formal devices are requests for assistance submitted under mutual legal assistance treaties (MLATs) and letters rogatory (Brenner & Schwerha, 2002). An investigator's first step is determining if an MLAT encompassing the evidence to be sought is in effect between the United States and the country where the evidence is located. Using an MLAT is much faster than the letter rogatory procedure (U.S. Department of Justice, 1999). If an MLAT is in effect, the investigator must prepare a request for assistance pursuant to the treaty; it contains essentially the same information as that used for a letter rogatory, which is described below, except for the promise of reciprocity (U.S. Department of Justice, 1999). If an MLAT is not in effect, the investigator will have to resort to the letter rogatory process.

A letter rogatory is a request from a U.S. judge to a judge in another country requesting the performance of acts that would be illegal without local judicial approval (U.S. Department of Justice, 1999). The investigator must complete the letter rogatory and have it transmitted to authorities in the country from which assistance is being sought (U.S. Department of Justice, 1999). Letters rogatory are usually transmitted through diplomatic channels, which is one reason why they are such a time-consuming method of obtaining assistance; the Department of Justice warns federal prosecutors it may take a year or more to obtain assistance through a letter rogatory (U.S. Department of Justice, 1999).

Formal methods of obtaining evidence are far too time consuming to be effective in cybercrime cases, and informal methods, even when supplemented by the efforts of Interpol and the G8, can be unreliable (U.S. Department of Justice, 1999). This is part of a larger problem, namely that the laws of varying nations are inconsistent.

That was the problem in investigating the Love Bug virus, which spread around the world in May 2000 (Brenner & Schwerha, 2002). U.S. experts traced the virus to the Philippines; when FBI agents arrived there, they worked with local authorities to investigate Onel de Guzman, the primary suspect. Informal cooperation between the officers worked splendidly; the problem came with the Philippine legal system (Brenner & Schwerha, 2002). At that time, the Philippines criminal code did not criminalize hacking or the dissemination of viruses; laws to that effect were enacted after this incident. This presented several problems: investigators had difficulty getting a warrant to search de Guzman's apartment because warrants authorize searches for evidence of "crimes" and virus dissemination was not then a crime (Brenner & Schwerha, 2002). The officers eventually got the warrant and conducted the search, but then they had to decide what to charge de Guzman with. He was charged with fraud and theft, but the charges were dismissed (Brenner & Schwerha, 2002). Because de Guzman could not be prosecuted locally, he could not be extradited for prosecution elsewhere; no one was ever prosecuted for the damage caused by the Love Bug (Brenner & Schwerha, 2002).

Many believe the only way to achieve an internationally effective response to cybercrime is to harmonize national laws so they are consistent in how they (a) define cybercrime offenses and (b) specify what law enforcement officers can and cannot do in gathering evidence in cybercrime investigations (Brenner & Schwerha, 2002). So far, the most notable achievement in this effort is the Council of Europe's Convention on Cybercrime. Parties to the Convention, which is not limited to European nations, agree to take such "legislative or other measures" as are necessary to outlaw certain types of computer-facilitated criminal activity (Brenner & Schwerha, 2002). They also agree to take similar measures to ensure that they can preserve and collect evidence and provide assistance in cybercrime investigations even when no MLAT is in force between the requesting country and the requested country (Brenner & Schwerha, 2002). So far, 34 countries, including the United States, Canada, and Japan, have signed the Convention (Brenner & Schwerha, 2002). It goes into effect when it has been ratified by 5 countries, 3 of which are members of the Council of Europe; it has been ratified by 3 countries, all of which are members of the Council of Europe (Brenner & Schwerha, 2002).

CONCLUSION

Cybercrime presents challenges not only for the U.S. legal system: because cybercrime so easily and so often transcends national borders, cybercriminals can take advantage of gaps or inconsistencies in national law in an effort to evade apprehension and/or prosecution. It will not be easy to resolve the challenges cybercrime presents for the criminal justice system, here and abroad. As this chapter demonstrates, cybercrime requires the extrapolation of legal principles that were developed to deal with activity occurring in the real, tangible world; it will also, no doubt, require the articulation of new principles that are especially designed to deal with the novel ways criminal activity can manifest itself in the online world.

GLOSSARY

Affirmative Defense A legal doctrine that lets a defendant avoid liability even though he or she committed a crime; self-defense is an example.
Bench Trial A trial in which the judge, not a jury, acts as the finder of fact; in a bench trial the judge decides whether the defendant is guilty or innocent.
Beyond a Reasonable Doubt The standard of proof in criminal trials; the prosecution must prove beyond a reasonable doubt that the defendant committed the crime(s) charged; if the prosecution fails the finder of fact must acquit the defendant.
Computer Virus Computer program code that copies itself and spreads by attaching itself to a another computer program; a virus can alter or delete data or interfere with the operation of a computer.
Council of Europe Created in 1949, the Council of Europe brings together 45 European countries; among other things, the Council works to standardize social and legal practices across its member countries.
Cyberstalking The use of a computer and the Internet to stalk or harass someone, often by sending them harassing e-mails.
Double Jeopardy A constitutional prohibition that bars a government from trying someone more than once for the "same offence."
G-8 The major industrial democracies (the United States, Britain, Germany, France, Japan, Italy, Canada, and Russia) have joined together to address the political and economic issues they all face; officials from the member countries meet periodically to discuss these issues and formulate policies.

Hacking Gaining access to a computer or computer system without authorization; hacking is analogous to trespassing in the real world.
Intellectual Property In most countries, laws give the creators of intangible products—such as books, movies, and software—property rights in those products; the property rights can be sold or licensed, but they have the same legal status as ownership of tangible property, such as a house or a car.
Intellectual Property Crime In most countries, it is a crime to take someone's intellectual property without their permission or to use intellectual property in a way that is not authorized by the owner.
Interpol Interpol is an international police organization that was created in 1923; it is financed by its 181 member countries and coordinates law enforcement efforts around the world.
Jury Trial A trial in which a group of civilians, usually twelve in number, act as the finder of fact; in a jury trial these jurors decide whether the defendant is guilty or innocent.
Plea Bargain An arrangement in which a defendant pleads guilty, usually to a crime of lesser severity than that charged in the indictment; typically, plea bargains include a requirement that the defendant cooperate with the government by providing evidence against others.
Preponderance of the Evidence The standard of proof in civil trials; in civil trials, the plaintiff must present proof that establishes that her case is "more likely than not" to be true.
Sentencing Guidelines Rules adopted in the federal system and in most states that guide what judges can do in sentencing someone for an offense; they tend to require that a judge impose a specific sentence, based on various factors, instead of setting a range of time someone must serve.
Victim Impact Statement A statement submitted as part of the sentencing process; it is designed to show how the crime impacted on the victim's life and, where appropriate, on the victim's family.

CROSS REFERENCES

See *Cyberlaw: The Major Areas, Development, and Information Security Aspects; Cyberterrorism and Information Security; Law Enforcement and Computer Security Threats and Measures; Online Stalking; Privacy Law and the Internet.*

REFERENCES

American Bar Association. (2003). *Model rules of professional conduct*. Washington, DC: American Bar Association.
American Bar Association Task Force. (1998). *The federalization of criminal law*. Washington, DC: American Bar Association.
Ashcroft v. Free Speech Coalition. 535 U.S. 234. (2002).
Auditor Acquitted. (2003). *Computer cops*. Retrieved December 18, 2003, from http://www.computercops.biz/article2946.html

Bean, M. (2003). The Trojan horse: A viral defense? Retrieved December 18, 2003, from http://www.cnn.com/2003/LAW/08/12/ctv.trojan/

Beauprez, J. (2003, November 3). New rules cut hackers less slack. *Denver Post*. E01

Brenner, S. W. (2001). State cybercrime legislation in the United States of America: A survey. *Richmond Journal of Law & Technology, 7*, 28–36.

Brenner, S. W., & Schwerha, J. J., IV (2002). Transnational evidence gathering and local prosecution of international cybercrime. *John Marshall Journal of Computer and Information Law, 20*, 347–394.

California Penal Code. §502(b)(1). (2003).

Daubert v. Merrell Dow Pharmaceuticals, Inc. 509 U.S. 579. (1993).

Dean, S. W. (2003). Government surveillance of Internet communications: Pen register and trap and trace law under the Patriot Act. *Tulane Journal of Technology and Intellectual Property, 5*, 97–113.

Ditzion, R., Geddes, E., & Rhodes, M. (2003). Computer crimes. *American Criminal Law Review, 40*, 285–336.

Electronic Communications Privacy Act, Pub. L. No. 99-508, 100 Stat. 1848. (1986).

Esbenshade, P. W. (2002–2003). Hacking: Juveniles and undeterred recreational cybercrime. *Journal of Juvenile Law, 23*, 52–64.

Federal Bureau of Investigation, Infragard, http://www.infragard.net/.

Feldmeier, J. P. (2003). Close enough for government work: An examination of congressional efforts to reduce the government's burden of proof in child pornography cases. *Northern Kentucky Law Review, 30*, 205–227.

Goldman, A. (1995, July 2). Computer hacker agrees to plea bargain, lawyer says. *Los Angeles Times B3*.

Hans, V. P. (2002). U.S. jury reform: The active jury and the adversarial ideal. *St. Louis University Public Law Review, 21*, 85–96.

Hine, K. D. (1998). Vigilantism revisited: An economic analysis of the law of extra-judicial self-help. *American University Law Review, 47*, 1221–1253.

H.R. 5211. (2002). A Bill to Amend Title 17 of the U.S. Code (107th Congress, 2d Session).

Kahn, M. A. (2004). May the best merchandise win: The law of non-trademark uses of sports logos. *Marquette Sports Law Review, 14*, 283–317.

LaFave, W. R. (2003). *Substantive criminal law*. St. Paul, MN: West Group.

LaFave, W. R., Israel, J. H., & King, N. J. (1999). *Criminal procedure*. St. Paul, MN: West Group.

Loomis, C. (2001). Appropriate response: More questions than answers. Retrieved December 16, 2003, http://www.securityfocus.com/infocus/1516

Miami Electronic Crimes Task Force. (2003). Retrieved December 10, 2003, from http://www.facci.org/usss_ectf.htm

Mueller, C. B., & Kilpatrick, L. C. (2003). Federal evidence.

National Association of Attorneys General—Computer Crime. Retrieved December 12, 2003, from http://www.naag.org/issues/20010724-cc_list_bg.php

National Association of Criminal Defense Lawyers, Electronic Frontier Foundation & Sentencing Project.

(2003). Commentary on Homeland Security Act of 2002. Retrieved December 18, 2003, http://www.eff.org/Legislation/CFAA/1030_Comments_3-17-03.pdf

New York v. Ferber 458 U.S. 747. (1982).

Nicholson, L., Shebar, T., & Weinberg, J. (2000). Computer Crimes, *American Criminal Law Review, 37*, 207–259.

Questions cloud cybercrime cases. (2003). BBC News. Retrieved December 18, 2003, from http://news.bbc.co.uk/1/hi/technology/3202116.stm

Reuters Wired News. (2003). Helpful hacker will surrender. Retrieved December 12, 2003, from http://www.wired.com/news/privacy/0,1848,60334,00.html

Right to jury trial. (2003). *Georgetown Law Journal, 91*, 489–512.

Roberts, P. (2003). Homeless hacker heads to court. PC World.com. Retrieved December 11, 2003, from http://www.pcworld.com/news/article/0,aid,112442,00.asp

Romano, L. (2004, February 29). New Trial of 1995 Oklahoma Bombing to Open. Washington Post A15.

Smith v. Hooey 393 U.S. 374. (1969).

State v. Perry 83 Ohio St.3d 41, 697 N.E.2d 624. (Ohio 1998).

State v. Schwartz 173 Or. App. 301, 21 P.3d 1128 (Or. App.). (2001).

The Trojan horse defense in child pornography. (2003). NewsMax.com. Retrieved December 18, 2003, from http://www.newsmax.com/archives/articles/2003/8/12/204345.shtml

Trust me, I'm an IT expert. (2003). Silicon.com. Retrieved December 18, 2003, from http://www.silicon.com/comment/0,39024711,10006460,00.htm

United States Constitution, Amendment IV.

U.S. Department of Justice. (1999). U.S. Attorney's Manual. Retrieved December 17, 2003, from http://www.usdoj.gov/usao/eousa/foia_reading_room/usam/title9/1mcrm.htm

U.S. Department of Justice Computer Crime and Intellectual Property Section. (2001). Prosecuting intellectual property crimes manual. Retrieved December 10, 2003, http://www.cybercrime.gov/ipmanual.htm

U.S. Department of Justice Computer Crime and Intellectual Property Section. (2002). Searching and Seizing Computers and Obtaining Electronic Evidence in Criminal Investigations. Retrieved from http://www.cybercrime.gov/s&smanual2002.htm

U.S. Sentencing Commission. (2003). Increased penalties for cyber security offenses. Retrieved December 18, 2003, from http://www.ussc.gov/r_congress/cybercrime503.pdf

United States v. Czubinski 106 F.3d 1069 (1st Circuit). (1997).

United States v. Hicks 46 F.3d 1128 (4th Circuit). (1995).

United States Secret Service. (2004). Electronic crime task forces. Retrieved March 18, 2005, from http://www.ectaskforce.org/Regional_Locations.htm

Universal City Studios, Inc. v. Corley 273 F.3d 429 (2d Circuit 2001). (2001).

Vitiello, M. (1991). Reconsidering rehabilitation. *Tulane Law Review, 65*, 1011–1054.

Ying-Cheng, J. (2001, February 21). Man pleads "self-defense" after hacking. *Taipei Times*.

Cyberterrorism and Information Security

Charles Jaeger, *Southern Oregon University*

INTRODUCTION

In the past several years, the world has come face to face with terrorists who are becoming more extreme. At the same time, the world has become increasingly dependent on using computers and networks to manage the way we work, communicate, and live. Terrorism, used throughout human history in one form or another, has found a powerful new weapon.

Although most terrorist organizations remain either national or regional, cyberspace gives them tools to become global in reach and coordination. A cyberattacked nuclear power plant meltdown, a massive air traffic control shutdown, a dam spillway opened to flood downstream cities, or other cyber-based terrorist acts could entail even greater loss of life than the September 11, 2001, attacks. Cyberterrorists—an unknown, unseen enemy who strike from anywhere, anytime, and disappear like a vapor trail and is difficult to trace and bring to justice, with devastation potentially as destructive as poison gas, deadly diseases, truckloads of explosives, and atomic radiation—may evoke even more dread and terror than the conventional terrorist.

This chapter asks whether it is reasonable to conclude that global terrorism and cyberspace will converge in this deadly intersection. It attempts to present a balanced view of what constitutes cyberterrorism and the extent of the threat. It addresses how cyberattacks are possible on physical infrastructure or other vital facilities and explores the support role of cyberspace in conventional terrorism. It discusses how government, businesses, institutions, schools and universities, private interest groups, and individuals can each play a role in combating cyberterrorism.

Academic research on cyberterrorism is in its early stages. In the fast-moving world of cyberspace, formal research lags behind current events. Information sources for this chapter include scholarly journals and survey data where available, with up-to-date information from news reports and government or institutional Web sites.

The chapter begins by introducing potential terrorist acts and assessing sometimes confusing levels of threat. It asks whether fears of cyberterrorism are exaggerated and proceeds to formulate working definitions of cyberterrorism, which set a foundation for discussing how terrorism in cyberspace occurs and its relationships to asymmetric response and cyberwarfare. It follows this by showing some of the things individuals, companies, organizations, and government can do and how they can work together to help control the cyberterrorism threat.

The Cyberterrorism Threat

On August 14, 2003, 50 million people in the northeastern United States lost electrical power—the biggest electrical blackout in U.S. history—including the core of America's financial network. Police responded to 80,000 emergency (911) calls on September 11, 2005 (9/11), more than double the usual number, and firefighters made more than 800 elevator rescues (Kaplan, 2003). Some in the media speculated that Al Qaeda and other terrorists were beginning a wave of cyberattacks to disable the country's physical infrastructure; 50 million victims would be a big story. It played on conspiracy theory in a post-9/11 world.

On September 14, 2004, an air traffic blackout in the Los Angeles Air Route Traffic Control Center created chaos in much of the western United States, including reported near misses and "almost near-mid-air collisions . . . as helpless controllers watched in disbelief" (Associated Press, 2004). Communication was lost with some 800 airplanes in flight (Wald, 2004). Could cyberterrorists be on the attack?

Responsible news organizations soon ruled out terrorism in both cases. The electrical blackout was attributed to faulty tree trimming and vulnerable design deficiencies in an aging grid infrastructure (Reuters, 2003). The air traffic problems resulted from neglected computer maintenance. In the long term, however, these incidents make people think: Was there a reasonable basis for concern that terrorists could compromise the power grid or other vital physical infrastructure through cyberattacks? Could they do something even worse?

Acts That May Be Cyberterrorism

In 1996, Barry C. Collin, who takes credit for coining the term *cyberterrorism* in the mid-1980s, wrote, "This enemy does not attack us with truckloads of explosives, nor with briefcases of Sarin gas, nor with dynamite strapped to the bodies of fanatics. This enemy attacks us with ones and zeros." He listed some potentially deadly acts of the cyberterrorist:

• Remotely changing the pressure in gas lines, causing valve failures, explosion, and fire.
• Placing computerized bombs around a city, all simultaneously transmitting unique numeric patterns, each bomb receiving each other's pattern. If any of the set of bombs stops transmitting, all the others detonate simultaneously, which effectively prevents disarming any of the bombs.
• Attacking future air traffic control systems to cause civilian jets to collide.

Cyberterrorists might open a dam's spillway to inundate downstream communities or cause a meltdown of a nuclear power plant. They might cause trains to crash into each other. These "ones and zeros" attacks, Collin said, could have violent and fearful physical effects equally or more devastating than those caused by truckloads of explosives, dynamite, or poison.

Collin included several acts in cyberspace that do *not* have devastating physical effects on a large scale but clearly have the potential to create widespread chaos and fear in offices, homes, and on the streets:

• Remotely accessing the processing control systems of a cereal manufacturer to alter the formula and sicken children.
• Disrupting banks and international financial institutions and stock exchanges, with resulting loss of confidence in the economic system.
• Remotely altering formulas of medication at pharmaceutical manufacturers, resulting in ineffective or potentially harmful medications.
• Shutting down the electrical grid, causing widespread chaos.

"In effect," Collin (1996) concluded, "the cyber-terrorist will make certain that the population of a nation will not be able to eat, to drink, to move, or to live. In addition, the people charged with the protection of their nation will not have warning, and will not be able to shut down the

terrorist, since that cyber-terrorist is most likely on the other side of the world."

In 1998, Michael Vatis, director of the National Infrastructure Protection Center (NIPC), reportedly told a Senate subcommittee, "Tracing cyber-attacks is like 'tracking vapor'" (Christensen, 1999). Unknown and unseen, an enemy difficult to bring to justice connotes a lack of control that may make people more fearful.

Parks (2003) notes that attacks need not be confined to critical infrastructure, offering the example that a hacker could change the composition of vitamins at manufacture to include increasing an ingredient to a lethal level, and asks, "What if the cyber-terrorists were able to...attack...several hundreds of common products at the same time?"

Haimes (2002) separates cyberterrorism risks into three categories: (a) risk to critical cyberphysical infrastructure; (b) risk to organizational/societal infrastructures; and (c) risk to human lives and to individual property, liberty, and freedom. Physical infrastructure includes "manmade engineered systems that include telecommunications, electric power, gas and oil, transportation, water treatment plants, water distribution networks, dams, and levees." Threats include a list of potentially crippling adverse effects on society and loss of confidence in government institutions that could create chaos.

Other Warnings about Cyberterrorism

These warnings raise questions about our vulnerability to cyberterrorism. Fears were heightened by the September 11, 2001, attacks. In December 2001, a Luntz Research survey reported that 74% of Americans were concerned that a cyberattack could target critical infrastructure assets such as telephone networks or power plants. Harris Miller, president of the Information Technology Association of America (ITAA) said, "The attacks of Sept. 11...destroyed peace of mind for many people using the Internet [and] is generating high anxiety in cyberspace" (Greenspan, 2002a; CyberAtlas, 2001).

In June 2002, the *Washington Post* published an article titled "Cyber-attacks by Al Qaeda Feared, Terrorists at the Threshold of Using Internet as Tool of Bloodshed." It reported that the FBI, working with experts at the Lawrence Livermore National Laboratory, had been tracing a "suspicious pattern of surveillance against Silicon Valley computers by unknown browsers," mostly emanating from the Middle East and South Asia, targeting digital systems used to manage Bay Area utilities and other physical infrastructure. "Routed through telecommunications switches in Saudi Arabia, Indonesia and Pakistan, the visitors studied emergency telephone systems, electrical generation and transmission, water storage and distribution, nuclear power plants and gas facilities." The article said that additional information turned up on computers seized from Al Qaeda and on sympathetic Web sites. Roger Cressey, then chief of staff of the President's Critical Infrastructure Protection Board reportedly said, "Al Qaeda spent more time mapping our vulnerabilities in cyberspace than we previously thought. An attack is a question of when, not if" (Gellman, 2002).

The same article reported that in 1998 a 12-year-old hacker had taken "complete command" of Arizona's Roosevelt Dam and the system controlling floodgates holding back 489 trillion gallons of water, enough to flood Phoenix, Mesa, and Tempe (accurate facts are given later in this chapter). In a separate incident in the early 1990s, a man reportedly had "turned his vehicle into a pirate command center" for the sewage treatment center in Queensland, Australia, and used the digital controls to release thousands of gallons of sewage into parks and streams. Manuals for the digital control systems, the article said, were available on the Web, and "nearly identical systems run [U.S.] oil and gas utilities and many manufacturing plants." The North American power grid, described as "the most complex machine ever built," was identified as a potential target.

In October 2001, Richard Clarke, then White House security advisor and chairman of President Bush's Critical Infrastructure Protection Board, had claimed that cyberattacks on the nation's critical information technology infrastructure could cause "catastrophic damage to the economy" akin to the "functional equivalent of 767's crashing into buildings" (Johnson & Radcliff, 2001). In February 2002, testifying to the U.S. Senate, Clarke had warned, "Every sector of the U.S. economy and government has moved onto network systems...and nothing can operate unless the networks are functioning correctly. However, none of these things were designed with 'security in mind'" (Wynne, 2002).

In July 2002, the U.S. Naval War College and Gartner had carried out a "digital Pearl Harbor" war game to test the vulnerability of the U.S. infrastructure to a cyberterrorist attack. In a postgame survey, 79% of the participants said that a strategic cyberattack is likely within the next 2 years (Gartner, 2002).

Clarke had used the term *digital Pearl Harbor* in 1997 during operation "Eligible Receiver," a military exercise in which 35 hackers hired by the National Security Agency simulated attacks on the U.S electronic infrastructure and reportedly achieved "root-level" access in 36 of the Department of Defense's 40,000 networks, "turned off" sections of the U.S. power grid, "shut down" parts of the 9-1-1 emergency response network in Washington, DC, and other cities, and broke into computer systems aboard a Navy cruiser at sea (Christensen, 1999).

At the National Cyber Security Summit in December 2003, Secretary Tom Ridge of the Department of Homeland Security (DHS) cautioned, "A vast electronic nervous system operates much of our nation's physical infrastructure. Everything from electricity grids to banking transactions to telecommunications depends on secure, reliable cyber networks. These networks and the infrastructures they support present an attractive target for terrorists. They know, as we do, that a few lines of code could ultimately wreak as much havoc as a handful of bombs" (CERT, 2003b).

A leading journal reported a finding by the Center for Strategic & International Studies that "all it would take to decimate the technological infrastructure of the U.S. economy is fewer than 30 computer hackers strategically placed around the world and a budget of less than $10 million." It noted that research firm IDC estimated "there are 1.3 million people worldwide who possess the skills needed to launch a cyber attack" (*Information Management Journal*, 2002b).

This background, Collin's warnings, and incidents such as the electrical grid failure in 2002 and the shutdown of the air traffic control in 2004 raise questions about our vulnerability to cyberterrorism. But a media hungry for attention, agencies seeking increased budgets, and security products vendors all have something to gain. Other voices question whether the cyberterrorism threat is exaggerated.

Exaggerated Threats?

In an overview of the cyberterrorism threat, Lemos (2002) investigated facts surrounding the *Washington Post* story about the 12-year-old hacker who allegedly had control of Arizona's Roosevelt Dam and its 489 trillion gallons of water. Lemos reported that the hacker was 27, not 12, and the incident occurred in 1994, not 1998. Furthermore, "While clearly trespassing in critical areas, the hacker never could have had control of any dams—leading investigators to conclude that no lives or property were ever threatened." The Australian incident, it turns out, involved a former employee with access to a stolen copy of the control software.

Lemos (2002) notes that experts agree that it is easier to bomb a target than hack into a control system, and the results are more dramatic. He points out that the Digital Pearl Harbor exercise team determined that a successful effort would need significant resources—$200 million, high-level intelligence, and 5 years of preparation time—and may not result in enough high-value devastation. Those same participants who predicted a likely strategic cyberattack within the next 2 years finally concluded that "such an offense could cripple communications in a heavily populated area but would not result in deaths or other catastrophic consequences."

Denning (2001) supports that logic. "Although cyber terrorism is certainly a real possibility, for a terrorist, digital attacks have several drawbacks. Systems are complex, so controlling an attack and achieving a desired level of damage may be harder than using physical weapons. Unless people are killed or badly injured, there is also less drama and emotional appeal."

Lemos (2002) concludes that cyberterrorism "has become a catch-all buzzword that evokes nightmare images that can be exploited to support political agendas," including increased police power and funding for government departments and programs. He adds, "While warnings pervade government and the media, doomsday scenarios of cyberterrorism that result in massive deaths or injury remain largely the stuff of Hollywood scripts or conspiracy theory."

The *Wall Street Journal* used the term *terrorism-industrial complex* in reporting on the Digital Pearl Harbor exercise, saying, "It is the aim of this cluster of interests both to define 'terrorism' as a technological problem...and to convince everyone that various tech tools hold great promise in combating terrorism. Billions of dollars of federal 'homeland security' dollars are at stake" (Gomes, 2002).

Green, commenting on Richard Clarke's statements of alarm, Collin's predictions, the *Post* article, and other dire warnings says:

> There's just one problem: There is no such thing as cyberterrorism—no instance of anyone ever having been killed by a terrorist (or anyone else) using a computer. Nor is there compelling evidence that al Qaeda or any other terrorist organization has resorted to computers for any serious destructive activity. . . . It is virtually impossible to use the Internet to inflict death on a large scale, and many scoff at the notion that terrorists would bother trying. (Green, 2002)

He quotes a former Clarke colleague: "Dick has an ability to scare the bejusus out of everybody."

So, should cyberterrorism be considered a serious threat?

Lemos (2002) concedes that, although Collin's more extreme scenarios are unlikely, the threat of a cyberattack is real. "Many power companies and water utilities are operated with networks of computer-controlled devices, known as supervisory control and data acquisition (SCADA) systems, which could be hacked." These systems, which can dramatically lower the cost of network maintenance, provide a window for hackers and cyberterrorists, who might use them to attack the network and the devices attached to it.

Academic researchers support the media reports and heighten the concern. "Some of these [computer hackers] are aligning themselves with terrorists like bin Laden. While the vast majority of hackers may be disinclined towards violence, it would only take a few to turn cyber terrorism into reality. Further, the next generation of terrorists will grow up in a digital world, with even more powerful and easy-to-use hacking tools" (Denning, 2001).

In a typical lottery, although the odds of winning are very low, someone eventually gets the right numbers. Hackers, even with the odds stacked against them, sometimes succeed. Cyberterrorists, using common hacking techniques or soliciting hacker help, could penetrate secure systems, too. In a comprehensive discussion of risk assessment applied to cyberterrorism, Haimes (2002) asserts that the traditional paradigm of expectancy value risk assessment does not apply to potential cyberterrorism acts. A high-probability event with a low negative effect is far different than a low probability event with a high-negative effect, even though the two might score identically in a multiplicative model. "Because terrorism is asymmetric, it defies conventional benefit–cost analysis." Thus, if the potential negative effects are devastating, it is critical to bring the probability to near zero (Haimes, 2002).

Hensgen, Desouza, Evaristo, and Kraft (2003), in a game theory article calling cyberterrorism a "bastard stepchild to physical terror attacks [in a] 'virtual,' non-real world," note that "the virtual is transformed to actual by the execution of a keystroke" (Hensgen et al., 2003).

Following the 2002 electrical grid failure, Kaplan (2003) called it an "overloaded, archaic, unevenly managed electrical-transmission system." He cited a spokesman for the North American Electric Reliability Council saying, "Hackers try to intrude on some aspect of the grid's computer network on a daily basis" (Kaplan, 2003). We could be a keystroke away from disaster. Gordon and Ford (2002) conclude, "Unless steps are taken to significantly reduce risks, disaster is inevitable."

At the National Security Summit in December 2003, Tom Ridge, Secretary of the DHS said, "Eighty-five percent of our nation's critical infrastructure, including the cyber network that controls it, is owned and operated by the private sector" (CERT, 2003b), and there is little oversight to their direct and indirect paths to the Internet. Lemos (2002) cited a survey of 50 utilities that found that 40% of water facilities allowed their operators direct access to the Internet, and 60% of them could be dialed into by modem. Even after 9/11, many of these systems have not been updated. Newer technologies, such as KVM (shared keyboard, video, mouse) that simplify network management and make SCADA attacks even more attractive, may increase the risks by encouraging wider adoption of network access.

DEFINING CYBERTERRORISM

Definitions are required for counting and quantifying incidents of cyberterrorism, or the numbers are difficult to interpret. Laws and regulations depend on specific underlying definitions, otherwise they are unenforceable. This section explores some formal definitions used by government, private organizations, and academic researchers. Many of these definitions are inconsistent and imprecise. It gives examples of incidents in cyberspace that might be considered when defining cyberterrorism and leads to an extended definition of cyberterrorism. It also discusses how terrorists use the Internet in support roles. Multilevel operational definitions are presented, including a five-layer model. Later in the chapter, the ideas of asymmetric response and cyberwarfare are discussed in relation to the definitions.

Definitions in Use

In the United States, government agencies implement laws by formulating regulations, which may define specific terms such as *cyberterrorism*. Ultimately, a court establishes a case law determination for a given situation. Changes require new legislation or regulations, and the process begins anew. In the coming years, cyberterrorism issues and definitions will be clarified as case law evolves, but they are likely to be made more complex as new threats and other unforeseen activities arise outside precedents.

Government departments and agencies use the term *cyberterrorism*, but none have formulated a definition that is binding outside their sphere of influence. In 2001, the NIPC called cyberterrorism an "evolving concept" and stated, "the definition of terrorism must evolve to reflect the type of activity that goes beyond traditional physical violence" (NIPC, 2001b; Vatis, 2001).

Howard Schmidt, then vice chairman of the Critical Infrastructure Protection Board, defined cyberterrorism at a conference early in 2002 as "anything that disrupts or causes mistrust about the security of computers and networks" (Moran, 2002). This is a broad definition, as terrorism is usually thought of as including some element of politically motivated coercion, intimidation, fear, confusion, uncertainty, or violence directed at civilians or other noncombatants.

In congressional testimony, J. T. Caruso, deputy executive assistant director of the FBI's Counterterrorism and Counterintelligence unit, defined cyberterrorism as *"the use of* cyber tools to shut down critical national infrastructures . . . for the purpose of coercing or intimidating a government or civilian population" (emphasis added; Caruso, 2002; Greenspan, 2002b).

The NIPC's Analysis and Information Sharing Unit (2001b) proposed the following:

> Cyberterrorism is a criminal act perpetrated by *the use of* computers and telecommunications capabilities resulting in violence, destruction and/or disruption of services to create fear by causing confusion and uncertainty within a given population, with the goal of influencing a government or population to conform to a particular political, social, or ideological agenda. (emphasis added)

Mark Pollitt (2002), of the FBI Laboratory in Washington, DC, constructed a "working definition" as follows:

> Cyberterrorism is the premeditated, politically motivated attack *against* information, computer systems, computer programs, and data which result in violence against noncombatant targets by sub national groups or clandestine agents. (emphasis added)

The definitions have important differences. The NIPC and Caruso emphasize *the use of* computers in creating terror, focusing on the act itself. Pollitt emphasizes the *target* or victim(s) of the act. They generally agree on some element of politically motivated coercion, fear, confusion, uncertainty, violence, intimidation, or intent. Gordon and Ford (2002), in a comprehensive review of government definitions, make a similar distinction between the "tool" and the "target" and introduce "the concept of 'pure' cyberterrorism," which is carried out "entirely (or primarily) in the virtual world."

Hensgen et al. (2003) in discussing definitions and game theory, include both the use of computers and the target of the act in a working definition for cyberterrorism:

> A purposeful act, personally or politically motivated, that is intended to disrupt or destroy the stability of organizational or national interests, through *the use of* electronic devices which are *directed at* information systems, computer programs, or other electronic means of communications, transfer, and storage. (emphasis added)

Their definition is relatively broad. It can apply to both national and organizational interests in the virtual or physical worlds. However, it does not include elements commonly associated with terror.

More research needs to be done on establishing a definition of cyberterrorism that is consistent with definitions of conventional terrorism. Dictionary definitions of *terror* commonly include intense fear, extreme fright, dread, or panic. Terrorism includes violence or threatened violence, an ideology intended to cause harm, and some form of collective intent, usually with a political or ideological objective, directed at noncombatants.

The CIA's Counterterrorist Center refers to Title 22 of the U.S. Code, Section 2656f(d), in defining terrorism as "premeditated, politically motivated violence perpetrated against noncombatant targets by sub national groups or clandestine agents, usually intended to influence an audience" (DCI Counterterrorist Center, CIA, 2002). The FBI defines terrorism as "the unlawful use, or threatened use, of violence by a group or individual . . . to intimidate or coerce a government, the civilian population, or any segment thereof, in furtherance of political or social objectives" (Watson, 2002). The FBI's definition of terrorism could include *threats*, whereas the CIA specifies actual *acts*. Both involve political motivation or activities.

Dorothy Denning (2001), director of the Institute for Information Assurance, Georgetown University, offers a discussion of cyberterrorism that includes many of the elements that would lead to terror: fear, confusion, uncertainty, violence, or intimidation. "The attack should be sufficiently destructive or disruptive to generate fear comparable to that from physical acts of terrorism. Attacks that lead to death or bodily injury, extended power outages, plane crashes, water contamination, or major economic losses would be examples."

Compared to conventional terrorism, defining cyberterrorism is complicated by the nature of cyberspace. Traditionally, laws deal with acts that are defined to occur in time and space. Acts in cyberspace may have physical effects in time and place, but some of their causal factors reside in a virtual reality, mostly independent of time and space. Defining (and prosecuting) cyberterrorism acts will need to take these factors into account, and it will take time to develop applicable case law. Many other nations have similar interpretation problems, and work needs to be done to reach international consensus. A more detailed discussion of problems in formal cyberterrorism definitions is given in the *Internet Encyclopedia* (Jaeger, 2003).

Extended Definitions

Cyberterrorism often is defined loosely. President Clinton, in December 2000, said, "One of the biggest threats to the future is going to be cyberterrorism—people fooling with your computer networks, trying to shut down your phones, erase bank records, mess up airline schedules, do things to interrupt the fabric of life." Clinton's examples include many acts that do not qualify under FBI, CIA, and other definitions that include the terror component.

Gordon and Ford (2002) discuss extended definitions of cyberterrorism, which involve wide-ranging means of using cyberspace to further terrorism. They cite self-interest motives (media attention, budget, power) in a section on "terrorism as theater." Arguing for an extended definition, they maintain, "those who do insist on treating only 'pure cyberterrorism' as cyberterrorism are completely missing the true threat posed by the addition of acts in the virtual world to the terrorists' playbook."

Making a definition too restrictive may omit acts that should qualify. An overly broad definition, in contrast, will include so many acts that "terrorism" would become meaningless. Many ordinary crimes, vandalism, and hacking would be classified as terrorism. Even repeated "spam" might be terrorism if it intimidates or coerces people into purchasing or otherwise acting on an offer. Let us consider some examples.

In November 1999, a Tampa, Florida, man was charged in federal court with using the Internet to threaten to destroy the reputations of six young women and girls unless they engaged in phone and cybersex, charges investigated by a task force that included the FBI (FBI, 1999). Also in 1999, U.S. Web government sites were defaced in the name of China. The White House Web site was shut down for 3 days by massive amounts of e-mail. Pro-Chinese hackers hacked 165 Taiwanese Web sites to protest the Taiwanese presidential elections (Jane's Information Group Ltd., 1999). In 2000, pro-Pakistani hackers defaced more than 500 Indian Web sites. In 2001, U.S. Web sites were attacked after a Chinese fighter jet collided with a U.S. reconnaissance plane (Tang, 2001). Pro-Korean hackers attacked computers and Web sites of various Japanese organizations following their approval of a new history textbook (NIPC, 2001a). In July 2002, CNN reported that Yale University experienced 18 unauthorized Web site log-ins—traced back to computers at Princeton (CNN.com, 2002c). The Terrorism Research Center's Information Warfare Database lists over 50 "incidents" dating back to 1982 targeting the North American Air Defense Command, NASA, U.S. military sites, the White House, the U.S. Department of Defense, and others vital to U.S. and world security (Information Warfare Database, 2002).

These acts, and many other activities in cyberspace, are annoying and may cause monetary or other damages, but are they cyberterrorism? Some are intended to punish a country or other political entity for the purpose of influencing policy, but many do not involve large-scale or otherwise disastrous physical consequences.

In fact, only the cybersex case resulted in charges of cyberterrorism. That event had no political motivation or unauthorized break-ins, affected relatively few people, and created virtually no property damage or direct monetary losses. (The FBI called the attacks "large scale," and Frank Gallagher, special agent in charge of the Tampa division, described them as "cyberterrorism" because of the fear created in the recipients.) The case was resolved on charges other than cyberterrorism (FBI, 1999).

There is general disagreement on whether using the Internet in a support role should be considered cyberterrorism, especially where the objective is not immediately destructive and is designed to influence public policy or further a political cause.

In a 1999 article, Denning explored how Internet users can influence public policy. She separates their usage into three categories: activism, hacktivism, and cyberterrorism. Activism refers to the normal, nondisruptive use of the Internet for persuasion or information dissemination. Hactivism is where the activist uses hacking techniques for activities such as Web sit-ins or denial of service attacks, "with the intent of disrupting normal operations but not causing serious damage" against a target's Internet site. Cyberterrorism refers to a "convergence of cyberspace and terrorism [that is] politically motivated [and] intended to cause grave harm such as loss of life or severe economic damage" in influencing policy (Denning, 1999).

Support for Conventional Terrorism

Many experts believe that the most likely future attack scenario is for the cyberterrorists' bits and bytes to be combined with terrorists' bombs. This leads us to consider extended definitions of cyberterrorism, including support for conventional terrorism.

Gellman (2002) quotes Ronald Dick, then director of the FBI's NIPC, "The event I fear most is a physical attack in conjunction with a successful cyber-attack on the responders' 911 system or on the power grid," meaning that "the first responders couldn't get there . . . and water didn't flow, hospitals didn't have power. Is that an unreasonable scenario? Not in this world. And that keeps me awake at night."

The Digital Pearl Harbor study group dealing with the electrical network "envisioned a two-pronged attack: first, the physical destruction of key transmission bottlenecks, followed by sabotage through the Internet of the digital systems that allow supervisors to switch transmission flows, . . . thus blocking them from restarting the power after the attack" (Kaplan, 2003). With simultaneous attacks on water, rail, highway, air traffic, and other physical infrastructure and digital control systems, the cyberterrorist would compound and prolong physical attacks. Disruptions of banks, stock exchanges, and pharmaceutical and food manufacturing and distribution would compound the effects.

At the 2003 National Cyber Security Summit, Amit Yoran (2003), then director of the National Cyber Security Division of the DHS, warned "America's economic engine is fueled by efficiency . . . though the use of technology. . . . When we look at the vulnerability of cyberspace, there's no doubt in my mind that what we've seen so far in attacks is just the early stage of what could become a critical national weakness—if we don't aggressively address it."

Does the use of cyberspace to support conventional terrorism qualify as cyberterrorism? To the extent that it is premeditated, politically motivated, perpetrated against noncombatant targets to influence an audience, there is a reasonable argument for including such activity.

Communication in Terrorism

Under broad definitions, communication between terrorists and other cyberspace support for terrorist acts may be considered forms of cyberterrorism. The Web is a fast, easy, cheap, and powerful communication tool. Just as businesses, governments, military forces, and other individuals use the Internet to communicate and transfer files, so do terrorists. A December 2003 Al Qaeda video appeared on the Web to recruit new terrorists (Arena, 2003), and terrorists have used the Web for disseminating information about the Iraq war.

In February 2003, a University of Idaho graduate student was arrested and charged in U.S. district court with using his computer expertise between 1994 and 2003 to foster terrorism. Specifically, *United States of America vs. Sami Omar Al-Hussayen* charged that he "provided and conspired with others to provide material support and resources...by, among other things, creating and maintaining internet websites and other internet media designed to recruit mujahideen and raise funds for violent jihad in Israel, Chechnya and other places" (details are on www.findlaw.com).

After a 7-week trial and 7 days of deliberations, Al-Hussayen was found not guilty on three terrorism counts and a mistrial was declared on several other counts. The government agreed to drop the remainder of the charges after the defendant agreed to deportation to Saudi Arabia.

As early as 1999, Denning concluded, "It appears that virtually every terrorist group is on the Web," such groups are actively establishing alliances and coalitions via the Web, and this support role is the most common use of the Web in terrorism. She adds, "Forcing them off the Web is impossible, because they can set up their sites in countries with free-speech laws."

Cyberspace can become a conduit for terrorist intelligence gathering and calls-to-action, often using unprotected, hacked computers as open relays, planting spy devices, and reading the contents of computer hard drives in homes, businesses, or institutions anywhere in the world (security is covered in other chapters of this *Handbook*). Some of this activity is criminal, even if it does not result in terrorism.

A Five-Level Operational Model

Although a formal definition of cyberterrorism may remain obscure, it is useful to address the problem with a multilevel operational model that describes behavior. Tavani and other writers on ethics in cyberspace have separated cyberspace activities into variations of subsets, such as cybervandalism, cybertrespass, and cyberpiracy. Together, these activities capture a part of cyberterrorism, at least in the extended definition, but they are only elements in the destructive acts described by Collin and others. (Cybercrime, cybervandalism, hacking, and related topics are covered in other chapters of this *Handbook*.)

Conway (2002) described a general three-tiered schema, categorizing "fringe" activity on the Internet as "use, misuse, and offensive use." Use is normal and legal Internet usage—the same for terrorists as for anyone else—similar to Denning's activism. Misuse includes acts that disrupt or otherwise compromise other sites, including protests and vandalism typically associated with hackers. Most of the incidents described in this chapter fall

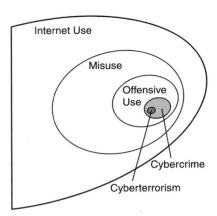

Figure 1: Categories of Internet usage related to terrorism.

into this category, similar to Denning's hacktivism. Offensive use entails actual damage, theft, fraud, extortion, or commercial espionage. Not all of these offensive uses are crimes. Some of them may be cyberterrorism.

Expanding Conway's general schema would include two additional subsets of offensive use: cybercrime and a subset of that, cyberterrorism. Cybercrime would be criminal acts using cyberspace that can be prosecuted. Cyberterrorism would include crimes with political motivations, grave harm, severe economic damage, and so on, consistent with dictionary definitions of terrorism, definitions of cyberterrorism in common use, and Denning's operational hierarchy (see Figure 1).

Many of what would be misuse and offensive use "incidents" are tracked by the Carnegie Mellon CERT Coordination Center. The incidents counts have increased exponentially since 1988 (CERT, 2004b) (see Figure 2).

Cyberterrorists seldom would engage in ordinary misuse or offensive use, unless such use supported their larger goals, as the potential risk of discovery would be counterproductive. Conversely, ordinary use of the Internet by terrorists to communicate and coordinate activities that support conventional terrorism is likely to be common.

HOW CYBERTERRORISM OCCURS

This section outlines how the convergence of the physical and virtual worlds creates vulnerabilities to cyberterrorism. It presents some of the tools and techniques available to cyberterrorists. It addresses the distributed nature of the generally unregulated Internet, which increases its vulnerability and creates limitations to how regulation can be applied. It discusses the concept of asymmetric response, its role in cyberwarfare, and its relationship to cyberterrorism.

Convergence of the Physical and Virtual Worlds

Cyberspace is a virtual world of combinations of ones and zeros with no appreciable mass, time, or space. Digits can represent the physical world but are not the physical object(s). With the attachment of stimuli and sensory interface devices, however, the flow of ones and zeros can

Number of Incidents

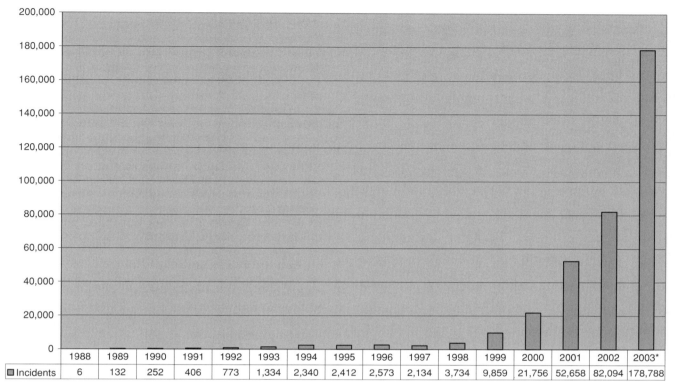

■ Incidents	1988	1989	1990	1991	1992	1993	1994	1995	1996	1997	1998	1999	2000	2001	2002	2003*
	6	132	252	406	773	1,334	2,340	2,412	2,573	2,134	3,734	9,859	21,756	52,658	82,094	178,788

Figure 2: Number of incidents (from www.cert.org/stats/). Asterisk indicates the 2003 estimate is based on 137,529 incidents reported through Q3.

control physical objects that exist in time and space. "It is now the intersection, the convergence, of these two worlds that forms the vehicle of cyberterrorism, the new weapon that we face" (Collin, 1996).

Collin (1996) discusses activities in the physical world that intersect with cyber-based systems through these vulnerable convergence points. Examples include food and pharmaceutical processing plants, electric and natural gas utilities, train crossings and traffic control systems, air traffic control systems, virtually all modern military equipment, and military, public safety, and civilian communications. Using readily available digital tools and freely available information from Internet Web sites, the cyberterrorist may exploit this "point of convergence" to achieve one or more of three goals: destruction, alteration, or acquisition and retransmission.

An electronic signal can be attacked if its rule-based behavior of ones and zeros can be determined and accessed. When remote administration of the physical device is used, illustrated by the discussion of SCADA devices at the beginning of this chapter, the Internet can be a conduit to the target device through standardized Internet rules [Internet protocols (IPs) and transmission or transfer control protocols (TCPs)] that enable worldwide communication. Each device has a unique IP address. Once terrorists access the IP address and learn the rules controlling the device itself, they have the potential to control it through cyberspace.

Hackers and terrorists may not need to know details of the physical structures in which the ones and zeros reside—usually a computer or system of computers with its associated network—or even the physical location of the device itself. If they know the processes used to maintain and control its action(s), the IP or other electronic address "where" it resides in cyberspace, and how its internal structure responds to electronic stimuli, the device is vulnerable.

The Internet was designed to be decentralized and unregulated, except through technical protocols, so there is little control over individual installations. There are no effective committees with official authority or tracking oversight based on content (although some countries such as China and France have laws regulating forbidden content). The terrorists' servers can reside in any country, sometimes in difficult-to-discover physical locations, and they can be moved easily.

Vulnerabilities: External, Internal, Other

Kevin Mitnick, "the condor," is perhaps the world's most notorious cybercriminal and the first to appear on the FBI's Most Wanted list. Mitnick stole tens of thousands of credit card numbers and copied millions of dollars worth of computer software beginning in the 1980s. He eventually served 5 years in prison and now is a consultant (Meriwether, 1995; Sargent, 2001).

Mitnick breaks vulnerability into four "access points": host, network, physical security, and people. He says the most common sources of vulnerability today are unpatched and misconfigured systems, their associated networks, and insufficient systems management education (*eWeek*, 2003). Hosts and networks can be protected with firewalls, improved passwords, encryption, and other technological shields, discussed later in this chapter and elsewhere in this book.

Mitnick says that systems operators—particularly those controlling physical infrastructure with SCADA devices—need more education, training, and awareness of the issues. "Unfortunately, a lot of enterprises believe that buying a firewall or an [intrusion detection system] is all they need to do. And they're lulled into a false sense of security." He is concerned that companies and organizations are not making the required commitment to long-term security. "A lot of our clients want a one-time . . . test to satisfy an auditor . . . or to get buy-in to get a security budget."

The 2004 "State of the CIO" survey found that the highest *technology* priority, after enhanced system performance, was ensuring data security and integrity. Data security did not make the top 10 of the CIO's *management* priorities (*CIO Magazine*, 2004).

In 2004, Deloitte's annual Global Security Survey of worldwide financial services firms reportedly found that 83% of respondents "acknowledged that their systems had been compromised in the past year, compared to only 39% in 2002." However, although 59% of the respondents "indicated security is a key part of their solution, only 10% . . . reported that their general management perceives security as a business enabler" (CCNMatthews, 2004).

Hinde (2003) supports the idea that technical solutions and other measures to keep outsiders from unauthorized access is only one part of the problem. "Internal security breaches and backdoors are a growing problem. Insider hacking represents about 70% of all malicious attacks, and costs US business over $1 billion annually in damages," he says. "Firewalls will not help against this." He recommends a 10-point plan for implementing an advanced intrusion detection system (IDT) that would address both internal and external threats.

There are conflicting estimates. The Carnegie Mellon CERT Coordination Center reports that a *CSO* magazine survey found 71% of attacks coming from outsiders, compared with 29% from insiders. Hackers were listed as the greatest security threat, followed closely by current or former employees or contractors (CERT, 2004a).

The CERT Center has tracked technical vulnerabilities since 1995. They have shown exponential growth until 2002, but there has been a gradual decline since then (CERT, 2004b) (see Figure 3).

Physical network architecture is vulnerable to traditional terrorism from the outside, too. In 2002, a story about Internet physical vulnerability reported how in San Jose, California, "any visitor can walk into the building and board the elevator unchallenged" and exit on the fifth floor location of MAE West, one of "about a dozen major U.S. peering points . . . where the wires of thousands of data networks intersect [in a] clustering effect" (Wylie, 2002). In a facility of this kind, a well-placed bomb might be coordinated with a cyberattack. Physical security at this and many similar facilities has been upgraded, but other locations have not.

Tools of Cyberterrorists

Hackers and cyberterrorists use similar tools and techniques: hardware, sophisticated software, and detailed knowledge of the technology, the targets, and the procedures used to maintain and control operations at target sites.

Today, hacking tools are more powerful, easier to use, and more plentiful than ever. Hacking software and documentation are easily obtained on the Internet. In discussing "the democratization of hacking," Christensen (1999) said, "The tools of mayhem are readily available. There are about 30,000 hacker-oriented sites on the Internet, bringing hacking—and terrorism—within the reach of even the technically challenged." He quotes a manager of technical security at a company that does business with the Pentagon: "You no longer have to have knowledge, you just have to have the time."

Hacking into secure sites may simply mean millions of iterations of new trial-and-error algorithms that ultimately discover the target device's secret passwords or defeat its other protective barriers. Even with a low probability of success, the documented cases of unauthorized entry are common.

In tracking attack sophistication versus intruder technical knowledge, Lipson (2002) asserts that in 1980, attack sophistication was low, but it required high intruder knowledge. By 2000, attack sophistication had become high, but the required intruder knowledge was low, and there was "widespread availability of exploit tools." An excellent graphic is included, showing the development of this relationship over time (Lipson, 2002).

Hackers typically work alone, but can gain power by working together. Obtaining the knowledge, hardware, software, and access to targets in cyberspace can be complex. Specialists can focus on a tiny problem that unlocks success in the broader venture. Acting together, even informally in loosely knit alliances, cyberterrorists can defeat barriers that would be impossible for any single individual. Networks of cyberterrorist hackers working together, perhaps in widely separated parts of the world, may one day unlock the keys to making Collin's doomsday scenarios reality.

BGP Tables, DNS Poisoning, and DDoS

Vulnerabilities exist in network traffic routing and in methods to track users. Snyder (2002) points out that the entire Internet depends on huge border gateway protocol (BGP) tables that detail the more than 100,000 routes information can travel. BGP4 is the protocol used to exchange routing information among providers and to propagate external routing information through autonomous networks. BGP-speaking routers "peer" with each other to exchange information about routes and improve data flow efficiency:

> In the early days, these tables were validated against routing registries that ensured bogus information could not be injected into the tables.

Vulnerabilities

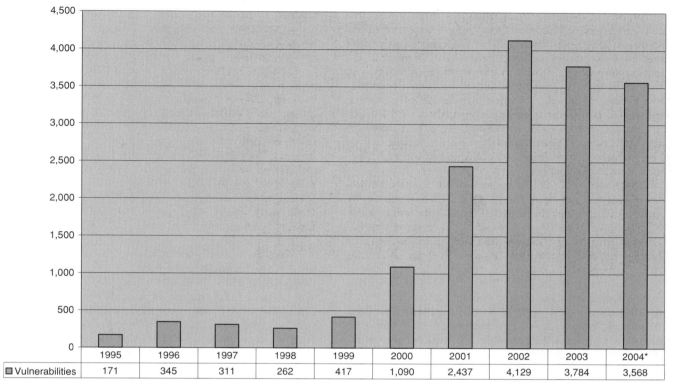

Vulnerabilities	1995	1996	1997	1998	1999	2000	2001	2002	2003	2004*
Vulnerabilities	171	345	311	262	417	1,090	2,437	4,129	3,784	3,568

Figure 3: Number of vulnerabilities (from www.cert.org/stats/). Asterisk indicates 2004 estimate is based on 1,740 vulnerabilities reported through Q2.

Nowadays, that doesn't happen. Keeping those routing registries updated and synchronized is just too expensive and inconvenient. The lack of a global routing registry means that it's fairly easy to create routes to nowhere.... If a determined attacker were to start injecting routes into the BGP tables, the ripple effects could be enormous.... [It] could cripple routers around the world.

Craig Labovitz, a border gateway protocol researcher, reportedly identified a 1997 event where a "serious weakness was discovered" by a network technician who changed two lines of code and "nearly brought down the global network" (Lemos, 2002).

The University of Oregon Route Views Project studies variations in core route table sizes and growth rates through regular BGP sessions with many routers spread throughout the world. They found that the number of routes in the Internet increased from approximately 15,000 in 1994 to approximately 115,000 by mid-2002, magnifying their vulnerability (Meyer, 2002).

Chakrabarti and Manimaran (2002), in their comprehensive taxonomy of Internet infrastructure security, say, "So far, the research in Internet security primarily focused on securing the information rather than securing the infrastructure itself." They note that attacks on BGP tables could create a "large amount of service disruption" and

"are very difficult to detect because the attacker is hidden," adding, "Such service disruption has already been noticed with . . . routing flaps due to Nimbda/Code Red" (their taxonomy discusses domain name system (DNS) hacking, routing table poisoning, packet mistreatment, and denial of service (DoS), using "masquerading," "cache poisoning," and other techniques).

Reviewing the DHS's National Strategy to Secure Cyberspace, Fisher (2003b) says, "While there is considerable space given to the need for reducing the number of vulnerabilities in . . . BGP (border gateway protocol), the Domain Name System and IP, the strategy makes little mention of how to go about fixing these problems, a key shortcoming."

Attacks on the are common. In March 2003, after Al-Jazeera's Web site showed pictures of dead or captured soldiers in Iraq, hackers posted the U.S. flag and the message "Let Freedom Ring" on Al-Jazeera's site. The suspected technique is called "DNS poisoning," which fools traffic-directing computers across the Internet (Associated Press, 2003a). A creative cyberterrorist might combine an attack on the DNS servers with BGP routing. If it is possible to use BGP tables to redirect messages by acquisition and retransmission to random or unknown locations, it might be possible to redirect them to a specific destination—its own control station—where the terrorist might alter the message contents and redirect it, thus taking control of critical physical devices without discovering the secret passwords and other barriers to these devices. A technique of this kind is unlikely but perhaps not impossible.

Internet DNS servers track users, referencing millions of user names. It is common to "ping" these and other address nodes by sending packets with a short query message that maintains communication with them and detects abnormalities. Normally, this traffic is minimal.

DoS attacks use packet flooding to overwhelm servers. In distributed denial of service attacks (DDoS), once a vulnerable computer is compromised, the worm infects that target, randomly or systematically selects new targets, and resends the exploit and propagation code to that host, which in turn launches coordinated attacks from their distributed locations.

On October 21, 2002, an estimated 6,000 computers worldwide swamped the Internet's 13 root servers in Japan, Europe, and the United States that control most of the Net's traffic. Eight were disabled to some degree. This massive "ping flooding" was part of a DDoS attack, "the biggest ever hacking attack on the Internet" (Naraine, 2002; Vickers, 2002).

These relatively new and effective tools in the cyberterrorist's toolkit are difficult to track. In the old days, it was possible to trace a message or command back to a guilty IP address. Today, with distributed attacks, the offending packets may originate in an otherwise innocent computer. (Details of DoS and DDoS attacks are in other chapters in this *Handbook*.)

The attacks may have resulted in no direct or lasting damage, but they are unsettling. One expert maintains that although there were few direct effects on Internet users, "as nations and critical infrastructure become more dependent on computer networks for their operation, new vulnerabilities are created—a massive electronic Achilles' heel" (Lewis, 2002).

On January 25, 2003, much of the Internet was shut down with a similar attack that used the "Slammer" worm (discussed later in this chapter and in other chapters of this *Handbook*). A security firm official predicted, "Slammer variants could emerge which are capable of being used in a blended threat scenario alongside physical attacks by radicals. This could achieve a significant multiplier effect" to prolong or worsen conventional terrorist attacks (Greenspan, 2003b).

RMA and Asymmetric Response

Asymmetric response (one sided; does not follow "rules") is a way for the weak to attack the strong. A rag-tag, poorly trained militia that is no match for a powerful state's army may use guerilla tactics, sneak attacks, bombings, or sniper attacks to harass and demoralize the superior force. As the balance tilts more and more toward the camp of the powerful adversary, asymmetric response becomes more likely. It can be highly effective, as witnessed by Russia's withdrawal from Afghanistan and the United States' departure from Somalia.

The industrialized nations have highly developed electronic infrastructure that drives knowledge-based economies and gives them advantages in business, government, and military power. Loren Thompson, a defense

analyst with the Lexington Institute in Arlington, Virginia, says, "Warfare is less and less about pushing men and machines around the battlefield and more and more about pushing electrons and photons" (CNN, 2003a). Attacking those assets through cyberspace, as a guerilla army might use suicide bombers and beheadings, to the degree that it creates chaos and panic, can be cyberterrorism.

The National Intelligence Council (NIC) has predicted asymmetric responses to an expected overwhelming military superiority brought about by a paradigm shift in the nature of warfare. This "revolution in military affairs" (RMA) will employ "a small, information-intensive, professional armed force [as] the model for a 21st century military," largely based on strength in information technology and smart weaponry (NIC, 1999). In October 2003, ministers from 19 NATO nations met to discuss "transformation of their armies" and held an exercise named Dynamic Response '07, designed to help formulate such a force of 5,000 international troops by October 2006 (CNN, 2003b).

When the U.S. military captured Saddam Hussein, they used digital technology, the Force 21 Base and Command Brigade and Below (FBCB2) system, for commanders to monitor and direct equipment and other war assets in real time. The Army Battle Command System (ABCS) helped run the war room to monitor the big picture. Voice radio, Internet controllers, and the global positioning system (GPS) added efficiency (Van Marsh, 2004). This expensive technology saves lives and gives the military a significant tactical advantage in physical warfare. Cyberterrorism—as an asymmetric response—may be the only way for an opposing force to counteract this overwhelming advantage.

Overill (2003), discussing the nature of asymmetric information warfare, observes that "the cost of defending an asset from attack is many orders of magnitude greater than the cost of attacking it." Regan (1999) points out, "Cyberterrorism allows terrorists...to inflict damage with no harm to themselves and little chance of being caught. It is a way for the 'weak' to attack the 'strong'."

The Associated Press reported that then-White House Technology Advisor Richard Clarke warned a Senate Judiciary subcommittee on cyberterrorism, "A serious cyber-attack is almost inevitable because it is cheaper and easier for a foreign country or a terrorist group than a physical attack" (Holland, 2002).

Cyberspace Warfare

Governments are becoming more interested in electronic warfare. In 2002, in testimony before a Senate Judiciary subcommittee on cyberterrorism, Richard Clarke named Iran, Iraq, North Korea, China, Russia, and other countries as "already having people trained in Internet warfare" (Holland, 2002). Previously, the NIC (1999) had said, "Iraq and Iran are examples of states that will likely explore the usefulness of information technology in pursuit of asymmetric conflict... including through the employment of information warfare and cyberterrorism."

The United States is not backing away from defensive— or offensive—use of cyberspace warfare tools. Fisher (2003a) cites the National Strategy to Secure Cyberspace:

"When a nation, terrorist group or other adversary attacks the United States through cyberspace, the U.S. response need not be limited to criminal prosecution. The United States reserves the right to respond in an appropriate manner, including through cyber warfare. The United States will be prepared for such contingencies."

The *Washington Post* reported that President Bush signed a National Security Presidential Directive 16 in July 2002, under which "The United States would launch cyber-attacks against enemy computer networks." The article said, "The Pentagon has stepped up development of cyber-weapons, envisioning a day when electrons might substitute for bombs and allow for more rapid and less bloody attacks on enemy targets" (Rasmussen, 2003). Mark (2003) reports that "the Pentagon is actively developing cyber-weapons to disable enemy radar, electrical grids and telephone systems."

In the 2003 buildup to the Iraq war, a CNN article had predicted a "fierce cyber war," saying, "Imagine Iraqi commanders getting misleading text messages on their cell phones. They appear to contain orders from Saddam Hussein but are actually sent by the U.S. military in disguise, directing Iraqi troops to a trap." CNN likened this to the Civil War, when signal flag messages were diverted, and in World War II, when German forces were deceived by "leaking" battle plans involving nonexistent troops. The article concluded that "the Internet makes deceptions easier" (CNN, 2003a).

SPONSORS AND SUPPORT

Terrorism traditionally has been sponsored by nations who provide financial resources and a safe haven. Cyberterrorism requires less funding. It uses fewer physical assets, so it is more mobile and can cross physical borders or operate simultaneously in many locations. Thus, nations that sympathize with cyberterrorists can support them without becoming a sponsor in the traditional sense. This section addresses different forms of terrorist groups and explores what it means to sponsor them in cyberspace. Cyberterrorism is an international issue, and perspectives from other parts of the world are explored.

Cyberterrorism Sponsors

Hackers and cyberterrorists can operate out of almost any physical location on Earth. Many undeveloped or emerging nations have daunting problems such as hunger, disease, political unrest, or traditional war, often to the extent that they are unable to address security issues or exert effective control over cyberspace. Although the number of computers may be relatively few in these countries, many offer adequate electronic infrastructure and sometimes—knowingly or not—harbor terrorists.

In simpler times, conventional terrorists required a sponsoring organization, often state sponsorship, to obtain sufficient funding and connections. Traditional organizations and state sponsors had a fixed infrastructure. They were comparatively easy to monitor to determine who was pulling strings and causing consequences. Today, terrorists can pursue extreme agendas with more powerful tools than ever before, leaving no easy-to-follow trail.

Low-cost cyberspace tools reduce the need for large-scale money transfers, and because physical currency need not be exchanged, following a money trail is more complex.

CNN quotes M. J. Gohel of the Asia-Pacific Institute in London, who describes many of these terrorist organizations as "autonomous with their own leadership, with their own funding, their own personnel. And they have their own plots, as it were. But they're all bonded together by a common ideology" (Arena, 2003). This fragmentation makes them and their funding difficult to track.

Caruso separated the international terrorist threat into three categories: (a) traditional, clearly defined terrorist organizations; (b) the radical international jihad movement; and (c) state sponsors of international terrorism, specifically identifying Iran, Iraq, Sudan, and Libya (Iraq subsequently has changed governments, and Libya has taken steps to limit terrorism; this list will likely undergo continual change). Many of the terrorist groups are not identified with a sponsoring country (Caruso, 2002).

Cyberterrorists acting alone or in small groups can pursue extreme agendas either through volunteer labor or by relatively small amounts of money disbursed from wealthy individuals, foundations, fund raising organizations, or almost any rogue country's intelligence unit. Regan (1999) quotes Dr. Harvey Kushner, chairman of the criminal justice department at Long Island University:

> We have moved away from state-sponsored terrorism. The old model of the hierarchical or "organized crime" group, no longer exists. These days, terrorists move in loose groups, constellations with free-flowing structures. So these days terrorism—both the traditional kind and cyberterrorism—is more the act of the freelancer or the individual. This is true both internationally and nationally.

The Associated Press, reporting on a London-based study, quotes author Kevin Rosser, "What we're beginning to see is a much more disparate movement of people who are sometimes coordinating and sometimes not, but who are inspired by the example of Al Qaeda, . . . so we see the threat becoming much more elusive and . . . much harder to track" (Associated Press, 2003b). However, if these groups coalesce into relationships with each other through Al Qaeda or other known organizations, better visibility could result, and tracking, with worldwide participation, could become more effective.

The Worldwide Perspective

Although there are differences between the way individual nations and the world community view cyberterrorism, there is general agreement that it is a global problem. Nations have become more aware of their vulnerability and are beginning to work together to counter the threat.

In 2003, European Union (EU) ministers agreed to "require all 15 EU member states to adopt a new criminal offence: illegal access to, and illegal interference with an information system," recommending "jail terms of at least two years in serious cases" (*The Information Management Journal*, 2003).

A Manila conference of Southeast Asian telecommunications ministers reported "facing a computer security threat following the 11 September terror attacks in the United States." They implemented "stricter measures to counter cyberterrorism" and "urged the United Nations to come up with a universally accepted definition" (BBC Worldwide Monitoring, 2002).

The United Nations (UN) understands the cyberterrorism connection. "The same Internet that has facilitated the spread of human rights and good governance norms has also been a conduit for propagating intolerance and has diffused information necessary for building weapons of terror" (Annan, 1999). Following the September 11, 2001, attack on the World Trade Center, the 56th regular session of the UN General Assembly declared that cyberspace threats are a weapon against UN goals and unanimously passed a resolution condemning terrorism and cyberterrorism.

On November 23, 2001, the first-ever international treaty on criminal offenses committed against or with the help of computer networks was signed in Budapest, Hungary, by 26 member states of the Convention on Cyber-crime, a part of the Council of Europe. Four nonmembers who helped draft the document, Canada, Japan, South Africa, and the United States, also signed to pursue "a common criminal policy aimed at the protection of society against cyber-crime" (Convention on Cyber-crime, 2001a). Christian Kruger, deputy secretary general of the council, announced that "the Convention would give national legal systems ways of reacting together to crimes committed against or through computer networks, especially those related to terrorism" (Convention on Cyber-crime, 2001b).

Although struggling to cooperate, some nations of the world are reluctant to give up sovereignty. Beyond prosecuting international war criminals charged with physical atrocities, international justice efforts have made only minimal progress. International law and bilateral treaties rarely adjudicate conflicts between companies, individual entities, or public/private disputes. Entities such as the World Trade Organization set rules for engaging in trade and commerce, but their judicial branch only settles differences in trade matters between nations. Formal international agreements usually deal with physical presence and events, not cyberspace activities.

Many developed nations have their own international security agencies, many of which operate anywhere in the world—and often in the virtual world. Nations with such agencies generally work with each other through informal agreements. Since the mid-1990s, cooperation has been on the upswing, and the 9/11 attacks and other international terrorism incidents have added urgency. Although it is rarely discussed publicly, this is a very active area of international relations.

CONTROLLING CYBERTERRORISM

This section begins with general strategies for fighting back against unauthorized attacks, including cyberterrorism. Subsections follow that focus on specific actions that government, businesses, organizations, higher education institutions, and individuals can do. Privacy concerns, especially where government regulations may limit freedom of speech or use confidential information, are addressed.

General Strategies

Many general steps can be taken by individuals, businesses, organizations, and government to reduce the risk of unauthorized intrusion into computer systems and electronically controlled infrastructure. Many of these are technical. Scholarly journals have raised issues of how we view the problem strategically.

Overill discusses the "protect, detect, and react" paradigm and outlines strategic issues associated with various types of reactive strategy. He separates defenses into technical possibilities, legal aspects, and ethical considerations. Technical responses range from benign (notifying the system operator) to aggressive (launch a retaliatory malicious software strike). Many of these are becoming part of built-in computer system "active defense" capabilities in organizational settings (Overill, 2003).

Marcella, Roth, and Espersen (2003) advocate moving "from a reactive posture to a proactive approach to crisis management," adding, "Assessing an organization's weaknesses may require the assessor . . . to think like a cyber criminal or terrorist might think." If management has not established a formal crisis management team, they say, "internal auditors . . . can come together as a proactive team to assist in mitigating exposures."

Although these strategies apply primarily in organizational settings, individuals and other noninstitutional users can take steps to help prevent unauthorized entry into their computer systems that could be used in DDoS attacks or other cyberattack activities. The National Cyber Security Alliance (NCSA) is a public/private partnership sponsored by computer hardware and software companies, ISPs, and others "focused on promoting cyber security and safe behavior online." The NCSA issues guidelines directed toward individuals, home users, and small businesses. It sponsors an October National Cyber Security Awareness Month (see http://www.staysafeonline.info). Their 10-point guidelines include operating systems upgrades and patches, antivirus software, password protocols, and other safeguards that most Internet users can apply. Some of these are simple enough to be applied by nontechnical users, whereas others require the guidance of information technology (IT) or other professionals.

Information Technology Professionals

Large business and government organizations usually have IT professionals that make critical decisions about safeguarding their computer systems from cyberattacks and how much information flexibility is built into their systems. Too much filtering screens out important information, whereas too little may risk penetration by intruders. Those that maintain systems connected to SCADA systems controlling vital infrastructure have a higher stake in cybersecurity.

In a journal article overview of how IT professionals can help safeguard their organizations, Hinde (2003) points out that "it may be difficult to differentiate between legitimate operations, intrusive marketing, hacker mischief, competitor attack, criminal activity and cyberterrorism," concluding that "for a truly secure computer, ban users and connectivity." He gives nine technical steps IT professionals can take to "become proactive in defending our computer systems," including IDSs and lock downs.

IT professionals install patches for viruses and worms such as "SQL Slammer" and the "W.32.Bugbear." On January 25, 2003, many of the more than 200,000 computers running Microsoft SQL Server 2000 were vulnerable to the Slammer attack that severely disrupted Internet traffic because required "patches" had not been installed (Fisher, 2003b). Dow Jones reported that Slammer was responsible for "generating a billion attacks an hour at its peak" and "is so virulent that a vulnerable machine—one that hasn't been patched for a particular flaw—is compromised within three minutes of coming online."

In December 2002, Fisher reported, "Security researchers have discovered a set of vulnerabilities in . . . the SSHv2 protocol that could give an attacker the ability to execute code on remote machines. The new flaws are especially dangerous in that they occur before authentication takes place. Attackers could, in some cases, run code on remote machines or launch denial-of-service attacks" (Fisher, 2002). IT professionals implement protective actions against such security flaws.

IT professionals also can help provide feedback to software vendors. In 2002, an average of 50 new software vulnerabilities were reported per week, and a SANS (SysAdmin, Audit, Network, Security) Institute official was quoted as saying, "What this illustrates is that a program that expects end users to patch their systems is futile," adding, "The only solutions are to make software developers, such as Microsoft, responsible for supplying safe, automatic updates or for companies to do much more aggressive filtering of traffic into their networks" (Richmond, 2003).

The Microsoft patches reportedly "were so difficult to install or so poorly publicized that some of Microsoft's own database administrators failed to install them." Database administrators "were required to manually stop each instance of the software running in their organizations, rename or remove some files, and paste the patch files into various directories in each instance." Microsoft released a self-installing patch in November 2002, shortly after the October 21, 2002, attack that swamped the Internet's 13 root servers in Japan, Europe, and the United States, "but it was given only to customers who contacted Product Support Services" (Vaas, 2003). In 2004, Microsoft released Service Pack 2 for XP that has been widely used and closes many of the potential illicit access points.

Professional IT organizations such as the ITAA helped formulate the National Strategy to Secure Cyberspace and participated in the National Cyber Security Summit. ITAA publishes newsletters and maintains an Information Sharing and Analysis Center (ISAC) to disseminate security information among its members and help organizations that do not have adequate resources to maintain their own security. It helped establish the I-ACERT security certification program (Miller, 2003).

The National Cyber Security Division of the DHS works with IT professionals in businesses, universities, and other organizations to promote the new IPv6 Internet protocol, which comes with an improved security framework promising fewer networking vulnerabilities (Fisher & Carlson, 2003). Anticipating its adoption, the updated IPv6 protocol is being implemented by many operating systems, some of which have already begun shipping.

Michael Rasmussen (2003), vice president for Standards and Public Policy for the Information Systems Security Association, says "If we can build the ideal and perfect IT security architecture—we will still have information security and privacy incidents. That is because we have people involved who are human, make mistakes, and succumb to greed and other motives." Regardless of how good technical security becomes, there will always be the chance of human error or inside complicity allowing access to secure IT resources.

Business and Industry

Some companies control vital physical infrastructure and have much to lose through cyberattacks, but there is wide variation in how they have taken protective action—and their attitudes toward the problem. Prior to 9/11, many companies were not taking effective steps to protect themselves from cyberattacks, and many were not sharing what they learned. Often, from a purely business point of view, it makes more sense for a company to deal with the issue internally than to report it to police or other investigative agencies. "Corporate leaders, in many instances, simply never tell the outside world they've been victimized, to avoid spooking investors or customers" (O'Connor, 2000).

An April 2002 CNN.com report on the seventh annual Computer Crime and Security Survey noted, "About 90 percent of the respondents detected a security breach within the last 12 months. However, only 34 percent reported the intrusions to law enforcement officials." It added, "There is much more illegal and unauthorized activity going on in cyberspace than corporations admit to their clients, stockholders and business partners or report to law enforcement." It quoted an FBI assistant director, "Now, more than ever, the government and private sector need to work together to share information and be more cognitive of information security so that our nation's critical infrastructures are protected from cyber-terrorists" (Sieberg, 2002).

Some companies have been lax in applying even modest protective measures. In February 2002, Richard Clarke, then the White House advisor on Cyberspace Security, gave the U.S. Senate a figure that has been widely quoted as short of meeting the need for security. "In the private sector," said Clarke, "the amount of money spent on IT security is roughly .0025% of total revenue. That is less than the amount of money spent on coffee in the same companies" (Wynne, 2002). New figures show that is changing.

In October 2002, the Associated Press reported on the W.32.Bugbear virus, calling it "the worst computer security outbreak in the world" (Associated Press, 2002a). Once a computer is infected, the hacker can steal and delete information. The worm lasted well into 2003 because many users did not realize that their computer was infected. Incidents such as these, although destructive in the short term, have a beneficial effect in prodding laggard businesses. "The expectation is that shareholders will eventually hold boards accountable for security breaches, and, in turn, boards will hold security officials responsible" (Carlson, 2002b).

A leading journal reported that a 2004 *CSO* magazine survey found that "online criminals... cost business an estimated $666 million in 2003." In a reversal of earlier surveys, 40% named outside hackers as the biggest cybersecurity threat, compared with 28% citing internal threats, such as disgruntled employees. The magazine concluded, "Auditing firms should include cybersecurity readiness as part of the criterion for determining whether companies have adequate internal and financial safety controls" (*The Information Management Journal*, 2004).

Many CIOs dispute Collin's or Clarke's extreme threat scenarios against physical infrastructure attacks. For example, Berinato examines safeguards in place at the Massachusetts Water Resource Authority (MWRA) and concludes that a cyberterrorist would need to penetrate firewalls and SCADA control barriers through two "very narrow access points," have insider knowledge of how the system operates, and then successfully "plant surreptitious code that would allow remote control of the chemical distribution or even the flow of water itself" and assume that the changes would go undetected long enough to have severe negative effects. An MWRA director calls them "ridiculous barriers." The article concludes, "The real threat is to critical data, not to property" (Berinato, 2002).

In recent years, companies have increased IT spending, much of it for improved security against viruses and worms (discussed elsewhere in this *Handbook*), aimed at loss of valuable data of computing systems. The 2004 "State of the CIO" survey shows that IT headcount increased in 37% of firms and decreased in only 17%. IT's budget as a percentage of organizational revenue ranged from 13.8% for financial firms down to 2.6% for manufacturers, with an average of 5.6% for all firms. The highest technology priority, after enhanced system performance, was ensuring data security and integrity (*CIO Magazine*, 2004).

Haimes (2002) and others emphasize a "holistic" approach to cyberthreats, using systems analysis that includes understanding the system's nature and improving the decision-making process. *The Information Management Journal* (2002a) reports that experts recommend educating personnel, establishing a crisis management team, and enforcing a "total risk management program."

Part of the holistic approach is to become more conscious of all types of threats. The journal points out, "A corporate Web site is a virtual gold mine for competitive intelligence gatherers." Especially when companies control SCADA devices or other physical infrastructure, cyberterrorists can use that information to help plot attacks. Preventive measures include using search engines to periodically check on who is linking to your company's site, not revealing too much information on job postings, and keeping "to a minimum the strategic information filed with government agencies" (*The Information Management Journal*, 2002c).

Companies face a balancing act in information sharing. They want to avoid the bad publicity associated with having had their systems and facilities compromised by a cyberterrorist; they want to protect proprietary information from scrutiny by agencies that would turn it into public record through the Freedom of Information Act; they are concerned that if they work too closely with competitors, they may be accused of antitrust violations; and many fear that they will be required to spend more time on assessment and managing security than on productive work.

Although America's largest buyer—the federal government—has no power to directly force business and industry into cooperation, it is using its purchasing power to force better security standards, establish configuration benchmarks, and encourage information sharing and cooperation through the National Cyber Security Summit and other initiatives (Fisher & Carlson, 2003). The National Strategy to Secure Cyberspace business sector strategy calls for a heightened awareness and responsibility within companies and promotes company-wide corporate security councils to integrate all aspects of security, including cybersecurity—a mostly voluntary emphasis. Some say it should be mandatory.

In the United States and many other economically advanced countries, 70% of the GNP is services. Although most large, information-intensive organizations have their own IT resources, many smaller entities cannot justify maintaining technical staffs, so it makes sense to outsource. In the past several years, an entire service industry has grown up around the idea of helping companies with cybersecurity.

Creating an internal security unit may be costly, require the recruitment of specialized personnel, entail substantial start-up time, and risk isolation from new developments. Service providers have highly trained people able to leverage their information and knowledge over several businesses.

Companies are investing in software, firewalls, virtual private networks (only minimally connected to the Internet), and other security components with a high services content. Global investment in e-security services were expected to total $14.5 billion in 2005, with North America accounting for 58% of the global total (McMahon, 2002). Some of these service companies have evolved as for-profit branch organizations of private interest groups that disburse information or other resources for counteracting cyberterrorism.

Government

The 9/11 attack was a "wakeup call" that helped galvanize support around the world for stronger government measures against terrorism, including cyberterrorism. In the United States, these include protection of government cyberspace activities, proactive coordination, and aggressive laws allowing an expansion of wiretapping and other surveillance.

Introspection and Protection
Compared to private business, government security has lagged. An ITAA survey in September 2002 found that 77% of respondents felt the private sector was more advanced

Vulnerability Notes

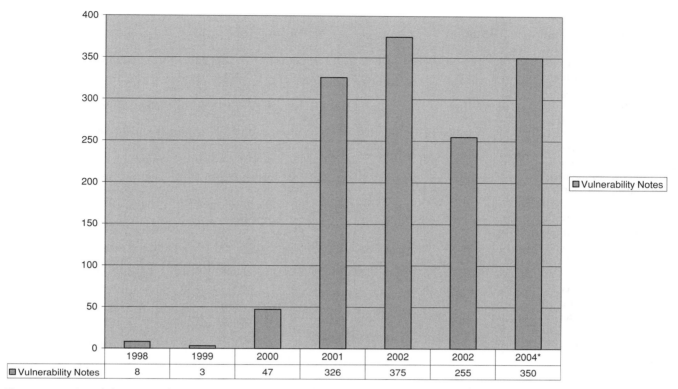

Vulnerability Notes	1998	1999	2000	2001	2002	2002	2004*
	8	3	47	326	375	255	350

Figure 4: Vulnerability notes (from www.certs.org/stats/). Asterisk indicates the 2004 estimate is based on 175 notes reported through Q2.

in hardening information systems than the public sector (Miller, 2003). This may be explained, in part, because "Government...staffs are paid less and don't have access to the latest software and hardware defenses" (Weiss, 2001).

In December 2002, President Bush signed the Federal Information Security Management Act (FISMA), which mandates that government agencies develop annual reports and risk assessments, configuration guidelines, continuity plans, security policies, and inventories of systems. Graded A–F on the security state of their cybersystems, including software security, employee training, and other factors, most agencies failed.

Agencies counter that the grades are "unfair" because "the self-evaluation the agencies must perform can cost hundreds of thousands of dollars, depending on the size of the network," and they simply have had "difficulty finding money in their budgets to comply" (Fisher & Carlson, 2003).

The situation is improving. In 2003, although the government received an overall D grade, it was up from an overall F in 2002. In 2003, 14 of the 24 agencies that were evaluated improved their year-over-year scores, although the DHS still received a failing grade. The Nuclear Regulatory Commission improved to an A from a C, and the National Science Foundation improved to an A- from a D- (Greenspan, 2003a).

Successful attacks on U.S. government systems are declining, having peaked in 2001 (Greenspan, 2003a). The

Cert Center publishes vulnerability notes that capture similar incidents. These increased dramatically in 2001, but have been relatively steady since then (CERT, 2004b) (see Figure 4).

Coordination

In September 2002, a draft of the President's National Strategy to Secure Cyberspace addressed ISPs, wireless networks, and other information security points of convergence for business and home Internet users. A final plan was released in February 2003. The report included 60 recommendations for government, companies, institutions, and individuals in the United States and other nations, including five priorities: (a) a national cyberspace security response system, (b) threat and vulnerability reduction, (c) security awareness and training, (d) securing government cyberspace, and (e) international cooperation (Fisher, 2003a).

Recommendations for government included improving federal cybersecurity, early warning and crisis management plans, and partnering to help develop new security technologies in science and industry. It "strives to ensure that any interruptions will be infrequent, brief, manageable, geographically isolated, and minimally detrimental to the welfare of the United States" (Porteus, 2002).

Many of these initiatives were merged into the DHS, established in November 2002. The DHS absorbed 22 federal agencies, including five cybersecurity offices and programs, and expanded the government's powers to obtain information from telephone and Internet service providers. About $3 billion was reserved for technology in the DHS 2003 and 2004 budgets, each approximately $30 billion. "One important DHS priority will be to examine the vulnerabilities found in security systems. The emphasis will be on catastrophic terrorism—threats to the security of our homeland that could result in large-scale loss of life as well as triggering major economic repercussions" (DHS, 2003).

In December 2003, the DHS and leading industry associations, including the U.S. Chamber of Commerce, the Business Software Alliance, the ITAA, and TechNet, hosted the National Cyber Security Summit. This "first forum of its kind since the release of the President's Strategy" brought together leaders from the public and private sectors to "support the National Cyber Security Division's efforts to improve the security of cyberspace, to strengthen the country's ability to prevent and respond to cyber attacks, and to cultivate and sustain a public-private partnership for cyber-security" (CERT, 2003a).

The government continues to pursue public/private cyberspace security initiatives, including ISACs such as CERT for "sharing information on cyber-attacks, vulnerabilities, countermeasures, and best practices" (ISAC, 2003). The ISACs deal with telecommunications, financial, chemical, energy, information technology, water, transportation, aviation, and food (Porteus, 2003). Other government activities include collaborating with organizations developing the more powerful and secure IPv6 Internet protocol, sponsoring simulations such as Digital Pearl Harbor, promoting ties with legitimate businesses investigating potential security risks, and improving surveillance.

Surveillance and Investigation

On October 26, 2001, the Patriot Act (Providing Appropriate Tools Required to Intercept and Obstruct Terrorism) was signed into law by President Bush. Tracking cyberterrorists and terrorists in cyberspace is a key objective of the act, which gives authorities broad powers to investigate terrorism. That same month, the President's Critical Infrastructure Protection Board was created. The Patriot Act is being reviewed by Congress in 2005, and it is likely it will be continually modified in future years.

In a broad sense, cyberspace surveillance systems are weapons that rely on prevention rather than actively destabilizing terrorist networks. The FBI was already experimenting with a controversial electronic surveillance system called Carnivore, which looked for suspicious activity in cyberspace, and had other tools under development. Through the Patriot Act, the DHS has been assigned additional powers of obtaining investigatory information from ISPs and other cyberspace service providers.

Opponents of these systems maintain that they are intrusive and do not warrant the increased invasion of privacy. The uses of commercial databases in data collection, along with many of the new surveillance tools, DHS reporting requirements for ISPs and other cyberspace service providers, and increased aggressive investigatory techniques, are being challenged by the American Civil Liberties Union (ACLU) and privacy organizations

(discussed later in this chapter and in other chapters in this *Handbook*).

The government maintains that the Patriot Act of 2001 and other surveillance and investigative powers have materially improved security and prevented attacks in both government and private entities. In December 2002, FBI Director Robert Mueller reported that in the period of just over a year since the World Trade Center attack, "tens of attacks, probably close to a hundred around the world" have been detected and stopped through improved surveillance (Associated Press, 2002b).

At the end of 2003, increased cyberspace "chatter" by suspected international terrorists triggered additional security at airports and other vulnerable points. Such "data mining" from programs similar to the FBI's Carnivore project is designed to identify potential threats using cyberspace patterns—which we might call *cybermetrics* or digital forensics.

The government has been aggressive in investigating other potential security threats. In late August 2002, the Associated Press reported an FBI raid on the offices of a San Diego consulting firm, which claimed that, motivated to expose a need for better security, it had "identified 34 military sites where it said network security was easily compromised" (CNN.com, 2002d).

On December 5, 2002, federal agents raided a Quincy, Massachusetts, company "that provides critical software to major U.S. agencies and is suspected of having ties to Osama bin Laden and Al Qaeda terrorists.... Officials suspected 'back doors' may have been built into the software to enable terrorist access to federal computers." Customers included the Department of Energy, the FBI, the U.S. Air Force, the Naval Air Systems Command, the Federal Aviation Administration, the House of Representatives, and NATO (Fox News, 2002).

In 2004, inbound international airline traffic was repeatedly interrupted for additional passenger screenings, based on intelligence information. In January 2004, the United States began photographing and fingerprinting noncitizens entering the country, implementing the U.S. Visitor and Immigrant Status Indicator Technology (US-VISIT), which uses "biometrics"—technology that identifies people using digitized biological traits. That program was extended to other nations in September 2004. The proposed new Computer Assisted Passenger Pre-Screening (CAPPS-2) and Automated Commercial Environment (ACE) were designed to use digital technology to collect and analyze data. Although these programs are not specifically targeted at cyberterrorists, data from them could be cross referenced with information about individuals engaged in cyberterrorist activities.

Legal and Privacy Concerns

Privacy advocates and cyberterrorism fighters often are on a collision course. One side is for maximizing personal liberties, whereas the other wants to minimize terrorism. It is probably impossible to satisfy both sides. Other nations face similar issues.

Rowland, discussing a balance between anonymity and "strategic lawsuits against public participation" (SLAPPs), points out that U.S. and international laws in this area have only recently begun to consider the issue in cyberspace (cyberSLAPPs). She asks, "To what extent will the law protect those who use anonymity ... to enable them to engage in public debate without the fear of reprisal and recrimination?" When it is relatively easy to hide an identity in cyberspace and asymmetric response is potentially devastating, "the fear of cyberterrorism ... provides another rationale for intervention and regulation" (Rowland, 2003). That debate will continue.

For years, the FBI and CIA were constrained in what they could do with respect to human intelligence—actual agents on the street. In response, they developed Carnivore, Magic Lantern, and other electronic surveillance technologies to monitor worldwide telephone conversations, e-mail, and other correspondence, all of which are intrusive.

A May 2004 magazine reported that the General Accounting Office (GAO) "enumerates nearly 200 data mining initiatives in operation or in the works," and many of these "rely on data purchased from the commercial sector" (Carlson, 2004). The Pentagon's Total Information Awareness project—renamed Terrorism Information Awareness (TIA)—was blocked in Congress following privacy objections (TIA details are on the DARPA Web site, www.darpa.mil). There are critics on both sides.

The ACLU and small but vocal private interest groups argue that electronic eavesdropping and the Patriot Act and other new antiterrorism laws violate fundamental rights guaranteed by the Constitution and the Bill of Rights, especially when they purchase data from commercial firms. They contend that the resulting loss of freedom is not worth the security benefits, the ends do not justify their means, and the government has too much power over individuals.

The other side argues that the National Strategy to Secure Cyberspace is not forceful enough, and we need more laws and regulations allowing increased oversight. Mark Rosh, formerly the Justice Department's top computer crimes prosecutor said, "You need to put some teeth into some of the proposals" (CNN.com, 2002a). Many who advocate more aggressive government monitoring recommend that private-sourced data be integrated into government surveillance programs.

Former Justice Department attorney Orrin Kerr maintains, "The law is a lot more balanced than people thought. The government ended up introducing a law that didn't really take any major steps." Under the Patriot Act, noncitizens are investigated by intelligence agencies with broad powers, but citizens are handled by the FBI, which is much more restricted. They can monitor online communications, but as with wiretapping or other surveillance, agents must get judicial permission to obtain message content (Borland & Bowman, 2002).

The new strategy, new laws, and new technology increase government and companies' ability (and perhaps willingness) to collect personal data. In an interview with the *Boston Globe*, Richard Hunter discussed companies' data collection policies and excerpts from his book, *World Without Secrets*: "Information is constantly recorded and made available to almost anyone who wants it, regardless of intent.... The amount of information that's out there, and readable, is already huge" (Denison, 2002). Companies already have most of the data, and the government can get it.

Data that the government controls is subject to the Privacy Act of 1974 and other restrictions, and information brokers have generally resisted selling to federal law enforcement agencies. Although the numbers are still low, as of 2002, it was reported, "The FBI's use of commercial databases has grown 9,600 percent over the last decade" (Carlson, 2002a).

Institutions, Organizations, and Conferences

Not-for-profit and private institutions typically do not have the same security needs as commercial companies. It would be rare for them to have control over nuclear power plants, electrical grids, dams, or other vital infrastructure. However, in many cases they hold considerable financial and information resources that may be vulnerable to cybercrime and terrorism, especially with extended definitions.

Although institutions seldom have enough in-house expertise to combat potential cyberterrorism, many of the security techniques companies are using apply equally to institutions. They are good candidates for private security firms, but resource constraints make it difficult to afford the needed services. This is an area that will benefit from closer attention.

Not-for-profit and private institutions are included in government initiatives such as the National Strategy to Secure Cyberspace. Many private and semiprivate groups that combat cybercrime and cyberterrorism now are connected in some way to the DHS. In addition, many operate programs to disseminate information about potential cyberterrorist threats. For example, the Carnegie Mellon Software Engineering Institute's CERT Coordination Center, which tracks cyberspace "incidents" and "vulnerabilities," publishes a stream of security notes designed to help businesses, organizations, educational institutions, government, and technical individuals. Organizations without full-time IT staffing can access these reports on the Internet and use them as indicators for when to consider contracting for needed services. Security notes rose dramatically beginning in 2001 (CERT, 2004b).

The SANS Institute together with the FBI publishes a top 20 list of security threats. The list is "especially intended for those organizations that lack the resources to train, or those without technically advanced security administrators" (Wagner, 2002).

The Critical Infrastructure Protection Project (CIP), part of the George Mason University School of Law, is associated with the DHS and over 30 local, state, and national associations, including the Association of Metropolitan Water Agencies (AMWA), the North American Electric Reliability Council (NERC), and the ITAA. It publishes reports to Congress and a monthly newsletter, *The CIP Report*, for constituents "who have an interest in critical infrastructure protection."

The NIC publishes papers on global trends under the aegis of the National Foreign Intelligence Board and the Director of Central Intelligence, sometimes together with other government or private centers. It sponsors conferences such as the Future Threat Technologies Symposium and The Global Course of the Information Revolution: Technological Trends (NIC, 2000). The National Infrastructure Protection Center (NIPC) and the

National Association of State Chief Information Officers (NASCIO) have partnered to form an ISAC "to disseminate intelligence quickly and prevent unauthorized and destructive infiltrations" (Greenspan, 2002b).

Some of these conference organizations sell business services to commercial, nonprofit, and government entities. Many participate in, sponsor, or promote conferences that call attention to cyberterrorism issues and cybercrimes. Some have become partnered with the DHS or otherwise help in implementing the National Strategy to Secure Cyberspace and other governmental programs. In all, they are an important component in counteracting cyberterrorism.

Higher Education Institutions

Higher education institutions have many of the same resources and opportunities as other organizations. In addition, they usually have considerable in-house expertise. Colleges and universities were Internet pioneers. Long before the graphical World Wide Web existed and before business was allowed to use the Internet for commercial purposes, the academic community was file sharing and facilitating group research using the Internet.

Many higher education institutions became leaders in developing security skills and experience with the UNIX operating system and its associated Internet protocols, TCP/IP. Individuals in higher education have a tradition of working long and hard in making UNIX and Internet tools robust—often with little or no compensation. Many of them are working on cyberterrorism issues.

Today, public and private universities, community colleges, and specialized institutions such as the American Military University develop innovative technologies and popular new courses to counteract terrorism and cyberterrorism. In a letter to alumni, John Hennessy, President of Stanford University said, "Professor William Perry, former Secretary of Defense, was one of the many faculty members who made extraordinary efforts to accommodate students in oversubscribed classes. Bill's class on 'Technology in National Security' swelled from an enrollment of 145 in the fall of 2000 to 329 students this past year!" (Hennessy, 2002).

In September 2002, it was reported that Congress approved National Science Foundation (NSF) grants for 7 large projects and 240 smaller projects. Between $500,000 and $13.5 million will go to each recipient organization, many of which are higher education institutions (Legon, 2002b). Many of these support antiterrorism initiatives.

Small Business and Individuals

In the past several years, the number of individuals using cyberspace has skyrocketed, and they are included in the National Strategy to Secure Cyberspace and other cooperative initiatives. E-mail is the most common application, and many users participate in chat rooms, instant messaging, or contribute Web content through Web logs (blogs) and other forums.

Most individuals become exposed to hackers or cybercriminals—not cyberterrorists—through credit card fraud, identity theft, or property crimes. Programs such as ISpyNOW, SpyBuddy, and Cute Spy enable hackers to monitor computer keystrokes and create logs that pick up e-mail messages, passwords, and other confidential information. Some can be installed remotely, potentially through back doors. Programs such as SpyCop have been used to detect the spy, tell when it was installed, and optionally disable it.

Many small business and individuals use digital cable or DSL lines for high-speed access through an ISP, often remaining connected 24 hours per day. Hackers can gain access to connected computers that have no firewall or if the firewall is ineffective against "back door" access points. Home and small business users may lack the technical expertise to configure these access points to protect against intrusion. The "I Love You" virus caused an estimated $4 billion in damages to individuals and international systems (Information Warfare Database, 2000). Hackers also plant worms or other invasive programs to hijack the computer and use it to send spam or to carry out DDoS or other forms of cyberattacks, a potential contributor to cyberterrorism.

PC Magazine listed 10 "bad guys" of cyberspace, including DDoS attacks, worms, viruses, e-mail attachments, open network or TCP ports, and "persistent connections" (usually 24/7). The article gives often-attacked filenames, discusses strengths and weaknesses of hardware or software firewalls, offers nine safety tips, details specific information about instant messaging hazards, and names vulnerable ports hackers exploit (Karagiannis & Sarrel, 2002). These data are somewhat more detailed than the NCSA guidelines (see http://www.staysafeonline.info).

The National Strategy to Secure Cyberspace makes simple recommendations to private users to regularly update antivirus and operating systems, turn off computers at night, and install firewall software or physically disconnect when offline. In addition, the strategy recommends that users apply caution in opening e-mail attachments that may contain viruses, worms, or other invasive components. Other common preventive measures include using strong passwords that mix characters and numbers, disabling unnecessary applications and services, maintaining proper browser security settings, and relentless vigilance.

WHO WILL WIN THE BATTLE OF CYBERTERRORISM?

This chapter is about the terrorist threat as it can best be seen from today, with the benefit of no hindsight. A long struggle with cyberterrorism may be just beginning. It could be a battle of minimization, not elimination. In the days following the 9/11 attacks, Secretary of Defense Donald Rumsfeld said of the war on terrorism:

> The cold war, it took 50 years, plus or minus. It did not involve major battles. It involved continuous pressure. It involved cooperation by a host of nations. And when it ended, it ended not with a bang, but through internal collapse. It strikes me that might be a more appropriate way to think about what we are up against here. (*World Almanac and Book of Facts*, 2002)

Richard Clarke adds, "We reserve the right to respond in any way appropriate: through covert action, through military action, any one of the tools available to the president" (Holland, 2002). This could indicate the future of counteracting cyberterrorism.

IT professionals in government, business, institutions, schools and universities, and private interest groups are interconnected through cyberspace. Each will play a role in combating cyberterrorism. Many government programs have been designed to bring these groups together, help secure systems from outside attack, monitor internal usage, and detect suspicious activity. Working together, they will become more effective in counteracting cyberterrorism.

In the coming years, cyberterrorists will have more powerful tools at their disposal. At the same time, government, businesses, institutions, and individuals will work together to craft strategies to counteract it. Although that effort seems to be making progress in protecting critical infrastructure, networks, and computer systems, continued vigilance will be required as terrorists obtain new tools.

How actively should governmental intervention policies regulate vulnerabilities in cyberspace? Parks (2003) takes the aggressive position, suggesting codification and compliance. "When we were approaching Y2K, also known as 'the end of the world,' the federal government required that all public companies disclose to their shareholders what measures had been taken to prevent predicted disruptions and failures in their systems, [and we] should implement information security regulations along those same lines." Others advocate cooperative, voluntary approaches that can react quickly to flexible threats and conditions, without rigid legal requirements.

People will need to learn to live with cyberterrorism and minimize its impact. Some individuals have resigned themselves to some loss of freedoms to counteract terrorist threats. Others have remained committed to preserving individual privacy. This will be an important issue in the next several years.

One thing seems clear: as cyberterrorism becomes increasingly global, governments worldwide and international governing organizations will need to participate in what is almost certain to be a long-term commitment. Balancing control with individual rights will take on an increasingly global perspective, and what was initially perceived to be a threat may become an opportunity to establish increased overall cooperation.

The strong level of disagreement between extreme points of view, such as those of Richard Clarke, who predicts doom and gloom, and opponents who do not see great danger, is an obstacle to effective policy. At least, in our changing environment, it should make people think and debate. Hopefully, the dialectic will lead to effective solutions.

GLOSSARY

9/11 The World Trade Center and Pentagon attacks, which occurred on September 11, 2001.

24/7 An activity that can occur 24 hours per day 7 days per week, as do many broadband Internet connections.

Asymmetric Response A one-sided response and a generic explanation why cyberterrorists behave as they do. Unable to achieve their objectives through conventional means, an extremist may strike against the "enemy" with a one-sided act of terror.

Border Gateway Protocol (BGP) Tables that detail the more than 100,000 routes information can travel over the Internet. BGP routers exchange information about routes and improve data flow efficiency.

Cybercrime Activity in cyberspace usually associated with fraud, commercial espionage, or theft of intellectual property, identity, or private data that can result in loss of data or corruption of computer files.

Cyberspace/Digital World/Virtual World The world of discrete mathematical values, usually ones and zeros at its lowest level, that powers computers and networks and can be used to represent the physical world. It is generally outside time and space, unless it is applied to a physical object through an interface to the analog world.

Cyberterrorism An evolving body of activity that includes both acts *in* cyberspace and *using* cyberspace tools to create fear or panic, often done by subnational groups or clandestine agents and directed toward intimidating or coercing a government or some segment of the noncombatant civilian population, usually in furtherance of political or social objectives; differs from hacking and cybervandalism in its intent and the degree of severity of the attacks.

Denial of Service (DoS) Attack A condition under which a Web site or other Internet resource is disabled by an attack from an overwhelming number of inbound messages. A distributed denial of service (DDoS) attack has the inbound messages coming from multiple computers.

Department of Homeland Security (DHS) Signed into law in November 2002, the DHS absorbed 22 federal agencies, including five cybersecurity offices and programs.

Graphical User Interface (GUI) Typically used to describe the graphical interface between a computer's display and the internal hardware workings or the interface between a computer's display and images served up on the Web.

Hacker A person who gains unauthorized entry into computers or other digital devices through cyberspace, usually for the purpose of minor damage or annoyance, such as defacement of a Web site or observation of data.

Hardware Physical devices that process mathematical ones and zeros. Hardware has an interface to the physical world, such as a keyboard or monitor display. SCADA devices include hardware.

Information Sharing and Analysis Centers (ISACs) Formal or informal groups that share information on cyberattacks, vulnerabilities, countermeasures, and information services best practices relating to telecommunications, financial, chemical, energy, information technology, water, transportation, aviation, food, and so on.

Physical World/Analog World The world of physical objects and forces in time and space. The analog world is continuous. It can be represented in cyberspace by devices that use digital ones and zeros.

SCADA Systems Supervisory control and data acquisition systems used in networks of digital computer-controlled devices for physical infrastructure.

Software Programming code that, at its basic level, delivers ones and zeros that can be used to control the operation and function of hardware devices, including SCADA systems.

Transmission Control Protocols/Internet Protocols (TCPs/IPs) The set of rules by which the Internet operates and communicates among devices.

World Wide Web (a.k.a. Web) The graphical overlay that resides on top of the Internet and allows graphics to be served and browsed.

CROSS REFERENCES

See *Cybercrime and the U.S. Criminal Justice System; Cyberlaw: The Major Areas, Development, and Information Security Aspects; Hackers, Crackers, and Computer Criminals; Hacktivism.*

REFERENCES

Annan, K. (1999). *Report of the Secretary General on the work of the organization* (A/54/1/, para. 254). Retrieved from http://www.un.org/Docs/SG/Report99/toc.htm

Arena, K. (2003, December 5). Al Qaeda tape likely used to rally, recruit. Retrieved December 5, 2003, from http://www.cnn.com/2003/US/12/05/holiday.terror.threat/index.html

Associated Press (AP). (2002a, October 7). Stealthy e-mail worm bores into computers in a dozen countries. *Medford Mail Tribune.*

Associated Press (AP). (2002b, December 16). FBI Director: 100 terror attacks thwarted. Retrieved December 16, 2002, from http://www.foxnews.com/story/0,2933,73122,00.html

Associated Press (AP). (2003a, March 27). Al-Jazeera Web site hacking. Retrieved March 27, 2003, from http://www.foxnews.com/printer_friendly_story/0,3566,82375,00.html

Associated Press (AP). (2003b, November 10). Report: New terrorists harder to track. Retrieved November 11, 2003, from www.foxnews.com/printer_friendly_story/0,3566,102728,00.html

Associated Press (AP). (2004, September 15). FAA radio outage affects airports, flights in West. *Medford Mail Tribune*, p. A6.

BBC Worldwide Monitoring (2002, August 31). "Southeast Asian nations agree tougher measures to counter cyberterrorism," Radio Australia, Melbourne. Retrieved November 7, 2002, from http://www.lexis-nexis.com

Borland, J., & Bowman, L. (2002, August 27). *E-terrorism: Liberty vs. security.* Retrieved December 19, 2003, from http://zdnet.com.com/2100-1105-955493.html

Carlson, C. (2002a). Data search stirs concern. *eWeek, 19*(32), 22.

Carlson, C. (2002b). Feds pitch cyber-fence. *eWeek, 19*(36), 18.

Carlson, C. (2004, May 27). *GAO report reveals rampant federal data mining.* Retrieved May 28, 2004, from http://www.eweek.com/print_article/0,1761,a=128302,00.asp

Caruso, J. (2002, March 21). *On combating terrorism: Protecting the United States.* FBI Press Room, testimony to U.S. House of Representatives. Retrieved August 8, 2002, from www.fbi.gov/congress/congress02/caruso032102.htm

CCNMatthews (2004, May 17). *World's top financial institutions struggle to fend-off escalating security threats, Deloitte study finds.* Canadian Corporate Newswire. Retrieved September 24, 2004, from http://www.lexis-nexis.com

CERT. (2003a). *Homeland Security announces the National Cyber Security Summit.* Carnegie Mellon CERT Coordination Center. Retrieved December 19, 2003, from http://www.cert.gov/press_room/detail/summit.html

CERT. (2003b). *Remarks by Secretary Tom Ridge at the National Cyber Security Summit.* Retrieved December 19, 2003, from http://www.cert.gov/press_room/detail/RidgeSummitSpeech.html

CERT. (2004a). *2004 E-crime watch survey shows significant increase in electronic crimes.* Carnegie Mellon CERT Coordination Center. Retrieved September 13, 2004, from http://www.cert.org/about/ecrime.html

CERT. (2004b). *CERT/CC statistics 1988–2004.* Carnegie Mellon CERT Coordination Center. Retrieved September 13, 2004, from http://www.cert.org/stats/cert_stats.html

Chakrabarti, A., & Manimaran, G. (2002). Internet infrastructure security: A taxonomy. *IEEE Network, 16*(6), 13–21.

Christensen, J. (1999, April 6). *Bracing for guerrilla warfare in cyberspace.* Retrieved July 25, 2002, from http://www.cnn.com/TECH/specials/hackers/cyber-terror/

CIO Magazine. (2004, October 1). *State of the CIO: The survey.* Retrieved October 4, 2004, from http://www.cio.com/archive/100104/survey.html

Clinton, W. (2000, December 11). *A foreign policy for the global age.* Address at the University of Nebraska. Retrieved August 14, 2002, from http://usembassy.state.gov/islamabad/wwwh00121101.html

CNN.com. (2002a, September 18). *Cyber-security plan avoids call for new rules.* Retrieved September 18, 2002, from http://www.con.com/2002/TECH/internet/09/18/cyber-security.ap/index.html

CNN.com. (2002b, October 25). *FBI: Al Qaeda operatives may target U.S. railroads.* Retrieved October 25, 2002, from http://www.cnn.com/2002/US/10/25/railroad.warning/index.html

CNN.com. (2002c, July 5). *Yale accuses Princeton of hacking.* Retrieved July 25, 2002, from http://www.cnn.com

CNN.com. (2002d, August 23). *FBI raids firm after military hacking claim.* Retrieved August 23, 2002, from http://www.cnn.com/2002/TECH/internet/08/23/computer.security.ap/index.html

CNN.com. (2003a, March 3). *Fierce cyber war predicted.* Retrieved March 3, 2003, from http://www.cnn.com/2003/TECH/ptech/03/03/sprj.irq.infro.war.ap/index.html

CNN.com. (2003b, October 18). *NATO needs rapid-response force.* Retrieved October 19, 2003, from http://

www.cnn.com/2003/WORLD/europe/10/18/nato.defense/index.html

Collin, B. C. (1996). *The future of cyberterrorism: Where the physical and virtual worlds converge.* Paper presented at 11th Annual International Symposium on Criminal Justice Issues. Retrieved July 23, 2002, from www.afgen.com/terrorism1.html

Convention on Cyber-crime. (2001a). *30 States sign the Convention on Cyber-crime at the opening ceremony.* Retrieved December 23, 2002, from http://press.coe.int/cp/2001/875a(2001).htm

Convention on Cyber-crime. (2001b). *The Convention on Cyber-crime, a unique instrument for international co-operation.* Retrieved December 23, 2002, from http://press.coe.int/cp/2001/893a(2001).htm

Conway, M. (2002, November). Reality bytes: Cyberterrorism and terrorist "use" of the Internet. *First Monday, 7*(11). Retrieved December 20, 2002, from http://firstmonday.org/issues/issue7_11/conway

Cyberatlas. (2001, December 13). *Internet, computer security concerns Americans.* Retrieved July 23, 2002, from http://cyberatlas.internet.com/big_picture/geographics/article/0,,5911_939161,00.html

DCI Counterterrorist Center, CIA. (2002). *The war on terrorism: A call to action.* Retrieved August 14, 2002, from http://www.cia.gov/terrorism/ctc.html

Denison, D. C. (2002, May 19). "Smart" stats: business at the speed of a fastball. *The Boston Globe.*

Denning, D. (1999, December 10). *Activism, hacktivism, and cyberterrorism: The Internet as a tool for influencing foreign policy.* Retrieved September, 2004, from http://www.nautilus.org/gps/info-policy/workshop/papers/denning.html (Denning's publications are available at http://www.cs.georgetown.edu/~denning/publications.html)

Denning, D. (2001, November 1). *Is cyber terror next?* Retrieved December 20, 2002, from http://www.ssrc.org/sept11/essays/denning.htm

DHS. (2003). *Department of Homeland Security Web site.* Retrieved December 19, 2003, from http://www.dhs.gov/dhspublic/display?theme=26&content=46&print=true

eWeek. (2003, February 26). *Mitnick: Leaving the dark side.* Interview transcript. Retrieved February 28, 2003, from http://www.eweek.com/print_article/0,3668,a=37623,00.asp

FBI. (1999, November 10). News release, Tampa, FL Retrieved August 6, 2002, from http://tampa.fbi.gov/pressrel/1999/11_10_99.htm

Fisher, D. (2002, December 16). Researchers warn of serious SSH flaws. *eWeek.* Retrieved February 4, 2003, from http://www.eweek.com/article2/0,1759,1657019,00.asp

Fisher, D. (2003a, February 4). Cyber-security plan counts on private sector's input. *eWeek.* Retrieved February 4, 2003, from http://www.eweek.com/print_article/0,3668,a=36580,00.asp

Fisher, D. (2003b). New dangers exposed in the wake of Slammer. *eWeek, 20*(5), 1.

Fisher, D., & Carlson, C. (2003, December 15). Feds unite on security benchmarks. *eWeek, 20*(50), 1.

FOX News. (2002, December 6). *Feds raid software company suspected of terror ties.* Retrieved December 6, 2002, from http://www.foxnews.com/story/0,2933,72345,00.html

Gartner. (2002, August 13). *Cyber-attacks: The results of the Gartner/U.S. Naval War College Simulation.* Transcript of conference call. Retrieved December 19, 2003, from www3.gartner.com/2_events/audioconferences/dph/dph.html

Gellman, B. (2002, June 26). Cyber-attacks by Al Qaeda feared, terrorists at the threshold of using Internet as tool of bloodshed. *Washington Post.*

Gomes, L. (2002, December 16). Digital Pearl Harbor is more marketing ploy than a real threat. *Wall Street Journal.*

Gordon, S., & Ford, R. (2002). Cyberterrorism? *Computers & Security, 21*(7), 636–647.

Green, J. (2002, November). *The myth of cyberterrorism.* Retrieved September 13, 2004, from http://www.washingtonmonthly.com/features/2001/0211.green.html

Greenspan, R. (2002a, September 27). *Computers still insecure.* Retrieved September 28, 2002, from http://cyberatlas.internet.com/big_picture/applications/article/0,1323,1301_1472111,00.html

Greenspan, R. (2002b, August 31). *Cyberterrorism concerns IT pros.* Retrieved September 28, 2002, from http://cyberatlas.internet.com/big_picture/geographics/article/0,,5911_1448291,00.html

Greenspan, R. (2003a, December 11). *U.S. gov't computers get barely passing grade.* Retrieved January 9, 2004, from http://cyberatlas.internet.com/big_picture/geographics/print/0,,5911_3288101,00.html

Greenspan, R. (2003b, January 16). *2003: Year of the worm?* Retrieved January 31, 2003, from http://cyberatlas.internet.com/big_picture/applications/print/0,,1301_1577811,00.html

Haimes, Y. (2002). Risk of terrorism to cyber-physical and organizational-societal infrastructures. *Public Works Management & Policy, 6*(4), 231–240.

Hennessy, H. L. (2002). Letter to alumni, Stanford University, August 2002.

Hensgen, T., Desouza, K., Evaristo, J., & Kraft, G. (2003). Playing the "cyber terrorism game" towards a semiotic definition. *Human Systems Management, 22*(2), 51–61.

Hinde, S. (2003). Cyberterrorism in context. *Computers & Security, 22*(3), 188–192.

Holland, J. (2002, February 13). *White House expert says US may retaliate with military if terrorists try cyberterrorism.* Retrieved July 31, 2002, from http://www.lexis-nexis.com

Information Management Journal. (2002a). A megabyte of prevention. *Information Management Journal, 36*(4), 10.

Information Management Journal. (2002b). Cyber security: Key to homeland security. *Information Management Journal, 36*(4), 10.

Information Management Journal. (2002c). Virtual vulnerabilities. *Information Management Journal, 36*(4), 11.

Information Management Journal. (2003). Cyber crime code could punish online protesters. *Information Management Journal, 37*(3), 10.

Information Management Journal. (2004). Online crime costs rising. *Information Management Journal, 38*(4), 14.

Information Warfare Database. (2002). *The Terrorism Research Center, in cooperation with Georgetown University.* Retrieved October 2, 2002, from http://www. terrorism.com/iwdb/incidents.asp

ISAC. (2003). *World Wide Information Sharing and Analysis Center, v1.51.* Retrieved December 19, 2003, from www.wwisac.com/aboutus.cfm and www.wwisac.com/ faq.cfm

Jaeger, C. (2003). Cyberterrorism. In *The Internet Encyclopedia* (pp. 353–371). New York: John Wiley & Sons, 2003.

Jane's Information Group Ltd. (1999, October 21). *China–Taiwan hacker wars.* Retrieved from http://www. infowar.com/hacker/99/hack_10299a_j.shtml;Internet

Johnson, M., & Radcliff, D. (2001, November 9). *Cybersecurity czar: Protect IT infrastructure.* Retrieved July 31, 2002, from http://www.cnn.com/2001/TECH/ internet/11/09/infrastructure.protection.idg/index.html? related

Kaplan, F. (August 15, 2003). *The Al-Qaeda question.* Retrieved December 19, 2003, from http://slate.msn. com/id/2087037

Karagiannis, K., & Sarrel, M. (2002, November 19). Keep hackers out: Part one, personal edition. *PC Magazine.* Retrieved December 2, 2002, from http://www. pcmag.com/print_article/0,3048,a=32564,00.asp

Legon, J. (2002a, October 23). *FBI seeks to trace massive Net attack.* Retrieved October 24, 2002, from http:// www.cnn.com/2002/TECH/internet/10/23/net.attack/ index.html

Legon, J. (2002b, September 27). *New net project aims to avoid hacking.* Retrieved September 28, 2002, from http://edition.cnn.com/2002/TECH/internet/09/27/iris. internet/

Lemos (2002, August 26). *What are the real risks of cyberterrorism?* Retrieved August 29, 2002, from http://zdnet.com.com/2100-1009_22-955293.html

Lewis, J. A. (2002, December). *Assessing the risk of cyber terrorism, cyber war and other cyber threats.* Center for Strategic & International Studies, Washington, DC. Retrieved from http://www.csis.org/tech/0211_lewis. pdf

Lipson, H. F. (2002, November). *Tracking and tracing cyber-attacks: Technical challenges and global policy issues.* Retrieved December 23, 2002, from http://www.cert.org/archive/pdf/02sr009.pdf

Marcella, A., Jr., Roth, J., & Espersen, D. (2003). A question of preparedness. *Internal Auditor*, October, 67– 69.

Mark, R. (2003, February 7). *Report: Bush considering cyber warfare.* Retrieved February 7, 2003, from http://dc.internet.com/news/article.php/1580981

McMahon, T. (2002, June 13). *Terrorist attacks mean big e-security spending.* Retrieved December 23, 2002 from http://www.europemedia.net/shownews.asp?ArticleID= 10960

Meriweather, D. (1995). *Takedown.* Retrieved August 14, 2002, from http://www.takedown.com

Meyer, D. (2002). *University of Oregon route views project.* Retrieved December 23, 2002, from http://www. antc.uoregon.edu/route-views

Miller, H. (2003, November). *Information security: The long campaign.* The CIP Report, p. 4. Retrieved December 19, 2003, from http://techcenter.gmu.edu/programs/ cipp/cip_report.html

Moran, J. M. (2002, February 5). Eye on cyberterrorism. *The Hartford Courant.*

Naraine, R. (2002, October 23). *Massive DDoS attack hit DNS root servers.* Retrieved October 25, 2002, from http://www.internetnews.com/ent-news/article. php/1486981

NIC. (1999, October 14). *Buck Rogers or rock throwers?* Conference report. Retrieved August 14, 2002, from http://www.cia.gov/nic/pubs/conferenece_reports/ buck_rogers.htm

NIC. (2000, December). *Global Trends 2015: A dialogue about the future with nongovernment experts.* Retrieved August 14, 2002, from http://www.cia.gov/nic/pubs/ 2015_files/2015.htm

NIPC. (2001a, October). *CyberProtests: The threat to the U.S. information infrastructure.* National Infrastructure Protection Center. Retrieved July 25, 2002, from www.nipc.gov

NIPC. (2001b, June 15). *Cyberterrorism: An evolving concept.* National Infrastructure Protection Center. Retrieved July 25, 2002, from www.nipc.gov

O'Connor, R. (2000, November 6). Cracker jacked! Feds losing battle against cyberintruders. *Interactive Week, 7*(45), 14–16.

Overill, R. (2003). Reacting to cyber-intrusions: The technical, legal, and ethical dimensions. *Journal of Financial Crime, 11*(2), 163–167.

Parks, C. (2003). Cyber terrorism: Hype or reality? *The Journal of Corporate Accounting & Finance, 14*(5), 9– 11.

Pastore, M. (2001, April 17). *Cyber-crime worries Americans, with good reason.* Retrieved July 23, 2002, from http://cyberatlas.internet.com/big_picture/ hardware/article/0,1323,5921_744811,00.html

Pollitt, M. M. (2002). *Cyberterrorism—Fact or fancy?* Retrieved August 14, 2002, from http://www.cs. georgetown.edu/~denning/infosec/pollitt.html

Porteus, L. (2002, September 19). *White House releases cyber-security plan.* Retrieved September 19, 2002, from http://www.foxnews.com/story/0,2933, 63452,00.html

Porteus, L. (2003, March 26). *Government creates its own private cyber network.* Retrieved March 26, 2003, from http://www.foxnews.com/printer_friendly_story/0,3566, 82273,00.html

Rasmussen, M. (2003, December 5). *The cyber-security challenge.* Transcript from Live Online discussion. Retrieved December 19, 2003, from www. washingtonpost.com

Regan, T. (1999, July 1). When terrorists turn to the Internet. *Christian Science Monitor*, p. 17. Retrieved August 14, 2002, from http://csmweb2.emcweb. com/durable/1999/07/01/p17s1.htm

Reuters. (2003, November 19). *Tree root cause in U.S., Canadian blackout.* Retrieved September 24, 2004, from www.cnn.com/2003/US/11/19/blackout.report.reut

Richmond, R. (2003, January 27). *Companies continue to wrestle with Slammer computer worm*. Retrieved January 28, 2003, from www.schwab.com

Rowland, D. (2003). Privacy, freedom of epression and CyberSLAPPs: Fostering anonymity on the Internet? *International Review of Law Computers & Technology, 17*(3), 303–312.

Sargent, M. (2001). *Twisted list: Five most notorious hackers ever*. Retrieved August 14, 2002, from http://www.techtv.com/screensavers/twistedlist/story/0,24330,3321221,00.html

Sieberg, D. (2002, April 7). *Cyber-crime rising, yet fewer companies reporting incidents*. Retrieved July 31, 2002, from http://www.cnn.com/2002/TECH/internet/04/07/cyber-crime.survey/index.html?related

Snyder, J. (2002, June 28). Could the next terror target be the Internet? *Canadian Business and Current Affairs*. Retrieved July 31, 2002, from http://www.lexis-nexis.com

Springer, D. (2002). *Electronic voting worries add to booth tensions*. Retrieved October 24, 2002, from http://www.foxnews.com/story/0,2933,66562,00.html

Tang, R. (2001). *China–U.S. cyber war escalates*. Retrieved August 14, 2002, from http://www.cnn.com/2001/WORLD/asiapcf/east/04/27/china.hackers

Vaas, L. (2003). Laborious updates leave SQL databases unpatched. *eWeek, 20*(5), 12.

Van Marsh, A. (2004, January 6). *How the Army used tech to nab Saddam*. Retrieved January 6, 2004, from www.cnn.com/2004/TECH/ptech/01/06/sprj.nirq.troop.tech/index.html

Vatis, M. (2001). *Interview with Michael Vatis, chief of National Infrastructure Protection Center (NIPC)* [Television Broadcast]. New York and Washington, DC: Public Broadcasting Service. Retrieved July 25, 2002, from http://www.pbs.org/wgbh/pages/frontline/shows/hackers/interviews/vatis.html

Vickers, A. (2002, October 25). FBI hunt megahackers who blitzed Internet. *The Mirror*. Retrieved November 7, 2002, from http://www.lexis-nexis.com

Wagner, J. (2002, October 2). *SANS/FBI names top 20 network threats*. Retrieved October 2, 2002, from http://www.internetnews.com dev-news/article.php/1474281

Wald, M. (2004, September 15). Radio failure in west disrupts air traffic. *The New York Times*, p. 18A.

Watson, D. L. (2002). *The terrorist threat confronting the United States*. Retrieved August 6, 2002, from http://www.fbi.gov/congress/congress02/watson020602.htm

Weiss, T. R. (2001). *Denial-of-service warning issued by FBI*. Retrieved July 31, 2002, from http://www.cnn.com/2001/TECH/internet/05/08/dos.warning.idg/index.html

World Almanac and Book of Facts, 2002. Notable quotes in 2002, (2000) Retrieved July 31, 2002, from http://www.lexis-nexis.com

Wylie, M. (2002, November 1). No safety net—Stopping hackers is one thing, but who guards the actual networks? *The Star Ledger*, p. 45.

Wynne, J. (2002). *White House advisor Richard Clarke briefs Senate panel on cyber-security*. Retrieved December 20, 2002, from http://usinfo.state.gov/topical/global/ecom/02021401.htm

Yoran, A. (2003). *Amit Yoran, NCSD director speaks at the summit*. Retrieved December 19, 2003, from http://www.uscert.gov/events/summit/YoranSummitSpeech.html

Online Stalking

David J. Loundy, *Devon Bank University College of Commerce*

WHAT IS ONLINE STALKING?
Definition

What is online stalking, often referred to as *cyberstalking*? The answer depends on whom you ask—there is no agreed upon definition. The term is usually defined based on an analogy to the crime of traditional stalking. Traditional stalking involves a form of repeated harassment that generally involves following the victim. It is harassment that leaves the victim with the fear that he or she will be physically harmed. Because "stalking" is an emotionally charged term, and one that often has specific legal implications, it is important to define the term properly.

"Cyberstalking" does not refer to annoying e-mail. It does not apply to irritating instant messages. It does not refer to defamatory message board posts. It does not refer to identity theft. All of these types of behavior, however, may fit into an overall pattern of conduct exhibited by stalkers. Online stalking is conduct similar to traditional stalking but carried out online. For instance, sending e-mail messages detailing the recipient's day-to-day activities and implying or threatening harm to the recipient may be a case of online stalking.

Various countries and states may have laws against stalking specifically or against various actions that may be part of a stalker's course of conduct. Service providers also may be willing to help customers who are being stalked online, or they may be willing to terminate the service of their own customers who are stalking others. Conduct that is merely irritating, however, may simply be seen as a natural part of life, and complaints about such conduct often will not be taken seriously by the law or a service provider.

What Is "Traditional" Stalking?

"Stalking" as a distinctly defined crime is fairly new, first appearing in the statute books in the early 1990s. It generally involves repeated contact with the victim—contact that makes the victim fear for his or her physical safety. An example of a stalking statute (California Civil Code, 2001) provides the following:

(a) A person is liable for the tort of stalking when the plaintiff proves all of the following elements of the tort:

(1) The defendant engaged in a pattern of conduct, the intent of which was to follow, alarm, or harass the plaintiff. In order to establish this element, the plaintiff shall be required to support his or her allegations with independent corroborating evidence.

(2) As a result of that pattern of conduct, the plaintiff reasonably feared for his or her safety, or the safety of an immediate family member. For purposes of this paragraph, "immediate family" means a spouse, parent, child, any person related by consanguinity or affinity within the second degree, or any person who regularly resides, or, within the six months preceding any portion of the pattern of conduct, regularly resided, in the plaintiff's household.

(3) One of the following:

(A) The defendant, as a part of the pattern of conduct specified in paragraph (1), made a credible threat with the intent to place the plaintiff in reasonable fear for his or her safety, or the safety of an immediate family member and, on at least one occasion, the plaintiff clearly and definitively demanded that the defendant cease and abate his or her pattern of conduct and the defendant persisted in his or her pattern of conduct.

(B) The defendant violated a restraining order, including, but not limited to, any order issued pursuant to Section 527.6 of the Code of Civil Procedure, prohibiting any act described in subdivision (a).

Stalkers are generally motivated by a desire to control their victims. Stalking is seen as a problem because it implies an intentional and concerted effort to place the victim in fear of bodily harm rather than mere casual but unwelcome contact. Thus, accidentally running into a former boyfriend at a restaurant may be an annoyance but such an encounter by itself would not constitute stalking.

Conversely, running into a former boyfriend every night in the parking lot of a different restaurant, as if he is following the woman around and waiting in the dark, could indicate conduct venturing into the realm of stalking. Stalking laws generally will not provide a remedy for the accidental encounter, but they will assist where there is a pattern of activity intended to instill a sense of fear in the victim. (Check with local legal authorities to determine what conduct is prohibited and what remedies are available in your local area.)

How Does Online Stalking Differ from Traditional Stalking?

Online stalking is a form of harassment, but it is more pointed, as is traditional stalking. It occurs through the use of a computer, and it may have more specific motivations than other forms of harassment. One way in which traditional stalking differs from online stalking is in some jurisdictions' specific requirement that the stalker "follow" the victim. How do you follow someone around in cyberspace? Such a spatial requirement may preclude the application of a specific stalking statute to online-only conduct. Second, because stalking statutes generally require a fear of bodily harm, it is less likely that an e-mail message will convey the same fear that a personal encounter would create. With an e-mail message, there is no way to know if the sender is even on the same continent as the recipient, much less a legitimate threat. Online stalking may lack the immediacy that is present with "real-world" encounters. For electronically received communications, a threat of harm may be more remote or less reasonable than, for example, a personal encounter. Additionally, online stalking adds a level of anonymity that may be missing in a real-life encounter. This anonymity also may have the side effect of emboldening stalkers who are more willing to attack or harass than they would be if their conduct was more readily traceable.

Why Does the Definition Matter?

Harassing conduct may be annoying, but it is conduct for which there are only limited remedies available under the law. Although, on the one hand, the extent or availability of any remedy varies depending on applicable laws in your country or state of residence, as a general rule you have no right to be protected from being annoyed—especially when the source of your annoyance is someone else's protected speech. Stalking, on the other hand, may be a criminal offense in many jurisdictions for which there are specific legal remedies. The law does not punish the speech *per se,* but punishes the use of speech as a weapon intended to cause harm in much the same way as hate speech or defamation may be outlawed because of the harm it causes rather than for the substance of the message. Stalking is essentially seen as a form of assault rather than an attempt to communicate.

The law is slow to keep up in many areas with changing technology, including in the area of addressing aspects of online harassment. Traditional stalking law may not help a victim if the online conduct does not fit within a particular statute's definition of stalking. Thus a statutory definition of stalking affects whether a particular stalking law applies to the unwelcome conduct. An example of an online-specific law is Illinois' Cyberstalking (2001) law, which reads as follows:

Sec. 12–7.5. Cyberstalking.

(a) A person commits cyberstalking when he or she, knowingly and without lawful justification, on at least 2 separate occasions, harasses another person through the use of electronic communication and:

  (1) at any time transmits a threat of immediate or future bodily harm, sexual assault, confinement, or restraint and the threat is directed towards that person or a family member of that person, or

  (2) places that person or a family member of that person in reasonable apprehension of immediate or future bodily harm, sexual assault, confinement, or restraint.

(b) As used in this Section: "Harass" means to engage in a knowing and willful course of conduct directed at a specific person that alarms, torments, or terrorizes that person. "Electronic communication" means any transfer of signs, signals, writings, sounds, data, or intelligence of any nature transmitted in whole or in part by a wire, radio, electromagnetic, photoelectric, or photo-optical system. "Electronic communication" includes transmissions by a computer through the Internet to another computer.

(c) Sentence. Cyberstalking is a Class 4 felony. A second or subsequent conviction for cyberstalking is a Class 3 felony.

However, even in the absence of a specific online stalking law, there may be other less obvious laws that provide a remedy, as well as technical options that also provide an adequate remedy to online harassment.

Defining conduct as stalking is also important because it provides a means to frame the discussion. Stalking is a concept that many people have encountered, at least via the media, and can therefore understand. By framing the online conduct in terms of traditional stalking, it may produce greater sensitivity to the effects of the unwelcome conduct. Merely calling the police and telling them that you are "receiving unwelcome instant messages" may be greeted with the suggestion that you simply turn off your computer. Obviously, such a dismissive reaction will not be of much comfort to a victim, because it shows no acknowledgment of the real harm that can result from a stalker's interests. If the police do not understand what an instant message is, at least they can be educated to the point that they understand the message sender could be a legitimate stalker intent on causing the same harm that any other stalker sending the same message via a more traditional medium could intend.

Who Is a Stalker?

A 2002 unscientific study done by Working to Halt Online Abuse (WHOA), an organization started by a former online stalking victim, describes the profile of an online stalker as follows:

- Seventy-one percent of cases reported to WHOA involved female victims, although there is no indication if women are harassed more frequently or are instead more likely to seek help with harassment.
- Forty-nine percent of people who contacted WHOA for help reported their ages as between 18 and 30.
- Fifty-two percent of cases reported to WHOA involved harassment by a male, 35% of the harassers were female, and 13% were of unknown gender.
- More than half of those reporting to WHOA had some previous contact with their harassers, most commonly as a result of a prior relationship or due to an online encounter.
- Nearly 2% of all online harassment (as distinguished from other contact) began via e-mail.
- Thirty-four percent of online stalking cases reported to WHOA included some form of offline harassment as well.

The study is unscientific because the responses are self-selected responses of those who decided to contact the organization. In the absence of scientifically valid survey data, however, it provides useful anecdotal information that helps define the problem.

What motivates a stalker? As discussed by Howard (1999) in *Cyber-Stalking: Obsessional Pursuit and the Digital Criminal,* there are four basic types of cyberstalkers:

1. **Simple Obsessional:** The largest category; typically involves a victim and a perpetrator who have a prior relationship. This group also poses the biggest threat to the victim. The motivation behind the stalking is often to restart a relationship—or seek revenge for the ending of a relationship—through the inducement of fear.
2. **Love Obsessional:** Such stalkers generally have no prior relationship with the victim. Victims are often encountered through the media or the Internet. A large percentage of such stalkers may be suffering from a mental disorder. A typical example of a love obsessional stalker is the "obsessed fan" of a celebrity.
3. **Erotomanic:** Similar to the love obsessional category, these stalkers go a step further and possess the delusion that their target is in love with them.
4. **False Victimization Syndrome:** This group accuses another person of stalking, either real or imaginary, to foster sympathy and support from those around them.

HOW MUCH OF A PROBLEM IS ONLINE STALKING?

Online stalking earns media attention, but how serious is the problem? This question is open to debate. A 1999 report prepared by the U.S. Department of Justice (1999), and later reports that merely respun the same content, stated that the problem is pervasive and, using "back of the envelope," calculations theorized that online stalking could be a crime with tens or hundreds of thousands of victims. The report, however, is sparse in actual support for these claims. In fact, it even cites a study conducted at the University of Cincinnati, of which the authors have

stated does not measure the statistics that the Department of Justice cites the study to support (Koch, 2000). Essentially, there are no empirical scientific studies or data as to the scope of the problem.

Although the media, legislatures, and other interested groups may provide more than a fair amount of hype for the topic, online stalking and other forms of online harassment are a legitimate concern, especially for victims. As more and more daily activities move online, a statistical analysis is not required to see that more harassing conduct likely will move online as well—an assumption supported at least by anecdotal evidence.

Examples of Online Stalking

Andrew Archambeau has the distinction of being the first person convicted of "cyberstalking," although his actions extended into the "real world" as well (Eckenweiler, 1996). The real-world aspects of his conduct are rarely mentioned in discussions of online stalking, however; only the fact that he harassed his victim by e-mail is discussed at any length. Archambeau had met a woman through a video dating service in early 1994, and they went out on two dates. Apparently he thought more of the relationship than she did, because she sent him an e-mail message saying that she did not want to see him again. Over the next few weeks, he sent her approximately 20 e-mail messages and also left her telephone messages (including one saying, "I stalked you for the first time today"). Requests to leave her alone were ignored. Unfortunately for him, he lived across the street from the school where she worked, thus making it appear that he was waiting outside her workplace. After he ignored a police warning to leave her alone, criminal charges were filed against him for violating Michigan's stalking law. After mounting an unsuccessful challenge to the statute's constitutionality, he finally pleaded no contest (Ellison & Akdeniz, 1998). Archambeau's conduct was obviously objectionable, and even absent the e-mail messages sent to his victim, he may have run afoul of the stalking law because of his real-world actions.

Another incident that had a much stronger online component, yet still included a variety of real-world contacts involved two law students at the University of Dayton who had begun dating. The woman decided to end the relationship, but the man wasn't willing to accept this proposition. Over winter break, he began sending his former love interest notes about how he was starving himself to death, including the details of the pain he was to suffer in the process. The two reconciled—briefly. After recovering from a suicide attempt provoked when the woman broke off the relationship a second time, Mr. Davis, the former boyfriend, sent the woman numerous e-mail messages stating that he had been researching her hometown and regularly spending time in a park near her apartment. The notes did not contain explicit threats of harm, but Davis's tone "fluctuated between despair over the break-up, anger, threats to commit suicide, a desire to see [the woman] in pain, and blaming [her] for ruining Davis' life" (*Dayton v. Davis,* 1999). Davis also included in his e-mail messages information that led to the belief that he had been watching the woman, such as knowing what she had watched on television, as well as a link to the Web site he had created. Davis Web site "portrayed, among other things, the image of [her] head transforming into a skull amidst flames, dripping blood, and charging horses ridden by robed skeletons. Interspersed with these images were quotations from the Bible and other sources in which the common theme was love, death, and destruction. On another Web page, Davis had posted pictures of [her] home town . . . although when questioned . . . Davis denied ever having been to the town" (*Dayton v. Davis*). Davis was charged by the authorities with violating the Ohio State law against menacing by stalking (R.C. 2903.211) and aggravated menacing R.C.G.O. 135.05(A). He defended himself by arguing that he had never actually threatened the woman. The court found that he had still succeeded in knowingly placing her in fear of serious physical harm, as evidenced in part by her moving out of her apartment and eventually transferring schools. Intentionally creating such fear, rather than making threats, is what the statutes prohibited. Davis was convicted and sentenced to 180 days in detention.

The first person convicted under the California state online stalking statute was Gary S. Dellapenta (Miller & Maharaj, 1999), a 50-year-old security guard who decided to generate some unwanted notoriety for his former girlfriend. In this case, the stalker's conduct was purely online, although it generated real-world consequences. Dellapenta posted messages on America Online and sent e-mail messages purportedly from the woman stating that she had "rape fantasies"—and soliciting assistance in living out those fantasies. The messages included her home telephone number, address, and instructions on how to disable her home security system. Six people decided to take up "her" offer and dropped by her apartment (she was not physically harmed by these visitors). Criminal charges were brought against Dellapenta for stalking, computer fraud, and solicitation of sexual assault, and he was sentenced to 6 years incarceration (Brenner, 2001). A similar false impersonation case in Korea that involved the culprit forging offers of sexual services in the name of the victim resulted in a warrant for the arrest of a man on criminal slander charges (Soh-Jung, 2001).

People v. Kochanowski (2000) involved a man who asked a coworker to help set up a Web site. The site contained suggestive photographs of his former girlfriend, along with her address and telephone numbers. The page also contained what the court described as "express references to intimate body parts and attributed to [the girlfriend] an infatuation with sex" (*People v. Kochanowski*, p. 462). The woman then began receiving disturbing calls at work. The court found that the former boyfriend was guilty of violating the New York statute prohibiting "aggravated harassment" [New York State Penal Law §240.30(1)] that prohibited certain intentionally annoying or alarming communications. Kochanowski argued in his defense that he had not made the alarming calls, which would have been a violation of a protective order the woman had obtained prohibiting the man from communicating with her. The court found it sufficient under the aggravated harassment statute, however, that he had intentionally caused such alarming communications to be made by others (although the court did not

find the specific terms of the protection order violated by Kochanowski's Web site).

Other examples demonstrate the international reach of online harassment—it may be just as easy to stalk someone on the other side of the planet as it is to stalk someone up the street. In the case of Rhonda Bartle, international online harassment did lead to an attempted real-world encounter (Hubbard, 2001). Bartle, a New Zealand author, started exchanging e-mail messages with Peggy Phillips, an American writer living in California. When the 84-year-old Phillips showed that she was interested in a deeper relationship than Ms. Bartle wanted, Ms. Bartle decided to end the relationship. Ms. Phillips commented about feeling suicidal and then took a plane to New Zealand. Bartle told the local taxi company not to take anyone to her house. When Phillips attempted to order a cab, the taxi company called the police, who then served Phillips with a trespass notice. After returning home, Phillips continued sending her unwanted e-mail messages (which, for the most part, were automatically filtered out of Bartle's e-mail). Because New Zealand did not have online stalking laws at the time, Bartle contacted the Orange County, California, police in an effort to have them enforce the California law against Phillips. (Unfortunately, news accounts did not state whether this proved productive.) Australian courts have also been faced with a jurisdictional fight over where an online stalking case can be heard against an Australian man who stalked a Canadian actress by e-mail (Cant, 2001).

WHAT CAN YOU DO IF YOU ARE A VICTIM?

According to information provided to members of the CyberAngels who may assist victims of online stalking:

> The victim is often embarrassed and does not seek help till the situation becomes out of hand. Why do you think this happens? They often know the stalker in some way. May even have had a relationship with them to some degree. Maybe online boyfriend and girlfriend. Maybe the victim had sought out the person first. Maybe they have given personal identifying information that has come back to haunt them. So they are embarrassed and ashamed and don't know what to do. The victim naturally will try to reason with the stalker, to get them to back off. It rarely works. Any attention given to a stalker is still attention and empowers them. If they can't have your love they will take your hate, anger and fear. (CyberAngels, n.d.)

In other words, asking a stalker to stop is not likely to be effective—although it is the first place to start. One of the most important things a victim can do is to document the situation. Save e-mail messages. Capture chat sessions. Document everything. Although the details on how to capture this information are beyond the scope of this article, the need is clear. This information is what allows you to make a case—be it with a service provider, law enforcement, or in court. Beyond this basic record keeping, there are a few places to seek help.

Service Providers and Technical Fixes

One remedy that may be available is to have the Internet access of a stalker eliminated. According to WHOA's statistics, most frequently cases reported to the organization were resolved after complaints to the sender's Internet service provider (ISP; WHOA, 2002). The vast majority of ISPs have some sort of "terms of service" agreement or "acceptable use policy." These are generally contracts with the service providers and their users that restrict the use of the service providers' systems. Although these policies generally do not create a legal remedy on behalf of a victim, they do provide a means for the service provider to terminate someone who is abusing people via the service provider's system. A service provider is often willing to terminate "problem users" because it does not want to be seen as contributing to the continuation of abusive activities, it actively wants such conduct removed from the Internet, or it simply does not want the hassle of dealing with a user who generates complaints and the possibility of (expensive) legal hassles. As a result, if a victim can trace a stalker back to his or her Internet service provider, it is always sensible to look at the service provider's Web site to see if the provider has an acceptable use policy or terms of service agreement that is being violated by the stalker's actions. This policy then can be brought to the service provider's attention when describing the actions of the provider's user. In the course of dealing with a stalker, however, although this line of action may be effective, having his or her Internet access shut down is likely to provoke anger, possibly producing more harmful behavior in the end (either through a different service provider or through real-world contacts) rather than eliminating the threat altogether.

Tracing the source of online harassment may be straightforward, or it may be almost impossible. A harasser may make no effort to hide his or her identity or the service provider being used to originate harassing messages. In such a case, contacting a service provider is a fairly simple process. In addition to looking to see if the provider has a Web site with contact information, many providers maintain an e-mail account intended for abuse complaints—generally in the form of "abuse@[serviceprovider.com]" or the like. In addition, the domain name registration for a service provider will usually have contact information. Domain name registration information can be checked from a Web site such as http://www.allwhois.com/.

It may not be easy to track the source of harassing communications because of the ease of anonymously communicating on the Internet. In addition to services that specifically provide for anonymous communication by stripping identifying information from e-mail messages and other public posts, it is also possible to forge routing information. Although tracing such forgeries is beyond the scope of this article and techniques change with advances in the technology involved, good resources can be found online. (For e-mail, see the SPAM-L FAQ in the Further Reading section.) Of course, even if you can trace a

message back to its source, it may be the case that the originating account was opened with false information.

If one can identify a service provider but not the real name of the user, the provider is not likely to be helpful in turning over its user's identity. Often a service provider will insist on some sort of subpoena or court order before turning over identity or contact information about one of its users, even in a case where it is willing to cancel that same user's account. (Some jurisdictions make it relatively easy to file a suit or otherwise compel the release of information possessed by an ISP that identifies a harasser. Some jurisdictions will allow the filing of a "John Doe" lawsuit for the purpose of discovering who the true target of the suit should be.) It is worth noting that in some jurisdictions the service provider may be immune from any liability itself for harboring an online stalker, but this is not likely to extend to protections from criminal liability where it is earned, and it does not mean a service provider is exempt from turning over useful information when presented with a court order.

In some cases a remedy can be obtained by the victim simply changing e-mail addresses. However, this will obviously not be effective in cases where there is ongoing contact between the victim and the stalker, either in the offline word or in some online forum where the stalker will be able to learn the victim's new contact information.

Without resorting to help from a service provider, there are some steps that victims can take for themselves. The most obvious is to avoid unwanted contact. Delete or "kill file" messages from the stalker, either manually or through an automatic filter that most popular e-mail programs and newsreaders allow users to establish. Avoid logging on to chat rooms at times when the stalker is likely to be logged on as well.

The Law

If you are being stalked, a typical response is to call the police. For traditional stalking, this may result in gaining the assistance one needs to stop the stalker's conduct. According to WHOA's (2002) statistics, referring a matter to law enforcement was the most frequent solution to a stalking incident if contacting a service provider or changing e-mail addresses proved insufficient. Unfortunately, in the case of online stalking, the response from the police is not always useful. Many people who call the police are unable to obtain redress for their problem. As found in the Department of Justice (1999) report, training of law enforcement officers to handle online stalking is erratic and, in large measure, insufficient. Depending on location, the type of law enforcement to contact may vary—for instance, are state or federal authorities the best resource? In the United States, a victim could try contacting the local or state police, the Federal Bureau of Investigation, or the Secret Service—all of which may handle some types of online crimes. The amount of coordination and awareness between law enforcement groups is growing. The level of technical sophistication and resources devoted to computer crime–related issues is also improving. In some cases, such improvements are required by legislation. Often the agency contacted may not know how to help but will know to whom the victim should be referred.

Victims who do not get a knowledgeable response may want to try a different law enforcement entity.

Another concern with contacting law enforcement is a matter of resource allocation. Simply put, law enforcement resources are limited, and there may be no one capable of taking time to help a victim of online harassment if other matters that affect more than a single victim or that appear likely to result in more immediate harm are consuming available resources. There may also be a lack of investigative tools with which to pursue a matter even if there is sufficient interest in the case.

Finally, contacting law enforcement may result in either a very public or a very private investigation. The fact that a police report has been filed, for instance, is a matter of public record in many jurisdictions and may attract media attention. Conversely, the details of an investigation undertaken by law enforcement may be confidential, even from the victim who reported the incident and stands to benefit from the results of any investigation. An investigation by law enforcement is generally out of the hands of the victim because it becomes the government's rather than the victim's case.

Another means of using the law to provide a remedy is through the hiring of a private attorney. The ability of an attorney to provide assistance will be dictated by where the victim and the stalker are located. This will determine, in part, the applicable laws, which will determine if a "private cause of action" exists. In other words, an individual generally cannot sue someone for violating a criminal law. Generally, only the government can sue someone to enforce the criminal law. Some statutes do, however, provide a private cause of action or some other civil remedy that will allow a victim to go after a stalker directly, without assistance from the government. The results of such a suit could include injunctive relief which, for example, would require the stalker to leave the victim alone or provide for recovery of monetary damages.

What kinds of laws are there? As mentioned, traditional stalking laws may apply to cyberstalking cases. These are generally criminal statutes that require law enforcement assistance. These statutes generally require multiple incidents of harassment that cause the victim to fear for his or her physical safety. Sometimes the safety of family members is also covered under these statutes. The statute may also dictate a specific behavioral requirement, such as the stalker's having physically followed the victim. Some jurisdictions have expanded or clarified their laws in recent years to provide a remedy specific to online stalking. These laws may acknowledge certain harmful uses of technology in defining the offense or merely serve to remove obstacles contained in traditional stalking statutes containing physical requirements that do not apply in the online world.

Some jurisdictions address stalking-like behavior with traditional harassment law or laws prohibiting intimidation. Harassment and intimidation laws may cover a broader range of conduct than traditional stalking laws, but they may have other sorts of obstacles to overcome to ensure that only egregious conduct is prohibited as unlawful harassment. Hurdles, for example, may include requirements that a harasser has the intent to cause harm, or they may require a certain level of damage before providing a remedy. These statutes may be technology dependent, such as harassing telephone call statutes, although use of modems to connect to the Internet may fit within the statutes' coverage.

If messages from a stalker contain actual threats, many jurisdictions have statutes that provide a remedy for the transmission of credible threats. One famous online "stalking" case, the "Jake Baker" case (*U.S. v. Alkhabaz*, 1997), involved a student at the University of Michigan who posted to Usenet news a piece of "erotic fiction" describing the sexual torture of a woman, a woman who was given the name of one of his classmates. The man was arrested and initially held in jail as a threat to society pending a psychiatric evaluation. The court held that the man's actions were not criminal, because no evidence was presented that his actions were anything more than a sick fantasy. Because there was no evidence that he would really act out his fantasy, there was no credible threat, and thus the federal statute at issue was not violated. Some jurisdictions may have different standards for threats made to certain types of people, such as the U.S. prohibition of threats made against the president (18 U.S.C. §871).

Statutes that address specific conduct such as identity theft, false attribution of origin of the messages, or eavesdropping may also come to bear in a cyberstalking case. Some "common law" concepts—traditional legal concepts that have evolved through court decisions and for which there may be no statute—may also provide a mechanism for legally attacking a stalker. For instance, assault (where a victim is placed in fear of bodily injury); intentional infliction of emotional distress; or, depending on the particular actions, defamation, trespass, or fraud-type arguments may also allow for a remedy. Depending on the law of a particular jurisdiction, "family law" remedies such as restraining orders and orders of protection, often aimed at keeping away ex-spouses or love interests, may be relevant.

CONCLUSION

Online stalking is a problem of unknown proportions. Just as traditional stalking is a concern for its victims, however, so, too is the online equivalent. As more people live more of their lives online, all forms of online crime are likely to increase. Although this will produce more claims of online stalking and other forms of online harassment, it will also force law enforcement to be more prepared to address the needs of victims. In the case of legislators, they will also be required to ensure that the laws have evolved to address the concerns of victims—without having undue impact on legitimate, but perhaps heated, interactions. Because of the international nature of the Internet, cooperation between governments will be essential to address foreign harassers. Efforts are already being put into place to aid in the international enforcement of criminal laws, as evidenced by the Council of Europe's Cybercrime Convention (Howard, 1999) that requires all signing countries to outlaw certain types of objectionable conduct and to provide international assistance in enforcing other countries' laws that prohibit this minimum level of criminal conduct. It is reasonable to expect that the more egregious forms of online stalking are likely to be sufficient to result in some degree of international cooperation.

GLOSSARY

Acceptable Use Policy An Internet service provider's rules describing what one of its customers may and may not do with or through the provider's computer system.

Criminal Lawsuit A lawsuit brought by the government against an individual. Unlike a private or civil lawsuit, a criminal lawsuit could involve jail time or other more serious sanctions depending on what remedies are contained in the applicable law.

Cyberstalking Another name for online stalking (see below).

Harass To engage in an intentional course of conduct directed at a specific person that alarms, torments, or terrorizes that person.

Injunctive Relief Relief granted by a court to a victim that generally orders another person not to do something, such as ordering a stalker to stay away from a victim, or to do something, such as remove objectionable material from a Web site.

John Doe Lawsuits Lawsuits filed against an unknown person. Once the lawsuit is filed, the party filing the suit can try to obtain more information on the person being sued.

Kill Files Filters in many e-mail programs that are used to block messages sent from people or addresses listed in the kill file (also called bozo filters). These are used so that e-mail or other electronic communications from a harasser can be deleted by the victim before they appear in the inbox.

Online Stalking A form of computer-mediated harassment analogous to traditional stalking.

Private Cause of Action or Private Right of Action The ability to sue a person engaging in objectionable conduct without the need for government involvement to enforce the law.

Restraining Orders Orders issued by a judge that may prohibit someone from contacting another person. What these orders may cover varies by jurisdiction.

Stalking A form of harassment generally targeted at a specific individual that causes fear of physical harm. As a legal term, this definition varies by jurisdiction.

CROSS REFERENCES

See *Cyberlaw: The Major Areas, Development, and Information Security Aspects; Legal, Social, and Ethical Issues of the Internet; Privacy Law and the Internet.*

REFERENCES

Brenner, S. (2001, June). "Cybercrime investigation and prosecution: The role of penal and procedural law. *E Law—Murdoch University Electronic Journal of Law, 8.* Retrieved Mar. 23, 2003, from http://www.murdoch. edu.au/elaw/issues/v8n2/brenner82_text.html

California Civil Code §1708.7—Stalking (2001).

Cant, S. (2001, March 27). Courts wrangle over cyberstalking. *The Age*, p. 3.

Council of Europe Convention on Cybercrime. (2001, November 23). Retrieved Mar. 23, 2003, from http://conventions.coe.int/Treaty/en/Treaties/Html/185.htm

CyberAngels (n.d.). Retrieved prior to June 1, 2002, from the CyberAngels Web site (no longer available).

Cyberstalking [Illinois Criminal Statute] 720 ILCS 5/12–7.5 (2001).

Dayton v. Davis, 735 N.E.2d 939 (Ohio App. 2 Dist., Nov. 24, 1999).

Eckenweiler, M. (1996, February 1). Net law. *NetGuide*, p. 35.

Ellison, L., & Akdeniz, Y. (1998, December). Cyberstalking: The regulation of harassment on the Internet. *Criminal Law Review* [Special Edition: *Crime, criminal justice and the Internet*], pp. 29–48.

Howard, C. (1999). *Cyber-stalking: Obsessional pursuit and the digital criminal. Stalking typologies and pathologies.* Retrieved Mar. 23, 2003, from http://www.crimelibrary. com/criminal_mind/psychology/cyberstalking/3.html? sect=19

Hubbard, A. (2001, June 24). When truth is stranger than fiction. *Sunday Star-Times*, p. A7.

Humphreys, L. (2001, June 20). NP author won't give in to stalker. *Daily News* (New Zealand).

Koch, L. (2000, May 25). Cyberstalking hype. *Interactive Week*, reprinted in Loundy, D., *Computer Crime, Information Warfare & Economic Espionage.* Carolina Academic Press, 2003, pp. 303–305.

Miller, G., & Maharaj, D. (1999, January 22). N. Hollywood man charged in 1st cyberstalking case. *Los Angeles Times*.

People v. Kochanowski, 719 N.Y.S.2d 461 (Sup. Ct. App. Term, NY, October 18, 2000).

Soh-Jung, Y. (2001, July 6). Internet stalker punishable for libel. *The Korea Herald*.

U.S. v. Alkhabaz, 104 F.3d 1492 (6th Cir. 1997).

U.S. Department of Justice. (1999, August). *Report on cyberstalking: A new challenge for law enforcement and industry.* A report from the Attorney General to the Vice President. Retrieved Mar. 23, 2003, from http://www. usdoj.gov/criminal/cybercrime/cyberstalking.htm

Working to Halt Online Abuse. (2002). http://www. haltabuse.org/resources/index.shtml

FURTHER READING

1999 Report on Cyberstalking: A New Challenge for Law Enforcement and Industry: http://www.usdoj. gov/criminal/cybercrime/cyberstalking.htm

CyberAngels (Initially a project of the Guardian Angels neighborhood watch organization, on June 1, 2002, the group splintered and divided into the CyberAngels and WiredPatrol.org): http://www.CyberAngels.org/

Lucke, K., Reading E-Mail Headers: http://www. stopspam.org/email/headers/headers.html

The SPAM-L FAQ: http://www.claws-and-paws.com/ spam-l/tracking.html

WiredPatrol.org Cyberstalking Index: http://www. wiredpatrol.org/stalking/index.html

Working to Halt Online Abuse: http://www.haltabuse.org/

Electronic Attacks

Thomas M. Chen and Jimi Thompson, *Southern Methodist University*
Matthew C. Elder, *Symantec Corporation*

INTRODUCTION

In today's society, computer systems are valuable, and often invaluable, for innumerable business and personal uses. Computer systems and networks are also very tempting as targets, shown by statistics that track the frequency and prevalence of cybercrimes. For example, Symantec Corporation estimates that organizations were hit by an average of 11 attacks daily during the first half of 2004 (Turner, 2004).

Part of the temptation is the ease of electronic attacks. Although not every attack takes advantage of vulnerabilities, it is widely known that computer systems have numerous vulnerabilities. In early 2004, about 48 new vulnerabilities were discovered weekly on average (Turner, 2004). Moreover, 96 percent of them were serious enough to be rated as moderately or highly severe. Attackers are keenly aware of new vulnerabilities because it takes time for organizations to set up adequate protection, e.g., software patching. In early 2004, exploits for new vulnerabilities appeared on average only 5.8 days after announcement of the vulnerability.

Electronic attacks have also become easier since virtually all computers are interconnected by the Internet or private networks. Moreover, mobile and handheld devices with Internet connectivity have steadily grown in popularity. This extensive network environment facilitates remote attacks and makes attacks more difficult to track to their sources. The growing number of networked machines also means more targets to attract attacks.

This chapter gives an overview of electronic attacks, highlighting the basic steps involved in attacks seeking to compromise computer systems. Most of the emphasis here is on network-enabled attacks, but this is not meant to imply that all electronic attacks are carried out through the network. This chapter also describes large-scale attacks such as viruses, worms, denial of service, and spam.

Types of Attackers

Attackers can be categorized in a number of different ways. One distinction often made is the relationship of the attacker to the target, either internal or external. Insider attacks from within an organization are believed to be the most common and most critical in past years. A commonly cited statistic in the late 1990s attributed 70 percent of all attacks to insiders. Insiders have certain advantages that can increase the likelihood of a successful attack, such as the trust of an organization and knowledge regarding systems and their defenses. However, with ubiquitous network connectivity today, external attacks are more likely than ever before (CERT, 2004).

Attackers can also be categorized as either amateurs or professionals. Many people probably visualize an attacker as the stereotypical male teenage "hacker" or "script kiddie" with too much free time. This stereotype has been perpetuated by fictional characters in films such as *War Games* as well as real-life arrested hackers. For example, the most recent case was the arrest of 18-year-old Sven Jaschan in May 2004. He is being prosecuted for writing the four most damaging worms of 2004, including the Netsky and Sasser worms, which accounted for 70 percent of the worms received in the world in the first half of 2004 (Sophos, 2004).

While teenage vandals are undoubtedly responsible for a substantial fraction of electronic attacks, it appears from recent trends that cybercrimes are being increasingly carried out by professionals and organized crime. Professional crimes tend to be more sophisticated and larger scale than amateur crimes. Attacks designed for identity theft and profit are becoming more prevalent. There are growing number of channels used for buying and selling lists of compromised computers and stolen identity data. Other professionals known to be involved in electronic attacks include national governments, military agencies, and industrial spies.

Attacker Goals and Motivations

The motivations for electronic attacks depend on the attacker. Because there are many different types of attackers, motivations can be almost anything, ranging from fun and fame to extortion, profit, espionage, revenge, or a political agenda.

The stereotypical teenage hacker is believed to be usually interested in gaining fame or notoriety. For example, according to some media accounts, Sven Jaschan appeared primarily motivated by curiosity and perhaps good intentions, writing Netsky. A worm to combat two other worms, MyDoom and Bagle.

On the other hand, messages encoded in the Bagle worm suggested that its authors were professionals motivated by profit. This is supported by the worm's actions, including installation of backdoors for remote access (Symantec, 2004).

An increasingly common goal is invasion of privacy or theft of confidential data. This is evident from the escalation of spyware and phishing attacks (described later in this chapter).

Attack Targets

An electronic attack will have specific targets depending on the attacker's goals. The target could be particular information on a single machine, or the target could be as broad as the entire network infrastructure.

A recent survey showed that 70 percent of organizations were hit by some type of electronic attack (CERT, 2004). E-commerce was the most frequently targeted sector, as many attackers now are motivated by financial gain (Turner, 2004).

Attack Phases

An electronic attack is commonly carried out through a progression of steps, analogous to the steps of a physical attack (Chirillo, 2002; McClure, Scambray, and Kutz, 2001; Skoudis, 2002). The first step is reconnaissance to collect the necessary intelligence in preparation of the actual attack. The second step is the actual attack, which could have many different goals. During and after the attack, the attacker may try to take actions to avoid detection.

RECONNAISSANCE PHASE

If an attacker wants to compromise a specific computer system, it would obviously be wise to prepare for an attack by first discovering everything possible about the target. The reconnaissance phase can reveal a variety of information—account names, addresses, operating systems, perhaps even passwords—that could increase the success of an attack. Moreover, most reconnaissance techniques are not viewed as malicious or illegal, and may be carried out without a high risk of alarming a potential target.

As one might imagine, many different reconnaissance techniques are possible, and attackers do not follow a unique sequence of steps. Here we outline three general steps to progressively discover more information about a potential target.

Footprinting

The initial step in discovery is called footprinting, fingerprinting, or enumeration. An abundance of information is readily available on the Web. These databases can be interrogated by a number of utilities such as *nslookup* or *dig*.

The whois databases contain information about the assignment of Internet addresses, registration of domain names, and individual contacts. Domain names such as www.mycompany.com are registered through the Internet Network Information Center (InterNIC), a consortium of several companies and the U.S. government. For a domain name, the InterNIC whois database can provide the registrant's name and address, domain servers, and contact information.

For information about ownership of ranges of IP addresses, the American Registry for Internet Numbers (ARIN) database provides a mechanism for finding contact and registration information for resources including IP addresses, autonomous system numbers, and registered organizations in the Americas. European IP address assignments can be discovered from Réseaux IP Européens Network Coordination Centre (RIPE NCC). Likewise, Asian IP address assignments are maintained by the Asia Pacific Network Information Center (APNIC).

Another useful database is the domain name system (DNS). DNS is a hierarchy of servers used to associate domain names, IP addresses, and mail servers. The hierarchy extends from the root DNS servers down to DNS servers for individual organizations and networks. These DNS servers contain information about other low-level DNS servers and IP addresses of individual hosts.

Scanning

Armed with information gained from footprinting, an attacker may know names and addresses for potential targets, and perhaps specific host system information. Footprinting is similar to looking up names and numbers in a telephone book. Scanning is a more active step to learn about potential targets from their responses. There are many different ways to conduct scans.

War Dialing. The most primitive though still useful type of scanning is war dialing. War dialers are simply automated machines for dialing a set of phone lines to find accessible modems. A telephone number within an organization is usually easy to find through the Internet or telephone books, then an attacker could dial a surrounding range of numbers. The results will reveal phone lines with modems. War dialers can include a nudging function that sends a predefined string of characters to a modem to see how it responds. The response may reveal the lack of a password, the type of platform, and perhaps a remote access program (e.g., the popular pcAnywhere).

Although war dialers have been in use for decades, they can still be effective in attacks when a modem is not properly secured. Obviously, modems without password protection are completely vulnerable. In addition, modems can be attacked by guessing the password (see the section below on password attacks). A successful attack through an unsecure modem can lead to compromise of an entire organization's network, effectively bypassing firewalls and other sophisticated defenses.

Ping Sweeps. Internet control message protocol (ICMP) is part of the Internet protocol to enable notification of troubles and other control functions. Ping consisting of a pair of ICMP messages called Echo Request and Echo Reply are designed to verify that a specific host is operational. An IP-addressable host should reply to an ICMP Echo Request with an ICMP Echo Reply.

Ping is frequently used by attackers to scan a block of IP addresses for live hosts. Any number of tools can easily perform a ping sweep. However, since ping sweeps can be noticed, organizations will sometimes block ICMP messages. TCP packets to well known ports will also work, prompting a TCP SYN-ACK reply.

Network Mapping. Traceroute is a widely used utility for mapping a network topology. It cleverly takes advantage of the time-to-live (TTL) field in the IP packet header. The TTL field is set to the maximum time allowed for delivery of an IP packet. Each router decrements the TTL field by the time spent by the packet in that router, but routers typically forward packets quickly and are then forced to decrement the TTL by the minimum unit of one. Thus, the TTL field essentially serves as a hop count, where each router decrements the TTL field by one. If the TTL field reaches a value of zero, a router should discard the packet and send an ICMP Time Exceeded message back to the source IP address in the discarded packet.

Traceroute sends out a series of UDP packets, starting with a TTL field value of one and incrementing the value by one for each successive packet. When ICMP Time Exceeded messages are returned, they reveal the addresses of routers at various distances. An example of traceroute is shown in Figure 1. Similarly, ICMP messages could be used instead of UDP packets.

Port Scanning. TCP and UDP packets are sent to and received at specific ports indicated in the TCP and UDP headers. The headers allow a range of 65,535 TCP and 65,535 UDP ports. Certain "well known" port numbers are pre-assigned to common protocols. For example, Web servers listen for HTTP requests on TCP port 80. The other ports may be used dynamically as needed.

An attacker is very often interested to discover which ports are open on a potential target, i.e., which services are listening. However, probing every possible port manually would be very tedious. A port scanner is an automated tool for sending probes to a set of specific ports to see which ports are open. An example of a port scan is shown in Figure 2.

Operating System Detection. Knowledge of a host's operating system and its version is valuable to attackers because specific vulnerabilities are known for different operating systems. One technique used by attackers is TCP stack fingerprinting, implemented in the popular Nmap tool. While the TCP protocol is standardized in terms of its three-way connection establishment handshake, the standards do not cover responses to various illegal combinations of TCP flags. Operating systems can differ in their implementations of responses to illegal TCP packets. The idea of TCP stack fingerprinting is to probe for these differences with various illegal TCP packets until the operating system, even its particular version, can be identified (Fyodor, 2002).

Scanning Tools. Plenty of free and commercial scanning tools are available. Many of these are used for legitimate purposes by system administrators.

Sam Spade is a combination of useful reconnaissance tools, wrapped behind a Windows graphical user interface, including ping, whois, IP block whois (ARIN database query), nslookup, traceroute, and a function to verify email addresses on a specific mail server. A version of Sam Spade is available as a Web-based tool. Many other Web-based scanning tools can be found easily, such as a Web portal run by Mixter that includes ping, traceroute, whois, and port scans.

Other examples of free toolkits include CyberKit and Cheops. Cheops is a popular, easy-to-use tool for network mapping that automatically draws out a network topology based on discovered hosts and distances; it also discovers active services through port scanning and identifies operating systems by TCP stack fingerprinting.

An example of a commercial tool, NetScanTools Pro includes ping, port scans, traceroute, netscanner (ping sweep), custom ICMP packet generation, whois, nslookup, IP packet capturing, email address validation, and operating system identification. It uses an unusual method for operating system identification based on observing responses to four types of ICMP messages and variations of them. WildPackets' iNetTools is another commercial tool providing many of the functions as other scanners.

Finally, probably the most widely used tool for port scanning is the open-source Nmap shown in Figure 3. Nmap is perhaps the most capable port scanner, providing options for many different types of scans. Possible scans include TCP Connect, TCP SYN, TCP FIN, Xmas Tree, Null, TCP ACK, and UDP. Other interesting options in Nmap include: scanning for RPC (remote procedure calls) services on a target machine; sending decoy scans with fake source addresses; sending scans with different timing options to avoid detection; and identifying a computer's operating system via TCP stack fingerprinting.

Vulnerability Scanning

Using general network scanning, an attacker can discover a broad range of information about a potential target, such as host addresses, network topology, open ports, and operating systems. The next step in reconnaissance is to scan for specific vulnerabilities that might be exploited for an attack. It is possible to manually scan for vulnerabilities, but would be obviously time consuming to check

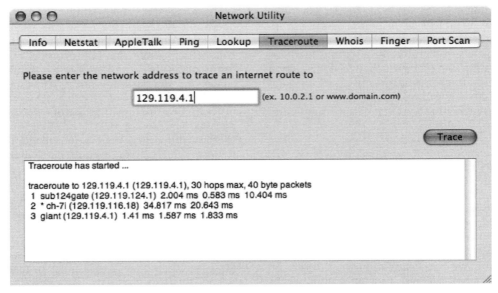

Figure 1: Example of traceroute output.

many machines for hundreds or thousands of vulnerabilities. Many automated vulnerability scanners are available and often used by system administrators to evaluate the security of an internal network.

Types of Vulnerabilities. Several types of vulnerabilities are usually sought by scanners:

• Default configuration weaknesses: Many operating systems and service applications ship with default accounts and passwords. These are intended to help ease the installation process, or simplify troubleshooting in case of lost passwords. Naturally, default passwords should be changed but are sometimes overlooked or ignored. Attackers look for the existence of default configurations

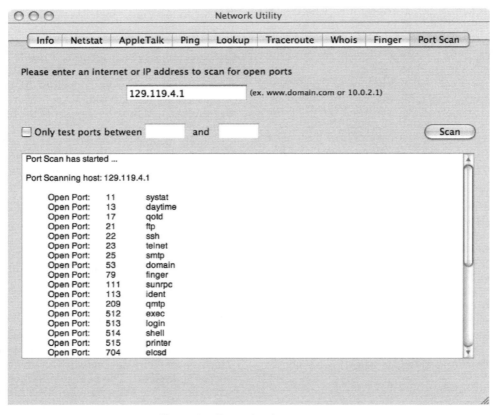

Figure 2: Example of a port scan.

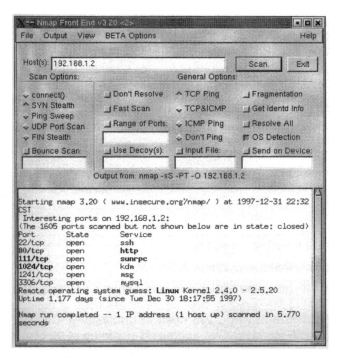

Figure 3: Nmap graphical user interface.

because they offer an easy way to compromise a system.

• Misconfiguration errors: Networking equipment requires expertise to configure properly. Obviously, incorrect configuration settings can defeat any security offered by networking equipment. An example is a misconfigured firewall that could be too permissive in allowing incoming packets.

• Well-known system vulnerabilities: New vulnerabilities are being constantly discovered in operating systems and applications. The most critical are often published by vendors with a patch. However, it requires a great deal of time and effort for organizations or individuals to keep up with security bulletins and patches. The time between the publication of a security vulnerability and the installation of patches leaves a window of opportunity for attackers to exploit that vulnerability.

Vulnerability Scanning Tools. A vulnerability scanner is an automated program generally consisting of a vulnerability database to check; a user interface to allow control of the scanner; scanning engine to send and receive packets; knowledge base to track the current scan; and a recording and reporting tool (Skoudis, 2002). Many open-source and commercial vulnerability scanners can be found easily.

Most vulnerabilities scanner operate in a similar way. They first discover live hosts within a given address range using ping or similar utility. Then they run a basic set of scans to discover open ports and active services running on the hosts. Based on this information, they proceed to more customized probes for vulnerabilities. In the final step, they generate output in the form of a report. Some vulnerabilities scanners include a function for network mapping as a byproduct.

The Security Administrator's Tool for Analyzing Networks (SATAN) was an early well-known vulnerability scanner developed in 1995. While SATAN is still freely available, it has two updated descendents, the open-source Security Auditor's Research Assistant (SARA) and the commercial Security Administrator's Integrated Network Tool (SAINT). SARA enhances SATAN's security engine and program architecture by providing an improved user interface and up-to-date vulnerability tests. SARA can discover information about hosts by examining various network services. It can also find potential security flaws, such as misconfigured network services, well-known system vulnerabilities, or poorly chosen policies. It can generate a report of these results or execute a rule-based program to investigate any potential security problems.

Nessus is a popular open-source vulnerability scanner. It works in a client-server architecture, where the client and server may run on the same machine. The client consists of a tool for user configuration and a tool for recording and reporting results. The server consists of a vulnerability database, a knowledge base to keep track of the current scan, and a scanning engine. Nmap is included as the built-in port scanning tool. The vulnerability database is designed to be modular in the form of plug-ins, each plug-in to check for a specific vulnerability. Nessus contains over 500 plug-ins, and a large user base continually contributes new ones. Vulnerabilities are rated and classified into categories such as finger abuses, Windows-related vulnerabilities, backdoors, CGI (common gateway interface) abuses, RPC vulnerabilities, firewall misconfigurations, remote root access, FTP, and SMTP (mail server vulnerabilities).

Commercial vulnerability scanners include TigerTools' TigerSuite Pro, McAfee's CyberCop ASaP, ISS's Internet Scanner, eEye Digital Security's Retina Network Security Scanner, and Cisco Systems' Secure Scanner.

ATTACK PHASE

The actual attack phase can take many different forms and serve different purposes, such as stealing confidential data, tampering with the integrity of data, compromising the availability of a resource, or obtaining unauthorized access to a system. As mentioned previously, these specific attack types can be directed at either specific targets or the general network infrastructure. Quite often, large-scale, indiscriminate attacks have the effect of widespread disruption of computers and networks, even if that is not the real intent. They have widespread effects because they are carried out through a network toward a large number of targets.

The major types of attack covered here include sniffing, session hijacking, password attacks, exploits, social engineering attacks, Trojan horses, spyware and adware, viruses and worms, spam, and denial-of-service (DoS) attacks. The list is not meant to be exhaustive, but rather highlights of important attack types seen today.

These attack types are not mutually exclusive—in fact, many times they are combined in so-called blended threats. For example, social engineering can be a component of many e-mail worms. Some spyware is included

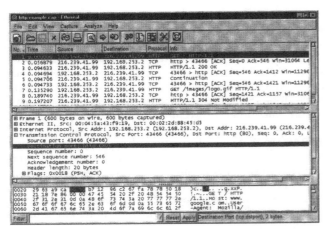

Figure 4: Example of Ethereal output.

as a Trojan horse in seemingly harmless software. Viruses can spread via spam, and so forth.

Sniffing

Sniffing is a form of passive attack that enables the compromise of confidential information. Sniffers, traditionally used by network administrators for traffic monitoring and LAN troubleshooting, have become one of the most commonly used attack tools. An example from the Ethereal sniffer is shown in Figure 4. On a LAN, hosts see all traffic broadcast on the LAN medium but normally ignore the packets that are addressed to other hosts. A sniffer program puts the network interface of a host into promiscuous mode to capture all packets seen at the interface. Thus, the sniffer can eavesdrop on everything transmitted on the LAN including user names, passwords, DNS queries, e-mail messages, and all types of personal data.

Many free and commercial sniffers are available, including tcpdump, windump, Snort, Ethereal, Sniffit, and dsniff.

Session Hijacking

Session hijacking is a combination of sniffing and address spoofing that enables the compromise of a user's remote login session, thus providing an attacker unauthorized access to a machine with the privileges of the legitimate user. Address spoofing in IP is quite simple because the sender of an IP packet writes in the IP source address in the packet header. Attackers can send packets with any fake IP source address.

If a user is currently engaged in an interactive login session (e.g., through telnet, rlogin, FTP), a session hijacking tool allows an attacker to steal the session. When most hijack victims see their login session disappear, they usually just assume that the cause is network trouble and try to login again, unaware of the hijacking attack.

Popular session hijacking tools include Juggernaut and Hunt. The hijacking attack begins with the attacker sniffing packets of an interactive session between two hosts, carefully noting the TCP sequence numbers of all packets. To hijack the session, the attacker injects packets with a source address spoofing one of the hosts. The proper TCP

sequence numbers must be used for the attack to work, because the receiving host must be convinced to accept the faked packets from the attacker.

Password Attacks

Password attacks enable unauthorized access to a machine or other resource with the privileges of the user associated with the compromised password. Passwords continue to be very frequently used for access control, despite their major weakness: if a password is guessed, an attacker could gain complete access. The most well protected systems could be compromised by a single weak password. Understandably, many attacks are often directed at guessing or bypassing passwords.

The easiest passwords to guess are the default passwords installed by many operating systems and service applications. Extensive lists of default accounts and passwords are not hard to find by searching on the Web, and sometimes they are overlooked or ignored by system administrators.

Another easy password attack is a dictionary attack that, as the name suggests, takes advantage of the natural human instinct to choose passwords that are common words or names. The chance of finding passwords that are common words may not be as likely as in the past though, because modern systems are usually programmed with rules to prevent users from choosing easily guessable passwords. More sophisticated hybrid password guessing tools combine dictionary attacks with limited brute-force attacks. They begin with guesses of common words but then methodically add characters to words to form new guesses.

The most powerful password attacks, called password cracking, can be performed if the attacker can obtain the password file (Shimonski, 2002). Computer systems store a list of user accounts and passwords in a password file, but the information is encrypted or hashed for protection against attackers. If an attacker can obtain the password file, the attacker has the advantage of time (translating into more CPU cycles) to crack the passwords by brute force (i.e., attempting all possible combinations of legal characters). A few examples of password cracking tools include John the Ripper, Cain and Abel, Crack, Lincrack, L0phtcrack, Nutcracker, PalmCrack, and RainbowCrack.

A variation and extension of password attacks involves guessing usernames as well as passwords. Even if an attacker does not know a username associated with a given resource prior to beginning a password attack, many systems include commonly named accounts such as "Administrator" or "Guest". Automated attacks in particular, such as self-propagating worms, can incorporate password attacks that will guess both usernames and passwords when attempting to compromise a resource.

Exploits

Exploits of vulnerabilities are a means of attack that enable unauthorized access to a system. Vulnerabilities are continuously discovered in operating systems and application software. A vulnerability is a description of a problem, which is not dangerous in and of itself. The danger comes when an exploit is written that takes advantage of a vulnerability to compromise the security of the operating system or application. Usually vulnerabilities are announced at the same time with a patch for fixing the vulnerability. A vendor has knowledge of the vulnerability but holds the information from the public at large until there is a fix for the problem. However, the vulnerability is sometimes announced prior to a patch, in which case there is an important race to devise and distribute a patch prior to the creation of an exploit taking advantage of that vulnerability. In general, the time between the announcement of a vulnerability and the appearance of a corresponding exploit is shrinking (Turner, 2004).

One of the most common types of exploit, used particularly often by worms, is a buffer overflow attack. Attackers are drawn to this exploit because many applications and operating systems do not perform proper bounds checking and are thus vulnerable to a buffer overflow. Furthermore, if successful, a buffer overflow attack could lead to complete control of a target machine.

A well-known instance is a stack-based buffer overflow, or "smashing the stack" (AlephOne, 1996). During a function call, various pieces of data are pushed onto the program stack: function-call arguments, return pointer, frame pointer, and local variables. Normally, at the end of the function call, the pieces of data are popped off the stack, and the return pointer is used to resume execution of the main program. A stack-based buffer overflow depends on inputting more data than expected into the local variables. The excess data is written into the allocated buffer space and then overwritten onto the frame pointer and return pointer. If the excess data can be crafted carefully enough, the overwritten return pointer can be made to point back into the stack somewhere in the data input by the attacker. Hence, when the main program resumes execution, the attacker's data (malicious code) will be run.

It might be observed that a buffer overflow attack requires careful coding and significant technical knowledge about the target processor architecture. Hence, buffer overflow attacks are not easy to craft from scratch, but pre-written exploits can be found and used even by novice attackers.

Social Engineering

Social engineering is a time-tested, low-tech approach that continues to be effective for both the reconnaissance and the actual attack phases. A social engineering attack refers to a human interaction where social skills are used to trick the victim into a compromising action, such as revealing personal information or opening an infected e-mail message. Social engineering can be combined with many of the other attack types to compromise security for just about any purpose. Although social engineering attacks are simple in concept, they can be surprisingly effective if executed well.

In the past, the telephone was a favorite avenue for social engineering attacks. Attackers would call an organization posing to be an employee, customer, supplier, or auditor, trying to obtain proprietary information. Today, many social engineering attacks are carried out through e-mail, due to the low risk and low cost of mass e-mailing. Also, e-mail works across different computing platforms

and various types of devices (including handheld mobile devices). E-mail became the preferred medium after the success demonstrated by mass e-mailing viruses, such as the 2000 Love Letter and 2001 Anna Kournikova viruses. E-mail viruses typically offer a provocative reason to entice the recipient into opening (executing) an e-mail attachment, which results in a virus infection. More recently, e-mails might pretend to be security bulletins, bounced e-mail, notifications from an ISP or system administrator, or other official-looking messages.

Recently, a type of social engineering attack called phishing (password harvesting fishing) has escalated in frequency. Phishing attacks begin with e-mail seemingly from a reputable credit card company or financial institution that requests account information, often suggesting that there is a problem with an account or a transaction. These e-mails are carefully crafted to appear official and often include corporate graphics. The e-mails typically include a link directing the victim to a Web site that appears to be genuine, but is actually a facsimile. The purpose of the Web site is to capture any account or personal information submitted by the victim. An example of a phishing e-mail appearing to be sent from eBay is shown in Figure 5.

Trojan Horses

Trojan horses are malicious programs that appear to be benign (analogous to the Greek wooden horse in the Trojan War). The purpose of the disguise is to entice a user into installing and executing the program. If executed, Trojan horses are capable of doing anything that other programs can do, running with the privileges of the associated user. Similar and related to social engineering attacks, Trojan horses can be combined with many of the other attack types to compromise security for just about any purpose. Today, Trojan horses are distributed by any number of stealthy ways including virus and worm payloads, peer-to-peer file sharing, and Web site downloads. Victims are often unaware of their installation.

The most worrisome Trojan horse may be backdoor programs, sometimes called remote access Trojans (RATs) because backdoors allow an attacker to remotely access a victim's machine. Backdoors circumvent the usual access control security (e.g., login with password). Many backdoor Trojans are known and some are promoted for legitimate administrative uses, including Sub7, Back Orifice 2000, and Virtual Network Computer (VNC).

Adware and Spyware

Adware is software to monitor and profile a user's online behavior, typically for the purposes of targeted marketing. Adware is often installed at the same time as other software programs; when this occurs without the user's knowledge, the adware (and the software with which it is bundled) is an instance of a Trojan horse. Even when the user is alerted to the presence of the adware (often buried in the ignored licensing agreement), adware can represent an attack on the privacy of the user and the confidentiality of the user's data when information about the user is communicated back to a marketing organization. Adware is primarily an annoyance,

From: eBay <eBay@eBay.com>
Subject: **Account Violate The User Policy Second Notice**
Date: December 1, 2004 5:25:40 AM CST
To:

Welcome to eBay

Dear valued customer   ⑦ Need Help?

We regret to inform you that your eBay account could be suspended if you don't re-update your account information. To resolve this problems please click here and re-enter your account information. If your problems could not be resolved your account will be suspended for a period of 24 hours, after this period your account will be terminated.

For the User Agreement, Section 9, we may immediately issue a warning, temporarily suspend, indefinitely suspend or terminate your membership and refuse to provide our services to you if we believe that your actions may cause financial loss or legal liability for you, our users or us. We may also take these actions if we are unable to verify or authenticate any information you provide to us.

Due to the suspension of this account, please be advised you are prohibited from using eBay in any way. This includes the registering of a new account. Please note that this suspension does not relieve you of your agreed-upon obligation to pay any fees you may owe to eBay.

Regards, Safeharbor Department eBay, Inc
The eBay team.
This is an automatic message. Please do not reply.

Announcements | Register | Shop eBay-o-rama | Security Center | Policies | PayPal
Feedback Forum | About eBay | Jobs | Affiliates Program | Developers | eBay Downloads | eBay Gift Certificates
My eBay | Site Map
Browse | Sell | Services | Search | Help | Community

Copyright © 1995-2004 eBay Inc. All Rights Reserved.
Designated trademarks and brands are the property of
their respective owners.
Use of this Web site constitutes acceptance of the
eBay User Agreement and Privacy Policy.

Figure 5: A fraudulent phishing e-mail pretending to be from eBay.

sometimes causing pop-up marketing windows during Web surfing.

A more serious and growing concern is another type of software that profiles and records a user's activities, called spyware. Similar to adware, spyware can sometimes be installed with a user's or system administrator's knowledge. For example, commercial versions of spyware are sold as means to monitor and regulate the online actions of children or an organization's employees. Often though, spyware can be installed stealthily on a machine as a Trojan horse or as part of a virus or worm compromise. Spyware can record keystrokes (also known as keystroke loggers), Websites visited, passwords, screenshots, and virtually anything done on a computer. After capturing data, spyware can communicate the stolen data by various channels (e.g., e-mail, FTP, upload to the Web, or Internet Relay Chat) to an attacker. Spyware, like adware, is an attack on user privacy, but spyware is also more likely to compromise confidential data for identity theft.

Viruses and Worms

Viruses and worms are software with the key characteristic of self-replication (Grimes, 2001; Harley, Slade, & Gattiker, 2001). While there is some debate and blurring of distinctions between viruses and worms, common traditional definitions are the following:

• Viruses are program code that replicate by modifying (infecting) a normal program or file with a copy of itself.

• Worms are stand-alone programs that replicate by spreading copies of themselves to other systems through a network.

Traditional viruses are not complete programs themselves. When the host program or file is executed, the virus code is executed and takes over control to copy itself to other files. Usually human action is needed to execute the host program, so viruses are sometimes characterized as requiring human action to replicate. Although viruses were far more common than worms around ten years ago, worms have become predominant in the past few years. The increase in worms has coincided with the growth of computer networks. Today virtually all computers are connected to private networks or the Internet, which is an environment naturally friendly to worms. In particular, the widespread popularity of e-mail has made it easier for worms to spread across different computing platforms. E-mail continues to be the most popular vector for worm propagation today, though typically e-mail worms require user intervention to propagate.

Viruses have evolved in their complexity over the years, often in response to countermeasures put in place by antivirus vendors. The first viruses often simply added their code to either the beginning or the end of the host file. In order to evade simple detection, viruses later began to intersperse their code throughout the host file. Another technique that viruses have adopted to evade detection is to encrypt their code within each host file instance, thus making it more difficult for a signature of the virus to be developed. When antivirus programs began keying on the decryption algorithm as the signature, viruses became polymorphic, changing their decryption algorithm with each copy. Taking it one step further, some viruses have become metamorphic, i.e., they change their logic (not just the decryption algorithm) with each infection instance.

Worms that are standalone files have not had to evolve in the same way as file-infecting viruses. Functionally, a worm program must carry out a few specific steps to spread to another target after infection of a victim host.

First, an algorithm chooses candidates for the next targets. The simplest algorithm, which is used by quite a few worms, is to choose an IP address (32-bit number) at random. This is not efficient because the IP address space is not populated uniformly. More sophisticated target selection algorithms choose addresses within the same networks as the victim because local networks have shorter propagation delays to allow faster spreading. Other target selection algorithms may choose targets discovered from a victim's e-mail address book, mail server, DNS server, or countless other ways.

Second, many (but not all) worms will perform scanning of selected targets, for the same purpose as scanning done by human attackers. Scanning prompts responses from the potential targets that indicate whether the worm's programmed exploits can be successful. This process identifies suitable targets among the selected candidates.

The third step is the actual exploit or attack to compromise a suitable target. A common attack is to send e-mail to the target, usually carrying an infected attachment that has to be executed. More sophisticated e-mail worms are activated when their message is just previewed or read. Other worms might attack via file sharing, password guessing, or any number of exploits. It is also common for worms to combine multiple exploits or propagation vectors (blended threats) to increase the likelihood of success and rate of spreading.

The fourth step after successfully gaining access is to transfer a copy of the worm to the target. Depending on the exploit, a copy of the worm might have been transferred during the exploit (e.g., by e-mail). However, some exploits only create a means of access, such as a backdoor or shell. The worm takes advantage of the access to transfer a copy of itself via any number of protocols including FTP, TFTP, or HTTP.

An optional last step is execution of the worm's payload, if there is one. The payload is the part of the worm's program that is directed at an infected victim and not related to its propagation. The payload could be virtually anything, and not necessarily destructive. In recent cases, payloads have included: opening backdoors allowing remote access; installing spyware; downloading worm code updates from the Internet; or disabling antivirus software.

Both viruses and worms are becoming easier to generate with the introduction of virus and worm toolkits. For example, the VBSWG (Visual Basic Script Worm Generator) toolkit simplified the process of creating e-mail worms for attackers—the Anna Kournikova worm in 2001 was produced using this toolkit. Other toolkits are easily found searching the Internet. Toolkits enable advances in malicious code technology to become commodities, easily reused by less experienced attackers for their own purposes.

Finally, there is a convergence occurring between viruses, worms, and other forms of malicious code. For example, there are instances of malicious code that both infect files like a virus and drop standalone copies of itself like a worm. Viruses and worms often possess characteristics of a Trojan horse, especially when they use social engineering to trick a user into aiding propagation. And viruses and worms can be used to enable the other forms of attack discussed next, both spam and denial of service (DoS) attacks.

Spam

Spam, the e-mail equivalent of unsolicited junk mail, has been a growing problem over the past few years. E-mail addresses are harvested from the Internet or generated randomly. They typically advertise a product, service, or investment scheme (which may well turn out to be fraudulent). E-mail is an attractive advertising medium in economic terms. Spammers can send enormous volumes of e-mail at much less cost than postal mail. The necessary equipment is modest: a PC, software, and an Internet connection. Even if the response rate is very small, a sizable profit can be made easily.

At the very least, spam wastes network resources (bandwidth, memory, server processing) and necessitates spam filtering at ISPs and organizations. It also wastes users' time to read and delete. The seriousness of the problem has steadily grown as the volume of spam has escalated.

A growing concern with spam is evidence of collaboration between spammers, virus/worm writers, and organized crime. A substantial number of worms have been used as a delivery vehicle for Trojan horses that set up "bots." Bots listen for instructions from a remote attacker or allow backdoor access. A number of bots under coordinated control is a bot net. Bot nets are being used for distributed DoS attacks or spamming. Moreover, spam is increasingly being used for phishing (as described earlier). Phishing attacks attempting identity theft with increasing sophistication suggests the involvement of organized crime.

Denial of Service

Most people tend to think of DoS attacks as flooding, but at least four types of DoS attacks can be identified:

- starvation of resources (e.g., CPU cycles, memory) on a particular machine
- causing failure of applications or operating systems to handle exceptional conditions, due to programming flaws
- attacks on routing and DNS
- blocking of network access by consuming bandwidth with flooding traffic.

There are numerous examples of DoS attacks. A "land attack" is an example of starvation. On vulnerable machines with Windows NT before service pack 4, the land attack would cause the machine to loop, endlessly consuming CPU cycles. The "ping of death" is an ICMP Echo Request message exceeding the maximum allowable length of 65,536 bytes. It caused earlier operating systems to crash or freeze (that programming flaw has been remedied in later operating systems).

The "Smurf" attack is an example of an indirect flooding attack, where the ICMP protocol is abused to cause many response packets to be sent to a victim machine in response to a broadcast packet. It is indirect because real attacker's address is not seen in any packets. It is also interesting as an example of amplification: a single attacker's packet is multiplied into many packets by the recipients of the broadcast.

The most harmful flooding attacks take advantage of amplification through a distributed DoS (DDoS) network (Dittrich, 2004). A famous DDoS attack occurred in February 2000 against several Web sites including Yahoo, eBay, e*Trade, and others. Examples of automated DDoS tools include Trin00, TFN (tribe flood network), TFN2K, and Stacheldraht. In addition, viruses and worms have been known to infect victims with DDoS agents.

DDoS attacks generally proceed in two phases. The first phase is stealthy preparation of the DDoS network. The attacker attempts to compromise a large number of computers, often home PCs with a broadband connection, by installing a DDoS agent (i.e., a Trojan horse). DDoS tools such as Trin00 and TFN set up a two-level DDoS network. A small fraction of compromised machines are designated as "masters", waiting for commands from the attacker. The remainder of compromised machines are "daemons" waiting for commands from masters. The daemons carry out the actual flooding attack to a specified target.

DETECTION AVOIDANCE PHASE

During reconnaissance or an attack, an attacker would naturally prefer to avoid detection, which could trigger defensive actions. After a successful attack gaining access or control of a target, an attacker would like to hide evidence of the attack.

Evading Intrusion Detection Systems

Intrusion detection systems (IDSs) are designed to alert system administrators about any signs of suspicious activities. They are analogous in function to burglar alarms, a way to react in case intruders are able to penetrate preventive defenses (e.g., firewalls). Network-based IDSs monitor the network traffic and might be a stand-alone device or integrated in firewalls or routers. Host-based IDSs are processes that run on hosts and monitor system activities. IDSs are now commonly used by organizations. Naturally, an intelligent attacker would want to avoid detection by IDSs.

Without special precautions, an attacker could be easily detected by an IDS during reconnaissance because scanning tools are noisy. A port scan might involve thousands of packets, while a vulnerability scan could involve hundreds of thousands of packets. These scans may have an obvious impact on normal traffic patterns in a network. Moreover, these scans are exactly the signs that IDSs are designed to look for.

Most commercial IDSs attempt to match observed traffic against a database of attack signatures (i.e., misuse detection). Hence, an attacker could try to evade a signature match by changing the packets or traffic pattern of an attack. One approach to changing the appearance of an attack is to take advantage of IP fragmentation. An IDS must be able to reassemble fragments in order to analyze an attack. An IDS without the capability for fragment reassembly could be evaded by simply fragmenting the attack packets. An IDS might also be overwhelmed by a flood of fragments or unusual fragmentation.

IDS evasion is also possible at the application layer. For example, an IDS may have a signature for attacks against known weak CGI scripts on a Web server. An attacker may try to evade this signature by sending an HTTP request for a CGI script, but the HTTP request is carefully modified to not match the signature but still run on the Web server.

Another strategy for evading detection by IDSs, or other monitoring products, is to simply overload them with common, unimportant events to mask the actual attack. "Flying under the radar" of an IDS is easy to do when thousands of meaningless port scans and ping sweeps are filling the operators' consoles and logs, while a more sophisticated attack is executed.

Covering Up

Covering up evidence after an attack is particularly important if an attacker wants to maintain control of the victims. One of the obvious methods is to change the system logs on the victim's computers. Unix machines keep a running system log about all system activities, which can be viewed by system administrators to detect signs of intrusions. Likewise, Windows NT/2000/XP systems maintain event logs including logins, file changes, communications, and so on.

An attacker needs to gain sufficient access privileges, such as root or administrator, to change the log files. It is unwise to simply delete the logs because their absence would be noticed by system administrators searching for unusual signs. Instead, a sophisticated attacker will try to carefully edit system logs to selectively remove suspicious events, such as failed login attempts, error conditions, and file accesses.

Rootkits

Rootkits are known to be one of the most dangerous means for attackers to cover their tracks. Rootkits are obviously named for the root, the most prized target on Unix systems because the root user has complete system access. If an attacker has gained root access, it is possible to install a rootkit designed to hide signs of a compromise by selectively changing key system components. The rootkit cannot be detected as an additional application or process; it is a change to the operating system itself. For example, Unix systems include a program *ifconfig* that can show the status of network interfaces, including interfaces in promiscuous mode (or a sniffer). A toolkit could modify *ifconfig* to never reveal promiscuous interfaces, effectively hiding the presence of a sniffer. Another program *find* is normally useful to locate files and directories. A toolkit could modify *find* to hide an attacker's files.

Kernel-level rootkits have evolved from traditional rootkits. In most operating systems, the kernel is the fundamental core that controls processes, system memory, disk access, and other essential system operations. As the term implies, kernel-level rootkits involve modification of the kernel itself. The deception is embedded at the deepest level of the system, such that no programs or utilities can be trusted any more.

Covert Channels

Although logs and operating systems can be modified to escape detection, the presence of a system compromise might be given away by communications. For example, system administrators might recognize the packets from an attacker trying to access a backdoor. Clearly, an attacker would prefer to hide his communications through covert channels.

A common method used to hide communications is tunneling, which essentially means one packet encapsulated in the payload of another packet. The outer packet is the vehicle for delivery through a network; the receiver has to simply extract the inner packet. The outer packet is usually IP for routing through the Internet. Also, ICMP messages and HTTP messages have been used. Since the inner packet has no effect on network routing, any type of packet can be carried by tunneling.

CONCLUSION

Computer systems are common targets for a wide range of electronic attacks. Instead of an exhaustive catalog, this chapter has attempted a quick tour of the most pressing types of attacks in preparation for later chapters with more details.

An understanding of attacks is necessary in order to design strong electronic defenses. This chapter has not addressed electronic defenses, which will be covered by other chapters. We have seen that attacks can be viewed as a sequence of phases proceeding from reconnaissance to attack to covering up. An understanding of the methods and tools used in each attack phase can be helpful in fortifying cyber defenses.

GLOSSARY

Adware A type of software to monitor and profile a user's online behavior.

Backdoor A means for an attacker to remotely access a system.

Buffer overflow An attack on programs without bounds checking that allows arbitrary attack code to be executed remotely on a target system.

Denial of service A type of attack on the proper operation of a system or service through exhaustion of system resources, exhaustion of bandwidth, exploitation of programming bugs, or attacks on routing and DNS.

Firewall A security system intended to protect an organization's internal network against threats from an external network, using configurable filtering rules.

Footprinting The initial process of discovering and identifying potential targets.

Intrusion detection system A device to monitor network traffic or system activities to search for signs of intrusions.

Pfishing A social engineering attack luring e-mail victims to a fake Website for the purpose of stealing personal data, such as account passwords.

Port scan A probe to TCP or UDP ports to discover whether a service is listening.

Reconnaissance The process of collecting information about potential targets in preparation for an attack.

Rootkit Tools to change system components to evade detection of an intrusion.

Session hijacking An attack to eavesdrop on an active session and take over control by impersonating one of the hosts.

Sniffer A program to passively intercept and copy network traffic typically on LANs.

Social engineering An attack attempting to persuade or trick victims into a compromising action, such as revealing

Spam Unsolicited junk e-mail, usually sent in bulk to many addresses.

Spyware A type of software to attack privacy by stealing personal data.

Trojan horse A program appearing to be useful but actually containing malicious functions.

Virus Program code that executes during the execution of an infected host program to copy itself to other programs.

Vulnerability A weakness or flaw that may be exploited by an attack to compromise a system or service.

Worm A self-replicating program that automatically attempts to copy itself to other systems across a network.

CROSS REFERENCES

See *Computer Viruses and Worms; Denial of Service Attacks; Hoax Viruses and Virus Alerts; Hostile Java Applets; Spam and the Legal Counter Attacks; Trojan Horse Programs.*

REFERENCES

Aleph One, "Smashing the stack for fun and profit," available at http://www.insecure.org/stf/smashstack.txt (date of access: Oct. 1, 2004).

CERT, "2004 E-crime watch survey shows significant increase in electronic crimes," available at http://www.cert.org/about/ecrime.html (date of access: Oct. 1, 2004).

Chirillo, J. (2002). *Hack Attacks Revealed*, 2nd ed. Indianapolis, IA: Wiley Publishing.

Dittrich, D., "Distributed denial of service (DDoS) attacks/tools," available at http://staff.washington.edu/dittrich/misc/ddos/ (date of access: Oct. 1, 2004).

Fyodor, "Remote OS detection via TCP/IP stack finger-printing," available at http://www.insecure.org/nmap/nmap-fingerprinting-article.html (date of access: Oct. 1, 2004).

Grimes, R. (2001). *Malicious Mobile Code: Virus Protection for Windows*. Sebastopol, CA: O'Reilly.

Harley, D., Slade, D., and Gattiker, U. (2001). *Viruses Revealed*. New York: McGraw-Hill.

McClure, S., Scambray, J., and Kutz, G. (2001). *Hacking Exposed*. 3rd ed. New York: McGraw-Hill.

Shimonski, R., "Introduction to password cracking," available at http://www-106.ibm.com/developerworks/library/s-crack/ (date of access: Oct. 1, 2004).

Skoudis, E. (2002). *Counter Hack: A Step-by-Step Guide to Computer Attacks and Effective Defenses*. Upper Saddle River, NJ: Prentice Hall PTR.

Sophos, "Suspected Sasser worm author caught; could trigger more arrests,: available at http://www.sophos.com/virusinfo/articles/sasserarrest.html (date of access: Oct. 1, 2004).

Symantec Corp., "W32.Beagle.B@mm," available at http://securityresponse.symantec.com/avcenter/venc/data/w32.beagle.b@mm.html (date of access: Oct. 1, 2004).

Turner, D., et al. (2004). *Symantec Internet Security Threat Report: Trends for January 1, 2004–June 30, 2004*. available at http://www.symantec.com (date of access: Oct. 1, 2004).

FURTHER READING

A number of Web sites contain information and software related to the attack tools mentioned in this chapter:

- Packetstorm, available at http://www.packetstorm security.org
- Operation:Security, available at http://www.operationsecurity.com
- Insecure.org, available at http://www.insecure.org/tools.html

Well-known Web sites with literature and advisories about vulnerabilities include

- CERT, available at http://www.cert.org
- SANS, available at http://www.sans.org

Antivirus corporate Web sites are a good source of information about malicious code:

- McAfee, available at http://www.mcafeee.com
- Sophos, available at http://www.sophos.com
- Symantec, available at http://www.symanec.com
- TrendMicro, available at http://www.trendmicro.com

Wireless Information Warfare

Randall K. Nichols, *The George Washington University & University of Maryland University College*

INTRODUCTION

Warfighting, as experienced on today's battlefields, demands that soldiers have not only timely information but also the ability to move that information from place to place. Weapon systems and decision-making commanders, using this information, may be constrained by *communications bandwidth and data-flow rates*. Soldiers require large communications "pipes." It may be difficult to predict the precise nature of the future battlefield, but we may be certain that it will continue to be built on a complex array of digital and analog communication networks. Those networks will integrate hardwired and wireless links, as well as satellite and line-of-sight signals. Whereas infantry-based armies of the ancient world depended on roads and couriers to move messages, future armies will rely on redundant communications networks to move their messages (Leonard, 2000).

Protecting one's own information, while trying to capture information from the enemy, is the crux of information warfare (IW). This modern type of warfare may be thought of in terms of "command, control, communications, computers, intelligence and recognition" or C4IR. The aspects of command and control (C2), embodied in this acronym, involve opposing forces attacking each other's information systems and processes while protecting their own. This is the foundation of information warfare; the intent is to create a condition in which the friendly side can obtain, assess, and disseminate important information to perceive the battlefield, control its forces effectively, and act decisively while denying the enemy to do likewise.

Probably the greatest amount of skepticism, regarding the future of information warfare, concerns the vulnerability of information technologies to actions by the enemy. This is especially true with *wireless* communications links because the extent of their operations has no borders; they are inherently insecure. The fear of someone hacking into battlefield computer networks, jamming a key signal node, or spoofing our vital GPS position-location devices is borne of a healthy regard for the extreme complexity of digitization and the use of commercial off-the-shelf (COTS) products. For example, the U.S. Army's combat divisions employ a vast array of computers, communications, sensors, and networks to achieve situational awareness and information dominance. With this complexity, comes vulnerability (Nichols & Lekkas, 2001).

This chapter focuses on the wireless side of warfare. We consider the *uniqueness* of wireless information warfare (WIW). Sources, taxonomies, and defenses of WIW are examined. We also incorporate a real attack/defense (A/D) scenario on a corporate "soft" target to emphasize the security concerns and the role of wireless information links.

DEFINITION OF WIRELESS INFORMATION WARFARE

To understand WIW, it is first necessary to define the broader category of information warfare (IW). Information warfare has been defined in numerous ways by entities such as the United States Joint Chiefs of Staff (JCS) and the United States Department of Defense (DoD) and by experts such as Edward Waltz. Edward Waltz explains that IW covers the acquisition, processing, and dissemination of information or the exploitation of information to achieve dominant awareness in the battlespace (Waltz, 1998). The JCS expands on the definition to state that "Information warfare includes actions taken to preserve the integrity of one's own information systems from exploitation, corruption, or disruption, while at the same time exploiting, corrupting or destroying an adversary's information systems and in the process achieving an information advantage in the application of force" (JCS, 2004). The DoD definition continues the expansion to include the effect on processes and networks, in this definition of IW: "Actions taken to achieve information superiority by affecting adversary information, information-based processes, information systems, and computer-based networks while defending one's own information, information-based processes, information systems, and computer-based networks" (Office of the Under Secretary of Defense for Acquisition and Technology, 1996).

Waltz uses the term *battlespace* in his definition of IW and although this term brings up military images, it should be recognized that the term *applies equally well* to military, commercial, and, to a lesser degree, private interactions with the outside environment. When such interactions occur via wireless means (e.g., radio, cellular phones, wireless networks, and wireless modems), then IW has entered the wireless arena and become WIW.

A former DoD definition of IW also delineates three central aspects of IW conflicts at the national level: information dominance, information attack, and information protection. DoD Directive Number 8100.2, April 14, 2004, specifically considers all of these aspects in terms of wireless technology, development, and deployment in detail (DoD, Number 8100.2, 2004).

Because of the complexity of both wireless communications and information warfare and definitions, background information and classification taxonomies for both of these topics are discussed in the following sections.

TAXONOMIES OF INFORMATION WARFARE

The three primary classifications of IW covered in this document include classifications based on domains of information aggression; classifications based on confidentiality, integrity, and availability; and classifications based on exploitation and attack/defense. Each of these taxonomies is described below.

Information warfare taxonomies provide a framework to develop and categorize the elements of a given attack or defense plan, including the countermeasures, their respective countercountermeasures, and the effects of both on the target systems. Evaluation of the effects on target systems is particularly important on wireless systems, because wireless systems include an additional area of impact—*degradation of performance*. Blocking or jamming a wireless system degrades system information performance (technical degradation or destruction) and effectiveness (utility or impact on downstream users of the information system under attack). Simple overloading can cause collisions in the delivery system.

Commercial firms and the public sector have a major impact on the development of IW concepts and IW weapons (e.g., countermeasures and countercountermeasures), partly because very few information-related technologies are export controlled in the United States or elsewhere. Information technologies include products or techniques such as network computing, intelligent mobile agents to autonomously operate across networks, multimedia data presentation and storage, and push/pull information dissemination. Information creation technologies are capable of creating synthetic and deceptive virtual information (e.g., morphed video, fake imagery, and duplicate virtual realities). Information security technologies include survivable networks, multilevel security, network and communications security, digital signatures, public key infrastructure (PKI), authentication technologies, wireless security end-to-end firmware, ASICS, and software. By understanding a taxonomy of IW it becomes possible to identify when and how to use the above tools and technologies that are so readily available.

Classification by Domain of Information Aggression

Waltz presents a taxonomy based on domains of information aggression. Information resources may be attacked and must be defended across all three of these domains: national, corporate, and private. Table 1 provides specific examples of information warfare within each domain.

Classification by Confidentiality, Integrity, and Availability

An alternative taxonomy may be constructed based on information warfare objectives, targets, attack objectives, countermeasures, and the responses of the targeted information infrastructures, all of which affect the capability of the information infrastructure to maintain the confidentiality, integrity, and availability of the data involved. Figure 1 shows the standard confidentiality, integrity, availability (CIA) requirements, and the associated objective of the countermeasures for each security requirement (Waltz, 1998).

The required security capability of any information system is to ensure the confidentiality, the integrity, and the availability of the information stored, used, or transmitted on the system. Any given IW operation on a wireless infrastructure or transmission vehicle may involve single, multiple, or complex combinations of specific tactical elements to achieve the basic IW objectives of disruption of availability, corruption of integrity, and exploitation of confidentiality.

Table 1 Taxonomy of Domains of Information Aggression

Domains of Conflict	Representative Examples
National (global, public, military sector)	Network warfare Economic warfare Political warfare Command-and-control warfare
Corporate (business sector)	Network-based information espionage, sabotage, and source intelligence Inside-agent espionage or sabotage Precision physical attack on information systems (EMP, etc.) Destruction of magnetic media Notebook computer theft Exploitation of former employees and competitor product, analysis Competitor trash capture and analysis Arson, other nonprecision attacks on information systems
Private (personal sector)	E-commerce fraud Net impersonation, spoofing, e-mail harassment, spamming Wiretapping and cell phone intercept Bank card impersonation, bank card and credit card theft Telephone harassment, "shoulder surfing," and PIN capture Credit card and database theft Computer destruction

Reprinted with permission from Waltz, Edward (1998), *Information Warfare: Principles and Operations*, Artech House, Norwood MA.

- **Disruption:** Disruption of information or denial-of-service (DoS) may be achieved by causing a loss or temporary delay in the information content or services. Jamming, overloading, and electromagnetic (EM) or physical destruction of wireless links or processors are examples of countermeasures (i.e., attacks) in this category.
- **Corruption:** Corruption of integrity may include changing (e.g., replacing or removing) or inserting information to achieve effects such as deception, disruption, or denial. Examples of specific countermeasures in this category include viruses with corruption engines and payloads, database worms, man-in-the-middle (MIM) attacks on cryptographic protocols, and sensor spoofers.
- **Exploitation:** Exploitation of confidentiality may be accomplished at external levels (passive observation) or internal levels (gaining access to internal sensitive

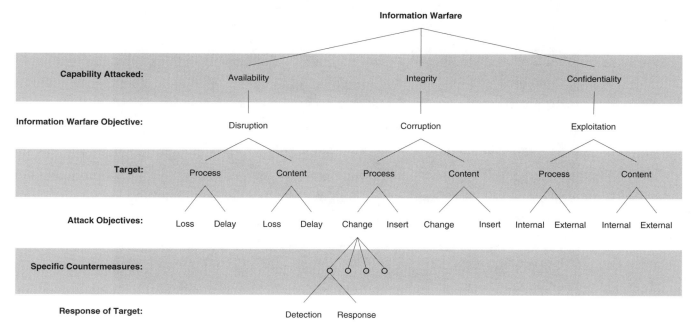

Figure 1: Classification by confidentiality, integrity, and availability [reprinted with permission from Waltz, E. (1998) *Information Warfare: Principles and Operations*, Artech House, Norwood, MA].

information or services by breaching security services) to gain information intended to remain confidential.

These objectives are achieved by targeting a process or the content via a specific tactical element of attack objective. To achieve the attack objective, specific countermeasures (e.g., attacks) are selected and applied. As seen in Figure 1, the degree of effect of each countermeasure may be categorized by the response of the targeted information system, in terms of the detection of the attack and the response to the attack, as follows.

- **Detection:** (1) undetected by the target, (2) detected on occurrence, or (3) detected at some time after the occurrence.
- **Response:** (1) no response (unprepared), (2) initiate audit activities, (3) mitigate further damage, (4) initiate protective actions, or (5) recover and regroup.

From the standpoint of a wireless system and infrastructure, this taxonomy includes only the *first effects*. One attack, even undetected, may have minor or political consequences, whereas another attack may bring immediate and cascading (second- and third-order) consequences. Figure 2 shows the interrelationships among the transmitting media (*x* axis), network layers (*y* axis), and major wireless services (*z* axis). It is conceivable that an attack at the lower intersecting layers could devastate the communication defenses of a given country because their services are not protected at the lower levels and multiple services are available (not separated) on the same computer systems (Nichols & Lekkas, 2001).

Relationship to Asymmetric Warfare

Figure 2 illustrates the importance and complexity of the concept of asymmetric warfare applied in the wireless arena. To fully understand its implications, we must make the mental bridge from the art and science of war in the kinetic world (where attrition is a prime driving force) to war in the digital world (in which a multitude of interrelated effects reign). Because information and knowledge are so critical for making good and timely decisions, the asymmetric tool of *information operations* will supplant the heavy reliance on traditional kinetic (bullets, bombs, and attrition) perspectives of conflict in the 20th century. Military and commercial services must prepare for future conflicts and transformation of war having an invisible, intangible, cerebral nature. People must consider and decide what information they need to make decisions faster and better than their enemies. People will need to determine how they access and use information and how they relate to the ends they seek—they must understand how to collect, process, and visualize information for its maximum usefulness. Autonomous intelligence agents ("cyberbots") will provide the help that cyberstrategists need to identify critical variables and potential second- and third-order effects (Hall, 2003).

New opponents will increasingly use asymmetric strategy, tools, and tactics. They will design their actions to lead to effects (outcomes) that cut across social, political,

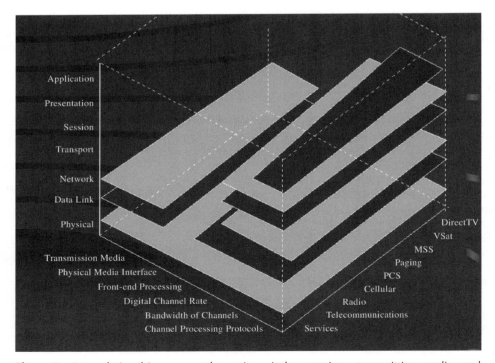

Figure 2: Interrelationships among the major wireless services, transmitting media, and network layers. [Reprinted with permission from Nichols, Randall K., Daniel J. Ryan and Julie J. C. H. Ryan (2000). *Defending Your Digital Assets against Hackers, Crackers, Spies and Thieves*, New York, McGraw Hill.]

military, commercial, financial, informational, and ecological systems. Their goal is to create the greatest second- and third-order effects possible, effects that eventually cause the country's will to implode. Asymmetric warfare involves intangibles—achieving offsets through surprise, shock, and ability to *influence information sources* to create aggregate effects in command and control systems, decision making of leaders, and the will of the public to support them (Hall, 2003).

Turning to Figure 2 again, and thinking about the asymmetric foes of the future, the author asserts that they will perform a sophisticated analysis of the stronger opponent's centers of gravity. They will seek to affect those centers of gravity indirectly but with significant impact, thereby affecting command and control (C2) to the point of decision—paralysis and creating conditions that make responses oscillate between impossible and inappropriate. Such an effort would be particularly powerful if the opponent timed such activities to occur at the moment of maximum vulnerability. An example of this idea would be to attack or manipulate a place (physical or more likely cyberspace) in which a confluence of communications, collection, automation, thinking and planning, and decision making occurs and whose role in activities is so important that if lost or adversely affected would seriously jeopardize security.

The United States has many vulnerability centers of gravity ranging from military command posts and headquarters to state and local emergency operations centers to incident command centers. Many of these vulnerabilities have arisen because of the need for mobility and wireless devices in the military. The situation is graver in the commercial organizations. Profit economics has tended to push commercial operations to group their wireless services (e.g., telecommunications, paging, cellular, radio, and TV) on the same enterprise servers and switches. Wireless security requires thoughtful analysis and involves many layers of defense. In general, it is not understood or performed competently. Knock out an enterprise server which coordinates multiple services and a foe brings on the second- and third-order effects that cascade and provide leverage (Nichols & Lekkas, 2002).

Wireless information operations could very well be the centerpiece of future asymmetric warfare and conflict. Why? People are more dependent on information and attendant communications to move the information, manipulate the data, and turn the information into learning. We are becoming wireless junkies, carrying multiple devices, requiring constant connections to the Web for our business, military, economic, and personal decisions. Wireless is the very reason we are so mobile and a prime reason we are so vulnerable. Adaptive foes cannot help but notice these vulnerabilities and will come at them with guile, cunning, and force.

Classification by Exploitation and Attack/Defense

An alternate classification of IW explores the two main operational objectives that can be applied to wireless systems: (1) exploitation of information and (2) attack and defense of information.

Information exploitation operations are defined as the acquisition, transmission, storage, or transformation of information that enhances the employment of military forces. This objective is the same for commercial and private forces to a lesser degree or scope. Two actions are possible: (1) direct, such as interception of adversary communications to locate or extract information, or (2) indirect, such as surveillance and reconnaissance sensors with subsequent intelligence analysis (e.g., from eyes in the sky to private eyes).

Attack and defense of information objectives have four categories that apply to wireless systems (especially infrastructure): (1) deception, (2) security, (3) electronic warfare, and (4) information corruption, as defined below:

- **Deception:** misleading the enemy about actual capabilities and intentions. It is indirectly accomplished by conducting misleading (military, commercial, illegal) operations that hint at incorrect future plans or intentions. For example, millions of wireless messages were sent out over-the-air (OTA) before the Normandy invasion and a month-long electronic warfare campaign was carried out prior to the ground engagement by a coalition of troops during the first Gulf War.

- **Security:** fundamental measures used to keep the enemy from learning our capabilities or intentions. May be applied directly as defensive countermeasures such as INFOSEC countermeasures designed to deny direct access to wireless (or wired) networks or may be applied indirectly such as COMSEC and CI.

- **Electronic warfare:** the denial of accurate information to the enemy (or target) using the electromagnetic spectrum. Electronic warfare (EW) is accomplished directly by using electromagnetic energy to couple deceptive information into an information system. It can also be accomplished indirectly via jamming or by deceiving a radar or RF sensor through the transmission of spurious waveforms to affect the receiver. Another method is to knock out the synchronization of a cryptographic transmission over a wireless media.

- **Information corruption:** a potentially devastating attack because it is normally done without visibly changing the physical entity within which it resides. This is a direct attack using malicious logic by penetrating security boundaries of an associated wireless (or wired) network to gain unauthorized access. The effect is a force multiplier if the target relies on the corrupted information (Ryan, 2000).

TAXONOMIES OF WIRELESS NETWORKS

The primary raison d'être for wireless communications is to enable mobility. Mobility means different things in the commercial and military worlds. Within the commercial/Internet community, the current notion of supporting host (user) mobility is via "mobile IP." Mobile IP supports host "roaming," where a roaming host may be connected through various means to the Internet. However, at no time is a host more than "one hop" (i.e., a wireless link, dial-up modem line, etc.) from a fixed network.

Supporting host mobility requires address management and protocol interoperability enhancements, but core network functions such as routing still occur within the fixed network.

The military vision of mobile IP is to support host mobility in wireless networks via mobile routers. Such networks are envisioned to have dynamic, rapidly changing mesh topologies consisting of bandwidth-constrained wireless links. These characteristics create a set of underlying assumptions for protocol design, which differs from those used for the higher speed, fixed topology Internet. These assumptions lead to somewhat different solutions for implementing core network functionality such as routing, resource reservation, and most importantly security (Feldman, 1998). Frater and Ryan (2001) provide recent treatment of the subject.

Two classification schemes for the mobility aspect of communications systems/networks are the network architecture classification and the mobility classification.

Network Architecture Classifications

Wireless networks fall into four categories based on characteristics of the supporting infrastructure and network architecture:

Wireless systems with a fixed supporting infrastructure. (Most existing wireless systems fall into this category.) A mobile user connects to a base station, access point, or satellite gateway; the remainder of the communications path (assuming mobile-to-fixed communications) passes over wired networks. Wired connections refer to anything that is not wireless, including the twisted pair wiring in telephone local loops, coaxial cable, and optical fibers. Examples include cellular phone systems, cordless phones, and some satellite networks. In the case of the cellular and cordless phones, the path from a mobile user to the public switched network (or vice versa) involves one wireless "hop" (transmission/reception pair). Cellular telephony requires a fixed supporting infrastructure that includes base stations and landlines that connect the base stations to each other and to the rest of the public switched network (PSN). For a small satellite terminal, such as the mobile phones used with the geostationary American Mobile Satellite (AMSAT), a mobile user connects to a gateway in two hops—one hop up to the satellite repeater and a second hop down to the gateway terminal (Earth station). The gateway provides a connection into the PSN.

Wireless systems in which users communicate directly through a satellite or satellites. Military satellite networks such as the Defense Satellite Communications System (DSCS) use large satellite terminals. Mobile terminals having sufficient EIRP (effective isotropic radiated power) and G/T (ratio of antenna gain to effective system noise temperature) and lying within the same satellite antenna footprint can communicate directly to one another through the satellite repeater via two hops. Until recently, communications between small mobile satellite terminals required four hops—two hops to reach a satellite hub and another two hops (again using the satellite as a repeater) to reach the destination terminal. Access to a gateway is required when a connection is being established for purposes of authentication and authorization.

Wireless data networks that are fully mobile (i.e., any supporting infrastructure) is also mobile. No such commercial wireless data networks currently exist. The U.S. military is currently investigating wireless network concepts involving repeaters on UAVs (unmanned aerial vehicles). A major advantage of the UAV-based relays over satellites is that they can be moved to any location where communications are needed. Furthermore, UAV relays would probably be under the control of the theater commander, whereas satellites are not. Geostationary satellites may be moved to support a local surge in demand (or to fill a void caused by the failure of another satellite), but this is generally not standard practice and should not be counted on (because of the expenditure of station-keeping fuels, reduction in the useful lifespan of the satellite, and the impact on the other users of the satellite; Feldman, 1998). Another concept involves cellular base stations on mobile vehicles; each vehicle would carry an antenna on a tall (e.g., 10-m-high) mast and would provide connectivity to users in its vicinity. High-capacity microwave trunks could be used to interconnect the mobile base stations, which would be necessary to provide connectivity to users served by different base stations. The high-capacity trunks would form a mobile network backbone; mobile-to-mobile connections would involve a single hop into or out of the backbone at each end. The base station vehicles would move with their forces but might have to stop moving to operate.

Wireless systems with no supporting infrastructure other than the mobile nodes themselves. Such fully mobile networks are called either mobile peer-to-peer networks or mobile mesh networks. New technologies such as Bluetooth and WiFi extend this taxonomy.

Mobility Classifications

Wireless can also be classified based on the *extent of mobility*. Consider the general problem of providing connectivity to mobile users through a supporting infrastructure of base stations. One could use a single base station capable of covering the entire area or a number of base stations, each covering a smaller area. To make a network with multiple base stations perform like a network with only a single base station, one must interconnect the base stations and design the network so that connections are maintained when users move across the boundaries of base station coverage regions ("cells"). The transfer of user connections from one base station to another is called a handover. Base stations must track mobile user locations even when they are not connected so that connections can be established at any time. All of this implies considerable complexity. Cellular telephone networks best illustrate untethered mobility with a fixed base station infrastructure.

Cordless telephones represent an extreme form of tethered mobility in which the handset can only be used near a specific base station (i.e., it cannot communicate with other base stations). Using a single base station to cover the entire area of interest offers significant advantages in terms of reduced protocol complexity (no need for handovers) and reduced computational load. However, several major drawbacks outweigh these benefits:

- As the size of the area to be covered increases, the required base station antenna height increases (to achieve line-of-sight to the mobile users). If the area to be covered is sufficiently large, then it might be necessary to put the base station on a satellite.
- As the size of the area to be covered grows, the EIRP requirements of the base station and of the mobile users increase.
- In a military network, a single base station that covers a large area becomes a critical node, as well as a high-value (and highly visible) asset that can be an attractive target for the enemy.

UNIQUE ASPECTS OF WIRELESS INFORMATION WARFARE

Traditional threats to wireless communications exist in three areas: (1) interception, (2) illegal access to mobile services, and (3) interference in wireless networks. Interception attacks include data interception on the air interface, loss of confidentiality of user data, loss of confidentiality of signaling information, and loss of confidentiality of user identity information. Illegal access to mobile services generally revolves around some scheme to masquerade or impersonate a subscriber while using system services. Interference in wireless networks includes jamming, denial of service, and radio frequency disruption (Nichols & Lekkas, 2001). Because wireless networks have significant vulnerabilities, the question of wireless security naturally arises.

Why Is Wireless Security Different?

There are *five fundamental differences* for wireless services: (1) bandwidth, (2) allowable error rates, (3) latency, (4) variability, and (5) power constraints. Many of these differences are seen at the network levels. Wireless networks are generally based on mobile devices that communicate via an electromagnetic transmission and reception method: (1) radio-frequency (RF) networks [HF, VHF, UHF (3MHz–3GHz)], (2) satellite communications (SAT) [SHF, EHF (3–300 GHz)], and (3) infrared (IR) (IrDA).

Wireless networks are generally characterized by low quality of service (QoS). Many employ small size devices with low power and low bandwidth options. Wireless networks are relatively more unreliable than wired networks, as packet losses occur more frequently in wireless networks. They exhibit high latency and variability because of retransmissions. Network limitations necessitate efficient communications and security protocols. Wireless designers consider a whole battery of variables in their designs: user expectations, interference, error rates, throughput, protocol overhead, compression, latency, battery life and energy-saving protocols, unknown network connectivity, "out of coverage," "one way coverage," chatty

applications/protocols, and "keep-alive messages." The Internet has made the problem more complex, because wired Internet protocols (e.g. IPSec, SSL, or SSH) are typically not optimized for wireless networks. They are too chatty and carry too much overhead and the timeouts are too tight (Nichols & Lekkas, 2001).

We must recognize that secure mobile devices will have the following:

- Relatively low computing power (compared to desktop PCs).
- Limits on the type of cryptographic algorithms a device can support.
- Limited storage capacity.
- Power conservation requirement (imposed by functionality limitations).
- Fundamental restrictions on: bandwidth, error rate, latency, and variability.
- Small footprint and compact Input/Output interfaces:
- Limited display capabilities (graphical user interfaces are a challenge to implement across multiple display form factors).
- Limits on usability and user experience issues.
- Throughput sensitivities to protocol overhead and compression.

Most existing security technologies, protocols, and standards have been designed for the wired/high bandwidth environment. In many cases, they are not well suited for the wireless mobile environment because they have too much overhead and exhibit tight timeouts. Thus we redefine successful implementation of wireless security to mean: (1) adaptation and integration of existing solutions and infrastructure, (2) promotion of consistency and interoperability among a diverse spectrum of mobile and wireless devices, and (3) provision for a high level of security without detrimental impact on the user experience. In a wireless network, security features greatly differ between each of the protocol stacks, and security policy implementation and enforcement are dependent on the carrier. For example, Table 2 lists some representative differences/features in the OSI layer implementation used by wireless.

The bearer layers are used to secure the OTA link to prevent eavesdropping threats. The transport layer incorporates security for goals of confidentiality and authentication. However, the implementation is discontinuous because of the numerous transition points between wireless and wired protocols. Application level security provides for access control, authentication, confidentiality, and nonrepudiation.

Designing security into wireless services means that we require wireless communications/transactions to exhibit high levels of authentication, confidentiality, data integrity, and nonrepudiation. Companies offering wireless services infrastructure must provide customers high levels of assurances that their communications/transactions are secure. This becomes a nontrivial challenge when dealing with an assortment of networks, protocols, and devices.

Table 2 Representative Differences and Features of Wireless OSI Layer Implementations

Layer	Representative Differences and Features
Physical	Provides signal scrambling for over-the-air (OTA) eavesdropping protection, using current technologies based on splitting the bit stream into small fragments called radio frames and then applying some form of frequency based scrambling technique. The radio frames travel on a spread spectrum of frequencies where each fragment is identified by a digital code known only to the device and the base station and no other device can receive the transmissions. For each connection, there are billions of code combinations available (example: CDMA network security).
Data Link and Network	Some protocols such as CDPD and GSM provide data confidentiality in these layers. CDPD applies encryption to each segmented datagram(s) prior to transmission. GSM uses a SIM (subscriber identity module) card to store a symmetric key known only to the mobile and the authentication center (AuC) at the carrier site. The key is used in both authentication and ciphering TDMA frames prior to transmission.
Transport	Secure Socket Layer (SSL): used extensively in Internet applications to secure TCP/IP connections. Public keys (e.g., RSA) are used to exchange a session key (e.g., RC4 or other algorithms) for bulk encryption. Incorporates an elaborate session/connection management protocol for session establishment, resumption, and termination. Designed for high-bandwidth connections; it is not optimized for high-latency networks. Enables client and server authentication via X.509 certificates. Unfortunately X.509 certificates have a large footprint and require significant computing power to process. SSL is not well suited for wireless applications.
Application	Application specific user authentication User ID and password Challenge-response authentication protocols Biometrics Message integrity Hashing of a shared secret and some message specific data to produce a unique MAC. (SHA1, MD5) Application level encryption: RC5, Triple 3DES, Rijndael, and so on Application level digital signatures for non-repudiation and authentication. (PKI), RSA, ECDSA (ECC).

Translating into mobile end-to-end security requirements, there must be confidentiality between mobile device and organization/user. Organizations must be able to authenticate sensitive transactions that have been signed by the user of the mobile device and vice versa. In addition, no intermediate entity (such as a mobile operator/carrier or middle-tier service provider) should be able to view, intelligently hear, alter, or store any of the confidential data/voice elements that make up the message or transaction. End-to-end security entails protecting voice/data with minimal cost, delay, complexity, and bandwidth overhead. Mobile and base stations must authenticate each other and allow distinct keys in a variety of environments. Two-way authentication is more effective using end-to-end encryption. Because no one organization can control the entire infrastructure, end-to-end connectivity needs to be independent of the underlying infrastructure. More and more functionality needs to be moved from the core and the perimeters of the networks to the edge devices. This needs to be done within a spectrum of emerging standards (IEEE 802.1b and family, wireless application protocol, WEP, Bluetooth, Future narrow band digital terminal, and so on (Nichols & Lekkas, 2001). Noonan provides a capable framework for hardening network wireless infrastructures from hacking (Noonan, 2004).

Performance Measures and Key Design Trade-Offs

The performance of a communications system depends on design parameters whose values can be selected by the system designer and environmental parameters over which the designer may have no control. The relationship between these parameters and performance metrics of interest is usually complex. Changing any single design parameter tends to affect all performance metrics and simultaneously changing multiple designs parameters typically affects performance metrics in ways that cannot be predicted from knowledge of the single parameter effects alone.

The goal of the design process is to select the design parameters that achieve specific performance levels (or the best performance possible) subject to constraints on system cost. Cost is commonly viewed as a major performance metric. Speed to deploy and/or market is another constraint. Some of the choices the designer must make are essentially discrete or integer valued, that is, a selection among a small (or at least finite) set of alternatives. The three-way divide among narrowband, direct sequence spread spectrum, and frequency hop spread spectrum is an example of a situation wherein such a choice must be made. Other design parameters are essentially real valued. For example, antenna size and transmitter output power can take on values from a continuum. Performance requirements of communications networks may also depend on a variety of other factors, including the types and quantities of traffic to be carried, the required availability and responsiveness of the system, the operating environment, and acceptable costs for the infrastructure and user equipment segments of the network. Some performance measures are specific to certain types of networks, or to certain types of traffic, and are inappropriate in other contexts.

Feldman (1998) shows why the wireless system design problem is difficult, for several reasons:

1. The designer is faced with a huge design space (each design parameter can be thought of as one dimension in a multidimensional space). Exhaustive exploration of this space is typically impractical. Thus, the designer must rule out many alternatives early in the design process based on experience to consider a smaller, more manageable set of alternatives that can be evaluated via simulation.

2. Current simulation tools at best tend to accurately model either the ISO physical layer (layer 1) on a single-link basis or the middle ISO layers (2–4) for networks involving multiple nodes but not both at the same time.

3. Even without detailed modeling of the physical layer, high-fidelity simulations of large networks tend to require large amounts of computation. One cannot scale down networks for purposes of performance evaluation because the behavior of networks involving small numbers of nodes may be very different.

4. The external environment in which a system must operate is often highly uncertain. Terrain type, presence of interfering equipments, jamming, and other external factors can all impact performance, but are difficult to accurately characterize and model. In the case of jamming, uncertainty about the threat is a major issue.

Military and commercial communications systems designers tend to choose different design approaches and thus reach different results primarily because (1) the expected operating environments are different, (2) the business practices and economics (including economies of scale) are different, and (3) robustness against jamming and low probability of detection (LPD) are of concern only for the military.

Military-Unique System Requirements

The military has unique requirements that drive the design of military communications systems toward solutions that are markedly different from commercial systems. The most important of these involve (1) low probability of detection, (2) resistance to jamming, (3) *precedence* and *perishability*, (4) electromagnetic compatibility, (5) interoperability with legacy systems, and (6) security.

Low probability of detection (LPD): This is critical for activities such as reconnaissance because it reduces the risks to forward spotters, and it is important in any situation where the enemy might employ direction-finding equipment to advantage.

Resistance to jamming: Although jamming of mission critical communications may have significant cost in both the commercial and military sectors, it is in the military arena that lives and equipment are most likely to hang in the balance and drive the need for jamming resistant communications.

Precedence and perishability: Military networks must be able to offer different grades of service to traffic based on *precedence level (priority)*, which indicates importance, and *perishability*, which indicates when the information must be received to be of value. Optimal handling of precedence and perishability information is especially important when a network becomes congested. In packet-switched networks (Internet) network status and control information are not privileged. In general, commercial providers have rejected the idea of different grades of service. Commercial vendors do not provide for either precedence or perishability. Guaranteed QoS makes sense for wired networks with stable topologies and constant link capacities but is almost certainly unrealistic for fully mobile wireless networks, even without the added factor of hostile enemy actions such as destruction of nodes and jamming of links. Furthermore, guaranteed QoS requires admission control, which is unacceptable on the battlefield, except as a last resort. In critical situations, the ability to get something intelligible through in a timely fashion is probably the most important tactical user communication requirement.

Electromagnetic compatibility: For some military platforms, for command posts and for vehicles moving in formation, electromagnetic compatibility (EMC) can be a problem because of interference between equipment operating in close proximity (possibly on the same platform). This is the so-called co-site interference problem.

Interoperability with legacy systems: The military tends to retain computer and communications equipment in the inventory for relatively long periods. In the commercial world, users are expected to upgrade or replace equipment every 2–4 years. Because volumes of military systems tend to be much smaller than those of commercial systems, the costs of R&D, software, and testing have a much greater impact on the final per-unit cost of military systems than they do for commercial products. These higher costs in turn force the military to try to retain the systems for as long as possible. In addition, spectral efficiency is much more important to the commercial designer because of the cost factor. Higher spectral efficiencies tend to reduce the cost of equipment (Feldman, 1998).

Differences in frequencies of operation, waveforms, modulation and error control coding protocols, and message formats prevent the different military systems (e.g., radios) from interoperating. Interoperability is a prevalent problem in separate-service efforts that do not address the need for communications interoperation between services and between our allies for joint and combined operations. The opposite is often true with commercial radios and upgrades.

Because cryptographic and ECCM algorithms in tactical radios have been implemented in hardware, and because the relevant devices and specifications are generally not made available to our allies, encrypted and jam-resistant tactical communications are problematic for combined operations.

Part of the solution for this problem may be software-based encryption; this permits one to change not only the keys but also the underlying algorithms. Software-based encryption is practical except perhaps at the highest data rates. Secrecy with respect to the encryption algorithms used in tactical radios is almost certainly a mistake. If we trust the algorithms, then there can be no harm in making them public. If we do not trust them, then scrutiny by academic researchers is one of the best ways to find flaws. This same basic reasoning about the secrecy of encryption algorithms can be applied to the pseudorandom sequence generators used in frequency hopping and direct sequence spread spectrum, but it does not apply to ECCM algorithms in general. The ECCM algorithms are not available to allies or enemies alike (Nichols & Lekkas, 2001).

Security: Security is often cited as an additional military-unique performance requirement. This is not accurate, however, because the business world is becoming increasingly concerned about the protection of information, and widespread commercial use of strong encryption and authentication (digital signatures) is increasing. There are, however, requirements unique to the military. Even if all user data are encrypted, transmission security is needed to protect traffic. Without this, an eavesdropper could perform traffic analysis. The commercial world rarely worries about this, even if data are protected by encryption. Secure multicast with frequent changes of multicast group membership may require mechanisms that are more complex for key generation, distribution, and authentication. The commercial world also needs to solve the problem of authenticating users who join a multicast, otherwise it would be impossible to have private conferences, pay-per-view events, and the like. However, the military authentication requirements are more complex. Military wireless networks must be capable of surviving in the event of the capture of equipment and software by the enemy (Feldman, 1998).

SECURE COMMUNICATIONS SYSTEM DESIGN

The integration of security features into developing communications systems is by no means limited to encryption and key management. Beginning with denial of physical access to facilities and direct observation of critical displays of information (e.g., monitors, control panels, cipher mechanisms, even user keyboards and other input devices), proximity detection devices and alarm/alert systems are of primary importance. Design includes tamper-proof manufacturing techniques, automatically zeroizing of circuits processing sensitive databases (e.g., encryption

keying devices), and specification of trusted systems and software in accordance with established operational procedures. Truly trusted systems must be designed at the factory, secured during transit, assembled/installed within a secured area, and maintained by specially cleared personnel. The design must accommodate configuration management of its hardware and software components as well as sustain periodic security audits.

OFFENSIVE INFORMATION OPERATIONS

Offensive information operations are malevolent acts conducted to meet the strategic, operational, or tactical objectives of authorized government bodies; legal, criminal, or terrorist organizations; corporations; or individuals. The operations may be legal or illegal, ethical or unethical, and may be conducted by authorized or unauthorized individuals. The operations may be performed covertly, without notice to the target, or they may be intrusive, disruptive, and even destructive. The effects on information may bring physical results that are lethal to humans. Waltz defines offensive operations as uninvited, unwelcome, unauthorized, and detrimental to the target; therefore, we use the term *attack* to refer to all such operations (Waltz, 1998).

For these reasons, this section must be considered within the context of *understanding offense to prepare for defense*: an understanding of the attacks it must face must precede security design. This section precedes the final section on defensive operations, developing the spectrum of attacks, whereas the next provides the complementary elements of protection and reaction.

Offensive information attacks have two basic functions: (1) to *capture* or (2) to *affect* information. Information may refer to processes or to data/information/ knowledge content. These functions are performed together to achieve the higher level operational and perceptual objectives. Functions, measures, tactics, and techniques of offensive operations relating to the wireless component of IW are of immediate interest.

Functions: The fundamental functions (capture and affect) are used to effectively gain a desired degree of control of the target's information resources. Capturing information is an act of theft of a resource if captured illegally. Affecting information is an act of intrusion with intent to cause unauthorized effects, usually harmful to the information owner. The functional processes that *capture and affect information* are called *offensive measures*, designed to penetrate operational and defensive security measures of the targeted information system (Waltz, 1998).

Tactics: The operational processes employed to plan, sequence, and control the countermeasures of an attack. These tactics consider tactical factors, such as attack objectives, desired effects (e.g., covertness, denial or disruption of service and destruction, modification, or theft of information), degree of effects, and target vulnerabilities.

Techniques: The technical means of capturing and affecting information of humans—their computers, communications, and supporting infrastructures—are described as techniques. In addition to these dimensions, other aspects, depending on their application, may characterize the information attacks.

Motive: The attacker's motive may be varied (e.g., ideological, revenge, greed, hatred, malice, challenge, and theft). Though not a technical characteristic, motive is an essential dimension to consider in forensic analysis of attacks.

Invasiveness: Attacks may be passive or active. Active attacks invade and penetrate the information target, whereas passive attacks are noninvasive, often observing behaviors, information flows, timing, or other characteristics. Most cryptographic attacks may be considered passive relative to the sender and receiver processes but active and invasive to the information message itself.

Effect: The effects of attacks may vary from harassment to theft, from narrow, surgical modification of information to large-scale cascading of destructive information that brings down critical societal infrastructure.

Ethics and legality: The means and the effects may be legal or illegal, depending on current laws. The emerging opportunities opened by information technology have outpaced international and U.S. federal laws to define and characterize illegal attacks. Unlike real property, information is a property that may be shared, abused, or stolen without evidence or the knowledge of the legitimate owner (Nichols, Ryan, & Ryan, 2000). There are two issues of concern in the wireless arena. These are the network (computer) attacks and attacks on protective cryptography.

Taxonomy of Attack Operations

The following may be considered malevolent at the functional level (Waltz, 1998)

- Target level of the IW model: perceptual, information, or physical
- Attack category: capture or affect

The attack matrix is divided into the two avenues of approach available to the attacker:

1. **Direct, or internal, penetration attacks:** Where the attacker penetrates a communication link, computer, or database to capture and exploit internal information, or to modify information (add, insert, delete) or install a malicious process.
2. **Indirect, or external, sensor attacks:** Where the attacker presents open phenomena to the system's sensors or information to sources (e.g., media, Internet, and third parties) to achieve counterinformation objectives. These attacks include insertion of information into sensors or observation of the behavior of sensors or links interconnecting fusion nodes.

The object of attack defines two categories of attacks that affect information:

1. **Content attacks:** The content of the information in the system may be attacked to disrupt, deny, or deceive the user (a decision-maker or process). Content attacks are focused on the real-time data and the derived information
2. **Temporal attacks:** The information process may be affected such that the timeliness of information is attacked. Either a delay in the receipt of data or insertion of false data and passed on as legitimate.

Components of Howard's process-based taxonomy are presented in Table 3 (reported in Waltz, 1999).

Howard constructed the taxonomy such that any simple attack can be categorized as a process, composed of the flow through the elements in the taxonomy (Howard

Table 3 Howard's Process-Based Taxonomy

Taxonomy		Description	
Attackers		Six categories of attackers are identified: hackers, spies, terrorists, corporate, criminals, and vandals.	
Tools		The levels of sophistication of use of tools to conduct the attack are identified.	
Access		The access to the system is further categorized by four branches.	
	Vulnerability exploited	Design, configuration (of the system), and implementation bugs are all means of access that may be used.	
	Level of intrusion	The intruder may obtain unauthorized access, but may also proceed to unauthorized use, which has two possible subcategories.	
		Use of processes	The specific process or service used by the unauthorized user is identified as this branch of the taxonomy.
		Use of information	Static files in storage or data in transit may be the targets of unauthorized use.
	Results	Four results are considered: denial of service, theft of service, corruption of information, or theft (disclosure) of information.	
	Objectives	The objective of the attack (often closely correlated to the attacker type).	

& Longstaff, 1998). Illustrated is the process thread of a network attack (state-supported agents are attackers) in which distributed (multiple-site) tools are used to exploit implementation vulnerabilities to gain use of the system. A specific system process is used to corrupt information in data packets in transit through the targeted computer to achieve a political objective of the supporting nation state.

This taxonomy clearly distinguishes the source (who), the objective (why), and the result (what) from the means (how). Each of these components is required to effectively detect, understand, and respond to attacks. The taxonomy is useful for real-time detection systems and is necessary for investigation and prosecution of attackers.

Cryptographic Attacks

The most devastating attacks on a wireless system are those that compromise the cryptographic security of the system or network. The analysis and "breaking" of encryption is performed to penetrate cryptographic information security to

- Gain one-time access to information that has been encrypted (this information may represent knowledge, electronic funds, certification, or many other information representations)
- Commit one-time security forgery (e.g., to create a secure authentication)
- Spoof a user by presenting a valid authentication intercepted and copied from a valid user
- Fully understand an encryption and keying process to permit repeated and full access to traffic on the targeted system

Cryptanalysis attacks seek to locate vulnerabilities of the general cryptographic system. A fundamental tenet of cryptographic algorithm design is that a strong algorithm's security rests entirely in the key and not the design details of the algorithm. A general rule of encryption security—Kerchoffs principle—is to assume that the attacker may know the encryption/decryption algorithms, but the system must remain secure by the strength of the method and security of the key. Cryptographic attacks against strong, known cryptosystems therefore seek to acquire or guess keys and understand the algorithms of unknown cryptosystems as follows:

- Key management systems are attacked to acquire keys or reduce the search space for brute force key searches.
- Key generators that format key variables and the distribution systems may be exploited if weaknesses occur in their design, implementation, or security.
- Random number generators that randomly select seed numbers to generate keys may be exploitable if they are pseudorandom and a repetitive (deterministic) characteristic can be identified. If deterministic sequences can be identified, key sequences can be predicted.
- Encryption system may be attacked if any portion of the path (plaintext or ciphertext) can be intercepted to perform an analysis.

Chapters "Public Key Algorithms" and "Elliptic Curve Cryptography" provide a description of the most basic cryptographic attack techniques, which include cryptanalysis and deception methods. Methods for attacking symmetric and asymmetric encryption systems differ. They are covered adequately in Chapters "Digital Watermarking and Steganography" and "Forensic Computing." Chapter "Side-Channel Attacks" discusses interesting wireless threats and cryptographic attacks.

DEFENSIVE INFORMATION OPERATIONS

Defensive information measures are also referred to as information assurance. Information operations protect and defend information and information systems by ensuring their availability, integrity, authentication, confidentiality, and nonrepudiation. This includes providing for the restoration of information systems by incorporating protection, detection, and reaction capabilities.

This definition distinguishes protection of the infrastructure by prevention of unauthorized access or attack (proactive measures) and defense of the infrastructure by detecting, surviving, and responding to attacks (reactive measures). The assurance includes the following component properties and capabilities (collectively known as CIA):

- Availability provides assurance that information, services, and resources will be accessible and usable when needed by the user.
- Integrity assures that information and processes are secure from unauthorized tampering (e.g., insertion, deletion, destruction, and replay of data) via methods such as encryption, digital signatures, and intrusion detection.
- Authentication assures that only authorized users have access to information and services on the basis of controls: (1) authorization (granting and revoking access rights), (2) delegation (extending a portion of one entity's rights to another), and (3) user authentication (reliable corroboration of a user, and data origin). (This is a mutual property when each of two parties authenticates the other.)
- Confidentiality protects the existence of a connection, traffic flow, and information content from disclosure to unauthorized parties.
- Nonrepudiation assures that transactions are immune from false denial of sending or receiving information by providing reliable evidence that can be independently verified to establish proof of origin and delivery.
- Restoration assures information and systems can survive an attack and that availability can be resumed after the impact of an attack.

Information assurance includes the traditional functions of information security (INFOSEC), which is defined at two levels. At the policy level, INFOSEC is the system of policies, procedures, and requirements to protect information that, if subjected to unauthorized disclosure, could reasonably be expected to cause damage. At the technical level, INFOSEC includes measures and controls that protect the information infrastructure against:

- Denial of service
- Unauthorized (accidental or intentional) disclosure
- Modification or destruction of information infrastructure components and data

INFOSEC includes consideration of hardware and software functions, characteristics, features, operational procedures, accountability procedures, and access controls at the central computer facility, remote computer, and terminal facilities; management constraints; physical structures and devices; and personnel and communication controls needed to provide an acceptable level of risk for the infrastructure and for the data and information contained in the infrastructure.

INFOSEC includes the totality of security safeguards needed to provide an acceptable protection level for an infrastructure and for data handled by an infrastructure. INFOSEC includes five components within communications security (COMSEC): emanations security (EMSEC), electronics security (ELSEC), transmission security (TRANSEC), computer security (COMPUSEC), and cryptographic security (COMSEC).

More recently, the aspect of survivability (the capacity to withstand attacks and functionally endure at some defined level of performance) has been recognized as a critical component of defenses included under the umbrella of INFOSEC and information assurance.

WIW IN PRACTICE: VULNERABILITIES OF A SUBURBAN HOSPITAL

To put theory into practice, an assault on a suburban hospital (a vital commercial target) is presented in this section. This assault involves a unique hopping attack across the hospital's wireless local area network (WLAN). The assault incorporated three separate wireless attack scenarios. A "soft" commercial target was deliberately chosen to remind the reader that WIW applies to more than just military targets. *WIW may be described in terms of military goals and objectives but in practice, it can be used just as effectively in the private theater. The attack described is feasible and remarkably effective on both private sector and military installations.* The target hospital is a full service regional 1000-bed medical center that serves a major county in a U.S. state, providing services of all types, including cardiac, respiratory, and organ transplant operations, maternity and pediatric care, emergency treatment, and outpatient services. To protect the facility, we have removed pertinent identifications from this chapter (references to people, locations, and certain applications software). We have advised the security officers at this installation, prior to publication of our findings, of the vulnerabilities in their system. We have been advised that appropriate measures have been put in place to hamper these attack scenarios. Our purpose is to show that WIW is a highly effective means of leveraging effort in terms of damage to the target (in *any* arena employing wireless devices and communications).

Security Measures for the Hospital

The hospital administrators are acutely aware of the precariousness of the open environment of a major hospital. Their primary attention is focused on three aspects of protection: (1) physical security, (2) personnel security, and (3) information security. These three aspects when integrated complement each other and provide a cumulative level of protection.

The main threat to the hospital is not focused on external or internal forces, though these areas are a primary concern. The hospital administration views the main daily threat to its information systems as a potential inability to keep up with maintenance and service to the information systems that support its health and life-saving mission. The largest part of the information management annual budget is for repair costs, supplies, and maintenance. The attitude of the administrators is that the information technology is mainly a means of functioning. The most recent risk assessments emphasized personnel and physical security as the primary countermeasures to human initiated attacks on the system. However, threats to information systems have been implemented regarding physical, personnel, and information processing and storage.

Hospital administrators are responsible for protecting patients' medical records as required by the Health Insurance Portability and Accountability Act (HIPAA). Although the primary intent of HIPAA is to improve access to health insurance, it is also concerned with healthcare fraud and abuse. One of its most important tenets for healthcare providers is proscriptions on how medical information may be used, disclosed, and accessed. The healthcare provider is responsible for the safeguarding of medical information while it is being stored and/or transmitted. There are significant penalties, both civil and criminal for the most severe cases of negligence or abuse (e.g., fines up to $250,000 and 10 years imprisonment). Violation of HIPAA provisions may result in potential financial losses and may damage the hospital's standing within the community it serves and within the medical community. It is important that hospital administrators realize that the security and privacy issues of HIPAA impact both the business processes of the medical center operation and the information systems used therein.

Target Wireless Operations

Each physician's area and nurses' station area is configured for wireless LAN operation. Use of 802.11g standards allows maximum usage of this feature, which is identification (ID) and password protected. The system transmitter-receiver supports bandwidth up to 54 Mbps and operates in the 2.4-GHz frequency range as an FCC Part 15 (low powered, unlicensed device). The radiating elements are fixed length whip antennas, vertically polarized, affording coverage over practically all of the hospital (including the cafeteria) except for the information systems area. Access to the Internet from an individual's laptop is accomplished by using a removable network card compatible with 802.11g standards. The hospital is transitioning toward replacing laptops with hand held wireless PDA type devices and Tablet PCs for e-mail, messaging, and paging. Physicians, nurses, and other essential personnel were the first to be equipped with these devices, which affected a savings over separate pager, cell phone, and laptop costs. This move to a smaller size form-factor increases the problems with theft, loss through neglect, and unauthorized use when left unattended.

When using the WLAN, security is provided in primarily in two ways. The first is media access control (MAC) address access control lists. The MAC of the wireless network adapter used by a computer must be in the access point (AP) MAC database before the computer is allowed to connect to the AP (and therefore the WLAN). In addition, use of 64-bit (or 128-bit) wireless encryption protocol (WEP) provides for confidentiality of data as they traverse the WLAN. The newer Wi-Fi Protected Access (WPA) is planned as a near future upgrade, but no resources have been allocated for its purchase, installation, and maintenance at this time. Voice-over Internet protocol (VoIP) is not currently available in the hospital, mainly because of the adequacy of the present phone system; in any event, use of VoIP will increase the security challenges significantly.

The wireless transceivers (AP and antennae) are scattered in strategic areas of the hospital, including the cafeteria. They are categorized as "low" and "high" powered. Between buildings, the hospital uses a laser transmission and receiving system in a line-of-sight arrangement. The data rate is high, about 100 Mbs, thus allowing a seamless interconnection of information systems without reverting to cable with its attendant problems, such as deterioration due to aging. This system's reliability has been proven in the past 3 years since its installation.

VLAN Operations and Servers

The hospital operates an intranet that is divided into four subnets using virtual local area networks (VLAN). The VLAN supports approximately 240 users. Three of the VLANS are intentionally kept nonspecific in terms of functionality, thus the failure of a single subnet will not wipe out a given hospital function. Historically, the hospital has added additional VLANs as the existing systems exceeded their capacity. All of the VLANs are protected by a single LAN firewall. Access to particular servers is controlled by particular VLANs and thus there is some sharing of resources across the different VLANs. All workstations are connected to a 100-MB backbone to the servers located in a secure separate facility. Two of the VLANs have Internet capability as well as availability of a virtual private network (VPN) capability.

The hospital requires many different types of servers on its network: an e-mail server, Internet servers, a firewall server, database servers, and application servers are spread out across various floors. The hospital uses a heterogeneous network with five different types of Unix (SCO, Solaris AIX, HPUX, and Linux), as well as three other operating systems (Windows, Novell, and Tandem).

Main servers carry the hospital core applications previously described. Department servers are used for nonstandard applications, such as tracking physicians' certifications. Because of the integration of these systems, medical information constantly flows across the network.

The Wireless Attacks

In this A/D simulation, the attack team (AT) posed as highly motivated and highly skilled terrorists with multiple objectives. The AT members are considered "long-term" assets whose objectives are to continue small, focused attacks against specialized targets to reduce public confidence in the infrastructure and public institutions. The AT does not mind being electronically "seen" because they want publicity related to how often/easy these attacks were, but they do not want to be "caught" (e.g., arrested). The AT is much more experienced than the average hacker or script-kiddie, who uses tools prescribed by more experienced people.

The AT attacks perpetrated against this hospital follow a standard methodology recognized within rogue groups of hackers, and professional penetration testers, as the "de facto" process for finding and exploiting vulnerabilities. This process may be used in both the logical/cyberenvironment and the physical world. Figure 3 illustrates the process flow, which is described below (Scambray, McClure, & Kurtz, 2001).

- **Footprinting:** This step includes target address range and naming acquisition as part of the overall information gathering process; the attacker attempts to gather as much data about the IT devices, network, and infrastructure as possible.
- **Scanning:** This step includes target assessment and identification of listening services and possible security vulnerabilities that may allow system access.
- **Enumeration:** This step includes more in-depth probing of systems and devices to identify valid user accounts and poorly protected resource shares.

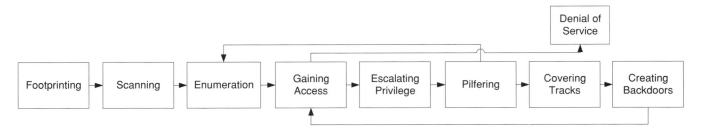

Adapted from *Hacking Exposed: Network Security Secrets and Solutions Second Edition*, by Stuart McClure, Joel Scambray, and George Kurtz. Osborne/McGraw-Hiill 2002

Figure 3: De facto methodology for wireless hacks.

- **Gaining Access:** This step is the exploitation of vulnerabilities to access the target once enough information has been gathered.
- **Escalating Privilege:** Once initial access is achieved the attacker attempts to gain full control of the system (administrator or root access).
- **Pilfering:** This step involves gathering information on a compromised system to gain access to other systems.
- **Covering Tracks:** This step involves backing out of a system leaving no proof that malicious activity occurred.
- **Creation of Backdoors:** This step involves leaving methods of gaining privileged access to systems for future actions on compromised systems.
- **Denial of Service:** This step involves preventing access to a target system, device, or service.

Each of the process flow items may be repeated in a "loop" fashion to continue building upon previous attacks. For example, once access is gained to a device more information about the system may produce additional vulnerabilities. Therefore, the attacker may go back to the footprinting, scanning, or enumeration phases. For each target, specific vulnerability *types* are targeted using automated and manual methods. Generally, the vulnerability types fall into eight categories:

1. **Kernel Flaws:** The kernel is the core of an operating system; it enforces the overall security model for the system. Any security flaw that occurs in the kernel puts the entire system in danger.
2. **Buffer Overflows:** A buffer overflow occurs when programs do not adequately check input for appropriate length, usually because of poor programming practice. When this occurs, arbitrary code can be introduced into the system and executed with the privileges of the running program. This code often can be run as root on Unix systems and SYSTEM on Windows systems.
3. **Symbolic Links:** A symbolic link or symlink is a file that points to another file. Often there are programs that will change the permissions of a file. If these programs run with privileged permissions, a user could strategically create symlinks to trick these programs into modifying or listing critical system files.
4. **File Descriptor Attacks:** File descriptors are nonnegative integers that the system uses to keep track of files rather than using specific filenames. Certain file descriptors have implied uses. When a privileged program assigns an inappropriate file descriptor, it exposes that file to compromise.
5. **Race Conditions:** Race conditions can occur when a program or process has entered into a privileged mode but before the program or process has given up its privileged mode. A user can time an attack to take advantage of this program or process while it is still in the privileged mode. If an attacker successfully manages to compromise the program or process during its privileged state then the attacker has won the "race." Common race conditions include signal handling and core file manipulation.

6. **Configuration Management:** File and directory permissions control which users and processes have access to what files and directories. Appropriate permissions are critical to the security of any system. Poor permissions could allow any number of attacks, including the reading or writing of password files or the addition of allowable hosts and users in access control databases or list files (e.g., rhost files). Configuration management includes the documentation of removing/disabling/changing default accounts and passwords.
7. **Trojans:** Trojan programs include programs such as BackOrifice, NetBus, and SubSeven or they can be custom built. Kernel root kits could also be employed once access is obtained to allow a backdoor into the system at anytime.
8. **Social Engineering:** Social engineering is the technique of using persuasion and/or deception to gain access to, or information about, information systems. It is typically implemented through human conversation or other interaction. The usual medium of choice is telephone but can also be e-mail or even face to face. Social engineering generally follows two standard approaches. In the first approach the attacker (or the information assurance tester) poses as a user experiencing difficultly and calls the organization's help desk to gain information on the target network or host, obtain a login ID and credentials, or get a password reset. The second approach is to pose as the help desk and call a user to get the user to provide his/her user id(s) and password(s). This technique can be extremely effective.

In practical example, we follow three different basic scenarios (e.g., attack vectors): (1) remote attacks on a wireless network, (2) attacks via trusted agents, and (3) attacks via public access pathways. Each scenario contains several different and specific methods of achieving the attack goal.

EXAMPLE ATTACK: REMOTE ATTACK ON A WIRELESS NETWORK (VLAN HOPPING)

Many risks are associated with this attack scenario, including being spotted by hospital employees/patrons, detection by IT staff (because of the amount of probes/scans), and detection by passing police patrols. This attack scenario required the attack team to spend considerable time performing a site survey of the hospital (i.e., war driving/walking); the AT started with the footprinting process to bound the scope of our attack by detecting all devices, which gave us the sum of all possible targets of evaluation (TOE). To do this the AT used specialized hardware and software to monitor the 802.11 frequency spectrum—in this case, a 15-db directional yagi antenna, a 5-db omnidirectional antenna, a laptop running Fedora Core 1 Linux (http://fedora.redhat.com/), a PCMCIA Orinoco-based 802.11 Network Interface Card (NIC), and the wireless application Kismet (http://www.kismetwireless.net/). The site survey first involved patrolling the outside perimeter of the hospital in

Figure 4: Hospital AP and associated ranges.

a car equipped with the magnetic mount omnidirectional antenna. After using the omnidirectional antenna to survey all the operating wireless devices, the AT used the 15-db directional yagi antenna to probe further into the hospital (for interior devices). Figure 4 shows the approximate range of each one of the wireless devices that we were able to find; each name (color) represents a different hospital AP and the circles represent the range of the signal. Of the 85 access points listed in this image, at least 9 were APs unprotected by wired equivalency protocol (WEP).

Additionally, the AT pinpointed those devices identified with the omni that have the greatest number of clients so they could capture the highest number of Internet protocol packets; the more packets captured, the faster the AT could crack the hospital WEP protections. During this step, the team also captured all traffic between the detected APs and client devices and downloaded the AP router tables using Kismet. To do this the AT was required to spend more time sniffing the network to gain the AP service set identifier (SSID) because the hospital had the AP set not to broadcast their SSID (the AT must have the SSID to connect to the AP later and attack internal devices). Capturing all the data traffic also allowed the AT to determine which devices were "static" or generally present on the network, which devices were AP/routers/repeaters, and which devices were transient clients (roaming doctors, nurses, etc.). In this step, the AT also built a logical diagram of the TOE; they gathered as much data about the wireless IT devices, network, and infrastructure as possible. The intent was to determine the interconnection and dependencies of devices.

When the AT finished the footprinting step, it tried unsuccessfully to connect to multiple APs. Because the AT had already cracked the hospital WEP key, it knew that MAC (media access control) filtering was enabled.

Only specified wireless clients were allowed to connect to a given AP. To bypass this protection the team picked the MAC of several authorized transient clients and connected once the transient devices disconnected from the network or moved to another AP. The AT then began the scanning step using NMAP (http://www.insecure.org) in "paranoid mode" with packet fragmentation (to help with IDS evasion) to identify logical ports and services available on each internal device connected to the AP (e.g., the wireless devices used by doctors and nurses). [The AT was aware that the hospital IDS might see the scan traffic and alert the sysadmins, who would in turn kick the MAC off the network. However, it should be noted that this did not occur. It is arguable that a better approach would be to deploy a passive network enumerator such as p0f found at http://lcamtuf.coredump.cx/p0f.shtml. However, passive enumerators such as p0f do not have as large an OS "fingerprint" database (because there is a smaller user base) and are not as accurate as active tools; therefore they are a tool of last resort]. The AT also started sniffing the traffic between AP and client devices to look for username/password combinations traversing the network unencrypted (using dsniff); they also cataloged associated vulnerabilities they found for later exploitation. To accomplish the scanning step the AT used tools such as nessus, superscan, nmap, and other general-purpose automated vulnerability tools so that they could identify vulnerable interfaces, such as WWW, FTP, SMB, and NETBIOS. Again, the AT was concerned about detection, so they also used the passive RNA scan to identify vulnerable interfaces. For the enumeration step the AT began in-depth probing of devices to determine accounts and poorly protected resources (e.g., file systems and network shares). During this stage tools such as smbgetusers, smbbf, nikto, whisker, and other specialized-/single-purpose tools were used. It was during this step in which it was determined that the hospital AP were acting as network bridges between the wireless network and the hospital local area network (LAN); once they had access to the AP the team was able to connect to the "wired" hospital network segments and numerous VLANs.

Once the AT finished the enumeration step, it had a baseline of possible targets and attack vectors for devices connected to the hospital wireless network. Their first attempt at attacking the attached systems was to probe the network segments looking for devices, which could be classified as some type of a server. Regrettably, each time the AT scanned a server their connection to the server was abruptly broken.

The AT assumed that the hospital has some sort of IDS/IPS protecting the servers. Therefore, the AT began concentrating on other devices such as portable monitoring stations, laptops, PDA/PED, and some mobile workstations. Here they used username/passwords obtained via our sniffer on the wireless network and root-level exploits (such as the RPC-DCOM vulnerability that allowed us administrator access to an unpatched Windows 2000/XP workstation). The AT systematically performed a search of storage devices (local and networked shares) for .doc, .xls, .jpg, .wpd, and so on and cataloged the directory trees; this information will be used for further exploitation/access and possible social engineering.

For each workstation compromised, the AT also introduced a backdoor (Trojan) and key-logger package. The purpose was to gather additional usernames/passwords for other systems; whenever someone used our compromised systems to access another area, the key-loggers captured their username and password (even if the system is on another "wired" segment or VLAN). Once the AT finished attacking the Windows-based workstations, the team began application-level attacks against Linux/Unix servers with the purpose of introducing malicious code into the hospital network (including viruses, rootkits, and key loggers). In particular, they attacked the hospital e-mail server by attempting to send unauthenticated e-mail to hospital employees.

The AT purpose was twofold: (1) to impersonate hospital help desk/system administrators with the goal of using e-mail to perform password harvesting from users and (2) to introduce both destructive and nondestructive viruses/worms into the hospital systems via the primary e-mail server. For their first goal, the AT exploited vulnerabilities in the hospital e-mail server in which no authentication was required to send e-mail to anyone within the hospital domain. The AT was successful in this endeavor and gained multiple passwords from almost a dozen users before system administrators notified their users.

For the second goal the AT attempted to use the same vulnerability in the e-mail server to attach a virus to an e-mail prior to sending it out to hospital users; they were unsuccessful in this attack because the hospital had an antivirus program for e-mail servers installed on the system. However, while doing the enumeration of the internal network VLAN on which the AT were connected (via the AP and compromised hosts) the AT discovered a Solaris and HP-UX computer that had the POSTFIX mail transport agent (MTA) enabled with a default configuration. Using these computers the AT were able to successfully send out e-mail to domain users containing viruses and use these systems to send e-mails for password harvesting.

The last attack using the wireless system was a two-stage attack to gain access to sensitive and protected systems; the first stage was done earlier where the team gained administrative-level access to a Windows 2000/XP system on the LAN. The second stage of the attack was to use that system to gain access to the VLAN containing sensitive systems. To accomplish this, the AT installed a Trojan and specialized tools on the workstation that enabled them to launch attacks directly from the workstation targeting the VLAN switches. The AT used tools to sniff the wired network to find the VLAN switches and created a logical map. Once they had the TOE identified, the AT began scanning with Nmap, SNMPwalk, and so on to identify vulnerable ports and services. It was able to find multiple switches with default simple network management protocol (SNMP) interfaces (community names). The AT then used these interfaces to change the switch configurations so that the VLAN is supertrunked across interfaces (the VLAN the AT computer is connected to now has access to all VLANs). Once the team had access to the protected VLAN, they were able to identify a vulnerable Windows 2000 server with generic cardiology software containing doctor id numbers, patient records, and other sensitive information.

Attack via Trusted Agents

This scenario uses vulnerabilities found in the hospital IT interconnections to trusted sources such as remote employees, state/local systems, and transient employees (such as interns and volunteers). Each attack vector within this scenario required multiple stage attacks, each one building upon the previous until the result is gained (access to the internal hospital systems). Again, the intent is to determine the interconnection and dependencies of devices. For this scenario the AT extensively researched public information sources such as the hospital Web site (including the teaching/research areas), doctors associated with the hospital, and federal/state/local programs related to hospitals and hospital research. The attack team attempted to determine what the physical and logical bounds are of IT devices and what security controls may be in place for those devices. It used the information to determine where IT devices are located (what doctor's offices, where students and researches keep their laptops, etc.).

The attack scenario involved multiple preparatory stages of research before launching the footprinting, scanning, and enumeration activities. The first stage was defining the targets: the AT scoured the hospital public Web pages, newsgroups, and university pages for information. The AT was looking for any information that could tell them which doctors were related to the hospital, how interns/volunteers work at the hospital, and what types of research are performed. For the second preparatory stage of the attack, they did the same thing for the doctor's offices (including physical reconnaissance) and university-based research areas (areas on the university campus that dealt with work performed at the hospital). The third and final preparatory stage required team members to "interview" interns, volunteers, and nurses (at related doctor's offices) to gather information. Interviews took the form of casual chitchat and "formal" interviews for the "purpose" of writing school reports or newspaper articles.

Once the AT finished the research stage, it used the information to begin footprinting, scanning, and enumeration of the federal, state, and local government interconnects. The interconnects include fractional T1, 56k leased lines, and dial-up connections to federal, state, and local government agencies. The AT was able to gain very little information about the systems associated with the interconnects; either no information was available about the systems on the other end (e.g., they had their banners turned off) or the connections were repeatedly dropped. Attempting to identify vulnerabilities on these connections was an arduous task and each time the team failed.

Next, the AT began targeting remote access for doctors. It started this attack by performing information gathering off the hospital Web site (i.e., they manually scoured the site looking for doctor names, addresses, and phone numbers). The AT then performed Internet searches on those doctors to find personal or doctor office Web sites; each

site was then scanned/enumerated for vulnerabilities. The original plan dictated that once these attack vectors have been attempted they would then begin site reconnaissance of the doctor's offices to determine the possibility of a wireless Ethernet attack or physical break-in and local compromise of computers, which may provide information/access to hospital systems. However, during the enumeration of the public hospital Web site the AT found numerous entry points for remote access. Of these, the AT found a custom portal (a Web page created by hospital IT staff), which allowed access to the generic remote access application. The portal was vulnerable to a cross-site-scripting attack (XSS), which then allowed the team read access to doctor and patient records contained in the remote access software.

The AT's last effort in attacking via trusted agents was to surreptitiously obtain an intern laptop from the intern "sleep room." Although this was extremely risky, an AT member was able to dress in hospital "scrubs" and walk freely into the room itself. The AT person spent several hours posing as an external exchange student (a student from a different hospital and school) visiting the teaching hospital for a 2-day "familiarity" tour. During this visit, the AT member spent time talking to other interns gaining their trust and eventually asked to borrow one of the intern's computers when the intern went back to work. Once the AT intruder had access to the system, he booted into a bootable operating environment (Knoppix-STD), copied off all documents and data (including password files, etc.) onto an external USB drive and installed a keylogger/Trojan with the ability to send information to the AT via its own e-mail engine.

Attack via Public Access Pathways

The AT used public Internet interfaces and remote access gateways to perform these attacks. When the AT members first began the footprinting, scanning, and enumeration steps against the public Web servers, their connections were dropped and eventually the team could no longer connect to the servers with those IP addresses. From this, the AT determined that some type of IDS/IPS was in place, which prevented initial attempts. Because of this, the AT changed the settings on their tools to "IDS Evasion" so that the scanning process would not be detected as quickly. This worked for a time but the AT found it was still being detected and eventually dropped/blocked from connecting. After several days of no activity, the AT launched a distributed denial of service (DoS) attack against the primary Web server. While this attack was being performed, the AT began footprinting, scanning, and enumerating the other servers. Because the system administrators and IDS/IPS were busy tracking the DoS, the team was able to continue uninterrupted. The AT performed the same basic process of scanning and enumerating these access paths as in prior scenarios in order to find vulnerabilities and exploit them. The AT used information from the other scenarios, including all hospital owned/related IP address space information, and footprinted all devices associated with the address space. Once the devices were footprinted, the AT began the scanning and enumeration process and attempted to exploit vulnerabilities such as cross-site scripting (XSS), application-level vulnerabilities, and weak passwords.

The AT's first attack was again focused on the public hospital Web server. Here it found another custom portal allowing access into the remote access application. Because the AT was only able to obtain read access to an application on the Web server (the remote access application), the AT was unable to introduce any malicious code onto the server.

The AT again accessed the hospital e-mail server, this time from the Internet, and was able to send out e-mail posing as system administrators and help desk employees. Although the system administrators caught on to this faster this time, the AT was still able to get passwords from a couple of users. However, the users changed their passwords before the AT could take advantage of the vulnerability.

Last, the AT tried to gain access to protected systems by using VLAN exploitations against the switches and routers facing the Internet. Each time their connections were dropped/blocked and eventually the AT could not connect using their IP addresses. The AT assumed that the hospital IDS/IPS had automatically detected their exploits and was configured to drop the connection, and then the IP altogether, after successive malicious attempts.

EXAMPLE DEFENSE: METHODS OF DEFENSE

The defense team (DT) reviewed the AT findings, failures, and successes and recommended the following computer security countermeasures be installed or hardened.

Host-Based Intrusion Detection System (h-IDS)

Host-based intrusion detection system upgrades and installation were deemed an effective method of intrusion detection as compared to network-based intrusion detection systems. This is based partly on the fact that data transmitted over the hospital information system are encrypted; therefore, network-based IDS will not be as effective in identifying intrusion signatures. By configuring IDS in host-based mode, activities of each host (e.g., the various hospital servers) can be monitored. IDS within the IS has been configured to monitor the following (Peikari & Fogie, 2002):

In packet level

- Unexpected signature
- TCP/IP violations
- Packets of unusual size
- Low TTL (time-to-live)
- Invalid checksum

In application level

- CPU usage
- Disk activity
- User login
- File activity
- Number of running services
- Number of running applications
- Number of open ports
- Log file size

When any abnormality is detected, an alert should be sent to the centralized console in real time. This method has high sensitivity but unfortunately generates a great deal of data. It is important to carefully craft detection signatures to weed out what are called "false positives."

Other properties of IDS are log file monitoring and integrity monitoring. Log file monitoring that is used is Swatch (Simple Watcher; http://www.SourceForge.net), which can scan log entries and report in real time. An integrity monitor watches key system structures for change. For example, a basic integrity monitor uses system files or registry keys as "bait" to track changes by an intruder. The integrity monitor software used is Tripwire (http://www.tripwire), which can monitor the following (Peikari & Fogie, 2002):

- File additions, deletions, or modifications
- File flags (hidden, read-only, archive, and so on)
- Last access time
- Last write time
- Create time
- File size
- Hash checking

In addition, IDS can be configured for signature scanning and anomaly detection. The hospital now uses Snort for much of their IDS signature scanning (Snort 2.0). Caswell has written an excellent reference on Snort 2.0 (Caswell, Beale, Foster, & Posluns, 2003). Anomaly detection involves establishing a baseline of normal system or network activity and then sounding an alert when a deviation occurs. Because network traffic is constantly changing, such a design lends itself more to host-based IDS rather than network IDS (Peikari & Fogie, 2002): Snort also serves as an intrusion prevention system (IPS). At the time of detection, the system administrator can use Snort to block suspect IP addresses and kill the connections.

To maximize the effectiveness of a monitoring infrastructure, the DT recommended that everything be centralized within a few servers. This means using software that is modular enough to allow for different types of monitoring. Some of the most common programs used for this type of centralized monitoring include "HP OpenView" (Hewlett-Packard), "Netcool" (Micromuse), "Big Brother" (Quest Software), "WhatsUp Gold" (Ipswitch), and "Nagios" (Nagios). It was recommended that the system administrator plug in only those monitoring tools required by the hospital security policies to develop modules to accommodate needs (Liska, 2002) and to provide a means for real-time audit log monitoring.

Firewall

In addition to the host-based IDS, the DT recommends that the network be protected by firewalls that are configured in "invisible" mode. This set up adds another layer of security to the network. The disadvantage to a typical firewall is that it is a destination on the network. A traditional firewall has a public and a private network, so it has addresses that can be attacked. An intruder can attempt to launch a DoS attack against the firewall directly. If the firewalls are set up so that if the firewall application crashes, the server underneath simply becomes a router—directing traffic from the public to the private network, which introduces great vulnerability. If an attacker successfully launches a DoS attack against the firewall and is able to crash the application, that attacker now has full access to the network. The invisible mode helps to counteract some of these vulnerabilities and exhibits the following advantages (Liska, 2002):

- It is more difficult to build a network map, because the firewall does not provide an attacker with an IP address, therefore it is more difficult to find vulnerable devices on the network.
- The lack of a public IP address also makes it more difficult for an attacker to determine the type of firewall in place—making it harder to exploit weaknesses in the firewall.
- It is easier to add a firewall to an existing network, because invisible mode requires no change in network settings.

The main disadvantage to this mode is the increased difficulty in network troubleshooting. The firewalls act as a device on the network that is directly impacting traffic but do not show up as network nodes. This can sometimes create confusion and make spotting network problems more difficult. Firewall software used in the target hospital information systems are Checkpoint FW-1, Raptor, and Netscreen.

The hospital is using a hybrid system because it offers both packet filtering and a proxy firewall. Additional features suggested and recommended for the firewall are as follows (Bhasin, 2002):

- Incorporate tunneling functionality to implement a site-to-site encryption solution
- Log the activities of the network so that administrators can track events of the day
- Inclusion of built-in high-availability and graceful degradation to handle network risks that may arise due to unexpected breakdowns; this feature enables firewalls to transfer their operations to backup firewalls if there is a breakdown.
- Inclusion of mechanisms that can trap intruders; one such mechanism is the use of a honey pot, which entices intruders by displaying data that is not valid.

Defenses for Wireless Networks

Attacks are performed systematically. There are steps that an attacker takes to gain access over the network eventually. There are countermeasures in place, which may safeguard the information system in each level. These countermeasures may result in either the attacker running out of resources or becoming psychologically discouraged in pursuing his or her attacks against the target.

Physical security measures represent a first line of defense against physical surveillance by any attacker who attempts to roam around the hospital either during business hours or during nonbusiness hours. In either case, the physical security such as security guards and surveillance cameras may spot him. Security personnel patrol hospital premises on a regular basis. Any suspicious activity will be reported to the security office of the hospital. Depending on the circumstances, local law enforcement may be contacted. Closed circuit cameras are present both in the hospital and in the parking lot. Any suspicious activity spotted by the surveillance will be reported to the security office. The physical countermeasures will provide means to limit access to the hospital information system. This is called threat decomposition.

The data transmitted over the network are encrypted as an additional line of defense. Unfortunately, the data on a given machine are not encrypted, which is vulnerability. If an attacker cannot access the physical machine, he has to break many security measures to get access to the machine. The most common countermeasures in place for wireless networks are WEP and MAC address filtering. WEP is based on four 64-bit (or one 128-bit) encryption keys, which is not strong encryption per se. Coupled with MAC address filtering, it adds another layer to the security. WEP is a shared key protocol meaning both ends of the link use the same key. In WEP mode, a packet is added to the data called integrity check value (ICV) and the packet is encrypted via an RC4 encryption method. Key IDs (for decryption) and initialization vector (IV) are added to the packet in unencrypted form and sent to the receiver (Edney & Arbaugh, 2003). Hospital policies require daily review of audit logs to detect any malicious activities. In case of malicious activity detection, system administrators are charged with changing the WEP keys and blocking all the MAC addresses until the spoofed MAC has been detected and blocked.

Considering the mechanics of WEP, it is not a secure protocol. WEP is vulnerable to many attacks.

- **Challenge Response Mechanism:** WEP authentication relies on a challenge/response mechanism. First, the AP sends a random string of numbers. Second, the mobile device encrypts the string and sends it back. Third, the AP decrypts the string and compares it to the original string. It can then choose to accept the device and send a success message. The key used for this process is the same WEP key used for encryption. The operation does not authenticate the access point to the mobile device. Therefore, a rogue access point can pretend it was able to check the encrypted string and send a success message without ever knowing the key. There is no token provided to validate subsequent transactions, making the whole authentication process rather ineffective. In addition, during authentication the access point sends a random string of 128 bytes. The mobile station encrypts the string and sends it back. WEP encryption involves generating a sequence of pseudorandom bytes called the key stream and XOR-ing it with the plaintext. So anyone watching this transaction now has the plaintext challenge and the encrypted response. Therefore, simply by XOR-ing the two together, the attacker has a copy of the RC4 random bytes (Edney & Arbaugh, 2003).

- **Frame Capture:** An attacker with a wireless sniffer that is able to capture all the frames sent between an access point and a mobile device. At the time of log in, the server sends a login message and a legitimate user enters a username and password. The attacker cannot see the file because it is encrypted; however, at a later time, the attacker can send a copy of the message the legitimate user sent to the server (replay). The access point passes the message to the login server, which accepts it as a valid log in, because it was encrypted by the correct key. The attacker can thus successfully log into the network and the server. WEP has no inherent protections against a replay attack (Edney & Arbaugh, 2003).

- **Direct Key Attack:** This is a weakness inherent in RC4 encryption, which is often referred to as a "weak key" vulnerability. WEP does not protect against this weakness. An attacker can directly attack a WEP encryption key and, within a short period, reconstructs the key.

The following are a list of methods to protect against WEP vulnerabilities. However, these methods are not perfect. WEP is still far from a reliable security countermeasure.

- Use of a combination of SSID (with broadcast disabled), WEP, and MAC address filtering to secure wireless network.
- Segmentation of wireless LAN traffic. If possible, all access points plug into the same switch or group of switches. Keeping WLAN traffic segmented in this manner helps to limit the damage an attacker can do, if the WLAN security is breached (Liska, 2002).
- Changing of WEP keys on a periodic basis or whenever the system administrator detects probing into the network.
- Limitations on the number of copies of a message that can be accepted. This is a function of the wireless security protocol.
- Termination of the wireless network when not in use.
- Changing of all the hardware default passwords like routers and switches.
- Modification of WEP key lengths from 64 bits to 128 bits.

It should be expected that a determined attacker would break WEP and get access to the wireless network. The countermeasures in place to protect the wireless network will likely fail. However, other countermeasures in place will assist in protecting the network and detecting the attacker.

To better secure the wireless network, an upgrade of the hardware and software to WAP or even better to RSN (robust security network) is recommended. Another technique, which can add security to the network, is the use of

a DMZ (demilitarized zone). By doing this, WLAN is in a semitrusted zone that is expected to be attacked by hackers. By operating with the mentality that the WLAN could already be owned, a more appropriate plan can be taken about who and what is allowed to access the internal network. However, although this type of protection can help protect internal resources, it will not protect the wireless network users. Therefore, the DMZ should be just one part of a wireless security plan (Peikari & Fogie, 2002).

Configuring access points to use RADIUS/LEAP to authenticate users can further enhance wireless network security. A user connects to an access point and the network card authenticates using SSID, WEP, or both. A RADIUS request is then forwarded from the access point to a RADIUS server. The RADIUS server authenticates the user, who is now able to pass traffic across the network. For redundancy, a second RADIUS server can be added to the access point. If the primary server fails, users will be automatically forwarded to the secondary server (Liska, 2002). Using RADIUS in conjunction with a VPN is a powerful, but expensive, solution to the problems associated with WEP. In this configuration, the 802.11 link is used simply as a transport mechanism. Network access, user authentication, and data encryption are handled by the VPN.

Defense against Information Pilfering

An attacker can penetrate the network by breaking WEP and spoofing a MAC address and start probing the network. Correct IDS monitoring configuration will detect these probes. Assuming the attacker gains access to the network via a spoofed MAC address, if the attacker attempts during business hours to probe the IS, his behavior may deviate from the norms. Because the legitimate user is using his or her account to perform daily activities, there are chances that an attacker can be detected by employees or system administrators because of unfamiliar behavior. Each user will only have access to particular sections of the IS. Unusual behavior such as accessing areas where the user would not normally access may cause an IDS alarm if the traffic patterns are unusual enough. If an attacker attempted to perform his probing at night, it would be easier for system administrators to detect the probe via time restricted login policies and the typically lower amounts of network traffic. As expected, appropriate monitoring policies that are enforced present a formidable deterrence to an attacker. All server activities are monitored because of hospital policy. As a result, an attacker will have a hard time searching through network and local shares to catalog directory trees. If the spoofed MAC address is not permitted to perform these activities, the IDS will set a flag to the system administrator in real time. The system administrator will detect and block the IP address and kill the connection. Therefore, for this attack, the countermeasures in place will effectively defend against the attack and the attacker will be stopped.

In our example, however, the AT occupied the system administrators with the DoS attack on the primary Web server and has already gained access to the secondary Web server. The IDS has been distracted by the DoS attack. Thus, the system administrator has ignored the activity logs on the secondary Web server. The attacker can continue his DoS attack on the primary server and possibly keep his activities on the secondary server undetected. Therefore, the attacker may be successful in his attack.

Defense against Malicious Code Introduction

In this attack, the attacker tries to introduce malicious code into the system by installing RAT backdoors. There are countermeasures in place to prevent the attacker from succeeding in this attack. The attacker can get access to the primary mail server and sends out e-mail from that server because the mail server does not require SMTP authentication. While the attacker uses the mail server to send out his e-mail with malicious codes as attachment, the antivirus software installed on the mail server (Sophos mail server A-V software) will detect and stop the e-mail. There are especially virulent attacks possible and the DT was familiar with Young and Yung's work on Malicious CryptoVirology (Young & Yung, 2004)

There are different methods to secure mail servers in the hospital (Liska, 2002).

- To enhance the security of an MTA (mail transfer agent), the system administrator should limit the range of IP addresses that can use MTA as a mail relay. An MTA cannot be closed off to all outside connections, because it has to be reachable by other servers that are sending legitimate mail to users on the network. Only users within the hospital network should be able to send e-mail to remote mail servers using the MTA. The administrator should use the domain name as the determining factor, allowing users to relay mail through the mail server if the "from address" matches the hospital's domain name. However, it is too easy to bypass this security measure by forging the originating address in the mail program.
- Another method of MTA security is POP-before-relay. Before a user can connect to send mail, he or she must first connect to the POP mail server and authenticate against it. If authentication is successful, that user's IP address will be allowed to relay for a set period, usually 5–15 min.
- All the unnecessary accounts on the mail server have to be removed. In addition, the number of accounts on the mail server has to be restricted. Administrator should create a group on the mail server that is reserved for mail users. The group should have no access privileges to the server, only the ability to check e-mail. If the mail group is tightly controlled, with very restricted access, then none of the users should be able to cause any damage to the server.
- To increase security for the mail servers, the hospital mail server can be switched from mail authentication to authenticated post office protocol (APOP). APOP functions in the same manner as POP mail, but it encrypts the user's password using the MD5 one-way hash algorithm. APOP also requires a separate authentication database, so that even if a user's password is compromised, an attacker will not be able to gain access to the rest of the network.
- A more secure solution for POP or IMAP (Internet message access protocol) sessions is to connect over a TLS (transport layer security) session. TLS is a form of encryption, based on Netscape's SSL. A certificate is generated and submitted to a certificate authority. Afterward, the certificate is installed on the mail server. The mail clients are configured to use TLS (or SSL, depending on the client) encryption when connecting to the mail server. Using this method, not only is the password encrypted, but the entire session is encrypted as well. This provides the greatest level of security. TLS-encrypted POP and IMAP sessions operate in the same manner that HTTPS-based encryption does. The disadvantage of TLS encryption for POP or IMAP is the extra load of the network by continuously encrypting and decrypting POP or IMAP sessions. To solve this problem, a larger-user network with TLS should implement an SSL accelerator from Intel, Nortel, and Cisco. Using an SSL accelerator in conjunction with TLS authentication of POP or IMAP sessions will increase security without negatively affecting the server's performance.
- The hospital's policy must implement restrictive mail scanning. Currently, all the attachments of the e-mails are scanned for viruses or worms. Hospitals should also scan e-mails for UBE (unsolicited bulk e-mail, also referred to as SPAM). The administrator has to perform checks to determine false-positive and false-negative rates by using UBE scanning. In addition, the system administrator should review blacklists that are publicly available to set restrictions for receiving e-mails. Hospitals can stipulate policies for content scanning to assure avoidance of information theft by hospital employees.

Attacker Identification

Pipkin provides the following advice on attacker identification:

> A system that has been compromised is likely to be attacked again. Monitoring the restored systems will help verify that the improvements deter future attacks and can assist in the gathering of information about the attacker if he returns. The monitoring should include the services that were compromised, the processes that were used to compromise the system originally, and the connections for other systems that were compromised. The restored system should be placed at the highest level of monitoring for a period of time after the attack to help restore confidence in the system. (Pipkin, 2002).

Defense from Attack via Trusted Agents

These attacks are performed remotely. The hospital cannot control the access points that an attacker uses to penetrate into the hospital information system because there is no control of those resources from the hospital. If an attacker can break into the third-party machine and gain access to the hospital's system, he can easily bypass all the security measures in the hospital.

Defense against Remote Doctor Offices

The DT noted that remote access to the hospital information system was gained through Web-based one-way SSL. Remote connections are based on username and password. There are computer policies that passwords have to contain a certain number of letters and numbers. System administrators can program the "passfilt.dll" file in Windows NT or 2000 to increase the security of passwords. In addition to creating policies for passwords, the hospital information system is equipped with "Passfilt Pro (Altus Net)" software, which increases the security of the passwords on the network so the attacker cannot brute-force the passwords or, if he does, it will take him a much longer time to break the password. However, if the attacker again gains access and harvests the password from the remote machine, he can easily bypass the SSL and all the password protection countermeasures. In this attack, the attacker will gain access to the system and break into the remote machine. He will obtain the password and gain access from the hospital remote access system. Because the attacker intrudes as a legitimate user, countermeasures fail to prevent or detect intrusion and his presence is undetected.

To mitigate the risk of intrusion via remote connections, the hospital can upgrade the system to robust authentication methodology. The hospital IS can be accessed remotely via hardware token VPN or usage of PKI. Either method requires a token for the user to access the network remotely. The hospital can implement products such as "RSA SecureID (RSA)" for remote connection.

Defenses against Attacks via Public Access Pathways

In this scenario, the attacker is taking advantage of one of the weakest links in the hospital information system: Web servers. With the present architecture of the Web servers in the hospital, the attacker can easily gain access to the IS. The only countermeasures on the Web servers are IDS and firewalls. The attacker can bypass the firewall, create a distraction for the IDS, and bypass the IDS as well. In this scenario, the attacker realizes that Web servers are protected by IDS. Thus, he will run a DoS attack on the primary Web server. The effort of the system administrators will be focused on blocking and stopping the DoS attack and bringing the system back online. Meanwhile, the attacker has gained access to the secondary Web server and accessed the databases.

There are architectures and methodologies that can improve the security of the Web servers (Liska, 2002).

• The Web server should be a single-use server. Only personnel who absolutely need access should have it. A staging server can be used for further restricting access to the actual Web server. The staging server is a replica of the Web server. It should have the same operating system, same patches, same file structure, and all of the same software as the Web server. Content destined for the Web server is loaded to the staging server and then pushed to the Web server using software like "RedDot Solution's Content Management Server (CMS) (RedDot)." Different users or departments in the hospital are given accounts on the staging server. The accounts are used to upload content to the staging server. The content is pushed from the staging server to the actual Web server using a separate account to which the users do not have access. The Web server is configured to only allow the staging account access from the IP address of the staging server. The staging server should be placed on a separate VLAN than the Web server. The staging server should be part of a private VLAN that is not accessible through the firewall. This will prevent an attacker who does gain access to the Web server from getting to the staging server and using it to launch additional attacks. Because the staging server is the only machine that will send content to the Web server, hospital administrators can restrict the ways of accessing the server. Content can be uploaded using either Secure Copy (SCP) or Secure FTP (SFTP). Standard FTP ports should be disabled on the server. If other forms of access are required, they should only be allowed from the staging server, and those ports should be blocked to the server through the firewall.

• Content on the Web server should be stored on a separate partition from the operating system files. The default files from programs installed to assist in serving Web pages (i.e., Apache, Internet Information Server, and ColdFusion programs) should be deleted. If the content of a Web site is largely static, there should be restriction on HTML pages and setting the file permissions as readable but not writable and not executable. If Web site content is dynamic and database driven, the files will have to be readable and executable but not writable.

• One of the weaknesses for the Web servers is possible exploitation of cross-site scripting (XSS). The hospital should implement script security to mitigate this vulnerability. This can be performed by three computer policies: A script should never accept unchecked data; all inputs should be validated; scripts should not rely on path information assembled from the server. "Administrator should hard code data paths directly into the scripts. Hard coding path information into a script prevents an attacker from manipulating the PATH variable to display files on the web server" (Liska, 2002). (It is arguable that the trade-off between security and usability will tip the scale in favor of usability in many situations. A more reasonable approach might be teach the hospital's developers to code securely or to use a Web-based application scanner or red-team to audit the Web applications.)

• Clustering and network load balancing: A cluster is a series of servers that act as a single server. The servers communicate either with each other or with a cluster controller to process requests as they are made. The cluster is assigned an IP address. The individual servers are also assigned unique IP addresses, which allow for server management and communication between the servers. Clusters add security to the Web server by increasing its availability and by increasing the difficulty of launching an attack against the server. Each time a request to the Web site is made a different server may respond to the request. An attacker engaged in a complicated break-in attempt will need to restart the process each time a request is made because there is no way to guess which server will respond. If a private network is used to maintain the servers, there is no public address for the attacker to complete an attack. It provides extra time for the administrator to catch the alarm, track down the attacker, and stop the attack before it is successful. Network load balancing uses a switched device [such as "Cisco CSS11500 (Cisco)," "Nortel Network Alteon 184 (Nortel)," "Extreme Network SummitPx1 (Extreme)," or "F5 Network BIG-IP 5000 (F5)"] to direct traffic between multiple servers. Web site requests are forwarded to the appropriate server based on load balance. If a server fails, it is taken out of service rotation by the load balancer and an alert is generated. No traffic is lost as the load balancer simply redirects requests to another server. It is recommended that two network balancers be used in a pair. In case the first one is down from a DoS attack, the second one directs the traffic. The advantage of using clustering and network load balancing is that even if the site is offline because of a DoS attack, the Web server is secure.

Incident Response

After the system administrator stops the DoS attack, blocks the IP address, and kills the connection, it is time for the incident response process: isolating the system, securing the system, data integrity check and recovery, repairing the vulnerability, system recovery, monitoring for additional signs of attacks, gathering jnformation (counterintelligence), and documentation.

The system administrator (SA) examines other systems for any unusual activity. The SA correlates the attack time logs with databases access times. He or she will notice unauthorized activities on the secondary server. Thus, the SA will isolate the Web server, run integrity checks on the databases on the secondary Web server, and compare it with backup results to determine any modification. Again, if there have been alterations, entire databases will be recoverable from backups. As a minimum, however, the confidentiality of the data has been compromised. The secondary Web server will stay offline until the vulnerability is fixed and the data has been recovered.

Principle of least privilege (access as well as trust relationships with other servers/network resources), shutting down unneeded services, removing all data not needed on public servers, and replacing default scripts, accounts, and so on move the Web root to a different partition to avoid directory transversal attacks are all potential solutions that could be implemented.

To mitigate this risk, the hospital can implement more secure Web server architecture as mentioned above. Another recommended solution would be running vulnerability assessments on the server periodically or after any major change. The hospital can use vulnerability scanners such as Retina (eEye), NetRecon (Symantec), ISS Internet Scanner (ISS), Cybercop Scanner (Network Associates), The Open Source Nessus Project (Nessus), and Whisker (Open Source).

Defense against VLAN Hopping

On this attack, the DT noted that the attacker would gain access to the system and exploit the VLAN hopping vulnerability. The access entry for the AT for the target hospital was the cardiology system. The system administrator could catch the attacker on the VLAN via h-IDS and audit log monitoring. He can detect the attacker and can block the IP address and kill the connection. However, detection is often too late and comes after there has been an information leak in the system. As a minimum, information confidentiality has been breached. The integrity of data should be checked in the incident response process.

Once the security incident has been determined, the severity of the security incident has to be reported to the incident response team (team consists of system administrators). The incident should be communicated to management immediately. Computer-based communications such as e-mail, electronic notes, or instant messaging programs should not be used, because they may not be secure. Management should be contacted via telephone, pager, or in person. Because the hospital information is sensitive, in a security incident situation, law enforcement (FBI) will also be informed.

Because an intrusion has occurred through the cardiology system, the system cannot be trusted anymore. The network that the attacker has compromised should be blocked to outside access. Network connections to the system and any other remote connections that can be used to provide access to the intruder must be removed. It is critical to kill the attacker's connection and block the IP address before he or she can try to cover his or her tracks by destroying the file systems of the machine. The services for the network must be blocked to stop attacker to gain access to other systems.

After the SA stops the DoS attack, Snort anomaly detector will identify the IP address of the attacker. Snort is IPS as much as it is IDS. The IP address of the attacker will be blocked and the connection will be terminated. Therefore, the attacker will be stopped from accessing to the other VLANs. The defense on this attack depends on the speed of stopping the DoS attack and identifying the attacker's IP address on the secondary attack. Time is a critical factor in this defense. If the attacker is undetected for long time, he or she will gain access to more VLANs and it is harder to identify the damages. After the attacker is stopped, data integrity checks have to be practiced to assure no data modification. In practice the VLAN hopping attack is devastating and is undetected until the end game.

CONCLUSIONS

The author chose a commercial entity rather than a military target for our attack via wireless media. It was felt that this would provide an instructive example to which most readers can relate. WIW attacks and defenses represent trade-offs in security. Perhaps the two best books on the subject are by wireless experts Nichols and Lekkas (Nichols & Lekkas, 2001) and by cryptography guru Bruce Schneier (Schneier, 2003). The former book focuses on the methodologies for designing secure wireless communications systems. There is a special section on security for WIW embedded systems. The latter book details not only the cryptography trade-offs involved but looks at the entire security process holistically. The same processes that are used in a military arena apply to commercial theaters too—and perhaps more effectively. The results of the AT/DT WIW hospital scenario bear out the security best practices espoused in these aforementioned references.

The results of the hospital attacks and defenses above prove that a defense in depth implementation can be very useful in keeping out the wireless hackers. However, it also proves that a determined enough hacker with extensive resources will work long enough to find the weak links in the system. Arquilla warned that networks would become the next battlefield (Arquilla & Ronfeldt, 2001). Networks are ubiquitous. They are also the wireless hackers' playground.

Security is not 100% effective in preventing all vulnerabilities from being exploited by determined hackers—especially in wireless based networks. There are always new vulnerabilities from the evolution of software and hardware to newer versions. In our example, critical systems and network that are used for hospitals cannot afford to be slack with security measures as lives are dependent on the security of the network. It is not inconceivable that a hacker could gain access to the systems that nurses use to consult on what medications to give to their patients.

The AT executed essentially three attacks. The first attack (via VLAN hopping) showed the ease with which the AT was able to map the wireless access points for a hospital. The hospital security management should conduct a risk assessment of the hospital networks to determine the vulnerabilities in the hospital network. Through the analysis, they will have better knowledge of the priority vulnerabilities that need mitigation and will be able to spend their security budget more wisely. Although this attack was shown to not totally succeed, it could very well succeed where the network administrators are less aware of and less trained in security. Furthermore, a huge amount of *information* was developed. Clearly, WEP is inadequate for decent degree of security, but it is better than no wireless security at all. The advent of the WPA using the 802.11x standard would afford a definite improvement in securing WLANs that should be implements as soon as possible. A wireless IDS using passive sensors would also be another important consideration for organizations as upgrades are considered.

The second attack (via trusted agents) showed that they succeed in some of the stages of the attack dealing directly with people but they fail to gain the necessary access to the network. The conclusion here is the same as for the first attack, *information* gained helped the AT to be successful on the final breach of the network.

The third attack (via public access pathways) showed the AT succeeding in gaining access through the Web server. The hospital needs to beef up the Web security as there are medical databases with Web access that are weak points to the network as discussed in the introduction.

The attack successes came about as a direct result of the effectiveness of the VLAN hopping technique. The defense successes were directly attributable to the defense-in-depth principle. This bifunctionality is the nub of WIW. Attackers are able to access the various wireless nodes in the system, crack the weak cryptography or identify the APs, develop a TOE and from that exploit the weakest links to the heart of the network. The defenders must develop a defense in depth, be always monitoring activities, prepare to respond to incidents and constantly upgrade their systems to improve their security posture.

Other possible scenarios might have included Software Defined Radio technology with user enable programming and dual/triple mode chipsets that could permit security breaches between media domains, real problems that were not included in this scenario of a typical hospital found in a large city area at this time mainly because they would not typically be found in an urban hospital at this time. In the near future, however, as businesses increase their security awareness, the impact of these and emerging technologies will have to be considered.

GLOSSARY

Access Point (AP) A hardware device or software that acts as a communication hub for users of a wireless device to connect to a wired LAN. APs are important for providing heightened wireless security and for extending the physical range of service, a wireless user has access to.

Analog A characteristic of a circuit or device having an output that is proportional to the input.

Asynchronous Transfer Mode (ATM) A technique for dispatching data in packets or cells of a fixed size over a network. The advantage is that video, audio, and files can be transmitted over the same network without one type of data transmission seizing the line for an excessive time.

Asymmetric Warfare The strategy, tactics, and tools a weaker adversary uses to offset the superiority of a foe by attacking the stronger force's vulnerabilities, using both direct and indirect approaches to hamper vital functions or locations for the explicit purpose of seeking and exploiting advantages.

Attack/Defense Scenario (A/D) a team simulation pedagogical tool that allows a team to explore wireless network construction, information systems, and information assurance. Teams construct networks, impose policies, and explore cyber intrusion techniques. Team members role-play both attacker and defender positions for a chosen wireless target. Teams explore interrelationships between people, procedures, hardware, software, and data and how each of these factors impacts on the target wireless network design and security. The A/D deliverable is an After Action Report which represents the group's collective evaluation on the success or failure of the attack and defense in depth. Attacks and defenses are normally multi-tiered.

Authenticated Post Office Protocol (APOP) A post office protocol (see POP), which encrypts the user's password using the MD5 one-way hash function.

Cellular Digital Packet Data (CDPD) An open data transmission specification supporting access up to 19.2 KB to the Internet as well as other packet switched networks in the 800–900-MHz band.

Cellular Phones A mobile radiotelephone, usually hand held, used in an area divided into small sections (cells), each with its own fixed base-station transmitter/receiver allowing access to the public telephone system. These may use analog or digital transmission techniques. Base stations support handovers so that users can move from one cell (region supported by a given base station) to another cell.

CI The abbreviation for counterintelligence.

Code Division Multiple Access (CDMA) A digital wireless technology that uses a spread spectrum technique to scatter a radio signal across a wide range of frequencies. CDMA is a 2G technology. WCDMA, a 3G technology, is based on CDMA.

Command, Control, Communications, Computers, Intelligence, and Recognition (C4IR) Integrated systems of doctrine, procedures, organizational structures, personnel, equipment, facilities, communications, intelligence, and identification designed to support a commander's exercise of command and control across the range of military operations.

Commercial-off-the-Shelf (COTS) An item, such as software or hardware, available for sale in the private sector and usually immediately available.

Communications Security (COMSEC) The protection resulting from all measures designed to deny unauthorized persons information of value that might be derived from the possession and study of telecommunications, or to mislead unauthorized persons in their interpretation of the results of such possession and study. Communications security includes cryptosecurity, transmission security, emission security, and physical security of communications security materials and information. (a) Cryptosecurity: The component of communications security that results from the provision of technically sound cryptosystems and their proper use. (b) Transmission security: The component of communications security that results from all measures designed to protect transmissions from interception and exploitation by means other than cryptanalysis. (c) Emission security: The component of communications security that results from all measures taken to deny unauthorized persons information of value that might be derived from intercept and analysis of compromising emanations from cryptoequipment and telecommunications systems. (d) Physical security: The component of communications security that results from all physical measures necessary to safeguard classified equipment, material, and documents from access thereto or observation thereof by unauthorized persons.

Computer Security (COMPUSEC) The protection resulting from all measures to deny unauthorized access and exploitation of friendly computer systems.

Confidentiality, Integrity, and Availability (of Data) (CIA) Factors of a data processing system and its files that must be protected. Confidentially protects the existence of a connection, the traffic flow, and information content from disclosure to unauthorized partied. Integrity is the assurance that information and processes are secure from unauthorized modifications by use of cryptography, digital signatures, and intrusion detection. Availability is the degree that information, data processes, and resources are usable when needed.

Cordless Phones For most types of cordless phones, a single base station supports each mobile user. A user cannot move from one base station to another while a call is in progress.

Cross-Site Scripting (XSS) A security breach that takes advantage of dynamically generated Web pages. In an XSS attack, a Web application is sent with a script that activates when it is read by an unsuspecting user's browser or by an application that has not protected itself against cross-site scripting. Because dynamic Web sites rely on user input, a malicious user can input malicious script into the page by hiding it within legitimate requests. Common exploitations include search engine boxes, online forums, and public-accessed blogs. Once XSS has been launched, the attacker can change user settings, hijack accounts, poison cookies with malicious code, expose SSL connections, access restricted sites and even launch false advertisements. The simplest way to avoid XSS is to add code to a Web application that causes the dynamic input to ignore certain command tags.

Cryptanalysis The steps and operations performed in converting encrypted messages into plain text without initial knowledge of the key employed in the encryption.

Cryptography The science that deals with hidden, disguised, or encrypted communications. It includes communications security and communications intelligence.

Deception Those measures designed to mislead the enemy by manipulation, distortion, or falsification of evidence to induce the enemy to react in a manner prejudicial to the enemy's interests.

Denial of Service (DoS) A loss of the ability of a data processing system to provide satisfactory service with respect to confidentiality, integrity, and/or the availability of its data. This loss may be temporary, as in a delay, or it may be long lasting enough have a catastrophic effect on an enterprise.

Digital Description of or relating to a device that can read, write, or store information that is represented in numerical form.

EIRP Equivalent isotropically radiated power. EIRP represents the total effective transmit power of the radio, including gains that the antenna provides and losses from the antenna cable. In the United States, the FCC (Federal Communications Commission) defines power limitations for wireless LANs in FCC Part 15.247. Part 15.247 provides details on limitations of EIRP.

Electromagnetic Compatibility (EMC) Ability of systems, equipment, and devices that use the electromagnetic spectrum to operate in their intended operational environments without suffering unacceptable degradation or causing unintentional degradation because of electromagnetic radiation or response. It involves the application of sound electromagnetic spectrum management; system, equipment, and device design configuration that ensures interference-free operation; and clear concepts and doctrines that maximize operational effectiveness.

Electronic Counter Counter Measures (ECCM) Term used as an alternative to "electronic protection." ECCM is to ensure continued friendly use of the electromagnetic spectrum despite adversaries, electronic attack (EA) and electronic support (ES). Countering EA efforts is the focus of electronic protection although some electronic protection techniques are also designed to make adversary ES more challenging.

Electronics Security (ELSEC) Protection resulting from all measures designed to deny unauthorized persons information of value that might be derived from their interception and study of noncommunications electromagnetic radiations (e.g., radar).

Electronic Warfare Denial of accurate information to an unauthorized party by use of the electromagnetic spectrum.

Emanations Security (EMSEC) Control of electromagnetic emissions that may compromise internal information.

Exploitation Taking full advantage of any information that has come to hand for tactical, operational, or strategic purposes.

Firewall A system, hardware or software based, that is designed to block unauthorized access to or from a specified network. Its effectiveness is dependent on the degree of proper configuration.

Forward Line of Own Troops (FLOT) A line that indicates the most forward positions of friendly forces in any kind of military operation at a specific time. The forward line of own troops (FLOT) normally identifies the forward location of covering and screening forces. The FLOT may be at, beyond, or short of the forward edge of the battle area. An enemy FLOT indicates the forwardmost position of hostile forces.

Global System for Mobile (communications) (GSM) The most widely used of the three digital wireless telephone technologies (TDMA, GSM, and CDMA), and it supports voice, data, text messaging, and cross-border roaming. The SIM (subscriber identification module), a removable plastic card that contains a users data, is an essential element in a GSM network.

Handover A transfer of a user connection or function from one base station to another.

Health Insurance Portability and Accountability Act of 1996 (HIPAA) A federal law that allows persons to qualify immediately for comparable health insurance coverage when they change their employment relationships. Title II, Subtitle F, of HIPAA gives Health and Human Services, the federal department that has overall responsibility for implementing HIPAA, the authority to mandate the use of standards for the electronic exchange of health care data; to specify what *medical* and *administrative code sets* should be used within those standards; to require the use of national identification systems for health care patients, providers, payers (or plans), and employers (or sponsors); and to specify the types of measures required to protect the security and privacy of personally identifiable health care information. Also known as the Kennedy–Kassebaum Bill, the Kassebaum–Kennedy Bill, K2, or Public Law 104-191.

Information Based Warfare (IBW)/Information Operations (IO) Actions taken to affect adversary information and information systems while defending one's own information and information systems.

Information Security (INFOSEC) The protection of information and information systems against unauthorized access or modification of information, whether in storage, processing, or transit, and against denial of service to authorized users. Information security includes those measures necessary to detect, document, and counter such threats. Information security is composed of computer security and communications security.

Information Warfare (IW) Definition I Information operations (IO) conducted during time of crisis or conflict to achieve or promote specific objectives over a specific adversary or adversaries. IW actions may induce denial of service, corruption of data, and/or exploitation of the information obtained.

Information Warfare (IW) Definition II Actions taken to achieve information superiority by affecting adversary information, information-based processes, information systems, and computer-based networks while defending one's own information, information-based processes, information systems, and computer-based networks. (DoD96, 1996)

Information Warfare (IW) Definition III The offensive and defensive use of information and information systems to deny, exploit, corrupt, or destroy, and adversary's information, information-based processes, information systems, and computer-based networks while protecting one's own. Such actions are designed to achieve advantages over military or business adversaries. (Goldberg, 2001)

Internet Message Access Protocol (IMAC) An agreed-on format for transmitting e-mail data between two devices.

Intrusion detection System (IDS) Inspects all inbound and outbound network activity and identifies suspicious patterns that may indicate a network or system attack from someone attempting to break into or compromise a system. A secure form is the h-IDS or host based IDS, which allows online monitoring of activities.

Line-Sight Radios Connections are limited to line of sight because of operation at frequencies above HF, the need for high data rates, lack of hardware and protocol support for multihop transmission, or some combination of these factors. There are two types: (1) fixed or transportable, high capacity systems for point-to-point trunking (multiple streams of data and digital voice are multiplexed together over a single connection) and (2) mobile, semimobile (stop to transmit or receive), or transportable low-capacity radios that are designed primarily for handling single two-way (typically push-to-talk), voice connections.

Low Probability of Detection (LPD) A relative indication of a poor chance of an event being noticed.

Mail Transfer Agent (MTA) Software used by the mail server.

Media Access Control (MAC) A system of addressing defined by IEEE that uniquely identifies each node of a network.

Mobility Ability of a host (user) of a network to connect in various ways, such as by using a roaming host or routers.

Over The Air (OTA) (or Over-The-Air) A standard for the transmission and reception of application-related information in a wireless communications system. The standard is supported by Nokia, SmartTrust, and others.

OTA is commonly used in conjunction with the Short Messaging Service, which allows the transfer of small text files even while using a mobile phone for more conventional purposes. In addition to short messages and small graphics, such files can contain instructions for subscription activation, banking transactions, ringtones, and Wireless Access Protocol settings. OTA messages can be encrypted to ensure user privacy and data security.

Packet Radio Networks The radios in these networks are digital and exchange information in a store-and-forward fashion, so that a source and destination that are not able to communicate directly may nevertheless be able to exchange information. Packets are routed through the network, and may take one or more hops to reach the destination.

Pagers These include conventional pagers, alphanumeric pagers, and two-way pagers.

Peer-to-peer network A system in which each workstation has equivalent capabilities and responsibilities rather than certain computers dedicated to performing tasks for others (as in a client server system).

Post Office Protocol (POP) An older format for transmitting e-mail data between two devices.

Precedence A designation assigned to a message by the originator to indicate to communications personnel the relative order of handling and to the addressee the order in which the message is to be noted. Time standards are specified for each precedence's processing. The most immediate to least designations are as follows: flash, immediate, priority, and routine.

Quality of Service (QoS) A relative measure of satisfaction of an act performed for a user

Radio Frequency Identification Devices (RFID) Devices, passive or active, that are typically attached to objects for purposes of inventory, location, and/or description of contents (for containers). The RFID responds to queries.

RC4 A stream cipher developed by RSA laboratories circa 1987.

Satellite Earth Terminals In a satellite link, one of the nonorbiting communications stations that receives, processes, and transmits wireless signals between itself and a satellite. Note: Earth terminals may be mobile, fixed, airborne, or waterborne.

Secure Set Identifier (SSID) A 32-character stream included in a packet header that functions as a password, differentiating one WLAN from another. Because an SSID can be sniffed in plain text from a packet, it does not supply any security to the network. Also known as *network name*.

Security (of Information) With respect to classified matter, the condition that prevents unauthorized persons from having access to official information that is safeguarded in the interests of national security.

Social Engineering Deceptive techniques involved by persons pretending to have authorization to obtain information or entry into a facility for which they are not authorized.

Subscriber Identification Module (SIM) A removable plastic card that contains a user's data, usually for security purposes to confirm the user is authorized to access a system or data files.

Target A file, device, or any type of location to which data is moved or copied (including the entire enterprise system or backbone of communications.

Targets of Evaluation (TOE) the explicit enumeration of all possible wireless targets of interest to an attack team. TOE also defines the spectrum of wireless targets that must be considered by a defense team. In essence the TOE defines the scope of wireless warfare for both teams.

Taxonomy The study of the general principles of scientific classification.

Tethered Mobility A condition in which a system can only be used within a given range of a specific node (e.g., a cordless telephone)

Time Division Multiple Access (TDMA) A technology used in digital cellular telephone communication to divide each cellular channel into three time slots to increase the amount of data that can be carried. GSM and D-AMPS use TDMA in one form or another.

Transmission Security (TRANSEC) The protection of transmissions ("externals") from traffic analysis, disruption, and imitative deception typically by encryption means. See Communications Security (COMSEC).

Trojan A malicious program that presents itself as being of a nondestructive nature. A characteristic that distinguishes them from viruses is that Trojans do not replicate themselves.

Unsolicited Bulk E-mail (UBE) Commonly known as a type of spam.

Virtual Local Area Network (VLAN) A network of computers that behave as if they are connected to the same wire even though they may actually be physically located on different segments of a LAN. VLANs are configured through software rather than hardware, which makes them extremely flexible. One of the biggest advantages of VLANs is that when a computer is physically moved to another location, it can stay on the same VLAN without any hardware reconfiguration.

Virtual Private Network (VPN) A network in which some of the parts are connected using the public Internet, but the data sent across the Internet are encrypted, so the entire network is virtually private. An example might be a company network where there are offices in different cities. Using the Internet, the offices merge their networks into one network. The data are encrypted to ensure that only the offices can see the data on the Internet link.

Virus Apparently innocuous program or other software that, when loaded, becomes destructive in nature. Viruses replicate. They are created for a specific destructive purpose.

Wi-Fi Protective Access (WPA) An interim standard (to be replaced by IEEE 802.11i) that is an improvement over the security features of WEP, including improved data encryption and user authentication.

Wired Equivalency Privacy (WEP) A security protocol for WLANs defined in the 802.11b standard and designed to provide the same level of security as that of a wired LAN, usually through encrypting data.

Wireless Information Warfare (WIW) Information warfare focusing on data processed over radio and light systems.

Wireless Local Area Network (WLAN) A local area network that employs radio waves instead of wires to transmit and receive data. It enables fast data transmission through a wireless connection at relatively low cost. Particularly suitable for organizations such as hospitals and schools as well as businesses; also refers to wireless networks between computers within one building or a group of buildings. WLANs may use infrared or radio techniques. The IEEE standard for WLANs is 802.11. Well-known further WLAN proposals come from the competing groups Bluetooth and Home-RF.

Wireless Modems A modem that accesses a private wireless data network or a wireless telephone system.

Wireless Security Implementation (1) Adaptation and integration of existing wireless solutions and infrastructure; (2) promoting consistency and interoperability among a diverse spectrum of mobile and wireless devices; (3) providing a high level of security without detrimental impact on the user experience. In a wireless network, security features greatly differ between each of the protocol stacks, and security policy implementation and enforcement are dependent on the carrier (Nichols & Lekkas, 2001).

CROSS REFERENCES

See *Bluetooth Security; Computer Network Operations (CNO); Computer Viruses and Worms; The Legal Implications of Information Security: Regulatory Compliance and Liability; WEP Security; Wireless Threats and Attacks.*

REFERENCES

Altus Network Solutions Inc., http://www.altusnet.com/passfilt/overview.htm

Arquilla, J., & Ronfeldt, D. (2001). *Networks and netwars.* National Defense Research Institute. Rand.

Bhasin, S. (2002). *Web security basics.* Premier.

Caswell, B., Beale, B., Foster, J. C., & Posluns, J. (2003). *Snort 2.0: Intrusion detection.* Sebastopol, CA: Syngress.

Check Point Software Technology Inc., http://www.checkpoint.com

Cisco System Inc., www.cisco.com/en/US/products/hw/contnetw/ps792/

DoD Directive 8100.2 (2004). Use of commercial wireless devices, services, and technologies in the department of defense (DoD) Global Information Grid (GIG). Retrieved April 14, 2004.

Edney, J., & Arbaugh, W.A. (2003). *Real 802.11 Security: Wi-Fi Protected Access and 802.11i.* Boston, MA: Addison-Wesley.

eEye Digital Security, www.eeye.com

Extreme Networks, www.extremenetworks.com/services/resources/smpx1.asp

F5 Networks Co., www.f5.com/f5products/bigip/BIGIP5100/

FCC, Federal Communication Commission, http://www.fcc.gov/

FCC Part 15.27, retrieved from: http://www.wi-fiplanet.com/news/article.php/1136171

Fedora Core 1 Linux, (http://fedora.redhat.com/)

Feldman, P. M. (1998). *Emerging commercial mobile wireless technology and standards: Suitable for the Army?* Rand.

Flickenger, R. (2003). *Wireless hacks: 100 industrial-strength tips and tools.* Sebastopol, CA: O'Reilly.

Frater, M. R., & Ryan, M. J. (2001). *Electronic warfare for the digitized battlefield.* Boston, MA: Artech House.

Goldberg, A. (2001, June 30) Institute for the Advanced Study of Information Warfare. Retrieved from http://www.psycom.net/iwar.1.html

Grimes, R. A. (2001). *Malicious mobile code: Virus protection for Windows.* Sebastopol, CA: O'Reilly.

Hall, W. M. (2003). *Stray voltage: War in the information age.* Annapolis, MD: Naval Institute Press.

Hewlett-Packard Inc., www.openview.hp.com

Howard & Longstaff (1998). see http://www.cert.org/research/taxonomy_988667.pdf

Huddleston, M. *HIPAA: What, Why, and Where?* Fairfax (VA) Department of Information technology, presentation given to the Fairfax County Information Technology Policy Advisory Committee on June 27, 2002.

Ipswitch Inc., http://www.ipswitch.com/Products/WhatsUp

Internet Security Systems, Inc., http://www.iss.net

Kismet wireless application (http://www.kismetwireless.net/).

Leonhard, R. R. (2000). *The principles of war for the information age.* Novato, CA: Presidio.

Liska, A. (2002). *The practice of network security: Deployment strategies for production environments.* Upper Saddle River, NJ: Prentice Hall.

Micromuse Inc., www.micromuse.com/index.html

Nagios. www.nagios.org

Nessus. http://www.nessus.org Network Associates, Inc., http://www.nai.com

Nichols, R. K. (1999). *The ICSA guide to cryptography.* New York: McGraw-Hill.

Nichols, R. K., & Lekkas, P. C. (2002). *Wireless security: Models, threats, solutions.* New York: McGraw-Hill.

Nichols, R. K., Ryan, D. J., & Ryan, J. C. H. (2000). *Defending your digital assets against hackers, crackers, spies and thieves.* New York: McGraw-Hill.

NMAP scanning tool, http://www.insecure.org

Noonan, W. J. (2004). *Hardening network infrastructures: Bulletproof your systems before they get hacked.* New York: Osborne.

Nortel Networks, www.nortelnetworks.com/products/01/alteon/webswitch/techspecs.html

Open source-rfp labs, http://www.wiretrip.net/rfp/

Peikari, C., & Fogie, S. (2002). *Maximum wireless security.* Indianapolis, IN: Sams.

Pipkin, D. L. (2002). *Halting the hacker: A practical guide to computer security*, 2nd ed. Upper Saddle River, NJ: Prentice Hall.

p0f, P0f v2 is a versatile passive OS fingerprinting tool, found at: http://lcamtuf.coredump.cx/p0f.shtml

Quest Software Inc (formerly BB4 Technologies Inc), www.bb4.com

RedDot Solution Corp., www.reddot.com

RNA Sourcefire passive scanning tool from: http://www.sourcefire.com/products/rna.html

RSA Security Inc., www.rsasecurity.com/products/securid/tokens.html

Ryan, D. (2001). From INFOSEC Lecture at George Washington University, Washington, DC.

Ryan, M. J., & Frater, M. R. (2002). *Tactical communications for the digitized battlefield*. Boston, MA: Artech House.

Schneier, B. (2003). *Beyond fear: Thinking sensibly about security in an uncertain world*. Copernicus.

Scambray, J., McClure, S., & Kurtz, G. (2001). *Hacking exposed: Network security secrets & solutions*, 2nd ed. Berkley, CA: Osborne.

Snort TM, www.snort.org

SourceForge.net, http://www.oit.ucsb.edu/~eta/swatch/

Symantec, http://enterprisesecurity.symantec.com/

Tripwire IDS. http://www.tripwire.com

Waltz, E. (1998). *Information warfare: Principles and operations*. Boston, MA: Artech House.

Young, A. L., & Yung, M. (2004). *Malicious cryptography: Exposing CryptoVirology*. New York: John Wiley & Sons.

FURTHER READING

Denning, D. E. (1999). *Information warfare and security*. Boston, MA: Addison-Wesley. It is the primer on IW.

Hall, W. M. (2003). *Stray voltage: War in the information age*. Annapolis, MD: Naval Institute Press. A stunning look at future asymmetric warfare and information operations.

Hurley, C., Thornton, F., Puchol, M., & Rogers, R. (2004). *Wardriving: Drive, detect, defend*. Sebastopol, CA: Syngress. A guide to wireless "insecurity."

Parker, T., Shaw, E., Stroz, E., Devost, M. G., & Sachs, M. H. (2004). *Cyber adversary characterization: Auditing the hacker mind*. Sebastopol, CA: Syngress.

Schleher, D. C. (1999). *Electronic warfare in the information age*. Boston: Artech House. Deep and heavy reading.

Schwartau, W. (2000). *Cybershock: Surviving hackers, phreakers, identity thieves, Internet terrorists and weapons of mass disruption*. New York: Thunder's Mouth. A prophet in the area received well by some.

Skoudis, E. (2004). *Malware: fighting malicious code*. PTR. State-of-the-art information and defenses.

Computer Network Operations (CNO)

Andrew Blyth, *University of Glamorgan, Pontypridd, United Kingdom*

INTRODUCTION

Computer network operations (CNO) is primarily about the management of computer and networks within a corporate environment so as to allow the organization to maintain/achieve a competitive advantage. Within a commercial organization CNO is used to refer to the ability to access information hosted on information systems in a timely manner so as facilitate the functioning of the organization.

When this definition is applied to information security and information assurance we can interpret CNO as follows:

> Computer network operations are about identifying cyber-based attacks targeted against your information technology infrastructure. This is achieved through a process of data integration and data function of security related information from multiple disparate heterogeneous systems.

To understand information security and how it relates to electronic commerce we need to have a precise set of definitions as to what we mean by: threat, threat agent, and vulnerability (Denning, 1999; Waltz, 1998).

- Threat. The *Concise Oxford Dictionary* defines the word *threat* as follows:

> Declaration of intention to punish or hurt; menace of bodily hurt or injury to reputation or property, such as may restrain a person's freedom of action; indication of something undesirable coming.

For the purposes of this report threat is a function of an adversary's motivation, their capability, the opportunity, and the impact that a successful attack would have on an organization.

Threat = Function (Motivation, Capability, Opportunity, Impact)

Each of the terms utilized in the threat function are defined as follows:

- Motivation. The *Concise Oxford Dictionary* defines the word motivation as follows:

> Supply a motive to cause a person to act in a particular way. In the context of a threat, motivation is considered to be identification of both the reasons why someone would launch an attack and a measure of the degree to which the attack would be pressed home.

For the purpose of this chapter we consider motivation to be the degree to which an aggressor is prepared to implement a threat. The motivational factors are the specific real-world elements that drive a hacker to consider penetrating a computer system. There are a variety of features that are worth considering in the question of motivation. First, motivation provides the *impetus* for the hacking attempts; it determines how persistent the hacker will be in his or her attempts; it determines how much effort (time, money) the hacker is prepared to expend on the attempt. It determines, in short, just how much we should be concerned about the hacker. This aspect is examined further below.

A second feature of importance in motivation is the *continuity* that it implies. A strong and focused motivation—say in pursuit of animal rights or Irish liberation—will suffuse much of the individual's offensive activity. A recreational motivation will lead predominantly to a recreational approach to hacking attempts—though it is of course important to understand that recreational motivations can easily translate under certain circumstances such as duress into more sinister activities. This indeed leads to the third important feature of the motivation, which we can classify as its *flavor*. For example, is the hacker motivated by the opportunity for financial gain? Is the motivation ideological, personal, or even trivial in nature? Is the hacker (like Levin) perhaps motivated by external coercion? This flavor of motivation is important because it has a bearing on persistence, but also because it has a bearing on the selection criteria that the individual will apply (Jones, Kovacich, & Luzwick, 2002). Levin was reputed to be the principle author of a successful attack against Citibank (Neumann, 1995).

Motivational factors in and of themselves cannot be *detected* by intrusion detection systems technology—at least, not with the current state of the art. However, important motivational elements can be observed in the records that are collected and maintained by a variety of network security systems; they represent important information that can and should be analyzed. Abstracting such profiles is part and parcel of the objective of this new-generation IDS technology, allowing confident identification of individuals to be supported (Rehman, 2003).

Capability. The *Concise Oxford Dictionary* defines the word capability as meaning the power to do something. In terms of information security the term capability is used as a measure of (1) the availability of a number of tools and techniques to implement an attack and the ability to use the tools and techniques correctly and (2) the availability of education and training to support the correct use of various tools and techniques.

For the purposes of this chapter we use the term *capability* to mean the degree to which an aggressor is able to implement a threat.

- Opportunity. The *Concise Oxford Dictionary* defines the word opportunity as meaning, a favorable occasion for action. Sun Tzu stated: "The good fighters of old first put themselves beyond the possibility of defeat, and then waited for an opportunity of defeating the enemy" (Griffith, 1971).

Consequently, for a threat agent to bring its capability to bear against a target they must have the correct conditions to do so, and for their capabilities to be effective and have an impact on the target, the target must be vulnerable to attack.

- Impact. The term *impact* is used to denote the concept of effect that an attack can have against a computer-based system, company, individual, and so on. The measurement of an attack can be made in direct and indirect terms. For example, we can measure impact directly as follows: duration of unavailability of service/drop in share price and loss of commercial confidence/loss of trust.
  - Threat agent. The term *threat agent* is used to denote an individual or group that can manifest a threat.
- Vulnerability. The *Concise Oxford Dictionary* defines the term *vulnerability* as "susceptible to damage." Vulnerability has been defined as follows: (1) a point where a system is susceptible to attack, (2) a weakness in the security system that might be exploited to cause harm or loss, or (3) some weakness of a system that could allow security to be violated.

A threat agent is an individual or organization that has the potential to realize a threat against a specific target. Consequently, threats and threat agents are unique to the target and must be considered in the context of the environment, be that commercial or political that the target functions in. Modern threat agents such as hackers, organized crime, terrorists, and so on have all adopted and utilized computer network operations to help them achieve their objectives.

NETWORK DEFENSE AND NETWORK ATTACK

To understand network defense or network attack we must first develop an understanding of what we mean by network and security. The term network is used to denote a TCP/IP infrastructure.[1,2] In the area of information security (IS) and information assurance (IA) there are two basic models of security that allow us to understating and implement information assurance. The first model is called the confidentiality, integrity, and availability (or CIA) model. This basic model defines security in simple terms (Pfleeger & Pfleeger, 2003).

Confidentiality means that the assets of the system are accessed only by authorized parties. Another aspect in confidentiality is that the traffic flow is also protected by any kind of "outside" analysis. This requires that an attacker will not be able to identify any asset in a transaction, such us the sender, the receiver, and the context. Integrity means that the assets of the system can be modified by authorized parties only and in authorized ways. Here there is a concept of "inside" and "outside" integrity. We not only want the "outsiders" not to be able to modify system data but also the insiders not to be able to participate in any sort of malicious operations with the system data. Availability means that the assets of a system are always available to the authorized parties. Having one or two of the above goals achieved is relatively easy. The difficulty lies in achieving all three of them as each one is going "against the other" in some sort of manner.

The second model defines information security in terms of detect, deter, protect, react, and recover (DDPRR). Detect means the ability to identify an attack whether it is a cyber-based intrusion or social engineering. Deter means the ability to show that this system is well protected and monitored so try some place else. Most hackers are opportunistic and once they realize that a system is protected they will move onto the next target. Protect means the ability to know what assets we possess and what assets we need to defend. React means that once an attack is detected, we have the ability to respond in a defensive manner to safeguard the asset. Defense actions can include actions such as redefining the rules on a firewall or phoning the police. Recovery is the ability to take an asset that has been compromised by an intruder and restore that asset to a safe and secure state. So, for example, it can mean taking a computer system and formatting the hard disk, reinstalling the operating system, and applying all of the security patches to bring the system into a secure state.

Computer network operations encompasses computer network attack (CNA) and computer network defense (CND). The term *computer network attack* is used to mean the art by which a computer network is subverted via cyber means, whereas the term computer network defense refers to how a computer network is protected from a computer network attack (Blyth & Kovacich, 2001).

NATO, Europe, the United States, and Canada now view computer network operations as an integral part

---
[1] See *The Handbook of Information Security, Volume I, Key Concepts, Infrastructure, Standards and Protocols*. Chapter 37, "Internet Architecture."
[2] See *The Handbook of Information Security, Volume I, Key Concepts, Infrastructure, Standards and Protocols*. Chapter 38, "TCP/IP."

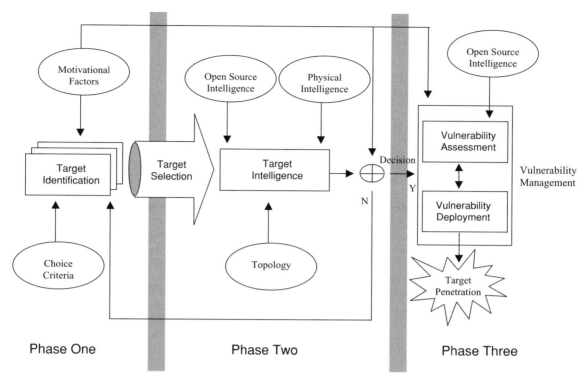

Figure 1: The CNA process.

of military operations during peacetime, war, and crisis. Within the commercial sector, the rise in extortion and industrial espionage attacks targeted against corporate IT infrastructure has resulted in the need for organizations to protect themselves. This process of protection is not the simple deployment of technology such as intrusion detection systems and firewall; rather, it is a process that centers on the role and function of the individual within the organization and makes use of technology, policy, and education/awareness (Rathmell, 2001). It is also reputed that both Koreas and Israel have this capability.

A MODEL OF COMPUTER NETWORK ATTACK

Threat agents when employing CNA will operate in a characteristic fashion, performing a set of analytic, probing, and exploitive behavior with computer systems or networks.[3] This behavior is identifiable and, to an extent, predictable. Within this element of the work package, the authors have constructed a general-purpose model of hackers' activity—a model that can be applied not simply to the recreational, low-skill "Kiddie Script" hacker aimlessly exploring computer networks but also to the more determined professional criminal. Central to this model is the recognition of a sequence of activities, but crucially incorporating a sense of *expenditure* on the part of the intruder—in terms of time, equipment, finance, and commitment. Using this model, we can address the most fundamental of our questions for consideration: *"How do hackers penetrate computer networks and systems?"*

Figure 1 provides a flowcharted model for the individual decision points and activities that are common to all intrusion attempts.

The CNA process model is a simple, general-purpose one, in which hackers of any persuasion perform a series of increasingly refined actions against an increasingly focused set of target computer systems. Figure 1 shows the basic process that an intruder would go through when penetrating a system. This process is divided up into three distinct phases. The first phase is concerned with the processes by which an intruder identifies and selects the machine(s) and network(s) to be penetrated. The second phase is concerned with the processes by which an intruder would gather intelligence about the machine(s) and network(s) to be penetrated. Phase three is concerned with the processes by which a computer system is penetrated. This phase involves the selection and deployment of a set of vulnerabilities against a set of target machine(s) and network(s).

Target Identification

The world contains untold millions of computer systems, each of which might be a potential target for a hacker, depending on the criteria that the hacker applies in selecting computers for attention.

For some hackers, every one of these millions of systems is indeed a potential target: they are as likely to attack any one as any other, with a selection criterion that is essentially opportunistic. For others, the total set of systems can be more finely subdivided into systems in which they have a very specific interest and a determination to perform a more focused sequence of activities.

In the target identification section of the model, we uncover the decisions and activities the hacker has applied

---

[3] See *The Handbook of Information Security, Volume III, Threat, Vulnerabilities, Prevention, Detection and Management.*

in uncovering the specific types of computer system of interest to them: all government computers, computers belonging to animal testing organizations, Irish republican newspaper sites, all banking computer networks, and so on. This represents a subdivision of the universal set of computers, with decisions made by the hacker based on two important elements: (1) their determination to penetrate the computer and (2) the specific criteria to be applied.

Motivational Factors

The motivational factors are the specific real-world elements that drive a hacker to consider penetrating a computer system. Analysis of computer criminals suggests that the primary motivations include the following, sometimes in combination (Blyth & Kovacich, 2001; Jones et al., 2002):

- The need to resolve intense personal problems such as job-related difficulties, mental instability, debt, drug addiction, loneliness, jealousy, and the desire for revenge
- Peer pressure and other challenges, for example, among malevolent hackers
- Idealism and extreme advocacy, for example, by espionage agents and terrorists
- Financial gain

There are a variety of features that are worth considering in the question of motivation. Firstly, motivation provides the *impetus* for the hacking attempts; it determines how persistent the hacker will be in his attempts; it determines how much effort (time, money) the hacker is prepared to expend on the attempt. It determines, in short, just how much we should be concerned about the hacker. This aspect is examined further below.

A second feature of importance in motivation is the *continuity* that it implies. A strong and focused motivation—say, in pursuit of animal rights or Irish liberation—will suffuse much of the individual's offensive activity. A recreational motivation will lead predominantly to a recreational approach to hacking attempts—although it is of course important to understand that recreational motivations can easily translate under certain circumstances such as duress into more sinister activities.

This indeed leads to the third important feature of the motivation, which we can classify as its *flavor*. For example, is the hacker motivated by the opportunity for financial gain? Is the motivation ideological, personal, or even trivial in nature? Is the hacker (like Levin) perhaps motivated by external coercion? This flavor of motivation is important not only because it has a bearing on persistence but also because it has a bearing on the selection criteria that the individual will apply.

Motivational factors in and of themselves cannot be *detected* by IDS technology—at least, not with the current state of the art. However, important motivational elements can be observed in the records that are collected and maintained by a variety of network security systems: they represent important information that can and should be analyzed. Abstracting such profiles is part and parcel of the objective of this new-generation IDS technology, allowing confident identification of individuals to be supported.

Choice Criteria

Driven by the motivation factors, hackers will apply their individual choice criteria to the universal set of computer systems, abstracting the (possibly still large) set of targets in which they have an interest. The choice criteria have several aspects to them.

First, there is the question of criteria *freedom*: does the hacker in fact have any say in the specific criteria applied, or is the choice predetermined by an external agency? Again, this element of target selection can be observed as a feature that we can think of as *persistence*: how determined does the intruder seem to be in the face of real or perceived security measures?

Second, there is the question of criteria *flexibility*: will the selected set of targets evolve over time, perhaps compromising choice as the difficulty of hitting specific targets becomes obvious—or are the criteria immutable?

Third, what is the *breadth* of criteria? How many systems are considered? Where are they located? How are the choice criteria effectively articulated?

Self-evidently, there is an interaction between motivational and choice aspects, leading to the determination, the persistence, the precision, and so on with which the hacker approaches the subsequent stages of his activity. The target identification stage provides the hacker with a set of potential victims to be considered: a set from which the specific targets are then selected.

Target Selection and Intelligence

The selection of specific targets from the broad set of potential victims is driven by a variety of elements. First and most obviously, there is an opportunistic element to even the most highly focused attacks: a range of systems might be scanned in a particular order or a more intelligent set of choices might be made, based on what intelligence the hacker gathered about the system. Some of this intelligence is also available to the *defender* of the system, although it is unlikely that more than a subset of this will be feasibly obtained by the IDS itself.

Open Source Intelligence

Hackers will attempt to perform a review of open source material in an attempt to gather intelligence on the network topology for a target organization or network. This can include such diverse elements as newsgroup postings referring to problems operating a particular type of computer and evidence showing with whom the employees of the target normally communicate. For example, a hacker could:

- Perform a Web search on related names and terms using Web search engines
- Analyze postings by users of target systems and target organizations on Usenet
- Analyze various open source exploit databases
- Analyze various other open source material

- Use remote domain name system (DNS) mining tools
- Connect to various computer underground servers and acquire the password file for the target system

It should be noted that from the perspective of an outsider penetrating a computer network, a review of open source literature is an activity that an intrusion detection system is unlikely to detect. However, from the perspective of an employee within an organization, it is possible that by logging all out-bound traffic an administrator would be able to identify an insider accessing various types of open source intelligence. This type of analysis of traffic generated by employees within a system can be used as an early-warning system.

The creation of a global information infrastructure (GII) means that a threat agent can mount a computer network attack against a target from any place on the planet. Understanding the CNA process model can allow us to create an understanding of how to implement computer network defense. Standards such as Common Criteria and BS 7799/ISO-17799 allow administrators to deploy technologies within a network environment that will stop, delay, hinder, or detect an attack.

Deploying/Exploiting a Vulnerability

Within the context of computer network operations, a threat to a system can be defined as follows (Summers, 1997): "Some weakness of a system that could allow security to be violated."

Vulnerability assessments are concerned with the identification of the weakness that may be exploited. In general, vulnerabilities exist throughout the information systems processes, software, hardware, information, business processes, and people. Software can be vulnerable to interruption of execution, deletion, interception of software in transit, and modification. Hardware is vulnerable to theft and interruption of service. Finally, information is vulnerable to interruption (loss), interception, modification, and fabrication. In essence, there are seven types of vulnerabilities that can exist in any system, and these are as follows:

1. *Physical Vulnerabilities*: intruders can break into computing facilities. Once in they can sabotage and vandalize computers and steal hardware, diskettes, printouts, and so on.
2. *Natural Vulnerabilities*: computers may be vulnerable to natural disasters and to environmental threats. Disasters such as fire, flood, earthquakes, and power loss can wreck your computer and destroy information.
3. *Hardware/Software Vulnerabilities*: certain kinds of hardware and software failures can compromise the security of a computer system. Software failures of any kind may cause systems to fail and may open up systems to penetration or make systems so unreliable that they cannot be trusted.
4. *Media Vulnerabilities*: disk packs and tapes can be stolen or damaged by such mundane perils as dust and ballpoint pens.

Table 1 External Misuse

Mode of Misuse	Description
Visual spying	Observation of keystrokes or screen.
Misrepresentation	Deceiving operators and users.
Physical scavenging	Dumpster diving for printouts, floppy disks, and so on.

5. *Emanation Vulnerabilities*: all electronic equipment emits radiation that can be intercepted.
6. *Communication Vulnerabilities*: if your computer is attached to a network then its message can be intercepted and possibly modified or misrouted.
7. *Human Vulnerabilities*: the people who administer and use your computer facilities represent the greatest vulnerability of all. They may be vulnerable to greed, revenge, blackmail, and the like.

With regard to computer network operations these vulnerabilities can manifest themselves via the following types of misuse.

External misuse of an information system is related to the creation, manipulation, and destruction of information by a user within the organization. This type of misuse forces one to examine how, when, where, and by whom information is created, manipulated, and destroyed. This type of analysis is primarily concerned with the physical environment within which the users execute the business processes. Generally nontechnological and unobserved, external misuse is physically removed from computer and communications facilities. It has no direct observable effects on the systems and is usually undetectable by the computer information assurance systems. Types of external misuse are listed in Table 1 and include the following:

- *Visual spying*: for example, remote observation of typed key strokes or screen images.
- *Deception*: various forms of deception external to computer systems and telecommunications. For example, social engineering (having one act in a manner conducive to another's needs; e.g., release their password).
- *Physical scavenging*: for example, collection of waste paper or other externally accessible computer media, so-called dumpster diving.

Hardware misuse of an information system is primarily concerned with the information assurance of the physical devices that form the physical infrastructure of the organization's information system. Table 2 shows types of misuse. It is important to note that this type of misuse also includes theft of removable storage media such as printout and electromagnetic tapes and other electronic removable media. In essence there are two types of hardware misuse: passive and active.

- *Passive Hardware Misuse*. This tends to have no immediate side effect on hardware or software behavior and includes the following:

Table 2 Hardware Misuse

Mode of Misuse	Description
Logical scavenging	Examining discarded/stolen media.
Eavesdropping	Intercepting electronic or other information.
Interference	Jamming, electronic or otherwise.
Physical attack	Damaging or modifying equipment or power.
Physical removal	Removing equipment and storage media.

- Logical scavenging (such as the examination of discarded computer media)
- Electronic or other types of eavesdropping that intercept signals, generally unbeknownst to the victims; for example, picking up emanations, known as TEMPEST (telecommunications electronics material protected from emanating spurious transmissions)
- Planting a spy-tap device in a terminal, workstation, mainframe, or other hardware subsystem.
- *Active Hardware Misuse*. This generally has noticeable effects and includes the following:
  - Theft of computing equipment and physical storage media
  - Hardware modifications, such as internally planted Trojan horse hardware devices
  - Physical attacks on equipment and media, such as interruption of power supplies. This type of attack can also make use of electromagnetic pulse (EMP) weapons

Masquerading misuse of an information system is primarily concerned with the authentication of information, its source, its destination, and its users. Masquerading attacks, listed in Table 3, include the following:

- *Impersonation of the identity of some other individual or computer subject*. For example, using a computer identifier and password to gain access to a computer system. The computer identifier and password may belong to a person or a computer demon.

Table 3 Masquerading

Mode of Misuse	Description
Impersonation	Using false identities external to the computer system
Piggybacking attacks	Usurping communication lines and workstations
Spoofing attacks	Using playback, creating bogus nodes and systems
Network weaving	Masking physical whereabouts or routing

Table 4 Pest Programs

Mode of Misuse	Description
Trojan horse attacks	Implanting malicious code, sending letter bombs.
Logic bombs	Setting up time or event bombs.
Virus/worms attacks	Attaching to programs and replicating.

- *Piggyback attacks*. For example, an unauthorized user may hijack a communication channel to a computer.
- *Spoofing attacks*. For example, using the identity of another machine on a network to gain unauthorized access. Types of attacks include IP spoofing, machine spoofing, and demon spoofing.
- *Playback attacks*. For example, the playback of network traffic in the attempt to recreate a transaction.
- *Network weaving to hide physical whereabouts*. A person connects through several machines to a target machine.

Pest programs, briefly described in Table 4 are primarily concerned with the availability of information systems services, and the expected behavior of services.

- *Trojan Horse*: a Trojan horse is an entity (typically a program, but not always) that contains code or something interpretable as code that, when executed, will have undesirable effects, such as the clandestine copying of information or the disabling of the information system.
- *Letter bomb*: a letter bomb is a peculiar type of Trojan horse attack whereby the harmful agent is not contained in a program but rather is hidden in a piece of mail or information. The harmful agent usually consists of special characters that are only meaningful to a particular mail agent. This bomb is triggered when it is read as a piece of electronic mail.
- *Logic bomb*: a logic bomb is a Trojan horse in which the attack is detonated by the occurrence of some specified logical event such as the first subsequent login by a particular user.
- *Time bomb*: a time bomb is a logic bomb in which the attack is detonated by the occurrence of some specified time-related logic event (e.g. the next time the date is 18 December).
- *Virus/worms*: viruses and worms often attack the Internet and other networks. For example: in May 2000, the "I Love You" e-mail virus was released. When the worm executes, it will search for certain types of files and make changes to those files depending on the type of file. For files on fixed or network drives, it will take the following steps: Files with the extension *vbs* or *vbe* are overwritten with a copy of the virus, and files with the extension *mp3*, *mp2*, *js*, *jse*, *css*, *wsh*, *sct*, *jpg*, *jpeg*, or *hta* are overwritten with a copy of the virus and the extension is changed to *vbs*.

Because the modified files are overwritten by the worm code rather than being deleted, file recovery is difficult and

Table 5 Bypasses

Mode of Misuse	Description
Trapdoor attacks	Utilizing existing flaws in the system and misconfigured network programs
Authorization attacks	Password cracking and so on

may be impossible. By May 10, 2000, it was estimated that the viruses had infected 600,000 machines in the United States alone and had cost American business $2.5 billion in damages and lost income.

Bypasses, listed in Table 5, are a type of misuse of an information system primarily concerned with authorization and configuration management. A *trapdoor* is an entry path that is not normally expected to be used. There are several types of trapdoors:

- Inadequate identification, authentication, and authorization of users, tasks, and systems (e.g., the Sendmail debug option that was used by the Internet worm)
- Improper initialization; many bypasses are enabled by systems being incorrectly configured, so that when they are initialized IA features can be bypassed
- Improper finalization; when a program terminates it must ensure that it disposes of all secure information properly—if not, improper finalization occurs
- Incomplete or inconsistent authentication and validation can be caused by improper argument validation (e.g., the Internet worm used a bug in the *get* function located in the finger demon to gain root access); the bug was that the *get* function did not do a bounds check on the number of arguments
- Improper encapsulation of the internals of a system can allow a user to access information or functions that they are not authorized to access

Authorization attacks are attacks where an attacker attempts to guess a user's password. This type of attack can be computerized and tools such as John-the-Ripper and L0pht-Crack have been developed. It is estimated that L0pht-Crack can perform a complete search of the Windows NT password search space on a 1.0-GHz PC in 3 and a half days.

Active misuse of an information system is primarily concerned with modifying information or entering false or misleading information. Table 6 describes types of active misuse. The following are also examples of active misuse:

Table 6 Active Misuse

Mode of Misuse	Description
Basic active attack	Creating, modifying, entering false or misleading information
Incremental attack	Using salami attacks
Denial of service	Perpetrating saturation attacks

Table 7 Passive Misuse

Mode of Misuse	Description
Browsing	Making random and selective searches
Inference, aggregation	Exploiting database inferences and traffic analysis
Covert channels	Exploiting covert channels or other information leakage

- A box office supervisor cancelled tickets, which had been sold, and then later resold the tickets, keeping the cash. The box office supervisor falsified the audit trail, but this was detected after problems with the software were investigated. The employee was prosecuted and given six months' imprisonment.
- The World Wide Web provides a vehicle through which organizations and people can communicate and disseminate information. Hundreds, if not thousands, of businesses and government agencies have had their Web sites attacked. The general effect of unauthorized alteration of a Web site is a loss of public confidence in the agency's ability to protect its information systems and often a public relations nightmare.

In addition, this type of misuse is concerned with the denial of service (DOS). For example, a company that specializes in trading on the Internet is exposed to the threat that if the Internet connection is lost then the ability for the company to conduct business is lost and the supply chain is broken.

Passive misuse of an information system is primarily concerned with exploiting the information within the system so as to conduct analysis and make inferences about the existence of sensitive information. Table 7 lists types of passive misuse.

Inactive misuse of an information system is primarily concerned with willfully failing to perform expected duties or committing errors of omission. Table 8 describes inactive misuse.

Indirect misuse of an information system is primarily concerned with preparing for subsequent misuses, as in offline preencryption matching, factoring large numbers to obtain private keys, autodialer scanning. Table 9 describes indirect misuse.

TECHNOLOGIES FOR COMPUTER NETWORK DEFENSE

The three most common types of technologies that get deployed to protect a computer network from attack are intrusion detection systems, firewalls, and honey-pots.

Table 8 Inactive Misuse

Mode of Misuse	Description
Inactive misuse	Willfully failing to perform expected duties, or committing errors of omission

Table 9 Indirect Misuse

Mode of misuse	Description
Indirect misuse	Preparing for subsequent misuses, as in offline preencryption matching, factoring large numbers to obtain private keys, autodialer scanning

- Intrusion detection systems come in two flavors: misuse detection and anomaly detections. Misuse detection makes use of expert system technology to detect attack. This type of technology is very good at detecting known forms of attack and thus has a very low false positive rate, whereas it is very poor at detecting new forms of attacks. Anomaly detection focuses on the rule of statistics to the identification of an attack and makes use of key technologies such as byzantine network, neural network, and genetic algorithms. Such technologies are very good at identifying new attacks but can generate a lot of false positive assessments when identifying known attacks.

- The most common forms of firewalls on a network will be either a packet filtering firewall or a proxy firewall. A packet filtering firewall uses the contents of the TCP/IP packet to decide if a packet is allowed onto the network or not. A proxy firewall uses a proxy service to relay messages to systems located behind the firewall that are not visible inform of the firewall. Computer network defense will make use of vast quantities of audit data such as IDS logs, firewall logs, router logs, and other system type logs. Technologies such as INCH, IODEF, and IDMEF are all XML-based solutions to the problem of data integration, data fusion, and data sharing (Rehman, 2003).

- The development of deception technologies such as honey-pots and honey-nets are designed to divert an attack from a critical part of the network to a non-critical part of the network. The goal when deploying these technologies is to tempt a threat agent into wasting time, money, and other precious resources into trying to compromise systems that have no impact on the

effectiveness in operational terms of the organization. In fact, while a threat agent is attacking a honey-pot, a defending organization can deploy a set of countermeasures to apprehend the threat agency.

SURVIVABILITY

Survivability is about detecting, recovering, and tolerating an attack. In terms of computer network defense (CND) it means defense in depth. Figure 2 illustrates this principle. The threat is made manifest via a threat agent and the attack is detected. The detection process can involve technologies such as intrusion detection systems (e.g., Snort) or the simple education of users to look for erroneous behavior. Once an attack is detected, the computer system then has to operate while under attack.

The computer system is required to recover from the attack and mount a defensive response. As in many countries, such as the UK, United States, Canada, Australia, and New Zealand, where hacking is illegal, it is a point of legal, ethical, and moral debate as to under what conditions it is acceptable to mount an offensive response. A defensive response can mean reconfiguring a firewall in real time to stop an intruder from penetrating a network further or deploying technologies that aid in deceiving an intruder and thus luring the attacker away from the real system (Blyth & Kovacich, 2001).

DECEPTION

Deception in information security is something that is now starting to attract attention (Grazioli & Jarvenpaa, 2003). Technologies such as honey-potting have matured and commercial products are now available. The model of using deception in information security is based on the concept of defense in depth. When using deception in computer network operations we should implement deception in layers, understand that intruders will fall prey to deception differently, depending on their knowledge, experience, capabilities, determination, resources, and so on and deploy deception accordingly, and use the information gathered in an intelligence gathering capacity to

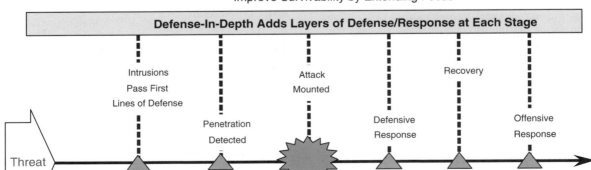

Improve Survivability by Extending Focus

Figure 2: Survivability.

understand intentions, interests, capabilities, and modus operandi.

When using deception in information security the goal is to increase the survivability of your critical information systems by allowing an adversary to expend time and resources attacking false systems. From a defensive point of view our goal is to protect our own command and control systems, as the loss of these systems could function as a force multiplier for an adversary.

When deploying deception we need to appreciate that deception will affect different people in different ways, consequently we need to understand the following: what deception can mean and how and why deception works on different types of people.

The *Concise Oxford English Dictionary* defines the term *deception* as meaning "Deceiving or being deceived; thing that deceives, trick, sham" and defines the term *deceives* as "persuade of what is false, mislead purposely."

In terms of information assurance the goals of using deception are as follows (Dearth, 1998; Gerwehr & Glenn, 2000):

- *To condition a target's belief*
- *To influence the target's actions*
- *For the deceiver to benefit from the target's actions*

The most common form of this type of information assurance activity is called perception management and propaganda (Waltz, 1998). The goal of perception management is to control the way that an adversary sees the world through their belief system. Propaganda is using information to convince people that your view of the world is the correct view of the world. Propaganda is not new and forms part of commercial advertising that we see on television and the Internet today. Many terrorist organizations make use of the Internet as a tool for propaganda (Johnson, Grazioli, & Berryman, 2001). The problem that many governments now face is that the Internet allows people direct access to a population. Before the Internet a government could disrupt radio signals, but censorship on the Internet is a far more difficult subject.

The goal of using deception in a defensive capacity is to control and direct the actions of an adversary so as to protect your own assets and ensure that mission/safety critical information systems are protected and continue to function while under attack. An example of using computer-based deception would be to create a fake network and IP addresses space within which an adversary would seek to find nonexistent information. Consequently, by getting the adversary to seek for nonexistent information, we are forcing them to commit their resources to an activity that will fail; thus we are weakening our opponent. In addition, we can also monitor the activities of the adversary and use this monitoring as a vehicle for gathering intelligence on their capabilities. We may also wish to create fake network and vulnerable computer systems as a mechanism for leaking information to an adversary that we would wish them to have. Thus intelligence and counterintelligence have a role to play in any deception operation.

DECEPTION TAXONOMY

The following is a taxonomic framework that can be used to develop an understanding of the way in which cyberdeception can function:

- Feint, diversion, display, decoy, dummy, camouflage, concealment, cover, mimicry, spoofing, dazzling, sensory-saturation, disinformation, and conditioning
- Static, dynamic, adaptive, and premeditated
- Host-based and network-based
- Offensive deception operations and defensive deception operations
- Phases of a deception operation
- Dissimulation and simulation
- Deceit, denial, disruption, distraction, and development

We now examine each of these in turn in more detail. The types of deception acts that can be used in information warfare are as follows:

1. Feint/diversion. The aim of a feint/diversion attack is to overload another network service while attacking another. For example, a feint/diversion attack would begin to deploy resources in mounting an attack against it. The attack could be anything from intelligence gathering to denial of service, including mounting a denial of service attack against one server while using a specific root-level remote exploit against another.
   - On January 10, 1992, ABC's "Nightline" reported that a virus had been shipped in a printer to the Iraqi government. The virus named AF/91 never existed and was part of a disinformation campaign designed to stop the Iraqi government from using computer equipment.
2. Display/decoy/dummy. The aim of a display/decoy/dummy attack is to induce a belief in an adversary that they have correctly identified your main networks and servers.
3. Camouflage/concealment/cover. The aim of a camouflage, concealment, and cover attack is either to insert information into an adversary's information system without them realizing it or to covertly observe an adversary without them realizing it. For example, directing a network based attack via a compromised third party.
4. Mimicry/spoofing. The aim of a mimicry/spoofing attack is to induce a belief in an adversary that they have received information from an agent, when in fact the agent did not send it. Examples of mimicry and spoofing attacks include the following:
   - Sending fake e-mails and reports from a person/agent
   - Creating a fake node on a network using IP spoofing. This type of attack was used by Mitnick against Shimomura (Shimomura & Markoff, 1996)
5. Dazzling/sensory-saturation. The aim of a dazzling/sensory-saturation attack is to overload the sensing capability and processes capability of adversaries with so much data that they are blinded for a period of time.

6. Disinformation. The aim of a disinformation attack is to provide an adversary with false information from a credible in such a manner so as to influence/control their behavior. Sun Tzu (Griffith, 1971), talks about such stratagems such as providing agents with deliberately false information. Modern examples include the following:
   - On December 16, 1999, federal prosecutors charged two men with posting false messages about a company on Internet bulletin boards in an effort to bolster the company's stock prices. The pair were accused of posting phony stories over a 2-day period in November about NEI Webworld, a Dallas-based printing services company. The bogus postings pushed the price of NEI's stock up from 13 cents to more than $15 per share.

7. Conditioning. The aim of a conditioning attack is to induce a belief in an adversary that is incorrect. For example, making a server unstable by resetting it, thus conditioning the administrator into believing that there is some hardware fault.

The static, dynamic, adaptive, and premeditated types of deception that can be used in information assurance are as follows:

1. Static deception is where a deception method is in place irrespective of state activity or history of either deceiver or target.
2. Dynamic deception is where the deceiver employs a deception method when a strict set of circumstances occurs.
3. Adaptive deception is where a deception method is triggered as in dynamic deception, but the method or triggering event may be modified by feedback.
4. Premeditated deception is where a deception method is designed and implemented by the deceiver based on experience, knowledge of own vulnerabilities/strengths, and observations of the target.

The host-based and network-based types of deception that can be used in information warfare are as follows:

1. Host-based deception is deception that is based on a target computer that an intruder has access to. This type of deception can include modification of tools such as ls and ps on UNIX to provide false information (Cheswick, 1992) or the creation and location of false information on the computer so as to misinform an adversary (Stoll, 1989).
2. Network-based deception is deception that makes use of a computer network or computer system to create the illusion of a fake computer network. For example, simulating multiple operating systems on a single computer.

The types of offensive deception operations and defensive deception operations that can be used in information security are as follows:

1. Offensive deception is where a deception method is designed to enhance the effectiveness of offensive acts while reducing an adversary's effectiveness in both offense and defense.
2. Defensive deception is where a deception method is utilized that is designed to enhance the effectiveness of defensive acts while reducing an adversary's effectiveness in both offense and defense.

With regard to information security the phases of a deception operation can be viewed as being cyclic in nature progressing through seven stages/phases defined as follows:

1. Phase/Stage 1: Defining and reviewing operational objectives that the deception operation is required to achieve.
2. Phase/Stage 2: Evaluating your own and the adversary's capabilities and other situational factors. This will draw on intelligence gathered in other operations. In a commercial setting it could include market research and competitive analysis. From a computer-based perspective it could include a technical assessment of an adversary's capability and resource utilization.
3. Phase/Stage 3: Developing the concept of operations and set of actions that will implement the operation and achieve the objectives defined in Phase/Stage 1.
4. Phase/Stage 4: Allocation of resources required. This could include physical resources such as people, technologies, finances, and computers, but it could also include logical resources such as information.
5. Phase/Stage 5: Coordinating the plan relative to other plans. Often a deception operation will form part of a larger strategic plan of a campaign. Thus, to avoid it adversely interacting with other operations it needs to be coordinated and synchronized with other plans.
6. Phase/Stage 6: Performing a risk and feasibility assessment. This involves assessing the potential for success and failure and examining the strategies and costs that need to be put in place to ensure success. The assessment can also include a calculation of the cost if the deception operation fails. Cost can be calculated not only in monetary value but also in the loss of prestige and trust.
7. Phase/Stage 7: Review adherence to strategic and tactical objectives. The deception operation needs to be viewed as integrated into a strategic whole if the strategic objectives are to be achieved.

We can also view deception in terms of dissimulation and simulation.

1. The term *dissimulation* is used to refer to the concept of hiding the real. Dissimulation includes the following:
   - Masking: hiding some or all of the real target by making it invisible to an adversary's sensor capability.
   - Repackaging: hiding the real target by disguising it so that the adversary's sensor capability sees the repackaged artifact.
   - Dazzling: hiding the real target by confusing/overloading an adversary's sensor capability.
2. The term *simulation* is used to refer to the concept of showing the false. Simulation includes the following:

- Mimicking: showing false to adversary's sensor capability through imitation.
- Inventing: showing false by creating a different reality for an adversary's sensor capability to detect.
- Decoying: showing false by diverting the attention of an adversary's sensor capability.

We can also view deception in terms of deceit, denial, disruption, distraction, and development.

- Deceit is fabricating, establishing, and reinforcing incorrect or preconceived beliefs, or creating erroneous illusions.
- Denial is masking operations for protection or to achieve surprise in an attack operation.
- Disruption is creating confusion and overload in the decision making process.
- Distraction is moving the focus of attention toward deceptive actions or a way from authentic actions.
- Development is creating a standard pattern of behavior to develop preconceived expectations for subsequent exploitation.

In general terms, however, deception is used to encompass a number of concepts concern with misinformation and perception management. In military terms deception is used to *camouflage, conceal, deceive, imitate, disinform, keep secret, secure, feint,* and *divert*. But how are these concepts being embraced within modern military doctrine and information warfare?

STRATEGIES AND POLICIES FOR COMPUTER NETWORK OPERATIONS

Strategies for CNO and in particular CND must function at the strategic, tactical, and operational levels. At the strategic level, we must focus on developing an understating of the risks and threats faced both in terms of CND and CAN (Rathmell, 2001). Questions arise about the capabilities and motivations of threat agents faced. At the strategic level both the attacker and defender must build strategic alliance with other parties.

In tactical terms, there is a need to focus on the clear identification of operational procedures and responsibilities, along with system planning and acceptance and business continuity planning (Pfleeger & Pfleeger, 2003). These must be tested and continually revised if they are to be effective. Whereas at the operational level we must focus on the use and deployment of up-to-date technologies and systems to hinder an attack.

IMPLEMENTING COMPUTER NETWORK OPERATIONS

When we consider CNO at an international level we can use the security models of CIA and DDPRR to create a framework within which a integrate approach can be formulated.

- *Deterrence*: Multilateral initiatives to deter a threat agent from mounting a CNA. Such an approach must include

the harmonizing of cybercrime legislation and the sharing of evidence and intelligence.
- *Prevention*: Multilateral initiatives to prevent CNA by promoting the correct specification, design, implementation, and deployment of secure systems. Such an approach must include the sharing of security related information such as vulnerabilities and patches. Deception technologies such as honey-pots also allow for an attack to be diverted to a fake target thus preventing the attack on the real target.
- *Detection*: Multilateral initiatives to detect CNA that focus on enhanced cooperation of organization and agencies at both a professional and technical level. The development and deployment of intrusion detection systems and deception technologies such as honey nets allow for an intruder to be detected.
- *Reaction*: Multilateral initiatives to react and survive a CNA. Such initiatives must include the creation of computer network infrastructure that is capable of surviving and tolerating attacks. Initiatives must also include cooperation among criminal justice agencies, government agencies, and the public.

In short, for CNO to function we require an integrated approach that supports cooperation and the exchange of information across organization and political boundaries.

GLOSSARY

Capability   The ability of an adversary to perform an action.

Computer Network Attack   The art of breaking into a computer network.

Computer Network Defense   The art of defending against someone breaking into a computer network.

Computer Network Operations   Both computer network attack and computer network defense.

Computer Security   The protection resulting from all measures to deny unauthorized access and exploitation of friendly computer systems.

Confidentiality, Integrity, and Availability (of data)   Factors of a data processing system and its files that must be protected. Confidentially protects the existence of a connection, the traffic flow, and information content from disclosure to unauthorized parties. Integrity is the assurance that information and processes are secure from unauthorized modifications by use of cryptography, digital signatures, and intrusion detection. Availability is the degree that information, data processes, and resources are usable when needed.

Cryptanalysis   The steps and operations performed in converting encrypted messages into plain text without initial knowledge of the key employed in the encryption.

Cryptography   The science that deals with hidden, disguised, or encrypted communications. It includes communications security and communications intelligence.

Deception   Those measures designed to mislead the enemy by manipulation, distortion, or falsification of evidence to induce the enemy to react in a manner prejudicial to the enemy's interests.

Denial of Service A loss of the ability of a data processing system to provide satisfactory service with respect to confidentiality, integrity, and/or the availability of its data. This loss may be temporary, as in a delay, or it may be long-lasting enough have a catastrophic effect on an enterprise.

Exploit A specific technique that allows for the security of a system to be compromised.

Information-Based Warfare/Information Operations Actions taken to affect adversary information and information systems while defending one's own information and information systems.

Information Security The protection of information and information systems against unauthorized access or modification of information, whether in storage, processing, or transit and against denial of service to authorized users. Information security includes those measures necessary to detect, document, and counter such threats. Information security is composed of computer security and communications security.

Information Warfare Definition I Information operations conducted during time of crisis or conflict to achieve or promote specific objectives over a specific adversary or adversaries. Information warfare actions may induce denial of service, corruption of data, and/or exploitation of the information obtained.

Information Warfare Definition II Actions taken to achieve information superiority by affecting adversary information, information-based processes, information systems, and computer-based networks while defending one's own information, information-based processes, information systems, and computer-based networks.

Information Warfare Definition III The offensive and defensive use of information and information systems to deny, exploit, corrupt, or destroy an adversary's information, information-based processes, information systems, and computer-based networks while protecting one's own. Such actions are designed to achieve advantages over military or business adversaries.

IP The Internet protocol.

Risk The level of threat posed by an adversary.

Security (of Information) With respect to classified matter, the condition that prevents unauthorized persons from having access to official information that is safeguarded in the interests of national security.

Social Engineering Deceptive techniques involved by persons pretending to have authorization to obtain information or entry into a facility for which they are not authorized.

Threat A function of motivation, capability, opportunity, and impact that describes a threat agent.

Threat Agent A hacker, cracker, criminal, spy, and so on.

Transmission Control Protocol

Trojan A malicious program that presents itself as being of a nondestructive nature. A characteristic that distinguishes them from viruses is that Trojans do not replicate themselves.

Vulnerability A method that allows for the security of a system to be compromised.

CROSS REFERENCES

See *Active Response to Computer Intrusions; Hackers, Crackers and Computer Criminals; Network Attacks; The Use of Deception Techniques: Honeypots and Decoys.*

REFERENCES

Blyth, A. J. C., & Kovacich, G. L. (2001). *Information assurance: Surviving in the information environment*. Berlin: Springer-Verlag.

Cheswick W. R. (1992). *An evening with Berferd, in which a cracker is lured, endured and studied*. USENIX Conference, Winter, 1992.

Dearth, D. H. (1998). Deception, human factors and information operations. In A. D. Campen & D. H. Dearth (Eds.), *CyberWar 2.0: Myths, mysteries and reality*. London: AFCEA International Press.

Denning, D. E. (1999). *Information warfare and security*. Boston: Addison-Wesley.

Gerwehr, S., & Glenn, R. W. (2000). *The art of darkness: Deception and urban operations* (Rep. No. MR-1132-A). Santa Monica, CA: The RAND Corporation.

Grazioli, S., & Jarvenpaa, S. (2003). Deceived! Under target on line. *Communications of the ACM, 46*(12), 196–205.

Griffith, S. B. (1971). *Sun Tzu—The art of war*. Oxford, UK: Oxford University Press.

Johnson, P. E., Grazioli, J. K., & Berryman, G. R. (2001). Detecting deception: Adversarial problem solving in a low base rate world. *Cognitive Science, 25*(3), 355–392.

Jones, A., Kovacich, G. L., & Luzwick, P. G. (2002). *Global information warfare: How businesses, governments, and other achieve objectives and attain competitive advantages*. Fort Lauderdale, FL: Auerbach.

Neumann, P. (1995). *Computer related risks*. Washington, DC: ACM Press.

Pfleeger, C. P., & Pfleeger, S. L. (2003). *Security in computing*, 3rd ed. Upper Saddle River, NJ: Prentice Hall.

Rathmell, A. (2001). Controlling computer network operations. *Journal of Information and Security, 7*, 121–144.

Rehman, R. U. (2003). Intrusion detection with snort. Upper Saddle River, NJ: Prentice Hall.

Shimomura, T., & Markoff, J. (1996). *Takedown*. New York: Hyperion.

Summers, R. C. (1997). *Secure computing: Threats and safeguards*. New York: McGraw-Hill.

Stoll, C. (1989). *The cuckoo's egg*. New York: Doubleday.

Waltz, E. (1998). *Information warfare: Principles and operations*. Norwood, MA: Artech House.

Electronic Protection

Neil C. Rowe, *U.S. Naval Postgraduate School*

INTRODUCTION

The term *electronic protection* has been used inconsistently in the literature to mean several things related to information security. We interpret it here in the strict sense of methods of protecting information systems from attacks that do not require an electrical or software connection to the target but exploit electromagnetic effects of electronics. Unfortunately, electrical connections to a target system are not necessary to have serious security problems. We do not consider here other important aspects of this considered elsewhere in the *Handbook*, such as radio frequency and wireless communications security, wireless information warfare, hacking techniques in wireless networks, mobile devices and protocols, and smart card security. We also do not consider primarily nonelectronic physical attacks on computer systems and networks such as explosions of conventional munitions (see Physical Security Threats).

The two main threats addressed by electronic protection are people trying to steal your secrets (spies) and people trying to vandalize your hardware or prevent it from working (saboteurs). These threats are more associated with military information systems than civilian systems and are particularly serious in battlefield situations (Friedman, 1983), so much of the research has been done by military organizations. Spies in a military setting are trying to get intelligence, and if they get it from electronic signals, they are doing signals intelligence (SIGINT; Zorpette, 2002). But spying and sabotage are also an increasing problem for businesses; secrets of competitors can be worth considerable money and effort. Incidents may be underestimated because it is of little advantage for either the military or business to report them. Electronic spying and sabotage are usually illegal; in the United States, U.S. Code Section 2511 prohibits real-time acquisitions of electronic communications in transit, and many countries have similar laws. But this has not stopped determined spies when key government, military, or business secrets are at stake.

Like all security measures, electronic protection must be cost-effective. One needs to assess the likelihood of an attack and how serious the results of that attack might be. It is thus important to do a risk assessment (see Risk Assessment and Risk Management) before committing to the protection methods to be discussed.

ELECTRONIC EMANATIONS FROM COMPUTER TECHNOLOGY

We first consider the problem of information leakage from a computer system or network through the electromagnetic radiation it produces. This has been termed *emanations security* or *emissions security* in the military literature.

The Physics of Electronic Emanations

It was discovered in the 19th century by Oersted, Faraday, and Henry and formulated in Maxwell's equations that changing electrical currents induce changing magnetic fields and magnetic fields induce changing currents. Computers use patterns in currents for operations and communication. These changes induce a changing magnetic field that propagates as an electromagnetic wave through surrounding space. This field can be picked up by electrical conductors in the vicinity, and in bad cases can impede operations of other electronic devices via *electromagnetic interference*. Thus an antenna with an amplifier can pick up a considerable amount of signal from a nearby computer and can reconstruct the generating electrical signals. Electromagnetic signal strength or intensity is the amplitude of the electromagnetic field waveform at some point in space (also called the electric flux density) and is the major factor affecting detectability of the signal. Signal intensity generally decreases as the square of the distance from the radiation source. Bugging devices within computers can pick up signals more successfully than remote ones can.

Electronic protection has not improved as the speed of computer technology has increased. With clock times now below nanoseconds, computers are radiating signals whose base frequencies are in the range of microwave radiation. As with microwave ovens, microwaves have good penetrating power for many kinds of materials. (The higher the frequency, the more energy the radiation has; however, penetration ability varies considerably with the chemistry of the material.)

Matters are made worse by the use of abrupt changes between two levels of voltage in digital hardware. The more abrupt a transition, the more high-frequency components in its spectrum. A sine wave has only one frequency; a square wave consisting of alternation between two voltages has a frequency spectrum of odd multiples of a base frequency where the amplitude of the components is inversely proportional to the frequency. High-frequency components of a waveform are refracted less by materials than low-frequency components, making them easier to detect if they are not absorbed. Furthermore, materials that one frequency poorly penetrates may be much more transparent to another—and the harmonics of an abrupt transition can be significant over quite a range of frequency. A spy may need only find one frequency to recognize the transition of a digital signal.

Several additional factors affect the intensity of signals emanating from a computer system:

- Higher currents produce stronger signals than lower currents. Most parts of computers run on relatively low currents, but an important exception is a cathode ray monitor, which requires hundreds of volts. Consequently, their screen images are easier to detect than most computer signals.
- Slower signals are often easier to detect than faster signals because they stand out better from the background noise. Therefore cables connecting to a modem are more susceptible to eavesdropping than a cable to a fast digital telephone line. However, faster signals may also radiate better.
- Periodic signals are easier to detect than irregular or one-time signals because signal energy can be summed for corresponding parts of each period, greatly helping detection. Important periodic signals occur in many places in computers, especially in the central processing unit (CPU) cycle, the monitor screen refresh process, and the loop that monitors the keyboard for key depressions.
- "Unbalanced" signals are easier to detect than balanced signals. Signals are balanced when pairs of opposite currents occur on adjacent wires. Balance is a problem for some kinds of cables.
- Many sophisticated techniques from electrical engineering can help detect signals in the presence of noise, even nonrandom noise (Garth & Poor, 1994).
- Electronic circuits have resonant frequencies. An external signal can be broadcast to a computer system to induce it to resonate at one its natural frequencies. This has the effect of modulating normal signals of the computer, making them easier to detect by demodulation.

However, the effect is weak and it is difficult to control what kind of information you obtain.

- If a spy can plant a Trojan horse on a computer system, it could deliberately create periodic loops in code to make stronger electromagnetic signals, providing a covert channel for transmission of information (see Side Channel Attacks).

Electronic Eavesdropping Technology

An electronic eavesdropper uses bugs consisting of the following:

- A device for picking up signals, as large as possible and as close as possible to the source while maintaining concealment; this can be an antenna at a distance or an induction loop around an electronic component
- An amplifier for the signals from the antenna
- A receiver (electronic filtering to extract the signal from the noise); the emanations of a computer are not designed for easy separation like radio stations are, but good filters can be effective
- Either a recording device (which may be hard to conceal given the amount of data recorded) or a retransmission device; retransmission is commonly by radio at a specific frequency, but could also be done by digitizing and connecting to a computer network (if the signal picked up is video, it could be retransmitted to another screen nearby).

Bug technology continues to decrease in size for the same performance (Murray, 2003). Intelligence agencies use bugs camouflaged as all kinds of everyday objects, so do not expect them to be easy to recognize. They may not need to be camouflaged much anyway—most people rarely look inside the cabinet of their computer. Even chips could be bugs because many computers leave empty slots during manufacture to permit later expansion. Good places to put bugs are on the display and keyboard drivers to enable reading of everything the user is doing. People who like to be suspicious have claimed bugs are widespread (Thomas, 2004), but one must be skeptical of much of what one reads about bugs on the Internet.

Points of Weakness for Electromagnetic Emanations in Computer Systems

We enumerate here some particular sources of signals that spies could exploit for electronic eavesdropping.

Cathode Ray Monitors

The traditional television-style monitor screen is a big source of emanations. Van Eck (1985) stimulated a great deal of interest by showing how easy it was to duplicate the display of a traditional cathode ray monitor on a nearby monitor using just the radiated signal. Reception is aided by high currents used by such devices. In addition, screen display follows a consistent periodic sequence: Each line of the screen is drawn from side to side, and the standard VGA format uses exactly 480 lines with exactly 640 pixels per line. This means one can reconstruct the screen signal by an easy guess as to the vertical sync (the time to draw all lines) and the horizontal sync (the time to draw one line) (Kuhn & Anderson, 1998). Liquid-crystal displays such as those found in most laptops do not use this mechanism but still give some weaker emanations nonetheless, especially the back-lit ones common today.

Keyboard

Another weakness is the keyboard-handling software. Usually the keys are sampled periodically by a keyboard driver to see if they have been depressed. This produces a near-periodic signal that can be compared between cycles to detect key depressions. However, it involves transitory changes and lower currents than those of the monitor.

Cables

Electrical cables connecting a computer to other devices can be a source of signal because of their similarity to antennas (which are long wires, too). Cables can use higher currents than CPUs because of the need to reduce transmission losses. Modem cables in particular are desirable targets because of their low data rates and the possibility of picking up passwords and keys in the clear. Furthermore, modems often use serial (one-at-a-time) character transmission, which reduces the number of signals that need to be distinguished by the eavesdropper.

Most cables are shielded to reduce the electromagnetic interference on their signal from other devices. (Exceptions include many telephone cables that are unshielded twisted pairs.) This means that the main conductor is surrounded but separated from an electrically conductive covering that carries the ground (or comparison) voltage. In principle, this should reduce emanations substantially. But in practice, not all cables are properly grounded (grounding can be difficult), not all shielding is effective (good cabling costs money), and there is a source of signal at each end where the cable connects to other electronics. Smulders (1990) showed a surprising ability to pick up signals from a modem cable with a standard radio receiver.

Power and Ground Voltages

Electrical devices using varying amounts of power create transients in the power and ground connections that they use. The effect is visible on any device sharing the same power connections, as within a building. This effect is often seen when large motors turn on and can be seen to a lesser extent with computer peripherals, especially a cathode ray monitor. But the signals produced are very noisy because everything attached to the power line or ground can also produce an effect.

Magnetic Disks

Magnetic hard disks rotate continually even when not being read. If the disk head remains over a particular track on the disk, it will generate a periodic signal representing the bits on that track. But this is uninteresting data most of the time, and the signal may be so weak because of shielding that it would be easier to directly connect to the associated computer system.

Optical Signals

Light is also electromagnetic and we need to prevent reading of computer screens through windows with telescopes. Just ensuring that the screen is unreadable at a reasonable distance is insufficient with cathode ray monitors, because the changes over time in the total diffused light from a monitor can carry enough information to enable reconstruction of characters (Kuhn, 2002). Many computers and peripherals also have light-emitting diodes (LEDs) intended to give operators a simple summary of what the devices are doing. However, LEDs can switch on and off at a rate up to 10 ns, far beyond what people can detect, and this could be a covert channel to signal information to a confederate (Loughry & Umpress, 2002).

Error Correction

Detected electromagnetic emanations have considerable noise, because the transmission of information is neither engineered nor intended. A variety of error-correction methods can be used by the eavesdropper. Conventional electronic filtering can be done when the signal has a primary frequency, or a strong known unwanted frequency can be filtered out. Video signals have a variety of specialized correction techniques that have been developed to aid copying of video. Research in optical character reading (Liu, Babad, Sun, & Chan, 1991) has developed a variety of robust techniques for correcting noisy images of characters.

As for digital data, error-correcting codes and checksums in network transmissions can be picked up by the eavesdropper to correct some reception errors (Forouzan, 2003). But even without such codes, a spy eavesdropping on text can exploit knowledge of an alphabet or language used to rule out most errors. For instance for English, 20,000 words is a common vocabulary size for a native speaker, and the average word is eight letters long. Yet there are 200 billion possible eight-letter words, so most of the one-character errors in interpreting an eight-letter English word are easy to correct. Kukich (1992) gives a comprehensive overview of algorithms for such corrections. For other kinds of data, knowledge of the typical symbols can be formulated from experience (Moulin & O'Sullivan, 2003).

The frequent predictability of software can be exploited by an eavesdropper. For instance, encryption algorithms often start execution with the same sequence of code; an eavesdropper could learn to recognize the signals corresponding to that code and then zero in on the plaintext key typed next. The eavesdropper could learn the necessary patterns by obtaining and running their own copy of the encryption software.

REDUCING THE THREAT OF ELECTRONIC EMANATIONS

In the face of these threats, several techniques can prevent or reduce eavesdropping, as summarized in Table 1.

The most obvious techniques are concealment of the emanations themselves by reducing their intensity. This was the idea behind the TEMPEST standards adopted by the U.S. government in the 1960s to reduce emanations from their important computers (McNamara, 2004). Although the quantitative details of TEMPEST

Table 1 Summary of the Suitability of Electronic Protection Methods for Attack Targets

Threat	Monitor	Keyboard	Cables	Power and Ground	Disks	Optical Signals
Electromagnetic shielding	Yes	Yes	Yes	No	Yes	No
Source Suppression	Yes	No	Yes	Yes	No	Yes
Noise generation and encryption	Yes	Yes	Yes	Yes	Yes	Yes
Signal irregularity	Yes	Yes	Yes	Yes	No	Yes
Deliberate deception	Yes	No	Yes	No	Yes	Yes
Bug detectors	Yes	Yes	Yes	Yes	Yes	No

specifications are still secret (i.e., they are classified), the basic principles are available in the open literature. TEMPEST has not been as important since a 1991 report of the U.S. Central Intelligence Agency concluded it was not cost-effective, especially within the United States in protecting against foreign spies. TEMPEST hardware for computers, peripherals, and cables typically costs two to three times that of equivalent unprotected commercial hardware. There are so many software-based ways of stealing secrets that electronic eavesdropping is less threatening than it once was. Nonetheless, TEMPEST standards are still important for U.S. military and diplomatic computers that have important secrets.

Electromagnetic Shielding

Electromagnetic emanations can be reduced or even suppressed entirely by use of appropriate electromagnetic shielding. Gauss's law says the surface integral of a closed contour surrounding an object is only proportional to the charge enclosed. If that contour is unbroken and electrically conductive, an internal electrical field with no net charge will cancel itself out so there will be no net electrical field outside the contour. This also means that any electrical charge on a closed conductive surface resides entirely on the outside of the surface.

Therefore, to eliminate emanations, we should put computers in metal boxes (Faraday cages) made of conductive materials such as copper, aluminum, or steel. A variety of materials and forms (solid metals, conductive coatings, adhesive foils, conductively filled materials, etc.) suffice (Molyneux-Child, 1997). However, perfect protection assumes the conductive enclosure is unbroken. Because there usually must be gaps for ventilation, power lines, keyboards, and network connections, these gaps may permit signals to leak out (Warne & Chen, 1992). Consequently, significant gaps must be minimized. A key factor is the ratio of the diameter of the gap to the wavelength of the signal frequency one wishes to suppress (Hoffman Enclosures Inc., 2003). As a rule of thumb, it has been suggested this should be 1/10th or less to prevent significant radiation from escaping, and 1/100th to provide 60-db reduction (Molyneux-Child, 1997). Waveguides in the form of conductive pipes through the gaps can further reduce the emanations at these gaps, as can making the gaps into meandering channels. Power lines through these gaps can be filtered, and fiber optic cables through the gaps can supply communications signals without providing an electro-

magnetic channel. Monitor screens can be coated with a conductive film, but keyboards are tricky to protect. A number of vendors supply such specialized hardware. Such shielding is difficult to do on laptop computers, where weight and space are at a premium.

To simplify construction, the conducting box is often constructed with a grid of wires like a cage. This works well if the gaps between the wires fulfill the wavelength constraints, and it permits better ventilation than a closed surface. Rooms and even buildings can be built using these conductive grids (Hemming, 1992).

Cables provide special problems for shielding because an unshielded and unbalanced electrical cable can be much like an antenna. Fiber optic cables are the best solution although they are more expensive per unit length than electrical cables. They have no electromagnetic emanations along their bodies because they are coated to prevent the escape of light. Their only weakness is on their ends where light is converted to and from electrical signals. Long fiber optic cables such as long-distance telephone lines also need to be periodically boosted electronically along their length, and the booster is susceptible to eavesdropping.

Optical signals from cathode ray monitors and LEDs can be suppressed by covering room windows and otherwise controlling their light, even the reflected light. Kuhn (2002) also suggests increasing light noise by using significant broad-frequency illumination for the computer room by incandescent or high-frequency fluorescent lights to cover the frequencies of the monitor light. Good design for LEDs should ensure they do not change any faster than humans can follow them.

Source Suppression

Another goal should be to reduce emanations from the computer itself. A good compact design of the machine will help. This means a relatively small chassis and short cables to reduce electrical dipoles that cause emanations. Devices used to measure electromagnetic interference can help locate possible emanation problems (Masuda et al., 2003). Generally speaking, the intensity of a signal decreases as the square of the distance from the source, so one can estimate how close an enemy must be to pick up a signal.

For conventional electrical cables of either the twisted-pair or coaxial type, ferrite beads or disks on the ends can reduce emanations. Ferrites are ferromagnetic materials that dissipate high-frequency magnetic fields as small amounts of heat with magnetic eddy currents. They are useful for frequency over 100 MHz, in the range of computer signals, but require some care to use effectively because they must be matched to appropriate electrical hardware. In-line capacitors can also achieve the effects of ferrite beads but can involve more power dissipation.

Because high frequencies tend to be easier to pick than low frequencies, it is desirable to lower the high-frequency emanations by slowing the switching times between low and high voltages in signals. This is difficult with the CPU but makes sense for the cables, particularly the video and keyboard cables that do not need fast transition times. This can be done by running the signals through a suitably designed low-pass filter, something done routinely to reduce electromagnetic interference. Kuhn and Anderson (1998) also designed special "Tempest fonts" for monitor screen display that have reduced high-frequency components but are still legible, making them harder for an eavesdropper to pick up.

Another approach to source suppression is to move the source about as in a mobile device. That way any fixed-location eavesdropper cannot obtain all the information. But this is possible only with a few applications.

Noise Generation and Encryption

Another way to make eavesdropping more difficult is to broadcast noise at the same time. Noise can be just many signals at the same time. It is difficult to eavesdrop on a single computer in a busy office with many computers, and similarly, it is difficult to eavesdrop on the signals of a CPU because there are so many in a small space. Noise, however, can create electromagnetic interference if too strong. Realism requires that noise start and stop and eavesdropping could be done while it is off. Also, it is important to create sufficiently complex noise that cannot be easily filtered out. Analog white noise, for instance, noise of a uniform mixture of frequencies, is just added to the frequencies already present and its uniform height can be easily subtracted from the frequency spectrum. So digital noise is needed that looks like real computer operations from a number of simultaneous sources. Even noise sources that are obviously fake can create a difficult combinatorial problem for the attacker in assigning bits to each signal if the sources are located near one another.

The effect of noise can be created by omitting error-correcting bits transmitted in network protocols so attackers have a more difficult time fixing errors in reception. Because their error rate will be higher than that of the system they are monitoring, this creates added problems for them. However, this may give only a mild effect and also hurts the system if its own error rate is nonnegligible. So it is hard to justify against rare threats.

A systematic way to accomplish noise is to encrypt much of the digital activity of the computer. This is a good practice for files and network communications anyway when secrecy is important, so it can be extended to other aspects of the computer when electromagnetic emanations are a concern. Strong encryption methods are now easily available (see PKI and PGP). Unfortunately,

the keyboard depressions and the monitor display cannot ultimately be encrypted, so other techniques are necessary for them. It will help to avoid displaying passwords and keys on the screen because the screen contents are easy to pick up. Steganography is not as useful as encryption because activities and files are difficult to conceal completely.

Even when data are encrypted, spies may learn something from when and where it is being used. Spies can do traffic analysis to determine the flow of information between sites; for a hierarchical organization, this may be sufficient to identify the flow of information. To prevent this, it is useful to send dummy (noise) messages periodically between sites; if an equal number of messages are sent between each pair of sites on the average, a spy cannot infer any structure of the sites.

Signal Irregularity

Because eavesdropping is easier with periodic signals, another idea is to insert deliberate random delays in transmission of signals to avoid periodicity. This can be done by changing the operation of the lowest layers of the OSI network transmission protocols (Forouzan, 2003), the physical and data link layers. Because slow transmissions such as those with keyboards, monitors, and modems are the easiest to eavesdrop, and the EIA-232 (also called RS-232) protocol and associated cable hardware are used for these on most computers, it is desirable to add irregularity to that protocol. Transmissions with EIA-232 can be synchronous (with a clock signal) or asynchronous (without); synchronous transmissions are paradoxically best suited to creating irregularity because the clock signal can be supplied irregularly to indicate when the signal level should be sampled.

Irregularity can also be created at higher levels of network protocols. At the data link layer, gaps in time between bursts of data (frames) can be made random. Although bursts may be deciphered, it will be hard to string them into packets, particularly when similar signals on other electronic equipment are being generated at the same time. Buffering at the receiving end can regularize the data as needed to enable normal computer operations. Asynchronous transfer mode (ATM), important for the Internet, already supports irregular handling of its small packets.

Random delays can also be done in drawing the screen of the monitor. Also, the monitor does not need to draw the lines on the screen in vertical order but could draw them in an order determined by a secret time-varying key. Then an eavesdropper not knowing the key would see only a scrambled mess. But they could try orders at random until they hit on the right one because 480 lines in the standard VGA format is not many. Similarly, keyboard sampling to recognize key depressions could randomly delay between cycles and does not need to check the keys in the same order every time. Keyboard rates now are so slow compared to CPU processing times that a more complex keyboard-sampling method makes no difference to interaction speed. As for periodicity of a magnetic disk, the disk head can be moved when not in use to a blank portion of the disk.

Trojan horses that deliberately create periodic signals to facilitate eavesdropping can be found by the usual methods for finding Trojan horses (see Trojan Horse Programs) such as comparing checksums on executables to previous checksums and looking for statistically anomalous run-time behavior. Their broadcast may be detected by monitoring the emanations of the hardware for unusual frequencies.

Deliberate Deception

Deception is a classic military technique for exploiting modest resources for a major gain. Deception could be done in electronic emanations to plant disinformation with the eavesdropper. For instance, dummy computers could transmit false information made especially easy (in intensity or accessibility) for the eavesdropper to pick up. This is easiest if one can replay old signals that are no longer secret, with date and detail changes. Routine data such as transmission headers are easy to fake.

Deception can help confirm eavesdropping. One can plant some information and see if an eavesdropper reacts; if they do, then deception can be tailored to them more specifically. Counterintelligence uses methods like these. Honeypots (see Use of Deception Techniques: Honeypots and Decoys) also use deception to collect information about attackers and their attacks. They can pretend to have resources that attackers want such as unencrypted (but ineffective) passwords to waste the time of the attacker. Deception can often be more effective than concealment because the enemy can recognize that you are concealing something and redouble his or her efforts to get it, whereas deception may make him or her go away.

Bug Detectors

If eavesdropping is suspected, one can try to locate the eavesdropping hardware and remove it (Ferrand, 1988; Tolces, 1986). If the countermeasures discussed have already been employed, any useful bug must be nearby. A variety of electronic bug detectors are available, but a purchaser must be cautious because there is much competition among vendors and little regulation. Some vendors promise more than they can deliver, and some are outright scams. Careful testing of products is essential.

There are two approaches to bug detection. One is to focus on the eavesdropping device itself. Because nearly all use electronics, one can exploit properties of electronics. For one thing, they dissipate some heat, so an infrared camera may be able to see bugging devices hidden unexpectedly in everyday objects such as light fixtures and telephones. Another idea is to take advantage of the nonlinearity of many transistors by irradiating the area with a strong microwave signal and looking for distinctive reradiation patterns at different frequencies than the excitation (Yost, 1985). This is usually what is meant by sweeping an area for bugs. It requires a very pure frequency generation because the detectable signals can be small, and good amplification for the sensitive signals after filtering out the excitation signal. Almost any bug will need to contain transistors, but this will not work for MOSFET circuits nor transistors with very small input leads. It will also not find bugs next to legitimate electronic hardware nor those electromagnetically shielded.

Another approach is to focus on bug transmissions. Because most bugs collect too much data to store at the bug (concealment is important, and the bug may need to remain untouched in place a long time to prevent suspicion), retransmission of data by electromagnetic waves to a more convenient location is usual. So frequency-scanning bug detectors, or frequency analyzers, look for unusual frequencies in the electromagnetic spectrum that could represent bug transmissions. It helps that it is easier for a spy to use off-the-shelf hardware for transmitters and receivers to take advantage of frequently used parts of the spectrum. These include the citizen's band at 25–50 MHz, the frequency modulation radio band at 88–120 MHz, the police band at 150–174 MHz, and the gap between UHF and VHF television at around 470 MHz (Yost, 1985); the antenna size required ranges from a few feet for the first to an inch for the last. So a bug detector frequency scanner should focus on those ranges. Techniques for detecting signals in nonrandom noise can help (Garth & Poor, 1994). Additional tricks may be necessary to detect signals of highly motivated adversaries such as military enemies (Stephens, 1996).

Spies can use several additional techniques to conceal bug transmissions: (1) a wide-spectrum broadcast, (2) frequency hopping in the broadcast, (3) double modulation using subcarrier frequencies, and (4) frequencies close to legitimate signals such as radio stations ("snuggling"). But each of these leaves clues in the frequency spectrum. Wide-spectrum and frequency-hopping behavior will give a distinctive "smear" pattern; double modulation will give two equal peaks; and snuggling will give two distinct but very close peaks. It may help to keep records of the frequencies observed at a location to better notice changes created by new transmissions, analogously to using checksums for detecting changes to a file system. Frequency detection is not foolproof as it does not work when bug is turned off; a bug could be designed for only occasional transmissions.

Bugs can also be detected by nonelectronic inspection by noticing unusual changes to objects, such as repair work or abrasions where none should be expected, new objects or building materials, and so on. Counterintelligence training (Shulsky, 1993) provides many suggestions.

PROTECTING AGAINST OFFENSIVE SIGNALS

Now let us turn to the use of electromagnetic signals as weapons against computer systems for sabotage or harassment.

Damage Mechanisms for Electromagnetic Signals

A disadvantage of the decreasing size of computer and network hardware is that they are becoming increasingly vulnerable to electronic attacks as they become less able to dissipate large amounts of power. So a high voltage suddenly created within modern circuitry can more easily create permanent damage. High voltages induce high current flows that can melt electrical conductors, causing electrical breaks or shorts deep inside chips that are virtually impossible to repair. This heat can also melt the packaging and create toxic fumes or start fires. In addition, even moderate levels of heat can destroy the essential dielectric properties of the semiconductors that are the building blocks of integrated circuits, making them useless.

Several methods can damage circuitry without a direct electrical connection. High-frequency electromagnetic waves can be used that have powerful penetration capabilities. A short burst of such frequencies can be created by a nuclear explosion high in the atmosphere, an electromagnetic pulse (U.S. Government Printing Office, 1998). Such pulses are serious threats to international security because they can destroy digital hardware over a wide area. Smaller pulses can also be created from spark gaps, and they can be effective against specific targets.

Microwave radiation can also be used to attack computer hardware. Because microwave ovens can cook food, higher power microwaves can be focused to overheat particular targets. Such weapons can be either narrow band or broadband. Narrow band can be more effective if one knows the natural frequencies of an electronic device and can stimulate the device at those frequencies, amplifying the damage, but that requires detailed knowledge of the device. The former Soviet Union is alleged to have been the world leader in developing offensive electromagnetic weapons as an inexpensive way to attack the combat systems of the more technologically advanced West.

Countermeasures for Damaging Electromagnetic Signals

The same electromagnetic shielding discussed above as a protection against spying can also protect against electromagnetic attacks, as Gauss's law applies to both incoming and outgoing signals (Kopp, 1997; Podgorski, 1990). But for perfect protection, the device must be perfectly enclosed in a conductive material. If there are any gaps in the surrounding material, they will permit penetration by radiation of frequencies less than the width of the gap unless countermeasures are used. Centimeter-sized gaps are sufficient for microwaves, but not for the X rays and gamma rays that occur with a nuclear explosion. More complex shielding designs can address this. Press (1990) proposes convoluted corridors that twist and turn for the necessary gaps as a way to significantly attenuate radiation traversal.

Shielding can also be at the level of the integrated circuit. "Radiation-hardened" integrated-circuit chips are available for military and space applications (Hughes & Benedetto, 2003) to protect against high-frequency radiation. They cost 10–1,000 times more than regular hardware because of their difficulty of manufacture but provide a number of techniques for protecting the chip. These include special thinness of the circuit layers (to reduce the effect of charged layers), extra width of critical electrical channels, fabrication at lower temperatures to reduce chemical weaknesses that radiation can exploit

and more complex design methods. However, they are generally designed for continuous radiation (as in nuclear and space applications) rather than for the short pulses of radiation typical of an attack.

Traditional methods of electronic protection against voltage spikes (because of lightning, power problems, etc.) can also provide some protection for electronic circuitry if they are significantly upgraded from usual practice. Press (1990) recommends protection for up to 10,000 volts on power lines and 20,000 volts on phone lines (albeit for only a few nanoseconds); special devices such as varistors can accomplish that. A fuse is the oldest and most familiar method, but is no protection for a voltage surge over every conductor. Fuses must also be replaced once they have been blown and must be chosen to have a faster delay than the damage time of the circuit they are protecting. Circuit breakers involve a gap across which a high-voltage spike could jump, so they are not appropriate for powerful electromagnetic attacks. Fiber optic cables are useful along input lines because they cannot be overloaded.

Surge protectors and transient protection devices are another traditional way of protecting electronic equipment against current spikes on its power or signal lines. They use large resistors to dissipate energy as heat and capacitors to even out the current supplied to a device. However, capacitors become less effective the higher the frequency of the signal they are protecting against, and they cannot react effectively against a nuclear electromagnetic pulse. Surge protectors have a rated delay, and useful ones need to have delays on the order of picoseconds.

As with emanations protection, the danger decreases with the square of the distance from the source. Thus if you can keep your enemy outside a given perimeter around your computer systems, you can estimate the closest they could get, the strength of their electromagnetic weapons, the strength of your protections, and the possible damage.

Electromagnetic Noise to Interfere with Computer Systems

Another way to interfere with electronics is to deliberately produce electromagnetic interference to impede operations. Jamming is an example, where supplying a strong signal at the same frequency as a narrow band signal such as radio will prevent listeners from receiving the signal. Jamming works best with analog voltages, where adding to an existing signal changes the meaning of the signal. This could affect the video monitor of a computer or analog input devices. But it is less a problem for digital communications where there are only two voltage levels, because moderate noise does not increase ambiguity unless it changes the voltage enough to go from low to high or vice versa. This inherent noise protection is, in fact, a main justification for the shift from analog to digital electronics that has been occurring since the mid-1950s. Some protection against electronic noise can be obtained by filtering it out using appropriate circuitry. If the noise has distinctive frequencies, appropriate electronic filters can be designed, even automatically, in response to observed signals.

CONCLUSION

Electronic threats to computer systems and networks are often overlooked in the concerns over the myriad of security problems with the new software technologies. Nonetheless, electromagnetic threats remain serious problems for high-security systems, and everyone concerned with information security should be aware of them and the variety of measures available to combat them.

GLOSSARY

Bug Detector　Electronic device for detecting electronic or audio eavesdropping devices.

Counterintelligence　Methods used to impede the collection by your enemy of intelligence about you.

EIA-232　Commonly used physical-level network protocol and associated hardware specifications for slow communications like those for keyboards, monitors, and modems; originally called RS-232.

Electromagnetic Interference　Electromagnetic waves that are sufficiently strong to induce significant voltages and thereby interfere with operations of electronic devices.

Electromagnetic Pulse　A burst of high-voltage electromagnetic radiation, created by a special device or a nuclear explosion.

Electromagnetic Shielding　Electrically conductive material placed around electronic devices to reduce their electromagnetic emanations and reduce their susceptibility to electromagnetic pulses.

Electronic Filter　An electronic device that amplifies some frequencies more than others, useful in reducing electromagnetic emanations.

Emanations (Emissions) Security　Issues in the protection of computers and networks from eavesdropping on the electromagnetic signals they inadvertently generate.

Faraday Cage　Perfect electromagnetic shielding with no gaps.

Ferrites　Ferromagnetic materials which can used for reducing high-frequency magnetic fields.

Ground　The comparison voltage for electronic circuitry, usually electrically connected to the earth through an electrical plug and appropriate building wiring.

Intelligence　Information about an enemy obtained by surreptitious means.

Signals Intelligence (SIGINT)　Gathering of intelligence data by intelligence agencies from electromagnetic signals.

Source Suppression　Reduction of electromagnetic emanations from a computer or network by reducing its generated signals.

TEMPEST　Secret U.S. Government standards for computer hardware with reduced electromagnetic emanations, used for military and diplomatic systems.

CROSS REFERENCES

See *Cryptographic Hardware Security Modules; Electronic Attacks; Encryption Basics; Hacking Techniques in Wireless Networks; Mobile Devices and Protocols; Physical Security Measures; Physical Security Threats; Radio Frequency and Wireless Communications Security; Smart Card Security; Wireless Information Warfare.*

REFERENCES

Ferrand, M. K. (1988). Hidden electronics detection. *Proceedings of the Microwave Symposium Digest*, IEEE MTT-S International (vol. 2, pp. 1035–1038).

Forouzan, B. (2003). *Data communications and networking* (3rd ed.). New York: McGraw-Hill.

Friedman, R. S. (1983). Intelligence and the electronic battlefield. In W. V. Kennedy, *Intelligence warfare* (pp. 76–95). New York: Crescent.

Garth, L. M., & Poor, H. V. (1994). Detection of non-Gaussian signals: A paradigm for modern statistical signal processing. *Proceedings of the IEEE, 82*(7), 1061–1095.

Hemming, L H. (1992). *Architectural electromagnetic shielding handbook*. New York: IEEE Press.

Hoffman Enclosures Inc. (2003). *Electromagnetic compatibility (EMC)*. Retrieved June 11, 2004, http://www.hoffmanonline.com/PDFCatalog/SpecifiersGuide/ChAp20_22.pdf.

Hughes, H., & Benedetto, J. (2003). Radiation effects and hardening of MOS technology: Devices and circuits. *IEEE Transactions on Nuclear Science, 50*(3), 500–521.

Kopp, C. (1997, February). *Information warfare—Part 2: Hardening your computing assets*. Asia/Pacific Open Systems Review. Retrieved October 9, 2004, from www.globalsecurity.org/military/library/report/1997/harden.pdf.

Kuhn, M.G., & Anderson, R. J. (1998). Soft TEMPEST: Hiding data transmission using electronic emanations. In D. Aucsmith (ed.), *Lecture in computer science, vol. 1525: Information hiding 1998* (pp. 124–142). Berlin: Springer-Verlag.

Kuhn, M. G. (2002). Optical time-domain eavesdropping risks of CRT displays. In Proceedings of the *IEEE Symposium on Security and Privacy* (pp. 3–18).

Kukich, K. (1992). Techniques for automatically correcting words in text. *ACM Computing Surveys, 24*(4), 377–439.

Liu, L.-M., Babad, Y. M., Sun, W., & Chan, K.-K. (1991). Adaptive postprocessing of OCR text via knowledge acquisition. In *Proceedings of the ACM Computer Science Conference* (pp. 558–569).

Loughry, J., & Umpress, D. (2002). Information leakage from optical emanations. *ACM Transactions on Information and Systems Security, 5*(3), 262–289.

Masuda, N., Tamaki, N., Kuriyama, T., Bu, J. C., Yamaguchi, M., & Arai, K.-T. (2003). High-frequency magnetic near-field measurement using planar multi-layer loop coil. In Proceedings of the *IEEE Electromagnetic Compatibility Symposium* (vol. 1, pp. 80–85).

McNamara, J. (2004). *The complete, unofficial TEMPEST information page*. Retrieved June 8, 2004, from www.eskimo.com/~joelm/tempest.html.

Molyneux-Child, J. W. (1997). *EMC shielding materials: A designer's guide* (2nd ed.). Boston: Oxford.

Moulin, P., & O'Sullivan, J. (2003). Information-theoretic analysis of information hiding. *IEEE Transactions on Information Theory, 49*(3), 563–593.

Murray, K. D. (2003). *Electronic eavesdropping and industrial espionage.* Retrieved June 11, 2004, from http://www.spybusters.com/mbsc3.html.

Podgorski, A. (1990). Composite electromagnetic pulse threat. In *Proceedings of the IEEE Symposium on Electromagnetic Compatibility* (pp. 224–227).

Press, J. (1990). EMP response of a generic ground-based facility. In *Proceedings of the IEEE Symposium on Electromagnetic Compatibility* (pp. 74–79).

Shulsky, A. N. (1993). *Silent warfare: Understanding the world of intelligence* (2nd ed.). Washington, DC: Brassey's.

Smulders, P. (1990). The threat of information theft by reception of electromagnetic radiation from RS-232 cables. *Computers and Security, 9*(1), 53–58.

Stephens, J. P. (1996). Advances in signal processing technology for electronic warfare. *Proceedings of the IEEE National Aerospace and Electronics Conference* (vol. 1, pp. 129–136).

Thomas, K. (2004). *PROMIS and computer paranoia.* Retrieved June 11, 2004, from www.disinfo.com/archive/pages/article/id905/pg1/.

Tolces, R. (1986, September). *Wiretap and bug detection.* California Association of Licensed Investigators Newsletter. Retrieved June 11, 2004, from www.bugsweeps.com/info/wiretap_detection.html.

Van Eck, W. (1985). Electromagnetic radiation from video display units: An eavesdropping risk? *Computers and Security, 4*(4), 269–286.

Warne, L. K., & Chen, K. C. (1992). A simple transmission line model for narrow slot apertures having depth and losses. *IEEE Transactions on Electromagnetic Compatibility, 34*(3), 173–182.

U.S. Government Printing Office. (1998). *Joint Economic Committee hearing: Radio frequency weapons and proliferation: Potential impact on the economy.* Retrieved June 10, 2004, from www.house.gov/jec/hearings/02-25-8h.htm.

Yost, G. (1985). *Spy-tech.* New York: Facts on File.

Zorpette, G. (2002). Making intelligence smarter. *IEEE Spectrum, 39*(1), 38–43.

Information Assurance

Peng Liu, *Pennsylvania State University*
Meng Yu, *Monmouth University*
Jiwu Jing, *Chinese Academy of Sciences Beijing, China*

INTRODUCTION

As society increasingly relies on digitally stored and accessed information, traditional information security technologies, policies, management, and practices are found more and more limited in satisfying the security and assurance needs of modern information systems and applications, for several reasons. In general, addressing only the protection of information against unauthorized disclosure, transfer, modification, or destruction, traditional information security cannot deliver the level of information assurance that modern applications require. In particular, first, as applications increasingly rely on digitally stored and accessed information, they increasingly rely on the availability of this information and the reliability of the corresponding information system. However, availability and reliability are largely neglected by traditional information security.

Second, although information confidentiality, privacy, and integrity protection are certainly crucial in meeting the security needs of modern applications, not all attacks can be prevented and some attacks do succeed. (Readers can refer to Volume III of this handbook for a detailed discussion of the threats and vulnerabilities to modern information systems.) These attacks can cause substantial confidentiality and privacy loss (via unauthorized disclosure of information), substantial integrity loss (via unauthorized modification of information), substantial availability/reliability loss and serious denial-of-service (via destruction of some critical components of the information system), and substantial nonrepudiation loss (via destruction of evidence and audit data). When applications were lightly dependent on digitally stored and accessed information, such information security losses might be able to be tolerated. But as applications increasingly rely on digitally stored and accessed information, such security losses can be disastrous and may no longer be able to be tolerated. Hence, another fundamental limitation of traditional information security is how to address these successful attacks or intrusions.

As a result, to meet the security and assurance needs of modern information systems and applications, a broader perspective is introduced, saying that, in addition to preventing information from being disclosed, modified, or destroyed, intrusions should be detected; countermeasures (e.g., responses) to intrusions should be planned and deployed in advance; security and fault tolerance mechanisms should work together to ensure confidentiality, privacy, integrity, nonrepudiation, authenticity, availability, and reliability in the presence of attacks; and the damage caused on the information and the information system should be repaired and restored (or recovered). In this literature, this is referred to as *information assurance*. For example, from the military perspective, information assurance must address the delivery of authentic, accurate, secure, reliable, timely information, regardless of threat conditions, within the distributed and heterogeneous computing and communication environment.

The basic meaning of information assurance is well captured by the definition from the *National Information Systems Security Glossary*, which is as follows:

> **Information Assurance (IA)**: Information operations that protect and defend information and information systems by ensuring their availability, integrity, authentication, confidentiality, and non-repudiation. This includes providing for restoration of information systems by incorporating protection, detection, and reaction capabilities. [*National Information Systems Security (INFOSEC) Glossary, NSTISSI No. 4009, Aug. 1997*]

Compared with the concepts of information security and information systems security, whose definitions are quoted below, it is not difficult to see that the concept of information assurance is much broader than that of information security. In particular, (a) the focus of information security is on protection or prevention, whereas the focus of information assurance is on integration of protection, detection, and reaction; (b) intrusion detection and reaction are not a major concern of information security, but they are certainly crucial for information assurance; (c) attack recovery or restoration may be a topic out of the scope of information security, but it is certainly a critical component of information assurance; (d) the goal of information security technologies is to prevent attacks from happening, whereas the goal of information assurance is to ensure that even if some attacks intrude into an information system, certain levels of availability, integrity, authentication, confidentiality, or nonrepudiation can still be guaranteed.

Information security: The protection of information against unauthorized disclosure, transfer, modification, or destruction, whether accidental or intentional.

Information systems security (INFOSEC): [The] protection of information systems against unauthorized access to or modification of information, whether in storage, processing or transit, and against the denial of service to authorized users, including those measures necessary to detect, document, and counter such threats.

It is no doubt that information assurance involves many disciplines and has a variety of aspects, such as the policy, legal, ethical, social, management, evaluation, and technical aspects of information assurance. Compared with traditional information security practices, information assurance involves not only the design and development of a variety of new security technologies but also a variety of emerging policy, legal, ethical, social, economical, management, evaluation, and assurance issues as information assurance evolves people's practices of information security in an ever quicker pace. Nevertheless, to make this chapter more tangible, it focuses primarily on the technical aspect of information assurance, though some relevant policy, management, and evaluation issues are also addressed. Readers can refer to Security Policy Guidelines and Security Policy Enforcement for a detailed discussion on the policy aspect. Readers can refer to Managing a Network Environment for detailed discussion on the management aspect. Readers can refer to Common Criteria for detailed discussion on the evaluation aspect. Readers can refer to the Social and Legal Issues part of Volume II for a detailed discussion on the social, ethical, and legal aspects of IA.

The rest of this chapter is organized as follows. Overview of Information Assurance Technologies presents an overview of IA technologies. Three generations of IA technologies are identified and summarized. Third generation IA technologies are classified into two categories: intrusion masking technologies and defense in depth technologies. In Section 3, we survey intrusion masking technologies. In Section 4, we survey defense in depth technologies. In Section 5, we conclude the chapter.

OVERVIEW OF INFORMATION ASSURANCE TECHNOLOGIES

In this section, we give a comprehensive overview of information assurance technologies, with a focus on the emerging third generation information assurance technologies and their relation with more established intrusion prevention and detection IA technologies.

Three Generations of IA Technologies

In general, existing IA technologies can be "clustered" into three generations as shown below. There is a natural evolution or maturing that has occurred in the IA community, and these generations offer evidence of the evolution.

- **First generation: prevent intrusions.** The goal is to prevent attacks from succeeding. The representative technologies are trusted computing base, access control and physical security, multiple levels of security, and cryptography.
- **Second generation: detect intrusions.** Because not all attacks can be prevented, intrusions will occur. Hence, the goal of second generation IA technologies is to detect intrusions. Some representative technologies are firewalls, intrusion detection systems, and boundary controllers.
- **Third generation: operate through attacks (or survivability).** Because some attacks will succeed, we need the third generation IA technologies. The goal is to enable information systems to continue delivering essential services with security assurance in the presence of sustained attacks. Some representative technologies are real-time situation awareness and response, real-time trade-off of performance, functionality and security, intrusion tolerance, and graceful degradation. It should be noticed that the third generation IA technologies are not simply focusing on the availability domain; their dimensions are much broader. In particular, without delivering such security assurance as confidentiality (privacy), integrity, authenticity and nonrepudiation, essential services cannot be continuously delivered under sustained attacks. In general, survivability means not only availability under attacks but also confidentiality (privacy), integrity, authenticity, and nonrepudiation under attacks. Moreover, in many situations, survivability implies reliability.

It should be noticed that among the three generations of IA technologies, each generation is crucial in achieving the goals of information assurance, and no one can replace another. (The second generation IA technologies do not subsume the first generation IA technologies, and the third generation IA technologies do not subsume the second generation IA technologies either.) In particular, the first generation IA technologies build the foundation for information assurance because without strong protection of information confidentiality, privacy, integrity, authenticity, and nonrepudiation, there can be too many successful attacks for the information system to survive, which in fact makes survivability infeasible. Moreover, intrusion prevention, intrusion detection, and intrusion tolerance (or survivability) actually share primarily the same goal (i.e., to ensure the information confidentiality, privacy, integrity, availability, authenticity and nonrepudiation in the face of attacks). A highly trusted and assured information system should be able to prevent as many attacks as possible from breaking into the system, detect the attacks that could not be prevented with accuracy and agility, and robustly operate through and recover from these successful attacks without losing availability, reliability, and accountability. Second, the third generation IA technologies are largely dependent on the second generation IA technologies, because many third generation IA technologies assume that the intrusions can be detected in a timely manner with good accuracy (e.g., low false positive rate and false negative rate).

Nevertheless, in this chapter we focus on the third generation IA technologies, because the first and second generation IA technologies are well covered by the other chapters of this handbook. In particular, we survey the technologies for developing survivable (networked) information systems. Readers can refer to Secure Public Networks, IPsec, SSL/TLS, Secret Key Cryptography, Database Security, Medical Record Security, Access Control: Principles and Solutions, PGP (Pretty Good Privacy), P3P (Platform for Privacy Preferences Project), Anonymity and Identity in the Internet, Privacy Law, Privacy Issues in Wired and Wireless Networks, and Medical Record Security for detailed discussions of first generation IA technologies. Readers can refer to Intrusion Detection: Detection Technology and Techniques, Intrusion Detection Systems Basics, Host-Based Intrusion Detection Systems, and Network-Based Intrusion Detection Systems for detailed discussions of second generation IA technologies.

Third Generation IA Technologies

Related to the fault tolerance concept and drawing from that discipline is the area of intrusion tolerance or survivability. Intrusion tolerance is emerging as one of the most important R&D areas in cyberoperations today because the systems and networks we depend on must continue to operate through intrusions and keep operating, although in a degraded mode, in spite of a sequence of successful cyberattacks.

Classification of Survivability Technologies

We can classify existing survivability technologies into two categories: intrusion masking and defense in depth. Note that well-known intrusion tolerance projects include the MAFTIA (Information Society Technologies, 2004) and OASIS (Information Processing Technology Office, 2004) projects.

Intrusion Masking

From the design perspective, one system design can be inherently much more *attack resilient* than another. The goal of intrusion masking is to redesign a regular vulnerable computer system with enough redundancy so that the new survivable design can function correctly even when part of the system is hacked. In this sense, we say the new survivable design can *mask* intrusions. Techniques in this category focus on how to enhance the inherent resilience of a secure system, and their effectiveness is typically much less sensitive to the agility and accuracy of intrusion detection than pragmatic, run-time intrusion response techniques. General principles in developing attack-resistant designs include but are not limited to (a) redundancy and replication (b) diversity (c) randomization (d) fragmentation and threshold cryptography and (e) increased layers of indirections. Techniques in this perspective include but not limited to Byzantine intrusion masking techniques (Castro & Liskov, 1999; Malkhi, Merritt, Reiter, & Taubenfield, 2003; Schneider, 1990; Sekar, Bendre, & Bollineni, 2001) that follow the redundancy and replication principle, threshold-cryptography-based attack resilient systems (Jing et al., 2003; Zhou, Schneider, & Renesse, 2002; Wylie et al., 2000) that follow the fragmentation principle, multipath routing (Vutukury & Garcia-Luna-Aceves, 2001) that follow the redundancy principle, and resilient overlay networks (Anderson, Balakrishnan, Kaashoek, & Morris, 2001) that follow the "increased layers of indirections" principle.

Defense in Depth

Instead of redesigning a system, the goal of defense in depth technologies is to arm the system with a set of attack that threat response facilities that, with the help of the intrusion detection, can respond to intrusions in such a way that the system can operate through attacks. Technologies in this category include (a) *boundary controllers* such as firewalls and access control (b) *intrusion detection* and (c) *threat/attack/intrusion response*. It is well known that boundary controllers cannot prevent every attack.

Intrusion detection (Lee, Stolfo, & Mok, 1999; Lunt, 1993; Jukherjee, Heberlein, & Levitt, 1994; Ning, Cui, & Reeves, 2002; Sekar et al., 2001; Debar, Cadier, & Wespi, 1999) is a key part of many survivable systems, but existing intrusion detection technologies in general suffer the high false positive (negative) rate problem, especially when the detection is anomaly based or specification based. Because intrusion detection techniques cannot guide us to respond to intrusions, existing defense-in-depth technologies focus on intrusion response, which can be classified into three categories as follows:

Type 1: Reactive response. Techniques in this category are activated only when an intrusion is identified and their effectiveness is highly dependent on the accuracy and latency of intrusion detection. For example, attack recovery techniques (Ammann, Jajodia, & Liu, 2002; Liu, Ammann, & Jajodia, 2000; Yu, Lium, & Zang, 2004) belong to this category. If the detection is quick and accurate, then the contaminated part of the system can be quickly repaired without causing serious integrity degradation. However, if there are many false alarms, a lot of clean elements could be corrupted by wrong "repairs." Some other Type 1 techniques include but are not limited to reactive one-phase damage containment techniques, detection-based (firewall) reconfiguration techniques, and patching techniques.

Type 2: Proactive response. Techniques in this category are activated in a proactive manner based on suspicious activities (or signs) before an intrusion is confirmed. Although proactive response may consume more resources, it may immunize the system from the damage caused by many attacks. Moreover, many proactive response mechanisms are transparent to users. Type 2 techniques include but are not limited to isolation (Liu, Jajodia, & McCollum, 2000), multiphase damage containment (Liu & Jajodia, 2001), and sandboxing (Malkhi & Reiter, 2000).

Type 3: Adaptive response. Feedback-based adaptation is a nice feature of many survivable systems, where the defense posture (i.e., security mechanism configuration) of the system is dynamically adjusted based on the changing environment. Adaptive response addresses the reconfigurable computing and communication aspect of survivable information systems. Type 3 techniques include but are not limited to the OASIS Willard project and adaptive ITDB (Luenam & Liu, 2002).

Because intrusion detection makes the system attack aware but not attack resilient, that is, intrusion detection itself cannot maintain confidentiality, integrity, and availability of information in the face of attacks, intrusion response is crucial is building survivable systems. Moreover, because the fundamental sciences, principles, and arts of survivable systems and networks are almost the same, we do not address systems and networks separately; instead, we focus on these common sciences, principles, and arts. Finally, malicious code defense is an important aspect of IA, but this aspect is not addressed in this chapter.

Survivability versus Fault Tolerance

As a core concept of the third generation IA technologies, survivability (Ellison et al., 1999) builds on the top of several related fields of study (e.g., security, fault tolerance, safety, reliability) and introduces new concepts and principles. In particular, because many survivability technologies are motivated by fault tolerance technologies, people may wonder about the differences between these two fields. In the following, we highlight three major differences between survivability and fault tolerance.

First, in fault tolerance, failures randomly happen; but in security, attacks are typically intentional and do not randomly happen. Moreover, attacks are more intelligent and active (i.e., more intentional and better planned) than failures, so more proactive tolerance techniques are needed for survivability.

Second, intrusion detection is typically much more complicated than failure detection. This is why there are so many new research challenges in intrusion detection.

Third, in the literature of fault tolerance, intrusions in many cases are modeled and tolerated as Byzantine faults, or arbitrary faults. Therefore, if a system is Byzantine fault tolerant, it is able to tolerate intrusions in some degree. BFT (Castro & Liskov, 1999), a practical Byzantine fault tolerant system, can tolerate both faults and intrusions. However, it should be noticed that not all damages to the system are caused by faults and not all intrusions can be modeled as Byzantine faults. For example, successful intrusions at the application level (e.g., corrupted transactions of database systems) and data corruption usually do not appear as faults and cannot be handled by Byzantine fault tolerance.

INTRUSION MASKING TECHNOLOGIES

In this section, we survey four representative intrusion masking technologies, namely survivable storage systems, intrusion masking distributed computing, attack resistant certification authority, and survivable network systems.

Survivable Information Storage Systems

As society increasingly relies on digitally stored and processed information, supporting the availability, integrity, and confidentiality of this information is crucial. We need systems in which users can securely store critical information, ensuring that it persists, is continuously accessible, cannot be destroyed, and is kept confidential. A *survivable storage system* would provide these guarantees over time and despite malicious compromises of storage node subnets.

In Deswarte, Blain, and Favre (1991) and Wylie et al. (2000), how to build a survivable distributed information storage system (e.g., a distributed file storage system) has been investigated. Current distributed file systems are not survivable; whenever a node is hacked, the attacker can not only know the content of the files stored on that node but also modify or destroy them. In Deswarte, Blain, and Favre (1991), a fragmentation-based survivability design is proposed, where (a) every file is fragmented into a set of *fragments* before it is stored on a storage node (b) fragments are replicated to yield more availability and (c) fragment *replicas* of a file are carefully scattered across the network of storage nodes in such a way that when a node is broken, the attacker can never get a complete set of the fragments for this file. Moreover, to prevent the attacker from getting partial information about the file from the fragments he captures after breaking into a node, each file is encrypted before fragmentation and the ciphertext fragments are made interdependent on each other (using such technique as CBC mode encryption), and the ensemble order among the fragments for the file is kept confidential. In this way, when the attacker captures a set of encrypted fragments, even if he or she knows the key, he or she is still unable to decrypt these fragments (in most cases).

In Wylie et al. (2000), a different secret-sharing-based survivable design, called PASIS, is proposed, although the goal is also to develop a survivable information storage system. The PASIS architecture, shown in Figure 1, flexibly and efficiently combines decentralized storage systems, data redundancy and encoding, and dynamic self-maintenance to achieve survivable information storage. A PASIS system applies threshold cryptography schemes (Shamir, 1979) to spread information across a decentralized collection of storage nodes. Client-side agents communicate with the collection of storage nodes to read and write information, hiding decentralization from the client system. Automated monitoring and repair agents on storage nodes provide self-maintenance features.

In particular, in PASIS an $m - n$ secret sharing scheme is used to break a data object (e.g., a file) into n *shares* so that (a) every shareholder (i.e., a storage node) has one of the shares (b) any m of the shareholders can reconstruct the object but (c) a group of fewer than m shareholders cannot gain any information about the object. Note that

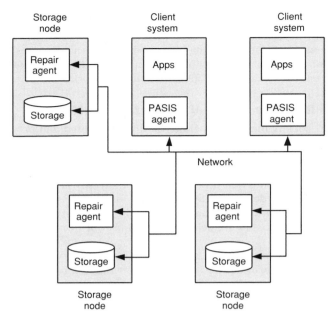

Figure 1: The PASIS architecture. Client systems and storage nodes are attached to the network. Client applications interact with a PASIS storage system through a PASIS agent. Storage devices and repair agents that monitor system status comprise the storage nodes.

a share in Wylie et al. (2000) and a fragment in Deswarte, Blain, and Favre (1991) are very different. A (cleartext) fragment can tell the attacker partial information about the corresponding data object, but a share could tell the attacker nothing about the data object. This nice property of secret-sharing schemes allows PASIS to achieve the same amount of security as Deswarte, Blain, and Favre (1991) without doing any encryption.

Correspondingly, the read and write operations need to be redesigned in PASIS. In particular, when a client reads a file, first, the client will look up, in the directory service, the names of the n shares that comprise the file. Second, the client sends read requests to at least m of the n storage nodes. Third, the client collects the responses. Fourth, the client reconstructs the file. Conversely, when a client writes a file, the client needs to a set of operations similar to those involved in a read except that the write operation does not complete until at least $n - m + 1$ (or m, whichever is greater) storage nodes have stored their shares.

In summary, the PASIS architecture illustrates the following ideas in building survivable storage systems. First, use *decentralized storage systems* to partition information among nodes. "Using data distribution and redundancy schemes commonly associated with disk array systems such as RAID (redundant array of independent disks) ensures scalable performance and fault tolerance" (Wylie et al., 2000). "Elimination of single failure points provides a starting point for developing survivable storage systems" (Wylie et al., 2000).

Second, exploit *data redundancy and encoding*. Threshold or secret-sharing schemes provide both information confidentiality and availability. "These schemes encode,

replicate, and divide information into multiple pieces (or shares) that can be stored at different storage nodes" (Wylie et al., 2000). The system can only construct the information when enough shares are available. Third, perform *dynamic self-maintenance*. "Over time, all systems need maintenance. Truly survivable systems automatically perform some self-maintenance includes regular monitoring for potential problems, such as failed or compromised nodes, performance bottlenecks, and denial-of-service attacks" (Wylie et al., 2000).

Finally, accomplish good trade-offs among information confidentiality, information availability, and storage requirements. Different threshold schemes will yield different confidentiality, availability, and storage requirements trade-offs. For example, as n increases, information availability increases (it is more probable that m shares are available), but the storage required for the information increases (more shares are stored) and confidentiality decreases (there are more shared to steal).

Intrusion Masking Distributed Computing

As businesses and applications are becoming more and more distributed (on the Internet), distributed computing and distributed software are more and more popular. To satisfying the IA needs of these distributed businesses and applications, survivable distributed computing is in urgent need. Nevertheless, distribution of computing can make information systems more vulnerable because the hacker will have more choices regarding where and when to enforce the attack; and any local breach may lead to serious global compromise through the interdependencies among distributed operations.

Distributed software is often structured in terms of clients and services. Each service comprises one or more servers and exports operations that clients invoke by making requests. Although using a single centralized server is the simplest way to implement a service, the resulted service can only be as secure and reliable as that server. If this level of fault and intrusion tolerance is unacceptable, then multiple servers that fail independently must be used. Usually, replicas of a single server are executed on separate processors of a distributed system, and protocols are used to coordinate client interactions with these replicas. Moreover, to make a replicated system more resilient to attacks, various *diversifying* technologies such as diverse operating systems can be used.

The *state machine (replication) approach* (Schneider, 1990) is a general method for implementing an intrusion-masking service by replicating servers and coordinating client interactions with server replicas. In this approach, an intrusion-masking server (modeled as a state machine) is implemented by replicating that server (i.e., both services and data) and running a (server) *replica* on each of the nodes in a distributed system. In the state machine approach, given the same sequence of requests (from probably a set of clients) to each replica, a group of nonfaulty replicas that start consistent (i.e., having the same state) will remain consistent (after the sequence of requests are processed). Hence, when a group of server replicas is serving a set of clients, if the requests of the clients can be delivered to the replicas in such a way that the same sequence of requests will always be received by each replica, then if the group has $2t + 1$ replicas, it can *mask t* intruded replicas, because each client can use majority voting to identify both the correct and the malicious responses.

Ensuring that the same sequence of requests (i.e., the same messages and the same order) will be delivered to each replica is, however, fairly difficult, because of the complexities of the networking environment and the fact that any node or (communication) link in a distributed system could be faulty or vulnerable. For one example, if we let a replica be the (designated) *sender* that transmits the clients' messages (or requests) to the other replicas, then if the sender is faulty, the group of replicas can receive inconsistent requests. Conversely, even if the sender is not faulty, communication failures can still cause replicas to receive inconsistent or differently ordered requests. For another example, if we let each client directly send its requests to each replica, then even if nothing is faulty, two replicas could receive two requests from two clients, respectively, in different orders, because of delay and competition. According to Schneider (1990), two requirements need to be satisfied to achieve this goal: (a) *consistency*, whereby every nonfaulty server replica receives every request, and (b) *total order*, whereby every nonfaulty replica processes the requests it receives in the same relative order. Developing the protocols that can satisfy these two requirements has raised a tremendous amount of interests, and fortunately as a result, a family of reliable totally ordered group communication services that can satisfy the two requirements are developed (e.g., Reiter, 1994). And these protocols (or services) have naturally become a key component of a typical implementation of the state machine approach. Because the state machine approach can handle arbitrary Byzantine faults such as software bugs, operator mistakes, and malicious attacks, the corresponding systems (services) built using this approach are also called Byzantine fault tolerant distributed systems (services). Nevertheless, to guarantee correctness and security, in general these reliable totally ordered group communication services require that fewer than one-third of replica group members be faulty. Therefore, a survivable distribute computing system built using the state machine approach actually uses $3k + 1$ or more server replicas to mask k intruded replicas.

Although many solutions for state machine replication have been proposed, state machine replication has not been widely deployed in the real world primarily because of the fact that most of these solutions have significant performance overhead (another reason might be that once one replica is compromised, it is fairly easy to compromise the remaining replicas). To mitigate this problem, in Castro and Liskov (1999) a new practical algorithm for state machine replication called *BFT* is proposed, which can be used to build highly survivable systems that tolerate Byzantine faults. BFT shows how to build Byzantine fault tolerant systems that can be used in practice to implement real services because they do not rely on unrealistic assumptions and they perform well. Many existing solutions for state machine replication rely on *synchrony*

assumption for correctness (i.e., rely on know bounds on message delays and process speeds, which is dangerous in the presence of malicious attacks). An attacker may compromise the safety of a service by delaying nonfaulty nodes or the communication between them until they are tagged as faulty and excluded from the replica group. Such a denial of service attack is generally easier than gaining control over a nonfaulty node.

In contrast, BFT works in *asynchronous* environments such as the Internet, it incorporates mechanisms to defend against Byzantine faulty replicas, and it recovers replicas proactively. The recovery mechanism allows the algorithm to tolerate any number of faults over the lifetime of the system provided less than *one-third* of the replicas become faulty within a small window of vulnerability. The window may increase under a denial of service attack but the algorithm can detect and respond to such attacks and it can also detect when the state of a replica is corrupted by an attacker. BFT has been implemented as a generic program library with a simple interface. The BFT library provides a complete solution to the problem of building real services that tolerate Byzantine faults. The library is used to implement the first Byzantine fault tolerant NFS file system, BFS. The BFT library and BFS perform well because the library incorporates several important optimizations. The most important optimization is the use of symmetric cryptography to authenticate messages. Public key cryptography, which was the major bottleneck in previous systems, is used only to exchange the symmetric keys. The performance results show that BFS performs 2% faster compared to 24% slower than production implementations of the NFS protocol that are not replicated. Therefore, the BFT library is believed to be able to be used to build practical systems that tolerate Byzantine faults. Accordingly, in Yu, Liu, and Zhang (2003) BFT is extended to build practical Byzantine fault tolerant two-phase commit protocols (BFT-2PC) to tolerate both malicious coordinator and malicious participants in distributed transaction processing.

Finally, although BFT is quite efficient when the replica group is relatively small, BFT may not scale well for large groups. To improve scalability, a technology called *Byzantine Quorum* is proposed (Malkhi & Reiter, 1998), where quorum replication techniques are applied to achieve Byzantine fault tolerance in asynchronous systems. This technology may provide more scalability because each operation is processed by only a subset of replicas instead of every replica. Nevertheless, this approach to scalability is fairly expensive: it requires $n > 4f + 1$ to tolerate f faults; each replica needs a copy of the state; and the load of each replica decreases slowly with n (it is $O(1/\sqrt{n})$).

Attack Resistant Certification Authority

In a public key infrastructure, a *certificate* specifies a binding between a name and a set of attributes especially the public key. Certificates are the core of PKI technologies. "Over time, public keys and attributes can change: a private key might be compromised, leading to selection of a new public key, for example. The old binding and any certificate that specifies that binding then become *invalid."* A *certification authority* (CA) attests to the validity of bindings by issuing digitally signed certificates that certify these bindings and by providing a means for clients to check the validity of certificates. "With an online CA, principals can check the validity of certificates just before using them" (Zhou et al., 2002). An online CA needs not only to be secure (the CA's private key cannot be compromised) but also to be available and reliable, which is exactly the goal of survivable CA.

COCA (Cornell certification authority) (Zhou et al., 2002) is a fault tolerant and secure online certification authority that has been built and deployed both in a local area network and on the Internet. Extremely weak assumptions characterize environments in which COCA's protocols execute correctly: no assumption is made about execution speed and message delivery delays (i.e., COCA assumes asynchrony, channels are expected to exhibit only intermittent reliability and with $3t + 1$ COCA servers up to t may be faulty or compromised). These extremely weak assumptions inversely make COCA extremely resilient to malicious attacks. COCA is the first system to integrate a Byzantine quorum system (Malkhi & Reiter, 1998; used to achieve availability and scalability) with threshold cryptography and proactive recovery (used to defend against mobile adversaries which attack, compromise, and control one replica for a limited period of time before moving on to another). In addition to tackling problems associated with combining fault tolerance and security, COCA develops new proactive recovery protocols and gives a quantitative evaluation on its cost and effectiveness.

The idea of COCA has four major aspects. First, the CA service is supported by a set of replicated COCA servers, but the private key of the CA service (namely the signing key) is held by no COCA server. Instead, different shares of the key are stored on each of the servers, and threshold cryptography is used to construct signatures on responses and certificates. To sign a message from a client, each COCA server generates a *partial signature* from the message and that server's share of the service private key, some COCA server combines these partial signatures and obtains the signed message. In this way, even when several COCA servers are compromised, the private key will still not be disclosed if the number of compromised servers is below the threshold of the scheme.

Second, to be resilient to server failures and provide more availability, every client request is processed by multiple servers and every certificate is replicated on multiple servers. (Note that COCA supports two types of requests: a query request retrieves a certificate, whereas an update request creates, updates, or invalidates a certificate.) The replication is managed as a dissemination Byzantine quorum system (Malkhi & Reiter, 1998), where servers are organized by COCA into sets, called *quorums*, and, accordingly, each client request is processed by a quorum instead of every replica server. However, because a client making a request cannot authenticate messages from a COCA server (because in COCA clients do not know server public keys) and therefore cannot determine whether a quorum of servers has processed that request, COCA let some servers become *delegates* for each request. A delegate presides over the processing of a client request and

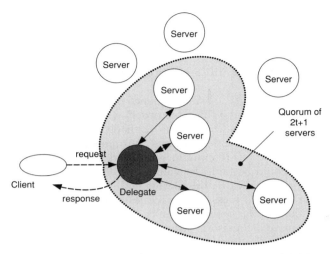

Figure 2: Overview of client request processing in COCA.

assembles the needed partial signatures from other COCA servers. A client request is handled by $t + 1$ delegates to ensure that at least one of the delegates is correct.

Figure 2 gives a high-level overview of how COCA operates by depicting one of the $t + 1$ delegates and the quorum of servers working with that delegate to handle a client request. The figure shows a client making its request by sending a signed message to $t + 1$ COCA servers. Each server that receives this message assumes the role of delegate for the request. A delegate engages a quorum of servers to handle the request and constructs a response to the request based on the responses (i.e., partial signatures) received from that quorum. The delegate then assembles these responses into a signature signed by the CA service. After receiving this signature, the client checks that the response is correctly signed by the service and incorrectly signed responses will be discarded.

Third, a mobile adversary might compromise $t + 1$ servers over a period of time and, in doing so, collect the $t + 1$ shares of the service private key. To counter this attack, COCA employs a proactive secret-sharing (PSS) protocol to refresh these shares, periodically generating a new set of shares for the service private key and deleting the old set. New shares cannot be combined with old shares to construct signatures. Fourth, to support the asynchrony assumption, COCA develops an asynchronous PSS protocol.

COCA is motivated by an earlier work denoted Ω ("Omega") (Reiter, Franklin, Lacy, & Wright, 1996). Ω is a survivable key management service for open networks whose goal is to provide flexible and powerful interfaces to meet the demands of an ever widening range of applications. Ω provides the flexibility of an online server without incurring the fault tolerance or security vulnerabilities usually associated with such servers. Ω is built on top of the Byzantine quorum technology, but it does not involve threshold cryptography. Finally, in addition to distributed survivable CA such as COCA and Ω, in Jing et al. (2003) a centralized attack resilient CA called ARECA is proposed that is built on the top of threshold cryptography and a new *two-phase signature generation* technique.

Survivable Network Systems

In Anderson et al. (2001) resilient overlay network architectures are addressed. A "Resilient Overlay Network (RON) is an architecture that allows distributed Internet applications to detect and recover from path outages and periods of degraded performance within several seconds, improving over today's wide-area routing protocols that take at least several minutes to recover" (Anderson et al., 2001). "A RON is an application-layer overlay on top of the existing Internet routing substrate. The RON nodes monitor the functioning and quality of the Internet paths among themselves, and use this information to decide whether to route packets directly over the Internet or by way of other RON nodes, optimizing application-specific routing metrics" (Anderson et al., 2003). It is clear that a RON can mask such attacks as distributed denial of service attacks and attacks on routers and physical communication links.

Results from two sets of measurements of a working RON deployed at sites scattered across the Internet demonstrate the benefits of the RON architecture. For instance, over a 64-hr sampling period in March 2001 across a 12-node RON, there were 32 significant outages, each lasting over 30 min, over the 132 measured paths. RON's routing mechanism was able to detect, recover, route around all of them, in less than twenty seconds on average, showing that its methods for fault (and intrusion) detection and recovery work well at discovering alternate paths in the Internet. Furthermore, RON was able to improve the loss rate, latency, or throughput perceived by data transfers; for example, about 5% of the transfers doubled their TCP throughput and 5% of transfers saw their loss probability reduced by 0.05.

RON node is sufficient to overcome faults or intrusions and improve performance in most cases. These improvements, particularly in the area of fault detection and recovery, demonstrate the benefits of moving some of the control over routing into the hands of end systems.

DEFENSE IN DEPTH TECHNOLOGIES

Compared with intrusion masking technologies, where many attacks may be masked without causing any system security (e.g., integrity and availability) degradation, defense in depth technologies usually would introduce certain level of system security degradation. Conversely, the advantage of defense in depth technologies is that (a) they do not require the system to be redesigned and can be directly applied to legacy systems and (b) their overhead is typically smaller than intrusion masking technologies.

The key issues and problems in developing defense in depth technologies are as follows:

- How to quickly *contain/isolate* the intrusions so that their infection will not be too serious to operate through.
- How to quickly distinguish the damaged part for the undamaged part of the system.
- How to quickly repair the contaminated part of the system without bringing it offline.
- How to handle the impact of false alarms, undetected intrusions, and the detection latency.

- How to make the intrusion response facilities adaptive and proactive.
- How to validate the cost effectiveness of defense in depth technologies.

In the rest of this section, we break the possible defense in depth technologies into subsections. In the first subsection, we discuss phases of in-depth defense. In the second subsection, we use an intrusion tolerant database system to illustrate some important techniques of defense in depth.

Phases of Defense in Depth

In the literature, defense in depth is usually referred to as information warfare defense. Information warfare defense does everything possible to prevent attacks from succeeding, but it also assumes that not all attacks will be averted at the outset. This places increased emphasis on the ability to live through and recover from successful attacks. Information warfare defense must consider all phases of the attack and recovery process. These phases, and the activities that occur in each, are proposed in Ammann, Jajodia, McCollum, and Blaustein (1997) and quoted as follows:

- *Prevention*: the defender puts protective measures in place.
- *Intelligence gathering*: the attacker observes the system to determine its vulnerabilities and find the most critical functions or data to target.
- *Attack*: the attacker carries out the resulting attack plan.
- *Detection*: the defender observes symptoms of a problem and determines that an attack may have taken place or be in progress.
- *Containment*: the defender takes immediate action to eliminate the attacker's access to the system and to isolate or contain the problem, preventing it from spreading further.
- *Damage assessment*: the defender determines the extent of the problem, including failed functions and corrupted data.
- *Reconfiguration*: the defender may reconfigure to allow continued operation in a degraded mode while recovery proceeds.
- *Repair*: the defender recovers corrupted or lost data and repairs or reinstalls failed system functions to reestablish normal operations.
- *Fault treatment*: to the greatest extent possible, the defender identifies weaknesses exploited in the attack and takes steps to prevent a recurrence.

Some phases, such as prevention, intelligence gathering, detection, containment, reconfiguration, and repair, lend themselves to automated mechanisms and support within the system being attacked. Others, such as fault treatment and some aspects of damage assessment, typically require human intervention.

It should be noticed that the above phases are motivated by the life cycle of fault tolerance. Fault tolerance is a natural approach for dealing with information attacks because it is designed to address system loss, compromise, and damage during operation. Traditional fault tolerance approach phases include detection, containment, adaptation, and recovery. Fault semantics for information attacks differ from the traditional fault tolerance model because in such cases faults are intentionally introduced and malicious, and some attacks may be disguised to appear like normal operations. Therefore, semantics for countermeasures must differ correspondingly, as mentioned under.

The information warfare defender's goal is to keep the system operating to support as much critical processing as possible, even if the system is contaminated (or infected) by an attack. One way to ensure continued service is to explicitly address integrity losses caused to the systems in the presence of information warfare attacks. To some degree, real systems lack integrity most of the time. These integrity losses do not always prevent the systems from achieving their critical objectives. The challenge in information warfare is to anticipate acceptable integrity losses and design systems to operate in these degraded modes.

Survivable Database Systems

Existing survivable database technologies can be roughly broken into two categories: *transaction-based* database survivability (Ammann et al., 2002; Liu et al., 2004; Smirnov & Chiueh, 2004), which enables a database to operate through attacks via identifying and "rolling back" malicious and affected transactions, and *data-object-based* database survivability (Panda & Giordano, 1998), which enables a database to operate through attacks via identifying and repairing each corrupted data object. In this section, we use ITDB (Intrusion Tolerant Data Base) to illustrate the design principles of survivable database systems.

ITDB (Ammann et al., 2002; Liu, 2002; Liu et al., 2000a, 2000b, 2004) is a transaction-level self-healing database framework. Because preventing malicious transaction from being executed is in general not a realistic solution, ITDB focuses on how to enable a database to *heal* itself under sustained malicious transaction attacks in such a way that the database can continue delivering (to a large extent valid) transaction-processing services in the face of such attacks.

ITDB focuses on the intrusions enforced by authorized but malicious transactions. ITDB views a database as a set of data *objects*. At a moment, the *state* of the database is determined by the values of these objects. The database is accessed by transactions for the ACID properties. A *transaction* is a partial order of *read* and *write* operations that either *commits* or *aborts*. The execution of a transaction usually transforms the database for one state to another. Moreover, ITDB models the (usually concurrent) execution of a set of transactions by a structure called a *history*.

ITDB focuses on the *damage* caused by malicious, committed transactions. Because an *active*, malicious transaction will not cause any damage before it commits (due to the *atomicity* property), it is theoretically true that if we can detect every malicious transaction before

it commits, then we can roll back the transaction before it causes any damage. However, this "perfect" solution is not practical for two reasons. First, transaction execution is, in general, much quicker than detection, and slowing down transaction execution can cause very serious denial of service. For example, the Microsoft SQL Server can execute over 1000 (TPC-C) transactions within 1 s, whereas the average anomaly *detection latency* is typically in the scale of minutes or seconds (because of the difficulty of anomaly detection).

Hence ITDB is motivated by the following practical goal: "After the database is damaged, locate the damaged part and repair it as soon as possible, so that the database can continue being useful in the face of attacks." In other words, ITDB wants to provide sustained levels of data integrity and availability to applications in the face of attacks. The major components of ITDB are shown in Figure 3. Note that all operations of ITDB are on-the-fly without blocking the execution of (most) normal user transactions. The job of the *intrusion detector* is to identify malicious transactions. In the rest of this section, we give an overview of the jobs that the other ITDB components do.

The complexity of ITDB is mainly caused by a phenomenon called *damage spreading*. In a database, the results of one transaction can affect the execution of some other transactions. Informally, when a transaction T_i reads an object x updated by another transaction T_j, T_i is directly *affected* by T_j. If a third transaction T_k is affected by T_i, but not directly affected by T_j, T_k is indirectly affected by T_j. It is easy to see that when a (relatively old) transaction B_i that updates x is identified malicious, the damage on x can spread to every object updated by a *good* transaction that is affected by B_i, directly or indirectly. The job of the *damage assessor* is to identify every affected good transaction. The job of the *damage repairer* is to recover the database from the damage caused on the objects updated by malicious transactions as well as affected good transactions. In particular, when an affected transaction is located, the damage repairer builds a specific *cleaning* transaction to clean each object updated by the transaction (and not cleaned yet). Cleaning an object is simply done by restoring the value of the object to its latest undamaged version. This job gets even more difficult as the execution of new transactions continues because the damage can spread to new transactions and cleaned objects can be redamaged. Therefore, the main objective of ITDB is to guarantee that damage spreading is (dynamically) controlled in such a way that the database will not be damaged to a degree that is useless.

The developers of ITDB believe the single most challenging problem in developing practical, cost-effective self-healing database systems (e.g., ITDB) is that during the detection latency, a tremendous amount of damage spreading can be caused. This is because of the fact that intrusion detection is in general much slower than transaction processing. So when a malicious transaction is detected, a lot of affected transactions may have already been committed. Therefore, a practical, cost-effective self-healing database system must be able to live with substantially longer detection latency relative to transaction processing.

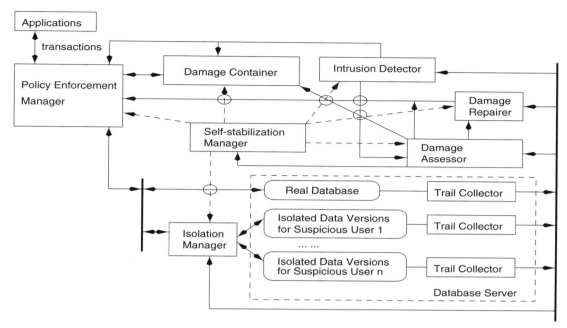

Figure 3: The ITDB architecture.

A unique technical contribution of ITDB is that it can live with long detection latency without suffering serious damage spreading. Allowing long detection latency not only lowers ITDB's requirement on detection agility, but also indirectly lowers ITDB's requirements on detection rate and false alarm rate, because in many cases, longer detection latency can lead to higher detection rate and lower false alarm rate.

However, living with long detection latency is not an easy task. In ITDB, the impact of detection latency is threefold as follows: (1) during the detection latency, the damage can spread to many objects; (2) a significant *assessment latency* can be caused, and during the assessment latency the damage can further spread to many more objects; (3) significant assessment latency can cause ineffective—to some degree at least—damage containment. These three aspects of impact can cause the database to be too damaged to be useful. The job of the isolation manager and the damage container is to mitigate this impact.

It is easy to see that if every malicious transaction B_i can be identified just after it commits, very little damage can spread, and damage assessment can be done quickly. However, with significant detection latency, when B_i is identified, in the history there can already be many good transactions following B_i and many of them may have already been affected by B_i. Damage assessment at this situation can cause substantial delay, because as shown in (Ammann et al., 2002) damage assessment can spend substantial computation time to scan a long subhistory log for identifying the affected transactions.

Significant assessment latency could cause ineffective damage confinement. At first glance, it seems that to prevent damage spreading during repair, containing the damage that is located by the damage assessor is a good idea. However, in this approach damage will not be contained until an object is identified by the damage assessor as damaged. Hence damage containment depends on damage assessment. As a result, when there is a significant latency in locating a damaged object x, during the latency many new transactions may read x and spread the damage on x to the objects updated by them. As a result, when x is confined many other objects may have already been damaged, and the situation can feed on itself and become worse because as the damage spreads the assessment latency could become even longer. This clearly contradicts with our original motivation of damage containment.

ITDB tackles the three challenges through two novel techniques: attack isolation and multiphase damage containment. Although working toward the same goal, the isolation manager and the damage container take two very different approaches. And these two approaches compensate each other. In particular, the damage container takes a novel *multiphase* damage containment approach that first instantly contains the damage that might have been caused by an intrusion as soon as the intrusion is identified and then tries to uncontain the objects that are previously contained by mistake. Multiphase damage containment can ensure that no damage will spread during the assessment latency, although with some availability lost. However, the damage container can do nothing to reduce the damage caused during the detection latency. In contrast, the isolate manager can reduce the damage caused during the detection latency (thus it indirectly reduces the damage caused during the assessment latency) by isolating the execution of a *suspicious* transaction that is very likely to cause damage later on. Isolation immunizes the database from the damage caused by the set of suspicious transactions without sacrificing substantial availability, because if an isolated user turns out to be innocent, most—if not all—of his or her updates can be merged back to the real database.

Finally, the job of the *self-stabilization manager* (SSM) is to dynamically reconfigure the other ITDB components based on (a) the current attacks, (b) the current workload, (c) the current system state, and (d) the current defense *behavior* of ITDB, in such a way that stabilized levels of data integrity and availability can be provided to applications in a cost-effective way. Factors (a), (b), and (c) are called the *environment* of ITDB. The jobs of the *policy enforcement manager* (PEM) are to proxy user transactions and enforce systemwide intrusion tolerance policies. For example, a policy may require the PEM to reject every new transaction submitted by a user as soon as the intrusion detector finds that a malicious transaction is executed by the user. Intrusion response policies and security manager interfaces are certainly a crucial aspect of ITDB. In summary, ITDB develops a family of novel defense in depth techniques, such as on-the-fly attack recovery, multiphase damage containment, attack isolation, and rule-based adaptive intrusion tolerance.

From the self-healing perspective, ITDB considers recovery from malicious but committed transactions. Traditional recovery mechanisms do not address this problem, except for complete *rollbacks* to a previous *checkpoint*, which undo the work of good transactions as well as malicious ones, and compensating transactions, whose utility depends on application semantics. ITDB develops two attack recovery mechanisms: on-the-fly repair and history rewriting. For on-the-fly repair, instead of rolling back the database to the latest checkpoint, the *write–read dependency* between transactions is analyzed on the fly to determine which good transactions are affected by a bad transaction, directly or indirectly. Then a specific *cleaning transaction* is composed to clean the infection caused by each malicious or affected transaction, and the concurrency control algorithm is adapted in such a way that new user transactions can be executed simultaneously together with cleaning transactions without affecting the correctness of repair. Finally, when an on-the-fly repair terminates with all the damage repaired, ITDB can detect the termination in a timely manner.

For history rewriting, ITDB rewrites execution histories for the purpose of backing out malicious transactions (Liu et al., 2000b). Good transactions that are a directly or indirectly, by malicious transactions complicate the process of backing out undesirable transactions. The prefix of a rewritten history produced by the algorithm serializes exactly the set of unaffected good transactions. The suffix of the rewritten history includes special state information to describe a good transactions as well as malicious transactions. ITDB can extract additional good transactions from this latter part of a rewritten history. The latter processing saves more good transactions than is possible with a dependency graph based approach to recovery.

Finally, in Yu et al. (2004), a self-healing workflow system is proposed. Compared with ITDB, Yu et al. (2004) considers more types of dependency relations and introduces a set of theorems to trace damage spreading, construct repairing tasks, and create execution orders between recovery and normal tasks in such a way that correct, on-the-fly workflow attack recovery can be achieved.

CONCLUSION

As society increasingly relies on digitally stored and accessed information, applications have increasingly higher requirements on supporting the availability, integrity, and confidentiality of this information, and traditional information security technologies are increasingly limited in satisfying the security requirements of applications because of their inability to survive successful attacks. As a result, information assurance technologies are introduced to not only prevent information from being disclosed, modified, or destroyed, but also detect intrusions and operate through attacks in such a way that a certain level of information security can be ensured in the presence of attacks. In this chapter, we survey the natural evolution of information assurance technologies. Three generations of IA technologies are summarized, and the newest generation of IA technologies is discussed in detail. In summary, this chapter takes the first steps to give a comprehensive overview of the scope of IA technologies, the relation between the emerging survivability technologies and the more established IA technologies such as information security and intrusion detection technologies, the characteristics of survivability technologies, and the representative ideas, principles, and techniques of survivable systems development.

Although a variety of emerging IA technologies have been developed recently to ensure a certain level of information security in the presence of attacks for applications, existing IA technologies are still at their earlier stage and limited in many aspects, and advanced IA technologies have not been widely deployed in the real world so far. Hence, a lot of existing new IA technologies and practices are yet to come. Here we to mention several new research and development directions in IA technologies, which are illustrated as follows:

- The *threat* aspect of survivability. Without a tangible and accurate threat model, a highly assured information system cannot be developed. To build a good threat model, both the system's vulnerabilities and the attacks' characteristics (e.g., intent) are crucial. Some preliminary research has been done in analyzing the attacker's intent and strategies (e.g., Liu & Zang, 2003), but more research is certainly needed. Risk analysis is a relevant topic and readers can refer to Risk Assessment and Risk Management for information on this topic.

- Survivability requirements analysis. Without a clear specification of the users' *survivability requirements*, a survivable system may either overreact to attacks (and threats) or be not proactive enough, and the effectiveness of survivability mechanisms could not be well evaluated. Survivability requirements analysis is a challenging problem, especially when quantitative requirement specifications are expected.

- Survivability *metrics* and measurements. Information assurance metrics are scarce and qualitative. Given the need to determine the information assurance posture for a given organization under given conditions, users in the field require a means to determine the relative degree of assurance associated with the information assets under their control. Likewise, developers of survivable systems require metrics to measure the degree to which they are employing engineering practices during the system development process. The use of IA metrics would permit establishing trust in a system built from untrusted components, determining sufficient levels of security for the specific tactical situation and condition, and assessing system vulnerabilities. IA metrics enable quantitative tradeoffs between security and performance (degradation).

- *Service survivability*. Existing IA technologies largely focus on system survivability, but in many cases system survivability does not imply service survivability, and additional service survivability facilities and controls are needed. Service survivability are application oriented and at a higher level than system survivability.

- Wireless Information assurance. A key piece of the large-scale information enterprise is the wireless information assurance segment. Wireless networks must exhibit the same functional and IA attributes as wired networks. They must be protected; attacks against these networks must be detected; specifics of successful attacks must be assessed and finally appropriate responses must be carried out. As we move to more and more wireless components becoming a part of the larger network and as wireless networks proliferate, we need to be aware that these networks, if improperly understood and configured, could provide a "back-door" into our protected wired enterprise. Intrusion detection for wireless networks must be addressed as well as recovery of wireless services after adversary disruption/denial destruction of friendly networks.

- Using intrusion tolerant middleware (Courtney et al., 2003; Ramasamy, Pandey, Lyons, Cukier, & Sanders, 2002; Singh, Cukier, & Sanders, 2003) to facilitate the development of intrusion tolerant applications. In this way, developers may be relieved from substantial IA design and development issues.

ACKNOWLEDGMENT

This work was supported by NSF ANI-0335241, NSF CCR-0233324, and Department of Energy Early Career PI Award.

GLOSSARY

Assurance (a) The degree of confidence that a target of evaluation adequately fulfills the security requirements. (b) A measure of confidence that the security features and architecture of an automated information system accurately mediate and enforce the security policy. Note: The two main aspects of assurance are effectiveness and correctness or development and evaluation assurance.

Authenticity The ability (a) to establish the validity of a claimed identity and (b) to provide protection against fraudulent transactions by establishing the validity of a message, station, individual, or originator.

Availability (a) The ability to access a specific resource within a specific time frame as defined within the IT product specification. (b) The ability to use or access objects and resources as required. The property relates to the concern that information objects and other system resources are accessible when needed and without undue delay. (c) The prevention of the unauthorized withholding of information or resources.

Byzantine Fault Tolerance A Byzantine fault is one in which a component of some system not only behaves erroneously but also fails to behave consistently when interacting with other components. Correctly functioning components of a Byzantine fault tolerant system will be able to reach the same group decisions regardless of Byzantine faulty components.

Certificate A certificate is a document that attests to the truth or ownership of something. A digital certificate is a digital document that serves the same purpose. Most specifically, it attests to the truth that you are who you say you are and that you own the particular public key specified in the certificate.

Certification Authority A trusted third party who confirms the identity of an organization or individual (an entity).

Confidentiality Assurance that information is not disclosed to inappropriate entities or processes.

Fault Tolerance The ability of a system or component to continue normal operation despite the presence of hardware or software faults.

Integrity (a) Correctness and appropriateness of the content and/or source of a piece of information. (b) The prevention of the unauthorized modification of information. (c) Sound, unimpaired, or perfect condition.

Intrusion Detection A security service that monitors and analyzes system events to find and provide real-time or near-real-time attempt warnings to access system resources in an unauthorized manner. This is the detection of break-ins or break-in attempts by reviewing logs or other information available on a network.

Nonrepudiation An attribute of communications that seeks to prevent future false denial of involvement by either party. *Nonrepudiation with proof of origin* provides the recipient of data with evidence that proves the origin of the data.

Survivability The ability of a network computing system to provide essential services in the presence of attacks and failures and recover full services in a timely manner.

Vulnerability A hardware, firmware, communication, or software flaw that leaves a computer processing system open for potential exploitation, either externally or internally, thereby resulting in risk for the owner, user, or manager of the system.

CROSS REFERENCES

See *Active Response to Computer Intrusions; Electronic Attacks; Intrusion Detection Systems Basics.*

REFERENCES

Ammann, P., Jajodia, S., & Liu, P. (2002). Recovery from malicious transactions. *IEEE Transactions on Knowledge and Data Engineering, 15*(5), 1167–1185.

Ammann, P., Jajodia, S., McCollum, C. D., & Blaustein, B. T. (1997). Surviving information warfare attacks on databases. In *Proceedings of the IEEE Symposium on Research in Security and Privacy* (pp. 164–174).

Anderson, D. G., Balakrishnan, H., Kaashoek, M. F., & Morris, R. (2001). Resilient overlay networks. In *Proceedings of the 18th ACM Symposium on Operating Systems Principles*.

Castro, M., & Liskov, B. (1999). Practical Byzantine fault tolerance. In *Proceedings of the OSDI*.

Courtney, T., Lyons, J., Ramasamy, H. V., Sanders, W. H., Seri, M., Atighetchi, M., Rubel, P., Jones, C., Webber, F., Pal, P., Watro, R., Cukier, M., & Gossett, J. (2003). Providing intrusion tolerance with ITUA. In *Supplemental Volume of the 2002 International Conference on Dependable Systems & Networks (DSN-2002)* (C-5-1 to C-5-3).

Debar, H., Dacier, M., & Wespi, A. (1999). Towards a taxonomy of intrusion detection systems. *Computer Network, 31*, 805–822.

Deswarte, Y., Blain, L., & Fabre, J.-C. (1991). Intrustion tolerance in distributed computing systems. In *Proceedings of the IEEE Symposium on Research in Security and Privacy* (pp. 110–121).

Ellison, R. J., Fisher, D. A., Linger, R. C., Lipson, H. F., Longstaff, T. A., & Mead, N. R. (1999). Survivability: Protecting your critical systems. *IEEE Internet Computing, 3*(6), 55–63.

Information Processing Technology Office. (2004). *OASIS demonstration, integration and validation*. Retrieved January 2, 2005, from http://www.darpa.mil/ipto/programs/oasis_demval/

Information Society Technologies. (2004). *What was MAFTIA?* Retrieved January 3, 2005, from http://www.maftia.org/

Jing, J., Liu, P., Feng, D. G., Xiang, J., Gao, N., & Lin, J. Q. (2003). ARECA: A highly attack resilient certification authority. In *Proceedings of the ACM First Workshop on Survivable and Self-Regenerative Systems*.

Lee, W., Stolfo, S., & Mok, K. (1999). A data mining framework for building intrusion detection models. In *Proceedings of the IEEE Symposium on Research in Security and Privacy*.

Liu, P. (2002). Architectures for intrusion tolerant database systems. In *Proceedings of the 2002 Annual Computer Security Applications Conference* (pp. 311–320).

Liu, P., Ammann, P., & Jajodia, S. (2000). Rewriting histories: Recovery from malicious transactions. *Distributed and Parallel Databases, 8*(1), 7–40.

Liu, P., & Jajodia, S. (2001). Multi-phase damage confinement in database systems for intrusion tolerance. In *Proceedings of the 14th IEEE Computer Security Foundations Workshop* (pp. 191–205).

Liu, P., Jajodia, S., & McCollum, C. D. (2000). Intrusion confinement by isolation in information systems. *Journal of Computer Security*, 8(4), 243–279.

Liu, P., Jing, J., Luenam, P., Wang, Y., Li, L., & Ingsriswang, S. (2004). The design and implementation of a self-healing database system. *Journal of Intelligent Information Systems, 23*(3), 247–269.

Liu, P., & Zang, W. (2003). Incentive-based modeling and inference of attacker intent, objectives and strategies. In *Proceedings of the ACM CCS 2003*.

Luenam, P., & Liu, P. (2002). The design of an adaptive intrusion tolerant database system. In *Proceedings of the IEEE Workshop on Intrusion Tolerant Systems*.

Lunt, T. F. (1993). A survey of intrusion detection techniques. *Computers & Security, 12*(4), 405–418.

Malkhi, D., Merritt, M., Reiter, M. K., & Taubenfeld, G. (2003). Objects shared by Byzantine processes. *Distributed Computing, 16*(1), 37–48.

Malkhi, D., & Reiter, M. (1998). Byzantine quorum systems. *Distributed Computing, 11*, 203–213.

Malkhi, D., & Reiter, M. (2000). Secure execution of Java applets using a remote playground. *IEEE Transactions on Software Engineering, 26*(12).

Mukherjee, B., Heberlein, L. T., & Levitt, K. N. (1994). Network intrusion detection. *IEEE Network*, 26–41.

Ning, P., Cui, Y., & Reeves, D. S. (2002). Constructing attack scenarios through correlation of intrusion alerts. In *Proceedings of the ACM International Conference on Computer and Communications Security*.

Panda, B., & Giordano, J. (1998). Reconstructing the database after electronic attacks. In *Proceedings of the 1998 IFIP WG11.3 Working Conference on Database and Applications Security* (pp. 143–156).

Ramasamy, H. V., Pandey, P., Lyons, J., Cukier, M., & Sanders, W. H. (2002). Quantifying the cost of providing intrusion tolerance in group communication systems. In *Proceedings of the International Conference on Dependable Systems and Networks (DSN-2002)* (pp. 229–238).

Reiter, M. (1994). Secure agreement protocols: Reliable and atomic group multicast in rampart. In *Proceedings of the 2nd ACM Conference on Computer and Communications Security* (pp. 60–80).

Reiter, M., Franklin, M. K., Lacy, J. B., & Wright, R. N. (1996). The Ω Key Management Service. In *Proceedings of the ACM CCS, 1996*.

Schneider, F. B. (1990). Implementing fault tolerant services using the state machine approach: A tutorial. *ACM Computing Surveys, 22*(4).

Sekar, S., Bendre, M., & Bollineni, P. (2001). A fast automaton-based method for detecting anomalous program behaviors. In *Proceedings of the IEEE Symposium on Research in Security and Privacy*.

Shamir, A. (1979). How to share a secret. *Communications of the ACM*, 612–613.

Singh, S., Cukier, M., & Sanders, W. H. (2003). Probabilistic validation of an intrusion-tolerant replication system. In *Proceedings of the 2003 International Conference on Dependable Systems and Networks (DSN-2003)* (pp. 615–624).

Smirnov, A., & Chiueh, T. (2004). A portable implementation framework for intrusion-resilient database management systems. In *Proceedings of the 2004 IEEE International Conference on Dependable Systems and Networks*.

Vutukury, S., & Garcia-Luna-Aceves, J. J. (2001). MDVA: A distance-vector multipath routing protocol. In *Proceedings of the IEEE INFOCOM, 2001*.

Wylie, J., Bigrigg, M., Strunk, J., Ganger, G., Kiliccote, H., & Khosla, P. (2000). Survivable information storage systems. *IEEE Computer*.

Yu, M., Liu, P., & Zang, W. (2004). Self healing workflow systems under attacks. In *Proceedings of the 24th IEEE International Conference on Distributed Computing Systems*.

Yu, M., Liu, P., & Zhang, W. (2003). Intrusion masking for distributed atomic operations. In *Proceedings of the 2003 IFIP International Information Security Conference*.

Zhou, L., Schneider, F. B., & Renesse, R. V. (2002). COCA: A secure distributed online certification authority. *ACM Transactions on Computer Systems, 20*(4).

PART 2

Social and Legal Issues

The Legal Implications of Information Security: Regulatory Compliance and Liability

Blaze D. Waleski, *Fulbright & Jaworski LLP*

INTRODUCTION

Modern business is all but dependent upon information technology (IT), and reliance on the exchange of electronic information is rapidly becoming entrenched in our day-to-day personal lives (e.g., through the Internet, wireless devices, and other interactive means of data transfer). To an ever greater degree, business relies on technologies that connect with its customers, and with other businesses, for example, to streamline supply routes, control inventory, and minimize time to market, exchange services and products in business-to-business trade platforms, enhance distribution channels, boost sales through e-commerce, improve fulfillment operations, and enrich customer databases with valuable information concerning customer spending patterns and the like. There are, in fact, companies, such as Axciom Corporation, Abacus Direct, Equifax, Experian, and InfoUSA, that focus on compiling and aggregating consumer-related data.

The Internet has been the foremost catalyst of this business evolution, precipitating a global interconnectivity of computer systems that permits ready access by businesses and individuals to vast amounts of corporate and consumer information, which, thanks to advancements in IT, are becoming increasingly easy to access, search, and retrieve. A by-product of this evolving global electronic business model is the interdependence on the access to and sharing of data. IT—through software applications, hardware and communications equipment, networking systems, and the many related services—facilitates this access to and sharing of data.

Rethinking the Security of Data in Light of Modern IT

Modern IT, and particularly the Internet, has caused a rethinking of how corporate data and personal information should be handled. Most of that information is now in electronic form. It is quite common now for a business's key information to reside in an electronic data format, sometimes never being transformed into paper hardcopy at all. Because it can be easily accessed, copied, and widely distributed in electronic form, via the Internet for example, and often as easily as by typing a few keystrokes, concerns of security are greater than ever. With the efficiencies brought about by modern IT have come greater risks—risks that often involve undesired, or even illegal, use of, access to, and disclosure of sensitive data.

Public awareness of these risks, at least with regard to personal information, has raised the bar for information security by putting pressures on business to assure consumers of the security of their information. To allay consumer concern, many Web sites display a privacy policy aimed at reassuring consumers hesitant about uploading their personal information online and have taken steps to secure that data. Today's business also operates with an understanding that a security breach could cause echoing negative public relations. For example, *In the Matter of Eli Lilly and Co.* (2002), Eli Lilly had offered users of several drugs, including the antidepressant medication Prozac, an e-mail reminder service that would allow each user to receive personal e-mail messages to remind them to take or refill their medication. On June 27, 2001, Lilly sent an e-mail to all 669 subscribers of the e-mail service, but listed each of their e-mail addresses in the "To:" field of the e-mail, thereby unintentionally disclosing to each individual subscriber the e-mail addresses of all other subscribers. Lilly's privacy policy included statements such as "Eli Lilly and Company respects the privacy of visitors to its Web sites, and we feel it is important to maintain our guests' privacy as they take advantage of this resource." The Federal Trade Commission (FTC) alleged that Lilly's claim of privacy and confidentiality was deceptive because it "failed to maintain or implement internal measures appropriate under the circumstances to protect sensitive consumer information," as evidenced by its June 27, 2001, disclosure.

Public concern has also prompted lawmakers to enact legislation affecting how certain personal information is handled. Those laws can impact a business's implementation of IT, can create regulatory compliance obligations, and may pose the potential for liability to third parties if the data are mishandled. The new regulatory environment and its corporate compliance issues, coupled with corporate concern for negative public relations, the potential for civil liability, and the heightened risks brought about by advancements in IT, have caused businesses to pay closer attention to IT security practices and to look at how IT may be used to both satisfy compliance obligations and minimize liability.

WHAT IS AT RISK?
Corporate Data and Personal Information

Corporate data are often a valuable asset. Trade secrets, confidential business information such as customer lists, and other sensitive business information such as internal operating procedures are guarded with great care, are protected from unauthorized disclosure to outsiders, and should be secured.

Additionally, the personal information of employees and consumers (sometimes referred to in legal texts as nonpublic personal information, personally identifiable information, or simply personal data), such as contact information, financial data and transaction records, and personal health information, is generally viewed as private and confidential to the individual and therefore protected against unauthorized access by and disclosure to third parties. It is not uncommon for a business to invest in the security of human management and payroll systems to ensure adequate protection of information about employees. Nor is it unusual for a business to safeguard consumer information, not only because its unauthorized disclosure may pose a risk of regulatory noncompliance, but also because such information may be considered a valuable asset, the disclosure of which could result in a competitive loss in the marketplace.

Nature of the Data

Data of little commercial value, or that are not highly private to an individual, may pose little risk. However, data that may pose a distinct risk if subject to a security breach, and that may result in liability, could include sensitive information such as the following:

1. Company trade secrets, which may include customer lists or business methods. Rights in trade secrets are governed by state law (*Roton Barrier, Inc. v. Stanley Works*, 1996). The Restatement of Torts acknowledges that a customer list may be a trade secret (see Restatement of Torts §757, Comment b). A business must protect the secrecy of a trade secret to retain its trade secret status (see *Defiance Button Machine Co. v. C&C Metal Products Corp.*, 1985, in which rights in a customer list were forfeited because information was not kept confidential).

2. Information that may not necessarily be a trade secret, but which a business nonetheless considers to be confidential (e.g., price lists, internal policy manuals) and does not want disclosed to certain other parties (e.g., competitors) or publicly (see *Overholt Crop Insurance Service Co. v. Travis*, 1991, in which the court enforced a company's rights in its customer information that had been revealed under a confidential relationship, even if the information was "technically not a trade secret").

3. Confidential information of a business partner, of a contracting entity, or of a business customer and of which an organization is in possession and for which the organization has agreed to keep confidential (e.g., through a contract, such as a nondisclosure agreement).

4. Information collected from or about a consumer (such as contact information, demographic information, transaction records, credit report data, purchasing habits, or Web site surfing activity), which may be subject to:
   (a) Specific laws governing redisclosure and use of consumer information, such as financial information and medical records. Examples of such laws include the Financial Services Modernization Act of 1999 (more commonly known as the Gramm-Leach-Bliley Act or GLB), which governs the protection of "personally identifiable financial information," and the Health Insurance Portability and Accountability Act (HIPAA), which governs the protection of "protected health information." In Europe, the Data Protection Directive (1995) governs generally the protection of "personal data."
   (b) More general consumer protection laws governing personal information of consumers. Examples of such laws include the Federal Trade Commission Act (FTCA, 1914) and individual state consumer protection laws.
   (c) A commitment by the business to keep the consumer's information private, such as in a Web site privacy policy or in a legally required privacy notice (such as a GLB notice).

In many instances, the nature of the data will determine whether certain statutory or regulatory obligations are triggered and thus whether the data are subject to regulatory compliance requirements (e.g., HIPAA pertains only to "protected health information," a statutorily defined term). The nature of the data may affect the risk in two ways: (1) highly sensitive data, such as trade secrets, customer credit card information, and consumer financial account information, will be a target for hackers, increasing the likelihood of unauthorized disclosure by intrusion, and (2) in the event of a breach, more sensitive data may pose a greater degree of harm and perhaps result in a public relations fiasco as well.

Attendant Risks

It is important to understand how the data are used and what therefore could happen to them (or, if a breach has occurred, what has happened to the data). Key to this understanding is knowing how the data are gathered, transmitted, used, and stored and where in that process the data might be (or have been) compromised in one way or another. This exercise pinpoints where the integrity of those data may be (or was) compromised.

Why is this important? Certain regulatory obligations specifically address the handling of data (e.g., GLB prohibits an unauthorized disclosure to a nonaffiliated third party). In terms of devising an appropriate compliance program, it is necessary to understand fully how the data are to be used, and what access, use, and disclosure restrictions need to be placed on those data. Moreover, the potential for liability to others will depend to a large extent on how the data are handled (e.g., liability might attach under a negligence theory if the data were handled in an unreasonable fashion). The implementation of appropriate IT infrastructure and data security policies and procedures can often help to satisfy compliance obligations and to mitigate the potential for liability.

At the preventive stage, there are several security considerations, the evaluation of which provides a good framework for assessing and testing security controls:

Physical security. Physical security refers to the security measures in place to prevent unauthorized physical entry to the location at which computer equipment is located and may include such relatively simple measures as locked entryways and access to central computing rooms via authorized identification card only or more sophisticated measures such as biometric screening systems such as fingerprint or retinal scan recognition. Ordinarily, locked entryways and access restricted to authorized identification cards would suffice, but other measures may be considered when highly sensitive data are at issue.

Technical security. Technical security encompasses the use of logical security, which includes implementation of hardware and software designed specifically to secure data. Logical security has been defined as "security measures for controlling access to electronic information resources through logical means (e.g., via software or network controls), procedural controls related to software development and change control, security of data, communications, and reduction of risk from harmful and intrusive computer software." See "University of Central Florida" (2001). It contemplates controls within software that limit access by a secure means of authentication and authorization. Logical security includes issuance and maintenance of user identifications and corresponding passwords and other software-related protocols for identifying authenticity. Extranets, virtual private networks, and remote access typically employ varying degrees of logical security. Logical security also involves securing networks and securely integrating applications and systems by using software and hardware designed specifically to secure or otherwise prevent risk to data. Examples include software firewalls, virus and monitoring applications, and hardware firewalls and routers. Software that is implemented should be regularly updated (e.g., with current security patches). Virus scanning software should be regularly updated with current virus definitions. Technical security may also include adequate contingency plans, including routine backup and archiving of data, to minimize the risk in the event of data loss.

Personnel and administrative security (employee and consultant policies and procedures). The nature of the data may warrant that they be accessed by a limited number of personnel having higher security clearance. Moreover, personnel with access should be trained as to the business' policies and procedures with regard to the use and disclosure of such data. There should also be fail checks built into the system, or some sort of counterintelligence mechanisms, to identify individuals who may not follow procedures or who may, themselves, seek to access, copy, steal, or release data improperly. Background checks may be made on persons being considered for hire as employees or to be retained as consultants who are expected to have access to sensitive data or to the systems that store or transmit such data. Adequate training and ongoing support may minimize the risk of data being inadvertently deleted or altered by human error or ignorance. Adequately trained personnel should administer the business' security policies and procedures.

Operational security. The overall operations of the business should be guided by a security policy that takes into account the unique risks and vulnerabilities associated with the attendant business practices, which will include several of the foregoing security concerns. Certain laws (e.g., GLB) require a business to implement a security program suitable for its size, business practices, risks, and vulnerabilities.

As shown below, failures in the foregoing may lead to regulatory noncompliance and also may give rise to third-party liability. Security breaches that may trigger regulatory obligations, or generate the potential for third-party liability, include unauthorized access, use, or disclosure of data or systems and destruction, loss, or corruption of data.

Unauthorized Access, Use, and Disclosure. Information of a sensitive nature—for example, corporate trade secrets, confidential information of a business partner, or personal information of consumers—poses a distinct risk of liability if it is not properly safeguarded. Most organizations recognize that this information should be kept confidential. Not all organizations, however, appreciate how their IT infrastructure and policies impact the potential for liability.

Liability may arise when the information is accessed by an unauthorized person, such as a hacker. A common fear in the corporate sector is that an intruder will infiltrate the organization's systems and steal valuable data. The intruder, who may be an outsider, a contractor, or even an internal employee, may seek to blackmail the organization, threatening to publicly disclose the data unless the organization pays a sum of money. At times, a business may want to avoid the negative implications of a public disclosure and heed the intruder's demands. Other times, law enforcement will intervene, but the intruder is not always apprehended, and the news of the security breach may not be well received by customers or shareholders. In other instances, the hacker may, unbeknownst to the business, use or sell the stolen information for illegitimate purposes, such as identity theft.

Although the threat of an intruder is typically recognized by an organization's risk management, liability for unauthorized access, use, or disclosure of data may arise in other contexts, such as with inadvertent disclosures caused by human error or by a technology snafu. For example, data may be misdirected or transferred to the wrong destination (e.g., in e-mail) or unintentionally released or displayed (e.g., on a Web site), any of which could result from technological failure or human oversight.

Employee unawareness of legal obligations may also lead to regulatory noncompliance and third-party liability. An employee may not know that certain data should not be disclosed. For example, under GLB, a financial institution may not use or disclose nonpublic personal information except as set forth in the institution's privacy notice, and then, in certain regards, only to the extent that the consumer has not opted out of specific disclosures. If, for example, the marketing arm of a firm has access to customer information, such as via the firm's customer relations management software, but has not been informed of the regulatory restrictions, or of any consumer opt-outs, it might improperly share the data with third parties in marketing campaigns in violation of GLB. Personnel not familiar with the applicable data restrictions might unwittingly misuse the data, causing an organization to be noncompliant with regulatory requirements.

In other situations, an organization may contract to use data for certain limited purposes, such as in a data supply agreement or in a service provider relationship in which either the service provider or the customer commits contractually to limit its use and disclosure of the data it receives. Usage or disclosure of the data outside the contract parameters may result in a breach of the contract. Proper IT implementation and practices, including adequate personnel training and education, should help to avoid such problems.

There are also risks associated with unauthorized access to computer systems, even where data are not accessed or compromised. For example, a denial of service attack could render business operations ineffective, creating potential business loss and third-party liability. Unauthorized access to a network could likewise create potential losses and liability.

Corruption, Destruction, or Loss of Data. Liability may also arise from the corruption, destruction, or loss of data. Where a business has contracted with another to process certain data, implicit in which is the maintenance or preservation of those data, or where a business expressly agrees to preserve data (such as where a contract contemplates routine backup of data), the corruption or loss of those data may lead to contractual liability. Adequate procedures with respect to the handling of the data, as well as backup and disaster recovery practices, should mitigate the potential for such loss.

Data may be destroyed, lost, or corrupted due to a number of factors, including viruses, Trojan horses, worms, or other harmful software code; ill-intentioned efforts by intruders; software errors, malfunctions and bugs; failed hardware or media; telecommunications glitches and failure; noncompliance with internal procedures; or natural disaster, terrorism, an act of God, or other force majeure events. None of the foregoing may be absolutely avoidable, but the likelihood of an occurrence, or of data being destroyed, lost, or corrupted in the event of an occurrence, may be mitigated by proper precautionary measures. Many businesses employ a backup regimen, for example. The procedures vary from company to company, depending upon the nature and value of the data and the attendant risks. It is fairly common for a business to employ a nightly backup of all transactions that occurred during the day onto tapes that are stored offsite periodically. Certain data may warrant more elaborate, and costly, backup procedures involving duplicate or redundant systems that copy data daily, hourly, or at other assigned times or that mirror data immediately. Frequent backups should lessen the amount of data that could be lost and would therefore need to be restored, thus reducing the potential for liability.

When data are destroyed, lost, or corrupted, a business faces both (1) additional costs and expenses for its internal efforts, and perhaps for external services to assist, in restoring the data and (2) potential liability to third parties, such as, for example, where the security of the data was entrusted to that party and the data cannot be fully restored or cannot be restored in a timely manner, causing an interruption in the other party's business operations. Steps taken to avoid events that may compromise the data will obviously lessen a business's risk. Moreover, adequate backup and disaster recovery programs will minimize the extent of data lost, and thus the potential financial exposure, in the event that data are compromised.

Risks Incumbent With the Internet and Subcontracting

The makeup of an organization's IT infrastructure may impact the risk of a security breach and the potential for liability. It may also affect the organization's regulatory compliance. The IT upon which a business depends typically involves a mix of internal technology, such as owned or leased computer equipment and networking systems, licensed or proprietary software, and IT personnel responsible for the smooth operation of the business's IT systems and, to a varying degree, technology solutions offered by one or more IT service providers, such as managed network servicers, telecommunications providers, application service providers, hosting companies, and outsourcing providers. Many of those services are provided remotely, through the Internet, or otherwise contemplate access via the Internet. How an organization's IT infrastructure is deployed may influence whether a particular statutory or regulatory obligation is triggered and may affect the potential for third-party liability.

Web Sites and the Internet
An overriding consideration in any legal assessment is whether the data are collected from or accessible to the outside. Where an organization collects information through a Web site or stores data on a server connected to the Internet, the potential for unauthorized access and disclosure to someone outside the organization may be greater than with a closed system. Furthermore, data that are transmitted or stored unencrypted are at greater risk if intercepted or otherwise accessed by an intruder.

Consumer data collected via a Web site may also subject a business to certain obligations under consumer protection laws, or perhaps contractual liability under the business's own privacy policy if the terms in that policy are not followed.

Outsourcing and Subcontracting

Utilizing third-party service providers may be an attractive option where such providers are, given the efficiencies created by their niche expertise or their economies of scale, capable of providing a service at reduced costs when compared with supporting the service in-house. In other instances, there may be no alternative to engaging an IT service provider, as is typically the case with a telecommunications provider. Furthermore, vendors that concentrate on providing a particular service may have expertise in an area that may be difficult to replicate in-house. A hosting company is a good example. Many hosting companies maintain large server farms on which they host many Web sites for their customers. A hosting company often negotiates favorable terms with hardware and software providers, and with an Internet Service Provider (ISP) or telecommunications provider for Internet access, and can build those savings into its offering to its customers. A hosting company can also reduce costs by using shared servers and allocating personnel to multiple accounts.

When IT is handled primarily in-house, the organization has direct control over its IT operations and can usually achieve an acceptable comfort level with its risk and liability assessments by review and enforcement of its own internal policies and procedures, and through the periodic undertaking of internal compliance audits. However, when a business elects to engage a third-party vendor to provide certain of its IT services, a number of legal issues arise that are more difficult to assess. When certain aspects of the IT program are outsourced or otherwise entrusted to a third party, direct control over some or all of the IT operations, and the security of its data, is lost. The business is then dependent, to an extent, on the vendor (and its subcontractors) to ensure that adequate security policies and procedures are in place, monitored, and enforced (e.g., to meet the business's regulatory obligations and to minimize the potential for liability).

Allowing third parties access to corporate and personal data and the business's IT systems obviously poses a level of risk that should be considered when looking to engage any vendor. Some amount of due diligence should be conducted to gain a satisfactory level of comfort with the vendor (e.g., reference checks, background checks, and Dunn & Bradstreet financial checks). Moreover, the contract between the vendor and the customer should clearly spell out the expectations of the parties, including who is responsible for what (e.g., in the event of a security breach), how data are to be handled (e.g., which restrictions attach to which data), which types of security are to be implemented, and who is liable for what. In certain instances, engaging a subcontractor will trigger regulatory obligations with regard to the subcontract itself (e.g., HIPAA requires that a subcontractor sign a business associate agreement that must satisfy certain express regulatory requirements).

Service provider contracts will often attempt to disclaim liability for these types of events (e.g., in a force majeure clause, in general or specific disclaimers, in disclaimers of damages, or in limitations of liability). From the customer's perspective, such disclaimers may be acceptable so long as they are qualified as being outside the service provider's reasonable control, not reasonably avoidable with proper due diligence and foresight, and the contract elsewhere affirmatively requires the provider to undertake steps to maintain the security and integrity of the data.

STATUTORY AND REGULATORY COMPLIANCE

The Impact of the Law: Determining Regulatory Obligations and Assessing the Potential for Liability

Security breaches may pose liability under a number of different legal theories, depending upon the nature of the data and the circumstances surrounding the breach. They may also create noncompliance situations with regulatory obligations, subjecting the organization to penalties and possible enforcement actions by government regulators. This section looks at statutory and regulatory obligations and the potential for liability for failures to comply with those obligations. The remainder of this chapter looks at the potential for third-party liability under contract and tort theories.

As an introduction, it is worthy to note that there is a body of decisional law in the United States premised upon an individual's right to privacy in certain information. It has been held, for example, that an individual has a constitutional right to privacy in the very intimate aspects of his or her personal life, such as with certain medical information. It has also been held that an individual may maintain an action in tort for an invasion of his or her privacy, which could, for example, include the privacy of financial information. See *McNally v. The Pulitzer Publishing Co.* (1976), which differentiated between the constitutional right of privacy and the common law right recognized by state tort law. The failure to safeguard such information may give rise to claims of a violation of either a constitutional right or of a tort involving the invasion of privacy. Although possible claims in tort are discussed in a later section of this chapter, the concept of this right to privacy has influenced, and continues to influence, the development of statutes and regulations that impose upon organizations an obligation to safeguard certain personal information.

Damages

Certain statutes may provide for statutory remedies (e.g., a dollar figure for violations or treble damages). To the extent that a statute imposes a duty to maintain the security of data, and allows a private claim to be brought for a breach of that statutory duty, unless otherwise provided in the statute, the claimant will likely need to demonstrate that he or she suffered some actual damage to recover under the statute (*Doe v. Chao*, 2004). In the *Doe v. Chao* case, the plaintiff alleged a violation of the Privacy Act of 1974, which requires federal agencies not to disclose data, because the Department of Labor had disclosed his Social Security number on public documents. The Privacy Act states that a claimant who suffered damages as a result of a violation of the act may receive "actual damages sustained by the individual... but in no case shall a person entitled to recovery receive *less than* the sum of $1,000" (5 U.S.C. §552a(g)(4)(A)). In declining to award the statutory $1,000, the Court held that the plaintiff's assertions "that he was 'torn... all to pieces' and 'greatly concerned and worried' because of the disclosure of his Social Security number and its potentially 'devastating' consequences" was insufficient to establish that he had, in fact, suffered actual damage (2004 U.S. LEXIS at *8).

In many instances, it may be difficult for a claimant to establish any damages arising from an unauthorized disclosure of his or her personal information. This topic is further addressed in the discussion about remedies under the next section of this chapter. It would be ill-advised, however, to assume that damages may never be assessed in respect of disclosures of consumer data.

Legislative Developments

The growing concern for privacy in recent years has prompted legislative action both in the United States and abroad requiring organizations to protect the privacy of personal information. The statutory approach in the United States is often referred to as sectoral in nature because the laws are drawn along industry lines; that is, they pertain to specific information gathered by organizations in specific industries (namely financial and medical). Unlike the Data Protection Directive, for example, which has been adopted in European countries and which imposes restrictions on the collection, use, and disclosure of personal information generally, regardless of the context of the relationship in which the information was collected—whether financial, medical, or otherwise, the United States has no comparable broad stroke law that restricts generally the collection, use, or disclosure of personal information (see Data Protection Directive, 1995).

The U.S. approach, therefore, creates one anomaly in that the same information collected via different relationships could in one instance be subject to statutory and regulatory restrictions and in another instance not be regulated at all. Moreover, in some instances the information could be subject to more than one statutory scheme (e.g., information might fall under both HIPAA and GLB, raising the issue of which regulation should govern—GLB regulators have addressed this by suggesting that the applicable regulation be the one more protective to the consumer). See Privacy of Consumer Financial Information; Final Rule, 65 Fed. Reg. 35,164 (2000). Whether specific information is governed by regulation requires a thorough understanding of the statutory scheme.

U.S. Federal Law

Two U.S. federal statutes that directly address IT security are the Financial Services Modernization Act of 1999 (more commonly known as the GLB) and HIPAA (1996). These two statutes, and their accompanying regulations,

focus on the privacy of certain personal information, but also specifically address the security of data. Neither statute concerns corporate data (e.g., corporate trade secrets or confidential information), unless that information includes the personal information of individuals that is protected by the statute. The following takes a close look at the regulatory obligations imposed on data security by these statutes, but by no means is an exhaustive review of all the regulations. Neither statute allows for a civil cause of action (enforcement would be brought by the applicable federal agency or state authority), but the security requirements set out in the regulations might reflect standards that a court could consider in addressing a liability claim brought by a private party.

GLB. Although it is limited to "nonpublic personal information" collected by "financial institutions," GLB is a good example of statutory and regulatory initiatives that directly impact IT operations and data security procedures. It is worthy to note that GLB applies broadly to many businesses that handle financial data in one way or another and not just banks. GLB was enacted in 1999.

What Are Financial Institutions?

GLB applies only to financial institutions, a term broadly defined by the statute. The term *financial institution* means "any institution the business of which is engaging in financial activities as described in section 1843(k) of title 12" (Financial Services Modernization Act, 1999, 15 U.S.C. §6809(3)(A)). 12 U.S.C. §1843(k) describes a long list of activities as being financial in nature. 12 U.S.C. §1843(k) includes a list of entities that includes the more traditional financial institutions, such as lending institutions, banks, insurance companies, underwriters, investment companies, financial advisors, and funds and broker-dealers. In addition to the traditional financial activities identified in 12 U.S.C. §1843(k), the term *financial activities* includes activities that the Federal Reserve Board has found, by regulation, order, or interpretation, to be either closely related to banking (12 U.S.C. §1843(k)(4)(F)) or usual in connection with the transaction of banking or other financial operations abroad (12 U.S.C. §1843(k)(4)(G)).

Activities that are "closely related to banking" are identified at 12 C.F.R. §225.28 and 12 C.F.R. §225.86(a), and include, in certain circumstances, brokering or servicing loans; leasing real or personal property (or acting as agent, broker, or adviser in such leasing) without operating, maintaining, or repairing the property; appraising real or personal property; check guaranty, collection agency, credit bureau, and real estate settlement services; providing financial or investment advisory activities including tax planning, tax preparation, and instruction on individual financial management; management consulting and counseling activities (including providing financial career counseling); courier services for banking instruments; printing and selling checks and related documents; community development or advisory activities; selling money orders, savings bonds, or traveler's checks; and providing financial data processing and transmission services, facilities (including hardware, software, documentation, or operating personnel), databases, advice, or access to these by technological means.

Activities that are "in connection with the transaction of banking or other financial operations abroad" are identified at 12 C.F.R. §211.5(d) and 12 C.F.R. §225.86(b), and include leasing real or personal property (or acting as agent, broker, or adviser in such leasing), where the lease is functionally equivalent to an extension of credit; acting as fiduciary; providing investment, financial, or economic advisory services; and operating a travel agency in connection with financial services.

Given the broad definition of financial institution, many organizations that were not traditionally thought of as financial institutions may nonetheless be subject to GLB and therefore required to comply with its security and privacy regulations.

Who Are the Regulators?

GLB provides the statutory framework but instructs the relevant federal and state agencies and authorities to promulgate regulations governing the application of the statute for those entities within their respective jurisdictions. Accordingly, the Securities and Exchange Commission (SEC) issued a Privacy Rule that incorporates its Security Rule (17 C.F.R. §248.30) and implements GLB's statutory requirements with regard to the entities governed by the SEC (investment advisers registered with the SEC, brokers, dealers (broker-dealers), and investment companies (funds); 17 C.F.R. Part 248; See Final Rule: Privacy of Consumer Financial Information (Regulation S–P) (SEC), 65 Fed. Reg. 40,334 (2000)). Similarly, the various banking agencies—the Federal Reserve System, Federal Deposit Insurance Corporation, Office of Comptroller of the Currency, Department of the Treasury, and the Office of Thrift Supervision, Department of the Treasury—issued a Joint Privacy Rule and Joint Security Guidelines (12 C.F.R. Part 40) governing the various banking institutions under their jurisdiction. The National Credit Union Administration (NCUA) issued regulations (12 C.F.R. Parts 716 and 741) governing credit unions that it regulates. For insurance companies, GLB regulations are implemented by the applicable state insurance department or authority of the state in which the person is domiciled. The National Association of Insurance Commissioners has proposed a model regulation for adoption by the states (See *What's happening with privacy*, n.d.).

For all those entities that do not otherwise fall under the jurisdiction of the federal agencies identified above, or the state insurance departments or authorities, but nevertheless are financial institutions under the broad statutory definition of that term, GLB authorizes the FTC to regulate such entities with regard to GLB compliance. The FTC issued its Privacy Rule (16 C.F.R. Part 313) and Security Rule (16 C.F.R. Part 314) in 2000.

Restrictions on Handling of Data

GLB limits the disclosure of nonpublic personal information. Nonpublic personal information is defined as "personally identifiable financial information provided by a consumer to a financial institution resulting from any transaction with the consumer or any service performed for the consumer or otherwise obtained by the financial institution" (Financial Services Modernization Act, 1999, 15 U.S.C. §6809(4)(A)). This is broadly construed to "encompass any information that 'is requested by a financial institution for the purpose of providing a financial product or service,' 65 Fed. Reg. at 33,658, inasmuch as all such information can be fairly characterized as 'relating to finance and financiers'" (*Trans Union LLC v. Federal Trade Commission*, 2002). Accordingly, information collected in connection with a financial transaction would be subject to GLB's security and privacy requirements, even if the information itself is not necessarily financial in nature (nonpublic personal information would therefore include, e.g., any name, address, telephone number, e-mail address, Social Security number, contact information, or other information supplied by a consumer in connection with an application for a financial product or service).

Precisely how GLB limits the use of nonpublic personal information can be a bit complicated under the statutory and regulatory scheme. In essence, however, GLB requires a financial institution to disclose clearly to consumers in a privacy notice its policies and procedures with regard to the collection, use, and disclosure of nonpublic personal information. The notice must clearly indicate what information is collected, how it is used, and to whom it is disclosed and, in certain instances, the consumer must be afforded an opportunity to opt out of disclosures of the information to nonaffiliated third parties. The institution must ensure that it complies with its notice and any opt-out elections made by a consumer. Failure to do so may result in a regulatory enforcement action and civil penalties.

Security Obligations

GLB requires each agency to establish appropriate standards relating to administrative, technical, and physical safeguards:

- to ensure the security and confidentiality of customer records and information;
- to protect against any anticipated threats or hazards to the security or integrity of such records; and
- to protect against unauthorized access to or use of such records or information which could result in substantial harm or inconvenience to any customer (Financial Services Modernization Act, 1999, 15 U.S.C. §6801(b)).

Each agency issued its own security guidelines or regulations. The following outlines the security guidelines promulgated by the banking agencies. The FTC's security rule is found at 16 C.F.R. §314; the Securities and Exchange Commission's security rule is included in its privacy regulations (Regulation S-P) at 17 C.F.R. §248.30.

A financial institution must develop and implement "a comprehensive written information security program that includes administrative, technical, and physical safeguards" (a) designed to protect the security and confidentiality of "customer information" and (b) to assess, manage and control risks pertaining to the institution's "customer information systems" (12 C.F.R. Part 30, Appendix B, ¶ II.A-C). Customer information is "any record containing nonpublic personal information, as defined in §40.3(n) of this chapter, about a customer, whether in paper, electronic, or other form, that is maintained by or on behalf of the bank" (12 C.F.R. Part 30, Appendix B, ¶ I.C.2.c). This includes "data, files, or other information" about the consumer. It includes records that may contain other than nonpublic personal information, even records that contain very little nonpublic personal information. Records that contain little nonpublic personal information are still customer information under the guidelines; this fact may be a factor in determining the appropriate level of protection. See Interagency Guidelines Establishing Standards for Safeguarding Customer Information (Banking Agencies), 66 Fed. Reg. 8,618 (2001). "Customer information systems" are "any methods used to access, collect, store, use, transmit, protect, or dispose of customer information." This includes "electronic or physical" methods. A "financial institution's responsibility to safeguard customer information continues through the disposal process" (12 C.F.R. Part 30, Appendix B, ¶ I.C.2.d).

The guidelines do not impose specific requirements in terms of the administrative, technical, and physical safeguards to be adopted by an organization. They are, instead, intended to be flexible, permitting an institution to develop a program "appropriate to the size and complexity of the bank and the nature and scope of its activities" (12 C.F.R. Part 30, Appendix B, ¶ II.A).

Assess Risks

The guidelines allow an organization latitude in developing an information security program appropriate for its business. The organization must assess the risks that customer information may be compromised (e.g., disclosed, misused, altered, or destroyed), taking into consideration internal and external threats, the likelihood and potential damage of these threats (including the sensitivity of the customer information), and the arrangements in place to control the risks. There is no requirement that all organizations afford the same degree of protection to all customer information. Rather, the guidelines permit the organization "the discretion to determine the levels of protection necessary for different categories of information" (Interagency Guidelines Establishing Standards for Safeguarding Customer Information (Banking Agencies), 66 Fed. Reg. 8,621 (2001)).

For example, sensitive data that are stored on or transmitted through "systems that are accessible through public telecommunications networks... may require more and different protections, such as encryption, than if it were located in a locked file drawer" (Interagency Guidelines Establishing Standards for Safeguarding Customer Information (Banking Agencies), 66 Fed. Reg. 8,621 (2001)). Such data may include customer account numbers and access codes because they are more at risk of being targeted by a hacker and their disclosure would cause the customer considerable harm.

Manage and Control Risks

The information security program must be appropriate for an organization's activities, considering the risks stated above. A number of security measures that are to be considered and, if appropriate, adopted are identified at 12 C.F.R. Part 30, Appendix B, ¶ III.C.1.a through h. They include the following:

1. Access controls (e.g., passwords for customers to access their information electronically, identification criteria to be used by employees before providing account information, procedures to guard against pretext calling).

2. Access restrictions at physical locations (to permit access by authorized personnel only to computer facilities, record storage facilities, etc.).

3. Encryption of customer information (in electronic format while in transit or while residing on electronic storage devices, in either case where access may be gained by unauthorized individuals).

4. Review of updates and upgrades to customer information systems (to ensure continued integrity of the financial institution's information security program).

5. Dual control procedures, segregation of duties, and employee background checks for employees with responsibilities for or access to customer information. Dual control procedures "refers to a security technique that uses two or more separate persons, operating together to protect sensitive information. Both persons are equally responsible for protecting the information and neither can access the information alone." (Interagency Guidelines Establishing Standards for Safeguarding Customer Information (Banking Agencies), 66 Fed. Reg. 8,622 (2001)).

6. Monitoring of customer information systems (to detect attempted and actual attacks and intrusions).

7. Response procedures (specifying actions to take when it is suspected or verified that unauthorized individuals have accessed the financial institution's customer information systems, including, when appropriate, reports to law enforcement and regulatory agencies).

8. Contingency plans and measures to protect against loss of or damage to customer information (e.g., due to fire, water damage, or technological failures).

The information security program should include training "designed to train employees to recognize, respond to, and report unauthorized attempts to obtain customer information" (12 C.F.R. Part 30, Appendix B, ¶ III.C.2). Staff should be properly informed about the organization's procedures for reporting suspicious activities (such as suspicious activity reports [SARs]) and other federal reporting requirements. An institution regulated by the FRS must file an SAR with the Financial Crimes Enforcement Network of the Department of the Treasury "when it detects a known or suspected violation of Federal law, or a suspicious transaction related to a money laundering activity or a violation of the Bank Secrecy Act" (12 C.F.R. §208.62). The NCUA also requires federally insured credit unions to file similar reports (see 12 C.F.R. §748.1(c)).

Systems Testing

An information security program should include regular testing of key controls, systems, and procedures. There is no requirement that an organization apply specific tests to evaluate the key control systems of its program; the organization must determine the frequency and nature of the testing based on its risk assessment. The tests should be conducted or reviewed by independent third parties or by staff independent of those that develop or maintain the security programs or operate the customer information systems.

Adjustments to Security Program

Adjustments should be made to the information security program "as necessary to reflect changes in both internal and external conditions" (Interagency Guidelines Establishing Standards for Safeguarding Customer Information (Banking Agencies), 66 Fed. Reg. 8,623 (2001); see 12 C.F.R. Part 30, Appendix B, ¶ III.E). An organization must adjust, as appropriate, the program "in light of any relevant changes in technology, the sensitivity of its customer information, and internal or external threats to information security" (12 C.F.R. Part 30, Appendix B, ¶ III.E). This would include analyzing the risks to customer information posed by new technology before adopting that technology to ascertain whether any adjustments to the security program are necessary. The program should also be adjusted to reflect an organization's "own changing business arrangements, such as mergers and acquisitions, alliances and joint ventures, outsourcing arrangements, and changes to customer information systems" (12 C.F.R. Part 30, Appendix B, ¶ III.E).

Service Providers and Subservicers

An organization may, in the course of its business, outsource certain business functions or otherwise engage service providers to handle certain business operations that would necessarily require or permit their access to customer information. Such activities create additional risks to the security and confidentiality of the information and, to protect against such risks, the "institution must take appropriate steps to protect information that it provides to a service provider, regardless of who the service provider is or how the service provider obtains access" (Interagency Guidelines Establishing Standards for Safeguarding Customer Information (Banking Agencies), 66 Fed. Reg. 8,618 (2001)). An organization is responsible for customer information accessed by its service providers. Service providers are broadly defined and include "any person or entity that maintains, processes, or otherwise is permitted access to customer information through its provision of services directly to the bank" (12 C.F.R. Part 30, Appendix B, ¶ I.C.2.e). A service provider does not include a person or entity, such as a subservicer, that indirectly provides services to a financial institution. A subservicer that is retained by a primary service provider would not be a service provider to the organization that engaged the primary service provider, because it has no contractual relationship with the subservicer. A subservicer is "any person who has access to an institution's customer information through its provision of services to the service provider and is not limited to mortgage subservicers" (Interagency Guidelines Establishing Standards for Safeguarding Customer Information (Banking Agencies), 66 Fed. Reg. 8,619, fn. 8 (2001)).

An organization must exercise due diligence in selecting a service provider, which would include a review of the (a) measures taken by a service provider to protect customer information and (b) controls the service provider has in place to ensure that any subservicer used by the service provider will be able to meet the objectives of the guidelines. An organization should enter into a contract with its service providers that requires the provider to implement appropriate security measures designed to meet the objectives of the guidelines.

An organization must exercise an appropriate level of oversight over each of its service providers to ensure that the provider is implementing the security measures for which it has been contracted. The oversight responsibilities should be consistent with the organization's own risk assessment procedures. Not all outsourcing arrangements need be monitored or monitored in the same fashion. Where, for example, a service provider is also a regulated financial institution or subject to other legal and professional standards that require it to safeguard customer information, it may be reasonable to rely on the fact that the provider must comply with such restrictions, and therefore it may not be necessary to provide as much oversight.

The service provider may be monitored through periodic review of audits, summaries of test results or other equivalent measures of the service provider. The contract with the service provider should call for the receipt of copies of audits and test result information adequate to confirm that the service provider is implementing security measures consistent with the provider's contractual obligations. A contract may call for the service provider to submit to periodic audits of its security measures.

Liability and Enforcement Actions

The banking rule is not intended to impose absolute liability for a financial institution that has a security breach. This is evident in the qualification in 12 C.F.R. Part 30, Appendix B, ¶ II.B that a security program is to be *designed* to accomplish the statutory objectives set out at 15 U.S.C. §6801(b).

Under certain of the guidelines, if an agency determines that an organization has failed to satisfy the security standards set forth in the guidelines, the agency may request the institution to submit a compliance plan that sets out the steps it will take to correct the deficiency and how long those steps will take. If the organization fails to submit or implement a compliance plan, the agency shall, by order, require the institution to correct the deficiency and may take further actions. If the organization fails to comply with an order, the agency may seek enforcement and a civil money penalty in court.

HIPAA. HIPAA was enacted in August 1996. In accordance with HIPAA, the United States Department of Health and Human Services (HHS) promulgated regulations titled Standards for Privacy of Individually Identifiable Health Information (the HIPAA Privacy and Security Rule), which became effective in April 2003 and established national standards for the privacy and security of health information (45 C.F.R. Parts 160 and 164. See 65 Fed. Reg. 82462; 67 Fed. Reg. 53182).

Who and What Are Regulated by HIPAA?

HIPAA applies to covered entities, which include health plans, health care clearinghouses, and certain health care providers. A health plan is an individual or group plan that provides, or pays the cost of, medical care. Health plans include group health plans, health insurance issuers, health maintenance organizations, Parts A and B of the Medicare program, a Medicaid program, Medicare supplemental insurers, and certain long-term care insurers. A health care clearinghouse is an entity that processes, or facilitates the processing of, health information into a standard format or standard data elements, receives health information in a standard format and process, or facilitates the processing of that information into a nonstandard format or nonstandard content. A health care provider is broadly defined and includes all persons and organizations who furnish, bill, or are paid for providing health care, services, or supplies related to the health of an individual, in the normal course of business. If the health care provider transmits health information electronically in connection with certain transactions, it is a covered entity under the HIPAA Privacy and Security Rule.

HIPAA pertains to protected health information (PHI), which includes medical records and other health information that identifies or could be used to identify an individual, regardless of its form (electronic, paper, or oral), that are created or received by a covered entity or its business associate. PHI includes, for example, any information about payment for health care.

Outsourcing and Vendors

The HIPAA Privacy and Security Rule imposes specific regulatory obligations on outsourcing and other vendor relationships. Where a covered entity engages a third-party contractor, HIPAA requires the covered entity to secure specific contractual commitments from the contractor, which the HIPAA Privacy and Security Rule refers to as a "business associate" (45 C.F.R. §160.103). A business associate may be a subcontractor, an outsourcer or any party that (a) performs a function or activity on behalf of the covered entity and that function or activity involves the use or disclosure of PHI (for example, claims processing, data analysis, utilization review, and billing functions) or (b) provides certain specified services to a covered entity (namely legal, actuarial, accounting, consulting, data aggregation, management, administrative, accreditation or financial services).

The HIPAA Privacy and Security Rule requires covered entities to have business associates execute a business associate agreement. Among other things, the business associate agreement may not permit the business associate to use or disclose PHI in any manner that would violate the HIPAA Privacy and Security Rule if done by the covered entity, must limit the use of PHI only for the purpose for which the business associate is engaged, and must provide assurances that the business associate will safeguard the PHI from misuse. For example, the business associate agreement must

- Require the business associate to use appropriate safeguards to prevent the unauthorized use or disclosure of PHI (the HIPAA Privacy and Security Rule does not define the appropriate safeguards; 45 C.F.R. § 164.504(e)(2)(ii)(B)).
- Report to the covered entity any unauthorized use or disclosure of PHI of which it becomes aware (45 C.F.R. § 164.504(e)(2)(ii)(C)).
- Ensure that any agents of the business associate, including any subcontractor, to whom the business associate provides PHI agree to the same conditions and restrictions that apply to the business associate with respect to the PHI (45 C.F.R. § 164.504(E)(2)(ii)(D)).
- Permit access to PHI to satisfy the covered entity's obligations to allow individuals to amend their PHI or to provide individuals with an accounting of the disclosures of their PHI (45 C.F.R. § 164.504(e)(2)(ii)(E)-(G)).
- Return or destroy all PHI received from or created or received by the business associate on behalf of the covered entity or ensure its continued protection upon the termination of the contract (45 C.F.R. § 164.504(e)(2)(ii)(I)).

The business associate agreement may permit the business associate to disclose PHI as required by law (e.g., court orders, court-ordered warrants, a civil or an authorized investigative demand, subpoenas or summonses issued by a court, a governmental or tribal inspector general or an administrative body authorized to require the production of information, Medicare conditions of participation with respect to health care providers participating in the program, and statutes or regulations that require the production of such information if payment is sought under a government program), so long as the business associate obtains certain assurances from the person to whom the PHI is disclosed.

Security

HIPAA imposes general requirements on covered entities to maintain the security of PHI. For example, the HIPAA Privacy and Security Rule requires covered entities to

- Ensure the confidentiality, integrity, and availability of all electronic PHI the covered entity creates, receives, maintains, or transmits.
- Protect against any reasonably anticipated threats or hazards to the security or integrity of such information.
- Protect against any reasonably anticipated uses or disclosures of such information that are not permitted or required under the rule (45 C.F.R. §164.306(a)).

As with GLB, HIPAA allows flexibility in determining the approach to ensuring security. The following factors must be considered in devising a security program appropriate for a particular organization:

- The size, complexity, and capabilities of the covered entity.
- The covered entity's technical infrastructure, hardware, and software security capabilities.
- The costs of security measures.
- The probability and criticality of potential risks to electronic PHI (45 C.F.R. §164.306(b)(2)).

The HIPAA Privacy and Security Rule implements these statutory requirements by setting out a fairly lengthy list of administrative, physical, technical, and organizational safeguards that a covered entity must institute (or, in certain instances, must consider instituting) to protect the integrity of PHI. Those safeguards are detailed at 45 C.F.R. §§164.308-164.314 and include the following:

Administrative Safeguards

Risk analysis. Conduct accurate and thorough assessment of the potential risks and vulnerabilities to the confidentiality, integrity, and availability of electronic PHI held by the covered entity.

Risk management. Implement security measures sufficient to reduce risks and vulnerabilities to a reasonable and appropriate level.

Information system activity review. Implement procedures to regularly review records of information system activity, such as audit logs, access reports, and security incident tracking reports.

Assigned security responsibility. Identify the security official who is responsible for the development and implementation of the policies and procedures required by the rule.

Workforce security. Implement policies and procedures to ensure that all members of the workforce have appropriate access to electronic PHI and to prevent those workforce members who do not have access from obtaining access to electronic PHI.

Security awareness and training. Implement a security awareness and training program for all members of the workforce (including management).

Protection from malicious software. Procedures for guarding against, detecting, and reporting malicious software (e.g., viruses, worms, or Trojan horses).

Log-in monitoring. Procedures for monitoring log-in attempts and reporting discrepancies.

Password management. Procedures for creating, changing, and safeguarding passwords.

Security incident procedures. Implement policies and procedures to address security incidents.

Response and reporting. Identify and respond to suspected or known security incidents; mitigate, to the extent practicable, harmful effects of security incidents that are known to the covered entity and document security incidents and their outcomes.

Contingency plan. Establish (and implement as needed) policies and procedures for responding to an emergency or other occurrence (for example, fire, vandalism, system failure, and natural disaster) that damages systems that contain electronic PHI.

Data backup plan. Establish and implement procedures to create and maintain retrievable exact copies of electronic PHI.

Disaster recovery plan. Establish (and implement as needed) procedures to restore any loss of data.

Emergency mode operation plan. Establish (and implement as needed) procedures to enable continuation of critical business processes for protection of the security of electronic PHI while operating in emergency mode.

Testing and revision procedures. Implement procedures for periodic testing and revision of contingency plans.

Applications and data criticality analysis. Assess the relative criticality of specific applications and data in support of other contingency plan components.

Physical Safeguards

Facility access controls. Implement policies and procedures to limit physical access to its electronic information systems and the facility or facilities in which they are housed, while ensuring that properly authorized access is allowed.

Facility security plan. Implement policies and procedures to safeguard the facility and the equipment therein from unauthorized physical access, tampering, and theft.

Access control and validation procedures. Implement procedures to control and validate a person's access to facilities based on their role or function, including visitor control and control of access to software programs for testing and revision.

Maintenance records. Implement policies and procedures to document repairs and modifications to the physical components of a facility that are related to security (for example, hardware, walls, doors, and locks).

Workstation use. Implement policies and procedures that specify the proper functions to be performed, the manner in which those functions are to be performed, and the physical attributes of the surroundings of a specific workstation or class of workstation that can access electronic PHI.

Workstation security. Implement physical safeguards for all workstations that access electronic PHI to restrict access to authorized users.

Device and media controls. Implement policies and procedures that govern the receipt and removal of hardware and electronic media that contain electronic PHI into and out of a facility and the movement of these items within the facility.

Technical Safeguards

Unique user identification. Assign a unique name or number for identifying and tracking user identity.

Emergency access procedure. Establish (and implement as needed) procedures for obtaining necessary electronic PHI during an emergency.

Automatic logoff. Implement electronic procedures that terminate an electronic session after a predetermined time of inactivity.

Encryption and decryption. Implement a mechanism to encrypt and decrypt electronic PHI.

Audit controls. Implement hardware, software, or procedural mechanisms that record and examine activity in information systems that contain or use electronic PHI.

Organizational Safeguards

Business associate contracts. The contract between a covered entity and a business associate must provide that the business associate will do the following:

- Implement administrative, physical, and technical safeguards that reasonably and appropriately protect the confidentiality, integrity, and availability of the electronic PHI that it creates, receives, maintains, or transmits on behalf of the covered entity.

- Ensure that any agent, including a subcontractor, to whom it provides such information agrees to implement reasonable and appropriate safeguards to protect it.
- Report to the covered entity any security incident of which it becomes aware.
- Authorize termination of the contract by the covered entity, if the covered entity determines that the business associate has violated a material term of the contract.

The HIPAA Privacy and Security Rule also requires a covered entity to designate a privacy official responsible for the development and implementation of its PHI policies and procedures. Those policies and procedures must be updated as necessary and appropriate to comply with changes in the law, including any changes in the HIPAA Privacy and Security Rule. A covered entity's workforce must be trained about its policies and procedures with respect to PHI, as necessary and appropriate for the workforce members to carry out their duties. A covered entity must have and enforce appropriate sanctions against members of its workforce who fail to comply with its privacy and security policies and procedures.

HHS may pursue violations of HIPAA and the HIPAA Privacy and Security Rule. Violations carry a civil penalty of not more than $100 for each such violation, except that the total amount imposed on the person for all violations of an identical requirement or prohibition during a calendar year may not exceed $25,000.

Other Laws. Other U.S. statutes are relevant to the discussion of IT security insofar as they may impose obligations with regard to data security or give rise to liability in the event of a security breach. Given that steps to ensure privacy of information in electronic format will depend, in large part, upon adequate information security measures, some laws may indirectly impact IT security by imposing obligations to maintain the privacy of personal information.

Consumer Protection Laws

Federal Trade Commission Act

Consumer protection law at the U.S. federal level may be found in the Federal Trade Commission Act (1914). Under Section 5 of the FTCA, the FTC is authorized to take action against businesses involved in unfair or deceptive acts or practices in or affecting commerce. The FTC is permitted a fair amount of latitude under the FTCA in determining what constitutes "unfair or deceptive acts or practices." (See *FTC v. Colgate-Palmolive Co.*, 1965: "This statutory scheme necessarily gives the Commission an influential role in interpreting §5 [of the FTCA as to what are deceptive practices] and in applying it to the facts of particular cases arising out of unprecedented situations . . . the Commission is often in a better position than are courts to determine when a practice is 'deceptive' within the meaning of the Act.")

The FTC has taken the position that a misrepresentation as to the handling of personal information is a violation of Section 5 of the FTCA. For example, in the complaint filed by the FTC in *In the Matter of Geocities*

(1998), the FTC alleged, "The acts and practices of respondent as alleged in this complaint [that Geocities misrepresented its information collection practices] constitute unfair or deceptive acts or practices in or affecting commerce in violation of Section 5(a) of the Federal Trade Commission Act" (Complaint at ¶ 20). Geocities had allegedly misrepresented that the personal information it collected from its users would not be disclosed to third parties without the user's consent when Geocities actually disclosed it to third-party marketers.

The FTC may consider a promise to safeguard personal information—in a Web site privacy policy or in some other commitment made by a company—as a representation by that company that the personal information will be safeguarded in the manner promised. For example, in *In the Matter of Guess?, Inc.*, the FTC asserted that

> since at least October 2000, Guess' Web site has been vulnerable to commonly known attacks such as "Structured Query Language (SQL) injection attacks" and other web-based application attacks. Guess' online statements reassured consumers that their personal information would be secure and protected. The company's claims included "This site has security measures in place to protect the loss, misuse, and alteration of information under our control" and "All of your personal information, including your credit card information and sign-in password, are stored in an unreadable, encrypted format at all times." In fact, according to the FTC, the personal information was not stored in an unreadable, encrypted format at all times and Guess' security measures failed to protect against SQL and other commonly known attacks. In February 2002, a visitor to the Web site, using an SQL injection attack, was able to read in clear text credit card numbers stored in Guess' databases, according to the FTC.

The FTC alleged that Guess misrepresented "the extent to which it maintains and protects the security of personal information collected from or about consumers" (In the Matter of Guess?, Inc., 2003).

In *In the Matter of Microsoft Corporation* (2002), the FTC asserted that Microsoft's Passport service "collects personal information from consumers and allows them to sign in at any participating website with a single name and password." According to the FTC, "Microsoft's Passport privacy policies included statements such as, 'Passport achieves a high level of Web Security by using technologies and systems designed to prevent unauthorized access to your personal information.'" After an investigation, the FTC alleged, among other things, that "Microsoft falsely represented that [i]t employs reasonable and appropriate measures under the circumstances to maintain and protect the privacy and confidentiality of consumers' personal information." (See also Muris, 2001, who stated, "Having encouraged commercial Web sites to post these notices, the FTC needs to ensure compliance. Privacy promises made offline should be held to the same standard.")

The failure to comply with such a representation in a privacy policy may be declared a violation of the FTCA for which the FTC may take action. Under the FTCA, the FTC may seek preliminary and permanent injunctive relief to remedy "any provision of law enforced by the Federal Trade Commission" whenever the FTC has "reason to believe" that a party "is violating, or is about to violate" a provision of law enforced by the FTC (15 U.S.C. §53(b)).

If the conduct were such as "a reasonable man would have known under the circumstances was dishonest or fraudulent," the FTC may also pursue consumer redress in the form of "rescission or reformation of contracts, the refund of money or return of property, the payment of damages, and public notification respecting the rule violation or the unfair or deceptive act or practice," or such other "relief as the court finds necessary to redress injury to consumers or other persons, partnerships, and corporations resulting from the rule violation or the unfair or deceptive act or practice" (15 U.S.C. §57b). Under the FTCA, the FTC may also seek civil penalties when the violator had "actual knowledge or knowledge fairly implied on the basis of objective circumstances that such act is unfair or deceptive and is prohibited by such [unfair or deceptive acts or practices] rule" under Chapter 2 of the FTCA (15 U.S.C. §45(m)(1)). The civil penalty is capped at $10,000 per violation.

Electronic Communications Privacy Act

An amendment to the Wiretap Act, the Electronic Communications Privacy Act (ECPA, 1986) prohibits anyone from intentionally accessing, using, or disclosing stored communications, such as e-mail or stored voice messages, without authorization. Violations of the ECPA are punishable by fines, imprisonment, or both. The ECPA allows for a civil cause of action and recovery of actual damages but not less than $1,000 per violation of the statute, plus the costs and reasonable attorneys' fees in pursuing the action. If the violation were willful or intentional, the court may assess punitive damages (18 U.S.C. §2707(c)).

The ECPA also expressly prohibits providers of "electronic communication" or "remote computing services" from knowingly divulging the contents of a communication in electronic storage, except under certain enumerated circumstances (18 U.S.C. §2702(a)). The following disclosures are excepted from the statutory prohibition: (a) to intended recipients and their agents; (b) with the consent of the originator or the recipient of the communication, and in the case of remote computing services, the subscriber to the service; (c) to a person employed or authorized to forward the communication to its destination; (d) as necessarily incident to providing a service or to protecting the rights or property of the service provider; (e) to a law enforcement agency, if the communication was inadvertently obtained and appears to pertain to criminal activity; and (f) as otherwise authorized by law (18 U.S.C. §2702(b)).

Electronic communication services are defined as "any service which provides to users thereof the ability to send or receive wire or electronic communications" (e.g., an ISP) or telephone company that offers digital services (18 U.S.C. §2510(15)). Remote computing services are defined as "the provision to the public of computer storage or processing services by means of an electronic communications system" (e.g., application service providers and certain Web-based services that provide services to the public; 18 U.S.C. §2511(2)).

The ECPA does not address security of data per se; however, to the extent it prohibits certain disclosures, organizations must be cognizant that such disclosures are not intentionally or knowingly made without authorization (e.g., providers of electronic communication or remote computing services need to ensure that such disclosures are not knowingly made unless expressly permitted by the ECPA). Where, for example, an employee or agent intentionally or knowingly discloses a stored communication (e.g., because he or she did not appreciate the restrictions on disclosure of such information or otherwise failed to follow privacy or security procedures), under certain circumstances the act of the employee or agent may be imputed to the employer, in which event the employer could be liable under the ECPA.

In *Muskovich v. Crowell* (1996), the court held that a telephone company did not knowingly disclose an unlisted telephone number (which the court assumed fell within the definition of electronic communication). There, an MCI employee, in violation of MCI's employee policies, obtained a subscriber's unlisted number and made a number of harassing phone calls to her. Finding that "the term knowingly means that the Defendant was aware of the nature of the conduct, aware of or possessing a firm belief in the existence of the requisite circumstances and an awareness of or a firm belief about the substantial certainty of the result," the court held that since "MCI trained Crowell in policies requiring confidentiality of customer information and prohibiting profanity and personal use of company facilities, services or customer information" and the defendant "violated MCI's express policies by making personal use of confidential information he obtained from customer records," without MCI's actual knowledge, MCI had not violated the ECPA by knowingly disclosing such information (*Id.* at *12-14).

The Uniting and Strengthening America by Providing Appropriate Tools Required to Intercept and Obstruct Terrorism Act (USA Patriot Act) amended the ECPA to expressly allow organizations to cooperate with law enforcement as part of a legitimate investigation and to permit the voluntary disclosure of stored communications in certain instances. The ECPA also permits the disclosure of stored communications with the consent of the originator or addressee of the stored communication. Such consent may be obtained, for example, through an appropriate employee manual, workplace policy, terms of use, or other agreement with the originator of the stored communication.

Sarbanes-Oxley Act

The Sarbanes-Oxley Act (SOX) was enacted in July 2002 in response to the corporate accounting scandals in the 1990s. The law has far-reaching implications on the disclosures and accounting practices of public companies and applies generally to companies (whether organized in the United States or elsewhere) that have registered equity or debt securities with the SEC under the Securities Exchange Act (SEA). Although SOX does not directly impose security requirements, it requires, among other things, that chief executive officers (CEOs) and chief financial officers (CFOs) of public companies provide a written statement with each periodic report certifying that the report fully complies with the requirements of Section 13(a) or 15(d) of the SEA and that the information contained in the report fairly presents, in all material respects, the financial condition and results of operations of the company. A CEO or CFO who provides such certification knowing that the report does not meet those standards may be fined up to $1 million, imprisoned for up to 10 years, or both. A CEO or CFO who willfully provides the certification knowing that the report does not meet those standards may be fined up to $5 million, imprisoned for up to 20 years, or both.

SOX also requires, through SEC rules, that the principal executive officers and principal financial officers of public companies certify the following in each annual and quarterly report:

1. the certifying officer has reviewed the report;
2. based on the knowledge of the officer, the report does not contain a material misstatement or material omission and the financial statements and other financial information included in the report fairly present, in all material respects, the financial condition and results of the operations of the company; and
3. each certifying officer (a) is responsible for establishing and maintaining effective internal controls; (b) has designed such internal controls to ensure that material information relating to the company is made known to him or her; (c) has evaluated the effectiveness of those controls as of a date no more than 90 days before filing the report; (d) has presented in the report his or her conclusions about the effectiveness of those controls; (e) has disclosed to the outside auditors and to the audit committee any significant deficiencies in those controls and any fraud involving management or other employees who have a significant role in the company's internal controls; (f) has identified to the outside auditors any material weaknesses in those controls; and (g) has stated in the report whether or not there were significant changes in the internal controls that could affect those controls, including any corrective actions.

SOX therefore imposes upon the directors and officers of a public company direct responsibility for corporate accounting practices and reporting and oversight over the company's internal controls relating thereto. The requirements placed upon directors and officers by SOX have had an indirect impact on security measures as increasingly auditing firms and other entities realize that the integrity of financial data cannot be ensured without an adequate security program and periodic audits thereof. SOX should therefore indirectly impact a company's use of IT by creating incentives to deploy adequate IT security solutions, and internal control measures, that will ensure and protect the integrity of corporate data comprising the company's SEC disclosures and reporting.

Furthermore, to the extent that any business maintains records in electronic format, and the data in those records is used in preparing corporate tax filings or SEC disclosures, the business may be required to later reproduce those data to support the accounting in the tax filings or the representations made in the disclosures. Accordingly, adequate safeguards should be undertaken to protect the integrity of that data.

Uniform Computer Information Transactions Act

The Uniform Computer Information Transactions Act (UCITA, 1999) was drafted by the National Conference of Commissioners on Uniform State Laws (NCCUSL) and was originally proposed as an amendment to the Uniform Commercial Code (UCC) in the form of a new article (UCC Article 2B). Fundamental disagreement over the substance of the language caused the project to be dropped as a proposed amendment to the UCC and recast as a stand-alone model act that could be adopted by each of the states. Approved by NCCUSL on July 29, 1999, only two states—Virginia and Maryland—have adopted UCITA as state law, and each has adopted the model act with some modifications.

Although UCITA attempted to establish uniform laws governing the licensing and use of software, it has been criticized on a number of grounds. For example, UCITA essentially validates shrink-wrap or click-through licenses—the standard, take-it-or-leave-it licenses that are often tied to software. A trap for any business would be the downloading and installation by employees of software onto company computers, where the software is accompanied by click-through licensing terms. In such instances, the business could be subject to those terms, even though the terms were not formally reviewed and accepted by the legal department.

UCITA also validates stop code, or software code, mechanisms that may deactivate the functionality of the software automatically over time, switch off use of the software for other reasons (e.g., if installed on a replacement computer), or otherwise allow the vendor to shut down the software remotely through a back door (e.g., through an Internet connection). The implications of such stop code are obvious, particularly where incorporated within mission critical software.

Anyone doing business in a jurisdiction that has recognized UCITA should consider the implications of that act. Furthermore, in negotiating any licensing or IT agreement, the parties should also be aware of a contract clause that attempts to apply any or all of the provisions of UCITA to the terms of the agreement.

Computer Fraud and Abuse Act

The Computer Fraud and Abuse Act (CFAA, 1986) is intended to reduce hacking of commercial computer systems and prohibits, among other things, anyone from intentionally accessing a computer without authorization and thereby improperly obtaining information from the computer (18 U.S.C. §1030 et seq.). The CFAA applies to computers (a) storing certain financial information, (b) storing information from any department or agency of the United States, and (c) used in interstate or foreign commerce or communication (18 U.S.C. §1030(a)(2)).

Violation of the CFAA is punishable by imposition of a fine, imprisonment, or both (18 U.S.C. §1030(c)). The CFAA permits, under certain circumstances, a person damaged by reason of a violation of the CFAA to bring a civil cause of action for compensatory damages and injunctive or other equitable relief (18 U.S.C. §1030(g)).

Although the CFAA requires intent to access a computer without authorization, instances may arise in which, for example, overzealous employees seek, intentionally, to obtain information from competitors to obtain a competitive advantage in the marketplace or in which a software tool is used, intentionally, to crawl, mine, or extract data from Web sites and databases available online, however, in doing so circumvent authorization requirements for legitimate access to that data. Such conduct could run afoul of the CFAA and risk civil liability, in addition to fines and, in certain instances, imprisonment of the violator.

Other U.S. Federal Statutes

Other U.S. statutes that impact data security from one angle or another (some of which apply only to government agencies) and are worth mentioning include the following:

1. The Privacy Act of 1974 which, in relevant part, provides that "no [government] agency shall disclose any record which is contained in a system of records by any means of communication to any person, or to another agency" (5 U.S.C. §552a).
2. The Computer Security Act of 1987 (amended by the Clinger-Cohen Act of 1996 and the E-Government Act of 2002), which requires the government to promulgate standards for computer security, train relevant employees in computer security and establish plans for the security and privacy of computer information. In relevant part, the act requires that

> each federal agency shall provide for the mandatory periodic training in computer security awareness and accepted computer security practice of all employees who are involved with the management, use or operation of each Federal computer system within or under the supervision of that agency ... [and] establish a plan for the security and privacy of each Federal computer system ... that is commensurate with the risk and magnitude of the harm resulting from the loss, misuse, or unauthorized access to or modification of the information contained in such system. (40 U.S.C. §1441)

3. The Clinger-Cohen Act (1996; formerly known as the Information Technology Management Reform Act), which directs executive agencies of the government to establish the position of chief information officers (CIO) and places responsibility on the CIO for

> providing advice and other assistance to the head of the executive agency and other senior management personnel of the executive agency to ensure that information technology is acquired and information resources

are managed for the executive agency ...; developing, maintaining, and facilitating the implementation of a sound and integrated information technology architecture for the executive agency; and promoting the effective and efficient design and operation of all major information resources management processes for the executive agency, including improvements to work processes of the executive agency. (40 U.S.C. §1401)

4. The Trade Secrets Act (2000), which criminalizes unauthorized government disclosure of trade secrets.
5. The Uniform Trade Secrets Act (1985), which has been adopted by a majority of the states in one form or another and which protects certain confidential information receiving the status of a trade secret under the terms of the act.
6. The Fair Credit Reporting Act (1970), which limits the disclosure and use of certain credit information appearing on a consumer's credit bureau report.
7. The Children's Online Privacy Protection Act (1998), which prohibits the online collection and use of information from children under the age of 13 without parental consent.
8. The Controlling the Assault of Non-Solicited Pornography and Marketing Act of 2003, which places certain restrictions on the transmittal of commercial e-mail.

See *Cobell v. Norton* (2001).

U.S. State Laws. There is a growing trend among the states, undoubtedly prompted by increasing public concern for such things as identity theft and misuse of private information, to enact privacy laws that would supplement the protections afforded by federal law. California, for example, has enacted a number of privacy-driven statutes, among them being the California Information Practices Act.

California Information Practices Act

California passed a unique law, effective July 1, 2003, requiring notification of security breaches. An amendment to the California Information Practices Act (2003), and titled Notice of Security Breach, the law requires any business or California state agency that maintains unencrypted computerized data that include personal information to notify any California resident of a security breach involving his or her personal information (CA Civil Code §§1798.29 and 1798.82–1798.84). The purpose of the law is to give affected individuals the opportunity to take steps to protect themselves from identity theft.

Under the California Act, personal information refers to "an individual's first name or first initial and last name in combination with any one or more of the following data elements, when either the name or the data elements are not encrypted" (CA Civil Code §1798.82(e)):

- Social Security number.
- Driver's license number or California identification card number.

- Account number, credit or debit card number, in combination with any required security code, access code, or password that would permit access to an individual's financial account.

" 'Breach of the security of the system' means unauthorized acquisition of computerized data that compromises the security, confidentiality, or integrity of personal information maintained by the person or business" (CA Civil Code §1798.82(d)). The law states that

> any person or business that *conducts business in California*, and that owns or licenses computerized data that includes personal information, shall disclose any breach of the security of the system following discovery or notification of the breach in the security of the data to any resident of California whose unencrypted personal information was, *or is reasonably believed to have been*, acquired by an unauthorized person. (CA Civil Code §1798.82(a); emphasis added)

Because the law applies to any business or person that *conducts business in California*, it has the potential to affect many businesses located outside the state of California (i.e., even if the business does not have a physical presence within the state), particularly companies that conduct business through a Web site via the Internet. Furthermore, because the law requires a business to notify affected individuals if a security breach is *reasonably believed* to have occurred, businesses that believe they may have been subject to a breach will need to make a prompt assessment of the situation to determine whether notification is required under the law.

To the extent applicable, the owner or licensee of the information must also be notified (CA Civil Code §1798.82(b)). For example, where a data processor or outsourcer is handling data on behalf of another organization and the data processor's systems are breached, and the other organization is deemed the owner of the data, the data processor will need to notify the organization of the security breach. The statute allows for a private cause of action, thus permitting those who have been injured by a violation of the statute to seek redress in a lawsuit (CA Civil Code §1798.84).

Because many organizations shy away from public disclosure of security breaches, largely because of the public relations fallout, the California law has caused a fair amount of commotion. The law will require, at least when the personal information of California residents is concerned, that organizations immediately notify such individuals (and perhaps the organization's business associates, if they own the data) when there is reason to believe that their personal information has been compromised due to a breach of the organization's (or its subcontractor's) IT systems. At least one lawsuit, seeking class action status, has been filed under the California law (see *Hamilton v. Microsoft Corp.*, 2003). The complaint alleged that Microsoft's response to security vulnerability, in respect of its Windows operating system and other software

products, is not sufficient to protect important and vital information and data.

State Consumer Protection Laws

Given its limited resources, the FTC has not often pursued privacy violations of the sort mentioned in the foregoing section. State attorneys general may pursue claims under state consumer protection laws whether or not the FTC pursues the matter under the FTCA. For example, in the FTC Toysmart action (*Federal Trade Commission v. Toysmart.com, LLC*, 2000), the FTC proposed a settlement with Toysmart, but the attorneys general of 47 states rejected that settlement, filing an objection to the FTC's application to enter the settlement (see *In re Toysmart.com, LLC*, 2000).

There are a number of state consumer protection laws that resemble the FTCA in addressing false, misleading, or deceptive business practices. In some states, the language of the state consumer protection law parallels that of Section 5 of the FTCA. See *Vermont v. International Collection Service, Inc.* (1991), in which "fourteen states have adopted this version [of the Unfair Trade Practices and Consumer Protection Law as proposed by the FTC], commonly known as the mini-FTC act." State consumer protection laws are typically enforced by the office of the state attorney general but may allow for a private cause of action by consumers. See *Florez v. Linens 'n Things, Inc.* (2003), in which California consumer protection law permits private action regarding retailer's collection of personal information from customer.

Attorneys general have already shown an indication that they will pursue action where the security of personal information is compromised. For example, the New York State Office of the Attorney General (NYOAG) announced a multistate agreement with technology publisher Ziff Davis Media Inc. to "redress an Internet security breach that exposed the personal information of thousands of magazine subscribers online." According to the NYOAG,

> a magazine promotion Ziff Davis ran on its website in November of [2001]...allowed a computer file of approximately 12,000 subscription orders for Electronic Gaming Monthly to be accessed by anyone surfing the Internet. Personal data was exposed, including credit card information, which resulted in some subscribers becoming victims of identity theft.

The NYOAG noted that Ziff Davis's "privacy policy promised reasonable security, but it was not effective in this case" (Office of New York State Attorney General Eliot Spitzer, 2002).

In October 2003, the NYOAG settled a claim against Victoria's Secret Direct, LLC that the company's Web site allowed users to view online order information of other users, including personal information such as name, billing address, and items ordered. The NYOAG noted that

> the published privacy policy for Victoria's Secret indicated that: "Any information you provide to

us at this site when you establish or update an account, enter a contest, shop online or request information...is maintained in private files on our secure web server and internal systems...." (Office of New York State Attorney General Eliot Spitzer, 2003)

Where a private cause of action is allowed, an aggrieved consumer may sue to recover his or her damages or, if permitted by the statute, statutory damages, treble damages, or both.

Foreign Laws. The security of data may be impacted by laws outside the United States. For example, the European Union follows a Data Protection Directive that imposes various limitations and restrictions on the access, use, and disclosure of personal information (European Parliament, 1995). The Data Protection Directive is implemented as national law by the member countries of the European Union. The directive requires certain security measures to be taken:

1. The organization having control of the personal data (the controller) must implement appropriate technical and organizational measures to protect personal data against accidental or unlawful destruction or accidental loss and against unauthorized alteration, disclosure or access, in particular where the processing involves the transmission of data over a network, and against all other unlawful forms of processing. Having regard to the state of the art and the costs of their implementation, such measures shall ensure a level of security appropriate to the risks represented by the processing and the nature of the data to be protected (European Parliament, 1995, Article 17, ¶ 1).
2. The "controller must, where processing is carried out on his behalf, choose a processor who provides sufficient guarantees in respect of the technical security measures and organizational measures governing the processing to be carried out and must ensure compliance with those measures" (European Parliament, 1995, Article 17, ¶ 2).
3. The carrying out of processing by a processor must be governed by a contract binding the processor to the controller and stipulating in particular that (i) the processor shall act only on instructions from the controller, and (ii) the obligations set out in paragraph 1 above shall also apply to the processor (European Parliament, 1995, Article 17, ¶ 3).

The Data Protection Directive also restricts the transfer of certain information outside the European Union to countries that do not provide adequate safeguards to ensure the privacy and security of the data. See European Parliament (2002). As of March 2004, the United States was not considered to be a country that provides adequate safeguards. Thus, under the directive, personal data (e.g., employee data collected by human resource departments, customer information, and prospective client lists) cannot normally be transferred from the European office of a company to its U.S. office or to any other person or entity

in the United States. There are three mechanisms in place, however, to legally effectuate such a transfer:

1. Where the individual consents to the transfer of his or her data.
2. Where the parties enter into a contract incorporating model clauses approved by the European Commission in which the transferee agrees to safeguard the data in accordance with those clauses (see "Model contracts," n.d.).
3. For data transferred to the United States, where the U.S.-based business registers for and adheres to the Safe Harbor, a set of rules developed by the U.S. Department of Congress and approved by the European Commission (see "Safe harbor overview," n.d.).

Under certain local European laws, the transfer of personal data must be registered with a designated local authority. The failure to adhere to the restrictions of the Data Protection Directive could result in a violation of European law.

CONTRACTUAL LIABILITY

Liability may arise under a breach of contract claim. There are at least two distinct categories of contracts that could be impacted by a security breach:

1. Business-to-business contracts, such as vendor agreements, outsourcing agreements, facility management agreements, independent contractor agreements, application service provider agreements, service bureau agreements, transaction fulfillment agreements, hosting agreements, co-location agreements, and agreements for contingency planning, backup, and disaster-recovery services—in all of which one party is being entrusted with responsibility for, or has access to, sensitive data of the other party.
2. Consumer contracts, which may arise in varying contexts, such as through a Web site click-through agreement, privacy policy, terms of use, subscriber agreement or user agreement, or, perhaps, where statutorily mandated, such as for financial information governed by GLB and health information covered by HIPAA or in any other context in which an organization has made a representation to the consumer with respect to the privacy or security of his or her personal information.

Requirements of a Binding Contract

There must be mutual intent of the parties for there to be a binding contract, including an offer, acceptance, and consideration. See generally, Restatement (Second), Contracts, ch. 3, 4; see also *Maher v. United States* (2002). These requirements are almost always satisfied with a written agreement signed by at least two parties, particularly in a commercial setting in which the agreement is usually entered into by relatively sophisticated parties and often reviewed by attorneys. Although a contract need not necessarily be in writing to be binding, it is customary for many to be written instruments.

In the absence of an express agreement, a promise may nonetheless be enforceable under the theory of promissory estoppel or implied contract.

> The elements of promissory estoppel are: (1) a promise unambiguous in its terms; (2) reliance on such promise by the party to whom it is made; (3) this reliance is expected and foreseeable by the party making the promise; and (4) the one to whom the promise is made must rely on the promise to his injury. (*Cohabaco Cigar Co. v. United States Tobacco Co.*, 1999)

A "standardized contract, which, imposed and drafted by the party of superior bargaining strength, relegates to the subscribing party only the opportunity to adhere to the contract or reject it" is referred to as a contract of adhesion (Armendariz v. Foundation Health Psychcare Services, 2000) (citations and internal quotation omitted); see also *Farnsworth on Contracts* §4.26 (2001). ("The form may be a take-it-or-leave-it proposition, often called a contract of adhesion, under which the only alternative to complete adherence is outright rejection.") An online agreement, for example, may be a contract of adhesion since the end user may either accept or reject it, but has no power to negotiate its terms (Comb v. PayPal, Inc., 2002, for reviewing online agreement in terms of a contract of adhesion). If there were unequal bargaining power in the formation of a contract, as is true with a contract of adhesion, courts are likely to interpret any ambiguity in the contract against the drafter and in favor of the nondrafting party (*Farnsworth on Contracts* §4.26 (LEXIS 2001); *Comb*, 2002, 218 F. Supp. 2d at 1172). Furthermore, the fact that a contract is one of adhesion may sway the court that a provision of the contract is unconscionable and thus unenforceable (*Comb*, 2002, 218 F. Supp. 2d at 1172).

There is case law that supports the view that a cause of action may be maintained in contract for an unauthorized disclosure of personal information. For example, in *Peterson v. Idaho First National Bank* (1961), the Idaho Supreme Court dismissed the plaintiff's invasion of privacy claim but held open the possibility that the bank had breached an implied contractual duty of confidentiality. In that case, the plaintiff's manager had asked the bank to inform him when any of his employees did anything to discredit his company. A bank official informed the manager that the plaintiff had written several bad checks. The plaintiff brought suit against the bank for its unauthorized disclosure of his personal information. The court focused on the relationship of the parties and the nature of the information in finding that "it is implicit in the contract of the bank with its customer or depositor that no information may be disclosed by the bank or its employees concerning the customer's or depositor's account, and that, unless authorized by law or by the customer or depositor, the bank must be held liable for breach of the implied contract" (*Id.* at 290; see also *Barnett Bank of West Fla. v. Hooper*, 1986, acknowledging that a bank may have an implied contractual duty not to disclose information regarding a customer's account absent special circumstances such as fraud; and *Suburban Trust Co. v. Waller*, 1979,

recognizing a bank's implied contractual duty to keep private information concerning its customer's account).

Remedies

Damages

In a breach of contract action, the normal remedy for the aggrieved party is to recover his or her actual damages attributable to the breach. Where personal information has been disclosed due to a security breach, it may, however, be difficult to quantify the damages. In fact, a consumer may have no provable damages. For example, it has been held that a person suffered no quantifiable damage when his personal information was sold to third parties for marketing purposes (*Dwyer v. American Express Co.*,1995, in which the plaintiffs did not suffer damages by credit card company's disclosure of cardholders' credit card purchases and contact information; and *Smith v. Chase Manhattan Bank, USA, N.A.*, 2002: "Thus, the 'harm' at the heart of this purported class action, is that class members were merely offered products and services which they were free to decline. This does not qualify as actual harm.").

However, if the disclosure results in identity theft, there could be some level of real damages incurred. A survey by CalPIRG and the Privacy Rights Clearinghouse in May 2000 found that the average consumer identity theft victim spends 175 hours and $800 resolving identity theft problems and that it takes 2 to 4 years for victims to resolve all the resulting problems ("Identity theft," n.d.). Thus, there could be a quantifiable amount of actual damages in which a breach results in the disclosure of personal information of many individuals. Furthermore, it would be naïve to assume that any unauthorized disclosure of personal information would result in no damage, especially in light of the changing legal climate concerning the privacy and security of such information.

Consumer harm aside, in the commercial context the disclosure or loss of corporate data could have a substantial financial impact. For example, an unauthorized disclosure of trade secrets or customer information could put a business at a significant competitive disadvantage and, in some cases, ruin the business. Most commercial contracts will contain disclaimers of certain damages and limitations of liability. Depending on which side of the contract you are on, this may or may not be reassuring. For example, many contracts disclaim liability for consequential damages. Whereas direct, or compensatory, damages usually equate to the amount of money to put the aggrieved party in as good a position had the breaching party not breached (e.g., the amount of money that a customer had agreed to pay), indirect, or consequential, damages reflect the natural and probable consequences flowing from the breach and can be significantly more than the direct damages. Examples of damages that, depending upon the nature of the contract, tend to be consequential in nature include lost profits, loss of business, and loss of goodwill.

Damages that are consequential may not be recoverable if the parties have contracted to exclude them from liability in the event of a breach. Thus, if the disclosure of a trade secret or some other confidential information causes a business to lose a competitive edge in the marketplace, results in a public relations fiasco possibly driving down the stock, or if the loss or corruption of data leads to a loss of business or loss of clients, to the extent the damages are consequential in nature, the injured party may not be able to recover. Some contracts, however, exclude from the disclaimer of damages certain breaches of the contract or conduct of a party, such as a breach of an obligation to maintain the confidentiality of confidential information, a breach of a security requirement, or for reason of a party's negligence, recklessness, willful misconduct, or intentional conduct. Such exceptions could allow for recovery for such losses under certain circumstances.

Additionally, commercial contracts often limit the amount of liability to a dollar figure or a fixed amount, such as the total fees paid or a multiple thereof. Some contracts will limit the amount to the fees paid during a particular term of the contract, such as 1 year preceding the accrual of the claim. Unless there is an express carve out from the limitation of liability, the dollar cap would typically apply to any claim under the contract, including a claim for breach of confidentiality or breach of security (unless, for example, the applicable jurisdiction recognizes a tort claim for gross negligence or willful misconduct in such instance or otherwise, for public policy reasons, would disregard the contractual limitation of liability given the reckless or intentional conduct of the breaching party). The limitation of liability and disclaimers of damages are therefore very important aspects of any IT-related contract because, depending on which side of the contract a person is on, these clauses will greatly impact his or her financial risk in the event of a security breach. Accordingly, the precise wording of these clauses should be carefully considered during the contract negotiations.

Many contracts also include some type of indemnity, which can likewise affect financial liability arising from a security breach. For example, a clause that requires Party A to indemnify Party B for third-party claims arising out of a breach of a representation or warranty, or for Party A's or its subcontractors' negligence, recklessness, or willful misconduct, could make Party A contractually obligated to defend, indemnify, and hold harmless Party B should Party B become involved in a claim based on Party A's unauthorized disclosure of Party B's confidential information. The indemnity there could be triggered where, for example, the contract contained a representation or warranty regarding the confidentiality, privacy, or security of information or a representation or warranty against viruses, Trojan horses, worms, or other malicious code. It could also be triggered if Party A were negligent in, for example, exercising adequate safeguards to protect the information (e.g., in failing to use suitable firewalls or encryption, failing to screen employees and subcontractors and to do background checks, failing to provide adequate employee training, or failing to utilize reasonable physical and logical security).

Where there is a stream of providers of technology services, it is wise to ensure that the contractual chain is not broken at some point, thereby exposing one party to unnecessary liability. It is not at all uncommon to have various contracts and subcontracts involving multiple providers of IT services. In many instances, it is desirable to have the contracts contain similar obligations—particularly concerning liability—flowing upstream. For example, a provider that assumes responsibility to its customer in a contract, and then subcontracts out some or all of its obligations to another party, should take care to ensure that the contract with its subcontractor contains obligations similar to those in its customer contract. If there are gaps in the contractual obligations, the provider may, in the event of a breach, find itself in between its customer and its subcontractor with no contractual recourse against its subcontractor. This is particularly acute when the provider has agreed to indemnify its customer, but has failed to secure the same indemnity from its subcontractor. If, for example, the subcontractor releases customer data without authorization, thereby triggering the provider's indemnity to its customer, the provider may have to indemnify its customer, but not have a reciprocal right to obtain indemnity from the subcontractor. Thus, to the extent feasible, contractual obligations, particularly those affecting liability (e.g., indemnities, warranties, and disclaimers), should flow upstream.

It is worth noting that the value of any indemnity is tied directly to the financial wherewithal of the party giving it. That is, if the indemnifying party should become insolvent, the indemnity may be worthless. The contracting parties may therefore wish to explore, in addition to an indemnity provision, specific insurance commitments in the agreement.

It is also prudent to recognize downstream liability. For example, a provider of certain data may restrict the usage of data it provides to another service provider which, in turn, may offer those data bundled with other products and services to an end user. The end user may be bound, through its contract with the service provider, to adhere to the data provider's restrictions. In the absence of such a contract, the data may be protected by copyright or other intellectual property rights. Accordingly, the end user should be aware of potential liability it faces for any misuse of the data.

Equitable Relief

Equitable relief may be available where damages will not adequately compensate the injured party. If there is a contract, a court may order that the nonbreaching party specifically perform its obligations under the contract (see *Marquardt and Roche/Meditz and Hackett, Inc. v. Riverbend Executive Center, Inc.*, 2003, in which "the specific performance remedy is a form of injunctive decree in which the court orders the defendant to perform the contract"). In the context of a promise not to disclose personal information, a court may order the business to perform its promise not to disclose the information or to cease an ongoing disclosure. The burden rests with the party seeking equitable relief to show that there is no adequate remedy at law (see *Marquardt*, 74 Conn. App. at 421, 812 A.2d at 182, in which "a party seeking injunctive relief has the burden of alleging and proving irreparable harm and lack of an adequate remedy at law").

As a practical matter, to prevent the business from disclosing the information while the merits of the case are adjudicated, the claimant would seek interim relief in the form of a preliminary injunction. To obtain a preliminary injunction, the claimant must show that he or she will be irreparably harmed if the action is not enjoined (*Chicago Research & Trading v. New York Futures Exchange, Inc.*, 1982, in which "injunctive relief will be afforded only in those extraordinary situations where the plaintiff has no adequate remedy at law and such relief is necessary to avert irreparable injury.").

Web Sites

The Internet presented a new twist to traditional contract theory. In the online context, such as with a Web site terms of use, there is a written document (albeit in electronic form) but no signatures by the parties (at least not in the traditional penmanship sense; there may be electronic signatures for purposes of logging a transaction). Nonetheless, a business that posts an online terms of use or privacy policy on its Web site may be bound to the promises made in those terms or that policy. A terms-of-use or privacy policy may be a binding contract, enforceable by the customer against the organization that posted the terms or policy on its Web site. The enforceability of an online contract depends essentially upon basic contract principles. An online contract has been held enforceable (see *Hughes v. America Online, Inc.*, 2002, in which enforcing forum selection clause in an online click-through terms-of-service agreement; see also *Comb v. PayPal, Inc.*, 2002, in which a binding online agreement may shown by the assent of the parties).

The FTC has urged businesses to clearly inform consumers of their information collection practices. See, for example, FTC's Fair Information Practice Principles (n.d.). Although posting a privacy policy on a Web site is not legally required, it has become common practice. A carefully drafted privacy policy might be considered a proper means of disclosing to consumers a business's information collection, use, and disclosure practices and thereby fend off claims by consumers that they were unaware that, by uploading their personal information to a Web site, the information would be used or disclosed in various ways. In that regard, so long as the privacy policy accurately reflects an organization's practices, and the organization follows those practices, the policy might be used as a means to head off potential consumer confusion and complaints. An organization must, however, adhere to the statements in its policy. (According to Simpson, 2001, "Amazon.com and its Alexa Internet subsidiary probably made deceptive statements about their privacy practices ... [by] surreptitiously collecting personal data on customers through its Alexa system, which is designed to assist shopping and other activities online.")

Terms of Use and Privacy Policies

As a general principle, a Web site agreement will be enforceable against the end user if there is mutuality, that is, if the end user has assented to its terms. Courts have enforced online terms of service where the end user had to view the terms and affirmatively accept them (e.g., by clicking an I Accept button). The evolving case law indicates that where a business seeks to enforce its online terms against the end user, it must demonstrate that the end user affirmatively assented to the terms. See, for example, *Hughes v. America Online, Inc.*, 2002, which upheld the forum selection clause in a click-wrap agreement governing use of an e-mail service; *Groff v. America Online, Inc.*, 1998, which enforced the click-through choice of law clause in online terms of service agreement where user clicked "I agree" not once but twice; and *Caspi v. Microsoft Network, LLC*, 1999, which enforced forum selection clause in a click-through agreement for use of Internet service. See also *Stomp, Inc. v. Neato*, 1999, which commented that "'clickwrap agreement' allows the consumer to manifest its assent to the terms of a contract by 'clicking' on an acceptance button on the website."

Conversely, it would appear evident that the terms should be enforceable against the owner of the Web site who actually posted them. Under basic contract theory, the posted terms would, in essence, be an offer of a contract. If the end user accepts, there should be a binding contract. The end user, however, must have accepted the terms for them to be binding. See, for example, *Gibson v. United States*, 2003, in which elements of a contract must be shown to be entitled to a reward; and *Otworth v. The Florida Bar*, 1999, in which an offer for a reward is contractual and a "claimant must allege 'knowledge of existence of the offer of reward' to be entitled to the benefits of such reward." It has been held that an individual need only have been aware of the terms, and not have relied upon a particular term or even have read the terms, of a contract for it to be binding upon him or her (*Reuben H. Donnelley Corp. v. American Protective Services Corp.*, 1986, in which "this court agrees and holds that APS [American Protective Services] cannot avoid the contracts on the basis that it chose not to read them"). Where a Web site has posted terms, and an end user alleges he or she was aware of the terms, the owner of the Web site will be hard pressed to argue that it is not contractually bound to those terms. If a terms-of-use or privacy policy makes overly broad claims about maintaining the privacy or ensuring the security of personal information, it is conceivable that an end user may bring a breach-of-contract claim if there is a security breach that discloses his or her personal information. Identity theft resulting from an unauthorized disclosure is one area of significant concern and may generate such claims.

Two important considerations regarding privacy policies are (1) amendments to a privacy policy and (2) the sale of assets that include information collected under an existing privacy policy. If an organization desires to amend the terms of a privacy policy, and wishes the amendment to apply retroactively to information it had collected under the earlier privacy policy, it should notify all those whose information it had already collected of the amendment. This may be done by e-mail or, perhaps, by posting notice of the amendment on its Web site, so long as the organization has reason to believe that the affected individuals will receive notice in that manner. If an individual objects to his or her information being used in the manner set forth in the amendment, the organization should respect the individual's request and take appropriate measures, such as removing his or her information from the database or otherwise tagging that information for restricted use or disclosure. In addition to raising contracting concerns (e.g., such as an unconscionable term in a contract of adhesion), a failure to follow these steps could run afoul of the FTCA or state consumer protection laws as improper use of a consumer contract or possibly a misrepresentation to the consumer.

Where assets subject to purchase in a business transaction include information collected under an existing privacy policy, the acquiring business may have difficulty obtaining the information if it were collected under a privacy policy that indicated that such information would not be disclosed to third parties. For example, in 2000 the FTC and state attorneys general attempted to block the transfer of customer information collected by failed online toy retailer Toysmart.com LLC in a bankruptcy asset sale because the company had collected the information under a privacy policy that stated that personal information "is never shared with a third party." In response to the Toysmart matter, many businesses amended their privacy policies to state that they could transfer information in event of bankruptcy or an acquisition, merger, or sale of the company's assets. The FTC has indicated that a business obtaining such personal information should continue to respect the commitments made in the privacy policy under which the information was collected, unless it seeks to amend the terms of the privacy policy.

Privacy Seal Programs

Some private companies offer, for a fee, to certify that a privacy policy and the privacy practices of a business are trustworthy. Two companies that maintain seal programs are TRUSTe and BBBonline. If the policy and practices are certified, the business is permitted to display the sponsor's privacy seal. An organization may enter into an agreement with the sponsor of a seal program to display the seal on its Web site. The agreement will likely require, in addition to compliance with the organization's own posted policies and procedures, adherence to certain other policies regarding personal information that is required by the seal sponsor. Should the organization fail to comply with the terms of its agreement with the sponsor, due to a security breach or otherwise, it may find itself in breach of its contractual obligations to the sponsor. For example, in the Toysmart bankruptcy, TRUSTe intervened to enjoin the sale of Toysmart's customer list, asserting that the sale would be in breach of its seal licensing agreement with Toysmart. See Objection of Trusted Universal Standards In Electronic Transactions (TRUSTe) To Motion To Approve Stipulation, *In re Toysmart.com, LLC*, 2000.

TORT LIABILITY

A tort is "a legal wrong committed upon the person or property independent of contract" (Garner, 1983). In certain instances, the law will impose upon a person a duty of care. If the person fails to fulfill that duty, he or she may be liable to another person who has suffered damage as a result of the failed duty. Liability under tort theory may apply where there is no contract between two parties. Negligence, gross negligence, willful misconduct, and strict liability are common tort theories of liability.

Elements of a Tort

A party may be liable under a tort theory if

- the law recognizes a duty of care (e.g., to maintain the security of data or to prevent security breaches);
- there is a breach of that duty;
- there is a proximate relationship between the breach of the duty and the injury; and
- actual loss or damage is incurred as a result of the breach.

There is presently no clearly established duty of care with regard to the security of data under tort law. A leading case discussing when a tort duty should be imposed is *United States v. Carroll Towing Co., Inc.*, 1947. That case assessed whether a duty should be imposed based upon several factors: (1) the probability that harm will occur, (2) the gravity of the resulting harm, and (3) the burden of adequate precautions (*Id.* at 173). Under that rationale, a duty should exist if the probability of harm occurring and the magnitude of that harm outweigh the burden of avoiding the harm.

A handful of cases may offer guidance as to whether there exists such a duty. For example, in the banking context, it has been held that a bank has a duty to keep certain information confidential (*DJowharzadeh v. City Nat'l Bank & Trust Co.*, 1982). In that case, a bank customer provided to the bank's loan officer certain confidential information about a proposed real estate purchase, which the loan officer then disclosed to other individuals who used the information to the customer's detriment. Stating that the "customer's cause of action is, with these special facts, properly framed in terms of tortious conduct," the court held that the "bank's relationship to a loan applicant implicitly imposes the duty to keep the contents of loan applications confidential. This duty has existed traditionally and continues to exist, if not specifically in the law books, at least in the mind of the public in general and within the banking community in particular" (*Id.* at 620).

On the other hand, in *Stevens v. First Interstate Bank of California* (2000), the court held that a bank does not have a duty to safeguard personal information. In that case, the court framed the issue as follows:

> Where a third party misappropriates personal or credit information that a depositor had provided to a bank, and that misappropriation is the result of the bank's failure to adequately protect the information from such misappropriation, is the bank liable for the depositor's resulting emotional distress? (*Id.* at 285–286)

Viewing the bank–customer relationship in that case as "more analogous to a merchant-customer relationship in which the customer, in transacting a credit card or other noncash purchase, provides certain information to the merchant," the court concluded that the relationship between the parties had no element of a trust in it (e.g., in holding money in trust for someone) and, therefore, did not give rise to a duty on the part of the bank to protect the information from misappropriation (*Id.* at 288).

At least one case has found a duty to secure sensitive records accessible via the Internet under the theory that the party responsible for trust fund records had a fiduciary duty to protect them from unauthorized disclosure (*Cobell v. Norton*, 2001). In *Cobell*, the Department of the Interior (DOI) held or created in systems managed and administered by the Bureau of Indian Affairs Office of Information Resources Management certain Indian trust funds and individual Indian trust records. The information was kept on systems that were accessible to the Internet without firewalls, encryption, or other means of reasonable security. In a scathing report, the special master criticized the DOI for failing to employ adequate safeguards and recommended that the court intervene to take control over the DOI's IT systems. The special master found that the DOI had a fiduciary duty to safeguard information relating to the trust and that the DOI had derogated that duty by failing to implement satisfactory IT security safeguards (*Id.* at *141).

The fiduciary relationship in the *Cobell* case arose because of the special nature of the data—trust fund records—the special duty for which was already well established in common law. See *Rippey v. Denver U.S. Nat. Bank* (1967), in which "it is generally agreed that a trustee owes a duty to his beneficiaries to exercise such care and skill as a man of ordinary prudence would exercise in safeguarding and preserving his own property." Absent such a relationship, however, it is not clear that a duty would exist to safeguard sensitive information such as names, addresses, telephone numbers, or Social Security numbers. The lack of clear precedent either way—whether in favor of a duty or declining to recognize any duty—renders the notion of a tort claim for data security somewhat uncertain. The issue will undoubtedly present itself, and may, for example, arise in the context of an individual whose personal information was allegedly not adequately safeguarded, for example, after he or she uploaded that information through a Web site.

What Is Reasonable?

Were a court to find that a tort duty exists, the duty of care could vary depending upon the circumstances. Generally, however, the law will apply a duty to exercise *reasonable* care. A person who fails to exercise a reasonable duty of care is said to have been negligent. In tort cases, courts routinely determine what is reasonable under the circumstances drawing upon what has been learned in past cases and evidence offered in the current case. The oft-quoted measure in assessing reasonableness is what would a reasonable person have done under the circumstances. Of course, the issue of reasonableness is often open to debate and the subject of intense disagreement during a litigation.

Perhaps one of the most significant hurdles in a claim of negligence regarding data security is ascertaining what would be reasonable. Many people—courts included—lack a good understanding of the technical nuances that comprise IT and information security. A genuine lack of familiarity with the subject makes it extraordinarily difficult to assess reasonableness because one would have to defer to others' experiences as to what may or may not

be reasonable on an otherwise foreign subject. Moreover, like IT in general, security technologies are ever in flux, rapidly changing as computer technologies change. What may be reasonable one day may not be a short time later.

There is also a wide range of security needs, depending upon the nature of the data and the perceived risks. For example, sensitive personal information that a business considers a valuable asset and that represents a would-be target for thieves might require greater levels of security than similar, but less sensitive, information of little interest to hackers. Thus, there could be widely divergent security standards that are, nonetheless, reasonable under differing circumstances.

Because there are many differing approaches to security, the idea of one reasonable standard that could be applied across the board may be difficult to accept. Indeed, a single common standard for data security might even prove undesirable insofar as it could actually make hacking easier if would-be hackers knew that most security systems adhered to a similar common technical standard. However, it may be prudent to have certain general principles governing policies and procedures regarding security, but allow the technical implementation of security devices, applications, and systems to differ across individual business enterprises. Following the example in the HIPAA Privacy and Security Rule, for example, it may be acceptable to establish administrative, physical, technical, and organizational standards for safeguarding data, leaving the implementation of those standards to each organization (this, of course, would not completely solve the issue as there would still need to be some level of determination as to whether the standards were reasonably implemented within the parameters established).

For torts commonly seen by courts, there is ample case law to draw upon in assessing what would be reasonable. Where there is no well-established standard, as appears currently true for data security, a court may look to several factors in its attempt to assess what would have been reasonable under the circumstances. For example, a court may consider an argument concerning the costs to implement certain levels of security in relation to the risks involved. A plaintiff may be able to proffer a convincing argument that, where the risks substantially outweigh the costs or where the costs are relatively insignificant to a corporate budget, a business acted unreasonably in not applying more rigid, but costly, security protocols. A court may also entertain expert testimony concerning the security policies and procedures of other similarly situated organizations, the thinking being that if certain policies and procedures are being exercised by a number of a defendant's counterparts, it would be reasonable for the defendant to have followed similar policies and procedures.

A court may also consider industry standards to the extent there is some agreement within an industry as to what those standards are. In this regard, a court may look to examples in organizations that proffer security standards or otherwise audit security risks. It may also consider evidence of relevant statutory language and the requirements set out in regulatory pronouncements, such as GLB and HIPAA, that speak to the security of data.

Establishing a Standard

A judicially construed standard may be drawn from various sources. The following offers examples of sources that could be given weight in arriving at such a standard.

Statutes and Regulations

A statute that was enacted in 2002, the Federal Information Security Management Act (FISMA), may provide guidance as to what steps an organization should take in safeguarding. FISMA applies to government agencies and is therefore binding upon them. It is not binding upon private sector companies, but its principles may serve to establish standards applicable to private business. FISMA was enacted to

(1) provide a comprehensive framework for ensuring the effectiveness of information security controls over information resources that support Federal operations and assets;

(2) recognize the highly networked nature of the current Federal computing environment and provide effective government wide management and oversight of the related information security risks, including coordination of information security efforts throughout the civilian, national security, and law enforcement communities; (3) provide for development and maintenance of minimum controls required to protect Federal information and information systems; [and] (4) provide a mechanism for improved oversight of Federal agency information security programs. See 44 U.S.C. § 3541(1)-(4).

It is intended to provide a framework for government agencies to improve security and risk management processes by mandating reporting on security compliance with a set of standard internal controls. FISMA makes government agencies accountable for implementing defensible security measures and requires greater reporting on these security activities. The intent is to show government regulators an agency's security benchmark, how each agency is progressing against this benchmark, and how they continue to improve agency security measures on a year-over-year basis.

Among other things, FISMA focuses on (1) developing and overseeing the implementation of information security policies; (2) requiring agencies to identify and provide information security protections commensurate with the risk and magnitude of the harm resulting from the unauthorized access, use, disclosure, disruption, modification or destruction of information or information systems used by or on behalf of an agency (including systems operated by agency contractors); and (3) coordinating the development of standards and guidelines under the National Institute of Standards and Technology (NIST) Act with agencies and offices operating or exercising control of national security systems (including the National Security Agency) to ensure, to the maximum extent feasible, that such standards and guidelines are complementary with standards and guidelines developed for national security systems (see 44 U.S.C. §3543(1)-(3)). FISMA requires that each federal enterprise information security program be placed under the CIO and mandates an independent information security program audit function which is assigned to each agency's Office of Inspector General. Because the program is placed under the CIO, it can be fully and completely integrated into the budget process to ensure that information security is adequately addressed throughout the life cycle of any and all IT-related programs. This framework allows for budget integration and independent audit functions and, by way of such, is intended to result in an effective security program.

Other statutes, such as GLB and HIPAA, which outline requirements for information security, might also be considered in developing broader security standards for corporate and personal information.

Government and Industry Standards

The Bush administration outlined a plan to enhance security of IT systems known as *The National Strategy to Secure Cyberspace* (2003). In conceptual terms, it articulates five national priorities for security; identifies eight major actions and initiatives to reduce threats and related vulnerabilities; identifies four major actions and initiatives for awareness, education, and training; identifies five major actions and initiatives for the securing of governments' cyberspace; and identifies six major actions and initiatives to strengthen U.S. national security and international cooperation. Although the concepts are general in nature, and are not necessarily binding on anyone (they are set out in a strategy), they may be one of several things that factor into broad security standards.

In December 2003, the president signed Homeland Security Presidential Directive-7 (HSPD-7) titled "Critical Infrastructure Identification, Prioritization, and Protection." Based on that directive, the Department of Homeland Security has chartered the National Cyber Security Division (NCSD), and that office is responsible for implementing the national strategy. NCSD chartered the U.S. Computer Emergency Response Team (US CERT).

Guidance may also be gleaned from organizations that propose standards for IT security. For example, Statement on Auditing Standards (SAS) No. 70 is an auditing standard developed by the American Institute of Certified Public Accountants (AICPA). SAS 70 requires service organizations to disclose their control activities and processes to their customers and their customers' auditors in a uniform reporting format. The purpose of an SAS 70 examination is for a service organization to have its control objectives and control activities examined by an independent accounting and auditing firm that will issue an auditor's opinion ("About SAS 70," n.d.).

Implementation and Security Risk Analysis ISO 17799 is a detailed security standard offered by the International Organization for Standardization (ISO). ISO is a nongovernmental organization that develops standards for a variety of applications, particularly technical standards. ISO 17799 is intended to counteract interruptions to business activities and to critical business processes from the effects of major failures or disasters. It sets out a number of standards concerning business continuity planning, system access control, system development and maintenance, physical and environmental security, compliance, personnel security, security organization, computer and operations management, asset classification and control, and security policies ("ISO 17799: What Is It?" n.d.).

Another agency that promulgates guidelines relevant to IT security is the NIST. NIST "works with industry, research, and government organizations to make [information] technology more usable, more secure, more scalable, and more interoperable than it is today" (*Cobell v. Norton*, 2001, *34, fn. 21, quoting Dr. William O. Mehuron, "Information Technology Laboratory: What ITL Does," n.d.). Pursuant to the Information Technology Management Reform Act (Public Law 104-106), the secretary of commerce approves standards and guidelines that are developed by the NIST for federal computer systems. These standards and guidelines are issued by NIST as the Federal Information Processing Standards (FIPS) for government use. "NIST develops FIPS when there are compelling federal government requirements such as for security and interoperability and there are no acceptable industry standards or solutions" (*Cobell*, 2001, at *35, fn. 22, citing "General Information," n.d.). NIST standards are now mandated for federal agencies by FISMA.

The Computer Emergency Response Team Coordination Center (CERT/CC), a federally funded research and development center operated by Carnegie Mellon University, also provides a great deal of information regarding systems security and vulnerability (see http://www.cert.org). CERT/CC offers a method for evaluating security risks, security practices that an organization can implement (including evaluating security architecture to detect and respond to intrusions), and training courses for managers and technical personnel. The security practices developed by CERT/CC and other organizations may prove helpful in assessing what practices an organization should reasonably undertake to safeguard data. CERT/CC has a relationship with the US CERT.

Security Certifications

There are also organizations that offer to audit and certify IT systems from a security standpoint. For example, SysTrust is a certification program sponsored by the AICPA that is intended to audit and certify IT systems for availability, security, integrity, and maintainability (see "What is SysTrust," 2001). TruSecure is a private company that also offers a security certification program ("TruSecure Programs," n.d.). The knowledge and efforts of these organizations may help contribute to a standard.

The foregoing provides only a few possible examples from which to draw upon a legal standard for IT security. In developing a legal standard for any duty of care, a court, for example, may look to one or more of the above, or to other resources, in formulating what is reasonable and appropriate under the circumstances.

Damages

The damages typically recoverable for a tort are those that are reasonably foreseeable and are proximately caused by the act or omission of the wrongdoer. Some jurisdictions do not permit a tort plaintiff to recover economic losses in the absence of physical damage. This economic loss rule was typically applied to claims for pain and suffering or emotional distress where there was, in fact, no actual physical harm. In the case of unauthorized disclosure of information, the rule might prohibit recovery of any damages, because the loss would be essentially economic in nature without any underlying physical harm. Nonetheless, a number of courts now recognize an exception to this rule. See, for example, *People Express Airlines v. Consolidated Rail Corp.* (1985). Given the climate for data privacy and security, it would not be surprising for the exception to apply to security breaches. Whether the damages are quantifiable is another issue (as discussed above), but one not to be lightly taken.

CONCLUSION

Advancements in IT are rapidly changing the way business is done and how we conduct our personal lives. IT has, in many ways, made the world a smaller place by making information readily accessible. As a result, sensitive corporate and personal information, in electronic form, is at all times vulnerable to compromise, whether by human error, technical fault, ill-intent, or otherwise. Organizations that rely on or process such data may have legal obligations to maintain the security of the data and may face potential liability in the event of a security breach.

Given the increasing concern among businesses, consumers, and lawmakers for hackers, breaches of data systems and networks, identity theft, and the security of information generally, it is prudent to take steps to review existing security practices and to anticipate the potential for liability under current and evolving laws. Because data security is a relatively new area for the law, an organization would do well to keep advised of statutory, regulatory, judicial, and other legal developments as they arise, and to adapt its security practices accordingly. The risk of regulatory noncompliance and of potential third-party liability may be mitigated by the implementation of adequate IT infrastructure and practices based on a proper understanding of the legal framework affecting an organization.

GLOSSARY

Application Service Provider A business that offers remote access to and use of software application services, often through the Internet.

Click-wrap Agreement An agreement setting forth the terms and conditions for use of intellectual property or a service (e.g., a Web site), which must be assented to by the user by an affirmative action such as clicking an I Accept button or the equivalent.

Confidential Information Any information deemed confidential and having pecuniary value and that is protected from unauthorized disclosure to others.

Customer Relations Management Software Software designed to aggregate, compile, organize and sort data relating to a business's customers.

Equitable Relief Relief in the form of an injunction or specific performance, instead of money damages, that may be ordered by a court.

European Commission (formally the Commission of the European Communities) The executive of the European Union, whose primary roles are to propose and enact legislation and to act as guardian of the treaties that provide the legal basis for the European Union.

Federal Trade Commission (FTC) U.S. federal agency established in 1914 by the Federal Trade Commission Act to enforce, among other things, federal consumer protection laws by investigating complaints against individual companies.

Financial Services Modernization Act of 1999 (more commonly known as the Gramm-Leach-Bliley Act [GLB]) U.S. federal legislation enacted in 1999 governing the privacy and security of personally identifiable financial information.

Force Majeure An act of God or an event outside the reasonable control of a person or entity.

Health Insurance Portability and Accountability Act (HIPAA) U.S. federal legislation enacted in 1996 governing the privacy and security of heath information.

Hosting Company A business that offers services that host Web sites on computer servers and keep those Web sites available for access through the Internet.

Information Technology (IT) The technology required for processing information and the use of computers and computer software to convert, store, protect, process, transmit, and retrieve information.

Internet Service Provider (ISP) A business that offers users access to the Internet and related services.

Managed Network Servicer A business that manages and oversees an organization's computer networks.

Outsourcing The act of a business in subcontracting to a third party the responsibilities for certain services or equipment, which may include computer systems or software or the responsibilities for operating and maintaining such computer systems or software.

Privacy Policy A disclaimer placed on a Web site informing users about how the website collects, uses and shares the user's personal information.

Privacy Seal A seal of approval issued by a private company, which may be displayed on a Web site, certifying that the Web site has agreed to adhere to certain standards for the privacy and security of data transferred through the site.

Risk Management The total process of identifying, controlling, and mitigating risks.

Security Certification A certification issued by a private auditing firm certifying that an IT system adheres to certain minimum security requirements.

Terms of Use A set of rules set up by the owner of intellectual property or a service (e.g., a Web site) to govern its use and is often a contract between the owner and the user.

Tort Under common law, a civil wrong for which the law provides a remedy.

Trade Secret A confidential practice, method, process, design, or other information used by a company to compete with other businesses, which is protected from general disclosure to others.

Uniform Commercial Code (UCC) One of the uniform acts, dealing with sales and commercial transactions, that attempts to harmonize the law of the 50 U.S. states.

Web Site A collection of Web pages accessible via hypertext transfer protocol through the Internet.

CROSS REFERENCES

See *Cyberlaw: The Major Areas, Development, and Information Security Aspects; Digital Identity; Online Contracts; Privacy Law and the Internet; Risk Management for IT Security.*

REFERENCES

About SAS 70 (n.d.). Retrieved March 11, 2004, from http://www.sas70.com/about.htm

Armendariz v. Foundation Health Psychcare Services, 24 Cal. 4th 83, 113 (2000).

Barnett Bank of West Fla. v. Hooper, 498 So. 2d 923, 925 (Fla. 1986).

California Information Practices Act, CA Civil Code §1798 (1977). Retrieved March 11, 2004, from http://www.privacyprotection.ca.gov/code/cc1798.291798.82.htm

Caspi v. Microsoft Network, LLC, 323 N.J. Super. 118, 126 (1999).

Chicago Research & Trading v. New York Futures Exchange, Inc., 446 N.Y.S.2d 280, 282, 84 A.D.2d 413, 416 (N.Y. App. Div. 1982).

Children's Online Privacy Protection Act 15 U.S.C. §§6501–6506 (1998).

Clinger-Cohen Act, 40 U.S.C. §1401 (1996).

Cobell v. Norton, U.S. Dist. LEXIS 20453, *24–27 (D.C. 2001).

Cohabaco Cigar Co. v. United States Tobacco Co., 1999 U.S. Dist. LEXIS 17210, at *27 (N.D. Ill. 1999).

Comb v. PayPal, Inc., 218 F. Supp. 2d 1165, 1172 (N.D. Ca. 2002).

Computer Fraud and Abuse Act, 18 U.S.C. §1030 *et seq.* (1986).

Computer Security Act, 40 U.S.C. §1441 (1987).

Controlling the Assault of Non-Solicited Pornography and Marketing Act, Pub. L. 108–187 (2003).

Defiance Button Machine Co. v. C&C Metal Products Corp., 759 F.2d 1053, 1063 (2d Cir. 1985).

DJowharzadeh v. City Nat'l Bank & Trust Co., 646 P.2d 616 (Okla. Ct. App. 1982).

Doe v. Chao, 124 S. Ct. 1204, 2004 U.S. LEXIS 1622 (2004).

Dwyer v. American Express Co., 273 Ill. App. 3d 742, 750, 652 N.E.2d 1351, 1357 (App. 1995).

Electronic Communications Privacy Act, 18 U.S.C. § 2701 *et seq.* (1986).

European Parliament. (1995, November 23). Directive 95/46/EC of the European Parliament and of the Council of 24 October 1995 on the protection of individuals with regard to the processing of personal data and on the free movement of such data. *Official Journal of the European Communities L, 281*, 31–50. Retrieved March 11, 2004, from http://europa.eu.int/smartapi/cgi/sga_doc?smartapi!celexapi!prod!CELEXnumdoc&lg=EN&numdoc=31995L0046&model=guichett

European Parliament. (2002, July 31). Directive 2002/58/EC of the European Parliament and of the Council of 12 July 2002 concerning the processing of personal data and the protection of privacy in the electronic communications sector (directive on privacy and electronic communications). *Official Journal of the European Communities L, 201*, 37–47.

Fair Credit Reporting Act, 15 U.S.C. §§1681, 1681a–1681v (1970).

Fair information practice principles. (n.d.). Retrieved March 11, 2004, from http://www.ftc.gov/reports/privacy3/fairinfo.htm

Farnsworth on Contracts §4.26 (LEXIS 2001).

Federal Information Security Management Act, 44 U.S.C. §3541 *et seq.* (2002).

Federal Trade Commission Act, 45 U.S.C. §45 *et seq.* (1914).

Federal Trade Commission v. Toysmart.com, LLC, No. 00-11341-RGS (D. Mass., 2000).

Final Rule: Privacy of Consumer Financial Information (Regulation S–P) (SEC), 65 Fed. Reg. 40,334 (2000).

Financial Services Modernization Act (Gramm-Leach-Bliley Act), 15 U.S.C. §§6801–6809 (1999).

Florez v. Linens 'n Things, Inc., 2003 Cal. App. LEXIS 641, *6–7 (2003).

FTC v. Colgate-Palmolive Co., 380 U.S. 374, 385, 85 S. Ct. 1035, 1043 13 L. Ed. 2d 904, 914 (1965).

Garner, B. A. (Ed.). (1983). *Black's law dictionary* (5th ed.). Eagan, MN: West. General information. (n.d.). Retrieved March 11, 2004, from http://www.itl.nist.gov/fipspubs/geninfo

Gibson v. United States, 55 Fed. Appx. 938, 2003 U.S. App. LEXIS 2368, *3 (App. Fed. Cir. 2003).

Groff v. America Online, Inc., No. 90-8077, 1998 R.I. Super. LEXIS 46, at *13 (1998).

Hamilton v. Microsoft Corp., No. BC303321, Cal. Super. Ct. (October 1, 2003). Retrieved March 11, 2004, from http://www.computerbytesman.com/security/hamilton_v_microsoft_complaint.htm

Health Insurance Portability and Accountability Act, 42 U.S.C. §§1301 *et seq.* (1996).

Hughes v. America Online, Inc., 204 F. Supp. 2d 178, 181 (D. Mass. 2002).

Identity theft. (n.d.). Retrieved March 11, 2004, from http://www.privacy.ca.gov/cover/identitytheft.htm

Information Technology Laboratory: What ITL does. (n.d.). Retrieved March 11, 2004, from http://www.itl.nist.gov/itl-what_itl_does.html

Interagency Guidelines Establishing Standards for Safeguarding Customer Information (Banking Agencies), 66 Fed. Reg. 8,618 (2001).

In re Toysmart.com, LLC, No. 00-13995-CJK (Bankr. D. Mass., 2000).

In the Matter of Eli Lilly and Co., FTC File No. 0123214 (2002). Retrieved March 11, 2004, from http://www.ftc.gov/opa/2002/01/elililly.htm

In the Matter of Geocities, FTC File No. 982 3051 (1998). Retrieved March 11, 2004, from http://www.ftc.gov/os/1998/08/index.htm

In the Matter of Guess?, Inc., FTC File No. 0223260 (2003). Retrieved March 11, 2004, from http://www.ftc.gov/opa/2003/06/guess.htm

In the Matter of Microsoft Corporation, FTC File No. 0123240 (2002). Retrieved March 11, 2004, from http://www.ftc.gov/opa/2002/08/microsoft.htm

ISO 17799: What is it?" n.d.). Retrieved March 11, 2004, from http://www.iso17799software.com/what.htm

Maher v. United States, 314 F.3d 600, 606 (Fed. Cir. 2002).

Marquardt and Roche/Meditz and Hackett, Inc. v. Riverbend Executive Center, Inc., 74 Conn. App. 412, 421, 812 A.2d 175, 182, n.2 (Ct. App. 2003).

McNally v. The Pulitzer Publishing Co., 532 F.2d 69, 76 (8th Cir. 1976).

Model contracts for the transfer of personal data to third countries. (n.d.). Retrieved March 11, 2004, from http://europa.eu.int/comm/internal_market/privacy/modelcontracts_en.htm

Muris, T. J. (2001, October 4). *Protecting consumers' privacy: 2002 and beyond.* Remarks of FTC Chairman Timothy J. Muris at The Privacy 2001 Conference, Cleveland, OH. Retrieved March 11, 2004, from http://www.ftc.gov/speeches/muris/privisp1002.htm

Muskovich v. Crowell, 1996 U.S. Dist. LEXIS 22634 (S.D. Iowa 1996).

National Institute of Standards and Technology Act, 15 U.S.C. 278g-3.

The National Strategy to Secure Cyberspace. (2003). Washington, DC: Government Printing Office. Retrieved March 11, 2004, from http://usinfo.state.gov/journals/itgic/1103/ijge/gj11.htm

Office of New York State Attorney General Eliot Spitzer. (2002, August 28). Major tech publisher reaches agreement with attorney general on e-commerce security standards [Press release]. New York: Author. Retrieved March 11, 2004, from http://www.oag.state.ny.us/press/2002/aug/aug28a_02.html

Office of New York State Attorney General Eliot Spitzer. (2003, October 21). Victoria's Secret settles privacy case [Press release]. New York: Author. Retrieved March 11, 2004, from http://www.oag.state.ny.us/press/2003/oct/oct21b_03.html

Otworth v. The Florida Bar, 71 F. Supp. 2d 1209, 1215 (M.D. Fla. 1999).

Overholt Crop Insurance Service Co. v. Travis, 941 F.2d 1361, 1368 (8th Cir. 1991).

People Express Airlines v. Consolidated Rail Corp., 495 A.2d 107, 116 (N.J. 1985).

Peterson v. Idaho First National Bank, 367 P.2d 284 (Idaho 1961).

Privacy Act of 1974, 5 U.S.C. §552a(g)(4)(A), 2004 U.S. LEXIS at *8.

Privacy of Consumer Financial Information, Final Rule, 65 Fed. Reg. 35,164 (2000).

Reuben H. Donnelley Corp. v. American Protective Services Corp., No. 85 C 9086, 1986 U.S. Dist. LEXIS 23252, at *6 (N.D. Ill. July 2, 1986).

Rippey v. Denver U.S. Nat. Bank, 273 F. Supp. 718, 735 (D.C. Colo. 1967).

Roton Barrier, Inc. v. Stanley Works, 79 F.3d 1112, 1116 (1996).

Safe harbor overview (n.d.). Retrieved March 11, 2004, from http://www.export.gov/safeharbor/sh_overview.html

Sarbanes-Oxley Act, 15 U.S.C. §78 *et seq.* (2002).

Simpson, G. (2001, May 29). FTC: Amazon "deceptive" about privacy policy. *Wall Street Journal Online.*

Smith v. Chase Manhattan Bank, USA, N.A., 2002 N.Y. App. Div. LEXIS 3790, *5 (N.Y. App. Div. 2d Dept. 2002).

Stevens v. First Interstate Bank of California, 167 Ore. App. 280 (Or. Ct. App. 2000).

Stomp, Inc. v. Neato, LLC, 61 F. Supp. 2d 1074, 1081, n.11 (C.D. Cal. 1999).

Suburban Trust Co. v. Waller, 408 A.2d 758, 763–64 (Md. Ct. Spec. App. 1979).

Trade Secrets Act, 18 U.S.C. §1905 (2000).

Trans Union LLC v. Federal Trade Commission, 353 U.S. App. D.C. 42, 51, 295 F.3d 42, 51 (Ct. App. D.C. 2002).

TruSecure programs. (n.d.). Retrieved March 11, 2004, from http://www.trusecure.com/solutions/programs/index.shtml

Uniform Computer Information Transactions Act, 17 U.S.C. §107–109 (1999).

Uniform Trade Secrets Act (1985).

United States v. Carroll Towing Co., Inc., 159 F.2d 169 (2d Cir. 1947).

University of Central Florida Administrative Data, Information, and Computer Security Guidelines. (2001, April 5). Retrieved March 11, 2004, from http://ucf.edu/ADICSG.html

Vermont v. International Collection Service, Inc., 156 Vt. 540, 547, 594 A.2d 426, 430 (Vt. 1991).

What is SysTrust. (2001). Retrieved March 11, 2004, from http://www.systrustservices.com/fs_whatis.html

What's happening with privacy at the NAIC and in the states? (n.d.). Retrieved March 11, 2004, from http://www.naic.org/privacy/

Hackers, Crackers, and Computer Criminals

David Dittrich, *University of Washington*
Kenneth Einar Himma, *Seattle Pacific University*

INTRODUCTION

Early on, the threat posed by hackers, crackers, and computer criminals was comparatively minor. For starters, most people lacked sufficient access to the new information technologies to be affected in any significant way by computer crime. Equally important, most computer intruders lacked the skills and expertise to do significant damage to affected individuals.

Much has changed in the past 20 to 25 years. An ever-increasing number of people are coming to rely on e-mail, Web access, and other digital information technologies for social, personal, and commercial purposes, and those who lack direct access to these technologies frequently depend on commercial and governmental institutions that incorporate these technologies into key operations. In consequence, the increasing number of computer intrusions implicates, at least indirectly, the interests of the vast majority of people in the industrial world and a growing number of people in the developing world.

Moreover, computer criminals have been developing a more sophisticated (and dangerous) palate of tools for committing intrusions. Partly because computer technologies are so sophisticated, computer criminals tend to be more intelligent and more focused than other criminals. Not surprisingly, they have worked hard to hone their skills at breaking into computer systems and concealing their presence in those systems.

These efforts have paid off. Over time, scripts and programs have been improved to automate more and more of the various processes involved in staging a digital attack or intrusion. These new technologies can employ multiple attack vectors, install backdoors, disable antivirus and firewall software, disable and wipe log files, alter the operating system to run them at every reboot, and do all of this in a matter of seconds.[i]

The result is that hackers, crackers, and computer criminals now pose a serious threat to individuals, commercial firms, and state institutions. Because sophisticated intruders can command hundreds of thousands of computers to stage attacks against innocent persons and institutions, they can cause catastrophic harm. A sustained attack taking down a commercial Web site, for example, can result in the loss of millions of dollars in revenue—and potentially the loss of jobs. It is not overstating matters to characterize computer crime as one of the most important problems facing law enforcement today.

DEFINITIONS AND EXAMPLES
Defining the Terms: Hacking and Cracking

The words "hacker" and "cracker" are contentious terms, meaning different things to different people. Many people in the programming community, especially those who were programming in the seventies and eighties, view the word "hacker" as a term of approbation. Indeed, the original *Hacker's Dictionary*[ii], maintained for years by students at the Massachusetts Institute of Technology (MIT), defines "hacker" in terms that naturally lend themselves to such an interpretation:

---

[i] To get a sense for how much the computer criminal's tools and tactics have improved, consider this: ten years ago, it would take an expert hacker weeks, and even months, to break into several hundred systems; today, an expert hacker can compromise many more computers in a matter of days. For an example of the former, see Mann and Freedman (1998).

[ii] http://www.dourish.com/goodies/jargon.html

HACKER n. 1. A person who enjoys learning the details of programming systems and how to stretch their capabilities, as opposed to most users who prefer to learn only the minimum necessary. 2. One who programs enthusiastically, or who enjoys programming rather than just theorizing about programming. 3. A person capable of appreciating hack value (q.v.). 4. A person who is good at programming quickly. Not everything a hacker produces is a hack. 5. An expert at a particular program, or one who frequently does work using it or on it; example: "A SAIL hacker". (Definitions 1 to 5 are correlated, and people who fit them congregate.) 6. A malicious or inquisitive meddler who tries to discover information by poking around. Hence "password hacker", "network hacker".

According to the first five clauses of this early definition, the term "hacker" is used to pick out a class of people with a variety of intellectual virtues, including special expertise in computer and network systems. On this usage, the term applies only to persons of distinction—whether in virtue of their special skills or in virtue of their passion for intellectual pursuits. Indeed, as defined here, the term's connotation is sufficiently positive that it was bestowed as an honor: to be a hacker was to possess extraordinary programming ability and intellectually virtuous character traits.

Definition 6 comes closest to expressing the current use of the term "hacker" that is now irrevocably associated with computer crime. A hacker, on this usage, is a malicious or inquisitive meddler who pokes around to discover information. The use of "malicious," "meddler," and "poking around," at the very least, evokes the contemporary idea that a hacker is someone who intrudes upon the computer systems and networks of other people.

The different definitions reflect the history of hacking and the associated terms, which arguably extend as far back as the mainframe computer. Taken together, the various historical treatments of hacking distinguish a number of different classes or generations of persons who have been characterized as hackers. These classes include (1) the original MIT hackers who worked with mainframe computers in the 1950s and 1960s; (2) the hardware hackers of the so-called personal computer revolution of the 1970s; (3) the software hackers of the 1980s who developed new architectures for computer games; (4) so-called microserfs who have abandoned the original hacking culture to join large corporate firms as programmers and developers; (5) open source programmers; (6) hacktivists who commit computer intrusions for the purpose of advancing social and political causes; and (7) the hackers and crackers who commit computer intrusions for other malicious and nonmalicious purposes.[iii]

But, for better or worse, Definition 6 comes closest to capturing the meaning of the word as currently used in the community at large. Although many persons in the computer industry continue to use the term "hacker" to pick out programmers of distinction, the term "hacker" is now used by most persons only to pick out persons who intrude upon systems and machines belonging to other people without any meaningful authorization (whether through the consent of the owners or through the legal process). Anyone who trespasses upon someone else's system or network qualifies under this definition as a hacker according to this common usage.

In consequence, the term has lost its normative connotations (at least outside the computer industry). To the general population, it no longer connotes either expertise in programming or intellectual virtue of any kind. The media, for example, typically use the term, to the chagrin of many who lament these changes in conventional usage, to refer to the most unskilled intruders, including so-called script kiddies who simply take the most primitive hacking tools off the Web and use them without any understanding or creativity.

Even so, many persons attempt to distinguish intrusions motivated by malicious purposes (e.g., to destroy someone else's files) from intrusions motivated by benign purposes (e.g., to investigate security flaws in some operating system). Hacking that is motivated by a malicious intent to cause damage or harm is called "cracking" (or "black-hat hacking").[iv] Persons who distinguish hacking from cracking reserve the term "hacking" (or "white-hat hacking") for intrusions not associated with destructive or malicious purposes.

Motivations and Examples

Given the problems associated with hacking and cracking, it is important to understand the motivations of those who engage in such behaviors. Hacking and cracking, by definition, involve unauthorized intrusions upon the computers (and hence property) of other persons; as such, these behaviors are fairly characterized as antisocial. As is true of other antisocial behaviors, the problems associated with computer misconduct cannot be successfully addressed without some understanding of what motivates it.

Fame

It is not surprising that one very common motivation for hacking and other forms of computer misconduct is a desire for fame and notoriety. Fame and notoriety, after all, are common motivations in many other walks of life. Given the amount of media attention devoted to successful large-scale computer attacks and to such hacker celebrities as Kevin Mitnick, it is clear that hacking, cracking, and computer crimes are all viable paths to fame.

Hackers motivated by such considerations are primarily concerned with achieving recognition within the hacker community and have publicized their exploits among fellow hackers in a variety of ways. Early hackers, for example, discussed their exploits on special bulletin boards or print publications devoted to hacking, such

---

[iii] These classifications owe to several different historical treatments of hacking. See Levy (1984), Taylor (1999), and Taylor and Jordan (2004). I am indebted to an anonymous reviewer for drawing my attention to the importance of this point.

[iv] The term *cracking* is sometimes used to refer to people who produced high-quality programs for circumventing copywrite-protection technologies. See, for example, *Interview with Mike Hudack* (n.d.)

as *2600*. Contemporary hackers can discuss their exploits on Web logs (blogs) and in Internet chat rooms. In both cases, the idea was to find a comparatively private forum in which hacker exploits could be shared among a sympathetic community without incurring a risk of prosecution.

Even so, a hacker's desire for fame sometimes proves to be his or her undoing.[v] As former Justice Department Internet crimes prosecutor Marc Zwilleger put it, "[For t]he kind of people who do this, fame and notoriety are the primary motivation. They don't derive financial benefit from releasing a worm. If they can't claim credit, what's the point?"[vi] Indeed, many hackers who would otherwise have gotten away with their attacks have been caught because they claimed credit for an attack on a bulletin board or in a chat room.

Curiosity

Some intrusions are motivated by nothing more sophisticated than curiosity. Robert Tappan Morris wrote and released the first Internet worm in 1998 simply to satisfy curiosity. Morris did not intend the damage the worm eventually caused and did not anticipate that many sites would choose to shut off their Internet connections entirely because of the ensuing disruption to affected systems.[vii] Indeed, he had no developed sense of what the worm would do or how people might respond: he released the worm, in essence, just to see what would transpire.

Boredom

A desire to relieve boredom is another common motivation. Adrian Lamo wandered through the networks of WorldCom, Microsoft, Excite@Home, Yahoo!, and the *New York Times* partly out of boredom. Lamo entered a variety of networks, sometimes gaining access to sensitive information. After entering the *New York Times* network, he viewed employee records and Social Security numbers, as well as accessed the contact information for the newspaper's sources and columnists, including former U.S. president Jimmy Carter, former Marine colonel Oliver North, and hip-hop artist Queen Latifah. Somewhat sheepishly, Lamo attributed his behavior to boredom: "I was looking for something to do."[viii]

Intellectual Challenge

One of the most widely cited motivations, and the one most typically associated with the stereotype of the hacker as a social nerd, is the intellectual challenge involved in finding a way into a system. For example, Kevin Mitnick stole the source codes for Sun Microsystems' operating system, Nokia's cell phones, and Motorola's cell phones. In testimony before the U.S. Senate Committee on Governmental Affairs, Mitnick explained his motivations as follows:

> My motivation was the quest for knowledge, the intellectual challenge, the thrill and also the escape from reality—kind of like somebody

who chooses to gamble to block out things that they would rather not think about. My hacking involved pretty much exploring computer systems and obtaining access to the source code of telecommunication systems and computer operating systems, because my goal was to learn all I can about security vulnerabilities within these systems.[ix]

Such motivations presumably echo the intentions of many younger hackers who are eager to learn more about the relevant technologies, as well as to improve their own skills.

To Help Secure Systems

Hackers are sometimes motivated by a desire to improve the security of affected systems. For example, when the MSBlaster worm infected millions of computers in 2001, an unknown hacker wrote and released a counterworm that attempted to install a patch disabling MSBlaster. Although this counterworm was christened the Good Samaritan Worm for the salutary motivations of its creator, many experts feared that it might have more undesirable than desirable effects.

Indeed, computer intruders frequently lament that their victims do not seem to welcome their assistance. For example, an anonymous intruder to the National Aeronautics and Space Administration (NASA) expressed disappointment when his help was not accepted:

> I would email the system administrators sometimes and tell them that their computers were vulnerable. I would tell them how to break in, and how to fix the problems. I'd give them advice, and they would never follow it. Three weeks later I would go in and I *still* had access to their computers.[x]

These hackers believe that their efforts are legitimate because they are motivated by the best of intentions—the desire to help secure systems.

Financial Gain

Not surprisingly, some intrusions are motivated by financial gain. In 1994, Russian Vladimir Levin used stolen passwords to transfer an estimated $10 million out of Citibank into accounts around the world. Levin reportedly used stolen account names and passwords to make the transfers. All but $400,000 was recovered.[xi]

Russian hackers Vasily Gorshkov and Alexey Ivanov broke into a number of corporate networks and Internet

---

[v] It is worth noting, despite the use of "his or her" in this context, that the world of computing technology has been largely dominated by males. This is no less true of the hacking community: hackers are nearly always male.

[vi] See "Few Clues in Web Worm Whodunit" (2003).

[vii] See ftp://coast.cs.purdue.edu/pub/doc/morris_worm/

[viii] Lemos (2001).

[ix] http://www.pbs.org/wgph/pages/frontline/shows/hackers/whoare/testimony.html Mitnick turned out to be a master at using information to trick employees at these companies into giving him full access to the systems that contained the source code he sought (see the Social Engineering section for a discussion of such tactics). Mitnick went on to say, "The human side of computer security is easily exploited and constantly overlooked. Companies spend millions of dollars on firewalls, encryption, and secure access devices and it's money wasted because none of these measures address the weakest link in the security chain: the people who use, administer, operate and account for computer systems that contain protected information." *Id.*

[x] *Id.*

[xi] See http://www.pbs.org/wgbh/pages/frontline/shows/hackers/whoare/notable.html

service providers, looking for credit card numbers.[xii] If they were unsuccessful in finding credit card numbers, they would extort money from the victims to "fix" the holes. But if they were successful, they would use the numbers to purchase nonexistent items they sold on eBay, subsequently laundering the purchases through PayPal and fake e-mail accounts. The two reportedly caused an aggregate loss of more than $25 million.[xiii]

The U.S. Federal Trade Commission reported that, in 2003, $437 million was lost in online fraud.[xiv] These losses resulted from identity theft involving stolen credit cards and attacks aimed at inducing individuals, by fraudulent means, into giving out personal and financial information.[xv]

Financially motivated distributed denial of service attacks (DDoS) have also increased.[xvi] These attacks, which frequently involve a large number of innocent agent machines, threaten to deny customers access (or deny service) to online materials and services unless victims pay a substantial sum. Many attacks have affected online transaction-processing services[xvii]; the British Association of Real-time Gambling Operators (ARGO) reported, for example, that their members had paid over $73 million to extortionists between January and June 2004.[xviii] There is even a case (the first of its kind) in the United States involving someone allegedly hired to attack business competitors.[xix] This trend is growing at an alarming rate worldwide and is becoming a major focus of international law enforcement resources.

Political Activism (Hacktivism)

Some unauthorized intrusions are motivated by political and expressive purposes. In 1999, political activists sought to buttress the protests against the World Trade Organization (WTO) by striking at the WTO Web site. U.K.-based E-hippies, an activist group, attempted to shut down a WTO Web site hosted by Conxion by overwhelming it with requests for information. Similarly, in early 2000, a number of activists launched similar attacks against a variety of commercial Web sites, including Amazon.com and eBay.com, as a means of protesting the increasing commercialization of the Web. These self-styled activists viewed their attacks as a form of civil disobedience justified by the justice of the causes they sought to advance. These politically motivated attacks have come to be known as hacktivism.

Revenge

Some unauthorized intrusions are motivated as revenge for some sort of perceived slight.[xx] Convinced that he was

not being fairly compensated, Roger Duronio resigned from his position at Paine Webber as a system administrator. He planted a logic bomb (i.e., a program designed to take malicious action at a particular point in time) on 1,000 of PaineWebber's approximately 1,500 networked computers around the country, attempting to profit from the resulting damage.[xxi] Duronio purchased $21,000 of put options on stock in UBS, the parent company of PaineWebber, in the hope that the logic bomb would cause the value of UBS stock to drop, thereby increasing the value of his options. Although the logic bomb was successfully activated on March 4, 2002, causing an estimated $3 million in damages to PaineWebber, the anticipated drop in the price of UBS's stock did not occur.[xxii]

TACTICS, TECHNOLOGIES, AND TECHNIQUES

Hackers, crackers, and computer criminals have a growing palate of tactics and technologies that can be used to achieve their purposes. Common tactics include sniffers that harvest passwords from unsuspecting computer users connecting over the network; stepping stones that conceal the ultimate source of an intrusion; and stolen disk space to serve as caches for, among other things, attack programs, password files, or stolen credit card numbers. Attackers often use more than one of these tactics depending on their skill sets, timelines, and available bandwidths for targeting hosts. These and other tactics are discussed below.

Sniffers

Sniffers are the digital analog to wiretap devices in the telecommunications context. Whereas a wiretap is a physical device that records the analog transmissions of voice communications over a telephone line, a sniffer is a program that allows one to "see" and record the packets of data that contain the communication between people using computers. Just as a wiretap must be placed on one of the lines being monitored, sniffing can occur only on local area network segments (which include aggregator switches and backbone networks).[xxiii] It is not possible either to sniff traffic from multiple network hops (i.e., network interconnections) away from the target network or to tap a phone line physically located inside a building that the would-be wiretapper cannot enter.

Computer criminals frequently use sniffers to harvest passwords from unsuspecting computer users connecting over the network. These passwords can subsequently be used to gain access to valuable information that is stored on the user's network in e-mail and other files. Passwords can be obtained by sniffing the traffic associated with login authentication or by looking for passwords transmitted as part of text messages, such as e-mail, chat, or instant messages. (For this reason, users should be wary of transmitting very sensitive information on any channel that does not encrypt the transmissions.)

xii http://www.usdoj.gov/criminal/cybercrime/gorshkovconvict.htm

xiii http://www.usdoj.gov/criminal/cybercrime/ivanovSent.htm

xiv Naraine (2004).

xv These attacks have become known as phishing attacks. See the Social Engineering section for more detailed discussion of such attacks.

xvi See the Denial of Service section for a more detailed description and discussion of such attacks.

xvii Sullivan (2004).

xviii See Bullough (2004). The ARGO submission to the UK All Party Internet Group can be found at http://www.apig.org.uk/ARGO%20Evidence.doc

xix See Poulson (2004). See also the indictment against the suspects: http://www.reverse.net/operationcyberslam.pdf

xx These most frequently occur in the context of an employer–employee relationship that has gone bad. See http://abcnews.go.com/sections/business/TechTV/techtv_employee_revenge_020604.html

xxi See http://www.cybercrime.gov/duronioIndict.htm

xxii As of the date of this writing, there has been no resolution to this case. See http://www.usdoj.gov/criminal/cybercrime/cccases.html

xxiii For a more detailed description of network sniffers, see Dittrich (1998).

Internet Protocol Spoofing

The exchange of data between computers on the Internet is made possible through the use of various protocols. These protocols are layered in what is known as a stack, with lower level protocols handling transmission over physical media or wireless transmission and higher level protocols responsible for routing packets between networks. The latter eventually leads up to application-level protocols or higher.

For example, applications that use the Internet for communication rely on either the unreliable datagram protocol (UDP), which is used for quick but unreliable transmissions, or the transmission control protocol (TCP), which is used for more reliable transmissions. Applications using UDP typically send simple request/reply packets (somewhat like electronic versions of postcards) without the overhead associated with ensuring that packets actually make it from one computer to the intended destination. Applications that must ensure the integrity of the data being transferred can use TCP, which manages the process of establishing connections by tracking the number of bytes sent and received through use of sequence numbers and by checking to ensure they are transmitted without error through the use of checksums. This is part of the state information about transmissions maintained by the TCP portion of the TCP/Internet protocol (IP) stack.

Both TCP and UDP rely on a lower level routing protocol to get packets from one Internet host to another (sometimes through a dozen or more intermediary routers) known as the IP. Communication at the IP layer is handled by transmitting individual packets of data (known as datagrams) from sender to receiver and back again. Packets in transit are identified by several attributes, specified by fields in the packet's header, including their source and destination IP addresses. IP addresses are 4-byte values that are represented by dotted quads that consist of four decimal values between 0 and 255 separated by periods; these addresses specify the locations, so to speak, of the various computers and networks making up the Internet (an example of a dotted quad IP address is 192.168.0.1).

As may be evident, the exclusive use of numeric IP addresses for users to identify computers on the Internet is impractical in one important respect: sequences of up to 12 digits separated by three decimal points are very difficult for people to remember. To circumvent the need for people to remember these source addresses, methods of mapping names to IP addresses were developed. The Internet relies today on the domain name system (DNS) to map these decimal sequences to more easily remembered names. For example, the MIT computer housing the GNU Open Source software repository in California is named "prep.ai.mit.edu" in DNS and has the IP address 199.232.41.9. (The trailing period is just there to make that a valid English sentence. IP addresses do not end in periods.)

Unfortunately, the most widely used version of the Internet protocol (IPv4)[xxiv] is vulnerable to being exploited because IPv4 lacks any mechanism for guaranteeing the reliability of source addresses. It is possible for someone to generate a series of bytes forming a valid IP packet, inject it into the network, and route it to some unknowing receiving host. For example, a computer that tries to communicate with prep.ai.mit.edu might wind up exchanging information with a computer pretending to be 199.232.41.9.[xxv]

The problem is that it is quite difficult for a user to ascertain whether he or she is connecting to the intended source or to an imposter. File transfer protocol (FTP), Telnet,[xxvi] and hypertext transfer protocol (HTTP) browsers provide no way for the user to determine that he or she is not connecting to some imposter site. With some basic protocols (UDP services, for example, or the Berkeley "r" utilities), especially on TCP/IP stacks using predictable sequence numbers, someone can forge an entire series of packets and, as long as they reach the victim host before replies reach the host being faked, the victim will respond to them.

This unreliability in the validity of IP source addresses leads to several types of spoofing attacks. Blind spoofing attacks generally target stateless protocols, such as UDP, that do not employ any mechanism for authenticating clients or servers.[xxvii] These attacks are typically staged from one or more network hops from the targeted network and proceed by forging packets that make it appear that the targeted network is communicating with some acceptable host network; they are characterized as blind because they do not require that the attacker have visibility of the packets being sent back and forth to trick the target host.[xxviii]

Another common use of IP spoofing is in connection with denial of service (DoS) attacks. As will be discussed in more detail in the Denial of Service section, a DoS attack attempts to shut down a targeted network by overwhelming it with more traffic than it can handle. Perpetrators of such an attack frequently spoof a source address on the packets to either make it more difficult for the victim to identify the flooding hosts or make it more difficult for network operators to find and clean up the affected host.

Session Hijacking

Intruders can take over a user's session by deflecting traffic from its intended destination and interjecting their own

---

xxiv The newest version of the Internet Protocol, Version 6 (IPv6), includes features for cryptographic authentication and encapsulation that are intended to make address forgery and sniffing attacks impossible. As of this writing, IPv6 is still not in widespread use in the United States, although it is becoming very popular in some Asian and European countries.

xxv There are various types of attacks that involve IP spoofing, some more difficult than others, depending on where the attacker is located—in network terms—in relation to the victim. For more on IP spoofing attacks, see http://www.securityfocus.com/infocus/1674.

xxvi Even though clear-text password vulnerabilities have existed in programs such as FTP and Telnet for decades, some vendors still distribute these programs in their operating systems, and some people still continue to use them. This is most common behind firewalls or in home local area network environments, where users believe they are secure. Many sites ban these programs by policy and instead try to provide users with cryptographically secure services that do not expose passwords on the network, such as SSH or SSL.

xxvii Some protocols don't keep any state whatsoever and, in consequence, may respond to a reply that is received by a system that never even initiated a request. One such attack on the address resolution protocol compromises the mapping of IP addresses to the physical (e.g., Ethernet or MAC) addresses of network cards.

xxviii A more complex nonblind spoofing attack is described below in the Session Hijacking section.

traffic into the user's stream of communication. For example, someone making a connection to an FTP server or using Telnet will likely have an account on the server that would not exist if someone was simply impersonating the server. To circumvent this obstacle, intruder tools have been developed that act as a man in the middle and relay all traffic to and from the real server until the victim has logged in. The attacker can then interject packets into the stream with the client's forged source address and effectively take over the session.

This tactic has come to be known as *session hijacking*. By displacing the victim's traffic with his or her own, the attacker hijacks the victim's session. The victim will notice that the session has hung or died and may simply kill the session and start again, thinking that some relevant application has malfunctioned.

Simple forms of session hijacking can be defeated by using more secure communication methods, such as Secure Socket Layer (SSL) or SSH, which employ cryptographic certificate or key pair mechanisms to verify the authenticity of one or both ends of the connection and which encrypt the content of the communication. This effectively defeats the simple forms of session hijacking because, in ordinary cases, the attacker will not have access to the proper keys to get past the encryption used.

Certain man-in-the-middle attacks on SSL and SSH remain possible, but these can succeed only if users ignore warnings that encryption keys have changed since their last use or that certificates either do not match expectations or are not signed by proper certificate authorities. The weakest point is the first time a user connects to a site using a new SSL certificate or uses a new client to connect to an SSH server; at this point, the user must verify that a fingerprint matches to determine whether he or she is connecting to the real server or whether he or she is being tricked by a man-in-the-middle attack. Many users are not trained to do this fingerprint verification, and many sites do not provide users with a secure means to verify the fingerprint in the first place. Thus, even though strong encryption is available, it may be used improperly and only provide a false sense of security and be easily defeated by an intruder.

Buffer Overflows

Buffer overflows take advantage of a decades-old class of programming errors involving low-level languages such as C that use pointers to data structures in memory and do not take into consideration the size of those data structures. Programmers frequently make themselves vulnerable by defining a buffer to be of some small, fixed size—say 32 bytes—and then calling a function to read an arbitrary amount of data from a network socket. This programming error enables an intruder to attack by feeding a much larger amount of data into the socket, say 4,096 bytes, which effectively overwrites the 32 bytes (typically located on the stack, surrounded by other variables such as function call return addresses, frame pointers, etc.). This makes it possible for the intruder to inject binary machine language code and manipulate return addresses on the stack, tricking the computer into executing code that the intruder has injected.

Buffer overflow conditions can be identified by examining source code, by writing programs to generate large strings and examining their effect on a program using a debugger or by reverse-engineering the program using a disassembler. When, for example, Microsoft confirmed that source code to parts of its Windows NT and 2000 operating systems had been leaked on the Internet, the immediate fear of many security experts was that this would result in a slew of new exploits.

John the Ripper and Password-Cracking Techniques

A variety of techniques have been used to store passwords on systems for the purpose of authenticating users. For example, the UNIX operating system formerly combined the user's password and a two character "salt" to produce a scrambled string, which was stored on the system in a file visible to all applications and users.[xxix] The system would authenticate the user by combining the same two salt characters with the password provided by the user; if the result was the same as the stored string, then the same password was given.[xxx] If not, access was denied. The encrypted passwords were deemed to be safe in visible form, since computers at the time were not sufficiently powerful to attack the encryption mechanism or to use brute-force methods to try to determine the passwords (an attack known as password cracking). More recently, systems use hashing algorithms[xxxi], such as Message Digest 5 (MD5), that produce output with a much larger number of bits, making brute-force comparisons against longer pass phrases much more difficult.

John the Ripper is one of the most commonly used password cracking programs. Its popularity derives from its flexibility in handling many types of password hashing or encrypting mechanisms, its dictionary-attack techniques, and its functions for restarting interrupted sessions. It operates by detecting weak UNIX passwords and is compatible with a variety of different platforms, including DOS, Win32, BeOS, and Open VMS.

John the Ripper's core strength rests in using predefined dictionaries of words that are algorithmically permuted in ways commonly used by people choosing passwords, such as replacing letters such as "O," "A," and "S" with the digits "0," "4," and "5"; adding digits or punctuation as a prefix or suffix to words, and so forth. By allowing the selection of targeted dictionaries, an attacker

---

[xxix] For a discussion of how Unix passwords are encrypted, the role of a salt value in password encryption, weaknesses in the original crypt algorithm, password cracking attacks, and some proposed ways to harden Unix passwords, see "The Ambitious Amateur vs. crypt(3) or Pondering the Lifespan of Visible Passwords against Brute Force Attack," http://personal.stevens.edu/~khockenb/crypt3.html

[xxx] At the time, programmers believed that the algorithm was sufficiently complex that no risk would result from allowing all users to see the encrypted password.

[xxxi] Hash functions take a variable length input and convert it to a fixed length output. The kinds of hash functions used for passwords are known as cryptographic hash functions. Properly used, such functions should make it difficult for an attacker to find the same input (i.e., the user's password or pass-phrase) that resulted in the hash value stored in the password hash file. For more details, see http://en.wikipedia.org/wiki/Cryptographic_hash_function

can increase the likelihood of cracking weak user passwords. For example, if an attacker knows the password file comes from a system used by chemists, he or she can increase the chances of cracking the system's passwords by using a dictionary that includes chemical terms, names of famous chemists, and chemical companies (over one, say, that includes European poets or figures in African history). Dictionaries exist for all common fields of study and professions–hence the common admonishment to refrain from using words or names found in dictionaries or encyclopedias, even if they are foreign words or names.

There are a number of defenses against password cracking. Systems can defend against such attacks by securing the password hash file, requiring that users select hard-to-guess passwords and change them frequently, or using some form of *second-factor authentication* mechanisms (i.e., adding to the username or password another authentication challenge, such as a one-time password or key fob or card that generates random numbers).

In any event, intruders can obtain passwords without attempting to decrypt them or reverse hashing functions (assuming this is even theoretically possible). In many cases, they can simply attack the password authentication mechanism itself (i.e., the login/password challenge presented by the system) by attempting to predict a person's choice of password (people are not very good at generating randomness in passwords) or by taking advantage of weaknesses in the hashing algorithms themselves. The simple dictionary attack similar to the one used by John the Ripper, if targeted and sorted according to the frequency of occurrence of commonly used terms, can often break passwords in seconds.[xxxii]

These kinds of attacks (which do not require access to the stored password file) are becoming very popular against Windows computers running Windows remote access services, file-sharing services, as well as against SSH servers on non-Windows platforms. Programs such as Phatbot[xxxiii] implement remote dictionary-based attacks against Windows computers using over 100 popularly chosen passwords.[xxxiv] It is very successful in identifying hosts using these weak passwords. Informing users how

to form strong passwords can prevent Phatbot from entering systems using this method.

Up to this point, this portion of the chapter has discussed only tools and techniques for gaining entry to a computer system. In addition to gaining entry, it should come as no surprise that attackers typically wish to maintain access to the system they have compromised by avoiding detection over time as well as minimizing the chances they will be caught if and when they are detected. To accomplish these goals, the attackers must destroy evidence of the intrusion, conceal their presence in the system, and hide their true locations and identities. The next section discusses some of these techniques.

Postintrusion Concealment Using Rootkits

Rootkits are programs designed to conceal an intruder and his or her files, directories, or programs by making an operating system lie to its owner. The term *root* relates to the system administrator account, but also serves as a verb in the hacker vernacular referring to the act of gaining system administrator rights on a system ("Betty rooted that Unix system"). The term *kit* refers to the programs that are bundled by an attacker into a neat and easy-to-distribute and install package form (often a *tar* archive file).

Rootkits come in a few distinct types:

1. Straight replacements of, or modifications to, basic operating system programs that are designed to filter out strings based on rules or configuration;
2. Kernel modules that are loaded into the running operating system kernel that perform filtering and privilege escalation at a level below the operating system commands; and
3. Modifications to the kernel's run-time memory that alter system call tables, execution paths within system calls, or the return values of security checks to bypass intended access control mechanisms.

Rootkits elevate privileges on demand, provide continual unfettered (and nonlogged) access, and conceal the intruder's presence in a computer system. Although these methods generally leave some kind of trace in the system's file system,[xxxv] they all make the job of intrusion response

---

[xxxii] Sadly, many people do not try to choose passwords that either have the appearance of randomness or are hard-to-guess words or phrases. One recent study showed that the most frequently used password is "password." See, e.g., bCentral (2005) http://www.bcentral.co.uk/issues/technology/networks/securityconsiderations.mspx

[xxxiii] LurHQ (2005) http://www.lurhq.com/phatbot.html

[xxxiv] One version of Phatbot uses the following list of passwords: admin, Admin, password, Password, 1, 12, 123, 1234, beer, !@#$, asdfgh, !@#$%, !@#$%^, !@#$%^&, !@#$%^&*, WindowsXP, windows2k, windowsME, windows98, windoze, hax, dude, owned, lol, ADMINISTRATOR, rooted, noob, TEMP, share, r00t, freak, ROOT, TEST, SYSTEM, LOCAL, SERVER, ACCESS, BACKUP, computer, fucked, gay, idiot, Internet, test, 2003, 2004, backdoor, whore, wh0re, CNN, pwned, own, crash, passwd, PASSWD, iraq, devil, linux, UNIX, feds, fish, changeme, ASP, PHP, 666, BOX, Box, box, 12345, 123456, 1234567, 12345678, 123456789, 654321, 54321, 111, 000000, 00000000, 11111111, 88888888, fanny, pass, passwd, database, abcd, oracle, sybase, 123qwe, fool, server, computer, Internet, super, 123asd, ihavenopass, West, godblessyou, enable, xp, 23, 2002, 2600, 0, 110, 2525, newfy, 111111, 121212, 123123, 1234qwer, 123abc, 007, alpha, 1776, newfie, patrick, pat, root, sex, god, foobar, 1778, a, aaa, abc, test, temp, win, pc, asdf, secret, drugs, qwer, yxcv, zxcv, home, xxx, owner, login, Login, west, Coordinatore, Administrador, Verwalter, Ospite,

administrator, Default, administrador, admins, teacher, student, superman, wmd, supersecret, kids, penis, wwwadmin, database, changeme, dope, test123, user, private, 69, root, 654321, xxyyzz, asdfghjkl, mybaby, vagina, pussy, leet, metal, work, school, mybox, box, werty, baby, porn, homework, secrets, x, z, bong, qwertyuiop, secret, Administrateur, abc123, password123, red123, qwerty, admin123, zxcvbnm, poiuytrewq, pwd, pass, love, mypc, texas, Texas, Washington, washington, Tennessee, tennessee, jackdaniels, whisky, whiskey, azerty, poiut, mouse, ordinateur, souris, imprimeur, cederom, cédérom, bière, biere, moonshine, athlon, oil, opteron, écran, ecran, reseau, carte, merde, mince, ami, amie, copin, copine, 42, harry, dumbledore, hagrid, potter, hermione, hermine, gryffindor, azkaban, askaban, cauldron, buckbeak, hogwarts, dementor, quidditch, madre, switch, mypass, pw. It also attempts to use an empty password, which also is a surprisingly popular choice of passwords, even for the administrator account.

[xxxv] Nevertheless, it is important to note that modifications of kernel memory space are considerably less likely to leave detectable traces than the other methods.

more difficult because the system appears completely normal to the unwitting system owner or administrator. In many cases, the presence of a rootkit can be confirmed only by monitoring and analyzing network traffic from outside the system, as the intruder must get packets over the network to remotely control the computer.

Log Alteration

Once inside a computer system, attackers will often begin by disabling, deleting, or modifying logs to eliminate traces of their break-in and subsequent access to the system. A computer system contains two basic types of logs that intruders can alter to eliminate evidence of their presence in the system:

1. Binary logs that require a program or special application programming interface (API) to process and convert the logs to human readable text form. Examples of binary log files are Windows Event logs and Unix *wtmp/utmp/lastlog* files.
2. Text logs from services and applications that have already been converted to human readable form and simply need to be viewed. Examples of text log files are Apache Web server *access_log* and Unix *syslog* log files.

Use of Stepping Stones

The concept of a stepping stone is helpfully explained in terms of a physical analogy. If someone wishes to move from a point on one side of, say, a placid Japanese water garden to a point on the other side, he or she must find a series of solid and dry stones that can be used to step or hop from one side to the other. These *stepping stones* provide a safe path from one point to another point. If the number and proximity of these stepping stones is great enough, a person can make repeated trips across the water using different combinations of stones such that the path is not predictable and is possibly never repeated in the exact same sequence. Like physical stepping stones, digital stepping stones make it possible for a user to move from one machine location on the Internet to another.

The analogy, however, breaks down in one crucial respect. Digital stepping stones are used for the purpose of concealing the starting point of an intruder's path—and not for the purpose of moving from one location to another. Unlike physical stepping stones, digital stepping stones are not bound by physical constraints of movement; an attacker can conceivably move from any stone to any other stone—including from starting stone to destination stone; this means that intermediate stones are not necessary to enable the user to travel from a starting location to the final destination.

Digital stepping stones conceal the starting point of an attack from the ultimate victim.

To compromise a machine or network for use as a stepping stone, the attacker must gather intelligence about it.[xxxvi] A sophisticated attacker will typically spend considerable time reconnoitering a network to identify its

structure, the trust relationships[xxxvii] between hosts, the points of vulnerability, and the alarms and access controls in place. These efforts aim at identifying weaknesses that can be exploited to use the machine or network as a stepping stone.

Intruders sometimes exploit trust relationships between systems by gaining access (frequently through firewalls) to a host within the network perimeter and then masquerading as a trusted insider to hop from this system to other systems. If an attacker can install the SucKIT rootkit on a Linux server, for example, he or she can do two things: (1) harvest passwords by sniffing terminal sessions after they have been decrypted (i.e., even SSH sessions will be sniffed and passwords logged) and (2) use the back doors provided by SucKIT and bundled intruder tools to bounce from this system to others on the network.

Unfortunately, most networks have neither flow-level monitoring capabilities that detect new services showing up on a compromised host (e.g., the back doors) nor mechanisms for detecting and correlating connections involving the stepping stone (i.e., coming in from and bouncing to other systems). This typically means the operators or network administrators at a site have no idea when, how, or from where they are being attacked.

It is worth noting that stepping stones are frequently located in countries other than the ultimate target of the attack. For example, an attacker might start in the United States, bounce through a system in South Korea or Germany (both in different time zones and with different native languages), and then come back into the United States to a stepping stone within another network, moving finally into the targeted system. These stepping stones can literally be anywhere in the world, making it nearly impossible to tell where the attack originates. Four, five, or even more hops are feasible if the network latency is sufficiently low that keystroke delay does not become an issue. As network bandwidth increases worldwide, the attacker's ability to maintain anonymity and untraceability over the Internet also improves.

Antiforensics

As a general matter, forensic science is concerned with identifying and classifying information that will assist in investigating crimes. *Computer forensics* is concerned with gathering information about computers that will provide or lead to information about computer crimes. One of the first published white papers on computer forensics, "Basic Steps in Forensic Analysis of Unix Systems," explains the term "computer forensics" as follows:

[xxxvi] The same, of course, is true about the ultimate target of an attack.

[xxxvii] A trust relationship is formed between two systems when there is a shared authentication mechanism, like the same login name and password, or some other means of getting from one system to another. Trust is also found in external access control mechanisms, such as hardware or software firewalls. When trust relationships exist, an attacker who gains access to a single account on a single host may have actually gained access to hundreds or even thousands of other systems that trust the initially compromised host. In addition to the added reach of the intrusion, these trust relationships make great stepping stones to make it harder to detect or trace the attacker, and to make it easier to extend the attacker's reach into the network as if he or she were now an insider (which, for all intents and purposes, he or she now is.)

The science [of computer forensics involves] methodical, premeditated actions to gather and analyze evidence. The technology, in the case of computers, are programs that suite particular roles in the gathering and analysis of evidence. The crime scene is the computer and the network (and other network devices) to which it is connected.[xxxviii]

Accordingly, computer forensics is concerned with the preservation and analysis of the available data for the purpose of allowing a victim of computer attack to determine the extent of damage or intrusion and to take actions to remediate and bring back under the victim's control all computer and network resources compromised by the attacker. Computer forensics can either be employed by official law-enforcement agencies or by the victim in gathering information about a computer attack. In every case, however, it is concerned with determining the facts about the attack.

Antiforensics measures, in contrast, seek to alter evidence on a computer system to defeat defensive incident-response and law-enforcement investigations; such measures may include destroying existing evidence or planting false evidence. Although it is very difficult to go entirely undetected on a computer system,[xxxix] an attacker with full control of a computer and its operating system kernel can affect all time stamps, attributes, and memory contents. This can make it significantly more difficult for victims and law enforcement to detect intrusions and determine their ultimate sources.

Some techniques that have been discussed publicly and implemented include the following:

1. Deletion of all *i-node* attributes (including file name). I-nodes are data structures in Unix file systems that articulate the attributes of files, such as the file's owner, permissions, time stamps, location of blocks on a disk holding the file contents, and so forth. Directory entries then associate file names, and implicitly the path to the file within the file system (e.g., */home/users/bob/foo.tar.gz*), to the blocks on the disk where the contents of that file are stored. File systems, such as the Linux EXT3 file system, destroy the information that links the I-node to the blocks on the disk holding the file contents, but leave the file name, ownerships, time stamps, and so forth intact. Antiforensics tools wipe out these data to eliminate as much

information as possible about the files that have been deleted.[xl]

2. Encryption provides a means of concealing the true contents of a file. Most computer users are familiar with encryption as a means of hiding a password or an e-mail message from unintended eyes. But programs can also be encrypted, a feature that enables an attacker to defeat analysis of surface features (e.g., embedded strings, command prompts) and of the program while it runs using debuggers. Encryption can also effectively lock the program so that it can be run only by someone who knows a password. By encrypting portions of the program on disk, only to decrypt them at run time, and by exploiting other weaknesses in debugging APIs (e.g., the ptrace system call) and debugging applications (such as GNU, gdb, or objdump), attackers can make it more difficult to analyze or control the execution of malicious programs.[xli]

3. Kernel-system call-table modification can be used to conceal running programs, stored files, and network connections and to disable logging. By affecting the operating system's functioning at the level of the kernel's own memory image, rather than through replacement of programs that implement external commands, these measures make possible more comprehensive concealment. Taking over the exec system call, for example, can allow an attacker to control which programs are run, thereby providing one behavior for normal accounts and giving elevated privileges for special accounts. The SucKIT rootkit, described earlier, implements these features.

Covert Channels

The use of *covert channels* is intended to conceal the attacker's use of a compromised computer. Although an attacker can hide his or her presence within a computer system without much trouble, the act of communicating with the compromised system requires transmission of packets to and from that compromised system. In cases where these transmissions pass through other network devices not under the attacker's control, the attacker's use of the compromised computer can, in principle, be detected (by, e.g., a network operator, a security operator, an investigator, or even another attacker) while communications are in transit on the network. A covert channel is a mechanism for concealing the attacker's traffic by either hiding it or making it appear legitimate to third parties.

The Department of Defense's Trusted Computer System Evaluation Criteria defines a *"covert channel"* as "any communications channel that can be exploited by a process to transfer information in a manner that violates the system's security policy."[xlii] In practical terms, covert channels involve the use of some communication method that avoids the standard methods supported by the system

---

[xxxviii] See http://staff.washington.edu/dittrich/misc/forensics/. The authors go on to describe the job of the computer forensic scientist as follows: "Your job, as a forensic investigator, is to do your best to comb through the sources of evidence—disc drives, log files, boxes of removable media, whatever—and do two things: make sure you preserve as much of this data in its original form, and to try to re-construct the events that occurred during a criminal act and produce a meaningful starting point for police and prosecutors to do their jobs."

[xxxix] The reason for such difficulties is that computer intrusions necessarily involve changes to the system that leave traces, and the operating system must have some visibility of these changes to continue running the attacker's programs while functioning in a stable manner. To eliminate every single change to the system is nearly impossible, but it is certainly possible to hide from all but the most skilled system administrators and incident responders.

[xl] The grugq's *The Defiler's Toolkit* implements these techniques. See http://www.phrack.org/phrack/59/p59-0x06.txt

[xli] Programs like TESO's *burneye* encryption engine and Neel Mehta's and Shaun Clowes's *shiva* (see http://www.securiteam.com/tools/5XP041FA0U.html) implement these techniques.

[xlii] See Department of Defense (1985) http://www.radium.ncsc.mil/tpep/library/rainbow/5200.28-STD.html

and does so in a way that avoids logging or detection. For example, files may be transferred out of a system by encoding them in packets using the TCP sequence number or ID fields.[xliii]

These techniques make it difficult for victims and law enforcement to detect malicious software. The operation of malicious software blends in with normal traffic, getting lost in the massive volume of traffic on large networks. If network operators have little understanding of what normally flows over their networks, these techniques can be highly effective. (For example, there are 255 possible IP protocol values, only about half of which are even defined at this time, yet most networks route all of them. Some network monitoring tools will only look for TCP, UDP, ICMP (Internet Control Message Protocol), and Multicast, and lump everything else into one bucket called "other.")

Covert channels pose unique difficulties for anti-intrusion efforts. First, they are quite easy to use. Second, they can be implemented in many ways that use a forged source address together with directly routed traffic between sender and receiver to bounce packets off a third-party computer as a means of concealing the true source of network traffic (such as implemented by Simple Nomad's ncovert tool, released at BlackHat 2003).

Viruses, Trojan Horses, and Worms

Viruses, Trojan horses, and worms are malicious programs that pose a growing problem for computer users.[xliv] A *virus* is a program that infects computers by attaching itself to programs accessed by the affected computer (from its own file storage system or from remotely mounted file systems on a file server or network storage device).[xlv] Viruses are usually contrived to inflict damage on the victim while distributing themselves to as many other victims as possible through one or more available *infection vectors*, such as e-mail attachments or the boot block on removable media.

As the name suggests, a *Trojan horse* is an innocent-looking program that performs malicious functions that alter the victim's system without his or her knowledge. For example, an attachment to an e-mail message that purports to be a screen saver but actually creates a back door on the system through which it installs malicious software is a Trojan horse. Unlike viruses, Trojan horses generally attempt to deceive the user into running the attachment and hence rely on a form of social engineering (described in the next section).

A *worm* is a program that compromises a system by way of a remotely accessible vulnerability and then uses the infected host to distribute the worm to other hosts with the same vulnerability. Worms are usually malicious, but there have been worms, like the so-called Good Samaritan Worm, that attempted to close some existing vulnerability in compromised machines.

Attackers will sometimes use combinations of these programs to compromise a site. In cases where a direct attack against a firewall is not possible but e-mail is allowed into the site, an attacker can, for example, send e-mail messages to victims inside the network with an attachment containing a program that makes a connection to the attacker's Web site. If the victim opens the attachment, the connection is treated by the firewall as a legitimate connection initiated by the victim inside the network; in this way, attackers can circumvent the network's firewall protection to achieve a connection to the computer inside the firewall.

Another way to combine these tools begins with the release of a worm that opens a back door in infected machines. The attacker can then use a scanner or other malicious software to find and use these systems at a later date. An example of this is the program Phatbot, which looks for and takes control of systems infected by Bagle or MyDoom viruses.

Social Engineering

Although the term *social engineering* has a number of meanings,[xlvi] crackers use it to refer to social mechanisms (e.g., threats or fraudulent misrepresentations) that deceive a victim into doing what the attacker wants him or her to do. One especially effective form of social engineering is a *phishing scam*.[xlvii] Phishing involves the transmission of a message reporting to be from a security department of a popular bank, online auction site (such as eBay), or other online financial service (such as PayPal). The message claims that hackers have broken into the victim's account and that the victim must connect to the site to verify his or her personal information. The Web site is designed to appear legitimate to induce the victim to disclose information that can be used to steal his or her identity. In some cases, the attacker's site will even link back to the legitimate site for any number of subpages other than the authentication page, which is redirected to a Web server under the control of the attacker.

Denial of Service

A *denial of service attack* is a digital attack calculated to crash or shut down a Web site, server, or network either by exploiting a vulnerability in the system or by overwhelming it with more traffic than it can handle (e.g., in the form of sham requests for information).[xlviii] DoS attacks are distinguished from many of the attacks described previously in that they are directed not at the confidentiality or

---

[xliii] See, for example, Rowland (1996).

[xliv] Not every such program is motivated by a malicious purpose. Some viruses, Trojan horses, and worms have been developed to serve some legitimate purposes. For example, system administrators at the Xerox Palo Alto Research Center (PARC) developed a worm that would, among other things, clean up the Altos computers on their network. Unfortunately, such salutary intentions can have very bad results, as the users of PARC's network found out one morning in 1978 when a worm written by two PARC administrators rendered all 100 workstations useless due to a bug in the worm. See Lemos (2001) http://ecoustics-cnet. com.com/Year+of+the+Worm/2009-1001_3-254061.html and Hiltzik (1999).

[xlv] Viruses can also infect documents that support macro languages (which effectively incorporate programs into those documents).

[xlvi] It is sometimes used, for example, to refer to the use of the law to encourage socially desirable practices and attitudes among citizens.

[xlvii] US-CERT (2004) http://www.us-cert.gov/cas/tips/ST04-014.html

[xlviii] For a more complete description of denial of service, see Mirkovic, Dietrich, Dittrich, and Reiher (2005).

integrity of information systems, but rather at the availability of information systems. The point is not to gather confidential information, but instead to shut down the target and render its contents unavailable to its legitimate users.

The most potent form of a DoS attack is a *distributed denial of service* (DDoS) attack. DDoS attacks are usually staged from a large number of innocent machines that have been compromised without the owners' knowledge. Attackers install on these machines special attack software designed to overwhelm the target Web site, network, or server with requests for information; the attack is launched from these machines when the programs are simultaneously activated.

The use of compromised agent machines in DDoS attacks not only allows the attacker to direct more force at the target than could be deployed through a simple DoS attack, but also makes the identity of the culpable attacker much more difficult to ascertain. The use of innocent agent machines interposes, as it were, a layer of insulation between the target and the culpable attacking party, making it more difficult for the victim or law enforcement agencies to trace the attack path back to the originating source.

It is worth noting that DDoS attacks frequently employ a form of IP spoofing. Some DDoS programs forge a large number of random addresses, thereby making the attack appear to the user as if it came from everywhere on the Internet. Sites that do not filter packets, leaving their network with addresses that do not exist within the network (*egress filtering*), or do not filter packets entering their network with addresses from inside the network (*ingress filtering*) are particularly vulnerable and can make an attacker's job much easier by making it harder for a victim to trace the ultimate sources of the attack.

Unfortunately, the intensity of DDoS attacks has increased dramatically since they first appeared on the Internet landscape in 1999. Although the first DDoS attacks involved no more than 2,000 to 5,000 compromised attacking computers[xlix], more recent DDoS attacks have involved as many as just under half a million hosts.[l] The increasing number of attacking machines makes these latter DDoS attacks particularly effective in making unavailable the contents of target sites.

THE COMMON MORALITY ON HACKING AND CRACKING

This section considers whether and to what extent various types of computer intrusions by private persons[li] are ethically permissible according to what Bernard Gert, in an influential article on computer ethics, calls the "common

morality."[lii] The common morality, as Gert defines it, is "the [shared] *moral system* that people use . . . in deciding how to act when confronting moral problems and in making their moral judgments" (Gert, 1999, p. 58). As Gert points out, there is much more agreement among persons in any given culture on moral issues than there is disagreement; though it is quite natural to focus energy on what we disagree upon, "such controversial matters form only a very small part of those matters about which people make moral decisions and judgments" (Gert, 1999, p. 57).

This section attempts to identify those principles of the common morality that are relevant with respect to evaluating the various computer intrusions. Such principles include general norms protecting moral rights to property, privacy, intellectual property, autonomy, and free speech as well as certain norms encouraging the promotion of such social benefits as knowledge. Accordingly, the analysis in this section purports, following Gert, to be grounded in principles that are widely accepted in cultures such as this one—though some of these principles, such as those protecting intellectual property, have themselves come under increasing scrutiny within the past few years.

This is, of course, not the only worthwhile framework for evaluating ethical issues. There is a wide variety of general theoretical approaches to ethics, which include deontological ethical theories such as Kantian theories, virtue theories, theories of care, and an array of utilitarian theories (including hedonistic, preference, and welfare versions of act and rule utilitarianism). There is also a wide variety of more specific approaches to computer ethics—including Deborah Johnson's *global information ethics*, James Moor's *just consequentialism*, and Luciano Floridi's *conception of information as having moral standing*. But none of these frameworks, as is evident from the sheer number of them, commands general assent among either theorists or informed laypersons.

Fortunately, these theoretical approaches tend to agree on most moral principles. All mainstream theoretical approaches, deontological and consequentialist, afford substantial moral protection to our interests in life, liberty, property, physical security, and privacy. Indeed, the vast majority of these are fairly characterized as defining moral rights to life, liberty, property, physical security, and privacy that can be justifiably infringed only by reference to some other right that is at least as important. Accordingly, insofar as these theories all agree on these widely accepted principles of the common morality, hacking and cracking can be fruitfully evaluated by appealing to principles of the common morality.[liii]

Two final preliminary observations are in order. First, as articulated here, the common morality may presuppose a deontological (or duty-based) framework. Many theorists think that act utilitarianism is inconsistent with the existence of rights as this notion is commonly understood. On this line of reasoning, any act that maximizes utility

---

xlix The first public analyses of DDoS attack tools were published by David Dittrich in December 1999. See http://staff.washington.edu/dittrich/misc/trinoo.analysis.txt; http://staff.washington.edu/dittrich/misc/tfn.analysis.txt; and http://staff.washington.edu/dittrich/misc/stacheldraht.analysis.txt.

l See http://www.securityfocus.com/news/8573.

li Public acts (i.e., those performed by state agencies) raise radically different issues. States are frequently permitted to do things that private individuals are not—such as incarcerating persons.

lii See Gert (1999).

liii The arguments in this section parallel those made by Spafford in his classic article "Are Computer Hacker Break-ins Ethical?" (2001). Though Spafford does not explicitly characterize his analysis as grounded in the common morality (not surprising given that Spafford's article was written long before Gert's), he relies on principles that he takes to be largely uncontroversial among all but act-utilitarian theories.

is morally required by utilitarianism regardless of what kind of interest it might infringe. Critics of act utilitarianism have, for example, charged that killing an innocent person would wrongly be required by act utilitarianism if doing so were, all things considered, to maximize utility in a particular situation.

It is not entirely clear whether this criticism succeeds, as some act utilitarians deny these counterexamples, but the following analysis presupposes in any event that morality affords strong protection to our interests in life, liberty, property, physical security, and privacy. To the extent that act utilitarianism is inconsistent with the existence of moral rights and, as seems clear, the common morality presupposes the existence of moral rights (such as rights to life and liberty), the analysis of the common morality is deontological in character in the sense that it presupposes that our ethical principles are grounded in general rules that establish at least some duties that cannot justifiably be infringed to secure some set of desirable consequences.[liv]

Second, many of the principles of the common morality are directly challenged by hackers through their activities; hackers, for example, reject traditional views regarding the protection of property[lv] and privacy rights that ground many of the arguments that will be described further. Even so, it is important to realize that the burden rests on dissenters to make some sort of articulate case for rejecting these principles precisely because the various moral theories all tend to agree on these ordinary views.[lvi] Because there is so much agreement on the basic principles, it is not enough simply to deny them.

In any event, the analysis in this section should be understood as a plausible attempt to identify the implications of these common commitments. Because the analysis here does not seek to defend these common commitments or the moral theories that validate them, it cannot provide the final word. It is safe to say that the debate will continue.

The Case against Cracking

The moral case against cracking is straightforward according to the common morality.[lvii] Cracking involves unauthorized computer intrusions that are intended to cause harm or damage to the victims. According to the common morality, it is wrong for one person to deliberately cause harm to another person. Indeed, as Gert (1999) points out, many of our more specific moral commitments (as well as those commitments identified by most general theories) could be summed up in the rule "Do not cause harm."

Of course, the rule "Do not cause harm" is not absolute.[lviii] Although there are certain principles that can rebut the presumption of impermissibility, these principles do not apply to cracking in ordinary cases. For example, principles allowing punishment of wrongdoing do not apply because they justify only the state in carrying out a punishment; punitive measures by private individuals are almost universally condemned in Western cultures as wrongful vigilantism. Likewise, the principles that allow use of force in self-defense are clearly inapplicable in ordinary cases of cracking because those cases are not responses to attacks on others.

Nevertheless, principles of common morality allow for the possibility that cracking might be morally justified in highly exceptional cases if done without malicious purpose to bring about a great moral good. For example, someone who knows that stolen sensitive information about persons is about to be wrongfully published on a known terrorist Web site might, according to the common morality, be justified in attempting to destroy that information as a means of preventing the great harm that would result—provided that there is no other way to prevent the harm.

But it is doubtful that any cracking case has involved circumstances like the highly unusual ones described here. Indeed, such cases are sufficiently exceptional that it is reasonable to conclude that ordinary cracking is always wrong under the common morality—and the extent of the wrong is determined in part by the extent of the harm that is actually caused and in part by the extent of the harm that is intended by the cracker. The more malicious the intent, the worse the moral transgression involved in cracking. The garden-variety cracker, then, is guilty of committing a serious moral wrong under the common morality.

The Case against Hacking

The case against hacking seems no less straightforward under the common morality. Although the more malicious

---

[liv] It is worth noting that this does not imply that all moral rules are absolute. Some deontologists, like Kant, have taken this position; Kant, for example, believed that it is always wrong to lie—even when necessary to save someone's life. See, for example, Immanuel Kant, *Groundwork for the Metaphysics of Morals*; available at http://www.swan.ac.uk/poli/texts/kant/kantcon.htm. Most deontologists, however, have taken the position that less important duties are qualified by more important duties when they conflict. Thus, for example, if the duty to respect property comes into conflict with the duty to refrain from deliberately killing innocent persons, the former is qualified by the latter. The rule defining the duty to respect property is limited by the rule defining the duty not to kill innocent persons. See, for example, Ross (1930). As the latter view seems more in line with the common morality, I will presuppose it.

[lv] The term *property* here should not be construed as including intellectual property. It is meant here to pick out only concrete entities, such as land and computers, that are traditionally thought to receive moral protection.

[lvi] There have been various attempts to describe a hacker ethic, but these attempts have not really engaged the basic assumptions about property and privacy. Some of these efforts, as discussed further, are intended to justify certain intrusions by describing their benefits and motivations. But these arguments generally assume that such considerations win out over any moral interests people might have in their property and privacy. What is needed, however, is a sustained defense of this assumption.

Indeed, it is worth noting that much that has been written about the hacker ethic has been concerned to describe a work ethic that involves a profound commitment of time and energy to understanding hard and soft computing technologies. See, for example, chapter 1 in Himanen (2001). These efforts, however, do not even purport to engage these assumptions, which have nothing to do with describing a work ethic.

[lvii] Two preliminary observations about usage should be made at the outset. First, this entry uses *hacker* and related terms to refer to persons who commit unauthorized intrusions and the intrusions themselves. Second, as used here, the terms *hacker* and *hacking* encompass only unauthorized computer intrusions *not* intended to cause damage, whereas *cracker* and *cracking* encompass only unauthorized computer intrusions intended to cause damage.

[lviii] See Note 52, above.

intrusions involve serious transgressions because of the harm they are intended to cause, all unauthorized intrusions are morally objectionable because they wrongfully impinge upon the morally protected interests of their victims.

First, unauthorized intrusions impinge upon property interests that are clearly legitimate under the common morality. Someone who gains access to my computer without my permission has gained access to a physical entity in which I have a legitimate property interest; it is, after all, my computer—and I have, at the very least, a presumptive moral right, under the common morality, to exclude other people from appropriating my computer.[lix] Indeed, an unauthorized entry into some other person's network seems straightforwardly analogous to a trespass onto the real property of another person. According to the common morality, such trespass is morally wrong regardless of whether it results in damage because it violates the owner's property right to exclude other people from the use of his or her belongings.[lx]

Second, unauthorized intrusions can result in harm even when they are not intended to do so. Even skillful hackers who intend no damage can inadvertently cause significant damage to files and programs in which the victim has legitimate property interests under the common morality. The likelihood of causing such accidental damage is an additional factor that supports thinking that hacking is morally wrong.

Third, unauthorized intrusions impinge upon privacy interests that are clearly legitimate under the common morality.[lxi] Someone who gains access to my computer without permission is gaining access to space in which I have a legitimate privacy interest. If it is true that I may legitimately exclude others from use of an access to my computer, then it is not unreasonable to regard my computer as a private space in which I can store sensitive information. Even benign intrusions impinge, then, upon these legitimate privacy interests.

Accordingly, the common morality seems straightforwardly to condemn even benign intrusions because they impinge upon legitimate privacy and (physical) property interests—and this is true regardless of whether any actual damage is caused to the victim or the victim's property.

Hacker Attempts to Justify Hacking

Not everyone is convinced that hacking is wrong. Many hackers believe that, at the very least, nonmalicious intrusions are morally permissible and have offered a number of arguments purporting to justify such intrusions (and hence to qualify or limit the rules governing property and privacy rights). Some argue, for example, these intrusions are justified because they result in an increase in humanity's stock of knowledge about the relevant technologies. Others argue that any barriers to information are morally

illegitimate and hence deserve no respect. This section explains and critically evaluates these arguments under the common morality.

The Social Benefits of Benign Intrusions

Hackers argue that benign intrusions increase our technological knowledge in a couple of ways. First, by gaining insight into the operations of existing networks, hackers develop a base of knowledge that can be used to improve those networks. Second, the break-ins themselves call attention to security flaws that could be exploited by crackers or, worse, cyberterrorists. Thus, electronic trespass is distinguished from other forms of trespass in that it inevitably conduces to the public's benefit.

Neither consideration, however, justifies benign intrusions under the common morality. Even if the privacy and property interests of computer owners might sometimes yield to such considerations, these arguments are problematic because these social benefits can be achieved in other ways that do not infringe upon any legitimate interests.

Hackers can, for example, develop the techniques that enable them to break into other systems in settings where the consent of all parties has been obtained. In cases where hackers seek entry to the machines of ordinary users, they can solicit the consent of other like-minded users to allow them to attempt to circumvent the relevant security measures. In cases where hackers seek entry to the machines of large commercial users, they can seek employment at those firms or provide advice to employees of those firms.[lxii] It seems impermissible to infringe privacy and property interests to achieve benefits that can be achieved without infringing those interests.

Moreover, the social benefits arguments fail to take into account the social costs of hacking. The continuing threat of hacker attacks force companies to invest capital into security that they would otherwise invest in more productive areas. Hacker attacks may contribute to improving security technologies, but these technologies could arguably be developed at a much lower cost if hackers would cooperate with companies in developing these technologies—instead of forcing companies to develop them in an ongoing process of having to defend against such attacks.

There is, however, a deeper problem with these arguments. According to the common morality, the privacy and property interests of computer owners rise to the level of moral rights.[lxiii] But it is part of the very concept of a right that the infringement (as opposed to violation) cannot be justified by an appeal to the resulting good. The mere fact that someone could do a lot of social good by stealing, say, a billion dollars from Bill Gates cannot justify stealing that sum if Gates has a property right in that money. As Ronald Dworkin famously puts the point, rights trump consequences.[lxiv]

[lix] It should be noted that a computer is physical property and not intellectual property; for this reason, the argument does not rely on any contested claims about intellectual property.

[lx] Eugene Spafford, for example, characterizes hackers as "trespassers" and "burglars," which presupposes that hackers are violating property rights of some kind. See Spafford (1992, pp. 335, 340).

[lxi] See, e.g., Spafford (1992, p. 336).

[lxii] As Spafford (1992, p. 337) puts this point, "People wishing to report a problem with the security of a system need not exploit it to report it.... [O]ne does not set fire to the neighborhood shopping center to bring attention to a fire hazard in one of the stores."

[lxiii] It should be noted that this argument will not satisfy an act utilitarian who takes the position that there are no moral rights.

[lxiv] See, for example, Dworkin (1978).

The social benefits arguments, then, fail because they are the wrong kind of arguments under the common morality. The property and privacy rights that computer owners have in their machines can justifiably be infringed by an unauthorized intrusion only if required to secure some more important right that outweighs those privacy and property rights. If rights trump consequences, then hackers must identify some stronger right that justifies an intrusion: the appeal to social benefits, by itself, is insufficient to do so. Such an argument is considered in the next section.

Benign Intrusions as Free Expression
Hackers have also attempted to defend benign intrusions as free expression. On this line of reasoning, hacking is sometimes justifiable as an exercise of the moral right to free expression; in certain circumstances, hackers are morally entitled to intrude upon the computers of others—as long as they do nothing reasonably calculated to cause harm. The assumption here is that the hacker's right to free speech is more important than and hence qualifies (or limits) the victim's privacy and property rights.

The Free Flow of Information
This line of argument is grounded in the idea that the moral right to free expression is such that there should be no restrictions on the free flow of information; as this latter idea is sometimes put, information *wants* to be—or, better, *ought* to be—free.[lxv] If, on this reasoning, it is true that any restrictions on the free flow of information are morally wrong in virtue of violating the right to free expression, then security measures designed to keep hackers out of networks violate their rights to free expression because they inhibit the free flow of information.[lxvi] As long as hackers do no harm, it is morally permissible for them to intrude into networks to gain information.[lxvii]

The claim that there are no morally legitimate restrictions on the free flow of information is inconsistent with two widely accepted principles of the common morality. First, it is inconsistent with there being a right to informational privacy that entitles persons to exclude others from information in which they have a reasonable expectation of privacy; efforts that exclude others from information, by definition, impede the free flow of information.[lxviii]

Second, it is inconsistent with the claim that people have at least some moral right to control the disposition of their intellectual creations.[lxix] On this line of analysis, people have some intellectual property interest in their creations because such creations are the result of their labor and express their personality.[lxx] If, as most people

believe, at least one of these commonly held judgments is correct,[lxxi] then it is false that the right of free expression entails that there are no legitimate restrictions on the flow of information.

But even if it were true that there are no legitimate restrictions on the free flow of information, it doesn't follow that, as an ethical matter, people have carte blanche to get information. For example, it would clearly be wrong, under the common morality, for someone to break into my house to gain information about what books I buy. Similarly, if hacking violates the legitimate property interests of a person in his or her computer, then it is wrong regardless of whether the hacker is otherwise entitled to information on the victim's computer.

Hacking as Political Activism
Mark Manion and Abby Goodrum argue that politically motivated hacking is morally justifiable as civil disobedience as long as it results in neither harm to the victims nor profit to the hackers.[lxxii] If civil disobedience is morally justifiable to protest against injustice, it is sometimes justifiable to commit benign intrusions to protest injustice.[lxxiii] Insofar as it is permissible to stage a sit-in in a commercial or governmental building to protest, say, laws that violate human rights, Manion and Goodrum argue that it is sometimes permissible to benignly intrude upon commercial or government networks to protest such laws.

The problem with this argument is that hacking is not like ordinary civil disobedience in one very important respect under the common morality. Benign and malicious digital intrusions tend to inflict significantly greater harm than sit-ins or other ordinary forms of civil disobedience. For example, a DDoS attack that shuts down a large commercial Web site can result in millions of dollars in losses to that site and potentially in losses of livelihoods and it seems clear, under the common morality, that the infliction of such harms on ordinary people cannot be justified as a form of political activism or expression.

Here it is important to note that civil disobedience is typically motivated by a moral view that is deeply contested in the culture; in many cases, the view motivating civil disobedience is one that is held by a small percentage of people in the culture. Because there is no reliable way to determine which side of the view is correct, there are moral limits on what sorts of harm or inconvenience can justifiably be inflicted on persons who are not morally responsible for the policy being protested. Hacking that can result in the loss of jobs is always problematic, but is especially so when grounded in views that have not been adequately defended—as is all-too-frequently the case.

[lxv] See, for example, Barlow (n.d.). For a detailed analysis and criticism of this idea, see Himma (in press).

[lxvi] For a critical discussion of this claim, see Spafford (1992, pp. 41–47).

[lxvii] Accordingly, this argument does not even address, much less justify, cracking.

[lxviii] See Spafford (1992, p. 336).

[lxix] It is important to note, however, that the idea that people have intellectual property rights in various kinds of content has become increasingly controversial in recent years. For this reason, it is not entirely clear whether there is something fairly characterized as a *common morality* on this issue. Nonetheless, I include the argument here for the sake of completeness.

[lxx] For a discussion of these views, see, for example, Hughes (1988).

[lxxi] There is, of course, much controversy about whether and to what extent intellectual property rights are morally legitimate. See, for example, Hettinger (1989)

[lxxii] See Manion and Goodrum (2000). Though Manion and Goodrum do not explicitly refer to the common morality, their argument purports to be grounded in widely shared moral judgments about certain kinds of cases and is also fairly characterized as an argument that appeals to the common morality.

[lxxiii] Civil disobedience is typically justified as a form of political expression, a means of expressing one's political conscience and of bringing unpopular political ideas to the attention of an unsympathetic populace and government. See, for example, Dworkin (1978, chap. 9).

Thus, hacktivism will generally be unjustified under the common morality because there are no widely accepted principles that allow persons to inflict great harm on ordinary innocent parties as a means of expressing a political view or protesting injustice.

Benign Intrusions as Avoiding Waste

Hackers have also defended benign intrusions on the grounds that they make use of computing resources that would otherwise go to waste. On this line of reasoning, it is morally permissible to do what is needed to prevent valuable resources from going to waste; benign hacking activity is justified on the strength of a moral principle that condemns squandering valuable resources in a world of scarcity in which there are far more human wants than resources to satisfy them.

This argument also fails under the common morality. According to ordinary judgments, if one person has a property right in some object X, it is wrong for other persons to appropriate X without permission to prevent X from being wasted. As Spafford aptly puts this point:

> I am unable to think of any other item that someone may buy and maintain, only to have others claim a right to use it when it is idle. For instance, the thought of someone walking up to my expensive car and driving off in it simply because it is not currently being used is ludicrous. Likewise, because I am away at work, it is not proper to hold a party at my house because it is otherwise not being used. The related positions that unused computing capacity is a shared resource, and that my privately developed software belongs to everyone, are equally silly (and unethical) positions.[lxxiv]

If such reasoning is correct, hacking cannot be justified under the common morality to prevent waste.

THE LEGALITY OF HACKING

Whatever doubts one might have about whether some intrusions are ethically permissible, most are unambiguously prohibited by the law in most Western industrialized nations. This section discusses the law of the United States, Canada, and the European Union.

The United States

The primary federal law in the United States that covers unauthorized access and damage to computer systems is the Computer Fraud and Abuse Act (CFAA; i.e., 18

U.S.C. §1030.)[lxxv] The CFAA defines a number of crimes. Of particular relevance is Section 1030(a)(5), which provides as follows:

> Whoever . . . (A)(i) knowingly causes the transmission of a program, information, code, or command, and as a result of such conduct, intentionally causes damage without authorization, to a protected computer; (ii) intentionally accesses a protected computer without authorization, and as a result of such conduct, recklessly causes damage; or (iii) intentionally accesses a protected computer without authorization, and as a result of such conduct, causes damage; and (B) by conduct described in clauses (i), (ii), or (iii) of subparagraph (A), caused (or in the case of an attempted offense, would, if completed, have caused)—(i) loss to 1 or more persons during any 1-year period . . . aggregating at least $5,000 in value; (ii) the modification or impairment, or potential modification or impairment, of the examination, diagnosis, treatment, or care of 1 or more individuals; (iii) physical injury to any person; (iv) a threat to public health or safety; or (v) damage affecting a computer system used by or for a government entity in furtherance of the administration of justice, national defense, or national security . . . shall be punished as provided in subsection (c) of this section.

Subsection (c) authorizes fines and imprisonment of up to 20 years for specified violations of the quoted provision.

Although the relevant provisions apply only to protected computers, the definition of protected computers is potentially quite broad. In particular, the category of protected computers includes government computers and computers used by financial institutions, but also includes any "computer . . . used in interstate or foreign commerce or communication." Construed literally, this latter provision would include any computer used to send an e-mail from a person in one state to a person in another state or used to access any Web page published on a server physically located in a different state from the user. If so, this would include the vast majority of computers capable of being hacked because they are connected to a network; it is hard to imagine that any person who is connected to a network long enough to be hacked has not used his or her computer in one of these ways.

Although this subsection clearly applies to intrusions that cause or are intended to cause significant damage, it also potentially applies to benign intrusions. All that is required for liability is that the user gain unauthorized access to a machine that causes specified kinds or levels of damage. As long as the intrusion is deliberate and unauthorized, the damage need not be intended. Since even

---

[lxxiv] Spafford (1992, p. 340). Nevertheless, it is worth noting that the law sometimes permits a person to take possession of property through a wrongful act of trespass. According to the law of adverse possession, a person may come into possession of land by openly and notoriously occupying the land in a way that is clearly adverse to the owner's interests for an extended period of time; if the owner takes no action to halt the adverse possession, the land becomes the trespasser's after the end of the prescribed period (which may vary from one jurisdiction to the next). The justification for this rather counterintuitive law is that the community has an interest in ensuring that a scarce resource like land does not lie fallow. See, for example, http://www.propertylawuk.net/adversepossessionsquatters.html for a discussion of these interesting issues.

[lxxv] The Department of Justice maintains a Web page that lists recent computer crime cases. This site is primarily concerned with violations of the CFAA (18 U.S.C. §1030). But there is some information at the bottom of the page on other laws that were cited in various cases. See http://www.cybercrime.gov/cccases.html

benign intrusions run an obviously foreseeable risk of causing significant damage to protected machines, hackers can be held liable under this act for recklessly causing damage during a putatively benign intrusion.

In addition, benign intrusions may also violate legal rights to privacy—though such violations are perhaps more likely to give rise to civil, rather than criminal, liability—or state laws that criminalize unauthorized computer intrusions. Indeed, a growing number of states are enacting statutes that criminalize various forms of computer misuse which include, but are not limited to, unauthorized computer intrusions.

The relevant federal privacy statutes in the United States are collectively known as the Electronic Communications Privacy Act (or ECPA, for short). The ECPA is made up of the Wiretap Statute (18 U.S.C. §§2510-22), the Pen Register/Trap and Trace Statute (18 U.S.C. §3121) and the Stored Communications Statute (18 U.S.C. §2701). These statutes were further amended in 2001 by the Uniting and Strengthening America by Providing Appropriate Tools Required to Intercept and Obstruct Terrorism (USA PATRIOT) Act. The most likely to be used for prosecuting computer intrusions involving sniffers or keystroke monitors would be the Wiretap Statute.

As described earlier, a recent trend in computer crime is the use of very large (using perhaps as many as half a million compromised computers[lxxvi]) DDoS networks to cause disruption of online gambling sites in the United Kingdom to extort money from these sites. A total of $73 million were lost to extortion by these online gambling sites in the first part of 2004.[lxxvii] Three suspects were arrested by the British National High Tech Crime Unit in June 2004 for these attacks.[lxxviii] Had the victims been in the United States, such attacks could violate several other federal statutes, such as the following:

- 18 U.S.C. §1951—Extortion that affects commerce
- 18 U.S.C. §875—Threats transmitted in interstate commerce
- 18 U.S.C. §876—Mailing threatening communications
- 18 U.S.C. §877—Mailing threatening communication from a foreign country
- 18 U.S.C. §880—Receipt of the proceeds of extortion

Other possible violations of law include the following acts. Using a sniffer to steal account and password combinations for the purpose of using these stolen accounts can be prosecuted under the Fraud and Related Activity in Connection with Access Devices Statute (18 U.S.C. §1029). The willful and malicious destruction of data or systems used for communications can be prosecuted under the Communication Lines, Stations, or Systems Statute (18 U.S.C. §1362).[lxxix]

Canada

Section 342.1 of the Canadian Consolidated Statutes and Regulations defines the general framework that applies to hacker attacks. In particular, Subsection (1) provides the following:

> Every one who, fraudulently and without colour of right (a) obtains, directly or indirectly, any computer service, (b) by means of an electromagnetic, acoustic, mechanical or other device, intercepts or causes to be intercepted, directly or indirectly, any function of a computer system, (c) uses or causes to be used, directly or indirectly, a computer system with intent to commit an offence under paragraph (a) or (b) or an offence under section 430 in relation to data or a computer system, or (d) uses, possesses, traffics in or permits another person to have access to a computer password that would enable a person to commit an offence under paragraph (a), (b) or (c) is guilty of an indictable offence and liable to imprisonment for a term not exceeding ten years, or is guilty of an offence punishable on summary conviction.

On its face at least, Section 342.1 seems to create a more stringent standard protecting against unwanted computer intrusions. In contrast to the U.S. Computer Crime and Fraud Act, Section 342.1 lacks a damage requirement and hence appears to prohibit both malicious and benign computer intrusions.

In addition, Section 430 of the Canadian criminal law prescribes penalties for the crime of mischief, which occurs when one party, without authorization, intentionally damages, destroys, or renders less valuable the property of another person. Subsection 1.1 specifically defines damage to data as criminal mischief subject to specified penalties:

> Every one commits mischief who willfully (a) destroys or alters data; (b) renders data meaningless, useless or ineffective; (c) obstructs, interrupts or interferes with the lawful use of data; or (d) obstructs, interrupts or interferes with any person in the lawful use of data or denies access to data to any person who is entitled to access thereto.

Section 430 (1.1), then, creates additional liability for malicious intrusions (i.e., cracking) that result in damage.

The European Union

The Council of Europe has demonstrated a firm commitment to adopting a unified approach to dealing with computer misuse. On November 8, 2001, the Committee of Ministers of the Council formerly adopted the Convention on Cybercrime, which states guidelines for the various members of the European Union in formulating laws

---

[lxxvi] According to ARGO, 518,000 IP addresses were implicated in DDoS attacks associated with extortion demands. See http://www.apig.org.uk/ARGO%20Evidence.doc

[lxxvii] See Bullough (2004) http://www.usatoday.com/tech/news/internetprivacy/2004-07-28-russian-hackers_x.htm

[lxxviii] See http://zdnet.com.com/2100-1105_2-5278046.html

[lxxix] For a list of current and recent computer crime prosecutions under these federal statutes in the United States, see the Computer Crimes and

---

Intellectual Property Section Web page of the Department of Justice at http://www.cybercrime.gov

regarding computer misuse.[lxxx] The council observes the following in an explanatory note:

> The fast developments in the field of information technology have a direct bearing on all sections of modern society. The integration of telecommunication and information systems, enabling the storage and transmission, regardless of distance, of all kinds of communication opens a whole range of new possibilities.... By connecting to communication and information services users create a kind of common space, called "cyber-space", which is used for legitimate purposes but may also be the subject of misuse. These "cyber-space offences" are either committed against the integrity, availability, and confidentiality of computer systems and telecommunication networks or they consist of the use of such networks or their services to commit traditional offences.... The criminal law must therefore keep abreast of these technological developments which offer highly sophisticated opportunities for misusing facilities of the cyber-space and causing damage to legitimate interests.[lxxxi]

Section 1 of Chapter II of the convention states guidelines for formulating substantive criminal law as it pertains to unauthorized access of computers, unauthorized interception of data, data interference, system interference, misuse of computing devices, computer fraud, child pornography, and copyright infractions. Article 2 of the convention is of particular relevance for this entry as it defines the relevant guidelines for criminalizing unauthorized access to computers and associated technologies. Article 2 provides as follows:

> Each Party shall adopt such legislative and other measures as may be necessary to establish as criminal offences under its domestic law, when committed intentionally, the access to the whole or any part of a computer system without right. A Party may require that the offence be committed by infringing security measures, with the intent of obtaining computer data or other dishonest intent, or in relation to a computer system that is connected to another computer system.[lxxxii]

Insofar as the defining characteristic of a hacker attack is the attempt to gain unauthorized access, Article 2 purports to guide the adoption of criminal laws regarding hacker attacks. The clear intent, of course, is that unauthorized intrusions be prohibited by law.

Presumably, every member nation of the European Union already has laws on the books prohibiting hacking activities. Although these laws probably differ in particulars, it is reasonable to think that they satisfy the spirit of Article 2's general call to prohibit unauthorized intrusions.

[lxxx] Council of Europe (2001).
[lxxxi] Council of Europe (2001).
[lxxxii] See Council of Europe (2001)

CONCLUSIONS

It is reasonable to hypothesize that incidents of computer misconduct will continue to increase as hackers, crackers, and computer criminals progress in developing more sophisticated and destructive techniques and technologies for intruding upon and attacking the computers and networks of innocent persons. These new techniques will, in turn, give rise to new ethical issues and policy challenges as lawmakers struggle to keep abreast with the latest technologies. Unfortunately, at this time, legislators, policy makers, and law enforcement agencies have not been able to keep pace with the increasing incidence of hacking, cracking, and computer crimes. This chapter has attempted to provide an overview of the relevant technological, ethical, and legal challenges posed by the problem of computer crime.

GLOSSARY

Agent Machines   Machines belonging to innocent parties that are compromised by an attacker and used to stage a digital attack or intrusion of some kind.

Antiforensics   Measures that seek to alter evidence on a computer system to defeat defensive incident-response and law-enforcement investigations; such measures may include destroying existing evidence or planting false evidence.

Cracker   Someone who trespasses onto the computers or networks of other persons without authorization and with an intent to harm.

Cybercrime   Criminal activity that involves unauthorized use of computer technology in an essential way.

Cyberterrorism   Hacking activity that attempts to harm innocent persons and thereby create a general sense of fear or terror among the general population for the purpose of achieving a political agenda.

Denial of Service   A digital attack that is calculated to shut down a Web site, server, or network, usually by overwhelming it with sham requests for information.

Digital Intrusion   An act intended to gain unauthorized access to the digital contents (e.g., files or programs) of another person. Such access can be for comparatively benign purposes (e.g., merely to look at files) or for malicious purposes (e.g., to destroy files).

Hackers   Persons who attempt to gain unauthorized entry to network servers or other computers. Hacking is usually distinguished from cracking in that the latter, unlike hacking activity, is intended to cause harm to innocent persons.

Intrusion Response   Measures adopted by the victim of a digital intrusion intended to investigate, repel, or punish the intrusion.

Internet Protocol (IP) Spoofing   The use of a false IP address for the purpose of deceiving the user about the source of incoming packets.

Logic Bomb   A program designed to take malicious action at a particular point in time.

Rootkits   Programs designed to conceal an intruder and his or her files, directories, or programs by making an operating system lie to its owner.

Session Hijacking   Hijacking that occurs when an intruder deflects traffic from the user's intended destination and interjects its own traffic into the user's stream of communication.

Sniffers Programs that are designed to monitor network traffic on local area network segments.

Stepping Stones Chains of login sessions across multiple computers, often in different countries and time zones.

Trojan Horse A program that appears innocuous, but actually performs malicious functions that alter the victim's system without his or her knowledge.

Virus A malicious program (i.e., one intended to cause damage) that infects computers by attaching itself to programs accessed by the affected computer and attempts to distribute itself to as many other victims as possible through one or more available infection vectors, such as e-mail attachments.

Worms Programs that compromise a system by way of a remotely accessible vulnerability and then use the infected host to distribute the worm to other hosts with the same vulnerability.

CROSS REFERENCES

See *Computer Viruses and Worms; Cybercrime and the U.S. Criminal Justice System; Cyberterrorism and Information Security; Denial of Service Attacks; Electronic Attacks.*

REFERENCES

Barlow, J. P. (n.d.). *The economy of ideas.* Retrieved May 24, 2005, from http://www.eff.org/~barlow/EconomyOfIdeas.html

Bullough, O. (2004, July 28). Police say Russian hackers are increasing threat. Retrieved May 24, 2005, from http://www.usatoday.com/tech/news/internetprivacy/2004-07-28-russian-hackers_x.htm

Council of Europe. (2001). *Convention on cybercrime.* Retrieved May 24, 2005, from http://conventions.coe.int/Treaty/en/Reports/Html/185.htm

Dittrich, D. (1998). One sniff and your password is stolen. *Windows on Computing, 21.* Retrieved May 24, 2005, from http://www.washington.edu/tech_home/windows/issue21/password.html

Dreyfus, S. (1997). *Underground: Tales of hacking, madness and obsession on the electronic frontier.* Sydney: Random House Australia.

Dworkin, R. (1978). *Taking rights seriously.* Cambridge, MA: Harvard University Press.

Few Clues in Web Worm Whodunit. (2003, January 29). WiredNews.com. Retrieved May 24, 2005, from http://www.wired.com/news/infostructure/0,1377,57462,00.html

Gert, B. (1999). Common morality and computing. *Ethics and Information Technology, 1,* 57–64.

Hettinger, E. C. (1989). Justifying intellectual property. *Philosophy and Public Affairs, 18,* 31–52.

Hiltzik, M. (1999). The worm that ate the Internet. In *Dealers of lightning: Xerox PARC and the dawn of the computer age.* New York: Harper Collins.

Himanen, P. (2001). *The hacker ethic.* New York: Random House.

Himma, K. E. (in press). Information and intellectual property protection: Evaluating the claim that information should be free. *APA Newsletters on Philosophy and Computing.*

Hughes, J. (1988). The philosophy of intellectual property. *Georgetown Law Review, 77,* 287.

Interview with Mike Hudack. (n.d.). Retrieved May 24, 2005, from http://uit.no/breifilm/4276/7

Lemos, R. (2001, December 6). *Hacker had WorldCom in his hands.* Retrieved December 6, 2001, from http://news.com/Hacker+had+WorldCom+in+his+hands/2100-1001_3-276711.html

Levy, S. (1984). *Hackers: Heroes of the computer revolution.* New York: Penguin-Putnam.

Manion, M., & Goodrum, A. (2000). Terrorism or civil disobedience: Toward a hacktivist ethic. *Computers and Society, 30,* 14–19.

Mann, C. C., & Freedman, D. H. (1998). *At large: The strange case of the world's biggest Internet invasion.* New York: Simon & Schuster.

Mirkovic, J., Dietrich, S., Dittrich, D., & Reiher, P. (2005). *Internet denial of service: Attacks and defense mechanisms.* Englewood Cliffs, NJ: Prentice Hall.

Naraine, R. (2004, January 23). FTC: Online fraud losses hit $437M. Retrieved May 24, 2005, from http://www.clickz.com/stats/sectors/finance/article.php/5961_3303041

Poulson, K. (2004). FBI busts alleged DDoS mafia. Retrieved May 24, 2005, from http://www.securityfocus.com/news/9411

Ross, W. D. (1930). *The right and the good.* Oxford: Oxford University Press.

Rowland, C. H. (1996). Covert channels in the TCP/IP Protocol suite. Retrieved May 24, 2005, from http://www.firstmonday.dk/issues/issue2_5/rowland/

Slatella, M. (1996). *Masters of deception: The gang that ruled cyberspace.* New York: Perennial.

Spafford, E. (1992). Are computer hacker break-ins ethical? *Journal of Systems Software 17,* 41–48.

Stoll, C. (2000). *The cuckoo's egg.* New York: Pocket Books.

Sullivan, B. (2003, August 20). *Sobig variant floods inbox.* Retrieved May 24, 2005 from http://msnbc.msn.com/id/3078590/

Sullivan, B. (2004). Experts fret over online extortion attempts. Retrieved May 24, 2005, from http://www.msnbc.msn.com/id/6436834/

Taylor, P. (1999). *Hackers: Crime in the digital sublime.* New York: Routledge.

Taylor, P., & Jordan, T. (2004). *Hacktivism and cyberware: Rebels with a cause?* New York: Routledge.

Hacktivism

Paul A. Taylor, *University of Leeds, United Kingdom*
Jan Ll. Harris, *University of Salford, United Kingdom*

INTRODUCTION

Elsewhere (Jordan & Taylor, 2004; Taylor, 1999; Taylor, 2001), we have provided detailed accounts of both hacking and the attendant phenomenon of hacktivism. The purpose of this chapter is to provide a more succinct account of the way in which the key attributes of hacking have been adopted by new social movements that have pressed them into the service of the burgeoning antiglobalization movement. In carrying out this task, we will explore the points of contact and divergence that exist between traditional hacking and the recent emergence of hacktivism, the latter defined as the deployment of hacking tactics within the context of an explicit political agenda. Although hackers tend to be much more politically motivated than their hacker predecessors, their innovative acts are in fact very much in keeping with the original hacker ethic of using technology in the most ingenious manner possible. Hacking has, almost from its first emergence, been marked by a certain politics. However, this politics has revolved around the problem of the freedom of information and access to technology. The innovative feature of hacktivism is the way it takes this preexisting hacker ethic and applies it to the field of specific social protest movements whose concerns are not solely technological. Because hacktivism attempts to wrest control of the technologies of globalization from the hands of the state and corporations and to turn them against the very order that developed and deployed them, it can be said, to continue a trend in computer culture which, from the 1960s onward, hacktivists have sought to challenge the assumption that technology is intrinsically the tool of capitalism and the state.

This chapter begins with an introduction to the key ethical aspects of hacking and offers a schema that traces the evolution of hacking as a concept and practice through various generations. Although a more traditional and apparently politically neutral hacking culture is still extant, we will show how hacktivism, under the impetus of the antiglobalization movement, has emerged as a separate and distinct practice. Despite the common perception of hacking as a computer-related act, the term in its earliest use described a particular, playfully innovative,

and irreverent attitude toward any technology or associated system. The gradual reduction of the term solely to the field of computing is, it will be argued, commensurate with apparent erosion of the hacker ethic as reflected in Microsoft's corporate co-optation of gifted programmers and their culture, a takeover whose stakes are encapsulated in the term *microserfs*. From a radical political perspective, the microserf generation is shown to represent a particularly low point, and the political nature of hacktivism, as described through the notion of electronic civil disobedience and examples of specific hacktivist groups, is presented as a revival of hacking's early political promise. The uses to which these groups put the hacker ethic is then contrasted with the open-source (OS) movement, which despite lacking hacktivism's clear agenda, nevertheless retains a strong fidelity to the original aims of hacking. The chapter concludes with an analysis of the global trends that hacktivism and the OS movement simultaneously challenge and utilize.

THE CULTURE AND FOUNDING ETHICS OF HACKING

> Access to computers—and anything which might teach you something about the way the world works—should be unlimited and total. Always yield to the Hands-On Imperative!
>
> All information should be free
> Mistrust Authority—Promote Decentralisation
> Hackers should be judged by their hacking,
>   not bogus criteria such as
> degrees, age, race, or position.
> You can create art and beauty on a computer.
> Computers can change your life for the better.
> (Levy, 1984, pp. 40–45)

So runs Levy's (1984) summary of the hacker ethic. First-hand research among various groups of hackers (Taylor, 1999) suggests that central beliefs in the overarching value of technological ingenuity and a fascination with the innate complexity of systems should be added to Levy's ethical commandments. It is important to emphasize that it is only in relatively recent years that hacking became associated just with computers. When carrying out firsthand empirical research, hackers provided examples of their favorite hacks that included a number of different artifacts ranging from coffee machines to parking meters and a diverse range of systems encompassing the abstractions of the legal establishment (from a hacker who worked on his own legal defense in jail) and the labyrinthine practicalities of phone networks. Perhaps at its most basic level the term invokes a sense of *bricolage*, that is, a sort of creative or Puckish tinkering with technologies and systems so that they exhibit proprieties and display functions beyond those intended by the designers.

Himanen (2001) offers another perspective on the hacker ethic, arguing that hackers can be distinguished from their ambient culture by their overdeveloped work ethic. They have broken with the Protestant work ethic, in which regulated labor as the cornerstone of a virtuous life finds its reward in material remuneration and a clear conscience. Hackers, although by no means adverse to work, labor in a nonalienated fashion; their hours are irregular and determined by the waxing and waning of their own interest rather than by external dictates. Hackers do not value labor in itself, but rather their specific labor; their enthusiasm is not for the material rewards of work, but for the task itself. In this light, hacking at its most basic level is a joyous, playful, or creative activity. In this respect, the work ethic of the hacker is close to that of the creative artist or the academic, both of whom (ideally) work for the sake of the work (Moody, 2002, p. 154). But in the case of the latter there is a tendency toward individualism, an autonomous even solipsistic aspect that is absent in hacking. Such a formulation may appear paradoxical, given the popular image of the hacker as a socially maladroit loner, happier with code than people. Yet, although this stereotype is not without a grain of truth, it nonetheless fails to recognize the deeply social nature of hacking. To quote Marvin Minsky, "Contrary to popular belief, hackers are more social than other people" (as cited in Himanen, 2001, p. 52). Hackers, although perhaps solitary as individuals, are as a group or collective highly social. Peer recognition, and a desire to produce tools that are socially useful, is the lifeblood of their endeavor. Thus, hackers harness the traits of creativity and enthusiasm associated with highly individualized forms of production toward communal or collaborative projects. This social aspect is perhaps most clear in the activities of the open-source/free software communities but can be observed even in the more questionable activities of hackers.

All these ethical values emerged in the earliest days of computing and are perhaps most readily associated with Levy's further classification of the first three generations of hackers:

"True" hackers: these pioneers made their name experimenting with the large mainframe computers at such U.S. universities as the Massachusetts Institute of Technology during the 1950s and 1960s.

Hardware hackers: these were the entrepreneurial innovators of the 1970s who played a key role in making computing accessible to the masses by both facilitating and promoting the personal computing revolution and its much smaller, decentralized computing hardware.

Game hackers: in the 1980s, building upon the hardware successes of the personal computer (PC) revolution, the game hackers were responsible for the development of popular gaming software applications.

In view of the development of computer culture since Levy's analysis, four additional categories should be added to these earlier generations:

Hacker/cracker: from the mid-1980s to the present day, these terms are used (frequently interchangeably) to describe a person who illicitly breaks into other peoples' computer systems. The choice of term tends to vary depending upon the moral interpretation used by a commentator for acts that tend to be essentially the same. *Hacker*, for example, tends to be used by those sympathetic to the values of the computer underground, whereas *cracker* tends to be used by those who have a much sterner interpretation, such as the computer security industry that has grown up over time in response to such unsolicited intrusions.

Microserfs: this is the phrase used in Douglas Coupland's novel (1995) of the same name to describe those computer programmers, who, while exhibiting various obsessive and independent-minded traits of the hacker subculture, nevertheless became sucked into the corporate world of bonds and the desire to vest them.

Open source/free software hackers: A breed of hacker who self-consciously differentiates themselves from the both the corporate microserf and the deviant cracker. Based primarily around the open source GNU/Linux operating system, they can be seen as a return to the original spirit of the 1960s and 1970s. Indeed, there is a direct link in the form of Richard Stallman, whom Levy described in his 1984 volume as *the last hacker*. Stallman, in particular through the concept of *copyleft* and its adoption by Linus Torvalds, has operated as an intergenerational bridge, perpetuating the original hacker ethic. Unlike hacktivists, the open-source community are political by circumstance rather than by choice, that is, to the degree that their working methodology proves a challenge to the monopolistic agenda of Microsoft and the like.

Hacktivists: the mid-1990s marked a pivotal point at which previous, largely apolitical hacking activity was incorporated into a much more overtly political form. The political activity of the previous generations tended to be limited to securing freer access to computing facilities rather than questioning too deeply the political purposes for which the equipment could be used. The rise of hacktivism fundamentally changed this political blind spot and continues to integrate global networks of information technologies to object against the perceived excesses of global capitalism.

It should be noted that these generations represent a conceptual schema and that the real history of hacking and hacktivism is inevitably more complex, offering overlaps and concurrencies that problematize a simple subdivision of hacking into the previous generations. Notwithstanding these limitations, the schema nevertheless provide a useful overview of the way in which there has been a move away from, and then a return (in the form of open source and free software) to, key aspects of the original hacker ethic:

engagement with systems

hands-on curiosity applied to *any* technology

a desire to reverse the original purposes of an artifact or system.

Before looking at the sophisticated and self-reflexive politics of hacktivism that has sought to revisit and reapply these values, it is necessary to trace the decline in the political potential of early hacker groups and their subsumption within the corporate takeover of the information revolution.

FROM HACKING TO MICROSERFDOM

> These were the radical or guerrilla hackers, who were destined to give the computer a dramatically new image and a political orientation it could never have gained from Big Blue [IBM] or any of its vassals in the mainstream of the industry. At their hands, information technology would make its closest approach to becoming an instrument of democratic politics. (Roszak, 1986, p. 138)

In support of the above claim from Roszak, it is possible to trace a line of influence from the radicalized student population of the 1960s to the computer culture of the 1970s, for instance at the University of California Berkeley, famous as a breeding ground for both hackers and radical politics. This impression is reinforced by a number of influential texts, for instance Ivan Illich's *Tools for Convivality* (1973) and Ted Nelson's *Computer Lib/Dream Machines* (1974). Both books made an explicit connection between an emancipatory politics and an emancipated technology. Nelson's text, in appearance a sort of smazidat publication resembling the *Whole Earth Catalog*, was particularly prophetic. It offered the nebulous but inspiring vision of a *hypertextual* (this term's first appearance) system called Xanadu that would connect every document with every other document in a universal database. Perhaps more important was the fact that Nelson's vision was couched in a revolutionary rhetoric that argued that computing should be accessible to all and not the preserve of corporations or academics. Nelson's text thus assigned the hobbyist and the underground hacker "a noble role in the battle for humanity's future and recruited them for the rebellion they were witnessing on their college campuses" (Wolf, 1995, p. 8). Similarly, Illich argued for the liberation of the design of technology so that the principles were accessible to all, the *convivial* tool aimed to dissolve the distinction between user and producer. His thesis inspired members of the Homebrew Computer Club, such as Lee Felstein, whose "TV Typewriter or Tom Swift Terminal" was an early attempt to hack a monitor/interface using a keyboard and television and produce a "convival cybernetic device" inspired by Illich's vision of a convival technology (Levy, 1984, p. 210; see also Felsentein, 1995) and in this manner Illich's ideas were part of the matrix that spawned the PC revolution.

Thus, on the one hand, a hacker's belief in the ingenious use of technology offered an immediate potential for countercultural activity. If you see subversion in every object placed before you, it is likely that you will develop tendencies that can easily be viewed as subversive by those in authority. On the other hand, however, any radicality within the early generations tended to be mostly confined to issues of access. In other words, hackers could be radical but only tended to be so to gain time for hands-on experimentation with the artifacts and systems that they loved so much. The early radical wing of the hacking ethos was reflected in the advent of the *Youth International Party Line* an underground newsletter run by Abbie Hoffman established in 1971 and which changed its name in September 1973 to the *Technological American Party* (TAP). Newsletters were produced that vividly manifested the ubiquity of the pure hacker hands-on imperative with their raft of detailed technical information on such issues as how to phone-phreak (obtain free phonecalls through the technical manipulation of the phone system) and reengineer a large range of artifacts and techniques including burglar alarms, lock picking, pirate radio, and gas and electric meters.

TAP ceased publication in 1984, but its mantle was quickly assumed with the launch of the phone-phreak/hacker magazine *2600* whose anti-Big Brother government bent was immediately indicated by the editor's choice of the nom de plume Emmanuel Goldstein (the oppressed protagonist of George Orwell's *1984*). Meanwhile, in 1981 in Europe, a German hacker group established the Chaos Computer Club. It directly expressed the digitally correct implications of the original hacker ethic, "All information wants to be free," in the following declaration:

> A development into an "information society" requires a new Human Right of worldwide free communication. The Chaos Club … claims a border-ignoring freedom of information which deals with the effects of technologies on human society and individuals. It supports the creation of knowledge and information in this respect. (As cited in Bowcott and Hamilton, 1990, p. 53.)

We shall see in our subsequent discussion of hacktivism how this emphasis upon the primacy of informational flows lies behind the major schism between human rights and digital rights-orientated hacktivists (see Jordan & Taylor, 2004, for more details). Notwithstanding this perennial tension with the computer counterculture between radical politics and pragmatic issues of access, the first and second generations both exhibited a form of electronic populism. Their subversive desire to hack and the attempt to make technology more universally available were complementary facets of the same hacker agenda.

The earliest hackers had noncorporatist values to the extent that they inhabited cloistered university environments and were motivated by pure intellectual curiosity rather than business applications. With the more outward-looking second generation of hackers, a certain explicit anticorporate ethos, as evinced in the names of some of the early start-up companies such as the *Itty-Bitty Machine Company* (a parody of IBM) and *Kentucky Fried Computers* (Jordan & Taylor, 2004, p. 142). Likewise, the Apple computer company chose its symbol because of its "whole earth" connotations. This countercultural spirit was not to last, however, and the initial socially liberating potential of such computers increasingly became subordinated to their status as mere commodities: "all the bright possibilities seem so disturbingly compatible with corporate control and commercial exploitation" (Jordan & Taylor, p. 155). This corporate appropriation of the original hacker ethic was most dramatically illustrated by Apple's famous 1984 television commercial (directed by Ridley Scott) that culminated with the anti-Orwellian image of a woman sprinting across the screen to launch a huge hammer at a menacingly glowering Big Brother.

As computing technology developed within the ever-widening circles of commercially sponsored dissemination, the commodity view of information gained pace over the countercultural desire for a more politically engaged democracy fueled by the exponential increase in the accessibility of information. Thus the perennial tension between hacking's potential radicalism and the affinity of its code-loving tendencies to economic libertarianism was increasingly resolved in favor of the latter: the countercultural hopes pinned upon the computer as vehicle for antiestablishment values floundered as the *wunderkinds* of the 1970s became the software giants of the 1980s. Given the intrinsically commercial dimension of their activity, the second generation of game hackers was naturally primed to take advantage of the subsequent dot-com boom, whereas the third generation of crackers/hackers increasingly found an outlet for their idiosyncratic skills in the deliberately collegiate atmosphere of Microsoft's headquarters. The early hackers' desire to promote free access to computers and information as a means of facilitating an informed, and thereby empowered, demos had quickly retreated to a self-serving concern with access to computing for its own sake.

Thus the youthful, antiauthoritarian attitudes within the early generations of hacking were soon sublimated into a frustrated desire to consume computing resources (see Taylor, 1999, pp. 53–56) such that teenage hackers came to "resemble an alienated shopping culture deprived of purchasing opportunities more than a terrorist network" (Ross, 1991, p. 90). The nadir of this process was vividly portrayed in Douglas Coupland's (1995) geist-busting "factional" account of the lifestyles of the young programmers working at Microsoft's Seattle headquarters in *Microserfs*. The hacker/cyberpunks' willingness to immerse themselves in the labyrinthine matrices of code was easily co-opted to the creation of a particularly extreme form of *homo economicus*:

> In the 1980s corporate integration punctured the next realm of corporate life invasion at "campuses" like Microsoft and Apple—with the next level of intrusion being that borderline

between work and life blurred to the point of unrecognizability. *Give us your entire life or we won't allow you to work on cool projects*. In the 1990s, corporations don't even hire people anymore. People become their own corporations. It was inevitable. (Coupland, p. 211 [emphasis in the original].)

Microsoft's subsumption of hacker culture has been so successful because traits such as "high productivity, maverick forms of creative work, energy, and an obsessive identification with on-line endurance (and endorphin highs)" (Ross, 1991, p. 90) from the outset blurred the boundaries between work and play, labor and creativity. Thus it engineered an environment in which these qualities, which might have proved problematic in a traditional structure, served solely to valorize "the entrepreneurial codes of silicon futurism" (Ross, p. 90). In this manner, hacking's apparent political potential was diffused and business as usual had restabilized its hegemony. This was arguably because an essential part of the specific act of hacking is its love of the technical means rather than the political or philosophical end. Thus, although the hacking mentality could theoretically be applied to a multitude of artifacts, in practice it was limited to the joy of the hack and the technological means by which it is effected. In other words, an appreciation of the relation of the hacked artifact to the overarching technological system and the possibility of hacking as a subversive intervention in this system tends to be an underdeveloped dimension of hacking.

Similarly, from a political point of view, such a close attachment to the technological system results in a necessary convergence with the aims of the wider social systems that sustain it; to quote the Critical Art Ensemble (CAE),

> The hacker is generally obsessed with efficiency and order. In producing decentralized technology, a fetish for the algorithmic is understandable and even laudable; however, when it approaches a totalising aesthetic, it has the potential to become damaging to the point of complicity with the state (1994, p. 137).

This was demonstrated in one of the authors' (Taylor, 1999) early research into the original hacking communities where, in addition to the moral judgments about hacking made by external groups such as the computer security industry and law enforcement officers, hackers themselves readily expressed their ethical disapproval of those who engaged in destructive acts of electronic trespass. This was because it drew attention to, and thereby endangered, their otherwise harmless engagement with both artifacts and systems. Put another way, hackers did not want to alienate themselves unnecessarily from the society upon which they were dependent for their technological sandpits. Thus, in confirmation of the manner in which many hacker traits appear fundamentally ambiguous with respect to the wider political questions, the peculiar mixture of individuality and communality that characterized hacking culture proved a limitation on its political possibilities. Thus, while hacking produced novel forms of collective endeavor (e.g., live-in mini-gangs, conferences, chat room groups), the narrow activity itself remained fundamentally solitary, even solipsistic.

This is reflected in some of the cultural aspects of the early hacker communities. For example, the Electronic Frontier Foundation (EFF) was an interest group that although not specifically devoted to hacking per se, was, as its name suggests, closely akin to the hacker demand for unfettered access to the digital plains. This appeal to imagery of the Wild West tapped into a deep stratum of the American psyche and finds its echo in the influential fictional genre of cyberpunk that gave us the epochal term *cyberspace*, wherein suitably glamorized hacker protagonists are referred to as *console cowboys*. These tropes of rugged individualism in both cyberpunk depictions and organizations such as the EFF indicate how readily the original hacker ethic was elided with a libertarian, laissez-faire economic ideology. Rather than the socially inclusive dream of an informatically enabled populace that motivated some of those involved in the first wave of the PC revolution, computer networks were increasingly seen as an unprecedented, technologically facilitated opportunity to create virtual social conditions unencumbered by the regulatory weight of real-world government interference. Thus, the key significance of hacktivism and elements of the free software movement is the way in which they, by virtue of a reassertion of a revised set of countercultural values, challenge this apparently total surrender of every aspect of social life to the values of the market. Moreover, this challenge does not occur outside of the market, but rather within the context of the technologies that have played no small role in creating this situation.

HACKTIVISM, TACTICAL MEDIA, AND THE VIRTUAL SIT-IN

As hackers become politicized and as activists become computerized, we are going to see an increase in the number of cyber-activists who engage in what will become more widely known as Electronic Civil Disobedience. The same principles of traditional civil disobedience, like tresspass and blockage, will still be applied, but more and more these acts will take place in electronic or digital form. The primary site for Electronic Civil Disobedience will be in cyberspace (Wray 1998: 3).

As with the hackers before them, there are competing definitions of which activities and people deserve the terms *hacktivism* and *hacktivists*. The conceptual categories offered in this chapter thus inevitably involve simplification of blurred, if not contested, terminological boundaries. Thus, there may be examples of online individuals or groups who use hacking techniques for destructive activities while claiming a political motivation and as a consequence various interpretations can be made as to whether such people should be classed as hacktivists, hackers, or even the pejorative term *crackers*. Denning's comprehensive analysis of hacktivism provides a useful distinction between it, an online activism that simply uses new technologies, and the more sinister cyberterrorism: "Activism refers to normal, non-disruptive use of the Internet in support of an agenda or cause... hacktivism refers to the marriage of hacking and activism... cyberterrorism refers to the convergence of cyberspace and terrorism" (Denning, 1999, p. 2). Recently, within the post-9/11 context, the Uniting and Strengthening America by Providing Appropriate Tools Required to Intercept and Obstruct Terrorism (USA PATRIOT) Act has collapsed hacktivism, cyberterrorism, and the more traditional activities of crackers. All, in the eyes of U.S. law at least, can constitute cyberterrorism, and because that act allows for the extradition of cyberterrorists thus defined, it is has implications for any group considering adopting hacktivist strategies.

Out of these definitions this chapter focuses on the fusion of hacking and activism and its points of contact with the free software movement, which in concert offer the most theoretically interesting and legitimate direct challenge to the commercial paradigms that have dominated the Internet in recent years. In view of this terminological uncertainty, *tactical media* is a useful generic phrase that can be used largely synonymously with hacktivism, the following definition of which is offered by the Critical Art Ensemble:

> The term "tactical media" refers to a critical usage and theorization of media practices that draw on all forms of old and new, both lucid and sophisticated media, for achieving a variety of specific noncommercial goals and pushing all kinds of potentially subversive political issues. (The organizers of the 1993 Amsterdam event Next Five Minutes, as cited in CAE, 1994, p. 5.)

The definition by some of its practitioners (one of whose number has been recently detained under the USA PATRIOT Act, see www.caedefensefund.org) demonstrates its fidelity to the original hacking ethic's emphasis upon the ingenious reappropriation of *any* technological artifact or system. The other key feature of this definition is the inclusive phrase of "a variety of specific noncommercial goals." This is the main unifying feature of hacktivists: their self-reflexive political perspective. Again, in keeping with the original hacking ethic, they seek imaginative methods to reengineer the purpose of a system: in this case the global capitalist system of communication and commodity flows. They also reengineer concepts of protest so that conventional notions of civil disobedience are redesigned for the digital age. Most prominent among these techniques is that of the *virtual sit-in*:

> A virtual sit-in is little more than a collective, simultaneous requesting of a Web site. If one requests a Web site faster than it can be transferred and built up on the end user's screen, the server receives, on the one hand, a message telling it that the first request is no longer valid, and on the other hand, the new request. Scripts running on one's own computer or on go-between servers automate this process, and after a certain number of requests, the server under attack begins to suffer under the strain. One has to differentiate very specifically between knocking out a server

for private motives and a political action openly disrupting a Web site for clearly formulated reasons and for a limited time. That's when it becomes comparable to a warning strike during wage negotiations, a means of civil disobedience signalling that one side has the willingness and courage to fight (Grether, 2000, p. 5).

A practical example of this theory of electronic civil disobedience was provided in 1998 when a group known as the Electronic Disturbance Theater (EDT) coordinated a series of Web sit-ins in support of the Zapatistas, a Mexican antigovernment group largely made up of indigenous people from the Chiapas region. The sit-ins used an automated piece of software called Flood Net. The idea behind this program is that once downloaded onto a computer, it helps users to automatically connect their computer to constantly request access to a preselected Web site and renew the request every 7 seconds. If thousands of people use Flood Net on the same day, the combined effect of such a large number of activists will severely disrupt the operations of a particular site. The particular way in which Flood Net was used illustrates the important distinction to be made between pure hacktivism and the early hacking mentality that arguably lives on in the form of digitally correct hacktivism (see Jordan & Taylor, 2004). The overriding concern of digitally correct hacktivism is the maintenance of bandwidth functionality and the technical elegance of a hack. In contrast, the political success and strength of the Flood Net action was the very fact that it was not a highly sophisticated and largely automated program. It was relatively simple from a technological point of view and this meant that it required the mass participation of willing volunteers. This gave it a political credibility it would not otherwise have had. Before moving on to analyze further the political motivations and implications of hacktivism, it is helpful at this point to review some brief examples of hacktivist groups and their actions.

FURTHER EXAMPLES OF HACKTIVIST ACTIONS
Electronic Pressure Group Actions: The Etoy Campaign

> Despite all the naysaying, the Net is offering individuals new opportunities to take action and giving ideas a better shot at taking hold. It allows and even encourages cooperation in virtual groups, and in the best of situations, a self-organizing countermatrix as well that can make short work of a highly organized and powerful corporation (Grether, 2000, para. 2).

Grether (2000) provides a full account of the 1999 Etoy campaign by activists created in response to the court action initiated by a commercial company in an attempt to remove an art collective's Web site domain name (*etoy*) because it was too close to their own (*etoys*). The company's action was implemented despite the fact the art collective had been operating under its name first and generated enough online ill will to generate a highly coordinated campaign that incorporated various hacktivist (e.g., the Flood Net program) and public relations initiatives (e.g., mass mailings, countercourt actions, satirical mirror Web sites). The campaign was successful and the company was forced to retreat from its aggressively litigious stance. The incident illustrated the extent to which online actions can produce an unprecedentedly effective degree and speed of coordination constituting an important, new countervailing power to corporate influence.

Culture Jamming

> One two-dollar can of spray can reverse a hundred-thousand-dollar media campaign (Rushkoff, 1994, p. 281).

Although usually considered separately, culture jamming fits enough of this chapter's schematic requirements to be considered a form of hacktivism. Its basic purpose is to hack the symbolic codes of what its practitioners perceive to be an excessively commodified culture. It can be considered as a semiotic form of aikido, in so far as it seeks to use a minimum of effort to turn the strength of commercial culture back on itself (see also Klein, 2001, pp. 279–309). The Adbusters group, for example, uses techniques known as billboard banditry and subverting to make small, but hugely significant, changes to hugely expensive advertising campaigns. One vivid example of this technique was the use of cheap spray cans on the giant billboard figures of gamine Calvin Klein models. In this case culture jammers used the hacker technique of reverse engineering to give the models on the posters "zipper mouths" and blacked out eyeballs and a consequently skeletal appearance. As the above quote demonstrates, this practice is not intrinsically technological; nevertheless, the new media and the algorithmic manipulability that underwrites them provide a range of novel possibilities for culture jamming. Thus, common hacktivist tactics such as *Web redirects*, in which Web sites are hijacked and their users redirected to politically significant sites (for instance Nike.com redirected to a site concerned with worker's rights), and *Web site defacements*, such as those that proliferated at the start of the Iraq war and around the long-running Palestinian–Israel conflict, which were directed at a range of targets (Al Jazeera, the U.S. military, etc.) by a range of interest groups (both for and against the action and its various participants) (Allen & Demchack, 2003), can be seen as examples of technologically driven forms of culture jamming.

To this cultural jamming we might also add forms of intervention at the level of both software and hardware. In the case of hardware, this can take the form of a reverse engineering of artifacts that deliberately shut out or artificially delimit the options of their users. For instance, Microsoft's entry in the game console market, the X-Box, contained a fairly decent Windows-only computer. Users, through the addition of a mod chip, were able to release this computer, install an alternative operating system, and use it in a manner of their choosing. Such hacking is political only to the extent that it asserts a freedom to modify over a proprietorial vision of technology, in the case of a joint project carried out by CAE and the

Carbon Defense League, a similar technological detournement of the Nintendo Game Boy was implemented for explicitly political purposes, in this case to draw attention to the ideological programming inherent in game design (http://www.carbondefense.org/writing_4.html).

Perhaps of greater significance than this reverse engineering are attempts to develop forms of software that challenge or embody political positions, examples of which might include programs such as *Freenet*—an entirely decentered and encrypted person-to-person network whose raison d'etre is the prevention of any form of control or censorship, which attempts to enshrine at the level of code the values of free speech—and a range of software developed to override attempts by various governments and other organizations to delimit access to the Internet on the behalf of their populations. On a more general level, the proliferation of hacks to evade state and commercial control over the flow and ownership of data, software, and hardware can be seen as a form of cultural jamming in that they attempt to preserve the decentralized free flow of information that for many is the Net's most important dimension (Deibert, 2003).

Precision Targeted Satire: RTMark and the Yes Men

> To restate a situationist expression, rather than "fighting alienation with alienated methods" (bureaucracy, political parties, militancy, deferment of pleasure), one uses derision, irony, laughter— all underground strategies which undermine the process of normalization and domestication which are the goals of the guarantors of the external and hence abstract order. (Maffesoli, 1996, p. 50)

The emphasis upon performance has been given a sustainedly satirical treatment by such groups as RTMark and The Yes Men. RTMark's name stems from the phrase *registered trademark* and its distinctive mode of operation rests upon its pastiche of corporate organizational forms. For example, in an imitation of the conventional stock market, it offers investments in imaginative stocks. The investments are made in the form of such countercultural stunts as the switching of the voice boxes in GI Joes and Barbie dolls by a group calling themselves the Barbie Liberation Organisation. The Yes Men have recently released an independent film of their stunts and have particularly focused their attentions upon the global economic policies of the World Trade Organization by misleadingly carrying out satirical presentations at various high-profile public events while pretending to be World Trade Organization representatives. Another example of this precision-directed satire was offered by re-code.com, which aimed at exposing the fallacy of the empowered consumer (perpetrated by sites such as priceline.com). It lets consumers dictate the price of purchase by providing users of the online site with the ability to access and manipulate the barcodes of popular products sold. Users were able to modify, download, and print barcodes that could then be attached to their item of choice. Although the creators of this site stressed that its purpose is solely

satirical, a number of companies, including Wal-Mart, took a less charitable view of its activities and currently re-code.com is the subject of a legal action.

OPEN SOURCE AND FREE SOFTWARE: THE REBIRTH OF THE HACKING ETHIC?

Within the context of the issues under discussion, the emergence in the 1990s of the free software/open-source movement both confirms and consolidates many of the trends displayed by hacktivism, while also highlighting the perennial problems that plague the politicization of hacking. As stated above, the free software movement serves as a bridge between the ideals of the early generation of hackers and a new movement that has emerged in direct response to the increasing commodification of software and the Internet. We have spoken of tactical media as a synonym for hacktivism, and in this light, hacktivism can be seen as operating at the level of the message rather than the medium. In contrast, free software offers the possibility of an intervention in the structure of the medium because it renders the medium's design political. However, the politics of free software are a fraught matter, not least because the movement contains within itself a number of conflicting tendencies. Unlike hacktivism, which is irreducibly political, the politics of free software are in some respects extrinsic, that is to say the result of its context rather than a product of an explicit agenda. This resembles the problems faced by the first generations of hackers, with their predominant concern over the question of access, and like that generation the resolution of its immediate arena of conflict would possibly neutralize any wider political charge that the movement might possess. Certainly there are hackers among this community who see their work in political terms, not only as a challenge to the proprietorial model and monopolistic ethos of Microsoft and the like but also as a defense and assertion of fundamental freedom. But equally many of those who contribute to the project regard it simply in terms of an effective means for software design.

As a result, in 1998 the movement fractured into two factions when the Open Source Initiative, led by Eric Raymond, split from Richard Stallman's Free Software Foundation. The former claims to offer open-source software without "ideological tub-thumping" and a "losing attitude and symbolism" (http://www.opensource. org/advocacy/faq.html), arguing that OS is primarily a successful methodology for the development of software and as such is entirely compatible with the aims of big business. It has deliberately sought to meliorate those aspects of the movement that prove objectionable to corporate clients (not least a propensity toward long hair, beards, woolly hats, and comic T-shirts). In contrast, the free software faction has upheld the original hacker ethic and remains firm in the belief that free software partakes of a fundamental intellectual freedom. It argues that software should evolve in the way that science evolves, through the free exchange of information, for free software information should always be free (although as Stallman repeatedly points out the freedom he talks of is that of "free speech rather than free beer"). Despite these differences, their common methodology is in direct conflict with that practiced by Microsoft. Indeed, the color of the rhetoric the latter has used to describe OS indicates the threat this model represents; thus, Steve Ballmer of Microsoft has described it as "un-American" and a "cancer." Such pathological metaphors reveal the magnitude of the stakes involved, as do the infamous Halloween documents, a series of internal reports produced by Microsoft that describe free software as "long term credible" and a direct threat to Microsoft's revenues (http://www.opensource.org/halloween/links.php). The crux of the contention is the question of source code. Microsoft and a range of other software developers uphold a proprietorial model in which the codes that underpin their software are unavailable to its users or rivals.

The core principles to which both factions of the free software movement subscribe and that have provoked such strong reactions can be summarized as follows (see Cramer, 2000):

Free Software may be freely copied.

Not only the executable binary code, but also the program source code, are freely available.

The source code may be modified and used for other programs by anyone.

There are no restrictions on the use of Free Software. Even if Free Software is used for commercial purposes, no license fees have to be paid.

There are no restrictions on the distribution of Free Software. Free Software may be sold for money even without paying the programmers.

Free software is not freeware or shareware; that is to say, it can be sold. However, even if this is the case, the source code remains available and open to modification by the user or other programmers. These principles, known collectively as copyleft, have rapidly evolved within the context of the Internet and accommodate its open architecture into the very process of software design. Indeed, much of this architecture was written as free software, not for ideological reasons but because it predates the commodification of code that took place in the 1980s. Free software emerged as a response to this process, and attempted to preserve within a legislative framework (the GNU License) the freedoms threatened by this model. In this manner the open architecture of the Internet, constructed in part from nonproprietorial code, created an environment that facilitated the collaborative production of software. Thus the GNU/Linux system has been developed entirely online through the medium of e-mail and bulletin boards. In Microsoft's words "the ability of the OSS [open-source software] process to collect and harness the collective IQ of thousands of individuals across the Internet is simply amazing." In OS development, a multitude of unpaid console cowboys participate in a vast collaborative project, a system of cybernetic feedback in which the divisions between work and play and between user and consumer are continually transgressed for the sake of the product. This collectivism challenges both the self-serving mythos of the free market and the lone hacker, as well as the dictatorial hierarchy of conventional

project development. Moreover, as Cramer (2000) notes, it constitutes an archive that cannot be erased: the code, once written, is in the public realm and can be drawn upon by anyone. In this respect it offers an intimation of collective intelligence or, in Microsoft's phrase, a "mindshare."

The relation of open source to wider political questions is complex. Terranova (2000) argues that its breakdown of the distinction between consumer and producer reflects an extension of the market into every aspect of contemporary existence. DeLanda (2001) argues that despite its insistence on freedom, "the very fact that the [GNU] license acts as an 'enforcement mechanism' for openness shows how far its function is from one of just promoting 'freedom' (that is, Stallman's original intention)" (para. 7). Eric Raymond (n.d.) argues for open source as gift economy, but as Richard Barbrook notes this economy exists within an inescapable relation to a commodity economy: "money commodity and gift relations are not just in conflict with each other, but also co-exist in symbiosis" (Barbrook, 1997, p. 137). Similarly, Stefan Merten, one of the organizers of the Wizards of OS conferences that have been held on a yearly basis in Berlin since the late 1990s, argues for the emergence of a General Public License society in which "immaterial," intellectual, or "affective" labor would be exchanged along an open-source model (Merten, 2001). This immateriality and free software's association with it has been the source of critique regarding the ultimate significance of open source. According to Matteo Pasquinelli,

> Softwares are immaterial machines.... Free Software... [in] its immateriality... often fails to clash with the real world. Even if we know that it is a good and right thing, we ask polemically: what will change when all the computers in the world will run free software? The most interesting aspect of the free software model is the immense cooperative network that was created by programmers on a global scale, but which other concrete examples can we refer to in proposing new forms of action in the real world and not only in the digital realm? (Pasquinelli, 2004, p. 3)

The supposed immateriality of contemporary labor is the product of a Western myopia that fails to see that material labor, rather than having disappeared, has merely been outsourced to number of developing countries. In these regions, the division between producer and consumer remains firmly entrenched, because many of the goods manufactured by the coolies of global economy remain beyond the economic reach of their producers. However, it is worth pointing out that free software (for sound economic reasons) has found a welcome in developing countries, for instance India, where a large number of skilled programmers are contributing to a range of OS projects (Moody, 2002, p. 317).

Such contradictions might suggest that open source, like the politicized hacking of the 1970s, is too mired in the contradictions of its milieu to constitute a viable challenge to the values of late capitalism. But, to the extent that it exists and produces a technically superior product using methods that implicitly challenge the dominant values of contemporary economic thought, it stands as an index of possibilities. It demonstrates that the Internet can indeed support new productive relations and thus offers a positive model for movements such as hacktivism.

ALL THAT IS SOLID MELTS INTO AIR

Marx and Engels famously declared in the *Communist Manifesto* that under capitalism:

All fixed, fast-frozen relations, with their train of ancient and venerable prejudices and opinions, are swept away, all new-formed ones become antiquated before they can ossify. All that is solid melts into air, all that is holy is profaned, and men at last are forced to face . . . the real conditions of their lives and their relations with their fellow men (Marx & Engels, 1977, p. 46).

This prophetic articulation of the dematerializing qualities of commodity culture has recently found its echo in the titles of a spate of pro-business books that celebrate the putative weightlessness of the digital economy. For example, business books such as *Living on Thin Air, The Weightless World*, and *The Empty Rain Coat* are all premised upon an acceptance of, if not excitement about, the spatial disorientation created by globalization, and the new information technologies that have brought about these conditions. As stated previously, radical protest movements have sometimes been suspicious of too close an involvement with the technologies of their perceived enemies. The hacktivist groups and activities highlighted in this chapter represent a much more positive engagement with the realities of an increasingly networked world. Rather than rail against the enframing and circumscribing qualities of global systems, these movements have recognized, in Lash's words, that "there is no escaping from the information order, [and] thus the critique of information will have to come from inside the information itself" (Lash, 2002, p. vii). There is thus a growing recognition among new social movements that any desire for change to the social order will have to make use of, but also change the nature of, its present communication channels. They have chosen to concentrate upon the concluding part of Marx and Engel's pellucid assertion, that is, a recognition with "sober senses" of the "real conditions of their lives and their relations with their fellow men."

From the critical antiglobalization perspective, the increased efficiency of communication flows enabled by the new information technologies is part of both the problem and the solution. The same trends that result in the phenomenon of the *maquiladoras* (swallow factories— named after the way the fast-moving bird touches down momentarily before swooping off again) also provide such opportunities for global cooperation as that practiced by the EDT and their high-tech support for otherwise fragmented and globally disparate groups of people. What is important here is the to-and-fro movement of co-optation and counterresponse that takes place between corporate and anticorporate philosophies. Just as the hacker ethic became co-opted for the corporate requirements of Microsoft, so those wishing to oppose commercial forces do so in an adopt-and-adapt element of a system they oppose: free software is at once outside capitalism and within, where hacktivists in detourning the tools of economic globalization both challenge and acknowledge the reality of the system. In this light, Pasqunielli's (2004) dichotomy between the immateriality of cyberspace and the harsher conditions of the material world is too bald; it is a question not of testing one against the other, but of discovering the shifting and unstable alliances and the sudden conversions and adaptations that take place between the two.

CONCLUSION

This chapter has provided a brief overview of the main features, protagonists, and underlying philosophy of a number of emergent technologically orientated challenges to the current informational hegemony. Perhaps it was only a matter of time before anticorporate protestors saw globalization as an opportunity as well as a threat, but as much as its techniques involve new high-tech means they are essentially in keeping with both the original hacker ethic and conventional Marxist analysis of capitalism in which it is asserted that commercial power contains the seeds of its own downfall. In less polemical terms, more mainstream economic analysis also recognizes some of the inherent tensions created in the increasingly immaterial new economy that has spawned hacktivism. The fact that commodities are becoming increasingly immaterial means that it can be difficult to assert proprietary rights over them. This is a problem that both the music and the film industries are presently grappling with as they attempt to deal with the implications of the growth of online file sharing. Yet the sublimation of fixed values described by Marx and Engels a century and a half ago has still not resulted in capital's downfall: the market's powers of recuperation are robust. The basic situation faced by commercial and radical groups alike is that the online world creates conditions of flux. The "space of flows" of the information society (Castells, 2000) creates opportunities and challenges for resistance and capital alike, and in the case of open source these two vectors meet in a single praxis. This chapter has shown that, in contrast, hacktivism's most striking feature is not so much its imaginative reappropriation of technological methods and infrastructures, but its determination to apply such techniques for a social, rather than merely a technical, end. In the past, protest movements have been ill-equipped to do little more than reactively berate the worst aspects of changing social conditions whereas their corporate opponents have surfed the wave of change. The various generations of hackers have produced resources for different beasts; new sharks may now be in the water.

GLOSSARY

Antiglobalization/Anticapitalism Movements A new generation of protest movements that challenge the current neoliberal hegemony and attempt to draw attention to the intrinsically exploitative reality of free trade. They are distinguished by their decentralization, a lack of coherent ideology beyond what they oppose, and a willingness to engage in new methods of political protest.

Culture Jamming An attempt to overturn or expose the hidden agenda of cultural products by subverting their messages through low-tech means; rather than an external critique, it operates immanently at the level of specific cultural artifacts.

Free Software Software that includes its source code, which is available to all users who in principle can modify or contribute to its development. It is free as in "free speech" and not "free beer." This freedom is ensured by the use of licenses, which preserve the freedom of the code.

Hacker Ethic The belief that information sharing and technical innovation is in itself a positive act and that it should not be constrained or artificially delimited.

Hacking The ingenuity-driven activity of manipulating or modifying technologies without respect to their original functions, which should be distinguished from *cracking*, a more destructive or transgressive form of hacking.

Hacktivism The adoption of various procedures drawn from hacking for explicitly political ends; more generally, a recognition that political struggle in the 21st century necessarily includes information technologies.

Microserfs Term adopted from Douglas Coupland's eponymous novel, which describes the lives and frustrations of Microsoft employees in the mid-1990s.

Open-Source Movement A faction of the free software movement, that embraces the distribution of source code, but that views this freedom in terms of market choice and a rejection of centralized state control in favor of a free-market model. The most vocal proponent of this vision is Eric S. Raymond.

Source Code Source code is written in the higher programming languages that allow programmers to manipulate and assemble binary codes. This source code is not necessary for computers to run programs.

Virtual Sit-in A virtual sit in, like its physical counterpart, aims to immobilize a target by obstructing its services. The coordinated deployment by numerous users to bring down Web sites by accessing them several times a minute until the site collapses is an example of a virtual sit-in.

CROSS REFERENCES

See *Cyberterrorism and Information Security; Hackers, Crackers and Computer Criminals; Legal, Social and Ethical Issues of the Internet.*

REFERENCES

Allen, D. P., & Demchack, C. (2003, March–April). The Palestinian-Israel cyberwar. *Military Review*. Retrieved May 14, 2005, from http://www.findarticles.com/p/articles/mi_m0PBZ/is_2_83/ai_106732244

Barbrook, R. (1997). The digital economy. Retrieved from www.nettime.org

Bowcott, O., & Hamilton, S. (1990). *Beating the system:*

Hackers, phreakers & electronic spies. London: Bloomsbury.

Castells, M. (2000). *The rise of the network society*. Oxford, UK: Blackwell.

Coupland, D. (1995). *Microserfs*. London: Flamingo.

Cramer, F. (2000). *Free software as collaborative text*. Retrieved May 14, 2005, from http://www.netzliteratur.net/cramer/free_software_as_text.html

Critical Art Ensemble. (1994). *The electronic disturbance*. New York: Autonomedia.

Deibert, R. J. (2003). Black code: Censorship, surveillance, and militarization of cyberspace. *Millennium: Journal of International Studies, 32*(3).

DeLanda, M. (2001). *Open-source: A movement in search of a philosophy*. Retrieved May 14, 2005, from http://www.cddc.vt.edu/host/delanda/pages/opensource.htm

Denning, D. (1999). Activism, hacktivism, and cyberterrorism: The Internet as a tool for influencing foreign policy. Retrieved May 14, 2005, from http://www.nautilus.org/gps/info-policy/workshop/papers/denning.html

Felsenstein, L. (1995). Convivial cybernetic devices: From vacuum tube flip-flops to the singing Altair: An interview with Lee Felsentein. *The Analytical Engine: Newsletter of the Computer History Association of California, 3*, 3–14.

Grether, R. (2000, January). How the Etoy campaign was won. *Telepolis*. Retrieved May 14, 2005, from http://www.heise.de/tp/english/inhalt/te/5843/1.html

Himanen, P. (2001). *The hacker ethic and the spirit of the information age*. London: Secker and Warburg.

Illich, I. (1973). *Tools for conviviality*. New York: Harper & Row.

Jordan, T., & Taylor, P. (2004). *Hacktivism & cyberwars: Rebels with a cause?* London: Routledge.

Klein, N. (2001). *No logo*. London: Flamingo.

Lash, S. (2002). *Critique of information*. London: Sage.

Latour, B. (1988). *The prince* for machines as well as for machinations. In B. Eliot (Ed.), *Technology and social process* (pp. 20–43). Edinburgh: Edinburgh University Press.

Levy, S. (1984). *Hackers: Heroes of the computer revolution*. New York: Bantam Doubleday Dell.

Maffesoli, M. (1996). *The time of the tribes: The decline of individualism in mass society*. Sage: London.

Marx, K., & Engels, F. (1977). *Manifesto of the Communist Party*. Moscow: Progress.

Merten, S. (2001). Free software & GPL society: Stefan Merten of Oekonux interviewed by Joanne Richardson. Retrieved May 14, 2005, from http://subsol.c3.hu/subsol_2/contributors0/mertentext.html

Moody, G. (2002). *Rebel code: Linux and the open source revolution*. London: Penguin Books.

Nelson, T. (1974). *Computer lib/dream machines*. Sausalito, CA: Mindful Press.

Pasquinelli, M. (2004). *Radical machines against the techno-empire: From Utopia to network*. Retrieved May 14, 2005, from http://www.republicart.net/disc/empire/pasquinelli01_en.pdf

Raymond, E. S. (n.d.). *Open source F.A.Q.* Retrieved May 14, 2005, from http://www.opensource.org/advocacy/faq.html

Ross, A. (1991). *Strange weather*. London: Verso.

Roszak, T. (1986). *The cult of information: The folklore of computers and the true art of thinking*. New York: Pantheon.

Taylor, P. A. (1999). *Hackers: Crime in the digital sublime*. London: Routledge.

Taylor, P. A. (2001). Hacktivists: In search of lost ethics? In D. Wall (Ed.), *Crime and the Internet*. London: Routledge.

Terranova, T. (2000). Free labour: Producing culture for the digital economy. *Social Text 63, 18*(2), 33–57.

Wolf, G. (1995). The curse of Xanadu. *Wired, 3*(6), 158–202.

Wray, S. (1998a). Transforming Luddite resistance into virtual Luddite resistance: Weaving a World Wide Web of electronic civil disobedience. Retrieved May 14, 2005, from http://www.thing.net/~rdom/ecd/luddite.html

Wray, S. (1998b). *On electronic civil disobedience*. Paper presented to the Socialist Scholars Conference. Retrieved from http://www.nyu.edu/projects/wray/oecd.html

Corporate Spying: The Legal Aspects

William A. Zucker, *Gadsby Hannah LLP*
Scott Nathan, *Independent Consultant*

INTRODUCTION

When we think of spying, we think of James Bond or the characters in a John LeCarre novel. It is always covert. Its justifications are found in global national concerns and values. However, spying in the most traditional sense is no longer confined to covert operations between nations. Our government under the rubric of national security and the Uniting and Strengthening America by Providing Appropriate Tools Required to Intercept and Obstruct Terrorism (USA PATRIOT) Act is empowered to and does spy on its citizens, in their private and business lives. And we, its citizens, spy on each other.

The world searches for intelligence. Constantly. Governments pursue intelligence to better serve and protect their constituents. For-profit organizations seek intelligence to create better mousetraps, provide better services, and, in any event, enhance the balance sheet and shareholder value. Individuals seek intelligence to help themselves or others, to fend off or perpetrate an injustice, or simply to satisfy curiosity. The reasons people want to know would take a congressional library to catalog.

Business intelligence has many levels. Businesses need to understand the regulatory environment in which they must operate. They also must continuously develop and refine the kinds of products and services they offer to targeted consumers or customers. Enterprises also need

fully to understand how to create and maintain workplace environments that motivate employees to work hard and stay focused on the company's interests. And in this world of competition, knowing thy opponent is as good as knowing thyself, so millions of dollars are spent each year in the quest to learn everything about one's competitors. Much of the intelligence referred to here is called research and involves gathering information from diverse sources within the public record or that can be accessed once appropriate authority is obtained. Information begets databases that become profiles, are used to plot trends, and are mined for comparisons and potential advantages, all as part of determining a business' potential strategies and courses of action.

Spying, in fact, is the search for intelligence overtly as well as covertly. Although we tend to think of corporate spying as that which occurs on a business-to-business (B2B) level, B2B competitive intelligence is only one aspect of corporate spying. Businesses that spy on their employees by gathering information on computer usage, Internet access, Web sites visited, and e-mails sent and received. Some businesses also keep track of employees who access sensitive company information. Conversely, employees spy on their employers, sometimes secreting information about company operations for use as a whistleblower (a form of spying that is encouraged by public policy because it serves a greater good) or to aid the company's competitors (which, more often than not, also serves the personal interest of the employee who shares company information with the competition).

There are many consequences of corporate spying. There are, of course, the fundamental ethical concerns. Legitimacy concerns, which arise from those ethical ones, may limit the deployment of spying in the individual and business community. Whether those legitimacy concerns will hold as our society increasingly becomes more global and less personal is an open question and beyond the scope of this chapter. We know that spying occurs. As a practical matter, companies spend vast sums of money erecting barriers to unauthorized access to sensitive information. We can expect that such expenditures will also increase. We can also expect that as a countermeasure to spying, like the flotsam and jetsam used by aircraft to misdirect guidance systems, companies will disseminate misinformation—at what societal cost? Spying becomes more personal as it targets individuals and invades our sense of, and right to, privacy. Where, if at all, does privacy exist in the corporate environment? Under what circumstances, if at all, is it permissible to read the private communications between an employee and family members or medical care providers? When can someone listen to your phone calls?

These are not easy questions to answer. Without ignoring the fundamental philosophical and ethical issues that are raised, we must ask first what parameters are permitted by the law. As a practical matter, the law sets the stage for whatever drama may unfold. The purpose of this chapter is to acquaint the reader with the law as it pertains to each type of spying so that the reader can have a better idea of what is permissible and what plainly is not, and help the reader decide whether there are some forms of spying that may not be spying after all. The authors hope that this knowledge of the law will help inform the reader's choices including the reader's decisions about what safeguards or defenses he or she may wish to erect.

A SERIES OF QUESTIONS AND A HYPOTHETICAL

A Harvard law professor, who later was to become a federal judge, was fond of teaching the law by asking his students the following question: "ask yourself what your mother would have done and that is probably what the law requires." There are problems of course with this question, not only because it is an oversimplification, but also because it assumes an objective reasonable mother who may or may not exist for any of us. It does, however, show that the law is often rooted in our own visceral sense of right and wrong. Answering a few hypothetical questions will help you grapple, in real terms, with the kinds of circumstances in which the law will be applied.

Everyone today uses the Internet to research and gather information. When, however, does that use become spying? Let's test out your views with the following questions. Keep track of your answers.

Question	Yes	No
1. Is it spying to gather information using software that searches the Internet?		
2. Does your answer change if the search software gains access to an area of a Web site by cracking a protected code?		
3. Does your answer change if the information is not publicly available on the site?		
4. Is it spying when a company's Web site inserts a cookie in the computer of each visitor to the Web site for the purpose of gathering personal identifying information about each visitor?		
5. Is it corporate spying to create a mirror image of the data in a Web site and the code that is used to create the Web site when those data and code are released publicly?		
6. Does your answer to the last question change if the company that is copying the data and code is a direct competitor of the owner and host of the Web site?		

As discussed in the Introduction, corporate intrusion on an individual's entitlement to privacy is a paramount issue. Let's explore that issue and your views with a hypothetical fact pattern, pieced together from actual events.

Lorraine works for a company that tracks, retrieves, warehouses, and returns consumer goods. Its operations include a call center that makes and receives calls from the customers of its clients for a variety of reasons, including tracking defective inventory. Lorraine signs a nondisclosure agreement when she begins her employment and, over the course of 2 years, develops casual relationships with employees of her employer's customers as well as some retail customers from whom goods have been retrieved. Lorraine's attitude about her employment and her employer begins to sour; coincidentally, she takes an extended sick leave.

One morning she attempts to return to work, staying less than 2 hours. During that time, however, she copies to a disk the contact information for some of the people with whom she began developing casual relationships. She also sent this same information by e-mail from her computer in the office to her personal e-mail address accessible from her home computer. Lorraine never returns to work. In the days immediately after her departure, Lorraine's supervisor reviews the log of Lorraine's e-mails and the content of Lorraine's voice mail messages and discovers that the company's contact information has been taken by Lorraine for personal use. In response, the company sends two supervisors to Lorraine's house, demanding immediate access to Lorraine's home computer to search for any information belonging to the company, which Lorraine refuses.

When can companies monitor employees? When can information accessible to an employee while on the job become usable by the employee outside of work? Can employees give away their right to keep certain communications private?

We will attempt to answer all of these as well as other questions in this chapter.

THE COMMON LAW REMEDIES AND APPROACHES

The law in the United States has evolved over time. We act against a backdrop of judicial decisions that extend back hundreds of years. These decisions form a body of law known as the common law. It differs from statutes in that there is often no legislative enactment that describes the boundaries of rightful or wrongful conduct. The common law, although there are consistent trends and approaches, varies in nuance from state to state. Accordingly, what is set forth in this chapter are the broad strokes of the common law as they pertain to the issue of corporate spying.

The Concept of Proprietary Rights: Trade Secrets

For many years, unless an idea was patentable, the primary protection for internal business data, confidential or proprietary information, and computer code was through the common law doctrine of trade secrets (*Kewanee Oil Co. v. Bicron Corp.*, 1974). Generally, a trade secret might be considered any internal, nonpublished manufacturing know-how, drawings, formulas, or sales information used in a trade or business that has commercial applicability and that provides a business with some strategic advantage. Such information, so long as it was (a) not published or disseminated to others who were not obligated to maintain its confidentiality,[1] and (b) maintained in confidence with the protecting organization, could be protected as a trade secret.

The law of trade secret thus recognized a business's ownership or proprietary interest in such information, data, or processes. There are, however, important practical limitations on the application of trade secret protection. First and foremost, for any product sold in the market the law does not protect against a competitor seeing the product and then using it to figuring out how to manufacture like or similar items. Competitors are therefore free to *reverse engineer* a product so long as the reverse engineering is done wholly independently.

The second caveat is that an organization has to prove not only that the information qualifies for trade secret protection, but also that it protected the secrecy of the information as required by the law of the applicable jurisdiction. This means that ownership will be a matter not of record but of case-by-case proof, making enforcement of trade secret protection time consuming and expensive later on. Generally, the proof required consists of showing that there was an active security program in place that was sufficient to protect the information as confidential. Various programs may be deemed adequate, depending on the circumstances, but usually such programs have the following in common:

- An inventory of trade secret information that is periodically updated
- A security program to protect the technology at issue, often on a need-to-know basis with clear marking of information as confidential, access restricted
- A written description of the security program that is provided to all employees
- An enforcement officer or oversight procedure
- An enforcement program, including litigation, if necessary, to enjoin unauthorized access or distribution

In the field of computing, these principles often mean that source code or other readable formats should be secured in a locked file and marked confidential. All representations of the code as stored on magnetic or other medium should be marked confidential and secured. Computerized information should be password protected with restrictions on circulation of the password and periodic password changes.[2] A notice of confidentiality should be displayed as soon as access to the program is obtained, with appropriate warnings on limitation of use. Levels of access should be controlled so that privileges to copy, read, and write are appropriately restricted. Surveillance of entries and log-on should be routinely conducted to verify that there has been no unauthorized entry. Finally, periodic audits should be conducted to test and substantiate the security procedures.

Security and trade secret law are forever linked together. A trade secret cannot exist without such security. The watchwords "Eternal vigilance is the price of liberty," which have often been attributed to Thomas Jefferson, in the context of business information protection should be restated as "Eternal vigilance is the price of trade secret protection." It is not as catchy a phrase, but it is the price each business must pay if it relies in whole or in part on trade secret law for protection.

The Employee and the Concept of Fiduciary Duty

An Employee's Fiduciary Duty

Mobility of employees is a hallmark of today's business world. Job expectations are defined not in years, but in months. Employees may be hired for specific projects in which employment is a form a consulting, lasting only as long as the special assignment. But it was not always so. Out of a different era came the notion that an employee owes to his or her employer the fiduciary duty of utmost loyalty. As part of that fiduciary duty, an employee was prohibited from using any property that belonged to his or her employer in competition with the employer or for personal gain. An employee, however, was entitled to retain and use for whatever purpose his or her own skill and knowledge, which arguably could include contacts that he or she developed over the course of his or her employment if such contacts were not trade secrets.

Although the doctrine of fiduciary duty is a starting point, the limits of the doctrine can spawn endless

---

[1] The need to protect the information from general dissemination is what, in part, has given rise to the practice of nondisclosure agreements.

[2] Given the increasing use of outsourcing, protecting computer information and databases as trade secrets calls for even more elaborate programs. One should be especially careful regarding access to passwords.

arguments and lawsuits. The first step to giving the concept of fiduciary duty real teeth is to educate one's employees about what is protected information, what is treated as confidential, what is a trade secret, and the security measures that the employee must observe. The education process should begin with an employee handbook or a manual that is dedicated to the topic of the company's confidentiality and security program.

Contractual Additions

But education alone is not enough. Especially when we are dealing with technology, a system of contractual system of checks and balances needs to be built in. On its simplest level, an employee who creates a product for a company can be motivated to maintain the proprietary nature of that product by rewarding the employee for its financial success. But what of other employees, who have access to the same proprietary data in the ordinary course of their employement but do not directly share in the rewards from the success of the product? And what of the first employee who, while creating the first product, also learned of ways to develop another competing product that will accomplish the same task but cheaper or quicker?

The answer to these concerns has been to require an employee, when he or she is most highly motivated at the start of any employment, to sign an agreement to maintain the confidentiality of business information and not to compete for some agreed on period of time on the termination of his or her employment. Such restrictive covenants usually have to be supported by consideration—some quid pro quo. When people are first hired, employment is normally sufficient consideration. Because these covenants are viewed as anticompetitive, some states will not enforce covenants not to compete and others will blue pencil them, lining out provisions that a judge views as unreasonable. Particularly for significant employees, an employer should consider augmenting the consideration to strengthen the enforceability of the restrictive covenants. The most commonly used devices are bonuses tied to the restrictive covenants or posttermination severance that is also paid in exchange for the employee honoring the covenants.

Although most of these types of restrictive covenants focus on protection of the employer's information, that is, the obligation not to disclose the information to anyone who is not authorized by the employer to receive it, one commonly overlooked clause is disgorgement of employee generated information. This is especially important for technology-driven business. Such clauses generally require that the employee (a) disclose to the employer all discoveries, know-how, improvements, inventions, and the like during the term of his or her employment (and sometimes after if his or her employment served as a springboard) and (b) assign over to the employer all rights to the ownership of such intellectual property.[3] Any provisions that seek to reach beyond the term of employment must be reasonable in scope and thus must clearly relate to the employee's activities and the work assignments during the employee's employment.

Trespass

Trespass is a common law concept that we are all familiar with when applied to land. We've all seen and probably at some point in our youth violated the no-trespassing signs that were posted on an unfriendly neighbor's property. Trespass is also a concept that can apply to computers and informational databases. Courts have been taking older concepts and reapplying them to new situations.

In *eBay, Inc. v. Bidder's Edge, Inc.* (2000), the federal district court granted eBay an injunction forbidding Bidder's Edge from using a software robot to scrape information from eBay's Web site. The court based the injunction on its finding that accessing the Web site in a manner that was beyond eBay's posted notice (there were actual letters of objection) constituted a trespass. The court reasoned that the "electronic signals sent by Bidder's Edge to retrieve information from eBay's computer system [were] sufficiently tangible to support a trespass cause of action." The court further viewed the ongoing violation of eBay's fundamental right to exclude others from its computer system as creating sufficient irreparable harm to warrant an injunction. Thus, it was not necessary that eBay prove that the access actually interfered with the operation of the Web site. Rather, proof of the "intermeddling with or use of another's personal property" was sufficient to establish the cause of action for trespass. What is significant here is that eBay did permit others to access its Web site under license, and the court viewed conduct that exceeded the licensed use, on notice to the violator, to be a trespass.

However, the applicability of trespass to unauthorized computer activity is not settled. Where trespass involves an object, rather than land, there must not only be improper use, but also some harm to the physical condition or value of the object or the misuse must deprive the rightful owner of the use of the object for a substantial period of time. The two must be causally related. In *Intel v. Hamidi* (2003), the California Supreme Court reversed a lower court's banning a former employee from sending unsolicited e-mails on the grounds of trespass. The court thought that the reach of the doctrine had been extended too far, concluding that bad analogies (i.e., viewing servers as houses and electronic waves as intrusions) create bad law. The court declined to view computers as real property. Rather, finding that they were like other personal property, the court found that this communication was no different than a letter delivered by mail or a telephone call. In short, the court declined to find a trespass because there was an "unwelcome communication, electronic or otherwise" that had fictitiously caused an "injury to a communication system." Here there was no injury to the computer system, although Intel claimed injury to its business.

---

[3] One should also be aware of the concept of a *work for hire* as it applies in the field of copyrights to works that are created within the scope of employment and that are specially commissioned. The corollary doctrine is that of shop rights. The shop right doctrine usually applies to works made within the scope of employment or to products created using the resources, such as facilities, of the employer. The effect of the shop rights doctrine is to give the employer a nonexclusive license, but not ownership, to use the employee's work.

Intel v. Hamidi (2003) simply warns against overbreadth of application of the concept of trespass. If injury to the computer system can be demonstrated, then the concept of trespass does lie as a tool in the arsenal of remedies assuming that the trespasser can be identified.

Terms of Use

Terms of use can constitute a contract with respect to Web site usage. Thus, in any situation where electronic access is requested or permitted, the terms and conditions of use, together with an acknowledgement that such terms have been seen and consented to, can be enforced as restricting usage. In *Register.com, Inc. v. Verio, Inc.* (2004), the Second Circuit upheld an order enjoining Web site access primarily on the issue of contract. There, as described by the Second Circuit, the defendant Verio, against whom the preliminary injunction was issued, was engaged in the business of selling a variety of Web site design, development, and operation services. In the sale of such services, Verio competes with Register's Web site development business. To facilitate its pursuit of customers, Verio undertook to obtain daily updates of the WHOIS information relating to newly registered domain names. To achieve this, Verio devised an automated software program, or robot, which each day would submit multiple successive WHOIS queries through the port 43 accesses of various registrars. Upon acquiring the WHOIS information of new registrants, Verio would send them marketing solicitations by e-mail, telemarketing, and direct mail. To the extent that Verio's solicitations were sent by e-mail, the practice was inconsistent with the terms of the restrictive legend Register attached to its responses to Verio's queries.

Register at first complained to Verio about this use and then adopted a new restrictive legend on its Web site that undertook to bar mass solicitation "via direct mail, electronic mail, or by telephone." The court concluded that Verio's conduct formed a contract, like buying an apple at a roadside fruit stand, which Verio breached:

> We recognize that contract offers on the Internet often require the offeree to click on an "I agree" icon. And no doubt, in many circumstances, such a statement of agreement by the offeree is essential to the formation of a contract. But not in all circumstances. While new commerce on the Internet has exposed courts to many new situations, it has not fundamentally changed the principles of contract. It is standard contract doctrine that when a benefit is offered subject to stated conditions, and the offeree makes a decision to take the benefit with knowledge of the terms of the offer, the taking constitutes an acceptance of the terms, which accordingly become binding on the offeree. See, e.g., Restatement (Second) of Contracts §69 (1)(a) (1981) ("Silence and inaction operate as an acceptance . . . where an offeree takes the benefit of offered services with reasonable opportunity to reject them and reason to know that they were offered with the expectation of compensation.")

* * * *

> Returning to the apple stand, the visitor, who sees apples offered for 50 cents apiece and takes an apple, owes 50 cents, regardless whether he did or did not say, "I agree." The choice offered in such circumstances is to take the apple on the known terms of the offer or not to take the apple. As we see it, the defendant in Ticketmaster and Verio in this case had a similar choice. Each was offered access to information subject to terms of which they were well aware. Their choice was either to accept the offer of contract, taking the information subject to the terms of the offer, or, if the terms were not acceptable, to decline to take the benefits

Id., at 403; and was also a trespass because

> The district court found that Verio's use [**31] of search robots, consisting of software programs performing multiple automated successive queries, consumed a significant portion of the capacity of Register's computer systems. While Verio's robots alone would not incapacitate Register's systems, the court found that if Verio were permitted to continue to access Register's computers through such robots, it was "highly probable" that other Internet service providers would devise similar programs to access Register's data, and that the system would be overtaxed and would crash. We cannot say these findings were unreasonable.

Id., at 405. The court declined to reach the issue if such conduct also violated the Computer Fraud and Abuse Act.

Similarly, although in a different setting, in *ProCD v. Zeidenberg* (1996), ProCD sold a compact disk with noncopyrightable data. Access to the data, however, was controlled by a license agreement; if there was no acceptance, there was also no access. The license agreement prohibited the use of the data for any commercial use. Zeidenberg took the data and posted it on a Web site that he used commercially to sell advertising. Thus, the data were being used to attract visitors. The court found the license limitation on use enforceable.

The importance of this decision is that so long as the owner prominently specifies the limitations, the restrictions can become a contract that is accepted by accepting the benefits of access and be one safeguard against misuse of the access.

THE WIRETAP ACT

When we think about spying of any kind, we think about listening to or reading communications transmitted between people whom we believe are conveying information that we need. The question is whether, and to what extent, government agencies, corporations, and individuals can intercept those communications while they are being transmitted or retrieve them from either a temporary or a permanent destination. The answer to this question is influenced substantially by federal laws concerning wiretaps.

Electronic Communications

The Omnibus Crime Control and Safe Streets Act of 1968, generally referred to as the federal Wiretap Act, established the general parameters for permitted interception of communications by law enforcement. As originally crafted, the Wiretap Act covered only "wire and oral communications." In 1986, Congress enacted the Electronic Communications Privacy Act (ECPA), which amended the Wiretap Act and created the Stored Communications Act (SCA) to "update and clarify federal privacy protections and standards in light of changes in computers and telecommunication technologies" (Senate Report No. 99-541, 1986).

The critical update for our current purposes extended the Wiretap Act's coverage to include "electronic communications," which is defined as "any transfer of signs, signals, writing, images, sounds, data, or intelligence of any nature transmitted in whole or in part by a wire, radio, electromagnetic, photo-electronic or photo-optical system" (Wiretap Act, 1968, §2510(12)). "Intercept" is defined as "the aural or other acquisition of the contents of any wire, electronic, or oral communication through the use of any electronic, mechanical, or other device" (Wiretap Act, §2510(4)). Consequently, the Wiretap Act now makes it an offense to "intentionally intercept ... any wire, oral, or electronic communication" (Wiretap Act, §2511(1)(a), emphasis added; *Konop v. Hawaiian Airlines, Inc.*, 2002).[4]

For corporate and governmental spies, all was not lost. Under the consent of a party exception, it is permissible to intercept communications where "one of the parties to the communication has given prior consent to such interception" (Wiretap Act, 1968, §2511(2)(d)).[5] The requisite consent may be express or implied from the surrounding circumstances.[6] Furthermore, an employer may obtain consent by informing the employee of the monitoring practices in an employment contract or an employee handbook.[7]

Under the provider exception, a provider of electronic communication services "whose facilities are used in the transmission of a wire or electronic communication, [may] intercept, disclose or use that communication in the normal course of his employment while engaged in any activity which is a necessary incident ... to the protection of the rights or property of the provider of that service" (Wiretap Act, 1968, §2511(2)(a)(i) (Supp. 2003)). This exception may allow an employer to lawfully intercept communications to detect an employee's unauthorized disclosure of trade secrets to third parties.[8]

The Contemporaneous Transmission Requirement

The Wiretap Act only prohibits interceptions of electronic communications" (Wiretap Act, 1968, §2511(1)(a)), a term that has been more narrowly defined by the courts than the definition in the act might suggest. The definition of interception provides that an individual intercepts a wire, oral, or electronic communication "merely by *acquiring* its contents, regardless of when or under what circumstances the acquisition occurs" (*Konop v. Hawaiian Airlines, Inc.*, 2002, 302 F.3d at 876, emphasis added). In the context of this section, a serious question arose about the legality of intercepting electronic communications as they were being transmitted and once they were stored, either temporarily or permanently. Although "Congress intended to liberalize one's ability to monitor wire communications while it sought to make the monitoring of electronic communications more difficult" (*Konop v. Hawaiian Airlines, Inc.* 2002, 302 F.3d at 876), courts have consistently held that Congress intended to make acquisitions of electronic communications unlawful under the Wiretap Act "*only if* they occur *contemporaneously with* their transmissions."[9]

In recent years, the courts have attempted to apply the contemporaneous transmission requirement to various situations. For example, cookies used to recover personal data from visitors to a Web site constitute an interception of a contemporaneous electronic communication and a violation of the Wiretap Act (*In re Pharmatrak, Inc.*, 2003). Noting that electronic communications are generally in transit and in storage simultaneously, the court reasoned that users communicated simultaneously with the pharmaceutical client's Web server and with the software company's Web server and, thus, the information was acquired contemporaneously with its transmission.

---

[4] Noting the legislative history of the ECPA indicates that Congress wanted to protect electronic communications that are configured to be private, such as e-mail and private electronic bulletin boards.

[5] One should note, however, that as a result of the USA PATRIOT Act, an order from a U.S. or state attorney general is sufficient to permit the government to install a device to record electronic transmissions for up to 60 days when related to an ongoing criminal investigation. The Federal Bureau of Investigation (FBI) has in its arsenal a program know as Carnivore that essentially tracks a target's online activity. Recently, freedom of information inquiries by the Electronic Privacy Information Center suggests that the FBI has discontinued use of Carnivore because Internet service providers, in light of the USA PATRIOT Act, may be providing information regarding a user's Internet traffic directly to the government.

[6] According to *Griggs-Ryan v. Smith* (1990), holding consent may be implied where the individual is on notice of monitoring of all telephone calls.

[7] Federal law allows states to enact their own wiretapping statutes provided that the state statutes are at least as strict as the federal counterpart. Bernabei (2003) notes that most states have adopted statutes that mirror the federal statutes and that at least 10 states, including Massachusetts, require the consent of both parties before the employer can record a conversation.

[8] According to *Briggs v. Am. Air Filter Co.* (1980), a holding employer could monitor employee's communication "when [the] employee's supervisor [had] particular suspicions about confidential information being disclosed to a business competitor, [had] warned the employee not to disclose such information, [had] reason to believe that the employee is continuing to disclose the information, and [knew] that a particular phone call is with an agent of the competitor."

[9] See, for example, *Wesley Coll. v. Pitts* (1997; holding that the act criminalizes only the interception of electronic communications contemporaneously with their transmission, not once they have been stored); *Payne v. Norwest Corp.* (1995; holding the appropriation of voice mail or a similar stored electronic message does not constitute an interception under the Wiretap Act); *Steve Jackson Games, Inc. v. United States Secret Service* (1994; holding that the government's acquisition of e-mail messages stored on an electronic bulletin board system, but not yet retrieved by the intended recipients, was not an interception under the Wiretap Act).

Where electronic transmissions are found in random access memory or on the hard drive, they are stored communications and can be retrieved because they are outside the Wiretap Act.[10] Similarly, an e-mail that is recovered after it has been sent and received does not satisfy the contemporaneous transmission requirement and therefore has not been intercepted under the Wiretap Act (*Eagle Investment Systems, Corp. v. Tamm*, 2001). Perhaps in response to these and other decisions, in 2001 Congress amended the Wiretap Act to apply the contemporary transmission requirement to wire communications that could not be retrieved, thereby permitting the recovery of stored wire communications.[11]

Konop v. Hawaiian Airlines, Inc.

The *Konop* decision appears to be the most oft-cited case on the issue of interception under the Wiretap Act. Konop, the plaintiff, was an airline pilot who created and maintained a Web site where he posted bulletins critical of his employer, Hawaiian Airlines, Inc., and the airline union. Konop controlled access to his Web site by requiring visitors to log in with a user name and password and by creating a list of authorized users.

An officer of Hawaiian Airlines asked one such authorized user for permission to use his name to access the Web site. The officer logged on several times, and another officer, using the same technique, also logged on to view the information posted on Konop's bulletin. Konop eventually filed suit against Hawaiian Airlines, alleging that it violated the Wiretap Act when its officer gained unauthorized access to Konop's Web site.

The court first reiterated that the act only prohibits interceptions of electronic communications. Interception, the court held, requires that the party acquire the information contemporaneous with its transmission and not while it is in electronic storage. In this case, the court concluded that the employer did not violate the Wiretap Act because the officers accessed an electronic communication located on an idle Web site, which did not satisfy the contemporaneous transmission requirement.

THE STORED COMMUNICATIONS ACT

Unlike the Wiretap Act, the SCA, as its name suggests, establishes the limitations of access to stored communications (i.e., communications accessed *after* their transmission) (Bernabei, 2003, p. 2). Specifically, the SCA makes it unlawful to "intentionally access... without authorization a facility through which an electronic communication service is provided... and thereby obtain..., alter..., or prevent... authorized access to a wire or electronic communication while it is in *electronic storage*" (18 U.S.C. §§2701(a)(1), 2707(a); emphasis added). The SCA defines "electronic storage" as "(A) any temporary,

intermediate storage of a wire or electronic communication incidental to the electronic transmission thereof; and (B) any storage of such communication by an electronic communication service provider for purposes of backup protection of such communication" (18 U.S.C. §2510(17), incorporated by 18 U.S.C. §2711(1)). The SCA exempts from liability conduct "authorized... by the person or entity providing a wire or electronic communications service" (18 U.S.C. §2701(c)(1)) or "by a user of that service with respect to a communication of or intended for that user" (18 U.S.C. §2701(c)(2)).

Electronic Storage: Backup Files

The essential element that separates the SCA from the Wiretap Act is that the accessed communications reside in electronic storage. Therefore, the first question is what constitutes electronic storage. In *Theofel v. Farey-Jones* (2004), the U.S. Court of Appeals for the Ninth Circuit attempted to answer this question.

In *Theofel*, overzealous lawyers for Farey-Jones secured, through a subpoena issued to an Internet service provider (ISP), e-mails sent and received by their opponents in the lawsuit, a company called Integrated Capital Associates (ICA). The subpoena requested from the ISP virtually every e-mail ever sent or received by ICA and its employees. In response, the ISP posted a smattering of the e-mails on a Web site accessible to Farey-Jones and its lawyers. When ICA learned of these activities, they sued Farey-Jones for, among other things, violation of the SCA.

According to the court in *Theofel*, Congress recognized that users of ISPs have a legitimate interest in protecting the confidentiality of communications in electronic storage at a communications facility. Moreover, this legitimate interest cannot be overcome by fraud or by someone who knowingly exploits a mistake that permits him or her access to what is otherwise protected. The court found that the use of the subpoena to access ICA's e-mails when it was reasonably plain, at least to counsel, that the subpoena was invalid, negated any apparent authority that Farey-Jones and its lawyers may have had to view ICS's e-mails.

Farey-Jones claimed that the ICA e-mails were not in electronic storage and therefore no violation of the SCA occurred. The court disagreed. As stated above, electronic storage exists when messages are stored on a temporary, intermediate basis as part of the process of transmitting the message to the recipient and when messages are stored as part of a backup process. In this instance, the court found that the e-mails, which had apparently been delivered to their recipients, were stored by the ISP as part of its backup process for retrieval after initial receipt. Access to those e-mails was therefore protected by the SCA, which Farey-Jones and its lawyers violated.

Electronic Storage: Temporarily Stored Communications

Recent cases interpreting the meaning of "temporary, intermediate storage... incidental to" transmission of the communication have adhered to the letter of the law more than its spirit. In two cases involving the installation of cookies that were subsequently accessed by software

---

[10] In *United States v. Councilman* (2003), a Wiretap Act count was dismissed against an e-mail service provider who was charged with attempting to use electronic communications passing through his service for commercial gain.

[11] USA PATRIOT Act §209, 115 Stat. at 283 (2001); *Konop v. Hawaiian Airlines, Inc.*, 302 F.3d at 876–878 (2002; "The purpose of the recent amendment was to reduce the protection of voice mail messages to the lower level of protection provided other electronically stored communications.").

companies for commercial gain, the courts have held that cookies are permanently (or at least indefinitely) installed in the consumer's hard drive and therefore cannot be considered "temporary, intermediate storage" (*In re DoubleClick, Inc. Privacy Litigation*, 2001; *In re Toys R US, Inc. Privacy Litigation*, 2001). The *Doubleclick* decision also emphasized that the temporary, intermediate storage element of the SCA means what it says, that is, that the prohibited conduct involves only the unauthorized access to communications while they are being temporarily stored by an intermediate and does not include access to stored messages after they have been received. In the context of an employer's right to examine an employee's e-mails, the employee will have no claim that his or her employer has violated the SCA when the employer opens e-mails sent or received by the employee once the e-mail has been either received or discarded (*Fraser v. Nationwide Mut. Ins. Co.*, 2003).

THE COMPUTER FRAUD AND ABUSE ACT
Prohibited Behavior and Damages

In 1984, Congress passed the original version of the Computer Fraud and Abuse Act (CFAA). The general purpose was to protect federal interest computers by criminalizing intentional and unauthorized access to those computers that resulted in damage to the computers or the data stored on them. The statute was substantially amended in 1986 (Pub. L. 99-474) and again in 1996 (National Information Infrastructure Protection Act of 1996, Pub. L. 104-294) and now contains both criminal and private civil enforcement provisions.

The statute proscribes the following activities:

(a) Knowingly accessing a computer without authority or in excess of authority, thereafter obtaining U.S. government data to which access is restricted and delivering, or attempting to deliver, the data to someone not entitled to receive them

(b) Intentionally accessing a computer without authority or in excess of authority and thereby obtaining protected consumer financial data

(c) Intentional and unauthorized access of a U.S. government computer that affects the use of the computer by or for the U.S. government

(d) Accessing a computer used in interstate commerce knowingly and with the intent to defraud and, as a result of the access, fraudulently obtaining something valued in excess of $5,000

(e) Causing damage to computers used in interstate commerce by (i) knowingly transmitting a program, code, and so forth that intentionally causes such damage, or (ii) intentionally accessing the computer without authority and causing such damage[12]

(f) Knowingly, and with the intent to defraud, trafficking in computer passwords for computers used in interstate commerce or by the U.S. government

(g) Transmitting threats to cause damage to a protected computer with the intent to extort money or anything of value

The lynchpin among the relevant decisions concerning access to data under the CFAA is whether the access is without authority or in excess of authority. The factors considered by the courts include the steps taken by the owner of the information to protect against disclosure or use, the extent of the defendants' knowledge regarding their authority to access or use the data, and the use(s) made of the data after gaining access. The legislative history indicates that the statute was intended to "punish those who illegally use computers for commercial advantage" (S. Rep. No. 104-357, pp. 7–8).

Broadly speaking, there are two sets of circumstances to consider. In the first instance, is the actual access authorized either expressly or impliedly? In the Internet context, in which there is a presumption of open access, the site or data owners must show that they took some steps to protect the contents of their site and to limit access to the data at issue (*Register.com, Inc. v. Verio, Inc.*, 2000). Once those steps are taken, the protection constitutes a wall through which even automated search retrieval systems may not go without express permission. Without the wall, there must be some evidence of an intent to access for an impermissible purpose, as when Intuit inserted cookies into the hard drives of home computers.[13]

Second, has the authorized access been improperly exceeded? Generally speaking, those who use their permitted access for an unauthorized purpose to the detriment of the site or data owner have violated the CFAA. Examples include employees who obtain trade secret information and transmit it via the employer's e-mail system to a competitor for which the employee is about to begin work (*Shurgard Storage Centers, Inc. v. Safeguard Self Storage, Inc.*, 2000); using an ISP subscription membership to gain access to and harvest e-mail addresses of other subscribers to transmit unsolicited bulk emails (*America Online, Inc. v. LCGM, Inc.*, 1998); and using access to an employer's email system to alter and delete company files (*U.S. v. Middleton*, 2000).

The criminal penalties range from fines to imprisonment for up to 20 years for multiple offenses. As discussed in the Piracy section below, the CFAA has become a prominent element of claims by the U.S. government and private parties seeking to protect data that are not always protected by other statutory schemes.

Its Application to WebCrawling and Bots

Web robots or *bots* have become widespread to scrape data from Web sites. All of those data are generally available to the public. That is, any individual can access the same information but not with the speed or accuracy of

---

[12] See *Hotmail Corporation v. Van$ Money Pie, Inc.*, 1998.

[13] *In Re Intuit Privacy Litigation* (2001). But see *U.S. v. Czubinski* (1997), where the Court of Appeals found that an Internal Revenue Service (IRS) employee who accessed private tax information in violation of IRS rules but did not disclose the accessed information could not be prosecuted under 18 U.S.C. 1030(a)(4) because he lacked an intent to deprive the affected taxpayers of their right to privacy.

a Web spider. But when does such scraping run afoul of the CFAA? To what extent does the law protect site operators or company data from penetration by an outside third party?

The key to the analysis under the CFAA is to ask whether the data are in fact publicly available. Are there technical barriers such as passwords or codes that have to be circumvented? Do the terms of use prohibit access or use other than by an individual consumer? These questions are critical to making a determination whether the access either exceeds authority or is without authority under the CFAA.

If the answer to either one of these questions (or similar questions) is yes, one needs to consider access carefully because such access and downloading of data are likely to violate the CFAA. In *EF Cultural Travel v. Zefer Corporation*, Zefer designed a Web bot to scrape trip and pricing information from the Web site of EF Cultural Travel (EF) for use by a competitive travel Web site. The bot, designed by Zefer, downloaded the information by calling repetitive uniform resource locators on which each separate trip and pricing information was stored, reading the source code for the key features, and storing the information on a spreadsheet. The bot did so in a fashion not to burden or interfere with EF's Web site. Once gathered, the information was turned over to a competitor who used the information to adjust price and trip information it offered. Zefer's scraping did not occur continuously, but only on two dedicated occasions. EF sued, claiming that a violation of the CFAA had occurred. The First Circuit Court of Appeals disagreed, refusing to read into what is or is not authorized under some "reasonable expectations" standard, instead requiring the Web site operator to expressly state any limitations on access in its terms and conditions. On remand to the Federal District Court, the court, following the First Circuit, granted summary judgment for Zefer.

Simple Preventive Measures

Not surprisingly, there are several methods for preventing unauthorized access in the first instance and, if unsuccessful nonetheless, prevailing in any subsequent claim arising under the CFAA. Perhaps the most obvious measure, and one that the First Circuit Court of Appeals underscored, is to make sure that each visitor to a Web site is adequately notified that the owner of the site intends only limited use or access to the data on the site. The notice can take many forms.

For example, a detectable message easily identifiable on a home page warning visitors that the posted information is available only for viewing and not for use in any manner adverse to the host's interests would do the trick. Understandably, most Web hosts are reluctant to post such a blatant limitation—it's not necessarily good for business. For those interested in an equally effective but less direct message, an increasingly common practice is to compel site visitors to register before gaining access to links and other pages available through the home page. The more difficult the registration process, the greater the host's apparent intent to restrict access to and use of the information that will be accessible after registration is completed.

Those hosts that require the payment of money, some kind of membership, or an access agreement before providing access establish what, for purposes of statutes such as the CFAA that criminalize unauthorized access, will most often be seen as providing sufficient notice of the limits of authorized access. In the case of membership sites, the presumption is that each registrant is prequalified and therefore authorized to view and use the more restricted data, at least for purposes consistent with the terms of access. Enforceable click-wrap access agreements establish not only notice of access limitations, but they also secure each visitor's agreement to use the Web site and the data therein within the stated limitations.

Securing Web-based data against unauthorized use or users is, in some sense, antithetical to the information-sharing intent and purpose of the Web. In this regard, however, the decision to post information on the Web differs little from each organization's decision to facilitate its business at the risk of allowing competitors or adversaries to use our proprietary information against its interests. The greater the concern, the more likely that each host will have to either limit the data posted on the Web or increase each visitor's awareness of the rules of access.

ECONOMIC ESPIONAGE ACT OF 1996

Prior to 1996, the Trade Secrets Act (TSA) was the only federal statute prohibiting trade secret misappropriation. The TSA, however, was of limited utility because it did not apply to private sector employees and provided only limited criminal sanctions.[14] To combat an increase in computer crimes, Congress enacted the Economic Espionage Act (EEA) of 1996, which provided greater protection for the proprietary and economic information of both corporate and governmental entities against foreign and domestic theft.[15]

The EEA criminalizes two principal categories of corporate espionage: economic espionage and theft of trade secrets. Section 1831 punishes those who steal trade secrets "to benefit a foreign government, foreign instrumentality, or foreign agent." Section 1832 is the general criminal trade secret provision. The EEA criminalizes stealing, concealing, destruction, sketching, copying, transmitting, or receiving trade secrets without authorization or with knowledge that the trade secrets have been misappropriated, as well attempts to and conspiring to do any of these acts.

What Are Trade Secrets?

The EEA defines trade secret as

> all forms and types of financial, business, scientific, technical, economic or engineering information, including patterns, plans, compilations,

---

[14] See Trade Secrets Act; see also Chamblee (2003). Other federal statutes, such as the National Stolen Property Act, were likewise of marginal utility in combating the rising problem of economic espionage. See Chamblee, p. 2.

[15] Uhrich (2000/2001) observes that the FBI investigated over 200% more economic espionage cases in 1996 than it had in 1994.

program devices, formulas, designs, prototypes, methods, techniques, processes, procedures, programs, or codes, whether tangible or intangible, and whether or how stored, compiled, or memorialized physically, electronically, graphically, photographically, or in writing if—(A) the owner thereof has taken reasonable measures to keep such information secret; and (B) the information derives independent economic value, actual or potential, from not being generally known to, and not being readily ascertainable through proper means by the public. (18 U.S.C. §1839(3)[16]

Although one might assume that this definition is relatively straight forward, not everything is as it appears. In a case of domestic trade secret theft, the Court of Appeals for the Seventh Circuit examined what the EEA means when it says that the data or material "derives independent economic value, actual or potential, from not being generally known to, and not being readily ascertainable through proper means by, the public" (*United States v. Lange*, 2002; emphasis added). Noting that others had assumed that the word *public* meant the general public, the court in *Lange* astutely observed that this was not, in fact, the case. Moreover, the standard for measuring the persons who might readily ascertain the economic value of (in this case) the design and composition of airplane brake assemblies is not the average person in the street, for this assumes (as the court mentions) that not any person can understand and apply something as arcane as Avogadro's number. Instead, the definition of the term *the public* should take into account the segment of the population that would be interested in and understand the nature of that which has allegedly been misappropriated.

What About Multinationals?

The international reach of the EEA is limited, extending outside of the United States only if

> (1) the offender is a natural person who is a citizen or permanent resident alien of the United States, or an organization organized under the laws of the United States or a State or political subdivision... or (2) an act in furtherance of the offense was committed in the United States. (18 U.S.C. §1839)

Few defendants have been charged under the act since its passage in 1996, so the precise reach has yet to be tested. Having said this, the language of the EEA makes it clear that corporations with headquarters or operations subject to U.S. jurisdiction can be prosecuted or sued under the EEA. Similarly, some of the few existing decisions

involve the prosecution of agents of "foreign instrumentalities" who took steps in the United States in furtherance of their attempt or conspiracy to steal or transfer a trade secret can be prosecuted here (*United States v. Hsu*, 1998; *United States v. Yang*, 2002). Subsequent editions of this work will undoubtedly benefit from further developments in this area.

THE DIGITAL MILLENNIUM COPYRIGHT ACT

In 1998, Congress passed the Digital Millennium Copyright Act (DMCA) to address concerns raised by the Internet and copyright issues in the context of our increasingly technological society. The DMCA creates a civil remedy for its violation, as well as criminal penalties starting after October 2000. One of the purposes of the DMCA is to protect the integrity of copyright information. Removal of copyright notice, or distribution knowing that such copyright has been removed, is now actionable. Both civil and criminal remedies also now exist if one circumvents "a technological measure that effectively controls access to a work protected" by the Copyright Act (17 U.S.C. §1201(a)).

The criminal penalties for violation of the DMCA can be quite severe. If the violation is willful for commercial gain, the first offense bears a fine of up to half a million dollars or 5 years imprisonment. Subsequent violations bear fines of up to $1 million or 10 years imprisonment. Civil remedies include an order to restrain the violation, damages for lost profits, damages for recovery of the infringer's profits, or statutory damages for each violation. Depending on the section of the DMCA at issue, each violation can generate fines of up to $2,500 or $25,000. Because each act of infringement can constitute a violation, the statutory fines can become quite substantial.

Circumventing Technology Measures

As mentioned above, efforts to circumvent access limitations on copyrighted software are now punishable under the DMCA. In addition, it is a civil violation and a crime to "manufacture, import, offer to the public, provide or otherwise traffic in any technology, product, service, device, component, or part thereof," that "is primarily designed or produced for the purpose of circumventing a technological measure that effectively controls access to a work protected" under the Copyright Act (17 U.S.C. §1201(a)(2)).

A technological measure effectively controls access to a work if the measure, "in the ordinary course of its operation, requires the application of information or a process or a treatment, with the authority of the copyright owner, to gain access to the work" (DMCA, 1998, 17 U.S.C. §1201(a)(3)). One circumvents such a technology measure if one uses a means "to descramble a scrambled work, to decrypt an encrypted work, or otherwise to avoid, bypass, remove, deactivate, or impair a technological measure," without the authority of the copyright owner (DMCA, 1998, 17 U.S.C. §1201(a)(3)).

A spate of recent legal actions demonstrates that this legislation will be strictly enforced by the courts and that the technologically savvy will be in no better position

---

[16] This definition protects a wider variety of information than most federal and state civil laws. In *United States v. Hsu* (1998), "the EEA defines a 'trade secret' to expressly extend protection to the misappropriation of intangible information for the first time under federal law."

to gain access to protected technology than anyone else. In *RealNetworks, Inc. v. Streambox, Inc.* (2000), Streambox distributed software that enabled users to bypass the authentication process employed by RealNetworks, which distributes audio and video content over the Internet. Thus, Streambox users could get the benefit of the RealNetworks streaming audio and video content without compensating the copyright owners. The U.S. District Court in Washington State found that the Streambox software has a technological measure that was designed to circumvent the access and copy control measures intended to protect the copyright owners.

In a case involving DVD encryption, a U.S. District Court in New York found that posting links to sites where visitors may download the decryption program was trafficking in circumvention technology, and was a violation of the DMCA (*Universal City Studios, Inc. v. Reimerdes*). In *Universal City Studios, Inc. v. Reimerdes*, the court rejected an argument that the use of the decryption software constituted free expression protected by the First Amendment of the U.S. Constitution.[17] And in a direct challenge to the constitutionality of the statute, several professors who responded to an open invitation from the Secure Digital Music Initiative Foundation (SDMIF) to find ways to penetrate copyright protection measures have sued for the right to publish the results of their work (*Edward Felten, et al v. Recording Industry Association of America, Inc., et al*, 2001). Edward Felten, Bede Liu, and others accepted SDMIF's invitation and successfully cracked the copyright security measures employed to protect digital music files. When the professors attempted to deliver a paper describing their success, SDMIF and others threatened litigation based on the anticircumvention provisions of the DMCA. The *Felten* lawsuit challenges the constitutionality of the DMCA in these circumstances.

Exceptions to the Prohibitions on Technology Circumvention

Fair Use and Reverse Engineering

The DMCA, however, explicitly carves out all defenses to copyright infringement, including the doctrine of fair use, as being unaffected by the passage of the DMCA. In some circumstances fair use can include reverse engineering.

Within the field of computer software, recent cases have considered whether dissection to reverse engineer the program is a violation of the copyright. To those involved in protecting software programs, the answer appears to be that reverse engineering in the form of disassembly does not constitute an infringement, because of the doctrine of fair use.[18] The Ninth Circuit in *Sega*

Enterprises Ltd. V. Accolade, Inc. (1992) found as a matter of law that

> where disassembly is the only way to gain access to the ideas and functional elements embodied in a copyrighted computer program and where there is a legitimate reason for seeking such access, disassembly is a fair use of the copyrighted work. (977 F.2d at 1527-28)

The Ninth Circuit is not the only circuit that has upheld reverse engineering against a copyright claim. The federal circuit reached a similar conclusion regarding reverse engineering of object code to discern the ideas behind the program in *Atari Games Corp. v. Nintendo of America, Inc.* (1992). The fair use rationale of *Sega* was also adopted by the Eleventh Circuit in *Bateman v. Mnemonics, Inc.* (1996) on the grounds that it advanced the sciences. Thus, one can spy through reverse engineering still without running afoul of copyright protection or the DMCA.

However (and there usually is a however in the law), in *Bowers v. Baystate Technologies, Inc.* (2003), a split federal Circuit Court of Appeals found that a shrink-wrap license prohibiting reverse engineering was enforceable against the licensee who had reverse engineered Bowers' CAD Designer's Toolkit to develop a competing product. The Bowers court found that the contractual language trumped the fair use permitted under the Copyright Act. The Fifth Circuit reached the opposite result in the earlier decision of *Vault Corp. v. Quaid Software, Ltd.* (1988), specifically finding that the copyright act preempts state law that attempts to prohibit disassembly and holding a mass distribution license agreement unenforceable.

Thus, the extent to which *Bowers* may be followed is still uncleares but it suggests a course business, can at least attempt to follow to curtail reverse engineering. If *Bowers* becomes widely accepted, the United States will be in conflict with the European Union on this issue. In its 1991 Software Directive, the European Union set forth a right to reverse engineer that is consonant with fair use under the Copyright Act. The Software Directive also provided that the right cannot be waived by contract. So, until Bowers is settled, if a shrink-wrap license prohibits reverse engineering, it would be best to consider having it done abroad.

Other Exceptions

The DMCA also creates an important exception that recognizes the right to reverse engineer if (a) the person has lawfully obtained the right to use a copy of a computer program or (b) the sole purpose of circumventing the technology measure is to identify and analyze "those elements of the program that are necessary to achieve interoperability of an independently created computer program with other programs" (17 U.S.C. §1201(f)(1)). The DMCA creates a similar exemption for circumvention for the purpose of "enabling the interoperability of an independently created computer program with other programs, if such means are necessary to achieve such interoperability" (17 U.S.C. §1201(f)(2). The term "interoperability" is defined to encompass the "ability of computer programs to

---

[17] *Reimerdes* is currently on appeal to the Second Circuit Court of Appeals, which has heard oral argument and requested additional briefing.

[18] There is an open issue as to whether copyright protects the format for interfacing between application and data. Competitors particularly in the area of gaming look to reverse engineer the interface format to make new modules compatible with existing hardware. Such reverse engineering has been held not to violate the copyright laws, so long as the new product does not display copyrighted images or other copyrightable expressions. Thus, the nonprotectable interface may be protected if such copyrighted images or expressions are embedded in the display.

exchange information and of such programs mutually to use the information which has been exchanged" (17 U.S.C. §1201(f)(4). The information acquired through these permitted acts of circumvention may also be provided to third parties so long as it is solely used for the same purposes.

Exempt from the DMCA, as well, are good faith acts of circumvention for which the purpose is encryption research. A permissible act of encryption research requires that (a) the person lawfully have obtained a copy, (b) the act is necessary to the research, (c) there was a good faith effort to obtain authorization before the circumvention, and (d) such act does not constitute an infringement under a different section of the Copyright Act or under the Computer Fraud and Abuse Act of 1986. With the caveat that it must be an act of good faith encryption research, the technological means for circumvention can be provided to others who are working collaboratively on such research. The issue of good faith encryption research looks to what happened to the information derived from the research. If it was disseminated in a manner that was likely to assist infringement, as opposed to reasonably calculated to advance the development of encryption technology, then the act still falls outside the exemption. Other factors that go into the determination of good faith are whether the person conducting the research is trained, experienced, or engaged in the field of encryption research and whether the researcher provides the copyright owner with a copy of the findings.

The DMCA also has a bias against the collection or dissemination of personally identifying information. Thus, it is not a violation of the DMCA to circumvent a technology measure that essentially protects, collects, or disseminates personally identifying information, provided that the circumvention has no other effect and provided that the program itself does not contain a conspicuous notice warning of the collection of such information and a means to prevent or restrict such collection.

Finally, insofar as relevant to this chapter, the DMCA also excludes security testing from its scope. The DMCA grants permission to engage in security testing that, but for that permission, would violate the terms of the DMCA. If the security testing, for some reason, violated some other provision of the Copyright Act or the Computer Fraud and Abuse Act of 1986, then it is still an act of infringement. The DMCA, in part, considers whether a violation occurred by how the information was used. The factors to be considered include if the information was used to promote the security of the owner or operator of the computer network or system, was shared with the developer, and was used in a manner that would not facilitate infringement. For purposes of the DMCA, security testing means accessing either an individual computer or network for the purpose of "good faith testing, investigating, or correcting, a security flaw or vulnerability, with the authorization of the owner or operator" (17 U.S.C. §1201(j)(1)).

Impact of Recent RIAA and Other Litigation

The primary drafters of and advocates for passage of the DMCA were media companies and their industry trade associations, including the Recording Industry Association of America (RIAA) and the Motion Picture Industry Association of America. Their motivation was the perceived need to combat the technology that made free transfer of copyrighted work easier to accomplish. Advances in technology provided the entertainment industry with the incentive to propose and support some of the changes to the DMCA referred to above. Using the ample tools, Congress graciously provided and armed with claims that they were losing billions of dollars in sales revenues to the free sharing of electronic music files over the Internet, the RIAA and various individual recording industry giants have gone to court.

The initial target of their enmity was Napster, which created and made freely available the software that made music file transfers easy. In response to lawsuits filed by A&M Music and the RIAA, against the backdrop of the DCMA, federal trial and appellate courts found that the software and centralized internet-based distribution system offered by Napster violated the copyright law by, among other things, transferring copyrighted work for other than personal use. The first result of this litigation was the demise, by court injunction and later by acquisition by one of the media companies, of Napster.

To avoid a similar fate, other peer-to-peer file sharing companies, such as KaZaA and Morpheus, distributed software that enabled users to directly access the computer files of other users rather than offering a central library of protected work for each user to download. Efforts by the RIAA and others to prevent this kind of file sharing met with a different result in court. As a result, the RIAA decided to pursue users directly.

Beginning in late 2003, the RIAA opened a four-pronged approach to reduce unauthorized file sharing. First, it worked with Apple, Microsoft, and other software and hardware manufacturers and distributors to create a system for electronically distributing music to hardware that permitted the download of individual songs from extensive online libraries on a price-per-song basis. This spawned Apple's iPod and iTunes, among others.

Second, the RIAA began investigating and pursuing unauthorized music downloads by individuals. Using the powers provided by the DMCA, the RIAA obtained and served subpoenas on ISPs to secure the personal identification information of people sharing music files over the Internet. The RIAA has met with mixed success in this effort; a recent appeal by Verizon seeking to quash the RIAA's subpoena was successful (*Recording Industry Association of America, Inc. v. Verizon Internet Services, Inc.*, 2003).

Third, using the information gathered from various sources about the identity of file sharers, it has filed lawsuits against hundreds of individuals alleging violations of the DMCA and seeking damages, sometimes in the thousands of dollars. The defendants have included teenagers and people in their 60s, as well as occasional and prolific file sharers from all walks of life. Some of the cases were settled using written agreements in which the users promised not to violate the DMCA in the future. As long as the RIAA and media companies believe that electronic file sharing is diminishing industry revenues, there is reason to believe that lawsuits against individual file sharers will continue.

Finally, the RIAA has engaged in a public awareness campaign that portrays the artists as the victims of unauthorized file sharing. Interestingly, the response to this campaign generally and within the entertainment industry has been mixed. For example, a growing number of famous and fledgling musicians who object to the control of their work and their industry by the record publishing companies are supporting the use of the Internet for free file sharing as the best method for publicizing their work without relinquishing control of the work to the record publishers.

CORPORATE SPYING ON THE INDIVIDUAL
Competing Interests: Businesses and Individuals

Within today's corporate environment, employers' and employees' interests in protecting information are simultaneously harmonious and conflicting. Companies, with help from their employees, protect trade secrets, financial data (at least for companies whose stock is not publicly traded), customer lists, customer data, marketing strategies, intellectual property (computer source code, inventions), and information about mergers and acquisitions. They also work together to protect sensitive employee data concerning medical insurance, medical care, bank account numbers, social security payments, unemployment, marital and custodial issues, and sometimes employee credit information.

Conversely, there are data that employers and employees believe ought to be beyond the reach and dissemination of the other. When tobacco companies knowingly violate state and federal law concerning deceptive trade practices, the companies want to avoid disclosure of their knowledge that they violate those laws, whereas some employees may see it as their civic duty to expose that conduct. Not surprisingly, the tobacco companies have a different view of the disclosure of such sensitive information. On the other hand, employees believe that communications regarding intimate relationships either with other employees or persons outside the company are of no concern to their employers. Employers take the position that their communication equipment is intended for use solely in furtherance of the company's business interests and cannot and should not be used for intimate personal communications.

E-mail, Internet access, and voice mail are facts of life in any business. As useful as these technologies are, the possibilities of misuse are endless. Unmonitored Internet access (usually from points outside of the office firewall) can pick up viruses that will breach the security of the office system. Data can readily be transmitted to unauthorized recipients. Employees can broadcast libelous statements using a company Internet address to thousands of recipients. Intellectual property can be copied and distributed almost without detection. The question is where do the inviolable rights of employers and employees begin and end?

In a different context, businesses seek to understand the buying patterns and other habits of existing and prospective consumers. One way to secure this information without asking for it directly is to use spyware, which has been defined as everything from hacker's software to programs that merely track consumer patterns through keystroke monitoring. A more formal definition of spyware might be "any software that covertly gathers information about a user while he/she navigates the Internet and transmits the information to an individual or company that uses it for marketing or other purposes" (www.dictionary.com).

A growing number of consumers seeking to protect themselves against the wave of promotional information that permeates their mailboxes have raised a hue and cry about spyware and lawmakers have responded. In California, the Consumer Protection Against Spyware Act took effect on January 1, 2005. The CPASA outlaws software that secretly steals personal information such as user names and passwords, sends viruses, or takes control of infected systems as part of a distributed denial-of-service attack. Nationally, the House of Representatives has twice considered and once passed the SPY ACT, which prohibits a whole range of spyware- and adware-style activities, including keyboard logging, home page hijacking, and persistent on-screen ads. This legislation would require user permission before data collection could occur, among other things. Violators could face civil fines up to $3 million and, according to a follow-on bill, would criminalize the use of software, including spyware, to commit a crime including logging keystrokes or stealing confidential information.

Electronic Surveillance and Privacy: Reasonable Expectations

The definition and scope of the modern right of privacy emanates from several decisions by the U.S. Supreme Court over the past 40 years. In *Griswold v. Connecticut* (1965), the Supreme Court was asked to decide whether states had the authority to outlaw the private use of contraceptives, even among married couples. Declaring the existence of a zone of personal activity that even the framers of the Constitution would have deemed beyond the reach of governmental control, the Court held that consenting married adults had a reasonable expectation that certain activities would be private, among them the use of contraceptives in the privacy of their bedrooms.

In the famous case of *Roe v. Wade*, the Supreme Court extended the notion of a reasonable expectation of privacy to a woman's decision to abort a pregnancy, at least in the first trimester. Most recently, in *Lawrence v. Texas* (2003), the Court held that consenting male adults may not be charged with violation of antisodomy laws when they engage in such acts in the privacy of their own home. In these and other cases, the Court has focused on the liberties underlying the founding of this country and that such liberties import some protection against invasion by the government.

The reasonable expectation is not absolute in all circumstances and is certainly limited in its application in the workplace. Any e-mail can be monitored where consent is given and consent can be a condition of employment. Alternatively, an employer has the right to reasonably monitor electronic communications if it can show a business reason for doing so. Such reasons abound in today's environment, from prevention of theft of information to simple system misuse.

But employees nonetheless view such efforts by employers as spying. They view their electronic communications by e-mail in the same way as telephone calls—sacrosanct from third-party eavesdropping. Several states have considered requiring that employees be notified of any monitoring.[19] Many states have now enacted privacy statutes that make invasion of privacy a civil wrong. Our home state of Massachusetts, for example, has a statute that protects against substantial interference with a person's privacy. But is there in fact a reasonable expectation of privacy in today's environment?

The answer appears to be "no." In *Garrity v. John Hancock Mutual Life Insurance Co.* (2002 U.S. Dist. LEXIS 8343 (D. Mass. 2003), the employer fired employees who shared sexual material through the company's e-mail system. The employer knew by reviewing the e-mail messages stored in the employer's computer system. The Court concluded that there was no invasion of privacy because there was no expectation of privacy. The employees knew of Hancock's electronic communications policy and Hancock's retention of the right to review e-mails. In an earlier case, *Smyth v. Pillsbury Co.* (1996), the Court ruled that no expectation of privacy exists for employees using the company's e-mail system and made such a finding even although there was no company policy manual in place.

Looking at these two results, the conservative approach for businesses wanting to spy on their employees is to put a policy in place that permits inspection and monitoring of employee e-mails, especially given the vagaries of state law on the subject. Other judicial decisions uphold employer monitoring where such a policy is in place. *TBG Insurance Services Corp v. Superior Court* (2002) found no reasonable expectation of privacy as the employee had consented to having his home computer monitored by signing the company's electronic communications policy. *Muick v. Glenayre Electronics* 280 (2002)[20] reached the same conclusion where the issue was the employee's reasonable expectation of privacy in a laptop computer in light of the employer's policy permitting the employer to inspect at any time. A contrasting result was reached in *United States v. Slanina* (2002), where in the absence of such a policy, an employee was found to have a reasonable expectation of privacy because the employer had no policy in place and did not otherwise inform the employee that employees' computers were routinely accessed.

GOVERNMENT SPYING AND BUSINESSES: THE USA PATRIOT ACT

The USA PATRIOT Act was conceived, drafted, revised, and signed into law 45 days after 9/11 and alters at least 15 federal statutes. Some contend—perhaps correctly—that this mammoth legislation is merely an instinctive reaction to the events of 9/11: a natural response to an act of war. The USA PATRIOT Act responds in several ways to the kinds of activities likely to support acts of terrorism. First, it enhances the government's ability to investigate domestic criminal and foreign intelligence activity, broadening the scope and nature of communications that can be seized and reducing the barriers to seizing those communications. It also increases the likelihood of receiving assistance from corporate and individual citizens that may lead to arrests and convictions by, among other things, protecting those who provide that assistance. Whether, and to what extent, the heightened intrusion into our business and personal lives will withstand scrutiny by the Courts is the untold but unfolding story.

Terrorism and Financial Institutions

Title III of the USA PATRIOT Act, also known as the International Money Laundering Abatement and Anti-Terrorist Financing Act of 2001, expands the already considerable ability of the federal government to control money laundering, which is the flow of cash or other valuables derived from or intended to facilitate the commission of a crime. Among other things, the USA PATRIOT Act expands the list of businesses that are required to file reports with the government noting suspicious activities involving the flow of money. The expanded list now includes securities brokers and dealers, commodity merchants, advisors, and pool operators. These reports must be filed with the U.S. Treasury Department and, in some cases, the Internal Revenue Service. Because the vast majority of these transactions are electronic, there is a direct impact on the monitoring and reporting obligations of information technology departments in these companies.

Due diligence requirements also have been imposed on all domestic financial institutions concerning the opening and use of financial accounts. The USA PATRIOT Act requires financial institutions to verify the identity of any person seeking to open an account, maintain verification records, and consult published lists of known and suspected terrorists to determine if any person seeking to open an account appears on those lists. This means that all new customers and existing customers opening new accounts must be screened by the bank, presumably through the use of electronic databases. In addition, the act imposes strict time limits for responding to Justice and Treasury Department subpoenas.

The consequences of failing to adequately monitor and report such activity, as well as failing to adhere to the proscription against transmitting funds derived from illegal activities, were realized by PayPal, the online payment system owned by eBay, which was charged by the U.S. Attorney for the Eastern District of Missouri with transmitting funds received from online gambling. In the indictment, the government is seeking all revenues realized by PayPal from online gambling during the preceding 9 months, plus interest. PayPal may also

---

[19] This is the flip side of consent and is generally a good idea regardless of statutory requirements.
[20] Noting that intrusive surveillance might infringe the right of privacy.

receive criminal penalties. Presumably, PayPal would not have engaged in such activity had it adequately monitored the sources of the funds being transmitted over its system.

Compulsory and Voluntary Cooperation Between Business and Government

The Electronic Communications Privacy Act of 1986 was implemented to create some protections against the overzealous use of wiretaps on telephones. As part of that framework, the protections were extended to network services and a few exceptions were established. The authority necessary to obtain a wiretap depended on the level of content to be intercepted. An administrative agency order, which required a minimal showing of cause by law enforcement, did not permit law enforcement to obtaint message content, while a court-authorized subpoena, which required a court's acknowledgment of the existence of probable cause, permitted the recovery of much wider scope of information.

The USA PATRIOT Act changes the ECPA in several ways. First, it permits law enforcement to obtain routing information—such as the information appearing in the header of an e-mail—with a lower level of judicial scrutiny and based only on a certification by the government that the information is related to a criminal investigation. For example, the subject line of an e-mail, which might otherwise appear content oriented, may now be open to law enforcement without the usual demonstration of probable cause.

In addition, the USA PATRIOT Act clarifies the ECPA by permitting law enforcement to collect content traffic information (i.e., more than just a telephone number or Internet protocol address) from multiple forms of electronic communications—specifically the Internet—through the use of pen registers and the so-called trace and trap statute. Prior law permitted government access to the content of e-mails and communications records in the possession of third parties that have been stored for more than 180 days; the act adds government access to credit card and bank account numbers.

Further, the USA PATRIOT Act provides for the voluntary disclosure of certain electronic communications when a provider of electronic communications to the public (an ISP, for example) determines with its reasonable judgment that an emergency involving death or serious physical injury requires disclosure without delay. This permits disclosure of e-mails that appear serious to the service provider whether or not they are in fact serious (e.g., bad jokes sent by e-mail). Similarly, communications network owners who believe that a computer trespass (defined as accessing a protected computer without authority) has occurred may request an investigation by law enforcement, whether or not the network owner's concern is well founded. In this context, it has been suggested that government investigators who believe they need access to a computer network are free to initiate calls to network owners on the pretext of investigating a crime or a potential terrorist act for the purpose of gaining access to the network.

CONCLUSION

In today's world, we can all be spies and are all subject to being spied upon. The issue of what is fair game and what is private or protected personal property has become increasingly complex. The gray world of the spy now intrudes open all of our lives. Boundaries have become difficult to define. Information flows seamlessly and globally. What is good and what is bad—even when asking whether your mother would approve—is not always easily discernable. There is a real bramble of legal regulations within the United States. Add on another layer of complexity for global transactions.

As complicated as the subject is today, it is only going to become more complex in the future. Large corporations have the luxury of creating a new position—the corporate privacy officer—who is the hired specialist. Individuals can only read chapters such as this one and utilize Web sites such as http://www.epic.org/privacy/privacy_resources_faq.html to find resources that speak to their particular issues or concerns. Both help for the routine issues but not for the novel ones or for those that are factually complex where the real concerns may not be readily apparent.

The concerns about, and behind, corporate spying lie at the heart of the issues that confront us in the 21st century. We all need our "007" to help us put things rights. But in this context, it is to act as a guide to let us know what is permissible and what simply is not. This chapter is only a start. It should not be read as legal advice because all legal advice ultimately depends on the facts and individual or corporate goals. Rather, it should be read as raising questions that need to be considered as each of us works our way through issues that are pivotal to our rights as individuals as well as to corporate survival. We recognized the limitations in this chapter when we began the task of writing it. We hope it has prompted a concern to investigate and define these issues as they affect each of our lives and business. To that end, we would be glad to help the reader in the search for answers to the questions that affect their lives and futures.

GLOSSARY

Common Law The common law refers to the evolution of the law through cases and appellate decision, which establish the law through precedent and respected judicial reasoning and thought, as opposed to statutes, which are legislative enactments.

Computer Fraud and Abuse Act (CFAA) The Computer Fraud and Abuse Act, originally passed in 1984 and amended in 1986 and 1996, has civil penalties for unauthorized access to computers and is a major weapon in prosecuting theft of computer data.

Contract An agreement, usually in writing, which is demonstrated by some form of mutual assent to the terms and conditions.

Digital Millennium Copyright Act (DMCA) The Digital Millennium Copyright Act was enacted by Congress in 1998 and created civil and criminal penalties to enhance the protection of copyright information in the context of the Internet and to update protections in light of new technologies.

Economic Espionage Act (EEA)   The Economic Espionage Act of 1996 applies to corporate and governmental entities and creates criminal penalties for corporate espionage that involves either economic espionage or theft of trade secrets.

Electronic Communications Privacy Act (ECPA)   The Electronic Communications Privacy Act became law in 1986 and is codified in Title 18 of the United States Code. It created the Stored Communications Act to state as a matter of legislation federal privacy protections and standards as applied to computers and telecommunication technologies.

Fiduciary Duty   A duty that arises out of a relationship of trust and is generally described as imposing the utmost good faith and fair dealing.

Terms of Use   Terms of use are terms posted on a Web site that attempt to define the conditions under which a user can have access to the site. Some terms of use actually require a user to accept them before entry is permitted to that portion of the Web site. They may be viewed as akin to signage on property.

Trade Secrets   The concept of trade secrets has developed through the common law and describes proprietary business information usually that has some commercial usage.

Trespass   The concept of trespass is part of the common law of torts or civil wrongs and connotes entry onto property without right and without permission.

Uniting and Strengthening America by Providing Appropriate Tools Required to Intercept and Obstruct Terrorism Act (USA PATRIOT Act)   The USA PATRIOT Act was conceived after September 11, 2001, and passed without too much consideration of its effect. The USA PATRIOT Act, while giving the government a freer hand to investigate terrorism, may have vitiated key protections against unwarranted governmental intrusion and is likely to be a subject of growing debate as its erosion of civil liberties has united libertarians, whether of the left or right persuasion.

CROSS REFERENCES

See *Copyright Law; Information Leakage: Detection and Countermeasures; Legal, Social and Ethical Issues of the Internet; Privacy Law and the Internet; The Digital Millennium Copyright Act; The Legal Implications of Information Security: Regulatory Compliance and Liability; Wireless Information Warfare.*

REFERENCES

America Online, Inc. v. LCGM, Inc., 46 F. Supp. 2d 444 (E.D. Va. 1998).

Atari Games Corp. v. Nintendo of America, Inc., 975 F.2d 832 (Fed. Cir. 1992), *petition for rehearing denied,* 1992 U.S. App. Lexis 30957 (1992).

Bateman v. Mnemonics, Inc., 79 F.3d 1532 (11th Cir. 1996).

Bernabei, L. (2003). *Ethical and legal issues of workplace monitoring of employee communications.*

Bowers v. Baystate Technologies, Inc., 320 F.3d 1317 (Fed. Cir. 2003).

Briggs v. Am. Air Filter Co., 630 F.2d 414 (5th Cir. 1980).

Chamblee, J. M. (2003). *Validity, construction, and application of Title I of Economic Espionage Act of 1996,* 177 A.L.R. Fed. 609, *.

Computer Fraud and Abuse Act, Pub. L. 98-474, codified at 18 U.S.C. §1030 (1984).

Digital Millennium Copyright Act, 17 U.S.C. §1202 (1998).

Eagle Investment Systems, Corp. v. Tamm, 146 F. Supp. 2d 105, 112-113 (D. Mass. 2001).

eBay, Inc. v. Bidder's Edge, Inc., 100 F. Supp. 2d 1058 (N.D. CA 2000).

Economic Espionage Act, 18 U.S.C. §§1831-1839 (1996).

Edward Felten, et al v. Recording Industry Association of America, Inc., et al, U.S.D.C. Civil Action No. CV-01-2660 (D.N.J.)(First Amended Complaint filed June 26, 2001).

EF Cultural Travel v. Zefer Corporation.

Electronic Communications Privacy Act, Pub. L. No. 99-508, 100 Stat. 1848 (1986) (codified throughout scattered sections of 18 U.S.C.).

Fraser v. Nationwide Mut. Ins. Co., 2003 U.S. App. LEXIS 24856, *19 (3rd Cir. 2003).

Garrity v. John Hancock Mutual Life Insurance Co., 2002 U.S. Dist. LEXIS 8343 (D. Mass. 2003).

Griggs-Ryan v. Smith, 904 F.2d 112, 117 (1st Cir. 1990).

Griswold v. Connecticut (381 U.S. 479, 85 S. Ct. 1678, 14 L. Ed. 2d 510 (1965).

In re DoubleClick, Inc. Privacy Litigation, 154 F. Supp. 2d 497 (S.D.N.Y. 2001).

In re Intuit Privacy Litigation, 138 F.Supp. 2d 1272 (2001).

In re Pharmatrak, Inc., 329 F.3d 9, 21 (1st Cir. 2003).

In re Toys R US, Inc. Privacy Litigation, 2001 U.S. Dist. LEXIS 16947 (N.D. Ca. 2001).

Intel v. Hamidi, 30 Cal. 4th 1342; 71 P.3d 296; 1 Cal. Rptr. 3d 32 (2003).

Kewanee Oil Co. v. Bicron Corp., 416 U.S. 470, 473, 94 S. Ct. 1879, 40 L.Ed.2d 315 (1974).

Konop v. Hawaiian Airlines, Inc., 302 F.3d 868, 875 (9th Cir. 2002).

Lawrence v. Texas (539 U.S. 558, 123 S. Ct. 2472, 156 L. Ed. 2d 508 (2003).

Muick v. Glenayre Electronics, 280 F.3d 741 (7th Cir. 2002).

National Information Infrastructure Protection Act, Pub. L. 104-294 (1996).

National Stolen Property Act, 18 U.S.C. §2314.

Omnibus Crime Control and Safe Streets (Wiretap Act), 18 U.S.C. §§2511(1)(a) and 2502(a) (1968).

Payne v. Norwest Corp., 911 F. Supp. 1299, 1303 (D. Mont. 1995).

ProCD v. Zeidenberg, 86 F.3d 1447 (7th Cir. 1996).

RealNetworks, Inc. v. Streambox, Inc., 2000 U.S. Dist. LEXIS 1889 (W.D. Wash. 2000).

Recording Industry Association of America, Inc. v. Verizon Internet Services, Inc., 351 F.3d 1229 (D.C. Cir. 2003).

Register.com, Inc. v. Verio, Inc., 126 F.Supp. 2d 238 (S.D.N.Y. 2000).

Register.com, Inc. v. Verio, Inc., 356 F.3d 393 (2d. Cir. 2004).

S. Rep. No. 99-541, at 1 (1986) (reprinted in 1986 U.S.C.C.A.N. 3555, 3555).

S. Rep. No. 104-357.

Sega Enterprises Ltd. V. Accolade, Inc., 977 F.2d 1510 (9th Cir. 1992), amended, *Sega Enterprises Ltd. v. Accolade, Inc.,* 1993 U.S. App. Lexis 78.

Shurgard Storage Centers, Inc. v. Safeguard Self Storage, Inc., 119 F.Supp. 2d 1121 (W.D. Wash 2000).

Smyth v. Pillsbury Co. 914 F. Supp. 97 (E.D. Pa. 1996).

Steve Jackson Games, Inc. v. United States Secret Service, 36 F.3d 457, 461-62 (5th Cir. 1994).

Stored Communications Act, 18 U.S.C. §2701 *et seq.*

TBG Insurance Services Corp v. Superior Court, 96 Cal. App. 4th 443; 117 Cal. Rptr. 2d 155; 2002 Cal. App. LEXIS 1839 (Cal. App. 2d Dist. 2002).

Theofel v. Farey-Jones, 359 F.3d 1006 (9th Cir. 2004).

Trade Secrets Act, 18 U.S.C. §1905.

Uhrich, C. L. (2000/2001). The Economic Espionage Act: Reverse engineering and the intellectual property public policy. *Mich. Telecomm. Tech. L. Rev., 7,* 147–.

United States v. Councilman, 245 F. Supp. 2d 319 (D. Mass. 2003).

United States v. Czubinski, 106 F.3d 1069 (1st Cir. 1997).

United States v. Hsu, 155 F.3d 189, 196 (3d Cir. 1998).

United States v. Lange, 312 F.3d 263 (7th Cir. 2002).

United States v. Middleton, XXX F.3d (9th Cir. 2000).

United States v. Slanina, 283 F.3d 670 (5th Cir. 2002).

United States v. Yang, 281 F.3d 534, 543 (6th Cir. 2002).

Uniting and Strengthening America by Providing Appropriate Tools Required to Intercept and Obstruct Terrorism (USA PATRIOT) Act, §209, 115 Stat. at 283 (2001).

Universal City Studios, Inc. v. Reimerdes

Vault Corp. v. Quaid Software, Ltd., 847 F.2d 255 (5th Cir. 1988).

Wesley Coll. V. Pitts, 974 F. Supp. 375, 386 (D. Del. 1997).

Law Enforcement and Computer Security Threats and Measures

Mathieu Deflem and J. Eagle Shutt, *University of South Carolina*

INTRODUCTION

In the context of democratic societies, policing always involves a delicate task to provide security while also maintaining liberty. With the rapid expansion of computerized technologies and the Internet, this problem is posed even more acutely, for communication methods have not only expanded sharply, but the development of Internet technology has also brought about increased anonymity and freedom in communications. This situation creates a significant law enforcement problem as the same technologies that guarantee anonymity in legitimate transactions also provide new means to violate laws and to hide the identities of lawbreakers. Because of the cross-border nature of computers linked through networks, also, threats against computer security are often global in nature. By the very nature of the Internet as a border-transcending phenomenon, cybercrimes know no geographic boundaries.

From a legal and law enforcement viewpoint, measures against computer security threats pose problems of jurisdictional authority. National legal systems and their enforcement agencies are formally bound to nationally defined borders, whereas even a single transmission of computerized information over a network may pass through a dozen or more types of carriers, such as telephone companies, satellite networks, and Internet service providers, thereby crossing numerous territorial borders and legal systems (Aldesco, 2002). The cross-border nature of threats to computer security justifies the need for international cooperation and the development of global frameworks of law and law enforcement. In this chapter, we review the most important law enforcement efforts that have been taken at selected national and international levels to respond to the challenges affecting computer security.

COMPUTER SECURITY, THE INTERNET, AND CYBERCRIMES

With the advent and the exponential growth of the Internet and computerized transactions, the modern world has witnessed not only an expansion of new means of communication and the creation of virtual communities among people in disparate geographical locales, but it has also brought about new and unprecedented opportunities for illegitimate conduct (Ditzion, Geddes, & Rhodes, 2003; Maher & Thompson, 2002; Sinrod & Reilly 2000; Sussman, 1999; Wall 2001a). Cybercrimes have become a permanent factor in the current era of the globalization of information and communications. The negative implications of such crimes can be far-reaching in economic and other respects. The total amount of money involved with credit card theft, for example, is estimated at $400 million annually, whereas stolen patents and trademarks involve $250 billion a year (Aldesco, 2002; Baron, 2002).

Cybercrimes are relatively easy to execute and require little technical expertise. Toolkits and handbooks to commit cybercrimes are available on the Internet. Estimates show that nearly 50% of all U.S. companies were attacked by a computer virus, worm, or other Internet-related means in 2001. The computers of the Pentagon are attacked about 22,000 times a year. By 2000, intellectual property theft was already estimated to cause American companies losses in excess of $ 1 trillion (Barr, Beiting, & Grezeskinski, 2003). The so-called Love Bug worm that spread via e-mails to millions of computers in the spring of 2000 led to an estimated $8.7 billion in damages and may have cost as much as $10 billion in lost productivity (Bellia, 2001). The U.S. Defense Department reported that the worm had contaminated at least four classified U.S. military computer systems. The Philippine-based college dropout who caused the havoc could not be prosecuted in the United States as there was no applicable cybercrime law in the Philippines at that time, for which reasons he could also not be extradited (Cesare, 2001).

At least two types of crimes involving computer security can be distinguished (Goodman & Brenner, 2002). In a first category of offenses, the computer is the target of the crime by means of attacks on network confidentiality, integrity, and availability. Among the examples are unauthorized access to and illicit tampering with systems, programs, or computer data. In a second category of cybercrimes, traditional offenses, such as fraud, theft, and forgery, are committed by means of computers, networks, and other information and communications technology. The latter category of offenses is not novel or unique to the era of the Internet, yet it has qualitatively altered in kind by means of the use of advanced technologies, with important implications for legal policy and law enforcement practices.

Besides the high-tech nature of cybercrimes and the anonymity that the Internet affords, the border-transcending nature of the cyberworld is another outstanding characteristic of computer security since the late 20th century. "An international element is often present, not only when a computer system is the target of a crime," Bellia argues, "but also when a system merely facilitates online forms of traditional crimes or serves as a repository for evidence of a crime" (2001, p. 38). The targets of cybercrime, likewise, can be varied in nature, ranging from illicit gambling to the conveying of threats, the transmission of pornography, and attempts to lure children into sexual conduct to fraud and violations of intellectual property. The Internet has also grown in popularity across the globe and is affecting people of various ages, ethnic backgrounds, and class structures. As a result, the potential impact of cybercrimes can be exploited in a more organized manner that is akin to the existing traditional forms of organized crime, enabling the emergence of so-called cybercrime Mafias (Brenner, 2002). The complexity of cybercrime necessitates the development of new legal frameworks at the national and international levels.

ESTABLISHING COMPUTER SECURITY THROUGH NATIONAL LAWS

The appearance of new social ills in society will typically invoke the passing of new laws designed to prevent or treat the consequences of such problems. Until recently, the spread of computer crimes was unmatched by the development of proper criminal law statutes (Barr et al., 2003; Rustad, 2001). But the sharp rise in intellectual property crimes over the Internet and other crimes related to information in a highly computerized society has led the governments of many nations across the world to enact new criminal statutes specifically tailored to adequately respond to the changing conditions. This chapter will review these legal developments, focusing primarily on the United States and a selection of other nations.

In the United States, laws to protect computer security are primarily based on two pieces of legislation: the

Economic Espionage Act of 1996 and the National Stolen Property Act, which dates as far back as 1934 (Barr et al., 2003). These laws were invoked with renewed vigor because intellectual property crimes by means of the Internet were rising sharply. As the threat of civil action was an insufficient deterrent to thwart the theft of trade secrets and the infringement of trademarks, patents, and copyrights, U.S. Congress passed the Economic Espionage Act in 1996 to criminalize the theft of trade secrets. Other acts have been passed to adequately respond to specific nature of crimes committed in cyberspace. For instance, in 1997, the No Electronic Theft Act was passed to broaden criminal liability for copyright infringement even when no financial gain is involved (Rustad, 2001). The act was passed after an Massachusetts Institute of Technology student had been acquitted for distributing copyrighted software on the Internet because he had received no financial gain from his distribution activities.

The National Stolen Property Act provides criminal sanctions for the transmission of goods and moneys that are known to have been stolen or taken by fraud. Although the act was not designed to apply to theft by computerized means, U.S. federal courts have held that the act can be applied in this circumstance. Originally, the stolen item had to be physically removed for an offense to be prosecutable under the act, but more recently some courts ruled that electronic transmission may be sufficient.

Legal responses at the national level toward the protection of computer security are sometimes only of limited value, because their application and enforcement is limited to jurisdictional borders (whereas cybercrimes are not). The U.S. Copyright Felony Act, the No Electronic Theft Act, and the Digital Millennium Copyright Act, for example, all distinctly focus on computerized information, but they cannot be applied in an extrajurisdictional context. The Economic Espionage Act, however, also applies to economic espionage that occurs overseas, at least when it involves an offender who is a U.S. citizen or corporation or as long as some part of the illegitimate activity is connected to the United States (Barr et al., 2003, pp. 777–778).

The cross-border nature of many computer crimes need not necessarily be addressed by extending national laws to apply to extrajurisdictional territories. Providing there is some degree of coordination among national legal systems, an option toward effective criminalization is provided by cooperation across nation-state borders (Brenner & Schwerha, 2002). Such cooperation is legally secured through mutual legal assistance treaties among nations. The United States, for example, maintains some 40 bilateral mutual legal assistance treaties with foreign nations. These treaties provide both legal and practical means by which one country can seek or provide legal assistance from or to another country (Department of Justice, 2001). Legal cooperation across nations, however, requires that all participating countries have developed similar statutes.

A discussion of all national legal frameworks on computer security is beyond the scope of this chapter. But by reviewing a useful selection, it can be noted that many nations have developed explicit criminal codes against cybercrimes (Schjolberg, 2003). In the Americas, the Mexican penal code specifies that anyone who destroys or causes loss of information contained in computer systems or computer equipment protected by security measures shall be liable to punishments involving imprisonment or fines. Brazil has since July 2000 criminalized the entry of false data into information systems. Other Latin American countries, such as Venezuela and Chile, have passed similar legislation.

The Canadian Criminal Code criminalizes any attempts to fraudulently obtain a computer service or intercept any function of a computer system. In Australia, federal legislation was enacted with the Cybercrime Act of 2001, which criminalizes unauthorized access to, or modification of, data held in a computer to which access is restricted. Among the first nations to enact new laws to protect computer security, the United Kingdom passed a Computer Misuse Act in 1990 to penalize unauthorized access to computer materials. Also in Europe, the French penal code that went into effect in March 1993 provided for the criminalization of attacks on systems for automated data processing. The code criminalizes fraudulent access to an automated data processing system, as well as hindering the functioning of such systems and the fraudulent introduction or modification of data therein. Italy's penal code includes articles on the unauthorized access into computer or telecommunication systems. Similar regulations to protect data were introduced in Germany, Greece, and other European countries. In Belgium, for example, the national parliament in November 2000 adopted legal articles on computer crimes such as computer forgery, computer fraud, computer hacking, and sabotage.

Outside of Europe, China passed new legislation as early as 1994, when regulations were enacted concerning measures to protect the safety of computer information. India passed the Information Technology Act of 2000 that specifies regulations against the hacking of computer systems. Similarly, Japan introduced an Unauthorized Computer Access Law that went into effect in February 2000. In 2002, South Africa enacted an Electronic Communications and Transactions Act, which penalizes cybercrime as the unauthorized access to, interception of, or interference with computerized data.

THE ENFORCEMENT OF NATIONAL LAWS CONCERNING COMPUTER SECURITY

Passing appropriate laws is a necessary step to respond to crimes, but without effective police operations, such laws would remain inconsequential (Rustad, 2001). The policing of laws related to computer security poses several special problems, not least of all because of the enormous popularity of the Internet and the widespread use of computers. Already by the late 1990s, it was estimated that a global population of some 19 million computer users would have the necessary skills to mount a cyberattack should they choose to use their proficiency for such illegitimate purposes (Cilluffo, Pattak, & Salmoiraghi, 1999). The expansion of the Internet itself has contributed to the growing availability of the tools and skills necessary

to carry out a cybercrime. Moreover, the relative lack of technological expertise among enforcement agencies—at least until recently— initially posed serious limitations to the adequate implementation of any law enforcement plans (O'Neill, 2000). The technological characteristics of cybercrimes also affect the nature of appropriate police actions. The anonymity of the communicator and the methods used to shield one's true identity create considerable problems for the enforcement of any law concerning information and identity theft (Davis, 2003).

The strategies to police cyberspace that were implemented in recent years in the United States provide a good example of the value and limitations of jurisdictionally confined enforcement (Ditzion et al., 2003). Police actions to enforce laws concerning computer security were first stepped up during the Clinton administration. U.S. Congress expanded the scope of the Computer Fraud and Abuse Act, originally passed in 1986 in response to the so-called war games epidemic, to lower the punishable standard of criminal intent in cases of unauthorized computer access, ensuring that a broad class of hackers would be accountable under the statute and broadening the category of protected computers.

In the United States, a leading role in computer-related law enforcement efforts has been adopted by the Federal Bureau of Investigation (FBI), which established so-called computer crime teams in its various field offices across the U.S. states (Wolf, 2000). The FBI also set up the National Infrastructure Protection Center to function as a national law enforcement investigation and response entity for critical infrastructure threat assessment, warning, and vulnerability (Gravell, 1999). These activities have not been without consequences, as many prosecutions of computer criminals evolved from FBI stings operations (Barr et al., 2003).

Besides the operations by the FBI, relevant criminal enforcement strategies in the United States are also undertaken by a host of other agencies. The Central Intelligence Agency (CIA) is involved in securing computer communications through the monitoring of communications (Baron, 2002). In the Justice Department, the Computer and Telecommunication Coordinator (CTC) Program has been set up since 1995 at the recommendation of the Computer Crime Unit, now called the Computer Crime and Intellectual Property Section (CCIPS) in the Criminal Division (http://www.cybercrime.org). Every U.S. attorney's office has designated at least one CTC and over 35 districts have two or more. A total of 137 U.S. attorneys are presently working in the CTC Program. The CTCs have responsibility to prosecute computer crimes, serve as technical advisors to other U.S. attorneys, act in liaison with attorneys in other districts, and provide training and guidance to other attorneys and to federal and local agencies in their districts. More recently, since July 2001, additional Computer Hacking and Intellectual Property (CHIP) units of prosecutors have been established to work in collaboration with the FBI and other agencies. Likewise, the FBI organized a cyberbanking initiative in cooperation with the Departments of Justice and the Treasury as well as financial regulatory agencies to examine the risks associated with electronic banking technology (*Cyber Crime*, 1998).

Also established by the U.S. Department of Justice was the National Cybercrime Training Partnership (NCTP) to collaborate with all levels of law enforcement and develop a long-range strategy for high-tech police work, including interagency cooperation, networking, and training (Williams, 1999). At present, NCTP activities are in hiatus pending the formation and initial meeting of a new body, the Cybercrime Advisory Board, under the direction of the National White Collar Crime Center (NW3C). The latter center also runs the Internet Fraud Complaint Center (IFCC) in partnership with the FBI to address fraud committed over the Internet. The IFCC acts as a central repository of fraud complaints for the law enforcement community and provides an easy-to-use reporting mechanism for fraud victims. Another way for citizens to get involved in computer security is through the Cyber Citizen Partnership, a program set up by the Department of Justice and the Information Technology Association of America that involves a Web site to teach children about the right ways to use the Internet.

As is the case in matters of national legal systems, law enforcement measures on computer security have been implemented in many countries across the world. In Canada, a Tech Crime Unit has been established in the Royal Canadian Mounted Police. The Federal Police in Australia has Electronic Forensic Support Teams in most of the country's major cities. In the United Kingdom, a National Hi-Tech Crime Unit was established in 2001. By 2003, the unit's investigations had led to more than 100 arrests in over 40 operations. Special attention is paid to the unit's collaboration with the cybercrime police in other countries. Other countries in Europe, indeed, have similar specialized units set up in their respective police forces. Outside of Europe, the situation is no different as specialized "cybercop" teams are set up in many countries across the globe. For example, the Central Bureau of Investigation in India has established a unit to police Internet communications and cooperate with Indian portals to safeguard against cyberattacks. Special emphasis is placed on the training of officers to serve in such units, as their skills are very different from those needed in a more traditional police role.

BUILDING A GLOBAL LEGAL ORDER TO PROTECT COMPUTER SECURITY

Similar to the problems associated with legal frameworks, enforcement activities are especially affected by the cross-border nature of computer security-related activities in cyberspace (Calkins, 2000). Yet, among legal scholars there is disagreement on the value of international legal systems in the case of computer security and related Internet activities (Bellia, 2001; Berman, 2002). Some argue that laws regulating online activities crossing national borders are always ineffective because they are to be implemented in nations with limited jurisdiction. Other, however, suggest that the Internet is no less subject to extraterritorial authority than other forms of international activities that had already been regulated by international law for many years before the advent of the Internet. The reality is that the development of cyberspace

as a decidedly global phenomenon has instigated a host of legal initiatives at the international level. Mirroring the development of international police cooperation from the 19th century onward (Deflem 2002a, 2002b), technological advances are typically addressed at overcoming barriers of space and time, and criminal law and law enforcement respond in kind to internationalize their range and activities.

The history of the regulation of illegitimate conduct in cyberspace shows a steady expansion of applicable laws and an increasing involvement of various international bodies to tackle the cross-border nature of cybercrime (Goodman & Brenner, 2002; Grabosky & Smith, 2001; Norman, 2001; Wall, 2001b). Among the key players are the Organization for Economic Cooperation and Development (OECD), the Council of Europe, the European Union, and the United Nations.

Pertinent activities of the OECD date back to 1983 when the organization was assigned to secure a harmonization of European computer crime legislation. In the mid-1980s, the Select Committee of Experts on Computer-Related Crime of the Council of Europe thereupon drafted a recommendation to provide for an adequate and quick response to cybercrime by harmonizing existing legislation in the EU countries and improving international legal cooperation. By the mid-1990s, the Council of Europe had issued several reports detailing appropriate surveillance activities and methods of investigation in the realm of information technology.

Many international bodies were involved in developing an international regulation of cyberspace. In 1990, the United Nations first addressed some of the international legal issues associated with cybercrime. The U.N. Congress then urged the world's nations to step up their efforts to legally respond to computer crime and promote the development of an international legal framework. Also during the 1990s, international agreements were reached that specifically concerned trade secrets and the manner in which business information is to be protected. In 1994, the Uruguay Round Agreement presented Trade-Related Aspects of Intellectual Property Rights (TRIPs), and the OECD stipulated Guidelines on Security and Information Systems in 1992 and Guidelines for Cryptography Policy in 1997. Under the TRIPs agreement, enforcement of intellectual property rights can be obligated, whereas the OECD agreements are guidelines that do not attach binding obligations.

In 1997, the Justice and Interior Ministers of the Group of Eight (G8) met in Washington, D.C., and adopted a set of principles to combat high-tech crimes as well as an Action Plan to Combat High-Tech Crime (Bellia, 2001). The G8 agreement provides for national governments to pass legislation that enables international cooperation to keep pace with the development of technology and its use for illegitimate purposes.

The G8 action plan was a significant development in the internationalization of computer security law, for it inspired the Council of Europe to prepare a Convention on Cyber-Crime that has been favorably received in many countries since the convention was complete in 2001 (Aldesco, 2002; Baron, 2002; Davis, 2003; see also Brenner, 2002; Keyser, 2003; Marler, 2002). The primary goal of the convention is to pursue a cross-national policy against the threat of cybercrime by developing appropriate legislation and enhancing international cooperation (Aldesco, 2002, p. 93). The convention includes a harmonization of laws to prevent and suppress computer(-related) crimes by establishing a common standard of offenses. This legislation should cover a variety of related areas such as the illegal interception of and interference with computer data, computer-related forgery and fraud, child pornography, and violations of copyright.

The Convention on Cyber-Crime was the first formalized international treaty on criminal offenses conducted against or by means of a computer and computer networks. With initial preparations going back to the late 1980s, the convention was formally signed in November 2001 by 26 member states of the Council of Europe as well as by the United States, Canada, Japan, and South Africa. The United States had been involved in the elaboration of the convention in its capacity as an observer at the Council of Europe. Not all of the signing countries ratified the convention, although the convention finds broad support. Heralded as the only multilateral treaty to address the problems of computer-related crime and electronic evidence gathering, U.S. President Bush in November 2003 asked the U.S. Senate to ratify the convention. These and other international legal frameworks have distinct implications for law enforcement.

COMPUTER SECURITY AND INTERNATIONAL POLICING

From an international policing viewpoint, potential threats against computer security relate intimately to the specific means and object matter of computerized information. Computer security threats often concern multiple national jurisdictions. Police activities, in response, have to concentrate on locating the source of the communication to connect the traces of a cybercrime with a real person in the physical world. The infrastructure of the Internet does not provide a ready mechanism for tracing this "electronic trail" (Aldesco, 2002) that leads from the effects of a crime back to its perpetrator. Special strategies at an international level are needed to police threats against computers in a manner that is both effective and appropriate relative to applicable laws. Three basic models can be identified in the international policing of cybercrime: trans-border police actions involving unilaterally conducted investigations abroad, bilateral agreements among countries or their law enforcement agencies, and the establishment of multilateral regimes (Deflem, 2002a; see also Bellia, 2001).

Variations of Global Policing

In the case of transnational police activities on foreign soil, it is striking to note that the legal systems of some nations allow for extraterritorial police activities, even without a corresponding legal system in the country in which cross-border activities take place. Such transnational police activities often take place without the knowledge or consent of the host country. Some states assert a legal right to conduct "remote cross-border searches" (Bellia, 2001, p. 39) by using computers located within their jurisdiction to examine data that are stored outside of their jurisdiction. For example, in 2000, FBI agents downloaded data from Russian computers as part of an investigation of a ring of Russian hackers who had been targeting several U.S. companies.

International cooperation among police agencies can occur without explicit legal agreements, instead relying on an autonomously developed professional police culture among security and intelligence agencies across national borders (Deflem, 2002a). Law enforcement agencies in the United States and other countries can independently cooperate and undertake joint efforts in the policing of cyberspace. For instance, the Cybersmuggling Center operated by the U.S. Customs Service has been involved in cyberinvestigations concerning money laundering and child pornography distribution in cooperation with police from Germany, Indonesia, Italy, Honduras, Thailand, and Russia (President's Working Group, 2000).

When computer security-related crimes are subject to laws in one country but not in another, cooperation to investigate pertinent crimes may be hampered and extradition may be unlikely. Yet this limitation is not always in place, because some mutual legal assistance treaties among countries allow for assistance when illegitimate conduct is considered a crime in the state that requests extradition even though that conduct is not criminalized in the state from which assistance is requested (President's Working Group, 2000). Most often, however, especially in the more sensitive area of searches and seizures, a condition of dual criminality must exist whereby a particular type of conduct is considered a crime in both countries involved in a bilateral cooperation agreement.

Bilateral cooperation among nations is precarious, not only because each country involved in cooperation would have to develop similar laws, but also because each country would have to entertain agreements with all other nations of the world. As a perfect consensus about international policing of computer security among all of the world's nations is unlikely, the planning and implementation of multilateral strategies can be a more effective way to develop adequate global law enforcement. Because the Internet now connects virtually every country in the world, the law enforcement challenges posed by this global communication system also have to respond globally. Thus, the international legal frameworks that have been developed on matters of cybercrime carry implications for international law enforcement, especially at the level of each participating nation state and how its law enforcement agencies cooperate with one another. The Council of Europe's Convention on Cyber-Crime, most clearly, has distinct implications for international policing activities. As the convention seeks to harmonize procedures of mutual assistance among nations, special provisions are accorded to law enforcement to aid the investigation of cybercrimes (Aldesco, 2002). The nations that have signed the convention are required to ensure that special police measures are available, such as the realtime collection of traffic data and the interception of content data. The convention also enables police agencies of one nation to collect evidence related to cybercrimes for the police agency of another country and to establish a permanent communications network to provide international assistance with ongoing investigations. Under the provisions of the convention, also, police in a country are now authorized to request "that their counterparts abroad collect an individual's computer data, [and] have the individual arrested and extradited to serve a prison sentence abroad" (Aldesco, 2002, p. 95).

The Role of Interpol and Europol

The international dimensions of law enforcement also include multilateral organizations that have been set up among police agencies. Such international police organizations enable participating agencies to cooperate in the form of direct police-to-police information exchange, even when no formal intergovernmental accords have been reached (Deflem, 2002a). Among the most important of these organizations are the International Criminal Police Organization, better known under its abbreviation Interpol, and the European Police Office, called Europol.

Interpol is an international organization aimed at providing and promoting mutual assistance among criminal police agencies within the limits of their respective national laws and the Universal Declaration of Human Rights (Deflem, 2002a). Originally formed in Vienna in 1923, Interpol is not a supranational police agency, but a collaborative structure among law enforcement agencies from various nations that are linked via specialized national bureaus with a central headquarters in Lyon, France. Presently, Interpol involves police agencies from 181 national states. Interpol has been involved in efforts to combat information technology-related crime for a number of years through a system of so-called working parties on information technology crime that have been set up in various regions of the world (Goodman & Brenner, 2002; *Interpol's contribution*, n.d.). The European Working Party on Information Technology Crime was the first to be set up under this provision in 1990. It compiles a computer crime manual, organizes training courses in Internet-related crimes, and has set up a rapid information exchange system to transmit relevant information swiftly among the member agencies. The other working parties, which have been set up in the Americas, Africa, and Southern Asia, similarly work toward increasing the flow of information on computer security-related matters among its various agencies.

At a global level including all of its member agencies, Interpol has also instigated a number of activities. The Steering Committee for Information Technology Crime has been established to coordinate and harmonize the initiatives of the various regional working parties. Interpol also organizes international conferences on computer crime to share relevant information among its members (Goodman & Brenner, 2002). Initiatives have also been taken to secure coordination with private ventures geared at securing information. In 2000, for instance, Interpol agreed to provide intelligence to the private Web site Atomic Tangerine, which in return would pass on to Interpol information gathered from its monitoring of the Internet. Atomic Tangerine operates a Net Rader service that had on earlier occasions informed police authorities of a Pakistani Internet service provider that had been hacked into as a base to launch other Web site attacks.

Establishment of Europol was agreed upon in the Maastricht Treaty on the European Union in 1992 (Europol website; Rauchs & Koenig, 2001). Based in The Hague, The Netherlands, Europol started limited operations in January 1994 in the form of the Europol Drugs Unit (EDU). After the Europol Convention was ratified by all member states, Europol commenced the full scope of its activities in July 1999. The aim of Europol is to improve the effectiveness and cooperation among the competent authorities of the member states in preventing and combating serious international organized crime. Europol's areas of investigation include illicit drug trafficking, terrorism, child pornography, financial crimes, and cybercrime.

In matters of computer security and cybercrime in the European Union, Europol is involved only when an organized criminal structure is involved and two or more member states are affected (Computer Fraud and Security 2002; Europol website). Europol has set up a network of cybercrime units among its participating agencies, a centralized monitoring center at Europol headquarters, and a working group to establish cooperation with the private sector. In October 2002, Europol formed a High Tech Crime Center, a task force that has as its mission the coordination of cross-border cybercrime investigations in the European Union. In 2003, Europe's policing activities against cybercrimes were stepped up by the creation of a European-wide rapid reaction force against attacks on vital computer networks in the form of a single round-the-clock information exchange system against cyberattacks.

COMPUTER SECURITY, LAW ENFORCEMENT, AND THE BALANCE OF ORDER AND LIBERTY

With respect to the law enforcement aspects of computer security, a number of interesting issues and problems are revealed. The cross-border nature of computerized information exchange highlights the limits of national laws and law enforcement strategies and reveals the need for a coordination of law and law enforcement across jurisdictions. At the same time, continued efforts have to be made to protect liberty, privacy, and other democratic values that are promoted in an open and free society.

The Coordination of Law and Law Enforcement

A central concern with the existence of diverse national legal systems on computer security is that for national laws to be enforceable, the jurisdictional authority of a nation has to be recognized by other states (Berman, 2002; Speer, 2000). Consensus among the standards of law across nations would alleviate this problem, but there are difficulties with harmonizing various approaches to computer security issues such as copyright infringement and intellectual property theft. International treaties are surely a worthwhile ideal (Weber, 2003), but they cannot be effective unless the participating nations already resemble one another in social, cultural, and economic respects and it is precisely this condition of egalitarianism that is often not met. The cultures of nations, for instance, differ widely in terms of the emphasis they place on privacy, appropriate law enforcement strategies, and the very notion of jurisdictional sovereignty (Davis, 2003; Fischer-Hubner, 2000; Mayer-Schonberger, 2003).

An ironic consequence of the difficulties to establish a global legal order in matters of computer security (and other important legal issues) is that the lack of formal international agreements increases the likelihood of certain countries trying to exert extraterritorial jurisdiction on other countries (Podgor, 2002). Federal U.S. agencies, in particular, have often sought to assert federal extraterritorial jurisdiction in the prosecution of computer fraud activities that take place or originate from outside the borders of the United States. However, other countries might in turn resist such intrusive attempts that are seen as interfering with the national jurisdictional authority (Deflem, 2001, 2004a). Conflicts over extraterritorial claims cannot aid toward the development of coordinated legal and law enforcement strategies.

Some of the concerns that have been raised surrounding the European Convention on Cyber-Crime nicely illustrate the difficulties that international treaties on computer security face. Some members of the U.S. Congress, for instance, have criticized the European Convention because its widespread implementation would ultimately mean that the European data protection laws, which are considered too strict, might become the world's unitary privacy standard (Davis, 2003). As such, the convention raises resentment from nations on whose support it must ultimately rely. Related concerns have been expressed against the chilling effect the provisions of the convention might have against business enterprises, based in the United States or in other countries, whose commercial interests reach well beyond their respective national home bases.

More countries agreeing to the provisions of the European convention might lead other countries to also join in this international effort (Oddis, 2002). Yet, it can also be argued that adherence to the convention will violate jurisdictional and constitutional authority problems, because the individual states of the United States would not be allowed to create any conflicting or superceding laws to an agreed upon international treaty (Fisher, 2001; Hopkins, 2003). Even if such jurisdictional issues are cleared, there would still be a considerable problem with the fact that the enforcement and prosecution of the agreed upon international laws are left to the various participating states (Mayer-Schonberger, 2003). As Bellia (2001, p. 59) argues, an international agreement still leaves "in the hands of the state where the data is physically stored the power to search or seize the data in question."

Policing Technology, Maintaining Liberty

Some cybercrimes involve criminal offenses that also exist in "realspace" (O'Neill, 2000) but that can now be executed with more speed and efficiency. The technological sophistication of threats to computer security change the nature of appropriate law enforcement activities, as detection and prosecution become considerably more difficult. As such, the policing of computer security relates

intimately to the ever-evolving relationship between technology and law and the continued need to find the most efficient and appropriate way to handle concerns of law and law enforcement in a technologically advanced world. Because of the speed with which technological advances are made and the intrinsic complexity of modern technologies, existing systems of law and law enforcement are often outdated soon after they have been planned and implemented (Skibell, 2003).

The technologically sophisticated nature of computer crimes means that law enforcement must recruit and train computer specialists and place priority on cooperation and intelligence sharing (McFarlane, 2001). But the technological nature of computer security might also imply that a strategy of law enforcement is needed that shifts the burden of protection of the technology to the manufacturer. This burden-shifting approach would target the design flaws that can lead to securityrelated failures (Katyal, 2003; Pinkney, 2002). Although not everybody will agree with this strategy, it is clear that cooperation between the government and its agencies, on the one hand, and the private sector, on the other, is needed (Coleman & Sapte, 2003). The fact that attacks against computer security also create economic damage provides at least a commercial incentive for active cooperation from the private sector. Strategies of security are not free, but neither are the consequences of insecurity (Hinde, 2003).

Debates surrounding the protection of privacy rights are virtually concomitant with the rise of new technologies. In matters of computer-related crimes, civil libertarians have argued that police actions should always remain mindful of the legitimate transactions that are conducted over the Internet and other technological communication systems (Brenner, 2003; Huie, Laribee, & Hogan 2002; Tountas, 2003). Aldesco (2002), for instance, argues that law enforcement has a legitimate interest in combating computer crimes, but that government agencies should not invade the privacy of legitimate communications. Although the anonymity afforded by the Internet can be abused, it is also an important value in a society committed to the free development of communications (Marx, 2001).

Newly developed law enforcement methods to ensure computer security are often less concerned with protecting the liberties granted in a democratic constitutional state (Kennedy, 2002). The European Convention on Cyber-Crime, for instance, empowers law enforcement agencies with the authority to search and seize information that is stored on computer systems, at least when such activities are part of a particular investigation into a cybercrime. By giving new powers to law enforcement to investigate cybercrimes, even outside of their respective jurisdictions, an imbalance may be created when there are no increasing protections for personal privacy. It is to be noted that such issues of individual rights are also important to consider relative to foreign nationals who commit cybercrimes and who are then subject to computer searches and other investigative procedures by law enforcement (Young, 2003). Given the disparity in the recognition of liberty and civil rights across the world, the inhabitants of some countries will be more likely to face dire consequences than will others (Huie et al., 2002), further enhancing inequality on an international scale.

CONCLUSION

Law enforcement is an important and necessary component among the efforts to maintain computer security. Because of the rapid and widespread expansion of computerized technologies and because of the border-transcending nature of computers linked through networks, the policing of threats against computer security presents a challenge to traditional means of crime detection and investigation on an international scale. Existing notions of jurisdictional authority have to be redefined to meet the global needs of information security. Trying to avert cybercrimes and the economic and social harm they can cause, many nations across the world have developed new legislation. Extending these legislative efforts are international systems of law, such as the European Convention on Cyber-Crime, to respond to the need for international legal cooperation and more adequately address cybercrimes and related cross-borders threats against computer security.

Without adequate law enforcement, laws remain ineffective. In the case of computer security, law enforcement agencies have instituted specialized computer crime teams to focus on the ways in which crimes can be perpetrated against or with the aid of computers. As with their accompanying legal systems, pertinent law enforcement activities often extend beyond the reach of jurisdictional boundaries, whether via cooperation among the police forces of different nations or through unilaterally enacted police actions abroad. International police operations pose special problems of coordination among the law enforcement agencies of various countries and they also lead us to rethink the need for police to preserve liberty and legitimate computer transactions while seeking to police computer crimes effectively.

Law enforcement efforts against threats to computer security do not respond merely to technological developments, but also take shape in specific sociohistorical circumstances. Since the terrorist attacks of September 11, 2001, many dimensions of law enforcement have undergone considerable changes, not only in terms of counterterrorism strategies but also with respect to other aspects of crime and crime control (Deflem, 2004b). The policing of computer security issues has also been altered since 9/11 because scores of systems relating to security, means of transportation and communication, and other public facilities rely heavily on computerized systems (Birnhack & ElkinKoren, 2003; Brenner & Goodman, 2002; Raghavan, 2003). Given contemporary society's heavy reliance on computers, it is possible, for instance, for a terrorist group or individual to hack into the computers that oversee the subway system of a city or the railway network of a country. Following the attacks of 9/11, interest in and concern for computer security has skyrocketed, especially in connection with cyberterrorism. To be sure, cyberterrorism does not fully equate with cybercrime, but there is some overlap. For example, the initial stages of the offenses may be similar (e.g., sending out a computer virus), so that the response from a law enforcement viewpoint can be similar as well. But cybercrime and cyberterrorism differ in the harm they may cause and the motivation that is involved. In practice, however, the legislative responses—on both the national level and the international level—often confuse between the two offenses and have thus sped up the development of new means to police cybercrimes.

The strongest indicator of the changes affecting cyber-related matters in the post-9/11 era is the Uniting and Strengthening America by Providing Appropriate Tools Required to Intercept and Obstruct Terrorism (USA PATRIOT) Act in the United States (Berkeley Technology Law Journal, 2004; Copeland, 2004). Among other provisions, the act gives authorities new powers by means of expanded options for wiretaps and technological systems of cybersurveillance (Ventura, Miller, & Deflem, in press). Relatedly, also, the National Cyber Security Division was created in the Department of Homeland Security in June 2003 as part of the National Strategy to Secure Cyberspace. Similar such new laws and the means to enforce them are now being set up in many other countries. Cyberlaw and law enforcement are a rapidly expanding reality. Ongoing developments indicate that, after several years of slowly responding to the threat of cybercrime, the events of 9/11 have served as an important catalyst to step up efforts to provide computer security through law and law enforcement. Although most cybercrimes do not relate to terrorism, the terrorist events of 9/11 may have provided the strongest impulse to develop new coordinated means against all types of cybercrime.

GLOSSARY

Computer Security Threats Potential and actual violations of law that either involve attacks on the security of computers or that use a computer to commit an illegal act.

Convention on Cyber-Crime An international treaty initiated by the Council of Europe that involves a harmonization of legislation and an enhancing of international cooperation to prevent and suppress computer-related crimes.

Cross-Border Law Enforcement Activities of law enforcement agencies that transcend the jurisdictional authority of national states.

Cybercop Units Popular term for specialized units in law enforcement agencies that deal with cybercrimes and criminal activities associated with computerized information systems.

Cybercrimes Criminal activities involving the use of the Internet, including such criminal acts as fraud, identity theft, and cyberterrorism.

International Policing Police activities that involve citizens of other national states by means of international cooperation with foreign police, transnational police operations in foreign countries, or supranational crime developments affecting police in more than one country.

Law Enforcement The formal institutions of national states, and the functions that are associated with them, to enforce compliance to laws and investigate violations of law.

Legal Systems The whole of laws formally enacted by governing bodies, including the governments of national states and international governing agencies. Legal systems are accompanied by enforcement agencies and typically comprise civil and criminal laws.

CROSS REFERENCES

See *Combating the Cyber Crime Threat: Developments in Global Law Enforcement; Cyberterrorism and Information Security; Law Enforcement and Digital Evidence; Privacy Law and the Internet.*

REFERENCES

Aldesco, A. I. (2002). The demise of anonymity: A constitutional challenge to the convention on cyber crime. *Loyola of Los Angeles Entertainment Law Review, 23,* 81–123.

Baron, R. M. F. (2002). A critique of the international cyber crime treaty. *CommLaw Conspectus, 10,* 263–278.

Barr, K., Beiting, M., & Grezeskinski, A. (2003). Intellectual property crimes. *American Criminal Law Review, 40,* 771–823.

Bellia, P. L. (2001). Chasing bits across borders. *University of Chicago Legal Forum, 2001,* 35–101.

Berkeley Technology Law Journal. (2004). Cyberlaw: additional developments. *Berkeley Technology Law Journal, 19,* 543–553.

Berman, P. S. (2002). The globalization of jurisdiction. *University of Pennsylvania Law Review, 151,* 311–432.

Birnhack, M. D., & ElkinKoren, N. (2003). The invisible handshake: The reemergence of the state in the digital environment. *Virginia Journal of Law and Technology, 8.* Retrieved March 24, 2004, from http://www.vjolt.net/vol8/issue2/v8i2_a06-Birnhack-Elkin-Koren.pdf

Brenner, S. W. (2002). Organized cyber crime? How cyberspace may affect the structure of criminal relationships. *North Carolina Journal of Law & Technology, 4,* 1–50.

Brenner, S. W. (2003). Complicit publication: When should the dissemination of ideas and data be criminalized? *Albany Law Journal of Science & Technology, 13,* 273–429.

Brenner, S. W., & Goodman, M. D. (2002). In defense of cyberterrorism: An argument for anticipating cyberattacks. *University of Illinois Journal of Law, Technology & Policy, 2002,* 1–57.

Brenner, S. W., & Schwerha, J. J., IV. (2002). Transnational evidence gathering and local prosecution of international cyber crime. *John Marshall Journal of Computer & Information Law, 20,* 347–395.

Calkins, M. M. (2000). They shoot Trojan horses, don't they? An economic analysis of anti-hacking regulatory models. *Georgetown Law Journal, 89,* 171–224.

Cesare, K. (2001). Prosecuting computer virus authors: The need for an adequate and immediate international solution. *Transnational Lawyer, 14,* 135–170.

Cilluffo, F. J., Pattak, P. B., & Salmoiraghi, G. C. (1999). Bad guys and good stuff: When and where will the cyber threats converge? *DePaul Business Law Journal, 12,* 131–168.

Coleman, C., & Sapte, D. W. (2003). Securing cyberspace: New laws and developing strategies. *Computer Law and Security Report, 19,* 131–136.

Copeland, R. A. (2004). War on terrorism or war on constitutional rights? Blurring the lines of intelligence gathering in post-September 11 America. *Texas Tech Law Review, 35,* 1–31.

Computer Crime & Intellectual Property Section of the Criminal Division, Department of Justice. (n.d.). Retrieved May 14, 2005, from http://www.cybercrime.gov/compcrime.html

Cyber crime, transnational crime, and intellectual property theft: Testimony before the Joint Economic Committee, United States Congress (1998) (testimony of J. N. Gallagher).

Cyber Security Research and Development Act, Pub. L. 107–305, 107th Congress (2002).

Davis, E. S. (2003). A world wide problem on the World Wide Web: International responses to transnational identity theft via the Internet. *Washington University Journal of Law & Policy, 12,* 201–227.

Deflem, M. (2001). International police cooperation in Northern America: A review of practices, strategies, and goals in the United States, Mexico, and Canada. In D. J. Koenig & D. K. Das (Eds.), *International police cooperation: A world perspective* (pp. 71–98). Lanham, MD: Lexington Books.

Deflem, M. (2002a). *Policing world society: Historical foundations of international police cooperation.* Oxford, UK: Oxford University Press.

Deflem, M. (2002b). Technology and the internationalization of policing: A comparative-historical perspective. *Justice Quarterly, 19,* 453–475.

Deflem, M. (2004a). The boundaries of international cooperation: problems and prospects of U.S.-Mexican police relations. In M. Amir & S. Einstein (Eds.), *Police corruption: Challenges for developed countries–Comparative issues and commissions of inquiry* (pp. 93–122). Huntsville, TX: Office of International Criminal Justice.

Deflem, M. (Ed.). (2004b). *Terrorism and counterterrorism: Criminological perspectives.* Oxford, UK: Elsevier Science.

Department of Justice, Computer Crime and Intellectual Property Section (CCIPS). (2001). *Seizing computers and obtaining electronic evidence in criminal investigations.* Washington, DC: U.S. Department of Justice.

Ditzion, R., Geddes, E., & Rhodes, M. (2003). Computer crimes. *American Criminal Law Review, 40,* 285–336.

Fisher, J. (2001). The draft convention on cyber crime: potential constitutional conflicts. *UCLA Law Review, 32,* 339–361.

Fischer-Hubner, S. (2000). Privacy and security at risk in the global information society. In D. Thomas & B. D. Loader (Eds.), *Cyber crime: Law enforcement, security, and surveillance in the information age* (pp. 173–192). New York: Routledge.

Goodman, M. D., & Brenner, S. W. (2002). The emerging consensus on criminal conduct in cyberspace. *UCLA Journal of Law & Technology, 3.* Retrieved March 22, 2004, from http://www.lawtechjournal.com/articles/2002/03_020625_goodmanbrenner.php

Grabosky, P., & Smith, R. (2001). Telecommunication fraud in the digital age. In D. S. Wall (Ed.), *Crime and the Internet* (pp. 29–43). New York: Routledge.

Gravell, W. (1999). Some observations along the road to "national information power." *Duke Journal of Comparative & International Law, 9,* 401–426.

Hinde, S. (2003). The law, cyber crime, risk assessment and cyber protection. *Computers and Security, 22*, 90–95.

Hopkins, S. L. (2003). Cyber crime convention: A positive beginning to a long road ahead. *Journal of High Technology Law, 2*, 101–121.

Huie, M. C., Laribee, S. F., & Hogan, S. D. (2002). The right to privacy in personal data: The EU prods the U.S. and controversy continues. *Tulsa Journal of Comparative & International Law, 9*, 391–469.

Interpol's contribution to combating information technology crime. (n.d.). Retrieved January 23, 2004, from http://www.interpol.int/Public/TechnologyCrime/default.asp

Jackson, M. (2000). Keeping secrets: International developments to protect undisclosed business information and trade secrets. In D. Thomas & B. D. Loader (Eds.), *Cyber crime: Law enforcement, security, and surveillance in the information age* (pp. 153–172). New York: Routledge.

Katyal, N. K. (2003). Digital architecture as crime control. *Yale Law Journal, 112*, 2261–2289.

Kennedy, D. C. (2002). In search of a balance between police power and privacy in the cyber crime treaty. *Richmond Journal of Law & Technology, 9.* Retrieved March 24, 2004, from http://law.richmond.edu/jolt/v9i1/article3.html

Keyser, M. (2003). The Council of Europe convention on cyber crime. *Journal of Transnational Law & Policy, 12*, 287–326.

Maher, M. K., & Thompson, J. M. (2002). Intellectual property crimes. *American Criminal Law Review, 39*, 763–816.

Marler, S. L. (2002). The convention on cybercrime: Should the United States ratify? *New England Law Review, 37*, 183–219.

Marx, G. T. (2001). Identity and anonymity: some conceptual distinctions and issues for research. In J. Caplan & J. Torpey (Eds.), *Documenting individual identity* (pp. 311–327). Princeton, NJ: Princeton University Press.

Mayer-Schonberger, V. (2003). The shape of governance: Analyzing the world of Internet. *Virginia Journal of International Law Association, 43*, 605–673.

McFarlane, J. (2001). Transnational crime, corruption, and crony capitalism in the twenty-first century. *Transnational Organized Crime, 4*, 1–30.

Norman, P. (2001). Policing 'high-tech' crime within the global context: The role of transnational policy networks. In D. S. Wall (Ed.), *Crime and the Internet* (pp. 184–194). New York: Routledge.

Oddis, D. I. (2002). Combating child pornography on the Internet: The council of Europe's convention on cyber crime. *Temple International and Comparative Law Journal, 16*, 477–518.

O'Neill, M. E. (2000). Old crimes in new bottles: Sanctioning cyber crime. *George Mason Law Review, 9*, 237–288.

Pinkney, K. R. (2002). Putting blame where blame is due: Software manufacturer and customer liability for security-related software failure. *Albany Law Journal of Science & Technology, 13*, 43–82.

Podgor, E. S. (2002). International computer fraud: a paradigm for limiting national jurisdiction. *U.C. Davis Law Review, 35*, 267–317.

President's Working Group on Unlawful Conduct on the Internet. (2000). *The electronic frontier: the challenge of unlawful conduct involving the use of the Internet.* Washington, DC: U.S. Department of Justice.

Raghavan, T. M. (2003). In fear of cyberterrorism: an analysis of the congressional response. *University of Illinois Journal of Law, Technology & Policy, 2003*, 297–312.

Rauchs, G., & Koenig. D. J. (2001). Europol. In D. J. Koenig & D. K. Das (Eds.), *International police cooperation* (pp. 43–62). New York: Lexington.

Rustad, M. L. (2001). Private enforcement of cyber crime on the electronic frontier. *Southern California Interdisciplinary Law Journal, 11*, 63–116.

Schjolberg, S. (2003). *The legal framework: Unauthorized access to computer systems: Penal legislation in 44 countries.* Retrieved July 6, 2004, from http://www.mosstingrett.no/info/legal.html

Sinrod, E. J., & Reilly, W. P. (2000). Cyber-crimes: A practical approach to the application of federal computer crime laws. *Santa Clara Computer and High Technology Law Journal, 16*, 177–232.

Skibell, R. (2003). Cybercrimes & misdemeanors: A reevaluation of the computer fraud and abuse act. *Berkeley Technology Law Journal, 18*, 909–944.

Speer, D. L. (2000). Redefining borders: The challenges of cyber crime. *Crime, Law and Social Change, 34*, 259–273.

Sussman, M. A. (1999). The critical challenges from international high-tech and computer-related crime at the millennium. *Duke Journal of Comparative and International Law, 9*, 451–489.

Tountas, S. W. (2003). Carnivore: Is the regulation of wireless technology a legally viable option to curtail the growth of cyber crime? *Washington University Journal of Law & Policy, 11*, 351–377.

Ventura, H. E., Miller, J. M., & Deflem, M. (in press). Governmentality and the war on terror: FBI project Carnivore and the diffusion of disciplinary power. *Critical Criminology.*

Wall, D. S. (2001a). Cybercrimes and the Internet. In D. S. Wall (Ed.), *Crime and the Internet* (pp. 1–17). New York: Routledge.

Wall, D. S. (2001b). Maintaining order and law on the Internet. In D. S. Wall (Ed.), *Crime and the Internet* (pp. 167–183). New York: Routledge.

Weber, A. (2003). The Council of Europe's convention on cyber crime. *Berkeley Technology Law Journal, 18*, 425–446.

Williams, W. P. (1999). The national cybercrime training partnership. *The Police Chief.* Retrieved July 6, 2004, from http://www.wjin.net/Pubs/3417.htm

Wolf, J. B. (2000). War games meets the Internet: Chasing 21st century cybercriminals with old laws and little money. *American Journal of Criminal Law, 28*, 95–117.

Young, S. M. (2003). Verdugo in cyberspace: boundaries of fourth amendment rights for foreign nationals in cybercrime cases. *Michigan Telecommunication and Technology Law Review, 10*, 139–174.

Combating the Cybercrime Threat: Developments in Global Law Enforcement

Roderic Broadhurst, *Queensland University of Technology*

INTRODUCTION

The rapid development of computer connectivity and the role of the Internet in the emergence of new e-commerce markets are key generators of the processes of globalization and have compelled national governments and international agencies to address the need for regulation and safety on the information superhighways. These astonishing tools have eroded the traditional barriers to communication, compressed our concepts of time and place, and changed the way a large part of the world does business. Although the process of globalization continues to accelerate, a fully global response to the problems of security in the digital age has yet to emerge and efforts to secure cyberspace have been reactive rather than proactive.

The convergence of computing and communications and the exponential growth of digital technology have brought enormous benefits, but with these new benefits come greater risks. The new opportunities created in cyberspace have also enhanced the capacity for criminal enterprises to operate more efficiently and effectively both domestically and across borders. Law enforcement agencies in many jurisdictions have been unable to respond effectively and even in the most advanced nations, 'play catch-up' with cybersavvy criminals (Sussmann, 1999). As never before and at little cost, a single offender can inflict catastrophic loss or damage on individuals, companies, and governments from the other side of the world. With these risks has come the awareness that information security is no longer a matter for the technical and computer specialist, but for millions of people who now engage these new media every day for business, communications and leisure. The basic issue of how to police this new arena, cyberspace, is the focus in this chapter (for related discussion of cybersecurity systems for military purposes or asymmetric warfare see chapters "Online Stalking," "Wireless Information Warfare," and "Information Assurance").

The role of digital and information technologies in the generation of national wealth now means that the new risks associated with these changes require continued attention on all fronts: national, regional, and international. At the international level, two new treaty instruments provide a sound basis for the essential cross-border law enforcement cooperation required to combat cybercrime and are briefly discussed. The first is the purpose-built Council of Europe's (CoE) Cybercrime Convention, which, although it was designed as a regional mechanism, has global significance. The second is the United Nations Convention against Transnational Organized Crime (TOC Convention), which is global in scope but indirectly deals with cybercrime when carried out by criminal networks in relation to serious crime. A further UN draft resolution in 2003 "Cybersecurity and the Protection of Critical Information Infrastructures," cosponsored by Argentina, Bulgaria, Canada, Ethiopia, and the United States, was presented at the 58th session of the General Assembly. If adopted, it invites member states and all relevant international organizations to take into account the need to protect critical information structures from possible misuses, including tracing attacks and, where appropriate, the disclosure of tracing information to other nations (Redo, 2004).

At the international level, the role of agencies such as the United Nations Office of Drug Control and Crime Prevention (UNDCP), Interpol, the Organization for Economic Cooperation and Development (OECD), and the G8 group of nations and regional bodies such as the European Union (EU), Organization of American States (OAS), Association of South East Asian Nations (ASEAN), and the Asia Pacific Economic Council (APEC) provide the political and technical expertise necessary to effect cross-border cooperation in policing. As digital technology becomes more pervasive and interconnected, ordinary crime scenes will contain some form of digital evidence. Crucially many cybercrimes take place across jurisdictional boundaries with offenders routing attacks through various jurisdictions that can only be countered by a cross-border and international policing response.

The digital divide between nation states is growing rapidly and the role of advanced information technology-based economies in bridging this divide is essential. Most developing countries do not have a telecommunications sector capable of supporting information and communication technologies (ICT). In 2000, the United Nations reported that only about 4.5% of the global population had network access, but that 44% of North Americans and 10% of Europeans did, whereas rates for Africa, Asia, and South America ranged from 0.3 to 1.6%. Currently, more than 98% of global Internet protocol bandwidth, at the regional level, connects to and from North America. Fifty-five countries account for 99% of worldwide spending on information technology production. A fifth of the world's people living in the highest-income countries have 86% of the world's gross domestic product (GDP) and 93% of Internet users, whereas the bottom fifth have 1% of GDP and only 0.2% of Internet users (United Nations, 2003, as cited in Redo, 2004—see also volume II, chapter 88).

The need for reliable and efficient mechanisms for international cooperation in law enforcement matters has never been more urgent. As noted, the international community has taken a number of significant steps to facilitate cross-border cooperation in criminal matters, including in the investigation and prosecution of cybercrime. This chapter considers some of the avenues for cooperation. However rapid the growth of ICT may be, it is unlikely to continue its apparently exponential trajectory unless the digital divide is broken and poorer nations and neighbors are included.

There is also growing concern about the potential for misuse of information technology (IT) by terrorists. This has made cyberterrorism a major strategic issue in the prevention of terrorism because the technologies themselves may be attacked and can also be used to support terrorism in the same way ITs are used by predatory cybercriminals. The use of computers by terrorists to plan, organize, and communicate is well documented and counterterrorism agencies have commonly identified high-tech media such as cellular and satellite telephones and Internet-based communications. Cases have also been reported in which hacking, physical thefts, or the corruption of officials have been used to gain access to sensitive law enforcement information (see International Narcotics Control Board, 2001). The global reach of terrorism prompted the UN General Assembly in its resolution 51/210, to note the risk of terrorists using electronic or wire communication systems to carry out criminal acts (Redo, 2000, 2004).

CRIMINALITY AND COMPUTER CRIME

With government, industries, markets, and consumers increasingly dependent on computer connectivity, they are prone to an array of threats. The most notable have been the widely publicized computer viruses, which have increased in both virulence and velocity since 2000. The beginning of 2004 saw the development of increasingly complex malicious code in the form of the MyDoom or Norvag worm. It combined the effects of a worm, spreading rapidly across the Internet, with that of a distributed denial of service attack in which computing power is directed at a target system with a view toward shutting it down. In other words, infected computers were remotely commandeered and directed against the target computer. The risks now posed by the release of malicious codes of increasing complexity (often specifically targeted against either a significant commercial or government site) were substantial and could threaten the viability of e-commerce (Moore, Shannon, Voelker, & Savage, 2003; Semple, 2004; Staniford, Paxson, & Weaver, 2002; see also volume III, part 1).

The U.S. Federal Bureau of Investigation (FBI) has also stressed that critical infrastructure protection is a priority in the United States. Given that most elements of critical infrastructure such as power generation, telecommunications, transport, and financial institutions are owned by the private sector, cooperation between law enforcement and the private sector is obvious. To help bridge the public–private gap, the FBI has introduced its Infraguard Program with over 4,000 members (Iden, 2003). There is also a crucial role for the communications and IT industries in designing products that are resistant to crime and that facilitate detection and investigation.

What Is Computer Crime?

The scope of criminal activities and their social consequences can be summarized by a typology of computer-related crime that comprises the following: conventional crimes in which computers are instrumental to the offense, such as child pornography and intellectual property theft; attacks on computer networks; and conventional criminal cases in which evidence exists in digital form. The kinds of criminality encompass the following list (by no means exhaustive—see Part 2 for further details):

- Interference with lawful use of a computer: cyber-vandalism and terrorism; denial of service; insertion of viruses, worms, and other malicious code.
- Dissemination of offensive materials: pornography or child pornography, online gaming or betting, racist content, treasonous or sacrilegious content.
- Threatening communications: extortion, cyber-stalking.
- Forgery or counterfeiting: ID theft; internet protocol (IP) offenses; software, CD, DVD piracy; copyright breaches; and so forth.
- Fraud: payment card fraud and e-funds transfer fraud; theft of Internet and telephone services; auction house and catalog fraud; consumer fraud and direct sales (e.g., virtual snake oils); online securities fraud.
- Other: Illegal interception of communications, commercial or corporate espionage, communications in

furtherance of criminal conspiracies, electronic money laundering.

Many of these risks appear to mimic traditional criminal exploitation, albeit often executed with unprecedented ease, speed, and impact across jurisdictions and thus the appropriate response is guided by new technological disciplines. The tasks of identifying cybercriminals and bringing them to justice pose challenges to law enforcement agencies across the globe and require a degree and timeliness of cooperation that has been until only recently regarded as impossible to achieve. However, computer intrusion is now more likely a predicate to a more serious offense. Forensic computing and evidence preservation protocols are essential to effective investigation and prosecution, especially given the trans-border nature of evidence collection (Pollitt, 2003; and see volume II, part 3, chapters 124–129). In most cases it is unlikely that a computer expert will be available at the crime scene and the risks of contaminating the evidence are high. Consequently, as with other types of crime, the emphasis is on following the traditional chain-of-evidence rules and ensuring that command and control assigns the relevant expertise promptly to the task at hand. Frequently this will require drawing on expertise in the private sector or academia.

Leading crime prevention scholars Newman and Clarke (2003) provide a review of crime prevention in the e-commerce context. In online situations, the theft of information and the manipulation of identity and trust are the key. In their approach, crime is an *opportunity* that occurs when the following conditions combine in time and place: the presence of motivated and tempted offenders and attractive and tempting targets in the absence of effective guardians. When this situation arises, crime will occur providing the offenders also have appropriate resources to undertake the crime. Consequently, efforts to reduce online offenses and e-commerce crime need to recognize these basic ingredients and the numerous pathways or opportunities for crime in the online rather than face-to-face environment. A crucial factor is how trust is acquired and maintained when merchants must be more intrusive about their (unseen) customers' identity and credit risk and the apparent ease in which trust is manipulated by fraudsters and others operating online. Risk-aversive systems of e-commerce therefore needed to be far more integrated than conventional environments and require more than passing attention to what the information security engineers like to call social engineering (see also volume III, part 2).

TRANSNATIONAL POLICING AND CYBERCRIME

The transnational nature of cybercrime reflects the process of globalization, which has intensified over the past two decades. The emergence of e-commerce, as well as the social dimension of the Internet and associated cybercrimes, is a striking example of the challenges to the independent capability of nation states to regulate social and economic order within their territories. Radical versions of globalization go further and suggest that the nation-state system of international relations no longer provides an effective methodology for regulating either domestic or transnational activity, especially international trade. In either version of globalization, substate actors, such as large commercial institutions, play a crucial role in the emergence of what Sheptycki (2000) terms a transnational-state system. Consequently the role of public–private police partnerships in the marketplace and the emergence of civil society on the Internet combined with public awareness are essential to contain cybercrime among ordinary users.

Although there now exist international conventions and treaties expressly designed to inhibit serious criminal networks or offenders operating across borders, the reach of these instruments is limited by the speed and scale of domestic ratification and consequential enabling laws. In dealing with IT crime, law enforcement is at a disadvantage because of the remarkable speed in which cybercrimes unfold against the typically low-speed cooperation offered by traditional forms of mutual legal assistance. The role of multinational agencies such as Interpol and the United Nations has never been more essential. Yet globally the results fall far short of creating a seamless web of bilateral or multilateral agreements and enforcement that would ensure a hostile environment for cybercriminals. The compatibility of criminal activity with these global changes is illustrated by the expansion and convergence of the profitable business of smuggling of humans, narcotics, or other illicit commodities with the development of communication infrastructure and trade.

The passage of the Council of Europe's Cybercrime Convention in December 2001 and its activation in July 2004 provides an international legal mechanism for cooperation in law enforcement and harmonization of laws (see Cross, 2003; Csonka, 2005; Esposito, 2004, Sato 2004), although 37 states have signed the convention and the "First Additional Protocol to the Convention on Cybercrime on the Criminalisation of Acts of a Racist or Xenophobic Nature Committed through Computer Systems" has been signed by 22 states but is yet to be ratified (see "Additional Protocol to the Convention on Cybercrime," 2003).

The convention, apart from enhancing mutual legal assistance (MLA), provides comprehensive powers to expedite preservation of stored computer data and partial disclosure of traffic data, to make production orders, to search computer systems, to seize stored computer data, to enable the real-time collection of traffic data, and to intercept the content of questionable electronic data. A number of countries outside the Council of Europe (United States, Mexico, Japan, Canada, and South Africa) were involved from the outset and have signed the convention, and many other countries, notably in South America, are considering similar model legislation (see OAS, n.d., for recommendations on an inter-American cybercrime instrument). The convention is also open to any nonmember state wishing to join (via a request to the Committee of Ministers of the Council of Europe). Given the pressing need for a broader multilateral structure for cross-border cooperation in the computer crime area, every effort should be made to open up the convention for accession by a wide number of signatories as soon as is practicable (Bullwinkel, 2005). Indeed many jurisdictions in the Asian region, Thailand in particular, have looked at the convention for guidance in formulating national laws.

These developments are mirrored by the increasing transnational activities of corporate and private security. Indeed, given the role of (self-) regulatory approaches by corporations, especially multinational enterprises, the role for transnational private policing is already significant and widespread (Johnston, 2000). For example, private security is the major provider in the payment card industry, intellectual property investigations, and airline security. The sheer volume of potential global cybercrime activity compels police partnerships with banks, telecommunication providers, and corporations. Partnerships also raise real issues of shared intelligence in environments of trust. Thus, the mobilization of so-called private police and non-governmental organizations in partnership with public police are essential if cybercrime is to be contained. Crime exploits the gaps in the sovereign state system of international relations and unless that is recognized in communities of shared fate, coordinated forms of regulatory endeavor (free, for example, from unduly strict or pedantic definitions of dual criminality) may be the only means to curtail cybercrime and its inevitable cross-border dimension.

United Nations Convention against Transnational Organized Crime

Since the early 1990s, beginning with the Eighth UN Congress on the Prevention of Crime and the Treatment of Offenders (1990), the United Nations, with its network of institutes on crime prevention and criminal justice, has been actively involved in addressing problems of transnational crime and cybercrime. The scope of computer-related crime affects every country in the United Nations, and the UN General Assembly in 2001 promoted new international efforts to assist member states in dealing with computer-related crime. The General Assembly, in the "Plans of Action for the Implementation of the Vienna Declaration on Crime and Justice: Meeting the Challenges of the Twenty-first Century" (General Assembly resolution 56/261), devoted a special section to "Action against High-Technology and Computer-Related Crime," in which it provided action-oriented policy recommendations for the prevention and control of these crimes. In 2002, the General Assembly again addressed the Vienna Plan of Action (General Assembly resolution 57/170) and through the Commission on Crime Prevention and Criminal Justice recommended that the Eleventh United Congress on Crime Prevention and Criminal Justice consider the plan. In 2001, the UN secretary-general explored various options for further work on high-technology and computer-related crime and considered the following four questions: whether a global treaty, if any, should be normative or legally binding; what relationship, if any, this would have to the UN Convention against Transnational Organized Crime; how a treaty, once concluded, could be kept up to date; and how it may accommodate issues such as privacy,

freedom of expression, and other human rights and commercial interests (Redo, 2004).

Although not specifically directed at cybercrime, the complementary role of the TOC Convention is a highly relevant global instrument for addressing some of the more nefarious aspects of cybercrime. The TOC Convention was introduced in December 2000 in Palermo, Italy. The TOC Convention has been signed by 147 states (and 82 parties) and came into force on September 23, 2003 (see "United Nations Convention," n.d.). The TOC Convention significantly extends the reach of the 1988 Vienna Convention against Illicit Traffic in Narcotics and Psychotropic Substances. The TOC Convention enables MLA between states and establishes several offense categories: participation in an organized criminal group, money laundering, corruption and obstruction of justice, as well as protocols in respect to trafficking in women and children (117 states and 64 parties with effect from December 25, 2003); illicit manufacturing and trafficking in firearms (52 states and 22 parties but not yet in force); and smuggling of migrants (112 states and 57 parties with effect January 28, 2004). Serious crime is defined broadly (conduct attracting punishment of four or more years' imprisonment). The basis of the framework is one that yields such flexibility in the definitions of both organized and transnational crime that it may serve as a generic legislative model across diverse common law and continental systems. In addition, the TOC Convention expressly refers (Article 29(2)) to methods for combating the misuse of computers and telecommunications networks; refers to provisions for training and materials, especially assistance for developing countries; and places obligations on capable states. The convention also establishes a number of principles and arrangements for international cooperation, which may be taken as an example of a potent global instrument against cybercrime, in line with Article 13.1(a) of the UN Charter emphasizing the progressive development of international law. They include regulations limiting the rule of double criminality for mutual assistance purposes and introduce enterprise responsibility.

The scope of the TOC Convention includes particular offenses signatories are obliged to criminalize (Articles 5, 6, 8, and 23) as well as serious crime (as defined in the Convention), "where the offence is transnational in nature and involves an organized criminal group" (see Article 3(1)). Importantly, the definitions of *serious crime* and *organized criminal group* reflect an understanding that organized criminal activity is no longer confined to a relatively narrow range of offenses traditionally associated with organizations such as Triads and the Cosa Nostra. The TOC Convention defines an offense as "transnational" if it is (a) committed in more than one state; (b) committed in a single state but planned, prepared, directed, or controlled in another state; (c) committed in one state but involving an organized group whose activities cross national boundaries; or (d) committed in a single state but has "substantial effects" in another state (see Article 3(2)). Many of the most common forms of cybercrime therefore qualify as serious crime because such offenses usually affect more than a single jurisdiction, often involve at least three or more actors, and are committed with the aim of achieving some financial or material benefit.

Article 27 deals with police-to-police cooperation and reflects the types of assistance routinely provided among police officials in the absence of a formal agreement and reflects international consensus on the need for close coordination between law enforcement authorities and to achieve this goal, states are encouraged to promote the exchange of personnel and other experts, including liaison officers. Additionally, signatories are required to "make full use of agreements or arrangements, including international or regional organisations, to enhance the cooperation between their law enforcement agencies" (Article 27(2)). With respect to formal MLA, Article 18 contains provisions nearly as lengthy and detailed as a comprehensive bilateral MLA treaty. States may seek assistance in connection with taking evidence or statements from persons, executing searches and seizures, obtaining business or government records, and identifying and tracing the proceeds of crime. A requested state has the discretion to decline assistance on the ground of the absence of dual criminality—a potentially significant limitation in the cybercrime context, as many countries do not have fully developed legislation in this area. The TOC Convention also provides for extradition (Article 16) even where a state party makes extradition conditional on the existence of a bilateral treaty. Article 16 represents a major step forward because its effect is to incorporate into existing bilateral treaty relationships the numerous offenses covered by the convention (Article 16(3)). Thus, where two states' parties have relied on outdated and narrow extradition agreements (such as a list-based treaty providing for extradition only in relation to a specified list of offenses), the TOC Convention will substantially expand the range of extraditable offenses between them (Bullwinkel, 2005; Cross, 2003).

THE COUNCIL OF EUROPE CYBERCRIME CONVENTION

The Council of Europe, founded in 1949, comprises 45 countries, including the members of the European Union (a distinctly separate entity), as well as countries from Central and Eastern Europe. Headquartered in Strasbourg, France, the CoE was formed as a vehicle for integration in Europe, and its aims include agreements and common actions in economic, social, cultural, legal, and administrative matters. As one of the two principal supranational organizations in Europe (the other being the European Union), the CoE is responsible for creating and implementing a wide variety of measures aimed at international crime and has adopted a number of widely used conventions on interstate cooperation in penal matters. In 1996, the CoE's European Committee on Crime Problems established a committee of experts to address cybercrime, which completed its work late in 2001.

The resulting Cybercrime Convention has three aims: to lay down common definitions of certain criminal offenses—nine are mentioned in the convention—thus enabling relevant legislation to be harmonized at national level; to define common types of investigative powers better suited to the information technology environment, thus enabling criminal procedures to be brought into line between countries; and to determine both traditional and new types of international cooperation, thus enabling cooperating countries to rapidly implement the arrangements for investigation and prosecution advocated by the convention in concert, for example by using a network of permanent contacts. The convention has received strong support from lawmakers and practitioners throughout Europe and beyond. But both the convention and its additional protocol have been criticized on various grounds by a number of associations, particularly those active in the protection of freedom of expression and also by industry elements (Csonka, 2005).

The CoE Convention on Cybercrime obligates signatories to criminalise a minimum list of specific offenses for which there was consensus and thus harmonized offenses to eliminate problems of dual criminality. The basic structure and content of the convention is outlined below.

Computer-Related Offenses

Title 1 addresses offenses against the confidentiality, integrity, and availability of computer data such as (1) illegal access of a computer system; (2) interception of nonpublic transmissions of computer data to, from, or within a computer system; (3) interference with computer data; (4) interference with computer systems, such as computer sabotage; and (5) the misuse of computer-related devices (e.g., hacker tools), including the production, sale, procurement for use, import, or distribution of such devices. Criminalizing illegal access, that is, hacking, cracking, or computer trespass, sends a clear signal that this conduct is illegal in itself and will be prosecuted: such intrusions may give access to confidential data (including passwords and information about the targeted system) and secrets or to free use of the system and might encourage hackers to commit more dangerous forms of computer-related offenses, such as computer-related fraud or forgery. The criminalization of illegal interception protects the privacy rights of data communication, seeks to deter the tapping and recording of communications between persons, and applies this principle to all forms of electronic data transfer, whether by telephone, fax, e-mail, or file transfer. The provision on data interference aims at providing computer data and computer programs with protection similar to that enjoyed by corporeal objects against intentional infliction of damage. Conduct such as damaging, deteriorating, or deleting computer data reduces the integrity or content of data and programs and also captures malicious codes and viruses (e.g., Trojan horses).

The convention criminalizes acts of computer sabotage and covers the intentional hindering of the lawful use of computer systems, including telecommunications facilities, by using or influencing computer data (system interference). The section covering misuse of devices establishes a separate criminal offense including some specific conduct (production, distribution, sale, etc.) involving access devices, which were primarily designed or adapted for misuse. Devices that are designed and used for legal purposes are not included. This offense therefore requires a particular purpose: that is, committing any of the other offenses against the confidentiality, integrity, and availability of computer systems or data.

Title 2 covers the traditional offenses of fraud and forgery when carried out through a computer system. For forgery, the intent of this provision is to protect computer data in the same manner as tangible documents, where such data may be acted upon or used for legal purposes (Esposito, 2004). Chapter 5 obliges signatories to criminalize the attempt to commit certain offenses on which the convention imposes a criminalization obligation, as well as aiding and abetting the commission of offenses, and also provides for the liability of legal persons.

Content-Related Offenses

Title 3 seeks to control the use of computer systems as a vehicle for the sexual exploitation of children and acts of a racist or xenophobic nature. This category of offenses concerns the subject or contents of computer communications and focuses on offenses related to children. The convention makes various acts (from the possession to the intentional distribution of child pornography) criminal offenses, thus covering all links in the chain. This provision criminalizes various aspects of the electronic production, possession, and distribution of child pornography. Most states already criminalize the traditional production and physical distribution of child pornography, but with increasing use of the Internet as the main method to distribute such material specific provisions were essential to combat this new form of exploitation. Other types of illegal content, such as racist propaganda, have also been included but in the form of an additional protocol criminalizing racist propaganda. Esposito (2004) notes that cybercrime is now defined as crimes committed against and through computer systems. The CoE's Cybercrime Convention was originally intended to cover only the first category, although there is a growing consensus, at least in Europe, of the need to address the second category (e.g., Article 9 of the Cybercrime Convention on cyber-pedopornography and the additional protocol on the fight against racism and xenophobia on the Internet).

Offenses Related to Copyright Infringement

Title 4 criminalizes willful infringements of copyright and related rights when such infringements have been committed by means of a computer system and on a commercial scale. This section targets the large-scale distribution of illegal copies of works protected by intellectual property rights (IPR). Infringements of IPR, in particular of copyright, are among the most commonly committed offenses on the Internet and cause concern both to copyright holders and to those who work professionally with computer networks.

Jurisdiction

Among the various important matters addressed by the convention was the question of jurisdiction in relation to information technology offenses, for example to determine the place where the offense was committed and which law should accordingly apply, including the case of multiple jurisdictions and the question of how to solve jurisdictional conflicts. This provision establishes criteria under which contracting parties are obliged to establish jurisdiction over the criminal offenses in the convention. The provision concerning jurisdiction also requires states exercising jurisdiction to coordinate when victims are located in different countries.

Procedural Powers

The procedural part of the convention, which also applies to the additional protocol, aims to enable the prosecution of computer crime by establishing common procedural rules and adapting traditional measures such as search and seizure and creating new measures, such as expedited preservation of data, to remain effective in the volatile technological environment. As data in the IT environment is dynamic, other evidence collection relevant to telecommunications (such as real-time collection of traffic data and interception of content data) has also been adapted to permit the collection of electronic data in the process of communication.

GLOBAL AND REGIONAL COOPERATION

Cybercrime creates an unprecedented need for concerted action from government and industry, but also unprecedented challenges to effective international cooperation. As noted, it is not always clear where computer-related offenses take place for the purpose of determining criminal jurisdiction. An offense may produce victims in many countries, as in cases involving virus attacks, copyright violations, and other offenses carried out globally through the Internet. This in turn may result in cross-border conflicts regarding which jurisdiction(s) should prosecute the offender and how such prosecutions can be carried out to avoid inconvenience to witnesses, duplication of effort, and unnecessary competition among law enforcement officials (Bullwinkel, 2005, and see volume II, part 2, chapters 92 and 93).

Most countries have domestic statutes relating to legal assistance and extradition and these sometimes enable extensive cross-border cooperation even in the absence of a formal treaty relationship. However, domestic legislation, while helpful for certain types of cooperation, is not a substitute for well-developed bilateral (or multilateral) agreements. For example, in the absence of a treaty establishing a direct relationship between legal authorities, requests for legal assistance must often be transmitted through the cumbersome and time-consuming diplomatic channel and this method is too slow to meet the challenges of cybercrime. Bilateral agreements such as MLA treaties and extradition treaties are more reliable means for international cooperation in criminal matters. Extradition treaties fall into two general categories: so-called list treaties and more modern dual criminality treaties.

In the case of list treaties, the contracting parties are bound to extradite only those offenses specified in the agreement. This may be a significant limitation, particularly in cases involving newer forms of crime (including many cybercrimes). The trend in modern treaty practice is to provide for extradition for offenses punished by imprisonment for more than a year under the laws of both parties. These dual criminality extradition treaties are as broad as the criminal laws of the requesting state but extradition for cyberoffenses may prove difficult, because some jurisdictions have not yet criminalized the conduct. When this occurs the requested state should follow the practice, accepted in international law, of interpreting the treaty in favor of extradition. The advantages of a bilateral treaty are that they limit the requested state's discretion to refuse assistance. In bilateral MLA treaties, the parties will in most cases be required to execute the request unless the request relates to a political offense or to an offense under military law that would not be an offense under ordinary criminal law or when the request would prejudice the requested state's security or similar essential interests. Subject to limited exceptions and the overall scope of the agreement, bilateral treaties ordinarily oblige the signatories to provide a wide measure of assistance and often the requested assistance must be provided even in the absence of dual criminality (Bullwinkel, 2005).

The various measures now operating within the European Union, the Council of Europe's convention, the establishment of Europol, and a European Judicial Network provide examples of greater law harmonization and fewer opportunities for transnational criminals to exploit jurisdictional and legal loopholes between nations. Thus international law enforcement has shifted from a peripheral to a central role within otherwise domestically focused law enforcement agencies. In addition, the lines between the policing function and national security appear less distinct, and considerable overlap now routinely occurs between the agencies countering threats such as cybercrime, low-intensity warfare, and terrorism.

Regional efforts outside of Europe are also underway via OAS, ASEAN and the APEC forum. Such developments have yet to evolve into fully institutionalized forms of cross-border legal cooperation or to determine the response of states within the region. There are now significant regional forums for police and other law enforcement officials and there is routine exchange of consular police liaison officers (Aiziwa, 2001). The leading organizations, apart from the United Nations and the Council of Europe, involved in developing international and regional efforts against cybercrime are briefly described in the following sections.

G8 Senior Experts Group on Transnational Organized Crime

The Group of Eight (comprising Canada, Germany, France, Italy, Japan, the United Kingdom, the United States and, since 1995, Russia), although originally established to coordinate economic policy, has also developed initiatives to combat international crime. At the Halifax Summit in 1995, G8 heads of state established a cross-disciplinary group of senior government experts (the Lyon Group) to address methods of combating transnational organized crime. In 1996, the Lyon Group devised 40 recommendations aimed at increasing the efficiency of collective action against transnational organized crime via two interrelated goals: strengthened capacity in the investigation and prosecution of high-tech crime and more effective regimes for cross-border cooperation in criminal matters.

The 40 recommendations cover a range of issues and emphasized the need to eliminate delay in respect to traditional forms of cross-border assistance (such as informal police cooperation, mutual legal assistance, and extradition) and a coordinated approach in tackling high-tech crime. As a consequence of these recommendations, the Lyon Group's High-Tech Crime Subgroup was established and quickly thereafter the 24/7 computer security network, which has now expanded to countries outside the G8. As of 2004, 39 countries participated in the global 24/7 cybercrime response network. Later, G8 ministers endorsed a set of principles and an action plan to respond to transnational cybercrime cases that included provision of adequate personnel and training to fight high-tech crime; domestic laws that criminalized cybercrime and ensure that relevant evidence, including traffic data, could be preserved and obtained expeditiously; and coordination with industry to ensure that new technologies are developed in a way that will facilitate law enforcement action against cybercriminals. The 1999 Moscow meeting later endorsed principles on transborder access to stored computer data and called for a comprehensive response to Internet fraud and more industry coordination. Most recently, a joint communiqué of the G8 home affairs ministers meeting in Washington on May 10, 2004, noted, given the activation of the Council of Europe's Convention on Cybercrime, that action was required "to encourage the adoption of the legal standards it contains on a broad basis" and "all countries must continue to improve laws that criminalize misuses of computer networks and that allow for faster cooperation on Internet-related investigations" (G8 Justice and Home Affairs Communiqué 2004).

ASEAN

ASEAN comprises 10 nations: Brunei Darussalam, Cambodia, Indonesia, Laos, Malaysia, Myanmar, Philippines, Singapore, Thailand, and Vietnam. Although ASEAN has provided a limited pan-Asian approach, it does form a basis for developing a wider regional forum for considering matters of MLA. Its approach, even given the developing nature of the region, mirrors the methodology of the European Union, but the cultural and economic diversity of Asia makes the process of multilateralism fraught with difficulty (Khoo, 2003). Yet understanding the different capacities and perspectives of how each state could contribute was an essential first step. The endorsement in October 2000 of the action plan of the ASEAN and China Cooperative Operations in Response to Dangerous Drugs in partnership with the UNDCP illustrates the quickening of MLA responses to transnational crime such as cybercrime. ASEAN has conducted four ministerial meetings on problems of transnational crime (Manila 1997, Yangon 1999, Singapore 2001, and Bangkok 2003). These meetings oversee the work of the Annual Senior Officials Meeting on Transnational Crime and consider the deliberations of meetings of the ASEAN National Chiefs of Police (ASEANAPOL) and their cooperative efforts to combat transnational crime. At the Second ASEAN Ministerial Meeting on Transnational Crime (held in Myanmar in 1999), ASEAN ministers issued another ambitious communiqué outlining a broad plan of action to enhance collective efforts against the many forms of organized criminality in the region. A group of senior government officials (referred to as the Senior Officials Meeting on Transnational Crime, or SOMTC) has been tasked to assist in the execution of ministerial initiatives and directives.

The theme of greater cooperation carried over to the Third and Fourth ASEAN Ministerial Meetings on Transnational Crime, at which ASEAN ministers reiterated their commitment to collaborate further in the battle against computer-related crime and called for a stronger partnership between ASEAN and other partners and agencies, including Interpol and the United Nations ("Joint Communique of the Third ASEAN Ministerial Meeting," 2001). As noted, the ASEAN anticrime institutions, particularly SOMTC, mimics the G8's Lyon Group, indicating the relevance of such frameworks for collective government action. Particularly significant is that ASEAN's law enforcement experts group reports directly to ministers and thus, like the G8's Lyon Group, has the capacity to develop policies with support at the highest levels.

The European Union and Europol

The 1957 Treaty of Rome established the European Economic Community, which in turn evolved into the European Union, established under the Treaty of Maastricht in 1992. The European Union has 28 member states and recently completed the accession of 13 countries in eastern and southern Europe (with some new members joining on May 1, 2004). It includes supranational institutions that address international crime by adopting joint positions, directives, and other instruments addressing a wide variety of criminal activities. Among the most important in respect to the coordination of law enforcement are the adoption of a common position on negotiations relating to the CoE Cybercrime Convention and EU conventions on mutual assistance in criminal matters and extradition (see European Union, Judicial Cooperation in Criminal Matters, 1998 and see generally http://europa.eu.int/scadplus/leg/en/s22004.htm visited May 9, 2005), the establishment of a European Judicial Network consisting of liaison magistrates and representatives responsible for international judicial cooperation, and tasked with facilitating cross-border cooperation (Decision establishing Eurojust, 2002). Further strengthening of MLA is contained in the April 19, 2002, "Proposal for a Council Framework Decision on

Attacks against Information Systems", adopted in June 2003 (European Union, 2003)

Included within the EU is the European Police Office or Europol, dedicated to increasing the efficiency of cooperation among the police agencies of EU member states, with an emphasis on targeting organized crime. Based in Brussels, Europol is accountable to the EU's Council of Ministers for Justice and Home Affairs. The organization is comprised of European liaison officers (who represent national law enforcement agencies across the European Union, including police, customs, and immigration officials) and Europol staff officers. Like Interpol, Europol's primary function is to support the operational activities of national law enforcement officials and was recently extended to include the fight against cybercrime. In furtherance of this, its representatives facilitate the exchange of information, provide analyses of criminal intelligence, generate strategic reports on trends and patterns of criminal activity, and provide technical expertise for ongoing investigations within the European Union. In addition, it is likely Europol will eventually assume a greater investigative and operational role.

The Organization for Economic Cooperation and Development

Established in Paris in 1960 by 20 countries (now 30 members), the OECD aims to promote economic and social welfare throughout the OECD by helping member states to coordinate their efforts to aid less developed nations. The OECD has established a presence in law enforcement, for example, by establishing the Bribery Working Group, whose efforts ultimately led to the adoption of a convention against commercial bribery. The OECD has been active in the area of cybercrime and online security, especially in regard to encryption technology, evaluating the balance between law enforcement and privacy concerns, and the means by which member states can coordinate encryption policy and in 1997 issued a series of guidelines addressing these issues. More recently, in the wake of the terrorist attacks of September 11, 2001, OECD governments developed a series of guidelines designed to counter cyber-terrorism, computer viruses, hacking, and related threats ("OECD Governments Launch Drive," 2002). Although the recommendations are not legally binding, they reflect consensus among key jurisdictions on issues affecting the security of the online environment.

A highly effective approach to intergovernmental law enforcement coordination that offers a template for transnational cooperation against cybercrime is the Financial Action Task Force (FATF) established at the G7 Paris Summit in 1989 and based in the OECD. FATF is a policy-making body whose aim is the implementation of legislative and regulatory reforms needed to combat money laundering. In 1990, FATF issued a series of 40 recommendations addressing ways to combat and deter money laundering. The recommendations are grouped into three broad categories (criminal law, banking law, and international cooperation) and serve as the basis for its activities. As a result of awareness-raising activities undertaken by FATF, a number of FATF-style organizations have also developed at the regional level including, in the Asian-Pacific region, the Asia/Pacific Group on Money Laundering, established in 1997, which operates in a manner similar to FATF and, in 2000, began to undertake a FATF-style mutual evaluation. A novel feature of FATF is that members are subject to peer review, a two-part process by which the group assesses implementation of the 40 recommendations. First, each FATF member conducts an annual self-assessment using a standard questionnaire. Second, periodically members are subject to a process of mutual evaluation, involving a site visit by three or four experts from other member governments. Mutual evaluation has proved effective in persuading governments to take steps to fill gaps in anti-money laundering (see generally http://www.oecd.org/fatf/AboutFATF_en. htm).

Interpol

The International Criminal Police Organization, or Interpol, consists of 181 member states. Headquartered in Lyon, France, Interpol coordinates its activities through national central bureaus in individual countries. Its mission is to support law enforcement organizations throughout the world, in particular by facilitating the exchange of information, coordinating joint operational activities of member states, and developing and sharing expertise and best practices covering a wide range of criminal offences (see generally http://www.interpol.int/Public/icpo/Guide). Nearly half of Interpol's member countries lack the infrastructure for online communication (Noble, 2003) and thus in respect to IT crime, Interpol has recognized the need for law enforcement officials to acquire specialized knowledge and has developed international training courses and manuals providing useful guidance for investigators working on computer-related crime (see http://www.interpol.int/Public/TechnologyCrime/ WorkingParties/Default.asp#steeringCom).

Interpol's General Secretariat has also supported the formation of regionally organized working groups comprising local experts in computer-related crime who meet periodically to share experiences and develop best practices (Noble, 2003). An example is the Asia-South Pacific Working Party on Information Technology Crime that currently meets annually and has undertaken projects relating to the handling of digital evidence, forensic tools, and training. Interpol has also endeavored to build close ties to existing regional structures in Asia, including ASEANAPOL, in an effort to build on regional cooperation by facilitating the development of regional intelligence databases and the wide dissemination of data through Interpol's extensive telecommunications network. Interpol has also stressed financial and high-technology crime as two of Interpol's top five priorities (along with drugs, terrorism, people smuggling, and organized crime). In addition, Interpol has increased its focus on intellectual property-related crime, because sophisticated and well-financed organized criminal groups increasingly carry out these offenses on a global scale. Interpol hosted an initial meeting of its Intellectual Property Crime Action Group in July 2002 (see generally http://www.

interpol.int/Public/FinancialCrime/IntellectualProperty/ Default/.asp).

Generic problems of forgery and counterfeiting were the focus of Interpol's exemplary efforts in establishing a Universal Classification System for Counterfeit Payment Cards secure Web site. This secure site provides up-to-date information on trends and techniques with respect to the forgery of payment cards and fraud and enables law enforcement officials around the world to retrieve forensic data as well as general intelligence. Payment card industry representatives working in the anti-fraud area will also have access to the otherwise closed system. Apart from illustrating how Interpol's unique clearing-house function can be adapted to meet new problems, it showed that with support from the payment card industry the law enforcement community can be better trained and equipped. This cooperation strengthens police capacity to respond to the theft of payment cards and other computer-related crimes that reduce the integrity of the market and limit the social benefits of Internet communications. As well as serving as an example of how international agencies can assist with essential tasks such as secure shared intelligence, it also exemplifies the role of private non-state actors in the prevention of crime (Newton, 2004).

APEC

Founded in 1989 in Canberra, Australia, for the purpose of promoting economic growth among member states, APEC now consists of 21 member economies. APEC is a consensus body that meets annually at the ministerial level and historically has focused on trade, but increasingly its members look to it as a vehicle for cross-border police cooperation. APEC's work over the past several years has also evolved (as with the G8 and OECD) into a number of areas relevant to cybercrime enforcement, including an Intellectual Property Rights Working Group, an Electronic Commerce Steering Group (ECSG; see generally http://www.apecsec.org.sg/workgroup/e-commerce. html) and the work of the Council for Security Cooperation Asia and Pacific (2004). The objective of the ECSG, established in 1999, is to coordinate APEC-related activities in the area of e-commerce. Thus far, the ECSG has not directly addressed law enforcement issues in an e-commerce environment, but enforcement also connects to APEC's general interest in improving consumer trust and confidence in e-commerce. Further, the ECSG's increasingly detailed work in the areas of privacy and security in the online environment implicates law enforcement concerns.

At their meeting in Los Cabos, Mexico, in October 2002, APEC leaders noted the threat of global terrorism and the importance of increasing the protection of global infrastructures and that global communications are only as secure as its weakest link, and collectively committed to enact comprehensive cybersecurity laws, on a par with existing international standards, particularly the CoE Cybercrime Convention and UN General Assembly Resolution 55/63 of 2000; identify or create national cybercrime units and international high-technology assistance contact points; and establish computer emergency response teams that exchange threat and vulnerability assessments and information. They also called for closer cooperation between law enforcement officials and businesses in the field of information security and fighting computer crime by endorsing the APEC Cyber-security Strategy. The elements of the strategy cover legal developments, information sharing and cooperation, security and technical guidelines, public awareness, training and education, and wireless security. APEC's Telecommunications and Infrastructure Working Group has been most active in sponsoring projects to increase the ability of APEC member economies to more effectively address cybercrime, including through greater intergovernmental and public–private sector cooperation (see http://www.apectelwg.org/apecdata/telwg/28tel/estg/telwg28-ESTG-09.htm).

Urbas (2005) observed, in concluding an overview of legislation in Asia, that the development of legislation designed to counter intellectual property offenses and cybercrime showed that although some states had enacted new laws, many remained ill-equipped to deal with the cross-border nature of these offenses. Orlowski (2004) also reported an APEC cybercrime legislation survey involving 14 nations that found all had some legislative provisions to address cybercrime and to support law enforcement (see http://www.apectel28.com.tw/document/webword/estg/telwg28-ESTG-07.doc). However, mutual legal assistance, extradition arrangements, and provision of cross-border information in respect of computer offenses were found in only half the countries surveyed. The survey noted that the main concerns related to the difficulties in requesting the collection and preservation of evidence in real time, issues relating to jurisdiction for offenses and offenders, and lack of, or limitations in, mutual assistance and extradition arrangements. APEC has called for further work to develop laws and procedures that facilitate the investigation and prosecution of cross-jurisdictional cybercrime. As noted above, it is essential to continually monitor progress and where necessary provide assistance and encouragement to ensure that MLA is not impeded.

Summary of Measures for Regional Cooperation

Given the diversity of the above activities aimed at improving regional and international cooperation, the basic ingredients for a global approach can be deduced. Grabosky and Broadhurst (2005) outlined the basic elements of an effective regime for regional cooperation in combating cybercrime that include the following:

- Improve security awareness by providing adequate resources to secure transactions and equip system operators and administrators
- Improve coordination and collaboration by enabling systematic exchanges between the private sector and law enforcement including joint operations
- Take steps to ensure that technology does not outpace the ability of law enforcement to investigate and enact substantive and procedural laws adequate to cope with current and anticipated manifestations of cybercrime

- Broadly criminalize the conduct (including juvenile offenders) and focus on all violators big and small
- Strengthen international initiatives by updating existing treaties and agreements to recognize the existence, threats, and transnational nature of high-tech computer-related crimes and strive for legal harmonization
- The development of forensic computing skills by law enforcement and investigative personnel and mechanisms for operational cooperation between law enforcement agencies from different countries, that is, 24/7 points of contact for investigators.

In the future, organized crime may be expected to recruit IT specialists, intimidate corporate insiders to obtain access to IT systems, and use anonymizers and encryption in furtherance of cybercrime. In addition, there is evidence of the deployment of intelligent malicious software designed to elude detection by antivirus software. Automated intelligent computer and network attack capabilities allow remote initiation of attacks to be directed at any computer or network on the Internet while making it more difficult to identify the actual source of the attack. These advanced forms of intrusion code enable users to gain competitive advantage by extracting sensitive economic data from competitors and provide data (such as customers' records) for extortion and denial-of-service offenses. Most significant, attacks are instantaneous and often remote, disregarding national sovereignty. Whether they are the work of a 14-year-old, a terrorist, a foreign intelligence service, or an organized criminal may not be immediately apparent; all must be investigated. However, digital technology also affords new opportunities for individual citizens to communicate efficiently with police. An example is the Internet Fraud Complaint Center, which operates in the United States and receives online information from members of the public relating to questionable online activities that are evaluated and referred to the appropriate agency or jurisdiction.

Digital footprints are fragile or ephemeral, so swift action is often required. This becomes very difficult when an attack transits multiple jurisdictions with different regimes for preserving evidence. Traditional methods of law enforcement are therefore no longer adequate. A slow formal process risks losing evidence, and multiple countries may be implicated. Following and preserving a chain of evidence is a great challenge. Among the challenges faced by investigators is the enormous increase in storage capacity in today's computers and the challenge to effective and efficient searches that this entails. Almost every case will soon require computer forensics, and evidence will be located in multiple places. The challenge faced by investigators will be one of *information management* (Pollitt, 2003). Even local crimes may have an international dimension, and assistance may be required from all countries through which an attack was routed.

Many nations and regional bodies such as the Council of Europe have addressed the problem of cybercrime and laws exist that criminalize the unauthorized access and unlawful use of computers, but such laws are neither universal nor uniform. Concerns remain focused on the weakest links in the supposedly seamless security chain necessary to prevent cybercrime by predatory criminal groups. Comity thus can only be ensured if wealthy states and affected industries are prepared to extend aid to those less capable states or agencies. Consensus is the best strategy, for the suppression of computer-related crime entails a mixture of law enforcement, technological, and market-based solutions. It can be argued, however, that a strict enforcement agenda is usually not feasible because of the limited capacity of the state. It is also feared that overregulation could stifle commercial and technological development. Those skeptical of a heavily interventionist approach also argue that the marketplace may at times be able to provide more efficient solutions than the state to the problems of computer-related crime.

Although there is consensus about the risks of computer-related crime, apart from criminalizing the conduct at a global level, there is much less consensus about what might be done to prevent it. There is concern that the technological solution to information security is a mirage, more hope than reality, and that dependence on the promise of a technology fix is an approach fated to fail. So also is the faith in a deterrence-based approach in which the criminal law is deployed as the principal instrument of prevention. Deterrence is unlikely to succeed in all or even some circumstances, and experience with conventional crime suggests that over reliance on the law, as a deterrent or moral educator alone, is unlikely to help substantially even if legitimately supported by the community.

Fundamentally systems can be designed to lessen their vulnerability to criminal exploitation. Cybercrime is often facilitated by vulnerable software, much of which is designed with user-friendliness and convenience in mind rather than security. The common industry response is for manufacturers to structure their licence conditions to avoid potential liability and then to make patches available as vulnerabilities become apparent later on. Whether market forces will eventually drive the widespread development of truly secure software remains to be seen. Commercial enterprises may be in a position to achieve more protection than poorly resourced law enforcement agencies could deliver. Microsoft Corporation has now, it seems, reflected on its failure to lead the market in respect to consumer safety and to recognize that the market demands a secure and trusted environment if computers and information technology are to realize their full potential.

In conclusion, controlling crime involving digital technology and computer networks will require a variety of new networks: networks between police and other agencies within government, networks between police and private institutions, and networks of police across national borders. Over the past five years, considerable progress has been made within and between nations to develop the capacity of police to respond to cybercrime. But the pace of technological change will continue unabated and the adaptability of cybercriminals will continue to pose challenges for law enforcement. The extent of transnational law enforcement cooperation achieved thus far, promising though it may be, can only be regarded as a beginning.

GLOSSARY

Comity   An association of civility and mutual benefit among nations, especially in regard to the recognition of the laws and customs of other nations.

Dual Criminality   A rule governing or limiting the reach of a bilateral or multilateral treaty or convention, or a cross-border law enforcement that authorizes assistance only if the offense is criminalized in the law of both states.

Extradition   The formal arrangements between nations that allow fugitives, suspects, or witnesses in one country to be transported to the country in which the crime was committed.

List Treaty   A bilateral or multilateral treaty providing extradition or other legal assistance such as the seizure and preservation of evidence that is limited to the list of offenses.

Mutual Legal Assistance   The general term for all informal and official forms of police, legal, and criminal justice cooperation between states usually provided on a reciprocal basis.

Social Engineering   The manipulation of human behavior for the purposes of revealing passwords, source code, and other confidential information without recourse to unauthorized access to a computer system by means of exploiting or intrusion software.

CROSS REFERENCES

See *Cyberterroism and information Security; Global Aspects of Cyberlaw; Law Enforcement and Computer Security Threats and Measures; Law Enforcement and Digital Evidence; Privacy Law and the Internet.*

REFERENCES

Aizawa, K. (2001). Current mechanisms for international cooperation in criminal matters: Mutual legal assistance and extradition, 24/7 points of contact network, and training in the field of computer crime. In R. Broadhurst (Ed.), *Proceedings of the Asia Cyber Crime Summit*. Hong Kong: Centre for Criminology, University of Hong Kong, pp. 133–140.

Bullwinkel, J. (2005). International cooperation in combating cyber-crime in Asia: Existing mechanisms and new approaches. In R. Broadhurst & P. Grabosky (Eds.), *Cyber-crime: The challenge in Asia*, pp. 269–302. Hong Kong: University of Hong Press.

Council of Europe. (2003, January 28). *Additional Protocol to the Convention on cybercrime on the criminalisation of acts of a racist or xenophobic nature committed through computer systems*. Retrieved August 9, 2004, from http://conventions.coe.int/Treaty/en/Treaties/Html/189.htm

Council for Security Cooperation Asia and Pacific. (2004). *Cybercrime and its effects on the Asia Pacific region: Report of the Transnational Crime Working Group*. Retrieved August 4, 2004, from http://www.police.govt.nz/events/2001/e-crime-forum/cybercrime_and_its_effects.html

Cross, I. (2003). Enforcement and prosecution strategies in the 21st century: Combating multi-jurisdictional crime. In R. Broadhurst (Ed.), *Bridging the GAP: A global alliance on transnational organised crime*, pp. 25–36. Hong Kong: Hong Kong Police Printing Department HKSAR.

Csonka, P. (2005). The Council of Europe Convention on Cybercrime: A response to the challenge of the New Age? In R. Broadhurst & P. Grabosky (Eds.), *Cyber-crime: The challenge in Asia*, pp. 303–326. Hong Kong: University of Hong Press.

Decision establishing Eurojust (2002, 28 February). Retrieved May 9, 2005, from http://europa.eu.int/scadplus/leg/en/lvb/l33188.htm

Esposito, G. (2004). The Council of Europe Convention on Cyber-crime: A Revolutionary Instrument? In R. Broadhurst (Ed.), *Proceedings of the 2nd Asia Cyber Crime Summit*. Hong Kong: Centre for Criminology, University of Hong Kong, pp. 54–64.

European Union, (2003). Framework Decision. Retrieved May 9, 2005, from http://europa.eu.int/information_society/eeurope/2005/all_about/mid_term_review/security/index_en.htm

European Union (1998 June, 29) Judicial Cooperation in Criminal Matters. Retrieved May 9, 2005 from http://europa.eu.int/scadplus/leg/en/lvb/l33055.htm

G8 (2004, May 11), Justice and Home Affairs Communiqué, Washington. Retrieved December 11, 2004 from www.g7.utoronto.ca/justice/justice040511_comm.htm

Grabosky, P., & Broadhurst, R. (2005). The future of cyber-crime in Asia. In R. Broadhurst & P. Grabosky *(Eds.), Cyber-crime: The challenge in Asia*, pp. 347–360. Hong Kong: University of Hong Kong Press.

Iden, R. L. (2003). Cyber crime: What's the threat, the challenge, and the policing response. In R. Broadhurst (Ed.), *Bridging the GAP: A global alliance on transnational organised crime*, pp. 69–73. Hong Kong: Hong Kong Police, Printing Department HKSAR.

International Narcotic Control Board. (2001). *Report of the International Narcotic Control Board 2001* (UN E/INCB/2001/1). Vienna, Austria: Author.

Johnston, L. (2000). Transnational private policing: The impact of global commercial security. In J. W. E. Sheptycki (Ed.), *Issues in transnational policing*, pp. 21–42. London: Routledge.

Joint Communique of the Third ASEAN Ministerial Meeting on Transnational Crime. (2001, October 11). Retrieved November 21, 2003, from http://www.aseansec.org/5621.htm

Khoo, B. H. (2003). Police cooperation in fighting transnational organised crime: An Asian perspective. In R. Broadhurst (Ed.), *Bridging the GAP: A global alliance on transnational organised crime*, pp. 44–50. Hong Kong: Hong Kong Police, Printing Department HKSAR.

Moore, D., Shannon, C., Voelker, G. M., & Savage, S. (2003). *Internet quarantine: requirements for containing self-propagating code*. Paper presented at the meeting of the IEEE INFOCOM, San Francisco, CA.

Newman, G., & Clarke, R. (2003). *Superhighway robbery: Preventing E-commerce crime*. Devon, UK: Willan.

Newton, J. (2004). Interpol and the cards industry: Global partnerships to deliver local solutions. In R. Broadhurst (Ed.), *Proceedings of the 2nd Asia Cyber Crime Summit*. Hong Kong: Centre for Criminology, University of Hong Kong, pp. 124–127.

Noble, R. (2003). Interpol's new approach: A return to basics. In R. Broadhurst (Ed.), *Bridging the GAP: A global alliance on transnational organised crime*, pp. 37–43. Hong Kong: Hong Kong Police, Printing Department HKSAR.

OECD *governments launch drive to improve security of online networks*. (2002, August 7). Retrieved from http://www.oecd.org/document/53/0,2340,en_2649_201185_1946997_1_1_1_1,00.html

Organization of American States. (n.d.). *Group of experts and cyber crime*. Retrieved October 11, 2004, from http://www.oas.org/juridico/english/cyber.htm

Orlowski, S. (2004). APEC activities to address cybercrime through public/private cooperation. In R. Broadhurst (Ed.), *Proceedings of the 2nd Asia Cyber Crime Summit*. Hong Kong: Centre for Criminology, University of Hong Kong, pp. 37–45.

Pollitt, M. (2003). Digital evidence in Internet time. In R. Broadhurst (Ed.), *Bridging the GAP: A global alliance on transnational organised crime*, pp. 82–85. Hong Kong: Hong Kong Police, Printing Department HKSAR.

Redo, S. (2000). Crime as the growing international security threat: The United Nations and effective countermeasures against transnational economic and computer crime. UNAFEI Resource Material Series No. 55, Tokyo, Fuchu, Japan, pp. 117–139.

Redo, S. (2004). The UN. In R. Broadhurst (Ed.), *Proceedings of the 2nd Asia Cyber Crime Summit*. Hong Kong: Centre for Criminology, University of Hong Kong, pp. 18–29.

Sato, T. (2004). Countermeasures against cyber-crime in Japan. In R. Broadhurst (Ed.), *Proceedings of the 2nd Asia Cyber Crime Summit*. Hong Kong: Centre for Criminology, University of Hong Kong, pp. 139–145.

Semple, K. (2004, January 27). E-mail worm snarls computers around globe. *New York Times*. Retrieved January 28, 2004, from http://www.nytimes.com/2004/01/27/technology/27CND-VIRU.html

Sheptycki, J. W. E. (Ed.). (2000). *Issues in transnational policing*. London: Routledge.

Staniford, S., Paxson, V., & Weaver, N. (2002). How to own the Internet in your spare time. In *Proceedings of the 11th USENIX Security Symposium (Security '02)*. Retrieved December 9, 2003, http//www.icir.org/vern/papers/cdc-usenix-sec02/

Sussmann, M. A. (1999). The critical challenges from international high-tech and computer-related crime at the millennium. *Duke Journal of Comparative and International Law, 9*, 451–473.

United Nations. (2003). *World public sector report 2003: E-government at the Crossroads, Sales No. E.03.II.H.3*. New York: Author.

United Nations convention against transnational organized crime. (n.d.). Retrieved August 9, 2004, from http://

www.undcp.org/crime_cicp_signatures_convention.
html, visited August 9, 2004.

Urbas, G. (2005). Cyber-crime legislation in the Asia-
Pacific region. In R. Broadhurst & P. Grabosky (Eds.),
Cyber-crime: The challenge in Asia, pp. 207–242. Hong
Kong: University of Hong Press.

European Union, http://www.europa.eu.int/scadplus/leg/
en/lvb/114015b.htm; visited December 11, 2003.

European Union, http://www.europa.eu.int/scadplus/leg/
en/lvb/133055.htm; visited December 11, 2003

Interpol, http://www.interpol.int/Public/FinancialCrime/
IntellectualProperty/Default/.asp

Digital Identity

Drummond Reed, *OneName Corporation*
Jerry Kindall, *Epok, Inc.*

WHAT IS DIGITAL IDENTITY?

As an emerging technology, the meaning of *digital identity* depends to a large extent on who is talking about it. In general, the term refers to the class of technologies, standards, services, and applications that enable a real-world identity to be represented digitally on a network, manage the data related to the identity (its *attributes*), and control access to various network resources. Technically, any addressable resource on a network has identity; in many circles, though, the term is most meaningful when describing how an individual user's personal identity and personally identifiable data are modeled, represented, controlled, and shared on the network.

Digital identity touches on issues of trust, privacy, security, and interoperability that are becoming vital to the evolving Internet. As e-commerce and e-business become everyday realities, consumers want to control information about themselves, while at the same time being able to share it with trusted parties. For their part, businesses want to serve consumers better by knowing more about them, while at the same time being required to respect consumer privacy concerns and comply with regulations. And from a technology standpoint, the rapidly growing Web services infrastructure requires a way to authenticate users that is not tied to network location or device. The solutions to these problems are all aspects of digital identity.

DIGITAL IDENTITY AND PRIVACY

Public awareness of privacy issues has been steadily increasing over the past decade, in large part to the increasing use of the Internet and its ability to permit data sharing on a scale never possible before. Telemarketing, junk faxes, and unsolicited bulk e-mail (spam) are small but annoying signs of the growing erosion of privacy. Consumers have begun to reject this erosion, not only by calling for legislation (e.g., in the United States, 2003's Controlling the Assault of Non-Solicited Pornography and Marketing (CAN-SPAM) Act and the Federal

Trade Commission's Do Not Call list), but also by demanding products and services to protect their privacy. A good example is telephone services. Phone companies used to offer only one privacy service (an unlisted phone number). Now most offer caller ID, which lets subscribers see who is calling before picking up the phone; caller ID blocking, which lets subscribers keep people who have caller ID from finding out who they are; and finally anonymous call blocking, which automatically rejects calls from people who use caller ID blocking. There are plans afoot to bring something similar to the caller ID model to e-mail.

In the United States, civil libertarians have long been sounding the alarm about the amount of personal data stored in databases owned by corporations and the government. After September 11, 2001, many Americans have said they are willing to sacrifice some privacy to feel more secure, but to others, the existence of government surveillance systems such as Carnivore and Echelon point to an Orwellian future. What worth is security, they argue, echoing Franklin, if it comes at the cost of important constitutional protections? Some fear that safeguards against misuse of information are insufficient. They warn that employers, for example, might eventually use medical records to deny employment to those with unfavorable health conditions (or, as DNA testing becomes more precise, even to those with the *potential* to develop such conditions) by partnering with health insurers and hospitals to share this information.

These concerns have spurred a flurry of legislative action internationally. In the United States, the Gramm-Leach-Bliley Act (GLBA) makes financial institutions provide their customers with a written privacy policy, regulates how they can share their customers' personal data for marketing purposes, and requires them to allow consumers to opt out of marketing from nonaffiliated third parties. Also in the United States, the Health Insurance Portability and Accountability Act is intended to guarantee the security and privacy of personally identifiable health information, while requiring that standard data formats be used to allow these data to move with the patient among health care and insurance providers. In the United Kingdom, the Data Protection Act requires firms to tell consumers on request exactly what personal data about them they have in their files and also establishes guidelines for collecting, storing, and sharing this information. The European Data Directive establishes a clear and stable regulatory framework for the movement and framework of personal data for the entire European Union.

What impact will digital identity technology have on privacy issues? The long-term effects of any new technology are impossible to predict, of course, but there are reasons to believe that many of the effects will be positive. Digital identity technologies allow individual users to set the terms under which their personal data can be shared with others and for what purpose these data may be used. Unless the requester of the data agrees to respect these terms, the protocol does not allow the data to be shared. In this scenario, digital identity provides a way for organizations to demonstrate compliance with emerging privacy regulations. In fact, in the coming years, the authors believe that a key role of government will be to make agreements between digital identities legally binding, which has the potential to strengthen consumer privacy significantly.

The other, potentially more troubling, side of the digital identity coin is the technology's ability to link data stored in numerous databases into a coherent virtual view of an entity. Corporations and governments have, collectively, amassed thousands of pieces of information about every customer and citizen. Currently, this information is in thousands of separate databases, which makes it a limited threat to privacy. Digital identity has the potential to unify these databases not just within a single organization, but also across organizational boundaries—meaning that the data kept about consumers by different companies might eventually be compared and coordinated. The technical and business challenges involved in this kind of consolidation of personal data are not trivial, given the competitive nature of business, and digital identity is hardly a silver bullet for solving them; the threat is not necessarily imminent. Clearly, though, there is a vital role for government here, with a *minimum* requirement being legislation requiring companies to tell consumers on request what personal data they keep, where it comes from, and who else it will be shared with. A stronger solution would be to require corporations to disclose any data held by a corporation about an individual to that individual on request, much as mandated by the U.K.'s Data Protection Act. This is an area in which consumer lobbies and civil liberties watchdog groups could have significant leverage by educating the public on the issues—and now is the time to start.

The government, in addition to regulating digital identity, will also become a significant user of this new technology. In the United States, the federal government alone maintains thousands of databases in its hundreds of agencies; each of the 50 states (plus territories) also has a government, and there are thousands of county and municipal governments below them, each with their own databases about the citizenry. Consolidating all these bits of data could save billions of taxpayer dollars and enable a new level of government effectiveness and service. The United States' new Department of Homeland Security is also interested in digital identity technology as a means of allowing the country's various local, state, and federal intelligence, law enforcement, and emergency response agencies to aggregate the data each agency has, until now, maintained separately. Until relatively recently, it was routine for wanted criminals to be able to renew a driver's license or even receive public assistance without catching the eye of the police, because each government agency had its own database. Linking some of these records has made law enforcement efforts dramatically more effective and has helped many agencies become more responsive to their constituency's needs, and this trend will only be accelerated by digital identity.

But there's a darker side as well. Homeland Security has already expressed its intent to also aggregate information collected by other parties (e.g., library checkout records, credit histories, travel itineraries). There is no serious technical barrier to doing so. Certainly this would be of tremendous value in identifying and locating criminals, but it also carries obvious potential for abuse. Generally speaking, post-9/11 America is significantly more receptive to such ideas than it was just a few years ago, and there is a real danger that fear will permit unwise policy to be made and to stand unchallenged. Civil libertarians point to some of the provisions of the Uniting and Strengthening America by Providing Appropriate Tools Required to Intercept and Obstruct Terrorism (USA PATRIOT) Act as examples.

Once information about citizens has been aggregated, it can be mined to look for patterns deemed suspicious by the authorities, and any individuals identified could then be subjected to closer scrutiny. Of course, this can be (and is being) done to an extent without digital identity technology, but because the entire purpose of digital identity is to model individuals and aggregate their data, digital identity makes data mining much easier and more effective. Any intelligence-gathering technique based on data mining will inevitably result in innocent people being put under surveillance, even if the information gathered never reaches human eyes. This possibility should concern us deeply.

Law enforcement is, to be fair, involved in an ever-escalating information arms race. Criminals are becoming more and more sophisticated in their use of technology. There have already been reports, for example, of organized crime using data mining to identify and assassinate informants in their ranks. Must we as a society deny the police techniques that may be the only way to root out the worst criminals and terrorists? By analogy, few Americans would dream of barring police from carrying firearms, even though a gun is also a tool ripe for abuse. When criminals are heavily armed, the public recognizes that the police require equal firepower if society is not to be overrun by criminals. Thus, the authors believe that law enforcement and intelligence-gathering organizations will, in the end, be allowed to use data mining, although we likewise expect that this use will be strictly controlled and limited. Citizens must continue to demand due process and accountability from their governments and must remain vigilant for even the possibility of abuse.

At minimum, data mining should be held to the same legal standards and privacy expectations as other permitted forms of surveillance, such as wiretapping, although due to the nature of the technology, even stricter controls may be appropriate.

DIGITAL IDENTITY AND IDENTITY THEFT

In identity theft, an individual's personal information (often stolen from a wallet or snatched from the mail) is used to impersonate that person for the purposes of fraud. For example, an identity thief might obtain enough personal information to obtain credit or write bad checks in another person's name. Victims of identity theft often face years of frustrating harassment from creditors as they try to clear their record.

Identity theft has become a problem due to the fact that most people simply do not know the people with whom they do business very well. Indeed, this is utterly impractical in modern society. The cashier at the local grocery store must trust that the customer's identification is valid before accepting her check. Similarly, the customer must trust that the grocery store clerk will not steal her identity using the information on her check and driver's license. Anyone who can copy identity credentials can pretend to be someone else, taking advantage of the victim's good reputation to obtain lines of credit, pass bad checks, and commit other forms of fraud. In recent years, the situation has been aggravated by the Internet, where it is trivial to assume a fictitious identity and fraud of all types has flourished.

Before 1998, the year in which identity theft was made a federal crime in the United States, it was difficult to prosecute identity theft cases. The U.S. Department of Justice's identity theft Web site recounts the case of one notorious fraudster who ran up $100,000 worth of credit card debt, obtained a mortgage, and bought homes, motorcycles, and handguns using a stolen identity—and then called the victim to taunt him. This brazen scammer eventually declared bankruptcy in the victim's name. The identity thief, who had a previous felony conviction, served a brief sentence for violating firearms laws, but was not made to pay restitution to the victim, whereas the victim and his wife spent more than 4 years and $15,000 of their own money to rehabilitate their damaged credit and reputation.

Although identity thieves can now be punished, the authorities still have to catch them. Meanwhile, the victim's credit report rapidly accumulates negative information, affecting his or her ability to obtain not just loans but also utility service, insurance, and housing. Due to their artificially poor credit scores, identity theft victims must pay more for many things or are forced to make larger deposits or down payments and may even find it more difficult to find employment.

Thanks to the Internet, credit ratings are only one way scammers wreak havoc. If an identity thief obtains illegitimate access to a victim's eBay auction account, for example, the thief can use the account's reputation to defraud dozens of buyers before enough negative feedback accumulates to make buyers reluctant to bid. If a thief obtains the password to an online brokerage or banking account, the victim's finances are put directly at risk.

Often, Internet identity credentials are obtained using a technique called *phishing,* in which the criminal sends an official-looking e-mail to hundreds of potential victims claiming to be from, say, eBay or their bank and telling them that their password has expired. A link in the message directs them to a Web page that also looks official but is run by the scammer; if the victim falls into the trap and enters his or her credentials on this bogus Web page, they are sent directly to the identity thief.

Beyond the possible financial consequences are social ones, which can be no less disastrous. When someone learns another user's password and impersonates him or her in an online forum, where people know him or her only by the words he or she has typed, the impersonator can quickly ruin a hard-won reputation, and the legitimate user could lose his or her account or even, in extreme cases, be sued for libel. Even e-mail is not immune; the technique of sending out bulk e-mail with a victim's address in forged reply headers (such that the victim receives all the bounces and complaints and gains a reputation as a spammer) is common enough to have its own jargon name among mail administrators: the "Joe job."

Another new technological threat to identity is hacking. The businesses with which customers share personal information often keep it on file. Even assuming that access to this information is properly controlled and that the employees who do have access are trustworthy, both big assumptions, it is still possible that personal information could be compromised by a security breach. Sadly, bank computers do not seem to be nearly as secure as bank vaults; in one widely reported incident, a hacker obtained 8 million credit card numbers from a credit card processor.

Although identity fraud cases resulting in financial loss are crimes and can be prosecuted, the consequences even in nonfinancial cases are such a hassle that it makes sense to avoid becoming a victim. Here are some commonsense things you can do to protect your identity from being stolen:

- It should go without saying, but keep a close eye on your wallet or purse—these are still the most common vectors of identity theft. When traveling, take only the cards needed for the trip and keep them in a place where they will be hard for a pickpocket to get to, such as a front pocket.
- Check the mailbox regularly so sensitive information (such as financial documents) does not sit waiting for identity thieves. When going on vacation, have the mail held. If mail suddenly stops coming, check to make sure a fraudulent change of address has not been filed with the post office or the bank. Drop off sensitive mail in a locked mailbox or at the post office rather than leaving it out for the letter carrier.
- Keep vital documents with your social security number (SSN), driver's license number, credit card number, and other sensitive information in a safe place—preferably *literally* in a safe—especially if you have roommates or

have hired help, such as a maid service, in your home on a regular basis.

- Use a crosscut shredder to destroy documents with sensitive personal information, including expired credit cards, before throwing them away.

- Never write down personal identification number (PIN) codes or other passwords. Avoid using the same passwords for more than one thing (e.g., do not use the same PIN for voice mail and an ATM card), and avoid using easily guessed passwords. Change passwords regularly.

- Guard your SSN carefully, as it is an important identity credential. With legitimate exceptions such as your employer and creditors, always ask why the person who is requesting it needs it. The SSN is not intended as a general-purpose identification number, and companies should not use it as one. Avoid doing business with companies that ask for a SSN but do not actually need it, and never have it printed on checks.

- Sign up for a credit monitoring service, and check your credit report and your bank statements regularly for errors and signs of fraud.

- Ask the companies you do business with not to keep personal details on file and ask for a reason if they insist on doing so. Prefer businesses that are willing to respect your wishes in this regard.

- Do not give out any personal information on the phone to anyone who calls, even if they say they are with your bank or another company with which you do business. (Be especially suspicious if they say they are from "the bank" or "the phone company" but do not identify which one by name.) If you are interested in buying a product or service offered by phone, ask that the offer be sent in the mail, or request a phone number at which to call the seller, and check the company's reputation with the Better Business Bureau before proceeding.

- Many banks ask for your mother's maiden name when you open an account, so that later they can ask you for it as a means of confirming your identity. Don't use your mother's *real* maiden name, as it is easily obtained from public records.

- Use encryption to secure the personal information and Web passwords stored on a computer, especially if you use a laptop. Do not set up the computer to log in automatically to this program when it is turned on. This way, if your computer is hacked or stolen, the intruder or thief will get only gibberish rather than the information needed to steal your identity.

- Use a firewall program to keep the computer from being hacked and antivirus software to protect you from malicious e-mail attachments that attempt to steal personal information and send it elsewhere. Do not open e-mail attachments sent by unknown senders. Use the computer's update feature regularly to obtain security updates as they become available.

- Be wary of any e-mail or other electronic message that claims you need to reset your password or enter a new credit card number, even if it looks official. Call the company or go to their Web site by typing in the uniform resource locator (URL), rather than using the link provided in the e-mail.

- When submitting sensitive information to a Web site, look for the small lock icon in the browser that indicates a secure connection. This icon not only means that information will be transmitted securely, but it also means that the site is the one it claims to be in the URL. Be suspicious if the browser displays a message about an expired or invalid certificate or if the URL does not begin with "https" or has an @ sign in it.

- Be aware of the privacy policies of the companies you deal with so as to know who will have access to your personal information. If it is unclear, ask. Most legitimate companies have privacy policies posted on their Web sites.

- Shield the keyboard when entering a PIN or password, or make sure no one is close enough to see what you enter.

- Before selling or disposing of a computer or a hard disk, be sure to remove all personal information from it. Simply deleting the files or reformatting is not enough; use a "wipe" or "secure delete" program that overwrites the disk several times with gibberish and then reformat and do a fresh install of the programs that came with the computer.

The role of digital identity in combating identity theft is a supporting one. One important feature of digital identity technology is that all personal information is under the owner's control and is only shared with others under contract. Links allow companies access to your information when they need it, without requiring that this information be stored in their systems; this makes it much more difficult for a hacker to, for example, obtain millions of credit card numbers by breaking into one card processor's computer. Identity service providers may offer logging features that record exactly who accessed your personal information, and when, which will help to keep tabs on its use.

From the other side, identity technology will help large companies secure their systems by allowing them to require explicit contracts between customer data and the employees and departments that access it, helping to protect personal information from misappropriation by employees and business partners of the company. As mentioned earlier, businesses are already under regulatory pressure to protect customer information and ensure privacy, but the mishmash of systems in a typical large business makes it difficult to demonstrate compliance. By enforcing permissions at a protocol level, digital identity makes it possible to prove the security of a company's systems and implement rigorous privacy controls throughout an organization.

In the United States, the Fair and Accurate Credit Transactions Act of 2003 provides some additional measures to help prevent identity theft. For example, merchants are now prohibited from printing more than five digits of your credit card number on a receipt, and consumers are entitled to a free credit report every year to check it for signs of fraud. Financial institutions are now mandated to look for patterns common to identity theft and credit reporting agencies must flag credit files whose owners have reported identity theft. But as before, vigilance will remain the most important component of any strategy to avoid becoming a victim of identity theft. Tools for monitoring access to private consumer data will not help if consumers do not use them; technology to help businesses become more accountable will not help unless businesses are actually held accountable. Ultimately, everyone pays the price for identity fraud losses, so it is everyone's responsibility to minimize them.

DIGITAL IDENTITY AND WEB SERVICES

The increasing prominence of Web services as a new way to achieve cross-application and cross-domain data integration also highlights the need for digital identity. Because Web services are almost as new as digital identity, it is worth taking a brief look at the technology now.

Unfortunately, the term *Web services* has caused a lot of confusion among the uninitiated. Most Internet users have bought something at Amazon.com, searched the Web using Google, or used their bank's Web site to check their checking account balance. These are services available on the Web, but they are not Web services. *Web services* is a technical term that applies in a very specific way to automated application-to-application communications—it is an extension of the similar use of the term *services* in a local computing environment. Many operating systems offer services that applications can call on for messaging, checking spelling, displaying Web pages, and so forth. Web services are a way to use another computer's services using Web protocols.

To further explain the difference between the Web and Web services, we will compare the two directly. A Web site is designed to be used by humans, and it includes site-specific formatting and graphics for, among other things, branding purposes. For example, Bank of America's Web site looks nothing like Citibank's, and neither looks anything like Bank One's. This is inconvenient if a computer program, rather than a person, wants to access a service offered by a Web site. Suppose, for example, a user of a personal finance program wants to automatically import a checking register into the program from a bank's Web site. To do this, the personal finance program would need to know how to find that information on every bank's Web site. That would require the developers of personal finance programs to provide a different interface module for every bank in the world, and this is completely impractical. A much better answer is a standard interface for all bank Web sites that lets personal finance software, once properly authenticated, retrieve a customer's checking register.

The Web services paradigm is an attempt to address this problem and others like it, which are legion. Four key standards are involved. First, the extensible markup language (XML) is an established World Wide Web Consortium (W3C) format for data representation. The simple object access protocol (SOAP) is a W3C specification that defines how programs running on one computer can request that certain operations be performed on another. The Web services description language (WSDL) is an XML schema for describing a Web services interface in a standard, machine-readable format. Lastly,

Universal Description, Discovery, and Integration (UDDI) allows a Web site to automatically discover which services are available from a given provider and determine how they should be accessed. All of these are either already open standards or are in the process of being standardized, and an overwhelming number of major industry players (including IBM, Microsoft, Sun Microsystems, Hewlett-Packard, and BEA Systems) have thrown their weight behind the concept.

With Web services, applications and portable devices can access specific information and services over the Internet without a full-fledged Web browser. When a harried traveler is checking a flight departure time on his cellular phone, he or she does not want the whole American Airlines Web site, and he or she does not want to try to use Internet Explorer on his or her phone's tiny screen. He or she just wants to punch in the flight number and find out whether he or she is going to make his or her flight or not. This is a perfect application for Web services. At the same time, Web services allow services on the Internet to begin communicating directly with each other, as well as with users. For example, a Web portal might use Web services to retrieve top headlines from a news site and then format them according to the portal's own look and feel before displaying them on the site.

As with Web sites, some Web services are public, whereas others are accessible by subscription only or only to certain users (e.g., a company might operate some Web services only for its employees). It is necessary to authenticate users before allowing them to use these restricted services. Requiring separate credentials for each service quickly becomes a headache, especially when a single user might access the service from a mobile device, from one or more Web portals, and from a desktop application. What is needed is some way to ascertain the identity of users no matter how they access a given Web service, to model users as independent digital entities rather than only representing the devices they use. This is digital identity.

To complete the circle, digital identity services can themselves be provided as one or more Web services, making them widely available to users everywhere.

DIGITAL IDENTITY ILLUSTRATED

A simple example will serve to illustrate the basic model of digital identity. When modeling an information system, a common object-oriented methodology involves thinking of the system in terms of actors who engage in transactions with each other. For example, when a customer withdraws money from an ATM, there are three actors: the customer, the ATM, and the bank mainframe with which the ATM communicates to verify the customer's balance before dispensing money. The actors and the actions between them can be represented using a sequence diagram like that in Figure 1.

In this scenario, the ATM has interactions with the user in which it asks for information such as a PIN and the amount to be withdrawn. The ATM also has interactions with the bank mainframe, asking it to verify the account's current balance and telling it to record the withdrawal. (For simplicity, this diagram does not show exceptions,

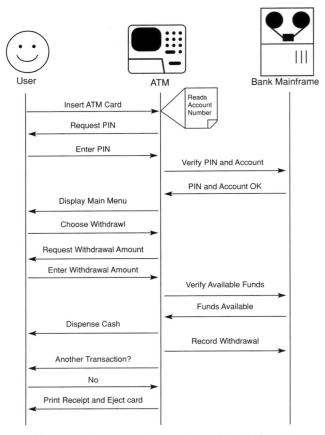

Figure 1: Sequence diagram for ATM withdrawal.

such as what happens when there is not enough money in an account to fulfill a request.) These various interactions are possible because the bank owns all the data involved in the transaction. The bank balance is stored in its computer (along with a PIN), and although the account number is stored on the ATM card that the customer carries, that number is issued by, and thus in that sense belongs to, the bank.

The bank has plenty of other information on its customers, too: their mailing addresses for statements, their SSNs for reporting interest income to the Internal Revenue Service, and their complete transaction histories. Though it describes customers, this information, too, belongs to the bank in the sense that customers do not have the authority to change it, even though they are the source of much of it. If a customer wants to change the address to which his or her statements are mailed, for example, the customer must provide the new address to the bank so it can be entered into its systems.

The ATM system works because all the actors involved in ATM transactions trust each other, and they trust each other because the bank controls all the information involved. The ATM knows that it can trust the balance data, because it knows it is connected to the bank's mainframe and not to some other computer. The bank's mainframe knows that it can trust the ATM, because it has provided credentials that prove it is an ATM owned by the same bank. And the ATM and bank know that they can trust

the customer, because the customer has inserted a card with an account number issued by the bank and entered the correct PIN for that account. In digital identity terminology, the bank's ATM system comprises a single *trust domain*. All the information in the system is owned by a single entity, and all the components of the system are deemed trustworthy. The bank considers the other information customers have given them (such as mailing address and SSN) to be trustworthy as well, because it is in their systems and thus under their control.

To keep the above scenario simple, it was assumed that the bank that owns the ATM is the bank at which the customer has an account. In the real world, of course, banks join ATM networks; customers can use their card at any ATM in a network that their bank is a member of (although the bank that owns the ATM may charge a fee). To achieve this, the member banks have had to agree on a common protocol for exchanging data. Each bank has had to decide what credentials they will accept from other banks' ATMs to verify that they are in fact legitimate ATMs and which credentials the users of these ATMs will have to provide. They have also had to agree on what data will be provided over the network, and they have taken steps to protect the security and integrity of the data as they flow from point to point. In doing so, the banks have enlarged their trust domain to encompass all banks on the network, at least for ATM-related transactions.

With digital identity standards, trust domains can be expanded even further. In other words, what if not just banks but *every person and business in the world* could communicate and exchange their data with anyone, just like the member banks of an ATM network? What is necessary to establish trust between all these entities? And what will such a world be like?

DIGITAL IDENTITY AND THE CONSUMER

Consumer digital identity applications are the obvious place to start exploring digital identity, as these have received the lion's share of media attention. Microsoft Passport, the Liberty Alliance, and the Extensible Name Service (XNS) from the XNS Public Trust Organization (XNSORG), all initially led with consumer-facing applications.

The digital wallet is perhaps the most common example. A typical digital wallet contains a customer's mailing address, preferred shipping addresses, and information about the credit cards frequently used for online purchases. When using a digital wallet to check out at an electronic storefront, the customer simply chooses the address and credit card to be used for the order from a pop-up list, rather than being forced to enter this information at each new store. Even more conveniently, when the customer moves or is issued a different credit card number, he or she simply changes the appropriate fields in the wallet—once. The simpler a site makes the purchase process, the more likely it is to close the sale (Amazon's patented One-Click ordering is a case in point), so the digital wallet is potentially a big win for both consumers and merchants—as well as for banks, who earn a fee on credit card transactions.

Single sign-on (or SSO) is another consumer service. SSO lets users log on, or *authenticate,* at one Web site and then use that authentication at other participating Web sites. For example, after users log into a Microsoft Passport account, they can get access to Hotmail, the Microsoft Network, Expedia, eBay, and other Web sites without having to enter their password again. It is particularly convenient to combine this with the digital wallet feature, making the wallet even more attractive for users.

Microsoft Passport is the most widely deployed single sign-on and digital wallet service at present, although adoption by consumers, vendors, and content providers has been slower than Microsoft had hoped, and a large percentage of the sites that accept Passport are owned by or affiliated with Microsoft. Part of the reason for the slow uptake is that Passport was designed as a centralized service. Microsoft stores all Passport data, including transaction records, on its own servers. Early technology adopters tend to be just the sorts of users who will insist on the privacy and security of their personal information, and Microsoft will have to provide more than convenience to win their trust. (Microsoft settled with the Federal Trade Commission in 2002 over complaints about the privacy and security of Passport subscriber data.)

The Liberty Alliance specifications and XNS both support a feature called *federation,* where users can choose from a number of hosts for their personal data and cooperating sites can share authentication seamlessly, much like an ATM network. Microsoft has announced that Passport will also move to this model.

But while digital wallets and SSO are part of digital identity, they are by no means the whole picture. It is, in fact, possible to implement these sorts of applications without even really modeling the underlying identity. A more robust conception of digital identity provides an infrastructure for a wide variety of applications.

THE IDENTITY WEB

To better understand the emerging vision of digital identity, we will look at the characteristics of a hypothetical full global identity infrastructure. Keep in mind that no such thing exists yet, and no one organization will build it. Instead, people and companies will begin using smaller identity-related applications as these applications become compelling. In fact, at first, users might not even realize they are using something called *digital identity*. But as more and more people use identity services, they will naturally want these services to work together, further increasing their value in a classic network effect. This in turn makes additional identity applications more and more compelling, which brings more users into the identity fold, which further increases the network effect. This eventually results in the *identity web*—a global interlinked digital identity community, the virtual world in which, with the proper permissions, everyone can share anything with anyone.

To benefit from the network effect, naturally, identity applications must be interoperable, which means that a standard identity protocol must be adopted by all players.

As of this writing there are two key digital identity standards emerging: extensible resource identifier (XRI) and XRI data interchange (XDI) and Liberty Alliance Project. Both are open public standards. XRI and XDI are two separate but related standards being developed by technical committees at the Organization for the Advancement of Structured Information Standards (OASIS), a global not-for-profit consortium that already maintains many of the key XML interoperability standards. These two standards are the successors to XNS, an early identity technology; key players in the development of XNS are also involved in XRI and XDI.

The Liberty Alliance is currently publishing its own specifications, though it may eventually contribute its work to another established standards body (some public reports have mentioned OASIS). Liberty's 65 members include American Express, MasterCard, Visa, America Online, Intuit, RSA Security, Sony, Sun Microsystems, Verisign, Fidelity Investments, Novell, Citigroup, Hewlett-Packard, Nokia, Vodafone, General Motors, Cisco Systems, Bank of America, PriceWaterhouseCoopers, EDS, Cisco Systems, Earthlink, OneName, and many others. This impressive array of members demonstrates the importance of interoperability to major corporations and provides enterprise customers with the assurance that Liberty standards will be viable from both a technical and a business standpoint.

The following sections draw on concepts from both of these emerging standards, with a particular focus on XNS, XRI, and XDI—largely because the authors are coauthors of the XNS specifications, but also because XNS reflects the broadest vision of digital identity available in the marketplace to date.

IDENTITY DOCUMENTS AND ADDRESSING

The core concept of digital identity is the *identity document,* an XML document that stores the data for which any given real-world entity is authoritative. People own their name and address, for instance, so this information would best be stored in an individual's personal identity document. An identity document can represent a person, a corporation or other organization, a software application, a server, or a directory category. Applications can query an identity document for just the attributes they are interested in; it is not necessary to retrieve and parse an entire document.

The identity document is hosted by an *identity service provider* on an *identity server.* As with Web hosting services, in the identity web there would be a multitude of identity service providers a user could choose to host his or her identity. Strong encryption would be used to ensure that only authorized users have access to the information in the identity document. Because digital identity is by its nature peer to peer (any identity can talk to any other identity), particularly savvy users could even choose to host their identity on their own computer for additional peace of mind.

To access the identity document itself and link to the information stored in it, an addressing scheme is needed.

Standard uniform resource identifiers (URIs) such as hypertext transfer protocol (HTTP) URLs, which are used to address documents on the Web, do not have the full range of functionality required by digital identity infrastructure. For example, links between identities should continue to work even if a digital identity moves to another host. (The details of how links are used to share data will be revealed shortly, but for now it suffices to note that broken links would render some shared data inaccessible, limiting the utility of sharing data in the first place.) To provide this higher level of functionality, XNS introduced a new addressing scheme that can contain identity IDs or identity names. An *identity ID* is a string of numbers and other characters that forms a permanent address for an identity. An identity ID resolves to the URI where the given identity is hosted, and although the identity ID never changes, the URI it resolves to can change if the identity is moved to a different host. Each attribute stored in an identity document, as well as the identity document itself, has an ID, and this ID, too, is the same as long as the object exists. In XNS, document and attributed IDs are assigned and resolved by the ID service.

Identity IDs, however, are assigned more or less arbitrarily and are structural rather than semantic. Typically, they are not very user friendly. Just as the domain name system (DNS) was invented to allow human-friendly host names to be assigned to computer-friendly Internet protocol (IP) addresses, so digital identity needs a way to make identity IDs easier for people to use. Enter the *identity name*. The XNS name service allows any object with an identity ID (i.e., an identity document or an attribute stored in it) to be assigned any number of names, which can be changed at the identity owner's whim. The naming service also allows an identity owner to organize the attributes stored in his or her identity document into categories or folders. For instance, phone numbers could be stored in a collection called "phone," allowing a cellular phone number to be named something like "=JohnSmith/phone/mobile." It is important to remember that although an identity document or an attribute might be located by name initially, when a link is established, it always uses the unbreakable ID.

The XRI builds on the concepts introduced in XNS addressing, while making addresses more like URIs. Version 1.0 of the XRI specification divides an address into two parts: the *authority portion* and the *local access portion*. The authority portion is analogous to the hostname portion of a URI (although the XRI specification does not specify what the authority portion points to, typically in identity applications it points to an identity document or to an identity host). Within each portion, an XRI can contain persistent segments (analogous to XNS's IDs), reassignable segments (analogous to XNS's names), or a mixture of both. Once the authority segment has been resolved, the identified authority can be passed to the local access segment to retrieve the desired resource. The authority identified by the authority segment does not need to be given the local access segment, and vice versa, enhancing privacy.

In the beginning, it is likely that organizations will operate their own resolution services for customers and partners. For example, a bank might offer identity services to its customers, which would work with the bank's merchants but with no one else. In other words, the bank would provide resolution services only for its customers and merchants. The identities that can be located through a single resolution service are referred to as a *community*. Using the process of federation, mentioned earlier, communities can agree to share these services and thereby merge their smaller communities into larger ones. As identity services become more popular, a demand will eventually arise for *global community services* that, like the global Internet's DNS, allow any identity in the world to be found by its XRI or similar address.

IDENTITY LINKING

Once attributes have been stored in identity documents that can find each other by ID, name, or XRI, the stage is set for letting these identities share data. *Linking* is the way information from one identity is shared with another. Links are almost always made using persistent identifiers such as XNS IDs, and because IDs never change over the life of an object, links between IDs never break while the linked object exists. When one identity needs information that is controlled by another identity, the first identity simply links to the data in the second. Then the two identities agree as to how those shared data will be kept current in the second identity—that is, how they will be synchronized.

An example will make the linking concept clearer. A person's mailing address, for all practical purposes, belongs to the person. (Street addresses are actually assigned by the city, but the city rarely changes them. More commonly, people change their own addresses—by moving. Thus, a mailing address can reasonably be treated as an attribute of an individual's identity.) The bank needs a mailing address to send statements, so the customer gives them this information, and the bank puts it into its system. As noted earlier, however, the bank controls that copy of the address. When customers move, they must ask the bank to change it—even though it is *their* address! Change-of-address forms are so unremarkable that it barely seems that this is a problem worthy of solving. But just envision all the copies of information that people and companies keep about other people and companies; a vast amount of storage is used for redundant copies of all this information, and an equally vast amount of effort is expended on keeping all the copies current.

In the identity web, the bank would simply link to a mailing address stored in the customer's identity document, using the address's immutable ID. To the bank's systems, it looks just like a copy of the customer's mailing address is stored in their database. However, the customer's copy of his or her mailing address, stored in the customer's identity document, is *authoritative*, meaning the customer can change it and the bank has to go along. When the customer moves, he or she simply updates the address stored in his or her identity document, and the customer's identity service provider would then send a digitally signed copy of the updated address to his or her bank. Their system would verify the digital signature to make sure the update was genuine and then automatically store the new address in the customer database. In essence, by eliminating redundancy, digital identity turns the world into an object-oriented, distributed, well-normalized database.

Of course, some of the technical details have been glossed over here. The XNS protocol actually gives the bank in this scenario several options for synchronizing with a customer's identity data. For example, instead of having updates pushed to them, the bank could retrieve a copy from the customer's identity document any time they needed it by sending a digitally signed request. Or the bank could just be notified that the address has changed and use some other method to update its database (for example, mailing a change-of-address form to the new address to verify that it is correct). The exact details of how the updates are handled are implementation specific, but regardless of how they are accomplished, linking of identity data is arguably the most important concept in the sphere of digital identity.

Linking also provides the means to consolidate multiple digital identities that represent the same real-world entity. For example, a bank maintains a digital representation of each customer's account balance and activity. This information actually is part of an individual person's identity—it is the customer's account, and the customer's money, and the customer's transactions—but, for security reasons, the bank must maintain the authoritative copy. (It just wouldn't do to let people change their own account balances!) In an identitycentric world, the bank might do this by creating an identity document on its identity server for each of its customers. The attributes of these documents would be customers' various accounts, and each account would have a balance and a transaction history associated with it, among other things. So an individual's bank-hosted identity represents the real-world person just as much as that person's personal identity, hosted elsewhere, that contains his or her mailing address. One is a person's financial identity and the other is a household identity. By creating a link between a person's financial identity and his or her household identity, this customer can create a single *virtual* identity document that allows him or her to view all personal information (including the portions maintained by the customer, the customer's bank and doctor, and other parties) in one place. Any number of third-party digital representations of a single real-world identity may be linked in this fashion.

A final application for linking is to intentionally split a single identity's attributes into two or more locations for security reasons, for much the same reason the bank maintains account balances rather than allowing customers to do so. For example, using linking, a cellular phone can become a digital wallet. By storing credit card numbers on a smart card inside the phone and configuring the phone to require its owner to unlock it using a PIN before it releases a credit card number, users can enjoy increased security for online shopping. To complete an online purchase, the phone must be turned on, it must have the user's (encrypted) smart card installed, and the user must approve the purchase by entering the PIN. This makes it very difficult for anyone but the legitimate owner to use a digital wallet for purchases without the owner's knowledge or approval. Using linking, however, users could still see this information as part of their main identity and update it as easily as any other information in their profile.

DATA SHARING PERMISSIONS AND CONTRACTS

As described so far, digital identity is a framework for sharing everyone's identity data freely with everyone else. Most people, however, simply are not willing to share all of their personal data with everyone who might want them. Indeed, people are very discriminating with their personal information. They only give out their credit card information to stores they feel are trustworthy. They only give out their direct e-mail addresses to others if they believe they will not get more junk mail by doing so. They pay extra to have their telephone number not listed in the white pages. Therefore, one of the central principles of digital identity is to give control of private data to the people and organizations to whom it belongs. A digital identity infrastructure must support flexible privacy control at the protocol level to gain the trust of users (Figure 2).

XNS's digital identity infrastructure handles privacy through a data structure called a *contract* that defines the terms under which data may be shared. For example, a contract between a personal identity and a merchant identity might specify that the following:

- The shipping address stored in the identity document will be used only to fulfill the current order and not to mail advertising
- The merchant will not retain the address in its systems any longer than is necessary for the purposes of shipping the order
- The merchant may not share the address with any other parties without customer consent

How are contracts established? Generally, they are negotiated automatically. The XNS Negotiation service, which is used to establish contracts, is an implementation of the Privacy Framework developed by the International Security, Trust, and Privacy Alliance (ISTPA). In a transaction between a customer and a merchant, the merchant identity would present to the customer identity a proposed contract indicating what information is needed, what it will be used for, how long it will be kept, and whom it may be shared with. If the customer has previously told his or her identity service provider what terms are acceptable and provided preferred values for the kinds of data the merchant wants, negotiation could be completed entirely without human intervention. More commonly, the customer would insist on having the opportunity to review and approve the terms and select the data to be shared before finalizing the transaction. The resulting contract records the mutually agreed-on terms and governs the links between the two identity documents between which the data will be shared. When a permission requirement has been established on a data attribute stored in an identity document, it becomes impossible for other identities to access that data without first agreeing to a contract.

Because the resulting data structure is called a *contract*, the obvious next question is whether it is legally binding. The law in most countries is moving steadily toward

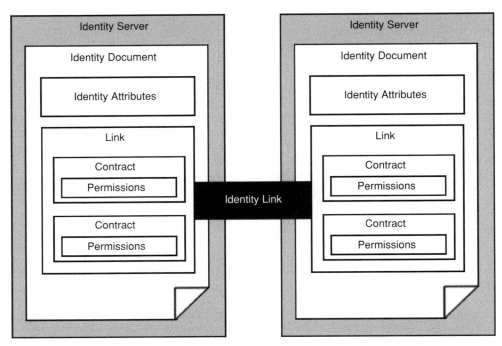

Figure 2: Identity link between two identity documents.

accepting digital signatures as legal proof of assent. The United States passed the Electronic Signatures in Global and National Commerce Act (popularly known as E-Sign) in 2000. Using established cryptographic techniques, it is possible to provide reasonable proof of the identities of the parties agreeing to the contract and to prevent repudiation. Still open, however, is the question of whether contracts automatically negotiated by software agents on behalf of the signers are legally binding. The authors expect such contracts to be affirmed in the coming years.

Even without the weight of the law behind them, data-sharing contracts make it easier for consumers to access and update the personal information that businesses keep about them, as well as allowing consumers to hold businesses more accountable for the ways they use their customers' data. Although some companies might not care for this level of accountability at first, eventually businesses will embrace it wholeheartedly, because contract-based data sharing provides a foundation of trust for building closer, more profitable relationships with customers, employees, suppliers, and partners.

OTHER DIGITAL IDENTITY SERVICES

Being able to locate identity documents and forge permission-protected data-sharing links between them makes a wide variety of digital identity applications possible. This is the foundation of XNS and XDI and also of Liberty Phase 2. Indeed, analysts predict that data sharing will be the single largest purpose for which digital identity technology will be used in the near term. Beyond sharing, however, digital identity enables other services that will make the Internet and many common communications functions safer, easier, and faster.

Many of these are *trust services*—services that make it easier to perform trusted digital transactions. For

example, an *authentication* service is needed to prove that a digital identity represents a real-world principal and to assert that real-world identity across trust domains. Once a user logs into his or her digital identity, in other words, other services can tell that person is the same person who created the identity, and therefore they can be assured that they are dealing with a single individual at all times. This enables single sign-on and customization features and also supports the creation of contracts between identities.

Certification service allows digital identities to make assertions about the truth of the data stored in them. A third party, called a *certifying authority,* provides a cryptographic signature that essentially claims that it has inspected the data in question and found them to be complete and accurate. A real-world example is a driver's license. It would be much better to keep a digitally signed version of a driver's license in an identity document rather than just including the raw data the license contains; the digital signature from the issuing government would allow this credential to be used as proof of age, for instance. Certification supports the mapping of real-world identity credentials into the digital realm and thus gives digital contracts their force.

A *session* service combines authentication and certification to support a browser-based SSO solution. The third party in this case is a *session server,* which issues a cryptographic token certifying that acceptable credentials were presented to begin a session. This *session token* is then either accepted by various Web resources in place of traditional credentials (such as a user ID and password) or is transparently mapped to acceptable local credentials. The Liberty Alliance version 1.0 protocols are essentially a federated session service.

A *hosting* service allows one identity to host another. When an identity document is hosted by an identity server, the hosting service is the service responsible for establishing the new identity's persistent address. In XNS, the identity server itself is represented by an identity document. Identities hosted by a server are registered with the server's *host identity* so that they can be located by name, ID, or XRI.

Finally, in an extensible identity protocol, some way must be provided for applications to discover new identity services they do not know about. In XNS, this is accomplished with the discovery service, which designates a *publishing identity* for each service's definition and allows the service's data formats and message descriptions to be retrieved in standard formats including XML Schema (XSD) and WSDL. The discovery service allows anyone to define new identity services that are completely interoperable with existing identity applications.

In XNS 1.0, the 10 services ID, name, discovery, hosting, data, folder, authentication, certification, session, and negotiation—plus the core service, which defines data formats and an abstract base class for messages—comprise the base services. These are, in the authors' estimation, the absolute minimum requirements for a fully functional identity infrastructure. Other potentially useful services include the following:

- *Reputation* service to allow the trustworthiness of an unknown identity to be evaluated based on the opinions of other identities
- *Introduction* service to allow two identities that currently link to a third identity to cut out the intermediary and link directly—essentially a three-way negotiation or friend-of-a-friend service
- *Directory* service to provide the ability to register and locate participating identities not just by name and ID but by certain attributes (e.g., locating all identities at a specific company or in a particular area)
- *Address translation* services allow popular identifiers such as e-mail addresses and phone numbers to be used as identifiers for identity documents, with full delegation capability

DIGITAL IDENTITY AND ENTERPRISE APPLICATION INTEGRATION

Large companies contain vast repositories of identity data. A lightweight directory access protocol directory server contains identity data; so does a customer relationship management system, an accounting system, or an order processing system. Even a network management tool, an e-mail server, or a collaboration server could be viewed as containing identity data. (Anything that stores and manages data about entities can be considered as an identity application in a loose sense.) None of these tools are designed to talk to each other, even though the benefits of doing so might be enormous.

The problem is compounded in obvious ways when companies join forces; it is not uncommon for a large enterprise to have several separate, incompatible information systems performing the same functions for its various divisions, like a fossil record of the company's merger history. It is the redundancy problem from this chapter's very first example—the same information stored in many places, wasting vast amounts of storage and requiring enormous effort to keep in sync—writ *very* large. The biggest corporate giants have hundreds or even thousands of different mission-critical databases stored in mutually incompatible systems around the world.

Addressing these issues in a comprehensive way all at once can be mind-bogglingly expensive and time consuming. Designing, implementing, and testing just data format conversions can take thousands of engineer-hours. Then there is the expense of replacing the legacy systems with more modern software and the inevitable headaches that come with trying to tie it all together, not to mention the additional time required for retraining employees on the new systems.

Reenvisioning digital identity as an integration layer on top of existing enterprise information systems makes it possible to undertake enterprise data integration in small, easily managed pieces. The legacy systems are kept intact and remain authoritative, with the data needed for a given application transparently mapped into identity documents using *adapters*, software modules that serve as a bridge between the identity server and the legacy systems. Using this approach, new integration applications can be built on top of the identity layer rather than talking directly to the enterprise layer and can be developed with modern object-oriented methodologies, with the legacy systems treated more or less as black boxes. Companies can begin with the proverbial low-hanging fruit—the most obvious enterprise integration projects with the clearest potential for substantial return on investment (ROI) or the best chance to achieve a new competitive edge (Figure 3). As these projects prove themselves out, more projects can be undertaken with increasing confidence, until at some point the network effect comes into play and the ROI of identity solutions already implemented increases exponentially by allowing new connections to be made. In the coming identitycentric world, it will eventually become a competitive disadvantage to store identity-related data in places where it cannot be shared (given appropriate permissions) with others.

An example will serve to illustrate how digital identity can be used for integration. Suppose two mail-order companies merge into one bigger company that now has two separate systems for processing orders and for mailing catalogs. An identity-based approach to integrating these systems, to allow customer service representatives to access all data stored in both systems without even having to know that there *are* two separate systems, would be to create an identity document to represent each customer. By means of adapters, individual data elements in these identity documents would be retrieved from the existing systems. The identity document stores any record keys necessary for finding the appropriate data in the two systems. When an application asks the identity server for the catalog mailing address from a customer's identity document, the identity server retrieves this data on the fly from the mailing list application. Requesting the last order date causes the identity server to query the order processing system for this bit of information. If the customer's entire identity document were requested, all the information needed from all systems involved would be retrieved behind the scenes, by means of adapters, and stitched

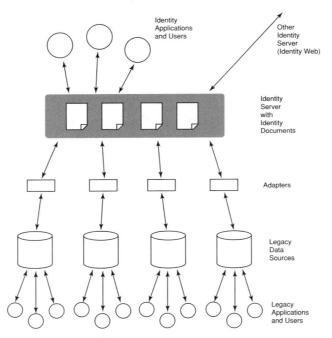

Figure 3: Digital identity as an enterprise integration layer.

together into an identity document conforming to the syntax required by the standard (e.g., XML). When an application changes something in the identity document, the adapters write the changes back out to the legacy systems. Adapters can also take care of any necessary protocol details (e.g., interfacing with the desired network stack), do encoding conversions (e.g., Extended Binary-Coded Decimal Interchange Code to Unicode), and provide caching services and even encryption and decryption.

The application never needs to know or care that any of this is happening; it uses the same simple, standardized object-oriented methods to read or write data regardless of where it is stored and how it must be accessed. Existing applications that are used with the legacy data systems can remain authoritative or can even be run simultaneously with the identity-based applications. In fact, if desired, the legacy systems can even be switched out from under the identity layer—suppose they need to be upgraded for other reasons—and, assuming the appropriate adapters have been written for the new systems, the identity-based applications will never notice. The adapter approach makes it possible for system integrators to build generic solutions for common integration problems; for each installation, they need only to write adapters and perform the specific customization necessary to get the new applications running on top of whatever legacy data stores a particular client has installed.

Once a data source becomes identity enabled, it is easy to add functionality incrementally. The first step might be to integrate the order processing and mailing list systems of two merged companies, as described above, so that customer data are more accurate and customer service staff can work more efficiently. The next step might be to add a Web interface to the system so that customers can

access and update this information on their own, reducing staffing needs for the call center. Next, the accounting system might be integrated to allow customers to see and pay their invoices online. Then the company might offer to integrate its order processing system with its identity-savvy institutional customers' inventory systems, so that their stock can automatically be replenished when it runs low. Each step adds real value, each has measurable ROI, and each can be accomplished in a relatively short time with relatively few development resources thanks to the standardized identity programming interface.

Stunning feats of integration such as these can be accomplished without digital identity—Wal-Mart's integration of its suppliers into its own data-processing operations is a textbook example. However, doing it the old-fashioned way requires expenditures of money and development resources in direct proportion to the amount of data already stored in legacy silos, and it is difficult for enterprises to justify the expense of many such projects on an ROI basis. Identity-oriented development promises to do for enterprise systems integration what object-oriented programming did for software engineering: make it simpler, quicker, less error prone, and less resource intensive. Suddenly, many projects that did not originally make financial sense look feasible, and they look even more attractive in light of the network effect made possible by open standards.

Our prediction is that the enterprise is where most identity-related development will occur over the next few years. Consumers will come to rely on identity-based services provided by these companies more and more, often without knowing (or needing to know) that these services are in fact founded on digital identity technologies. For example, companies will start allowing customers to share their account information with their strategic partners. Meanwhile, grass roots understanding of privacy issues will slowly but inexorably lead to consumer demand for identity applications and for true control over their own data. Consumer protection legislation and regulations will drive enterprises to adopt technologies with strong privacy safeguards, lending additional weight to the benefits of digital identity. Network effects will, finally, lead to the identity web, a global hyperlinked collection of personal data shared, by mutual agreement, between entities. By the end of this decade, the most compelling reason to use identity-based solutions in the enterprise will be that customers, vendors, partners, and competitors are already using them.

THE IDENTITY PLAYERS

This chapter has already touched on the efforts of XN-SORG, OASIS, and the Liberty Alliance in the realm of digital identity, as well as Microsoft's Passport. We can characterize these efforts as pure identity plays.

XNSORG, having launched XNS, turned over the reins to OASIS, where the XRI and XDI standards are the successors to XNS. Version 1.0 of the XRI specification is already available, and XDI is under development.

Liberty's Phase I specification defines an SSO service based on the security assertion markup language, wherein existing accounts at multiple sites that have agreed to share authentication can be linked. Sun Microsystems is already supporting Liberty Phase 1 in its directory server. Phase 2, released early in 2003, is a more sophisticated protocol that allows any Liberty-compliant service to federate with any other—without preexisting partnerships—and to share more attributes between accounts.

Microsoft's Trustworthy Computing initiative, popularly known by its code name Palladium, aims to add permissions to document sharing of all kinds through a combination of security and identity technologies. The industry perceives Trustworthy Computing as being driven in large part by the desire of content providers (e.g., the music and motion picture industries) to control how their content is being used and protect it from piracy, but Microsoft recognizes that consumers will not use a system with such restrictions unless it also provides compelling benefits for them as well. The carrot Microsoft offers with Palladium is to give *everyone* the ability to apply the same industrial-grade restrictions to information *they* create. As part of Palladium, Microsoft will also provide wider access to their Passport technology—including, in an unusual move for Redmond, sharing Passport Manager source code with selected partners and customers. (Passport Manager is the software module that allows a Web site to join the Passport network and access shared user data.) The next Passport will support federation.

These three are not the only players, though—only the most visible. Enterprise software vendors are also moving into digital identity. Much of the identity data in the enterprise is housed in directory servers, which are used to control access to corporate network resources as well as to store contact information. Manufacturers of directory and access management products have a natural interest, therefore, in providing their customers with the integration and data-sharing tools they will need in an identity centric world. Not surprisingly, vendors of access-control products—including IBM, Microsoft, Netegrity, Novell, Oblix, and Sun—are already beginning to tout digital identity functionality and interoperability for their products.

Current directory products do not scale well across trust domains—meaning that they are better suited to controlling access within an enterprise than across multiple enterprises—but some vendors already offer *metadirectory* products that can consolidate enterprise directories into one virtual directory. This monolithic approach does not offer the advantages of the Web architecture that will eventually evolve with digital identity; however, enterprises will continue to turn to these working solutions in the short term while identity standards shake out. At that point, it would be natural for these vendors to begin adding support for standards-based distributed identity.

As described earlier, digital identity has the potential to introduce a major paradigm shift in the enterprise integration category. Where the traditional integration approach is monolithic and expensive, the digital identity approach offers low upfront cost and incremental deployment. These are such powerful advantages that it is likely that vendors such as BEA, SeeBeyond, TIBCO, and webMethods will eventually be compelled to use this approach and may in time become leading vendors of identity solutions.

THE FUTURE OF DIGITAL IDENTITY

This chapter has presented the authors' vision of how digital identity will, through links between identities that share data, eventually form an identity web similar to the current World Wide Web (WWW) of documents. The initial growth of the identity web will be driven, like the early stages of the WWW, by early adopters, though early on, more businesses than consumers will see and exploit the potential of digital identity.

As digital identity infrastructure grows, it will have progressively wider applications in many product categories. For example, e-mail vendors could use digital identity protocols to provide permission-based mail filtering. Senders of mail would have to prove their identity and agree to a privacy contract before being permitted to send mail to a given address, potentially putting an end to spam once and for all. By the end of the decade, any product category that involves sharing information is likely to include digital identity features, particularly if it involves digital rights management.

Despite the possible privacy and civil liberties pitfalls, which continue to require vigilance, the concepts embodied by digital identity have the potential to have enormous net positive social and technological impact in the coming years. It is unfortunate that the word *revolutionary* has been tarnished by its application to so many lackluster technologies, because if ever a new technology deserved that adjective, it is digital identity.

GLOSSARY

Adapter   In Enterprise Data Integration, a software module that serves as a bridge between an integration layer and legacy systems.

Authentication   The process of proving that a user is an authorized user of a network resource by presenting credentials such as a user ID and password (colloquially known as logging in).

Community   The group of identities that can be located through a given address resolution service.

Contract   A list of mutually agreed permissions for sharing data between identities via an identity link.

Digital Identity   An emerging technology and application category that revolves around the logical modeling of real-world actors (e.g., people and companies) and their attributes and the permission-based sharing of these attributes between actors on a network.

Extensible Name Service (XNS)   An open, extensible markup language-based digital identity protocol licensed by the not-for-profit XNS Public Trust Organization (XNSORG).

Extensible Resource Identifier (XRI)   A new type of standard identifier that provides the functionality necessary for addressing identity documents.

Federation   The process whereby separate communities share address resolution services, thus merging two or more communities into a larger one and giving users a choice of which provider to use.

Global Community Services   A publicly accessible address resolution service that allows any digital identity to be located by any other, like the domain name service.

Host Identity   The identity that represents the identity service and is responsible for hosting other identities.

Identity Document   A document, stored on an identity server, which stores the attributes of some real-world actor (e.g., a person, a company, a device, or an application).

Identity ID   An immutable, machine-readable identifier that resolves to the network endpoint where an identity document is stored; identity IDs never change as long as the document exists and are the foundation of identity links.

Identity Link   A pipe between two identities for the two-way synchronization of shared attributes.

Identity Name   A human-readable semantic identifier for an identity document that can be resolved to an identity ID.

Identity Server   Software that stores identity documents and provides identity services for those documents.

Identity Service Provider   An organization that provides storage for identity documents.

Identity Web   The global interlinked digital identity community (see *Community*).

Liberty Alliance   An industry consortium founded by Sun Microsystems to deliver and support federated network identity solutions for the Internet.

Negotiation   The process of agreeing on a contract for sharing data between identities via an identity link.

Passport   Microsoft's consumer digital identity service based on the Kerberos authentication protocol.

Publishing Identity   The identity that makes available the definition of an identity service so that the service can be discovered by identity-savvy applications.

Trust Domain   Technically, a set of network resources, the access to which is controlled by a given directory server; in practice, the network resources a user can access with a single set of credentials; more generally, a set of network resources that trust each other, such as an ATM network.

Trust Services   Identity services that make it easier to perform trusted digital transactions; examples include authentication and certification.

Web Services   A new model for interapplication communication over the Internet using standardized protocols (XML, SOAP, WSDL, UDDI); the extension of the concept of local computing services to the Web.

XRI Data Interchange (XDI)   An effort to develop a protocol for permission-based data exchange based on extensible resource identifiers.

CROSS REFERENCES

See *Computer and Network Authentication; Legal, Social and Ethical Issues of the Internet; Password Authentication; Privacy Law and the Internet.*

FURTHER READING

Digital Identity World: http://www.digitalidworld.com/
Digital identity news site and "hub of the digital identity industry." Also organizes the Digital Identity World conferencet.

Electronic Frontier Foundation (EFF): http://www.eff.org/
Grass roots organization focused on protecting civil liberties at the interface where law and technology collide, including privacy issues.

Electronic Privacy Information Center (EPIC): http://www.epic.org/
Public interest research center in Washington, D.C., focusing on emerging civil liberties and privacy issues.

Federal Trade Commission Identity Theft Guide: http://www.ftc.gov/bcp/conline/pubs/credit/idtheft.htm
Official U.S. government publication on identity theft.

International Security, Trust, and Privacy Alliance (ISTPA): http://www.istpa.org/
Industry alliance working to clarify and resolve existing and evolving issues related to security, trust, and privacy; creators of ISTPA Privacy Framework.

Liberty Alliance: http://www.projectliberty.org/
Industry consortium founded by Sun Microsystems to deliver and support a federated network identity solution for the Internet.

Microsoft Passport: http://www.passport.net/Consumer/default.asp?lc=1033

Microsoft Security & Privacy: http://www.microsoft.com/security/
Information about Microsoft's consumer identity, security, and privacy initiatives, including Trustworthy Computing (Palladium).

Organization for the Advancement of Structured Information Standards (OASIS): http://www.oasis-open.org/

Industry consortium driving the development, convergence, and adoption of e-business standards, including many used in Web services and digital identity.

U.S. Department of Justice Internet Fraud Site: http://www.usdoj.gov/criminal/fraud/
Official U.S. government Web site on Internet fraud, including identity theft.

U.S. Federal Trade Commission Privacy Initiatives: http://www.ftc.gov/privacy/
Official U.S. government Web site on privacy and digital identity issues, including GLBA.

World Wide Web Consortium (W3C): http://www.w3c.org/
Industry forum for the development of interoperable technologies "to lead the Web to its full potential," including XML, SOAP, and the Platform for Privacy Preferences (P3P).

XNS Public Trust Organization: http://www.xns.org/
Not-for-profit custodian of extensible name service (XNS), an open, XML-based digital identity protocol.

Digital Divide

Jaime J. Davila, *Hampshire College*

INTRODUCTION

While the origin of the term "'digital divide'" is difficult to determine, by the mid-1990s conversations about the issues that define it were present at the highest levels of the U.S. federal government. On October 10, 1996, President Bill Clinton and Vice President Al Gore addressed the public at the Knoxville Auditorium Coliseum (Clinton & Gore, 1996). The main topic of their presentation was the government's effort to build "a bridge to the 21st century." During the conversation, they address the existing digital divide, referring to varying levels of access to the Internet available to different demographic groups in the United States. During this same federal administration, several reports were published by the National Telecommunications and Information Administration that quantified these differences. In addition, important federal programs were put in place with the goal of guaranteeing access to the Internet to all members of U.S. society.

By 2002, under a new federal administration, reports published by the same agency announced that the gap between the "haves" and the "have-nots" was quickly closing, and predicted that it would only be a matter of (short) time before the differences disappeared altogether. Almost at the same time, a number of researchers working with the Internet from various perspectives described a new type of digital divide, which went further than simple access to machines connected to the network; factors such as absence of adequate literacy levels, the nonexistence of relevant content, lack of ability to become creators of content (and not only "consumers of content") were placing demographic groups at risk of being unable to take advantage of the medium.

This chapter discusses how the meaning of the term "digital divide" has changed through time. It also explores new dimensions of the problem actively being studied and argues that even the original definitions of the problem are far from being solved.

THE ORIGINAL DEFINITION

The National Telecommunications and Information Administration (NTIA), a branch of the U.S. Department of Commerce, originally published data and analysis of who was using the Internet in 1996 and 1998. Under the title of *Falling Through the Net*, these reports outlined how typically disenfranchised groups were lacking connectivity to the Internet. White people were more connected than people of color, member of high income brackets were more connected that the poor, and so on. The problem was thought to be important enough to warrant direct governmental intervention. In 1996, the U.S. federal government created the E-rate program. Under this program, taxes were to be added to telephone bills to fund projects providing connectivity at schools and libraries. Although the government was not expecting to provide a connected computer to each household, access would be provided for all at places of public access. Table 1 presents the percent of households with online service for several important demographic groups in 1997 (NTIA, 1998).

"PROBLEM SOLVED"

By the beginning of the 21st century, many researchers and government officials declared that the problem of the digital divide had practically disappeared. The U.S. federal government, after changing from a Democratic to a Republican administration, reflected this attitude by changing the title of its recent findings from *Falling Through the Net* to *A Nation Online* (NTIA, 1999b). There were two main arguments for this position: first, that online connectivity was penetrating into general society slowly (but surely), in what is typically known as an

Table 1 Internet Use for Different Demographic Groups

Group	Percent Online
Race	
White, not Hispanic	21.2
Black, not Hispanic	7.7
Hispanic	8.7
Income	
Under $5,000	7.2
$5,000–9,999	3.9
$10,000–14,999	4.9
$15,000–19,999	7.0
$20,000–24,999	9.0
$25,000–34,999	13.9
$35,000–49,000	20.8
$50,000–74,999	32.4
$75,000+	49.2
Education	
Elementary	1.8
Some high school	3.1
High school or general educational development diploma	9.6
Some College	21.9
Bachelor's degree or higher	38.4

S-curve pattern of diffusion; second, that many Americans were gaining access to the Internet from places other than their households. Although these arguments are important (and presented here for a complete understanding of the digital divide problem and the dialogue around it), later sections of this chapter present data that contradict both of these arguments.

The S-curve Pattern of Diffusion

The theory of the S-curve pattern of technology diffusion argues that new technologies are never adopted with equal speed by all members of society. Early on, only a few try the new technology. Later, once the technology starts to become popular, it is quickly adopted by a greater number of people. Finally, after reaching a saturation point, the number of participants remains close to constant, ideally including a high percentage of the population. Figure 1

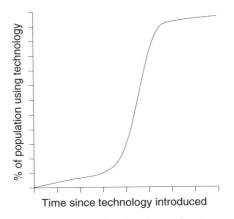

Figure 1: Typical technology adoption curve.

shows a typical technology adoption curve. Such trends have been seen for many technological innovations, including televisions, VCRs, microwave ovens, automobiles, and others. Internet penetration has moved faster than any recent technology, reaching 25% of the U.S. population in only 7 years. This is faster than the rate of diffusion for technologies that have reached close to 100% penetration, such as radio, television, and electricity (National Center for Policy Analysis, 1998). If the S-curve for Internet adoption is steep enough, the argument goes, soon everyone who wants to be connected, will be connected, making any current demographic difference a temporary part of the diffusion process (see, for example, Compaine, 2001).

Access Outside of Homes

In 2001, the year that *A Nation Online* was published by the NTIA, access to the Internet was defined as being able to connect to this medium from home, work, or school. This, in part, continued the idea introduced by the previous administration, which created the E-Rate program to facilitate people gaining access to the Internet from publicly accessible spaces. Defined in that way, connectivity numbers are as presented in Table 2, which includes numbers from 1997 to facilitate a comparison (1997 numbers are still defined in terms of access at home).

"A Problem Among Many"

Although it is not a claim of Internet diffusion, social scientists present at least one more rationale for not allocating great amounts of money to ameliorate the digital divide. This rationale argues that not being connected to the Internet is only one of many problems that affect those who are disenfranchised from fully participating in what society has to offer. In addition, not being connected is not one of the most serious problems, which warrants placing more attention elsewhere. Others question why society should pay so much attention to this one problem in light of so many others (Compaine, 2001). This issue is reexamined later in this chapter.

NEW DEFINITIONS

Parallel to reports that the whole nation was online, social scientists identified necessary requisites for taking advantage of the Internet, other than simply having access to connected machines. Broadly speaking, these have to do with each user's preparation and the context in which the Internet is used. This section explores some of those requirements more closely.

Literacy

Carvin (2000) identified six types of literacy skills needed by a user to take full advantage of the Internet: basic literacy (the ability to read and write), functional literacy (the ability to apply basic literacy to everyday tasks), occupational literacy (the skills necessary to succeed in a professional setting), technological literacy (the ability to use technological tools), information literacy (the ability to determine the quality of informational sources), and adaptive literacy (the ability to develop new skills). Some

Table 2 Reported Internet Connectivity

Group	Percent Online (1997)	Percent Online (2001)
Race		
White not Hispanic	21.2	59.9
Black not Hispanic	7.7	39.8
Hispanic	8.7	31.6
Income/year		
Under $5,000	7.2	25% for those earning
$5,000–9,999	3.9	$15,000/year or less
$10,000–14,999	4.9	
$15,000–19,999	7.0	33.4% for those earning between
$20,000–24,999	9.0	15,000–25,000
$25,000–34,999	13.9	44.1
$35,000–49,000	20.8	57.1
$50,000–74,999	32.4	67.3
75000+	49.2	78.9
Education		
Elementary	1.8%	12.8% for those with
Some high school	3.1%	< high school
High school or general educational development diploma	9.6%	39.8%
Some College	21.9%	62.4%
Bachelor's or more	38.4%	80.8%

of these types of literacy depend on or facilitate each other. For example, technological literacy is easier to acquire for those with adequate functional and adaptive literacy. Functional literacy, at the same time, strongly depends on basic literacy. These relationships point toward basic academic skills as a prerequisite of taking advantage of the Internet. They also point toward the need for proper training on how to use technology. All of these types of literacy are crucial for effective participation. As an example, Lazarus and Mora (2000) found that although 22% of the population of the United States does not have proper "everyday" literacy skills, most of the text available online is written assuming that the audience has at least an average level of literacy.

Data analysis also indicates that college-educated individuals derive greater occupational and educational benefit from the Internet (Robinson, DiMaggio, & Hargittai, 2003). This places in question the claim that the Internet can serve as a social equalizer, instead rendering it an exacerbating force for social inequalities.

Relevance

The Internet is heralded as an important communication medium because of its ability to facilitate flow of information. Therefore, for this new medium to be useful to all citizens, the information flowing has to be of relevance and interest to all. If the information available online turns out to be of little relevance to disenfranchised citizens, they will be less likely to participate with the medium. An audit performed by the Children's Partnership revealed that technologically underserved U.S. citizens found the Internet lacking in local information and cultural diversity (Lazarus & Mora, 2000). Servon (2002) argued that this is caused in part by the fact that the Internet was

originally "populated" by White, middle- and upper-class males who created the type of content that would interest them (Servon, 2002). This can lead to a dangerous cycle of exclusion: some demographic groups fail to connect because of the lack of information available online that interests them, and information they are interested in is not created because there is no present demand for it.

Ability to Create Content

Because of the Internet's power as a communication tool, those who can generate content for it are able to project their message in new and powerful ways. Therefore, being left out of the opportunity to generate Internet content is another way that population groups can be marginalized by this new technology. The Pew Internet Project, through a national phone survey, found great discrepancies in the levels of Internet content that had been created by various demographic groups. This included content creation through Web site creation, Web cams, weblogs, file sharing, and newsgroups. Table 3 summarizes their findings.

The Disabled

Serious consideration should be given to the way in which disabled people access the Internet. Those who are visually impaired or who have problems working with a mouse as an interface device, for example, can have great difficulty navigating and taking advantage of the opportunities offered by technology as a communication medium. In 2000, the NTIA reported that although 56.7% of U.S. citizens accessed the Internet (either from inside or outside their homes), only 28.4% of people with disabilities did. Only 22.5% of people with difficulty using their hands and 21.1% of people with vision problems used the Internet. In

Table 3 Web Content Creators

Group	Percent Online
Race	
White, not Hispanic	77
Black, not Hispanic	9
Hispanic	9
Income	
Under $30,000	19
$30,000–50,000	21
$50,000–75,000	17
$75,000+	31
Education	
Did not graduate from high school	6
High school graduate	19
Some College	29
Bachelor's degree or higher	46
Gender	
Male	51
Female	49
Age	
18–29	28
30–49	48
50–64	20
65+	4

Table 4 Percent of Internet Users With Access to Broadband Versus Dialup

Group	Broadband Access (%)	Dial-Up Access (%)
Race		
White, not Hispanic	85	79
Black, not Hispanic	4	8
Hispanic	5	9
Income		
Under $30,000	6	17
$30,000–50,000	14	24
$50,000–75,000	20	19
$75,000+	45	24
Education		
High school or less	13	37
Some college	28	28
Bachelor's Or more	59	35
Age		
18–24	11	15
25–34	20	22
35–44	28	27
45–54	26	21
55+	14	15
Gender		
Male	56	49
Female	44	51
Community Type		
Urban	29	24
Suburban	60	51
Rural	11	25

September 2000, President Clinton assigned $16 million to the Department of Education to promote technology programs for the disabled, and an additional $9 million to Americorps volunteers working with Internet for the disabled. In addition, modifications made to the U.S. Rehabilitation Act now require government Web pages to meet certain criteria to make them more accessible to people with disabilities (CNN, 2000). At the same time, government Web sites do not, in fact, fully satisfy these requirements. In a study commissioned by the Benton Foundation and the New York State *Forum of the Rockefeller Institute of Government*, Darell West (2003) reported that only 22% of federal Web sites, 24% of state government sites, and 13% of city sites complied with Section 508 of the U.S. Rehabilitation Act.

Broadband

Although, in theory, information available on the Internet is not dependent on the connection speed, some Web sites are designed to be accessed via high-speed connections. Many of these sites are rich on graphics and multimedia, suggesting that they are oriented more toward entertainment and less toward vital information. At the same time, a recent study by the Pew Internet Project found that access to high-speed Internet connectivity allows users to engage in the following three online patterns: content creation, wide ranging queries, and multiple Internet activities on a daily basis (Horrigan, 2002). The study also found discrepancies in the access that different groups have to high-speed Internet connections, as summarized in Table 4.

As can be seen by this data, discrepancies exist based on almost every category reported, with the possible exception of age.

A LOOK AT RECENT DATA

Although most people now agree that efficient access to the Internet involves more than simply access to a connected computer, the question of who has access to connected computers is still valid. To restate arguments discussed earlier, many consider that at least part of the digital divide problem has been solved, mostly because of access in public spaces and the quick diffusion that the Internet has shown. Recent data fail to back up these arguments. A study published by the Pew Internet Project in 2003 indicates that 63% of Americans make use of the Internet. Taken together with the 41.5% and 50.5% reported for 2001 and 2002, respectively, it might seem like the nation is still on the upswing of the diffusion curve (NTIA, 2002). In reality, each NTIA report uses numbers obtained in the previous year, and most of the access growth occurred in 2000 and early 2001 (Madden, 2003). We seem to have reached the flat upper part of the diffusion curve at around 60% to 65% penetration. If this is the case, we should not expect the number of Internet users to increase much more. More important, data suggest that we have reached this point of the S-curve for all demographic groups (Madden, 2003). That is, it does not seem to be the case that the number of White people online is now constant while the number of people of color is increasing on a separate S-curve. Table 5 summarizes who currently has

Table 5 Internet Use by Group, vs. Percent of U.S. Population

Group	Percent of Those Online	Percent of U.S. Population
Race		
White, not Hispanic	77	75
Black, not Hispanic	8	11
Hispanic	9	10
Income		
Under $30,000	18	28
$30,000–50,000	23	21
$50,000–75,000	18	14
$75,000+	26	18
Education		
Not a high school graduate	5	14
High school graduate	23	35
Some college	34	25
Bachelor's or higher	37	26
Age		
18–29	29	23
30–49	47	42
50–64	18	20
65+	4	15
Gender		
Male	50	48
Female	50	52
Community Type		
Urban	26	26
Suburban	52	48
Rural	21	26

access to the Internet, compared with their percentages in the general population. Differences based on race, gender, and geographic location have either shrunk or disappeared, but those based on income and education are still very much present. Smaller sets of data seem to suggest that Blacks and Whites have close to the same level of Internet knowledge and sophistication (Alvarez, 2003). With regard to disabilities, 38% of U.S. citizens with disabilities use the Internet, as opposed to around 60% of all Americans who do (Lenhart et al., 2003).

The hope that access at public spaces would provide for those unable to connect from their households has fallen short of the goal. Internet access at public spaces has grown, but this has not managed to provide efficient connectivity to the economically disadvantaged. Although most of the people who say they depend on libraries to connect to the Internet live in households making less than $30,000 per year, they are infrequent users of the medium (Harwood & Rainie, 2004).

THE INTERNATIONAL DIVIDE

A look at international data clearly shows dramatic differences in level of access to the Internet in different nations. The number of Internet users per 10,000 inhabitants is as low as 5.64 for Myanmar and as high as 6,747 for Iceland (International Telecommunications Union, 2004). The United Nations, during a World Summit on the Information Society held in 2003, declared its intent to harness technology to improve the human condition around the globe (United Nations, 2003a). UNCTAD, the United Nations Conference on Trade and Development, looked at data gathered and reported by several other agencies and developed a ranking methodology that measures not only current connectivity, but also the existence of infrastructure and political climate considered optimal for future growth. The following section lists the criteria used for this ranking and discusses them in light of research done by others regarding this topic.

Definition of United Nations Technology and Communications Index

The Information and Communication Technologies Task Force of the United Nations has designed an information and communications index to describe national conditions with regard to technology and communications (United Nations, 2003a). This index takes into account not only the number of people using the Internet, but also broader characteristics that describe how well each nation has taken advantage of technology and how much of the needed infrastructure for future development has been established. These characteristics are divided into connectivity, access, and policy environment.

Connectivity

The United Nations consideration of connectivity includes four components. PCs (personal computers) per capita, telephone lines per capita, mobile subscriber per capita, and Internet hosts per capita. In many countries, we see a close correlation between the number of computers per person and the number of people accessing the Internet. On one end of the spectrum are nations such as the United States and Sweden, with 65.89 and 62.13 computers per 100 inhabitants. On the other end are regions such as Africa, where there are 1.38 computers and .14 people connected per 100 inhabitants (International Telecommunications Union, 2003).

In many nations, a strong correlation is found between access to the Internet and access to telephone lines. In the United States, there are 62.13 telephone lines per 100 inhabitants. Canada has 65.84 per 100 inhabitants, and Sweden 72.16 per 100 inhabitants. Ethiopia, which has only 1.1 Internet users per 10,000 citizens, has only 0.63 telephone lines per 100 habitants (International Telecommunications Union, 2003).

Mobile subscribers per capita are included as a reflection of connection methods that might increase in importance in the future.

Internet hosts per capita looks at how many computers have an assigned IP (Internet protocol) address assigned to it. This includes both full- and part-time connections (such as the ones typically used by dial-up connections). Obtaining an accurate number for this variable is not always simple or possible, given that there is no necessary correlation between host names and the nations where they are located.

Access

The United Nation's model defines access in terms of number of Internet users per capita, literacy, gross domestic product (GDP) per capita, and cost of placing local calls.

In countries where telephone calls are accrued on a per-minute basis, the cost of placing local calls become part of the cost of connecting to the Internet. The Organization for Economic Cooperation and Development (2001) has found strong correlations between the price per minute for telephone calls and the number of Internet hosts in different countries.

Policy

The last indicator used by the United Nations in its indices is policy environment, which tries to document a general national framework conductive to the integration of technology into everyday life. This indicator includes the presence of Internet exchanges, competition in the telecommunications field, and competition in the ISP (Internet service provider) market.

Internet exchanges are defined as installations capable of exchanging traffic among Internet providers. The United Nations includes this indicator because it believes the existence of such an installation diminishes the dependency on international links and might reflect a proactive policy outlook.

Competition among telecommunication providers and among ISPs is desirable as a market force to increase quality and decrease the cost to consumers.

Quantitative National Differences

Based on the factors just outlined, great discrepancies are evident in national levels of technology preparedness. National indices go from as high as 1 for the United States to as low as 171 for Eritrea (these values are normalized based on the best performing nation and grow higher with decreasing performance). Although there are individual success stories of nations advancing in their ranking (such as Costa Rica and China), rankings seem to be consistent over time. Regional analysis also reveals that those nations at the extremes of the Internet connectivity distribution curve are in fact moving further apart from each other. Although Organization for Economic Cooperation and Development countries continue to improve, sub-Saharan African countries continue to fall behind. Not surprisingly, nations in the "high-income" grouping had an average connectivity ranking 77 places higher than "middle-income" nations. Finally, it is important to point that the UNCTAD study found correlations between local policies and national connectivity.

Other Potential Factors of the International Digital Divide

Norris (2001) analyzed data on Internet usage for Portugal, Greece, Germany, Spain, France, Belgium, Austria, Ireland, Italy, the United Kingdom, Luxembourg, Holland, Finland, Denmark, and Sweden. In all these countries, income, educational level, gender, age, and type of occupation (managerial vs. manual work) was a strong indicator of Internet connectivity. The problem of a gender-based digital divide, now mostly absent in the United States, is a major problem in countries outside Europe. Of the total number of people connected to the Internet, only 22%, 38%, and 6% are women from the regions of Asia, Latin America, and the Middle East, respectively (Hafkin & Taggart, 2001).

There are also drastic domestic differences within developing countries. Income, education, geographic location, and gender all seem to influence connectivity (Grace, Kenny, & Qiang, 2001).

THE IMPORTANCE OF CLOSING THE DIGITAL DIVIDE

The advantages provided by the Internet are many, but they can be generalized to the ability to acquire and communicate information. How these advantages are put to use vary depending on the user and his or her location. In the United States, for example, 53.9% of unemployed people who use the Internet from their homes and 29.8% of unemployed people who use the Internet from outside their homes use it to look for new jobs (NTIA, 1999a). Additionally, between 36% and 38% of people who use the Internet from any location are either taking online courses or doing academic research.

For countries around the world, taking advantage of new technological opportunities can be crucial for national economic development. Campbell (2001) found a strong correlation between the number of technology users and the percentage of growth in employment.

Citizens of a connected nation can follow the work of their elected representatives more closely. Many elected government officials, at both the state and federal levels, can be contacted via the Internet. Web sites not only provide information, they also allow for easier contact with elected officials. Information about government rules, regulations, and benefits can be found online. In fact, the chief executive officer of the U.S. Government Printing Office recently commented that within 5 years, 95% of all documents that are part of the Federal Depository Library Program would be available online (James, 2003). This depository includes all of the information published by U.S. federal government agencies.

Local governments have implemented Web sites through which a number of clerical tasks can be satisfied. For example, in Massachusetts citizens can renew their drivers licenses or car registrations from any computer with access to the Web, and all across the United States people can fill out and submit their income taxes electronically, receiving valuable guiding information for a process usually classified as arduous and complicated. Although the subject of e-government is discussed elsewhere in this encyclopedia, it should be clear from these examples that the Internet is making it easier for connected citizens to participate in governmental discussions and fulfill standard paperwork requirements.

Labor unions now use the Internet to inform and organize their members (CNN, 2000b). Union members are thus kept better informed and are in closer contact with the people they elect to act as their representatives.

As of 2002, the Pew Internet Project reported that 73 million Americans have looked for health information online, and 63 million had done education related research (Madden, 2003). High school technology education programs are training young programmers living in urban neighborhoods, allowing them to enter the workforce and command salaries of up to $150 per hour (Clewley, 2001). This offers a group of typically disenfranchised citizens skills that are in high demand, turning technology into an engine capable of propelling people into higher income jobs. In Sierra Leone, a local entrepreneur created a program in which young rebel soldiers were able to trade their arms for computer training, with the goal of turning them into the center of a software outsourcing business within 3 years (Hermida, 2002). In China, citizens successfully used the Internet to change the course of political action. After a wealthy car driver received what was considered to be an extremely soft sentence for killing a poor farmer with her car, massive online protests led to government officials reopening the case (Ni, 2004).

Examples such as these are too numerous to list all of them here. Although each has a different flavor and approach, what they and others like them have in common is their use of the Internet as a powerful communication mechanism. As such, they can serve as tools for increasing equality, bringing new opportunities to disadvantaged communities. If the divide between those who have access to the Internet and those who do not is not closed, it may well serve as a mechanism to exacerbate economic and social differences between the haves and the have-nots. Although many social scientists argue that access to the Internet is not the most pressing social problem to be addressed, others argue that so-called second-order resources such as the Internet are required to assist those in need to accumulate assets that allow them to exit from and remain out of poverty (Servon, 2002).

COMPLEX SOLUTIONS FOR A COMPLEX PROBLEM

The digital divide has proved to be a hard problem to solve, and with good reason. It includes many dimensions, and effective solutions will need to be multidimensional as well. Although defining a complete solution for this problem is outside the context of this chapter, we can point toward elements that such a solution must incorporate.

Solutions to the digital divide cannot be based simply on providing machines connected to the Internet, as was demonstrated by the "hole in the wall" experiment in New Delhi; computer kiosks were installed in a poor neighborhood, and no instructions were provided. With unrestricted 24-hour access, children learned rudimentary manipulation of the equipment (clicking and dragging with a mouse, etc.), but they spent most of their time playing computer games or using painting programs (Warschauer, 2003). Absent of guidance and purpose, connected machines fail to provide users with much of a chance to better their social positions.

It is not sufficient to place computers in schools, or even in coursework. Warschauer (2000) documented the different educational outcome of two classrooms in Hawaii where technology was being used. Although both schools used technology to improve the educational opportunities available to their students, differences were evident. The school in the more economically affluent community used computers to develop academic and scientific skills, whereas the students in the poorer school were involved with tasks directed more toward the workforce. This difference was matched by a series of goals and expectations set by the teachers at each of the schools. The context where the technology was used clearly affected the way in which it was experienced, integrated, and used.

Many Americans from disenfranchised groups experience technology within communal settings. The type of activity these experiences take place has implications for the impact and success of these exposures to technology. Based in local communities, community technology centers (CTCs) have the ability to integrate use of the Internet with other activities of high relevance to this population. Organized technology projects, as opposed to individualized access points, can serve as a focal point for the common efforts of a community group. Technology can also serve as a source of information and resources for the group, as well as a method to establish communications with other groups with common interests in different geographic locations (Warschauer, 2003). These centers typically offer programs that not only teach their participants how to access the Internet, but also teach them how to create content and how to develop their employability (Servon, 2002).

Although in theory, libraries and schools can both create programs that involve citizens in technology projects similar to the ones offered by CTCs, this is not their main mission. Frequently sparse economic resources and different central agendas make it more difficult for this type of institution to be as effective as CTCs in providing efficient Internet connectivity to the disadvantaged. If enough funds are allocated to design and implement proper technology projects, these public spaces can assist in providing access to those that cannot gain it from within their households.

Government participation needs to be strong to close the divide. As outlined earlier, governments are key players in establishing many of the prerequisites for strong e-readiness. The E-rate program in the United States has helped wire public spaces for access to the Internet. This is a good start, but the program does not provide for any type of training or programmatic support. It also makes funds available only to libraries and schools, and not to CTCs or other types of community groups.

Governments are also central in establishing economic incentives for e-commerce and in making sure infrastructure elements such as telephones lines are widely available. Public and private institutions can also be strong collaborators in training programs at different levels. Partnerships between communities and the information technology sector can both make useful skills available to participants, and provide a well-trained workforce to employers. In Seattle, for example, programs between community groups and Microsoft, Boeing, Cisco, and AT&T have all helped make technology available to typically marginalized groups (Servon, 2002).

Various national governments have implemented a variety of plans to reduce their domestic digital divide. The one common thread among all of them is their signaling that access to the Internet is an important national issue. In 2000, President Clinton presented a budget that included several key items designed to increase Internet access across the nation. Among other things, his proposal called for $2 billion in tax incentives for private companies donating hardware and training to technology centers; $150 million to train new teachers in the best ways to use technology; $100 million to create community technology centers; $25 million to encourage the private installation of Internet connectivity to underserved communities; and $10 million to train native Americans for careers in information technologies. In Brazil, the government put into place aggressive programs to provide Internet terminals at post offices in cities with 6 million or more habitants, and to provide Internet-ready home computers for as little as $15 per month. The Australian government has put in place a series of initiatives to bring both connectivity and training to all of its population, at a total cost of close to $426 million.

Potential Internet users need to understand what they have to gain from using the medium, and they need to know how to access its features. Both national governments and private institutions can play important parts in delivering this knowledge to citizens. Many of these types of initiatives share the common thread of being partnerships between public, private, and educational institutions.

A final characteristic for successful national Internet inclusion is the ease with which companies can establish electronic commerce and transactions. Murasoli Maran, secretary-general for the Asian Productivity Organization, argues that this benefits nations in three ways: It provides additional avenues for job creation and national economic development; it stimulates local and international entrepreneurs to assist with other items necessary for generalized Internet participation because they gain from an increase in online customers, and it provides incentives for citizens to acquire training in information technologies, because companies will now require a trained workforce (Maran, 2000).

Solving the international digital divide will require participation from players across national borders. The United Nations has called for national environments that encourage international cooperation and direct foreign investment. This will require efforts to "correct market failures, ... to maximize economic and social benefits, and to serve national priorities" (United Nations, 2003b).

In this way, then, connectivity, government leadership, computer infrastructure, a trained local workforce, and a positive electronic commerce climate form the cornerstones of Internet development for any country. All these factors feed off each other in a systemic process. For example, local governments have the primary responsibility of providing connectivity, but they usually come into partnerships with private industries to facilitate the rigorous task of wiring a nation. Private industries, at the same time, take advantage of government subsidies in exchange for providing hardware and training to the general population.

CONCLUSION

The digital divide is a problem that threatens to leave a considerable portion of the potential users of the Internet disconnected. Given the Internet's potential as a tool for social change and improvement, aggressive steps should be put in place to close this divide. While the digital divide has changed in nature and complexity since it was identified, the original problem is still present. Community groups, national and local governments, private industry, international bodies, and individual citizens will all need to come together in carefully crafted plans to design and implement effective solutions.

GLOSSARY

Broadband Normally understood to refer Internet connections faster than those provided by standard telephone lines. The Federal Communications Commission defines broadband as a medium that provides for communication faster than 200 Kb in each direction. Current examples include ISDN (integrated services digital network), cable, ADSL (asymmetric digital subscriber line), satellite, local wireless, and power broadband.

Community Technology Centers (CTC) Facilities and programs designed to provide free or low-cost computer access as well as training. Usually located in public housing developments, libraries, or other types of public access places.

Federal Communications Commission (FCC) It is the branch of the U.S. federal government that oversees the telecommunications and media industries.

General Educational Development (GED) The GED test measures how well someone has mastered the knowledge expected of a high school graduate.

CROSS REFERENCES

See *Digital Economy; Internet Basics; Legal, Social and Ethical Issues of the Internet; The Legal Implications of Information Security: Regulatory Compliance and Liability.*

REFERENCES

Alvarez, A. (2003). Behavioral and environmental correlates of digital inequality. *IT & Society*, 1, 97–140.

Campbell, D. (2001). Can the digital divide be contained? *International Labour Review*, 1, 119–141.

Carvin, A. (2000). More that just access: Fitting literacy and content into the digital divide equation. *Educause Review, 35*, 38–47.

Clewley, R. (2001). *Programming a way out of poverty.* Retrieved June 2, 2004, http://www.wired.com/news/school/0,1383,45922,00.html

CNN. (2000). Clinton pushes to help disabled bridge "digital divide. Retrieved June 2, 2004, http://www.cnn.com/2000/ALLPOLITICS/stories/09/21/clinton.digital

Compaine, B. (2001). *Information gaps: Myth or Reality?* In Compaine, B. (Ed.), *The digital divide: Facing a crisis or creating a myth.* Cambridge, MA: MIT Press.

Compaine, B., & Weinraub, M. J. (2001). *Universal access to online services: An examination of the issue.* In

Compaine, B. (Ed.), *The digital divide: Facing a crisis or creating a myth*. Cambridge, MA: MIT Press.

Grace, J., Kenny, C., & Qiang, C. (2001). *Information and communication technologies and broad-based development: A partial review of the evidence*. Washington, DC: World Bank.

Hafkin, N., & Taggard, N. (2001). Gender, information technology, and developing countries: An analytic study. Washington, DC: U.S.AID Office of Women in Development.

Harwood, P., & Rainie, L. (2004). PIP data memo: Use of the Internet in places other than home or work. Retrieved June 3, 2004, from the Pew Internet Project Web site: http://www.pewinternet.org/reports/toc.asp?Report=115

Hermida, A. (2002). Child soldiers to swap guns for PCs. Retrieved June 2, 2004, from the BBC News Web site: http://news.bbc.co.uk/hi/english/sci/tech/newsid_1886000/1886248.stm

Horrigan, J., & Rainie, L. (2002). The broadband difference: How online Americans' behavior changes with high-speed internet connections at home. Retrieved June 2, 2004, from the Pew Internet Project Web site: http://www.pewinternet.org/reports/toc.asp?Report=63

International Telecommunications Union. (2003). Main telephone lines, subscribers per 100 people. Retrieved June 3, 2004, from http://www.itu.int/ITU-D/ict/statistics/at_glance/main03.pdf

International Telecommunications Union. (2004). Internet indicators: Hosts, users and number of PCs. Retrieved June 3, 2004, from http://www.itu.int/ITU-D/ict/statistics/at_glance/Internet03.pdf

James, B. (2003). Keynote speech at the E-Government for All Conference. Retrieved June 4, 2004, from http://egov4all.gjhost.org/egovr/swebsock/0026727/0880529/CC44/main/viewitem.cml?9+4+10+1+0+0+1+x#here

Lazarus, W., & Mora, F. (2000). *Online content for low-income and underserved Americans: The digital divide's new frontier*. Santa Monica, CA: The Children's Partnership.

Lenhart, A., Horrigan, J., Rainie, L., Allen, K., Boyce, A., Madden, M., & O'Grady, E. (2003). The ever-shifting Internet population: A new look at Internet access and the digital divide. Retrieved June 3, 2004, from the Pew Internet Project Web site: http://www.pewinternet.org/reports/toc.asp?Report=88

Madden, M. (2003). America's online pursuits: The changing picture of who's online and what they are doing. Retrieved June 2, 2004, from the Pew Internet Project Web site: http://www.pewinternet.org/reports/toc.asp?Report=106

Maran, M. L. (2000). *International conference on productivity in the e-age, inaugural address*. Retrieved June 3, 2004, from http://www.apo-tokyo.org/sgstatem/0a_sg_20001122.htm

National Center for Policy Analysis. (1998). *Technology and economic growth in the information age*. Retrieved June 1, 2004, from http://www.ncpa.org/bg/bg147/bg147.html

National Telecommunications and Information Administration. (1995). *Falling through the Net: A survey of the "have nots" in rural and urban America*. Retrieved June 1, 2004, from the U.S. Department of Commerce Web site: http://www.ntia.doc.gov/ntiahome/fallingthru.html

National Telecommunications and Information Administration. (1998). *Falling through the Net II: New data on the digital divide*. Retrieved June 1, 2004, from the U.S. Department of Commerce Web site: http://www.ntia.doc.gov/ntiahome/net2/falling.html

National Telecommunications and Information Administration. (1999a). *Fact sheet: Americans using Internet for many tasks*. Retrieved June 2, 2004, from the http://www.ntia.doc.gov/ntiahome/digitaldivide/factsheets/usage.htm

National Telecommunications and Information Administration. (1999b). A nation online: How Americans are expanding their use of the Internet. Retrieved June 3, 2004, from http://www.ntia.doc.gov/ntiahome/dn/index.html

Ni, C. (2004, January 17). Incensed Chinese wield Internet clout to press for justice. *Los Angeles Times*, p. A3.

Norris, P. (2001). *Digital divide: Civic engagement, information poverty, and the Internet worldwide*. Cambridge, UK: Cambridge University Press.

Organization for Economic Cooperation and Development. (2001). *Working party on telecommunications and information services policies, pricing and e-commerce*. Retrieved June 3, 2004, from http://www.olis.oecd.org/olis/2000doc.nsf/LinkTo/DSTI-ICCP-TISP-(2000)1-FINAL

Robinson, J., DiMaggio, P., & Hargittai, E. (2003). New social survey perspectives on the digital divide. *IT & Society*, 1, 1–22.

Servon, S. (2002). *Bridging the digital divide: Technology, community, and public policy*. MA: Blackwell.

United Nations. (2003a). Information and communication technology development indices. Retrieved August 30, 2004, from http://www.unctad.org/en/docs/iteipc20031_en.pdf

United Nations. (2003b). Declaration of principles, World Summit on the Information Society. Retrieved August 30, 2004, from http://www.itu.int/dms_pub/itu-s/md/03/wsis/doc/S03-WSIS-DOC-0005!!PDF-E.pdf

Warschauer, M. 2000. *Technology and school reform: A view from both sides of the track*. Education Policy Analysis Archives, 8, Arizona State University.

Warschauer, M. (2003). *Technology and Social Inclusion. Rethinking the Digital Divide*. Cambridge, MA: MIT Press.

West, D. (2003). *Achieving E-Government for All: Highlights from a National Survey*. Benton Foundation and the New York State Forum of the Rockefeller Institute of Government. Retrieved June 2, 2004, from http://www.benton.org/publibrary/egov/access2003.html

Legal, Social, and Ethical Issues of the Internet

Kenneth Einar Himma, *Seattle Pacific University*

INTRODUCTION

Use of the networked world has resulted in many social and individual benefits. The World Wide Web, for example, makes it possible for people to access a wealth of information from the comfort of their own homes. E-mail capabilities enable individuals to communicate information from one country to another at a fraction of what it would cost to do so by making an international telephone call. Bulletin boards and discussion lists provide large groups of like-minded persons with a forum in which they can exchange ideas. All of these media are fully available to the user at any time of the day.

The unique capabilities of these new technologies, however, have also given rise to novel legal, social, and ethical problems. The ability to communicate information to potentially millions of people facilitates socially desirable expression, but it also facilitates expression of questionable morality and legality. Because, for example, the harm to an individual's reputation caused by defamation is a function of how many people receive the defamatory material, the capabilities of the Web increase a user's potential for causing harm by publishing defamatory material. Similarly, because the economic loss to a copyright holder caused by the unauthorized distribution of copyrighted materials is also determined by how many people receive those materials, the capabilities of the Web also increase a user's potential for causing harm by sharing copyrighted materials.

These new information technologies, then, can be used in ways that implicate a wide variety of interests of legal, social, and ethical significance. These interests include interests in privacy, free speech, security, economic well-being, and property. This chapter discusses some of the important ways in which these technologies have unfavorably implicated these interests, although it should be emphasized that the selection of issues here, of necessity, falls well short of being complete.[1]

FREE SPEECH ON THE INTERNET

While the establishment of the World Wide Web has greatly enhanced the ability of ordinary individuals to receive and communicate information and ideas, online speech also poses ethical and social problems. Unfortunately, the Internet has been used not only to seek information and truth, but also to defame, defraud, sexually exploit, and incite other people. It is not surprising, then, that such conduct is giving rise to much controversy about the scope of the right to free speech and its application to online activity.

Legal Protection of Free Speech

There is a consensus in Western nations that citizens have a moral right to free speech that is sufficiently important to deserve legal recognition and protection. A number of nations, including Canada and the United States, have formal constitutions that explicitly create a right of free speech limiting state restrictions on the free flow of ideas. The Canadian Charter, for example, provides that "Everyone has the following fundamental freedoms: (a) freedom of conscience and religion; (b) freedom of thought, belief, opinion, and expression, including freedom of the press and other media of communication; (c) freedom of peaceful assembly; and (d) freedom of association."[2] The First Amendment to the U.S. Constitution provides that "Congress shall make no law . . .

---

[1] A number of important topics cannot be discussed here because of space limitations. Notable examples include e-commerce, the digital divide, data quality, and e-learning.

[2] Canadian Charter of Rights and Freedoms, Part I, Section 2, "Fundamental Freedoms"; available at http://laws.justice.gc.ca/en/charter/.

abridging the freedom of speech, or of the press; or the right of the people peaceably to assemble, and to petition the Government for a redress of grievances."[3]

European nations also regard the free flow of information among individuals as a fundamental value. For example, Article 5 of the German constitution (*Grundgesetz*) guarantees the right of free speech and expressly prohibits censorship of any kind.[4] Similarly, a recent draft of the proposed Charter of Fundamental Rights of the European Union includes a provision establishing a right of free speech: "Everyone has a right to freedom of expression. This right shall include freedom to hold opinions and to receive and impart information and ideas without interference by public authority and regardless of frontiers."[5] Free speech is also protected by the courts in many European nations as an "implied right."

Moral Legitimacy of Free Speech Rights

Utilitarian justifications for legal protection of speech emphasize the benefits of free speech to the common good. John Stuart Mill (1989), for example, argued that allowing people the freedom to speak their minds and express their creative abilities promotes human happiness in several ways. First, allowing speech conduces to the speaker's well-being by facilitating the development of his or her critical faculties. Second, allowing creative expression promotes the ideological and technological betterment of humanity. Third, and most important, allowing free debate increases the likelihood that the truth will be discovered—and knowing the truth always conduces, on Mill's view, to human well-being.

Deontological justifications argue that there are strict moral limits on the extent to which one person may justifiably interfere with the autonomy of another person. Nozick (1977) argues, for example, that every autonomous moral agent has a "natural" right to liberty that includes the right to express her views free of coercive interference. Since people have natural rights in virtue of their status as moral persons and not in virtue of their status as citizens of some state, the operation of natural rights is not limited to obligating other individuals; even the state must respect a person's natural rights. Indeed, so important are these rights that Nozick (1977) notes that the state's only legitimate function is to protect them.

Contractarian theorists argue that the state's legitimate lawmaking authority depends entirely on the consent of citizens and that citizens consent only to limited restrictions on free speech. Although classical contractarian theories require that citizens *actually* consent, whether expressly or tacitly, to state authority, the most influential modern approach focuses on what citizens *would* consent to under certain counterfactual circumstances. John Rawls argues that a just state is bound by those principles that rational self-interested agents would choose if they had to select principles constraining the government without having any specific information about their

own particular preferences, abilities, and social circumstances.[6] On Rawls's view, citizens behind such a "veil of ignorance" would protect themselves from oppression by choosing a principle of personal liberty that defines a right to free speech.

Internet Issues
Web Pornography and Children

Pornographic material on the Web is both plentiful and easy to come by. A search of the word "sex" on any mainstream search engine will produce not only links to scientifically and medically useful information on sex, but also links to pornographic Web sites. Entering http://www.sex.com into a Web browser will take the user to a portal that provides links to various types of pornographic material, ranging from standard sexually explicit material to material that appeals to various fetishes. As is evident, the word "sex" can be used in a variety of Web-based devices to locate Web sites specializing in graphic sexual content.

This raises the worry that children who are emotionally unprepared for pornographic content may encounter it while surfing the Web. Although it is fair to say that the effects of pornography on adults remain unclear, child development experts agree that chronic exposure to pornographic materials can have long-lasting and harmful effects on children (see, e.g., Benedek & Brown, 1999). Such materials can affect the way in which children view sex, relationships, and women; they can also diminish the prospects for successful love relationships and might even raise the likelihood of sexual violence. Richard Spinello (2000, p. 57) eloquently described the concern:

> Given the power of sexuality in one's life, the need for carefully integrating sexuality into one's personality, and the unfortunate tendency to regard others as sexual objects of desire (rather than as human beings), there is a convincing reason for fostering a climate in which impressionable children can be raised and nurtured without being subjected to images of gross or violent sexual conduct that totally depersonalize sexuality, exalt deviant sexual behavior, and thereby distort the view of responsible sexual behavior.

The ease with which such materials can be accessed on the Web creates the possibility of such exposure in children—and its harmful consequences.

Legislators on both sides of the Atlantic share concerns about the potential impact of Web pornography on the emotional well-being of children. The European Parliament (1997), for example, strongly advocates legislation that would protect children from access to inappropriate sexual material on the Web. It formally resolved that "minors should be protected as soon as possible against access, via the new networks and services, to material which may harm their physical and psychological development."

It is unclear, however, what sorts of restrictions on Web pornography should be enacted by legislators. Although

---

[3] United States Constitution, First Amendment; available at http://caselaw.lp.findlaw.com/data/constitution/amendment01/.

[4] For an English translation of the German constitution, see http://www.psr.keele.ac.uk/docs/german.htm.

[5] Draft of the Charter of Fundamental Rights of the European Union, Chapter 2, Article 11; available from http://www.europarl.eu.int/charter/pdf/text_en.pdf.

[6] In particular, Rawls stated that citizens would choose a principle (the Liberty Principle) that grants each agent as much freedom as is compatible with like freedom for all other agents.

the legitimacy of concerns about minors is undeniably a point in favor of legal regulation of Web pornography, there are legitimate concerns militating against it. Any restriction on Web pornography is likely to impact socially desirable forms of speech and will thereby have the effect of limiting the access of adults to legitimate content and thereby violating their moral rights to free speech. As a historical matter, censors have typically tended to err on the side of restricting too much content in the name of sexual morality, frequently attempting to censor books and paintings that are now regarded as literary and artistic masterpieces. The effect on moral rights to free speech, had such efforts been successful, would have been significant.

Part of the problem here is that any restriction on sexually explicit content on the Web will have to be couched in abstract terms that admit of varying degrees of vagueness. Terms such as "obscene," "indecent," "pornography," and "sexually explicit" are all vague at the margins and admit of very different interpretations, depending on what background assumptions are incorporated into the interpretation. Some people, for example, would characterize explicit instructions about how to use a condom as "indecent" or "sexually explicit." Indeed, it is the very vagueness of these terms that makes it likely that too much, rather than too little, material will be censored.

Complicating the difficulty of trying to balance these competing interests is the issue of how much responsibility society should collectively bear to assist parents in raising children. On one view, society bears minimal responsibility; the primary responsibility for raising children rests with parents. On another, society has much at stake in how children are raised because the social costs of poorly raised children can be significant; accordingly, citizens must be prepared to make some sacrifices to increase the likelihood that children are raised in a way that ensures they become productive, well-adapted adults.

The various positions on how to balance these competing considerations are being debated not only by citizens, but also by legislative and judicial officials. Consider, for example, the controversy in the United States attending the enactment of statutes like the Communications Decency Act (CDA). The CDA prohibited the "transmission of any comment, request, suggestion, proposal, image, or other communication which is obscene or indecent, knowing that the recipient of the communication is under 18 years of age" and the "knowing [transmission] to a specific person or persons under 18 years of age . . . [of] any comment, request, suggestion, proposal, image or other communication that, in context, depicts or describes, in terms patently offensive as measured by contemporary community standards, sexual or excretory activities or organs." The CDA authorized a prison sentence of up to 2 years for violations.

Although the CDA struck the balance in favor of children, the U.S. Supreme Court struck the balance in favor of speech, striking down the CDA on the ground that it would restrict the constitutionally protected speech of adults (see *Reno v. ACLU*, 1997, at 2329). Crucial to the Court's decision was the observation that the Web is entitled to greater First Amendment protection than television and radio because one must take a series of affirmative

steps to view specific content online. Children are far less likely to be exposed accidentally to sexually explicit material on the Web than on television because they cannot randomly sample Web pages simply by changing channels. Although curious children can seek out such materials, it is the "ease with which children may obtain access to broadcasts" that, according to the Court, "justifie[s] special treatment of indecent broadcasting" (see *Reno v. ACLU* at 2342).

In response, critics argue that the difference between television and broadcasting is a difference in degree that does not justify treating the two media differently—and not a difference in kind. Although the likelihood that a child will accidentally encounter inappropriate content on the Web is lower than the likelihood he or she will accidentally encounter inappropriate content on television, the likelihood of the former is still morally significant; after all, a few mistaken keystrokes (e.g., inadvertently clicking on a link from a search) will expose a child to pornographic content. If the harm associated with such content is substantial enough to justify restricting it on television, then it is also substantial enough to justify restricting it on the Web, as long as there is a theoretically significant probability of accidentally encountering it there.

Perhaps persuaded by such reasoning, Congress subsequently enacted the Child Online Protection Act (COPA), which makes it illegal for commercial Web sites to allow persons under 17 to view sexually explicit materials that are "harmful to minors." Although the drafters of COPA deliberately attempted to avoid the constitutional problems of the CDA by restricting the speech of only commercial Web sites, a federal appeals court recently struck it down on the ground that it is unconstitutionally overbroad in two respects. First, the court held that "COPA's definition of 'material harmful to minors' impermissibly places at risk a wide spectrum of speech that is constitutionally protected" (*Ashcroft v. ACLU*, 2003, at 267). Second, it held that its definition of "minor" reaches material that is clearly protected for adults and is not obscene to older minors (*Ashcroft v. ACLU*, at 268).

Whether enactments such as COPA achieve a proper balance between the speech rights of adults and the social interests in the well-being of children remains hotly debated, but this much is clear: the interests in speech and the well-being of children are both legitimate and important in the sense that they both deserve some level of governmental protection. One can expect European and American nations to continue to invest considerable resources to working out the proper balance between the two interests.

Online Hate Speech

There are a growing number of racist, anti-Semitic, and heterosexist Web sites worldwide that advocate violent measures to achieve hate-inspired political agendas. White supremacist Web sites, for example, frequently call for "race wars." Extremist antiabortion Web sites feature photographs of women coming to or leaving abortion clinics. The most infamous of these sites once posted a "Wanted List" of abortion doctors and currently features an editorial advocating the arrest (which it describes as "an act of love") of all persons with a same-sex sexual preference.[7]

Online hate speech creates a host of social problems. To begin with, the anonymity of online communications has emboldened racists, anti-Semites, and homophobes to create more hate sites with increasingly egregious content. Further, the worldwide availability of such content enables bigots to find one another with unprecedented ease and to more easily reach people whose educational and economic circumstances make them susceptible to content that identifies an "Other" as scapegoat. Finally, many hate sites explicitly encourage terrorism to achieve their political agendas. These considerations point in the direction of restricting online hate speech.

Yet, as was true of pornography, there are considerations militating against regulation of such speech. Some opponents argue that restrictions on hate speech will not reduce racism, anti-Semitism, or heterosexism. On this line of analysis, such restrictions simply drive bigotry underground where it can fester until it results in serious social problems that will be far more difficult to address. Restricting hate speech, then, runs the risk of chilling legitimate speech ("hate speech" is as vague as, say, "indecency") without producing the intended desirable consequences. The best response to hate speech, as the point is sometimes put, is more speech, not less.

Reflecting the difficulties in balancing such considerations is the fact that various nations have adopted different approaches to online hate speech. (For an outstanding analysis of the social and legal issues presented by hate speech, see Stuart Biegel, 2001.) Legislation restricting hate speech is not feasible in the United States. According to prevailing interpretations of the U.S. Constitution, hate speech does not fall into the traditional categories of unprotected speech and is hence protected by the First Amendment. For this reason, laws targeting online hate sites on the basis of their content are constitutionally impermissible in the United States.

The United States is unique among Western industrial nations in this regard. Many European nations, such as Germany, have laws criminalizing certain forms of hate speech. Indeed, the Council of Europe (n.d.) is currently preparing legislation that would prohibit posting or distributing racist or xenophobic material through a computer system. For its part, Canada has already enacted extensive legislation against online hate. The Canadian Human Rights Act (n.d., Section 13) prohibits the communication over computer networks of "any matter that is likely to expose a person or persons to hatred or contempt by reason of the fact that that person or those persons are identifiable on the basis of a prohibited ground of discrimination."

Spam

Unsolicited mass e-mailings ("spam") are ethically problematic because they impose significant costs on Internet users. First, spam consumes scarce network resources (e.g., time and disk space) for which recipients must pay. Second, recipients must expend time and energy to deal with unsolicited mailings; as Spinello (2000, p. 63)

points out, "If a vendor sends out 6 million messages and it takes 6 seconds to delete each one, the total cost of this one mailing is 10,000 person hours of lost time." Third, Internet service providers (ISPs) and consumers are harmed because large quantities of spam can overload networks, slowing response rates and causing downtime. Spam raises ethical issues because these costs are typically imposed on consumers without their consent.[8]

Intentionally deceptive spam raises additional issues. Many senders attempt to ensure that recipients view their mailings by concealing their commercial nature. Such practices are ethically problematic not only because they are dishonest, but also because they deliberately attempt to frustrate the intent of consumers who wish to save time online by deleting spam mailings without viewing them. When such spam is of a graphically sexual nature, the risk that children and adults are exposed to unwanted and potentially harmful pornographic images is dramatically increased.

Western nations agree on the need to restrict spam but disagree on what restrictions are legitimate. The European Union recently adopted a directive requiring spammers to obtain the consumer's consent before sending unsolicited commercial e-mail (Saunders, 2002). Although such legislation is not possible in the United States because commercial speech is protected by the First Amendment, intentionally deceptive commercial speech can be prohibited. Indeed, Congress recently enacted the CAN-SPAM Act (i.e., the Controlling the Assault of Non-Solicited Pornography and Marketing Act), which prohibits many deceptive practices that have become common among spammers. CAN-SPAM prohibits, among other things, transmitting multiple commercial e-mails with the intent to deceive and intentionally falsifying header information before transmitting multiple commercial e-mails. The act became law in the United States on January 1, 2004.[9]

Whether such restrictions are ultimately efficacious in reducing objectionable spam, however, remains to be seen. First, there are a variety of increasingly sophisticated techniques that enable spammers to conceal their ultimate location. An increasing amount of spam, for example, is sent from innocent agent machines to which spammers have surreptitiously gained access because owners have unwittingly downloaded programs allowing backdoor access to their machines. Second, spam received in one country frequently originates from a different country. These factors make it difficult to enforce legal restrictions on spam and hence reduce the deterrent effects on potential spammers.

---

[7] The infamous Nuremberg Files Web site can be found at http://www.christiangallery.com.

[8] The proliferation of pop-up advertisements on the Web raises some similar issues. For example, the consumer must expend time and effort to close a pop-up ad; in this respect, pop-up ads are like spam. Even so, there is one fundamental difference between the two: to receive a particular pop-up ad, one must perform a specific cyberact—namely, direct a Web browser to retrieve the contents of a particular Web site. Receipt of spam, in contrast, does not require any specific act on the part of the user (apart from having an e-mail account).

[9] CAN-SPAM supplements the preexisting efforts of many states to legislate spam. In 1998, for example, the Washington State Legislature prohibited the transmission of unsolicited commercial e-mail to Washington state residents that contains false sender addresses or deceptive subject lines. Washington's Unsolicited Commercial Electronic Mail Act was upheld by the state's highest court in 2001.

Filtering Devices

A number of products filter objectionable content online. Individual filtering programs, for example, can be installed on a user's personal computer to block access to Web sites using certain sexually explicit terms or featuring images with a disproportionate quantity of fleshtones. Additionally, an increasing number of Web sites, although still a comparatively small percentage of total Web sites, participate in the PICS (Platform for Internet Content Selection) ratings system, which suppresses Web sites that rate themselves for mature audiences, as well as Web sites that decline to be rated.

The most contentious issue regarding such products involves their use by public libraries. Although many people believe public libraries should install such devices out of respect for the values of the communities they are intended to serve, library professionals and associations frequently oppose their use on two grounds. The first is that filtering programs are imprecise at this point in time— they sometimes fail to block access to pornographic content and sometimes block access to unobjectionable scientific or health-related content. The second is that there is a concern about whether it is ever appropriate for a library to censor content. The American Library Association, for example, takes the position that "A person's right to use a library should not be denied or abridged because of origin, age, background, or views." On this view, any form of censorship is inconsistent with the duty of libraries to ensure the free flow of information to individuals of all ages.

The U.S. Congress recently entered the filtering controversy with the enactment of the Children's Internet Protection Act (CIPA) in 2002, which requires public libraries to use filtering devices as a condition for receiving certain federal funds. Although a federal appellate court struck down CIPA on the ground that filtering devices typically screen out protected content (*American Library Association v. United States*, 2002), the U.S. Supreme Court recently upheld CIPA. Because CIPA requires library personnel to disable filtering devices on the request of an adult, the Court held that it leaves open alternative channels for adults to receive blocked content (*United States v. American Library Association*, 2003).

Search Engines

Search engines are an indispensable tool for sifting through the approximately 8 billion pages now on the Web (Suzukamo, 2002).[10] If the user knows (a) which sites contain the needed information and (b) the precise URL addresses of those particular sites, he or she can simply enter the addresses into the browser and it will call up those sites. If, as is more often the case, the user does not know where to go to find the needed information, he or she must rely on a search engine to find appropriate Web sites; navigating the Web without the use of a search engine can be a time-consuming process that fails to produce appropriate sites.

A search engine imposes order on the Web by creating a large database that contains an index of each page's URL, along with a fairly substantial list of key words describing its contents. When the user submits particular key words to a search engine, the engine returns a ranked list of URLs containing those key words. Search engines structure the Web by, in effect, characterizing each indexed page in terms of its content (as indicated by the appropriate key words).

Search engines, then, determine which pages users are likely to visit in two ways. First, search engines make available only those pages they have indexed—and there is currently no engine that has indexed every page on the Web.[11] For many people, a page that is not listed on any of the search engines doesn't exist; as Introna and Nissenbaum (2000) put the matter, "to exist is to be indexed by a search engine." Second, users are more likely to visit only highly ranked pages. Anecdotal evidence suggests that users are likely to visit only the top 10 to 20 pages (or "hits") returned by a search engine (Introna and Nissenbaum). If a low-ranked page exists for users, its existence is far less substantial than that of a highly ranked Web site.

Insofar as the criteria that determine the inclusion and ranking of pages determine how frequently a Web site is visited, they have two consequences of ethical significance on speech rights. First, they determine to what extent a particular publisher's Web speech is received. Second, they determine what content is ultimately available to persons seeking information on the Web. Given these critical effects, it is reasonable to think that search engines ought to employ ranking and inclusion criteria that satisfy ethical and technical standards.

Most search engines employ criteria that do not *explicitly* favor any particular class of publishers over another for reasons unrelated to merit. Web sites are usually either manually submitted to search engine editors who decide whether they are suitable for indexing or are retrieved by "spiders" that crawl the Web automatically indexing pages. A page's rank is usually determined by either the number of times a particular key word appears in the page or the number of other pages that contain links to the page.[12]

Some search engines, however, use economic criteria that favor firms willing to pay. Some engines, for example, allow a Web site to pay for expedited indexing, a process that can otherwise take months. Some engines permit firms to buy advertising linked to key words; any search using a particular key word will turn up a screen with an advertisement from a company that sells a related product or service. Some search engines have gone so far as to allow firms to bid on their top rankings.

Although some believe that market-driven search engine criteria are no more problematic than market-driven criteria for production of any other goods, critics have objected to economic criteria on three grounds. First, economic criteria rank content on the basis of characteristics that are irrelevant with respect to the quality or utility of the information; the ability or willingness of a Web site

---

[10] In 1999, Lawrence and Giles estimated that there were 800 million Web sites. If these estimates are accurate, the number of sites on the Web was 10 times as large in 2002 (Suzukamo, 2002) as it was 3 years earlier.

[11] Google, one of the most comprehensive search engines, states that it has indexed approximately 3 billion Web pages. See http://www.google.com/help/features.html (retrieved November 1, 2003).

[12] Some newer search engines attempt to evaluate a page's "authority." Teoma, for example, ranks a site based on the number of same-subject pages, as opposed to general pages, that reference it. The goal is to be able to identify pages that are regarded as "expert" among a particular subject community. See www.teoma.com.

owner to pay has nothing to do with the quality of the information contained in the site. Second, as Introna and Nissenbaum (2000) put the point, economic criteria compromise the ideal of the Web as a public good insofar as the Web "fulfills some of the functions of other traditional public spaces—museums, parks, beaches, and schools" and thereby contributes to the common good. On this view, selling influence on the Web is as ethically problematic as selling influence in a museum or school; in neither case should the common good be sold to the highest bidder. Third, failure to disclose that a Web site has bought its rank may mislead search engine users to believe the site's rank was determined by characteristics having to do with the quality and utility of the site.

INTELLECTUAL PROPERTY

The Web impacts the intellectual product of content creators and publishers in a variety of ethically significant ways. The Web provides them with another legitimate means to distribute intellectual product to an appropriate class of persons, but it also makes it possible for persons to distribute intellectual product to large numbers of persons without the authorization of those who claim to have property rights in that product. Since mass distribution of content on the Web can obviously reduce the economic market for the product, such distribution raises issues concerning the extent to which persons have legitimate property interests in content.

Legal Protection of Intellectual Property

Western nations generally offer three types of legal protection for intellectual property. First, patent law protects a person's interests in his or her own inventions, which includes newly designed useful processes.[13] A patent protects an invention by granting the inventor a limited monopoly power over the invention. This allows a patent holder the right to prevent other firms and persons from making or marketing it. Similar protections ("design patents" in some nations, "designs" in others) are also available for various aspects of a product's ornamental design.

Second, trademark law protects the right of a product or company owner to use marks that distinguish its goods and services from others. Trademark infringement generally occurs when a firm or individual uses a mark that is likely to confuse a reasonably intelligent consumer about the source or sponsorship of a good or service. Many nations allow a firm to establish a trademark simply by using it, but formal registration is frequently available as well.

Third, copyright law protects the original expression of ideas and facts—the particular form, language, and structure of articulated ideas, as opposed to the facts and ideas themselves, which are never protected.[14] Originality of expression requires the introduction of something new to the world; a person who simply copies the expression of someone else has not produced anything original that can

be protected by copyright. Copyright protection applies to original literary works (including computer programs), musical works, dramatic works, choreographic works, artistic works, sound recordings, and architectural works.

Copyright law typically defines two intellectual property rights. First, it grants to the author an exclusive right to reproduce, modify, distribute, perform, and display the protected work. Second, it grants to the author certain moral rights of authorship. Such entitlements may include the right to claim authorship in the protected work; the right to prevent someone from attributing a work to the author that he or she didn't create; the right to prevent someone from attributing a work to the author that diverges significantly from a protected work; the right to prevent intentional distortion, mutilation, or modification of a protected work that would detract from the author's reputation; and the right to prevent intentional or grossly negligent destruction of a protected work.

Most nations include an exception for "fair" uses.[15] Copyrighted material may be used for news, educational, and research purposes, provided that such material is not directly used for material gain. In determining whether a use of copyrighted material is fair or not, courts may look to the purpose of the use (e.g., whether it is commercial), the nature of the copyrighted material, the amount of material used relative to the copyrighted work as a whole, and the effect of the use on the market for the work. The last factor is especially important insofar as copyright is intended to protect an author's right to collect the economic value of his or her expression.

Moral Legitimacy of Intellectual Property Rights

Theorists have produced three main lines of justification for legal protection of intellectual property. The first line is grounded in the Lockean view that persons have natural moral (as opposed to merely social) property rights in their bodies and labor. Because the particular sequence of words or symbols chosen by an author to express an idea or fact is the product of his or her labor, the author acquires an exclusive property right to that particular sequence of words or symbols—as long as no one else has a prior right to that sequence. The Lockean argument can roughly be summarized as follows: he or she made it; therefore, he or she owns it.

The second line of justification for intellectual property rights is grounded in the Hegelian view that creators use symbols, words, and sounds to express their person. As an expression of personhood, an original creative work realizes and *extends* the creator's person. Because no one but the author has a protected interest in his or her person, the author acquires a protected interest in his or her expression because such expression is, in some vague but morally significant sense, an extension of his or her person. Roughly put, this line of argument can be summarized as follows: it is part of him or her; therefore, it is his or hers.

The third principal line of justification is utilitarian in character. Protection of intellectual property rights is

---

[13] The intellectual property statutes of various English-speaking nations are available at the following Web sites: Canada—http://strategis.gc.ca/sc_mrksv/cipo/welcome/welcom-e.html; United States—http://www.law.cornell.edu/topics/topic2.html; United Kingdom—http://www.intellectual-property.gov.uk/.

[14] Thus, others are free to express the same ideas and facts as long as they do not intentionally duplicate the author's original expression.

[15] See, for example, the "Fair Dealing" exception to Canadian copyright law beginning at Section 29 of the Canadian Copyright Act (R.S. 1985, c. C-42); and the "Fair Use" exception to U.S. copyright law beginning at 17 U.S.C. Section 107.

justified because such protection conduces to the common good. People will be far more likely to invest time and energy in creating the intellectual products that contribute so much to human happiness, flourishing, and well-being if they are granted an exclusive property right in their original creations. Roughly put, this line of argument is as follows: giving it to him or her benefits all of society; therefore, it is his or hers.

These justifications, however, are vulnerable to serious objections. Critics have argued, for example, that the utilitarian line of argument is problematic in a couple of important respects. First, it presupposes that the primary motivation for creation of content is material, but this presupposition is difficult to reconcile with the success of "open-source software." Open-source software is generally characterized by two features: (a) it is available either free of charge or at a purely nominal price, and (b) the source code of such software is made readily available to users who are free to improve the software by fixing bugs as they are identified. Although proponents of open-source software agree on the undesirability of strong copyright protection for software, they disagree on the reasons. Some proponents, such as Richard Stallman (e.g., 2002), argue that ownership of software is morally illegitimate, whereas others argue that such protection is undesirable because it discourages innovation and improvement: allowing users access to the source code ultimately results in superior software. In any event, the fact that there are many high-quality open-source software products available to users (e.g., Linux) seems to refute the idea that the primary motivation for content creation is material.[16]

Second, the utilitarian argument assumes that the social benefits of intellectual property protection can be achieved by no less restrictive measure than granting extended exclusive rights to intellectual property. Even if the primary incentive for content creation were material in character, there are other ways to protect it: a society could, for example, pay a salary or a fee to content creators. After all, software companies have enjoyed considerable success paying employees a salary for creating software.

Opponents of strong intellectual property protection also argue that intellectual objects are different from physical objects in two ways that diminish the force of the Lockean and Hegelian natural rights arguments. First, intellectual objects, unlike physical objects, are not scarce; one person's consumption of, say, a recipe does not reduce the supply of the recipe available for other persons. Second, intellectual objects, unlike physical objects, can be simultaneously consumed by all persons; whereas a hairbrush can be used by one person at a time, every person can simultaneously use the same recipe. Although this makes sense, on this line of reasoning, to assign exclusive rights to scarce objects that can be consumed by only one person at a time, it is problematic to assign traditional property rights to objects that can simultaneously be consumed by every person without reducing the amount of the object potentially available to others.

Some theorists also worry that the increasing willingness of online users to infringe copyright law undermines the social legitimacy of protecting intellectual property in cyberspace. On this line of analysis, which is roughly grounded in social contract theory, the legitimacy of any particular law depends on its being acceptable to those whose behavior it purports to govern. The growing tendency, however, especially among younger online users, to reproduce and distribute copyrighted works without permission calls into question whether intellectual property protection continues to enjoy widespread acceptance and support among citizens. Insofar as there is no longer a consensus on the legitimacy of such laws, the contractual basis for protecting intellectual property is arguably deteriorating.

Finally, some critics argue that advancements in information technology have made intellectual property rights morally obsolete. For example, Barlow argues that existing intellectual property laws have no proper application in cyberspace. First, Barlow (1996) believes that cyberspace is a distinct metaphysical reality that lies beyond the proper jurisdiction of any nation: "Your legal concepts of property, expression, identity, movement, and context do not apply to us. They are all based on matter, and there is no matter here." Second, Barlow (1992–1993) argues that information is itself a life form that, like any other life form, is entitled to some moral standing. On Barlow's view, information has a morally protected interest in freedom: "information," as he has notoriously put the matter, "wants to be free."

Internet Issues

Domain Names. Every computer on a network has its own Internet protocol (IP) address consisting in a unique sequence of numbers and dots (e.g., 213.57.66.938) that defines its location on the Web. When a user accesses a particular Web site, the contents of that site are sent from the host server's IP address to the IP address of the user's computer. In effect, then, IP addresses make it possible for networked computers to find each other, enabling users to access the contents of Web sites hosted at other locations on the network.

In most cases, users need not know a complicated IP address to access a Web site. Most Web sites have a natural language domain name (e.g., http://www.sporting-goods.com) assigned to their IP addresses that permits easier and more intuitive access to their contents. The user simply types in the natural language domain name, and the ISP either looks for the corresponding IP address or submits a request to a "root server" that serves as a digital directory associating IP addresses and domain names. Once the ISP has determined the corresponding IP address, the desired site is accessed.

Domain names can be valuable commodities. An intuitive domain name saves consumers time and energy; it is much easier to find a site with an intuitive domain name than with a long IP address that is difficult to find and remember. The resulting convenience to users can naturally translate into economic benefits; the easier it is to access

---

[16] It is worth noting that the open-source spirit is finding expression in other ways on the Internet. The free online encyclopedia, *Wikipedia*, for example, allows users to add and edit entries as they see fit. See http://www.wikipedia.com.

a commercial Web site, the more likely users are to visit and buy from that site.[17]

In consequence, there have been conflicts over the use and ownership of domain names. Early in the development of the Web, some people registered domain names featuring the trademarked names of large firms in the hope that the firms would buy those names whenever they decided to go online. Although a few such "cyber-squatters" made a quick profit for their trouble, courts now treat the practice of speculating on domain names incorporating trademarks as actionable trademark infringement (see, e.g., *Panavision v. Toeppe*, 1998).

More commonly, a slightly modified version of a popular Web site's domain name is used to capture some of its traffic. One commercial pornographic Web site in the United States, for example, uses the domain name "www.whitehouse.com." Users who type "www.whitehouse.com" instead of "www.whitehouse.gov" into their browsers—a common mistake—will access sexually explicit material instead of the U.S. president's official Web site. By such means, a person can dramatically increase traffic to his or her site.

Although such practices appear deceptive, they can facilitate legitimate purposes of free expression. A user who mistakenly types "www.gwbush.com" instead of "www.georgebush.com" will access a site criticizing George Bush's views and policies instead of his personal Web site. While the commercial use of a domain name similar to a trademarked name can dilute the value of the trademark and is hence unethical, the politically motivated use of a domain name to express legitimate criticism is arguably unobjectionable—as long as users are not likely to be confused about the origin of the site.

Illicit Copying Over the Internet

No case better exemplifies the clash between the intellectual property rights of copyright holders and the increasingly libertarian spirit of online users than the proliferation of MP3 file sharing over the Web. The development of the MP3 format was the first significant step in realizing the Internet's latent potential for online dissemination of music files. Earlier technologies offered little incentive to share music files; the files were too large to be uploaded and downloaded quickly, and their sound quality was generally inconsistent. MP3 technology, however, permits the compression of nearly perfect digital reproductions of sound recordings into small files that are efficiently transmitted from one user to another.

Napster augmented MP3's capabilities by introducing true peer-to-peer (P2P) file sharing. Whereas users of earlier file-sharing technologies had to download previously uploaded files from a central Web site or file transfer protocol (FTP) site, Napster users could simply take music files directly from the computers of other users. Although a central server was needed to keep a searchable list of all the available MP3 files, its purpose was limited to helping Napster users find each other. Because users could share music files online without anyone needing to take the time to upload music files to some central server, Napster made it easier than ever before for large groups of users to share their sound recordings.

Napster's P2P networking capabilities also inhibited the efforts of recording companies to stop reproduction and distribution of their copyrighted materials. When music files had to be transmitted through a central server, recording companies could demand that the server's owner destroy copyrighted files or litigate an expensive civil suit. Because Napster eliminated the need for centralized storage of such files, however, there was no one entity that could be pressured by copyright holders. Not surprisingly, the music industry viewed Napster as a grave threat to the value of its copyrights.

The conflict came to a head when a group of music companies sued Napster for "indirect" violations of U.S. copyright law. Because Napster's role was limited to enabling users of Napster's MusicShare software to gain access to the hard drives of other users, the company could not be held liable for direct infringements. Instead, the plaintiffs sought to hold Napster liable for contributory infringement (i.e., knowingly assisting others in directly infringing a copyright) and vicarious infringement (i.e., benefiting financially from infringements when it has the ability to supervise and terminate users).

Although the litigation did not settle the legal issues, it resulted in a preliminary injunction forcing Napster off the Web temporarily. A U.S. federal court issued an injunction prohibiting Napster from assisting users in sharing copyrighted materials without the express permission of the owners (*A&M Records v. Napster*, 2000). The court based its injunction on a prediction (as opposed to a final judgment) that Napster would lose at trial because (a) users were deriving an unfair economic benefit from using Napster by saving the cost of the relevant recordings and (b) Napster use was decreasing CD sales among users (*Napster*, 2000 at 1017). Napster recently returned to the Web offering music downloads for sale after negotiating contract agreements with five major record labels and hundreds of independent labels (see http://www.napster.com/about_us.html).

Because the litigation never resulted in a final judgment on the issue of file sharing, music-sharing technologies and Web sites have continued to proliferate,[18] apparently cutting into industry profits by reducing CD sales ("Downloads Blamed," 2002). In a controversial response, the Recording Industry Association of America recently started suing individuals, instead of music-sharing Web sites, for making music files available on these sites ("Recording Industry Begins Suing," 2003; "RIAA Strikes Back," 2003). These lawsuits have targeted not only adult users, but also the parents and grandparents of children users (RIAA Leaning on Kids' Parents, 2003). Although such tactics have been passionately criticized, they seem to have succeeded, according to recent reports, in reducing illegal file sharing—at least temporarily (Borland, 2003).

---

[17] Compaq reportedly paid more than $3 million to purchase the domain name www.altavista.com from the former owner of Alta Vista Technology after acquiring the company. Until Compaq purchased the domain name, it was forced to use the ungainly www.altavista.digital.com (Kornblum, 1998).

---

[18] Indeed, http://www.afternapster.com lists 32 file-sharing Web sites, many of which improve on the P2P networking capabilities of Napster.

Plagiarism

The availability of so much information on the Web has especially benefited students. First, students have access to far more written academic materials than ever before; the availability of academic writings on the Web is a welcome supplement to the offerings of school and public libraries. Second, student research efforts are no longer tied to the operating hours of libraries; students can access a wide range of materials at any time from wherever they happen to be with their computers. A student with a cellular modem does not even need to be near land-based telephone lines.

The Web also makes student plagiarism much more tempting, however. It not only provides easy online access to an abundance of quality writings, but also produces it in a form that is easy to plagiarize. Formerly, a plagiarist had to take the time to copy a text sentence by sentence onto a medium that could be turned in as her or his own; not infrequently, this involved hours of time typing or writing the text. Now a plagiarist can take someone else's text with a few keystrokes: one need do no more than highlight the relevant text, enter the appropriate keystrokes to copy and paste it into a word processing document, and unethically claim authorship in the work.

Student plagiarism also raises third-party ethical issues, because there are a number of Web sites offering original research papers for sale. One such Web site boasts: "Our 80 full-time researchers are available 24 hours a day, 7 days a week. Order now, and we will write your term paper within your specified deadline."[19] Although students must accept moral responsibility for initiating the sequence of acts that culminates in plagiarism, Web sites offering term papers for sale are not beyond ethical reproach because the operators must be aware there is a high likelihood that students will claim the work as their own.

Indeed, these sites seem to invite student plagiarism. After all, the only writing that is appropriately characterized as a "term paper" is writing that is being turned in as coursework; thus, advertising a piece of writing as a "term paper" is not unreasonably construed as a claim that the work is suitable to be turned in for a grade. If, as seems reasonable, knowingly aiding someone in committing an ethical violation is unethical, then offering term papers for sale in such a suggestive manner is also unethical.[20]

INFORMATION PRIVACY

The networked world has had ethically significant impact on information privacy. Internet users have a variety of ways to produce communications that are anonymous in principle or in effect, thereby empowering them to engage in more legitimate speech-related activities without fear of reprisal. Such anonymity also facilitates socially undesirable behavior, however: The lower the risk of being caught for criminal activity, the less effective the social consequences will be in functioning as a deterrent.[21] It is, for example, much easier to make anonymous threats over the Internet than by, say, telephone; whereas one can find a variety of ways to conceal one's identity in cyberspace from the comfort of one's own computer, it is virtually impossible for one to fully conceal one's identity by a telephone call made from one's home or cell phone.

Legal Protection of Information Privacy

The various constitutions differ with respect to how much protection they provide to privacy. The Canadian Charter and U.S. Constitution both contain a number of provisions that can be construed as concerned with protecting privacy. Each contains clauses protecting freedom of speech, thought, conscience, and religious worship, as well as freedom from unreasonable searches and seizures.[22] Such protections are reasonably construed as being concerned to establish a zone or sphere of privacy in which a person's movements are protected against state intrusion.

Neither the Canadian Charter nor the U.S. Constitution, however, contains a provision that explicitly defines a privacy right in personal information or data. While the U.S. Supreme Court has grounded a general right of privacy in the "penumbras" of the various protections mentioned above, the constitutional right to privacy in the United States has most commonly been cited as a justification for invalidating laws that restrain reproductive freedom.[23] What protections there are in Canada and the United States for personal information are defined largely by statute and common law.

In contrast, a recent draft of the Charter of Fundamental Rights of the European Union provides explicit privacy protection for personal information. Article 8 provides that "(1) Everyone has a right to the protection of personal data concerning him or her [; and] (2) Such data must be processed fairly for specified purposes and on the basis of the consent of the person concerned or some other legitimate basis laid down by law. Everyone has the right of access to data which has been collected concerning him or her, and the right to have it rectified."

It is worth noting that European statutory law provides comprehensive protection of a person's interest in information privacy. The European Parliament and Council of October 24, 1995, have issued a general directive governing the processing of personal information.[24] Chapter 1, Article 1 provides that "Member states shall protect the

---

[19] Retrieved September 7, 2002, from http://www.term-paper-time.com. It should be noted that the site also states in ironically ungrammatical fashion: "We always urge them not to use the work as their own. Although the work we do is completely original and cannot be found anywhere else on the Web" (http://www.term-paper-time.com/html/aboutus).

[20] There are now a number of Web-based products that assist instructors in detecting student plagiarism. Such products can be found at www.canexus.com/eve/index3.shtml, www.plagiarism.com, and www.powerresearcher.com. Nevertheless, it should be noted that these products will assist only in detecting instances of cut-and-paste plagiarism; they will not help in detecting instances where students have purchased specially written papers.

[21] For an empirical and normative analysis of the positive and negative effects of the anonymizing capabilities of the Internet, see Kling, Lee, Teich, & Frankel, 1999; Teich, Frankel, Kling, & Lee, 1999.

[22] See the First, Third, Fourth, Fifth, and Ninth Amendments to the U.S. Constitution; see Sections 2, 7, 8, 9, 11, and 13 of the Canadian Charter of Rights and Freedoms.

[23] See, for example, *Griswold v. Connecticut*, 381 U.S. 479 (1965); and *Roe v. Wade*, 410 U.S. 113 (1973).

[24] The full text of the directive is available from http://www.privacy.org/pi/intl_orgs/ec/final_EU_Data_Protection.html.

fundamental rights and freedoms of natural persons, and in particular their right to privacy, with respect to the processing of personal data."[25] Among other things, the directive limits the purposes for which personal information on an individual may be collected to "specified, explicit and legitimate purposes" and guarantees a right of access of the individual to such data.

In contrast, the U.S. approach to protecting information privacy has been somewhat uneven. On the one hand, pursuant to the Health Insurance Portability and Accountability Act (HIPAA; 1996), the U.S. Department of Health and Human Services (2000) promulgated the first federal standards for protecting the privacy of medical records. On the other hand, the U.S. PATRIOT Act, which was enacted in response to the terrorist attacks of September 11, 2001,[26] expands the surveillance capacities of the government in a number of ways. Section 213, for example, allows the government to conduct a search without notifying the subject that a warrant has been executed if "the court finds reasonable cause to believe that providing immediate notification of the execution of the warrant may have an adverse result." Similarly, Section 216 allows the government to monitor an individual's movements on the Web upon a showing that "the information likely to be obtained . . . is relevant to an ongoing criminal investigation." If the expansion of such investigative capacities arguably promotes citizens' security interests, it does so at some (possibly justified) cost to privacy interests.

Moral Legitimacy of Information Privacy Rights

Consequentialist theories justify privacy rights as necessary for a person's happiness and well-being. James Rachels (1975) argued, for example, that protection of privacy rights is justified by our need to control the structure of our social relationships: "If we cannot control who has access to us, sometimes including and sometimes excluding various people, then we cannot control the patterns of behavior we need to adopt . . . or the kinds of relations with other people we will have." Moreover, it is commonly believed that protection of privacy rights is justified by a concern to prevent the embarrassment or offense that would be caused to a person by disclosure of certain facts.

Deontological theories of privacy, in contrast, take the position that private facts about a person are "nobody else's business," regardless of what the consequences of disclosure might be. Privacy should be respected, on this line of reasoning, not just because it conduces to well-being, but also because persons are intrinsically valuable beings entitled to be treated as autonomous ends in themselves. The intrinsic value of each person, then, requires that certain facts be treated as private and subject to the

control of that person, even if those facts turn out to be extremely useful to other people.

Some theorists, however, caution that legal protection of privacy should be narrowly crafted to avoid unnecessarily restricting the free flow of information. Singleton (1998), for example, argued that the collection and dissemination of consumer information from business to business should not be restricted by privacy protections. Business dissemination of consumer information, on her view, is not morally distinguishable from ordinary gossip. Inasmuch as a legal ban on ordinary gossip would violate the right to free speech, so, too, would a ban on the dissemination of ordinary consumer information. Thus, she concludes, "[any] country that takes the freedom of information seriously cannot properly prohibit one business from communicating information about real events and real people to other businesses."[27]

Public and Private Information

The general claim that personal information ought to be protected by law does not, by itself, tell us much about how to determine what information about a person deserves legal privacy protection. For example, the altogether plausible consequentialist claim that protection of information is justified by a personal need to control the structure of various social relationships says little as to what information about a person ought to be protected by the law. For this reason, general justifications of privacy rights, such as those discussed in the last section, represent only a starting point in determining what content privacy law ought to have.

It is reasonable to think that whether a person ought to have a protected privacy right in a piece of information depends in part on the character of that information. Some facts about a person are generally accepted as private facts in which a person has a legitimate expectation of privacy. Because, for example, I am entitled to draw my drapes to prevent people from viewing what is going on in my home, the facts about what is going on my home are private—at least when the drapes are drawn[28] and my behavior is lawful. Thus, I have a legitimate expectation of privacy in aspects of my behavior that I may rightfully prevent people from viewing; these aspects of my behavior define private facts.

Some facts, however, should be regarded as private in virtue of their intimate character. It is almost universally accepted that certain physical functions, such as those involving the sexual and excretory organs, express private facts because of their felt intimate character. Information regarding a person's physical and emotional health is also widely regarded as private information that he or she should be entitled to control; indeed, so intimately vital

---

[25] "Processing of personal data" includes "collection, recording, organization, storage, adaptation or alteration, retrieval, consultation, use, disclosure by transmission, dissemination or otherwise making available, alignment or combination, blocking, erasure or destruction." Chapter 1, Article 2(b).

[26] The text of the USA PATRIOT Act is available from http://www.eff.org/Privacy/Surveillance/Terrorism_militias/20011025_hr3162_usa_patriot_bill.html. For a critical evaluation of the implication of the act on information privacy, see http://www.eff.org/Privacy/Surveillance/Terrorism_militias/20011031_eff_usa_patriot_analysis.html.

[27] Nevertheless, it should be noted that the U.S. Financial Services Modernization Act (Pub. L. 106–102) requires financial institutions (a) to inform customers of their policies regarding the collection, use, and dissemination of customer information and (b) to honor customers' requests not to have their information disseminated to third-party businesses. Although this, of course, does not amount to a ban on such practices, it significantly restricts what Singleton characterizes as the privacy equivalent of gossip.

[28] I can, of course, always voluntarily make private facts public by leaving my drapes open.

are these facts that medical professionals are charged with a legal duty of confidentiality.

Although many privacy issues concern private facts, others are concerned with information of a significantly different character. Some information contained in public records concerns matters that most individuals would regard as sensitive. For example, many people are reluctant to make their debt history readily available to anyone who happens to be curious about it—and this is especially so if that history includes a bankruptcy. Likewise, many people who have paid their debt for criminal offenses are reluctant to make their criminal records easily available out of a concern that such information would be used to discriminate against them.

The issue of whether a person has a moral right to control a particular piece of information that ought to be protected by the law thus depends on a variety of considerations. It will depend not only on broad theoretical arguments regarding the general justification of information privacy, but also on the character of the particular piece of information and how that information might be used by other persons. Such determinations present difficult issues of policy and ethics.

Internet Issues
Corporate Use of Personal Information

Many commercial firms collect information from visitors to their Web sites, which is stored in small data files called "cookies" and deposited on the visitors' own computers. These files typically contain information—such as passwords, on-site searches, dates of previous visits, and site preferences—that can be used by the firm to customize the user's experience when revisiting its site. For example, a bookselling Web site might store a list of previous searches on the user's computer so it can be accessed by the site on subsequent visits to generate a list of books to recommend to the user. This enables the site to provide what it considers to be better service by tailoring the user's Web environment to his or her preferences as expressed in previous visits to the site.

Although the use of cookies thus has a plausible business rationale, it raises ethical issues. Typically, cookies are transmitted from the user's hard drive to the site and retransmitted (possibly with modifications) from the site to the user's hard drive in a way that does not interrupt the user's browsing experience. This means that, in many cases, the user's hard drive—that is, his or her physical (as opposed to intellectual) property—is being modified without his or her consent. Although the legitimacy of intellectual property rights may be controversial, the legitimacy of personal property rights in physical objects is not (at least not in mainstream theorizing). The idea that someone else can, in essence, modify the user's physical property without his or her consent raises, to begin with, ethical issues concerning the user's property rights over the contents of his or her computer.

Moreover, some theorists worry that the use of cookies to keep information on the consumer raises privacy issues. As Spinello (2000, p. 111) puts the matter, "cookie technology is analogous to having someone follow you through the mall with a video camera." In both cases, the

technology keeps information on where you have gone, what you have looked at, and what you have purchased. To the extent that one has a legitimate expectation that one's movements in a public mall not be recorded, it can reasonably be argued that one also has a legitimate expectation that one's movements in cyberspace not be recorded.

Although it is possible for users to set up their browsers to refuse cookies or to alert them whenever a site attempts to store a cookie, this can cause inconvenience to the user. Refusing all cookies restricts the user's options in cyberspace because some Web sites cannot be viewed without accepting cookies. Setting a browser to ask before accepting cookies can result in frequent interruptions that radically change the quality of the browsing experience. Many users who restrict cookies find that the disutility associated with such frequent interruptions outweighs, at least in the short run, their privacy concerns and restore their browsers to the default setting that allows for unrestricted cookies.

There is thus a sense in which users who decline to configure their browsers to refuse cookies can be presumed to consent to cookies, but such consent is of questionable ethical significance. If the initial choice between A and B is not an ethically acceptable one, then the fact that a person voluntarily chooses A does not *logically imply* consent to A. For example, the fact that I voluntarily choose giving a robber my money if my only other choice is being shot does not entail that I have, in any ethically significant way, consented to give the robber my money. Consent is ethically significant only to the extent that it is rendered in an antecedent choice situation that is ethically acceptable. Thus, *if* the choice between accepting cookies and not being able to browse a Web site efficiently is not an ethically acceptable choice to impose unilaterally on a user, then the user's choice to accept cookies does not entail ethically meaningful consent. For this reason, the issue of whether accepting cookies amounts to meaningful consent depends on the issue of whether the choice to accept cookies or accept an inferior browsing experience can permissibly be imposed on users.

More troubling to privacy advocates than the data kept by any one firm, however, is the possibility that it could be combined with the information of other firms to create a comprehensive file about a user. To continue Spinello's analogy, this is analogous to having your movements in *every* store and mall recorded by a video camera and then keeping all those recordings in one central location that can be accessed by other persons. The more information about an individual that is centrally located and available for use by other persons and firms, the more likely it is to strike individuals as involving a breach of their privacy.

Notably, there are economic forces pushing in that direction. Businesses realize that consumer information is a valuable commodity and have evinced a growing willingness to sell it. Information about a consumer's buying and browsing habits can be used to tailor advertisements and mailings to his or her particular tastes and preferences, arguably serving both the consumer and the firm. It is not surprising, then, that trading in information itself is becoming an increasingly profitable venture—not only for firms specializing in information commerce, but also for ordinary firms specializing in other areas, and hence increases the likelihood that businesses will compile comprehensive files of personal information on individuals.[29]

State Databases

State databases raise a different set of issues because they contain only information that is "public" in an ethically meaningful sense. In most cases, what is at issue is the disposition of information that the public has a right to collect through its official state representatives. Thus, the information contained in state databases, if there legitimately, is information to which the public has some sort of antecedent claim. This distinguishes privacy issues involving state information from privacy issues involving corporate use of information that is not public in this sense.

Although state information is a matter of public record, privacy advocates believe that governments should take strong steps to protect the privacy of driver's license numbers, birthdates, official identification numbers (e.g., social security numbers), and other identifying information frequently used to access sensitive information about a person. This kind of information is uniquely subject to abuse: all that an identity thief in the United States, for example, needs to obtain credit cards in another person's name is her social security number and date of birth. With those two pieces of information, an identity thief can inflict long-term damage to a person's financial health and credit record.

The online dissemination of information already available to the public also raises privacy concerns. As noted earlier, privacy advocates are opposed to posting a person's public records online on the ground that such information can be used for discriminatory purposes. The availability of criminal records on the Web, for example, increases the likelihood that employers will discriminate against persons with criminal histories who have paid their debts to society.[30] Indeed, even a person's marital history can be used to discriminate against her or him. A landlord might refuse to rent to an older person who has never been married out of a suspicion that he or she might be gay. It is the possibility of such discrimination that, on this line of reasoning, requires granting a protected privacy interest in information that is admittedly public in one sense.

Such records have always been available to the public, but the risk of misuse increases with the ease with which these records can be obtained. As a general matter, most persons are not willing to incur the inconvenience of visiting a courthouse and asking for a person's criminal or marital records. Because posting such information on the Web eliminates such inconvenience, it dramatically increases the likelihood that people will seek such information and, a fortiori, the likelihood that people will

abuse it. For this reason, privacy advocates oppose posting this sort of public information on the Web.

These concerns are exacerbated by the amount of information that might be made available online. When it comes to privacy, the qualitative difference between what is and isn't ethical is sometimes a matter of quantity. As Spinello's mall analogy suggests, many people believe it would violate a person's legitimate interests in privacy to have his or her movements in a mall recorded and publicized. In relating this analogy to the issue of whether public records should be made available on the Web, it is crucial to emphasize that information about a person's movements around a mall is, in some sense, "public" information that is freely available to whoever might happen to be there.

Such worries are further increased by the ease with which various records might be obtainable on the Web. Indeed, some companies sell software that purports to enable people to obtain, among other things, public records that include criminal history, debt history, real property acquisitions, and marital records.[31] The idea that so much sensitive information about an individual can be obtained with just a few keystrokes makes many people rightly uncomfortable because of its susceptibility to being misused. Accordingly, privacy advocates argue that the easy availability of such information poses a significant threat to an individual's legitimate interests in information privacy.

Encryption Programs and Public Policy

A user's privacy can be violated online in yet another way. Ordinary means of communicating over the Internet are surprisingly insecure. E-mail messages are typically routed through many servers en route to their final destination. This raises the possibility that such messages could be intercepted and read by persons other than the intended recipient. For example, hackers or even system administrators could breach a user's privacy rights by reading his or her confidential e-mail.

One means for preventing these violations of privacy is the use of encryption programs. The most popular encryption programs function by means of an electronic binary "key" that maps strings of linguistic symbols into unintelligible code that can be deciphered only by someone who has the key. Senders and recipients who share a viable key, then, can communicate privately by means of encrypted messages.

Although encryption programs vary in sophistication, some programs enable encryption that is impossible to decode without the appropriate key. Although programmers have enjoyed considerable success in breaking even more sophisticated encryption programs, a "strong encryption" program incorporating a 128-bit algorithm (i.e., 2^{128} possible values) is, at least at this juncture, virtually unbreakable. For all practical purposes, then, an e-mail communication encrypted with a 128-bit algorithm cannot be deciphered and understood by anyone lacking the

---

[29] Online privacy services, such as Trust-E and BBB Online Privacy Program, rate various Web sites according to whether they agree to disclose their policies regarding the collection and dissemination of personal information by businesses. Trust-E is located at http://www.truste.org/; BBB Online is located at http://www.bbbonline.org/.

[30] Indeed, the ready availability of such information on the Web could increase the probability of recidivism. If employers unfairly refuse to hire persons with criminal records, they are likely to reoffend.

[31] One Web site boasts of a program, which it calls "the Internet's best selling spy software," that will allow persons to find "driver's records, lawsuits, criminal records, asset identification, ... tax liens, ... and court documents." http://www.oddworldz.com/landoh34/learn.html?. Other Web sites offering spy software include http://www.spy-patrol.com and http://www.spectorsoft.com.

key. Such communications are, given existing technologies, perfectly secure.

Some U.S. legislators and citizens favor legislation that restricts the export of such sophisticated encryption programs employing 128-bit keys. There have been a number of proposals, ranging from outright bans to restrictions that allow the state some sort of access to the keys. For example, the so-called Clipper computer chip, which was originally intended for encrypting telephone communications, came encoded with an algorithm enabling law enforcement agencies to decode encrypted communications. One half of the decryption key was given to each of two law enforcement agencies, thus requiring that one obtain the consent of the other to decrypt communications.

Supporters of such regulations have stressed security interests. On this line of reasoning, the interest in, or right to, security is the most important interest or right in the moral hierarchy and hence trumps other interests and rights in the event of a direct conflict. Supporters argue that restrictions on strong encryption are morally legitimate because they are necessary to ensure that intelligence and law enforcement agencies have sufficient resources to protect the public's security interests against the serious threat posed by the activities of terrorists and international criminals.

Opponents have stressed both privacy and speech interests. Restrictions on encryption that allow the state access to keys chill the exercise of legitimate speech interests because, under such restrictions, citizens must worry about whether the state can eavesdrop on encrypted communications. Privacy and speech rights require, on this view, that citizens feel (and be) utterly free to communicate with selected individuals without having to worry about whether the state can listen in on their private communications. Moreover, many believe that the continuing expansion of e-commerce, and the economic growth it makes possible, also depends on consumers feeling their transactions are protected against governmental eavesdropping.

COMPUTER SECURITY

The term "security" is something of a catch-all term. In its broadest use, the term connotes nothing more specific than "freedom from danger,"[32] but "danger" itself is a broad term appropriately used to characterize *any* serious threat to a morally significant interest. On this usage, then, any law that protects life, liberty, or property is fairly characterized as attempting to ensure a person's "security."

This portion of the chapter, however, is concerned only with legal and ethical issues as they arise in connection with *computer* security, "computer security" being construed to mean "freedom from unauthorized computer intrusions." Accordingly, this section is concerned with legal protections against unauthorized computer intrusions, the justification for such protection, and the challenge posed to such justifications by hackers.

Legal Protection of Computer Security

Security from unauthorized computer intrusions has become a priority for lawmakers. Most, if not all, developed nations have laws prohibiting unauthorized computer intrusions. In the United States, for example, the Computer Crime and Fraud Act (18 U.S. Code Section 1030) authorizes fines and imprisonment of up to 20 years for, among other things, "knowingly caus[ing] the transmission of a program, information, code, or command, and as a result of such conduct, intentionally caus[ing at least $5,000 in] damage without authorization, to a protected computer." Similarly, Section 342.1 of the Canadian Consolidated Statutes and Regulations authorizes imprisonment for up to ten years for, among other things, the fraudulent and wrongful "intercept[ion], direct[] or indirect[], [of] any function of a computer system."

The European Union has also endorsed strong protections against unauthorized computer intrusions. Article 2 of the European Convention on Cybercrime requires member nations to "adopt such legislative and other measures as may be necessary to establish as criminal offences under its domestic law, when committed intentionally, the access to the whole or any part of a computer system without right."[33] The clear intent of Article 2 is that unauthorized intrusions be prohibited by law.

Moral Legitimacy of Computer Security Rights

At first glance, laws prohibiting unauthorized computer intrusions seem easy to justify on ethical grounds. Although the more malicious intrusions involve serious ethical transgressions because of the harm they are intended to cause, all seem morally objectionable for two reasons. First, they appear to constitute an electronic form of trespass onto the *physical* property of another person. To obtain unauthorized entry into some other person's network or computer seems, from an ethical perspective, straightforwardly analogous to uninvited entry onto the real property of another person. Even if it turns out that there are no natural moral rights to intellectual property, it seems clear that persons have property rights in their computers and networks (which are, after all, material objects and not intellectual objects). Such trespass is widely regarded as morally wrong, regardless of whether it results in damage or harm, because it violates the property right of the owner to control the uses to which his or her property is put and hence to exclude other people from its use. Similarly, hacking into someone else's computer or network is wrong, regardless of whether it results in damage, because it violates the owner's property right to exclude others from using his or her computer or network equipment.

Second, such computer intrusions seem to violate the legitimate privacy rights of the victims. If it is true that persons have a property right in their physical hardware, then it is reasonable to think that they have privacy rights in the documents and files they store on that hardware. If I know that I may legitimately exclude you from appropriating my computer, then I have a reasonable expectation

---

[32] See, for example, Merriam-Webster Online Dictionary; available from http://www.m-w.com/.

[33] See http://conventions.coe.int/Treaty/en/Reports/Html/185.htm.

that I may exclude you from the files and documents that I store on my hard drive. On this second line of reasoning, hacking into someone else's hardware is wrong because it violates the legitimate privacy expectations of the owners. This is true regardless of whether owners actually store sensitive information on those machines: breaking into my home involves a violation of my privacy even if the perpetrator acquires no private information about me.

It is worth noting here that considerations having to do with the legitimacy of intellectual property rights do not play a general role in justifying laws prohibiting unauthorized computer intrusions. The reason for this is that unauthorized intrusions need not involve infringement on those interests protected by intellectual property law; there is nothing in the nature of such an intrusion that entails, say, the infringement of interests that are protected by a patent or by trademark law. In contrast, unauthorized computer intrusions seem, by definition, to impinge on someone's property rights in their computer hardware and hence on reasonable privacy expectations.

Internet Issue: Hackers

There are a growing number of well-publicized incidents in which hackers obtain unauthorized entry into a firm's or state agency's servers. Some of these incidents involve comparatively innocuous exploration of a network's structure; in such cases, hackers look around and leave without altering the system. Others involve the commission of computer pranks; one such famous incident involved an insulting message left by hackers on the *New York Times* Web site (see, e.g., Nutall, 1998). Yet others involve the commission of cyberterrorism that threatens national security, as when a hacker breaks into a government network that stores classified material, or individual well-being, as when a hacker breaks into a corporate server and takes credit card and bank account numbers.[34]

Many hackers reject the claim that all unauthorized computer intrusions can legitimately be prohibited to protect moral interests in property and privacy, arguing that some hacking activity can be justified in terms of its social benefits, at least when it results in no damage or harm to innocent persons. These computer intrusions, they point out, contribute to increasing our technological knowledge in a number of ways. First, by gaining insight into the operations of existing networks, hackers develop a base of knowledge that can be used to improve those networks. Second, the very break-ins themselves call attention to security flaws that could be exploited by malicious hackers or, worse, terrorists. Thus, electronic trespass is distinguished, according to proponents, from other forms of trespass in that it inevitably conduces to public benefit.

Certain hacking activities have also been defended as a form of free expression in two ways. First, the permissibility of benign break-ins appears to be a consequence of the claim that "information wants to be free." If it is true, as an ethical matter, that all information should be free, then security measures designed to keep hackers out of networks are morally objectionable on the ground that they inhibit

the free flow of information.[35] Second, some writers have argued that benign break-ins can be defended as a form of protest or political activism ("hacktivism"). On this line of reasoning, such incidents express legitimate outrage over the increasing commercialization of the Web. Politically motivated hacking, according to these writers, should be permitted as long as it results in neither harm nor profit (Manion & Goodrum, 2000).

E-VOTING

Central to the legitimacy of democratic governance is the right to vote. At the foundation of all democratic theories is the idea that every competent person has a right to autonomy that entitles her or him to participate actively in his or her own governance and hence has a right to participate in the political decision-making process. The right to participate protects a variety of activities other than voting; for example, it entitles competent persons to run for elected office. Its centerpiece is the right to vote in elections that determine either the content of the law or the persons who will serve as legislators or judges.

The traditional mechanism for exercising the right to vote is the paper ballot. Up until now, the vast majority of votes have been cast on paper or punch-card ballots; citizens indicate the candidate of their choice by making a physical mark of some kind on the ballot, either by writing a mark of some kind or punching a hole next to the appropriate candidate's name. Although these ballots have usually been counted by hand, a process that is highly vulnerable to abuse and error, election precincts in many countries are now using new automated technologies for counting votes.

There are a variety of new and developing technologies that fall under the rubric of e-voting. A number of companies have developed technologies enabling citizens to vote merely by touching a computer screen that is located at their precincts; votes can then be counted at the precinct by a local automated mechanism or can be transmitted via the Internet to a central location where votes from different precincts can be counted by a machine. Many proponents of e-voting envision a day when every voter can vote via his or her personal computer from the convenience of his or her own home.

These new and developing technologies implicate the right to vote in a variety of ethically significant ways. This section explores the various social and ethical issues that arise in connection with the application of these information technologies to the democratic process.

Legal Protection of Voting

Because the right to vote is the foundation of democratic governance, it is not surprising that democratic nations typically afford strong legal protection to the right to vote. Article I of the U.S. Constitution provides that federal legislators be democratically elected by citizens according to certain prescribed procedures (which may be defined in part by the states).[36] Similarly, Section 3 of the

---

[34] Some people distinguish "hacking" from "cracking." Cracking, unlike hacking, involves a malicious purpose; the intent is to gain entry to a network to cause harm or damage. In contrast, hacking is motivated primarily by curiosity.

[35] For a critical discussion of this claim, see Spafford (1992).

[36] The Fifteenth and Nineteenth Amendments prohibit restricting any person's right to vote on grounds having to do with race, color, gender, or previous servitude.

Canadian Charter provides that "Every citizen of Canada has the right to vote in an election of members of the House of Commons or of a legislative assembly and to be qualified for membership therein." Finally, Article 39 of the European Charter of Fundamental Rights states that "Every citizen of the Union has the right to vote and to stand as a candidate at election to the European Parliament."

The centrality of the right to vote is underscored by the fact that the justification for other fundamental rights is frequently couched in terms of the contribution they make toward democratic governance. The legal right to free speech, which is protected in North America and Europe, is frequently justified in terms of its contribution toward producing an informed and responsible electorate. Without free speech, on this line of reasoning, citizens would lack information that is essential to being able to exercise the right to vote in an ethically meaningful way.

Moral Legitimacy of E-Voting

The legitimacy of adopting e-voting technologies will largely depend on a number of factors. For starters, the legitimacy of such technologies depends on how accurate and how secure they are; the less accurate or secure a technology is, the less justified a state would be in adopting it. Further, the legitimacy of such technologies depends upon their effects on the voting behaviors of citizens. To the extent that adopting such technologies would result in a decrease in significant turnout among some important segment of the population, such technologies "chill" the exercise of the right to vote among members of the affected segment. For example, excessive polling taxes are illegitimate because they make it harder for less affluent citizens to exercise that right and thus violate their rights to vote. This section surveys some of the arguments that have been made on both sides of the issue.

Ethical Arguments for E-Voting
Accuracy of Technologies.
Arguments for the adoption of the new E-voting technologies usually focus on the effects of such technologies on various aspects of the election process. For example, newer technologies make it possible to determine the results of an election more quickly than is possible using hand counting or the older automated technologies, which require the physical transportation of ballots from voting box to the counting technology. Accordingly, these newer technologies dramatically reduce the waiting period associated with traditional technologies.

Proponents of e-voting technologies also argue that fully automating the voting process will improve the accuracy of the counting process by eliminating human judgment. Proponents point to the problems that arose in connection with counting ballots cast in Florida during the 2000 U.S. presidential election. Fallible and potentially biased human beings had to sort through a large number of ambiguously marked ballots and attempt to discern the voter's intent in marking the ballot. Fully automating the process takes elections out of the hands of human beings, replacing them with a much faster and more reliable technology.

Effects on Voter Turnout

These features of the new technologies, according to proponents, will help to improve turnout for elections by restoring voter confidence in the electoral system. For example, the problems with the 2000 presidential election have led to continuing debate about the legitimacy of the Bush presidency and weakened confidence among citizens in the U.S. electoral process, which presumably operates to reduce voter turnout. Because the new technologies are more securely insulated from human judgment—and hence from human fallibility and bias—citizens are more likely to trust the results and hence to participate in elections.

Proponents argue that future Web-based technologies will boost turnout by making it easier than ever for citizens to express their political views and preferences through the voting process. Citizens who own a personal computer with an Internet connection is, other things being equal, more likely to vote if they can reliably vote using the personal computer from the privacy of their home than if they can vote only by traditional means (which, it should be noted, include absentee ballots). It is true, of course, that not every citizen owns a personal computer, but this, proponents insist, is an argument for retaining other voting technologies and not an argument against adopting Web-based voting technologies as they are developed. As long as such voters are not unfairly disadvantaged by the adoption of newer technologies, it is ethically permissible and socially desirable to adopt these technologies.

Web-based technologies, on this line of reasoning, are especially likely to boost turnout among citizens who have disabilities that severely limit their ability to travel away from home. Appropriately adapted Web-based voting technologies ensure that severely disabled citizens (who own personal computers and have an Internet connection) can exercise their right to vote with far less inconvenience than is involved for them in using the traditional voting technologies.

To appreciate fully the force of these arguments, it is important to realize that the legitimacy of an election requires that all eligible citizens be in a position to meaningfully exercise their right to vote without incurring significant costs. It is clear, for example, that an election system requiring an expensive fee to vote is illegitimate because less affluent voters will be far less likely to vote. In consequence, elected officials are considerably less likely to take their wishes and needs into account in the lawmaking process. If the point of democracy is to ensure that all constituencies are fairly represented, then voting fees (or polling taxes) defeat democracy's very point.

Putting citizens in a position to be able to participate meaningfully in elections presumably requires not only that they receive sufficient education to minimally understand the issues, positions, and candidates, but also that elections be staged in a way that enables each citizen to exercise his or her right to vote without the sort of inconvenience that is likely to deter his or her from voting. Although it may sometimes be accurate to construe a citizen's failure to vote as indifference on his or her part, this is not necessarily true: it is reasonable to hypothesize that many persons who would like to vote are not able to do so because of the costs or inconveniences associated with traditional voting technologies.

Ethical Arguments Against E-Voting

Discriminatory Effects on Poor. There are a number of arguments against the adoption of e-voting technologies. Some opponents have grounded arguments against the adoption of technologies that would allow Internet-based voting in considerations having to do with economic justice. On this line of reasoning, the adoption of such technologies discriminates against people who cannot afford a personal computer and broadband access. Although the adoption of such technologies is likely to increase turnout among wealthier (and hence technologically savvy) voters, they are also likely to have the effect of reducing turnout among less affluent persons. Even if less affluent persons can still vote by traditional means or by using computers in public schools and libraries, the use of such means could be stigmatized (in much the same way, for example, that inhabitants of public housing projects are stigmatized), thereby reducing voter turnout among less affluent voters who do not have a personal computer. As a matter of economic justice, such discrimination is unfair.

Such disproportionate effects on turnout are objectionable from the standpoint of democratic principles as well. In theory (if not in practice), full voter turnout ensures that the interests of all persons will be adequately represented in the lawmaking process and hence that the content of the law will protect and advance those interests; a lack of participation, then, by any theoretically significant constituency makes it far less likely that the content of the law will adequately protect the interests of that constituency. If the adoption of Internet-based e-voting technologies is likely to increase turnout among wealthy voters but decrease turnout among less affluent voters, then the adoption of such technologies is objectionable on democratic principles as well as on principles of economic justice. By diminishing turnout among the poor, the adoption of these technologies would operate to ensure that their interests are not fairly represented in the lawmaking process.

Unreliability of Existing E-Voting Technologies

Although e-voting proponents believe that automating voting procedures is likely to increase the accuracy of results, opponents can point to a number of instances in which existing e-voting technologies produced inaccurate results.[37] In a 2002 election primary in Clay County, Kansas, for example, an automated counting technology falsely indicated that a candidate for county commissioner had lost by a slim margin of 4 percentage points, when a hand recount showed that he had actually won by a landslide with 76% of the votes (Harris, 2004; "Mayo Won by a Landslide," 2002). A "bad chip" was apparently to blame for a mistaken win by two Republican candidates for county commissioner in Scurry County, Texas; a recount using a new chip indicated that the Democratic candidates had won by a large margin ("Ballot glitches," 1998; Harris, 2004).

Mistaken election results are ethically problematic for at least two reasons. First, undiscovered mistakes can result in a losing candidate's holding a legislative office to which he or she was not elected and hence not entitled to hold. In such instances, the official's acts are politically illegitimate and not, strictly speaking, binding as a matter of law, but are nonetheless treated as being legally binding, something that is especially problematic when the acts involve paradigmatic lawmaking activities. Second, the proliferation of such errors is likely to diminish the confidence of citizens in the voting system procedures and is hence likely to reduce voter turnout in elections.

Security Concerns

Perhaps the most significant concern with adopting Internet-based e-voting technologies has to do with the insecurity of networks on the Internet. Hackers are continually becoming more sophisticated and better able to find gaps in even the most secure Internet-based systems. Not only can the best hackers find ways to circumvent the most sophisticated security technologies, they are also becoming better at minimizing the likelihood that they will be detected during an intrusion and subsequently apprehended. It is probably true that it is not possible to break into a system without leaving some physical trace (or record) of the intrusion, but it is also true that a more sophisticated hacker can take steps to diminish the number of traces he or she leaves.

For this reason, it is reasonable to worry about the security of Internet-based e-voting technologies. One concern is, of course, the worst-case scenario in which a highly sophisticated hacker changes the results of an election without ever being detected. Another concern is that the mere possibility of such a scenario is enough to significantly diminish the electorate's confidence in election results and the integrity of the voting process. The potential consequences of such a decrease in confidence range from widespread suspicion among citizens about closely contested elections to a dramatic reduction in voter turnout.

Although many reasonable persons believe that, at this point, the security problems outweigh the potential benefits of Internet-based e-voting technologies, it is important to keep in mind that this need not always be the case. The magnitude of the relevant security risks of e-voting is a function of both the state of the security technologies intended to protect the process and the state of the technologies available to hackers. As the states of both these technologies evolve over time, we should expect that an assessment of the relevant risks and benefits will vary over time. At any given time, then, an assessment of the risks and benefits will require an empirical analysis of the states of all the relevant technologies. This leaves open the possibility that if it is true, as opponents believe, that Internet-based e-voting technologies are not yet secure enough, they might someday be.

CONCLUSION

Although the advent of the Internet age has empowered ordinary citizens in novel ways, it has also created a number of equally novel ethical and social problems. Indeed, as is generally true, the very capabilities that increase a

---

[37] For a detailed account of many of these incidents involving elections in the United States, see chapter 2 of Harris (2004).

person's ability to promote public and private interests also increase his or her ability to harm other people. To the extent that, for example, the Internet enables the ordinary citizen to reach a worldwide audience, it dramatically improves his or her ability to propagate unethical and dangerous ideas.

We should expect that the social and ethical issues of the Internet are no less complicated than the remarkable technology that engenders them. For every argument that invokes traditional ethical and social values in defending a position about online behavior, there is a countervailing argument that resists the application of these values to a technology that seems so radically different from what has preceded it. The debates on these fascinating issues will fill the pages of academic and popular publications for the foreseeable future.

GLOSSARY

Consequentialism The class of ethical theories that determine the moral goodness or badness of an action entirely in terms of its consequences.

Cookies Small files deposited by a Web site on a user's computer for the purpose of enabling the Web site to track the user's preferences.

Copyright Legal device that grants an exclusive right to the holder to reproduce and distribute fixed, original expression.

Cyberterrorism Hacking activity that attempts to harm innocent persons and thereby create a general sense of fear or terror among the general population for the purpose of achieving a political agenda.

Deontologism Ethical theories that take the position that the moral goodness or badness of some actions is determined, not by their consequences, but by their intrinsic features.

Domain Names Natural language phrase (e.g., www.sportinggoods.com) that is associated with a Web site's Internet protocol address.

Encryption The translation of data (including that transmitted in e-mail messages) into code that cannot be deciphered and read by unintended recipients.

File Transfer Protocol (FTP) A device that allows a user to transfer files from his or her personal computer to a central network server and conversely.

Filters Programs designed to prevent a user from accessing Web sites with content that is deemed inappropriate.

Hackers Persons who attempt to gain unauthorized entry to network servers or other computers. Hacking is usually distinguished from "cracking" in that the latter, unlike hacking activity, is intended to cause harm to innocent persons.

Hacktivism Hacking activity motivated by a desire to express a political view or agenda. For example, a hacktivist might target a corporate Web site as a means of protesting the increasingly commercial character of the Web.

Intellectual Property Mental and abstract entities considered as property. Intellectual property includes music, expression of ideas, and designs.

MP3 Files Digital files using a format that permits the compression of nearly perfect digital reproductions of sound recordings into small files that can efficiently be transmitted from one user to another.

Patent Legal device that grants an inventor monopoly power over the design of his or her invention.

Peer-to-Peer (P2P) File Sharing A file-sharing device that allows Web users to directly access files that are stored on the computers of other Web users.

Spam E-mail sent indiscriminately without the recipient's consent or against the recipient's wishes.

Trademark Legal device that grants a firm an exclusive right to use a mark that distinguishes its goods and services from those of other firms.

Utilitarianism A consequentialist moral theory that holds that the goodness or badness of an action is determined entirely by its consequences on well-being, happiness, the number of preferences satisfied, or pleasure in the community.

CROSS REFERENCES

See *Copyright Law; Electronic Speech; Internet Censorship; Privacy Law and the Internet; Secure Electronic Voting Protocols.*

REFERENCES

A & M Records v. Napster, 114 F. Supp. 2d 896 (2000).

American Library Association v. United States, 201 F.Supp.2d 401 (2002).

Ashcroft v. ACLU, 322 F.3d 240 (2003).

Ballot glitches reverse two election results. (1998, September 3). *Houston Chronicle*

Barlow, J. P. (1992–1993). A taxonomy of information. Retrieved from http://www.eff.org/~barlow/EconomyOfIdeas.html.

Barlow, J. P. (1996). A declaration of the independence of cyberspace. Retrieved from http://www.eff.org/~barlow/Declaration-Final.html.

Benedek, E., & Brown, C. (1999). No excuses: Televised pornography harms children. *Harvard Review of Psychiatry, 7,* 236–240.

Biegel, S. (2001). *Beyond our control? Confronting the limits of our legal system in the age of cyberspace.* Cambridge, MA: MIT Press.

Borland, J. (2003, July 15). File-sharing down after music industry crackdown. *Silicon.com.* Retrieved November 1, 2003, from http://www.wired.com/news/digiwood/0,1412,59756,00.html.

Canadian Human Rights Act, Section 13. Retrieved from http://laws.justice.gc.ca/en/H-6/28764.html#rid-28778.

Council of Europe. (n.d.). Retrieved from http://www.coe.int/T/E/Communication_and_Research/Press/Theme_Files/Cybercrime/Index.asp.

Department of Health and Human Services. (2000). Standards for privacy of individually identifiable health information. Retrieved from http://www.hhs.gov/ocr/combinedregtext.pdf.

Downloads Blamed for Low CD Sales. (2002, August 26). *Wired News.* Retrieved November 1, 2003, from http://www.wired.com/news/business/0,1367,54767,00.html.

European Parliament. (1997). Resolution on the Commission Green Paper on the protection of minors and human dignity in audiovisual and information services (COM(96)0483-C4-0621/96). Retrieved from http://www.gilc.org/speech/eu/ep-minors-resolution-1097.html.

Harris, B. (2004). *Black box voting*. Tallon. Retrieved from http://www.BlackBoxVoting.org.

Health Insurance Portability and Accountability Act. Pub. L. No. 104-191 (1996). Text available at http://aspe.hhs.gov/admnsimp/pl104191.htm.

Introna, L. D., & Nissenbaum, H. (2000). Shaping the Web: Why the politics of search engines matter. *Information Society, 16*, 169–186.

Kling, R., Lee, Y.-C., Teich, L., & Frankel, M. S. (1999, February). Assessing anonymous communication on the Internet: Policy deliberations. http://www.indiana.edu/~tisj/readers/full-text/15-2%20kling.pdf.

Kornblum, J. (1998, August 11). Compaq buys AltaVista domain. CNET News.com. Retrieved from http://news.com.com/2100-1023-214326.html?legacy=cnet.

Lawrence, S., & Giles, C. L. (1999). Accessibility and distribution of information on the Web. *Nature, 400*, 107–109.

Manion, M., & Goodrum, A. (2000). Terrorism or civil disobedience: Toward a hacktivist ethic. *Computers and Society, 30*, 14–19.

Mayo won by a landslide—election reversed. (2002, August 22). *Wichita Eagle*.

Mill, J. S. (1989). *On liberty*. Cambridge University Press.

Nozick, R. (1977). *Anarchy, state, and utopia*. New York: Basic Books.

Nuttall, C. (1998, September 17). Hackers Hit *New York Times*. BBC Online Network. Retrieved from: http://news.bbc.co.uk/1/hi/sci/tech/170999.stm.

Panavision v. Toeppe, 141 F.3d. 1316 (1998).

Rachels, J. (1975). Why privacy is important. *Philosophy and Public Affairs, 4*, 323–333.

Rawls, J. (1999). *A theory of justice* (rev. ed.). Cambridge, MA: Harvard University Press, 1999.

Recording industry begins suing P2P file sharers who illegally offer copyrighted music online. (2003, September 8). Retrieved November 1, 2003, from the Recording Industry Association of America Web site: http://www.riaa.com/news/newsletter/090803.asp.

Reno v. ACLU, 117 S.Ct. (1997).

RIAA Leaning on Kids' Parents. (2003, July 24). *Wired News*. Retrieved November 1, 2003, from http://www.wired.com/news/digiwood/0,1412,59756,00.html.

RIAA strikes back at music pirates in 2003. (2003, October 21). Retrieved the Recording Industry Association of America Web site: November 1, 2003, from http://www.riaa.com/news/newsletter/102103.asp.

Saunders, C. (2002, May 31). EU OKs spam ban, online privacy rules. *Internet News*. Retrieved from http://www.internetnews.com/IAR/article.php/1154391.

Singleton, S. (1998, January 22). Privacy as censorship: A skeptical view of proposals to regulate privacy in the private sector. Cato Institute Policy Analysis No. 295 Retrieved from http://www.cato.org/pubs/pas/pa-295es.html.

Spafford, E. (1992). Are computer hacker break-ins ethical? *Journal of Systems Software, 17*, 41–47.

Spinello, R. (2000). *Cyberethics: Morality and law in cyberspace*. Sudbury, MA: Jones and Bartlett.

Stallman, R. M. (2002). *Free software, free society: Selected essays*. Boston: GNU Press.

Suzukamo, L. B. (2002, September 7). Have you Googled yet? *Seattle Times*, C7.

Teich, A., Frankel, M. S., Kling, R., & Lee, Y.-C. (1999). Anonymous communications policies for the Internet: Results and recommendations from the AAAS Conference. *The Information Society* 15(2). Retrieved from http://www.indiana.edu/~tisj/readers/full-text/15-2%20teich.pdf.

United States v. American Library Association, 123 S. Ct. 2297 (2003).

FURTHER READING
Books

Johnson, D. (2001). *Computer ethics* (3rd ed.). Upper Saddle River, NJ: Prentice Hall.

Tavani, H. T. (2004). *Ethics and technology: Ethical issues in an age of information and communication technology*. New York: Wiley.

Anthologies

Baird, R. M., Ramsover, R., & Rosenbaum, S. E. (Eds.). (2000). *Cyberethics: Social and moral issues in the computer age*. New York: Promethius Books.

Hester, D. M., & Ford, P. J. (Eds.). (2001). *Computers and ethics in the cyberage*. Upper Saddle River, NJ: Prentice Hall.

Johnson, D. J., & Nissenbaum, H. (Eds.). (1995). *Computers, ethics and social values*. Upper Saddle River, NJ: Prentice Hall.

Langford, D. (Ed.). (2000). *Internet ethics*. London: MacMillan.

Spinello, R., & Tavani, H. T. (Eds.). (2001). *Readings in cyberethics*. Sudbury, MA: Jones & Bartlett.

Journals

Ethicomp Journal. Online journal available at http://www.ccsr.cse.dmu.ac.uk/journal/.

Ethics and Information Technology. Published by Kluwer Academic. Web site: http://www.kluweronline.com/issn/1388-1957.

Journal of Information, Communication, and Ethics in Society. Published by Troubador. Web site: http://www.troubador.co.uk/ices/default.asp.

International Journal of Information Ethics. Online journal available at http://ijie.zkm.de/.

Surveillance and Society. Online journal available at http://www.surveillance-and-society.org.

Anonymity and Identity on the Internet

Jonathan Wallace, *DeCoMo USA Labs*

INTRODUCTION

The loose structure of the Internet dictates that it is somewhat difficult to determine a user's true identity; correspondingly, a weak degree of anonymity is easily available. Complete anonymity, or a high level of assurance of the identity of another user, both require work. Technical solutions exist to help with both problems. U.S. constitutional law and common law precedents show a high degree of reverence for anonymous discourse, which has played a significant role in the British and U.S. political systems. The Supreme Court has repeatedly referred to this history in affirming, in recent years, the right of U.S. citizens to speak anonymously on political and social matters. Cases involving anonymity on the Internet began with the passage of a Georgia law banning anonymous email. Most of the case law since then has involved public companies suing anonymous individuals who posted messages accusing the companies of stock fraud or poor management. These court decisions all have held that the same protections apply to anonymity online as apply to the authors of pamphlets, people obtaining signatures on campaign petitions, or distributing religious material door to door. Nonetheless, there is a vocal minority of law professors and other commentators calling for a change in the Internet's architecture to require that a sender's identity be associated with his message.

The Internet's architecture is very supportive of anonymous discourse—and, correspondingly, very unconcerned about verifying the identity of any communicator. Optimized for ease of messaging and widespread, rapid distribution, the Internet does not care very much about the source of a message. Originally based on an easygoing philosophy of trust not enforced by the architecture, the early Internet community relied highly on people being, at least approximately, who they said they were.

Of course, from the earliest years of the Internet community, tricksters, con artists and criminals delighted in exploiting the system's open architecture. In 1985, Joan, mute and crippled as a result of a terrible automobile accident, built an worldwide community of supporters online, whose sympathy turned to venom and rage when Joan was revealed to be Alex, a male psychiatrist who was not crippled (Rheingold, 1993). Such spectacles are still reenacted routinely today; it is a truism that anyone flirting with strangers in e-mail or chat should be (but often is not) highly suspicious as to whether any correspondent is actually the gender that the e-mail name indicates.

Sociologists and other social commentators have seen in the ambiguities of Internet identity a healthy opportunity for the human persona to develop, exploring alternative pathways and even genders in an atmosphere of healthy play. Virtual identities, says Massachusetts Institute of Technology (MIT) psychologist Sherry Turkle (1994), are "evocative objects for thinking about the self...experiences in virtual space" that compel us "to pay greater attention to what [we] take for granted in the real." The flip side, of course, is the huge mistaken investment of time, energy, friendship, and even money others may make based on the false representations of an alternate, "playful" identity.

Although it was never safe in e-mail to assume that anyone was exactly who they said they were, in the first years of Internet communication you could at least get a significant level of comfort from an e-mail address. "Tom@mit.edu" was at least *probably* involved with MIT in some capacity, as a student, professor, staff member, or alumnus.

Today such assumptions are completely untenable. With viruses and spammers routinely spoofing the e-mail addresses of unwitting third parties, Internet users, to protect themselves effectively, should assume that any message, regardless of who it appears to be from, is unwanted or actively dangerous. The offline equivalent would be if you needed to call the bomb squad to investigate every time you received an envelope from anyone—friend or stranger—in the mail.

MECHANICS OF ANONYMITY AND IDENTITY ON THE NET

For e-mail users, the Web provides a significant level of functional anonymity at the entry level. Anyone can open an account with a mass service such as Hotmail, using any available name on that system. Suppose you receive an e-mail from someone calling himself brickchurch@hotmail.com. For starters, you do not know whether this is actually a person's name or a variation (maybe Frank Church whose nickname is Brick?) or a hobbyist (who travels the world photographing brick churches everywhere) or someone who picked a name out of thin air. The Hotmail architecture is easygoing and does not care whether the e-mail address you pick has anything to do with your name.

Loose identity is true of most systems that are geared toward, or encourage, use for personal, nonbusiness purposes. These systems, however, fall into two major categories: Internet service providers (ISPs) that are relaxed about *apparent identity* but have stricter rules tracking *real identity* and nonISPs (such as Hotmail) that don't care about either.

If you receive e-mail from YouGoGirl@aol.com, you may have no idea who this is, but the chances are good that AOL knows (they have to bill her [or his?] credit card every month for the use of the system). Because Hotmail, as a free service at the entry level, has little concern for user identity, it will rarely (if ever) have verified knowledge about the identity of a nonpaying user. However, unless he takes measures to obtain a higher degree of anonymity (discussed later), the user may still leave some personal information on the Hotmail site, such as his originating IP address.

Another class of users with stronger identity rules are large corporations. Most Fortune 500 companies have internal company rules mandating the format of an e-mail address, along the lines of firstname_lastname@ fortunecompany.com. The Internet is oblivious to these rules, however, and therefore, the most this kind of self-policing does these days is to tell you that, *if the message actually came from fortunecompany.com,* it is likely from an employee with the name given in the e-mail header. These days, however, the message could just as easily be a virus or spam with a spoofed header, and not actually have passed anywhere near the fortunecompany.com mail server.

Entry-level anonymity is not highly resistant to attempts to determine the user's real identity. If Tracey Smith, who is YouGoGirl@aol.com, opened the brickchurch@hotmail.com account and always accesses it from that address, law enforcement authorities looking into the use of the Hotmail account for a confidence scheme will not have too much trouble tracing Tracey. If Tracey only accessed the Hotmail account from Internet cafes, where she (or he) paid cash or used a stolen credit card, determining the real identity of brickchurch@hotmail.com may be difficult or impossible.

When it comes to maintaining anonymity, surfing the Web presents a different problem than the mere sending of e-mail. An Internet user visiting a Web site leaves behind a record of the user's IP address. A user whose ISP assigns a permanent IP address may change his or her proper name in the header. The permanent IP address will follow him everywhere he goes.

Some ISPs do not assign users a permanent IP but give the user one of a collection of available IP addresses just as he or she sets out from the home network to surf the Internet. In this case, the trail again becomes much more difficult to follow; the same IP address may have been used by Tracey Smith at 1 p.m., John Adams at 3, and Jane Goodloe at 5 p.m., for example.

HOW DO WE KNOW WHO ANYONE IS ON THE NET?

It is difficult to know who anyone is on the Net. If you receive e-mail from britney_spears@hotmail.com, chances are good that you haven't just heard from the singer. If your correspondent, a stranger, claims to be a mining expert, or a professor of engineering, or a person looking for a long-term romantic relationship, how do you know what his or her bona fides are?

Little in the nature of e-mail or in the architecture of the Internet helps us in this attempt. Most of us probably use the same instincts to make these determinations that we do offline. Does a stranger claiming to be an engineering professor look like the real thing (insofar as we have an image of the real thing with which to compare him in our minds)? Does he or she sound knowledgeable about the field? Does your correspondent remember, from conversation to conversation, the information he or she relayed previously, such as education, state of birth, the names of siblings? Are there unexplained gaps in the information? Does the correspondent have anything to gain in a relationship or transaction with you by claiming to be something he or she is not? Are there revealing body language cues, such as an unusual nervousness or eagerness when certain topics come up?

In an e-mail exchange we can evaluate much of the same information, although we are deprived of important visual cues. This lack is offset to some extent, however, by the fact that the data is all there in writing. We are not challenged by possible inaccuracies of memory ("Didn't she say she was from Ohio last time?")

In an age of spam and viruses, the majority of the e-mail that many of us receive is automatically assigned to a "useless or dangerous" category and deleted. Several categories of correspondents send mail that is important, or potentially important, to us. The first, and the easiest to verify the identity of, are our offline friends and relatives. Years ago, your brother told you his new e-mail address was brickchurch@hotmail.com (the name he acquired playing football in high school). You are comfortable that whenever you send e-mail to, or receive e-mail from, that address, you are communicating with your brother.

Every once in a while, though, a virus spoofs your brother's e-mail address, and you get a communication apparently from him with a tagline such as, "Is that you naked in the picture!!!!?????" and an attachment. You immediately know this is a virus and did not originate from Brick because Brick wouldn't ask you a question like this, eschews the use of exclamation points and multiple question marks, and never sends you attachments.

A much higher level of difficulty arises when we receive unsolicited e-mail. The famous Nigerian scams (so called because most originate from that country) involve an e-mail that purports to be from the financial manager, wife, or son of a dead African politician or businessman. He or she has 10 or 15 million dollars in an account that the corrupt authorities of his country will steal if it is not expeditiously transferred out of the country. Will you help, in return for a fat commission? At some point along the way, you will be asked to put up some money of your own, as an earnest of your good faith. That money will, of course, disappear, and you will never receive the multimillion-dollar transfer. These con artists succeed if you allow your greed to overcome your suspicion. Each of these mails relies on a plausible-sounding story and e-mail address but probably would not resist much offline investigation. (Of course, the effect is diluted when you find yourself receiving 10 or 15 similar messages a day—what are the odds that the grieving relatives and business associates of 10 different African public figures would all be contacting you?)

The Internet does not only routinely confound expectations as to identity; its open architecture also startles people who think they have achieved anonymity. For example, an author who had written a progressive political essay published on the Web recently received an aggressive, insulting unsigned e-mail. A Google search disclosed that the correspondent had a minimal Internet footprint—only five or six messages left on a Web site devoted to guns.

Based on the original e-mail and this extremely minimal footprint, it was possible to develop a significant profile of the writer. His ISP was located in Colorado, and his e-mail address was the name of the adjacent town to the one where his ISP was based. His messages on the Web site were signed with a nickname (which probably referred to a physical feature of the individual) and disclosed that he was a military veteran who had served in a war, probably Vietnam, that he had been a sniper, and that he owned a particular kind of sniper rifle, favored a particular bullet, and prepared his own black powder for the rifle. All of this information—which the writer would most likely have been shocked to discover was so easy to gather in a few minutes of searching—would probably be sufficient to identify this individual in the real world.

TECHNICAL SOLUTIONS TO IDENTITY AND ANONYMITY

Approaches to verifying identity on the Internet fall into three basic categories (Kent & Millett, 2003): the user offers proof of something the user *knows* (such as a password or his mother's maiden name), something the user *is* (a fingerprint or signature), or something he or she *has* (a smart card or digital token).

The venerable password has, since the Internet's inception, been the entry-level guarantee that a user is who he or she claims to be. The inconvenience of remembering numerous passwords for different systems, plus the ease of guessing, reverse-engineering, or simply stealing passwords has always made this approach a necessary but insufficient condition for identity verification.

Digital signatures and public encryption keys allow the recipient to feel a high level of security that a message comes from the same person who communicated with his previously using that signature or key. That's all these measures ensure. however: They communicate nothing about the original bona fides of the sender, which the recipient must have obtained by other means. If the sender is your brother, "Brick" Church, then a key or a signature helps to assure you that your brother really sent the most recent message. If a Nigerian con artist is using strong encryption to communicate with you, the key will only assure you that you are dealing with the same con artist as before. In the last analysis, digital assurances of identity must still be backed up by instinct and offline inquiries or by reputation systems such as credit reports or the evaluation system used by Ebay.

Smart cards and digital tokens represent assets that can be stolen and therefore are often used in conjunction with passwords or other means of verifying identity. Biometric approaches using fingerprints or retinal patterns are expensive, require sophisticated hardware, and are somewhat inconsistent with the Internet's governing philosophy of speed and ease of communication.

Because of the serious problem of fraud in online transactions, the e-commerce industry has developed a variety of solutions to make transactions more secure, using SSL (secure sockets layer), Web site authentication certificates, and ways of verifying the identity of customers via passwords, signatures, specialized information or tokens. The reputation solution pioneered by Ebay, of allowing the users of a commerce system to evaluate each other, provides a high (but not infallible) level of confidence that a particular seller will not cheat you because he has dealt fairly with others. In a case currently being prosecuted by the Justice Department, however, a man sold $150,000 worth of electronics at very low prices, acquiring a host of favorable evaluations. He then leveraged his new reputation to sell another $700,000 of equipment that he never delivered.

Solutions to anonymity have taken two basic forms, one for e-mail and the other for Web surfing. In the 1990s, there were a number of anonymous remailers, Web sites from which you could send a message that would reach the recipient stripped of any identifying information whatever. The flaw in the design was that the Web site itself was a single point of vulnerability on which law enforcement and disturbed e-mail recipients could exert pressure. Virtually all of these remailers, led by the famous anon.penet.fi, had shut down by the end of the decade, after being raided by police, subpoenaed, or sued. They have been replaced by a new generation of remailers, such as dizum.com, which, used together with encryption software and front-end software such as Quicksilver and Mixmaster, all but eliminate the traceability of a message. These front-end anonymity solutions code your message in multiple layers of encryption, then send them through a series of remailers.

> Messages are multiply encrypted and formatted so as to appear identical to other Mixmaster messages. Messages are sent through chains of remailers. Each remailer removes one layer of encryption, and forwards the message. When the final remailer delivers the decrypted message to the recipient, it is impossible to find out where it came from, even if part of the remailers in the chain are dishonest. (Dizum.com Remailer)

Although the new generation of remailers has introduced a level of complexity that their predecessors lacked, somewhere in the chain there is still presumably at least one remailer that knows the identity of the sender—and that is therefore vulnerable to law enforcement pressure.

There are many solutions, commercial and free, to the problem of anonymous surfing. Sites such as The Anonymizer (www.anonymizer.com) present you with a form, or browser-within-a-browser, in which you enter the URL (uniform resource locator) of the site you wish to visit anonymously. The site comes up on your screen, but the Internet protocol (IP) address left in its log is that of the intermediary site, not yours. Anonymity-supporting sites such as these are routinely blocked by software filters ("censorware") because they represent an easy method of bypassing the filter's list of banned sites.

One ISP recently offered a well-received anonymous DSL (digital subscriber line) service. The user is assigned a dynamic IP address, of which the company keeps no record. A spokesman for the ISP is quoted as saying, "[we] cannot supply information we do not possess" (Bangeman, 2004). A Google search on "Internet Anonymity" produces sponsored links (ads) for numerous other commercial sites that promise anonymous surfing via an untraceable IP address.

A 2001 (Greene, 2001) article on "do it yourself anonymity," widely circulated on the Internet, suggests setting up an account using wholly fictitious information with a free ISP such as NetZero, masking caller ID on your home phone, and then identifying a Socks proxy server in a remote country through which you can send e-mail and surf. With the Socks software, the originating IP address on your e-mail, or recorded by the sites you visit, should be that of the proxy. Socks servers also do not keep cached copies of the sites you visit. For extra protection, the article recommends accessing the Anonymizer with all these measures in place.

Free software available from a German university project rather inauspiciously named JAP uses a variation on dynamic IP (JAP Project Web site: http://anon.inf.tu-dresden.de/index_en.html). All users share a single IP address, so it is impossible to determine which user accessed which site. Users access the service via an encrypted link, shared with other users, which passes through a series of intermediary sites. The project's coordinators warn, however, that "this version does not yet achieve the full security and anonymity that we strive for. It does not protect you against an adversary who has the capability to observe all communication links on the Internet."

As with e-mail, anonymous surfing is available through effective "low-tech" solutions, such as paying cash to surf in an Internet café.

A Reverence for Anonymity in U.S. Political Tradition

Anonymity in Internet discourse is founded in an old and honorable tradition of anonymous political communication. As such, online anonymity is entitled to the full protection of the First Amendment.

Anonymous speech on controversial political and moral topics was a common phenomenon in 18th- and 19th-century Great Britain and in pre-Revolutionary America. In 1720, two British men, John Trenchard and Thomas Gordon, published a highly influential series of political essays under the name Cato. Their work was reprinted by Benjamin Franklin and cited by John Adams and Thomas Jefferson.

The famous John Peter Zenger trial, in New York in 1735, involved Zenger's prosecution for publishing pseudonymous essays attacking the British-appointed governor of the colony. (Zenger had also republished several of Cato's essays.) Zenger's defense attorney asked the jury to protect the right of "exposing and opposing arbitrary power.... by speaking and writing truth." Zenger's subsequent acquittal helped to end the arbitrary prosecutions of American publishers and writers under British common law.

Thomas Paine's *Common Sense*, which was the touchstone for intense American feeling in support of separation from Great Britain, was first published under the pseudonym "An Englishman." The Federalist Papers, in which Alexander Hamilton, John Jay and James Madison laid out, and defended, the structure of the proposed U.S. Constitution, was jointly published by the three men under the single name, Publius. The Anti-Federalists replied with essays attributed to "Candidus," another "Cato," and "A Federal Farmer."

The inception of the American republic did not end the need for anonymity to protect the circulation of controversial speech. Before the Civil War, many abolitionists, aware of the unpopularity of their views and the possibility of severe physical danger to themselves, wrote under names such as "A Colored Baltimorean," "Communipaw," "Magawisca," and "Zillah."

When members of political administrations wish to float new ideas without triggering the assumption that they are speaking officially on behalf of the administration—or losing their jobs because the boss disagrees—they have frequently utilized anonymity in U.S. political life. In other cases, an elected politician may wish to send out a trial balloon without being held accountable for it. In 1947, George Kennan, an official in the Truman administration, published an essay titled "The Sources of Soviet Power." This work, which became the blueprint for the Cold War strategy of containment, was signed "X."

During the McCarthy era, blacklisted screenwriters frequently continued to work under pseudonyms. In 199_, the best-selling novel *Primary Colors* was published attributable only to Anonymous, although the author was shortly after revealed to be journalist Joe Klein. In 2004, the nonfiction work *Imperial Hubris* was published pseudonymously by a CIA case officer, critiquing U.S. intelligence gathering activities. Today hardly a day goes by without an article in the *New York Times, Washington Post, Chicago Tribune*, or other pillar of the mainstream press attributing a significant assertion to "a senior State Department official" or "White House staffer" (Wallace, 1994).

THE SUPREME COURT SPEAKS

The United States Supreme Court has repeatedly affirmed that anonymous communication is protected by the First Amendment. Starting in the 1950s, the Court held that the National Association for the Advancement of Colored People could keep its membership list secret from state investigators. In the following decade, reviewing a remarkable history of state harassment and dirty tricks directed at the Socialist Workers' Party, the Court exempted it from an Ohio requirement that it disclose its list of contributors. In *Talley v. California*, the Court invalidated a Los Angeles ordinance prohibiting distribution of anonymous leaflets. It held that "Anonymous pamphlets, leaflets, brochures and even books have played an important role in the progress of mankind."

In the 1995 case of *McIntyre v. Ohio Elections Commission*, Margaret McIntyre had been fined for handing out anonymous leaflets during a local school board campaign. Citing its holding in *Talley* about the importance of anonymous works in human progress, the Court noted that speakers may seek anonymity for a number of valid reasons: "The decision in favor of anonymity may be motivated by fear of economic or official retaliation, by concern about social ostracism, or merely by a desire to preserve as much of one's privacy as possible."

The Court recalled the newspaper right-of-reply law it had invalidated in the 1974 case of *Miami Herald Publishing Co. v. Tornillo*. Like the Ohio ordinance under review, that law had required speakers to add their names to their work. "The identity of the speaker," said the Court, "is no different from other components of the document's content that the author is free to include or exclude." They noted that anonymity "provides a way for a writer who may be personally unpopular to ensure that readers will not prejudge her message simply because they do not like its proponent."

The Court concluded that under the Constitution, "anonymous pamphleteering is not a pernicious, fraudulent practice, but an honorable tradition of advocacy and of dissent. Anonymity is a shield from the tyranny of the majority."

Since 1995, the Supreme Court has issued two more opinions elucidating the law pertaining to anonymous communications. In *Buckley v. American Constitutional Law Foundation*, the court examined a Colorado requirement that the circulators of political petitions wear an identification badge. Justice Ruth Bader Ginsburg delivered the majority opinion. The Court began by noting that the state did not require individuals collecting signatures on political nominating petitions to wear badges. Those advocating for ballot initiatives alone were singled out for this requirement.

The Court was impressed by trial testimony about harassment of signature seekers and the chilling effect of having to wear a badge, which made some people afraid to participate. The Court found the Colorado requirement even more onerous than the Ohio ordinance it struck down in *McIntyre*. The Court noted that the signature of a petition requires more sustained one-on-one interaction than the handing out of a leaflet. "[T]he badge requirement compels personal name identification at the precise moment when the circulator's interest in anonymity is greatest." Citing *McIntyre*, the Court struck down the Colorado law, holding that the badge requirement "discourages participation in the petition circulation process by forcing name identification without sufficient cause."

In *Watchtower Bible and Tract Society v. Village of Stratton*, the court reviewed an Ohio village ordinance requiring anyone soliciting door-to-door to obtain a permit. Among the various disturbing aspects of the practice, the Court, citing *McIntyre* and *Buckley*, noted the impact on the right of anonymity:

> First, as our cases involving distribution of unsigned handbills demonstrate, there are a significant number of persons who support causes anonymously. The requirement that a canvasser must be identified in a permit application filed in the mayor's office and available for public inspection necessarily results in a surrender of that anonymity.... The badge requirement that we invalidated in *Buckley* applied to petition circulators seeking signatures in face-to-face interactions. The fact that circulators revealed their physical identities did not foreclose our consideration of the circulators' interest in maintaining their anonymity. In the Village, strangers to the resident certainly maintain their anonymity, and the ordinance may preclude such persons from canvassing for unpopular causes. [citations omitted]

The Court did, however, recently set a significant limit to anonymity: It held that an individual stopped by the police during the investigation of a crime cannot refuse to give the police his name (*Hiibel v. Sixth Judicial Circuit Court of Nevada*, 2004).

INTERNET ANONYMITY AND THE LAW

Courts deciding on the law pertaining to new technologies must work by analogy. Is the telephone a new type of telegraph or something different? Are records like sheet music or unrelated to them? Strong analogies make for strong decisions; cases in which the courts disregard or veer away from analogies tend to result in confused law.

The key question in deciding on the level of constitutional protection for anonymity in cyberspace is whether an e-mail message is fundamentally similar in its nature to Mrs. McIntyre's pamphlet. So far courts have cautiously answered this question in the affirmative.

In 1996, the Georgia legislature, apparently oblivious to the *Mcintyre* decision of the year before, passed H.B. 1630, an amendment to the state's computer security law, making it a misdemeanor to "knowingly transmit any data through a computer network [using] any individual name ... to falsely identify the person ... transmitting such data." The American Civil Liberties Union (ACLU), acting on behalf of a group of Web publishing plaintiffs including the author of this chapter, brought the case of *ACLU v. Miller* (1997) in U.S. district court challenging the law as an infringement of the freedom of speech. The court granted a preliminary injunction preventing enforcement of the new law pending the trial. It held that "the statute's prohibition of Internet transmissions which 'falsely identify' the sender constitutes a presumptively invalid content-based restriction" under *McIntyre*. The court concluded that the statute was unconstitutional over-broad because it was

> not drafted with the precision necessary for laws regulating speech. On its face, the act prohibits such protected speech as the use of false identification to avoid social ostracism, to prevent discrimination and harassment, and to protect privacy[,] ... a prohibition with well-recognized First Amendment problems.

Georgia decided not to appeal the ruling, and therefore H.B. 1630 was ripped from the law books without more litigation or any utterance by a higher court. Presumably, someone in authority read *McIntyre* and decided the case was a lost cause.

ANONYMITY DURING WARTIME

Even before September 11, 2001, a climate of fear of terrorism, coinciding with law enforcement's fear of the Internet as a medium for hard-to-trace communication, led to several U.S. legal initiatives with the potential for undoing the less complex levels of anonymity.

In 1994, Congress passed the Communications Assistance for Law Enforcement Act (CALEA), which mandated that the telephone companies design their digital networks in a manner that would explicitly permit and support surveillance of electronic communications including e-mail. The new law allowed federal investigators to obtain addressee information more easily (addresses of the recipients of e-mail) and the contents of e-mail. In a recent "Notice of Proposed Rulemaking," the government has now signaled its intention of expanding CALEA to cover broadband transmissions and certain Voice over Internet Protocol (VoIP) communications as well. CALEA had always excluded data in the custody of "information service" providers or traveling on the Internet; e-mail was only vulnerable under the law when residing, or arriving, on the phone company's server. However, because many broadband and VoIP providers are ISPs, not phone companies, civil libertarians fear that adoption of the proposed CALEA rules will blur the distinction and lead to widespread law enforcement interference with ISPs.

CALEA is unique because it requires the system architecture to be designed with surveillance in mind. The Electronic Freedom Foundation (n.d.) states that a carrier receiving a court order or subpoena, must be able to "quickly isolate all wire and electronic communications to and from a targeted person.... quickly isolate call-identifying information (numbers they've called and calls they've received) of a targeted person" and "carry out intercepts unobtrusively, so targets are not made aware of the electronic surveillance."

In 2000, the Federal Bureau of Investigation (FBI) announced its use of Carnivore, specialized servers that could be attached to an ISPs server to monitor communications. The existence of Carnivore caused great concern in the civil liberties community because Internet communications are not segregated in the same way as phone calls. Although a surveillance device can easily trace one phone call from among hundreds of others, e-mail is sent divided into multiple individual packets that are mingled with packets from thousands or millions of other unrelated communications. To capture all of the packets of a particular suspect communication, the FBI would have to filter though all the other innocent packets being transmitted at the same time. Civil libertarians feared this would lead to wide-scale illegal monitoring of innocent communications. The FBI compounded these fears by refusing to release the source code of, or even a lot of specific information about, Carnivore (Captain, 2000; Harrison, 2000).

The author of a Carnivore FAQs (frequently asked questions), drawing some inferences about the likely functioning of the system, maintains that Carnivore is likely to be easy to defeat with more advanced levels of anonymous communication. Because Carnivore searches for the suspect's name and e-mail address in the "From:" line of a communication, the system may be thrown off the track by simple forgery of the message header. "When sending e-mail, simply change your name. Since Carnivore will never see your e-mail address go across the wire, it cannot capture the e-mail nor record the fact that it was even sent." Similarly, the use of multiple remailers, coupled with encryption software such as Quicksilver, should be sufficient to evade Carnivore.

After September 11, Congress passed the Patriot Act (H. R. 3162), containing numerous provisions intended to facilitate the investigation and apprehension of suspected terrorists. Under the Patriot Act, federal authorities could obtain information on a subscriber's e-mail merely by serving an ISP with a document called a National Security Letter (NSL). In a lengthy decision issued in September 2004, a federal district court sitting in New York City invalidated this use of NSLs, partly on the ground that they violate users' constitutionally protected rights of anonymity.

> Every court that has addressed the issue has held that individual internet subscribers have a right to engage in anonymous internet speech.... No court has adopted the Government's argument here that anonymous internet speech or associational activity ceases to be protected because a third party ISP is in possession of the identifying information.... the Court rejects the invitation to permit the right of internet anonymity and association to be placed at such grave risk. (*Doe v. Ashcroft*, 2004)

SUBPOENAS SEEKING THE IDENTITY OF ANONYMOUS SPEAKERS

The majority of the litigation pertaining to online anonymity has dealt with several closely related scenarios. A party, usually a corporation, is claiming it has been harmed by the accusations made by anonymous participants in online forums. In some cases, a company is seeking to blame these speakers for a drop in its stock price. In others, it is defending itself against a lawsuit, government investigation, or administrative proceeding and claims that the anonymous speakers are in a position to provide it with useful evidence for its defense.

Matters come to a head when the litigant serves an ISP with a subpoena requiring it to disclose the identity of a subscriber. Although some ISPs routinely give out this information without notifying the subscriber (and even sometimes without a subpoena), others have resisted disclosing the information or have given the subscriber enough notice to permit him to do so.

In *Doe v. 2themart.com Inc.* (2001), the corporate defendant in a shareholders' derivative suit served Infospace, a Seattle ISP, with a subpoena seeking the identity of John Doe, an anonymous poster on the "Silicon Investor" bulletin board. Infospace notified Doe of the subpoena's existence, and he contested it in court. The parties stipulated that Doe would be permitted to proceed anonymously while fighting the subpoena. The court said, "When an individual wishes to protect their First Amendment right to speak anonymously, he or she must be entitled to vindicate that right without disclosing their identity." The court first recognized that a subpoena, although issued by a private party, is governmental action because it is backed by the contempt power of the court. Therefore, the subpoena power is subject to the limitations of the First Amendment.

The court acknowledged that the "right to speak anonymously was of fundamental importance to the establishment of our Constitution." On the Internet, the right to speak anonymously "facilitates the rich, diverse and far-ranging exchange of ideas." If Internet users can be "stripped of that anonymity by a civil subpoena enforced under the liberal rules of civil discovery, this would have a significant chilling effect on Internet communications and thus on basic First Amendment rights."

The court then created a series of tests to be applied to determine the circumstances under which the identity of an anonymous communicant must be disclosed:

1. whether the subpoena has been issued "in good faith and not for any improper purpose";
2. whether the information sought relates to the core claim or defense of the party seeking the information;
3. whether the identifying information is "directly and materially relevant" to the claim or defense; and
4. whether information sufficient to establish or disprove that claim or defense "is unavailable from any other source."

The court then applied this test to the facts before it, holding that the information sought by 2themart did not relate to a core defense, and that the identity of the speakers (as opposed to their statements) was not of great importance either. "[T]heir identity is not needed to allow the litigation to proceed." Their statements on Silicon Investor were a matter of public record and, if in fact they had affected the company's stock price, they had done so anonymously. Their identities, unknown to the public at the time they made their statements, were not relevant now.

2themart argued that it wanted to correlate the statements on Silicon Investor to stock trades made by the individual speakers to determine whether they had profited from changes in the stock price caused by their allegations. The court responded that such innuendos of stock manipulation "do not suffice to overcome the First Amendment rights of the Internet users."

The court, granting Doe's motion to quash the subpoena, concluded that "the constitutional rights of Internet users, including the First Amendment right to speak anonymously, must be carefully safeguarded."

In *Global Telemedia International Inc. v. Doe1* (2001), the plaintiff corporation was publicly traded over the counter. The defendants were anonymous individuals who had posted derogatory statements about the plaintiff on the Raging Bull Web site. Plaintiff sued for libel, and the case was removed by the anonymous defendants to federal court. Defendants moved to dismiss the case under the California SLAPP (Strategic Lawsuit Against Public Participation) law. The court held that the SLAPP law was applicable because the plaintiff had made itself a matter of public interest "by means of numerous press releases issued since 1999."

The court noted that "Unlike many traditional media, there are no controls on the postings.... No special expertise, knowledge or status is required to post a message or to respond." This lack of status militated in favor of the defendants, by making their postings clearly their own opinions, rather than statements of verifiable fact. Only a false fact statement can be libelous; opinions cannot be. The court stated: "Given the general context of the postings, the colorful and figurative language of the individual postings, the inability to prove the statements true or false.... the postings are opinions." The court found that the anonymous defendants' postings were "an exercise of their free speech in connection with a public issue." Although the decision vindicates the right of anonymous Internet communication, it is a less than complete victory, because (in contrast to the result in *Doe v. 2themart*) the defendants' identities were disclosed in the course of the proceedings.

AN ANONYMOUS DOMAIN REGISTRANT

In *Columbia Insurance Inc. v. Seescandy.com* (1999), the plaintiff was the assignee of various trademarks pertaining to See's Candies. The defendant was an anonymous individual who had registered the seescandy.com domain. Plaintiff sued for trademark infringement, seeking an injunction against use of the See's Candies mark and also sought cancellation of the domain registration. The plaintiff was unable to serve the complaint because it couldn't identify the defendant.

The court began by recognizing a substantial, First Amendment–protected interest in anonymous communication, which it described as

> a legitimate and valuable right to participate in online forums anonymously or pseudonymously.... This ability to speak one's mind without the burden of the other party knowing all the facts about one's identity can foster open communication and robust debate.

The court simultaneously recognized that with the advent of the Internet, there came the ability to commit old torts, such as trademark infringement, in new ways: entirely online. The court then balanced the interests of the parties by creating a standard for determining when an anonymous litigant would be required to disclose its identity. It held that the plaintiff must identify the defendant with "sufficient specificity" to determine the "real person or entity who could be sued in federal court." The plaintiff must also describe all the steps it has taken on its own to identify the defendant, before invoking the court's power to do so. Finally, the plaintiff must establish to the court's satisfaction that the complaint would withstand a motion to dismiss to prevent the bringing of frivolous or groundless actions to force defendants to reveal their identity.

The court held that there was actual confusion here because potential customers visited the seescandy.com domain and attempted to order candy. It found that the plaintiff had accordingly met all three branches of the test—described the defendant adequately, made serious attempts to locate him, and established the merits of its trademark infringement claim. Accordingly, the court ordered the defendant to come forward and identify himself.

Dendrite International Inc. v. John Doe no. 3 (2001), closely followed *Seescandy*. Like *Global Media* and *2the-mart*, the case involved anonymous statements about a publicly traded company, made on an Internet message board. Plaintiff Dendrite was a software developer and publisher, with a specialty in pharmaceutical applications. John Doe no. 3 posted to a Yahoo! Message board dedicated to Dendrite and its stock. Like so many anonymous posters, John Doe no. 3 was extremely skeptical of the company's good faith and future prospects. Objecting to a change in Dendrite's revenue recognition procedure, Doe wrote:

> John's [(Dendrite president John Bailye)] got h is contracts salted away to buy another year of earnings—and note how they're changing revenue recognition accounting to help it.... Bailye has his established contracts structured to provide a nice escalation in revenue. And then he's been changing his revenue—recognition accounting to further boost his earnings.

Doe also alleged that Dendrite was looking for a larger company to acquire it. "[Dendrite] simply does not appear to be competitively moving forward. John knows it and is shopping hard. But Siebel and SAP already have turned him down. Hope Oracle doe s want in bad...."

Dendrite brought suit for libel, alleging that Doe's statements were false and harmed the company by driving down its stock price. The company then moved to conduct limited discovery for the purpose of determining John Doe no. 3's identity. The trial court denied the motion and the New Jersey Superior Court, Appellate Division, then considered the proper standard for deciding such a motion.

The trial court followed the *Seescandy* test, which as one of its prongs asks whether the plaintiff's case would survive a motion to dismiss. The court held that Dendrite had not made the minimum showing necessary to survive such a motion. The appeal court zeroed in on a conflict between the law applicable to motions to dismiss, and the strong First Amendment protection for anonymity. It pointed out that New Jersey procedure, like that of most

states, leans against the dismissal of cases at a preliminary stage, prior to the conduct of discovery. Therefore, a minimal showing of merit is required to defeat a motion to dismiss. However, if the same standard was applied to motions intended to identify anonymous speakers, the latter might find themselves too easily stripped of constitutional protections in cases which proved not to be very meritorious. Therefore, the appellate court favored a standard for anonymity determinations that was stronger and more demanding than that applied to motions to dismiss.

The appellate court found that Dendrite's complaint would have survived a motion to dismiss. To deny the motion to disclose Doe's identity, the trial court—although it never acknowledged it was doing so—properly applied a stricter standard, considering whether Dendrite would be able to prove any damages, a matter not usually considered on a motion to dismiss (where the court typically asks whether the plaintiff has properly alleged damage, not whether it will be able to prove it).

The appeals court agreed that Dendrite failed to show damage. Stock records

> indicate Dendrite experienced gains on 32 days, losses on 40 days, and no change on two days during that period, which overlaps the period when John Doe No. 3 w as posting his statements on the Yahoo! bulletin board. Dendrite 's total loss during this period was 29/3 2 of a point. Moreover, John Doe No. 3 made nine postings, two on the same day. On three of the days that immediately followed a posting by John Doe No. 3, Dendrite 's stock value decreased. However, on five of the days that immediately followed a posting by John Doe No. 3, Dendrite's stock value increased. The net change in Dendrite's stock value over those seven days was actually an increase of 3 and 5/8 points.

Accordingly, the court affirmed the dismissal of the motion, leaving John Doe's identity unknown. An interesting sidelight to the case is that the trial court allowed Dendrite to discover the identity of two other John Does, who did not come into court to defend themselves. John Doe no. 3 was the only defendant who appeared. The moral of the story is that people who wish to communicate anonymously must be willing to defend their right to do so.

Contrarians

Despite the lack of a court case at any level holding that *McIntyre* does not apply in cyberspace, there has been no shortage of commentators calling for limitations on online anonymity. Some of them have advanced legal arguments, and others have called for structural solutions (changes in the architecture of the Internet). The one thing all have in common is a failure to address *McIntyre* and the lack of a persuasive argument as to why Mrs. McIntyre's pamphlet should be treated one way if printed on paper and another if embodied in an e-mail or a Web page.

"[T]o achieve a civilized form of cyberspace," wrote David Johnson, "we have to limit the use of anonymous communications" (Johnson, 1994). In a student note published in the *Columbia Law Review* the year of the *McIntyre* decision, Noah Levine called for a "simple statute... requiring administrators of anonymous remailers to maintain records of users in a manner which allows for the identification of the senders of specific messages" (Levine, 1996).

In interpreting the First Amendment's simple words, "Congress shall make no law... abridging the freedom of speech, or of the press," the Supreme Court established a default rule of little permissible regulation for anything that comes from the printing press or which it finds analogous to printed matter. The Court has had to make a much broader analogous jump to find (for example) that movies are like print than to hold that the same exact essay, on the screen of your computer, should be treated the same way it would be in the pages of a magazine. In the seminal case of *Reno v. ACLU(1997)*, the first time it considered the First Amendment's applicability to the Internet, the Court (without promising always to follow this analogy, as indeed it has not) held evocatively that the Net allows any user to "become a pamphleteer."

Over the years, the court has created a couple of loopholes allowing other communications technologies to receive more restrictive treatment than print media. The best established of these is the "scarcity" doctrine, which states that, because there are a limited number of broadcast television and radio frequencies available, speech over these can be regulated to a higher degree than in the "nonscarce" print media. Later, in the *Pacifica* ("Seven Dirty Words") decision, the Court created an apparently independent justification for censorship that could (although the case involved radio) potentially be applied to a nonscarce medium: It held that there could be stronger regulation of "pervasive" media (which come into the house uninvited).

Although the pervasiveness doctrine, never fully explained, has continued to have a sort of half-life (Wallace, 1998), the Court boldly held in *Reno* that the Internet is neither scarce nor pervasive, cutting the legs out from under the proponents of Internet censorship, who have had to turn to other arguments that have received less Supreme Court attention. An important and particularly insidious argument made by some critics of Net speech is that the latter is more dangerous than Mrs. McIntyre's leaflet because it reaches much larger audiences. Cass Sunstein (1996), a respected law professor and frequent commentator on First Amendment issues, is a leading proponent of the idea that the Internet is dangerous because it reaches more people. A speech advocating an act of violence, said Sunstein, may not motivate anyone among a small number of listeners to act, but of the millions of people who can imaginably read the speech on the Internet, "one, or two, or ten, may well be provoked to act." This idea, that controversial speech is acceptable as long as it reaches only a few people, flies in the face of Justice Oliver Wendell Holmes's (in dissent; *Abrams v. United States*, 1919) governing metaphor for the First Amendment that "the best test of truth is the power of the thought to get itself accepted in the competition of the market." Sunstein argued the opposite, that is, if a "bad" thought is about to succeed in the market by reaching a wide audience, the government and courts should intervene to stop it.

A related argument is that anonymous speech is more dangerous on the Internet because of the lack of gatekeepers such as publishers, editors, or television producers who presumably will know the anonymous speaker's identity and in any event will refuse to publish really bad speech. This is a highly antidemocratic argument insofar as it holds that speech is only acceptable when prescreened by an informed elite. Attorney Lee Tien, in an article about the applicability of *McIntyre* to cyberspace, wrote that "Such an elitist attitude should not be part of modern free speech philosophy" (Tien, 1996). After all, no gatekeeper stood between Mrs. McIntyre and her intended audience. To reconcile *McIntyre* with the "gatekeeper" argument, it is necessary to drag Sunstein's "volume" argument back into the debate: Mrs. McIntyre's anonymous speech is acceptable only because her audience was very small. Now you have a doubly undemocratic gloss on the modern philosophy of freedom of speech. The Supreme Court has not as of yet given any credence to the gatekeeper or volume arguments.

CONCLUSION

The architecture of the Internet by its nature offers users weak proof of identity and also weak anonymity. Technological and practical solutions allow users higher assurances both of correct identity and of complete anonymity. Both are a good thing. Sometimes the most routine business cannot be safely transacted without some assurances of identity. The *Seescandy* case illustrates the difficulties caused by the defendant's ability to register a domain without proving his own identity to the registration authority. On the other hand, anonymous political speech has a long and honorable history and should be not simply permitted, but encouraged.

GLOSSARY

Anonymous DSL A DSL (digital subscriber line) connection provided by an Internet service provider that assigns the user a "dynamic" (temporary) Internet protocol address and then keeps no records of which user has been assigned which address.

Anonymous Surfing Site A Web site, such as The Anonymizer, that allows users to view other sites remotely while leaving in their logs only the identifying information of the intermediate site, rather than that of the user.

Digital Signature An unforgeable electronic "watermark" added to an e-mail message to assure the recipient of the identity of the sender.

Encryption Key A distinguishing digital feature of a message encrypted under certain software systems such as "pretty good privacy" (PGP). "Public keys" can be distributed by the sender to recipients of his mail and allow them to decrypt messages encrypted with the sender's "private key," which is known only to him or her. This approach incidentally provides a high degree of assurance that the sender is, at least, the same person who previously sent the mail using the same key.

Remailer A system, usually a Web site, set up to receive mail, strip it of its identifying elements, and forward it to its ultimate recipient as an anonymous message.

Remailer Software Software, such as Mixmaster, that works by encrypting a message and then sending it through a random series of remailers, each of which remove one layer of encryption. The last remailer in the chain forwards the message to the ultimate recipient. In theory, the path of the message across the Internet is untraceable.

Secure Sockets Layer (SSL) A protocol for the encryption of Internet communications, widely used in electronic commerce applications.

Socks Server Web proxy server software that promotes anonymity via features including a lack of logs identifying users who have used the system to send messages or to access other sites.

CROSS REFERENCES

See *Digital Identity; Digital Signatures and Electronic Signatures; E-Mail and Instant Messaging; Encryption Basics; Secure Sockets Layer (SSL); Spam and the Legal Counter Attacks.*

ACKNOWLEDGEMENTS

I am indebted to Michael Green, Esq., who assisted greatly with the research for this chapter.

REFERENCES

Abrams v. United States, 250 U.S. 616; 630 (1919).

ACLU v. Miller, 977 F.Supp. 1228 (Northern District of Georgia 1997).

Bangeman, E. (2004, March 18). Anonymous DSL. Retrieved August 2004 from the Ars Technica Web site: http://arstechnica.com/news/posts/1079646226.html

Buckley v. American Constitutional Law Foundation, 525 U.S. 182 (1999).

Captain, S. (2000, August 24). Encryption could starve Carnivore: Developers make server-level technology that could hamper law enforcement's e-mail surveillance. Retrieved from http://www.pcworld.com/news/article/0,aid,18209,00.asp

Columbia Insurance Co. Inc. v. Seescandy.com, 185 F.R.D. 573 (N.D. California, 1999).

Dendrite International Inc. v. John Doe no. 3, 342 N.J. Super. 134, 775 A.2d 756 (2001).

Doe v. Ashcroft, 2004 WL 2185571 (S.D.N.Y. Sept. 28, 2004).

Doe v. 2themart.com Inc., 140 F.Supp.2d 1088 (W.D. Washington 2001).

Electronic Frontier Foundation. (n.d.). CALEA FAQ. Retrieved from http://www.eff.org/Privacy/Surveillance/CALEA/faq.php

FCC v. Pacifica Foundation, 438 U.S. 726 (1978).

Global Telemedia International Inc. v. Doe1, 132 F.Supp.2d 1261 (C.D. California, 2001).

Graham, R. (2001, October 6). Carnivore FAQ—version 3. Retrieved from http://www.robertgraham.com/pubs/carnivore-faq.html

Greene, T. C. (2001, November 14). Do it yourself Internet anonymity. Retrieved from http://www.theregister.co.uk/2001/11/14/doityourself_internet_anonymity/

Harrison, A. (2000, July 17). ACLU challenges FBI E-Mail Taps: Feds say "Carnivore" e-mail snooping is a rare but necessary security measure. *Computerworld.* Retrieved from http://www.pcworld.com/news/article/0,aid,17655,00.asp

Hiibel v. Sixth Judicial Circuit Court of Nevada, 124 S. Ct. 2451 (2004).

Johnson, D. (1994, March 4). The unscrupulous diner's dilemma and anonymity in cyberspace. Retrieved from http://www.eff.org/Privacy/Anonymity/anonymity_online_johnson.article

Kent, S. T., & Millett, L. I. (Eds.). (2003). *Who goes there? Authentication through the lens of privacy.* Committee on Authentication Technologies and Their Privacy Implications, National Research Council. Retrieved from http://books.nap.edu/html/whogoes/ch5.html

Levine, N. (1996, October). Note: Establishing legal accountability for anonymous communication in cyberspace. 96 *Colum. L. Rev.* 1526.

McIntyre v. Ohio Elections Commission, 514 U.S. 334 (1995).

Miami Herald Publishing Co. v. Tornillo, 418 U.S. 241 (1974). Reno v. ACLU, 521 U.S. 844 (1997).

Rheingold, H. (1994). *The virtual community: Homesteading on the electronic frontier.* New York: Harper-Perennial.

Sunstein, C. (1996). Constitutional caution. *U. Chi. Legal F.* 361.

Talley v. California, 362 U.S. 60 (1960).

Tien, L. (1996, Spring). Who's afraid of anonymous speech? Mcintyre and the Internet. *Oregon Law Review, 75,* 117.

Turkle, S. (1995). *Life on the screen: Identity in the age of the Internet.* New York: Simon & Schuster.

Wallace, J. (1999, December 8). Nameless in cyberspace: Anonymity on the Internet (Briefing Paper no. 54). Washington, DC: Cato Institute.

Wallace, J. (1998, February 12). The specter of pervasiveness: *Pacifica,* new media and freedom of speech (Briefing Paper no. 35). Washington, DC: Cato Institute.

Watchtower Bible and Tract Society v. Village of Stratton, 536 U.S. 150 (2002).

Spam and the Legal Counter Attacks

Charles Jaeger, *Southern Oregon University*

INTRODUCTION

Spam and "Junk Mail"

Businesses, charitable organizations, politicians, special interest groups, and many others send millions of unsolicited "junk mail" pieces every month to your postal mailbox—cards, letters, leaflets, or almost anything they want. It's legal. Companies make money with it. You may have done it yourself.

Internet e-mail has become the new frontier of junk mail, with offers of every kind—sometimes hundreds per day—going to almost every e-mail address in the world. Businesses, charitable organizations, politicians, and special interest groups send it. Unsolicited e-mail is similar to postal junk mail, except it arrives in your e-mail box. Most people call it "spam" and most people hate it.

Ronald Scelson (2004)—known as the "Cajun Spammer"—is a high-volume spammer. On May 21, 2003, testifying before the United States Senate Commerce Committee, he boasted to the senators, "I send out between 120 million and 180 million e-mails every 12 hours." He added, "I'm probably the most hated person in this room" (Krim, 2003). Scelson reportedly earns $30,000 to $40,000 "in a good month" (Swartz, 2003a).

The volume is substantial. In January 2004, one report said that 700 billion unsolicited e-mail messages were sent—more than three per day for every person on the planet (Ray, 2004). In 2003, eMarketer estimated that 2.3 billion spam messages were sent daily (Powell, 2003). At the end of 2004, one report said that "spam accounted for 88% of e-mail sent in November (Rodgers, 2004).

Not only do unsolicited and unwanted messages clog up incoming e-mail boxes, they drive up prices for everyone who communicates with e-mail, costs that are passed through to consumers. Spam costs money for businesses to process and sort. It takes valuable resources from Internet service providers. It takes time from individuals; it lowers their trust in legitimate marketers who may have products they want or need; it harms economic growth.

E-mail, once "the next new thing" that would revolutionize ubiquitous low-cost communication, is threatened by its own technical magic in the hands of unscrupulous marketers, porn purveyors, political hucksters, and others with self-interests in communicating with you and me.

A new term, "spam rage," has evolved. On November 24, 2003, Reuters reported that Silicon Valley programmer Charles Booher said his computer "had been rendered almost unusable for about two months by a barrage of pop-up advertising and e-mail." Booher was arrested for "threatening to torture and kill employees of the company he blames for bombarding his computer with Web ads promising to enlarge his penis" (Reuters, 2003c).

In Paddy Chayefsky's classic film *Network*, a frustrated Howard Beale shouts, "I want you to get up right now, and go to the window, open it, and stick your head out, and yell: 'I'm as mad as hell, and I'm not going to take this anymore!'" As technology moved into the New Millennium, "There oughta be a law!" rang loudly through state and federal congressional chambers. Howard Beale, welcome to spam!

Costs of Spam

Business, government, not-for-profit organizations, and individuals are being battered by spam that lowers productivity and costs money in several other ways. The estimates vary widely, but regardless of who is counting, all are agreed that the lost productivity is substantial.

In November 2004, CNN reported that Bill Gates was the "world's most spammed person," receiving some 4 million e-mails per day, most of them spam. The company CEO said, "Microsoft has special technology that just filters spam intended for Gates," and "practically an entire department [is] dedicated to ensuring that nothing unwanted gets into his inbox" (CNN, 2004a).

Some high-profile companies suffer overall spam rates as high as 79%, according to a July 2003 CyberAtlas survey (Greenspan, 2003). Pressing the delete key may only take a second—much quicker than saying "no" to a telemarketer—but judgments about message validity, origin, and other factors soak up valuable time and energy in processing the messages.

Workers may sift through hundreds of e-mails per day in search of vital information. The survey listed 36% of respondents who spend between 10 and 30 minutes per day dealing with unwanted e-mail and another 32% spending between 30 and 60 minutes. At 60 minutes per day, an employee would be giving up 12.5% of the normal workday. Counting 5 days per week, it calculates to an annual loss of up to six 40-hour workweeks.

CyberAtlas calculated that 79% of respondents think unwanted e-mail should be legally limited or banned; 74% say there should be a federal "do not e-mail" list; and 59% would like to see spammers punished. In the survey, unwanted e-mail was rated equally with telemarketing as the most annoying marketing practice (Greenspan, 2003).

The Radicati Group says spam cost U.S. companies $20.5 billion in 2003; by 2007, the figure is expected to reach nearly $200 billion, or about $180 for every American. BellSouth says spam will add $3 to $5 to each customer's monthly bill (Sullivan, 2003a; Swartz, 2003b).

A 2004 American Management Association survey found that "e-mail and inbox management has become the number-one office task. The average employee now spends 25% of the workday on e-mail" (Swartz, 2004c).

A 2004 Nucleus Research survey said spam will cost large U.S. companies nearly $2,000 per employee in lost production. According to the United Nations, spam and antispam protection cost computer users $25 billion worldwide in 2003 (Swartz, 2004b).

A Ferris Research study determined that the overall cost to U.S. business in 2003 was $8.9 billion, including additional costs generated by requiring more powerful servers, more bandwidth, and "help desk support to annoyed users." On the average, it concluded, it takes 4.4 seconds to deal with a message (Swartz, 2003a).

A spam-costs calculator on the Web shows that for a company of 100 employees who spend 4.4 seconds per message dealing with 50 spam a day, nearly 59 workdays would be lost per year. If the average salary is $25 per hour, it totals over $35,000 in lost productivity (iHateSpam, 2004).

Spam creates other problems that cost business—and ultimately consumers—money. Sometimes legitimate communications are mistakenly screened out and deleted. Jupiter Research reported that the cost of "mistakenly blocked permission-based e-mails" will increase 82.2% between 2003 and 2008 ("Around the Block,", 2004).

These "false positives" can have devastating consequences for vital account management or customer service. If the client interprets them as being ignored by the company, whole chunks of revenue and profit can disappear. Consequently, companies are reluctant to use automated filters or other technology to screen out spam. Someone needs to read and delete each message, much as "practically an entire department" does at Microsoft.

Spam costs legitimate marketers money in other ways, too. In 2004, Gratton, in an overview of global spam, reported a survey finding that "52% of respondents are shopping less on the Internet or not at all because of concerns about receiving spam" (p. 3)

Storage is another cost. "Between one-third and one-half of all electronic communication kept in company storage systems are irrelevant. Most of these communications are personal mails and spam. Companies have a tendency to store everything in the fear that not doing so will put them in breach of regulations" (Swartz, 2004a).

Leaving monetary cost aside, most users consider spam a serious problem simply because of the annoyance. There are strong opinions on all sides.

A Balanced Viewpoint

The polarized opinions about spam include those who would prohibit it entirely, those who would allow it without limits, and the in-between. Interested parties include the spammer, who believes it is a right to send unsolicited mail; the consumer who may or may not want to receive that mail; the Internet service provider who finds its valuable bandwidth consumed by unwanted messages; the information technology (IT) professional who may be called on to control spam; organizations polarized around or advocating for or against unlimited e-mail or tight restrictions; law enforcement; and legitimate businesses that want to communicate with prospects.

From a public policy point of view, accommodating the myriad viewpoints is an example of the classic "macro–micro dilemma," where what is good for the individual or firm may be in conflict with what is good for society.

Government has a legitimate interest in controlling activities that are harmful to consumers, but it is also concerned with allowing businesses reasonable access to potential customers. The Federal Trade Commission (FTC) has concluded that "spam poses a serious threat to electronic commerce because deception and fraud characterize the vast majority of spam" (Privacy/Internet, 2004a). The dispute arises about the degree to which the government should limit such activity and where to draw the boundaries in a legal counterattack. The FTC has announced that it "planned to be largely hands-off, market driven," but aggressively prosecute spammers under existing laws (Porcelli, Selby, Bagner, & Sonu, 2002, p. 24).

This chapter is focused on the legal counterattack against spam. Although the chapter discusses freedom of speech, due process, abuse or trespass of chattels, the Commerce Clause, and enforcement problems, it is not intended to be a detailed legal review but simply presents perspectives on the issues in a way that a reader of scholarly texts can understand and use to make intelligent decisions about the role of a legal counterattack on spam in an information-based society. In the framework of rapidly changing legislation, it focuses on providing a foundation for understanding the issues in the legal counterattack of state and federal laws, including the federal CAN-SPAM Act that became effective January 1, 2004.

The legal counterattack is only one component in bringing spam under control. IT professionals working in colleges and universities at every level help make marketers, government, and organizations more aware of spam and its supporting technologies. The San Diego Super Computer Center at the University of California at San Diego, for example, publishes data on antispam databases used by "black lists." The United States Computer Emergency Readiness Team (US-CERT) center at Carnegie Mellon University monitors hacking techniques used in cyberterrorism and makes recommendations about making the communication infrastructure more secure (Jaeger, 2003). Many hacking techniques are used in spamming, and technical solutions help support a legal counterattack on spam. Laurence Lessig's (1999) classic article, "The Law of the Horse: What Cyberlaw Might Teach," from the *Harvard Law Review* is cited to illustrate a multidimensional approach that includes markets, social norms, and architecture, or "code," which may regulate interaction with cyberspace.

Specialized legal training is beginning to receive attention. Cyberspace is so new that it is difficult to keep up with its progress. In the summer of 2003, Chicago's John Marshall Law School offered "the first law school course devoted to the subject of unsolicited commercial e-mail" to "investigate legal and policy issues raised by e-mail marketing and spam" (Festa, 2003). Many more will come.

Scholarly research about spam is relatively scarce. This chapter supplements material from peer reviewed sources with up-to-date news and other media reports. The latter are sometimes inconsistent or even contradictory, but in the fast-moving world of cyberspace, they are essential to establishing an understanding of current issues.

The chapter concludes that the legal counterattack may not be effective on its own, but it will provide a foundation of rules to complement other approaches, including technology that individuals, companies, higher education institutions, Internet service providers (ISPs), special interest groups, and advertisers can use to control spam at their respective levels.

"SPAM" AND "SPAM"

The uppercase SPAM is a registered trademark for the world's leading canned meat product, made of spicy pork and ham. It is popular in some areas (e.g., parts of Hawaii), yet despised in others. The lowercase spam refers to e-mail messages.

It is widely believed that the first use of the term "spam" came about as a result of the Monty Python comedy skit in a restaurant that describes the frustration a woman endures while trying to order a meal. The restaurant serves SPAM with everything, and she wants none of it! Subsequently, a group of Vikings sing a chorus of "SPAM, SPAM, SPAM" in an increasing crescendo, drowning out

other conversation. The analogy to e-mail spam is the drowning out of normal discourse on the Internet and the strong feelings on both sides of the issue (the skit and discussion can be found at http://www.detritus.org/spam/skit.html; also see http://www.uselessmoviequotes.com/umq_n001.htm; http://www.museum.tv; http://www.webopedia.com/TERM/s/spam.html).

The first reported case of blatant e-mail abuse appears to have occurred on May 2, 1978, where a user of Arpanet (which preceded the Internet) distributed a message about an open house at Digital Equipment Corporation (DEC). The user typed in the e-mail address of every known person on the Arpanet and sent the identical message to all. By most contemporary definitions, this e-mail broadcast to large numbers in a commercial format would be spam (details of the message can be found at http://www.templetons.com/brad/spamreact.html; discussions of definitions are later in this chapter).

Prior to the early 1990s, for-profit use of the Internet was generally banned (except for membership bulletin boards and other content services). Military, government, or education personnel occasionally engaged in mass e-mails to groups of colleagues, and there was little incentive for abuse. Once money became part of the equation, with the development of the dot-com suffix, people began to see that it was a fast and inexpensive way to reach large numbers of users. It costs about the same for a mailing to 10 or 1,000 people, so some marketers just sent it to everybody.

A popular Web dictionary likens spam to SPAM with three statements: "Nobody wants it or ever asks for it. No one ever eats it; it is the first item to be pushed to the side when eating the entrée. [However], sometimes it is actually tasty, like 1% of junk mail that is really useful to some people" (see http://www.webopedia.com/TERM/s/spam.html). Even a low 1% response rate can make spam profitable.

Why Do They Spam?
Closed Loop Marketing
In their landmark book, *The One to One Future*, Peppers and Rogers (1993) show how businesses, organizations, or government can establish a "closed loop" using directly addressable media—postal mail, telemarketing, fax, or personal visits—to build ongoing relationships that benefit customers.

E-mail is one of the most cost-effective elements in the communication mix and removes many of the time and space constraints of other interactive media. The direct feedback improves a company's ability to satisfy individual wants and needs and builds positive relationships with millions of individuals. Customers can send e-mail responses in a fraction of the time it takes to write or telephone—so they do it more often.

Organizations communicate their missions and attract donations and volunteer support. Governments keep their constituents informed and get information back to help improve policy. Retailers invite prospects to their stores and build community with current customers. Business-to-business transactions are increasingly online, lowering supply chain and distribution costs. Consumers get e-mail information about new products and services that satisfy their needs and wants.

A Jupiter Research overview of e-mail marketing reported that "The evolution of e-mail as a cost-efficient marketing medium, coupled with the desire for improved capabilities, has driven 64% of marketers to deploy e-mail marketing systems" (Daniels, 2003).

As postal mail became more expensive and other direct marketing came under increasing regulation, e-mail became more attractive. When telemarketing was restricted by the "no call" list, new rules restricted fax, and postage rates rose, advertisers could turn to e-mail. It's fast, easy, and cheap.

Spammers

A new breed of advertisers—spammers—discovered e-mail, too. By eliminating the cost of postal stamps, telephone lines, and call centers, or banks of fax machines, they could send out millions of messages. Because incremental mailings cost almost nothing, they could advertise almost anything to millions for almost the same cost as to thousands. Deceptive or fraudulent operators were difficult to find and prosecute. At the same time, spam was relatively new, and the law had not had time to catch up to the problem. Spam multiplied exponentially in this "perfect storm."

Some spammers have a political or social agenda, using e-mail for idea advertising, advocacy, or solicitation. Some social interest groups who complain loudly about spam use it liberally themselves. Politicians exempted themselves from most regulation.

With mailings in the millions, even less than 1% interest can add up to a lot of money. In fact, enough people read and respond to spam that spammers make money. Indiscriminate mailings with very low response rates can yield good profits—it works for the few, while everybody else suffers. At the end of 2003, CNN reported that Internet and e-commerce jumped into the top 10 areas for the most consumer complaints (CNN, 2003). Most spammers are driven by money. If spammers stopped making money, most spam would end almost overnight.

A 2003 consumer survey found that 4% "read suspected spam to see if it might interest them" (Morrissey, 2003). Other surveys range widely, but using this figure, it is easy to see how spammers and their clients make money. Four percent of 120 million messages equals 4.8 million readers. If these generate just 400 responses who "click-through" to an affiliated mortgage lender—a tiny .00033% inquiry rate—and the lender pays $10 per inquiry, the spammer just earned $4,000 for 12 hours of work. The lender, who makes an average profit of $500 on each transaction and "converts" just 10% of the click-through inquiries, clears $16,000.

How is that different from traditional direct-response media: direct mail, fax, or telemarketing? With these, care is usually taken to eliminate the names least likely to be interested in the offer (an application of the Pareto curve, which the Italian economist Vilfredo Pareto developed to model resource allocation). The cost of contacting the entire list is prohibitive, so the traditional direct mailer may eliminate the 9 out of 10 who have the least interest in the offer. If only the 12 million names received the e-mail (the

1 out of 10), the other 108 million would be spared the message.

The spammer simply sends out 120 million e-mails at about the same cost of sending only 12 million. The cost of editing the list outweighs the benefits. Because the spammer does not edit the list, it is almost guaranteed that most of the likely uninterested 108 million recipients will simply be annoyed.

"No Spam in Heaven" Marketing

Wouldn't it be a better world if you and I never—*ever!*—received another piece of junk mail, or telemarketing call, or spam that did not in some way interest or potentially benefit us? Of course!

The idea that "there is no junk mail in heaven" is the ultimate goal in direct marketing (Roberts & Berger, 1999). If senders had perfect information about everyone and perfect systems to implement mailings, they would e-mail only to interested parties. "Information security" would be meaningless, and everyone would use best practices because, of course, in heaven only legitimate organizations with benevolent motives exist. The concept applies equally to e-mail marketing. There would be no spam in heaven!

Because we are not in heaven, this scenario has problems. First, notorious spammers don't care. Unlike postal mail, it's just cheaper to send spam messages to everyone. No qualification. No filters. Second, perfect information about you and me is fundamentally in conflict with privacy concerns, because unscrupulous parties with other motives use it against us.

Defining the limits of privacy in relation to spam will be one of the landmark issues of the new millennium. Some privacy advocates argue against collecting any personal information. Marketers would disagree. Under the current system, most legitimate organizations maintain some control over their prospect lists and make reasonable attempts to send messages only to interested parties. Onerous prohibitions on information, marketers would argue, will simply lead to higher costs (likely passed through to consumers), loss of jobs, and economic harm.

A SMALL SHADOWY GROUP OF PROS

The FTC believes that it is approximately 300 prolific spammers who leave ordinary e-mail users drowning in unwanted e-mail. John Mozena, cofounder of the spam-fighting Coalition Against Unsolicited Commercial E-mail (CAUCE), puts the figure at 200 spammers who generate 90% of the spam (Schwartz, 2003, p. 39).

Ronald Scelson (discussed earlier) represents one of these prolific spammers. Other spammers have produced equivalent amounts of spam, or more. Alan Ralsky reportedly can send up to 1 billion e-mails per hour (Powell, 2003). Scelson is included in this chapter because he has been visible, and he has articulated the spammers' point of view, both before and after new federal legislation (more about this later).

He does it for money—and he is unapologetic. He thinks he should be allowed to broadcast his messages just as do speakers on street-corner soap boxes and junk mailers. He asks, is there a difference between junk mail and spam? Both use a communication channel with addressable media.

Much of his argument revolves around First Amendment issues. He wants his freedom of speech—a common defense by spammers—and complains that others are sending spam, so he should be able to do it, too. It's harmless, he argues. If you receive something that you do not want, you can ignore it, just as the person on the street is free to ignore a soap box speaker or a postal recipient is free to discard junk mail.

He maintains that AOL, MSN, and other ISPs are even bigger spammers. They continually send e-mail to their own members, and they promote affiliate products for which they earn a commission. When it is in their financial interest, he maintains, the ISPs look the other way.

Scelson and others claim that many legitimate marketers and other respected entities profit from spam, including some of the very companies that publicly condemn it. This is changing as the Internet matures, but it is useful to look at the details.

The Money Trail

There is money in spam—and it is not all being made by spammers. There has developed a collision of two forces: those who would control spam, versus those who continue to develop technology that can make more spam, protect and hide spammers, and frustrate efforts at control. Sometimes, the money trail is described by the "iceberg principle," with much more activity below the surface.

Big companies, ISPs, Web hosting companies, data providers, software vendors, and even the U.S. Postal Service have an interest in spam. In discussing "White Collar Spam," Lieb (2003) listed Kraft Foods, Palm, AT&T, and "countless major banks and lenders" as regular spammers. She says they insulate their name and brands, but "tend to engage henchmen (list outfits, renegade affiliates) to do the dirty work."

Sullivan (2003c) investigated a spam trail that led "from Alabama to Argentina . . . and right through big-name companies like Ameriquest, Quicken Loans, and LoanWeb." He traced through 15 layers to companies who claimed to be legitimate e-mail marketers—or even spam fighters—and uncovered names purchased from "lead generators," "affiliates," and other third-party spam facilitators. He concluded, "While the dirty work is done by secretive, faceless computer jockeys who are constantly evading authorities, lots of companies with names you know profit at least tangentially, from their efforts."

Scelson testified that "pink contracts" and other sweetheart arrangements protect known spammers who are sending bulk e-mail through ISPs. The big operators are simply on-the-take for extra profit, he says. Favored pink-list spammers pay rates higher than other commercial clients and are terminated only when the ISP is threatened by a lawsuit or "blacklisting" from an antispam organization.

In November 2000, Festa reported that a large ISP, PSINet, had signed a contract with Cajunnet that "would permit Cajunnet to send unsolicited e-mail 'in mass quantity' through PSINet's lines . . . for a nonrefundable, up-front payment of $27,000 'for PSINet's increased risks.'"

The person who handled the account for PSINet said, "If the complaints were too much, we would discontinue the arrangement" (Festa, 2000).

An antispam blog participant (Web log of informal postings), listed 12 of the biggest ISPs who have accepted these contracts and summarized:

> Internet Service Providers pretend to be on your side in the fight against intrusive spam, but in reality, many of them are only too willing to sell out your in-box for a buck. And at the same time that they're contributing to the spam problem, two to five dollars of your monthly ISP bill goes towards fighting spam in the form of abusive desk staff and filtering systems. It seems they can have their cake and eat it too. (Suespammers, 2001)

When Ronald Scelson filed for bankruptcy in 2003, court records reportedly showed that he owed $56,463 to Bell South for "circuits" and another $4,407 to Cable & Wireless as his "Internet provider." These same firms were reported entering into "pink contracts" with spammers some three years earlier (Sullivan, 2003c).

Today, pink contract arrangements are not as popular as they were earlier this decade, when these practices were exposed. Antispammers argue that abuses have declined markedly with the cooperation of ISPs and should not be used as an argument supporting spam. Spammers, in contrast, complain that a "wink and a nod" or other subtle arrangements have the same effect, and ISPs are still on the take.

If the major ISPs are getting out of the business, smaller firms seem ready to take up the slack. E-mail and web sites work together, or the spammer doesn't get paid.

> That's why spammers pay hundreds, and sometimes thousands of dollars a month for what's known as 'bullet-proof' hosts, . . . sites that won't get pulled down, even in the face of a deluge of complaints. Commonly advertised . . . as 'bulk e-mail friendly Web hosting services,' many . . . operate offshore. (Sullivan, 2003b)

In *America Online, Inc. versus Hawke*, AOL alleged, "Defendants also offered 'bulk friendly hosting' on servers located in China, Latin America, or other foreign countries." This is discussed later in the chapter.

Software vendors also profit from spam by developing utilities and tools to fight it. Microsoft is no longer supporting Windows 9x, and users are advised to upgrade to XP—at a price—partly because of hacking and spam. In November 2003, Microsoft unveiled SmartScreen, a new antispam engine for their exchange servers and e-mail programs, leading to the conclusion that "almost 85 percent of e-mail gateways will have been replaced between the beginning of 2003 and the end of 2004" (Kuchinskas, 2003b).

The big data providers such as Experian also have a financial interest in e-mail. Marketers use these firms to enhance their mailing list data with e-mail "append" services to better differentiate customers and increase the effectiveness of their mailings, just as they did with traditional interactive media (Peppers & Rogers, 1993 Roberts & Burger, 1999).

Direct mail is one of the biggest revenue generators for the U.S. Postal Service (USPS). The millions of pieces of postal mail sent to consumers and businesses fund many of the USPS programs and allow them to keep the costs of first class mail lower. The USPS might have an interest in stopping spam to increase marketers' reliance on postal mail for ordering, but the USPS gains other revenue through shipping products sold by direct marketers. Postal mail and e-mail can be complementary, and the USPS has explored developing cyberspace products of its own.

Law enforcement, too, has an interest in spam. Funding through grants and spam-fighting programs add to their overall budgets. The FTC estimates that "nearly one in eight U.S. adults has had their credit card hijacked, identity co-opted or credit rating pockmarked by identity thieves over the last five years." Working with hackers, spammers increasingly are using cyberspace for these purposes (Reuters, 2003a).

SPAM AND CRIME

Three relatively recent practices combine to make spammers an especially potent threat: spoofing, phishing, and using hijacked, or "zombie," computers. Often, this is facilitated by sending dangerous viruses, worms, spyware, and adware to local computers. Sometimes, it includes sabotage spam as a competitive business weapon. Much of this criminal activity is coming from offshore, complicating apprehension and prosecution. Dan Larkin, chief of the Federal Bureau of Investigation's (FBI's) Internet Crime Complaint Center, says, "United States citizens and businesses are very attractive targets for the world. We're getting clobbered" (Sullivan, 2004).

"Spoofing" uses a form of identity theft to seek sales, contributions, or confidential information by fraudulently claiming to be a known entity. Often, the message looks completely authentic, including company logos and trademarks. "Real-life spoofs" reported by *The Washington Post* include fraudulent messages purportedly from flowers.com, Sony, Microsoft, PayPal, and the FBI (Lieb, 2002). In January 2005, an unemployed painter from Pennsylvania was arrested for sending out more than 800,000 e-mail spoofs fraudulently soliciting donations for victims of the December 26 Asian tsunami (Betteridge, 2005).

With "phishing," the spoofing message elicits confidential information such as social security numbers, account numbers and balances, or other confidential information such as passwords into a stock trading or airline miles site. These are used by the spammer or sold to others. In 2005, it was reported that "phishing attacks have reached 57 million U.S. adults and compromised at least 122 well-known brands" through increasingly sophisticated methods, spyware, malicious code redirects, and attacks on company domain name servers (Reuters, 2005).

"Zombie" computers are another factor. Hackers working with spammers open "backdoors" to "hijack" computers connected to the Internet. They may read everyone in that computer's address book. Then, using those addresses, they send spam from that computer, making it appear that the owner is the sender and increasing the likelihood of the message being opened and read. Messages attributed to the wrong person are difficult to track and prosecute.

In February 2004, Bloomberg News reported that "as much as 15% [of spam] come from [hijacked] home PCs infected with computer viruses" (Ray, 2004). Hijacked computers are in government entities, organizations, and homes, and educational institutions, particularly colleges. Many are set as "open relays," which are sometimes used by legitimate companies in their networks. Bick (2004a) offered a complete discussion of the issue and how legitimate senders can maintain open relays and still comply with new laws described in this chapter.

The Legal Counterattack
War on Spam

Governments, politicians, businesses, organizations, and many individuals have mounted a "War on Spam." Some want unsolicited e-mail stopped entirely.

Feelings are passionate on both sides. Some free speech advocates—and spammers—argue there should be no limitation. The Cajun Spammer says, "I'm willing to die for what I believe in. Look at Martin Luther King, Jr. When they assassinated him, that's when everything changed" (Brunker, 2003). (The connection is obscure.)

However, the courts have ruled that freedom of speech has limits. Telephone and fax solicitations are already controlled by legislation, so why not e-mail? Like postal mail, telemarketing, and fax, e-mail costs the sender money, but unlike these traditional media, the cost burden shifts to the recipient. It costs the spammer almost nothing to send 120 million messages, but the recipients, ISPs, and everyone else in the communication channel must spend time, bandwidth, or other resources dealing with those messages.

Economic interests argue that legislation needs to take reasonable use into consideration. Business—or anyone, they argue—should be allowed to send you unsolicited e-mails if reasonable conditions are met, but once you tell them to stop, they should respect your wishes. If every unsolicited message is spam, and organizations are completely barred from sending unsolicited messages, they say it will have a profoundly detrimental effect on jobs and economic activity.

Legitimate businesses want at least one opportunity to contact prospects by e-mail (the "one bite" approach). Marketers contend that is minimally intrusive and gives consumers information they may want or need. Small businesses, in particular, who often lack resources to pay for traditional direct-mail advertising, say they would be hurt by overly restrictive regulation.

State and Local Legislation

Shortly after the Internet became commercial, states began writing legislation about commercial e-mail. In 1997, Nevada was the first state to enact specific legislation. By the end of 2003, some 37 states had enacted antispam laws ranging from relatively mild to highly restrictive.

Washington passed an antispam measure in 1998 and has been diligent in finding a legislative formula that satisfies the courts on interstate commerce issues and the limitation that most e-mail addresses do not have identifying geographic characteristics (compared with postal zip codes and telephone area codes). California, which had a previous law, enacted new legislation in 2003, with fines and other civil penalties designed to put spammers out of business. Virginia has been a leader in applying criminal penalties to computer crimes that use fraud or deception.

Johnson (2003) gave a broad overview of the various state attempts to regulate unsolicited commercial e-mail (UCE), or spam, from an Internet law point of view. Topics include current or prior relationship with sender, consent or request of recipient, advertisements in exchange for free use of an e-mail service, transmission to organizations, and misrepresentation, nondisclosure, and falsification. A summary table details laws and codes related to major provisions of 34 state statutes. He concluded, "There is little uniformity among these statutes in terms of the definition of UCE, the conduct regulated, or the remedies or penalties that may be imposed."

Culberg (2002) offers a similar overview of combating spam at the state level. In 2000, Sinrod and Reyna (2000) gave a comprehensive account of several state laws. Kelin (2001) is another source on state law issues.

Virginia's antispam legislation includes criminal penalties directed primarily at senders of "fraudulent claims." It "allows authorities to seize the assets of spammers and carries penalties of up to five years in prison." A person could be prosecuted for sending over 10,000 unsolicited, deceptive e-mails per day or 100,000 in a month. It defined "deceptive" as altering an e-mail header or other routing information.

California's new law was to take effect January 1, 2004. Highly restrictive with tough penalties, the law made it illegal for marketers to e-mail California residents (or California ISP subscribers, regardless of their location), unless the recipient had provided "direct consent" or had a "preexisting or current business relationship." Ignorance of a recipient's location was not an excuse. The California law set fines of $1,000 per spam message, up to $1 million, and unlike most laws, included fines for e-mail sent by mistake. An important provision empowered individuals to sue, which many business and trade associations viewed as a formula for chaos. Overall, marketers considered the law a substantial threat to the emerging field of e-commerce.

Legitimate marketers believed that the tough provisions of the California law would make it difficult to do business and that irresponsible spammers—the source of most spam—would continue to abuse the system. Consumers would be deprived of legitimate messages and convenient shopping, they argued, while still being inundated with spam. They contended that the California law—and others like it—would create more problems than it solved.

The Federal CAN-SPAM Act

The new California antispam law had just been enacted when federal legislators passed the Controlling the Assault of Non-Solicited Pornography and Marketing Act of 2003, commonly known as the "CAN-SPAM" Act.

The CAN-SPAM Act largely supersedes the hodgepodge of more-or-less-restrictive state laws, which although similar in many respects, placed the burden on direct marketers to interpret and comply with 37 state jurisdictions. Given the diversity of laws, an ever-shifting regulatory mix, and different methods of defining and enforcing, businesses had complained that confusion and uncertainty was inhibiting economic growth and progress—and they were fearful that the tough California law would become a model for other legislation.

Pink (2002, p. 11) reviewed other problems of state regulation, concluding "fundamental problems of states regulating activity on the Internet, which is a global communications network that transcends state borders and, in many cases, is more appropriately regulated at the federal level."

The CAN-SPAM Act was signed into federal law on December 16, 2003, and went into effect on January 1, 2004. Some antispammers complain that it was simply a "sellout" to marketing lobbyists, and most legitimate marketers hope it will allow them to conduct responsible, straightforward, honest marketing campaigns that benefit consumers.

Provisions of the CAN-SPAM Act

The act preempts all state laws that expressly regulate commercial e-mail, except to the extent that they prohibit falsity or deception. State laws not specific to e-mail, such as antifraud laws, are unaffected. Under the Act, unsolicited commercial e-mail follows the basic ground rules shown in Table 1.

Additional prohibitions include harvesting e-mail addresses obtained by "automated means," use of e-mail addresses created automatically by random substitution, and using unauthorized "zombie" computers for fraudulent or deceptive messages. The act recognizes "carve outs" that allow states wider discretion in enacting additional legislation to pursue spammers who use fraud or other illegal or deceptive practices.

The CAN-SPAM Act empowers the FTC to fine violators up to $11,000 per violation. The Department of Justice can charge up to $2 million in fines, and judges can triple that to $6 million if the violation is willful or meets other conditions. Violators could face up to five years in jail. FTC Chairman Tim Muris has predicted that "the criminal enforcement of the CAN-SPAM Act will ultimately prove to be more effective than civil enforcement" (Privacy/Internet, 2004b).

Commercial electronic mail message(s) are defined in the act as "any electronic mail message the primary purpose of which is the commercial advertisement or promotion of a commercial product or service." Although most definitions of spam include "bulk" e-mail, the CAN-SPAM Act does not. Even a single message can be spam, with *each* e-mail address counted as one violation. The number of messages sent is used only to set penalties.

The CAN-SPAM Act permits the "one bite" approach that allows legitimate marketers to contact prospects at least once. It allows most transactional or relationship messages arising from a preexisting or current business

Table 1 Major Provisions of the CAN-SPAM Act That Went into Effect on January 1, 2004, Superseding Most State Antispam Laws

Rule	Description
Header Information	The sender organization must not be disguised; "spoofers" who deceive recipients into sending confidential information to credit company imposters and the like are prohibited.
Subject Headings	Prohibits deceptive subject headings in the e-mail; pornographic spammers must include "sexually explicit" in the subject line.
Return Address	Sending address must remain active for 30 days to allow processing of remove requests and other responses.
Remove Request	Requests for removal from the list must be honored within 10 calendar days; $250 fine per e-mail for not complying; removal systems must remain active for 30 days after a mailing.
Identifier Inclusion; Opt-Out Opportunity; Physical Address	Advertising must be identified; pornographic spammers are required to label advertisements clearly; must give notice and opportunity to decline further mailings (e.g., "click here to remove my name from the list"); must include valid physical address of company (P.O. box is allowed)

relationship. These include first, the "transactional or relationship message," further defined as e-mails that would "facilitate, complete, or confirm a commercial transaction that the recipient has previously agreed to enter into with the sender," and second, e-mail that simply references the sender's company, Web site, or other commercial entity. The use of "proxy" computers is allowed, as long as they are not used for fraudulent purposes and clear identification of the sender is given through other means. Bick (2004a) offered an in-depth discussion of these issues from a legal perspective, including discussing some of the implementation questions yet to be addressed.

Implementation Questions

Implementation and codification of the act is evolving. The FTC will make detailed rulings on the definition of "commercial electronic mail message," language such as "misleading," and ambiguities in other issues. It will issue regulations "to determine the criteria to establish the 'primary purpose' of an electronic mail message" (Rembert, 2004, p. 8).

Fingerman (2004, p. 12), in a lengthy legal overview of the act, pointed out that the language relating to subject lines "is rather vague; it is hard to say, for example, whether a coy or humorous subject line would trigger liability as misleading."

Raysman and Brown (2004) asked whether e-mail newsletters are commercial e-mails and whether a friend could be referred?

Kuchinskas asked (2003c), if an advertiser has 10 days to remove a name that has opted out, how would the e-mail service or list provider report that back to the advertiser, and who would be responsible from removing the name? What about "viral marketing," a recent trend where the recipient is asked to forward the message to another person? Will the advertiser need to run that name through their filter first? If a customer asks an advertiser to stop sending a newsletter, does that mean that their billing cannot be e-mailed? What about two different business units

in the same company, or a wholesaler who pays retailers to advertise their goods?

Soltoff (2004) noted that the act holds not just advertisers liable, but "all parties involved in sending e-mail." He raises questions about how advertisers, affiliates, and e-mailers will be able to suppress names with consistency. Also, there is some question whether the required "valid postal address" would be that of the advertiser or some other member of the e-mail sending chain. The FTC has ruled that post office boxes are valid for the purpose of physical address identification.

Nettleton (2004) asked whether a message advertising Viagra addressed to an individual within a company is really sent to the individual, or to the company, which may have a prior relationship with the marketer?

Do-Not-Spam Lists

The CAN-SPAM Act directs the FTC to implement detailed regulations to address these and other questions, and it tells them to investigate a do-not-spam list, similar to the do-not-call list for telemarketers and the do-not-fax list.

Spam fighters ask, why not just implement a do-not-spam-list? Direct Marketing Association (DMA) members match their outbound postal mailings through the do-not-mail list, purging out names who do not want to receive mail. Telemarketers are required by law to check their telephone dialing lists against the federal do-not-call list. The FTC requires fax marketers to obtain a recipient's permission before sending faxes.

In December 2003, it was reported that "The majority of Americans [83%] would sign up for a do-not-spam list, were the Federal Trade Commissioner to launch one" (Parker, 2003). However, spam is fundamentally different from other direct-response media, and notorious spammers have little incentive to comply.

The FTC has ruled that a do-not-spam list is impractical to implement under current conditions and would "do little or nothing" to halt unsolicited commercial e-mail. In contrast to the telemarketing list, a do-not-spam registry "would be ineffective because spammers can constantly create new e-mail addresses and identities, and because it costs virtually nothing for a spammer to clog consumers' inboxes" (Mark, 2003a).

Investigators would be able to track down and close e-commerce sites maintained by legitimate marketers who have physical facilities, much as they can do with telephone and fax call centers, but prolific spammers would fight back. First, spammers could simply ignore the list. They are difficult to track and apprehend, and jurisdiction issues are complex. Second, given the global nature of the Internet, it is easy for them to pack up and move to a new location—frequently offshore in another country. Consumers would still get the spam, but would be deprived of legitimate marketing messages they may want or need.

In addition, a do-not-e-mail-list could be dangerous. Technically, it may be possible to prevent hacking and theft of a list, but human error—or payoffs—could open the door to spammers. An industry expert said, "[It] scares the hell out of me. If I were a spammer, it would be like the holy grail . . . millions of valid e-mail addresses. I can't think of a model the FTC would use that could prevent spammers from just getting a copy of it and going to town" (Mara, 2004b).

The FTC agrees. "Spammers would stop at nothing to obtain this list and misuse it to the detriment of consumers," it concluded (FTC, 2004).

Other problems would frustrate enforcement. Most people have multiple e-mail addresses. Compared with postal mail or telephone numbers, it is easy to change e-mail addresses, making list maintenance difficult. The length of the list would be enormous—and growing.

Instead of a do-not-e-mail list, the FTC recommended that "anti-spam efforts should instead focus on creating a robust e-mail authentication system" (Swartz, 2004b). These options are discussed in the conclusion of this chapter and in other chapters of this book.

List Restrictions

The European Union has enacted highly restrictive legislation on selling and trading names in traditional postal mail and telephone lists. Some U.S. antispam advocates argue for similar restrictions on selling or trading names, but legitimate marketers argue that only they would be hurt. The notorious spammers operate with an underground economy and network of their own that ignores or circumvents such restrictions. Severe penalties, they say, would simply drive more spammer activities offshore, with little reduction in spam.

Companies doing direct marketing in the European Union have contests and other promotions that encourage consumers to submit names. Given similar restrictions, legitimate marketers in the United States say they would build their own house lists, too, and in the long-term, marketing messages would ultimately reach nearly equivalent levels. Meantime, they maintain, it would be time-consuming and expensive, resulting in higher costs to consumers.

Legitimate marketers argue that although some regulation is essential, excessive regulation prevents businesses from being free to innovate and offer new goods and services. Consumers would lose, they say, and restrictions on list sharing would result in an immediate loss of jobs. Let the government demonstrate that they can enforce current laws, they say, before enacting new ones that would stifle business. Most legitimate marketers prefer to regulate through trade association restrictions that can be adapted more quickly to meet changing conditions. Antispammers say trade groups will not do enough to limit spam.

Industry Self-Regulation

Trade associations apply association regulations and a code of ethics to their member companies. They support restrictions on direct marketing, but they argue that government regulation, once enacted, is inflexible and stifles creativity, causing job losses and economic dislocations—and ultimately lowering benefits for consumers. In the narrow sense, trade association regulation is not part of the "legal" counterattack, but the restrictions have much the same effect.

The DMA represents the majority of legitimate catalog, mail, and telephone marketers. Part of their mission is public education, keeping consumers from adopting negative attitudes. They have had a "do-not-mail" list for years and cooperate in reducing unnecessary postal junk mail. Their members are bound to observe do-not-call and do-not-fax lists. They publish guidelines for their members to observe responsible e-mail practices that minimize needless and annoying spam.

They maintain that most legitimate business, government, and not-for-profit organizations are not interested in harassing people. Members are given guidance not to send unsolicited e-mail to those who are unlikely to have an interest in or benefit from the goods, services, or ideas. Many antispammers and politically active groups concerned with commercialization in cyberspace argue that industry self-regulation simply allows the profit motive to define cyberspace.

In 1998, the DMA merged with the Association for Interactive Marketing (AIM), a newer, smaller organization that represents electronic commerce. Founded in 1993, the AIM describes itself as "a non-profit trade organization devoted to helping marketers use interactive opportunities to reach their respective marketplaces" (AIM, 2003). In 1999, the DMA absorbed the Internet Alliance, a similar organization.

In 2003, AIM, working through the organization's Council for Responsible E-mail, created a "best practices" document for legitimate e-mail marketers. The draft was designed to "help facilitate and distinguish permission-based e-mail communications sent by legitimate marketers from spam." It included recommendations for six major topics: consent, delivery, content, hygiene and suppression, education, and dispute resolution. Permission marketing is a small part of e-mail marketing. The DMA adopted a broader policy focusing on fraudulent e-mail.

In 2003, the DMA announced "Operation Slam Spam," targeting the 300 or so notorious spammers whom they contend send the majority of fraudulent e-mails. Soliciting its approximately 4,700 members to work with the

FBI, regulators, and ISPs, the DMA hoped to "terminate distributors of spam" (Khan, 2003).

ENFORCEMENT AND PROSECUTION
Issues with CAN-SPAM and State Legislation

The CAN-SPAM Act passed the U.S. Senate without a single dissenting vote. The House of Representatives passed it 392 to 5. One representative voting against it said, "While Congress has spent literally years grappling with the definition of spam, too little time has been spent considering enforcement of whatever framework is adopted" (Mark, 2003c).

Fraudulent or deceptive advertising regulations logically extend into cyberspace on both federal and state levels, but the CAN-SPAM Act gives the federal government a new set of weapons to pursue spammers. However, the FTC, state prosecutors, and ISPs were pursuing spammers even before the act, especially where the activity involved deception or fraud.

Efforts at regulation raise several issues in both state and federal jurisdictions: freedom of speech, jurisdictional issues, due process, the Commerce Clause regulating interstate commerce, trespass on chattels, and practical aspects of the mechanics of implementation and enforcement. The definition of "place" takes on an entirely new meaning in cyberspace, one that case law is only beginning to address. As the decade proceeds, we can expect to see case law more clearly defined.

First Amendment

Should freedom of speech apply to e-mail? Anyone can stand on a street corner soap box and broadcast messages. Passersby can choose to listen or ignore it. Spammers and civil libertarians argue that spam is free speech, and restrictive legislation infringes on freedoms guaranteed by the First Amendment of the Bill of Rights. Direct marketers have almost no restrictions on postal mail. Why should e-mail be different?

It is commonly believed that "U.S. businesses have a First Amendment right to distribute unsolicited e-mail advertisements" (Swartz, 2003b, p. 20). However, anti-spammers can argue that e-mail shifts the burden of cost away from the sender and onto the consumer. Unlike other forms of direct marketing, spam costs almost nothing to the sender, but cumulatively more to the recipients. Under these conditions, they can say, free speech should give way.

In a commercial context, the freedom of speech issue is frequently seen as having unwarranted importance. Restrictions on direct marketing and other commercial messages already exist. In most jurisdictions, it is unlawful to sell or make sales pitches on the street without appropriate licenses or permissions. In February 2004, the federal do-not-call list was upheld by the 10th Circuit Court of Appeals. The do-not-fax list also has been upheld. Restricting e-mail, anti-spammers can conclude, is a reasonable extension to these regulations.

In 1997, *CompuServe versus Cyber Promotions, Inc.*, the U.S. District Court, citing case law, held that the First Amendment to the U.S. Constitution "provides no defense" for intentional unauthorized use of proprietary computer equipment. This is discussed further in Chattels, later in the chapter.

Specific content areas may be more problematical. For example, Fingerman (2004, p. 12; citing *Reno versus American Civil Liberties Union*, 521 U.S. 844 [1997]) observes that "the sexually oriented material provision [of the CAN-SPAM Act] may be difficult to defend if challenged under the First Amendment. It is content-based regulation of speech, which triggers strict scrutiny."

In December 2004, Microsoft filed seven lawsuits against "John Doe" spammers, alleging that they did not use "Sexually Explicit" in the subject line, sometimes called the "brown paper wrapper" rule (Naraine, 2004). In January 2005, the FTC filed suit against one individual and six companies who allegedly did not follow that rule (Associated Press, 2005a, 2005b). It will be interesting to see how those cases proceed through the legal system, with potential First Amendment and other challenges.

Jurisdiction and Due Process

If limits can be put on e-mail, what jurisdiction should do it? In the 1945 *International Shoe* decision, the U.S. Supreme Court determined that "To have proper jurisdiction, a defendant must have purposely availed itself of the privilege of doing business (i.e., traveling, selling, advertising, and so on) in a state, and these "connections" to that state must meet minimum levels of due process" (Powers, 2002, p. 129).

How do you determine "where" a company operates? In the United States and most of the world, laws are often based on physical presence: a "place" that is identifiable, physical, and addressable. Jurisdiction usually resides there. For example, where a car accident takes place or a descendent resides, the rules are fairly straightforward.

Today, case law avoids the notion that a physical presence is necessary for jurisdiction, but is based on "purposeful availment" of the benefits of the forum state. The jurisdictional standard of purposefully availing oneself of the privilege of doing business is met, for purposes of claims arising from the defendant's activities in a state, where there are numerous transactions with residents of the state. Thus, for example, in 2002, where a domain name registrant allegedly engaged in some 5,000 transactions with Ohio residents and its site was accessible in Ohio, the Sixth Circuit held in *Bird versus Parsons* that it was subject to Ohio's jurisdiction.

Still, the question has become more complex. The boundaries of cyberspace do not have the usual physical characteristics. A company may have its headquarters in Delaware, their sales office in Florida, their Web server in Virginia, and their e-mail server in California. Signals divided into packets travel to their destination through multiple routes, which can be anywhere. In 1945, in contrast, it was relatively easy to determine whether a company was doing business "in" a state.

The courts have held that "even if both sender and recipient are in the same state, the spam may still cross state lines before it reaches its destination and thus qualify as interstate commerce" (Kelin, 2001). In *American Libraries Association versus Pataki*, the judge addressed the position that such commerce might remain in-state and ruled that "no intrastate communications exist" in that matter.

Another issue in state law is whether jurisdiction would apply to residents in unusual circumstances. For example, would it apply when a resident opens his or her e-mail out-of-state? In two challenges to the Commerce Clause (discussed next), the court found that to be a "jurisdictional question not at issue in this case" (Pink, 2002, p. 13).

Additional citations for jurisdiction issues are given at the end of this chapter under "Additional Reading."

The Commerce Clause

The biggest challenge to states enforcing their antispam laws probably has been the Commerce Clause in the U.S. Constitution (U.S. Const., art. I, §8, cl. 3), which says, "Congress shall have power...to regulate commerce...among the several states." Because spam is commerce and interstate commerce is regulated by federal law, to what extent can it be regulated by the states?

The Commerce Clause generally prohibits states from legislating beyond their borders or enforcing laws and regulations on entities operating beyond their boundaries. The limitation is implied, and so it is commonly called the "dormant" Commerce Clause.

Several state laws recognize spam restrictions that have been held in case law to be compatible with the dormant Commerce Clause. The courts have looked at two factors: First, does the state law discriminate against interstate commerce? Second, does the legislation impose a burden on interstate commerce that is excessive in relation to the local benefits?

Most of the 37 states that have enacted antispam legislation have attempted to control fraud or deceptive practices—regardless of where they originated. In formulating their laws, for example, both Virginia and California employed a similar provision: It applied state law to spammers who live outside the state. In *State of Washington versus Heckel*, Washington's law, which carried the provision, was challenged and carried to the Washington Supreme Court in 2001.

The Washington Supreme Court upheld the state's antispam law, and the U.S. Supreme Court refused to hear an appeal, effectively returning the matter to the lower court for trial. The finding was that the dormant Commerce Clause "implicitly operates as a limitation on state laws when such laws unduly burden interstate commerce." However, "The law is not unconstitutional if it regulates evenhandedly to effectuate a legitimate local public interest, its effects on interstate commerce are only incidental, and the burden it imposes on interstate commerce is not clearly excessive in relation to its putative local benefits."

On the topic of consumer protection, it was held in *Heckel* that "a requirement that an advertiser transmitting advertising directly to consumers in their homes or offices be truthful about the source of the advertising and does not burden commerce so much as facilitate it, by eliminating fraud and deception." In responding to the complaint that e-mail addresses generally do not identify the physical address of recipients, the court found that a public registry of e-mail addresses maintained by Washington, defining what e-mail addresses belong to Washington residents, was acceptable. Thus, states considering drafting new antispam legislation may consider *Heckel* a blueprint for what has worked in applying laws and regulations compatible with the Commerce Clause.

A 2002 California antispam case also gives guidance on the requirements for states passing laws that can apply against out-of-state spammers. In *Ferguson versus Friendfinders* the Court found, "The state has a substantial legitimate interest in protecting its citizens from the harmful effects of deceptive UCE" (unsolicited commercial e-mail); and "A regulation serving an important public interest is upheld unless its benefits are outweighed by the burden imposed on interstate commerce."

Pink (2002) and others ("California Anti-Spam Law," 2002) give more details of the explanation in both *State of Washington versus Heckel* and *Ferguson versus Friendfinders*, and the issue has also been decided at the federal level.

In December 2003, a federal judge dismissed an action by America Online (AOL) against a Florida group on a jurisdiction technicality but allowed AOL to overcome the objection by refiling an amended complaint within the bounds of the Commerce Clause (Reuters, 2003b).

In March 2004, AOL filed two suits in the U.S. District Court for the Eastern District of Virginia alleging violations of Virginia's Computer Crimes Act. The defendants, Davis Wolfgang Hawke, his associates, and numerous John Does, were charged with sending millions of deceptive and fraudulent unsolicited bulk e-mails. In *America Online, Inc. versus Hawke, et al; America Online, Inc. versus Does*, AOL alleged that the defendants were responsible for "triggering hundreds of thousands of Member complaints," by using fraud or deception.

The solicitation included mortgage leads, business opportunities, subscriptions to adult content Web sites, penis enlargement pills, weight loss supplements, handheld devices advertised as "personal lie detectors," and a product called "The Banned CD."

The complaint alleged that the defendants used "header information that was materially false or materially misleading," failed to include a "From" line "that accurately identified any person who transmitted or procured the transmission of the message,...contained subject headings that defendants knew, or should have known, were likely to mislead a recipient,...with the intent to falsify or forge electronic mail transmission information or other routing information," and intended to "sell, give, or distribute software that is primarily designed or produced for the purpose of facilitating or enabling the falsification of electronic mail transmission information or other routing information."

Trespass and Nuisance Claims

ISPs have challenged spammers on several grounds, including trespass to chattels, conversion, service mark infringement or dilution, fraud, unfair trade practices, and unfair competition. Of these, chattel claims have been most receptive to the courts (Sinrod and Reyna, 2000).

In 1997, in *CompuServe versus Cyber Promotions*, the court addressed whether the defendants were trespassing on CompuServe's personal property and held, "Trespass to chattels has evolved from its original common law application, concerning primarily the asportation of another's tangible property, to include the unauthorized use of personal property."

"Its chief importance now," it continued, "is that there may be recovery . . . for interferences with the possession of chattels which are not sufficiently important to be classed as conversion" (the Court called it "a little brother of conversion"). Further, "electronic signals sent by computer have been held to be sufficiently physically tangible to support a trespass cause of action." Thus, "Plaintiff has a viable claim for trespass to personal property and is entitled to injunctive relief to protect its property."

A source at the Internet Law Group, in a 2003 review of legal counterattacks, believes indiscriminate e-mail is "already illegal in all 50 states" and should be prosecuted based on chattels law (Schwartz, 2003).

In 1999, in *Intel versus Hamidi,* a California trial court extended the reach of chattel claims to noncommercial bulk e-mail. A former employee, Kourosh Hamidi, allegedly sent e-mails critical of Intel to some 35,000 employees through Intel's systems. In 2004, the California Supreme Court overturned the trial court, holding that "Hamidi did not commit trespass because Hamidi did not damage the computers" (Oriez, 2004b, p. 2). Because commercial spam does not damage computers, this ruling seems inconsistent with the CompuServe ruling, and it demonstrates the intricacies of relying on chattels claims.

Mossoff (2004, p. 625) took the position that ISPs and others should sue the spammers for creating a nuisance.

Nuisance doctrine is superior to the currently favored "trespass to chattels" because it does not require courts to engage in unnecessary legal fictions or doctrinal somersaults in finding that spam has "dispossessed" a plaintiff from its computer network [through] unreasonably and substantially interfering with an ISPs commercial operations—a paradigmatic nuisance injury.

Citations for additional case law relating to trespass to chattels, trademark infringement and dilution, and breach of contract claims by ISPs are given at the end of this chapter under "Additional Reading."

Other Prosecutions

On December 10, 2003, two Florida mortgage scam operators—who were *not* national mortgage lenders, but were advertising "3.95% 30 Year Mortgages"—were required to post $1 million bonds before sending any more unsolicited commercial e-mail. In addition, they were barred from using or benefiting from personal information that was deceptively collected from consumers (Mark, 2003b). Their real purpose was to collect consumer information, including social security numbers, income, and assets—information that could be sold. This is a variation of "phishing," discussed earlier in this chapter.

In late 2003, the FTC brought action against a software company accused of spamming PC users with pop-up ads and e-mails promoting its spam-blocker software. "In essence, defendants bombard an individual consumer with a stream of repeated, unwanted pop up spam in an attempt to induce the consumer to pay defendants to stop the bombardment." The FTC called it "nothing short of extortion" (Callaghan, 2003; Saunders, 2003). In 2004, the company agreed to stop the practice and submit to FTC monitoring for 5 years.

The pop-ups exploited a "feature" in Microsoft Windows called Messenger Service (subsequently addressed in XP Service Pack 2). The company "allegedly claimed it could send pop-ups to as many as 135,000 Internet addresses each hour and had a database of 2 billion addresses" (Manning, 2004). On July 31, 2004, the company reached a settlement in U.S. District Court in Maryland specifying that the company "will no longer send pop-up ads using the Windows Messenger Service or sell software that blocks such ads." The company also was restricted from sending e-mail solicitations.

New York has relied on standard consumer protection laws to prosecute spammers. In late 2003, New York Attorney General Eliot Spitzer, who has aggressively pursued securities fraud and antitrust issues, teamed up with his old nemesis Microsoft to file $38 million in lawsuits, with a mission "to put [fraudulent] spammers out of business for good." Spitzer maintained, "We want to prove to others who are spammers that the penalties will make it financially unviable. When we catch you, we'll drive you into bankruptcy" (Naraine, 2003).

Sampling 8,000 e-mails between May 13 and June 13, 2003, Spitzer's team detected 40,000 fraudulent statements in "separate marketing campaigns that passed through 514 IP addresses around the world," including hijacked computers "belonging to a foreign government's defense ministry, . . . a hospital, and . . . elementary and high schools." The spam messages "used other people's sender names, false subject lines, fake server names, inaccurate and misrepresented sender addresses, or obscured transmission paths, all in violation of New York and Washington state law" (Naraine, 2004; Sears, 2003).

AOL has been active in pursuing spammers, with successful lawsuits against spammers in *Verizon versus Ralsky, AOL versus CN Productions,* and others. Recent AOL lawsuits have been part of a coordinated action by members of the Anti-Spam Coalition, formed in April 2003, including AOL, Earthlink, Microsoft, and Yahoo! The Coalition filed legal complaints in federal courts in California, Georgia, Virginia, and Washington State alleging that the defendants sent "a combined total of hundreds of millions of bulk spam e-mail messages" seeking deceptive solicitations (Business Wire, 2004). An AOL spokesman said, "Congress gave us the necessary tools to pursue spammers with stiff penalties, and we in the industry didn't waste a moment moving with speed and resolve to take advantage of the new law" (CNN, 2004b).

A list and description of AOL cases has been active at http://legal.web.aol.com/email/jeaol/index.html. Cases involving other ISPs may be found at http://www.jmls.edu/cyber/cases/spam.html#cs-cp.

In April 2004, FTC authorities filed criminal charges under the CAN-SPAM Act against four alleged spammers who were arrested in Detroit and accused of disguising their identities in sales pitches for fraudulent weight-loss products. The FTC also announced legal actions against an Australian company. It was reported that FTC Chairman Timothy Muris said, "These cases should send a strong signal to spammers that we are watching their operations and working together to enforce the law" (Associated Press, 2004).

Defining Spam

The ultimate interpretation of laws and regulations in the legal counterattack—and the basis for enforcement—resides in the courts. The system has served the United States well over the past 200+ years and is a model for democracy everywhere.

The legal system was designed in an era when things moved slowly. Fast-moving new events such as spam have not always fared well in a traditional court environment. Spam is so new that many of our legal institutions are learning as they go. Definitions are crafted laboriously, but inconsistently in different jurisdictions. Months or even years of delay are normal in deliberating and handing disputes.

With global communication at lightening speed, prolific spammers spite the slower moving court system, setting up shell corporations in far-flung locations and finding definitional loopholes to put them back in business. They use protections designed for an earlier, slower moving era or operate with untested methods that have not been codified into law. They push the limits of what is legal and ethical. Many simply ignore the law, hoping to evade apprehension and enforcement.

Enforcement requires definition. The CAN-SPAM Act leaves much of the implementation to the FTC, which will be tested in the courts. In the courtroom, laws and regulations rest on definitions in determining prosecution and conviction, a process that exposes grey areas. As case law related to spam progresses, definitions will be clarified. In the broader sense, how spam is defined will have enormous implications in the New Millennium for both consumers and marketers, as it creates standards against which ethical, moral, and legal behavior is judged.

Commonly Used Definitions

A definition can be restrictive or permissive. In November 2003, the Pew Internet & American Life Project (2003) reported that "92% of e-mail users agree that spam is 'unsolicited commercial e-mail from a sender they do not know or cannot identify,'" and 32% extend this to a sender with whom they "have already done business." E-mail is an invasion of privacy, they say. Let's allow e-mailing *only* to people who have specifically requested it. Businesses and freedom of speech advocates can counter that if consumers understood the economic implications, they would approve responsible, legitimate commercial messages—at least a "one bite" approach.

Let us consider four definitions of spam commonly used in legal counterattacks (Sullivan, 2003b). Two include *single* unsolicited e-mails, and the others specify "bulk."

1. UCE: *unsolicited commercial e-mail*, usually excluding unsolicited political messages
2. UBE: *unsolicited bulk e-mail*
3. UCBE: *unsolicited commercial bulk e-mail*
4. UEMS: *unsolicited electronic mail solicitations*

UBE is identified in AOL's 2004 filings (*America Online, Inc. versus Hawke, et al.* and *America Online, Inc. versus Does*). UCE and UBE have been used by courts in making spam rulings (*State of Washington versus Hecke*; see also *Verizon versus Ralsky*). UCE is compatible with the CAN-SPAM Act and avoids some interpretation questions.

For example, what is the numeric definition of "bulk?" Would it matter if the same e-mails were sent in smaller, multiple batches? How many could be sent within any hour or twenty-four-hour period, regardless if batch or individual? What is "unsolicited?" "Commercial?" Must it be selling a product? What about lead generation, or surveys, contests, service bulletins, electronic magazines and newsletters, news services, and other content? What about sending a message asking parents in your child's school to donate to the athletic fund? When does e-mail "misrepresent" an offer or the "originator" or attempt to "confuse" or "defraud" people? Each of these terms requires its own specification.

Is spam only e-mail? Pop-up ads, banners, animated graphics, voice messages, spyware, required forms or registration, and other Web clutter is electronic, unsolicited, and a lot like spam. What is their relationship to e-mail spam? Should these be included in legal definitions of spam? Privacy advocates can argue that all of these—and other undiscovered techniques and devices—are similar to an unwanted guest walking thorough a home's front door: an invasion of privacy.

It is not in the scope of this chapter to resolve these questions, but it is useful to present them. Under the CAN-SPAM Act, the Federal Trade Commission will formulate appropriate regulations, and states will add compatible provisions. It will be interesting to see how the court system deals with the issues discussed here in applying case law.

Restrictive Definitions

Restrictive definitions include the so-called zero-tolerance policy—"*any* unsolicited e-mail," or "*any* e-mail that is not relevant or interesting." This, it can be argued, effectively would prohibit *any* unsolicited communications, even the "one-bite" approach.

The operational deficiency is obvious: If I find Susan Kathleen in the white pages and send her an innocent e-mail to ask if she is the same person I dated in high school, oops! That's spam. To remedy this, some would include "any e-mail that is not relevant or interesting," again an unworkable solution (How will I know if the recipient will find it relevant or interesting?). Definitions that include "unwanted" would have similar problems. Because senders cannot know individual responses ahead of time, they would surely send spam.

Gratton (2004) reported on a suggestion from Australia's National Office for the Information Economy that would define spam as "a communication that could not be reasonably assumed to be wanted or expected by a recipient." The ambiguous language used for this judgment would likely be perplexing to and unevenly applied by courts, as penalties were to be applied.

Highly restrictive definitions are sometimes used to generate statistics quoted by the mass media. Companies that sell filtering software benefit from copy such as, "The bad news is that the tipping point has been reached, as [our filters] classified 50% of all measured e-mail as unwanted messages" (Greenspan, 2003). The definition being used is seldom reported in a media "sound bite."

Permissive Definitions

Free-speech advocates may argue that they want *no* restrictions beyond outright fraud. They would argue for permissive definitions, where people can ignore unwanted e-mail and decide for themselves what is objectionable. People, they can point out, sometimes want information about things they claim to despise.

In January 2004, half of the top ten affiliate program "clickthroughs" (*voluntarily* clicking on an ad to go to a Web site) were for health, dating, or vitamin sites, including an herbal Viagra alternative—commonly objects of spam e-mail (CyberAtlas, 2004).

Some users publicly denounce spam, but privately open the unsolicited commercial messages voluntarily—and the products sell. In June 2003, *USA Today* reported, "Commercial e-mail ads produce more than $7.1 billion in sales annually" (Swartz, 2003a). The October 2003 Pew Internet & American Life Project (2003) poll found that 7% of e-mailers, more than 8 million people, reported ordering a product or service originating in spam.

Some users want spam. The *Wall Street Journal* noted, "If everyone hated spam, it would disappear," and reported on Orlando Soto, who "routinely comes home to some 150 e-mail pitches, and he loves getting them all" (Mangalindan, 2004). Mr. Soto, the article said, buys aromatherapy oils, pharmaceuticals, mystery novels, home games, and other items. Spam, it seems, "helps him 'unwind' and 'lose the stress of the day.'...Good spam, he says, leaves him feeling blessed." Others, of course, feel cursed.

Opt In, Opt Out: Four Alternatives

Implementing any definition usually considers four alternatives. You may be prohibited from contacting anyone. At the other extreme—probably Mr. Soto's preference—you are free to contact everybody. Opt-in and opt-out are the two middle cases.

Opt in says that a marketer may only contact people who have expressed an interest in their product and given explicit permission to contact them. This means that marketers must have some initial contact and secured their permission prior to sending any e-mail messages. The "double confirmed opt in" is more restrictive. A user must opt in, and then after receiving an e-mail message, opt in again confirming the first opt in.

Opt out means that marketers may send unsolicited e-mail messages to prospects without prior permission. They may continue to do so until the recipient explicitly denies permission for more mailings. This is sometimes called the "one bite" approach. It is less restrictive than opt in, but more restrictive than free access.

Permission Marketing

In the past several years, "permission marketing," a special case of opt in, has become a buzzword. Consumers volunteer to receive product information. Otherwise, they are not contacted. Seminars, articles, and books have extolled the virtues of marketing only to individuals who

have explicitly expressed an interest and given their permission to be sent e-mail messages. In 2003, eMarketer estimated that "76 billion messages are sent out annually through legitimate opt-in marketing campaigns" (Powell, 2003).

In practice, most people do not opt in to permission marketing lists, but almost everyone unknowingly ends up on them. They seldom know they are subscribed or how to be removed.

Many offers, contracts, and terms-of-use agreements have obscure passages buried within them allowing the list owner to interpret "permission." Technically, a user may have "agreed" to receive e-mail at some time in the past from "associated organizations" or "affiliates," which can mean almost anything. Some opt-in arrangements mean that *any* future offers are thereby "solicited." These "opt-in" lists are sold or rented out by list compilers and brokers.

In addition, many are fraudulent. Lieb (2003) described "black hat developers [who] write bots that can opt you in again and again," using robotic crawler software to harvest e-mail addresses. Once a list is sold or otherwise passed on, it is difficult to trace how a person was placed on it.

Until the CAN-SPAM Act, there was no nationwide requirement for an opt-out button or a sender's address, so recipients couldn't get off the lists. When those buttons did appear, they were often used only to validate the address, and many e-mail users still are reluctant to try to opt out.

EFFECT OF THE LEGISLATIVE COUNTERATTACK

The CAN-SPAM Act is the beginning of what is likely to become a continual effort at regulation at the federal level. Like most legislation, the act is unlikely to please those with strong opinions on either side. It does not put an end to all unsolicited e-mail, and it puts limits on spammers and legitimate marketers.

The Government Perspective

A White House spokesman said that spam is "annoying to consumers and costly to our economy," and the act will curb abuses by "establishing a framework of technological [and] administrative civil and criminal tools" (Associated Press, 2004).

Senator Charles Schumer (D.-N.Y.), who maintains that 250 spammers are responsible for 90% of the e-mail being sent said, "We are saying to those 250, no matter where you are, or how you try to hide your spam, we will find you. This bill gives the FTC and the Justice Department the tools to go after you" (Gaudin, 2003).

The Spammer Perspective

In May 2004, at the invitation of Senator John McCain, Ronald Scelson, the Cajun Spammer, returned to the U.S. Senate to testify about the new regulations. Scelson (2004), who claimed to be following the law, said, "The act that is to curtail fraud is in fact curtailing our ability to engage in free enterprise." [It] "begins to look like small business against big business." Other spammers have similar complaints.

After working diligently to become "white listed" by AOL, Scelson says WorldCom, his ISP, worked behind his back to convince AOL to revoke that status based on a count of undeliverable e-mails. These "bounce-backs," he said, were from an old list, and "the only way to get the bad addresses out of the list was to deliver into AOL and pick up their nondeliverable reports back to us.... WorldCom stepped in and tried to shut me down even after AOL sent proof of our white list classification."

Scelson also complained that "blacklist" organizations have disregarded the CAN-SPAM Act, saying they "act like vigilantes now more than ever before. These groups will not remove the blacklist even if you prove to them that you are compliant with the new legislation.... They do not identify themselves like we do so pursuing legal action against them is nearly impossible. Many of these groups are not even on U.S. soil." Further, he says, they "use automated systems to generate multiple complaints to the Internet service providers."

The Antispammer Perspective

In mid-2004, Swartz (2004d) reported that e-mail users "have seen little reprieve in the amount of unsolicited e-mails that fill their inboxes each day." Advocates of the act say there has not been adequate time to change spammer behavior. Several lawsuits filed against alleged spammers by large ISPs have yet to work their way through the system.

Many antispammers call the CAN-SPAM Act a "flop." Often, these are advocates of a much more restrictive definition of spam. Although the Act permits ISPs to sue, it prevents individuals from suing spammers—a provision in the California law that legitimate marketers maintained would result in legal chaos. Ray Everett-Church of the ePrivacy Group said, "This is a pretty bad bill.... It actually legitimizes most forms of spam" (Gaudin, 2003). He assumed a restrictive definition.

Antispammers are concerned that relatively liberal access to prospects through list sharing and the CAN-SPAM Act's failure to allow individuals to sue leads to a "slippery slope" that will encourage reckless e-mail spam.

The Business Perspective

Legitimate marketers have welcomed a nationwide universal standard that they can observe, and they are "happy to comply with" the CAN-SPAM Act (Kuchinskas, 2003a). The act provides consistency and—what they believe Congress intended—a consideration for the concerns of both consumers and legitimate businesses that depend on communicating with customers.

Marketers maintain, "Laws against unwanted e-mails will have little effect on the real culprits—the mass spammers—[while] keeping track of e-mail addresses, permissions, and the documentation required to fend off lawsuits could become a major overhead headache for firms deploying e-mail" (Oliva, 2004).

Some businesses complain that the CAN-SPAM Act gives legitimacy to the argument that companies have an obligation to protect employees from spam. Oriez reported that "there have been a number of suits against employers by employees who allege that failing to block pornography created a hostile work environment" and discussed several cases (Oriez, 2004b, p. 3).

Established marketers and trade groups such as the DMA see overregulation as the "slippery slope" to be avoided. Although legitimate marketers may reduce or eliminate some mailings, most of them are expected to implement the act's legal provisions and continue what they consider to be ethical practices.

The States' Perspective

The 37 states that enacted legislation before 2004—and others such as New York that rely on conventional fraud and deceptive business practice law—have been upstaged by the CAN-SPAM Act. Although many of the states recognize the advantages in uniformity, lawmakers in states such as California that envisioned more restrictive measures have been disappointed. They have an opportunity to work with federal officials to strengthen the act, or they may devise additional provisions that are not in conflict with the act ("carve-outs," discussed elsewhere in this chapter), but their constituents are primarily bound by the federal rules.

THE GLOBAL PERSPECTIVE

While this chapter has focused primarily on the legal counterattack against spam in the United States, spam has a global presence. Consumers worldwide are receiving more and more unwanted spam, and many spammers have moved outside the United States to avoid laws, regulations, and enforcement.

The Movement Offshore

As the CAN-SPAM Act and state legislation has become more restrictive, many spammers simply ignore it or move offshore, outside the jurisdiction of federal and state courts. Even if they can be found, they usually do not comply with the dispute resolution methods. An industry insider said, "The law won't affect true e-mail abusers, against whom it was written" (Soltoff, 2004).

A February 2004 article quotes the director of the FTC's Bureau of Consumer Protection: "There certainly hasn't been any significant reduction in the number of spams that have been forwarded to our mail boxes" and concluded that "Spammers have already figured out quick ways to get around the rules" (Fox News, 2004).

After the act became law, a *Washington Post* article reported that AOL's spam fighting group determined the following: "Of the roughly 2.4 billion pieces of spam AOL blocks a day, there has been a roughly 10 percent shift in their origins to overseas-based Internet addresses" (Krim, 2004). That percentage is increasing.

Industry analyst Sara Radicati concluded, "The worst spam is being sent from offshore. It's malicious and there's tons of it.... This is going to have absolutely no effect on the most disruptive, the most offensive, the most hard to deal with spam" (Gaudin, 2003).

European Legislation

Spam in Europe has risen dramatically, prompting one writer to conclude, "Europe has overtaken North America as the most digitally attacked continent" (Greenspan, 2003). A 2003 study found that spam cost European businesses $2.5 billion (Swartz, 2003a). In response, the European Union has increased enforcement of cyberspace.

The European Union issued a Directive on Privacy and Electronic Communications 2002/58/EC requiring all member nations to enact antispam laws by October 31, 2003 (although only six complied on time). The regulations also cover direct marketing by telephone and fax, lists, Internet cookies, and other means and generally are more restrictive than in the United States. Europe is blaming "weak" U.S. laws for most of the spam in Europe (Gratton, 2004).

In December 2003, based on the Directive, the United Kingdom enacted antispam legislation (see Stokes & Bramwell, 2004, for details of the law). The tighter rules were found to have done little to control spam, and the U.K. compliance officer "received complaints in the hundreds from annoyed e-mail users disillusioned by the buildup to the law's enactment." An observer is quoted, "Unless there is a globally ratified act it is never going to be very effective" (Bishara, 2004).

Nettleton offered an in-depth analysis of problems in the U.K. implementation, including the statement that "the vast majority of spam originates from the USA and Asia, and hence the implementation of the Directive is likely to do little to cut down its volume" (Nettleton, 2004).

A journal report supports Nettleton's figures. "Several studies have revealed that at least 50% of all unsolicited e-mails originate in the United States" (Swartz, 2004c).

In January 2004, a report said the European Union Commission determined that "the new Directive . . . in many cases, is ineffective . . . [and] admitted that further action was needed to combat the problem of junk e-mail." Measures being considered include additional investigatory powers, allowing victims to claim damages, aggressive filtering, and international cooperation (Bennett, 2004).

The European Coalition Against Unsolicited Commercial E-mail (EuroCAUCE) is an outspoken advocate of making e-mail adhere to the same standards as postal, telephone, and fax marketing, including the bias toward opt in. It has helped the European Union develop opt-in regulations similar to those for their postal mail (EuroCAUCE, 2003).

EuroCAUCE published a proposed timeline of regulation extending through 2006 that includes a do-not-e-mail list. However, EuroCAUCE does not effectively address the widely debated differences between those media and e-mail that lead many to conclude that such a list will be ineffective or even dangerous (discussed earlier in this chapter).

Growing International Action

As definitions and enforcement become tighter in the highly developed nations, spammers are moving offshore, operating anywhere in the world. An April, 2004, Com-touch study reported that 71% of spammers' Web sites are hosted in China, and 60.5% of the global spam is sent from the United States, demonstrating that "spam is a global problem" ("China—Main Source of Spam E-mail," 2004, p.1).

Countries across the globe have been active in investigating or enacting new legislation, including Singapore, Taiwan, Thailand, and China. Korea reportedly is testing a fee-for-e-mail, based on the number of sent messages, which has resulted in a decline of spam (Charron, 2003).

In 2002, ISPs in China agreed to form a coalition to counter the distribution of spam and computer viruses over their servers, prompted by "press reports that, over the past year, servers in both North America and Europe have blocked all e-mail from China" (Fishman, Josephberg, Linn, Pollack, & Victoriano, 2002, p. 31). The coalition also proposed the establishment of the "China Anti Junk Mail Association" that would "disseminate information regarding servers that accommodate spammers."

In 2004, spam-blocking organizations reported that China and Korea each accounted for approximately 10% of spam traffic that could be identified by country of origin. Argentina and Brazil "seem to have fallen into disuse recently," perhaps because ISPs there are taking action (Oriez, 2004a, p. 29).

Canadian policy, in 1999, suggested that "specific antispam legislation was not needed," instead relying on existing fraud and consumer protections. As spam volume has risen, however, Canada is considering additional legislation (Gratton, 2004).

Effective January 1, 2001, e-mail addresses were defined as "personal information" under Canada's existing Personal Information Protection and Electronic Documents Act (PIPEDA). Swartz (2003b, p. 22) reported that under these rules, "Computer mischief offenses could apply in cases where spamming would interfere with or obstruct a person's access to data or use of a computer system and the sender was reckless in that he or she understood that this would likely occur." Punishment could be up to 10 years in prison.

Many observers feel that without multinational agreement, it is "unclear whether national laws will stop spam" (Raysman & Brown, 2004). Spammers can set up almost anywhere in the world. A legal newsletter concludes, "International measures may be necessary to truly eradicate fraudulent spam" (Bick, 2004b).

Kelin (2001, p. 435) observed,

> Spam is a nationwide, even worldwide, problem. Even if spam were outlawed in an entire country, it could still be sent into that country from elsewhere. Thus, outlawing spam in the United States may simply result in spam being sent via foreign ISPs that are not subject to U.S. laws.

The United Nations has announced that it would attempt to "standardize legislation to make it easier to prosecute senders of junk e-mail" (Swartz, 2004b). International action would include some form of defining and enforcing prohibitions. One of the barriers to agreement will be the difference of opinion on whether opt out or opt in will become the standard. The United States favors opt out, whereas Europe and much of the rest of the world prefer opt in (Swartz, 2003b).

In July 2004, an international conference in Geneva, sponsored by the United Nations International Telecommunication Union (ITU), was attended by UN officials and representatives from 60 countries. The need for legislation, new technology to control unsolicited e-mail, phishing and other forms of electronic fraud, and closer international cooperation and support from ISPs and other industry sources were included on the agenda. At the meeting, the UN agency said it would present "examples of anti-spam legislation that countries can adopt to make cross-border cooperation easier" (Lemke, 2004). Reportedly, part of the ITU solution involves "fundamentally changing the nature of the Internet and SMTP" (the technical specifications for simple mail transfer protocol; Wagner, 2004).

The Organization for Economic Cooperation and Development, which has attempted to regulate international handling of personal information since 1980 through the Code of Fair Information Practices, has published new "suggested guidelines" for dealing with spammers and "protecting consumers from cross-border fraud" (Gratton, 2004).

Currently, there is no effective international law or court system to deal with individual entities in commercial matters. It may be possible to approach spam through the World Trade Organization, IMF, or World Bank, where it would be in the economic interests of nations to participate in spam reduction or face sanctions.

CONCLUSION

Discussing what he calls "The Tragedy of E-mail," Charron (2003) cited Garrett Hardin's 1968 article titled "The Tragedy of the Commons." For assets shared in common (such as cyberspace), "The individual benefit of utilizing that asset always outweighs the more remote long-term harm in destroying the asset as a whole." With spam, "The cost of using the asset is zero, and individual benefits seem to outweigh the incremental destruction to the asset as a whole." In other words, the spammer takes short-term benefits, and society ultimately suffers.

The Internet evolved out of its military origin into a cooperative, loosely administered collection of collegial users who, for the most part, followed etiquette and reasonable rules designed to benefit all of the users. Primary domain names (.mil, .edu, .net, .gov) were designed to quickly identify types of users. Second-level domain names (.adv, .porn, etc.), if observed as intended, would make it easy for users to filter out unwanted communications. As the Internet became more mature, however, spammers and others with personal gain motives have ignored the informal conventions and codes of conduct. Instead, they exploit it to the detriment of the larger community.

Spam is a problem that took a relatively short time to develop, but may take considerable time to control. One observer notes, "While spammers are on the run, they are still winning the race against corporations and government officials trying to shut them down. For every spam-

mer put out of business by a lawsuit, probably hundreds of newbies are being trained in secretive 'spam clubs' around the Internet. For every account shut down for illegal activity, thousands more open up" (Sullivan, 2003b). The legal counterattack can help.

The legal counterattack on spam sets out a legislative game plan to mitigate the potential degradation of our collective cyberspace commons. The CAN-SPAM Act establishes, for the first time, a relatively consistent set of rules for senders of commercial e-mail. It standardizes, it sets a foundation, and it leaves room for legitimate marketing in cyberspace. It attempts to balance the macro–micro dilemma, although it is unlikely to satisfy extremes on either end of the issue. Other nations and economic unions have taken similar action, more or less restrictive.

Legislation is only one piece of the mosaic in the evolving counterattack on spam that will define society's interface to cyberspace. It is not a perfect world, and those who demand "There oughta be a law!" sometimes are chasing the chimera of a perfect legislative solution, which does not exist. As the evolution of opposing points of view and society's experience with cyberspace becomes more mature, a series of measured responses will reconcile the divergent interests of antispammers, commercial marketers, Mr. Skelson, Mr. Soto, privacy advocates, and others.

The legal counterattack is only one means of dealing with spam. Stanford law professor Lawrence Lessig, in his 1999 classic, "The Law of the Horse: What Cyberlaw Might Teach," said, "[of] the collection of tools that a society has at hand for affecting constraints upon behavior, . . . law . . . is just one of these tools." Lessig offered four interdependent "modalities of regulation in real space and cyberspace" that include law, social norms, markets, and architecture.

Today, the notorious spammers flout the Net's social norms. And, until profit is taken out of spamming, the market modality can make them money. By architecture, Lessig meant the physical world, including cyberspace structures. The architecture, or "code," he argues, can be changed. That would include "the software and hardware that make cyberspace the way it is." Government can "take steps to alter the Internet's design. It can take steps, that is, to affect the regulability of the Internet."

Just because the laws are written as they are, and understanding that the laws often lag technology, does not mean we have to wait for a legal counterattack to catch up. We can be proactive in other ways. Combating spam can be a unified goal, with many entities collaborating to accomplish the desired end result. For example, the law says that port scanning is legal (*Moulton versus VC3*), but we do not have to allow that activity to take place in our networks. Similarly, we know that looking at pornography is legal for adults, yet most companies have established rules (codes) about no pornography at work. Network administrators need effective processes to keep up with filtering on the border (of the local network), users need to notify administrators when spam comes through and when other e-mails do not, and the administrators need to notify the FCC and law enforcement who can track down spammers.

In September 2003, Lessig suggested that technologists be given more input into the debate. "We should be embarrassed by how extraordinarily poorly our legal system works" (Coffee, 2003). In January 2004, at the National Spam and the Law conference in San Francisco, Lessig said, "The [CAN-SPAM] Act won't stem the tide of spam" (Mara, 2004a). The legal counterattack game plan needs execution and control, but it needs technology, human-user actions, and other complementary solutions to help bring spam under control.

Schwartz (2003) outlined seven technology solutions, but says "technology alone will never win the war." He concluded that the legal counterattack needs to be coordinated with technology solutions and other means of controlling spam.

Technology solutions may include authentication, sophisticated filters that can use artificial intelligence and other learning techniques to reduce the false positives, better virus checking, more effective closing of "backdoor" access to computer intruders, more secure operating systems, and better service bureau tools. Webber (2004) offered several practical solutions along these lines that ordinary users can implement (Webber, 2004). A broad discussion of technology solutions is beyond the scope of this chapter, but they are promising in complementing the legal counter attack.

In 2004, the BBC News reported that an IBM scientist had developed an antispam filter inspired by the way scientists analyze generic sequence "that automatically learns patterns of spam vocabulary with a proven 96.5% success rate" (News Track, 2004). There will be other new developments, as yet undiscovered.

Better "data mining" technology—especially on an international basis—would allow faster and more effective detection and tracing of spammers, although these solutions are controversial. The Terrorism Information Awareness program, for example, may be a model for effectively tracking down notorious spammers, but it was stopped because of privacy concerns. Many provisions of the Patriot Act will be under review in 2005 for similar reasons.

If money is a motivator, it may also be a deterrent. Bill Gates, in a talk show interview January 27, 2004, "predicted a spam-free world by 2006," and a Microsoft spokesperson said, "We as a company believe that by a couple of years from now spam will be down to a very manageable level. It will be almost an afterthought" (Mara, 2004c). Gates mentioned several methods, including an electronic version of postage and authentication.

Competing proposals that shift costs to the sender are on the table from AOL, Earthlink, Yahoo, and others. ISPs could charge subscribers based on the bandwidth they use, a small per e-mail cost might be assessed, or bulk mailers might be required to post a bond that would include a "micropayment." The other side argues that these schemes are a tax in disguise and would create more problems than they solve. In May 2004, Microsoft reportedly agreed to "merge its [authentication] proposal" with AOL (Swartz, 2004b). Such agreements, although promising, are notoriously unstable.

The Internet probably has been the vehicle for the most fast-moving adoption and diffusion of new technology in human history. Many argue that the phenomenal growth of the Internet since the mid-1990s has resulted largely from the fact that it is not regulated or taxed, giving individuals and companies the freedom to find creative ways to use its still-to-be-discovered full potential. Many who are strongly opposed to spam also are against placing restrictions or taxation on Internet usage. Counterattacks that make senders of e-mail pay often are opposed as leading to too much central control.

Meantime, spammers will continue to challenge the legislative counterattack. New legislation and case law for issues relating to cyberspace are developing on a regular basis (see additional reading suggestions at the end of this chapter). The next generation is likely to address spam in libraries and other public meeting places, children's protection, e-mail and spam on cell phones and other wireless networks, and other issues that have only begun to be recognized—or are still undiscovered. Spam over instant messaging (spim) reportedly reached 500 million items in 2003 (Swartz, 2004d). Software engineers recently succeeded in spamming Internet telephone systems (voice over Internet Protocol), sending "voice messages to 1,000 targets per minute . . . the first known demonstration of . . . (spit)" (Jonietz, 2004).

Controlling new technology will involve strategic political decisions, legislation, and some implementation of Lessig's code architecture, social norms, and markets. There is a cyclical nature to the counterattack. We will need to ask ourselves, what is the vision of the future? What are people willing to give up in the way of personal and collective liberties to protect the commons? Will it be effective?

For the moment, at least, the balance may be shifting. At the end of 2004, AOL reported that a combination of the legal counterattack and technical measures had resulted in "a sharp decline in the amount of spam received and reported by members" (Rodgers, 2004). The decline was attributed to "improved security and spam blocking features, as well as the company's well-publicized legal action against spammers."

Progress in controlling spam will be measured objectively and subjectively in this changing environment. Perception is affected by expectations. Five years ago, spam was not much of a problem. Now, if it can be cut in half, most consumers will be pleased—even if the spam is still bad. Almost everyone hopes Bill Gates's prediction will be fulfilled.

GLOSSARY

Blacklist A list of e-mail addresses, domain names, or other identifiers in cyberspace that is used to identify and block spammers and potential spam activity.

Bots Robotic software crawlers that methodically seek Web pages and other areas of cyberspace to find key words and other information, including e-mail addresses that can be harvested and used by spammers.

Bounce E-mail messages that have been returned as undeliverable; useful in differentiating legitimate marketers from spammers, and sometimes used to determine whether an entity should be blacklisted.

CAN-SPAM Act Legislation in the United States that sets out rules for sending unsolicited commercial e-mail messages; formally the Controlling the Assault of Non-Solicited Pornography and Marketing Act of 2003; the full text of the law is available at http://www.congress.gov/cgibin/bdquery/z?d108:S. 877.

Data Mining Searching through data to find patterns of interest, for example, xxxx@yyyyyyy.com, a pattern for an e-mail address.

False Negative Failure to identify spam e-mail.

False Positive Misidentifying legitimate e-mail as spam.

Hijacked Computer *See* zombie computer.

One Bite Approach An approach that allows one commercial message to be sent to an e-mail address; the recipient may opt out of future messages.

Open Relays Mail servers that have been carelessly configured so that anyone on the Internet can send mail through them without needing a password; the messages appear to have come from an Internet service provider, not a spammer.

Opt In A recipient must specifically agree to receiving e-mail before any is sent.

Opt Out Messages may be sent; recipient must request removal from the mailing list.

Phishers Spammers who send fraudulent e-mail asking for confidential information such as social security numbers, bank accounts, or credit card numbers; often combined with spoofing to make it appear that the request is from a legitimate agency or business.

Pink Contracts An Internet service provider arrangement with e-mailers to permit borderline spam through payment of an extra charge.

Preview Window A window enabling a user to see into an inbound e-mail message without opening it; often used by spammers to present pornographic images or register validated e-mail addresses.

Spoofers Spammers who forge a sender's identity to make it appear that a message is from a different sender, often a friend or trusted company or agent; it can damage a company's brand or image; it can be used to deceive a spam filter.

UCE, UBE, UCBE, UEMS Acronyms for definitions of spam commonly used in legal proceedings. Further defined in the Commonly Used Definitions section.

White List A list of e-mail addresses, domain names, or other identifiers in cyberspace that is used to identify specific users and allow them to pass e-mail messages through the Internet and World Wide Web.

Zombie Computer A computer that has been "hijacked" or otherwise entered by hackers or spammers who use it to send out spam messages, often from the computer's e-mail address book; sometimes politely called "open proxies," which, if not hijacked, can perform valuable functionality in delivering legitimate Internet messages.

CROSS REFERENCES

See *Cyberterrorism and Information Security; E-Mail and Instant Messaging; Global Aspects of Cyberlaw; Legal, Social and Ethical Issues of the Internet.*

REFERENCES

Around the block. (2004, Jul/Aug). *Marketing Management, 13*(4), 7.

Association for Interactive Marketing. (2003). *About AIM: Overview*. Retrieved August 15, 2003, from http://www.interactivehq.org/about/

Associated Press. (2004, April 29). U.S. charges four under new law against "spam" e-mails. Retrieved April 29, 2004, from http://www.cnn.com/2004/LAW/04/29/internet.spam.ap/index.html

Associated Press. (2005a, January 12). F.T.C. files first legal case against sexually explicit spam. Retrieved January 13, 2005, from http://www.nytimes.com/2005/01/12/technology/12porn.html

Associated Press (2005b, January 11). FTC shuts down X-Rated spammers. Retrieved January 11, 2005, from http://www.foxnews.com/printer_friendly_story/0,3566,144022,00.html

Bennett, M. (2004, February 2). EC urges spam crackdown. VUU NET. Retrieved June 4, 2004, from Lexis Nexis.

Betteridge, I. (2005, January 18). Man admits to tsunami phishing scam. Retrieved January 21, 2005, from http://www.eweek.com/print_article2/0,2533,a+ 142829,000.asp

Bick, J. (2004a, May 10). A hole in the CAN-SPAM Act. *New Jersey Law Journal*. Retrieved June 4, 2004, from LexisNexis.

Bick, J. (2004b, February 2). Spam is still lawful. *New Jersey Law Journal*. Retrieved June 4, 2004, from LexisNexis.

Bishara, M. (2004, January 12). New anti-spam laws fail to bite. Retrieved February 17, 2004, from http://www.cnn.com/2004/TECH/internet/01/12/spam.continues/index.html

Brunker, M. (2003, August 7). In the trenches of the "spam wars." Retrieved August 15, 2003, from http://www.msnbc.com/news/945559.asp?0cb=-213171549

Business Wire. (2004, March 10). America Online, EarthLink, Microsoft, and Yahoo! team up to file first major industry lawsuits under new federal anti-spam law. *Business Wire*. Retrieved June 4, 2004, from LexisNexis.

California anti-spam law ruled constitutional. (2002, February). *Journal of Internet Law, 5*(8), 21.

Callaghan, D. (2003, November 6). FTC slams pop-up spammer. Retrieved November 7, 2003, from http://www.eweek.com/print_article/0,3048,a=111640,00.asp

Charron, C. (2003, December 16). Face the truth: It's time to charge for e-mail. Devices, Media, & Marketing First Look: Research & event highlights from Forrester electronic newsletter, December 16, 2003.

China—Main source of spam email. (2004, May 3). *Emerging Markets Economy*. Retrieved November 19, 2004, from Business Source Premiere.

CNN (2003, November 24). Ticking off consumers. Retrieved November 24, 2003, from http://money.cnn.com/2003/11/24/pf/consumer_complaints/index.htm?cnn=yes

CNN (2004a, November 18). Gates world's most spammed person. Retrieved November 19, 2004, from http://www.cnn.com/2004/TECH/internet/11/18/gates.spam.ap/index.html

CNN (2004b, March 10). ISPs sue over spam e-mails. Retrieved March 15, 2004, from http://money.cnn.com/LAW/03/10/spam.suits.ap/index.html

Coffee, P. (2003, October 6). Future of spam control. *eWeek, 20*(40), 38.

Culberg, K. (2002, September). Regulating the proliferation and use of spam. *Journal of Internet Law, 6*(3), 18–19.

CyberAtlas. (2004, February 3). *January's Top Affiliate Programs* [in electronic newsletter] (archives available at www.clickz.com).

Daniels, D. (2003, August 25) The state of e-mail marketing. Jupiter Research, Marketing Operations, Jupitermedia, New York.

EuroCAUCE. (2003). *E-Privacy Directive Proposal COM(2000)*. Retrieved December 9, 2003, from http://www.euro.cauce.org/en/timeline1.html

Festa, P. (2000, September 6). PSINet assailed as spam contract surfaces. Retrieved September 3, 2003, from http://news.com.com/2102-1023_3-248211.html?tag=ni_print

Festa, P. (2003, June 3). Lawyers begin anti-spam training. Retrieved December 9, 2003, from http://www.silicon.com/research/specialreports/thespamreport/0,39025001,10004459,00.htm

Fingerman, D. (2004, February). Spam canned throughout the land? Summary of the CAN-SPAM Act. *Journal of Internet Law, 7*(8), 10–17.

Fishman, R., Josephberg, K., Linn, J., Pollack, J., & Victoriano, J. (2002, July). International developments. *Intellectual Property & Technology Law Journal, 14*(7), 29–32.

Fox News (2004, February 10). FTC: "CAN-SPAM" law only a mild deterrent. Retrieved February 10, 2004, from http://www.foxnews.com/printer_friendly_story/0,3566,110910,00.html

Gaudin, S. (2003, December 10). Christmas comes early for spammers. Retrieved December 11, 2003, from http://www.internetnews.com/IAR/print.php/3287501

Gratton, E. (2004, June). Dealing with unsolicited commercial emails: A global perspective. *Journal of Internet Law, 7*(12), 3–13.

Greenspan, R. (2003, December 4). The deadly duo: spam and viruses. Retrieved December 11, 2003 from http://cyberatlas.internet.com

iHateSpam. (2004). The cost of spam. Retrieved February 24, 2004 from http://www.sunbelt-software.com/evaluation/931/web/ihs_roi.cfm

Jaeger, C. (2004). Cyberterrorism. *The Internet encyclopedia*. Hoboken, NJ: John Wiley & Sons, 353–372.

Johnson, C. (2003, September). Spammer beware! A survey of state statutes regulating unsolicited commercial email. *Journal of Internet Law, 7*(3), 1–7.

Jonietz, E. (2004, October). Talking Spam, *Technology Review, 107*(8), 25.

Kelin, S. (2001, Winter). State regulation of unsolicited commercial e-mail. *Berkeley Technology Law Journal, 16*(1), 435.

Khan, M. (2003, August 25). DMA plans operation slam spam. Retrieved September 3, 2003, from http://www.dmnews.com/cgi-bin/artprevbot.cgi?article_id=24841

Krim, J. (2003, May 22). A spammer speaks out. Retrieved May 23, 2003 from http://www.washingtonpost.com/ac2/wp-dyn/A23386-2003May21?language=printer

Krim, J. (2004, January 7). Spam still flows into e-mail boxes. *The Washington Post*. Reprinted January 7, 2004, in *Medford Mail Tribune*, p. 1D.

Kuchinskas, S. (2003a, November 26). Marketers relieved at CAN-SPAM bill's progress. Retrieved November 26, 2003, from http://www.internetnews.com/IAR/print.php/3113961

Kuchinskas, S. (2003b, November 20). Spam battle's shifting sands. Retrieved December, 2003, from http://www.internetnews.com/IAR/print.php/3287341

Kuchinskas, S. (2003c, November 20). SpamCop rescued from edge. Retrieved November 21, 2003, from http://www.internetnews.com/IAR/print.php/3112051

Lemke, T. (2004, July 8). Nations to release anti-spam guidelines. Retrieved July 18, 2004, from http://washingtontimes.com/business/20040708-094843-3455r.htm

Lessig, L. (1999, December). The Law of the Horse: What Cyberlaw Might Teach, *Harvard Law Review, 113*(2), 501–549.

Lieb, R. (2002, March 15). Spoofing: Identity crisis. Retrieved February 17, 2004, from http://www.clickz.com/experts/brand/buzz/print.php/992021

Lieb, R. (2003, November 21). The 10 biggest spam myths. Retrieved November 21, 2003, from http://www.clickz.com/feedback/buzz/print.php/3112021

Mangalindan M. (2004, March 15). For Orlando Soto, no day is complete without some spam. *Wall Street Journal*, p. A1.

Manning, S. (2004, July 31). San Diego firm loses pop-up ad battle [Associated Press]. *San Jose Mercury News*, p. 3C.

Mara, J. (2004a, January 23). Can-Spam Conference: How to comply with a "total failure." Retrieved January 23, 2004, from http://www.internetnews.com/IAR/print.php/3302811

Mara, J. (2004b, February 24). FTC requests vendor input on do-not-spam list. Retrieved February 24, 2004, from http://www.clickz.com/news/print.php/3316911

Mara, J. (2004c, January 27). Gates predicts death of spam. Retrieved February 3, 2004, from http://www.internetnews.com/IAR/article.php/3304201

Mark, R. (2003a, August 20). FTC Chief critical of proposed anti-spam bills. Retrieved August 20, 2003, from http://dc.internet.com/news/print.php/3066111

Mark, R. (2003b, December 11). FTC imposes $1M bonds on spam hustlers. Retrieved December 11, 2003, from http://dc.internet.com/news/print.php/3288001

Mark, R. (2003c, November 26). Spam bill is a turkey. Retrieved November 26, 2003, from http://dc.internet.com/bus-news/print.php/3113941

Morrissey, B. (2003, October 13). Study: Consumers get spam savvy. Retrieved October 13, 2003, from http://www.internetnews.com/IAR/print.php/3090961

Mossoff, A. (2004, Spring). Spam—oy, what a nuisance. *Berkeley Technology Law Journal, 19*(2), 625–666.

Naraine, R. (2003, December 18). Target spam: NY AG, Microsoft file $38M suits. Retrieved January 9, 2004, from http://www.internetnews.com/IAR/print.php/3290671

Naraine, R. (2004, December 2). Microsoft tests 'brown wrapper' porn rule with spam suits. Retrieved January 13, 2005, from http://www.eweek.com/print_article2/0,2533,a=140273,00.asp

National do not email registry—a report to Congress. (2004). Federal Trade Commission, 18. Retrieved April 26, 2005, from http://www.ftc.gov/reports/dneregistry/report.pdf

Nettleton, E. (2004, April). Electronic marketing and the new anti-spam regulations. *Journal of Database Marketing & Customer Strategy Management, 11*(2), 235–240.

News Track. (2004, November). Spam spotting the DNA way. *Communications of the ACM, 47*(11), 9.

Oliva, R. (2004, January/February). Spam! *Marketing Management, 13*(1), 50.

Oriez, C. (2004a, July/August). Spam and block lists update. *Information Executive, 8*(4), 26–29.

Oriez, C. (2004b, January/February). Spam in the courtroom. *Information Executive, 8*(1), 1–3.

Parker, P. (2003, December 23). Do-not-spam proves popular concept. Retrieved February 24, 2004, from http://www.clickz.com/news/print.php/3292361

Peppers, D., & Rogers, M. (1993). *The one to one future.* New York: Doubleday.

Pew Internet & American Life Project. (2003). *PEW Internet Project: Summary of findings.* Retrieved November 5, 2003, from http://www.pewinternet.org

Pink, S. (2002, April). State spam laws survive constitutional scrutiny, but should Congress enact a federal law? *Journal of Internet Law, 5*(10), 11–15.

Porcelli, N., Selby, S., Bagner, J., & Sonu, C. (2002, June). FTC settles first spam cases. *Intellectual Property & Technology Law Journal, 14*(6), 24–25.

Powell, W. (2003, April). Spam wars. *T+D, 57*(4), 22.

Powers, D. (2002). *The Internet legal guide.* New York: Wiley.

Privacy/Internet. (2004a, September). FTC report to Congress rejects national do not email registry creation. *Intellectual Property & Technology Law Journal, 16*(9), 12.

Privacy/Internet. (2004b, August). Sen. McCain urges FTC to step up enforcement against companies under anti-spam statute. *Intellectual Property & Technology Law Journal, 16*(8), 17.

Ray, T. (2004, February 18). E-mail viruses blamed as spam rises sharply [Bloomberg News]. *The Seattle Times,* p. E6.

Raysman, R., & Brown, P. (2004, May 10). CAN-SPAM act: Let the games begin. *New York Law Journal.* Retrieved June 4, 2004, from LexisNexis.

Rembert, L. (2004, Spring). Will CAN-SPAM affect you? *Marketing Research, 16*(1), 8.

Reuters. (2003a, September 4). FTC: ID theft strikes 1 in 8 adults. Retrieved September 4, 2003, from http://money.cnn.com/2003/09/04/news/economy/id_theft.reut/index.htm

Reuters. (2003b, December 31). Judge throws out AOL spam suit. Retrieved December 31, 2003, from http://money.cnn.com/2003/12/31/technology/aol_spam.reut/index.htm?cnn=yes

Reuters. (2003c, November 24). Male enlargement ads prompt spam rage. Retrieved November 24, 2003, from http://www.cnn.com/2003/TECH/internet/11/24/spam.rage.reut/indes.html

Reuters. (2005, January 20). Experts: 'Phishing' more sophisticated. Retrieved January 20, 2005, from http://www.cnn.com/2005/TECH/internet/01/20/tech.phishing.reut/index.html

Roberts, M., & Berger, P. (1999). *Direct marketing management.* Upper Saddle River, NJ: Prentice-Hall.

Rodgers, Z. (2004, December 27). At AOL, a drop in spam. Retrieved December 27, 2004, from http://www.clickz.com/news/print.php/3451971

Saunders, C. (2003, December 16). Messenger ads will continue, for now. Retrieved December 19, 2003, from http://www.instantmessagingplanet.com/public/print.php/3289801

Scelson, R. (2004, May 20). growing problem of spam. *Federal Document Clearing House Congressional Testimony.* Retrieved June 4, 2004, from LexisNexis.

Schwartz, E. (2003, July). Spam wars. *Technology Review, 106*(6), 32–39.

Sears, D. (2003, December 18). N.Y., Microsoft bring suit against spammers. Retrieved December 19, 2003, from http://www.eweek.com/print_article/0,3048,a=114888,00.asp

Sinrod, E., & Reyna, J. (2000, February). The eye of the high tech storm: The law of email, part 1. *Journal of Internet Law, 3*(8), 1–10.

Soltoff, P. (2004, January 12). CAN-SPAM: The reality. Retrieved January 13, 2004, from http://www.clickz.com/em_mkt/print.php/3297691

Stokes, S., & Bramwell, A. (2004, February). The push to can spam. *Managing Intellectual Property, Issue 136,* 27.

Suespammers. (2001). *ISPs with pink contracts.* Retrieved September 3, 2003, from Web log http://www.spamcon.org/pipermail/suespammers/2001-February/00837.html

Sullivan, B. (2003a, August 6). Spam wars: How unwanted e-mail is burying the Internet. Retrieved August 15, 2003, from http://www.msnbc.com/news/941040.asp?0cb=-113171549

Sullivan, B. (2003b, August 11). The secret tricks that spammers use. Retrieved August 15, 2003, from http://www.msnbc.com/news/940853.asp

Sullivan, B. (2003c, August 8). Who profits from spam? Retrieved August 15, 2003, from http://www.msnbc.com/news/940490.asp?0sl=-42

Sullivan, L. (2004, February 14). Internet scammers send their spam to the wrong cyber surfer. Reprinted from *The Baltimore Sun* in *The Medford Mail Tribune,* p. 1A.

Swartz, N. (2003a, March/April). Spam costs businesses $13 billion annually. *Information Management Journal, 37*(2), 9.

Swartz, N. (2003b, September/October). The international war on spam. *Information Management Journal, 37*(5), 18–24.

Swartz, N. (2004a, November/December). E-mails waste businesses' archive space. *Information Management Journal, 38*(6), 11.

Swartz, N. (2004b, September/October). FTC nixes "do-not-spam" list. *Information Management Journal*, *38*(5), 8.

Swartz, N. (2004c, March/April). The worldwide war on spam continues. *Information Management Journal*, *38*(2), 16.

Swartz, N. (2004d, May/June). What spam law? Next up...spim, *Information Management Journal*, *38*(3), 12.

Wagner, J. (2004, July 8). Experts question UN's anti-spam plan. Retrieved July 13, 2004, from http://www.internetnews.com/infra/print.php/3378241

Webber, R. (2004, November). Beam me up (and out of this email/virus mess). *Journal of Financial Service Professionals*, *58*(6), 44–48.

CITED CASES

American Libraries Association versus United States, 201 F. Supp. 2d 401 Civ. Act. No. 01-1303. 01-1322 (E.D. Pa. 2002).

America Online, Inc. versus Hawke, etal., Civ. Act. No. 259-A T9E (E.D. Va. 2004).

America Online, Inc. versus Does, Civ. Act. No. 260-A (E.D. Va. 2004).

Ferguson versus Friendfighters, Inc., 94 Cal. App. 4th 1255 (Cal. App. 2002).

Moulton versus VC3, Civ. Act. No. 1:00-CV-434-TWT (N.D. Ga. November 6, 2000).

State of Washington versus Heckel, 24 P.3d 404 (Wash. 2001).

Verizon Online Services, Inc. versus Ralsky, 203 F. Supp. 601, 606 (E.D. Va. 2002).

FURTHER READING

Spam and cyberspace are fast-moving areas of the law. More up-to-date case citations to the CAN-SPAM act, case law, and law reviews may be found on WESTLAW or LEXIS-NEXIS by typing in "CAN-SPAM" or, separately, "e-mail and spam," or other similar combinations.

Trespass to Chattels Claims

America Online, Inc. versus IMS, 24 F. Supp. 2d 548, 550-51 (E.D. Va. 1998).

America Online, Inc. versus LCGM, Inc., 46 F. Supp. 2d 444 (E.D.Va. 1998).

America Online, Inc. versus Prime Data Systems Inc, 1998 WL 34016692 (E.D. Va. 1998)

CompuServe, Inc. versus Cyber Promotions, Inc., 962 F. Supp. 1015, 1021-24 (S.D. Ohio 1997)

Hotmail Corp. versus Van$ Money Pie Inc., 47 U.S.P.Q. 2d 1020 (N.D. Cal. 1998) (finding likelihood of success on trespass claim against spammer).

Trademark Infringement and Dilution Claims

America Online, Inc. versus IMS, 24 F. Supp. 2d 548, 551 (E.D. Va. 1998).

America Online, Inc. versus LCGM, Inc., 46 F. Supp. 2d 444, 449-50 (E.D. Va. 1998).

America Online, Inc. versus Prime Data Systems Inc, 1998 WL 34016692 (E.D. Va. 1998)

Classified Ventures, L.L.C. versus Softcell Marketing, Inc., 109 F. Supp. 2d 898 (N.D. Ill. 2000).

Classified Ventures, L.L.C. versus Softcell Marketing, Inc., 109 F. Supp. 2d 898, 900-01 (N.D. Ill. 2000).

Hotmail Corp. versus Van$ Money Pie Inc., 47 U.S.P.Q. 2d 1020, 1023-24 (N.D. Cal 1998).

Breach of Contract Claims by ISPs

Hotmail Corp. versus Van$ Money Pie Inc., 47 U.S.P.Q. 2d 1020 (N.D. Cal. 1998).

Jurisdictional Claims and "Purposeful Availment" of the Benefits of the Forum State

Bird versus Parsons, 289 F.3d 865 (6th Cir. 2002); Neogen Corp. versus Neo Gen Screening, Inc., 282 F. 3d 883 (6th Cir. 2002) (passive web site available in Michigan, that also let Michigan residents use passwords to view blood test results, with at least 14 transactions with Michigan residents, constituted purposeful availment sufficient for jurisdiction; citing Zippo Mfg. Co, infra).

Gorman versus Ameritrade Holding Corp., 293 F.3d 506 (D.C. Cir. 2002) (a defendant's web site allowed Washington, D.C., residents to form contracts with it to buy securities and brokerage services).

Additional citations: Optinrealbig.com, LLC versus Ironport Systems, Inc., 323 F.Supp.2d 1037 (N.D. Cal. 2004) (sender tort action against ISPs where preliminary injunction is denied).

FTC versus Phoenix Avatar, LLC., 2004 WL 1746698 (N.D. Ill. July 30, 2004) (FTC CAN-SPAM enforcement action, one of many cases available online).

White Buffalo Ventures, LLC versus Univ. of Texas at Austin, 2004 WL 1854168 (W. D. Tex. Mar. 22, 2004) (discusses CAN-SPAM and 1st Amendment commercial speech claim);

In re Uhrig, 306 B.R. 687 (M.D. Fla. Bankr. 2004) (cites to $1.9 million judgment for wrongful transmission of spam emails).

"E-Nuisance: Unsolicited Bulk Email at the Boundaries of Common Law Property Rights," 78 So. Cal. Law Review 363 (Nov. 2004) (available on WESTLAW at 78 SCALR 363).

Cyberlaw: The Major Areas, Development, and Information Security Aspects

Dennis M. Powers, *Southern Oregon University*

INTRODUCTION

As the number of Internet users, Web connections, and personal computers increased exponentially, controversies and legal problems also accelerated in cyberspace without any specific statutes or case law at first to govern the inevitable conflicts. Despite solid preexisting legal foundation, no information medium ever had such an enormous appetite to leapfrog geographic territories and laws, in turn creating intense pressures on that system.

If somebody "ripped off" another's slogan or logo in "pre-Net" California, it was possible that a business located in Chicago would never know the difference. If one person wrote a defamatory article in a local Florida newspaper about someone in Oregon, the defamed person at that time could have died before reading that particular printed statement. Once the Internet came into existence, however, anyone with an Internet connection—whether living in Florida or in France—could stumble across that slogan or posting. Large organizations were caught napping when more nimble entrepreneurs registered their trademarks as domain names, and then offered to sell those registrations back for outrageous sums of money. Who could ever have predicted the rise of mass-copying technology such as Napster and Kazaa that bypassed the copyrights of the musicians, composers, and recording studios? Not to mention the countless rogue programmer attacks and security failures of information systems throughout the world.

The wide differences among the laws of wide numbers of states and other countries became quickly evident. Whether entered into by e-mail or not, a contract under certain facts could be fine in Georgia but void in California, and a copyright claim upheld in Japan but not in the United States, with its differing laws and "fair use" exception. Over time, court decisions confirmed that existing legal concepts were applicable to cyberspace, and legislatures enacted specific statutes to fill in the gaps. These basic legal concepts with later refinements proved adaptable to the Internet technology of the new millennium, just as they had during the dawning of new technologies in the past century, and as unfolds during the course of this chapter.

INTELLECTUAL PROPERTY

The rise of the Internet and its conflicts highlighted the entire subject of intellectual property. Although important in pre-Internet property matters, intellectual property considerations became dominant in protecting one's rights to their creations and the value of a site, its creations, and processes—whether by copyrights, trademarks, or patents.

Copyright Law

Your computer is a worldwide copying machine, and the Internet made it extraordinarily easy for nearly anything to be instantly copied, e-mailed, and printed out anywhere, regardless of the true copyright holder's rights. In response, the United States took the lead to enact legislation that complemented the basic law of copyrights and met this tension between competing interests.

The first major step taken was its enactment of the U.S. Digital Millennium Copyright Act of 1998 (DMCA). The online service provider section of the DMCA establishes the procedures for copyright owners to contact service providers with their complaints over a subscriber's improper online use of copyrighted material. This act mandates providers to remove materials used improperly once they reasonably determine there are, in fact, copyright infringements as alleged. If the subscriber files a counterprotest, however, then the provider must repost the material unless the complainant files a lawsuit against the infringer for copyright infringement over the offending use.

In effect, this legislation grants copyright owners an administrative tool to remove infringing material without having to litigate the problem, as well as a "safe harbor" against liability for U.S. online service providers. The definition of "service providers" is broad and includes not only Internet service providers (ISPs), Web hosting companies, wire and fiber transmission entities, and router services, but also corporations, universities, municipalities, governmental agencies, and other entities that "provide" online services. To receive the protection of this federal statute, an organization must register under the act with the U.S. Copyright Office and follow the DMCA's removal provisions. Check out http://www. loc.gov/copyright for the details on the DMCA.

The United States was the first country to enact DMCA legislation, and this statute took it into compliance with an international copyright treaty (the WIPO Copyright Treaty, 1996). As other countries imitate this general approach, the ability to cause infringing material to be removed without using expensive litigation will begin to become globally codified. For more information, please see the chapter on the Global Aspects of Cyberlaw in this *Handbook*. Another significant U.S. legislative enactment was the No Electronic Theft Act of 1997 (NET). Under the NET, criminal penalties can be imposed on people who exchange or barter unauthorized copies of software, videos, clips, or music, whether or not they receive money for it. The only requirement is that the value of the pirated material exceed $2,500 (for felonies) in a given 6-month period. Although enforcement of the NET Act has been limited to high-profile cases thus far, all users should be aware of its provisions.

Among other important copyright areas, cases have held that publishers must pay additional fees for pre-Net work completed by freelancers, including a U.S. Court of Appeals ruling that the National Geographic Society made an unauthorized use of pictures taken by a freelance photographer back in 1961 when it issued a CD-ROM years later of its back issues (*Greenberg v. National Geographic Society*, 2001). It was ordered to pay license fees for that use. The U.S. Supreme Court decided the issue when it later ruled that media companies must obtain the consent of their freelance writers and creators (as employees create "works for hire," their employers typically gain those copyrights) before any pre-Net text, picture, or creation could be posted or sold online, thus forcing royalties to be paid for that use (*New York Times v. Tasini*, 2001).

In the late 1990s, music lovers using a Website and software program called Napster began file-sharing music by swapping digital copies of recordings with one another. After lawsuits by recording industry groups effectively shut down Napster (*A&M Records v. Napster*, 2001), Internet users began sharing music files by using programs that allow them to search the computer libraries of other users. Rather than providing a centralized server where swappers could trade copyrighted material directly ala Napster, this technology allowed users to download software from sites such as Grokster and trade copyrighted music between themselves in an environment that didn't involve a central server. In 2004, the U.S. Court of Appeals for the Ninth Circuit in *MGM Studios v. Grokster* (2004) held that Grokster's use of such a decentralized environment was not a violation of applicable copyright laws as was Napster. On appeal, the U.S. Supreme Court heard oral arguments in 2005 on this case with its decision expected later in the year.

In addition to these aspects, other developments occurred as to the online copyright infringement issue, whether concerning books or music. The U.S. Supreme Court held in *Eldredge v. Ashcroft* (2003) that Congress had acted constitutionally in 1998 when it extended copyright protection for most works through the Sonny Bono Copyright Term Extension Act (Supp. 1999), retroactively increasing the copyright protection term from 50 years after an author's life by another 20 years to 70 in total. Various cases upheld the constitutionality of the DMCA, including its safe-harbor provisions for ISPs.

The federal courts also have apparently answered the issue as to whether the DMCA mandates ISPs to turn over customer information to the recording industry of those suspected of illegally trading music files. In *Recording Industry Association of America (RIAA) v. Verizon Internet Services* (2003), the U.S. Court of Appeals in Washington, D.C., overturned the District Court's decision and ruled that the RIAA could not use just subpoenas or simple notices under the DMCA to force ISPs to supply it with user names that it could only identify by their computer's online addresses. The RIAA would have to file a formal lawsuit, then after that filing of its "John Doe" complaint, request a subpoena to secure the identity from the ISP. Immediately after the decision, the RIAA filed four new lawsuits naming 532 "John Does" to show that this added cost to its litigation policy would not deter it. The Supreme Court refused to grant certiorari and rejected the appeal without comment.

Whether the situation concerns Napster imitators, video downloading, or copying overseas, the legal wrangling between copyright holders and the public over "fair use" considerations will continue unabated. As other countries enact their own cyber copyright and intellectual property laws, the likelihood of global jurisdictional disputes increases. Please consult the chapter on Copyright Law in this *Handbook* for an extensive treatment of these copyright areas.

Domain Names and Trademark Law

Trademark Law and Domain Names

For decades before the emergence of the Internet, trademark law was relatively straightforward. Trademarks and service marks abound, simply arising from a company's use of marks identifying certain products or services as being theirs (e.g., Apple with its rainbow apple and eBay's stylized logo). The concept of trade and service marks came about to keep businesses from "passing off" their products as being those of their competitors or of rightful owners, and the ownership of marks is another important intangible property right.

Then along came the Internet, domain names, and new Web sites that had registered the addresses of bona fide trademark and service-mark holders (i.e., Burger King vs. the "burgerking.com" registered by an individual). They knew that the domain name used to access any site was an important asset of identification, just as an entity's mark was important in the decision to purchase a product (or domain name selection). Because domain names must be registered to have any validity and registrars don't conduct background checks over an applicant's representations as to who owns the legitimate trademark rights, registration even today can be a race to the swiftest on a "first come, first serve" basis.

In the early and mid-1990s, "entrepreneurs" recognized this grand opportunity. In a style reminiscent of the old Gold Rush days, they raced to tie up as many of those good corporate names as they could, whether it was "harvard.net" or "burgerking.com." Later, they would send a demand letter to those entities and offer to sell their domain names back—at a tidy profit. Or the new owners would sit on their names and wait for that interest, conjuring up the concepts of "cybersquatting" and "cyberpirating." When one adds to this equation the various classifications (i.e., from ".com" and ".org" to the later introduced ".biz" and ".info") with the different country designations that are possible, it is easy to see the large opportunities created to tie up good corporate names at a good profit.

A brisk market in the buying and selling of domain names started—just hit the key word "domain name" in your search engines and see what arises. The people who registered general names, such as "business.com" or "loans.com," made excellent business decisions. One Houston businessman paid $150,000 in 1997 for the rights to "business.com," then sold that to a California company for a cool $7.5 million 2 years later. In 2000, mortgage.com was sold for $1.8 million and loans.com for $3 million.

Without any statutory guidance, the courts handed down mixed decisions as to when a mark holder would prevail, if at all, over a cybersquatter and a given domain name. The reason: The law was clear at the time that domain-name registrations and trademarks and service marks, whether registered or not, were two different concepts. Because there was no right by itself to use a mark as a domain name, owning one didn't necessarily convey any ownership rights to the other.

Anticybersquatting Consumer Protection Act (ACPA; 1999)

Before the passage of the ACPA, the Federal Trademark Dilution Act (FTDA, 1995) was the statutory alternative that trademark holders used to fight cybersquatters. The FTDA did not require proving a likelihood of confusion on the part of consumers on the use of a disputed mark, but that there was a "dilution" of that mark. This act provided a mark owner with injunctive relief against another's commercial use of one that diluted the distinctive quality of that distinctive mark. Dilution occurred when an unauthorized use lessened the ability of others to distinguish goods or services from the other, including if those actions cheapened that mark (i.e., one Billy Nike

establishes a bar called "Nike's Sleazy Palace" to which the sporting goods manufacturer, Nike, takes exception). The FTDA's effect was to protect famous marks—such as McDonald's or Goodyear—from the use of others that would "dilute" their value. *Panavision v. Toeppen* (1998) was one of the first cases to expand the FTDA's dilution protection of trademarks to domain names. In Panavision, the appellate court held that the defendant's actions diluted the value of Panavision's trademark because his registration of "panavision.com" (and attempts to sell that back to the company) weakened the ability of its potential customers to find Panavision on the Internet. So long as the defendant held the Internet registrations, he curtailed, or diluted, Panavision's value of its trademarks on the Internet, and the court upheld the injunction against that use. The problem was that entities had to prove that their trademark value had been diluted under the FTDA, as well as that this action could be ineffective and costly, when all that they wanted was to get their domain name back. Some states laws, in fact, were stronger than the FTDA. (Later, in *Moseley v. Secret Catalogue* (2003), the U.S. Supreme Court affirmed that actual harm must be proven before even FTDA injunctive relief can be obtained.)

In response, the United States passed its Anticybersquatting Consumer Protection Act, or ACPA, in late 1999. This act allows civil lawsuits to be brought for trademark and service mark violations against anyone, who with a "bad faith" intent to profit from a mark, registers, uses, or attempts to sell a domain name that's identical or confusingly similar to that protected mark. Factors indicating bad faith are whether the name owner actually diverted the trademark owner's customers, offered the registered name for sale without having used it, or registered multiple names. Under the Anticybersquatting Act, the courts can cancel a "pirated" domain name, assess attorney fees and costs, and levy penalties up to $100,000 against an infringer (depending on the level of bad faith and the actual damages). This act gave broad legal weapons for any mark holder to protect its trade or service mark, as well as more remedies and damages for any unauthorized use.

This legislation also made it illegal to register the name of any living person without that person's consent, while intending to profit by that action. Actors Brad Pitt and Kenny Rogers immediately filed suit on this provision alone, Kenny Rogers objecting to the "kennyrogers.com" registered to the Web site of a California wedding service. Both celebrities, among others, retrieved their "names."

ICANN's Dispute Resolution Process

ICANN instituted a procedure for resolving domain-name disputes. Under an agreement called the Uniform Domain-Name Dispute-Resolution Policy (UDRP), those with a dispute over a registered domain name involving their trademark or service mark have the alternative to file a complaint with an ICANN approved dispute-resolution service. Pursuant to these procedures, the service provides an arbitration panel that then rules which party has the legitimate right to that name, and if either party disagrees with the handed-down ruling, then that party can litigate the disputed matter further in court. The judge in the court case can review all of the facts and isn't necessarily bound by the review board's determination. Once a final decision is reached, the registrar then transfers the domain name as the court or administrative panel decided; for further details on this policy, see ICANN's site at http://www.icann.org.

Whether marks are registered or not, legitimate holders can take their case to different alternative dispute resolution centers under this process, and the United Nation's World Intellectual Property Organization (WIPO) hears most of these cases. (For more details, see its site at http://www.wipo.int/.) Basically, the claimant must prove (a) that the domain name very closely resembles a trademark registered or owned by that entity, (b) that the party that registered the domain name has no rights or legitimate interest in that name, and (c) that the domain name was registered and used for illicit purposes or in bad faith. This is an inexpensive process (a one-person panel for a case involving up to five domain names at the time of this publication costs the complainant $1,500, and a three-person panel costs $4,000); fast (the arbitrators' decision is normally rendered within 60 days); convenient (there is no hearing to attend; the arbitrator or panel reviews only the complaint, response, and supporting documents); and the decisions typically favor the trademark holder (some four fifths of the determinations favor the mark owner).

The initial decisions on domain names reached conclusions in favor of companies with recognizable names, such as the World Wrestling Federation, Stella D'Oro Biscuits (a Nabisco affiliate), and Telstra (the Australian telecom company), ordering their domain names transferred back to them. WIPO arbitration panels handed back the Web addresses bearing the names of the Corinthians (Brazilian soccer team), Dan Marino, Julia Roberts, Kevin Spacey, Yahoo!, ESPN, and Wal-Mart. However, Sting, Bruce Springsteen, the Reverend Dr. Jerry Falwell, and Ted Turner failed to prove that their personal names had been used in a trademark sense as a label of particular goods or services and did not prevail in their UDRP proceedings. ICANN's dispute-resolution policy, however, does not apply to all registrars—it applies to the TLDs (top level domains of ".com," "Net," ".biz," etc.) and not directly to the "ccTLDs" (individual country domains, such as ".cn" for China), unless that country agrees or has established its own dispute resolution board. A number of the ccTLDs have done so.

The Legal Weapon Tradeoffs

Entities with U.S.-based domain name/trademark conflicts must decide between using the Anticybersquatting Act, an ICANN proceeding, or both. ICANN gives a fast resolution, whereas ACPA litigation can take up to 2 years or more for a decision. Although the federal statutory-authorized lawsuit allows for a preliminary injunction, the opportunity to be awarded good damages, and transfer back of the domain name (which is all that an ICANN-UDRP procedure can do), this alternative is highly expensive with much more downtime, complexity, and legal dollars required. The ACPA is a final determination, whereas the extent to which an ICANN decision can be litigated further is currently being determined.

The rest of the world is not as restrictive as the United States or other developed countries, and the game is still being played in some fashion. Countries in Asia, the former Soviet Union, Eastern Europe, and others have not yet tightened their laws, although over time, they likely will. It may still be possible in small nations such as Moldavia (until they change) for cybersquatters to purchase domain names that aren't already reserved, and the question of conflicting laws always seems to rear up when lawsuits are brought to challenge ICANN administrative rulings.

For international protection, entities need to register their mark with the U.S. Patent and Trademark Office (PTO), and U.S. concerns need to file that registration with the appropriate agency of the foreign countries in which they operate. Although the granting of a registration by the PTO is not conclusive on the issue of who owns a mark, it is prima facie evidence of that ownership (see the PTO at http://www.uspto.gov for the details). Given the estimated numbers of domain names (escalating from present numbers to more than 100 million in 2 years by various estimates), the number of permutations, and various country designations, the volumes of conflicts, arguments, and opportunities for these disputes can only increase over time.

For more on this subject, see the chapter on Trademark Law in the *Handbook*.

Patent

Through patents, the United States by its Patent and Trademark Office grants an inventor the exclusive right to make, use, or sell an invention for 14 years (design patents) or 20 years (inventions). To obtain a patent, the inventor must meet certain requirements, such as novelty, usefulness, and nonobviousness. Computer hardware (i.e., the design of electronic components, handwriting recognition systems, and so on) is patentable, but software typically isn't brought into the process, because of the time it takes for a patent to be granted and contrary regulations in a few cases. The number of patent applications for Internet applications increased in recent years owing to court decisions (beginning with *State Street Bank v. Signature Financial Group*, 1998) upholding patents issued for Web site business processes and operating methods. Amazon.com (its "one-click" online purchasing system), Onsale (operating auctions), Cybersettle (its "double-blind bid" dispute resolution procedure), Priceline.com (conducting an online "reverse" auction), Microsoft (online shopping and merchandising), Sun Microsystems (Internet bill processing), Tumbleweed Communications (online greeting card delivery), E-Data Corporation (online selling to any point of sale location), and other e-commerce entities have received patents on their specific business or operational models. As expected, the court challenges from competitors over these patents have also increased, as competing entities battle over controlling important operational methods. The chapter on Patent Law in this *Handbook* goes into the details.

DEFAMATION

Cyberspace creates an inordinate ability to post defamatory comments quickly that injure another person's reputation and can be seen around the world. Those who post libelous comments, however, do not enjoy the anonymity in cyberspace that one might first expect. A cyber-defamation lawsuit is typically filed in the city where the chatroom provider or ISP is located and lists various "John Does" or "Jane Does." This is legal jargon for naming unknown parties to the lawsuit, whose actual names will be added later after discovering their true identities. The lawyer then files a subpoena (demanding that the desired information be released) against the provider to gain the identity of the particular John or Jane Doe who posted the inflammatory remarks.

Lawyers serve subpoenas daily on CompuServe, AOL, Yahoo, Microsoft, and others to retrieve some poster's identity. If the ISP doesn't turn over the demanded information, the attorney then goes to court to ask the judge to force the ISP to divulge the required data. The judge balances the right to protect someone's anonymity versus the injured party's right to be protected from harm. The plaintiff, or injured party, usually must prove that there's no other way to obtain relief without securing this specific information. If multiple servers are involved, the attorneys will follow the e-mail address back through that chain with multiple subpoenas.

A doctor at the Emory University School of Medicine in Atlanta, Georgia, came across a posting on a Yahoo message board. It falsely suggested that he had taken kickbacks from a urology company to give his department's pathology business to the company and had been forced to resign over this conflict of interest. The message was from "fbiinformant," who later was discovered to be a former employee at the urology company who disliked the doctor. In what was believed to be the first Internet defamation case to reach trial, a U.S. District Court judge awarded $675,000 to that doctor, all because of this one "anonymous" Internet message (see *Graham v. Oppenheimer*, 2000). Litigating defamatory e-mails, postings, and communications continued on unabated from there.

As to the online service providers, the court decisions have consistently upheld that there is no liability on their part for defamatory postings made by third parties. The Communications Decency Act of 1996 (CDA) bars tort-based claims or lawsuits against ISPs for defamatory, obscene, or other objectionable postings, provided there is no complicity by the ISP with that third party over those postings or other unreasonable behavior (the provider also must "actively" remove the objectionable material). Although portions of the CDA were later held to be unconstitutional (see *Reno v. American Civil Liberties Union*, 1997), these provisions continued in their legal validity and effect.

PRIVACY CONCERNS

At this time, there is no general, sweeping U.S. law regulating or requiring entities to disclose how they use sensitive financial and other personal information gained from their customers or users, nor how they gather that data. Notwithstanding recent U.S. Federal Trade Commission (FTC) high-profile proceedings against companies over their information practices, the FTC has had, in effect, a "self-policing" policy, promoting industry self-regulation in the fields of data collection and customer profiling. Congress did enact legislation as to the online privacy protection of children, however, when it enacted the Children's Online Privacy Protection Act (COPPA) in 1998. This statute requires that Web sites "earmarked" for

children, or who knowingly collect data on users under age 13, need to (a) obtain verifiable parental consent for any collection or use of their children's information (i.e., "no consent, no collection") and (b) on request, provide the parent with the ability to review any personal information that has been so collected. The FTC has issued administrative rules on COPPA to guide these "kiddie" Web sites on their compliance with this legislation (see http://www.ftc.gov for more on this subject). Additionally, the FTC has charged entities with violating COPPA and reached settlement with several of those Web sites.

Congress also passed the Gramm–Leach–Bliley Act (GLBA), known also as the Financial Services Modernization Act of 1999 and which applies to Internet transmissions and electronic data collection. This legislation basically requires that financial institutions (a) inform consumers of their privacy policies and (b) notify consumers before acquiring, transferring, or selling their private data to third parties, giving them the opportunity to "opt out" of such data-transfer practices.

Additionally, various states have passed privacy legislation both in the financial area and in preserving the confidentiality of sensitive medical records, including diagnosis, treatment, and prognosis. As with most state laws, these acts are not uniform—for example, depending on the subject area, some states require opt-in conditions before data can be collected or used, whereas others establish opt-out standards. Rules have also been enacted under the Health Insurance Portability and Accountability Act (HIPAA) of 1996 in this area (see the U.S. Dept. of Health and Human Services at http://www.os.dhhs.gov for more), and the court challenges on its implementation are underway.

The differences between the United States and other countries, such as Canada and the European Union (EU), couldn't be more pronounced than in the rights of privacy area. Canada's Personal Information Protection and Electronic Documents Act (S.C., 2000) implements a wide array of data protection, including a phase-in of "opt-in" provisions for its citizens. The EU's Data Protection Act came into effect in 1998, also using a completely different approach from that of the United States. Citizens there gained enhanced rights to prohibit their private data from being released, including requiring entities to secure "opt-in" permission in various situations before personal data can be acquired, sold, or shared. For further information, including on the "safe harbor" guidelines for U.S. companies with subsidiaries operating under the more stringent EU privacy laws, see the U.S. Department of Commerce Web site at http://www.commerce.gov, as well as the chapter on Privacy Law and the Internet in this *Handbook*.

CENSORSHIP

The First Amendment places strong limitations on the government's ability to censor, or unduly regulate, the rights to basic freedoms such as those of speech and expression, and the Internet is no exception. For example, Congress passed the Communications Decency Act of 1996 (CDA) which, among various provisions, essentially made it a crime for anyone to knowingly distribute obscene material for sale in cyberspace. Later in 1997, the U.S. Supreme Court in *Reno v. American Civil Liberties*

Union declared that most of the important provisions of the CDA dealing with obscenity were unconstitutional, holding that these provisions were so vague as to be void on their face. The fact that statutes applied to cyberspace didn't mean the constitutional tests applied were any less strict, and later legal battles over subsequent pornographic statutes have applied the same strict construction tests of the offline world.

For example, Congress in 1998 passed the Child Online Protection Act (COPA) as a successor to the struck-down CDA provisions in another attempt to stop children from gaining access to sexually explicit materials on the Internet. In 2002, the U.S. Supreme Court reviewed COPA and partially upheld it, adding further legal uncertainty. In *Ashcroft v. ACLU* (2002), the court ruled that the act's reliance on community standards to identify "material that is harmful to minors" did not by itself render the statute unconstitutional. The divided court kept alive the fight over whether the measure was unconstitutional, however, by affirming the appellate court's ban against COPA's enforcement, then returning the issue for further review on free-speech questions that the court felt had been left unresolved. Subsequently affirming the preliminary injunction on COPA's use, the U.S. Court of Appeals for the 3d Circuit in its decision, *Ashcroft v. ACLU* (2003), then rejected the U.S. Supreme Court's reasoning, finding that the law was not the least restrictive way to achieve the government's interest in protecting children. This panel of circuit judges said that the law was "vague, overbroad, and puritanical," and violated the First Amendment. The Justice Department again appealed. The U.S. Supreme Court then agreed with the appellate court in *Ashcroft v. ACLU* (2004) that enforcement of COPA should be enjoined because the statute likely violates the First Amendment, and that employing filters were a less restrictive way than COPA's mandated use of credit cards or other measures employed to restrict access. Yet, the Supreme Court remanded the case again to the lower court for consideration whether there are less restrictive ways to achieve the government's objectives. Whether in cyberspace or not, the complexities of First Amendment case law continue.

The U.S. Supreme Court in United States et al v. American Library Association (2003) held by a 6–3 majority that Congress could require public libraries to install mandatory filters on Internet computers as a condition of receiving federal technology grants and "e-rate" discounts, upholding the constitutionality of the Children's Internet Protection Act (CIPA, 2000). The Supreme Court later declined to review the "Nuremberg Files" case, in which an 11-judge U.S. Court of Appeals panel voted 6–5 in Planned Parenthood v. American Coalition of Life Activists (2002) to uphold a 1999 trial verdict against an antiabortion Web site that disclosed the names, addresses, and family information of physicians who performed abortions. The trial jury awarded punitive damages of $107 million against the coalition of activists, but the appellate panel remanded the damage amount back to the trial court to determine whether the award was excessive or not.

In a case in which the judge described was a dispute between the protection of trade secrets versus freedom of speech, a federal judge ruled a Web site operator could continue posting confidential Ford Motor Company documents on new car designs and other internal data (see *Ford Motor Co. v. Lane*, 1999). Lawsuits over employer Internet-use policies, however, provided the policies are reasonable with notice given to the employees, have generally been upheld in the employer's favor. An employer's use of Web filtering software (where worker e-mails are subject to scrutiny) also is under challenge, but most legal scholars believe that these challenges generally won't be sustained. Moreover, the courts so far have not been receptive to employee claims that work done on an employer's computer system is personal and entitled to constitutional protection. Please see the chapter on E-Mail and Internet Use Policies for more on this subject.

Courts have generally upheld the right of "suck.com" Web sites to criticize the operations of major businesses (e.g., "http://www.ballysucks.net"; see *Bally v. Faber*, 1998), although the complaining companies have had more luck in challenging these sites under ICANN domain name proceedings. For example, the Salvation Army filed an ICANN-UDRP proceeding over the name "salvationarmy-sucks.com", and the arbitrators ruled in favor of it, when evidence of offers to sell the name back to the Salvation Army came to light. Generally, provided the posted allegations are basically true or represent protectable opinion rather than false facts, the cases hold these expressions to be protected by the First Amendment. If you use a search engine with the descriptive word "suck.com" or type your favorite company name with a "suck.com" after it, watch the complaint Web sites surface that already are in existence.

Another growing First Amendment consideration involves its application in disputes where software sites collide with commercial trade interests. For example, the DVD Copy Control Association (DVDCCA) attempted to shut down Web sites, including that of California resident Andrew Bunner, which provided a link to DeCSS software code that unscrambled encrypted DVDs and allowed them to be played on unlicensed computers. A California Court of Appeals court (*DVDCCA v. Bunner*, 2001) overturned the trial judge's temporary injunction against Bunner's site as an unconstitutional prior restraint protected by the First Amendment. In reversing the appellate court, however, the California Supreme Court (*DVDCCA v. Bunner*, 2003) decided that computer source code is a form of speech that can be constitutionally protected, but that this injunction was appropriate because it was not based on the content of Bunner's speech—it was only protecting the DVDCCA's trade secrets. The court sent the issue back to the appellate court for a ruling on whether the injunction was warranted under the state's trade secret laws. The California Court of Appeal (*DVDCCA v. Bunner*, 2004) held that the facts did not support the injunction because the DeCSS software was so widely distributed before the injunction was requested. For more on the subject of censorship, please see the chapter on Internet Censorship in this *Handbook*.

CYBERFRAUD

Cyberfraud is a major problem on the Internet, owing to its anonymity, commercial reach, and speed in exchanging credit card data. Hackers abound, trying to exploit any weakness in a site's systems and database. The ease of entry onto the Internet makes it even easier for "fly by night" firms to race in, skim off money, and quickly disappear without leaving a trace. No matter where you live, the Web has indeed become global in when and how the unwary are fleeced. In the United States, the FTC is the federal agency charged with prohibiting unfair or deceptive commercial acts, including misleading advertising (fraudulent investments are handled by the Securities and Exchange Commission, or SEC). The FTC's rules and regulations against unfair or deceptive business practices specifically cover Internet transactions, and its Web site (http://www.ftc.gov) has pages with information about Internet fraud, complaints, and its fight against this problem.

The FTC has brought countless numbers of fraud and misleading advertising complaints to stop such unfair practices, both online and offline. In 2001, the FTC opened a Web site with statistics and information on primarily U.S. Internet fraud and identity theft. The site is called "Consumer Sentinel" (see http://www.consumer.gov/sentinel), and it started with a database of more than 300,000 complaints lodged with the FTC over the last several years. The site provides data on fraudulent transaction trends, as well as the ability to submit online complaints (as does the FTC with its Web site). From year to year, identity fraud is the overall top consumer fraud complaint from all sources received by the FTC and by a wide margin, followed by Internet auctions and Internet services/computer complaints. If you find online fraud problems involving different countries, then head to "econsumer" at http://www.econsumer.gov/, which has in place direct links to consumer fraud agencies in various countries and represents a coordinated world effort to work together on this global problem. This site also allows for the filing of international fraud complaints.

The Internet is an excellent tool both for investors with easy access to research sources, as well as for the shysters, hipsters, and con artists to get to the investors' and other people's money. Because anyone with a computer and modem can reach tens of thousands of potential investors simply by creating an attractive Web site and spamming, the U.S. SEC has had to become active on the Internet. It established a national cyberforce of attorneys, accountants, and analysts specifically trained to watch out for fraudulent online security transactions (see http://www.sec.gov for more information, including its reported Internet fraud cases).

For example, one case involved a company that used spam e-mail to announce an initial public offering (nearly all of us have received junk e-mail of this type), stating that it had been approved by the SEC and would realize at least $1 billion in eyewear sales. In fact, it had never been approved by the SEC and didn't even own an office or inventory. The owner of the company used the "invested" money for restaurants (eating meals), casinos (gambling), and adult entertainment clubs. The investors lost everything that they had invested—the usual and unfortunate result with fraudulent investments, regardless of whether the FTC or SEC intervenes later.

Regardless of the state or country, the law is clear with regard to cyberfraud: (a) any Web advertisement of illegal transactions under a particular country's or state's laws (e.g., gambling or usury) will be illegal there; (b) fraudulent, false, or materially misleading statements are illegal and unenforceable, no matter where you live; and (c) the regulatory agencies in different states and countries vary widely in their ability to crack down on misleading advertising, even when the customers or investors have lost all of their money. Remember: If the advertised "return" is too good to be true, then it usually is; and investors must be quite careful when reviewing potential investments of any kind, whether online or offline. (For more information, see the chapter on cyber crime and fraud.)

E-COMMERCE LAW
"Click" Contracts

Given the ease with which online contracts can be made, the tearing down of geographic barriers, and E-mail "proof" that lasts forever, basic contract law is even more important on the Net. From what is needed for a legitimate contract (i.e., mutual assent, consideration, capacity, and no legal defenses) to how duties are delegated and determining damages, all of the fundamental contract laws apply in cyberspace. (For an excellent discussion on this area, see *Cyberlaw, Text and Cases, Second Edition* by Ferrera, Lichtenstein, Reder, Bird, & Schiano, 2003.) As expected, e-contracts do have important aspects that stand out from offline contracts.

You can't discuss and then sign an e-contract with your handwritten name, as you can when you're in a face-to-face meeting with the other party. In place of this "personal touch," the law basically allows that you can agree to the terms and conditions of an electronic agreement when you click the "I agree," "I'll buy," or "Subscribe" button. The mouse click on that agreement button sets the approval to the conditions of your e-contract.

The courts generally have upheld these "click" contracts as being as valid as if you signed a written agreement on the dotted line. (See, for example, *Crispi v. The Microsoft Network*, 1999, and *Geoff v. AOL, Inc.*, 1998.) Any on-screen click, no matter where it's located (but provided it's reasonably identified as the "click" agreement button), will do. The legal premise is that the medium in which a signature or contract is created shouldn't affect its validity, and the transaction is enforceable, whether that medium is paper or electronic. There are limitations on when click contracts will be enforced, however, and this is discussed later in this section.

E-Signatures, Taxation, and Spam

The U.S. government and nearly all of the states have enacted a version of an electronic signature statute. The federal act (Electronic Signature in Global and National Commerce Act, 2000) ensures that electronic records, signatures, and contracts have the same legal effect as their ink-and-paper counterparts (including that electronic records satisfy statutes mandating that records be kept in writing), validating online commerce and allowing for the eventual recordation of documents such as deeds, mortgages, and bills of sale by accepting digital notarization. Along with its state counterparts, this legislation mandates that an e-signature is enforceable if both parties agree to its technological format (whether signature verification is based on encryption software, smart cards, mouse-pad technology, or whatever), and it provides that a signature may not be denied legal effect simply because it is in electronic form. It is an enabling statute that sets down standards that can be followed and allows states to enact their own but generally consistent legislation within this umbrella, prohibiting laws that limit permissible electronic signatures to one single technology. The states differ widely in their authorizations because numbers are applicable to all electronic transactions, whereas others can be more limited in their scope and effect. Internationally, many countries (from Brazil and Taiwan to the individual members of the EU) have enacted e-signature and e-commerce laws, simply because it is in their best interests to do so.

In 1998, the United States' Internet Tax Freedom Act capped taxes on online sales with a 3-year moratorium on any *new* state, local, or federal Internet taxes (as defined) to October 20, 2001; after an interim delay, the moratorium was extended for an additional 2-year period that then expired on November 1, 2003. It is a misnomer, however, that this statute generally ended Internet taxation. Among other allowed taxes (including "grandfathered" Internet taxes and taxes on Internet access) when the "moratorium" expired, 45 states charged sales tax on tangible products bought online, given that the seller had some form of a physical presence or "nexus" (i.e., a warehouse, retail store, office, or sales representatives) in that state—all as permitted under already existing tax law (see *National Bellas Hess v. State of Illinois*, 1976).

What was held in abeyance was the legal ability to tax an online purchase from a resident in a state where no such nexus or connection to the selling site's state was present. In late 2004, Congress finally approved the extension of these federal restrictions against taxing online sales transactions to November 1, 2007, and President Bush signed this legislation into law. Notwithstanding this, it is expected that the states and non-Internet merchants will continue to make the pleas to Congress to tax online sales as never before—and the lobbying will continue well past any further legislation that's enacted, whether the ban is made permanent or another short-term "moratorium" ensues.

As e-commerce expanded, huge increases in unwanted electronic solicitations (otherwise known as spam and junk e-mail) have also taken place. Given the Net's anonymity, enforcement difficulties, jurisdictional issues, and that more serious crimes are usually in line for prosecution, controlling spam legally will not be possible until the U.S. and the international community in general pass federal laws with strong enforcement mechanisms. Although the U.S. federal government passed an antispam bill, the CAN-SPAM Act of 2003, critics believe that this law doesn't go far enough. For example, there is no requirement of an "opt-in" provision, because the act allows e-marketers to continue spamming until the recipient responds with a required "opt-out" message (which also confirms that e-mail address). Further, this legislation legitimizes unsolicited e-mail as a marketing tool and is ineffective on those spammers who increasingly operate outside U.S. jurisdictional limits; this act also supersedes conflicting state antispamming laws that are stricter in cases. (Even given that nearly all U.S. states have enacted laws regulating spam, including fines and jail time as penalties, these laws are rarely or difficult to enforce. In numbers of states, no one has yet been prosecuted under those statutes.) In contrast to the U.S.'s position, countries from Australia to the European Union have passed strict antispam laws with "opt-in" provisions and varying effective dates. For the latest on antispam legislation and developments, see http://www.spamlaws.com.

For more on e-commerce law, taxation, and spam, please see the applicable chapters in this *Handbook*. Although beyond the scope of this chapter, the global e-commerce legal aspects are considerable and ever changing; please see the treatment of these international areas throughout this treatise.

"Terms of Use" Provisions

Many Web sites separate out the necessary purchasing information from their legal Terms of Use and Privacy policies. Although the general areas treated are similar, each site's provisions are different, depending on whether a particular location sells products, provides services, gives information, or some combination. Nonetheless, the general concepts covered are basically the same.

Given that the basic contract business terms (e.g., quantity, price, time for delivery, delivery mode, and so on) are present, what was once "just legal boilerplate" has now become more important: disclaimers of liability, limitations of warranty, indemnity, handling of disputes, applicable law, and dispute resolution, among other areas—and this is especially true when distant localities become involved.

The disclaimer-of-liability provisions typically limit a seller's liability for injury or loss incurred by the buyer to exchanging the product or a refund of the purchase price, all at the seller's option. This refund policy is usually coupled with a disclaimer of liability, such as the following: "Seller disclaims all liabilities and warranties, express or implied, including the warranties of merchantability and fitness for a particular purpose, and this Web company shall not be liable for any damages, whether consequential or incidental."

The intent of these provisions is for the seller to "duck away" from liability, leaving the manufacturer on the hook. Although not unanimous in their decisions, the courts generally uphold limitations on consequential damages (for example, a site's loss of data that results in a further loss to its users or customers) in business transactions, and it is well-settled law that two contractual parties in commercial situations can negotiate arms-length the extent to which either party's damages will be limited, given equal bargaining power (see *Robotic Vision Systems v. Cybo Systems, Inc.*, 1998). These provisions usually are not upheld if a personal injury is involved with an individual, however, such as when a customer is injured using a defective product that caused those injuries.

As a basic legal concept, no one can contract against the effects of strict product liability or one's own negligence, unless separately negotiated between two contracting businesses. If that were the case, then there could never be any product liability, because every manufacturer and retailer in the world would be contractually providing, "Sorry, if there's a problem with our product, even if it's entirely our fault, we don't accept that liability—you do." Depending on the circumstances, Web sites can be held completely responsible for a customer's damages, notwithstanding these one-sided contract provisions. For example, if a pharmacy Web site erroneously fills a prescription for high-blood pressure medication that severely worsens the problem, that Net retailer typically will have to compensate that injured person for his or her damages from those bad pills, regardless of any Terms of Use limitations to the contrary.

Standard Terms of Use agreements also provide for "tight" indemnity provisions (i.e., that the user is responsible for any damages), as well as favorable provisions on applicable law (typically the site's state law, if favorable), dispute location (the Web-site's hometown and state), copyright use (i.e., one must gain their written consent to any copying), privacy policies, and the like. Although courts tend to uphold these one-sided provisions, sites cannot be totally unfair in them, nor limit what the law already allows. For example, the United States provides for a "fair use" exception for copyrights, and the courts will generally not allow any such one-sided, restrictive statements to erode this long-standing doctrine. Just because a Web site operator says it's true doesn't necessarily make it legally so. However, any user must be aware that all Terms of Use provisions, including privacy policies, are agreements of legal significance and that it will take a successful court challenge to overturn their application. If possible with larger companies, it's better to negotiate out ahead of time the legal provisions, or boilerplate, that aren't in your favor.

Validity

Most courts uphold "take it or leave it," click e-agreements, provided (a) the terms are written in understandable English with readable print and not hidden from the user's view; (b) the user has the opportunity to read and understand these terms, all before having to make any purchase or use decision; (c) the provisions are reasonable; and (d) the user has to take some affirmative action to agree (such as clicking an "I agree" button). Because courts tend to enforce software shrink-wrap agreements (where the act of opening the software package is deemed to be acceptance of the included terms), they're doing the same with Web site Terms of Use "click" provisions, provided these elements are present.

If, however, the language used is hidden or not conspicuous, in small print, or wholly unreasonable in effect (e.g., "This Web site is not responsible for any of your damages, regardless of how much we are at fault"), then courts will generally not uphold them. There must be some knowledge (the terms are easily located and understood), prior decision-making (the user can decide before having to order), and facts showing at least mutual assent or an implied agreement (e.g., clicking on an icon to show your assent).

A leading Second U.S. Circuit Court of Appeals case, *Specht v. Netscape Communications Corp.* (2002), reviewed the standard terms and provisions applied when a user downloaded software. The standard terms provided that all provisions came into legal effect when any user simply downloaded or installed the software. However, users could directly download this software before coming or scrolling down to the "I agree" icon and any inspection of the terms of use that bound their decision. Applying standard contract law on mutuality of assent, the court upheld a lower court's decision and refused to enforce an arbitration clause in the Web site's forum state, holding that the required mutuality for contract assent was not present.

When the requisite criteria is present, courts will uphold these terms on a general, conceptual basis, provided additionally there is no blatant unreasonableness in those provisions. Based upon the Uniform Commercial Code's Section 2-302 (basic to most states' laws) that codifies the traditional common law doctrine of unconscionability, courts still have the ability to set aside those standard terms. The intentional misuse of a Web site by a user, however, can negate provisions that don't meet these standards. For example, in *Register.Com, Inc. v. Verio* (2000), a court held that when Internet users intentionally misuse a site's content, there is an implicit agreement to any terms of the Web site's legal notice that would prohibit that action.

A recent Northern California Federal District Court case, *Cairo v. Crossmedia Services* (2005), consistently applied both *Specht* and *Register* to a Web site's terms-of-use provisions that involved a forum-selection clause. Contrary to Crossmedia Services (CMS) forum clause that required lawsuits to be filed in Illinois, plaintiff Cairo filed a declaratory relief action in California. The federal court found that Cairo's use of CMS's Web pages in allegedly copying promotional materials was such an "actual or imputed knowledge" of those terms as to effectively bind Cairo to the forum selection clause mandating Illinois as the proper venue. CMS's motion to dismiss was granted.

INFORMATION SECURITY LEGAL LIABILITIES

Whether owing to electrical brownouts, software errors, or hacker interference, systems crash every minute with loss of data, inoperable equipment, and frozen software. Along with the reported cases, there are general rules of law that apply in deciding how and where liability for damages will reside. Basically, liability sits with the computer software and hardware manufacturers for their products' "inability to perform as promised," along with a growing Web operator liability when users lose data or incur damages—but along distinct legal lines.

Computer Software and Hardware Manufacturer Liabilities

The great majority of cases involving computer software or hardware defects are brought usually on contract, breach of warranty, fraud, and recession grounds, not on general tort grounds such as negligence or strict liability theories. As basic law, courts apply contract law to contract situations such as the purchase of computer software, errors, and breach of warranty problems, with tort law applied to noncontract situations (see, for example, *Grynberg v. Agri Tech, Inc.*, 2000).

Owing to an apparent general acquiescence of system malfunctions, vendor responses in solving their user's problems, insurance coverage, continuing technological improvements, responsive security safeguards (i.e., stronger firewalls, backing-up data, internal security procedures, etc.), and limitation of damage clauses, only a tiny fraction of security-related problems come to court and then most settle before trial. Two issues are common in these contractual disputes (and see the earlier discussion on "Terms of Use" and "Validity"): (a) Whether shrink-wrap (physically opening the plastic wrapping of a software box) or clickwrap (digital clicking on an Internet "I Agree" icon) acts are present, was there a valid contract entered into that included the standard Terms of Use provisions? (b) If so, was there a legally enforceable disclaimer of liabilities and/or damages?

Various courts have concluded that shrink-wrap and clickwrap licenses are a valid form of contracting, that a vendor may propose a contract of sale be formed, not in the store or over the phone, but after the customer has had a chance to inspect both the item and the terms in the box (or after "clicking" an "I Agree" button) as to standard, unchangeable terms. For example, see *ProCD, Inc. v. Zeidenberg* (1996); *Brower v. Gateway 2000, Inc.* (1998); *Mortenson Co. Inc. v. Timberline Software Corp.* (2000); *i.LAN Systems v. NetScout Service Level Corp.* (2002). Basically, if a shrink-wrap license agreement is enforceable with implicit contractual assent, then it is also correct to enforce a clickwrap agreement on the Internet.

Typically, these agreements contain limitation on liabilities, such as limiting any damages to a refund of the software price (or replacement of the hardware within a certain period) with no compensation for any out-of-pocket losses or ensuing damages. As mentioned in the previous section on e-commerce Terms of Use provisions, exclusionary clauses in purely commercial transactions—especially where the parties are of equal bargaining power and specifically negotiate their contractual terms—are generally upheld.

For example, in *Mortenson v. Timberline*, plaintiff Mortenson purchased a bid-analysis software package from defendant Timberline. After Mortenson used the software to prepare a bid that erroneously turned out to be nearly $2 million less than it should have been, Mortenson sued on breach of warranty grounds. The Washington Supreme Court affirmed the lower courts' holding that the limitation of damages contained in the vendor's shrink-wrap package was valid. Mortenson was limited to a refund of the cost of the software with no provision for the much larger damages it had incurred due to that software error.

Other courts, however, have gone in different directions on this issue. In *Amsan LLC v. Prophet 21 Inc.* (2001), for example, a federal judge in Pennsylvania ruled that the software licensee could avoid the limitation-of-liability clause in its license agreement and pursue its remedies under the UCC, holding that because the warranty had failed in its essential purpose, that the limitation clause had to also fail.

Except for the outstanding issue of these limiting provisions, however, it is clear there can be contractual liability if a software manufacturer warrants to anyone that its product will specifically perform in some way (i.e., "calculate mortgage payments to the penny") and doesn't. When a system crashes owing to no fault of the software provider (i.e., a hacker cracks through the site) at this time, the great majority of users generally seem to accept their fate. However, when an employee is responsible for that loss of data or security problem, the liability issues are clear.

Security-Related Liabilities (Employee)

Liability against others for security-related breaches and damages is dependent mainly on whether an employee or outside third party is responsible for creating the security breach. Employee-created liabilities, even if the intentional act or tort of that employee, creates liability for his or her employer based on common-law liability standards—regardless as to whether the Internet, information security, or online operations are involved. Under the doctrine of respondeat superior, an employer is held accountable for the damages created by its employee, provided that employee was operating at the time within the scope of the employment relationship.

When an intentional tort is involved, as opposed to just being negligent or at fault, liability is still found on various grounds, including that the particular employee's acts would have normally been furthering the employer's business or was within their job responsibilities—even given that the intentional act would not have been condoned by the employer (see also Bick, 2003). Employees can create this vicarious liability for their employers, whether it's hacking into confidential databanks, disabling protective software programs, or sending sexually harassing e-mail messages. In fact, as Continental Airlines found in *Blakey v. Continental Airlines* (2000), businesses have liability for the individual online harassing acts of their employees; in this case, other pilots posted sufficient harassing gender-based messages on the pilots' bulletin board (and only accessible by them) that the court found the employer liable for a hostile work environment.

When hackers and viruses unexpectedly show up, however, whether it's cracking passwords, exploiting software design flaws, or coordinating attacks on target computers and Web sites, the issue becomes expectedly more complicated.

Hackers, Crackers, and Viruses

Several large Web sites, such as Yahoo, Amazon.com, eBay, CNN, and Dell, in February 2000 were severely disrupted by distributed denial-of-service (DDoS) attacks. Later estimates of the lost business, data, and operational downtime ranged from $1.2 to $1.7 billion dollars. A 15-year-old teenager (known online as "Mafiaboy") living with his parents in Montreal, Canada, was responsible for the attacks. Despite the large-scale damages, Mafiaboy (Canadian law protects the anonymity of juveniles) received a sentence of 8 months in juvenile detention and a

$250 fine to charity. If a teenager could do this, think what a dedicated hacker might be able to do. Or an experienced cracker on subscriber passwords.

Just 3 months later, the "I Love You" virus infected 45 million computers around the world. This hacker virus imbedded itself in a computer's system files, causing system crashes and freezing, then ordered the "host" computer to forward an infected electronic mail attachment to all addressees in the user's e-mail address book. Depending on the estimate—and including nearly 30 copycat viruses that came into being in the next weeks, the "I Love You" virus cost between $6 and $10 billion in lost productivity. There were no reported major U.S. cases decided regarding these security-related breeches, although claims and litigation with insurers over their coverage occurred.

Newspapers still report all too frequently the disruption caused by worldwide Internet attacks by hackers on computers and, given its market domination, on Microsoft operating systems in the main, such as the 2003 'LovSan' virus. Given massive losses of data, or stolen identities, the question becomes just who is legally responsible for these problems—the software manufacturer(s), their Web site operator-customers, or the individual site users—and to what extent?

Clearly, hackers are subject to a variety of criminal and civil law sanctions (see generally Jacobson & Greene, 2002). Yet as seen so clearly in the Mafiaboy case, hackers—if they can be located at all—don't have the money to pay for damages. The problem escalates when the virus or attack is terrorist inspired, and it will be years before any final court decisions are handed down on the myriad legal questions inherent in the September 11, 2001, tragedy (i.e., the extent to which the victim, such as the airlines, can be held liable for the intentional and criminal acts by others).

Regardless of cause, Web site operators work hard to recreate lost data and mitigate damage to their users—or risk losing their customers. When users can't access a particular site or lose data, compensation is rarely given, however, and it isn't cost-effective in the great majority of cases to litigate over limiting damage provisions. In high damage cases, users look toward the software manufacturer or Web operator (or both) with insurance coverage on both sides playing a dominant role (see also the next section, "Insurance Law"). The tendency by all players is to "downplay" any system malfunctions, reporting little, if anything, to the authorities or their users, preferring to negotiate with their vendors over any business losses or with their insurance carriers.

However, lack of information-security practices, record-retention policies, or backup procedures can create numerous headaches with state and federal regulatory agencies (see generally Bick, 2001). For example, the SEC penalizes organizations that it deems not to be in compliance with its record-keeping directives. In 2003, the SEC announced in a settlement agreement that it had fined five large, reputable businesses with broker-dealer operations—Deutsche Bank, Goldman Sachs, Morgan Stanley, Salomon Smith Barney, and U.S. Bancorp Piper Jaffray—a total of $8.25 million ($1.65 million each) for failing to have in place adequate procedures to retain e-mails and keep them accessible, all in violation of

record-keeping procedures (*Deutsche Bank*, 2002). Not having generally reasonable procedures for storing data, backup systems, or online and offline storage facilities can create problems when in litigation; courts are not accepting of excuses when discovery requests are thwarted by lack of data, and this violation can lose you a lawsuit (Buford, 2003). Further, state professional ethics bodies can and will intervene if, for example, a law firm or physicians group doesn't adequately protect its electronic records with backup files.

To What Extent Is the Victim Liable?

The question then becomes to what extent is the victim liable to its own customers? Generally speaking, an organization or individual is not liable to its customers for the unanticipated, independent tort of a third party. Presently, Web sites and their users seem to generally accept their losses from hackers and viruses, whether the software manufacturer could have anticipated the rogue programming or not—even when a protecting software patch against the computer virus was available and the site operator didn't quite get around to employing it.

Legal experts maintain (for example, see Pinkney, 2002, and de Villiers, 2003) that common-law negligence and strict-liability grounds should be available, whether a patch was actually in existence or not. The theory of negligence involves proving four separate elements: a duty to a third party, the breach of that duty, proximate cause (or some "connection" or foreseeability between the breach and any ensuing damages), and damages that occur. Strict product liability is where liability is basically imposed regardless of fault on any merchant who introduces into commerce a good or product that is "unreasonably dangerous" when in a "defective condition." To the extent that the software manufacturer and Web operator are not completely at fault, an offset to any user damages could be available. In both cases, end users can be compensated to the extent that any resulting losses are not their fault. By applying a standard of reasonableness or not being "unreasonably dangerous" with strict product liability, this line of reasoning implies that there is a duty or standard on the part of Web operators and the software and hardware manufacturers to create "information-secure" sites.

Victims of a computer virus infection, consequently, under current negligence theory and these arguments can sue the providers, distributors, and operators of infected software for their damages. Proof of specific negligence can be straightforward when the circumstances involve a familiar virus strain that could have been cost-effectively prevented. In cases involving complex and novel strains, however, these evidentiary standards may not be available and such direct proof not exist. Even in these cases, circumstantial evidence based on the doctrine of "res ipsa loquitur" (and see further, de Villiers, 2003) can be used to prove one's case. (The theory of res ipsa loquitur, or "the thing speaks for itself," allows an inference of negligence based on the mere occurrence of an accident and its surrounding circumstances, not requiring the proof of specific negligence.) Another de Villiers' article (de Villiers, 2004) analyses the use of a negligence cause of action in the inadvertent transmission of a computer virus and discusses these liability parameters within a virus infection context.

The same line of reasoning can be applied in hacker attacks that involve multiple computers. When DDoS attacks take place, the hacker typically has accessed a "master" computer that enslaves multiple numbers of other "zombie" computers in marshalling their systems to act in concert and flood the target system with massive amounts of e-mails, requests, and traffic, in an attempt to cause that system to crash or deny service to legitimate users. If a patch is available to protect these computers from being so enslaved, then using a negligence or strict liability standard can conceivably bring even these outside systems into the sphere of liability (Radin, 2001, 2002).

To do this, the courts will need to carve an exception to the general rule that disappointed expectations and economic damages (i.e., lost business profits, customers, and personnel downtime) under a "sour" contract are not recoverable, as well as the application of limiting Terms of Use liability and damage provisions, because negligence or strict product liability concepts in the great number of cases are not applied to these factual situations that don't involve tortuous physical harm to persons or property (see *Springfield Hydroelectric Company v. Copp*, 2001; *Gus' Catering, Inc. v. Menusoft Systems*, 2000).

When basic contract law and the UCC is applied instead of torts or strict liability, as we have seen, there is a much higher likelihood that limitation-of-liability and damage clauses will be upheld. In tort actions, courts go the other way and generally disregard these limitations (i.e., those providing that any damages are limited to just a refund of the product's purchase price), holding that as a general policy individuals and organizations should not be allowed to contract against their own negligence.

Contractually, larger companies and entities with greater bargaining power negotiate with their software providers to insert protective language into their licenses in place of these limiting damage provisions. For example, their contracts may directly provide that the software companies are liable for any costs of security breaches and hacker attacks that exploit software weaknesses (i.e., the costs of data replacement, cleanup, and lost business). If the software provider wants the business, then it may very well accept this different language.

Smaller users are typically protected, if a hacker or thief steals a credit card number and uses this to charge for goods, whether online or offline: The customer is protected under current law for losses exceeding $50, provided he or she doesn't unreasonably delay in their notification of the credit card company after learning of the loss. In response, Mastercard, Visa, and American Express, among others, are understandably working with their banks and merchants to increase online information security with time lines to institute safeguards or else the participating institutions bear the cost of any chargebacks for purchases made from stolen credit cards and identities.

As leading court decisions are awaited, state agencies and legislatures are beginning to make the first inroads. In 2003, the New York attorney general's office cited Ziff Davis ("ZD"), the New York–based print and online publisher of computer magazines such as *PC Week*, for failing to provide reasonable computer security standards. In an offering of free limited subscriptions to a computer gaming magazine, ZD and its Web host failed to take precautions to protect consumer data, including leaving unencrypted subscriber data in the open on a publicly accessible server with no authentication controls. Hackers immediately gained access to the subscriber list, soon gaining the credit card information of 50 holders and posting the names and e-mail addresses of some 12,000 of its readers. Ziff Davis agreed to pay a $100,000 fine to the states of New York, California, and Vermont, along with $500 to each of the 50 subscribers whose credit card information was so accessed. Additionally, the settlement agreement provided that ZD would store data on protected servers, encrypt data in protected files, and use automated security tools (i.e., firewalls and intrusion detection systems), in addition to undertaking other safeguards. Organizations that fail to implement reasonable security systems and procedures are at risk for similar governmental action should a hacker break in.

Additionally, companies risk needing to call in the Federal Bureau of Investigation (FBI) or Justice Department under the Homeland Security Act (2002), if a hacker intrudes into sensitive information. For example, Data Processors International (DPI) is a U.S. firm that processes credit card information for Visa, MasterCard, American Express, and Discover. To its chagrin, DPI discovered that a hacker in February 2003 had accessed some 8 million credit card numbers. DPI called in the FBI to conduct a criminal investigation.

On July 1, 2003, California became the first state to pass a database privacy and antihacker act. This legislation requires that state agencies and companies with databases must notify their California customers when user personal information is illegally accessed from that computer network (California Legislative Service, 2002). If they don't so notify their users or customers quickly and without unreasonable delay, then the company assumes the damages incurred by its users. Californians can bring civil actions for damages and injunctive relief. The law is intended to help consumers protect against identity theft by requiring businesses, wherever located, to disclose quickly any breach in their security system of personal information that is not encrypted. At this time, there is no comparable federal law. Unlike the California law, however, the federal U.S. Homeland Security Act makes the disclosure of these breeches voluntary.

The present lack of statutory and court direction will change, however, when a massive hacker attack involves a nuclear power plant, worldwide identity thefts, airline controller traffic, or some terrible act of injury. The resulting damage and noninsured liabilities will create an unfortunate climate mandating the standards as to who will pay for those liabilities and under what circumstances. Courts then will hand down decisions on negligence, strict liability, and the comparative negligence parameters. Legislatures will be forced to get down to business.

INSURANCE LAW

With the technological sophistication of rogue programmers, the risks of operating on the Internet can be substantial. Whether hackers or employees destroy data systems, intercept stored or transmitted personal information (identity loss), commit computer fraud, or order DDoS attacks, there are multiple risks of data loss and damages. Where a loss is uninsured, the risks increase that affected sites will need to compensate, one way or another, a large user's losses or accept that loss of business or even a lawsuit. A critical issue is whether Internet insurance risk coverage is present, and several basic considerations need to be analyzed first.

Unless a special rider or policy is purchased, the typical homeowner's policy does *not* cover an individual's losses for loss of data or other Internet damages, although it will generally cover the destruction of that computer. If you're running a business, then your personal insurance policies (whether fire, homeowner's, or car) in nearly all cases will not insure against loss when you're conducting your business operations—whether your activities are online or offline. You will need business or commercial insurance generally for such commercial protection.

Two basic insurance areas for any business are first-party property coverage (i.e., insuring your buildings and personal property against loss) and third-party liability coverage (i.e., lawsuits brought by third parties against you due to your operations). A separate commercial general liability (CGL) insurance policy typically covers third-party customer or user claims. CGL, excess liability, and other liability policies protect the policyholder against liability, including outside claims of "property damage" or "physical damage to the tangible property of others" from your acts.

Pre-cyberspace, the notion of "direct physical loss" was easy to recognize because this involved specific identified risks such as fire, slip-and-fall incident, or an automobile accident. The legal question was whether a given policy covered the submitted asset loss or third-party liability claim. The problem then came about when these decades-defined incidents under standard policy provisions now involved the loss of electronic data, as the Internet Age created new forms of loss. The question was just how "physical" were these intangible, millions of bits of information.

Insurance companies understandably took the position that their standard commercial CGL, E & O (errors and omissions), BPP (business owner's package policy), and other policies did not cover most Internet risks, arguing generally that loss of access, data, and the use of information systems was not the equivalent of a direct physical loss. Although the majority of cases held that these pre-Net policies did *not* cover electronic data losses from hacker attacks or crashed sites (see *Lucker Manufacturing v. Home Insurance Co.*, 1994), a few courts have taken a broad policy look at the issue and held for the insured (see *American Guarantee & Liability Insurance Co. v. Ingram Micro, Inc.*, 2000). In *Ingram Micro*, an Arizona federal district court made a basic policy decision that coverage "must exist" for these type of losses in the light of the realities of the modern Internet world.

In very specific areas other than loss of data, standard umbrella and CGL insurance policies can provide some small Internet insurance coverage—but discuss these provisions with your insurance agent or manager in detail. For example, claims stemming from a policyholder's

online advertising activities that, in turn, involve defamation, libel, slander, violation of privacy rights, or copyright infringement can generally be covered (provided the insurer didn't change that language later). CGL policies also generally provide coverage for the "oral or written publication of material that slanders or libels a person or organization (including product disparagement)," including the "publication of material that violates a person's privacy." Although some professionals recommend that businesses review their CGL policy for such coverage or negotiate with their insurer, legal experts believe that the better approach is to purchase specific Internet policies (i.e., media Internet operations)—and to be sure there is stated, definite coverage for your particular Net operations and risks.

Insurance companies then developed specific Internet data loss and third-party liability policies specifically covering the risks of loss from hackers, computer viruses, employee hacking, and much of the Internet privacy and intellectual property claims that clearly were not covered under traditional CGL, E & O, excess liability, and other pre-Internet policies. Supplemental e-commerce first-party property policies now can cover loss of electronic data, while digital error and omission policies can protect an insured from liability in defined areas, such as the above-mentioned advertising/personal liability, electronic data transmission, security lapses, and even copyright infringement (see, for example, Savetz, 2002). Web operators anticipating losses from Internet security problems can consider insurance coverage from their inland marine policies, fidelity policies, computer crime policies, and any other ones that have specific insurance coverage for these anticipated claims (see generally Gold, 2002). That's the good news.

The bad news is that insurance companies already are eliminating the provisions in their CGL policies that could infer coverage (such as in the advertising and privacy areas) that withstood court scrutiny and are tightening up sections to exclude Internet operations specifically. With the advent of worldwide virus attacks, such as the Code Red worm (an estimated $2 billion in damages in 2001) and "Slammer" worm (some $1 billion in lost global productivity in 2003), various insurance companies have raised premiums for Internet coverage or simply excluded certain Net coverage, such as that caused by computer viruses. Where reasonable coverage is possible, insurance companies are requiring that companies take strong preventive loss measures (i.e., strong firewalls, frequent backing-up of data, use of encryption, smart cards, electronic keys, and data restoration equipment plus procedures to secure their online systems), along with requiring stand-alone hacker policies—or go unprotected. The horrors of September 11 further compounded the question with the specter of terrorists unleashing viruses and the need for vulnerable industries to implement security procedures plus acquire adequate insurance to cover these risks (if affordable).

The bottom line is that it's a much better idea to discuss what Internet and security coverage is possible and at what cost with your insurance agent or risk manager before you incur an online loss. Read the policy provisions closely and, if possible, obtain a letter from your insurer that specifically outlines your coverage. Litigating against your insurance company and agent over a denied claim—especially when that includes your customer's or user's complaints against you—is not a good alternative. You may be better off paying the higher premiums of specific Internet loss coverage or knowing, alternatively, that you are "self-insured": the euphemism that in return for not paying premiums, you know you're absorbing all of your and your users' losses. For more on this subject, please see Security Insurance and Best Practices in this *Handbook*.

THE CLASH OF LAWS

Given the numbers of cyberlaw conflicts, a key issue is whether a court in the plaintiff's geographical area can hear and decide the case. Simply put, if the problem is big enough, you want your understandable laws to apply, eat and sleep in your own home, work in your office when not in court, and not have to hire an expensive attorney in a different state or foreign country. People involved in a court case don't want jetlag, bad food, unfamiliar surroundings, a strange language, and being away from their family for weeks on end, which is why jurisdiction and conflicts of law is such a large, cyberlaw issue.

Jurisdiction over a nonresident Web site or Internet transaction in the United States is normally based on a local state's long-arm statute. These laws provide that a state can assert jurisdiction over a nonresident defendant who commits a tort, transacts business, or has some connection with that state. When a state court asserts jurisdiction over a particular controversy to render a binding decision, for the most part it will also be constitutionally permitted to apply its laws, given sufficient connections with that dispute. (Federal courts apply the appropriate state substantive law when relevant to their decisions).

The U.S. Supreme Court's landmark *International Shoe Company v. Washington State* (1945) decision established the law in this area. For a court to have proper jurisdiction, defendants must have purposely availed themselves of the privilege of doing business in that particular state (i.e., traveling through, selling there, advertising in, or other contacts in that state), and these "minimum contacts" must meet sufficient levels of due process so as not to offend our "traditional concepts of fair play and substantial justice."

For example, if a Wyoming rancher died and willed his ranch to his Wyoming son, it would offend our sense of "fair play" if a second son, who happened to live in Alabama, could sue and haul that Wyoming brother into an Alabama court. There are no connections with Alabama to this case, so the only court with jurisdiction should be Wyoming—and that court would apply Wyoming law (the property is there, the decedent and his heir lived in the state, the will was probated there, and so on).

When it comes to jurisdiction on the Net, U.S. courts generally look at a Web site's level of Internet activity, drawing distinctions between passive and active locations—and this distinction will be drawn more in foreign courts, although it is not a trend overseas. Called the "Zippo sliding scale," this test was set down in *Zippo Manufacturing Co. v. Zippo Dot Com, Inc.* (1997).

At one end of the spectrum, Web sites that enter into contracts with out-of-state residents involving repeated contacts, e-mails or other correspondence, and selling appreciable amounts of products or services into that state are held to be "active" Web sites. These active sites can be sued in the state of their customers, or in those out-of-state residents, as various U.S. cases have held. Given the existence of these sufficient contacts, a local court could (depending on the facts) disregard a contrary Terms of Use condition of the Web site that provided it could only be sued in its home state.

On the other side of the equation, sites that only advertise or post information about their business on the Internet—not taking any orders or conducting business through that Net site—are held to be "passive" Web sites. These Internet "informational" sites generally cannot be sued out of state and dragged from their home base into foreign courts, simply because they maintain a virtual presence. To hold differently would be to subject Net operators to being sued anywhere in the world that allowed an Internet connection to be made.

In between are Net sites that provide more connections between their state and out-of-state customers—and it usually takes more than having an e-mail capability and a toll-free number to confer that jurisdiction. With these same facts, e-mailing questions about a potential purchase (without more) doesn't suffice either, although some courts view this as borderline and "getting very close." If a defendant Web site displays a downloadable mail-in order form, toll-free telephone number, and e-mail address but no orders are ever made there, then these facts are not normally good enough. Given a finding that a passive site was involved, the upset user then must travel to the Web site's home state to sue. As indicated, a factual decision needs to be made in each case as to whether these minimum connections for due process reasons are present.

Some courts have developed an "effects"-based approach exception to the Zippo sliding scale. When using this approach, the court focuses its analysis on the actual effect that a Net site had in its state or the defendant's intent, not on how interactive the Internet location was. This test derives from the U.S. Supreme Court's *Calder v. Jones* (1984) decision, in which jurisdiction was found over a nonresident defendant newspaper, based on its intentional conduct outside the forum state that was deemed to cause defamatory injury to the plaintiff resident in that state—even though strong factual connections weren't otherwise present. Although courts tend to apply the "effects" test in cases involving intentional torts, such as defamation or trademark infringement cases, they do differ on what conduct constitutes the kind of "express" aiming or effect that's required to satisfy the test. Applying the "effects" test can find jurisdiction when there aren't sufficient contacts of the type called for under the *Zippo* sliding scale.

In a closely followed case, the California Supreme Court in *Pavlovich v. Superior Court* (2002) overruled a Court of Appeals decision involving the application of the effects test. Pavlovich had posted his programming adaptation of DeCSS software, a technology allowing the scrambling system in DVDs to be rendered ineffective and

THE CLASH OF LAWS

their contents copied. The appellate court held that California had jurisdiction over Pavlovich, a Texas resident but who was an engineering student at Purdue University in Indiana at the time. Although the defendant's actions didn't come close to meeting the *Zippo* test, the appeals court held that because there was an "effect" in California from Pavlovich's "intentional tortuous" actions, that California had jurisdiction, could apply its long-arm statute, and force the defendant to come there and defend himself. The California Supreme Court, however, reversed this decision on a 4–3 vote. It held that under the *Zippo* test, the Web site was merely an informational one and there was no evidence that the defendant had expressly hurled his activities at California. It ruled that a defendant's knowledge or foreseeability alone of harmful effects ensuing in a specific state (California) is not sufficient by itself to establish any "purposeful availment" of that state's law under the effects test. There must be more than that.

As can be seen, these can be complicated cases, whether the issue involves e-commerce differences, sales tax assessments, or defamation cases. Further, not only can a business (or wrongdoer) be a resident of one state, or even offshore from the United States, his server may be located physically in a different state, the connecting routers in others, and the end user or complaining party in another completely different one.

Keep in mind that the U.S. Supreme Court hasn't yet ruled on this area of virtual personal jurisdiction, nor what happens when a Web site's Terms of Use provisions are different from the reviewing court's laws—and courts, domestic and foreign alike, can and do give "wild" judgments that don't seem to meet any tests or analysis. For example, Australia's highest court ruled in *Dow Jones v. Gutnick* (2002) that a publisher could be sued for defamation in whatever country an individual's reputation has allegedly been harmed. This case arose when an Australian businessman, Joseph Gutnick, sued U.S.-based Dow Jones & Co. for comments made about him in an article posted on the Internet in *Barron's Online*. This court found that because damage to the plaintiff's reputation had occurred in Victoria where the article was downloaded and read, it was appropriate for Gutnick to seek damages in that Australian forum. If other countries follow the Gutnick decision, let's say Canada, then it is entirely likely that if a defamatory digital publication is read in Canada, that there can be a sufficient nexus to maintain a defamation action in Canada, regardless that the publisher and server of that entity is located entirely in the United States—not an appealing legal proposition for that publisher.

Because laws vary greatly from country to country, what's prohibited by one nation can be entirely permissible in another. Unless an international treaty governs (e.g., the United Nation's Contracts for the International Sale of Goods [CISG]), countries are free to apply their own, quite different laws. The court that feels it has the greatest "connections," or the greatest interest in protecting its citizens, can and will take charge. It is quite possible that the courts in two countries could reach two entirely different results—and this has happened numbers of times. The basic question then is the extent to which the laws of one country may be enforced against Web sites and hosts located in others.

As one example, a French judge ordered U.S.-based portal Yahoo to block Web surfers in France from an auction where Nazi memorabilia were sold, including a fine of 100,000 francs ($13,700 U.S. dollars) for every day of noncompliance. Although Yahoo's offering sales of Nazi items was legally protected in the United States under the U.S. Constitution, it voluntarily banned the sale of these items in response. Arguing that the French court had no jurisdiction over it, however, Yahoo quickly countersued in a California Federal District Court to overturn that decision's effect in the United States.

In late 2001, the U.S. court ruled that Yahoo didn't have to comply with the French court's order (*Yahoo! v. La Ligue Contre le Racisme et L'Antisemitisme*, 2001). It held that a U.S. court cannot enforce a foreign order that violates the U.S. Constitution by "chilling protected speech that occurs simultaneously within our borders." Thus, the U.S. court held that Yahoo didn't have to comply with all the laws in other countries that conflicted with those of the United States. French civil rights groups appealed this decision to the Ninth Court of Appeals. (In 2003, a French court acquitted Yahoo of criminal charges that it had violated French criminal law by previously allowing the online sale of Nazi memorabilia from its U.S. Web servers.)

The appellate court in the United States, however, reversed the District Court's order (*Yahoo! v. La Ligue Contre le Racisme et L'Antisemitisme*, 2004), concluding that there was no basis for general jurisdiction in this case because the French groups did not have the continuous and systematic contacts with the forum state to support a finding of general personal jurisdiction. A key issue was that the French groups had never tried to collect on their judgment. Instead, Yahoo had filed a pre-emptive lawsuit against the groups, and in a split 2-1 decision the majority didn't reach the First Amendment issue, holding that Yahoo would have to wait on that question until the French litigants came to the United States to enforce their judgment. The Ninth Circuit Court of Appeals then decided to rehear the case "en banc" (the full court), but whatever its final decision, an appeal to the U.S. Supreme Court is expected.

The problem is not simple: Given other countries entering this fray, which court is right, when, and under or with what final authority? Because no international Supreme Court exists to adjudicate private disputes, there is no real way to settle this problem unless the parties later agree to those procedures. If the parties had negotiated the applicable law and forum before that dispute arose, then that agreement would control.

Fundamental differences among the various countries abound that affect basic principles, whether it's the United States and its First Amendment or EU countries with their basic consumer privacy protections. France mandates the use of the French language for numbers of documents in that country, whereas the EU and Japan have enacted strong antispam laws. Germany provides for a 2-week right of recession on online purchases, the U.S. to the contrary in this situation, as well.

One way to solve these questions is for countries to pass an international jurisdiction treaty that binds the signatory states. The Hague Conference on Private

International Law with over 60 member countries presently has established the "Hague Convention on Jurisdiction and Enforcement of Judgments in Civil and Commercial Cases." (For more on the Hague Convention and its jurisdictional efforts, see its Web site at http://www.hcch.net.) The Hague's jurisdictional treaty legislation is in the works but will take years to finalize—and this state of affairs is the reason why alternative dispute resolution is growing in e-importance. For further treatment of international cyberlaw areas, see the appropriate chapters in this *Handbook*.

CYBERLAW DISPUTE RESOLUTION

One cyberlaw fact of life stands out: Resolving disputes arising from the Internet's global reach through litigation is complex, expensive, and loaded with unclear results. In response, the Net community is actively pursuing alternative dispute resolution techniques (ADRs) such as mediation and arbitration—both offline and online. Given their low cost, confidentiality, limited negativity, and speed in resolving cyberdisputes, the use of ADRs is accelerating among users.

Web sites and online operators actively promote ADRs in their agreements and Terms of Use provisions. ADRs have been used to settle all types of Internet disputes, whether between Web partners, competing sites, domain name holders, ISPs and their subscribers, copyright holders and copiers, and many other Net matters. Credit card companies use an ADR form when they use "chargebacks" to end a customer's complaint with an online seller. As discussed before, ICANN has established a worldwide arbitration procedure to resolve domain name "cybersquatting" disputes. The U.S. Digital Copyright Act basically provides for an administrative procedure in resolving copyright disputes.

One of the striking ADR advances has been the rise of online cybermediators who work primarily online. For example, one party contacts the cybermediator about the problem and the parties' inability to solve it; the mediator then contacts the second party. If both parties agree to use a mediated approach and accept the ground rules, the online mediation begins. Typically, each party e-mails the mediator with his or her position or an acceptable settlement amount. The mediator then intercedes, shuttling back and forth electronically to reach a settlement. Although the experience has been that not having an actual presence between the mediator and parties (i.e., not experiencing body language and "real-time" emotions with words having a stronger unanticipated impact when made by e-mail) can be a drawback of online mediation, the 24/7 availability at any time, low cost, and no need to travel have proven to be advantageous.

Online resolution has particular advantages with lower monetary claims. In financial disputes, each party e-mails the amount at which they would settle their claim. In these "mediations," the agreed rules can provide for three rounds or more of settlement offers. Each party has also agreed to lower its demands by an agreed percentage—let's say 10%. By the third round, if the sides are close (let's say within 20%, or by some other formula), then that difference is halved and a deal struck. This is a brilliantly

simple, mathematically oriented solution with special advantages for low-figure disputes.

The leading player in providing this "double-blind bid" procedure is Cybersettle.com, which was awarded a U.S. Patent (among other countries) for that process. Other ADR service providers in cyberspace are ClickNsettle.com, SquareTrade.com, InternetNeutral, American Arbitration Association (adr.org), and SettleOnline, to name a few, and there are over fifty online dispute resolution Web sites at this time. Rather than being caught up in establishing expensive legal precedents over simply the issue of which law applies, where, and when—and then the main legal case must be fought—more and more parties are settling their disputes on or off the Net by using ADRs.

THE LAW OF LINKING

The World Wide Web depends on linking for its very existence, because this makes the Internet what it is. With the Net's maturity, however, the previous unconditional freedom to link has evolved into a framework of commonsense legal and netiquette rules that dictate limits on this freedom.

The general rule is that one doesn't need permission to link directly to another site, provided there is no commercial gain or some competitive informational advantage brought about by that linkage (even for a nonprofit institution). It is clear, moreover, that users should receive permission when they are "deep linking" or "framing," if only as a courtesy—and whether one should ask permission before any linking is a question of cyberethics, quite distinct from the law and any of its requirements. Clearly, any stated or implied representation by linking that another's work is yours would be trade or service-mark infringement (e.g., using its logo in conjunction with a trade or service), unfair competition and libel (e.g., saying something is yours when it's not), or a violation of the covenant of "good faith" that's implied in netiquette. Linking to illegal content by itself can also be illegal; in *Universal City Studios v. Reimerdes* (2000), the court enjoined the defendants from creating links from their court-prohibited site to numbers of other "mirror" sites.

When links bypass home pages, connecting instead to a page deep within that site, additional considerations become present. Lawsuits have been filed and settled in the plaintiff's favor in which the plaintiff complained over "deep links" bypassing the advertising on their home page, decreasing the "hit count" (users surf past the "count" page), diminishing their site's value, and allowing the defendant to "pass off" that information as its own.

The U.S. legal community, for example, watched closely when the owners of a newspaper, the *Shetland Times* in Scotland, brought a lawsuit against the *Shetland News*, a startup news service located in the same town. The *Shetland Times* published a daily online version of its newspaper, and the *News* was the first local daily to publish solely on the Web. It linked directly into the *Times* for news, and the *Shetland Times* went to court. The court granted the *Times* a temporary restraining order against the *News* and its linking practice (*Shetland Times v. Shetland News*, 1996), and the case soon settled out of court.

One well-publicized framing case was the lawsuit brought by various media companies (CNN, Time Warner, *USA Today*, the *Washington Post*, etc.) against Total News for its framing strategy. The media argued that the use of those frames, whereby Total News showed news stories taken from the plaintiffs with only its advertising displayed, violated their copyright and trademark rights. Total News reached a settlement before trial, agreeing not to frame any content and paid to link to their sites in a separate window (*Washington Post Co., et al. v. Total News*, 1997).

An accelerating Net phenomenon has been the rise of linking agreements in which a linked site pays for the exposure. These situations occur in two ways: (a) the linkage is in reality an advertising contract or customer referral agreement (see Amazon.com's "Associate" program); (b) the linked site commercially profits or otherwise benefits from a deep link. In both cases, a written linking agreement is essential.

Commercially profiting by deep linking or sophisticated software without the other site's permission is another growing legal area. Known as "robots," "bots," "spiders," or "crawlers," these automated software systems steam past home pages deep into data banks, gathering information and transporting copies of whatever is desired back to the host site. If done frequently enough, these "hits" can create a near simultaneous look at whatever data is out there.

The largest Internet auction service, eBay, filed a lawsuit in late 1999 against Bidders Edge, one of several Net auction search services. It had been accessing eBay's site up to 125,000 times daily (as much as 1.53% of the total daily requests to eBay) in searching out what was going on specifically at eBay's auctions, and eBay promptly sued after not being able to work out a license agreement with Bidders Edge to pay for this continuing access.

The judge granted an injunction, agreeing with eBay's contention that Bidder's Edge and its robots were trespassing on eBay's site by using and diminishing the resources of eBay's computer systems without permission (*eBay v. Bidder's Edge*, 2000). Bidder's Edge quickly appealed, but just before the appellate court issued its decision, the two companies agreed to settle their lawsuit. Later, eBay reported that the settlement prohibited Bidder's Edge from sifting through its site for information and that Bidder's Edge agreed to pay an undisclosed amount of money.

Internationally, a Danish court in *Danish Newspaper Publishers Association v. Newsbooster.com* (2002) ordered an online news site, Newsbooster.com, to remove links from its site to articles on the Web sites of various newspapers, on the ground that the links violated the EU Database Directory and bypassed the newspapers' home pages—following past precedent, both U.S. and a growing international law.

The directions of the law of linking are clear: (a) The general rule is that users do not need permission to link directly to the home page of another site, provided they don't disparage, misrepresent, or misappropriate; (b) given that these facts aren't present, framing and deep linking as opposed to linking will more likely constitute a violation; and (c) deep linking in commercial situations, as opposed to noncommercial ones, are likely to be violations in which (1) direct competitors are involved, (2) there is an advantage being taken by that linkage, and (3) there is an element of "unfairness" or bad faith on the part of the linking party. Furthermore, if data are being misappropriated, misused, or passed off by another as its own, even nonprofit or noncommercial sites may have valid causes of action.

CYBERCRIME

Cybercrime flourishes on the Internet, whether it is fraud, phony investments, hackers and poppers, pornography, rigged auctions, computer stalking, or prohibited gambling (and see http://www.cybercrime.gov for more). The advantages of the Net for all users can quickly turn into disadvantages for law enforcement. The ease of entry and ability to disconnect from the Web allow criminals to appear and disappear within seconds with their ill-gotten gains. Arresting criminals is further complicated by the myriad jurisdictions that cybercriminals can cross so quickly, the protection of rogue nations, and differing state or national laws that can make extradition difficult. In turn, the authorities have had to add technology patrols to their arsenal of weapons, and Net users must be ever on the alert.

Although nations add protective laws over time (e.g., the United States with its Access Device Fraud Act, 18 U.S.C. 1029 [1984]; Computer Fraud and Abuse Act, 18 U.S.C. 1030 [1986]; Trademark Counterfeit Act, 18 U.S.C. 2320 [1984]; and the various others mentioned previously), the question of jurisdiction and enforcement is always raised in this context. With criminal statutes, states and countries look at jurisdiction from the point of view of their laws and interest in protecting their citizens. For example, if gambling is illegal in State A but not State B, then a Web site in State B could be prosecuted by State A for its allowing the residents of State A to use that site. The reasoning is that every Web operator has the ability to be in compliance with State A's laws by simply refusing to allow A's residents to break their state's laws (i.e., by filtering out State A users).

Enforcement is always another question. Located in the Bahamas or other locations where activities such as gambling are legalized, just how do you enforce State A's judgment penalizing another in a foreign state or country, not to mention the inherent personal jurisdiction and conflicts of laws question (i.e., the Yahoo Nazi memorabilia decisions)? Unless there's increased cooperation among the differing authorities and criminal justice treaties agreed to, the First Amendment legal considerations by themselves will be voluminous. When property rather than an individual's freedom is concerned, courts seem to have less problems in determining rights, especially as to property that has already been seized (see, for example, *U.S. v. $734,578.82 in U.S. Currency*, 2002).

The horrors of September 11 brought other considerations of Internet crime to the forefront, given the ability of terrorists to communicate, raise money, and transfer assets over the Net. Among various legislative proposals, the enactment of the Uniting and Strengthening America by Providing Appropriate Tools Required to Intercept and

Obstruct Terrorism Act of 2001, or the "USA PATRIOT Act," illustrates these new thrusts. Among other provisions, the USA PATRIOT Act requires key financial sectors to implement programs that prevent their services from being used to launder money or finance terrorism. Entire new industries, such as operators of credit card systems, money transfer companies, check cashiers, security firms, insurance companies, and even casinos—whether online or not—now are encompassed by strict regulations that once included only banks. This act also amended various provisions of the U.S. Code to allow broad interceptions of electronic communications and seizure of customer records (and also controversial). Other nations have or are enacting similar legislation. Their courts, including those of the United States, are currently being asked to rule on just how legal these restraints are on individual privacy and constitutional rights. See the chapter on cybercrime and fraud, among other chapters on cyberterrorism and the criminal justice system in the U.S.

CONCLUSION

Hold onto your hats, the Internet hurricane of change is still howling—but inside your office or study. Legally, as well as technologically, there are more vibrant areas of change coming. For example, professional associations these days face Web sites that give information out to potential patients, clients, and customers on a global basis. From medicine and accounting to lawyering and filling drug prescriptions, state licensing boards are taking issue with this "practice without a required state license." This area continues to be well litigated.

Another area involves the ability of the Internet to "cut out the middleman." Because this medium allows consumers to contact suppliers directly, the old ways of conducting business are being seriously challenged in the courts. Travel agents sue airlines, wine distributors litigate with wineries that sell direct (in effect, suing their own customers or suppliers), and offline textbook distributors sue online retailers, not to mention the ever-increasing numbers of other industries that are litigating these types of developments. Although the consumer has benefited, it's clear that the legal industry also has.

A U.S. Supreme Court decision (*Granhold v. Heald*, 2005) ruled that laws dating back to post-Prohibition days were unconstitutional that allowed in-state wineries to ship directly to adult consumers within their borders, but then prohibited out-of-state wineries from shipping to the same accounts. The court ruled that restricting the ability of out-of-state wineries to ship directly to consumers in today's Internet Age violated the Commerce Clause, despite the 21st Amendment (which repealed Prohibition) which basically established that wine entering a state typically must be sold through a three-tier system of "producer to wholesaler to retailer" before reaching the consumer. If a state chooses to allow direct shipments of wine, then it must now do so on "evenhanded terms"—and the traditional wholesaler lost economic power again.

International price competition, courtesy of the Internet, is another litigious trend. For example, the Food and Drug Administration, citing safety concerns and regulatory violations, has sued U.S. companies that solicit drug prescriptions in the United States, then fax them to Canadian or other overseas suppliers, which then fill the orders and mail them back to their U.S. customers—at prices much lower than those available in the United States, owing to price regulations in effect overseas. These overseas Internet competitive developments will only increase over time, including the accompanying legal issues, battles, and legislative developments.

There's no question that the megasites and huge portals (such as AOL and Yahoo) dominate the Internet, and that the question of antitrust will rear its head even higher in the future. From AOL's acquisition of gigantic Time Warner to the Covisint cyberventure between the world's six largest car manufacturers and their suppliers, the Web trend continues toward greater concentrations of power.

With the increase in cyberlaw actions over time, the rise and accepted use of cybercourts will also become a reality, along with more jurisdictions and courts converting to public accessible, electronic record keeping and filing. The federal government has instituted a PACER (Public Access to Court Electronic Records) system, which is an electronic public access service that allows users to obtain case and docket information from Federal Appellate, District and Bankruptcy courts, including a U.S. Party/Case Index. Links to almost all of these courts are available by registering with PACER, the judiciary's centralized registration, and a relatively inexpensive fee is assessed for usage (see http://pacer.psc.uscourts.gov/ for more on this). States have also instituted their own digital-access court information systems and procedures, some more advanced than others, and check out yours with a search engine.

In this direction, Michigan became the first state to create a specific cybercourt (Mich. Pub. Acts, 2001). When funded and operational, the new cybercourt under this legislation could become a model for other states. This court would have concurrent jurisdiction over commercial litigation in disputes where the amount in controversy exceeds $25,000. All filings are to be made electronically, whereas all actions, depositions, and court appearances are by "electronic communications," such as streaming video, audio, and Internet conferencing; the intent is that there will be no paper transmitted or physical interface between judge, litigants, or witnesses. Appeals are to be made either to a new cybercourt of appeals or through a normal appellate court. See http://www.michigancybercourt.net for the details and background of this approach.

Internationally, countries from England and Australia to Singapore already are experimenting with cybercourt systems and procedures. The Singapore Supreme Court, for example, has established a successful Technology Court allowing video conferencing for pre-trial conferences, ex-parte applications, and other "noncontentious" applications, thus allowing lawyers to have their applications heard and decided by the court without the need to appear personally. Further, a digital filing service, service of process, notification system, and other electronic systems are in place, making this a model for the future (and see http://www.supcourt.gov.sg/ for more).

Regardless of the new Internet legal controversies that will rise up further in this new millennium, three realities exist: (a) The legal concepts already in place have proven to be quite adaptable to these challenges; (b) the concepts of fair play, common sense, and netiquette are filling in the gaps through court decisions and statutes; and (c) the use of ADRs on the Net will continue to grow over time because of the inappropriateness of litigation to solve the cyberdisputes among the citizens of the world.

The Internet has enhanced our lives and challenged our laws. The legal system is continuing to meet the challenge, including the impact of information security issues, but our world is never again going to be the same.

GLOSSARY

Anticybersquatting Consumer Protection Act (ACPA) A U.S. statute (15 U.S.C. 1125, 1999) that protects trademark or service mark holders (including the names of famous people) from those who register a mark's domain name or its equivalent with a bad faith intent to profit from that act (e.g., cyberpirates). It allows the trademark or service mark holder to sue for actual or statutory damages (when actual damages are difficult to prove) and force the domain name to be transferred back.

"Click" or "Clickwrap" Contracts An agreement whereby a party agrees to the terms and conditions of an online agreement by clicking on a space reading "I agree," or some wording to that effect, to indicate the requisite mutual assent to those conditions and understanding.

Communications Decency Act Section 230 of this act (47 U.S.C. 223, 1996) provides that an online service provider is not to be treated as a publisher for purposes of liability for defamatory postings by third parties, nor liable for defamation in such cases.

Cyberlaw The emerging body of law that governs cyberspace transactions and disputes, otherwise known as the "Law of the Internet."

Cyberpirates Persons or entities who register a domain name that is the valid trademark or service mark of another, intending to sell that registered domain name back to the legitimate mark holder at a profit. This term is similar to "cybersquatters" who register domain names ahead of such interest but wait (or "squat") on those names until offers to buy back those names are received from others.

Defamation A false statement made by some person or entity about another, either orally or in writing, that is published to a third party and wrongfully harms the injured party's reputation.

Digital Millennium Copyright Act (DMCA) The 1998 act that amended U.S. copyright law and included (a) a section prohibiting circumvention of encryption or security protections on copyrighted software to violate its copyright (17 U.S.C. 1201–1204) and (b) a section on online service provider liability (17 U.S.C. 512). The online provider provisions set down an administrative proceeding that is used to resolve copyright disputes over third-party postings with online servers and establishes a "safe harbor" liability protection for those providers.

Distributed Denial of Service (DDoS) Attack A simple denial of service ("DoS") attack typically involves one computer making repeated connection requests in trying to overpower the target system. In a DDoS attack the connection requests originate from a large number of computers, making it difficult to distinguish attacking traffic from legitimate ones. To launch a DDoS attack, a hacker accesses a computer system without authorization and inserts a software program that renders the system a "master," able to control other computer systems. The hacker places software code then on numbers of other computer systems, causing them to operate as "agents" or "zombies" of the master system. The master system instructs its zombies to produce a flood of simultaneous requests to connect to the target system, overwhelm its capabilities, and attempt to thwart legitimate connection requests.

Fair Use The U.S. Copyright Act provides that the "fair use" of copyrighted works involving purposes such as criticism, comment, news reporting, teaching, scholarship, or research is not copyright infringement. Thus, some copying or copyright use is legally permissible in the United States that ordinarily would not be allowable in other countries.

Intellectual Property Property that the mind creates from intellectual, creative processes, whether music, books, inventions, poetry, software, trademarks, domain names, or even trade secrets. Depending on the form of intellectual creation, such property is protectable by copyrights (i.e., music, software, or a Web site's "look and feel"), trademarks (i.e., distinctive marks, whether identifying products or service), patents (i.e., inventions and Internet business-procedures), and trade secrets (i.e., customer lists, Coca-Cola's formula, and so on).

Internet Corporation for Assigned Names and Numbers (ICANN) The nonprofit organization that oversees a wide range of Internet functions (once the responsibility of the U.S. government) and is now managed by an international board of directors. Among other functions, ICANN promulgates policy on the registration of domain names, accreditation of new registrars, and implementation of domain-name dispute resolution policies.

Jurisdiction The power of a court or governmental agency to hear a case and decide the rights of the people or entities that appear before it. This jurisdiction can be *in personam* (determining the rights of people or entities, wherever they reside) or *in rem* (determining the ownership rights to property that is located within the court's territorial limits, regardless of where the disputing parties reside).

Long-Arm Statute U.S. state statutes that authorize a local court to assert personal jurisdiction over a nonresident defendant located outside that state, given certain factual circumstances being present, such as causing injury within that state by an act that takes place within it (i.e., a car accident).

Netiquette An informal, essentially noncodified doctrine of "Web manners," courtesy, and cyberethics aimed at creating a system establishing what is or isn't acceptable conduct on the Net, regardless of what the law provides.

No Electronic Theft Act (NET)   A U.S. act (17 U.S.C. 506(a), 1997) that provides there is an illegal infringement when pirated copyrighted material has a value of $1,000 (a misdemeanor) or $2,500 (a felony), even though there is no monetary gain or economic incentive on the part of the infringer.

"Opt In" and "Opt Out"   The two distinct privacy policies used by Internet firms and Web sites, which may or may not be codified. With "opt-out" provisions, the user must take the affirmative step to say "no" or refuse permission to a Web site's collection and transmission of financial and other sensitive consumer information. With "opt-in" policies, the Web site must take the steps to gain the positive approval of a user before it can collect, transmit, or sell such private information. Marketing firms prefer "opt-out" policies or laws, because these are less marketing restrictive and put the burden on the user, not the site.

Prima Facie Evidence   Evidence presented that indicates a strong presumption the given fact or evidentiary assertion is factually true.

Service Mark   A word, name, logo, mark, device, or some combination used by any person or entity to identify and distinguish services performed by it from those of another (e.g., Priceline.com's name and logo).

"Shrink-wrap" Agreement   An agreement whereby a party agrees to the terms and conditions of the contract, the provisions contained inside the box in which the goods are packaged, by opening the wrapper, or plastic shrink-wrap, that encloses the entire package. The act of opening the plastic, or box, indicates the requisite mutual assent to those conditions and understanding.

Terms of Use   The legal provisions that govern anyone's use of a particular Web site, including purchasing its product or service, and typically include disclaimers of liability, indemnity, handling of disputes, applicable law, dispute resolution, copyright and trademark notices, linking conditions, among other areas. Terms of Use provisions generally are located at the bottom of the home page with an icon of the heading, "Legal Provisions," or some similar identification. They can also include privacy provisions, although these provisions are typically set out separately.

Tort   The breach of a legal duty to exercise reasonable care that proximately causes injury or damage to another. This is a civil wrong that does not arise from a breach of contract.

Trademark   A word, name, logo, mark, device, or some combination used by any person or entity to identify and distinguish its goods from those of another (e.g., McDonalds' golden arches or Nike's winged shoe).

U.S. Copyright Office   The U.S. agency that oversees the registration and regulation of copyrights (see http://www.loc.gov/copyright).

U.S. Patent and Trademark Office (PTO)   The U.S. agency that oversees the registration and regulation of patents and trademarks/service marks (see http://www.uspto.gov for further information).

World Intellectual Property Organization (WIPO)   The specialized United Nations agency and intergovernmental organization that is responsible for promulgating and administering major international intellectual property conventions.

CROSS REFERENCES

See *Copyright Law; Cyberterrorism and Information Security; Hackers, Crackers and Computer Criminals; Internet Censorship; Patent Law; Privacy Law and the Internet; Security Insurance and Best Practices; Trademark Law.*

REFERENCES

A&M Records, Inc. v. Napster, Inc., 239 F.3d 1004 (2001).

American Guarantee & Liability Insurance Co. v. Ingram Micro, Inc., 2000 U.S. Dist. Lexis 7299, D. Ariz. (2000).

Amsan LLC v. Prophet 21 Inc., No. 01-1950, 01-1954, (E.D. Pa.), U.S. Dist. LEXIS 16698 (2001).

Anticybersquatting Consumer Protection Act, 15 U.S.C. 1125(d) (1999).

Ashcroft v. American Civil Liberties Union, 535 U.S. 564 (2002).

Ashcroft v. American Civil Liberties Union, 322 F. 3d 240 (2003).

Ashcroft v. American Civil Liberties Union, 124 Sup. Ct. 2783 (2004).

Bally v. Faber, 29 F. Supp.2d 1161 (1998).

Bick, J. (2001). Securities law. Avoiding the violations risked by companies that use the Web to disseminate information. *The Internet Newsletter.* 6(7), 1.

Bick, J. (2003). Are you breaking the law? *The Internet Newsletter, 1*(6), 1.

Blakey v. Continental Airlines, 164 N.J. 38, 751 A.2d 538 (2000).

Brower v. Gateway 2000, Inc., 246 A.D.2d 246 (1998).

Buford, D. (2003). Cyberspace is being discovered, and employers may be footing the bill. *New York Employment Law Letter, 10*(7).

Cairo v. Crossmedia Services, 2005 WL 756610, 2005 U.S. Dist. LEXIS 8450 (N.D. Cal., April 1, 2005).

Calder v. Jones, 465 U.S. 783 (1984).

California Legislative Service, Ch. 915, S.B. 1386 (2002).

Children's Internet Protection Act, 20 U.S.C. 9101 (2000).

Children's Online Privacy Protection Act, 47 U.S.C. 231 (1998).

Crispi v. The Microsoft Network, L.L.C., 323 N.J. Super. 118 (N.J. App. Div., 1999).

Danish Newspaper Publishers Association v. Newsbooster.com, Bailiff's Court of Copenhagen, Denmark (July 5, 2002).

Deutsche Bank, In the Matter of, SEC No. 3-10957 (2002).

de Villiers, M. (2003). Virus Ex Machina: Res Ipsa Loquitur. *Stanford Technology Law Review,* (1).

de Villiers, M. (2004). Computer Viruses and Civil Liability: A Conceptual Framework. *Tort & Insurance Law Journal, 40*(123).

Dow Jones v. Gutnick, 2002 HCA 56 (2002).

DVD Copy Control Association, Inc. v. Bunner, 93 Ca. App. 4th 648 (6th Dist., 2001).

DVD Copy Control Association, Inc. v. Bunner, 75 P. 3d 1 (2003).

DVD Copy Control Association, Inc. v. Bunner, 116 Cal. App. 4th 241 (2004).

eBay v. Bidder's Edge, 100 F. Supp.2d 1058 (2000).

Eldredge v. Ashcroft, U.S. Sup. Ct. No. 01-618 (2003).

Electronic Signatures in Global and National Commerce Act, 15 U.S.C. 7001 (2000).

Federal Trademark Dilution Act, 15 U.S.C. 1125(c) (1995).

Ferrera, G., Lichtenstein, S., Reder, M., Bird, R., & Schiano, W. (2003). *Cyberlaw: Text and Cases* (2nd ed.). Cincinnati, OH: South-Western.

Financial Services Modernization Act, 15 U.S.C. 6801 (1999).

Ford Motor Co. v. Lane, E.D., Michigan, No. 99–74205 (1999).

Geoff v. AOL, Inc., No. PC 97–0331, R.I. Super. Ct. (1998).

Gold, J. (2002). Insurance coverage for Internet and computer related claims. *The Computer & Internet Lawyer*, *19*(4), 8.

Graham v. Oppenheimer, No. 3:00cv57, E.D. Va. (2000).

Granhold v. Heald, U.S. Sup. Ct. (Docket No. 03-1116, decided May 16, 2005).

Greenberg v. National Geographic Society, 244 F. 3d 1267 (2001).

Grynberg v. Agri Tech, Inc., 10 P.3d 1267 (2000).

Gus' Catering, Inc. v. Menusoft Systems, 762 A.2d 804 (2000).

Health Insurance Portability and Accountability Act, Pub. L. No. 104-191 (1996).

Homeland Security Act of 2002, U.S. Pub. L. Nos. 107-296, 116 Stat. 2135 (2002).

i.LAN Systems v. NetScout Service Level Corp., 183 F. Supp.2d 328 (2002).

International Shoe Company v. Washington State, 66 U.S. Sup. Ct. 154 (1945).

Jacobson, H., & Green, R. (2002). *Computer crimes. American Criminal Law Review*, *39*(273).

Lucker Manufacturing v. Home Insurance Co., 23 F.3d 808 (1994).

MGM Studios, Inc. v. Grokster, Ltd., 380 F. 3d 1154 (2004).

Mich. Pub. Acts 262 (2001).

Mortenson Co. Inc. v. Timberline Software Corp., 140 Wa.2d 568, 998 P.2d 305 (2000).

Moseley v. Secret Catalogue, Inc., 537 U.S. 418 (2003).

National Bellas Hess v. State of Illinois, 386 U.S. 753 (1976).

New York Times v. Tasini, 533 U.S. 483 (2001).

Panavision International, L.P. v. Toeppen, 141 F.3d 1316 (1998).

Pavlovich v. Superior Court (DVD Copy Control Association, real party in interest), 29 Ca. 4th 262 (2002).

Pinkney, K. R. (2002). Putting blame where blame is due: Software manufacturer and customer liability for security-related software failure. *Albany Law Journal of Science & Technology*, *13*(43).

Planned Parenthood v. American Coalition of Life Activists, 290 F.3d 1058 (2002).

ProCD, Inc. v. Zeidenberg, 86 F.3d 1447 (1996).

Radin, M. J. (2001). Distributed denial of service attacks: Who pays? (part I). *Cyberspace Lawyer*, *6*(no.9), 2.

Radin, M. J. (2002). Distributed denial of service attacks: Who pays? (part II). *Cyberspace Lawyer*, *6*(no.10), 2.

Recording Industry Association of America v. Verizon Internet Services, 240 F. Supp. 2d 24 (2003).

Recording Industry Association of America v. Verizon Internet Services, 351 F. 3d 1229 (2003).

Register.Com, Inc. v. Verio, 126 F. Supp.2nd 238 (2000).

Reno v. American Civil Liberties Union, 521 U.S. 844 (1997).

Robotic Vision Systems v. Cybo Systems, Inc., 17 F. Supp.2d 151 (1998).

Savetz, K. (2002, May 1). Lawsuits, downtime, data that has been stolen or destroyed—data insurance helps tech companies recoup unexpected losses. *New Architect*, p. 32.

Shetland Times v. Shetland News, Scottish Outer House, 1997 S.C. 604 (1996).

Sonny Bono Copyright Term Extension Act, 17 U.S.C. 101, 302-305 (Supp. 1999).

Specht v. Netscape Communications Corp., 306 F.3d 17 (2002).

Springfield Hydroelectric Company v. Copp, et al, 779 A.2d 67 (2001).

State Street Bank v. Signature Financial Group 149 F.3d 1368 (1998).

Universal City Studios v. Reimerdes, 82 F. Supp.2nd 211 (2000).

U.S. v. $734,578.82 in U.S. Currency, 286 F.3d 641 (2002).

United States, et al v. American Library Association, 123 S. Ct. 2297 (2003).

Uniting and Strengthening America by Providing Appropriate Tools Required to Intercept and Obstruct Terrorism Act of 2001, Pub. L. No. 107-56, 115 Stat. 272 (2001).

Washington Post Co., et al v. Total News, 97 Civ. 1190, S.D.N.Y. (1997).

WIPO Copyright Treaty, 36 I.L.M. WIPO Treaty, WIPO Doc. CRNR/DC/94 (1996).

Yahoo! v. La Ligue Contre le Racisme et L'Antisemitisme, 169 F. Supp.2nd 1181 (2001).

Yahoo! v. La Ligue Contre le Racisme et L'Antisemitisme, 379 F. 3d 1120 (2004).

Zippo Manufacturing Co. v. Zippo Dot Com, Inc., 952 F. Supp. 1122 (1997).

FURTHER READING

Ambrose, S. F., Jr., & Gelb, J. W. (2003). Consumer privacy regulation, enforcement, and litigation in the United States. *The Business Lawyer*, *58*, 1181.

American Civil Liberties Union et al. v. Ashcroft, 322 F. 3rd 240 (2003).

Ashcroft v. American Civil Liberties Union, 124 S. Ct. 399 (2003-1).

Bensusan Restaurant v. King, 937 F. Supp. 295 (1996).

Child Online Protection Act, Pub. L. No. 105-277, Title XIV (1998).

Consumer Sentinel, for the latest on primarily U.S. fraud protection and online complaint procedures: http://www.consumer.gov/sentinel

Controlling the Assault of Non-Solicited Pornography and Marketing Act of 2003 (CAN-SPAM Act), Senate No. 877 (passed November 25, 2003; signed into law, December 16, 2003).

Department of Commerce, for latest developments including EU "safe harbor" privacy guidelines: http://www.commerce.gov

Econsumer.gov, for data on international fraud protection and online complaint procedures: http://www.econsumer.gov/

For EU rights developments, including its copyright directive: http://eurorights.org

FTC site, for data on COPA, consumer protection, and latest developments in other areas: http://www.ftc.gov

ICANN, for information on its domain name dispute resolution process, registration, and accepted registrars: http://www.icann.org

International Money Laundering Abatement and Financial Anti-Terrorism Act, U.S. Pub. Laws No. 107–56, Title III (2001).

Kelly v. Arriba Soft Corp., 280 F.3d 934 (2002).

PACER, for information on Federal Appellate, District and Bankruptcy courts, including a U.S. Party/Case Index: http://pacer.psc.uscourts.gov/

Powers, D. M. (2002). *The internet legal guide: Everything you need to know when doing business online.* New York: Wiley.

Securities and Exchange Commission, for information on securities and investment fraud: http://www.sec.gov

Spamlaws.com, for the latest developments on anti-spam laws, both in the United States and globally: http://spamlaws.com

U.S. Copyright Office information, including DCMA and registration data: http://www.loc.gov/copyright/

U.S. Dept. of Justice, for overall and latest information on computer-related crimes: http://www.cybercrime.gov

U.S. Patent and Trademark Office, for information on trademarks, service marks, and patents: http://www.uspto.gov

Vir, Monica (2003). The Blame Game: Can Internet Service Providers Escape Liability for Semantic Attacks? *Rutgers Computer and Technology Law Journal,* 23(193).

Global Aspects of Cyberlaw

Julia Alpert Gladstone, *Bryant University*

INTRODUCTION

As we stand firmly in the 21st century, we can see that the Internet has transformed from a research network into a viable commercial marketplace. The legal framework of the Internet has also undergone significant changes from the time when John Perry Barlow declared:

> Governments of the Industrial World, you weary giants of flesh and steel, I come from Cyberspace, the new home of the Mind. On behalf of the future, I ask you of the past to leave us alone. You are not welcome among us. You have no sovereignty where we gather. (Barlow, 1996)

There has been much debate as to whether national laws should apply to cyberspace, or whether a different regulatory system that better accounts for the borderless nature of the medium should be implemented. It was initially argued by some that lack of geographical borders in cyberspace turned cyberspace into its own distinct sovereignty beyond the scope of territorial law (Johnson & Post, 1996). Although this viewpoint was not universally accepted, "the belief in the virtually insurmountable legal complications created by bordered laws mapped onto a borderless Internet became a truism amongst many observers" (Geist, 2003).

During the economic prosperity of the 1990s, the Clinton administration was happy to step aside and yield development of Internet policy largely to private sector and self-regulatory initiatives. A report that outlined this policy on the Internet was set out in the Framework for Global Electronic Commerce (1997). It emphasized private sector leadership and minimal government regulation. The European Declaration, issued within one month of the Framework, also noted the special cross border characteristics of the Internet and called for private sector dominance.

Today, spurred by business interests and as each nation seeks to protect its citizens and preserve its sovereignty, governments are taking more actions to establish the rules and regulations for cyberspace. This marks a shift in attitude and policy that can be attributed to the strengthening of national powers. This shift toward regulation through national laws has given rise to increased conflicts over which national law applies to a global Internet transaction, as well as the extent to which national laws can be applied extraterritorially.

This chapter reviews the major national and international laws in the areas of jurisdiction, privacy, electronic signatures, and encryption as well as copyrights and patents that presently affect cyberspace activity to suggest that there is an incongruence between nations in many areas. The author suggests that action be taken both in the private sector and by governments around the globe to synchronize laws in these areas. Certainty and consistency of laws are critical to the functioning of any society. The continued growth and development of the Internet will depend on whether a legal climate of predictability and reliability can be achieved.

This chapter begins by exploring the fundamental question of who, if anyone, has the legal authority to regulate the Internet. In the context of transnational law, this is, in essence, the issue of personal jurisdiction. The second section reviews the challenges that are often raised against a nation's exercise of power beyond its borders and moves on to review the current status of jurisdiction jurisprudence for cyberspace. Concern about the protection of personal information threatens the growth of commerce on the Internet. The third section, "Privacy," examines the national laws and international laws and treaties that loosely form a privacy policy in cyberspace. Commerce is the major growth area on the Internet that depends on reliable contracts. The use of encryption and digital signatures to ensure the enforceability of electronic contracts is discussed in the fourth section, "Encryption and Electronic Signatures," together with an analysis of the current global status of electronic signature legislation.

Our definitions and understanding of rights to ownership in intellectual property have been challenged in response to the movement of information onto the Internet, and nations have responded to these changes in various ways. The final section, "Intellectual Property," reviews the principal international and national rules in the areas of patent and copyright infringement as they have been influenced by and have responded to the activity in cyberspace. Trademark issues are not included because this is a matter that is closely tied to the issue of registration of domain names; this has developed into its own specialty with the development of the Internet Corporation for Assigned Names and Numbers (ICANN) and is best left for a separate chapter.

The lack of uniformity in approach to legislation in many substantive areas is evident from the analysis presented in this chapter, and I suggest that policymakers remove their national blinders in order to foster e-commerce.

JURISDICTION
Jurisdiction—An Overview

Legal certainty and predictability is an essential element for electronic commerce to evolve profitably and efficiently. Compliance with rules is impossible without an understanding of whose law is applicable and the corollary to this is where the legal dispute, if it were to arise, will be resolved (ABA Project, 2000). These are questions of personal and prescriptive jurisdiction, which a century and a half ago were resolved easily when most people lived and died in relatively small geographic areas and the law of that place applied. Under traditional legal systems, the sovereign power of the state, which legitimizes the enforcement of its laws, is based on territoriality. There is a general correspondence between physical borders and legal borders. National borders have formed the sovereignty paradigms for regulatory authority and decision making. When parties to the action lived and the activities in dispute occurred in a single state, that state's courts and laws were the only obvious and uncontested jurisdictional choice (Mody, 2001).

Generally speaking, a state can only enforce its laws against a defendant when there is a local presence or when there are assets within the local jurisdiction (ABA Project, 2000). The Internet's architecture allows information to flow without bounds, and therefore, the individual or organization supplying the information cannot control where that content will end up. There are no physical barriers or cues to notify the provider; therefore, an activity, which may be lawful in Belize, for example, may be easily accessed in New York where it is unlawful (Mody, 2001). Individual states invest time, money, and effort to protect the welfare of its citizens and, naturally, legislate

accordingly. There is an apparent conflict between a state's sovereign interest to protect its citizens and a foreign content provider's ability to carry on its lawful activity. The main criticism that transnational cyberspace breaks jurisdictional rules is based on the notion a state may not act beyond its own territorial borders.

Fundamental Jurisdictional Principles Under International Law

Jurisdiction can be broken down into two categories: prescriptive jurisdiction, which addresses the authority of a state to apply its own laws to regulate conduct, and enforcement jurisdiction, which is the executive's authority to compel compliance with these laws. The focus of this chapter is on prescriptive jurisdiction, although issues of enforcement jurisdiction are raised in the discussion of *Yahoo! Inc., v. La Ligue Contre le Racisme et l' Antisemitisme* (2001).

The threshold matter of "jurisdiction to prescribe" means that the substantive laws of the forum country are applicable to the particular persons and circumstances (Restatement[3rd] of the Foreign Relations Law of the U.S. sections, 300–450). When a country has jurisdiction to prescribe, it can appropriately apply its legal norms to conduct. Simply stated, a country has jurisdiction to prescribe law with respect to (a) conduct that, wholly or in substantial part, takes place within its territory; (b) the status of persons, or interests in things, present within its territory; (c) conduct outside its territory that has or is intended to have substantial effect within its territory; (d) the activities, interests, status, or relations of its nationals outside as well as within its territory; and (e) certain conduct outside its territory by persons who are not its nationals that is directed against the security of the country or against a limited class of other national interests (RESTATEMENT[3rd] OF THE FOREIGN RELATIONS LAW OF THE U.S. sections, 300–450).

Jurisdiction to adjudicate or to enforce means that the tribunals of a given country may resolve a dispute to enforce a judgment where the country has jurisdiction to prescribe the law. The exercise by a country of jurisdiction to enforce is subject to the requirement of reasonableness. States exercise jurisdiction to adjudicate on the basis of various links, including the defendant's presence, conduct, or, in some cases, ownership of property within the country. Exercise of judicial jurisdiction on the basis of such links is on the whole accepted as "reasonable"; reliance on other bases, such as the nationality of the plaintiff or the presence of property unrelated to the claim, is generally considered "exorbitant" (RESTATEMENT[3rd] OF THE FOREIGN RELATIONS LAW OF THE U.S. sections, 300–450).

Although historically a sovereign's power was tied to its geography, a state's power to regulate activity that originates outside the country but causes local harms has been recognized for many years. One of the first cases to recognize that a state's regulatory authority may extend to an extraterritorial activity was decided in the Permanent Court of International Justice (PCIJ) in 1927. *In the Case of S.S. Lotus* (1927), the court held that the state of Turkey could apply its criminal law to a foreigner who acted outside of Turkey when committing the offense so charged and that prejudiced Turkey and its citizens, provided the foreigner was arrested in Turkey. This was an application of the law to a person or act outside the territory of Turkey, which had a local effect. This early case applied the "effects principle" to expand the authority of a state. This is a logical extension of control by a state outside of its territory to protect its citizens from actions taken by a defendant, which had an "effect" or impact within the state. A state's territorial borders were no longer the sole determination of rule making authority.

In the more famous case of the *United States v. Aluminum Company of America* (ALCOA), (1945), the U.S. Second Circuit Court of Appeals considered whether the United States could apply the antitrust provisions of the Sherman Act to a Canadian company. The anticompetitive acts took place in Canada, but the material effects were experienced in the United States; the court ultimately did apply U.S. rules to this Canadian company. Thus, with the ALCOA case, the presumption of extra territoriality had been overcome.

Classic U.S. Jurisdiction Principles

In the United States, assertion of jurisdiction over the person must satisfy the standard of constitutional due process. States enact long-arm statutes to exercise jurisdiction legitimately over nonresidents. Initially to establish personal jurisdiction over a defendant, a U.S. court will apply the relevant long-arm statute to see whether it permits the exercise of personal jurisdiction. Second, the court will apply the precepts of the Due Process Clause. A standard inquiry for whether due process has been satisfied focuses on whether the defendant has "minimal contacts" within the forum such that assertion of jurisdiction does not offend the "traditional notions of fair play and substantial justice" (*World-Wide Volkswagen Corp. v. Woodson*, 1980).

Under the Due Process Clause of the Constitution, one must look at the relationship between "the defendant, the forum and the litigation" (Aciman & VoVerde, 2002). Physical presence is not required, rather the plaintiff must show that the defendant has purposefully directed its activities toward the forum state, or otherwise "purposefully availed itself of the privilege of conducting activities within the forum State, thus invoking the benefit and protection of its laws" (*Hanson v. Denckla*, 1958).

Questions of jurisdiction in cyberspace have generated lengthy court decisions and caused much global debate because of the unique nature of Internet information dissemination. The current global jurisdictional case law though voluminous and inconsistent suggests that two principal tests are being used to ascertain jurisdiction (Rice and Gladstone, 2002). One is the "*Zippo* test" which is named after the case that first articulated it, *Zippo Manufacturing Co. v. Zippo Dot Com, Inc.* (1997), and the other is the "effects test," which is based on a standard developed from a U.S. Supreme Court case that arose in the context of print media, *Calder v. Jones* (1984).

The "*Zippo* test" establishes jurisdiction over a nonresident defendant based on the degree of interactivity between the Web site and the forum. Mere access to the non-resident's Web site is the least interactive; under the "*Zippo* test" a passive Web site is not sufficient to establish specific jurisdiction. District Judge McLaughlin explained that whether jurisdiction could be properly asserted in a case was to be based on the nature and quality of the commercial activity that an entity conducts over the Internet. Jurisdiction cases fall somewhere on a sliding scale or spectrum on which the likelihood that personal jurisdiction can be constitutionally exercised is directly proportionate to the nature and quality of the commercial activity that an entity conducts over the Internet.

The primary difficulty that arises in applying the *Zippo* sliding-scale standard to jurisdiction cases in cyberspace has been in determining the degree of "interactivity." Similar fact patterns have lead to different jurisdictional findings in different courts. In addition, whether a Web site has been integral in a forum often turns more on a court's perception than on real differences in the manner in which the user employs the Internet. For example, a judge in the Southern District of New York in 2000 found that the mere availability of the defendant's Web site in New York made it "intuitively apparent" that defendant's services were used by New York residents (*Cable News Network, L.P. v. GoSMS.com, Inc.*, 2000). The judge therefore found grounds for jurisdiction even though he acknowledged that plaintiff's allegations that defendants' mobile telephone and two-way e-mail services allegedly used in New York were "factually unsupported."

Jurisdiction Based on "Effects"

The first instance when "purposeful direction" arose was in the context of traditional media, and it has become the basis for all U.S. cases applying the "effects test." In *Calder v. Jones* (1984), Florida residents who had essentially no physical contacts with California wrote and edited an article in the *National Enquirer* that defamed Shirley Jones, a well-known movie actress residing in California. The *Enquirer* had greater circulation in California than in any other state, and the material was based on California sources. The U.S. Supreme Court found jurisdiction, holding that California was the focal point both of the story and the harm suffered. The Court held that the defendants' acts were intentional, that they were aimed at California, and that its effects took place in California.

The first use of the "effects test" in asserting jurisdiction against a defendant in an Internet context was the cybersquatting case of in *Panavision Int'l. L.P v. Toeppen* (1998). Toeppen, an Illinois defendant, had intentionally registered the California plaintiff's trademark as his domain name, namely Panavision. When attorneys for Panavision contacted Toeppen to demand that he stop using the name, he responded by offering to sell the name for $13,000 and promising not to acquire any other similar names. Unwilling to be bribed, Panavision sued Toeppen in California District Court where Toeppen objected on jurisdictional grounds. The court found jurisdiction appropriate under the "effects" test because the defendant had intentionally directed its conduct toward California knowing the effect of his registering the domain name would be felt in California. The Ninth Circuit agreed, analogizing cybersquatting to an intentional tort and found that "the brunt of the harm to Panavision was felt in California."

In a recent Australian libel case, the "effects" test was applied to assert jurisdiction to protect a Melbourne citizen. The Victorian Supreme Court found jurisdiction over Dow Jones, a United States company, based on its *Wall Street Journal* Web site, which carried an allegedly libelous article about Joseph Gutnick, an American businessman who lived in Melbourne, Australia. The Australian Court found the publication occurred and thus had its impact whenever the article was downloaded, thereby dismissing Dow Jones' argument that the court lacked jurisdiction because the information was not published in Australia. Again, the impact and effect was felt in Australia (*Gutnick v. Dow Jones*, 2001) VSC 305.

Several leading cyberspace commentators have suggested that the effects test is a more useful mechanism than the *Zippo* test for establishing jurisdiction in Internet cases. In fact, the effects test has been refined into two parts: a "Strict Effects" test, which looks to the intent of defendant acting outside the jurisdiction to establish a connection and a looser, and a "Soft Effects" test, which focuses more simply on the impact within the jurisdiction (Rice & Gladstone, 2002). The former has been employed mostly in tort and intellectual property cases. Indeed, cases of defamation lend themselves easily to finding jurisdiction under the Strict Effects test because intent to harm is an essential element of the underlying cause of action. At the present time, it is likely that a court dealing with the issue of jurisdiction over a nonresident based on his or her online activity will start its inquiry by using *Zippo* but continue the analysis by applying the effects test. Therefore, attorneys who advocate jurisdiction in a particular forum would be best advised to consider both tests because the effects test may apply where the *Zippo* test does not.

Fundamental Principles of Jurisdiction Under European Law

In the European Union (EU), the primary source of law on jurisdiction, recognition and enforcement of judgments law has been the Convention on Jurisdiction and the Enforcement of Judgments in Civil and Commercial Matters September 30, 1968 (the Brussels Convention). Under the Brussels Convention, jurisdiction is based on the defendant's domicile, Art.2. Alternative jurisdictional grounds are available so long as there is a close link between the court and the action or if the "sound administration of justice" would be facilitated. In contract matters the place of performance would govern the jurisdiction decision (Art.5.1), although there are special provisions for consumer contracts. In tort matters, jurisdiction would lie in the place where the harmful event occurred (Art.5.3).

The Brussels Convention was modified effective March 2002 as the EU issued the so-called Brussels Regulation (2000). In contrast to a convention or directive, a "regulation" of the EU becomes binding immediately after its adoption upon the 15 member states without the need for further implementation. The economic drive of electronic commerce created the need for certainty and uniformity of jurisdictional rules early on; therefore, the EU found it efficient to proceed quickly with a mere regulation.

Although the Brussels Regulation does not alter the main structure of the Brussels Convention, it effectuates certain changes that are to take account of the new technological developments that result from e-commerce. Most importantly, the Brussels Regulation is consumer-centered, establishing that the courts of the consumer's domicile will have jurisdiction over a foreign defendant if the latter "pursues commercial or professional activities in the Member State of the consumer's domicile or, *by any means*, directs such activities to that Member state … and the contract falls within the scope of such activities." This language expands the range of situations in which the consumer can sue in his or her place of domicile.

The phrase "by any means" was included to broaden the scope of jurisdiction to reach Internet-based transactions (European Commission, 1999). The Brussels Regulation equates doing business or the offer of goods and services via the Internet with an invitation or advertising by businesses which by any means directs its activities toward that member state. In essence, the Brussels Regulation provides that an unintended effect in a member state can be the basis for jurisdiction. Because jurisdiction in European countries is not limited by U.S. Constitutional principles of due process as it is in the United States, the Brussels Regulation does not require notice or "minimum contacts."

The Brussels Regulation was controversial; the negotiations reflected the tension between business and consumer groups. Industry groups claimed it would hinder the growth of e-commerce by making small to medium-size businesses reluctant to set up Web sites for fear of being subjected to the jurisdiction of the courts of too many countries. Alternatively, the EU Commission believed that without strong consumer protection the negative impact on consumer confidence would hurt the unified European market (European Commission, 2000). If, as a result of consumer's reluctance to venture into the World Wide Web to shop, they were to stay within their own country, the commission believed the EU e-commerce sector would be put at a significant competitive disadvantage to the United States; this is based on the belief that the United States has stronger consumer protection laws.

The EU Parliament has also passed its Electronic Commerce Directive, which provides a more restrictive jurisdictional doctrine to legal disputes, restricting plaintiffs to a "country of origin" approach, Art.3. Under the Electronic Commerce Directive "the law of the country of origin (which is the seller's place of business) would govern the cross-border disputes." Although this may provide more certainty to businesses, it provides consumers with much less confidence in their business dealings (Boam, 2001). There are several exclusions from the Electronic Commerce Directive, including "contractual obligations concerning consumer contracts." It is therefore uncertain how these exclusions will work together with the Brussels Convention as amended and will require case-by-case examination of jurisdictional issues in the short run.

Enforcement Jurisdiction and the Yahoo! Case

The recent French lawsuit by the International League Against Racism and Anti-Semitism and the Union of

French Law Students against Yahoo! (the Yahoo! Case), which received so much attention in the popular press, summarizes many of the fundamental principles and issues that remain to be resolved in the area of international jurisdiction. In April 2000, two French groups, the Union of French Law Students and the International League Against Racism and Anti-Semitism, filed suit against Yahoo! for hosting auctions that displayed and sold Nazi propaganda. The memorabilia auctions were accessible only via the English-language site, Yahoo.com. Direct access through Yahoo.fr was not possible. Yahoo! argued in French court that the court did not have jurisdiction over Yahoo! That plea was denied, and in November 2000, a French court ruled that Yahoo! must put filtering systems in place to block users in France from access to Nazi-related goods or pay fines of approximately $13,000 per day (Rice, 2002). Only a watered-down version of the soft effects test could be seen to apply to the French court's decision in this case, and because Yahoo! was not targeting France, which is a key element in the effects test, the assertion of jurisdiction arguably violates the due process requirement of U.S. law (Rice & Gladstone, 2002).

Yahoo! chose not to appeal the French court's judgment but rather challenged the enforcement of the order in the United States. In December 2000, Yahoo! filed a lawsuit in the U.S. District Court of Northern California, seeking a declaratory judgment that any final judgment of a French court would not be enforceable in the United States. Before the California court could address the merits of the case, in a bit of an ironic twist, the French defendants motioned the California court to dismiss the declaratory judgment suit due to lack of jurisdiction. The U.S. court denied the motion to dismiss, finding jurisdiction based on the effects theory. The court ruled that the defendant knowingly engaged in the activities and intended to have an effect on the United States citizens, for example, the use of U.S. marshals to serve Yahoo! officers in California. Clearly, the French citizens purposely availed themselves of the benefits of the United States.

A state can only enforce its laws against a defendant in a forum where the defendant can be found or where there are assets belonging to the defendant. Enforcement of a judgment rendered by another forum, however, requires its recognition by another court to enforce it. If it is the judgment of a court in a state in the United States, the Full Faith and Credit Clause of the Constitution requires that it be recognized by another state. When recognition of a judgment of a foreign court is sought in the United States, it depends on the principle of "comity" (ABA Project, 2000). Comity is not a matter of absolute obligation, but it is the recognition that one nation allows within its territory to the legislative, executive, or judicial acts of another nation (ABA Project, 2000). National procedures required for recognition and enforcement of judgments vary widely around the globe. In the United States, comity is generally upheld unless to do so would violate due process, personal jurisdiction, or some public policy.

To determine the enforcement jurisdiction of the French court over Yahoo!, the Federal District Court for the Northern District of California found the issue to be whether it was consistent with the Constitution and the Laws of the United States for another nation, namely France, through their court order, to curtail the Yahoo! Web site. The French therefore would be regulating speech by U.S. residents within the United States on the basis that such speech could be accessed by Internet users in France. The court was mindful of the extent to which the United States is governed by the "comity of nations" but did not believe that comity was a matter of absolute obligation. The court decided the case in accordance with the Constitution, finding that the French order violated the U.S. Constitution, thereby recognizing that it was necessarily adopting the position that "certain judgments embedded within this enactment including the fundamental judgment expressed in the First Amendment that it is preferable to permit non-violent expression of offense viewpoints then to impose viewpoint based government regulation upon speech."

The court rendered judgment in favor of Yahoo! in a summary judgment motion that they requested on the declaratory judgment action to find the French order in violation of the First Amendment. This finding of a threat to constitutional rights by the court was the grounds by which it effectively rendered the order unenforceable and demonstrates the limits of perspective jurisdiction. This case suggests the disharmony that continues to exist among nations on questions of jurisdiction.

It appears that courts and legislatures have found legitimate grounds for asserting prescriptive jurisdiction over defendants based on actions taken in cyberspace, but that may have little importance when the plaintiff seeks a restorative remedy. Enforcement jurisdiction, which requires the injured party to attach either the defendant or his or her tangible assets, becomes an issue of comity or state's recognition of its obligation to enforce a law. Questions of comity have not been resolved sufficiently to ensure smooth enforcement on the Internet. Policymakers and governments will need to address this higher level of enforcement jurisdiction to foster predictability and certainty necessary for the growth of commerce on the Internet.

PRIVACY

Society has not previously experienced the technological efficiencies that characterize the Internet—namely, transparent dissemination, collection, and aggregation of information. Although the facility of data collection has economic benefits, it compromises the individual's right to privacy. The Internet is the largest electronic infrastructure that allows public access to a nearly infinite resource of information, and as such it holds the current greatest threat to personal privacy. In recent years, many sectors of the global community have been directing time and resources to resolve the inherent tension that has developed between seeking the economic benefits from modern data collection practices and ensuring human dignity that is threatened by modern surveillance (Gladstone, 2000b).

The mechanisms used to protect that information fall into three categories: self-regulatory, statutory, and technology approaches. The self-regulatory or market-dominated approach, which is adopted in the United States, is based on industry-developed norms, policies, and contracts, rather than statutory legal rights to protect the privacy interests of its citizens. The statutory or rights-dominated approach, which is developed in the

European models and recently adopted in Asia, New Zealand, and India, relies on statutory and common laws to establish rights to information privacy (Reidenberg, 2000). Technology is used globally in varying degrees in different sectors. Data flows on the Internet are international, and these divergent data protection policies and rules confront each other with increased frequency. Attempts at harmonization have been enacted , most notably the International Safe Harbor Privacy Principles (1999), which were adopted to implement the EU Privacy Directive, but further work toward uniformity is needed.

This section begins with a description of two examples of how one's privacy is threatened on the Internet. The first example reviews data collection practices that threaten consumer privacy and is followed by a review of the laws in the United States that have been passed to prevent inadvertent exposure to pornography on the Internet. The section continues by exploring the differences that underlie the United States' versus the other nations' approaches to privacy, which suggests reasons for difficulties in finding a common ground. The *EU Privacy Directive—Explained* discusses the background and scope of the Council Directive 95/45/EC (EU Privacy Directive, 1995), including a discussion of the strategies for U.S. compliance, namely, the Safe Harbor rules, the Model Contract Terms, and derogations or exceptions allowed under national law.

The technology that drives the Internet is based on an open architecture, which has a natural default to expose information about people's actions on the Internet, whether it be the World Wide Web or e-mail. Several surveillance initiatives or technologies by the U.S. government have drawn on this open architecture to retrieve personal information about citizens. After the September 11, 2001, terrorist attacks in the United States, threats of terrorism have lead the U.S. government to increase surveillance of foreigners as well as its own citizens. The passage of the USA PATRIOT Act (2001) and the Total Information Awareness Act (2003) have broadened the powers of the United States to investigate into the lives of individuals beyond the limits guaranteed by the U.S. Constitution. The expansion of privacy intrusion is developing at the same time that European initiatives to increase privacy rights and domestic proprietors who are looking to sell protective schemes are announcing the harms caused by privacy intrusions.

Threats to Privacy Posed by the Internet

The expansion of digital computers and networking technology, with the Internet being the most prime example, has moved much of our social, educational, and commercial activities into an electronic environment. The technology that has enabled integrated global networks facilitates the creation of digital records of what an individual has spent time looking at, the time spent at a particular site, messages sent, and purchases made. This "electronic footprint" is created through a variety of processes that can be generated by simple browsing the Web (Piera, 2001). Activity of the user within the Web site provides "click stream data," which includes the time spent on each page and the information that has been retrieved. Technology is available that can collect and organize all this information

into data packets; these are referred to as *cookies* and are stored on the user's hard drive. A cookie is assigned a unique identifying code, and each time the user goes back to the Web site, the cookie is retrieved, which then tailors the second visit according to the previous behavior at the Web site. This invisible data collection is primarily conducted by business. The warehousing of transaction information and profiling of online users has become a critical component for e-commerce business models. The behavioral information enables sites to characterize users and offer them content of personal interest. Internet revenue is generated through target advertising that has become especially efficient as a consequence of the design of technological infrastructures that enable the global network.

This economic efficiency comes at the cost of lost privacy to the consumer. Studies indicate that Internet users choose not to make an online purchase due to privacy interest issues. In fact, some argue that consumers have lost total control over their personal privacy choices.

Inadvertent exposure to online pornography presents another example of how privacy is threatened by the borderless and anonymous world of cyberspace. Internet pornography is big business comprising 11% of the entire $9 billion e-commerce sector in 1998, with industry experts projecting that e-porn will generate more than $3 billion by 2003 (Alexander, 2002).

Many of the sites are free and serve as teasers to lure people into commercial sites; consequently children and adults alike may enter a pornographic Web site inadvertently. Such accidental exposure is common particularly because Web site addresses are often misspellings of desired Web sites. In addition, the open architecture of the Internet where all material is equally accessible means that sex-related materials are not segregated on the Internet as they may be in the material world. This exposure violates one's right to be left alone. Sexually explicit materials on the Internet range from the commonplace pornographic still frame to live broadcasts of couples losing their virginity.

The general public in the United States has voiced a desire to restrict the dissemination of pornography on the Internet, and Congress has responded with at least three major legislative reforms. Congress' top-down attempts to regulate have not been successful because in each instance a federal court has invalidated the statute based on constitutional grounds.

The first and most significant act that Congress passed to eradicate online pornography was the Communications Decency Act (CDA), which covered a wide variety of activity. The operative provisions found in Section 502(a) prohibited the "knowing transmission of obscene or indecent messages to any recipient under 18 years of age" and criminalized the "knowing, sending or displaying of patently offensive messages in a manner that is available to a person under 18 years of age." In *ACLU v. Reno* (1997), in upholding the decision of the three-judge panel the Supreme Court found that provisions of the CDA were impermissible content-based restrictions on speech. In addition, the Court found that the language was facially overbroad and vague, which would create an unacceptable chilling effect on the speech of adults using the Internet.

The subsequent two laws that Congress passed were more specifically directed toward children. The Child Online Protection Act (COPA) followed the tone of the CDA by criminalizing Web publishers who used the World Wide Web to make harmful material available to minors. COPA provided broad affirmative defenses if a Web publisher had restricted access to minors with the use of credit cards or other age verifying technology. COPA was found to be unconstitutional because of the impermissible burden placed on protected adult speech. The District Court found that COPA was neither narrowly tailored nor were the least restrictive means used to protect children from harmful materials. Finally, the Children's Internet Protection Act (CIPA) required that all public schools and libraries with Internet access install filtering software to block access to sexually explicit Web sites. A U.S. district court in Philadelphia found the CIPA unconstitutional because the filtering software would "block access to a substantial amount of speech that was both constitutionally protected and fails to meet even the filtering companies' own blocking criteria."

As of the time of this writing, the regulation of Internet pornography continues to present a challenge to Congress that remains unresolved. Access to the Internet, which is truly a unique marketplace of ideas, presents tensions among several fundamental rights. Our freedom of expression must be protected while at the same time one's right to be left alone or one's right to privacy must also be respected. To balance the right of privacy against other rights or practices such as data collection, one must first examine the much more important question: What is the value of the right to privacy?

Views of Privacy

In the United States, the government has taken a restrained approach to protecting personal privacy, in contrast to the governments of many other nations. Since the American Revolution, many Americans have tended to fear a strong government. The U.S. Constitution gives the federal government only certain enumerated powers, leaving all others to the states. The first ten Amendments to the Constitution (the Bill of Rights) assure Americans additional freedoms, which most covet. The protection of privacy is not a fundamental right stated in the U.S. Constitution because it can impose restrictions on other fundamental rights. The First Amendment free speech guarantee limits government regulation of the flow of information including personal data. In nearly every country within the EU, the privacy right is expressly granted in the Constitution. In the entire history of the United States, the position of chief counselor for privacy was created for only 2 years, whereas in Europe there are entire parliamentary departments and "privacy czars" devoted to data protection and privacy concerns. The American reluctance to grant power to the government in this area is also reinforced by the country's laissez-faire market economy.

It would be inaccurate, however, to suggest that Americans desire privacy less than other members of the global community; rather they have a holistic view of their rights. This can be evidenced by the language used in the United State to describe data privacy. Americans use the term *privacy* by which they can refer to the right to be free from the gaze of a peeping Tom or the right not to disclose one's name on a website. Europeans use the term *data protection*, which very specifically addresses information generated by an individual's overt activity.

Despite these different privacy orientations, a major international accord that addressed personal data protection, the Organisation for Economic Cooperation and Development (OECD; 1980) Privacy Guidelines of 1980 (the OECD Privacy Guidelines) was adopted in 1980. The OECD Privacy Guidelines have been adopted by all 25 member nations, and although they are not binding, they serve as suggestions for member countries and others in developing their domestic legislation. The OECD Privacy Guidelines established eight basic principles that govern the handling of personal information, referred to as *fair information principles*. They are collection limitation, data quality, purpose, specification, use limitation, security safeguards, openness, individual participation, and accountability. These are internationally accepted principles that pertain to all types of data processing by both the public and the private sector. Application of the OECD Privacy Guidelines is based on a loose reciprocity model of enforcement whereby personal data can flow freely between countries that provide equivalent protection.

EU Privacy Directive—Explained

The most recently enacted and extensive statement of information privacy principles is the EU Privacy Directive. The EU Privacy Directive is a full-fledged system for the protection of personal data that requires the establishment of rights for data subjects and obligations for those who process personal data. It also provides monitoring by an independent body and sets out sanctions for offenders. The goal of the EU Privacy Directive is to increase the free flow of information, and it is designed to allow personal data to be sent or processed on the same terms within the EU and throughout the world. More than 15 member countries have passed their legislation to implement the EU Privacy Directive, and to date only France has not passed such laws. The EU Privacy Directive is broken into seven chapters that contain a total of 32 articles. The following overview of key provisions of the EU Privacy Directive illustrates the intensive focus on information privacy taken by the member states, which reflects a greater concern for data protection than typically found under U.S. law.

Article 2 of the EU Privacy Directive contains the operative definitions of the EU Privacy Directive, which include *personal data, processing of personal data, personal data filing system, controller, processor, third party,* and *recipient*. The EU Privacy Directives employs the terms *controller* and *data subject*, which creates a top-down assumption of computer networks, not necessarily personal or individual use of computers. These assumptions are less applicable or useful in a world of personal computers where people are browsing on the Internet.

Articles 6 and 7 of the EU Privacy Directive provide the general rules on the lawfulness of the processing of personal data. Article 6 establishes data quality principles by requiring that personal data must be processed fairly and lawfully and that such data be accurate, kept up to date, and kept in a form that permits identification of data subjects for no longer than necessary. Lawful and fair processing is further defined by requiring that the data be collected for explicit, legitimate purposes. In addition, there can be no "secondary use" or "sharing" of data. Affiliate sharing or secondary use of personal data is allowed in the United States under the Financial Services Modernization Act of 1999, the U.S. law that provides the most comprehensive privacy protections for consumers to date (Gladstone, 2000b). Once again, this highlights the differences in privacy policies between the United States and Europe.

There are provisions in the EU Privacy Directive that allow data processing if the data subject "unambiguously gives consent." A data subject can give his consent either by "opting in" or "opting out." A data processor may disclose on its Web site that personal data disclosed by the consumer may be further distributed for purposes of research or marketing. The Web site may offer the viewer to choose not to allow the Web site to engage in this practice; this is opting out. It is unclear whether opting out satisfies the criteria of "unambiguously giving consent" or whether only an opting-in alternative whereby the Web site disseminates the data only if the viewer clicks "yes" to such a practice is sufficient (Gladstone, 2000b).

Article 7 also allows the processing of data that is needed to execute a task carried out in the public interest or for the exercise of the official authority vested in the controller. As in Article 3, the focus of the EU Privacy Directive is to protect data from abuse by private hands; the EU Privacy Directive deference to the government or an official authority is unlike the American approach, which seeks to minimize government involvement.

Articles 25 and 26 govern the transfer of personal data outside the EU to third countries such as the United States. The EU Privacy Directive bars the export of European personal data to countries that do not have "adequate" personal data protection regimes. The EU Privacy Directive sets out specific derogations whereby personal data may be exported despite adequate protection. These exemptions include where there has been consent by the subject, if it is necessary to the completion of a contract, or if it is in the public interest or for the vital interest of the subject. Information on the Internet crosses geographic and political borders on a continuous basis, and therefore all countries connected to the Internet are subject to the extraterritorial application of the EU Privacy Directive. Many U.S. companies have been concerned about the impact of the directive's "adequacy standards" on their privacy policies and practices.

Safe Harbor Compliance

The initial response of the United States to comply with the adequacy standards of the EU Privacy Directive resulted in the establishment of the International Safe Harbor Principles. After protracted negotiations, the United States government and the European Commission jointly agreed to principles to satisfy the "adequacy standards" of the EU Privacy Directive. Organizations that seek to benefit from the Safe Harbor Principles must self-certify

their compliance with the U.S. Department of Commerce, thereby agreeing to terms of data handling practices, compliance, and dispute settlement. The Safe Harbor mechanism allows voluntary commitment by U.S. companies, which builds on the United States-self regulatory approach to privacy. In 2003, there were 300 U.S. firms that had agreed to join the Safe Harbor program.

The Safe Harbor principles comprise two documents, list of seven "critical" elements dealing with data processing and a list several frequently asked questions (FAQs). Organizations may choose to adhere precisely to the specific provisions of the Safe Harbor Principles to obtain the benefits of the Safe Harbor and publicly declare that they do so. Alternatively, organizations may develop their own self-regulatory privacy program provided it conforms to the Safe Harbor Principles or join a self-regulatory privacy program that adheres to the Safe Harbor Principles. Organizations that have agreed to comply with the Safe Harbor principles are subject to Section 5 "unfair and deceptive" practices of the Federal Trade Commission Act or air carriers are subject to the equivalent statute of the Department of Transportation. There are several industries such as the telecommunications and financial services industries that are not eligible for the Safe Harbor or whose business practices are incompatible with the provisions.

The seven critical elements of the Safe Harbor are notice, choice, onward transfer, security, data integrity, access, and enforcement. At least five of the critical elements directly address the provisions in Articles 2 through 14 of the EU Privacy Directive. From the perspective of ensuring the same high level of privacy protection as the EU Privacy Directive, the Safe Harbor principles appear to fall short in several areas, which again reflects the trade-off between privacy and other fundamental rights in the United States. Under the Safe Harbor criteria of providing notice, individuals must be informed in clear and conspicuous language: (a) the purpose for which an organization collects and uses information, (b) the types of third parties to which an organization discloses the information; and (c) how to make inquiries or complaints. This Safe Harbor requirement follows the requirements of Articles 10 and 11 of the EU Privacy Directive, but Articles 10 and 11 require information be given to the subjects *before* the collection of personal information. The Safe Harbor notice requirement provides more leeway because such notice may be given before personal information is received or "as soon thereafter as practical." This delayed notice was undoubtedly fashioned to encourage easy compliance with the EU Privacy Directive, but abuse of this option could effectively negate one of the key privacy protection mechanisms of the EU Privacy Directive. If an organization finds that prior notice is too costly, under Safe Harbor Principles it may routinely opt for giving notice after the fact. In addition, the Safe Harbor notice requirement does not require that data subjects be explicitly informed of their right of access to personal data (Gladstone, 2000). This is another disparity with the EU Privacy Directive, and it diminishes the underlying goals of the EU Privacy Directive.

Article 14 of the directive grants the data subject rights to object to the processing of data that the controller anticipates as being processed for direct marketing and is incompatible with the purpose for which it was collected. The Safe Harbor gives individuals the opportunity to choose, opt out, in deciding whether and how personal information will be disclosed to third parties for a purpose other than that for which it was originally collected. Under EU Privacy Directive, the data subject must be given the opportunity to object before the data is disclosed for the first time to a third party. The Safe Harbor opt-out "choice falls short of the prior choice requirements in Article 14 of the EU Privacy Directive (Gladstone, 2000b). Article 6 of the EU Privacy Directive sets out the principle of the quality of the data, which may be collected and prohibits further processing of that personal data in a way that is incompatible with "legitimate purpose for which it was collected." The parallel provision of Safe Harbor Principles, titled "Data Integrity," once again allows an organization more freedom in collecting and maintaining data because an organization is not prohibited from further processing data as long as it takes "reasonable steps to ensure the data is accurate, complete and current."

Article 25 of the EU Privacy Directive prohibits the transfer of personal data to a third country that lacks an adequate level of protection, and Article 26 offers certain limited exceptions to this prohibition. The onward transfer provision of the Safe Harbor requires that disclosure of personal information to a third party be consistent with the principles of notice and choice; an organization is liable if it knows or has reason to know that a third party will process the information improperly. Under the Safe Harbor Principles, however, an organization is in compliance when transferring data to a third party, even if the third party does not subscribe to the Safe Harbor Principles or the EU Privacy Directive, as long as that third party signs an agreement to protect the data. This flexibility could easily create of a data haven and effectively subvert the EU Privacy Directive even if one were to comply with the Safe Harbor, thereby essentially frustrating the purpose of the EU Privacy Directive (Reidenberg, 2000).

Model Contract Clauses

In an effort to offer more flexibility for compliance with the EU Privacy Directive, in December 2001 the EU Commission adopted Commission Decision 2002/16 (Contract Clause Decision), which sets out standard contract clauses for the transfer of personal data to processors in non-EU countries that have not been recognized as providing "adequate protection" for data. Under these standardized contract clauses, an EU company exporting data can and must treat the data with the full respect of the EU data protection requirements. The terms of these standard privacy contract clauses can be appended to existing licenses or contracts and offer a guarantee that the necessary security measures for privacy protection are in place.

The companies that choose to comply with the Safe Harbor provisions are subject to the enforcement jurisdiction of the U.S. Federal Trade Commission. Under the standard contract clauses, an entity becomes subject to the European Data Authority, and the standard contract creates a private right of action in Europe. In addition, the terms of the standard contract are rigid and may impose criminal penalties.

The EU Privacy Directive, which has set the standard for privacy protection for international transfer of data, can be satisfied in several ways. The means of compliance that varies from joining the Safe Harbor to drafting model contract clauses will depend on the nature of one's organization and how one's data are collected.

Technological Responses to Privacy Protection

The legal and self-regulatory instruments just described have legitimately received substantial public support in their effort to protect privacy. The fundamental flaw with these privacy programs or legislation is a lack of understanding of the premise underlying the technological structure of computer networks, in particular the Internet. Loss of control over one's personal data or relinquishment of one's privacy is a direct result of the technology or infrastructure of the Internet. Network computer systems are designed to have identifiable transactions; every time one logs on to the Internet, an electronic record is created (Lessig, 1991).

The ease with which privacy is sacrificed as a result of the openness of the infrastructure of the Internet has recently been brought to the attention of the public as the Federal Bureau of Investigation (FBI) has widely implemented Carnivore, an efficient surveillance technology that captures Internet conversations. Carnivore is a software technology that was developed to intercept e-mail messages based on code words (Electronic Privacy Information Center, 2000). Carnivore is the term used for an entire system, which is a computer running on Microsoft's Windows 2000 operating system and software that scans and captures packets, the standard unit of Internet traffic as they travel through an Internet service provider's (ISP's) network.

The FBI can install a Carnivore unit at an ISP's network station and configure it to capture e-mail going to or from the person under investigation. Under the USA PATRIOT Act, discussed later, to obtain a court order to install Carnivore, a law enforcement agent must simply certify to a judge that the information is "relevant to an ongoing criminal investigation." In addition to the fact that the warrant requirements are lowered under the USA PATRIOT Act, the packet-switching technology that drives the Internet has allowed the FBI to gather more information than a prescribed search warrant would allow. This compromises the privacy of all persons who have any interaction with the targeted suspect. Questions have been raised regarding the mechanics of the Carnivore system. When the Electronic Privacy Information Center filed a Freedom of Information Act (1999) request for Carnivore's source code, the inner workings of how the device functioned, the FBI refused to disclose this information. This persistent refusal for full disclosure has led to several lawsuits against the FBI, which has created the impression in the eyes of the public that law enforcement is taking away rights rather than protecting them (Van Bergen, 2002).

Any discussion of privacy recognizes that a balance must be struck between the interests of privacy and security. The U.S. Department of Justice has been arguing with civil liberties groups and privacy advocates for several years over amendments to federal statutes that would expand law enforcement wire tapping and electronic surveillance operations. Congress had been reluctant to expand law enforcement surveillance activities with respect to the Internet, citing privacy concerns. After the September 11 terrorist attacks, the USA PATRIOT Act passed through Congress swiftly; Congressional reluctance and public opposition, as measured by consumer polls, to expanded surveillance diminished.

The USA PATRIOT Act is a long and complex statute that made changes to more than 15 U.S. statutes, several of which directly affect Internet communications. Section 216 of the act addresses pen/trap orders, which were initially defined under the Electronic Communications Privacy Act as including a device attached to a telephone line to trace and trap telephone numbers. Since about September 2000, the FBI had been routinely applying pen/trap devices to computer communications, and thus under the USA PATRIOT Act, the pen/trap provisions apply to computer communications so that all e-mail addresses, Web addresses visited by a target, Internet protocol addresses, and other routing information can be obtained. The contents of the message has never been retrievable under a pen/trap order, but telephone numbers can be easily separated from telephone message; e-mail addresses are not so easily separated from e-mail contents or e-mail subject headings in particular.

The USA PATRIOT Act amends the Foreign Intelligence Surveillance Act (FISA), which historically had separated domestic criminal investigations from foreign investigations. Domestic surveillance was governed by Title III of the Omnibus Crime Control and Safe Streets Act of 1968, which provided for adequate safeguards for basic constitutional rights such as the Fourth Amendment probable cause requirements and judicial review. Foreign intelligence, which was governed by FISA, grants the attorney general the power to treat an alien as an agent of a foreign power, and therefore that person is not entitled to constitutional rights. The boundaries between these two laws are blurred under the USA PATRIOT Act, a fact that is most evident from the expanded definitions of *terrorist*. Consequently, under the USA PATRIOT Act's pen/trap provisions, an ISP must respond to a court order as long as the law enforcement agent certifies that the surveillance "is relevant to an ongoing investigation." The Fourth Amendment requirements of probable cause when conducting wiretaps have been lowered. In addition, pursuant to the same lowered standard, any business may now be served with an order for the production of "any tangible thing," not just a business record. Clearly ISPs, cable subscribers, and businesses in general ought to review their privacy policies and confidentiality agreements to ensure that they accurately reflect their new obligations under the USA PATRIOT Act.

There are significant differences in the regulations surrounding the protection of personal information in the United States and in Europe. These differences will likely impede global e-commerce and international agreements, and negotiations are needed to enable nation states' policies to develop in harmony. Joel Reidenberg (2001) suggested the promotion of negotiations of a General Agreement on Information Privacy (GAIP) in connection with the World Trade Organization (WTO). Reidenberg recommends this type of a treaty organization because it places data protection in a trade arena rather than a political arena; by placing GAIP within the WTO, it would add social protection norms to a trade treaty. The GAIP would include many signatory countries and focus on an institutional process of norm development to facilitate near-term standards for informational privacy. The WTO could define cost standards for data protection that could be incorporated into a multilateral trade agreement (Reidenberg, 2001).

ENCRYPTION AND ELECTRONIC SIGNATURES

The expansion of Internet technology has allowed people to use the Internet as a platform for worldwide business, and therefore contracts are being formed among parties with no prior relationships. Parties want to rely exclusively on online communications; thus, a reliable system of authentication is needed to ensure the success of e-commerce (Winn, 2001). The ability to transmit information secretly over distances has been accomplished using cryptography for decades. Digital signatures and encryption are the two key aspects of cryptography that have been recognized as essential tools for security and trust for electronic commerce. This section begins with an explanation of the current global regulation regarding the control of exportation of encryption. The most popular form of encryption in use today is public key asymmetric cryptography (private key infrastructure; PKI), which is used in digital signatures. *Electronic Signatures-Technical Overview* distinguishes digital signatures from electronic signatures before offering an overview of the PKI technology. *Regulatory Models* explains the three legislative models that have been developed for the regulation of electronic signatures.

Cryptography is the art of using code to keep information secret and encryption is the technique to encode or scramble communications. Most nations regulate the exportation of encryption technology because of the fear that abuse of the technology by terrorists or criminals would impede the ability of national security and law enforcement to do their jobs. Privacy advocates and free speech proponents in the United States agree that restrictions on exports of encryption infringe on individuals rights to informational privacy and on Fourth Amendment and First Amendment rights. Members of the high-tech and software industries complain that such restrictions are anticompetitive vis-à-vis foreign nationals.

Encryption Exportation Regulation; United States Law and International Treaties

Under the Arms Export Control Act of 1978 (2000), the U.S. State Department decides whether an item is dual purpose, which is a category that includes commercial products with military application. Control over the licensing and export of dual-purpose products is transferred to the Department of Commerce (DOC; Paik, 2000). The DOC under the EAA now regulates the export of all general-purpose encryption devices and software. The

DOC Export Administration Regulations 15 C.F.R. 730-74 (2000) include source code and object code in the definition of software subject to regulation and exportation which includes "downloading or causing the downloading of such software ... or making such software available from electronic bulletin boards" (Paik, 2000). During the years of the Clinton administration, there was significant discussion regarding the requirement that software companies create key recovery systems, one which was recommended by the government was known as the Clipper Chip. That requirement was not adopted, and current regulations allow U.S. citizens to ship any retail encryption product around the world to commercial concerns after a one-time technical review by an interagency panel (Paik, 2000).

The Wassenaar Agreement is an international agreement that addresses controls on encryption exports to which 33 countries, including the United States, subscribe ("What Is the Wassenaar Arrangement," n.d.). The agreement, which was designed to promote cooperation among its members, was amended in 1998 to impose export control on export software for keys above 64 bits and to eliminate record keeping for low-level encryption. Several countries, including Israel, South Africa, India, and China, however, are not members. Therefore, there is not harmonization in the global encryption export market (Paik, 2000).

Electronic Signatures—Technical Overview

An electronic signature is any method that logically associates an electronic representation of the identity of a person with the content of an electronic document or record. It implies acknowledged authorship or agreement, but there are times, with e-mail programs, for instance, when an electronic signature can be applied automatically. Generally, with electronic records the goal is to protect the integrity of the content, and a generic electronic signature provides little assurance that documents have not been altered. Digital signatures are a special subset of electronic signatures which can provide this assurance (Ballon, 2001).

Digital signatures serve three essential functions: authentication, integrity, and nonrepudiation. Authentication means that the party is who he or she claims to be. Integrity means that the communication has not been tampered with (i.e., it is in its original form), and nonrepudiation prevents the party from retreating from the transaction in the event a dispute arises. A digital signature denotes an electronic imprint that is created using public key encryption (PKI). Public key encryption is also referred to as asymmetric encryption because two keys are used, a private key and a public key. The two keys are mathematically related so that when the message is encrypted with the private key and sent off to the recipient, the recipient must use the sender's public key to decrypt it. Each user has a different public–private key pair (Berman, 2001).

A digital signature is not a digitized version of a person's handwritten signature, but a "message digest" of the document that is being encrypted or sent. The message digest is created by processing the document through a unique computer generated code known as a *hash*. Once the hash is created, the signer types in a personal identification number (PIN) that allows the private key to generate a long series of numbers and letters, which is the digital signature. The sender uses a one-way hash function to encrypt the message he or she wants to sign and then sends it off. The computer generated signature and the hash result are unique to the message. Every time the message passes through the hash function, the same message digest is produced. To verify the signature of a digitally signed message, the receiver reverses the process with the public key.

For a digital signature system to function, the parties must be assured that the public keys that they obtain actually belong to the person he or she purports to be and not to a forger. The way to achieve this confidence is with a CA, which is an entity, either public or private, that attests to the integrity of the system. CAs issue certificates of authenticity as to the ownership of the keys. There have been several proposals as to the best solution to the problem of authentication (Zemmick, 2001). At the present time, several banks offer this service.

The intention in all jurisdictions that have enacted electronic signature laws is to encourage the development of e-commerce, but there is a large disparity in their treatment of electronic signatures. According to Smedinghoff and Ruth (1999), "predictability is a watch word for the growth of commerce and law can play a role in providing this valuable commodity," and yet the most striking feature of the various electronic signature laws enacted around the world is their lack of uniformity (Fischer, 2001). As we saw with the various privacy policies, failure of policymakers to remove national barriers will hinder successful global e-commerce and possibly widen the digital divide.

Regulatory Models

Electronic signature legislation can be seen as based on one of three models. The first is known as the *mandatory* or *prescriptive model* because it mandates a specific technology (Fischer, 2001). Alternatively, the *minimalist legislative approach* is technology neutral; and the third *hybrid approach* suggests a favored technology that affords presumptions under the law. Proponents of the prescriptive model, which include Germany, Italy, Malaysia, and Russia, mandate specific technology when authorizing electronic signatures as an alternative to pen and paper. PKI, the digital signature that is currently the most sophisticated technology, is required. In addition, this mandatory or prescriptive approach often outlines specific criteria for the trusted third party or CA. The rationale given for this approach is that the requisite security for e-commerce can only be obtained with these constraints. In addition, it is believed that these requirements will ensure legal certainty, which is essential for public trust. Critics of this approach point out that this not only grants economic advantages for a particular existing technology, it is shortsighted because although the "best" technology in 2002 may be PKI, better, more sophisticated techniques may become available.

In addition, this mandatory or prescriptive approach often outlines specific criteria for the trusted third party

(CA) and usually overly limits the liability of the CA. Typical prescriptive digital signature laws place the burden for loss or theft of a private key on the consumer if there was a failure to exercise reasonable care. The consumer will bear the entire loss, thus insulating the CA from any liability. This structure of liability seems to burden the consumer unfairly in an effort to create a less risky role for the CA in which the CA could more efficiently protect itself.

The hybrid model, which was adopted under the E.U. Signature Directive of 1999 (European Parliament and Council Directive, 2000) by the European Union, is often referred to as a two-tier model because it grants basic validity to all electronic signatures but provides special treatment to certain advanced signatures. Under this hybrid approach, an electronic signature cannot be denied legal effectiveness solely because it is electronic, but some technologies are given presumptions of authenticity if the signature meets certain requirements. At the present time, the only technology that meets these heightened standards is PKI.

The rights and duties set out for the parties to an electronic transaction under the hybrid model reflect a market driven philosophy. Unlike under the prescriptive approach, CAs will be found liable in damages for harm caused to someone that has reasonably relied on a certificate for the accuracy of the information unless it can be proven that the CA was not negligent. The presumption is in favor of the consumer. CAs under the hybrid approach can limit their liability by contract, however, before entering into the transaction.

The minimalist, wholly technology-neutral approach provides that no electronic signature of whatever type may be denied legal effect, validity, or enforceability because it is in electronic form. The United States Electronic Signatures in Global and National Commerce Act of 2000 (E-SIGN) endorses this approach. Australia and the United Kingdom have also enacted minimalist legislation, and New Zealand is considering a law similar to that of Australia (Fischer, 2001). The philosophical principles on which it is based foster technological advancements by allowing the market to decide which technology is best. It also allows several systems to be developed simultaneously. E-SIGN was drafted and enacted swiftly in the United States, in part as a response to the factious division among the several states in adopting various versions of electronic signature legislation.

The major criticism of E-SIGN is that it is too vague, and its lack of certainty will hamper electronic commercial growth. Critics of E-SIGN suggest that the nonrestrictive legislation might lead to parties being held liable for contracts that they did not actually authorize (e.g., if a party somehow failed to protect the security of his or her signature device). Although the liability may be severe, the "liberty to contract" concept prevails, which leaves the parties free to be bound or reject the contract.

The electronic signature legislation that has been passed in countries around the world reflects the contrasting views of minimalist and the prescriptive approach. The global initiative by the United Nations Commission on International Trade Law (UNCITRAL) working group on electronic commerce is not expected to have a significant impact on existing or proposed legislation because business lost confidence in the proposal during negotiations due to the parties' insistence on a prescriptive approach mandating a PKI (Fischer, 2001). The future of commerce will not take place on paper, and it is important for the law to grow to facilitate the development of e-commerce. Attention needs to be given to harmonize the differences among nations that exist in the area of electronic signatures, possibly through revision of the work produced by UNCITRAL.

INTELLECTUAL PROPERTY

Technology has had a profound impact on the perception of intellectual property and the appropriate distribution of the rights traditionally attached to trademark, patent, and copyright in the global context. Although technological advances have created unprecedented opportunities for economic prosperity in the area of intellectual property, legal systems have had to adapt to maintain firm standards while fostering financial growth. Consistency in legal paradigms across national borders, which is crucial to establish the Internet as a reliable conduit for successful global commerce, has been relatively successful in the area of intellectual property. International intellectual property conventions have been consolidated under the auspices of Convention Establishing the World Intellectual Property Organization (WIPO). The Agreement on Trade Related Aspects of Intellectual Property (TRIPs) has formed a WTO-WIPO union by integrating much of WIPO's law into WTO's trade regime (Mort, 1997). Trends in practice also suggest a tendency toward uniformity. This section reviews substantive provisions of the WIPO Copyright Treaty (1996), key terms of the Digital Millennium Copyright Act (DMCA), the European Copyright Directive, and the Electronic Commerce Directive, particularly as they reflect the guidelines for ISP copyright liability.

Digital transmissions allow infringers to obtain and disseminate information quickly without being detected. The Internet presents difficult challenges for copyright owners to identify and stop infringement. Locating a financially sound ISP to end the copying activity is the surest route for the copyright owner. This section also examines the discrepancies that exist between the U.S. and the EU approaches to database protection and business method software protection.

ISP Liability for Third-Party Copyright Infringement

Intellectual property conventions that predated WIPO's creation in 1967 historically operated independently without institutional oversight (Mort, 1997). WIPO, which was designed as a specialized agency to administer major international conventions under the leadership of the United Nations director general secretariat, had difficulty enforcing rights and resolving conflicts. Serving as the sole international authority for more than two decades, WIPO lacked the necessary enforcement powers to eliminate piracy of intellectual property. In 1986, as part of the Uruguay Round Negotiations, intellectual property protections were integrated into the General Agreement on Tariffs and Trade (1947) in 1994. TRIPs was established and a symbiotic institutional relationship between the WTO and WIPO was formed (Mort, 1997). There was a simple integration of intellectual property protection into a trade based sanction regime. In 1995, a cooperative agreement was signed between the two bodies to coordinate their efforts.

In 1996, WIPO concluded two treaties covering the protection of copyright and rights in digital environments, the WIPO Copyright Treaty and WIPO Performances and Phonograms Treaty. The WIPO Copyright Treaty established a distribution, rental, and communication right in creative works to the public. This distribution right under the WIPO Copyright Treaty may be accomplished through sale or other means of transferring ownership, but the right is limited to fixed tangible copies capable of circulation (Soma & Norman, 2000). There was no agreement between the delegates on the scope of the doctrine of exhaustion for "first sale" rights, so this was left to be defined by each adopting nation. Another important provision of the WIPO Copyright Treaty related to the exhaustion of rights is that the right of public communication permits copyright holders to make their works available by wire or wireless means. Included in this right is the ability to make works available to the public so that they can access them as they choose. In the event communication permits recipients to reproduce a tangible copy, national law must define liability for infringement.

The implications of this broad access right is that ISPs could be liable for direct and contributory copyright infringement causes of action that may be brought by the copyright owner against the ultimate recipient. The right created in the WIPO Copyright Treaty leaves details about liability for third-party copyright infringement to the contracting parties. This has caused much concern among telecommunications companies and ISPs, because such a broad interpretation of the treaty could lead to lawsuits from copyright owners (Mort, 1997).

Under case law in the United States, the issue of determining ISP liability for third-party copyright infringement starts with an examination of the type of service the ISP provides in relationship to the infringement claim. The categorization of the ISP is based on the level of knowledge the ISP had of infringing activity, the control of the ISP, the length of time the material is stored on the ISP server, and any financial benefit received by the ISP. When defined according to function, one will analyze and apply liability to the ISP based on the traditional common carrier versus publisher or distributor model (Soma & Norman 2000).

In the United States, the DMCA limits ISP liability for third-party copyright infringement when the ISP complies with a detailed system of notice and removal. When an ISP acts as a mere conduit for data, the DMCA will limit liability of the ISP relating to these transitory communications.

The recently passed EU Copyright Directive follows a similar logic as the DMCA in that it exempts ISPs from liability when they play a passive role as a mere conduit of information from third parties. An ISP cannot modify the work in any manner; the ISP must comply with industry standards for transmission and storage and must remove infringing materials expeditiously to avoid copyright infringement liability. A third-party copyright infringement case would not be successful unless the ISP had been warned to remove it and did not do so (Mcdonald, 2001). Finally, the Electronic Commerce Directive, which is similar to the DMCA and the EU Copyright Directive, sets out guidelines for liability for ISPs where they play a passive role as a mere conduit of information from third parties. Similarly, the Electronic Commerce Directive limits ISPs from liability for other intermediary activities such as storage of information or caching.

Databases

Database protection presents a controversial area of legislation in the global arena. A database, which is a compilation of information, is not protected under copyright law in the United States unless the arrangement or selection rises to a sufficiently high level of originality or uniqueness in its selection or arrangement. Database protection was limited by the U.S. Supreme Court in *Feist Publications Inc. v. Rural Tel. Serv. Co.* (1991) in which the court held that a white pages telephone directory, which consisted of preexisting factual material, lacked the requisite originality in selection coordination and arrangement of data to garner copyright protection. The simple listing of subscribers in alphabetical order by surname lacked originality, despite the excessive time, effort, and energy expended to organize it. Feist struck down the "sweat of the brow" doctrine, which some U.S. courts had used to find copyright protection. Opponents of greater legal protection for databases believe that the balance between control over information and allowing information into the public domain is best met with few legal restrictions imposed. "Information is meant to be free" is the ideology expressed in support of a reduced role of government.

The European countries believe that there are sound economic justifications for affording protection to owners of databases based on the "sweat of the brow" theory and in 1996 passed the EC Directive No. 96/9, on the Legal Protection of Databases (the Database Directive). The *sui generis* protection granted to databases under the Database Directive is based on a property concept, which bestows exclusive rights of ownership to the database compiler. The provisions to afford database protection was dropped from the WIPO Copyright Treaty over objections by members of the academic and scientific community, but debate over this issue remains in the United States. Several legislative bills have been introduced in Congress based on the belief that such protection would make the United States more competitive in foreign markets. None of these bills have passed as of the time of the writing of this chapter.

Software Patents

The topic of patenting software and, in particular, business methods has received a lot of attention from the pubic because of the economic success of several e-commerce entrepreneurs (Gladstone, 2002). The EU and American approaches to protection of software have traditionally been reported as divergent but, on closer examination, the two policies appear to be converging, particularly in light of the decline of the heated electronic commerce boom. Historically, intellectual property and software was limited to copyright protection on the grounds that it was written in code, thus it was a literary work, and hence copyright protection was appropriate. In *Diamond v. Diehr* (1981), however, the U.S. Supreme Court held that a process for monitoring the temperature inside a synthetic rubber mold using a computer and the Arrhenius equation for measuring cure time as a function of temperature and other variables was patentable subject matter. The court focused on the "postsolution activity" that resulted from the computer program (Cohen & Lemley, 2001). The lesson from the *Diehr* decision was to include a physical element or step in any future patent application that might recite a "mental process." This theory was adopted and clarified by the federal circuit in *In re: Alappat* (1994), which established that an "otherwise statutory process or apparatus requirement may be satisfied by drafting claims to include a general purpose computer or standard hardware or memory element that would be necessary for any useful application of the algorithm." The logic of these cases did not include claims reading on computer programs themselves, as opposed to programs implemented in a machine or system (Mcdonald, 2001). This obstacle was overcome in the *In re: Boureguard* (1995); while an appeal was pending, the U.S. Patent and Trade Office established that software stored in memory media is patentable as an article of manufacture.

Article 52 of the Convention on the Grant of European Patents of the European Patent Convention (EPC) indicates that computer programs "as such" are not patentable and that programs for computers shall not be regarded as inventions. The European Patent Office, estimates, however, that they have issued more than 20,000 patents on computer programs. In late 2000, there was a Diplomatic Conference to revise the EPC to change Article 52, bringing it in line with actual practice and with TRIPs, making it clear that patent protection would be available to technical inventions of all kinds (Mcdonald, 2001). This measure did not pass, however. The reversal and decision to hold on to the old position is interesting in that it reflects a rebellion against the rushed commercialization reflected in the e-commerce boom.

Critical in any discussion of intellectual property rights is finding the correct balance between creating incentives to encourage innovation by inventors and the public's right to access to information and knowledge. The trend in the United States to grant exclusive patent rights to software involving Internet technology continued unabated to the point where the U.S. Patent Office was granting patents on "how to get a business method patent." Beginning with the case of *State Street Bank & Trust vs. Signature Financial* (1998) in which Signature Financial was granted a patent for a data processing system to implement an investment structure, the court endorsed business methods providing they comply with other requirements for a patent, thus laying to rest "the ill conceived exception to the law" that business methods were not patentable. U.S. patents have been issued on numerous technological processes; the "single click" patent covering a method and system for placing purchase orders via a commercial network that was granted to Amazon.com

and contested by Barnesandnoble.com is one of the more controversial and publicly known cases to be litigated. Although Amazon.com initially was granted an injunction to prevent Barnesandnoble.com from using the process, the patent is still being challenged (Shulman, 2000).

The U.S. trend to grant patents on software for business methods informed the discussion within the Diplomatic Conference of the European Commission regarding their policy toward granting patents on software. It is likely that the concern over the inseparability of business methods from software patents in general may have encouraged no change in the EPC. Proponents of LINUX, the open-source software that encourages sharing of ideas to promote innovation, began campaigning against software patents in general in Europe in the late 1990s. This development may also have influenced the change in the EPC outcome (Mcdonald, 2000).

The economic downturn of the late 1990s, which hit technology companies and Internet startups particularly harshly, likely also contributed to the slowdown in Internet-related business method patent filings. Nonetheless, the curtailment of the public's endorsement of companies whose sole or main asset was a business method patent was a key factor. Empirical evidence which demonstrates the withdrawal of funds from these "idea factories" (Shulman, 2000) suggests that the flurry of business method patents may not have been based on solid economic grounds. The multibillionaire entrepreneur Jay Walker, whose company Walker Digital claimed 70 business method patents with 400 pending before the U.S. Patent Office, had to lay off 80% of its workforce within a few short years of establishing itself (Shulman, 2000). The profusion of new software business method patents was exciting but, in fact, it had a chilling effect on e-commerce; when put to the Wall Street test, most of these companies did not fare well. Although parties are still applying for business method patents, often these are an offensive or a defensive act taken to prevent others from gaining market share rather than with an expectation of employing the patent. The recent decline in enthusiasm of business method software patents in the United States suggests that the EU position to proceed cautiously before modifying laws to broaden individuals' rights at the expense of the public's access to information may be the better approach (Gladstone, 2002).

CONCLUSION

The Internet reaches around the globe, and it may be unrealistic to expect symmetry between nations. Nonetheless, policymakers must continue to strive for a common ground. There is sufficient legal and empirical evidence to support a nation's asserting jurisdiction and enforcing its laws beyond its borders, but enforcement jurisdiction and questions of comity present additional difficulties, as seen recently with the internationally recognized Yahoo! case. In the areas of privacy and electronic signatures, discrepancies between countries remain apparent, and these variances are rooted in fundamental cultural, social, and philosophical differences. The Internet has become a medium for widespread commercial activity, but continued expansion will require agreement regarding mechanisms to regulate in all areas of human activity. Global consensus to limit ISP liability for copyright infringement, the reduction in the business method patent application surge, and the reluctance in the United States to pass a *sui generis* database protection law suggest a concerted global effort not to limit public access to information and to allow the Internet to serve as a conduit of knowledge dissemination. There is clearly a trend toward common ground in several areas of intellectual property law in cyberspace. Harmonization in all areas of the law is the goal to strive for, because without seamless predictable systems, businesses and consumers will be reluctant to enter into transactions.

GLOSSARY

Cyberspace Functionally, cyberspace is where messages and Web pages are posted for everyone in the world to see. In *Reno v. ACLU* (1997) the first opinion about the Internet by the U.S. Supreme Court, it was stated that "Taken together, these tools constitute a unique medium—known to its users as 'cyberspace'— located in no particular geographical location but available to anyone, anywhere in the world, with access to the internet."

Cybersquatting The practice in which a person or an entity registers a domain name with no intention to use the name for a useful purpose; rather, the sole purpose is to thwart the ability of the rightful owner or trademark holder to obtain the name.

Data Protection The right provided for under the Council Directive 95/45/EC of the European Parliament and of the Council of the European Union of Oct. 24, 1995, also known as the EU Privacy Directive.

Electronic Signatures in Global and National Commerce Act (E-SIGN) A U.S. law that was passed in 2000 that recognizes the legal effect of an electronic signature in whatever form it is made.

Encryption The conversion of data into a form, called ciphertext, that cannot be easily understood by unauthorized people.

International Safe Harbor Principles The regulatory response of the United States government to the "adequacy standards" of the EU Privacy Directive, agreed on by the European Commission.

Privacy The right to be left alone

CROSS REFERENCES

See *Copyright Law; Digital Signatures and Electronic Signatures; Encryption Basics; Patent Law; Privacy Law and the Internet.*

REFERENCES

ABA Project (2000). Achieving Legal and Business Order in Cyberspace; A Report on Global Jurisdiction Issues Created by the Internet.

Aciman, C., & VoVerde, D. (2002, January). *Redefining the Zippo Test: New trends on personal jurisdiction for internet activities.* The Computer and Internet Lawyer.

ACLU v. Reno, 521 U.S. 844 (1997).

Agreement on Trade-Related Aspects of Intellectual Property Rights. (1994, April 15). Marrakesh Agreement Establishing the World Trade Organization, Annex 1C, Legal Instruments—Results of the Uruguay Round vol. 31, 33 I.L.M. 81 (1994).

Alexander, M. (2002). The First Amendment and problems of political viability; the case of Internet pornography. *Harvard Journal of Law & Public Policy, 25,* 977.

Arms Export Control Act of 1978, 102, 22 U.S.C.S. 2799aa-1 (2000).

Ballon, C. I. (2001). *E-commerce & Internet law: A legal treatise with forms.* Little Falls, NJ:Glasser Books.

Barlow, J. P. (1996). *A declaration of the independence of cyberspace.* Retrieved January 10, 2004, from http://www. eff.org/barlow/Declaration-Final.html

Berman, A. B. (2001). Note: International divergence: The "KEYS" to signing on the digital line—the cross-border recognition of electronic contracts and digital signatures. *Syracuse Journal of International Law and Commerce, 28,* 125.

Boam, C. P. (2001). The Internet, information and the culture of regulatory change: A modern renaissance. *CommLaw Conspectus, 9,* 175.

Brussels Convention. *Convention on Jurisdiction and the Enforcement of Judgments in Civil and Commercial Matters* (Sep. 30, 1968), 1998 OFFICIAL J. C027, 0001-0027.

Brussels Regulation. *Council Regulation (EC) 44/2001 of 22 December 2000 on Jurisdiction and the Recognition and Enforcement of Judgments in Civil and Commercial Matters,* 2001 O.J. (L 12) 1.

Cable News Network, L.P. v. GoSMS.com, Inc., WL 1678039 (SDNY 2000).

Calder v. Jones, 465 U.S. 783 (1984).

In The Case of S.S. Lotus (Fr. v. Turk), 1927 P.C.I.J. (Ser A) No. 10 (1927).

Child Online Protection Act Pub. L. No. 105- 277, 112 Stat. 2681-736 (1998).

Children's Internet Protection Act, Pub. L. No. 106-554, tit. Xii, 114 stat. 2763, 2763A-335 (2001).

Cohen, J. E., & Lemley, M. A. (2001). Patent scope and innovation in the software industry. *California Law Review, 8,* 1.

Communication Decency Act (CDA), Pub. L. No. 104-104,tit.V,110 Stat.56, 133.

Convention Establishing the World Intellectual Property Organization. (1967, July 14). 21 U.S. T. 1770, 828 U.N.T.S. 3 (WIPO).

Convention on the Grant of European Patents. (1973, October 5). 13 I.L.M. 270.

Diamond v. Diehr, 450 U.S. 175 (1981).

Digital Millennium Copyright Act. Pub. L. No. 105-304, 112 Stat. 2877 (1998) (codified as amended at 17 U.S.C. 1201 (2000).

Electronic Commerce Directive (EC Directive) Regulations 2002 (SI 2002 N2013)

Electronic Communications Privacy Act (ECPA) (18 U.S.C. 3121-3127).

Electronic Privacy Information Center. (2000). *Evolution of Carnivore.* Retrieved May 8, 2002, from http://www. epic.org/privacy/carnivore/#documents

EU Privacy Directive. (1995, October). Council Directive No. 95/46/EC of 24 October 1995 on the Protection of Individuals with Regard to the Processing of Personal Data and on the Free Movement of Such Data, art. 2(c), Official Journal of the European Community, L281/31.

European Commission. (1999). Explanatory Memorandum to the Proposal for a Council Regulation on Jurisdiction, COM 348 of 14 July 1999. Retrieved from http://www.europa.eu.int/comm/justice_home/pdf/com 1999-348-en.pdf

European Commission. (2001). Decision 2002/16 EC of 21 Dec 2001, Contract Clause Decision, Retrieved August 14, 2002, from http://europa.eu.int/comm/internal_market/en/dataprot/modelcontracts/02-16_en.pdf

European Commission. (2000, October 26). Explanatory Memorandum to Amended Proposal for Council Brussels Regulation, COM (2000) 689.

European Council. (2000, June 8). Council Directive 00/31 of 8 June 2000 on certain legal aspects of information society services, in particular electronic commerce, in the International Market (Directive on Electronic Commerce), [2000] O.J. L. 178/1.

European Council. (2001). Copyright Directive. Council Directive 01/29,2001 O.J. (L 167/10).

European Council. (1996). Directive No. 96/9, O.J. L. 77/20, on the Legal Protection of Databases.

European Parliament and Council Directive. (2000). 1999/93, 2000 O.J. (l 13) 12 at Art 2 (20), E.U. Signature Directive.

Export Administration Regulations, 15 C.F.R. 730-74 (2000).

Federal Trade Commission Act, 15 U.S.C. 45.

Feist Publications Inc. v. Rural Tel. Serv. Co., 499 U.S. 340 (1991).

Financial Services Modernization Act of 1999, Gramm-Leach-Bliley Act, Pub. L. No. 106-102, 113 Stat 1338 1999.

Fischer, S. F. (2001, January). Saving Rosencrantz and Guildenstern in a virtual world? A comparative look at recent global electronic signature legislation. Presented at the Association of American Law Schools 2001 Annual Meeting Section on Law and Computers, San Francisco, California. Boston University Journal of Science and Technology Law, 7, 229.

Foreign Intelligence Surveillance Act, 50 U.S.C. 1841–1846.

Framework for Global Electronic Commerce. (1997, July 1). Retrieved January 19, 2004, from http://www.ta.doc. gov/digeconomy/framewrk.htm

Freedom of Information Act, 5 U.S.C. 552 (1994 & Supp. 1999).

Fromholz, J. M. (2000). Berkeley Technology Law Journal Annual Review of Law and Technology; VI. Foreign & International Law. The European Union Data Privacy Directive. Berkeley Technology Law Journal, 15, 461.

General Agreement on Tariffs and Trade. Oct. 30, 1947, 61 Stat. A-11, T.I.A.S. 1700, 55 U.N.T.S. 194, art. IX.

Geist, M. (2003). Cyberlaw 2.0, 44B.C.L.Rev 323.

Gladstone Alpert, J. (2000a). Survey of Cyberspace Law An Introduction Keeping Pace. Business Lawyer, 56, 1.

Gladstone Alpert, J. (2000b). The U.S. privacy balance and the European privacy directive: Reflections on the United States privacy policy. Willamette Journal of International Law and Dispute Resolution, 7.

Gladstone Alpert, J. (2002). Why patenting information technology and business methods is not sound policy: Lessons from history and prophecies for the future. Hamline Law Review, 25, 2.

Gutnick v. Dow Jones (2001) VSC 305.

Hanson v. Denckla, 357 U.S. 235 (1958).

In the Case of S.S. Lotus (Fr. v. Turk.) 1927 P.C.I.J. (Ser A) No. 10 (1927).

In re: Alappat, 33 F.3d 1526 (1994).

In re: Boureguard, 53 F.3d 1583 (Fed Cir. 1995).

International Safe Harbor Rules. (1999). Retrieved May 8, 2002, from: http://www.ita.doc.gov/td/ecom/shprin.html

Johnson, D. J., & Post, D. (1996). Law and borders—the rise of law in cyberspace. Stanford Law Review, 48, 1367.

Lessig, L. (1991). Code and other laws of cyberspace.

Mcdonald, B. (2001). International intellectual property rights. Retrieved May 8, 2002, from: http://www.wrf.com

Mody, S. S. (2001). National cyberspace regulation: Unbundling the concept of jurisdiction. Stanford Journal of International Law, 37, 365.

Mort, S. A. (1997). The WTO, WIPO & the Internet: Confounding the borders of copyright and neighboring rights. Fordham Intellectual Property, Media & Entertainment Law Journal, 8, 173.

Organisation for Economic Cooperation and Development. (1980). Guidelines on the Protection of Personal Data. Retrieved from http://www.oecd.org/dsti/sti/it/secur/prod/PRIV-EN.HTM#4

Paik, J. L. (2000). NOTE: The encryption export tax: A proposed solution and remedy to the issues and costs associated with exporting encryption technology. Cornell Journal of Law and Public Policy, 10, 161.

Panavision Int'l. L.P v. Toeppen, 141 F.3d 1316 (9th Cir. 1998).

Pastore, M. (2002). Economic downturn slows B2B commerce. Retrieved May 8, 2002, from http://cyberatlas.internet.com/markets/b2b/article/0,1323,10091_719571,00.html

Piera, F. (2001). International electronic commerce: Legal framework at the beginning of the XXI century. Currents: International Trade Law Journal, 10, 8.

Reidenberg, J. R. (2001). E-Commerce and Privacy Institute for Intellectual Property & Information Law Symposium: E-Commerce and Trans-Atlantic Privacy. Houston Law Review, 38, 717.

Reidenberg, J. R. (2000). Cyberspace and privacy: A new legal paradigm? Resolving conflicting international data privacy rules in cyberspace (Symposium). Stanford Law Review, 52, 1315.

Restatement (3rd) of the Foreign Relations Law of the U.S. sections, 304, 401,402, 421,431.

Rice, D., & Gladstone J. (2002). Can a single test be used to establish jurisdiction in cyberspace? An assessment of the effects test in American jurisprudence. Business Lawyer.

Rice, D. & Gladstone, J. (2003). An Assessment of the Effects Test in Determining Personal Jurisdiction in Cyberspace. *Business Lawyer, 58* (2), 601–654

Safe Streets Act of 1968 (18 U.S.C. 2510-22).

Shulman, S. (2000). *Software patents tangle the Web*. Retrieved May 8, 2002, from http://www.technologyreview.com/articles/shulman0300.asp

Smedinghoff, T., & Bro, R. (1999). Moving with change: Electronic signature legislation as a vehicle for advancing e-commerce. *John Marshall Computer and Information Law, 17,* 723.

Soma, J. T., & Norman, N. A. (2000). International takedown policy: A proposal for the WTO and WIPO to establish international copyright procedural guidelines for Internet service providers. *Hastings Communications and Entertainment Law Journal, 22,* 391.

State Street Bank & Trust v. Signature Financial, 149 F.3d 1368 (Fed Cir. 1998).

Title III of the Omnibus Crime Control and Safe Streets Act of 1968, (18 U.S.C. 2510-22).

Total Information Awareness (2003). Report to Congress regarding the Terrorism Information Awareness Program, Consolidated Appropriations Resolution, 2003, Pub. L. No. 108-7, Division M, $ 11 1(b).

United States v. Aluminum Company of America (ALCOA). 148 F.2d 416 (2d Cir.1945).

United States Electronic Signatures in Global and National Commerce Act of 2000 (E-SIGN), 15 U.S.C. 7001-06, 7021,7031 (West 2000).

USA PATRIOT ACT (Uniting and Strengthening America by Providing Appropriate Tools to Intercept and Obstruct Terrorism Act of 2001), Pub. L. No. 107-56, 115 Stat 272 (2001).

Van Bergen, J. (2002, April). *Repeal the USA Patriot Act*. Retrieved August 12, 2002, from http://truthout.com/docs_02/04.05D.JVB.Patriot.htm

What Is the Wassenaar Arrangement? (n.d.). Retrieved July 17, 2001, from http://www.wassenaar.org/docs/talkpts.html

Winn, J. K. (2001). The emperor's new clothes: The shocking truth about digital signatures and Internet commerce. *Idaho Law Review, 37,* 353.

WIPO Copyright Treaty. (1996, December 20). Retrieved May 8, 2002, from http://www.wipo.org/eng/iplex/index.htm

WIPO Performances and Phonograms Treaty. (1996, December 20). Retrieved May 8, 2002, from http://www.wipo.org/eng/iplex/index.htm

World-Wide Volkswagen Corp. v. Woodson. 444 U.S. 286 (1980).

Yahoo! Inc., v. La Ligue Contre Le Racisme Et L' Antisemitisme, 169 F.Supp. 2d 1181 (2001).

Zemnick, S. R. (2001). Student note. The E-Sign Act: The means to effectively facilitate the growth and development of e-commerce. *Chicago-Kent Law Review, 76,* 1965.

Zippo Manufacturing Co. v. Zippo Dot Com, Inc., 952 F. Supp. 119 (W.D. Penn. 1997).

FURTHER READING

Aaron, D. The Second Annual Privacy & Data Security Summit. Retrieved (August 14, 2002) from http://www.privacyassociation.org/docs/aaron-020201.pdf

Electronic Frontier Foundation. (2001). *EFF Analysis of the Provisions of the USA PATRIOT Act*. Retrieved May 8, 2002, from http://www.eff.org/Privacy/Surveillance/Terrorism_militias/20011031_eff_usa_patriot_analysis.html

Geist, M. (2001). Is there a there there: Toward greater certainty for internet jurisdiction. *PLI/Pat, 661,* 561.

Global information networks: Realising the potential. (1997, July). Ministerial Declaration from European Ministerial Conference, Bonn, Germany.

Godwin, M. (2001, September). ALERT: Ask Congress to legislate to improve security not eliminate freedoms. Retrieved from the Electronic Frontier Foundation Web site: http://www.eff.org/effector/HTML/effect14.24.html#I

Rice, D. (2002). Refining the *Zippo* test: New trends on personal jurisdiction for internet activities. *Prentice Hall Law & Business. The Computer & Internet Lawyer.*

Privacy Law and the Internet

Ray Everett-Church, *PrivacyClue LLC*

INTRODUCTION

Understanding privacy is a true challenge, in no small part due the difficulty in defining the concept of privacy itself. The textbook definition of privacy only begins to scratch the surface of a deeply complex issue, made all the more complex because of the strong personal feelings evoked by privacy breaches. Accounting for privacy concerns can be a daunting task, especially when one is building Internet-based services and technologies whose success can depend on not offending consumers' mercurial sensibilities about the value of their privacy versus the value of those services that depend on free-flowing personal data.

This chapter discusses the roots of privacy law, including the different ways privacy matters are dealt with under constitutional law, statutes, and common law. With the fundamentals established, the rest of this chapter will discuss how many of those principles have come to be applied in today's Internet-oriented privacy terrain, and how businesses must prepare for doing business in this new environment.

PRIVACY LAW BASICS
Privacy Defined

The Merriam-Webster Dictionary of Law defines **privacy** as "freedom from unauthorized intrusion: state of being let alone and able to keep certain especially personal matters to oneself." Within this broad "state of being let alone," particular types of privacy intrusion have been recognized under law. How one defends themselves against intrusions differs, however, based on who it is doing the intruding.

Constitutional Privacy

Even though you will find no trace of the word "privacy" in the U.S. Constitution, a series of Supreme Court decisions beginning in the 1920s began to identify the modern concept of privacy. As the Court refined its views on privacy, it found the idea of privacy within the spirit of the Constitution's protections, if not in the plain language of the document. In 1928, in a landmark wiretapping case *Olmstead v. United States*, 277 U.S. 438 (1928), Supreme Court Justice Louis Brandeis articulated these ideas in some of the most important words ever written about privacy:

"The makers of our Constitution undertook to secure conditions favorable to the pursuit of happiness. They recognized the significance of man's spiritual nature, of his feelings and of his intellect. They knew that only a part of the pain, pleasure and satisfactions of life are to be found in material things. They sought to protect Americans in their beliefs, their thoughts, their emotions, and their sensations. They conferred, as against the Government, the right to be let alone—the most comprehensive of rights and the right most valued by civilized men" (Brandeis dissenting, *Olmstead* at 478).

Brandeis's phrase, "the right to be let alone," is one of the most often-repeated ideas in privacy and has influenced the court's inquiry beyond the plain words of the Bill of Rights to find other privacy rights that are logical extensions of the meaning contained in the original words, including

- The First Amendment right of free speech has been read to include the right to speak anonymously. Free speech has also been interpreted in reverse: you have the right to not be forced to say certain things.

- The First Amendment right of free association means that you can join clubs and affiliate yourself with anyone you choose. Inherent in that right, according to the court, is the right not to say whom you're associating with.
- The Fourth Amendment prohibits the government from searching your home and property and from seizing your papers or possessions, except under very specific circumstances. The Fourth Amendment has also been read to give certain rights against government wiretaps and surveillance.
- The Fifth Amendment includes various rights of due process, which means that if the government is interested in depriving you of any of your rights—throwing you in jail, for example—it must first follow strict procedures designed to protect your rights. Among those is the right against being forced to incriminate yourself.
- The equal protection clause of the Fourteenth Amendment requires that both sexes, all races, and all religions be given equal protection under all the laws of the United States and all the laws of every state. This protection comes despite other amendments that can be read to permit some types of discrimination.

But these rights aren't absolute, for example:

- The government can set up wiretaps, perform surveillance, and perform searches and seizures if they have the reasonable belief ("probable cause") that a crime has been committed and if given permission (a "warrant") by a judge;
- The government can establish secret wiretaps and surreptitiously search your home or car, without a normal warrant, if you are suspected of being a terrorist or an "agent of a foreign power;"
- It can be illegal to keep certain materials in your home, such as drugs or child pornography;
- Certain public organizations (like the Jaycees, which was the subject of a lawsuit that established this precedent) cannot use the First Amendment right of free association to exclude protected classes of people, such as women or certain minorities. On the other hand, at the time this book was written, the Boy Scouts could discriminate against gay people.

But the Constitution only affects privacy issues involving the government. What are your rights against people who are not part of the government, such as individuals and corporations? That's where a patchwork of common law privacy protections and several statutes comes into play.

Common Law Privacy

The common law is a set of rights and obligations first recognized by courts rather than by legislatures. Just because it is "judge-made" law, though, one cannot discount the common law as being less forceful. In fact, many common-law rights have been enforced for centuries and are some of the most powerful precedents in our legal system. They are rarely overturned by legislatures, and many state and federal laws are simply codifications of common-law ideas that have been around for hundreds of years.

In a groundbreaking law review article in 1960, William Prosser set out four broad categories of common law that underlie privacy-related torts:

- Intrusion into one's seclusion;
- Disclosure of private facts;
- Publicizing information that unreasonably places one in a false light; and,
- Appropriation of one's name or likeness. (Prosser, 1960)

Intrusion. The tort of intrusion recognizes the value of having your own private space, and provides relief from those who would seek to violate it. Eavesdroppers and "peeping toms" are two examples of activities considered intrusion.

Disclosure. The tort of disclosure recognizes that making public certain private facts can cause harm to an individual. For example, disclosures about someone's health status, financial records, personal correspondence, and other kinds of sensitive personal information can cause harm if made public.

False Light. The tort of false light is similar to libel in that it involves publicizing falsehoods about someone, but it is subtly different. One famous case of false light, *Cantrell v. Forest City Publishing Co.*, 419 U.S. 245 (1974), involved a family who was inaccurately portrayed in a news article in a humiliating fashion that brought shame and embarrassment. Another, *Douglass v. Hustler Magazine*, 769 F.2d 1128 (1985), involved a model who posed nude for a popular pornographic magazine, which were instead published with embarrassing captions by a notoriously vulgar magazine instead.

Appropriation. This tort involves using the name or likeness of someone for an unauthorized purpose, such as claiming a commercial endorsement by publishing someone's image (or even that of a look-alike impersonator) in an advertisement.

In this age of modern technology, there appear to be many new ways of violating these centuries-old privacy torts. The prevalence of miniature "Web-cams," highly sophisticated digital photo editing applications, and the vigorous online trade in pornographic imagery, have each added to the ways in which individual privacy can be violated.

PRIVACY LAWS IN THE UNITED STATES AND ABROAD

In a 1973 report to Congress, the U.S. Department of Health, Education and Welfare (HEW) outlined four tenets of fair information practices. These guidelines were groundbreaking in that they set forth four characteristics that any fair policy regarding the collection and use of personal information had to take into account. The four tenets were

Notice. Details of information practices and policies should be disclosed to data subjects.

Choice. Data subjects should be given the ability to exercise choices about how data may be used or disclosed.

Access. Data subjects should be permitted access to data gathered and stored about them.

Security. Holders of personal data should be responsible for providing reasonable levels of security protection for data in their possession (HEW, 1973).

Since then, there have been a number of laws enacted in the United States dealing with individual privacy. The standard U.S. approach is, however, to focus on particular types of information used by or about specific sectors:

Banking Records. Your personal banking information is protected by law, up to a point, including under provisions of a new law called the Financial Services Modernization Act (also known by its authors as the Gramm-Leach-Bliley Act).

Credit Reports. The Fair Credit Reporting Act (FCRA) requires that credit bureaus handle your data in certain ways.

Medical and Health Insurance Records. Laws and regulations governing how medical records can be used have been in place for several decades, and provisions of a new law called the Health Insurance Portability and Accountability Act (HIPAA) are creating new rights for patients to protect and access their own health information (HHS 2002).

Government Records. The Privacy Act of 1974, which included the original tenets outlined in the HEW report, sets limits on how government agencies can collect and use personal information, while laws like the Freedom of Information Act of 1966 require government to give all citizens access to certain government records, provided that the government also take precautions not to breach privacy when making that information public.

Children's Privacy. While not limited to one business sector, a law called the Children's Online Privacy Protection Act (COPPA) places restrictions on online organizations that seek to collect data from one sector of the public: children under the age of 13. COPPA requires the publication of a privacy policy to explain data practices relating to children's information, requires verifiable parental consent before any personally identifiable information may be collected from children over the Internet, and limits companies ability to share children's information with third parties.

International Privacy Law

The recognition of privacy rights in international law goes back to December 10, 1948, when the United Nations adopted the Universal Declaration of Human Rights. Article 12 of that document says: "No one shall be subjected to arbitrary interference with his privacy, family, home or correspondence, nor to attacks upon his honour and reputation. Everyone has the right to the protection of the law against such interference or attacks" (UN, 1948).

Building on that foundation, and applying the four tenets articulated in 1973 by the U.S. government, in 1980 the multinational Organization for Economic Cooperation and Development (OECD), of which the United States is a member, issued its eight Principles of Fair Information Practices. These principles consisted of:

Collection Limitation. There should be limits to the collection of personal data, and any such data should be obtained by lawful and fair means and, where appropriate, with the knowledge or consent of the data subject.

Data Quality. Collection of personal data should be relevant to the purposes for which they are to be used, and, to the extent necessary for those purposes, should be accurate, complete and kept up to date.

Purpose Specification. The purposes for which personal data are collected should be specified not later than at the time of data collection and the subsequent use limited to the fulfillment of those purposes or such others as are not incompatible with those purposes and as are specified on each occasion of change of purpose.

Use Limitation. Personal data should not be disclosed made available or otherwise used for purposes other than those specified in accordance with principle of purpose specification, unless done with the consent of the data subject or by authority of law.

Security Safeguards. Personal data should be protected by reasonable security safeguards against such risks as loss or unauthorized access, destruction, use, modification, or disclosure of data.

Openness. There should be a general policy of openness about developments, practices and policies with respect to personal data. Means should be readily available of establishing the existence and nature of personal data, and the main purposes of their use, as well as the identity and usual residence of the data controller.

Individual Participation. An individual should have the right to obtain from a data controller confirmation of whether data are held about the individual, to be given access to the data in an intelligible form, and to have the data erased, rectified, completed, or amended.

Accountability

A data controller should be accountable for complying with measures which give effect to the principles (OECD, 1980).

The European Union has taken the OECD principles and incorporated them into a sweeping Data Privacy Directive that establishes these principles in law. The directive mandates the following minimum standards in all countries that are members of the European Union:

- Companies can only collect information needed to complete the transaction, and must delete it after the transaction is over, unless they have explicit permission.
- Consumer's personal information must be kept up to date, or deleted.
- The purpose for collecting data must be given at the time that data are collected.
- An individual's personal information cannot be used for any other purpose (e.g., mailing catalogs or coupons) unless they have explicit permission.
- Companies must have appropriate security safeguards in place to guarantee privacy of any data in their possession.
- Companies must keep consumers advised in a clear and open manner about their data practices and how consumer's privacy will be impacted by any changes.
- Consumers must be permitted to see any information a company has on file about them, must be permitted to correct any errors, and must be allowed to delete data unless there's a legally mandated reason for keeping it.
- Companies who keep consumer information must have someone in the company accountable for assuring that the privacy laws are being adhered to.
- Companies may not transfer data outside the E.U. unless the country to which the data is being transferred has privacy laws as strict as those in the E.U. (EC, 1995)

It should also be noted that these restrictions apply to all data in a company's possession, whether customer data or employee data. And these are minimum standards; individual member countries can—and have—enacted laws that are even stricter.

To enforce their privacy laws, many E.U. member countries have established data protection authorities—government agencies whose mandate is the policing of data practices within, and crossing, national borders. These authorities often require corporations who possess personally identifiable information about any citizen of their nation to register with the agency and file detailed statements of what data are collected and how it is utilized.

In addition, while U.S. law focuses on certain categories of information, such as financial or healthcare data, holders of the data such as credit bureaus, or categories of data subjects such as children, the E.U. law gives special consideration to data about:

- Race
- Religious Affiliation
- Membership in Political Parties and Trade Unions
- Criminal Records

These topics are of particular concern to Europeans, in part because of how records containing information about race, religion, and trade union memberships were gathered and used by the Nazi regime in Germany and in their occupied countries to decide who should be shipped off to concentration camps. For Europeans, the threat of private information being misused is more than a test of wills between marketers and consumers, but meant the difference between life and death for the parents and grandparents of today's European lawmakers.

Cross-Border Data Flow

The issue of cross-border data flow has been particularly vexing for U.S. corporations, especially given the number of Internet-based firms with operations in the E.U. that depend upon data flows from the E.U. back to the United States Because the United States does not have broad privacy-protecting statutes on par with the E.U., U.S. corporations face the prospect of being unable to communicate customer data, or even personnel records, back to U.S.-based facilities.

Recognizing the potential for numerous disputes, the United States and E.U. entered into a series of negotiations in the late 1999 and 2000, culminating in an agreement to create a **Safe Harbor** program. This program permits U.S. corporations to assert their adherence to an array of basic privacy requirements, with the assumption that those who certify compliance and bind themselves to enforcement measures in the event of misbehavior will be permitted to continue transferring data from the E.U. into the United States (DOC, 2000).

BALANCING PRIVACY AND LAW ENFORCEMENT

In post-"September 11" America, a great deal of public concern centers around the extent to which new antiterrorism intelligence gathering will negatively impact the privacy of average citizens. While few individuals will ever believe they merit the kind of surveillance activities implemented for mafia dons, drug kingpins, or terrorists, many are concerned that ubiquitous surveillance capabilities will result in less privacy for everyone, average citizens and mafia dons alike. Therefore, it is appropriate to briefly discuss the kinds of issues raised by increasing surveillance capabilities, and to discuss a number of programs and laws that are adding to the pressures on personal privacy. More significantly, given the extent to which American business is increasingly becoming the repository of detailed information about the lives and business transactions of individuals, it is also appropriate to discuss how businesses are increasingly being called on to aid law enforcement in their investigatory efforts, and why businesses need to exercise some judgment in deciding when and how to comply with law enforcement requests.

Surveillance, searches, and wiretaps raise extremely complex legal and technical issues that are impossible to cover in this brief space. Should these issues arise in your personal or professional activities, it will not be possible for you to deal with them without the assistance of qualified legal counsel. There are, however, some things to keep in mind that will help you to understand how an organization may be affected.

Most domestic wiretapping is governed by the Electronic Communications Privacy Act of 1986 (ECPA). In addition, the Foreign Intelligence Surveillance Act of 1978 (FISA) governs wiretaps and surveillance of those considered "agents of a foreign power." Both the ECPA and the FISA were modified, clarified, and in some cases expanded significantly, by the Uniting and Strengthening America by Providing Appropriate Tools Required to Intercept and Obstruct Terrorism Act of 2001, or "USA PATRIOT Act" for short. While some provisions of the USA PATRIOT Act were due to expire in 2004, some portions have been further expanded upon by more recent acts of Congress and remain an issue of much contentious debate.

ECPA

The ECPA generally prohibits providers of communications services (e.g., Internet service providers) from disclosing the contents of an electronic communication, whether it is in transmission or in storage, to any person other than the intended recipient. However, the ECPA also contains a number of exceptions, some of which include:

- Service providers may make disclosures to law enforcement, if proper warrants are presented. The ECPA explains those procedures in some detail.
- The ECPA's limitations only apply to services offered to the public, not to operators of, for example, an internal corporate system.
- The ECPA does not restrict the collection, use, or disclosure to non-governmental entities, of transactional information such as email addressing and billing information.
- Disclosures to private parties pursuant to subpoenas issued by civil courts may also be permitted.

In addition, the ECPA permits the government to request "dialing and signaling" information from telephone companies. Under these so-called "trap and trace" orders, law enforcement can use devices known as "pen registers" to capture the numbers being called and other information about the communications, short of the actual contents of the calls themselves. The contents of the calls can also be gathered, but only under a separate warrant that requires much more rigorous procedures and additional judicial review.

FISA

In cases where information is sought about the activities of agents of foreign powers, such as terrorists or spies, law enforcement may seek disclosure of information relevant to an investigation through a special warrant procedure. There are two noteworthy differences between standard warrants and FISA warrants: First, the FISA creates a system of special "FISA courts" in which judges meet, hear evidence, and issue warrants in total secrecy. Second, FISA warrants are much more sweeping than normal warrants and are not required to meet the same evidentiary standards as normal warrants. These differences raise significant Constitutional questions that have been raised in recent challenges to the activities of the FISA courts. Ironically, the FISA courts themselves have not been oblivious to the questions their seemingly unchecked powers have raised: a recently released decision of the FISA appeals court—the first document ever released publicly by the body—cited dozens of cases in which law enforcement provided deceptive or outright false information to the court in support of wiretap applications. Appealing to the

US Supreme Court, the Bush Administration successfully overrode the FISA appeals court's objections to expanded wiretap procedures (EPIC FISA Archive, 2003).

Concerns about state-sponsored collection of data about individuals are nothing new. Privacy watchdogs and investigative journalists have widely publicized programs like the FBI's "Carnivore" (a device for intercepting and recording Internet-based communications) (EPIC Carnivore Archive, 2001), "Magic Lantern" (a piece of software that can be surreptitiously installed on a targeted computer, allowing law enforcement to capture every keystroke) (Sullivan, 2001), and the rumored international wiretapping consortium called "Echelon" (EU Parliament, 2001).

In 2002, the U.S. Department of Defense sought funding of an anti-terrorism program called "Total Information Awareness" which would have compiled electronic records on nearly every business, commercial and financial transaction of every U.S. citizen. The massive database would then be analyzed in an effort to uncover transactions and patterns of behavior that could be deemed suspicious. While the Total Information Awareness program was stripped of most of its funding by Congress in early 2003, the Department of Defense has vowed to keep researching the issues and technologies needed to undertake such a program (EPIC TIA Archive, 2003). In a September 10, 2003, op-ed piece for the *New York Times*, Department of Defense official (and controversial figure from the Reagan Administration's Iran-Contra affair) Admiral John Poindexter defended the rechristened "Terrorism Information Awareness" program (Poindexter, 2003). However, as of this writing, the program has not regained support, or funding, in Congress.

Business Issues Under Wiretap Laws

The wiretap activities under the ECPA and the FISA have until recently been relatively limited in their effects on businesses. Aside from telephone companies and some Internet service providers, few businesses were affected by these procedures. But under recent changes to the FISA made by the USA PATRIOT Act, law enforcement is now permitted to request business records from nearly any business to assist it in foreign intelligence and international terrorism investigations.

Previously, the FISA only allowed law enforcement to request business records from certain categories of businesses, such as common carriers, hotels, and car rental facilities. But under the new rules, subpoenas can be issued without limit to particular categories, including banks, retailers, and any other entity within the government's reach. The USA PATRIOT Act also expanded the search and seizure from merely "records" to "any tangible things," such as computer servers.

The pen register and trap/trace provisions of the ECPA have been expanded under the USA PATRIOT Act to add "routing" and "addressing" to the phrase "dialing and signaling," making it clear that these activities now include Internet traffic, not just telephone calls. The act does specify that the information retrieved through this process "shall not include the contents of any communication." There will undoubtedly be significant litigation in coming years to define where the dividing line falls between "content" and "addressing." For example, entering a search term or phrase into a search engine may cause the content of that search to be embedded in the address of the Web page on which the results are displayed.

PRIVACY ISSUES FOR BUSINESSES

Similarly, the Society for Human Resource Management (SHRM) reported in January 2004 that 57 percent of HR professionals are somewhat or very concerned about workplace violence in part as a result of the terror incidents of September 11, 2001. Eighty percent of human resources professionals now say they conduct background checks on employees, up 29 percent from a similar survey in 1996, and 35 percent conduct credit checks to screen potential employees, an increase of 16 percent from 1996. Eighty-two percent of human resources professionals report their organizations investigate the background of potential employees, up from 66 percent in 1996 (SHRM, 2004).

Workplace privacy concerns do, however, predate the September 11 security concerns. For example, in a widely published 2000 survey of over 2,000 U.S. corporations, the American Management Association (AMA) discovered that 54 percent of companies monitor their employees' use of the Internet, and 38 percent monitor their employees' e-mail. In a follow-up survey in 2001, the percentage of companies doing Internet monitoring rose to 63, with 47 percent monitoring e-mail (AMA, 2001). The rise in monitoring tracks with the rise in potential problems that can flow from providing access to the Internet. Along with the ability to work more efficiently, companies are now finding themselves held responsible when bad things find their ways into employees' desktops. In the same AMA study, 15 percent of the companies surveyed have been involved in some kind of legal action concerning employee use of e-mail and/or Internet connections. In several noteworthy cases, companies have been held liable for sexual harassment-related claims from

- harassment occurring over employer-operated message boards;
- employees leaving pornographic images on computer monitors; and,
- employees distributing sexually explicit jokes through office e-mail.

In response to these concerns, many companies have installed filtering mechanisms on their e-mail traffic looking for unacceptable language. Other companies have implemented software that blocks pornographic Web sites. Still others have opted for the low-tech approach of implementing zero-tolerance policies regarding the use of office computers for anything inappropriate.

Unfortunately in some instances, these measures have resulted in confusion and in some cases have wound up creating problems for both innocent and not-so-innocent people. For example, it was widely reported in 1999 that 23 employees of the *New York Times* were fired for trading dirty jokes over the office e-mail system (Oakes, 1999).

Yet, in other cases, recipients of unsolicited e-mail have opened the fraudulently labeled mail and been subjected to a barrage of pornographic images and salacious Web pop-up ads (Levine et al., 2002).

Because Web monitoring logs and filtering systems may not be able to differentiate between Web pages viewed accidentally and those viewed purposefully, innocent workers can (and have) been left fearing for their jobs. For these reasons, companies are beginning to adopt internal privacy policies that help set better guidelines and establish reliable procedures for dealing with trouble when it arises.

Employee Privacy Policies

In most circumstances, there are very few legal restrictions on what employers can do with their own computers and networks, up to and including monitoring of employee's communications. While some firms quietly implement employee monitoring policies and wait to catch unsuspecting employees in unauthorized activities, many firms give notice to their employees that they may be monitored. Still others require employees to relinquish any claims of privacy as a condition of employment.

Increasingly, however, companies are recognizing the negative impact of paternalistic monitoring practices on employee morale. So to engender trust, rather than inspire fear, increasing numbers of firms have begun providing their employees with privacy statements in their corporate employee handbooks, or by publishing policy statements on company-internal Web sites. According to the AMA's 2001 survey, four out of five respondent firms have a written policy for e-mail use, and 77 percent for Internet use; 24 percent have training programs to teach these policies to employees, and an additional 10 percent plan one (AMA, 2001).

As noted earlier with regard to the European Union's Data Privacy Directive, companies with operations in the E.U. are already familiar with the mandate to provide data subjects—in these cases, employees—with information about the company's data gathering and usage policies. While there is currently no U.S. equivalent to these requirements, a growing number of firms are proactively recognizing that a well-defined set of privacy policies and practices can avoid misunderstandings and can even provide the basis of a legal defense in cases where companies are accused of failing to act on claims of Internet-based sexual harassment.

Developing an Employee Privacy Policy

The creation of a privacy policy for internal use in an organization can be as simple or as complex as the organization itself. Most companies collect information from their employees in the form of personnel records. Firms may also collect personal information from customers or clients. An internal privacy policy should address acceptable practices with regard to each type of information maintained by the company.

A good internal privacy policy should define what standards of behavior are expected of those who have responsibility over the data held by the company—including both employee data and the personal data of a company's customers—and should inform employees about the consequences of noncompliance. Additional topics that can be covered in a privacy policy include procedures for reporting breaches, procedures for allowing employees to access and correct their own personnel records, procedures regarding access to proprietary records such as customer lists, and procedures for auditing compliance and for training employees how to comply with the company's guidelines.

CONSUMER INTERNET PRIVACY

Before the Web existed, companies gathered whatever information they could get about their customers from a variety of sources, such as real estate transaction records, credit bureaus, court documents, and motor vehicle records. But for many companies, among the most elusive, and hence the most valuable information—what you are interested in buying and exactly when you are ready to buy—was largely unavailable. Occasionally, a clever marketer could devise an algorithm or a statistical model that might be used to infer some purchase preference from the tidbits of information that might be gathered about a customer from scattered sources. But the Internet has made such information gathering much more commonplace.

Browser Privacy Issues

Much of the average computer user's online activities revolve around the two most popular Web browsers, Internet Explorer and Netscape. Browsers continue to evolve and improve, especially where privacy and security issues are involved. However, even the most recent versions have some fundamental privacy problems that arise not by accident but by design. In many cases, there are default settings that permit the collection and storage of usage data. These include

- Browsers regularly tell Web sites what kind of browser it is, what version, what operating system it running on, and even what Web site "referred" you to the current page you are visiting.
- Some browsers have settings that permit users to automatically capture and enter user IDs and passwords for Web sites, as well as other personal information such as credit card numbers. These "wallet" features provide convenience, but also present a privacy risk should anyone gain access to that machine and use it to log into sites or access your personal information.
- Browsers can be instructed by Web sites to store little text files, called **cookies**, on your local hard drive. Cookies can be used to store personal information or to assign unique identifiers that allow sites to identify you individually on future visits.
- Browsers can keep a log of every Web site you visit and may even keep copies of the pages and images you have viewed. The "history" function can log this data for days, weeks, or even months. Depending on the size of the hard drive and the default settings for a browser, it may also store days or weeks of Web page files and images in a "cache" folder.

Internet Explorer and Netscape have their own built-in privacy settings and controls. However they do vary in the level of control they allow over elements like cookies. The Help file that comes with each browser explains the browser's privacy settings and describes how to control them.

IP Addresses and Browser Data

In 1990, an engineer at a Swiss physics laboratory, Tim Berners-Lee, invented a new data exchange standard in an effort to speed the sharing of information between researchers at widely dispersed locations. His creation was the hypertext transport protocol, or http, and it made data sharing across the Internet literally as easy as point-and-click (Cailliau, 1995).

But when the first Web servers and Web browsers were developed, not much attention was paid to subjects like security and privacy. Because Berners-Lee and other engineers needed to troubleshoot their fledgling Internet connections, they built many automatic reporting features, that would let them easily get to the root of the problem when something went haywire. This need for information such as browser type, version, operating system, and referring page, was built into the earliest browsers and persists there today.

While not a tremendous privacy concern, the collection of this browser data is a standard function of most web server software. Most sites collect this data for troubleshooting purposes and then delete it after some period of time, mostly because it can become very voluminous very quickly, and its usefulness diminishes over time.

One element of the data that is also captured in the process of requesting and serving Web pages is the **IP address** of the user's computer. An IP, or Internet Protocol, address is a formatted string of numbers that uniquely identifies your computer out of all of the other computers connected to the Internet. IP addresses, which look something like 192.168.134.25, are assigned in blocks to Internet service providers, who in turn dole them out to their customers. With most dial-up Internet access accounts, users are assigned a "dynamic" IP address, meaning that the IP address assigned to your computer changes every time you log onto your ISP, and gets tossed back into the ISP's pool of addresses when you disconnect. By contrast, dedicated servers and some desktop computers in corporate or academic settings may have a "static" IP address, which is unique to that machine and may persist for the life of the equipment.

But in this age of always-on Internet connections, such as those provided by DSL or cable modem services, it is possible for an average user's computer to have the same IP address for days, weeks, or months on end. From a privacy perspective, a static IP address can compromise one's privacy because an unchanging IP address make it easier for the truly determined to track an individual's Internet usage. For example, a site that collects IP addresses in their server logs may be able to correlate with other transactional records (e.g., purchase history or search parameters) to associate a unique IP address with a unique user and their online activities.

Given that most consumers use Internet service providers that regularly use dynamic IP addressing (as most of the DSL and cable modem providers claim), IP addresses are not considered a very reliable means of allowing Web sites or online advertisers to track users uniquely. However, this lack of reliability should not be confused with anonymity. As a routine bookkeeping matter, many service providers log which IP address was allocated to which user's account at a given period of time. These connection records are frequently sought by prosecutors investigating criminal activities perpetrated via the Internet and by parties in private lawsuits over online activities. In recent years, dozens of companies have successfully uncovered the identities of "anonymous" critics by obtaining court orders for the release of user identities. Not every Internet service provider has willingly provided that information; in 2002, Verizon Internet fought attempts by the Recording Industry Association of America to release records identifying users accused of illegally trading music files. As of this writing, the federal district court in Washington, DC, held that Verizon was required to reveal the user's identity, however Verizon has appealed (McCullagh, 2003). Ultimately courts ruled that the recording industry needed court approval for subpoenas seeking the identity of alleged music pirates (Borland, 2003).

Cookies

Connections made using http are called "stateless," which means that after your computer receives the content of a requested page, the connection between your computer and the far-away Web server is closed. Rather than maintain a constant open connection "state," each file that makes up the page (e.g., each of the graphics on a page) creates a new and separate connection. This is why, for example, it is sometimes possible to receive all the text of a Web page, but not the images; if the Web browser breaks the connection, or the distant server is too busy, it will not be able to open additional connection to receive the additional data.

The benefit to a stateless connection is simple: it enables one machine to serve a much higher volume of data. However, the downside to a stateless connection is that on occasion it might be helpful for a server to remember who you are. For example, when someone logs onto their stock portfolio, privacy and security dictate that the server not reveal your account information to anyone else, however, efficiency demands that every time you load a page, you should not have to reenter your user ID and password for every new connection your browser makes to the remote computer. So how do you make a server remember who you are? You do so by creating a constant state in an otherwise stateless series of connections. And the method for doing this is the cookie.

Cookies contain a piece of data that allows the remote Web server to recognize a unique connection as having a relationship to another unique connection. In short, the cookie makes sure that the server can remember a visitor through many steps in a visit or even when time has passed between visits. As a basic security measure, it should be noted that cookies are designed to be read only by a server within the same domain that created it. So, for example, only a server in the yahoo.com domain can read cookies set by a server in the yahoo.com domain.

Cookies enable a myriad of helpful features, such as the ability to personalize a Web site with your choice of colors, or language, or stock symbols on a stock ticker. It also enables features such as shopping carts on e-commerce Web sites, permitting you to select multiple items over the course of a long visit and have them queued for purchase at the end of your visit.

Not all cookies are used for collecting or retaining information over a long period of time, such as those used by advertisers. For example, many Web sites contain a great deal of frequently changing content and generate their Web pages from large databases of text. In some of these cases, the Web servers require cookies to help determine, for example, what page it should serve up to you based upon the search terms that you entered into a search engine.

A special type of cookie, called a **session cookie**, is set to be automatically deleted after a relatively short period of time, usually within about 10 minutes after you leave a site. This type of cookie is typically used for remembering information over a short duration, such as what you may have stored in a shopping cart. Because session cookies are so short lived, they do not have quite the same privacy implications as their longer-lived cousin, the **persistent cookie**. Persistent cookies often have expiration dates set many years in the future.

Most web browsers have settings that allow a user to accept or reject certain cookies. For example, an alternative brand of Web browser called Opera, favored among the privacy community, allows users to accept or reject cookies based on whether it is a **first-party cookie** being set by the site the user is actively visiting, or whether it is a **third-party cookie**, being set by some other entity, such as an advertising service via an ad banner appearing on the site.

Web Bugs

Another popular technology for tracking users' activities online is the **Web bug**, also called "Web beacons," "1-by-1 pixels," or "clear GIFs." (GIF, which stands for Graphics Interchange Format, is a particular type of file format for images.)

Web bugs are special links embedded in Web pages, or other HTML-coded documents such as some types of email, that allow the link's creator to track every instance in which the document is viewed (Smith, 2001). As discussed earlier, every time a Web page is loaded, images on the page are loaded in a separate transaction with the Web server. When a Web bug is programmed into a Web page, its code looks similar to the code for just about any graphic image appearing on that page. In reality, though, it has three differences:

- The Web bug graphic can be called from any site, most often from a third-party site, allowing that site to record deals about your visit.
- The Web address used to call in the Web bug graphic is often encoded with specific data relating to the page being visited, or in the case of HTML email, it

may be encoded with information about your e-mail address.

- The graphic image associated with the Web bug is deliberately made to be so tiny that it is invisible to the naked eye.

Most Web bugs are the size of a single screen pixel. What is a pixel? Every image on a computer screen is comprised of very tiny dots. The smallest unit of dot on your computer screen is the pixel. But even a single pixel can still be visible, so Web bug images are often made of a graphic image called a clear GIF, or a transparent GIF, which allows the background color or image to show through it, rendering it effectively invisible.

Because Web bugs can be embedded in any Web page or HTML document, they can also be included in e-mail, allowing sites to track details about when a message is read, and to whom the message might be sent. This versatility is why Web bugs have become so widely used. It is also why an industry group called the Network Advertising Initiative, which represents a growing category of online advertising firm called **ad networks**, responded to pressure from privacy advocates and legislators by agreeing to a set of guidelines for notice and choice when Web bugs are in use.

Ad Networks

Some sites rent out space on their Web pages to third parties, often for placement of advertisements. Along with those ad banners, many third-party advertising companies also try to set their own cookie on your browser. These cookies can be used for things like managing ad frequency (the number of times an advertisement is shown to a particular individual), and to track users movements between the many sites on which the advertising companies place their cookies. These ad networks are a type of advertising agency that rents space on dozens or hundreds of websites, and frequently uses cookies placed on all of the sites in their network to build a profile about the kinds of Web sites a particular user likes to visit.

What is increasingly a marketer's paradise is becoming a consumer's nightmare: the deluge of commercial messages in e-mail inboxes, parades of pop-up advertisements, and even solicitations arriving by cellular phone and pager are making consumers leery of the alleged benefits of this ubiquitously wired world. In response to growing consumer concerns, companies have sought to develop privacy polices that help consumers better understand how their information is gathered and used.

PRIVACY POLICY FUNDAMENTALS

According to the Federal Trade Commission (FTC), if a company makes a promise that it does not deliver on, that is considered an unfair or deceptive trade practice, for which the offender can be fined up to $11,000 per violation, in addition to other legal remedies (FTC OGC, 2002). Central to the FTC's advocacy of greater consumer privacy protections has been the call for companies to adopt privacy policies that provide consumers with useful information about how their personal information is

gathered and used. While there are no federal laws that require the publication of a privacy policy, except where data collection from children is involved, it is widely considered an industry "best practice" to publish a privacy policy on any public Web site.

Considering the liability created by writing a privacy policy that a company cannot deliver on, the drafting of a privacy policy is not something to be undertaken lightly or without advice of legal counsel. However, good privacy policies tend, at minimum, to address those elements contained in the widely accepted fair information principles, which have also been endorsed by the FTC: notice, choice, access, and security. We will discuss the FTC's role in policing privacy matters later in this section, but it should also be noted that legal actions by state Attorneys General, as well as private lawsuits, are also driving companies toward some level of uniformity in privacy disclosures.

Those privacy policies cited by privacy advocates as being "best of class" also include the elements of the OECD's principles of fair information practices. There are also a number of online privacy policy generators that allow you to create policies by picking and choosing from predefined language based on the applicable situation. According to the privacy organization, TRUSTe, their recommended Model Privacy Statement has several key elements that echo the OECD principles:

- What personally identifiable information the company collects.
- What personally identifiable information third parties collect through the Web site.
- What organization collects the information.
- How the company uses the information.
- With whom the company may share user information.
- What choices are available to users regarding collection, use and distribution of the information.
- What types of security procedures are in place to protect the loss, misuse or alteration of information under the company's control.
- How users can correct any inaccuracies in the information. (TRUSTe, 2004)

Once a company has surveyed their data practices and articulated them clearly in a privacy policy document, the next most important task is to assure that the company lives up to its promises. There are three ways to do this: manage privacy matters internally, look to industry-sponsored groups for guidance on compliance, or wait for law enforcement to come after you.

Chief Privacy Officers

As the importance of privacy has grown in the corporate setting, and as the risks from privacy problems have increased, companies have begun to create a new management position, the Chief Privacy Officer (CPO), as the designated point-person for managing privacy policies and practices.

Since the first CPO position was created in 1999 at the start-up Internet advertising firm AllAdvantage.com, the CPO job description (if not always the title) has been rapidly adopted across corporate America; by the end of 2000, a significant number of Fortune 100 firms had a CPO-type position, often reporting to the seniormost levels of the organization. According to the Privacy Working Group of the advocacy group Computer Professionals for Social Responsibility, there are many benefits to appointing a CPO:

> A talented and properly-positioned CPO will add value across corporate divisions from development to customer relations, from liability mitigation and risk management to increased market share and valuation. Perhaps most importantly, the Chief Privacy Officer promotes an essential element of new economy corporate citizenship—Trust. (Enright & McCullough, 2000)

The CPO has both an internal and an external role at his or her company. The internal role includes participation in companywide strategy planning, operations, product development and implementation, compliance monitoring and auditing, and employee training and awareness. The external role of the CPO involves enhancing the company's image as a privacy sensitive organization, through fostering positive relationships with consumers and consumer groups, privacy advocates, industry peers, and regulators.

In many respect, the CPO becomes the focal point for a company's privacy activities, and in turn can become the company's public face on the privacy issue. The position is most effective if it is perceived as objective, with ombudsman-like qualities, serving as a protector of consumer interests while seeking balance between those interests and the interests of the company. Yet there are other organizations offering assistance in the ombudsman role: trustmark organizations.

Trustmarks

There are several independent, industry-sponsored organizations that will certify a company's privacy policy in order to improve consumer perceptions. Upon certification, they permit sites to use their "seal of approval," sometimes referred to as a **trustmark**, to demonstrate to the public their commitment to privacy concerns. The most popular privacy seal programs—BBBOnline, CPA WebTrust, and TRUSTe—certify the validity of the policies on many thousands of Web sites. And the growing use of these trustmarks does seem to be having an effect: an August 1999 study found that 69 percent of Internet users said that they recognize the TRUSTe seal, the most widely adopted of the privacy seal programs.

Seal programs verify that a Web site's privacy policy covers certain privacy topics (e.g., the use of cookies and sharing data with third-party marketers). However, the seals do not set any specific quality standards, benchmarks, or specific data handling practices. As such, a site could, theoretically, earn a seal for making the required disclosures, even if in the course of the disclosure it reserves for itself the right to make whatever use of personal information it sees fit. This has been one of the criticisms leveled at the seal programs, as has their dependence on licensing fees from those entities they are asked to police.

Federal Trade Commission

Under their broad legislative mandate to proscribe deceptive and unfair trade practices, the FTC began reviewing online marketing practices back in 1996. Soon the FTC's investigators were uncovering evidence of what they felt was egregious behavior by a few online marketers. Major corporations quickly distanced themselves from the alleged "bad actors," but acknowledged that privacy was a growing concern for online consumers, and promised the FTC that the industry would do better at policing itself.

After numerous public controversies over well-known corporations continuing to abuse consumer privacy, and despite repeated pledges to adhere to standards promulgated and policed by the industry itself, surveys have continued to show that consumer perceptions of the potential for privacy abuses (whether perceived or actual) by online marketers continues to be a factor in consumer hesitance to fully embrace Internet commerce. In response, the FTC has sought on numerous occasions to assist companies in adopting practices that are more conducive to consumer confidence. These efforts have focused on the well-worn mantra: notice, choice, access, and security.

In December 1999, the FTC convened an Advisory Committee on Online Access and Security to provide advice and recommendations to the agency regarding implementation of these basic fair information practices. The committee, consisting of representatives from the online industry, trade groups, academia, and privacy advocates, sought to provide guidance on how to solve the last two elements of fair information practices: access and security. Their report outlines many of the problems with setting universal standards for access and security, and in the end came to few conclusions (FTC ACOAS, 2000).

Some six years after first looking into online privacy issues, the FTC is still warning online companies that if they do not clean up their act, stricter measures might be required. During the intervening years, however, the FTC has not been completely idle:

- In 1998, the FTC reached a settlement with GeoCities, a personal Web site hosting service, over charges that it misrepresented how user information would be used and engaged in deceptive practices relating to its collection of information from children. Part of the settlement required GeoCities (now owned by Yahoo!) to post, "a clear and prominent Privacy Notice, telling consumers what information is being collected and for what purpose, to whom it will be disclosed, and how consumers can access and remove the information." The notice, or a link to it, was required on the Web site's home page and on every page where information was collected (FTC, 1998).

- In 1999, the FTC issued regulations implementing the Children's Online Privacy Protection Act, which requires online businesses to seek permission from parents before gathering personally identifiable information from children under age 13. It has since brought several enforcement actions to punish Web sites that have ignored those regulations (FTC "Kidz Privacy," 2003).

- In recent years, the FTC has filed numerous actions against Internet-based fraudulent schemes, get-rich-quick scams, and quack medical remedies promoted via e-mail and on the Web.
- In 2000, the FTC intervened in the bankruptcy sale of a customer list belonging to defunct online toy retailer Toysmart.com. The basis of the action was to prevent the list from being used in any way inconsistent with the privacy policy under which it was gathered (FTC, 2000).
- In 2001, the FTC settled with pharmaceutical firm Eli Lilly and Company over an e-mail that improperly disclosed the e-mail addresses of hundreds of users of a prescription reminder service at the Web site Prozac.com, in violation of the site's privacy policy (FTC, 2002).
- In 2003, the FTC settled with clothing manufacturer Guess? Jeans, Inc., over security breaches in the database associated with their online sales Web site. The FTC claimed that Guess? Jeans had failed to use reasonable measures to protect the privacy of consumers' credit card and other personal information when they failed to implement a security patch to remedy a well-known security vulnerability in their database software (FTC, 2003).

The FTC has steadfastly refused to seek greater legislative authority than its already broad mandate under the Federal Trade Act to police unfair or deceptive trade practices. However the agency has threatened the industry that it will indeed seek more specific privacy-oriented enforcement authority if companies do not improve their self-regulatory efforts. It must also be noted that the FTC is just one governmental authority with the ability to prosecute privacy violations: most state Attorneys General have state versions of the Federal Trade Act that enable them to seek remedies similar to those available to the FTC. Indeed, Attorneys General in Michigan, Washington, California, and Massachusetts, have all been active in undertaking privacy-related enforcement actions, and the National Association of Attorneys General has held many seminars on investigating and prosecuting Internet privacy matters (NAAG, 2001).

CONCLUSION

Consumers and businesses alike are grappling with the complex privacy concerns that the Internet era has brought to the fore. This chapter is a necessarily brief overview of the privacy landscape. Indeed, entire books can—and have—been written about the ways Internet technologies have created new challenges to the average person's desire to "be let alone." But as this chapter has shown, there are a number of concepts that find their way into privacy-related policies and practices. Among them, the fundamental principles of notice, choice, access, and security, are driving both consumer expectations and business planning. Keeping these principles in mind, many who are called on to seek privacy solutions in their own particular business or personal context have a conceptual framework within which to arrive at their own conclusion.

GLOSSARY

Ad Network A consortium of Web sites linked together by an advertising agency for purposes of aggregating advertising placements and tracking consumers movements among and between member sites.

Cookies A small file saved by your Web browser, at the direction of a Web site, containing data that may be later retrieved by that Web site. See also persistent cookies, session cookies, third-party cookies.

COPPA Children's Online Privacy Protection Act of 1998. Legislation that limits operators of commercial Web sites and online services from collecting personal information from children under age 13.

ECPA Electronic Communications Privacy Act of 1986. Legislation governing the use of wiretaps for domestic law enforcement activities.

FISA Foreign Intelligence Surveillance Act of 1978. Legislation governing the use of wiretapping and physical searches in investigations involving terrorists and agents of foreign powers.

GLB Gramm-Leach-Bliley Act, also known as the Financial Services Modernization Act. Legislation that instituted major changes to the U.S. banking system. In pertinent part, GLB requires that organizations providing financial services disclose their data collection practices to customers, and to provide the ability to opt-out of those practices.

HIPAA Health Insurance Portability and Accountability Act of 1996. Legislation that instituted a number of changes to health insurance practices. In pertinent part, HIPAA included privacy-related provisions applicable to health information created or maintained by health care providers, health plans, and health care clearinghouses.

Internet Protocol (IP) Address The unique numerical address assigned to each computer connected to the Internet. An address may be assigned temporarily (called a dynamic IP address) or may be assigned for long periods (called a static IP address).

OECD Organization for Economic Cooperation and Development. A group of 30 democratic, market economy countries working collaboratively on economic, social, and trade issues.

Persistent Cookies Cookie files designated to be stored for long periods, sometimes as long as 10 years.

Privacy Freedom from unauthorized intrusion. A state of being let alone and able to keep certain especially personal matters to oneself.

Safe Harbor A legal concept which permits an entity to reduce and/or avoid legal liability by agreeing to adhere to certain standards or procedures. In the context of Internet privacy, Safe Harbor refers to an agreement between the United States and the European Union that permits U.S. companies to certify that they adhere to the stricter privacy standards required by European law, thereby avoiding a more burdensome set of country-by-country registration procedures.

Session Cookies Cookie files designated to be stored for only the duration of a visit to a Web site; usually ten minutes or less.

Third-Party Cookies A cookie file set by some entity other than the operator of the Web site being visited by the user. Third-party cookies are often used by advertising services to track user movements between multiple Web sites over periods of times.

Trustmark A symbol used to identify those Web sites who have subjected their privacy policy to review by a third-party watchdog organization.

Web Bugs (also called Web Beacons, 1-by-1 Pixels, or Clear GIFs) Special links embedded in Web pages, or other HTML-coded documents such as some types of email, that allow the link's creator to track every instance in which the document is viewed.

CROSS REFERENCES

See *Copyright Law; Cryptographic Privacy Protection Techniques; Legal, Social and Ethical Issues of the Internet; The Legal Implications of Information Security: Regulatory Compliance and Liability.*

REFERENCES

American Management Association (AMA) (2001). 2001 Workplace Monitoring and Surveillance: Policies and Practices. Available at: http://www.amanet.org/research/pdf/ems_short2001.pdf (Date of access: August 21, 2005).

Borland, J. (2003). Court: RIAA Lawsuit Strategy Illegal. News.com. Available at: http://news.com.com/2100-1027-5129687.html (Date of access: February 8, 2004)

Cailliau, R. (1995). A Little History of the World Wide Web. Available at: http://www.w3c.org/History.html (Date of access: February 8, 2004)

Cantrell v. Forest City Publishing Co., 419 U.S. 245 (1974). Available at: http://laws.findlaw.com/us/419/245.html (Date of access: February 8, 2004)

Children's Online Privacy Protection Act. (15 U.S.C. §§ 6501–6506) Available at: http://www.ftc.gov/ogc/coppa1.htm (Date of access: February 8, 2004)

Douglass v. Hustler Magazine, 769 F.2d 1128 (1985)

Electronic Communications Privacy Act of 1986. (18 U.S.C. § 2701) Available at: http://www4.law.cornell.edu/uscode/18/2701.html (Date of access: February 8, 2004)

Electronic Privacy Information Center (EPIC) Carnivore Archive. (2002) Available at: http://www.epic.org/privacy/carnivore/ (Date of access: February 8, 2004)

Electronic Privacy Information Center (EPIC) Foreign Intelligence Surveillance Act (FISA) Archive. (2003) Available at: http://www.epic.org/privacy/terrorism/fisa/ (Date of access: February 8, 2004)

Electronic Privacy Information Center (EPIC) "Terrorism" Information Awareness (TIA) Archive. (2003) Available at: http://www.epic.org/privacy/profiling/tia/ (Date of access: February 8, 2004) (Editing note: the strikethrough text is on the original Website title)

Enright, K. P. and McCullough, M. R. (2000). Computer Professionals for Social Responsibility Privacy Working Group: CPO Guidelines. Available at: http://www.privacylaw.net/CPO_Guidelines.pdf (Date of access: December 3, 2002)

European Commission (EC). (1995). Directive 95/46/EC of the European Parliament and of the Council of 24 October 1995 on the protection of individuals with regard to the processing of personal data and on the free movement of such data. *Official Journal L.*, *281*, 31. Available at: http://europa.eu.int/comm/internal_market/privacy/index_en.htm (Date of access: February 8, 2004)

European Union (EU) Parliament. Temporary Committee on the ECHELON Interception System Report. (2001) Available at: http://www.europarl.eu.int/tempcom/echelon/pdf/prechelon_en.pdf (Date of access: February 8, 2004)

Fair Credit Reporting Act. (15 U.S.C. §§ 1681–1681(u), as amended) Available at: http://www.ftc.gov/os/statutes/fcra.htm (Date of access: February 8, 2004)

Federal Trade Commission (FTC). (1998). In the Matter of GeoCities, File No. 982 3051. Available at: http://www.ftc.gov/os/1998/08/geo-ord.htm (Date of access: February 8, 2004)

Federal Trade Commission (FTC). (2000). FTC v. Toysmart.com, LLC, and Toysmart.com, Inc. (District of Massachusetts) (Civil Action No. 00-11341-RGS). Available at: http://www.ftc.gov/opa/2000/07/toysmart.htm (Date of access: February 8, 2004)

Federal Trade Commission (FTC). (2002). In the Matter of Eli Lilly and Company, File No. 012 3214. Available at: http://www.ftc.gov/opa/2002/01/elililly.htm (Date of access: February 8, 2004)

Federal Trade Commission (FTC). (2003). In the Matter of Guess?, Inc., and Guess.com, Inc., File No. 022 3260. Available at: http://www.ftc.gov/opa/2003/06/guess.htm (Date of access: February 8, 2004)

Federal Trade Commission (FTC) Advisory Committee on Online Access and Security (ACOAS). (2000). Final Report. Available at: http://www.ftc.gov/acoas (Date of access: February 8, 2004)

Federal Trade Commission (FTC) "Kidz Privacy" Education Campaign Site. (2003) Available at: http://www.ftc.gov/bcp/conline/edcams/kidzprivacy/news.htm (Date of access: February 8, 2004)

Federal Trade Commission (FTC) Office of the General Counsel (OGC). (2002). "A Brief Overview of the Federal Trade Commission's Investigative and Law Enforcement Authority." Available at: http://www.ftc.gov/ogc/brfovrvw.htm (Date of access: February 8, 2004)

Foreign Intelligence Surveillance Act of 1978. (codified at 50 U.S.C. §§ 1801–1811, 1821–1829, 1841–1846, 1861–62, as amended) Available at: http://www4.law.cornell.edu/uscode/50/1801.html (Date of access: February 8, 2004)

Freedom of Information Act of 1966. (5 U.S.C. § 552) Available at: http://www.usdoj.gov/oip/foia_updates/Vol_XVII_4/page2.htm (Date of access: February 8, 2004)

Gramm-Leach-Bliley Act. (Codified in relevant part at 15 U.S.C. §§ 6801–6809) Available at: http://www.ftc.gov/privacy/glbact/glbsub1.htm (Date of access: February 8, 2004)

Levine, J. R., Everett-Church, R., & Stebben, G. (2002). Internet Privacy for Dummies. New York: Wiley Publishing, Inc.

McCullagh, D. (2003). Labels, Verizon DMCA Battle Rages. ZDNet News. Available at: http://zdnet.com.com/2100-1104-983896.html (Date of access: February 8, 2004)

National Association of Attorneys General (NAAG). (2001). 39 Attorneys General, the District of Columbia Corporation Counsel, and the Georgia Governors Office of Consumer Affairs Submit Comments to FCC Urging Better Privacy Protections For Consumers. Available at: http://www.naag.org/issues/pdf/20011228-signon-fcc.pdf (Date of access: February 8, 2004)

Network Advertising Initiative (NAI). (2001). Web Beacons: Guidelines for Notice and Choice. Available at: http://www.networkadvertising.org/Statement.pdf (Date of access: February 8, 2004)

Oakes, C. (1999). 23 Fired for Email Violations. Wired News. Available at: http://www.wired.com/news/politics/0,1283,32820,00.html (Date of access: February 8, 2004)

Olmstead v. United States, 277 U.S. 438 (1928) Available at: http://laws.findlaw.com/us/277/438.html (Date of access: February 8, 2004)

Organization for Economic Cooperation and Development (OECD). (1980). Guidelines on the Protection of Privacy and Transborder Flows of Personal Data. Available at: http://www.oecd.org/document/25/0,2340,en_2649_34255_1888153_1_1_1_1,00.html (Date of access: February 8, 2004)

Poindexter, J. M. (2003) Finding the Face of Terror in Data. New York Times. Available at: http://www.nytimes.com/2003/09/10/opinion/10POIN.html (Date of access: February 8, 2004)

Privacy Act of 1974. (5 U.S.C. § 552A) Available at: http://www.usdoj.gov/foia/privstat.htm (Date of access: February 8, 2004)

Prosser, W. L. (1960). Privacy. California Law Review, 48, 383

Smith, R. M. (2001) FAQ: Web Bugs. Available at: http://www.eff.org/Privacy/Marketing/web_bug.html (Date of access: February 8, 2004)

Society for Human Resource Management. (2004). SHRM Finds Employers Are Increasingly Conducting Background Checks To Ensure Workplace Safety. Available at: http://www.shrm.org/press_published/CMS_007126.asp#P-5_0 (Date of access: February 8, 2004)

Sullivan, B. (2001). FBI Software Cracks Encryption Wall. MSNBC News. Available at: http://www.msnbc.com/news/660096.asp (Date of access: February 8, 2004)

TRUSTe. (2004). Model Privacy Statement. Available at http://www.truste.org/webpublishers/pub_modelprivacystatement.html (Date of access: February 8, 2004)

United Nations. (1948). Universal Declaration of Human Rights. Available at: http://www.un.org/Overview/rights.html (Date of access: February 8, 2004)

Uniting and Strengthening America by Providing Appropriate Tools Required to Intercept and Obstruct Terrorism (USA PATRIOT) Act of 2001. (Pub. L. No. 107-56) Available at: http://www.epic.org/privacy/terrorism/hr3162.html (Date of access: February 8, 2004)

U.S. Department of Commerce. (2000) Safe Harbor. Available at: http://www.export.gov/safeharbor (Date of access: February 8, 2004)

U.S. Department of Health and Human Services (HHS). (2002). Medical Privacy—National Standards to Protect the Privacy of Personal Health Information, Office for Civil Rights. Available at: http://www.hhs.gov/ocr/hipaa/ (Date of access: February 8, 2004)

U.S. Department of Health, Education and Welfare (HEW). (1973). Records, Computers and the Rights of Citizens. Available at: http://aspe.hhs.gov/datacncl/1973privacy/tocprefacemembers.htm (Date of access: February 8, 2004)

Internet Censorship

Richard A. Spinello, *Boston College*

INTRODUCTION

This chapter discusses the controversial topic of censorship in cyberspace. Censorship is sometimes undertaken in the name of securing a local network and client systems from the insidious exogenous influences emanating from the global Internet. Censors often seek to protect impressionable or vulnerable individuals from objectionable forms of speech that might be laced with pornographic images, xenophobia, or racism. Digital technology has enabled the privatization of censorship because it can be carried out not only by government authorities but also by private parties, including corporations and private schools, or libraries. Censorship can be achieved through public law or through software programs that constrain expression more opaquely than the law. As a result, to some degree censorship has become easier to achieve in cyberspace thanks to the use of such programs.

Although I refrain from reaching any normative conclusions about the use of censorship, this chapter argues that it should not be confused with security. Censorship is triggered by content that is unwelcome for various ideological reasons, but the goal of digital security should not be limitations on expression for the sake of its content. Rather, the purpose of security should be protection against the physical impact of another's conduct, which can result from malicious code, denial of service attacks, hacking, or trespass. Arguably, a country that filters out unwanted sexual images or political speech is engaged in censorship and should not attempt to justify such activities under the pretext of providing "security" for its citizens. Given that the tools used to secure the network from alien influences are the same ones used to censor that network, it is all too easy for countries and organizations to align their security procedures with a censorship agenda.

WHAT IS CENSORSHIP?

Censorship is a value-laden term that defies a simple formulation. It has been broadly defined by philosophers, however, as the intentional suppression or regulation of expression based on its content (Williams, 1998). Also, according to Williams, the activity in question "has at least to be publicly recognized in order to count as censorship." Thus, it is usually associated with a government or a "legally constituted" authority's prohibition of a publication or speech that has a certain content. However, censorship should include any act that is intended to restrict, encumber, limit, or deter in some way the expression of another. It is possible to restrict and limit another's expression in a nontransparent fashion, especially given the tools of digital technology. It is also possible for private individuals or organizations to suppress expression. Therefore, a modification of the traditional definition seems appropriate: Censorship is the public or covert suppression or regulation of speech based on its content conducted by a legally constituted authority or by private parties.

In addition to direct censorship or suppression of content, there is *circumstantial censorship* defined as "any factor that restricts or suppresses desired communications." Such indirect censorship encompasses a person's lack of resources or the problematic material conditions (such as economic structures) that hinder one's ability to engage in speech (Baker, 1996). Although this form of circumstantial censorship is important, the primary concern of this chapter is with direct intentional censorship originating from either the public or private spheres (see the chapter on the digital divide).

The Net's distributed and anarchic architecture makes it a medium strongly resistant to government regulation including conventional types of censorship. Distributed peer-to-peer networks such as the ones used for the sharing of music files (KaZaA or Gnutella) are particularly difficult to control. FreeNet, for example, is a *darknet* a—Web site used to avoid Internet surveillance and censorship. It is a fully distributed network that relies on strong encryption to protect the privacy of its users as they share information and is considered to be "almost perfectly ungovernable" (Vaidhyanathan, 2004). Nonetheless, in most cases, thanks in part to certain software and hardware architectures, governments have found ways to censor this medium, often under the pretense that they must regulate access to "protect" their citizens from corrupting foreign influences located in cyberspace.

THE FIRST AMENDMENT

Any discussion of censorship would be incomplete without understanding the scope of the right to free speech as expressed in the First Amendment of the U.S. Constitution. That amendment simply states:

> Congress shall make no law respecting the establishment of religion, or the free exercise thereof; or abridging the freedom of speech or of the press; or the right of the people peaceably to assemble, and to petition the Government for a redress of grievances.

The purpose of this amendment is to protect freedom of individual thought and expression and to encourage a robust "marketplace of ideas" that serves the common good. Free speech is also regarded as important for one's self-fulfillment and autonomy: "the value of free expression . . . rests on its deep relationship to self-respect arising from autonomous self-determination without which the life of the spirit is meager and slavish" (Richards, 1974).

Although the right to free speech has broad scope in the United States, it is by no means absolute. Since the Constitution was written, a number of free speech principles have emerged that articulate when the government can intervene in speech issues. Those guidelines help to define the limits of protected free speech. Here is a concise overview of some of the key principles:

> Courts have focused not only on what forms of speech are protected but on the means of restriction that are "constitutionally permissible;" in accordance with the over breadth, vagueness, and prior restraint doctrines courts may "invalidate restrictions on expression . . . even though the particular speech at issue might constitutionally be restricted by other means." (Stone, Seidman, Sunstein, Tushnet 2001)

> Government restrictions on the "time, place, and manner" in which speech is allowed are constitutional only if they meet these three conditions: they must be "content neutral" (that is, limit expression without regard to its content); they must leave other opportunities for speech to occur; they must be "narrowly tailored" and "serve a significant state interest." (Fisher, 2001)

> Content-based government restrictions on speech are regarded as unconstitutional unless they serve a "compelling state interest";

> Although some forms of expression have a privileged status (such as literary, artistic, and political expression), several forms of low value speech are not fully protected by the First Amendment:
> — Speech that will likely induce "imminent lawless action"
> — "Fighting words," that is, insulting words apt to start a fight or a conflict of some sort
> — Obscenity: speech that depicts or describes sexual conduct in a "patently offensive" way, appeals to "prurient interests," and "taken as a whole, lacks serious literary, artistic, political, or scientific value" (*Miller* v. *California*, 1973).

> — Child pornography
> — Material harmful to minors
> — Defamatory statements defined as communication that tends to harm the reputation of another so as to lower his or her esteem in the eyes of the community (Fisher, 2001; Spinello, 2002).

> Commercial speech has an intermediate status. According to Justice Powell, commercial speech should be "afforded . . . a limited measure of protection, commensurate with its subordinate position in the scale of First Amendment values" (*Ohralik v. Ohio State*, 1978). Thus, such speech can be banned if it is misleading or if it is associated with illegal products.

The First Amendment protects citizens only from the government's attempts to impose restrictions on free speech rights. According to this "state action" doctrine, the limits of the First Amendment apply to the government but not to private agents. An Internet service provider (ISP), for example, may decide to install filters to screen out pornographic content. If such a policy were mandated by the government or if the ISP were assuming "government-like powers," it would most likely constitute "state action" and trigger First Amendment issues. Some scholars disagree with this interpretation of the First Amendment and believe that the Internet should prompt us to reconsider this "state action" philosophy. They reason that ISPs, search engines, and other intermediaries now have the means to place restrictions on speech, and yet the First Amendment would not apply to their restrictive activities. Fried (2000), however, pointed out the downside of turning to such a revisionist doctrine, despite the growing influence of the Internet and the accretion of power by ISPs:

> By limiting the First Amendment to protecting citizens from government (and not from each other), the state action doctrine enlarges the sphere of unregulated discretion that individuals may exercise in what they think and say. In the name of First Amendment 'values,' courts could perhaps inquire whether I must grant access to my newspaper to opinions I abhor, must allow persons whose moral standards I deplore to join my expressive association, or must remain silent so that someone else gets a chance to reach my audience with a less appealing but unfamiliar message. . . . I am not convinced that whatever changes the Internet has wrought in our environment require courts to mount this particular tiger.

The Internet has surely been a major challenge for First Amendment jurisprudence. But in the United States and in other democratic countries, good faith efforts have been made to treat the Internet fairly as another medium of communication and to ensure that it enjoys the same amount of free speech protection without special privileges (see the chapter on electronic speech).

HARMFUL FORMS OF SPEECH

The Internet has made it easier for individuals to speak with anonymity and with greater impact, and it has provided a valuable space for new virtual communities. As a result, it has become a positive force for social and political change in many countries. There is, however, a dangerous side to this proliferation of speech. The Internet is a borderless global technology that cannot be easily controlled. It sometimes delivers offensive material that can range from child pornography to racist diatribes.

The use of censorship tools is most often induced by these many forms of harmful speech that have appeared in cyberspace alongside of constructive and healthy speech. Categories of speech that have been deemed harmful by various countries and governments include pornographic or obscene speech, hate speech, virtual threats, online incitement, defamation, and even spam (or junk e-mail). While those who pioneered Internet technology have consistently asserted that the right to free expression in cyberspace should have as broad a scope as possible, the increased use of the Internet especially among more vulnerable segments of the population (such as young children) has forced some public policy makers to rethink this laissez-faire approach.

In the United States, the result has been a concerted effort to control pornographic forms of speech, although the definition of this type of speech is notoriously difficult to express concisely. Nonetheless, pornographic speech appears to include speech that is obscene for everyone and speech that is harmful to minors, that is, "defined to be obscene on the basis of its appeal to [children] whether or not it would be obscene to adults" (*Ginsberg* v. *U.S.*, 1966). The penthouse.com Web site would fall into the latter category whereas child pornography would be included in the former one. Islamic countries such as Saudi Arabia have also expressed grave concerns about the abundance of pornography in cyberspace, and they, too, have initiated censorship measures to block this type of expression.

Other countries such as Germany and France, however, have been more preoccupied with extirpating hate speech from Web sites viewed by their citizens. There are stringent anti-hate laws in Europe that must be followed even in cyberspace. In Germany, for example, carefully defined laws forbid the posting of Nazi propaganda or other racist and anti-Semitic material. According to the European Convention for the Protection of Human Rights, "the right to free speech does not extend to speeches that threaten, deny or even lead to the destruction of human dignity and human integrity" (Rorive, 2003).

But extremist hate sites are more commonly hosted on servers in the United States, where hate speech is protected by the First Amendment unless it rises to the level of a specific threat, or in developing countries. The Internet's global nature makes possible this type of arbitrage opportunity, whereby individuals locate their servers in a different jurisdiction to evade certain regulations. Although some regard regulatory arbitrage as problematic, others contend that its "effects will tend to promote democratic values of openness and freedom more than they will detract from what most consider to be the modern states' legitimate regulatory powers" (Froomkin, 1997).

One of the most pernicious and pervasive forms of speech is spam, which is most properly defined as automated unsolicited bulk e-mail. Spam is usually some form of commercial e-mail, but noncommercial enterprises can also communicate by means of bulk e-mail. However, should *all* unsolicited bulk e-mail be considered as nuisance spam mail? Given the need to respect and protect speech of public concern, this would depend on the nature of the speech, the volume of the mailings, and frequency of transmission. Regardless of how we define it, however, the economics of spam are highly attractive because the marginal cost of sending another electronic message is virtually zero. Yet spam imposes costs on the recipients and the ISPs who must deliver this mail. Users are burdened by the need to delete an endless stream of messages. Given the costs of spam, it is no surprise that organizations and ISPs seek to block it to protect their servers from a burdensome overload of unauthorized e-mail messages (see the chapter on spam and the legal counter attacks).

These various forms of harmful speech that proliferate in cyberspace represent the primary motivation for the use of censorship tools. Of course, some countries, such as China, Cuba, and Saudi Arabia, go further and seek to censor dissenting political discourse as well. In China, for example, the Chinese company QQ filters words such as "democracy" and "Falun Gong" from its instant messaging service in compliance with government regulations (Hutzler, 2004). The Chinese government has also jailed some individuals for promoting political dissent on the Web. Such actions are considered repressive and an unambiguous violation of human rights according to the standards set by international bodies such as the United Nations.

TOOLS OF THE CENSORS

What sorts of tools do the censors have at their disposal? I have already alluded to some of these tools, but Lessig (1999) provided a framework that can answer this question more comprehensively. In the physical world, argued Lessig, we are regulated or constrained in four basic ways: laws, social or ethical norms, the market, and physical architectures. We are also constrained in cyberspace by the same four modalities of regulation: law, code (such as software applications), social norms, and the market. Laws, such as those that provide copyright and patent protection, regulate cyberspace behavior by proscribing certain activities and by imposing *ex post* sanctions for violators. According to Lessig, "law functions in two different ways: when its operation is direct, it tells individuals how to behave and threatens punishment if they deviate from that behavior; [w]hen its operation is indirect, it aims at modifying one of the other structures of constraint (95)" For example, law might dictate that car manufacturers make cars that will not start without a seatbelt fastened, and it thereby brings a significant architectural change. Markets regulate behavior in various ways—the pricing policies of ISPs will determine who can afford access to the Internet, and e-commerce Web sites come and go depending on their marketplace acceptance.

The counterpart of architectural constraint in the physical world is code: "not the code at its most basic level of

Internet exchange [the transmission control protocol/IP protocols], but the applications (both in hardware and software) that use or implement those protocols" (Lessig, 1999). They, too, constrain and control our activities. These programs are often referred to as the "architectures" of cyberspace. Code, for example, limits access to certain Web sites by demanding a username and password; encryption code is used to protect data from thieves and snoops, and software programs such as CyberPatrol filter out pornographic material from an end user's computer. All of these "architectures" constrain behavior and have regulatory impact. According to Lessig (2004), "the code of cyberspace is itself a kind of sovereign ... [and] thus competes with the regulatory power of local sovereigns."

Finally, there are norms that regulate cyberspace behavior, including Internet etiquette and social customs. For example, "flaming" is considered "bad form" on the Internet, and those who do it will most likely be disciplined by other members of the Internet community. Those who misrepresent themselves in a chat room also violate those norms, and they too will be reproved if their true identity is revealed. Just as in real space, cyberspace communities rely on shame and social stigma to enforce cultural norms.

Censorship is most effectively accomplished by the use of code and law, and sometimes by reliance on the combined forces of code and law—that is, code backed up by law. Consider the Digital Millennium Copyright Act (DMCA) of 1998, which forbids circumventing technological measures that protect copyrighted material. It also prohibits making or "trafficking in" anticircumvention devices. In this case, law and technology work together as a potent constraint to protect online digital content. The DMCA was invoked to halt the dissemination of a decryption program known as DeCSS that was written to decode encrypted DVD files. The defendants in this case were forbidden from posting this code on their Web site and from linking to other sites where the DeCSS program could be found (see the chapter on the Digital Millennium Copyright Act).

The primary theme of Lessig's analysis for our purposes is that code creates new opportunities for the censor, who can now suppress unwelcome speech in nontransparent ways by means of software filters, firewalls, and similar mechanisms. According to Mitchell (1995), "control of code is power," and we might add that control of code is control of content because it can structure what we see and read in cyberspace and thereby facilitate the work of the censor. Code also makes private censorship possible. Censorship can be "private" in two ways: it can be implemented in the private sector by parents or organizations (private schools and libraries, corporations, etc.) and it can be accomplished in a nonpublic or clandestine manner because users do not always know when their access to certain information is being restricted.

SECURITY, CENSORSHIP, AND "POINTS OF CONTROL"

Thanks to the Internet, computers are connected to one another in a "single cloud-like global network" ("Securing the Cloud," 2002). Despite the benefits of easy connectivity, which include international commerce opportunities, greater efficiency, and remote access, there are costs as well. One such cost is the elevated risk of security breaches. Networks are vulnerable to attack and susceptible to unwanted data or intrusive activities.

The linkage of countries throughout the world to the global information infrastructure (GII) has also created many sources of friction. These countries are obviously anxious to participate in the benefits of connectivity, but they keenly recognize the costs sometimes associated with that connectivity. Countries such as Singapore and China aspire to be key players in the global economy, but they also want to protect their cultures from dehumanizing influences and antisocial Web sites. Foremost among these concerns is the need to prevent exposing users to sexually explicit content. Censorship has become a primary means of dealing with such material. In 1995, for example, the German government raided the offices of CompuServe's German subsidiary, accusing the company of failure to block access to pornographic material in violation of German law. Countries want to protect their citizens from objectionable content, and this objective is often seen as a vital element of an overall security plan. Thus, censorship is often justified as one way of "securing" or protecting national cultures from certain forms of unwelcome content.

The primary purpose of network security is to prevent unauthorized intrusions such as hacker attacks and the diffusion of malicious code or even Internet infrastructure attacks. Malicious code includes Trojan horses, viruses, worms, and other "malware" often hidden in legitimate programs. A worm, for example, resembles a virus because it is a self-replicating program, but unlike a virus, it requires no host system to propagate. These parasitic programs can lead to destruction of data or to prolonged downtime (see the chapter on computer viruses and worms).

Firewalls are the principal means of keeping these infectious programs and other forms of malware away from computers or networks. A firewall is usually a combination of hardware and software that sits between the Internet and an internal network (see the chapter on firewall basics). Its task is to examine the stream of network traffic (and service requests) and to follow certain rules about which data are to be allowed into and out of that internal network. According to Ellis (1997), "A simple firewall may consist of a filtering router, configured to discard packets that arrive from unauthorized addresses."

But these security tools can also be used to facilitate the goal of censorship. Firewalls represent code that can also function as digital fences, keeping out unwanted forms of speech such as sexually explicit content. Organizations can protect themselves from the Internet with proxy servers that typically reside inside a firewall between the Web browser and the true server. A proxy server can help an organization stop its users from accessing undesirable Web sites, and it can protect the internal network from being identified by the public. This "alias" keeps the network anonymous from the outside world and makes it harder for hackers to identify and attack client systems.

Thus, there is a strong temptation to use the code that has been developed to enhance security as an instrument of censorship. The purpose is often to enforce local laws and to achieve the goal of security, broadly conceived. Some countries seek to "secure" client systems against any objectionable communication from the Internet. This may include malicious viruses, but it might also include speech considered to be harmful such as pornography. Saudi Arabia, for example, attempts to block Internet pornography at the national level as a means of "protecting" its citizens. In some Eastern or Islamic cultures the definition of "pornography" is fairly broad and includes material considered merely erotic or romantic in the West.

Organizations may be anxious to keep out viruses, but they also want to keep out pornography and spam. Spam has been classified by corporate plaintiffs in some cases as a form of "trespass to chattels," that is, an illicit interference with one's property (Spinello, 2003; *Intel* v. *Hamidi*, 1999). Many companies and ISPs seek to suppress this form of commercial speech for the sake of the viability of their systems and integrity of the network. Censors, therefore, erect "barbed wire" or digital fences on this electronic frontier that restrict the free flow of information in cyberspace as a means of protecting their internal network.

Finally, it is instructive to consider the various "points of control" where censors are most likely to exert influence (Zittrain, 2003). Data on the Internet passes from one node or computer system ("source") to another node ("destination") through intermediaries. A packet of data is transmitted from the source computer with the Internet protocol (IP) address of the destination computer. It usually passes through the source node's ISP to the ISP serving the destination node which in turn delivers it to that node. According to Zittrain, the movement of data on the Internet passes through five distinct phases: the data begins at the (1) source node and passes through (2) the source ISP; "it continues through transit and/or peering through (3) the cloud, is handled by (4) the destination ISP and then arrives at (5) the destination [node] (120)." All of these represent points of transmission simultaneously represent points of control for the data that pass over this system. Censorship (or security) can take place at any of these crucial junctures.

GOVERNMENT CENSORSHIP

Governments' efforts to restrict Internet speech they regard as dangerous have varied greatly. Islamic countries have focused on pornography and some forms of political speech. Some liberal Western democracies, such as the United States, have sought to censor or suppress sexually explicit speech, and others, such as France and Germany, have concentrated on virulent hate speech. It is instructive to consider the concerted efforts of the United States to restrict sexually explicit speech in cyberspace by means of command and control legislation.

The United States government first sought to deal with the pervasive problem of Internet pornography with a piece of legislation called the Communications Decency Act of 1996 (CDA). This ill-fated law criminalized the "knowing" transmission over the Net of "obscene or indecent" material to anyone under the age of 18. Shortly after the CDA was signed into law, a lawsuit was immediately filed by the American Civil Liberties Union (ACLU) and several other groups, claiming that the CDA violated the First Amendment. One year after its passage, the Supreme Court struck down the law because it interfered with the First Amendment rights of adults to access sexually explicit sites. According to the majority opinion in *Reno v. ACLU* (1997) the act "suppresses a large amount of speech that adults have a constitutional right to receive and to address to one another." Moreover, the law's reference to "indecent" material was considered to be unconstitutionally vague.

In October 1998, however, Congress tried again, passing the Child Online Protection Act (COPA), which was immediately challenged by the ACLU. COPA was more precisely written than the CDA. It required Web site operators to restrict access to any material deemed to be "harmful to minors." Such material had to be obscene or meet a new federal harmful-to-minors standard with three requirements (for example, the material "depicts, describes, or represents, in a manner patently offensive with respect to minors, an actual or simulated sexual act or sexual conduct . . . or lewd exhibition of the genitals").

The ACLU also challenged COPA and won its case in Federal District Court in Philadelphia and in the U.S. Court of Appeals for the Third Circuit. In 2002, the U.S. Supreme Court remanded the case to the Third Circuit, which again found COPA unconstitutional because it did not satisfy the First Amendment's "least restrictive means" test. However, the case *Ashcroft* v. *ACLU* was appealed once again to the Supreme Court. That Court decided in 2004 to keep in place the district court's order blocking the enforcement of COPA, but it remanded the case to the district court for yet another hearing (Greenhouse, 2004).

Despite these setbacks, Congress did not abandon its efforts to contain the spread of pornography in cyberspace. In 2000, it passed the Children's Internet Protection Act (CIPA), which was signed into law by President Bill Clinton just before his departure from office. With CIPA, the government sought to implicitly mandate the use of filters. It hoped to rely on private surrogates, libraries, and schools to regulate speech harmful to minors. According to Lessig's paradigm, this regulatory regime is a clever combination of code and law.

CIPA is linked to the federal government's e-rate program, which provides an opportunity for schools and libraries to be reimbursed for the costs of connecting to the Internet or to be subsidized for other telecommunications expenses. The law mandates that computer terminals used by all library patrons (i.e., adults and children) must have filters that block Internet access to visual images that are obscene or involve any sort of child pornography. In addition, library computer terminals used by children under 17 must filter out these two categories of material plus any visual material that is harmful to minors. Public schools seeking e-funds must implement the same type of filtering scheme.

In April 2001, a group of libraries and library associations initiated a lawsuit against the government, claiming that CIPA was unconstitutional. The plaintiffs argued that filters were imprecise and "blunt" instruments, inadvertently blocking out many Web pages that did not contain sexually explicit material. Some of the sites blocked by typical filters included those having to do with sex education, and others were related to health issues, including Columbia University's question-and-answer site. Also, as the plaintiffs pointed out, technology protection measures cannot block access to *all* the material that is obscene, child pornographic, or harmful to minors

In the summer of 2002 a federal judicial panel of the U.S. District Court for the Third Circuit struck down the law. The court concluded that sections of this law were "invalid under the First Amendment." The federal government appealed the case to the Supreme Court, and in late June 2003, that court vacated the district court's ruling and upheld CIPA. In its 6–3 decision, the Supreme Court concluded that limitations imposed by CIPA on Internet access were equivalent to limitations on access to books that librarians choose to acquire or not acquire. There was consensus that filters are inaccurate instruments for restricting the access of children to pornographic material because those filters sometimes block sites that adults have a right to see. Nonetheless, the majority of the Supreme Court concluded that First Amendment rights were not being infringed by this law, as long as adults could request that the filters be disabled, without unnecessary delay.

Other countries have taken more extreme and direct steps to protect their citizens from objectionable content. In some countries, comprehensive restrictions on Internet traffic have been imposed for social and political purposes. Saudi Arabia, China, Singapore, and a host of other countries have put into effect countrywide filtering systems by blocking content, usually at the level of the destination ISP. In Saudi Arabia, all Internet traffic is routed through a proxy server that weeds out certain Web sites based on filtering criteria determined by the state. The blocked sites included pornographic sites along with those that might offend the sensibilities of its citizens. This would include content critical of the Islamic religion or political discourse critical of the Saudi regime. Political dissent is not tolerated in Saudi Arabia, and government officials wanted to be sure that the Web would not provide a forum to foment such dissent. In addition, many other sites, "including anonymizers and translators which might themselves be easy launching pads to otherwise-blocked sites" are filtered out as well (Zittrain & Edelman, 2002).

Although China has embraced digital technology and has tried to extend Internet usage among its citizens, it seeks to keep out the "foreign 'flies'—from liberalism to democracy to pornography—that will come in with the Internet" ("Wired China," 2000). China requires ISPs to install routers capable of blocking problematic IP addresses. Thus, routers across the country have been skillfully configured to delete packets that have objectionable content. China's filtering software blocks many mass media Web sites such as those operated by the BBC, CNN, and the *Washington Post* (Zittrain & Edelman, 2003). Private companies that offer Internet access in China must abide by the same rules. All service providers and media companies operating in China must sign the Public Pledge on Self-Discipline, promising not to produce or make available information that would violate the country's censorship

laws. As a consequence, "if someone in Shanghai uses Yahoo! China to query the term 'Taiwan independence,' the search will yield no results" (Scanlon, 2003).

India, a democratic state, has also implemented Internet content filtering on a countrywide basis. The Open Net Initiative (2004) reports that Indian Ministry of Communications & Information Technology has ordered Indian Internet Service Providers to block sites such as Yahoo!Group kynhun and HinduUnity.org. The latter site was ordered blocked because it contains "inflammatory anti-Islamic material." The Open Net Initiative reported that the Indian ISPs complied with the order in a way that "result[ed] in collateral blocking of thousands of newsgroups."

Thus, the Internet is subject to various forms of censorship at the national level. The firewalls and filtering mechanisms used for this purpose are far from foolproof, but they make it much more difficult for Internet users to retrieve sought after information. They also "represent the most effective point of blockage along the path of data from faraway places into the personal computers of Internet users within those countries" (Zittrain, 2003).

PRIVATE CENSORSHIP

Given the difficulty of regulating content on the borderless Internet at a national level (by code or law), a more decentralized approach to censoring cyberspace may be more feasible. When government action fails, the burden falls on private "regulators" such as parents, private schools, and corporations. Of course, reliance on such a decentralized mode of censorship is made possible through code, the same filtering architectures that are a surrogate for ineffectual laws.

Popular blocking programs for individual systems or local area networks (LANs) include Cyber Patrol, N2H2 Internet Filtering, Websense Enterprise, and SmartFilter. These programs generally function by relying on preset categories of objectionable speech. Categories might include Adult/Sexually Explicit, Nudity, Pornography, and so forth. Once the categories are determined, filtering companies use automated systems (such as a spider) to examine Web sites and determine candidates for each category. Thus, a bot such as a spider might visit the penthouse.com Web site and based on key words or textual data at that site classify it as "Adults Only/Pornography." For some companies, the final categorization is made without human intervention; others rely in part on human reviewers to make the final determination. If a parent installs a filtering program such as N2H2 with categories such as "Adults Only/Pornography" activated, anyone trying to access the penthouse.com site will be prevented from doing so by the software (Spinello, 2003).

In addition to private schools, and parents, corporations also assume the dubious role of private censors. Most workers have come to accept ongoing monitoring as part of the new reality for the 21st-century work environment. Companies monitor the network activities of workers through software that detects access to Web sites providing pornography, gambling, music or streaming video. For example, products such as Websense permit employers to set which Web site categories are permitted for particular categories of employees. It blocks content and generates detailed reports on Web site visits. Or software such as MIMEsweeper may be employed to monitor and restrict internal and external e-mail messages and to screen e-mail for viruses, malicious programs, or attachments that violate file size limits. MIMEsweeper can also be used to review e-mail content based on key word searches, checking for objectionable content such as obscene words. Once such e-mail is detected it is prevented from being sent or delivered.

Finally, as we have seen, Internet intermediaries such as ISPs and search engines are being called on to stop the flow of objectionable content such as pornography and hate speech. ISPs have traditionally been regarded as passive conduits, unaccountable for the online activities of its customers. In some contexts, however, they might be asked to "co-regulate [harmful] content in collaboration with public authorities" (Rorive, 2003). Warner (2002) reported that "industry groups, with the help of law enforcement authorities, are succeeding in getting ISPs to take down sites that violate laws regarding . . . speech and standards of decency." Some search engines such as Google, on the other hand, voluntarily restrict the flow of problematic information. This strategy flows from the company's idealistic "do no evil" philosophy. According to McHugh (2003), Google "has begun filtering its own servers to block users in Germany, France, and Switzerland from accessing sites carrying material likely to be judged racist or inflammatory in each country." Google also offers its users a version of its search engine functionality that omits sites containing "pornography and explicit sexual content."

Many reasons are given for some of this extensive censorship, but the validity of restricting information flows is a matter of great debate. Employers worry about their liability if a worker transmits objectionable content over their network, and search engine providers may not want to abet young children searching for pornography to download. Countries such as India and Iran are also attempting to protect their cultural values. However, censorship involves collateral damage because accurate filtering is difficult to achieve. Edelman (2004) reports that Google's SafeSearch "blocks at least tens of thousands of web pages without any sexually explicit content . . . includ[ing] sites operated by educational institutions, non-profits, news media, and national and local governments." Filters used to block pornography have also been criticized for both overblocking nonpornographic material and underblocking (that is, failing to block such material).

In addition, there should be a clear distinction established between the activities of censorship and security. As I have argued in this chapter, censorship is suppression of content based on its nature. Fencing off users from pornographic material or virulent hate speech is not the same as protecting servers, clients, and networks from damaging viruses, denial of service attacks, or illicit acts of trespass. The purpose of digital security should be clarified as the protection against the *physical impact* of another's conduct and not the potential ill effects of another's expression, however odious that expression may be.

This is not always an easy line to draw, however, and so there will be some ambiguous cases, such as the blocking of spam. Is the filtering of spam equivalent to securing servers and networks from the potential physical impairment or is it censorship? A case can surely be made that bulk e-mail transmissions are tantamount to trespass because they can be a burden on server equipment and on networks. Blocking such e-mail, however, would not be censorship as long as the intention is not to suppress a particular type of content but to protect those servers and networks from the burden of processing vast amounts of unsolicited e-mail. In the case of *CompuServe v. Cyber Promotions, Inc.* (1997), the service provider CompuServe alleged that the heavy volume of spam transmitted by Cyber Promotions was a burden on its equipment and thereby impaired that system. A federal court agreed and analogized that the transmission of unwanted spam was no different from throwing unsolicited newspapers onto someone's property.

CONCLUSIONS

This chapter has shown that the goal of a secure network or the protection of computer systems can lead organizations and even countries to engage in the activity of censorship, that is, the suppression of objectionable content. Some countries have relied on technical means such as software filters and proxy servers to make the Net safe for children and to protect their citizens from exposure to indecent images. Sometimes that censorship is repressive, however, because it includes valuable political speech.

This chapter has eschewed taking a position on the merits of censorship or delineating its possible parameters. Repressive forms of political censorship obviously deserve condemnation. Yet given the diversity of cultures involved in the use of the Internet and the need to be wary of cultural imperialism, it is difficult to reproach countries for blocking Internet traffic containing hate speech or what they regard as pornographic material. Suffice it to say that democratic governments like the United States prefer to suppress only the most harmful forms of speech (such as child pornography) and never political speech that is in the public interest. Other cultures, of course, do not give the same preeminence to free speech rights. The primary problem with any form of censorship is the difficulty of separating constructive speech from problematic speech. As Barlow (1996) wrote, "We cannot separate the air that chokes from the air upon which wings beat." Efforts to make this distinction all too often lead to the suppression of legitimate forms of expression. The collateral damage associated with the use of blunt instruments such as filtering software is proof enough of that proposition.

Thanks to digital technology censorship seems to be more ubiquitous because it can be undertaken by both the public and private sectors. Censorship is triggered by content that is unwelcome for various ideological reasons. I maintain, however, that security should not be confused with censoring data based on ideology. The goal of security should not be limitations on expression for the sake of its content. Rather, the goal of digital security should be protection against the negative physical impact of another's conduct, which can result from malicious code, hacking, or denial of service attacks. Countries and organizations may end up using security tools such as proxy servers and firewalls for the purpose of censorship. But they should not justify censorship under the pretext of Internet security, and all citizens of cyberspace should keep this critical distinction clearly in mind.

GLOSSARY

Censorship   The intentional suppression or regulation of expression based on its content.

Code   Hardware and software applications that use Internet protocols and can function as a regulatory constraint.

Content Filtering   Software that restricts access to Internet content by scanning that content based on key word searches.

Darknet   A Web site used to avoid Internet surveillance and censorship.

Firewall   An electronic barrier restricting communications between two points of control on the Internet.

Hate Speech   Any form of speech that threatens, denies, or leads to the destruction of human dignity and human rights.

Pornography   Includes indecent and obscene sexually explicit material that appeals to the prurient interest in sex.

Proxy Server   An Internet server that controls client computers' access to the Internet.

Spam   Unsolicited, automated electronic mail.

CROSS REFERENCES

See *Electronic Speech; Firewall Basics; Legal, Social and Ethical Issues of the Internet; Spam and the Legal Counter Attacks*.

REFERENCES

Baker, E. (1996). New media technologies, the First Amendment, and public policies. *Communications Review, 1*, 315–333.

Barlow, J. P. (1996). A declaration of the independence of cyberspace. Retrieved May 10, 2004, from http://www.eff.org~barlow/Declaration-Final.html

CompuServe v. Cyber Promotions, Inc. (1997). 962F. Supp. 1015 [S. D. Ohio].

Edelman, B. (2004). Empirical analysis of Google Safe-Search. Retrieved June 7, 2004, from http://cyber.law.harvard.edu/people/edelman/google

Ellis, J. (1997). Security of the internet. In J. Froehlick & P. Kent (Eds.), *Encyclopedia of telecommunications* (pp. 231–255). New York: Marcel Dekker.

Fisher, W. (2001). Freedom of expression on the internet. Retrieved November 24, 2002, from http://eon.law.harvard.edu/ilaw/speech

Fried, C. (2000). Perfect freedom or perfect control. *Harvard Law Review, 14*, 606–675.

Froomkin, M. (1997). The Internet as a source of regulatory arbitrage. In B. Kahin & C. Nesson (Eds.), *Borders in cyberspace* (pp. 129–163). Cambridge, MA: MIT Press.

Ginsberg v. United States (1966). 383 U.S. 463.

Greenhouse, L. (2004, June 30). Court blocks law regulating Internet access to pornography. *New York Times*, p. A1.

Hutzler, C. (2004, September 1). China finds new ways to restrict access to the Internet. *Wall Street Journal*, pp. B1–2.

Intel Corp. v. Hamidi (1999). No. 98A505067 [Cal Super Ct.].

Lessig, L. (2004). The laws of cyberspace. In R. A. Spinello & H. Tavani (Eds.), *Readings in cyberethics*. (2nd ed., pp. 134–144). Sudbury, MA: Jones and Bartlett.

Lessig, L. (1999). *Code and other laws of cyberspace*. New York: Basic Books.

McHugh, J. (2003, January). Google sells its soul. *Wired*, 131–135.

Miller v. California (1973). 413 U.S. 15.

Mitchell, W. J. (1995). *City of bits: Space, place and infobahn*. Cambridge, MA: MIT Press.

Ohralik v. Ohio State Bar (1978). 436 U.S. 447.

Open Net Initiative (2004). Internet content filtering in India. Retrieved June 1, 2004, from http://www.opennetinitiative.net/bulletins/003

Reno v. ACLU (1997). 521 U.S. 844.

Richards, J. (1974). Free speech and obscenity law: Toward a moral theory of the First Amendment. *University of Pennsylvania Law Review, h1123*, 45–89.

Rorive, I. (2003). Strategies to tackle racism and xenophobia on the internet: Where are we in Europe? *International Journal of Communications Law and Policy, 7*, 110–118.

Scanlon, J. (2003, August 31). 7 ways to squelch the Net. *Wired* 31.

Securing the Cloud. (2002, October 26). A survey of digital security. *The Economist*, S1–S20.

Spinello, R. (2003). *Cyberethics: Morality and law in cyberspace* (2nd ed.). Sudbury, MA: Jones and Bartlett.

Spinello, R. (2002). *Regulating cyberspace: The policies and technologies of control*. Westport, CT: Quorum Books.

Stone, G., Seidman, L., Sustein, C., Tushnet, M. (2001). *Constitutional law*. New York: Aspen.

Vaidhyanathan, S. (2004). *The anarchist in the library*. New York: Basic Books.

Warner, B. (2002, Jun 17). Hackers, porn and pirates add to ISP liability woes. Reuters News Service, June 17 Retrieved May 18, 2004 from http://digitalmass.boston.com/news/2002/06/17/isp-woes.html

Williams, B. (1998). Censorship. In R. Chadwick (Ed.), *Encyclopedia of applied ethics* (Vol. 1., pp. 433–436). San Diego, CA: Academic Press.

'Wired China.' (2000, July 22). *The Economist*, 25.

Zittrain, J. (2003). Internet points of control. *Boston College Law Review*, 43, 118–139.

Zittrain, J., & Edelman, B. (2003). Empirical analysis of internet filtering in China. Retrieved May 31, 2004, from http://cyber.law.harvard.edu/filtering/china

Zittrain, J., & Edelman, B. (2002). Documentation of internet filtering in Saudi Arabia. Retrieved May 31, 2004, from http://cyber.law.harvard.edu/filtering/saudiarabia

Copyright Law

Randy Canis, *Greensfelder, Hemker & Gale, P.C.*

COPYRIGHT FUNDAMENTALS

Introduction

This chapter is meant to provide readers with a fundamental understanding of the core concepts of U.S. copyright law as they apply to the digital realm; these concepts are expanded further in the chapter in this handbook, The Digital Millennium Copyright Act. As copyright law is complex and ever changing, this chapter should be used for informational purposes only. It should not be relied upon as a source of legal advice; instead the reader should contact a lawyer who practices in the field of copyright law to determine whether the particular issues of concern are lawful and/or appropriate given the current state of the law.

Copyright as Intellectual Property

Intellectual property rights include trademarks, copyrights, patents, and trade secrets. These intellectual property rights share a common characteristic in that the rights granted are intangible; there is no physical embodiment of such rights that can be provided to another to transfer ownership of these rights. For example, a plastic chair is a physical asset and is personal property, whereas the method of manufacturing and assembling the chair is intellectual property. Rights in intellectual property are secured by adherence to various legal mechanisms that have been adopted and used nationwide since the ratification of the Constitution. However, the United States was not the first country to recognize intellectual property rights, and at present the vast majority of foreign countries provide similar and complementary protection schemes.

The desire for intellectual property protection in the United States originated during the Constitutional Conventions. The Founding Fathers debated to what extent various types of monopolies should be permitted in their new nation. They decided to distance themselves from some of the practices of England, one of which was the monarchy's practice of granting valuable monopolies to produce certain well-known items throughout the British Empire. Such monopolies did not encourage the development of new technologies or provide enhanced rights to the citizenry; instead, they provided certain select citizens who were friends of the monarchy with financial windfalls by giving them protection from competition. England altered some of its long-standing monopolistic practices in 1710 when Parliament enacted the Statute of Anne. This statute was intended to limit the perpetual rights of publishers to a fixed number of years, after which other publishers could produce the work.

The Founding Fathers ultimately agreed that Congress should have the authority to promulgate legislation to protect works and inventions. Article I, Section 8, Clause 8 of the U.S. Constitution provides that "Congress shall have Power...[t]o promote the Progress of Science and useful Arts, by securing for limited Times to Authors and Inventors the exclusive Right to their respective Writings and Discoveries." This clause provided Congress with a constitutional basis for the development of federal copyright and patent law. The Founding Fathers intended these rights to spur development of new ideas and creations by providing creators with a financial incentive to make such developments. However, these rights are not without limitation in that ultimately consumers must benefit from the provision of the additional rights to the authors and inventors. The balance between the right of authors and inventors to profit and the consumers to receive a benefit as a result of the right is a key element that Congress considers when altering the scope of protection for creations and inventions.

Copyright law fits in the scheme of intellectual property rights by enabling authors to protect their particular manner of expressing an idea. Examples of works in the digital realm that are subject to copyright protection include digital photos, Web sites, and e-books. Patent law, the intellectual property scheme most similar to copyright law, protects the underlying applied idea irrespective of its expression in a particular embodiment. Examples of various inventions that are subject to patent protection include Internet shopping carts, methods of processing digital images, and microprocessor improvements.

Trademark law enables consumers to identify and distinguish the products and services offered from one source to that offered by another and protects against consumer confusion by use of a device, such as a mark. Examples of marks that are subject to trademark protection include COCA-COLA® soft drink, YAHOO!® Internet services, and EXPRESS PERSONNEL SERVICES® employment and personnel services. Trade secret law enables persons to protect information from being taken without authorization so long as access to the information is limited. Examples of information that is subject to trade secret protection include customer lists, the names of key employees, and new product development information that has not yet been made public.

Copyright law has significantly evolved since the passage of the first Congressional set of copyright laws in 1790. Congress passed substantial revisions to the Copyright Act in 1831, 1870, 1909, 1976, and 1998 to reflect technological advances and changes in the scope of protection. Copyright law continues to adapt to the changing environment of computers and the Internet and is likely to undergo further development over the coming years as a result. Nonetheless, this chapter should provide a strong basis for understanding the basic concepts of copyright law, as well as the current state of the law.

Subject Matter of Copyright

Before the Copyright Act of 1976, copyright protection for a particular work was based on when the author first made his or her work available to the public by publishing it. Prior to publishing, the work was subject to a so-called common law copyright under the Copyright Act of 1909.

By refusing to publish, the author had unlimited rights at common law to control the work so as to prevent others from utilizing it without permission. After publishing, the common law copyright was extinguished, and the statutory copyright (i.e., under the 1909 Act) governed the copyright rights in the work to which the author was entitled. However, under the 1976 Act copyright protection begins upon fixation in a tangible form as opposed to publishing. Despite the change in law, the 1909 Act is still relevant because works that entered the public domain name before the effective date of the 1976 Act (i.e., January 1, 1978) may not be protected thereunder.

COPYRIGHT REQUIREMENTS
Introduction

For an author to have a valid copyright in a particular work, the work must (1) be original, (2) remain fixed in a tangible medium of expression, and (3) have involved a minimum degree of creativity. For example, if the students in a classroom each drew a representation of the St. Louis Arch on a piece of paper, each would have a copyright in their respective drawings regardless of their artistic abilities. The aforementioned requirements for having a valid copyright are explained in greater detail in the sections below.

Originality

Copyright protection under the 1976 Act extends to original works of authorship that are fixed in a tangible medium of expression. To be protected, the creation must be an original work of the author, originating from the author claiming copyright, and not copied from another source.

There are several significant aspects of the originality requirement. Artistic merit is irrelevant to the ability to copyright the work. Without such a limitation, only works that were judged to have merit (by the Register of Copyrights) would be imbued with protection, and other such works deemed unworthy would leave the author with no such rights. This limitation would thereby encourage various types of works while discouraging others that could be unrecognized masterpieces or otherwise significant to a smaller class of people. Ultimately, appointing a person or an agency to distinguish "good works" from "bad works" is unnecessary because the public buys or supports what it likes and ignores that which it does not. As the Supreme Court stated in *Bleistein v. Donaldson Lithographing Co.* (1903),

> It would be a dangerous undertaking for persons trained only to the law to constitute themselves final judges of the worth of pictorial illustrations, outside of the narrowest and most obvious limits. At the one extreme some works of genius would be sure to miss appreciation. Their very novelty would make them repulsive until the public had learned the new language in which their author spoke. It may be more than doubted, for instance, whether the etchings of Goya or the paintings of Manet would have been sure of protection when

seen for the first time. At the other end, copyright would be denied to pictures which appealed to a public less educated than the judge. Yet if they command the interest of any public, they have a commercial value—it would be bold to say that they have not an aesthetic and educational value—and the taste of any public is not to be treated with contempt. It is an ultimate fact for the moment, whatever may be our hopes for a change. That these pictures had their worth and their success is sufficiently shown by the desire to reproduce them without regard to the plaintiffs' rights.

In addition, the underlying idea of the work is not subject to copyright protection. Copyright law does not provide a monopoly on an idea (e.g., the process of formatting a digital image), but rather on the expression of that idea by a particular author (e.g., the way a programmer implements his or her process of formatting a digital image). Accordingly, two different authors could write stories about the friendship and similarities between a computer scientist who becomes a patent attorney and his friend who is an ambitious and famous rock drummer, and each author would be entitled separately to copyright protection for his or her stories.

Works must have some minimal degree of creativity to be original, such that the author must contribute something to the work for it to be entitled to a copyright. The author must demonstrate substantial creative input or variation; the work must be more than a trivial (i.e., insubstantial) variation or a mere reproduction of prior works. Thus, a painter who makes a hand-painted reproduction of a prior painter's work would not be entitled to copyright protection; however, a second painter's drawing of the same subject matter using different lighting, different materials, and a different view would be entitled to copyright protection. Works that fail to have the minimal degree of creativity are denied copyright protection.

Originality is not equivalent to the novelty requirement of patent law, as it is a lower standard in which the author must only create the work independently. The ideas and themes contained in a particular work may have appeared in earlier works, but so long as the work originates with the author, copyright protection is still available. For example, consider how many movies include police officers performing the good cop/bad cop scenario. None of these movies can claim the exclusive rights to such a scenario and limit the others' expression of the same. In contrast, a first entity can infringe a second entity's patent even if the first entity was not aware of the second entity's patent and had created invention independently. The comparison of the two standards frequently arises, because computer software was generally not considered patentable until the State Street Bank case as discussed in the chapter, Patent Law, found elsewhere in this handbook.

With respect to computer software and other works that may use both copyright and patent law for protection, a copyright is more likely to be found valid in a court case than a patent because of the types of challenges available to third parties. With copyright law, copying another's work is needed to demonstrate copyright infringement, whereas such information is not needed in patent law. However, the scope of protection with copyright is less in that it only protects against copying and not the underlying idea. Accordingly, companies typically seek both patent and copyright protection on their computer software.

Works of Authorship

Works of authorship define the type of "writings," as used in the Constitution, for which copyright protection is available. Congress has broadly interpreted "writings" to define these categories for works of authorship: (1) literary works; (2) musical works, including any accompanying words; (3) dramatic works, including any accompanying music; (4) pantomimes and choreographic works; (5) pictorial, graphic, and sculptural works; (6) motion pictures and other audiovisual works; (7) sound recordings; and (8) architectural works. These categories were meant by Congress to be nonexclusive so as to encompass new technologies, which include computer software and the "look and feel" of a Web site.

Unprotectible Works

Certain types of work are not subject to copyright protection because protection of those works would prevent others from using the underlying idea. To the extent that the expression cannot be delivered in another author's form, the expression is unprotectible because the underlying idea has merged with the expression. Accordingly, if there was only one way to implement an online shopping cart system, no one could claim exclusive copyright rights to such an implementation of the system, but yet the same system could be subject to patent rights. In addition, copyright protection does not extend to ideas, procedures, processes, systems, operational methods, concepts, principles, or discoveries, but rather is limited to the manner in which the creation is expressed by the author.

Works consisting of words and short phrases, such as names, titles, and slogans; familiar symbols or designs, mere variations of typographic ornamentation, lettering or coloring; and the mere listing of ingredients or contents are not subject to copyright law. For example, a list of ingredients for chocolate chip cookie mix is unprotectible. However, a book of recipes for various kinds of chocolate chip cookies may be entitled to protection as a compilation, and a particular recipe could also be subject to trade secret protection. Certain words and short phrases may still be subject to trademark protection. For example, LET'S GET READY TO RUMBLE® is a registered service mark used by Michael Buffer to promote various boxing matches.

Works that consist entirely of public domain information are also not protectible, including standard calendars, height and weight charts, tape measures and rulers, schedules of sporting events, and lists or tables taken from public documents or other common sources. Such works fail to demonstrate the more than trivial level of creativity that is necessary for copyright protection. However, even though a map consists of public information, the generation of such a map involves substantial selection and arrangement and is therefore eligible for copyright protection. For example, Internet users cannot utilize a map generated from Yahoo! or Mapquest.com in their Web site without properly obtaining a license from these companies by following the terms and conditions posted on their respective Web sites.

Other works that are not subject to copyright include typefaces, ideas, plans, methods, systems, or devices, as distinguished from the particular manner in which they are expressed or described in a writing. Thus, a translation of an existing work to another format or another language is ineligible for copyright protection as a work of a new author, whereas copying the underlying idea but utilizing new expression is eligible for such protection. However, the utilitarian aspects of such creations are protectible under patent law, such as a system for communicating digital information over a network.

Blank forms, such as time cards, graph paper, account books, diaries, bank checks, scorecards, address books, report forms, order forms, and the like, which are designed for recording information and do not in themselves convey information, are also not subject to copyright protection. The underlying facts and the methods of recording information are not protectible, but the textual information that accompanies the blank forms if significant enough may have enough originality and creativity to make the work subject to copyright protection.

Fixation

Works must be fixed in a tangible medium of expression to be protected under the Copyright Act. Without the fixation requirement, it would be difficult to determine what a particular author considered to be his or her work. In addition, the Copyright Office would be unable to review and consider whether a work should be entitled to a copyright registration. Material objects that qualify as media of expression include canvas, paper, audio and video cassettes, DVDs, CDs, and computer disk drives.

Works must be embodied in a tangible form that is "sufficiently permanent or stable to permit it to be perceived, reproduced, or otherwise communicated for a period of more than transitory duration." Accordingly, a digital image that is electronically transmitted over a computer network and is never retained in a storage medium is not subject to copyright protection. The requirement for fixation is met when the work can either be perceived directly or with the aid of a machine or other device. Unfixed works, such as extemporaneous utterances, unchoreographed dance performances, and unwritten jazz and musical performances, are all subject to common law copyright and are not covered under the federal Copyright Act because they do not meet the fixation requirement. However, when these works are recorded they may then be eligible for copyright.

TERM OF COPYRIGHT
Background of Term

The author and the author's heirs enjoy a period of exclusivity in which they can reap the financial rewards from the author's creation of the work. However, the length of the copyright per the Constitution is only for a "limited" time. Upon expiration of the term of the copyright, the work is dedicated to the public, which is then free to use it without authorization from or compensation to the author.

Term Under the 1909 Act

Under the 1909 Act, the duration of the copyright for published works was 28 years, with a single 28-year renewal term, for a maximum of 56 years. The duration under the 1909 Act was set with the intention that the author would be able to have exclusive rights to the work during his or her lifetime. Works that were not published were subject to common law copyright, and the authors (and the author's heirs) could indefinitely protect the work from copying by refusing to publish the work. If the work was ultimately published, its limited period of protection was the aforementioned two terms.

Term Under the 1976 Act

Since the adoption of the 1976 Act, works that are fixed in a medium of expression are protectible under statutory copyright, regardless of whether the work is published or unpublished. The term for such works under the 1976 Act was for the life of the author plus 50 years; for anonymous and pseudonymous works and for works made for hire the term was for 75 years from publication or 100 years from creation, whichever expired first. Accordingly, the term under the 1976 Act was meant to enable the author to have exclusive rights during his or her lifetime and for the next generation. However, the term was extended by Congress in 1988, as described below.

Sonny Bono Copyright Term Extension Act of 1998

The passage of the Sonny Bono Copyright Term Extension Act of 1998 (the Sonny Bono Amendment) extended the terms in the 1976 Act by 20 years, not only for newly created works but also for works already subject to the previous terms. Upon passage, critics complained that the Sonny Bono Amendment's retroactive effect would effectively prevent a plethora of works from entering the public domain name for an additional 20 years.

The Sonny Bono Amendment was challenged in a series of court decisions resulting in the 2003 Supreme Court case of *Eldred v. Ashcroft*. In this case, the petitioner asserted that the Sonny Bono Amendment was unconstitutional under the Copyright Clause because it extended the duration of the copyright for preexisting works, as opposed to only newly created works. The Court ruled that the amendment was constitutional because (1) the precise duration of a federal copyright has never been fixed at the time of the initial grant, (2) Congress has routinely applied new definitions or adjustments of the copyright term to both future works and existing works not yet in the public domain, and (3) the amendment did not create a perpetual copyright.

The effect on consumers of this ruling is that few works will enter into the public domain for the next 20 years, thereby preventing people such as Eldred from making such works available over the Internet for free. Copyright owners assert that consumers will receive additional benefits because copyright owners are able to reap financial rewards over a longer time period. Despite the courts' allowance of the Sonny Bono Amendment to stand, unlimited extensions for preexisting works still would appear to violate the Constitutional mandate that protection for works only be awarded for a limited time.

FORMALITIES
Copyright Notice

The accession by the United States to the Berne Convention in 1989 removed the requirement that works must contain a notice of copyright. Works protected by copyright may now optionally contain a notice of the copyright on publicly distributed copies. When used, the Copyright Act dictates that the form of the notice comprise three elements: (1) the symbol © (the letter C in a circle), or the word "Copyright" or the abbreviation "Copr."; (2) the year of first publication of the work; and (3) the name of the owner of the copyright in the work. For example, the copyright notice used with the DVD movie, "The Usual Suspects," is © 1996 Polygram Video.

The copyright notice, if affixed, must be done so in a manner and location to provide a person with reasonable notice of the copyright. Although notice of the copyright is optional on works after the accession to the Berne Convention, its inclusion in a copyright infringement case where the defendant had access to the work effectively eliminates the defendant's innocent infringement defense as described in greater detail below. For works prior to the accession to the Berne Convention, the copyright can be lost if the notice was omitted and the omission was not properly cured. Accordingly, it behooves most authors to include copyright notices on their works. For example, the author of a particular Web site can place a suitable copyright notice at the bottom of each of the Web pages by using footers on every page.

Registration with the Copyright Office

To have a copyright in a work, it is not a prerequisite to register the copyright with the Copyright Office. Rather, copyright is established upon fixation in a tangible medium of expression so long as the underlying work is original. Registration of a copyright for a work may occur at any time. However, registration is a perquisite to obtaining statutory damages, putting third parties on constructive notice of the copyright registration, and having a *prima facie* presumption of validity of the copyright. Because damages are often difficult to prove in copyright infringement suit, the ability to recover statutory damages not only greatly benefits the plaintiff's case but also increases the likelihood of a favorable settlement.

The Copyright Office provides various forms to enable copyright owners to register their copyrights: form TM for nondramatic literary works, form PA for works of performing art, form SR for sound recording works, form VA for works of visual arts, and form SE for serial works, including newspapers, magazines, newsletters, annuals, and journals. All these forms are available for free download at the Copyright Office Web site at http://www.copyright.gov. Each form generally is a double-sided page and often includes the option of providing instructions on additional pages. Despite the apparently simplicity of the documents, issues including authorship and ownership of the work can often confuse a layperson and cause him or her to complete these forms incorrectly. The author urges that persons seeking to register their works first consult an attorney who practices in the field of copyright law prior to filling.

OWNERSHIP
General Ownership

Copyright ownership provides its owner with various exclusive rights as described in greater detail below. Ownership differs from a license, as a license may only provide its user with a limited right to use a particular copy in possession of the user; for example, the usage may be for a limited time, within a set geographical area, or in a certain manner. Ownership traditionally vests with the author or jointly among a group of authors, and assignment of copyright is possible.

Work Made for Hire

One of the fundamental issues in copyright law for companies is whether a worker is the author of a particular work that was created. Unlike patent law in which inventorship cannot be altered based on employment or agreements, authorship of a particular work may vest with another, depending on the nature of the relationship between the worker and the employer and whether an agreement governs the creation of the work. If a work is considered a *work made for hire*, the employer will be considered the actual author of the work instead of the employee who created the work. For example, the work made for hire issue frequently arises when companies hire outside developers to create a Web site or write code for a computer program on behalf of the company. When the company wants to modify the Web site or distribute the software program and the developer objects without the payment of additional fees, the company frequently learns that it did not have all rights that it had anticipated in the particular work. Companies often rely on the faulty logic that if they paid a lot of money for the work, then they must own all rights to it. However, that is not a legitimate basis for determining whether a work qualifies as a work made for hire.

A work made for hire is defined differently for employees and nonemployees (i.e., contractors). For an employee's work to be considered to be a work for hire, the work must be prepared within the scope of the employee's employment. For a nonemployee, the work must be (1) specially ordered or commissioned; (2) for use as a contribution to a collective work, a part of a motion picture or other audiovisual work, a translation, a supplementary work, a compilation, an instructional text, a test, answer material for a test, or an atlas; and (3) in a written instrument signed by the parties that states the work shall be considered a work made for hire.

With employees, the key question is whether the work is within the scope of employment. If so, the work is deemed authored by the employer, and the employer will have all exclusive rights associated with the work. If the work falls outside the scope of employment, the work is deemed authored by the employee, and the employer will simply have a license to use the particular embodiment of the work without the exclusive rights associated with the work. Under the 1909 Act, whether a worker was considered an employee was based on the traditional employment relationship. However, under the 1976 Act, the determination as to whether a worker is an employee was modified as discussed in *Cmty. for Creative Non-Violence v. Reid* (1989) below.

With nonemployees, the first issue is whether the work is specially ordered or commissioned. Thus, purchasing an "off the shelf" object at a store cannot be considered a work made for hire. The second issue is whether the work falls within the defined statutory classes, which include contributions to collective works, parts of a motion picture or other audiovisual work, translations, supplementary works, compilations, instructional texts, tests, answer material for tests, and atlases. If the work falls outside these defined classes, such as is the case with computer software, it cannot be considered a work made for hire. The third issue is whether there is a properly written agreement between the parties that the work shall be considered a work made for hire. Without such a written agreement, the work will fail to qualify as a work made for hire.

In *Cmty. for Creative Non-Violence v. Reid* (1989), the Supreme Court considered whether James Earl Reid, an artist, or the Community for Creative Non-Violence (CCNV), an organization that hired Reid to produce a sculpture, owned the copyright in a sculpture. Reid agreed to donate his services to create the sculpture, and CCNV paid for the materials. However, there was no written agreement between the parties, and copyright ownership was not discussed. When the parties disagreed on how the work should be preserved and presented, communication between the parties broke down, and a lawsuit ensued.

In this case, the Supreme Court acknowledged that the copyright in a work initially vests in the author or authors of a work, subject to the important work made for hire exception. This exception provides that "'the employer or other person for whom the work was prepared is considered the author' and owns the copyright, unless there is a written agreement to the contrary." Because a sculpture is not specifically listed within the class of specially commissioned works included in the definition of work made for hire, the Court first considered whether an employee within the scope of employment made the sculpture.

The Court held that the author is an employee under the common law understanding of agency law. The factors that the Court considered to support this ruling include "the hiring party's right to control the manner and means by which the product is accomplished[,]...the skill required; the source of the instrumentalities and tools; the location of the work; the duration of the relationship between the parties; whether the hiring party has the right to assign additional projects to the hired party; the extent of the hired party's discretion over when and how long

to work; the method of payment; the hired party's role in hiring and paying assistants; whether the work is part of the regular business of the hiring party; whether the hiring party is in business; the provision of employee benefits; and the tax treatment of the hired party."

Despite the apparent definiteness that work made for hire may seem to provide, circumstances with workers change that could affect whether a particular worker is still considered an employee. In addition, there may be questions as to whether a particular work is within the scope of the employee's employment. Therefore, it is always a best practice to create an employment agreement that clearly defines the scope of the employee's employment and a fallback assignment clause that provides that works will be assigned to the employer if they fail to qualify as a work made for hire.

RIGHTS GRANTED
Exclusive Rights

The copyright laws of the United States grant the author of a copyrighted work certain exclusive rights in the work, including the right to (1) reproduce the copyrighted work in copies or phonorecords; (2) prepare derivative works based upon the copyright work; (3) distribute copies or phonorecords of the copyrighted work to the public; (4) publicly perform literary, musical, dramatic, and choreographic works, pantomimes, and motion pictures and other audiovisual works; (5) publicly display literary, musical, dramatic, and choreographic works, pantomimes, and pictorial, graphic and sculptural works, including individual images from a motion picture or other audiovisual work; and (6) publicly perform sound recordings by means of a digital audio transmission. Of the six rights, the first two are infringed by an act performed publicly or privately, whereas the remaining four are infringed only when occurring publicly.

The copyright owner can transfer or license these rights in full or in part to others. The language used to provide these rights to another should be unambiguous so that there is no dispute as to what rights are being transferred or licensed, and a transfer of copyright rights must be in writing to be valid. For example, a court found that a transfer of "all right, title and interest" to computer programs and software was not merely a license to use the software, but rather a transfer of the copyright embodied in the computer programs and software.

Public Performance

Under the Copyright Act, performing a work publicly means either to (1) perform or display it at a place open to the public or at any place where a substantial number of persons outside a normal circle of a family and its social acquaintances are gathered or (2) to transmit or otherwise communicate a performance or display of the work to a place previously specified or to the public, by means of any device or process, regardless of the place and time it is received by the public. Thus, the presentation of a movie at a movie theater and a performance of a song at a music club are both considered public performances. With respect to the Internet, a Web conference between two parties would not be considered a public performance, but a worldwide WEBEX presentation to clientele would be considered a public performance.

For-profit performances of works require a license from the copyright owner. Such performances include those for which an admission fee is charged or performances that enhance the related profit-making activity of the entity. Nonprofit performances also require a license unless the performance is exempted by the fair use doctrine or the public performance is exempted under the Copyright Act. The exempted performances include some teaching activities and religious assemblies when no admission is charged or when the profit is used for educational, religious, or charitable purposes, unless the public performance is objected to by prior written notice. Public performances occur in places that are open to the public or where a substantial number of persons outside the normal circle of family and social acquaintances are gathered.

The Copyright Act does, however, provide some limitations for certain types of performances that are not infringements of copyright. These performance include performance or display of a work by instructors or pupils in face-to-face meetings and in certain proscribed circumstances: such performances include digital transmissions between such persons, performance of a nondramatic literary or musical work or of a dramatico-musical work of a religious nature or display of a work in the course of services at a place of worship or other religious assembly, and performance of a nondramatic literary or musical work otherwise than in a transmission to the public without any purpose of direct or indirect commercial advantage and without payment of any fee in certain proscribed circumstances.

Public Display

Public display is the copyright owner's exclusive right to show other people the copyrighted work. The receipt of a fee is irrelevant to whether a party displaying the work constitutes a public display. An example of when the copyright owner's exclusive right to display a copyrighted work publicly is violated includes when Internet users are allowed to view copyrighted images from a Web site upon the payment of a fee without a license from the owner of the copyrighted image and when preview clips consisting exclusively of scenes taken from full-length copyrighted feature films are presented on a Web site.

Reproduction

Phonorecords are defined as material objects in which sounds, other than those accompanying a motion picture or other audiovisual work, are fixed by any method now known or later developed, and from which the sounds can be perceived, reproduced, or otherwise communicated, either directly or with the aid of a machine or device.

The exclusive right of reproduction allows the copyright owner to prevent others from reproducing the work in the form of a copy or phonorecord. Copies are defined broadly under the Copyright Act and include all material objects, excluding phonorecords, in which a work is fixed by any method now known or later developed and from which the work can be perceived, reproduced or otherwise communicated, either directly or with the aid of a machine or device. Copies include downloading reproduced thumbnail and full-sized images taken from an Internet newsgroup to a user's hard drive.

Distribution and the First Sale Doctrine

Copyright owners are provided with the exclusive right to distribute copies of phonorecords of their works, which includes posting a work on a Web site for download by Internet users. The distribution right is limited to the first transfer of ownership, because under the Copyright Act the ownership of the copyright is distinct from ownership of a material object in which the copyright is embodied per the First Sale Doctrine as described in greater detail below.

Under the *First Sale Doctrine*, the copyright owner's right to control distribution is exhausted by the first sale of each lawfully made copy. The owner of such a copy has the right of resale or transfer, and the copyright owner has no control over resale or transfer of a particular copy. Mere possession of the copyright object by rental, lease, loan, or otherwise is insufficient to trigger first sale rights. For example, as discussed in *Adobe Sys. v. One Stop Micro, Inc* (2000), a copyright owner does not forfeit the right of distribution by entering into a distribution agreement by which it licenses off-the-shelf software; the owner can therefore prevent an educational version of a software program from being resold as a full retail version.

TYPE OF WORK
Derivative Work

A copyright owner has the exclusive right to create or authorize the creation of a work based in part on his or her underlying work. A *derivative work* is a work based upon one or more preexisting works in which the original work is recast, transformed, or adapted. The derivative work copyright protects only new materials contributed by the author and does not affect or enlarge the scope, duration, ownership, or subsistence of any copyright protection in the preexisting material. Examples of various types of derivative works include translations, musical arrangements, dramatizations, fictionalizations, motion picture versions, sound recordings, art reproductions, abridgments, and condensations. Cases involving derivative works include copying and using specific functions from a preexisting computer software in a new software program, creating a descrambler to obtain access to otherwise protected video programming content by copying portions of the original access program, and utilizing portions of source code in a computer game to create a new computer game. In addition, a work consisting of editorial revisions, annotations, elaborations, or other modifications, which, as a whole, represent an original work of authorship, is a derivative work.

Joint Work

A *joint work* is a work prepared by two or more authors with the intention that their contributions be merged into inseparable or interdependent parts of a unitary whole and for which the intent to merge the work into a unitary whole must exist at the time of creation. The second author must contribute more than the suggestions of ideas and minor bits of expression, as each author's components must be independently copyrightable. The joint owners can independently exploit the work without consent of the other joint owners, but must account to the other joint owners for such exploitation. The duration of the copyright is the life of the last author to die plus 70 years.

Composite Work

A *composite work* is a work prepared by two or more authors without the intent to merge their contributions into a unitary whole. Each part of the composite work must be licensed and terminated separately, and each part has its own copyright duration.

Compilation

A *compilation* is a work formed by the collection and assembling of preexisting materials or of data that are selected, coordinated, or arranged in such a way that the resulting work as a whole constitutes an original work of authorship. Therefore, it is not the underlying materials or data that are protected by copyright, but rather the selection, coordination, or arrangement of the work that is entitled to a copyright. Thus, although a standard program call or database read is not subject to copyright protection, the series of such calls and reads in the context of a computer program may be subject to copyright protection for the work as a compilation.

In *Feist Publications, Inc. v. Rural Telephone Service Co., Inc.* (1991), the Supreme Court addressed whether a telephone directory was subject to copyright protection. Rural Telephone Service Company issues an annually updated telephone directory comprising both white pages and yellow pages for northwest Kansas. Feist Publications publishes telephone directories that cover a wider area. Both companies distribute their directories free of charge and compete vigorously for yellow page advertisements. Of further significance is that Rural Telephone had access to subscriber information pursuant to its monopoly and was required to issue a directory as part of its monopoly agreement; however, it refused to license the directory information to Feist Publications so that it could maintain a monopoly on yellow pages listings. Feist Publications then copied the listings without authorization from Rural Telephone and a lawsuit ensued.

In its decision, the Supreme Court balanced the tensions between the two established propositions of the law that "facts are not copyrightable [and that] . . . that compilations of facts generally are." The Court found that the facts did not meet the requisite level of originality because the "first person to find and report a particular fact has not created the fact; he or she has merely discovered its existence." The Court considered that the author of a compilation "chooses which facts to include, in what order to place them, and how to arrange the collected data so that they may be used effectively by readers." The Court then held that the copyright protection of the compilation

only extended to the components of the work that are original to the author and that others were free to copy the facts so long as any expression used to express the facts was not copied. Accordingly, regardless of the effort expended, copyright does not protect generic selection, order, or arrangement such as is used with telephone white pages.

COPYRIGHT INFRINGEMENT
Civil Infringement

When someone violates any one of the author's exclusive rights, the person commits *copyright infringement*. Infringement may be found for both intentional and unintentional (i.e., innocent) acts, such as subconsciously copying a song written by another. The owner of the copyright is entitled to various remedies including an injunction to stop the infringing behavior and actual or statutory damages. The statute of limitations for bringing a civil action is 3 years.

To establish infringement, a party must establish ownership of a copyright and that there was impermissible copying. Ownership of the copyright is established by presenting the registration certificate received from the Copyright Office. As for copying, infringement is proven easily when actual portions of the work are copied. However, usually infringement is shown through circumstantial evidence, such as by the combination of a substantial similarity of the copied work to the original work and access by the author to the original work.

Willful Infringement

In *Playboy Enters. v. Webbworld Inc.* (1997), defendant Webbworld had implemented software that scoured Internet newsgroups for adult-oriented images and posted them on its Web site for viewing by paying customers. Playboy filed suit over images that had been taken from its magazines and posted on Webbworld's Web site. The district court found in favor of Playboy on the grounds of copyright infringement, as the posted images were found to violate Playboy's exclusive rights for reproducing, distributing, and displaying the copyrighted images. In addition, the court found that Webbworld had acted willfully despite its implementation of a "compliance program" because it copied the images from a newsgroup whose title "centerfolds" suggested that it might have copyrighted works in it. In addition, after receiving notice of infringement from Playboy, it continued to obtain infringing images from the same newsgroup. Accordingly, Internet users who receive notice of an accusation of copyright infringement should take the notice seriously and consult their attorney to determine what, if any, remedial actions should be taken.

Criminal Infringement

Any person who infringes a copyright willfully may be punished criminally for up to 10 years in prison and fined. Conduct that does not give rise to civil copyright infringement (i.e., money damages) cannot give rise to criminal infringement. The statute of limitations for the government to bring such a criminal action is 5 years.

Historically, there has been an additional requirement for criminal infringement. For an infringement to rise to a criminal level, it must be (1) for purposes of commercial advantage or private financial gain, or (2) the reproduction or distribution during any 180-day period of one or more copies or phonorecords of one or more copyrighted works must have a total retail value of more than $1,000. However, the 1997 NET Act amended the Copyright Act to make the showing of intent to create a profit to be irrelevant.

Compensatory and Statutory Damages

The copyright owner is entitled to recover the actual damages suffered as a result of the infringement, as well as any additional profits of the infringer. As an alternative to seeking actual damages and profits, the copyright owner can seek statutory damages in a lawsuit at any time before a final judgment is rendered. Statutory damages are awarded per work and range from $750 to $30,000 as the court considers just, unless there is innocent infringement or if the infringer is a nonprofit in which case the amount is reduced to $250. Finally, statutory damages may be increased to $150,000 if the infringement is willful.

Vicarious Infringement

Vicarious infringement occurs when a defendant has the legal right and physical ability to supervise the infringing activity and has a direct financial interest in those activities. Accordingly, if vicarious infringement is found, the defendant can be liable as though he or she were the party actually committing the infringement. In a typical case involving vicarious infringement, a music club owner is found liable when he or she hires a band that performs various works and the right holders to the works are not compensated.

Contributory Infringement

Contributory infringement is found when a party with knowledge of the infringing activity induces, causes, or materially contributes to the infringing conduct of another. The contribution must be more than the mere passive providing of premises, the supply of staple items of commerce, or the supply of material that can also be used for lawful activities. When contributory infringement is found, the defendant can be liable as though he or she were the party actually committing the infringement. For example, the storage on a defendant's system of infringing copies of copyrighted image files and retransmission to other servers do not constitute a direct infringement by a bulletin board system (BBS) operator of the exclusive right to reproduce the images where such copies are uploaded by an infringing user; however, those actions may be considered contributory infringement, notwithstanding defenses available to the BBS operator under the Digital Millennium Copyright Act (DMCA). The chapter in this *Handbook* on the DMCA describes more fully Congress's

response to the problems associated with transmitting digital information over global networks.

LIMITATIONS ON EXCLUSIVE RIGHTS
Fair Use

The exclusive rights of a copyright owner are subject to certain limitations and exceptions under which some acts that would otherwise be considered an infringement are exempted under the doctrine of *fair use*. Whether a particular use of a work is fair depends on a balancing of four factors: (1) the purpose and character of the use, including whether such use is of a commercial nature or is for nonprofit educational purposes; (2) the nature of the copyrighted work; (3) the amount and substantiality of the portion used in relation to the copyrighted work as a whole; and (4) the effect of the use upon the potential market for or value of the copyrighted work. Whether a use qualifies as fair is determined by balancing the exclusive rights of the copyright owner against the rights of another to use the copyright material in a reasonable manner without the owner's consent. For example, the copying by a professor of an article from a newspaper for in-class distribution is much more likely to be found a fair use than the commercial copying and reselling of copyrighted music.

The balancing test for fair use is fact specific and requires a case-by-case analysis. Because the finding of whether a use is fair turns on the facts of each particular case, no bright line test is available to determine whether such use will be considered fair.

The fair use doctrine thereby permits courts in limited circumstances to prevent the stifling of creativity brought about by rigid interpretation of the Copyright Act. Ultimately, this means that cases will test the bounds of whether a certain use qualifies for a fair use or whether it is an infringement. Such decisions can have a significant impact on the markets available to a certain product, such as portable digital music players.

Fair use allows certain uses of copyrighted works for such purposes as criticism, commentary, news reporting, teaching, scholarship, and research.

With respect to the first factor of the fair use test—the purpose and character of the use—courts typically are less willing to deem a use fair when it is commercial and profit seeking in nature. Yet, uses involving nonprofit educational purposes, such as copying textbooks for students, can still be found to be infringing as such use would destroy the market for the textbooks and eliminate the incentive for authors and publishers to update their works.

Courts often favorably consider the first factor of the fair use test when the use of a work is transformative, such that the use of the work adds something new; alters the original work with new expression, meaning, or message; or is otherwise for a different or further purpose than the original work.

With regard to the second factor—the nature of the copyrighted work—the law generally recognizes a greater need to disseminate factual works than creative works, and therefore a finding of fair use is more likely with a factual work. In addition, the use of published works is more likely to qualify as a fair use because the first appearance of the artist's expression has already occurred.

For the third factor—the amount and substantiality of the portion used—it inherently makes sense that the more portions of a work that are used, whether qualitatively or quantitatively, the less likely it is that the use of such portions will be considered fair. However, taking essential parts of the original work, even when they are only a small portion of the original work, can still be found to be substantial when they are at the heart of the work. In contrast, in some cases, wholesale copying can still be considered fair use, such as copying digital images in their entirety in a reduced format for an online image search engine.

With respect to the fourth factor—the effect of the use on the market or value of the work—when the use is a commercial use, market harm is presumed and must be rebutted by the defendant. When market harm cannot be presumed, the copyright holder has the burden of proof to demonstrate the market effect. Market harm would occur when the new use of the work would become widespread, adversely affecting the market for the copyrighted work, such that it would substitute for the original. The court may also consider possible adverse affects on the potential market for derivative works.

In *Sony Corp. of America v. Universal City Studios, Inc.* (1984), the Supreme Court addressed whether the manufacture and sale of video tape recorders (VTRs) by Sony violated any copyright rights of Universal City Studios, the owner of a number of copyrights on broadcast television shows. Universal City Studios sought to find Sony liable for vicarious and contributory infringement in that Sony "sold equipment with constructive knowledge of the fact that its customers may use that equipment to make unauthorized copies of copyrighted material." The Court applied the staple article of commerce doctrine, by which the sales of copying equipment "does not does not constitute contributory infringement if the product is widely used for legitimate, unobjectionable purposes . . . [or if] . . . it [is] . . . capable of substantial noninfringing uses." The Court also considered whether unauthorized time-shifting was fair use.

The Court found that the predominant use of the VTRs was to time-shift programming, such that a viewer could watch a televised program at a later and more convenient time because he or she was unable to view the program when broadcast. The Court ultimately ruled that VTRs were capable of a substantial noninfringing use and that home time shifting is fair use, thereby enabling many companies to sell video tape records without concern of facing massive damages for copyright infringement.

The Ninth Circuit Court addressed whether reverse engineering was a fair use in *Sony Computer Entertainment, Inc. v. Connectix Corp.* (2000). Sony produces and markets Sony Playstation gaming units on which users play Sony PlayStation games. Connectix makes and sells a software emulator program called Virtual Game Station that enables computer owners to play Sony PlayStation games on their computers. Although the Virtual Game Station does not contain any of Sony's copyright material, in the process of producing Virtual Game Station Connectix repeatedly copied Sony's copyrighted BIOS so as to determine how the Sony Playstations gaming units operated.

The Ninth Circuit found that "the methods by which Connectix reverse-engineered the Sony BIOS were necessary to gain access to the unprotected functional elements within the program." The court ruled that the "copies made and used by Connectix during the course of its reverse engineering of the Sony BIOS were protected fair use, necessary to permit Connectix to make its noninfringing Virtual Game Station function with PlayStation games." However, decisions by courts have held that such reverse engineering may still be a violation of an applicable license agreement such as where the right to reverse engineer was waived.

Audio Home Recording Act of 1992

The Audio Home Recording Act of 1992 amended the Copyright Act to prevent the importation, manufacture, or distribution of digital audio recording devices and digital audio interface devices that did not conform to the serial copy management system (SCMS). The purpose of this Act was to prevent the making of digital copies of already copied works by most consumers and provided some recourse to copyright owners by providing them with royalty payments from the sale of digital audio records and digital audio media. Although the Act's provisions for digital audio tape recorders and associated media were not controversial, the Recording Industry Association of America's attempt to prohibit the distribution of MP3 players that did not read the SCMS code resulted in a lawsuit that ultimately decided the future availability and desirability of MP3 players in the United States.

In *Recording Indus. Ass'n of Am. v. Diamond Multimedia Sys.* (1999), the Ninth Circuit considered whether the Rio portable music player was a digital audio recording device subject to the restrictions of the Audio Home Recording Act of 1992. The court considered that with the Rio player the digital audio files had to be created on a hard drive of a personal computer, and not on the player itself. Ultimately the court found that both the Rio player and computers were not digital audio recording devices within the meaning of the act and that, even when used in combination, neither where required to recognize the SCMS code.

File Sharing

In *A&M Records v. Napster, Inc.* (2001), the Ninth Circuit addressed, among other issues described in the DMCA chapter, whether persons who transmitted and received copyrighted digital music files over a computer network without authorization from the copyright owner were making a fair use of copyrighted music. With respect to the first factor in the fair use doctrine, the court found that the use was commercial, as the plaintiff demonstrated by showing that repeated and exploitative unauthorized copies of copyrighted works were being made to save the expense of purchasing authorized copies. The court determined that the copyrighted music was creative in nature, which cuts against a finding of fair use under the second factor. The court found that the third factor weighed against a finding of fair use because Napster users transmitted and downloaded copyrighted music in its entirely as opposed to portions thereof. Finally, with regard to the fourth factor, the court concluded that Napster harmed the market in at least two ways: it reduced audio CD sales among college students and raised the barriers to plaintiffs' entry into the market for the digital downloading of music. Therefore, the court ruled that the users who transmitted and received copyrighted digital music files over the computer network were not making a fair use of the copyrighted music. Additional issues involving the foregoing case are discussed at length in the DMCA chapter with respect to Napster's contributory and vicarious infringement in light of the DMCA.

In addition, a Supreme Court case issued after the drafting of this chapter held that companies that were created for the purpose of facilitating copyright infringement cannot avoid being liable for infringement themselves.

Quotations

Quotations from works can be made without consent of the author under the fair use doctrine, such as for new stories and historical analysis. However, the amount of the quotations cannot be unreasonably large and cannot destroy the marketability of the source by the copyright owner.

Innocent Infringement

The innocent infringement defense, when invoked successfully by a defendant in a copyright infringement suit, reduces the amount of damages for which the defendant could otherwise be liable. To be successful, the defendant has the burden to prove that he or she was unaware of the copyright owner's copyright and had no reason to believe that the acts constituted copyright infringement. The copyright owner can eliminate the innocent infringer defense by marking copies or phonorecords of the copyrighted work with a copyright notice.

CONCLUSION

Copyright law attempts to strike a balance between allowing authors to control and profit from their work while still providing the public with certain rights. Ultimately, the public benefits from copyright law because it encourages further creations and allows the public to enjoy the fruits of these creations. Copyright law will continue to face challenges with respect to computers and the Internet, and further significant changes to the law should be expected.

GLOSSARY

BBS An electronic bulletin board system.
Common law Law that has not been enacted by a legislature, but rather has been derived and developed from judicial decisions.
Compilation A work formed by the collection and assembling of preexisting materials or of data that are selected, coordinated, or arranged in such a way that the resulting work as a whole constitutes an original work of authorship.

Contributory Infringement The knowing contribution to another's infringing activity.
Derivative Work A work based on one or more preexisting works where the original work is recast, transformed, or adapted.
DMCA The Digital Millennium Copyright Act.
Fair Use A use that would ordinarily violate an exclusive right, but is nonetheless found to be noninfringing and permissible.
Infringement Violating any of the exclusive rights of the copyright owner.
Joint Work A work prepared by two or more authors with the intention that their contributions be merged into inseparable or interdependent parts of a unitary whole.
License An authorization from the copyright owner to use one or more exclusive rights of a work; licenses are normally negotiated and recorded in a written document that includes a variety of other terms.
Phonorecords LPs, CDs, and cassette tapes.
Public Performance A performance or display at a place open to the public or at any place where there are a substantial number of persons outside a normal circle of a family and its social acquaintances, whether in person or by means of a digital transmission.
Reverse Engineering Determining the functional aspects of a software program by monitoring the input and output of the software program.
RIAA The Recording Industry Association for America (www.riaa.org).
Statutory Law Law that has been enacted by the legislature.
VTR Video tape recorders are Betamax video recorders as discussed in the Sony case, but also include standard video cassette records (VCRs).
Work Made for Hire A work that, despite being created by one author, is considered to be authored by another.

CROSS REFERENCES

See *Legal, Social and Ethical Issues of the Internet; Patent Law; The Digital Millennium Copyright Act; The Legal Implications of Information Security: Regulatory Compliance and Liability; Trademark Law and the Internet.*

REFERENCES

A&M Records v. Napster, Inc., 239 F.3d 1004 (9th Cir. 2001).
Adobe Sys. v. One Stop Micro, Inc., 84 F. Supp. 2d 1086 (N.D.CA 2000).
Bleistein v. Donaldson Lithographing Co., 188 U.S. 239 (1903).
Cmty. for Creative Non-Violence v. Reid, 490 U.S. 730 (1989).
Eldred v. Ashcroft, 537 U.S. 186 (2003).
Feist Publications, Inc. v. Rural Telephone Service Co., Inc., 499 U.S. 340 (1991).
Playboy Enters. v. Webbworld Inc., 991 F. Supp. 543 (N.D.TX 1997).

Recording Indus. Ass'n of Am. v. Diamond Multimedia Sys., 180 F.3d 1072 (9th Cir. 1999).

Sonny Bono Copyright Term Extension Act of 1998. (1998). Retrieved from http://www.copyright.gov/ legislation/s505.pdf

Sony Computer Entertainment, Inc. v. Connectix Corp., 203 F.3d 596 (9th Cir. 2000); cert denied 531 U.S. 871 (2000).

Sony Corp. of America v. Universal City Studios, Inc., 464 U.S. 417 (1984).

FURTHER READING

Aalmuhammed v. Lee, 202 F.3d 1227 (9th Cir. 1999).

Baltimore Orioles, Inc. v. Major League Baseball Players Asso., 805 F.2d 663 (7th Cir. 1986).

Bitlaw. (n.d.). *International copyright*. Retrieved from http://www.bitlaw.com/copyright/international.html

Black, J. (2002, September 27). *A case to define the digital age: A Supreme Court ruling on a 20-year extension of copyright protection could decide much of what Web surfers get to see, hear, and share*. Retrieved from http://www.businessweek.com/technology/content/ sep2002/tc20020927_7367.htm

Bridgeport Music, Inc. v. Rhyme Syndicate Music, 376 F.3d 615 (6th Cir. 2004).

Campbell v. Acuff-Rose Music, 510 U.S. 569 (1994).

Central Point Software v. Nugent, 903 F. Supp. 1057 (E.D.TX 1995).

Dogan, S. (n.d.). *Copyright in cyberspace: Requirements for copyrightability*. Retrieved from http://www. cyberspacelaw.org/dogan/dogan2.html

Ebay, Inc. v. Bidder's Edge, 100 F. Supp. 2d 1058 (N.D.CA 2000).

Engineering Dynamics v. Structural Software, 26 F.3d 1335 (5th Cir. 1994).

F.E.L. Publications, Ltd. v. Catholic Bishop of Chicago, 214 U.S.P.Q. (BNA) 409 (7th Cir. 1982).

Home Recording Rights Coalition. (n.d.). *Betamax: The inside story*. Retrieved from http://www.ari.net /hrrc/html/inside_betamax.html

MacMillan, R. (2003, January 15). *Eldred v. Ashcroft: A primer*. Retrieved from http://www.washingtonpost.com/ wp-srv/technology/articleseldredprimer_100902.htm

MGM Studios, Inc. v. Grokster Ltd., 380 F.3d 1154 (9th Cir. 2004).

National Football League v. McBee & Bruno's, Inc., 792 F.2d 726 (8th Cir. 1986).

NFL v. Primetime 24 Joint Venture, 131 F. Supp. 2d 458 (S.D.NY 2001).

Quality King Distributors, Inc. v. L'anza Research Int'l, Inc., 523 U.S. 135 (1998).

Sega Enters. v. Accolade, Inc, 1993 U.S. App. LEXIS 78; 93 Daily Journal DAR 304 (9th Cir. 1993).

Shaul v. Cherry Valley-Springfield Cent. Sch. Dist., 363 F.3d 177 (2d Cir. 2004).

Smith, T. (2001, March 15). *Sony buys PlayStation emulator*. Retrieved from http://www.theregister.co.uk /2001/03/15/sony_buys_playstation_emulator/

Sprenger, P. (1999, June 15). *Rio rolls Over RIAA*. Retrieved from http://www.wired.com/news/politics /0%2C1283% 2C20235%2C00.html

Three Boys Music Corp. v. Bolton, 212 F.3d 477 (9th Cir. 2000).

Ty, Inc. v. Publ'ns Int'l, 292 F.3d 512 (7th Cir. 2002).

U.S. Copyright Law. (n.d.). Retrieved from http://www. copyright.gov/title17/

Xoom, Inc. v. Imageline, Inc., 323 F.3d 279 (4th Cir. 2002).

Patent Law

Gerald Bluhm, *Tyco Fire & Security*

INTRODUCTION

This chapter introduces the fundamental concepts of patent law, both in the United States and internationally, with some focus on software and Internet-related issues. Patents are exclusionary monopolies for a limited term, granted in exchange for inventors disclosing how to make or use their inventions. With the promise of such monopolies, inventors are encouraged to invent and thus reap the rewards made possible by the rights accorded. Competitors must either obtain a license to make or use a patented invention or discover new ways that circumvent a patented invention as defined by the patent claims.

Some have rejected the use of the word "monopoly" to describe patents. Regardless of whether one uses that term, certain rights are granted to the owner of a patent. For example, in the United States, the owner of a patent has the right to *exclude* others from making, using, selling, or offering for sale the invention in the United States, importing the invention into the United States, or importing into the United States something made by a patented process. Other countries convey similar rights for patents issued in those countries. What may not be obvious is that a patent does not grant its owner the right to make, use, sell, offer for sale, or import the patented invention. In fact, many patented inventions are improvements to existing patented work and, if made, used, or sold, would constitute infringement of the earlier patent.

GENERAL CONSIDERATIONS
Why Get a Patent?

There are many reasons why obtaining patent protection is beneficial, and the brief discussion presented here is not intended to be all inclusive. One reason for obtaining a patent is to protect one's intellectual property. That is, the holder of the patent may be able to prevent competition by preventing others from taking advantage of the invention. Because of the patent, others may decide not to compete at all in the particular area or may decide to spend significant amounts of time and money developing processes or products that do not infringe on it. Alternatively, if both sides are willing, the patent holder may license all or part of the patent to another party for a fixed fee, a royalty, or some combination of the two. A license is basically an agreement between a licensor (patent holder) and licensee that the licensor will not sue the licensee for what would otherwise constitute infringement of some or all of the patent claims.

Another reason for obtaining a patent is more defensive. For example, company B may be reluctant to sue company A for infringement of company B's patent, if company B thinks that company A may countersue for infringement of company A's patents. Such a situation may result in cross-licensing between the two parties, in which each agrees not to sue the other for infringement of all or part of each other's patents.

Yet another reason for obtaining a patent, especially for start-up companies, is to attract investment. Investors like to know that intellectual property has been protected and exclusive rights are controlled, providing value in their investment. The existence of one or more patents (or even pending patent applications) may be an indication of a company's viability.

Patent Term—How Long Does a Patent Last?

Patent protection begins on the day a patent is issued. Because of a change in law in 1994 to conform to the Uruguay Round of the General Agreement on Tariffs and Trade (GATT), when a U.S. patent expires depends on when the application was filed. Before the change in law, the term of a U.S. utility patent was 17 years from the issue date. Now, however, any U.S. utility patents issuing from an application filed on or after June 8, 1995 are valid for 20 years from the priority date; that is, the date of the earliest application to which the application claims priority (the earliest filing date in a chain of continuation and divisional applications). Utility patents that were still in force on June 8, 1995, and applications filed before that date but still pending receive the best of both worlds (with regard to patent terms): either 17 years from the issue date or 20 years from the priority date, whichever is later. Various adjustments and extensions may be available under certain conditions, although a discussion of these conditions is beyond the scope of this chapter. The patent terms discussed above pertain to U.S utility and plant patents. U.S. design patents expire after 14 years from the issue date.

In most other countries, a utility patent expires 20 years from the priority date.

Types of Patents

In the United States, there are three types of patents: utility patents, design patents, and plant patents. Utility patents are the most familiar type. They may be obtained for "any new and *useful* process, machine, manufacture, or composition of matter, or any new and useful improvement thereof" (35 U.S.C. §101).

Design patents may be obtained for new, original, and ornamental designs for manufactured articles. A design patent protects the way an article looks, as depicted in the drawings. Design patents have a term of 14 years from the issue date. They may be obtained for computer-generated icons, including full-screen displays and individual icons. The U.S. Patent and Trademark Office's (USPTO) *Manual of Patent Examining Procedure* (MPEP), section 1504.01(a) provides "Guidelines for Examination of Design Patent Applications for Computer-generated Icons" (see U.S. Design Patent D453,769 for an example of a design patent for a computer-generated icon). According to MPEP section 1504.01(a).1.A, to satisfy the manufactured article requirement, such an icon may be claimed as "a computer-generated icon shown on a computer screen, monitor, other display panel, or a portion thereof" or with similar language. The icon must also be fundamentally ornamental, rather than functional. Fonts may also be patented with design patents (for an example, see U.S. Design Patent D454,582).

The Plant Patent Act of 1930, now codified as 35 U.S.C. § 161, allows "plant patents" for plants that are reproduced asexually. Tubers, such as potatoes, are excluded (i.e., they are not patentable). To be patentable, a plant must have been found in an uncultivated state (e.g., *not* in a garden). A plant patent includes the right to exclude others from causing the plant to reproduce asexually or using, offering for sale, or selling the plant (or parts of the plant) in the United States, or importing the plant into the United States if it was asexually reproduced (see 35 U.S.C. §§ 161–164).

Despite the availability of plant patents, utility patents may also be obtained for both sexually and asexually reproduced plants (see *J.E.M. AG Supply Inc, dba Farm Advantage, Inc., et al. v. Pioneer Hi-Bred International, Inc.,*

1996). The requirements for obtaining a plant patent are more relaxed than those for obtaining a utility patent, however.

Outside the United States, many countries provide for patents that are not given full-blown examinations and that do not receive full-blown benefits. Germany, Spain, and France, for example, have "petty" (or "utility model") patents. Australia has an "innovation" patent, and Indonesia has a "simple" patent. These patents are typically for shorter terms and may not be required to satisfy the nonobviousness standard.

PATENT LAW IN THE UNITED STATES
Constitutional Basis

The U.S. Constitution grants to Congress the power "to promote the Progress of . . . useful Arts, by securing for limited Times to . . . Inventors the exclusive Right to their respective . . . Discoveries" (Article I, Section 8, Clause 8). In accordance with this power, Congress has over time enacted several patent statutes. In particular, in 1952, the present patent law, codified under Title 35 of the United States Code (35 U.S.C.; available on the Web at http://uscode.house.gov/title_35.htm), was enacted, although it has been amended many times over the years.

U.S. Patent & Trademark Office

Almost every country has a patent or intellectual property or industrial property office. In the United States, the USPTO (http://www.uspto.gov) processes patent applications and ultimately issues or grants patents. During the processing of an application (a process known as *patent prosecution*), the application is reviewed by an examiner who is familiar with the specific technology field of the invention described in the application. The examiner will reject one or more of the claims of the application if he or she feels that, when compared with prior art (existing knowledge possessed and/or information accessible by those in the subject technology field), there is nothing novel or nonobvious about the invention as claimed. The examiner may also object to the written description of the application if he or she feels that it does not satisfy the disclosure requirements of the statutes. Patent prosecution typically involves communications back and forth between the examiner and the inventor (or the inventor's patent attorney or agent) in which the inventor or attorney clarifies how the invention is in fact novel and nonobvious in relation to the prior art and is disclosed adequately by the application.

Inventors can represent themselves before the USPTO. Alternatively, an inventor or the assignee to whom the inventor assigns ownership of an invention may use an attorney or agent registered to practice before the USPTO. Both patent attorneys and patent agents must have technical backgrounds in a science or engineering field and have taken and passed a registration examination administered by the USPTO. In addition, patent attorneys must have graduated from law school and be admitted to practice law in at least one jurisdiction, whereas patent agents are not attorneys.

What Is Patentable?

An inventor may obtain a patent for "any new and useful process, machine, manufacture, or composition of matter, or any new and useful improvement thereof" (35 U.S.C. §101). In a landmark U.S. Supreme Court case in which whether a live, human-made microorganism could be patented was at issue, the Supreme Court unequivocally stated that "anything under the sun that is made by man" is patentable (*Diamond v. Chakrabarty*, 1980).

What is not patentable? Generally speaking, laws of nature, physical phenomena, and abstract ideas per se are not patentable. For example, the Supreme Court stated,

> "a new mineral discovered in the earth or a new plant found in the wild is not patentable.... Likewise, Einstein could not patent his celebrated law that $E = mc^2$; nor could Newton have patented the law of gravity." (*Diamond v. Chakrabarty*, 1980)

Of course, a practical application of some physical phenomena may be patentable. For example, although a new plant found in the wild is not patentable, its medicinal use may be. In *Diamond v. Chakrabarty* (1980), the Supreme Court clearly stated that even living things, in this case microorganisms produced by genetic engineering, are patentable. In fact, all that matters is whether the living matter is the result of human intervention.

In particular, Internet-related inventions are patentable and can be protected with method claims, apparatus claims, so-called Beauregard claims, embedded signal claims, and the like, all of which are discussed later in the chapter. Many Internet-related inventions are protected by "business method" patents.

Business Methods

Prior to the *State Street Bank & Trust Co. v. Signature Financial Group, Inc.* (1998) decision by the Court of Appeals for the Federal Circuit (CAFC), there was some uncertainty as to whether methods of doing business were patentable. Although the invention claimed was technically a "machine" that implemented business methods, this decision is cited for confirming that indeed business methods themselves are patentable.

In the *State Street Bank* case, Signature was the assignee (owner) of U.S. Patent No. 5,193,056. The claimed invention was a system in which mutual funds pool their assets into an investment portfolio to take advantage of economies of scale in administering investments. State Street Bank had been negotiating a license with Signature Financial to use that invention. When negotiations broke down, State Street Bank sought a declaratory judgment that the patent was invalid because it described a business method. The court, however, concluded that business methods are patentable subject matter.

When is a method a business method? This is not always clear. For example, Amazon.com received a patent (U.S. Patent No. 5,960,411) for its one-click process. Although the invention has been labeled a method of doing business by some, Amazon itself has asserted that its one-click patent is not a business method patent.

The USPTO has established a classification system made up of more than 400 classes that are further divided into subclasses. Every application is assigned to a class and subclass according to the technology of the invention. In general, methods that fall into the USPTO's Class 705 ("Data processing: financial, business practice, management, or cost/price determination") are considered to be business methods. The first few subcategories of Class 705 include health care management; insurance; reservation, check-in, or booking display for reserved space; staff scheduling or task assignment; market analysis, demand forecasting or surveying; and so on; see http://www.uspto.gov/web/patents/classification/USPC705/def5705.htm for a complete list of Class 705 categories.

For those inventions that are considered to be business methods, some special rules apply both during prosecution of a business method patent application and with respect to infringement. Whereas most patent applications undergo examination by a single examiner, business method applications may be subjected to multiple reviews. Extra reviews were added in part as a response to numerous complaints made in the popular press and elsewhere that many business method patents were being issued on inventions that were not patentable.

Furthermore, accused infringers of issued business method patents have at their disposal an extra defense against the accusation that infringers of other types of patents do not have. For example, for most patents, if party A receives a patent for an invention and party B has been practicing the invention prior to issuance of the patent, party B must stop its practice or obtain a license once the patent is issued. After the *State Street* decision, however, Congress added Clause § 273 to Title 35 of the U.S. Code as part of the American Inventor's Protection Act of 1999; this clause provides for "intervening rights" to protect parties who may not have applied for a business method patent based on the misconception that such patents were unobtainable. The details of § 273 are beyond the scope of this article, but basically it provides, in certain situations, a defense to an infringement claim for a party that was using the patented business method before the patent was issued.

Requirements for Patentability

An invention must meet four basic requirements before it can be patented in the United States: the invention must be (1) patentable subject matter; (2) novel; (3) nonobvious in view of the current state of the art and with respect to a person knowledgeable or "of ordinary skill" in the art; and (4) useful.

Novelty is statutorily provided for in 35 U.S.C. § 102, which describes several conditions in which a patent may not be obtained: if the invention was known or used by others in the United States prior to the patent applicant's date of invention (this could happen, for example, when two people separately invent the same invention, each unaware of the other's activity or accomplishment) or if the invention has been patented or described in a printed publication anywhere in the world. "Printed publications" may include any information that is freely accessible via the Web, even though a Web page is not technically printed in hard copy. It is not necessary that the publication be in English.

Even an inventor's own actions or writings can be held against him or her in rejecting the novelty claim. An inventor has 1 year in which to file a patent application in the United States if the invention was patented by the inventor or described by the inventor in a printed publication anywhere in the world or if the invention was in public use or on sale in the United States.

The prohibition against obviousness is statutorily provided for in 35 U.S.C. § 103(a), which states in essence that even if the invention is not disclosed in a single prior art document or is in use or on sale, if the difference between the invention and prior the art, (including use, or sale) is obvious, a patent cannot be obtained. Examiners often reject applications based on their sense that it would be obvious to combine two or more published patents or other publications that complement each other. Of course, such a combination must be obvious to a person having ordinary skill in the art, and it must have been obvious at the time the invention was made.

Often, by the time a patent is issued, which may be 2 or 3 years after the application was filed, or even at the time when the application is filed, it may seem to be obvious in light of the prior art. However, the critical time to examine obviousness is when the invention was made. As many court decisions show, it is not always easy to cast away current knowledge and place oneself back to the time the invention was made to determine whether it was obvious. Thus, assertions as to whether an invention is obvious or not in view of the cited art can be highly subjective.

Section 35 U.S.C. § 101 requires that an invention be useful, concrete, and tangible. At least three categories of subject matter have been identified by the Supreme Court as not, by themselves, patentable: laws of nature, natural phenomena, and abstract ideas. For example, the CAFC stated in the State Street Bank ruling that mathematical algorithms by themselves are unpatentable because "they are merely abstract ideas constituting disembodied concepts or truths that are not 'useful.'"

Generally speaking, the requirement that an invention be useful is an extremely low bar to patentability. Nonetheless, an invention can fail the usefulness test if an applicant fails to explain adequately why the invention is useful or if an assertion of utility is not credible. For example, the invention considered in *Newman v. Quigg* (1989) was considered to be a perpetual motion machine and thus found to be inoperative (as going against the laws of thermodynamics). It therefore did not meet the usefulness standard.

In addition to these requirements, a specification is required in the patent application that includes a written description and at least one claim. The written description must describe the invention and teach enough about it in sufficient detail so as to enable "any person skilled in the art" to make or use the invention without undue experimentation. The written description must also describe the "best mode" (i.e., the best way to carry out the invention) known to the inventor, although there is no requirement to point out a specific embodiment of the invention as the best mode. The first paragraph of 35 U.S.C. § 112 discusses the requirements of the written description.

The specification must conclude with at least one claim, which is the legal statement defining the subject matter over which the patent will confer the right to exclude. Courts look to the claims when determining whether an accused party is infringing a patent. Claims are discussed in more detail later in the chapter. Finally, 35 U.S.C. § 113 sets forth the particular requirements for drawings, which must be supplied as needed to provide an understanding of the invention.

Patent Prosecution

The process of obtaining a patent—from filing a patent application, to responding to office actions from the USPTO, to paying the issue fee—is referred to as *patent prosecution*. The first step in the patent prosecution process, other than the invention itself, is often a "prior art" search. There is no obligation on the part of an applicant to do a search, although there is an obligation to report known material information to the USPTO. Nonetheless, performing a search is often a good idea. If search results show that the invention is not novel, one can avoid a long, costly, and ultimately unsuccessful prosecution process. If the invention appears to be novel in view of the search results, often the search—by exposing those aspects that are well known or that have been described in the references uncovered in the search—will then enable the person who ultimately drafts the patent application to focus on those parts that are novel.

For example, a cursory search for U.S., Japanese, and European patents and published patent applications can be performed using, respectively, the online search facilities of the USPTO, the Japanese Patent Office (in English at http://www.ipdl.jpo.go.jp/homepg_e.ipdl), and the European Patent Office (EPO), which also enables Japanese patent searches (http://ep.espacenet.com). Most patent offices in other countries have their own Web sites that can be searched. A list of these sites can be found at either the USPTO's or the EPO's Web sites. In addition, many useful documents and news items may be found on the Web using standard Web searching facilities. More extensive (and expensive) searches may be conducted using proprietary databases that may contain articles from hundreds or thousands of trade journals, professional publications, newspapers, magazines, and so on. An online search may be quite limited in scope, and when possible one should use an experienced searcher to conduct an accurate and comprehensive search.

The next step is preparing or drafting the patent application. A patent attorney or agent ordinarily prepares the application, although inventors can represent themselves before the USPTO. The application is then filed with the USPTO. Once received by the USPTO, an application is assigned an application number, and if it is not a provisional application, it will eventually be assigned to an art group consisting of examiners who are familiar with the particular field to which the application/invention pertains. Finally, the application is assigned to a specific examiner in the art group.

That examiner reviews the application in light of both the results of his or her own prior art search and any material information submitted by the applicant. Typically, the examiner objects to one or more aspects of the application and, in an *office action*, rejects one or more of the claims based on the prior art. Or the examiner may object to unclear language in the specification or an informality in the submitted drawings. An office action is mailed to the applicant (or his or her attorney), and the applicant must reply within a certain time frame or the application will be considered abandoned.

The applicant can reply to the office action in several ways. He or she can point out the differences between the invention as claimed and the prior art cited by the examiner in the office action, emphasizing that the invention is not taught or even suggested by knowledge of the prior art. The applicant can cancel claims, amend claims for clarity, narrow claims to overcome the examiner's rejections, or even broaden claims. New claims may also be added (at least in response to a first office action). Corrections to the specification or drawings may also be made, but in any case, the applicant is never allowed to introduce new matter into the application.

The examiner often makes a subsequent office action *final*. Certain rules apply when the applicant replies to a final office action—for example, new claims cannot normally be added, and only certain amendments of a limited nature are permitted—but a final office action is not as "final" as it sounds.

If some claims are allowed in an office action, an applicant can, in the reply, cancel the rejected claims, permitting a patent to be issued with the allowed claims. A new application, called a *continuation*, can then be filed with the rejected claims. (Note that this continuation application must be filed while the parent application is pending; that is, before the parent application is issued as a patent with the allowed claims.)

Alternatively, if no claims are allowed, the applicant, in response to a final office action, may file a *Request for Continued Examination* (RCE). For the equivalent cost of filing a new application, the applicant is allowed to continue prosecution without the finality of the final office action. In older cases, those filed before May 29, 2000, the applicant may, while the first application is pending, file a continuation-type application, called a *Continued Prosecution Application* (CPA), and allow the first application to become abandoned.

During the course of prosecution, it may be desirable to file a new set of claims while allowing the original application to proceed. For example, the applicant may determine that aspects of the original application not previously claimed may be worth pursuing and may file the same specification with a different set of claims, claiming priority to the first application. This continuation application has its own filing date, but because it claims priority to the first application, it will expire (under the current statute) 20 years from the filing date of the first application (or the filing date of the earliest application in the priority chain). If new matter is added to the specification of a continuation—for example, an improvement or a new configuration—the new application is called a *continuation-in-part* (CIP). A patent issuing on a CIP application, like other utility patents, expires 20 years from the filing date of the first application to which the CIP claims priority.

In some cases, an examiner may determine that the claims of an application define two or more different inventions, each requiring its own prior art search. In this case, the examiner may issue a *restriction requirement* in which the various claims are divided into different groups, each pertaining to a different invention. The applicant is then required to select one of the groups and to cancel or amend the remaining claims. The canceled claims can be filed (while the original application is still pending) in one or more applications known as *divisional* applications. As with continuations, each divisional application has its own filing date, but each must claim priority to the parent and therefore has a term of 20 years from the filing date of the parent (or the earliest filed application in the priority chain).

Eventually, the applicant hopes, each application (including parent, continuations, CIPs, and divisionals) is allowed. For a given allowed patent application, the applicant must pay an issue fee; soon thereafter the patent is issued and is then in force. Although the term of a patent is currently 20 years from the priority date, maintenance fees must be paid at specific intervals from the date of issue or the patent will expire. These intervals are 3 years and 6 months; 7 years and 6 months; and 11 years and 6 months from the date of issue. A 6-month grace period is available for a surcharge.

Appealing an Examiner's Decision

If the applicant is dissatisfied with the examiner's conclusions as to unpatentability, the applicant can appeal to the Board of Patent Appeals and Interferences within the USPTO. Each appeal is heard by at least three members of the board. An applicant who is unhappy with the board's decision may make a further appeal to the U.S. Court of Appeals for the Federal Circuit (CAFC). The CAFC makes a decision based only on the record from the appeal to the board. Alternatively, an unhappy applicant may file a civil suit against the Director of the USPTO in the U.S. District Court for the District of Columbia. Unlike appeals to the CAFC, new evidence may be presented in these civil suits in addition to the record from the appeal to the board.

Publication and Provisional Rights

Applications filed on or after November 29, 2000 are published roughly 18 months from the priority date, unless the applicant specifically requests that they not be published, certifying at the same time that the invention has not been and will not be the subject of an application filed in another country. Early publication can be requested. Applications filed before November 29, 2000 but still pending as of that date are not typically published, but publication may be requested.

If a published application eventually issues as a patent, with a claim that is "substantially identical" to a claim published in the application publication, the owner of the patent may be entitled to a reasonable royalty, from the time of the publication date up to the issue date, from someone who makes, uses, offers for sale, or sells an infringing device as against that claim in the United States or who imports an infringing device into the United States and who has "actual notice" (currently a matter of some dispute) of the published patent application. The rights to these royalties are known as *provisional rights*.

How to Read a Patent

A patent is organized into four sections: a cover sheet, drawings, a specification, and claims. The cover sheet includes bibliographical information, a short abstract that describes the invention briefly, and usually a copy of one of the drawings considered to be representative of the invention. Drawings must be provided when necessary for understanding the invention.

The specification includes a background, a summary, a brief description of the drawings, and a detailed description of the invention. The background section describes prior art or the state of the art prior to the patented invention. The summary provides a short synopsis of the invention and often is a regurgitation of the claims in plainer language. A brief description of the drawings typically follows. Next comes a written description of one or more embodiments of the invention. As previously mentioned, the written description must enable any person skilled in the art to make and use the invention. It must also set forth the "best mode" contemplated by the inventor, although this best mode need not be pointed out as such.

In the final section, a set of claims are provided that point out and distinctly claim the protected subject matter. Each claim is written as a single sentence and typically includes a preamble, a transitional phrase, and a set of limitations. For example, claim 1 of U.S. Patent No. 6,004,596 ("Sealed crustless sandwich") appears as follows:

I claim:

1. A sealed crustless sandwich, comprising:
   a first bread layer having a first perimeter surface coplanar to a contact surface;
   at least one filling of an edible food juxtaposed to said contact surface;
   a second bread layer juxtaposed to said at least one filling opposite of said first bread layer, wherein said second bread layer includes a second perimeter surface similar to said first perimeter surface;
   a crimped edge directly between said first perimeter surface and said second perimeter surface for sealing said at least one filling between said first bread layer and said second bread layer;
   wherein a crust portion of said first bread layer and said second bread layer has been removed.

In this example, the *preamble* is the phrase: "A sealed crustless sandwich." The transitional phrase is "comprising." These elements are followed by five limitations: "a first bread layer," "at least one filling," "a second bread layer," "a crimped edge," and the condition "wherein a crust portion . . . has been removed." For this claim to be infringed, an unauthorized party must make, use, sell or offer to sell, or import into the United States a sandwich product that satisfies every one of these limitations. It is irrelevant that another crustless sandwich may have other components not described in the claim; for example, a

cherry on top. As long as some food product meets every one of the limitations listed in claim 1, that product is said to infringe claim 1. On the other hand, if a sandwich is lacking some element, such as the crimped edge, it cannot literally infringe (but see below regarding the doctrine of equivalents).

A first claim is typically written broadly, to cover a wide range of variations. Narrower claims often follow that include the limitations of the broad claim, plus additional limitations that limit the scope of the invention recited by these narrower claims. Narrower claims are often written as dependent claims.

For example, claim 1 above is an independent claim. Claim 2 in the same patent reads as follows:

2. The sealed crustless sandwich of claim 1, wherein said crimped edge includes a plurality of spaced apart depressions for increasing a bond of said crimped edge.

Claim 2 is called a dependent claim because it *depends from* claim 1. That is, it includes all of the five limitations of claim 1, plus the further limitation that the crimped edge includes "spaced apart depressions." For a sandwich to infringe this claim, it must meet all of the limitations of claim 1 *and* claim 2. One reason for providing additional narrower claims is that often, during litigation of a patent suit, some claims may be found to be invalid. Even though a claim may be invalidated in a court of law (for example, if a publication is presented that predates the patent's priority date and that teaches or suggests one or more of the claims), a narrower claim with additional limitations may still be valid, even if it depends from the invalidated claim.

Another reason for providing additional narrower claims is the so-called doctrine of claim differentiation, under which "two claims of a patent are presumptively of different scope" (*Kraft Foods, Inc. v. Int'l Trading Co.*, 2000). According to this doctrine, if a dependent claim includes a narrowing definition of some limitation of a base claim, then the base claim is presumed to encompass not only the narrow definition but other embodiments as well. For example, claim 2 above may help support the proposition that claim 1 covers crustless sandwiches that do not have depressions that are spaced apart as well as crustless sandwiches that have other kinds of bonding mechanisms.

First-time readers of claims are often puzzled by their seemingly bizarre language and grammar. Sometimes this language results from the statutory requirement that claims particularly point out and distinctly claim the subject matter that the inventor or applicant regards as his or her invention. Thus, use of a definite article such as "the" is typically not allowed unless it refers to something already defined in the claim (i.e., there is an "antecedent basis" for the thing being referred to). For this reason, one often sees *a* number of (things)," whereas in normal usage one would say "*the* number of (things)."

In addition, use of the word "or" is generally frowned upon as it leaves options open and is therefore not considered to distinctly claim an invention. Thus, one often sees in claims the following wording—"at least one of [Choice A], [Choice B], *and* [Choice C]" or "any of

[Choice A], [Choice B], *and* [Choice C]"—whereas in normal speech, one might say "either [Choice A], [Choice B], *or* [Choice C]." Similarly, instead of stating "one or more of," claims will more often state "a plurality of" or "at least one of," leading to even more confusing language later in the claims, such as "the at least one of." Although such language may at first be confusing, an understanding of why these terms are used may help in reading and interpreting a claim.

Another aspect of claims that can be confusing to the layperson is that often very similar language is used in two different claims. For example, a patent typically will have a method claim and an apparatus (or system) claim that use parallel language. Remember, however, that the scope of the right to exclude may be different between a method and an apparatus or composition of matter.

A limitation in an apparatus claim may also be expressed as a means or step for performing a specified function without the recital of any specific structure. Although such a limitation is not always triggered by "means for" (also called "means-plus-function") language and may even be triggered in the absence of such language, such claims are often added to a patent. A "means for" limitation is construed to cover the corresponding structure, material, or acts described in the specification and their equivalents (see 35 U.S.C. § 112, sixth paragraph).

In addition to the more or less standard apparatus, method, and "means-for" claims, computer- and software-related inventions are often additionally recited in so-called Beauregard claims and signal claims. As the USPTO states, a computer program is merely a set of instructions, capable of being executed but is not itself a process (see section 2106(a) of the *Manual of Patent Examining Procedure*). To be patentable, a computer-readable medium or an "article of manufacture" comprising a computer-readable or useable medium is claimed, having therein a computer program that performs some steps of a process. These types of claims have been called Beauregard claims after the inventor of one of the first patent applications to use such claims (see U.S. Patent No. 4,962,468).

Another type of claim one might encounter is the so-called propagated signal claim. Such a claim might appear as follows:

1. A computer data signal embodied in a carrier wave for [doing something], the computer data signal comprising:
   program code for [performing a first action];
   program code for [performing a second action]; etc.

Such claims are thought to protect against the unlicensed transmission of a computer program over a network such as the Internet or through modems. Of special concern with claims directed to client/server applications is the fact that a single party may not be performing or using all of the limitations of a claim. In other words, if a claim states actions taken by both the server and the client, which are controlled by two independent parties, then neither party can be an infringer. Therefore, it may be desirable in a patent to have one set of claims directed to the overall invention, another set of claims directed to actions taken at the server (possibly in response to messages received from a client), and yet another set of claims directed to actions taken by a client (possibly in response to messages received from a server).

Protecting Patent Rights
What Rights Are Conferred on a Patentee?
A patent confers specific "exclusive" rights on the owner of a patent. That is, the owner of a patent is granted the right to exclude other parties from various acts, including making, using, offering to sell, or selling the patented invention (as set forth in the claims) within the United States or importing the patented invention into the United States. When a process is patented as opposed to an apparatus or composition of matter, the patentee is similarly granted the right to exclude others from using, offering to sell, or selling in the United States or importing into the United States any product made by the claimed process. Note that a patent does not give an owner the right to practice the invention recited in the patent; another (broader) patent may exclude the owner from practicing the invention. These rights begin when the patent is granted—that is, when the patent is issued—and last until the patent expires.

Infringement
When someone performs one of the restricted acts described above without permission of the patent owner, the claims of the patent are said to be infringed. There are three types of infringement: direct infringement, active inducement to infringe, and contributory infringement. *Direct infringement* occurs when someone performs one of the restricted acts; that is, makes, uses, sells the invention (as set forth in at least one claim of the patent), or offers it for sale in the United States or imports it into the United States. Note that direct infringement does not require knowledge by the infringer that the invention is prohibited, nor does it require that the infringer intentionally perform the act. All that is required for direct infringement is the act.

Active inducement to infringe occurs when someone induces another to infringe. If there is no direct infringement, there cannot be an active inducement to infringe, no matter how hard someone tries to induce infringement. Of course, there could be other legal issues in this case.

Contributory infringement occurs when a component of a patented invention is sold or offered for sale in the United States or imported into the United States by a party who is aware that the component is especially made or adapted for an infringing use. As with active inducement to infringe, there cannot be any contributory infringement unless there is direct infringement by some party. Note that because use must occur within the United States, in an Internet-related patent, there may be no infringement where either a server or a client outside the United States performs some of the elements of a patent claim.

Doctrine of Equivalents
Under the *doctrine of equivalents*, a patent claim may be infringed even if the accused device does not literally

infringe the claim, but the differences between the claims of the patent and the accused device are insubstantial. This means that the accused product can infringe a patent's claims if it performs the same function to achieve the same result in substantially the same way as the patent claim.

Prosecution history estoppel, however, may limit the scope of equivalents of a patent. Prosecution history estoppel applies when an applicant amends the patent claims to overcome an examiner's rejection or makes arguments during patent prosecution that help interpret the claims. After amending the claims, the applicant cannot recapture that which was given up or surrendered by narrowing the scope of the patent claim, and the applicant is estopped from claiming that he or she could not have reasonably been expected to have drafted a claim that would have literally encompassed the alleged equivalent (see *Festo Corporation v. Shoketsu Kinzoku Kogyo Kabushiki Co., Ltd*, 2002).

Remedies
When the owner of a patent believes another party is infringing on it, the owner typically seeks one of two things: (1) to have the accused party cease from engaging in the infringing acts and collect damages for past infringement and/or (2) to license the invention to the accused party in order to collect future royalties. An owner typically files a lawsuit seeking one or more remedies if he or she does not wish to license the invention, or if license negotiations break down, or to "persuade" the accused party to obtain a license. The patent owner can seek an injunction against the accused party, wherein the court can order a cessation of the infringing act. A court can also award monetary damages to compensate the owner for the infringement. These damages can be the patentee's lost profits due to lost sales or can be a reasonable royalty for the use of the invention and may include interest and other costs, if the court so decides. A court may increase these monetary damages up to three times where willful infringement is found. In exceptional cases, a court may award attorney fees for either party, whichever prevails.

Defending Against an Accusation of Infringement
There are two main ways a party accused of infringement can avoid liability: the party can assert that (1) its product does not infringe the patent(s) in question or that (2) the patent in question is invalid of when forceable, based on any one of a number of reasons (i.e., lack of novelty, obviousness, incorrect inventorship, inequitable conduct, etc.). Issuance of a patent by the USPTO creates a presumption of validity of the patent. Nonetheless, a court may rule, based on the patent itself, the prosecution history of the patent application, and/or new evidence, that the patent is not valid. Generally speaking, damages cannot be obtained for infringements that occurred more than 6 years before the filing of the suit.

Independent of the statutory time frame, an infringement suit may be barred by *laches*; for example, if the patent owner deliberately delayed bringing the suit for an unreasonable time, knowing that the delay would work to the detriment of the accused infringer. In 2002, the CAFC confirmed the existence of *prosecution laches*, in which an unreasonable delay during prosecution of the application, together with harm to the other party caused by the delay, can result in unenforceability of a patent (*Symbol Technologies, Inc. al. v. Lemelson Medical, Education & Research Foundation, Limited Partnership*, 2002).

Court Jurisdiction in Patent Cases
Because patent law is federal law (as opposed to state law), federal courts have jurisdiction over all patent-related cases. Furthermore, although there are many federal courts of appeal, Congress, in seeking to establish a single interpretation of the patent laws, established the Court of Appeals for the Federal Circuit (CAFC) to hear all patent-related appeals (but see the discussion below of *Holmes Group, Inc.*).

Typically, a three-judge panel hears and decides an appealed case. On occasion, that decision may be appealed. One of the parties may ask for an *en banc* rehearing in which all or most of the judges from the CAFC rehear the case. If a party is not satisfied with the final ruling, it may appeal to the U.S. Supreme Court. However, very few patent cases are ever heard by the Supreme Court, typically 1 or 2 a year, if that.

One case that was heard by the Supreme Court recently was *Holmes Group, Inc. v. Vornado Air Circulation Systems, Inc.* (2002). In this case, Holmes filed a complaint seeking a declaratory judgment that its products did not infringe Vornado's *trade dress*. Trade dress is another form of protection that does not involve patents. Although the original complaint did not involve patents, Vornado filed a counterclaim alleging patent infringement. After an appeal to and decision by the CAFC, the Supreme Court heard the case.

The Supreme Court ruled that the CAFC does not have jurisdiction over a case that involves questions of patent law where the party bringing the suit did not, in its complaint, assert any patent law issues. Thus, although the CAFC was created in part to form a uniform interpretation of patent law across the country, where the original complaint does not assert any patent law issues, the CAFC may not have jurisdiction, even where patent issues are later asserted in a counterclaim.

Provisional Applications

A provisional application must have a written description and drawings sufficient to teach the invention to one skilled in the art. However, a provisional application is not examined and thus will never issue into a patent. No claims are required, although it may be preferable to include some claims for reasons beyond the scope of this article. A provisional application is relatively inexpensive to file and provides a priority date for any application filed within a year claiming the benefit of the provisional application, as to the matter disclosed in the provisional application. Note, however, that a provisional application is automatically abandoned 1 year from its filing date, unless it is converted into a nonprovisional application within that time. To receive the benefit of the filing date, within a year either a provisional application must be converted to a nonprovisional application, or more commonly a nonprovisional application must be filed. Although a provisional application establishes a priority date, the 20-year term of an issued patent claiming the benefit of the provisional application begins on the filing date of the first nonprovisional application in the priority chain.

NON-U.S. PATENTS
General Information

Patents are, of course, available outside the United States. One may file a first application almost anywhere in the world and follow up with applications in other countries within 1 year of filing the first application, maintaining the first application's filing date as a priority date.

As the USPTO's *Manual of Patent Examining Procedure* (MPEP) states, the right to rely on a foreign application is known as the *right of priority* in international patent law. The right of priority originated in a multilateral treaty of 1883, known as the Paris Convention for the Protection of Industrial Property, or more simply as the Paris Convention. The treaty is administered by the World Intellectual Property Organization (WIPO) at Geneva, Switzerland.

In addition to filing in individual countries, applications can be made in several regional areas, including the European Patent Convention (EPC; http://www.european-patent-office.org/index.en.php), the African Intellectual Property Organization (OAPI; http://www.oapi.wipo.net) made up of French-speaking African countries, the African Regional Industrial Property Organization (ARIPO; http://www.aripo.wipo.net) comprising English-speaking African countries, and the Eurasian Patent Organization (EAPO), (http://www.eapo.org/) which includes former republics of the Union of Soviet Socialist Republics.

For protection in EPC member countries, an application is filed at the European Patent Office (EPO) in Munich, Germany, designating some or all EPC member countries. Only one application needs to be filed and prosecuted to obtain coverage for any or all of the member countries. The application can be filed and prosecuted in English up to the point of issuance. A separate national patent is issued for each selected country, and each patent is subject to the patent laws of the country in which it is issued (and could ultimately be invalidated in some countries but not others). A separate European Community Patent may become available in the next few years, wherein an application filed under this regime would issue as a single community-wide patent, subject to a single jurisdiction with regard to various legal claims.

Patent Cooperation Treaty

Yet another alternative is to file an application according to the Patent Cooperation Treaty (PCT; see http://www.wipo.int/pct/en/). A PCT application serves as an application in each country that is designated. The process begins when an applicant from a member country files a PCT application in a designated receiving office (such as the USPTO). This begins the "international stage." The application is published approximately 18 months after the priority date. A search is performed and a search report sent to the applicant.

PCT procedures have undergone significant changes as recently as January 2004. For applications filed before January 1, 2004, at the request (i.e., a "Chapter II Demand") of the applicant, a preliminary examination may be performed and a written opinion is issued. This is similar to patent prosecution in the United States. However, the applicant typically has only one opportunity to respond to the written opinion and to amend the claims. Ultimately, an International Preliminary Examination Report is issued. Thirty months (31 months for some countries) from the priority date, or 20 months for some countries if the preliminary examination has not been requested, the application must enter the "national stage" in those countries or regions in which protection is sought. Prosecution of the application then continues independently in each country or region until the patent is granted.

For applications filed on or after January 1, 2004, the search authority issues, in addition to the search report, a written opinion, whether or not requested by the application in a Chapter II demand. Except in a very few countries, the national stage may be entered at 30 months regardless of whether a Chapter II Demand was made. If a Chapter II Demand is not made, the written opinion is transformed into a Chapter I "international preliminary report on patentability." For these applications, a Chapter II Demand must be made by the later of 22 months from the priority date or 3 months from the international search report.

Applications filed prior to January 1, 2004 had to designate, at filing, those countries or regions from which the applicant might later elect to enter into the national stage. Although many applicants often designated all countries just to be safe (after paying for a certain number of designated countries, the rest were free), for applications filed on or after January 1, 2004, all countries and regions are designated automatically unless expressly excluded.

Filing patent applications in multiple jurisdictions can be very expensive. To keep costs down, applicants typically file only in those jurisdictions where the invention is likely to be used most frequently and where meaningful enforcement can be achieved. A PCT application enables an applicant, for a relatively low cost, to delay for up to 30 months (31 months in some cases) both the designation of particular countries or regional jurisdictions and the costs of entering in those countries and regions.

Other Considerations

Although many procedures and rights are similar in various countries and regions, there are differences, some of which may be somewhat significant. It is not the intent of this chapter to cover the particulars of the patent laws and procedures of every nation. The number of countries is too numerous, and laws and procedures are always changing. Nevertheless, it is instructive to discuss some details to give an idea of the subtle and not-so-subtle differences among countries or regional organizations. Thus, although this section does not provide a comprehensive comparison of patent procedures and rights throughout the world, it offers an instructive examination of several different aspects employed around the world.

Although novelty, nonobviousness, and usefulness form the cornerstone in obtaining a U.S. patent for an invention, in most of the rest of the world, the requirements are stated differently. For example, a claim in a PCT application must be novel, involve an "inventive step," and be "industrially applicable."

A few countries, such as Australia, Canada, Colombia, and the United States, provide a 1-year grace period after publication of a document describing an invention during which an application for the invention may be filed. In most other countries, such a disclosure before the filing of an application is an absolute bar to obtaining a patent.

Another difference is that in the United States, when two inventors claim to have invented the invention independently, the patent is awarded to the first to invent (with some caveats). Of course, the precise instance of invention may be difficult to discern and to prove, leading to a complicated procedure known as an interference proceedings. The rest of the world follows a "first-to-file" policy, in which a patent for an invention is awarded to the first applicant to file, regardless of who invented it first.

In the United States, a computer program is patentable if it produces a "useful, concrete, and tangible result," as specified in the State Street ruling. However, in many foreign countries, software per se is explicitly barred from being patentable. Nonetheless, "thousands of patents for computer-implemented inventions have been granted by the European Patent Office (EPO) and by national patent offices," according to the Commission of the European Communities (2002).

Another notable difference is that in the United States the applicants must be the inventors (though they can assign their rights), whereas in other countries, applicants may be either the inventor or the assignee, which can be an individual or a corporation.

In the United States, examination of a patent application by an examiner is automatic. However, in many other countries, examination must be requested within some time period from the filing date. For example, in Japan, the examination must be requested within 3 years for patent applications filed on or after October 1, 2001. For applications filed before October 1, 2001, the request must be made within 7 years. In Canada, a request for examination must be filed within 5 years.

Before filing a foreign application, a foreign filing license is required for any invention *invented* in the United States, even by a non-U.S. citizen. Filing a "foreign" application without a foreign filing license could lead to invalidation or unenforceability of a patent. Italy similar requirements, although many other countries do not.

Patent prosecution procedures for the EPO are governed by the European Patent Convention (EPC; see http://www.european-patent-office.org/legal/epc/index.html). There are currently 31 member countries of the EPO and 5 "extension" countries that are expected to become members. About 18 months after the priority date, an application is published or "laid open" to public inspection. A prior art search is performed and a search report is generated, in which an examiner may cite references that show that certain claims are either not novel or do not have an inventive step (i.e., the claims are obvious in view of the prior art). The search report is typically published along with the application. (If the application was originally filed as a PCT application and the search report was performed by the EPO, then a second search is not performed.) Within 6 months of the search report, the applicant must file a request for examination.

In the United States, during patent prosecution, claims can usually be broadened or new broader claims added in an amendment. It is usually sufficient that the narrower (prebroadening) claims are supported in the specification. In the EPO, in contrast, claims typically cannot be broadened unless the claimed (broader) invention is specifically described in the specification.

EPO applications can be very expensive as the number of claims exceeds 10. Typically only one of each type of independent claim (e.g., apparatus, method) is allowed.

Types of Patent Applications

In foreign countries, the term "divisional" application covers both divisional applications and continuations. If the parent application is an innovation patent, a divisional application can be filed as either an innovation patent or as a standard patent. Australia provides for "patents of addition" for improvements and modifications to an invention (somewhat akin to U.S. CIPs) and for divisionals.

Some countries have equivalents to U.S. provisional applications. For example, in Great Britain and Canada, one can file an "informal" application without claims. Such an informal application acts, as does a U.S. provisional application, to preserve the priority date. However, the informal application is not provisional in that claims must be added within 1 year to formalize the application. Australia, in contrast, provides for a "provisional" application that must be followed within 12 months by either a "complete" or international (PCT) application. New Zealand also provides for a provisional application, with 12 months to file a regular application or up to 15 months with a 3-month extension.

Time Limits in Patent Prosecution

In both the EPO and USPTO, there is no time limit to the prosecution process, and prosecution can theoretically last for a very long time. Certain countries, however, do impose limits. For example, Great Britain requires that an application be put in order within 4-1/2 years of the priority date. At most, a 1-month extension is available. This process includes the PCT international stage and the EPO prosecution if any.

Employed Inventor Laws and Shoprights

In the United States, absent agreement otherwise, an employer has a nonexclusive, nontransferable right to use an employee's patented invention for its own use if the employee used the employer's materials or facility to develop the invention. Such rights are known as *shoprights*. Conversely, some countries, such as Germany and Japan, have "employed inventor laws." Under such laws, if an employer fails to file an application for an invention within a certain time frame, the employee can file an application in his or her own name. To protect themselves in such cases, employers may file petty patents.

Provisional Rights

Though not necessarily called by that term, many countries provide the equivalent of U.S. provisional rights. For example, in Canada, after the granting of a patent, a patentee may be entitled to reasonable compensation for infringement occurring in Canada as of the date the application was laid open.

Compulsory Licenses and U.S. March-in Rights

According to 35 U.S.C. § 203 (*march-in rights*), a federal agency that has funded development of an invention to which a small business or nonprofit organization has acquired patent rights has the right to require a contractor, an assignee, or exclusive licensee of the invention to grant a license in any field of use.

In the United States, state and federal governments and their agencies are immune from certain types of suits for infringement under the doctrine of sovereign immunity. Essentially, states may be enjoined, but not sued for damages. The federal government may be sued for a "reasonable royalty" before the U.S. Court of Federal Claims pursuant to its limited waiver of sovereignty embodied in 28 U.S.C. § 1498. Most other countries apply at least some form of sovereign immunity.

In many foreign countries, a patented invention must be manufactured or otherwise worked or exploited in that country within a certain period, typically 3 years, or the patent could be invalidated; alternatively, a compulsory license may be granted. In Canada, a compulsory license may be granted to remedy certain abuses of patent rights. Such abuses, which are beyond the scope of this article, cannot be considered until 3 years after the grant.

CONCLUSION

Patents can be valuable assets for any business, large or small, or they can be a waste of money. In return for disclosing the invention, the patentee is granted a limited term (typically 20 years from filing) in which the competition cannot use the patented device or method. The competition therefore must research and develop noninfringing alternatives, a process that could be costly, timely, and in some cases, even futile, therein giving the patentee a substantial advantage. Alternatively, the patentee may choose to license the patented technology in return for a royalty or some other consideration. A patent does not give the owner the right to practice the invention.

GLOSSARY

Claim The part of a patent that defines the actual intellectual property protected by the patent; that is, the inventive subject matter protected by the patent.

Dependent Claim A patent claim that incorporates by reference the limitations of another patent claim. Such a claim typically begins with language such as, "The device of Claim X, further comprising . . . ," which has the effect of incorporating by reference the limitations of Claim X.

Doctrine of Claim Differentiation A doctrine under which claims of a patent are presumptively of different scope, so that if a dependent claim includes a narrowing definition of some limitation of a base claim, then the base claim is presumed to encompass not only the narrow definition but other embodiments as well.

Doctrine of Equivalents A doctrine by which, even if a device or process does not exactly match every limitation of a patent's claim, the device may still infringe the patent if the differences are, to a "person of ordinary skill in the art," insubstantial (as determined by a judge or jury during an infringement hearing).

Element Although "element" and "limitation" are sometimes used interchangeably, the term "element" is used more frequently by the courts to refer to aspects of an allegedly infringing device or method. In an infringement case, the elements of the alleged infringing device or method are compared with the claim limitations of the patent allegedly being infringed. Note, however, that the U.S. statute (35 U.S.C. § 112) refers to both an "element in a claim" (sixth paragraph) and "limitations of [a] claim" (fourth and fifth paragraphs).

Independent claim A patent claim that does not incorporate any other patent claim by reference.

Infringement When a device or method has all of the limitations of a claim (which may be interpreted differently under the patent laws of individual countries), the device or method is said to infringe the claim. Various remedies may be available to the owner of the infringed patent.

Laches An equitable principle whereby a party is estopped (not allowed) from bringing a lawsuit after an unreasonable or unexplained delay that has had a detrimental effect on the party being sued.

Limitation A claim limitation is a part of a claim that defines a particular aspect of the invention (i.e., an aspect of the invention that must be practiced if the invention is to be infringed). Every claim has at least one limitation, and most claims have two or more limitations.

Means plus function A particular claim limitation may be written in "means plus function" language, wherein the limitation is recited as a means or a step for performing a specified function, without reciting the particular structure, material, or acts, which are thus construed to be those described in the specification (and equivalents). "Means plus function" claim limitations are specifically authorized by U.S. statute. In some countries, "omnibus" claims serve a similar purpose.

Nonobvious One of the basic requirements in obtaining a patent is that the invention be nonobvious to one of ordinary skill in the particular art concerned, in view of the known (prior) art.

Novelty One of the basic requirements in obtaining a patent is that the invention be novel. Legally, in the United States, this means that a claim may be barred if any of the conditions stated in 35 U.S.C. § 102 hold true; that is, a description has been published anywhere in the world, the invention has been sold or offered for sale or otherwise placed in the public domain, etc. Similar conditions apply in other countries; however, certain grace periods apply in some countries for certain types of prior disclosure.

Patent A grant that gives the holder of a patent certain rights to exclude others from practicing, (i.e., making), using, selling, offering for sale, importing, etc., a claimed invention, in the country in which the patent has been granted and for the term during which the patent is valid.

PCT The Patent Cooperation Treaty under which an applicant of a member country can file a single international patent application that may designate one, many, or all of the member countries. The PCT does not provide for the granting of patents; that occurs at the "national stage."

Prior art The accumulated knowledge of those skilled in the particular art concerned, which can bar issuance of a patent if the claims are not novel or nonobvious in view of the prior art.

Prosecution The process of obtaining a patent, from the filing of an application to the issuance of the patent (or abandonment of the application).

Prosecution laches An equitable principle in which unreasonable delay during prosecution of a patent application, together with harm to another party caused by the delay, can result in unenforceability of the issued patent.

Provisional application A particular type of patent application that is never examined but serves to provide a priority date for a future, nonprovisional application, subject to the requirement that the provisional application describes the invention fully.

Provisional rights The rights of a patent owner to a reasonable royalty for an infringing device or method, covering the period between publication of a patent application and the granting of the patent with substantially identical claims as those in the published application.

Right of priority The right to rely on another application.

U.S. Patent and Trademark Office (USPTO) The U.S. governmental agency authorized to issue patents, as well as to register trademarks (see Trademark Law in this handbook).

CROSS REFERENCES

See *Copyright Law; Legal, Social and Ethical Issues of the Internet; The Legal Implications of Information Security: Regulatory Compliance and Liability; Trademark Law and the Internet*.

REFERENCES

Commission of the European Communities (2002). *Proposal for a directive of the European Parliament and of the Council on the Patentability of Computer-implemented Inventions*. Retrieved from http://europa.eu.int/comm/internal_market/en/indprop/comp/com02-92en.pdf

Diamond v. Chakrabarty, 1980

Festo Corporation v. Shoketsu Kinzoku Kogyo Kabushiki Co., Ltd., 535 U.S. 722 (2002).

Holmes Group, Inc. v. Vornado Air Circulation Systems, Inc., 535 U.S. 826 (2002).

J.E.M. AG Supply Inc, dba Farm Advantage, Inc., et al. v. Pioneer Hi-Bred International, Inc., 1996

Kraft Foods, Inc. v. Int'l Trading Co., 2000

Newman v. Quigg (1989)

State Street Bank & Trust Co. v. Signature Financial Group, Inc. (1998). Retrieved from http://www.ll.georgetown.edu/Fed-Ct/Circuit/fed/opinions/97-1327.html

Symbol Technologies, Inc. al. v. Lemelson Medical, Education & Research Foundation, Limited Partnership, 2002

U.S. Patent and Trademark Office. (2000, June 30). *U.S. Patent Classification System—Classification definitions*. Retrieved from http://www.uspto.gov/web/offices/ac/ido/oeip/taf/def/705.htm

FURTHER READING

Albert, G. P., Jr. et al. (1999). *Intellectual property law in cyberspace*. Washington, DC: BNA Books.

Chisum, D. (2002). *Chisum on patents, a treatise on the law of patentability, validity and infringement*. New York: M. Bender. Available at LexisNexis.com

Chisum, D., Nard, C., Schwartz, H., Newman, P., & Kieff, F. S. (2004). *Principles of patent law* (3rd ed.). New York: Foundation Press.

Donner, I. H. (1999). *Patent prosecution, practice & procedure before the U.S. Patent Office* (2nd ed.). Washington, DC: BNA Books.

Faber, R. C. *Landis on mechanics of patent claim drafting* (4th ed.). New York: Practicing Law Institute.

Harmon, R. L. (2001). *Patents and the Federal Circuit* (5th ed.). Washington, DC: BNA Books.

Miller, A. R., & Davis, M. H. (1990). *Intellectual property— Patents, trademarks and copyright in a nutshell*. St. Paul, MN: West Publishing Co.

Stobbs, G. A. (1995). *Software patents*. New York: John Wiley & Sons.

Web sites

American Bar Association: http://www.abanet.org/intelprop/comm106/106general.html

American Intellectual Property Law Association: http://www.aipla.org/

CAFC opinions may be found at:

http://www.law.emory.edu/fedcircuit/ (Emory University)

http://www.ll.georgetown.edu/federal/judicial/cafed.cfm (Georgetown University)

http://www.fedcir.gov/ (CAFC)

Cornell University: http://www.law.cornell.edu/topics/patent.html

Findlaw: http://www.findlaw.com/

Intellectual Property Owners Association http://www.ipo.org

Intellectual Property Today: http://www.iptoday.com/

IPWatchdog.com: http://www.ipwatchdog.com/patent.html

Nolo: http://www.nolo.com/

PatentLawLinks.com: http://www.patentlawlinks.com/

U.S. Patent and Trademark Office: http://www.uspto.gov/

WIPO Collection of Laws For Electronic Access (CLEA): http://www.wipo.int/clea/en/index_netscape.jsp

U.S. Supreme Court: http://www.supremecourtus.gov/

Trademark Law and the Internet

Ray Everett-Church, *PrivacyClue LLC*

INTRODUCTION

Trademark law is a fascinating subject for many people, in part because most everybody in our society understands and appreciates the power of popular trademarks, such as Lexus, Pokemon, Yahoo!, and Safeway. Trademarks are such an integral part of our language and culture that we all have a vested interest in their protection. Because trademarks are all about meaning, trademark disputes are a kind of spectator sport: they involve popular cultural icons and turn on questions such as whether the average person is likely to be confused if a trademark is used improperly. So in many respects, everybody gets to have an opinion on trademark issues, and that opinion more often than not counts for something in the final calculus of trademark disputes.

In this chapter, we will look at the fundamental ideas that underlie the protection of trademarks and we will look at ways in which trademarks can be infringed and protected. Once that groundwork has been laid, we will then look at how these fundamentals have been applied to the unique and significant disputes that have arisen in the Internet context. In many respects, trademark law has been turned upside down by the Internet, so we will look at how the principles of trademark law are being applied in today's Internet-oriented business environment.

TRADEMARK DEFINED

Merriam-Webster's Dictionary of Law defines **trademark** as "a mark that is used by a manufacturer or merchant to identify the origin or ownership of goods and to distinguish them from others and the use of which is protected by law."

In practice, a trademark is any word (Sun), name (Calvin Klein), symbol (golden arches), device (the Energizer Bunny), slogan ("Fly the Friendly Skies"), package design (Coca-Cola bottle), colors (FedEx purple and orange), sounds (the five tone Intel Corporation sound) or any combination thereof that identifies and distinguishes a specific product or service from others in the marketplace.

As trademark law has evolved, the field has become an important subset of the larger category known as **intellectual property** law. As the name implies, intellectual property law (which also includes patent, copyright, and trade secret law) treats these rights as a kind of property right, protecting the rights of owners to exploit the property for their own benefit while prohibiting unauthorized use by others. But unlike real estate or personal property law, intellectual property law concerns ownership of intangible things such as ideas, words, and meanings, rather than physical things.

The legal protections afforded by trademark law also extend to the related concepts of **service marks** and **trade dress**. Service marks differ from trademarks in that they are marks used to identify a particular service, or to distinguish the provider of a service, rather than a tangible product. For example, the name of a consulting firm, or the name of a proprietary analytical process used by that consulting firm, might be more properly identified as a service mark. Trade dress is the overall image of a product, composed of the nonfunctional elements of its design, packaging, or labeling. This could include specific colors or color combinations, a distinctive package shape, or specific symbols or design elements.

Many people confuse trademark with copyright. Copyright is a person's exclusive right to benefit from the reproduction or adaptation of an original work of authorship, such as a literary, artistic, or musical work. Trademark differs from copyright in that trademark law does not prohibit the reproduction or adaptation of the creative products of an author. Rather trademark law seeks to prevent confusion over words or other characteristics used to uniquely identify the source or quality of a product or service. For example, Paul Simon's 1973 song "Kodachrome" refers to a trademark owned by Eastman Kodak Company even though Simon holds the copyright on his work.

The relative strength of a particular trademark depends upon where it falls within a range of five categories: fanciful, arbitrary, suggestive, descriptive, or generic. The greatest protection comes for fanciful marks consisting of invented words like Xerox, Kodak, or TiVo. The next strongest protection comes for arbitrary marks, which are commonplace words used in a manner that is unrelated to their dictionary meaning, such as Apple for computers or Shell for gasoline. Suggestive marks are familiar words or phrases that are used in an inventive way to "suggest" what their product or service really consists of, such as Home Box Office for a movie channel or Mail Boxes Etc. for a postal services franchise. The least protection comes for descriptive marks which do little more than describe the characteristics or contents of the product, such as the publication Automotive Industry News, or Cellphone Center for a cellular telephone retailer. Finally, generic names, which merely state what the product or service is, cannot function as trademarks. Some marks, such as aspirin, linoleum, escalator, or nylon, were once trademarks but became generic because the trademark holder failed to police unauthorized use.

FEDERAL TRADEMARK LAW

For trademarks used in interstate commerce, U.S. law provides protection under the Trademark Act of 1946, known more commonly as the **Lanham Act**. The Lanham Act also created a registration process for trademarks, and legal and procedural incentives for trademarks to be registered with the U.S. Patent and Trademark Office (USPTO). Many States within the U.S. also afford trademarks protections under their State's laws.

The Lanham Act provides a functional definition of what is eligible to be registered as a trademark. Potentially anything can be registered as a trademark if it functions among consumers to distinguish a specific product from other products in the marketplace. The Lanham Act does, however, prohibit certain marks, including anything immoral, deceptive, scandalous, disparaging towards an institution or national symbol, falsely suggests a connection to a person, consisting of a flag other governmental insignia, using a name or portrait of a deceased President of the United States during the life of his widow without her consent, and numerous other limitations. Once registered, a mark may also be cancelled if it has become generic, has been abandoned, was obtained through fraud, or is otherwise prohibited by the aforementioned conditions.

One important limitation on registration comes when the mark is part of the product's functionality. An aspect of the product may meet the definition of a trademark and may even be recognized as a trademark by consumers, but it cannot be registered if it is essentially a functional aspect of the product. For example, a company might sell a computer monitor that has a unique shape that is immediately recognizable to the public and distinguishes the monitor from the products of competitors. Under the functional definition of a trademark, the unique shape

may be registered. However, if the shape is actually a functional aspect of the product, for example the shape is responsible for improved resolution, the shape cannot be registered as a trademark. (In such a case, though, the manufacturer may be able to seek patent protection for the unique design.)

The USPTO registers trademarks and service marks that are used in interstate commerce. Trademarks need not be registered for an owner to enforce his or her rights in court, however federal registration provides numerous legal benefits to a trademark owner at a reasonable expense. For example, once a mark is registered, the registration establishes the validity of the registrant's claims of ownership and places the world on constructive notice that the owner has exclusive rights to use the mark in commerce. If the holder of a registered trademark establishes infringement under the Lanham Act, they can not only enjoin any misuse of a mark, but they may also be able to recover statutory damages and in some cases, attorneys' fees.

Federal registration on the principal register gives nationwide protection from infringement, while common law protects the mark only in the specific geographical area in which the mark is used in commerce; and state law protects the mark only within the state where the mark is registered. Thus, another benefit of federal registration is the establishment of rights across a larger geographical area than under common law and state law.

In fact, the scope of protection for a federally registered mark is usually broader than under common law or state law. For example, under common law and many state trademark registration statutes, trademark protections may be restricted to those specific products or services for which the mark has explicitly been used, while federal law allows a mark to be protected even when used in conjunction with a wider array of related products or services, such as a family of services offered under an umbrella trademark. Finally, the Lanham Act provides legal remedies that go beyond those available at common law including, for example, treble damages against a "willful" infringer, as well as reimbursement of attorney fees in exceptional cases. It is important to note, however, that unlike many areas in which federal law supercedes state law, state and federal trademark law often co-exist well and aggrieved parties can frequently bring legal actions using both state and federal law to equal effect.

The Lanham Act's protections flow equally to trademarks and service marks. Trade dress is also protected by the Lanham Act, provided it is not a functional part of the product and is distinctive, has acquired secondary meaning as being uniquely associated with the product, and there is a likelihood of confusion on the part of the consumer if a competing product were to possess similar trade dress.

Trademark Registration

First, it is important to note that there are legal protections under trademark law for marks that have not been registered with the USPTO. Section 43(a) of the Lanham Act permits legal action against anyone who falsely makes use of a trademark word, name, or symbol in a manner that is likely to cause confusion or misrepresents the nature or origins of the product or service. This protection is not predicated on the registration of a mark with the USPTO. In addition, as noted elsewhere in this article, state laws may also provide protections as well. However, the Lanham Act, and many state laws, provide significant incentives for registration, giving additional remedies and rights to those who have availed themselves of the registration process.

For those who do choose the registration route, the USPTO maintains two types of trademark registries, the Principal Register and the Supplemental Register. The Principal Register is where a "registered trademark" is registered. There are three ways a trademark or service mark may be registered with the USPTO. The first method, called an "in use" application, is for an applicant who is already using a mark in commerce. The second method is an "intent to use" application, for marks that are not yet in use, but which the applicant is preparing to use. The third method is based upon certain international agreements, by which applicants outside the United States can file an application based upon applications or registrations in another country.

The Supplemental Register is where marks that are descriptive in nature but have not yet established secondary meaning are maintained. Marks on the Supplemental Register can use the ® symbol, and if the mark is continuously used and unchallenged for five years, the holder may file another application and claim such use presumptively establishes secondary meaning under Section 2(f) of the Lanham Act, and thereby move the mark onto the Principal Register.

The registration process itself is relatively straightforward. The application documents must be filed by the owner of the mark, usually through the services of an attorney concentrating in trademark law. (For brevity we will focus only on an "in use" application and will not further discuss the "intent to use" application.) The application contains information about the individual or corporation who owns the mark, an exact representation of the mark (in text or in image form) as well as several specimens of the mark in actual use, information about the date of first use and date of first use in commerce of the mark, a description of the goods or services used in conjunction with the mark, and the "classification" of the goods or services according to a standardized list of 42 pre-defined classifications. Some goods and services may be registered in multiple classes, with the application fees increasing accordingly.

Once received, the USPTO makes an initial review of the application to determine if the application contains all the information necessary to be considered "filed." If the application is complete, a "filing date" is issued along with a serial number and sent to the applicant. Several months after filing, an examiner at the USPTO reviews the application in more detail, researches the information provided, and makes a determination as to whether the mark should be registered. If it cannot be registered, the examiner will issue a notice called an "office action" which explains the grounds for refusal, including any deficiencies in the application itself. In some cases, only minor adjustments might be necessary in order to permit registration and sometimes the application can be corrected over the phone. Applicants have six months to respond to an office action or else the application will be considered abandoned. If the applicant cannot overcome the examiner's objections, a final office action is issued, at which point the applicant may appeal to the Trademark Trial and Appeal Board. Should the applicant be unsuccessful there, they may appeal that decision to federal court.

If there are no objections to the application, or the applicant overcomes the objections, the examiner will approve the mark for publication in the Official Gazette, a weekly publication of the USPTO. The applicant is notified of the date of publication through an official Notice of Publication.

Anyone who believes the registration harms them or is otherwise in violation of the Lanham Act has 30 days from publication to file an opposition to the registration or seek an extension of time to do so. At this point the administrative proceeding is *inter partes* (meaning between two parties, in contrast to an *ex parte* proceeding before the examiner only) and is known as an "opposition." The opposition proceeding determines the validity of the objections. If no objection is received, the mark will be registered. After the registration is issued, anyone who believes they have been harmed by the registration may begin a "cancellation proceeding," which is similar to an opposition proceeding except that it takes place after registration. In an opposition, the applicant bears the ultimate burden of establishing registerability; in a cancellation, the party seeking the cancellation bears the burden of proving the registration was improvidently issued. Opposition and cancellation proceedings are held in a formal, trial-like hearing before the Trademark Trial and Appeal Board, a division of the USPTO.

A mark will be registered only after it has been published and the opposition period has expired. Once registered, federal trademark registrations run for ten years, with renewal terms lasting ten years. Between the fifth and sixth year, however, the registrant must file an affidavit to confirm the mark is still in use. If that affidavit is not filed, the registration is cancelled. Thus, a trademark must remain in use or its registration may be cancelled, but if a mark is in continual use and that use is properly demonstrated as required by law, the registration could remain effective forever.

After five years, the owner of a registered mark may request that the mark be deemed "incontestable." Under the Lanham Act, incontestability means that certain legal avenues of challenging the mark—such as a claim that the mark is not distinctive, lacks secondary meaning, is confusingly similar to another mark, or the mark is purely functional—are no longer available. The term "incontestable" is somewhat misleading in that there remain certain circumstances in which the mark may be challenged and have the registration cancelled, such as an assertion that the mark was improperly registered in the first instance.

The Differences Between ®, ™ and ℠

Once registered, the registration symbol, ®, may be used. It is considered trademark misuse to display the registration symbol at any point before the USPTO issues the final registration notice to the applicant. In contrast, anyone who wishes to claim rights in a mark may use the ᵀᴹ(trademark) or ˢᴹ (service mark) designation along side the mark. Use of ᵀᴹ or ˢᴹ alerts the public to the claim of ownership and exclusive use. It is not necessary to have a registration, or even a pending application, to make use of these designations, and consequently the claim may or may not have any validity. In short, use of ᵀᴹ or ˢᴹ tells the world that you are prepared to put up a fight.

STATE STATUTES AND COMMON LAW

Many states also have trademark registration statutes that allow registration of marks used in intrastate commerce, using procedures that function similarly to the USPTO process defined by the Lanham Act. In addition, all states protect unregistered trademarks under some combination of state statute and common law. For the sake of brevity, this section will not detail trademark protections in all fifty US states.

In most states, the common law recognizes ownership of a trademark. Ownership under common law is most often established by demonstrating when the mark was first used in commerce, but unlike federal law, common law protections extend only to those areas or markets in which the mark is actually used. In contrast, federal registration of a trademark gives a basis under federal law for a suit for infringement, in addition to any common law claims that might be available. While it is possible to protect one's rights using only common law or state statutory protections, the benefits that flow from federal registration make it highly desirable.

INFRINGEMENT AND DILUTION

There are two main rights that trademark owners will assert: **infringement** and **dilution**. Infringement of a trademark usually involves the use of the mark in a way that is so similar to the owner's usage that the average purchaser will likely be deceived, will mistake the infringing goods for the original, or will likely experience confusion. Dilution is a lessening of the value of a trademark caused by an unauthorized use of the mark, regardless of whether any actual confusion, deception, or mistake occurred.

Infringement

Under the Lanham Act the standard for determining whether a mark is infringing is whether there is a "likelihood of confusion" over the mark in a particular usage context. More specifically, infringement comes when a consumer is likely to be confused over the source, sponsorship, or approval of the goods bearing the mark.

In deciding whether consumers are likely to be confused, courts have previously looked at a number of factors, including:

- Similarity between the two marks (such as any visual, phonetic, or contextual similarities);
- Similarity of the goods or services being offered;
- Proximity of the goods in a typical retail setting;
- Strength of the plaintiff's mark as exemplified by how well known the mark is to the public at large;
- Evidence of any actual confusion by consumers;

- Evidence of the defendant's intent in using the mark;
- Likely level of care employed by consumer in the purchase of that type of product; and,
- Likely growth or expansion of the product lines.

Of these eight factors, the first two are arguably the most important. For example, using an identical mark on an identical product is a clear case of infringement, such as a company other than Ford manufacturing a midsized automobile and calling it a Taurus. Similarly, calling the vehicle a Taurius would run into problems. (This use of similarly spelled names is of particular concern in the Internet domain name context, which will be discussed in a later section.)

But mere similarity is not always determinative of infringement. For example, it is possible to find Delta Faucets just a few aisles away from Delta power tools at your local home improvement store. While made by different companies, the similarity in trademark does not constitute infringement because consumers are not very likely to mistake a belt sander for a shower head.

Dilution

To further clarify the distinction between normal trademark infringement and dilution, in 1995 Congress amended the Lanham Act by passing the Federal Trademark Dilution Act (FTDA). This legislation expanded protections granted to famous and distinctive trademarks under the Lanham Act. Unlike infringement, dilution does not require evidence of a likelihood of confusion. Instead, the plaintiff must demonstrate that their mark is "famous," that it is being used in commerce by another party, and that the use causes the dilution of the "distinctive quality" of the mark.

The FTDA says that in determining whether a mark is "famous," a court may look at factors including the length of time a mark has been used, how widely and in what geographic areas it as been advertised, how recognizable the mark is to the public, and other factors. Highly distinctive long-used and well known marks, such as Coca-Cola or Kodak are examples of famous marks. Once a plaintiff establishes the fame of a mark, the owner can seek an injunction against further use of the mark in a manner that dilutes the distinctive qualities of that mark.

There are two types of dilution of a mark: **blurring** and **tarnishment**.

Blurring. Blurring is the weakening of a mark through its identification with dissimilar goods. For example, marketing Kleenex brand refrigerators would not likely confuse someone looking for bathroom tissue to accidentally purchase a refrigerator, however the use of the trademark would dilute the marks distinctiveness as representing personal care paper products.

Tarnishment. Tarnishment is the use of a mark in an unflattering light, through associating it with either inferior or distasteful products. For example, in the case *Toys 'R' Us v. Akkaoui*, 40 USPQ.2d 1836 (N.D. Cal. 1996), the toy retailer brought a successful tarnishment claim against a pornographic web site "adultsrus.com."

Other Trademark Claims

Although dilution claims and infringement claims based upon likelihood of confusion are the two most common trademark-related causes of action, there are a number of other bases for bringing suits. Many states have enacted unfair competition laws that prohibit a range of activities known as **passing off**, **contributory passing off**, **reverse passing off**, and **misappropriation**.

Passing off. Passing off occurs when a defendant attempts to "pass off" their product as if it were the mark owner's product. For example, affixing a Dell nameplate to computers actually made in someone's basement would constitute passing off.

Contributory passing off. Contributory passing off occurs when a defendant induces a retailer to pass off a product. For example, bribing a computer store to sell computers with a fake Dell nameplate would be contributory passing off.

Reverse passing off. Reverse passing off takes place when someone tries to market someone else's product as their own. If a computer store purchased Dell computers, replaced the nameplate with its own store brand nameplate, and attempted to sell the computers, they would have engaged in reverse passing off.

Misappropriation. Misappropriation, a privacy-related tort, is traditionally defined as using the name or likeness of someone for an unauthorized purpose, such as claiming a commercial endorsement by publishing someone's image (or even that of a look-alike impersonator) in an advertisement. In the trademark context, using a mark without authorization can violate federal and state law prohibitions on certain unfair trade practices, including the unauthorized use of marks in inappropriate ways.

Parody and Fair Use

Aside from challenging the validity of a trademark claim or attacking the elements of the infringement claim, defendants in trademark infringement or dilution cases can also claim two affirmative defenses: parody and fair use.

Parody. Certain uses of a trademark for purposes of humor, satire, or social commentary, may be permissible if they are not very closely tied to commercial use. The theory underlying the protection of parody is that artistic and social commentary are valuable contributions to the society, therefore some deference to the First Amendment's protection of these types of speech is in order, even when balance against the detriment to a trademark owner. The protections vary, however. For example, in the highly amusing case of *Hormel Foods Corp. v. Jim Henson Productions*, 73 F.3d 497 (2d Cir. 1996), the use of a pig-like character named "Spa'am" in a Muppet movie was found not to violate Hormel's rights in the trademark "SPAM." However, in *Coca-Cola Co. v. Gemini Rising, Inc.*, 346 F. Supp. 1183 (E.D.N.Y. 1972), the printing of posters with a stylized slogan and logo reading "Enjoy Cocaine" were found to violate the rights of Coca-Cola in the stylized slogan and logo "Enjoy Coca-Cola."

Fair Use. Fair use occurs when the public benefit of allowing the use is perceived to override any perceived harm to the trademark owner. For example, in the case *Zatarains, Inc. v. Oak Grove Smokehouse, Inc.*, 698 F.2d 786 (5th Cir. 1983), the defendant's use of "fish fry" to describe a batter coating for fish was not an infringement of the plaintiff's mark "Fish-Fri." The court held that fair use prevents a trademark owner from monopolizing a descriptive word or phrase to the exclusion of anyone else who seeks merely to accurately describe their goods. The defense of fair use is only available, however, when the mark at issue is descriptive, and then, only where the descriptive term is used descriptively. Federal trademark statute also contains a right to fair use limited to usage in comparative advertising.

POLICING TRADEMARK ON THE INTERNET

Along with the tremendous growth in the usage of the Internet for both commercial and personal use, there has been a similar expansion in the number of trademark-related disputes involving the Internet. In a later section we will discuss the complex legal issues arising from trademark disputes over Internet domain names. But first there are a number of trademark issues that arise just from the very nature of the Internet as a facilitator of ubiquitous information sharing and access.

Perhaps the most important reason behind the growing amount of trademark-related litigation is that uncovering instances of trademark violations can be as simple as typing your trademark into an Internet search engine. Just a decade ago, a trademark owner in Maine might have no idea that his trademark might be in use by someone in Oregon. But with the ability to quickly and cheaply search the Internet, trademark owners are quickly able to perform searches that might have been impossible—or just impossibly costly—a few years ago.

The ability to so easily discover trademark infringement, both intentional and unintentional, has catapulted trademark law into one of the most active areas of litigation in the Internet arena. But the nature of trademark law itself has also added to the litigation explosion. As noted above, failure to properly police a mark can result in it becoming generic, and thus unprotected. Therefore, the same ease with which a trademark owner might uncover infringement may require that a trademark owner keep policing the Internet routinely and bring enforcement actions: If an infringement is known—or could be discovered through basic due diligence—and goes unchallenged, the trademark owner could lose control of its mark.

The requirement of constant policing of trademarks has, however, caused the unfortunate side effect of a growing number of heavy-handed actions against inexperienced web users, and still more enforcement actions that are brought in cases where a finding of infringement or dilution is highly unlikely. In many of these cases, well-intentioned individuals have been bullied by corporations over trademarks appearing on personal web pages. In some cases that have received significant media attention, sites created by fans of rock groups, automobiles, and movie stars have been threatened by the very entities that the sites were set up by their creators to honor.

Meta Tags

In recent years, several disputes have arisen over the use of trademarks in **meta tags** on Internet web pages. Web pages on the Internet are coded using a type of programming language called Hyper Text Markup Language, or HTML. The codes that are embedded in HTML documents, called tags, tell the browser how to display the information contained on the page, such as when to display words in bold, when to change fonts or font sizes, how to align tables, or where to place images. Web page designers can also include meta tags, which are special tags that contain information about the contents of the web page. Meta tags are used by search engines to find and rank pages so that more relevant search findings are displayed before less relevant ones.

In one of the first lawsuits over meta tags, *Oppedahl & Larson v. Advanced Concepts, et al.*, Civ. No. 97-CV-1592 (D.C. Colo., 1997), a Colorado law firm discovered that the defendants had put the law partners' names, "oppedahl" and "larson," in meta tags on several web pages. This was presumably done in hopes that searches for the respected law firm's name would gain more attention for the defendants' web pages. Suing under both the Lanham Act and the Federal Trademark Dilution Act, as well as state and common law unfair trade practice actions, the law firm won a permanent injunction against any further use of their names in meta tags on the defendants' web sites. Since that case, a number of other disputes have tested the extent to which trademarks may be used in meta tags and have largely resulted in prohibitions against uses by entities seeking to enhance site traffic by using the marks of competitors.

One of the issues that has arisen in meta tag disputes is the concept of "initial interest confusion." Initial interest confusion occurs when the use of another's trademark is done so in a manner reasonably calculated to capture initial consumer attention, even though no actual sale is finally completed as a result of the confusion. The case of *Brookfield Communications, Inc., v. West Coast Entertainment Corp.*, 174. F.3d 1036 (9th Cir. 1999), illustrates the issue. Brookfield operated a web site, MovieBuff.com, containing a movie database. West Coast, a video retailer, used the term "moviebuff" in meta tags on its web site. A court held that West Coast's use of term in meta tags led to "initial interest confusion," in which search engine users looking for MovieBuff.com's site might visit West Coast's site and stop looking for MovieBuff.com, even though there might never be any confusion over sponsorship of the two sites.

Not all cases in which meta tags were at issue have resulted in a ban on their use. For example, in the case of *Playboy Enterprises, Inc. v. Terri Welles*, 162 F.3d 1169 (9th Cir. 2002), a model who had posed as a Playboy Playmate of the Month was permitted to use "Playboy" and "Playmate" as meta tags for her web site. But new uses

have created more confusion in this area. For example, in late 2003 and early 2004, several courts issued diverging opinions on the usage of trademarks to trigger various advertising "pop-up" advertisements and targeted advertisements keyed to trademarks appearing in search engines. Many of these cases are ongoing at the time this article is being written, and it is likely that confusion will continue until higher courts weigh in.

Deep Linking

Fundamental to the functioning of web pages on the Internet is the concept of a link. A link, short for hyperlink, is a tag coded within a web page that turns a piece of text (or in some cases an image) into a pointer to another document or page. Clicking on that link will typically cause the browser to follow the link and open the new page. While a simple link to the homepage of a web site will not typically run into trademark issues, some sites choose to create links to pages many levels down within a site. For example, instead of linking to the home page of a manufacturer, a web site designer might choose to create a link that goes directly to a page displaying one of the manufacturer's products. This practice is called **deep linking**.

Some site owners object to deep linking because it allows visitors to quickly bypass other contents of a web site, including advertisements, which they would normally see if they had to navigate step-by-step through the contents of a site. In several court cases, plaintiffs have charged that deep linking deprives them of the full benefits of having visitors explore their site, and have argued a variety of copyright, trademarks, and unfair competition claims. Proponents of deep linking counter that deep links are no different than footnotes or bibliographies, permitting readers to jump quickly to precise information. There are few clear court decisions on the trademark implications of deep linking, however many of the suits have focused on evidence of a defendant's bad faith, such as any appearance that the deep linking is intended to take unfair advantage of the other site's content, which will cut strongly in favor of the plaintiff.

In a related issue, there have been numerous disputes over the practice of "framing" Internet content. Framing is a technique in which content from one site is displayed within a "frame" appearing on another unrelated site. The use of framing often makes it appear that the content is owned or otherwise presented by an entity other than its actual owner or authorized user. Most disputes regarding framing have centered on copyright implications of unauthorized framing of content, however trademark issues also arise when there might be confusion as to the source of the content or its relationship to advertisements and other affiliations which might be suggested by the way in which the framed material appears.

DOMAIN NAMES

With the explosive growth of the Internet, both in its importance to global commerce and in the effect it has had on all aspects of our society, the importance of the domain names used on the Internet cannot be understated. The academic and non-commercial roots of the Internet caused many of its key functions, such as the Domain Name System, to be designed without some important safeguards. For example, domain names could then—and in many cases can still—be registered by anyone willing to pay the registration fee. In the early days of the Internet this fact caused something of a "land grab" mentality in which speculators rushed to purchase the rights to domain names that were expected to become valuable. Indeed, the domain name WallStreet.com, registered for under $100, was reportedly sold for over $1 Million (Bicknell, 1999).

Unfortunately however, some speculators also rushed in and purchased domain names that were identical (or in some cases merely similar) to valuable brand names. These so-called "cybersquatters" sought to gain financially by occupying the "virtual" real estate of someone else's trademark translated into a domain name. Because a domain name has become such an important part of a company's marketing identity, trademark owners have been forced to wage legal battles to retake control of their trademarks in cyberspace. Cybersquatting is discussed in detail in a later section, but it may be useful to look first at how domain names work and why they have become a trademark law battleground.

Domain Name System Basics

Generally speaking, each computer connected to the Internet requires a unique address, called an Internet Protocol ("IP") address, in order to distinguish it from all the other computers on the Internet. When computers communicate across the Internet, they use IP addresses in order to ensure that when a user on a particular computer requests data from another computer, the data gets delivered to the right place.

IP addresses are not very friendly to human eyes. Looking something like "192.168.27.145," it was quickly determined that it would be easier to assign names to stand in for those numbers, because many humans find it easier to remember names than to remember numbers. Thus, the designers of the early Internet developed the Domain Name System ("DNS") to permit the reliable association of names with IP addresses. As a result, with the help of DNS, when you tell your web browser that you want to check out the latest news at CNN.com, it is able to correctly direct your query to 64.236.16.116, which is one of the many web servers that answer to the busy CNN.com domain name.

Domain names, and their underlying numbers, are controlled by the Internet Corporation for Assigned Names and Numbers ("ICANN"). ICANN controls not only the allocation of IP addresses and the network of domain name registrars who control all domain names, but also delegate operation of the Root Servers. The Root Servers, the heart of the Domain Name System, are a collection of servers operated around the globe that manage all requests for information about the top level domains ("TLDs"). TLDs are simply a means of organizing domain names into broad categories.

As of this writing, there are 14 generic TLDs in which entities or individuals can register secondary domains, in some cases subject to certain restrictions. They include:

- .com for commercial sites
- .net for networks
- .org for non-profit organizations
- .gov for U.S. federal government sites
- .edu for educational institutions
- .int for entities created by international treaties
- .mil for U.S. military sites
- .biz for businesses
- .info for general use
- .name for personal use by individuals
- .pro for professional fields such as lawyers and accountants (this TLD was still inactive as of February 2003)
- .aero for the aerospace industry
- .coop for cooperatives
- .museum for museums

There are also over 200 country code TLDs (ccTLD), based upon the two-letter country codes for the worlds recognized nations. Examples include:

- .us for the United States
- .uk for the United Kingdom
- .ca for Canada
- .mx for Mexico
- .de for Germany
- .jp for Japan

When you enter a domain name into your browser (for purposes of this example we will use www.example.com) here is—in theory—how the Domain Name System works to assure you get to the web site you want:

- Your browser communicates your request for www.example.com, via your Internet connection, to the Domain Name Servers designated for your use by your Internet service provider.
- Your service provider's Domain Name Servers in turn ask the upstream DNS servers (and if necessary, eventually, the Root Servers) to search their database for the IP address of the Domain Name Servers that are authoritative for the TLD "com."
- Your query is then passed to the Domain Name Servers for "com," which then search their database for the IP address of the Domain Name Servers that are authoritative for the second-level domain "example" within the top level domain "com."
- Your query is then passed to the Domain Name Servers for "example.com," which then searches their database for the IP address of the server that answers to the subdomain "www" within that second-level domain.
- Once it locates the correct IP address, it tells your web browser what IP address to connect to, whereupon that server recognizes your request for a web page and transmits the appropriate data back to your computer.

This is "in theory" because in reality, this process can be simpler, or more complex, depending upon how your ISP chooses to manage its DNS requests. For example, some ISPs keeps a record of previous DNS requests in a "cache" file so that it can better manage time lag and server load issues by serving up IP addresses that it trusts are probably still correct since the looking them up a few hours earlier.

Domain Name Registration

The first challenge in registering a domain name is to identify a domain name that is suitable for your needs. Depending on the intended use of the domain name, there are many considerations, beginning with the choice of TLD that best suits your vision for your domain. Once you have decided on the TLD, you may have a choice of registrars delegated by ICANN to manage the process of domain name registration. For example, as of this writing there are several hundred ICANN-accredited registrars, not counting the designated registrars for all the country code TLDs.

Once you have selected a registrar, you will communicate to them what second-level domain you wish to register. In most cases, they will check their records and determine whether the domain name requested is already registered, or might have previously been reserved. Presumably you will have checked to see if there is a web site already operating at the domain name you have selected, however the absence of an active site is not determinative, as it is possible for a domain name to be registered, but not in active use.

If the second-level domain name you desire has not been previously registered, you will likely be given the choice of registering it. Upon providing contact and billing information, and paying the registrar's fee of course, you will also be asked to provide the IP addresses of a primary and a secondary Domain Name Server for your domain. While some registrars offer you the option of also hosting the domain on their own servers, you may need to have previously arranged with an ISP to establish the technical details necessary for operating DNS, web, and email services for your newly-chosen domain name. If you have set up these services in advance, however, then it is possible to have your new domain fully functional within just a matter of minutes or hours after completing the registration process.

Internet Domain Disputes

Far and away the greatest amount of trademark-related controversy on the Internet concerns use of domain names. Because of both the value of trademarks themselves, and the value of memorable domain names for maximizing the marketing and sales power of online operations, using popular trademarks as domain names has been an important issue for businesses beginning to make use of the Internet. Much to their consternation however, many companies have attempted to register domain names related to their company name or their trademarks only to discover that someone else has already registered those domain names.

In the course of many legal disputes over domain names, some consensus among the courts has developed. Most courts have applied trademark law in much the same fashion as they would in any other trademark dispute. For example, marks are assessed for the extent to which they are fanciful, arbitrary, suggestive, descriptive or generic. Disputes have also been judged on whether there is evidence of bad faith on the part of either party. In the Oppedahl & Larson case discussed above, there was no reasonable basis for the defendant to be making use of "Oppedahl" and "Larson" other than their desire to garner traffic attracted by someone else's mark.

The most common method of using a trademark in a domain name is the verbatim use of the mark in conjunction with the TLD, such as Pepsi.com. But a related form of trademark infringement comes in dilution through the registration of similar domains, or domains containing misspellings or common typographical errors. Disputes over domains such as "amazom.com" (instead of amazon.com), gateway20000.com (instead of gateway2000.com), and micros0ft.com (microsoft.com with the second letter "o" replaced with a zero), have almost uniformly resulted in court decisions or settlements transferring domain ownership to the aggrieved party. These and other cases of infringement have resulted in a new area of law—and even of legislation—focused on resolving trademark-related domain name disputes.

Cybersquatting

In the mid-1990s, Dennis Toeppen registered some 250 domain names that were either similar or identical to popular trademarks, including deltaairlines.com, eddiebauer.com, neiman-marcus.com, northwestairlines.com, and yankeestadium.com. In two cases considered pivotal among domain name trademark disputes, *Intermatic Incorporated v. Toeppen*, 947 F.Supp. 1227 (N.D. Ill. 1996), and *Panavision Int'l, L.P. v. Toeppen*, 945 F. Supp. 1296 (C. D. Cal., 1996), the plaintiffs successfully forced Toeppen to relinquish control of the domains intermatic.com and panavision.com, respectively.

The Panavision case in particular illustrates how many of the cybersquatting disputes play out. In 1995, Toeppen registered the domain name www.panavision.com and created a web site that contained photographs taken around the city of Pana, Illinois. When contacted by Panavision, a maker of motion picture cameras and photographic equipment, Toeppen offered to sell the domain name for $13,000. Panavision declined and brought suit under the Federal Trademark Dilution Act.

As discussed in an earlier section, the FTDA requires plaintiffs to demonstrate that their mark is "famous" and that the defendant is using a mark in commerce in a fashion that could cause dilution of the mark's distinctiveness. While Toeppen claimed that his use of the mark was non-commercial, the court held that having offered the domain name for sale indicated that he intended that the domain name itself be a commercial offering.

In the Intermatic case, Toeppen originally operated a web page at the intermatic.com address which described a piece of software he claimed to be developing called "Intermatic," later replacing it with information about Champaign-Urbana, Illinois, the community in which Toeppen lived. The Intermatic court held that despite these non-commercial uses, the registration of the domain name itself was dilutive of Intermatic's mark.

Anticybersquatting Consumer Protection Act

As the problem of cybersqatting grew throughout the 1990s, Congress responded in 1999 by enacting the Anti-cybersquatting Consumer Protection Act ("ACPA"), which amended the Lanham Act to include protections specific to Internet domain names. One change from past practice under the Federal Trademark Dilution Act, however, was the ACPA's removal of the requirement that the mark be used in commerce. This greatly expanded plaintiffs' ability to take control over domain names that had merely been registered but were not actually in use.

The ACPA states that cybersquatting occurs when the person registering a domain name containing a trademark "has a bad faith intent to profit from that mark" and "registers, traffics in, or uses" a domain name that is "identical or confusingly similar to or dilutive of that mark." The Act includes nine factors that courts may take into consideration when determining the existence of bad faith intent:

- the trademark or other intellectual property rights of the person, if any, in the domain name;
- the extent to which the domain name consists of the legal name of the person or a name that is otherwise commonly used to identify that person;
- the person's prior use, if any, of the domain name in connection with the bona fide offering of any goods or services;
- the person's bona fide non-commercial or fair use of the mark in a site accessible under the domain name;
- the person's intent to divert consumers from the mark owner's online location to a site accessible under the domain name that could harm the goodwill represented by the mark, either for commercial gain or with the intent to tarnish or disparage the mark, by creating a likelihood of confusion as to the source, sponsorship, affiliation, or endorsement of the site;
- the person's offer to transfer, sell, or otherwise assign the domain name to the mark owner or any third party for financial gain without having used, or having an intent to use, the domain name in the bona fide offering of any goods or services, or the person's prior conduct indicating a pattern of such conduct;
- the person's provision of material and misleading false contact information when applying for the registration of the domain name, the person's intentional failure to maintain accurate contact information, or the person's prior conduct indicating a pattern of such conduct;
- the person's registration or acquisition of multiple domain names which the person knows are identical or confusingly similar to marks of others that are distinctive at the time of registration of such domain names, or dilutive of famous marks of others that are famous at the time of registration of such domain names, without regard to the goods or services of the parties; and,
- the extent to which the mark incorporated in the person's domain name registration is or is not distinctive and famous.

The Act then indicates that bad faith cannot be found if the defendant "believed and had reasonable grounds to believe that the use of the domain name was a fair use or otherwise lawful."

The recent dispute over the domain name Nissan.com gives some insight into how courts are applying the ACPA and other aspects of traditional trademark law analyses. The domain name is at the center of a dispute between Nissan Motor Co., Ltd., a popular car manufacturer, and Nissan Computer Corporation, a small business in North Carolina operated by Mr. Uzi Nissan. In *Nissan Motor Co., Ltd v. Nissan Computer Corp.*, 61 U.S.P.Q.2d 1839 (C.D. Cal., 2002), the court noted that the defendant registered the domain in 1994 and has been operating his firm under the Nissan name since 1985. While the court found that the initial registration of the domain name was not in bad faith, the court did take issue with several aspects of Mr. Nissan's behavior, including his initial response to Nissan Motors complaint: an offer to sell the domain name for several million dollars. More recently, the court ordered Mr. Nissan to cease any commercial activities involving the site when it was discovered that Mr. Nissan was advertising automotive-related products on the site, despite his business being unrelated to automobiles. (Officialspin. com, 2002)

One of the innovative aspects of the ACPA is the way it deals with jurisdictional matters. Traditionally, legal disputes have always been subject to jurisdictional boundaries and national borders, and either the physical presence of the parties within those boundaries or evidence of the parties' contacts with the jurisdiction. Recognizing that in many cases cybersquatters go to some lengths to hide their identity or their location, the ACPA permits the trademark owner to take action against the domain name itself, rather than the domain owner personally. This permits aggrieved parties to locate the registrar and, although the registrar itself cannot be held liable for an infringing domain it permitted to be registered, the domain name itself can be attacked.

ICANN Domain Name Dispute Process

While the ACPA's jurisdictional elements have simplified matters somewhat for trademark owners with domains that have been registered within the United States, the global nature of the Internet has required a less geocentric dispute resolution process. To that end, ICANN as developed a Uniform Domain Name Dispute Resolution Policy ("UDRP") the provisions of which are in many respects similar to those of ACPA.

The UDRP process relies upon third-party, private dispute resolution mechanisms rather than the more expensive prospect of litigation in a court of law. For trademark owners who are seeking a quicker and cheaper resolution of domain disputes, the UDRP route has proven to be extremely popular, even though no monetary damages or injunctions are available. Indeed, the only remedies available under the UDRP are the cancellation or transfer of the domain name. Thus, for instance where the injury to the trademark owner is more serious, traditional litigation may yet be necessary.

The World Intellectual Property Organization ("WIPO") has attempted to define cybersquatting, and to establish guidelines for dispute resolution. In a 1999 report on the

Management of Internet Names and Addresses, the WIPO delegates discuss at great length the phenomenon of registering trademarks as domain names with the intent of profiting from the ownership, either by capitalizing on traffic brought in through the confusion, or by selling the domain to the trademark owner. In the end, WIPO's recommendations are very similar to those contained in the ICANN UDRP and the ACPA.

The UDRP, WIPO's recommendations, and the operations (and even the very existence) of ICANN are currently the subject of tremendous international debate. While the details of these arguments are too lengthy for inclusion in this brief article, many web sites (including ICANNWatch.org and UDRPinfo.com) chronicle the legal, technical, and political arguments over this emerging field.

CONCLUSION

As the Internet becomes an even more critical channel for businesses to reach out to consumers, the value of a well leveraged trademark has never been higher. At the same time, the pressures on trademark owners from infringing activities is requiring them to be ever more vigilant in their policing and prosecution of violators. In response to these pressures, courts and lawmakers have expanded and clarified traditional trademark protections, adding greatly to the remedies available to trademark owners who feel their rights have been violated. In this chapter we have covered the fundamentals of trademark law, and seen them applied to the unique new situations presented by Internet technologies. While the trademark space will continue to evolve, it is clear that the value of trademarks is as well-recognized as ever in the history of commerce.

If there is one conclusion to be drawn, it is that trademark is a very complex field of law and procedure, requiring expert guidance in order to provide maximum opportunity and protection. While this article may provide readers with a general overview of many current issues in trademark law, it is not a substitute for qualified legal counsel. As has been noted repeatedly throughout this article, successful use of trademark law depends upon many detailed analyses, procedural hurdles, and requires a significant commitment of time and resources in order to take full advantage. Trademark law provides robust protections to those who, with assistance from talented counsel, seek to protect their goods and services in the marketplace.

GLOSSARY

Blurring   At type of dilution in which the distinctiveness of a mark is weakened through its identification with dissimilar goods.

Deep linking   Creating a web page link that is tied directly to a document deep within the page hierarchy of a web site, rather than simply linking to the main home page of the site.

Dilution   A lessening of the value of a famous trademark caused by an unauthorized use of the mark, regardless of whether any actual confusion, deception, or mistake occurred.

Distinctiveness   The ability of a mark to distinguish the goods and services of the mark from the goods and services of another.

Domain Name   An alphanumeric electronic address on the Internet.

Famous Trademark   A court-determined trademark designation under 35 USC §1125(c).

Lanham Act   Also known as the Trademark Act of 1946, it created a set of federal rules for governing the process of registering trademarks and established certain nationwide legal protections for trademark

Likelihood of Confusion   The test of trademark infringement under the Lanham Act. A likelihood of confusion exists if a substantial number of reasonably prudent consumers are likely to be confused as to the source of the goods or services.

Infringement   Use of a trademark in a way that is so similar to the owner's usage that an average consumer will be deceived, will mistake the infringing good for the original, or will experience confusion over the nature or origin of the product.

Initial Interest Confusion   The use of another's trademark in a manner reasonably calculated to capture initial consumer attention, even though no actual sale is finally completed as a result of the confusion.

Intellectual property   The concept of legal recognitions for property rights in intangible things such as ideas and intellectual creations.

Meta tags   Hidden codes embedded in web pages that contain keywords related to the contents of a particular page, designed to only be seen by search engines.

Secondary meaning   An association that has developed in the public's mind between the mark or trade dress of a product and owner of the mark or product.

Service mark   A mark that is used to identify a service or the provider of a service rather than a tangible product, such as the name of a consulting firm, or the name of a proprietary analytical process used by that consulting firm.

Tarnishment   A type of dilution in which the mark is used in an unflattering light, such as by associating it with inferior or distasteful products or services.

Trademark   A mark that is used by a manufacturer or merchant to identify the origin or ownership of goods and to distinguish them from others and the use of which is protected by law.

Trade dress   The overall image of a product, composed of the nonfunctional elements of its design, packaging, or labeling, including specific colors or color combinations, a distinctive package shape, or specific symbols or design elements.

U.S. Patent and Trademark Office (USPTO)   The federal agency charged with managing the nationwide issuance of patents and registration of trademarks.

CROSS REFERENCES

See *Copyright Law; Legal, Social and Ethical Issues of the Internet; Patent Law; The Legal Implications of Information Security: Regulatory Compliance and Liability.*

REFERENCES

Bicknell, Craig (1999). Making a Mint on Wallstreet.com. Wired News. Available at: http://www.wired.com/news/business/0,1367,19285,00.html (Date of access: February 8, 2004)

Coca-Cola Co. v. Gemini Rising, Inc., 346 F. Supp. 1183 (E.D.N.Y. 1972)

Hormel Foods Corp. v. Jim Henson Productions, 73 F.3d 497 (2d Cir. 1996)

ICANN Uniform Dispute Resolution Policy (UDRP). Available at: http://www.icann.org/udrp/udrp.htm (Date of access: February 8, 2004)

Intermatic Incorporated v. Toeppen, 947 F.Supp. 1227 (N.D. Ill. 1996) Available at: http://www.loundy.com/CASES/Intermatic_v_Toeppen (Date of access: February 8, 2004)

Nissan Motor Co., Ltd v. Nissan Computer Corp., 61 U.S.P.Q.2d 1839 (C.D. Cal., 2002)

OfficialSpin.com (2002). Nissan Computer Corporation keeps domain name, for now. Available at: http://www.officialspin.com/main.php3?action=recent&rid=405 (Date of access: February 8, 2004)

Oppedahl & Larson v. Advanced Concepts, et al., Civ. No. 97-CV-1592 (D.C. Colo., 1997) Available at: http://www.patents.com/ac (Date of access: February 8, 2004)

Panavision Int'l, L.P. v. Toeppen, 945 F. Supp. 1296 (C.D. Cal. 1996) Available at: http://www.techlawjournal.com/courts/avery/19980417.htm (Date of access: February 8, 2004)

Playboy Enterprises, Inc. v. Terri Welles, 7 F. Supp. 2d 1098 (S.D. Ca. 1998), aff'd. in part, reversed in part, 162 F.3d 1169 (9th Cir. 2002)

Toys 'R' Us v. Akkaoui, 40 USPQ.2d 1836 (N.D. Cal. 1996).

Trademark Act of 1946 (also called the Lanham Act). (15 U.S.C. § 1051) Available at: http://www4.law.cornell.edu/uscode/15/1051.html (Date of access: February 8, 2004)

United States Patent and Trademark Office. Trademark Information. Available at: http://www.uspto.gov/main/trademarks.htm (Date of access: February 8, 2004)

Zatarains, Inc. v. Oak Grove Smokehouse, Inc., 698 F.2d 786 (5th Cir. 1983)

Online Contracts

G. E. Evans, *Queen Mary Intellectual Property Research Institute, UK*

INTRODUCTION

The global organization of networked computers that we call the Internet has given contracts a new role and dimension. Contracts have become the very building blocks of electronic commerce. Not only do they perform an essential function as the purveyors of software and content licenses, but they also provide the core infrastructure for the exchange of informational products in networked markets. In fact, one of the five key principles of the *A Framework for Global Electronic Commerce* (White House, 1997) relies on the establishment of a legal environment based on a contractual model of law. In a renaissance of freedom of contract, licensors are charged with the freedom to order contractual relationships as they see fit to market their products online and, in so doing, advance the growth of the new economy. One of the clearest indications of the new economic trajectory may be seen in the significant returns of the software sector. The actual and estimated return of the combined hardware, software, and services sectors was $536.8 billion for the U.S. economy during 2003 (U.S. Department of Commerce, 2003).

Since the idea of open-architecture networking was first introduced in 1972, the Internet has revolutionized the communications world in an unparalleled manner.

Whether we are talking about selling intangible or tangible goods, the Internet has dramatically changed not only business–customer relations but also the way in which products are distributed and exchanged. Computer networks make possible new vertical and horizontal business relationships between producers, users, consumers (P2P), and suppliers (B2B). In response, Internet business models, whether virtual or clicks-and-mortar, are assuming an increasing variety of forms, including the following: brokerage, advertising, informediary, merchant, manufacturer, affiliate, community, subscription, and utility (Afuah & Tucci, 2000). Moreover, the supply of goods and services directly between supplier and consumer has given rise in turn to new classes of business intermediaries. From the business communities of aggregators to the online auctions, all rely on contracts to provide stable online trading markets, a trading venue defined by clear rules, industrywide pricing, and open market information for buyers. eBay.com, for example, was among the first successful sites to provide a framework where consumers could trade a wide variety of goods and services with each other (consumer-to-consumer, C2C) and with business (consumer-to-business, C2B).

Arguably, we might think of shrink-, click-, or browsewrap agreements as a new kind of *lex mercatoria* or merchant-designed law to facilitate the online exchange of goods and services in consumer markets. In contrast to traditional contracts, there is a far greater degree of uncertainty as to online contracts' validity and enforceability, particularly in the areas of jurisdiction, contract formation, identification of the terms and statutory issues relating to signature, and other evidentiary requirements. For example, vendors and merchants question how an offer should be made and acceptance given. Buyers are concerned that one false click might result in their being ensnared into entering a binding contract.

Through a combination of mercantile custom, common law, and legislative developments, the classic principles of contract law are being adapted and supplemented to accommodate the needs of electronic commerce. The aim of this chapter is to provide the reader with an overview of the law relating to the formation and validity of electronic contracts and to offer some recommendations concerning the measures that might be taken to create an enforceable electronic contract. The first part of this chapter describes the problems pertaining to contracting online, including the maintenance of security of electronic transactions and the integrity of electronic documents. The next part considers the legal framework for electronic contracting, notably with respect to the provision of standards and procedures for electronic signature. The next section examines the enforceability of clickwrap and browsewrap licenses that the software industry has pioneered to facilitate online transactions of its products and to give additional security to its intellectual property. In a medium where it is all too easy to include unduly harsh terms, this section also discusses the doctrine of unconscionability, which may subsequently render a contract unenforceable, and how to guard against such a contingency. The chapter then discusses the vexed question of contractual restrictions in end user license agreements, including limitations on the fair use of software, the means of dispute resolution, and the forum in which licensees can bring suit. The next section examines the problems that have arisen with respect to the licensing of digital information and sales law, particularly warranties concerning the fitness and merchantability of informational goods, such as software. The chapter then considers the developments that have taken place with respect to consumer rights online, in particular the ability of consumers to enjoy the legal protection offered by their home states. The chapter concludes with some tips and suggestions for contractors as to how, given the current state of the law, they might best offset the risks of contracting online. Although this chapter generally deals with contractual issues associated with the security of online commerce, other security-related considerations that also affect the validity of online contracts are beyond its scope and are covered in other parts of this handbook: network security (Volume I, Part 2: Infrastructure for the Internet, Computer Networks and Secure Information Transfer), protocol standards (Volume I, Part 3: Standards and Protocols for Secure Information Transfer), and security management (Volume II, Part 3: Foundations of Information, Computer, and Network Security).

MAINTAINING THE SECURITY OF ELECTRONIC TRANSACTIONS
Problems Concerning the Authenticity and Integrity of Electronic Documents

Authenticity is concerned with the source or origin of a document or message ([Fed. R. Evid. 901]). Integrity is concerned with the accuracy and completeness of the communication. In a paper-based world, a contracting party can rely on numerous indicators of trust to ensure the authenticity and integrity of a document. These indicators include using paper, perhaps with a letterhead or watermarks, or other indicia of trust, to which the message is attached and not easily altered; handwritten ink signatures; sealed envelopes for delivery via a trusted third party, such as the postal service or a courier service; or personal interaction between the parties. However, with electronic documents and electronic communications conducted remotely over the Internet, none of these indicia of trust is possible. To all intents, a communication in binary code can be copied and modified easily without discovery. In addition, although a handwritten signature can be readily verified to authenticate the identity of the signer and the source of a document, online there is an additional risk that the party contracting may not be who they claim or that the substance of the communications used to form an agreement may be subject to alteration.

Party Authentication and Message Integrity

Moving transactions to an electronic environment has two important consequences. First, in many cases it may be difficult to know when one can rely on the authenticity and integrity of an electronic message. Authentication issues, although rare in the real world, become increasingly important in the virtual world (see the chapter in this handbook, Anonymity and Identity on the Internet). On the Internet, how do we decide whether Jane Doe is who she says she is? Those decisions that involve entering into contracts, shipping products, making payments, or otherwise incurring financial risk are difficult to make when relying on an electronic message. Second, in the event of legal action, this lack of reliability can make it extremely difficult to prove the validity of the contract in court. For example as an evidentiary matter, if the defendant denies making the "signature" that is attached to an electronic document, it may be impossible for the plaintiff to prove the authenticity of that electronic signature, in the absence of additional evidence (e.g., *U.S. v. Eisenberg*, 1986; *U.S. v. Grande*, 1980).

The concern regarding integrity arises from the fact that electronic documents are easily altered in a manner that is not detectable. Further, because every copy of an electronic document is a perfect reproduction, the original of an electronic document does not exist. How then are we to know whether the document the recipient received is the same as the document that the sender sent? How do we know whether the document has been altered either in transmission or storage?

If users are to have trust in the electronic medium, recipients of electronic messages must be confident of the communication's accuracy (Smedinghoff, 2002). The question of integrity is critical when it comes to the negotiation and formation of contracts online, the licensing of digital content, the making of electronic payments, and the verification of the authenticity of these transactions at a later date. For example, a contractor who wants to receive tenders from bidders online must be able to verify that the messages containing the bids have not been altered. In that situation, the use of cryptographic algorithms, accompanied by digital signatures, is the best means of detecting any alteration in an electronic document.

If the commercial world is to benefit from the advantages of online contracts, both buyers and sellers need to be assured that online contracts are secure insofar as the identity of the parties and the certainty of the terms are concerned. The Statute of Frauds, which requires that certain contracts, such as those dealing with transfers of land, be in writing, was designed to overcome the problem of fraud with respect to oral contracts. Although the principle is still a sound one, to condition the enforceability of an online contract on a requirement for pen-and-paper writing would present a barrier to the effective use of the electronic medium (Prefatory Note to the Uniform Electronic Transactions Act, 7a, Part I, U.L.A. 17 (supp. 2000)).

THE LEGAL FRAMEWORK FOR ELECTRONIC CONTRACTING
United Nations Model Law on Electronic Commerce

With a view to removing barriers to electronic transactions, the United Nations Commission on International Trade Law (UNCITRAL) Model Law on Electronic Commerce of 1996:

- establishes rules and norms that validate and recognize contracts formed through electronic means
- sets default rules for contract formation and governance of electronic contract performance
- defines the characteristics of a valid electronic writing and an original document
- provides for the acceptability of electronic signatures for legal and commercial purposes
- supports the admission of computer evidence in courts and arbitration proceedings

U.S. Laws Covering Electronic Transactions

These principles were implemented in the United States in 1999, when the National Council of Commissioners on Uniform State Laws (NCCUSL) approved the Uniform Electronic Transactions Act (UETA), 7A, Part I, U.L.A. 17 (Supp. 2000), which facilitates the use of electronic documents and electronic signatures. As of June 2004, 46 states have enacted the UETA (see http://www.ncsl.org/). In addition, the Uniform Computer Information Transactions Act (UCITA), also approved by NCCUSL in 1999, among its substantive provisions on electronic contracts, includes articles validating electronic transactions for the "licensing" of computer data (National Conference

of Commissioners on Uniform State Laws, 2001b). Concerned at the slowness and lack of consistency with which UETA was being adopted by state legislatures, in 2000 Congress stepped in to enact the Electronic Signatures in Global and National Commerce Act (E-SIGN; Pub. L. No. 106–229, 114 Stat. 464 (2000)).

Finally, Article 2 of the Uniform Commercial Code (UCC), which has governed the sale of goods since its promulgation in 1951, has recently been amended to accommodate electronic commerce and to reflect the development of business practices, changes in other law, and interpretive difficulties of practical significance (National Conference of Commissioners on Uniform State Laws, 2002). Adopted on May 13, 2003 by the NCCUSL and the American Law Institute (ALI), the amended Article 2, section 2-108(4) is intended to modify, limit, and supercede E-SIGN. In addition to the potential difficulties of application concerning its interface with E-SIGN, amended Article 2 (Sales) is not a revolution in sales law. The provisions of amended Article 2 include substitution of the word "record" for "writing" throughout amended UCC Article 2 and the adoption of new language concerning contract formation in amended UCC 2-204, 2-211, 2-212, and 2-213. In states that do not adopt amendments to UCC Article 2, E-SIGN (or UETA to the extent that it preempts E-SIGN) will apply to transactions subject to Article 2. In states that do adopt amended UCC Article 2, E-SIGN will not govern transactions subject to Article 2.

Formation and Validation of Electronic Contracts

As a matter of general principle, there is no requirement that the parties to a contract must indicate their consent to be bound by signature. In fact, the law provides that a contract for sale of goods may be made in any manner sufficient to show agreement, including conduct by both parties that recognizes the existence of such a contract (UCC § 2-204). Similarly, E-SIGN provides that "a contract . . . may not be denied legal effect, validity, or enforceability solely because an electronic signature or electronic record was used in its formation" (§ 101(a)(2)). In addition, UETA provides that "a contract may not be denied legal effect or enforceability solely because an electronic record was used in its formation" (§ 7(b)). Finally, the UNCITRAL Model Law on Electronic Commerce is even more explicit in providing that "an offer and the acceptance of an offer may be expressed by means of data messages" and "where a data message is used in the formation of a contract, that contract shall not be denied validity or enforceability on the sole ground that a data message was used for that purpose" (Article 11(1)).

As a general rule, offers to contract may be made orally, in writing, or by conduct. There is no reason in principle therefore why an offer that is electronically transmitted should be any less effective than a written one. The problem is largely one of evidence. Questions may arise concerning the reliability of electronic communications, which may make it more difficult to introduce evidence in court. To be valid, an offer must communicate to the person receiving it that, once the offer is accepted, a contract is created. An offer may be accepted "in any manner and by any medium reasonable in the circumstances" (UCC 2-206(1)(a)). Online offers may be accepted by e-mail or other form of electronic message, by electronic agent, and by conduct, such as clicking on a button or downloading content. Thus, if an offer is made by e-mail, one should be able to accept it by the same means unless the offer states otherwise (Restatement (Second) of Contracts § 65).

Although, generally speaking, an acceptance does not necessarily have to be sent the same way as the offer (*Market Development Corp. v. Flame-Glo Ltd.*, 1990), UETA provides that an electronic record is considered received only when it enters a computer system "that the recipient has designated or uses for the purpose of receiving electronic records of the type sent" (§15(b)(1)). Consequently, if the parties have regularly corresponded in the past by e-mail, an e-mail acceptance sent to the offerer's e-mail address will presumably be effective. The purpose of the UETA requirement is to assure that recipients can designate the e-mail address or system to be used in a particular transaction in the event the parties have multiple e-mail addresses.

When Is an Electronic Record Sent or Received?

Issues surrounding the timing of electronic records may be essential for resolving questions as to whether a binding contract has been created, as in the case where the offeror sets a deadline for acceptance. In addition, electronic transmissions may pose similar problems to cases where the offer and acceptance were exchanged by fax or other means of communication in which the interaction is not immediate. In the case where a message is sent from one computer system to another, UETA provides that the time at which an electronic record is considered to have been sent is the time that the record "enters an information processing system outside the control of the sender"; in the case where a message is sent from one person to another on the same system, such as where both parties are using the same Internet service provider, it is the time that the record "enters a region of the information processing system designated or used by the recipient which is under the control of the recipient" (§ 15(3)). An electronic record is considered to have been sent as of that time, provided that it is addressed properly to an information-processing system that the recipient has designated or uses for the purpose of receiving electronic records and from which the recipient is able to retrieve the electronic record, and provided further that it is in a form capable of being processed by that system (UETA § 15(a)(1) and 15(a)(2)).

Conversely, UETA provides that an electronic record is considered received by the intended recipient when it enters an information processing system that the recipient has designated or uses for the purpose of receiving electronic records of the type sent and from which the recipient is able to retrieve the electronic record, and is in a form capable of being processed by that system (§ 15(b)). It is also important to note that an electronic record is considered received even if no individual is aware of its receipt. That is, as with the postal service, once the message is delivered, it makes no difference whether the addressee actually opens it.

Automated Transactions

Can a computer be said to have entered into a contract? Generally speaking, it may do so, depending on the circumstances. Certainly, a computer is capable of generating an offer. Inventory systems for example, are designed to calculate when supplies are low and automatically generate an electronic purchase order to the vendor. By analogy, case law indicates the validity of such contracts (*State Farm Mutual Auto. Ins. Co v. Bockhorst*, 1972). The law accepts that the computer operates in accordance with the information and directions supplied by its programmers. Similarly, a computer-generated acceptance, as distinct from a mere acknowledgment of receipt, may serve to create a binding contract (*Corinthian Pharmaceutical Systems v. Lederle Labs*, 1989). Accordingly, an electronic data interchange (EDI) message, such as a purchase order acknowledgment, would be considered an appropriate acceptance.

With respect to the related question of the enforceability of contracts formed via electronic agents, both E-SIGN and UETA expressly recognize the validity of such contracts. An electronic agent is defined as a computer program or other automated means used to initiate an action or respond to electronic records or performances in whole or in part without review or action by an individual at the time of the action or response (E-SIGN § 106(3); UETA § (2)(6)).

E-SIGN provides that a contract or other record relating to a transaction may not be denied legal effect, validity, or enforceability solely because its formation, creation, or delivery involved the action of one or more electronic agents so long as the action of any such electronic agent is legally attributable to the person to be bound (§ 101(h)). Similarly, UETA recognizes that a contract may be formed by the interaction of electronic agents of the parties, even if no individual was aware of or reviewed the electronic agent's actions or the resulting terms and agreements (§ 14(1)). In addition, UETA recognizes that a contract may be formed by the interaction of an electronic agent and an individual (§ 14(2)). Likewise, UCITA provides for the making of contracts bymeans of an "electronic agent" (s.102) and provides for the validation of electronic contracts to the extent that it validates contracts made by "electronic agents" or preprogrammed computer programs (ss. 107 and 206).

Notice and Consent Requirements

Because electronic contracts involve additional risks when compared with traditional transactions, both E-SIGN and UETA expressly require that the parties agree to enter into their transaction electronically before it will be considered enforceable. Conversely, as there is no obligation on the parties to do so, they are entitled to refuse to enter into the transaction in electronic form (E-SIGN, 15 U.S.C. § 7001(b)(2); UETA §s 5(a)). As to the question whether the parties have "agreed to conduct transactions by electronic means" (UETA § 5(b); E-SIGN, 15 U.S.C. § 7001 (c)), their agreement may be either express or implied and is to be objectively determined from the surrounding circumstances, including the parties' conduct (UETA § 5(b)). Although some state enactments of

UETA—for example, that of California—require such consent to be in electronic form in order to provide greater certainty, in other states consent may be implied from conduct. For example, in the event one party launches a Web site that is capable of entering into electronic transactions and the other party accesses that Web site and proceeds to enter into an electronic contract with the first party, there is a strong inference that the parties have implicitly agreed to conduct business electronically.

E-SIGN's Consumer Consent Provisions

Whereas the provisions of UETA concerning consent to transact electronically apply equally to commercial and consumer transactions, E-SIGN contains special requirements for businesses that want to use electronic records or signatures in consumer transactions. It requires businesses to obtain from consumers electronic consent or confirmation to receive information electronically that is required by law to be in writing. This would be the case for example, with laws requiring written disclosure of interest rate charges in consumer loan transactions. The act went into effect in October 2000 (15 U.S.C. § 7001(c)). Section 101(c)(1) of the act provides that information required by law to be in writing can be made available electronically to a consumer only if he or she affirmatively consents to receive the information electronically and the business clearly and conspicuously discloses specified information to the consumer before obtaining his or her consent. Moreover, Section 101(c)(1)(C)(ii) states that a consumer's consent to receive electronic records is valid only if the consumer "consents electronically or confirms his or her consent electronically, in a manner that reasonably demonstrates that the consumer can access information in the electronic form that will be used to provide the information that is the subject of the consent." Presumably, the obligation to "reasonably demonstrate" ability to access the information may be met if the consumer merely states in an electronic message that he or she can access the electronic records in the specified formats or otherwise acknowledges or responds affirmatively to an electronic query that asks whether the consumer can access the electronic record (Federal Trade Commission, 2001; Consumer Consent Provision in Section 101(C)(1)(c)(ii)).

Signature Requirements

The requirement that the parties sign their transaction has three purposes: (1) the signature serves as an expression of intent, (2) it may be required by law, and (3) it may be necessary for the security of the transaction. With respect to the first purpose, a signature provides *prima facie* evidence of the signer's intent with respect to the document signed. Of course, the nature of the signer's intent varies with the transaction and in most cases can be determined only by looking at the surrounding circumstances in which the signature was made. For example, a signature may indicate an intent to be bound to the terms of a contract, the approval of a request by an employee or person designate for funding of a project, authorization to a bank to transfer funds, or simply that the contents of a document have been made known and that the other party has had an opportunity for review.

Concerning the second purpose, a signature is often the means employed to satisfy a law that requires the fact of signature before the document will be considered legally binding. The Statute of Frauds is probably the best known of the numerous federal and state statutes that require certain types of transactions, such as the sale of land or contracts for the sale of goods in excess of the stipulated monetary limit (Amended Article 2 (Sales), 2002, increases the threshold amount to $5,000), to be documented in writing and to be signed. In this regard, the increasing weight that courts tend to be placing on e-mail communications and electronic signatures should put buyers on their guard. Prospective buyers should ask themselves whether they are willing to be contractually bound by offers that are made by e-mail, because the e-mail sender's act of typing his or her name at the bottom of the e-mail may be sufficient to manifest intention to authenticate the transmission for Statute of Frauds purposes. The copy of the e-mail in question submitted as evidence of an intention to contract has been held sufficient for the purpose. In the case of *Rosenfeld v. Zerneck* (2004), for example, the plaintiffs had e-mailed the defendant, confirming their offer to purchase the defendant's home for $3.5 million. The defendant accepted the offer via e-mail. The typed signature at the bottom of the defendant's e-mail was held to satisfy the requirement that a "writing be subscribed under New York State's general Statute of Frauds" (General Obligations Law § 5-701), for the New York legislature had amended that provision to allow for the subscription of electronically transmitted memoranda.

Finally, a signature often functions as a means of security, in the sense that it can be used either to authenticate a document, notably for the purposes of identifying the source of the document, or to ensure the integrity of the document to the extent that it has not been altered by an unauthorized source. It is for this reason, for example, that parties to a multipage contract sometimes initial each page of the contract. In the electronic environment, certain types of signatures (e.g., cryptographically created digital signatures) can play an important role in verifying the integrity of the entire document.

Definition of Electronic Signature

Traditionally, the law has allowed any symbol (e.g., the notorious "x"), that is made with the intent to sign a document to qualify as a legally valid signature. Hence, the definition of "signed" in the Uniform Commercial Code includes "any symbol" as long as it is "executed or adopted by a party with present intention to authenticate a writing" (Article 1, § 1-201(39) (1999)). The law is chiefly concerned with the signer's "intention to authenticate" the document by affixing her signature and thereby indicating her intention to be legally bound.

Both E-SIGN and UETA extend the traditional approach of the law to the concept of an electronic signature. To be enforceable, they require that an electronic signature meet the following three criteria (E-SIGN, 15 U.S.C. § 7006(5) and UETA § 2(8)):

1. be a sound, symbol, or process.
2. be attached to or logically associated with an electronic record. This requires that the parties implement

an electronic recordkeeping process that is capable of providing evidence that a specific signature was applied to or used in connection with a specific document. The easiest way to comply with this requirement is to have the signature incorporated as part of the electronic record that is stored.

3. be made with the intent to sign the electronic record to the end that the signature relates to a specific document and to evidence the signer's intent with respect to that document.

The European Union (EU) Electronic Signature Directive uses a similar definition of an electronic signature. Under the directive, an electronic signature must also meet three criteria: (1) be data in electronic form, (2) be attached to or logically associated with other electronic data, and (3) serve as a method of authentication (Electronic Signature Directive, Article 2(1) AA). For the majority of transactions electronic signatures that meet these requirements will be considered legally enforceable as substitutes for handwritten signatures (UETA §s 2(8) and 7(d); E-SIGN, 15 U.S.C. § 7001(a) and 7006(5)).

Methods of "Signing" an Electronic Record

The definition of an electronic signature acknowledges that there are a variety of methods by which an electronic record may be signed. Although an electronic signature, by its nature, must be represented digitally—that is, in binary code—it can take many forms and can be created using a variety of different technologies. Well-known examples of electronic signatures that satisfy E-SIGN and UETA include the following:

- a name typed at the end of an e-mail message by the sender (*Shattuck v. Klotzbach*, 2001)
- a digitized image of a handwritten signature that is attached to an electronic document
- a PIN number that identifies the sender to the recipient
- a unique biometrics-based identifier, such as a fingerprint
- a mouse click as illustrated by the ubiquitous "I accept" button
- a "digital signature" created through the use of public key cryptography

"Digital Signatures" Created by Public Key Cryptography

There is a considerable difference, however, between an electronic signature that merely satisfies the requirements of E-SIGN and UETA and a trusted, certified electronic signature. As we have noted, when transactions are automated and carried out remotely, using digital technology that can easily alter the record, it becomes critical to have a means of ensuring the identity of the parties and the integrity of the document. Merely clicking on an "I accept" button or typing a name on an e-mail message offers no evidence as to the authenticity of the signature.

Because most legally recognized electronic signatures provide only a weak level of authentication, they have to be accompanied by certification procedures. Parties who wish to conduct their business by electronic means would be well advised to use the services of one of the many certification authorities. VeriSign, Baltimore Technologies, RSA Security, and Pretty Good Privacy are some of the companies that offer digital signature technologies and certification services. A digital signature is the sequence of bits that is created by running an electronic message through a one-way hash function to create a unique digest (or "fingerprint") of the message and then using public key encryption to encrypt the resulting message digest with the sender's private key.

Encryption technology through public key infrastructures (PKI) is employed to enhance security. Public key cryptography employs an algorithm using two different but mathematically related cryptographic keys: one for creating a digital signature or transforming data into a seemingly unintelligible form and the other key for verifying a digital signature or returning the message to its original form (American Bar Association Section of Science and Technology Electronic Commerce Division Information Security Committee. Digital Signature Guidelines. August 1, 1996. Available at: http://www.abanet.org/scitech/ec/isc/dsgfree.html.) Such digital signatures allow the sender of a document or a message to encrypt that message or document with a unique, private key. The message recipient is then able to decrypt the document using a related public key.

Most governments have undertaken initiatives to promote the use of digital signature and encryption technology in the public and private sector. In contrast with E-SIGN, the EU Directive for example provides a comprehensive regulatory framework. It envisions the growth of a complex network of competing and complementary PKIs providing electronic certificates to customers that, in turn, can be used by these customers to sign documents electronically.

Record Accessibility Requirements

Another key requirement for the enforceability of electronic transactions is that the documents that comprise the transaction should be communicated in a form that can be retained and reproduced accurately by the receiving party. E-SIGN legislation provides that the legal effect, validity, or enforceability of an electronic record "may be denied if such electronic record is not in a form that is capable of being retained and accurately reproduced for later reference by all parties or persons who are entitled to retain the contract or other record" (15 U.S.C. § 7001(e)). Similarly, UETA provides that "if a sender inhibits the ability of a recipient to store or print an electronic record, the electronic record is not enforceable against the recipient" (§ 8(c)).

That is not to say that this requirement limits electronic transactions to those parties that possess the technical capability for downloading or printing documents. Rather, the focus is on the form of the document as communicated by the sender and essentially requires that the sender do nothing to inhibit the ability of the recipient to download, store, or print the applicable record. The fact that the recipient may choose to use a device without such capabilities, such as a PDA or other handheld device without a print capability, should not affect the enforceability of the transaction. On the other hand, such provisions clearly call into question the form of clickwrap agreement typically used on many Web sites in which the agreement is displayed in a separate window from which it cannot be downloaded or printed.

Record Retention Requirements

An essential element for the enforceability of all transactions is record keeping. In the event of a dispute, it is necessary to produce reliable evidence documenting the terms of the transaction and the agreement made by the parties. For electronic transactions, this issue raises questions as to whether the keeping of electronic records is sufficient to satisfy the applicable statutes, regulations, or evidentiary rules and, if so, what requirements must be met for acceptable electronic records. Both E-SIGN and UETA address this issue directly and impose similar requirements. In essence, storage of an electronic record will satisfy legal record retention requirements if the stored copy of the electronic record meets the following two criteria:

1. accurately reflects the information set forth in the record (E-SIGN, 15 U.S.C. § 7001(d)(2); UETA § 12(b))
2. remains accessible for later reference to all persons who are entitled to access by law, for the period required by the relevant statute and in a form that is capable of being accurately reproduced for later reference, whether by transmission, printing, or otherwise (UETA § 12(a); E-SIGN, 15 U.S.C. § 7001(d))

With respect to evidentiary rules, both E-SIGN and UETA also provide that if a rule of evidence or other rule of law requires a record relating to a transaction to be provided or retained in its original form, this obligation is satisfied by meeting the accuracy and accessibility requirements listed above (E-SIGN 15 U.S.C. § 7001(d)(3); UETA § 12(d)). These provisions also make clear that records can be kept in electronic-only form. Furthermore, they provide considerable flexibility to the parties in terms of how they store the records, when and whether they wish to store the records on new media, and how to meet applicable evidentiary requirements.

ENFORCEABILITY OF ONLINE CONTRACTS
Characterizing Shrink-, Click-, and Browsewrap Agreements

Clickwrap agreements may be seen as analogous to shrinkwrap agreements, the original character and form of which are generally attributed to software producers and their desire to find a satisfactory method of distributing software held on CDs or diskettes and sold in packaged form. Likewise, clickwrap agreements are online contracts that invite users to scroll through their terms and conditions before manifesting their assent to contract by clicking on a button that states "I accept" or "I agree." A third form of online contract that is rapidly gaining favor because of its user friendliness is the browsewrap agreement. In this form of agreement, a notice is simply placed on the Web page informing users that they are subject to a license agreement, which is available for online viewing at any time.

The enforceability of clickwrap and browsewrap agreements and the security of the intellectual property they purport to protect are of critical importance, in view of the fact that such agreements have become the common means of exchange for consumer goods in networked markets worldwide. Although the intention to contract might be signaled by the user's clicking on the "I accept" button, the validity and hence the security of clickwrap agreements are by no means as easily assured. Intention is but one of the essential elements necessary to the formation of a legally binding contract. As a matter of general principle, the law also requires one party, usually the seller, to make an offer setting out the terms of the proposed contract to another party, the buyer. A valid contract is formed when an unequivocal acceptance of the offer is communicated to the offeror or seller.

Manifesting Assent to Clickwrap and Browsewrap Agreements

If a clickwrap or browsewrap agreement is implemented properly, it should operate to create a valid and binding online contract between buyer and seller. Both E-SIGN and UETA explain that the "process" of clicking a mouse can qualify as a signature if the other applicable requirements are also present. As the Reporter's note to UETA explains, "this definition includes as an electronic signature the standard webpage click-through process. For example, when a person orders goods or services through a vendor's web site, the person will be required to provide information as part of a process which will result in receipt of the goods or services. When the customer ultimately gets to the last step and clicks 'I agree,' the person has adopted the process and has done so with the intent to associate the person with all the record of that process" (§ 2, comment 7). More broadly, with respect to the formation of such contracts, the courts are guided by the principles of sales law as contained in Article 2-204 of the UCC (Uniform Commercial Code), which states that "a contract for sale of goods may be made in any manner sufficient to show agreement, including conduct by both parties which recognizes the existence of such a contract."

The classic case on the validity of such contracts is *ProCD v. Zeidenberg* (1996), where the Seventh Circuit held that software shrinkwrap license agreements are a valid form of contracting under Wisconsin's version of the Uniform Commercial Code. In ringing affirmation of the recent trend to also uphold clickwrap contracts, the federal district court of Minnesota in *I-Sys Inc. v. Softwares Inc.* (2004) rejected an argument that clickwrap acceptance of a software license under protest did not bind the defendants. According to the terms of the license, installation and use of the software with the license attached constituted acceptance of the 1995 and 1998 license terms. The 1995 and 1998 licenses were shrinkwrap agreements, meaning that a file was installed together with the software containing a license document instructing users that by using the software they were accepting the license terms. Subsequently, in 2001 software updates were distributed by means of a clickwrap license that required users to accept the terms by clicking through a series of screens before they could access the software. Plaintiff software developers contended that, by not returning the software with a 1995 or 1998 license and by clicking through the 2001 license, the defendants had accepted the terms of the license and were bound by it. The defendant software distributors argued that they were unaware of the 1995 and 1998 licenses and only "accepted" the 2001 license under protest because they needed the updated software that came with it. The court rejected the defendants' argument that they did not truly "accept" the license terms, but clicked through only because they needed the software to upgrade earlier, unsatisfactory versions. It found that references to the licenses in invoices and in the software development agreements gave the defendants sufficient notice of them.

Until recently, the enforceability of browsewrap agreements, in which the terms and conditions are typically posted on the Web site by way of a hyperlink, had been in some doubt. Courts had generally been reluctant to enforce the terms of an agreement that lacks any formal indication that the user has read and agreed to the terms of the contract (*Pollstar v. Gigmania Ltd.*, 2000; *Ticketmaster Corp. v. Tickets.com, Inc.*, 2000). However, in a landmark decision affirming the enforceability of browsewrap licenses, the U.S. Court of Appeal for the Second Circuit found Verio Inc., having accepted the plaintiff's terms of use, to be in breach of contract (*Register.com Inc v Verio Inc.*, 2004). Register.com derived its authority to act as a registry for the issuance of domain names from a standard form agreement with the Internet Corporation for Assigned Names and Numbers (ICANN), a nonprofit corporation established by the U.S. government to administer the domain name system. Under the agreement with ICANN, Register was required to maintain a publicly available 'WHOIS' database of registrants' contact information and was not to impose restrictions on the use of this data, except in relation to mass solicitations by e-mail or spamming. Register established a WHOIS database, which it updated on a daily basis, and provided a free public inquiry service for the information contained therein. Register's responses to WHOIS queries were captioned by a legend stating that by submitting a query, the user agreed not to use the data to conduct mass solicitations of business by e-mail, direct mail, or telephone. Contrary to the terms of use, Verio developed an automated software program or robot to access the WHOIS database and compile substantial lists of new domain name registrants whom Verio then proceeded to bombard with unsolicited marketing by e-mail, direct mail, and telephone. Register demanded that Verio cease the practice, but Verio complied only in part—ceasing the e-mail solicitations but continuing to promote its services by direct mail and telephone.

When Register brought suit for breach of contract, Verio argued that because they had not received adequate notice, they could not be said to have consented to the restrictive terms and were therefore not contractually bound to comply with them. In this case notice of the restrictive conditions did not appear until after Verio had submitted the query and received the WHOIS data. Contrary to the Ticketmaster case, the Court of Appeals found that online contracts do not always require formal acceptance by the offeree. Rejecting the need for a requirement that users click an "I agree" icon, the Court of Appeals drew on the general principles of contract law to find that the terms of use in Register's browsewrap agreement, combined with Verio Inc.'s conduct in repeatedly utilizing the WHOIS database, constituted a valid offer and acceptance, thereby resulting in a legally enforceable contract with Verio. Of course, had Verio's utilization of the database been irregular or occasional, it might not have been deemed to have accepted Register's terms of use. In the event, however, the Court upheld the preliminary injunction enjoining Verio Inc. from either utilizing a search robot to obtain information from the plaintiff's database or utilizing information derived from it for mass solicitation.

The Court of Appeals distinguished the facts in Register.com from its former decision in *Specht v. Netscape Communications* (2002). In that case the question for the court was whether plaintiffs were bound by an arbitration clause in the agreement. The Second Circuit held that under the terms of the license agreement to which plaintiffs agreed, governing their use of Netscape's browser, they were under no obligation to arbitrate the claims they raised in the litigation. The software in question could be downloaded from a page on defendant Netscape's Web site by clicking on a button that said "download." When plaintiffs proceeded to initiate installation of the Communicator, they were automatically shown a scrollable text of that program's license agreement and were not permitted to complete the installation until they had clicked on a "Yes" button to indicate that they accepted all the license terms. However, the terms of the license agreement were not contained on this Web page, and the only notice users received of the license agreement was found on a portion of the Web page below the download button. Typically, this notice appeared "below the fold" and was not on that portion of the page that first appeared on the user's screen when he or she proceeded to download the program. This notice informed users that their use of the software would be governed by the terms of a license agreement, which could be seen by clicking on a link provided on the Web page. Once the program was downloaded, the user received no further notice of either the license agreement or its terms. The Second Circuit Court of Appeals found that the plaintiffs were not bound by the terms of the license agreement because they had neither had reasonable notice of the restrictive terms nor had they adequately manifested their assent to be bound by them.

Notice of Unusual or Onerous Terms

Although the general trend at both the legislative and judicial spheres is, in principle, to endorse the validity of clickwrap contracts, that does not mean that the contract is necessarily enforceable. Case law reveals that problems can arise in two areas in particular: the form of assent and the reasonableness of the contractual terms. The legal problems associated with such agreements concern the conditions for the formation of a valid contract and the identification of contractual terms. A contract's terms and conditions are fixed at the moment the contract is formed. Contractual provisions will form part of the agreement only if the other party has reasonable notice of them before agreeing to contract.

Reasonable notice for unusual and onerous provisions requires greater time than does reasonable notice for normal provisions. This is a particularly significant issue since the clickwrap license is commonly used to unilaterally set out the sellers' terms to the purchaser. Thus the standard software license tends to include a conspicuous notice of title retention in the seller, restrictions on transfer and modification, prohibition of reverse engineering, limited copying provisions, and a forum selection or arbitration clause.

In *Forest v. Verizon Communications Inc*. (2002), the question was whether a forum selection clause mandating that claims be brought in a particular jurisdiction should be applied to a class action suit involving plaintiffs' attempts to register for and use Verizon's broadband service. The subscribers argued that Verizon had not provided sufficient notice of the forum selection clause or its consequences. To become broadband subscribers, users had to agree to all the terms of the agreement, including the forum selection clause. The clause was found in the final part of the agreement, which was available for viewing in a scroll box; however, the box was only large enough to enable users to view a small portion of the document at any time. Users were on notice to 'read the following agreement carefully.' The contract was entered into by the subscriber clicking an "Accept" button below the scroll box. The District of Columbia Court of Appeals found that users were provided with adequate notice of the forum selection clause, stating that "the general rule is that absent fraud or mistake, one who signs a contract is bound by a contract which he has an opportunity to read whether he does so or not." The court noted that in reading through the agreement before it was accepted, users would have inevitably discovered the forum selection clause. Nevertheless, it pointed out that the use of a "scroll box" that displays only part of the agreement at any one time is detrimental to the provision of adequate notice (see also *Caspi v. Microsoft Network*, 1999; *CompuServe, Inc v. Patterson*, 1996; *I Lan Systems v. Netscout Service Level Corp.*, 2002, concerning the incorporation of a clause limiting liability).

Similarly in the earlier case of *Hill v. Gateway 2000, Inc*. (7th Cir. Jan. 6, 1997), the Seventh Circuit Court of Appeals held that the "accept-or-return" agreement was effective, stating "competent adults are bound by such documents, read or unread." Although it is not necessary for the buyer to have read the agreement to be bound by it, clearly failure to read the terms can result in substantial loss. Thus, in *M.A. Mortenson Co., Inc. v. Timberline Software Corp.* (2000), the plaintiff sought recovery of $1.95 million, based on an alleged software malfunction that resulted in a project bid of $1.95 million lower than intended. The court followed the reasoning of *ProCD* and *Hill* to find that Mortenson's use of the software constituted its assent to the agreement, including the license terms.

Contracts Voidable for Unconscionability

The enforceability of contracts generally may be affected by particularly onerous or unconscionable terms in standard consumer contracts. The common law of contract has traditionally been able to provide relief when one party is so clearly incapable of looking after his or her interests; in other words, that to enforce the contract would be unconscionable or against all conscience. This principle is codified in Section 2-302 of the UCC, which provides that where a court finds the contract or any clause of the contract to have been unconscionable at the time it was made the court may refuse to enforce the contract, or it may enforce the remainder of the contract without the unconscionable clause, or it may so limit the application of any unconscionable clause as to avoid any unconscionable result. The courts do not set aside private bargains lightly, and the test of unconscionability is notoriously difficult to satisfy. The terms of an unconscionable transaction must suggest that one party took unfair advantage of the party with the disability. Thus, offering to buy a Picasso drawing at a rock-bottom price from a 92-year-old impecunious widow who is unaware of its true market value would be *prima facie* unconscionable.

Nonetheless, in a medium where it is all too easy to create unrealistically one-sided commercial contracts, drafters of online contracts should bear in mind the doctrine of unconscionability to ensure that particularly onerous or unusual (and potentially "unfair") terms are brought to the attention of the persons with whom they are contracting with or risk a court later determining such contracts to be unenforceable. Moreover, even if incorporated properly into a contract, certain terms, such as unreasonable exclusion clauses or limitations of liability, may nevertheless not be enforced against buyers who agreed to a contract of adhesion or standard form contract.

Almost all unconscionability cases have elements of both procedural and substantive unconscionability. Procedural unconscionability involves the manner and process by which the terms become part of the contract. For example, these practices are unconscionable: the use of incomprehensible or legalistic fine-print standard form contract provisions; binding the buyer to additional written terms after the contract is signed; switching contract documents at the last moment to include non-negotiated, one-sided terms; and pressuring the client to sign a contract before reading it. Substantive unconscionability involves the terms of the contract themselves that are unreasonably, unacceptably, or unfairly harsh and against good conscience. Potentially unconscionable clauses would include those authorizing venue or jurisdiction in distant forums, disclaimer of warranties, and limitations or waiver of remedy clauses.

The following case is illustrative: in Comb v. PayPal, Inc., (ND Cal. 2002), plaintiffs successfully claimed that even if they had concluded the user agreement, this agreement, and in particular its arbitration clause, was unconscionable. The court held that PayPal's user agreement was a contract of adhesion, and hence procedurally unconscionable, because it was a form agreement drawn by PayPal, a party of superior bargaining power, and offered to its customers on a take-it-or-leave-it basis. The court also found that the user agreement and its arbitration provisions were substantively unconscionable. In reaching this conclusion, the court pointed to several provisions contained in the agreement, including the following:

- PayPal could amend the agreement at any time without notice to users, and these amendments would be binding on them.
- PayPal could freeze all of the funds in a customer's account pending its resolution of any dispute.
- The arbitration provisions mandated arbitration pursuant to the commercial rules of the American Arbitration Association (AAA), which was cost prohibitive, in light of evidence that such a procedure would cost $5,000, whereas the average PayPal transaction was $55.
- The arbitration provision required all arbitrations to proceed in Santa Clara County, California, where PayPal was headquartered, whereas PayPal's customers resided throughout the United States.
- The arbitration provision prohibited joinder of claims among individuals, requiring each instead to proceed individually.

Taken as a whole, these provisions rendered the user agreement and its arbitration provisions unconscionable. The court accordingly denied PayPal's motion to compel arbitration.

CONTRACTUAL RESTRICTIONS ON THE USE OF SOFTWARE
Copyright Preemption, Fair Use, and Reverse Engineering

It is common practice among software companies to study competitors' products in order to improve their own offerings. In this context, the legality of *reverse engineering*, a procedure that generally involves converting machine code back to source code, was recently called into question after the U.S. Supreme Court denied leave to appeal in *Bowers v. Baystate Technologies Inc.* (2003). The Supreme Court's denial of Baystate's petition tends to implicitly affirm the decision of the Federal Court of Appeals that private parties can indeed contract to prohibit the reverse engineering of their intellectual property. A divided Appeals Court found that the federal Copyright Act does not preempt state contract law that allows parties to impose a ban on reverse engineering.

In this controversial case, Harold Bowers had obtained patent and copyright protection for computer-aided design (CAD) software that he distributed under a shrinkwrap licensing agreement that prohibited reverse engineering. Baystate then developed a competing product, which incorporated features of Bowers' software. Bowers alleged Baystate had not only infringed his copyright but also breached the end use license agreement (EULA) by reverse engineering his software in order to modify its own competing software package. For its part, defendant Baystate claimed that it had only evaluated a competitor's product in order to improve its CAD software and that it had not violated encrypted source code. Moreover, Baystate argued that federal copyright law preempts terms that limit the use of copyrighted materials.

Copyright law permits fair use of the work in the form of clean room reverse engineering. Section 117 of the Copyright Act permits an owner of a computer program to make an adaptation of that program provided that the adaptation is either "created as an essential step in the utilization of the computer program in conjunction with a machine" ($\S\S 117(1)$) or "is for archival purpose only" ($\S\S 117(2)$). The Court of Appeals found that federal copyright law does not preempt the terms of the contract and upheld the shrinkwrap license. Its decision of January 2003 upheld the decision of the lower court in awarding the plaintiff US$5.27 million for breach of contract and patent infringement.

Nonetheless, contractual prohibitions on reverse engineering remain controversial (Reichman, 1999). In Bower's case the Appeal Court was split, the dissenting judge finding that with respect to nonnegotiated contracts such as shrinkwrap licenses, the contract claim was indeed preempted by federal copyright law. Judge Anthony Dyk chose to follow the decision of the Fifth Circuit in *Vault Corp. v. Quaid Software Ltd.* (1988). He took the view that restrictions on reverse engineering represented the thin end of the wedge. If today software developers were permitted to eliminate the fair use defense, then tomorrow they could also restrict a purchaser from asserting the "first sale" defense, embodied in 17 U.S.C. $\S 109(a)$ or any other of the protections Congress has afforded the public in the Copyright Act.

In the case cited, Quaid reverse engineered Vault's program in order to create its own program, called RAMKEY, which disabled PROLOK's copy protection. In the course of writing RAMKEY, Quaid loaded the PROLOK program into its computer memory. The court rejected Vault's claim of copyright infringement. The plaintiff's principal claim was founded in Louisiana law. Quaid breached its license agreement by decompiling or disassembling Vault's program in violation of the Louisiana state licensing law that permits a software producer to impose a number of contractual terms upon software purchasers when the license agreement accompanies the producer's software (La.Rev.Stat.Ann. $\S\S\S\S 51:1963$ & 1965). Enforceable terms include the prohibition of (1) any copying of the program for any purpose and (2) modifying and/or adapting the program in any way, including adaptation by reverse engineering, decompilation, or disassembly (La.Rev.Stat.Ann. $\S\S 51:1964$).

Although the restrictions in Vault's license agreement were consistent with the state statute and *prima facie* enforceable under Louisiana's License Act, the District Court found that it conflicted with several areas of federal copyright law. First, although the License Act authorizes a total prohibition on copying, the Copyright Act allows archival copies and copies made as an essential step in the utilization of a computer program (17 U.S.C. $\S\S 117$). Second, although the License Act authorizes a perpetual bar against copying, the Copyright Act grants protection against unauthorized copying only for the life of the author plus (then) 50 years (17 U.S.C. $\S\S 302(a)$). Third, although the License Act places no restrictions on programs that may be protected, under the Copyright Act, only "original works of authorship" can be protected (17 U.S.C. $\S\S 102$. Vault, 655 F.Supp. at 762-63).

With respect to the questions of the preemption of federal law based on section 301 of the Copyright Act, the Federal Appeals Court found that the provision in Louisiana's License Act, which permits a software producer to prohibit the adaptation of its licensed computer program by decompilation or disassembly, conflicts with the rights of computer program owners under §§ 117 and clearly "touches upon an area" of federal copyright law. Because Louisiana's License Act "touched upon the area" of federal copyright law, its provisions were pre-empted or superseded by the fair use provisions of the Federal Copyright Act. As a result Vault's efforts to prohibit this activity under Louisiana law was illegal. This finding was consistent with the Supremacy Clause of the U.S. Constitution and its role in precluding any state laws that conflict with expressed federal policy in fields where the federal government exercises substantial control (*Bonito Boats, Inc.v. Thunder Craft Boats, Inc.*, 1989; *Kewanee Oil Co. v. Bicron Corp.*, 1974).

To allow software vendors unilaterally and without restriction to impose terms that prohibit reverse engineering is inimical to the free flow of ideas and information and would frustrate the policy of encouraging the creation of innovative and interoperable software products. Yet, how can small software developers stay in business if larger companies can simply reverse engineer the product before they have been able to recover their investment? Software vendors and content providers rely on contracts to reinforce their intellectual property rights in the digital environment where the risk of unauthorized reproduction and distribution is so much greater. Bower's company, HLB Technology, epitomized the small to medium-sized enterprise driven out of the market by big business. The defendant had not only incorporated features of Bower's product but, having acquired the company with which Bower's held a distribution agreement, it also proceeded to repudiate the contract.

The problematic state of the relationship between copyright and contract is a reflection of the difficulty the licensor has in monitoring licensee use of software and in distinguishing between licensees likely to breach terms of the license essential to the protection of valuable intellectual property (Nimmer, 1998). In the earlier case of *ProCD* the Court of Appeals for the Seventh Circuit also dealt with the preemption issue as to whether federal copyright law disallowed enforcement of the contractual restrictions on use of informational content. The question for the court in *ProCD* was whether the buyer's promise not to make commercial use of the uncopyrightable data in the plaintiff's directory interfered with the balance drawn in the Copyright Act. Previously in *Feist Publications v. Rural Telephone Service Co.* (1991), the U.S. Supreme Court had ruled that the unoriginal compilation of data, such as white pages listings in telephone directories, was unprotectable by copyright law. The Supreme Court's decision seemed to regard such information, once published, as being in the public domain and therefore able to be appropriated freely. A mass-market license term prohibiting the redistribution of telephone listings was ostensibly contrary to the Supreme Court's ruling.

Hence in *ProCD v. Zeidenberg* the defendant argued that the Copyright Act preempts the enforcement of such

contracts. The appellate court, however, disagreed. Judge Easterbrook, writing for the majority, found no problem of preemption once he differentiated between contractual rights that are good against the parties to the agreement only, and property rights that are good against the world. Because there was an "extra element" of agreement, the state contract claim was not "equivalent" to a copyright claim. Hence, federal policy did not preempt enforcement of the contractual restrictions.

The issue remains a live one. The migration of software distribution systems to networked environments poses both new risks and new possibilities of risk management for licensors. To the extent that access controls can be placed on software and brought within the Digital Millennium Copyright Act framework (1998), the large corporate licensors have been successful in gaining new tools for controlling the volume of infringing activities. As a matter of technical self-help, the ability to monitor the use of software is also increasing and provides licensors not only with more information about potentially infringing activities but also with the necessary foundation for new pricing models.

SALE OF GOODS LAW AND DIGITAL INFORMATION TRANSACTIONS
Is a Computer Information Product a "Good" or a "License"?

Case law shows that contracts for the transfer of intangible property test the very limits of established law concerning the sale of goods. As a threshold matter, its application is problematic because the product involved is a transaction of "goods," as defined in UCC Article 2 to mean "all things (including specially manufactured goods) which are movable at the time of identification to the contract for sale." To distinguish between transfers that consist largely of intangible as opposed to tangible property, proposed amendments to the Uniform Commercial Code (UCC) in Article 2, section 2-103 (2003), state that the term "goods" expressly excludes "information." However, neither Revised Article 2 nor Revised Article 1 defines the term "information" (National Conference of Commissioners on Uniform State Laws, 2001a, 2002), The Official Comment to § 2-103 declares, "This article does not directly apply to an electronic transfer of information, such as the transaction in *Specht v. Netscape* (2002)."

Revised Article 9 clarifies that software is ordinarily not a good and is a "general intangible" except in some limited cases of embedded software. Consequently, although Article 2 would not apply directly to a download of software or digital content, the sale of "smart goods" such as an automobile would be covered fully by Article 2, even though it incorporates many computer programs. In the case of *Specht*, the Second Circuit Court of Appeals observed that downloadable software "is scarcely a tangible good." It chose instead to base its decision on the common law of contracts of California and the Restatement (Second) of Contracts, as it declined to enforce the terms of a license concerning mandatory arbitration that appeared below the "Download" button on a portion of the

Web page that was not visible on most visitors' screens until they scrolled to the bottom of the page.

Whether and to what extent Revised Article 2 applies to a transaction that includes both goods and information are to be determined from all the facts and circumstances. In effect, the amendments to Article 2 leave the courts to sort out in individual cases the UCC's application to computer and software licensing transactions. Generally speaking, with respect to the question whether an online transaction should be characterized as a "sale" or a "license," courts have been accustomed to looking at the totality of the circumstances of the transaction, including such factors as whether a single copy or multiple copies are transferred, whether the transaction involves the physical movement of goods, how the payment is structured, the duration of the agreement, who retains title to the copy for purposes of loss, and the tax treatment of the transaction (*Applied Info. Mgmt. Co. v. Icart*, 1997). In allowing the common law to develop an appropriate body of principles for informational transactions online, the Uniform Computer Information Transactions Act (UCITA), promulgated expressly with the aim of bringing uniformity and certainty to the rules that apply to software transactions, is likely to play its most influential role to date. In view of the problems that may be associated with characterizing software as goods or services, business and software vendors would be well advised to address this distinction expressly in the terms of the contract.

Warranties as to Fitness and Merchantability

Sales and consumer law traditionally protects the buyer's legitimate expectation that the goods will be of merchantable quality (UCC 2-314: implied warranties of merchantability) and fit for the purpose for which they were bought (UCC 2-315: fitness for a particular known purpose). Additionally, revised Article 2 would considerably expand the risk of liability for breach of the warranty of good title. Current law makes sellers liable if they actually do not have "good title"; Revised Article 2-312 creates liability any time that a third party makes a "colorable claim" to title.

In the information economy, however, the problem the law has to confront is that software vendors and content providers, by typically characterizing the transaction as a license to use the software or content and not a sale as such, thereby purport to preclude the application of the UCC's implied warranties. Should the licensor wish to disclaim all implied warranties in a mass-market license, it is sufficient to state the following: "except for express warranties stated in this contract, if any, this information is being provided with all faults, and the entire risk as to satisfactory quality, performance, accuracy, and effort is with the user, or words of similar import." In addition, under current law licensors appear to have the advantage where computer viruses are concerned—that is, destructive computer instructions designed to damage or destroy intangibles—insofar as the principal basis for liability is a warranty of merchantability, which is routinely disclaimed in both negotiated and mass-market licenses. Thus, in *Specht* for example, the terms of the

communicator license agreement included a complete disclaimer of warranties ("as is"), an entire-risk clause, and a limitation of liability clause for consequential and other damages. Again, in *Mortenson Company, Inc. v. Timberline Software Corporation* (2000), Timberline's license agreement provided the usual warranty disclaimers, together with a disclaimer for damages or liability. When the plaintiff nonetheless brought suit for breach of express and implied warranties, alleging the software was defective, Timberline moved for summary judgment, arguing the limitation on consequential damages in the licensing agreement barred Mortenson's recovery. Moreover, Revised Article 2 tends to sanction this practice by purporting to exclude informational products from the scope of the UCC.

Warranties for Informational Products under UCITA

The Uniform Computer Information Transactions Act (UCITA, formerly UCC Draft Article 2B), is founded upon the conceptual framework for commercial transactions in Article 2 of the UCC, which regulates the sale of goods. UCITA creates a standard framework of rules applicable to software and other computer information licensing transactions. "Information" includes computer programs, "computer information" means information in electronic form, and "computer information transaction" includes license agreements (§ 102(35), (10), and (12)).

UCITA contains several innovative provisions drafted to accommodate issues unique to transactions in information. These provisions address such controversial questions as the validity of adhesion contracts, warranties for information products, problems associated with breach, and the remedies for breach. Other issues addressed by the provisions are express warranties (s. 402) and implied warranties of quiet enjoyment and noninfringement, merchantability and quality of the computer program's informational content, licensee's purpose, and system integration (ss. 403-5).

Although UCITA contains implied warranties that reflect those found in sales law, these warranties have been adjusted and expanded to meet the unique character of information products. For example, merchantability for mass-market licenses consists of five minimum performance standards, including the contract description, fitness for the ordinary purposes, and the functionality of a computer program (ss. 403-5). The warranty that the goods will be fit for purchaser's purpose is the same as in sales law if the transaction is to deliver a product; however, UCITA creates a standard to distinguish this warranty from a services contract. Although sales law has no implied warranty that services will give a result consistent with the transferee's purpose, UCITA warrants that the services will not fail of the purpose because of a lack of effort. Again, where necessary, UCITA extends the nature and scope of implied warranties, as in the case of the warranty that the system components will work in integration (s. 405).

In sum, warranties for informational products are still at a formative stage. Although two states have enacted UCITA (Maryland and Virginia), five states (Iowa, West

Virginia, New York, Oregon, and Ohio) have enacted anti-UCITA "bomb shelter" legislation that would protect their residents from the application of UCITA in a transaction subject to the laws of states that have enacted it. Given the extent of the controversy, UCITA was significantly amended by NCCUSL in 2002 in response to substantive recommendations made by a Working Group on UCITA appointed by the American Bar Association. Absent statutory provisions, it is likely that courts will base their decision-making on the common law of contracts and the Restatement (Second) of Contracts as the case of *Specht* illustrates. Consequently, taking account of the problematic state of warranties for fitness, for purpose, and for merchantability of software and content, buyers would be well advised to seek warranties from the supplier wherever possible and to the extent feasible to ensure that the software will operate under certain conditions and that it will have the functionality the business needs.

CONSUMER PROTECTION ONLINE
Caveat Emptor

As consumer groups have argued, under the terms of UCITA it is relatively easy for the licensor to eliminate any warranty or representation in mass-market licenses. In fact, because of the strength and concentration of the software and content industries, there has been international interest in ensuring that consumers have adequate redress against defective products (Evans, 1999). The Organization for Economic Cooperation and Development (OECD) *Guidelines for Consumer Protection in the Context of Electronic Commerce* (1999) are designed to help ensure that consumers are no less protected when shopping online than they are when they buy from local stores or order from catalogues. By setting out the core characteristics of effective consumer protection for online business-to-consumer transactions, the guidelines are intended to help eliminate some of the uncertainties that both consumers and businesses encounter when buying and selling online. The guidelines reflect existing legal protection available to consumers in more traditional forms of commerce; encourage private sector initiatives that include participation by consumer representatives; and emphasize the need for cooperation among governments, businesses, and consumers. Their aim is to encourage fair business, advertising, and marketing practices; clear information about an online business's identity, the goods or services it offers, and the terms and conditions of any transaction; a transparent process for the confirmation of transactions; secure payment mechanisms; fair, timely, and affordable dispute resolution and redress; privacy protection; and consumer and business education.

Choice of Law

Although the ability to market and sell products and services from a single site to an unlimited geographic market is one of the advantages of electronic commerce, it also poses a major challenge for consumer protection online (*American Libraries Ass'n. v. Pataki*, 1997). When transactions cross the jurisdictional boundaries defining legal communities, there must be a workable method of coordinating the rights and liabilities of the parties. Fair, timely, and affordable dispute resolution is not possible if consumers are unable to benefit from the protection they have come to expect. One of the key issues for policymakers is developing a practicable and reasonably predictable set of rules to determine which jurisdiction's laws will apply to consumer contracts and which courts will have the authority to adjudicate and enforce disputes. UETA and, to a lesser extent E-SIGN provide little guidance with respect to these issues. UETA provides, as a default rule, that an electronic record is deemed to be sent from the sender's place of business and to be received at the recipient's place of business (§ 15(d)) or residence (§ 15(d).) UCITA, which allows the choice of any U.S. forum (including a foreign one) for the convenience of the producer, is criticized for allowing a too flexible choice of law and forum in mass-market transactions to the detriment of consumer interests.

Insofar as the sale of goods (as distinct from information), is concerned, Revised Section 1-301 of the UCC represents a significant rethinking of the choice of law issues addressed in current UCC Section 1-105. Current law allows the parties to the transaction to designate a jurisdiction whose law is to govern, if the transaction bears a "reasonable relation" to that jurisdiction. Revised Article 1 deviates from this unified approach by providing different rules for consumer transactions than for "business to business" transactions. Revised Article 1 requires no such relationship between the transaction and the chosen jurisdiction, unless one of the parties to the agreement is a consumer. It proposes a choice of law rule that would afford greater autonomy to each party, but with certain safeguards to protect consumer interests. On the one hand, Revised Article 1-301 purports to allow vendors the ability to choose the law of any state to apply to their contracts. On the other hand, Revised Article 1-301(2) provides that a choice of law agreement cannot alter the applicability of a consumer protection law of the state in which the consumer habitually resides. Thus, if ComCo has its headquarters in New York, I am a resident of California, and I purchase a microwave oven from a ComCo store in Ohio, then a provision in the sales agreement subjecting all disputes to the law of Texas would not be binding because I am a consumer. However, if Comco purchased the microwave for resale from Panacook, located in North Carolina, and had it shipped directly to the California store, then a provision in the Comco-Panacook agreement subjecting all disputes to Texas law would be binding because neither party is a consumer.

Needless to say, the proposed choice of law rule has given rise to controversy concerning the scope of party autonomy on the part of both business and consumer interests (National Association of Manufacturers, 2004). Many businesses find the notion that they should be expected to comply with the various regulatory regimes in which consumers happen to be located expensive and unrealistic (Americans for Fair Electronic Commerce Transactions, 2004; National Conference of Commissioners on Uniform State Laws, 2001a). The revision is sufficiently problematic that none of the small number of states that have enacted Revised Article 1 to date has enacted Section

R1-301 as drafted. Virginia's version of Revised Article 1 (effective July 1, 2003) rejects the uniform version's choice of law provision, opting to retain the basis of former Section 1-105, which requires some reasonable relation between the state whose law the parties choose by agreement and the transaction the parties choose to subject to that law. In view of the novelty and potentially problematic nature of consumer contracts online, revised UCC Article 2 gives the courts the right to overrule the statute in contracts involving consumers. Hence, Revised § 2-108(1)(b) is subordinate to any judicial decision "that establishes a different rule for consumers."

BEST PRACTICE FOR ONLINE CONTRACTS

The foregoing review of statute and case law has provided some pertinent indications as to how online vendors, in particular software vendors and content providers, might utilize clickwrap agreements to protect their rights and promote consumer confidence. In the absence of national standards and given the sometimes divergent decisions of the courts respecting these issues, online business should keep in mind three general criteria with regard to the enforceability of clickwrap and browsewrap agreements:

1. Agreements that are clear and conspicuous and require some proof of acceptance by the user are more likely to be enforced by the courts.
2. Browsewrap and clickwrap agreements potentially face challenges on two separate grounds: procedural challenges based on the manner in which the mutual assent is made and substantive challenges as to the terms of the agreement itself. Thus, even if the agreement is enforceable overall, particular terms might not be enforceable.
3. The enforcement of clickwrap and browsewrap agreements is likely to differ depending on the law in the jurisdiction where the contract is construed.

Consequently, when drafting an online agreement on behalf of the vendor, best practice involves two chief points:

1. To increase the site's chances of having any such agreement enforced against site visitors, the agreement should be set up so as to create a "contract." This means that, in addition to the issues about validity of consideration, there must be an offer that is set forth in the respective agreement, terms of service and, for the issues related to this chapter, a valid "acceptance" of the terms of that offer. Hence, there must be prominently displayed on the site, preferably on the home page, a link to the respective agreement in large, bold type. This link must take the visitor to the agreement, and there must be a mechanism whereby the visitor affirmatively clicks on an "I accept" button, having been given an opportunity to review the terms and conditions, before being able to proceed through the site. This latter procedure—blocking access to the site until there is an affirmative response from the visitor—is what the courts seem most likely to look for in determining whether there has been a valid acceptance. Equally, vendors should make sure that the buyer has the opportunity to reject the transaction upon review of the terms.
2. Vendors should make sure warranty disclaimers and limitations of damages are conspicuous by placing them in a large, bolded font and making sure that the purchaser does not have to scroll down to see them. Equally, it is not advisable to place additional terms where they can only be viewed through a "disclaimer" link or at another location on the Web site.

In summary, by ensuring that the terms and conditions are readily accessible, that the purchaser has certain clear rights upon receipt and review of these provisions, and not least by keeping records to prove assent, vendors can minimize the possibility that a court may conclude that they are unenforceable.

Even if best practice is followed, it is still possible that a purchaser may dispute his or her consent to terms and conditions that appear in a shrinkwrap or clickwrap agreement. In such an event, in an attempt to bring the dispute settlement into familiar home territory, consider adding an arbitration clause. Alternatively, an agreement might attempt to invoke laws more favorable to software and content providers, such as those of California, or to have recourse in a choice of law clause to the law of those states where UCITA applies such as Virginia.

Given the unsettled state of the law, whether you are an individual user or in a business, software licenses may need more careful attention than simply clicking "I accept." Falling into the clickwrap trap can leave buyers vulnerable to costly upfront fees and products that are not fit for the intended purpose. Those in business would be well advised to protect their company's intellectual property by taking the time to negotiate all software licenses, even those involving off-the-shelf software. Readers now cognizant of the uncertain state of the law, who take the time to read the entire clickwrap agreement, may well decide they want to buy on very different terms!

CONCLUSION

The law relating to the enforceability of contracts online is still in its formative stages. Early legislative intervention in the form of electronic signature legislation has largely accomplished two goals: first, it has removed the initial barriers to e-commerce, and second, it has promoted the uptake of electronic commerce by helping establish the "trust" and the "predictability" needed by the parties if they are to enter into contracts online. Likewise, the courts have followed suit in seeking to validate the clickwrap and browsewrap agreements used by vendors to distribute their goods online. Yet, now that in the United States alone there are 46 enactments of electronic signature legislation, not to mention the national variations that exist worldwide, the very predictability that governments are seeking to establish is at risk. Consequently, with the aim of continued harmonization, the United Nations Commission on International Trade Law (UNCITRAL) is constructing a *Draft Convention On [International] Contracts Concluded Or Evidenced By Data Messages* (2002). It includes provisions dealing with the substantive rights and obligations of the parties in the context of contract formation by electronic means.

In sum, the continued development of electronic commerce depends on how problems are resolved relating to the formation and enforceability of contracts online. Rules regarding offer and acceptance, place of formation, and certainty of terms are still not perfectly transferable to the online environment. As far as the individual parties are concerned, those who contract autonomously and in the course of an ongoing business relationship can simply agree to the particular rules that are to govern their transactions. However, where standard form, mass market contracts are concerned, given the failure of UCITA to gain widespread acceptance, it remains largely up to the courts to adapt the law of contract to the online environment.

GLOSSARY

Assent/Consent In law, the active acquiescence or silent compliance by a person legally capable of consenting (see age of consent). It may be evidenced by words or acts or by silence when silence implies concurrence. Actual or implied consent is necessarily an element of every contract and every agreement. In criminal charges, the consent of the party injured (if not obtained by fraud or duress) is a defense for the accused, unless a third party or the state is injured.

Browsewrap license A "browsewrap agreement" appears on a web site, but does not require the user to take any action to express consent. The terms of the agreement are displayed to users only if they click on the hyperlink that brings up the "terms and conditions" page.

Clickwrap License A window containing the terms of a clickwrap agreement commonly appears on the downloading, installation, or first use of a software application. The user is asked to click either "I agree" or "I do not agree." If the user does not agree, the process is terminated.

Contract For a contract to be valid, both parties must indicate that they agree to its terms. This is accomplished when one party submits an offer that the other accepts within a reasonable time or a stipulated period. If the terms of the acceptance vary from those of the offer, that "acceptance" legally constitutes a counteroffer; the original offering party may then accept it or reject it. At any time before acceptance, the offer may be rescinded on notice unless the offering party is bound by a separate option contract not to withdraw.

Copyright A property right by an author in an original work that has been fixed in a tangible medium, including literary, musical, artistic, photographic, or film works. The holder of a copyright has the exclusive right to reproduce, distribute, perform, and display the work.

Electronic Contract An electronic contract is an agreement created and "signed" in electronic form—in other words, no paper or other hard copies are used.

Electronic Signature An electronic sound, symbol, or process attached to or logically associated with a contract or other record and executed or adopted by a person with the intent to sign the record.

Fair Use An exception under the U.S. Copyright Act that allows one who does not own a copyright to make "fair use" of the copyrighted work for such purposes as criticism, comment, news reporting, teaching, scholarship, or research without being liable for copyright infringement.

Internet The international computer network linking together thousands of individual networks at military and government agencies, educational institutions, nonprofit organizations, industrial and financial corporations of all sizes, and commercial enterprises (called gateways or service providers) that enable individuals to access the network.

Law Merchant (or *Lex Mercatoria*). Originally a body of rules and principles relating to merchants and mercantile transactions, developed by merchants themselves for the purpose of regulating their dealings. The law merchant owed its origin to the fact that the civil law was not sufficiently responsive to the growing demands of commerce, as well as to the fact that trade in medieval times was in the hands of those who might be termed cosmopolitan merchants, who wanted a prompt and effective jurisdiction.

License Licensing is a branch of the law of contracts. The contract is a specific form of agreement and strictly speaking embodies a license; that is, a permission from an owner of a right given to another to use part of that right. The other side of the contract is the obligation assumed by the receiver of the permission (i.e., the licensee) in return for the permission.

Online The state in which a computer is connected to another computer or server via a network; in other words, a computer communicating with another computer.

CROSS REFERENCES

See *Copyright Law; Digital Signatures and Electronic Signatures; Internet Basics; Legal, Social and Ethical Issues of the Internet; The Legal Implications of Information Security: Regulatory Compliance and Liability.*

REFERENCES

Afuah, A., & Tucci, C. (2000). *Internet business models and strategies*. Boston: McGraw-Hill.

Americans for Fair Electronic Commerce Transactions. (2004). *Proposed UCITA-related legislation*. Retrieved September 15, 2004, from http://www.affect.ucita.com/Legislation.htm

American Libraries Ass'n v. Pataki, 969 F. Supp. 160 (S.D.N.Y., 1997).

Applied Info. Mgmt. Co. v. Icart, 976 F. Supp. 149, 155 (E.D.N.Y. 1997).

Bonito Boats, Inc. v. Thunder Craft Boats, Inc. 489 U.S. 141, 109 S.Ct. 971 (U.S.Fla., 1989).

Bowers v. Baystate Technologies Inc., 320 F.3d 1317 (C.A.Fed. (Mass.), 2003).

Caspi v. Microsoft Network, L.L.C., 732 A.2d 528 (N.J.Super.A.D., 1999).

Comb v. PayPal Inc., 218 F.Supp.2d 1165 (N.D.Cal., 2002).

Commission of the European Communities (1999). *Proposal for a Directive of the European Parliament and of the Council on the Community Framework for Electronic Signatures.*

CompuServe, Inc. v. Patterson, 89 F.3d 1257 (C.A.6 (Ohio), 1996).

Corinthian Pharmaceutical Systems v. Lederle Labs, 724 F. Supp. 605 (S.D. Ind. 1989).

Digital Millennium Copyright Act framework Pub. L. No. 105-304, 112 Stat. 2860 (Oct. 28, 1998).

Evans, G. E., (1999). Opportunity costs of globalizing information licenses. *Fordham University Journal of Intellectual Property, Arts and Entertainment Law, 10*(1), 267.

Federal Trade Commission. (2001, June). *Report to Congress on The Electronic Signatures In Global And National Commerce Act: The consumer consent provision in Section 101(c)(1)(C)(ii).* Retrieved September 15, 2004, from http://www.ftc.gov/reports/#2001

Feist Publications v. Rural Telephone Service Co, 111 S.Ct. 1282 (U.S.Kan., 1991).

Forest v. Verizon Communications Inc. 2002 D.C. App. LEXIS 509.

Hill v. Gateway, Inc., 105 F.3d 1147 (C.A.7 (Ill.), 1997).

I Lan Systems v. Netscout Service Level Corp., 183 F.Supp.2d 328 (D.Mass., 2002).

I-Sys Inc. v. Softwares Inc., Civil No. 02-1951, 2004 WL 742082 (D. Minn. 2004).

Kewanee Oil Co. v. Bicron Corp. U. S. Supreme Court 416 U.S. 470, 94 S.Ct. 1879 (U.S. Ohio 1974).

M.A. Mortenson Co., Inc. v. Timberline Software Corp., 998 P.2d 305 (Wash., 2000).

Market Development Corp. v. Flame-Glo Ltd., 1990 WL 116319 (E.D. Pa. August 8, 1990).

National Association of Manufacturers. (n.d.). *Industry concerns about Final Article 2 Revisions.* Retrieved September 15, 2004, retrieved June 5, 2005 from http://www.nam.org/s_nam/doc1.asp?CID=200173&DID=223242

National Conference of Commissioners on Uniform State Laws. (2001a). *Drafts of Uniform and Model Acts: Uniform Commercial Code, Revision, Article 1.* Retrieved September 15, 2004, from http://www.law.upenn.edu/bll/ulc/ulc.htm

National Conference of Commissioners on Uniform State Laws. (2001b). *Uniform Computer Information Transactions Act (formerly Uniform Commercial Code Draft Article 2B).* Retrieved September 15, 2004, from http://www.law.upenn.edu/bll/ulc/ucita/ucita01.htm

National Conference of Commissioners on Uniform State Laws. (2002). *Drafts of Uniform and Model Acts: Uniform Commercial Code, Revision, Article 2.* Retrieved September 15, 2004, from http://www.law.upenn.edu/bll/ulc/ulc.htm

Nimmer, R. (1998). Breaking barriers: The relationship between contract and intellectual property law. *Berkeley Tech LJ, 13,* 827.

Organization for Economic Cooperation and Development (OECD). (1999). *Guidelines for consumer protection in the context of electronic commerce.* Retrieved September 15, 2004, from http://www1.oecd.org/publications/e-book/9300023E.PDF

Pollstar v. Gigmania Ltd., 170 F.Supp.2d. 974 (E.D. Cal. 2000)

ProCD v. Zeidenberg, 86 F.3d 1447 (C.A.7 (Wis.), 1996)

Register.com Inc. v. Verio Inc., 356 F.3d 393 (C.A.2 (N.Y.), 2004)

Reichman, J. R. (1999). Privately legislated intellectual property rights: Reconciling freedom of contract with public good uses of information. 147 U. Pa. L. Rev. 875.

Rosenfeld v. Zerneck, 776 N.Y.S.2d 458 (N.Y.Sup., 2004).

Shattuck v. Klotzbach, 2001 Mass. Super. LEXIS 642 (December 11, 2001).

Smedinghoff, T. J. (2002). *The legal requirements for creating secure and enforceable electronic transactions.* Retrieved September 15, 2004, from http://www.bakernet.com/ecommerce/etransactionsarticle.pdf

Specht v. Netscape Communications Corp., 150 F.Supp.2d 585 (S.D.N.Y., 2001), aff'd.–306 F.3d 17 (C.A. 2 (N.Y.) 2002).

State Farm Mutual Auto. Ins. Co v. Bockhorst, 453 F.2d 533 (C.A.10, 1972).

Ticketmaster Corp. v. Tickets.com, Inc., 2Fed.Appx. 741 (C.A.9 (Cal.) 2001).

U.S. v. Eisenberg, 807 F.2d 1446 (8th Cir. 1986)

U.S. v. Grande, 620 F.2d 1026 (4th Cir. 1980), cert. denied, 449 U.S. 830, 919 (1980).

United Nations Commission on International Trade Law (UNCITRAL). (1996). *Model law on electronic commerce.* Retrieved September 15, 2004, from http://www.uncitral.org/english/texts/electcom/ml-ecomm.htm

United Nations Commission on International Trade Law (UNCITRAL). (2002). *Preliminary draft convention on [international] contracts concluded or evidenced by data messages.* Retrieved September 15, 2004, from http://www.law.gov.au/agd/seclaw/electronicpaper.html

U.S. Department of Commerce. (2003). Information technology producing industries—Hopeful signs in 2003. *Digital Economy, 2003.* Retrieved September 15, 2004, from https://www.esa.doc.gov/reports/DE-Chap1.pdf

Vault Corp. v. Quaid Software Ltd., 847 F.2d 255, 261 (C.A. 5 (La.), 1988).

White House. (1997, July 1). *A framework for global electronic commerce.* Retrieved September 15, 2004, from http://www.technology.gov/digeconomy/framewrk.htm

Electronic Speech

Seth Finkelstein, Consulting Programmer, *SethF.com*

INTRODUCTION

The Internet is fundamentally a mechanism for communication. By lowering the costs of copying and distributing information, it created a revolution in electronic speech. That in turn led to a host of issues stemming from the new methods of reaching an audience. Suddenly, old equilibriums and economics between speaker and listener were disrupted. One famous aphorism stated, "The Net interprets censorship as damage, and routes around it." This was then rebutted by the question, "What if censorship is in the router?"

The conflict between social and technological constraints is a key part of the evolution of electronic speech. It is conceivable that speakers and listeners could route around censorship laws by using various electronic networks. However, a router, a device that connects different networks (facilitating speech), may contain within it technological censorship programs that do not permit certain types of speech to either be made or received. Thus, contrary to purely utopian or dystopian views, there is no inevitable outcome in terms of a freer or more constrained ability to speak or be heard.

These new speech issues can be viewed as aspects of information or signal processing or as previous problems in new contexts. The positive results of gains in speech ability have been matched by potentially negative effects stemming from those gains in speech ability.

SOCIAL SIGNAL PROCESSING

There is a saying, "If a tree falls in the forest, and nobody hears it, does it make a sound?" If someone writes an article, and nobody reads it, has the author communicated anything? Or, how does one get heard over the noise? The idea of free speech coexists with an understanding that usually there is no guarantee of listeners. Thus, there is an imbalance between those seeking to speak and those who wish to hear. This differential leads to specific patterns of modulating the exchange between writers and readers. By an analogy with the issues of electronic signal processing communications, this might be thought of as social signal processing, with comparable structural issues. Many vocabulary terms, such as broadcasting, channel, communication, filtering, noise, receiver, transmitter, and so on, have applicability in overlapping contexts.

Commons Models

The commons model is a common model of interaction, similar to the idea of a "speaker's corner" in a public park. In this configuration, every speaker communicates with every listener in a collective, many-to-many arrangement. The writers individually send their messages to a system that then by default distributes it to every other member of the system. In the simplest form, each member has equal access to every other member. Usenet newsgroups or open mailing lists follow this model: "Usenet is a worldwide distributed discussion system. It consists of a set of 'newsgroups' with names that are classified hierarchically by subject. 'Articles' or 'messages' are 'posted' to these newsgroups by people on computers with the appropriate software . . . [T]hese articles . . . are then broadcast to other interconnected computer systems via a wide variety of networks" (Spafford, 1993).

This system does not scale well as the number of writers increases. As more messages compete for the fixed amount of reading time available, the expected utility of each message often decreases. Moreover, a well-known hazard is that a few participants can engage in a protracted series of exchanges that generate objections from other members, as Nagel (1996) points out, "Discomfort with diversity (the number of messages increases dramatically; not every thread is fascinating to every reader; people start complaining about the signal-to-noise ratio; person 1 threatens to quit if *other* people don't limit discussion to person 1's pet topic; person 2 agrees with person 1; person 3 tells 1 and 2 to lighten up; more bandwidth is wasted complaining about off-topic threads than is used for the threads themselves; everyone gets annoyed)."

These stresses on the commons system lead to ad hoc methods of managing list conduct. Participants viewed as deviating from group norms may be admonished by others, with varying degrees of politeness and subsequent success (it can be said that personal attacks are a form of governance of open mailing lists). Readers are often advised to shun problematic writers by simply ignoring them or automatically deleting their messages via sorting software known as "killfiles" (Phillips, 1995).

However, these methods of speech management often fail, at least from the viewpoint of those practicing them. Personal attacks on recalcitrant writers may just not work. Not everyone wants to maintain killfiles or uses a message-reading system that supports such features. Moreover, messages may be distributed in a collected digest form, which is not amenable to killfiles as a solution.

This tragedy of the commons leads to a search for a more tightly controlled environment.

Moderator Models

In the moderated model of electronic speech, a few selected authorities exercise value judgments on the contributions. These individuals read every message submitted and perform an editorial function of selecting contributions for approval, possibly even adding additional explanatory material. Often the authority is a single person due to the proprietary nature of the group or list or the moderator's interest (McKeon, 1997).

> There are 280+ moderated groups in the 8 Usenet hierarchies, mostly in comp., soc., sci., and rec.; and about 80+ in alt.*

> Some parallel models for moderation are:

> - a refereed scientific journal;
> - publication with a small subscriber base and an unpaid editor;
> - restaurant with a polite but determined doorman.

This arrangement almost always produces results: the selected material is overall of much higher quality than that in the commons model. However, that higher quality comes at several costs. The editor may have notable biases and prejudices or may even use the position to engage in personal attacks, to which the target cannot reply to the same audience. Submitters may feel discouraged if they have devoted time to composing a message only to have it rejected.

There is typically no direct payment for the editor. So the return for the effort may only be from professional service (such as building a record for tenure committees), prestige, self-promotion, or influence. The time demands of sorting through the material can be burdensome. Delays in approving messages can make a fast-moving discussion impossible or result in messages being old news when finally distributed.

The scaling limit here is the number of messages that can be processed effectively by the selecting authority or authorities. To alleviate some of the workload, automated assistance has been developed to try to handle some of the most common cases programmatically. A notable example is the software program, Secure Team-based Usenet Moderation Program (STUMP). This software has such features as the ability to create a list of contributors who will have contributions immediately accepted, another list for immediate denial, and management of evaluation of the rest (Chudov, 2004). Yet, substantial human effort is still necessary.

Given the demands on a single person or even a small group of people, the editorial burdens have led to explorations of more elaborate ways to distribute the workload.

Distributed Models

A distributed model seeks to address the evaluation issues by spreading the necessary work among as large a group as possible. Web discussion forums, such as the sites http://slashdot.org/ or http://www.kuro5hin.org/, are popular examples of this model. These community sites have thousands of members, many of whom write small comments about an article. To select comments of greater value (according to varying definitions of value), there is a system of rating the comments, and the ratings work is spread among the site members themselves.

This distributed system can scale to numbers of comments previously unmanageable by earlier methods. However, the problems scale up as well. A highly rated comment may be popular, but not accurate, whereas a low-rated comment may be accurate but not popular. Methods are needed to prevent small groups from "gaming" the system. The site administrators themselves may put a thumb on the scales in the ratings, using their authority to override results of the group selection (Jobi, 2002). Even when unfair moderating is not taking place, lack of accountability in the process may lead to a perception of unfairness, or inversely, abusive moderating can be given a cloak of plausible deniability.

Engineering and tuning these distributed evaluation systems (as well as examining their often complex unintended consequences) are currently fertile areas of research, as Lampe and Resnick (2004) note:

> Closer analysis, however, revealed that it often takes a long time for especially good comments to be identified. We also found that incorrect moderations were often not reversed, and that later comments, comments not at top-level, and comments with low starting scores, did not get the same treatment from moderators as other comments did. These findings highlight tensions among timeliness, accuracy, limiting the influence of individual moderators, and minimizing the effort required of individual moderators. We believe any system of distributed moderation will eventually have to make tradeoffs among these goals.

Thus, the tradeoffs required in community moderation can subtly define the overall feel and utility of the community. It is important to distinguish between "reader-fair" versus "writer-fair" results. An outcome which is "reader-fair" is one where all highly rated comments are worth reading. An outcome which is "writer-fair" is one where all comments that are worth reading are highly rated. While a system which was perfectly writer fair would then be reader fair, it's possible to have an overall reader fair result along with many individual cases which are not writer fair. Reader fair globally is not the same as writer fair locally. A site's economic survival may depend on achieving a large measure of reader fairness, but individual contributors may be more concerned with writer fairness (especially for their own comments). Too many writer unfair outcomes would eventually produce reader unfairness. However, it may be entirely viable for a community to have a maltreated minority as long as there is a satisfied majority. In this way, distributed systems generate problems familiar to any analysis of social governance.

Power Laws

With the expansion of the Internet and the availability of simple Web site publishing tools, there has been a concomitant growth of small-scale electronic speech outlets–first e-mail, then mailing lists, then newsgroups, and then Web sites. As of this writing, much interest has been generated around Web-hosted chronologically updated pages that are updated frequently, known as *blogs* (from the word "Web-logs").

Initially, the rise of the Internet as a means of distribution of electronic speech was often greeted with great optimism because of its prospects for equality. "The world of computer communications, however, has turned out to be the great equalizer. Suddenly anyone can become a publisher, reporter, or editorialist. What's more, each of us has as good a chance of being heard as anyone else in the electronic community" (Godwin, 1993).

Yet, it is a fallacy to assume that production equals audience. The empirical experience has been virtually the opposite, as Perseus (2003) points out:

> Nanoaudiences are the logical outcome of continued growth in blogs. Assume for a moment that one day 100 million people regularly read blogs and that they each read 50 other peoples' blogs. That translates into 5 billion subscriptions (50 * 100 million). Now assume on that same day there are 20 million active bloggers. That translates into 250 readers per blog (5 billion/20 million)—far smaller audiences than any traditional one-to-many communication method. And this is just an average; in practice many blogs have no more than two dozen readers.

More simply, everyone cannot have a million readers. Just because of time constraints, there will only be available a very few high readership ecological niches. Or, more broadly, only a relatively small number of high-influence positions can exist, if influence is defined nontrivially.

The words "equality" or "democracy" have two different, somewhat contradictory meanings. They can signify that all participants have equal power ("one person, one vote"), or they each may have an abstractly equal chance of achieving vastly unequal power ("anyone can be President"). Electronic speech often promises the former in theory and delivers the latter in practice.

There are solid mathematical reasons for extreme inequalities. One extensively discussed phenomenon is the power-law distribution. Shirky (2003) writes, "In systems where many people are free to choose between many options, a small subset of the whole will get a disproportionate amount of traffic (or attention, or income), even if no members of the system actively work towards such an outcome. This has nothing to do with moral weakness, selling out, or any other psychological explanation. The very act of choosing, spread widely enough and freely enough, creates a power-law distribution."

Power-law distribution formalizes the pyramids of influence concept, in which there are a few powerful members at the top and many much less influential participants below. The counterintuitive nature of this result, of replicating the influence structures present in older media, often comes as a disappointment to almost everyone involved. Note, however, that there is some variation as to the magnitude of the effect within specialties: "NEC researchers discovered that the degree of 'rich get richer' or 'winners take all' behavior varies in different categories and may be significantly less than previously thought. A new model has been developed which can be used to predict and analyze competition and diversity in different communities on the Web" (Pennock, Flake, Lawrence, Glover, & Giles, 2002).

The gulf between initial estimation and the realities of implementation has an intriguing similarity to the difficulties of effective computational parallel processing. Ideally, if one processor can do one unit of work, N processors working in parallel should do N units of work. Yet, scaling the computational work is known to be extremely complex in practice because of coordination limits. Similarly, N voices of electronic speech often simply thrash at each other, producing nothing but the equivalent of process contention.

Whatever the gross equivalences, there will always be deep functional distinctions among one horse, a dozen dogs, a hundred cats, and a million ants.

INEQUALITY AND PUBLIC POLICY

The structural inequalities described above have profound implications for political speech, as Hindman, Tsioutsiouliklis, and Johnson (2003) point out:

> Claims about the Web and politics have commonly confounded two different things: retrievability and visibility, the large universe of pages that could theoretically be accessed versus those that citizens are most likely to encounter. While the governing assumption of much previous work has been that retrievability would translate inexorably into visibility, we cast doubt on that claim.... Online political communities on the Web thus seem to function as "winners take all" networks, a fact that would seem to have widespread implications for politics in the digital age.

Rather than democracy, the natural organization of Web communities in electronic speech apparently tends to a form of oligarchy. As some sites become more well known, they capture the attention of the population, becoming a common reference for the group. Less well-known sites are then less able to compete for share, receive less attention, and thus have (all other factors being equal) correspondingly diminishing influence. This effect inverts the naive conception of electronic speech as a level playing field. Instead, it has a few kings of the hill.

Journalist A. J. Liebling famously observed "Freedom of the press is guaranteed only to those who own one." And although electronic speech has naively been hailed as everyone owning a press, as has been noted above, inequality of audience can span a difference of many orders of magnitude: "it is clear that in some ways the Web functions quite similarly to traditional media. Yes, almost anyone can put up a political Web site. But our research suggests that this is usually the online equivalent of hosting a talk show on public access television at 3:30 in the morning" (Hindman et al., 2003).

If one assumes this inequality is at least worthy of examination, the question then arises as to potential methods of redress. The general issue of imbalances of distribution of communication ability has been addressed by various laws and court decisions. In the United States, the case *Miami Herald v. Tornillo* (1974) overturned a "right of reply" law applied to newspapers (FindLaw, 2004):

> The Court was unanimous in holding void under the First Amendment a state law that granted a political candidate a right to equal space to answer criticism and attacks on his record by a newspaper. Granting that the number of newspapers had declined over the years, that ownership had become concentrated, and that new entries were prohibitively expensive, the Court agreed with proponents of the law that the problem of newspaper responsibility was a great one. But press responsibility, while desirable, "is not mandated by the Constitution," while freedom is. The compulsion exerted by government on a newspaper to print that which it would not otherwise print, "a compulsion to publish that which "reason" tells them should not be published," runs afoul of the free press clause.

When discussing electronic speech, there is often confusion regarding legal ideas of regulation that apply to broadcast television or radio, based on the inaccurate lumping together of all media that have any association with electronic equipment. These legal ideas of representation include such concepts as the (obsolete) "fairness doctrine" or "indecency." When electronic speech is transmitted through wireless networks, there may be an attempt to invoke government control of the public airwaves. However, again in the United States, the Supreme Court concluded, in *Reno* v. *ACLU* (1997), there is "no basis for qualifying the level of First Amendment scrutiny that should be applied to this medium." That is, electronic speech is more like a print publication than a radio show.

Other countries have different approaches. As of the writing of this chapter, the Council of Europe (2004) has received extensive commentary on a draft recommendation addressing issues of "the right of reply in the new media environment." Principle 1 of this draft document states, "The right of reply, and in particular the principles of Resolution (74) 26, should apply not only to the press, radio and television, but also to professional on-line media."

An idea that new media will intrinsically cure inequality is merely a restatement of the hope of a technological solution to a social problem.

SPEECH-RESTRICTING ARCHITECTURES

The action of a large number of people who want to speak necessarily generates an opposite reaction from those who do not want them to be heard (see the chapter, Internet Censorship, in this *Handbook*). The battle between speakers and censors has profound implications for Internet architecture (Lessig, 1999).

One difficulty in this area is the overloading of the word "filter." This word has at least three different meanings:

1. Prohibition—An authority forbids another person to read the content.
2. Killfiling—The reader wishes not to read the content.
3. Personalization—The reader wants to affirmatively obtain selected content.

Confusion over these varying meanings can lead to mixing ideas primarily associated with one meaning with another. Prohibition of content assumes a willing reader attempting to seek out that material and an external directive to forbid it.

It should be emphasized that debates over the justifications for electronic speech restrictions need to distinguish between arguments over values and arguments over implications. What content a government can prohibit from its citizens is a statement of values. That the method of prohibition works equally well on any kind of content is a statement of implications. Moreover, if a method works for parents with regard to teenagers in America, it will certainly work for a government against citizens in China. Inversely, if the effects of electronic speech are such that citizens can escape the control of government in China, then teenagers will be able to avoid the control of parents in America.

Private Blacklists

The most common speech-restricting architecture is the compilation by a private entity of *blacklists* of prohibited sites and key words, or alternately *whitelists* of permitted sites. Although this practice is often termed "filtering," the possibility of confusion with other applications of the word makes the alternate, more precise term "censorware" a better choice for these programs. Moreover, a filter is associated with removing toxic material that the user does not wish to have. These speech restrictions pertain to a third party, an authority controlling what another person is permitted to read.

The essential mechanism of the restriction is conceptually simple (Finkelstein & Tien, 2001). Every time a reader wishes to connect to any electronic speech, the request is examined programmatically against the lists of sites and/or key words. The system may be configured in a manner that whatever is not explicitly permitted is forbidden (whitelisting) or whatever is not explicitly forbidden is permitted (blacklisting). Depending on whether or not the request is considered acceptable, the reader is then either allowed or prohibited from obtaining the content.

Given this framework, the checking of acceptable speech requests can be done at any level of detail. Entire sites can be uniformly prohibited, or the restrictions can be on partial portions of Web sites (directories) or specific items (file). Alternately, any content that has a particular pattern in its name can be prohibited (e.g.,).

Although the most common area of blacklisting is sexual material, the principle is general, and a product usually has a collection of blacklists, which cover various subjects that are to be forbidden. Some other typical forbidden topics are drug-oriented material or music-trading sites.

Virtually all private blacklists are encrypted and considered as highly secret intellectual property of the censorware company (the exceptions to this rule have a very small market share). Decrypting the blacklist can subject an investigator to a lawsuit on the grounds of violating copyright, trade secret, breach of shrinkwrap license contract, and more. The right to circumvent the encryption of censorware blacklists has also been one of the few exemptions granted, for a limited time, to the anti-circumvention prohibition of the Digital Millennium Copyright Act.

Government Blacklists

Given the simplicity and straightforwardness of the blacklist system, it translates naturally into an application of direct government censorship. In this implementation, the government simply commands all Internet service providers (ISPs) in the country to attempt to suppress the speech by disallowing network connections to any of the sites on the blacklist. In the case of undemocratic regimes, this is straightforward (Edelman & Zittrain, 2003).

However, for democratic countries, attempts at direct prohibition are problematic. In the United States, one contentious instance has been a Pennsylvania law where, according to the Center for Democracy and Technology (2003), "The law provides that the state Attorney General or any country district attorney can unilaterally apply to a local judge for an order declaring certain Internet content may be child pornography, and requiring any ISP serving Pennsylvania citizens to block the content."

In the United States, measures taken to implement such speech restrictions involve such issues of law as prior restraint and acceptable burdens to enforce such a law. Because some sites may share Internet protocol address locations with other sites (virtual hosting), denying access to a targeted site might also deny access to the speech of many innocent sites.

In the United Kingdom, the Internet Watch Foundation (IWF) has begun providing a small blacklist of various prohibited, highly illegal sites (IWF, 2004): "One of the services the IWF offers its members is access to a database of child abuse website URLs so they can help protect children and the public from inadvertent exposure to abusive images of children online. These URLS are for websites which contain child abuse images and are collated from the reports we receive via our [I]nternet hotline."

Other governments may try to follow this lead.

Government Classification Bureaus Applied to the Internet

In contrast to blacklists, a classification or labeling approach typically leads to proposing a speech-suppression architecture that is optimized to the complex needs of encoding government law and social customs. Such an approach relies on the existence of elaborate databases maintained either implicitly or explicitly by force of law and then may layer exemptions, special treatment, or elaborate joins on top of those databases. There is even a research area of specification languages devoted to expressing censorship policy, much like the computer language Fortran is devoted to mathematical calculations and Java to object-oriented modeling. For example, consider the following fragment of the PICSRules specification (Evans, Feather, Hopman, Presler-Marshal, & Resnick, 1997).

```
11 Policy (RejectByURL ("http://*www.badnews.com:*/*"
   "http://*@www.worsenews.com:*/*"
   "*://*@18.0.0.0!8:*/*"))
12 Policy (AcceptByURL "http://*rated-g.org/movies*")
```

...

11 Reject any HTTP URLs from the www.badnews.com and www.worsenews.com hosts, and all URLs that specify a host whose ip address has 18 as its first eight bits (these are the addresses corresponding to mit.edu).

12 Accept URLs whose domain names end in rated-g.org and whose pathnames begin "movies", but only if no username or port number is specified. For example "http://www.mystuff.rated-g.org/movies/hello" would be accepted, but neither "http://joe@www.mystuff.rated-g.org/movies/hello" nor "http://www.mystuff.rated-g.org:8009/movies/hello" would be accepted at this point in the rule processing (although they might be accepted by one of the subsequent policy statements).

Although such specifications were popular at the start of the growth of the Internet in the mid-1990s, maintaining the labeling database in any distributed form has proved to be less efficient than simple private blacklists. The primary interest in this area at the time of this writing seems to be in the European Union. These systems are theoretically a method for potentially resolving the cultural conflicts of member states over the problems of electronic speech and worldwide interconnection, in terms of the potential to subvert local censorship regulations.

Yet, even though they have not been implemented widely, such systems are already present in prototype form, complete with sample code for demonstration products. Too often the concept is naively reinvented by people unfamiliar with the state of the art as it has been developed. For example, the Internet Content Rating Association (ICRA) advocates a system with several rating descriptors, which are arguably both elaborate and confusing (ICRA, 2004):

> Nudity and sexual material, Erections and female genitals in details, Male genitals, Female genitals, Female breasts, Bare buttocks, Explicit sexual acts, Obscured or implied sexual acts, Visible sexual touching, Passionate kissing, None of the above.

> Context: this material . . . appears in an artistic context and is suitable for young children, appears in an educational context and is suitable for young children, appears in a medical context and is suitable for young children.

Note that the concerns of certain Islamic states, where censorship may be applied even to the clothed depiction of the female anatomy, are not addressed by this framework. Further, same-sex interactions and opposite-sex interactions seem to have the same rating, a decision that may be contentious.

Moreover, determining what is "passionate," "artistic," and "suitable for young children" is left as an exercise for the reader. Determining such ratings accurately for a Web site that publishes hundreds of pages every day, some perhaps generated by site members without editorial control, is left as another exercise for the reader.

Third-Party Sites

The extensive relaying and copying aspects of many electronic speech systems produce an architectural effect that has profound implications for attempts at control. It is not enough merely to suppress the speaker or to direct paths of speech distribution. All indirect distribution paths must be cut as well.

Ordinarily, little attention is given to the architecture of connection between a speaker and a listener. In public speaking, the connection is via sound waves, leading to the problem of the "Heckler's Veto." That is, physically, a heckler injects competing sound waves into the communications channel, creating channel noise that overrides the intended signal. For publication, censorship is designed to prevent the speaker from generating the message in the first place and then others from further spreading that message.

However, for networked speech, there are sites that act upon other sites. These third-party sites provide services on speech, such as archiving material from other sites ("The Internet Archive"), keeping a local copy that may be more accessible than the original (Google cache), or providing privacy and anonymity by stripping personally identifying details from the connection (Finkelstein, 2002). By providing these services, these sites thus constitute a loophole in any system of speech suppression. That is, a reader might be able to obtain prohibited content by connecting to one of these sites and using it as a relay to reach the contraband content. Even scanning the packets at the reader's point of origin might not help, as the connection could be encrypted. Mere compression of content in transport, often done for efficiency as opposed to secrecy, can frustrate packet monitoring. This issue has

now been acknowledged by various censorware companies themselves (N2H2, 2003).

> Loopholes

> Sites filtered because they open a loophole that can be exploited to access pages which would otherwise be filtered out from your service. Unless this category is selected, the system's Internet Content Filtering protection can be compromised.

> Examples:
> http://www.kaza.com
> www.triangleboy.com
> http://www.google.com/search?q=cache

In particular, the need to prohibit access to privacy and anonymity sites sets up a profound conflict between social expectations which are common, at least in Western society, and requirements of law enforcement within the system. While there are many contexts where a person is made aware that his or her actions may be subject to monitoring by authorities, it is yet a further step to prohibit conduct which might impede that monitoring.

SPEECH-RESTRICTION THEORIES: CONTROL RIGHTS VERSUS TOXIC MATERIAL

Participants in debates about the architectural restriction of electronic speech sometimes approach the topic using different conceptual frameworks. Unexamined incompatibilities in the theoretical grounding of the restrictions can lead to significant problems with their implications. For example, lawyers and policy analysts are often concerned with the right of control in an environment and determining the chain of authority via control of property:

> The burden should be on the filterer to justify the denial of another person's access. The most plausible justifications for restricting access are that the third party owns the computer or that the third party has a relation of legitimate authority over the user. For privately-owned computers, the brute fact of ownership may often be a good enough reason, although a relation of legitimate authority will often also be present. Thus parents may restrict their children's use of their computers. . . . Private employers may restrict employees' use based on ownership of the computer and legitimate relations of authority and workplace control. Nevertheless, restricting employee access may involve technological surveillance and invasions of privacy. These are separate questions that must not be overlooked (Balkin, Noveck, & Roosevelt, 1999).

So the focus here may be said to be control rights. However, discussing the issue of parents restricting their children in terms of relationship or computer ownership can obscure the possible rationale used by the parents themselves. In a competing framework, the primary considerations are potential exposure to speech that is regarded as harmful and its conjectured negative effects. In this system, the focus may be said to be on toxic material. These theories can be seen, for example, in one court case where a mother sued a public library in an attempt to force it to restrict the speech available on its computers: "Parents in the community generally do not know that the library allows children to view obscene and pornographic material on library computers and believe that the library is a "safe" place where children will not be harmed by library resources.... Children such as Brandon P. who view obscenity and pornography on the library's computers can and have sustained emotional and psychological damage in addition to damage to their nervous systems. It is highly likely that such damage will occur given the library's policy" (Millen, *Kathleen R. v. City of Livermore*, 1998).

According to this viewpoint, the harmful result would presumptively be the same no matter who owned the computer. Indeed, an implication here is that the untoward effect would be identical if the material was viewed as a side effect of someone else obtaining it, even if that other reader had a legal right to acquire it:

> How I train my children and what moral values I impart to them doesn't do much good if they're simply walking by a computer in the reference area while an adult male is accessing hard-core pornography, which has been a very common occurrence at our library. What gives the library or anyone else that right, especially in a public institution, to take away the innocence of my child? We get frequent phone calls from distraught parents ... who are being responsible parents with their children in the library and suddenly being exposed to the most vile material (Thornburgh & Lin, 2002).

Alternately, the presumed toxicity of the speech can be deemed a type of environmental effect, a kind of pollution, where the influence is considered a civil rights violation. One library's policy viewed the issue of restriction of speech in terms of sexual harassment (Loudoun County Public Library, 1997):

> Title VII of the Civil Rights Act prohibits sex discrimination. Library pornography can create a sexually-hostile environment for patrons or staff. Pornographic internet displays may intimidate patrons or staff, denying them equal access to public facilities. Such displays would transform the library environment from one of reading and scholarship to one which invites unwelcome sexual advances and sexual harassment. Permitting pornographic displays may constitute unlawful sex discrimination in violation of Title VII of the Civil Rights Act. This policy seeks to prevent internet sexual harassment.

Note that this rationale has no factor regarding the age of the reader. That is, minors and adults are not differentiated in terms of basis for the restriction.

Thus, for best results, policy debate participants should carefully examine the ideology they are using in their own approaches and be aware of possible conflicts with those who hold other theories. A parent who believes the toxic material theory is unlikely to be sympathetic to a lawyer's argument about the limits of government authority (under the First Amendment of the U.S. Constitution) to restrict speech in a public library. On the other hand, civil libertarians, who try to accommodate public concern about children and sexual material by focusing on speech restrictions that are permissible at home under the control rights theory, could find their conceded restrictions extended far past the proposed initial domain when government authorities focus on the material itself. These are fundamental differences in viewpoint that are not amenable to simple resolution.

UNINTENDED CONSEQUENCES

Given the expansive reach of electronic speech, undesired effects that once were limited to wreaking a small amount of possible damage now have much greater possible effects. Negative results from hostile use and archiving of one's speech are well known throughout history. However, the increased potential for positive applications comes with a similar gain in the potential for negative applications.

Search Engine

The ability to easily research decades-old statements, formerly a problem mostly for long-term politicians and such, has been democratized. That is, although opposition research previously required significant expense and so limited the application to targets worth that cost, the commodification of information has greatly lowered the threshold for performing an investigation. With large databases of indexed writing, especially of the small-scale electronic publishing discussed earlier, comes the ability to readily locate perhaps embarrassing or untoward content created by a person. As one old cartoon depicted it (Farley, 1996), "Suddenly, just as Paul was about to clinch the job interview, he received a visit from the Ghost of Usenet Postings Past."

As the amount of available speech increases, the applications of a search become more widespread. Romantic dates, academic applications, business partners can be cheaply, and perhaps unreliably, researched in this manner. Often this is termed "Googling" a person, after the most popular way of conducting this research, with the Google search engine. Such searches have become a matter of ethical debate:

> The Internet is transforming the idea of privacy. The formerly clear distinction between public and private information is no longer either/or but more or less. While the price of a neighbor's condo may be a matter of public record, it's a very different kind of public if it's posted on the Internet than if it's stored in a dusty filing room open only during business hours. This distinction does not concern the information itself but the

ease of retrieving it.... With this change comes a paradoxical ethical shift where laziness, or limiting yourself to insouciant Googling, is more honorable than perseverance, as in hauling yourself down to the municipal archives, say (Cohen, 2002).

As noted, the very ease with which research can be accomplished requires rethinking the ethics to be applied to it.

E-mail Embarrassment

Complementing the issues of being able to pull speech from archives is the speech hazard that exists in which speech that was not intended to be distributed extensively can be disseminated widely to an audience far beyond expectations. The most well-known examples are those that have a sexual appeal. The http://snopes.com Urban Legends site has verified several examples of this effect:

> Don't send messages describing your sexual exploits from your employer's e-mail system (especially if you work for a staid professional firm), no matter how much you trust the recipients. One invocation of the 'forward' command by any of the recipients is all it takes to start a chain reaction that will send your e-mail on its way to thousands of e-voyeurs, land your name (accompanied by an embarrassingly graphic story) in the newspapers, and possibly get you fired from your job (Mikkelson & Mikkelson, 2001).

Of course, the forwarding of interesting documents has occurred since copying existed. What is notable is the increased ease of the communication. The overall effect is that items that would otherwise be of minor interest can achieve more renown. In one case, a long letter from a journalist describing a World Economic Forum conference eventually appeared on a popular community discussion site. This conflicts with some social expectations that have been developed previously, leading to what has been called "accidental privacy spills":

> In crudely mechanistic terms, going from paper to bits lowers the cost of copying and forwarding. It takes a pretty important letter to be worth the bother of Xeroxing, stamping, and mailing, but even an infinitesimally small benefit is worth the minimal cost of clicking on the forward button and typing in a few addresses. People who wouldn't have forwarded a letter will forward an email—and they'll forward it to more people (Grimmelmann, 2003).

So practical expectations of privacy, which formerly existed from different thresholds of information flow, now need to be reconsidered.

Spam

Spam (unsolicited bulk e-mail) is an extensive topic in itself (see the *Handbook* chapter, Spam and the Legal

Counter Attacks). However, in some ways spam is an electronic speech problem and a classic unintended consequence. If electronic speech becomes very cheap, then there is an economic incentive to indulge in mass solicitations. The financial basis is that by shifting the costs of processing the solicitation onto the receiver, a mass of unwilling listeners can be ignored and profit made from a very few interested targets. From this perspective, the problem of spam is created because it is too easy to speak to other people, spawning electronic sales efforts that are the equivalent of doorbell-ringing of whole cities at once.

This mass solicitation then creates an interest in the idea of a right NOT to listen or in what permissions, implicit or explicit, must be present before an attempt to contact another person is acceptable (especially to make a sales pitch). The idea of being able to speak by default, unless told otherwise, in all contexts, quickly yields an unworkable implication of being required to opt out of an endless stream of individual product advertisements. Yet, requiring too strict a permission system risks criminalizing casual, though arguably commercial, contacts.

Anti-spam efforts can become electronic speech issues in and of themselves. One common system is to create a blacklist of Internet addresses, which might be of addresses that send spam, or Web sites devoted to products advertised in spam, or much more aggressively, sites that are deemed to be "spam-support" under some criteria. Even further, some blacklists go into the realm of a secondary boycott, containing addresses that have no connection to spamming whatsoever, except that they share ISP service with an ISP that has spammers. Note that the extensive blacklisting in this secondary boycott case differs from overbroad censorware blacklisting, in that the expansive spam blacklisting is not an error, but a deliberate and intentional pressure tactic.

The spam blacklists efforts are often defended as electronic speech themselves, as an opinion for the purposes of association. For example, one spam blacklist organization, the Spam Prevention Early Warning System (SPEWS), compares itself to the *Consumer Reports* magazine (SPEWS, 2004).

Q10: Isn't SPEWS censorship?

A10: No, SPEWS is a list of areas of the Internet that some people do not wish to communicate with. Think of it as one group's *Consumer Reports* review of portions of the billions of Internet addresses. These are the ones SPEWS members have a poor opinion of. SPEWS is not anti-commerce and fully supports the USA's First Amendment and other nations' free speech protections. In fact, the USA's Supreme Court agrees with the SPEWS view. The creators of SPEWS are its main users and who it was designed for, if others decide to also use its data, they are exercising their own rights. No one is forced to use SPEWS.

In this framework, the argument regarding the use of the blacklist is over issues of causality and responsibility of speech. After all, in the case of the crime of blackmail, a blackmailer is only providing information to the community, and ideally the information used for the blackmail is completely truthful. All other community members who use the data provided by the blackmailer are then exercising their own rights. The moral dispute is not resolvable by an appeal to speech rights.

CONCLUSION

Many of the issues arising from electronic speech are generated by the effects of more efficient information exchanges. However, this gain is independent of the assumed social value of the speech. A change that spreads politics also spreads pornography. An improved ability to research product reviews goes hand in hand with an improved ability to research people's history. An inexpensive way to connect with long-lost relatives is also a cheap way for many new best friends to send solicitations. The copyright status of any particular message is generally completely irrelevant to its technical ease of propagation.

Moreover, increasing speech production, while listening ability remains relatively unchanged, causes a need for techniques to better allocate the finite span of attention. This then creates new environments for monopolization and marginalization of speech distribution. It's all a matter of implications, rather than values. The bits don't know why they shouldn't flow.

GLOSSARY

Blacklist A list of items intended to be stigmatized or marginalized.

Blog A frequently updated, reverse-chronologically ordered set of Web pages, often written by one person (though it can be a group effort). Also termed Weblog or Web-log.

Censorware Software designed and optimized for use by an authority to prevent another person from sending or receiving information.

Moderation A system for selecting among speech based on imputed value.

Power Law Also known as Zipfian distribution, an arrangement where the occurrence of each element in a ranking of elements falls off with an exponential frequency.

Spam Unsolicited bulk mail, typically commercial in nature.

CROSS REFERENCES

See *Internet Censorship; Legal, Social and Ethical Issues of the Internet; Privacy Law and the Internet; Spam and the Legal Counter Attacks.*

REFERENCES

Balkin, J., Noveck, B., & Roosevelt, K. (1999, September 15). *Filtering the Internet: A best practices model*. Retrieved September 6, 2004, from http://www.copacommission.org/papers/yale-isp.pdf

Center for Democracy and Technology. (2003, February). *The Pennsylvania ISP Liability Law: An unconstitutional prior restraint and a threat to the stability of the Internet*. Retrieved September 6, 2004, from http://www.cdt.org/speech/pennwebblock/030200pennreport.pdf

Chudov, Igor (2004). *STUMP Secure Team-based Usenet Moderation Program*. Retrieved September 6, 2004, from http://www.algebra.com/~ichudov/stump/

Cohen, R. (2002, December 15). The Ethicist : Is Googling O.K.? *The New York Times*. Retrieved September 6, 2004, from http://www.nytimes.com/2002/12/15/magazine/15ETHICIST.html

Council of Europe. (2004, January 21). *Compilation of comments on the draft recommendation on the right of reply in the new media environment* (MM-S-OD (2003)011 rev). Retrieved September 6, 2004, from http://www.coe.int/t/e/human_rights/media/7_links/MM-S-OD(2003)011rev%20E%20Right%20of%20reply.asp

Edelman, B., & Zittrain, J. (2003, March 20). *Empirical analysis of Internet filtering in China*. Retrieved September 6, 2004, from http://cyber.law.harvard.edu/filtering/china/

Evans, C., Feather, C., Hopman, A., Presler-Marshal, M., & Resnick, P. (1997, December 29). *PICSRules 1.1: W3C recommendation* (REC-PICSRules-971229). Retrieved September 6, 2004, from http://www.w3.org/TR/REC-PICSRules

Farley, D. (1996, January 24). *Doctor fun*. Retrieved September 6, 2004, from http://www.ibiblio.org/Dave/Dr-Fun/df9601/df960124.jpg

FindLaw. (n.d.). *Governmental regulation of communications industries*. Retrieved September 6, 2004, from http://caselaw.lp.findlaw.com/data/constitution/amendment01/17.html#7

Finkelstein, S. (2002, November). *BESS's Secret LOOPHOLE (censorware vs. privacy & anonymity)*. Retrieved September 6, 2004, from http://sethf.com/anticensorware/bess/loophole.php

Finkelstein, S., & Lee, T. (2001). *Blacklisting bytes*. Retrieved September 6, 2004, from http://www.eff.org/Censorship/Censorware/20010306_eff_nrc_paper1.html

Godwin, M. (1993). *A new frontier for freedom of expression*. Retrieved September 6, 2004, from http://www.cpsr.org/conferences/cfp93/godwin.html

Grimmelmann, J. (2003, February 19). *Accidental privacy spills: Musings on privacy, democracy, and the Internet*. Retrieved September 6, 2004, from http://research.yale.edu/lawmeme/modules.php?name=News&file=article&sid=938

Hindman, M., Tsioutsiouliklis, K., & Johnson, J. (2003, July 28). *"Googlearchy": How a few heavily-linked sites dominate politics on the Web*. Retrieved September 6, 2004, from http://www.princeton.edu/~mhindman/googlearchy–hindman.pdf

Internet Content Rating Association (2004). *The ICRA vocabulary and definitions*. Retrieved September 6, 2004, from http://www.icra.org/vocabulary/

Internet Watch Foundation. (2004, June 7). *IWF child abuse website database—BT project*. Retrieved September 6, 2004, from http://www.iwf.org.uk/media/news.archive-2004.39.htm

Jobi (2002, January 18). *Trouble over At slashdot*. Retrieved September 6, 2004, from http://www.kuro5hin.org/story/2002/1/17/21155/1564

Lampe, C., & Resnick, P. (2004). *Slash(dot) and burn: Distributed moderation in a large online conversation space*. Retrieved September 6, 2004, from http://www. si.umich.edu/%7Epresnick/papers/chi04/index.html

Lessig, L. (1999). *Code and other laws of cyberspace*. New York: Basic Books.

Loudoun County Public Library (1997, October 20). *Policy on Internet sexual harassment*. Retrieved September 6, 2004, from http://www.techlawjournal.com /courts/loudon/71020pol.htm

McKeon, D. (1997, March 11). *Moderated newsgroups FAQ*. Retrieved September 6, 2004, from http://www. faqs.org/faqs/usenet/moderated-ng-faq/

Miami Herald Pub. Co. v. Tornillo, 418 U.S. 241 (1974). Retrieved September 6, 2004, from http://caselaw.lp. findlaw.com/scripts/getcase.pl?court=US&vol=418& invol=241

Mikkelson, B., & Mikkelson, D. P. (2001, May 24). *Urban legends reference pages: Risqui business (Chung King)*. Retrieved September 6, 2004, from http://www. snopes.com/risque/tattled/chung.htm

Millen, M. (1998, November 3). *First amended complaint for injunctive relief*. Kathleen R. v. City of Livermore, Case No. V-015266-4. (2001). Retrieved September 6, 2004, from http://www.techlawjournal.com/courts/ kathleenr/19981103.htm

N2H2. (2003, April 16). *Filtering categories list*. Retrieved from http://web.archive.org/web/20030416154546/ http://www.n2h2.com/products/categories.php

Nagel, K. (1996, May). *The natural life cycle of mailing lists*. Retrieved September 6, 2004, from http://www. psicopolis.com/psicopedia/Psychology%20of%20 Cyberspace/psycyber/lifelist.html

Pennock, P., Flake, G., Lawrence, S., Glover, E., & Giles C. (2002, April). Winners don't take all: Characterizing the competition for links on the web. *Proceedings of the National Academy of Sciences, 99*(8), 5207–5211.

Perseus (2003). *The blogging iceberg*. Retrieved September 6, 2004, from http://www.perseus.com/blogsurvey/ thebloggingiceberg.html

Phillips, L. (1995, October 21). *rn KILL file FAQ*. Retrieved September 6, 2004, from http://www. faqs.org/faqs/killfile-faq/

Reno v. ACLU, 521 US 844 (1997). Retrieved September 6, 2004, from http://laws.findlaw.com/US/000/96- 511.html

Shirky, C. (2003, February 8). *Power laws, Weblogs, and inequality*. Retrieved September 6, 2004, from http:// www.shirky.com/writings/powerlaw_weblog.html

Spafford, G. (1993). *What is Usenet?* Retrieved September 6, 2004, from http://www.faqs.org/faqs/usenet/what- is/part1/

SPEWS (2004). *Frequently asked questions, comments and answers*. Retrieved September 6, 2004, from http:// www.spews.org/faq.html

Thornburgh, D., & Lin, H. S. (2002). *Youth, pornography, and the Internet*. Washington, DC: National Research Council.

Software Piracy

Robert K. Moniot, *Fordham University*

INTRODUCTION

Paper tape, floppy disk, CD-ROM, and now the Internet: whatever the medium in which software has been provided as technology has progressed, pirates have found ways to copy it illicitly. The software industry regards piracy as a major problem. In recent years, an estimated 35% of all copies of packaged PC software applications installed worldwide were pirated, having a retail value of some US $30 billion annually. If all software categories were included, this total would be even larger. Illicit copying of software has existed for a long time, and the new modes of copying enabled by the Internet have made it much harder for the software industry to combat it.

MODES OF SOFTWARE PIRACY

Software piracy is any copying of software in contravention of its license. One of the biggest obstacles to reducing piracy is the widespread ignorance of what actions constitute piracy. Here are some ways that piracy can occur:

- downloading proprietary software from an unauthorized Internet bulletin board or Web site or directly from another user via a peer-to-peer file-sharing program
- purchasing counterfeit software in a store or at an Internet Web site or auction
- borrowing the medium containing an application purchased by an employer for use at one's place of work and installing it on a personal computer at home
- borrowing a program from a friend, co-worker, or a library and installing it on one's own computer
- selling or giving away an old version of a program after receiving an upgrade
- leaving an installed program on an old computer after installing it on a new computer without purchasing a new copy of the program
- installing more copies of a program on the computers in an enterprise than the license allows or installing it on a server for use over a local area network if this is not permitted by the license

Note that it is always permissible to make a copy of software for backup or archival purposes, but any such copy must be destroyed if the user no longer can legitimately use the program. In addition, users may sell or give away programs they legitimately own to someone else, provided they do not retain their copies. For instance, users can leave installed software on old machines that they sell or give away if they purchase new computers with new software preinstalled.

The term "piracy" has long been used to mean acts of infringement of copyright. Thus, it was natural to adopt the term to include the illicit copying of software, even before the application of copyright law to software was clarified fully. However, piracy is a broad term encompassing many diverse forms of infringement, only some of which are listed above. Each of these forms has its own legal and ethical ramifications, as well as distinct perceptions by its practitioners. One important distinction is between copying for private use only or end-user piracy, and copying for sale. Many people consider copying for personal use to be either acceptable or having only minor ethical significance, whereas most recognize copying for sale as both unethical and illegal. Another distinction is between small-scale and large-scale piracy. Although each act of small-scale piracy is relatively minor, the aggregate effect is quite large. In fact, small-scale copying for personal or corporate use is said to be the most widespread form in practice, accounting for over half the total value of pirated software (Software and Information Industry Association, 2000). The growth of the Internet as a medium for exchange of software has greatly facilitated this form of piracy.

End-User Piracy

Small-scale piracy mainly takes the form of *softlifting*, which means unauthorized copying by individuals for their own personal use. Softlifting can be done in a wide variety of ways. Probably the most common method is to borrow the installation media from a friend or co-worker. Or instead of borrowing the original media, one might obtain an unauthorized or "bootleg" copy. Sharing of software over the Internet is also common. Before the advent of the World Wide Web, individuals often posted software on Usenet newsgroups or on bulletin board systems. Today, there are thousands of Web sites that post "warez," contraband software, for download. More recently, peer-to-peer systems have been developed that allow individuals to share software with each other directly.

Renting software and not uninstalling it after use was once a fairly common mode of softlifting. For this reason, the unauthorized renting of software was made illegal in the United States in 1990. Web sites offering software rental can still be found on the Internet, but it does not seem that this is a prevalent mode of softlifting today. The law permits libraries to lend software, provided that the package contains a clear copyright notice. Quite likely these loans are often used for softlifting.

Closely related to softlifting is *softloading* or the installation of a legitimately purchased program onto more machines than for which the software is licensed. It can also involve the installation of the software onto a server for use by multiple client machines in a local area network. Softloading usually occurs in a corporate setting, which can be a business, a nonprofit institution such as a university or hospital, or a government agency. It can occur inadvertently, if the information technology staff does not keep proper records of licenses and the number of installed copies of each software application.

Commercial Piracy

Bootlegging is the reproduction of pirated software for sale. Frequently this software is a cracked version of a commercial product, but it may also be an illicit duplicate of a legitimately acquired copy. Bootlegging is called counterfeiting if it is done in such a way as to make the product appear to be authentic, so that it can be sold for a price that is comparable to the normal retail price. Counterfeiters take care to duplicate the appearance of the media, the packaging, and even the documentation as closely as possible. In some cases, the purchaser may be unaware that the product is not genuine and will be unpleasantly surprised to find it is not entitled to support, such as upgrades from the manufacturer. Or there may be telltale indications that the software is not legitimate, such as poorly reproduced artwork, misplaced logos, misspellings, or a missing authenticity hologram. In other cases, the bootleggers make no attempt to conceal the pirated status of the product, and it is sold for an extremely low price. Often, a number of bootleg applications with a market value of hundreds of dollars are bundled together on a single CD that may sell for $20 or less.

Bootlegging is the easiest form of piracy for software producers to combat, provided there is support from the authorities in the host country. This is because bootlegging resembles most closely traditional forms of copyright or patent infringement, for which legal remedies are well established. Furthermore, the offender is often identified readily, and a lawsuit is likely to yield a substantial return in the form of damages and penalties. However, it must be recognized that in many countries, especially in Eastern Europe and Asia, enforcement is lax and bootleggers often sell their wares quite openly.

Original equipment manufacturers (OEMs) produce personal computers that are typically sold fully loaded with an operating system and a suite of applications. The OEMs typically enter into licensing agreements with the software producers to authorize the installation of this software. However, OEMs or hardware dealers sometimes illegally load software onto more machines than authorized, or they may load software that was not included in the license agreement as a way of making the computers more attractive for sale. This practice is called *hard-disk loading*. *Unbundling* is the sale of OEM-version software items separately from the computer system for which they are authorized. *Mischanneling* is the diversion of specially discounted software, intended for academic institutions, government agencies, and other high-volume customers, for sale to others who do not qualify for these discounts.

MOTIVATIONS FOR SOFTWARE PIRACY

Why does an individual choose to pirate software? Conversely, if obtaining an illicit copy of a software application is so easy and cheap, why does anyone purchase the legitimate article? Probably the reader can think of several likely motivations on either side, but a number of studies have been done in an effort to provide well-founded answers to these questions (see, for instance, Cheng, Sims, & Teegen, 1997; Peace, Galletta, & Thong, 2003; Simpson, Banerjee, & Simpson, 1994; Taylor & Shim, 1993). These studies are not always directly comparable, because they take different approaches and use different models of softlifting attitudes and intentions. They also vary in the ways they validate the measures used and control for various biases. Despite these differences in methodology, the results of these studies are generally consistent, supporting their overall validity.

Of course, studies of this nature inevitably have some limitations. For instance, most are based on surveys of students and business executives. Although these groups are important in the softlifting scene, they may not be representative of softlifters generally. In addition, the studies do not measure piracy activity directly. Rather, they measure perceptions and motivations—subjective factors that nonetheless should be significant predictors of behavior. It is also possible that some of the reasons given by the survey participants may be rationalizations, rather than true motives. So long as these limitations are kept in mind when interpreting the results, the studies can still provide useful guidance toward identifying measures that could affect softlifting behavior.

Probably the most important reasons for softlifting identified by these studies are economic: the software is seen as overpriced, or the individuals cannot afford it. Another commonly given reason is the desire to try out the software before buying it or to use it for only a short time. Reasons for purchasing software, in contrast, include the perception that it will be useful for schoolwork or on the job, and the expectation that it will be used frequently. Another motive for purchasing is the availability of user manuals and technical support. A significant finding of the studies is that the perception of softlifting as unethical, illegal, or against school or company policy has little effect on the decision to softlift. However, a perception that soft-lifting is acceptable and prevalent among one's peers increases the likelihood of softlifting.

Other studies have tried to identify cultural and socioeconomic indicators that are predictors of software piracy rates (see, for instance, Depken & Simmons, 2004; Husted, 2000; Marron & Steel, 2000; Ronkainen & Guerrero-Cusumano, 2001). These studies have the advantage of using software industry estimates of piracy rates, rather than relying on self-reporting in surveys, which is not as reliable an indicator of actual behavior. However, these studies perforce use data at the level of whole nations and so necessarily average out the differences among individuals or among regions within a given country. It should be noted that the piracy data on which these studies are based include only business software. However, because there is probably a strong correlation between business and personal copying of software in each country, the results should be applicable to rates of individual softlifting as well. These studies found that lower piracy rates are associated with higher levels of economic development (per capita gross domestic product [GDP] or income), with greater disparities in income within a country (implying a smaller middle class), and with stronger institutions to enforce contracts and protect property from expropriation. They also found that individualist cultures—those that value individual rights and ownership—have lower piracy rates than more collectivist ones that put greater value on mutual help and sharing.

These results are reasonable. Higher levels of economic development mean that individuals and businesses are more able to pay for software. In countries with greater income inequalities, the lower classes are unable or barely able to afford computers at all, and so most technology purchasing is done by the wealthy who can easily afford to pay for it. It is the members of the middle class, often struggling to make ends meet, who are the most likely to seek to cut costs by pirating software.

Alternative Views of Softlifting

Economic factors alone are not able to explain the disparities among nations with respect to the acceptability of unauthorized copying (Depken & Simmons, 2004; Kini, Ramakrishna, & Vijayaraman, 2004). For instance, Hong Kong's per capita GDP is one of the highest in the world, yet its software piracy rate is nearly twice that of Switzerland. Strong institutional protection of property and contract rights is primarily a feature of Western cultures that emphasize individualism and competition. Other cultures, particularly those of southern and eastern Asia, have a different tradition that deemphasizes rights of individual ownership in favor of the duties of cooperation and sharing of the fruits of one's creativity for the benefit of society. Anti-American sentiment or local nationalism could also be significant factors favoring piracy in some countries.

The reader should keep in mind that, although the Western paradigm of copyright protection is the basis for the laws governing the dissemination of most software, such protection is a particular legal framework corresponding to a particular era and society and is not a universal ethical norm. The use of the term "piracy" in this chapter should not be taken to imply that all unauthorized copying is unethical or that those who practice it are behaving immorally. In many countries, the imposition of copyright protection for software is seen as an effort by the West to strengthen and maintain its dominance in technology. Even in countries where such protection is provided by law, this legal framework often must compete in the moral sphere with strongly held traditional values of community and solidarity, which may lead individuals to judge that it is ethical to copy software in some circumstances.

Hackers and Crackers

There is another category of individuals whose motivations need to be examined: the *warez doodz*. In the typology of Loper (2000), these are hackers who specialize in trading pirated software. Like other types of hackers, they are fascinated with learning the inner workings of software systems and reject conventional norms regarding ownership of intellectual property when it is in electronic form. Some warez doodz are "crackers," highly skilled programmers who can analyze and neutralize sophisticated software copy protection mechanisms. Many are relatively unskilled and are limited to following the instructions of others to crack or distribute software. Some warez doodz engage in this activity for profit, but very often they do not, nor do they need or use the software themselves. Instead, they are motivated by the intellectual challenge involved, the feeling of power and control, and the desire to enhance their reputation (McCandless, 1997). Rehn (2004) has pointed out the similarities between the "warez scene" and classical gift economies or potlatch rituals, phenomena that are normally associated only with archaic communities.

Implications of the Studies

The findings of all the studies cited above carry some implications for software publishers' efforts to reduce the rates of software piracy. First, it seems that educational programs aimed at increasing individuals' awareness of the illegality of softlifting or persuading them to regard it as unethical are of only limited effectiveness. The studies show, perhaps surprisingly, that simple awareness of the illicitness of softlifting has little effect on behavior. Technical copy protection mechanisms (discussed in a later section) can deter casual copying, but cannot stop all piracy. They are inevitably defeated by clever crackers who enjoy the challenge they present. In contrast, perceived consequences, in terms of benefits as well as penalties, are important factors in most individuals' decisions whether or not to softlift. The studies indicate that increasing the likelihood of being caught and punished would deter softlifters. However, it is impractical to prosecute individual softlifters, and in addition, an overly aggressive enforcement program could backfire by creating an adverse public reaction.

Hence, although a gently applied "stick" consisting of user education and relatively unobtrusive technical copy-protection measures, such as product activation, can be of some use, software publishers will obtain more effective results with a "carrot" by making their products more affordable through attractive pricing options (perhaps charging different prices for different categories of customers) while enhancing the perceived value of their products by providing user manuals, technical support, and inexpensive upgrades. The studies cited above show that, if individuals value the software for its usefulness and value the support provided by the vendor, they will be more willing to pay for it. In fact, many software makers are already using some or all of these options to good effect.

The validity of these arguments is confirmed by the observation that the Linux operating system and its accompanying utility and application software from the GNU organization and elsewhere are sold successfully by a number of vendors, even though the software is all legally obtainable for free over the Internet. These vendors succeed in charging money for the software because they provide valuable support services, including documentation and help lines. Firms that depend on computer systems for their daily operations willingly pay for such support because they want to have someone to turn to for help when something fails.

Organizations that Combat Software Piracy

There are two main trade organizations that represent the software industry in its efforts to counter the illicit traffic in software. The Business Software Alliance (BSA; http://www.bsa.org) is an international organization representing major software and e-commerce developers. Its membership includes such flagship companies as Microsoft, Apple, and Adobe. Founded in 1988, its mission is to educate computer users about copyrights, to lobby for intellectual property legislation, and to combat software piracy. The Software and Information Industry Association (SIIA; http://www.siia.net) is a coalition of software and electronic content producers. It was formed in 1999 from the merger of the Software Publishers Association (SPA; founded in 1984) and the Information Industry Association (IIA). Its membership includes some members of BSA, but also includes many smaller software and information technology companies. Its mission is to promote the interests of the software and digital information industry, to provide knowledge resources to member companies, and to fight software piracy. SIIA still uses the name SPA for its anti-piracy arm.

SCOPE AND IMPACT OF PIRACY
Estimated Piracy Rates

Estimating the extent of software piracy is not a simple task. Obviously, many of the transactions whereby people obtain illicit copies of software are conducted in secrecy, and Internet warez sites do not usually keep careful records of downloads. Consequently any estimates of piracy rates must be indirect. One of the most widely cited estimates of piracy rates and of the economic impact of piracy has been produced by the International Planning and Research Corporation (IPR) and later by the International Data Corporation (IDC), which are specialized consulting firms. These studies, referred to hereafter as "the

BSA studies," have been commissioned annually since 1994 by the BSA and SIIA.

The basic quantity estimated in the BSA studies is the annual piracy rate, calculated by dividing the number of illicit copies of software applications newly installed each year by the total number of copies installed in the same year. Thus, a piracy rate of zero would mean that all software was acquired legitimately, whereas a piracy rate of 100% would mean that all software was pirated. The BSA studies estimate the piracy rate globally, as well as on a regional and country-by-country basis (Business Software Alliance, 2005). Up until 2002, the BSA studies considered only business software applications. Beginning in 2003, the studies have encompassed all packaged PC software, including operating systems and typical home-use applications, such as recreational, educational, and personal finance software. Therefore the piracy rates calculated from 1994 through 2002 cannot be directly compared to those for 2003 and later, although they show considerable similarity.

For the first 6 years of the studies, the global piracy rate showed a slow but steady decline from about 50% in 1994 to 36% in 1999. This trend was probably due to several factors, including the efforts made by the software industry and national governments to educate the public about copyright laws and to enforce those laws. In addition, during that time, U.S. software companies made efforts to increase their presence in overseas markets, including providing better user support, while software prices generally declined. These developments made the option of purchasing software legitimately more attractive in those countries. After 1999, the global piracy rate increased slightly, fluctuating near 40% with no clear trend evident. This increase may be due to the increased competitive pressures during a period of slower economic growth, which led businesses to be more willing to pirate software to cut costs. If this explanation is correct, then we may expect to see piracy rates resume their decline once worldwide economic conditions improve. The global piracy rates for 2003 and 2004, based on the expanded set of categories of software, were 36% and 35% respectively, too small a difference to infer a trend at this time.

The BSA studies also estimate the retail "dollar losses" due to software piracy, calculated by multiplying the number of pirated copies by the average market price of a copy. (This is a simplistic calculation, but it provides a rough measure of the amount, as distinct from the proportion, of pirated software.) The global dollar losses showed little variation over the first 9 years of the BSA studies, varying between a low of US $11 billion and a high of US $13 billion, with no overall trend. The reason for the low degree of variation in this quantity is that the growth of the software market during this period has been accompanied by decreases in both the piracy rate and the price of software. These figures increased substantially, to about US $30 billion annually, in 2003 and 2004 due to the larger number of categories of software included.

Regional and country-by-country piracy data from the BSA studies are not analyzed in detail here for reasons of space, but a few broad patterns are noted. North America, with a rate of 22% in 2004, has had the lowest piracy rate of any region for every year of the study. Western

Europe regularly comes in second, with a rate of 35% in 2004. Despite their relatively low piracy rates, these two regions have some of the highest dollar losses. This seeming paradox is explained by the fact that these two regions are the largest consumers of software. Eastern Europe, with a piracy rate for 2004 of 71%, has consistently had the highest rate of any region. The other regions have intermediate piracy rates; in 2004, their rates were as follows: Asia/Pacific, 53%; Latin America, 66%; and Middle East/Africa, 58%. The largest dollar loss among these regions is found in Asia/Pacific, where a substantial piracy rate is combined with a large consumption of software, resulting in a dollar loss that is comparable to that for Europe or North America.

With the exception of Eastern Europe, all of the countries with piracy rates over 70% are Third World countries. In most of these countries there is little indigenous software production, and so for them piracy has a net economic benefit without adversely affecting their own local industry. In this regard it is noteworthy that India, which has become a major player in the software industry, reduced its piracy rate significantly from 79% in 1994 to a low of 61% in 1999. The rate has, however, climbed again, to 74% in 2004, erasing much of this gain. China's piracy rate, meanwhile, has remained very high, only declining from 97% in 1994 to 90% in 2004. China was seeking membership in the World Trade Organization during much of this period and was consequently under pressure to improve its protection of intellectual property rights, but its efforts in this direction have evidently had little effect. An alternative interpretation could be that enforcement efforts succeeded to some extent, but were offset by increases in piracy as China's economy grew very rapidly and became more open in this period.

As mentioned, Eastern Europe has consistently had the highest piracy rate of the six regions of the BSA studies. However, if we exclude Russia and most other countries of the former Soviet Union, the rest of the Eastern European countries (including the Baltic States) have made substantial progress recently, reducing their software piracy rates by at least 15 percentage points during the period from 1994 to 2002. However, their current piracy rates still have room for improvement, ranging from a high of 74% (Romania) to a low of 41% (the Czech Republic) and averaging about 53%. The large reductions in piracy rates in these countries probably reflect the emergence of free-market economies, a process that is normally accompanied by increased protection of intellectual property (Software and Information Industry Association, 2000). This transition has apparently not happened in the countries of the former Soviet Union, which had a combined piracy rate of 87% in 2004.

Methodology of the Study

To calculate the piracy rate for a given country or region, the analyst needs to determine the number of pirated copies and the number of legitimately purchased copies of software applications installed in that region. The BSA has access to proprietary sales information from the BSA member companies, and so the figures for legitimate software sales are obtained readily. The number of pirated copies is inferred as the difference between this number and the "demand" for software (i.e., the number of application programs that one would expect to be loaded onto the computers in use). The BSA uses hardware sales data to determine the number of new machines sold each year. To obtain an estimate of the number of machines currently in use, a correction is applied for turnover as older machines are taken out of service and replaced by new ones. From this figure the demand is calculated based on the average number of application programs that would normally be installed on each computer. The BSA studies' calculation of demand takes into account differences between new and replacement machines, between home and business computers, and among the various categories of software, as well as different levels of technological development in different regions.

Freeware and shareware are taken into account in the study by estimating the demand for this type of software and assuming it is fulfilled completely. Freeware is software that its producer makes available free of charge, and shareware is software that is distributed for free with a request that users who like it should send the author a contribution. Because there are no sales records for these applications, supply is difficult to measure, but this uncertainty has little impact on the study's conclusions because freeware and shareware currently represent an insignificant fraction of the packaged PC software market.

Despite all of the uncertainties involved, the BSA piracy estimates are probably the best obtainable under the circumstances. Marron and Steel (2000) performed a regression of the BSA estimated piracy rates on an independently estimated measure of patent protection in various countries and found a strong correlation, as would be expected. This test gives some confidence in the basic validity of the BSA data. In addition, because the BSA uses a consistent methodology globally and from year to year (except for the above-mentioned expansion of software categories beginning in 2003), trends and inter-regional comparisons should be reasonably reliable.

Financial Impact of Piracy

The most recent BSA calculations of lost revenue include all packaged (as opposed to custom or in-house developed) PC software applications. Therefore, the roughly US $30 billion in estimated annual losses probably represents the majority of the revenue losses experienced by the industry.

Of course, calling these revenues "losses" implicitly assumes that all software now pirated would be purchased through legitimate channels at current prices if all piracy were stopped. However, it is likely that, if piracy were somehow made impossible, some users who currently pirate software would choose not to purchase the software at all. In addition, very probably prices would change in such an altered market. Thus, it is more precise to refer to this quantity as the "market value" of the pirated software.

More realistic economic models have been developed to consider the overall effect of illicit copying on software producers' revenues. Slive and Bernhardt (1998), among others, describe how, in some situations, piracy of a software product can actually increase the total profits of its manufacturer through what economists call *network externalities*. In essence, the value of a particular software product is increased by having a large community of users. For instance, the users enjoy the convenience of being able to interchange files in the format used by the application. They may also invest considerable time in learning to use the application and can then move more easily to a new employer where the same software is in use than to one that uses some other product. In this context, piracy can be viewed as a form of price discrimination (the practice of charging different prices to different customers) in which the software is effectively sold at zero price to some customers. The resulting increase in the size of the user community enhances the value of the software, leading to increased sales and possibly also allowing the vendor to charge higher prices to those customers who will pay.

A key element of network externalities is the existence of two distinct populations of users. Home users generally place less value on software than businesses do and are less likely to be willing to pay for it. Businesses value the software more and are also likely to pay for it for the sake of reliability and support. Businesses and other organizations are also targeted more easily by anti-piracy campaigns. Hence, the software companies may find it in their best interest to turn a blind eye to home-use softlifting, knowing that it is helping them build market share that pays dividends in the more lucrative business market.

For small firms attempting to enter the software market, it is unlikely that the positive network effects of piracy will be sufficiently strong to compensate for the revenue losses. This is especially the case for non-U.S. software producers. They have an inherent advantage in their home countries in producing certain types of applications, such as manufacturing, banking, and financial software, areas that are the most dependent on local laws and business practices. However, this advantage is defeated if they are forced to compete against extremely low-cost pirated copies of software produced in the United States (PricewaterhouseCoopers, 1999).

MECHANISMS FOR PROTECTION OF SOFTWARE

Softlifting has been going on ever since there was anything to softlift. The very first consumer application produced by Microsoft was a Basic language interpreter for the Altair microcomputer that appeared in 1975. A paper tape containing a demo version of the interpreter was stolen, and soon the demo was circulating widely among the Altair user community. Subsequent software products have fared no better. Industry efforts at education and persuasion have met with only limited success. Consequently, the industry turned to legal and technical measures to protect its interests.

Legal Protection Mechanisms
Goals of Legal Protection Mechanisms
Historically, one can identify three main distinct philosophical frameworks on which theories of intellectual property rights have been based. The natural rights view, prominent in European legal theory, finds a right of

ownership to arise from the investment of one's labor in the creation of the product. Another viewpoint considers information to be a public good, which cannot be owned by anyone. This view has prevailed in socialist systems, which reserved the creation and control of intellectual goods to the state. Third, the utilitarian view considers intellectual property as one element of an economic balance sheet that is to be optimized for the maximum benefit to society (Maskus, 2000). This viewpoint has predominated in the United States and has guided the formulation of its legal mechanisms of copyrights and patents.

The basic tradeoff involved in intellectual property rights laws is between stimulating innovation and creation of new inventions and creative works, on the one hand, and allowing access to and utilization of those inventions and works, on the other. This tradeoff is complex, depending on such factors as the state of development of creative industries in the country, its market structure, the educational level of its citizens, and so forth. Finding the right balance becomes even more problematic on a global scale among a diversity of interacting countries with widely different levels of economic development. For a thorough discussion of this topic, see Maskus (2000). Here we simply observe that the essential element of copyright and patent mechanisms is the granting to the creator of a work a temporary monopoly on its production and sale. This permits the owner of the monopoly to charge a price substantially above the marginal cost of reproducing the work (which is often quite low) so as to recover the costs of development, and it also provides an incentive for innovation. The monopoly protection is made contingent on the publication of the idea or its expression, so that others can build on the idea in further creative works.

Some have argued that existing legal conceptions of intellectual property are not adequate for dealing with software (Davis, Samuelson, Kapor, & Reichman, 1996). Copyright laws have traditionally been applied only to writings and other forms of expression that are not industrially useful, whereas patents were applied only to useful ideas and inventions. Yet, software is precisely a useful object that happens to be expressed as a writing. The application of copyright protection to software can also be criticized because of the very long term of protection, usually at least 50 years. For software such a long period is effectively infinite because a program will be completely useless after that time. Furthermore, the manner in which software is published, as binary code that is meant to be read only by machines while the source code is treated as a trade secret, effectively does not amount to disclosure in the traditional sense. Thus, others are unable to build on or improve upon the works, which is contrary to the aim of fostering innovation. For such reasons as these, many observers consider copyright to be overly protectionist of the interests of the software makers. Notwithstanding these objections, the existing legal framework has been adapted to deal with software by a process of relatively narrowly focused changes to existing legislation accompanied by court decisions to establish precedents, just as happened with earlier technological innovations, such as audio and video recorders.

Still, it should be kept in mind that this legal framework is only one of several possible solutions to the problem of ensuring for society an abundant supply of creative works. It is a solution that is situated within the Western tradition of protection for intellectual property. Other solutions, such as state support for software producers or a system of shared royalty payments funded by hardware or media sales, can be imagined. The *open source* software movement promotes an alternative mode of software production in which widely dispersed programmers contribute to the development of an application, the source code of which is freely available. However, to date none of these alternatives has provided a viable mechanism for funding the work at the levels that would be required to support the current software establishment.

In what follows, the discussion of legal issues is mainly in terms of U.S. law. This is reasonable because most software is produced in the United States, and various international treaties have established a legal climate that is substantially the same in most countries. These treaties include the Berne Convention for the Protection of Literary and Artistic Works, the Universal Copyright Convention, and the General Agreement on Tariffs and Trade (GATT) accord on Trade-Related Aspects of Intellectual Property Rights (TRIPs; see, for instance, *Harvard Law Review*, 2003, for a discussion of these developments.)

Software Copyright and Licensing

Because a program must be copied from a distribution medium to a computer's hard drive to be installed, and then copied again from the hard drive to the working memory (RAM) to run, copyright in principle gives the software maker almost complete control over the use of its product. According to this view, the customer does not purchase the software, but only pays for a license to use it, under whatever terms the maker chooses to dictate. Exceeding the scope of the license grant is thus tantamount to a violation of copyright, though whether this is always an act of piracy is debatable. In practice, the strictness of this view is tempered by market pressures and by the recognition in law that the customer is entitled to certain basic rights. For instance, licenses that disclaim any liability for defects in the software are generally considered to be unenforceable (Kaner & Pels, 1998). In addition, the making of legitimate backup copies of software is explicitly permitted by U.S. copyright law (17 USC 117) and the European Software Directive (Section 5(b)). Today, most packaged software carries a notice on the outside of the package saying that the purchaser indicates acceptance of the license by the act of opening the package. However, because the license is inside the shrinkwrapped package, there is no way the customer can read it first in order to decide whether to accept it. In the United States and elsewhere, court cases such as *ProCD* vs. *Zeidenberg* (1996) have generally upheld the enforceability of these shrinkwrap licenses, provided that the terms of the license fall within ordinary expectations, but the question is still controversial among legal scholars.

Fair Use

One legal question that should be addressed is whether individual copying of software for personal use might fit within the parameters of the fair use doctrine, which permits the duplication of copyrighted material under some conditions. A determination of fair use must consider four factors: (1) the purpose or character of the use (whether commercial or productive); (2) the nature of the use (whether one is primarily availing oneself of the uncopyrightable factual content of the work or of its expression); (3) the substantiality of the use (whether the work is copied in its entirety or only in part); and (4) the effect of the action on the market for the work. Hornik (1994) argues persuasively that softlifting fails to meet these four criteria for fair use:

1. Although the software is not being copied for sale and even though it may be used in ways that benefit the rest of society (the main aim of fair use), it is also likely to be used directly or indirectly for financial gain.
2. What the softlifter is primarily interested in is the "expression" of the software; that is, its embodiment in code.
3. In softlifting, the entire work is duplicated.
4. Although some softlifters would choose not to buy the software if the choice were to pay or to do without, the practice probably decreases sales at least to some extent.

Hence, a fair use defense of softlifting as it is typically practiced would probably not stand up in court.

Enforcement Efforts

One area in which the software industry has had some success in improving compliance with licensing and copyright laws has been in pressing its case against corporate softloaders. On behalf of their member companies, BSA and SIIA have undertaken programs of voluntary audits of large firms, inspecting their computers to determine whether software has been loaded onto them in violation of license agreements. When the organization receives a reliable report (usually from an employee of the firm) that softloading is occurring, the firm is sent a letter giving it a choice of permitting the audit or being sued for infringement. Most firms choose the audit to avoid the adverse publicity that a lawsuit would entail. They may also have favorable software licensing arrangements that would be at risk if they failed to cooperate. If the audit reveals violations, the firm must destroy the infringing software, purchase replacements for it, and pay a fine. In return, the firm is released from all further legal claims for prior acts of infringement.

Stopping bootlegging, on the other hand, requires different measures. As discussed above, the development of an indigenous software industry is a key element for gaining the strong support of local governments for the enforcement of intellectual property laws. Even so, the U.S. dominance of the software industry means that, for most other countries, enforcement of laws protecting software nearly always imposes a net cost on their economies. Hence, efforts to increase compliance with these laws have involved tying them to other aspects of trade relations (Shadlen, Schrank, & Kurtz, 2003).

Internet piracy presents greater obstacles to legal enforcement. Suppose someone downloads a software package that has been illicitly placed on a Web site. A software producer that wishes to bring suit to redress this action faces several practical difficulties (Christensen, 1997). First it must decide whom to sue: the downloader, the intermediary (the service provider hosting the Web site), or the person who uploaded the software in the first place. Next it must decide where to sue: because each of the three parties involved in the action could be located in a different country, the choice of an appropriate venue can be complicated. Finally, assuming the prosecution is successful, the software producer must attempt to recover damages.

Prosecution of an individual downloader is difficult in all of these respects. Web sites usually do not maintain logs of download activity for very long. Even with access to these logs, it can be difficult to identify the downloader, and savvy pirates can masquerade as different users. The downloader may be located in a foreign country that may have weaker intellectual property laws than those in the software producer's home country. Although suit may be brought against foreign nationals in a domestic court, enforcement of the judgment can be difficult. Finally, the amount of damages that can be assessed for a single count of softlifting may not cover the costs of litigation, and the guilty party may not have the means to pay the damages anyway.

In the United States, the 1997 No Electronic Theft (NET) Act addressed this last issue by increasing civil penalties and for the first time providing for criminal penalties for copyright infringement that is not for financial gain, provided the value of the stolen works is at least $1,000. These measures have made it more likely that an action against an individual softlifter could result in significant penalties, including jail time. Recently some high-profile actions have been brought against particularly flagrant softlifters in hopes of making examples of a few in order to deter others. However, because of the difficulties, as well as for public relations reasons, software companies have historically tended to avoid legal action against individual softlifters.

A more suitable target for legal action may be the uploader. A single upload can be responsible for thousands of downloads, so the damages that can be claimed can be quite large. Furthermore, if the uploader acted for profit, the penalties are even greater. However, many uploaders post software on warez sites simply for the enjoyment of sharing with others and thumbing their noses at powerful software companies. Identification of the uploader can also be difficult, for the same reasons as with downloaders. Finally, even if the legal action is successful, an individual uploader may not have the means to pay the penalties, and the software company would have to be satisfied with a moral victory.

Prosecution of the online service provider (OSP) used as an intermediary for software piracy may be a viable option. The term "OSP" is used here to distinguish such a provider from an Internet service provider (ISP) that merely provides a connection to the Internet. OSPs operate the computers on which reside bulletin board systems (BBSs), Web pages, newsgroups, and chat rooms, all of which can be used to exchange pirated software. Courts have held OSPs responsible for the copyright infringement activities of their customers under the notions of contributory or vicarious liability (Hayes, 2002).

Contributory liability is applicable if the OSP knew about the infringing activity and encouraged or facilitated it. Vicarious liability can apply if the OSP controlled the means to commit infringements, even if it did not monitor or encourage the infringing activity itself, so long as it benefited financially from it. In response to the threat of legal action, many OSPs now publicize and enforce strict policies against infringing activities by their users, although undoubtedly much pirating activity still goes undetected.

Prosecution of the OSP has several practical advantages from the point of view of the software maker: the OSP is an established firm that can be identified easily, the amount of damages that can be sought is large, and in the event of a successful suit the OSP is likely to have the resources to pay the judgment.

A recent development that makes prosecution of the intermediary harder is peer-to-peer (P2P) file sharing. The novel idea behind a P2P service is that the files to be downloaded do not reside on a central server, but on the computers belonging to the users of the service. The central server, if there is one, only acts as a go-between by maintaining lists of what files the users have made available for download by others. Once a user has located a particular file on another user's machine, the file is exchanged directly from one machine to the other without any further involvement on the part of the server. P2P file sharing was pioneered by Napster, which was originally designed to allow users to share music files in MP3 format. Napster's free service was shut down following a lawsuit brought by the music industry (*A&M Records, Inc., et al. vs. Napster, Inc.*, 2002). The success of this suit hinged on the fact that Napster maintained lists of available titles on a central server and thus participated actively in the process of file sharing, although it did not store any music files itself. Successors to Napster, such as KaZaA and Morpheus, have adopted more decentralized structures that are less susceptible to legal action. However, suits have been brought against them; see *Metro-Goldwyn-Mayer Studios, Inc. et al., vs. Grokster, Ltd.* (2003). These newer services also provide facilities for sharing other types of files in addition to MP3s, including software.

Technical Protection Mechanisms

Because legal protections alone have not sufficed, software makers have devised various technical mechanisms to prevent the unauthorized copying of their products. The most commonly used protection mechanisms rely on a special key code that must be entered by the user during the installation process. Typically this key code is provided along with the installation medium in each software package. Key codes do not prevent softloading, because there is nothing to prevent the user from installing the same software on multiple machines. However, the user can at least be limited to using the software on one machine at a time by means of a key disk or a dongle. A key disk is a special diskette or CD, provided along with the software, which must be inserted into the disk drive during operation of the application program. The program queries the key disk from time to time to verify the user's authorization. For the key disk to be effective, of course, it must be difficult to copy by the means at a typical user's disposal.

A drawback of key disks is that they prevent the disk drive from being used for other purposes while the application is in use. A related alternative is the dongle, a device that attaches to the parallel, serial, or USB port of the computer. As with a key disk, the application queries the dongle as it runs. Dongles are relatively expensive, typically adding $20 to $30 to the cost of an application, so they are only practical for high-end software.

Media-limited installations are a way to prevent softloading. In these schemes, the installation program counts how many times the application has been installed and refuses to exceed the limit. This method requires the installation medium or at least a component of it to be writeable. In addition, for the protection to be effective, the medium must be difficult to copy by standard means.

Such mechanisms as key disks and media-limited installations were suitable during the 1980s when most software was distributed on floppy disks. As applications grew in size and distribution on CDs became the norm, these methods became less appropriate. In addition, any copy-protection scheme that would prevent legitimate uses, such as making archival backup copies or reinstalling the software after a hardware failure, irritated customers. Because of the consumer backlash against copy protection, by the early 1990s, relatively few packaged software applications that were being sold included any protection other than an installation key code.

Protection measures that rely on special hardware, whether key disk, uncopyable medium, or dongle, are not well suited to today's environment in which much of the software is distributed via the Internet. Often, the software can be downloaded freely, but contains a "time bomb" that will deactivate it after a trial period, such as 30 days. Before that period expires, the customer must register and pay for the software, obtaining a key code that renders the installation permanent.

Unfortunately for the software producers, all of the methods that they have invented to deter the unauthorized use of their products can be cracked or circumvented. Copy-protection schemes suffice to keep the average user, who has no knowledge of the inner workings of software, honest. It is virtually impossible to devise a scheme that a skilled and dedicated cracker cannot defeat.

Cracking a program typically involves reverse engineering the binary code, taking it apart to find where the key code is checked or the dongle is interrogated, and bypassing or disabling these sections. If the protection scheme involves cryptography, this only adds to the challenge. Cryptography is the science of scrambling the contents of a file in such a way that it can be unscrambled only by using a secret, randomly chosen key. It is a practical impossibility to crack a well-designed modern cryptographic system by sheer guesswork, even using the fastest available computers. However, a fundamental problem facing any cryptographic copy-protection method is that the software itself must contain a decryption routine including the key, which a clever cracker can in principle discover no matter how well it is hidden.

Recent Developments

The battle against online piracy is no longer the province of the software producers alone. The entertainment media industry is getting involved because of the increasingly digital nature of their products. Their lobbying efforts in the United States bore fruit in the 1998 adoption of the Digital Millennium Copyright Act (DMCA), which greatly strengthened the copyright protection of digital information. Perhaps the most controversial aspect of the DMCA is its prohibition of all acts of circumvention of copy-protection mechanisms. Critics argue that these provisions of the law have primarily been used to silence those who disclose weaknesses in these mechanisms, rather than to stop copyright pirates.

Hollywood has also lobbied for new legislation that would require copy-protection mechanisms to be embedded in every digital device and in all pieces of software that will be produced in the future. The new measures being advocated go even farther than the software industry wishes. Some of the proposed protection mechanisms will interfere with the legitimate duplication of software by OEMs and may prevent computer users from performing legitimate tasks. It is not clear at this time where these efforts will lead, but it is unlikely that they will be any more successful than previous measures in stopping piracy completely.

CONCLUSION

Piracy costs the software industry billions of dollars annually in lost revenues. The precise cost cannot be ascertained, because there are many economic factors that would change if the illicit copying could somehow be stopped entirely. Softlifting and softloading probably account for the largest proportion of the activity, and the Internet is an increasingly important medium for the exchange of "warez."

Technical means of enforcing copy protection can always be defeated. Veterans of the struggle against crackers recognize that, at best, copy protection only slows pirates down and puts some obstacles in the softlifters' path, so that enough people will purchase the product for it to be profitable. Furthermore, copy protection, if it is too intrusive, annoys customers and can even backfire by spurring more circumvention efforts. Consequently, most software producers have decided not to rely solely on technical means, but to undertake a campaign of user education, coupled with high-profile legal action, to try to persuade customers to obey the laws protecting software. These efforts have borne fruit, reflected in a slow but steady decline in piracy rates in most countries. The biggest reductions in piracy rates have occurred in countries that have been making the transition to free-market economies and developing their own indigenous software industries. Although software piracy will probably never be eliminated completely, there are good reasons to hope that in coming years it will decline to levels that are tolerable for the software industry.

GLOSSARY

Crack As a verb, to circumvent technical measures intended to prevent the unlicensed operation of a program. As a noun, a program that has been cracked so that it can be used by unauthorized users.

Dongle A specialized hardware device that attaches to a computer's parallel, serial, or USB port and that is queried by a program during operation to verify the user's authorization to use the program.

Hard-disk loading The installation of unauthorized software on computers being prepared for sale by original equipment manufacturers or other computer vendors.

Mischanneling The selling of software intended for academic, government, or other special categories of customers to those who do not belong to the intended group.

Softlifting The unauthorized copying of software by an end user for his or her own use, rather than for sale.

Softloading The copying of software by an end user onto more machines than permitted by the license, or the unauthorized loading of software onto a server for use by client machines in a local area network.

Unbundling The selling of software that is licensed only to be sold as part of a package as a separate item.

Warez Slang term for pirated software, usually referring to items made available on the Internet.

CROSS REFERENCES

See *Copyright Law; Legal, Social and Ethical Issues of the Internet; Patent Law; The Legal Implications of Information Security: Regulatory Compliance and Liability.*

REFERENCES

A&M Records, Inc., et al. vs. Napster, Inc. *Federal Reporter 3rd Series, 284,* 1091; U.S. Court of Appeals, 9th Cir (2002).

Business Software Alliance (2005). *Second annual BSA and IDC global software piracy study.* Retrieved June 1, 2005, from http://www.bsa.org/usa/research

Cheng, H. K., Sims, R. R., & Teegen, H. (1997). To purchase or to pirate software: An empirical study. *Journal of Management Information Systems, 13*(4), 49–60.

Christensen, K. D. (1997). Fighting software piracy in cyberspace: Legal and technological solutions. *Law & Policy in International Business, 28,* 435–475.

Davis, R., Samuelson, P., Kapor, M., & Reichman, J. (1996). A new view of intellectual property and software. *Communications of the ACM, 39,* 21–30.

Depken, C. A., & Simmons, L. C. (2004). Social construct and the propensity for software piracy. *Applied Economics Letters, 11,* 97–100.

Harvard Law Review (2003). Tackling global software piracy under TRIPS: Insights from international relations theory. *Harvard Law Review, 116*(4), 1139–1160.

Hayes, D. L. (2002). Copyright liability of online service providers, a three-part series. *The Computer and Internet Lawyer, 19*(10), 1–27 (Part I); (11), 15–30 (Part II); (12), 12–34 (Part III).

Hornik, D. M. (1994). Combating software piracy: The softlifting problem. *Harvard Journal of Law & Technology, 7,* 377–417.

Husted, B. W. (2000). The impact of national culture on software piracy. *Journal of Business Ethics, 26,* 197–211.

Kaner, C., & Pels, D. (1998). *Bad software: What to do when software fails.* New York: Wiley.

Kini, R. B., Ramakrishna, H. V., & Vijayaraman, B. S. (2004). Shaping of moral intensity regarding software piracy: A comparison between Thailand and U.S. students. *Journal of Business Ethics, 49,* 91–104.

Loper, D. K. (2000). *The criminology of computer hackers: a qualitative and quantitative analysis.* Unpublished doctoral dissertation, Michigan State University.

Marron, D. B., & Steel, D. G. (2000). Which countries protect intellectual property? The case of software piracy. *Economic Inquiry, 38,* 159–174.

Maskus, K. E. (2000). *Intellectual property rights in the global economy.* Washington: Institute for International Economics.

McCandless, D. (1997, April). Warez wars. *Wired Magazine.* Retrieved May 3, 2002, from http://www.wired.com/wired/archive/5.04/ff_warez_pr.html

Metro-Goldwyn-Mayer Studios, Inc. et al., vs. Grokster, Ltd. (2003). *Federal Rules Decisions* 218, 423; U.S. Court of Appeals, 9th Circuit.

Peace, A. G., Galletta, D. F., & Thong, J. Y. L. (2003). Software piracy in the workplace: A model and empirical test. *Journal of Management Information Systems, 20*(1), 153–177.

PricewaterhouseCoopers (1999). *Contributions of the packaged software industry to the global economy.* Retrieved June 1, 2005, from http://www.bsa.org/usa/ (search on pricewaterhousecoopers)

ProCD vs. Zeidenberg (1996). *Federal Reporter 3rd Series, 86,* 1447; U.S. Court of Appeals, 7th Circuit.

Rehn, A. (2004). The politics of contraband: The honor economies of the warez scene. *The Journal of Socio-Economics, 33,* 359–374.

Ronkainen, I. A., & Guerrero-Cusumano, J.-L. (2001). Correlates of intellectual property violation. *Multinational Business Review, 9*(1), 59–65.

Shadlen, K., Schrank, A., & Kurtz, M. (2003). The political economy of intellectual property protection: The case of software (Working paper no. 03-40). *Development Studies Institute, London School of Economics and Political Science.* Retrieved May 23, 2004, from http://www.lse.ac.uk/collections/DESTIN/pdf/WP40.pdf

Simpson, P. M., Banerjee, D., & Simpson, C. L., Jr. (1994). Softlifting: A model of motivating factors. *Journal of Business Ethics, 13,* 431–438.

Slive, J., & Bernhardt, D. (1998). Pirated for profit. *Canadian Journal of Economics, 31,* 886–899.

Software and Information Industry Association (2000). *SIIA's report on global software piracy 2000.* Retrieved June 1, 2005, from http://www.siia.net/estore/GPR-00.pdf

Taylor, G. S., & Shim, J. P. (1993). A comparative examination of attitudes toward software piracy among business professors and executives. *Human Relations, 46,* 419–433.

Internet Gambling

Susanna Frederick Fischer, *Columbus School of Law, The Catholic University of America*

INTRODUCTION: SECURITY RISKS AND OTHER CHALLENGES OF INTERNET GAMBLING

The U.S. General Accounting Office has defined Internet gambling as "any activity that takes place via the Internet and that includes placing a bet or wager" (U.S. General Accounting Office, 2002, p. 1). Many types of gambling activity take place online, including casino-style games (like blackjack, poker, or roulette), pari-mutuel wagering (such as wagering on horse races, dog races, or jai alai), lotteries, sports wagering, and bingo. Nonexistent before the mid-1990s, Internet gambling is now easily available to anyone with access to a computer hooked up to the Internet. As Internet gambling has become more widespread, it poses security and privacy risks for an increasing number of people. The next section of this chapter describes the phenomenal growth of Internet gambling.

Gambling has always been a financially hazardous activity, but gambling online may increase the dangers. Some gambling Web sites have serious security problems. They may close down without paying out winnings, use software to unfairly manipulate outcomes so bettors cannot win, or commit identity theft. Some online gambling operations have been vehicles for money laundering by criminals or terrorists. Gambling online may also imperil the privacy of personal information. Some unscrupulous Internet gambling operations may sell or steal personal data, which may end up in the hands of spammers or criminal entities. Online bettors often have little effective legal recourse against illegal or offshore gambling operations. As with other forms of e-commerce, nefarious third parties pose added security risks, such as hackers diverting online gambling payments. Online casinos may also be at risk of loss from cheaters who break into computer systems or interfere with random number generators. The third section of this chapter discusses these security and privacy problems in more detail.

From a regulator's perspective, Internet gambling poses difficult challenges. Some regulators advocate the wholesale prohibition of Internet gambling, not just because of security and privacy problems but also because of the risk of other social harms, including organized crime, money laundering, global terrorism, fraud, pathological or addictive gambling, and underage gambling. Another concern is that offshore Internet gambling causes economic harm to local communities by drawing away customers, jobs, tax revenues, and profits from local land-based casinos.

Others contend that the prohibition of Internet gambling is neither necessary nor effective. Some believe that a type of more limited regulation will be sufficient to avert the dangers associated with Internet gambling. One argument that is often cited against prohibition is that a wholesale ban on Internet gambling is effectively impossible because some gambling operators are unscrupulous, do not respect the law or other forms of regulation, are based offshore beyond the reach of regulators, and can use fast-developing technologies to evade any regulation that may be imposed. The fourth section considers this debate over the regulation of Internet gambling in greater depth.

As a result of social and moral concerns, including fears of security and privacy abuses, some jurisdictions prohibit online gambling. For example, the current position of the U.S. government is that offshore operators who offer online gambling services to U.S. residents violate federal law. Other jurisdictions, such as Antigua and Barbuda, have embraced Internet gambling on the theory that it will boost their local economies by creating jobs, especially for young people who might otherwise turn to crime. The fifth section surveys the current regulatory landscape for online gambling, showing its complexity, variation, and uncertainty.

Applying the law to Internet gambling activities involves difficult issues. Gambling laws enacted before the

advent of online gambling raise problems of interpretation. Technology is moving so swiftly in this area that even laws that specifically address online gambling may still be difficult to apply to technologies that did not exist when they were enacted. Another complexity is that even jurisdictions that clearly permit some types of Internet gambling may prohibit others or may limit some gambling activity to their own residents. Moreover, even when a server hosting a gambling Web site is located in a jurisdiction that has legalized Internet gambling, it may not be legal for that gambling operation to accept bets from a computer located in a jurisdiction that prohibits Internet gambling.

Jurisdictional rules often impose significant limitations on the ability to enforce domestic gambling laws directly against offshore online gambling operators. As a result, some American federal and state authorities have chosen to pursue some offshore gambling operations indirectly by pressuring financial institutions to block credit card and other payments relating to Internet gambling. In turn, some online gamblers have increased this pressure on financial institutions by claiming that their unpaid credit card debts cannot be legally enforced as a matter of public policy. In response to these developments, many American banks that issue credit cards have implemented policies to block Internet gambling transactions. This move has in turn sparked conflict among World Trade Organization members over its trade and development ramifications.

Internet gambling raises two central problems for regulation of the Internet generally. The first is the proper relationship between law and technology as sources of regulation. The second is whether one jurisdiction's regulatory regime can legitimately affect online activity by people who are physically outside that jurisdiction's borders. Other difficult issues involving these problems are spam, online infringement of intellectual property rights, and the spread of computer viruses around the world (see these chapters in this *Handbook*: Hackers, Crackers, and Computer Criminals; Developments in Global Law Enforcement; Spam and the Legal Counter Attacks; and Cybercrime and the U.S. Criminal Justice System.

PHENOMENAL GROWTH OF INTERNET GAMBLING

Although reported statistics vary somewhat, observers generally agree that the online gambling industry has exploded since its start in the early 1990s. According to a major U.S. government study, the number of Internet gamblers doubled between 1997 and 1998, increasing from 6.9 million to 14.5 million (National Gambling Impact Study Commission [NGISC], 1999). One prominent online gambling analyst, Christiansen Capital Advisors, has reported that global online gambling industry revenue grew by more than 42% between 2002 and 2003, to over $US 5.6 billion (CCA, 2003). It has estimated that global revenue from online gambling will increase to over $18 billion by 2010 (Figure 1).

Although a definitive tally of Internet gambling sites is not currently available, one widely quoted estimate provided by a U.S. Department of Justice official (Internet gambling, 2003) stated that by the end of 2003 there would be around 1,800 casino-style online gambling sites.

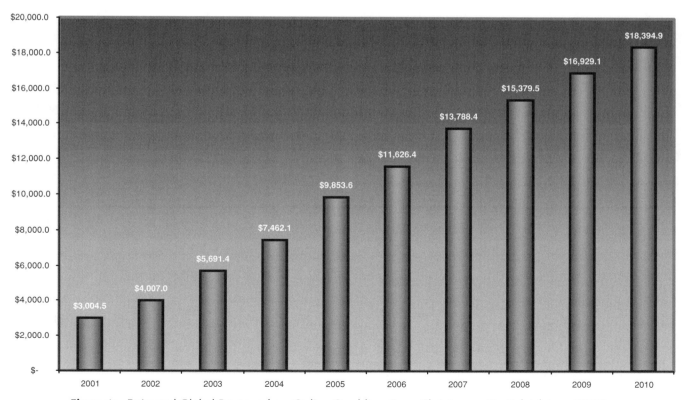

Figure 1: Estimated Global Revenue from Online Gambling. From Christiansen Capital Advisors (2004).

The growth of Internet gambling parallels a similar trend in gambling generally, which has recently been increasing significantly in the United States. The American Gaming Association has reported that from 1992 to 2002 gross gambling revenue (GGR) more than doubled from all forms of gaming, including casinos, lotteries, pari-mutuel wagering, legal bookmaking, charitable gaming and bingo, Indian reservations, and card rooms. Over this decade, GGR increased from $US 30.4 billion to $US 68.7 billion. Christiansen Capital Advisors reported that GGR increased to over 72.8 billion in 2003 (CCA, 2003).

Many online gambling operations use software developed by gaming software providers, such as Microgaming, CryptoLogic, Playtech, or Odds on Gaming. Some of these software providers own and operate their own online gambling operations. Others just license their software to third-party casinos. Security and privacy are significant issues for all types of online gambling operations.

SECURITY AND PRIVACY ISSUES FOR INTERNET GAMBLING

Opponents of online gambling (Internet gambling, 2003; Kindt & Joy, 2002) contend that it spawns crime and is increasingly being used to further organized crime. There are certainly very serious security and privacy problems associated with some online gambling operations. Criminal acts associated with Internet gambling include identity theft, fraud, extortion, money laundering, and cheating. Some online gambling operations fail to protect the privacy of players' financial and other personal data, which may violate the law of some jurisdictions. Even where the disclosure of such data is not itself illegal, it may put players at risk of being defrauded if that information is provided to criminal enterprises or individuals.

Security Problems

The NGISC Final Report (1999) warns that unscrupulous Internet gambling operators can easily close down at will, and they do so frequently, pocketing payments made to them without paying out winnings. Many bettors who have provided online gambling sites with credit card or bank account information have suffered identity theft or have been defrauded, either by the online gambling operator or by a third-party hacker.

Another danger for those wagering on Internet gambling sites is dishonest software. For example, a rigged software-based random number generator can be used to cheat players. When rogue gambling operations or hackers are based offshore, they are often beyond the reach of regulatory bodies, leaving bettors unprotected from fraud. Concerns about fraud are a major reason for recent attempts by U.S. authorities to block the financial transactions used to pay for Internet gambling transactions (see below).

Even if an online gambling site is legitimate, players may still be at risk for a type of identity theft known as "black-holing" (Germain, 2004). Criminals hijack a gambling Web site, causing those who attempt to link to the hijacked site to be redirected without their knowledge to another, apparently identical site run by the hijackers.

When visitors log in to the fake site, the hijackers collect their user IDs and passwords. The thieves then redirect visitors to the real gambling site so that they will believe that they never left it. Another risk for players at legal online gambling sites is the possible lack of adequate reserves to pay out winnings (Cabot, 2004).

Online bettors are not the only ones who may suffer harm from security violations. Criminals have also targeted online gambling operations. Cyberextortionists have sent online gambling operators e-mails threatening distributed denial of service (DDOS) attacks if they fail to accede to demands for payment (Germain, 2004). The amounts demanded by such cyberprotection rackets are typically small, designed to ensure that the threatened sites can afford to pay them. Although some gambling sites, such as the large British betting chain William Hill, have refused to accede to such threats (Leyden, 2004), many other sites have chosen to comply, rather than risk serious harm to their businesses. For example, BetWWTS.com, a sportsbook licensed by the Government of Antigua and Barbuda, paid $30,000 to hackers who had attacked its site (Swartz, 2004). Because online gambling sites rely on transactions with customers every few seconds, just a few hours offline during a popular betting event like the Superbowl could strike a devastating financial blow. Some gambling sites have gone out of business after DDOS attacks (Swartz, 2004).

One study (U.S. GAO, 2002) reports that many American law enforcement officers are seriously worried about the potential of Internet gambling to foster money laundering in an age of global terrorism, because of the anonymity of the Internet, the availability of encryption, and remote access. Officials at many U.S. government agencies have frequently voiced concern about links between online gambling and organized crime. One Department of Justice official (Internet gambling, 2003) has pointed out that offshore online gambling operations are attractive to money launderers, because their location is effectively beyond the reach of American regulators. Other features that attract criminals are the high volume and speed of Internet gambling transactions, as well as the difficulty in tracing anonymous gambling transactions.

Along with the security problems of identity theft, extortion, and money laundering, online gambling operations also face the problem of cheating by players. This is a common problem for land-based casinos as well. As depicted in the television drama *Las Vegas,* bricks-and-mortar gambling businesses often use overhead cameras to survey an entire casino for cheaters. Such businesses may even employ facial recognition technology in an effort to match players with known cheaters. The anonymity of the Internet makes the pursuit of cheaters an even greater challenge for online gambling operations. No existing technology can provide absolute protection against cheating.

Nor is there yet any completely effective technological means to secure gambling sites against hacking or identity theft. Many online gambling sites use encryption technologies, such as the Secure Sockets Layer (SSL) protocol to protect personal information and credit card numbers from being viewed as they travel across the Internet. A variety of other measures have been deployed to combat hackers and intruders, including firewalls, hardware and software detection units, monitoring by humans and custom-designed monitoring scripts, and filtering technologies designed to identify and block attack packets. Many sites also take precautions against hardware failure or data loss, including using power backups and emergency generators, tape backups, offsite storage for backups, network monitoring, and hardware redundancy. But none of these security technologies can provide an absolute bar to intruders or identity thieves. Clever hackers have always found ways to evade new security technologies as quickly as they are developed. The arms race between security technology and intruder technology is likely to continue for the foreseeable future.

Privacy Violations

An issue that is closely related to security is personal privacy. Some online gambling operations have sold or provided personal and financial data to other entities, which have included telemarketers, spammers, and fraudulent businesses. Privacy laws vary considerably among jurisdictions and often fail to protect many kinds of personal information (see these chapters in this *Handbook*: Anonymity and Identity on the Internet and Privacy Law and the Internet).

Some online gambling sites have posted privacy polices specifying the circumstances and extent to which the site may sell or transfer customers' personal data to third parties. Any such policy should be read carefully before providing any personal information to a site. Unfortunately, the mere existence of a privacy policy is no guarantee that it will be followed. If a site violates its own privacy policy, its operators may be liable for unfair or deceptive practices, depending on applicable laws (see Privacy Law and the Internet in this *Handbook*).

Protecting Yourself from Security and Privacy Violations

Although some online gambling sites are honest and legitimate, it is often very difficult to know which particular sites are trustworthy. Anyone wishing to gamble online should thoroughly investigate an online gambling site before placing any bets. The Web site should provide information on the operator, the jurisdiction where the operation is licensed, the rules and guidelines governing it, and its cash policies. Players should test the validity of a site's contact information by trying out its customer support and checking the validity of its contact information before playing. Of course, security risks may still exist, such as the risk of a site closing down and disappearing before paying out winnings. Players should therefore be careful not to wager more than they can afford to lose.

Some online gambling sites have received the seal of approval of respected self-regulatory gambling watchdog organizations, such as the Gambling Commission (http://www.gamblingcommission.com), which conducts random remote audits throughout the year to ensure the fairness, integrity, and randomness of the casino's software, as well as to confirm that the casino follows its own posted rules, is truthful in advertising its payout

odds and percentages, honors wagers even if there is a power failure, has sufficient cash reserves to pay winners, handles players' disputes swiftly and accurately, maintains thorough logs of player transactions, and has customer service representatives available to discuss players' accounts. Other respected gambling watchdogs are the Canadian-based Interactive Gaming Council (IGC; http://www.igcouncil.org/) and the United Kingdom-based E-Commerce and Online Game Regulation (eCOGRA; http://www.ecogra.org). Even if a gambling Web site displays the seal of approval of one of these watchdog organizations, it is a good idea to confirm that the site is actually included in the list of members on the watchdog organization's Web site.

A useful American resource for victims of online fraud is the Internet Fraud Complaint Center (IFCC), a partnership between the FBI and the National White Collar Crime Center. The IFCC's mission is to address fraud committed over the Internet. Complaints can be filed at its Web site at http://www.ifccfbi.gov. The U.S. Federal Trade Commission also has a Web site at http://www.ftc.gov with when complaints of fraud, identity theft, or privacy violations can be lodged. If a fraudulent Internet gambling Web site is based in another country, victims should find and contact the appropriate regulatory or law enforcement agency for the country where the gambling operation is based. However, there is no guarantee that doing so will prove effective. Even if the appropriate body can be found, it can provide players with little assistance if the offending Web site has closed down or disappeared or if the governing law provides no recourse.

DEBATE OVER PROHIBITION OR REGULATION

There is considerable disagreement over whether Internet gambling should be prohibited or regulated. Supporters of prohibition point not only to the security and privacy problems discussed above but also contend that online gambling leads to a host of other social, moral, and economic harms. Although some opponents of prohibition agree that Internet gambling is associated with serious dangers, they believe that some more limited system of regulation will be effective to combat them. Others oppose prohibition on the basis that online gambling has social benefits and is consistent with American constitutional values. Still another point of view is that wholesale prohibition of online gambling is effectively unenforceable. This section considers this debate in more detail.

The Case for Prohibition of Internet Gambling

Many commentators, such as Kindt and Joy (2002), support the prohibition of Internet gambling because of its social, moral, and financial dangers, including security and privacy violations, fraud, pathological and underage gambling, bankruptcy, crime, and economic harm to local communities. One major government study on the social and economic impact of gambling in the United States recommended that the U.S. federal government should prohibit all online gambling that is not already authorized in the United States or between gamblers in the United States and offshore operations (NGISC, 1999). It also concluded that states should not allow the expansion of home gambling. The same study also supported the enactment of state and federal law to prohibit wire transfers to Internet gambling operations and to bar the collection of credit card debts arising from Internet gambling. It also called on the U.S. government to "take steps to encourage or enable foreign governments not to harbor Internet gambling organizations that prey on US citizens" (pp. 5–12).

One frequently voiced concern about Internet gambling is the need to protect consumers from fraudulent online gambling operations (see above). Critics of Internet gambling, such as Kindt and Joy (2002) and Schwartz (1999), fear that it causes gambling addictions leading to the squandering of family assets and bankruptcies. The NGISC (1999) reported that online gambling is likely to be especially attractive to pathological gamblers because of the instant gratification it provides, as well as the privacy, ease, convenience and 24-hour availability of gambling from home. A 2002 University of Connecticut study categorized 74% of the online gamers surveyed as pathological or problematic gamblers (Ladd & Petry, 2002). The American Psychiatric Association has issued a mental health advisory on Internet gambling, which states: "Internet gambling, unlike many other forms of gambling activity, is a solitary activity, which makes it even more dangerous: people can gamble uninterrupted and undetected for unlimited periods of time" (p. 1).

Another social concern is that Web sites facilitate gambling by underage children, who may use their parents' credit cards to gamble, thereby causing financial problems for their families. The NGISC (1999) reported that the anonymity of the Internet permits underage children to gamble online and that most gambling Web sites rely on users to provide their real age, without requiring any independent verification. A recent survey found that 7% of adolescents had gambled online, a significant rise over previous studies that reported that only 1% to 2.7% of adolescents had gambled online (Annenberg Public Policy Center, 2003). There is evidence of increased gambling addictions among young people as Internet access spreads rapidly across the globe and most online gambling sites continue to lack effective age verification controls (Kindt & Joy, 2002). A 2002 Federal Trade Commission survey of 100 Internet gambling sites found that most were easy for children to access, lacked adequate or any warnings for minors about the laws prohibiting underage gambling, and did not have any effective way to prohibit access by minors. The same survey also reported that children were exposed to ads for online gambling sites on other Web sites (Federal Trade Commission, 2002).

Additionally, some advocates for prohibitions on virtual casino gambling, such as Craig (1998), fear that Internet gambling causes economic harm to local communities. Craig argues that offshore casinos are likely to draw bettors away from local casinos, harming jobs and profits and reducing tax revenue. According to Craig, online casinos based on local servers are unlikely to create many new jobs, except for a handful of computer programmers.

The Case Against Prohibition: A More Limited Regulatory Approach

Some commentators, such as Friedrich (2003) and Loscalzo and Shapiro (2000), oppose the wholesale prohibition of Internet gambling while agreeing with prohibitionists that Internet gambling poses some serious social and moral dangers. These opponents of prohibition argue that the better course is some more limited regulation of online gambling. A variety of regulatory regimes have been proposed, ranging from industry self-regulation to several types of governmental regulation.

Proponents of regulation do not always agree on which social and moral dangers are valid concerns for online gambling. For example, Loscalzo and Shapiro (2000) agree that fraud and addiction are serious concerns, but dispute the argument that children's use of parental credit cards for Internet gambling is likely to result in family bankruptcies. They point out that there are liability limits for the unauthorized use of credit cards and contracts with minors are likely to be voidable and unenforceable.

Other supporters of more limited regulation argue that prohibition will not work. Friedrich (2003) believes that gambling is now so widespread in American society that attempts to wipe out online gambling will be as ineffective as the constitutional prohibition of alcohol was against drinking in 1920s America. According to this view, the unintended consequence of the wholesale prohibition of Internet gambling is likely to be more illegal gambling and related unlawful activity. A similar argument, made by Loscalzo and Shapiro (2000) and by Kelly (2001), is that such prohibition will encourage online gambling operations to move offshore, putting them beyond the reach of U.S. regulators.

If a society elects to regulate rather than prohibit Internet gambling, it must decide what type of regulatory regime to adopt. One commentator (Craig, 1998) enumerates several approaches short of prohibition that policymakers can take to regulate Internet gambling. These include (1) a "decriminalization" model, which tolerates Internet gambling regardless of whether the current law on the books prohibits it; (2) a "gambler protection" model, which permits some Internet gambling while attempting to ensure that online gambling operations provide fair and honest gambling services and keep criminal elements out of gaming; and (3) a "government protection" model, under which a government sponsors certain forms of gambling to generate revenue for a local community. Craig advocates the application of different regulatory models to different types of Internet gambling. He supports decriminalization of online sports gambling, a government protection model for online lotteries, and a gambler protection model for pari-mutuel wagering. Craig also argues for the prohibition of virtual casino gambling, on the basis that its social cost outweighs its social gain.

The Case Against Prohibition: A Market-Based Approach

In his list of regulatory models, Craig (1998) also includes a nongovernmental approach. This libertarian "government-neutral" model would allow the market to determine the extent of Internet gambling. Some opponents of prohibition favor this model. For example, Bell (1999) contends that legalization of Internet gambling is inevitable. Echoing the classic cyberlibertarian position famously trumpeted by John Perry Barlow in his 1996 manifesto, "A Declaration of the Independence of Cyberspace," Bell argues that effective prohibition of Internet gambling is impossible. According to Bell, the architecture of the Internet provides the technological means to evade laws prohibiting Internet gambling. Moreover, the global nature of the Internet makes purely domestic prohibitions on Internet gambling ineffectual in stopping online gambling activity. Jurisdictional and sovereignty rules limit the ability of national authorities to regulate or control offshore gambling activity. According to this view, it is pointless to enact unenforceable laws prohibiting online gambling.

Moreover, Bell argues that legalizing Internet gambling is socially beneficial. He believes that Americans enjoy gambling and will fight to continue to gamble online. According to Bell, the right to gamble is enshrined in fundamental rights and values guaranteed by the Founding Fathers, including the right to dispose of one's property as one wishes and the inalienable right to the pursuit of happiness. Another benefit, in Bell's view, is that online gambling operations will spur the development of better software and networking technology, which can be used to benefit e-commerce more broadly. He also contends that gambling at home provides a more "wholesome environment" (1999, p. 11) than that of real-world casinos. Although Bell opposes wholesale prohibition, he does not argue against all regulation, but suggests that, to be effective, it will be sufficient for such regulation to be minimal.

One possible market-based approach is industry self-regulation. As noted above, there are several watchdog organizations with the mission of furthering self-regulation of the Internet gambling industry, generally by setting standards for online gambling operations. For example, the IGC has a code of conduct requiring its members to, *inter alia*, ensure compliance with applicable laws and regulations, maintain accountability and proper record-keeping, ensure truth in advertising, prohibit access by minors, control compulsive gamblers, ensure adequate financing for prize payouts, assure customer privacy, and deter fraud. The IGC also has drafted Responsible Gaming Guidelines, which attempt to deal more specifically with the problems of addicted gamblers and underage gamblers. Some online gambling watchdogs also test, through the use of audits or other means, that their members actually adhere to their standards (see above). For example, the Gambling Commission conducts random ongoing audits on its members and also obtains information on its members through player feedback, independent research, phone interviews, and insider news and tips.

As Loscalzo and Shapiro (2000) point out, a self-regulatory model must rely heavily on the market policing itself. Such a model would not bar unregulated operations from offering online gambling services, but assumes that the market will operate to support only trustworthy and responsible operations.

The debate over whether Internet gambling should be prohibited or regulated continues. There is disagreement both over what the proper extent of regulation should be and the extent to which current law regulates or prohibits online gambling.

CURRENT REGULATION OF INTERNET GAMBLING

Both in the United States and worldwide, the application of the law to the relatively new phenomenon of Internet gambling varies widely and is accompanied by great uncertainty. This section broadly surveys the current state of the law in this area and also considers other kinds of regulation of Internet gambling.

Legal Regulation of Internet Gambling in the United States

Americans are heavily involved in online gaming and generate between 50% and 70% of online gaming revenues (U.S. GAO, 2002). Whether American players are violating U.S. federal and/or state law is a complex question because there is a patchwork of different laws regulating gambling, and most of these do not specifically address online gambling.

Federal Law

Although under the U.S. Constitution, the regulation of gambling is primarily left to state law, the Commerce Clause permits the federal government to regulate gambling that affects interstate commerce. Most Internet gambling can thus be federally regulated as long as bets are placed and received in different states or between a state and a foreign country (Gottfried, 2004).

There has been ongoing debate over whether U.S. federal law prohibits Internet gambling. Most commentators agree that federal law bans online sports betting (Miller & Claussen, 2004); the legality of casino gambling under federal law is subject to greater dispute. The Bush Administration has often repeated the assertion made in a January 2004 letter sent by the U.S. Department of Justice to the Chair of the Virgin Islands Casino Control Commission that existing federal law prohibits all types of Internet gambling, including casino-style gambling (Kelly, Mignin, & Saxman, 2004). According to this view, if an offshore gambling site accepts bets from customers in the United States, it would violate various federal laws, including the federal Wire Wager Act (Wire Act).

The Wire Act was enacted during the Kennedy Administration at a time long before the existence of online gambling. This statute, part of a series of antiracketeering laws designed to combat organized crime, specifically prohibits a person "engaged in the business of betting or wagering" from knowingly using "a wire communication facility for the transmission in interstate or foreign commerce of bets or wagers or information assisting in the placing of bets or wagers on any sporting event or contest, or for the transmission of a wire communication which entitles the recipient to receive money or credit as a result of bets or wagers, or for information assisting in the placing of bets or wagers" (Wire Act §1084(a)).

The U.S. Department of Justice has prosecuted several Internet gambling operators under the Wire Act. Some courts have found the Wire Act applicable to Internet gambling. For example, in 2000, a New York federal court convicted Jay Cohen, an American citizen, of Wire Act violations arising from his operation of a lucrative offshore Internet sports betting operation, World Sports Exchange (WSEX). Though WSEX was based in Antigua, its advertising targeted U.S. residents. Cohen voluntarily returned to the United States to fight the charges against him, though his business associates continued to operate WSEX in Antigua beyond the reach of American regulators.

Cohen unsuccessfully argued that the Wire Act's safe harbor in §1084(b) applied to Internet gambling. The safe harbor exempts transmissions from liability where (1) betting is legal in both the place of origin and the destination of the transmission and (2) the transmission is limited to mere information that assists in the placing of bets, as opposed to including the bets themselves. The U.S. Court of Appeals for the Second Circuit upheld Cohen's conviction on appeal, finding that betting was indisputably illegal in New York, and the U.S. Supreme Court refused to review this decision (*United States v. Cohen* (2001/2002)).

Cohen was sentenced to a 21-month prison term. He served 17 months at a federal minimum-security prison camp in Las Vegas and then a brief period at a halfway house in Oakland, CA before being released in May 2004 on probation for two years (Free Jay Cohen!, 2004). Cohen has continued to fight against his conviction, both by posting his views on a Web site (http://www.freejaycohen.com) and appealing the dismissal, by a New York federal district court, of his habeas corpus petition to vacate his conviction and sentence (Aronovitz & Schopper, 2004). This appeal was unsuccessful (*Cohen v. U.S.*, 2005).

Another successful Wire Act prosecution was brought in January 2000 by the U.S. Attorney's Office for the Eastern District of Missouri against the owners of Paradise Casino, an offshore sportsbook based in Curacao (U.S. Department of Justice, 2001). The owners, Marc Meghrouni and Scott Shaver, were also charged with tax fraud, and their casino was charged with money laundering. Each of these defendants entered guilty pleas to all of the charges against them and agreed to forfeit a million-dollar condominium and a 1995 Lamborghini.

The Department of Justice's view that the Wire Act prohibits all types of online gambling is controversial. A different interpretation of this law is that it applies only to Internet sports betting and not to other types of online gambling. In the only reported ruling on this issue to date, a federal appellate court in New Orleans agreed with this narrower interpretation. In November 2002, in *In Re Mastercard International Inc. Internet Gambling Litigation*, the U.S. Court of Appeals for the Fifth Circuit endorsed a federal trial court's holding that the Wire Act's statutory language clearly applies only to online gambling on sporting events or contests and not to casino-style Internet gambling. As a result, the Fifth Circuit upheld the trial court's dismissal of the complaint in the lawsuit, a class action brought under racketeering laws by Internet gamblers seeking to avoid credit card debts incurred at online casinos.

Another open question, on which courts have been divided, is whether the Wire Act covers gambling activity in which information assisting bets or wagers is received but not actually sent. For example, in *United States v. Stonehouse* (1971), the U.S. Court of Appeals for the Seventh Circuit held that the Wire Act did not apply to a situation in which the defendant used a Western Union ticker tape machine only to *receive* interstate communications that assisted in the placing of bets, because the machine did not permit him to *send* such information. Other courts have disagreed with this approach. For example, the U.S. Court of Appeals for the Eighth Circuit found, in *United States v Reeder* (1980), that the word "transmission" in the statute covered both the sending and receiving of wagering information and thus applied to the defendant's interstate telephone calls to an out-of-state sports information service. No court has yet ruled on this issue in the context of Internet gambling.

The Wire Act's requirement that a defendant be "engaged in the business of betting or wagering" (§1084(a)) appears to exclude individual casual gamblers. Courts considering the meaning of this phrase have supported this interpretation. For example, in *United States v. Baborian* (1981), the U.S. District Court for the District of Rhode Island held that Congress did not intend for social bettors to be subject to prosecution under the Wire Act, regardless of how sophisticated an individual bettor might be or how large the amount of money being wagered. In keeping with this approach, federal prosecutors have not pursued individual players for merely placing bets online.

However, Wire Act prosecutions relating to Internet gambling have not been limited to the operators of online casinos and sportsbooks. Prosecutors have also targeted online payment services for processing gambling payments. For example, the U.S. Attorney's office for the Eastern District of Missouri accused the online payment service PayPal of violating the Wire Act and the Patriot Act for processing gambling payments to offshore gambling casinos and sportsbooks between October 2001 and November 2002 (U.S. Department of Justice, 2003a). The Patriot Act, enacted in 2001, strengthens existing federal money laundering laws and prohibits money-transmitting businesses in interstate or foreign commerce from transmitting either funds derived from criminal offenses or funds intended to promote or support unlawful activity (18 U.S.C. §1960). In the PayPal case, the prosecution sought a settlement from eBay, which acquired PayPal in 2002, including payment of all earnings derived from Internet gambling over the 9-month period. In July 2003, eBay agreed to pay the U.S. Attorney's Office a settlement of $10 million and to undergo a corporate compliance program. eBay has now ceased the processing of gambling payments.

Other federal laws may apply to Internet gambling, including the Racketeer Influenced and Corrupt Organizations Act (RICO), the Travel Act, the Wagering Paraphernalia Act of 1961, and the Illegal Gambling Business Act. The RICO Act imposes both civil and criminal penalties for receiving and using or investing income from "a pattern of racketeering activity," including illegal gambling as well as the collection of unlawful debt, such as a debt incurred in connection with unlawful gambling activity (18 U.S.C. §1962(a)).

Federal prosecutions have been brought successfully under racketeering laws against Internet gambling operations and operators. For example, an Internet sportsbook based offshore on the island of Curacao in the Netherlands Antilles, Gold Medal Sports, pleaded guilty to racketeering in December 2001 in a federal district court in Madison, WI (U.S. Department of Justice, 2001). Gold Medal Sports agreed to cease operating and to forfeit criminal earnings of more than $3 million. The two primary owners of Gold Medal Sports also pleaded guilty to violating the Wire Act and filing false tax returns. They were each sentenced to 5 years in prison and paid fines of $100,000 each, as well as back taxes cumulatively amounting to over $1.4 million (U.S. Department of Justice, 2002). Five others involved in Gold Medal Sports, including two accountants and two attorneys, were also indicted on federal charges. Three pleaded guilty, and one became a fugitive from justice. The fifth was later convicted at trial (Thompson, 2003).

Internet gambling operations have also been prosecuted for violations of the federal Travel Act, which criminalizes interstate travel or use of the mail or any facility with intent to distribute the proceeds of illegal gambling activity, to commit any crime of violence to further such activity, or to otherwise promote or carry on such activity. In *People v. World Interactive Gaming Corporation* (1999), a New York state trial court found that the operator of an Internet casino that offered online gambling to New York residents was guilty of violating both the Travel Act and the Wire Act. Because the defendants knowingly violated New York's antigambling laws, they had conducted "unlawful activity" under the Travel Act. The defendant, a Delaware corporation that operated an online casino based in Antigua, was enjoined from conducting business in New York and also had to pay restitution, penalties, and damages.

Another indictment involving Travel Act violations arising out of Internet gambling activities was announced in October 2003 by the U.S. Attorney's Office for the Northern District of California (U.S. Department of Justice, 2003b). Four individuals and two businesses controlled by them were indicted on various conspiracy, money laundering, and Travel Act charges. According to the indictment, the defendants allegedly formed one of the companies, Gold Chips Technologies, to develop Internet gaming software for virtual casinos.

Some Internet gambling transactions may be subject to the Wagering Paraphernalia Act, which prohibits anyone except common carriers from knowingly carrying or sending "in interstate or foreign commerce any record, paraphernalia, ticket, certificate, bills, slip, token, paper, writing, or other device used or to be used, or adapted, devised or designed for use in (a) bookmaking; or (b) wagering pools with respect to a sporting event; or (c) in a numbers, policy, bolita, or similar game" (18 U.S.C. §1953(a)). Violators are subject to fines or imprisonment for up to 5 years. Although the Wagering Paraphernalia Act contains an exception for "the transportation of betting materials to be used in the placing of bets or wagers on a sporting event into a State in which such betting is legal" (18 U.S.C. §1953(b)), this provision has been found to be inapplicable to the transportation of lottery tickets to a foreign country where betting is legal (*United States v. Baker,* 1966). Although the Wagering Paraphernalia Act was subsequently amended to add a specific exception for such activity, it may still prohibit many other types of offshore Internet gambling transactions. It was held to be violated in *People v. World Interactive Gaming Corporation* (1999), in which records of gambling activity were sent from Antigua to New York and computers used for gambling were sent from New York to Antigua. Some commentators, such as Schwartz (1999), have contended that the Wagering Paraphernalia Act, the Travel Act, and the Wire Act should all be interpreted broadly to apply to online gambling because of the common purpose underlying all these statutes, namely to prohibit the use of interstate commerce for immoral or illegal purposes.

The Illegal Gambling Business Act prohibits illegal gambling businesses. An illegal gambling business is defined as a gambling business that violates the local law where it is conducted; involves at least five people in its conduct, financing, management, supervision, direction, or ownership; and has been in substantially continuous operation for more than 30 days or has a gross revenue of at least $2,000 in any single day (18 U.S.C. § 1955(b)(1)).

Another federal statute that is relevant to Internet gambling is the Indian Gaming Regulatory Act (IGRA). IGRA permits some gambling on Indian reservations, providing that certain types of games are subject to the agreement of a tribal-state compact. IGRA could apply to Internet gambling if it takes place on tribal lands. The Eighth Circuit considered this issue when the Missouri Attorney General sought to bar the Coeur d'Alene Indian Tribe (the Tribe) in Idaho from accepting money from Missouri residents using home computers to play an Internet lottery run by the Tribe under an IGRA compact with Idaho. The Tribe claimed that IGRA preempted Idaho from regulating the lottery. In *Missouri ex rel Nixon v. Coeur D'Alene Tribe* (1999), the Eighth Circuit ruled that the federal district court had erred in its finding that IGRA completely preempted the field of Internet gaming, and it instructed the federal district court to determine whether the lottery was on Indian lands. Only if it was would IGRA completely preempt the state's right to regulate or prohibit the lottery. The U.S. Supreme Court denied certiorari (1999). The case was eventually settled without clearly resolving this issue.

The Tribe has shut down its Internet lottery, but it may not be offline forever. A recent Ninth Circuit decision may have provided the Tribe with a ray of hope for its online lottery. This case arose out of a dispute over interstate toll-free phone service, which the Tribe had sought to obtain for the lottery from various services, including AT&T. When, under pressure from various state attorneys general, AT&T refused to provide toll-free telephone service for the lottery, the Tribe successfully sued in Coeur d'Alene Tribal Court to force AT&T to do so. AT&T then filed suit in federal district court in Idaho, arguing that the Tribal Court lacked jurisdiction. The district court ruled that, although the lottery's administration occurred on tribal lands, because some lottery participants were buying their tickets when off the Tribe's reservation IGRA did not govern the lottery, and thus the Tribal Court's ruling was erroneous as a matter of law. This ruling mooted AT&T's

jurisdictional challenge. However, the district court also granted AT&T declaratory relief, ruling that the telephone company was not required to provide toll-free telephone service from any state that notified AT&T that the lottery violated that state's law. On appeal, the Ninth Circuit ruled in *AT&T v. Coeur d'Alene Tribe* (2002) that the tribal court did lack jurisdiction, but AT&T was not the proper challenger. Because the National Indian Gaming Commission had approved the Tribe's lottery, the states should have filed the action. AT&T decided not to petition the Supreme Court for review, but left it to the states to mount further legal challenges to the lottery. At the time of this writing, the states have not yet acted and the Tribe has not yet restarted the lottery.

Another federal statute, the Interstate Horseracing Act (IHA) has been viewed by some, including the World Trade Organization's Dispute Settlement Body, as permitting the extension of some legal gambling operations to the online environment. Congress enacted the IHA to regulate interstate pari-mutuel wagering on horse races. In pari-mutuel wagering, the bets are pooled. The winning bettors take approximately 80% of the pool, and the remainder goes to the jockeys, racetrack owners, and the state government licensing the horserace. The IHA prohibits interstate off-track wagers except where certain consents have been obtained, including from the host racing association, the host racing commission, the off-track racing commission, and, in most circumstances, all racetracks operating within 60 miles of where the wager is accepted. The statute defines an "interstate off-track wager" as a "legal wager placed or accepted in one State with respect to the outcome of a horserace taking place in another State and includes pari-mutuel wagers, where lawful in each State involved, placed or transmitted by an individual in one State via telephone or other electronic media and accepted by an off-track betting system in the same or another State, as well as the combination of any pari-mutuel wagering pools" (15 U.S.C. §3002).

This language, which was amended in 2000 over objections by the U.S. Department of Justice, appears to permit wagering on horses over the Internet, subject to the required consents. Although the Department of Justice stated in 2000 that it considered the offering of bets on horses over the Internet to violate the Wire Act regardless of this amendment (Bishop, 2000-2001), at the time of this writing no state-licensed horse racing tracks have been prosecuted for conducting Internet betting.

Excluding horse racing, dog racing, and jai alai, most sports betting is now prohibited by the federal Professional and Amateur Sports Protection Act of 1992 (PASPA). This law prohibits the establishment of state-sponsored gambling operations for betting or wagering on amateur and professional sports. However, PASPA contains some exceptions for certain preexisting legal sports wagering, including Nevada's state sports pools and Oregon's sports lottery, as well as exemptions for horseracing, dog racing, and jai alai. PASPA's opponents included the Department of Justice, which considered the law to intrude excessively on states' rights (Senate Report, 1991). A contrary position was offered by the National Gambling Impact Study Committee, which criticized PASPA for not being strong enough (NGISC, 1999). The NGISC recommended that state exemptions should be removed

entirely for collegiate and amateur sporting events. Some commentators, such as Cabot and Faiss (2002), have criticized PASPA for its ineffectiveness in deterring sports gambling, which is widespread and broadly socially accepted and amounts to a significant proportion of Internet gambling.

This brief survey of federal law relating to Internet gambling has sought to show its complexity and lack of clarity. Even if the Justice Department is correct in its contention that federal law clearly prohibits online gambling, there would still be jurisdictional and enforcement barriers to suing offshore gambling operations successfully. In recognition of these barriers, most recent federal enforcement efforts against offshore Internet gambling have targeted such operations indirectly by pursuing companies that service offshore gambling operations, including advertisers, consultants, and Web portals.

In 2003, the Department of Justice launched an initiative, spearheaded by the U.S. Attorney's Office for the Eastern District of Missouri, against broadcasters and other media outlets, warning them that running ads for online casinos and offshore sportsbooks amounted to "aiding and abetting" violations of federal law for which they would risk prosecution (Walters, 2004). Since then, federal law enforcement officials have continued to take even more aggressive action against advertisers and promoters of online gambling operations. Their efforts have included the use of investigative subpoenas seeking information and documents about media companies' ties to offshore gambling operations, as well the seizure of millions of dollars from one media company, Discovery Communications (Discovery), which had placed television ads for an offshore gambling operation, Costa-Rican-based Tropical Paradise (Richtel, 2004). Tropical Paradise later sued Discovery for breach of contract. The case was dismissed without prejudice in June 2004.

This latest federal enforcement effort has had significant results. Major search engines Google and Yahoo, as well as broadcasters Infinity Broadcasting and Clear Channel Communications, have stopped taking the placement of ads for online gambling operations (Richtel). Nevertheless, the First Amendment's protection for commercial speech makes the Justice Department's "aiding and abetting" argument legally controversial. The U.S. Supreme Court recently held in *Greater New Orleans Broadcasting Association, Inc. v. United States* (1999) that the government's ability to regulate gambling is not necessarily coextensive with its ability to regulate the advertising and marketing of gambling, but the precise extent of constitutional protection for online gambling advertising has not yet been resolved definitively by the courts (Walters, 2004).

The operator of several portal websites on online gambling, Casino City, Inc. (Casino City) attacked the Justice Department's enforcement actions by filing suit in August 2004 in the United States District Court for the Middle District of Louisiana, seeking a declaratory judgment that it has a constitutional right, under the First Amendment, to sell and run advertising for online gambling operations based in jurisdictions that have legalized such activity (*Casino City v. United States Dep't of Justice* (2004)). In February 2005, the court dismissed the case on the basis that Casino City lacked standing, finding that Casino

City's self-described conduct could not amount to aiding and abetting federal law, and that Casino City was subject to no credible threat of prosecution. Additionally, the court found that Casino City had not established a valid right under the First Amendment, which did not guarantee the right to advertise unlawful activity. Casino City's appeal against this ruling is currently pending. Advertising for online gambling thus remains yet another area of uncertainty for the applicability of existing federal law to online gambling activities.

Proposed Federal Legislation

None of the existing federal laws discussed above specifically addresses the legality of Internet gambling. Since 1995, several bills have been introduced to more clearly prohibit or regulate Internet gambling. None of these has yet been enacted into law. In June 2003, the House of Representatives did pass one piece of proposed legislation, the Unlawful Internet Gambling Funding Prohibition Act, sponsored by Representative Spencer Bachus, an Alabama Republican. This bill sought to choke off the financial transactions, including credit card payments and electronic fund transfers, used by Americans to pay for Internet gambling at offshore casinos. This proposed law, gave federal regulators 6 months to draft regulations to restrict such financial transactions. The bill provided that these restrictions must be "reasonably designed to identify and prevent" such transactions (H.R. 2143, §3(a) (2003)). Transactions with lawful state-sponsored gambling operations, including horse racing, dog racing, and lotteries, were exempted.

In July 2003 the Senate Banking Committee voted to report an amended form of a somewhat similar legislative proposal, the Unlawful Internet Gambling Prohibition Act of 2003 (S. 627), to the Senate for consideration. Senator Jon Kyl, an Arizona Republican, originally introduced this bill. Like its House of Representatives counterpart, S. 627 would prohibit gambling businesses from accepting credit cards or other bank instruments in connection with Internet gambling (S. 627 §3 (2003)), though it differed from the Bachus bill by including criminal sanctions and eliminating the exemption for state online lotteries. Congress never had to reconcile the two bills because the full Senate never acted on S. 627. Even though these particular legislative proposals have not been enacted, many observers believe that federal legislation specifically regulating Internet gambling legislation is now likely. However, there is little agreement on when this will happen or the form it will take.

State Law

The Constitution leaves the regulation of gambling largely to the states through the exercise of their police power. In *United States v. Edge Broadcasting* (1993), the U.S. Supreme Court stated: "While lotteries have existed in this country since its founding, States have long viewed them as a hazard to their citizens and to the public interest, and have long engaged in legislative efforts to control this form of gambling" (p. 421). Another U.S. Supreme Court decision, *Greater New Orleans Broadcasting Association, Inc. v. United States* (1999), stated "[t]hat Congress has generally exempted state-run lotteries and casinos from

federal gambling legislation reflects a decision to defer to, and even promote, differing gambling policies in different States" (p. 187).

Each state can decide whether to allow any gambling within its borders and, if so, which kind of gambling operations to permit. Although there is considerable variation in the extent to which different states regulate gambling, most states license or permit at least some forms of gambling. Only two states, Utah and Hawaii, entirely prohibit gambling.

The gambling laws of most states do not specifically address online gambling. One state, Nevada, has passed legislation that would legalize Internet gambling, but implementation is currently stalled due to the hostility of certain U.S. federal authorities to the law, including the Justice Department (Kelly, Mignin, & Saxman, 2004). An American territory, the Virgin Islands, has also enacted legislation to legalize Internet gambling, but federal authorities consider it to violate federal law (Kelly et al.). Several states, including Illinois, South Dakota, Nevada, Louisiana, and Oregon, have passed laws specifically prohibiting Internet gambling. Many of these state laws have carve-outs for existing forms of legal gambling. For example, the Illinois law contains exceptions for, *inter alia*, state-licensed pari-mutuel wagering, certain games of bingo, Illinois-sponsored state lotteries, certain raffles, certain riverboat gambling, and certain charitable games (720 Ill. Comp. Stat. Ann. 5/28-1(b)(2005)). South Dakota's prohibition on Internet gambling is not applicable to the South Dakota lottery (S.D. Codified Laws §22-25A-15 (2004)). Louisiana's prohibition on Internet gambling is inapplicable to, *inter alia*, certain riverboat gambling, certain pari-mutuel wagering, certain charitable gaming, and Louisiana state-licensed lotteries (Louisiana Revised Statutes 14: 90.3 (F) (2005)).

Perhaps oddly, the states that have enacted specific Internet gambling prohibitions have not actively enforced them. This may be attributable to constitutional hurdles posed by the "dormant Commerce Clause," which bars a state statute from applying to commerce taking place entirely outside the state's borders, even if the commerce has effects within the state (Kelly, Mignin, & Saxman, 2004). However, other states that lack specific prohibitions for Internet gambling have launched enforcement efforts against online gambling.

The attorneys general of several states, including Florida, Indiana, Kansas, Louisiana, and Texas, have issued opinions that Internet gambling is generally illegal under state law, with few exceptions (Kelly, Mignin, & Saxman, 2004). The attorneys general of other states, including Arizona and Colorado, have sought to regulate online gambling by requesting media entities not to broadcast advertising for it (Kelly et al.). Some state attorneys general have prosecuted gambling operations that have permitted residents of their states to bet on the Internet.

New York Attorney General Eliot Spitzer has been particularly aggressive in enforcing New York's antigambling laws. All types of gambling except pari-mutuel wagering and the state lottery are illegal in New York (*United States v. Cohen*, 2001), and there have been successful prosecutions of online gambling operators in New York state and federal courts, including the Wire Act prosecution discussed above against Jay Cohen, the American operator of an Internet casino based in Antigua that took bets from residents of New York. No doubt aware of how difficult it is to prosecute offshore enterprises, Spitzer has taken action successfully against financial institutions in an effort to block the payments used for online wagering.

Spitzer launched an investigation of Citibank's Internet gambling transaction policy and threatened the credit card giant with civil or criminal actions for advancing or profiting from illegal gambling activity. In response, Citibank agreed to introduce a policy, lasting for 5 years, to block transactions coded by Visa and Mastercard that indicate that a customer has engaged in online gambling (Attorney General of the State of New York Internet Bureau, 2002a). Apparently fearing investigations by other states' attorneys general, Citibank agreed to block transactions for customers in all 50 states. Another Spitzer investigation led to a 2002 agreement with online payment service PayPal, under which PayPal agreed not to process payments by PayPal's New York members for online gambling transactions prohibited by New York law (Attorney General of the State of New York Internet Bureau, 2002b). As noted above, PayPal was subsequently acquired by eBay, which has terminated the processing of online gambling payments.

Other state attorneys general have also been active in pursuing those they believe to be operating unlawful Internet gambling enterprises. For example, in 2001, then New Jersey Attorney General John Farmer brought several civil lawsuits against various operators of offshore Internet casinos and sports betting operations, as well as suppliers, such as Cryptologic, a gaming software developer. In 2002, two of these lawsuits were settled on terms that included the agreement of the online betting operations not to accept bets from people located in New Jersey and that of the suppliers to use their best efforts to prevent their customers or licensees from accepting online bets from people in New Jersey (Kelly et al., 2004; New Jersey Office of Attorney General, 2002).

Missouri Attorney General Jay Nixon, also an active opponent of online gambling brought the first successful prosecution of an Internet gambling operation in 1998, obtaining guilty pleas from a Pennsylvania business, Interactive Gaming & Communications (IGC), as well as from its president, Michael Simone, for violating Missouri law by accepting gambling wagers over the Internet from a Missouri resident. Both Simone and IGC pleaded guilty. As part of Simone's plea, he agreed to pay a $2,500 fine. IGC agreed to pay a $5,000 fine, as well as a $20,000 payment for the costs of the prosecution (Missouri Attorney General's Office, 1998).

In 1995, then Minnesota Attorney General Hubert Humphrey III filed a lawsuit for injunctive relief under Minnesota consumer protection law against Granite Gate Resorts, Inc., a Nevada corporation that provided online advertising for a planned Internet sports wagering service, WagerNet, which was to be run out of Belize. Humphrey alleged that Granite Gate's advertising in Minnesota that Internet gambling was lawful amounted to deceptive trade practices, consumer fraud, and false advertising. Ruling on Granite Gate's challenge to the Minnesota court's jurisdiction, a Minnesota state trial court judge refused to dismiss the case. The Court of Appeals of Minnesota subsequently affirmed the trial court's decision, finding that, Granite Gate had sufficient contacts with Minnesota that the lawsuit did not offend due process by reason of its Internet advertising directed to a nationwide market, including Minnesota residents, as well as its solicitation of Minnesota residents. An equally divided Supreme Court of Minnesota later affirmed the decision of the Court of Appeals (*State by Humphrey v. Granite Gate Resorts*, 1998). The case was settled in 1999 (Kelly et al., 2004).

Attorneys general from Missouri and Wisconsin have also taken action to stop Indian tribes from offering Internet gambling to residents of their states. As discussed above, when the Idaho Coeur d'Alene tribe set up a national Internet lottery, the Attorney General of Missouri filed suit in 1998 to stop this service being offered to Missouri residents. Later, then Wisconsin Attorney General Jim Doyle, also sued to block the lottery, claiming it violated Wisconsin law. The U.S. District Court for the District of Wisconsin ruled that Wisconsin could not regulate Internet gambling by Indian tribes because of their sovereign immunity (Kelly, 2000). However, the contractor hired by the technology company to operate its online lottery, Unistar Entertainment, was not protected by sovereign immunity. The Wisconsin lottery case was later settled. Other lawsuits brought by the state of Wisconsin against online gambling operations have also ended with settlements (Kelly, 2000).

Targeting Gambling Payments

State attorneys general have not been the only ones to target Internet gambling payments, as discussed above. Some online gamblers have sought to prevent collection on their Internet gambling debts by claiming that credit card companies and card-issuing banks have facilitated illegal gambling. One example is a California state court case, *Providian National Bank v. Haines* (1998). The defendant, Cynthia Haines, used credit cards to rack up $70,000 in Internet gambling charges, but did not pay her credit card bills. When one of the banks that had issued Haines with a credit card, Providian National Bank (Providian), sued her, she counterclaimed that Providian's efforts to recoup the debt violated California law because online gambling transactions were illegal, unfair, and unenforceable. She also added claims against Visa and MasterCard, alleging that they had acted unlawfully in allowing her to use her credit card for illegal Internet gambling. Both MasterCard and Visa eventually settled with Haines (Anastasio, 2001).

Under the settlements, Haines did not have to pay back her debts herself. The online gambling sites would cover the payments with the card-issuing banks, and Visa agreed to pay the banks, including paying Providian the almost $5,000 that Haines had accrued using a Providian-sponsored card (Macavinta, 1999). The settlements also required MasterCard to implement a new policy that required gambling sites accepting its cards to post notices that Internet gambling was illegal in some jurisdictions (Anastasio, 2001). These gambling sites also had to ask gamblers where they were located. Visa agreed to send its cardholders nationwide notices stating that Internet gambling was illegal in some jurisdictions and that their credit cards could only be used for legal transactions (Macavinta, 1999).

Some courts have been hostile to Internet gamblers who have attempted to evade their gambling debts. For example, in 1999, the U.S. District Court for the Western District of Wisconsin dismissed a class action lawsuit brought by an Internet gambler, Ari Jubelirer, against MasterCard and MBNA America Bank seeking a declaratory judgment that the defendants had violated federal racketeering law by paying credit card charges to illegal gambling operators (*Jubelirer v. Mastercard International, Inc.*, 1999). Jubelirer sought to prevent collection of his $20 online gambling loss, as well as a $4.95 processing fee. Ordering Jubelirer's complaint dismissed for disclosing no viable cause of action, District Judge John C. Shabaz wrote, "However broadly worded, the RICO statute is not to be applied to 'situations absurdly remote from the concerns of the statute's framers'" (p. 1053 [citation omitted]).

Despite the outcome in *Jubelirer*, after the *Haines* settlement many credit card companies remain concerned about lawsuits founded on claims that they are facilitating unlawful gambling activity. They are also worried about fraudulent charges. The full-service credit card companies, American Express Company and Discover Financial Services, have instituted policies prohibiting the use of their cards for Internet gambling and have also implemented procedures designed to ensure that Internet gambling operations do not become merchants for their credit cards (U.S. GAO, 2002). Both of the major credit card associations, Visa and MasterCard, now have policies and a coding system that allow members to deny authorization for Internet gambling transactions, although they do not require members to do so (U.S. GAO, 2002). The voluntary nature of these policies may be attributable to the fact that many of these association's members are located in areas of the world where Internet gambling is legal.

Member banks that are authorized to issue credit cards often attempt to block Internet gambling transactions, sometimes using third-party processors to assist them. These banks are waging a continuous battle with Internet gambling sites, some of which attempt to disguise gambling transactions or to mask where payments are going through the use of online payment providers like NETeller. Many of the largest American member banks that issue credit cards, as well as most small community bank issuers, have started to block online gambling transactions (U.S. GAO, 2002). These banks include Bank of America, Fleet, Direct Merchants Bank, MBNA, Chase Manhattan Bank, and Citibank. American acquiring banks that are members of credit card associations try not to acquire Internet gambling operations as merchants, although some non-U.S. acquiring banks do not attempt to restrict such operations from becoming merchants (U.S. GAO, 2002).

Regulation of Internet Gambling in the Rest of the World

The discretionary nature of the credit card associations' Internet gambling policies is the result of wide variation in the regulation of Internet gambling around the world. In contrast to the prohibitionist stance of the U.S. federal government, around 75 jurisdictions have legalized various types of online gambling (Schneider, 2004). Antigua and Barbuda, Belgium, Belize, Dominica, Gibraltar, Isle of Man, Liechtenstein, the Netherlands Antilles, and dozens of other jurisdictions currently permit some type of Internet gambling, although a detailed discussion of their laws is outside the scope of this relatively brief overview.

Worldwide regulatory approaches to online gaming include a prohibitionist model, a gambler protection model, and a government protection model (Cabot, 2004). As discussed above, the U.S. Justice Department takes a prohibitionist stance toward online gambling, although there is debate over the extent to which federal law actually prohibits online gambling. The theory underlying the gambler protection model of regulation is that gambling cannot be effectively prohibited, even if it is a potentially harmful activity (Cabot). Governments regulating on this basis issue gambling licenses subject to restrictions designed to protect against the social harms discussed above, such as security violations, problem gambling, underage gambling, and the use of gambling operations to launder money. An example is Antigua and Barbuda's Gaming Regulations of 2001 (Antigua and Barbuda, 2003). A third type of regulation, the government protection model, permits at least some online gambling because of its economic and social benefits, such as generating tax revenues, contributing to charities, and promoting employment (Cabot). An example of this type of regulation is the online lottery sponsored by the government of Liechtenstein at http://www.interlotto.li/.

Some less developed countries have legalized online gambling as a means to stimulate economic development by generating government revenue in license fees and taxes and increasing employment. In 1999 the small Caribbean nation of Antigua and Barbuda, with a population of less than 100,000, had 119 licensed online "remote access" gambling operators employing approximately 3,000 citizens and generating approximately 10% of its gross domestic product (Antigua and Barbuda, 2003).

However, between 1999 and 2003 there was a considerable reduction in the number of Antiguan-based online gambling operations, decreasing by more than three-quarters to 28, and also a very significant drop in number of their employees, from around 3,000 to fewer than 500. The Government of Antigua and Barbuda has charged that a "material factor" in this decrease is the "increasingly aggressive" action that the U.S. has taken against offshore gambling operations that it views as unlawful (Antigua and Barbuda, 2003, pp. 1–2).

This decline in Antiguan online gaming operations has generated an international trade conflict. In 2003, the Government of Antigua and Barbuda submitted a dispute to the World Trade Association (WTO), contending that existing and proposed American federal and state laws prohibiting cross-border Internet gambling, as well as executive and judicial acts taken against offshore gambling operations, put the United States in violation of its treaty obligations under the WTO's General Agreement on Trade in Services (GATS), including its market access and national treatment commitments, because the United States measures treated foreign suppliers of cross-border gambling services less favorably than domestic providers of gambling services. Antigua's position was that the fundamental issue is international development, specifically the development of global e-commerce, which the United States pledged to foster at a 2001 WTO ministerial conference in Doha, Qatar (Directorate of Offshore Gambling, 2003; Doha Declaration, 2001; Sanders, 2003).

Antiguan officials argued that the online casino industry helps provide much-needed employment to Antigua's young people, helping deter them from turning to unlawful means of livelihood, such as the drug trade. They also argued that concerns about crime and money laundering are unfounded because the online casino industry in Antigua and Barbuda is tightly regulated and supervised by the government (Antigua and Barbuda, 2003). Although, as noted above, the extent to which U.S. federal law, as well as state law, bars cross-border Internet gambling is a complex and uncertain question, Antigua argued that the United States conceded that it has measures that totally prohibit cross-border Internet gambling services from Antigua. In support of this argument, Antigua relied, *inter alia*, on various U.S. government statements that it is always illegal for foreign operators to provide cross-border Internet gambling services anywhere in the United States.

In response, the United States criticized Antigua's characterization of American federal and state law as cumulatively amounting to a complete prohibition of cross-border Internet gambling, contending that Antigua had not satisfied the burden it bore as complainant to establish a *prima facie* case that some specific regulatory measure is not consistent with U.S. obligations under GATS. Additionally, the United States denied that cross-border gambling services are within its commitments under GATS and argued that even if they were, Antigua had not proved that any U.S. measure is inconsistent with its GATS obligations. In support of the latter argument, the United States argued that remote online gambling poses serious financial and social dangers, such as crime, money laundering, and problem or addictive gambling (United States, 2003).

In July 2003, the Dispute Settlement Body of the WTO agreed to establish a dispute resolution panel (WTO, 2003). In the spring of 2004, the WTO panel assigned to this case issued a confidential report on the dispute (Georgi, Vlaemminck, & Alberda, 2004). Although this report was not immediately made publicly available, it was widely reported to be in favor of Antigua's position, and the United States immediately stated its intention to appeal to the WTO's Appellate Body (Georgi et al., 2004).

In late June 2004, the WTO panel agreed to a suspension of the dispute until August 23, 2004, giving the parties time to attempt to resolve the dispute through negotiations (WTO, 2004a). The panel subsequently agreed to two additional extensions, the first until early October 2004 and the second until mid-November 2004 (WTO, 2004b, WTO, 2004c). Antigua requested the resumption of the proceedings in November 2004, and the United States did not object.

The WTO panel made its report public on November 2004 (WTO, 2004d). The panel found that the United States had made specific commitments under GATs with regard to gambling and betting services and, rejecting the argument that Antigua had failed to make out a prima facie case that specific U.S. measures violated these obligations, also found that certain U.S. federal and state laws, including the federal Wire Act, Travel Act, and Illegal Gambling Business Act, as well as the Louisiana and South Dakota prohibitions on Internet gambling, amounted to GATS violations. The panel also found that the United States had not been able to establish that the laws were justified under an exception in GATS permitting WTO members to adopt measures necessary to protect public morals or maintain public order, because the United States had failed to consult with Antigua before imposing its prohibitions on the cross-border supply of gambling and betting services The panel additionally found that Antigua had failed to show that these U.S. measures were not administered in a reasonable, objective and impartial manner in violation of other provisions in GATS.

The United States appealed to the Appellate Body in January 2005 (WTO, 2005a). Antigua also appealed on some issues. In April 2005, the Appellate Body circulated its report (WTO, 2005b; WTO, 2005c).

Both sides' appellate arguments had mixed success in the Appellate Body's 145-page report. The Appellate Body rejected the United States' argument that Antigua had failed to sufficiently identify particular federal measures that it alleged to be in violation of GATS, finding that Antigua had made out a *prima facie* case of inconsistency for the Travel Act, the Wire Act, and the Illegal Gambling Business Act. But the Appellate Body found that Antigua had not done so for the state laws reviewed by the panel.

The Appellate Body also rejected the contention of the United States that it had not excluded gambling and betting services from its commitments under GATS. Nevertheless, the Appellate Body agreed with the United States that it could restrict gambling if it was necessary to protect public morals or maintain public order. The Appellate Body found that the United States had succeeded in showing that there was a connection between Internet gambling and danger to the American public, but it rejected the claim that remote gambling was linked to organized crime. It disagreed with the panel's finding that the United States had failed to show that the three statutes were necessary based on the lack of consultation with Antigua. As a result, the Appellate Body concluded that it was legitimate for the United States federal government to legislate the prohibitions in the Travel Act, the Wire Act, and the Illegal Gambling Business Act to protect American residents, provided that such laws did not discriminate against foreign businesses. But the Appellate Body also found that the United States had failed to establish that the prohibitions in the three statutes were applied equally to both domestic and foreign suppliers of gambling services. Another federal statute, the Interstate Horseracing Act, appeared, on its face, to exempt certain domestic suppliers from the prohibitions under the three federal statutes on the provision of remote pari-mutuel betting on horseracing. The Appellate Body did not find it necessary to rule on whether the IHA in fact had this discriminatory effect.

The Appellate Body's report recommended that the Dispute Settlement Body request the United States to bring its laws into conformity with its obligations under GATS. On April 25, 2005, the Dispute Settlement Body adopted the Appellate Body's report (WTO, 2005d). In May 2005, the United States stated that it would require a reasonable period of time to comply with the Dispute Settlement Body's recommendations and rulings, but could not agree with Antigua on what a reasonable period would be (WTO, 2005e) Antigua requested that this dispute be resolved through binding arbitration under WTO dispute settlement rules by July 19, 2005.

The rulings and recommendations of the WTO Dispute Settlement Body have no immediate effect on U.S. law, which can be changed only by Congress. The current administration is unlikely to support legislation to permit foreign gambling operators to provide services to U.S. residents. But the horseracing lobby is likely to oppose legislation to ban all online gambling on horseracing. Rather than amending its law, the United States could opt to pay compensation or be subject to trade sanctions by Antigua and Barbuda (Georgi, Valemminck, & Alberda, 2004). Such sanctions might, ironically, inflict less harm on the United States than the small Caribbean nation.

However until this international trade law dispute is ultimately resolved, its existence demonstrates that Internet gambling has become a significant trade and development issue. It also highlights the global aspect of the controversy over online gambling. Because the Internet lacks geographical borders, the regulatory systems adopted by one jurisdiction to control online activity are likely to have significant effects elsewhere in the world. This makes the effective regulation of Internet gambling even more of a challenge than for offline forms of gambling.

CONCLUSION: THE FUTURE OF INTERNET GAMBLING

The future of the Internet gambling industry and how it will be regulated are uncertain. Some recent events seem to be harbingers of a future decline for the industry, such as the decision by some major financial institutions not to get involved with online gambling, as well as the recent crackdown by U.S. federal authorities on some media companies for placing advertisements for Internet gambling operations. Other recent technological developments, including alternate payment systems and wireless gambling systems, seem to point in the opposite direction.

The recent actions taken by American credit card-issuing banks to block Internet gambling transactions did put serious financial pressure on some online gambling operations. During 2001 and 2002, many online gambling operations experienced a decline in revenues by up to 70 or 80%, and some smaller operations did not survive this downturn (Cabot & Balestra, 2004). However, the industry as a whole is continuing to experience growth. Many commentators believe that the future of the online gambling industry will depend on the success of alternate digital payment systems, such as e-cash or smart cards. If such new types of payment systems become widespread, a perverse long-term effect of Internet gambling regulation by U.S. federal and state authorities may be an increase in the fraud and money laundering that such regulation is designed to prevent, because the greater anonymity of e-cash and similar alternate payment systems makes it more difficult to trace payments.

New wireless hand-held gambling technology is being developed, which seems likely to foster the growth of the industry by allowing players to make wagers anywhere they happen to be, whether in the street, at the bank, at the post office, in a café, in a store, or elsewhere. Wireless wagering devices are already used quite widely in Asia, where over 100,000 Hong Kong bettors own them, but they have been slower to reach the American market (Finley, 2004). However, in 2004, the online horseracing wagering company Youbet introduced a wireless subscription wagering service for American consumers in many states using certain pocket PC phones. This service was developed by Digital Orchard, which maintains a Youbet Anywhere website at http://products.digitalorchid.com/youbet/. There are plans to add live video streaming to enable customers to watch and bet on races as they are being run, no matter where those customers may be (Finley, 2004).

Across the globe, the law is having great difficulty in keeping pace with technological development. As discussed above, many gambling laws were drafted so long ago that they do not make any specific provision for online gambling. Even as new laws are drafted that deal with online gambling specifically, digital gambling technologies are evolving so rapidly that these new laws may be obsolete in many respects by the time they are enacted. This situation poses a serious challenge to the rule of law. The law must find a way to function effectively in this climate of technological change if it is to retain its central importance in society. If the law permits technology to trump its regulatory effect, it will lose its power to affect human behavior and ultimately to shape a just society. How the law should deal with this problem is one of the central problems of our Internet age.

A second central problem that is implicated by Internet gambling is whether one jurisdiction's regulatory regime can legitimately affect online activity by people who are physically outside that jurisdiction's borders. The WTO dispute between Antigua and the United States exemplifies this difficult problem.

Regulators confronting the security and privacy problems of Internet gambling must bear both of these central problems in mind when seeking to craft a regulatory framework for Internet gambling. This has already proved to be a very difficult challenge, and there is little likelihood that the immediate future will see an end to the many conflicts over gambling online.

ACKNOWLEDGMENTS

The author would like to express her gratitude to Stan McCoy, Assistant General Counsel, Office of the U.S. Trade Representative, and Kay C. Georgi, a partner in the Washington D.C. office of Coudert Brothers LLP, for providing expert advice on the international trade dispute between Antigua and the United States.

GLOSSARY

Black-holing The hijacking of a gambling Web site.
Casino A place where games of chance are played.
Cyberlibertarian An ideology of regulation for cyberspace that frowns on any intervention by national

governments and encourages the free flow of information over the Internet.

Distributed denial of service (DDOS) attack The flooding of computer servers with packets of data by malicious Web users, who are typically exploiting the vulnerability of insufficiently secured computers. The goal of a DDOS attack is to shut down targeted systems and to deny legitimate users the ability to access and use these systems.

Extortion Blackmail, or an offense that includes the illegal taking of money by anyone who employs threats or other illegal use of fear or coercion; commonly punishable as a felony.

Fraud A knowing misrepresentation made with the intent of causing another to detrimentally rely on it; can be punishable as a crime.

Internet gambling Gambling in which the Internet is used to place bets or wagers. Many courts require three elements–a prize, consideration, and chance–for an activity to be considered gambling.

Jurisdiction The legal authority of a court to hear and decide a case; the geographical area over which a court has authority to decide cases.

Money laundering The process whereby criminals conceal illicitly acquired funds by converting them into seemingly legitimate income.

Pari-mutuel gambling A form of gambling in which the gambler bets against other gamblers, not the house (as in casino gambling); frequently offered at certain sporting events, including horse and dog racing; often state regulated and legally available in many places where most or all other forms of gambling are illegal.

Pathological gambling The inability over a period of time to control or resist the compulsion to gamble, despite what may be serious negative consequences of this behavior.

Random number generator A software program that determines the outcome of online casino games by using algorithms to generate sequences of numbers that are indistinguishable from random coin flips or dice throws. A random number generator that is not rigged or biased should produce numbers that are unpredictable and not correlated with each other. Random number generators pose a difficult problem for computer science because computers cannot generate truly random numbers but only numbers that appear to be random.

Regulation The act of controlling or directing through the use of rules or standards.

Secure sockets layer protocol (SSL) A security protocol developed by Netscape for transmitting private data over the Internet, providing data encryption, server authentication, message integrity, and optional client authentication for a TCP/IP connection. Major Web browsers, including Internet Explorer, support SSL.

Sovereignty The principle that a state exercises power over its territory, system of government, and population.

Underage gambling Gambling by children or teenagers. It is illegal in many jurisdictions; although the age limit varies, it is often 18 or 21.

World Trade Organization (WTO) An international organization that regulates trade and tariffs between nations. Most nations have ratified the WTO's trade agreements that set rules for international commerce.

CROSS REFERENCES

See *Cyberlaw: The Major Areas; Development, and Information Security Aspects; Cyberterrorism and Information Security; Internet Basics Legal; Social and Ethical Issues of the Internet; Privacy Law and the Internet.*

REFERENCES

American Gaming Association. (n.d.) *Gaming revenue: 10-year trends.* Retrieved June 19, 2005, from http://www.americangaming.org/Industry/factsheets/statistics_detail.cfv?id=8

American Psychiatric Association. (n.d.). *APA advisory on Internet gambling.* Retrieved June 19, 2005, from http://www.psych.org/news_room/media_advisories/internetgamblingadvisory11601.pdf

Anastasio, M. (2001). The enforceability of Internet gambling debts: laws, policies, and causes of action. *Virginia Journal of Law and Technology, 6,* 6. Retrieved June 19, 2005, from http://www.vjolt.net/vol6/issue1/v6i1a06-Anastasio.html

Annenberg Public Policy Center. (2003, April 14). *Majority of adolescent males have gambled for money.* Retrieved June 19, 2005, from http://www.upenn.edu/researchatpenn/article.php?652&soc

Antigua and Barbuda (2003, October 8). *United States.-Measures affecting the cross-border supply of gambling and betting service, First submission of Antigua and Barbuda, Executive Summary* (WT/DS285). Retrieved June 19, 2005, from http://www.antigua-barbuda.com/business_politics/pdf/Antigua_FirstSubmission_ExecutiveSummary.pdf

Aronovitz, C. & Schopper, M. D. (2004). US case law. In A. N. Cabot & M. Balestra, (Eds.), *Internet gambling handbook* (7th ed., pp. 305–330). St. Charles, MO: River City Group LLC.

AT&T v. Coeur d'Alene Tribe, 295 F.3d 899, 902–910 (9th Cir. 2002).

Attorney General of the State of New York Internet Bureau. (2002a, June 21). *In the Matter of Citibank (South Dakota), Inc.: Assurance of discontinuance.* Retrieved June 19, 2004, from http://www.oag.state.ny.us/press/2002/jun/citibank.pdf

Attorney General of the State of New York Internet Bureau. (2002b, August 16). *In the Matter of PayPal, Inc.: Assurance of discontinuance.* Retrieved June 19, 2005, from http://www.oag.state.ny.us/ internet/litigation/paypal.pdf

Barlow, J. P. (1996). *A declaration of the independence of cyberspace.* Retrieved June 19, 2005, from http://www.eff.org/~barlow/Declaration-Final.html

Bell, T. W. (1999). *Internet gambling: Popular, inexorable, and (eventually) legal* (Policy Analysis No. 336). Washington, DC: Cato Institute. Retrieved June 19, 2005, from http://www.cato.org/pubs/pas/pa-336es.html

Bishop, M.S. (2000–2001). Note, and they're off: The legality of interstate pari-mutual wagering and its impact on the thoroughbred horse industry. *Kentucky Law Journal, 89,* 711–741.

Cabot, A. (2004). Challenges for Internet gambling. In A. N. Cabot & M. Balestra, (Eds.), *Internet gambling handbook* (7th ed., pp. 25–32). St. Charles, MO: River City Group LLC.

Cabot, A. N., & Balestra, M. (Eds.). (2004). *Internet Gambling handbook* (7th ed.). St. Charles, MO: River City Group LLC.

Cabot, A. N., & Faiss, R. D. (2002). Sports gambling in the cyberspace era. *Chapman Law Review, 5,* 1–45.

Casino City, Inc. v. United States Department of Justice, No. 04-557-B-M3 (M. D. La. filed Aug. 9, 2004). Retrieved June 19, 2005, from http://online.casinocity.com/firstamendment/legaldocuments.cfm

Christiansen Capital Advisers. LLC (2003). *The gross annual wager of the United States: 2003.* Retrieved June 19, 2004, from http://www.cca-i.com/Primary%20Navigation/Online%20Data%20Store/Free%20Research/2003%20Revenue%20by%20Industry.pdf

Craig, A. (1998). Gambling on the Internet. *Southern Methodist University School of Law Computer Law Review & Technology Journal,* 63–104.

Directorate of Offshore Gaming of Antigua and Barbuda (2003, July 9). *Antigua's impudence: Challenging the US in the WTO.* Retrieved June 19, 2005, from http://www.antiguagaming.gov.ag/press/press_release_16.asp

Doha Declaration (2001, November 20). *Ministerial declaration on the TRIPS agreement and public health* (WT/MIN(01)/DEC/1). Retrieved June 19, 2005, from http://www.wto.org/english/thewto_e/minist_e/min01_e/mindecl_e.htm

Federal Trade Commission (2002, June 26). *FTC warns customers about online gambling and children.* Retrieved June 19, 2005, from http://www.ftc.gov/opa/2002/06/onlinegambling.htm

Finley, B. (2004, June 22). Wireless wagering ready for debut. *ESPN.com.* Retrieved June 19, 2005, from http://espn.go.com/horse/columns/misc/1826323.html

Free Jay Cohen! (2004). *Free Jay Cohen!* Retrieved June 19, 2005, from http://www.freejaycohen.com

Friedrich, T. J. (2003). Comment, Internet casino gambling: The nightmare of lawmaking, jurisdiction, enforcement and the dangers of prohibition. *CommLaw Conspectus, 11,* 369–388.

Georgi, K., Vlaemminck, P., & Alberda, R. (2004). International law. In A. N. Cabot & M. Balestra, (Eds.), *Internet gambling handbook.* 7th ed., pp. 243–252). St. Charles, MO: River City Group LLC.

Germain, J. (2004, March 23). Global extortion: Online gambling and organized hacking. *TechNews World.* Retrieved June 19, 2005, from http://www.technewsworld.com/story/33171.html

Gottfried, J. (2004). The Federal framework for Internet gambling. *Richmond Journal of Law and Technology, 10,* 26. Retrieved June 19, 2005, from http://law.richmond.edu/jolt/v10i3/article26.pdf

Greater New Orleans Broadcasting Association, Inc. v. United States, 527 U.S. 173, 176, 187, 191 (1999).

Illegal Gambling Business Act, 18 U.S.C. §1955 (West 2005).

Indian Gaming Regulatory Act, 25 U.S.C. §2701 *et seq.* (West 2005).

Internet gambling: Hearings before Committee on Banking, Housing, and Urban Affairs, U.S. Senate (2003, March 18) (testimony of John G. Malcolm, Deputy Assistant Attorney General, Criminal Division, U.S. Department of Justice). Retrieved June 19, 2005, from http://www.cybercrime.gov/malcolmTestimony318.htm

Interstate Horseracing Act, 15 U.S.C. §3001 *et seq.* (West 2005).

Jubelirer v. Mastercard Int'l, Inc., 68 F. Supp. 2d 1049 (W. D. Wis. 1999).

Kelly, J. M. (2000). Internet gambling law. *William Mitchell Law Review, 26,* 117–177.

Kelly, J., Mignin, R., & Saxman, S. (2004). US policy. In A. N. Cabot & M. Balestra, (Eds.), *Internet gambling handbook* (7th ed., pp. 257–304). St. Charles, MO: River City Group LLC.

Kindt, J. W., & Joy, S. W. (2002). Internet gambling and the destabilization of national and international economies: Time for a comprehensive ban on gambling over the World Wide Web. *Denver University Law Review, 80,* 111–153.

Ladd, G. T., & Petry, N. M. (2002). Disordered gambling among university-based medical and dental patients: A focus on Internet gambling. *Psychology of Addictive Behaviors, 16*(1).

Leyden, J. (2004, Mar. 17). Online extortionists target Cheltenham. *The Register.* Retrieved June 19, 2005, from http://www.theregister.co.uk/2004/03/17/online_extortionists_target_cheltenham/

Loscalzo, T. E., & Shapiro, S. J. (2000). Internet gambling policy: Prohibition versus regulation. *Villanova Sports & Entertainment Law Forum, 7,* 11–27.

Macavinta, C. (1999, October 14). Visa affiliates clear online gambling debt. *C/net News.com* Retrieved June 19, 2005, from http://news.com.com/2100-1040-231449.html?legacy=cnet

In Re Mastercard International Incorporated Internet Gambling Litigation, 313 F.3d 257, 262–63 (5th Cir. 2002).

Miller, L. K., & Claussen, C. L. (2001). Online sports gambling—Regulation or prohibition? *Society for the Study of the Legal Aspects of Sport and Physical Activity Journal of Legal Aspects of Sport, 11,* 99–130.

Missouri Attorney General's Office. (1998, September 22). Nixon obtains first criminal conviction in country for Internet gambling, guilty pleas today in Springfield. Retrieved June 19, 2005, from http://www.ago.state.mo.us/newsreleases/1998/92298.htm

Missouri ex rel. Nixon v. Coeur D'Alene Tribe, 164 F.3d 1102, 1109 n. 5 (8th Cir.), cert. denied, 527 U.S. 1039 (1999).

National Gambling Impact Study Commission (NGISC) (1999). *Final report.* Retrieved June 19, 2005, from http://govinfo.library.unt.edu/ngisc/reports/fullrpt.html

New Jersey Office of the Attorney General (2002, June 11). New Jersey settles Internet sports betting suits. Retrieved June 19, 2005, from http://www.state.nj.us/lps/ge/2002news/internet_settlement.htm

People v. World Interactive Gaming Corporation, 185 Misc.2d 852, 862 (N.Y. Sup. Ct. 1999).

Professional and Amateur Sports Protection Act of 1992, 28 U.S.C. §3701 et seq. (West 2005).

Providian National Bank v. Haines, No. CV 98–858 (Cal. Super. Ct. Marin Cty, filed July 13, 1998).

Racketeer Influenced and Corrupt Organizations Act, 18 U.S.C. §1961 et seq. (West 2005).

Richtel, M. (2004, June 1). U.S. seizes cash in online gambling crackdown. Las Vegas Sun.

Sanders, R. (2003, June 24). Statement to the Dispute Settlement Body of the WTO. Retrieved June 18, 2005, from http://www.antigua-barbuda.com/business_politics/wto/sirronald_wto_statement.asp

Schneider, S. (2004). The market—An introduction. In A. N. Cabot & M. Balestra, (Eds.), Internet gambling handbook (7th ed., pp. 47–54). St. Charles, MO: River City Group LLC.

Schwartz, J. M. (1999). The Internet gambling fallacy craps out. Berkeley Technology Law Journal, 14, 1021–1070.

Senate Report No. 248, P.L.102-559 Professional and Amateur Sports Protection Act, 102nd Cong., 1st Sess. (1991).

State by Humphrey v. Granite Gate Resorts, 568 N.W.2d 715 (Ct. App. Minn. 1997), aff'd, 576 N.W.2d 747 (Minn. 1998).

Swartz, J. (2004, March 9). Online betting sites fight cyber extortion. USA Today.

Thompson, L. (2003, June 17). U.S. attorney laundered millions in Bahamian accounts. The Nassau Guardian. Retrieved June 19, 2005, from http://www.thenassauguardian.net/business/287861705843030.php

Travel Act, 18 U.S.C. §1952 (West 2005).

United States. (2003, November 14). United States measures affecting the cross-border supply of gambling and betting services (WT/DS285). Retrieved July 18, 2004, from http://www.ustr.gov/enforcement/briefs.shtml

United States v. Baker, 364 F.2d 107, 110 (3d Cir.), cert. denied, 385 U.S. 986 (1966).

United States v. Baborian, 528 F. Supp. 324, 328–29 (D.R.I. 1981).

United States v. Cohen, 260 F.3d 68 (2d Cir. 2001), cert. denied, 536 U.S. 922 (2002), post-conviction relief denied, 2005 U.S. App. LEXIS 7094 (2d Cir. Apr. 22, 2005).

United States v. Edge Broadcasting, 509 U.S. 418, 421 (1993).

United States v. Reeder, 614 F.2d 1179, 1184–85 (8th Cir. 1980).

United States Stonehouse, 452 F.2d 455, 456-57 (7th Cir. 1971).

Unlawful Internet Gambling Funding Prohibition Act, H.R. 2143, (108th Cong., 1st Sess. (2003).

U.S. Department of Justice. (2001, December 3). Internet sports bookmakers plead guilty; will forfeit $3.3 million in criminal earnings. Retrieved June 19, 2005, from http://www.usdoj.gov/criminal/cybercrime/goldmedalPlea.htm

U.S. Department of Justice. (2002, October 22). Florida lawyer charged in offshore sports betting case. Retrieved June 19, 2005, from http://www.usdoj.gov/criminal/cybercrime/tedderIndict.htm

U.S. Department of Justice. (2003a, July 24). Paypal, Inc. pays $10 million to the Justice Department to settle forfeiture allegations involving Paypal's aiding illegal offshore gambling activities.

U.S. Department of Justice. (2003b, October 3). Press release. Retrieved June 19, 2005, from http://www.usdoj.gov/usao/can/press/html/2003_10_03_tedeschi.html

U.S. General Accounting Office. (2002). Internet gambling: An overview of the issues (GAO-03-89). Retrieved June 19, 2005, from http://www.gao.gov/new.items/d0389.pdf

Wagering Paraphernalia Act of 1961, 18 U.S.C. §1953 (West 2005).

Walters, L. G. (2004). Advertising and US law. In A.N. Cabot & M. Balestra, (Eds.), Internet gambling handbook (7th ed., pp. 331–348). St. Charles, MO: River City Group LLC.

Wire Act, 18 U.S.C. §1084 (West 2005).

World Trade Organization. (2003, August 26). United States—Measures affecting the cross-border supply of gambling and betting services. Constitution of the panel established at the request of Antigua and Barbuda—Note by the secretariat (WT/DS285/3). Retrieved June 19, 2005, from http://www.wto.org/english/tratop_e/dispu_e/dispu_status_e.htm#2003

World Trade Organization. (2004a, June 28). United States—Measures affecting the cross-border supply of gambling and betting services. Communication from the chairman of the panel (WT/DS285/5). Retrieved June 19, 2005, from http://trade-info.cec.eu.int/doclib/cfm/doclib_section.cfm?sec=202&lev=2&order=date\

World Trade Organization (2004b, August 20) United States-Measures affecting the cross-border supply of gambling and betting services.—Communication from the chairman of the panel (WT/DS285/5/Add.1). Retrieved June 19, 2005, from http://www.wto.org/lenglish/tratop_e/dispu_e/dispu_status_e.htm#2003

World Trade Organization (2004c, October 11). United States—Measures affecting the cross-border supply of gambling and betting services—Communication from the chairman of the panel (WT/DS285/5/Add.2). Retrieved June 19, 2005, from http://www.wto.org/english/tratop_e/dispu_e/dispu_status_e.htm#2003

World Trade Organization, (2004d, November 10) United States—Measures affecting the cross-border supply of gambling and betting services—Report of the panel (WT/DS285/R). Retrieved June 19, 2005, from http://www.wto.org/english/tratop_e/dispu_e/dispu_status_e.htm#2003

World Trade Organization (2005a, January 13). United States—Measures affecting the cross-border supply of gambling and betting services—Notification of an appeal By the United States (WT/DS295/6). Retrieved June 19, 2005, from http://www.wto.org/english/tratop_e/dispu_e/dispu_status_e.htm#2003

World Trade Organization (2005b, April 7) United States—Measures affecting the cross-border supply of gambling *and betting services—Communication from the appellate body* (WT/DS285/9). Retrieved June 19, 2005, from http://www.wto.org/english/tratop_e/dispu_e/dispu_status_e.htm#2003

World Trade Organization (2005c, April 7) *United States—Measures affecting the cross-border supply of gambling and betting services—Report of the appellate body* (WT/DS295/AB/R). Retrieved June 19, 2005, from http://www.wto.org/english/tratop_e/dispu_e/dispu_status_e.htm#2003

World Trade Organization (2005d, April 25) *United States—Measures affecting the cross-border supply of gambling and betting services—Appellate body report and panel report action by the dispute settlement body* (WT/DS285/10). Retrieved June 19, 2005, from http://www.wto.org/english/tratop_e/dispu_e/dispu_status_e.htm#2003

World Trade Organization (2005e, June 9) *United States—Measures affecting the cross-border supply of gambling and betting services—Request from Antigua and Barbuda for arbitration under article 21.3(c) of the DSU* (WT/DS285/11). Retrieved June 19, 2005 from http://www.wto.org/english/tratop_e/dispu_e/dispu_status_e.htm#2003

The Digital Millennium Copyright Act

Seth Finkelstein, *SethF.com*

INTRODUCTION

In 1998, citing the United States' obligations under World Intellectual Property Organization (WIPO) copyright treaties, Congress passed the Digital Millennium Copyright Act (DMCA). The DMCA is a wide-ranging addition to copyright-related law, encompassing such topics as take-down procedures in copyright infringement disputes and safe-harbor defenses for Internet service providers (ISPs). This chapter focuses on the aspects of the DMCA that have particular relevance to research by academics and professionals: the portions that define offenses such as "circumvention" or "trafficking."

BASICS AND CRITICAL PROVISIONS

The DMCA is structured as a set of prohibitions, followed by various qualifications and exemptions to those prohibitions. The initial provisions are very broad and far reaching. It is a matter of much controversy whether subsequent interpretations and legal holdings will sufficiently constrain the scope of what constitutes a violation. The law in this area is very unsettled, with new cases being argued regularly. Significant judicial opinions are expected for years to come, and in response to those rulings, various legislative modifications and amendments will be proposed. Although it is always good practice to check for the most recent work, the subject matter in this instance is evolving particularly rapidly.

Circumvention

The first provision of this type is §1201(a)(1), defining circumvention violations. It reads:

> (a) Violations Regarding Circumvention of Technological Measures.—(1)(A) No person shall circumvent a technological measure that effectively controls access to a work protected under this title.

Circumvention is a new offense, one created by the DMCA. It is not copyright infringement, which is an infraction against a different set of rights, most commonly the making of copies in violation of copyright law. Rather, the §1201(a)(1) circumvention offense itself is obtaining unauthorized access to copyrighted material ("work protected under this title"). This new offense can be confusing to those who have formed their idea of copyright law from earlier incarnations. One common reaction is to repeat the defenses to infringement, such as fair use. However, circumvention is not infringement so the defenses that apply to infringement do not apply to circumvention. Indeed, this difference in defenses is one of the most significant aspects of the DMCA.

It should be stressed that *access* is not necessarily *copying*. Obtaining unauthorized access may involve nothing more than viewing encrypted video on an operating system that does not have a licensed (authorized) decryption player. Inversely, copying is not necessarily access. Encrypted copyrighted material can be reproduced while still encrypted. However, often these two actions are necessarily intertwined.

Technological Measure and "Effectively Controls Access"

The DMCA goes on to define the terms used in the circumvention offense as follows:

> (A) to "circumvent a technological measure" means to descramble a scrambled work, to decrypt an encrypted work, or otherwise to avoid, bypass, remove, deactivate, or impair a technological measure, without the authority of the copyright owner; and

> (B) a technological measure "effectively controls access to a work" if the measure, in the ordinary course of its operation, requires the application of information, or a process or a treatment, with the authority of the copyright owner, to gain access to the work.

It is important to take note of the phrase, "effectively controls access." This is often misunderstood by scientists or engineers as meaning that a measure successfully controls access, implying perhaps a necessity to use strong cryptography. No such requirement is present. In fact, the access control can be very weak in technological terms. Possibly the best analogy is the phrase used to characterize the criminal offense, "breaking and entering." This offense does not require anything to be damaged physically, which is one ordinary sense of the word "breaking." Even opening a closed door would qualify. That the open door is not a broken object, in the English sense of the word, is irrelevant. The argument that "effectively controls access" has a paradoxical meaning has been both attempted repeatedly in court and strongly ruled incorrect by judges.

The judicial failure of "effectively" as a limiting argument cannot be overemphasized. Technologists often reinvent and propose that interpretation. To give one important rejection, in *Universal City Studios Inc. v. Reimerdes* (2000), the trial court wrote at length regarding how the definition cannot be viewed as self-defeating:

> Finally, the interpretation of the phrase "effectively controls access" offered by defendants at trial—viz., that the use of the word "effectively" means that the statute protects only successful or efficacious technological means of controlling access—would gut the statute if it were adopted. If a technological means of access control is circumvented, it is, in common parlance, ineffective. Yet defendants' construction, if adopted, would limit the application of the statute to access control measures that thwart circumvention, but withhold protection for those measures that can be circumvented. In other words, defendants would have the Court construe the statute to offer protection where none is needed but to withhold protection precisely where protection is essential. The Court declines to do so. Accordingly, the Court holds that CSS effectively controls access to plaintiffs' copyrighted works.

When the case was appealed, *Universal City Studios Inc v. Corley* (2001), the appeals court accepted the above reasoning regarding what constitutes effectiveness. In *321 Studios v. Metro Goldwyn Mayer et al.* (2004), the trial court rejected a challenge to the concept of effective control stemming from widespread availability:

> 321, in a footnote, questions whether CSS is an effective control or protection of DVDs, since the CSS access keys are widely available on the internet. However, this is equivalent to a claim that, since it is easy to find skeleton keys on the black market, a deadbolt is not an effective lock to a door.

Further, in the case *RealNetworks, Inc. v. Streambox, Inc.* (2000), merely setting a bit flag (called there a "Copy Switch") was held by the district court to qualify as effective protection when combined with an authentication scheme:

> 8. In conjunction with the Secret Handshake, the Copy Switch is a "technological measure" that effectively protects the right of a copyright owner to control the unauthorized copying of its work. See 17 U.S.C. §1201(b)(2)(B) (measure "effectively protects" right of copyright holder if it "prevents, restricts or otherwise limits the exercise of a right of a copyright owner"); . . . To access a RealMedia file distributed by a RealServer, a user must use a RealPlayer. The RealPlayer reads the Copy Switch in the file. If the Copy Switch in the file is turned off, the RealPlayer will not permit the user to record a copy as the file is streamed. Thus, the Copy Switch may restrict others from exercising a copyright holder's exclusive right to copy its work.

A password has been also been ruled to meet the standard of an effective technological measure. However, the unauthorized use of a password has been held *not* to be circumvention within the meaning of the DMCA, in a district court case, *I.M.S. Information Management Systems, LTD. v. Berkshire Information Systems, Inc.* (2004):

> Defendant is alleged to have accessed plaintiff's [password] protected website without plaintiff's authorization. Defendant did not surmount or puncture or evade any technological measure to do so; instead, it used a password intentionally issued by plaintiff to another entity. As an analogy to Universal Studios, the password defendant used to enter plaintiff's webservice was the DVD player, not the DeCSS decryption code, or some alternate avenue of access not sponsored by the copyright owner (like a skeleton key, or neutralizing device). Plaintiff, however, did not authorize defendant to utilize the DVD player. Plaintiff authorized someone else to use the DVD player, and defendant borrowed it without plaintiff's permission. Whatever the impropriety of defendant's conduct, the DMCA and the anti-circumvention provision at issue do not target this sort of activity.

In sum, the standard is legal, not cryptographic. The key element is not the computational strength of a cipher or any type of certification to an industry standard or best practices procedure. Rather, only a minimal effort is needed. Just meeting a simple test concerning the procedure by which access to the work is obtained will trigger the application of the law.

Trafficking

Building on the prohibition of circumvention itself, a second provision, §1201(a)(2), forbids various types of trafficking:

(2) No person shall manufacture, import, offer to the public, provide, or otherwise traffic in any technology, product, service, device, component, or part thereof, that—

And then the law sets out a qualifying test, which is important to understand in terms of implications:

(A) is primarily designed or produced for the purpose of circumventing a technological measure that effectively controls access to a work protected under this title;

(B) has only limited commercially significant purpose or use other than to circumvent a technological measure that effectively controls access to a work protected under this title; or

(C) is marketed by that person or another acting in concert with that person with that person's knowledge for use in circumventing a technological measure that effectively controls access to a work protected under this title.

As circumvention is different from infringement, trafficking is different from circumvention. One need not do any circumvention oneself in order to violate the trafficking provision, and no infringement need be done in either case. Trafficking provisions concern tools and are sometimes analogized to laws against burglary tools. This analogy has problems though, as many burglary tools are often legal in and of themselves, with related offenses requiring an intent to commit burglary.

Although trafficking is often discussed in terms of devices, the text of the law specifically forbids "any technology." This has been held to encompass the source code of computer programs (*Universal v. Reimerdes*, 2000, footnote 135). A very controversial question is whether it also extends to academic research papers (Liu, 2003).

The test to qualify as a circumvention tool addresses certain frequent objections to the concept of prohibited devices. For example, a general-purpose debugging program would not qualify because it is not "primarily designed" for circumvention, nor does it have "only limited commercially significant purpose or use" except for circumvention.

Closely related to §1201(a)(2) is another trafficking provision, §1201(b)(1). Although §1201(a)(2) is concerned with a technological measure that effectively protects "*access,*" §1201(b)(1) addresses trafficking regarding "*a right of a copyright owner.*" Except for this change, the language of §1201(b)(1) is otherwise parallel to that of §1201(a)(2).

Fair Use Implications

As has been discussed above, the offenses defined by the DMCA are distinct from the concept of copyright infringement. These differences, particularly fair use rights, are mentioned in a provision of the DMCA, §1201(c), which begins:

(c) Other Rights, Etc., Not Affected.
(1) Nothing in this section shall affect rights, remedies, limitations, or defenses to copyright infringement, including fair use, under this title.

This is an especially subtle statement, going to the heart of the debates over the meaning of fair use. The logical problem is an interpretation that, as a legal matter, because the DMCA offenses are not copyright infringement, by definition defenses to copyright infringement such as fair use are not affected. This view holds that if a prohibition against circumvention of access controls makes impossible any unauthorized use at all, that does not affect the ability to argue fair use as a defense to copyright infringement. More simply, if a copy could be made, fair use could be argued as a defense to copyright infringement. However, the fact that the copy might not be able to be made in the first place, without violating access controls, is deemed irrelevant.

One way to think of this problem is as a conflict about whether fair use is a reflection of a substantive right, grounded in the First Amendment, or merely one particular defense to one specific part of copyright law having to do with infringement. The legal results so far have supported the latter viewpoint. In the case *Universal v. Corley* (2001), the court stated:

> We know of no authority for the proposition that fair use, as protected by the Copyright Act, much less the Constitution, guarantees copying by the optimum method or in the identical format of the original. Although the Appellants insisted at oral argument that they should not be relegated to a "horse and buggy" technique in making fair use of DVD movies, [Footnote 36] the DMCA does not impose even an arguable limitation on the opportunity to make a variety of traditional fair uses of DVD movies, such as commenting on their content, quoting excerpts from their screenplays, and even recording portions of the video images and sounds on film or tape by pointing a camera, a camcorder, or a microphone at a monitor as it displays the DVD movie. The fact that the resulting copy will not be as perfect or as manipulable as a digital copy obtained by having direct access to the DVD movie in its digital form, provides no basis for a claim of unconstitutional limitation of fair use.

The court concluded: "Fair use has never been held to be a guarantee of access to copyrighted material in order to copy it by the fair user's preferred technique or in the format of the original."

The footnote 36 in the passage above is notable in itself:

> 36. In their supplemental papers, the Appellants contend, rather hyperbolically, that a prohibition on using copying machines to assist in making fair use of texts could not validly be upheld by the availability of "monks to scribe the relevant passages."

These interpretations are another instance where the legal reasoning strikes many technologists as paradoxical if not incomprehensible. One might ask, in what sense can a right be said to exist, if the means to exercise it are heavily constrained? The judicial resolution of this quandary, via strict theoretical partitioning of the concepts, invites repeated challenges because of the practical connections. Yet, so far, all rulings on this issue have been consistently along the above lines. For example, in *321 Studios v. MGM* (2004),

> This Court agrees with this analysis in Corley: ["optimum method" conclusions repeated]
> The fact that the resulting copy will not be as perfect or as manipulable as a digital copy obtained by having direct access to the DVD movie in its digital form, provides no basis for a claim of unconstitutional limitation of fair use.

These rulings all demonstrate how complex and counterintuitive are the fair use issues in view of the DMCA's constraints on access and copying tools.

MAJOR EXEMPTIONS

Despite not having a general defense for fair use, the DMCA does exempt various activities. These exemptions are notably restrictive and narrow, but some are worthy of discussion for academic or scientific applications.

Reverse Engineering

The §1201(f) provision contains a limited right to engage in circumvention (§1201(a)(1)) for the purpose of reverse engineering, specifying the qualifications as follows:

> (f) Reverse Engineering.—(1) Notwithstanding the provisions of subsection (a)(1)(A), a person who has lawfully obtained the right to use a copy of a computer program may circumvent a technological measure that effectively controls access to a particular portion of that program for the sole purpose of identifying and analyzing those elements of the program that are necessary to achieve interoperability of an independently created computer program with other programs, and that have not previously been readily available to the person engaging in the circumvention, to the extent any such acts of identification and analysis do not constitute infringement under this title.

The most important portions of this provision are the "sole purpose" aspect and the clause "to the extent... not constitute infringement." These narrow the range of the defense considerably in practice. It is critical to keep in mind that these determinations may be affected by the court's view of the overall value of the activity and of the character of the defendants. In *Universal v. Reimerdes* (2000), the court ruled very unfavorably on the "sole purpose" aspect of this provision, with notable comments:

> Finally, it is important to recognize that even the creators of DeCSS cannot credibly maintain that the "sole" purpose of DeCSS was to create a Linux DVD player. DeCSS concededly was developed on and runs under Windows—a far more widely used operating system. The developers of DeCSS therefore knew that DeCSS could be used to decrypt and play DVD movies on Windows as well as Linux machines. They knew also that the decrypted files could be copied like any other unprotected computer file. Moreover, the Court does not credit Mr. Johansen's testimony that he created DeCSS solely for the purpose of building a Linux player. Mr. Johansen is a very talented young man and a member of a well known hacker group who viewed "cracking" CSS as an end in itself and a means of demonstrating his talent and who fully expected that the use of DeCSS would not be confined to Linux machines. Hence, the Court finds that Mr. Johansen and the others who actually did develop DeCSS did not do so solely for the purpose of making a Linux DVD player if, indeed, developing a Linux-based DVD player was among their purposes.
>
> Accordingly, the reverse engineering exception to the DMCA has no application here.

Yet, the ability to conduct reverse engineering is deeply affected by the development of tools to aid in the process. The exemption addresses that trafficking prohibitions by providing a limited ability to make and communicate such tools. As §1201(f) goes on to state,

> (2) Not withstanding the provisions of subsections (a)(2) and (b), a person may develop and employ technological means to circumvent a technological measure, or to circumvent protection afforded by a technological measure, in order to enable the identification and analysis under paragraph (1), or for the purpose of enabling interoperability of an independently created computer program with other programs, if such means are necessary to achieve such interoperability, to the extent that doing so does not constitute infringement under this title.
>
> (3) The information acquired through the acts permitted under paragraph (1), and the means permitted under paragraph (2), may be made available to others if the person referred to in paragraph (1) or (2), as the case may be, provides such information or means solely for the purpose of enabling interoperability of an independently created computer program with other programs, and to the extent that doing so does not constitute infringement under this title or violate applicable law other than this section.

Note though, that the permissions are again constrained by the qualifiers as to "solely for the purpose" and "not constitute infringement." It is especially important to observe that although §1201(f)(1) permits a person to circumvent, and §1201(f)(2) allows them to develop tools, §1201(f)(3) restricts distribution of the fruits of these efforts to apply only to the person who has done them in the first place. Therefore, against what would be a prevailing conception, third-party republication is not within this exemption. Again, in *Universal v. Reimerdes* (2000), Judge Kaplan said: "First, Section 1201(f)(3) permits information acquired through reverse engineering to be made available to others only by the person who acquired the information. But these defendants did not do any reverse engineering. They simply took DeCSS off someone else's web site and posted it on their own."

Judge Kaplan went on to say, "Defendants would be in no stronger position even if they had authored DeCSS. The right to make the information available extends only to dissemination "solely for the purpose" of achieving interoperability as defined in the statute. It does not apply to public dissemination of means of circumvention, as the legislative history confirms. [footnote 151] These defendants, however, did not post DeCSS 'solely' to achieve interoperability with Linux or anything else."

In a different case, (*Lexmark International Inc. v. Static Control Components, Inc.*, 2003) the district court said quite bluntly: "Sections 1201(f)(2) and (3) of the DMCA are not broad exceptions that can be employed to excuse any behavior that makes some device "interoperable" with some other device." However, a successful appeal resulted in a more robust view, where the appeals court opinion stated "the statue is silent about the degree to which the "technological means" must be necessary, if indeed they must be necessary at all, for interoperability."

Encryption Research

The exemption of most interest to the academic reader is certainly the §1201(g) provision, which provides a DMCA framework for "permissible acts of encryption research." It lays out a complex series of definitions and tests that must be met to qualify for the exemptions. The term "encryption research" is defined as

o (1) Definitions.—For purposes of this subsection—

(A) the term "encryption research" means activities necessary to identify and analyze flaws and vulnerabilities of encryption technologies applied to copyrighted works, if these activities are conducted to advance the state of knowledge in the field of encryption technology or to assist in the development of encryption products; and

(B) the term "encryption technology" means the scrambling and descrambling of information using mathematical formulas or algorithms.

Note the clause requiring activities to be "conducted to advance the state of knowledge." It provides fertile ground for argument over what qualifies as proper research. Although much security research is conducted within an unquestioned academic context, not all such activity is necessarily sympathetic to the courts or public opinion.

The text of the exemption specifies further conditions— that one must have "lawfully obtained the encrypted copy," have "made a good faith effort to obtain authorization before the circumvention," and not otherwise have violated any laws. Then it enumerates complicated

qualifying conditions. These conditions warrant detailed study, as they are most relevant to avoiding being the target of litigation:

o (3) Factors in determining exemption.—In determining whether a person qualifies for the exemption under paragraph (2), the factors to be considered shall include—

+ (A) whether the information derived from the encryption research was disseminated, and if so, whether it was disseminated in a manner reasonably calculated to advance the state of knowledge or development of encryption technology, versus whether it was disseminated in a manner that facilitates infringement under this title or a violation of applicable law other than this section, including a violation of privacy or breach of security;

+ (B) whether the person is engaged in a legitimate course of study, is employed, or is appropriately trained or experienced, in the field of encryption technology; and

(C) whether the person provides the copyright owner of the work to which the technological measure is applied with notice of the findings and documentation of the research, and the time when such notice is provided.

This might be seen as an attempt to codify a distinction between "black hats" and "white hats" (crackers versus scientists) in terms of research. Yet, given the arguments over practices and methods of disclosure of security vulnerabilities, there is certain to be ample room for debate over who will be protected under the above criteria.

CRIMINAL PROVISIONS

Although copyright law is commonly thought of in terms of monetary damages and civil lawsuits, there has always been a criminal law component. The DMCA criminal offenses are at §1204:

> Sec. 1204.—Criminal offenses and penalties
>
> (a) In General.—
>
> Any person who violates section 1201 or 1202 willfully and for purposes of commercial advantage or private financial gain—
>
> (1) shall be fined not more than $500,000 or imprisoned for not more than 5 years, or both, for the first offense; and
>
> (2) shall be fined not more than $1,000,000 or imprisoned for not more than 10 years, or both, for any subsequent offense.

Note all violations of section 1201 are included, encompassing §1201(a)(1) circumvention offenses and §1201(a)(2) and §1201(b)(1) trafficking offenses.

The critical element in the above provisions is *"for purposes of commercial advantage or private financial gain."* Satisfying this provision turns out to be much easier than one might think. In particular, it does not require any money to be exchanged, contrary to intuitive expectations. In a comparable copyright law provision (No Electronic

Theft Act, 1997), the US Department of Justice sample language for jury instructions regarding this element is that "the Government need not prove that the defendant actually received a profit from the infringement. The Government need only show that the defendant acted with the hope or expectation of some commercial advantage or financial gain."

The Department Of Justice Criminal Resource Manual (1997a, b) states clearly, "Emphasis should be placed on the word 'purpose,' because it is not necessary to prove that any profit was realized." Later in the document, the manual stresses with emphasis that the key word in the requirement is *"purpose"* (emphasis in original): "Evidence of discrete monetary transactions (i.e., the selling of infringing goods for a particular price) provides the clearest evidence of financial gain, but such direct evidence should not be a prerequisite to prosecution. Such a stringent requirement would ignore the plain wording of the statute, which requires only the showing of commercial or financial *purpose*."

The overall requirement seems to be construed broadly (bartering, being an employee, etc.), encompassing "expressed or implied intent of the parties." This aspect of being an employee was seen very specifically in the *United States v. Elcom Ltd.* (2002) "Sklyarov" case, discussed below.

EXEMPTION PROCESS— ANTICIRCUMVENTION RULEMAKING

Section 1201(a)(1)(C) of the DMCA provides a process by which users of a "class of works" can apply for an exemption from the §1201(a)(1) circumvention prohibitions. These exemptions specifically do not apply to any trafficking prohibitions. This process takes places every 3 years, starting from 2000. All exemptions last for only one 3-year cycle and must be reargued from the start at every rulemaking.

Note these exemptions do not affect any other laws that might be used against a researcher. In particular, copyright infringement, trade secret law, and shrinkwrap license prohibitions against reverse engineering are all potential legal problems (Copyright Office, 2003).

Although this process does have an effect, it also has notable limitations. As outlined in the "Statement of the Librarian of Congress Relating to Section 1201 Rulemaking" (Billington, 2003; see Library of Congress, 2003)

> It is important to understand the purposes of this rulemaking, as stated in the law, and the role I have in it. The rulemaking is not a broad evaluation of the successes or failures of the DMCA. The purpose of the proceeding is to determine whether current technologies that control access to copyrighted works are diminishing the ability of individuals to use works in lawful, non-infringing ways. The DMCA does not forbid the act of circumventing copy controls, and therefore this rulemaking proceeding is not about technologies that control copying. Some of the

people who participated in the rulemaking did not understand that and made proposals based on their dissatisfaction with copy controls. Other participants sought exemptions that would permit them to circumvent access controls on all works when they are engaging in particular non-infringing uses of those works. The law does not give me that power....

Despite these restrictions, the anticircumvention rulemaking is one of the few avenues where researchers can attempt to ameliorate the effects of the DMCA in even the smallest way. Participation does not require a law degree, being part of a lobbyist organization, or access to Congressional legislative staff. As stated in the "Recommendation of the Register of Copyrights" (Peters, 2003) regarding one particular exemption (censorware): "The Register's recommendation in favor of this exemption is based primarily on the evidence introduced in the comments and testimony by one person, Seth Finkelstein, a nonlawyer participating on his own behalf."

It is possible for a researcher to be heard (Finkelstein, 2002, 2003).

Classes of Works Exempted (2003)

At the time of the writing of this chapter, the 2003 rulemaking process had recently been completed. The following exemptions were granted:

(1) Compilations consisting of lists of Internet locations blocked by commercially marketed filtering software applications that are intended to prevent access to domains, websites or portions of websites, but not including lists of [spam or viruses].

(2) Computer programs protected by dongles that prevent access due to malfunction or damage and which are obsolete.

(3) Computer programs and video games distributed in formats that have become obsolete and which require the original media or hardware as a condition of access.

(4) Literary works distributed in ebook format when all existing ebook editions of the work...contain access controls that prevent the enabling of the ebook's read-aloud function and that prevent the enabling of screen readers to render the text into a specialized format.

However, these exemptions did not come close to covering all the various areas of research that have been affected by the DMCA.

MAJOR CASES

Much of the meaning of the DMCA is being shaped by judicial interpretation. This is an ongoing process, as various questions are considered and ruled on. The law may change, and the reader must keep that in mind. The material below is accurate as of mid-2004.

Universal City Studios, Inc. v. Reimerdes (DeCSS)

The most significant case of litigation under the DMCA is arguably *Universal City Studios, Inc. v. Reimerdes*, aka the DeCSS case. Many movie and TV shows available on DVD format disks are encrypted with a process known as content scramble system (CSS). This encryption restricts the material to access only on authorized DVD players, which are licensed to decrypt the content. Notably, commercial-grade bit-for-bit copying of the DVD disks can proceed whether or not the content is encrypted with CSS. However, it is of little use to exchange the encrypted data over file-sharing networks. Moreover, tying viewing the DVD video to licensed players enforces a geographical market segmentation scheme known as "region coding." Each DVD can have a region assigned to it, which makes it viewable only on players that are coded to the corresponding region.

DeCSS is a program that decrypts the CSS encryption. The unencrypted files can then be viewed on unlicensed players and exchanged over networks, and region coding becomes irrelevant. Making the DeCSS program available quickly led to lawsuits. One lawsuit branch involved trade secret law (*DVD-CCA v. Bunner* and *DVD-CCA v. Pavlovich*, California DeCSS cases), and is not discussed here. The *Universal v. Reimerdes* case (New York DeCSS case, later appealed as *Universal v. Corley*, has become the leading law on the DMCA. These are two different phases of the same case. At the trial level, in district court, Reimerdes was the main defendant. Later, after an adverse decision, Corley appealed to the U.S. Court of Appeals for the Second Circuit, which decided that case.

Contrary to many newspaper reports, it is not accurate that a 15-year-old Norwegian teenager (Jon Johansen) broke the encryption code. Perhaps the best account of the origin of DeCSS can be found in the testimony of Jon Johansen during the trial (Johansen, 2000, p. 619).

Q. Who wrote DeCSS?

A. I and two other people wrote DeCSS.

…

Q. Mr. Johansen, what did you do next towards making DeCSS?

A. We agreed that the person who I met would reverse engineer a DVD player in order to obtain the CSS algorithm and keys.

….

Q. Thank you very much. Now, you testified on direct that a German person, I think, had reverse-engineered the Xing DVD player, is that correct?

A. Yes, that is correct.

Q. And that person goes by the nick Ham?

A. Yes, that's correct.

Q. And it's Ham who wrote the source code that performed the authentication function in DeCSS, is that correct?

A. No, that is not correct. He did not write the authentication code. He wrote the decryption code.

…

Q. And it was Ham's reverse engineering of the Xing DVD player that revealed the CSS encryption algorithm, am I right?

A. Yes, that's correct.

Q. Reverse engineering by Ham took place in or about September 1999?

A. Yes, I believe it was late in September of 1999.

Q. And you testified that it was this revelation of the CSS encryption algorithm and not any weakness in the CSS cipher that allowed MORE to create DeCSS, is that correct?

A. Yes, that's correct.

Q. You obtained the decryption portions of the DeCSS source code from Ham, correct?

A. Yes, that's correct.

Q. You then compiled the source code and created the executable?

A. Well, in the form I received it, it was not compatible.

The actual writer of the DeCSS decryption code remains anonymous to this day. Given that Jon Johansen was criminally prosecuted in Norway for his role in the creation of the DeCSS code, the consequences for the programmer behind the decryption would certainly be severe.

Johansen was tried on charges related to a Norwegian law concerning data security and was acquitted. However, Norwegian law allowed the prosecutor to appeal the case. Johanson was then retried and reacquitted.

However, the litigation in the U.S. case was not concerned with creation of a program, but rather with its distribution. At issue was the right to publish the decrypting programs, not liability for their production. As software involves speech issues, several constitutional principles were at stake. However, the eventual court ruling went completely against publication rights (*Universal v. Reimerdes*, 2000).

The District Court, Kaplan, J., held that [sic]: (1) posting decryption software violated DMCA provision prohibiting trafficking in technology that circumvented measures controlling access to copyrighted works; (2) posting hyperlinks to other web-sites offering decryption software violated DMCA; (3) DMCA anti-trafficking provision was content-neutral as applied to computer program; (4) DMCA did not violate First Amendment as applied to defendants and decryption software; (5) defendants failed to establish anti-trafficking provision was overly broad on grounds that it prevented noninfringing fair use of movies; (6) application of anti-trafficking provision to enjoin defendants from hyper-linking to other web-sites offering decryption software did not violate First Amendment; and (7) plaintiffs were entitled to injunction enjoining defendants from posting decryption software or hyperlinking to other web-sites that made software available.

As the leading case authority on the DMCA, this decision has been cited repeatedly for the manner is which it interprets the various controversies.

United States v. Elcom (Dmitry Sklyarov, eBooks)

Many people believe that DMCA criminal sanctions will be applied only to large-scale commercial copyright infringers. The case of Dmitry Sklyarov, the first programmer to be arrested and face criminal charges under the DMCA, shows that the reach of the law is much further than assumed. Dmitry Sklyarov was a Ph.D. student at the Bauman Moscow State Technical University. Working for the Russian company ElcomSoft, he developed software (Advanced eBook Processor; AEBPR) to decrypt the encrypted eBook format developed and marketed by the document technology platform company, Adobe Systems.

While attending a conference in the United States, Skylyarow was arrested for violating DMCA provision §1201(b)(1), under a theory of trafficking in copy-control circumvention tools. Contrary to the popular conception, he was not arrested for anything he said at the conference itself. Rather, his appearance there presented an opportunity for the United States to exercise jurisdiction. The facts that the AEBPR program itself was sold commercially and he had been listed at one time as the copyright owner were taken to be sufficient for criminal liability (*U.S. v. Sklyarov Criminal Complaint*, 2001).

Notably, it was not necessary for any actual infringement to have taken place. A ban on merely selling a circumvention tool itself (which fell under the DMCA's standards) was ruled to be a reasonable prohibition (*U.S. v. Elcom*, 2002, aka *Elcomsoft*):

> Pirates and other infringers require tools in order to bypass the technological measures that protect against unlawful copying. Thus, targeting the tool sellers is a reasoned, and reasonably tailored, approach to "remedying the evil" targeted by Congress. In addition, because tools that circumvent copyright protection measures for the purpose of allowing fair use can also be used to enable infringement, it is reasonably necessary to ban the sale of all circumvention tools in order to achieve the objectives of preventing widespread copyright infringement and electronic piracy in digital media.

The arrest of a programmer at a conference caused widespread public concern, especially within the security and cryptography communities. Protest rallies were held, and the case attracted interest that publicized problematic aspects of the DMCA. Eventually the charges were dropped against Sklyarov in return for his testimony against his employer. Finally, ElcomSoft was acquitted in a jury trial (Bowman, 2002). There has been extensive argument regarding what implications should be drawn from both the initial prosecution and the subsequent acquittal (Liu, 2003).

321 Studios v. MGM

321 Studios makes and sells programs called DVD Copy Plus and DVD-X COPY. These programs are marketed for the purpose of making a personal, archival backup copy of content on a DVD, even of CSS-encrypted content, such as a commercial movie. 321 Studios sought a declaratory judgment that, in distributing these programs, it was not in violation of the DMCA. It was opposed by members of the Motion Picture Association of America (MPAA).

The eventual ruling thoroughly rejected the claims of 321, on summary judgment (i.e., ruling that simply as a matter of a law, 321 was in violation of the DMCA). The court found prior cases—*Universal v. Reimerdes* (2000), *Universal v. Corley* (2001), *United States v. Elcom* (2002)—"dispositive on many of the same issues" of fair use and application of the DMCA: "This Court finds, as did both the Corley and Elcom courts, that legal downstream use of the copyrighted material by customers is not a defense to the software manufacturer's violation of the provisions of §1201 (b)(1)."

Though the case was appealed, 321 Studios was driven out of business by legal costs from being the target of many lawsuits (Cowley, 2004).

Felten et al. v. RIAA

Princeton University Computer Science professor Edward Felten is a researcher in the field of information security. His research group participated in a challenge by the Secure Digital Music Initiative (SDMI) to evaluate vulnerabilities in digital watermarking systems for music files. When the group (Felten, Scott Craver, Bede Liu, Min Wu, Dan Wallach, Ben Swartzlander, Drew Dean, and Adam Stubblefield) planned to present a paper detailing its research results showing weaknesses in the various technologies, Professor Felten was threatened with legal liability by the Recording Industry Association of America and the SDMI, on the grounds of violating a "click-through agreement" and the DMCA (Oppenheim, 2001):

> In addition, because the public disclosure of your research would be outside the limited authorization of the Agreement, you could be subject to enforcement actions under federal law, including the DMCA. The Agreement specifically preserves any rights that proponents of the technology being attacked may have "under any applicable law including, without limitation, the U.S. Digital Millennium Copyright Act, for any acts not expressly authorized by this Agreement." The Agreement simply does not "expressly authorize" participants to disclose information and research developed through participating in the Public Challenge and thus such disclosure could be the subject of a DMCA action.

Although later statements from the RIAA and SDMI denied there was a legal threat, a "declaratory judgment" suit was brought against them to establish that such scientific research would not be chilled by the fear of litigation. However, the court was not convinced that there was an actual case or controversy qualifying for a legal opinion. The paper in question had been published after the issue was publicized widely, and further judicial action was ruled premature.

This case is notable for the implication that the reach of the DMCA extends to "information and research," at least to the extent of generating a formal letter regarding legal action from organizations that object to the dissemination of the material.

EXAMPLE CONTROVERSY— MEDIAMAX CD3

Although not a legal case, this widely publicized conflict between a company and a graduate student is additionally instructive regarding what academic researchers may face and how the issues can be phrased.

SunnComm is a company that manufactures a copy-restriction system for CD music, MediaMax CD3. John Alex Halderman was a Princeton Ph.D. student studying computer security with, interestingly enough, Edward Felten as his advisor. Halderman published a report, "Analysis of the MediaMax CD3 Copy-Prevention System," detailing vulnerabilities of SunnComm's technology. SunnComm reacted with nationally publicized threats to sue on various grounds, including the DMCA (SunnComm, 2003a; Vance, 2003).

Although SunnComm was widely reported to be angered that its copy-control technology could be disabled by the use of the shift key (Borland, 2003), deeper examination indicates that the most contentious issue was publishing details of its MediaMax drivers (Halderman, 2003):

Next, follow these additional steps to disable Media-Max:

1. Select the SbcpHid driver from the Device Manager list and click "Properties" from the Action Menu.
2. Click the Driver tab and click the Stop button to disable the driver.
3. Set the Startup Type to "Disabled" using the dropdown list.

A little-noted part of the SunnComm press release explained the basis under which SunnComm considered it had grounds for a lawsuit under the DMCA (SunnComm, 2003a):

> In addition, SunnComm believes that Mr. Halderman has violated the Digital Millennium Copyright Act (DMCA) by disclosing unpublished MediaMax management files placed on a users computer after user approval is granted. Once the file is found and deleted according to the instructions given in the Princeton grad students report, the MediaMax copy management system can be bypassed resulting in the copyrighted protected music being converted or misappropriated for potentially unauthorized and/or illegal use. SunnComm intends to refer this possible felony to authorities having jurisdiction over these matters because: 1. The author admits that he disabled the driver in order to make an unprotected copy of the discs contents, and 2. SunnComm believes that the authors report was disseminated in a manner which facilitates infringement in violation of the DMCA or other applicable law.

One commentator in a discussion forum, who claimed to be a SunnComm employee, put the issue as follows (AfterDawn.com, 2003):

> Just out of complete curiosity, do you guys *really* think that the shift key/autorun issue was what the problem was about?
>
> …do you guys *really* believe..and i mean **really** believe that the shift key 'escaped' notice, going thru the various dev cycles, testing 3rd party testing etc etc??? *especially* if the autorun feature was going to be used???
>
> Just a little FYI for all..the issue was about disclosing file names, locations and circumvention directions, which, if i read the DMCA correctly could be construed as a possible violation..
>
> …
>
> were we *ever* gonna sue over the shift key? jeez..are you guys serious? that makes us laugh every time we see it, in big bold headline stories, such as at the top of this one..
>
> btw, he didn't get sued, we decided not to go after him, and not because of the shift key, but because ultimately, the media's 'spin' would eventually become bigger (and badder) than the actual inital problem....

Translated from the informal phrasing, the commentator argues that SunnComm considered charging Halderman with violating the §1201(a)(2) trafficking provisions, under the theory that the details in his paper constituted *technology* for circumvention (not that the shift key was a circumvention device). Likely a §1201(a)(1) circumvention access violation was intended as well.

Although these theories are expansive, it is notable how the language of the press release is directed toward countering the §1201(g) research exemption. The "disseminated in a manner which facilitates infringement" phrasing is a direct reference to the §1201(g)(3)(A) factor "in determining if a person qualifies for the exemption" for performing "permissible acts of encryption research." Further, other parts of the press release seem aimed to delegitimize Halderman with regard to the §1201(g)(3)(B) "legitimate course of study" factor. It is possible to see an attack on the §1201(g)(3)(C) "notice" factor too. If this construction was intended, SunnComm had designed its press release to set the terms of public debate in a way that would nullify Halderman's obvious defenses.

SunnComm (2003b) quickly retracted its legal threats in the wake of an enormous amount of bad publicity. However, all researchers cannot count on having such favorable publicity.

CODE AS SPEECH

Consider the following text (Winstein & Horowitz, 2001)

```
s"$/=\2048;while(<>){G=29;R=142;if((@a=unqT="C*",_)
[20]&48){D=89;_=unqb24,qT, @ b=map{ord qB8,unqb8,
qT,_^$a[--D]} @INC;s/... $/1$&/;Q=unqV,qb25,_;H=73;O=$b[4]<<9
|256|$b[3];Q=Q>>8^(P=(E=255)&(Q>>12^Q>>4^Q/8^Q))<<17,
O=O>>8^(E&(F=(S=O>>14&7^O)^S*8^S<<6))<<9,_=
(map{U=_%16orE^=R^=110&(S=(unqT,"\xb\ntd\xbz\x14d")
[_/16%8]);E^=(72,@z=(64,72,G^=12*(U-2?0:S&17)),
H^=_%64?12:0,@z)[_%8]}(16..271))[_]^((D>>=8)+=P+(~F&E))
for@a[128..$#a]}print+qT,@a}';s/[D-HO-U_]/\$$&/g;s/q/
pack+/g;eval
```

Above is a series of symbols that form a program in the computer language Perl. In this sentence, the words are a series of symbols that convey meaning in the language English. Though more people are familiar with the latter than the former, can there be said to be an intrinsic, or practically sustainable, distinction? As noted in one legal brief (Tyre, 2001): "If '$plain_text = $file_key^$xor_block' seems unapproachable, consider what those not trained in the language of legal citation would make of '111 F.Supp.2d 294, 326 (S.D.N.Y. 2000).' Each is meaningless to those unfamiliar with the language; but each is more precise and compact for those who do understand than would be an English narrative equivalent."

As a further example, consider the following different explanations of a simple cipher:

> The ROT13 algorithm explained ("Caesar Cipher"):
> 1) The decryption algorithm for ROT13 is to take the range of letters from a-z, and for those twenty-six letters, replace the first thirteen of them with the range of letters from n-z and the second thirteen of them with the range of letters from a-m
> 2) To un-ROT13, do a tr/a-z/n-za-m/ over each character in the file
> 3) perl -pe 'tr/a-z/n-za-m/;' < infile > outfile
> Where was the line crossed, from "speech" to "code"?

The potential narrative equivalence between English and computer language will undoubtedly be a subject of much contentious litigation over the boundaries of permissible expression (Touretzky, 2000). Possible disputes are foreshadowed in *Universal v. Reimerdes* (2000) where the court remarked

> During the trial, Professor Touretzky of Carnegie Mellon University, as noted above, convincingly demonstrated that computer source and object code convey the same ideas as various other modes of expression, including spoken language descriptions of the algorithm embodied in the code.... He drew from this the conclusion that the preliminary injunction irrationally distinguished between the code, which was enjoined,

and other modes of expression that convey the same idea, which were not, id., although of course he had no reason to be aware that the injunction drew that line only because that was the limit of the relief plaintiffs sought. With commendable candor, he readily admitted that the implication of his view that the spoken language and computer code versions were substantially similar was not necessarily that the preliminary injunction was too broad; rather, the logic of his position was that it was either too broad or too narrow.... Once again, the question of a substantially broader injunction need not be addressed here, as plaintiffs have not sought broader relief.

Arguably, that "broader relief" would have been requested by SunnComm versus Halderman had the controversy proceeded to a lawsuit as threatened. Strategic considerations on this matter may have been one reason for the withdrawal by SunnComm.

However, because new languages and ways of expressing computational concepts are continually being invented, the exact reach of the DMCA will remain unclear for the foreseeable future. The DeCSS algorithm has even been expressed in Haiku format poetry (Schoen, 2004).

HOW NOT TO GET SUED UNDER THE DMCA

Given the potential for the DMCA to chill cryptography and security research, many professionals are concerned with what they can do to reduce their risk of prosecution. Dmitry Sklyarov's arrest and criminal charges show that the problem is not in the realm of fantasy.

Surveying the behavior of plaintiffs in many DMCA cases, the critical variable seems to be the perception of the character of the defendant. Although a corporation might have the legal ability to bring DMCA charges against a university professor, any prospect of setting an unfavorable legal precedent with a sympathetic defendant results in the withdrawal of threats. Conversely, an unsympathetic defendant appears not to do well in the judicial process (Bowman, 2001): "As soon as the judge says 'hacker,' you know you've lost," University of Minnesota law Professor Dan Burk said. "There is an attempt to paint defendants as unsympathetic, low-priority, on the fringe— to make it seem like nobody respectable is going to be harmed except for weird hacker types."

In view of this, the best practice is arguably to have as much professional and institutional backing as is possible. Consulting staff counsel, if available, can help with specific situations.

Keeping in mind the text of the §1201(g) exemption, preliminary notification of parties adversely affected by the research should not be done casually or without prior legal consultation. The fact that such notification is an element of a DMCA defense means it will affect how a court views any potential case. Pragmatically, it presents an opportunity for one to be the target of a legal threat aimed at chilling the presentation of results. This topic is extensively covered in Liu's 'The DMCA and the Regulation of Scientific Research" (2003), and the interested reader should consult that paper for further discussion.

CONCLUSION

The DMCA has profoundly unsettled the delicate balance that existed earlier in copyright law. Advances in technology, which have vastly increased the ability to make copies, have been in direct conflict with the imperative of copyright-concerning controls on content. The compromises of fair use and ability to produce and market technology if the technology has substantial noninfringing use may be irreconcilable in practice with the offenses of circumvention itself and the broad prohibitions against trafficking in circumvention technology. Moreover, the interpretation of contraband technology to encompass computer programs (even source code), and hence perhaps technical speech itself, greatly extends the reach of copyright-related regulation. Potentially the effects could lead to a chilling effect on academic research.

Various proposals have been made to ameliorate the negative effects of the DMCA. However, there is a fundamental clash between the needs of copyright owners to suppress information regarding copy-controlling encryption algorithms and the needs of the free exchange of methodology and validation of results for any research. This clash may ultimately be unsolvable.

GLOSSARY

1201(a)(1) The DMCA provision prohibiting the act of *circumvention* of a *technological protection measure* that effectively controls *access* to a copyrighted work.

1201(a)(2) The DMCA provision prohibiting trafficking in "any technology, product, service, device, component" for *circumvention* of a *technological protection measure* that effectively controls *access* to a copyrighted work.

1201(b)(2) The DMCA provision prohibiting trafficking in "any technology, product, service, device, component" for *circumvention* of a *technological protection measure* that effectively protects a right of a copyright owner (usage controls).

Circumvention To "descramble . . . decrypt . . . , or otherwise to avoid, bypass, remove, deactivate, or impair a technological measure, without the authority of the copyright owner." This is legally and conceptually distinct from *infringement*. Note that circumvention encompasses much more than decryption.

CSS Content scramble system, an encryption algorithm used to control access to content on DVD format disks. Although CSS does not affect commercial-grade duplication of a DVD, it prevents meaningful consumer copying and peer-to-peer file sharing.

DeCSS A program that decrypts the CSS encryption created by a team of three programmers (not, as commonly believed, the work of one teenager). Lawsuits concerning DeCSS have been the most prominent DMCA litigation.

Effectively A legal standard for content restriction. A technological protection measure "effectively controls access" if it, "in the ordinary course of its operation, requires the application of information, or a process or a treatment, with the authority of the copyright owner, to gain access to the work." A technological protection measure "effectively protects a right of a copyright owner" if it "in the ordinary course of its operation, prevents, restricts, or otherwise limits the exercise of a right of a copyright owner."

Fair Use In law, a defense against copyright infringement, allowing legal use of copyrighted material for such purposes as criticism, comment, news reporting, teaching, scholarship, or research. More philosophically, a safety valve for resolving the conflicts between copyright's restrictions on the use of speech and the U.S. Constitution's First Amendment provision concerning freedom of speech.

Infringement A violation of any of certain exclusive rights granted by copyright law. Some examples of these rights are reproduction, making of derivative works, performance, and display. This is legally and conceptually distinct from *circumvention*. Fair use is one defense against infringement.

Reverse Engineering In legal terms, "to study or analyze (a device, as a microchip for computers) in order to learn details of design, construction, and operation, perhaps to produce a copy or an improved version." (see *Bowers v. Baystate Technologies Inc.*, 2002)

Trafficking To "manufacture, import, offer to the public, or otherwise traffic in any technology, product, service, device, component, or part thereof" that violates the relevant DMCA provision. It is important to note that devices are just one part of this term, as it also encompasses the very broad idea of technology (which is extended to computer program source code).

CROSS REFERENCES

See *Copyright Law; Cybercrime and the U.S. Criminal Justice System; Encryption Basics; Legal, Social and Ethical Issues of the Internet.*

REFERENCES

321 Studios v. Metro Goldwyn Mayer et al., No. C 02-1955 SI (N.D. Cal. Feb. 19, 2004). Retrieved June 21, 2004, from http://www.eff.org/IP/DMCA/MGM_v_321Studios/20040219_Order.pdf

AfterDawn.com (2003, October 9). *Student uses Shift key, gets sued (discussion).* Retrieved June 21, 2004, from http://www.afterdawn.com/news/archive/4569.cfm

Billington, J. H. (2003, October 28). *Statement of the Librarian of Congress relating to Section 1201 rulemaking.* Retrieved June 21, 2004, from http://www.copyright.gov/1201/docs/librarian_statement_01.html

Borland, John (2003, October 7). Shift key breaks CD copy locks. *CNET News.com.* Retrieved June 21, 2004, from http://news.com.com/2100-1025-5087875.html

Bowers v. Baystate Technologies Inc., 64 USPQ2d 1065 (CA FC 2002).

Bowman, L. M. (2001, May 2). Putting a kind face on copyright battles. *CNET News.com.* Retrieved June 21, 2004, from http://news.com.com/2100-1023-256912.html

Bowman, L. M. (2002, December 17). ElcomSoft verdict: Not guilty. *CNET News.com*. Retrieved June 21, 2004, from http://news.com.com/2100-1023-978176.html

Copyright Office (2003). *Rulemaking on Anticircumvention web page*. Retrieved June 21, 2004, from http://www.copyright.gov/1201/

Cowley, S (2004, August 10). 321 Studios reaches postmortem deal with MPAA. *The Industry Standard*. Retrieved June 14, 2005 from http://www.thestandard.com/article.php/20040810194622938

Department of Justice. (1997a, August 20). *Federal prosecution of violations of intellectual property rights, sample language for jury instructions, 18 U.S.C.S., §2319*. Retrieved June 21, 2004, from http://www.usdoj.gov/criminal/cybercrime/intell_prop_rts/app_h.htm

Department of Justice. (1997b, October). *United States Attorneys' Manual Title 9, §1851*. Retrieved June 21, 2004, from http://www.usdoj.gov/usao/eousa/foia_reading_room/usam/title9/crm01851.htm

Digital Millennium Copyright Act (DMCA) of 1998, Pub. L. 105-304, 17 U.S.C.S. §1201 (2004). Retrieved June 21, 2004, from http://www4.law.cornell.edu/uscode/17/1201.html

Digital Millennium Copyright Act (DMCA) of 1998, Pub. L., 17 U.S.C.S. §1204 (2004). Retrieved June 21, 2004, from http://www4.law.cornell.edu/uscode/17/1204.html

DVD-CCA v. Bunner and *DVD-CCA v. Pavlovich* archives. Retrieved June 21, 2004, from: http://www.eff.org/IP/Video/DVDCCA_case/

Finkelstein, S. (2002). *How to win (DMCA) exemptions and influence policy*. Retrieved June 14, 2005, from http://www.eff.org/IP/DMCA/finkelstein_on_dmca.html

Finkelstein, S. (2003, April 11). *DMCA anticircumvention hearing testimony*. Retrieved June 21, 2004, from http://sethf.com/anticensorware/hearing_dc.php

Halderman, J. A. (2003). Analysis of the MediaMax CD3 copy-prevention system. *Princeton University Computer Science Technical Report* (TR-679-03). Retrieved June 21, 2004, from http://www.cs.princeton.edu/~jhalderm/cd3/

I.M.S. Inquiry Management Systems, LTD. v. Berkshire Information Systems, Inc, 307 F.Supp. 2d 541 (S.D.N.Y. 2004).

Johansen, J. (2000). *Testimony in Universal City Studios Inc. v. Reimerdes*. Retrieved June 21, 2004, from http://www.eff.org/IP/Video/MPAA_DVD_cases/20000720_ny_trial_transcript.html

Lexmark International Inc. v. Static Control Components, Inc. 253 F.Supp. 2d 943 (E. D. Ky. 2003), reversed, 387 F.3d 522 (6th Cir. 2004). Retrieved June 14, 2005, from http://www.eff.org/legal/cases/Lexmark_v_Static_Control/

Library of Congress. (2003, October 21). *Copyright Office exemption to prohibition on circumvention of copyright protection systems for access control technologies* 68 Fed. Reg. 62,011 (to be codified at 37 C.F.R. pt. 201). Retrieved June 21, 2004, from http://www.copyright.gov/fedreg/2003/68fr2011.html

Liu, J. (2003). The DMCA and the regulation of scientific research. *Berkeley Technology Law Journal, 17,* 501. Retrieved June 21, 2004, from http://papers.ssrn.com/sol3/papers.cfm?abstract_id=457742

No Electronic Theft Act of 1997, PL 105-147 (HR 2265), codified at 17 U.S.C.S. §506 (2004).

Oppenheim, M. (2001, April 9). *RIAA/SDMI legal threat letter*. Retrieved June 21, 2004, from http://www.eff.org/IP/DMCA/Felten_v_RIAA/20010409_riaa_sdmi_letter.html

Peters, M. (2003, October 27). *Recommendation of the Register of Copyrights in RM 2002-4; Rulemaking on exemptions from prohibition on circumvention of copyright protection systems for access control technologies*. Retrieved June 21, 2004, from http://www.copyright.gov/1201/docs/registers-recommendation.pdf

RealNetworks, Inc. v. Streambox, Inc., No. 2:99CV02070, 2000 WL 127311 (W. D. Wash. 2000). Retrieved June 21, 2004, from http://www.law.uh.edu/faculty/cjoyce/copyright/release10/Real.html

Schoen, S. (2004). *The history of the DeCSS haiku*. Retrieved June 21, 2004, from http://www.loyalty.org/~schoen/haiku.html

SunnComm. (2003, October 9). *SunnComm CEO says Princeton report critical of its MediaMax CD copy management technology contains erroneous assumptions and conclusions*. Retrieved June 21, 2004, from http://www.sunncomm.com/press/pressrelease.asp?prid=200310091000

SunnComm. (2003, October 10). *SunnComm Technologies reverses decision to bring legal action against Princeton researcher*. Retrieved June 21, 2004, from http://www.sunncomm.com/press/pressrelease.asp?prid=200310101150

Touretzky, D. S. (2000). *Gallery of CSS descramblers*. Retrieved June 21, 2004, from http://www-2.cs.cmu.edu/~dst/DeCSS/Gallery/

Tyre, J. S. (2001, January 23). *Programmers' & Academics' Amici Brief in "MPAA v. 2600" Case, Brief of Amici Curiae in Support of Appellants and Reversal of the Judgment Below (Jan. 26, 2001); Universal v. Reimerdes (Jan. 26, 2001) 00-9185*. Retrieved June 21, 2004, from http://www.eff.org/IP/Video/MPAA_DVD_cases/20010126_ny_progacad_amicus.html

U.S. v. ElcomSoft & Sklyarov Archive. Retrieved June 21, 2004, from http://www.eff.org/IP/DMCA/US_v_Elcomsoft/

United States v. Elcom LTD., 203 F. Supp.2d 1111 (ND Cal. 2002). Retrieved June 14, 2005, from http://digital-law-online.info/cases/62PQ2D1736.htm

United States v. Sklyarov Criminal Complaint (2001, 2001). United States District Court, Northern District Of California. Retrieved June 21, 2004, from http://www.eff.org/IP/DMCA/US_v_Elcomsoft/20010707_complaint.html

Universal City Studios Inc. v. Reimerdes, 2000 Copr.L.Dec. P 28,122, 55 U.S.P.Q.2d 1873 111 F.Supp.2d 294, United States District Court, S.D. New York. affirmed, Universal City Studios, Inc. v. Corley, 273 F.3d 429 (2nd Cir. 2001), amended January 29, 2002. Retrieved June 14, 2005, from http://cyber.law.harvard.edu/openlaw/DVD/NY/trial/op.html

Universal City Studios Inc. v. Corley, No. 00-9185 November 28, 2001, 273 F.3d 429, 60 USPQ2d 1953, U.S. Court of Appeals, Second Circuit, amended January 29, 2002. Retrieved June 14, 2005, from http://www.eff.org/IP/Video/MPAA_DVD_cases/20011128_ny_appeal_decision.html

Vance, A. (2003, October 16). SunnComm CEO demands to be called a "laughing stock." *The Register*. Retrieved June 21, 2004, from http://www.theregister.co.uk/2003/10/16/sunncomm_ceo_demands/

Winstein, K., & Horowitz, M. (2001). *qrpff (see Touretzky, 2000, Gallery of CSS descramblers)*. Retrieved June 21, 2004, from http://www-2.cs.cmu.edu/~dst/DeCSS/Gallery/qrpff.pl

Digital Courts, the Law and Evidence

Robert Slade, *Vancouver Institute for Research into User Security, Canada*

INTRODUCTION

Computer and system security professionals traditionally deal with issues of technology, but may be called upon to investigate when security is breached and to support forensic investigations and legal proceedings. Conversely, members of the legal profession are increasingly called upon to bring cases based upon, and present in court, information obtained from computer, network, and other technical systems.

To both groups, let me point out that this chapter is an overview and not an encyclopedia itself. Subfields of forensic science can produce very fat books, and the law produces entire libraries. Technical experts are not going to find details of file system internals here, nor are lawyers going to find case law.

LEGAL SYSTEMS

In dealing with legal issues, we have an immediate problem in that different countries not only have distinct laws but possibly even diverse legal systems. There are different approaches to what constitutes law and legal proceedings, and these will have an impact in regard to what constitutes evidence permissible in court.

Those from Britain, the Commonwealth countries, and the United States will be most familiar with the *common law* system, based on the presumption of laws that uphold the common good, from an originating charter document and case law precedents laid down over the years. (Common law is also the system under which a suspected criminal is presumed to be "innocent until proven guilty.") In some of those countries there are specific laws that would make, for example, malicious software illegal. In Canada, a relevant section of the Criminal Code states that anyone "who, without authorization, modifies data, or causes data to be modified" is guilty of an offense, which would seem to cover it nicely. However, most common law systems also have provisions against mischief or vandalism, so malicious software could probably be prosecuted even in the absence of a specific law. (Successful prosecution is quite another matter, the requirements for which this chapter covers at length.) Common law systems have, in fact, two different standards of legal evidence and proof, which are described below.

Most other countries have *code law* or *civil law* systems. Under these systems, an activity is not illegal unless there is a specific law against it. (In access control terms, everything is permitted unless it is forbidden.) Therefore, under such systems, it may be perfectly legal to write and distribute malicious software (or break into computer systems, or sell pirated copies of copyright-protected software) simply because there are no laws prohibiting such activities: the lawmakers haven't caught up with the times. ("Black hat" who break into computer systems, need not think they can get off freely by moving to such countries: if they travel in or to a country where the activity is illegal, they can be prosecuted there and sometimes even extradited.)

Common law and code law systems are not the only types of legal systems. There are religious legal systems, and you may also encounter systems based on socialist theories of social and economic structures. Of these additional systems, possibly the most important, in terms of evidence, are the religious systems.

The religious legal systems that most people will have heard about are probably the systems of *Shariah*, or Islamic law. These systems are generally stated to be based on the holy book of Islam, the Koran or Qu'ran. In broad outline this statement is true, but with certain provisos. Possibly the most important aspect of religious legal systems is that the clergy hold very special rights and powers. Although this is true of all religious legal systems, it has been amply demonstrated recently in a variety of Islamic jurisdictions. Koranic scholars have noted that the Taliban regime in Afghanistan upheld a variety of laws (dealing, for example, with the cutting of beards and the position of women in society) that had little or no basis in Islamic religious writings. Under religious systems, therefore, the clergy may also have extraordinary powers of determining what may constitute evidence.

Differences within Common Law

Just to make the situation even more obscure (given lawyers, what else did you expect?), beware of confusing the two different uses of the term "civil." Common law and code (civil) law are two different types of legal systems. Under the common law system, there are criminal cases, tort (or civil) cases, and regulatory cases, governed by different types of law. Criminal cases involve criminal laws and possibly jail time. Civil cases involve some form of tort, or injury (which only has to be a hurt—it does not have to be a wound) to someone. Once again, under the common law system, even if you cannot, for some reason, prosecute someone as a criminal for writing malicious software, if you can prove that what he or she did hurt you in some way (cost you money, lost you something, or even just got people to make fun of you) then you can launch a civil action, or lawsuit, against that person. You cannot put that person in jail, but you may be able to get some money. (Well, you can get a decision that he or she owes you something. Collecting actual money may be an entirely different issue, indeed.)

There is an additional point to be made about the difference between civil and criminal cases under common law systems, and it is directly relevant to forensic studies and digital evidence. The test of evidence and proof is not the same in the two types of cases. A criminal case must be proven "beyond a reasonable doubt." If a case can be made, and accepted by reasonable people, that the events in question could have occurred without illegal activity on the part of the accused, then the case must fail. Civil cases only require that a decision be made on the balance of the probabilities. The most famous example of this difference was in the trials surrounding the death of Nicole Simpson. The trial for murder was a criminal case, and the defense raised sufficient doubt of guilt that O. J. Simpson was found to be not guilty. The case for wrongful death was a civil case, and O. J. Simpson was found, in regard to the same event and on the basis of the same evidence, to be guilty. (It is interesting to note that DNA evidence, a technical and at that time novel form of identification, played a large part in that trial.) Thus, evidence for a criminal trial must be presented much more carefully than for civil cases.

Jurisdiction

When dealing with information and telecommunications systems, jurisdictional issues may play a role; that is, determining who has the right to try the case and under what system of law. For example, if a Canadian, living in Canada, started a business writing malware that was created and distributed from a machine in the United States and that malware affected someone in Britain, it is possible that the person responsible for creating the malicious software could be prosecuted in any or all of the three countries. A greater problem arises when the activity could be legal in one jurisdiction, but is against the law in another. This has become a major issue recently in regard to privacy. For example, the European Union has a set of directives in regard to privacy. One of the principles is that personally identifiable information about European citizens cannot be transferred by a third party to a jurisdiction where similar protections do not apply. Because the United States has no consistent privacy regulation on a federal level, special arrangements must be made by American companies to safeguard data relating to European customers.

Jurisdictional issues can be extremely complex, and everyone involved in Internet activities should be aware of the potential problems. Courts are increasingly willing to allow cases to proceed even if the activities of an individual or site are intended for a specific area and are legal in that locale, simply because they are available on the Internet and may be illegal elsewhere.

A similar, but unrelated concept is that of venue, the particular place where the trial is conducted. In many cases a great deal of effort and maneuvering are done to ensure that a trial proceeds at a specific location, either for the convenience of one side or to increase the cost and difficulty, in relation to attendance and the production of witnesses, for the other.

Digital Court

In discussing the law and issues of evidence with regard to technology, the topic of the *digital court* will likely arise. Unfortunately, this term is used in a variety of ways. To the general public, the term probably evokes the idea of courts that may act entirely within the realm of cyberspace, possibly being held as an activity on a Web site. Although this may be an end goal for this concept, the current reality tends to be more limited.

In general, courts now use a number of technologies. Most courts now accept the practice of remote depositions or testimony, with examinations being made by types of teleconference or videoconference. Some specialty courts, with limitations on the size or importance of disputes, may conduct most or all activities, including motions and judgments, by e-mail messages and/or file attachments. (A recent study in the Canadian province of British Columbia, for example, demonstrated that cryptographically robust digital signatures of land title documents precluded a common form of mortgage fraud.)

Another use of the term "digital court" arises in relation to legal training. There are companies that provide simulated courts, using a variety of technologies, furnishing the ability to "play out" cases and then examine the activities and results.

At present, the term "digital court" is used most frequently in regard to court reporting. More and more courts are dispensing with fully trained and experienced court stenographers who can provide a real-time transcript of the proceedings. Such reporters require a significant amount of education and experience, and increasing demands on the court system are placing such activities out of reach. Therefore, technology is being used in a variety of ways to reduce the need for real-time transcripts. In some cases, the verbal activity in the court is recorded as sound files, and a stenographer creates a transcript later. In others, the sound file is recorded, but no transcript is made if the case is not appealed.

Returning to the broadest definition of the term as a full court conducted entirely online, this activity is currently problematic and will require much greater study before it is to be realized. The activities of a court are highly complex, and the greatest probity and confidentiality must be maintained. Note that even in such a simple matter as an election, the use of fully digital technology is far from being universally accepted. A number of issues of security, availability, authentication, confidentiality, and acceptability must be dealt with before a fully digital court can be realized.

EVIDENCE

Simply by including the word "forensic" along with "computer" (or "digital," "network," or "software"), we have indicated that we are primarily concerned with evidence. That being the case, we need to know what items the law and the courts consider to be evidence.

Types of Evidence

Many types of evidence can be offered in court. The most common forms are direct, real, documentary, and demonstrative evidence.

Direct evidence is the normal statement from a witness that we are all familiar with from television dramas. Knowledge is obtained from any of the witness's five senses and is, in itself, proof or disproof of a fact. Direct evidence is called to prove a specific act or occurrence. Because direct evidence relates to a person, digital evidence is not involved.

Real evidence, also known as associative or physical evidence, is made up of tangible objects. Physical evidence includes such things as tools used in the crime, fruits of the crime (possession of stolen goods or even a suddenly acquired pile of cash), or possibly perishable evidence that we may be able to reproduce. Often the purpose of the physical evidence is to link the suspect to the scene of the crime. It is this evidence that has material existence and can be presented to the view of the court and jury for consideration. Digital evidence is unlikely to be real evidence, although certain pieces of computer hardware may be real evidence.

Documentary evidence is material presented to the court in the form of business records, manuals, printouts, and so forth. Much of the evidence submitted in a computer crime case—and almost everything that can be considered digital evidence—is documentary, and there are special considerations for this type of material that are described below.

Finally, demonstrative evidence is evidence used to aid the jury. It may be in the form of a model, experiment, chart, or an illustration offered as proof. It should be noted that demonstrative evidence is being used more often to aid the court and the jury, especially in the form of simulation and animation. In regard to computer, network, software, or digital forensics, there will be increasing significant requirements for demonstrative evidence as the courts come to accept the process as reliable. Explanations of how software forensics works, how information is laid down on disks or tape, how characteristics are obtained and analyzed, and the reliability of the procedures (including error rates) are all forms of demonstrative evidence.

There are many mathematical algorithms used in linguistic or software forensic analysis that must either be stipulated or proven to the court to be completely accurate. It is generally more difficult to admit a simulation as evidence because of the substantive nature of the process. Simulations must make a great many assumptions about what is important in the real world, and it is unlikely that the opponent in litigation would allow such assumptions to go unchallenged.

Computer animation, in contrast, is simply a computer-generated sequence, illustrating an expert's opinion. (This chapter discusses, in more depth, the requirements for expert testimony in later sections.) Animation does not predict future events, but merely supports the testimony of an expert witness through the use of demonstrations. An animation of a hard disk spinning while the read/write heads are reading data can help the court or jury understand how a disk drive works. There are no mathematical algorithms that must be proven. The key to having animation admitted as evidence is a strong expert witness. It is very important to understand the difference between these two types of evidence because it affects the standard of admissibility (discussed in the next section).

Rules of Evidence

The specific rules of evidence may vary among jurisdictions, but some principles are fairly standard. Some are common sense, whereas others are not quite as obvious and may direct specific actions that must be taken in regard to the collection, preparation, and presentation of exhibits.

First of all, evidence must be *relevant*. Although the assessments that are done on hardware or software may be technically interesting, the court will not want to hear about results unless the data have a bearing on the matter at hand. The fact that a given program uses a particular programming trick is not necessarily evidence. In contrast, the fact that the trick is used in this program, and only in programs written by one particular author, *is* evidence. Analysis of software can provide information about what a program does, what it was intended to do, and possibly who wrote it, but generally to turn this information into evidence, there needs to be additional data (possibly about the programming environment). On the other hand, a comparative analysis of the code of two programs can probably provide evidence of whether one copied from another and which came first.

Another concept in evidence is what is called a *foundation of admissibility*. This is somewhat more technical and deals with the reliability or acceptability of the evidence as something upon which the court can base a decision. It partly relates to specific procedures for what is called the chain of evidence or chain of custody and also the matter of expert testimony, both of which are examined below.

Any information presented as evidence should have been obtained by legal means. The results of illegal searches or surveillance will not (with some provisos) be accepted in court. Some recent laws may have interesting ramifications in this regard. The U.S. Digital Millennium Copyright Act holds that it is illegal to break into any technology intended to protect copyrighted material. Programmers are held to have copyright on the programs that they produce. Therefore, if the programmer even does a simple self-encryption on the program code, it may be illegal to do a decryption in order to analyze the software.

Hearsay and Business Documents

An additional factor in the admissibility of evidence is the concept of *hearsay*. As a witness in court, you may be asked to say what you did or witnessed directly. Except in very unusual circumstances, you will not be asked and will not be allowed to say what someone else told you that he or she did or saw. This "second-hand" testimony is called hearsay and is pretty much automatically suspect. If the court is to accept evidence other than directly from the source, there has to be corroborating testimony.

Business documents are all considered to be, in some sense, hearsay. This is because they are all, in a way, information about a transaction, rather than direct evidence of a transaction. This characterization is particularly true in relation to electronic data. When presenting printouts or other representations of digital information, there must be testimony about how the information is stored and handled, whether there are regular procedures for doing so, whether there was any kind of departure from regular procedures in this particular instance, what protections are in place to ensure the integrity of the data, who has access and the ability to change the data, and so forth.

Whether related to a business or not, all computer and digital records are regarded as hearsay in this light. In a sense, this point is going to lie at the heart of every examination of digital evidence. In addition, digital evidence is suspect because of the ease with which it can be created, destroyed, or altered.

Digital Frailty and the Chain of Evidence

Digital information is extremely fragile. A change of a single bit in a megabyte file can radically alter its implications, meaning, or outcomes. Although operating systems generally track changes to some extent, even if only the last time a file was changed, it is quite possible to alter data without leaving any trace that a modification has been made or indicating by whom. Therefore, it is vitally important, in terms of admissibility, to be able to prove that the analyst has not made any changes to the system while studying it. This is so important that the G-8 nations commissioned an initiative for a set of proposed international principles for computer evidence. The standards state that actions taken in seizing digital evidence should not change the evidence, that any person accessing the evidence should be forensically competent, and that all actions in regard to the evidence should be documented fully.

Of course, not every single-bit change to a massive file has any significance. In fact, there are situations in which identical files are stored in different ways, without any meaningful change having taken place at all. For example, text files in DOS and Windows systems are stored with two characters (a carriage return and a line feed) at the end of every line. UNIX file systems store text files with only a single character indicating the end of the line. Therefore, for identical text files stored on different file systems the hash value, digest, or digital signature would detect a difference (because they are designed to indicate a variation even in a single bit) and declare the files to be different. Thus, computer forensics must sometimes deal with the issue of *canonicalization*, which ensures that the digital material being marked to determine changes is limited to those sections where changes are relevant. Obviously, the concept of canonicalization itself needs to be presented carefully in court, if relevant, to ensure that the significance and reliability of the procedure are understood.

An important concept in the presentation of any physical evidence is the chain of custody. The court will need to know who had access to the evidence and what they did to it. The court will also need to know that nobody other than the people listed could have had access to the material. If there is any possibility that the evidence might have been tampered with, even if there is no specific reason to suspect that something was done to the items in question, then there is a reasonable doubt that the evidence actually does support what we assert.

Remember also the point about competence in regard to the handling of data. Even without the G-8 standards, the existence of an incompetent person in the chain of custody could raise doubts about the validity of the results obtained in any testing. In the case of a criminal case, this fact could be sufficient to cause the case to fail.

In the case of digital and electronic data, the identification and preservation of the information are absolutely vital. Digital data are fragile and can be modified easily; once modified, there is almost no way to determine that a change was made, when the change was made, and who made it. Therefore, the establishment of an iron-clad chain of custody is crucial.

The chain of custody for computer, network, or software forensics uses procedures very similar to those for other forms of electronic evidence. There will have to be identification and preservation of the original system. Either the computer itself or the electronic media will need to be labeled and secured. Access to these original items must be restricted. (In some special circumstances, of course, the material to be studied will be available only in the memory of the computer, and therefore the original physical representation cannot be preserved. In that case, the procedures involved in recovering the material and maintaining it thereafter must be documented.)

The original material should not be studied, because the tools used to study the files can also be used to modify them. Therefore, printouts and/or message digest calculations should be created as soon as possible to be able to demonstrate that the data studied or presented are the same as the original. In most cases, it is a good idea to have a videotape of the original procedures of seizing and recovering the computer. Rather ironically, any videotaping should be analog, not digital to avoid the suggestion that the digital video was itself edited or modified.

Providing Expert Testimony

For the foreseeable future, digital forensics is going to be an arcane art that is presented in court, if at all, by an expert. Therefore, the rules governing expert witnesses are also germane to this discussion.

Despite the aphorism attributed to Mark Twain that an expert is simply some guy from out of town, it is not necessarily possible to walk into court and simply state that you are an expert in a field. The court will decide (or the other side will challenge) whether you have sufficient education and training, experience, or skill to support your conclusions and whether there is a "reasonable basis" for the conclusions you reach. If you are not an expert, you can present the uninterpreted results of your analysis. However, masses of unexplained data are likely to be judged irrelevant to the case. If you do obtain the status of an expert witness, then you are also able to present your opinion about what the results mean.

Assessment of expertise in cases involving information technology has been and continues to be difficult. Unlike other professions such as medicine, civil engineering, or accounting, there is no organized, licensed professional college, organization, institute, or other body involved in the regulation, censure, and discrimination of specific expertise. (Or, at least, no universally recognized one—As the old joke has it, the nice thing about computer standards is that there are so many of them.) Given the novelty of the field of software forensics, the requirements for education and training are likely to be even more problematic. After all, there is no certificate, diploma, or degree program in software forensics, although there are some courses available in the data recovery procedures of computer forensics. Some individuals are working on various aspects of the field, but academic research in isolated areas is unlikely to be accepted as sufficient training, at least not in and of itself.

The expert need not have complete knowledge about the field in question, need not be certain, and need not be unbiased: the expert must only be able to aid the jury in resolving a relevant issue. Although the level of expertise may affect the weight accorded to the expert's opinion, it does not affect admissibility. It has been held that the court cannot exclude testimony simply because the trial court does not deem the proposed expert to be the best qualified or because the proposed expert does not have the specialization the court considers most appropriate.

Again, experience is going to be difficult to assess in the immediate future. Experience as a low-level programmer analyzing and debugging code is likely to be a help, but not necessarily sufficient. Academic research on plagiarism and the similarity of code between programs could be relevant. Virus researchers, who are used to finding identifiable patterns in programs (as well as specific functions), could have an advantage. However, the experience of a specific software forensic practitioner will probably have to be matched with the particular case being pursued.

Skill is an interesting concept and is not necessarily simply related to training or experience. A peer group may very well adjudge an individual as being particularly skilled, even though there is little or no difference in training or experience between the skilled person and his or her colleagues. Therefore, we may be faced with the situation of bringing testimony, of one type or another, attesting to the skill of the expert being brought before the court. A demonstrated success rate may be said to be a measure of skill, but even this is going to be a rather subjective criterion because definitions of success will vary.

Of the different factors that make up the assessment as to whether or not a witness is expert, probably one that deserves a lot of attention is that of reasonable basis. It is not enough that we, as experts, can see a conclusion or finding. An expert's opinion must be reliable; that is, based on valid reasoning and reliable methodology, as opposed to subjective belief or unsupported speculation. If an expert opinion is based on speculation or conjecture, it may be stricken. An expert witness must be able to explain the reasoning leading to that conclusion at least to a judge

and possibly to members of a jury, who probably do not have any kind of technical background.

Software forensic evidence is likely to rely on statistical methods. Presentation of the evidence, therefore, will need to be accompanied by clear explanations not only of how the characteristics were determined but also of why they are important. The court must make an assessment as to whether the reasoning or methodology underlying the testimony is scientifically valid. To do so, the court should consider whether a method consists of a testable hypothesis, whether the method has been subject to peer review, the known or potential rate of error, the existence and maintenance of standards controlling the technique's operation, whether the method is generally accepted, the relationship of the technique to methods that have been established to be reliable, the qualifications of the expert witness testifying based on the methodology, and the nonjudicial uses of the method. All of these factors should be addressed in presenting expert testimony in court.

In the United States there is case law, known as the Daubert decision, which states that judges must decide not only whether a witness is truly expert but also on what the expert may testify about. This restriction of testimony on the part of the judge has become known as the *gatekeeper function*. In American courts an expert witness may find that restrictions are placed on the testimony that can be delivered. The court, even after having decided that a witness is an expert, may limit the areas of expertise that are acceptable.

An expert witness may play several roles in a case. First, there is the consulting expert who provides advice and information to counsel well in advance of the trial itself. At the time of the trial, the court's expert gives supposedly unbiased explanations to the court (usually the judge) about specialized technical matters bearing on the case. Then there is the testifying expert, which is the role most people think of in regard to expert witnesses. The testifying expert explains findings, discoveries, and their implications. However, the discoveries may be such that they could only be seen or made by the expert. In that case, the expert witness also functions as a witness to fact. It is important to ensure that the expert knows and does not confuse which of these roles he or she is being asked to undertake. The expert may, in fact, be asked to fulfill more than one of these roles in the course of the proceedings, and in such a situation maintaining the division between roles is vital. The function the expert is being asked to undertake will shape the work to be done and will possibly restrict the testimony that can be given.

In normal testimony, witnesses are only allowed to tell what they saw, heard, or in some way know to be a fact. Witnesses are not permitted to infer or extrapolate beyond direct observation. In contrast, experts are allowed to draw conclusions and even present opinions. This extension of the testimony of the professional is not unrestricted and is therefore more open to challenge by the opposing side.

One very common source of tension in obtaining and presenting technical testimony is the significant difference in mindset between the technical and legal worlds. Computer work generally involves finding an answer to a problem: if the code works, background study and documented analysis are generally irrelevant. The legal profession, on the other hand, depends absolutely upon advance preparation, and an answer is almost useless unless the reasoning, background, and process are not only chronicled but also obtained properly and legally. Both the legal counsel and the technical expert have to work to see the other's point of view. Lawyers, accustomed to carting around trunks full of papers for even the simplest case, will have to be prepared for the assumption that "it works" is sufficient proof. Techies will need to overcome their deep-seated aversion to any and all forms of documentation and shed the automatic assumption that all users are incapable of understanding technical concepts.

ETHICS

The topic of ethics is a very difficult one, and a complete discussion is beyond the scope of this chapter. Discussions of ethics, particularly in regard to information technology, tend to fail to provide useful direction. This deficiency is due in large measure to a breakdown in communication: the parties to such debates seldom agree even on the most basic definition of what ethics actually are. Some see ethics as fundamental guiding principles, whereas others assume that they are legalistic codes of conduct. Few can even agree on whether ethical standards are absolute or relative. This chapter does not pursue this deliberation, but rather addresses some related topics that are more directly relevant to digital forensics.

Disclosure

The concept of disclosure—how much information to provide about a potential security weakness—has become a major issue in security circles in recent years. In the early days of computer security work, a majority of practitioners came from a military or related background, with its strong emphasis on confidentiality. Thus, it was automatically assumed that limiting information was a good thing. Because nobody knew much about computers then, keeping the details quiet did provide a limitation on the number of people who could even attempt to penetrate systems. Later, this position became known as security by obscurity, or SBO.

Obscurity has now been found wanting. In the same way that writers cannot edit their own text (trust me on this), security planners and administrators are often blind to the faults in their own protective systems. Without some outside analysis of a setup or product, flaws can go undetected for years. In such a situation, the first time the existence of a problem becomes apparent is when someone uses it. The attackers and black hat will find weaknesses, even if nobody talks about them. The only people that obscurity keeps in the dark are those charged with protecting the systems.

Some experts advocate full disclosure. This means that anyone who discovers a security loophole should immediately publish all details in full, including instructions on how to use the vulnerability. However, because full disclosure requires that everyone be alert to every security warning that comes along, no matter how minor, most people are more comfortable with some level of partial disclosure. Partial disclosure usually involves limits, such as informing the publisher of a product problem before alerting the general public, to give the vendor time to come up with some way to fix the problem. Sometimes the information given to the public may be restricted to the existence of the issue, as well as suggestions about safety measures. Partial disclosure is not standardized in any way, and the definition of what it entails may vary from person to person.

The virus research community has frequently been accused of practicing a form of security by obscurity. Legitimate researchers refuse to distribute virus code unless they know that the person making the request is qualified and that the requester abides by the same code of conduct and will not give out copies of the software. This position may seem untenable in these days of e-mail viruses, when virus code may be obtained almost as easily as spam messages. The virus research community, however, believes that establishing a flexible line on distribution would be too complex and would inevitably lead to increased distribution and therefore chooses to err on the side of caution.

Black Hat Motivations as a Defense

Because some of these contentions may be used as a defense in court, it is important to examine the commonly presented justifications for the activities of the black hat community (system penetration, software piracy, virus writing, etc.) as arguments relating to the activity of digital forensics. Regardless of how we may consider them from an ethical standpoint, we may need to defend against them as legal debates.

One of the most frequently attempted justifications of black hat activity of all kinds is that it is protected under the concept of freedom of speech. The free speech defense may be an extremely strong one, particularly in nations under common law systems, where some form of freedom of expression is often a constitutional right. So far the courts still appear to be divided on the issue of whether or not computer code counts as "speech." A more reliable approach to dealing with the free speech argument is to examine the restrictions on freedom of speech, which restrict the right to create harm with speech. There are generally laws and precedents against slander, hate speech, and even shouting "fire" in crowded theaters.

Many individuals who practice system violation activity rationalize that they are following in the detective footsteps of the old-time hackers (system experts), who explored and discovered the capabilities of early computing devices. In many cases there is honest disagreement among individuals in regard to the legality of attempts to break into security systems for the purpose of strengthening those same systems. Some individuals who seem to have sincerely wanted to publicize security weaknesses, or offer their services as consultants, have found themselves facing criminal charges. There are two points to make in this regard. One is to ensure that the activity you are examining is malicious in intent. The other is to be very sure that, when investigating a system, you have permission to do so.

CONCLUSION

In today's interconnected computing environment, you may be faced with a variety of legal systems. Although you cannot know all the relevant laws around the globe, a general overview of the types of legal systems you may encounter can be helpful.

The digital forensic investigator is involved in collecting, analyzing, and presenting evidence. Note that there are very definite rules in regard to the collection and treatment of evidence. In particular, note the chain of custody concept that is so vital in the traditional data recovery side of computer forensics.

As a specialist in computer, network, or software forensics, you may be required to act as an expert witness in one or more roles. Be aware of the special demands and responsibilities of that function.

A number of issues will bear on your activities in the legal arena. Although the law and ethics are not identical, it is probably necessary to examine all activities from an ethical perspective while the legislation and precedents relating to software are being worked out.

GLOSSARY

Relevant terms may also be found in the security glossary at http://victoria.tc.ca/techrev/secgloss.htm or http://sun.soci.niu.edu/~rslade/secgloss.htm

Acceptable use policy (AUP) A written policy outlining the usage that may or may not be made of computing or network resources. Previously this applied primarily to institutions (such as universities) providing access to systems such as the Internet. Although not as widely used currently, AUPs should still be part of a company's security policy.

Accountability The property that enables activities on a system to be traced to individuals (or entities) who may then be held responsible for their actions.

Black hat Communities or individuals who either attempt to break into computer systems without prior authorization or who explore security primarily from an attack perspective. The term originates from old American Western genre movies where the "good guys" always wore white hats and the "bad guys" always wore black.

Computer forensics Originally the full means of obtaining legal evidence from computers and computer use, computer forensics is now apparently limited to the recovery of data from computers and computer media. Computer forensics has therefore become only one part of digital forensics.

Digital forensics Sometimes known as digital forensic research or digital forensic science, this has recently become the umbrella term for all forms of research and analysis of computers and computer use directed at obtaining evidence of intrusion, attack, or wrongdoing. The First Digital Forensic Research Workshop defined digital forensic science as "[t]he use of scientifically derived and proven methods toward the preservation, collection, validation, identification, analysis, interpretation, documentation and presentation of digital evidence derived from digital sources for the purpose of facilitating or furthering the reconstruction of events found to be criminal, or helping to anticipate unauthorized actions shown to be disruptive to planned operations." Three major fields of digital forensics are computer forensics, forensic programming (or software forensics), and network forensics.

Forensic programming Originally from the field of computer virus research, forensic programming involves the analysis of code for evidence of intent, program identity, or authorship. Outside the field of virus research, forensic programming is often referred to as code analysis, although code analysis may be limited to analysis of source code, whereas forensic programming frequently deals with object code when object code is the only evidence available. It is one of the major divisions of digital forensics.

Hacker Originally the term meant one who was skilled in the use of computer systems, particularly if that skill was acquired in an exploratory manner. Later, the term evolved to be applied to someone, skilled or unskilled, who breaks into security systems. Actually, you can determine people's level of technical expertise by how they use the term. Someone who uses hacker as meaning expert is someone who really does advanced technical work. Someone who uses hacker as a bad guy may have a technical background of some type or hold a technical job, but usually is nowhere near the "cutting edge."

Incident An occurrence that has been assessed as having an adverse effect on the security or performance of a system. Note that this definition is somewhat vague, particularly in regard to the level of assessment. Those from a law enforcement background tend to see incidents in terms of attacks with (potentially) identifiable intruders. Those from a systems administration or support background tend to see an incident as any anomaly in the system that might affect performance or service.

Incident response The reaction, generally by a predesignated team, to a detrimental incident. Currently, the incident response literature is primarily concerned with the collection and preservation of evidence in a manner appropriate for presentation in a court of law.

Network forensics The collection and analysis of evidence of intrusion or malfeasance from network activity and data. It is closely related to intrusion detection systems and one of the major divisions of digital forensics.

CROSS REFERENCES

See *Computer Forensic Procedures and Methods; Digital Evidence; Forensic Computing; Law Enforcement and Digital Evidence.*

FURTHER READING

Caloyannides, M. A. (2001). *Computer forensics and privacy*. Norwood MA: Artech House

CERIAS. (n.d.). Retrieved from http://www.cerias.purdue.edu/coast/coast-library.html

DFRWS. (n.d.). *Digital forensic research workshop*. Retrieved from March 15, 2005, http://www.dfrws.org/

Forensic Evidence.com (n.d.). *Forensic stylistics in the court*. Retrieved from http://www.forensic-evidence.com/site/ID/linquistics.html

Gordon, S. (2001). *Defining and questioning conventional wisdom: Papers*. Retrieved from http://www.badguys.org/papers.htm

Johnson, D. (1994). *Computer ethics*. Englewood Cliffs, NJ: Prentice Hall.

Kruse, W. G., & Heiser, J. G. (2001). Computer forensics. Boston, MA: Addison, Wesley.

QSUM. (n.d.). *The cumulative sum (cusum) technique for authorship analysis & attribution*. Retrieved March 15, 2005, from http://hometown.aol.com/qsums

Slade, R. (2004). *Software forensics*. New York: McGraw-Hill.

SWDGE and IOGE. (2000, April). Digital evidence: Standards and principles. *Forensic Science Communications, 2*(2). Retrieved March 15, 2005, from http://www.fbi.gov/hq/lab/fsc/backissu/april2000/swgde.htm

Taylor, P. A. (1999). *Hackers: Crime in the digital sublime*. London & New York: Routledge.

PART 3

Foundations of Information, Computer, and Network Security

Encryption Basics

Ari Juels, *RSA Laboratories*

INTRODUCTION

Encryption is the procedure of rendering a message into a concealed form so that it is decipherable exclusively by a particular recipient or recipients. The message in its original state is known as a *plaintext* (or *cleartext*); in its encrypted form, it is known as a *ciphertext*. Historically, the aim of encryption has been to enable two parties to exchange messages confidentially, even in the presence of an eavesdropper capable of intercepting most or all of their communications. The use of encryption has been confined chiefly to diplomatic and military circles in the past, but its scope in everyday life has broadened enormously in recent years. Thanks to the rise of the Internet, it is estimated that over half a billion personal computers are equipped today with strong encryption capabilities in their Web browsing software. This includes nearly every new computer sold today.

Active users of the Internet employ encryption on a regular basis. When accepting credit card information or processing other financial transactions, most Web servers initiate encryption sessions with clients. The form of encryption used to support sessions of this kind on the Web is very strong—so strong that it is generally believed to be effectively unbreakable by even the most powerful computers. In most browsers, the appearance of an icon representing a closed padlock on the bottom of the screen indicates the use of encryption in a protocol known as SSL (Secure Sockets Layer). By clicking on this padlock, a user can learn detailed information about the encryption session, much of which is explained in further depth in this chapter. Encryption also plays an important role in most important industrial communications systems, of course, such as networks used for banking transactions.

For the reader interested in a cursory introduction to encryption, without much of the detail provided in this chapter, it is possible to read the following sections as a more-or-less self-contained exposition: Some Basics, Symmetric-Key Encryption Today, the opening paragraphs of Public-Key Cryptography, The RSA Cryptosystem, and How Public-Key Encryption Is Used.

Some Basics

The science of constructing encryption algorithms and related systems is known as *cryptography*. That of analyzing and attempting to find weaknesses in encryption algorithms is called *cryptanalysis*. Together, the two complementary sciences are known as *cryptology*. Cryptologists like to explain their ideas in terms of a small troupe of fictional characters. Traditionally, Alice and Bob are the names assigned to the fictional parties wishing to exchange confidential messages with one another. The hypothetical eavesdropper on their communication is called Eve. We follow this nomenclature in our explanations in this chapter.

An encryption algorithm is considered to be secure when Eve cannot feasibly distinguish between the encryptions of two different plaintexts. This should hold even in cases where Eve has the ability to manipulate the messages transmitted between Alice and Bob in various ways. For example, suppose that Eve can cause Alice to generate and reveal ciphertexts A and B computed on messages X and Y in a random order. Eve should nonetheless be unable to tell whether A is an encryption of X or of Y.

The operational basis of an encryption algorithm, or cipher, is a piece of information known as a key. A key serves as input to the encryption process that Alice and Bob have agreed to use. The encryption process consists of a series of instructions on how Alice, for instance, should convert a plaintext into a ciphertext. The key serves as a parameter guiding the instructions. The reverse process, whereby Bob converts a ciphertext back into a plaintext, is also guided by a key, one that may or may not be the same as Alice's. The security of traditional ciphers, that is, the privacy of the messages they encrypt, depends on a shared key that is kept secret. For example, in one form of folklore encryption, Alice and Bob each have copies of the same edition of a particular novel. They share the identity of this novel as a secret between them. Alice encrypts a plaintext by finding a random example of each letter of her message in the novel. She writes down the page, line, and ordinal position of each of these letters in turn. The result of this process constitutes the ciphertext. Bob, of course, can reverse the process and obtain the original plaintext by referring to his copy of the shared novel. In this case, the novel itself serves as a key—one that is quite long, of course, running as it usually does to hundreds of pages. In the forms of cryptography used on computers today, the key is much shorter, typically the equivalent in length of several words or sentences.

A Brief Historical Note

An exciting subject of study in its own right, the history of cryptology is also intimately associated with the birth of the digital computer. During World War II, the efforts of British signals intelligence to break the German Enigma cipher led to the development of mechanical devices known as "bombes," so called because of the ticking sounds they made in testing possible cipher keys. The "bombes" and the later generation of Colossus machines arising from these efforts were important precursors of the modern computer. Moreover, the man overseeing the immensely successful Enigma break was Alan Turing, a progenitor of the field of computer science.

SYMMETRIC-KEY ENCRYPTION: INTRODUCTION

When Alice and Bob make use of the same key for encryption and decryption, as in our example above involving the novel, this is referred to as symmetric or symmetric-key encryption. Figure 1 gives a basic operational schematic of symmetric-key encryption.

Let us consider another folklore cipher, in which each letter of a message is replaced with another letter according to a fixed set of random, predetermined assignments. For example, the message, "MEET ME UNDER THE BRIDGE" might be encrypted as follows:

ZKKO ZK BWIKQ OPK UQMIFK.

This form of encryption is known as a substitution cipher. It is in fact quite easy for a skilled cryptanalyst—or even just a good puzzle solver—to break. Edgar Allen Poe, for instance, challenged readers of a newspaper in 1839 to submit English-language ciphertexts produced by letter substitution. He published the plaintexts of many such challenge ciphertexts in subsequent numbers of the

newspaper. Knowing, for example, that 'e' is the most common letter in the English language, one would be tempted—quite correctly—to identify the letter 'K', which appears most frequently in the above ciphertext, with the letter 'E' in the plaintext. More sophisticated cryptanalytic techniques for attacking substitution ciphers focus on the frequency statistics not just for single letters, but also for letter pairs and triples.

Knowing that their cipher is subject to cryptanalytic attacks of this kind, Alice and Bob might be tempted to use a different, perhaps more complex, cipher and to hide from Eve not just their key but also the workings of the cipher. This is equivalent in effect to making the choice of the cipher a part of the key itself. An important principle enunciated by the 19th-century cryptologist Kerckhoffs discourages this approach. Adhered to by contemporary cryptologists, this principle may be stated as follows: The security of a cipher should reside in the key alone, not in the secrecy of the process of encryption. The motivations behind Kerckhoffs's principle are several. First, widespread use of a good cipher requires that its workings be divulged in some form. Even if a cipher is disseminated only through software, for example, the underlying instructions can be reverse-engineered. Thus, it is fair to assume that an attacker can learn the mechanics of the cipher. Moreover, despite the oft-demonstrated inventiveness of the cryptographic community, there is time enough to devise and refine only a limited number of basic techniques for strong new ciphers. A poorly designed cipher, even when its workings are hidden from view, is vulnerable to attack by means of an arsenal of analytic techniques refined by the cryptanalytic community over many years. These techniques are roughly analogous in spirit to the idea that leads to the discovery of the letter 'E' in the example ciphertext above, but rely on more sophisticated forms of statistical analysis.

The basic unit of information in the computer and the fundamental unit for the encoding of digital messages is not the letter, but the bit. For this reason, contemporary symmetric-key ciphers operate through the manipulation of bits rather than lexicographic units. One of the earliest ciphers designed from this perspective is known as the one-time pad. Invented during World War I, the one-time pad is also of interest as the only cipher whose security is provable in the strictest mathematical sense. Formal understanding of its properties emerged in 1948–1949, with the publication of seminal work by Claude Shannon. (The security analysis of other ciphers, as we shall explain, has a strong, but less complete or rigorous mathematical basis.)

A one-time pad is a key shared by Alice and Bob consisting of a perfectly random string of bits as long as the message that Alice wishes to transmit to Bob. To encrypt her message, Alice aligns the pad with the message so that there is a one-to-one correspondence between the bits in both. Where the pad contains a '1', Alice flips the corresponding bit in her plaintext. She leaves the other bits of the plaintext unchanged. This simple process yields the ciphertext. As may be proven mathematically—and perhaps grasped intuitively—this ciphertext is indistinguishable to Eve from a completely random string. Indeed, from her perspective, it is a completely random string. This is to say

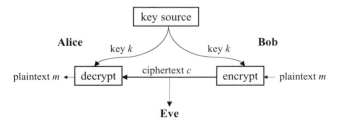

Figure 1: (Symmetric-key encryption): Bob wishes to transmit plaintext message m securely to Alice over a channel subject to eavesdropping. He encrypts it under shared symmetric key k to obtain ciphertext c, and transmits c. Eavesdropper Eve learns the ciphertext c, but should not learn m if the cipher is constructed and used properly.

that Eve can learn no information at all from the ciphertext, no matter how powerful her cryptanalytic capabilities. Apart from its requirement of perfect randomness, though, the one-time pad carries another strong caveat. The term *one-time* refers to the fact that if Alice uses the same key to encrypt more than one message, she loses the security properties of the cipher. This makes the one-time pad impractical for most purposes, as it requires that Alice and Bob generate, exchange, and store many random bits in advance of their communications. Nonetheless, the one-time pad has seen practical use. For example, the "hot-line" established between the United States and Soviet Union in the wake of the Cuban missile crisis employed a one-time pad system to ensure confidentiality, with tapes containing random keying material exchanged via the embassies of the two countries.

Symmetric-Key Encryption Today

The symmetric-key ciphers in common use today are designed to employ relatively short keys, typically 128 bits in length. Moreover, these ciphers retain their security properties even when individual keys are used to encrypt many messages over long periods of time. Indeed, a well-designed symmetric-key cipher should permit only one effective avenue of attack, described by cryptographers as exhaustive search or brute force. By this, it is meant that an attacker familiar with the cipher makes random guesses at the key until successful. If Eve wishes to mount a brute force attack against a ciphertext sent by Alice to Bob, she will repeatedly guess their shared key and try to decrypt the message until she obtains the correct plaintext.

Given use of a 128-bit-long key, Eve will on average have to make well more than a trillion trillion trillion guesses before she is successful! This is more, for example, than the total number of atoms composing all of the human beings in the world. The most powerful computers available today could not be expected to mount a successful brute force attack against a well-designed cipher employing a key of this length, even over the course of many years. It should be observed that the difficulty of breaking a key doubles for every additional bit in length. Thus, for instance, a 128-bit key is not twice as hard to break as a 64-bit key, but over a million trillion times harder.

The first widely embraced cipher employing the strong design principles in use today was the Data Encryption Standard or DES (pronounced "dehz"). Developed at IBM, the DES cipher was published as a federal standard in 1976 by what is now the National Institute of Standards (NIST) of the United States government. DES and security-enhanced variants are still widely deployed, particularly in the banking industry. DES employs a 56-bit key, operating on a basic unit of encryption consisting of a 64-bit block. This is to say that to encrypt a long message using DES, Alice first subdivides the message into 64-bit (i.e., eight-byte) blocks, each of which she enciphers individually. Ciphers that operate in this fashion are referred to as block ciphers.

Brute force attack on a 56-bit key requires substantial computational effort, very likely beyond the reach of most organizations at the time of invention of DES. Today,

however, such capability is attainable with networks of ordinary workstations. This was first demonstrated in 1997 when a successful attack was mounted against a DES-encrypted ciphertext by a network of thousands of computers over the course of 39 days, and subsequently duplicated by a single, special-purpose computer in less than a day. (It should be noted that even today, DES is still not easy to break without considerable resources.) Earlier concerns about the strength of DES had already prompted many organizations to employ a strengthened version involving application of DES operations not once but three times to each input block, and typically using two distinct DES keys. Known as triple-DES, this enhanced version offers considerably stronger security than DES, with what may be viewed as an effective key strength of up to 112 bits.

With DES in its basic form approaching the end of its serviceable lifetime, the cryptographic community began in 1999 to lend its efforts to the development of a new standard cipher to serve as a successor. The Advanced Encryption Standard or AES (pronounced letter by letter) emerged as the result of an open competition conducted by NIST. After a period of rigorous scrutiny by the research community and government agencies, a cipher known as Rijndael (of which one recognized pronunciation is "Rhine dahl") was selected as the AES. Designed by two Belgian researchers, Joan Daemen and Vincent Rijmen, the AES promises to see widespread deployment in the United States and internationally in coming years. Rijndael is a block cipher designed to accommodate key lengths of 128, 196, or 256 bits and operate on data blocks of 128, 196, or 256 bits in any of the nine possible combinations. Rijndael, like many contemporary symmetric-key ciphers, is capable of very fast encryption—substantially faster than triple-DES. On a Pentium III running at 1 GHz, implementations of AES with 128-bit keys are capable of achieving an encryption speed of 50 MB/s. The code sizes for such implementations can be less than 1 kB. The size of a basic ciphertext yielded by AES, as with any block cipher, is roughly the size of the plaintext. A little extra space—less than the block size—may also be needed to accommodate added randomness and the fact the plaintext generally cannot be divided into data blocks of exactly the right size. See the NIST AES Web site for further information and links (National Institute of Standards and Technology, 2005).

Another symmetric-key cipher deserving discussion is RC4. In contrast to the block ciphers described above, RC4 is known as a stream cipher. It does not operate by encrypting individual blocks of data. Rather, the only input to RC4 is a key, typically 128 bits in length. The output of this cipher is a string of random-looking bits. This string may be made as long as desired by the user. To encrypt a message for Bob, Alice inputs a shared key to RC4 and generates a string as long as the message. Although not a one-time pad, this string is used by Alice to encrypt the message in exactly the same manner as a one-time pad, i.e., using the same system of bit alignment and flipping. Additionally, the output string of RC4 for a particular key has the "one-time" restriction, which is to say that the string can be safely used for encryption only once. The fact that RC4 can generate a string of arbitrary length, however, means that different portions of the string can be used for different messages. Also, encipherment under RC4 is naturally capable of yielding a ciphertext identical in length to the plaintext.

This said, the output string of RC4 on a given key is not in fact a one-time pad, because it is not fully random. This may be seen in the fact that Alice and Bob know the process that generated the string, because they know their shared input key to RC4. In particular, they can write down a short set of instructions describing to someone else how to generate exactly the same output string from RC4. If k denotes their shared key, these instructions would simply say, "Give the key k as input to RC4." They could not do this in the case of a truly random string. Suppose, for instance, that Alice and Bob generated a shared random string, i.e., a one-time pad, by flipping a coin many times. If they gave the instructions "flip a coin" to Carol, it is almost certain that Carol, in following the same instructions, would generate a very different-looking string. Obviously, though, RC4 is much more convenient for Alice and Bob to use than a one-time pad, because it only requires of them that they share a key of, say, 128 bits in length. For all intents and purposes, this is true no matter how long the messages they wish to encrypt.

The security of the RC4 cipher comes from the fact that from the perspective of Eve, who does not know the key, the output of RC4 is indistinguishable from a one-time pad. This is to say that if Alice were to give an RC4 output string to Eve (rather than using it for encipherment), and were also to give Eve a truly random string of the same length, Eve would not be able to tell the difference. Thus, as far as Eve is concerned, when Alice and Bob encrypt their messages using RC4, they might as well be using a one-time pad. This, at any rate, is a rough expression of the conclusion that cryptanalysts have arrived at after many years of statistical study of the RC4 cipher. They express this belief by describing the output of RC4 as being pseudorandom. Strong block ciphers like AES are also believed to possess this property of pseudorandomness, but in a different form.

RC4 is of particular interest because it is one of the most commonly used ciphers in the world and included in the software in nearly every new PC sold today. It is generally a component of the SSL encryption system used for secure credit-card transactions on the Internet. In other words, the closed padlock on a browser screen mentioned earlier in this chapter indicates that the RC4 cipher is being used. RC4 was designed by Ronald L. Rivest, one of the co-inventors of the RSA cryptosystem, which we discuss later in this chapter. The letters "RC" stand for "Ron's Code," and the number '4' denotes Rivest's fourth cipher design. The design principal for RC4, like that of most symmetric ciphers, is a delicate sequencing of a few very basic mathematical instructions. In RC4, the operations are the swapping of integer elements in a small array representing a permutation and addition of small integers (in fact, modular addition, an operation explained later in this chapter). Others of Rivest's suite of cipher designs are also in common use, namely RC2, which forms the basis of many e-mail encryption programs, and also RC5. In addition to DES, triple-DES, AES, and the RC series,

there are a number of other popular ciphers used in various systems today. These include IDEA, CAST-128, and Blowfish, to name just a few.

More on the Security of Symmetric-Key Encryption

As already explained, cryptologists know of a truly complete mathematical proof of security only for the one-time pad. For DES, triple-DES, AES, RC4, and kindred ciphers, cryptographers have no such security proofs. Strong proof for these ciphers is not possible at present; belief in their security, however, rests on fairly well-explored (if heuristic) mathematical foundations.

Shortly after the publication of DES, two cryptologists named Eli Biham and Adi Shamir developed a technique called differential cryptanalysis. Roughly speaking, differential cryptanalysis involves statistical analysis of a cipher based on the way particular bits change (or do not change) in output ciphertexts when bits in certain positions are flipped in input plaintexts. The technique of differential cryptanalysis helped to confirm the strength of DES and to inform the design of later ciphers. (Some time after the academic development of differential cryptanalysis, it was publicly revealed that the technique had already been familiar to the government intelligence community and had indeed helped guide the design of DES.) Subsequently developed cryptanalytic techniques have further enhanced the collection of tools available to the cryptanalyst, influencing new cipher designs in the process.

We have thus far been describing Eve as an inert eavesdropper, attempting to decipher the messages sent between Alice to Bob by harvesting and analyzing the ciphertexts they exchange. In fact, cryptologists also consider a range of ways in which Eve might try to tamper with or otherwise influence what messages Alice and Bob exchange in the hope of learning additional information. For example, if Alice encrypts all of her e-mail, then Eve might send a note containing a petition to Alice and ask Alice to forward it to her friends. If Alice sends the petition to Bob while Eve is eavesdropping, then Eve learns a ciphertext for which she herself has selected the corresponding plaintext. In other words, Eve is able to perform active experimentation on the cipher. If Alice and Bob use a cipher that is poorly designed, then Eve may be able to gain information about their key in this way or about messages they have exchanged with one another. This type of attack is known as a chosen-plaintext attack. It is an example of one of the types of attack against which cryptographers must ensure that their cipher designs are resistant.

Even if a cipher is well designed, it must still be used with great care. Consider another example. Suppose that Alice and Bob always use a strong block cipher such as AES with a random 128-bit key to encrypt their communications. They perform encryption simply by dividing their messages into blocks and encrypting each block individually under their key. But suppose further that Eve knows that Alice and Bob exchange stock tips, and that these regularly take the form of simple buy and sell orders. Eve might then pass some stock tips to Alice, such as "Buy ABC, Inc." and "Sell DEF Corp.," and suggest that these be forwarded to Bob. If Eve eavesdrops while these stock tips are forwarded, then she learns what the corresponding ciphertexts look like. Thus, if Alice later sends the message "Buy ABC, Inc." to Bob, Eve will be able to recognize the ciphertext and identify the corresponding buy or sell order. In other words, even though Alice and Bob are using a very strong cipher, Eve will be able to identify (and, effectively, to decrypt) any of a small set of target messages!

The way that Alice and Bob use a block cipher is known as a mode of operation. The naïve example we just described is known as electronic code book (ECB) mode, a form whose use is avoided today in part because of the problem we have just described. To prevent Eve from learning what particular ciphertexts look like, Alice may adopt a mode of operation that involves the introduction of random bits into the message. One popular mode of operation today is known as cipher-block-chaining (CBC) mode. In this system, Alice divides her plaintext into blocks and inserts some freshly generated random bits at the beginning to serve as the first block. Alice then employs a principle of "chaining" in which the encryption of one block is affected by the encryption of the previous one, thereby causing the randomness in the first block to propagate through the ciphertext. Although the architectural motivations behind this mode are somewhat complex, its basic impact on message privacy is easy to understand. The fact that Alice introduces randomness into her ciphertexts means that the same plaintext is not encrypted twice the same way, and thus that Eve cannot trick Alice so as to recognize the stock tips or other plaintexts that Alice encrypts. Other modes of encryption aim at formally achieving additional security aims like message authentication. In particular, they enable Alice and Bob to ensure that the origin of messages is legitimate, and that the messages do not include spurious insertions or modifications made by Eve.

Encryption and Passwords

Symmetric-key ciphers are used not only to protect communications but also commonly to protect files against unauthorized access. Many users rely on encryption software to protect files on their hard drives against exposure to hackers or to protect sensitive data in case of laptop theft. For these purposes, it is common for the user to employ a password. The encryption software converts this password into a key for use with a standard symmetric-key cipher such as AES. Because users typically employ passwords consisting of or closely related to words in their native languages, there is generally less randomness in the key generated by a password than in a randomly generated symmetric key. One well-known means for a hacker to attack password-encrypted files in a particular encryption system, therefore, is to compile a large lexicon of common passwords. The hacker converts each entry in the lexicon into a symmetric key in the same manner as the encryption system and then uses each such key in a brute force attack against individual users employing that system. This is known as a dictionary attack. One way to reduce vulnerability to dictionary attacks is to use salt. This is a random string of bits generated for each password individually and combined with the password in the generation of a

symmetric key. The use of salt renders dictionary attacks more difficult, as it effectively forces an attacker to recompile the base lexicon for each target password. It should be understood nevertheless that salt is a limited countermeasure and does not compensate for poor selection of passwords.

Passwords are, of course, also the most common way for users to authenticate when logging into accounts over the Internet. In this context, however, the password is typically not used as an encryption key. Instead, the server to which the user is attempting to connect checks processed password information against a database entry for the requested account.

PUBLIC-KEY CRYPTOGRAPHY

Many years of research have led to the widespread deployment of strong symmetric-key ciphers capable of high encryption speeds. One might be tempted to believe that the basic problem of private communications has been solved and that the science of cryptology has run its course. Even if a symmetric-key cipher is unbreakable, however, there remains a fundamental problem. We have assumed in our discussion that Alice and Bob share knowledge of a secret key. The question is: How do they obtain this key to begin with?

If Alice and Bob can meet face to face, in the absence of the eavesdropper Eve, then they may generate their shared key by repeatedly flipping a coin, or Alice may simply hand Bob a key written on a piece of paper or stored on a floppy disk. What if Alice and Bob wish to communicate privately over the Internet, however, without ever meeting? Alternatively, what if a commercial site on the Web wishes to enable any customer, new or old, to submit an order and credit card number securely from anywhere in the world? The administrator of the Web site cannot possibly hope to communicate keys in private to all customers before they log in. To simplify the formidable difficulties that secure key distribution can pose, cryptographers have devised a form of mathematical magic known as public-key encryption or cryptography (also known as asymmetric-key cryptography, in contrast to symmetric-key cryptography). Using public-key cryptography, Alice and Bob can send each other encrypted messages securely, even if they have never met and even if Eve has eavesdropped on all of their communications!

In a public-key cryptosystem, Alice possesses not one, but two keys. The first is known as her public key. Alice makes this key known to everyone; she may publish it on her Web page, in Internet directories, or in any other public place. Her second, mathematically related key is known as a private key. Alice keeps this key secret. She does not divulge it to anyone else, even people she wishes to communicate with privately. Together, the public key and private key are referred to as a key pair. Bob sends a private message to Alice by performing a computation using her public key and perhaps a private key of his own as well.

Public-key cryptography is a powerful tool—indeed, one whose feasibility may at first seem counterintuitive. Even if Eve knows Alice and Bob's public keys, it is possible for Alice and Bob to communicate privately using public-key cryptography. Moreover, with public-key cryptography, not only Bob but Carol or any other party can achieve private communication with Alice over a public communication medium such as the Internet.

Diffie–Hellman Key Exchange

Public-key encryption was the brainchild of Ralph Merkle, who in 1974 conceived a plausible, but somewhat impractical, initial scheme. The idea saw its first practical form in 1976 in a seminal article by Whitfield Diffie and Martin Hellman entitled "New Directions in Cryptography." Diffie and Hellman proposed a system in which Alice can combine her private key with the public key of Bob, and vice versa, such that each of them obtains the same secret key. Eve cannot figure out this secret key, even with knowledge of the public keys of both Alice and Bob. This system has come to be known as Diffie–Hellman key exchange, abbreviated D–H.

Diffie–Hellman exploits a form of mathematics known as modular arithmetic. Modular arithmetic is a way of restricting the outcome of basic mathematical operations to a set of integers with an upper bound. It is familiar to many schoolchildren as "clock arithmetic." Consider a clock on military time, by which hours are measured only in the range from zero to 23, with zero corresponding to midnight and 23 to 11 o'clock at night. In this system, an advance of 25 hours on 3 o'clock brings us not to 28 o'clock, for example, but full circle to 4 o'clock (because $25 + 3 = 28$ and $28 - 24 = 4$). Similarly, an advance of 55 hours on 1 o'clock brings us to 8 o'clock (because $55 + 1 = 56$ and $56 - (2 \times 24) = 8$). In this case, the number 24, an upper bound on operations involving the measurement of hours, is referred to as a modulus. When a calculation involving hours on a clock yields a large number, we subtract the number 24 until we obtain an integer between 0 and 23, a process known as modular reduction. This idea can be extended to moduli of different sizes. For example, in the modulus 10, the sum of 5 and 7 would not be 12, which is larger than 10, but 2, because modular reduction yields $12 - 10 = 2$. We say that an arithmetic operation is modular when modular reduction is applied to its result. For example, modular multiplication is simply ordinary multiplication followed by modular reduction. We write mod p to denote reduction under modulus p. Thus, for example, it is easily seen that $3 \times 4 \bmod 10 = 2$.

Diffie and Hellman proposed a public-key cryptosystem based on modular multiplication or, more precisely, on modular exponentiation, i.e., the repeated application of modular multiplication. Their scheme depends for its security on the use of a modulus that is a very large number. In the systems used today, the modulus is typically an integer that is 1024 bits in length, i.e., a little more than 300 decimal digits. It is also generally prime, which is to say that apart from the number 1, it is not divisible by any smaller integers. There are some additional, technical restrictions on the form of the modulus that we do not explore here.

The security of D–H is based on the following idea. Suppose that p is a large modulus and g is an integer less than p (again, with some additional technical restrictions). Suppose that Alice selects a random integer a, also less than p. She then computes the integer $y = g^a \bmod p$ and gives the integers p, g, and y to Eve. It is believed by cryptologists that with this information alone, it is infeasible for Eve to figure out the value a. The task of figuring out a is known as the discrete logarithm problem, one that has been the subject of many years of study by mathematicians and cryptographers. Although the security of D–H is not directly based on the discrete logarithm problem, it is very closely related.

In D–H, the values p and g are standard, public values. They may be conveyed in some widely distributed piece of software, such as a browser. Alice selects a random integer a less than p as her private key and computes $y_{\text{Alice}} = g^a$ mod p as her public key, i.e., the key that she publishes. Bob similarly selects a random integer b, also less than p, as his own private key and computes $y_{\text{Bob}} = g^b$ mod p as his public key. Using her secret key a, Alice can take the public key y_{Bob} and compute a value $k = (y_{\text{Bob}})^a \bmod p$. Bob, similarly, can compute exactly the same value k using y_{Alice} in combination with his own private key b. In particular, it is also the case that $k = (y_{\text{Alice}})^b \bmod p$ (thanks to the commutative properties of modular exponentiation). Eve, however, cannot figure out the secret k. This, at least, is the belief of cryptologists, based on the idea that Eve knows neither of the private keys a or b and on the difficulty of the discrete logarithm problem. Thus, if Alice and Bob employ the secret k as the basis for private communication using a symmetric-key cipher such as AES, Eve will be unable to eavesdrop successfully on their communications. This is a capsule summary of the idea behind the Diffie–Hellman cryptosystem. There are other details involved in making D–H a secure, workable system, which we gloss over in this description. We also note in passing that an attractive feature of D–H is the fact that variants may be implemented over algebraic structures known as elliptic curves. This results in more compact key lengths and faster running times.

D–H is used, among other places, in some versions of PGP (Pretty Good Privacy), a popular piece of encryption software used to secure Internet communications such as e-mail and available as freeware in some versions.

The RSA Cryptosystem

A year after the publication of Diffie and Hellman's key exchange system, three faculty members at MIT proposed a new public-key cryptosystem. This cryptosystem is called RSA after its three inventors, Ronald Rivest, Adi Shamir, and Leonard Adleman. RSA is now the most widely deployed cryptosystem in the world (see RSA Laboratories, 2005).

Use of the RSA cryptosystem for encryption is very similar to that of D–H. One superficial difference is that in the RSA cryptosystem, Bob can send an encrypted message to Alice without having a public key of his own. In particular, Bob can encrypt a message directly under Alice's public key in such a way that Alice can decrypt the ciphertext using her private key. Figure 2 diagrams this operation of RSA and similar public-key encryption schemes. (Much the same functionality can be achieved with D–H by having Bob generate a temporary key pair on the fly and using this as the basis for encryption of a message for Alice.)

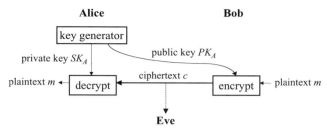

Figure 2: Public-key encryption (e.g., RSA). Alice generates for herself a private key SK_A and corresponding public key PK_A. Suppose then that Bob wishes to transmit plaintext message m securely to Alice over a channel subject to eavesdropping. Bob encrypts m under public key PK_A to obtain ciphertext c, which he transmits to Alice. Eavesdropper Eve learns the ciphertext c and may also learn PK_A, as it is a public value. If the public-key encryption algorithm is well constructed and properly used, however, Eve should be unable to learn m.

There are two rather more important differences between the two cryptosystems. The first lies in the speed of their respective operations. In RSA, encryption is a very fast operation; it generally requires less computational effort than a D–H key exchange. Decryption, however, is several times slower for RSA than key exchange in D–H. Another important difference between the two is a feature present in RSA. RSA can also be used to perform digital signing, an operation not covered in this chapter, but of central importance in cryptography. Digital signing achieves the goal of authenticating messages, i.e., proving their origin, rather than concealing their contents.

The RSA system employs modular arithmetic, the same type of mathematical basis as for Diffie–Hellman key exchange. In D–H, the modulus is a published value that may be used by any party to construct his or her key pair. In RSA, however, every party uses a different modulus, published as part of his or her public key. Thus, if Bob wishes to encrypt a message for Alice, he uses a modulus N_{Alice} unique to the public key of Alice; if he wants to encrypt a message for Carol, he uses a different modulus, N_{Carol}. The reason for the use of different moduli is the fact that the value of the modulus in the RSA cryptosystem relates directly to that of the private key.

A modulus N in the RSA cryptosystem has a special form. It is the product of two large prime integers, generally denoted by p and q. In other words, $N = p \times q$. The pair of primes p and q are treated as private values in the RSA cryptosystem; they are used to compute the private key for the modulus N. Thus the security of RSA is related very closely to the difficulty of determining the secret primes p and q given knowledge of the modulus N. This is known as the problem of factoring and is believed to be extremely difficult when p and q are large. In typical systems today, p and q are chosen to be primes of about 512 bits in length, so that N is an integer of about 1024 bits, the same length as generally selected for a Diffie–Hellman modulus. Factoring is the only effective method known for attacking RSA when the cryptosystem is used properly.

Among its many other uses, the RSA cryptosystem (along with RC4) is used as the basis for SSL, the encryption system in most Web browsers today, and also in some versions of PGP (Pretty Good Privacy) software.

More Technical Detail on RSA

We now describe in more mathematical detail how the RSA cryptosystem works. Unable as we are to delve further into the underlying mathematics, we provide only prescriptive formulae, without explaining the rationale behind them. For further information, the reader is directed to a good textbook (e.g., Menezes, van Oorschot, & Vanstone, 1996).

To compute her public key, Alice selects two random primes, p_{Alice} and q_{Alice}, both of roughly equal length in bits, e.g., 512 bits long. The product

$$N_{\text{Alice}} = p_{\text{Alice}} \times q_{\text{Alice}}$$

is the modulus used by Alice in her public key. She also selects a small odd integer e_{Alice}; generally, this value is more or less standardized in a given system, the integer 65535 being a common choice. An additional restriction on e_{Alice} is that it must not have a factor in common with $p_{\text{Alice}} - 1$ or $q_{\text{Alice}} - 1$, a criterion considered in the selection of primes. Together, the pair of values $(e_{\text{Alice}}, N_{\text{Alice}})$ constitutes Alice's public key. Her private key is computed as follows. Let $\Phi(N_{\text{Alice}}) = (p_{\text{Alice}} - 1) \times (q_{\text{Alice}} - 1)$. Alice computes her private key, generally denoted by d_{Alice}, in such a way that $e_{\text{Alice}} \, d_{\text{Alice}} = 1 \bmod \Phi(N_{\text{Alice}})$. The bit-length of the private key d_{Alice} here is typically quite close to that of N_{Alice}.

A message in the RSA cryptosystem consists of a positive integer m less than N_{Alice}. To encrypt m, Bob computes the ciphertext

$$c = m^{e_{\text{Alice}}} \bmod N_{\text{Alice}}.$$

As a technical restriction required to achieve good security, the plaintext m is formatted so as to be about equal in length to the modulus, resulting in a ciphertext that is similarly so. To decrypt the ciphertext, Alice applies her private key and computes the following:

$$m = c^{d_{\text{Alice}}} \bmod N_{\text{Alice}}.$$

An Example

Let us consider a small example to provide some flavor of how the RSA cryptosystem works. For illustrative purposes, we consider integers much smaller than those needed for true, secure use of RSA. Suppose that p_{Alice} and q_{Alice} are 5 and 11, respectively. Then $N_{\text{Alice}} = 5 \times 11 = 55$. Observe that $e_{\text{Alice}} = 3$ does not divide $p_{\text{Alice}} - 1$ or $q_{\text{Alice}} - 1$. Thus, Alice can use $(e_{\text{Alice}}, N_{\text{Alice}}) = (3,55)$ as her public key. A valid private key for Alice is $d_{\text{Alice}} = 27$, because $\Phi(N_{\text{Alice}}) = (p_{\text{Alice}} - 1) \times (q_{\text{Alice}} - 1) = (5 - 1) \times (10 - 1) = 40$ and $e_{\text{Alice}} \times 27 = 81 = 1 \bmod 40$.

To encrypt the message $m = 7$, Bob computes the ciphertext $c = 7^3 \bmod 55 = 343 \bmod 55 = 13$. Alice decrypts the ciphertext $c = 13$ by computing $13^{27} \bmod 55$. Using a pocket calculator, the reader can easily verify that the result of this decryption operation is indeed the original plaintext $m = 7$.

The security of RSA requires some special, technical restrictions on the value of m. In fact, as the RSA cryptosystem is generally employed, the message m is itself the key for a symmetric-key cryptosystem such as AES, and is specially formatted prior to encryption. Public-key cryptosystems are generally used in conjunction with symmetric-key cryptosystems, as we discuss below.

With a 1024-bit RSA modulus, a Pentium III running at 1 GHz can perform roughly 40 RSA decryption operations per second, and about 600 encryption operations per second under the public exponent $e = 65535$. (These speeds, of course, depend critically on the particular software implementation.)

As explained above, the security of the RSA cryptosystem is closely related to the difficulty of factoring the product of two large primes. Security guidelines for RSA thus depend on advances in the factoring problem made by researchers, as well as the cost and availability of computing power to a potential attacker. According to guidelines issued in 2003 by NIST, 1024-bit RSA moduli may be used to secure data whose privacy needs to be assured until the year 2015. For more sensitive data, a 2048-bit RSA modulus is recommended instead. Although there is substantial debate and uncertainty among cryptographers as to the exact ongoing security level afforded by RSA, there is general agreement as to the rough accuracy of these predictive guidelines. To avoid a common misconception, it should be emphasized that the mathematical basis for the RSA cryptosystem means that the recommended modulus lengths, and thus the public and private keys, are substantially longer than the 128- to 256-bit key lengths prescribed for symmetric-key ciphers.

How Public-Key Encryption Is Used

Encryption of a large quantity of data is generally much slower using a public-key cryptosystem than using a symmetric-key cipher. On the other hand, public-key encryption offers an elegant approach to the problem of distributing keys that is unavailable in symmetric-key ciphers. It is common in practice, therefore, to combine the two types of encryption systems to obtain the best properties of both. This is achieved by use of a simple principle known as enveloping. Enveloping involves use of a public-key cryptosystem such as RSA as a vehicle for transporting a secret key, which is itself then used for encryption with a symmetric-key cipher. To send a megabyte-long file to Alice, for example, Bob might select a random 128-bit RC4 key k and encrypt the file under k. He would then send this ciphertext of the file to Alice, along with an RSA encryption of k under Alice's public key. In effect, enveloping is a way of making a public-key cryptosystem faster. Enveloping yields much the same data flows as in Figure 2. The only difference is that a symmetric key k is encrypted rather than an ordinary plaintext m; in addition to the public-key ciphertext c, Bob also transmits a symmetric-key ciphertext c', namely the message m encrypted under k using a symmetric-key cipher.

As with symmetric-key ciphers, cryptologists aim to design public-key cryptosystems to withstand a wide range of possible attacks, including some very strong ones in which Eve can persuade Alice to decrypt a range of ciphertexts that Eve herself selects. Like symmetric-key block ciphers, when used in a naïve manner, RSA has a limitation in that encryption of the same plaintext always yields the same ciphertext; it also has the additional weakness of leaking some bits of a plaintext. Prior to encryption under RSA, therefore, it is common practice to subject a message to a special type of formatting that involves the addition of random bits. Loosely speaking, this incorporation of randomness serves much the same purpose as in the case of cipher-block chaining for symmetric-key block ciphers, as described above. Other aspects of the formatting process permit the RSA cryptosystem to withstand other forms of attack, and to do so with guarantees that are subject to rigorous mathematical justification.

Most public-key encryption systems have an additional advantage over symmetric-key systems in that they permit a flexible approach to distributed storage of the private key, known as secret sharing. This is a way of mathematically splitting a private key into a number of elements known as shares. To achieve a decryption operation, each of these shares may be applied individually to a ciphertext, without the need to assemble the shares themselves in a single place. Thus, a cryptosystem can be set up so that compromise of any one share does not expose the full decryption key itself. For example, Alice can divide her private key into, say, three shares, keeping one for herself and giving one each to her friends Bob and Carol. To decrypt a ciphertext, Alice can ask Bob and Carol to apply their shares and to send her the result. Alice can then complete the decryption with her own share, without Bob or Carol seeing the resulting plaintext. If an attacker breaks into Alice's computer and obtains her share, the attacker will still be unable to decrypt ciphertexts directed to Alice (without also obtaining the assistance of Bob and Carol). The system can even be set up so that decryption is possible given particular sets of shares. Thus, for example, Alice might be able to achieve decryption of her ciphertexts even if Bob or Carol is on vacation.

Despite its great flexibility, public-key cryptography does not directly address all of the challenges of key distribution. For example, we have said that Alice can safely disseminate her public key as widely as she likes, publishing it in Internet directories and so forth. But when Bob obtains a copy of Alice's public key, how does he really know it belongs to Alice and is not, for example, a spurious key published by Eve to entrap him? To solve problems of this kind, we appeal to a public-key infrastructure (PKI), as explained in detail in the chapter on that topic. Another issue worth mentioning—and a pitfall for many system designers—is the problem of finding an appropriate source of randomness for generating keys. Good generation of random bits is the cornerstone of cryptographic security and requires careful attention.

A final problem that encryption alone does not solve is that of message integrity. When Bob sends a message to Alice encrypted using, for example, RC4, he may be reasonably well assured of the privacy of his communication if he uses the cipher correctly. When Alice receives his message, however, how does she know that Eve has not tampered with the message en route, by changing a few bits or words? Indeed, how does she even know that Bob is the one who sent the message? For this type of assurance, some additional cryptographic apparatus is required in the form of a message authentication code or a digital signature. These are techniques for applying a key to a message to obtain an unforgeable "fingerprint" that shows evidence of any tampering.

CONCLUSION: FURTHER READING

The reader interested in more detailed treatment of the topics discussed here need go no further than this encyclopedia. Subsequent chapters offer details on symmetric-key cryptography, including the ciphers DES and AES, on public-key cryptography, and also on more advanced topics such as hash functions, elliptic curves, and identity-based cryptography. This encyclopedia also contains chapters on the selection and management of cryptographic keys, as well as the design of cryptographic protocols, that is, systems that build on encryption techniques to achieve complex aims such as electronic voting and digital rights management (DRM).

Two broad and accessible introductory books on the field of cryptology are *Applied Cryptography*, by Bruce Schneier (2002a), and the online compendium *Frequently Asked Questions About Today's Cryptography* (RSA Laboratories, 2005). A more detailed technical treatment of cryptographic techniques and concepts, along with an extensive bibliography, may be found in the excellent *Handbook of Applied Cryptography*, by Alfred J. Menezes, Paul C. van Oorschot, and Scott A. Vanstone (Menezes et al., 1996). Detailed information on the AES algorithm (Rijndael) is available in *The Design of Rijndael*, by Joan Daeman and Vincent Rijmen (2002).

Readers interested in the practical application of cryptography in real-world systems may wish to consult *Network Security: Private Communication in a Public World*, by Charles Kaufman, Radia Perlman, and Mike Speciner (2002), and *Cryptography and Network Security: Principles and Practice*, by William Stallings (2002). For a more comprehensive view of security engineering, an excellent work is Ross Anderson's *Security Engineering: A Guide to Building Dependable Distributed Systems* (2002). Of similar interest is Bruce Schneier's *Secrets and Lies* (Schneier, 2002b), which offers some caveats regarding the limitations of cryptography and other security tools.

A good introductory textbook of a more academic flavor is *Cryptography: Theory and Practice*, by Douglas Stinson (2002). For information on the foundational mathematics and theory of cryptology, an important work is *Foundations of Cryptography: Basic Tools*, an evolving series of volumes by Oded Goldreich (2000, 2004); a second volume, entitled *Foundations of Cryptography: Basic Applications* (2004), is forthcoming in 2004. For a historical overview of cryptology, the classic text is *The Codebreakers*, by David Kahn (1996). More up-to-date, although less exhaustive, is *The Science of Secrecy from Ancient Egypt to Quantum Cryptography*, by Simon Singh (2000).

The use and export of products containing strong cryptographic algorithms were at one time strongly restricted by regulations of the United States government and other nations. The United States government dramatically relaxed its restrictions in 2000, however, as did many other nations at around the same time. Some countries, such as China, still retain strong regulations around both domestic use and import and export of cryptographically

enabled products. Although regulations treating the use of cryptography are in frequent flux, readers may refer to the Electronic Privacy Information Center (2005) for historical and some current information on this topic.

Cryptologists continue to devote effort to the development of new symmetric ciphers and public-key cryptosystems, as well as the improvement of existing ones. Although encryption is the fountainhead of contemporary cryptology, it is by no means the only focus of the field. As is the case with many branches of science, cutting-edge inventions in cryptology often lie dormant for years or decades before their widespread use. The scope of cryptologic research today extends beyond the problems of message privacy and integrity to the goal of achieving fair play in electronic environments in a much broader sense. Secure electronic voting, online privacy protection, and digital rights management are just a few of the many areas where researchers in cryptography have made strides in recent years. At the frontiers of cryptology are ideas involving the use of quantum mechanics and even DNA for attacking ciphers. Many cryptologists are members of the International Association for Cryptologic Research (IACR), whose home page (IACR, 2005) lists publications and conferences devoted to advanced current research in cryptography and cryptanalysis.

GLOSSARY

AES The Advanced Encryption Standard, a symmetric-key cipher known as Rijndael, serving as successor to DES.

Asymmetric In the context of encryption, a type of cryptographic system in which a participant publishes an encryption key and keeps private a separate decryption key. These keys are respectively referred to as public and private. RSA and D–H are examples of asymmetric systems. *Asymmetric* is synonymous with *public-key*.

Ciphertext The data conveying an encrypted message.

Cryptanalysis The science of analyzing weaknesses in cryptographic systems.

Cryptography The science of constructing mathematical systems for securing data.

Cryptology The combination of the complementary sciences of cryptography and cryptanalysis.

Cryptosystem A complete system of encryption and decryption, typically used to describe a public-key cryptographic system.

Decryption The process of obtaining a readable message (a *plaintext*) from an encrypted transformation of the message (a *ciphertext*).

DES The Data Encryption Standard, an existing form of symmetric cipher in wide use today, often in a strengthened variant known as triple DES.

Diffie–Hellman (D–H) A public-key cryptosystem used to exchange a secret (symmetric) key.

Encryption The process of rendering a message (a *plaintext*) into a data string (a *ciphertext*) with the aim of transmitting it privately in a potentially hostile environment.

Enveloping A method for using a symmetric-key cipher in combination with a public-key cryptosystem to exploit simultaneously the advantages of the two respective systems.

Key A short data string parameterizing the operations within a cipher or cryptosystem, and whose distribution determines relationships of privacy and integrity among communicating parties.

Key pair The combination of a public and private key.

Plaintext A message in readable form, prior to encryption or subsequent to successful decryption.

Private Key In an asymmetric or public-key cryptosystem, the key that a communicating party holds privately and uses for decryption or completion of a key exchange.

Public Key In an asymmetric or public-key cryptosystem, the key that a communicating party disseminates publicly. In the context of encryption, a type of cryptographic system in which a participant publishes an encryption key and keeps private a separate decryption key. These keys are respectively referred to as public and private. RSA and D–H are examples of public-key systems. *Public-key* is synonymous with *asymmetric*.

RC4 A symmetric-key cipher of the type known as a stream cipher. Used widely in the SSL (secure sockets layer) protocol.

RSA A public-key cryptosystem in very wide use today, as in the SSL (secure sockets layer) protocol. RSA can also be used to create and verify digital signatures.

Symmetric A type of cryptographic system in which communicating parties employ shared secret keys. The term is also used to refer to the keys employed in such a system.

CROSS REFERENCES

See *Data Encryption Standard (DES); Symmetric-Key Encryption; The Advanced Encryption Standard.*

REFERENCES

Anderson, R. J. (2002). *Security engineering: A guide to building dependable distributed security systems*. New York: John Wiley & Sons.

Daeman, J., & Rijmen, V. (2002). *The design of Rijndael*. Berlin/New York: Springer-Verlag.

Electronic Privacy Information Center. (2005). Web page on cryptography policy. Retrieved 14 September 2005, from http://www.epic.org/crypto/.

Goldreich, O. (2000). *Foundations of cryptography: Basic tools*. Cambridge, UK: Cambridge University Press.

Goldreich, O. (2004). *Foundations of cryptography: Basic applications*. Cambridge, UK: Cambridge University Press.

Kahn, D. (1996). *The codebreakers: The story of secret writing*. New York: Simon & Schuster.

Kaufman, C., Perlman, R., & Speciner, M. (2002). *Network security: Private communication in a public world* (2nd ed.). Englewood Cliffs, NJ: Prentice Hall.

International Association for Cryptologic Research (IACR) home page. (2005). Retrieved 14 September 2005, from http://www.iacr.org

Menezes, A. J., van Oorschot, P. C., & Vanstone, S. A. (1996). *Handbook of applied cryptography*. Boca Raton, FL: CRC Press.

National Institute of Standards and Technology (NIST) Web page on the AES Algorithm (Rijndael). (2005). Retrieved 14 September 2005, from http://csrc.nist.gov/encryption/aes/rijndael

RSA Laboratories. (2005). *Frequently asked questions about today's cryptography*. Retrieved 14 September 2005, from http://rsasecurity.com/rsalabs/faq/index.html

Schneier, B. (2002a). *Applied cryptography: Protocols, algorithms, and source code in C* (2nd ed.). New York: John Wiley & Sons.

Schneier, B. (2002b). *Secrets and lies: Digital security in a networked world*. New York: John Wiley & Sons.

Singh, S. (2000). *The science of secrecy from ancient Egypt to quantum cryptography*. New York: Alfred A. Knopf.

Stallings, W. (2002). *Cryptography and network security: Principles and practice* (3rd ed.). Englewood Cliffs, NJ: Prentice Hall.

Stinson, D. (2002). *Cryptography: Theory and practice* (2nd ed.). Boca Raton, FL: CRC/C&H.

Symmetric Key Encryption

Jonathan Katz, *University of Maryland*

INTRODUCTION

Symmetric key encryption schemes (also variously known as *secret key*, *private key*, or *shared key* encryption schemes for reasons that will become clear in a moment) allow users who have previously agreed on a shared, secret key to ensure the secrecy of their communication. A prototypical example might be two soldiers who wish to communicate securely while they are in the battlefield. Before heading to the battlefield (say, while they are together on base), these two soldiers can generate and share a random key k, which they will keep secret from everyone else. Later, when they are in the battlefield, these soldiers can use the common key k they have shared to communicate securely. In particular, when one soldier (the "sender") wishes to send a message M (sometimes also called the *plaintext*) to the other (the "receiver"), she will *encrypt* M using some symmetric key encryption scheme and the shared key k; this results in a *ciphertext* C, which is transmitted to the receiver. When the receiver obtains C, he will *decrypt* it—again using the key k—to recover the original message M. Roughly speaking (and we will see more formal definitions later), a "good" encryption scheme satisfies the property that any passive eavesdropper who observes the transmitted ciphertext C learns nothing about the underlying message M (i.e., the secrecy of M is ensured).

A number of quick observations are in order. First, because both parties hold the same key that is used for both encryption and decryption, either party can send messages securely to the other party; there is thus no fundamental distinction between which party is the "sender" and which is the "receiver" (as either party may take on either role), and this motivates the terminology "symmetric key" encryption. Because the same key is used for both encryption and decryption, however, it is clearly crucial that the shared key be kept *completely secret* from any potential adversary or eavesdropper who might try to recover M from the observed ciphertext C. Less obvious, but still a consequence of the above, is that the shared key must be

chosen *completely at random*; otherwise, an eavesdropper can "guess" partial information about the key with high probability and then potentially learn some information about the underlying message M.

Symmetric Key Encryption Versus Public Key Encryption

It is instructive to compare symmetric key encryption to public key encryption and to discuss briefly the relative advantages of each. (The reader is referred to the Chapter "Key Management" for further discussion of public key algorithms.) In the public key setting, a potential receiver first generates a pair of keys (PK, SK): PK represents a public key that is widely disseminated, whereas SK is a secret key that is kept private by the receiver. To send a message M to this receiver, a sender encrypts M using PK to generate a ciphertext C, which is then transmitted to the receiver. The receiver decrypts C using SK to recover the intended message M.

A clear difference is that public key encryption is inherently *asymmetric*: the keys used by the sender and receiver are different, and thus secret communication can occur in one direction only. (This can be addressed in any of a number of ways, but the point is that a single invocation of a standard public key encryption scheme forces a distinction between one user who will act as a receiver and other users who will act as senders.) Furthermore, PK is not kept secret from a potential eavesdropping adversary— the message remains indecipherable to an eavesdropper who obtains C even if this adversary also knows PK. A summary of the differences between symmetric key and public key encryption is given in Table 1.

It may appear at first glance that public key encryption has a clear advantage over symmetric key encryption in that it does not require any secret distribution of keys prior to communication. More generally, any public key encryption scheme can be used as a symmetric key encryption scheme by simply having parties share (secretly) both PK and SK. However, symmetric key encryption has

Table 1 Summary of Differences Between Symmetric and Public Key Encryption.

Symmetric Key	Public Key
Key k shared by both parties	Key PK known by sender; key SK known by receiver
k used for encryption/decryption	PK used for encryption; SK used for decryption
Secrecy of k essential for security	Encryption "secure" even though PK not secret

at least two primary advantages as compared to public key encryption:

1. Perhaps most importantly, symmetric key encryption is roughly 2–3 orders of magnitude faster than public key encryption (it is difficult to give an exact comparison because the exact efficiency advantage depends on a number of implementation details). In fact, symmetric key encryption is essentially always used in practice *in the public key setting* to yield improved efficiency for the (public key) encryption of bulk data; this is discussed further under "Hybrid Encryption." A thorough understanding of symmetric key encryption is therefore crucial to fully appreciate how encryption (of either type) is implemented in practice.

2. Symmetric key encryption provides a simple and immediate way to establish a secure "point-to-point" channel between two parties. In particular, in addition to ensuring secrecy a symmetric key scheme potentially allows each party to ensure that the communications it receives indeed originate from the other party (as discussed briefly under "Stronger Definitions of Security"). Such functionality is somewhat more difficult to achieve in the public key setting.

In contrast, public key encryption does offer the following advantages:

- We have already mentioned that public key encryption solves (to some extent) the *key distribution problem* in that the communicating parties do not need to secretly share a key in advance of their communication. Thus, public key encryption is potentially more powerful in that it allows two parties to communicate secretly even if *all* communication between them is monitored.

- Consider the scenario in which it is desired to establish secure channels between every pair of users in a network of size n. Using symmetric key techniques, this will require a total of $\binom{n}{2} = O(n^2)$ keys (one for each pair of parties). If public key cryptography is used, however, this can be reduced to a total of only n keys.

Because the focus of this chapter is on the symmetric key setting, "encryption scheme" will be used to refer to a symmetric key encryption scheme unless explicitly stated otherwise.

Basic Notation and Definitions

The above discussion has been relatively informal and in particular has not included a careful and formal definition of what it means for a symmetric key encryption scheme

to be "secure." Before we turn to this problem in the sections that follow, we first introduce some basic definitions.

Let $\{0, 1\}^\ell$ denote the set of binary strings of length ℓ.

Definition 1 *A symmetric key encryption scheme is defined by a key space $\mathcal{K}$, a message space $\mathcal{M}$ with $|\mathcal{M}| > 1$, and two (efficient) algorithms: the* encryption algorithm $\mathcal{E}$ *and the* decryption algorithm $\mathcal{D}$. *The latter have the following functionality:*

- *The encryption algorithm $\mathcal{E}$ takes as input a key $k \in \mathcal{K}$ and a message $M \in \mathcal{M}$ and outputs a ciphertext C; this is denoted by $C \leftarrow \mathcal{E}_k(M)$.*

- *The decryption algorithm $\mathcal{D}$ takes as input a key $k \in \mathcal{K}$ and a ciphertext C and outputs a message $M \in \mathcal{M}$. We write this as $M := \mathcal{D}_k(C)$.*

We require that for all $k \in \mathcal{K}$ and all $M \in \mathcal{M}$ we have $\mathcal{D}_k(\mathcal{E}_k(M)) = M$.

Note that the above definition describes only the semantics of symmetric key encryption; it does not say anything about security.

Following the above notation, a symmetric key encryption scheme is utilized as follows: First, a key k is chosen uniformly at random from the key space $\mathcal{K}$ and shared by two parties. When one of these parties wants to send a plaintext message $M \in \mathcal{M}$ to the other party, this party computes $C \leftarrow \mathcal{E}_k(M)$ and transmits C. Upon receiving C, the second party recovers the initial message by computing $M := \mathcal{D}_k(C)$. As expected, because they use the same key k, the message recovered by the second party is the one intended by the first party.

A few remarks about the above definition are in order:

- Except for some "classical" encryption schemes and their weaknesses we make the simplifying assumption that the key space $\mathcal{K}$ consists of all binary strings of some fixed length; that is, $\mathcal{K} = \{0, 1\}^s$ for some s.

- In an effort to simplify more formal definitions (see, e.g., Bellare, Desai, Jokipii, & Rogaway, 1997; Goldreich, 2004; Katz & Yung, 2000), we do not define what it means for $\mathcal{E}$ and $\mathcal{D}$ to be "efficient." A number of other simplifications were also made, but the interested reader is referred to the listed references for more details.

- We have used the notation $C \leftarrow \mathcal{E}_k(M)$ to represent the fact that *the encryption algorithm may be randomized* (see further discussion under "A Stronger Notion of Security") and thus running $\mathcal{E}_k(M)$ multiple times may yield a different ciphertext each time. In contrast, we assume the decryption algorithm is deterministic without much loss of generality.

SOME "CLASSICAL" ENCRYPTION SCHEMES AND THEIR WEAKNESSES

It is instructive to begin with some examples of "classical" symmetric key encryption schemes, both to get a feel for how symmetric key encryption works as well as to see why constructing a "secure" encryption scheme is harder than it might first appear. In the descriptions that follow, we consider the alphabet Σ consisting of all capital English letters (i.e., $\Sigma = \{A, \ldots, Z\}$) and the message space will be all strings over this alphabet. We also use the fact that we can map letters in Σ in the natural way (i.e., $A = 0$, $B = 1$, etc.) to the numbers from 0 through 25, inclusive. The *shift cipher* is about the simplest scheme one might consider. In this scheme, the key is an arbitrary letter chosen from Σ. To encrypt a message $M = \sigma_1 \cdots \sigma_n$, where each $\sigma_i \in \Sigma$, we simply "add" the key to each letter of the message, working modulo $|\Sigma| = 26$ (so that, for example, $Z + B = A$). To decrypt, we simply reverse the process and subtract the key from each letter of the ciphertext. As an example, using this scheme to encrypt the message "HELP" with the key "D" gives the ciphertext "KHOS" and it is clear that decryption of this ciphertext using the same key will recover the original message.

It is not very difficult to see that the security provided by the shift cipher is quite weak. An adversary, faced with a ciphertext corresponding to some unknown message, can simply try decrypting this ciphertext using all possible values of the secret key. Because there are only 26 possible keys, this will not take exceedingly long. Furthermore, it is likely (especially for longer messages) that only one key will decrypt the ciphertext to a meaningful message (for instance, this is the case for the ciphertext "KHOS" considered above), in which case the adversary can determine with reasonable likelihood the message that was sent.

This type of attack—in which an adversary tries decrypting a ciphertext using all (or many) possible keys—is called an *exhaustive key-search attack*. Obviously, one way for a symmetric key scheme to be secure against such an attack is for the key space to be large enough so that searching through all keys is infeasible. A larger key space, however, is not enough to guarantee security of a scheme. To see this, consider the *substitution cipher* in which the key is an arbitrary permutation of Σ. A permutation of Σ can be given by simply listing the elements of Σ in two rows, once in the "regular" order and once in an arbitrary order, for example:

$$A \ B \ C \ \cdots \ Z$$
$$F \ T \ Z \ \cdots \ X$$

If the above represents a permutation π, then we have $\pi(A) = F$, $\pi(B) = T$, and so on. We can also compute the inverse mapping π^{-1}; for example, $\pi^{-1}(X) = Z$. In this scheme, encryption of a message $M = \sigma_1 \cdots \sigma_n$ using a key π results in the ciphertext $C = \pi(\sigma_1) \cdots \pi(\sigma_n)$. Decryption of a ciphertext $C = \sigma_1' \cdots \sigma_n'$ using key π is performed as one might expect by simply computing the message $M = \pi^{-1}(\sigma_1') \cdots \pi^{-1}(\sigma_n')$.

The number of permutations of Σ is 26! and so the key space of the substitution cipher is clearly much larger than the key space of the shift cipher. (Although it would not be difficult for a modern computer to search through 26! keys, it would be difficult to search through this many keys by hand.) Nevertheless, the substitution cipher is not very secure; indeed, the substitution cipher is used for making puzzle "cryptograms" in newspapers! In particular, one feature of this encryption scheme is that it preserves letter frequencies; that is, if a given letter x occurs some fraction of the time in the plaintext message, then there will be some letter $\pi(x)$ that occurs with the same frequency in the ciphertext. When the plaintext is reasonably long, this begins to "leak" information about the key and the message. For example, it is well-known that in normal English text the letter E occurs more often than any other letter. So, an adversary might guess that the letter occurring most often in the ciphertext corresponds to the plaintext letter E. Using additional information about English letter frequencies, as well as frequencies of digrams (consecutive letters) and trigrams (three consecutive letters), the adversary can gradually learn information about the message without the need to exhaustively search through all possible keys.

"PERFECT" SECRECY AND ITS LIMITATIONS

The brief discussion of some classical cryptosystems in the previous section generates the following observations and questions, which we hope will serve as motivation for the remainder of this chapter. First, *designing good cryptographic algorithms is hard*; for this reason, one should avoid designing "home-brew" cryptographic algorithms without having first developed the requisite expertise in cryptography. Moreover, the attacks described in the previous section raise another concern: *how does one identify when an encryption scheme is secure*? This is a fundamental question, as, clearly, it is undesirable to deploy an encryption scheme that might be broken by an adversary more clever than the designer of the scheme. This hints at a more basic question: *what does it mean for a scheme to be secure*? (Alternately, how do we know that the substitution cipher, say, does not qualify as a "secure" scheme?) Before we delve into the design of "secure schemes," we first more carefully study different definitions of what it might mean for a scheme to be "secure." It is important to stress here that a number of different security definitions are possible, and so—in general—saying that a scheme is "secure" is meaningless unless one also specifies the definition with respect to which security holds.

The most basic goal of an encryption scheme is to preserve the secrecy of M in the presence of an eavesdropping adversary who learns $C = \mathcal{E}_k(M)$ (but does not know k!). We stress that the adversary is assumed to know the full details of the encryption scheme used (i.e., the adversary knows the encryption algorithm $\mathcal{E}$ being used by the parties); the only information the adversary does *not* know is the secret key k. Indeed, following Kerckhoffs's rule (Kerckhoffs, 1883), a "good" encryption scheme should be secure even under this assumption; furthermore, designing a scheme to be secure "only" when the details of the scheme are not revealed to an adversary usually results in a weak scheme that is soon broken.

It remains only to formally specify what "preserving the secrecy of M" means. One, perhaps natural, possibility is to require that an eavesdropping adversary who observes C cannot determine the message M. However, this definition is easily seen to be too weak because an encryption scheme that completely reveals, say, the first half of M (but that "securely encrypts" its second half) would potentially meet this definition. Of course, when the first half of the message is the critical half such an encryption scheme is useless! Additionally, it is unclear what this definition requires in the case of small message spaces (or, equivalently, large message spaces but where the adversary has some *a priori* knowledge about what messages are likely to be sent). For the message space $\mathcal{M} = \{$"yes", "no"$\}$, for example, an adversary who simply guesses which message was encrypted will be correct half the time!

A much stronger definition of secrecy—termed *perfect secrecy*—was proposed by Shannon (Shannon, 1949) and forms the starting point for more modern definitions. Informally, a symmetric key encryption scheme achieves perfect secrecy if an eavesdropping adversary who observes the ciphertext C learns *no information whatsoever* about the communicated message M (note that this rules out schemes such as the one described earlier which leak the first half of M). In particular, even if the adversary knows in advance that the message is one of two possibilities (say, "yes" or "no" as above), the adversary does not learn which of these is the actual message upon observing C.

Because the original definition (Shannon, 1949). Is somewhat complex, we omit the details here. However, the following, simpler definition—which considers exactly the case in which the adversary "knows" that the message is one of two possibilities—can be shown to be equivalent to the original definition.

Definition 2 *An encryption scheme $(\mathcal{E}, \mathcal{D})$ over key space $\mathcal{K}$ and message space $\mathcal{M}$ achieves* perfect secrecy *if for all $M_1, M_2 \in \mathcal{M}$ and all eavesdropping adversaries A, the probability (over choice of key $k \in \mathcal{K}$) that A guesses "M_1" when it observes an encryption of M_1 is equal to the probability that A guesses "M_1" when it observes an encryption of M_2.*

That is, no eavesdropper A can distinguish between the case that M_1 is encrypted and the case that M_2 is encrypted, even when A knows that the message must be one of these possibilities.

Achieving Perfect Secrecy

Perfect secrecy can be achieved by the so-called *one-time pad* encryption scheme (Vernam, 1926), which is defined as follows. Let the message space $\mathcal{M}$ be identified with $\{0, 1\}^\ell$ (i.e., the set of all binary strings of length ℓ) for an arbitrary $\ell > 0$. The key space $\mathcal{K}$ is identical to the message space. To encrypt an ℓ-bit message $M \in \mathcal{M}$ using an ℓ-bit key $k \in \mathcal{K}$, the sender computes $C := M \oplus k$, where $\oplus$ denotes the bitwise exclusive-or (xor) operation (i.e., the ith bit of C is equal to the xor of the ith bits of M and k). To decrypt ciphertext C, the receiver computes $M := C \oplus k$. Note that this indeed recovers the original message because

$$C \oplus k = (M \oplus k) \oplus k = M \oplus (k \oplus k) = M,$$

where we use the fact that any string xor'ed with itself gives the all-zero string.

To prove that this scheme achieves perfect secrecy we need only observe that, over random choice of $k \in \{0, 1\}^\ell$, the ciphertext C is a uniformly distributed, ℓ-bit string regardless of the message being encrypted. In other words, for *any* $M \in \mathcal{M}$ the ciphertext C is uniformly distributed when k is chosen uniformly at random from $\mathcal{K}$. (As proof, let $\Pr_{k \in \{0,1\}^\ell}[C = \hat{C}|M]$ denote the probability, over choice of k, that the ciphertext C is equal to some arbitrary, fixed ℓ-bit string $\hat{C}$ when C is an encryption of M. Then for any $\hat{C}, M$ we have $\Pr_{k \in \{0,1\}^\ell}[C = \hat{C}|M] = \Pr_{k \in \{0,1\}^\ell}[k = M \oplus \hat{C}]$, and this last expression is equal to $1/2^\ell$ because k is uniformly distributed.) Because the (distribution of the) observed ciphertext C is independent of the message M being encrypted, the ciphertext reveals no information whatsoever about M and hence Definition 2 is satisfied for any algorithm A. A formal proof follows easily from this somewhat informal argument.

Limitations of Perfect Secrecy

The one-time pad encryption scheme, though it achieves perfect secrecy, does have a number of limitations. First, the shared key k is as long as the message M. In addition to being inefficient, this also requires the length of the message (or at least an upper bound on the message length) to be known in advance at the time the key is generated and shared. Furthermore, the one-time pad encryption scheme is *completely insecure* when it is used to encrypt more than one message using the same key (hence the name "one-time" pad): if an adversary intercepts $C_1 = M_1 \oplus k$ and $C_2 = M_2 \oplus k$, then the adversary can compute $C_1 \oplus C_2$, which is equal to $M_1 \oplus M_2$. Given this information, the adversary can then learn partial information about the two encrypted messages (and, in particular, learn the bit positions where M_1 and M_2 differ). Even worse, if the adversary happens to know M_1 (say, because of some *a priori* information) it can then derive the key by computing $k = C_1 \oplus M_1$ and then decrypt any messages sent in the future using the same key. This latter attack extends similarly even if the adversary knows only partial information about M_1 (in which case it may then learn corresponding partial information about M_2).

Unfortunately, the following theorem shows that the above limitations are inherent (Shannon, 1949):

Theorem 1 *Any encryption scheme achieving perfect secrecy requires the key space $\mathcal{K}$ to be at least as large as the message space $\mathcal{M}$. In particular, if keys and messages all have some fixed length then the key must be at least as long as the total length of all encrypted messages.*

Without giving a formal proof, we discuss the intuition which is quite straightforward. Consider the case of an encryption scheme with key space $\{0, 1\}^{\ell_1}$ and message space $\{0, 1\}^{\ell_2}$ with $\ell_2 > \ell_1$ and focus on the encryption of a single message. In this case, before observing the ciphertext an adversary may have no information about which message is being sent and thus all 2^{ℓ_2} messages are possible. After observing a ciphertext, however, an adversary can compute $M := \mathcal{D}_k(C)$ for all $k \in \mathcal{K}$ and thus narrow down the space of possible messages to only $2^{\ell_1} < 2^{\ell_2}$ possibilities. This means that the adversary has learned some information about the message, in contradiction of the stringent requirements of perfect secrecy.

We also remark that "perfect *secrecy*" does not imply "perfect *security*"! In particular, as discussed above, the one-time pad encryption scheme is *not* secure in the sense of Definition 5, below, which refers to secrecy following the encryption of multiple plaintext messages. Finally, the one-time pad encryption scheme is not at all secure with respect to even stronger definitions of security such as those briefly mentioned under "stronger definitions of security."

To summarize: we have introduced the notion of perfect secrecy, shown that the one-time pad encryption scheme achieves this notion, and then proved that this scheme is, in fact, optimal as far as perfect secrecy is concerned. Does this end our discussion of symmetric key encryption? Not by a long shot. Perfect secrecy is, on the one hand, too weak in that it does not ensure secrecy when multiple messages are encrypted (with the same key) and does not satisfy stronger notions of security such as those considered under "stronger definitions of security." On the other hand, perfect secrecy is too strong in that it requires secrecy even against *all* adversaries (and, in particular, even adversaries having arbitrarily high computational power), which is simply not necessary in practice. Indeed, we will see that by (slightly) relaxing the definition it is possible to circumvent the limitations outlined above. This is fortunate because the limitations of the one-time pad—especially the restriction that it is secure only when used to encrypt a single message—make it undesirable for use in almost all practical situations.

COMPUTATIONAL NOTIONS OF SECURITY

As discussed in the previous section, one of the drawbacks of the notion of perfect secrecy is that it requires secrecy to hold even against "all-powerful" adversaries having unbounded computational power and running for an unlimited amount of time. Here, we explore so-called *computational* notions of security that focus on ensuring security "only" against adversaries having some (reasonable) bound on their computational power and/or running time. First, let us establish some notation by reconsidering Definition 2. Fixing an encryption scheme and considering any particular eavesdropper A, let $\Pr_{k\in\mathcal{K}}[A(\mathcal{E}_k(M)) = 1]$ denote the probability (over random choice of key k) that A outputs "1" when it observes an encryption of the message M. Viewing an output of "1" as a "guess" that the encrypted message was M_1, we may rewrite Definition 2 as follows:

An encryption scheme over message space $\mathcal{M}$ is perfectly secure if for all $M_1, M_2 \in \mathcal{M}$ and for all adversaries A we have the following:

$$\Pr_{k\in\mathcal{K}}[A(\mathcal{E}_k(M_1)) = 1] - \Pr_{k\in\mathcal{K}}[A(\mathcal{E}_k(M_2)) = 1] = 0.$$

Note that this definition protects against *all* adversaries and ensures that all such adversaries learn *absolutely*

nothing about the message. In practice, however, it may well be sufficient to protect "only" against adversaries *running in some bounded amount of time* and to allow such adversaries to (potentially) learn at most a *very small amount* of information about the encrypted message (or to learn some information about the message but only with very small probability). Modifying the definition of perfect secrecy in this way, we obtain the following definition of computational secrecy:

Definition 3 *An encryption scheme over message space $\mathcal{M}$ is (t, ε) computationally secret if for all equal-length messages $M_1, M_2 \in \mathcal{M}$ and all eavesdropping adversaries A running in time at most t we have the following:*

$$\left|\Pr_{k\in\mathcal{K}}[A(\mathcal{E}_k(M_1)) = 1] - \Pr_{k\in\mathcal{K}}[A(\mathcal{E}_k(M_2)) = 1]\right| \le \varepsilon,$$

where the probabilities are over random choice of $k \in \mathcal{K}$, as well as any randomness used by A.

We remark that the requirement that M_1 and M_2 are equal-length messages is essential, because an encryption scheme cannot, in general (and is not, in general, intended to), hide information about the length of the encrypted message. We stress that the adversary A may potentially be randomized (as long as it does not run in time longer than t). Indeed, this will be the case for all definitions of security considered in this chapter, even if not explicitly stated. (We remark that for the case of Definition 2 we may assume without loss of generality that the adversary is deterministic because there are no limitations there on the amount of time the adversary may run and hence randomization does not provide any additional benefit to an adversary.) Note that $(\infty, 0)$ computational secrecy is equivalent to perfect secrecy.

The definition above allows for any choice of t, ε, and ultimately the desired level of secrecy—or, equivalently, the desired setting of these parameters—will depend on the application, the security requirements of the communicating parties, and the assumed abilities of any potential adversaries trying to learn information about the communicated message. Typical choices in practice might be $t = 1000$ years, $\varepsilon = 2^{-80}$ so that (informally) an eavesdropper would not learn anything about the encrypted message with probability better than 2^{-80} even after trying for 1000 years.

Beating the One-Time Pad

We show now how one of the limitations of the one-time pad—namely the restriction that the key must be as long as the message—can be overcome when computational secrecy is allowed. First, we introduce the notion of a *pseudorandom generator* (PRG) (Blum & Micali, 1984; Yao, 1982). Informally, a PRG is a deterministic function that expands a short, random "seed" into a longer, "random-looking" (i.e., pseudorandom) output. What does it mean for the output of a PRG to "look random"? This is defined in a manner analogous to the definition of computational secrecy, above, by requiring that no time-bounded adversary can distinguish the output of the PRG from a random string. We stress here that the adversary is not limited to any particular set of statistical tests—the only "restriction" is that the adversary is not allowed to run "too long." This important difference is what differentiates *cryptographic* PRGs (Blum & Micali, 1984; Yao, 1982), from PRGs used in noncryptographic contexts (see Knuth, 1997); the latter should never be used when the former are called for.

We now present the formal definition:

Definition 4 *Let G be an efficient, deterministic algorithm that takes an ℓ_1-bit string as input and returns an ℓ_2-bit string as output, with $\ell_2 > \ell_1$. We say G is a (t, ε) secure PRG if for all algorithms A running in time at most t we have the following:*

$$\left| \Pr_{x \in \{0,1\}^{\ell_1}}[A(G(x)) = 1] - \Pr_{y \in \{0,1\}^{\ell_2}}[A(y) = 1] \right| \leq \varepsilon.$$

In words, no adversary A running in time at most t can distinguish between the output string $G(x)$ (for randomly chosen input x) and a random ℓ_2-bit string y with probability better than ε. We remark that any PRG can be "broken" (namely its output can be distinguished from random) by simply performing an exhaustive search for the input string x. Thus (informally), at a minimum it must be the case that exhaustive search through all 2^{ℓ_1} possible input strings cannot be performed in time t.

Pseudorandom generators may be constructed based on a number of widely believed assumptions (Blum, Blum, & Shub, 1986; Blum & Micali, 1984; Goldreich & Levin, 1989; Håstad, Impagliazzo, Levin, & Luby, 1999; Yao, 1982). Stream ciphers, used extensively in practice, can be viewed as a generalization of PRGs and are discussed further under "block ciphers and stream ciphers" and "modes of encryption."

The existence of a PRG $G : \{0, 1\}^{\ell_1} \to \{0, 1\}^{\ell_2}$ suggests the following natural modification of the one-time pad encryption scheme: the shared key k is a randomly chosen string of length ℓ_1. To encrypt a message $M \in \{0, 1\}^{\ell_2}$, the sender computes $s := G(k)$ and then forms the ciphertext $C := M \oplus s$. To decrypt this ciphertext, the receiver computes $s := G(k)$ and then $M := C \oplus s$. It is not hard to see that this correctly recovers the original message. Note further that this scheme indeed improves upon the one-time pad encryption scheme in that the key length ℓ_1 is less than the message length ℓ_2.

What can we say about the security of this scheme? Arguing informally, the security of G implies that the string $s = G(k)$ computed by the sender during the process of encryption is pseudorandom and hence indistinguishable from a random string of length ℓ_2 for any adversary running in time at most t. Thus, from the point of view of any eavesdropping adversary (running in time at most t), an execution of the above encryption scheme is indistinguishable from an execution of the one-time pad encryption scheme. Perfect secrecy of the one-time pad thus implies computational secrecy of the above encryption scheme. More formally:

Theorem 2 *If G is a (t, ε) secure PRG, then the encryption scheme described above is $(t, 2\varepsilon)$ computationally secret.*

A Stronger Notion of Security

Although the above scheme does allow for a key that is shorter than the message, it still suffers from another drawback of the one-time pad encryption scheme in that it is secure only when used to encrypt a single message. Indeed, the same attacks shown previously for the case of the one-time pad apply here as well: for example, observing two ciphertexts $C_1 = M_1 \oplus G(k)$ and $C_2 = M_2 \oplus G(k)$ still allows an adversary to compute $C_1 \oplus C_2 = M_1 \oplus M_2$ and hence to learn partial information about the two messages. Also, if an adversary sees $C = M \oplus G(k)$ for a known message M then the adversary can compute $G(k)$ (but not the key k!) and then decrypt any ciphertexts intercepted in the future.

This discussion of various attacks motivates the following taxonomy of possible methods by which an adversary might try to learn information about an encrypted message (or messages):

Ciphertext-only attacks: Here, an adversary has observed a sequence of ciphertexts $C_1 = \mathcal{E}_k(M_1), C_2 = \mathcal{E}_k(M_2), \ldots$ encrypted with respect to the same key. In such a scenario, the adversary may try to learn information about the sequence of messages (say, whether $M_1 = M_2$) even if it cannot learn information about any particular message.

Known-plaintext attacks: Here, an adversary observes a sequence of ciphertexts $C_1, C_2, \ldots$ (again encrypted with respect to the same underlying key k) and may additionally *know* that C_1 is an encryption of M_1, and so on (say, because it has some *a priori* information about the messages). Then, it obtains a ciphertext $C = \mathcal{E}_k(M)$ for an unknown message M (more generally, it may obtain a sequence of ciphertexts as in the case of a ciphertext-only attack) and then tries to learn information about M.

Chosen-plaintext attacks: Stronger than the above is an attack in which the adversary obtains ciphertexts $C_1 = \mathcal{E}_k(M_1), \mathcal{E}_k(M_2), \ldots$ for messages $M_1, M_2, \ldots$ of the adversary's *choice*. This might occur, for example, if the adversary is an "insider" (mistakenly trusted by the sender and receiver) who has some influence over the messages sent by the parties. Then, as above, the adversary might obtain a ciphertext $C = \mathcal{E}_k(M)$ for an unknown message M (more generally, it may obtain a sequence of ciphertexts as in the case of a ciphertext-only attack) and then try to learn information about M.

The above attacks are certainly plausible in many practical situations, and one would therefore like to design an encryption scheme that is secure even in the face of such attacks. As has already been noted, however, neither the one-time pad encryption scheme nor the modified encryption scheme discussed in the previous section is secure against any of the above attacks. In fact, neither Definition 2 nor Definition 3 takes into account any of the above attacks, and thus a revised definition of security is needed.

It is possible to capture all the above attacks in an elegant way by imagining a mental experiment in which an adversary is given access to an *encryption oracle* $\mathcal{E}_k(\cdot)$. As the notation implies, this "oracle" represents a means by which the adversary can obtain encryptions of any message(s) of its choice; namely the adversary submits message M to this oracle and receives in return a corresponding ciphertext $C := \mathcal{E}_k(M)$. We stress that the adversary is allowed to access this oracle as many times as it likes, subject to the bound on its total running time. Definition 3 may then be modified as follows:

Definition 5 *An encryption scheme over message space $\mathcal{M}$ is (t, ε) secure against chosen-plaintext attacks if for all equal-length messages $M_1, M_2 \in \mathcal{M}$ and all eavesdropping adversaries A running in time at most t we have the following:*

$$\left| \Pr_{k \in \mathcal{K}}[A^{\mathcal{E}_k(\cdot)}(\mathcal{E}_k(M_1)) = 1] - \Pr_{k \in \mathcal{K}}[A^{\mathcal{E}_k(\cdot)}(\mathcal{E}_k(M_2)) = 1] \right| \leq \varepsilon,$$

where the probabilities are over random choice of $k \in \mathcal{K}$, as well as any randomness used by A. Note that the same key k used by the encryption oracle is also used to encrypt the unknown message M_1/M_2.

It follows directly from the definition that an encryption scheme satisfying the above does indeed ensure security against chosen-plaintext attacks in the informal sense discussed at the beginning of this section (when A then observes the encryption of a single unknown message M_1/M_2). Moreover, it can be shown (Bellare et al., 1997) that the above definition also implies security when A observes a sequence of ciphertexts corresponding to the encryption of a sequence of unknown messages; that is, the definition ensures security against ciphertext-only attacks as well (and also ensures security against the more general version of the chosen-plaintext attack in which the adversary observes a sequence of ciphertexts for unknown messages). We now make a simple—but extremely important—observation regarding the above definition:

Lemma 3 *No deterministic encryption scheme is secure against chosen-plaintext attacks.*

Proof. Let $(\mathcal{E}, \mathcal{D})$ be a deterministic encryption scheme, let $M_1, M_2 \in \mathcal{M}$ be arbitrary distinct messages of the same length, and consider an adversary A who does the following: it submits M_1 to its encryption oracle to obtain C_1 and then submits M_2 to its encryption oracle to obtain C_2. It then observes a ciphertext C and has to decide whether C represents an encryption of M_1 or M_2. If $C = C_1$ then A outputs "1", whereas if $C = C_2$ then A outputs "2."

Note that we must have $C_1 \neq C_2$ because otherwise the receiver would be unable to decrypt correctly. Furthermore, because $\mathcal{E}$ is deterministic it must be the case that either $C = C_1$ (if and only if C is an encryption of M_1) or $C = C_2$ (if and only if C is an encryption of M_2). Thus,

$$\left| \Pr_{k \in \mathcal{K}}[A^{\mathcal{E}_k(\cdot)}(\mathcal{E}_k(M_1)) = 1] - \Pr_{k \in \mathcal{K}}[A^{\mathcal{E}_k(\cdot)}(\mathcal{E}_k(M_2)) = 1] \right|$$
$$= 1 - 0 = 1,$$

which means that the scheme is not very secure (in the sense of Definition 5).

Although the above may seem a bit contrived (in the sense that rarely does a real-life adversary have full access to an encryption oracle in this way), it does point to an important practical limitation of deterministic encryption schemes: they reveal when the same message is encrypted more than once. Because it may often be desirable to keep even this information secret, deterministic encryption schemes are not recommended for use in practice.

Pseudorandom Functions and Security Against Chosen-Plaintext Attacks

Before showing a randomized encryption scheme that is secure against chosen-plaintext attacks, we first introduce the notion of a *pseudorandom function* (Goldreich, Goldwasser, & Micali, 1985). This primitive—which may be viewed as a more powerful generalization of a pseudorandom generator—is an efficiently computable, keyed function that "acts like a random function" from the perspective of anyone not knowing the key. In more detail, let $F : \{0, 1\}^s \times \{0, 1\}^\ell \to \{0, 1\}^\ell$ represent an efficiently computable, keyed function where for any $k \in \{0, 1\}^s$ we let $F_k : \{0, 1\}^\ell \to \{0, 1\}^\ell$ denote the function $F(k, \cdot)$ (we set the input and outputs lengths of F_k equal for convenience only; this is not essential). Informally, F is a pseudorandom function if the function F_k "looks like" a random function to any adversary who can observe the input/output behavior of F_k but does not know the value of the key k. This is formalized by giving an adversary access to some (imaginary) "black box" which contains either a completely random function (mapping $\{0, 1\}^\ell$ to $\{0, 1\}^\ell$), or an instance of F_k for a randomly chosen k. The adversary can "probe" this black box by submitting inputs of its choice and receiving the corresponding outputs. We say F is pseudorandom if no time-bounded adversary can distinguish between the two cases. Formally:

Definition 6 *Let F be as above, and let $\mathrm{Rand}^{\ell \to \ell}$ denote the set of all functions mapping $\{0, 1\}^\ell$ to $\{0, 1\}^\ell$. We say F is a (t, ε) secure pseudorandom function if for all algorithms A running in time at most t we have the following:*

$$\left| \Pr_{k \in \{0,1\}^s}[A^{F_k(\cdot)} = 1] - \Pr_{f \in \mathrm{Rand}^{\ell \to \ell}}[A^{f(\cdot)} = 1] \right| \leq \varepsilon.$$

In other words, A cannot distinguish between the case when it is given oracle access to F_k (for randomly chosen $k \in \{0, 1\}^s$) and the case when it is given oracle access to a completely random function f.

Pseudorandom functions may be constructed based on a any pseudorandom generator (Goldreich, Goldwasser, & Micali, 1986) and hence from any of a number of standard cryptographic assumptions. In practice, highly efficient *block ciphers* are assumed to be good pseudorandom functions; these are discussed further under "block ciphers and stream ciphers."

With the above definition in mind, we now show a simple encryption scheme secure in the sense of Definition 5 (Goldreich, Goldwasser, & Micali, 1985). The shared key k is a randomly chosen string of length s, and the message space $\mathcal{M}$ is $\{0, 1\}^\ell$. To encrypt a message $M \in \{0, 1\}^\ell$, the sender chooses a random $r \in \{0, 1\}^\ell$ and then sends the following ciphertext:

$$\langle r, F_k(r) \oplus M \rangle.$$

Decryption proceeds in the obvious way: given a ciphertext $\langle r, C \rangle$ the receiver recovers M by computing $C \oplus F_k(r)$.

Arguing informally about the security of this scheme, we may observe the following: because F is pseudorandom and an eavesdropper does not know the shared key k, use of the function F_k is indistinguishable from the use of a truly random function f as far as any adversary running in time at most t is concerned. We may thus analyze the security of the scheme assuming a truly random function f is used, and the adversary is given a ciphertext $\langle r, f(r) \oplus M \rangle$ for which $M \in \{M_1, M_2\}$. Letting $\langle r_1, C_1 \rangle, \ldots, \langle r_n, C_n \rangle$ denote the ciphertexts the adversary has received in return from the encryption oracle, there are two cases to consider:

1. If $r \notin \{r_1, \ldots, r_n\}$, then because f is a truly random function the value of $f(r)$ is completely random and hence the observed ciphertext is encrypted essentially as in the one-time pad scheme. Thus, in this case A learns nothing about the encrypted message.

2. If $r \in \{r_1, \ldots, r_n\}$, then A learns the value of $f(r)$ from one of the responses it received from its encryption oracle and hence can tell whether M_1 or M_2 was encrypted. (For example: assume $r = r_i$. Then if M_i is the ith message that A submitted to its encryption oracle, A learns that $f(r) = f(r_i) = C_i \oplus M_i$.) Because all the r_i's are chosen at random, however, the probability that this occurs is at most $n/2^\ell$, which is small when ℓ is reasonably large.

Because $n \leq t$ (where t is the running time of A), we obtain the following theorem.

Theorem 4 *If F is a (t, ε) secure pseudorandom function, then the encryption scheme described above is $(\mathcal{O}(t), \mathcal{O}(\varepsilon + t/2^\ell))$ secure against chosen-plaintext attacks.*

The above scheme immediately extends to allow encryption of arbitrarily long messages: given a message $M \in (\{0, 1\}^\ell)^n$, simply break it into a sequence of n blocks, each of length ℓ, and then encrypt each block using the above scheme (with independent choices of r each time). It follows from the definition of security against chosen-plaintext attacks that this too is secure in the sense of Definition 5.

SYMMETRIC KEY ENCRYPTION IN PRACTICE
Block Ciphers and Stream Ciphers

As mentioned briefly earlier, a pseudorandom function may be constructed based on quite general cryptographic assumptions (Goldreich, Goldwasser, & Micali, 1986). Yet what makes the notion of pseudorandom functions especially useful in practice is the existence of *block ciphers*: very efficient keyed functions that seem to be pseudorandom for all practical purposes. In fact, block ciphers satisfy the following even stronger property: they are efficiently invertible keyed *permutations*. That is, if F :

$\{0, 1\}^s \times \{0, 1\}^\ell \to \{0, 1\}^\ell$ is a block cipher, then for all keys $k \in \{0, 1\}^s$ the function F_k is a permutation over $\{0, 1\}^\ell$; furthermore, given k it is possible to efficiently compute F_k^{-1}. (Definition 6 may be appropriately modified in this case so that the comparison is now between F_k for random k and a truly random *permutation* f.) In addition, block ciphers are typically assumed to satisfy a stronger security property than that of Definition 6 in which the adversary is given access either to both F_k and F_k^{-1} or to both f and f^{-1} (where f now represents a random permutation as discussed earlier) and *still* cannot distinguish between these two cases.

Two popular and widely used block ciphers are the data encryption standard (DES) (Federal Information Processing Standards Publication 46, 1977) and the advanced encryption standard (AES) (Daemen & Rijmen, 2002). (These algorithms are covered in more detail in the Chapters "Hashes and Message Digests" and "Number Theory for Information Security," respectively). Triple-DES (which uses two or three independent DES keys and applies DES three times) may be viewed as a block cipher as well.

Though block ciphers are already quite efficient, when efficiency is at a premium a *stream cipher* is sometimes used. Perhaps the best way to view a stream cipher is as a pseudorandom function mapping a fixed-length input to an arbitrarily long output. The best-known stream cipher is RC4. This algorithm was designed by RSA Security and has never been publicly released by this company. Nevertheless, a purported description of the RC4 algorithm was posted anonymously to a newsgroup in 1994. See RC4 (2004) or Scheier (1995, Section 17.1) for further details.

Modes of Encryption

A stream cipher enables efficient instantiation of the encryption scheme discussed under "Pseudorandom Functions and Security Against Chosen-Plaintext Attacks": to encrypt an arbitrary length message M using a stream cipher F and key k, simply choose a random r and then compute the ciphertext $\langle r, F_k(r) \oplus M \rangle$. The only difference between this scheme and the one discussed under "Pseudorandom Functions and Security Against Chosen-Plaintext Attacks" is that now M may be arbitrarily long since the output of a stream cipher F is no longer a short, fixed length but is instead arbitrarily long.

In contrast, block ciphers operate only on short, fixed-length blocks. To encrypt arbitrary length messages using a block cipher a *mode of encryption* must be used. We have already seen that the scheme discussed under "Pseudorandom Functions and Security Against Chosen-Plaintext Attacks" may be used to encrypt arbitrary length messages using a block cipher; however, this results in a ciphertext that is twice as long as the message being encrypted and it is natural to wonder whether better efficiency is possible. In fact, three efficient modes of encryption secure against chosen-plaintext attacks were introduced as part of the DES standard (Federal Information Processing Standards publication 81, 1980): *cipher-block chaining* (CBC) mode, *cipher feedback* (CFB) mode, and *output feedback* (OFB) mode (a fourth mode of encryption discussed in the standard—*electronic codebook* (ECB)

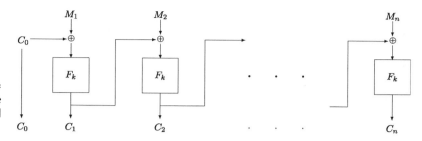

Figure 1: CBC mode encryption of message $M = M_1, \ldots M_n$ using key k and block cipher F. The initialization vector C_0 is chosen at random, and the output ciphertext is $C = C_0, C_1, \ldots, C_n$.

mode—is deterministic and thus not secure in the sense of Definition 5). Many other modes of encryption have since been proposed and offer some advantages; however, these are outside the scope of this survey.

In the descriptions that follow, we assume a block cipher F operating on ℓ-bit blocks and view the plaintext message M as a sequence of ℓ-bit blocks $M_1, \ldots, M_n$ (we assume for simplicity that the length of M is a multiple of ℓ). In CBC mode, the sender constructs the ciphertext as follows (see Figure 1):

> Choose $C_0 \in \{0, 1\}^\ell$ at random
> For $i = 1$ to n :
> $\qquad C_i := F_k(M_i \oplus C_{i-1})$
> Output $\langle C_0, C_1, \ldots, C_n \rangle$

The block C_0 is known as the *initialization vector* and is chosen at random each time encryption is performed. Decryption of ciphertext $\langle C_0, \ldots, C_n \rangle$ is done by reversing the above steps:

> For $i = 1$ to n :
> $\qquad M_i := F_k^{-1}(C_i) \oplus C_{i-1}$
> Output $M_1, \ldots, M_n$

(Note that decryption requires F to be efficiently invertible.) As mentioned above, it is known that CBC mode is secure in the sense of Definition 5 (Bellare et al., 1997). Note that the ciphertext is only ℓ bits longer than the message, a substantial improvement over the simple scheme discussed under "Pseudorandom Functions and Security Against Chosen-Plaintext Attacks." This feature will be shared by all the modes of encryption described here.

OFB mode can be viewed as a method for building a stream cipher out of a block cipher. Here, the sender computes the ciphertext in the following manner:

> Choose $C_0' \in \{0, 1\}^\ell$ at random
> Set $C_0 = C_0'$

> For $i = 1$ to n :
> $\qquad C_i' := F_k(C_{i-1}')$
> $\qquad C_i := C_i' \oplus M_i$
> Output $\langle C_0, C_1, \ldots, C_n \rangle$

The initialization vector $C_0' = C_0$ is used as a seed to generate a pseudorandom sequence $C_1', \ldots, C_n'$, which is then xor'ed with the message. In this way, OCB mode may be viewed as defining a stream cipher $G_k(C_0') = F_k(C_0')F_k^2(C_0') \cdots F_k^i(C_0')$ and then using this to encrypt as discussed earlier in this section. Decryption of ciphertext $\langle C_0, \ldots C_n \rangle$ is done as follows:

> Set $C_0' = C_0$
> For $i = 1$ to n :
> $\qquad C_i' := F_k(C_{i-1}')$
> $\qquad M_i := C_i \oplus C_i'$
> Output $M_1, \ldots, M_n$

We remark that OFB mode does not require that F be efficiently invertible or even a permutation.

CFB mode also generates a pseudorandom sequence which is xor'ed with the message, but this sequence now depends on the message itself and so CFB mode cannot be viewed as a "pure" stream cipher. Here, the sender generates the ciphertext as follows (see Figure 2):

> Choose $C_0 \in \{0, 1\}^\ell$ at random
> For $i = 1$ to n :
> $\qquad C_i' := F_k(C_{i-1})$
> $\qquad C_i := C_i' \oplus M_i$
> Output $\langle C_0, C_1, \ldots, C_n \rangle$

Decryption is done by reversing the above:

> For $i = 1$ to n :
> $\qquad C_i' := F_k(C_{i-1})$
> $\qquad M_i := C_i \oplus C_i'$
> Output $M_1, \ldots, M_n$

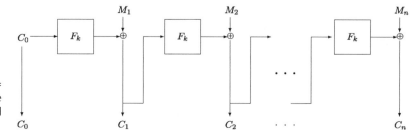

Figure 2: CFB mode encryption of message $M = M_1, \ldots M_n$ using key k and block cipher F. The initialization vector C_0 is chosen at random, and the output ciphertext is $C = C_0, C_1, \ldots, C_n$.

As in the case of OFB mode, CFB mode does not require that F be efficiently invertible or a permutation.

Hybrid Encryption

Throughout this chapter, we have assumed that the communicating parties share a secret key in advance of their communication. If this were the only instance in which symmetric key encryption could be used, its applicability would be rather limited. However, symmetric key encryption is used extensively in the public key setting as well, via a technique called *hybrid encryption*. Here, a public key encryption scheme is used to encrypt a randomly chosen symmetric key k that is then itself used—in conjunction with a symmetric key encryption scheme—for encryption of bulk data. In more detail, assume a receiver has generated keys (PK, SK) for some public key encryption scheme in which encryption is denoted by $\mathcal{E}$; let $\mathcal{E}'$ denote a symmetric key encryption scheme with key space $\mathcal{K}$. A sender who knows PK can encrypt a long message M by choosing a random key $k \in \mathcal{K}$, encrypting k using PK (and the public key encryption algorithm $\mathcal{E}$) to generate $C \leftarrow \mathcal{E}_{PK}(k)$ and then encrypting M using k and the symmetric key scheme to generate $C' \leftarrow \mathcal{E}'_k(M)$. The ciphertext transmitted to the receiver is simply $\langle C, C' \rangle$. Decryption can be done in the obvious way by reversing these steps: to recover the message, the receiver first recovers k using SK and then recovers M using k. Note that this achieves the functionality of public key encryption with the asymptotic efficiency of symmetric key encryption (i.e., when long-enough messages are encrypted). Furthermore, it can be shown that this construction is secure against chosen-plaintext attacks (under an appropriate analog of Definition 5 for the public key setting) as long as the underlying symmetric key and public key schemes are secure against chosen-plaintext attacks.

Stronger Definitions of Security

A notion of security that is stronger than that of Definition 5 is that of security against *chosen-ciphertext attacks*. Informally, such attacks correspond to scenarios in which an adversary may be able to obtain (partial) information about plaintexts corresponding to ciphertexts constructed by the adversary. More formally, Definition 5 is augmented by additionally giving the adversary access to a *decryption oracle* $\mathcal{D}_k(\cdot)$ that returns the decryption of any ciphertext(s) of the adversary's choice. (To make the definition nontrivial, the adversary is disallowed from submitting its input ciphertext—that is, the ciphertext C for which the adversary is trying to decide whether C corresponds to an encryption of M_1 or M_2—to the decryption oracle.) See Katz and Yung (2000b) for further details. Although such an attack may seem contrived, protecting against chosen-ciphertext attacks is crucial when encryption schemes are used as primitives within higher level protocols (e.g., authentication protocols), and this notion of security is now required of all modern-day encryption schemes. It is not hard to see that none of the encryption schemes discussed in this chapter is secure against chosen-ciphertext attacks, but further discussion of this issue (including descriptions of schemes that are secure against chosen-ciphertext attacks) is outside the scope of this survey.

More generally, one often wants to achieve secrecy in combination with *integrity* (that is, to prevent an adversary from undetectably modifying the messages sent between the two communicating parties). A crucial point is that, generally speaking, *encryption alone does not guarantee integrity*; in particular, an encryption scheme secure in the sense of Definition 5 does not necessarily (and, in fact, usually does not) provide any integrity whatsoever. This is evident from, for example, OFB mode encryption as discussed under "Modes of Encryption": it is not hard to see that an adversary can modify the ciphertext at will and the receiver will always decrypt any ciphertext as some valid message. Even worse, an adversary can potentially modify the ciphertext in such a way that it has a predictable effect on the underlying message *even though the adversary does not necessarily learn what that underlying message is*. Consider again the case of OFB mode encryption, for example, and assume an adversary observes a ciphertext C_0, C_1, C_2 (where these are a sequence of ℓ-bit blocks) that is an encryption of some unknown message $M = M_1, M_2$. If the adversary sets $C'_2 = C_2 \oplus 1^{\ell}$ and forwards C_0, C_1, C'_2 to the receiver, the receiver will recover a message M_1, M'_2 in which all the bits in the second message block have been flipped (i.e., $M'_2 = M_2 \oplus 1^{\ell}$)! This may be problematic in itself or may lead to other security problems (see, e.g., Katz & Schneier, 2000).

If one desires both secrecy and integrity, an *authenticated encryption scheme* must be used (Bellare & Namprempre, 2000; Katz & Yung, 2000a). Interestingly, an authenticated encryption scheme is automatically secure against chosen-ciphertext attacks (Bellare & Namprempre, 2000; Katz & Yung, 2000a). Recently, there have been a number of constructions of authenticated encryption schemes (see Black, 2005); these, however, are outside the scope of this survey.

FURTHER INFORMATION

Further information about symmetric key encryption, written in a manner that is accessible to nonspecialists, is available in books by Schneier (1995) and Ferguson and Schneier (2003). The *Handbook of Applied Cryptography* (Menezes, van Oorschot, & Vanstone, 2001) also contains detailed coverage of many aspects of symmetric key encryption. For further information about classical symmetric key encryption schemes and additional weaknesses of such schemes, the reader may consult the textbook by Stinson (2002). More advanced presentations of some of the material covered here are available in Stinson's book (2002), the online notes by Goldwasser and Bellare (2001) or Bellare and Rogaway (2003), and the second volume of Goldreich's graduate-level textbook (Goldreich, 2004).

The notion of computational security for encryption derives from the work of Goldwasser and Micali (1984) who first rigorously defined the notion for the case of public key encryption. Subsequent work concerning definitions of security for symmetric key encryption includes (Bellare et al., 1997; Katz & Yung, 2000b). Goldreich's first volume (Goldreich, 2001) contains much more information about pseudorandom generators and pseudorandom functions.

GLOSSARY

Block Cipher   A highly efficient keyed permutation operating on short blocks that is assumed to act as a pseudorandom permutation.

Ciphertext   The "garbled" output that results from encrypting a message.

Decryption   Application of a keyed procedure to a ciphertext to recover the underlying message.

Encryption   Application of a keyed procedure to a message with the intent of making the message unreadable to anyone who does not know the corresponding key enabling decryption.

Plaintext   Another word for the message, or data, to be communicated.

Pseudorandom Function   A keyed function whose input/output characteristics for a randomly generated key cannot be distinguished from a truly random function by anyone who does not know the underlying key.

Pseudorandom Generator   A deterministic function which expands a short "seed" to a longer, "random-looking" string.

Public Key Encryption Scheme   An encryption scheme in which the keys used for encryption and decryption are different and that is "secure" (in some appropriate sense) even if the encryption key is known.

Stream Cipher   A highly efficient keyed function that maps a short input to an arbitrary-length pseudorandom string.

Symmetric Key Encryption Scheme   An encryption scheme in which the same key is used both for encryption and decryption.

CROSS REFERENCES

See *Data Encryption Standard (DES); Encryption Basics; The Advanced Encryption Standard*

REFERENCES

Bellare, M., Desai, A., Jokipii, E., & Rogaway, P. (1997). A concrete security treatment of symmetric encryption. In *Proceedings of the 38th Annual Symposium on Foundations of Computer Science* (pp. 394–403). Los Alamitos, CA: IEEE Computer Society.

Bellare, M., & Namprempre, C. (2000). Authenticated encryption: Relations among notions and analysis of the generic composition paradigm. In *Advances in Cryptology—Asiacrypt 2000*, LNCS vol. 1976, (pp. 531–545). New York: Springer-Verlag.

Bellare, M., & Rogaway, P. (January, 2003). Introduction to modern cryptography. Retrieved January 1, 2004, from http://www.cs.ucsd.edu/users/mihir/cse207/classnotes.html

Black, J. (2005). Authenticated encryption. In *Encyclopedia of cryptography and security*, H.C.A. van Tilborg, ed. Springer-Verlag. Retrieved January 1, 2004, from http://www.cs.colorado.edu/~jrblack/papers/ae.pdf

Blum, L., Blum, M., & Shub, M. (1986). A simple and secure unpredictable pseudo-random number generator. *SIAM Journal on Computing, 15*(2), 364–383.

Blum, M., & Micali, S. (1984). How to generate cryptographically strong sequences of pseudorandom bits. *SIAM Journal on Computing, 13*(4), 850–864.

Daemen, J., & Rijmen, V. (2002). *The design of Rijndael: AES—The advanced encryption standard*. Berlin: Springer-Verlag.

Federal Information Processing Standards publication 46. (1977). Data encryption standard. Washington, DC: U.S. Department of Commerce/National Bureau of Standards.

Federal Information Processing Standards publication 81. (1980). DES modes of operation. Washington, DC: U.S. Department of Commerce/National Bureau of Standards.

Ferguson, N., & Schneier, B. (2003). *Practical cryptography*. New York: John Wiley & Sons.

Goldreich, O., (2001). *Foundations of cryptography, vol. 1: Basic tools*. Cambridge, UK: Cambridge University Press.

Goldreich, O. (2004). *Foundations of cryptography, vol. 2: Basic applications*. Cambridge, UK: Cambridge University Press.

Goldreich, O., Goldwasser, S., & Micali, S. (1985). On the cryptographic applications of random functions. In G. R. Blakley & D. Chaum (eds.), *Lecture Notes in Computer Science, vol. 196: Advances in Cryptology—Crypto '84*, vol. 196: (pp. 276–288). New York: Springer-Verlag.

Goldreich, O., Goldwasser, S., & Micali, S. (1986). How to construct random functions. *Journal of the ACM, 33*(4), 792–807.

Goldreich, O., & Levin, L. (1989). Hard-core predicates for any one-way function. *Proceedings of the 21st Annual ACM Symposium on Theory of Computing* (pp. 25–32). New York, NY: ACM Press.

Goldwasser, S., & Bellare, M. (August, 2001). *Lecture notes on cryptography*. Retrieved January 1, 2004, from http://www.cs.ucsd.edu/users/mihir/papers/gb.html

Goldwasser, S., & Micali, S. (1984). Probabilistic encryption. *Journal of Computer and System Sciences, 28*(2), 270–299.

Håstad, J., Impagliazzo, R., Levin, L., & Luby, M. (1999). A pseudorandom generator from any one-way function. *SIAM Journal on Computing, 28*(4), 1364–1396.

Katz, J., & Schneier, B. (2000). A chosen-ciphertext attack against several e-mail encryption protocols. In *Proceedings of the 9th USENIX Security Symposium* (pp. 241–246). Berkeley, CA: USENIX Association.

Katz, J., & Yung, M. (2000a). Unforgeable encryption and chosen-ciphertext secure modes of operation. In *Fast Software Encryption 2000 vol. 1978: Lecture Notes Computer Science* (pp. 284–299). New York: Springer-Verlag.

Katz, J., & Yung, M. (2000b). Complete characterization of security notions for probabilistic private-key encryption. In *Proceedings of the 32nd Annual ACM Symposium on Theory of Computing* (pp. 245–254).

Kerckhoffs, A. (1883). La cryptographie militaire. *Journal des Sciences Militaires, 9th Series*, February, 161–191.

Knuth, D. E. (1997). *The art of computer programming, vol. 2: Seminumerical algorithms* (3rd ed.). Boston: Addison-Wesley.

Menezes, A. J., van Oorschot, P. C., & Vanstone, S. A. (2001). *Handbook of applied cryptography*. Boca Raton: CRC Press.

RC4. (2004). Wikipedia encyclopedia entry. Retrieved January 1, 2004, from http://en.wikipedia.org/wiki/RC4

Schneier, B. (1995). *Applied cryptography: Protocols, algorithms, and source code in C* (2nd ed.). New York: John Wiley & Sons.

Shannon, C. E. (1949). Communication theory of secrecy systems. *Bell System Technical Journal, 28,* 656–715.

Stinson, D. R. (2002). *Cryptography: Theory and practice* (2nd ed.). Boston: Chapman & Hall.

Vernam, G. S. (1926). Cipher printing telegraph systems for secret wire and radio telegraphic communications. *Journal of the American Institute for Electrical Engineers, 55,* 109–115.

Yao, A. C. (1982). Theory and application of trapdoor functions. In *Proceedings of the 23rd IEEE Symposium on Foundations of Computer Science* (pp. 80–91). Los Alamitos, CA: IEEE Computer Society.

Data Encryption Standard (DES)

Mike Speciner, *Independent Consultant*

INTRODUCTION

The Data Encryption Standard (DES) is a widely deployed secret key encryption method standardized by the U.S. National Bureau of Standards in 1977. This chapter describes the method in detail, explains how it is used to encrypt long messages, and how it is used with multiple keys for better security.

HISTORY

DES was originally developed by an IBM team formed in the early 1970s in response to customer requests for a method to secure data. IBM submitted DES to the National Bureau of Standards, which published it as a standard in 1977. One of the members of the IBM team, Horst Feistel, had come up with the basic structure on which DES is built, and he and fellow teammate Don Coppersmith created the Lucifer cipher, the direct ancestor of DES. The U.S. National Security Agency provided guidance toward the final form of DES.

OVERVIEW

DES (see Figure 1) uses a 56-bit key to transform a block of 64 bits (called the plaintext) into another block of 64 bits (called the ciphertext). DES starts by rearranging (permuting) the bits of the plaintext. It then transforms the 64-bit block resulting from this initial permutation in a sequence of 16 identical rounds, each round using a different 48-bit round key derived from the 56-bit DES key. After the last round, it swaps the two 32-bit halves of the transformed block. Finally, it permutes the bits to produce the ciphertext. The final permutation is the inverse of the initial permutation; that is, if you started with a block of 64 bits and performed the initial permutation immediately followed by the final permutation (or vice versa), you would end up with what you started with.

This transformation from plaintext to ciphertext is called DES encryption. The inverse transformation, DES decryption, uses the same 56-bit key to transform the ciphertext into the plaintext. It turns out that DES decryption is identical to DES encryption but with the 48-bit round keys applied in reverse order.

PERMUTATIONS

The initial permutation can be specified as a sequence of 64 numbers that are the input bit numbers:

```
58 50 42 34 26 18 10 2
60 52 44 36 28 20 12 4
62 54 46 38 30 22 14 6
64 56 48 40 32 24 16 8
57 49 41 33 25 17  9 1
59 51 43 35 27 19 11 3
61 53 45 37 29 21 13 5
63 55 47 39 31 23 15 7
```

So, the first input bit (bit 1) gets moved to position 40, the second input bit (bit 2) to position 8, and so on (see Figure 2). Similarly, the final permutation is as follows:

```
40 8 48 16 56 24 64 32
39 7 47 15 55 23 63 31
38 6 46 14 54 22 62 30
37 5 45 13 53 21 61 29
36 4 44 12 52 20 60 28
35 3 43 11 51 19 59 27
34 2 42 10 50 18 58 26
33 1 41  9 49 17 57 25
```

KEY DISTRIBUTION/PER-ROUND KEYS

The 56-bit DES key is the source for the sixteen 48-bit round keys (also known as subkeys). DES key bits are numbered from 1 through 64, where bits 8, 16, 24, 32, 40, 48, 56, and 64 are not actually bits from the 56-bit key but rather the odd parity of the preceding 7 bits.

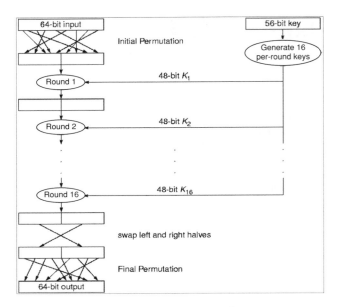

Figure 1: Basic structure of DES.

These parity bits are numbered but not used (other than for error detection when all 64 bits are transmitted).

First, the 56 bits of the key are permuted (see Figure 3) into two 28-bit halves, called C_0 and D_0:

C_0	D_0
57 49 41 33 25 17 9	63 55 47 39 31 23 15
1 58 50 42 34 26 18	7 62 54 46 38 30 22
10 2 59 51 43 35 27	14 6 61 53 45 37 29
19 11 3 60 52 44 36	21 13 5 28 20 12 4

Next, the round keys K_n are generated in 16 rounds. First each of C_{n-1} and D_{n-1} are rotated left to get C_n and D_n. In rounds 1, 2, 9, and 16, it is a single-bit rotate; that is, the bits are shifted left one position and the bit falling off the left end ends up at the right end. In the other rounds, it is a two-bit rotate. Twenty-four of the 28 bits of C_n (where the bits of C_n are numbered 1 through 28) are permuted to get the left half of K_n using the following permutation:

14 17 11 24 1 5 3 28 15 6 21 10 23 19 12 4 26 8 16 7 27 20 13 2,

and 24 of the 28 bits of D_n (where the bits of D_n are numbered 29 through 56) are permuted to get the right half of

K_n using the following permutation:

41 52 31 37 47 55 30 40 51 45 33 48 44 49 39 56 34 53 46 42 50 36 29 32.

This key distribution process contributes to the *diffusion* of the key.

A ROUND

(See Figure 4.) Round n takes its 64-bit input block considered as a 32-bit left half L_n and a 32-bit right half R_n, and, using the round key K_n, transforms these into two 32-bit halves L_{n+1} and R_{n+1} that are concatenated to produce its 64-bit output block. L_{n+1} is just R_n, whereas R_{n+1} is the bitwise exclusive or ($\oplus$) of L_n and a function of K_n and R_n. This function is the "mangler function," which we describe in the next section.

Note that if you feed round n its own output with the halves swapped (i.e., $R_{n+1}|L_{n+1}$), it produces its own input with the halves swapped, namely $R_n|L_n$. If you look at the structure of DES, what was a mysterious swapping of halves after the last round now makes complete sense, because it means that DES decryption is identical to DES encryption but with the round keys applied in reverse order. A cipher with this structure is known as a Feistel cipher.

THE MANGLER FUNCTION

The mangler function is the crucial part of DES algorithm. It is responsible for hiding the data by mixing it with the key. So the mangler function provides much of DES's *confusion*. It is also a source of *diffusion* that is amplified by successive rounds.

The mangler function produces a 32-bit result V from two input values: a 48-bit round key K and a 32-bit value R. First, it expands R to 48 bits (see Figure 5). Then it performs a bitwise exclusive or ($\oplus$) of K with the expanded R to get a value X. Then, it breaks up X into eight 6-bit chunks X_i and looks up X_i in a substitution table called S-box i, which produces a 4-bit result. Finally, the eight 4-bit results are concatenated into a 32-bit quantity whose bits are permuted to get V, the output of the mangler function. This permutation is as follows:

16 7 20 21 29 12 28 17 1 15 23 26 5 18 31 10 2 8 24 14 32 27 3 9 19 13 30 6 22 11 4 25.

The expansion of R to 48 bits is done by breaking R into eight 4-bit chunks and then expanding each of those chunks to 6 bits by taking the adjacent bit on each side the

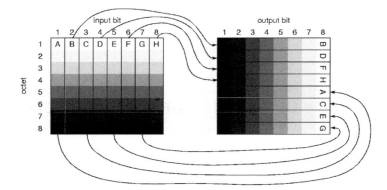

Figure 2: Initial permutation of data block (reverse the arrows for final permutation).

1	2	3	4	5	6	7
9	10	11	12	13	14	15
17	18	19	20	21	22	23
25	26	27	28	29	30	31
33	34	35	36	37	38	39
41	42	43	44	45	46	47
49	50	51	52	53	54	55
57	58	59	60	61	62	63

$\Rightarrow$

57	49	41	33	25	17	9
1	58	50	42	34	26	18
10	2	59	51	43	35	27
19	11	3	60	52	44	36
63	55	47	39	31	23	15
7	62	54	46	38	30	22
14	6	61	53	45	37	29
21	13	5	28	20	12	4

Figure 3: Initial permutation of key.

chunk and pasting them onto the chunk. For this process, the leftmost and rightmost bits of R are considered adjacent. The resulting 6-bit chunks are concatenated. (This expansion also goes by the name *expansion permutation*, although it is not a permutation at all.)

As described previously, each 6-bit chunk of X is turned into a 4-bit chunk using its associated S-box, and the resulting 4-bit chunks are concatenated into a 32-bit quantity. Numbering the bits of X from left to right as 1 through 48, and the bits of the 32-bit quantity as 1 through 32, the S-box lookup tables are shown in Figures 6–13.

The S-boxes were carefully crafted to make DES resistant to differential cryptanalysis. They are the only nonlinear portion of DES algorithm. [A function f transforming one fixed-length chunk of bits to another (of possibly different length) is linear if $f(a \oplus b) = f(a) \oplus f(b) \oplus f(0)$ for all a and b. For example, one of the simplest linear functions is the parity function that is 0 if its argument has an even number of 1s and is 1 otherwise.]

This completes the description of DES algorithm.

WEAK AND SEMI-WEAK KEYS

There are 16 DES keys with properties that make them suspect, and so their use is discouraged. These are the keys that have each of C_0 and D_0 being one of four values: all ones, all zeroes, alternating ones and zeroes, and alternating zeroes and ones. The weak keys have each of C_0 and D_0 being all ones or all zeroes; they are their own inverses in that encryption and decryption are identical. The remaining 12 possibilities are semi-weak keys; each is the inverse of one of the others in that encryption by one is identical to decryption by the other.

Whether weak and semiweak keys are actually less secure is not particularly important. Once particular values of a key are pointed out, they are likely to be tried first when attempting cryptanalysis. This is why it's probably also not a good idea to use keys with small numeric values. To avoid such "distinguished key" attacks, keys should have approximately equal numbers of 0s and 1s. Almost all potential keys are of this form anyway.

TRIPLE DES (3DES OR TDEA)

When DES was designed, its 56-bit key was at best barely good enough to keep data secure. These days, 56 bits is not nearly enough, and so TDEA (Triple Data Encryption Algorithm) was standardized. TDEA uses three successive DES operations, each with its own key, to encrypt a block. The first and third are DES encryptions, whereas the middle is a DES decryption. The main reason for this "EDE" scheme is so that a TDEA engine can emulate a DES engine by using the same DES key for all three operations. TDEA is often used with only two distinct keys, where the two DES encryptions use the same key, but it should be used with three distinct keys for maximum security. There is a known attack (although not a practical one) that suggests that TDEA with only two distinct keys is much less secure than would be expected from its 112-bit total key size.

As should be obvious, decrypting a TDEA-encrypted block also involves three successive DES operations. Here, the first and third are decryptions, whereas the middle is an encryption, with the keys being the same as those used for the TDEA encryption, but used in reverse order.

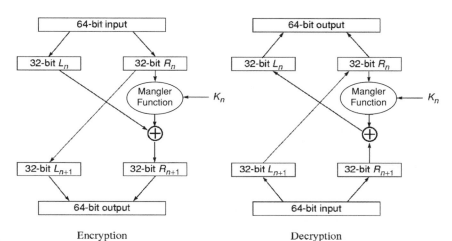

Figure 4: DES round.

Encryption   Decryption

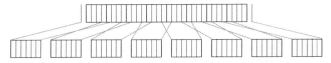

Figure 5: Expansion of R to 48 bits.

Input bits 1 and 6   Input bits 2 thru 5

↓	0000	0001	0010	0011	0100	0101	0110	0111	1000	1001	1010	1011	1100	1101	1110	1111
00	1110	0100	1101	0001	0010	1111	1011	1000	0011	1010	0110	1100	0101	1001	0000	0111
01	0000	1111	0111	0100	1110	0010	1101	0001	1010	0110	1100	1011	1001	0101	0011	1000
10	0100	0001	1110	1000	1101	0110	0010	1011	1111	1100	1001	0111	0011	1010	0101	0000
11	1111	1100	1000	0010	0100	1001	0001	0111	0101	1011	0011	1110	1010	0000	0110	1101

Figure 6: S-box 1, producing bits 1–4.

Input bits 7 and 12   Input bits 8 thru 11

↓	0000	0001	0010	0011	0100	0101	0110	0111	1000	1001	1010	1011	1100	1101	1110	1111
00	1111	0001	1000	1110	0110	1011	0011	0100	1001	0111	0010	1101	1100	0000	0101	1010
01	0011	1101	0100	0111	1111	0010	1000	1110	1100	0000	0001	1010	0110	1001	1011	0101
10	0000	1110	0111	1011	1010	0100	1101	0001	0101	1000	1100	0110	1001	0011	0010	1111
11	1101	1000	1010	0001	0011	1111	0100	0010	1011	0110	0111	1100	0000	0101	1110	1001

Figure 7: S-box 2, producing bits 5–8.

Input bits 13 and 18   Input bits 14 thru 17

↓	0000	0001	0010	0011	0100	0101	0110	0111	1000	1001	1010	1011	1100	1101	1110	1111
00	1010	0000	1001	1110	0110	0011	1111	0101	0001	1101	1100	0111	1011	0100	0010	1000
01	1101	0111	0000	1001	0011	0100	0110	1010	0010	1000	0101	1110	1100	1011	1111	0001
10	1101	0110	0100	1001	1000	1111	0011	0000	1011	0001	0010	1100	0101	1010	1110	0111
11	0001	1010	1101	0000	0110	1001	1000	0111	0100	1111	1110	0011	1011	0101	0010	1100

Figure 8: S-box 3, producing bits 9–12.

Input bits 19 and 24   Input bits 20 thru 23

↓	0000	0001	0010	0011	0100	0101	0110	0111	1000	1001	1010	1011	1100	1101	1110	1111
00	0111	1101	1110	0011	0000	0110	1001	1010	0001	0010	1000	0101	1011	1100	0100	1111
01	1101	1000	1011	0101	0110	1111	0000	0011	0100	0111	0010	1100	0001	1010	1110	1001
10	1010	0110	1001	0000	1100	1011	0111	1101	1111	0001	0011	1110	0101	0010	1000	0100
11	0011	1111	0000	0110	1010	0001	1101	1000	1001	0100	0101	1011	1100	0111	0010	1110

Figure 9: S-box 4, producing bits 13–16.

Input bits 25 and 30   Input bits 26 thru 29

↓	0000	0001	0010	0011	0100	0101	0110	0111	1000	1001	1010	1011	1100	1101	1110	1111
00	0010	1100	0100	0001	0111	1010	1011	0110	1000	0101	0011	1111	1101	0000	1110	1001
01	1110	1011	0010	1100	0100	0111	1101	0001	0101	0000	1111	1010	0011	1001	1000	0110
10	0100	0010	0001	1011	1010	1101	0111	1000	1111	1001	1100	0101	0110	0011	0000	1110
11	1011	1000	1100	0111	0001	1110	0010	1101	0110	1111	0000	1001	1010	0100	0101	0011

Figure 10: S-box 5, producing bits 17–20.

Input bits 31 and 36   Input bits 32 thru 35

↓	0000	0001	0010	0011	0100	0101	0110	0111	1000	1001	1010	1011	1100	1101	1110	1111
00	1100	0001	1010	1111	1001	0010	0110	1000	0000	1101	0011	0100	1110	0111	0101	1011
01	1010	1111	0100	0010	0111	1100	1001	0101	0110	0001	1101	1110	0000	1011	0011	1000
10	1001	1110	1111	0101	0010	1000	1100	0011	0111	0000	0100	1010	0001	1101	1011	0110
11	0100	0011	0010	1100	1001	0101	1111	1010	1011	1110	0001	0111	0110	0000	1000	1101

Figure 11: S-box 6, producing bits 21–24.

Input bits 37 and 42   Input bits 38 thru 41

↓	0000	0001	0010	0011	0100	0101	0110	0111	1000	1001	1010	1011	1100	1101	1110	1111
00	0100	1011	0010	1110	1111	0000	1000	1101	0011	1100	1001	0111	0101	1010	0110	0001
01	1101	0000	1011	0111	0100	1001	0001	1010	1110	0011	0101	1100	0010	1111	1000	0110
10	0001	0100	1011	1101	1100	0011	0111	1110	1010	1111	0110	1000	0000	0101	1001	0010
11	0110	1011	1101	1000	0001	0100	1010	0111	1001	0101	0000	1111	1110	0010	0011	1100

Figure 12: S-box 7, producing bits 25–28.

Input bits 43 and 48   Input bits 44 thru 47

↓	0000	0001	0010	0011	0100	0101	0110	0111	1000	1001	1010	1011	1100	1101	1110	1111
00	1101	0010	1000	0100	0110	1111	1011	0001	1010	1001	0011	1110	0101	0000	1100	0111
01	0001	1111	1101	1000	1010	0011	0111	0100	1100	0101	0110	1011	0000	1110	1001	0010
10	0111	1011	0100	0001	1001	1100	1110	0010	0000	0110	1010	1101	1111	0011	0101	1000
11	0010	0001	1110	0111	0100	1010	1000	1101	1111	1100	1001	0000	0011	0101	0110	1011

Figure 13: S-box 8, producing bits 29–32.

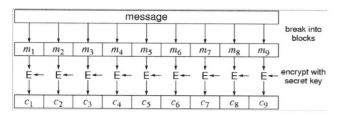

Figure 14: ECB. For decryption, just reverse the vertical arrows and replace encrypt (E) with decrypt (D).

MODES OF OPERATION: ENCRYPTING LONG SEQUENCES OF DATA

To encrypt a long sequence of data, a block encryption algorithm must break up the data into blocks with a block size specific to the encryption algorithm. In the case of DES, the data is broken into 64-bit blocks. Although each block could be encrypted with a different key, in practice a single key is used. The problem with just encrypting each block with the same key is that the same plaintext block is always encrypted into the same ciphertext block, which might help a forger or cryptanalyst.

We describe several techniques for encrypting long sequences of plaintext: electronic codebook (ECB), cipher block chaining (CBC), output feedback mode (OFB), cipher feedback mode (CFB), and counter mode (CTR). ECB, CBC, OFB, and CFB, when used with TDEA, are called TECB, TCBC, TOFB, and TCFB. TCBC-I, TOFB-I, and TCFB-P, where I stands for "interleaved" and P stands for "pipelined," are modifications specified by ANSI to take advantage of the availability of multiple (actually three) encryption engines.

Electronic Codebook (ECB)

This is the technique we just described: each block of plaintext is encrypted independently with the same key. (See Figure 14).

Cipher Block Chaining (CBC)

In this technique, each block of plaintext is ⊕ed with another quantity before being encrypted. The first block is ⊕ed with something called an initialization vector (IV), which must be known to the decrypter. It is normally a random number selected by the encrypter and kept with the ciphertext so that it is known to the decrypter. Each plaintext block after the first is ⊕ed with the ciphertext of the previous block before being encrypted. (See Figure 15).

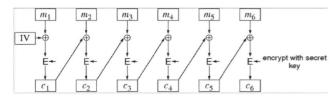

Figure 15: CBC. For decryption, just reverse the vertical arrows and replace encrypt (E) with decrypt (D).

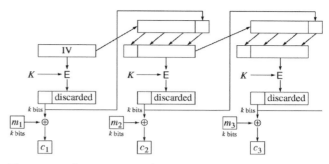

Figure 16: k-Bit OFB. For decryption, just reverse the arrows at m_1 and c_1.

Output Feedback Mode (OFB)

In this technique, the data to be encrypted is broken up into chunks of a size k less than or equal to the encryption algorithm's blocksize. The plaintext is not actually encrypted, but merely ⊕ed with a pseudorandom stream of k-bit chunks generated by repeated application of the encryption algorithm, starting with a k-bit initialization vector. Thus OFB encryption and decryption are identical operations.

To start the generation of the pseudorandom stream, the IV, padded on the left with zeroes, is written to a blocksize-length shift register. Then the following is repeated: the shift register contents are passed to the encryption engine. The leftmost k bits of the encrypted result form the next chunk of the pseudorandom stream and are also shifted into the shift register from the right. (See Figure 16).

A serious weakness of OFB is that someone who knows the plaintext associated with a given ciphertext can forge any same-length (or shorter) message by ⊕ing the ciphertext with the known plaintext ⊕ed with the forged plaintext.

Cipher Feedback Mode (CFB)

CFB is similar to OFB. The only difference is the k-bit value that is shifted into the shift register. For CFB, it is the just-generated chunk of ciphertext, which is the ⊕ of the newly generated pseudorandom stream chunk with the current plaintext chunk. (See Figure 17).

Counter Mode (CTR)

Counter mode generates a pseudorandom stream of chunks from an initialization vector by successively

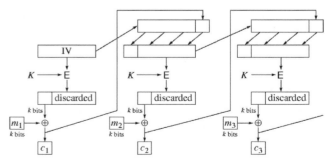

Figure 17: k-Bit CFB. For decryption, just reverse the arrows at m_1 and c_1.

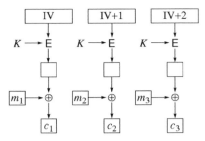

Figure 18: CTR.

encrypting IV, IV+1, IV+2, ... (see Figure 18). These chunks are $\oplus$ed with the plaintext chunks to form the ciphertext chunks. Thus CTR encryption and decryption are identical operations. CTR has the same weakness as OFB.

CRYPTANALYSIS

Various ideas have been used in an attempt to "break" DES, that is, to decrypt DES-encrypted data without knowing the key. What this really means is figuring out the key based on knowing the ciphertext and having some knowledge of the plaintext. At the very least, one has to be able to recognize when something is plaintext. Some of the techniques require much more knowledge, such as having a large number of plaintext–ciphertext pairs using the key or knowing the ciphertext associated with some carefully chosen plaintext. We mention exhaustive search, and differential and linear cryptanalysis in the following sections. Of these, the only really practical attack at present is exhaustive search, and it is the main reason that TDEA has replaced DES.

Exhaustive Search

The idea of exhaustive search is to try each possible key in turn until the correct key is discovered. On average, one has to try half of the 2^{56} keys (i.e., 2^{55} keys) before finding the correct one.

Differential Cryptanalysis

The idea of differential cryptanalysis is to correlate $p \oplus q$ with $c \oplus d$, where p, c and q, d are each plaintext–ciphertext pairs. This technique can be used to crack a DES key with about 2^{47} known plaintext–ciphertext pairs.

Linear Cryptanalysis

The idea of linear cryptanalysis is to look at linear relations between plaintext bits, ciphertext bits, and key bits. A linear relation just means that the $\oplus$ of the selected bits is zero (or one). This technique can be used to crack a DES key with about 2^{43} plaintext–ciphertext pairs.

SUMMARY

DES is the first commercial encryption scheme standardized by the U.S. government. It is a block encryption scheme with 64-bit blocks and 56-bit keys. It has been in use for over a quarter of a century and has withstood the test of time. Although it is not considered secure in its 56-bit key incarnation, it can be combined with itself in

TDEA to provide 112- or 168-bit key encryption. Although this seems to still be secure, a new block encryption algorithm called AES (Advanced Encryption Standard) has been standardized by the U.S. National Institute of Standards and Technology, which uses 128-bit blocks and 128-, 192-, or 256-bit keys and can be implemented much more efficiently in software than DES.

GLOSSARY

Bitwise Exclusive Or ($\oplus$) A function that takes two equal-length chunks of bits (the arguments) and produces another equal-length chunk of bits (the result) where a result bit is 0 when the corresponding two argument bits are equal and is 1 when they differ. Note that $\oplus$ has a number of interesting properties: it is commutative [$a \oplus b = b \oplus a$] and associative [$a \oplus (b \oplus c) = (a \oplus b) \oplus c$]; if 0 represents bitwise 0, $a \oplus a = 0$ and $a \oplus 0 = a$; as a consequence of these properties, if $a \oplus b = c$, then $a = b \oplus c$ and $b = c \oplus a$.

Block Encryption An encryption method that transforms a fixed-length block of plaintext into an equal-length block of ciphertext.

Ciphertext The result of encrypting the plaintext.

Confusion A property of a good block encryption technique where changing any subset of key and plaintext bits has a complex effect on the ciphertext.

Diffusion A property of a good block encryption technique where a single bit of the key or the plaintext affects many bits of the ciphertext.

Feistel Cipher A block encryption technique with a structure similar to DES: The plaintext block (after an initial permutation) is split into two halves, and then a sequence of identical rounds is performed where the right half becomes the new left half while the right half and the round key are combined by a mangler function [see below] whose result is then $\oplus$ed with the left half to produce the new right half. The halves from the final round are then swapped (and the inverse of the initial permutation is performed) to produce the ciphertext block. In a Feistel cipher, the only difference between encryption and decryption is the order in which the round keys are applied.

Key Distribution Within a block encryption algorithm with multiple rounds, the method by which the round keys are derived from the encryption key.

Mangler Function In a Feistel cipher, the part of the algorithm that provides the confusion. The mangler function, considered as a round key-dependent function of the right half, is not normally reversible.

Permutation A technique in which the bits in a chunk are rearranged according to a specific rule. In this chapter, we define a given permutation by a sequence of source bit numbers. So, for example, 3 1 2 would define the permutation that moves bit 3 to position 1, bit 1 to position 2, and bit 2 to position 3.

Plaintext The actual data to be encrypted.

Round In many block encryption techniques, a part of the algorithm that is repeated many times, with the output of one round used as the input to the next. Usually, a second input to a round is the round key, derived from the encryption key and often different for each round. Rounds are repeated to provide sufficient diffusion and confusion.

S-Box The part of an encryption algorithm such as DES that performs substitution.

Secret Key Encryption A method of encryption in which a single value (called a key) is used by both the encryption and decryption algorithms to map plaintext to ciphertext and ciphertext to plaintext, respectively.

Substitution A technique in which a chunk of bits is replaced by a different chunk of bits according to a specific rule. Also called table lookup.

Symmetric Encryption Another name for secret key encryption. The word *symmetric* refers to the fact that the same secret value (the key) is used for both encryption and decryption.

CROSS REFERENCES

See *Encryption Basics; Symmetric Key Encryption*.

REFERENCES

American National Standards Institute. *Triple Data Encryption Algorithm Modes of Operation*. ANSI X9.52-1998. As of 14 April 2005, may be purchased from http://webstore.ansi.org/ansidocstore/product.asp?sku=ANSI+X9%2E52%2D1998.

National Institute of Standards and Technology. Data Encryption Standard. *Federal Information Processing Standards Publication 46*, Retrieved 14 April 2005, from http://www.csrc.nist.gov/publications/fips/fips46-3/fips46-3.pdf

National Institute of Standards and Technology. DES Modes of Operation. *Federal Information Processing Standards Publication 81*, Retrieved 14 April 2005, from http://www.itl.nist.gov/fipspubs/fip81.htm

FURTHER READING

Coppersmith, D. (1994). The Data Encryption Standard (DES) and its strength against attacks. *IBM Journal of Research and Development, 38*(3), 243–250. Retrieved 14 April 2005, from http://www.research.ibm.com/journal/rd/383/coppersmith.pdf

Feistel, H. (1973). Cryptography and computer privacy. *Scientific American, 228*, 15–23.

Kaufman, C., Perlman, R., & Speciner, M. (2002). *Network security: Private communication in a public world*. Upper Saddle River, NJ: Prentice Hall.

Landau, S. (2000). Communications security for the 21st century: The advanced encryption standard. *Notices of the American Mathematical Society, 47*(4), 450–459. Retrieved 14 April 2005, from http://www.ams.org/notices/200004/fea-landau.pdf

Landau, S. (2000). Standing the test of time: The data encryption standard. *Notices of the American Mathematical Society, 47*(3), 341–349. Retrieved 14 April 2005, from http://www.ams.org/notices/200003/fea-landau.pdf

Merkle, R. C. (1981). On the security of multiple encryption. *Communications of the ACM, 24*(7), 465–467.

Schneier, B. (1996). *Applied cryptography: Protocols, algorithms, and source code in C* (2nd ed.). New York: John Wiley & Sons.

The Advanced Encryption Standard

Duncan A. Buell, *University of South Carolina*

HISTORY OF THE ADVANCED ENCRYPTION STANDARD PROCESS

In July 1977, the United States National Bureau of Standards (NBS, whose name was later changed to the National Institute of Standards and Technology, or NIST), promulgated Federal Information Processing Standard (FIPS) 46, the Data Encryption Standard, or DES, for ensuring secure communication, primarily with regard to financial transactions conducted electronically (NIST, 1999). DES had a rather controversial start; from the very beginning there were critics who pointed out that the technical capability for breaking DES was not entirely beyond 1980s technology. Diffie and Hellman argued in 1977 that by about 1987 a machine capable of an essentially brute-force attack on DES would cost only about $200,000 (Diffie, 1977). Indeed, DES was broken, using an approach similar to and at a cost similar to the projections of Diffie and Hellman, but not until 1998. A careful analysis of the nature of DES and its successors can be found in Landau (2000a, 2000b).

In part because of concerns about security, many of those using DES by the 1990s were using "Triple-DES," encrypting three times instead of just once. It was clear to NIST by the mid-1990s that a new encryption standard was necessary. To this end, a competition was announced in January 1997.

A number of NIST criteria were outlined in advance. The goal was a cryptosystem that was at least as secure as Triple-DES that was in moderately wide use, but a cryptosystem that was much more efficient than Triple-DES. The Rijndael/AES algorithm, for example, is strongly byte-oriented, making it clean and efficient in a high-level language on a standard processor but also relatively straightforward to implement on the kind of minimal-capability processor as might be found on a smart card. The NIST specification was for a block length of 128 bits and for key lengths of 128, 192, and 256 bits.

Finally, there were stringent standards set regarding intellectual property issues, in that NIST intended AES to be an open standard without encumbrances from patents or other claimed proprietary content.

A series of three conferences were held on proposals for AES, on 20–22 August 1998 in Ventura, California (NIST, 1998a; Roback, 1999), on 22–23 March 1999 in Rome, Italy (NIST, 1998b), and on 13–14 April 2000 in New York City (NIST, 2000a).

There were fifteen submissions that were accepted by NIST for the first round of the evaluation. These are (from Daemen and Rijmen, 2001) presented in Table 1.

In August 1999, the list of fifteen candidates was reduced to five—MARS, RC6, Rijndael, Serpent, and Twofish. An analysis of the study of the finalists can be found in Nechvatal et al. (2000), and summary can be found in Stallings (2003). The initial three criteria of security, cost, and implementation characteristics were modified somewhat during the evaluation process. Although security remained the primary concern, the analysis of the proposed algorithms resulted in a refinement of the other two criteria. The cost criteria included both software efficiency and the cost, both in general silicon area and in memory required, of a hardware implementation. Implementation characteristics included the specifics of implementation in silicon, in field programmable gate arrays, on general purpose processors with a high degree of instruction-level parallelism. Also considered were the flexibility of the algorithm to accommodate parameters outside the original requirements of AES (in case attacks on the original algorithm were discovered).

Finally, the selection of Rijndael as the AES was announced in a press release on 2 October 2000 and followed by the publication of FIPS 197 on 26 November 2001 (NIST, 2001). The security of all the finalists had been judged to be adequate. In general, the choice of Rijndael can be traced to the simplicity of the operations it requires and the byte orientation of those operations. These led to relatively high execution efficiency both in software and hardware, although the extensive use of memory tables results in a relatively large silicon area among the finalist

Table 1 The Original AES Candidates

Cryptosystem	Submitter(s)
CAST-256	Entrust (Canada)
Crypton	Future Systems (KR)
DEAL	Outerbridge and Knudsen (U.S.A. and Denmark)
DFC	ENS-CNRS (France)
E2	NTT (Japan)
Frog	TecApro (CR)
HPC	Schroeppel (U.S.A.)
LOKI97	Brown et al. (Australia)
Magenta	Deutsche Telekom (Germany)
MARS	IBM (U.S.A.)
RC6	RSA (U.S.A.)
Rijndael	Daemen and Rijmen (Belgium)
SAFER+	Cylink (U.S.A.)
Serpent	Anderson, Biham, Knudsen (UK, Israel, Denmark)
Twofish	Counterpane (U.S.A.)

algorithms. Finally, Rijndael as proposed incorporated the variations in key and block size beyond the original specifications for AES that would be needed in a flexible algorithm.

References

The best overall reference for AES as it has been adopted is probably the book by the AES inventors, Joan Daemen and Vincent Rijmen (2001). We have relied heavily on this reference in our description of AES. A NIST Web site points to its standards information on cryptographic matters (2003a); this Web site contains pages specifically on AES, the FIPS, and the process by which the standard was adopted (2001, 2003b). A number of additional Web sites contain links to articles describing implementations as well as attacks (Courtois, 2004).

AES and Rijndael

The original cipher proposed by Daemen and Rijmen was named Rijndael as a word created from the surnames of the authors. As is pointed out in their book (2001), the only difference between the the original Rijndael algorithm and the AES algorithm as selected is that the Rijndael algorithm can be used with a number of block lengths and a number of key lengths, but the AES, as a standard, fixes the block length at 128 bits and the key lengths at 128, 192, or 256 bits.

The only other distinction to be noted is in the labeling of the transformations of AES. We follow the labeling of the FIPS and of the inventors' book (Daemen & Rijmen, 2001) and not that of the original submission of Rijndael to the AES competition. For example, the original submission referred to a `ByteSub` and a `ShiftRows` transformation, and the FIPS now refers to `SubBytes` and `ShiftRows`.

BACKGROUND MATHEMATICAL CONCEPTS
Galois Field Arithmetic

The AES makes extensive use of arithmetic in the *finite field*, or *Galois field*, $GF(2^8)$ of $2^8 = 256$ elements. A background in finite field arithmetic can be found in Chapter 110 of these volumes. We do not attempt here to cover the theory of finite fields, but we do describe the computational structure of these fields as that structure is needed to understand AES.

For pedagogical purposes, we consider first $GF(2^3)$, a finite field of eight elements. Such a field can be realized using modular polynomial arithmetic and the primitive irreducible polynomial $x^3 + x + 1$. Consider the eight polynomials in an indeterminate x of degree less than or equal to 2 and with coefficients either 0 or 1:

$$GF(2^3) = \{0, 1, x, x + 1, x^2, x^2 + 1, x^2 + x, x^2 + x + 1\}.$$

We create a finite field of these eight polynomials by providing them with an *addition* operation as follows:

$$(a_2x^2 + a_1x + a_0) + (b_2x^2 + b_1x + b_0) = (a_2 \; XOR \; b_2)x^2 + (a_1 \; XOR \; b_1)x + (a_0 \; XOR \; b_0)$$

and a *modular multiplication* operation as follows:

$$(a_2x^2 + a_1x + a_0) * (b_2x^2 + b_1x + b_0) \equiv (a_2 \; AND \; b_2)x^4$$
$$\times [(a_1 \; AND \; b_2) \; XOR \; (a_2 \; AND \; b_1)]x^3$$
$$+ [(a_0 \; AND \; b_2) \; XOR \; (a_1 \; AND \; b_1) \; XOR \; (a_2 \; AND \; b_0)]x^2$$
$$+ [(a_0 \; AND \; b_1) \; XOR \; (a_1 \; AND \; b_0)]x$$
$$+ (a_0 \; AND \; b_0) +$$
$$\equiv c_4x^4 + c_3x^3 + c_2x^2 + c_1x + c_0 \pmod{x^3 + x + 1}.$$

The arithmetic modulo the polynomial $x^3 + x + 1$ proceeds as if we had the following equation:

$$0 = x^3 + x + 1.$$

If this were true, and once we have defined addition as above as a coefficient-wise XOR operation, we can add x^3 to both sides of the equation to get the following:

$$x^3 = x^3 + x^3 + 1 + x = (1 \; XOR \; 1)x^3 + x + 1 = x + 1.$$

We use this identity recursively if necessary to reduce the degree of a polynomial by two with every application. The modular reduction of the product polynomial above thus becomes the following:

$$c_4x^4 + c_3x^3 + c_2x^2 + c_1x + c_0$$
$$\equiv c_4(x^2 + x) + c_3(x + 1) + c_2x^2 + c_1x + c_0$$
$$\equiv (c_2 \; AND \; c_4)x^2 + (c_1 \; AND \; c_3 \; AND \; c_4)x + (c_0 \; AND \; c_3) \pmod{x^2 + x + 1}$$

$+$	0	1	x	$x+1$	x^2	x^2+1	x^2+x
0	0	1	x	$x+1$	x^2	x^2+1	x^2+x
1	1	0	$x+1$	x	x^2+1	x^2	x^2+x+
x	x	$x+1$	0	1	x^2+x	x^2+x+1	x^2
$x+1$	$x+1$	x	1	0	x^2+x+1	x^2+x	x^2+1
x^2	x^2	x^2+1	x^2+x	x^2+x+1	0	1	x
x^2+1	x^2+1	x^2	x^2+x+1	x^2+x	1	0	$x+1$
x^2+x	x^2+x	x^2+x+1	x^2	x^2+1	x	$x+1$	0
x^2+x+1	x^2+x+1	x^2+x	x^2+1	x^2	$x+1$	x	1

Figure 1: Addition table for $GF(2^3)$ arithmetic.

Thus, for example, we define the product of $x^2 + x + 1$ and $x^2 + x$ to be the following:

$$(x^2 + x + 1) * (x^2 + x) \equiv x^4 + x^3 + x^2 + x^3 + x^2 + x$$
$$\equiv x^4 + (1 \; AND \; 1)x^3 + (1 \; AND \; 1)x^2 + x$$
$$\equiv x^4 + x \equiv x(x + 1) + x \equiv x^2 + x + x$$
$$\equiv x^2 + (1 \; AND \; 1)x \equiv x^2 \quad (\bmod \; x^3 + x + 1). \qquad (1)$$

The reader can verify that the addition and multiplication tables for this arithmetic are given in Figures 1 and 2.

We observe that the following conditions for this arithmetic to make $GF(2^8)$ into a field are true:

- The addition and multiplication are commutative. That is, for all $p, q \in GF(2^3)$ we have the following:

$$p + q = q + p \quad \text{and} \quad p * q = q * p.$$

- There is an additive identity, namely the polynomial 0, such that

$$0 + p = p + 0 = p$$

holds for all $p \in GF(2^3)$.

- For every $p \in GF(2^3)$, there is an additive inverse, which we shall write $-p$, such that

$$p + (-p) = (-p) + p = 0.$$

We note that the additive inverse of a polynomial p is in fact p itself. This follows from the use of the coefficientwise XOR for polynomial addition in this field.

- There is a multiplicative identity, namely the polynomial 1, such that

$$1 * p = p * 1 = p$$

holds for all $p \in GF(2^3)$.

- For every $p \in GF(2^3)$, there is a multiplicative inverse, which we shall write p^{-1}, such that

$$p * p^{-1} = p^{-1} * p = 1.$$

- Multiplication distributes over addition.
- The seven nonzero polynomials of $GF(2^3)$ can be generated as the powers of a single polynomial, which for this field can be taken to be x, so that the set of powers

$$\{x^i \quad (\bmod \; x^2 + x + 1) \quad | \quad 1 \le i \le 7\}$$

is the full set of seven distinct nonzero polynomials of $GF(2^3)$. (This fact is crucial to doing fast arithmetic for AES.)

The Galois Field *GF*(2⁸) and AES

The above example used a polynomial of degree three to create a finite field of $2^3 = 8$ elements. For AES, we use the following polynomial:

$$m(x) = x^8 + x^4 + x^3 + x + 1$$

of degree eight and thus create a finite field of $2^8 = 256$ elements. Except for the level of tedium in computing the addition and multiplication tables, the arithmetic is entirely similar.

What we now note is that we can dispense with the polynomial notation and view the polynomials simply as bit strings, with the 8-bit byte that is the bit string $b_7 b_6 b_5 b_4 b_3 b_2 b_1 b_0$ being used as a shorthand notation for the degree-seven polynomial

$$b_7 x^7 + b_6 x^6 + b_5 x^5 + b_4 x^4 + b_3 x^3 + b_2 x^2 + b_1 x^1 + b_0 x^0$$

that is an element of the finite field of 256 elements defined by $m(x)$.

$*$	1	x	$x+1$	x^2	x^2+1	x^2+x	x^2+x+
1	1	x	$x+1$	x^2	x^2+1	x^2+x	x^2+x+
x	x	x^2	x^2+x	$x+1$	1	x^2+x+1	x^2+1
$x+1$	$x+1$	x^2+x	x^2+1	x^2+x+1	x^2	1	x
x^2	x^2	$x+1$	x^2+x+1	x^2+x	x	x^2+1	1
x^2+1	x^2+1	1	x^2	x	x^2+x+1	$x+1$	x^2+x
x^2+x	x^2+x	x^2+x+1	1	x^2+1	$x+1$	x	x^2
x^2+x+1	x^2+x+1	x^2+1	x	1	x^2+x	x^2	$x+1$

Figure 2: Multiplication table for $GF(2^3)$ arithmetic.

The AES makes extensive use of the fact that bit strings can be taken a byte at a time and interpreted in this way as coefficients of polynomials. What is crucial to the performance of AES is that the fact that the nonzero polynomials can be generated as powers of a single polynomial [x in the case of the example above, and $x + 1$ in the case of the field defined by $m(x)$]. This permits us to use the powers of the generator to create a table of logarithms and do multiplication in the Galois field by table lookup. In the case of our example (1) above, we have the following:

$$111 \leftrightarrow x^2 + x + 1 \equiv x^5 \pmod{x^3 + x + 1}$$

and

$$110 \leftrightarrow x^2 + x \equiv x^4 \pmod{x^3 + x + 1}$$

so the product is as follows:

$$(x^2 + x + 1) * (x^2 + x) \equiv x^5 * x^4 \equiv x^9 \equiv x^2$$
$$\pmod{x^3 + x + 1} \leftrightarrow 100,$$

because we know that $x^7 \equiv 1 \pmod{x^3 + x + 1}$.

More Polynomial Arithmetic

As part of the encryption and decryption processes, AES uses groups of four bytes to define polynomials $f(X)$ of degree three in an indeterminate X; each byte is taken to define an element of $GF(2^8)$ that is one of the coefficients of $f(X)$. The AES process then does arithmetic on these polynomials modulo the polynomial $X^4 + 1$. We write these polynomials as follows:

$$a_3 \odot X^3 + a_2 \odot X^2 + a_1 \odot X + a_0$$

and write the coefficients a_i in hexadecimal notation, so a specific coefficient $a_3 = x^5 + x^3 + 1 \leftrightarrow 00101001$ would be written as 29.

Although there is a mathematical basis for these operations, from a computational point of view we can regard this almost as a positional notation for the arithmetic. Because $X^4 \equiv 1 \pmod{x^4 + 1}$, multiplication of a polynomial $f(X)$ by $b \odot X$ modulo $X^4 + 1$ is really a coefficientwise multiplication by b in $GF(2^8)$ and a left circular shift of the coefficients as follows:

$$(b \odot X) \cdot (a_3 \odot X^3 + a_2 \odot X^2 + a_1 \odot X + a_0)$$
$$\equiv (b * a_2) \odot X^3 + (b * a_1) \odot X^2$$
$$+ (b * a_0) \odot X(b * a_3) \pmod{X^4 + 1}$$

where the multiplication $*$ of the coefficients takes place in $GF(2^8)$. It is in part to recognize this purely formal nature of these polynomials that we use the $\odot$ symbol for multiplication by the coefficients.

THE ADVANCED ENCRYPTION STANDARD ALGORITHM

This section closely follows the descriptions of Daemen and Rijmen (2001) and of the FIPS (NIST, 2001).

p_0	p_4	p_8	p_{12}
p_1	p_5	p_9	p_{13}
p_2	p_6	p_{10}	p_{14}
p_3	p_7	p_{11}	p_{15}

Figure 3: Byte-by-byte view of the 128 bits of a plaintext block.

The AES is a *key-alternating iterated block cipher*. A *block cipher* is a cipher in which bits are enciphered in blocks. That is, the *plaintext* is broken into equal-sized blocks, and each block is passed through an encipherment process to produce a block of *ciphertext*. In the case of AES, blocks are fixed at 128 bits. An *iterated block cipher* is one in which a fixed encipherment process, usually called a *round*, is applied a number of times to the block of bits. Finally, by *key alternating* we mean that the cipher key is XORed to the *state* (the running version of the block of input bits) alternately with the application of the round transformation.

The input to AES is the *plaintext*, a sequence of blocks of 128 bits each of the message to be encrypted, and the *key*, a block of $K = 128, 192$, or 256 bits, with the size an option of the user. The blocks of plaintext are encrypted using the key to produce a *ciphertext* of blocks of bits of 128 bits each. AES is a *symmetric* cipher, in that the ciphertext produced by plaintext and key is converted back to plaintext using the same key.

Viewed simplistically, AES is almost (but not quite) an outer loop of N_r iterations, each called a *round*, of bit transformations and an inner set of four stages of transformations per round. The current pattern of bits as input to or output from one of these transformations is referred to as the *state*.

The AES plaintext is 128 bits long. AES is strongly byte oriented; if we view the stream of bytes of both plaintext and key as being numbered in increasing order

$$p_0 p_1 \ldots p_{15}$$

and

$$k_0 k_1 \ldots k_{K/8},$$

then the bytes of both plaintext and key are usually viewed as a two-dimensional array in column-major order, shown for the plaintext in Figure 3; the key can be represented similarly.

A key would be arranged in a similar pattern of four rows and $K/32 = 4, 6$, or 8 columns, respectively, for the key lengths of $K = 128, 192$, or 256 bits.

The Outer Structure of the Rounds

The outer structure of AES is shown in Figure 4. For key lengths of $K = 128, 192$, and 256 bits, we use $N_r = 10, 12$, and 14 round transformations, respectively. (Note that the initial specification of Rijndael, as opposed to the adopted version for AES, permits various key lengths and plaintext block lengths and has a specification for N_r that varies accordingly. What we describe here is AES and not the more general Rijndael.)

```
Rijndael(State, CipherKey)
{
  KeyExpansion(CipherKey, ExpandedKey);
  AddRoundKey(State, ExpandedKey[0]);
  for( i = 1; i < Nr; i++)
    Round(State, ExpandedKey[i]);
  FinalRound(State, ExpandedKey[Nr]);
}
```

Figure 4: Outer transformation loop of AES.

The input key is first expanded with the KeyExpansion function to produce a key that is $N_r + 1$ times its original size. The expanded key is then taken in blocks of K bits at a time. One block is added to the state prior to the round iterations, $N_r - 1$ blocks are added in at the end of each of the rounds in the loop, and the final block is added in at the end of the FinalRound transformation. The rounds themselves are shown in Figure 5.

SubBytes

Encryption

The SubBytes step is nonlinear. Indeed, it is the only nonlinear step in AES. Each individual byte $a = a_7a_6a_5a_4a_3a_2a_1a_0$ (written as a string of bits) of the state is subjected (at least conceptually) to a two-stage transformation

$$a \to a^{-1} \text{ in } GF(2^8) \to f(a^{-1})$$

where $y = f(x)$ is the transformation of Figure 6 and the $GF(2^8)$ arithmetic is defined above.

Decryption

For decryption, the inverse operation to SubBytes, called InvSubBytes, is accomplished with the function f^{-1} of Figure 7 followed by a byte inversion in $GF(2^8)$.

The S_{RD} function

A crucial feature of AES is that its predilection for computation on bytes makes for efficient implementation. Although the SubBytes operation is conceptually a Galois field inversion followed by an affine transformation, these two can be combined and implemented with a 256-long table lookup, which is referred to later as the function

```
Round(State, ExpandedKey[i])
{
  SubBytes(State);
  ShiftRows(State);
  MixColumns(State);
  AddRoundKey(State, ExpandedKey[i]);
}

FinalRound(State, ExpandedKey[Nr])
{
  SubBytes(State);
  ShiftRows(State);
  AddRoundKey(State, ExpandedKey[Nr]);
}
```

Figure 5: Round transformations of AES.

$$\begin{pmatrix} 1 & 1 & 1 & 1 & 1 & 0 & 0 & 0 \\ 0 & 1 & 1 & 1 & 1 & 1 & 0 & 0 \\ 0 & 0 & 1 & 1 & 1 & 1 & 1 & 0 \\ 0 & 0 & 0 & 1 & 1 & 1 & 1 & 1 \\ 1 & 0 & 0 & 0 & 1 & 1 & 1 & 1 \\ 1 & 1 & 0 & 0 & 0 & 1 & 1 & 1 \\ 1 & 1 & 1 & 0 & 0 & 0 & 1 & 1 \\ 1 & 1 & 1 & 1 & 0 & 0 & 0 & 1 \end{pmatrix} \times \begin{pmatrix} x_7 \\ x_6 \\ x_5 \\ x_4 \\ x_3 \\ x_2 \\ x_1 \\ x_0 \end{pmatrix} \oplus \begin{pmatrix} 0 \\ 1 \\ 1 \\ 0 \\ 0 \\ 0 \\ 1 \\ 1 \end{pmatrix} = \begin{pmatrix} y_7 \\ y_6 \\ y_5 \\ y_4 \\ y_3 \\ y_2 \\ y_1 \\ y_0 \end{pmatrix}$$

Figure 6: The function $f(x)$ in SubBytes.

S_{RD}. For example, the byte 73 in hexadecimal represents the polynomial in $GF(2^8)$ whose inverse is represented by the byte 85. Computing $f(85)$, we get 8F, which would be stored in the 73_{16} location of the lookup table.

For high level language code or for implementation on any standard processor, this is almost certainly the most efficient approach, because the intraword bit manipulations of Galois inversion and the affine transformation are not supported by CPU instructions. For hardware implementations, implementation of the actual arithmetic is not out of the question, as discussed.

ShiftRows

Encryption

The second stage of the inner loop of AES is the ShiftRows operation. In this stage, the bytes of the four rows of the state are circularly shifted left. Row 0 of the state is not shifted; row 1 is shifted left one byte, row 2 shifted two bytes, and row 3 shifted left circularly by three bytes. A graphical tableau for ShiftRows is as shown in Figure 8.

Decryption

In decryption, the inverse of the ShiftRows step, referred to as InvShiftRows, is simply the appropriate right circular shift of the bytes of the state.

MixColumns

Encryption

In the SubBytes stage, The bits $b_7b_6b_5b_4b_3b_2b_1b_0$ of a byte were viewed as coefficients of a polynomial $b_7x^7 + b_6x^6 + b_5x^5 + b_4x^4 + b_3x^3 + b_2x^2 + b_1x^1 + b_0$ that represented an element of the finite field $GF(2^8)$, and this element was inverted in $GF(2^8)$. In the MixColumns stage, we carry that representation one step further. The four bytes of a column in the state are each viewed as elements of $GF(2^8)$ that are now coefficients of a cubic polynomial. For example, a column of state (with bytes written as two hexadecimal digits)

$$\begin{pmatrix} 0 & 1 & 0 & 1 & 0 & 0 & 1 & 0 \\ 0 & 0 & 1 & 0 & 1 & 0 & 0 & 1 \\ 1 & 0 & 0 & 1 & 0 & 1 & 0 & 0 \\ 0 & 1 & 0 & 0 & 1 & 0 & 1 & 0 \\ 0 & 0 & 1 & 0 & 0 & 1 & 0 & 1 \\ 1 & 0 & 0 & 1 & 0 & 0 & 1 & 0 \\ 0 & 1 & 0 & 0 & 1 & 0 & 0 & 1 \\ 1 & 0 & 1 & 0 & 0 & 1 & 0 & 0 \end{pmatrix} \times \begin{pmatrix} y_7 \\ y_6 \\ y_5 \\ y_4 \\ y_3 \\ y_2 \\ y_1 \\ y_0 \end{pmatrix} \oplus \begin{pmatrix} 0 \\ 0 \\ 0 \\ 0 \\ 0 \\ 1 \\ 0 \\ 1 \end{pmatrix} = \begin{pmatrix} x_7 \\ x_6 \\ x_5 \\ x_4 \\ x_3 \\ x_2 \\ x_1 \\ x_0 \end{pmatrix}$$

Figure 7: The function $f^{-1}(x)$ in InvSubBytes.

B_0	B_4	B_8	B_{12}
B_1	B_5	B_9	B_{13}
B_2	B_6	B_{10}	B_{14}
B_3	B_7	B_{11}	B_{15}

$\rightarrow$

B_0	B_4	B_8	B_{12}
B_5	B_9	B_{13}	B_1
B_{10}	B_{14}	B_2	B_6
B_{15}	B_3	B_7	B_{11}

Figure 8: Byte transformations of the `ShiftRows` step.

1F
3D
5B
79

would be taken to represent the polynomial

$$1\text{F} \odot X^3 + 3\text{D} \odot X^2 + 5\text{B} \odot X + 79$$

with, for example, the last coefficient $79 = 0111\ 1001$ being taken to mean the polynomial

$$0 \times x^7 + 1 \times x^6 + 1 \times x^5 + 1 \times x^4 + 1 \times x^3$$
$$+ 0 \times x^2 + 0 \times x^1 + 1 \times x^0$$

as an element of $GF(2^8)$.

The columns of the state, viewed as polynomials in X with coefficients in $GF(2^8)$, are multiplied by the following:

$$c(X) = 03 \odot X^3 + 01 \odot X^2 + 01 \odot X + 02$$

modulo $X^4 + 1$. The polynomial $c(X)$ is invertible modulo $X^4 + 1$, with inverse

$$d(X) = c^{-1}(X) = 0\text{B} \odot X^3 + 0\text{D} \odot X^2 + 09 \odot X + 0\text{E}.$$

Because this is more complicated than most of the stages of AES, we will go into somewhat more detail. Assume we have the following column of state:

a_3
a_2
a_1
a_0

The multiplication of `MixColumns` is as follows:

$$\left(a_3 \odot X^3 + a_2 \odot X^2 + a_1 \odot X + a_0\right)$$
$$\times \left(03 \odot X^3 + 01 \odot X^2 + 01 \odot X + 02\right),$$

which is rewritten as follows:

$$
\begin{aligned}
X^6 \cdot (&& && && 03 \odot a_3) \\
X^5 \cdot (&& && 03 \odot a_2 & +01 \odot a_3) \\
X^4 \cdot (&& +03 \odot a_1 & +01 \odot a_2 & +01 \odot a_3) \\
X^3 \cdot (03 \odot a_0 & +01 \odot a_1 & +01 \odot a_2 & +02 \odot a_3) \\
X^2 \cdot (01 \odot a_0 & +01 \odot a_1 & +02 \odot a_2 &) \\
X^1 \cdot (01 \odot a_0 & +02 \odot a_1 & &) \\
X^0 \cdot (02 \odot a_0 && &&)
\end{aligned}
$$

and which reduces to the following:

$$
\equiv
\begin{aligned}
X^5 \cdot (&& && 03 \odot a_2 & +01 \odot a_3) \\
X^4 \cdot (&& +03 \odot a_1 & +01 \odot a_2 & +01 \odot a_3) \\
X^3 \cdot (03 \odot a_0 & +01 \odot a_1 & +01 \odot a_2 & +02 \odot a_3) \\
X^2 \cdot (01 \odot a_0 & +01 \odot a_1 & +02 \odot a_2 & +03 \odot a_3) \\
X^1 \cdot (01 \odot a_0 & +02 \odot a_1 &&) \\
X^0 \cdot (02 \odot a_0 &&&)
\end{aligned}
$$

and then to

$$
\equiv
\begin{aligned}
X^4 \cdot (&& +03 \odot a_1 & +01 \odot a_2 & +01 \odot a_3) \\
X^3 \cdot (03 \odot a_0 & +01 \odot a_1 & +01 \odot a_2 & +02 \odot a_3) \\
X^2 \cdot (01 \odot a_0 & +01 \odot a_1 & +02 \odot a_2 & +03 \odot a_3) \\
X^1 \cdot (01 \odot a_0 & +02 \odot a_1 & +03 \odot a_2 & +01 \odot a_3) \\
X^0 \cdot (02 \odot a_0 &&&)
\end{aligned}
$$

and finally to

$$
\equiv
\begin{aligned}
X^3 \cdot (03 \odot a_0 & +01 \odot a_1 & +01 \odot a_2 & +02 \odot a_3) \\
X^2 \cdot (01 \odot a_0 & +01 \odot a_1 & +02 \odot a_2 & +03 \odot a_3) \\
X^1 \cdot (01 \odot a_0 & +02 \odot a_1 & +03 \odot a_2 & +01 \odot a_3) \\
X^0 \cdot (02 \odot a_0 & +03 \odot a_1 & +01 \odot a_2 & +01 \odot a_3),
\end{aligned}
$$

where the reduction is done modulo $X^4 + 1$.

The entire operation on columns of the state can thus be done as a matrix multiplication in $GF(2^8)$:

$$
\begin{pmatrix} b_3 \\ b_2 \\ b_1 \\ b_0 \end{pmatrix}
=
\begin{pmatrix}
03 & 01 & 01 & 02 \\
01 & 01 & 02 & 03 \\
01 & 02 & 03 & 01 \\
02 & 03 & 01 & 01
\end{pmatrix}
\begin{pmatrix} a_3 \\ a_2 \\ a_1 \\ a_0 \end{pmatrix}
$$

Decryption

The inverse to `MixColumns`, called `InvMixColumns`, is a multiplication of the columns by the inverse $d(X)$, all taken modulo $X^4 + 1$. As above, the operation can be condensed into a matrix operation on the columns of state as follows:

$$
\begin{pmatrix} a_3 \\ a_2 \\ a_1 \\ a_0 \end{pmatrix}
=
\begin{pmatrix}
0\text{E} & 0\text{B} & 0\text{D} & 09 \\
09 & 0\text{E} & 0\text{B} & 0\text{D} \\
0\text{D} & 09 & 0\text{E} & 0\text{B} \\
0\text{B} & 0\text{D} & 09 & 0\text{E}
\end{pmatrix}
\begin{pmatrix} b_3 \\ b_2 \\ b_1 \\ b_0 \end{pmatrix}
$$

Key Addition

The key addition step is labeled `AddRoundKey`. Because this is an XOR of bits of the expanded key with the state, the `AddRoundKey` step is its own inverse. The key addition is displayed in Figure 9.

Key Schedule

The key addition steps require significant numbers of bits of key. These bits are obtained from the initial key by an expansion process. Care must be taken, of course, when expanding an input key because the resulting key bits can

p_0	p_4	p_8	p_{12}
p_1	p_5	p_9	p_{13}
p_2	p_6	p_{10}	p_{14}
p_3	p_7	p_{11}	p_{15}

$\oplus$

k_0	k_4	k_8	k_{12}
k_1	k_5	k_9	k_{13}
k_2	k_6	k_{10}	k_{14}
k_3	k_7	k_{11}	k_{15}

$=$

p'_0	p'_4	p'_8	p'_{12}
p'_1	p'_5	p'_9	p'_{13}
p'_2	p'_6	p'_{10}	p'_{14}
p'_3	p'_7	p'_{11}	p'_{15}

Figure 9: `AddRoundkey` operating on the 128 bits of a plaintext block.

contain no more inherent randomness than is present in the initial key prior to the deterministic expansion.

With 10, 12, or 14 rounds in AES, the algorithm will need $128 \times 11 = 1408$, $128 \times 13 = 1664$, or $128 \times 15 = 1920$ bits of key to perform the `AddRoundKey` step. One 128-bit block of key is used prior to the iteration of the rounds, and then additional 128-bit blocks are used for each iteration within the rounds. The key bits are obtained via an `ExpandedKey` function that is applied to the initial key value.

For a version of AES with N_r rounds, the expanded key should be viewed as a two-dimensional array of four rows and $4 \times (N_r + 1)$ columns, which we subscript as $W[0..3][0..4 \times (N_r + 1)]$. If we set N_k to 4, 6, or 8 according as the key length is 128, 192, or 256 bits, then the first $4 \times N_k$ block receives the original key in column-major order as in Figure 10, and the key is then expanded by the application of the recursive function detailed below. Columns of bytes of key are produced recursively:

1. If the column subscript $j \geq N_k$ is neither 0 modulo N_k nor 4 modulo N_k for $N_k = 8$, then we have the following:

$$
\begin{bmatrix} W[0][j] \\ W[1][j] \\ W[2][j] \\ W[3][j] \end{bmatrix} = \begin{bmatrix} W[0][j - N_k] \\ W[1][j - N_k] \\ W[2][j - N_k] \\ W[3][j - N_k] \end{bmatrix} \oplus \begin{bmatrix} W[0][j - 1] \\ W[1][j - 1] \\ W[2][j - 1] \\ W[3][j - 1] \end{bmatrix}
$$

```
KeyExpansion(byte K[4][Nk], byte W[4][Nb*(Nr+1)])
{
  for(j = 0; j < Nk; j++) }
  {
    for(i = 0; i < 4; i++) }
    {
      W[i][j] = K[i][j];
    }
  }

  for(j = Nk; j < Nb*(Nr+1); j++) } /* expansion loop on columns */
  {
    if(0 == j mod Nk) /* if-then for bytes down columns */
    {
      W[0][j] = W[0][j-Nk] XOR S[W[1][j-1]] XOR RC[j/Nk];
      for(i = 1; i < 4 i++)
      {
        W[i][j] = W[i][j-Nk] XOR S[W[i+1 mod 4][j-1]];
      }
    }
    else
    {
      for(i = 0; i < 4 i++)
      {
        W[i][j] = W[i][j-Nk] XOR W[i][j-1];
      }
    } /* end if-then down columns */
  } /* end expansion loop on columns */
} /* end KeyExpansion */
```

Figure 10: Key expansion for 128- or 192-bit keys.

2. If $N_k = 8$ (256-bit keys) and the column subscript j is 4 modulo 8, then we XOR the $(j - N_k)$-th column not with the $(j - 1)$-st column but with the bits obtained by first applying S_{RD} to that column. That is, we have the bit operations below. In this, S_{RD} is the combined $GF(2^8)$ and affine transformation used in `SubBytes`.

$$
\begin{bmatrix} W[0][j] \\ W[1][j] \\ W[2][j] \\ W[3][j] \end{bmatrix} = \begin{bmatrix} W[0][j - N_k] \\ W[1][j - N_k] \\ W[2][j - N_k] \\ W[3][j - N_k] \end{bmatrix} \oplus \begin{bmatrix} S_{RD}(W[0][j - 1]) \\ S_{RD}(W[1][j - 1]) \\ S_{RD}(W[2][j - 1]) \\ S_{RD}(W[3][j - 1]) \end{bmatrix}
$$

3. If the column subscript i is 0 modulo N_k, then we have the bit operations below. In addition to the S_{RD} operation, we have a circular shift down of the bytes of column $j - 1$ before the application of S_{RD} and the XOR in byte 0 of a *round constant RC*, where

$$
\begin{bmatrix} W[0][j] \\ W[1][j] \\ W[2][j] \\ W[3][j] \end{bmatrix} = \begin{bmatrix} W[0][j - N_k] \\ W[1][j - N_k] \\ W[2][j - N_k] \\ W[3][j - N_k] \end{bmatrix}
$$
$$
\oplus \begin{bmatrix} S_{RD}(W[1][j - 1]) \oplus RC[j/N_k] \\ S_{RD}(W[2][j - 1]) \\ S_{RD}(W[3][j - 1]) \\ S_{RD}(W[0][j - 1]) \end{bmatrix}
$$

$$
\begin{aligned}
RC[1] &= x^0 \quad \text{that is, } 01 \\
RC[2] &= x^1 \quad \text{that is, } 02 \\
&\cdots \\
RC[j] &= x^{j-1} \quad \text{in} \quad GF(2^8).
\end{aligned}
$$

The `ExpandedKey[i]` value as used in the pseudocode description of the algorithm refers to columns $N_b \times i$ through $N_b \times (i + 1) - 1$ when viewed as columns or bytes $4 \times N_b \times i$ through $4 \times N_b \times (i + 1) - 1$ taken in column-major order. Thus, key bits are extracted from the `ExpandedKey` in blocks of 128 bits at a time, but the key bits are generated column by column as needed, not necessarily in blocks of 128 bits.

Specifically, for key lengths of 128 or 192 bits, the `ExpandedKey` is created with the function of Figure 10. For key lengths of 256 bits, the `ExpandedKey` is created with the function of Figure 11.

IMPLEMENTATION ISSUES

The AES was designed so that it would perform well on a range of processors, including smart cards with small 8-bit processors, fast standard processors, and even on special purpose hardware. Because the functions of AES are bit manipulations, and because many of these functions are not provided in the instruction set architecture (ISA) of a standard processor, some accommodation for the bit-processing must be made in an implementation on

```
KeyExpansion(byte K[4][Nk], byte W[4][Nb*(Nr+1)])
{
  for(j = 0; j < Nk; j++) }
  {
    for(i = 0; i < 4; i++) }
    {
      W[i][j] = K[i][j];
    }
  }

  for(j = Nk; j < Nb*(Nr+1); j++) } /* expansion loop on columns */
  {
    if(0 == j mod Nk) /* if-then for bytes down columns */
    {
      W[0][j] = W[0][j-Nk] XOR S[W[1][j-1]] XOR RC[j/Nk];
      for(i = 1; i < 4 i++)
      {
        W[i][j] = W[i][j-Nk] XOR S[W[i+1 mod 4][j-1]];
      }
    }
    else if(4 == j mod Nk)
    {
      for(i = 0; i < 4 i++)
      {
        W[i][j] = W[i][j-Nk] XOR S[W[i][j-1]];
      }
    }
    else
    {
      for(i = 0; i < 4 i++)
      {
        W[i][j] = W[i][j-Nk] XOR W[i][j-1];
      }
    } /* end if-then down columns */
  } /* end expansion loop on columns */
} /* end KeyExpansion */
```

Figure 11: Key expansion for 256-bit keys.

a standard processor. Conversely, AES has been designed so that these tweaks are relatively straightforward and so that high performance can be achieved even on relatively low-performance processors.

Just to review the operations necessary, we summarize the operations to be performed:

1. SubBytes: Mathematically, the computation in SubBytes includes the $GF(2^8)$ arithmetic followed by the affine transformation $f(x)$. Computationally, this can all be done by table lookup in a 256-long table and is referred to as the S_{RD} (or sometimes just S) function.
2. ShiftRows: This consists entirely of byte-oriented memory moves of the array of state.
3. MixColumns: Mathematically, the MixColumns operation involves modular polynomial operations using polynomials in X whose coefficients are elements of $GF(2^8)$. Compuationally, the polynomial arithmetic is just byte moves in memory following arithmetic on the coefficients in $GF(2^8)$. In the case of encryption, the coefficient arithmetic is very easy because one needs only to multiply coefficients by 1, x, and $x + 1$. In the case of decryption, the multipliers are more complicated and the arithmetic is thus harder to implement in hardware. In the case of a software implementation, neither is a complicated operation because the multiplication is usually done with a table lookup.
4. AddRoundKey: This operation is simply an XOR of the key for the round and the state.

5. KeyExpansion: Most of the key expansion operations are XORs. The other operation is the application of the S_{RD} function from SubBytes.

Software Implementations

The primary points of concern for any software implementation clearly are three computations:

1. The $GF(2^8)$ arithmetic appearing in several places.
2. The byte-oriented finite field operations in Mix-Columns.
3. The issue of memory storage and/or access for the expanded key bits.

Because AES operates entirely on bytes, we can ignore the XOR operations and the byte movements of the ShiftRows step; there are no operations here that are not well supported by the ISA of a standard processor.

We have already pointed out that the combined Sub-Bytes operation can be done by table lookup with the S_{RD} function. If not for this, then at other points in the computation one will need to be able to do arithmetic in $GF(2^8)$. Fortunately, this can be done with fixed arithmetic steps and does not need complex loops with decisions. The polynomial modulus is as follows:

$$m(x) = x^8 + x^4 + x^3 + x + 1,$$

so we have the following:

$$x \cdot \sum_{i=0}^{7} a_i x^i = \sum_{i=0}^{7} a_i x^{i+1}$$
$$\equiv a_6 x^7 + a_5 x^6 + a_4 x^5 + (a_3 \oplus a_7) x^4 + (a_2 \oplus a_7) x^3$$
$$+ a_1 x^2 + (a_0 \oplus a_7) x^1 + a_7 \pmod{m(x)}.$$

The modulus $m(x)$ is a nine-bit pattern 1 | 00011011. Multiplication of the eight-bit pattern $a_7 a_6 a_5 a_4 a_3 a_2 a_1 a_0$ produces the nine-bit pattern $a_7 | a_6 a_5 a_4 a_3 a_2 a_1 a_0 0$, so in the case that $a_7 = 1$ we XOR the right-hand eight bits with a mask 00011011 to perform the reduction modulo $m(x)$. In software, this can be implemented as a shift left that is possibly followed by an XOR with a mask 00011011. Multiplication by any element of $GF(2^8)$ can be accomplished by breaking that element down into its powers of x (in effect, by using the usual recursive doubling approach), so that the fundamental operation of multiplication by x (a.k.a. 02) is sufficient as a kernel.

One of the reasons for the choice of the polynomial $c(x)$ was that the coefficients 01, 02, and 03 allow for multiplication as a simple operation. Multiplication by 01 is in fact not multiplication; multiplication by 02 is the operation defined above, and multiplication by 03 is multiplication by 02 followed by an XOR. Unfortunately, the coefficients 09, 0B, and 0D, and 0E of the InvMixColumns step are not inherently so simple, if only because the nontrivial entries are more dense and the number of 1-bits greater, making for more bit operations required for the $GF(2^8)$ operation.

Fortunately, as pointed out by Daemen and Rijmen (2001), P. Barreto has observed that the InvMixColumn multiplication is separable into two matrix products as follows:

$$\begin{pmatrix} 0E & 0B & 0D & 09 \\ 09 & 0E & 0B & 0D \\ 0D & 09 & 0E & 0B \\ 0B & 0D & 09 & 0E \end{pmatrix} = \begin{pmatrix} 02 & 03 & 01 & 01 \\ 01 & 02 & 03 & 01 \\ 01 & 01 & 02 & 03 \\ 03 & 01 & 01 & 02 \end{pmatrix} \times \begin{pmatrix} 05 & 00 & 04 & 00 \\ 00 & 05 & 00 & 04 \\ 04 & 00 & 05 & 00 \\ 04 & 04 & 00 & 05 \end{pmatrix}$$

This permits the `InvMixColumns` to be implemented with the following preprocessing step followed by the same multiplication as used in `MixColumns`.

On 32-bit or larger processor platforms, the same intraword operations can be implemented as on 8-bit platforms, but the longer wordlength can be an advantage in that one can handle four-byte columns in a single step.

Software for AES is relatively straightforward to implement, and use of the software features mentioned above mitigates substantially any complexities because of ISA shortcomings. As part of the original AES competition and selection process, it was necessary for reference code for each algorithm to be submitted. Reference code by P. Barreto and V. Rijmen appears in Daemen and Rijmen (2001) and totals fewer than 350 lines of C, including four major tables for lookup of the $GF(2^8)$ arithmetic. Two other versions of reference code can be found at Daemen and Rijmen (2004).

Several authors have reported the processing rate of software implementations of AES. Timings are notoriously quick to become obsolete, and timings are often difficult to compare. Lipmaa reports (2004) 260 cycles (1.437 Gbits/s) for encryption and 257 cycles (1.453 Gbits/s) for decryption, with assembly language programs on a 3.05-MHz Pentium 4 processor and 319 cycles (0.861 Gbits/s) and 344 cycles (0.798 Gbits/s) for encryption and decryption, respectively, with C programs (gcc 3.0.2) on a 2.25-MHz Athlon processor. Other implementations are reported at between 226 and 376 cycles on lesser processors, with the faster implementations being in assembly language and the slower implementations in C or C++. Gladman reports (1999, 2000) similar timings.

It is worth pointing out that the speed of AES in software is somewhat, but not significantly, slower than either DES or triple-DES (Sanchez-Avila, 2001).

Hardware Implementations

The AES was designed so that it might be suitable for smart-card and similar applications. Thus, although software implementations are of interest, the various hardware or programmable-logic implementations of AES are of interest, and in addition to speed, issues of silicon resources and attendant power consumption become relevant. Many of the hardware implementations were done prior to the adoption of Rijndael as the AES, and the articles were published in the AES conference proceedings (NIST, 2000a). A number of these articles provide a comparative analysis of the five finalist algorithms. Some comparisons have also been published in other journals or conferences (Dandalis, 2000).

Hardware implementations of AES have been quite varied, in part because of the varied many different uses to which AES could be put. Many of these implementations

have been specific ASICs or ASIC designs; some have been architectural specifications for a processor that would support AES computations in a "native" mode (Kuo, 2001; Satoh, 2003; Sklavos, 2002). A large number of implementations have been made on field programmable gate arrays (FPGAs) (Chodowiec, 2001, 2003; Fischer, 2001, Gaj, 2001; Jarvinen, 2003; Kancharla, 2003; McLoone, 2001; Standaert, 2003; Weaver, 2002). Some work also continues on algorithmic means by which processing could be sped up under the assumption that one has, in hardware, substantial flexibility in how the bits are manipulated; among these studies are some on the best way by which the Galois Field arithmetic can be supported in hardware (Rudra, 2001).

Finally, there are corporate offerings of AES cores. Companies such as Helion or North Pole Engineering offer a range of AES cores, from tiny ASIC designs to large ASIC designs or FPGA implementations, with a throughput range of tens of megabits per second to claimed best-case rates in the tens of gigabits per second (Helion, 2004; North Pole, 2003).

Hardware implementations, although varied, can generally be said to address one or more of the following questions:

1. If one were designing an ASIC for AES, what design would yield the absolutely the fastest throughput?
2. If one were designing an ASIC for AES, what design would yield the the fastest throughput and use no more hardware than might be available on a smart card?
3. If one were designing an ASIC for AES, what design would yield the the fastest throughput and use no more hardware than might be available on a network interface card?
4. If one were implementing AES on reconfigurable hardware (FPGAs), what design would yield the absolutely the fastest throughput?
5. If one were implementing AES on reconfigurable hardware, what design would yield the the fastest throughput and use no more hardware than might be available on a smart card?
6. If one were implementing AES on reconfigurable hardware, what design would yield the the fastest throughput and use no more hardware than might be available on a network interface card?

The FPGA-based implementations add another dimension to the definition of "best" in that they permit designing an implementation with the look and feel of an ASIC, but they must be placed on specific commercial chips. Where software implementations are constrained by the ISA of the processor, the FPGA implementations are constrained by the size and nature of the FPGA resources. In most instances, the eventual constraint on throughput is not on the AES core but on the bandwidth through the device of which the FPGA is a part (Rudra, 2001).

Further, on either ASICs or FPGAs, there are methods either for improving performance or for decreasing size by rearranging the steps of the algorithm. If hardware size is not an issue, then the iterative loop of the rounds can be unrolled to pipeline the rounds themselves. This should permit increased throughput, at the cost of a latency that will not be noticed in steady state, but which will require hardware for each individual round instead of a single hardware module used repeatedly.

One effect of the loop unrolling is that the number of lookup tables might increase dramatically, because one would prefer to keep the tables physically close to the logic that uses the stored values. To avoid the hardware cost of the $GF(2^8)$ lookup tables, one can perform the arithmetic in hardware; one comparison (Kancharla, 2003) showed a very dramatic decrease in hardware utilization and an increase in speed when this change was made to a design. An additional benefit is that memory access is inherently going to be sequential, working against the parallelism of hardware, and the on-chip memory resources of FPGAs is not sufficient to provide for all the tables needed in a fully unrolled AES design.

Even if the outer loop of rounds cannot be fully unrolled, there is also the possibility in hardware for combining the flow of processing inside the rounds. In general, the larger the hardware circuit to be synthesized by design tools, the more efficient and higher performing the circuit will be (until the circuit is so large that the tools can no longer function properly). Larger designs provide more opportunity for synthesis tools to extract parallelism. Also, breaking a large design into modules often requires signals that must propagate from one module to another to be registered both on output and on input; if multiple modules are synthesized together, then such signals can be dealt without the artificial modularization.

SECURITY—THE FUTURE OF THE ADVANCED ENCRYPTION STANDARD

The primary reason for existence of a cryptographic algorithm is to maintain *confidentiality* of data, that is, to prevent disclosure of data to unauthorized parties. In its simplest application, a user would encrypt a data file so that it could be transmitted "in the clear" without fear that the contents could be read by someone not possessing the key. Conscious user action to encrypt the data can provide the security required, although in a corporate setting the data transmission software could be configured to make this transparent. Either way, the data need only be encrypted and decrypted once per transmission in this end-to-end method, and the management of keys is simplest of all the scenarios because keys need only be distributed to users.

A more complicated setting would exist if the goal were to encrypt the data payloads of individual packets after the transmission process has begun, and if the process of decryption and reencryption were to take place at every link along the path from sender to receiver. Because the number of packets and the number of links would normally each be much larger than the number of files transmitted, and because the process would now have to be completely transparent to the users involved, this situation requires a much higher speed of encryption and decryption. This also requires a much different standard for the integrity of the key distribution process because all the link-to-link connections must be provided with keys.

Regardless of the application, the fundamental question to be addressed with regard to any cryptographic algorithm is, "Is it secure?" The initial attempts at cryptanalysis, done as part of the AES evaluation process, are detailed in the NIST report (Nechvatal et al., 2000). There has been subsequent work attacking AES, and one summary of some of these attacks can be found at Courtois (2004). Courtois and Pieprzyk have shown (2002) that AES can be written as an overdefined system of multivariate quadratic equations and an attack developed on that basis; this approach has also been used by Murphy and Robshaw (2002). As of this writing and according to Courtois, no one has so far shown that this approach will not work, but no one has so far demonstrated by example that it does work.

Courtois is clearly skeptical about AES. In response to the NESSIE (New European Schemes for Signatures, Integrity and Encryption) press release (2003) that states that no weakness has been found in AES (or in 16 other algorithms submitted to the European competition), Courtois argue, "This is simply not true and such a recommendation could have serious consequences." Much more positive, or at least less skeptical, about the status of AES is Landau (2004), who writes, "The cryptography community is a rather contentious lot, but it has been virtually unanimous in its praise of NIST's AES effort and the choice of Rijndael as the Advanced Encryption Standard. This is high praise indeed."

Despite the complaints of Courtois, then, the future of AES seems assured. The NIST Web site (2000b), in the response to a frequently asked question, says that AES "has the potential to remain secure well beyond twenty years." It seems likely, then, that AES will continue to be an approved algorithm for U.S. government use for many years to come.

CROSS REFERENCES

See *Data Encryption Standard (DES); Encryption Basics; Symmetric-Key Encryption*.

REFERENCES

Chodowiec, P., Khuon, P., & Gaj, K. (2001). Fast implementations of secret-key block ciphers using mixed inner- and outer-round pipelining. In *Proceedings of the International Symposium on Field Programmable Gate Arrays* (pp. 940–102). New York: ACM Press.

Chodowiec, P., Khuon, P., & Gaj, K. (2003). Very compact FPGA implementation of the AES algorithm. In C. D. Walter, Ç. K. Koç & C. Paar (Eds.), *Lecture Notes in Computer Science 2779*: *Proceedings, Second International Workshop, Cryptographic Hardware and Embedded Systems* (pp. 319–333). Berlin: Springer-Verlag.

Courtois, N. T. (2004). *Is AES a secure cipher*. Retrieved May 4, 2004, from http://www.cryptosystem.net/aes

Courtois, N. T., & Pieprzyk, J. (2002). Cryptanalysis of block ciphers with overdefined systems of equations. In Y. Zheng (Ed.), *Lecture Notes in Computer Science 2501: Advances in Cryptology—ASIACRYPT 2002* (pp. 267–287). Berlin: Springer-Verlag.

Daemen, J., & Rijmen, V. (2001). *The design of Rijndael: AES, the advanced encryption standard*. Berlin: Springer-Verlag.

Daemen, J., & Rijmen, V. (2004). *Rijndael home page*. Retrieved April 30, 2004, from http://www.esat.kuleuven.ac.be/rijmen/rijndael

Dandalis, A., Prasanna, V. K., & Rolim, J. D. P. (2000). A comparative study of performance of AES final candidates. In Ç. K. Koç & C. Paar (Eds.), *Lecture Notes in Computer Science 1965*: Proceedings of the Second International Workshop, Cryptographic Hardware and Embedded Systems (pp. 125–140). Berlin: Springer-Verlag.

Diffie, W., & Hellman, M. E. (1977). Exhaustive cryptanalysis of the NBS Data Encryption Standard. *Computer*, *10*, 74–84.

Fischer, V., & Drutarovský, M. (2001). Two methods of Rijndael implementation in reconfigurable hardware. In Ç. K. Koç, D. Naccache, & C. Paar (Eds.), *Lecture Notes in Computer Science 2162*: Proceedings of the Third International Workshop, Cryptographic Hardware and Embedded Systems (pp. 77–92). Berlin: Springer-Verlag.

Gaj, K. (2001). *Home page*. Retrieved April 30, 2004, from http://ece.gmu.edu/crypto/rijndael.htm

Gladman, B. (1999). Implementation experience with AES candidate algorithms. In *Proceedings, of the Second AES Candidate Conference*. Rockville, MD: National Institute of Standards and Technology.

Gladman, B. (2000). *Home page*. Retrieved April 30, 2004, from http://fp.gladman.plus.com/

Helger Lipmaa, H. (2004). *AES candidates: A survey of implementations*. Retrieved April 30, 2004, from http://www.tcs.hut.fi/helger/aes

Helion Technologies, Inc. (2004). *AES (Rijndael) cores*. Retrieved April 30, 2004, from http://www.heliontech.com/core2.htm

Jarvinen, K. U., Tommiska, M. T., & Skytta, J. O. (2003). A fully pipelined memoryless 17.8Gbps AES encryptor. In *Proceedings of the International Symposium on Field Programmable Gate Arrays* (pp. 207–215). New York: ACM Press.

Kancharla, P. (2003). *The Advanced Encryption Standard on a reconfigurable computer*. Master's thesis, University of South Carolina.

Kuo, H., & Verbauwhede, I. (2001). Architectural optimization for a 1.82Gbits/sec VLSI implementation of the AES Rijndael algorithm. In Ç. K. Koç, D. Naccache, & C. Paar (Eds.), *Lecture Notes in Computer Science 2162: Proceedings of the Third International Workshop, Cryptographic Hardware and Embedded Systems* (pp. 51–64). Berlin: Springer-Verlag.

Landau, S. (2000a). Standing the test of time: The Data Encryption Standard. *Notices of the American Mathematical Society*, *47*, 341–349.

Landau, S. (2000b). Communications security for the twenty-first century: The Advanced Encryption Standard. *Notices of the American Mathematical Society*, *47*, 450–459.

McLoone, M., & McCanny, J. V. (2001). High performance single-chip FPGA Rijndael algorithm. In Ç. K. Koç, D. Naccache, & C. Paar (Eds.), *Lecture Notes in Computer Science 2162*: Proceedings, Third International Workshop, Cryptographic Hardware and Embedded Systems (pp. 65–76). Berlin: Springer-Verlag.

Murphy, S., & Robshaw, M. (2002). Essential algebraic structure within the AES. In M. Yung (Ed.), *Lecture Notes in Computer Science 2442: Advances in Cryptology—CRYPTO 2002* (pp. 1–16). Berlin: Springer-Verlag.

Nechvatal, J., Barker, E., Bassham, L., Burr, W., Dworkin, M., Foti, J., & Roback, E. (2000). *Report on the development of the Advanced Encryption Standard*. Retrieved April 30, 2004, from http://csrc.nist.gov/CryptoToolkit/aes/round2/r2report.pdf

NESSIE. (2003). *NESSIE project announces final selction of crypto algorithms*. Retrieved May 4, 2004, from http://www.cosic.esat.kuleuven.ac.be/nessie/deliverables/press_release_feb27.pdf

NIST. (1998a). *First AES Candidate Conference*. Retrieved April 30, 2004, from http://csrc.nist.gov/CryptoToolkit/aes/round1/conf1/aes1conf.htm

NIST. (1998b). *Second AES Candidate Conference*. Retrieved April 30, 2004, from http://csrc.nist.gov/CryptoToolkit/aes/round1/conf2/aes2conf.htm

NIST. (1999). FIPS 46-3: Data Encryption Standard (Reaffirmed). Retrieved April 30, 2004, from http://csrc.nist.gov/publications/fips/fips46-3/fips46-3.pdf

NIST. (2000a). *Proceedings, The Third Advanced Encryption Standard Candidate Conference*. Retrieved April 30, 2004, from http://csrc.nist.gov/CryptoToolkit/aes/round2/conf3/aes3conf.htm

NIST. (2000b). *Advanced Encryption Standard questions and answers*. Retrieved May 4, 2004, from http://www.nist.gov/public_affairs/releasesaesq&a.htm

NIST. (November 26, 2001). *FIPS 197: Announcing the Advanced Encryption Standard (AES)*. Retrieved April 30, 2004, from http://csrc.nist.gov/encryption/aes/index.html

NIST. (2003a). *Cryptographic toolkit*. Retrieved April 30, 2004, from http://csrc.nist.gov/CryptoToolkit

NIST. (2003b). *AES*. Retrieved April 30, 2004, from http://csrc.nist.gov/CryptoToolkit/aes/index.html

North Pole Engineering, Inc. (2003). *AES core user's manual*. Retrieved April 30, 2004, from http://www.northpoleengineering.com/aescore.htm

Roback, E., & Dworkin, M. (1999). Conference Report: First Advanced Encryption Standard AES Candidate Conference. *Journal of Research of the National Institute of Standards and Technology*, *104*, 97–105.

Rudra, A., Dubey, P. K., Jutla, C. S., Kuman, V., Rao, J. R., & Rohatgi, P. (2001). Efficient Rijndael encryption implementation with composite field arithmetic. In Ç. K. Koç, D. Naccache, & C. Paar (Eds.), *Lecture Notes in Computer Science 2162: Proceedings, Third International Workshop, Cryptographic Hardware and Embedded Systems* (pp. 171–184). Berlin: Springer-Verlag.

Sanchez-Avila, C., & Sanchez-Reillo, R. (2001). The Rijndael block cipher (AES proposal): A comparison with DES. *Proceedings of the 35th IEEE Carnahan Conference on Security Technology* (pp. 229–234). Piscataway, NJ: IEEE.

Satoh, A., & S. Morioka. (2003). Unified hardware architecture for 128-bit block ciphers AES and Camellia. In C. D. Walter, Ç. K. Koç, & C. Paar (Eds.), *Lecture Notes in Computer Science 2779: Proceedings, of the Second International Workshop, Cryptographic Hardware and Embedded Systems* (pp. 304–318). Berlin: Springer-Verlag.

Sklavos, N., & Koufopavlou, O. (2002). Architectures and VLSI Implementations of the AES-proposal Rijndael. *IEEE Transactions on Computers, 51,* 1454–1459.

Stallings, W. (2003). *Cryptography and network security: Principles and practice.* Upper Saddle River, NJ: Pearson.

Standaert, F.-X., Rouvroy, G., Quisquater, J.-J., & Legat, J.-D. (2003). Efficient implementation of Rijndael encryption in reconfigurable hardware: Improvements and design tradeoffs. In C. D. Walter, Ç. K. Koç, & C. Paar (Eds.), *Lecture Notes in Computer Science 2779: Proceedings of the Second International Workshop, Cryptographic Hardware and Embedded Systems* (pp. 334–350). Berlin: Springer-Verlag.

Weaver, N., & Wawrzynek, J. (2002). *High performance compact AES implementations in Xilinx FPGAs.* Retrieved April 30, 2004, from http://www.cs.berkeley.edu/ñweaver/papers/AES_in_FPGAs.pdf

Hashes and Message Digests

Magnus Daum and Hans Dobbertin, *Ruhr University Bochum, Germany*

INTRODUCTION

Modern asymmetric cryptology started with the invention of digital signatures (see Chapter 176, Digital Signatures and Electronic Signatures) in the mid-1970s, when Diffie and Hellman described properties of suitable mathematical mechanisms. Very shortly later Rivest, Shamir, and Adleman made this idea concrete by introducing their famous RSA scheme (see Chapter 111, Public Key Algorithms). Signing and verification in this scheme uses modular exponentiation, which is useful because of its algebraic properties. Conversely, modular exponentiation is relatively slow when applied to the bit sizes needed for RSA to be secure.

To implement digital signature schemes, in practice one needs an additional cryptographic primitive, a so-called (cryptographic) hash function. A hash algorithm computes an output (or hash value), which is a short string of fixed length—say n bits—as a function of the input (message), a bit string of arbitrary length.

In a digital signature scheme, when Alice wishes to sign a message, she hashes the message, signs the hash value with her *private key*, and sends both the message together with the signed hash value to Bob. To verify the signature, Bob also hashes the message (using the same hash function). Conversely, he recovers the hash value of the signed message from the signature using Alice's *public key*. Then he checks whether the two hash values are equal; if they are, the signature is valid (see Figure 1). (The latter applies to schemes such as RSA, whereas the verification in schemes like the NIST standard Digital Signature Standard (DSS); [Federal Information Processing Standard, 186-2, 2000] is a bit different. But a hash function is involved here in the same way.)

The reasons for using a hash function are (1) to save computation time (hash algorithms are significantly faster than asymmetric mechanisms—to be more precise, a hash function not meeting this requirement would be practically useless for real applications) and (2) to save

storage space and time for sending (signing without hashing would, at a minimum, double the size of a message).

Hash functions are nowadays also used in various cryptographic applications. For example, if one needs to preserve the integrity of a long message that is being sent, one can simply compute the hash value of the message and send it in addition to the message. Then, if one is able to preserve the integrity of this much shorter hash value, the receiver can check the integrity of the received message by simply computing the hash value of the received message and comparing it with the received hash value. Hash functions are also used in other cryptographic protocols such as, for example, protocols for payment or for broadcast authentication (see also Chapter 114, Cryptographic Protocols).

This chapter begins with general definitions and remarks. Then we describe some approaches to designing hash functions, and we give a description of general attacks, especially the birthday attack, followed by the main principle of *iterated compression* and the *Merkle–Damgård theorem*.

Almost all hash functions that appear today in practical applications are either in some sense derivatives of the hash function MD4, introduced by Ron Rivest, or in a minor part built from a block cipher by some general method. Therefore, in this chapter we focus on these classes of hash functions. We first present the compression functions of the most important MD4-type hash functions. Then we describe some techniques that were used to attack some of these functions and give an overview of the current status of these hash functions. Finally, we describe the general methods that can be used to construct hash functions from block ciphers and the most important construction of a message authentication code.

Definitions

In general, a hash function is a function that meets two requirements: (1) it is easily computable and (2) it

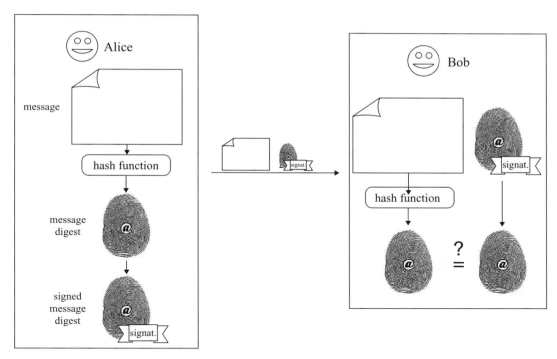

Figure 1: Hashing in a digital signature scheme.

compresses the input to some shorter output (hence the name).

Hash functions are also used in a noncryptographic framework, especially in connection with searching. In this context, a hash function is used to map the key of an object to a memory address at which the object is stored. For these kinds of hash functions it is desirable that collisions (i.e., keys with the same hash value occur very rarely). See Knuth's standard textbook [29] (1998) for more details and examples on this kind of hashing.

In this chapter, we deal with *cryptographic* hash functions. For a cryptographic hash function, the need to avoid collisions is much stricter; it has to be *collision resistant*.

Definition 1 *A hash function h is called* **collision resistant** *if it is computationally infeasible to find a collision, that is, a pair of two different messages X and X' with $h(X) = h(X')$.*

Of course the *existence* of collisions is unavoidable. Because of the compression, on average there are very many preimages to one hash value (i.e., very many messages which map to this hash value). The point is that in fact two such messages cannot be *found*. The reason for this requirement is that Eve could take advantage of a collision as follows (see Figure 2): suppose Eve would be able to produce two messages, X and X', that are mapped to the same hash value and whose contents differ significantly, for example, two contracts about buying something but with very different prices. Then Alice might be willing to sign X, which seems to be quite cheap to her. So Eve asks Alice for her digital signature on this contract and what she receives is not only a valid signature for X but also

for X'. The signature for X is also valid for X', because the verification process only refers to the (common) hash value of X and X'. This means, Eve can replace X by X' and claim that Alice signed X'.

Therefore it makes sense to require that security of a hash function means collision resistance.

Hash functions also occur as components in various other cryptographic applications (e.g., protection of pass phrases) where usually much weaker cryptological requirements are sufficient, namely *preimage resistance* and *second preimage resistance*.

Definition 2 *A hash function h is called*

- **preimage resistant** *if, given a hash value V, it is computationally infeasible to find a message X with $h(X) = V$*
- **second preimage resistant** *if, given a message Y, it is computationally infeasible to find a message $X \neq Y$ with $h(X) = h(Y)$.*

If both conditions (preimage resistance and second preimage resistance) are satisfied, then we say that h is *oneway*. If onewayness is violated, then the cryptographic defect is made even dramatically worse than in the case of a simple violation of collision resistance: Eve does not depend on the cooperation of Alice. If she obtains any message signed by Alice, then she will be able to replace it with a different message.

Let us take a look at some relationships between these properties of hash functions.

Theorem 1 *If h is a collision resistant hash function, then it is also second preimage resistant.*

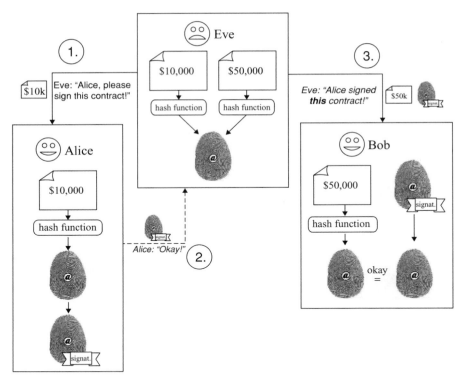

Figure 2: Forging a signature with a noncollision resistant hash function.

This is quite obvious, given the definitions above. Intuitively it seems to be quite clear as well that second preimage resistance implies preimage resistance: If we would be able to find preimages for given hash values than it seems to be clear intuitively that given some message Y with hash value $h(Y)$ it is possible to compute some preimage X that produces the same hash value. For common hash functions with a lot of compression this conclusion should be true, but formally there is some problem with this argument. It is not clear that the messages X and Y are different. This means that formally we can present a function that is second preimage resistant but not preimage resistant.

Example 1
The identity function is obviously not preimage resistant, but as there is only one preimage to each image, it is impossible to find a second message with the same hash value as any other message. Thus the identity function is second preimage resistant as well as collision resistant.

But if we ignore such "pathological" examples of hash functions that do not behave like a random function (what a good hash function should do), then, in fact, collision resistance implies preimage resistance and second preimage resistance.

We must admit that the above notions of collision resistance and onewayness are pragmatic and not formal mathematical definitions. In particular, the question What does *computationally infeasible* mean precisely? depends very much on the context being considered. For

example, computationally feasible may mean in polynomial time (asymptotically) or simple requiring less than some specified bound of computing time or space (e.g., 2^{80} steps).

It is possible to make these definitions more precise by introducing suitable formalisms, but often these definitions are not very useful in practice for the concrete hash functions we can construct today.

DESIGNING HASH FUNCTIONS

The design of hash functions is certainly one of the most difficult problems in cryptography. The difficulty is to find a design that is simultaneously fast and cryptographically strong. To be more precise, one needs to find an appropriate balance between performance and a complexity, which is estimated to be sufficient for collision resistance.

The first decision to make when designing a hash function is to choose the size of the hash values. Of course, for reasons of efficiency, it is desirable to make it as small as possible, but, conversely, it must be sufficiently large that the hash function can be considered collision resistant and (second) preimage resistant.

As mentioned earlier, these terms depend on the context in which the function is considered. But in the community it is well established that in the general case an attack needing at least 2^{80} steps can be considered computationally infeasible, today. To decide whether a certain hash function is secure in this context, one should be aware of possible general attacks on hash functions. The most important of these attacks is the Birthday attack.

Birthday Attack

The term *birthday attack* stems from the so-called birthday paradox. Strictly speaking this is not a true paradox but simply a surprising fact.

Fact 1 (Birthday Paradox) *In a group of 23 persons, the probability that 2 of them share the same birthday is greater than 50%.*

At first glance, the number of people required for this probability is surprisingly low. However, it can be confirmed as follows: For two persons, the chance that they share the same birthday is 1/365 (we are simplifying a little by ignoring leap years and other irregularities). Thus, the probability that they have different birthdays is $1 - 1/365 = 364/365$. Given that the first two persons have different birthdays, there are 363 "possible birthdays" left for a third person such that all three of them have different birthdays (i.e., the chance for this to happen is $364/365 \times 363/365$). A fourth person adds another factor of 362/365 to this probability and so on. This argument shows that, for k people, the probability that they all have different birthdays is as follows:

$$\frac{364}{365} \times \frac{363}{365} \cdots \cdots \frac{366 - k}{365} = \prod_{i=0}^{k-1} \frac{365 - i}{365} .$$

Hence, the probability that two of these k people share the same birthday is as follows:

$$1 - \prod_{i=0}^{k-1} \frac{365 - i}{365} .$$

Computing these values for 22 and 23 people, respectively, shows that the corresponding probabilities are approximately 47.6 and 50.7%, respectively (i.e., 23 is the smallest number of people for which the probability of two people in a group of k people having the same birthday is greater than 50%).

Another approach of understanding why the *birthday paradox* is not as surprising as it seems at first glance, is the following argument: The number of possible pairs of persons (and therefore possible instances of having the same birthday) is as follows:

$$\binom{23}{2} = \frac{23 \times 22}{1 \times 2} = 253$$

in this case. Considering the fact that the probability for each of these pairs for being of composed of two persons sharing the same birthday is 1/365, this result seems much less surprising.

In fact, for 30 people the probability of two of these people sharing the same birthday is greater than 70%, and, for more than 60 people, one can be almost sure, because then the probability is greater than 99%.

We give a precise analysis for a more general form of the paradox, stating the following:

Theorem 2 (Generalized Birthday Paradox) *Given a set of t pairwise distinct elements ($t \geq 10$), the probability that in a sample of size $k > 1.2\sqrt{t}$ (drawn with repetition) there are two equal elements is greater than $\frac{1}{2}$.*

Proof.

Let P be the probability that all k chosen elements are distinct. Then by analogy with the above argument, this probability is as follows:

$$P = \prod_{i=0}^{k-1} \frac{t - i}{t} = \prod_{i=0}^{k-1} \left(1 - \frac{i}{t}\right) = \frac{t!}{t^k(t - k)!} .$$

This is because, after drawing i elements, there are $t - i$ (of t) elements that can be drawn without producing two equal elements. Because $e^x \geq x + 1$, for all x, it holds that (with $x = -\frac{i}{t}$)

$$P \leq \prod_{i=0}^{k-1} e^{-\frac{i}{t}} = e^{\sum_{i=0}^{k-1} -\frac{i}{t}} = e^{-\frac{1}{t}\binom{k-1}{2}} = e^{-\frac{k(k-1)}{2t}} .$$

For $k > 1.2\sqrt{t}$ and thus $k > \frac{1}{2}(1 + \sqrt{1 + 8t \log 2})$ (for $t \geq 10$), it follows that

$$e^{-\frac{k(k-1)}{2t}} < e^{-\frac{\frac{1}{2}(\sqrt{1+8t \log 2}+1)\frac{1}{2}(\sqrt{1+8t \log 2}-1)}{2t}} = e^{-\frac{\frac{1}{4}(1+8t \log 2-1)}{2t}}$$
$$= e^{-\log 2} = \frac{1}{2}$$

and thus $P < \frac{1}{2}$, which means that the probability $1 - P$ that there are two equal elements is greater than $\frac{1}{2}$.

For cryptographic applications, it is more convenient to consider the following corollary:

Corollary 1 (Generalized Birthday Paradox; "Collision Version")

Suppose that $F : \mathcal{X} \to \mathcal{Y}$ is a random function where $\mathcal{Y}$ is a set of t values. Then one can expect to find a collision after about $\sqrt{t}$ evaluations of F.

It is interesting to notice that the number of evaluations mentioned in the corollary is some kind of "worst case" (for the attacker): If there was some bias in the considered function, that is, it is more probable that some value Y_1 is hit than some other value Y_2, then the expected number of required evaluations would decrease. For example, consider the extreme case that all the values from $\mathcal{X}$ are mapped to only one value in $\mathcal{Y}$. Then a collision will be found after evaluating F exactly twice, independent of the size of $\mathcal{Y}$.

Thus it is an important requirement for a hash function that it maps to all possible hash values with (nearly) the same probability.

An n-bit hash function can take on 2^n values. Thus after computation of hash values of about $2^{n/2} = \sqrt{2^n}$ messages we expect to find a collision.

Important research is addressing the problem of how to implement, practically, a collision search using the birthday paradox or variants of it. There are two questions that arise when implementing such an attack in practice: (1) Is it possible to construct a collision between *meaningful* messages? and (2) How can one actually *find* the collision (without having to do about 2^n comparisons)?

The answer to the first question is "yes"; the idea (Yuval, 1979) is the following: starting from two messages,

X_1 and X_2, whose hash values one wishes to collide, one produces about $2^{n/2}$ variants of each of these messages, having the same content. This seems to be impractical, but can be done easily by finding $n/2$ independent positions, in which the actual code of the text can be changed, without changing its contents, for example, by using synonymyous expressions, exchanging tabs for spaces (or vice versa), adding some blank lines and so on. Then, by a reasoning very similar to that of the birthday paradox, there is a good chance that there are two messages, X_1' (a variant of X_1) and X_2' (a variant of X_2), that generate the same hash value.

But the second question still holds: how to actually *find* those messages. Clearly, it is not a good idea to compare the hash values of all X_1 variants with those of all X_2 variants, as then about 2^n comparisons would be required. Yuval's answer to this is to first compute the hash values of all X_1 variants and to store them in some data structure, allowing inserting and finding elements in constant time. This is possible in practice, for example, using a "hash table" (see [29], Kunth, 1998 not to be confused with cryptographic hashing that is the subject of this chapter). With such a data structure it is possible [in time $O(2^{n/2})$] to check for all X_2 variants whether there is an X_1 variant with the same hash value.

The problem here is that the hash values of $2^{n/2}$ variants of X_1 need to be stored. Usually practical bounds on space are much stricter than on computing time, that is, if n is that large that a computing time of $2^{n/2}$ can only be considered *just* feasible, then the required storage space is too large to be feasible. For example, currently, a computing time of 2^{64} steps may be considered feasible by using extreme parallelization, but a required memory of 2^{64} bytes ($= 2^{34}$ GB $\approx$ 17 billion GB) is far beyond our current capabilities.

However, the required space can be reduced to "almost nothing," using an idea primarily known from Pollard's ρ-method for factorizing integers. Generally, this method works with a function f mapping some set onto itself and looks at sequences that are recursively defined by the following:

$$h_i := f(h_{i-1}).$$

As long as the set on which this function is defined, is finite, at some point this sequence will run into a loop, that is, there are natural numbers m, p with $h_m = h_{m+p}$. From that moment on the sequence behaves periodically, that is,

$$h_{m+l} = h_{m+l+kp}$$

for all $l, k \geq 0$. This is the reason for calling this method the ρ-method (see Figure 3).

In the following, let m be the minimal number with $h_m = h_{m+p}$. Then additionally (and most important), as long as $m > 1$, this also gives a collision: As m is defined to be minimal with $h_m = h_{m+p}$, we have the following:

$$h_{m-1} \neq h_{m-1+p},$$

but

$$f(h_{m-1}) = h_m = h_{m+p} = f(h_{m-1+p}).$$

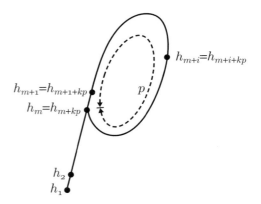

Figure 3: The ρ in Pollard's ρ-method.

To apply this method to find collisions in hash functions, the function f is defined on the set of all the hash values of all variants of X_1 and X_2 in the following way: It first maps an arbitrary hash value to one of the variants and then computes the hash value of this message. For usual hash functions we can assume that they behave (nearly) randomly and thus also this mapping f can be assumed to be a (nearly) random function. Hence, it is very probable that the cycles we find for this function, have $m > 1$ and thus directly lead to a collision.

The crucial observation (Floyd) is, that one needs to store only very few values to detect such cycles: Start with the pair (h_1, h_2) and iteratively compute the pairs (h_i, h_{2i}) until one finds a pair with $h_i = h_{2i}$. If p and m from above are minimal, the first time such a pair occurs is, when $i = p(\lceil \frac{m}{p} \rceil + 1)$ (i.e., for some $m \leq i \leq m + p$). From the generalized birthday paradox we can expect $m + p$ to be of order $O(2^{n/2})$, which means we essentially need to compute $O(2^{n/2})$ hash values to find a collision, but we must store only the current pair of hash values. For more details on implementation issues in connection with collision searching (see, e.g., van Oorschot & Wiener, 1999).

Meet-in-the-Middle Attack

Another kind of attack similar to the birthday attack is the "meet-in-the-middle" attack. This method does not attack collision resistance, but (second) preimage resistance, and is able to find (second) preimages in a time similar to that of the birthday attack.

However, it is not as general as the birthday attack because it cannot be applied to arbitrary hash functions but only to a certain class of "weak" hash functions: if one can fix some inner point in the computation of the hash value where some intermediate value is computed, such that the second part of the computation can be reversed (i.e., one can compute backward from the hash value to the intermediate value) and the inputs determining the computations in the two parts can be chosen independently, then the hash function is subject to a meet-in-the-middle attack.

The attack works as follows (very similar to Yuval's birthday attack): suppose the intermediate value has bit size n. Then generate $2^{n/2}$ initial parts (or "first halves") of messages X_1 (or, rather, as in the birthday attack, variants of some initial part of some fixed message) that can serve as input for the first part of the computation and generate $2^{n/2}$ endings (or "second halves") of messages X_2 for the second part of the computation. Then one obtains two sets of intermediate values, one set by computing from the beginning using the X_1's as inputs and one set by computing backward from some fixed hash value to the intermediate value using the X_2's as inputs. Similar to the argument used for the birthday attack after computing this many intermediate values one can expect to find a collision (i.e., one inital part X_1' and one ending X_2' that produces the same intermediate value). At this point, the concatenation of these two message parts gives a message whose hash value is the desired one.

Because such intermediate values in the computation usually have the same bit length as the hash value, this shows that, with an effort similar to that of finding collisions with the birthday attack (second) preimages can be computed (as long as the hash function is subject to this kind of attack). Note that the conclusion is *not* that computing preimages is as easy as finding collisions but that when designing a hash function, one has to ensure that the design is not subject to this kind of attack.

In general, these attacks show that, to prevent an attacker from finding collisions using a birthday attack, n should be large enough such that computing $2^{n/2}$ hash values is computationally infeasible. As mentioned earlier, today $n = 160$ is still considered to be sufficient, but recognizing the rapid increases in computing power suggests that one should consider using a larger value of n even today.

Hashing by Iterated Compression

All the hash functions we described in the rest of this chapter follow a certain design principle proposed by Merkle and Damgård (1990). The basic idea is that hashing, like encryption, should be done blockwise. The Merkle–Damgård principle defines how a hash function h with n-bit hash values can be built up from a compression function f—loosely speaking, a "small hash function." We assume that the computation of f is initialized by n-bit vectors, that f compresses input blocks of fixed size, say r bits, and returns n-bit outputs. (In particular, we have $n = 128$ and $r = 512$ for MD4 and MD5.) In the following, we denote the compression function f initialized with the value IV (initial value) by f_{IV}.

To be able to apply the Merkle–Damgård principle, we first must pad the message such that its length is a multiple of r. This can be done in different ways, for example, by simply appending some zeroes, but this would allow some special attacks (see, for example, Menezes, van Oorschot, & Vanstone, 1996, Remark 9.32). To avoid these attacks, it is necessary to at least append some block to the message during the padding that contains the binary representation of its original bit length.

Suppose that, after appropriate padding, a given message M is split into a sequence of s blocks of length r as follows:

$$M = M^{(1)}M^{(2)}\ldots M^{(s)}.$$

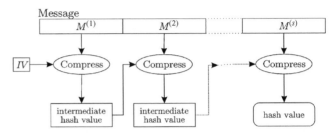

Figure 4: Merkle–Damgård principle, hashing by iterated compression.

The hashing process is initialized with some fixed n-bit initial value IV^*, which is a part of the specification of the hash algorithm. The hash value of M is then computed by an iterative application of f, where the $M^{(i)}$ are taken as inputs and each output of f is the initial value for the next application of f as follows:

$$H_0 := IV^*,$$
$$H_i := f_{H_{i-1}}(M^{(i)}), \quad i = 1, \ldots, s.$$

The hash value of M is defined to be the last output of the compression function f as follows:

$$h(M) := H_s.$$

Clearly, this general design principle can easily fall victim to a meet-in-the-middle attack, if the compression function is poorly designed: a meet-in-the- middle attack can be initiated if the compression function is invertible, in the sense that the initial value IV can be easily computed from the input message block $M^{(i)}$ and the output $f_{IV}(M^{(i)})$. Then one can simply choose some point between any two applications of the compression function as the collision point, and the corresponding intermediate hash value as the intermediate value needed in the meet-in-the-middle attack. This means, when designing a hash function using the Merkle–Damgård principle, it is important to avoid such poorly behaved compression functions. In many practical designs, this problem is solved by including some "feed-forward." This means at the end of the computation the IV used at the beginning of the computation is used again such that when computing backwards one would have to know the result in advance.

Using this common design principle, the hash functions considered in this chapter mainly differ in the compression function they use (in addition to different choices for some parameters). But before we can move on to the description of these different compression functions under Compression in MD4-like hash functions, we first need to discuss in more detail the term *collision*, in the context of the compression function ("Collisions and Pseudocollisions of the Compression Function"), and the relationship between collision resistance and the discrete log problem (Collision Resistance and the Discrete Log Problem).

Collisions and Pseudocollisions of the Compression Function

Suppose we have an iterated hash function h based on a compression function f. As the output $f_{IV}(M^{(i)})$ of the compression function actually has two inputs or at least depends on two parameters, the input message block $M^{(i)}$ and the initial value IV, we need to clarify the term *collision*.

A *collision* of the compression function consists of *one* initial value IV and two different inputs X and X' such that

$$f_{IV}(X) = f_{IV}(X').$$

It is important to observe that an attack leading to collisions of the compression function is already very close to collisions for the hash function. What remains is to extend the attack in a way that it is possible to prescribe the initial value above as the initial value IV^* of the hash algorithm.

Loosely speaking, we can state that collisions of the compression function are (instances of) collisions of the hash function with a wrong initial value.

Conversely, we use the more general term *pseudocollision* of the compression function if two initial values IV, IV' and inputs X, X' are given such that

$$f_{IV}(X) = f_{IV'}(X') \quad \text{and} \quad (IV, X) \neq (IV', X').$$

Thus we allow different initial values here.

The fundamental theoretical result of the Merkle–Damgård construction (hashing by iterated compression) is as follows:

Theorem 3 (Merkle–Damgård Theorem) *If the compression function f is pseudocollision resistant, then the derived hash function h is collision resistant.*

For a proof of this theorem, see Section 10 of Buchmann, 2002.

Unfortunately, we cannot apply this theorem to verify the collision resistance of MD4-like hash functions, either in the positive or in the negative sense. Finding pseudocollisions of f with different initial value does not necessarily imply any hint how to find collisions of h. (We do not have the converse of the Merkle–Damgård theorem.) Conversely, for the reasons discussed above, our present knowledge does not allow us to construct a practical compression function with provable pseudocollision resistance.

In contrast, collisions of the compression function are already close to hash collisions, only the initial value is wrong. Hence, to avoid misinterpretations of cryptanalytic results it is very important to distinguish between collisions and pseudocollisions of the compression function. (*Caution*: some authors call a collision what we call a pseudocollision; see, for instance, den Boer & Bosselaers, 1994.)

Collision Resistance and the Discrete Log Problem

For mathematical terms used in this section, we refer to Chapter 110, Number Theory for Information Security.

Suppose we have a finite cyclic group G generated by an element a as follows:

$$G = \{a^x : x = 0, 1, 2, \ldots, t - 1\},$$

where t is the order of G (i.e., G has t elements). Then the discrete log problem (DLP, see Chapter 111, Public-Key Algorithms) means that, given random $b \in G$, we have to find the integer x, smaller than the order t of G, such that

$$a^x = b.$$

Note that if $a^y = b$ for *any* integer y, then we get x as the remainder of y modulo t.

DLP looks like a preimage problem, for which we would need about t computations of a^x to match b. But DLP can be transformed into a collision-finding problem and can therefore be solved much more efficiently. The reason is that the mapping $x \mapsto a^x$ has a very special property, the "homomorphic" equation:

$$a^{x_1} a^{x_2} = a^{x_1 + x_2}.$$

In fact, we define the functions $E(x) = a^x$ and $F(x) = (a^x b)^{-1}$ for $x = 0, 1, \ldots, t - 1$. By a collision of E and F, we understand a pair of integers x_1, x_2, such that $E(x_1) = F(x_2)$. Such a collision leads to the solution $x = x_1 - x_2 \bmod t$ of $a^x = b$:

$$a^{x_1 - x_2} = E(x_1) F(x_2)^{-1} b = b.$$

Note that, conversely, if we have a solution of $a^x = b$, then x and 0 form a collision of E and F. After computing only about $\sqrt{t}$ many values of E and F, we have a good chance of finding a collision (see "Birthday Attack"). This connection between the DLP and collision detection makes it plausible that, for the following hash function by Chaum, van Heijst, and Pfitzmann, it is possible to show its collision resistance as long as the DLP is believed to be a hard problem:

Definition 3 (Chaum–van Heijst–Pfitzmann hash function) *Suppose q is a large prime, $p = 2q + 1$ is also prime and a, b are primitive elements of Z_p, the ring of integers modulo p. Then the hash function*

$$h : \{0, \ldots, q - 1\}^2 \to \mathbb{Z}_p^x$$

is defined as

$$h(x_1, x_2) = a^{x_1} b^{x_2} \bmod p.$$

Remark. Note that h is not a hash function in the proper sense because it can be applied only to messages of bit length $\leq 2\lceil \log_2 q \rceil$, whereas (in principle) a hash function has to be defined for arbitrarily long messages.

Theorem 4 *The above Chaum–van Heijst–Pfitzmann hash function h is collision resistant if and only if the DLP is solvable in the cyclic group $G = \mathbb{Z}_p \backslash \{0\}$ of integers modulo p, under multiplication.*

For the easy proof of this theorem, we refer to Section 7.4 of the standard cryptography book of Douglas Stinson (1995).

However, the Chaum–van Heijst–Pfitzmann hash function, like RSA, is based on modular arithmetic. Thus it does not meet our requirement of being fast. It remains a significant open challenge to find fast hash functions for which we can prove security, in the sense of collision resistance, relative to a mathematical problem that is believed to be hard.

As long as a solution to this problem is elusive, we must rely on ad hoc designs for practical hash functions. And here it can cause a pitfall to develop a design that allows us to derive a "provable security" in the sense that, for example, all hash values occur with about the same probability. Conversely, from the theoretical point of view it would be nice to have such a property. But experience has shown that we run the risk that the internal structure of such a design that allows us to prove a certain restricted aspect of security could, conversely, turn out to cause other weaknesses. As long as our theoretical knowledge is as limited, as it is today, we believe that, for practical applications, it is better to follow another approach—loosely speaking, trial and error. Proposals are discussed in the cryptographic community. Their analyzes lead to (partial) attacks, and in this way we obtain more insight into how to avoid the observed weaknesses. The survivors of this cryptographical evolution are the candidates for future standards. The design of practical block ciphers, in particular, the competition of candidates for the AES block cipher, is another example of this procedure.

COMPRESSION IN MD4-LIKE HASH FUNCTIONS

The compression functions described in this section have many things in common. They use word sizes of w bits ($w \in \{32, 64\}$) and operate on $4 \leq r \leq 8$ registers that are initalized with an IV (or intermediate hash value) of $r \times w = n$ bits. Then they are modified in 48–80 steps, using some function that depends on the 512 or 1024 bits of the message input. The output of n bits then consists of the final state of the registers, usually after adding the initial value again to include some "feed-forward" (see end of "Hashing by Iterated Compression"). Details on the parameters for certain hash functions can be found in Table 1. A survey of these functions is given in Figure 5.

The description of the compression functions can be split into two parts, the *message expansion*, in which the message is expanded to some longer bit string, which is then used as input to the second part, the *step operations* (compare Figure 6).

Message Expansion

In the message expansion part, the current message block $M^{(i)}$ used as input to the compression function is first split into (usually 16) words M_i. Then, from these M_i, some values W_i are computed, which are later used in the step operation to update the registers.

The compression functions considered here use two different kinds of message expansions to compute the W_i from the M_i, a "roundwise permutation," or some recursive definition.

Roundwise Permutation

Roundwise permutation means that we have some number of rounds (usually 3–5) consisting of as many steps as we have message words M_i (usually 16). Then, in every round, each of the message words is used once, that is, for each round k, we have a permuation σ_k such that $W_{16k+i} = M_{\sigma_k(i)}$.

This kind of message expansion is used in (extended) MD4, MD5, HAVAL, and the RIPEMD variants. Two concrete examples of such permutations are given in Tables 2 and 3.

These tables show that the permutations used are chosen to have "regular irregularities." For example, in the MD5 expansion, the index used in each round is increased by some fixed number (1 in the first round, 5 in the second, and then 3 and 7). These numbers are chosen such that they do not have common divisors, which means that there are only few other patterns in these sequences. There is no real, obvious reason for doing this, but heuristically it seems to be better, that is, harder, to attack if the message blocks are mixed well.

In the RIPEMD family, this is done in an even more systematic way. We describe it here, using the example of RIPEMD-160: first a permutation ρ is defined as in Table 4 and another permutation π is defined by setting $\pi(i) = 9i + 5 \bmod 16$. Table 5 gives the order of the message words.

These permutations were chosen such that there are as few patterns as possible and message words that are close in the left half are at least seven positions apart in the right half, not only within each round, but also between different rounds.

Recursive Message Expansion

Message expansion by recursive definition means that after choosing some starting values (usually $W_i = M_i$, $i = 1, \ldots, 16$) the following W_i are computed recursively from the preceding W_i. This kind of message expansion has the advantage that (nearly) all the W_i depend on (nearly) all the M_i, meaning that if just one of the words of the message is changed, most of the steps in the second phase of the computation are affected. This clearly makes it much harder to control what is happening. This kind of message expansion is typical for the hash functions of the SHA family. In SHA-0, the following recursive definition is used (for notation see Table 6):

$$W_i = W_{i-3} \oplus W_{i-8} \oplus W_{i-14} \oplus W_{i-16}, \quad i \in \{17, \ldots, 80\}.$$

But there is a flaw in this definition: the k-th bit of each word W_i is influenced only by the k-th bits of the preceding W_i. This means that this expansion causes much less diffusion than desireable. For example, the revised version SHA-1 uses the following message expansion that

Table 1 Parameters of Some Hash Functions

	Word Size (in bit)	Registers	Output Length (in bit)	Steps	Reference
MD4	32	4	$4 \times 32 = 128$	$3 \times 16 = 48$	Rivest (1991, 1992a)
Ext. MD4	32	2×4	$8 \times 32 = 256$	2×48	Rivest (1991)
MD5	32	4	$4 \times 32 = 128$	$4 \times 16 = 64$	Rivest (1992b)
HAVAL	32	8	128, 160, 192, 224, 256	$3 \times 32, 4 \times 32, 5 \times 32$	Vaudenay (1995)
RIPEMD-0$^{(*)}$	32	2×4	$4 \times 32 = 128$	2×48	RIPE Consortium (1995)
RIPMED-128	32	2×4	$4 \times 32 = 128$	2×64	Dobbertin et al. (1996)
RIPMED-160	32	2×5	$4 \times 32 = 160$	2×80	Dobbertin et al. (1996)
RIPMED-256	32	2×4	$8 \times 32 = 256$	2×64	Bosselaers Dobbertin et al. (1996)
RIPMED-320	32	2×5	$10 \times 32 = 320$	2×80	Bosselaers Dobbertin et al. (1996)
SHA-0$^{(*)}$	32	5	$5 \times 32 = 160$	80	Federal Information Processing Standard (FIPS) 180 (1993)
SHA-1	32	5	$5 \times 32 = 160$	80	Federal Information Processing Standard (FIPS) 180-2 (2002)
SHA-224	32	8	$7 \times 32 = 224$	64	Federal Information Processing Standard (FIPS)180-2 (2002)
SHA-256	32	8	$8 \times 32 = 256$	64	Federal Information Processing Standard (FIPS) 180-2 (2002)
SHA-384	64	8	$6 \times 64 = 384$	80	Federal Information Processing Standard (FIPS) 180-2 (2002)
SHA-512	64	8	$8 \times 64 = 512$	80	Federal Information Processing Standard (FIPS) 180-2 (2002)

Note: The functions marked by an asterisk have originally been proposed without the "−0" extension. This was added later to avoid confusion.

Table 2 Indices j with $W_{16r+i} = M_j$ in the MD4 Message Expansion

r \ i	0	1	2	3	4	5	6	7	8	9	10	11	12	13	14	15
0	0	1	2	3	4	5	6	7	8	9	10	11	12	13	14	15
1	0	4	8	12	1	5	9	13	2	6	10	14	3	7	11	15
2	0	8	4	12	2	10	6	14	1	9	5	13	3	11	7	15

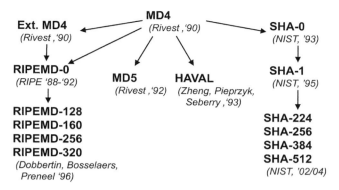

Figure 5: The MD4 family of hash functions.

achieves much more diffusion:

$$W_i = (W_{i-3} \oplus W_{i-8} \oplus W_{i-14} \oplus W_{i-16}) \lll 1, \quad i \in \{17, \dots, 80\}.$$

This means the message expansion of SHA-0 was just supplemented with a rotation by one bit, which causes the bits of these values to be mixed much more than before. In the later SHA versions, NIST decided to mix even more by using not only $\oplus$ and bit rotations but also bit shifts and modular additions in the message expansion. SHA-256 (and thus also SHA-224, which mainly consists in applying SHA-256 and ignoring 32 output bits) uses the following expansion rule:

$$W_i = \sigma(W_{i-2}) + W_{i-7} + \sigma_0(W_{i-15}) + W_{i-16},$$

where

$$\sigma_0(x) := (x \ggg 7) \oplus (x \ggg 18) \oplus (x \gg 3),$$
$$\sigma_1(x) := (x \ggg 17) \oplus (x \ggg 19) \oplus (x \gg 10).$$

Hence, the message expansion is no longer linear. The message expansion of SHA-512 (and SHA-384) is similar but uses 64-bit words and some adjusted σ_0 and σ_1.

Step Operation

The single steps in the compression process of all hash functions of the MD4-family are based on the following operations on words, where a word is a 32-bit (or in some cases 64-bit) quantity:

- Bitwise Boolean operations

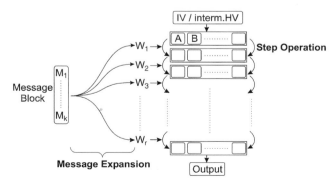

Figure 6: Interaction between message expansion and step operations.

- Addition modulo 2^{32} (or 2^{64}, respectively)
- Bit shifts and rotations

(For the notation of these operations see Table 6.)

These operations have been chosen, because they can be computed very rapidly on modern computer architectures and because the mixing of Boolean functions and addition is believed to be cryptographically strong.

As described earlier, the most distinctive differences between the compression functions described here lie in the different step operations, which describe how the chaining registers are updated. They have in common, that only one or two of the registers are updated in each step, using some function that is a mixture of the basic operations described above.

In the following, we describe some of the important features of each step operation. For details on the definitions of the complete hash functions, consider the references given in Table 1.

MD4

As an example, we take a closer look at the MD4 compression function to illustrate its internal structure. The 512-bit input $M^{(j)}$ and 128-bit initial value IV are split into words. The compression process operates on four word registers (chaining registers) A, B, C, D, which are initialized with IV. The compression algorithm has three rounds each consisting of 16 steps (i.e., in total 48 steps) in which the W_i resulting from the message expansion (see Table 2) are applied.

In every step, one of the chaining registers is updated. A typical step operation of the compression in MD4 is as follows:

$$A := (A + \Phi_i(B, C, D) + W_i + K_i \lll s_i,$$

where Φ_i is a round-dependent, bitwise defined Boolean function, K_i is a step-dependent constant, and the rotation amount s_i is also step dependent. The Boolean functions used in MD4 are as follows:

$$\Phi_i(X, Y, Z) := \text{ITE}(X, Y, Z) := XY \vee \overline{X}Z, \qquad 1 \le i \le 16,$$
$$\Phi_i(X, Y, Z) := \text{MAJ}(X, Y, Z) := XY \vee XZ \vee YZ, \quad 17 \le i \le 32,$$
$$\Phi_i(X, Y, Z) := \qquad\qquad\qquad X \oplus Y \oplus Z, \qquad 33 \le i \le 48.$$

They were chosen, as they have some important properties supporting an "avalanche effect" (this means that small differences in the registers are mapped to large differences after only a few steps). For example, these functions are balanced. Further, if the bits of X, Y, and Z are independent and unbiased, then also each output bit will be independent and unbiased, and last, changing one bit of the inputs changes the output in exactly half of the possible cases.

After processing the three rounds, the compression value is obtained by wordwise addition (modulo 2^{32}) of IV to the chaining registers.

MD5

The design of MD5 is quite similar to that of MD4. In addition to the ITE and the XOR function used in MD4, also the following two Boolean functions are used in MD5,

Table 3 Indices j with $W_{16r+i} = M_j$ in the MD5 Message Expansion

r \ i	0	1	2	3	4	5	6	7	8	9	10	11	12	13	14	15
0	0	1	2	3	4	5	6	7	8	9	10	11	12	13	14	15
1	1	6	11	0	5	10	15	4	9	14	3	8	13	2	7	12
2	5	8	11	14	1	4	7	10	13	0	3	6	9	12	15	2
3	0	7	14	5	12	3	10	1	8	15	6	13	4	11	2	9

which have similar properties:

$$\Phi(X, Y, Z) = XZ \vee Y\bar{Z} = \text{ITE}(Z, X, Y),$$
$$\Phi(X, Y, Z) = Y \oplus (X \vee \bar{Z}).$$

The step operation itself is very similar to that of MD4 with one primary difference: after the rotation, one of the registers is added to get the new register value:

$$A := B + ((A + \Phi_i(B, C, D) + W_i + K_i) \lll s_i).$$

For a visualization of this step operation, see Figure 7.

RIPEMD-128/-160/-256/-320

The most important difference in the compression functions of the RIPEMD functions is that the message is processed in two parallel lines. That means we have two sets of 4 (in RIPEMD-128/-256) or 5 (in RIPEMD-160/-320) registers, which are initialized with the same IVs and updated using the same step operation, but with different constants, different amounts of rotations and, most important—as seen above—different message schedules. After processing the full number of rounds, in the end the results of both lines are then combined together with the IV to produce the output.

The step operation in RIPEMD-128/-256 is the same as in MD4, and in RIPEMD-160/-320, a very similar function

$$A := ((A + \Phi_i(B, C, D) + W_i + K_i \lll s_i) + E$$

is used, in which, at the end, the value of the additional (fifth) register is added to the result. Additionally, in RIPEMD-160/-320, another register in updated in each step, namely $C := C \lll 10$. Of course, these functions, although appearing to be identical or similar to those above (for MD4/MD5), are different in the sense that in some of the steps they use other Boolean functions Φ and other constants for each step. For details on this, see Dobbertin, Bosselaers, and Preneel (1996).

The larger-sized functions RIPEMD-256 and RIPEMD-320 differ from their smaller brothers mainly at the end. Apart from some additional interaction between the two parallel lines, the only difference is, that in the end in RIPEMD-128/-160 the values of the register are added to-gether, whereas in RIPEMD-256/-320, the values are just concatenated to produce a longer output. For details on this, see Bosselaers and Dobbertin et. al. (1996).

SHA-0/1

In SHA-1 (and also formerly in SHA-0), the step operation is very similar to those above, just that the shift now uses a fixed value and operates only on one register instead of some intermediate result:

$$A := (A \lll 5) + \Phi_i(B, C, D) + E + W_i + K_i.$$

The Φ_i are some of those also used in MD4 and MD5 (see above) and again (as in RIPEMD-160) one additional register is updated in each step by rotating it, in this case by 30 bits. For a visualization of this step operation, see Figure 7.

SHA-224 and SHA-256

First of all, for these two hash functions notice that they are nearly identical or rather that SHA-224 is merely a shortened SHA-256. To compute a SHA-224 hash value, one performs exactly the same steps as for a SHA-256 hash value, but simply using another IV, and in the end, one truncates the output by using only the leftmost 224 bits. This is done to offer a bigger variety of standarized sizes of hash values because hash functions are usually only a building block in some bigger cryptographical protocol and often the size of the hash value is determined by the surrounding protocol.

For these two functions, the complexity of the step operation is increased by using two mechanisms, by using more (eight) registers, and by using a more complex step function. In each step, first two auxiliary values are computed as

$$T_1 := H + ((E \ggg 6) \oplus (E \ggg 11) \oplus (E \ggg 25)) + \text{ITE}(E, F, G) + W_i + K_i,$$
$$T_2 := ((A \ggg 2) \oplus (A \ggg 13) \oplus (A \ggg 22)) + \text{MAJ}(A, B, C),$$

and then two of the registers are updated with $E = D + T_1$ and $A = T_1 + T_2$. Here it is interesting to note that all 64 steps of the compression function use the same Boolean

Table 4 Permutation Used in the Message Expansion of RIPEMD-160

i	0	1	2	3	4	5	6	7	8	9	10	11	12	13	14	15
$\rho(i)$	7	4	13	1	10	6	15	3	12	0	9	5	2	14	11	8

Table 5 Permutations Used in the Message Expansion of RIPEMD-160

Line	Round 1	Round 2	Round 3	Round 4	Round 5
left	id	ρ	ρ^2	ρ^3	ρ^4
right	π	$\rho\pi$	$\rho^2\pi$	$\rho^3\pi$	$\rho^4\pi$

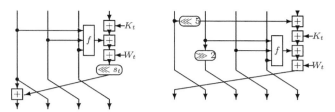

Figure 7: Step operations of MD5 (left) and SHA-0/1 (right).

function and differ only in the constant K_i and the message block W_i.

A consequence of this new, more complex, step operation is that it is slightly slower to compute than the ones described earlier, but it should also be much harder to cryptanalyze.

SHA-384 and SHA-512

The situation with SHA-384 and SHA-512 is similar to that of SHA-224 and SHA-256: SHA-384 is merely a shortened version of SHA-512 with a different IV. As mentioned above, these two functions use 64-bit words instead of the common 32-bit words so as to take advantage of modern 64-bit computer architectures. Apart from this, the step operation is nearly the same as in SHA-256 with just some constants adjusted to the larger word size.

HAVAL

HAVAL is a very interesting design. In general it uses the same structure as all the other functions here in the MD4 family, but there are also some important differences. Apparently, the most important difference is that, instead of the commonly used Boolean functions with three input variables as in all the other MD4-family hash functions, HAVAL uses Boolean functions with seven input variables. They are constructed in a very special way (which was first described in Seberry & Zhang, 1992), such that they have a number of properties, which are believed to make them cryptographically strong. These are, for example, the properties mentioned above for the three variable functions (e.g., balancedness) but also having high nonlinearity and being linearly inequivalent. For details on this, see Section 3 of (Vaudenay 1995) the original description of HAVAL.

Another difference in HAVAL is that the user can adjust the security level by choosing between different numbers (3, 4, or 5) of passes and thus can make a trade-off between efficiency and security.

Performance

It is difficult to measure the performance of hash functions objectively because it depends very much on actual implementations and on the platforms on which they are implemented. In this section, we try to give a rough overview at least of the relative performance of some hash functions by presenting two tables with performance data on two different platforms: Table 7 of Bosselaers shows the performance of some of the older members of the MD4-family on an old 90-MHz Pentium (for details see Bosselaers). Table 8 shows the performance of some of the newer hash functions on a 2.1-GHz Pentium 4, as they are implemented in the Crypto++ library (see Crypto++ 5.2.1 Benchmarks).

ATTACKS ON MD4-LIKE HASH FUNCTIONS

In what follows, we describe the status of the analysis of the MD4-like hash functions described above.

The first analyses of MD4 and MD5 were made by Merkle (unpublished), den Boer and Bosselaers (1992, 1993) and Vaudenay 1995. Then the second author developed a new general technique to attack MD4-like hash functions and applied it to RIPEMD-0, MD4, Extended MD4 and MD5 in a series of papers (1996–1998; Dobbertin 1995, 1996a, 1996b, 1997, 1998a). Later this technique was used by Kasselman & Penzhorn (Kasselman & Penzhorn 2000) to attack a reduced version of Haval and by van Rompay, Biryukov, Preneel, and Vandewalle (2003) to break the smallest full version of HAVAL (3 rounds, 128 bit output).

In 1998, Chabaud and Joux used a different method to show how SHA-0 could be broken theoretically. This was later extended by Biham and Chen (2004), who produced near-collisions of SHA-0 and collisions of reduced

Table 6 Notation

$a \vee b$	Bitwise or of the variables a and b
$\bar{a}$	Bitwise negation of the variable a
$a \ll b$	Leftwise shift of variable a over b positions
$a \gg b$	Rightwise shift of variable a over b positions
$a \lll b$	Leftwise rotation of variable a over b positions
$a \ggg b$	Rightwise rotation of variable a over b positions
$+$	Modular addition (the modulus is usually 2^{32})
$\oplus$	Exclusive-or

Table 7 Performance of Some Hash Functions on a 90-MHz Pentium (See Bosselaers)

Hash function	Performance (in megabytes per second)
MD4	23.90
MD5	17.09
RIPEMD-0	12.00
RIPEMD-128	9.73
SHA-1	6.88
RIPEMD-160	5.68

Table 8 Performance of Some Hash Functions on a 2.1-GHz Pentium 4 (See Crypto++ 5.2.1 Benchmarks)

Hash function	Performance (in megabytes per second)
MD5	216.67
HAVAL(3 rounds)	108.54
HAVAL (4 rounds)	69.28
SHA-1	67.98
HAVAL(5 rounds)	67.44
RIPEMD-160	52.60
SHA-256	44.46
SHA-512	11.39

versions of SHA-1 with it. Joux, Carribault, Jalby, and Lemuet (2004) then used this extension to produce real collisions of SHA-0.

Also in 2004 Wang, Feng, Lai, & Yu refined and extended some of these techniques to produce real collisions for MD4, MD5, RIPEMD-0, and HAVAL (3 round, 128 bit).

In this section, we first give a survey of the most important techniques used in these attacks and try to classify them in a common scheme. After that we describe the status of the hash functions that we described earlier.

General Attack Methods

In this section, we give a survey of the most important aspects of the techniques used in current cryptanalyses to find collisions for hash functions. For a more detailed analysis of these techniques, see Daum (2005).

All the current techniques have in common that they can be divided into at least two parts. In the first part, the general "attack strategy," a so-called difference pattern is chosen or determined. Usually in this part many steps are done by hand and are of a more theoretical nature. In contrast, the second part, in which the actual collisions are determined, usually requires a lot of time-consuming computations. The techniques used here include "brute force"–like searches but also more sophisticated algorithms.

Difference Patterns

All the methods described in this section are attacks on the collision resistance of a hash function. This means we are looking for two messages, X and X', that produce the same hash value. Therefore, we have to correlate the computations that are done when computing the hash value of X and the computations for the hash value of X'. A *difference pattern* is a sequence of differences, where each difference corresponds to one step in these computations. Each of the difference values is defined as a difference of a value from the computation for X and the corresponding value from the computation for X'.

We have to distinguish between *input differences*, which means differences in the messages, or rather in the values W_i after the message expansion, and *output differences*, that is, differences appearing in the register values after applying the step operations. Another important distinction is that between *modular differences*, that is, differences with respect to integer addition, usually

modulo 2^n (where n is the register size in bits), and $\oplus$ *differences*.

Usually one tries to choose the input differences in a way such that the output differences behave in some special way. Clearly, the most important goal in doing so is that the last output differences, which correspond to the output value of the compression function, are zero differences because that is what constitutes a collision. But generally more restrictions than this have to be imposed to find actual collisions in the end, and this is where the methods used in the attacks differ significantly.

In some sense, it is more natural to consider modular differences because most of the basic operations from which the step operations are built are modular additions. Especially the last operations applied in each step, which have the directest influence on the differences are modular additions. But one cannot analyze the function completely by considering only modular additions, because there are also operations which are not compatible with this kind of difference and it is not possible to deduce $\oplus$-differences directly from the modular differences.

Conversely, it is also not possible to analyze these functions completely by considering only $\oplus$ differences. Usually, when using mainly $\oplus$-differences, the operations that are not compatible with this kind of differences are approximated by other functions that are compatible. Then the algebraic structure of a vectorspace can be used and it is quite easy to analyze this approximative function with linear algebra techniques. However, one has the problem to transfer the results for the approximation to the real function.

Inner Collisions

The method used in Dobbertin (1995, 1996a, 1996b, 1997, 1998a) to attack RIPEMD-0, MD4, and MD5 uses a concept called "inner collisions" that consists of a very simple input difference pattern and only little restrictive output difference pattern. We describe the basic ideas of this technique using the example of the attack on MD5.

The method uses mainly modular differences and the following simple input difference pattern: we assume for the colliding message pair X, X' that all words coincide, with one exception, say X_{i_0} and X'_{i_0}:

$$X'_{i_0} = X_{i_0} + \Delta,$$

where Δ is some small value; in the actual attack it is chosen to be 1. This implies, because of the message expansion by roundwise permutation, that only four of the W_i (in the MD5 attack for $i \in \{15, 26, 36, 51\}$) and the corresponding step operations differ when processing X', in contrast to processing X. Thus, in the first 14 steps, exactly the same step operations are used to update the same register values, meaning that, initially, it suffices to start with step 15 in the cryptanalysis. Similarly, the last 13 steps (52–64) are the same, implying that finding a collision after 64 steps is equivalent to finding a collision after step 51. In other words, from this input difference pattern we can conclude that the output difference pattern has zeroes at the first 14 and at the last 13 steps. This situation is illustrated in the left diagram in Figure 8.

This limits the avalanche effect from taking effect over 64 rounds to only 37 rounds. To limit it even more, in this

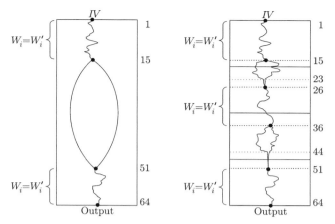

Figure 8: Overview of the attack on the compression function of MD5.

technique one restricts the desired collisions even more, by requiring that, during the processing of the two messages, so-called inner collisions appear. That means that, not only after step 51 but also after step 26, we require the contents of the registers to be equal when processing X and X', respectively. This leads to a situation (as shown on the right-hand side of Figure 8) where in steps 27 to 35 exactly the same things are happening (the output difference pattern has zeroes in these steps), meaning that the avalanche effect only takes place in two quite short ranges of 12 and 16 steps.

Inner Almost-Collisions
Another important approach used in this technique is to look for "inner almost-collisions" some steps before the required inner collisions.

The general problem with the approach of considering mainly differences of values (and not the values themselves) is that the difference propagation is not deterministic. That means, given differences for the register values and for the input value for one certain step, the difference of the values in the register, which is updated in this step, is, in general, not uniquely determined. It also depends on the actual values in the registers and not only on their differences.

However, for "small" differences, this behavior is quite predictable, meaning that the probabilities for certain output differences are significantly higher than for all the others. Here "small" does not mean the size of the actual integer value of the modular difference, nor the hamming weight of its binary representation, but mainly having a short signed representation. That means the difference can be written as a sum of very few values of the form $\pm 2^i$ (for details on this, see Daum, (2005).

Thus, if the output difference is quite small after some step—and this is what is called an "inner almost-collision"—there is a difference pattern for the next steps that is fulfilled with high probability for random register values. Therefore, the idea is to perform some kind of differential attack (modulo 2^{32}) on the steps immediately before the inner collisions to decide which differences in the registers are the most likely to lead to the desired inner collision.

Elementary Collisions
Chabaud and Joux (1998) use a different approach to dealing with this "nondeterministic difference propagation." They use only $\oplus$ differences, but the propagation of these differences in the actual step operation is as little deterministic as described earlier for the modular differences.

Thus their idea was to consider approximations of the step operations by some operation that has a deterministic difference propagation. Therefore, they replaced every nonlinear (with respect to the $\oplus$ operation) operation by some linear operation. For example, instead of the modular addition of two values they used the $\oplus$ sum of these values, which is the same as ignoring carry bits during the modular addition. As this results in a linear function the difference behavior of this approximative function, can be analyzed using linear algebra techniques.

The crucial idea then was to consider elementary collisions (or *local collisions* as they were called in Chaubaud & Joux, 1998) of this approximative function, that is, collision appearing after as few steps as possible. Therefore, they defined *perturbations* and corresponding *corrective patterns*. Making a perturbation simply means to change one bit in the input difference pattern at some arbitrary step. The corresponding corrective pattern than consists of some bits in the steps following the perturbated step, which lead to a collision in the approximated function after as few steps as possible.

For example, in SHA-0 the step operation is given by the following:

$$A := (A \lll 5) + \Phi_i(B, C, D) + E + W_i + K_i,$$

which can be approximated by the following:

$$A := (A \lll 5) \oplus (B \oplus C \oplus D) \oplus E \oplus W_i \oplus K_i.$$

This means, if we decide to change the k-th bit of W_i, then also the k-th bit of the updated register A is changed. In the next step, the values in the registers are changed cyclically, that is, B inherits the value and thus also the difference from register A. But before that, the new value of register A is computed by the formula above (with $i + 1$ instead of i) and to avoid another nonzero difference in this register, we have to change the $(k + 5)$-th bit of W_{i+1}, because the register A is rotated by 5 bits before being used. Thus the $(k + 5)$-th bit of step $i + 1$ is the first correction bit of the corrective pattern.

By analogous considerations, it can be determined which bits have to be changed in next four steps to avoid nonzero differences. Then, after six steps, this leads to a collision in the approximated function, a so-called elementary collision. It is called elementary, as it can be shown by arguments about the dimensions of the corresponding subspaces that all the collisions of the approximated function can be written as sums of these elementary collisions. Thus it is quite easy with methods from linear algebra to find such input difference patterns that lead to output difference patterns corresponding to a collision of the approximated function.

However, there are two drawbacks with this approach. First, the chosen input difference pattern, consisting of perturbations and corresponding corrective patterns, must be consistent with the message expansion. That is, one must be able to find messages (or rather message differences), which, after the expansion, result in the wanted input difference pattern. For SHA-0 (where this method was used) this is quite simple, because the message expansion itself is linear. Thus this requirement resulted simply in some additional linear conditions. To apply this method on hash functions with a nonlinear message expansion, one would have to use an approximation again.

The other problem is that, so far, the input difference pattern determined in this way only leads to output difference patterns corresponding to a collision if the approximated function is applied. If this should also be the case for the actual (nonlinear) step operations and thus result in a collision of the actual hash function, various additional conditions have to be met.

This leads directly to the second part of these attacks: how to find the actual collisions after having decided the difference patterns.

Randomized Searches

Usually the additional conditions mentioned above can be assumed to be (nearly) independent conditions, which are fulfilled for random messages with some probability. This probability can be deduced from a detailed view at the approximation. Thus the first, but quite naive, way of searching for collisions would simply be to produce random messages, apply the chosen input difference pattern, and hope that all the additional conditions are met such that the message results in a collision.

Usually the probabilities deduced from the additional conditions are so small that this approach is computationally infeasible. But there is some refinement, used in Chaubaud and Joux (1998), that makes this approach much more feasible: One starts, as before by choosing random messages and applying the input difference pattern, but first only the additional conditions for the first 15 steps (in which the first 15 of 16 message words are used) are considered. After having found a message producing the intended output difference pattern in the first 15 steps, one changes only the 16th message word for a while. This does not change the output difference pattern for the first 15 steps but produces a nearly random behavior for the remaining steps. Thus mainly the probability for these remaining steps is of importance for the overall complexity of this attack.

Chabaud and Joux (1998) describe a difference pattern that is fulfilled (in this sense) with a probability of 2^{-61}, which means their attack has a complexity of about 2^{61}.

Neutral Bits

Biham and Chen (2004a) refined this approach even more by looking for *neutral bits*.

Their idea is to increase this range of steps for which one tries to assure in advance (before the main part of randomized search) that the output difference pattern is as intended. Clearly, if one looks at more than 15 steps, it is no longer possible to change some message word arbitrarily without having to fear that the output difference pattern has changed. But this is where the *neutral bits* come into play. A bit of some message is called neutral if changing it does not prevent the message from fulfilling the intended output difference pattern for the chosen range of steps. One can also try to combine these neutral bits to larger sets of bits that often also have this property.

Biham and Chen observed that if many of such sets of neutral bits are combined, changing any subset of these bits does not change the output difference pattern with a quite high probability. Thus this technique can be used to produce a large amount of messages that fulfill the intended output difference pattern in advance for some more steps than 15, as in the technique used by Chabaud and Joux.

The more steps one tries to tick off in this way in advance, the fewer neutral bits will be found and thus the fewer messages can be produced. But increasing the number of steps will also increase the probability of success for the remaining steps. Thus it is crucial for this approach to find a suitable number of steps for which the probability of success and the number of producable messages are fitting.

Solving Systems of Equations

In the attacks used in Dobbertin (1995, 1996a, 1996b, 1997, 1998a), in which the difference pattern was chosen using the concept of *inner collisions* (see above), the second part of finding actual colliding messages is quite different from what we just described for the attacks by Chabaud/Joux and Biham/Chen.

In these attacks, we have to distinguish among three different kinds of (ranges of) steps. First, we have the areas in which the output difference is intended to be always zero. In the example of the MD5 attack (see Figure 8) this is the case for steps 1 to 14, 27 to 35, and 52 to 64. For the remaining steps (in which there is some nonzero output difference), we have to distinguish between areas with arbitrary differences and those with small differences, where the concept of *inner almost-collisions* (see above) is used.

The last mentioned areas (those with the inner almost-collisions) are dealt with in a way very similar to what we described earlier in the attack of Chabaud and Joux. As the output difference for these steps is fulfilled with a quite high probability for random register values, we simply need to produce a large amount of messages fulfilling the output difference pattern for the other areas and then with a high probability we will find one leading to a collision.

Thus the attack is reduced to mainly two computational parts: a part for finding inner collisions and a part for connecting them. Finding inner collisions means to find actual register values for the steps with nonzero output differences that can be achieved by some pair of messages and the chosen input difference, of course, taking into account the message expansion.

To achieve this, in this method the inner collisions are described by using systems of equations derived from the equations that describe the step operation. These equations usually include $\oplus$, modular additions, bitwise defined functions, and bit rotations simultaneously. As these operations are not very convenient to handle mathematically, it is not an easy matter to solve them efficiently, and very sophisticated methods have to be used to find solutions. Some examples of such techniques can be found in Dobbertin (1996a, 1997, 1998a). Refinements of these algorithms that can also be used to represent the sets of solutions of these systems of equations are described in Daum.

After having found such inner collisions, the last part of the attack is to connect them. This means that one has to find the paths (corresponding to actual register values), which are identical for X and X', between the (end of the) first inner collision and the point where the two paths drift apart again (compare the right-hand side of Figure 8). Additionally (at least to find a collision of the hash function and not only of the compression function), one also has to find a connection between the right initial value IV^* and the state at which the paths drift apart for the first time (which is in step 15 in MD5). Finding these connections again comes down to solving equations similar to those above used for finding inner collisions.

Status of Different Hash Functions

MD4: Three Rounds Are Not Enough

The most successful analytic result for MD4 is a collision consisting of two contracts as presented in Figure 9 (see "Alf swindles Ann"; Dobbertin, 1995). Here the asterisks represent 20 "random" bytes, which form a header. These two contracts generate the same MD4 hash value. Moreover, if the third round in the compression function of MD4 is cancelled, then it is shown in Dobbertin (1998b) how preimages can be constructed. This result brings even the onewayness of MD4 into question.

Another way of producing collisions for MD4 was found by Wang et al. (2004). They succeeded in producing collisions for MD4 with a complexity (after some precomputation) of only 4–64 runs of MD4. Despite these rather devastating analyses, it does not mean that the MD4 design principle is compromised. The moral is simple: three rounds in the compression function are not enough.

Extended MD4 and RIPEMD-0: Too Much Symmetry

The compression of Extended MD4 consists of two instances of a modified MD4 compression that run in parallel, with some interaction. Therefore, Extended MD4 compression has 6 rounds (2×3), but despite this, it is surprisingly weak. The reason for this weakness, which led, in 1996, to finding collisions of the compression function (Section 8 in Dobbertin, 1998a) can be clearly identified: the two parallel lines in the compression are too similar.

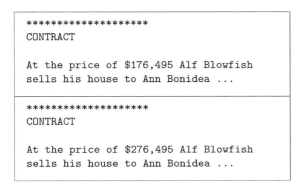

```
********************
CONTRACT

At the price of $176,495 Alf Blowfish
sells his house to Ann Bonidea ...

********************
CONTRACT

At the price of $276,495 Alf Blowfish
sells his house to Ann Bonidea ...
```

Figure 9: Two contracts producing the same MD4 hash value.

The ordering in which the words are applied in the single steps is identical. This allows an attack on both lines simultaneously, in parallel.

The 1993 design of RIPEMD (which we now call RIPEMD-0, to distinguish it from the newer RIPEMD versions) is modeled after Extended MD4, and unfortunately it inherited the same design defect. Thus, the second author was able to find attacks on two-round reductions of RIPEMD-0 (Dobbertin, H. [1997]). Later Wang et al. (2004) were even able to produce real collisions for the full (2×3-round) RIPEMD-0. In this attack, they also extensively use the strong symmetry in RIPEMD-0 by using the same differential patterns for both strings of RIPEMD-0.

MD5: Four Rounds Are Not Enough for Collision Resistance

As seen above, MD5 is a slightly modified version of MD4 with a four-round compression. In 1993, den Boer and Bosselaers (1994) found pseudocollisions for the compression function of MD5 with different initial values but common input. This result implies that the Merkle–Damgård theorem (Theorem 3), which derives the security of a hash function from its underlying compression function, cannot be invoked for MD5. This finding of pseudocollisions shows that the compression function, considered as a cryptographic primitive of its own, has a weakness. But, as already discussed above, the pseudocollisions alone do not lead us closer to collisions of the hash function.

In 1996, the second author (Dobbertin, 1996b) constructed collisions of the MD5 compression function, that is, MD5 collisions with a wrong initial value. This came close enough to collisions of MD5 (compare "Collisions and Pseudocollisions of the Compression Functions") to suggest that MD5 should no longer be used in applications such as signature schemes, where a collision-resistant hash function is required. Nevertheless, it was still used (or at least allowed to be used) in many applications.

In 2004, Wang et al. succeeded in producing real collisions for the full MD5 hash function. The new idea in their approach was to look for a collision after processing not one but two blocks of the message. This means they have the freedom to choose two difference patterns. They used this freedom by using two different difference patterns with the property that the resulting differences at the end of these patterns are additively inverse modulo 2^{32}. Then a combination of these two patterns leads to a collision because after applying the second difference pattern the initial value of this application of the compression function (and thus the resulting difference of the first pattern) is added again, nullifying the difference in the registers.

Although this attack clearly shows that MD5 is not collision resistant, it tells us nothing about the onewayness of MD5. The attack (as all the methods described under "General Attack Methods") directly aims at producing collisions and cannot be modified (at least in some obvious way) to compute preimages. Thus, using MD5 as a oneway function (as it done most of the time nowadays) can still be considered secure.

SHA-0: Too Much Linearity

The most remarkable design idea in SHA, which is essentially different from the design of all former MD4-like hash functions, is the recursive expansion of the sequence of input words for the compression, instead of multiple applications of input words in different rounds.

As mentioned under "Message Expansion," there was a flaw in the message expansion of SHA and this flaw caused NIST/NSA to replace SHA (later usually referenced as SHA-0) by SHA-1 in FIPS 180-1, which is now included in Federal Information Processing Standard 180-2 (2002). Details of this "flaw" found by the NSA were never published.

But, in 1998, Chabaud and Joux found an attack (see "General Attack Methods") on SHA-0 with an effort of about 2^{61}, which is not practical, but requires essentially less effort than the birthday attack. With their method of *neutral bits* Biham and Chen (2004) succeeded in actually finding collisions for SHA-0 variants with 65 and 82 steps, respectively (instead of 80 steps). Joux et al. (2004) then adopted this technique and used it to find an attack having a complexity of "only" about 2^{51}, which led—with the help of a supercomputer—to actual collisions of SHA-0.

HAVAL: Using Seven-Bit Inputs in the Boolean Functions Does Not Help Much

In 2000, using the technique of inner collisions (see "General Attack Methods"), Kasselman and Penzhorn (2000) cryptanalyzed a reduced version of three round HAVAL. Actually, they were able to find a collision for the last two out of three rounds of HAVAL.

Later, in 2003, van Rompay et al. described an algorithm that is able to produce collisions for the full three-round HAVAL with the apparently small complexity of about 2^{29} computations of the compression function of HAVAL. This attack is another example of the application of the technique of inner almost-collisions.

Then, in 2004, Wang et al. presented a technique (similar to the one which they applied also to MD4, MD5, etc.), which makes it possible to produce collisions for 3-round HAVAL with an effort of only about 2^6 computations of the compression function.

Thus, at least the small-sized versions of HAVAL are not collision resistant, and these results bring the collision resistance even of the larger-sized HAVAL versions into question as the attacks seem to be extendable to some degree.

SHA-1

In SHA-1, the revised version of SHA, the message expansion includes an additional rotation by one bit in each step of the recursion. This causes a significant increase in the diffusion of this hash function. But despite this additional security, Biham and Chen (2004b) succeeded in finding collisions for at least a strongly reduced variant of SHA-1 with 43 instead of 80 rounds. But although 43 rounds is a surprisingly large number of rounds, this is far from being a threat for the full SHA-1 as it is supposed to be used.

Thus, from what we know today, SHA-1 should still be considered as collision-resistant hash function.

RIPEMD-128/-160/-256/-320

The design of RIPEMD-128/-160/-256/-320 is based directly on RIPEMD-0 (and thus on Extended MD4, the 256-bit extension of MD4). However, conclusions from the results of analyses on these functions were taken into account (how to choose, or not to choose, certain parameters), and the number of rounds is extended from 3 to 4 and 5, respectively (for each of two parallel lines). That is, there are 128 and 160 steps, respectively.

So far, no attacks requiring less effort than the birthday attack are known on these hash functions.

SHA-224/-256/-384/-512

In the recently published new versions SHA-256 and SHA-512 (and thus also in the shortened versions SHA-224 and SHA-384), the effect of diffusion is increased by using a yet more complex design, for example, by using even a nonlinear message expansion.

Thus, so far, no attacks requiring less effort than the birthday attack are known on these hash functions.

BUILDING HASH FUNCTIONS FROM BLOCK CIPHERS

Comparing the common design of hash functions, as presented under "Hashing by Iterated Compression", with the different operation modes of block ciphers (see Chapter 106, Secret Key Cryptography) shows that there are many similarities. Thus, it is not surprising, that there have been many proposals on how to construct hash functions from block ciphers. Another reason for considering this topic is that there are many block ciphers whose security is well analyzed and well established, and the hope might be that it is possible to use this to construct secure hash functions.

All the common designs for building hash functions based on block ciphers use the principle of iterated compression (see "Hashing by Iterated Compression") and differ only in the way in which the compression function is built from the block cipher. To construct a hash function with an output length of n bits, one typically uses a block cipher with a block length of b bits, where b divides n. In most cases, the ratio $\frac{n}{b}$ is either 1 (*single-length* constructions, considered under "Single-Length Constructions") or 2 (*double-length* constructions, considered under "Double-Length Constructions"). Usually larger ratios are not used, as they would also lead to a larger number of calls of the encryption function of the block cipher and thus to a worse performance.

Actually, this number of calls to the encryption function during one call of the compression function is an important characteristic of such a design because it is a direct indicator for the performance of the design. If the encryption function is called s times during one call of the compression function, then the *rate* of this construction is defined to be $\frac{1}{s}$.

There are two reasons why in practice mostly dedicated hash functions (as in presented in the previous sections) and not hash functions based on block ciphers are used: first, despite being based on *well-analyzed* block ciphers, there are no proofs showing that the constructed

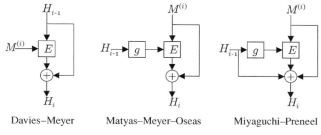

Figure 10: Typical single-length constructions of block cipher–based hash functions.

functions are secure *in practice* as hash functions and, second, usually the dedicated designs of hash functions are more efficient than the ones based on block ciphers.

Single-Length Constructions

There are three schemes that have all been proposed in the 1980s and can be considered the main examples of secure single-length constructions of hash functions from block ciphers. These are the Davies–Meyer, Matyas–Meyer–Oseas, and the Miyaguchi–Preneel constructions (see Figure 10).

If $E_k(m)$ stands for the encryption of the message m by applying the chosen block cipher using the key k, then the output of the compression function f following the Davies–Meyer scheme can be written as follows:

$$f_{H_{i-1}}(M^{(i)}) := E_{M^{(i)}}(H_{i-1}) \oplus H_{i-1}.$$

Having a close look at the designs of the dedicated hash functions described earlier shows that many of these hash functions were designed having the Davies–Meyer scheme in mind. The internal design of many dedicated compression functions, as described under "Hashing by Iterated Compression" is very similar to the design of a block cipher using a message block $M^{(i)}$ as a key and the intermediate hash value H_{i-1} as the message to be encrypted. The idea of later adding the intermediate hash value H_{i-1} again (as in the Davies–Meyer construction) is exactly what is done in many dedicated designs to include some "feed-forward" (compare "Hashing by Iterated Compression").

As can be seen in Figure 10, the other schemes are quite similar. The compression function in the Matyas–Meyer–Oseas scheme can be written as follows:

$$f_{H_{i-1}}(M^{(i)}) := E_{g(H_{i-1})}(M^{(i)}) \oplus M^{(i)},$$

and the compression function in the Miyaguchi–Preneel scheme is defined to be the following:

$$f_{H_{i-1}}(M^{(i)}) := E_{g(H_{i-1})}(M^{(i)}) \oplus M^{(i)} \oplus H_{i-1}.$$

In both cases, g stands for a function, which maps n-bit inputs to suitable keys for the encryption function and may be the identity function, if this is suitable.

Apparently, all these designs are very similar or rather can be written as follows:

$$f_{H_{i-1}}(M^{(i)}) := E_a(b) \oplus c,$$

with $a, b, c \in \{H_{i-1}, M^{(i)}, H_{i-1} \oplus M^{(i)}\}$ Preneel, Govaerts, and Vandewalle (1994) analyzed a more general constuction, where $a, b, c, \in \{vH_{i-1}, M^{(i)}, H_{i-1} \oplus M^{(i)}\}$ and v simply stands for some fixed value. They examined which of these constructions led to secure hash functions and found out that all but 12 of the 64 possible constructions cannot be considered secure and are subject to more or less severe attacks. The 12 constructions left over— to which also the three constructions described above belong—can be summarized to be of the following form:

$$f_{H_{i-1}}(M^{(i)}) := E_k(m) \oplus m[\oplus k],$$

where $k, m \in \{H_{i-1}, M^{(i)}, H_{i-1} \oplus M^{(i)}\}, k \neq m$, and the final addition of k is meant to be optional.

Although presented attacks for the weak constructions of this family, later Black, Rogaway, and Shrimpton (2002) analyzed these constructions again, focusing on proofs. They present proofs for all the 12 constructions mentioned above showing that these are secure at least in the black-box model (see Shannon 1949). This means that these proofs show only the absence of attacks on these schemes treating the block cipher as a black box, but they say nothing about possible attacks on these constructions that use some structural properties of the used block cipher. Additionally, they were able to figure out eight further constructions of the type defined above, which are probably (in the black-box model) as collision resistant as the first 12 functions, only their security as oneway functions is not as good. At this point, it is important to note that these proofs are only proofs in the black-box model, which is not "realistic" but an idealized model making it possible to prove anything. For a more detailed discussion, see Black et al. (2002).

The advantage of the single-length constructions is clearly their performance. Their speed is determined by the speed of the used block cipher and modern block ciphers usually come close to the effiency of modern dedicated hash functions. The problem is that there are hardly any block ciphers providing a block length sufficiently large to guarantee collision resistance. One would need a block cipher with a block length of at least 160 bits and many common modern block ciphers usually provide only 128 bits if not only 64 bits.

Double-Length Constructions

If one wants to construct a secure hash function based on a block cipher with a relatively small block length, one has to use double-length constructions. There are two widely used designs of such constructions, MDC-2 and MDC-4. They were designed by Brachtl et al. (1990) originally based on DES, and MDC-2 is part of the ISO/IEC standard 10118-2.

MDC-2

MDC-2 mainly consists of two parallel instances of the Matyas–Meyer–Oseas scheme with some additional interaction. It was originally designed to be used with DES, but it can be based on any block cipher with a block length of b bits, providing a hash value of $2b$ bits length. The message to be hashed is split into blocks of length b each. One of these message blocks $M^{(i)}$ together with two chaining variables H_{i-1}^L and H_{i-1}^R are used as inputs for the compression function, which is computed as follows: Apply the Matyas–Meyer–Oseas twice, each time using one of the chaining variables together with the message block as inputs and split the respective outputs into two halves:

$$E_{g(H_{i-1}^L)}(M^{(i)}) \oplus M^{(i)} =: A \parallel B,$$
$$E_{g(H_{i-1}^R)}(M^{(i)}) \oplus M^{(i)} =: C \parallel D,$$

where A, B, C, D are each of length $\frac{b}{2}$ bits. Then mix these values by switching the right parts to compute the new values for the chaining variables as follows:

$$H_i^L := A \parallel D,$$
$$H_i^R := C \parallel B.$$

This compression function is illustrated in Figure 11.

MDC-4

MDC-4 is designed to be mainly a "double MDC-2," a concatenation of two applications of MDC2. Therefore we need, as before, two chaining variables H_{i-1}^L and H_{i-1}^R and split the message into blocks of b bits each. Additionally, we need two auxiliary chaining variables $\tilde{H}_i^L$ and $\tilde{H}_i^R$, which are in a first step computed exactly as the original chaining variables in MDC-2:

$$A \parallel B := E_{g(H_{i-1}^L)}(M^{(i)}) \oplus M^{(i)},$$
$$C \parallel D := E_{g(H_{i-1}^R)}(M^{(i)}) \oplus M^{(i)},$$
$$\tilde{H}_i^L := A \parallel D,$$
$$\tilde{H}_i^R := C \parallel B.$$

Then in the second application of MDC-2 the auxiliary chaining variables are used instead of the original chaining variables, and the original chaining variables take the place of the message block:

$$A \parallel B := E_{g(H_i^L)}(\tilde{H}_{i-1}^R) \oplus H_{i-1}^R,$$
$$C \parallel D := E_{g(H_i^R)}(\tilde{H}_{i-1}^L) \oplus H_{i-1}^L,$$
$$H_i^L := A \parallel D,$$
$$H_i^R := C \parallel B.$$

This design is illustrated in Figure 12.

MESSAGE AUTHENTICATION CODES

A *message authentication code (MAC)* can be shortly described as a keyed hash function. This means it is a family of hash functions h_k, that is indexed by some key k. For each evaluation, depending on the key k, one function is chosen to produce the message digest $h_k(X)$ corresponding to the message X and the key k.

Comparing it with other cryptographical primitives, another way of describing a MAC would be to call it a "symmetric digital signature." Clearly, it is not possible to use MACs to sign contracts: if one is able to check the signature, one has to know the key and this means one could have signed it oneself. But, if two parties agreed on a secret key, they can use a MAC to authenticate messages to each other by signing the message with the key they agreed on.

The requirements for a MAC to be useful, are similar to those proposed for hash functions earlier with the addition that the dependance of the key has to fulfill some properties: Clearly, MACs should be efficiently computable and should also compress messages of arbitrary length to fixed length message digests. Additionally, MACs should have the property that given a message X it should be difficult to compute $h_k(X)$ without knowing the key k. This is formalized in the property of *computation resistance*: A MAC is called *computation resistant* if, given an arbitrary number of pairs $[X_i, h_k(X_i)]$

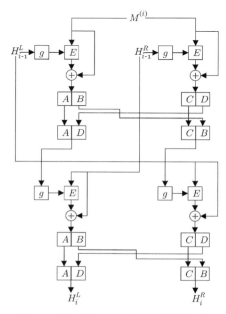

Figure 12: Construction of MDC-4.

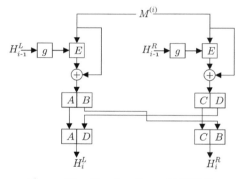

Figure 11: Construction of MDC-2.

of messages and corresponding message digests, it is computationally infeasible to compute $h_k(X')$ for any new $X' \neq X_i$.

MACs are used to authenticate messages, that is, to guarantee the origin and the integrity of a message. Therefore, they are useful in various cryptographic protocols. For details on applications of MACs, see Chapter 114 (Cryptographic Protocols) and Chapter 176 (Digital Signatures and Electronic Signatures).

In this chapter, we concentrate on the technical construction of MACs. There are several possible constructions for MACs, for example, several ways of constructing MACs from block ciphers or also dedicated designs. We focus here on a very important construction, which is used most often in practice and which can be carried out on some arbitrary hash function, the HMAC.

HMAC

The HMAC was proposed by Bellare, Canetti, and Krawczyk (1996b); a short introduction can be found in Bellare, Canetti, and Krawczyk (1996a).

The basic idea of the HMAC is to use some arbitrary hash function as a black box and build a MAC from it. As should be clear from the previous sections, hash functions do not use any kind of key, so the main question in the HMAC construction should be how to provide a hash function with a key.

The first, naive idea would be to simply prepend or append the key to the message and then hash the extended message $X\|k$ (or $k\|X$ respectively). This construction would fulfill the requirement of being a family of hash functions, which is efficiently computable. But it is not computation resistant, as there are many simple attacks on these constructions, such as birthday-style attacks or extension attacks (for details, see Example 9.64, 9.65 in Menezes et al., 1996).

Thus Bellare et al. decided to do a more sophisticated, nested construction: in the HMAC the key is used twice and it works as follows (as illustrated in Figure 13): let X be the message and k the key, which should be no longer than 64 bytes. If it is shorter, it is padded by appending

zeroes. Further, let

$$ipad = 0 \times 36 \text{ repeated 64 times,}$$
$$opad = 0 \times 5c \text{ repeated 64 times,}$$

be two bit strings used to mask the key.

Start with prepending $k \oplus ipad$ to the message and compute the hash value $h((k \oplus ipad)\|X)$ of this extended message by applying the chosen hash function h. Then prepend the bit string $k \oplus opad$ to this computed hash value and once again apply the hash function to compute the final output as follows:

$$h_k(X) = h((k \oplus opad) \| h((k \oplus ipad)\|X)).$$

At first glance, the complexity of this construction seems to be twice the complexity of the used hash function h because it is applied two times. But especially for quite long messages it is only marginally more complex than computing the simple hash value of the message, as the "message" used as input for the second application of h is very short, only about two blocks.

The most interesting aspect of this construction is, that it is provably secure, given some reasonable assumptions. In fact, what Bellare et al. (1996b) show is that, if it is possible for an attacker to break the HMAC construction, then this attacker would be able (with the same effort) to do one of two things: (1) find collisions in the hash function, even for a random or secret IV or (2) compute the output of the compression function even without knowing the IV.

It is very reasonable to assume that this is not possible for any hash function in practical use, or, in other words, a hash function failing to meet this requirements should also not be used in other cryptographical applications.

The HMAC construction was originally designed to be used with MD5 and is nowadays usually used in conjunction with SHA-1. It is a standard in many cryptographical protocols.

CONCLUSION

We can clearly state that the functions MD4, Extended MD4, RIPEMD-0, SHA-0, and MD5 are broken and must not be used in practical applications where security depends on the collision resistance.

We emphasize that the hash function RIPEMD-128 was designed only as a plug-in for RIPEMD-0. However, hash functions with 128-bit values are becoming more and more susceptible to the birthday attack in the near future. Some years ago, Van Oorschot and Wiener calculated that at a cost of $10 million one could build a "birthday attack" machine that could find MD5 collisions in about a month. As a result of Moore's law, we can suppose that today such a machine could be build for much less money and perhaps even be capable of finding the collisions faster.

The status of SHA-1 is not that clear. From what we know today, SHA-1 should still be considered collision resistant and therefore there is no need to replace it at the moment wherever it is used. But for future applications, it seems to be a better idea to use other hash functions, as it

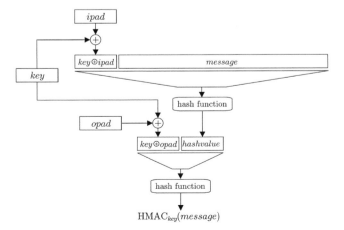

Figure 13: HMAC construction.

is difficult to estimate for how long SHA-1 will stay secure. One of the challenges presented to the crypto community in the crypto competition *Mystery Twister* is to find a collision for a 60-round SHA-1 version (see Mystery Twister, 2005).

Summarizing, we can recommend RIPEMD-160/-256/-320 and the new SHA versions SHA-224/-256/-384/-512 as collision resistant (and therefore oneway) hash functions. If merely a oneway hash function is needed, we also recommend MD5 because it is very fast.

GLOSSARY

Birthday Attack An attack that makes use of the *birthday paradox*; that is, it uses the fact that for collision problems one needs a surprisingly low number of attempts to find a collision by brute force.

Collision A pair of two messages producing the same hash value.

Collision Resistant Function A function for which it is computationally infeasible to find a *collision*.

Compression Function A function that compresses inputs of some fixed length to outputs of some smaller length; usually used as the main building block of a *hash function*.

Hash Function A function that compresses arbitrary long messages to a hash value or *message digest* of a fixed size.

MAC A "keyed hash function" or "symmetric digital signature" usually used to authenticate messages.

MD4/MD5 Two hash functions proposed by Ronald Rivest in 1990 and 1992, respectively. Archetype for a whole class of hash functions.

Message Digest Also called "digital fingerprint"; hash value of a message allowing in practice a unique identification of a message.

Oneway Function A function that is *preimage resistant* and *second preimage resistant*.

Preimage Resistant Function A function for which it is computationally infeasible to find a message mapping to a previously given value.

Pseudocollision A pair of two input pairs (IV, X), (IV', X') for a compression function mapping to the same output value. In contrast, for a real *collision* of a compression function we additionally require $IV = IV'$.

RIPEMD A family of hash functions based on the function RIPEMD-0. This function was proposed by the RIPE Consortium and originally simply called RIPEMD. Attacks on this function led to refinements and the definitions of the other, repaired versions RIPEMD-128/-160/-256/-320 in.

Second Preimage Resistant Function A function, for which it is computationally infeasible, given one message, to find another message mapping to the same value.

SHA A family of hash functions designed and proposed by NIST in the Secure Hash Standard. The first function of this family was originally simply called SHA (Secure Hash Algorithm) and is now usually referenced as SHA-0. This function was replaced as a standard bei SHA-1 in 1995, and in 2002/2004 the new and more complex variants SHA-224/-256/-384/-512 were proposed.

CROSS REFERENCES

See *Cryptographic Protocols; Encryption Basics.*

REFERENCES

Bellare, M., Canetti, R., & Krawczyk, H. (1996a). *The HMAC construction. CryptoBytes, 2*(1), 12–15.

Bellare, M., Canetti, R., & Krawczyk, H. (1996b). *Keyed hash functions for message authentication.* In *Lecture Notes in Computer Science: Advances in Cryptology—Crypto '96* (pp. 1–15). New York: Springer-Verlag.

Biham, E., & Chen, R. (2004a). *Near-collisions of SHA-0.* In *Lecture Notes in Computer Science, vol. 3152: Advances in Cryptology—Crypto '04.* New York: Springer-Verlag. [Also available under Cryptology ePrint Archive, Report 2004/146, http://eprint.iacr.org/2004/146]

Biham, E., & Chen, R. (2004b). *Near-collisions of SHA-0 and SHA-1.* Presented at SAC 2004, Waterloo, Canada. [available from http://www.cs.technion.ac.il/~biham/]

Black, J., Rogaway, P., & Shrimpton, T. (2002). *Black-box analysis of the block-cipher-based hash-function constructions from PGV.* In *Lecture Notes in Computer Science, Vol. 2442: Advances in Cryptology—Crypto '02* (pp. 320–335). New York: Springer-Verlag. [Full version available from http://www.cs.ucdavis.edu/~rogaway]

Boer, B. den, & Bosselaers, A. (1992). *An attack on the last two rounds of MD4.* In *Lecture Notes in Computer Science, vol. 576: Advances in Cryptology—Crypto '91* (pp. 194–204). New York: Springer-Verlag.

Boer, B. den, & Bosselaers, A. (1994). *Collisions for the compression function of MD5.* In *Lecture Notes in Computer Science, vol. 773: Advances in Cryptology—Eurocrypt '93* (pp. 293–304). New York: Springer-Verlag.

Bosselaers, A. *The RIPEMD-160 page.* Retrieved January 1, 2004, from http://www.esat.kuleven.ac.be/~bosselae/ripemd160.html.

Brachtl, B. O., Coppersmith, D., Hyden, M. M., Matyas, S. M., Meyer, C. H., Oseas, J., Pilpel, S., & Schilling, M. (1990). *Data authentication using modification detection codes based on a public one way encryption function.* U. S. Patent Number 4,908,861, March 13, 1990.

Buchmann, J. (2002). *Introduction to cryptography.* New York: Springer-Verlag.

Chaubaud, F., & Joux, A. (1998). *Differential Collisions in SHA-0.* In *Lecture Notes in Computer Science, vol. 1462: Advances in Cryptology—Crypto '98* (p. 56ff). New York: Springer-Verlag.

Chaum, D., van Heijst, E., & Pfitzmann, B. (1992). *Cryptographically strong undeniable signatures, unconditionally secure for the signer.* In *Lecture Notes in Computer Science, vol. 576: Advances in Cryptology–Crypto '91* (pp. 470–484). New York: Springer-Verlag.

Crypto++ 5.2.1 Benchmarks. http://www.eskimo.com/~weidai/benchmarks.html.

Damgård, I. B. (1990). *A design principle for hash functions.* In *Lecture Notes in Computer Science, vol. 435:*

Advances in Cryptology—Crypto '89 (pp. 416–427) New York: Springer-Verlag.

Daum, M. (2005) *Cryptanalysis of hash functions of the MD4-family*. Ph.D. thesis, Ruhr University Bochum.

Dobbertin, H. (1995). *Alf swindles Ann. CryptoBytes*, *1*(3), 5.

Dobbertin, H. (1996a). *Cryptanalysis of MD4*. In *Workshop, Lecture Notes in Computer Science, vol. 1039: Fast Software Encryption—Cambridge* (pp. 53–69). New York: Springer-Verlag.

Dobbertin, H. (1996b). *The status of MD5 after a recent attack. CrytoBytes, 2*(2), 1–6.

Dobbertin, H. (1997). *RIPEMD with two-round compress function is not collision-free. Journal of Cryptology, 10*, 51–68.

Dobbertin, H. (1998a). *Cryptanalysis of MD4. Journal of Cryptology, 11*, 253–274.

Dobbertin, H. (1998b). *The first two rounds of MD4 are not oneway*. Fast Software Encryption-Paris Workshop, Lecture Notes in Computer Science, vol. 1372, Springer-Verlag.

Dobbertin, H., Bosselaers, A., & Preneel, B. (1996). *RIPEMD-160: A strengthened version of RIPEMED*. In *Lecture Notes in Computer Science, vol. 1039: Fast Software Encryption—Cambridge Workshop* (pp. 71–82) New York: Springer-Verlag.

Federal Information Processing Standard 180. Secure hash standard (1993).

Federal Information Processing Standard 180-2. (August, 2002). *Secure hash Standard*. Retrieved January 1, 2004, from http://www.csrc.nist.gov/publications/fips/fips180-2/fips180-2withchangenotice.pdf

Federal Information Processing Standard 186-2 (2002). *Digital signature standard (DSS), January-2000, change notice 1, October 2001*. Retrieved January 1, 2004, from http://www.csrc.nist.gov/publications/fips/fips186-2/fips186-2-change1.pdf

Joux, A., Carribault, P., Jalby, W., & Lemuet, C. (2004). *Collisions in SHA-0*. Presented at the rump session of Crypto 2004.

Kasselman, P., & Penzhorn, W. (2000). *Cryptanalysis of reduced version of HAVAL*. Electronics Letters, *36*(1), 30–31.

Knudsen, L., & Preneel, B. (1997). *Fast and secure hashing based on codes*. In *Lecture Notes in Computer Science, vol. 1294: Advances in Cryptology—Crypto '97* (pp. 485–498). New York: Springer-Verlag.

Knuth, D. E. (1998). *The art of computer programming*. Boston, MA: Addison-Wesley-Longman.

Menezes, A., van Oorschot, P., & Vantone, S. (1996). *Handbook of applied cryptography*. Boca Raton, FL: CRC Press.

Mystery Twister Homepage. http://www.mystery-twister.com.

Preneel, B., Govaerts, R., & Vandewalle, J. (1994). *Hash functions based on block ciphers: A synthetic approach*. In *Lecture Notes in Computer Science, vol. 773: Advances in Cryptology—Crypto'93* (pp. 368–378). New York: Springer-Verlag.

RIPE Consortium. (1995). *Lecture Notes in Computer Science, vol. 1007: Ripe integrity primitives—Final report of RACE Integrity Primitives Evaluation (R1040)*. New York: Springer-Verlag.

Rivest, R. (1991). *The MD4 message digest algorithm*. In *Lecture Notes in Computer science, vol. 537: Advances in Cryptology—Crypto '90* (pp. 303–311). New York: Springer-Verlag.

Rivest, R. (1992a). *The MD4 message-digest algorithm, Request for Comments (RFC) 1320*. Internet Activities Board, Internet Privacy Task Force.

Rivest, R. (1992b). *The MD5 message-digest algorithm, Request for Comments (RFC) 1321*. Internet Activities Board, Internet Privacy Task Force.

Seberry, J., & Zhang, X.-M. (1992). *Highly nonlinear 0-1 balanced Boolean functions satisfying strict avalanche criterion*. In *Lecture Notes in Computer Science: Advances in Cryptology—Auscrypt '92*. New York: Springer-Verlag.

Shannon, C. (1949). *Communication theory of secrecy systems. Bell Systems Technical Journal, 28*(4), 656–715.

Stinson, D. R. (1995). *Cryptography: theory and practice*. Boca Raton, FL: CRC Press.

van Oorschot, P. C., & Wiener, M. J. (1999). *Parallel collision search with applications to hash functions and discrete logarithms. Journal of Cryptology, 12*, 000–000.

Van Rompay, B., Biryukov, A., Preneel, B., & Vandewalle, J. (2003). *Cryptanalysis of 3-pass HAVAL*. In *Lecture Notes in Computer Science, vol. 2894: Advances in Cryptology—Asiacrypt 2003* (pp. 228–245). New York: Springer-Verlag.

Vaudenay, S. (1995). *On the need for multipermutations: Cryptanalysis of MD4 and SAFER*. In *Lecture Notes in Computer Science, vol. 1008: Fast Software Encryption—Leuven Workshop* (pp. 286–297). New York: Springer-Verlag.

Wang, X., Feng, D., Lai, X., & Yu, H. (2004). *Collisions for hash functions MD4, MD5, HAVL-128 and RIPEMD*. Cryptology ePrint Archive, Report 2004/199. Retrieved January 1, 2004, from http://eprint.iacr.org/2004/199

Yuval, G. (1979). *How to swindle Rabin. Cryptologia, 3*, 187–189.

Zheng, Y., Pieprzyk, J., & Seberry J. (1993). *HAVAL—A one-way hashing algorithm with variable length and output*. In *Lecture Notes in Computer Science: Advances in Cryptology—Auscrypt '92* (pp. 83–104). New York: Springer-Verlag.

Number Theory for Information Security

Duncan A. Buell, *University of South Carolina*

INTRODUCTION

The mathematical basis for the algorithms used in public key cryptosystems (RSA, Diffie–Hellman, discrete logarithms, elliptic curves, etc.) relies on some moderately deep concepts and results from number theory, which is covered in the specific chapters on these topics elsewhere in this handbook. Underlying the deep results in number theory, however, are some fundamentals that are almost, but perhaps not quite, obvious. Our purpose in this chapter is to present those parts of the theory of numbers necessary for an understanding of the more advanced material. We begin our discussion with a look at the ordinary integers. Central to work in number theory is the nature of arithmetic (addition, multiplication, and the like) modulo prime numbers. For some purposes, specifically, for example, in elliptic curves and in the advanced encryption standard of the National Institute of Standards and Technology (NIST), it is necessary to go beyond the integers to look at the polynomial arithmetic modulo irreducible polynomials that is the analog of ordinary arithmetic modulo prime integers. Fortunately, the results from arithmetic modulo prime integers carry over almost exactly to polynomial arithmetic, so we can treat this latter topic largely by analogy to more familiar material.

REFERENCES

Most of this material can be found in any standard introductory text in number theory, such as the books by Hardy and Wright (1980), by Niven, Zuckerman, and Montgomery (1991), or by Rosen (2000). Although these references will be complete, they will also oversatisfy the needs of a reader interested only in cryptography. A detailed analysis of the computational complexity of algorithms in number theory can be found either in Bach and Shallit (1996) or in Cohen (1993). More condensed versions can be found as the introductory chapters in references on

cryptography by Buchmann (2001) or Koblitz (1987) or in the standard algorithms reference of Cormen, Leiserson, Rivest, and Stein (2003). For complexity and implementation issues of doing multiprecise arithmetic, there is still probably no better reference than Knuth (1998). The large book by Schneier (1996) presents a very brief introduction to and then relies on the material in this chapter. The standard reference on the large topic of finite fields is the book by Lidl and Niederreiter (1994). Further information can be found in Golomb (1982). Two background references on elliptic curves are Koblitz (1984) and Silverman and Tate (1992), although once again these cover much more material than is needed for this application. Two excellent references on elliptic curves in cryptography are the book by Menezes (1993) and the new book by Hankerson, Menezes, and Vanstone (2004). Further information on cryptography and on the elliptic curve recommendations of NIST can be found in their publications (Barker, 2000; NIST, 1999). Further information on the NIST AES can be found in Daemen and Rijmen (2001), from the Rijndael Web site (2003), or from NIST directly (NIST, 1998, 1999, 2000, 2001).

DIVISIBILITY

Most of elementary number theory concerns the *integers* $\mathbb{Z} = \{\ldots, -3, -2, -1, 0, 1, 2, 3, \ldots\}$. Occasionally, we refer to the *rational numbers* $\mathbb{Q} = \{a/b : a, b, \in \mathbb{Z}\}$.

If $a, b \in \mathbb{Z}$, and $b \neq 0$, then the *integer part* of a/b, written $[a/b]$, also referred to as the *floor* of a/b and written $\lfloor a/b \rfloor$, is the integer c such that $c \leq a/b < c + 1$. The *ceiling* of a/b, written $\lceil a/b \rceil$, is the integer c such that $c - 1 < a/b \leq c$.

We present these definitions to clarify the notation for negative values. The integer part function "truncates toward negative infinity" in that, for example,

$$[(-5)/4] = [5/(-4)] = -2 \cdot$$

An integer b is *divisible* by an integer a if there exists an integer c such that $b = ac$. We say that a is a *divisor* of b.

Notes

- We write $a|b$ or $a\nmid b$, read "a divides b" or "a does not divide b", according as b is or is not divisible by a.
- We note that $a|a$ always holds. If $a|b$ and $0 < a < b$, then we say that a is a *proper divisor* of b.
- We note also that $a|0$ holds for all integers a but that $0|b$ never holds for any nonzero integer b. The only instance in which $a|0$ would make sense would be in the expression $0|0$. By convention, we specifically exclude this relatively useless special case because permitting it would require the addition of extra qualifications on a large number of theorems.

Theorem 110.1. *The following hold for all integers:*

1. *If $a|b$, then $a|bc$ for any integer c.*
2. *If $a|b$ and $b|c$, then $a|c$.*
3. *If $a|b$, then $ac|bc$ for any integer c.*
4. *If $a|b$ and $b|a$, then $a = \pm b$.*
5. *If $a|b$ and $a|c$, then $a|(bx + cy)$ for any integers x and y.*
6. *If $a|b$, $a > 0$, and $b > 0$, then $a \leq b$.*

Proof. The proofs of these follow immediately from the definition.

One of the basic results of school arithmetic is that division of two integers yields a remainder that is smaller than the divisor. This is formalized in the following theorem.

Theorem 110.2. (The division algorithm). *If a and $b > 0$ are integers, then there exists a unique pair of integers q and r such that $a = bq + r$ and $0 \leq r < b$.*

Proof. Among the values

$$\ldots, a - 3b, a - 2b, a - b, a, a + b, a + 2b, a + 3b, \ldots$$

there is a value $r = a - qb$ that satisfies the required inequality. Indeed, taking negative numbers into account, if $q = [a/b]$, then $q \leq a/b < q + 1$, so $bq \leq a < bq + b$ and thus $0 \leq a - bq < b$, as desired.

To prove uniqueness, we consider two such representations

$$a = bq_1 + r_1 = bq_2 + r_2$$

where we assume without loss of generality that $q_1 > q_2$, which implies that $r_2 > r_1$. From this we get

$$b(q_1 - q_2) = r_2 - r_1 > 0$$

so that $b|(r_2 - r_1)$. But this then implies that $0 \leq b \leq r_2 - r_1 < r_2 < b$, which is a contradiction.

We refer to q and r as computed by the division algorithm as the *quotient* and *remainder*, respectively.

Given integers a and b, we say that an integer c is a *common divisor* of a and b if c divides a and c divides b. If a and b are not both zero, then among the common divisors of a and b we will refer to the largest as the *greatest common divisor*, written $\gcd(a, b)$.

We remark that the *greatest common divisor* is sometimes referred to as the *highest common factor*.

We note that the gcd is defined only for pairs of integers a, b not both of which are zero and that it is thus always positive.

In the case that $\gcd(a, b) = 1$, we say that a and b are *relatively prime* or *prime to one another*.

Theorem 110.3. *The gcd of integers a and b, $g = \gcd(a, b)$, is the least positive value of $ax + by$ as x and y range over all integers.*

Proof. Among all the values of $ax + by$ as x and y range over all integers, we choose the least positive value $m = ax_0 + by_0$, and we claim that this is $g = \gcd(a, b)$. Clearly, any common divisor, and especially the greatest common divisor g, must divide a and b and therefore m. If, then, we have that $m|a$ and $m|b$, then $g = \pm m$, and because both m and g are positive by assumption, we have that $g = m$.

So let us assume that $m \nmid a$, for example, and therefore that $a = qm + r$ with $0 < r < m$. But in that case we have $0 < r = a - qm = a - q(ax_0 + by_0) = a(1 - qx_0) + by_0$, which violates the choice of m as the *least* positive linear combination of a and b. We conclude that $m|a$. A similar argument shows that $m|b$, from which it follows that $m = g$.

Theorem 110.4. (The Euclidean algorithm). *If, given integers a and b, we make a repeated application of the division algorithm:*

$$
\begin{aligned}
b &= r_0, \\
a &= bq_1 + r_1, & 0 < r_1 < b \\
b &= r_1 q_2 + r_2, & 0 < r_2 < r_1 \qquad (1) \\
r_1 &= r_2 q_3 + r_3, & 0 < r_3 < r_2 \\
&\cdots
\end{aligned}
$$

then the process must terminate with $r_{j+1} = 0$ for some j and we have that $r_j = \gcd(a, b)$.

Proof. It is useful for intuitive purposes to notice that the Euclidean algorithm is a recursive algorithm: if we use the division algorithm to determine q and r such that $a = bq + r$ with $0 \leq r < b$, then

- either $r = 0$ and $b = \gcd(a, b)$
- or $r \neq 0$ and $\gcd(a, b) = \gcd(b, r)$.

To prove the theorem, we observe that the process must terminate because the remainders r_i are positive and decreasing with every step.

We further note that when the process stops with $r_{j+1} = 0$, then r_j must be a divisor of a and b because we have the following:

$$
\begin{aligned}
r_{j-1} &= r_j q_{j+1} + 0 & \text{and hence} & \quad r_j | r_{j-1}, \\
r_{j-2} &= r_{j-1} q_j + r_j & \text{and hence} & \quad r_j | r_{j-2},
\end{aligned}
$$

and so forth. Thus r_j is a common divisor of a and b. To see that r_j is the greatest common divisor $g = \gcd(a, b)$, we observe that g divides a and b and therefore divides r_1. Because g divides b and r_1, we have that g divides r_2, and so on, so that g must also divide r_j, from which we conclude that $g = r_j$.

Theorem 110.5. (The extended Euclidean algorithm). *The values x_0 and y_0 such that $\gcd(a, b) = ax_0 + by_0$ can be obtained by eliminating the r_i from Eq. (1).*

Proof. We can write Eq. (1) as matrix equations, with each successive equation obtainable from the previous equation by the application of a simple matrix:

$$\begin{pmatrix} 0 & 1 \\ 1 & -q_1 \end{pmatrix} \begin{pmatrix} a \\ b \end{pmatrix} = \begin{pmatrix} b \\ r_1 \end{pmatrix}$$

$$\begin{pmatrix} 0 & 1 \\ 1 & -q_2 \end{pmatrix} \begin{pmatrix} 0 & 1 \\ 1 & -q_1 \end{pmatrix} \begin{pmatrix} a \\ b \end{pmatrix} = \begin{pmatrix} r_1 \\ r_2 \end{pmatrix} \quad (2)$$

$$\cdots$$

$$\begin{pmatrix} 0 & 1 \\ 1 & -q_{j+1} \end{pmatrix} \cdots \begin{pmatrix} 0 & 1 \\ 1 & -q_1 \end{pmatrix} \begin{pmatrix} a \\ b \end{pmatrix} = \begin{pmatrix} r_j \\ r_{j+1} \end{pmatrix} = \begin{pmatrix} r_j \\ 0 \end{pmatrix}$$

If we then compute the matrix product of the last line, we obtain the needed values x_0 and y_0.

$$\begin{pmatrix} x_0 & y_0 \\ z & w \end{pmatrix} \begin{pmatrix} a \\ b \end{pmatrix} = \begin{pmatrix} 0 & 1 \\ 1 & -q_{j+1} \end{pmatrix} \cdots \begin{pmatrix} 0 & 1 \\ 1 & -q_1 \end{pmatrix} \begin{pmatrix} a \\ b \end{pmatrix}$$

$$= \begin{pmatrix} r_j \\ r_{j+1} \end{pmatrix} = \begin{pmatrix} r_j \\ 0 \end{pmatrix} \quad (3)$$

Example

We apply the Euclidean algorithm to the pair $a = 261$, $b = 48$. We get the following:

$$261 = 48 \times 5 + 21,$$
$$48 = 21 \times 2 + 6,$$
$$21 = 6 \times 3 + 3,$$
$$6 = 3 \times 2 + 0,$$

so the sequence q_1, q_2, q_3, q_4 is 5, 2, 3, 2. The matrix product of Eq. (3) is as follows:

$$\begin{pmatrix} 7 & -38 \\ -16 & 87 \end{pmatrix} \begin{pmatrix} 261 \\ 47 \end{pmatrix}$$

$$= \begin{pmatrix} 0 & 1 \\ 1 & -2 \end{pmatrix} \begin{pmatrix} 0 & 1 \\ 1 & -3 \end{pmatrix} \begin{pmatrix} 0 & 1 \\ 1 & -2 \end{pmatrix} \begin{pmatrix} 0 & 1 \\ 1 & -5 \end{pmatrix} \begin{pmatrix} 261 \\ 47 \end{pmatrix} = \begin{pmatrix} 3 \\ 0 \end{pmatrix}$$

from which we get the extended gcd as $7 \times 261 - 38 \times 48 = 3$.

PRIME NUMBERS AND FACTORING

We say that an integer $p > 1$ is a *prime number* if there are no positive divisors of p other than 1 and p. If p is not prime, then it is a *composite number*.

Theorem 110.6. *The following hold:*

1. *Every positive integer has a prime divisor.*
2. *If, for a prime p, we have $p|ab$, then either $p|a$ or $p|b$.*
3. *If, for a prime p, we have $p| \prod_{i=1}^{n} a_i$, then $p|a_i$ for some i.*

Proof. Let a be a positive integer. Then a has at least the divisors 1 and a. If there are no other divisors, then a is prime and part (1) is proved. If a has other divisors, then let p be the least among them. If p is prime, then part (1) is proved. If p is not prime, then it has some divisor $q \neq 1, p$. But now we have $1 < q < p < a$, and because $q|p$ and $p|a$, we must have $q|a$, contradicting the choice of p as the smallest divisor of a.

Now let ab be an integer that is divisible by a prime p, and let $g_1 = \gcd(a, p)$ and $g_2 = \gcd(b, p)$. Because g_1 and g_2 are both divisors of p, and because the only divisors of p are 1 and p, we must have, say, that $g_1 = 1$ and $g_2 = p$. This implies that $p|b$.

The proof of part (3) now follows by induction.

We now come to the main theorem of elementary number theory.

Theorem 110.7. (The Fundamental Theorem of Arithmetic). *Every positive integer $a > 1$ can be factored into a product of primes, and the factoring is unique up to order.*

Proof. To prove the first part, we see that if a is prime, then it is a product of primes with only one factor in the product. If a is not prime, it must have a a prime divisor a_1 and an integer **cofactor** $a_2 = a/a_1$, both of which are positive and smaller than a. We can repeat the above argument on the factors a_1 and a_2, but this process of splitting into factors can only go on for finitely many steps because the factors are all positive and smaller than a.

Now let us assume that we have $a = \prod_{i=1}^{n} p_i = \prod_{j=1}^{m} q_j$ be two factorings of a into products of primes. Because p_1 divides the first product, it must divide the second product, and therefore, it must divide q_j for some j. But q_j is prime, and therefore, $p_i = q_j$. We may now repeat this argument on a/p_1, and the argument must terminate with $n = m$ and all the p_i matched up in a one-to-one fashion with a q_j.

CONGRUENCES

Given integers a, b, and m, we say that a is *congruent* to b modulo m, which we write as $a \equiv b \pmod{m}$, if the difference $a - b$ is divisible by m. We refer to the integer m as the *modulus*. We note that divisibility, and thus the congruence relation, is independent of whether the modulus is positive or negative, so we usually restrict our attention to positive moduli m. By convention, a modulus m cannot be zero because that would require a divisibility condition $0|(a - b)$ that we have earlier declared impermissible.

We also note that it seems all too commonplace to find incorrect terminology in use. Although we say and write that a is congruent to b modulo m, the arithmetic of congruences is referred to as *modular* arithmetic, not (as is unfortunately often seen in publications in electrical engineering) *modulo* arithmetic.

Congruence arithmetic shares many properties with ordinary arithmetic, provided that we do not attempt arbitrary division.

Theorem 110.8. *Let a, b, c, and d be integers. Then*

1. $a \equiv b \pmod{m}$, $b \equiv a \pmod{m}$, *and* $a - b \equiv 0 \pmod{m}$ *are equivalent statements.*

2. *If* $a \equiv b \pmod{m}$ *and* $b \equiv c \pmod{m}$, *then* $a \equiv c \pmod{m}$.

3. *If* $a \equiv b \pmod{m}$ *and* $c \equiv d \pmod{m}$, *then* $a + c \equiv b + d \pmod{m}$ *and* $ac \equiv bd \pmod{m}$.

4. *If* $a \equiv b \pmod{m}$, *then there exists an integer k such that* $a = b + km$.

5. *If* $a \equiv b \pmod{m}$ *and if* $f(n)$ *is a polynomial in the variable n with integer coefficients, then* $f(a) \equiv f(b) \pmod{m}$.

As can be deduced from the theorem above, addition, subtraction, and multiplication with congruences is the same as for ordinary arithmetic. That division fails, however, can be seen from the following example. With conventional arithmetic, if we have $ax = ay$, for $a \neq 0$, then we can divide by a to obtain $x = y$. This fails in general in modular arithmetic. Consider $a = 7$, $x = 17$, $y = 5$, and modulus $m = 21$. Then certainly $119 = 7 \times 17 \equiv 7 \times 5 \equiv 35 \pmod{21}$. However, it is not true that $17 \equiv 5 \pmod{21}$. Because 7 divides 119, 35, and 21, we have only the weaker statement that $17 \equiv 5 \pmod{3}$.

Theorem 110.9. *Let a, m, r, and s be integers. We have* $ar \equiv as \pmod{m}$ *if and only if* $r \equiv s \pmod{m/\gcd(a, m)}$. *Specifically, if* $ar \equiv as \pmod{m}$ *and* $\gcd(a, m) = 1$, *then* $r \equiv s \pmod{m}$.

Proof. We have $ar \equiv as \pmod{m}$ if and only if some integer k exists so that $ar = as + km$. If $g = \gcd(a, m)$, then $a = ga'$, $m = gm' = g[m/\gcd(a, m)]$, and $a'(r - s) = km'$. Now, because $\gcd(a', m') = 1$, no prime dividing a' can divide m', and yet all the factors of a' must divide the right-hand side km'. We conclude that $a'|k$, so $k' = k/a'$ is an integer and we have $r - s = k'm'$, which is sufficient because of part (1) of the previous theorem.

If $a \equiv b \pmod{m}$, then we say that b is a *residue* of a modulo m. The *residue class* of a modulo m is the set $\bar{a} = \{n : n \equiv a \pmod{m}\} = \{a + \lambda m : \lambda \in \mathbb{Z}\}$. A complete residue system R modulo m consists of the integers 0 through $m - 1$, so that every integer a is congruent modulo m to some residue $r \in R$ and yet no members of R are congruent modulo m.

The fundamental theorem on the solution of congruences is discussed next.

Theorem 110.10. *Given integers a, b, and m, the congruence*

$$ax \equiv b \pmod{m} \qquad (4)$$

is solvable for integers x if and only if $\gcd(a, m)|b$. *If* $\gcd(a, m)|b$ *and* x_0 *is a solution, then all solutions of congruence (4) are given by* $x = x_0 + km$, *where k is any integer.*

Proof. If we have a solution x to the congruence, then we have an equality $ax = b + km$ for some integer k. Clearly, then, $\gcd(a, m)$ must divide b. Conversely, if $\gcd(a, m)|b$, then we can divide $\gcd(a, m)$ from a, b, and m and reduce the problem to one of solving the congruence (4) in the case $\gcd(a, m) = 1$.

In the simpler case of congruence (4) with $\gcd(a, m) = 1$, there must be integers t and u such that $at - mu = 1$. We can multiply by b to see that $a(bt) - m(bu) = b$, choose $x_0 = bt$ as a solution to congruence (4), and then notice that the values $x = bt + km$ for any integers k are an infinite set of solutions to (4) because we have $a(x_0 + km) - m(bu + ak) = b$.

It remains only to show that these are the only solutions, and it suffices to deal with the case with $\gcd(a, m) = 1$. Assume, then, that we have two solutions, x_0 and x_1, to (4) with $\gcd(a, m) = 1$. We then have $ax_0 \equiv b \pmod{m}$ and $ax_1 \equiv b \pmod{m}$; we subtract to get $a(x_1 - x_0) \equiv 0 \pmod{m}$, which is equivalent to $a(x_1 - x_0) = km$ for some integer k. Because a divides the left-hand side, it must divide the right-hand side, but because $\gcd(a, m) = 1$, we must have that $a|k$ and thus that $x_1 = x_0 + (k/a)m$ for some integer k/a, which is what we were trying to prove.

Examples

Let us solve the following:

$$60x \equiv 21 \pmod{69}. \qquad (5)$$

Because $\gcd(60, 69) = 3$, we divide through by 3 to get the equivalent congruence

$$20x \equiv 7 \pmod{23}. \qquad (6)$$

The congruence

$$20x \equiv 1 \pmod{23}$$

has solutions, found using the extended Euclidean algorithm, of $x = 15 + 23k$ for any k. The congruence (6) therefore has solutions $x = 105 + 23(7k) = 13 + 23(7k + 4)$, or $x \equiv 13 \pmod{23}$, and thus the congruence (5) has solutions $x = 39 + 69(7k + 4)$, or $x \equiv 16 \pmod{69}$.

To see an instance of a congruence with no solutions, consider the following:

$$60x \equiv 17 \pmod{69}.$$

To have solutions, we must have x such that $60x - 17 = 69k$ for some integer k. But by rearranging terms this becomes $60x - 69k = 17$, with 3 dividing the left-hand side but not the right-hand side, which is impossible.

GROUPS AND FIELDS DEFINED MOD PRIMES

Let S be a set on which a binary operation $\oplus$ is defined. The binary operation is *closed* on S if, for every pair $a, b \in S$, we have $a \oplus b \in S$. The operation is *associative* if, for every triple $a, b, c \in S$, we have $(a \oplus b) \oplus c = a \oplus (b \oplus c)$. Given a set S together with a closed associative operation on S, we say that $G = (S, \oplus)$ is a *group* if

- there exists an *identity* element e such that for all $a \in S$, $a \oplus e = e \oplus a = a$;
- for every element $a \in S$ there exists an *inverse* element a' such that $a \oplus a' = a' \oplus a = e$.

We note that inverses are unique: if a' and a'' are two elements for which

$$e = a \oplus a' = a \oplus a'',$$

then from $e = a \oplus a'$ we get $a'' = a'' \oplus (a \oplus a') = (a'' \oplus a) \oplus a' = e \oplus a' = a'$.

A group G is said to be *commutative* or *abelian* if for every $a, b \in G$ we have $a \oplus b = b \oplus a$.

A canonical example of a group, which happens to be an abelian group, are the integers $(\mathbb{Z}, +)$ under ordinary addition, for which the identity is the number 0 and the inverse of a is $-a$.

The nonzero integers under multiplication do not form a group because there are no integers with multiplicative inverses except for ± 1, but the nonzero rational numbers do form a group under multiplication. In this instance, the identity is the number 1, and the inverse of the nonzero rational number a/b is the rational number b/a.

A subgroup of a group $G = (S, \oplus)$ is a pair $G' = (S', \oplus)$ such that $S' \subseteq S$ and G' is itself a group under $\oplus$. The set of even integers, for example, forms a subgroup of the group of integers under addition.

We say that a set S with two closed associative operations, written $\oplus$ and $\otimes$, is a ring if S is an abelian group under $\oplus$ and if $\otimes$ distributes over $\oplus$. If the nonzero elements of S also form an abelian group under $\otimes$, then we say that S with its operations forms a field.

The canonical example of a ring is the set of integers under usual addition and multiplication, and the canonical example of a field is the set of rational numbers under usual addition and multiplication.

What we will now prove is central to the use of number theory for public key cryptography. We write $\mathbb{Z}_{(\text{mod } n)}$ to denote the set of integers modulo an integer n. This is always a ring, and if n is a prime, the next theorem shows that it is also a finite field of n elements.

Theorem 110.11. *The set $\mathbb{Z}_{(\text{mod } n)}$ of integers modulo a prime number p form a field under the usual operations of congruence arithmetic.*

Proof. Clearly, the integers modulo p under addition form an abelian group. The identity of the group under addition is the residue class congruent to 0 modulo p, and the inverse of any element a is just $-a$. Under multiplication, the identity must clearly be 1, and it

remains only to prove that any integer relatively prime to p has an inverse modulo p. This, however, is exactly the conclusion to be drawn from Theorem 110.10; for any a, the inverse is the residue b such that $ab \equiv 1 \pmod{p}$.

We note that $\mathbb{Z}_{(\text{mod } n)}$ for a composite number n is never a field. The only integers modulo a composite n that have inverses modulo n are those that are relatively prime to n. A *reduced residue system* is a set $S = \{s_i\}$ of residue classes modulo n for which

1. for all i, $\gcd(s_i, m) \equiv 1 \pmod{m}$;
2. for any $n \in \mathbb{Z}$, there exists an s_i such that $n \equiv s_i \pmod{m}$;
3. for no distinct subscripts i, j do we have $s_i \equiv s_j \pmod{m}$.

Modulo 21, for example, one reduced residue system is the set of residue classes $\{1, 2, 4, 5, 8, 10, 11, 13, 16, 17, 19, 20\}$. The integers $3k$ and $7k$, for k any integer, are zero divisors. In ordinary arithmetic, if we have a product $ab = 0$, then one of a or b must be zero. Modulo a prime number, there are no nontrivial zero divisors, but modulo a composite number n, such as 21, the integers a that are not relatively prime to n but not congruent to zero modulo n have a nontrivial cofactor b such that $ab \equiv 0 \pmod{n}$. For example, $3 \times 7 \equiv 0 \pmod{21}$ and $6 \times 7 \equiv 0 \pmod{21}$.

The Euler totient, also called the Euler phi function, is the function $\phi(n)$ equal to the number of integers modulo n that are relatively prime to n. We adopt the convention that $\phi(1) = 1$. The first and most important property of the Euler function is that it is multiplicative; that is, that for relatively prime integers m and n, we have $\phi(mn) = \phi(m)\phi(n)$.

Theorem 110.12. *If m and n are integers for which $\gcd(m, n) = 1$, then $\phi(mn) = \phi(m)\phi(n)$.*

Proof. Consider two complete sets of residue classes $R_m = \{a_i : i = 1, \ldots, \phi(m)\}$ and $R_n = \{b_j : j = 1, \ldots, \phi(n)\}$ of integers relatively prime to m and n, respectively. Let M and N be chosen so that $Mm \equiv 1 \pmod{n}$ and $Nn \equiv 1 \pmod{m}$. We form the $\phi(m)\phi(n)$ elements $a_i nN + b_j mM$ and claim that these are distinct and that they form a complete set of residues modulo mn. They are distinct because if we had for two such elements the congruence $a_{i_1} nN + b_{j_1} mM \equiv a_{i_2} nN + b_{j_2} mM \pmod{mn}$, then we could reduce modulo m and modulo n to get $a_{i_1} \equiv a_{i_2} \pmod{m}$ and $b_{j_1} \equiv b_{j_2} \pmod{n}$, which are contradictions. And if we choose any element c relatively prime to mn, then c reduced modulo m is prime to m and must be congruent to some a_i, and similarly for n, so that our system is complete.

Theorem 110.13. *If $n > 1$ is an integer, and $n = \prod_{i=1}^{k} p_i^{e_i}$ is the canonical factoring of n into a product of primes, then*

$$\phi(n) = \prod_{i=1}^{k} p_i^{e_i - 1}(p_i - 1) = n \prod_{p|n} \frac{p-1}{p}.$$

Proof. By the multiplicativity of the Euler function, we need show only the following:

$$\phi(p^e) = p^{e-1}(p-1)$$

for primes p, and the general formula will follow. To see this, we write each of the p^e integers 0 through $p^e - 1$ base p as

$$k = a_{e-1} \times p^{e-1} + \cdots + a_2 \times p^2 + a_1 \times p + a_0$$

with $0 \le a_i \le p - 1$ for all i. We observe that the integers that are *not* prime to p^e are exactly those for which $a_0 = 0$. There are p^{e-1} of these, so there are $p^e - p^{e-1} = p^{e-1}(p-1)$ such integers that *are* prime to p^e, and the theorem is proved.

Theorem 110.14. *For $n \ge 1$ we have $\sum_{d|n} \phi(d) = n$.*

Proof. We will prove this by induction on the number of distinct prime factors of n. For a prime power $n = p^e$ we have $\phi(p^e) = 1 + (p-1) + p(p-1) + \cdots + p^e(p-1)$, which telescopes. If now we have $\gcd(n, p) = 1$, then

$$\sum_{d|np^e} \phi(d) = \sum_{d|n} \phi(d) + \sum_{d|n} \phi(pd) + \cdots + \sum_{d|n} \phi(p^e d)$$

$$= 1 \times \sum_{d|n} \phi(d) + \phi(p) \times \sum_{d|n} \phi(d) + \cdots + \phi(p^e)$$

$$\times \sum_{d|n} \phi(d)$$

$$= n \times \sum_{d|p^e} \phi(d) = np^e.$$

Examples

- For $n = p$ a prime, we have $\phi(p) = p - 1$ and $\sum_{d|n} \phi(d) = 1 + (p-1) = p = n$, as required by Theorems 110.13 and 110.14.

- For $n = p^e$ the power of a single prime, we have $\phi(p) = p^{e-1}(p-1)$ and $\sum_{d|n} \phi(d) = 1 + (p-1) = p = n$, as required by Theorems 110.13 and 110.14.

- For $n = pq$ the product of two primes, we have $\phi(p) = p - 1$ and

$$\sum_{d|n} \phi(d) = 1 + (p-1) + p(p-1)$$

$$+ p^2(p-1) + \cdots + p^{e-1}(p-1)$$

$$= 1 + (p-1)\frac{p^e - 1}{p - 1} = p^e = n.$$

- For a more complicated $n = 2^3 \times 3^2 \times 5 = 360$, for example, we have

$$\phi(360) = \left[2^2(2-1)\right]\left[3(3-1)\right]\left[1(5-1)\right]$$

$$= 96$$

$$= 360\left(\frac{2-1}{2}\right)\left(\frac{3-1}{3}\right)\left(\frac{5-1}{5}\right).$$

A group $G = (S, \oplus)$ is *cyclic* if there exists a *generating element* a such that repeated application of $\oplus$ to a generates the entire set S as a, $a \oplus a$, $a \oplus a \oplus a$, and so forth. For

Table 1 Index Function for the Prime 11

Exponent	1	2	3	4	5	6	7	8	9	10
Residue	2	4	8	5	10	9	7	3	6	1

example, both the integers and the integers modulo p are generated by 1 under ordinary addition.

What is crucial to the utility of number theory in public key cryptography is that, modulo a prime p, the group of integers formed by multiplication is also generated by a single element, which we refer to as a primitive root. For example, the integers modulo 11 are generated by repeated multiplication by the primitive root 2:

$$
\begin{aligned}
2^1 &= 2 \times 1 &&\equiv 2 &&(\text{mod } 11), \\
2^2 &= 2 \times 2 &&\equiv 4 &&(\text{mod } 11), \\
2^3 &= 2 \times 4 &&\equiv 8 &&(\text{mod } 11), \\
2^4 &= 2 \times 8 \equiv 16 &&\equiv 5 &&(\text{mod } 11), \\
2^5 &= 2 \times 5 \equiv 10 &&\equiv 10 &&(\text{mod } 11), \\
2^6 &= 2 \times 10 \equiv 20 &&\equiv 9 &&(\text{mod } 11), \\
2^7 &= 2 \times 9 \equiv 18 &&\equiv 7 &&(\text{mod } 11), \\
2^8 &= 2 \times 7 \equiv 14 &&\equiv 3 &&(\text{mod } 11), \\
2^9 &= 2 \times 3 &&\equiv 6 &&(\text{mod } 11), \\
2^{10} &= 2 \times 6 \equiv 12 &&\equiv 1 &&(\text{mod } 11).
\end{aligned}
$$

We can convert the multiplicative arithmetic modulo 11 into additive arithmetic in the exponents by using the exponents as discrete logarithms as in Table 1.

We note that discrete logarithms function for arithmetic modulo primes in the same way as do ordinary logarithms in that multiplication modulo a prime can be accomplished by adding discrete logarithms. For example, we have

$$8 \equiv 30 \equiv 5 \cdot 6 \equiv 2^4 \cdot 2^9 \equiv 2^{13} \equiv 2^3 \equiv 8 \quad (\text{mod } 11).$$

With $p = 11$ and $\phi(p) = 10$, we have one element of order 2, namely $2^5 \equiv 10$ (mod 11) and four elements of order 5, namely $2^2 \equiv 4$ (mod 11), $2^4 \equiv 5$ (mod 11), $2^6 \equiv 9$ (mod 11), and $2^8 \equiv 3$ (mod 11). The multiplicative subgroup $\{1, 4, 5, 9, 3\} = \{2^0, 2^2, 2^4, 2^6, 2^8\}$ generated by $2^2 = 4$ is the same as the additive subgroup $\{0, 2, 4, 6, 8\}$ of even exponents modulo 10. And there are no other subcycles modulo 11. The four elements whose exponents 1, 3, 7, 9 are relatively prime to 10 are all primitive roots modulo 11.

Before we can prove the next main theorem, we must first digress to continue the discussion of solutions of congruences. We have already observed that linear polynomials $ax + b$ with coefficients taken from $\mathbb{Z}_{(\text{mod } p)}$ have no solutions or unique solutions in the field $\mathbb{Z}_{(\text{mod } p)}$; this is the meaning of Theorem 110.10.

In fact, we have the same strong theorem over finite fields that we have over the complex numbers.

Theorem 110.15. *Let $f(x) = a_n x^n + \cdots + a_0$ be a polynomial of degree n and not identically zero with coefficients in $\mathbb{Z}_{(\text{mod } p)}$. Then $f(n)$ has at most n distinct roots in $\mathbb{Z}_{(\text{mod } p)}$.*

Proof. We prove this by induction on n. The case $n = 1$ is Theorem 110.10.

We assume, then, that polynomials of degree $n - 1$ or smaller have no more roots than the degree of the polynomial, and we let $f(n)$ be a poly of degree n with coefficients in $\mathbb{Z}_{(\text{mod } p)}$. If $f(n)$ has as many as n roots $r_1, r_2, \ldots, r_n$, then we form the polynomial

$$g(n) = f(n) - a_n(x - r_1)(x - r_2) \cdots (x - r_n).$$

We have arranged for the x^n to disappear, so this is a polynomial of degree strictly smaller than n, but it has at least the n roots given explicitly above. This is contrary to our assumption unless the polynomial is identically zero when its coefficients are reduced modulo p. So $g(n)$ is identically zero, which means that for all integers r we have the following:

$$f(n) \equiv a_n(x - r_1)(x - r_2) \ldots (x - r_n) \quad (\text{mod } p).$$

If there were an $n + 1$-st root r_{n+1} of $f(n)$, we would have the following:

$$f(r_{n+1}) \equiv a_n(r_{n+1} - r_1)(r_{n+1} - r_2) \cdots (r_{n+1} - r_n) \equiv 0 \ (\text{mod} p).$$

We now utilize the fact that in a field there are no zero divisors in a field: if the product is zero modulo p, then one of the factors must be zero modulo p, which implies that we do not in fact have $n + 1$ distinct roots of $f(n)$.

The fact that we are working in a field is crucial to the truth of the theorem above, not just to the method by which we have proved it. The polynomial $x^2 + 3x + 2$, for example, taken modulo the composite number 6, is only of degree two but has the four roots 1, 2, 4, 5.

The next three theorems provide the structure of the multiplicative group modulo primes.

Theorem 110.16. (Fermat's Little Theorem). *If p is a prime, and a any integer with $\gcd(a, p) = 1$, then $a^{p-1} \equiv 1$ (mod p).*

We do not prove Fermat's Little Theorem because it follows from the stronger and more general theorem of Euler.

Theorem 110.17. (Euler's Theorem). *If a and m are integers with $\gcd(a, m) = 1$, then $a^{\phi(m)} \equiv 1$ (mod m).*

Proof. Consider a reduced residue system modulo m, $R_1 = \{r_1, \ldots, r_{\phi(m)}\}$ and let a be a integer relatively prime to m. We claim that R_1 is the same set, when reduced modulo m, as $R_2 = \{ar_1, \ldots, ar_{\phi(m)}\}$. This is true because $ar_i \equiv ar_j$ (mod m) implies that $r_i \equiv r_j$ (mod m).

We now observe the equality of the following products:

$$\prod_{i=1}^{\phi(m)} ar_i \equiv a^{\phi(m)} \prod_{i=1}^{\phi(m)} r_i \equiv \prod_{i=1}^{\phi(m)} r_i \quad (\text{mod } m);$$

the first product is taken over the set R_2 and the last is taken over the same set R_1.

Because these are a set of reduced residues, each is prime to m and we can divide out the product to get $a^{\phi(m)} \equiv 1$ (mod m).

Fermat's Little Theorem now follows as a special case of Euler's Theorem in the case that m is a prime p.

Theorem 110.18. *The multiplicative group of integers modulo a prime p is cyclic and can be generated by a primitive root. The number of primitive roots modulo p is $\phi(\phi(p))$.*

Proof. We have already seen in the case of the prime 11 what it is that we wish to prove is always true, namely that we can work additively with the exponents of a single element that generates the full cycle of reduced residues.

We will say that an integer a has order e modulo p if $a^e \equiv 1$ (mod p) and $a^f \equiv 1$ (mod p) holds for no f smaller than e. The crucial fact we just proved in the previous theorem is that there are at most $p - 1/e$ integers modulo p that have order e because all such are roots of the polynomial $x^e \equiv 1$ (mod p) and are not roots of $x^f \equiv 1$ (mod p) for any f smaller than e.

We first observe that if a has order e, then the powers $a, a^2, \ldots, a^e$ are all distinct modulo p. If they were not, and we had $a^j \equiv a^k$ (mod p), for $0 < j < k \le e$, $j \ne k$, then we would have $a^{k-j} \equiv 1$ (mod p) but $0 < k - j < e$, contrary to our choice of e.

We next observe that the order e of any element must divide $p - 1$. Because we have $a^e \equiv 1$ (mod p) and $a^{p-1} \equiv 1$ (mod p), we can conclude by doing arithmetic on the exponents that $a^{\gcd(e, p-1)} \equiv 1$ (mod p). But we cannot have $\gcd(e, p - 1) < e$ without violating our definition of e as the order of a. Hence $e | (p - 1)$.

If a is of order e, then $a, a^2, \ldots, a^{e-1}, a^e$ are distinct modulo p and are the solutions of $x^e \equiv 1$ (mod p). The $\phi(e)$ of these with exponents prime to e are actually of order e and not some smaller order. Thus for all divisors e of $p - 1$ there are either $\phi(e)$ residues or no residues of order e. If we let $\psi(e)$ be the number of residues of order e, for $e | (p - 1)$, then clearly $\psi(e) \le \phi(e)$ and

$$\sum_{e | (p-1)} \psi(e) = p - 1.$$

By Theorem 110.14 we have

$$\sum_{e | (p-1)} \phi(e) = p - 1,$$

so in fact

$$\sum_{e | (p-1)} (\psi(e) - \phi(e)) = 0.$$

But each summand is less than or equal to zero and hence must be equal to zero. In particular, then, $\psi(p - 1) = \phi(p - 1)$. Because $\psi(p - 1)$ is positive, so must be $\phi(p - 1)$, which means that a primitive root must exist.

Once we have verified the existence of an element g that generates the entire multiplicative cycle modulo p, it follows immediately by looking at the arithmetic with the exponents that all the powers g^j for j prime to $p-1$ must also generate the complete cycle.

THE CHINESE REMAINDER THEOREM

Theorem 110.19. *Let $m_1, m_2, \ldots, m_k$ be k integers that are relatively prime in pairs. Let $a_1, a_2, \ldots, a_k$ be any k integers. Then the congruences*

$$x \equiv a_1 \pmod{m_1}$$
$$x \equiv a_2 \pmod{m_2}$$
$$\cdots$$
$$x \equiv a_k \pmod{m_k}$$

have common solutions. All such solutions are congruent modulo $m_1 m_2 \ldots m_k$.

Proof. We will provide two proofs of this theorem. First, we shall construct a solution explicitly. Let $x_1 = a_1 + x_2 m_1$ for a variable x_2; the values x_1 certainly satisfy the first congruence. The second congruence now reads as follows:

$$a_1 + x_2 m_1 \equiv a_2 \pmod{m_2}$$
$$x_2 m_1 \equiv a_2 - a_1 \pmod{m_2}.$$

The existence of b_1 such that $b_1 m_1 \equiv 1 \pmod{m_2}$ is guaranteed because the moduli are pairwise relatively prime. Thus,

$$x_2 \equiv b_1(a_2 - a_1) \pmod{m_2}$$

provides simultaneous solutions

$$x_1 = a_1 + m_1 b_1(a_2 - a_1) + x_3 m_1 m_2$$

of the first and second congruences, with x_3 now the free variable. We continue one congruence at a time, and the conclusion is obvious.

Our second proof resembles Lagrange's interpolation formula. Let $M_j = \prod_{i \neq j} m_i$ for each j, and let b_j solve $b_j M_j \equiv 1 \pmod{m_j}$. Then the sum

$$a_1 b_1 M_1 + a_2 b_2 M_2 + \cdots + a_k b_k M_k$$

is a simultaneous solution to the congruences.

In general, because the simultaneous solution is congruent modulo the product of the moduli, one would need multiple precision arithmetic to compute the solutions exactly. The first method of proof minimizes the need for multiprecision arithmetic, although the precision must grow with each congruence. The second method of creating the solution requires full precision throughout and is thus not as computationally efficient.

POLYNOMIAL ARITHMETIC

Our goal in this chapter has been to provide a background in the number theory necessary to understand public key cryptography. Much of the necessary theory has to do with ordinary arithmetic, albeit with integers hundreds of bits in length. In one specific instance, however, that of elliptic curves used for cryptographic purposes, one must also be prepared to deal with arithmetic in binary finite fields. The NIST has described several elliptic curves suitable for use in cryptography by those who wish to use elliptic curves for cryptography (NIST, 1999). Some of these curves are defined modulo large prime integers, while some of them are defined over binary finite fields.

The arithmetic of binary finite fields, using polynomials, is entirely analogous to ordinary integer arithmetic modulo primes. Instead of integers, we deal with polynomials whose coefficients are defined modulo 2, and instead of prime numbers we use "irreducible" polynomials. In a deeper abstract sense, both kinds of arithmetic are just arithmetic in finite fields, but we will for concreteness develop the theory by analogy with the more familiar ordinary integers.

Polynomials

We will deal with *polynomials* in one variable, $f(x) = a_n x^n + \cdots + a_0$, $a_n \neq 0$, of *degree* $deg(f) = n$, whose *coefficients* a_i are integers taken modulo 2. The coefficient $a_n \neq 0$ and the term $a_n x^n$ are the *leading coefficient* and *leading term*, respectively, and the coefficient a_0 is the *constant term*. When one shifts to polynomial arithmetic, one also usually introduces some new terminology, and we will refer to any finite field of k elements as the *Galois field* $GF(k)$ of k elements, sometimes also written $\mathbb{F}_k$. One theorem that can be proved is that there is really only one finite field of k elements, so referring to "the" field is not incorrect. Thus, integer arithmetic modulo a prime p is arithmetic in the Galois field $GF(p)$, and we can refer to the polynomials as we have defined them here as polynomials *defined over $GF(2)$*, written $GF(2)[x]$.

We will, in this section, always mean "a polynomial in $GF(2)[x]$" whenever we refer to "a polynomial."

We note a few very simple (and convenient) facts about arithmetic in $GF(2)[x]$.

Theorem 110.20. *Let $f(x)$, $g(x)$, and $h(x)$ be polynomials in $GF(2)[x]$. Then the following are true:*

1. *The only constant polynomials are 0 and 1.*
2. *If $f(x) = \sum_{i=0}^{n} a_i x^i$, $g(x) = \sum_{i=0}^{n} b_i x^i$, and $h(x) = \sum_{i=0}^{n} c_i x^i = f(x) + g(x)$, then $c_i = XOR(a_i, b_i)$ for each i.*
3. *If $f(x) = \sum_{i=0}^{n} a_i x^i$, then $f(x) = \sum_{i=0}^{n} a_i x^{2i}$.*

Proof. The proofs of these follow from the definitions.

We note that arithmetic in polynomials modulo 2 is almost entirely analogous to the arithmetic in the integers. The two primary differences are the fact that the bit-level arithmetic is done with XORs and without carry bits (and is therefore much less complex at the bit level than ordinary arithmetic) and the fact that we bound the size of the operands with which we deal with the degree of the polynomial instead of with the magnitude of the integers. One other difference that is apparent with polynomials in $GF(2)[x]$ is that "plus is the same as minus": because $+1 \equiv -1 \pmod 2$, we also have $+x = -x$ in $GF(2)[x]$.

Divisibility

We say that a polynomial $f(x)$ is divisible by a polynomial $g(x)$ if there exists a polynomial $h(x)$ such that $f(x) = g(x) \times h(x)$. We say that $g(x)$ is a *divisor* of $f(x)$. As in the case of integers, we note that the zero polynomial is divisible by any polynomial, and we adhere to the convention that we do not consider the case $0|0$ that would be the only instance in which division by the zero polynomial would make sense. Given polynomials $f(x)$ and $g(x)$, we say that a polynomial $h(x)$ is a *common divisor* of $f(x)$ and $g(x)$ if $h(x)$ divides $f(x)$ and $h(x)$ divides $g(x)$. If the polynomials $f(x)$ and $g(x)$ are not both zero, then among the common divisors of $f(x)$ and $g(x)$ we will refer to the divisor of largest degree as the *greatest common divisor*, written $\gcd(f(x), g(x))$.

Remark: Our universe of discourse is simplified by the fact that we are dealing with coefficients that are either 0 or 1. If we were dealing with coefficients modulo 3, for example, then there might be a legitimate need to deal with an ambiguity beyond just the degrees of the polynomials— both x^2 and $2x^2$ could be said to be divisors of x^3 because we would have $x^3 = (x) \times (x^2)$ and $x^3 = (2x) \times (2x^2)$. With coefficients defined only modulo 2, however, no such ambiguity exists; there is only one possible nonzero coefficient. The following theorem is the analog of Theorem 110.1. We note two differences between integers and polynomials under prime numbers and factoring, and groups and fields defined mod primes.

Theorem 110.21. *The following hold for all polynomials in $GF(2)[x]$:*

1. *If $f(x)|g(x)$, then $f(x)|g(x)h(x)$ for any polynomial $h(x)$.*
2. *If $f(x)|g(x)$ and $g(x)|h(x)$, then $f(x)|h(x)$.*
3. *If $f(x)|g(x)$, then $f(x)h(x)|g(x)h(x)$ for any polynomial $h(x)$.*
4. *If $f(x)|g(x)$ and $g(x)|f(x)$, then $f(x) = g(x)$.*
5. *If $f(x)|g(x)$ and $f(x)|h(x)$, then $f(x)|(g(x)r(x) + h(x)s(x))$ for any polynomials $r(x)$ and $s(x)$.*
6. *If $f(x)|g(x)$, then $deg(f(x)) \leq deg(g(x))$.*

Proof. The proofs of these follow immediately from the definition.

Theorem 110.22. (The polynomial division algorithm). *If $f(x)$ and $g(x)$ are polynomials in $GF(2)[x]$, then there exists a unique pair of polynomials $q(x)$ and $r(x)$ such that $f(x) = g(x)q(x) + r(x)$ and $0 \leq deg(r) < deg(g)$.*

Proof. Our earlier proof of the analogous Theorem 110.2 was largely existential. We will for the sake of variety construct the polynomials that prove this theorem.

In the case that $deg(f(x)) < deg(g(x))$, we set $q(x) = 0$ and $r(x) = f(x)$.

In the case that $deg(f(x)) = deg(g(x))$, we set $q(x) = 1$ and $r(x) = f(x) + g(x) \equiv f(x) - g(x) \pmod{2}$.

Finally, if we have $deg(f(x)) = n > deg(g(x)) = m$, we set $q_1(x) = x^{n-m}$ and $r_1(x) = f(x) + x^{n-m}g(x)$, so that

$$f(x) = q_1(x) \cdot g(x) + r_1(x)$$

and $deg(r_1(x)) < deg(f(x))$. We repeat the above process with $r_1(x)$ and $g(x)$ replacing $f(x)$ and $g(x)$, obtaining perhaps $q_2(x) = x^{n'-m}$ and $r_2(x)$ so that

$$
\begin{aligned}
f(x) &= q_1(x) \cdot g(x) + r_1(x) \\
&= q_1(x) \cdot g(x) + q_2(x) \cdot g(x) + r_2(x) \\
&= (q_1(x) + q_2(x)) \cdot g(x) + r_2(x)
\end{aligned}
$$

and so forth.

This terminates with $q_k(x)$ so that

$$f(x) = \left(\sum_{i=1}^{k} q_i(x) \right) g(x) + r_k(x)$$

and $0 \leq deg(r_k(x)) < deg(g(x))$.

Uniqueness follows exactly as with the case of integers.

Greatest Common Divisor

Theorem 110.23. (The Euclidean algorithm). *If, given polynomials $f(x)$ and $g(x)$ in $GF(2)[x]$, we make a repeated application of the division algorithm:*

$$
\begin{aligned}
f(x) &= g(x)q_1(x) + r_1(x), & 0 < deg(r_1(x)) < deg(g(x)) \\
g(x) &= r_1(x)q_2(x) + r_2(x), & 0 < deg(r_2(x)) < deg(r_1(x)) \\
r_1(x) &= r_2(x)q_3(x) + r_3(x), & 0 < deg(r_3(x)) < deg(r_2(x)) \\
& \cdots &
\end{aligned}
$$

$$(7)$$

then the process must terminate with $deg(r_{j+1}(x)) = 0$ for some j, and we have that $r_j(x) = \gcd(f(x), g(x))$.

Proof. The proof in the case of polynomials mimics almost exactly the earlier proof for integers.

Theorem 110.24. (The extended Euclidean algorithm). *The values $r_0(x)$ and $s_0(x)$ such that $\gcd(f(x), g(x)) = f(x)r_0(x) + g(x)s_0(x)$ can be obtained by eliminating the $r_i(x)$ from Eq. (7).*

Proof. Again, the proof for polynomials mimics the earlier proof for integers.

Irreducible Polynomials

A polynomial $f(x)$ in $GF(2)[x]$ is called *irreducible* if it cannot be expressed as product $f(x)|g(x)h(x)$ with $g(x), h(x) \in GF(2)[x]$ and the degrees of $g(x)$ and $h(x)$ both smaller than that of $f(x)$.

As will be seen in the following theorems, the irreducible polynomials play a role in the formation of finite fields that is analogous to that of prime integers. Irreducible polynomials are normally defined in a manner slightly different from prime integers; instead of part (1) of Theorem 110.6, we have part (2) of the following analogous theorem.

Theorem 110.25. *The following hold:*

1. *The polynomial $f(x)$ is irreducible in $GF(2)[x]$ if and only if the only divisors of $f(x)$ are itself and 1.*

2. *Every polynomial of positive degree has an irreducible divisor.*

3. *If, for an irreducible polynomial $f(x)$, we have $f(x)|\prod_{i=1}^{n} g_i(x)$, then $f(x)|g_i(x)$ for some i.*

Proof. In essence, we mimic the proof for integers of Theorem 110.6, but we use the degree of the polynomial instead of the magnitude of the integer.

Let $f(x)$ be an irreducible polynomial of positive degree and assume that $g(x)$ is a divisor of least degree of $f(x)$. (We note in contrast to the integers that there are multiple polynomials of the same degree, and hence "a divisor" is correct and "the divisor" would be wrong.) Then we have $f(x) = g(x)h(x)$ for some $h(x)$ of degree at least 1. But this precisely contradicts the assumption that $f(x)$ is an irreducible polynomial because we have both $deg(g(x)) < deg(f(x))$ and $deg(h(x)) < deg(f(x))$, so neither $f(x)|g(x)$ nor $f(x)|h(x)$ can hold.

Conversely, let us assume that the only divisors of $f(x)$ are itself and 1, and let $f(x)|g(x)h(x)$ for two polynomials $g(x)$ and $h(x)$. Let $s(x) = \gcd(f(x), g(x))$, and let us apply the extended Euclidean algorithm to get the following:

$$s(x) = f(x) \times u(x) + g(x) \times v(x). \qquad (8)$$

We must by assumption have either $s(x) = f(x)$ or $s(x) = 1$. In the former case we have $f(x)|g(x)$. In the latter case we multiply (8) by $h(x)$ to get the following:

$$h(x) = f(x) \times u(x) \times h(x) + g(x) \times h(x) \times v(x),$$

from which we conclude that $f(x)|h(x)$, proving part 1.

To prove part 2, we observe that $f(x)$ has a divisor of least degree $g(x)$. Because this divisor can have no divisors of smaller degree except 1, then this divisor must be irreducible.

Part 3 follows by induction.

Theorem 110.26. (The fundamental theorem of arithmetic). *Every polynomial of positive degree $f(x)$ can be factored into a product of irreducible polynomials, and the factoring is unique up to order.*

Proof. Again, this proof mimics the proof for integers.

Congruences

Given polynomials $f(x)$, $g(x)$, and $m(x)$, we say that $f(x)$ is *congruent* to $g(x)$ modulo $m(x)$, which we write as $f(x) \equiv g(x) \pmod{m(x)}$, if the difference $f(x) - g(x)$ is divisible by $m(x)$.

The basic results on congruences (Theorems 110.8, 110.9, and 110.10) carry over precisely for polynomials in $GF(2)[x]$, and their proofs are entirely similar. We also, by our definition of divisibility, have prevented the zero polynomial from being a modulus for congruences. We do not, however, need to prevent the nonzero polynomial of zero degree, namely 1, from being a modulus.

Theorem 110.27. *Let $a(x)$, $b(x)$, $c(x)$, $d(x)$, $r(x)$, and $s(x)$ be polynomials in $GF(2)[x]$. Then*

1. $a(x) \equiv b(x) \pmod{m(x)}$, $b(x) \equiv a(x) \pmod{m(x)}$, and $a(x) - b(x) \equiv 0 \pmod{m(x)}$ *are equivalent statements.*

2. *If $a(x) \equiv b(x) \pmod{m(x)}$ and $b(x) \equiv c(x) \pmod{m(x)}$, then $a(x) \equiv c(x) \pmod{m(x)}$.*

3. *If $a(x) \equiv b(x) \pmod{m(x)}$ and $c(x) \equiv d(x) \pmod{m(x)}$, then $a(x) + c(x) \equiv b(x) + d(x) \pmod{m(x)}$ and $a(x)c(x) \equiv b(x)d(x) \pmod{m(x)}$.*

4. *If $a(x) \equiv b(x) \pmod{m(x)}$, then there exists a polynomial $k(x)$ such that $a(x) = b(x) + k(x)m(x)$.*

Theorem 110.28. *Let $a(x)$, $m(x)$, $r(x)$, and $s(x)$ be polynomials in $GF(2)[x]$. We have $a(x)r(x) \equiv a(x)s(x) \pmod{m(x)}$ if and only if $r(x) \equiv s(x) \pmod{m(x)/\gcd(a(x), m(x))}$. Specifically, if $a(x)r(x) \equiv a(x)s(x) \pmod{m(x)}$ and $\gcd(a(x), m(x)) = 1$, then $r(x) \equiv s(x) \pmod{m(x)}$.*

Theorem 110.29. *Given polynomials $a(x)$, $b(x)$, and $m(x)$ in $GF(2)[x]$, the congruence*

$$a(x)r(x) \equiv b(x) \qquad (\bmod\ m(x)) \qquad (9)$$

is solvable for polynomials $r(x)$ if and only if $\gcd(a(x), m(x))|b(x)$. If this is true, and $r_0(x)$ is a solution, then all solutions are given by $r(x) = r_0(x) + k(x)m(x)$, where $k(x)$ is any polynomial.

Example
Let $a(x) = x^4 + x^3 + x^2 + 1$, $b(x) = x^2 + x$, and $m(x) = x^5 + x^4 + x + 1$. We note that $a(x) = (x + 1)(x^3 + x + 1)$, $b(x) = x(x + 1)$, and $m(x) = (x + 1)^5$, and that $a(x)/(x + 1)$ is not divisible by $x + 1$. Thus, $\gcd(a(x), m(x)) = x + 1$ and this divides $b(x)$. We reduce the congruence

$$\begin{aligned}(x^4 + x^3 + x^2 + 1) \times r(x) \\ \equiv x^2 + x \ (\bmod\ (x^5 + x^4 + x + 1))\end{aligned} \qquad (10)$$

to

$$(x^3 + x + 1) \times r(x) \equiv x \ (\bmod\ (x^4 + 1))$$

by dividing by $x + 1$. If we follow the extended Euclidean algorithm for these polynomials, we have

$$\begin{aligned}
x^4 + 1 &= (x^3 + x + 1) \times (x) + x^2 + x + 1, \\
x^3 + x + 1 &= (x^2 + x + 1) \times (x + 1) + x, \\
x^2 + x + 1 &= (x) \times (x + 1) + 1, \\
x &= 1 \times (x) + 0,
\end{aligned}$$

so the sequence q_1, q_2, q_3, q_4 is (x), $(x + 1)$, $(x + 1)$, (x). The matrix product is as follows:

$$\begin{pmatrix} 0 & 1 \\ 1 & x \end{pmatrix} \begin{pmatrix} 0 & 1 \\ 1 & x+1 \end{pmatrix} \begin{pmatrix} 0 & 1 \\ 1 & x+1 \end{pmatrix} \begin{pmatrix} 0 & 1 \\ 1 & x \end{pmatrix} \begin{pmatrix} x^4+1 \\ x^3+x+1 \end{pmatrix} =$$

$$\begin{pmatrix} x^2 & x^3+x+1 \\ x^3+x+1 & x^4+1 \end{pmatrix} \begin{pmatrix} x^4+1 \\ x^3+x+1 \end{pmatrix} = \begin{pmatrix} 1 \\ 0 \end{pmatrix}$$

from which we get the extended gcd as follows:

$$(x^4 + 1)(x^2) + (x^3 + x + 1)(x^3 + x + 1) = 1.$$

We can choose $r(x) = x(x^3 + x + 1) = x^4 + x^2 + x$, and all solutions to Eq. (10) are given by the following:

$$r(x) = x^4 + x^2 + x + k(x)(x^5 + x^4 + x + 1),$$

where $k(x)$ is any polynomial.

Groups, Rings, and Fields Defined Modulo Polynomials

The basic structure of the integers modulo primes carries over to a basic structure of polynomials in $GF(2)[x]$ modulo irreducible polynomials, but for fairly obvious reasons the arguments about the number of elements must change.

For a prime p, the number of nonzero residues modulo p is $p - 1$, and the residues modulo p form a field of p elements (counting the zero) with a cyclic multiplicative group generated by any primitive root. The residues modulo p have multiplicative orders dividing $p - 1$. Further, because the absolute values of two different primes are different, each prime defines a different field with a different number of elements.

Given a polynomial $f(x)$ of degree d, then $f(x)$ can be written as a string of 0 and 1 coefficients $d + 1$ bits long, with the bit for the x^d term set. The 2^d residues modulo $f(x)$; that is, all the polynomials of degrees $d - 1$ and lower, correspond to the d-bit sequences of 0s and 1s, and the number of residues is the same for all moduli of the same degree. Indeed, for each degree d, there is a unique field of 2^d elements up to *isomorphism*, and this field can be obtained by considering polynomials modulo any irreducible polynomial of degree d.

Primitive Polynomials and Shift Register Sequences

The structure of the finite fields defined by polynomials with coefficients 0 and 1 is described in depth in Lidl and Niederreiter (1994) and in Golomb (1982).

Let $f(x)$ be a polynomial of degree d. If $f(x)$ is irreducible, then the polynomials of $GF(2)[x]$ form a field whose multiplicative group is cyclic, just like the field of integers modulo a prime integer. However, for computational reasons, we usually work not with the irreducible polynomials but with a more restrictive set of polynomials, the *primitive* polynomials.

Given a polynomial $f(x)$ of degree d with constant term 1, the *order* of $f(x)$, written $ord(f)$, is the least integer e such that $x^e \equiv 1 \pmod{f(x)}$. A polynomial with constant term 0 can be written $x^k g(x)$ for some integer k, and we say that the order of $f(x)$ is the order of $g(x)$. A polynomial $f(x)$ is called *primitive* if it has order $e = 2^d - 1$. The computational justification for our interest just in primitive and not in all irreducible polynomials is that being able to generate the multiplicative group with powers of x results in simpler electronic circuitry for the *shift register sequences* that are the coefficients of the residues (Golomb, 1982). Multiplication by x will be shown later to be simply a shift left followed possibly by an XOR; this is obviously simpler than multiplying by a polynomial having more than one nonzero coefficient.

Table 2 Irreducible Polynomials of Small Degrees

Degree	Irreducible Polynomials
1	$x + 1$
2	$x^2 + x + 1$
3	$x^3 + x + 1$
	$x^3 + x^2 + 1$
4	$x^4 + x + 1$
	$x^4 + x^3 + 1$
	$x^4 + x^3 + x^2 + x + 1$
5	$x^5 + 1$

The following theorems show that the notion of a primitive polynomial is well defined and that a primitive polynomial can always be found for any degree.

Theorem 110.30. *If $f(x)$ is a polynomial of degree d and constant term 1, then the order of $f(x)$ is finite and less than or equal to $2^d - 1$.*

Proof. Consider the sequence $S = \{x, x^2, x^3, \ldots\}$. Taken modulo $f(x)$, this sequence becomes a sequence of polynomials in $GF(2)[x]$ of degree less than or equal to d. None of these can be the zero polynomial: if a polynomial $g(x)$ has degree $\le d$, then $xg(x)$ has constant term 0 but $f(x)$ has constant term 1, so $xg(x) \equiv 0 \pmod{f(x)}$ is impossible. There are $2^d - 1$ such polynomials as elements of S reduced modulo $f(x)$, so eventually we run out of possibilities. Now if we have $x^r \equiv x^s \pmod{f(x)}$, then we have $x^{r-s} \equiv 1 \pmod{f(x)}$, because x and $f(x)$ are relatively prime.

Theorem 110.31. *The order of any irreducible polynomial $f(x)$ of degree d divides $2^d - 1$.*

Theorem 110.32. *For any degree $d > 0$, there exists a primitive polynomial of degree d.*

In fact, there are much stronger theorems that can be proved, but we will not prove them here. Theorem 110.32, however, is more than just the polynomial analog of the theorem that the integers modulo a prime integer form a cyclic group generated by a primitive root; it is the statement, in effect, that x can be taken to be that primitive root.

Examples

Irreducible Polynomials. A small effort shows that the irreducible polynomials of degrees up through 5 are as presented in Table 2.

Primitive Polynomials. There are eight polynomials of degree 4 over $GF(2)$ with constant term 1. With a small amount of trial and error, one can determine that many of them factor and are thus not irreducible. The factorings for the degree 4 polynomials are presented in Table 3.

We consider the sequence of powers of x modulo, for example, $f(x) = x^4 + x + 1$, and obtain Table 4.

Thus, $x^4 + x + 1$ is not only irreducible but also primitive. One can similarly show that $x^4 + x^3 + 1$ is primitive. This is an example of the following theorem that we will state but not prove.

Theorem 110.33. *Let* $f(x) = x^d + a_{d-1}x^{d-1} + \cdots + a_1 x + 1$ *be a primitive polynomial. Then its reverse* $f'(x) = x^d + a_1 x^{d-1} + \cdots + a_{d-1}x + 1$ *is also primitive.*

The polynomial $x^4 + x^3 + x^2 + x + 1$ is irreducible, but it is not primitive. In fact, the multiplicative cyclic group is generated by $x + 1$, as shown in Table 5.

We note that the progression in Table 5 of $1, x, x^2, x^3, x^3 + x^2 + x + 1, 1$ is the progression

$$\begin{aligned}
(x+1)^{12}, \\
(x+1)^{24} &= (x+1)^9, \\
(x+1)^{36} &= (x+1)^6, \\
(x+1)^{48} &= (x+1)^3, \\
(x+1)^{60} &= 1.
\end{aligned}$$

If we view the 0–1 coefficients as a sequence of bits, left to right in decreasing powers of x, so that the polynomial $f(x) = x^4 + x + 1$ is represented as 1|0011, then the residues modulo $f(x)$ can be written as four-bit sequences (with a temporary carry at the right), with x written as 0|0010. Multiplication by x is thus a shift left. If a 1 is shifted into the carry position, we XOR the pattern with 1|0011 to force the carry position back to zero. The elegant implementation in hardware is just that the bit shifted to the carry position is tapped and then always XORed (if it is a 0, this has no effect) with the lower bits as specified by the polynomial. Using this representation, Table 4 becomes Table 6.

BIT COMPLEXITY

There are two levels at which one might wish to analyze the time complexity of arithmetic and number-theoretic operations. For those whose interest is in software, the complexity of computation is normally measured in terms of the number of CPU instructions executed. Addition and subtraction instructions are far cheaper than multiplication, and division is normally so expensive that one avoids it if at all possible, so at the level of software and machine instructions one is usually counting multiplications to measure complexity. However, at the level of CPU instructions, one usually is not concerned about the *bit-level* complexity; the cost of adding two 14-bit numbers on a 64-bit machine is usually the same as the cost of adding two 35-bit numbers.

Oddly enough, for purely theoretical purposes and for the very practical purposes of hardware design, one needs to consider the actual bit-level complexity of arithmetic. In general, a naive analysis of the complexity is sufficient for our purposes, if only because any reasonably complicated computation in number theory will require general purpose arithmetic, and general purpose arithmetic will not be able to make use of the clever tricks that might speed up arithmetic in special cases.

Timing Costs of Arithmetic

We measure the cost in time of arithmetic in terms of the number of bit operations needed. For example, to add two integers $a = a_m a_{m-1} \ldots a_1 a_0$ and $b = b_n b_{n-1} \ldots b_1 b_0$ of bit lengths $m+1$ and $n+1$, respectively, where we assume $m > n$, the naive approach is the right-to-left ripple-carry schoolchild method that requires $m+1$ bit-adds (because m is assumed larger than n). Multiplication requires $(m+1) \times (n+1)$ bit-operations because there are that many products of bits $a_i \times b_j$ that have to be added in to the running sum at the correct bit location.

Table 4 Powers of x Modulo $x^4 + x + 1$

Power	Equivalent to	Reduces to
x	$\equiv x$	
x^2	$\equiv x^2$	
x^3	$\equiv x^3$	
x^4	$\equiv x^4$	$\equiv x + 1$
x^5	$\equiv x^2 + x$	
x^6	$\equiv x^3 + x^2$	
x^7	$\equiv x^4 + x^3$	$\equiv x^3 + x + 1$
x^8	$\equiv x^4 + x^2 + x$	$\equiv x^2 + 1$
x^9	$\equiv x^3 + x$	
x^{10}	$\equiv x^4 + x^2$	$\equiv x^2 + x + 1$
x^{11}	$\equiv x^3 + x^2 + x$	
x^{12}	$\equiv x^4 + x^3 + x^2$	$\equiv x^3 + x^2 + x + 1$
x^{13}	$\equiv x^4 + x^3 + x^2 + x$	$\equiv x^3 + x^2 + 1$
x^{14}	$\equiv x^4 + x^3 + x$	$\equiv x^3 + 1$
x^{15}	$\equiv x^4 + x$	$\equiv 1$

Table 3 Factorings for Degree 4 Polynomials

Polynomial	Factoring
$x^4 + 1$	$= (x+1)^4$
$x^4 + x + 1$	Irreducible
$x^4 + x^2 + 1$	$= (x^2 + x + 1)^2$
$x^4 + x^3 + 1$	Irreducible
$x^4 + x^2 + x + 1$	$= (x+1)(x^3 + x^2 + 1)$
$x^4 + x^3 + x + 1$	$= (x+1)^2(x^2 + x + 1)$
$x^4 + x^3 + x^2 + 1$	$= (x+1)(x^3 + x + 1)$
$x^4 + x^3 + x^2 + x + 1$	Irreducible

Table 5 Powers of $1 + x$ Modulo $1 + x + x^2 + x^3 + x^4$

Powers	Equivalent to	Power	Equivalent to
$(x+1)$	$\equiv x + 1$	$(x+1)^9$	$\equiv x^2$
$(x+1)^2$	$\equiv x^2 + 1$	$(x+1)^{10}$	$\equiv x^3 + x^2$
$(x+1)^3$	$\equiv x^3 + x^2 + x + 1$	$(x+1)^{11}$	$\equiv x^3 + x + 1$
$(x+1)^4$	$\equiv x^3 + x^2 + x$	$(x+1)^{12}$	$\equiv x$
$(x+1)^5$	$\equiv x^3 + x^2 + 1$	$(x+1)^{13}$	$\equiv x^2 + 1$
$(x+1)^6$	$\equiv x^3$	$(x+1)^{14}$	$\equiv x^3 + x$
$(x+1)^7$	$\equiv x^2 + x + 1$	$(x+1)^{15}$	$\equiv 1$
$(x+1)^8$	$\equiv x^3 + 1$		

Table 6 Powers of x Modulo $x^4 + x + 1$

Powers	Bit Pattern	Reduces to		
x	0|0010			
x^2	0|0100			
x^3	0|1000			
x^4	1|0000	$\rightarrow$ 1|0000	XOR	1|0011 = 0|0011
x^5	0|0110			
x^6	0|1100			
x^7	1|1000	$\rightarrow$ 1|1000	XOR	1|0011 = 0|1011
x^8	1|0110	$\rightarrow$ 1|0110	XOR	1|0011 = 0|0101
x^9	0|1010			
x^{10}	1|0100	$\rightarrow$ 1|0100	XOR	1|0011 = 0|0111
x^{11}	0|1110			
x^{12}	1|1100	$\rightarrow$ 1|1100	XOR	1|0011 = 0|1111
x^{13}	1|1110	$\rightarrow$ 1|1110	XOR	1|0011 = 0|1101
x^{15}	1|1010	$\rightarrow$ 1|1010	XOR	1|0011 = 0|1001

Division is perhaps actually easier to analyze as a bit-level operation than with a higher radix. The extremely naive view of division as repeated subtraction is in fact exactly what is useful when analyzing the bit complexity. To produce the quotient and remainder q and r from input operands a and b, so that $a = qb + r$, it is necessary to perform as many as $O(\lg a)$ subtractions. That this is logarithmic and not linear [that is, $O(\lg a)$ and not $O(q)$ subtractions] is because we can subtract not b from a but a subtrahend $2^k \times b$ chosen to align with the leftmost nonzero bit of the minuend. In this way, each subtraction reduces by at least one the length in bits of the minuend. The cost of subtracting $2^k \times b$ and not just b is lost in counting the costs of subtracting because we can initially align the bits of b with the leftmost and not the rightmost bit of a and then just shift right for each succeeding subtraction.

As stated, for general purpose arithmetic or for purposes other than purely theoretical analysis, one almost always is restricted to the naive complexity for arithmetic. Table 7, taken from Bach and Shallit (1996), presents in addition to the easily derived naive complexities the best-known asymptotic complexities for arithmetic, where the function $\mu(m, n)$ is $m(\lg n)(\lg \lg n)$ if $m \geq n$ and $n(\lg m)(\lg \lg m)$ otherwise.

For theoretical purposes, the asymptotic complexity at the bit level is no different from that at the software level of counting CPU instructions. The constants will change because of the aggregation of bits into words, but the inherent complexity will be the same.

Table 7 Bit-Level Complexity of Arithmetic

Operation	Naive complexity	Best-known complexity
$a \pm b$	$\lg a + \lg b$	$O(\lg a + \lg b)$
$a \times b$	$(\lg a)(\lg b)$	$O(\mu(\lg a, \lg b))$
$a = qb + r$	$(\lg b)(\lg q)$	$O(\mu(\lg q, \lg b))$

Worst Case of Greatest Common Divisor

A brief analysis of the greatest common divisor algorithm is illustrative of the nature of analysis of basic number-theoretic operations. We consider the Euclidean algorithm as the naive algorithm, and we observe that division is by far the most costly of the operations in the Euclidean algorithm.

Theorem 110.34. *The worst case of the naive Euclidean algorithm occurs with the computation of* $\gcd(F_{n+1}, F_n)$, *where* F_{n+1} *and* F_n *are consecutive Fibonacci numbers. Thus, the worst case of the naive Euclidean algorithm when given inputs A and B with* $1 \leq \lg A, \lg B \leq n$ *is that n divisions are required.*

Proof. The Euclidean algorithm requires the maximal number of division steps in the event that the quotients are 1 at every step. This is exactly what happens when the inputs are consecutive Fibonacci numbers because the Fibonacci recurrence $F_{n+1} = F_n + F_{n-1}$ is exactly the division algorithm $F_{n+1} = 1 \times F_n + F_{n-1}$ with $q = 1$ and $r = F_{n-1}$.

A more detailed analysis of the gcd, as given in Knuth (1998), shows that 41% of the quotients in the division step are 1, 16% of the quotients in the division step are 2, and 9% of the quotients in the division step are 3. This leads to an alternative gcd algorithm as follows: instead of dividing r_i by r_{i+1}, which is expensive, we subtract r_{i+1} from r_i as many as three times. If the values of r_i and r_{i+1} are known to be of the same number of bits, then 2/3 of the time we will be able to avoid the division at the cost of at most three subtractions. Although this algorithm is not necessarily suitable for operands longer than the register length of the CPU being used, it can be very effective for operands that fit into registers and on which single machine instructions can be used to perform the subtractions and tests (Buell, 1989).

BIT COMPLEXITY FOR MULTIPRECISE ARITHMETIC

The usual analysis of the complexity of arithmetic assumes that the operands are simply strings of bits. In a real computer, however, operands are measured in terms of the number of words they require for their representation, and an addition of very short operands is no faster than addition of longer operands provided that all operands and results fit in a single CPU register. We refer to operands and arithmetic as *multiprecise* if the operands must be represented as multiword arrays. For the most part, it is only the constant that changes; the asymptotic analysis of arithmetic is not affected by word size or the overhead of handling arrays instead of single operands.

Complexity of Integer Arithmetic

The bit complexity for multiprecise arithmetic is not different from ordinary arithmetic. The issue in multiprecise arithmetic has thus usually been with software implementations. A detailed analysis exists in Knuth

(1998). Probably the most common software package in common use is the gmp library by Granlund (2001).

Complexity of Polynomial Arithmetic

Virtually all the analysis for integer arithmetic, including multiprecise integer arithmetic, carries over for polynomial arithmetic in $GF(2)[x]$, with one major and crucial difference. Although the bit operation count is the same for polynomial arithmetic as for integers, there are no carries in polynomial arithmetic, so that the bit operations can be parallelized in hardware or vectorized in software.

Montgomery Multiplication

Much of the use of number theory in computer security and in cryptography relies on multiplication of long-word-length objects (both integers and polynomials in finite fields $GF(2^n)[x]$) modulo a *fixed* integer or polynomial modulus. A problem with this is that modular reduction is computationally expensive, costing roughly the same time as division. A clever technique for reducing the complexity of modular multiplication is because of Peter Montgomery (1985). This method has also been explored for implementation directly in hardware (Bajard, 1997; Eldridge, 1993). We remark that the Montgomery trick as presented below works *mutatis mutandis* for polynomial arithmetic.

The basic idea of Montgomery multiplication goes back to a standard trick that has been used for decades for arithmetic modulo Mersenne numbers. This trick is half the reason that the largest known prime numbers are usually Mersenne primes. (The other half is that a test exists that all prime numbers pass and most composite numbers fail. This test is useful in primality testing for eliminating most composites. If the numbers tested are generic numbers, then there are false positives that pass the test but are not prime. In the case of Mersenne numbers, however, the test is both "if and only if" in that all prime Mersenne numbers pass and all composite Mersenne numbers fail. The combination of a test that always works for Mersenne numbers coupled with the following trick for rapid computation modulo Mersenne numbers is why the largest known primes have usually been prime Mersenne numbers.)

Let $M_n = 2^n - 1$ be the n-th Mersenne number, a number of n bits, and assume that we are doing arithmetic modulo M_n. The crucial operation is multiplication: if A and B are integers reduced modulo M_n, that is to say, n-bit numbers, then the product $C = A \times B$ can be written as $C = C_1 \times 2^n + C_0$; C_1 and C_0 are the digits of the product C written with radix 2^n.

The computational trick is to observe the following:

$$
\begin{aligned}
C &= C_1 \times 2^n + C_0 \\
&= C_1 \times 2^n - C_1 + C_1 + C_0 \\
&= C_1 \times (2^n - 1) + C_1 + C_0 \\
&= C_1 \times M_n + C_1 + C_0 \\
&\equiv C_1 + C_0 \quad (\mathrm{mod}\ M_n).
\end{aligned}
$$

For example, if $n = 5$, so $2^n = 32$, and if we let $A = 17$ and $B = 11$, we have the following:

$$
\begin{aligned}
A \times B &= 17 \times 11 = 187 \\
&= 5(32) + 27 = 5(32) - 5 + 5 + 27 \\
&= 5(32 - 1) + 32.
\end{aligned}
$$

Modulo $2^5 - 1 = 31$, we have $A \times B \equiv 32$. On a binary computer, we split the 10-bit product 187 into its left half of $0101_2 = 5_{10}$ and right half of $1101_2 = 27_{10}$, add the halves, and then subtract 31 from 32 (because in this case the addition of the halves generated a carry) to get the correct answer of 1 modulo 31.

In general, instead of having to *divide* by M_n to produce the remainder, we only need to add the left half of the product to the right half of the product. If there is a carry left, there is an additional subtraction. These costs are small, however, relative to the cost of naive modular reduction. The left half of a $2n$-bit number contains n bits, and we should expect on average that half of these would be 1. Reducing the $2n$-bit product modulo an n-bit modulus would naively require n subtractions. The cost of one n-bit addition followed some of the time with an n-bit subtraction is small by comparison.

The Montgomery algorithm is based on the technique for Mersenne numbers, and it works in essence by converting a modulus N with a complicated bit pattern into a modulus that is a power of 2. What would have been costly arithmetic operations become reductions modulo a power of 2 (choosing the bits of the right half of a double-length product) and divisions by a power of 2 (selecting the bits of the left half of a double-length product). The algorithm requires conversion of all numbers into a "Montgomery" representation, but if we have a great deal of arithmetic modulo a single fixed N, the one-time conversion into Montgomery representation prior to the arithmetic and the cost of converting back to ordinary representation afterward is more than compensated for by the elimination of expensive modular division operations.

Given a modulus N, we choose a suitable k to make $R = 2^k > N$. We assume that R and N are relatively prime (if not, we divide out the common factor and solve this problem, multiplying back by the common factor at the end). We can then solve for R' and N' such that $RR' - NN' = 1$.

What we now do is multiply all the constants and values of variables by R. Then, instead of doing arithmetic with integers a and b, say, we will be doing arithmetic with integers aR and bR. At the very end of the computation, we multiply any result by R' and reduce modulo N. Because $RR' \equiv 1 \pmod{N}$, we thus recover the result we would have if we had done the arithmetic in the usual number representation.

Addition and subtraction of the Montgomery-transformed numbers are fine, because

$$
a + b = c \Leftrightarrow aR + bR = cR.
$$

The problem is with multiplication:

$$
aR \times bR = abR^2,
$$

which means that we have an extra factor of R. What we need is a function to which we can pass the product abR^2

and from which will be returned abR. We could do this by multiplying by R' and reducing modulo N, but that would be a multiplication modulo N, and it is exactly this that we are trying to avoid.

To convert a product $T = abR^2$ into its Montgomery representation cR, we apply the functions

$$m = (T \pmod R) \times N' \pmod R$$
$$t = (T + mN)/R \tag{11}$$

returning either t or $t - N$, whichever lies in the range 0 to $N - 1$.

We note the careful process of computing m and t. We begin with operands a and b each less than N, thus each less than R, thus each a k-bit number (we will call this "single-length"). We then convert to aR and bR modulo N as single-length operands. Then T is a double-length product of $2k$ bits. Computing $T \pmod R$ consists of taking the rightmost k bits, which is computationally cheap, and results in a single-length operand. The multiplication by N' really is a multiplication and results in a double-length product. Reduction mod R is once again the selection of the rightmost k bits to produce the single-length value m.

Computing mN requires a real multiplication. Adding the double-length T to the double-length mN is a genuine arithmetic operation, but it is inexpensive compared to the multiplications. Finally, division by R is merely shifting the sum right by k bits or else selecting the leftmost k bits. At the end, we may need one more genuine subtraction of N. The single modular reduction is accomplished at the cost of two multiplications, one or two addition/subtractions, and two bit shift/select operations. We note that the algebra has resulted in a value for $T + mN$ that is zero modulo R that is, for which the rightmost k bits are zero.

Example

Let $N = 79$, and instead of using a power of 2 for R, we use $R = 100$ for readability. This would then be an efficient algorithm on a computer operating in decimal on words of two decimal digits in length. By analogy with the binary operations of a standard computer, we assume for this example that choosing the right two decimals (reduction modulo 100) of a four-decimal digit product and choosing the left two decimals (division by 100, discarding the remainder) are cheap when compared with actual division.

We find that $64 \times 100 - 81 \times 79 = 1$, so we have $R = 100$, $R' = 64$, $N = 79$, $N' = 81$.

Let us assume we wish to multiply 61 and 5 modulo 79. To convert to Montgomery representation, we multiply both these numbers by $R = 100$ and reduce modulo $N = 79$, using the standard expensive operations: $61 \to 61 \times 100 \pmod{79} \equiv 17$ and $5 \to 5 \times 100 \pmod{79} \equiv 26$. In Montgomery representation, we multiply 17 times 26 to get $T = 442$. Modulo 79, we know that $442 \equiv 6100 \times 500 \pmod{79}$, but what we need to determine is the integer t that is the Montgomery representation for $442/100 \pmod{79}$.

We compute the following:

$$T \pmod R = 442 \pmod{100} \equiv 42$$

$$(T \pmod R) \times N' = 42 \times 81 = 3402$$
$$m = ((T \pmod R) \times N') \pmod R$$
$$= 3402 \pmod{100} \equiv 02$$
$$T + mN = 442 + 2 \times 79 = 600$$
$$t = (T + mN)/R = 600/100 = 6.$$

We convert from Montgomery representation by multiplying t by R' modulo N to get $6 \times 64 \pmod{79} \equiv 384 \pmod{79} \equiv 68$. Algebraically, we have the following:

$$61 \to 61 \times 100 \pmod{79} \equiv 17$$
$$5 \to 5 \times 100 \pmod{79} \equiv 26$$
$$68 \to 68 \times 100 \pmod{79} \equiv 6$$

and the result of the Montgomery multiplication of 17×26 is 6.

Theorem 110.35. *Montgomery multiplication, using Eq. (11), is correct. The cost of a single multiplication modulo N is approximately equal to the cost of three ordinary multiplications on integers of size equal to $\lg N$.*

Proof. We assume that value T is a product and hence is double length. Because we choose $R > N$ but not too much bigger, the products can be taken to be double length (plus a constant addend) in R.

The first modular reduction simply converts T to a single-length number modulo R. Modulo R, we have that $m = TN'$. Thus,

$$mN \equiv TN'N \equiv -T \pmod R.$$

When we then take $T + mN$, we get an integer that is zero modulo R, and we can legitimately divide out the R and get an integer quotient for t.

Now the fact that we get the correct quotient comes from the fact that

$$tR = T + mN \equiv T \pmod N$$

so that, modulo N, we have $t \equiv TR'$.

CROSS REFERENCES

See *Encryption Basics; PKI (Public Key Infrastructure); Public-Key Algorithms*.

REFERENCES

Bach, E., & Shallit, J. (1996). *Algorithmic number theory, volume 1: Efficient algorithms*. Cambridge: MIT Press.
Bajard, J.-C., & Dider, L.-S. (1997). An RNS Montgomery modular multiplication algorithm. *Proceedings of the IEEE Symposium on Computer Arithmetic*, 234–239.
Barker, E. (October 16, 2000). *NIST cryptographic toolkit*. Retrieved April 30, 2004, from http://csrc.nist.gov/encryption/index.html
Buchmann, J. A. (2001). *Introduction to Cryptography*. Berlin: Springer-Verlag.

Buell, D. A., & Ward, R. L. (1989). A multiprecise integer arithmetic package. *The Journal of Supercomputing, 3,* 88–107.

Cohen, H. (1993). *A course in computational algebraic number theory.* Berlin: Springer-Verlag.

Cormen, T. H., Leiserson, C. E., Rivest, R. L., & Stein, C. (2003). *Introduction to algorithms.* Cambridge: MIT Press/McGraw-Hill.

Daemen, J., & Rijmen, V. (2001). *The design of Rijndael* : AES, *the advanced encryption standard.* Berlin: Springer-Verlag.

Daemen, J., & Rijmen, V. (2003). Rijndael home page. Retrieved April 30, 2004, from *http://www.esat.kuleuven.ac.be/ rijmen/rijndael*

Eldridge, S. E., & Walter, C. D. (1993). Hardware implementation of Montgomery's modular multiplication algorithm. *IEEE Transactions on Computers, 42,* 693–699.

Golomb, S. (1982). *Shift register sequences.* Laguna Hills, CA: Aegean Park Press.

Granlund, T. (2001). *GNU MP: The GNU multiple precision arithmetic library.* Boston: Free Software Foundation, Inc. Retrieved April 30, 2004, from *http://www.swox.com/gmp*

Hankerson, D., Menezes, A., & Vanstone, S. (2004). *Guide to elliptic curve cryptography.* New York: Springer-Verlag.

Hardy, G. H., & Wright, E. M. (1980). *An introduction to the theory of numbers, fifth edition.* Oxford, UK: Oxford University Press.

Knuth, D. E. (1998). *The art of computer programming, vol. 2: Seminumerical Algorithms, Second Edition.* Reading, MA: Addison-Wesley.

Koblitz, N. (1984). *Introduction to elliptic curves and modular forms.* New York: Springer-Verlag.

Koblitz, N. (1987). *A course in number theory and cryptography.* New York: Springer-Verlag.

Lidl, R., & Niederreiter, H. (1994). *Introduction to finite fields and their applications, second edition.* Cambridge, MA: Cambridge University Press.

Menezes, A. J. (1993). *Elliptic curve public key cryptosytems.* Boston: Kluwer Academic.

Montgomery, P. L. (1985). Modular multiplication without trial division. *Mathematics of Computation, 44,* 519–521.

NIST. (1998). *First AES Candidate Conference.* Retrieved April 30, 2004, from *http://csrc.nist.gov/CryptoToolkit/aes /round1/conf1/aes1conf.htm*

NIST. (1998). *Second AES Candidate Conference.* Retrieved April 30, 2004, from *http://csrc.nist.gov/CryptoToolkit/aes/round1/conf2/aes2conf.htm*

NIST. (July, 1999). Recommended elliptic curves for federal government use. Retrieved April 30, 2004, from *http://csrc.nist.gov/csrc/fedstandards.html, http://csrc.nist.gov/encryption/dss/ecdsa/NISTReCur.pdf, http://csrc.nist.gov/publications/fips/fips186-2/fips186-2-hange1.pdf*

NIST. (2000). *Proceedings, The Third Advanced Encryption Standard Candidate Conference.* Retrieved April 30, 2004, from *http://csrc.nist.gov/CryptoToolkit/aes/round2/conf3/aes3conf.htm*

NIST. (November 26, 2001). *FIP197: Announcing the advanced encryption standard (AES).* Retrieved April 30, 2004, from *http://csrc.nist.gov/encryption/aes/index.html.*

Niven, I., Zuckerman, H. S., & Montgomery, H. L. (1991). *An introduction to the theory of numbers, fifth edition.* New York: John Wiley & Sons.

Rosen, K. H. (2000). *Elementary number theory and its applications, fourth edition.* Reading, MA: Addison-Wesley.

Schneier, B. (1996). *Applied cryptography, second edition: Protocols, algorithms, and source code in C.* New York: John Wiley & Sons.

Silverman, J. H., & Tate, J. (1992). *Rational points on elliptic curves.* New York: Springer-Verlag.

Public Key Algorithms

Bradley S. Rubin, *University of St. Thomas*

INTRODUCTION

It is hard to place ourselves back in the mid-1970s, when conventional cryptography using a shared, secret key was the only type available—and the only type thought possible. Although effective at providing such functions as privacy and authentication, conventional cryptography has an inconvenient requirement. If one party wants to communicate with another party in a secure fashion, they have to somehow get a secret key to that other party before they can securely communicate. How can the parties (let us call them Alice and Bob) perform this key distribution, which must be done in a secure manner? Well, maybe Alice could encrypt the secret key before it is sent to Bob. What secret key will Alice and Bob use to encrypt this secret key? We are caught in an infinite series of requirements for a secure distribution channel for the secret key. We must somehow figure out how to get Bob a secret key, ideally over an otherwise insecure channel.

There are conventional cryptography solutions that get a secret key from Alice to Bob, but none of them are particularly convenient. Alice could send Bob a key in the postal mail or with a courier who has a handcuffed briefcase, but this precludes immediate, private communication between parties who have met spontaneously. Alice could send the secret key on an alternative electronic communication channel, such as e-mail or fax, but she is betting that an attacker will not be listening in on that channel. We could have a trusted third party, Trent, who shares a secret key with Alice and another secret key with Bob and uses these keys to encrypt a new secret key to be sent to and used by Alice and Bob. But how does Trent get his initial secret keys to Alice and Bob in the first place? Making sure a Trent is around whenever Alice wants to talk with a new person is not convenient. We really have to trust Trent, because if Trent is compromised, then the stolen keys can decrypt not only new communications between Alice and Bob but also any old encrypted communications that were saved. If N parties want to be able to securely communicate with each other, they will need a total of $N \times (N-1)/2$ secret keys, which can grow to be a very big number and an associated management

headache. This number can be reduced to N keys if we use more sophisticated protocols to get temporary (session) keys from Trent, but Trent must be there when we need him and must respond quickly.

The key distribution requirements for parties that want to communicate spontaneously is a fundamental disadvantage for conventional cryptography. But this was the only form of cryptography available until the mid-1970s, so people made it work the best they could. Most experts, at that time, said that doing better was a fundamentally unsolvable problem. Then a number of people made a significant series of discoveries that culminated in the invention of public key cryptography, so now we all can surf to a Web site where we had no previous contact and perform tasks such as entering our credit card numbers over a newly created secure communication channel.

Furthermore, some public key algorithms, such as RSA, can be used for both encryption (providing privacy) and also for a very different function—digital signature. A paper signature identifies the originator of a document in a way that both authenticates the originator (proves they are who they say they are) and provides nonrepudiation (does not allow the originator to deny that they are the originator). Clearly, there are flaws with the paper signature process, but in general it works fairly well. We would like to have an analogous capability for digital transmissions. Conventional cryptography can provide the authentication function, partially meeting the signature requirement. If Alice sends an encrypted message to Bob, and Bob can determine that it decrypts properly, then Bob knows it came from Alice because she is the only other entity with the secret key. But Alice can deny she sent a given message because Bob could have sent it to himself, because he too has the secret key. So, in this scenario using conventional cryptography, we have authentication but not nonrepudiation.

Some types of public key cryptography can provide nonrepudiation capability, which is a stronger notion than just authentication, via digital signature. If Alice signs a message with her private key (using techniques discussed later), then Bob can verify the signature with Alice's public key. But now Alice cannot deny that she signed the message because she is the only one with her private key (unless she claims her private key was compromised). In this scenario, we have both authentication as well as the stronger notion of nonrepudiation, giving us digital signature.

Encryption alone provides privacy but not nonrepudiation. Digital signature alone provides nonrepudiation but not privacy. Encryption and digital signature can be combined to provide both characteristics. In this scenario, Alice and Bob each have two private and public key pairs, one for signing and one for encryption. It is a good practice to always sign a message before encrypting it, so we can always know the plaintext that we are signing. Alice can first sign a message with her private signing key and then encrypt that result with Bob's public encryption key. She sends this signed and encrypted message to Bob. Bob first decrypts the message with his private encryption key and then verifies the signature with Alice's public signing key. For best security, Alice and Bob should each have two different key pairs, one pair for encryption and the other pair for digital signature, to avoid certain attacks discussed later.

Public key cryptography, although a significant advance, has some shortcomings, such as performance and the need for revocation lists, and does not eliminate the need for conventional cryptography. In practice, systems protocols use a hybrid system of both conventional and public key cryptography.

The remainder of this chapter first reviews the breakthrough thought about public key cryptography in Ralph Merkle's puzzles and then looks at the knapsack algorithm, which was the first practical public key cryptosystem (now broken), and then the Diffie–Hellman key exchange algorithm, which is still used today, and a related public key cryptosystem called ElGamal. Finally, we examine the most popular and flexible public key cryptosystem, RSA, which can be used for both encryption and digital signature functions. We also look at some RSA implementation considerations and attacks.

Note that the algorithms and history discussed here are based on the public literature in cryptographic research. There is evidence that many of these ideas were previously discovered by the Communications Electronics Security Group (CESG) in Great Britain. See Levy (2001) and Singh (1999) for more details about this issue as well as some captivating accounts of the history of the invention, use, and politics surrounding public key cryptography.

Several references provide more detailed, yet broad, technical coverage of the topics in this chapter, such as a historical review by Diffie (1988); implementation considerations by Ferguson and Schneier (2003); a mathematics textbook by Garrett (2001); a mathematically oriented handbook by Menezes, Van Oorschot, and Vanstone (1996); a public key volume by Salomaa (1996); an applied handbook by Schneier (1995); and textbooks by Stallings (2003) and Stinson (2002).

MERKLE'S PUZZLES

The first to make a dent in the problems fundamental to public key cryptography was Ralph Merkle (1978). As a student, he wrote a paper for his computer security class describing a technique using puzzles to allow both Alice and Bob to obtain the same secret key by exchanging information over an insecure channel. Furthermore, an eavesdropping Eve, who monitors this insecure channel, cannot discover this secret key. Unfortunately, good communication of the idea between him and his professor did not occur, his professor did not recognize the value of his contribution, and Merkle dropped the course. He then wrote up his idea for publication, but it was rejected in the review process. Fortunately, he eventually found others who understood and enhanced the value of his initial contribution.

Here is Merkle's puzzle idea. If Alice wants to agree on a key with Bob, she first creates a large number of puzzles. A puzzle is a general term for something that can be solved with a large, but doable, amount of effort. Each puzzle contains a unique puzzle identifier and a key that is not visible until the puzzle is solved. Alice then sends these puzzles in random order to Bob. Bob picks one of these many puzzles at random and solves it, extracting the puzzle identifier and the key. Bob sends Alice the puzzle identifier and Alice looks up the corresponding key. Alice and Bob now both have a shared, secret key that they can use with conventional cryptography to exchange messages. Eve, our eavesdropper, is faced with the task of decrypting all the puzzles (or, on average, half of them) before the puzzle identifier that she sees passed from Bob to Alice has any meaning. As long as Alice and Bob finish using the key before Eve gets a chance to solve the puzzle that Bob chose, the communication is secure (unless Eve saves old encrypted messages, which she can now decrypt). Alice must generate a whole new series of puzzles before executing the protocol again or else Eve will eventually make enough progress to break all the puzzles.

Although the communication overhead for this scheme is too great to yield a practical solution, it represents the first rift in conventional wisdom that said that this was an impossible problem to solve. Merkle then worked with Martin Hellman and Whitfield Diffie after reading a draft paper by the two and finding they were thinking about the same issues. This work eventually led to the Merkle–Hellman knapsack algorithm (Merkle & Hellman, 1978), the first practical public key algorithm, which has now been broken, and the Diffie–Hellman key exchange algorithm (Diffie & Hellman, 1976b), which is still in use today. Later, Ron Rivest, Adi Shamir, and Len Adelman at MIT came up with another approach to public key cryptography and created the RSA algorithm (the initials of their last names) and the company by the same name (Rivest, Shamir, & Adelman, 1978). The RSA algorithm is the most widely used public key cryptography algorithm today and has the added advantage of providing digital signature functionality as well.

ONE-WAY FUNCTIONS

All public key algorithms rely on the notion of a trapdoor one-way function. A one-way function is easy to compute in one direction but hard to compute in the reverse direction. The term *easy*, in a computational complexity sense, means it can be performed in polynomial time or better.

In addition, the terms *hard, computationally infeasible,* or *intractable* mean it takes more than polynomial time (i.e., an exponentially more difficult amount of time) to execute as the size of the input data increases. Note that this is related to the computational complexity notions of P and NP, but complexity theory generally deals with the worst case. In cryptography, the average case behavior is more important.

Hash algorithms take a long sequence of bits and map them to another fixed length and smaller sequence of bits. Many, but not all, hash algorithms have this one-way function characteristic. It is very easy to hash a long string of bits into a small hash representation, but it is computationally infeasible, given an arbitrary small hash representation, to come up with a string of bits that hash to this value. However, some hash algorithms, such as checksum (an XOR of all the bytes to produce a single byte), are easy in both directions, so do not qualify as one-way functions. Cryptographic hashes, such as MD5 (IETF, 1992) and SHA-1 (NIST, 2002), have the one-way property.

But unlike a plain one-way function, a trapdoor one-way function can be easy to compute in the reverse direction if you know a secret. If you know the secret trapdoor, the reverse function can be computed in polynomial, or P, time. If you do not know the secret, it is computationally infeasible to compute. It turns out that these functions are very difficult to find. But they are the key ingredient for public key cryptographic algorithms.

Let us formalize the concepts we have seen so far into the four properties that Diffie and Hellman (1976a) described as necessary for a public key cryptosystem. The first three are required and the fourth is optional:

1. Applying a decryption process D to a message M that has undergone an encryption process E yields the original message M: $D[E(M)] = M$.
2. Both E and D are easily computable from the same random source.
3. If E is revealed to the world, it gives no information about D.
4. The reverse of property 1 holds as well: $E[D(M)] = M$.

A function E that satisfies properties 1 through 3 is a trapdoor one-way function. Some algorithms that are based on functions that satisfy these three properties can be used directly for encryption (such as knapsack, ElGamal, and RSA). These are called *public key cryptosystems*. Other algorithms cannot directly be used for encryption but can allow two parties to agree on a common key that can subsequently be used for conventional encryption. These are called *public key distribution systems* (such as the Diffie–Hellman key exchange algorithm). A function that also satisfies property 4 is said to be reversible and is a public key cryptosystem that can be used for both encryption and digital signature (such as RSA).

KNAPSACK ALGORITHM

The knapsack algorithm, created by Merkle and Hellman (1978), was the first practical public key cryptosystem algorithm and it can be used for both encryption and (with modifications) digital signature, but it has been broken. All attempts to fix it have been unsuccessful, so it is not a practical algorithm today (although there has been renewed interest in the knapsack problem in a newer area called lattice-based cryptography). But it nicely provides the intuition about how trapdoor one-way functions work, so we begin with the knapsack problem.

The Merkle–Hellman knapsack algorithm is based on a mathematical problem called the *subset sum* problem, which is illustrated as follows. Assume we have a knapsack that can hold only a certain maximum weight of groceries and we have a table full of groceries of different weights. Our goal is to select just the right items from the table of groceries to exactly reach the maximum weight allowed by the knapsack.

A Knapsack Algorithm Example

Assume that our table has five items that weigh 1, 3, 4, 6, and 10 pounds. Assume also that we have a knapsack that can hold a maximum of 21 pounds. With a little trial and error work, we find we can exactly fill the knapsack with the following items: 1, 4, 6, and 10. This seems like a simple problem, but when the number of items grows, the time it takes to find a solution grows exponentially, so this quickly grows from an easy problem to an impossibly difficult one. In computational complexity terms, it is an NP-complete problem.

But, there is a special kind of knapsack, called a *superincreasing knapsack*, which is trivial to solve. In a superincreasing knapsack, the items are not only in increasing order, but also each item weighs more that the sum of all the previous items in the list. For example, this is a superincreasing knapsack: 1, 3, 5, 10, and 20. Our original knapsack of 1, 3, 4, 6, and 10 is a nonsuperincreasing knapsack, because 4 is not greater than 1 + 3.

Superincreasing knapsacks have the interesting property that makes finding a solution very simple. To do this, we go through the knapsack weights in reverse order and subtract them from the target weight. If the result is negative, we do not include this weight in the solution and go on to the next weight. If the result is positive, we include this weight in the solution and subtract this weight from current weight and go on to the next weight. The final result is 0 if we have a solution that exactly matches the starting weight. For example, with our superincreasing knapsack of 1, 3, 5, 10, 20 we can find the result that matches a total weight of 26 as follows:

$$26 - 20 = 6 \quad \text{(positive, so use this weight)}$$
$$6 - 10 = -4 \quad \text{(negative, so skip this weight)}$$
$$6 - 5 = 1 \quad \text{(positive, so use this weight)}$$
$$1 - 3 = -2 \quad \text{(negative, so skip this weight)}$$
$$1 - 1 = 0 \quad \text{(zero, so use this weight and done)}$$

So our solution is 20, 5, 1.

We need one more piece of information before we can use knapsacks for encryption. For every superincreasing knapsack, we can transform it into a nonsuperincreasing knapsack with the following transformation. We first pick a number m that is greater than the sum of all the knapsack items. We then find an n that is relatively prime (shares no factors) to m. In this example, let us assume $m = 41$ and $n = 3$. We then multiply every weight in the superincreasing knapsack by n and take the result mod m.

$$1 \times 3 \bmod 41 = 3$$
$$3 \times 3 \bmod 41 = 9$$
$$5 \times 3 \bmod 41 = 15$$
$$10 \times 3 \bmod 41 = 30$$
$$20 \times 3 \bmod 41 = 19$$

So the superincreasing knapsack 1, 3, 5, 10, 20 transforms to the nonsuperincreasing knapsack 3, 9, 15, 30, 19. We call the former knapsack the private key and the latter knapsack the public key. Let us assume these are owned by Bob. Bob keeps the private key private and gives the public key to anyone who needs it to encrypt a message for Bob.

Putting these pieces together, assume Alice wants to send the message 01011 10111 00011 to Bob. Alice first encodes each group of binary plaintext by mapping them against Bob's public key by adding up all the weights that have a 1 value (indicating that the weight is present).

$$01011 = 9 + 30 + 19 = 58$$
$$10111 = 3 + 15 + 30 + 19 = 67$$
$$00011 = 30 + 19 = 49$$

We then treat 58, 67, and 49 as the ciphertext and send it to Bob. Bob first calculates one more number: he must find the modular inverse of 3 mod 41, in other words, x where $3 \times x \equiv 1 \pmod{41}$. Using the extended Euclidean algorithm (Knuth, 1981), he finds $x = 14$. We can check this by seeing that $(3 \times 14) \bmod 41 = 1$.

Now, Bob multiplies each ciphertext value by $x \bmod m$ as follows:

$$58 \times 14 \bmod 41 = 33$$
$$67 \times 14 \bmod 41 = 36$$
$$49 \times 14 \bmod 41 = 30$$

Finally, using his private key (the superincreasing knapsack), he finds these weights as the solution and converts them to binary by using a 1 for every weight present:

$$33 = 20 + 10 + 3 : 01011$$
$$36 = 20 + 10 + 5 + 1 : 10111$$
$$30 = 20 + 10 : 00011$$

So, Bob now knows the plaintext. An eavesdropping Eve would see only the ciphertext, the public key, and the nonsuperincreasing knapsack and so would be faced with solving a computationally infeasible problem.

Real world knapsacks need large values (on the order of 200 decimal digits) for many of the parameters. For more information on knapsack mathematics and implementation issues, see Garrett (2001) and Salomaa (1996). But not only has the original knapsack technique been broken, all known variants have also been broken (Odlyzko, 1990). So, this algorithm is no longer practical, but it remains important for its conceptual value.

KEY ESTABLISHMENT TECHNIQUES

Before we explore the next algorithms, it is important to distinguish between several kinds of *key establishment* techniques (Menezes, Van Oorschot, & Vanstone, 1996). When public key cryptography is used for encryption, it is often for the purpose of getting Alice and Bob the same secret key, which no one else knows. Once both parties have this shared secret key, they can then use conventional cryptography (algorithms such as DES, DESede, AES) to encrypt their communications. This is desirable because conventional cryptographic algorithms, such as AES and DES, perform a few orders of magnitude faster than public key algorithms, such as RSA. This hybrid approach allows systems to optimize the key distribution benefits of public key cryptography with the performance of conventional cryptography. It turns out that there are two fundamental ways to accomplish the goal of establishing this secret key between the communicating parties, *key transport* and *key exchange*.

With key transport, Alice uses public key cryptography to encrypt another secret key that she generates and then delivers this encrypted secret key to Bob. Alice does this by encrypting the secret key with Bob's public key. When Bob receives this encrypted key, he decrypts it with his private key. Then, Alice and Bob communicate privately using conventional cryptography and this secret key.

Key exchange is a different technique that also results in Alice and Bob having a shared secret key. But, instead of Alice generating that secret key, encrypting it, and sending it to Bob (as in key transport), Alice and Bob exchange several numbers as part of a protocol. At the end of this protocol, Alice and Bob agree on the shared secret key. The magic here is that if an eavesdropper listens to all the traffic between Alice and Bob, he or she does not end up with the secret key!

Key transport tends to be more useful in applications where one party is not online. For example, with e-mail, we want to send a message without requiring the receiving party to be online to execute a protocol with us. Key exchange can be used when the other party is online, in applications such as instant messaging or secure telephone communication. Algorithms like knapsack, ElGamal, and RSA can be used for key transport. Algorithms such as Diffie–Hellman can be used for key exchange. All of them can be used for key establishment.

DIFFIE–HELLMAN KEY EXCHANGE

The Diffie–Hellman key exchange algorithm (Diffie & Hellman, 1976b) was one of the first public key algorithms, and it is still in use today. Two parties exchange some information that results in both of them deriving the same value, which can be used as a key for subsequent use with a conventional cryptographic algorithm. Furthermore, an eavesdropping Eve can see all of the exchanged information but cannot derive the same key! It relies on the modular exponentiation, which is a computationally easy problem, and the discrete logarithm problem, which is an exponentially difficult problem. Modular exponentiation means finding the value of $g^x \bmod n$ when all values are known. For example, $3^4 \bmod 13 = 3$. The inverse problem, the discrete logarithm problem, asks for x, given $b = g^x \bmod n$. For example, solving for x in $5 = 3^x \bmod 13$. In this case, there is no solution for x. How about $9 = 3^x \bmod 13$? In this case, there are multiple values of x (2, 5, 8, 11) where this holds true.

To have a unique solution, we must find a value for g that is a primitive root, or generator, of 13 (Garrett, 2001). A number g is a primitive root of 13 if all of its powers of g between 1 and 12 (done mod 13) generate all the values between 1 and 12. For example, with $g = 2$ we obtain the following:

$$2^1 \bmod 13 = 2,$$
$$2^2 \bmod 13 = 4,$$
$$2^3 \bmod 13 = 8,$$
$$2^4 \bmod 13 = 3,$$
$$2^5 \bmod 13 = 6,$$
$$2^6 \bmod 13 = 12,$$
$$2^7 \bmod 13 = 11,$$
$$2^8 \bmod 13 = 9,$$
$$2^9 \bmod 13 = 5,$$
$$2^{10} \bmod 13 = 10,$$
$$2^{11} \bmod 13 = 7,$$
$$2^{12} \bmod 13 = 1.$$

So 2 is a primitive root or generator of 13. The complete set of generators are {2,6,7,11}. Knuth (1981) discusses the computation issue of finding generators. Picking the generator 7, for example, we know that $9 = 7^x \bmod 13$ has the unique solution, found through trial and error, of $x = 4$. There are other algorithms for solving this discrete logarithm problem that are more efficient, but still exponential, such as Pollard's Rho algorithm or the even more efficient index calculus methods (Menezes, Van Oorschot, & Vanstone, 1996).

A Diffie–Hellman Example

To start, either Alice or Bob picks a large, strong, prime number n (a method for doing this and the meaning of strong are discussed in a later section) and a value g that is a primitive root of n. These values are sent to the other party, and they can be seen by Eve. Alice and Bob each pick a large random number, a and b, which they keep private. Assume (keeping the numbers small and simple) that $n = 23$, $g = 11$, Alice's private number is $a = 30$, and Bob's private number is $b = 15$:

1. Alice computes $A = g^a \bmod n = 11^{30} \bmod 23 = 8$ and sends it to Bob.
2. Bob computes $B = g^b \bmod n = 11^{15} \bmod 23 = 10$ and sends it to Alice.
3. Alice then computes $k = B^a \bmod n = 10^{30} \bmod 23 = 2$.
4. Bob then computes $k = A^b \bmod n = 8^{15} \bmod 23 = 2$.

So, Alice and Bob have derived the same key value, 2! Eve saw n, g, A, and B. For her to calculate the key as well, she would have to solve $8 = 11^x \bmod 23$ or $10 = 11^x \bmod 23$. Both of these are discrete logarithm problems, which are exponentially difficult problems, meaning as the numbers get big enough, they are computationally infeasible to solve.

Diffie–Hellman Attacks

Although Diffie–Hellman is considered secure today, there are a variety of attacks that lead to some implementation considerations, only briefly mentioned here. More details are discussed in Ferguson and Schneier (2003) and Garrett (2001).

The protocol as presented in the example is vulnerable to a man-in-the-middle attack (Stallings, 2003), where a malicious intruder, Mallory, can listen to and respond to the protocol messages from Alice and Bob in a way where Mallory can learn all the keys and Alice and Bob are not aware of this breach. Also, certain values passed as the prime number n or its primitive root g can cause weakness and should be checked as part of a higher level protocol. The prime number n should be on the order of 6800 bits long.

ElGAMAL

The ElGamal public key cryptosystem created by Taher ElGamal (1985), like the Diffie–Hellman key exchange, is based on the discrete logarithm problem. But, unlike Diffie–Hellman key exchange, it can be used for encryption. Just as in Diffie–Hellman, the sender selects a large prime number n and g, a primitive root of n, and calculates a public key, which is sent to the receiver. The plaintext M has to be less than n. The sender also picks a random integer between 1 and $n - 1$, inclusive. Also, there are two ciphertexts created by the sender, one of which is used to represent the encrypted message key and the other that represents the encrypted message. The receiver uses the sender's public key to first recover the message key from the first ciphertext and then uses that message key to recover the plaintext message itself.

An ElGamal Example

Let us assume, as in the previous Diffie–Hellman example (keeping the numbers small and simple) that $n = 23$, $g = 11$, and Alice's private number is $a = 30$. Alice must also compute a random number k between 1 and $n - 1$, inclusive, for each encrypted block. We assume that $k = 10$ for this block. Let us also assume that the plaintext message $M = 13$:

1. Alice computes $A = g^a \bmod n = 11^{30} \bmod 23 = 8$ and sends it to Bob. This is her public key.
2. Alice computes $K = A^k \bmod n = 8^{10} \bmod 23 = 3$.
3. Alice computes a ciphertext $C_1 = g^k \bmod n = 11^{10} \bmod 23 = 2$ and sends it to Bob.
4. Alice computes a ciphertext $C_2 = K \times M \bmod n = 3 \times 13 \bmod 23 = 16$ and sends it to Bob.
5. Bob computes $K = C_1^A \bmod n = 2^8 \bmod 23 = 3$.
6. Bob computes the modular inverse, K^{-1}, of K. In other words, finding the value for x where $3 \times x \equiv 1 \bmod 23$. $x = 8$, using the extended Euclidean algorithm.
7. Bob then computes $C_2 \times K^{-1} \bmod n = 16 \times 8 \bmod 23 = 13$, the original plaintext message.

Note that in this algorithm, the size of the ciphertext is twice the size of the plaintext. Also, because of the random *k* value per message, we avoid having the same plaintext encrypting to the same ciphertext, thwarting dictionary attacks.

There is a form of the ElGamal algorithm that can be used for digital signature, but it is not a simple reversal of the encryption form of the algorithm. The ElGamal signature algorithm, with improvements by Schnorr, is the base for the U.S. government's Digital Signature Standard (DSS) (NIST, 1994). In DSS, the signature can be used only for digital signature and not encryption. This was a desirable property in the era when the U.S. government wanted to encourage the use of digital signatures for contract signing in international commerce but did not want to propagate the use of encryption, which could be used for criminal purposes.

RSA

Although the seminal Diffie–Hellman article described the characteristics of a public key cryptosystem that can be used for both privacy (encryption) and nonrepudiation (digital signature), it did not describe an actual algorithm that had the essential properties. This motivated the MIT team of Rivest, Shamir, and Adleman to discover an algorithm with these properties. After many false starts, they finally arrived at the algorithm we know today as RSA. For this accomplishment, they were awarded the 2002 Turing Award, the Nobel Prize of computer science (2002 A. M. Turing Award Winners, 2004).

RSA was difficult to discover, but it is easy to describe. Quoting their article:

> A message is encrypted by representing it as a number M, raising M to a publicly specified power e, and then taking the remainder when the result is divided by the publicly specified product, n, of two large secret prime numbers p and q. Decryption is similar; only a different, secret, power d is used, where $e \times d \equiv 1 \pmod{(p-1) \times (q-1)}$. The security of the system rests in part on the difficulty of factoring the published divisor, n.

An RSA Example

First, we choose two random, large, prime numbers p and q. For the sake of a simple example, we keep the numbers simple, so let us say that $p = 61$ and $q = 71$, both of which are prime. We then compute $n = p \times q = 61 \times 71 = 4331$. This is also known as the modulus. We discuss how to find large prime numbers in a later section.

We then compute something called the *Euler totient* of n, symbolized by $\phi(n)$. This is defined as the number of numbers less than n that are relatively prime to n. So $\phi(12) = 4$ because the numbers $\{1,5,7,11\}$ are relatively prime to 12. Because all numbers less than a prime number are relatively prime to it (otherwise it would not be prime), the totient of a prime number is just 1 less than the number. So $\phi(p) = p - 1 = 61 - 1 = 60$ and $\phi(q) = q - 1 = 71 - 1 = 70$. But, we want $\phi(p \times q)$, and it can be shown that this is equal to $\phi(p) \times \phi(q)$. So,

$$\phi(n) = \phi(4331) = \phi(61) \times \phi(71) = 60 \times 70 = 4200.$$

Now, we pick a random number e that is relatively prime to $\phi(n)$. Let us say that e is 1027. Then we find the corresponding d, which is the modular inverse of $e \bmod \phi(n)$. We can find d using the extended Euclidean algorithm as follows:

$$e \times d = 1 \bmod (\phi(4331)) \quad \text{or} \quad 1027 \times d = 1 \bmod 4200, \text{ or}$$
$$d = 1963$$

The public key is $\{e, n\}$ or $\{1027, 4331\}$ and the private key is $\{d, n\}$ or $\{1963, 4331\}$. Note that although each key is composed of more than just the modulus n, the RSA key size is conventionally stated as the size of just n in bits. Also, we must be sure to destroy p and q.

For this example, let us assume that Alice converts a plaintext message M into a series of decimal digits, such as 123, 456, and 789. Using Bob's public key, Alice computes the ciphertext $C = M^{1027} \bmod 4331$. So $123^{1027} \bmod 4331 = 62$, $456^{1027} \bmod 4331 = 2167$, and $789^{1027} \bmod 4331 = 3197$. Our ciphertext message is thus 62, 2167, 3197. Alice sends this ciphertext message to Bob.

Bob now needs to convert the ciphertext message to plaintext by using his private key. Bob computes the plaintext $M = C^d \bmod 4331$. So $62^{1963} \bmod 4331 = 123$, $2167^{1963} \bmod 4331 = 456$, and $3197^{1963} \bmod 4331 = 789$. The result is the original plaintext message 123, 456, 789.

RSA Digital Signatures

As previously discussed, RSA is reversible, so it can be used both for encryption (privacy) and digital signature (nonrepudiation). A digital signature would proceed similarly, except Alice would sign a message with her private key using $C = M^d \bmod n$ and Bob would verify the signature using Alice's public key using $C^e \bmod n$, which is $(M^d \bmod n)^e \bmod n$, which is $M^{de} \bmod n$, which is back to M.

Although the digital signature could be applied to the entire message, in practice it is applied to a cryptographic hash, or message digest, of the message as both a performance improvement and integrity check. This message digest is usually generated using an algorithm such as MD5 or SHA-1 (Stallings, 2003) and acts like a one-way fingerprint for the message. So, Alice would first generate the message digest of the message $MD(M)$ and sign it with her private key. She would then send the original message M and the signed message digest of M ($M + D_{\text{Alice-Private}}[MD(M)]$) to Bob. Bob would then recalculate the message digest of M using the same hash algorithm and then apply Alice's public key to the signature portion of the message yielding $MD(M)$, which should be the same as the $MD(M)$ that he just calculated if the signature verifies. More information about using RSA for digital signature can be found in Menezes, Van Oorschot, and Vanstone (1996).

Generating Large Prime Numbers

As we have seen, the RSA algorithm requires that we generate two random, large, prime numbers p and q. Because a prime number is one that has no factors other than 1 and itself, it may seem that generating a prime number is as difficult as factoring a number, which is the exponentially hard problem that RSA is based on in the first place.

It turns out that there are several algorithms that can test whether a random candidate number is prime more efficiently than factoring.

First, how many prime numbers are there? The Prime Number Theorem, which says that the number of primes smaller than a given number n is about $n/\ln(n)$, gives us this insight (Garrett, 2001). We can use this theorem to estimate the density of prime numbers around a given number. For 1024-bit RSA keys, p and q are on the order of 2^{512} each. So, about 1 of every $2^{512}/[2^{512}/\ln(2^{512})]$ or 355 numbers in this vicinity are prime. One way to generate a prime number of this size is to just generate a random number and test whether it is prime, and this will take on average 355 attempts for keys of this size. We can skip even numbers and drop this average in half.

One algorithm for testing primality is the Miller–Rabin algorithm (Stallings, 2003). It is a nondeterministic algorithm, meaning that it determines that a number is prime with an uncertainty. The algorithm can be run multiple times to decrease this uncertainty, until it achieves an acceptable level of uncertainty. Recently, a deterministic algorithm for primality testing, known as AKS (Agrawal, Kayal, & Saxena, 2002) was discovered, but it is slower than Miller–Rabin.

Some authors and standards recommend or require that p and q are *strong* primes. This means that $p - 1$ and $p + 1$ are divisible by a large prime number. Although this helped thwart some factoring attacks, it does not help increase security with more recent factoring methods.

RSA Attacks

Although RSA, with adequate key size, is considered secure today, there are a number of attacks that lead to some implementation considerations. In addition, if RSA is used improperly in security protocols, it can lead to vulnerabilities without breaking the RSA algorithm itself. This section gives just a few of the more common attacks and implementation considerations. For more details, see Boneh (1999), Ferguson and Schneier (2003), Garrett (2001), and Schneier (1995).

Fundamentally, a message M is encrypted via M^e mod n, so reverse this function and find M. This is known as taking the eth root mod n and is an apparently computationally hard problem (Garrett, 2001). However, this is not the only route to an attack against RSA.

An attacker can see e and n, because they form the public key, which is public. An attacker would like to get d, so they can either decrypt messages encrypted with e, or forge message signatures by signing them with d. One way to get d is to compute the modular inverse of e mod $\phi(n)$. But to get $\phi(n)$, we need to find p and q. This means we must factor n into its component primes p and q. But as n gets larger, this becomes exponentially more difficult. So the security of RSA is primarily based on the difficulty of factoring large numbers.

Table 1 (FactorWorld!, 2004) shows some history of factoring records, showing the decimal digit size, the year the factoring was completed, the amount of computing power required (expressed in millions of instructions per second-years) and the factoring algorithm used. MPQS stands for multiple polynomial quadratic sieve and GNFS

Table 1 Decimal Digit Factoring Records

Decimal digits	Year	MIPS-years	Algorithm
116	1990	275	MPQS
120	1993	830	MPQS
129	1994	5000	MPQS
130	1996	1000	GNFS
140	1999	2000	GNFS
155	1999	8000	GNFS
158	2002	?	GNFS
160	2003	?	GNFS
174	2003	13200	GNFS

stands for general number field sieve. Note the efficiency gained with the new algorithm.

For comparison, Table 2 shows the decimal equivalent for a variety of RSA key sizes. Note, in general, the sizes of keys for public key cryptography are much larger and not comparable to the sizes of keys for conventional cryptography. The 512-bit key size is already vulnerable. Most applications today select a key size of 1024 bits. Some applications are beginning to use greater key sizes. Lenstra and Verheul (2001) predict that a key size of 2048 bits will remain secure until the year 2022. As in any use of cryptography, one should use a key size that not only is appropriate for current needs but that will also remain secure for the length of time the data must be secure. This means we must anticipate both improvements in computing power (as Moore's law describes) and improvements in factoring algorithms. This can be as much an art as it is a science.

Another way of attacking RSA makes use of a plaintext–ciphertext pair. In this case, if an attacker knows M and the corresponding C, in addition to n, they can try to solve the equation $C = M^e$ mod n for the encryption key or $M = C^d$ mod n for the decryption key. But both of these problems are variations of the discrete logarithm problem, so we are back to another hard problem such as factoring, so this in infeasible as the numbers get large.

There are several other kinds of attacks that lead to some implementation considerations and constraints. For example, because of the *common modulus* attack one should never intentionally choose the same modulus, or n, for more than one user. At first, this might seem acceptable and desirable because it saves time as we do not have to generate another p and q. But if two users have the same n, then one of the users can use their own e and d along with n to find p and q. The user, with p and q, now takes the other user's public key e and calculates his or her private key d.

Table 2 RSA Key Size Decimal Equivalents

RSA key size	Decimal digits
512	155
1024	309
2048	617

There are numerous other implementation considerations. For example, the value for d should be larger than the square root of n, and the value for e is often selected to be 65537 to avoid some attacks. Also, as with any type of cryptography, good random number sources or pseudorandom number generation algorithms are critical.

RSA Protocol Attacks

It is possible to use RSA in an incorrect way, which can lead to vulnerability, without actually breaking the algorithm itself. In general, these are known as *protocol attacks* (Kaufman, Perlman, & Speciner, 2002). One example arises when an attacker gets an RSA implementation to sign a carefully chosen number. This can occur in a challenge response protocol, where a challenger generates a numeric challenge, asks the challenged entity using RSA to sign the challenge with its private key, and then applies the challenged entity's public key to authenticate the entity. If an attacker can get an entity to sign a message M', while the attacker's true agenda is to get the entity to sign a message M, they can generate a random number r and construct $M' = r^e M \bmod n$. After the entity signs M' and returns it, the attacker takes the result and divides by $r^e \bmod n$ and gets the entity's signature on the original message M. This attack is called *blinding* (Boneh, 1999). A related attack is to have the entity sign two messages, M_1 and M_2. They have inadvertently also signed $M_3 = M_1 \times M_2 \bmod n$.

In another signing-based attack, a malicious Mallory gets Alice to decrypt some ciphertext by signing a message. Mallory generates a random number r, where $r < n$. Mallory sends $y = (r^e \bmod n) \times c \bmod n$ to Alice, pretending it is a random number as part of a challenge/response authentication protocol, and Alice signs it with her private key d, giving $u = y^d \bmod n$ back to Mallory. Mallory then computes $(r^{-1} \bmod n) \times u \bmod n$, which is $r^{-1}r^e r^d c^d \bmod n$, or $c^d \bmod n$, which is just m, Alice's unencrypted message! This is one reason that the key pair used for digital signature should be distinct from the key pair used for encryption.

The RSA algorithm does not have a minimum block size, but if too small a block size is used, then an attacker can simply build a dictionary of all plaintext–ciphertext pairs. So, large block sizes are used in practice (usually the same size as the modulus). Short messages can be padded to meet this length. The standard PKCS1 is designed specifically for RSA to help do this padding in a way that resists attack (RSA Laboratories, 2001). Public key cryptosystems work best, in both a security and performance sense, with small (but not too small) random-appearing data, such as secret keys and one-way hash functions.

PROTECTING PUBLIC AND PRIVATE KEYS

The public key cryptographic algorithms we have discussed still leave open some higher level security considerations. First, as with any cryptographic application, the algorithm is only as good as the key protection. Private keys must be stored in ways that are inaccessible to attackers. Using passwords and passphrases that are weaker in entropy than the keys they protect defeats the intended security of the algorithm and is perhaps the biggest security weakness in systems that employ cryptography, public key or conventional. Other human-factor and systems issues are discussed in Schneier (2000).

We must also ensure that public keys purported to belong to an entity really do belong to them. We cannot always trust e-mail or public directory distributions of the public key. One common solution is to have a trusted third party, such as VeriSign, use their private key to sign a *digital certificate*, which contains an entity's public key and other identifying information. Then, users of that digital certificate can use the third party's public key (usually distributed with the operating system or browser) to validate the signature on the certificate. This authenticates that the public key really belongs to the entity.

There are several weaknesses with this approach to public key authentication, most notably with certificate revocation lists (CRLs) that must be checked (but usually are not) by applications to identify certificates that have been compromised. Gutman (2002) discusses these problems and potential solutions.

CONCLUSION

Table 3 summarizes the algorithms referenced in this chapter and their characteristics. Elliptic curve cryptosystems, discussed in another chapter, are also a type of public key cryptosystem based on the ElGamal family. For Java implementations of many of the algorithms and supporting numeric calculations discussed in this chapter, see Bishop (2003).

Public key cryptography is an amazing invention. It has transformed many core security functions and practices and is present today in protocols and applications such as SSL/TLS, SSH, S/MIME, and PGP. Arguably, e-commerce

Table 3 Public Key Algorithm Summary

	Public key cryptosystem	Public key distribution system	Encryption	Digital signature	Key establishment
Knapsack	X		X	X	X
Diffie–Hellman		X			X
ElGamal	X		X	X	X
ElGamal signature & DSS				X	
RSA	X		X	X	X

would not be possible without this technology, because it relies on private, authenticated communication between two spontaneously interacting parties. So, we are now all free to connect to a Web site without any preexisting business relationship, and in a few mouse clicks can ensure we are privately sending our credit card number to an authenticated server to purchase a product. This technology has brought us a rich variety of computer applications, opened the doors for many mathematical developments, and raised many interesting privacy and political issues. Even more amazing, just over 25 years ago, most thought that this would not be technically possible.

GLOSSARY

Certificate Authority A trusted third party that verifies public key owner identity and who then signs that public key with the certificate authority's private key, thereby authenticating that key and binding it to its owner.

Certificate Revocation List An online list, maintained by a certificate authority, which contains the serial numbers of all invalid certificates issued by that certificate authority.

Diffie–Hellman A public key distribution algorithm that leverages the discrete logarithm problem that is used for key agreement between two parties that have not previously exchanged secret information.

Digital Certificate The binding of a public key with the owner's identification and other fields, such as validity dates, that is digitally signed by a certification authority and validated with a public key, which is usually located in a browser or operating system. It is used to help prove that key owners are who they say they are.

Digital Signature The application of a private key to a message (or more typically to the message digest of a message) via a cryptographic algorithm to yield a signed message so that a receiver can apply the corresponding public key to the signed message via a cryptographic algorithm to yield the original message or message digest. This verifies that the message could only have been originally signed by the sender, providing both source authentication and the even stronger notion of nonrepudiation.

Discrete Logarithm Problem Given $b = g^x \bmod n$, find x.

ElGamal A public key cryptosystem that leverages the discrete logarithm problem, like the Diffie–Hellman algorithm, but unlike Diffie–Hellman, can be used directly to encrypt a message. Another part of this algorithm provides digital signature function.

Hash Algorithm A function that take a long sequence of bits and maps them to another, fixed length and smaller, sequence of bits.

Key Agreement Two (or more) parties exchange some data that results in both parties deriving a common key, in a way in which an eavesdropper cannot do so (as in the Diffie–Hellman algorithm). This common key can subsequently be used with a conventional cryptographic algorithm for private communication.

Key Transport One party creates a key and securely sends it to the other party using a previously established conventional key or using a public key algorithm like RSA.

Knapsack A public key cryptosystem that leverages the subset sum problem. This algorithm is now considered insecure.

Miller–Rabin Algorithm A nondeterministic algorithm that determines whether a number is prime with a degree of uncertainty.

Nonrepudiation Not allowing denial that an action was performed. An example is the use of a digital signature to allow a person to sign a message with a private key, which also means they cannot deny it was signed by them because only they know that private key.

One-Way Function A function that is easy to compute in one direction but hard to compute in the reverse direction.

Public Key Cryptography A cryptographic technique that uses both secret and corresponding public information that, depending on the specific algorithm, provides message privacy via encryption, nonrepudiation via digital signature, or key exchange to parties that have not previously exchanged secret information.

Public Key Cryptosystem A system that uses two related keys, a private key that must be kept secret and a public key that must be known to all message senders, that provide for encryption with the public key and decryption with the private key, providing message privacy.

RSA A public key cryptosystem that can also be used for digital signature that leverages the problem of factoring large numbers into their component prime numbers.

CROSS REFERENCES

See *Digital Certificates; Digital Signatures and Electronic Signatures; Encryption Basics; Key Management; PKI (Public Key Infrastructure)*.

REFERENCES

2002 A. M. Turing Award Winners. (2002). Retrieved July 1, 2004, from http://www.acm.org/awards/turing_citations/rivest-shamir-adleman.html

Agrawal, M., Kayal, N., & Saxena, N. (2002). PRIMES is in P. Retrieved July 1, 2004, from http://www.cse.iitk.ac.in/news/primality.html

Bishop, D. (2003). *Introduction to cryptology with Java applets*. Sudbury, MA: Jones and Barlett.

Boneh, D. (1999). Twenty years of attacks on the RSA cryptosystem. *Notices of the AMS, 46,* 203–213.

Diffie, W. (1988). The first ten years of public key cryptography. *Proceedings of the IEEE, 76,* 560–577.

Diffie, W., & Hellman, M. (1976a). New directions in cryptography. *IEEE Transactions on Information Theory, IT-22,* 644–654.

Diffie, W., & Hellman, M. (1976b). Multiuser cryptographic techniques. *Proceedings of the AFIPS National Computer Conference,* 109–112.

ElGamal, T. (1985). A public key cryptosystem and a signature scheme based on discrete logarithms. *IEEE Transactions on Information Theory, 31,* 469–472.

FactorWorld! (2004). Retrieved July 1, 2004, from http://www.crypto-world.com/FactorWorld.html

Ferguson, N., & Schneier, B. (2003). *Practical cryptography*. Indianapolis, IN: John Wiley & Sons.

Garrett, P. (2001). *Making, breaking codes: An introduction to cryptology*. Upper Saddle River, NJ: Prentice Hall.

Gutman, P. (2002). PKI: It's not dead, just resting. *IEEE Computer, 35*, 41–49.

IETF. (1992). The MD5 Message-Digest Algorithm. RSA Laboratories (2002). PKCS #1 v2.1: RSA cryptography standard. Retrieved July 1, 2004, from http://www.rsasecurity.com/rsalabs

Kaufman, C., Perlman, R., & Speciner, M. (2002). *Network security: Private communication in a public world* (2nd ed.). Upper Saddle River, NJ: Prentice Hall.

Knuth, D. (1981). *The art of computer programming: Vol. 2. Semi-numerical algorithms* (2nd ed.). Reading, MA: Addison-Wesley.

Lenstra, A., & Verheul, E. (2001). Selecting cryptographic key sizes. *Journal of Cryptology*, 255–293.

Levy, S. (2001). *Crypto: How the code rebels beat the government—Saving privacy in the digital age*. New York: Penguin Books.

Menezes, A., Van Oorschot, P., & Vanstone, S. (1996). *Handbook of applied cryptography*. Boca Raton, FL: CRC Press. Retrieved July 1, 2004, from http://www.cacr.math.uwaterloo.ca/hac

Merkle, R. (1978). Secure communications over insecure channels. *Communications of the ACM, 21*, 294–299.

Merkle, R., & Hellman, M. (1978). Hiding information and signatures in trap door knapsacks. *IEEE Transactions on Information Theory, IT-24*, 525–530.

NIST. (1994). Federal Information Processing Standards Publication 186: Digital signature standard (DSS). Retrieved July 1, 2004, from http://www.itl.nist.gov/fipspubs/fip186.htm

NIST. (2002). *Federal Information Processing Standards Publication 180–2: Secure hash standard*. Retrieved July 1, 2004, from http://csrc.nist.gov/publications/fips/fips180-2/fips180-2.pdf

Odlyzko, A. (1990). The rise and fall of knapsack cryptosystems. *PSAM: Proceedings of the 42th Symposium in Applied Mathematics, American Mathematical Society, 42*, 75–88.

Rivest, R., Shamir, A., & Adleman, L. (1978). A method for obtaining digital signatures and public key cryptosystems. *Communications of the ACM, 21*, 120–126.

RSA Laboratories. (2002). *PKCS #1 v2.1: RSA cryptography standard*. Retrieved July 1, 2004, from http://www.rsasecurity.com/rsalabs

Salomaa, A. (1996). *Public key cryptography* (2nd ed.). Berlin: Springer-Verlag.

Schneier, B. (1995). *Applied cryptography: Protocols, algorithms, and source code in C* (2nd ed.). New York: John Wiley & Sons.

Schneier, B. (2000). *Secrets and lies: Digital security in a networked world*. New York: John Wiley & Sons.

Singh, S. (1999). *The code book: The evolution of secrecy from Mary, Queen Of Scotsto quantum cryptography*. New York: Doubleday.

Stallings, W. (2003). *Cryptography and network security: Principles and practices* (3rd ed.). Upper Saddle River, NJ: Prentice Hall.

Stinson, D. (2002). *Cryptography: Theory and practice* (2nd ed.). Boca Raton, FL: CRC Press.

Elliptic Curve Cryptography

N. P. Smart, *University of Bristol, UK*

INTRODUCTION

Elliptic curves were first introduced into cryptography by Miller (1986) and Koblitz (1987). In recent years they have gained widespread interest because of their shorter key size compared to systems such as RSA, their superior efficiency in certain situations, and the smaller bandwidth that they require. These advantages are becoming more compelling as time progresses because of the increased use of smaller and smaller mobile computing devices with associated bandwidth and computational constraints.

However, probably the main driving force behind interest in elliptic curve based cryptography (ECC) is that as time progresses one needs to increase ECC key sizes more slowly than one needs to increase RSA key sizes. This is because the best known attacks against ECC are exponential in nature, whereas we already know that integer factorization has subexponential solutions.

In this chapter we aim to introduce the basics of elliptic curve cryptography. However, the literature is vast and we can only really touch on most subjects; more details can be found in the large number of books on the subject, such as Blake, Seroussi, and Smart (1999), Blake, Seroussi, and Smart (2004), and Washington (2003). We start by introducing the group law, which is the tool that allows one to convert traditional schemes such as Diffie–Hellman key exchange and ElGamal encryption into the elliptic curve setting. We then progress to explaining implementation issues, such as how one selects parameters and implements algorithms to ensure that elliptic curve-based systems run as fast as possible. Following this, we then go on to discuss the elliptic curve discrete logarithm problem (EC-DLP) on which the security results are based. In this section we also discuss how one generates secure elliptic curves, a procedure that is analogous to generating "safe" prime numbers in the traditional ElGamal system. After these sections, which introduce the mathematical foundations, we then begin to touch the surface of the large number of cryptographic protocols, which can be implemented using elliptic curves, concentrating on those most widely deployed. Then we discuss issues related to secure implementation on trusted tokens such as smart cards. Elliptic curves are particularly suited to smart cards, for the reasons mentioned above, but smart cards are vulnerable to so-called side-channel attacks and hence one needs to implement procedures that minimize leaked information.

Before ending this introduction it is worthwhile for the reader new to elliptic curves to understand that although their use in cryptography is relatively recent, they have in fact been studied in mathematics for many years. Indeed they form the testing ground for many conjectures and programs that aim to unify various areas of mathematics.

The chord-tangent process we discuss under Group Law was certainly known to Newton and Fermat. Indeed, the doubling algorithm is a special case of Fermat's method of ascent. The link with ellipses, and hence the name elliptic curve, comes via a route in the applied mathematics of the 19th century. In solving certain differential equations, which arise naturally in nature, one is led to the use of so-called elliptic functions. Whereas the traditional circular functions of sin and cos are related to properties of a circle and are periodic, that is:

$$\sin(z) = \sin(z + 2\pi) = \sin(z + 4\pi) = \cdots = \sin(z + n2\pi),$$

elliptic functions are related to the properties of ellipses and are doubly periodic, as complex functions, that is:

$$\Psi(z) = \Psi(z + n_1\omega_1 + n_2\omega_2), \quad \text{for } n_1, n_2 \in \mathbb{Z}.$$

Elliptic functions are considered the next class of functions after the elementary ones of sin, cos, sinh, and so on. In fact they are the result of the following integral:

$$\Psi(z) = \int_{-\infty}^{z} \frac{dx}{\sqrt{f(x)}},$$

where $f(x)$ is a cubic function. In general, such integrals cannot be expressed in terms of the elementary functions, hence the need to introduce a new class, which are called elliptic functions. An elliptic function is related to the function $\sqrt{f(x)}$, where $f(x)$ is a cubic polynomial, that is, to the following curve:

$$y^2 = f(x),$$

which is why such curves are called elliptic curves. The addition law, described under Group Law, is equivalent to the composition law for elliptic integrals used by in the study of some differential equations.

The study of diophantine equations of the follwing form:

$$y^2 = \text{cubic over } \mathbb{Z}, \qquad (1)$$

was started in earnest in the early 20th century. It was soon noticed that the group law made these curves a useful testing ground for problems and conjectures in number theory, in particular as elliptic curves essentially formed the most interesting class of one-dimensional number theoretic objects.

In 1929 Siegel (1966) showed that the set of integral solutions to Eq. (1) was finite. Siegel's proof was not algorithmic and it was not until 1970 that Baker and Coates (1970) provided a proof of this result that allowed one to find the solutions.

In 1922 Mordell (1922) showed that the set of rational solutions to Eq. (1) forms an abelian group of finite rank. Mordell's proof used a technique that meant it was not always possible to compute the rank of the group or the generators. In the late 1950s Birch and Swinnerton-Dyer (1963, 1965), in one of the first major machine computations in number theory, produced a conjecture that related the obstruction to Mordell's proof being algorithmic with the value of a certain function called an L-function. At about the same time Shimura, Taniyama (and later Weil) came up with a conjecture that related this L-function to an object in complex function theory called a modular form. As the 1960s progressed people found links between various areas of mathematics in this way, as they tried to prove the conjectures of Birch and Swinnerton-Dyer and Shimura-Taniyama-Weil. In 1986 Frey (1986) conjectured a link, made more precise by Serre and then proved by Ribet (1990), between Fermat's Last Theorem and elliptic curves that meant that if someone proved the Shimura-Taniyama-Weil conjecture then they could prove Fermat's Last Theorem. Finally in 1995 Wiles (1995) proved the conjecture of Shimura-Taniyama-Weil and so Fermat's Last Theorem was proved.

Elliptic curves have also been used in areas of computational number theory relevant to traditional factoring-based public key cryptography. In 1987 Lenstra (1987) generalized Pollard's (1974) $p - 1$ factoring method to the elliptic curve setting in much the same way as Miller and Koblitz generalized ElGamal public key systems to the elliptic curve setting. The resulting factoring method of Lenstra, called the elliptic curve method (ECM), is the most successful factoring algorithm for 100 decimal digit numbers in the sense that it will factor efficiently more 100 digit numbers than any other algorithm. However, it is particularly unsuited to the factoring of RSA style numbers that are the product of two primes of roughly the same size. Despite this drawback ECM is often used as a subprocedure in processing the output of the sieving stage in algorithms to factor RSA style numbers.

Elliptic curves also play a crucial role in the primality testing method of Goldwasser and Kilian (1986). This technique, usually called the elliptic curve primality proving method (ECPP), produces a very short primality certificate. Although it is not a deterministic primality testing algorithm, such as the recent breakthrough of Agrawal, Kayal, and Saxena (2003), the fact that it produces a simple certificate makes it a very useful procedure when you want to guarantee that you are using prime numbers.

As one can see, elliptic curves have had a great influence on mathematics and have been studied for many years. Many of the techniques developed for purely intellectual curiosity have been applied in practical situations in cryptography. Indeed, we shall see the names of Frey, Pollard, and Weil coming up later when we discuss the EC-DLP.

GROUP LAW

For cryptographic purposes we are interested only in elliptic curves defined over finite fields. We first need to select a finite field K; in practice this is usually either a field of characteristic two $K = \mathbb{F}_{2^p}$ or a field of large prime characteristic $K = \mathbb{F}_p$. The size of 2^p or p is closely related to the size of the final ECC key, as we shall see later, and so one should ensure that the size of the finite field is at least 160 bits long.

An elliptic curve over K is then defined as a nonsingular cubic curve over the field K. Various simplifications can be applied, which boil down to the fact that a curve can be written either as

$$E : Y^2 = X^3 + aX + b, \quad \text{in large prime characteristic}$$

or as

$$E : Y^2 + XY = X^3 + aX^2 + b, \quad \text{in characteristic two.}$$

The set of points on the curve $E(K)$ is then defined to be the set of all pairs $(x, y) \in K \times K$ that satisfy the equation, plus a special point $\mathcal{O}$ called the point at infinity. The point $\mathcal{O}$ is considered to lie infinitely far up the y-axis.

By a theorem of Hasse it is known that

$$\#K + 1 - 2\sqrt{\#K} \le \#E(K) \le \#K + 1 + 2\sqrt{\#K}.$$

Hence, the number of points on the curve is very closely related to the size of the underlying finite field.

The set $E(K)$ is in fact a finite abelian group, that is, we can add points to each other to form other points in such a way that the resulting addition law is associative, commutative, has an identity (the point at infinity $\mathcal{O}$), and for which every point has an additive inverse. Given such a finite abelian group we can then transfer traditional discrete logarithm based cryptographic protocols to the elliptic curve setting.

There are two equivalent ways to define the group law on an elliptic curve. The first is a geometric way, which, although intuitively easy, is hard to use in practice and makes more immediate sense for curves defined over the real numbers. This geometric definition can be made to be rigorous for finite fields, one just needs to be careful as to how one defines tangent, and so on. The second approach to defining the group law is to use formulae. These equations are very easy to use in practice, yet do not convey much intuition. We therefore opt to give both definitions.

Geometric Definition of the Group Law

We assume for this section that the curve is given by an equation of the following form:

$$Y^2 = \text{cubic in } X.$$

However, a similar geometric definition works in other cases, one just needs to change the process of "reflecting in the X-axis" mentioned below.

Let P and Q be two distinct points on E, both defined over K. The straight line joining P and Q, called a chord, must intersect the curve at one further point, say R, because we are intersecting a straight line with a curve of degree three. The point R will also be defined over K because the line, the curve, and the points P and Q are themselves all defined over K. If we then reflect R in the X-axis we obtain another rational point which we shall call $P + Q$ (see Figure 1 for a visualization over the real numbers).

Note, if one point Q is the point at infinity then the curve joining $\mathcal{O}$ with P intersects the curve at a point with the same x coordinate as P, but which has y coordinate equal to minus the y coordinate of P. If we then reflect this point in the x axis we return to the point P. Hence,

$$P + \mathcal{O} = \mathcal{O} + P = P.$$

In a similar way one can see that we have the following:

$$(x, y) + (x, -y) = \mathcal{O}$$

and so if $P = (x, y)$ then $-P = (x, -y)$.

The above definition is symmetric in the starting points P and Q, hence the resulting operation obviously satisfies

the following:

$$P + Q = Q + P$$

and so the operation is commutative. Showing the above addition law is also associative in that for all P, Q, and R we have the following:

$$(P + Q) + R = (P + Q) + R,$$

is a little more involved, see Cassels (1991).

To add P to itself, usually called doubling P, we take the tangent to the curve at P. Such a line must intersect the cubic curve in exactly one other point, which we denote by R. Again we reflect the point R in the x- axis to obtain a point that we call $[2]P = P + P$ (see Figure 2).

Note, that if the tangent to the point is vertical, it "intersects" the curve at the point at infinity and $P + P = \mathcal{O}$ (i.e., P is a point of order 2).

Algebraic Formulation of the Group Law

We now present the group law by formulae on points. Using a little algebra one can show that the following formulae are what one would obtain from applying the geometric definitions above. We divide into two cases, that of large prime characteristic and that of characteristic two. Although other cases are possible, we limit ourselves to these two because they are the cases of most interest to cryptographers.

$K = \mathbb{F}_p$

The formulae for the group law in characteristic $p > 3$, where the curve is of the form

$$Y^2 = X^3 + aX + b$$

are given by, for $P_i = (x_i, y_i)$, $-P_1 = (x_1, -y_1)$. If

$$P_3 = (x_3, y_3) = P_1 + P_2 \neq \mathcal{O},$$

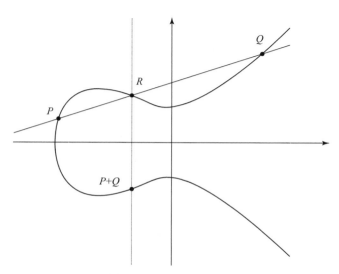

Figure 1: Adding two points on an elliptic curve.

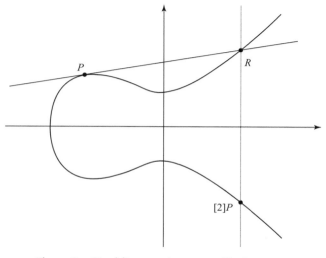

Figure 2: Doubling a point on an elliptic curve.

then x_3 and y_3 are given by the formulae

$$x_3 = \lambda^2 - x_1 - x_2,$$
$$y_3 = (x_1 - x_3)\lambda - y_1.$$

where if $x_1 \neq x_2$ we set

$$\lambda = \frac{y_2 - y_1}{x_2 - x_1},$$

and when $x_1 = x_2$, $y_1 \neq 0$ we set

$$\lambda = \frac{3x_1^2 + a}{2y_1}.$$

Two points sum to $\mathcal{O}$ if $x_1 = x_2$ and $y_1 = -y_2$, hence as a special case we have, if $(x, 0) \in E(K)$ that $2(x, 0) = \mathcal{O}$.

$K = \mathbb{F}_{2^n}$

The formulae for the group law in characteristic two, with a curve of the form,

$$Y^2 + XY = X^3 + a_2 X^2 + a_6$$

are given by, for $P_i = (x_i, y_i)$, $-P_1 = (x_1, y_1 + x_1)$. If

$$P_3 = (x_3, y_3) = P_1 + P_2 \neq \mathcal{O},$$

then x_3 and y_3 are given by the formulae

$$x_3 = \lambda^2 + \lambda + a_2 + x_1 + x_2,$$
$$y_3 = (\lambda + 1)x_3 + \mu$$
$$= (x_1 + x_3)\lambda + x_3 + y_1,$$

where if $x_1 \neq x_2$ we set

$$\lambda = \frac{y_2 + y_1}{x_2 + x_1}, \quad \mu = \frac{y_1 x_2 + y_2 x_1}{x_2 + x_1}$$

and when $x_1 = x_2 \neq 0$ we set

$$\lambda = \frac{x_1^2 + y_1}{x_1}, \quad \mu = x_1^2.$$

Two points sum to $\mathcal{O}$ if $x_1 = x_2$ and $y_2 = y_1 + x_1$, hence as a special case if $(0, y) \in E(K)$ then $2(0, y) = \mathcal{O}$.

Projective Coordinates

For positive integers k we write

$$[k]P = \underbrace{P + P + \cdots + P}_{k \text{ times}}.$$

This is extended to all integers $k \in \mathbb{Z}$ using the inverse $-P$ of a point. A lot of division operations in the field K are required if $[k]P$ is computed using the standard coordinate system above, where one uses two field elements to represent a point. However, division is a very expensive operation that leads one to introduce a different coordinate system where one can implement the addition formulae above but without the need for expensive divisions. In this section we introduce such a system, called projective coordinates, but for the sake of space we focus only on large prime characteristic p. However, a similar situation occurs in characteristic two.

To get some feeling for the operations in affine coordinates, so one can see the advantage of projective coordinates later, we now examine the operations defined above. In large prime characteristic, we can see that when $P_1 \neq P_2$, then the computation of $P_1 + P_2$ requires one inversion and three multiplications in K; we ignore additions in K because they are relatively cheap. We denote this computational cost by $1I + 3M$, where I and M denote, respectively, the cost of field inversion and multiplication. When $P_1 = P_2$, the cost of the point doubling operation can be seen to be $1I + 4M$.

The standard projective coordinates used in cryptography, often called Jacobian or weighted projective coordinates, represent a affine point (x, y) by a triple (X, Y, Z) on the following curve:

$$Y^2 = X^3 + aXZ^4 + bZ^6.$$

To map between the two coordinate systems we use the following:

$$(X, Y, Z) \longleftrightarrow (X/Z^2, Y/Z^3).$$

Notice, that many projective points correspond to a single affine point, a fact which is useful in some side-channel defences we mention later. The point at infinity $\mathcal{O}$ is represented by the triple $(1, 1, 0)$.

The following sequence of operations computes the sum $P_3 = (X_3, Y_3, Z_3)$ of two points $P_1 = (X_1, Y_1, Z_1)$ and $P_2 = (X_2, Y_2, Z_2)$ in projective coordinates, assuming $P_1, P_2 \neq \mathcal{O}$ and $P_1 \neq \pm P_2$:

$\lambda_1 = X_1 Z_2^2,$	$\lambda_2 = X_2 Z_1^2,$	$\lambda_3 = \lambda_1 - \lambda_2,$
$\lambda_4 = Y_1 Z_2^3,$	$\lambda_5 = Y_2 Z_1^3,$	$\lambda_6 = \lambda_4 - \lambda_5,$
$\lambda_7 = \lambda_1 + \lambda_2,$	$\lambda_8 = \lambda_4 + \lambda_5,$	$Z_3 = Z_1 Z_2 \lambda_3,$
$X_3 = \lambda_6^2 - \lambda_7 \lambda_3^2,$	$\lambda_9 = \lambda_7 \lambda_3^2 - 2X_3,$	$Y_3 = (\lambda_9 \lambda_6 - \lambda_8 \lambda_3^3)/2.$

Assuming division by 2 is performed by multiplication of a precomputed constant and multiplication by 2 is for free, one can then see that the cost of a point addition is given by $16M$, which will be faster than using affine coordinates when

$$16M < 1I + 3M$$

(i.e. when an inversion is slower than 13 multiplications). An important case is when one point, say P_1, is given in affine coordinates and the other one in projective coordinates (i.e. we have $Z_1 = 1$). This requires only 11 multiplications and so this "mixed" addition will be faster than a purely affine addition when a single inversion is slower than 8 multiplications.

We still need to consider point doubling in projective coordinates, that will turn out to be the operation that dominates the execution of cryptographic applications.

The formulae for doubling are given by the following:

$$\lambda_1 = 3X_1^2 + aZ_1^4, \quad Z_3 = 2Y_1Z_1, \quad \lambda_2 = 4X_1Y_1^2,$$
$$X_3 = \lambda_1^2 - 2\lambda_2, \quad \lambda_3 = 8Y_1^4, \quad Y_3 = \lambda_1(\lambda_2 - X_3) - \lambda_3.$$

This has a cost of $10M$, which reduces to $8M$ when one selects curves such that $a = -3$ as one often does. Hence, with this optimization the cost of a projective doubling is faster than an affine one when

$$8M < 1I + 4M$$

(i.e. when an inversion is slower than four multiplications). Note, for almost all implementations of large prime characteristic fields a field inversion will always take longer than four field multiplications.

Point Multiplication

As already mentioned the operation on which elliptic curve cryptography is built is the operation that takes an integer k and a point P and computes the point multiple as follows:

$$Q = [k]P = P + P + \cdots + P.$$

This is, for suitably chosen curves, a function that is believed to be hard to invert. The value k is called the (elliptic curve) discrete logarithm of Q with respect to the base P.

Point multiplication in elliptic curves is a special case of the general problem of exponentiation in an abelian group. Hence, all of the prior work on such algorithms for use in traditional discrete logarithm based cryptosystems can be applied in the elliptic curve setting. However, one has some advantages that can be exploited in the elliptic curve situation. For example, elliptic curve subtraction comes for essentially the same cost as addition, so we can use signed representations for the multiplier k.

The Binary Method

The simplest algorithm for point multiplication is the binary method, which relies on the binary representation of the number k. This comes in two variants; the right-to-left variant processes the bits of k from the least significant bit to the most significant bit, the left-to-right variant processes the bits in the reverse order. To understand both variants consider the multiplier k given by the follwing:

$$k = \sum_{j=0}^{\ell-1} k_j 2^j \quad k_j \in \{0, 1\},$$

where ℓ is the bit-length of k.

The right-to-left variant works as follows:

$$T \leftarrow P.$$
$$Q \leftarrow \mathcal{O}.$$
For $j = 0$ to $\ell - 1$ do.
    If $k_j = 1$ then $Q \leftarrow Q + T$.
    $T \leftarrow [2]T$.
Return Q.

The left-to-right variant works in the following manner:

$$Q \leftarrow \mathcal{O}.$$
For $j = \ell - 1$ to 0 by -1 do.
    $Q \leftarrow [2]Q$.
    If $k_j = 1$ then $Q \leftarrow Q + P$.
Return Q.

Both methods are often referred to as the double-and-add algorithm, because the inner workings of each loop consist of always doubling a point and a conditional addition. One should notice that the left-to-right variant does not use a temporary variable T, which is often useful in practical situations where memory is constrained. Also, because one only performs addition of the point P, in the step $Q \leftarrow Q + P$, one can perform a "mixed" addition by keeping Q in projective coordinates and P in affine coordinates. The left-to-right variant is also of theoretical importance because it is this variant which is generalized to the more efficient algorithms we shall see below.

Whichever variant one uses, the binary method always performs $\ell - 1$ point doublings and on average $\ell/2 - 1$ point additions. If we let D_A, resp. D_P, denote the number of affine, resp. projective, doublings performed and A_A, resp. A_M, denote the number of affine, resp. mixed, point additions performed, then the left-to-right binary method requires on average

$$\ell(A_M/2 + D_P)$$

operations.

The m-ary Method

The obvious generalization of the binary method is, instead of processing one bit of k at a time, to process r bits at a time. This results in the m-ary method, where $m = 2^r$, for some integer $r \geq 1$. In practice one would usually take $r = 4$ or 5. We first write k in its m-expansion as follows:

$$k = \sum_{j=0}^{d-1} k_j m^j, \quad \text{with } k_j \in \{0, 1, \ldots, m - 1\}$$

and we then precompute the multiples as follows:

$$P_i = [i]P \quad \text{for } i = 0, \ldots, m - 1.$$

So as to take advantage of mixed addition below, one often computes the P_i in affine form. The m-ary point multiplication algorithm is then given by the following:

$$Q \leftarrow \mathcal{O}.$$
For $j = d - 1$ to 0 by -1 do.
    $Q \leftarrow [m]Q$. (This requires r doublings.)
    $Q \leftarrow Q + P_{k_j}$.
Return Q.

It can be readily verified that the algorithm computes $[k]P$, following Horner's rule:

$$[k]P = [m](\ldots [m]([m]([k_{\ell-1}]P) + [k_{\ell-2}]P) + \cdots) + [k_0]P$$

Assuming projective coordinates are used for Q and affine coordinates for the P_i then:

- The number of projective doublings in the main loop of the m-ary method is $(d-1)r$.
- The number of mixed additions in the main loop is $d-1$.
- The preprocessing requires $m-2 \approx 2^r$ affine additions.

However, for an ℓ-bit number k, we have $d \approx \ell/r$, which means that the m-ary method requires approximately

$$2^r A_A + \ell(A_M/r + D_P)$$

operations. Hence, for the cost of a little preprocessing and some extra storage we have reduced the number of mixed additions that are needed to be performed when compared to the binary methods.

Window Methods

The m-ary method above can be regarded as a special case of a *window* method, where bits of the multiplier k are processed in blocks (windows) of length r. We can, however, improve things by using a variable length window and assuming each processed window starts with a set bit in the right most location. We think of this as the left hand edge of each window is allowed to slide leftwards, until it meets a set bit, thus giving the method its name. We first encode our multiplier as follows:

$$k = \sum_{i=0}^{d-1} k_i 2^{e_i},$$

where $e_i - e_{i-1} \geq r$ and

$$k_j \in \{1, 3, 5, \ldots, 2^r - 1\}.$$

We then precompute

$$P_i = [i]P \quad \text{for } i \in \{1, 3, 5, \ldots, 2^r - 1\}.$$

The value $[k]P$ if computed via the algorithm

$Q \leftarrow P_{k_{d-1}}.$
For $i = d-2$ to 0 by -1 do.
$\quad Q \leftarrow [2^{e_{i+1}-e_i}]Q.$
$\quad Q \leftarrow Q + P_{k_j}.$
$Q \leftarrow [2^{e_0}]Q.$
Return Q.

The analysis of this method is quite involved but essentially boils down to the fact that $d \approx \ell/(r+1)$. Hence, again assuming projective values of Q and affine values for the stored P_i:

- The number of projective doublings is around ℓ
- The number of mixed additions in the main loop is $\ell/(r+1)$.
- The preprocessing requires 2^{r-1} affine additions.

In total we therefore need about

$$2^{r-1} A_A + \ell(A_M/(r+1) + D_P)$$

operations. We therefore not only reduce the number of mixed additions, we also reduce the preprocessing and the amount of required storage.

Signed Digit Representations

We mentioned earlier that point subtraction has virtually the same cost as point addition on an elliptic curve group. This means we could make use of representations of the multiplier k that use negative, as well as positive, values of the window values k_i. First consider representing k in the following form:

$$k = \sum_{j=0}^{d-1} s_j 2^j \quad \text{where } s_j \in \{-1, 0, 1\}.$$

Such a representation is called a (binary) *signed digit* representation. Clearly, such a representation includes the standard binary representation, and the signed digit representation is not unique, as we can see from the example of representing the integer 3,

$$3 = 1 + 2 = -1 + 4 = 1 - 2 + 4 = \cdots.$$

One can, however, always select a signed digit representation which is particularly sparse, in that it has no adjacent nonzero digits (i.e. $s_j s_{j+1} = 0$ for all $j \geq 0$). Such a representation is called a *nonadjacent form* (NAF).

Given a NAF for k one can then compute a point multiplication, in a left-to-right form, via the following:

$Q \leftarrow \mathcal{O}.$
For $j = d - 1$ to 0 by -1 do.
$\quad Q \leftarrow [2]Q.$
$\quad$ If $s_j = 1$ then $Q \leftarrow Q + P.$
$\quad$ If $s_j = -1$ then $Q \leftarrow Q - P.$
Return Q.

A NAF usually has fewer nonzero digits than a binary representation, indeed the expected weight is around $\ell/3$. We therefore require, again assuming a projective representation for Q and an affine representation for P, around

$$\ell(A_M/3 + D_P)$$

operations, which is not as efficient as our m-ary method for windows of size $r = 3$ or our sliding window method for $r = 2$. However, one can achieve this improvement without the need for preprocessing and storage inherent in the window based methods.

A Signed m-ary Sliding Window Method

We can, however, combine the sliding window method with the signed digit method to obtain a new method which is often the method of choice for general elliptic curve point multiplications. We assume that the windows we will choose will be of length at least r, and we define

$$B = \{-2^{r-1} + 1, \ldots, -1, 0, 1, \ldots, 2^{r-1} - 1\}.$$

We then write the multiplier k as follows:

$$k = \sum_{i=0}^{d-1} k_i 2^{e_i} \quad \text{with } k_i \in B \setminus \{0\} \text{ and } e_i \in \mathbb{Z}_{\geq 0},$$

where $e_{i+1} - e_i \geq r$ for all $0 \leq i \leq d-2$. We do not explain how such a representation is computed, but see Blake et al. (1991) for details.

Once we have produced such a representation for k the algorithm is similar to those seen before. We need to precompute as follows:

$$P_i = [i]P \quad \text{for } i \in B \cap \mathbb{Z}_{\geq 0}.$$

Hence, we compute and store 2^{r-2} points, which is less than that needed for the unsigned sliding window method for the same sized windows. We then compute $[k]P$ via the following algorithm:

$Q \leftarrow P_{k_{d-1}}$.
For $i = d-2$ to 0 by -1 do.
$\quad Q \leftarrow [2^{e_{i+1}-e_i}]Q$.
$\quad$ If $k_i > 0$ then $Q \leftarrow Q + P_{k_i}$.
$\quad$ Else $Q \leftarrow Q - P_{-k_i}$.
$Q \leftarrow [2^{e_0}]Q$.
Return Q.

The expected number of operations performed by this method is, given our standard assumptions,

$$2^{r-2} A_A + \ell(A_M/(r+1) + D_P).$$

Hence, the improvement comes mostly in the precomputation and storage.

The exact choice of which algorithm to use such as m-ary, signed window method, NAF or signed sliding windows depends on various machine dependent parameters such as available memory, the relative costs of projective, mixed and affine point additions, and so on. The literature contains a number of other variants for use in elliptic curve systems that we do not have space to cover, but the above algorithms are the main ones and should form a starting point for the reader's own investigations.

Special Methods
The above methods are useful when one is presented with a general point P and one is asked to compute $Q = [k]P$. However, in many of the protocols we shall see later one needs to compute either $Q = [k]P$ for a fixed value of P over a number of runs of a protocol or $Q = [k_1]P_1 + [k_2]P_2$, a so-called multiple-exponentiation.

We present here algorithms for these special situations but giving only the most basic variants. A close examination of the research literature will reveal a large number of possible variants and improvements.

We start by considering the case of the multiplication $Q = [k]P$, where P is fixed over a number of runs of a protocol, a so-called fixed base method. In this situation one could do some precomputation using P, which could be too expensive if only one multiplication was to be performed but which is cheap if one considers a number are to be done.

We assume a window size of r bits and precompute as follows:

$$P_i = [2^{ri}]P$$

for $i = 0, \ldots, d = \lceil \ell/r \rceil$. If this is done in affine coordinates then this requires ℓD_A operations. Then on receiving a multiplier k one encodes it in base 2^r as follows:

$$k = \sum_{i=0}^{d-1} k_i 2^{ri},$$

with $k_i \in \{0, \ldots, 2^r - 1\}$. With this encoding one can perform the following algorithm:

$Q \leftarrow \mathcal{O}$.
$T \leftarrow \mathcal{O}$.
For $j = 2^r - 1$ to 0 by -1 do.
$\quad$ For $i = 0$ to $d - 1$ do.
$\quad\quad$ If $k_i = j$ then $T \leftarrow T + P_i$.
$\quad Q \leftarrow Q + T$.
Return Q.

For each value of k this requires

$$(2^r + \ell/r)A_M$$

operations. Hence, if we are performing s such point multiplications of the same point P then the above algorithm requires

$$\ell D_A + s(2^r + \ell/r)A_M$$

as opposed to

$$2^{r-2} A_A + s\ell(A_M/(r+1) + D_P)$$

for s applications of the signed sliding-window method.

We now turn to so called multiexponentiation, which really should be multimultiplication in the elliptic curve setting. The most elementary form of this is as follows, often called Shamir's trick, but actually because of Strauss. Suppose we wish to compute the following:

$$Q = [k_1]P_1 + [k_2]P_2.$$

We precompute

$$P_0 = \mathcal{O},$$
$$P_1 = [0]P_2 + [1]P_1 = P_1,$$
$$P_2 = [1]P_2 + [0]P_1 = P_2,$$
$$P_3 = [1]P_2 + [1]P_1 = P_1 + P_2.$$

Then, given the two multipliers k_1 and k_2, we write the binary representation of k_1 and k_2 in a $2 \times \ell$ matrix, with the least significant bits in the rightmost column. We let C_i denote the integer value obtained by taking the integer given by the binary representation in the i-th column of the matrix, where the top row is the least significant bit of C_i, and compute Q via the following:

$$Q \leftarrow \mathcal{O}.$$
$$\text{For } i = 1 \text{ to } \ell \text{ do.}$$
$$Q \leftarrow [2]Q.$$
$$Q \leftarrow Q + P_{C_i}.$$
$$\text{Return } Q.$$

This requires ℓ projective doublings and ℓ mixed additions (i.e., 2ℓ curve operations) and should be compared to the $\approx 3\ell$ curve operations needed on average to perform two binary multiplications followed by a projective addition. Even if using the signed sliding window method, one would require roughly

$$2\ell(A_M/(r+1) + D_P)$$

operations. Hence, even this naive method of multimultiplication is faster than the two signed sliding-window multiplications when

$$D_P > r A_M/(r+1).$$

As we mentioned before, a typical cost is $D_P \approx 8M$ and $A_M \approx 11M$. Hence, if one took window widths of $r = 3$ in the signed sliding window method then the multimultiplication method would be faster. The exact choice of method depends on various implementation details, such as the ratio I/M and the available memory.

Special Curves

There is a certain family of curves, which occurs quite frequently in elliptic curve cryptography, called the *Koblitz curves*. Originally this term was used for curves defined over a subfield k of K, where we consider the group of points over the larger field for cryptographic purposes. The reason for considering these curves was that they possess an endomorphism structure that allows an efficient implementation of the point multiplication algorithms.

Nowadays, especially in standards such as SEC (2000a, 2000b), the name *Koblitz curve* is used for any elliptic curve that possesses a special endomorphism structure that enables improvements to be made to the multiplication algorithms above.

There are two common classes of Koblitz curves:

1. The classical case of curves over $\mathbb{F}_2$ (sometimes called anomalous binary curves or ABC curves), which are given by the following:

$$Y^2 + XY = X^3 + aX^2 + 1,$$

where $a \in \{0, 1\}$. These curves are defined over $\mathbb{F}_2$ but we work in the group of points defined over the field $\mathbb{F}_{2^n}$.

2. The more recent case of Koblitz curves over a large prime field which have a suitable endomorphism.

We do not discuss these curves further in this article, but the interested reader is referred to the extensive literature on such curves.

THE ELLIPTIC CURVE DISCRETE LOGARITHM PROBLEM

The elliptic curve discrete logarithm problem (or EC-DLP) is the problem of reversing the point multiplication algorithm performed in the last section, that is, given $P, Q \in E(K)$ find the value of λ, if it exists, such that

$$Q = [\lambda]P.$$

For suitably chosen fields, curves and points this problem is believed to be computationally infeasible to solve. In the following we shall summarize the results in this area.

However, we should note that many elliptic curve based cryptographic protocols actually rely on weaker problems for their security, such as the elliptic curve Diffie–Hellman problem (EC-DHP) or the elliptic curve Decision Diffie–Hellman problem (EC-DDH).

The elliptic curve Diffie–Hellman problem is the problem of given P, Q, R such that

$$Q = [x]P \quad \text{and} \quad R = [y]P$$

to find the value S such that

$$S = [xy]P.$$

Clearly the EC-DHP is no harder a problem than than the EC-DLP because we can solve EC-DHP given an oracle to solve EC-DLP.

Given $P, Q, R,$ and S such that

$$Q = [x]P, \quad R = [y]P \quad \text{and} \quad S = [z]P,$$

the elliptic curve Decision Diffie–Hellman problem is the problem of determining whether $z = x \times y \pmod{l}$, where l is the order of the point P. Clearly, an oracle to solve EC-DHP can be used to solve EC-DDH, hence EC-DDH is the (potentially) easier problem.

In most cases it is believed that all three problems are very hard to solve, for suitably chosen parameters. However, we shall see later that there is one special class of curves for which there is a polynomial time algorithm to solve EC-DDH but only a subexponential algorithm to solve EC-DHP or EC-DLP.

Known Generic Attacks

We start by considering generic attacks against the EC-DLP. The name *generic* refers to the fact that such attacks will apply in any finite abelian group and not just an elliptic curve group. What makes elliptic curves particularly attractive is that for well-chosen parameter sets the generic attacks are the best one can currently perform. In the following cases we assume we have a discrete logarithm problem given by the following:

$$Q = [\lambda]P,$$

where P and Q are given and the goal is to find λ.

Exhaustive Search

This is the most elementary attack. One simply performs the following algorithm

$$R \leftarrow \mathcal{O}.$$
For $\mu = 0$ to $l - 1$ do.
     If $R = Q$ then output μ and stop.
     $R \leftarrow R + P.$
Output "No Solution".

This algorithm requires $O(1)$ storage, but requires $O(\#E(K))$ time in both the worst and average case.

Pohlig–Hellman

The discrete logarithm problem in a group G [for instance, $G = E(K)$] is only as hard as the discrete logarithm problem in the largest subgroup of prime order in G. This observation is because of Pohlig and Hellman (1978), and their method works in an arbitrary finite abelian group.

To explain the Pohlig–Hellman algorithm, suppose we have a finite cyclic abelian group G whose order is given by the following:

$$N = \#G = \prod_{i=1}^{t} p_i^{e_i}.$$

The case of noncyclic groups may be handled analogously. We assume that the number N can be factored (this assumption is valid for the EC-DLP because group orders for elliptic curve cryptography are rather small compared to current factoring records).

Now suppose we are given two points $P, Q \in G$ such that there exists an integer λ such that

$$Q = [\lambda]P.$$

Our aim is to find λ by first finding it modulo $p_i^{e_i}$ and then using the Chinese remainder theorem to recover it modulo N.

We can map the discrete logarithm in G to a discrete logarithm in a cyclic subgroup of prime power order C_{p^e} using the following map:

$$\phi_p : \begin{cases} G & \to & C_{p^e} \\ R & \longmapsto & [N/p^e]R \end{cases}$$

The map ϕ_p is a group homomorphism so if we have $Q = [\lambda]P$ in $\langle P \rangle$ then we will have $\phi_p(Q) = [\lambda]\phi_p(P)$ in C_{p^e}. But the discrete logarithm in C_{p^e} would only be determined modulo p^e. This gives the following algorithm:

Write $N = \#G = \prod_{i=1}^{t} p_i^{e_i}.$
For $i = 1$ to t do.
     $Q_p \leftarrow [N/p_i^{e_i}]Q.$
     $P_p \leftarrow [N/p_i^{e_i}]P.$
     Find $\lambda_i \in \mathbb{Z}/p_i^{e_i}\mathbb{Z}$ such that $Q_p = [\lambda_i]P_p.$
Using the Chinese remainder theorem find λ such that $\lambda = \lambda_i \pmod{p_i^{e_i}}.$

The only problem is that we have not shown how to perform the step of solving the EC-DLP in a subgroup of prime power order. We reduce this to the problem of solving EC-DLPs in subgroups of prime order as follows.

Suppose P and Q are of prime power order p^e such that

$$Q = [\lambda]P.$$

Clearly λ is defined only modulo p^e and we can write

$$\lambda = \lambda_0 + \lambda_1 p + \cdots + \lambda_{e-1} p^{e-1}.$$

We find $\lambda_0, \lambda_1, \ldots$ in turn, using the following procedure.

$$\lambda' \leftarrow 0.$$
For $t = 0$ to $e - 1$ do.
     $Q' \leftarrow Q - [\lambda']P.$
     $P' \leftarrow [p^t]P.$
     $Q'' \leftarrow [p^{e-t-1}]Q'.$
     $P'' \leftarrow [p^{e-t-1}]P'.$
     Find $\lambda_t \in \mathbb{Z}/p\mathbb{Z}$ such that $Q'' = [\lambda_t]P''.$
     $\lambda' \leftarrow \lambda' + p^t \lambda_t.$
Output $\lambda'.$

Note in the above algorithm that at the start of each loop we have, for some integer λ'',

$$\lambda = \lambda' + p^t \lambda''.$$

The points P' and Q' are defined to be of order p^{e-t} such that

$$Q' = [\lambda'']P'.$$

Hence, P'' and Q'' are of order p and are related by the following:

$$Q'' = [\lambda_t]P''.$$

All the steps in the above two subprocedures of the Pohlig–Hellman algorithm are very simple. The main difficulty therefore is in solving the EC-DLP in the cyclic subgroups of prime order. It therefore follows that the difficulty of the EC-DLP depends on the largest prime factor of the order of the group, say l. For efficiency we prefer that the subgroup of order l contains a large proportion of all the points on the curve. Hence, it is common to take an elliptic curve E over a finite field K such that

$$\#E(K) = N = h \times l,$$

where l is a large prime and h is very small, typically $h = 1, 2,$ or 4. We shall now assume that elliptic curves have been chosen to satisfy this constraint.

Baby-Step/Giant-Step

In our above discussion of the Pohlig–Hellman algorithm we assumed we had an algorithm to solve the discrete logarithm problem in cyclic groups of prime order. We shall now describe a general method of solving such problems that is more efficient than exhaustive search. This method is because of Shanks and is called the baby-step/giant-step method. Once again this is a generic method that applies to any cyclic finite abelian group.

Again we fix notation as follows. We have a public cyclic subgroup $G = \langle P \rangle$ of some elliptic curve group $E(K)$, which we can now assume to have prime order l. We are also given a point $Q \in G$ and are asked to find the value of λ modulo l such that

$$Q = [\lambda]P.$$

We assume there is some fixed encoding of the elements of G, so in particular it is easy to store, sort, and search a list of elements of G.

The principle behind the baby-step/giant-step method is a standard divide and conquer approach found in many areas of computer science. We first write the following:

$$\lambda = \lambda_0 + \lambda_1 \left\lceil \sqrt{l} \right\rceil.$$

Because $\lambda \leq l$ we have that $0 \leq \lambda_0, \lambda_1 < \lceil \sqrt{l} \rceil$. The goal is then to find λ_0 and λ_1.

In the first stage of the baby-step/giant-step method we compute the baby steps as follows:

$P_0 \leftarrow \mathcal{O}.$
For $i = 0$ to $\lceil \sqrt{l} \rceil$ do.
    Store (P_i, i) in a hash table T indexed by the first entry in the pair.
    $P_{i+1} \leftarrow P_i + P.$
Output T.

To compute and store the baby-steps clearly requires $O(\lceil \sqrt{l} \rceil)$ time, and a similar amount of storage. We now perform the second stage involving the giant-steps:

$P' \leftarrow \left[\left\lceil \sqrt{l} \right\rceil \right] P.$
$j \leftarrow 0.$
$Q' \leftarrow Q.$
While $(Q', i) \notin T$ for some i do.
    $j \leftarrow j + 1.$
    $Q' \leftarrow Q' - P'.$
Output $i + j \left\lceil \sqrt{l} \right\rceil.$

When this second stage terminates, which is guaranteed to happen after at most $\lceil \sqrt{l} \rceil$ steps, it outputs the discrete logarithm of Q with respect to P. To see this notice that on termination of the while loop we have $Q' = Q - [j]P'$ and there is a $(P_i, i) \in T$ such that $P_i = Q'$. When such a match occurs we have the following:

$$[i]P = Q - \left[j \left\lceil \sqrt{l} \right\rceil \right] P,$$

and so $\lambda_0 = i$ and $\lambda_1 = j$, that is,

$$\left[i + j \left\lceil \sqrt{l} \right\rceil \right] P = Q.$$

Notice that the time to compute the giant-steps is at most $O(\sqrt{l})$. Hence, the overall time and space complexity of

the baby-step/giant-step method is $O(\sqrt{l})$. This complexity is for both the worst and average cases of running the algorithm.

It is known, see Shoup (1997), that the baby-step/giant-step method is the fastest possible method for solving the discrete logarithm problem in a "black box" or 'generic' group. A black box group is a group modeled in such a way that the representations of group elements provides no structure. Of course in any particular group there may be a special purpose algorithm that works faster. The fact that for general elliptic curves the baby-step/giant-step method is the most efficient algorithm known for the EC-DLP has led some people to model elliptic curves as black box groups in security proofs.

In conclusion, combining the baby-step/giant-step method with the Pohlig–Hellman algorithm, if we wish a discrete logarithm problem in a group G to be as difficult as a work effort of 2^{80} operations, then we need the group G to have a prime order subgroup of order at least 2^{160}.

This means that for elliptic curve cryptography we select a curve such that

$$\#E(K) = N = h \times l,$$

where

$$l > 2^{160}.$$

Pollard Methods

The trouble with the baby-step/giant-step method is that, although its run time is bounded by $O(\sqrt{l})$, it also requires $O(\sqrt{l})$ space. This space requirement makes the algorithm infeasible in practice. Hence, it is desirable to reduce the large space requirement while still obtaining a time complexity of $O(\sqrt{l})$. Pollard achieved this (1978), but the method only has an expected running time rather than an absolute bound on the running time. The resulting algorithm is therefore of the "Las Vegas" type.

The methods for reducing the space complexity all make use of random walks, and a number of techniques exist in the literature almost all of which are because of Pollard (such as the rho, lambda, and kangaroo methods).

These algorithms were all developed for serial computers. In real life when one uses random walk-based techniques to solve discrete logarithm problems one uses a parallel version because of van Oorschot and Wiener (1994), using so-called distinguished points, which is easy to distribute over the Internet.

In 1997 Certicom announced a series of elliptic curve challenges, and the ones that have been successfully solved have all been done using the parallel Pollard method with distinguished points. At the time of writing the largest EC-DLPs attempted have been a curve over a binary field with group order of a 97-bit prime, a Koblitz curve with group order a 108-bit prime and a curve over a field of large prime characteristic with group order a 109-bit prime. The computational power needed to solve the 109-bit challenge utilized around $10,000$ PCs running 24 hr a day for 549 days, and as such was greater than the effort needed to factor a 512-bit RSA modulus.

In January 2003 NIST, the U.S. National Institute for Standards and Technologies, issued its recommendations on key establishment schemes (2003). In this document it presented the recommendations for various key sizes, which we give in the table below for both ECC-based systems and systems based on traditional discrete logarithms in a finite field $\mathbb{F}_p^*$. We assume the elliptic curve E has group order

$$\#E(K) = h \cdot l,$$

where l is a prime. We also assume for the finite field setting that the prime p satisfies $p - 1 = t \cdot q$ where q is a prime, one then considers protocols defined in a subgroup of order q of the finite field $\mathbb{F}_p^*$. The first row gives the equivalent block cipher strength.

Group	Bits of security	80	112	128	129	256
$E(K)$	$\log_2(l) \geq$	160	224	256	384	512
	$\log_2(h) \leq$	16	16	16	16	16
$\mathbb{F}_p^*$	$\log_2(q) \geq$	160	224	256	384	512
	$\log_2(p) \geq$	1024	2048	3072	8192	15360

Note that the size of p in finite field systems is usually comparable to the size of the modulus in an RSA system. Hence, the above says that to obtain the same security as a 256-bit block cipher one would require an elliptic curve size of around 512 bits or an RSA modulus of around 15360 bits.

In 2001 Lenstra and Verheul (2001) published a careful analysis comparing the best known algorithms for RSA factorization, traditional discrete logarithms, and elliptic curve discrete logarithms. Their analysis came up with the following comparisons where N is an RSA modulus

Bits of security	80	109
$\log_2(l) \geq$	165	206
$\log_2(q) \geq$	142	193
$\log_2(p) \geq$	1184	3392
$\log_2(N) \geq$	1513	4047

Although different from the NIST comparisons, the two works show that as time progresses and traditional public key algorithm key sizes increase, the benefit of ECC becomes more pronounced.

Known Special Attacks

We now consider attacks that apply to certain special classes of elliptic curves.

Weil Pairing and Tate Pairing Attacks

Menezes, Okamoto, and Vanstone (1993) were the first to show that the EC-DLP may be transformed into a discrete logarithm problem in a finite field. Their method used the Weil pairing. This method was generalized by Frey and Rück (1994) using the Tate pairing. We recall the Frey-Rück attack here.

Let $K = \mathbb{F}_q$ and let P and Q be points in $E(K)$ of order l. Suppose that l is coprime to q. Let k be a positive integer such that the field $\mathbb{F}_{q^k}$ contains the lth roots of unity [in

other words, $l | (q^k - 1)$ and k is the order of q in $\mathbb{Z}_l^*$]. We use the following notation, where $G = E(\mathbb{F}_{q^k})$ as follows:

$$G[l] = \{P \in G : [l]P = \mathcal{O}\},$$
$$lG = \{[l]P : P \in G\},$$
$$(\mathbb{F}_{q^k}^*)^l = \{\alpha^l : \alpha \in \mathbb{F}_{q^k}^*\}.$$

The Tate pairing is a mapping

$$\langle \cdot, \cdot \rangle : G[l] \times G/lG \to \mathbb{F}_{q^k}^*/(\mathbb{F}_{q^k}^*)^l,$$

which satisfies the following properties:

1. (Well defined) $\langle \mathcal{O}, Q \rangle \in (\mathbb{F}_{q^k}^*)^l$ for all $Q \in G$ and $\langle P, Q \rangle \in (\mathbb{F}_{q^k}^*)^l$ for all $P \in G[l]$ and all $Q \in lG$.
2. (Nondegeneracy) For each point $P \in G[l] - \{\mathcal{O}\}$ there is some point $Q \in G$ such that $\langle P, Q \rangle \notin (\mathbb{F}_{q^k}^*)^l$.
3. (Bilinearity) For any integer n, $\langle [n]P, Q \rangle \equiv \langle P, [n]Q \rangle \equiv \langle P, Q \rangle^n$ modulo l-th powers in $\mathbb{F}_{q^k}^*$.

The Tate pairing is used to attack the EC-DLP in the following way:

Choose $R \in_R E(\mathbb{F}_{q^k})$ until $\langle P, R \rangle \notin (\mathbb{F}_{q^k}^*)^l$.
$\zeta_1 \leftarrow \langle P, R \rangle$.
$\zeta_2 \leftarrow \langle Q, R \rangle$.
$\eta_1 \leftarrow \zeta_1^{(q^k-1)/l}$.
$\eta_2 \leftarrow \zeta_2^{(q^k-1)/l}$.
Find λ such that $\zeta_2 = \zeta_1^\lambda$.

Note that the index calculus algorithms for solving the discrete logarithm problem in $\mathbb{F}_{q^k}^*$ have subexponential complexity in terms of the field size q^k (their performance is comparable with integer factorization algorithms). Because the original problem is in a group of size q it is necessary that the subexponential complexity in terms of q^k be smaller than the complexity $O(\sqrt{q})$ of the Pollard methods. Hence, this strategy is practical only when k is relatively small.

It is known that supersingular curves are vulnerable to the Frey–Rück attack (because the value k is always less than or equal to 6). There are also nonsupersingular curves that are vulnerable to this attack (e.g., curves of trace two over $\mathbb{F}_q$). Hence, one should always choose elliptic curves such that

$$l \nmid q^k - 1$$

for all "small" values of k (e.g., $k \leq 30$). This test will eliminate all supersingular curves and curves of trace two, plus a few others. We emphasize that this test is trivial to perform and that the probability of a random nonsupersingular curve failing this test is negligible.

In practice one uses a slightly modified pairing, called the modified Tate pairing,

$$\langle \cdot, \cdot \rangle : G[l] \times G[l] \to \mathbb{F}_{q^k}^*/(\mathbb{F}_{q^k}^*)^l,$$

which is well-defined and bilinear and satisfies $\langle G, G \rangle \neq 1$ for all $G \neq \mathcal{O}$. The use of a modified pairing slightly simplifies the above attack and allows some interesting other applications to which we now turn.

Curves with small values of k, such as supersingular elliptic curves, are cryptographically interesting because they are an example of a group for which the best known algorithm to solve the Diffie–Hellman problem runs in subexponential time but for which there is a polynomial time algorithm to solve the Decision-Diffie–Hellman problem. Suppose we are given $P = [a]G$, $Q = [b]G$, and $R = [c]G$, and we are asked to determine if $ab \equiv c \pmod{l}$, this is the Decision-Diffie–Hellman problem. Using the (modified) Tate pairing, which can be computed in polynomial time when k is small, we only need to check that

$$\langle R, G \rangle = \langle [c]G, G \rangle = \langle G, G \rangle^c$$
$$= \langle G, G \rangle^{ab} = \langle [a]G, [b]G \rangle$$
$$= \langle P, Q \rangle.$$

The Tate pairing has now become interesting in a constructive sense because of various new applications. The first constructive applications were pairing based key agreement and signature schemes by Sakai, Ohgishi, and Kasahara (2000) and a tripartite Diffie–Hellman key agreement protocol of Joux (2000). However, the most interesting application was the development of an identity-based encryption scheme by Boneh and Franklin (2001).

The Anomalous Curves Attack

An elliptic curve E defined over a prime field $\mathbb{F}_p$ is said to be anomalous if it has exactly p points. In 1997 several researchers independently announced related methods to reduce the discrete logarithm problem on an anomalous elliptic curve $E/\mathbb{F}_p$ to the discrete logarithm problem in the additive group $\mathbb{Z}/p\mathbb{Z}$ of the integers modulo p. Smart (1999) posted an announcement on the internet briefly describing a method to solve this problem. At the same time a preprint appeared by Satoh and Araki (1998), which used identical methods. It then became known that Semaev (1998) had already submitted an article on this topic, and that Rück (1999) had generalized this method to deal with Abelian varieties.

The p-adic version of the method essentially uses the p-adic filtration of a lift of the elliptic curve to the p-adic numbers. The p-adic elliptic logarithm is then used to solve the EC-DLP. The fact that the method applies only to anomalous curves is because one requires $p = l$ so as to kill off the higher groups in the p-adic filtration.

We note that anomalous curves $E/\mathbb{F}_p$ are very rare. There is approximately $1/(4\sqrt{p})$ chance of a random curve being anomalous. Also, this phenomenon has no impact for the case of elliptic curves over fields of small characteristic. In the case of large odd characteristic one should always have

$$l \neq p.$$

We emphasize that this test is trivial to perform and that the probability of a random nonsupersingular curve failing this test is negligible.

Weil Descent

The technique of Weil descent to solve the EC-DLP was first proposed by Frey (1998). This strategy was detailed further by Galbraith and Smart (1999). These early ideas were initially sketchy, giving the basic approach, but were unable to solve the EC-DLP for specific curves. Then the work of Gaudry, Hess, and Smart (2002) provided techniques and efficient algorithms that would allow certain curves to be attacked in practice. The precise approach followed in the work of Gaudry, Hess, and Smart is now called the GHS attack, but it should not be confused with the general Weil descent methodology, which could be made to apply to other curves.

The basic method applies to elliptic curves over field extensions of the form $\mathbb{F}_{q^n}$, where q is a prime or prime power and $n > 1$. The principle is to transform the EC-DLP from $E(\mathbb{F}_{q^n})$ to a discrete logarithm problem on the Jacobian of a curve C over $\mathbb{F}_q$. Because subexponential algorithms exist for the discrete logarithm problem in high genus curves, this gives a possible method of attack against the EC-DLP.

In the basic GHS attack q is a Power of 2 and the curve C is a hyperelliptic curve. Menezes and Qu (2001) analyzed the GHS attack for cryptographically interesting cases and demonstrated that it did not apply to the case when $q = 2$ and n is prime. However, this did not preclude fields of the form $\mathbb{F}_{2^{155}}$, because 155 is composite, which could be approached using the GHS attack. Such fields are interesting because they allow fast computations and are used in certain standards.

In 2001 Smart examined the GHS attack for elliptic curves with respect to the field extension $\mathbb{F}_{2^{155}}/\mathbb{F}_{2^{31}}$ and concluded that such a technique was unlikely to work for any curve defined over $\mathbb{F}_{2^{155}}$. Jacobson, Menezes, and Stein (2001) also examined the field $\mathbb{F}_{2^{155}}$, this time using the GHS attack down to the subfield $\mathbb{F}_{2^5}$. They concluded that such a strategy could be used in practice to attack around 2^{33} isomorphism classes of elliptic curves defined over $\mathbb{F}_{2^{155}}$. Because there are about 2^{156} isomorphism classes of elliptic curves defined over $\mathbb{F}_{2^{155}}$, the probability of finding one where the GHS attack is applicable is negligible.

In 2002 Galbraith, Hess, and Smart extended the GHS approach via the use of isogenies. They were able to extend the attack to a much larger range of curves, but were still unable to attack all curves over the field $\mathbb{F}_{2^{155}}$. In 2003 Hess extended the approach still further by using different forms of Artin-Schreier extensions. Although the number of curves that can be attacked using the new method is much larger than the original GHS attack, one is still unable to apply the methodology to all curves over the field $\mathbb{F}_{2^{155}}$.

To avoid any possible security issues related to the GHS and the Weil descent methodology one can always take elliptic curves defined either over a large prime field of odd characteristic or curves over a field of order 2^p, where p is a prime.

Domain Parameter Generation

In using an elliptic curve system one needs to choose an elliptic curve. Taking all the above into consideration, the current security recommendations imply that choosing a curve should be done in the following manner

- Choose a finite field $K = \mathbb{F}_q$ of order $q = 2^p$ or $q = p$, where p is a prime such that $q \geq 2^{160}$.
- Choose an elliptic curve E over K and compute $N = \#E(K)$. Write $N = h \cdot l$, where l is a prime.
- Reject the curve if $h > 65536$ or $l < 2^{160}$.
- Reject if $q = p = l$.
- Reject if $q^k \equiv 1 \pmod{l}$ for some $k \leq 30$.

The only difficult part of this procedure is Step 2, where one is asked to compute $\#E(K)$. Traditionally this was a difficult problem, but because of the polynomial time algorithm of Schoof (1985) it can at least be solved in principle in polynomial time. In the 1980s and early 1990s improvements were made to the basic Schoof algorithm, mainly by Elkies and Atkin, to produce a reasonably fast algorithm to compute $\#E(K)$ in the two cases of interest, namely characteristic two and large prime characteristic.

The method of Schoof–Elkies–Atkin is called an l-adic method in that it works by computing the value of $\#E(K)$ modulo l for lots of small primes l and then combines this information using the Chinese remainder theorem to obtain the correct value of N.

In 2000 another method was proposed by Satoh (2000) for the case of curves defined over fields of small characteristic p, in this p-adic approach one lifts the curve to the p-adic numbers and then computes the value of N modulo a suitably high power of p. The method of Satoh, as improved by Skjernaa, Vercauteren, Harley, and Mestre, is now the method of choice for fields of characteristic two.

Although algorithms to compute the number of points on an elliptic curve over a finite field are now common, one very rarely needs them. Various standards bodies, for example NIST, ANSI, and SECG, specify a set of curves that have already been generated. This allows implementors to work with only a finite set and so improve both efficiency and interoperability. This restriction, to using in practice a small set of curves, is not known to introduce any security weaknesses.

PROTOCOLS

We now turn our attention to precisely which protocols one uses in elliptic curve cryptography. Although virtually any traditional discrete logarithm-based protocol can be converted into the elliptic curve setting, the three most important protocols are the elliptic curve variant of DSA (EC-DSA), the elliptic curve variant of Diffie–Hellman key agreement (EC-DH), and the elliptic curve variant of (a secure version of) ElGamal encryption (EC-IES). Hence, in this section we limit ourselves to discussing these three protocols only.

To specify elliptic curve protocols one requires a set of domain parameters, which consists of a finite field $K = \mathbb{F}_q$, an elliptic curve E over K, such that the group order $N = h \cdot l$ is known with l a large prime. One of course assumes that the curve is "secure" in that the discrete logarithm problem in the subgroup of order l is hard. Finally, one also requires a fixed base point G of order l.

EC-DSA

The elliptic curve variant of the digital signature algorithm, or EC-DSA, allows the owner of a private key $x \in \mathbb{F}_l^*$ to digitally sign a message m such that anybody who knows the corresponding public key $Y = [x]G$ is able to verify the signature on the message.

We let x-coord(T) denote the function that takes the x coordinate of the point T and then interprets its binary representation (in some standardized form) as an integer. When the field $\mathbb{F}_q$ is of large prime characteristic then we simply interpret the value of $x(T) \in \mathbb{F}_q$ as an integer. However, when $q = 2^p$ this requires both parties to agree on some standardized way of representing elements of $\mathbb{F}_q$. Almost all standards use the same representation so in practice this is no problem.

The signing algorithm for EC-DSA is as follows, where we let H denote a cryptographic hash function from messages of arbitrary length to elements of $\mathbb{F}_l^*$.

> Choose $k \leftarrow \{1, \ldots, l-1\}$.
> $T \leftarrow [k]G$.
> $r \leftarrow x$-coord$(T) \pmod{l}$.
> If $r = 0$ then return to the beginning.
> $e \leftarrow H(m)$.
> $s \leftarrow (e + xr)/k \pmod{l}$.
> If $s = 0$ then return the beginning.
> Output (r, s).

Note, that the signing algorithm always performs a point multiplication on the base point G only. Hence, if memory allows this can be made very efficient using one of the fixed base multiplication routines.

Given a message m, a signature (r, s), and a public key $Y = [x]G$, we verify the signature as follows:

> Reject if $r, s \notin \{1, \ldots, l-1\}$.
> $e \leftarrow H(m)$.
> $u_1 \leftarrow e/s \pmod{l}$, $u_2 \leftarrow r/s \pmod{l}$.
> $T \leftarrow [u_1]G + [u_2]Y$.
> Accept if and only if $r = x$-coord$(T) \pmod{l}$.

Note in the verification step we perform a simultaneous multiplication, for which we can use Shamir's trick, or we can use a special fixed base algorithm to compute $[u_1]G$ and a more general algorithm to compute $[u_2]Y$ followed by a point addition.

Like most efficient digital signature algorithms, very little can be proved about the security of EC-DSA in the standard model of computation. In fact even if we accept the random oracle model one still is unable to prove the security of EC-DSA. However, if one assumes the generic group model as a way of modeling the elliptic curve group then a proof of security has been given by Brown (2002). In this proof it is shown that any attacker against EC-DSA, in the sense of an active attacker trying to form an existential forgery, must break the hash function H to be able to perform a successful attack on EC-DSA. However, one should note that the generic group model assumption is controversial; see Stern, Pointcheval, Malone-Lee, and Smart (2002) for an example of a criticism of this approach.

Key Agreement

The first application of asymmetric cryptography was the protocol of Diffie and Hellman for two parties to agree a secret key over a public unsecured channel. However, one should note that one needs to combine the Diffie–Hellman protocol with (at least) authentication to obtain a secure key agreement protocol.

The elliptic curve variant of the Diffie–Hellman protocol consists of two parties, usually denoted Alice and Bob, deciding on two private ephemeral keys. Alice generates the private ephemeral key a and computes the corresponding public ephemeral key $P_A = [a]G$, which she sends to Bob. Bob generates the private ephemeral key b and sends to Alice the public ephemeral key $P_B = [b]G$. Alice can then compute the shared secret as follows:

$$K = [a]P_B = [ab]G,$$

whereas Bob computes the same shared secret as

$$K = [b]P_A = [ab]G.$$

On the assumption that the elliptic curve Diffie–Hellman problem is hard, then an eavesdropper is unable to compute K given P_A and P_B.

Various improvements/choices can be made on the basic protocol. One can add authentication by the use of each party digitally signing its message flow, or one can add key confirmation. Because, in the authenticated version the long-term static public keys are used only to authenticate the message flows the protocol is easily seen to be forward secure, a property that traditional SSL-like RSA key transport does not possess. If one party, say Bob, is offline then Alice could take Bob's static public key as his ephemeral public key; however, this would come at the expense of forward secrecy.

There is a protocol by Law, Menezes, Qu, Vanstone, and Solinas (2003), called MQV, which using the same message flows as the basic unauthenticated Diffie–Hellman protocol allows one to obtain an authentic key agreement scheme. This protocol is especially suited if bandwidth is constrained.

EC-IES

To use elliptic curves as a public key encryption scheme one adapts the basic ElGamal scheme. The changes from the basic ElGamal scheme are to ensure semantic security against adaptive chosen ciphertext attacks. The resulting scheme, EC-IES, was proved secure by Abdalla, Bellare, and Rogaway (2000).

To encrypt one makes use of a message authentication code (MAC), which one should think of as a keyed hash function and a symmetric cipher $E_k(m)$. In addition use is made of a key derivation function $KD(T, l)$, which takes a small key T and expands it to a key (or keys) of length l for use by a MAC or symmetric cipher.

Given message m and public key $Y = [x]G$ we produce the ciphertext (U, c, r) via the algorithm

> $U \leftarrow [k]G$.
> $T \leftarrow [k]Y$.
> $(k_1 \| k_2) \leftarrow KD(T, l)$.
> Encrypt the message, $c \leftarrow E_{k_1}(m)$.
> Compute the MAC on the ciphertext, $r \leftarrow MAC_{k_2}(c)$.
> Output (U, c, r).

Each element of the ciphertext (U, c, r) is important

- U is needed to agree the ephemeral Diffie–Hellman key T.
- c is the actual encryption of the message.
- r is used to avoid adaptive chosen ciphertext attacks.

Decryption of (U, c, r) to recover the message m via the private key x is performed via the sequence of steps.

> $T \leftarrow [x]U$.
> $(k_1 \| k_2) \leftarrow KD(T, l)$.
> Decrypt the message $m \leftarrow D_{k_1}(c)$.
> If $r \neq MAC_{k_2}(c)$ then output "Invalid Ciphertext".
> Output m.

Assuming the MAC and symmetric cipher meet some basic security properties, the above scheme is secure under an interactive hashed version of the DDH assumption (see Abdalla et al., 2002, for precise details of the exact assumption needed).

If one does not like the interactive hash DDH assumption then one can also prove security assuming the key derivation function is perfect and assuming the Gap-Diffie–Hellman problem is hard. This later problem is the problem of solving EC-DHP assuming one has an oracle to solve the EC-DDH.

For further details of the security proofs for EC-IES one should consult (Dent,). There are also a number of issues related to EC-IES related to various choices made by standards bodies. Some of these choices have very slightly weakened the security results provable for EC-IES.

DEFENCES AGAINST SIDE CHANNEL ATTACKS

Because elliptic curve cryptosystems are often used in potentially hostile environments their implementation is susceptible to side channel attacks such as those based on timing, power, or EM radiation. Such attacks were first introduced into the cryptographic community by Kocher, Jaffe, and Jun (1999).

It has proved possible, by examining the power trace, for example, to determine the operations performed by an algorithm. For example the sequence of double and add operations used in the point multiplication algorithm can be captured because the two operations are often distinguishable from different power traces. Such an attack is called simple power analysis (SPA). A more powerful attack, called differential power analysis (DPA), is when the adversary runs many runs of the protocol with different data and then uses statistical correlations between the side channel data (e.g., the power traces) to determine the secret key.

The need to provide defences against these attacks has resulted in a large amount of literature over the past few years within the elliptic curve community (e.g., see any of the proceedings of the CHES conference). The essential idea to defend against SPA is to stop the attacker being able to distinguish between double and additions or to decorrelate the observable operations from the private key. For defences against DPA one tries to randomise the data in such a way as to remove any statistical correlations in the side channel data.

Simple Power Analysis

If one uses the left-to-right binary exponentiation algorithm mentioned earlier then on observing the sequence of operations

$$D, A, D, A, D, D, A, D, D, D, A, \ldots$$

we know that the binary representation of the secret multiplier will be

$$1, 1, 0, 1, 0, 0, 1, \ldots$$

One way of stopping such attacks is to create exponentiation algorithms for which, even if you know the order of point additions and doublings, one cannot obtain the secret multiplier.

The problem with the left-to-right binary method is that each addition occurs only when a bit of the secret key is set. Hence, a possible defence is to always perform an addition no matter what the bit of the key is. Such an algorithm was given by Coron (1999):

$$Q \leftarrow \mathcal{O}.$$
For j from $\ell - 1$ to 0 by -1 do.
$\quad T[0] \leftarrow [2]Q.$
$\quad T[1] \leftarrow T[0] + P.$
$\quad Q \leftarrow T[k_i].$
Return Q.

This defence can be generalized to produce more efficient algorithms, we refer the reader to the extensive literature for more details (see Joye, for a survey).

Another defence against SPA is to make the side channel information from a point addition and the side channel information from a point doubling to be indistinguishable. An early idea of doing this was to add dummy operations into the procedures for addition and doubling. A more fundamental approach was proposed by Liardet and Smart (2001), who suggested using group law formulae that were the same for addition and doubling. This was first presented in the case of elliptic curves in Jacobi form and was quickly extended to Hessian form curves (Joye and Quisquater, 2001) and finally to curves in standard form by Brier and Joye (2002).

Differential Power Analysis

The above defences do not defend against differential power analysis. In a differential attack the attack is essentially using correlations between the differences in the power trace created by the exact data being computed rather than the operations themselves. Hence, none of the above defences will protect against differential attacks because on every protocol run they operate on the same data.

There are a number of possible defences against differential power attacks on elliptic curves, but the most elegant and simple one is to use randomized projective coordinates. This randomizes the data in the following way. Suppose we are given an affine point $P = (x, y)$ on the curve and are asked to compute $Q = [k]P$. We assume we are given a point multiplication algorithm that is secure against SPA and that operates on points in Jacobian projective coordinates. The randomized projective coordinates method then works as follows:

$$r \leftarrow K^*.$$
$$P' = (X_P, Y_P, Z_P) = (xr^2, yr^3, r).$$
$$Q' = (X_Q, Y_Q, Z_Q) \leftarrow [k]P'.$$
$$Q \leftarrow (X_Q/Z_Q^2, Y_Q/Z_Q^3).$$
Output Q.

Again we refer the reader to the Joye survey for further details of various defences.

CONCLUSION

Elliptic curves are of interest to cryptographers because they provide public key encryption in an efficient manner. The key size required to match a given level of symmetric cipher security is smaller compared to traditional systems such as those based on factoring or traditional discrete logarithms. The reduced key size means one requires less bandwidth or computational resources to implement an elliptic curve based system. In addition new applications such as identity based cryptography are enabled by elliptic curves in a way that is impossible with traditional public key constructions.

ACKNOWLEDGMENTS

The author thanks the following people for comments on earlier drafts of this article: Steven Galbraith, Dan Page, Martijn Stam, and Frederik Vercauteren.

CROSS REFERENCES

See *Cryptographic Protocols; Side-Channel Attacks; Smart Card Security.*

REFERENCES

Abdalla, M., Bellare, M., & Rogaway, P. (2000). DHAES: An encryption scheme based on the Diffie–Hellman problem. Submitted to *P1363a: Standard Specifications for Public-Key Cryptography, Additional Techniques.*

Agrawal, M., Kayal, N., & Saxena, N. (2003). Primes is in P. Preprint.

Araki, K., & Satoh, T. (1998). Fermat quotients and the polynomial time discrete logarithm algorithm for anomalous elliptic curves. *Commentarii Mathematici Universitatis Sancti Pauli, 47,* 81–92.

Baker, A., & Coates, J. (1970). Integer points on curves of genus 1. *Proceedings of the Cambridge Philosophical Society, 67,* 595–602.

Birch, B. J., & Swinnerton-Dyer, H. P. F. (1963). Notes on elliptic curves. I. *J. Reine Angew. Math., 212,* 7–25.

Birch, B. J., & Swinnerton-Dyer, H. P. F. (1965). Notes on elliptic curves. II. *J. Reine Angew. Math., 218,* 79–108.

Blake, I. F., Seroussi, G., & Smart, N. P. (1999). *Elliptic curves in cryptography.* Cambridge, UK: Cambridge University Press.

Blake, I. F., Seroussi, G., & Smart, N. P. (ed.) (2004). *Elliptic curves in cryptography II: Further topics.* Cambridge, UK: Cambridge University Press.

Boneh, D., & Franklin, M. (2001). Identity based encryption from the Weil pairing. In *Advances in cryptology—CRYPTO 2001* (pp. 213–229). New York: Springer-Verlag.

Brier, É., & Joye, M. (2002). Weierstrass elliptic curves and side-channel attacks. In *Public key cryptography—PKC 2002* (pp. 335–345). New York: Springer-Verlag.

Brown, D. (2002). *Generic groups, collision resistance, and ECDSA.* ePrint Report 2002/026. Retrieved January 1, 2004, from http://eprint.iacr.org/

Cassels, J. W. S. (1991). *Lectures on elliptic curves.* Cambridge, UK: Cambridge University Press.

Chudnovsky, D. V., & Chudnovsky, G. V. (1987). Sequences of numbers generated by addition in formal groups and new primality and factorization tests. *Advances in Applied Mathematics, 7,* 385–434.

Cohen, H., Miyaji, A., & Ono, T. (1998). Efficient elliptic curve exponentiation using mixed coordinates. In *Advances in cryptology—ASIACRYPT 98* (pp. 51–65). New York: Springer-Verlag.

Coron, J.-S. (1999). Resistance against differential power attacks for elliptic curves cryptosystems. In *Cryptographic hardware and embedded systems—CHES 1999* (pp. 292–302). New York: Springer-Verlag.

Dent, A. (2004). Proofs of security for ECIES. I. F. Black, G. Seroussi, & N. P. Smart (Eds.). *Advances In Elliptic Curve Cryptography* (pp. 41–67). Cambridge, UK: Cambridge University Press.

Frey, G. (1986). Links between stable elliptic curves and certain diophantine equations. *Annales Universitatis Saraviensis, 1,* 1–40.

Frey, G. (1998). *How to disguise an elliptic curve.* Talk at Waterloo workshop on the EC-DLP, 1998. Retrieved January 1, 2004, from http://cacr.math.uwaterloo.ca/conferences/1998/ecc98/slides.html

Frey, G., & Rück, H.-G. (1994). A remark concerning *m*-divisibility and the discrete logarithm problem in the divisor class group of curves. *Math. Comp., 62,* 865–874.

Galbraith, S.D., & Smart, N. P. (1999). A cryptographic application of Weil descent. In *Cryptography and coding, 7th IMA Conference* (pp. 191–200). New York: Springer-Verlag.

Galbraith, S. D., Hess, F., & Smart, N. P. (2002). Extending the GHS Weil descent attack. In *Advances in Cryptology—EUROCRYPT 2002* (pp. 29–44). New York: Springer-Verlag.

Gaudry, P., Hess, F., & Smart, N. P. (2002). Constructive and destructive facets of Weil descent on elliptic curves. *Journal of Cryptology, 15,* 19–46.

Goldwasser, S., & Kilian, J. (1986). Almost all primes can be quickly certified. In *Proceedings of the 18th STOC,* (pp. 316–329).

Hess, F. (2003). The GHS attack revisited. In *Advances in Cryptology—EUROCRYPT 2003* (pp. 374–387). New York: Springer-Verlag.

Jacobson, M., Menezes, A., & Stein, A. (2001). Solving elliptic curve discrete logarithm problems using Weil descent. *J. Ramanujan Math. Soc., 16,* 231–260.

Joux, A. (2000). A one round protocol for tripartite Diffie–Hellman. In *Algorithmic Number Theory Symposium—ANTS IV* (pp. 385–394). New York: Springer-Verlag.

Joux, A., & Nguyen, K. (2003). Separating Decision Diffie–Hellman from Diffie–Hellman in cryptographic groups. *Journal of Cryptology, 16,* 239–248.

Joye, M. (2004). Defences against side-channel analysis. In I. F. Black, G. Seroussi, & N. P. Smart (Eds.). *Advances In Elliptic Curve Cryptography* (pp. 87–102). Cambridge, UK: Cambridge University Press

Joye, M., & Quisquater, J.-J. (2001). Hessian elliptic curves and side channel attacks. In *Cryptographic hardware and embedded systems—CHES 2001* (pp. 402–410). New York: Springer-Verlag.

Koblitz, N. (1987). Elliptic curve cryptosystems. *Math. Comp., 48,* 203–209.

Kocher, P. C., Jaffe, J., & Jun, B. (1999). Differential power analysis. In *Advances in cryptology—CRYPTO '96* (pp. 388–397). New York: Springer-Verlag.

Law, L., Menezes, A., Qu, M., Solinas, J., & Vanstone, S. (2003). An efficient protocol for authenticated key agreement. *Designs, Codes and Cryptography, 28,* 119–134.

Lenstra, H. W. (1987). Factoring integers with elliptic curves. *Ann. Math., 126,* 649–673.

Lenstra, A., & Verheul, E. (2001). Selecting cryptographic keysizes. *Journal of Cryptology, 14,* 255–293.

Liardet, P.-Y., & Smart, N. P. (2001). Preventing SPA/DPA in ECC systems using the Jacobi form. In *Cryptographic hardware and embedded systems—CHES 2001* (pp. 391–401). New York: Springer-Verlag.

Menezes, A. J., Okamoto, T., & Vanstone, S. A. (1993). Reducing elliptic curve logarithms to a finite field. *IEEE Trans. Info. Theory, 39,* 1639–1646.

Menezes, A. J., & Qu, M. (2001). Analysis of the Weil descent attack of Gaudry, Hess and Smart. In *Progress in cryptology—CT-RSA 2001* (pp. 308–318). New York: Springer-Verlag.

Miller, V. (1986). Use of elliptic curves in cryptography. In *Advances in cryptology—CRYPTO 85* (pp. 417–426). New York: Springer-Verlag.

Mordell, L. J. (1922). On the rational solutions of the indeterminate equations of the third and fourth degrees. *Proceedings of the Cambridge Philosophical Society, 21,* 179–192.

NIST Special Publication 800-56. (2003). Recommendation on key establishment schemes. Version 2.0, http://www.nist.gov/

Pohlig, S., & Hellman, M. (1978). An improved algorithm for computing logarithms over $GF(p)$ and its cryptographic significance. *IEEE Transactions on Information Theory, 24*, 106–110.

Pollard, J. (1974). Theorems on factorization and primality testing. *Proceedings of the Cambridge Philosophical Society, 76*, 521–528.

Pollard, J. (1978). Monte Carlo methods for index computations mod p. *Math. Comp., 32*, 918–924.

Ribet, K.A. (1990). On modular representations of $Gal(\overline{\mathbb{Q}}/\mathbb{Q})$ arising from modular forms. *Invent. Math., 100*, 431–476.

Rück, H.-G. (1999). On the discrete logarithm in the divisor class group of curves. *Math. Comp., 68*, 805–806.

Sakai, R., Ohgishi, K., & Kasahara, M. (2000). Cryptosystems based on pairing. In *2000 Symposium on Cryptography and Information Security (SCIS2000).*

Satoh, T. (2000). The canonical lift of an ordinary elliptic curve over a finite field and its point counting. *J. Ramanujan Math. Soc., 15*, 247–270.

Schoof, R. (1985). Elliptic curves over finite fields and the computation of square roots mod p. *Math. Comp., 44*, 483–494.

Semaev, I. (1998). Evaluation of discrete logarithms in a group of p-torsion points of an elliptic curve in characteristic p. *Math. Comp., 67*, 353–356.

Shoup, V. (1997). Lower bounds for discrete logarithm and related problems. In *Advances in Cryptology—EUROCRYPT '97* (pp. 313–328). New York: Springer-Verlag.

Shoup, V. (2001). A proposal for an ISO standard for public key encryption, v2.1. Preprint.

Siegel, C. L. (1966). Über einige Anwedungen diophantischer Approximationen (1929). In *Collected Works* (pp. 209–266). New York: Springer-Verlag.

Smart, N. P. (1999). The discrete logarithm problem on elliptic curves of trace one. *Journal of Cryptology, 12*, 193–196.

Smart, N. P. (2001). How secure are elliptic curves over composite extension fields? In *Advances in Cryptology—EUROCRYPT '01* (pp. 30–39). New York: Springer-Verlag.

Standards for Efficient Cryptography. (2000a). *SEC1: Elliptic curve cryptography, version 1.0.* Retrieved January 1, 2000, from http://www.secg.org/

Standards for Efficient Cryptography. (2000b). *SEC2: Recommended elliptic curve domain parameters, version 1.0.* Retrieved January 1, 2000, from http://www.secg.org/

Stern, J., Pointcheval, D., Malone-Lee, J., & Smart, N. P. (2002). Flaws in Applying Proof Methodologies to Signature Schemes. In *Advances in Cryptology—CRYPTO 2002* (pp. 93–110). New York: Springer-Verlag.

van Oorschot, P., & Wiener, M. (1994). Parallel collision search with applications to hash functions and discrete logarithms. In *2nd ACM Conference on Computer and Communications Security* (pp. 210–218). ACM Press.

Washington, L. C. (2003). *Elliptic curves: Number theory and cryptography*. Boca Raton, FL: Chapman and Hall/CRC Press.

Wiles, A. (1995). Modular elliptic curves and Fermat's Last Theorem. *Ann. Math., 142*, 443–551.

IBE (Identity-Based Encryption)

Craig Gentry, *DoCoMo USA Labs*

INTRODUCTION

Adi Shamir, co-inventor of the first public key cryptosystem (RSA), introduced the notion of identity-based cryptography (IBC) in 1984 as a way to simplify public key infrastructure (PKI) (Shamir, 1985). (See Chapter 57 of this *Handbook* for a review of public key infrastructure.) His idea, at a high level, is simple and elegant: if public keys did not need to be *distributed*—if, instead, all public keys in the system were somehow known to all users—then much of the infrastructure needed to support public key cryptography (e.g., public key directories) would be unnecessary. For example, if a user's public key is its *identity* in some standardized format—e.g., an e-mail address—then a message sender needs only the user's e-mail address to e-mail the user an encrypted message; no separate mechanism is needed to distribute public keys.

High-Level Description of IBC

Since Shamir introduced this idea, cryptographers have discovered a wide variety of identity-based cryptosystems, but they share some common characteristics. Although user *public* keys can be any specified bit-string, user *private* keys are generated by a trusted third party, typically called a *private key generator* (PKG). Specifically, if the PKG's public/private key pair is (P_{PKG}, S_{PKG}) and a user's public "identity" string is ID, then the PKG generates the user's identity-based private key C_{ID} as a function of S_{PKG} and ID. To handle the possibility of revocation, the PKG typically includes the date (or some other time period) as part of the user's ID so that user private keys naturally expire; it issues new periodic private keys only to users that are currently legitimate. In the case of identity-based encryption (IBE), encryption and decryption typically proceed as follows:

- Encryption: Sender uses (P_{PKG}, ID, m) to compute c, a ciphertext for message m under the identity ID.
- Decryption: Recipient uses (C_{ID}, c) to recover m.

For identity-based signing (IBS), the algorithms are as follows:

- Signing: Signer uses (C_{ID}, m) to compute Sig, a signature on message m.
- Verification: Verifier uses (P_{PKG}, ID, m) to verify Sig.

Notice that, as advertised, the IBE sender (or IBS verifier) does not need to fetch a separate public key for the IBE recipient (or IBS signer). Although it is true that the identity-based sender (or verifier) still needs to obtain the *PKG's public key*, it is arguably much easier to distribute a few PKG public keys than (numerous) traditional user public keys (e.g., in some cases, it may even be a viable option to "embed" a PKG's public key in applications or user devices). By removing the need to distribute user public keys (and certificates), IBC can enable a key (and certificate) management system with much less infrastructure than traditional PKI.

IBC covers much more than just IBE and IBS. Other types of cryptosystems that have identity-based versions include key agreement, signcryption (i.e., signer efficiently signs and encrypts a message), blind signatures (i.e., signer blindly signs an unknown message), undeniable signatures (i.e., legitimate signature is verifiable only with signer's help, but signer cannot repudiate it), and ring signatures (i.e., signer signs anonymously as a member of an ad hoc group). In addition to briefly examining identity-based ring signatures later on, this chapter focuses primarily on IBE and IBS (especially IBE), their advantages and disadvantages, their closest alternatives, and some extensions.

It is important to emphasize that IBC has no significant advantages over traditional public key cryptography (PKC) in all contexts. In particular, IBC is not particularly advantageous when key and certificate distribution are already not a problem (e.g., in highly interactive protocols where one party could simply transmit its public and certificate to another party). In fact, this includes IBS, because a traditional public key signer can simply transmit its public key and certificate to a verifier along with its signature. (However, we hasten to add that IBS schemes still may have some performance advantages—in particular, because IBS users do not need to generate keys and because in IBS there is no separate public key or certificate to transmit, leading to a possible bandwidth reduction.)

Identity-based cryptography's advantage is perhaps clearest in the setting of noninteractive encryption (e.g., the sending of an encrypted email message), where the communication is initiated not by the owner of the public key and certificate, but by a sender that would otherwise (in a traditional public key encryption scheme) have to proactively fetch the recipient's public key and certificate before encrypting. Here, IBC reduces the load not only on senders but also on the trusted authority (the PKG) and its associated infrastructure, because no mechanism is needed to distribute public keys and certificates to encrypters. Identity-based cryptography has clear advantages in other contexts, as well (e.g., for ring signatures). We discuss these advantages in more detail later.

Identity-based cryptosystems can also have some disadvantages. In particular, the fact that the PKG generates the private keys of all of its users effectively gives the PKG *private key escrow* (i.e., the PKG can perform any private key operation that its users can, and therefore can, for example, decrypt its users' IBE-encrypted messages or forge its users' identity-based signatures). This disadvantage is particularly substantial for IBE, because a PKG can *passively* decrypt its clients' messages, whereas a certification authority (CA) in a PKI needs to mount an *active* attack. Another disadvantage is that the PKG must use *secure channels* to distribute the identity-based private keys, but this turns out to be a less serious problem. We compare identity-based cryptography with public key cryptography in the next section, focusing in more detail on these advantages and disadvantages.

The Development of Practical Identity-Based Schemes

Although the high-level "blueprint" for identity-based encryption and signature schemes is quite simple, this does not imply that constructing *concrete* identity-based cryptosystems is an easy task. Shamir (1985) provided the first IBS scheme in his initial article on IBC. The two most well-known IBS schemes are Fiat–Shamir (1986) and Guillou–Quisquater (1988), the latter of which we review later.

Constructing IBE schemes proved to be a much more difficult problem. Although there were some early efforts (e.g., by Maurer & Yacobi, 1991), versions of the first truly practical IBE scheme, which use "pairings" over elliptic curves or abelian varieties, were discovered independently by Sakai, Ohgishi, and Kasahara (2001) and

Boneh and Franklin (2001). Boneh and Franklin provided the more rigorous treatment, proving that the scheme, when combined with the Fujisaki–Okamoto transform, is secure in the "random oracle model" against adaptive chosen ciphertext attack assuming the hardness of the so-called "Bilinear Diffie–Hellman" problem. Cocks (2001) discovered a very different IBE scheme in 2001 based on the hardness of the quadratic residuosity problem modulo a number of unknown factorization, but this scheme has attracted much less attention because it suffers from significant ciphertext expansion (i.e., the ciphertext is many times longer than the plaintext). We review Cocks's scheme and the Boneh–Franklin scheme in later sections of this chapter.

More Than Just Identities

Identity-based cryptography is useful for more than just managing identities and simplifying PKI. In particular, the bit-string "ID" (as used in the high-level description of IBC) is not limited to containing someone's "identity"; it can contain any specified information.

For example, consider a scenario in which Bob performs the role of a PKG, generating a PKG public key P_{Bob} and issuing identity-based decryption keys to himself by setting ID to be a *date*; then Alice encrypts to Bob by applying an IBE scheme to (P_{Bob}, ID = *date*, m), as discussed in Boneh and Franklin (2001). Why is this arrangement useful? Suppose that Bob is going on a vacation, and he would like to use his laptop to decrypt his messages during this period, but he is concerned that his laptop may be stolen, compromising his private key. To address this problem, Bob can download a batch of "date-based" decryption keys to his laptop; if his laptop is stolen, the compromise is limited to the dates of his vacation. The "master" private key—the one he uses in his role as PKG—remains secure on his home computer.

Generally speaking, ID can be any sort of "*Incidental Data*" that an authorizer—in its capacity as a PKG—may (or may not) "sign" by issuing the corresponding decryption key. When we view IBE from this broader perspective, we see that by encrypting a message with ID and an authorizer's public key, an encrypter makes a recipient's ability to decrypt contingent on the recipient's acquisition of the authorizer's signature (in the form of an identity-based decryption key) on ID. In this sense, a more appropriate name for identity-based encryption might be "signature-contingent decryption." One can imagine a variety of scenarios, beyond the ordinary IBE scenario, where a content encrypter may want to make decryption (by one or more recipients) contingent on a release signed by a trusted authority. We discuss some of these scenarios toward the end of the chapter.

IBC VERSUS PUBLIC KEY CRYPTOGRAPHY

In this section, we discuss the advantages and disadvantages of identity-based cryptography relative to public key cryptography. As we explain, the differences between identity-based *signing* and public key *signing* (PKS) are not very significant; so we focus our comparison primarily on the trade-offs between identity-based *encryption* and public key *encryption* (PKE), which are more interesting. We also discuss "ring signatures" as another exemplary setting in which the advantages of IBC are compelling. Finally, we analyze some common objections to and misconceptions about identity-based cryptography.

Points of Comparison

Before delving into advantages and disadvantages, let us establish a "mapping" between the fundamental components of IBC and PKI-supported PKC that will allow us to compare them, focusing on the encryption case.

First, consider a traditional PKE scheme: after Bob creates a public/private key pair (P_{Bob}, S_{Bob}), Alice uses (P_{Bob}, m) to compute a ciphertext c for her message m, and Bob uses (S_{Bob}, c) to recover m. This traditional PKE scheme suffers from a key authentication problem: How does Alice know that the value of P_{Bob} that she has obtained is really Bob's public key rather than an impostor's? The essential purpose of PKI is to solve this key authentication problem. Typically, a PKI includes a certification authority (CA), which publishes its own public key P_{CA} and then performs several functions. First, the CA registers Bob and gathers information about him, including his public key P_{Bob}. If satisfied, the CA signs this information with its private signing key S_{CA}, thereby generating a "public key certificate" C_{Bob} on P_{Bob} for Bob. Thereafter, the CA may use an "infrastructure" to distribute P_{Bob} and C_{Bob} to people such as Alice, who must obtain and verify Bob's certificate before sending an encrypted message to Bob. Because Bob's public key may eventually become invalid (e.g., if his private key is compromised), the CA may also need to deploy infrastructure to distribute "certificate status" information to people such as Alice, so that they can check that Bob's certificate has not been revoked.

In an IBE scheme, a CA is replaced by a private dey generator (PKG), which publishes its public key P_{PKG},

and then performs somewhat analogous functions. Like a CA, the PKG registers Bob and gathers his identifying information ID_{Bob}, but Bob does not generate and send a public key (P_{Bob}) in an IBE scheme. If satisfied, the PKG "signs" ID_{Bob} using its private key S_{PKG}, thereby generating an identity-based decryption key C_{Bob} for Bob. The PKG must send C_{Bob} to Bob over a secure channel, because it is Bob's only secret. Alice uses (P_{PKG}, ID_{Bob}, m) to compute a ciphertext c for her message m, and Bob uses (C_{Bob}, c) to recover m. IBE is convenient from Alice's perspective, because she does not need to obtain and verify a certificate for Bob; rather, she knows that Bob (or an impostor) will be unable to decrypt her message unless he received the necessary identity-based decryption key (C_{Bob}) from the PKG (in effect, an *implicit certificate*). IBE is also convenient from the PKG's perspective, because the PKG does *not* need to deploy infrastructure to distribute Bob's public key to people such as Alice; rather, assuming Alice knows P_{PKG} and ID_{Bob}, she already has all the information she needs to encrypt. The PKG can address the "revocation" issue by including time periods of sufficient granularity into ID_{Bob} and issuing new private keys to Bob at the beginning of each time period; Alice incorporates the current time period as part of ID_{Bob} when encrypting. PKI often uses a period-based approach to revocation as well (e.g., periodic issuance of CRLs); to ease comparison, we focus primarily on this type of PKI.

To summarize, the PKG plays a role analogous to that of a CA in a PKI. An identity-based decryption key is analogous to a certificate, but it is sent over a secure channel to the specific client (Bob) rather than being sent over a public channel to various third parties (like Alice). Instead of verifying Bob's CA-issued certificate explicitly (as she would in a PKI), Alice "verifies" Bob's PKG-issued identity-based decryption key implicitly by generating a ciphertext that cannot be decrypted without it. Unlike the encryption key in a PKE scheme, Bob's identity-based encryption key is "transparent"; it is an identity that need not be separately *distributed or obtained*.

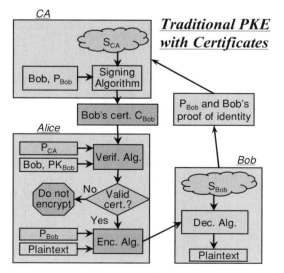

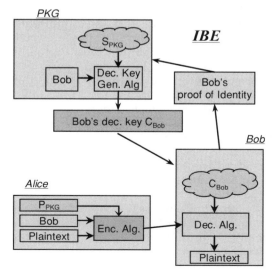

Figure 1: Comparison of PKI-supported PKE with IBE.

Advantages of IBC

The main advantage of IBE is that, unlike PKI-supported PKE, the sender does not need to obtain the recipient's public key and (periodic) certificate, via some mechanism, before sending an encrypted message. In PKI-supported PKE, the sender may obtain this information either from a server within the system's infrastructure or from the recipient itself. (Note: Fig. 1 omits the latter option for simplicity.) However, both of these options impose undesirable interaction and delay on the encrypter before it can send its message. Each option also has additional problems. Specifically, obtaining the information directly from the recipient may not be viable in high-latency applications (e.g., e-mail), and obtaining it from the system requires that the system always be online and have considerable infrastructure. (Conversely, the advantages of IBE become less compelling when such an infrastructure is not considered burdensome or in highly interactive applications where the recipient can simply relay its public key and certificate to the sender.)

Let us consider a typical PKI in detail, to better understand how IBE simplifies things. In a typical PKI, it is not the recipient's responsibility to distribute its own public key and fresh certificate; instead, the sender should be able to acquire the recipient's public key and certificate status from the CA or its servers. Thus, the CA must deploy infrastructure that can respond to *third-party queries*—i.e., queries by one party (which may not even be a client of the CA) regarding the public key or certificate of a different party (a client of the CA). Such third-party queries are difficult to handle for several reasons. First, because these queries can come from anywhere and concern any client, every server in the system must always be online and able to ascertain the certificate status of every client in the system. Contrast this with IBE, in which *the PKG does not need to respond to third-party queries;* it needs only to distribute (using a "push" model, if desired) the private keys of the clients that it serves. Second, third-party queries multiply the query processing costs of the CA and/or its servers. For example, if each client's certificate status is queried 10 times per day, then the system must process $10N$ queries (where N is the number of clients) rather than distributing just N daily identity-based private keys to clients. Finally, there is a business model and security consideration: if the CA must respond to queries from nonclients, it has less control over its costs and becomes more susceptible to denial of service (DoS) attacks. In short, by eliminating the need to deal with third-party queries, IBE can significantly reduce the costs and infrastructure needed to support encryption. Overall, IBE can be significantly more convenient both for encrypters and for the trusted authority.

A further advantage of IBE over PKI-supported PKE is that IBE is arguably more likely to propagate itself than PKI, whose adoption has been disappointingly slow. Using IBE, Alice can send Bob a message encrypted Bob's public key (his identity) even before Bob obtains his private key from the PKG; thus, Alice encourages Bob to adopt IBE. Conversely, PKI propagation is not as "viral;" instead, Bob must adopt PKI and generate a public key before

he can receive an encrypted message. In short, uptake of PKI technology for encryption can only be initiated by the intended recipient of a message, whereas uptake of IBE technology can be initiated also by the sender.

The advantages of IBS over PKS are less compelling. In fact, although some specific IBS schemes (e.g., the Guillou–Quisquater scheme, described later on) may have efficiency advantages, they *do not* have significant infrastructural advantages over traditional public key signing (PKS) schemes. The reason is that distributing public keys and certificates is much easier for PKS schemes than for PKE schemes: a PKS signer can simply distribute this information to the third-party verifier itself, sending its public key and certificate to the verifier along with its signature.

In terms of efficiency, however, IBS does allow users to avoid the expense to key generation. Also, IBS schemes may sometime have bandwidth advantages over PKS schemes—because an IBS signature may consume fewer bits than the combination of a PKS signature, PKS public key, and PKS certificate—but this may not always be the case. Besides, a similar bandwidth advantage can be achieved using other methods—for example, Boneh, Gentry, Lynn, and Shacham (2003) describe how multiple signatures, such as a PKS signature and PKS certificate— can sometimes be compressed into a single, short "aggregate" signature. In short, IBC greatly simplifies the management of encryption keys but performs little better than traditional PKI in managing basic signing keys (though it may have some efficiency advantages). (See Bellare, Namprempre, & Neven, 2004, for a comprehensive analysis and taxonomy of IBS schemes.)

IBC's infrastructural advantages are not limited to the encryption context, however; for example, another setting in which IBC has infrastructural advantages—that is, in which IBC removes the need for an infrastructure to distribute public keys and certificates—is *ring signatures*. In a conventional *public key* ring signature scheme, a signer A_i with public/secret key pair (P_i, S_i), who belongs to an arbitrary "ring" of users $R = (A_1, \ldots, A_t)$ with public keys $(P_1, \ldots, P_t)$, can use S_i and $(P_1, \ldots, P_t)$ to generate a "ring signature" Sig on a message m that will convince a verifier that *some* member of R signed m; however, the verifier— which is given m, Sig, $(P_1, \ldots, P_t)$, and possibly the t certificates for the t public keys—will not be able to determine *which* member generated the signature. This allows A_i to sign m *anonymously* as a member of the ring R. However, for ring signing to be truly anonymous, it is not reasonable for A_i to request the other ring members' public keys (and certificates) from the ring members directly, because the ring members potentially could break the anonymity of a ring signature by comparing their logs concerning who has made such requests. Thus, public keys must be distributed indirectly, though an *infrastructure*.

For *identity-based* ring signatures, the only information A_i needs about the other ring members is their identities; A_i does not need to separately obtain their public keys (since public keys are identities). Consequently, by making ring signatures identity-based, and assuming the PKG does not disclose the clients for which it has issued private keys, we can preserve anonymity while eliminating the need for a public key distribution infrastructure. Moreover, identity-based ring signing is more convenient for the sender (i.e., the signer), who does not need to fetch other parties' public keys. Finally, identity-based ring signing, unlike conventional ring signing, allows the actual signer to include users in its ring even if those users do not yet have private keys. (Notice how these advantages—elimination of infrastructure, convenience for the sender, and usability of public keys before private keys are generated—parallel those of IBE.)

Disadvantages of IBC

The primary disadvantage of IBC—and particularly of IBE—is private key *escrow* (i.e., the ability of the PKG to perform any private key operation, such as decrypting an IBE-encrypted message) that one of its clients can perform. Of course, escrow has advantages in some contexts. For example, giving private key escrow to law enforcement officials enables easier monitoring of suspected criminals. Also, within an enterprise, escrow allows a company to decrypt documents encrypted by an employee that has lost his decryption key or left the company. However, in many contexts, escrow will be completely undesirable.

How serious is escrow as a disadvantage relative to public key cryptography? Once again, the considerations are different for signing than for encryption. Unfortunately, for IBE, it is *unavoidable* that the PKG can *passively* decrypt its clients' messages, given IBE's basic premise that any specified string can act as a user's public key even if the user did not generate the string itself. To see why, notice that Bob cannot generate his own private key; if he could, then so could anyone else with equal computational power, because Bob is assumed to have no "privileged" knowledge about his identity string. So, Bob's private key must be generated by a third party (or a federation or "threshold" of third parties)—call it a "PKG"—as a function of Bob's string and information that is known only to the PKG—call it the PKG's private key. (See Boneh & Franklin, 2001 and Lee et al., 2004, for information regarding using multiple parties in the key-issuing process.) Because the only privileged information that Bob uses to decrypt comes from the PKG, the PKG can also decrypt. In PKI-supported PKE, the CA cannot mount this type of passive attack (though it can actively generate a fraudulent certificate for a "fake" key and relay it to a sender, hoping that the sender will encrypt with the fake key).

Escrow is not a significant disadvantage for IBS relative to PKS, because PKS suffers from an analogous problem—namely a CA can forge a user's signature by generating a "fake" public/private key pair, computing a certificate binding the fake public key to the user's identity, and then signing a given message with the fake private key. Clearly, neither public key signature schemes nor identity-based signature schemes are invulnerable to an active attack by the only "trusted" party in the system. Similarly, one can easily construct other types of identity-based cryptosystems that limit the PKG to active attacks—for example, a Diffie–Hellman key exchange authenticated

using IBS—thereby minimizing the disadvantage of escrow; however, in such cases, one should closely examine whether the identity-based scheme has any significant advantage over its traditional public key-based counterpart.

Another disadvantage of identity-based cryptography is that, if a PKG has a large clientele, private key generation can become computationally expensive. Suppose that the current date is included as part of client's public ID. Then, the PKG must generate a new private key for every client every day. Contrast this with a CA that issues a certificate revocation list (CRL) update every day. Most likely, the CRL update will require considerably less *computation*, because it needs to include only the small percentage of clients revoked on that day (though, as mentioned, the *communication* and *infrastructure* necessary for a CRL-based PKI may be much greater, because of third-party queries). To some extent, the computational problem of generating clients' daily private keys can be overcome by using *hierarchical* IBE, in which a root PKG offloads private key generation to lower level PKGs in much the same way as a root CA offloads certification to a hierarchy of CAs. We discuss hierarchical IBE later in this chapter.

Common Objections to IBC

Here, we list some other possible objections to identity-based cryptography and analyze them in detail. To avoid confusion, we focus exclusively on the encryption case.

Objection: Private Key Distribution Is Problematic: Before Bob gets his identity-based private key, he must have a secure channel with his PKG. This predicament seems to pose a "chicken-and-egg" problem: how can Bob secure a channel before receiving his private key? In reality, the setup phase of IBE is no more problematic than the setup phase of PKI. To allow the PKG to transmit his identity-based private key securely during the setup phase, Bob can simply generate an ordinary public/private key pair and give the PKG a public key P_{Bob} during the registration process, just as he would when registering with a CA. In either case, the PKG/CA needs to confirm that P_{Bob} is Bob's public key; this separate "chicken-and-egg" problem may be accomplished "out-of-band"—for example, by having Bob register in person. Thereafter, the PKG can use P_{Bob} to encrypt each of Bob's periodic identity-based private keys, until the PKG is notified that P_{Bob} is invalid (while analogously, in a PKI, the CA may periodically affirm its certification of P_{Bob}, until otherwise notified). Using such a temporary public key does not eliminate the advantages of IBE, because it is needed only for private key transmission; it does not need to be distributed to, or obtained by, third parties (such as Alice). (We note that private key distribution could obviously be handled in different ways; the above approach merely simplifies the comparison to traditional PKI.)

Objection: Key Revocation Is Problematic: Suppose Bob's identity-based private key is compromised. Does Bob then need to change his identity? If Alice wants to encrypt a message to Bob, how does she find out that Bob's key is no longer valid, given that the main advantage of

IBE is that the encrypter should not need to obtain extraneous information about the recipient beforehand? In short, handling key revocation in IBE seems problematic. However, the solution (which was noted earlier) is simple: just embed a time period t in Bob's encryption key $\text{ID}_{\text{Bob},t}$. The PKG sends Bob a new private key at the beginning of each time period (as long as his status remains valid), and it publishes its "schedule" of time periods as part of its public key P_{PKG}. Alice uses $(P_{\text{PKG}}, \text{ID}_{\text{Bob},t}, M)$ to encrypt M for Bob, knowing that Bob (or an impostor) cannot decrypt unless his decryption key is up to date. Revocation is not immediate—the granularity of revocation depends on the length of the time periods—but other common revocation solutions [such as certificate revocation lists (CRLs)] are also typically periodic. Online certificate status protocol (OCSP) and "mediated IBE" offer immediate revocation, but they have some disadvantages (discussed below).

Objection: The PKG Is a Vulnerability: A PKG can passively decrypt all client messages (because it has private key escrow); an attacker that compromises the PKG can do the same. Conversely, an attacker who compromises a CA cannot decrypt client messages unless an active attack is mounted (by giving Alice a "fake" certified public key for Bob). So, the consequences of a PKG compromise are more severe. However, the *probability* of a PKG compromise is arguably less than that of a CA compromise for certain PKI implementations, such as OCSP. In OCSP, the CA must always be online to respond to a certificate status queries by generating a fresh signature on the certificate's current status. If the OCSP CA is centralized, it becomes highly vulnerable to DoS attacks; if it is distributed and each server has its own secret key, then compromising any server compromises the entire system. A PKG's private key, which only needs to be used periodically, can (arguably) be more safely insulated. (Of course, again, OCSP has the advantage of offering immediate certificate revocation.)

Objection: IBE Does Not Really Eliminate Nonclient Queries: Suppose that Alice wants to encrypt to Bob, but that she is not a client of Bob's PKG; before encrypting, she must acquire the public key of Bob's PKG, perhaps by querying the PKG itself. However, the public key of Bob's PKG—which may include a "cryptographic" key, as well as "non-cryptographic" information, such as how a client's identity should be formatted to construct his public key, the PKG's schedule of time periods, and so on—is essentially static; thus, Alice's request for the PKG's public key is not a nonclient query requiring an *individualized* response. After obtaining its public key, Alice needs no further information from Bob's PKG to encrypt to Bob (because she can presumably obtain Bob's identity through alternative means).

Objection: Pervasive Computing Makes IBE Obsolete: One of the main advantages of IBE is that it allows Alice to encrypt to Bob without needing to interact with Bob or the CA to obtain Bob's public key and certificate status. This advantage is more pronounced when such interaction would be a burden—for example, when it would make the transaction slower, more expensive, or less reliable. However, if "pervasive computing" becomes sufficiently efficient, inexpensive, robust, and "pervasive," eliminating interaction becomes less of an advantage. In this situation, IBE indeed begins to lose its advantage over PKE. In short, IBE is less of a win for highly interactive transactions, or when a suitable distribution infrastructure is already deployed.

ALTERNATIVES TO IBE

We have already discussed one alternative to IBE: PKE supported by a PKI. Here, we discuss four other alternatives: Kerberos, mediated IBE, certificate-based encryption, and domain-based IBE.

IBE versus Kerberos

Kerberos is an authentication and key establishment protocol that uses only symmetric (secret key) cryptography. The protocol employs a trusted authority, called a key distribution center (KDC), that already shares pairwise secret keys with other parties in the system. When one party (say, Alice) wants to establish a shared secret key with a second party (Bob), Alice contacts the KDC. The KDC generates a session key K_{AB} for Alice and Bob to share and (to oversimplify things a bit) encrypts K_{AB} under the respective secret keys K_{KA} and K_{KB} that it shares with Alice and Bob, sending the two ciphertexts to Alice. In her first message to Bob, Alice relays the encryption of K_{AB} under K_{KB}; thereafter, Alice and Bob can use K_{AB} to encrypt and authenticate their communications.

Kerberos and IBE are similar in the sense that, in both, the trusted authority has "key escrow" because it generates all secret keys. However, the KDC must always be online to generate keys on demand. Moreover, the KDC generates potentially many more keys than a PKG—one for each *pair* of correspondents. Conversely, a KDC can generate symmetric keys quickly; a PKG needs much more computation to derive an identity-based decryption key.

There are also trade-offs from Alice's perspective. In IBE, Alice does not need to contact the trusted authority at all after obtaining its public key; she can encrypt to any of the PKG's clients during any time period without the PKG's assistance. In Kerberos, Alice must (at a minimum) contact the KDC every time she wants to communicate with someone new. She may need to contact the KDC even more frequently if she does not cache session keys that she receives from the KDC (which would consume memory), or if the session keys are valid for short time periods. Also, Alice's interaction with the KDC in Kerberos causes additional delay and bandwidth consumption and may make the protocol less reliable. Conversely, in Kerberos, Alice can find out immediately if Bob has been revoked; in IBE, Alice can only assume that Bob has been revoked if he does not respond appropriately (implicitly indicating that he cannot decrypt her message).

IBE versus Mediated IBE

Mediated IBE—introduced by Ding and Tsudik (2003)—is similar to IBE in that Alice needs only Bob's identity and the public key of Bob's PKG to encrypt. The essential difference is in how decryption is performed. In mediated IBE, the PKG splits the decryption key for Bob's identity between Bob and an entity called a "semitrusted mediator" (SEM). Bob must cooperate with his SEM every time he wants to decrypt a message; Bob cannot decrypt alone (nor can the SEM). The advantage of this arrangement over IBE is that it permits instant (as opposed to periodic) revocation; if Bob loses his decryption privileges, the SEM simply refuses to help him decrypt. The disadvantage of mediated IBE is that it's not very scalable; because an SEM must cooperate in every decryption operation and must store a partial decryption key for each of its clients, mediated IBE is perhaps best suited to "enterprise" settings in which the clientele is small. As in IBE, the PKG has private key escrow.

Libert and Quisquater (2003b) and Baek and Zheng (2004) describe how a concrete mediated IBE scheme can be derived from the Boneh–Franklin IBE scheme; the latter proves that the resulting scheme is chosen ciphertext secure.

In comparing mediated IBE with IBE, one question to consider is whether revocation really needs to be immediate. For enterprise settings, where a fired employee can cause significant damage if its privileges are not revoked promptly, the answer may be yes. For other settings, such as when a client wants to revoke its key after it realizes that it left its wireless device on the train *several hours ago*, immediate revocation may be overkill—that is, it may be a less significant consideration than mediated IBE's performance disadvantages (particularly its lack of scalability).

Also, in some contexts, mediated IBE may have few advantages over the following simple reencryption approach: Alice encrypts her message under the PKG's public key, and (if Bob is entitled) the PKG decrypts and then reencrypts under Bob's key. In both approaches, Alice needs only the PKG's public key and Bob's identity, whereas the PKG has private key escrow. The main difference is that, in mediated IBE, the PKG delegates partial decryption to an SEM rather than performing it itself. For a small clientele, where it may not make sense to have more than one SEM, delegation may not offer much advantage.

IBE versus Certificate-Based Encryption and Certificateless PKE

Certificate-based encryption (CBE), proposed by Gentry (2003), and certificateless PKE (CL-PKE), subsequently proposed by Al-Riyami and Paterson (2003), are designed to preserve some of the advantages of IBE while eliminating private key escrow.

In CBE, Bob generates his own public/private key pair (P_{Bob}, S_{Bob}), as in a regular PKI. Also, Bob obtains his certificate from his CA as he would in a regular PKI: he gives the CA P_{Bob} and his proof of identity, and the CA returns its digital signature on $(Bob, P_{Bob}, time_t)$ or something similar. The difference from PKI is that Bob's certificate $C_{Bob,t}$ also functions as a secondary decryption key, as in IBE. This "super-functional" certificate, which can be viewed as an identity-based decryption key on the identity $(Bob, P_{Bob}, time_t)$, allows the CA to simplify its infrastructure, as explained below.

To encrypt to Bob, Alice must know P_{Bob} and P_{CA}, as in a regular PKI. However, she does *not* need to obtain and verify Bob's certificate $C_{Bob,t}$ before encrypting to him. Instead, to oversimplify a bit, Alice doubly encrypts her message—once with P_{Bob} using standard PKE and once with the identity $(Bob, P_{Bob}, time_t)$ using an IBE scheme. To decrypt, Bob needs two decryption keys: S_{Bob} and $C_{Bob,t}$. Although Alice does not verify explicitly that Bob has an up-to-date certificate $C_{Bob,t}$, she verifies it implicitly by generating a ciphertext that cannot be decrypted without it. (Conversely, Alice is certainly welcome to obtain and verify $C_{Bob,t}$ explicitly before encrypting, if she desires.)

Because Alice must obtain P_{Bob} before encrypting to Bob anyway, it may not seem like much of an advantage that she does not need to obtain $C_{Bob,t}$ (see Fig. 2). However, notice that P_{Bob} is *long-lived* information (i.e., Bob will probably change his public key only rarely, perhaps once per year). Conversely, Bob's certificate status information should be *fresh* (e.g., updated daily or hourly); indeed, the frequency of certificate status updates determines the time granularity of revocation. Thus, from

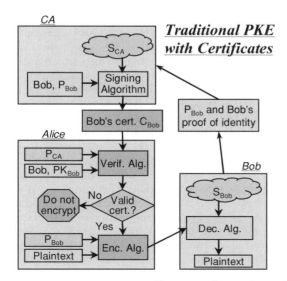

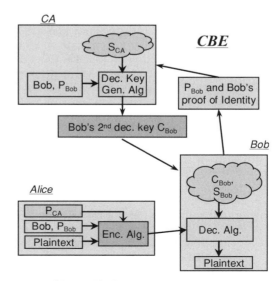

Figure 2: Comparison of PKI-supported PKE with CBE.

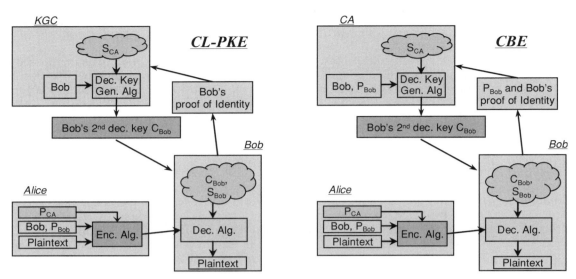

Figure 3: Comparison of CL-PKE with CBE.

Alice's perspective, CBE is more convenient that PKI-supported PKE. In CBE, Alice needs only to obtain new information about Bob when he changes his public key; in PKI-supported PKE, she must obtain new information about him for each new time period that she encrypts to him.

Similarly, CBE is more convenient than PKI-supported PKE from the C A's perspective. The CA does not need to set up infrastructure to distribute fresh certificate status information to third parties. Instead, like a PKG in IBE, the CA only needs to distribute certificates (i.e., identity-based decryption keys) to its clients, using a "push" model if desired. Overall, CBE allows a CA to enjoy many of the same infrastructural advantages as a PKG in IBE (discussed under "Advantages of IBE"), including reduced costs and infrastructure, a more sensible business model, and decreased susceptibility to DoS attacks.

Compared to IBE, CBE has the disadvantage that Bob's public key must be obtained and distributed. The main advantage of CBE is that, unlike the PKG in IBE, the CA in CBE does not have escrow; it cannot decrypt Alice's message to Bob because it does not know S_{Bob}. This is important from a privacy perspective. Also, because the CA does not have escrow, an attacker that compromises the CA cannot immediately decrypt messages sent to the CA's clients; thus, the consequences of a CA compromise in CBE are less severe than those of a PKG compromise in IBE. A final advantage is that, unlike an identity-based decryption key in IBE, the CA can send C_{Bob} to Bob over an insecure channel, because nobody can decrypt his messages without S_{Bob}. Gentry (2003) also provides a concrete CBE scheme that is a relatively straightforward and efficient adaptation of the Boneh–Franklin IBE scheme and describes how a CBE CA can arrange its clients in a hierarchical fashion to improve its efficiency and scalability.

CL-PKE, proposed by Al-Riyami and Paterson (2003), is quite similar to CBE (see Fig. 3). The main difference is that the trusted authority, which is called a key generation center (KGC) in their scheme, "signs" only

Bob's identity to generate C_{Bob} (which they call a "partial private key"). The main advantage of this arrangement is that Bob can use multiple public keys with the same identity without needing to get multiple values of C_{Bob} from the KGC. A disadvantage is that the KGC must send C_{Bob} via a secure channel, because otherwise Bob's identity could be usurped. As a corollary, C_{Bob} cannot also serve as a certificate that Alice has the option of explicitly verifying.

Al-Riyami and Paterson also provide certificateless signature and key agreement schemes, but the advantages of "certificateless PKC" are greatest in the encryption context (for reasons similar to those discussed in connection with IBC). Yun and Lee (2004) provide generic constructions of certificateless encryption and signature schemes. Kang, Park, and Hahn (2004) provide a certificate-based signature (CBS) designed to be compatible (in particular, it uses the same parameters) with Gentry's CBE scheme.

IBE versus Domain-Based IBE

Two papers—Chen, Harrison, Moss, Soldera, and Smart (2002) and Smetters and Durfee (2003)—suggest using hybrid PKI/IBE approach in which companies or domains have public keys that must be distributed and obtained, but these companies or domains use an IBE scheme to generate private keys for their employees or clients. To encrypt to Bob, Alice must obtain Bob's identity and the public key of Bob's company; a CA must distribute the public key of Bob's company to third parties.

As one would expect, the advantages and disadvantages of this hybrid approach, which we call domain-based IBE (DBIBE), lie in between those of PKI and IBE. DBIBE probably reduces the number of public keys relative to traditional PKI, but probably not so much that it becomes practical for users or applications to store these public keys locally. Thus, some infrastructure may be necessary to distribute public keys and certificates.

Unlike in IBE and CBE, the CA in DBIBE must distribute fresh certificate status information concerning the domain-based public keys to third parties for each time period. Thus, if Alice encrypts to the same person during different time periods using DBIBE, she can use the same domain-based public key, but she must recheck this public key's certificate status; this check is unnecessary in IBE and CBE. Conversely, if Alice encrypts to different people in the same domain during the same time period, Alice need not obtain new information when using IBE or DBIBE; in CBE, she must obtain the second person's public key.

Relative to an IBE scheme managed by a "global" PKG, DBIBE mitigates the key escrow problem somewhat; DBIBE PKGs have escrow only over clients in their respective domains. Relative to CBE, such domain-based escrow may be a disadvantage in some contexts [though it may be acceptable (or even desirable) in others—e.g., where a company may wish to have access to its employee's e-mails].

THE GUILLOU–QUISQUATER IBS SCHEME

At last, we describe some concrete IBC schemes. Although the advantages of IBS over PKS are not as significant as the advantages of IBE over PKE, this section describes an IBS scheme by Guillou and Quisquater (1988) that has some efficiency advantages over the widely used RSA PKS scheme, while achieving essentially identical security (in the random oracle model); although verifying a Guillou–Quisquater (GQ) signature takes longer than verifying a (low-public-exponent) RSA signature, GQ signature generation is faster. (As mentioned above, Shamir, 1985, described the first concrete IBS scheme in his initial article proposing the notion of IBC.)

The GQ signature scheme is as follows.

Setup: The PKG picks two large (e.g., 512-bit) primes p and q and sets $n = pq$. It also picks two cryptographic hash functions $H_1: \{0, 1\}^* \to Z/nZ$ (from arbitrary length bit-strings to integers modulo n) and $H_2: \{0, 1\}^* \to [0, 2^k - 1]$, where k bits is a suitable hash output size (e.g., 160 bits for SHA-1). Finally, it picks a prime number $e > 2^k$ that is relatively prime to $\varphi(n) = (p-1)(q-1)$ and computes d such that $ed \equiv 1 \pmod{\varphi(n)}$. The PKG keeps the values (p, q, d) secret; its public key includes (n, e, H_1, H_2) and possibly other information, such as the PKG's "schedule" for issuing private keys to its clients.

Private Key Generation: Given Bob's identity string $\text{ID}_{\text{Bob}} \in \{0, 1\}^*$, the PKG sets $s_{\text{Bob}} \equiv (H_1(\text{ID}_{\text{Bob}}))^d \pmod{n}$. It sends s_{Bob} to Bob via a secure channel.

Signing: To sign the message m, Bob:

- Generates a random number $r \in Z/nZ$ with uniform distribution
- Computes $R = r^e \pmod{n}$ and sets $c = H_2(m\|R)$
- Computes $S = rs_{\text{Bob}}^c \pmod{n}$ and sends the signature (S, c) to Alice

Verification: Alice computes $R' = S^e/(H_1(\text{ID}_{\text{Bob}}))^c$ $\pmod{n}$ and confirms that $c = H_2(m\|R')$.

In the GQ IBS scheme, Alice does not need to obtain an individual public key for Bob; instead, she needs only his PKG's public key and his identity IDBob. Also, for a 1024-bit modulus n, the signature in GQ is about $1024 + 160 = 1184$ bits for typical parameters, much shorter than the combination of an RSA signature, RSA public key and RSA public key certificate, which may be $3 \times 1024 = 3072$ bits overall. GQ's signing and verification time are each dominated by two exponentiations, with exponents about k bits apiece. Conversely, the RSA PKS scheme may use a small public exponent (e.g., $e = 3$), allowing very fast verification; however, signing exponent is typically very long (e.g., 1024 bits), making signature generation slower than in GQ.

COCKS'S IDENTITY-BASED ENCRYPTION SCHEME

Cocks's IBE scheme (2001) is fairly lightweight computationally, but it involves significant ciphertext expansion (i.e., the length of the ciphertext is many times the length of the plaintext). For this reason, and because pairings have turned out to be a remarkably versatile cryptographic tool, the Boneh–Franklin IBE scheme has received much more attention. However, we review Cocks's scheme for completeness.

Setup: The PKG picks two large (e.g., 512-bit) primes p and q satisfying $p \equiv q \equiv 3 \pmod{4}$ and sets $n = pq$. It also picks a cryptographic hash function $H: \{0, 1\}^* \to Z/nZ$. The PKG keeps the values (p, q) secret; its public key includes (n, H) and possibly other information, such as the PKG's "schedule" for issuing private keys to its clients.

Private Key Generation: Given Bob's identity string $\text{ID}_{\text{Bob}} \in \{0, 1\}^*$, the PKG determines the smallest i such that the Jacobi symbol of $a_i = H(i, \text{ID}_{\text{Bob}})$ modulo n is 1:

$$\left(\frac{a_i}{n}\right) = 1.$$

The PKG computes Bob's private key as $r_i = a_i^{(n+5-p-q)/8}$ $\pmod{n}$, which satisfies either $r_i^2 \equiv a_i \pmod{n}$ or $r_i^2 \equiv -a_i$ $\pmod{n}$, as described in (Cocks, 2001).

Encryption: To encrypt to Bob using n and ID_{Bob}, Alice first generates Bob's encryption key a_i. (Notice that she can compute the Jacobi symbol of a_i modulo n without knowledge of n's factorization.) Alice does not know whether Bob's private key is a modular square root of a_i or $-a_i$; thus, she must, in effect, generate two ciphertexts, the first of which she generates as follows. Alice generates a symmetric key k and encrypts the plaintext message m with it. She encrypts each bit of the symmetric key separately. To send a bit $b \in \{-1, 1\}$ of the symmetric key, she picks a random $t \in Z/nZ$ such that

$$\left(\frac{t}{n}\right) = b,$$

and sends the ciphertext $c \equiv t + a_i/t \pmod{n}$.

Decryption: To recover b from c, Bob computes $c + 2r_i \equiv t + 2r_i + a_i/t \equiv t(1 + r_i/t)^2 \pmod{n}$ and then computes the following:

$$\left(\frac{c + 2r_i}{n}\right) = \left(\frac{t}{n}\right) = b.$$

The two Jacobi symbols are identical because, modulo $n, c + 2r_i$ equals t times a quadratic residue. Bob must also perform the encryption procedure for $-a_i$, choosing a different random value of t. Once the complete symmetric key k is obtained, Bob can decrypt the plaintext message m.

In terms of performance, about $2 \times 128 \times \log n \approx 262144$ ciphertext bits are needed to encrypt a 128-bits AES key; thus, the communication complexity of Cocks's scheme is quite high. Bob needs to perform the decryption procedure only once for each bit of the symmetric key, depending on whether r_i is a modular square root of a_i or $-a_i$; because each decryption involves only a fast Jacobi symbol computation, Cock's scheme is quite practical in terms of computation.

Although Cocks's scheme has significant performance disadvantages relative to Boneh–Franklin, it has the advantage that its security is based on the quadratic residuosity problem (an old, well-established hard problem in cryptography), whereas the security of Boneh–Franklin is based on the comparatively new and less-studied "Bilinear Diffie–Hellman" problem. The quadratic residuosity problem is as follows: given a modulus n of unknown factorization and a number a whose Jacobi symbol modulo n is 1, decide whether there exists some $x \in Z/nZ$ such that $x_2 \equiv a \pmod{n}$ (i.e., whether a is a quadratic residue). Currently, the fastest known general algorithm for deciding quadratic residuosity, when n and a are generated as above, involves first factoring n.

Cocks proves the semantically security of his scheme assuming the hardness of the quadratic residuosity problem. When Cocks's IBE scheme is used in combination with certain transforms, such as that described in (Fujisaki & Okamoto, 1999), the resulting hybrid encryption scheme can be proven secure against chosen-ciphertext attacks in the random oracle model. (We discuss the Fujisaki–Okamoto transform more explicitly in connection with the Boneh–Franklin IBE scheme.)

IDENTIFY-BASED ENCRYPTION USING PAIRINGS

In 2001, Boneh and Franklin discovered a very practical IBE scheme that uses a mapping over elliptic curves (and, more generally, over abelian varieties) called a "pairing"; they also rigorously proved its security (in the "Random Oracle Model") against chosen-ciphertext attacks under the assumption that a certain number-theoretic problem, called the "Bilinear Diffie–Hellman Problem," is "hard" to solve. (Sakai, Ohgishi, & Kasahara, 2001, informally presented a similar pairing-based IBE scheme without chosen ciphertext security.)

Before discussing the Boneh–Franklin IBE scheme in detail, we provide some background on the relevant mathematical properties of pairings and discuss previous uses of pairings in cryptography.

Mathematical Background (on Pairings)

A "pairing" $\hat{e}: G_1 \times G_1 \to G_2$ is a mapping that takes two elements of a first cyclic algebraic group of order q and maps them to an element of a second cyclic algebraic group, also of order q. Modified Weil and Tate pairings (e.g., as described in Joux, 2000; Boneh & Franklin, 2001; or Barreto, Kim, Lynn, & Scott, 2002)—seem to be particularly useful for cryptography. They map two elements of a q-order subgroup of an elliptic curve or abelian variety $E(F_{p^k})$ to an element in a q-order subgroup of a finite field $F_{p^{k\ell}}$ (for some integer $\ell \geq 1$, which depends on the particular curve or variety). For convenience, we call a pairing "useful" if it also has the following desirable properties:

- *Bilinearity*: $\hat{e}(aQ, bR) = \hat{e}(Q, R)^{ab}$ for all $Q, R \in G_1$ and all $a, b \in Z$.
- *Nondegeneracy*: The map does not send all pairs in $G_1 \times G_1$ to the identity in G_2.
- *Computability*: An efficient algorithm exists to compute $\hat{e}(Q, R)$ for any $Q, R \in G_1$.

For certain curves and varieties (e.g., *supersingular* ones), modified Weil and Tate pairings are useful pairings.

Below, we review some cryptographic uses of pairings. See Barreto (2004) for a comprehensive list of references related to pairing-based cryptography. For information on the implementation and performance of pairing-based cryptography, see Barreto, Kim, Lynn, and Scott (2002). Because pairing-based cryptography is relatively new, however, do not be surprised to see performance enhancements subsequent to the publication of this *Handbook*.

Previous Uses of Pairings in Cryptography

The first significant use of useful pairings in cryptography was destructive—namely to cryptanalyze (or "break") cryptosystems that use supersingular elliptic curves. The security of elliptic curve cryptosystems often relies on the hardness of the elliptic curve discrete logarithm (DL) problem:

> *Discrete Logarithm (DL) Problem*: Given $P \in G_1$ and aP (for unknown randomly chosen $a \in Z/qZ$), compute a.

For certain elliptic curves, the DL problem is believed to be much harder than the DL problem for finite fields; this is basically why elliptic curve variants of common cryptosystems (e.g., Diffie–Hellman and ElGamal) can use smaller keys, making them faster and more efficient. However, Menezes, Okamoto, and Vanstone (1993) demonstrated that, because the Weil (and Tate) pairing $\hat{e}: G_1 \times G_1 \to G_2$ is efficiently computable when G_1 is a *supersingular* elliptic curve group (and G_2 is a subgroup inside a finite field), pairings allow the supersingular elliptic curve DL problem to be reduced to the finite field DL problem. Specifically, given (P, aP), one can efficiently compute $g = \hat{e}(P, P)$ and $g_a = \hat{e}(P, aP)$ and then use a subexponential index-calculus algorithms to compute the discrete logarithm of g_a with respect to g within the finite field.

Sakai, Ohgishi, and Kasahara (1999) and Joux (2000) were the first to discover significant *constructive* applications of pairings in cryptography. Joux proposed a scheme for "tripartite Diffie–Hellman"—that is, a one-round key agreement scheme analogous to Diffie–Hellman in which three (rather than just two) parties derive a shared secret. In this scheme, each of the three parties—say, Alice, Bob, and Carol—chooses a random value in Z/qZ—say, a, b, and c. Alice sends aP to Bob and Carol; similarly, Bob and Carol transmit bP and cP. At this point, each of the three parties can compute s $= \hat{e}(P, P)^{abc}$, their shared secret; for example, Alice—who knows a, bP, and cP—can compute s as $\hat{e}(bP, cP)^a$.

Sakai, Ohgishi, and Kasahara proposed, among other things, a *noninteractive* two-party key agreement protocol (Sakai, Ohgishi, & Kasahara, 2000). In their protocol, a trusted third party, which we call a PKG, generates a private key $s \in Z/qZ$ and publishes P, sP, as well as other relevant information (e.g., hash functions and key update schedules). Alice and Bob have public keys P_A, $P_B \in G_1$. These public keys may be identity based—for example, one may set $P_A = H(\text{ID}_A)$, where ID_A is Alice's identity string, and $H: \{0, 1\} \rightarrow G_1$ is a specified cryptographic hash function. After Alice and Bob receive their private keys—sP_A and sP_B, respectively—from the PKG, they may each compute their shared secret $\hat{e}(P_A, P_B)^s$ non-interactively; for example, Alice computes this value as $\hat{e}(sP_A, P_B)$.

Both of these early pairing-based cryptosystems rely on the hardness of the following problem.

> *Bilinear Diffie–Hellman (BDH) Problem*: Given a randomly chosen $P \in G_1$, as well as aP, bP, and cP (for unknown randomly chosen $a, b, c \in Z/qZ$), compute $\hat{e}(P, P)^{abc}$.

The BDH problem is analogous to the well-known Diffie–Hellman (DH) problem, which (over the group G_1) is defined as follows.

> *Diffie–Hellman (DH) Problem*: Given a randomly chosen $P \in G_1$, as well as aP, bP (for unknown randomly chosen $a, b \in Z/qZ$), compute abP.

Notice that, for the BDH problem to be hard, it must be hard to solve the DH problem over both G_1 and G_2. If the DH problem over G_1 is easy, one can efficiently compute abP from aP and bP and then compute $\hat{e}(P, P)^{abc} = \hat{e}(abP, cP)$. If the DH problem over G_2 is easy, one can efficiently compute $\hat{e}(P, P)^{abc}$ from $\hat{e}(P, P)^{ab}$ and $\hat{e}(P, P)^{c}$, after computing $\hat{e}(P, P)^{ab} = \hat{e}(aP, bP)$ and $\hat{e}(P, P)^{c} = \hat{e}(P, cP)$.

The Boneh–Franklin IBE scheme, which we now describe, also relies on the hardness of the BDH problem.

The Boneh–Franklin IBE Scheme

Setup: The PKG generates groups G_1 and G_2 of prime order q with a useful pairing $\hat{e}: G_1 \times G_1 \rightarrow G_2$, an arbitrary generator P of the group G_1, and two cryptographic hash functions $H_1: \{0, 1\}^* \rightarrow G_1$ and $H_2: G_2 \rightarrow \{0,1\}^k$. (The message space for the IBE scheme will be $\{0,1\}^k$, the set of k-bit strings.) The PKG then picks random $s \in Z/qZ$, keeping this value secret. Its public key includes $(G_1, G_2, \hat{e}, P, sP, H_1, H_2)$ and possibly other information, such as the PKG's "schedule" for issuing private keys to its clients.

Private Key Generation: Given Bob's identity string $\text{ID}_{\text{Bob}} \in \{0, 1\}^*$, the PKG computes Bob's private key as sP_{Bob}, where $P_{\text{Bob}} = H_1(\text{ID}_{\text{Bob}})$.

Encryption: To encrypt a k-bit message m to Bob using ID_{Bob} and the PKG's public key, Alice computes $P_{\text{Bob}} = H_1(\text{ID}_{\text{Bob}})$, generates random $r \in Z/qZ$, and computes the ciphertext $c = [rP, m \oplus H_2(g^r)]$, where $g = \hat{e}(sP, P_{\text{Bob}}) \in G_2$.

Decryption: To decrypt $c = [U, v]$, Bob computes, $v \oplus H_2(e(U, sP_{Bob}))$, which should equal m.

The above scheme is provably secure (in the random oracle model) against chosen-plaintext attacks assuming the BDH problem is hard, but it is not secure against adversaries capable of adaptive chosen-ciphertext attack. However, one can get a chosen-ciphertext secure scheme by applying the Fujisaki–Okamoto transform, as follows. The PKG includes two additional cryptographic hash functions $H_3: \{0, 1\}^{k+k_0} \rightarrow Z/qZ$ and $H_4: \{0, 1\}^{k_0} \rightarrow \{0, 1\}^{k_{sym}}$ within its public key, where k_σ is the length of a random string σ (e.g., 160 bits) used in the modified encryption procedure and k_{sym} is the length of a random key for a symmetric encryption scheme E (e.g., 128 bits for AES), also used in the modified encryption procedure. Also, H_2 is modified slightly so that its output is k_σ bits. Then, modified encryption and decryption proceed as follows.

Encryption: To encrypt message m to Bob using ID_{Bob} and the PKG's public key, Alice computes $P_{\text{Bob}} = H_1(\text{ID}_{\text{Bob}})$, generates random $\sigma \in \{0, 1\}^{k_0}$ and computes $r = H_3(m \| \sigma)$. She sets the ciphertext to be $m = [rP, \sigma \oplus H_2(g^r), E_{H_4(\sigma)}(m)]$, where $g = \hat{e}(sP, P_{\text{Bob}}) \in G_2$.

Decryption: To decrypt $c = [U, v, w]$, Bob sets $\sigma' = v \oplus H_2(e(U, sP_{Bob}))$, sets $m' = E^{-1}_{H_4(\sigma')}(w)$, and sets $r' = H_3(m' \| \sigma')$. Bob checks that $U = r'P$; if not, the decryption process fails. If so, Bob concludes that m' is the plaintext.

Pairing-Based IBE Without Random Oracles

Recently, Boneh and Boyen (2004) proposed a pairing-based IBE scheme that is provably secure *without random oracles* against adaptive chosen-ciphertext attacks, assuming the following problem is hard:

> *Decision Bilinear Diffie–Hellman (Decision BDH) Problem*: Let S_0 be the set of tuples (P, aP, bP, cP, g^d), where $P \in G_1; a, b, c \in Z/qZ; g = \hat{e}(P, P)$ and $d = abc \pmod{q}$. Let S_1 be the set of tuples (P, aP, bP, cP, g^d) without the restriction on d. Suppose that a tuple (P, aP, bP, cP, g^d) is selected by choosing $k \in \{0, 1\}$ uniformly and drawing a tuple uniformly from S_k. Given the tuple, decide whether k equals 0 or 1.

The Decision BDH problem is hard if it is computationally infeasible to decide correctly with probability nonnegligibly more than $1/2$. The scheme presented below has only semantic security (not chosen-ciphertext security); chosen-ciphertext security can be achieved through a transform by Canetti, Halevi, and Katz (2004). The scheme is described in a way that incorporates and generalizes a simplification by Waters (2004) that improves the efficiency of the Boneh–Boyen scheme.

Setup: The PKG generates $G_1, G_2, \hat{e}$, and P as before. For some integer d (Waters implicitly sets $d = 161$), the PKG also generates random $(P_0, \ldots, P_d) \in G_1$. Finally, it picks a random $s \in Z/qZ$ and stores sP_0 as its secret key. It publishes the key $(G_1, G_2, \hat{e}, P, sP, P_0, P_1, \ldots, P_d, V, \theta)$, where V is the description of a set of d-dimensional integer vectors and $\theta : \{0, 1\}^* \rightarrow V$ is a (collision-resistant) mapping of user identity strings to vectors in V. [Waters implicitly sets, $V = \{(z_1, \ldots, z_d) : z_1 = 1; \forall_{2 \leq i \leq d} z_i \in \{0, 1\}\}$, and suggests a collision-resistant hash function (such as SHA-1) to map identities to 160-bit strings $(z_2, \ldots, z_{161})$.] The PKG also may publish other information, such as its "schedule" for issuing private keys to its clients.

Private Key Generation: Given Bob's identity string $ID_{Bob} \in \{0, 1\}^*$, the PKG computes $(z_1, \ldots, z_d) = \theta(ID_{Bob}) \in V$. The PKG then generates a random $t \in Z/qZ$, and sets Bob's private key (S_{Bob}, T_{Bob}) according to $S_{Bob} = sP_0 + tP_{Bob}$ and $T_{Bob} = tP$, where $P_{Bob} = z_1 P_1 + \cdots + z_d P_d$.

Encryption: To encrypt $m \in G_2$, Alice computes $(z_1, \ldots, z_d) = \theta(ID_{Bob})$ and $P_{Bob} = z_1 P_1 + \cdots + z_d P_d$. She generates a random $r \in Z/qZ$, and sends the ciphertext $c = [rP, rP_{Bob}, m \cdot g^r]$, where $g = \hat{e}(sP, P_0) \in G_2$.

Decryption: To decrypt $c = [U, U_{Bob}, v]$, Bob computes $v \cdot \frac{e(T_{Bob}, U_{Bob})}{e(S_{Bob}, U)}$, which should equal m.

Using Waters's parameters, the PKG's public key is unfortunately quite large, because it includes of 164 elements of G_1. Although the details are omitted here, it turns out that one can use substantially smaller values of d (e.g., $d = 5$) while maintaining provable security if one allows the integers z_i to vary within a larger range than $[0, 1]$ (e.g., within $[0, 2^{160/(d-1)} - 1]$). This allows the PKG's public key to be substantially smaller. Either way, encryption and decryption are reasonably efficient, taking only about twice as much time as in Boneh–Franklin, even though Boneh–Franklin is known to be secure only in the random oracle model.

HIERARCHICAL IDENTITY-BASED ENCRYPTION

IBE lifts the public key and certificate management problem from the client level to the PKG level; to encrypt to Bob, Alice needs to obtain a public key (and possibly a public key certificate) only for Bob's PKG, not for Bob. This advantage of IBE is maximized when there are very few PKGs in the system. In this case, after Alice obtains and stores the public keys of these PKGs, she (ideally) need not fetch anyone's public key ever again.

However, a disadvantage of IBE is that private key generation can become computationally expensive for the PKG if it has a large clientele; particularly, if its chosen time granularity of key updates (and, hence, its time granularity of key "revocation") is very small. Of course, one way to solve this problem (and keep fine time granularity) is to have many PKGs, each with a clientele of manageable size, but this solution does not maximize the abovementioned advantage of IBE; if there are many PKGs, Alice may need to obtain many public keys.

In traditional PKI, this problem is addressed by having a hierarchy of certification authorities. In a hierarchical PKI, Bob is certified by a CA, which (in turn) is certified by another CA, and so on, up to a "root" CA; the result is a "certificate chain" connecting Bob to his root CA. Before encrypting to Bob, Alice must obtain Bob's certificate chain, along with his public key and the public keys of the intermediate CAs in his certificate chain. As long as Alice knows the public key of Bob's root CA beforehand, Alice can verify that Bob's public key and those of the intermediate CAs have been properly certified; she can then encrypt to Bob. From a CA's perspective, hierarchical PKI allows a CA to delegate its certificate generation to "lower level" CAs. This delegation is doubly advantageous; not only does it allow a CA to reduce its workload, but it also gives the task of checking the correctness of Bob's claimed identity information to a lower level CA that probably has a closer relationship with Bob.

To get the advantages of hierarchical PKI, but without the need to distribute and obtain certificate chains, Horwitz and Lynn (2002) introduced the notion of "hierarchical IBE"; they also described a hierarchical IBE scheme that is practical only for a two-level hierarchy. In hierarchical IBE, Bob's private key is generated by his *parent* PKG after it receives its private key from Bob's grandparent PKG, and so on, up to a "root" PKG. For example, if Bob's e-mail address is Bob@cs.univ.edu, then his corresponding "ID-tuple" is (edu,univ,cs,Bob), and his private key is generated by his computer science department [which has ID-tuple (edu,univ,cs)] after it receives its private key from the university. Alice can encrypt to Bob if she knows his identity [e.g., (edu,univ,cs,Bob)] and the public key of his *root* PKG. She does not need the public key of Bob's parent PKG; indeed, neither Bob nor any of his "ancestor" PKGs below the root has any public keys or certificates at all. Hierarchical IBE also enjoys the double advantage of delegable private key generation: local identity checking and better scalability. Once it gets its own private key, Bob's parent PKG (e.g., his computer science department, which probably has a close relationship with him) can generate Bob's private key without any interaction with higher level PKGs (thereby enhancing scalability).

A disadvantage of hierarchical IBE is that Bob's ancestors in the hierarchy have escrow (i.e., they can decrypt ciphertexts directed to Bob). This escrow problem is unavoidable (just as it is to nonhierarchical IBE); it is inevitably the case that the federation of entities that generates Bob's private key (the set of Bob's ancestors, in this case) will be able to decrypt Bob's mail. However, in some cases, one can limit escrow to a subset of Bob's ancestors. For example, Gentry and Silverberg (2002) describe a hierarchical IBE scheme in which Bob's ancestors do not have escrow if they are higher in the hierarchy than Alice's and Bob's lowest level common ancestor. For example, if Alice and Bob are in the same computer science department, the computer science department has escrow, but the university and higher level ancestors do not.

Another disadvantage of hierarchical IBE is that it might be difficult for the various entities in the hierarchy to coordinate their key update schedules. Like public keys, key update schedules need to be obtained; thus, they should ideally be included in the root PKG's public key, which is the only public key in the system. In this case, the root PKG's public key will become very large if lower level PKGs are permitted to have different key update schedules; conversely, limiting the lower level PKGs to a "global" key update schedule reduces flexibility.

Below, we describe a concrete hierarchical IBE scheme, from Gentry and Silverberg (2002), that efficiently enables a hierarchy with an arbitrary number of levels. Although the Gentry–Silverberg scheme devolves into the Boneh–Franklin scheme when the hierarchy is only one level, hierarchical IBE is not merely a recursive application of IBE; instead, private key generation must be holistically integrated from top to bottom in the hierarchy. The Gentry–Silverberg hierarchical IBE scheme is as follows.

Root PKG Setup: The root PKG sets up like a PKG in Boneh–Franklin.

Private Key Generation: Let E_t be an entity with ID-tuple $(\text{ID}_1, \ldots, \text{ID}_t)$, where $(\text{ID}_1, \ldots, \text{ID}_i)$ is the ID-tuple of E_t's ancestor at level i. Then, to generate E_t's private key, E_t's parent:

- Computes $P_t = H_1(\text{ID}_1, \ldots, \text{ID}_t) \in G_1$;
- Generates random $s_{t-1} \in Z/qZ$, and sets $Q_{t-1} = s_{t-1}P$;
- Sets $S_t = S_{t-1} + s_{t-1}P_t$, where $S_{t-1} \in G_1$ is part of E_t's parent's private key;
- Sends $(S_t, Q_1, \ldots, Q_{t-1})$ to E_t as E_t's private key.

As "base" values for this recursion, $S_0 = 0$ and $s_0 = s$ (the root PKG's secret). An intermediate PKG at level $i > 0$ can generate s_i randomly for each of its clients, or keep it fixed.

Encryption: To encrypt a k-bit message m to E_t using $(\text{ID}_1, \ldots, \text{ID}_t)$ and the root PKG's public key, Alice computes $P_i = H_1(\text{ID}_1, \ldots, \text{ID}_i) \in G_1$ for $1 \leq i \leq t$, generates random $r \in Z/qZ$, and computes the ciphertext $c = [rP, rP_2, \ldots, rP_t, m \oplus H_2(g^r)]$, where $g = \hat{e}(sP, P_1) \in G_2$.

Decryption: To decrypt $c = [U, U_2, \ldots, U_t, v]$, E_t computes

$$v \oplus H_2\left(\frac{e(U, S_t)}{\prod_{i=2}^{t} e(Q_{i-1}, U_i)}\right),$$

which should equal m.

As with Boneh–Franklin, the Fujisaki–Okamoto transform can be applied to the above hierarchical IBE scheme to make it secure (in the random oracle model) against adaptive chosen-ciphertext attacks, assuming the hardness of the BDH problem. Also, as noted by Boneh and Boyen (2004) and Waters (2004), one can construct a HIBE scheme that is provably secure without random oracles under the Decision BDH assumption by straightforwardly extending the techniques used for the nonhierarchical case.

As noted by Gentry and Silverberg (2002), when we take advantage of the observation (a recurring theme in this chapter) that an identity-based private key can also be viewed as the PKG's signature on that identity, the above secure HIBE scheme leads directly to a secure hierarchical IBS (HIBS) scheme, as follows. Root PKG setup and private key generation are the same as above. Then, to sign m, entity E_{t-1} generates a signature that looks like a private key on the tuple $(\text{ID}_1, \ldots, \text{ID}_{t-1}, m)$—that is, E_{t-1}:

- Computes $P_m = H_1(\text{ID}_1, \ldots, \text{ID}_{t-1}, m) \in G_1$
- Generates random $s_{t-1} \in Z/qZ$, and sets $Q_{t-1} = s_{t-1}P$

- Sets $S_m = S_{t-1} + s_{t-1}P_m$, where $S_{t-1} \in G_1$ is part of E_{t-1}'s private key
- Sends $(S_m, Q_1, \ldots, Q_{t-1})$ as its signature on m

The only proviso is that if one wants to treat private key generation and signing as distinct procedures, one should ensure that the message space (i.e., possible values of m) does not overlap with the identity space (i.e., possible values of ID_t)— for example, by appending a different prefix to m than to ID_t before applying H_1. To verify E_{t-1}'s signature on m, confirm the following:

$$e(S_m, P) = e(sP, P_1)e(Q_{t-1}, P_m)\prod_{i=2}^{t} e(Q_{i-1}, P_i),$$

where $P_m = H_1(\text{ID}_1, \ldots, \text{ID}_{t-1}, m)$ and $P_i = H_1(\text{ID}_1, \ldots, \text{ID}_i)$ for $1 \leq i \leq t - 1$.

The security of the HIBS scheme follows immediately from the security of the HIBE scheme, because an attacker that can generate a HIBS forgery can generate a HIBE private key to which it is not entitled. However, HIBS can be proven secure in the random oracle model under a weaker assumption than the hardness of BDH— namely the hardness DH in G_1 (cf. Bellare et al., 2004, and Libert & Quisquater, 2004).

MORE THAN JUST IDENTITIES: EXTENDING IDENTITY-BASED CRYPTOGRAPHY

Not surprisingly, the techniques that enable IBE (especially pairings) are useful for more than just managing identities. Barreto (2004) has collected numerous references on the uses of pairings in cryptography, covering everything from fast pairing computation algorithms, to pairing-based functions that are verifiably random, to public key multicast encryption, to schemes that allow limited third-party searches on encrypted data. In this section, we briefly survey a few other pairing-based protocols, especially those that can properly be considered applications or extensions of IBC.

Signature-Contingent Decryption

As mentioned under Introduction, IBE allows an encrypter to generate a ciphertext that is indecipherable until a specified authorizer signs some specified incidental data ID. Thus, one may view IBE as enabling "signature-contingent decryption" or "authorized decryption." We have already seen one example of a "signature" being used as a decryption key—namely CBE; in CBE, the "signature" is a certificate issued by a CA. This subsection mentions some other applications of the "signature-contingent decryption" concept, beyond the usual context of simplifying PKI.

Policy Enforcement and Controlling Workflow

Casassa Mont, Pearson, and Bramhall (2003) describe how IBE enables the creation of "sticky policies." In their scenario, the incidental data ID is the "policy" that the encrypter trusts that the authorizer will enforce before it issues the decryption key. As an example, they mention a DRM scenario: a content provider may encrypt its content such that a recipient device can decrypt it only if an authorizer confirms that the recipient's device has a compliant trusted platform. Using IBE, one can ensure that the encrypter's policy "sticks" to the encrypted content—that is, the authorizer must be aware of the policy before it can "sign" the policy by issuing the decryption key needed to recover the content.

Casassa Mont and Bramhall (2003) describe how IBE can be used to address the "late binding" problem, where it is not known beforehand exactly who will be the person filling a particular role. Using IBE, an encrypter can specify the role of a would-be decrypter; later, if the authorizer determines that a recipient satisfies that role, it "certifies" the recipient by giving it the appropriate decryption key, allowing the recipient to decrypt. Thus, IBE simplifies role-based access control.

Public Key Encryption with Keyword Search

Consider the following scenario. Bob has an e-mail account with a service provider that he does not completely trust, but he wants to enable his service provider to sort his e-mail to some extent, even if his e-mail is encrypted. For example, Bob may want his service provider to route all encrypted e-mails containing an encryption of the keyword "Project X" into a special folder, without the service provider learning anything beyond the fact that these e-mails contain this common plaintext term. Independently, two recent articles—Waters, Balfanz, Durfee, and Smetters (2004) and Boneh, Di Crescenzo, Ostrovsky, and Persiano (2004)—construct "searchable public key encryption" (SPKE) schemes by building on the Boneh–Franklin IBE scheme. Waters et al. focus on the application of constructing an encrypted but searchable audit log; the log encrypts its entries in such a way that an "audit escrow agent" can enable less trusted "investigators" to search the log for specified keywords.

Essentially, the approach they use for constructing a SPKE scheme from the Boneh–Franklin IBE scheme is as follows. Alice creates a (preferably short) list of keywords that her message contains. For each keyword W, she uses an IBE scheme that encrypts k-bit messages to encrypt 0^k (the string consisting of k zeros), using Bob's public key as the PKG's public key and using the keyword W itself as the identity. She appends the list of IBE ciphertexts to her encrypted message. If Bob wants to enable his service provider to distinguish which messages contain W, he behaves like a PKG and gives the service provider the identity-based decryption key (under his public key) for "identity" W, thereby effectively "signing" the keyword that can be searched. Then, the service provider can determine whether Alice included W in her list of keywords simply by attempting to decrypt each IBE ciphertext with the decryption key for the identity W; if one of the ciphertexts decrypts to 0^k, W is in Alice's list (with high probability).

Boneh et al. show that IBE is actually necessary for the existence of searchable public key encryption (SPKE) schemes and suggests that the converse may be false. An IBE scheme can readily be used to construct a SPKE scheme only if the IBE scheme has "public key privacy;"

for example, given an IBE ciphertext c that is the encryption of 0^k under identity W_1 or identity W_2, it should be hard to distinguish which is the case. Without such public key privacy, the service provider (and other parties) could extract more information about Bob's e-mails than he wishes to permit. Although the Boneh–Franklin IBE scheme is public key private, Cocks's IBE scheme is not (see Boneh et al., 2004).

Miscellaneous Applications

Next, we mention miscellaneous other extensions of IBC. These include using pairings to achieve key-insulated, forward-secure, and intrusion-resilient encryption, fuzzy IBE, secret handshakes, and simplified IPSec.

Key-Insulated, Intrusion-Resilient, and Forward-Secure Encryption

In a key-insulated, intrusion-resilient, or forward-secure encryption (or signature) scheme, a user may retain some measure of security even if its private key is compromised. In a key-insulated or intrusion-resilient scheme, the idea is that the user maintains two "modules" (e.g., a laptop and a phone). Although the user maintains a fixed *public* key, the two modules interact at the beginning of each time period to generate the time period's *private* key, which the second module can use to perform private key operations (e.g., decryption or signing). A scheme is called *key-insulated* (Dodis, Katz, Xu, & Yung, 2002) if an adversary that is given access to all of the second module's secrets for one or more time periods (e.g., when the adversary steals the user's phone) still cannot compromise the scheme's security for other time periods. Constructing a key-insulated cryptosystem from an identity-based cryptosystem is trivial: in time period t, the first module [which acts as a PKG with key pair (P_{PKG}, S_{PKG})] gives the second module the private key for identity "t"; then, taking key-insulated encryption as an example, the sender encrypts its message using P_{PKG} and t. (Unfortunately, unlike IBC, key insulation requires a private and authenticated channel to exist between the two modules *even after all secrets on the second module are compromised;* perhaps, in some circumstances, this difficult requirement could be met using a physical link.)

Strong key insulation and *intrusion resilience* offer even stronger security guarantees. A strongly key-insulated scheme is not only key-insulated but also retains its security against adversaries that compromise the first module but not the second. Bellare and Palacio (2002) construct a strongly key-insulated encryption scheme by starting with the trivial key-insulated encryption scheme derived from Boneh–Franklin and then splitting the PKG's secret key between the first and second modules. An intrusion-resilient scheme retains its security as long as the adversary does not compromise both modules in the same time period. Dodis, Franklin, Katz, Miyaji, and Yung (2003) describe an encryption scheme that achieves intrusion resilience (roughly speaking) by splitting the PKG's functionality between the two modules, which then proactively update their shares of the PKG's secret at the beginning of each time period. Like key-insulated schemes, strongly key-insulated and intrusion-resilient schemes suffer from the problematic secure channel requirement described above. The scheme of Dodis et al. also incorporates a technique to achieve forward security.

In a forward-secure scheme, a user maintains a fixed public key, but it evolves its private key forward in such a way that, if its private key for time period t is compromised, the attacker still cannot perform private key operations for time periods $t - 1$ or earlier. (However, all future time periods are compromised, because the attacker can now also evolve the private key forward.) Thus, although the user needs only one module, it obtains a weaker security guarantee than key insulation. Canetti, Halevi, and Katz (2003) constructed the first nontrivial forward-secure encryption scheme by adapting the HIBE scheme of Gentry and Silverberg (2002). At a high level, their idea is to arrange the time periods (for convenience, assume there are 2^k of them) from left to right as leaves in a binary tree, associate a HIBE identity tuple to each node (including interior nodes) in the tree depending on the node's position in the hierarchy, and have the user evolve its periodic private key by traversing the tree from left to right while generating (using the Gentry-Silverberg private key generation procedure) and caching the appropriate node private keys. To encrypt a message to Bob, Alice treats Bob's public key as if it were the public key of a root PKG in a HIBE scheme, expresses the time period as if it were a k-element ID-tuple, and then applies HIBE.

Fuzzy Identity-Based Encryption

For IBC to be practical, identity strings must be chosen in a systematic way that ensures (at least with high probability) the uniqueness of each identity. Traditional identities, such as names (e.g., John Smith), do not satisfy this criterion, although one could mitigate this problem by adding more information to the name-space (e.g., place of residence) or making it hierarchical. This chapter has used e-mail addresses as a running example of a name-space offering uniqueness, but one may prefer to use identity strings that are more closely and reliably tied to actual people. One option is to use biometrics, such as fingerprints or voice prints (or some combination), to construct globally unique personal identifiers. Unfortunately, the measured value of a biometric tends to vary each time the biometric is sampled.

To use biometrics as identities in IBC, a couple of solutions have been proposed. One is to treat the sampled biometric as a corrupted codeword in an error-correcting code. The PKG gives the user the identity-based private key corresponding to the codeword closest to the scanned value of its biometric. To encrypt to the user, a sender might first scan the user's the biometric and then encrypt using the closest codeword (which is hopefully the same as it was in the PKG's scan). Sahai and Waters (2004) propose a different approach, called "fuzzy IBE," that modifies Boneh–Franklin to allow a user to decrypt even if its decryption key corresponds to an identity ID that is different from the identity ID' that the sender uses to encrypt, as long as ID and ID' are sufficiently close under some metric, such as Hamming distance.

Secret Handshakes

Balfanz et al., (2003) describe a "secret handshake" scheme, which is also based on the Sakai–Ohgishi–Kasahara noninteractive key agreement protocol. If Alice believes Bob is a member of group B, and Bob believes Alice is a member of group A, their scheme allows Alice and Bob to confirm the correctness of these memberships; if either membership is incorrect, neither party learns which groups the other party *actually* belongs to.

Streamlined IPSec

Appenzeller and Lynn (2002) note that IPSec can be dramatically simplified by replacing an approach based on traditional public key cryptography with an approach that uses the Sakai–Ohgishi–Kasahara (2000) noninteractive key agreement protocol. Their modified version of IPSec simplifies key management, requires no notion of "sessions," needs no per-host state, and has minimal bandwidth overhead. A disadvantage is that, to use the noninteractive key agreement protocol, the parties must share a PKG.

Smetters and Durfee (2003) propose a less radical change to IPSec—namely using domain-based IBC (discussed above as an alternative to IBE). Unlike Appenzeller-Lynn, this approach permits the use of multiple PKGs (one for each domain). It also has the advantage over PKI of raising the problem of key and certificate management from the user level to the domain level.

CONCLUSIONS AND FURTHER READING

With the development of practical IBE schemes in 2001, IBC has been an especially active and exciting research area over the past few years, and likely will continue to be for the foreseeable future. Given that IBC is a rapidly moving target, the strategy of this chapter has been (1) to give newcomers to IBC a good high-level intuition for the advantages and disadvantages of, and alternatives to, IBC in general (and thereby to enable practitioners to consider IBC's usefulness in various settings) and (2) to provide concrete and useful details regarding IBE and IBS (especially IBE) as illustrative examples. We hope that the intuition, at least, has enduring value.

By necessity, much was omitted. For example, many other types of identity-based cryptosystems (e.g., identity-based signcryption, blind signatures, undeniable signatures, and key agreement) were not covered. Also, even for IBE and IBS, some technical material (e.g., an optimized algorithm for computing the Tate pairing of two points on an elliptic curve) was left out. These are areas of current research. The reader interested in current IBC research can find a wealth of information through the International Association for Cryptologic Research (IACR), whose homepage lists major cryptology conferences and links to the Cryptology ePrint Archive, where cryptologists often post recent research results.

Many chapters on topics related or relevant to IBC can be found in this *Handbook*. For example, there are infrastructurally oriented chapters on PKI, key management, and identity management. There are also more algorithmically oriented chapters on the basics of encryption, public key algorithms, number theory, and elliptic curves.

GLOSSARY

Certificate A digital signature generated by a trusted authority (often called a CA) that signs a public key and an identifier.

Certificate-Based Encryption Encryption scheme in which a personal secret key and a certificate are needed to decrypt.

Certificateless Public Key Encryption Encryption scheme in which a personal secret key and an identity-based secret key are needed to decrypt.

Certification Authority A trusted authority that issues certificate (or certificate status information).

Certificate Revocation List A list of certificates revoked before their anticipated expiration dates, which is signed by a Certification Authority.

Domain-Based Identity-Based Encryption Encryption scheme in which each domain has a PKG that publishes its public key and that issues identity-based decryption keys to clients in its domain.

Forward-Secure Encryption Encryption scheme in which a user evolves its private key forward such that, if it is compromised, previous time periods remain secure.

Hierarchical IBE IBE scheme in which the sender encrypts using an ordered (e.g., hierarchical) sequence of strings (e.g., an identity-tuple) and the public key of a PKG.

Identity-Based Cryptography The study of, or the collection of, cryptosystems in which any arbitrary string can serve as an identity-based public key, and an identity-based private key is generated using an identity-based public key and a PKG's secret key.

Identity-Based Encryption Encryption scheme within IBC, in which a sender encrypts using an identity-based public key and a PKG's public key.

Internet Protocol Security A set of security protocols developed by the Internet Engineering Task Force.

Intrusion-Resilient Encryption Encryption scheme using two modules that provides some security unless both modules are compromised in the same time period.

Kerberos An authentication and key agreement protocol using symmetric cryptography.

Key-Insulated Encryption Encryption scheme using two modules that provides some security unless the first module is compromised.

Mediated IBE Encryption scheme in which a user must collaborate with a semi-trusted mediator to decrypt.

(Useful) Pairing A non-degenerate efficiently-computable bilinear map that maps two elements of a first group to an element of a second group.

Private Key Escrow Ability of a PKG to perform any identity-based private key operations that its clients can.

Private Key Generator A trusted authority that uses its secret key to compute identity-based private keys corresponding to identity-based public keys.

Public Key Encryption A cryptographic protocol that uses two keys — a public key known to everyone (the public) and a private or secret key known only to the recipient (private party) of the message.

Public Key Infrastructure Infrastructure needed to distribute public keys and certificates (or certificate status information).

Random Oracle Model A false but useful heuristic employed in proofs of security, in which a cryptographic hash function is treated as if it is an oracle that, on a given input, outputs a consistent random response.

RSA A public key encryption and signature scheme.

Third-Party Query A query by one party requesting another party's public key public key or certificate (or certificate status information).

CROSS REFERENCES

See *Digital Certificates; Encryption Basics; Kerberos; PKI (Public Key Infrastructure).*

REFERENCES

Al-Riyami, S. S., & Paterson, K. G. (2003). Certificateless public key cryptography. In *Proceedings of Asiacrypt 2003*, LNCS 2894 (pp. 452–473). Berlin: Springer-Verlag.

Appenzeller, G., & Lynn, B. (2002). *Minimal overhead IP security using identity based encryption*. Preprint Retrieved January 1, 2004, from http://rooster.stanford.edu/~ben/pubs/

Baek, J., & Zheng, Y. (2004). Identity-based threshold decryption. In *Proceedings of PKC 2004*, LNCS 2947 (pp. 262–276). Berlin: Springer-Verlag.

Balfanz, D., Durfee, G., Shankar, N., Smetters, D. K., Staddon, J., & Wong, H. C. (2003). Secret handshakes from pairing-based key agreements. In *Proceedings of the IEEE Symposium on Security and Privacy* (pp. 180–196).

Barreto, P. S. L. M. (2004). *The pairing-based crypto lounge*. Retrieved January 2, 2004, from http://planeta.terra.com.br./informatica/paulobarreto/pblounge.html

Barreto, P. S. L. M., Kim, H. Y., Lynn, B., & Scott, M. (2002). Efficient algorithms for pairing-based cryptosystems. In *Proceedings of Crypto 2002*, LNCS 2442 (pp. 354–368). Berlin: Springer-Verlag.

Bellare, M., Namprempre, C., & Neven, G. (2004). Security proofs for identity-based identification and signature schemes. In *Proceedings of Eurocrypt 2004*, LNCS 3027 (pp. 268–286). Berlin: Springer-Verlag.

Bellare, M., & Palacio, A. (2002). *Protecting against key exposure: Strongly key-insulated encryption with optimal threshold*. Preprint. Retrieved January 1, 2004, from http://eprint.iacr.org/2002/078

Boneh, D., & Boyen, X. (2004). Secure identity based encryption without random oracles. In *Proceedings of Crypto 2004*, LNCS 3152 (pp. 443–459). Berlin: Springer-Verlag.

Boneh, D., & Franklin, M. (2001). Identity based encryption from the Weil pairing. In *Proceedings of Crypto 2001*, LNCS 2139 (pp. 213–229). Berlin: Springer-Verlag.

Boneh, D., Gentry, C., Lynn, B., & Shacham, H. (2003). Aggregate and verifiably encrypted signatures from bilinear maps. In *Proceedings of Eurocrypt 2003*, LNCS 2656 (pp. 416–432). Berlin: Springer-Verlag.

Boneh, D., Ding, X., Tsudik, G., & Wong, M. (2001). A method for fast revocation of public key certificates and security capabilities. In *Proceedings of 10th Usenix Security Symposium* (pp. 297–308). Retrieved January 1, 2004, from http://www.usenix.org/publications/library/proceedings/sec01

Canetti, R., Halevi, S., & Katz, J. (2003). A forward-secure public key encryption scheme. In *Proceedings of Eurocrypt 2003*, LNCS 2656 (pp. 255–271). Berlin: Springer-Verlag.

Canetti, R., Halevi, S., & Katz, J. (2004). Chosen-ciphertext security from identity-based encryption. In *Proceedings of Eurocrypt 2004*, LNCS 3027 (pp. 207–222). Berlin: Springer-Verlag.

Casassa Mont, M. C., & Bramhall, P. (2003). *IBE applied to privacy and identity Management*, HPL-2003-101. Retrieved January 1, 2004, from http://www.hpl.hp.com/techreports/2003

Casassa Mont, M. C., Bramhall, P., Dalton, C. R., & Harrison, K. (2003). *A flexible role-based secure messaging service: Exploiting IBE technology in a health care trial*. Presented at the 14th International Workshop on Database and Expert Systems Applications (DEXA).

Casassa Mont, M. C., Pearson, S., & Bramhall, P. (2003). *Towards accountable management of identity and privacy: Sticky policies and enforceable tracing services*, HPL-2003-49. Retrieved January 1, 2004, from http://www.hpl.hp.com/techreports/2003

Chen, L. Harrison, K. Moss, A. Soldera, D., & Smart, N. (2002). Certification of public keys with an identity based system. In *Proceedings of ISC 2002* (pp. 322–333). Berlin: Springer-Verlag.

Cocks, C. (2001). An identity based encryption scheme based on quadratic residues. In *Proceedings of Cryptography and Coding 2001*, LNCS 2260. Berlin: Springer-Verlag.

Ding, X., & Tsudik, G. (2003). Simple identity-based cryptography with mediated RSA. In *Proceedings of CT-RSA 2003* (pp. 193–210). Berlin: Springer-Verlag.

Dodis, Y., Franklin, M., Katz, J., Miyaji, A., & Yung, M. (2003). Intrusion-resilient public key encryption. In *Proceedings of CT-RSA 2003*, LNCS 2612 (pp. 19–32). Berlin: Springer-Verlag.

Dodis, Y., Katz, J., Xu, S., & Yung, M. (2002). Key-insulated public key cryptosystems. In *Proceedings of Eurocrypt 2002*, LNCS 2332 (pp. 65–82). Berlin: Springer-Verlag.

Fiat, A., & Shamir, A. (1986). How to prove yourself: Practical solutions to identification and signature problems. In *Proceedings of Crypto 1986*, LNCS 263 (pp. 186–194). Berlin: Springer-Verlag.

Fujisaki, E., & Okamoto, T. (1999). Secure integration of asymmetric and symmetric encryption schemes. In *Proceedings of Crypto 1999*, LNCS 1666 (pp. 537–554). Berlin: Springer-Verlag.

Gentry, C. (2003). Certificate-based encryption and the certificate revocation problem. In *Proceedings of Eurocrypt 2003*, LNCS 2656 (pp. 272–293). Berlin: Springer-Verlag.

Gentry, C., & Silverberg, A. (2002). Hierarchical ID-based cryptography. In *Proceedings of Asiacrypt 2002*, LNCS 2501 (pp. 548–566). Berlin: Springer-Verlag.

Guillou, L., & Quisquater, J.-J. (1988a). A practical zero-knowledge protocol fitted to security microprocessor minimizing both transmission and memory. In *Proceedings of Eurocrypt 1988*, LNCS 330 (pp. 123–128). Berlin: Springer-Verlag.

Guillou, L., & Quisquater, J.-J. (1988b). A "paradoxical" identity-based signature scheme resulting from zero-knowledge. In *Proceedings of Crypto 1988*, LNCS 403 (pp. 216–231). Berlin: Springer-Verlag.

Horwitz, J., & Lynn, B. (2002). Toward hierarchical identity-based encryption. In *Proceedings of Eurocrypt 2002*, LNCS 2332 (pp. 466–481). Berlin: Springer-Verlag.

Joux, A. (2000). A one round protocol for tripartite Diffie–Hellman. In *Proceedings of the 4th International Symposium on Algorithmic Number Theory (ANTS IV)*, LNCS 1838 (pp. 385–393). Berlin: Springer-Verlag.

Kang, B. G., Park, J. H., & Hahn, S. G. (2004). A certificate-based signature scheme. In *Proceedings of CT-RSA 2004*, LNCS 2964 (pp. 99–111). Berlin: Springer-Verlag.

Lee, B., Boyd, C., Dawson, E., Kim, K., Yang, J., & Yoo, S. (2004). Secure key-issuing in ID-based cryptography. In *Proceedings of the ACM Workshop on Australian Information Security, Data Mining and Web Intelligence, and Software Internationalisation* (pp. 69–74).

Libert, B., & Quisquater, J.-J. (2003a). New identity based signcryption schemes from pairings. In *IEEE Information Theory Workshop 2003* (pp. 155–158).

Libert, B., & Quisquater, J.-J. (2003b). Efficient revocation and threshold pairing based cryptosystems. In *Proceedings of PODC 2003* (pp. 163–171). New York: ACM Press.

Libert, B., & Quisquater, J.-J. (2004). *The exact security of an identity based signature and its applications*. Preprint. Retrieved January 2, 2004, from http://eprint.iacr.org/2004/102

Maurer, U., & Yacobi, Y. (1991). Non-interactive public key cryptography. In *Proceedings of Eurocrypt 1991*, LNCS 547 (pp. 498–507). Berlin: Springer-Verlag.

Menezes, A., Okamoto, T., & Vanstone, S. A. (1993). Reducing elliptic curves logarithms to logarithms in a finite field. *IEEE Transactions of Information Theory*, 39(5), 1639–1646.

Miller, V. (1986). *Short Programs for Functions on Curves*, unpublished manuscript.

Sahai A., & Waters, B. (2004). *Fuzzy identity based encryption*. Preprint, 2004. Retrieved January 2, 2003, from http://eprint.iacr.org/2004/086

Sakai, R., Ohgishi, K., & Kasahara, M. (1999). *Notes on ID-based key sharing systems over elliptic curve*. Technical Report of IEICE, ISEC99-57, Nov. 1999.

Sakai, R., Ohgishi, K., & Kasahara, M. (2000). Cryptosystems based on pairing. In *Symposium on Cryptography and Information Security* (SCIS), January, 2000.

Sakai, R., Ohgishi, K., & Kasahara, M. (2001). Cryptosystems based on pairing over elliptic curve. In

Symposium on Cryptography and Information Security (SCIS), January, 2001 (in Japanese).

Shamir, A. (1985). Identity-based cryptosystems and signature schemes. In *Proceedings of Crypto 1984*, LNCS 196 (pp. 47–53). Berlin: Springer-Verlag.

Smetters, D. K., & Durfee, G. (2003). Domain-based administration of identity-based cryptosystems for secure email and IPSEC. In *Proceedings of the 12th USENIX Security Symposium* (pp. 215–229).

Waters, B. (2004). *Efficient identity-based encryption without random oracles*. Preprint. Retrieved January 1, 2004, from http://eprint.iacr.org/2004/180

Waters, B., Balfanz, D., Durfee, G., & Smetters, D. K. (2004). Building an encrypted and searchable audit log. To appear in *Network and Distributed Security Symposium* (NDSS) 2004.

Yun, D. H., & Lee, P. J. (2004a). Generic construction of certificateless encryption. In *Proceedings of ICCSA 2004*, LNCS 3043 (pp. 802–811). Berlin: Springer-Verlag.

Yun, D. H., & Lee, P. J. (2004b). Generic construction of certificateless signature. In *Proceedings of ACISP 2004*, LNCS 3108 (pp. 200–211). Berlin: Springer-Verlag.

Cryptographic Protocols

Markus Jakobsson, *Indiana University, Bloomington*

INTRODUCTION: WHAT IS A PROTOCOL?

Here is a protocol we have all known since we were children: two children get one cake and need to share it in a way that they both agree to. It would easily create unfairness if one of them cuts the cake and then selects a piece. Instead, one child cuts the cake, then the other one gets to select a piece, and then the child who cut the cake gets the remaining piece.

One can think of a protocol as a step-by-step recipe for one or more chefs to cook a particular dish and make sure that nobody makes a mistake. More generally, a protocol is a sequence of steps taken by one or more participants wanting to achieve some goal. Often, and as above, it is important to construct the protocol in a way that makes the different participants behave in the wanted way; in the example above, this corresponds to cutting the cake into two equally large pieces. In the case of only one participant, of course, this does not apply, as if he or she were to cheat, he or she would simply cheat him- or herself.

In this chapter, we cover the fundamentals of how to design and understand a protocol, starting with understanding the problem to be solved, including the threat that an attacker poses. Therefore, given that the emphasis is on understanding how to design rather than what is being used, we do not survey common protocols, such as secure sockets layer, Internet security protocol, and so on. Instead, we give examples of useful cryptographic building blocks and some protocols that use these building blocks.

CLASSIFYING PROTOCOLS WITH RESPECT TO THE ADVERSARY

When one designs a protocol, it is important to understand what could go wrong if somebody were to cheat. First, it is important to think of who could cheat. The cake-cutting protocol is well designed so not much can go wrong (if we exclude cheating such as grabbing the whole cake and running away with it instead of cutting it). Conversely, if the person who cuts also got to choose first, it is easy to see how he or she could cheat: by cutting two very different-sized pieces and then selecting the largest. So in the general situation where two people want to fairly share a cake, it makes sense to think of these two people as possible cheaters, or adversaries, when considering whether the protocol one has designed is secure.

To see that there may be other types of adversaries, let us consider another type of protocol. Assume that there are two people and that one of these people wants to send a message to the other to suggest a meeting place for their upcoming rendezvous. Of course, the sender could cheat by writing down another place than the one where he or she wants to meet, but even though this is a form of cheating, it does not seem like a very appealing thing to do. Conversely, if a person working in the post office is very curious, he or she may want to get access to the letter and open it to learn the meeting place. This seems like a more reasonable type of cheating for this scenario. Therefore, this type of protocol should be designed to protect against some third party, but we may not have to worry about one of the principal participants cheating the other. One approach to avoid the "post office attack" might be to send several numbered messages, one for each letter of the meeting place, letting the intended recipient piece together the message from the many numbered messages received. At least, this would make it a little harder for the adversary we consider, as he or she would have to get access to a large portion of the numbered messages to be able to know what the meeting place is with a good probability.

Of course, if the two parties have access to some form of encryption, and have already exchanged keys, there would be much better approaches to secure the exchange of information. However, if the two parties have not agreed on what keys to use for the encryption and authentication, they need to do so first. The adversary may want to eavesdrop on this process, or even replace some of the messages going back and forth during this phase, with the goal of learning or replacing the keys the two main parties will use. At the same time, one of the two participants may want to trick the other into using a particular key, perhaps with some known weakness in. This could allow the cheater to leak some secret information that the other sent to him or her, and then claim that he or she did not, but rather that some unknown attacker intercepted the encrypted messages and managed to break the weak key. If it then could be shown that the key used really turned out to be weak, then this would hold the cheater free from responsibility. This example shows that several types of adversaries may coexist at the same time: both protocol participants and unknown third parties. It also suggests that protocol design could be rather complex, given all the bizarre ways of cheating that might exist.

For protocols involving two or more participants, it is important to determine all reasonable ways in which these could attempt to cheat and design the protocol in a way that allows the detection of or avoids any such cheating. A protocol is *secure* against a given type of adversary if this adversary cannot cause an incorrect output to be produced by the protocol without this being detected by the other protocol participants. Therefore, to make meaningful statements about the security of a protocol, it is important first to specify exactly what the adversary is able to do and what his or her goals might be.

A protocol can be thought of as a "recipe" to compute some information. Many protocols require interaction between the parties who hold the inputs that we want to compute the output from, but interestingly, this is not a requirement. In fact, a very common protocol, the Diffie–Hellman key exchange, requires no interaction at all. Given that this is a very straightforward protocol, it is well suited as a first real example of a cryptographic protocol.

We will assume that everybody who potentially wants to use the protocol knows the protocol and also knows some common system parameters. One of such parameters is a large prime value, which is often denoted p. Another value is what is referred to as a generator and is denoted g. We do not describe exactly how this is selected here but instead refer to the chapter on key establishment for more details. Each party selects a secret key. We refer to Alice's secret value as x_A, to Bob's as x_B, Cindy's as x_C, and so on. Each party computes a corresponding public key, as the value g raised to the secret key, modulo p. Thus, $y_A = g^x A \pmod{p}$, and $y_B = g^x B \pmod{p}$. If two parties, say Alice and Bob, wish to establish a shared key, then Alice will take Bob's public key y_B and raise to her own secret key x_A, whereas Bob will take Alice's public key y_A and raise to his own secret key x_B. Given how y_A and y_B are defined, we will have $y_B^x A = (g^x B)^x A = (g^x A)^x B = y_A^x B$ and therefore these two parties will have the same value. Now, the important thing is that they are the only two who can do this. Although Cindy, for example, has both y_A and y_B, she cannot compute the shared key that Alice and Bob computed given these values; she needs one of their secret keys for this.

Now, before we start looking at more complex protocols, it is important to first develop an understanding of what we hope to achieve when designing a given protocol. To do this, we need to start by understanding

what we want to prevent from happening. In other words, we need to understand what types of attacks our protocol is likely to have to withstand.

UNDERSTANDING THE ADVERSARY

What Are the Goals of the Adversary?

In many situations, it is likely to assume that it is not the goal of the cheating adversary to cause an arbitrary incorrect output to be produced by the protocol. Rather, he or she may have some particular goal, such as getting a bigger piece of cake, learning the secret messages, or being able to leak secret information without being held responsible. The first thing we must understand before starting to design a protocol is what the likely adversary will want to achieve.

For example, if we are designing a system that allows users to download and watch movies for a fee, we should naturally be concerned that an adversary will want to watch movies without paying or give others access to watch movies, whether for free or for a charge. We may also be concerned about privacy: to protect against an adversary who wants to determine who watches what movies. Conversely, we are likely to be less concerned about the location of a given subscriber, as long as the above security requirements are satisfied. Now, consider instead another example in which we want to design a system that allows legitimate users to access a corporate database. Here, we may require that nobody accesses the database from outside the office to make sure that employees are not forced to download sensitive documents by an outside kidnapper, so here location might matter. Privacy is likely to not matter much: if anybody within the company wishes to determine who downloads what files, that is probably okay. But just as in the movie download case, it is obvious that we want to make sure that only registered users get to download information. We do not want a visitor to the building to have access rights to the database. This shows us two situations that on the surface are very similar in one respect: protecting access to some resource. Given the big differences in adversarial goals, the protocols for the two situations are likely to be very different, though.

It is often reasonable to assume that the adversary is *rational* (i.e., he or she will only do things that benefit him or her), whereas a *malicious* attacker may do things even if they hurt him or her, as long as he or she reaches his or her goals. For example, a cell phone user may want to cheat (and send incorrect messages to a base station, for example) if this will lower the monthly bill and get him or her better coverage and service. He or she is not likely to cheat in this way if it makes it impossible for him or her to place phone calls, because he or she is rational. Conversely, a terrorist might want his or her cellular phone to send incorrect messages to base stations, no matter whether he or she can place phone calls, if this incorrect information were to cause the base station to drop connections of other users. This is because this second adversary is malicious.

One can even have many adversaries, each with different goals and abilities, and have different security guarantees against each one of them. We give an example of that below.

What Can the Adversary Do—And Not Do?

It is important to specify what an adversary is able to do to reach his or her goals. It is a common assumption that the adversary has some computational limitations. For example, it is commonly assumed that the adversary cannot factor large integers of certain forms (this is what the RSA signature and encryption techniques rely on). The reason people feel comfortable making this assumption is that nobody so far has specified a method that does factor large integers, and many people have tried.

In other situations, people may make no particular assumptions on the computational abilities of the adversary. In other words, even though nobody is known to have the ability to factor large numbers, one would assume that *the adversary* knows it (but won't tell anybody else). Clearly, such an adversary is more powerful that an adversary who cannot factor large numbers, and therefore, a protocol that is secure against this more powerful adversary is more secure than one that is only secure against an adversary who cannot factor. Of course, it may be difficult to design a protocol that is of the more secure kind or such a protocol may need expensive hardware to be run or may be very inefficient for the intended participants. It is therefore not always beneficial to offer the absolutely highest level of security at any cost but rather to offer the best level of security for a reasonable threat. This threat, of course, corresponds to the believed abilities of the adversary.

Let's consider the case of setup boxes for satellite TV. They may use some protocol that makes it difficult to clone them or make it difficult to watch a program by a person who has not paid his or her subscription to the service. We all know that it is not impossible to cheat in such systems, though. It may be expensive to reverse engineer the hardware and figure out what the protocol is, which acts as a deterrent of cheating. Conversely, once somebody has learned this, he or she could tell lots of other people or plainly build fake setup boxes en masse. If there is a way for the service provider to change the protocol occasionally, in a way that is automatically updated by "legal" decoders, that would then make illegal decoders less valuable and make it more difficult for the adversary to sell these. Similarly, if there would be a way to detect if a given decoder is legal or not—without physical access to it—that may allow the service provider to know the extent to which service is stolen and perhaps even who the adversary is. That, again, would make it less attractive to cheat. Although the service providers would clearly love to be able to produce a protocol that is secure against any adversary, such a method is not known to exist. Therefore, the question becomes: how much security can we obtain at a reasonable cost?

WHAT SHOULD A PROTOCOL DO—AND NOT DO?

Before designing a protocol for a given situation, it is crucial to consider all the things that the protocol should do to protect against the adversary. For example, it may be important for information to be encrypted so that the adversary cannot eavesdrop on it and learn secret information. Similarly, it may be important for protocol participants to be able to verify from whom a particular message originated and possibly to prove this to other participants. To end up with a good protocol, all of these requirements should be kept in mind when the protocol is designed. This is better than trying to add security features to an already existing protocol, as doing that is likely to complicate the protocol and the security analysis of the same.

It is also important to consider what the protocol should *not* do. For example, many wireless protocols attach a short tag to each message that is being broadcast, where this tags tells each recipient whether the message was intended for him or her. Many protocols also use a tag that specifies from whom the message was sent, allowing easy responses. Both of these types of tags are practical to make the protocol efficient (participants would not have to bother with messages that are not intended for them!) but also have drawbacks. Namely, it is possible for an eavesdropping adversary to determine who is communicating with whom—simply by monitoring the radio traffic! This may be contrary to the privacy wishes of the participants.

Another example showing that it is important to consider what protocols should not do—to potentially avoid this when designing them—can be found in the context of anonymous payment schemes. Payment schemes such as those proposed by Chaum (1983) or Brands (1994) have the nice feature that they allow users to spend money in a way that is not traceable by the bank or anybody else for that matter. However, it also allows criminals to do the same, of course, and if a criminal can force an honest user to withdraw money and pass it on to the criminal (in a blackmail attack, for example) then the funds are still impossible to trace: for the bank, for the legitimate user, and anybody else. That means that this type of crime may be encouraged, as the protocol allows for abuse of the privacy, and without any means of tracing or blocking the use of money that has been stolen in this manner.

Therefore, we must consider all possible types of attacks against a protocol, and make sure that the protocol itself does not give rise to new types of attacks—whether this attack benefits from too little privacy (as in the wireless example) or too much (as in the payment example.) This could be very challenging.

COMMON BUILDING BLOCKS

Although each setting and adversary may require a unique protocol to reach the wanted goal, there are many common building blocks that can be used by different protocols. We review some of these here and then describe how these can be used in various settings.

Proving Without Leaking: The Zero-Knowledge Protocol

A protocol is *zero knowledge* if it allows one participant (the prover) to convince another participant (the verifier) that some statement is true but without having to give out information that allows the verifier to know why the statement is true or to convince somebody else of this fact. To make this a little less abstract, consider a prover who wants to convince a verifier that he or she knows the secret key corresponding to a particular public key. Doing this would in effect prove that he or she is the person associated with the public key (assuming the secret key has not been compromised). Although the prover could simply send over the secret key to the verifier, allowing the verifier to check that it corresponds to the given public key, this would not be such a smart approach, as now, because the verifier would also know the secret key. It would be better if the prover can convince the verifier that he or she knows the secret key without giving any information at all—short of the fact that the prover knows the secret key.

There are many ways for a prover to convince a verifier that he or she knows the secret key without automatically leaking the same. For example, he or she could let the verifier select a random value, encrypt this with the prover's public key, and send this ciphertext to the prover. The prover would then decrypt the ciphertext, obtaining the random value, and send this to the verifier. The verifier would know that only he or she knew the random number and so the prover must have been able to decrypt the ciphertext! However, this is not zero knowledge: it leaks one piece to information to the verifier, namely a plaintext. The reason is that the verifier could cheat by not selecting a random plaintext and encrypting it, but instead send over a ciphertext that he or she would like to know the plaintext to. The prover would decrypt the ciphertext he or she received and send back the resulting plaintext, not knowing that the verifier did not already know this. This could be used by a cheating verifier to learn the plaintext to any ciphertext corresponding to the prover's public key, which could be disastrous for the prover.

A modification of the above protocol is as follows:

1. The verifier selects a random plaintext, call this R. He or she encrypts this with the prover's public key, obtaining a ciphertext C. He or she sends C to the prover.
2. The prover decrypts C, obtaining a value r (that should be equal to R). However, he or she does not send r to the verifier. Instead, he or she concatenates a portion of random bits to r, and encrypts the resulting value with his or her own public key (the public key of the prover). Call this new ciphertext c. He or she sends c to the verifier. Note that the verifier cannot decrypt c, so he or she cannot obtain r (or any portion thereof) from it.
3. The verifier sends R to the prover. The prover compares this to r. If they are the same, he or she knows that the verifier knew the plaintext corresponding to C. If not, then he or she knows that the verifier was trying to cheat, in which case he or she will abort the execution of the protocol.
4. The prover sends r and the random bits used to pad it, allowing the verifier to check that if he or she encrypts this, he or she would obtain c (which is the value that the prover sent him in step 2) and that r equals R (which means that the prover must know the secret key that allows him or her to decrypt). If both of these conditions hold, the verifier knows that the prover must know the secret key, but he or she does not learn anything else.

In the above protocol, the encryption technique used to encrypt r is referred to as a *commitment*. It can be seen as a form of encryption where one cannot decrypt or even replicate the ciphertext from its input plaintext unless the *entire* input is known—plaintext *and* random bits.

Why does this work? Because the verifier does not know the random bits used by the prover, he or she cannot obtain r without disclosing R. More specifically, he or she cannot verify whether the response he or she gets in step two is correct: he or she must continue by performing step 3 of the protocol. This allows the prover, in turn, to verify that the verifier did not cheat (by not knowing the plaintext of C). Finally, step 4 allows the verifier to check that the prover did not cheat (by performing the protocol without knowing the secret key needed for decryption of C).

The way one shows that the protocol is zero knowledge is by showing that the verifier could have produced the entire transcript of the protocol on his or her own, without the involvement of the prover. This can be done as follows: The verifier picks a random value R and encrypts this as in step 1, obtaining the ciphertext C. This is the information of step 1 of the protocol. Then, he or she sets $r = R$ and selects a random bit sequence to pad r with. He or she encrypts the padded value using the prover's public key, obtaining c. This is the information of step 2 of the protocol. He or she then produces the information of step 3 of the protocol. This is simply the value R, which he or she knows. Finally, he or she produces the information of step 4 of the protocol, namely the value r and the random bits appended to it. He or she knows these, of course, because he or she produced them by him- or herself. Now, the verifier has produced a complete transcript, which a third party cannot tell apart from a "real" transcript.

If the third party cannot tell a real transcript from a "faked" (or simulated) transcript, then one cannot leak any more information than the other. We know that the simulated transcript cannot leak any information about the secret key, simply because the verifier does not know this value (so how could the transcript he or she produces depend on this value?). Then, we must conclude that the real transcript also does not leak any information about the secret key. This is what we wanted to prove: that the protocol is zero knowledge.

But why does the real protocol manage to convince the verifier that he or she could have produced the transcript on his or her own? That is a valid question. The answer is simply that the real protocol convinces the verifier that the prover knows the secret key because the verifier knows that only he or she knows the plaintext R and that he or she is not trying to con him- or herself into believing that the prover knows how to produce this value from the resulting ciphertext C. In contrast, the third party does not know this: he or she sees the entire transcript, not knowing who knows R and who does not.

Another type of zero-knowledge protocol is the cut-and-choose protocol. This works using the same basic principles used by two people trying to share a cake in a fair way: there are two (or more) possible questions a verifier may ask. The prover prepares the answers to these and sends commitments to each answer. The verifier then selects what question to ask, and the prover has to "open up" the corresponding commitment. If he or she refuses to do so, or the answer it contains is incorrect, then the verifier rejects the proof. Otherwise, the verifier trusts the proof with some probability. The prover and verifier may repeat the above many times, until the verifier is convinced enough that the prover is not cheating. The protocol is designed such that knowing one of the answers does not give away the secret the prover claims to know, but knowing more than one would give away at least some portion of the secret. However, each round of the proof uses different randomness to make the exact questions and answers somewhat different from before, and so, the verifier will never learn two "matching" answers (and will therefore not learn the secret). We will give more concrete examples of this method later.

Proving Correct Exponentiation

In many situations, one protocol participant has a secret key, which is often a value x for which another value $y = g^x$ (modulo some known very large integer p) is known. Some other protocol participant may provide him or her with a value m and want him or her to compute $s = m^x$ (modulo p). But given s and y, this second participant will not be able to verify whether s was correctly computed because he or she does not know the value x. Therefore, the first participant has to act as a prover and convince the second participant (the verifier) that the correct exponent was used. There are many possible protocols to do this, we show one such from David Chaum (1991).

1. The verifier selects two random numbers, a and b, and computes $q = g^a m^b$ (modulo p). He or she sends this value q to the prover but does not reveal a or b. To simplify the notation, we do not write out the "modulo p" onwards.

2. The prover computes $w = q^x$. Note that this is equal to $g^{ax} m^{bx} = g^{xa} m^{xb} = y^a s^b$. He does not send this value to the verifier (as this would allow the verifier to cheat by sending an arbitrary value q and have q^x computed!). Instead, he or she commits to w and sends this commitment, call it c, to the verifier.

3. The verifier receives c and then reveals a and b to the prover.

4. The prover verifies that $q = g^a m^b$. If it is not, then he or she halts the protocol. Otherwise, he or she sends w to the verifier.

5. The verifier checks whether $w = y^a s^b$. If it does, then he or she accepts the proof, knowing that the prover could not have computed this quantity in step 2 (when he or she did not know a and b) without knowledge of x. If the equality does not hold, then he or she knows that the prover must have cheated.

Proving Correct Encryption/Reencryption

A common crypto system is El Gamal encryption. It works as follows: there is a secret key, x, that is only known by the owner of the corresponding public key $y = g^x$. A message m is encrypted by selecting a random value e and computing the pair $(y^e m, g^e)$. Call this pair (A,B), where A is the quantity $y^e m$ and B is the quantity g^e. Note that encryption can be done by anybody because it uses only public information. However, only the owner of the secret key can decrypt, which is done by computing $A/B^x = y^e m/(g^e)^x = y^e m/(g^x)^e = y^e m/y^e = m$.

In many cases, a protocol participant has some message m that needs to be encrypted as above and needs to convince a verifier that it is indeed encrypted correctly. This corresponds to proving that he or she used the same exponent e for the first and the second term. We may use the protocol for correct exponentiation to accomplish this task. More specifically, we can consider the quantity B as a public key corresponding to a secret key e known only by the prover. Then, the prover would show that the quantity A/m (for a known message m) equals y raised to the same exponent e—the "secret key." If you look at the protocol for proving correct exponentiation, you will see that this is sufficient for the verifier to be convinced that the prover performed a correct exponentiation and, therefore, a correct encryption of the known value m.

Another common method is what is referred to as reencryption. Here, a first participant receives an El Gamal ciphertext (A,B). He or she may not know the secret key to decrypt and may not know what message the pair corresponds to. He or she still wishes to produce a new and independent-looking ciphertext that corresponds to the same secret key and the same message. What he or she does is as follows: chooses a random value e' (which is not related to the value e above.) He or she then computes $y^{e'}$ and $g^{e'}$, and then $(Ay^{e'}, Bg^{e'})$. Note that because (A,B) equals $(y^e m, g^e)$ for some unknown value e, the new pair must equal $(y^{e+e'} m, g^{e+e'})$. Since we could rename e+e' as e", we see that this new pair, let us call it (A',B') is an encryption of the same message m as (A,B) is. Note again that m does not need to be known for this to be performed. We will demonstrate useful applications for this onwards.

Now, say that a verifier may want to know that the reencryption was performed correctly, that is, that (A,B) corresponds to the same (potentially unknown) plaintext m as (A',B') does. Again, this corresponds to showing that the factors multiplied in to (A,B) to obtain (A',B') were correctly formed. If we divide A' by A, and B' by B, we receive these. The prover will show that they use the same exponent, just as we did for correct encryption: by using one of them as a public key, and prove that the other one is consistently formed, using the protocol for correct exponentiation.

Proving Equivalence

There are two types of common equivalence proofs: a first type allows a prover to convince a verifier that the plaintexts of two different ciphertexts equal each other. The second type of equivalence test allows two players, each holding a secret value, to compare these two values to see if they are the same—of course, without revealing any other information about the values to each other. We describe how this can be performed next and later show uses of these techniques.

First, let us therefore consider how a prover can show that the plaintexts of two ciphertexts are the same. We again use El Gamal encryption and call the ciphertexts (A,B) and (A',B'). We assume for now that they are constructed using the same public key; this is not a necessary requirement but simplifies the protocol. Recall that $(A,B) = (y^e m, g^e)$ and $(A',B') = (y^{e'} m', g^{e'})$ for some values e, e', m, m'.

Both prover and verifier can compute $(A/A', B/B') = (y^{e-e'} m/m', g^{e-e'})$. If the plaintexts are equal to each other, this means that this quantity equals $(y^{e''}, g^{e''})$ for some value e''. If the prover knows e and e', then he or she will also know e'' and will be able to prove to the verifier that the "divided pair" is of the expected format, using the same techniques as shown before. Conversely, if the prover does not know both e and e', but does know x (where $y = g^x$), then he or she still can prove the relation. Namely that the divided pair is of the form $((g^{e''})^x, g^{e''})$, again using the same technique.

In the second variant of the comparison problem, the two protocol participants each have a value and want to compare these two values. They want to learn only whether the values are equal. This problem is referred to as the "socialist millionaires' problem" and was proposed by Jakobsson and Yung (1996). The reason for this is that there is another, more famous problem in which the two participants each have a value (representing their riches) and wish to compare these (to learn who is the wealthiest). The socialist millionaires wish to know only if they are equally wealthy. There are many possible protocols to let the two participants compare their values. We consider one with a similar structure to the protocols we have introduced—this is introduced to simplify the understanding of the protocol, but it should be noted that there are more efficient techniques.

We call the two participants P_1 and P_2, as they are both provers in a sense. P_1 has a value m_1, and P_2 has a value m_2. Furthermore, P_1 has a secret key x_1 and a corresponding public key $y_1 = g^{x_1}$; P_2 has a secret key x_2 and a corresponding public key $y_2 = g^{x_1}$, both using the same modulo p. Now, let $y = y_1 y_2$. This corresponds to a secret key $x = x_1 + x_2$, which is not known by either part on its own. The comparison protocol is as follows:

1. Both participants encrypt their value (m_1 and m_2) using the public key y and El Gamal encryption. This results in ciphertexts (A_1, B_1) and (A_2, B_2). They send these ciphertexts to each other.

2. Both participants compute $(A, B) = (A_1/A_2, B_1/B_2)$. Note that this is an encryption of the value 1 if and only if $m_1 = m_2$.

3. P_1 selects a random number r_1, and P_2 selects a random number r_2. They both keep their respective value secret.

4. P_1 computes $(A', B') = (A_1^r, B_1^r)$ and sends (A', B') to P_2. He or she proves to P_2 that the exponentiation of A uses the same exponent as the exponentiation of B. This can be done using the protocol for correct exponentiation that we have shown before.

5. P_2 computes $(A'', B'') = (A_2'^r, B_2'^r)$ and sends (A'', B'') to P_1. He or she proves to P_1 that the exponentiation of A' uses the same exponent as the exponentiation of B'.

6. P_1 partially decrypts the ciphertext by computing B''^{x_1}, sending this quantity to P_2. He or she also proves that he or she performed the correct exponentiation with respect to his or her public key. P_2 further decrypts the ciphertext by computing $(B''^{x_1})^{x_2}$ and proving this to be done correctly. If the plaintext equals 1, then the participants conclude that $m_1 = m_2$.

Note that (A'', B'') was an encryption of $(m_1/m_2)^{r_1+r_2}$. This equals 1 if and only if $m_1 = m_2$. Otherwise it is a random

value, and because neither participant knows both r_1 and r_2, they will not be able to say something about the other participant's secret value (m_1 or m_2) from this quantity.

You may ask yourself what the benefit of steps 3–5 is. To see this, assume that we always would set r_1 and r_2 to 1. Then, at least participant P_2 would learn m_1/m_2 in step 6. Because he already knows m_2, he would in fact learn m_1. This is not possible in the above protocol.

Secret Sharing and Proactive Secret Sharing

In section 5.4, we saw an example of a secret sharing scheme. The public key y corresponded to a secret key that was not known by either participant but rather was the sum of their individual shares. The secret shares, in other words, were x_1 and x_2, and the public key was $y = g^{x_1+x_2}$. This is referred to as a two-of-two secret sharing scheme. This means that there are two shares, and to reconstitute the secret key (or perform any function computation using it, such as the decryption performed in the section, "Proving Equivalence"), one needs both of those. In short, we write a two-of-two secret sharing scheme as a (2,2) secret sharing scheme. It is clear that using the same method, one can create a (3,3) or (4,4) secret sharing scheme or an (n,n) secret sharing scheme, where n is the number of shares.

Another type of secret sharing scheme does not require all shares to be used to reconstitute the secret. A (k,n) secret sharing scheme—pronounced a k-of-n secret sharing scheme—has the property that only k of the n shares are needed. For example, if $k = 2$ and $n = 3$, we only need two of three shares, and any two will work. The construction of such a secret sharing scheme follows a very simple and elegant principle, which we illustrate for the (2,3) case. Consider a line that intersects the y axis is some point $(x,y) = (0,y_0)$. Call y_0 the secret to be shared. Let (x_1,y_1), (x_2,y_2), and (x_3,y_3) be three points on the line. We call these the secret shares. If you know one of secret shares alone, you cannot say anything about where the line intersects the y axis (i.e., you cannot compute the secret). However, if you know two of the shares—any two!—that allows you to extrapolate the line to determine the intersection with the y axis, and therefore the secret. So there are three secret shares, and any two of them are sufficient to compute the secret. At the same time, one is not enough. We can easily expand this to a (2,4) scheme by producing another point (x_4,y_4) on the line: it is still the case that any two of the secret shares can be used to compute the secret. Now, a line is a degree-1 polynomial. If we instead of a line use a degree-2 polynomial, it is not sufficient to know two secret shares (points on the curve) to compute the secret (the intersection with the y axis.) However, three shares is enough. In general, we need $k + 1$ shares to determine where a curve intersects the y axis if the curve is a degree-k polynomial. This corresponds to a ($k+1$,n) secret sharing scheme. In our setting, all the points on the curve are represented by integers, and all arithmetic is modulo some integer as well; to perform the extrapolation in such a situation, one uses a LaGrange interpolation, which is covered in more detail in another chapter. The secret sharing scheme we have explained was invented by Shamir (1979) and is referred to as *Shamir secret sharing*.

Secret sharing can be used in many ways to enhance security. One of the most common ways is to distribute a secret key, such as the signing key for a certification authority (CA), so that an intruder who gains temporary access to one of the machines of the CA cannot learn the secret signing key. Instead, if the signing key is distributed between some n machines, and k out of these shares are necessary to reconstitute the key, the attacker would have to gain access to at least k of the machines. This, of course, is much more difficult than gaining access to only one machine. The primary reason why we do not set $k = n$ (which would require all shares to be present to compute the secret) is to avoid problems associated with temporary failures of some of the servers. For example, in a (2,3) secret sharing scheme, one can perform all the computation as long as only one of the servers does not respond. This gives security against attacks in which a small number of machines are targeted and brought down to prevent correct execution of the protocol.

As described above, a benefit of using a secret sharing scheme is to defend against an attacker that compromises a small number of machines. A proactive secret sharing scheme defends against a more aggressive attack, namely one in which the attacker gains access to some small number of machines during a first time period, some other machines during a second time interval, and yet some other machines in a third interval. It is assumed that the attacker is detected and "kicked out" from machines at the end of each time interval, and so he or she compromises only a given maximum number of machines at any point in time. When he or she compromises a machine, he or she copies all its information and sends it to some central site of his or hers. This site then obtains lots of shares over time. In fact, after the attacker has compromised all machines, it will have received shares from all of these.

To avoid that the secret can be reconstituted by the attacker after performing an attack of this kind, all the shares are "rerandomized" at the end of each time interval, but without affecting what point the new curve intersects the y axis in. This can be done by adding a curve to the old curve. The curve we add to it will intersect the y axis in (0,0) and will have the same degree as the first curve but otherwise be randomly selected. This creates a new curve that intersects the y axis in the same point as the old curve but where each share will be new and independent of the old shares. Therefore, as long as the attacker does not compromise k shares during any one point in time, he or she will not benefit from old shares he or she has obtained—they will not be on the same curve as newer shares will. This is referred to as *proactive secret sharing* and was introduced by Herzberg, Jarecki, Krawczyk, and Yung (1995).

Hash Functions, Signatures, and Message Authentication Codes

We now briefly describe hash functions, digital signatures, and message authentication codes (MACs). These three building blocks are described in much more detail in other chapters; we only briefly review them here for the convenience of the reader, given that some of the protocols we describe later use these constructions.

A hash function is a function that takes an arbitrarily long input and produces a fixed-length and relatively short output. The output is typically 128 bits (as for MD5)

or 160 bits (as for SHA-1). It is not possible to compute what could have been the input given an output value, and it is not possible to find two input values that produce the same output value. These collisions exist, as can be seen from the fact that the inputs can be of any length and, therefore, that there are more input values than output values. Still, given the construction of the hash function, it is computationally infeasible to find such collisions. Similarly, given an output, it is infeasible to find an input that would have generated this output. Hash functions are covered in much more detail in other chapters of this book, and we refer the interested reader to these.

A digital signature s on a message m is a value that can be produced only by somebody with knowledge of a particular secret key—the secret key of the signer. Once produced, the value s can be verified (relative to m) without knowledge of the secret key—the corresponding public key suffices. An example of a signature scheme using the same computational structures as we have used above is the *Schnorr signature*, named after its inventor, Claus-Peter Schnorr. There, a signer has a secret key x in an interval between 0 and q for some large prime number q and a corresponding public key $y = g^x$ modulo p. For details on the choice of the parameters p and q, we refer to the article by Schnorr (1991) and subsequent chapters in this book.

A signature is generated by selecting a temporary secret key, k, and computing $r = g^k$, which can be thought of as a temporary public key. Then, s is set to $s = xe + k$ modulo q, where $e = h(m, r)$. Here, h is a hash function, and m is the message to be signed. The pair (r,s) constitutes the signature on m.

To verify a triple (m, r, s), a verifier will check if $g^s = y^e r$, where e is computed as $e = h(m, r)$. Note that if the signature was correctly computed, then $g^s = g^{xe+k} = g^{xe}g^k = y^e r$. This is exactly what is verified. Variations of these equations exist and can be shown to be equivalent.

A MAC can be thought of as a digital signature, where the same key is used to produce and verify a "signature." This, of course, means that a MAC cannot be used to sign a contract, as anybody who can verify it could also have produced it. Conversely, MACs can be used between two participants who share a key, for these to be able to authenticate messages they send to each other. An eavesdropper will not be able to forge MACs because he or she does not know the key that is used. A MAC function can be implemented by using a hash function, in which case it is referred to as a HMAC. This is done by hashing the input to the MAC function along with the key of the MAC function, both to produce the MAC value and to verify it. For more details, we refer to the publication by Bellare, Canetti, and Krawczyk (1996) in which the concept was proposed.

SOME CRYPTOGRAPHIC PROTOCOLS
Payments, Micropayments, and Applications

Cryptographically secure payment schemes can be produced in many different ways. Two of the most popular are based on a digital signature or on hash functions alone. We review the principles of these.

A payment scheme can be based on a digital signature scheme. One solution is for a user to select a secret key and public key, and then perform a withdrawal from a bank by getting a bank signature on the public key along with a denomination. The user's secret and public key are used only for this withdrawal, and so each withdrawal uses new and random keys. Conversely, the keys used for signing are the same for every withdrawal—they are the keys of the bank. A bank signature on the message "y,\$1" corresponds to a withdrawal of \$1, where one needs the secret key associated with y to spend the funds. The user spends the funds (or parts thereof) by signing a message that states the amount. In other words, to spend 55 cents of the above dollar, he or she will sign a message saying "55 cents" using the secret key corresponding to y. The recipient of the money will verify the signatures (both that of the user and that of the bank on the public key of the user). He may later deposit the funds with a bank. This bank will then verify the signatures as well, and also verify that the user who withdrew the funds have not issued payments in excess of the withdrawn value. If this holds, then the bank credits the account specified by the participant performing the deposit.

The above payment scheme is best suited for payments that are not very small—55 cents may in fact be in the small range in view of the amount of work that has to be performed to verify the signatures, and so on. A scheme with smaller computational overhead is as follows:

The user selects a random value r_n and computes $r_{n-1} = h(r_n)$, where h is a hash function. He or she, then iteratively computes $r_i = h(r_{i+1})$ for $0 < i < n$. This results in a "hash chain" of length $n+1$ (i.e., one with a known endpoint and n values that are preimages to the endpoint. Let us assume that $n = 100$).

The user then obtains a bank signature on the end value r_1, and the value of the withdrawal, say \$1. He or she does not show the bank any of the other values of the chain.

To pay a recipient, the user gives him or her the preimage to r_1 (i.e., the value r_2). The recipient can verify whether this is correct by computing $h(r_2)$ and comparing this to r_1. This corresponds to a payment of 1 cent, because all $n = 100$ values together are worth \$1. To pay another cent, the user will reveal the value r_3, which can be verified by hashing it, and compare the result to the known value r_2. To pay 2 cents after that, he or she gives r_5. The recipient then applies the hash function twice and compares it to the last known value on the chain. The recipient can deposit a sequence of payments by sending the last one to the bank. The bank can then hash it the appropriate number of times and compare the result to r_1 (or the last deposited value on the chain). If they agree, then the bank credits the participant who performed the deposit with the corresponding amount. This scheme is referred to as PayWord and was proposed by Rivest and Shamir (1996).

In PayWord, the user will know that nobody can steal his or her money by forging payments on his or her behalf. This is so because nobody can find hash preimages to the values that are public, given the assumption on the hash function. In the above, we assume that the user stores all the values $r_1 \ldots r_n$. This is, in fact, not necessary: he or she can instead store only r_n and then compute the wanted value from this by applying a hash function the appropriate number of times. Note that he or she cannot compute a value r_2 from r_1, or r_3 from r_2, and so on, as this requires inverting the hash function. Whereas storing a long chain may be expensive in terms of storage, computing

consecutive preimages of a long chain will be computationally demanding. A solution that minimizes both of these costs was suggested by Coppersmith and Jakobsson. That construction is also a good example of a protocol that only involves only one participant—the participant who needs to generate the sequence of hashed values.

Achieving Privacy and Privacy Control
Payments Patterns
In the payment schemes described above, there is no privacy from the bank. In other words, if the bank issuing the funds also receives the deposit, it will know exactly where the user in question spent his or her money. This is so because it will know to what merchant account it was later deposited. At the same time, the bank will know who withdrew the funds—at least by a pseudonym—because the withdrawal needs to be done from an account, and the account holder needs to prove that he or she has access rights to it. Although pseudonyms can be helpful in hiding the real identity of the user, there are ways in which a pseudonym can be associated with the real identity. For example, anybody paying his or her phone bill is with a big likelihood revealing this link, because people typically pay their *own* phone bills and not that of others, and the phone number is associated with a name. Similarly, having anything shipped to your address will reveal the link. To offer a better degree of privacy for payment schemes, several solutions have been proposed.

One such solution uses what is called "blind signatures." A blind signature can be generated only by somebody who has the secret signing key. After it has been generated, it can be "unblinded" by the party who requested it. The result of the unblinding is a valid signature, but one that cannot be related to the blind signature. To the signer, a particular unblinded signature will be equally likely to correspond to the actual request during which it was generated as to another request. We do not describe how to generate blind signatures here but instead refer the interested reader to other chapters of this book and to the article by Chaum (1983), in which the concept was first proposed.

Using blind signatures, one can get perfect privacy. The user would identify him- or herself to withdraw money from his or her account and would then blind the message to be signed. This would be sent to the bank, who would debit the bank account and generate the blind signature. This would be unblinded by the user, who later can spend the money in the same way as described before. When the money gets deposited with the bank, the bank can verify the validity of the signature, but cannot determine from what withdrawal it stems.

One concern with the above proposal is that because the user specifies the message, he or she then blinds it. He or she could ask the bank to withdraw just a dollar from his or her account, but let the message state that the digital signature corresponds to \$100—or any amount for that matter. This would enable him to spend up to that amount while having only \$1 debited from his account. Of course, this is not very appealing to the bank. To avoid this, the bank could use different public and secret keys to sign messages. It would use one key pair for \$1 withdrawals, one for $5 withdrawals, one for $50, and so on. To withdraw $56, one would withdraw one of each of the above types or some other combination that adds up to the correct amount. Then, the value would not be part of the message; only the public key associated with the funds would. The user can state whatever message he or she wishes—this corresponds to the public key used only for spending the money, and if he or she "cheats" by using the "wrong" message, then he or she simply prevents him- or herself from spending the money.

Another, much more serious, concern is that a criminal would force an honest user to withdraw money from his or her account in a way that is blinded both from the bank and the honest user—but not to the attacker! That can be done simply by having the attacker prepare the message and the blinded version and then forwarding this to the honest user, who would (under threat) request to make a withdrawal, send the blinded message, and forward the resulting blinded signature to the attacker. The attacker would then unblind it and later be able to spend the money in a way that cannot be traced back to him or her or the attack. Many proposals have been made to avoid this type of threat; some of these are described by von Solms and Naccache (1992) and Jakobsson and Yung (1996).

Traffic Analysis
Encryption is used to prevent an eavesdropper from determining what two communicating parties say to each other. In many situations, though, it may not matter so much what people say as the fact that they are communicating. For example, if one person repeatedly communicates with a known criminal; this very fact is enough to suspect that he or she is also criminal—reading the plaintext messages may confirm this, but is not necessary to establish a suspicion. In this case, the "eavesdropper" may be law enforcement. The technique of determining who is communicating with whom is referred to as *traffic analysis*. There are other cases where the party attempting to do traffic analysis is on the other side of the law. Examples of this relate to finding out what electronic votes were cast by whom, determining what Web pages people browse, and determining purchase patterns. There are several ways of preventing traffic analysis by making it impossible for an eavesdropper to do any better than guessing when it comes to who originated a given message or what message a given person sent. We review some of these techniques next.

The Chaumian Mix
A mix network is run by a series of servers, each of which takes a collection of ciphertexts as input, reorders these and decrypts them, and output this new collection of items. These items are also ciphertexts, unless the process of decrypting, permuting, and forwarding has completed. They are given to the next server, who again permutes them and decrypts them. For each server, the order the appearance of the items changes—the latter because the removal of one layer of encryption. This way, an eavesdropper who sees all input items and all output items will not be able to determine their correspondence. That is, unless he or she corrupts the server that performed the operation on them—if he or she does, then he or she will know

the exact relation between them. However, because there are many servers that each operate on the collections of items, an attacker would need to corrupt all of them to determine the correspondence between inputs and outputs.

To take a little bit more detailed look at this technique, we assume that all messages to be sent are encrypted many times; first with a first public key and then with a second, a third, and so on up to an nth public key. The last public key used for encryption belongs to the first server in the line, the second to the last key belongs to the second server, and so on. Therefore, the last layer of encryption to be added is removed first and then the second to last. The last server in the mix network owns the first public key used, and he or she outputs the original message. Of course, and as described above, the servers also randomly reorder all items as they forward them.

Let us see how this can be used. Say that there are some large numbers of voters. Each voter specifies what candidate he or she wants to vote for and then encrypts this message. He or she then encrypts the resulting ciphertext and then encrypts *that* ciphertext and so on. In the end, each voter has an item that has been encrypted some specific number of times, say n times. Everybody encrypts their votes the same number of times, and this number is of course known by everybody. The public keys used for encryption correspond—in reverse order—to the public keys of the servers of the mix network. These multiply encrypted votes are then given to the first server, who permutes, decrypts, and sends the results to the second server and so on. In the end, the nth server outputs a collection of plaintext messages: these are the votes! Here, it is not possible to determine who voted for whom.

This type of mix network is sometimes referred to as a Chaumian mix, after the researcher who first proposed the idea, David Chaum (1981).

Reencryption Mixes
One drawback of a Chaumian mix is that each time an item is encrypted, it typically grows a little, and so the multiply encrypted message may become somewhat large. This is because one needs to attach a random pad before each encryption, or otherwise one could determine what inputs to the mix network corresponds to what outputs simply by encrypting the outputs. Another drawback is that all the public keys of the mix servers have to be used in the right order. If one of the servers is down or refuses to collaborate, then the mixing cannot complete unless its secret decryption key is collectively known by some other set of servers (i.e., it is *shared*, as was described before). However, probably the biggest drawback is that one server may decide to remove any number of items and replace them with items of a similar format. That way, he or she can encrypt the names of candidates he or she favors and replace the same number of (arbitrarily selected) ciphertexts with these. He or she would then decrypt, permute, and forward, and nobody would know about the replacement, assuming he or she added the appropriate number of "encryption layers" to the new votes. Of course, although this attack cannot be detected, people may suspect that it took place if all the votes are for one candidate, so the attacker would replace only a sufficient number of votes to swing the election in favor of his or her preferred candidate.

All of these problems can be addressed using what is sometimes referred to as a reencryption mix. In a reencryption mix, the inputs are only encrypted once; that is, there are not multiple layers of encryption. However, there is not one server who knows the corresponding secret key—this is shared between many servers. Also, instead of *decrypting* the input items, they perform *reencryption* (as described before). After all the servers have permuted and reencrypted, the resulting list of outputs are still ciphertexts: they have not been decrypted. They would then be decrypted by some set of servers, potentially the same set, but without the need for any permutation. The decryption would be performed in several steps, as the secret keys for decryption would be shared between several servers, possibly using a proactive secret sharing scheme as described above. The decryption process would be done similarly to how we showed in the last protocol in the section, "Proving Equivalence." One can see that the size of the input ciphertexts does not depend on the number of servers.

Note that the above approach does not address the problem with replacement of ciphetexts. Therefore, as servers reencrypt and permute the ciphertexts, they also have to prove equivalence between all input items and all output items, using a proof of correct exponentiation or reencryption. We have shown before how to do that to one given ciphertext. Here, the problem is a little bit more complex because the server needs to avoid showing the correspondence between input items and output items—otherwise there will be no protection against traffic analysis.

Many ways of doing this have been proposed. One of the conceptually simpler versions is that each server shows how some fraction of all inputs were operated on to produce the corresponding outputs. The correspondence between these items are therefore revealed, but not that of the remaining items. All the other servers together select what items a given server should "open up." That means that a server will not know beforehand what items will be audited and, therefore, he or she will be caught with a big probability if he or she tries to modify a large number of items. For example, in an election with 1 million voters, he or she can change exactly one vote and get a way with it with probability 50% (if half of all items are audited). He or she can cheat on 2 items with probability 25%, and on 10 items with probability less than 1 in a 1,000. Similarly, he or she can cheat on 20 items with a probability less than 1 in a million. This provides a very high degree of assurance that the election results are correct, given that it is likely to be necessary to corrupt much more than 20 votes to swing a standard election with a million voters. This scheme was proposed by Jakobsson, Juels, and Rivest (2002), and more details are provided in their article, along with a more detailed analysis of the failure probabilities. There are other, more complicated, solutions that make it impossible to replace even one of the ciphertexts without being detected (see, for example, the scheme by Abe, 1999).

Crowds

An alterative to mix networks is a system referred to as "crowds," a concept proposed by Reiter and Rubin (1998). You can think of that as a group of participants that want to protect each other's privacy. When one of them wants to send a message somewhere, he or she instead sends it to one of the members of the group. This member either sends it to its destination or passes it on to another group member. This third group member, in turn, sends it to either its destination or to a fourth group member and so on. The group members that messages are forwarded to are chosen randomly. This way, an outside observer will not know where a given message originated: it could be from anybody in the group. Similarly, group members would not know either, as they may get the message either from the originator or from somebody who just passed it on. Clearly, the size of the group impacts the degree of privacy offered by this solution in the same way as the number of messages input to a mix network affects the privacy of each message. If there are only two group members in crowds, an outsider would be able to guess who the originator is with 50% probability, and there would be no "internal" hiding of the origin within the group. However, for reasonably large groups (or crowds) of participants, the privacy is reasonable. Depending on the application this is used for, encryption or reencryption techniques may be used in conjunction with the above idea. It may not be practical for an election because it requires all group members (voters) to be available for each other, but it does suit applications such as Web browsing.

Fair Exchange

A fair exchange is a technique that allows two participants to exchange information in a manner that prevents one of them from cheating the other in a way that gets the cheater the information he or she wanted but leaves his or her victim without the information he or she expected. An example situation is where two participants want to sign a contract simultaneously. Neither participant wants the other to be able to walk away with a signed contract before he or she also has one. Another possible application is the exchange of (digital) money: one participant has a certain number of electronic dollar coins and the other a matching number of electronic yen coins. They want to exchange these for each another in a way that prevents either party from not fulfilling his or her part of the deal. In fact, this situation is technically very similar to the contract exchange example, because both an electronic coin and a contract typically would use a digital signature to authenticate its authenticity. The problem therefore often becomes one of exchanging digital signatures in a way that prevents one party from getting the other's signature without sending over his or her own.

The simplest solution to this problem is to involve a trusted third party who will receive both signatures, verify their correctness, and then send them out to their recipients at the same time. Sometimes, though, it is not reasonable to expect the existence of such a trusted third party, and other solutions are preferable. Another type of solution does involve a trusted third party, but only if something goes wrong. The main structure of such a protocol is as follows:

1. Participant A encrypts his or her signature s_A and a description of what he or she wants in return, using

the trustee's public key. He or she sends the resulting ciphertext to participant B.

2. Participant B sends his or her signature s_B to participant A.
3. Participant A sends his or her signature s_A to participant B.

Now, if participant A refuses to perform the third step, then participant B will send the ciphertext to the trusted party, along with s_B. The trusted party will decrypt the ciphertext and verify that s_B is the signature A wants in exchange. He or she will then send s_A to B and s_B to A.

In reality, the protocol is a bit more complicated. Namely one has to protect against A's cheating by producing a ciphertext on some useless information. Then he or she would stop intentionally at the end of the second step, successfully having cheated participant B. Therefore, A has to prove to B that the ciphertext "contains" the correct plaintext—but without revealing the exact contents of the ciphertext. (Doing so would allow B to cheat.) For more details on how this could be done, please see a detailed description in the article by Asokan, Shoup, and Waidner (1998).

Broadcast Authentication

In many situations, there is a small number of senders who wants to transmit data to a large number of recipients. The recipients want to know that the data are authentic, that is, that the data were indeed sent by the claimed sender.

One could use digital signatures for this purpose and let each sender digitally sign each message that he or she sends. However, digital signatures are relatively expensive to produce and verify, and the typical verifier in this kind of setting may not have a lot of computational power. Conversely, one may use MACs to authenticate each message. This is considerably less expensive because it uses only a symmetric cryptography operation as opposed to a asymmetric (or public key) operation. However, because each message is to be received by a very large number of participants, it is not convenient to attach one MAC for each recipient to each message. At the same time, one cannot send the same MAC to many recipients interested in verifying its correctness. The reason is that whoever can verify a MAC can also produce it. Giving the verification key to many recipients would therefore allow one cheating receiver to potentially impersonate the sender and make other recipients believe that fake messages were authentic.

A solution to the above problem is the TESLA protocol, introduced by Perrig, Canetti, Tygar, and Song (2002). In this, a large number of symmetric keys are produced as follows: first, an "end point" key is selected at random. Then, a one-way function (such as a hash) of this key is computed, and the result is a second key. A third key is produced by hashing the second key and so on. In this way, some n keys are produced. (This is therefore the same structure as is used in PayWord, as previously described.) This is all done by the participant who will later want to authenticate his or her messages. The last key to be produced, we may call this k_n, is made public.

To authenticate a first message, the sender uses key k_{n-1} to compute the MAC. He or she sends the message and the MAC to everybody, but nobody can verify it. Then, some time later, he or she sends the key k_{n-1} to everybody. Now, they can verify the MAC. They also verify that this key is correct by hashing it and comparing the result to key k_n. The next time the sender wishes to transmit an authenticated message, he or she uses key k_{n-2} to MAC it and later transmits this key as well. More specifically, each time interval (of, say, 5 s) is associated with one key used for MAC-ing. In this interval, the key two time intervals back is revealed (two steps as opposed to one to avoid synchronization problems). Because everybody will know the release schedule, nobody will accept an authentication that uses a key that has already been released. This is important, of course, because potentially anybody knows this key.

To do this, the sender can have stored all the keys in the sequence, which is referred to as a hash chain. Alternatively, he or she can store only one value: the one that was used to generate all the others. Then, when he or she needs a specific key, he or she would compute this from the "original" key by applying a hash function the appropriate number of times. The first approach has the drawback of requiring a potentially very large amount of storage, if the chain is long. The latter will force the sender to perform a lot of computation for each key he or she wishes to compute. This is so because he or she will have to compute keys in the reverse order they were initially produced, and hash functions are believed not to be invertible. Thus, he or she has to perform all the steps from the original key each time. If he or she stores some fraction of keys in between, he or she increases the storage by that number. In the end, the product of the amount of storage and the number of hash function computations remains more or less the same. An approach that avoids both the excessive computational requirements and the excessive storage requirements was described by Coppersmith and Jakobsson (2003). This way, TESLA remains highly efficient even for very long chains.

GLOSSARY

Adversary When designing a cryptographic protocol, we need to consider the ways in which it potentially can be abused. A common technique is to consider how one or more protocol participants, all controlled by one adversary, can cause the incorrect computation to be performed.

Authentication A way for one protocol participant to convince another of his or her identity. Typically, this is linked to a message sent between these two participants, in which case we say that this message is authenticated. There are authentication schemes that are symmetric (e.g., MACs), and there are those that are asymmetric (e.g., digital signatures.)

Ciphertext The data conveying an encrypted message.

Decryption The process of obtaining a readable message (a *plaintext*) from an encrypted transformation of the message (a *ciphertext*).

Diffie–Hellman A public key cryptosystem used to exchange a secret (symmetric) key.

El Gamal An encryption technique (named after its inventor) often used in mix networks.

Encryption The process of rendering a message (a *plaintext*) into a data string (a *ciphertext*) with the aim of transmitting it privately in a potentially hostile environment.

Fair Exchange A cryptographic technique to protect two or more protocol participants against each other's potential misbehavior, thereby ensuring that each participant obtains the information he or she expects at the end of the protocol execution.

Key A short data string parameterizing the operations within a cipher or cryptosystem, and whose distribution determines relationships of privacy and integrity among communicating parties.

Key Pair The combination of a public and private key.

Malicious An adversary may perform actions that hurt others even if they do not benefit him- or herself.

Mix Network An anonymity construction built from a series of mix servers, each of which perform some reordering and reencryption/encryption/decryption of input ciphertexts before passing the resulting ciphertexts on to the next mix server.

Plaintext A message in readable form, prior to encryption or subsequent to successful decryption.

Private Key In an asymmetric or public key cryptosystem, the key that a communicating party holds privately and uses for decryption or completion of a key exchange.

Public Key In an asymmetric or public key cryptosystem, the key that a communicating party disseminates publicly. In the context of encryption, a type of cryptographic system in which a participant publishes an encryption key and keeps private a separate decryption key. These keys are respectively referred to as public and private. RSA and Diffie–Hellman are examples of public key systems. *Public key* is synonymous with *asymmetric*.

Reencryption The process of generating a new ciphertext from an old ciphertext in a way that the two ciphertexts correspond to the same plaintext but look different. Here, different typically means that one cannot determine whether they correspond to the same plaintext without decrypting both.

RSA A public key cryptosystem in very wide use today, as in the SSL (secure sockets layer) protocol. RSA can also be used to create and verify digital signatures.

Secret Sharing A way to partition information so that a small portion of the pieces does not reveal the information in question, whereas a sufficiently large portion does. This required number of pieces is referred to as the threshold of the secret sharing scheme.

Symmetric A type of cryptographic system in which communicating parties employ shared secret keys. The term is also used to refer to the keys employed in such a system.

Traffic Analysis Determining who is communicating with whom. Often this type of analysis reveals plenty of information about the relationships between protocol participants, even to a party who cannot determine what plaintext messages are sent between the communicating parties.

Zero Knowledge A way of performing a cryptographic proof, guaranteeing that no secret information is leaked to the verifier of the proof. This is often proven by demonstrating a simulator of the proof; this is an algorithm that produces transcripts that cannot be distinguished from real protocol transcripts when inspected by a third party.

CROSS REFERENCES

See *Computer and Network Authentication Encryption Basics Hashes and Message Digests*.

REFERENCES

Abe, M. (1999). Mix-networks on permutation networks. In *Lecture Notes in Computer Science, vol. 1716: Advances in Cryptology—Proceedings of Asiacrypt '99* (pp. 258–273). New York: Springer-Verlag.

Asokan, N., Shoup, V., & Waidner, M. (1998). Asynchronous protocols for optimistic fair exchange. In *Proceedings of the IEEE Symposium on Research in Security and Privacy* (pp. 86–99). IEEE Press.

Bellare, M., Canetti, R., & Krawczyk, H. (1996). Message authentication using hash functions—The HMAC construction. *RSA Laboratories' CryptoBytes, 2*(1).

Brands, S. (1994). Untraceable off-line cash in wallet with observers. In Stinson, D. R. (ed.), *Lecture notes in computer science, vol. 773: Advances in Cryptology—Proceedings of Crypto '93* (pp. 302–318). New York: Springer-Verlag.

Chaum, D. (1983). Blind signatures for untraceable payments. In Chaum, D., Rivest, R. L., & Sherman, A. T. (eds.), *Advances in Cryptology: Proceedings of Crypto '82* (pp. 199–203). New York: Plenum Press.

Chaum, D. (1991). Zero-knowledge undeniable signatures. In *Lecture notes in computer science, vol. 473* (pp. 458–464). New York: Springer-Verlag.

Chaum, D. L. (1981). Untraceable electronic mail, return addresses, and digital pseudonyms. *Communications of the ACM, 24*(2), 84–88.

Coppersmith, D., & Jakobsson, M. (2003). Almost optimal hash sequence traversal. In *Lecture notes in computer science, vol. 2357: Financial cryptography* (pp. 102–119). New York: Springer-Verlag.

Herzberg, A., Jarecki, S., Krawczyk, H., & Yung, M. T. (1995). Proactive secret sharing or: How to cope with perpetual leakage. In *Lecture notes in computer science, vol. 963: Advances in Cryptology—Crypto '95* (pp. 339–352). New York: Springer-Verlag.

Jakobsson, M., Juels, A., & Rivest, R. (2002). *Making mix nets robust for electronic voting by randomized partial checking.* In Boneh, D. (ed.), *USENIX'02* (pp. 339–353).

Jakobsson, M., & Yung, M. (1996). Proving without knowing: On oblivious, agnostic and blindfolded provers. In *Lecture notes in computer science, vol. 1109: Advances in Cryptology–Crypto '96* (pp. 186–200). New York: Springer-Verlag.

Jakobsson, M., & Yung, M. (1996). Revokable and versatile electronic money. In Neuman, C. (ed.), *Proceedings of the 3rd ACM Conference on Computer and Communications Security* (pp. 76–87). ACM Press.

National Institute of Standards and Technology, U.S. Department of Commerce. (1995). *FIPS 180-1, Secure Hash Standard*. April 1995.

Perrig, A., Canetti, R., Tygar, J. D., & Song, D. (2002). The TESLA broadcast authentication protocol. *RSA Laboratories' CryptoBytes, 5*(2), 2–13.

Reiter, M. K., & Rubin, A. D. (1998). Crowds: Anonymity for Web transactions. *ACM Transactions on Information and System Security, 1*, 66–92.

Rivest, R. (1992). *The MD5 Message-Digest Algorithm*. RFC 1321.

Rivest, R. L., & Shamir, A. (1996). PayWord and MicroMint: Two simple micropayment schemes. In *Security Protocols Workshop* (pp. 69–87).

RSA Laboratories. (2004). *Frequently asked questions about today's cryptography*. Retrieved January 3, 2004, from http://rsasecurity.com/rsalabs/faq/index.html

Schneier, B. (1996). *Applied cryptography: Protocols, algorithms, and source code in C* (2nd ed.). New York: John Wiley & Sons.

Schnorr, C. P. (1991). Efficient signature generation by smart cards. *Journal of Cryptology, 4*(3) 161–174.

Shamir, A. (1979). How to share a secret. *Communications of the ACM, 22*(11) 612–613.

von Solms, S., & Naccache, D. (1992). On blind signatures and perfect crimes. *Computers and Security, 11*(6), 581–583.

FURTHER READING

The reader interested in more detailed treatment of the topics discussed here need go no further than this handbook. Subsequent chapters offer details on most aspects of cryptography. However, for the reader interested in other reading material, we recommend two introductory books on the field of cryptology, namely *Applied Cryptography* (Schneier, 1996) and the online compendium *Frequently Asked Questions About Today's Cryptography* (RSA Laboratories, 2004). Both describe common protocols, along with what these are intended to be used for. In addition, the reader interested in specific details in the protocols described in this chapter is recommended to look at the articles listed in the bibliography, many of which are relatively accessible to nonexperts.

Quantum Cryptography

G. Massimo Palma, *Università degli Studi di Milano, Italy*

INTRODUCTION

Quantum cryptography is the name under which are commonly known those techniques that make use of the laws of quantum mechanics to prevent the unauthorized access to secret information. The most celebrated of such protocols, whose description is the main scope of this section, is quantum key distribution, undoubtedly the most successful quantum information processing protocol from the technological viewpoint. Quantum key distribution is a scheme that allows two remote parties to share a common secret random string of bits even in the presence of an adverse party who tries to eavesdrop. As discussed shortly, it solves the problem of secure distribution of private cryptographic keys by allowing the detection of any eavesdropping.

Quantum key distribution is historically the first quantum information processing protocol. Some of the ideas behind it were implicitly suggested by Stefan Wiesner, who proposed "quantum tokens which cannot be forged," later published in Wiesner (1983). The first quantum cryptographic protocol, however, was put forward in 1984 by Charles Bennett and Gilles Brassard (Bennett & Brassard, 1984). In this protocol, the ingredients used to guarantee security are the use of single quanta to encode bits, the Heisenberg uncertainty principle, which implies the impossibility of knowing the polarization of a single photon along two different polarization axes, and the quantum no-cloning theorem (i.e., the impossibility of making a faithful copy of a single unknown quantum state; Wootters & Zurek, 1982). It is indeed the disturbance introduced by any eavesdropping on the signal used to encode the key bits that makes possible the detection of any intrusion. The use of a further ingredient, namely quantum entanglement, was first proposed by Ekert in 1991. Entanglement is the property of quantum systems composed of two or more subsystems to show stronger nonlocal correlation between its subsystems than compatible with the laws of classical physics. Although entanglement is not essential for the implementation of quantum cryptographic schemes its use allows new strategies for the detection of unwanted eavesdropping. Since the publication of the above seminal articles the field has reached an astonishing degree of sophistication in a very short time. Great progress has been made on both the theoretical side, with

very detailed analysis of eavesdropping strategies and of security criteria on both the two original protocols as well as on their several variations, and on the experimental side, with several preindustrial prototypes for the secure distribution of cryptographic keys in local networks of optical fibers of nearly 100 km. In the following pages, we describe the basic concepts and techniques of quantum key distribution for a readership with no previous knowledge of quantum mechanics and suggest the essential reading for further, more detailed, study.

The typical scenario of all quantum key distribution protocols is the following: two remote parties, traditionally called Alice and Bob, want to establish a secret random binary string to be later used as private cryptographic key. They have at their disposal a private quantum channel and a public classical channel. The private quantum channel is used to exchange a sequence of single quanta. Because of the properties of quantum systems any attempt to intercept and measure such quanta will modify their state. The public classical channel is used to exchange information and can be passively eavesdropped. The fact that eavesdropping on the public channel cannot be detected does not compromise the security of the protocol, as shown shortly. It is important, however, that the public channel must be authenticated (i.e. at some stage Alice and Bob must acknowledge each other as the legitimate parties). A malicious eavesdropper, traditionally called Eve in the literature, may "cut" the public channel pretending to be Bob with Alice and Alice with Bob. If such a man-in-the-middle attack were successful Eve would have two keys, one in common with Alice and the other in common with Bob. To prevent this Alice and Bob use an authentication procedure requiring the use of a previously shared short secret key. This may seem a sort of catch-22 situation in which a key is needed to establish a key. The situation is slightly different. It is true that Alice and Bob must initially share a short secret classical key, but this is needed only once. Indeed at the end of a successful quantum distribution session Alice and Bob share a key much longer than the one used for authentication and they can agree to keep a short part of it for authentication in a subsequent session. In this sense, quantum key distribution is a process of cryptographic key growth.

PUBLIC VERSUS PRIVATE KEY CRYPTOSYSTEMS

Cryptography is the art of concealing information in transit. In the typical scenario, the sender, Alice, wants to send a secret message, from now on called plaintext, to a legitimate receiver, Bob. To this goal Alice encrypts the plaintext into a cyphertext by mean of an encryption algorithm with the help of some secret additional information, called key. The cyphertext must be unintelligible to any unauthorized party and only Bob, who shares the key with Alice, should be able to recover the plaintext from the cyphertext by mean of a decryption algorithm.

Present-day cryptographic protocols can be divided into two categories: private key and public key cryptosystem. The basic idea behind public key cryptosystems, known also as asymmetric cryptosystems, is that the key used to encrypt the message need not be the same one used to decrypt it. One such protocol is RSA. The security of public key cryptosystem relies on the existence of problems that are difficult to solve—such as factoring large numbers—unless some additional information is available.

The security of public key cryptosystems is acceptable for most purposes. As their security is based on the unproved computational complexity of some problems (e.g., it is not known if no classical algorithm can solve the factoring problem in polynomial time), the degree of privacy they provide is acceptable when the time required to decrypt the cyphertext is longer than the time over which the information it contains is sensitive or when the value of the resources needed to decrypt the message is bigger than the value of the information gained. Furthermore, a quantum algorithm—the Shor algorithm—is known to solve the factoring problem in polynomial time. Although it is not yet foreseeable a date by which the first quantum computer will be on our desks, this is a potential danger when highly secret information must be protected.

Private key cryptosystems are used when Alice and Bob want to exchange highly sensitive information whose secrecy must be above doubt. In such cryptosystems, the keys used in the encryption and in the decryption algorithms are the same. The algorithms themselves are public and the security is guaranteed by the secrecy of the key. A description of the Vernam cipher or one time pad illustrates the idea. In this cryptosystem the plaintext is converted into a binary string. The key is also a (secret) random binary string and the encryption algorithm consists in the sum modulo two of the plaintext and the key. The decryption algorithm consists again in a sum modulo two of the cyphertext and the key. Because the sum modulo 2 is associative and the sum of any string with itself is identically zero, it is clear that the decryption algorithm gives back the plaintext. Three requirements are strictly necessary to guarantee security of the one time pad: the key must be (1) a truly random string of length equal to the plaintext, (2) used only once, and (3) secret.

If the above requirements are met then, as shown by Shannon (1946), the information gained by Eve when she intercepts the cyphertext is zero. This can be easily understood by noting that the XOR of any binary string with a random binary string of equal length is itself random. If the key is not random, or if it is used more than once, then some periodicity in the statistical properties of the cyphertext may appear, thus revealing some information about the key. If, for instance, the key is used twice, then Eve, by doing the XOR of two intercepted cyphertexts, can eliminate the key and obtain the XOR of two plaintexts, which is no longer random and contains valuable information. The above description of classical cryptosystems is a rather simple one and is aimed simply to setting the scenario for quantum cryptosystems. A more detailed description of classical cryptosystems can be found in other sections of the present *Handbook*, in particular in the chapters on encryption basics, symmetric key encryption, public key infrastructures, and data encryption standard.

It is clear that the difficult point in the implementation of public key cryptosystems is the key distribution. At some stage, before transmitting their secret messages, Alice and Bob must agree on a common secret key. In most circumstances, they exchange the key by means of a trustworthy courier. This procedure, however, is not without drawbacks. For instance, there is no guarantee that Eve has not read the key while it is being exchanged. Quantum key distribution provides a solution precisely to the key distribution problem, guaranteeing secrecy though the laws of quantum mechanics.

THE PHOTON POLARIZATION AND THE RULES OF QUANTUM MECHANICS

To introduce the principles and language of quantum mechanics used in quantum cryptographic protocols, we analyze the properties of the photon polarization. This choice is justified not only by the fact that the photon polarization is an excellent case study to introduce all the basic concepts of quantum mechanics but also by the fact that indeed quantum optical systems are the technology used to experimentally implement quantum key distribution.

Classical Polarization

In classical physics monochromatic light is an electromagnetic wave, characterized by an oscillating electric field perpendicular to the direction of propagation of the wave. The light polarization is the plane of oscillation of this electric field (see Figure 1). Linearly polarized light is characterized by a fixed plane of oscillation.

In Figure 2a and 2b a vertically and a horizontally polarized waves are pictorially shown. Because of the superposition principle, more general polarization states can be obtained by suitably superimposing vertically and horizontally polarized waves. For instance, the sum of a vertical and a horizontal wave of equal amplitude gives rise to a wave polarized at $+45°$ if the two waves are in phase or $-45°$ if their phase is opposite (Figure 2c and 2d). Circularly polarized waves (Figure 2e and 2f), in which the direction of the electric field rotates, are obtained by superimposing two orthogonal linearly polarized waves of equal amplitude with a phase difference of $\pi/2$, which means that the horizontal wave reaches is maximum when the amplitude of the vertical one has zero

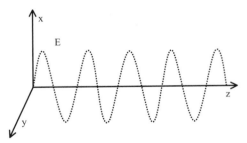

Figure 1: The polarization of an electromagnetic wave is the direction of oscillation of the electric field. Above is shown a vertically polarized monochromatic plane wave at a given time t. The wave propagates in the positive z direction, whereas the electric field E oscillates sinusoidally in the x direction.

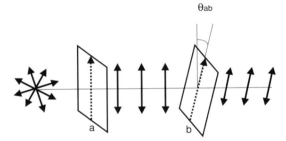

Figure 3: An unpolarized light beam shines on a first polarizer a. The light emerging from the polarizer is polarized along the polarizer axis—the vertical axis in the case of polarizer a. If a second polarizer b is inserted, the light intensity transmitted by b is a factor $\cos^2\theta_{ab}$ less intense than the light transmitted by a.

amplitude and vice versa. The most general polarization state, obtained by the superposition of two orthogonally polarized waves of arbitrary amplitude and phase difference is elliptical. The light emitted by common thermal sources, such as the sun or incandescence lamps, is unpolarized (i.e., its polarization is not fixed but fluctuates over time scales of a few nanoseconds).

A polarizer is an optical device made from a material with anisotropic absorbing properties. When a light beam crosses a polarizer with polarization axis n all the electric field perpendicular to the direction n is absorbed, whereas the field in the direction parallel to n crosses the polarizer entirely undisturbed. Consider now a light beam crossing two polarizers in sequence, with polarization axis a and b, respectively. The light emerging from the first polarizer is polarized along the a direction, whereas the light emerging from the second one is polarized along the b axis. If the angle between the a and b axis is θ_{ab}, the amplitude of the field transmitted by polarizer b is a factor $\cos\theta_{ab}$

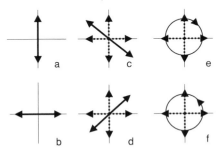

Figure 2: Various polarizations can be obtained by superimposing vertically (a) and horizontally (b) polarized waves. Superposing two waves of equal amplitude with a 0 or π phase difference produces a linearly polarized wave along the 45° (c) or −45° (d) direction. Analogously a left circular (e) or right circular (f) polarization is obtained by superimposing a vertical and a horizontal wave of equal amplitude with a phase difference of $\pi/2$ or $-\pi/2$ respectively.

smaller than the amplitude of the light transmitted by the first polarizer a. As the light intensity is proportional to the square of the electromagnetic field, we immediately obtain Malus's law: $I_T = I_0 \cos^2\theta$ (i.e., the intensity I_T of the light transmitted by a polarizer is equal to the incident intensity I_0 diminished by a factor $\cos^2\theta$, where θ is the angle between the polarization of the incident light and the polarizer axis).

Another interesting device is the beam splitter (BS). A light beam entering a BS is split into a transmitted and a reflected beam. Because of the conservation of energy, the sum of the transmitted and reflected intensities is equal to the intensity of the incident beam. Of particular interest is the 50% BS, in which the transmitted and reflected beams have equal intensity.

Finally, a polarizing beam splitter (PBS) is a beam splitter that reflects or transmits light depending on the polarization of the incident light. If the polarization of the incoming light is parallel to the PBS axis, the beam is transmitted, whereas if it is polarized in its orthogonal direction, it is reflected. In general, if θ is the angle between the polarization of the incoming light beam and the PBS axis n, the transmitted beam has an intensity $I_T = I_0 \cos^2\theta$ and is polarized along n, whereas the reflected light has an intensity $I_R = I_0 \sin^2\theta$ and is polarized along the direction perpendicular to n.

Quantum Polarization

In quantum terms, a light beam is described, crudely speaking, as a beam of indivisible massless particles called photons, all traveling at the speed of light c and with energy proportional to the frequency of the field. Here the term *particle* is not to suggest a material point but rather a quantum of energy. The intensity of the field is proportional to the number of photons in the beam. Each photon is characterized by its own polarization. A polarized light beam is one in which all photons have the same polarization, whereas in an unpolarized beam, the polarization of each photon is fixed in time but randomly distributed.

Photons polarized along a given axis cross undisturbed a polarizer with the same polarization axis, whereas they are absorbed by a polarizer with orthogonal polarization

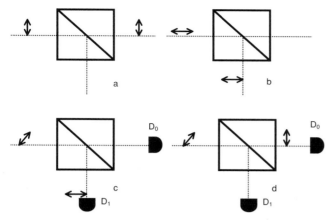

Figure 4: A polarizing beam splitter (PBS) with vertical axis is shown. In such a device a vertically polarized light beam is transmitted (a), whereas a horizontally polarized light beam is reflected (b). If a light beam with intensity I, polarized at an angle θ with respect to the vertical direction, is shone on the PBS, a vertically polarized fraction with intensity $I\cos^2\theta$ is transmitted, whereas a horizontally polarized fraction with intensity $I\sin^2\theta$ is reflected. At a single photon level, this means that each photon of the beam is either reflected (c) with probability $\sin^2\theta$ or transmitted (d) with probability $\cos^2\theta$. Note that in both cases the polarization of the incident photon, originally at an angle θ, changes abruptly, becoming either vertical if transmitted of horizontal if reflected. This is an example of projective quantum measurement.

axis. When a beam of N_0 photons polarized along axis a crosses a polarizer with axis b, a fraction $N_T = N_0 \cos^2\theta_{ab}$ of photons are transmitted, whereas all the others are absorbed. This is nothing but Malus's law, once the intensity is expressed in terms of photon number. Note that because photons are indivisible quanta, each photon is either transmitted or absorbed. The probability that a photon is transmitted is equal to $\cos^2\theta_{ab}$; however, the transmitted photon is no longer polarized in the a direction but in the b direction.

Similarly, a BS does not "split" photons; they are either reflected or transmitted and the conservation of energy becomes simply a conservation of photon number. Finally, when a beam of N_0 photons polarized along axis a enters a PBS with axis b, a fraction $N_T = N_0 \cos^2\theta_{ab}$ of photons is transmitted, whereas a fraction $N_R = N_0 0\sin^2\theta_{ab}$ is reflected. All transmitted photons are polarized along b, whereas all reflected photons are polarized in the direction orthogonal to b, as can easily be verified by placing a polarizer with axis along b in the path of the transmitted beam or with axis in the direction perpendicular to b in the path of the reflected beam.

A PBS can be viewed as a measurement device for photon polarization. Suppose that the beam is so weak that only a single photon at a time crosses a PBS with a photodetector at each output arm, as depicted in Figure 4. Each time a photon arrives either one or the other photodetector clicks, never both at the same time. When it clicks always the same photodetector, say D_0, it means that each photon is polarized in the direction parallel to the PBS axis. When it clicks always D_1, then all the photons

are polarized in the direction orthogonal to the PBS axis. When photons are polarized in any other direction it is not possible to predict which detector will click but only to assign the probability of each detector to click. From what we have said above, it should be clear that it is not possible to determine the polarization of a single photon—a beam with a large number of identical photons is needed to make a statistical analysis of the measurement results.

We now introduce the mathematical formalism needed to describe the quantum properties of photon polarization. To start with let us choose two linear orthogonal polarization axes and call them vertical and horizontal. The state of a single vertically polarized photon is labeled by the symbol $|V>$; the state of a single horizontally polarized photon is labeled by $|H>$. The general state of a single photon with polarization A is described by two complex numbers α_V, α_H and is written in the so-called Dirac notation, as $|A> = \alpha_V|V> + \alpha_H|H>$. The quantities α_V, α_H are called probability amplitudes because the probability that if we measure the photon polarization in the vertical/horizontal direction we obtain a positive answer (i.e., a click in the corresponding detector) that is equal respectively to $|\alpha_V|^2$; $|\alpha_H|^2$. Since either one of the two detectors will click, we must clearly have $|\alpha_V|^2 + |\alpha_H|^2 = 1$. In mathematical terms, therefore, the state of a quantum system, in our case the state of the photon polarization, is described by a complex vector of unit length. Any two orthogonal polarizations form a basis in terms of which the photon polarization state can be expressed. The choice of basis depends on which polarization measurement is made on the photon. For instance, linearly polarized photons along one of the two diagonal axes can be written respectively as follows:

$$|45°> = (|H> + |V>)/\sqrt{2};$$
$$|-45°> = (|H> - |V>)/\sqrt{2}$$

and vice versa

$$|H> = (|45°> + |-45°>)/\sqrt{2};$$
$$|V> = (|45°> - |-45°>)/\sqrt{2}.$$

From now on, we label $\{|H>;|V>\}$ as the (+) basis, whereas we label $\{|45°>;|-45°>\}$ as the (×) basis. It should be clear from the above discussion that, if we measure $|H>$ in the (+) basis, we will obtain always the answer H, whereas if we measure it in the (×) basis, we obtain randomly, with equal probability, $45°$ or $-45°$.

To conclude this section, we introduce the concept of inner product. Given two state vectors $|A> = \alpha_V|V> + \alpha_H|H>$, $|B> = \beta_V|V> + \beta_H|H>$ the inner product $<A|B>$ is defined as $<A|B> = \beta_V \alpha_V^* + \beta_H \alpha_H^*$. Physically $|<A|B>|^2$ is the probability that state $|A>$ will pass the test for being in state $|B>$. There exist linear operators U such that if all the state vectors are transformed by U, all the inner products are unaffected (for real three-dimensional vectors, any rotation operator has this effect). Such operators are called unitary. The time evolution of any closed quantum system (i.e., in the absence of dissipation) is represented by a unitary operator.

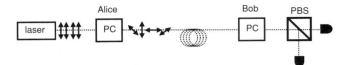

Figure 5: Experimental scheme of BB′84 quantum key distribution protocol. A laser emits a sequence of dim single-photon pulses. By means of a Pockels cell (PC), Alice changes randomly the photon polarization of the photons that are sent to Bob, typically via an optical fiber. Bob chooses randomly his measurement basis by means of a second PC and a PBS.

NONORTHOGONAL STATES QUANTUM KEY DISTRIBUTION PROTOCOLS

We have now all the ingredients to introduce the first quantum key distribution protocol, known as BB′84, after Bennett and Brassard who proposed it in 1984 (Bennett & Brassard, 1984). Here is the scenario: Alice wants to send a secret string to Bob by means of a sequence of polarized photons. To this end, she could use the following coding scheme:

$$0 \rightarrow |V>; 1 \rightarrow |H>,$$

choose randomly between 0 and 1, and send the correspondingly polarized photon to Bob (see Figure 5).

Bob receives the photon and measures its polarization. He can do it without errors, provided he knows in advance which polarization basis Alice has used, by means of a PBS and two photodetectors, as shown in Figure 4. If the axis of Bob's PBS is vertical then whenever he detects a transmitted photon, he knows that Alice has sent a 0, and whenever he measures a reflected photon he knows that Alice has sent a 1. The reader can easily find the weakness of the above scheme. A malicious eavesdropper, Eve, could intercept the photon, measure it, and resend a photon correspondingly polarized to Bob. There would be no way for Alice and Bob to detect the presence of Eve and therefore the above scheme would be totally insecure.

However, as first shown by Bennett and Brassard, the introduction of additional randomness into the protocol is enough to make it secure. Indeed it is enough for Alice not to encode her random bits always on the same basis but to switch randomly between the $\{|H>; |V>\}$ (+) basis and the $\{|45°>; |-45°>\}$ (×) basis. The protocol works as follows: Alice chooses a random string of bits and encodes

them choosing randomly between the (+) and the (×) basis. In other words, the qubits are coded as follows:

$$0 \rightarrow |45°>; 1 \rightarrow |-45°>,$$

or

$$0 \rightarrow |V>; 1 \rightarrow |H>,$$

according to the randomly chosen basis. The photons are then sent through a private quantum channel to Bob, who measures them. However, now Bob does not know which basis was randomly chosen by Alice and therefore he can only choose randomly how to align the PBS of his measuring apparatus. Half of the times his measurement basis will coincide with the basis chosen by Alice. In this case, the result of his measurement will coincide with the bit sent by Alice. Whenever Bob's measurement basis differs from Alice's, however, the results of his measurements are entirely uncorrelated with the bits sent by Alice. At this stage of the protocol, in the absence of Eve, Alice and Bob share two strings whose bits have a 50% chance of being correlated. To discard the uncorrelated bits, Alice announces on a public classical channel the basis used to encode her bits. Bob then announces publicly in which instances his measurement basis coincides with Alice's but keeps secret the result of the measurement. In the absence of Eve, at this stage of the protocol Alice and Bob share a secret random string of bits, known as sifted key. An example of possible sequence is shown in Figure 6.

Let us turn our attention now to the consequences of the presence of Eve. The simplest eavesdropping strategy, known as the intercept-and-resend strategy, consists in intercepting the photons Alice sends to Bob, to measure their polarization and then to resend to Bob a photon with the same measured polarization. Since Eve, like Bob, does not know which basis was randomly chosen by Alice to polarize her photons, she can only make a random choice of measurement basis. She has a 50% chance of measuring in the right basis, in which case Bob receives from Eve a photon with the same polarization originally chosen by Alice and therefore cannot detect Eve's presence. With a 50% chance, however, Eve's basis choice is wrong, in which case the result of her measurement has no correlation whatsoever with the polarization of Alice's photon. The consequences of this are twofold. First of all Eve gains no knowledge from her measurement. Furthermore, her measurement modifies irreversibly the state of Alice's photon and therefore even when Bob measures it

Alice's basis	+	+	×	+	×	+	×	+	+	+	×	+	×	×
Alice's bits	1	0	0	1	1	0	0	0	1	0	0	1	0	1
Alice's photons	H	V	45°	H	-45°	V	45°	V	H	V	45°	H	45°	-45°
Bob's basis	+	×	×	+	+	×	×	×	+	×	×	+	+	×
Bob's bits	1	0	0	1	0	1	0	1	1	1	0	1	0	1
Same basis?	Yes	No	Yes	Yes	No	No	Yes	No	Yes	No	Yes	Yes	No	Yes
Sifted key	1		0	1			0		1		0	1		1

Figure 6: An example of sequence of steps leading to the sifted key in the BB′84 protocol. Note that in this example we have assumed no eavesdropping. The presence of Eve would introduce discrepancies between Alice and Bob sifted keys.

in the correct basis his resulting bit is uncorrelated with Alice's. Suppose, for instance, that Alice sends a vertically polarized photon (i.e., a 0) and that Eve measures it in the ($\times$) basis, obtaining as a result the polarization $-45°$ (i.e., a 1). The best Eve can do is to send to Bob a photon with the same polarization she measured. If he measures in the ($+$) basis (i.e., the same used by Alice), then the chances of obtaining 0 and 1 are the same. This suggests the following strategy to detect Eve's presence: Alice and Bob select a random subset of their sifted key and compare the values of such bits over the public channel. In the absence of any eavesdropping, all the values of Alice and Bob bits should coincide. If, however, Eve has intercepted the photons sent over the private quantum channel, there is a 25% chance that the value of each such bit differs. If Alice and Bob compare a substring of length n the probability that Eve is not detected is equal to $(^3/_4)^n$, which, for sufficiently large n is basically negligible. Eve could reduce her chance to be detected by intercepting only a subset of the photons exchanged between Alice and Bob; this, however, also reduces her knowledge about the final key. In general, the more the information gained by Eve the more the noise she introduces over the private quantum channel (i.e., the more Alice's and Bob's raw keys will differ). Indeed from both the conceptual and the practical viewpoints eavesdropping and environmental noise at the quantum level are the same thing and therefore, to be on the safe side, any noise should be attributed to eavesdropping. Once Alice and Bob have detected Eve's presence they must estimate the amount of information she has gained on the key (i.e., the error rate she has introduced in the sifted key), known as QBER, for quantum bit error rate, and compare it with a security threshold (we discuss later how such a threshold can be established). If the QBER is below the security threshold, it is possible for Alice and Bob to distill a private key by means of a discussion over the public channel. Such part of the protocol is entirely classical and we only briefly describe it. If, however, the QBER is above threshold, then Alice and Bob must restart the protocol.

Here in summary are the steps of the BB'84 protocol:

Alice

- Chooses a random sequence of polarization basis, either ($+$) or ($\times$).
- Chooses a random binary string. Such bits are encoded as $0 \rightarrow V$ or $+45°$, $1 \rightarrow H$ or $-45°$ polarized photons, according to the random choice of basis made above.
- The photons are sent to Bob via a quantum private channel.

Bob

- Chooses a random sequence of polarization basis, either ($+$) or ($\times$).
- Measures the polarization of the photons sent by Alice according to the above choice of basis.

At the end of this stage Alice and Bob share a string of random bits called a raw key. The two raw keys differ because in 50% of cases they used a different a basis to randomly prepare/measure the photons.

Alice

- Announces on the public classical channel the basis used to polarize her photons but keeps secret the bits sent.

Bob

- Announces on the public channel which of his measurements were made in the same basis.

Alice and Bob.

- Discard all bits of their string whenever their basis disagree.

At the end of this stage Alice and Bob share a binary string known as a sifted key. In the absence of noise and eavesdropping their sifted keys should coincide.

Alice and Bob

- Select a substring of the sifted key, compare them over the public channel and make a statistical estimate the QBER (i.e., estimate the percentage of bits which disagree in their strings. Such substrings, used for a statistical estimate, are discarded.).
- Compare the QBER with the security threshold. If the noise is below threshold they correct the errors in their key obtaining the so called reconciled key.
- Distill a shorter secret key, the private key, out of the reconciled key.
- If the QBER is above threshold, they restart the protocol at some later stage.

The sequence of steps listed above is basically common, apart from minor details, to all quantum key distribution protocols.

The careful reader has probably noticed some redundancy in the above protocol. Indeed, the random use of two different polarization bases, i.e., of four states belonging to two nonorthogonal bases, is not necessary. Security can be obtained with the use of just two nonorthogonal polarization states, as shown by Bennett in 1992. In this protocol, Alice encodes her random bits on two nonorthogonal states, for example:

$$0 \rightarrow |V>$$
$$1 \rightarrow \cos\theta|V> + \sin\theta|H>.$$

Since these two states are not orthogonal, neither Bob nor Eve can, with a single measurement, determine the polarization of the photon. Bob's goal is not to maximize his mutual information of Alice's string, which is a statistical quantity, but to be sure that the bit value he detects is the same Alice has sent. To this purpose he performs what is known as positive operator value measure (POVM). The polarization measurement process using a PBS is an example of what is known in physics as projective measurement (or VonNeumann measurement). The reason for such a name is nearly obvious: the polarization of a photon that has crossed a polarizer is always along the polarizer's axis (i.e., it is projected on the polarization basis of the polarizer whatever the original polarization of the photon). The number of outcomes of a projective measurement is equal to the number of basis states—two orthogonal polarizations in the case of photons. In a POVM the number of possible outcomes is increased by making a joint projective measurement on the original system and an auxiliary system called ancilla. A mathematical description of POVM is entirely outside the scope of the present review. The interested reader can find a thorough description of POVMs in Peres (1993) and in Nielsen and Chuang (2000). For the present discussion, it will be enough to say that for the Bennett'92 protocol it is possible to devise a POVM with three possible outcomes: 0, 1, and ? (i.e., either Bob knows with certainty the bit value sent by Alice or he knows nothing about it). Here are the steps of the Bennett'92 protocol:

- Alice sends a random sequence of photons polarized in one of two nonorthogonal polarizations on a private quantum channel.
- Bob measures the photons with a POVM with outcomes 0,1,?
- Bob announces on the public channel which bits have not been identified (i.e., outcomes?).
- Alice discards from his string such bits.

At this stage Alice and Bob share a sifted key. The remaining steps leading to the secret private key are the same as in the BB'84 protocol. Again the presence of Eve is identified as nonzero error rate on the sifted key.

We should also briefly mention the existence of other quantum key distribution protocols that make use of a larger set of nonorthogonal states, such as the six-states protocol (Bruss, 1998). They do not differ conceptually from the protocols described so far, the only difference being in the details of their practical implementation and of eavesdropping detection.

Let us turn our attention to the security threshold. Once the sifted key has been established Alice, Bob and Eve have each a—generally different—random binary string. Let's call such strings X, Y, Z, respectively, and $P(X, Y, Z)$ their joint probability distribution. Under which condition such joint probability distribution can be established will be discussed in the next section. Alice and Bob can establish a secret key, using error correction and privacy amplification, if and only if $I(X,Y) \geq Max \{I(X,Z); I(Y,Z)\}$, where $I(X,Y)$ denotes the mutual information between the random variables X, Y (Csiszàr & Koerner, 1978). In other words, the requirement to establish a cryptographic key is that the information shared between Alice and Bob must be higher than the information Eve has on either Alice's or Bob's strings. The problem is that Alice and Bob must estimate $P(X, Y, Z)$ from the knowledge of X,Y (i.e., from the marginal distribution $P(X, Y)$ only). This requires a detailed analysis of the optimal eavesdropping strategies on the given

quantum key distribution protocol. Such analysis is rather complex and requires realistic assumptions about what Eve can do on the specific quantum channel used. Some aspects of quantum eavesdropping are described later.

The procedure, by which Alice and Bob can establish a key, once they have estimated that the QBER is below the security threshold, consists, as mentioned, of two steps. The first is error correction, at the end of which Alice and Bob share the reconciled key. According to Shannon's theorem, if the error rate is e, the number of bits that Alice and Bob must somehow make public to correct all errors in a string of length n is at least equal to $n[e \log_2 e + (1 - e)\log_2(1 - e)]$. The Shannon theorem is nonconstructive and therefore provides no explicit recipe to design such error correcting codes. Some codes with efficiency very close to the Shannon limit have been proposed: for a short discussion, see the review chapter on quantum cryptography contained in Bowmeester, Ekert, and Zeilinger (2000) and the review article by Gisin, Ribordy, Tittel, and Zbinden (2002).

The error correcting protocol discussion over the public channel will in general disclose to Eve some additional information about the reconciled key. To eliminate virtually all information Eve has on the reconciled key, Alice and Bob make use of a privacy amplification protocol. This protocol is again entirely classical and therefore here we simply illustrate the basic idea. Suppose that the probability that Eve's bit is the same as the reconciled key is $p = \frac{1}{2}(1 + \varepsilon)$. For $\varepsilon = 0$ Eve has no knowledge of the key as this amounts to choosing randomly her bit value. Assume now that Alice and Bob extract a shorter key by taking the parity bit of two consecutive bits, therefore halving the length of their reconciled key. The probability that each of Eve's bits now coincides with the corresponding one of this shorter key is reduced to $p' = \frac{1}{2}(1 + \varepsilon^2)$. It is not necessary to actually sacrifice every second bit as more efficient privacy amplification protocols have been developed (Bennett, Brassard, & Maurer, 1995).

What has been described above is a particular case of what is known as secret key agreement by public discussion (see Maurer, 1993). In this framework two important techniques should be briefly mentioned, namely advantage distillation and quantum privacy amplification. Advantage distillation (Maurer, 1993; Maurer & Wolf, 1999) is a classical protocol that allows Alice and Bob to share a secret key even if they start from a disadvantageous situation (i.e., when the information Eve has on Bob's or Alice's string is larger than the mutual information between Alice and Bob). The basic idea is that before starting the error correction and privacy amplification Alice and Bob distill, by means of two way communications (i.e., by means of feedback), a string on which Eve's information is smaller than their mutual information. Quantum privacy amplification (Deutsch et al., 1996) is a quantum protocol that can be used in entanglement based quantum key distribution, which is described below. The interesting point is that the QBER above which advantage distillation or quantum privacy amplification make possible the establishment of a secret key is the same, as shown by Gisin and Wolf (1999).

QUANTUM EAVESDROPPING

A correct estimation of the security threshold requires a detailed analysis of all the possible eavesdropping strategies on the private quantum channel used in a given quantum key distribution protocol. Alice and Bob, given their QBER, must estimate the information Eve has on their bit strings. The assumption is that Eve does not suffer of any technological limitation. In other words, to prove unconditional security one has to assume that the adverse party has at its disposal perfect technology. It must be said straight away that, although a complete theory of quantum eavesdropping is still missing, the field has reached a very high degree of sophistication and is rapidly becoming an area of research by itself. Here we simply illustrate some basic strategies and their limitations. In eavesdropping analysis, one considers various classes of eavesdropping strategies of increasing generality. The simplest and more realistic of such classes is the one of individual attacks, called also incoherent attacks. For such attacks, Eve lets each of the photons in transit interact with a separate probe system that is then individually measured. The interesting feature of this strategy, as illustrated in the previous section is that a joint probability distribution can be assigned for Alice, Eve, and Bob measurement outcomes. The simplest incoherent eavesdropping attack, namely the intercept-and-resend strategy, or opaque eavesdropping, has already been illustrated for the BB'84 protocol. For such strategy the only way by which Eve could reduce the chance of being detected is by reducing the number of photons intercepted and measured. This, however, will reduce also her knowledge on the sifted key. A factor that could reduce the chance to detect Eve's intrusion is the presence of more than one photon in the signal sent by Alice to Bob. The experimental realization of true single photon sources is very challenging. In the simplest experimental implementation, Alice uses faint pulses containing an average of about 0.1 photons. Since photons are indivisible quanta, an average of 0.1 photons simply means that most pulses contain no photons, some contain a single photon, and few pulses contain two or more photons. In this case, Eve could send the signal through a beam splitter, obtaining, sometimes, two single photon pulses. This allows Eve either to keep one of the photons for her measurement and send the other to Bob (who could not detect Eve's interception as his photon has not been measured on its way) or to perform a measurement on both single photon signals, increasing the amount of information gained from bits sent by Alice. Therefore, the use of sources that are as much as possible true single photon sources is of great importance.

The reader may wonder why Eve does not simply try to build a device able to make multiple copies of the photons sent by Alice. This would allow her to send the signal to Bob without modifying it and to perform her measurement on the photon "clones." One of the "oddities" of quantum mechanics that prevents this simple strategy is that an unknown quantum state cannot be faithfully copied, a fundamental fact known as "no-cloning theorem," first discussed by Wootters and Zurek (1982). In our specific discussion, this means that, if we are given a photon in an unknown polarization state, we cannot build any device able to produce for us two photons with the same such polarization. The theorem is straightforward to prove. Suppose we are given a vertically polarized photon and a device able to accept it as input and to produce two vertically polarized photons as output. The action of such device is described by a linear unitary operator as follows:

$$|V>|\text{blank}> \rightarrow |V>|V>,$$

where |blank> is a given fixed initial state of our device. Suppose also that the same apparatus can copy also a horizontally polarized photon:

$$|H>|\text{blank}> \rightarrow |H>|H>.$$

An apparatus able to do the above copying operation is perfectly feasible. Assume, however, that the input state is the arbitrary state $|A> = \alpha_V|V> + \alpha_H|H>$; by linearity we have the following:

$$(\alpha_V|V> + \alpha_H|H>)|\text{blank}> \rightarrow (\alpha_V|V>|V> + \alpha_H|H>|)$$
$$\neq (\alpha_V|V> + \alpha_H|H>)(\alpha_V|V> + \alpha_H|H>),$$

which shows how it is impossible to clone a photon in an unknown polarization state.

Much recent research in quantum information theory has investigated so-called approximate cloning (i.e., the design of machines able to clone), with the maximum possible fidelity, of states belonging to a given set. Although their description falls well outside the scope of this brief review their importance in the framework of eavesdropping strategies in quantum key distribution must be stressed. The important point is that approximate cloning modifies the state of the original signal and that, in general, the more the information of the original state is contained in Eve's copy, the more the original signal is disturbed. To see that Eve cannot make a copy of the original signal without modifying it, consider the following eavesdropping attack on the Bennet'92 protocol. Suppose Alice uses two states, $|s_0>$, $|s_1>$, to encode her bits and that Eve has built a machine M that makes copies of the signal states as follows:

$$|s_0>|\text{blank}> \rightarrow |s_0>|m_0>,$$
$$|s_1>|\text{blank}> \rightarrow |s_1>|m_1>,$$

where, as before, |blank> is a standard initial state of the machine. As the evolution of a quantum machine is described by a unitary operator, which preserves the inner product, we must have $<s_1|s_0><\text{blank}|\text{blank}> = <s_1|s_0><m_1|m_0>$. Because $<\text{blank}|\text{blank}> = 1$ this means that $<s_1|s_0> = <s_1|s_0><m_1|m_0>$. Note, however, that the signal states are nonorthogonal (i.e., $<s_1|s_0> \neq 0$), so the above condition can be satisfied only when $<m_1|m_0> = 1$. This, however, implies that Eve does not have any information on the signal states. Whenever $<m_1|m_0> \neq 0$ the signal states are modified; that is:

$$|s_0>|\text{blank}> \rightarrow |s_0'>|m_0>,$$
$$|s_1>|\text{blank}> \rightarrow |s_1'>, |m_1>,$$

614 QUANTUM CRYPTOGRAPHY

with $\langle s_1|s_0\rangle \neq \langle s_1'|s_0'\rangle$. This change in the direction of the signal change causes a change in the statistics of Bob's measurements outcomes, revealing Eve's presence. We stress again that in individual attack strategies described above the photons are intercepted and somehow measured individually. For the BB84 protocol, it can be shown (see Gisin et al., 2002) that, for QBER below 15%, a secret key immune against any individual attack can be established by means of error correction and privacy amplification. For QBER between 15% and 25%, the use of the advantage distillation protocol is necessary. However, such protocols are much less efficient than just error correction and privacy amplification.

To conclude this section, we mention the existence of more general classes of eavesdropping strategies known as coherent attack. In the most general coherent strategy, known also as joint attack, several photons are probed coherently and Eve performs a joint measurement on the probe after Alice and Bob have ended their public discussion. An intermediate class is that of collective attack, in which the photons are probed individually but the probes are measured collectively at the end of the public discussion. These strategies require that Eve can store coherently the probe states to delay as much as possible their measurement. We do not discuss such strategies here because on the one hand they are much less realistic than individual attack, whereas on the other hand, a complete theory of coherent eavesdropping is still missing. For a review of the state of the art see Gisin et al. (2002).

ENTANGLEMENT-BASED QUANTUM KEY DISTRIBUTION PROTOCOL

In 1991 Ekert proposed a new protocol in which a new quantum ingredient was introduced to guarantee the security of quantum key distribution: entanglement. To illustrate the concept of entanglement, which, as said in the introduction, is the property of quantum systems to show stronger nonlocal correlations than any classical system, consider the following two photons state:

$$|\psi\rangle = (|V\rangle_A|H\rangle_B - |H\rangle_A|V\rangle_B)\sqrt{1/2},$$

where the subscripts A and B mean that the first and second photon of the pair are in Alice's and Bob's hands, respectively (see Figure 7).

Suppose that Alice measures the polarization of her photon in the (+) basis and obtains as a result V. This will immediately modify the state of Bob's photon, which will instantaneously collapse into state $|H\rangle$. Analogously if Alice's measurement result is $|H\rangle$, then Bob's photon will collapse into state $|V\rangle$. In other words, as a result of her measurement in the (+) basis Alice can obtain, with equal probability, the result V or H; however, once her measurement is performed she can predict with certainty the outcome of Bob's measurement, provided he measures in the (+) basis as well. This kind of correlations could be explained in classical terms. Suppose, however, that Alice measures her photon in the (×) basis. The outcome of her measurement can be, with equal probability, ±45°. The astonishing fact is that Alice's outcome will again

determine Bob's. To see this it is enough to notice that given *any* two orthogonal polarizations N, $N_\perp$ the state $|\psi\rangle$ can be written as follows:

$$|\psi\rangle = (|N\rangle_A|N_\perp\rangle_B - |N_\perp\rangle_A|N\rangle_B)\sqrt{1/2}$$

and therefore Alice's and Bob's measurements outcome will always be correlated provided they use the same basis, whatever this is. No classical theory can explain such strong correlations.

It is straightforward to see how entanglement can be used to implement a quantum key distribution protocol. Since Alice's measurement on her photon can be seen as a random preparation of Bob's photon, the first steps of BB'84 protocol can be modified as follows: Alice and Bob choose randomly to measure their photons in the (+) or in the (×) basis. When they choose the same basis, which for random choice happens with 50% chance, the outcomes of their measurements are perfectly (anti-) correlated: when they measure in the (+), such outcomes will be, with equal probability, either Alice H Bob V or Alice V Bob H. When they both measure in the (×) basis, the possible equiprobable outcomes will be either Alice +45° Bob −45° or Alice −45° Bob +45°. Note that these outcomes are truly random, as they are determined by the laws of quantum mechanics. When Alice and Bob choose a different basis, the outcomes of their measurements will be two uncorrelated random bits.

The remaining discussion over the public channel leading to the sifted key and the detection of the possible presence of Eve is the same as in the BB'84 protocol. Entanglement, however, makes possible more sophisticated strategies to detect the presence of Eve. Such strategies were initially developed in the study of the foundations of quantum mechanics. The basic idea is that entanglement between Alice and Bob is destroyed by any measurement made by Eve and that any residual correlation between Alice and Bob measurements can, in this case, be accounted for by the laws of classical physics. Classical correlations can be statistically distinguished from quantum ones. A set of inequalities that would be satisfied by the statistical properties of a suitable set of measurement on two separate subsystems if these were classically correlated but would be violated by quantum correlated (entangled) systems have been proven by J. S. Bell (Bell, 1987). In

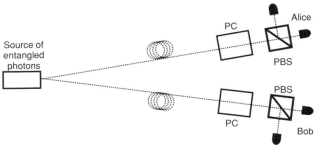

Figure 7: A source emits pairs polarization entangled photon. The first photon of the pair is sent to Alice, the second to Bob. By means of two Pockels cells and two PBS, they make random polarization measurement on their photons.

the Ekert'91 protocol Alice and Bob make their measurement along three polarization directions randomly chosen from a suitable set. This will be the step leading to the raw key. In the following public discussion, Alice and Bob announce their measurement bases. When the bases chosen by Alice and Bob are the same, their results should be perfectly correlated. The instances in which they have performed their measurements in different bases are not discarded but used to make a statistical test. If the data statistics violate a particular form of Bell inequality, then entanglement has not been disrupted by Eve and the key distribution session can continue with the reconciliation step, otherwise the degree of security must be estimated before proceeding with reconciliation. As already mentioned, quantum privacy amplification (Deutsch et al., 1996) allows one to distill a shorter string of entangled qubits out of the set disrupted by Eve. The basic idea is that Eve acquires information on the key bits by entangling her measurement apparatus with the entangled photons exchanged between Alice and Bob. However, entanglement is a "monogamous" quantity: the more Eve gets entangled with Alice and Bob, the lesser these two are entangled each other. The quantum privacy amplification protocol allows Alice and Bob to increase their mutual entanglement on a subset of their initial set of entangled pair of photons, therefore reducing virtually to zero their entanglement with Eve. However, the resources needed for such protocol are the same needed for quantum computation and therefore it is not discussed here.

SUGGESTIONS FOR FURTHER READING

This chapter simply touches the surface of the broad research now going on in quantum cryptography. In particular, we have emphasized the theoretical aspects of the topic while basically ignoring the experimental aspects. Furthermore, we have not discussed more specialized aspects of the field, such as quantum bit commitment, as they are at present less well established than quantum key distribution. We therefore conclude this chapter with some suggestion for further reading. The list is by no means complete and reflects the writer's tastes and interests. The first published popular article on quantum cryptography is Bennett, Brassard, and Ekert (1992), still a pleasant starting point. Other review articles, from gentle to more formal, can be found in Macchiavello, Palma, and Zeilinger (2001); see also LoMonaco (1998), Luetkenhaus (1999), Gisin and Brunner (2003), and the review chapter on quantum cryptography contained in Bowmeester et al. (2000). At present the most complete review article on the subject is that by Gisin et al. (2002), a very thorough presentation of all theoretical and experimental aspects of quantum key distribution, aimed to a readership with a reasonable familiarity with basic quantum mechanics and quantum optics. In this chapter, I have not discussed quantum cryptographic protocols based on continuous variables (see, for instance, Hillery, 2003; Grosshans et al., 2003). This choice is because of the fact that their description, although not adding conceptually anything to the above introductory overview, would require the use

of the language of quantum optics. This is well outside the aims of a tutorial review. To the reader interested in fundamentals of quantum mechanics, we suggest the classic lectures by Richard Feynman (1963). Quantum cryptography is often described within the broader contest of quantum computation and quantum information theory. The classical reference book in the field is Nielsen and Chuang (2000). More introductory lecture notes are available on the Web; in particular, we suggest the lecture notes by Preskill and by Mermin. The latter in particular are aimed at a computer science readership with no prior knowledge of quantum mechanics.

GLOSSARY

Asymmetric In the context of encryption, a type of cryptographic system in which a participant publishes an encryption key and keeps private a separate decryption key. These keys are, respectively, referred to as public and private. RSA and D-H are examples of asymmetric systems. *Asymmetric* is synonymous with *public key*.

Beam Splitter An optical device that partly reflects and partly transmits a light beam.

Ciphertext The data conveying an encrypted message.

Cloning The process of making an approximate copy of an unknown quantum state.

Cryptanalysis The science of analyzing weaknesses in cryptographic systems.

Cryptography The science of constructing mathematical systems for securing data.

Cryptology The combination of the complementary sciences of cryptography and cryptanalysis.

Cryptosystem A complete system of encryption and decryption, typically used to describe a public key cryptographic system.

Decryption The process of obtaining a readable message (a *plaintext*) from an encrypted transformation of the message (a *ciphertext*).

Eavesdropping The act of interception of the cyphertext and of its decryption by and adverse party.

Encryption The process of rendering a message (a *plaintext*) into a data string (a *ciphertext*) with the aim of transmitting it privately in a potentially hostile environment.

Entanglement The property of quantum systems composed by two or more subsystems to show stronger nonlocal correlation between its subsystems than compatible with the laws of classical physics.

Key A short data string parameterizing the operations within a cipher or cryptosystem, and whose distribution determines relationships of privacy and integrity among communicating parties.

Key Distribution A protocol for the distribution of cryptographic keys.

Photo Detector An optical device that measures the presence of a photon in a beam by absorbing it.

Photon An energy quantum of the electromagnetic field. One of the properties of photon is its polarization.

Plaintext A message in readable form prior to encryption or subsequent to successful decryption.

Polarization The plane of oscillation of the electric field of an electromagnetic wave.

Polarizer An optical device made from a material with anisotropic-absorbing properties. When a light beam crosses a polarizer with polarization axis n, all the electric field perpendicular to the direction n is absorbed, while the field in the direction parallel to n crosses the polarizer entirely undisturbed.

Polarizing Beam Splitter A beam splitter that reflects or transmits light depending on the polarization of the incident light. If the polarization of the incoming light is parallel to the PBS axis the beam is transmitted while if it is polarized in its orthogonal direction it is reflected.

Private Key In an asymmetric or public-key cryptosystem, the key that a communicating party holds privately and uses for decryption or completion of a key exchange.

Public Key In an asymmetric or public-key cryptosystem, the key that a communicating party disseminates publicly. In the context of encryption, a type of cryptographic system in which a participant publishes an encryption key and keeps private a separate decryption key. These keys are respectively referred to as public and private. RSA and D-H are examples of public key systems. *Public key* is synonymous with *asymmetric*.

Symmetric A type of cryptographic system in which communicating parties employ shared secret keys. The term is also used to refer to the keys employed in such a system.

CROSS REFERENCES

See *Encryption Basics; PKI (Public Key Infrastructure); Symmetric-Key Encryption.*

REFERENCES

Bell, J. S. (1987). *Speakable and unspeakable in quantum mechanics*. Cambridge, UK: Cambridge University Press.

Bennett, C. H. (1992). Quantum cryptography using any two non orthogonal states. *Physical Review Letters, 68,* 3121–3124.

Bennett, C. H., & Brassard, G. (1984). Quantum cryptography: Public key distribution and coin tossing. In *Proceedings of* IEEE *International Conference on Computer, Systems & Signal Processing*, Bangalore, India, December 10–12, 1984 (pp. 175–179).

Bennett, C. H., Brassard, G., & Ekert, A. K. (1992). Quantum cryptography. *Scientific American, 267,* 26–33.

Bennett, C. H., Brassard, G., & Maurer, U. M. (1995). Generalised privacy amplification. *IEEE Transactions on Information Theory, 41,* 1915–1923.

Bowmeester, D., Ekert, A., & Zeilinger, A. (2000). *The physics of quantum information*. New York: Springer-Verlag.

Bruss, D. (1998). Optimal eavesdropping in quantum cryptography with six states. *Physical Review Letters, 81,* 3018–3021.

Csiszàr, I., & Koerner, J. (1978). Broadcast channels with confidential message. *IEEE Transaction on Information Theory, IT-24,* 339–348.

Deutsch, D., Ekert, A., Jozsa, R., Macchiavello, C., Popescu, S., & Sanpera, A. (1996). Quantum privacy amplification and the security of quantum cryptography over noisy channels. *Physical Review Letters, 77,* 2818–2821.

Ekert, A. K. (1991). Quantum cryptography based on Bell's theorem. *Physical Review Letters, 67,* 661–663.

Feynman, R. (1963). *The Feynman lectures on physics, vol. 3.* Boston: Addison-Wesley.

Gisin, N., & Brunner, N. (2003). *Quantum cryptography with and without entanglement.* arXive:quant-ph/0312011, available at http://arxiv.org

Gisin, N., Ribordy, G., Tittel, W., & Zbinden, H. (2002). Quantum cryptography. *Review of Modern Physics, 74,* 145–195 see also arXive:quant-ph/0101098, available at http://arxiv.org]

Gisin, N., & Wolf, S. (1999). Quantum cryptography on noisy channels: Quantum vs. classical key agreement protocols. *Physical Review Letters, 83,* 4200–4203.

Grosshans, F., Van Assche, G., Wenger, J., Broul, R., Cerf, N. J., & Grangier, P. (2003). Quantum key distribution using Gaussian modulated coherent states. *Nature, 421,* 238–241.

Hillery, M. (2003). Code-breakers confounded, *Nature, 421,* 224.

LoMonaco, S. (1998). A quick glace at quantum cryptography, arXive:quant-ph/9811056 Available at http://arxiv.org

Luetkenhaus, N. (1999). Quantum key distribution: Theory for applications. *Applied Physics B, 69,* 395–400.

Macchiavello, C., Palma, G. M., & Zeilinger, A. (2001). *Quantum computation and quantum information theory.* Singapore: World Scientific.

Maurer, U. M. (1993). Secret key agreement by public discussion from common information *IEEE Transactions on Information Theory, 39,* 733–742.

Maurer, U. M., & Wolf, S. (1999). Unconditionally secure key agreement and the intrinsic conditional information. *IEEE Transactions on Information Theory, 45,* 499–514.

Mermin D. *Lecture notes on quantum computation.* Retrieved January 2, 2004, from http://people.ccmr.cornell.edu/~mermin/qcomp/CS483.html

Nielsen, M., & Chuang, I. (2000). *Quantum computation and quantum information.* Cambridge, UK: Cambridge University Press.

Peres, A. (1993). *Quantum theory: Concepts and methods.* Amsterdam: Kluwer Academic.

Preskill, J. *Lecture notes for physics 219: Quantum information and computation* http://www.theory.caltech.edu/people/preskill/

Shannon, C. E. (1946). Communication theory of secrecy systems. *Bell Systems Technology Journal, 28,* 656–715.

Wiesner, S. (1983). Conjugate coding. *SIGACT News, 15,* 78–88.

Wootters, W. K., & Zurek, W. H. (1982). A single quantum cannot be cloned. *Nature, 299,* 802–803.

Key Lengths

Arjen K. Lenstra, *Lucent Technologies Bell Laboratories and Technische Universiteit Eindhoven*

INTRODUCTION

In cryptographic context, 40, 56, 64, 80, 90, 112, 128, 155, 160, 192, 256, 384, 512, 768, 1024, 1536, 2048, and 4096 are examples of key lengths. What they mean and how they are and should be selected is the subject of this chapter.

Key lengths indicate the number of bits contained in a certain cryptographic key or related arithmetic structure. They are a measure for the security that may be attained. To the uninitiated, however, the relation between key lengths and security is confusing. To illustrate, key lengths 80, 160, and 1024, though quite different, may imply comparable security when 80 is the key length for a symmetric encryption method, 160 a hash length, and 1024 the bit length of an RSA modulus. Part of this correspondence follows immediately from the well-known "fact" that symmetric encryption with B-bit keys and

$2B$-bit cryptographic hashes offer the "same" security. But the correspondence with 1024-bit RSA is quite a different story that allows many variations. In the sequel, an attempt is made to view this and other key length issues from all reasonable perspectives.

Key lengths are often powers of 2 or small multiples thereof. This is not for any mathematical or security reason. It is simply because data is usually most conveniently processed and stored in chunks of 8 bits (bytes), 32 bits (words), 64 bits (blocks), and so on.

Symmetric Encryption and Cryptographic Hashing

Ideally, the long-term prospects of the relationship between key length and security should be well understood when key length decisions are made. In the case of symmetric encryption and cryptographic hashing methods, the decision is facilitated for most users by the following three facts:

1. There is broad consensus which symmetric key lengths and cryptographic hash sizes are "conservative" (i.e., have good prospects to offer very long term security).
2. Nowadays, for symmetric cryptosystems and cryptographic hash functions most default choices available on the marketplace are conservative.
3. The performance of symmetric cryptosystems and cryptographic hash functions is barely, if at all, affected by the key length choice.

Thus, for symmetric encryption and cryptographic hashing it suffices to make a reasonably well informed conservative choice.

Asymmetric Cryptosystems

As hinted at above, there is much less agreement about conservative choices for asymmetric cryptosystems such as RSA. Furthermore, for these cryptosystems the performance *does* deteriorate with increasing key lengths. Even if a consensual conservative choice could be made, it may not be a choice that is practically feasible. In practice most users of asymmetric cryptosystems follow the recommendations of the vendor community. But there is no guarantee that the vendor community always has sufficient business incentive to comply with the recommendations of the standards bodies or that the latter fully understand all relevant issues. The larger context is the overall cost/benefit picture and the fact that in all practical circumstances there are more pressing areas than key sizes to which industry is giving a higher priority when addressing security concerns. However, those issues are not addressed in this chapter. The main purpose of the present chapter is to offer unbiased advice to the more prudent users of asymmetric cryptosystems to help decide which of the available options may be adequate for their purposes.

Security in Practice

The security that corresponds to a key length choice for a cryptographic protocol measures the largest effort, that is, in principle, needed to attack the cryptosystem incorporating that protocol. The key length itself yields an upper bound for the security, namely the effort required for exhaustive key search. Cryptosystems are usually most efficiently attacked by exploiting other than cryptographic key-related weaknesses. Examples are imperfections in the underlying protocol, the implementation, the environment, or the users. Selecting appropriate key lengths may therefore be regarded as an academic exercise. It should be kept in mind, however, that inadequate key length choices do affect the security of a cryptosystem. In the remainder of this chapter, security-affecting issues other than key lengths are discussed no further.

Overview

This chapter is organized as follows. The section titled Security Level introduces the concept of security level and contains the general background for the remainder of the chapter. Key lengths for symmetric cryptosystems are discussed under Symmetric Cryptosystems and cryptographic hash function sizes under Cryptographic Hash Functions. An overview of asymmetric methods is given under Asymmetric Methods, which leads to the discussion of factoring based cryptosystems under Factoring-Based Cryptosystems and of discrete logarithm based cryptosystems under Discrete Logarithm-Based Cryptosystems. The reader who is not familiar with common cryptographic concepts such as symmetric and asymmetric cryptosystems may look them up in other chapters of this handbook.

In the sequel, $\log x$ denotes the natural logarithm of x and $\log_b x$ denotes the base b logarithm of x. As customary, $\exp(x) = e^x$.

SECURITY LEVEL
Generic Attacks

For symmetric cryptosystems, *generic attacks* are defined as attacks where the key has to be recovered from a known (plaintext, ciphertext) pair. Plaintext and ciphertext in case of block ciphers may consist of a number of blocks that is not too large. In the cryptographic literature such attacks are referred to as known plaintext attacks. It is assumed that the input pair uniquely determines the key or that correctness of the key can independently be verified. Refer to Brazier (2000) for a discussion of the latter point. For asymmetric cryptosystems generic attacks are defined as attacks where the private key has to be found given the public key.

Generic attacks exclude attacks where the attacker has access to any other data that can be generated only by means of the unknown key, such as in differential and linear cryptanalysis of block ciphers. In this chapter only generic attacks are considered because it is generally believed that they most closely correspond to real-life situations. Furthermore, given the cost of an attack effort as used in this chapter and as defined below, for most popular block ciphers generic attacks are the ones that are believed to have the lowest cost (cf. M. J. Wiener, personal communication, 2004; see Symmetric Cryptosystems for an exception).

Security Level

If a symmetric cryptosystem with λ-bit keys does not allow a generic attack that requires less effort than exhaustive key search, then it is traditionally said to have *security level* λ. Exhaustive key search for λ-bit keys may be expected to involve $2^{\lambda-1}$ different keys, with in the worst case up to 2^λ keys. In general, a cryptographic system offers security level λ if a successful generic attack can be expected to require effort approximately $2^{\lambda-1}$. How an attack effort is measured is explained in the next paragraph.

The Cost of an Attack Effort

A security level explicitly refers to an attack effort and not to the time that may be needed to realize it. All attacks discussed in this chapter are fully parallelizable in the following way. Assume an attack can be realized in d days by a device that costs c dollars. Then, for any reasonable w, the attack can be realized in d/w days by a device costing cw dollars. As first suggested in this context in Bernstein (2001), this implies that an appropriate way to measure an attack effort is obtained by multiplying the time required by the equipment cost; see also Lenstra, Shamir, Tomlinson, and Tromer (2002) and Wiener (2005) where this measure is referred to as the *throughput cost* and *full cost*, respectively. Below it is simply referred to as the *cost* of an attack effort and it will be measured in *dollardays*: the attack effort suggested above would cost dc dollardays. Exhaustive key search is an example of a fully parallelizable attack, because the search space can be arbitrarily divided over any number of processors that can work independently on the search range assigned to them.

This cost allows to leave unspecified if and how an attack effort is parallelized or distributed—all one has to do is make sure that full parallelization of an attack is possible. Note that this does not take into account large-scale (and possibly surreptitious) Internet-based calculations. For cryptographically relevant key lengths, however, effective attacks require such a huge computational effort that they will not go unnoticed when mounted using some type of Internet worm.

Relation Between Security Level and Security

To determine whether a cryptographic system offers adequate security or protection, it is not immediately useful to tie the definition of security level to symmetric cryptosystem key lengths. In the first place, the amount of time and money required to realize an attack effort decreases over time because computers become faster and cheaper. Thus, the amount of protection offered by a certain fixed security level is constantly eroded. A related point is that cryptanalytic progress over time may affect the security level of a cryptographic system not by lowering the cost to realize a certain attack but by proposing an improved attack method. Furthermore, the definition of security level involves an unspecified constant of proportionality— vaguely indicated by the "approximately $2^{\lambda-1}$"—and thus its meaning may vary from system to system. And finally, "adequate protection" is a vague term whose interpretation depends on the application one has in mind and is even then still subjective. In the remainder of this section, these issues affecting the relation between security levels and security are addressed, which allows selection of key lengths corresponding to any amount of protection one feels comfortable with.

Modeling the Relation

Although a cryptosystem's security level may not be indicative of its effectiveness, security levels allow comparison of the security offered by cryptosystems. Assuming identical constants of proportionality and environments, a cryptosystem of security level $\lambda + \mu$ may be expected to be 2^μ times harder to attack, and thus be 2^μ times more secure, than a cryptosystem of security level λ. Once it has been agreed that a certain security level offers an adequate amount of protection in a certain known (past) environment, twice the protection can be achieved in that environment by incrementing the security level by one (assuming other characteristics of the cryptosystem involved

are not affected by the change). And, more in general, an x times higher amount of protection follows, in that same environment, by adding $\log_2 x$ to the security level. If, additionally, the effect of changes in the environment is modeled, then a more general correspondence can be derived between security levels and amount of protection for any (future) environment. As indicated above, these environmental changes come in two flavors: changes in the computational environment that affect the amount of protection by lowering the cost at which the same attack can be realized but that leave the security level itself unchanged and changes in the cryptanalytic environment that allow a different type of attack thereby lowering the security level. The presentation below heavily relies on Lenstra and Verheul (2000) where this approach was first proposed.

Defining Adequate Protection

The data encryption standard (DES) is a symmetric cryptosystem with 56-bit keys, published in 1977 by the U.S. Department of Commerce (National Bureau of Standards, 1997) and was brought up for reaffirmation, like other Federal Information Processings Standards (FIPS), once every 5 years. There was some skepticism about the security level of the DES. But despite extensive cryptanalysis no better generic attack than exhaustive key search has been found and the security level is generally believed to be 56.

Because the DES was widely adopted, there must have been broad consensus that in 1982, the first year the DES would come up for review, it offered an adequate amount of protection for commercial applications. For that reason, and for the purposes of this chapter, *adequate protection* is defined as the security offered in 1982 by the DES. Disregarding the effect of the constant of proportionality, this is synonymous with *security level 56 in 1982*. In the remainder of this section, it is discussed what security level can be expected to offer adequate protection until the year of one's choice. It is left to the reader to determine how the definition of adequate protection compares to one's own security requirements and, if desired, to change the default choice made above. The paragraphs below may be helpful for this purpose.

The Cost of Breaking the DES

To put the definition of adequate protection in a different light, in 1980 it was estimated that, in 1980 money and technology, an exhaustive key search attack against the DES would require on average 2 days on a device that would cost approximately U.S.\$50 million to build. The design underlying this estimate is fully parallelizable as defined above: in 1980 the DES could be broken in approximately 100M dollardays. The cost does *not* include the one time overhead for the detailed design specifications.

Modeling the Effect of Changes in the Computational Environment

Technical progress had a profound effect on the security of the DES. In 1993 a DES key search engine was proposed that would require about 150K dollardays, down from the 100M dollardays required by the 1980 design (Wiener,

1993). And in 1998 a parallel hardware device was built for U.S.\$130K, including design overhead, and used to crack the DES in a matter of days (Electronic Frontier Foundation, 1998; Kocher, 1999). Thus, though security level 56 may have offered adequate protection for commercial applications in 1982, this is no longer the case in 2004.

The effect of changes in the computational environment is modeled using Moore's law. Traditionally, it says that the computing power per chip doubles every 18 months. To make Moore's law less technology dependent the following variant is adopted for this chapter:

Moore's law: The cost of any fixed attack effort drops by a factor 2 every 18 months.

This can be seen to be in reasonable correspondence with the various DES cracking devices referred to above. It follows that the 100M dollardays cost of the 1980 DES cracker would be reduced to 40M dollardays in 1982, because $40 \approx 100/2^{24/18}$.

Obviously, all estimates of this sort based on Moore's law have to be taken with a grain of salt and interpreted appropriately: the approximate values and growth rates matter, not the precise figures. General agreement on Moore's law, however, is impossible to achieve. As formulated above, it is an acceptable compromise between those who argue that this rate of progress cannot be sustained, and those who find it prudent to expect more rapid progress or that, based on economies of scale arguments, an even stronger version of Moore's law would apply when highly parallel devices are taken into account (cf. P. C. Kocher, personal communication, September 1999). Another argument in favor of more rapid progress is that cost according to the definition used in this chapter includes both time and the price of memory: speed may increase—traditionally the only effect taken into account in Moore's law—whereas simultaneously the price of memory may drop, combined with the fact that for asymmetric cryptosystem cryptanalysis larger memories may allow closer to optimal parameter selection and thereby make computations much more time efficient (cf. Lenstra et al., 2003 and Factoring-Based Cryptosystems). But arguing against it is the observation that memory speeds often lag behind, thereby affecting or possibly canceling the effect of processor speedups. Overall the choice made in this chapter must be seen as a compromise that attempts to take all processor speed and memory issues into account.

The Cost of Adequate Protection

Adequate protection was defined as the security offered by the DES in 1982. The cost to break the DES in 1982 is estimated as 40M dollardays. This leads to the following equivalent and more generally applicable definition of adequate protection. Irrespective of the speed or type of the cryptosystem, a cryptosystem is said to offer adequate protection until a given year if the cost of a successful attack measured in that year—and thus using the buying power of the dollar in that year—can be expected to be approximately 40M dollardays. See below how to change the cost figure corresponding to adequate protection from 40M to $x * 40$M if 40M is felt to be inadequate ($x > 1$) or

overkill ($0 < x < 1$) or if the effect of ination is not adequately taken into account by Moore's law. For reasonable values of x, the effect of the resulting corrections is mostly negligible because only the approximate values matter.

For asymmetric cryptosystems based on the factoring problem or the general problem of computing discrete logarithms in multiplicative groups of finite fields the 40M dollardays cost measure will be used to determine adequate protection. For other asymmetric cryptosystems based on the discrete logarithm problem, symmetric cryptosystems, and cryptographic hash functions one can instead use the approach based on security levels combined with Moore's law. To allow comparison with DES security levels, the effect of the constant of proportionality must be taken into account, at least in principle. Below it is shown how this is done.

The Effect of Moore's Law

It follows from Moore's law that to maintain the same amount of protection once every 18 months the security level should be incremented by 1, assuming the speed is not affected. Thus, assuming the same speed as the DES, a symmetric cryptosystem of security level $56 + 10 = 66$ would offer adequate protection in 1997, because 1997–1982 = 15 years covers 10 periods of 18 months. Under the same assumption, security levels 76 and 86 should be adequate until 2012 and 2027, respectively.

More in general, a symmetric cryptosystem of speed comparable to the DES would offer adequate protection until the year $y = 1982 + 15x$ if its security level is $\lambda = 56 + 10x$. Given a security level λ, the year $y(\lambda)$ until which it offers adequate protection is thus calculated as follows:

$$y(\lambda) = 1982 + \frac{3(\lambda - 56)}{2}. \tag{1}$$

Conversely, given a year y, the security level $\lambda(y)$ that offers adequate protection until year y is as follows:

$$\lambda(y) = 56 + \frac{2(y - 1982)}{3}. \tag{2}$$

Although this may be a reasonable model that leads to a useful computational tool, it would stretch the imagination to use it beyond, say, the year 2050. But it is, for instance, not unreasonable to conclude that the widely used security level $\lambda = 80$ offers adequate protection until the year

$$y(80) = 1982 + \frac{3(80 - 56)}{2} = 2018$$

[cf. Eq. (1)].

The Effect of the Constant of Proportionality

If a symmetric cryptosystem is $s > 0$ times faster than the DES, exhaustive key search and thus generic attacks are s times faster as well. To compensate for $s \neq 1$ without changing the year, $\log_2 s$ should in principle be added to the security level; or if the security level should be left unchanged, $1.5 \log_2 s$ must be subtracted from the year.

Ciphers faster than the DES ($s > 1$) require a higher security level or the same security level does not last as long. But for slower ciphers ($s < 1$) a lower security level suffices or the same security level lasts longer.

In theory, this correction based on the speed compared with the DES takes care of the unspecified constant of proportionality mentioned above. In practice, however, this correction should not be used. Not only is $|\log_2 s|$ typically small but also making such corrections would lead to a misleading sense of precision contradictory to the way these estimates should be interpreted.

Alternative Definitions of Adequate Protection

Defining adequate protection as the security offered by security level 56 in 1982 may be a reasonable compromise. But it is a subjective choice. If "security level 56 in year Y" better reflects one's feelings, then one should replace in the sequel all occurrences of 1982 by Y. Furthermore, in the "40M dollardays cost" associated with adequate protection, the 40 must be divided by $2^{2(Y-1982)/3}$. For instance, if the DES was still felt to offer adequate protection in the year 1990, replace 1982 by 1990 throughout, and 40M by $1M$, because $2^{2(1990-1982)/3} \approx 40$.

Similarly, if one is more comfortable with interpretation of cost figures and finds the "40M dollardays" inappropriate, replace the 40 in the sequel by $x * 40$ for any $x \neq 1$ of one's choice. As a consequence, all occurrences of the year 1982 must be replaced by $1982 - 1.5 \log_2 x$.

Modeling the Effect of Changes in Cryptanalytic Capabilities

Moore's law may act as a self-fulfilling prophecy by influencing and controlling the development of the steady stream of improvements required to sustain it. There is no similar mechanism controlling the rate of cryptanalytic progress.

Moore's law affects all cryptosystems across the board in the same way by lowering the cost of attacks (cf. discussion of Moore's law under Security Level). However, cryptanalytic progress usually affects the security level of one particular type of cryptosystem while leaving that of others untouched. An advance in factoring does not affect the security level of symmetric cryptosystems, and a newly found peculiarity in the design of an S-box used by some symmetric cryptosystem has no effect on the security level of RSA or of symmetric cryptosystems using nonaffected designs. Furthermore, the overall effect of cryptanalytic progress may vary from system to system. When a new weakness in a symmetric cryptosystem or cryptographic hash function is discovered, it may be possible to modify or simply retire it because relatively small modifications often render new attacks useless and, if not, there are enough equivalent alternative cryptosystems and functions to choose from. In the asymmetric case, the situation is different. The luxury of a quick switch to an alternative cryptosystem can generally not be afforded because there are not that many different equivalent schemes. As a result, adapting key lengths may be the only option to compensate for the effects of a new cryptanalytic insight such

as a new algorithm to solve the mathematical problem underlying an asymmetric cryptosystem.

There are cryptographic applications, however, where system modification or retirement and key length adaptations are not feasible, and where adequate protection must be maintained for an extended period of time, even in the presence of cryptanalytic progress discovered after the application was put to use. For instance, in long-term confidential data storage in an infrastructure that lacks appropriate physical protection, the fixed stored data must remain undecipherable as long as the confidentiality must last. With the present state of the art of cryptology disasters can always happen, and adequate long-term protection cannot be fully guaranteed. Barring disastrous cryptanalytic progress, however, proper application of suitably modeled cryptanalytic progress leads to an acceptable practical solution for long-term protection as well.

It remains to model cryptanalytic progress. A priori it is unclear how this should be done. However, because there is no reason to expect significant changes in the global research community that is interested in cryptanalysis, it is assumed that the rate of cryptanalytic progress in the future is the same as it was since cryptography became more of a mainstream public domain activity. Because past cryptanalytic progress varied considerably between different cryptographic systems, a specific cryptanalytic progress model is defined for each of the various cryptosystems. The details of each model are described in the relevant sections below.

SYMMETRIC CRYPTOSYSTEMS

Symmetric cryptosystems are encryption methods where sender and receiver share a key for encryption and decryption, respectively. Examples are block and stream ciphers. There is a great variety of such cryptosystems, but only a few of them are generally accepted and widely used. The popular block ciphers, with the exception of the original DES, can be expected to offer adequate protection (cf. Security Level) for the foreseeable future. If adequate protection until the year 2018 is desired the key generation method should use at least 80 random bits. With 90 random bits adequate protection until at least 2030 may be expected. Thus, from a pragmatic point of view, key length selection for block ciphers is hardly an issue as long as one sticks to widely used modern schemes. In this section, some issues are discussed concerning security levels and key lengths for a number of popular block ciphers.

Stream ciphers are more problematic. They are not considered here for a variety of reasons. Often their design is proprietary or their usage subject to licensing restrictions. Their cryptanalysis is too much in a state of flux and their security level influenced by the way they are used. For instance, the strong version A5/1 of a stream cipher used in the European cellphone industry can trivially be broken (Biryukov, Shamir, & Wagner, 2001) a similar application of the stream cipher RC4 was found to be completely insecure (Fluhrer, Mantin, & Shamir, 2001), and the stream cipher SEAL has been revised several times (Handschuh & Gilbert, 1997). Finally, all six stream ciphers submitted to the NESSIE initiative (New

Table 1 Common Block Ciphers

Name	Key Length	Block Length	Security Level
DES	56	64	56
Two key triple DES	112	64	112
Three key triple DES	168	64	123
DESX	120	64	120
IDEA	128	64	128
AES-128	128	128	128
AES-192	192	128	192
AES-256	256	128	256

European Schemes for Signatures, Integrity, and Encryption [NESSIE], 2000–2003.) were found to be too weak and none was selected, illustrating the apparent difficulty of designing stream ciphers.

Block Ciphers

Table 1 lists some common block ciphers along with their key length choices, block lengths, and the most up-to-date information about their security levels under generic attacks. The list is for illustrative purposes only and is not, nor is it meant to be, exhaustive. In- or exclusion of a cipher in no means indicates the author's support for that cipher or lack thereof. Although other types of attacks such as differential and linear cryptanalysis are not considered to determine the security level (cf. Security Level), the more recent block ciphers are designed to have strong resistance against those attacks as well.

Typically, key lengths of block ciphers are not variable parameters, so for a fixed block cipher iterated application is the only way to increase its security level. Double encryption using two independent keys is widely believed to add little to the security level (cf. Wiener, 2004) and is therefore not considered in Table 1. Triple encryption, however, has significant effect on the security level, as shown for the DES in Table 1. It turned out to be a convenient way to boost security by repeated application of an available cipher when replacement by a stronger one is not an option. Usually the middle encryption is a decryption operation for easy compatibility with the original single encryption. The two key variant uses the same key for the first and last iteration, but a different for the middle decryption iteration, whereas the three key variant uses three independent keys for the three iterations.

For triple-DES the security levels in Table 1 are based on the analysis in Wiener (2004). For two key triple-DES the security level of 112 assumes that the known plaintext consists of at most 2^{12} blocks; for instance, with 2^{30} known plaintext blocks the security level would be only about 100 (cf. M. J. Wiener, personal communication, 2004). Also, under a different attack model, where an unlimited number of chosen plaintexts is allowed, the security level drops even sharper, namely from 112 to about 75 (cf. M. J. Wiener, personal communication, 2004). For DESX (cf. Kilian & Rogaway, 1996) and IDEA (cf. Biham, Dunkelman, Furman, & Mor, 2004) the security levels are based on the fact that even after many years no effective cryptanalysis has been published, as far as generic attacks are concerned. For the advanced encryption standard (AES), they may be based on wishful thinking because at the time of writing of this chapter the AES has been scrutinized for only a few years. But this is combined with the expectation (based on the sudden replacement of SHA by SHA-1, see Cryptographic Hash Functions) that if anytime soon something serious affecting the AES would be found, a modification would be introduced. Table 1 shows that, other than for legacy reasons and if the security level is the only criterion, there is in principle no reason to settle for a cipher that offers a security level lower than its key length.

Performance Considerations

As indicated under Security Level, a proper interpretation and comparison of the security levels in Table 1 in principle requires knowledge of the relative speeds of the various block ciphers. It is also mentioned, however, that this type of "overprecision" has no practical relevance. This is illustrated here.

According to Eq. (1) under Security Level, security level λ offers adequate protection until the year $y(\lambda) = 1982 + 3(\lambda - 56)/2$, disregarding the effect caused by the speed relative to the DES. A block cipher of security level $\lambda \geq 128$ leads to an uncorrected year estimate of $y(128) = 2090$ and beyond. Proper interpretation of this result is that security level 128 should suffice for, say, the next 3 decades and probably even longer. Incorporation of the effect of the speed compared with the DES has no effect. For instance, IDEA and the DES have comparable hardware performance, but in software, IDEA is approximately twice faster (i.e., $s = 2$ in the notation presented under Security Level). So, in principle it would be "correct" and may be even believed to be prudent to subtract $1.5 \log_2 2 = 1.5$ from the year 2090, as set forth under Security Level. But the practical conclusion that IDEA should offer adequate security for the foreseeable future remains untouched by this correction. The same practical conclusion would be reached for block ciphers of security level 128 that would be a million times faster or slower than the DES.

Other Considerations

Another issue with block ciphers is their block length. With b bit blocks, and under reasonable assumptions regarding randomness of the inputs and the cipher's output behavior, a duplicate output block may be expected after about $2^{b/2}$ blocks have been encrypted. A duplicate generated with the same key may facilitate cryptanalysis and should be avoided.

When $b = 64$, this implies that the key should be refreshed well before 2^{32} blocks of 64 bits (i.e., 32 GB) have been encrypted—say after 10 gigabytes. When $b = 128$, the likelihood is negligible that duplicate blocks are encountered for any realistic amount of data properly encrypted with the same key.

Symmetric Key Lengths That Offer Adequate Protection

With the exception of the DES, all ciphers listed in Table 1 offer adequate protection with respect to generic attacks at least until the year 2030: even the weakest among them, two key triple-DES, may be expected to offer adequate security until 2066 because, according to Eq. (1), $y(112) = 1982 + 3(112 - 56)/2 = 2066$. Correction for the performance degradation compared with the DES (by $-\log_2 1/3$ resulting in $y(112) = 2067.5$ because s would be $1/3$) is meaningless because the precision suggested by the original calculation is overzealous already: the model is nowhere near precise enough to draw conclusions up to a specific year, let alone half a year, and certainly not if it is more than 50 years in the future.

Given the virtual lack of cryptanalytic progress with respect to generic attacks and assuming current cryptanalytic trends persist (i.e., that cryptanalysis remains relatively ineffective), the ciphers of security level ≥ 128 can be expected to offer adequate protection for any conceivable commercial application, including long-term data storage, and as long as anyone can reasonably predict. Thus, most ciphers from Table 1 with the exception of the DES can safely be recommended, as long as the amount of data that will be encrypted with a single key is limited. If the latter cannot be guaranteed, the AES should be used.

In Blaze et al. (1996), which dates back from 1996, it is recommended that for adequate protection for the next 20 years (i.e., until the year 2016) keys in newly deployed symmetric cryptosystems should be at least 90 bits long. According to the estimates presented here, security level $\lambda = 90$ would offer adequate security until the year $y(90) = 1982 + 3(90 - 56)/2 = 2033$ and security level $\lambda(2016) = 56 + 2(2016 - 1982)/3 = 78\frac{2}{3}$ would suffice until the year $y = 2016$ (cf. Eqs. [1] and [2]). Thus, the recommendation of Blaze et al. (1996) is conservative and can be followed without hesitation.

It may seem wasteful to use a key length such as 128 that leads to a security level that is so much larger than necessary. As far as the speed of symmetric cryptosystems is concerned, this is not an issue because key sizes have no major impact on their speed. If the "overlong" key is problematic because of other concerns such as cost of key exchange or storage, a sufficiently shortened but still adequately long version may be used and padded with a fixed sequence of bits known as *salt* (cf. Schneier, 1996). If used, salt should be applied with great care. For instance, in case of triple-DES care must be taken that it does not reduce the encryption to double encryption, thereby effectively almost halving the length of the already shortened key (cf. Wiener, 2004). Because algorithms are generally designed assuming the entire key is secret, as a general practice it is recommended to derive the actual key from the shortened version and the salt by hashing or a similar mixing operation.

CRYPTOGRAPHIC HASH FUNCTIONS

Given an input consisting of an arbitrary sequence of bits, a cryptographic hash function efficiently produces a fixed length output, the *hash* of the input. In this section H denotes the bit length of the hash. The output is intended as a "fingerprint" of the input in data integrity and authentication applications. Therefore, cryptographic hash functions must have a number of properties that make them suitable for these applications. In the first place given any output value for which the corresponding input is unknown, it must be computationally infeasible to find any input that hashes to that output. Second, for a known (input/output) pair, it must be computationally infeasible to find another input that hashes to the same output. Although these two properties suffice for many applications (cf. Bellare & Rogaway, 1997) it is common to assume a stronger version of the last property, namely that it must be computationally infeasible to find two distinct inputs that hash to the same output. This last requirement is often referred to as *collision resistance*.

The issue at discussion here are the requirements on H without which a cryptographic hash function cannot have the desired properties (i.e., the length requirements that must be met irrespective of any of the other properties of the hash function). Obviously, satisfying the requirements on H does not guarantee proper design of the hash function, it is just a necessary first step.

Assume that the output of a hash function behaves as a uniformly distributed random H bit value. It follows from the first two requirements that H must be chosen such that it is computationally infeasible to perform 2^H applications of the hash function (for random inputs). Thus, to achieve security level λ and to satisfy the first two requirements, it must be the case that $H \geq \lambda$.

The collision resistance requirement, however, has more severe consequences for H. If values are drawn at random from a set of cardinality C, then the expected number of draws before an element is drawn twice (a so-called collision) is approximately $1.25\sqrt{C}$. This fact is commonly known as the *birthday paradox*. If follows that if the hash is computed of different randomly selected inputs, a duplicate output can be expected after about $1.25 * 2^{H/2}$ attempts. This birthday paradox attack is fully parallelizable with cost, as defined under Security Level essentially proportional to $2^{H/2}$ (cf. Wiener, 2004). To achieve security level λ and to satisfy the third requirement, it must therefore be the case that $H \geq 2\lambda$.

The search for a collision as described above is commonly known as a *collision attack*. Resistance against exhaustive key search and collision attacks play comparable roles in the contexts of symmetric cryptosystems and cryptographic hash functions, respectively: well-designed symmetric cryptosystems do not allow generic attacks faster than exhaustive key search, and well-designed cryptographic hash functions do not allow discovery faster than by collision attacks of a distinct pair of inputs with identical outputs.

Cryptographic Hash Functions

Table 2 lists some common hash functions along with their output lengths and the most up-to-date information

Table 2 Common Cryptographic Hash Functions

Name	H	Security Level
RIPEMD-160	160	80
SHA-1	160	80
SHA-256	256	128
SHA-384	384	192
SHA-512	512	256

about their security levels under collision attacks (cf. Federal Information Processing Standard 180-2, 2000).

Cryptanalytic Developments

Well-known precursors of the cryptographic hash functions in Table 2 are MD4, MD5, and RIPEMD-128, all with $H = 128$, and SHA, with $H = 160$. Significant deficiencies were found in their design. MD4 is considered to be broken, and it is widely suspected that the security levels of MD5 and RIPEMD-128 are both lower than 64. Furthermore, a suficiently serious problem was found in SHA to replace it by SHA-1. For a discussion of these developments, see Chabaud and Joux (1998), Dobbertin, Bosselaers, and Preneel (1996), and Bosselaers (2004).

The results of those cryptanalytic findings were incorporated in the design of the cryptographic hash functions in Table 2. That is no guarantee that those functions do not allow faster attacks than collision attacks. But it indicates that the functions from Table 2 were designed with a great deal of care and that an unanticipated new weakness most likely requires new cryptanalytic insights. Given how infrequently such insights occur, it is reasonable at this point to assume that the security levels in Table 2 are accurate for the foreseeable future. This should be combined with a conservative choice of cryptographic hash function and, where possible, application of the methods from Bellare and Rogaway (1997) to design one's protocols in such a way that the cryptographic hash function does not have to be collision resistant (i.e., does not have to meet the third requirement). If the latter is properly done it effectively doubles the security level.

Performance Considerations

Whether a cryptographic hash function of hash length H offers adequate protection until a certain year, as defined under Security Level, in principle depends on the relative speed of the hash function compared to the DES. With inputs of comparable length, the speed of all common cryptographic hash functions is comparable to the speed of common block ciphers, such as the DES. Thus, the effect of incorporating the speed is negligible to begin with. Furthermore, as argued under Symmetric Cryptosystems, for the larger H values the effect is best neglected anyhow because it would lead to inappropriately precise interpretation of inherently imprecise figures.

Cryptographic Hash Lengths That Offer Adequate Protection

In combination with the findings under Security Level and Symmetric Cryptosystems, it follows that cryptographic hash functions with 2λ-bit hash values offer adequate protection until the year $y(\lambda) = 1982 + 3(\lambda - 56)/2$ (cf. Eq. [1]). More in particular, the above cryptographic hash functions with $H = 160$, assuming they remain unbroken, may be expected to offer adequate protection until the year $y(160/2) = 2018$. All functions listed in Table 2 can be expected to offer adequate protection at least until the year 2030, very conservatively estimated, under the proviso that the functions with 160-bit hash values

are used in combination with the methods from Bellare and Rogaway (1997). As a rule of thumb, hash lengths must be chosen to be twice longer than symmetric key lengths.

ASYMMETRIC METHODS
Private Key and Public Key

In asymmetric cryptosystems each user, say A, has its own pair of keys: A's private key s_A and the corresponding public key p_A. Typically, the public key p_A can be used by any party to encrypt information intended for user A, which can then be decrypted by A using s_A. Alternatively, A may use s_A to digitally sign documents, and any party can use p_A to verify the resulting digital signatures. For some cryptosystems, a single private/public key pair allows both en-/decryption and digital signatures, but great care has to be taken when doing so (cf. Davida, 1982; Desmedt & Odlyzko, 2003; Haber & Pinkas, 2001).

Performance Deterioration

For symmetric cryptosystems and cryptographic hash functions the number of realistic alternatives is fairly limited, and their speed hardly depends on the key or hash length one settles for. For asymmetric cryptosystems, the situation is different. There the performance of both the public operation (encryption or signature verification) and the private one (decryption or signature generation) deteriorates markedly, and possibly to different degrees, as the security level increases. Therefore, for asymmetric cryptosystems it is more important than for symmetric cryptosystems and cryptographic hash functions to determine the smallest key length that still offers the right amount of protection, thereby balancing security and performance requirements.

The Design of Asymmetric Cryptosystems

The design of all common symmetric cryptosystems and cryptographic hash functions is mostly based on a combination of hard-to-define ingredients such as experience, avoidance of common errors, incorporation of the latest cryptanalytic insights, taste, sound judgment, and luck. As argued in Landau (2004), the design of the AES is a first attempt to a more scientific, less artful approach to block cipher design. All common asymmetric cryptosystems, conversely, are based on a well-defined mathematical problem, if at all possible combined with a proof that solving the latter is equivalent to breaking the cryptosystem. The security of an asymmetric cryptosystem is then based on the hope and belief that the mathematical problem does not allow an eficient solution. Sometimes that hope turns out to be ill founded. For instance, the once popular trapdoor knapsack public key cryptosystems (cf. Merkle & Hellman, 1978) were found to be susceptible to attacks using lattice basis reduction. Efficient lattice basis reduction methods thus meant the end for trapdoor knapsack asymmetric cryptosystems. Refer to Nguyen and Stern (2001) for the extensive literature on these and related subjects.

Factoring and Discrete Logarithms

The two mathematical problems underlying the popular and by now "classical" asymmetric cryptosystems are integer factorization and computing discrete logarithms, as described below. Both these problems have been the subject of active research during the past few decades. Also, the cryptographic protocols they are embedded in have been widely studied, in various cases resulting in provable equivalence of breaking the protocol and solving the mathematical problem. Despite occasional jumps because of theoretical advances, it turned out that the practical implications of the solution methods for the mathematical problems underlying asymmetric cryptosystems so far always displayed a smooth pattern without jumps or unwelcome "surprises." The assumption that this same smooth pattern persists allows reasonably well-founded analyses of key lengths required for adequate protection in the future. These analyses are presented in the subsequent sections.

It should be understood, however, that a clearly discernable and well-established past pattern in practical cryptanalytic progress is no guarantee that the future pattern will be the same or that there will not be any surprising breakthroughs with immediate practical consequences. With the present state of the art there is no hard proof of the security of any of the popular asymmetric cryptosystems, simply because there are no proofs yet of the diffculty of any of the underlying mathematical problems: the only evidence of their difficulty is our failure to solve them. This is independent of any proofs of equivalence between a cryptosystem and its underlying mathematical problem. To refer to this provable equivalence as "provable security," as common in the cryptographic literature, may be misleading, because what it actually means is "provable equivalence to a problem of unproved hardness."

Roughly speaking, all common asymmetric cryptosystems are based on one of the following two problems, or a variation thereof:

Integer factorization. Given a composite integer $n > 0$, find integers $u > 1$ and $v > 1$ such that $n = uv$.
In RSA, the most common factoring based asymmetric cryptosystem, a user's public key contains the integer n, the corresponding private key contains (information equivalent to) u and v, and n is unique per user.

Discrete logarithm. Given an element g of a multiplicatively written group G and an element h in the subgroup $\langle g \rangle$ generated by g, find an integer k such that $g^k = h$. The smallest nonnegative such k is referred to as the discrete logarithm of h with respect to g and denoted $\log_g h$.
For additively written groups, one would look for an integer k such that $kg = h$. The smallest nonnegative such k is again referred to as $\log_g h$.
In discrete logarithm-based asymmetric cryptosystems, a user's public key contains g and h and the corresponding private key contains $\log_g h$. Different users may share the same g but use different h's.

The *traditional* discrete logarithm problem refers to the case where G is chosen as the multiplicative group $(\mathbf{F}_{p^\ell})^*$

of a finite field $\mathbf{F}_{p^\ell}$ of cardinality p^ℓ, for some prime p and positive integer ℓ.

Instances of these problems can easily be generated that are suitable for cryptographic applications and generally believed to be hard to solve. In the sections below, it is discussed how to do this in such a way that the corresponding cryptosystems offer adequate protection until a specified year, as defined under Security Level. This has certain consequences for the size of the integer n and its factors, for the cardinality $\#\langle g \rangle$ of the subgroup $\langle g \rangle$, and for the cardinality $p^\ell - 1$ of the group $G = (\mathbf{F}_{p^\ell})^*$ if the traditional discrete logarithm problem is used. Intuitively this is rather obvious, because small integers are easy to factor, small factors are easy to find, and discrete logarithms are easy to calculate if $\#\langle g \rangle$ is small. The requirements on n and its factors are discussed under Factoring-Based Cryptosystems and the same is done for g both for the case $G = (\mathbf{F}_{p^\ell})^*$ and for more general groups G under Discrete Logarithm-Based Cryptosystems.

Other Asymmetric Cryptosystems

There are quite a few asymmetric cryptosystems that are based on different mathematical problems than the currently popular ones mentioned above, but that have not yet gained general acceptance. The reason for the latter is related to the underlying mathematical problem, the cryptographic protocol it is embedded in, or a combination of these issues. There may be skepticism about the difficulty of the mathematical problem because it has not been studied long enough. Or the effectiveness of solution methods may be hard to judge or in a constant state of flux, making it difficult to recommend secure parameter choices. Also, cryptographic protocols that are provably equivalent to the mathematical problem may still be lacking, or the cryptosystem may simply be too impractical. Asymmetric cryptosystems that have any of these shortcomings are discussed no further in this chapter. Examples are the recently proposed lattice-based cryptosystems (cf. Nguyen & Stern, 2001), such as NTRU in Ajtai and Dwork (1997), Goldreich, Goldwasser, and Halevi (1997), and, in particular, Hoffstein, Pipher, and Silverman (1998) (even though it was not originally designed as a lattice-based cryptosystem). Although NTRU looks promising because of frequent protocol design tweaks, the dust has not settled yet and it is too early for a fair security assessment. The reader is recommended to consult the recent cryptology literature to find the latest updates on asymmetric cryptosystems that are not treated here.

FACTORING-BASED CRYPTOSYSTEMS

There are several types of asymmetric cryptosystems that rely for their security on the hardness of the integer factorization problem: if the integer factorization problem can be solved for a certain composite integer referred to as the *modulus* n, then the cryptosystem using that n can be broken. Thus, factoring the modulus suffces to break the cryptosystem. In this section, we discuss how n should be selected in such a way that the integer factorization problem for n offers adequate protection until a year of one's choice. It should be kept in mind, however, that for most common factoring-based cryptosystems (such as RSA) it has, in general, not been proved that factoring the modulus is also necessary to break them, although cryptosystems equivalent to factoring do exist. An example is Rabin's signature scheme (cf. Rabin, 1979).

Main Variants

The way the modulus is constructed depends on the factoring-based cryptosystem one uses. In the most common factoring-based cryptosystems, the modulus is the product of two primes of approximately the same size (cf. Rivest, Shamir, & Adleman, 1983). A variation, RSA multiprime (cf. Rivest, Shamir, & Adleman, 1983), improves the efficiency of the private operations by allowing more than two factors of approximately equal size in the modulus. Less common variants are RSA for paranoids (Shamir, 1995), where the private operations are performed modulo the smallest prime factor of the modulus, and variants where the modulus contains repeated factors. Requirements on the size of the modulus and its factors are discussed below. For any of the variants moduli can be constructed efficiently because primes of any practical size can be generated quickly.

Trial Division

The conceptually most straightforward way to factor a composite integer n is by trying if n is divisible by 2, 3, 5, 7, 11, 13,..., successively trying all primes until the smallest proper divisor is found. This process is known as *trial division*. It remains the method of choice of amateur factorizers. For that reason a detailed explanation of the cryptanalytic ineffectiveness of trial division is provided.

For randomly selected composites without known properties, and therefore not stemming from cryptographic applications, trial division is often a very efficient way to find a factor because for random composites the smallest factor can be expected to be small: half of the random composites are even, so the first trial division attempt will be successful in 50% of the cases, one-third of the remaining (odd) numbers is divisible by 3 and so on. It is very easy, however, to construct composites for which trial division is totally ineffective. This can be seen as follows.

According to the *prime number theorem* the number of primes up to x is proportional to $x/\log x$. This means that to find the smallest prime factor p of n using trial division on the order of $p/\log p$ smaller primes have to be tested before p is found. Because the cost of each attempt is at least proportional to the logarithm of the number tested and because the primes $\leq p$ can be generated in time proportional to p, the overall computational effort to find the prime factor p of n is proportional to p. Thus, if n is constructed as the product of two, say, b-digit primes, the computational effort to factor n using trial division is on the order of 10^b, which can be parallelized in any way one sees fit by distributing ranges of candidate factors. Even for moderate b such as 50 a computational effort of this magnitude is out of reach, also if any realistic level of parallelism is applied. Furthermore, there are other factoring methods that would factor such n much

faster. These other methods also allow arbitrary, but even much simpler, parallelization.

Another consequence of the prime number theorem is that the number of b-digit primes outnumbers the number of smaller primes. Thus, it does not help much, as often proposed, to exclude from the search in the example the primes having fewer than b digits thereby limiting the trial divisions to b-digit primes. This counting argument needs to be refined if binary as opposed to decimal length is used—amateur factorizers, however, are usually bit challenged and prefer decimal notation.

Exponential Time Factoring Algorithms

In the worst case, where n has two factors of approximately equal size, the computational effort to factor n using trial division is proportional to $\sqrt{n} = n^{1/2} = \exp((\log n)/2)$. With a constant multiple of the input length $\log_2 n$ in the exponent, it follows that trial division is an *exponential time algorithm*. There are exponential time factoring algorithms that are much faster than trial division. For instance, Pollard's rho method (Pollard, 1978) can be expected to find the smallest p dividing n after a computational effort that is not proportional to p but to $\sqrt{p}$ (i.e., proportional to $n^{1/2}$ in the worst case $p \approx \sqrt{n}$).

If exponential time algorithms were the fastest factoring algorithms, it would be possible to select moduli n in such a way that $\log_2 n$ is proportional to the desired security level: if Pollards rho would be the best factoring algorithm, then 4λ-bit moduli would offer security level λ. Unfortunately, for cryptographic applications of factoring-based asymmetric cryptosystems, exponential-time algorithms are by no means the best that can be done for factoring. As indicated above, much faster factoring algorithms exist. As a consequence, the required modulus bit length grows much faster than a linear function of the desired security level. In particular, modulus sizes grow much faster than symmetric cryptosystem key sizes and cryptographic hash function sizes.

Polynomial Time Factoring Algorithms

On the opposite side of the spectrum from exponential-time algorithms are the *polynomial time algorithms*: a polynomial time factoring algorithm would require computational effort proportional to at most $(\log n)^c$, for some constant c. Although a polynomial time factoring algorithm has been published in Shor, 1994, it requires a not-yet-existing type of computer, a so-called quantum computer, to run it on. If the engineering problems of building a large enough quantum computer can be solved, factoring may be done in polynomial time, which will most likely mean the end for factoring-based asymmetric cryptosystems. Even a very modest prototype quantum device whose factoring capabilities would be non-trivial but well below those of an ordinary PC, for instance a device that would be able to factor a 128-bit RSA modulus in half an hour, would suffce to shake our confidence in the practical difficulty of integer factorization. Most popular number theory based asymmetric cryptosystems would be affected to the same dramatic extent. The effect on symmetric cryptosystems and cryptographic hash functions would be less significant.

Alternatively, development of a polynomial time factoring algorithm that would run on a traditional computer, a possibility that cannot yet provably be excluded, would have the same consequence. Even if the method has complexity $O((\log n)^{12})$ and will not be a practical threat, its mere existence would be devastating for most current asymmetric cryptosystems—irrespective of future improvements and eventual practical applicability of the method.

At this point, there is not sufficient reason to suspect that practical polynomial time factoring is a realistic prospect. The possibility of practical polynomial time factoring is therefore not included in the analysis below.

What can realistically be done, however, is something that lies between exponential time and polynomial time factoring. These so-called subexponential time factoring algorithms are further discussed below.

Subexponential Time Factoring Algorithms

The computational effort required for an exponential time factoring algorithm is bounded from above by a constant positive power of

$$n = \exp(\log n).$$

For a polynomial time method the required computational effort would be bounded from above by a constant power of

$$\log n = \exp(\log \log n).$$

To express the computational effort of algorithms that are faster than exponential time but not as fast as polynomial time, both possibilities are captured in a single formula in the following way. Let

$$L[n, r, \alpha] = \exp(\alpha (\log n)^r (\log \log n)^{1-r}).$$

Exponential time is characterized by $r = 1$, polynomial time by $r = 0$, and everything in between (i.e., $0 < r < 1$) is referred to as *subexponential time* (with, in all cases, α a positive constant).

There are many factoring algorithms for which the computational effort is expected to be $L[n, 1/2, 1 + o(1)]$ for $n \to \infty$ (i.e., asymptotically for n to infinity, the value of α approaches 1). For most of these algorithms the analysis is based on heuristic arguments, for some it can rigorously be proved. Note that, on the scale from $r = 0$ to $r = 1$ suggested above, $L[n, 1/2, 1 + o(1)]$ (i.e., $r = 1/2$) is halfway between exponential time and polynomial time—this is just a curiosity of this parameterization and should be taken with a grain of salt. One example is the quadratic sieve factoring algorithm (QS), which can heuristically be expected to factor n, irrespective of any properties its factors may have, for a computational effort that behaves as $L[n, 1/2, 1 + o(1)]$ for $n \to \infty$ (cf. Pomerance, 1983). Another example is the elliptic curve method (ECM), which can heuristically be expected to find a factor p of n for a computational effort $(\log n)^2 L[p, 1/2, \sqrt{2} + o(1)]$ (cf. Lenstra, 1987); in the worst case $p \approx \sqrt{n}$ this becomes $L[n, 1/2, 1 + o(1)]$.

Number Field Sieve

Because so many quite different methods all share essentially the same expected computational effort $L[n, 1/2, 1 + o(1)]$, this was suspected by some to be the "ultimate" complexity of factoring, although the author is unfortunately not aware of any published conjectures. In 1988 these cryptographic dreams were shattered by John Pollard's invention of a new factoring algorithm (cf. Lenstra & Lenstra, 1993). The blow was, however, softened considerably by credible-looking evidence that the new method would become practical only beyond key sizes that were then employed in practice. Even though as a result of Pollard's invention long-term expectations suddenly changed significantly, the practical impact turned out to fit smoothly on the anticipated cryptanalytic curve. The credible-looking evidence later turned out to be wrong—if the new algorithm had immediately been as effective as it turned out to be, its practical impact would have been alarming, too.

The original version of the new factoring algorithm, now referred to as the *special number field sieve* (SNFS), was intended to factor the ninth Fermat number $F_9 = 2^{2^9} + 1$, a number that was indeed completely factored in 1990 (Lenstra, Lenstra, Manasse, & Pollard, 1993). The SNFS can be applied to numbers that allow a particularly "nice" polynomial representation, such as F_9. Based on heuristic arguments the expected computational effort is $L[n, 1/3, 1.526 + o(1)]$. The generalized version, now referred to as the *number field sieve* (NFS), factors any number n for a (heuristic) expected computational effort $L[n, 1/3, 1.923 + o(1)]$ (cf. Lenstra & Lenstra, 1993), which was later improved to $L[n, 1/3, 1.902 + o(1)]$ (cf. Coppersmith, 1993).

On the scale from exponential time ($r = 1$) to polynomial time ($r = 0$) the NFS represents substantial progress from the halfway point ($r = 1/2$) in the direction of polynomial time algorithms. Because the invention of the NFS no progress affecting the current best $r = 1/3$ value has been published (with the exception of $r = 0$ for quantum computers).

The Cost of the NFS

Let the cost function be as defined under Security Level, that is, the product of time (or, equivalently, computational effort) and equipment cost. The NFS has two major stages, the relation collection stage and the matrix stage. As shown in Bernstein (2001) and Lenstra et al. (2002), the cost of the NFS depends on the way the relation collection stage is carried out. If a memory-intensive approach based on sieving is used the overall NFS cost behaves as $L[n, 1/3, 2.852 + o(1)]$ for $n \to \infty$. An ECM-based approach is asymptotically considerably less costly: just $L[n, 1/3, 1.976 + o(1)]$ if the matrix step is done on a mesh of processors and $L[n, 1/3, 2.080 + o(1)]$ if the matrix is done using more traditional methods, and both for $n \to \infty$.

NFS Results

Compared with the older $L[n, 1/2, 1 + o(1)]$ methods, the NFS is conceptually complicated and, originally, suffered from rather large $o(1)$ values. Therefore, it was believed by some that the NFS had only theoretical but no practical value (cf. Dagstuhl Seminar 9226, 1992). However, a lot of progress has been made to improve the method, thereby lowering the $o(1)$s. As a result the NFS eventually surpassed the older methods also from a practical point of view. At the time of writing of this chapter, the NFS is the method of choice for actual large-scale distributed factorization experiments (cf. Cavallar et al., 2000; J. Franke, personal communication, 2004) and special purpose factoring hardware design proposals such as TWINKLE and TWIRL (cf. Lenstra & Shamir, 2000; Shamir & Tromer, 2003; Shamir, 1999). The following results have been obtained using the sieving-based approach:

- **Software implementation**: a 576-bit modulus has been factored using the NFS in about 12 years of computing time on a 1-GHz Pentium III processor (J. Franke, personal communication, 2004). In reality the attack made use of the full parallelizability of the main part of the attack: it was done on m processors in $12/m$ years of computing time per processor, for some large m. Assuming the essential parts of a single 1-GHz Pentium III processor can be obtained for, say, U.S.\$100, a software attack on a 576-bit RSA modulus would cost less than 0.5M dollardays.

- **Special purpose hardware design proposal:** using 90-nm VLSI technology, it can be expected that factorization of a 1024-bit modulus takes at most one year using TWIRL, a special purpose hardware device that takes at most U.S.\$1 million to build (Lenstra et al., 2003). It follows that in 2004, at the time of writing this chapter, the cost of an attack on a 1024-bit RSA modulus using dedicated hardware can be estimated as at most 400M dollardays.

    The earlier 130-nm version of the same device has a cost that is 10 times as high. The relatively large cost reduction is because of the fact that the larger memory of the later 90-nm design allowed much better parameter choices and thus led to a more than proportional speedup. This is an example of the effect that was noted in the discussion of Moore's law under Security Level. This remark is solely meant to explain why the 90-nm data point is so much better than the previous 130-nm one, it does not influence Moore's law or the way it will be used for asymmetric crypto systems,

Actually, these results refer to just the relation collection step, in practice the most cumbersome stage of the NFS factoring process. The other major stage, the matrix step, although in theory equally costly, is in practice negligible compared to the relation collection stage (cf. Bernstein, 2001; Lenstra et al., 2002).

Using $L[n, 1/3, \ldots]$-based estimates (as shown below) it can be seen that dedicated hardware is substantially more cost-effective than a software implementation. This implies that the hardware estimates lead to larger, more conservative RSA moduli. The estimates below are therefore based on the hardware figures.

Extrapolation to Other Modulus Lengths

The 400M dollardays cost to factor 1024-bit moduli in the year 2004 is combined with the asymptotic cost estimates for NFS to estimate the cost of factoring b-bit moduli in 2004 as follows:

$$\frac{L[2^b, 1/3, \alpha]}{L[2^{1024}, 1/3, \alpha]} \times 400\text{M dollardays},$$

with $\alpha = 2.852 + o(1)$. For the sake of simplicity—and because no better alternative is available—it is assumed that upon substitution the two $o(1)$s cancel. From a theoretical point of view, this assumption is hardly acceptable, but for limited range approximations the results of this compromise approach have been satisfactory, so far. Although the 400M dollardays for 1024-bit moduli is based on the sieving-based approach, the author found that rough estimates for the ECM-based approach are not that much different. Therefore, one may alternatively replace 2.852 by 1.976 or 2.080 in the above estimate. For key length estimate purposes, $\alpha = 1.976 + o(1)$ is a more prudent choice than the other two choices because $\alpha = 1.976 + o(1)$ results in lower factoring costs and therefore larger and more conservative choices for key lengths achieving adequate protection.

As an example, 1248-bit moduli are roughly expected to be between

$$\frac{L[2^{1248}, 1/3, 1.976]}{L[2^{1024}, 1/3, 1.976]} \approx 250,$$

and

$$\frac{L[2^{1248}, 1/3, 2.852]}{L[2^{1024}, 1/3, 2.852]} \approx 3000$$

times costlier to factor than 1024-bit ones. Similarly, 1536-bit moduli are between 137K and 26M times costlier and 2048-bit moduli are at least 2 billion times costlier to factor than 1024-bit ones.

These extrapolation arguments are mostly useful to get a quick first impression of the cost of breaking a certain modulus size. If a more accurate estimate is needed, the much more cumbersome approach from Lenstra et al. (2003) can be used.

Cryptanalytic Developments

During the past 3 to 4 decades, there has been a steady stream of developments in integer factorization algorithms. The practical performance of the best-existing algorithms such as the NFS and the ECM is still constantly fine-tuned and improved. This smooth progress is, less frequently, combined with more substantial advances such as, most importantly, the invention of an entirely new method or, less dramatic but often with important practical consequences, better ways to handle certain steps of existing methods. It is reasonable to assume that the trend as observed so far will continue for the years to come.

Combining the occasional jumps and the regular smooth progress, the effect of cryptanalytic progress on the difficulty of the integer factorization problem turns out to be very similar to Moore's law: overall, and on the same equipment, the cost of factoring drops by a factor 2 every 18 months. According to Moore's traditional law as formulated under Security Level, the equipment cost also drops by a factor 2 every 18 months. These two effects, cryptanalytic progress and hardware advances, have in the past been independent and it is reasonable to assume that they will remain to be so. As a result of the combination of these two independent effects, the decrease in the cost of factoring is modeled in the following way:

Double Moore factoring law: The cost of factoring any fixed modulus drops by a factor 2 every 9 months.

As an example, in 2.5 years it can be expected that the cost of factoring a 1024-bit modulus is reduced to the following:

$$\frac{400\text{M}}{2^{2.5} \times 12/9} \approx 40\text{M dollardays}.$$

Similarly, over a period of 6 years it is expected that the factoring cost drops by a factor $2^{6 \times 12/9} = 256$. Thus, it would be conservative to expect that factoring a 1248-bit modulus in 2010 would cost about the same as a 1024-bit modulus in 2004.

Note that the double Moore factoring law consists of equal technology and algorithmic components. If one argues that because of economies of scale and high parallelism a double Moore law already applies to the technology component alone (cf. P. C. Kocher, personal communication, September 1999), then one should consider a triple instead of double Moore factoring law. This is not done here.

Small Factors

In regular RSA, the modulus is chosen as the product of two primes of approximately equal sizes. Asymptotically, and for all regular RSA moduli commonly in use, the most efficient published method to factor such moduli is the NFS. As cited above, there are at least two variants of RSA where the modulus n may have one (RSA for paranoids) or more (RSA multiprime) prime factors that are substantially smaller than $\sqrt{n}$. Currently, the asymptotically fastest method to find small factors, if there are any, is the ECM. Therefore, care must be taken to select the factors in such a way that finding them using the ECM can be expected to be at least as hard as factoring n using the NFS. The reader is referred to Lenstra (2001) for a further discussion of this point.

RSA Modulus Lengths That Offer Adequate Protection

According to the definition discussed under Security Level, an RSA modulus offers adequate protection until year y if the factorization cost in that year can be expected to be at least 40M dollardays. Thus, 1024-bit RSA moduli offer adequate protection for 2.5 more years from the year 2004, when this chapter was written. More in general, by combining the above extrapolation to other modulus lengths with the double Moore factoring law it can be determined—to the best of the current knowledge—if a b-bit RSA modulus offers adequate protection until the year y: it does if

$$\frac{L(2^b, 1/3, \alpha)}{L(2^{1024}, 1/3, \alpha)} \times 400 \geq 40 \times 2^{4(y-2004)/3},$$

where, again, $\alpha = 1.976$ leads to a conservative, relatively large b value and $\alpha = 2.852$ to a less prudent smaller one. All estimates are conservative in the sense that the base-point of the extrapolation is the cost of an attack on a 1024-bit modulus using the dedicated hardware described in Shamir and Tromer (2003) as analyzed in Lenstra et al. (2003).

Table 3 lists the resulting RSA modulus bit lengths for both choices for α and for several years, and Table 4 lists the years until which several common RSA modulus bit lengths offer adequate protection, again for both α-values. For each year y in the two tables the security level $\lambda(y) = 56 + 2(y - 1982)/3$ that offers adequate protection until year y, rounded upward to the nearest integer, is given between parentheses (cf. Eq. [2]). Note that $\lambda(y)$ corresponds to the minimally required symmetric key length in year y.

It follows from the tables that 2048-bit RSA moduli offer adequate protection at least until the year 2030, and even until 2040 if one is less prudent and confident that ECM-based factoring devices will not be able to outperform the sieving-based approach before the year 2040.

Although this type of estimate is the best that can be done at this point, it should be understood that actual factoring capabilities may follow an entirely different pattern. Any prediction more than a few decades away about security levels is wishful thinking. The figures in the tables should be properly interpreted, namely as today's best estimates that may have to be revised tomorrow. Anyone using factoring based asymmetric cryptosystems should constantly monitor and stay ahead of the developments in the research community.

Table 3 Minimal RSA Modulus Bit Lengths for Adequate Protection Until a Given Year

Year y ($\lambda(y)$)	(Optimistic) Bit Length for $\alpha = 2.852$	(Conservative) Bit Length for $\alpha = 1.976$
2010 (75)	1112	1153
2020 (82)	1387	1569
2030 (88)	1698	2064
2040 (95)	2048	2645
2050 (102)	2439	3314

Table 4 Years Until Which Common RSA Modulus Bit Lengths Offer Adequate Protection

Modulus Bit Length	(Conservative) Year y_c for $\alpha = 1.976$ ($\lambda(y_c)$)		(Optimistic) Year y_o for $\alpha = 2.852$ ($\lambda(y_o)$)	
1024	2006	(72)	2006	(72)
1280	2014	(78)	2017	(80)
1536	2020	(82)	2025	(85)
2048	2030	(88)	2040	(95)
3072	2046	(99)	2065	(112)
4096	2060	(108)	2085	(125)
8192	2100	(135)	2142	(163)

DISCRETE LOGARITHM-BASED CRYPTOSYSTEMS

Let $g \neq 1$ belong to some group G and let $h \neq 1$ be an element of the subgroup $\langle g \rangle$ of G generated by g. It is assumed that the order $\#\langle g \rangle$ of g is known, but the order of h is unspecified. The cryptographic application of the generator g imposes a representation for each element of $\langle g \rangle$. Given these representations the group operation and inversion can be performed efficiently. Using multiplicative notation for the group operation the element g^k can for any k be computed in $O(\log |k|)$ group operations plus a single inversion if $k < 0$. Conversely, because of the cryptographic application, g and G must be chosen such that the "reverse" problem of computing $\log_g h$ offers adequate protection until a year of one's choice. The resulting requirements on g and G are discussed in this section.

The discrete logarithm problem can be solved either in the subgroup $\langle g \rangle$ directly or in the group G in which $\langle g \rangle$ is embedded. For adequate protection, it must be infeasible to solve the problem using either approach. Of particular practical interest is the traditional discrete logarithm problem where $G = (\mathbf{F}_{p^\ell})^*$.

Unsuitable Groups

There are groups in which discrete logarithms are not hard to compute. An example is the additive group of integers modulo a positive integer, where computing discrete logarithms is equivalent to modular division. Obviously, such groups must be avoided in cryptographic applications. Unfortunately, this is not always as easy as it sounds. There are examples of groups where at first sight the discrete logarithm problem looks hard, but where, after closer scrutiny by the research community, the problem turned out to be easier than expected. For instance, a certain type of elliptic curve based groups as proposed for cryptographic applications in Miyaji (1993) was shown to allow trivial discrete logarithm computation in Satoh and Araki (1998), Semaev (1998), and Smart (1999). Interestingly, these groups were offered as an alternative to another class of elliptic curve based groups where the discrete logarithm problem allowed an undesirable reduction to the traditional case $G = (\mathbf{F}_{p^\ell})^*$ (cf. Frey & Rück, 1994; Menezes, Okamoto, & Vanstone, 1993).

Accidents of this sort are impossible to avoid. But, as a general advice, cryptographic application of newly proposed groups should be postponed until the mathematical and cryptanalytic communities have scrutinized the proposed groups and failed to "break" them. In the sequel, it is implicitly assumed that the groups in question do not allow other attacks than the ones described below. If $G = (\mathbf{F}_{p^\ell})^*$, discrete logarithms in G can be calculated using a method that is similar to the NFS algorithm for integer factorization discussed under Factoring-Based Cryptosystems. Roughly speaking, computing discrete logarithms in $(\mathbf{F}_{p^\ell})^*$ is about as hard as factoring an integer n with $\log n \approx \log p^\ell$ using the NFS. Thus, to achieve adequate protection until a given year the size requirements on n as presented under Factoring-Based Cryptosystems imply the same size requirements on p^ℓ.

This is a rough estimate in the sense that it somewhat underestimates the difficulty of computing discrete logarithms in $(\mathbf{F}_{p^\ell})^*$ and thereby overestimates the p^ℓ values that would suffice for adequate protection. An often encountered argument is that the matrix step (cf. Factoring-Based Cryptosystems) as required for the discrete logarithm version of the NFS, is much harder than the one for the regular factoring NFS. It is true that the matrices, assuming comparable dimensions, are harder to deal with. But, in the first place, compared with factoring the cost will not increase by more than a factor $(\log \#\langle g \rangle)^2$, which is, relatively speaking, only a minor effect. In the second place, the actual cost of the relation collection stage (cf. Factoring-Based Cryptosystems) may still far outweigh the matrix step cost, further diminishing the effect of the more expensive matrix step on the overall cost of the computation. Given the granularity of finite field sizes that are available in practice, there is no practical need for more precise estimates.

Reduction to Prime Order Subgroup

Because of the Pohlig–Hellman algorithm, the problem of computing $\log_g h$ can efficiently be reduced to the problem of computing $\log_g h$ modulo each of the prime divisors of $\#\langle g \rangle$ and their powers (cf. Pohlig & Hellman, 1978). Therefore, and because the complete factorization of $\#\langle g \rangle$ may be unknown and hard to find (cf. Factoring-Based Cryptosystems), it is assumed that $\#\langle g \rangle$ has at least one prime divisor that satisfies the size requirements specified further below and, if applicable, the structural requirements set forth in the next paragraphs. For convenience of presentation and without loss of generality, it is assumed that $\#\langle g \rangle$ itself is prime, implying that the order of h, the element whose discrete logarithm is sought, equals the same prime. If $G = (\mathbf{F}_{p^\ell})^*$ with $\ell \geq 2$, this prime $\#\langle g \rangle$ must be carefully chosen, as shown in the next paragraphs.

The Discrete Logarithm Problem in a Subgroup of $G = (\mathbf{F}_{p^\ell})^*$

The generator g belongs to $G = (\mathbf{F}_{p^\ell})^*$ and thus has (prime) order dividing $p^\ell - 1$. For $\ell > 1$, however, the number $p^\ell - 1$ has factors that should be avoided in the sense that if $\#\langle g \rangle$ divides such a factor, the difficulty of the discrete logarithm problem in $\langle g \rangle$ may be affected: g must be chosen such that $\#\langle g \rangle$ does not divide $p^d - 1$ for any d less than and dividing ℓ. This is explained below. Readers not interested in the justification of the choice of $\#\langle g \rangle$ can skip to its size requirements.

Justification of Choice of Subgroup of $(\mathbf{F}_{p^\ell})^*$

For each positive integer d dividing ℓ the finite field $\mathbf{F}_{p^\ell}$ has a subfield $\mathbf{F}_{p^d}$ and the multiplicative group $G = (\mathbf{F}_{p^\ell})^*$ has a subgroup $(\mathbf{F}_{p^\ell})^*$ of order $p^d - 1$ dividing $p^\ell - 1$. If the order $\#\langle g \rangle$ of g divides $p^d - 1$ for a d less than and dividing ℓ, then g belongs to the true subgroup $(\mathbf{F}_{p^d})^*$ of the multiplicative group $G = (\mathbf{F}_{p^\ell})^*$ of the finite field $(\mathbf{F}_{p^\ell})$, and thereby g belongs to the true subfield $\mathbf{F}_{p^d}$ of $\mathbf{F}_{p^\ell}$. Representations of such subfield elements of $\mathbf{F}_{p^\ell}$ can efficiently be mapped back and forth to direct representations in the finite field $\mathbf{F}_{p^d}$ itself. As a result, the discrete logarithm problem in $\langle g \rangle$ can be solved in the true subfield $\mathbf{F}_{p^d}$, which is a substantially easier problem than in the "large" field $\mathbf{F}_{p^\ell}$: in the notation presented under Factoring-Based Cryptosystems it reduces the cost of computing discrete logarithms from $L[p^\ell, 1/3, \alpha]$ to $L[p^d, 1/3, \alpha]$, for some constant $\alpha > 0$.

It follows that g should be chosen in such a way that its order $\#\langle g \rangle$ does not divide $p^d - 1$ for any d less than and dividing ℓ. This is achieved as follows. The dth cyclotomic polynomial $\Phi_d(X)$ is recursively defined by the following:

$$X^d - 1 = \prod_{t \text{ dividing } d} \Phi_t(X).$$

For instance, $\Phi_1(X) = X - 1$, $\Phi_2(X) = X^2 - 1/X - 1 = X + 1$, $\Phi_3(X) = X^3 - 1/X - 1 = X^2 + X + 1$, and so on. Thus, g must be chosen in such a way that $\#\langle g \rangle$ divides $p^\ell - 1$ but does not divide $\Phi_d(p)$ for a d less than and dividing ℓ. This condition is satisfied if g is chosen so that $\#\langle g \rangle$ is a prime divisor larger than ℓ of $\Phi_\ell(p)$, the "last" cyclotomic factor of $p^\ell - 1$ (cf. Lenstra, 1997). For instance, if $\ell = 2$ the order $\#\langle g \rangle$ of g must be chosen as a sufficiently large prime divisor of $\Phi_2(p) = p + 1$; and of

$$\Phi_6(p) = \frac{p^6 - 1}{(p - 1)(p + 1)(p^2 + p + 1)} = p^2 - p + 1$$

if $\ell = 6$.

Size Requirements

Under the general representation assumptions specified at the beginning of this section (and avoiding unsuitable groups), the best methods to solve the discrete logarithm problem in $\langle g \rangle$ require approximately $\sqrt{\#\langle g \rangle}$

group operations. There are essentially two methods that achieve this operation count, Shanks's baby-step/giant-step method (Knuth, 1998, Exercise 5.17) and Pollard's rho method (Pollard, 1978). Shanks's method requires a substantial amount of memory. This implies that the cost of an attack effort (as defined under Security Level) by means of Shanks's methods is much larger than $\sqrt{\#\langle g \rangle}$: according to Wiener (2004) it is approximately $(\#\langle g \rangle)^{2/3}$.

Pollard's rho method requires just a constant amount of memory when run on a single processor. Although this implies an attack effort cost of approximately $\sqrt{\#\langle g \rangle}$, an attack of this sort does not have any practical significance because the original algorithm imposes a long serial computation that cannot be parallelized. However, a variation of Pollard's rho method allows efficient parallelization with the same cost (cf. Pollard, 1978). Therefore, both from a theoretical as practical point of view, the cost of Pollard rho based attack effort is approximately $\sqrt{\#\langle g \rangle}$.

It follows that the discrete logarithm problem in an order $\#\langle g \rangle$ subgroup g offers security level approximately $\log_2 \sqrt{\#\langle g \rangle} = \frac{1}{2} \log_2 \#\langle g \rangle$. To decide whether a certain discrete logarithm security level offers adequate protection as defined in Section 2, the relative speed of the group operation compared to the DES must in principle be taken into account. Because in any standard application the DES will be at least as fast as the group operation, and considerably faster if $g \in (\mathbf{F}_{p^\ell})^*$, neglecting this effect will only increase the level of protection offered by the discrete logarithm based cryptosystem.

Cryptanalytic Developments

Concerning cryptanalytic methods that directly attack the subgroup discrete logarithm problem, the most recent substantial cryptanalytic development was the parallelization of Pollard's rho method, as referred to above. This influenced the practical significance of a Pollard rho based attack, but had no theoretical effect on the cost. As far as the choice of the subgroup size $\#\langle g \rangle$ is concerned, it is therefore reasonable to assume that for the foreseeable future the cost of subgroup attack efforts will not be different from the current cost of $\sqrt{\#\langle g \rangle}$ group operations. This cost corresponds to the provable lower bound for the computation of discrete logarithms in generic groups (cf. Nechaev, 1994; Shoup, 1997).

There has been a steady stream of improvements to the NFS method for factoring that may have comparable effects on the version of the NFS that applies to the computation of discrete logarithms in $(\mathbf{F}_{p^\ell})^*$. As under Factoring-Based Cryptosystems it is reasonable to assume that in the foreseeable future there will not be major variations in the rate of cryptanalytic progress observed over the last few decades.

Choices of $\#\langle g \rangle$ and p^ℓ That Offer Adequate Protection

Summarizing the above conditions on g, it is assumed that g is chosen in such a way that $\#\langle g \rangle$ is prime so that the discrete logarithm problem in $\langle g \rangle$ cannot be reduced to a discrete logarithm problem in a smaller group (of order a proper divisor of $\#\langle g \rangle$). Furthermore, if $g \in (\mathbf{F}_{p^\ell})^*$

it is assumed that #⟨g⟩ is a prime divisor larger than ℓ of $\Phi_\ell(p)$ to make sure that g cannot be embedded in a smaller multiplicative group $(\mathbf{F}_{p^d})^*$ for some $d < \ell$.

Under these restrictions, g must be chosen such that the discrete logarithm problem in ⟨g⟩ offers adequate protection until the year of one's choice. Combining the attack effort cost of $\sqrt{\#\langle g\rangle}$ with Moore's law it follows that a subgroup of prime order #⟨g⟩ offers adequate protection until the year

$$y\left(\frac{1}{2}\log_2 \#\langle g\rangle\right) = 1982 + \frac{3\left(\frac{1}{2}\log_2 \#\langle g\rangle - 56\right)}{2}$$

[cf. Eq. (1)]. This "double growth" compared with symmetric key lengths leads to the same rule of thumb as given at the end of Cryptographic Hash Functions for hash function lengths. Because the collision attack presented under Cryptographic Hash Functions and Pollard's rho-based attack here are both based on the same birthday paradox technique, this is hardly a surprise.

If $g \in (\mathbf{F}_{p^\ell})^*$ adequate protection until year y also requires to select p^ℓ in such a way that

$$\frac{L(p^\ell, 1/3, \alpha)}{L(2^{1024}, 1/3, \alpha)} \times 400 \geq 40 \cdot 2^{4(y-2004)/3},$$

with α either 1.976 (prudent) or 2.852 (optimistic) as under Factoring-Based Cryptosystems. This is the same requirement as on regular RSA moduli.

It follows that the U.S. government's digital signature algorithm (DSA), standardized in FIPS Publication 186 (cf. Federal Information Processing Standard 186, 1994), with #⟨g⟩ ≈ 2^{160} offers adequate protection against subgroup attacks until the year

$$y\left(\frac{1}{2}\log_2 \#\langle g\rangle\right) \approx y\left(\frac{1}{2}\log_2 2^{160}\right) = y(80) = 2018.$$

But the fact that the DSA prescribes usage of $g \in (\mathbf{F}_{p^\ell})^*$ with $\log_2 p \leq 1024$ undermines the security level and implies that the DSA offers adequate protection only until 2006 (cf. Table 4). FIPS Publication 186 is currently being revised to support larger key sizes for the DSA. ECDSA (cf. Johnson & Menezes, 1999) does not suffer from an embedding in a finite field and is believed to offer adequate protection until 2018 when 160-bit prime order subgroups are used.

CONCLUSION

To summarize, adequate protection was defined as the security offered in 1982 by the DES. It was argued that a cryptosystem offers adequate protection until a given year if the cost of a successful attack in that year is at least 40M dollardays: a computation that lasts x days on possibly parallelized or distributed equipment that costs $40/x$ million dollars to build (for any reasonable x).

Given this definition and using conservative dedicated hardware cost estimates, for the most common cryptographic systems the following general key length recommendations can be made:

- **Symmetric cryptosystems:** A symmetric cryptosystem with $(56 + b)$-bit keys and no known weaknesses offers adequate security until year $1982 + y$ only if $3b \geq 2y$.
- **Cryptographic hash functions:** A cryptographic hash function of bit-length $112 + b$ and without known weaknesses offers adequate security until year $1982 + y$ only if $3b \geq 4y$.
- **Factoring-based asymmetric cryptosystems:** Refer to Table 3 for modulus bit lengths that should offer adequate protection until year $2000 + 10i$ for $0 < i \leq 5$. Refer to Table 4 for the year until which several common modulus bit lengths can be expected to offer adequate protection.
- **Discrete logarithm-based asymmetric cryptosystems:** A subgroup ⟨g⟩ offers adequate security until year $1982 + y$ only if

$$3\left(\frac{1}{2}\log_2 \#\langle g\rangle - 56\right) \geq 2y.$$

If $g \in (\mathbf{F}_{p^\ell})^*$, then $\log_2 p^\ell$ must satisfy the same requirements as modulus bit lengths for factoring based asymmetric cryptosystems. Furthermore, stay away from newly proposed groups.

Finally, it was shown how the definition of adequate protection can be tuned to one's own perception of security and how this changes the key length recommendations.

ACKNOWLEDGMENT

This chapter benefited greatly from enlightening e-mails from Michael Wiener and insightful and detailed comments and suggestions by anonymous reviewers. The first version of this chapter was written while the author was employed by Citigroup, N.A.

GLOSSARY

AES (Advanced Encryption Standard) A block cipher with 128-bit blocks and keys of 128, 192, or 256 bits, successor of the DES.

DES (Data Encryption Standard) A block cipher with 64-bit blocks and keys of effectively 56 bits, replaced in favor of the AES.

DESX (Data Encryption Standard XORed) Strengthened version of the DES where the input plaintext is bitwise XORed with 64 bits of additional key material before encryption with DES and the output is also bitwise XORed with another 64 bits of key material.

DSA (Digital Signature Algorithm) A standardized digital signature algorithm that relies for its security on the hardness of computing discrete logarithms in 160-bit prime order subgroups of the multiplicative group of a 512 to 1024-bit prime field.

ECDSA (Elliptic Curve Digital Signature Algorithm) As DSA, except that the multiplicative group is replaced by the group of point of an appropriately chosen elliptic curve.

ECM (Elliptic Curve Method) An integer factorization method that makes use of elliptic curves.

FIPS (Federal Information Processing Standards) Standards and guidelines that are developed by the USA National Institute of Standards and Technology (NIST) for Federal computer systems and approved by the USA Secretary of Commerce.

GHz (Gigahertz) A unit of alternating current or electromagnetic wave frequency equal to one thousand million hertz.

IDEA (International Data Encryption Algorithm) A block cipher with 64-bit blocks and 128-bit keys.

MD (Message Digest) A digital fingerprint serving as a compact representative image of an input string of arbitrary length.

NESSIE (New European Schemes for Signature, Integrity, and Encryption) A European project to put forward a portfolio of strong cryptographic primitives that has been obtained after an open call and been evaluated using a transparent and open process.

NFS (Number Field Sieve) An integer factoring algorithm that makes use of algebraic number fields and sieving.

QS (Quadratic Sieve) An integer-factoring algorithm that makes use of quadratic polynomials and sieving.

RACE (Research and Development in Advanced Communications Technologies in Europe) A European program for the preparation and promotion of an integrated broadband communication system in Europe.

RC4 (Ron's Cipher 4) A proprietry stream cipher with variable key size.

RIPEMD (RACE Integrity Primitives Evaluation Message Digest) A 160-bit cryptographic hash function.

RSA (Rivest Shamir Adleman) A public key cryptosystem that relies for its security on the hardness of the integer factorization problem.

SEAL (Software-Optimized Encryption Algorithm) A binary additive stream cipher with 160-bit keys, designed for efficient software implementation on 32-bit processors.

SHA (Secure Hash Algorithm) A 160-bit cryptographic hash funcation.

TWINKLE (The Weizmann Institute New Key Location Engine) A proposed special purpose optoelectronic device for the factorization of integers.

TWIRL (The Weizmann Institute Relation Locator) A proposed special purpose pipelined hardware device for the factorization of integers.

XOR (Exclusive or) A function of two bits that produces zero if the two inputs bits are identical and that produces one if the two input bits are different.

CROSS REFERENCES

See *Cryptographic Protocols; Encryption Basics; Hashes and Message Digests; Key Management; Symmetric-Key Encryption.*

REFERENCES

Ajtai, M., & Dwork, C. (1997). *A public-key cryptosystem with worst-case/average-case equivalence.* Proceedings 29th STOC, ACM 1997, 284–293.

Bellare, M., & Rogaway, P. (1997). *Collision-resistant hashing: Towards making UOWHFs practical.* In *Lecture Notes in Computer Science, Vol. 1294:* Proceedings Crypto'97 (470–484). New York: Springer-Verlag.

Bernstein, D. J. (2001). *Circuits for integer factorization: A proposal.* Retrieved January 1, 2004, from cr.yp.to/papers.html#nfscircuit

Biham, E., Dunkelman, O., Furman, V., & Mor, T. (2004). *Preliminary report on the NESSIE submissions Anubis, Camelia, IDEA, Khazad, Misty1, Nimbus.* Retrieved January 1, 2004, from https://www/cosic.esat.kuleuven.ac.be/nessie/reports

Biryukov, A., Shamir, A., & Wagner, D. (2001). *Real time cryptanalysis of A5/1 on a PC.* In *Lecture Notes in Computer Science, Vol. 2001: Proceedings of FSE 2000.* (pp. 1–18). New York: Springer-Verlag.

Blaze, M., Diffie, W., Rivest, R. L., Schneier, B., Shimomura, T., Thompson, E., & Wiener, M. (January, 1996). *Minimal key lengths for symmetric ciphers to provide adequate commercial security.* Retrieved January 1, 2004, from www.bsa.org/policy/encryption/cryptographers_c.html

Bosselaers, A. (2004). http://www.esat.kuleuven.ac.be/~bosselae/ripemd160.html

Brazier, J. R. T. (2000). *Possible NSA decryption capabilities,* jya.com/nsa-study.htm

Cavallar, S., Dodson, B., Lenstra, A. K., Lioen, W., Montgomery, P. L., Murphy, B., & te Riele, H. J. J., et al. (2000). *Factorization of a 512-bit RSA modulus.* In *Lecture Notes in Computer Science, Vol. 1807: Proceedings Eurocrypt 2000* (pp. 1–17). New York: Springer-Verlag.

Chabaud, F., & Joux, A. (1998). *Differential collisions in SHA-0.* In *Lecture Notes in Computer Science, Vol. 1462: Proceedings Crypto'98* (pp. 56–71). New York: Springer-Verlag.

Coppersmith, D. (1993). *Modifications to the number field sieve. Journal of Cryptology,* 6, 169–180.

Dagstuhl Seminar 9226. (June 1992). Algorithms in number theory.

Davida, G. (1982). *Chosen signature cryptanalysis of the RSA (MIT) public key cryptosystem,* TR-CS-82-2, Dept. of EECS, Univ. of Wisconsin, Milwaukee.

Desmedt, Y., & Odlyzko, A. M. (2003). *A chosen text attack on the RSA cryptosystem and some discrete logarithm schemes.* Retrieved January 1, 2004, from www.dtc.umn.edu/~odlyzko/doc/arch/rsa.attack.pdf

Dobbertin, H., Bosselaers, A., & Preneel, B. (1996). *RIPEMD-160, a strengthened version of RIPEMD.* In *Lecture Notes in Computer Science, Vol. 1039*: Fast Software Encryption (pp. 71–82). New York: Springer-Verlag.

Electronic Frontier Foundation. (1998). *Cracking DES.* San Francisco: O'Reilly.

Federal Information Processing Standard 186. (1994). Digital signature standard (DSS). Retrieved January 1, 2004, from www.itl.nist.gov/fipspubs/fip186.htm

Federal Information Processing Standard, 180-2. (2000). *Secure hash standard.* Retrieved January 1, 2004, from csrc.nist.gov/publications/fips/fips180-2/fips180-2withchangenotice.pdf

Fluhrer, S., Mantin, I., & Shamir, A. (2001). *Attacks on RC4 and WEP. RSA Laboratories' Cryptobytes,* 5(2)

26–34. [Also at www.rsasecurity.com/rsalabs/crypto bytes]

Franke, J., personal communication, January 2004.

Frey, G., & Rück, H.-G. (1994). *A remark concerning m-divisibility and the discrete logarithm problem in the divisor class group of curves.* Mathematics of Computer, *62*, 865–874.

Goldreich, O., Goldwasser, S., & Halevi, S. (1997). *Public-key cryptosystems from lattice reduction problems.* In *Lecture Notes in Computer Science, Vol. 1294: Proceedings Crypto'97.* New York: Springer-Verlag.

Haber, S., & Pinkas, B. (2001). *Securely combining public-key cryptosystems.* In *Proceedings of the 8th ACM conference on computer and communications security* (pp. 215–224).

Handschuh, H., & Gilbert, H. (1997). X^2 *Cryptanalysis of the SEAL encryption algorithm.* In *Lecture Notes in Computer Science, Vol. 1267: Proceedings of FSE 1997.* New York: Springer-Verlag (pp. 1–12).

Hoffstein, J., Pipher, J., & Silverman, J. H. (1998). *NTRU: A new high speed public key cryptosystem.* In *Lecture Notes in Computer Science, Vol. 1423: Proceedings ANTS III*, (pp. 267–288). New York: Springer-Verlag.

Johnson, D., & Menezes, A. (1999). *The elliptic curve digital signature algorithm (ECDSA),* CACR Technical report CORR 99-31, University of Waterloo.

Kilian, J., & Rogaway, P. (1996). *How to protect DES against exhaustive key search.* In *Lecture Notes in Computer Science, Vol. 1109: Proceedings Crypto'96.* (pp. 252–267). New York: Springer-Verlag.

Knuth, D. E. (1998). *The art of computer programming, vol. 2: Seminumerical Algorithms* (3rd ed.). Addison-Wesley.

Kocher, P. C. (1999). *Breaking DES. RSA Laboratories' Cryptobytes, 4*(2), 1–5. [also at www.rsasecurity.com/rsalabs/cryptobytes]

Landau, S. (2004). *Polynomials in the nation's service: Using algebra to design the advanced encryption standard. The Mathematical Society of America Monthly, 111,* 89–117.

Lenstra, A. K. (1997). *Using cyclotomic polynomials to construct efficient discrete logarithm cryptosystems over finite fields.* In *Lecture Notes in Computer Science, Vol. 1270: Proceedings ACISP'97* (pp. 127–138). New York: Springer-Verlag.

Lenstra, A. K. (2001). *Unbelievable security.* In *Lecture Notes in Computer Science, Vol. 2248: Proceedings Asiacrypt 2001* (pp. 67–86). New York: Springer-Verlag.

Lenstra, A. K., & Lenstra, H. W., Jr. (eds.). (1993). *The development of the number field sieve.* In *Lecture notes in mathematics, Vol. 1554.* New York: Springer-Verlag.

Lenstra, A. K., Lenstra, H. W., Jr., Manasse, M. S., & Pollard, J. M. (1993). *The factorization of the ninth Fermat number.* Mathematics of Computation, *61,* 319–349.

Lenstra, A. K., & Shamir, A. (2000). *Analysis and optimization of the TWINKLE factoring device.* In *Lecture Notes in Computer Science, Vol. 1807: Proceedings Eurocrypt 2000* (pp. 35–52). New York: Springer-Verlag.

Lenstra, A. K., Shamir, A., Tomlinson, J., & Tromer, E. (2002). *Analysis of Bernstein's factorization circuit.* In *Lecture Notes in Computer Science, Vol. 2501: Proceedings Asiacrypt 2002* (pp. 1–26). New York: Springer-Verlag.

Lenstra, A. K., Tromer, E., Shamir, A., Kortsmit, W., Dodson, B., Hughes, J., & Leyland, P. (2003). *Factoring estimates for a 1024-bit RSA modulus.* In *Lecture Notes in Computer Science, Vol. 2894: Proceedings Asiacrypt 2003* (pp. 55–74). New York: Springer-Verlag.

Lenstra, A. K., & Verheul, E. R. (2000). *Selecting cryptographic key sizes.* In *Lecture Notes in Computer Science, Vol. 1751: Proceedings PKC 2000,* LNCS1751 (pp. 446–465). New York: Springer-Verlag. *Journal of Cryptology, 14,* 255–293. [Available from www.cryptosavvy.com]

Lenstra, H. W., Jr. (1987). Factoring integers with elliptic curves. *Annals of Mathematics, 126,* 649–673.

Menezes, A. J., Okamoto, T., & Vanstone, S. A. (1993). Reducing elliptic curve logarithms to a finite field. *IEEE Transactions on Information Theory, 39,* 1639–1646.

Merkle, R., & Hellman, M. (1978). Hiding information and signatures in trapdoor knapsacks. *IEEE Transactions of Information Theory, 24,* 525–530.

Miyaji, A. (1993). *Elliptic curves over F_p suitable for cryptosystems.* In *Lecture Notes in Computer Science, Vol. 718: Proceedings Auscrypt 92* (pp. 479–491). New York: Springer-Verlag.

National Bureau of Standards. (January, 1997). NBS FIPS PUB 46: Data Encryption Standard. Washington, DC: National Bureau of Standards, U.S. Department of Commerce.

Nechaev, V. I. (1994). *Complexity of a determinate algorithm for the discrete logarithm. Mathematical Notes, 55,* 155–172; translated from *Matematicheskie Zametki, 55*(2), 91–101; this result dates from 1968.

New European Schemes for Signatures, Integrity, and Encryption. (NESSIE). (2000–2003). Retrieved January 1, 2004, from https://www.cosic.esat.kuleuven.ac.be/nessie/

Nguyen, P. Q., & Stern, J. (2001). *The two faces of lattices in cryptology.* In *Lecture Notes in Computer Science, Vol. 2146: Proceedings of CALC 2001* (pp. 146–180). New York: Springer-Verlag.

Pollard, J. M. (1978). *Monte Carlo methods for index computation (mod p).* Mathematics of Computation, *32,* 918–924.

Pohlig, S. C., & Hellman, M. E. (1978). An improved algorithm for computing logarithms over GF(p) and its cryptographic significance. *IEEE Transactions on Information Theory, 24,* 106–110.

Pomerance, C. (1983). *Analysis and comparison of some integer factoring algorithms.* In *Computational methods in number theory* (H. W. Lenstra, Jr., & R. Tijdeman, eds.) Math. Centre Tracts 154, 155, Mathematisch Centrum, Amsterdam (1983), pp. 89–139.

Rabin, M. O. (1979). *Digital signatures and public-key functions as intractable as factoring.* MIT Laboratory for computer science, Technical report, MIT/LCS/TR-212, January 1979.

Rivest, R. L., Shamir, A., & Adleman, L. M. (1983). *Cryptographic communications system and method,* U.S. Patent 4,405,829, 1983.

Satoh, T., & Araki, K. (1998). Fermat quotients and the polynomial time discrete log algorithm for anomalous elliptic curves. *Comentari Mathematics University Sancti Pauli, 47,* 81–92.

Schneier, B. (1996). *Applied cryptography* (2nd ed.). New York: John Wiley & Sons.

Semaev, I. A. (1998). Evaluation of discrete logarithms on some elliptic curves. *Mathematics of Computation, 67*, 353–356.

Shamir, A. (1995). RSA for paranoids. *RSA Laboratories' Cryptobytes, 1*(3), 1–4.

Shamir, A., & Tromer, E. (2003). Factoring large numbers with the TWIRL device. In *Lecture Notes in Computer Science, Vol. 2729: Proceedings Crypto 2003* (pp. 1–26). New York: Springer-Verlag.

Shamir, A. (1999). Factoring large numbers with the TWINKLE device. In *Lecture Notes in Computer Science, Vol. 1717: Proceedings CHES'99*. New York: Springer-Verlag.

Shor, P. W., (1994). Algorithms for quantum computing: Discrete logarithms and factoring. In *Proceedings of the IEEE 35th Annual Symposium on Foundations of Computer Science* (pp. 124–134).

Shoup, V. (1997). Lower bounds for discrete logarithms and related problems. In *Lecture Notes in Computer Science Vol. 1233:* Proceedings Eurocrypt'97 (pp. 256–266). New York: Springer-Verlag.

Smart, N. P. (1999). The discrete logarithm problem on elliptic curves of trace one. *Journal of Cryptography, 12*, 193–196.

Wiener, M. J. (1993). *Efficient DES key search*. Manuscript, Bell-Northern Research, August 20.

Wiener, M. J., (2004). The full cost of cryptanalytic attacks. *Journal of Cryptography, 17*, 105–124.

Key Management

Xukai Zou and Amandeep Thukral, *Purdue University*

INTRODUCTION

Cryptography plays a fundamental role in information security to provide confidentiality, authentication, and data integrity, even authorization. The most critical element in any cryptographic system is (cryptographic) *key*, and *key management* is the most important and difficult issue in cryptosystems. The security of a cryptosystem relies on secrecy of the keys and not on the secrecy of the encryption/decryption algorithms. Selection of keys with large size precludes the attempt of determining a key by brute force (see the chapter for key length in this book). Thus, breaking a cryptosystem comes to try to break the key management scheme.

Key management refers to generation, distribution, updating, and revocation of keys. *Key generation* is generally implemented by a (pseudo)-random number generator (with proper seeds) to enforce that the keys generated will be uniformly distributed in the key space, thus preventing attackers from guessing (Bishop, 2003). The issue of who is responsible for generating the key is dependent on cryptosystems/key management schemes (as discussed for each of key management schemes in the following sections). *Key distribution* refers to securely distributing a pregenerated key to corresponding communicating parties over insecure channels. Different key distribution schemes have been proposed and are discussed in the following sections. In some schemes, the key generation is accomplished by the participation of all communicating parties and the generated key contains the shares of all parties and is computed by each of the parties, thus there is no further need for distributing the key. In this case, key generation and key distribution become one task, called *key agreement*. The combination of key generation and key distribution is also called *key establishment*

(Boyd & Mathuria, 2003). *Key updating* refers to changing/regenerating and redistributing the key. Whether there is a need for key updating or how to perform key updating depends on security systems and is discussed in the following sections. *Key revocation* refers to destroying the key. One way is to discard/remove the key from its storage after its usage. Another way is to set an expiration date for a key and to treat the key as invalid once the key expires.

Key management can be typically classified as secret key management for two-party communication, public key management (certificate) (they are for secret key cryptosystems and public key cryptosystems respectively), and group key management for secure multiparty (group) communication. It is well known that the biggest problem with secret key cryptosystems is how to distribute securely the shared secret key to two communicating parties ahead of data communication. Unless the two parties meet face to face and tell each other their shared secret key, any other way of distributing the shared secret key, such as by e-mail, phone, or postal mail, may result in the interception/disclosure of the shared secret key during its transmission. Another problem with secret key cryptosystems is the large number of keys ([i.e., $n(n-1)/2$]). Suppose there are n people in a related communication setting such that any two people may communicate. Each individual needs $n-1$ keys, one with each of other $n-1$ people. The total number of keys needed in this setting is $n(n-1)/2$. When n is large, it is a problem. Several secret key management schemes for two-party communication have been proposed and they are discussed under Secret Key Management for Two-Party Communication. The invention of public key cryptosystems aims to eliminate the key distribution completely because the public key of an individual will be made public and the private key is just kept secret to the individual. However, the following problem arises: when someone, say, Bob, obtains the public key of an individual, say, Alice, from her personal home page, her e-mail, or a public key dictionary, how can Bob be assured that the public key Bob received is really Alice's and not a masquerader's? It is very possible that Alice's public key was modified/replaced during its storage or transmission (which is generally not secured). The solution for binding an individual's public key with its identity is *public key certificates* and *trusted certificate authority*, which are discussed under "Public Key Certificate."

In contrast to two-party communication, *secure group communication* (SGC) involves multiple (more than two) parties. SGC is becoming increasingly important because broad critical applications, such as teleconferencing, multipartner military action, and cyberforensics in critical fields, such as government, military, and law enforcement, resort to SGC to provide confidentiality and integrity. Other typical SGC applications include collaborative work, telemedicine, distributed interactive simulations, interactive games, and grid computing. As in two-party communication, the confidentiality of group communication is achieved by encrypting group messages with a shared secret, which is called *group key*. Only the group members can access the group key and thus are able to decrypt the messages. Therefore, the first issue facing SGC is *group key management*. The main difficulty for group key management is *group dynamics*. Unlike in two-party communication where the communication will terminate if either party leaves or stops the communication, the group communication continues even when the members join or leave the group communication dynamically. Whenever members join and/or leave the group, the group key needs to be changed to guarantee *backward secrecy* and *forward secrecy*. Backward secrecy means that when a member joins a group, the group key needs to be changed so that the new member cannot obtain the old group keys to decrypt previous messages (in case he or she has intercepted and stored such earlier messages). Forward secrecy means that whenever a member leaves a group, the group key needs to be changed so that the ex-member does not possess the current group key; otherwise, he or she would be able to decrypt future group messages. Because group dynamics is a typical behavior of group communication, key updating (also called rekeying) is a typical feature of group key management. There has been considerable research on group key management and the book *Secure Group Communication over Data Networks* (Zou, Ramamurthy, & Magliveras, 2004) provides a comprehensive survey of SGC and group key management. Group Key Management for Secure Group Communication gives a brief introduction of group key management so that readers could sense the flavor of group key management for SGC.

SECRET KEY MANAGEMENT FOR TWO-PARTY COMMUNICATION

Two-party key management refers to the situation where there are two people communicating and the key management procedure involves sharing keys between them.

Typically, there are three classes of key management schemes for two-party communication: public key cryptosystems, Diffie–Hellman key exchange, and trusted central authority. They are discussed in this section.

Secret Key Establishment With Public Key Cryptosystems

Assume two users, Alice and Bob, wish to communicate using a secret key. Let P_B and S_B be Bob's public key and private key respectively. Let us further assume that Alice wishes to start the communication with Bob. Alice would generate an ephemeral session key k and then encrypt it under Bob's public key and send it across. This way only Bob (who holds the corresponding private key) would be able to decrypt the message to obtain the secret key. The steps are depicted below.
Alice to Bob:

$$y = \{k\}_{P_B}.$$

Bob:

$$k = \{y\}_{S_B}.$$

Thus, Alice and Bob obtain a common secret key that they can use for secure communication.

It is worth pointing out that the public key cryptosystems is much slower than the secret key cryptosystems, thus the public key cryptosystem is generally used to encrypt and distribute a secret key (which is short) and the secret key cryptosystem to encrypt and transmit data messages (of random length). This kind of combination between secret key encryption and public key encryption results in an efficient yet secure scheme, called *hybrid encryption*. Here is an example. Suppose Alice wants to send messages to Bob securely. Alice first generates a secret session key SK, encrypts a message m with SK (by a secret key encryption algorithm), encrypts SK with Bob's public key (by a public key encryption algorithm), and transmits both the encrypted message and the encrypted session key to Bob. After receiving the transmission, Bob first decrypts the session key (with his private key) and then decrypts the message with the session key. The advantages of hybrid encryption are obvious. The (long) messages of random lengths are encrypted using a secret key encryption algorithm, which is efficient. The session key is encrypted by a public key encryption algorithm and can be securely transmitted to the receiver over insecure channels. Compared to messages, a session key is very short. Thus the public key encryption of the session key will not be an efficiency problem.

Secret Key Establishment With a Diffie–Hellman Key Agreement

In 1976, Diffie and Hellman proposed an elegant protocol for two parties to achieve a shared secret key over an insecure channel. This is the well known Diffie–Hellman key exchange/agreement protocol (Diffie & Hellman, 1976). The protocol is based on discrete logarithm problem (DLP). The DLP problem and Diffie–Hellman key exchange are discussed below.

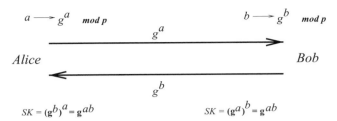

Figure 1: Diffie–Hellman key agreement.

Suppose n is a positive integer. $\mathbb{Z}_n^*$ is defined as the set of numbers in $\mathbb{Z}_n$ that are relatively prime to n, that is, $\mathbb{Z}_n^* = \{a \mid 1 \leq < a \leq n-1 \text{ and } \gcd(n,a) = 1\}$. Let p be a large prime and $\alpha \in \mathbb{Z}_p$ a primitive element (i.e., generator) of $\mathbb{Z}_p^*$ ($= \{1, 2, \cdots, np-1\}$). Given $a \in [0, p-2]$, computing $\beta \equiv \alpha^a \pmod{p}$ is efficient, but the reverse is not. The related DLP can be stated as follows: given any $\beta \in \mathbb{Z}_p^*$, find the unique integer a, $0 \leq a \leq p-2$ such that $\alpha^a \equiv \beta \pmod{p}$. We denote the integer a by $\log_\alpha \beta$.

The Diffie–Hellman key agreement protocol can be described as follows. Suppose p is a large prime and g is a generator of $\mathbb{Z}_p^*$ such that the DLP problem in $\mathbb{Z}_p^*$ is intractable. Both p and g are publicly known. Suppose two members, Alice and Bob, want to establish a shared secret. Alice selects a random number $a \in [1, p-2]$, computes $p_a = g^a \bmod p$, and sends p_a to Bob over the insecure channel. Similarly, Bob selects a random number $b \in [1, p-2]$, computes $p_b = g^b \bmod p$, and sends p_b to Alice. As a result, each of Alice and Bob is able to compute the shared secret key $\text{SK} = (p_b)^a = g^{ab} = (p_a)^b \bmod p$ (see Figure 1). However, any other individual cannot compute SK even if he or she intercepts the public components p_a and p_b and can compute g^{a+b}. a (or b) is called the Diffie–Hellman private share or simply private share of Alice (or Bob), and $p_a \bmod p$ (or $p_b \bmod p$) the Diffie–Hellman disguised public share or simply public share of Alice (or Bob). We call the derived secret key $\text{SK} = g^{ab} \bmod p$ a DH key.

It is worth pointing out that the DH key agreement method should never be used in the basic form described here, as it is vulnerable to a man-in-the-middle attack (see "The man-in-the-middle Attack in Diffie–Hellman Key Exchange"). Furthermore, in practice, the derived DH key is rarely used as a secret key but rather as a (long term) shared secret that enters into the computation of the (short term) session keys (see key utilization).

Secret Key Establishment With a Trusted Central Authority

As mentioned in the introduction, one problem with secret key cryptosystems is $n(n-1)/2$ keys for a group of n people. A solution to the problem is using a trusted central authority. Suppose there is a trusted central authority Trent and every individual has one unique shared secret key with Trent. For example, Alice has a shared secret key with Trent K_{AT} and Bob has a shared secret key K_{BT}. Whenever Alice and Bob want to communicate, the following steps show a typical scenario to establish a shared secret key (called session key and just used in one communica-

tion session) between them:

$$\text{Alice} \rightarrow \text{Trent: } \{A, B\}_{K_{AT}}.$$
$$\text{Trent} \rightarrow \text{Alice: } \{k_{AB}, \{A, k_{AB}\}_{K_{BT}}\}_{K_{AT}}.$$
$$\text{Alice} \rightarrow \text{Bob: } \{A, k_{AB}\}_{K_{BT}}.$$

Alice wants to talk to Bob and sends a message encrypted with key K_{AT} to Trent. Then Trent selects a random number as session key K_{AB} and sends an encrypted message back to Alice. The message contains the session key along with a ticket $\{A, k_{AB}\}_{K_{BT}}$ and was encrypted with K_{AT}. Finally, Alice sends the ticket to Bob. As a result, Alice and Bob obtain a shared secret key k_{AB}. Kerberos (Kohl & Neuman, 1993; Steiner, Neuman, & Schiller, 1988) is an example of this kind of system.

PUBLIC KEY MANAGEMENT

Public key cryptosystems are based on the existence of a key pair for each user. Every user in the system has a public key and a corresponding private key. To transmit a message securely, it is encrypted with the recipient's public key. The recipients uses its private key to decrypt the message. Because the private key is never required to be transmitted to or shared with other individuals, the need for sharing secret information is eliminated. The major issue in public key management essentially changes to one of authentication: how to verify the authenticity of the public key.

Public key cryptosystems have become very popular for transmitting of information securely over the Internet. The reason for the popularity is the security offered and the fact that they are relatively simple to use. The major disadvantage with public key cryptosystems is that they are relatively a lot slower than the secret key cryptosystems. As a result, in practice usually a hybrid scheme is used. Still the issue of authentication of the public key still remains. Public key management is implemented through the concept of a *public key infrastructure* (PKI) (Brands, 2000; Choudhary, Bhatnagar, & Hague, 2002; Lloyd & Sams, 1999; Nash, Duane, Joseph, & Brink, 2001), which consists of *public key certificate* and *certificate authority*.

We discuss these concepts below.

Public Key Certificate

Public key certificates can be thought of as digital documents that bind a public key to an individual or an entity. An analogy could be a notary seal that binds a person's identity to the signature in a way that is verified by the notary. The notary could be thought of as a trusted third party. Certificates help in the verification of claims that a certain public key indeed belongs to a specific individual. This helps in providing authentication of users and also helps avoid attacks where someone could impersonate a valid user.

A basic certificate contains the public key and the name of the owner. Generally, it also includes an expiration date, which would help in revocation of the keys. Additionally, the certificate might also include the name of the certifying authority, the serial number and other information.

The most commonly and widely accepted standard in public key certificate is the X.509 standard. It is an International Telecommunication Union standard for defining digital certificates, will be discussed leter in this section.

Certificate Authority

A certificate authority (CA) is a third-party organization that vouches for the authenticity of the public keys belonging to subjects or other certification authorities. The certification authority is responsible for issuing and managing digital certificates of authenticity, which are electronic records that a user holds the private key corresponding to the public key enclosed. The CA usually has some kind of agreement with a financial institution (also known as *registration authority* (RA)), which provides the CA with the necessary information used to confirm a user's identity.

The major roles of a CA are as follows:

- Issues public/private keys to those users who do not wish to generate their own keys
- Issues certificates to users that carry its signature; the signature ensures that it is impossible for anyone to modify the contents of the certificate without being noticed
- Publishes the user's certificates
- Manages the published certificates
- Issues information regarding revocation of certificates in the form of certificate revocation lists

The CA acts as the central agent for trust in the PKI. As long as the users can trust the CA, they can be assured about the distribution, management, and revocation of public keys in the system. The signed digital certificates issued by the CA give the users the required trust for the authenticity and integrity of the public keys contained in them.

The registration authority is responsible for the identification and authentication of the certificate subscribers. It records and verifies all the information regarding the users that the CA needs to issue a certificate. The RA does not issue or sign any certificate on its own. It acts as an intermediary between the CA and users.

The RA is a place where users must go to verify their identity and apply for a certificate. The verification can be done in a number of ways. For example, any valid identity card that the user hold could be one of the ways to authenticate the user's identity. The functions of a RA are listed below.

- Accept user request for the issuance of a certificate
- Validate the user
- Send the request to the CA
- Receive the processed and signed certificate from the CA
- Send the certificate to the correct user

Hierarchical Certificate Authorities

With the rapid increase in the number of users on the Internet over the past few years, it has practically become infeasible for a single certification authority to be able to handle the needs of certificates for all the users. As a result, multiple CAs exist over the Internet, VeriSign, and Thawte being some examples. Most of the CAs exist in noncooperative domains, such as financial, health, and business. When two users share the same CA, they are assumed to know its public key. But in cases where they do not get their certificates from the same CA, a hierarchy of the CAs is required. A certification hierarchy provides scalability and ease of administration.

The hierarchical CA model was proposed in late 1980s and was initially employed in the privacy enhanced mail standard. In the hierarchical CA model, the trust between CAs flows from the root. It uses certificates linking members of the hierarchy to validate other CAs. The root CA is trusted by all users. Also known as the root authority, it has a self-signed certificate. The child CAs of the root CA are known as subordinate certification authorities. Each CA in the hierarchy has certificates for clients (forward) and for parents (backward). These certificates might contain the certification for the client (user) or may contain certificates that certify other CAs. Each intermediate node trusts the certificates issued by its parents. It can be considered as a big tree like structure where the end user is placed at the leaf node. The validity for the leaf's certificate is verified by tracking backward from its certifier, to other certifiers, until a trusted root certificate is found.

Figure 2 explains how the hierarchical trust model works. In the figure, CA $<< U >>$ implies the certificate issued by the certification authority for U. Note that U could be an end user (U_1, U_2, and U_3) or other CAs (B,C,D,E,F). When a user wants to obtain and/or verify the certificate (of another user), the certificate chain is used to trace the authenticity of certificates. For example, when U_3 hope to verify U_1's certificate, U_3 follows $E << C >>$ $C << B >>$ $B << D >>$ $D << U_1 >>$.

Revocation of Public Key Certificate

Certificate revocation is a process by which the binding between the identity and the public key is made invalid. Although certificates have a period of validity, they can be revoked before expiry. There can be a number of reasons

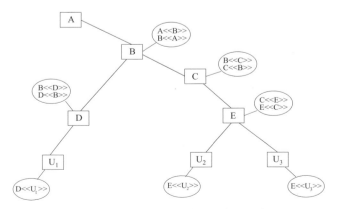

Figure 2: Certificate authority hierarchy.

why key revocation could be invoked, some of which are mentioned below:

- The private key of the user is compromised.
- CA's certificate is compromised.
- The CA may no longer certify the user.

There are many approaches to certificate revocation. We discuss a few of them here.

- Certificate revocation lists: a CRL contains outdated or compromised certificates from a certificate authority. The CA generates such lists periodically and publishes them to a directory. The CRL contains the serial number and date of issue for every compromised key that has a valid expiration date. The major advantage of using such a scheme is that it is very simple. The trouble with CRLs is the fact that it requires that the CA or some other source of CRLs to be online at all times. Without access to a recent CRL, the user would not be able to know if the certificate is valid. Another issue comes with the frequency with which the CRLs are released by the CA. If the CRLs are issued infrequently, then the amount of time vulnerable to compromise increases. Conversely, issuing the CRLs frequently reduces the vulnerability period but increases the network traffic generated.
- Online Certificate Status Protocol (OSCP): an alternative to CRLs is based on online validation services that currently leverage RFC 2560—the online certificate status protocol (Myers, Ankney, Malpani, Galperi, & Adams, 1999). The protocol requires the user to contact an online server about whether a certificate is valid. The answer obtained from the server is digitally signed.
- Certificate revocation tree: based on the Merkle hash trees, the certificate revocation tree (CRT) was proposed in 1998 (Merkle, 1989). The scheme allows a user to attain a short proof of validity for a certificate based on its serial number. The serial numbers of the revoked certificates are stored as leafs. A Merkle hash tree is later constructed with the leaves, the root of which is signed by the CA. It takes $O(\log n)$ time for a proof that a given serial number is not in the leaves. The tree changes with each new certificate revocation.

X.509 Certificate Standard

A public key infrastructure uses certificates to provide authentication. With the widespread use of PKIs all across the globe, certain standards had to be laid to ensure global compatibility between the certificates. The X.509 is a PKI standard that is accepted worldwide [RCF 2510 (Adams & Farrel, 1999) and RCF 2459 (Housley, Ford, Polk, & Solo, 1999)]. It defines the standards for the format of the certificates, what information goes in them and the way the CRLs are implemented.

X.509 assumes a strict hierarchical system of certificate authorities for issuing certificates. It describes a model for cross-certification of certificates from multiple CAs. It supports a number of protocols such as Privacy Enhance Email (PEM), Secure Hyper Text Transfer Protocol (S-HTTP), and SSL for providing security to the privileged information stored in the certificates. In addition to the CAs signature, a X.509 certificate consists of the following information:

- Version: describes the version of the certificate that has been issued
- Serial number: each certificate is issued a unique identifier by the CA that is called the serial number
- Signature algorithm identifier: an identifier for the algorithm that the CA uses to sign the certificate
- Issuer name: specifies the name of the CA who as issued the certificate
- Validity period: signifies the time for which the certificate is valid; it has the date of issue and also the date when the certificate expires
- Subject (user) name: the name of the user with whom the public key is identified
- Subject public key information: this field has the public key of the user along with the algorithm with which the key is used

There have been three versions of X.509 that have come out to date, with version 3 being the latest. The first two versions were developed primarily to be used for interorganizational operations. These versions had several structural restrictions with regard to the policy association and the utility of these certificates was restricted. X.509 version 3 introduced the concept of *extensions* in 1996. Extensions provide methods for associating additional attributes with users and the public keys. It provides organizations with the option of adding additional information such as employee id apart from their common name. X.509 version 3 allows for private extensions that can be used to carry information unique to communities. Each extension in a certificate can be classified as critical or noncritical. If a system that uses certificates with extensions encounters a critical extension that it does not recognize, it rejects it. Conversely, a noncritical extension could be ignored. Some of the extensions of X.509 version 3 are discussed below:

- Alternate name: an alternate name refers to a name that identifies a user in an organization. It can be an e-mail address or an employee id. The advantage of using such alternate names in the X.509 certificates is that it helps to identify the user entity without referring to the X.500 directory.
- Subject directory attributes: this extension allows for the certificate to contain attribute values for the user entity in addition to its name.
- Certification path constraints

We know certificates have a validity period associated with them but they may have to be revoked prior to their expiry date for a number of reasons discussed above. X.509 standard defines a method for certificate revocation wherein the CA periodically issues a CRL. We know that the CRL consists of a list of the revoked certificates and is freely available in a public directory.

Public Key Infrastructure

Public key infrastructure refers to the framework and services that provide for the generation, production, management, and accounting of public key certificates. The PKI encompasses certificate management and registration functions. The PKI is a coherent structure of CAs. Most of the PKIs adopt the hierarchical structure discussed above. The main functions of a PKI are as follows:

- Authentication: implies that the sender is he or she claims to be
- Confidentiality: implies that the information is readable only by the intended receiver
- Integrity: implies that the receiver is able to confirm (through the use of) certificates that the message has not been modified during transmit
- Nonrepudiation: implies that the sender/receiver cannot disavow what he or she has done

A PKI brings the required trust from the physical world into the electronic world with the use of public key certificates and certification authorities. Based on the number of CAs in an arrangement, a PKI can be classified as one of the three types.

1. Single CA architecture: the most basic of the architecture, it consists of a single CA that issues the certificates and CRLs to all the users. All users in the system use the certificates issued by this central CA. The major advantage of such a system is that it is simple to deploy and certificate revocation becomes easy. Scalability becomes a major hurdling issue in the use of such kind of system. Although the single CA scheme is very suitable for a small enterprise, for a big firm, the single CA would not be able to serve all the users.

2. Enterprise CA architecture: the scalability factor leads us to design a decentralized framework of CAs for enterprises with large number of users. This requires the distribution of operations of certificate issuing, management and revocation of a single CA to multiple CAs. The ways in which these CAs are organized in the PKI leads to the following two models of enterprise CA architecture:
   - Hierarchical PKI architecture: the hierarchical PKI architecture is the most common PKI and is deployed by many organizations. Unlike the single CA architecture, here a number of CAs coexist and provide the PKI service. The system consists of a root CA and its subordinates. More about the architecture and functioning can be found in the section on hierarchical certification authorities.
   - Mesh architecture: in the mesh architecture multiple CAs exist in a peer-to-peer model. Each CA is an independent entity and there is no superior–subordinate relationships among the CAs. Each CA is a trusted entity and because the CAs can issue certificates to one another, they share a bidirectional relationship. Because in a mesh PKI, all CAs need to cross certify each other, it becomes quite complex than the corresponding hierarchical model. The advantage that is gained is because of the fact that multiple trust paths exist and the certification path from a user's certificate to a trust point is nondeterministic.

3. Hybrid CA architecture: the need for a hybrid CA architecture comes in when two organizations having different public key infrastructures need to interact among themselves. A hybrid CA architecture allows organizations with different PKIs to interact and interoperate with each other in a trusted environment.

GROUP KEY MANAGEMENT FOR SECURE GROUP COMMUNICATION

Secure group communication refers to that scenario of group communication in which the members of a group can communicate with one another in a way that outsiders (any user who is not a member of the group) cannot glean any information even when they are able to intercept the messages. Secure group communication has been an active area of research because of the need to maintain privacy and integrity in group oriented applications.

Based on the mechanism employed by the group members to obtain the common shared key, the group key management schemes for SGC can be broadly classified into three main classes: centralized key distribution, decentralized key management, and distributed (Contributory) key agreement. The book (Zou et al., 2004) offers a comprehensive overview of group key management and here we just highlight the main ideas of these schemes.

Centralized Key Distribution

Most of the early key management schemes proposed for SGC had the notion of a trusted central authority, which is responsible for the generation and distribution of the group key. The central entity is also known as group controller or key distribution center (KDC). Assume that there is a secure channel between the central entity and each of the members. The central entity generates the group key and distributes it to each of the members via the secure channel between them.

The naive group key management scheme works as follows. Whenever a member joins, the group controller generates a new group key, encrypts the new key with the old key, and multicasts to the group. At the same time, the group controller also sends the new key to the joining member via the secure channel between the joining member and the group controller. Whenever a member leaves, the group controller generates a new group key and sends the key to each of the remaining members one by one. The naive scheme is, of course, unscalable for the member leaving operation. An elegant scheme, called key tree, was proposed, which treats the join operation and leave operation in the same way and is discussed next.

It is worth pointing out that being responsible for the generation and distribution of the group key, the group controller is obviously a single point of failure. The entire group would be affected if the security of the group controller is compromised. It also becomes a performance bottleneck in situations where the group controller also performs the task of rekeying the keys on membership change.

Key Tree Based Scheme

The key tree based scheme is a powerful group key management scheme and was developed independently by several research groups (Caronni, Waldvogel, Sun, &

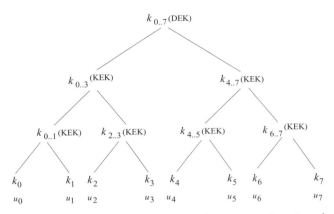

Figure 3: Key tree based scheme: each group user is assigned the keys from its leaf to the root.

Plattner, 1998; Noubir, 1998; Wallner, Harder, & Agee, 1998; Wong, Gouda, & Lam, 1998). In this scheme, the group users and keys are organized in the form of a logical tree with the view of reducing the number of messages required for rekeying (see Figure 3). Each node in the tree is assigned a key and each group user is placed at a leaf node of the tree. Each group user is assigned keys along the path from its leaf to the root. For example, u_3 is assigned the keys $k_{2..3}, k_{0..3}, k_{0..7}$. Leaf keys are owned by individual users and shared between the group controller and each of group users. The internal keys are shared by subsets of group users are used to encrypt other keys, and called key encryption keys (KEK). The root key is shared by all of the group users and is utilized as the group key for encrypting data message and thus, it is also called data encryption key (DEK). (Note: it is a common practice that the root key is not used directly as the group key but used to derive the group key.) When a group user leaves, all the keys the leaving user knows (i.e., all the nodes from the parent of the leaving user to the root) need to be changed. Every changed key is then encrypted by its two child keys and broadcast to the group. When a user joins the group, a similar procedure applies after the user is authenticated. The group controller decides where the user is to be placed in the tree and determines the keys for the joining user (i.e., the ones from the root to the new user's leaf). The group controller sends the new user's leaf key to the new user securely (it is assumed that there is a secure channel between the group controller and each of the group users). The the group controller changes these keys, encrypts them with its two child keys, and broadcasts them to the group. Suppose n is the group size and the key tree is a balanced binary tree, then the maximum number of keys held by any user at any given time is $\log_2(n) + 1$. The number of keys that need to be changed for a join or leave is of the order of $O(\log(n))$ and so is the number of rekeying messages.

Decentralized Key Management

The decentralized approach involves splitting up a large group into small subgroups with a view of distributing the load of key management to different levels in the system. The approach minimizes the concentration of work at any centralized place and also helps in providing better fault

tolerance. A typical decentralized scheme is IOLUS and is discussed below.

IOLUS

Mittra proposed a framework for scalable secure multicasting (Mittra, 1997). The scheme splits a large group into small subgroups. Each of such subgroups is managed by a *group security agent* (GSA). The security of the system is managed at different levels that can be viewed as a hierarchy. The GSA at the highest level is also called a *group security controller* (GSC). GSC may control the division of subgroups and the selection of GSAs. Each of the subgroups have different independent keys for communication. A GSA will have not only its own subgroup key but also its parental subgroup key. In this way, when a GSA receives a message from one subgroup (encrypted with the subgroup key), it can decrypt the message, encrypt the message with the key of the other subgroup, and send to the other subgroup. This independence of the keys has an advantage that member join and leave can now be treated locally. The system tends to be scalable and the fault tolerance is also improved because of the absence of a central controller. Despite being scalable and fault tolerant, IOLUS suffers from the increased communication costs during actual data exchanges. This happens because of the fact that the message gets encrypted and decrypted several times when it is sent from a user in one subgroup to another. The GSA may possibly become a performance bottleneck. Figure 4 shows an example. When a member from subgroup S_4 sends a message M encrypted with key K_4, the GSI between S_1 and S_4 will decrypt M and reencrypt M with key K_1. All the members in subgroup S_1 can recover M. The GSI between S_1 and S_5 will reencrypt M with K_5 and thus the members in S_5 will recover M. Similarly, the GSI between S_0 and S_1 will reencrypt M with K_0, so all members in S_0 will recover M. At this stage, the message will continue to be transmitted to other subgroups S_2 and S_3 and finally to $S_6, \ldots, S_9$.

Distributed (Contributory) Key Agreement

Distributed key agreement schemes involve an equal participation by all the members of a group toward key management. Each member provides its share toward the shared key. The group key is a function of all the shares provided by the users. Being contributory in nature, each user should be aware of the other users in the group to make sure the protocol is robust. A few of the distributed key agreement protocols have been proposed in the literature and we discuss the Burmester and Desmedt protocol below.

Burmester and Desmedt Protocol

Burmester and Desmedt proposed a contributory key agreement scheme in 1995 (Burmester & Desmedt, 1995, 1996). The protocol involves two rounds of broadcast per user and hence a total of $2n$ broadcast messages. The protocol is explained below.

Suppose that p (a large prime) and g (a generator of $\mathbb{Z}_p^*$) are the public components and the group size is n. Let the members in the group be $m_0, m_1, m_2 \ldots m_{n-1}$ and the members are treated cyclically. The following steps are performed to obtain the common shared secret:

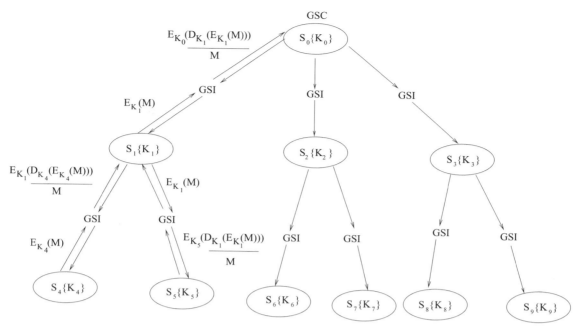

Figure 4: Subgroups and GSAs in Iolus scheme.

Step 1 Every member m_i generates a random exponent s_i and broadcasts $b_i = g^{s_i}$ (b stands for blinded secret). This is the first round of broadcast.

Step 2 Every member m_i then computes and broadcasts $X_i = (b_{i+1}/b_{i-1})^{s_i}$. This is the second round of broadcast.

Step 3 Every member m_i can now obtain the shared key by computing $K_i = b_{i-1}^{ns_i} \times X_i^{n-1} \times X_{i+1}^{n-2} \cdots X_{i-2} \bmod p$.

The group key so obtained is $K = g^{s_0 s_1 + s_1 s_2 + \cdots + s_{n-2} s_{n-1} + s_{n-1} s_0}$.

AUTHENTICATED KEY MANAGEMENT

As discussed above, security functions (such as encryption algorithms and MAC algorithms) are public and the security of a system depends on the secrecy of keys. Thus the attacker targets breaking keys, in particular key management schemes. One common attack is the *man-in-the-middle* attack in the sense that the attacker sits in the middle of two communicating parties and cheats both parties but the two parties have no sense that an attacker is in the middle who is capturing all the communications. This kind of attacks is most dangerous yet hidden. To defend against the man-in-the-middle attack, there is a need for mutual authentication during the key management process (Boyd & Mathuria, 2003). Two scenarios are discussed below.

The Man-in-the-Middle Attack in Diffie–Hellman Key Exchange

The Diffie–Hellman key agreement is a wonderful protocol but it suffers from the man-in-the-middle attack. As shown in Figure 5, when Alice and Bob are conducting key exchange and data communication, Carol is sitting in between secretly. The exchanged values $p_a = g^a \bmod p$ and $p_b = g^b \bmod p$ are replaced with $p_c = g^c \bmod p$ by Carol. The key computed by Alice (or Bob) becomes $g^{ac} \bmod p$ (or $g^{bc} \bmod p$) and is mistaken to be the secret key shared

between Alice and Bob. When Alice transmits messages that were encrypted with $g^{ac} \bmod p$ and directed to Bob, Carol intercepts the messages, decrypts them, reencrypts them using $g^{bc} \bmod p$, and sends them to Bob. As a result, Carol obtains all the messages in cleartext form, whereas Alice and Bob are totally unaware that their communications have been compromised.

To defend against the man-in-the-middle attack, authentication should be involved in the key exchange procedure, called authenticated Diffie–Hellman (Kaufman, Perlman, & Speciner, 2002). In this setting, Alice and Bob know some sort of secret in advance with which they can conduct mutual authentication. This shared secret can be used to prove that it was they who generated the Diffie–Hellman public shares. The proof can be performed in the following ways:

- Encrypt the Diffie–Hellman public shares using the shared secret and transmit the encrypted shares

- Encrypt the Diffie–Hellman public shares with each other's public key, that is, authentication using public key encryption

- Sign the Diffie–Hellman (public) share and send the share, the participants' signature, and their public key

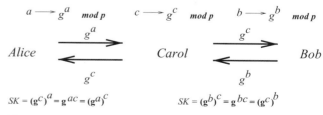

Figure 5: Man-in-the-middle attack in Diffie–Hellman key exchange.

certificate, that is, authentication using public key signature.

Another way to defend against the man-in-the-middle attack in the Diffie–Hellman key exchange is using published Diffie-Hellman shares (Kaufman et al., 2002). In this scenario, every individual has a publicly known, permanent, unforgeable, public share, which can be achieved using public share certificates, as public key certificates do.

The Man-in-the-Middle Attack in Public Key Cryptosystems

Public key cryptosystems can also suffer from the man-in-the-middle attack. For example, when Alice is transmitting the public key P_A to Bob (or Bob is retrieving Alice's P_A from Alice's personal home page or a public key directory), an attacker, Carol, intercepts the transmission and replaces P_A with her own public key P_C. Bob will mistake P_C as Alice's public key, P_A, encrypt messages with P_C, and send them to Alice. Carol intercepts the messages, decrypts them using her private key, reencrypts them with P_A, and sends the reencrypted messages to Alice. This is caused by separation of an individual's identity and its public key. The problem can be solved by public key certificates that bind a public key with its owner (see "Public Key Certificate"). Public key certificates are in fact an authentication method via certificate authority.

KEY UTILIZATION

There are different kinds of keys that can be utilized in different security functions.

Secret Key

A secret key is a shared secret between two communicating parties. A secret key is primarily used for encryption/decryption in a secret key cryptosystem. In this case, the secret key is both the *encryption key* and the *decryption key*.

A secret key can also be used for user authentication, an example of which is the following. Suppose K_{AB} is a secret key shared by Alice and Bob and Bob wants to authenticate Alice before data communication. Bob initiates the authentication by sending a challenge (a nonce R) for Alice to respond. Bob then checks the response (decrypts it using K_{AB} and compares it with R) and verifies that it is really Bob in the other end. The challenge/response procedure is as follows:

Bob → Alice: R //Bob sends a nonce (i.e., a random value)
Alice → Bob: $\{R+1\}_{K_{AB}}$ //Alice responses with $R+1$ encrypted by K_{AB}.

Finally, a secret key can also be used for data integrity such as computing message authentication code (MAC). In this case, the secret key can also be called an MAC key. The sender computes the MAC for a message, sends the MAC along with the message. The receiver recomputes the MAC after receiving the message, and compares the computed MAC with the received MAC. If matched, the message was intact, otherwise, the message was modified during its transmission.

Public Key and Private Key

A public key is an individual's key in a public key cryptosystem and is made public, whereas a private key is an individual's key in a public key cryptosystem and must be kept secret to the individual itself. The public key is used for encryption of messages and thus is the encryption key, whereas the private key is used for decryption and thus is the decryption key. As discussed previously, because of the high computation cost, the public key is generally used to encrypt a secret key before data communication. The public key and private key can also be used in digital signature: Alice signs a message using her private key (so signature key) and then anybody else (to say, Bob) can verify Alice's signature using her public key (so verification key). If the verification successes, then both the message and the message sender are authenticated (i.e., the message is intact during its transmission and the message sender is indeed Alice). Similar to the secret key based user authentication, the private key and public key can be used for user authentication in a challenge–response manner. Suppose Alice's public key is P_A and private key S_A and Bob wants to authenticate Alice. In this case, the private key S_A is used by Alice for encryption and thus an encryption key and the public key P_A is used for decryption by Bob and thus a decryption key. The challenge and response procedure is as follows:

Bob → Alice: R //Bob sends a nonce (i.e., a random value)
Alice → Bob: $\{R+1\}_{S_A}$ //Alice responses with $R+1$ encrypted by S_A.

Key Granularity and Derivation

A common practice is that one key is just used for one purpose, thus making it harder for an attacker to compromise keys. For example, when confidentiality is required, a secret key is used for encryption (as well as decryption) or a public key and its corresponding private key are used for encryption and decryption. For data integrity, an independent MAC key (different from the encryption/decryption key) is used for computing MAC. For authentication using digital signature, a new pair of public and private keys, which is different from the pair of public and private keys used for encryption and decryption, are generated for signature generation and verification.

In most implementations of secure communication systems, two participants first establish a shared secret, called a master key, and then, derive other keys from the master key. For example, in SSL, six different keys are derived from the master key with three in each direction: encryption key, initialization vector, and MAC key.

Another good practice is separating a long term secret key from short-term session keys. Once two communicating parties establish a long-term shared secret key via some methods, the long-term key is used to generate/encrypt/distribute short-term session keys for different communication sessions and the short-term session keys are used for the encryption of data in sessions. There are several reasons for doing this. First, if data are encrypted with different keys, instead of a single key, the likelihood of an attacker being able to break the ciphertext/key will be reduced (Bishop, 2003). Second, the replay attacks will be less effective (Bishop, 2003). Finally, the compromise of one session key will only cause the encrypted data in this session to be revealed. Furthermore, even though the long term secret key is compromised, the previous communications data can be still protected because the data was encrypted with the session keys, unless the transmissions of session keys were also captured and stored, resulting in the session keys being discovered.

KEY STORAGE, RECOVERY, AND ESCROW

As discussed above, there are mainly three kinds of keys: secret key, public key, and private key. The issue with public key is to protect the key's integrity. Public key certificate will suffice. Conversely, the issue with secret key (for secret key cryptosystems) and the private key (for public key cryptosystems) is to protect their confidentiality (Bishop, 2003).

People may protect keys' confidentiality by remembering them or writing them on a notebook. The first method is painful because the key can be quite large. Furthermore, memorization may be lost. The second method is not reliable because the notebook may be destroyed or stolen. Therefore, key storage is a serious issue. One simple choice is to put the key in a file (or a key database) and protect the file by some access control mechanism. However, access control mechanisms can often be defeated (Bishop, 2003). Another attempt is encrypting the key file with a new key. This will result in the same problem: how to store the new key. Furthermore, the key is entered to decrypt the file, the key and file contents will reside in memory at some point, which provides a chance for an attacker to eavesdrop the key. The attacker can also record the keystrokes used to decrypt the file and replay them at a later time, thus compromising the key (Bishop, 2003). One feasible alternative is to manufacture the key onto physical devices such as ROM or smart cards. To encrypt or decrypt a message, the smart card is inserted into a computer and the key is read from the smart card into a computer register, used for encrypting the message, and then discarded, thus the key will never be exposed at any point. The main problem with the smart card solution is that the smart cards may be lost or stolen. One remedy is to split the key into two pieces (such as key = key1 $\oplus$ key2) and to put each piece into an independent device.

Now matter how careful a person is, there is a possibility that the key was lost. Once a key is lost, there is a need to recover the key. For (careless) individuals, it is advisable for you to keep your key in a safe place. In case your key is misplaced or lost, you can retrieve a copy of your key rather than conceding that all your important data (encrypted with your key) are irretrievably lost (Kaufman et al., 2002). As discussed above, storing all users' keys unencrypted somewhere is a big security risk and storing the users' keys in a key database encrypted with a key K needs to expose K to the database server. This would mean that all the keys are exposed to anyone who has access right to the server. The feasible and secure way is to have a trusted third party store and recover keys.

Key escrow is a key recovery system in which a third party can recover the key (Bishop, 2003). Key escrow is primarily applied to legal and law enforcement settings. The objective of a key escrow system is to provide encryption of data traffic such that the properly authorized third parties can obtain the traffic encryption keys (Menezes, Oorschot, & Vanstone, 1996). This grants the authorized third parties the capability to decrypt the traffic if needed (Menezes et al., 1996). A key escrow system contains three components (Bishop, 2003): (1) the user security component, performing encryption/decryption and supporting the next component; (2) the key escrow component, managing key storage and utilization of recovery keys; and (3) the data recovery component, performing data recovery. There are five desirable properties for a key escrow system (Bishop, 2003): (1) independence on the encryption algorithm; (2) complete protection of users' privacy and data confidentiality unless the escrowed keys are used; (3) requirement of legal/business process mapping into the key exchange protocol, thus preventing users from bypassing the escrow system; (4) requirement of authenticating all participating parties; (5) requirement of the escrowed key's valid time being exactly matched with the message's observable time.

Currently, there are two typical key escrow systems (Bishop, 2003): Clipper Chip and the Yaksha escrow system. Clipper Chip is the U.S. government's escrowed encryption standard (EES) and Yaksha is based on RSA cryptosystem and utilizes a central escrow server.

CONCLUSION

This chapter discussed key management issues and techniques for three different settings: secret key management, public key management, and group key management. Key management deals with the issues as key generation, key distribution/key agreement, key updating, and key revocation. Secret key management can be based on public key cryptosystems, Diffie–Hellman key exchange, or a trusted central authority. Public key management mainly deals with preventing forgery/replacement of a public key and utilizes public key certificates and certificate authority to bind the identity of an individual with its public key. Group key management can be centralized, decentralized. or distributed. The article also discussed relevant issues such as authenticated key management, key utilization, key storage, and key escrow.

ACKNOWLEDGMENT

We thank anonymous reviewers for their constructive suggestions.

GLOSSARY

Certificate Authority A third-party organization that vouches for the authenticity of the public keys belonging to subjects.

Certificate Revocation A process by which the binding between the identity and the public key is made invalid.

(Digital) Signature A value computed for a message based on a user's private key such that a recipient of the message can verify, based on the public key of the user, that the message is really from the user.

Key Agreement One class of key management methods, by which the shared secret key is agreed upon by all participants and contains the shares of all participants.

Key Escrow A key recovery system in which a third party can recover the key.

Key Management The technique to deal with generation, distribution, updating, and revocation of keys.

Message Authentication Code An authenticator that is a hash function of both the data to be authenticated and a secret key. In other words, MAC is a keyed hash function. It is also referred to as a cryptographic checksum.

Public Key Certificate Binding of a public key with the identity of its owner, signed by a trusted certificate authority. It is used to obtain the authentic public key of a user or verify the authenticity of a claimed public key by a user.

Public Key Infrastructure The framework and services that provide for the generation, production, management, and accounting of public key certificates.

Secure Group Communication A scenario of group communication in which the members of a group can communicate with one another in a way that outsiders (any user who is not a member of the group) cannot glean any information even when they are able to intercept the messages.

CROSS REFERENCES

See *Digital Certificates; Digital Signatures and Electronic Signatures; Encryption Basics; Key Lengths; PKI (Public Key Infrastructure); Symmetric-Key Encryption*.

REFERENCES

Adams, C., & Farrell, S. (1999). *Internet X.509 public key infrastructure certificate management protocols. RCF 2510.* Retrieved January 2, 2004, from http://www.faqs.org/rfcs/ rfc2510.html

Bishop, M. (2003). *Computer security: Art and science.* Boston, MA: Pearson.

Boyd, C., & Mathuria, A. (Eds.). (2003). *Protocols for authentication and key establishment.* New York: Springer-Verlag.

Brands, S. A. (Ed.). (2000). *Rethinking public key infrastructure and digital certificates.* Cambridge, MA: MIT Press.

Burmester, M., & Desmedt, Y. (1995). A secure and efficient conference key distribution system. In *Lecture notes in computer science, vol. 950: Advances in Cryptology—EUROCRYPT'94* (pp. 275–286). New York: Springer-Verlag.

Burmester, M., & Desmedt, Y. G. (1996). Efficient and secure conference-key distribution. In *Security protocols workshop* (pp. 119–129).

Caronni, G., Waldvogel, K., Sun, D., & Plattner, B. (1998). Efficient security for large and dynamic multicast groups. In *Proceedings of the Seventh IEEE International Workshop on Enabling Technologies: Infrastructure for Collaborative Enterprises (WETICE '98),* (pp. 376–383).

Choudhury, S., Bhatnagar, K., & Haque, W. (Eds.). (2002). *Public key infrastructure implementation and design.* New York: John Wiley & Sons.

Diffie, W., & Hellman, M. E. (1976). Multiuser cryptographic techniques. *AFIPS Conference Proceedings, 45,* 109–112.

Housley, R., Ford, W., Polk, W., & Solo, D. (1999). *Internet X.509 public key infrastructure certificate and CRL profile. RCF 2459.* Retrieved January 2, 2005, from http://www.faqs.org/rfcs/rfc2459.html

Kaufman, C., Perlman, R., & Speciner, M. (2002). *Network security: Private communication in a public world.* Upper Saddle River, NJ: Prentice Hall.

Kohl, J., & Neuman, C. (1993). *The Kerberos network authentication services (v5). RCF 1510.*

Lloyd, S., & Sams, C. A. (Eds.). (1999). *Understanding the public-key infrastructure: Concepts, standards, and deployment considerations.* New York: Macmillan.

Menezes, A., Ooschot, P. V., & Vanstone, S. (Eds.). (1996). *Handbook of applied cryptography.* Boca Raton, FL: CRC

Merkle, R. C. (1989). A certified digital signature. In *Proceedings of Crypto '89, Lecture notes in computer science, vol. 435.* (pp. 234–246). New York: Springer-Verlag.

Mittra, S. (1997). Iolus a framework for scalable secure multicasting. *Journal of Computer Communication Reviews, 27,* 277–288.

Myers, M., Ankney, R., Malpani, A., Galperin, S., & Adams, C. (1999). *Internet X.509 public key infrastructure online certificate status protocol—OCSP. RCF 2560.* Retrieved January 7, 2004, from http://www.faqs.org/rfcs/rfc2560.html

Nash, A., Duane, W., Joseph, C., & Brink, D. (Eds.). (2001). *PKI—Implementing and managing e-security.* New York: Osborne/McGraw-Hill.

Steiner, J., Neuman, C., & Schiller, J. (1988). Kerberos: An authentication service for open network systems. In *Proceedings of the 1988 Winter USENIX Conference* (pp. 191–202).

Wallner, D. M., Harder, E. J., & Agee, R. C. (1998). Key management for multicast: Issues and architectures. In *Internet draft (work in progress), Internet engineering task force.* Retrieved January 4, 2004, from draft-wallner-key-arch-01.txt

Wong, C. K., Gouda, M., & Lam, S. S. (1998). *Secure group communications using key graphs. (Technical report TR 97-23,* pp. 68–79). Austin: *University of Texas at Austin.*

Zou, X., Ramamurthy, B., & Magliveras, S. S. (Eds.). (2004). *Secure group communications over data networks.* New York: Springer-Verlag.

Secure Electronic Voting Protocols

Helger Lipmaa, *Cybernetica AS and University of Tartu, Estonia*

INTRODUCTION

Since the early 1990s, one of the global buzzwords (or, rather, buzz-letters) has been *"e,"* short for *electronic*, which signifies almost everything connected with (inter-)networking. The ubiquity of *"e"* is caused by the global penetration of the Internet and, in many places of the world, by easier availability of Internet-based services, compared to the traditional services. Numerous e-processes are already taking place, starting from e-banking and ending with (in some countries) e-government. This had led to the situation where one wants to "e-ize" most of the processes and services that can be found in a modern society. After all, moving to the e-services helps one to cut down costs and save time. Additionally, it makes it possible for more and more people to become a part of the global society and to benefit from its services.

Not surprisingly, also "e-izing" (nationwide or local) elections promises to give measurable benefits. The very basic idea of the elections is to give every citizen of a country (or some other political unit) an equal right when deciding about the future of their country. To guarantee equal rights, it is essential to achieve a high voter turnout. As the most extreme case, let us look at an imaginary political system that has only two parties in an election where "the winner takes all." If only 51% of the voters vote and the winning party collects 51% of the participating votes, the resulting government does not necessarily represent the majority of the citizens.

This is exactly where e-voting could help: it is at least one's hope that when voting is made more convenient, considerably more voters will turn out. And what could be more convenient than voting at your own home by using your own personal computer? Or your laptop when traveling—or even your mobile phone when you do not have access to the Internet? Moreover, if votes are submitted electronically, vote counting could be almost instantaneous—in the contemporary world, quick vote counting is unfortunately an important issue. And last but not least, e-voting could make it cheaper and easier to organize elections.

But, alas, convenience is not everything. Traditional voting booths have been designed to prevent vote coercion. But how can coercion be prevented when a user votes from home? How can that voter's computer functions be correctly ascertained (no viruses, Trojan horses, or keyboard sniffers)? How can that voting center's computer functions be correctly ascertained (e.g., denial of service attacks and insider attacks)? Asking from a voter's—who may not know anything about how a computer or the Internet works—point of view, can one guarantee the correctness and robustness of the elections? And what about privacy? Can one protect the voter against coercers?

The answer is "partially, yes." Under some feasible *cryptographic* assumptions, privacy can be protected, although the voter still needs to trust his or her *voting platform* (e.g., a computer or a mobile phone) and other pieces of hardware that are not under his or her own control. (But see also Further Research Topics). If, additionally, special hardware is used, one can design coercion-free elections. The use of secure cryptographic protocols together with fault-tolerant, well-organized, sufficiently duplicated, and constantly verified voting infrastructure *might* also guarantee robustness. The necessary cryptography is already out there, together with a developing understanding of what are (at least some of) the specific requirements on the infrastructure and on the voters. Real understanding cannot come before people have gone through many trials and errors that result from electronic elections with significant, nonduplicated, and nonreputable outcomes. It is our feeling that these real-life requirements will never be satisfied, even if some new breakthrough in cryptography makes some of the requirements obsolete.

Before going further, some warnings. e-voting means at least two quite different things: *Internet voting* (voting over the Internet, as discussed above, by using a personal computer or mobile device with the possible help of minimal additional specialized hardware) or *kiosk voting* (voting in some fixed location, such as a library or kiosk, by using special hardware). Kiosk voting also includes the current practice of some countries to use electronic or mechanical devices—such as optical scans—in the voting stations. Kiosk voting can be easier to organize—there is no question about the untrusted operating system on the voter's computer, for example—but it does not allow for convenient "anywhere voting." (However, note that a diligent user can analyze software, running on his or her computer, whereas software, running in a kiosk is most likely going to be nonaccessible.) Still, kiosk voting might increase the voter turnout—and definitely decreases vote counting time. In this survey, by e-voting we refer primarily to Internet voting. All the protocols that we present can also be used in the case of kiosk voting, although some of their features might be overkill. Conversely, even in the case of kiosk voting, the current cryptographic solutions—even if used 100% correctly, which is rarely the case—are not yet completely satisfying.

In this chapter, we are going to present in detail several (under appropriate definitions) secure and (relatively) efficient cryptographic e-voting protocols. We discuss the level of security achieved by the described protocols and also their efficiency. We stop on the requirements on the infrastructure that seem to be necessary for the state of the art cryptographic e-voting protocols to fulfill their promise. Finally, we outline some important open questions and further research directions.

Notation. Let cands be the number of candidates, somehow enumerated by integers from 0 to cands $- 1$. Let $V = (V_1, \ldots, V_{\text{voters}})$ be the set of eligible voters. Let $V' \subseteq V$ be the set of eligible voters who turned up and voted. Let v_i be the vote as cast by V_i; we assume $v_i = \bot$ if V_i did not vote. Let μ be the concrete voting mechanism that is being used.

VOTING: GENERAL OVERVIEW

During an election of, for example, a national or local government, voters cast votes to a number of candidates. After the voting phase, the winning candidate(s) are computed from the set of votes. There are many game theoretically sound (or just validated by practice) *voting mechanisms* for the latter part. Next, we briefly summarize some of the well-known voting mechanisms (in all cases, the candidate with the most points wins). As in the rest of the chapter we assume that there are voters (voters) and candidates (cands). In all four cases, every voter outputs an ordered list of cands candidates.

1. **Plurality:** A candidate receives 1 point for every voter that ranks it first. (Here, it is sufficient for the voter to output only the top choice.)
2. **Borda:** For each voter, a candidate receives cands $- 1$ points if it is the voter's top choice, cands $- 2$ if it is the second choice, ..., 0 if it is the last.
3. **Single transferable vote (STV):** The winner determination process proceeds in rounds. In each round, a candidate's score is the number of voters that rank it highest among the remaining candidates, and the candidate with the lowest score drops out. The last remaining candidate wins. (A vote transfers from its top remaining candidate to the next highest remaining candidate when the former drops out.)
4. **Maximin:** A candidate's score in a pairwise election is the number of voters that prefer it over the opponent. A candidate's number of points is the lowest score it gets in any pairwise election.

If a mechanism μ is used, let $\mu(v_1, \ldots, v_{\text{voters}})$ be the result of the election given votes v_i.

Exactly how the voting process is organized depends largely on the individual country and sometimes also on the individual county or even the village. However, an election tends to have at least the following phases, where the specifics of every phase may vary wildly:

- **Voter registration:** All/most of the/some of the citizens are automatically registered as voters. The rest must register themselves as eligible voters.
- **Voting:** During a few preannounced days, every registered voter can cast his or her vote. At some a priori known time moment, the voting phase will be over. Voting period may depend on the individual tallier. (Thus, this model includes absentee voting.)
- **Tallying:** After the end of voting phases, talliers count their tallies that are then mixed together to obtain the final result. (This phase depends heavily on the voting mechanism, the size of the country, etc.)

In practice, plurality and Borda elections are somewhat easier to organize than STV and Maximin because in them only the total count of points for every candidate is needed for every candidate. This total count can just be incremented as more and more votes from different voting stations become counted. This also means that when there are many talliers (e.g., corresponding to different counties) different subtallies can just be added up.

E-VOTING: GENERAL SETTING

Different countries implement elections in different ways to comply and cope with their own traditions, definition of democracy, size of the country, and so on. E-voting must take all such considerations into account and thus, just to make e-voting understandable to the voters, at least at first, e-voting must largely mimic conventional voting. In particular, e-voting should have a registration phase, a voting phase, and a tallying phase. Only later, when voters have become used to the e-voting, could one change the election process to better suit the specifics of e-voting.

Thus, we think of e-voting as just a method to make voting more convenient by enabling both the voters and the talliers to use technology to speed up their part of the process. Maybe later changes caused by e-voting will cause a revolution in the voting process—and thus in the whole society. Currently, the change offered by e-voting is (or at least, in our opinion, should be) rather evolutionary.

How would (evolutionary) e-voting look like in an ideal world? First, the voters enter their votes to the *voting platform* (e.g., a computer). Then, the votes get transmitted to a central machine (the *tallying platform*) that computes the winner by using a fixed voting mechanism. Finally, the talliers output the name of the winner (or winners) with other auxiliary information that may be necessary (e.g., the number of votes of every candidate). In such an ideal world, all parts of the system function correctly. In particular, ideal e-voting has two important properties:

1. **Correctness:** The output of the elections is $\mu(v_1, \ldots, v_{voters})$. That is, the election outputs a correct result, meaning that only the votes of legitimate voters count.

2. **Privacy:** During the election, nobody will gain new information about any of v_i-s—except what follows from $\mu(v_1, \ldots, v_{voters})$ and their own private inputs. This includes the next subgoals: (a) voter's preferences remain private, (b) voting is coercion free (even if you choose so, you are not able to later prove your vote), and (c) independence (voter should know his or her vote).

All mentioned subgoals correspond to the necessity of avoiding certain attacks. For example, imagine a simple voting protocol where every voter sends its encrypted vote to the tallier. Bob, a huge fan of a singer named Alice, just copies her encrypted vote and enters this to the voting platform. Or may be, Bob is able to manipulate the ciphertext so that his vote is the opposite of Alice's vote. This does not violate Alice's privacy (only under very special circumstances, Bob gains any information about Alice's vote!) but it creates undesirable situations where voters vote as their idol does—or as their hated one does not. This means that Bob must know his vote.

Next, we give the definition of a secure electronic voting protocol. The definition is not fully formal because, in practice, it is not clear what is meant by "security." Moreover, some of the electronic voting protocols, presented in the following sections, do not satisfy the ideal security definition.

Assume that we have a fixed voting mechanism μ, such as Plurality or Borda. Let Φ_μ be the function that, given votes of participating voters, computes some intermediate result that is necessary for finding the winner. For example, $\Phi_{\text{Plurality}}(v_1, \ldots, v_{voters})$ is usually a function that returns a vector $(w_1, \ldots, w_{cands}, w_\perp)$, where $w_i = \sharp\{j : v_j = i\}$ is the number of voters V_j that voted for the ith candidate. It is possible to define $\Phi_{\text{Plurality}}(v_1, \ldots, v_{voters}) = w$, where w is the name of the winner. However, such solutions are not usually considered in the case of paper ballot voting, because the privacy of losing candidates is usually hard to implement. The concrete definition depends on the voting traditions of an individual country. For example, if the number of seats in the parliament is proportional to the number of votes every party achieves, the full vector $(v_1, \ldots, v_{voters})$ must be revealed.

As in a conventional election, an e-voting protocol consists also of the registration phase, the voting phase, and the vote counting phase. In the registration phase, the legitimate voters obtain the right to participate in e-voting. How this is done depends heavily on the

traditions and technological infrastructure. For example, in some countries, the voters may be able to register by using their ID cards. This is largely a political issue, and we will just assume that legitimate voters will be able to vote and obtain necessary information (such as the public keys of the authorities) in an authenticated manner.

In the voting and tallying phase, we make a comparison with the "ideal world." In the ideal world e-voting protocol, the trusted third party $\mathcal{T}$ keeps a database of votes. Every voter V_i casts a vote v_i that may be equal to $\perp$. The third party $\mathcal{T}$ stores the vote in her database. (A voter might be able to vote several times, but then only the result of the last vote counts.) After the end of the voting phase, $\mathcal{T}$ computes $\psi = \Phi_\mu(v_1, \ldots, v_{voters})$. In the tallying phase, the value ψ is published. The tallier $\mathcal{A}$ finds the winner(s) of the election, based on ψ, by using rules, induced by the mechanism μ. (This part of the election is repeatable and verifiable by everybody.)

It is required that at the end of the protocol, the participants should have no information about the private inputs and outputs of their partners, except for what can be deduced from their own private inputs and outputs. In particular, V_i has no information about the value of v_j for $j \neq i$, and $\mathcal{A}$ has no information about the value of v_i for any i, except what they can deduce from their own private inputs and outputs. In practice, it usually means that it is required that the voting center gets to know how many voters voted for every candidate but not how did every single voter vote.

In an ideal world, exactly three types of attacks are possible (Goldreich, 2004): a party can (a) refuse to participate in the protocol, (b) substitute his or her private input to the trusted third party with a different value, or (c) abort the protocol prematurely. In our case, attack (c) is irrelevant, because V_i has no output in the voting phase and $\mathcal{T}$ has no output in the tallying phase. (Attack [c] models the case when the first party halts the protocol after receiving his private output but before the second party has enough information to compute her output.)

Therefore, in an ideal world e-voting protocol, we cannot protect against a participant, who (a) refuses to participate in voting (*nonparticipation attack*) or (b) enters a vote that differs from his or her preference (may correspond to vote manipulation). No other attacks should be possible. Neither (a) nor (b) is traditionally considered an attack in the context of voting. The argument here is game theoretical and the solutions must be proposed by mechanism design (and politics!) instead of cryptography: namely a nonmanipulable mechanism (e.g., the algorithm with what the election winner is determined from all the collected votes) must be designed so that answering against one's true preference (or nonparticipation) would not give more beneficial results to the respondent than the truthful answer.

Conversely, as we stated, no other attacks should be allowed. This requirement is very strict, so we explain why it is necessary in the voting context. Clearly, one must protect the privacy of voters: it is required that in democracy, one should be able to vote according to his or her true preferences. There are many cases where nonprivate voting could damage the interests of the individual voter (starting from a quarrel with his or her significant other and ending with the possibility of getting discriminated by the new government, against whom one just voted).

It is also necessary to protect the privacy of $\mathcal{A}$, although the reason here is more subtle. Namely if V_i obtains any additional information about ψ before the end of the elections, he or she might halt the protocol or change his or her vote. This might always happen because by a classical result of voting theory, all nondictatorial voting mechanisms can be manipulated (Gibbard, 1973; Satterthwaite, 1973). As an easy example, a voter can decide to vote for his or her second preference, when the first preference has no chance to win. (Halting the e-voting protocol while having no information on ψ is equivalent to the nonparticipation attack.) The third requirement on the protocol, of course, is that $\mathcal{A}$ either halts or receives $\Phi_\mu(v_1, \ldots, v_{\text{voters}})$.

In a real-world implementation, we want to replace $\mathcal{T}$ by a cryptographic protocol $\Pi = (V_1, \ldots, V_{\text{voters}}; \mathcal{A})$ between V_i and $\mathcal{A}$. This protocol $(V_1, \ldots, V_{\text{voters}}; \mathcal{A})$ is assumed to be "indistinguishable" from the ideal-world protocol, that is, with a high probability, it must be secure against all attacks except (a) and (b). "Secure" means that the privacy of V_i (resp. $\mathcal{A}$) must be protected if V_i (resp. $\mathcal{A}$) follows the protocol and that $\mathcal{A}$ either halts or receives the value $\Phi_\mu(v_1, \ldots, v_{\text{voters}})$. Note that in particular this means that all messages between voters and $\mathcal{A}$ bust be authenticated by say using digital signatures.

Ideally, the security of the voters should be information theoretical (that is, even an omnipotent adversary should not be able to violate the privacy of voters), whereas the security of tallier $\mathcal{A}$ can be computational (that is, a computationally bounded adversary should not be able to force $\mathcal{A}$ to accept an output that is not equal to $\Psi_\mu(v_1, \ldots, v_{\text{voters}})$). This is because the voters, if they cheat, must do it online, whereas the adversary has all the eternity to violate voters's privacy. However, it is much easier to design e-voting with computational voter security. In particular, all protocols that are described in the next sections provide only computational voter privacy.

In a majority of existing secure e-voting protocols, every participant proves in zero knowledge (Goldwasser, Micali, & Rackoff, 1989) that he or she behaved correctly. (Sometimes, it is sufficient to have weaker guarantees, e.g., to present witness indistinguishable proofs.) Every voter must be able to verify the correctness of the zero-knowledge proofs and thus can verify that his or her vote was counted. In this case, one talks about *voter-verifiable (or voter-verified) electronic elections*. If the zero-knowledge correctness proofs are not only verifiable by the designated verifier but for everybody, including the casual observers, one talks about *universally verifiable electronic elections*. In practice, it is important that electronic (including both Internet and kiosk) elections were universally verifiable. Without universal verifiability, there is no hope of having any reliable "vote recounting" in the case of overvoting or undervoting, and no hope of correcting the errors in current kiosk voting. See, for example, (Verified Voting Foundation, 2004) for a high-profile campaign for universal verifiability.

Finally, note that the security requirements of e-voting schemes are different from the requirements of say electronic banking. One could assume that e-banking is at least to some extent reliable, because in the case of cheating, bank would get out of business. However, the sitting government will get out of business when it loses the election and, moreover, has means to influence operators of e-voting systems. This is one of the reasons why universal verifiability is a must in the case of e-voting.

CRYPTOGRAPHIC PRELIMINARIES

A public key cryptosystem is a triple $\Pi = (\text{Gen}, \text{Enc}, \text{Dec})$ where Gen is the key generation algorithm that generates a private/public key pair (sk, pk), Enc is the encryption algorithm, and Dec is the decryption algorithm. For a fixed Π and public key sk, we denote the corresponding plaintext space by $P = P(\Pi, \text{pk})$, randomness space by $R = R(\Pi, \text{pk})$, and ciphertext space by $C = C(\Pi, \text{pk})$. Denote the encryption of a message $m \in P$ as $\text{Enc}_{\text{pk}}(m; r)$, where pk is the used public key and $r \in R$ is the used random coin. Throughout this chapter, let κ denote the security parameter.

IND-CPA Secure Homomorphic Cryptosystems

Define

$$
\text{Adv}_{\Pi, \kappa}^{\text{pkcsem}}(A) := |\Pr[(\text{sk}, \text{pk}) \leftarrow \text{Gen}(1^\kappa), (m_0, m_1)
$$
$$
\leftarrow A(1^\kappa, \text{pk}), b \leftarrow_r \{0, 1\}, r \leftarrow_r R :
$$
$$
A(1^\kappa, m_0, m_1, \text{pk}, \text{Enc}_{\text{pk}}(m_b; r)) = b] - \frac{1}{2}| .
$$

We say that Π is *IND-CPA secure* if $\text{Adv}_{\Pi, \kappa}^{\text{pkcsem}}(A)$ is negligible in κ for any probabilistic polynomial time machine A. That is, Π is IND-CPA secure if it is difficult for a polynomially bounded adversary to distinguish between random encryptions of two elements chosen by him- or herself.

Assume that the C (resp. P) is a group with group operation $\cdot$ (resp. $+$). Assume that R is a groupoid with groupoid operation $\circ$. Π is *homomorphic* when $\text{Enc}_{\text{pk}}(m_1; r_1) \text{Enc}_{\text{pk}}(m_2; r_2) = \text{Enc}_{\text{pk}}(m_1 + m_2; r_1 \circ r_2)$ for any valid public key pk, plaintexts m_i, and random coins r_i.

The first well-known IND-CPA secure homomorphic cryptosystem ElGamal was proposed by El Gamal (1984). In the conventional ElGamal, one fixes two large primes p and q, s.t. $q \mid (p - 1)$, and let G_q be the unique subgroup of $\mathbb{Z}_p^*$ of order q. Let g be a generator of G_q. Private key is a random element sk $\leftarrow_r \mathbb{Z}_q$. The corresponding public key is $h \leftarrow g^{\text{sk}}$. Encryption is defined as $\text{Enc}_{\text{pk}}(m; r) := (g^r; mh^r)$. A ciphertext (c, d) can be decrypted by $m \leftarrow d/c^{\text{sk}} = mh^r/g^{\text{skr}}$. Because $\text{Enc}_{\text{pk}}(m_1; r_1)\text{Enc}_{\text{pk}}(m_2; r_2) = \text{Enc}_{\text{pk}}(m_1 m_2; r_1 + r_2)$, P is the multiplicative group $(G_q, \cdot)$. ElGamal is IND-CPA secure under the decisional Diffie–Hellman assumption (Tsiounis & Yung, 1998).

In several e-voting protocols, one needs an additively homomorphic cryptosystem, that is, where $P = (\mathbb{Z}_n, +)$ for some (possibly key dependent) n. One can modify ElGamal to behave like an additively homomorphic cryptosystem by defining $\text{Enc}_{\text{pk}}(m; r) := (g^r; g^m h^r)$, but in this case decryption is feasible only when m is known to belong to some relatively small set (e.g., $m \in \{0, 1\}$).

Paillier's cryptosystem Paillier (Paillier, 1999) is the first well-known IND-CPA secure additively homomorphic cryptosystem. Its IND-CPA security is based on the decisional composite residuosity assumption (Paillier, 1999). Paillier's cryptosystem was extended by Damgård and Jurik to allow encryption of large messages (Damgård & Jurik, 2001). In the Damgård–Jurik cryptosystem DJ01, $n = pq$ is the public key and its factorization (p, q) is the secret key. One sets $\mathsf{Enc}_{\mathsf{pk}}(m; r) := (1 + n)^m r^{n^s} \bmod n^{s+1}$, where $s \geq 1$ can be freely chosen after n is generated. Here, $m \in \mathbb{Z}_{n^s}$ and $r \leftarrow_r \mathbb{Z}_n^*$. (In practice, $r \leftarrow_r \mathbb{Z}_n$ suffices.) For decrypting, one first computes $\mathsf{Enc}_{\mathsf{pk}}(m; r)^{(p-1)(q-1)} = (1 + n)^{m(p-1)(q-1)} r^{\varphi(n^s)} \bmod n^{s+1} = (1 + n)^{m(p-1)(q-1)} \bmod n^{s+1}$ and recovers m from that by using an algorithm from Damgård and Jurik (2001).

Another similar cryptosystem, DJ03, was proposed by Damgård and Jurik in 2003 (Damgård & Jurik, 2003). DJ03 is slower and has longer ciphertexts than DJ01, and its IND-CPA security is based on both the decisional Diffie–Hellman and the decisional composite residuosity assumptions being true. Conversely, it has a simpler threshold version than DJ01.

Threshold Homomorphic Cryptosystems

The goal of a threshold cryptosystem $\Pi = (\mathsf{Gen}, \mathsf{Enc}, \mathsf{Dec})$ is to make it possible to share the private key among a set of receivers, so that only authorized sets of servers can decrypt messages. As always, Gen is the key generation algorithm, Enc is the encryption algorithm, and Dec is the decryption algorithm. In the case of a threshold cryptosystem, the key is generated jointly by all participants so that everybody knows the public key pk, and all servers will have shares of the private key sk. Decryption is done by an authorized set of servers without explicitly reconstructing the private key. Conversely, encryption algorithm is mostly used by outsiders who might not know that decryption is done in a threshold manner.

Next we describe the *threshold ElGamal Cryptosystem*, mostly because of its simplicity. A description of the more complicated threshold DJ01 and DJ03 cryptosystems can be found from Damgård and Jurik (2001, 2003). Let Gen be a subgroup of $\mathbb{Z}_p^*$ of order q, where q and p are large primes. To generate a secret key $s \in \mathbb{Z}_p$, every server Server$_j$ generates a share s_j as in Shamir's secret sharing scheme (Shamir, 1979). That is, $s_j = f(j)$ for some polynomial f that is unknown to any single server. There exists exactly one polynomial f of degree k such that $s_j = f(j)$ for $j \in \{1, \ldots, k\}$. Server$_j$ commits to her share s_j by publishing the value $h_j \leftarrow g^{s_j}$. As in Shamir's secret sharing scheme, the secret s is equal to $s = f(0)$.

By the Lagrange interpolation formula, given k points (x_i, y_i), s.t. $y_i = f(x_i)$, $i = 1, \ldots, k$, $f(x) = \sum_{i=1}^k y_i \prod_{j=1, j \neq i}^k (x - x_j)/(x_i - x_j) \pmod{p}$ (here, $x_j = j$ and $y_j = s_j$) and thus $s = f(0) = \sum_{i=1}^k c_i s_i \pmod{p}$, where $c_j := \prod_{j=1, j \neq i}^k -j/(i - j) \bmod p$.

Therefore, g^s can be computed as $\prod_{j \in X} h_j^{c_j}$ from the public values h_j only, where X is any subset of k authorities. Then, $h = g^s$ is announced as the public key. No collection of $<k$ servers learns s, but note that s is only computationally hidden (w.r.t. the discrete logarithm problem).

To decrypt $(x, y) = (g^r, mh^r)$, the servers Server$_j$ perform the following steps: (a) each Server$_j$ broadcasts $w_j = x^{s_j}$ and proves in zero-knowledge that $\log_g h_j = \log_x w_j$; (b) let X be any subset of k authorities who passed the zero-knowledge proof. The plaintext can be recovered by X as $m' \leftarrow y/\prod_{j \in X} w_j^{c_j}$. Really, $w_j^{c_j} = x^{c_j s_j} = g^{r c_j s_j}$, thus $m' = mg^{rs}/\prod g^{r c_j s_j} = m$.

How to Prove Equality of Discrete Logarithms?

Chaum and Pedersen (1992) proposed the following protocol, where A proves that $x = g^\mu \wedge y = h^\mu$ for some μ: (a) prover generates a random $r \leftarrow_r \mathbb{Z}_q$ and sends $(a, b) \leftarrow (g^r, h^r)$ to verifier, (b) verifier sends a random $e \leftarrow_r \{0, 1\}^t$, $t \geq 80$, to prover, (c) prover sends $z = r + \mu e \bmod q$ to verifier, and (d) verifier checks that $g^z = ax^c$ and $h^z = by^c$.

Commitment Schemes

A commitment scheme is a function $C : X \times R \rightarrow Y$ from the plaintext space X and random coin space R to the commitment space Y. A commitment scheme C is (a) *statistically hiding* if the commitment $y = C(m; r)$ leaks a statistically insignificant amount of information about the plaintext m and the coin r and (b) *computationally binding* if, given commitment $y = C(m; r)$ to some element r from the plaintext space, it is hard to find $m' \in P$, $m' \neq m$ and an r', s.t. $y = C(m'; r')$. For the best-known commitment schemes (e.g., Pedersen 1991), the plaintext space is equal to $\mathbb{Z}_n$ for some n. Therefore, $C(m; r) = C(m + n; r)$ and such commitment schemes are not binding over the integers.

Fujisaki and Okamoto (1999) proposed an *integer commitment scheme* that is binding over the integers. Their scheme was later improved by Damgård and Fujisaki (2002). The Damgård–Fujisaki integer commitment scheme is computationally binding and statistically hiding, given some reasonable cryptographic assumptions. Moreover, one can construct a very efficient honest-verifier statistical zero-knowledge (HVSZK) argument of knowledge that given three commitments c_1, c_2, and c_3, the prover knows such integers μ_1 and μ_2 and corresponding random coins ρ_1, ρ_2, and ρ_3, that $c_1 = C(\mu_1; \rho_1)$, $c_2 = C(\mu_2; \rho_2)$, and $c_3 = C(\mu_1 \mu_2; \rho_3)$.

The homomorphic property of integer commitment schemes together with the efficient HVSZK argument of knowledge for the multiplicative relation can be used to construct efficient HVSZK arguments of knowledge of type $c_1 = C(\mu_1; \rho_1) \wedge \cdots \wedge c_n = C(\mu_n; \rho_n) \wedge c_{i+1} = C(\mu_{i+1}; \rho_{i+1}) \wedge \mu_{i+1} = p(\mu_1, \ldots, \mu_n)$, where p is an arbitrary polynomial $p \in \mathbb{Z}[X_1, \ldots, X_n]$. Lipmaa (2003) proposed a uniform methodology for constructing efficient HVSZK arguments of knowledge for a relatively large class $\mathcal{D}$ of languages; it is conjectured but not known that $\mathcal{D} = \mathcal{NP}$. Given a statistically hiding and computationally binding integer commitment scheme with efficient HVSZK arguments of knowledge for additive and multiplicative relations, one can argue in HVSZK that she knows an auxiliary (suitably chosen) witness ω, such that $\mathfrak{R}_S(\mu; \omega) = 0$, where $\mathfrak{R}_S$ is the representing polynomial of

S (Matiyasevich, 1993; Lipmaa, 2003). In particular, this results in an subquadratic-length *Diophantine argument system* for all languages from the class L_2 of bounded arithmetic.

The *range argument* $y = C(\mu; \rho) \wedge \mu \in [L, H]$ has an HVSZK argument of knowledge with linear length $\Theta(|\mu|)\kappa$ (Lipmaa, 2003). It is based on the famous theorem of Lagrange that every nonnegative integer μ can be represented as $\omega_1^2 + \cdots + \omega_4^2$ for some integers ω_i. The corresponding values ω_i can be computed efficiently (Lipmaa, 2003). (See Groth, 2004, for a slight refinement.)

Efficient RAIE

In the next, we need an honest-verifier zero-knowledge proof of knowledge that the prover has encrypted a value of form voters^j where $j \in [0, \text{cands} - 1]$ for some publicly known constants voters and cands. This is called a *range argument in exponents* (RAIE). The currently most efficient honest verifier computational zero-knowledge (HVCZK) RAIE was proposed by Lipmaa, Asokan, and Niemi (2002). The resulting RAIE has communication $\Theta(\max(k, \text{cands} \log \text{voters}) \cdot \log \text{cands}) = \Theta(\text{cands} \cdot \log \text{voters} \cdot \log \text{cands})$. For RAIE, one can use another function $a^{[\![i]\!]}$ instead of the exponentiation a^i(Lipmaa, 2003). The function $a^{[\![i]\!]}$ is defined as follows. All nonnegative integral solutions (x, y) of the equation $x^2 - axy - y^2 = 1$ are equal to either $(a^{[\![i+1]\!]}, a^{[\![i]\!]})$ or $(a^{[\![i]\!]}, a^{[\![i+1]\!]})$, $i \geq 0$, where $a^{[\![i]\!]}$ can be computed by using the next recurrent identities (Matiyasevich, 1993): $a^{[\![0]\!]} := 0$, $a^{[\![1]\!]} := 1$, and $a^{[\![i+2]\!]} := aa^{[\![i+1]\!]} - a^{[\![i]\!]}$ for $i \geq 0$. Thus, $\{a^{[\![i]\!]}\}_{i \in \mathbb{N}}$ is a Lucas sequence. When $a > 2$ and $i > 0$ then $(a-1)^i \leq a^{[\![i+1]\!]} \leq a^i$. Also, $a^{[\![i]\!]}$ can be computed almost as efficiently as a^i.

Bulletin Board

A bulletin board is a public broadcast channel with memory where a players write information that any party can read. See, for example, Cramer, Gennaro, and Schoenmakers (1997).

HOMOMORPHIC E-VOTING SCHEMES

Assume that the election uses the Plurality mechanism. (Implementing other mechanisms by using the next approach is also possible, although much more cumbersome.) Then, secure e-voting can be achieved as follows by using a secure homomorphic threshold cryptosystem $\Pi = (\text{Gen}, \text{Enc}, \text{Dec})$ (Cramer, Gennaro, & Schoenmakers, 1997; Damgård & Jurik, 2001): Let a be the upper limit to the number of voters. Let $\tau \geq 1$. There is $2\tau + 1$ servers that share a public key pk and a private key sk so that everybody can encrypt a message by using pk, but only $\geq \tau + 1$ collaborating servers can jointly decrypt the ciphertext. Assume $v_i \in [0, \text{cands} - 1]$ corresponds to the preferred candidate. The ith voter encrypts voters^{v_i} by using the key pk and sends it to the servers. The servers collect all ciphertexts and return receipts to the voters. The list of all encrypted votes is written on the bulletin board. After the end of the election, the servers multiply all ciphertexts, getting $y = \text{Enc}_{\text{pk}}(\sum_i \text{voters}^{v_i}) = \text{Enc}_{\text{pk}}(\sum \alpha_j \text{voters}^j)$, where

α_j is the number of voters who voted for the candidate j. Thus, the servers can jointly decrypt y, and then compute the coefficients α_j. The value y together with the vector $(\alpha_1, \ldots, \alpha_{\text{cands}})$ is published.

Next, we will look into the details of this generic *homomorphic e-voting* protocol.

Guaranteeing Correctness

To guarantee the correctness of this protocol, all voters must prove or argue in zero knowledge that they encrypted a value of form a^j, where $j \in [0, \text{cands} - 1]$. This corresponds to the RAIE. The function $a^{[\![i]\!]}$ is exactly as suitable as a^i to be used as the encoding function that the voters use in the homomorphic e-voting scheme (Lipmaa, 2003). Because $(a^{[\![i]\!]})^2 - aa^{[\![i]\!]}a^{[\![i+1]\!]} - (a^{[\![i+1]\!]})^2 = 1$, there is a $\Theta(\text{cands} \log \text{voters})$-bit HVSZK argument of knowledge to prove that a voter voted correctly. Lipmaa, Asokan, and Niemi (2002) proposed an alternative RAIE that is also based on the methodology from (Lipmaa, 2003). Instead of the function voters^i (or voters$^{[\![i]\!]}$), it uses the function b^i, where b is the least prime $b \geq$ voters. Because voters is fixed a priori and publicly known, b can be computed before the electronic voting starts. This RAIE is approximately as efficient as the RAIE based on the Lucas sequences: the arguer must argue that the committed value μ is such that $b^L \leq \mu$ and $\mu \mid b^H$. As later shown in (Damgård, Groth, & Salomonsen, 2002), one can simplify the argument even more by assuming that $b = p^2$ for a prime p: then one has to argue the knowledge of an ω, for which $(\omega \mid p^{H-L}) \wedge (\omega^2 p^{2L} = \mu)$. The RAIE is the single most communication-consuming subprotocol of the homomorphic voting scheme. Therefore, the use of HVSZK arguments results in a $\Theta(\log \text{cands})$-fold decrease of total communication.

Server's correctness can be verified by every voter by multiplying all the votes on the bulletin board, checking that their own votes are there, that the product is equal to y, and, finally, that $\sum \alpha_j \text{voters}^j$ is a correct decryption of y (by verifying another zero-knowledge proof).

Multicandidate Voting

The homomorphic e-voting scheme is especially efficient when used together with the additive variant of ElGamal. However, this is true only when voters^{cands} is relatively small: the decryption results in $g^{\sum \alpha_j \text{voters}^j}$, from which $\sum \alpha_j \text{voters}^j \in [0, \text{voters}^{\text{cands}} - 1]$ can be found by solving the restricted discrete logarithm problem. The realistic value of voters is in $\{1, \ldots, 10^8\}$, depending on the elections. In the two-candidate case, when cands $= 2$, and assuming that voters $= 10^7$, voters$^{\text{cands}} \leq 10^{14} \leq 2^{47}$. Finding the corresponding discrete logarithm can be done in time $O(\sqrt{\text{voters}^{\text{cands}}}) \leq 2^{24}$, which is still realistic in most of the cases. However, for cands > 3, we must look at alternatives to ElGamal.

The DJ01 cryptosystem can serve as a natural alternative. By using DJ01, the servers directly recover $\sum \alpha_j \text{voters}^j$, and thus the costly discrete logarithm computation can be avoided. Moreover, values up to say voters$^{\text{cands}} \approx 2^{4096}$ (this corresponds to say voters $\leq 10^8$ and cands ≤ 150) can be tolerated without significant performance loss. Conversely, the threshold DJ01 cryptosystem is slower and less convenient than the threshold ElGamal cryptosystem. Some compromise is offered by the DJ03 cryptosystem. However, at this moment, the choice of existing IND-CPA secure homomorphic cryptosystems is not completely satisfying.

The currently most efficient multicandidate homomorphic voting protocol is described in Damgård, Groth, and Salomonsen (2002).

VERIFIABLE SHUFFLE-BASED E-VOTING SCHEMES

In the verifiable shuffle-based approach (initiated by Chaum, 1981), every voter encrypts his or her vote v_i by using a public key cryptosystem $\Pi = (\text{Gen}, \text{Enc}, \text{Dec})$ that must be IND-CPA secure, allow certain efficient zero-knowledge proofs of knowledge and be reblindable. Reblindability means that there must exist a function blind, such that for every ciphertext c, $\text{blind}_{\text{pk}}(c; R) = \text{Enc}_{\text{pk}}(\text{Dec}_{\text{sk}}(c); R)$ as distributions, where R is the domain of random coins of Π. Clearly, every homomorphic cryptosystem is reblindable because then one can define $\text{blind}_{\text{pk}}(c; r) := c \cdot \text{Enc}_{\text{pk}}(0; r)$.

In this approach, the encrypted votes, $c_{0i} = \text{Enc}_{\text{pk}}(v_i; r_i)$ are posted on the bulletin board together with the zero-knowledge proof of knowledge that $\text{Dec}_{\text{sk}}(c_{0i})$ corresponds to a valid candidate. This zero-knowledge proof of knowledge may not be necessary and can be replaced by a potentially simpler proof of knowledge that the voter knows $\text{Dec}_{\text{sk}}(c_{0i})$. At the end of the voting phase, the values c_{0i} will be mixed by ℓ, $\ell > 1$, mix-servers $\text{MixServer}_1, \ldots, \text{MixServer}_\ell$. The jth mix-server MixServer_j receives a list of voters encrypted votes $(c_{j-1,1}, \ldots, c_{j-1,\text{voters}})$, $c_{j-1,i} = \text{Enc}_{\text{pk}}(v_{\chi_{j-1}(i)}; r'_{j-1,i})$, where χ_{j-1} is some permutation and $r'_{j-1,i}$ is some random number. She then randomly reblinds all ciphertexts and permutes them. That is, she generates a random permutation π_j and for every $i \in [1, \text{voters}]$ she creates a random blinding factor r''_{ji}. She defines the following:

$$c_{ji} := \text{blind}_{\text{pk}}(c_{j-1,\pi_j^{-1}(i)}; r''_{ji}) \tag{1}$$

and writes $(c_{j1}, \ldots, c_{j\text{voters}})$ on the bulletin board. This must be accompanied by a proof of correctness that for some permutation π_j and for some random r''_{ji}, holds.

Every mix-server must verify the proofs of knowledge up to her round. At the end of ℓ rounds, all servers (and voters) must verify the correctness of all proofs of knowledge on the board. After that, everybody can be sure that $(c_{\ell 1}, \ldots, c_{\ell\text{voters}})$ is an encryption of some permutation of $(v_1, \ldots, v_{\text{voters}})$. Thus, the only thing left is to decrypt the ciphertext tuple. This can be done in a threshold manner, assuming that $\frac{1}{2}\ell + 1$ servers have to collaborate to decrypt this tuple. At the end of this section we describe some alternative possibilities.

How can we prove efficiently that Eq. (1) is true for some π_j and $\{r''_{ji}\}_i$? Next, we give a brief description of two existing verifiable shuffle protocols. (See Neff, 2001, for the third.)

Furukawa-Sako Protocol

Represent the permutation π_j by the permutation matrix M^j, with $M^j_{ab} = 1$ if $\pi_j(a) = b$ and $M^j_{ab} = 0$ otherwise. A nice way of using this matrix representation to achieve efficient zero-knowledge proofs is described in Furukawa and Sako (2001) and Furukawa (2004). It is based on the next fact (Furukawa, 2004): Let δ_{ij} be 1 if $i = j$ and 0 otherwise. Let δ_{ijk} be 1 if $i = j = k$ and 0 otherwise. Let q be a large prime. An voters × voters matrix M is a permutation matrix if

$$\sum_h M_{hi} M_{hj} = \delta_{ij} \tag{2}$$

and

$$\sum_h M_{hi} M_{hj} M_{hk} = \delta_{ijk}. \tag{3}$$

Thus, instead of Eq. (1), one could prove that $c_{ji} = \text{blind}(\prod_{i=1}^{\text{voters}} c_{j-1,i}^{M_{ji}}; r''_{ji})$ and that Eqs. (2) and (3) are true.

Equation (2) can be verified by defining $s_i = \sum_{j=1}^{\text{voters}} M_{ij} e_j$, for e_j chosen randomly by the verifier, and then checking that $\sum_{i=1}^{\text{voters}} s_i^2 = \sum_{i=1}^{\text{voters}} e_i^2$. Because of Eq. (2), $s_i^2 = \sum_{j=1}^{\text{voters}} M_{ij} M_{ik} e_j e_k = \sum e_{\chi(i)}^2$ and $\sum_{i=1}^{\text{voters}} s_i^2 = \sum_{i=1}^{\text{voters}} e_{\chi(i)}^2 = \sum_{i=1}^{\text{voters}} e_i^2$. Analogously, Eq. (3) is verified by checking that $(\sum M_{ij} e_j)^3 = \sum e_i^3$. Some more care has to be taken to achieve complete security (Furukawa, 2004; Furukawa & Sako, 2004).

In this approach, the prover must make approximately 8 voters exponentiations, and the verifier must make approximately 10 voters exponentiations. When $|p| = 1024$ and $|q| = 160$, it takes about 5280 voters bits to communicate the proof of knowledge.

Groth's Verifiable Shuffle

An alternative, somewhat more efficient, verifiable shuffle was proposed by Groth (2003). It assumes the use of an IND-CPA secure homomorphic cryptosystem Π (e.g., ElGamal, Paillier, or DJ01) and a compatible homomorphic commitment scheme. In this verifiable shuffle, the prover first commits to the shuffle. The verifier picks a vector of random integers, and the prover proves that the scalar product of this vector and the vector of encrypted votes is preserved after the shuffling. In more details, Groth's verifiable shuffle is as follows:

- Prover: For $j \in \{1, \ldots \text{voters}\}$, commit to $C_{1,i} \leftarrow C_{\text{pk}}(\pi(j); r_{2,j})$. Send $C_{1,i}$, together with a proof of correct shuffle, to the verifier.
- Verifier: For $j \in \{1, \ldots, \text{voters}\}$, generate a random t_j and send t_j to the prover.
- Prover: For $j \in \{1, \ldots, \text{voters}\}$: $C_{2,i} \leftarrow C_{\text{pk}}(t_{\pi(j)}; r_{tj})$. Send $\{C_{1,i}\}_i$, together with a proof of correct shuffle and that this shuffle was the same as on step 1, to the verifier.
- Prover proves in zero knowledge that $\text{Dec}_{\text{sk}}(\prod c_{ji}^{t_{\pi(i)}}) = \text{Dec}_{\text{sk}}(\prod c_{j-1,i}^{t_i})$

The three first proofs of knowledge can be executed jointly by proving that for a random λ, chosen by the verifier, $\{C_{1,i} C_{2,i}^\lambda\}$ commits to $\{i + \lambda t_i\}$. The proof that $\{c_i\}$ commits to $\{m_i\}$ can be done as follows: Prover sets $c_m = C_{\text{pk}}(m; 0)$, for m generated by the verifier, and proves that the multiplication of the contents of $c_1 c_m^{-1}, \ldots, c_{\text{voters}} c_m^{-1}$ is equal to $\prod_{i=1}^{\text{voters}} (m_i - m)$. All (or at least a significant fraction) of the resulting voters zero-knowledge multiplication proofs can be done in parallel by using multicommitments.

In this approach, the prover must perform approximately 6 voters exponentiations, and the verifier must perform approximately 6 voters exponentiations. When $|p| = 1024$ and $|q| = 160$, it takes about 1184 voters bits to communicate the proof of knowledge.

Security Model and Strengthening

By using a verifiable shuffle-based scheme as described above, both the privacy of the voters and the correctness will hold if at least $\tau + 1$, where $\ell = 2\tau + 1$, servers are honest. It is, however, possible to achieve a better result. Assume that Π is the ElGamal cryptosystem and that every mix-server MixServer_j has additionally her own private key sk_j and public key $h_j = g^{\text{sk}_j}$. Every voter encrypts his vote v as

$$(a_0, b_0) \leftarrow (g^r; v \cdot (h_1 \cdot \ldots \cdot h_\ell \cdot h)^r)$$

for $r \leftarrow_r R$. The first mix-server generates a random number r_1 and computes the following:

$$(a_1, b_1) \leftarrow (a_0 \cdot g^{r_1}, b_0 \cdot a_0^{-\text{sk}_1} \cdot (h_2 \ldots h_\ell \cdot h)^{r_1}) \ .$$

Then $(a_1, b_1) = (g^{r+r_1}, v \cdot (h_2 \ldots h_\ell \cdot h)^{r+r_1})$, that is, the first mix-server has peeled off encryption by his own key. He will then shuffle the result and accompany it with a proof of correct reencryption and shuffling. This can be done efficiently (Furukawa, 2004), although the proof will not be zero-knowledge but "permutation hiding." The second mix-server behaves analogously, by generating a random number r_2, and computing $(a_2, b_2) = (g^{r+r_1+r_2}, v(h_3 \ldots h_\ell \cdot h)^{r+r_1+r_2})$ and sending the results—in a shuffled form, accompanied with correctness proofs—to the third server. The last server outputs the set $\{(g^{r+r_1+\cdots+r_\ell}, vh^{r+r_1+\cdots+r_\ell})\}$ of encrypted votes. After that, $2t + 1$ servers collaborate to recover $\{v\}$. Here, the privacy of any voter is preserved if at least one of the mix-servers is honest. At least $\tau + 1$ servers must be honest to recover $\{v\}$ from the shuffle. (See Groth, 2004, for a different approach.)

COMPARISON AND PRACTICAL CONSIDERATION

We briefly described two main approaches to cryptographic e-voting: one that is directly based on IND-CPA secure homomorphic encryption and the other based on verifiable shuffles. (We did not describe the third major approach, based on blind signatures, because of the lack of universal verifiability. There are also potentially other problems with this approach. See, e.g., Fujioka, Okamoto, & Ohta, 1992, for one possible blind-signature-based protocol.) Of these two approaches, the first one is more efficient, but the second one is more universal. The verifiable shuffle-based approach becomes more efficient when the number of candidates is large (in the hundreds), when there is a need to support write-ins or

different voting mechanisms (e.g., Borda). Moreover, in the verifiable shuffle-based e-voting, the voters do not have to perform zero-knowledge proofs of vote validity: it suffices to encrypt and sign the vote; invalid votes will be detected by servers anyhow. This is important in practice, since it decreases the complexity of software that needs to be installed in voters machines. Last and not least, the privacy of voters is guaranteed if at least one of the mix-servers is honest (given that the reencryption techniques are used), while the correctness of elections is guaranteed when at least the fraction of $\frac{1}{2}$ of the servers is honest. This compares favorably to the homomorphic approach, where also the privacy depends on the threshold trust. This means, in particular, that in the case of verifiable shuffle-based solution, less servers could be used.

On the other hand, in the homomorphic e-voting protocols, the job of talliers is considerably simpler, and it is simpler to achieve universal verifiability. In the verifiable shuffle-based protocols, every mix-server has to perform C voters exponentiations (shuffle verification and correctness proof, reencryption, etc), where $C \approx 20$ is a small constant. In the homomorphic protocols, the servers must just multiply the encryptions and then jointly decrypt the result. The verification of voter's correctness proofs can be distributed among different servers so that every server verifies only a fraction of them. This means that it is likely that homomorphic protocols are faster at least by an order of the magnitude. However, one must first test this in practice. It is also likely that continuous research in both directions will result in even faster protocols. Only since 2002 have we started to see really efficient cryptographic protocols for e-voting [e.g., protocols used in homomorphic e-voting from Damgård & Jurik (2001), Damgård et al. (2002), Lipmaa (2003), and Lipmaa et al. (2002) and verifiable shuffle protocols from (Furukawa (2004), Furukawa & Sako (2001), Groth (2003), and Neff (2001)]. The recent breakthroughs in both directions are at least partially caused by the recently developed efficient IND-CPA secure homomorphic cryptosystems (Damgård & Jurik, 2001, 2003; Naccache & Stern, 1998; Okamoto & Uchiyama, 1998; Paillier, 1999) and the relatively new concept of integer commitment schemes (Damgård & Fujisaki, 2002; Fujisaki & Okamoto, 1999).

FURTHER RESEARCH TOPICS

All described e-voting protocols have some flaws in common. Next, we outline some major problems in e-voting protocols and propose some initial solutions. An efficient solution to any of the following problems would be a major advance in the state of the art. Note that some of (or even, most of) the problems in e-voting cannot have cryptographic solutions, and we do not discuss them at all.

Information-Theoretic Privacy for Voters

As mentioned before, ideally the privacy of voters should be information theoretical. However, all the described approaches only guarantee computational privacy. To somewhat improve the situation, one could use public key encryption with really high security parameter (say, ElGamal in $\mathbb{Z}_p$ with $|p| = 4096$ and $|q| = 256$). Many zero-knowledge proofs in a voting protocol can be done by using statistically hiding commitment schemes; because of statistical hiding, such proofs may executed by using moderate security parameters. Alternatively, one could try to devise protocols that really are information theoretically secure (in a suitable trust model). At this moment the corresponding solutions are inefficient (Otsuka, 2004).

Alternatively, *real* information theoretical security can be obtained by using *cryptographic randomized response techniques (cryptographic RRTs)* (Ambainis, Jakobsson, & Lipmaa, 2004). Here, every voter randomizes his or her vote by using a publicly known probability; the result of randomization does not say anything about the real preference of the voter. If a large number of votes are "summed" together, one can obtained an unbiased estimate to the actual voting result with a very small error margin. Cryptographic RRT of Ambainis, Jakobsson, and Lipmaa (2004) should be used to guarantee that the voters randomise their votes correctly. Whether this solution is politically acceptable, is unclear. However, it seems to be currently the only efficient way to guarantee unconditional vote privacy.

Eliminating the Random Oracle Assumption

Almost all e-voting protocols use honest-verifier zero-knowledge proofs (or arguments) of knowledge that are known to be intrinsically interactive in the standard model (i.e., without any assumptions of the existence of a random oracle or a common reference string). However, for universal verifiability, the correctness proofs must be noninteractive. Honest-verifier zero-knowledge proofs of knowledge are usually made noninteractive—in the random oracle model—by using the Fiat-Shamir heuristic (Fiat & Shamir, 1986) by first proving that the protocol is secure when using a random oracle and then the random oracle with a hash function such as SHA1. Unfortunately, it is known that there exist natural-looking protocols that are secure in the random oracle model but that cannot be instantiated with any function. There is no guarantee that this is not the case with the existing voting e-protocols.

The common reference string (CRS) model seems to be much more realistic, and in efficiency, protocols in the CRS model rival with the protocols in the random-oracle model. As a short example, Damgård (2001) has proposed the next general methodology of transforming three-round honest-verifier zero-knowledge proofs to noninteractive zero-knowledge proofs in the CRS model. Assume that all participants have an access to a trapdoor commitment public key of a central authority (e.g., the CA who is needed anyways). Then given a three-round honest-verifier zero-knowledge protocol with messages (a, e, z), the prover will first transfer a trapdoor commitment to a, obtain e, and only then return (a, z). (See Damgård, 2001, for a complete protocol.)

In electronic voting, we however need noninteractive zero knowledge. The current noninteractive zero-knowledge proofs in the CRS model are not that efficient, unless one wants to use nonstandard assumptions. For example, Groth (2004) proposes efficient noninteractive zero-knowledge proofs in the CRS model, where the security assumption is that the concrete protocol is sound. It is an important open problem to design efficient noninteractive zero-knowledge proofs in the CRS model that rely only on standard computational assumptions.

Moreover, we think that the CRS model is almost realistic, but it would still be desirable to do without it. The implication of noninteractive witness-indistinguishable protocols, obtained by, say, derandomization (Barak, Ong, & Vadhan, 2003), to e-voting is something that must still be studied.

Achieving Coercion Resistance

As noted before, an e-voting system should be secure against coercing (and vote buying). A lot of relevant cryptographic research has been focusing on verifiability; that is, making it impossible for a voter to prove that he or she obeyed the coercer. However, as noted in Juels and Jakobsson (2002), verifiability is insufficient. To be really coercion resistant, an e-voting protocol should additionally be secure against the randomization attack (coercer forces the voter to submit invalid vote), forced-abstention attack (coercer forces the voter to refrain from voting), and simulation attack (coercer buys the secret key of the voter and simulates the voter by using this key). Juels and Jakobsson proposed a *coercion-resistant e-voting protocol* (Juels & Jakobsson, 2002) that is secure against the mentioned attacks. However, their—yet formally unpublished—solution is not very efficient. It would be very important in practice to improve upon their protocol.

Finally, note that the next simple administrative procedure helps significantly. Allow parallel kiosk voting and Internet voting such that for voters who have voted both ways, only their kiosk vote will be counted. However, this solution has also clear drawbacks. First, ideally, one would like to organize e-voting without any kiosk voting at all, to decrease costs. Parallel voting would instead increase the costs. Second, an invalid or a closely guarded individual is not able to go to a kiosk polling station.

Human-Oriented Verifiability

One huge problem with all described e-voting protocols is that they are hardly verifiable by an average Joe. To increase the trust in e-voting, it should be possible for every voter to verify that their own vote is counted correctly. There are yet no completely satisfying solutions to this problem. See Malkhi, Margo, and Pavlov (2002) and Chaum (2004) for some recent work in this direction and Damgård and Jurik (2002) for another approach that does not require trust in the equipment.

ACKNOWLEDGMENTS

We thank anonymous referees for very useful comments. This work was partially supported by the Finnish Defence Forces Research Institute of Technology.

GLOSSARY

Electronic Voting   Paperless voting by using any electronic or mechanical voting.

Homomorphic Public Key Cryptosystem A public-key cryptosystem where group operations on ciphertexts result in group operations on plaintexts.

Internet Voting Voting over the Internet using personal computing devices.

Kiosk Voting Electronic voting in predestined locations (e.g., libraries and schools).

Public Key Cryptosystem A triple (Gen, Enc, Dec), where Gen is an efficient key generation algorithm that generates a public and a secret key, Enc is an efficient encryption algorithm that uses the public key, and Dec is an efficient decryption algorithm that uses the secret key.

Universal Verifiability An election is said to be universally verifiable if anybody, not only the voters, can verify that the election winner has been determined correctly.

Verifiable Shuffle A permutation of ciphertexts, such that nobody but the permuter can distinguish the used permutation, but anybody can verify that some permutation was used.

Voting Mechanism A rule to determine election winner from the votes of the voters.

CROSS REFERENCES

See *Cryptographic Protocols; Digital Certificates; Digital Signatures and Electronic Signatures; Encryption Basics; Legal, Social and Ethical Issues of the Internet.*

REFERENCES

Ambainis, A., Jakobsson, M., & Lipmaa, H. (2004). Crptographic randomized response techniques. In F. Bao, R. H. Deng, & J. Zhou (Eds.), *Lecture notes in computer science, vol. 2947: Public Key Cryptography 2004* (pp. 425–438). New York: Springer-Verlag.

Barak, B., Ong, S. J., & Vadhan, S. P. (2003). Derandomization in cryptography. In D. Boneh (Ed.), *Lecture notes in computer science, vol. 2729: Advances in Cryptography—CRYPTO 2003* (pp. 299–315). New York: Springer-Verlag.

Cramer, R., Gennaro, R., & Schoenmakers, B. (1997). A secure and optimally efficient multiauthority election scheme. In W. Funny (Ed.), *Lecture notes in computer science, vol. 1233: Advances in Cryptography—EUROCRYPT 1997* (pp. 103–118). New York: Springer-Verlag.

Chaum, D. (1981). Untreaceable electronic mail, return addresses, and digital pseudonyms. *Communications of the ACM, 24*(2), 84–88.

Chaum, D. (2004). Secret ballot receipts: True voter verifiable elections. *IEEE Security and Privacy, 3*(1), 39–47.

Chaum, D., & Pedersen, T. P. (1993). Wallet databases with observers. In E. F. Brickell (Ed.), *Lecture notes in computer science, vol. 740: Advances in Cryptography—CRYPTO '97* (pp. 89–105). New York: Springer-Verlag.

Damgård, I. (2001). Efficient concurrent zero-knowledge in the auxiliary string model. In B. Pfitzmann (Ed.), *Lecture notes in computer science, vol. 2045: Advances in Cryptography—EUROCRYPT 2001* (pp. 418–430). New York: Springer-Verlag.

Damgård, I., & Fujisaki, E. (2002). An integer commitment scheme based on groups with hidden order. In Y. Zheng (Ed.), *Lecture notes in computer science, vol. 2501: Advances in Cryptography—ASIACRYPT 2002* (pp. 418–430). New York: Springer-Verlag.

Damgård, I., Groth, J., & Salomonsen, G. (2002). The theory and implementation of an electronic voting system (pp. 77–99). Amsterdam: Kluwer.

Damgård, I., & Jurik, M. (2001). A generalization, a simplification and some application of Paillier's probabilistic public-key system. In K. Kim (Ed.), *Lecture notes in computer science, vol. 1992: Public Key Cryptography 2001* (pp. 119–136). New York: Springer-Verlag.

Damgård, I., & Jurik, M. (2002). Client/server tradeoffs for online elections. In D. Naccache & P. Paillier (Eds.), *Lecture notes in computer science, vol. 2274: Public Key Cryptography 2002* (pp. 125–140). New York: Springer-Verlag.

Damgård, I., & Jurik, M. (2003). A length-flexible threshold cryptosystem with applications. In R. Safavi-Naini (Ed.), *Lecture notes in computer science, vol. 2727: The 8th Australasian Conference on Information Security and Privacy* (pp. 350–364). New York: Springer-Verlag.

El Gamal, T. (1985). A public key cryptosystem and a signature based on discrete logarithms. In G. R. Blakley & D. Chaum (Eds.), *Lecture notes in computer science, vol. 196: Advances in Cryptography—Proceedings of CRYPTO '84* (pp. 10–18). New York: Springer-Verlag.

Fiat, A., & Shamir, A. (1987). How to prove yourself: Practical solutions to identification and signature problems. In A. M. Odlyzko (Ed.), *Lecture notes in computer science, vol. 196: Advances in Cryptography—Proceedings of CRYPTO '84* (pp. 10–18). New York: Springer-Verlag.

Fujioka, A., Okamoto, T., & Ohta, K. (1992). A practical secure voting scheme for large scale elections. In J. Seberry & Y. Zheng (Eds.), *Lecture notes in computer science, vol. 178: Advances in Cryptography—AUSCRYPT 1992* (pp. 186–194). New York: Springer-Verlag.

Fujisaki, E., & Okamoto, T. (1999). Statistical zero-knowledge protocols to prove modular polynomial relations. *IEICE Transactions of Fundamentals of Electronic Communications and Computer Science, E82-A*(1), 81–92.

Furukawa, J. (2004). Efficient, verifiable shuffle decryption and its requirements of unlinkability. In F. Bao, R. H. Deng, & J. Zhou (Eds.), *Lecture notes in computer science, vol. 2947: Public Key Cryptography 2004* (pp. 319–332). New York: Springer-Verlag.

Furukawa, J., & Sako, K. (2001). An efficient scheme for proving a shuffle. In J. Kilian (Ed.), *Lecture notes in computer science, vol. 2139: Advances in Cryptography—CRYPTO 2001* (pp. 368–387). New York: Springer-Verlag.

Gibbard, A. F. (1973). Manipulation of voting schemes: A general result. *Econometrica, 41,* 597–601.

Goldreich, O. (2004). *Foundations of cryptography: Basic applications.* Cambridge, UK: Cambridge University Press.

Goldwasser, S., Micali, S., & Rackoff, C. (1989). The knowledge complexity of interactive proof systems. *SIAM Journal of Computing, 18*(1), 186–208.

Groth, J. (2003). A verifiable secret shuffle of homomorphic encryptions. In Y. Desmedt (Ed.), *Lecture notes in computer science, vol. 2567: Public Key Cryptography 2003* (pp. 145–160). New York: Springer-Verlag.

Groth, J. (2004). *Honest verifier zero-knowledge arguments applied.* Ph.D. thesis, University of Århus, Denmark.

Juels A., Catalano, D., & Jakobsson, M. (2002). *Coercion-resistant electronic elections.* Retrieved November 5, 2002, from http://eprint.iacr.org/2002/165

Lipmaa, H. (2003). On Diophantine complexity and statistical zero-knowledge arguments. In C. Sung Laih (Ed.), *Lecture notes in computer science, vol. 2894: Advances in Cryptography—ASIACRYPT 2003* (pp. 398–415). New York: Springer-Verlag.

Lipmaa, H., Asokan, N., & Niemi, V. (2002). Secure vickrey auctions without threshold trust. In M. Blaze (Ed.), *Lecture notes in computer science, vol. 2357: Financial Cryptography—Sixth International Conference* (pp. 87–101). New York: Springer-Verlag.

Malkhi, D., Margo, O., Pavlov, E. (2002). E-voting without 'cryptography'. In M. Blaze (Ed.), *Lecture notes in computer science, vol. 2357: Financial Cryptography—Sixth International Conference* (pp. 1–15). New York: Springer-Verlag.

Matiyashevich, Y. (1993). *Foundations of computing: Hilbert's tenth problem.* Cambridge, MA: MIT Press.

Naccache, D., & Stern, J. (1998). A new public key cryptosystem based on higher residues. In *5th ACM Conference on Computer and Communications Security* (pp. 59–66). New York: ACM Press.

Neff, C. A. (2001). A verifiable secret shuffle and its application to e-voting. In *8th Conference on Computer and Communications Security* (pp. 116–125). New York: ACM Press.

Okamoto, T., & Uchiyama, S. (1998). A new public-key cryptosystem as secure as factoring. In K. Nyberg (Ed.), *Lecture notes in computer science, vol. 1403: Advances in Cryptography—EUROCRYPT '98* (pp. 308–318). New York: Springer-Verlag.

Otsuka, A. (2004). An unconditionally secure electronic voting scheme. In *DIMACS Workshop on Electronic Voting—Theory and Practice.*

Paillier, P. (1999). Public-key cryptosystems based on composite degree residuosity classes. In J. Stern (Ed.), *Lecture notes in computer science, vol. 1592: Advances in Cryptography—EUROCRYPT '99* (pp. 223–238). New York: Springer-Verlag.

Pedersen, T. P. (1992). Non-interactive and information-theoretic secure verfiable secret sharing. In J. Feigenbaum (Ed.), *Lecture notes in computer science, vol. 576: Advances in Cryptography—CRYPTO '91* (pp. 319–332). New York: Springer-Verlag.

Satterthewaite, M. A. (1973). *The excitence of strategy-proof voting procedures: A topic in social choice theory.* Ph.D. thesis, University of Wisconsin, Madison.

Shamir, A. (1979). How to share a secret. *Communications of the ACM, 22*(11), 612–613.

Tsiounis, Y., & Yung, M. (1998). On the security of ElGamal-based encryption. In H. Imai & Y. Zheng (Eds.), *Lecture notes in computer science, vol. 1431: Public Key Cryptography 1998* (pp. 117–134). New York: Springer-Verlag.

Verified Voting Foundation. (2004). Verified voting—Campaign to demand verifiable voting results. Retrieved January 1, 2004, from http://www.verifiedvoting.org

Digital Evidence

Robin C. Stuart, *Digital Investigations Consultant*

DEFINITION

We know that evidence is an offer or support of proof: the latent fingerprint, the bloodstains on the carpet, the smoking gun. How does digital evidence fit into this landscape? And what constitutes "digital evidence"?

What Is Digital Evidence?

According to *Merriam-Webster's Dictionary of Law*, the word *evidence* means, "something that furnishes or tends to furnish proof." In 1998, the Scientific Working Group on Digital Evidence defined the term *digital evidence* as ". . . any information of probative value that is either stored or transmitted in digital form."

In plain English, and as tested and defined in various United States courts, digital evidence is an offer of proof generated, stored, or transmitted in electronic form. This proof could originate from sources such as a cell phone, a pager, a personal digital assistant (PDA), or a computer; basically, any device that can be used to transmit and store data in binary form. For example, text messages, e-mail, databases, or Web server logs.

How Is Digital Evidence Used?

Digital evidence is useful in a court of law in criminal or civil cases ranging from cyberstalking to industrial espionage. However, given the high volume of legal actions filed in the United States, cases involving digital evidence are no different from those involving more traditional forms of evidence; they may never reach the trial phase. This in no way makes the handling or veracity of the evidence any less formal or important. In fact, the digital evidence you gather and analyze today may be used in a civil lawsuit years from now. For this reason, all digital evidence should be treated as if it were to come under legal scrutiny.

The most frequent uses of digital evidence tend to be policy or employment related, or related to breaches of security on corporate computer systems. Such cases may include employee misuse of company resources, such as surfing Internet pornography sites from company workstations or illegally downloading or copying software. Security breaches could originate from external sources, such as an outsider who exploits a vulnerability to find a way into a company's private network. Or breaches could originate inside the company itself, for example, an employee attempting to gain entry into resources of sensitivity beyond their privilege level.

Careful isolation and examination of digital evidence is key in identifying whether suspected information security or criminal activity occurred and the extent of damages incurred. This is discussed in detail below.

ADMISSIBILITY

The Federal Rules of Evidence provide guidance on the question of what constitutes admissible evidence, that is, evidence that may be presented in a court of law. Regardless of form, evidence is considered admissible if it is relevant, material, and competent. Accordingly, evidence is deemed relevant and material if it may make the fact in question more probable. The competency of evidence is based on precedents regarding its reliability.

Let us take a look at the standards as they pertain to digital evidence.

United States Standards

Digital records as proof are offered under the Best Evidence Rule. The Federal Rules of Evidence, under section 1001, includes "electronic recording, or other form of data compilation," in its definition of legally admissible "Writings and Recordings."

Rule 1002 requires that the evidence be an "original," which may pose a problem in that a true original of digital evidence is in binary form and therefore not humanly readable. Rule 1001(3) addresses this problem by stating in its definition of *original* the following: "If data are stored in a computer or similar device, any printout or other output readable by sight, shown to reflect the data accurately, is an 'original.'"

The onus is on the presenter of the digital evidence to prove that the data are reflected accurately. Authenticating the evidence, accounting for the handling of the evidence, and providing assertions of the integrity of the evidence is of paramount importance.

Another method that digital records are successfully introduced as evidence is under the Federal Rules of Evidence's Hearsay Exception, Rule 803(6), which provides an exception to the inadmissibility of hearsay for business records (i.e., kept or generated in the regular course of business). According to the Department of Justice in their document "Searching and Seizing Computers and Obtaining Electronic Evidence in Criminal Investigations," "...the business record exception is the most common hearsay exception applied to computer records."

International Standards

The British Standards Institution (BSI) has published a series of guidelines and procedural steps to, if not ensure, at the minimum heighten the probability of computer records as admissible evidence. The standards have gained international acceptance and cover the proper handling and storage of digital data from its creation to discovery in legal proceedings. The recurring theme is an audit trail or, more specifically, methods to provide accountability, authentication, and nonrepudiation of the records so as to be admissible as evidence.

These themes are similar to the United States' standards of proper care and handling of evidence under the Best Evidence Rule; authentication of the evidence, accountability for the handling of the evidence, and proving the integrity of the evidence before and after examination.

PRESERVATION OF EVIDENCE

To present digital evidence, it must be examined. Before the examination, it must first be preserved. How the data are identified, collected, and handled is the single most important piece of information when presenting digital evidence. Remember, for the evidence to be deemed admissible, it must be shown as relevant and material. Any doubt that can be raised as to the integrity of the evidence and its handling could impact a showing of relevance.

Preserving digital evidence should be thought of as similar to preserving a crime scene; document everything, take photos, and thoroughly record as much information as possible regarding the state of the evidence at the time it was found. If the evidence is a running computer, volatile data are easily and irretrievably lost.

The following sections highlight key areas of preserving the scene to ensure the relevance and materiality of digital evidence.

Chain of Custody

The prevailing rule in gathering, handling, and dealing with digital evidence is to document absolutely everything. Write down anything and everything that you see, do, or think from the moment the word "evidence" is first uttered.

One of the strongest documents in the investigator's cadre of notes and records is the chain of custody document. An accurate reflection of evidence handling is essential to providing a testament to the integrity of the evidence, should the veracity of the evidence or its handling ever be called into question. The chain of custody documentation is the single most important record in the event that the evidence will be used in court. If the evidence is intended for use in an administrative, criminal, or civil action, the integrity of the evidence will be the first point of interrogation by an opposing party.

The chain of custody is a written record describing how the evidence was identified, collected, stored, and handled and by whom, when, and for what purpose. According to the RFC 3227, "Guidelines for Evidence Collection and Handling," the chain of custody should provide the following:

- Where, when, and by whom the evidence was discovered and collected
- Where, when, and by whom the evidence was examined and handled
- Who had possession of the evidence, how was it stored, and when
- When the evidence changed hands and when and how did the exchange occur (this category includes shipping)
- Physical description of the evidence (make and model, serial number, drive size, etc.)
- Hash values, if applicable/available (described under "Preserving Evidence Integrity" below)

Volatile versus Nonvolatile Evidence

Volatility of the evidence source is of prime consideration when collecting, securing, and examining digital evidence. The term *volatility*, in this context, means "subject to change." In other words, the integrity and availability of the evidence can be compromised easily and possibly destroyed.

Something as simple as shutting down the suspect device may jeopardize potentially valuable information residing in memory; half-finished or deleted files, opened files, e-mails or fragments of opened files and e-mails, passwords, user names, Web addresses or Web page fragments, and program fragments or characteristics are just a few of the items that may be found in an examination of the random access memory (RAM) space. Some malicious programs load and run entirely in memory space to avoid detection during a hard drive examination. All of this information is irretrievably lost when the host system is shut down or the power removed. Additionally, by removing power or shutting down a machine, information such as running processes, data residing in swap or page-file space, and network connection information are lost. Therefore, all of these information sources are regarded as volatile.

Nonvolatile evidence refers to data or information that, although still subject to change as far as date and time stamps, and associated user information, the data itself remain substantively intact, regardless of the power or connectivity status of the machine. This typically refers to the data residing on the hard drive or removable media such as floppy disks, compact discs (CDs), or

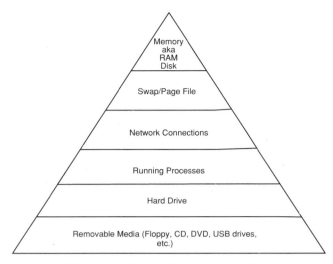

Figure 1:   Order of evidence volatility.

digital video discs (DVDs) or the floppy, CD-ROM, and DVD drives themselves.

The generally accepted order of volatility, from most volatile evidence source to least, is as shown in Figure 1.

Validation and examination of volatile, as well as non-volatile, evidence helps "tell the story" with regard to the state of the evidence at the time of collection. In cases of memory-resident malicious code, it may contain the entire story, otherwise missed in an examination of only nonvolatile evidence.

Evidence Handling Guidelines

Evidence gathering and preservation should be clearly documented for the sake of organization. The more consistent the approach to evidence collection, the more likely the evidence will stand tests to its credibility.

The first and foremost rule of evidence handling is to document absolutely everything. Whether the examiner maintains a log by hand or electronically, it is imperative that a "paper trail" be established and maintained, attesting to everything from the first point of contact between the examiner and the requestor of his or her services right up until the evidence is presented in court or destroyed. This is similar to the chain of custody but differs in that it should be a diary of the examination steps and procedures. Key elements of a handler's log are as follows:

- Date
- Time
- Examiner's name
- Examiner's company name
- Detailed description of the evidence (i.e., hard drive, laptop, PDA, etc.) that includes model, make, serial number(s)
- Detail description of any and all actions. If the actions involve physical handling of the evidence, include details of what was handled, how, and why
- Date and time the action or activity concluded

- Date, time, and physical location where the examiner stored the evidence upon conclusion of handling, preferably in a locked, fireproof safe.

Preserving Evidence Integrity

The value of evidence is earned only if its integrity survives challenge. You must be able to prove that the evidence is intact, in exactly the same state as it was found and collected. The popular method of offering such proof is a mathematical checksum, such as MD5 or SHA-1. A checksum operation calculates a unique "hash" value, which can serve as a sort of fingerprint. The hash value is represented by a 16-character hexadecimal value, calculated against the contents of a file or drive. Once an original hash is calculated, the hashing operation should produce the identical value every time against that same piece of evidence, so long as that evidence did not change. Even a minor change, such as opening a file on a Windows machine, may change the state of the evidence by altering its date and time stamp and, thus, reflect a new hash value at the next checksum operation identifying a change.

Any form of digital evidence can be hashed, including a volatile evidence dump file, a logical drive, a physical hard drive, or a digital camera's memory card. Prior to collection of volatile evidence or physically removing a hard drive to be used as evidence from a computer, a checksum should be calculated against the hard drive to use as the litmus against tampering. This hash value should be noted in the chain of custody form.

Likewise, a checksum operation should be performed on the contents of a memory card, if the evidence in question is a digital photograph. The hash and the images can be burned to a CD to provide an assurance that any photographs introduced as evidence have not been tampered with or electronically altered. Some higher-end digital camera makers have built in a "watermarking" system on images to add an additional layer of integrity checking.

Volatile evidence can be collected onto a write-once/read-many format, such as a CD-ROM. To avoid making changes to the state of the hard drive, which itself may and probably will be considered evidence, volatile evidence should be collected using a trusted binary run from a CD or floppy disk. This method provides the least amount of interaction with the suspect host while still allowing an investigator(s) to collect the evidence. At the time the volatile evidence is written to the CD-R disk, a hash value should be calculated as the final step. Again, this hash should be noted on the chain of custody form as a characteristic of the volatile evidence collected.

Once nonvolatile evidence, such as a hard drive, is collected as evidence by physical removal, another process is needed to ensure the integrity of the original evidence. This process is a bit-level copy of the evidence drive. Using one of many tools, both freeware and commercial, a physical drive can be duplicated, bit for bit. This is superior to a copy operation in that the bit-level duplicate is absolutely identical to the original, whereas a copy is just that, with its own new date and time stamps and user and file statistics. Such a copy is immediately tainted by virtue of the fact that it is inherently unlike the original.

Again, this duplication process is proved by a checksum. The hash value of the bit-level duplicate should match that of the original. Both hashes should be noted in the chain of custody.

Finally, the examination of the evidence should only occur on the bit-level duplicate, never the original. The original evidence should be stored in a static-free container, in a tightly controlled environment, preferably locked in a safe that only one person controls. The storage of the original media should, again, be noted in the chain of custody.

Examination Guidelines

As stated above, the examination of the evidence should be carried out only on the duplicate of the evidence. This protects the original evidence from any alterations. This also protects the examiner; if a change is accidentally made to the duplicate, that copy can be destroyed and another duplicate made.

The media on which the duplicate is made should be absolutely "clean," in other words, new, unformatted disks. If the only medium available for an examination copy is a reused drive, the drive should be "wiped," or written over using a disk wiping utility, several times over. As of this writing, the Department of Defense standard for writing over a used drive is to wipe it seven times. Wiping a used drive, or designating a new, unformatted drive, ensures that the bit-level duplicate will be free from leakage from previous data. Any such data leak would be easily identified by the hashing operation at the completion of the duplication process.

The duplicate should be treated as the original evidence in that any actions involving the examination copy should be noted in the chain of custody, including the examination itself. Tools used to examine the data should be noted, and those tools should involve as little interaction with the digital evidence as possible. Hardware write blockers should be employed at all times during an examination. Software write blockers are not always 100% effective, and an examiner wants as little room for doubt as possible as to the integrity of both the examination and the evidence. Remember, any changes to the examination duplicate will alter the hash value, thus creating a question as to the integrity of the examination and, potentially, the evidence itself.

Occasions may arise where the examination must be carried out on the original media. An example of this would be collection of the volatile memory or RAM disk. Even the act of acquiring the data in memory will change the contents as any action that appears on a monitor screen is recorded, albeit temporarily, in memory. In this instance, the examiner should checksum the resultant data as soon as possible after the data acquisition and then follow the above steps of duplication so as to preserve the state of the data. Additionally, every step in the collection process should be recorded in the examiner's log, including key strokes. Some operating systems will record your interaction for you by default, such as the Linux bash history. Whenever possible, such logs of shell activities should be harvested along with the evidence and kept with the evidence, as well as included in the examiner's log.

PRESENTATION

Presenting digital evidence is easier than it sounds. First, the actual evidence is the preserved hard drive, handheld device, memory card, or a CD containing the volatile evidence collected. The actual pieces of a computer or other digital device are not glamorous, nor are they human-readable. The physical evidence is shown, but that's not the end of the story. The examination records—the chain of custody, autogenerated reports (available in commercial forensic analysis software), printed logs, and so on—become stand-ins for the physical evidence. Recall that U.S. law supports human-readable records excerpted from digital media, discussed previously in this chapter.

As you may have already ascertained, the presentation is what the careful documenting of evidence handling is all about. The chain of custody, the checksum hashes, and the examiner's report support the integrity of the evidence, the thoughtfulness of the care and handling of the evidence, and the results of the examination of the evidence. Key factors in sustaining the admissibility and relevance of digital evidence are validation, authentication, and non-repudiation.

Validation

The chain of custody and evidence handling hash values may be presented as forms of validating that the evidence presented is unaltered. Each provides a layer of support that the evidence, as presented and examined, is in the same state as it was when it was originally identified, collected, duplicated, and examined. In other words, that the forensic process did not impact or alter the evidence in any way.

The chain of custody validates the integrity of the evidence by its detailed mapping of the handling of both the original evidence and any examination copies throughout the lifespan of the investigation.

The hash values, which should appear on the chain of custody document, may be highlighted to illustrate that the evidence's "fingerprint" never changed during the course of collection and examination. Thus, it can be extrapolated that the evidence itself never changed.

Authentication

Authenticating digital evidence is no different from any other form of evidence. Authentication is typically a human act, whereby one attests to the authenticity of the evidence. In simple terms, it is stating, "This is what I found, here's where I found it, and this is what I did with it." The investigator and/or examiner are the central players in the authentication process. Sworn affidavits, depositions, discovery responses, and expert testimony are legal methods of authenticating evidence that may involve the person who collected and/or examined the digital evidence at issue.

The chain of custody plays a role here, as well as in validation, by establishing who touched the evidence, when, how, and why. Again, these acts are supported by sworn statements by the person or people who appear on the log.

Nonrepudiation

The term *nonrefudiation* means indisputable proof that evidence is what it claims to be. The proof must be complete, and it must be tamper proof. In the technical community, it is typically applied to discussions of digital certificates, which provide proof of origin or proof of receipt in transactions. In this discussion, nonrepudiation may be applied to the evidence itself. The act of locking away the original piece of equipment in evidence is an act to support nonrepudiation of the integrity of the evidence. The evidence is stored in a tamper-proof manner.

The examination copies of evidence can be encrypted by the examiner, which does not necessarily make evidence tamper proof, merely tamper resistant by anyone other than the holder of the encryption key. Encrypting working copies does add a level of control to support the investigator's authentication of their work. But encryption is not, in and of itself, nonrepudiable. It is up to the authentication and validation efforts to provide sufficient proof that the subsequent examination of the evidence did not tamper with the integrity of that evidence. File system time stamps on the encrypted file help support claims of nonrepudiation.

RETENTION/DESTRUCTION

After collecting the evidence, how long should it be kept? When is it safe to dispose of the evidence and should it be disposed of properly?

Regulated industries must adhere to legal retention requirements such as Sarbanes-Oxley, discussed below. Nonregulated entities also have a duty to retain evidence, but requirements are usually triggered and spelled out by a court-issued protective order. Those entities not embroiled in litigation, however, should document historical records that have been destroyed—what was destroyed, when, how, why, and by whom. In other words, entities who dispose of historical data are well advised to be ready to present evidence as to why they do not have the evidence, should they ever be served with a discovery request or preservation request.

As a business matter, everyone should have a documented retention and destruction policy. Moreover, that policy should be reviewed on an annual basis for relevancy and compliance.

Retention Guidelines

There are two reasons to retain digital evidence, regulatory compliance, or litigation. Businesses under the watchful eye of their respective state or federal government should be well versed in their duties. For instance, publicly held companies and their supporting industries are subject to the document retention guidelines under the Sarbanes-Oxley Act (SOX; 2002). SOX requires that documents, including digital records, be preserved for 7 years, under penalty of prison for no less than 10 years for company management and a hefty fine, up to $5 million.

Those unaffected by industry regulation need to be concerned with record retention requirements if such records are, or are likely to be, the target of discovery motions in litigation. Failure to preserve data in this case is referred to as "spoliation of evidence." Evidence spoliation carries potentially severe sanctions, up to and including default judgment or criminal punishment, if the destruction of evidence is shown to be willful. In other words, if your company has been issued a discovery or preservation of data request and, subsequent to the receipt of that request, opposing counsel can show that records responsive to that request were destroyed. Negligent destruction of data, records that were destroyed by accident, typically carry less severe sanctions. The punishment could be monetary fines or attorney's fees.

To avoid evidence spoliation claims, record retention policies should be in place and routinely reviewed. Compliance audits should always be part of scheduled policy reviews.

Destruction of Evidence

The nature of digital evidence, residing or written in digital form to magnetic media, makes disposal of some forms of evidence as difficult as recovering it was simple. Data that are "deleted" from a hard drive are not actually gone. Rather, it is simply designated as available space, the previous file system pointers to the data removed from the drive's file map. Once written to a magnetic surface, such as the platters of a hard drive, it is nearly impossible to actually physically remove. Therefore, there are two options to properly dispose of digital evidence: reusing or recycling the media, and physical destruction.

Reuse/Recycling

The decision to reuse or recycle media on which sensitive data, such as that used as evidence, should be considered carefully. Some forms of media are economically more feasible to simply destroy. For example, CDs or DVDs are relatively inexpensive. If used to gather evidence that may be considered confidential or valuable, such as intellectual property, it is not worth the risk to reuse rewritable disks.

But what about hard drives? Large capacity drives can get expensive. Tape drives can also be costly. Both types of media are intended for reuse.

The question then becomes how to protect the data previously preserved. In other words, how to "destroy" the evidence without destroying the media. The answer is to overwrite the data. There are several programs available, both commercial and freeware, that write over the entire contents of a drive with random 0s and 1s, rendering the data unobtainable. This is more than merely reformatting. Reformatting a drive is similar to deleting in that it merely reassigns the available data surface. The data are still there and readable. Overwriting the entire disk assures that the data are obscured.

Overwriting, or disk wiping, is an operation that should be performed several times over to prevent any data leakage. Wipe utilities are typically configurable to allow the user to specify the number of overwriting operations. A minimum of three wipes is considered best practice, although the higher the number of overwrites, the better. As of this writing, the United States Department of Defense standard is to wipe a drive seven times before media is allowed to be reused.

Media Destruction

The only truly safe way to dispose of data is to physically destroy the media on which it resides. This is relatively simple for floppy disks, CDs, DVDs, tapes, USB drives, and zip drives. Hard drives are bit more involved. Technically, unless each platter is completely shattered, someone somewhere can probably recover data from it. The methods to recover data get more expensive, the worse the condition of the drive, but it is still possible. Therefore, the only way to be absolutely certain that data on a hard drive are absolutely gone is to destroy it absolutely.

Incineration of the entire drive is one method. Opening up the hard drive and then removing and shattering each platter individually is another method. There are also media destruction and disposal services available, although contracting out such actions may be against your organization's data handling policy, depending on the sensitivity of the data residing on the media.

As with all aspects of digital data and evidence handling, media destruction should be carefully documented. Have a policy and procedure in place to ensure that the media are truly destroyed and that the evidence is truly irretrievable. In addition, close out your investigation or examination documentation with the date, time, manner, and identity of the actual person who destroyed the media.

CONCLUSION

Digital evidence is similar to any other form of legal proof; it must withstand challenges to its integrity, its handling must be carefully tracked and documented, and it must be authenticated by the handler(s) and examiner(s). The fact that the evidence resides on or is generated by a digital device only means that a skilled digital forensics examiner should be involved in the handling process to ensure that any material facts may be properly preserved and introduced.

GLOSSARY

Admissible Capable of being allowed or conceded.
Authentication To prove that an item of evidence is genuine for the purpose of establishing admissibility.
Chain of Custody Written record describing how the evidence was identified, collected, stored, handled, by whom, when, and for what purpose.
Digital Evidence Information of probative value stored or transmitted in electronic form.
Media Physical repository of electronically generated, stored, or transmitted data.
Nonrepudiation Ability to ensure that initiator, creator, or sender of digital information is unable to deny being the initiator, creator, or sender, or that the recipient of digital information is unable to deny being the recipient.
Volatility Subject to change.

CROSS REFERENCES

See *Computer Forensic Procedures and Methods; Digital Courts, the Law and Evidence; Forensic Computing; Law Enforcement and Digital Evidence.*

REFERENCES

British Standards Institute. (1999). *A code of practice for legal admissibility and evidential weight of information stored electronically* (2nd ed.). London: British Standards Institute.

The Electronic Evidence Information Center. (2004). *Legal reference material*. Retrieved June 22, 2004, from http://www.e-evidence.info/legal.html

Merriam-Webster. (1996). *Merriam-Webster's dictionary of law*. New York: Merriam-Webster, Inc.

Request for Comment. (2002). *RFC 3227, guidelines for evidence collection and archiving*. Retrieved February 16, 2004, from http://www.faqs.org/rfcs/rfc3227.html

Sarbanes-Oxley Act of 2002. (2002). Retrieved February 16, 2004, from http://www.legalarchiver.org/soa.htm

United States Department of Justice. (2002). *Searching and seizing computers and obtaining electronic evidence in criminal investigations*. Retrieved February 16, 2004, from http://www.usdoj.gov/criminal/cybercrime/s&smanual2002.htm

U.S. House Judiciary Committee. (2002). *Federal rules of evidence*. Retrieved February 16, 2004, from http://www.house.gov/judiciary/Evid2002.pdf

Digital Watermarking and Steganography

M. A. Suhail, *University of Bradford, UK*
B. Sadoun, *Al-Balqa' Applied University, Jordan*
M. S. Obaidat, *Monmouth University*

INTRODUCTION: DIGITAL INTELLECTUAL PROPERTY

Information is becoming widely available via global networks. These connected networks allow cross references among databases. The advent of multimedia is allows different applications to mix sound, images, and video and interaction with a large amount of information (e.g., in e-business, distance learning, and human-machine interface). The industry is investing to deliver audio, still image, and video data in electronic form to customers, and broadcast televisions companies, major corporations, and photo archivers are converting their archive contents from analog to digital form. This movement from traditional media, such as paper documents, analog recordings, to digital media is due to the several advantages of digital media over the traditional media. Among these advantages are (Swanson, Kobayashi, & Tewfik, 1998; Tirkel et al., 1993):

- The quality of digital signals is higher than that of their corresponding analog signals. Traditional assets degrade in quality as time passes. Analog data require expensive systems to obtain high-quality copies, whereas digital data can be easily copied without loss of fidelity.
- Digital data (audio, still image, and video signals) can be easily transmitted over networks (e.g., the Internet). A large amount of multimedia data is now available to users all over the world. This expansion will continue at a rapid rate, especially with the widening availability of advanced multimedia services such as e-commerce, e-government, advertisement, interactive TV, digital libraries, and many others.
- Exact copies of digital data can be easily made. This is very useful but it also creates problems for the owner of valuable digital data like precious digital images. Replicas of a given piece of digital data cannot be distinguished and their origin cannot be confirmed. It is not easy to determine which piece is the original and which is the copy.
- It is possible to hide some information within digital data in such a way that data modifications are undetectable for the human senses.

E-Commerce

Modern electronic commerce (e-commerce) is a new activity that is the direct result of a revolutionary information technology, digital data and the Internet. E-commerce is defined as the conduct of business transactions and trading over a common information systems (IS) platform such as the Web or Internet. The amount of information being offered to public access grows at an amazing rate with current and new technologies. Technology used in e-commerce is allowing new, more efficient ways of carrying out existing business, and this has had an impact not only on commercial enterprises but also on social life. The e-commerce potential has become a reality with the development of the World Wide Web (WWW) in the 1990s.

E-commerce can be divided into e-tailing, e-operations, and e-fulfillment; all supported by an e-strategy. E-tailing involves the presentation of the organization's selling wares (goods and services) in the form of electronic catalogs (e-catalogs). E-catalogs are an Internet version of the information presentation about the organization, its products, and so on. E-operations covers the core transactional processes for production of goods and delivery of services. E-fulfillment is an area within e-commerce, which still seems quite blurred. It complements e-tailing and e-operations as it covers a range of postretailing and operational issues. The core of e-fulfillment is payment systems, copyright protection of intellectual property, security (which includes privacy), and order management (i.e., supply chain, distribution, etc.). In essence, fulfillment is seen as the "fuel" to the growth and development of e-commerce.

The owners of copyright and related rights are granted a range of different rights to control or be remunerated for various types of uses of their property (e.g., still images, video, and audio). Among these is the right to exclude others from reproducing the property without authorization. The development of digital technologies, permitting transmission of digital data over the Internet, has raised questions about how do these rights apply in the new environment? How can the digital intellectual property be made publicly available while guaranteeing ownership of the intellectual rights?

Copyright Protection of Intellectual Property

An important factor that slows down the growth of multimedia networked services is that authors, publishers, and providers of multimedia data are reluctant to allow the distribution of their documents in a networked environment. This is because the ease of reproducing digital data in their exact original form is likely to encourage copyright violation, data misappropriation, and abuse. There is the problem of theft and distribution of intellectual property. Therefore, creators and distributors of digital data are actively seeking reliable solutions to the problems associated with copyright protection of multimedia data.

Moreover, the future development of networked multimedia systems, in particular on open networks such as the Internet, is conditioned by the development of efficient methods to protect data against unauthorized copying and redistribution of the material put on the network. This will guarantee that the owners' rights are protected and their assets are properly managed. Copyright protection of multimedia data has been accomplished by means of cryptography algorithms to provide control over data access and to make data unreadable to unauthorized users. However, encryption systems do not completely solve the problem because once encryption is removed there is no more control on the dissemination of data.

DIGITAL WATERMARKING

The concept of digital watermarking arose while trying to solve problems related to the copyright of intellectual property in digital media. It is used as a means to identify the owner or distributor of digital data. Watermarking is the process of encoding hidden copyright information because it is possible today to hide information messages within digital audio, video, still images, and texts by taking into account the limitations of the human audio and visual systems.

Digital Watermarking: What, Why, When, and How?

Digital watermarking has proved to be an efficient technique to protect intellectual property from illegal copying. It provides a means of embedding a message in a piece of digital data without destroying its value. Digital watermarking embeds a known message in a piece of digital data as a means of identifying the rightful owner of the data. These techniques can be used on many types of digital data, including still imagery, movies, and music. In this chapter, we focus on digital watermarking for images and in particular invisible watermarking.

What Is Digital Watermarking?

A digital watermark is a signal permanently embedded into digital data (audio, still images, video, and text) that can be detected or extracted later by means of computing operations to make assertions about the data. The watermark is hidden in the host data in such a way that it is inseparable from the data and so that it is resistant to many operations that do not degrade the host document. Thus by means of watermarking, the work is still accessible but permanently marked.

Conversely, watermarking is not like encryption. Watermarking does not restrict access to the data, whereas encryption has the aim of making messages unintelligible to any unauthorized persons who might intercept them. Once encrypted, data cannot be retrieved except by a reverse process called encryption. A watermark is designed to permanently reside in the host data. If the ownership of a digital work is in question, the information can be extracted to completely characterize/identify the owner.

Why Digital Watermarking?

Digital watermarking is an enabling technology for e-commerce strategies: conditional and user specific access to services and resources. Digital watermarking offers several advantages. The details of a good digital watermarking algorithm can be made public knowledge. Digital watermarking provides the owner of a piece of digital data the means to mark the data invisibly. The mark could be used to serialize a piece of data as it is sold or used as a method to mark a valuable image. For example, this marking allows an owner to safely post an image for viewing, but legally provides an embedded copyright to prohibit others from posting the same image. Watermarks and attacks on watermarks are two sides of the same coin. The goal of both is to preserve the value of the digital data. However, the goal of a watermark is to be robust enough to resist attack but not at the expense of altering the value of the data being protected. Conversely, the goal of the attack is to remove the watermark without destroying the value of the protected data. The contents of the image can be marked without visible loss of value or dependence on specific formats. For example a bitmap (BMP) image can be compressed to a JPEG image. The result is an image that requires less storage space but cannot be distinguished from the original. Generally, a Joint Picture Experts Group (JPEG) compression level of 70% can be applied without humanly visible degradation. This property of digital images allows insertion of additional data in the image without altering the value of the image. The message is hidden in unused "visual space" in the image and stays below the human visible threshold for the image.

When Did the Technique Originate?

The idea of hiding data in another media is very old as described in the case of steganography. Nevertheless, the term *digital watermarking* first appeared in 1993, when Tirkel et al. (1993) presented two techniques to hide data in images. These methods were based on modifications to the least significant bit (LSB) of the pixel values.

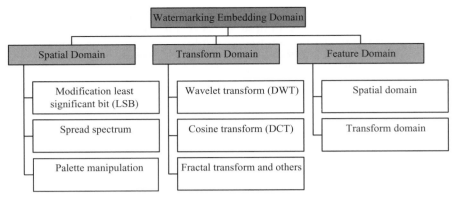

Figure 1: Classification of watermarking algorithms based on domain used for the watermarking embedding process.

How Can We Build an Effective Watermarking Algorithm?

The following sections provide a detailed answer to this question. However, it is desired that watermarks survive image-processing manipulations such as rotation, scaling, image compression, and image enhancement. Taking advantage of the discrete wavelet transform properties and robust features extraction techniques is the new trends that are used in the recent digital image watermarking schemes. Robustness against geometrical transformation is essential because image-publishing applications often apply some kind of geometrical transformations to the image, and thus, an intellectual property ownership protection system should not be affected by these changes.

Digital Watermarking Concept

In this section, we try to provide a theoretical background of watermarking. We focus mainly on digital images and the principles by which watermarks are implemented. We discuss the requirements needed for an effective watermarking system and show that the requirements are application dependent: however, some of them are common to most practical applications. The challenges facing researchers in this field are reviewed from viewpoint of the digital watermarking requirements. Swanson et al. (1998) sheds some light on this matter.

Visible Versus Invisible Watermarks

Digital watermarking is divided into two main categories: visible and invisible. The idea behind the visible watermark is very simple. It is equivalent to stamping a watermark on paper, and for this reason is sometimes said to be digitally stamped. An example of visible watermarking is provided by television broadcasting channels, such as BBC, CNN, and TV5, whose logos are visibly superimposed on the corner of the TV picture frame. Invisible watermarking, conversely, is a far more complex process and concept. It is most often used to identify copyright data such as author, distributor, and source.

Though a lot of research has been conducted in the area of invisible watermarks, much less has been done for visible watermarks. Visible and invisible watermarks both serve to deter theft but they do so in very different ways.

Visible watermarks are especially useful for conveying an immediate claim of ownership (Mintzer, Braudaway, & Yeung, 1997). Their main advantage, in principle at least, is the virtually elimination of the commercial value of a document to a would-be thief, without lessening the document's utility for legitimate, authorized purposes. Invisible watermarks, conversely, are more of an aid in catching a thief than for discouraging theft in the first place (Mintzer et al., 1997; Swanson et al., 1998). This chapter focuses on the latter category, and the phrase *watermark* is taken to mean the invisible watermark, unless otherwise stated.

Watermarking Classification

There are different classifications of invisible watermarking algorithms. The reason behind this is the enormous diversity of watermarking schemes. Watermarking approaches can be distinguished in terms of watermarking host signal (still images, video signal, audio signal, integrated circuit design), the availability of original signal during extraction (nonblind, semiblind, blind). Also, they can be categorized based on the domain used for watermarking embedding process, as shown in Figure 1. The Watermarking application is considered one of the criteria for watermarking classification. Figure 2 shows the subcategories based on watermarking applications.

Digital Watermarking Application

The four main digital watermarking applications are

- Copyright protection
- Image authentication
- Data hiding
- Covert communication

Figure 2 shows the different applications of watermarking with some examples for each of these applications. Moreover, digital watermarking has been proposed for tracing images in the event of their illicit redistribution. The need for this has arisen because modern digital networks make large-scale dissemination simple and inexpensive. In the past, infringement of copyrighted documents was often limited by the unfeasibility of large-scale

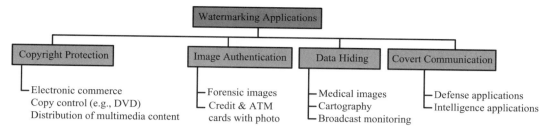

Figure 2: Classification of watermarking technology based on applications.

photocopying and distribution. In principle, digital watermarking makes it possible to uniquely mark each image sold. If a purchaser then makes an illicit copy, the illegal duplication may be convincingly demonstrated (Swanson et al., 1998). Such discussion on watermarking applications leads us to explain the difference between robust and fragile watermarks.

Robust Versus Fragile Watermarks. Robust and fragile watermarks are also two categories of watermarking; it all depends on what you want to do with the watermark (application). A robust watermark is difficult to be removed from the object in which it is embedded in. It is used for ownership assertion (proof of ownership). The main properties of this kind of watermark are as follows:

- Robustness against all kinds of image distortion (difficult to remove)
- Does not have good localization properties
- Should distinguish malicious and nonmalicious modifications
- The watermark can be embedded using spread spectrum or frequency domain techniques
- Watermark pattern must be perceptually transparent
- Watermark depends on a secret key

Conversely, the fragile watermark, which is also known as a tamper-proof watermark, is easy to alter. Such watermarks are destroyed by data manipulation. It is used for content authentication (good for integrity checks). The main properties of this class of watermarking are as follows:

- Break easily (remove easily)
- Computationally cheap
- Good localization properties
- Too sensitive for redundant data
- Embedded in spatial domain

Watermark Embedding

Generally, watermarking systems for digital media involve two distinct stages: (1) watermark embedding to indicate copyright and (2) watermark detection to identify the owner (Swanson et al., 1998). Embedding a watermark requires three functional components: a watermark carrier, a watermark generator, and a carrier modifier.

A watermark carrier is a list of data elements, selected from the unwatermarked signal, which are modified during the encoding of a sequence of noiselike signals that form the watermark. The noise signals are generated pseudorandomly, based on secret keys, independent of the carrier. Ideally, the signal should have the maximum amplitude, which is still below the level of perceptibility. The carrier modifier adds the generated noise signals to the selected carrier. To balance the competing requirements for low perceptibility and robustness of the added watermark, the noise must be scaled and modulated according to the strength of the carrier (Swanson et al., 1998; Tirkel et al., 1993).

Embedding and detecting operations proceed as follows. Let I_{orig} denote the original multimedia signal (an image, an audio clip, or a video sequence) before watermarking. Let W denote the watermark, which the copyright owner wishes to embed, and I_{water} denote the signal with the embedded watermark. A block diagram representing a general watermarking scheme is shown in Figure 3. The watermark W is encoded into I_{orig} using an embedding function E as follows:

$$E(I_{\text{orig}}, W) = I_{\text{water}}. \qquad (1)$$

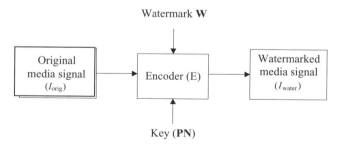

(a) Watermarking embedding system

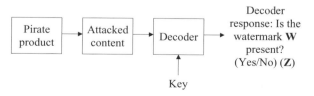

(b) Watermarking detecting system

Figure 3: Embedding and detecting systems of digital watermarking.

The embedding function makes small modifications to I_{orig} related to W. For example, if $W = (w1, w2, \ldots)$, the embedding operation may involve adding or subtracting a small quantity a from each pixel or sample of I_{orig}. During the second stage of the watermarking system, the detecting function D uses knowledge of W, and possibly I_{orig}, to extract a sequence W' from the signal R undergoing testing:

$$D(R, I_{\text{orig}}) = W'. \qquad (2)$$

The signal R may be the watermarked signal I_{water}, it may be a distorted version of I_{water} resulting from attempts to remove the watermark, or it may be an unrelated signal. The extracted sequence W' is compared with the watermark W to determine whether R is watermarked. The comparison is usually based on a correlation measure, ρ, and a threshold, λ_o, used to make the binary decision (Z) on whether the signal is watermarked. To check the similarity between W, the embedded watermark and the extracted one (W'), the correlation measure between them can be found using the following expression:

$$\rho(W, W') = \frac{W \cdot W'}{\sqrt{W' \cdot W'}}, \qquad (3)$$

where WW' is the scalar product between these two vectors. However, the decision function is

$$Z(W', W) = \begin{cases} 1, & \rho \geq \lambda_0 \\ 0 & \text{otherwise} \end{cases}, \qquad (4)$$

where ρ is the value of the correlation and λ_0 is a threshold. A 1 indicates that a watermark was detected, whereas a 0 indicates that a watermark was not detected. In other words, if W and W' are sufficiently correlated (greater than some threshold λ_0), the signal R has been verified to contain the watermark, which confirms the author's ownership rights to the signal. Otherwise, the owner of the watermark W has no rights over the signal R. It is possible to derive the detection threshold λ_0 analytically or empirically by examining the correlation of random sequences. Figure 4 shows the detection threshold of 600 random watermark sequences studied and only one watermark, which was originally inserted, has a significantly higher correlation output than the others. As an example

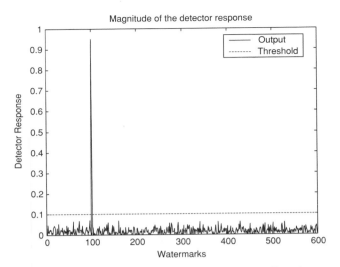

Figure 4: The detection threshold experimentally of 600 random watermark sequences studied; only one watermark, which was originally inserted, has a higher correlation output above others. Threshold is set to be 0.1 in this graph.

of an analytically defined threshold, τ can be defined as follows:

$$\tau = \frac{\alpha}{3N_c} \sum^{N_c} | I_{\text{water}}(m, n)|, \qquad (5)$$

where α is the weighting factor and N_c is the number of coefficients that have been marked. The formula is applicable to square and nonsquare images (Voyatzis, Nikolaidis, & Pitas, 1998). One can even just select certain coefficients (based on a pseudorandom sequence or a human visual system [HVS] model). The choice of the threshold influences the false positive and false negative probability. Voyatzis et al. (1998) proposes some methods to compute predictable correlation thresholds and efficient watermark detection systems.

A Watermarking Example

A simple example of the basic watermarking process is described here. The example is very basic and meant to illustrate the main concept. The discrete cosine transform (DCT) is applied on the host image, which is represented by the first block (8×8 pixel) of the "trees" image shown in Figure 5. The block is given by the following:

$$B_1 = \begin{bmatrix} 0.7232 & 0.8245 & 0.6599 & 0.7232 & 0.6003 & 0.6122 & 0.6122 & 0.5880 \\ 0.7745 & 0.7745 & 0.7745 & 0.7025 & 0.7745 & 0.7025 & 0.7745 & 0.7025 \\ 0.7745 & 0.7745 & 0.7025 & 0.7745 & 0.7745 & 0.7025 & 0.7025 & 0.7025 \\ 0.7025 & 0.7025 & 0.7025 & 0.7025 & 0.7025 & 0.7745 & 0.7025 & 0.7025 \\ 0.7745 & 0.7025 & 0.7745 & 0.7025 & 0.7025 & 0.7025 & 0.7025 & 0.7025 \\ 0.7025 & 0.7025 & 0.7025 & 0.7745 & 0.7025 & 0.7745 & 0.7025 & 0.7025 \\ 0.7025 & 0.7745 & 0.7025 & 0.7025 & 0.7745 & 0.7025 & 0.7745 & 0.7025 \\ 0.7025 & 0.7025 & 0.7745 & 0.7745 & 0.7745 & 0.7025 & 0.7025 & 0.7025 \end{bmatrix}.$$

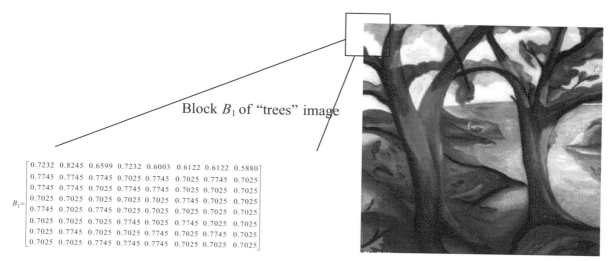

Block B_1 of "trees" image

$$B_1 = \begin{bmatrix} 0.7232 & 0.8245 & 0.6599 & 0.7232 & 0.6003 & 0.6122 & 0.6122 & 0.5880 \\ 0.7745 & 0.7745 & 0.7745 & 0.7025 & 0.7745 & 0.7025 & 0.7745 & 0.7025 \\ 0.7745 & 0.7745 & 0.7025 & 0.7745 & 0.7745 & 0.7025 & 0.7025 & 0.7025 \\ 0.7025 & 0.7025 & 0.7025 & 0.7025 & 0.7025 & 0.7745 & 0.7025 & 0.7025 \\ 0.7745 & 0.7025 & 0.7745 & 0.7025 & 0.7025 & 0.7025 & 0.7025 & 0.7025 \\ 0.7025 & 0.7025 & 0.7025 & 0.7745 & 0.7025 & 0.7745 & 0.7025 & 0.7025 \\ 0.7025 & 0.7745 & 0.7025 & 0.7025 & 0.7745 & 0.7025 & 0.7745 & 0.7025 \\ 0.7025 & 0.7025 & 0.7745 & 0.7745 & 0.7745 & 0.7025 & 0.7025 & 0.7025 \end{bmatrix}$$

Figure 5: The "trees" image with its first 8 × 8 block.

Applying DCT on B_1, results in DCT(B_1):

$$\text{DCT}(B_1) = \begin{bmatrix} 5.7656 & 0.1162 & -0.0379 & 0.0161 & -0.0093 & -0.0032 & -0.0472 & -0.0070 \\ -0.0526 & 0.1157 & 0.0645 & 0.0104 & -0.0137 & -0.0114 & -0.0415 & -0.0336 \\ -0.0354 & 0.0739 & -0.0136 & -0.0410 & -0.0081 & -0.0187 & -0.0871 & 0.0063 \\ -0.0953 & 0.0436 & 0.0379 & -0.0090 & -0.0394 & 0.0182 & -0.0031 & -0.0589 \\ -0.1066 & 0.0500 & 0.0034 & -0.0355 & -0.0093 & 0.0147 & 0.0526 & -0.0278 \\ -0.0790 & -0.0064 & 0.0088 & 0.0240 & -0.0200 & -0.0361 & -0.0586 & -0.0731 \\ -0.0422 & 0.0366 & -0.0460 & -0.0150 & 0.0518 & 0.0141 & 0.0105 & -0.0980 \\ 0.0025 & 0.0697 & 0.0327 & -0.0140 & 0.0286 & -0.0084 & -0.0422 & 0.0329 \end{bmatrix}.$$

Notice that most of the energy of the DCT of B_1 is compact at the DC value (DC coefficient = 5.7656).

The watermark, which is a pseudorandom real number generated using a random number generator and a seed value (key), is given by the following:

$$W = \begin{bmatrix} 1.6505 & 0.2759 & -0.8579 & -1.6130 & -1.0693 & 0.2259 & -0.4570 & 0.7167 \\ 0.7922 & -0.6320 & 0.8350 & -0.3888 & 0.4993 & 0.2174 & -1.6095 & -0.9269 \\ 0.7319 & 0.7000 & 1.6191 & -0.0870 & 0.7859 & 0.1870 & -0.3633 & 2.5061 \\ 0.9424 & 0.8966 & -0.0246 & -1.4165 & 0.5422 & 0.1539 & -1.1958 & 0.0374 \\ 0.2059 & 1.8204 & 0.5224 & -0.9099 & -1.6061 & -0.7764 & -0.8054 & -1.0894 \\ -0.1303 & -0.3008 & 1.6732 & -1.1281 & -0.3946 & 0.8294 & -0.0007 & -0.7952 \\ 0.0509 & -1.7409 & 1.1233 & 0.3541 & 0.1994 & -0.0855 & 0.1278 & -0.6312 \\ -0.1033 & -1.7087 & 0.5532 & 0.2068 & 2.5359 & 1.7004 & -0.6811 & -0.7771 \end{bmatrix}.$$

Applying DCT on W results in DCT(W) as shown below:

$$\text{DCT}(W) = \begin{bmatrix} 0.2390 & 1.5861 & 0.1714 & 0.7187 & -0.3163 & -1.0925 & 2.6675 & 1.3164 \\ 0.1255 & 0.8694 & 2.8606 & -0.2411 & 0.6162 & -1.1665 & -0.1335 & -0.8266 \\ 0.0217 & -1.4093 & -1.3448 & 1.3837 & 1.3513 & 1.0022 & 0.8743 & 0.3735 \\ -1.7482 & 0.8337 & 1.5394 & -0.0076 & -1.7946 & 1.1027 & -0.4434 & -0.5771 \\ -0.7653 & 0.5313 & 0.9799 & 1.2930 & -0.0309 & -0.9858 & -0.9079 & -0.8152 \\ 0.4222 & -0.9041 & 1.2626 & -0.0979 & 0.6200 & 0.1858 & -0.1021 & 0.1452 \\ 1.4724 & -1.1217 & 0.7449 & -0.2921 & -0.3144 & -0.7244 & 0.4119 & 0.0535 \\ 0.4453 & 0.0380 & 0.9942 & -1.5048 & 0.0656 & 0.4169 & -0.7046 & -0.5278 \end{bmatrix}.$$

B_1 is watermarked with W as shown in the block diagram in Figure 6 according to the following formula:

$$f_w = f + \alpha \cdot w \cdot f, \qquad (6)$$

where f is a DCT coefficient of the host signal (B_1), w is a DCT coefficient of the watermark signal (W), and α is the watermarking energy, which is taken to be 0.1 ($\alpha = 0.1$). The DC value of the host signal is not modified, thereby minimizing the distortion of the watermarked image. Therefore, the DC value will be kept un-watermarked.

The above equation can be rewritten in a matrix format as follows:

Security

Effectiveness of a watermark algorithm cannot be based on the assumption that possible attackers do not know the embedding process that the watermark went through. The robustness of some commercial products is based on such an assumption. The point is that by making the technique very robust and making the embedding algorithm public, this actually reduces the computational complexity for the attacker to remove the watermark. Some of the techniques use the original nonmarked image in the extraction process. They use a secret key to generate the watermark for security purpose (Swanson et al., 1998).

$$\mathrm{DCT}(B_{1w}) = \begin{cases} \mathrm{DCT}(B_1) + \alpha \cdot \mathrm{DCT}(W) \cdot \mathrm{DCT}(B_1) \ for \ all \ \text{coefficient} \ except \ DC \ value \\ \mathrm{DCT}(B_1) \, for \ DC \ value, \end{cases} \qquad (7)$$

where B_{1w} is the watermarked signal of B_1. The result after applying the above equation can be calculated as follows:

$$\mathrm{DCT}(B_{1w}) = \begin{bmatrix} 5.7656 & 0.1346 & -0.0386 & 0.0172 & -0.0090 & -0.0028 & -0.0598 & -0.0079 \\ -0.0532 & 0.1258 & 0.0830 & 0.0101 & -0.0145 & -0.0101 & -0.0409 & -0.0308 \\ -0.0355 & 0.0635 & -0.0117 & -0.0467 & -0.0092 & -0.0206 & -0.0947 & 0.0066 \\ -0.0786 & 0.0472 & 0.0438 & -0.0090 & -0.0323 & 0.0202 & -0.0029 & -0.0555 \\ -0.0984 & 0.0527 & 0.0037 & -0.0400 & -0.0092 & 0.0132 & 0.0478 & -0.0255 \\ -0.0823 & -0.0058 & 0.0099 & 0.0238 & -0.0212 & -0.0368 & -0.0580 & -0.0742 \\ -0.0485 & 0.0325 & -0.0494 & -0.0146 & 0.0502 & 0.0131 & 0.0109 & -0.0985 \\ 0.0026 & 0.0700 & 0.0360 & -0.0119 & 0.0288 & -0.0088 & -0.0392 & 0.0312 \end{bmatrix}.$$

Notice that the DC value of $\mathrm{DCT}(B_{1w})$ is the same as the DC value of $\mathrm{DCT}(B_1)$. To construct the watermarked image, the inverse DCT of the above two-dimensional array is computed to give B_{1w} as follows:

$$B_{1w} = \begin{bmatrix} 0.7331 & 0.8361 & 0.6609 & 0.7228 & 0.5991 & 0.6026 & 0.6175 & 0.5922 \\ 0.7818 & 0.7809 & 0.7735 & 0.7011 & 0.7712 & 0.6955 & 0.7755 & 0.6998 \\ 0.7734 & 0.7746 & 0.6973 & 0.7682 & 0.7663 & 0.7002 & 0.6956 & 0.6920 \\ 0.7064 & 0.7093 & 0.7045 & 0.7037 & 0.7013 & 0.7692 & 0.6986 & 0.6933 \\ 0.7872 & 0.7100 & 0.7789 & 0.7081 & 0.7067 & 0.7012 & 0.7013 & 0.6996 \\ 0.7051 & 0.7032 & 0.7026 & 0.7801 & 0.7078 & 0.7741 & 0.7015 & 0.6978 \\ 0.7017 & 0.7765 & 0.7002 & 0.7067 & 0.7765 & 0.7026 & 0.7736 & 0.6992 \\ 0.6877 & 0.7048 & 0.7712 & 0.7800 & 0.7793 & 0.7001 & 0.7044 & 0.6974 \end{bmatrix}.$$

It is easy to compare B_{1w} and B_1 and see the very slight modification because of the watermark.

Robust Watermarking Scheme Requirements

In this section, the requirements needed for an effective watermarking system are introduced. The requirements are application dependent, but some of them are common to most practical applications. One of the challenges for researchers in this field is that these requirements compete with each other. Such general requirements are listed below. Detailed discussions of them can be found in references (Ruanaidh, Dowling, & Roland, 1996; Voyatzis et al., 1998).

Invisibility

Perceptual Invisibility. Researchers have tried to hide the watermark in such a way that watermark is impossible to notice. However, this requirement conflicts with other requirements such as robustness, which is an important requirement when facing watermarking attacks. For this purpose, the characteristics of the HVS for images and the human auditory system (HAS) for audio signals are exploited in the watermark embedding process.

Statistical Invisibility. An unauthorized person should not detect the watermark by means of statistical methods. For example, the availability of a great number of digital

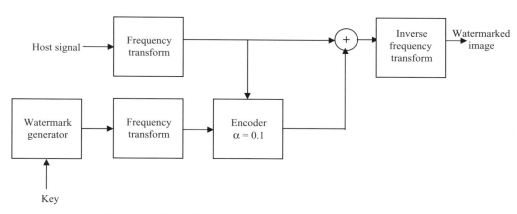

Figure 6: Basic block diagram of the watermarking process.

works watermarked with the same code should not allow the extraction of the embedded mark by applying statistically based attacks. A possible solution is to use a content dependent watermark (Voyatzis et al., 1998).

Robustness

Digital images commonly are subject to many types of distortions, such as lossy compression, filtering, resizing, contrast enhancement, cropping, rotation, and so on. The mark should be detectable even after such distortions have occurred. Robustness against signal distortion is better achieved if the watermark is placed in perceptually significant parts of the image signal (Ruanaidh et al., 1996). For example, a watermark hidden among perceptually insignificant data is likely not to survive lossy compression. Moreover, resistance to geometric manipulations, such as translation, resizing, rotation, and cropping, is still an open issue. These geometric manipulations are still very common.

Watermarking Extraction: False Negative/Positive Error Probability

Even in the absence of attacks or signal distortions, false negative error probability (the probability of failing to detect the embedded watermark) and of detecting a watermark when, in fact, one does not exist (false positive error probability), must be very small. Usually, statistically based algorithms have no problem in satisfying this requirement.

Capacity Issue (Bit Rate)

The watermarking algorithm should embed a predefined number of hidden bits in the host signal that depends on the considered application. There is no general rule for this. However, in the image watermarking, the possibility of embedding into the image at least 300–400 bits should be guaranteed. In general, the number of bits, which can be hidden into data, is limited. Capacity issues were discussed by Servetto, Podilchuk, and Ramchandran (1998).

One can understand the challenge to researchers in this field because the above requirements compete with each other. The important test of a watermarking method would be that it is accepted and used on a large, commercial scale and that it stands up in a court of law. None

of the digital techniques have yet to meet all of these requirements. In fact the first three requirements (security, robustness, and invisibility) can form sort of a triangle (Figure 7), which means that if one is improved, the other two may be affected.

Digital Watermarking Algorithms

Current watermarking techniques described in the literature can be grouped into three main classes. The first includes the transform domain methods, which embed the data by modulating the transform domain signal coefficients. The second class includes the spatial domain techniques, which embed the watermark by directly modifying the pixel values of the original image. The transform domain techniques have been found to have the best robustness, when the watermarked signals are tested after having been subjected to common signal distortions. The third class is the feature domain technique, which takes into account region, boundary, and object characteristics. Such watermarking methods may present additional advantages in terms of detection and recovery from geometric attacks, compared with previous approaches.

The algorithms in this survey are organized according to their embedding domain, as indicated in Figure 1. These are grouped into spatial domain techniques, transform domain techniques, and feature domain techniques. We highlight the main features of these techniques. The wavelet domain is the most efficient domain

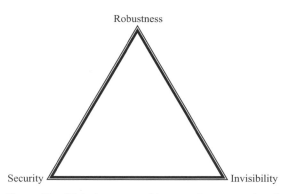

Figure 7: Digital watermarking requirements triangle.

for watermarking embedding so far. However, our review considers some other techniques, which serve the purpose of giving a broader picture of the existing watermarking algorithms. Some examples of spatial domain and fractal based techniques are reviewed as well.

Spatial Domain Techniques

This section gives a brief introduction to the spatial domain technique. Many spatial techniques are based on adding fixed amplitude pseudonoise (PN) sequences to an image. In this case, E and D, as introduced earlier, are simply the addition and subtraction operators, respectively. Pseudonoise sequences are also used as the "spreading key" when considering the host media as the noise in a spread spectrum system, where the watermark is the transmitted message. In this case, the PN sequence is used to spread the data bits over the spectrum to hide the data. When applied to the spatial or temporal domains, this approach modifies the LSB of the host data. The invisibility of the watermark is achieved on the assumption that the LSB data are visually insignificant. The watermark is generally recovered using knowledge of the PN sequence (and perhaps other secret keys, like watermark location) and the statistical properties of the embedding process. Two LSB techniques are described in reference (Schyndel, Tirket, & Osborne, 1994).

Transform Domain Techniques

Many transform-based watermarking techniques have been proposed. To embed a watermark, a transformation is first applied to the host data, and then modifications are made to the transform coefficients. The works presented in Ruanaidh et al. (1996), Servetto et al. (1998), Schyndel et al. (1994), Bors and Pitas (1996), Nikolaidis and Pitas (1996), and Pitas (1996) can be considered to be the pioneering efforts that utilize the transform domain for watermarking process. These articles were published at early

stages of development of watermarking algorithms, so they represent the basic framework for this research area. This section has three main parts, including discussions of wavelet-based watermarking, DCT-based watermarking, and fractal domain watermarking.

Digital Watermarking Using Wavelet Decomposition. Many articles have proposed to use the wavelet transform domain for watermarking because of a number of advantages that can be gained by using this approach. The works described in Wei, Qin, and Fu (1998), Zhu, Xiong, and Zhang (1998), Suahil and Obaidat (2001), and Suhail, Obaidat, Ipson, and Sadoun (2003) implement watermarking in the wavelet domain. As an example, a perceptually based technique for watermarking images is proposed in Wei et al. (1998). The watermark is inserted in the wavelet coefficients and its amplitudes are controlled so that the watermark noise does not exceed the just-noticeable difference of each wavelet coefficient. Meanwhile, the order of inserting watermark noise in the wavelet coefficients is the same as the order of the visual significance of the wavelet coefficients (Wei et al., 1998). The invisibility and the robustness of the digital watermark may be guaranteed.

Discrete Cosine Transform-Based Digital Watermarking. Several watermarking algorithms have been proposed to utilize the DCT. However, Cox, Kilian, Leighton, and Shamoon (1997) and the Koch and Zhao (1995) algorithms are the most well known DCT-based schemes. Cox et al. (1997) proposed the most well-known spread spectrum watermarking schemes. Figure 8 shows the block diagram of the Cox et al. algorithm. The image is first subjected to a global DCT, and then the 1,000 largest coefficients in the DCT domain are selected for watermarking. They used a Gaussian sequence of pseudorandom real numbers of length 1,000 as a watermark. This

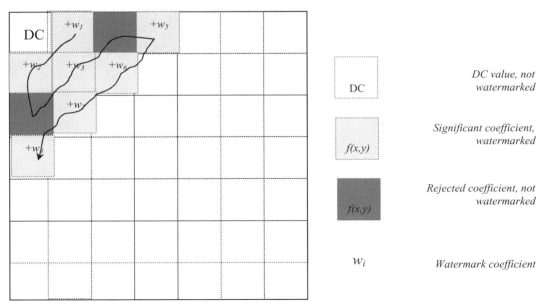

Figure 8: Cox embedding process, which classifies DCT coefficients into significant and rejected coefficients.

approach achieves a good robustness against compression and other common signal processing attacks. This is a result of the selection perceptually significant transform domain coefficients. However, the algorithm is in a weak position against the invariability attack proposed by Craver, Memon, Yeo, and Yeung (1997). Also, the global DCT employed on the image is computationally expensive. The DCT has been applied also in many other watermarking algorithms (Suhail & Obaidat, 2003).

Fractal Transform Based Digital Watermarking.

Though a lot of work has been done in the area of invisible watermarks using the DCT and the wavelet-based methods, relatively few references exist for invisible watermarks based on the fractal transform. The reason for this might be the computational cost of the fractal transform. Discussions of fractal watermarking methods are presented in Puate and Jordan (1996). Puate and Jordan (1996) used fractal compression analysis to embed a signature in an image. In fractal analysis, similar patterns are identified in an image and only a limited amount of binary code can be embedded using this method. Because fractal analysis is computationally intensive and some images do not have many large self-similar patterns, the techniques may not be suitable for general use.

Feature Domain Techniques (Second-Generation Watermarking)

First-generation watermarking (1GW) methods have been mainly focused on applying the watermarking on the entire image/video domain. However, this approach is not compatible with novel approaches for still image and video compression. JPEG2000 and MPEG4/7 standards are the new techniques for image and video compression. They are region or object based, as can be seen in the compression process. Also, the 1GW algorithms proposed so far do not satisfy the watermarking requirements.

Second-generation watermarking (2GW) was developed to increase the robustness and invisibility and to overcome the weaknesses of 1GW. The 2GW methods take into account region, boundary, and object characteristics and give additional advantages in terms of detection and recovery from geometric attacks compared with first-generation methods. This is achieved by exploiting salient region or object features and characteristics of the image. Also, 2GW methods may be designed so that selective robustness to different classes of attacks is obtained. As a result, watermark flexibility will be improved considerably.

Kutter et al. used feature point extraction and the Voronoi diagram as an example to define region of interest (ROI) to be watermarked (Kutter, Bhattacharjee, & Ebrahimi, 1999). The feature extraction process is based on a decomposition of the image using Mexican hat wavelet mother, as shown in Figures 9 and 10. However, the stability of the method proposed depends on the features points. These extracted features have the drawback that their location may change by some pixels because of attack or during the watermarking process. Changing the location of the extracted feature points will cause problems during the detecting process.

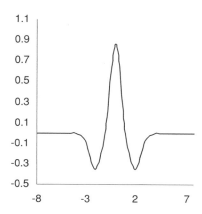

Figure 9: Mexican hat mother wavelet function for 1D.

From the literature review in this section, it is apparent that digital watermarking can be achieved by using transform techniques, embedding watermark data into the frequency domain representation of the host image or by directly embedding the watermark into the spatial domain data of the image. The review also shows there are several requirements that the embedding method has yet to satisfy. Creating robust watermarking methods is still a challenging research problem. These algorithms are robust against some attacks but not against most of them. As an example, they cannot withstand geometric attacks such as rotation or cropping. Also, some of the current methods are designed to suit only specific application, which limits their widespread use.

Moreover, there are some concerns in the existing algorithms associated with the watermark embedding domain. These concerns vary from system to system. Watermarking schemes that modify the LSB of the data using a fixed magnitude PN sequence are highly sensitive to signal processing operations and are easily corrupted. Some transform domain watermarking algorithms cannot survive most image processing operations and geometric manipulations. This will limit their use in large numbers of applications. Using fractal transforms, only a limited amount of binary code can be embedded. Because fractal analysis is computationally expensive, and some images do not have many large, self-similar patterns, fractal-based algorithms may not be suitable or practical for general use. Feature domain algorithms suffer from problems of stability of feature points if they are

Figure 10: The 2D Mexican hat mother wavelet function in spatial domain (left) and in transform domain (right).

exposed to an attack. For example, the method proposed in Kutter's work (Kutter et al., 1999) depends on the stability of extracted features whose locations may change by several pixels because of attack or because of the watermarking process. This will cause problems during the decoding process. Security is an issue facing most of the existing watermarking algorithms.

STEGANOGRAPHY

Steganography is one of the fundamental ways by which data can be kept confidential. It is an effective method of hiding data that has been used throughout history. This section will give an introductory discussion of steganography: what it is, how it can be used, and how the steganography implications can have on information security.

What Is Steganography?

Steganography has been around since the times of ancient Rome. Steganography (also known as *steg* or *stego*) is the art of writing in cipher, or in characters, that are not intelligible except to persons who have the key; it is a type of cryptography (Johnson, 2004; Radcliff, 2003). In computer terms, steganography has evolved into the practice of hiding a message within a larger one in such a way that others cannot distinguish the presence or contents of the hidden message. Steganography has evolved into a digital strategy of hiding a file in some form of multimedia, such as an image, an audio file (such as a .wav or mp3), or even a video file.

However, image steganography is defined as hiding a secret message within an image in such a way that others cannot distinguish the presence or contents of the hidden message. For example, a message might be hidden within an image by changing the LSB to be the message bits. By embedding a secret message into a carrier image, a stego image is obtained. It is important that the stego image contains no easily detectable artifacts because of message embedding that could be detected by electronic surveillance.

Steganographic History

Steganography appeared before cryptography (Kahn, 1967). Throughout history, people have hidden information by a multitude of methods and variations. For example, in ancient Rome and Greece, text was traditionally written on wax that was poured on top of stone tablets. If the sender of the information wanted to obscure the message—for purposes of military intelligence, for instance, they would use steganography: the wax would be scraped off and the message would be inscribed or written directly on the tablet. Wax would then be poured on top of the message, thereby obscuring not just its meaning, but its very existence (Johnson, 2004). Another ingenious method was to shave the head of a messenger and tattoo a message or image on the messenger's head. After the hair grew back, the message would be undetected until the head was shaved again.

Recent times have yielded more advanced techniques, such as the use of invisible ink, where messages are written using substances that subsequently disappear. The hidden message is later revealed using heat or certain chemical reactions. Invisible inks offered a common form of invisible writing, especially during the early years of World War II. A seemingly innocent letter could contain a very different message written between the lines with invisible ink.

Other methods may employ routine correspondence, such as the application of pinpricks in the vicinity of particular letters to spell out a secret message. Advances in photography produced microfilms that were used to transmit messages via carrier pigeon. Further developments in this area improved film and lenses that provided the ability to reduce the size of secret messages to a printed period. Because of the advances in technology today, moving communications to electronic means, digital multimedia signals, typically audio, video, or still image, are being used as vehicles for steganographic communication.

Steganography Applications

Like many information security tools, steganography can be used for a variety of reasons, some not so good. Steganography can be used to maintain the confidentiality of valuable information to protect the data from possible sabotage, theft, or unauthorized viewing such as in the case of military applications. Steganography can also be used as a way to make a substitute for a one-way hash value (where you take a variable length input and create a static length output string to verify that no changes have been made to the original variable length input) (Schneier, 1996). Further, steganography can be used to tag notes to online images (like Post-it notes attached to paper files) (Radcliff, 2003).

Unfortunately, steganography can also be used for illegitimate reasons. For instance, if someone was trying to steal data, they could conceal it in another file or files and send it out in an innocent looking e-mail or file transfer. Furthermore, persons with a hobby of saving pornography on their hard drives may choose to hide the evidence through the use of steganography. As was pointed out, it can be used as a means of covert communication. Of course, this can be both a legitimate and an illegitimate application.

Steganography Tools

There are many good and different tools that are available for steganography. An important distinction that should be made among the tools available today is the difference between tools that do steganography and tools that do steganalysis, which is the method of detecting steganography and destroying the original message. Steganalysis focuses on this aspect, as opposed to simply discovering and decrypting the message, because this can be difficult to do unless the encryption keys are known. For more comprehensive discussion of steganography tools, see Johnson (2004).

Algorithms and Systems

There are several different steganographic systems that can be used to embed hidden messages into JPEG images. The statistical distortion depends on the steganographic system that inserted the message into the image. Because of this different distortions associated with the different systems, it is possible to identify the signatures left by each system and allow for the identification of which system was used. Three popular steganographic programs available on the Internet that hide information in JPEG images are JSteg, JSteg-Shell, JPHide, and OutGuess. All three of these examples use a form of least significant bit embedding and are detectable by using statistical analysis. LSB manipulation is a quick and easy way to hide information but is vulnerable to small changes resulting from image processing or lossy compression. Such compression is a key advantage that JPEG images have over other formats. High-color quality images can be stored in relatively small files using JPEG compression methods. JPEG files are well known for being efficient carriers of image information, often achieving compression gains of about 90%, according to simple comparisons of JPEGs. During compression, the steganographically hidden message delicately embedded usually within the LSBs of the color information is easily destroyed. A generally acceptable image quality is preserved when steganographically embedding a maximum of 15% of the cover image's file size. These file sizes limit the amount of message data in the average GIF to approximately 150 to 450 bytes and the average JPEG image to anywhere from 3 to 150 KB.

JPEG images use the discrete cosine transform to achieve compression that is called a lossy compression transform because the cosine values cannot be calculated exactly, and repeated calculations using limited precision numbers introduce rounding errors into the final result. Also, images can be processed with Fast Fourier and wavelet transformations (Xia, Boncelet, & Arce, 1997). Other image properties such as luminance can also be manipulated. Patchwork (Bender et al., 1996) and others use *redundant pattern encoding* or spread spectrum methods (Cox et al., 1997) to scatter hidden information throughout the cover images. These approaches may help protect against image processing such as cropping and rotating, and they hide information more thoroughly than by simple masking. They also support image manipulation more readily than tools that rely on LSB. In using redundant pattern encoding, you trade off message size against robustness. A small message may be painted many times. A large message may be inserted only once because it would occupy a greater portion of the image area.

Moreover, some techniques *encrypt and scatter* the hidden data throughout an image. Scattering the message makes it appear more like noise. Proponents of the approach assume that even if the message bits are extracted, they will be useless without the algorithm and stego-key to decode them. For example, the White Noise Storm tool and frequency hopping, which scatters message throughout the image, are based on spread spectrum (SS) technology. Instead of having channels of communication that are changed with fixed formula and passkey, White Noise Storm spreads eight channels within a random number generated the previous window size and data channel. Scattering and encryption helps protect against hidden message extraction but not against message destruction through image processing. A scattered message in the image's LSBs is still as vulnerable destruction from

lossy compression and image processing. Steganography's niche in security is to supplement cryptography, not replace it. If a hidden message is encrypted, it must also be decrypted if discovered to provide another layer of protection.

Statistical Analysis

One of the more common tests that can reveal that an image has been modified by steganography is by determining that an image's statistical properties are different from the normal. Some tests just measure the entropy of the redundant data and are independent on the data format. It can be expected that images with hidden data will have higher entropy than those images without.

Simple tests are used to measure the correlation toward one. These tests are not able to decide automatically if an image contains a hidden message. One property of encrypted data is that the 1 and zero bit are equally likely. When using the method to LSB embed encrypted data into a GIF image that contains color two more often than color three, color two is changed more often to color three than the other way around. As a result, the difference in color frequency between two and three is reduced by the embedding. The χ^2-test can be used to determine whether an image shows distortion from embedding hidden data. Because the test uses only the stego medium, the expected distribution for the χ^2-test has to be computed from the image. The probability of embedding information into different parts of the image is computed. For an image that does not contain any hidden information, it is expected that the probability of embedded information is zero everywhere.

Attacking Steganography

The only way to detect/attack steganography is to be actively looking into specific files or to get very lucky. Sometimes an actively enforced security policy can provide the answer. Detecting the movement and behavior of traffic on your network may also be helpful to attack steganography. However, network intrusion detection systems can help administrators to gain an understanding of normal traffic in and around the network and can thus assist in detecting any type of attack on the network. If the administrator is aware of this sort of anomalous activity, it may warrant further investigation.

Steganalysis is the comparison among the carrier (cover), stego image, and the hidden message. The various methods used to analyze stego images are termed attacks and include *stego-only*, where the attacker has access only to the stego image; *known cover*, where the attacker has access only to the carrier; *known message*, where the attacker has access only to the message; *chosen stego*, where the attacker has access to both the stego image and stego algorithm; and *chosen message*, where the attacker generates a stego image from a message using an algorithm, looking for signatures that will enable him to detect other stego images.

The stego-only attack is the most important attack against steganographic systems because it will occur most frequently in practice. In general, there are two mechanisms to attack steganography, which really are also methods of detecting it. Theses are the visual attack and the statistical attack. The visual attack finds out the differences in the files that are encoded where it relies on the capabilities of the human visual system. However, the statistical attack is to compare the frequency distribution of the colors of a potential stego file with the theoretically expected frequency distribution for a stego file where it performs statistical tests on the stego file.

The Stego-Only Visual Attack

The visual attack is a stego-only attack that exploits the assumption of most authors of steganography programs that the LSBs of a cover file are random. This is done by relying on a human to judge if an image presented by a filtering algorithm contains hidden data. The filtering algorithm removes the parts of the image that are covering the message. The output of the filtering algorithm is an image that consists only of the bits that potentially could have been used to embed data. The filtering of the potential stego image is dependent on the steganographic embedding function that is analyzed. This form of steganography borrows from spread spectrum techniques employed in radio communication, especially the embedding of information in the LSBs, whose values are essentially lost in the noise of the image.

The Stego-Only Statistical Attack

Regarding visual attacks, statistical attacks exploit the fact that most steganography programs treat the LSBs of the cover file as random data and therefore assume that they can overwrite these bits with other random data (the encrypted secret message). However, in "A Survey of Steganography" by S. Hetzl past examples have proven that the LSBs of an image are not random (Hetzl, 2002). When a steganography program embeds a bit through overwriting the LSB of a pixel in the cover file, the color value of this pixel is changed to an adjacent color value in the palette, or in the RGB cube if the cover file is a true color image. The volume within the RGB cube represents all possible colors identified as a combination of red, green, and blue, each with intensity from 0 to 255. When overwriting the LSBs of all occurrences of one of these color values with a bit from the secret message, the frequencies of these two color values will essentially be the same. This happens because the data being embedded are encrypted and therefore equally distributed. The essence of the statistical attack is to measure how close to identical the color frequency distributions of the potential stego file are. This results in a measure for the probability that the analyzed file contains a hidden message. This statistical attack is implemented using a χ^2-test. In successive steps, increasing areas of the potential stego file are analyzed, starting with the first percentage of data, then the first two percentages of data, and so on until 100% of the data have been analyzed.

LSB encoding is only one popular method of information hiding. Another method that is described as "frequency domain experimentation" is frequency domain encoding that inserts messages into images by working with two-dimensional Fast Fourier transform (2D FFT) of the carrier image (Schneier, 1996).

Steganography and Security

Steganography is an effective means of hiding data, thereby protecting the data from unauthorized or unwanted viewing. But stego is simply one of many ways to protect the confidentiality of data. It is probably best used in conjunction with another data hiding method. When used in combination, these methods can all be part of a layered security approach. For example, encryption is one of the good complementary methods. Encryption is the process of passing data or plaintext through a series of mathematical operations that generate an alternate form of the original data known as ciphertext. The encrypted data can only be read by parties who have been given the necessary key to decrypt the ciphertext back into its original plaintext form. Encryption does not hide data, but it does make it difficult to read!

CONCLUDING REMARKS

The term *information hiding* relates to both watermarking and steganography. There are three different aspects to an information hiding system that contend with one another: capacity, security, and robustness (Chen & Wornell, 2001). Capacity refers to the amount of information that can be hidden. Security refers to the inability of an eavesdropper to detect hidden information, and robustness refers to the amount of modification the cover medium can withstand before the hidden information is destroyed.

The differences between the watermarking and steganography are often questioned or debated. The underlying technology to implement both of them may be the same, but the objectives are different. In the watermarking technique, the object of the communication channel is the carrier. The embedded information (watermark) can be thought of as an attribute of the carrier as it conveys additional information about the carrier such as copyright, ownership, distribution, tamper detection, and so on. Many watermarking techniques require a certain amount of robustness to carrier distortion (an exception is fragile watermarks). The payload size (size of the embedded information) is typically small. However, from an attack point of view, a successful attack against a watermarking system is to make the watermark unreadable or unintelligible. However, discovery of the fact that a watermark exists is not necessarily considered an attack.

In the case of steganography, the object of the communication channel is the embedded information. The carrier is simply an envelope that should conceal the existence of the embedded message. The main goal of steganography is secretive communication. Most steganographic techniques are fairly fragile to carrier disruptions and the payload size is relatively large when compared with watermarks. An attack against a steganographic system is the detection that an embedded message exists. Another attack is similar to watermarking, which includes disruption of the communication channel.

The techniques employed to encode information in both watermarking and steganography may be similar; however, the primary differences are in the application of the embedded information and the relationship to the carrier.

GLOSSARY

Algorithm   A set of steps used to solve a problem or perform an operation.

Compression   This is a process used to represent data with less data. This can be done by removing redundant information. Another technique is to represent the most frequently occurring datum in a data stream with a shorter datum.

Contrast   The variation in brightness between the darkest and lightest regions of an image.

Correlation   It is a measure of similarity between two signals. The degree of similarity is often expressed as a number between zero and one. One indicates a perfect match.

Digital Watermarking   It is an identification code carrying information (an author's signature, a company logo, etc.) about the copyright owner, the creator of the work, the authorized consumer, and so on. It is permanently embedded into digital data to indicate copyright and provide a means for checking if the data have been modified.

Discrete Cosine Transform   A transform used in many applications, including image compression. It breaks an image down into additive real sinusoidal components.

E-Commerce   It is the conduct of business transactions and trading over a common information systems platform such as the Web or Internet.

Fast Fourier Transform   An algorithm for computing the Fourier transform with fewer computations.

Fourier Transform   A method of transforming image information from the spatial domain to the frequency domain.

Fragile Watermark   Fragile watermarks are also known as tamper-proof watermarks. Such watermarks are destroyed by data manipulation.

Frequency Domain   A representation of a signal according to its basic frequency components.

Image Compression   The class of techniques used to reduce the amount of data necessary to represent an image.

Image Enhancement   A class of techniques used as selective emphasis and suppression of information in an image. The ultimate goal is to increase the image's usefulness. Enhancements may include such operations as sharpening or contrast modification.

Information Hiding   Information hiding deals with communication security, which comprises encryption and traffic security. Encryption protects the content during distribution over an open network such as the Internet. The traffic security pertains to concealing its sender, its receiver, or its very existence.

Intensity   Amplitude or power of light.

Invisible Watermarking   It refers to the embedded digital watermark that is nonseeable. It is hidden in the content. It can be detected by an authorized agency only. It is most often used to identify copyright data, such as author, distributor, and so on.

JPEG   Joint Picture Experts Group. JPEG usually refers to the image compression standard developed by that group. This type of image compression can be either lossless or lossy, depending on the application.

MPEG   Motion Picture Experts Group. It has developed an algorithm to compress video sequences. Typically, references to MPEG refer to the compression algorithm.

MPEG-4   It is an International Standard Organization (ISO)/International Electromechanic Commission (IEC) standard (ISO / IEC 14496). It provides an audiovisual coding standard for very low bit rate channels. Such channels are found in the Internet and mobile applications.

Noise   A random variation in signal value occurring during digitizing, transmission, or other processes in a digital system.

Pixel   A picture element. An image is composed of many tiny dots. These dots are called pixels.

RGB   The additive color space consisting of the primaries red, green, and blue. This color model is used in most computer graphics display hardware

Scaling   The geometric process that enlarges or shrinks an image.

Spatial Domain   The normal domain of image data intensity as a function of position.

Steganography   It is a subdiscipline of information hiding. Here, secret information is hidden in an innocuous (harmless) message. Such an innocuous message is also known as cover message.

Visible Watermarking   It is an extension of the concept of logos. Such watermarks are applicable to images only. These logos are inlaid into the image, but they are transparent. It is sometimes called digitally stamped. An example of visible watermarking is provided by television channels, such as CNN, BBC, and TV5, whose logos are visibly superimposed on the corner of the TV picture frame.

Watermarking Invisibility   Imperceptibility requires that the marked data and the original data should be perceptually indistinguishable.

Watermarking Robustness   Robustness refers to the fact that the embedded information should be reliably decodable after modifications of the marked data.

Watermarking Security   Security here refers to the difficulty of extracting or removing the embedded watermark without knowledge of the secret key (or keys).

Wavelet Transform   A transform that decomposes a signal into very simple basis functions.

CROSS REFERENCES

See *Computer and Network Authentication; Copyright Law; Electronic Commerce; Forensic Computing.*

REFERENCES

Bender, W., Gruhl, D., Morimoto, N., & Lu, A. (1996). Techniques for data hiding. *IBM Systems Journal, 35*(3/4), 313–336.

Bors, A., & Pitas, I. (1996). Image watermarking using DCT domain constraints. *International Conference on Image Processing Proceedings, ICIP 96* (vol. 3, pp. 231–234), Lausanne, Switzerland.

Chen, B., & Wornell, G. W. (2001). Quantization index modulation: A class of provably good methods for digital watermarking and information embedding. *IEEE Transactions on Information Theory, 47*(4), 1423–1443.

Cox, I., Kilian, J., Leighton, F. T., & Shamoon, T. (1997). Secure spread spectrum watermarking for multimedia. *IEEE Transaction Image Processing, 6*(12), 1673–1687.

Craver, S., Memon, N., Yeo, B., & Yeung, M. (1997). On the invertibility of invisible watermarking techniques. In *International Conference on Image Processing Proceedings, ICIP 97* (pp. 540–543).

Hernadez, J., & Gonzalez, F. (1999). Statistical analysis of watermarking schemes for copyright protection of images. In *Proceeding of the IEEE, Special Issue on Protection of Multimedia Content* (pp. 1142–1165).

Hetzl, S. (2002). *A survey of steganography*. Retrieved January 2, 2005, from http://www.rn.inf.tu-dresden.de/westfeld/attacks.html

Johnson, N. F. (2004). *Steganography*. Retrieved January 3, 2005, from http://www.jjtc.com/stegdoc/sec202.html

Kahn, D. (1967). *The codebreakers*. New York: Macmillan.

Koch, E., & Zhao, J. (1995). Towards robust and hidden image copyright labeling. In *Proceeding of IEEE Nonlinear Signal Processing Workshop* (pp. 452–455).

Kutter, M., Bhattacharjee, S. K., & Ebrahimi, T. (1999). Towards second generation watermarking schemes. In *International Conference on Image Processing Proceedings, ICIP 99* (vol. 1, pp. 320–323).

Mintzer, F., Braudaway, G. W., & Yeung, M. M. (1997). Effective and ineffective digital watermarks. In *International Conference on Image Processing Proceedings, ICIP 97* (vol. 3, pp. 9–12).

Nikolaidis, N., & Pitas, I. (1996). Copyright protection of images using robust digital signatures. In *Proceeding of IEEE Conference Acoustics, Speech & Signal Processing '96* (pp. 2168–2171).

Pitas, I. (1996). A method for signature casting on digital images. In *International Conference on Image Processing Proceedings, ICIP 96* (vol. 3, pp. 215–218).

Puate, J., & Jordan, F. (1996). Using fractal compression scheme to embed a digital signature into an image. In *Proceedings of SPIE Photonics East'96 Symposium*. Retrieved January 2, 2005, from http://iswww.epfl.ch/~jordan/watermarking.html

Radcliff, D. (2003). *Steganography: Hidden data*. Retrieved January 3, 2005, from http://www.computerworld.com/securitytopics/security/story/0,10801,71726,00.html

Ruanaidh, J. O., Dowling, W. J., & Boland, F. M. (1996). Watermarking digital images for copyright protection. *IEEE Proceedings on Vision, Signal and Image Processing, 143*(4), 250–256.

Schneier, B. (1996). *Applied cryptography*. New York: John Wiley & Sons.

Schyndel, R. G., Tirkel, A. Z., & Osborne, C. F. (1994). A digital watermark. *Proceeding of IEEE International Conference on Image* (vol. 2, pp. 86–90).

Servetto, S. D., Podilchuk, C. I., & Ramchandran, K. (1998). Capacity issues in digital image watermarking. *International Conference on Image Processing, ICIP 98* (vol. 1, pp. 445–449).

Suhail, M. A., & Obaidat, M. S. (2001). On the digital watermarking in JPEG 2000. In *The 8th IEEE International Conference on Electronics, Circuits & Systems (ICECS2001)* (pp. 871–874).

Suhail, M. A., & Obaidat, M. S. (2003). Digital watermarking-based DCT and JPEG model. *IEEE Transaction Instruments and Measurements, 52*(5), 1640–1647.

Suhail, M. A., Obaidat, M. S., Ipson, S. S., & Sadoun, B. (2003). A comparative study of digital watermarking in JPEG and JEPG2000 environments. *Elsevier Information Sciences Journal, 151*, 93–105.

Swanson, M. D., Kobayashi, M., & Tewfik, A. H. (1998). Multimedia data-embedding and watermarking technologies. *Proceedings of the IEEE, 86*(6), 1064–1087. http://www.tsi.enst.fr/~maitre/tatouage//icip2000.html

Tirkel, A., Rankin, G., Schyndel, R., Ho, W., Mee, N., & Osborne, C. (1993). Electronic watermark. *Proceedings of Digital Image Computing, Technology and Applications, DICTA 93*, 666–673.

Voyatzis, G., Nikolaidis, N., & Pitas, I. (1998). Digital watermarking an overview. In *Proceedings EUSIPCO '98*, Rhodes, Greece, September.

Wei, Z. H., Qin, P., & Fu, Y. Q. (1998). Perceptual digital watermark of images using wavelet transform. In *IEEE Transactions on Consumer Electronics* (vol. 444, pp. 1267–1272).

Xia, X.-G., Boncelet, C. G. & Arce, G. R. (1997). A multiresolution watermark for digital images. In *International Conference on Image Processing* (vol. 1, pp. 548–551).

Zhu, W., Xiong, Z., & Zhang, Y. (1998). Multiresolution watermarking for images and video: A unified approach. In *International Conference on Image Processing Proceedings, ICIP 98*, (vol. 1, pp. 465–468).

Law Enforcement and Digital Evidence

J. Philip Craiger and Jeff Swauger, *University of Central Florida*
Mark Pollitt, *DigitalEvidencePro*

DIGITAL EVIDENCE AND DIGITAL FORENSICS

One of the by-products of the growth of information technology has been the proliferation of the "computer criminal." Forensic evidence at a crime scene that once was limited to physical items and attributes (carpet fibers, tool marks), and biological matter (hair, blood, fingerprints) now often includes *digital evidence*. In 1999, the Scientific Working Group on Digital Evidence (www.swgde.org) defined digital evidence as:

Information of probative value stored or transmitted in binary form.

Examples of digital evidence would include common application files (word processing, spreadsheets, etc.), graphical files, audio and video recordings and files, server logs, and application executables.

Like other forensic disciplines, digital forensics has its origins in the legal system. Digital forensics can be described as a technical solution to what is principally a legal problem. This statement is true for all of the forensic sciences. As a result, the law has had an equal, if not greater, influence on the practice of digital forensics than has computer science or engineering. The admissibility of digital forensic processes and products is the ultimate goal.

Law enforcement's view of digital forensics is driven by the premise that anything done to an item collected as evidence is subject to presentation in court. This simple fact has tremendous impact, not only on law enforcement's view of digital forensics but also on the development and regulation of processes. Regardless of the scientific virtue of anything discovered, the value of these discoveries is constrained by the requirements of the legal system.

Who Should Read This Chapter?

We wrote this chapter for semitechnically literate professionals at small or medium-sized law enforcement agencies (or businesses) who are involved in the processing of digital evidence. Agencies of this size make up the majority of law enforcement agencies in the United States.

From our many discussions with personnel from these agencies, we have found that the person most often placed in charge of digital forensics examinations was selected because they were the most technically literate person in the agency. It is atypical for these personnel to have degrees in IT-related fields (e.g., computer science, management information systems, or information technology) or years of experience in computer-related fields.

Furthermore, we did not assume that these agencies have access to digital forensics experts or that they have large budgets for training or technology, which is typical for the majority of small law enforcement agencies with which we are familiar. The descriptions and demonstrations in our chapter were written at a level that a semi-technically literate person should be able to follow without too much trouble. For the more technical demonstrations, interested readers may wish to refer to the resources listed in our reference section for more information. A very good source on the use of the Linux operating system in digital evidence cases, written specifically for law enforcement, is Grundy (2004). Readers should also refer to other chapters in this volume, including Computer Forensics Procedures and Methods, Forensic Computing, Forensic Analysis of Windows Systems, and Forensics Analysis of UNIX systems.

This chapter is not a step-by-step "how-to" guide but rather a primer to create an understanding of the challenges, combined with descriptions and pointers on what is available, in terms of technologies and methods, to assist agencies in dealing with these challenges. Our reference section contains dozens of books and pointers that further elaborate on the solutions we describe in this chapter.

Challenges to Law Enforcement

In this chapter, we provide an introduction to several challenges that agencies face during digital evidence investigations. We selected these challenges based on discussions with local, state, and national law enforcement agencies and our own personal experience. Because of space limitations, we have not included every conceivable problem that agencies may encounter. Rather we selected a subset of problems that have demonstrated an ability to hinder computer crime investigations. In fact some of the problems may not be widespread at the moment. For instance, encryption is used in a small percentage of digital evidence cases; however, when used it can greatly impede an investigation.

We present these challenges in the following order:

- Data obfuscation
  - Encryption
  - Steganography
- Forensic tool validation
- Forensic countermeasures
- Large quantities of evidence
- Diversity of digital devices and media

For each challenge we describe potential solutions for dealing with the problem. We begin this chapter with the most technical subject first, techniques for obfuscating (hiding) digital files.

Data Obfuscation

Criminals who use computers to conduct illegal activities often attempt to hide the fruits of their crimes and often hide the very tools used in the commission of the crime (e.g., software tools). Hiding files on a computer can take on many forms, ranging from simply changing a file's three-letter extension to more technical methods such as file encryption and steganography. Each of these technologies has the potential to impede severely the recovery of digital evidence. We discuss encryption and steganography in turn below and describe potential methods of coping with each.

Encryption

This section provides sufficient detail on encryption so that the semitechnical reader can understand the problems that may be encountered during digital forensic examinations involving encryption. Readers interested in more detailed information on encryption are urged to review chapters in Volume II, Part 3 of the Handbook of Information Security: Encryption Basics, Symmetric-Key Encryption, Hashes and Message Digests, and Public-Key Algorithms. We include several important resources on encryption at the end of this chapter.

In simple terms, encryption takes a digital artifact (text, picture, audio, video, etc.) and transforms it so that it is unreadable. The transformation process requires a cipher—mathematical encryption algorithm—and a key. Frequently, the key is a password. The cipher takes the file and key and performs the necessary calculations to make the file unreadable. To decrypt requires reversing the transformation process so that the file is once again readable. This requires knowing which cipher was used, and most importantly, the key that was used in the transformation process.

Encryption is used legitimately and legally by business, industry, governments, military, and individuals, to ensure privacy of information by keeping it hidden from those not authorized to read the information. Unfortunately, it can also be used by criminals to hide the fruits of their crimes.

There are two major classes of encryption algorithms: symmetric (or secret key), and *asymmetric* (or public key). Symmetric key algorithms use a single key for encryption and decryption. Asymmetric key encryption algorithms use two keys: a public key and a *private* key. The public key is freely shared and is used by senders to encrypt a message that is meant for the recipient only.

Assuming the encryption works as intended, the encrypted message can only be decrypted with the recipient's private key. Often the keys are interchangeable; that is, if the public key encrypts the message, the private key can decrypt it, and if the private key encrypts a message, the public key can decrypt it. Although keys are often interchangeable, this is not required for asymmetric encryption. The private key may also be used in digital signatures as a means of authenticating the source of a message. A "digital signature" encrypted with the sender's private key may be attached to a message. Any message recipient can prove the message is authentic by decrypting the signature using the sender's public key, assuming the sender's private key has not been compromised.

A symmetric cipher (i.e., mathematical formula or algorithm) combines the password and the message and encrypts them into "ciphertext," essentially an unreadable scrambled message. To "decipher" the message (i.e., recover the text) requires knowledge of the cipher.

With public key algorithms, a separate mathematical function is used to create the public/private key pair. The private key is protected by encrypting it with a symmetric key cipher and a password. Knowledge of the encryption algorithm and the password used to encrypt the private key is required to recover the text.

Symmetric and public key algorithms are not directly comparable because the process underlying the encryption cipher differs dramatically. The current U.S. government standard for symmetric encryption is the Advanced Encryption Standard, which has key lengths of 128, 192, or 256 bits. In contrast, public key algorithms such as the RSA public key algorithm use keys containing 1024, 2048, or 4096 bits. The longer the key length, the more secure the encrypted message is for both symmetric and asymmetric encryption. As of 2004, symmetric key lengths of 128 bits or more are considered secure, as are public key lengths of 1024 bits or more.

Public key encryption is a slow process compared with symmetric key encryption because more computation is required. Because of this, a third form of encryption is

```
                        pc@gheera:~/documents/examples

File  Edit  View  Terminal  Tabs  Help
[pc@gheera examples]$ file *
craiger.hotel.request2.doc:  PGP armored data message
craiger.hotel.request.doc:   Microsoft office Document
hotels.doc:                  data
linux.2.6.8.1.uml:           ELF 32-bit LSB executable, Intel 80386, version 1 (SY
SV), for GNU/Linux 2.2.5, statically linked, stripped
nutcake.recipe.txt:          data
WORMPAPER2.pdf:              data
WORMPAPER.pdf:               PDF document, version 1.2
[pc@gheera examples]$ ▮
```

Figure 1: UNIX file command run against several files.

sometimes used. This form of encryption is a hybrid technique that combines symmetric and public key encryption. Examples include PGP (Pretty Good Privacy, http://www.pgpi.org) and its open source counterpart, GPG (GNU Privacy Guard, http://www.gnupg.org). These hybrid algorithms create randomly generated session keys that are used to encrypt messages with a symmetric cipher (DES, Triple-DES, CAST, AES, etc.). The session key is then encrypted with a public key, and the encrypted session key is sent, with the encrypted message to the recipient of the message. The recipient uses his or her private key to decrypt the encrypted session key, which may then be used to decrypt the message. Hybrid methods are attractive because they combine the best of both symmetric and public key encryption algorithms. As an additional measure of security, the recipient's private key is encrypted with a symmetric cipher and requires a password to decrypt. This extra layer of encryption of the private key provides an added layer of security.

What Information Can Be Encrypted?

Suspects can encrypt any digital files, from an individual file to an entire hard drive. Regardless of what data is encrypted, it is necessary to know both the cipher used for encryption and the password in order to decrypt the ciphertext.

Individual File Encryption

Before investigators can decrypt and analyze encrypted information, the encrypted files must be detected and identified for further analysis. Many digital forensic tools can determine whether a file has been encrypted by evaluating the file's header information. Header information is digital information contained within the beginning of a file that indicates the file type. Unfortunately, this method

only works if the file headers have not been modified and whether the file has a recognizable header.

There is no single, simple, 100 percent accurate way of determining whether an individual file is encrypted, or whether the file merely resembles an encrypted file. In the following example, four of the files in the directory (Figure 1) are encrypted:

- request2.doc: GPG Public-key ASCII encrypted
- football.sch   GPG Public-key binary encrypted
- WORMPAPER2.pdf   GPG Symmetric key encrypted file
- shoppinglist.txt   PGP Symmetric key encrypted file

Additionally, the file hotels.doc is a compressed—using zip compression—file whose header information was removed. When the header information is removed from a file, applications can no longer correctly determine the file type. It also means that the file is corrupted and most likely cannot be opened by the application that created it.

We ran the UNIX file command against all of the files in this directory. The file command reads a file's header information and compares it against a known list of headers to determine the type of file. As Figure 1 demonstrates, the file command contains enough information to conclude that request2.doc is as an encrypted file of type PGP armored. For the remaining encrypted files, however, the headers do not contain enough information to determine the type of file by using the file command.

We replicated this experiment using the same files and a commercial forensics tool. As Figure 2 demonstrates, we achieved the same results (under the column "File Type").

It is impossible to determine whether a file is encrypted merely by "eyeballing" its contents. As Figures 3–5

	File Name	File Type	Ext	Full Path
☑	WORMPAPER.pdf	Acrobat Portable Document Format (P...	pdf	final\NO NAME-FAT12\WORMPAPER.pdf
☑	request.doc	Microsoft Word 97 Document	doc	final\NO NAME-FAT12\request.doc
☑	request2.doc	PGP Encrypted Message	doc	final\NO NAME-FAT12\request2.doc
☑	shoppinglist.txt	Plain Text Document	txt	final\NO NAME-FAT12\shoppinglist.txt
☑	football.sch	Unknown File Type	sch	final\NO NAME-FAT12\football.sch
☑	WORMPAPER2.pdf	Unknown File Type	pdf	final\NO NAME-FAT12\WORMPAPER2.pdf

Figure 2: Results for commercial forensic toolkit.

```
pc@gheera:~/documents/examples
File  Edit  View  Terminal  Tabs  Help
0010810:  24a6 beff 7c7b 4e18 0f9e 358b 9826 c134    $...|{N...5..&.4
0010820:  24a5 9284 7b13 f21f cee1 0acf 23ce 30d2    $...{.......#.O.
0010830:  97e4 e0d9 b84d 2223 2d0c 2318 2c3e 448a    .....M"#-.#.,>D.
0010840:  00a8 f6ab ae18 5994 cd9e 88fb 5d37 3d25    ......Y....]7=%
0010850:  2ff6 1680 bd9b 80f7 308f e2e1 3098 0c6a    /.......0...O..j
0010860:  19c8 7b39 22ca 5c61 8c8c 5e7b 96b2 0aa5    ..{9".\a..^{....
0010870:  798c be22 570e 7e89 9a5a 3a19 958b 921a    y.."W.~..Z:.....
0010880:  d050 47d5 d10e 1a1e 06e3 5496 096a 252a    .PG.......T..j%*
0010890:  1019 601b b33d ce72 5f8b d782 d433 bcb4    .. `..=.r_.....3..
00108a0:  875c 9eaa e693 3529 899b 3d0b d685 b836    .\....5)..=....6
00108b0:  6463 f0f8 b35d aad8 d40a 656a 67d5 13b4    dc...]....ejg...
00108c0:  b1d6 1953 48df 7a46 2116 f7ba fbb8 cfcb    ...SH.zF!.......
```

Figure 3: Symmetric cipher encrypted file.

demonstrate, the contents of an encrypted file may appear very similar to other files such as binary executables and compressed files (e.g., zipped files). To demonstrate, we created a symmetric key encrypted file (Figure 3), a compressed file (Figure 4), and a binary executable (Figure 5). Clearly, there are no visually identifiable differences that allow an investigator to determine the type of file through a mere visual examination.

File System-Level Encryption

There exist several applications that can encrypt a volume (partition) or even an entire hard drive. These applications are available for several operating systems, including Windows, Linux, and Macintosh. These applications work the same as individual file encryption, using a cipher and a key to encrypt data.

Some of these applications can leave visible clues that a suspect is running hard drive encryption. For instance, we found that several Windows-based encryption applications display their icon in the Window's taskbar. Figure 6 shows the icon displayed—floppy disk with yellow key underneath—for the BestCrypt encryption application (www.jetico.com). (There is no guarantee that a volume or disk encryption application will place its icon in the Window's taskbar. Therefore, lack of an icon does not guarantee that the file system is not encrypted. An investigator can be certain a file system or disk is encrypted if the investigator attempts to access files and is presented with dialog box requesting a password for file access.)

When the user attempts to access a file on an unmounted encrypted file system, the encryption program will ask the user for the password. If the user does not have the correct password, the encrypted file system remains unmounted and the files cannot be accessed. However, if the encrypted file system is mounted, then the files can be accessed. (Mounting a file system makes the files on the media accessible to the operating system and applications.)

Windows Encrypted File System (EFS)

The Windows 2000, XP, and 2003 Server operating systems have the capability of encrypting volumes using Microsoft's Encrypted File System (EFS). EFS is a hybrid method that uses a symmetric algorithm for data encryption and a public-key for protecting the symmetric key. Access to the public key is protected via a password. While Windows 2000 defaults to 56-bit Digital Encryption Standard (DES), XP and 2003 Server defaults to the Advanced Encryption Standard (AES) with a 256-bit key, a much more secure cipher than either 56-bit DES or 3DES.

EFS supports third-party data recovery through the concept of a Data Recovery Agent (DRA). A DRA is a designated authority—most often a security or network administrator but could be anyone—whose private key is used to protect the data in addition to the primary's public key (i.e., the original data owner's public key).

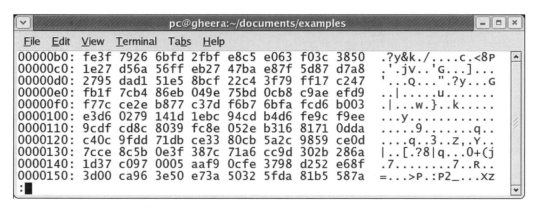

Figure 4: Compressed file with modified header.

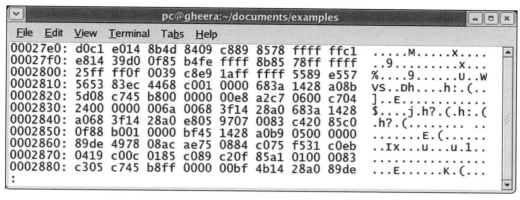

```
                 pc@gheera:~/documents/examples
 File  Edit  View  Terminal  Tabs  Help
00027e0: d0c1 e014 8b4d 8409 c889 8578 ffff ffc1   .....M.....X....
00027f0: e814 39d0 0f85 b4fe ffff 8b85 78ff ffff   ..9.........X...
0002800: 25ff ff0f 0039 c8e9 1aff ffff 5589 e557   %....9......U..W
0002810: 5653 83ec 4468 c001 0000 683a 1428 a08b   VS..Dh....h:.(..
0002820: 5d08 c745 b800 0000 00e8 a2c7 0600 c704   ]..E...........
0002830: 2400 0000 006a 0068 3f14 28a0 683a 1428   $....j.h?.(.h:.(
0002840: a068 3f14 28a0 e805 9707 0083 c420 85c0   .h?.(.......... ..
0002850: 0f88 b001 0000 bf45 1428 a0b9 0500 0000   .......E.(......
0002860: 89de 4978 08ac ae75 0884 c075 f531 c0eb   ..Ix...u...u.1..
0002870: 0419 c00c 0185 c089 c20f 85a1 0100 0083   ................
0002880: c305 c745 b8ff 0000 00bf 4b14 28a0 89de   ...E......K.(...
:
```

Figure 5: Binary executable without header.

Consequently, in a networked environment data recovery of an EFS encrypted partition is very possible as long as someone has been designated as a third-party DRA. If a DRA does not exist, then the only person capable of decrypting the data is the primary owner. Should this be the case, other methods are required to gain access to the public key's password. Some of these methods are described in a later section.

How to Determine Whether Files Are Encrypted

How does one determine whether a file is encrypted? Unfortunately, this sometimes requires trial-and-error attempts to decrypt the files, using a variety of encryption applications. This is demonstrated below with GPG and PGP encryption applications.

An investigator should run a forensic application that uses header information against all files on a hard drive first to determine whether any files are obviously encrypted. As demonstrated previously, accurately determining the type of file can be hit-or-miss depending on what type of encryption is used. If an investigator has on good authority that the suspect is known to use encryption, then some trial-and-error involving attempts to decrypt the files with a variety of encryption applications may be necessary.

Below we demonstrate this with GPG and PGP encryption applications. (Some applications append their own three letter extension when encrypting files, such as .gpg or .pgp. A user can remove the extension to remove that clue.)

Figure 7 demonstrates a trial-and-error attempt to decrypt files using GPG. Figure 8 demonstrates this process using PGP. The total experimental results are presented in Table 1.

Table 1 indicates how PGP and GPG performed in determining whether or not a file was encrypted. The Ys under the "GPG" and "PGP" headings indicate that the application correctly determined whether the file

was encrypted. For this simple example, the applications were 100% accurate. GPG and PGP correctly determined that files encrypted with the other applications were encrypted, as well as determining whether the cipher used for encryption was a symmetric or public key cipher.

Real-world situations are much more complex than this example; however, this simple demonstration shows the type of experiments one might have to conduct in order to determine which files, if any, are encrypted.

Breaking Encryption

Several techniques that can be used to recover digital evidence are described. Each of these methods relies on recovering the password used for encryption.

Asking the Suspect and Social Engineering

The simplest and easiest method of overcoming encryption is to ask the suspect for the password(s). This technique can be very effective, particularly if it is used immediately after law enforcement serves a search warrant on the suspect. This is the time when suspects may be psychologically weak, confused, or frightened, and are therefore more psychologically amenable to answering questions. We know of numerous examples of suspects who openly shared passwords, and other relevant information, upon being served with a search warrant.

Another approach that relies on psychology is "social engineering." Social engineering is a term commonly used to describe how computer criminals gather information by tricking people (e.g., secretaries, network administrators, help-desk personnel, regular users, etc.), into divulging information necessary to break into a computer. In social engineering, the investigator attempts to use knowledge of the suspect to obtain the password, either by direct inquiry or by educated guessing based on information provided by the suspect. For example, suspects can often be induced to reveal private information about them that can be used to guess passwords. For example, often words such as pet's names, children's names, and football team names are used as passwords. The effectiveness of social engineering is highly dependent on the interpersonal skills and insight of the investigator. Examination of the suspect's home and other details about their life can also be useful in searching for information relevant to the suspect's passwords.

Figure 6: Icon displayed in task bar for BestCrypt encryption program.

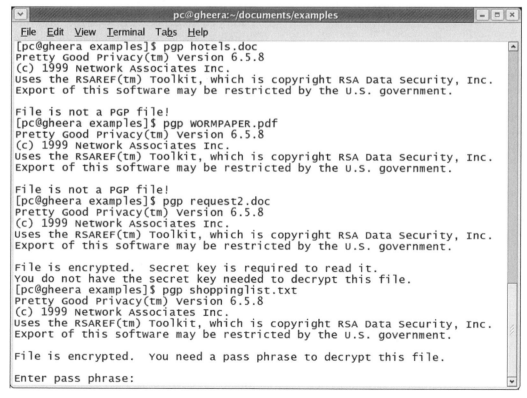

Figure 7: Attempting to decrypt files with GPG.

If a suspect refuses to divulge his or her passwords, three other options are available. One is to use "password cracking" software. A second method is to search the suspect's computer, in the hope that the suspect's password is located somewhere on the computer. Finally, investigators may attempt to recover passwords from other accounts used by the suspect, in the hope that the suspect has used the same password on more than one account. Each of these methods is described.

Automated Tools: Password Crackers

Password cracking is a term that implies an automated method of guessing passwords. There are three commonly employed modes of password guessing: (a) heuristic or rule-based attacks, (b) dictionary attacks, and (c) brute force attacks. These are described in order of the complexity and amount of time it typically takes to perform the attack.

Figure 8: Attempting to decrypt files with PGP.

Table 1 Experimental Results

File	File Results (based on header)	Actual File Type	GPG	PGP
hotel.doc	Data	Compressed file	Y	Y
request.doc	MS Word	MS Word	Y	Y
request2.doc	PGP armored	PGP Public-key armored	Y	Y
WORMPAPER.pdf	PDF file	PDF file	Y	Y
WORMPAPER2.pdf	Data	Symmetric key encrypted	Y	Y
shoppinglist.txt	ASCII text	PGP symmetric key encrypted	Y	Y
football.sch	Data	Public-key encrypted	Y	Y
linux	Binary	Binary	Y	Y

Rule-Based Attacks

Rule-based attacks make use of numerous rules of thumb that users often follow when creating passwords. Rule-based attacks can be based on information retrieved through social engineering, as mentioned earlier. The reason these attacks are so effective is that human behavior is often predictable: users often create passwords that are meaningful to themselves personally because these passwords are easy to remember. Examples include birthdays, anniversaries, names of children, simple keyboard combinations ('qwerty,' 'abc123,' etc.), names of pets, and commonly used passwords such as the word "password" or the username.

Organizational password policies often mandate that users create passwords composed of upper- and lowercase letters, numbers, and special characters in order to increase the difficulty of guessing passwords. Despite these policies, some users create password combinations that follow a formula that is guessable. For instance, a username followed by a number or special character, such as 'lmcbride1,' or 'lmcbride!' are common.

A rule-based attack generates passwords using a defined set of characters. Thus, guesses for a username 'lmcbride' might include: lmcbride1, lmcbride2, lmcbride3...lmcbride*, lmcbride/, and so on. Rule-based attacks work remarkably well because passwords that are created from a truly random set of characters are very difficult to remember. When passwords are difficult to remember, users often write their passwords down, and these passwords may be located through other procedures.

Dictionary Attack

A *dictionary attack* uses a list of words from a dictionary as the basis for guessing passwords. If the suspect uses a word contained in the dictionary, it will be guessed fairly quickly, no matter how long the word: "Antidisestablishmentarianism" will be guessed more quickly than "cat" because it comes prior to it in a dictionary. Depending on the size of the dictionary and the speed of the computer, in many cases, a dictionary attack may run through all the words in the dictionary in less than a minute.

Dozens of dictionaries can be downloaded from the Internet, including specialized dictionaries containing names of cartoon characters, sports teams, or mythical or fictional characters from TV shows, movies, or literature. Dictionaries are also available in multiple languages. We suggest that law enforcement agencies download several sets of dictionaries, including some of the largest dictionaries available, and use all of these dictionaries before moving to the more time-consuming brute force attack.

Brute Force Attack

The most time-consuming type of password attack is the brute force attack. A brute force attack looks at combinational possible combinations of letters, numbers, and special characters, and uses them in guessing the password. A password eight characters in length that uses upper- and lowercase letters (52), numbers (10), and special characters (32), means there are 94^8 or 6,095,689,385,410,816 possible combinations. Brute force attacks on passwords more than eight characters in length are generally unfeasible. Use brute force attacks as a last resort only.

Passwords on Disk

Accessdata's Password Recovery Toolkit (PRTK) is a commercial password cracker (www.accessdata.com) that works for many encryption problems. PRTK has a very interesting password cracking methods that works in concert with Accessdata's Forensic Toolkit (FTK). This method is based on the fact that the user's password may appear somewhere on the suspect's hard drive. For instance, the suspect may have included the password in a document, or an ill-behaved encryption application placed the password in RAM, and was subsequently written to a swap or hibernation file. FTK will extract and index every word on a hard drive and output this list to a text file, which can is then imported into PRTK and used as a dictionary. If the password appears anywhere on the hard drive, in allocated, unallocated, or slack space, then the PTK will break the password.

Break Other Accounts

Humans are creatures of habit, as they saying goes. Most users employ the same password for many different accounts: Why remember 10 passwords for 10 accounts when I only have to remember one! A careful user may use multiple passwords, but to reduce cognitive load, select passwords that fall into a category that is meaningful to the user, for instance, characters from Star Trek, a pet's name, and so on. It may be useful for an agency to attempt to (legally) break passwords for other accounts to which the suspect has access to determine whether the suspect uses a guessable pattern, for example, ckirk!, mspock!, msulu! (i.e., Star Trek characters).

Commercial and Freeware Tools

There are commercial and freeware tools that perform password cracking. There are several free password crackers that are very good and widely used, including John the Ripper (www.openwall.com) and Crack (ftp.cerias.purdue.edu/pub/tools/unix/pwdutils/crack). One of the best-known and efficient applications is L0phtCrack, a commercial tool from @stake (atstake.com). Password dictionaries may be found at several locations on the Internet and are easily located by using Google to search for "password cracking dictionary."

Steganography

Steganography is a term that means "covered writing." Steganographic algorithms take the bits that comprise a message and embed these bits within another file. The most common example is hiding text within a graphical image, which is demonstrated below.

There are several steganographic algorithms. One of the more common uses the least significant bit of a byte from the file to be hidden; exchanging that bit with the least significant bit from a byte within the cover medium, or file the data is to be hidden in. On average, no more than 50 percent of the bits from the cover medium (also called the receptacle image) are changed in this process. Because they are the least significant bits, very little of the receptacle will display an obvious change.

For example, in order to hide the letter A, we first convert it to the ASCII character 65 in decimal, or 1000001 in binary form. We need eight bytes of data to hide the ASCII value of "A." If we have the following eight bytes of data, inserting the ASCII character A will yield:

```
1110101  →  1110101
1101101  →  1101100
1001100  →  1001100
0110110  →  0110110
0010111  →  0010110
0101000  →  0101000
0000001  →  0000001
```

Here we have hidden the character A, which in this case only required changing two of the least significant bits in the 8 bytes of data we selected. We can of course recover the hidden text by stripping the least significant bit from each byte and piecing them back together.

Steganographic Demonstration

Various steganographic algorithms and programs will hide digital data within almost any other form of digital data. Evidence can be hidden in audio files, various types of graphical images, text files, and other files in Figure 9. We illustrate hiding the text from the Declaration of Independence (9629 characters, a lengthy document) within a NASA graphic image.

This is a large image, 1280 × 1024 pixels, therefore, we are hiding a large document; therefore, we need a large number of bits in which to exchange the bits to be hidden. The example below uses the freeware steganographic program Outguess to hide the text of the Declaration of Independence and save the new file as "hidden.jpg."

Figure 9: Original Image—Buzz.jpg.

A password was also used to make it more difficult to extract the contents of the file.

```
# outguess -k 'password' -d dofi.txt  buzz.jpg hidden.jpg
Reading buzz.jpg....
JPEG compression quality set to 75
Extracting usable bits: 266613 bits
Correctable message size: -5457 bits, 1610934.89%
Encoded 'dofi.txt': 74152 bits, 9269 bytes
Finding best embedding...
   0: 37202(50.1%)[50.2%], bias 34881(0.94),  saved: -15, total: 13.95%
   1: 37126(50.0%)[50.1%], bias 34887(0.94),  saved: -6, total: 13.93%
   2: 37143(50.1%)[50.1%], bias 34822(0.94),  saved: -8, total: 13.93%
   4: 37277(50.2%)[50.3%], bias 34644(0.93),  saved: -25, total: 13.98%
   5: 37059(50.0%)[50.0%], bias 34530(0.93),  saved: 2, total: 13.90%
   8: 37043(49.9%)[50.0%], bias 34440(0.93),  saved: 4, total: 13.89%
  45: 36987(49.9%)[49.9%], bias 34448(0.93),  saved: 11, total: 13.87%
 122: 36796(49.6%)[49.6%], bias 34630(0.94),  saved: 35, total: 13.80%
 135: 36922(49.8%)[49.8%], bias 34458(0.93),  saved: 19, total: 13.85%
 164: 36678(49.4%)[49.5%], bias 34136(0.93),  saved: 49, total: 13.76%
 164, 70814: Embedding data: 74152 in 266613
Bits embedded: 74184, changed: 36678(49.4%) [49.5%], bias: 34136, tot:
266499, skip: 192315
Foiling statistics: corrections: 12996, failed: 494, offset: 118.798470
+- 250.581476
Total bits changed: 70814 (change 36678 +  bias 34136)
Storing bitmap into data...
Writing hidden.jpg....
```

Note that there is some loss of information because of the transposition of bits, which causes degradation in the quality of the image. However, this is typically not discernible to the human eye. Figure 10 shows the resulting image, which contains the hidden text.

Figure 10: Stegoed Image: hidden.jpg.

To demonstrate that the files are distinct, we calculate the MD5 cryptographic hash of each file:

```
# sha1sum buzz.jpg hidden.jpg
f131e22ca580183d9767f91379074d9d1ec43029  buzz.jpg
75a6fed4bf9e929b096b6ac65e830e902c53bec4  hidden.jpg
```

Note that the two cryptographic hashes of the original and hidden file are different, indicating that the two files have distinct content.

In order to recover the hidden text from the graphic file it is necessary to know the application that was used to hide the image because different applications may use different algorithms to hide data.

If someone attempts to extract the hidden content but does not know the password, the extraction process essentially fails. Below is an example of results obtained when an incorrect password is used.

```
# outguess -k 'mypassword' -r hidden.jpg declaration.txt
Reading hidden.jpg....
Extracting usable bits: 266613 bits
Steg retrieve: seed: 51622, len: 63321
Extracted datalen is too long: 63321 > 33327
```

File Recovery

We recover the steganographic content by supplying the correct password.

```
# outguess -k 'password' -r hidden.jpg declaration.txt
Reading hidden.jpg....
Extracting usable bits: 266613 bits
Steg retrieve: seed: 164, len: 9269
```

We successfully recovered our text. The length of the text is 9269 bytes (characters), which is the same number of bytes that was contained within the original document. We can determine whether anything has changed in the recovered file by calculating a cryptographic hash of the file and comparing it to the hash of the original file.

```
# sha1sum declaration.txt dofi.txt
ca2c56c043d7da0fea8ae31891bcff0d289034ca  declaration.txt
ca2c56c043d7da0fea8ae31891bcff0d289034ca  dofi.txt
```

As is obvious from the hashes, the recovered file is identical to the original file.

Coping with Steganography

A major problem for law enforcement with respect to steganography is that the information is "hidden in plain sight." A document can be embedded in an MP3 file or a graphical image, and if the MP3 is played or the graphical image is viewed by an investigator, it will not be obvious that information is hidden within the medium. A Web page may contain dozens or hundreds of graphic images, any of which may or may not contain an embedded message. It is impossible to determine through visual examination whether a graphic file contains vital evidence embedded as hidden data.

The best clue that a suspect has used steganography is often provided by a search for steganography tools on a suspect's computer. If steganographic tools or applications are located, the next task is to determine which files contain embedded information. The first and best option is to ask the suspect at the outset which files contain hidden information. If the suspect refuses to divulge that information, there are two options. First is to use automated tools that can detect, albeit imperfectly, hidden information. Second is to conduct trial-and-error experimentation as described in the prior section on encryption.

Several automated tools are available to evaluate the frequency of bits within a file to determine whether the file has embedded steganographic information. Stegdetect (www.outguess.com) is a freeware application that calculates statistics on a graphic as a means of determining whether an image contains hidden information.

The listing below demonstrates the use of Stegdetect to determine if steganographic content is present in several files:

```
# Stegdetect *.jpg
testimg.jpg : jphide(***)
testimgp.jpg : jphide(***)
testorig.jpg : jphide(***)
testprog.jpg : jphide(***)
travel.jpg : negative
```

In the listing above, we used Stegdetect to determine that four of the five files contain steganographic contents, and it includes the name of the application that was most likely used to hide the content. In this example, JPhide, a popular Windows-based steganography program, was identified. Stegdetect correctly identified the files that contain steganographic content, as well correctly determining that travel.jpg did not contain any embedded information.

Various other tools are available that use similar calculations to determine whether a file has hidden information. We have found that these tools are not foolproof; they can miss files with embedded information.

Manual Methods of Determining Steganographic Content

A suspect may leave clues as to files with steganographic content. For instance, in the presence of steganography programs, one should conduct a visual search for all graphical files. Two graphical files that appear to be the same visually but have different cryptographic hashes may be evidence of embedded information. The graphic file with the latest creation or modified date and time is more likely to the file with embedded content.

Steganography programs often use a password to increase the difficulty of extracting the hidden content. As discussed in the section on encryption, there are several avenues one can pursue for recovering passwords. The first and easiest is simply to ask the suspect for any passwords he or she uses. It may come as a surprise how often suspects freely provides passwords when asked.

DIGITAL FORENSIC TOOL VALIDATION

Digital forensic techniques and tools, as with all other forensic disciplines, must meet basic evidentiary and scientific standards to be allowed as evidence in legal proceedings. The requirements for the admissibility of scientific evidence and expert opinion were outlined in the precedent setting U.S. Supreme Court decision in the case of *Daubert v. Merrell Dow Pharmaceuticals, Inc.*, 509 U.S. 579 (1993). In order to be admissible, evidence or opinion derived from scientific or technical activities must come from methods that are proven to be "scientifically valid." Scientifically valid techniques are capable of being proven correct through empirical testing. In practice, this means that the tools and techniques used in digital forensics must be validated and that crime laboratories, including digital forensic labs, should be accredited or otherwise proven to meet such scientific standards. Obviously strict and accurate validation testing of new forensic tools is required if the results from such applications are to be acceptable as evidence in criminal cases.

In the United States, the American Society for Crime Lab Directors/Lab Accreditation Board (ASCLD/LAB: www.ascld-lab.org) is the official body that accredits crime labs. The board has developed numerous standards relating to establishing the validity and acceptability of forensic techniques, tools, and accreditation of individual crime labs. ASCLD/LABs criteria for accreditation consist of standards covering crime lab management and operations, personnel, and physical plant. Each standard is labeled as desirable, important, or essential, depending on its importance and requirement for meeting ASCLD/LAB specifications. Labs seeking accreditation must meet 100% of the essential criteria, 75% of the important criteria, and 50% of desirable criteria.

With respect to forensic tools and techniques, ASCLD/LAB standard 1.4.2.6 addresses the required scientific validation of procedures used in crime labs:

1.4.2.6 ARE NEW TECHNICAL PROCEDURES SCIENTIFICALLY VALIDATED BEFORE BEING USED IN CASEWORK AND IS THE VALIDATION DOCUMENTATION AVAILABLE FOR REVIEW?

Standard 1.4.2.6 is an essential standard, indicating the importance of scientific validation of tools and techniques. In the context of digital forensics labs, this standard requires that software (and hardware) must be validated prior to its use in examinations.

In the context of digital evidence, the Scientific Working Group for Digital Evidence (SWGDE) defines the term validation as "An evaluation to determine if a tool, technique or procedure functions correctly and as intended" (SWGDE, p. 2). Software validation has long been an important component of software design and development. However, it plays a crucial role in digital forensics because the potential consequence of denying a defendant's constitutional rights to life and liberty:

> Validation testing is critical to the outcome of the entire examination process. Validation, based on sound scientific principles, is required to demonstrate that examination tools (hardware and software), techniques and procedures are suitable for their intended purpose. Tools, techniques and procedures should be validated prior to initial use in digital forensic processes. Failure to implement a validation program can have detrimental effects. (SWGDE, p. 2)

Validation Testing Challenges

The National Institute for Standards and Technology's (NIST) Computer Forensics Tool Testing (CFTT: www.cftt.nist.gov) division is one government entity that formally tests computer forensics software. CFTT performs extremely rigorous scientific tests to validate software tools used in digital forensic examinations. CFTT has and continues to perform testing on numerous computer forensic software applications and has identified various problems that have been addressed by the software vendors. Unfortunately, the ability of one organization to examine all forensic software products and their variations is limited because of the sheer magnitude of the task. For example, software should be revalidated when either a major new release occurs or when a patch or update is released to add features or correct previously existing problems. Such retesting is called regression testing. In addition, revalidation should occur when significant changes are made to the operating system on which the software will run. Updates to operating systems have the potential to change the operation of software that was previously found to work correctly on an earlier version of the operating system. Most people have experiences from attempting to run software under an operating system change that was guaranteed to be "backward compatible" that will make this requirement self-evident.

As mentioned previously, the forensic community cannot rely on a single certifying body to test and evaluate all forensic software, as the sheer pace of change and number of software products is overwhelming. In addition, software tools written by forensic examiners that are not commercial products, often provide additional functionality examiners find useful. Such software, unless it is widely distributed and used, will not rise to the attention of major validation organizations. Consequently, the onus of validation testing is placed on individual examiners who often have no training in software validation testing. Validation is thus often an ad hoc measure that suffices for the moment. Care must be taken in such testing to insure that sufficient scientific rigor is applied to prevent the invalidation of the tool and the evidence it produces.

Validation Testing Approaches

There are various ways to validate a forensic software tool, some of which are more rigorous than others. The most rigorous involves both testing and a detailed examination of the source code, called a code walkthrough. As its name implies, code walkthroughs require that the actual source code is available and also requires programmers, software engineers, and managers with technical expertise. In addition to knowledge of software coding techniques and languages, expertise must also include detailed understanding of the task being performed, in this case forensic examination of computer files and hardware (e.g., hard drives). Code walkthroughs may take months or even years to conduct on large software applications. Obviously, such testing will not be possible for all applications of interest.

From the standpoint of a forensic investigator, there is a more practical and informal approach, black-box testing. This is where much validation of digital forensic software occurs due to both the complexity and time required for code reviews and due to the fact that commercial companies are usually unwilling to share source code (which is rightly considered valuable proprietary intellectual property). Black-box testing is an attractive alternative because it does not require programming and software engineering expertise or source code, while allowing the testing of software in a less expensive and quicker fashion. It does, however, require that the testing be designed by personnel with domain knowledge of digital forensics and computer hardware/software standards (i.e., understanding of the processes to be tested). In black-box testing, the software is treated without regard for its internals (code), only the ability of the tool to function correctly and as intended is evaluated. The software code is treated as a "black box" the internal functioning of which is unknown.

Black-box testing of forensic tools can be accomplished in several ways. One way is to exercise a tools capability against a known standard. For instance, say that we wish to test the keyword search capability of hypothetical Tool A. To do this, we need a known sample (e.g., a hard drive) that contains known and defined instances of the text for which we will search. Tool A's search function is tested by searching our known sample for instances of the keyword. In this example, we search for the term "coke_buddy" on the hard drive as in previous examples. For completeness and fidelity to the real world, our known instances must include the keyword in common formats such as 16-bit UNICODE and 7-bit ASCII, as both formats are used by

the operating system to store data on the hard drive. We then use Tool A to perform a search for the keyword and record the results.

Another accepted method of black-box testing is to compare the validation results between more than one tool that performs the same function (i.e., Tools A, B, and C). This method is useful when we do not have a known sample to test, that is, we do not have a validated reference data source. This approach can provide particularly strong evidence of validation if one or more of the tools (A, B, or C) have been validated previously.

This approach allows us to perform validation testing in the absence of a known sample, unlike the testing procedure above that requires the contents of the test data to be known *a priori*. If we run the search and all three tools return the same results, then we have supporting evidence that the software functions as intended. This result is strongest when Tools B and C have both been validated, and Tool A returned the same results. The claim is weaker if the only one of the other tools has been validated. If none of the other tools have been validated, the confidence is the weakest, although the fact three tools created by three separate programming teams returned the same results can be interpreted as triangulating on the results. Care must be taken, however, to exercise the tools over their full range of user selectable parameters and against a number of different data sets or test samples. While one or two tests may show excellent results, there can always be situations where the tool will fail that are unusual enough to have not been tested or addressed by the designers. Some peculiar combination of set-up parameters, operating criteria, or type of files being searched may reveal a hidden error that, while rarely occurring, is sufficient to invalidate the tool.

Test Samples

Selecting or creating test samples is one of the most challenging aspects of validation testing. The test sample should consist of a number of heterogeneous examples that replicate conditions that will be found in the real world. In addition to common types of data, the test samples must include boundary cases. These boundary cases are conditions or examples of things the tool must be capable of detecting even if they are very uncommonly found in most situations. If the tool correctly reports the results from real-world examples as well as boundary cases, then we can say with some authority that the software functions as expected.

A test sample for validation testing would ideally be a sample prepared by the tester containing a complete set of variables and data to thoroughly exercise the application under test. The advantage of running the tool against a known sample is that the results are known a priori given that the examiner knows what exists on the source media. The disadvantage is that time and effort to create the known sample, which can be extensive, and the potential lack of knowledge about the range of variables that can exist. When preparing a hard disk for testing a tool for text searching, for example, both common formats (16-bit UNICODE and 7-bit ASCII) must be included. If the preparer of the test sample does not know about or forgets to include 16-bit UNICODE examples in the sample, the sample will not exercise the tool sufficiently to evaluate its performance. In the creation of test samples for computer forensic applications, this requires that the sample be developed by experts with extensive knowledge of both computer hardware and operating system standards. Such expertise is required to ensure that the test sample does not overlook important conditions or data which would hamper the validation tests thoroughness.

As mentioned previously, it is not always possible to generate a complete and thorough test sample, and in such a case a variety of real-world data sets may be used. A sufficient number of diverse data sets must be used to adequately test the application. Selection should be made from a number of possible operating systems and including a variety of different data types produced by a number of different applications. Careful selection of such data sets can produce a test sample sufficiently varied to give confidence in the validation testing performed. One option is to use test samples consisting of data from previous forensic examinations where the results of the examination are already known. This is preferable to an unknown test sample, and is much less time consuming and difficult than deliberately generating a new test sample. Test samples derived from previous, extensive forensic examinations have the advantage of being known samples; that is, the examiner has a good idea of what exists on the disk, higher confidence coming from the most thorough of previous investigations. Regardless of how the test sample is selected, care must be taken to ensure the samples exercise the boundary conditions.

Analysis of Results

In the Daubert decision, the court found that in evaluating a scientific technique, known or potential rates of error, and error type should be considered. Two error types are of particular interest, Type I and Type II errors. Type I errors occur when a tool or process falsely identifies a positive result when none is present (i.e., a false positive). Type II errors occur when a tool or process does not identify results that are actually there (i.e., a false negative). Identification of what type of error is present is of particular importance due to the legal implications of using such results in a court proceeding. Therefore, if the forensic tool does not function as intended and returns erroneous results, it is important to identify the type of error that occurred.

Returning to our example involving the search for the keyword "coke_buddy," we know that our sample hard drive contains instances of our keyword as we prepared the test drive. Tool A's performance is evaluated by comparing the tools search results with our expected results. The tool should find all known instances of the keyword, if Tool A's search function works as expected. Table 2 shows the result of a test where Tool A found all instances of the keyword.

Table 2 Search Results for Tool A

Format	Location (byte offset)	Found
UNICODE	14432	Y
ASCII	212178	Y
ASCII	242966	Y
UNICODE	7663911	Y

In this example, Tool A has passed the test by detecting all instances of the keyword and not returning any errors. If, for example, the test results had turned out as in Table 3.

Table 3 Search Results for Tool B

Format	Location (byte offset)	Found
UNICODE	14432	N
ASCII	212178	Y
ASCII	242966	Y
UNICODE	7663911	N

In this instance, Tool A did not find the keyword when present in UNICODE format. This is a Type II error, the return of a false negative. If, for example, the test sample hard drive only contained the keyword in ASCII format, and we recorded the following results in Table 4 below:

Table 4 Search Results for Tool C

Format	Location (byte offset)	Found
UNICODE	N/A	Y
ASCII	212178	Y
ASCII	242966	Y
UNICODE	N/A	Y

In this example, Tool A falsely identified the keyword as being present in a case where it was not and is an example of a Type I error, a false positive.

Of course there are other combinations of results that can occur, such as if the tool misidentifies the contents of the drive, identifying a UNICODE instance as an ASCII instance. The larger the number of different types of data to be identified, the more convoluted the results can become. The larger the number of test samples, or the larger the number of relevant data in the test sample, the higher the confidence in the results of the test.

In an actual tool validation, we would have included several more stringent tests, including keywords that overlapped contiguous sectors and keywords that overlapped noncontiguous (fragmented) sectors. These two circumstances are typically considered two of the most strenuous tests for a search tool.

In the case of a test failure, it is important to determine, if possible, why the tool did not function as intended. In the example where the tool failed to identify the UNICODE keyword, it could be that the keyword crossed noncontiguous cluster boundaries, that is, part of the keyword was situated in one cluster, and the remaining part was in another cluster that was not contiguous with the first (which occurs due to file fragmentation). In this instance one would continue testing to determine whether any other situations caused a failure to report the correct results. A single failure does not necessarily discredit the use of the software in its entirety. The failure needs to be interpreted in light of the remaining test results. Regardless of the outcome, validation testing requires extensive and thorough documentation, identifying all test conditions, variables used, hardware and associated software used in the test, and all test results. In the case of test failures, the results and conditions that resulted in the error should be especially well documented, and the examiner may wish to consider contacting the company or individual that created the software and inform them of the anomaly.

A tool doesn't have to meet 100% success to be validated. There are cases where it may be impossible, for various reasons, to achieve perfect results. For instance, the ability of a password cracker to break encryption is determined by many factors, one of which is time (every password is crackable, given enough time). Therefore, in some cases, a more realistic goal of less than 100% results may be used.

Summary

As can be seen, while there are numerous methods by which validation testing may be performed, all of them require careful thought, preparation, and documentation to test the application as completely as possible. Documentation is one of the most important activities in validation testing, as it allows others to both understand and to repeat the examiners experiments. Replication of experimental results by other examiners is one of the foremost requirements for acceptance of scientific testing.

FORENSIC COUNTERMEASURES

Our population as a whole is becoming more computer literate, and so are criminals. Criminals who use computers to conduct illegal endeavors are learning techniques that allow them to cover traces of these criminal acts. The term "forensic countermeasures" and "anti-forensics" have been used to describe the techniques performed on digital media in order to reduce the likelihood that digital evidence will be recovered. Forensic countermeasures include a collection of disparate techniques, such as encryption and steganography (covered previously), file compression, media formatting, file wiping, and even wholesale destruction of media. Criminals may combine these techniques for added effect, for instance, encrypting a document and then wiping the original file from the media. In this section, we will concentrate on the topic of file wiping as forensic countermeasure primarily because several commercially available applications advertise the ability to remove all traces of evidence from magnetic media.

Although forensic countermeasures can be used in criminal endeavors, there are legitimate and legal uses of these techniques. For example, disposing of old computer hardware and media can be problematic because residual sensitive information can remain on media. We are not making a value judgment regarding the uses of these techniques but rather are merely describing what we know to be true with regard to computer criminal behavior.

File Wiping

A number of commercially available tools promise to remove all traces of "evidence" on a computer. These tools, and their freeware cousins, write a series of characters, 1's, 0's, or random characters over a file several times. This overwriting technique eliminates law enforcement's opportunity to recover the file's contents because the contents have been overwritten, destroying all previously written data. This file-overwriting technique is commonly

referred to as "wiping" a file. Although these wiped files may be recovered using special techniques such as magnetic force microscopy, the tools required are expensive enough that only the best-funded agencies have access to such equipment.

The following Linux command line will write a series of zeros over every sector on a floppy disk:

```
# dd if=/dev/zero of=/dev/fd0
```

This command will wipe not only the file contents but also the file system areas (master boot record, FAT, and root directory entry), as well as the unaddressable space at the end of the disk (i.e., disk space that cannot be used by the file system).

Several companies advertise their products' ability to purge unwanted files (evidence) from magnetic media (floppy disks, hard drive, etc.) We have tested several of these applications in our lab, and none appear to work perfectly without some investigation, and trial-and-error experimentation. Some of these tools are simple command line tools that do a respectable job of overwriting files but fail to wipe the directory entries that contain information such as file names, attributes, date and times, and file size.

Many GUI-based tools are extensively configurable. When we ran these tools with the default settings, we were able to recover some information that we surmised would have been wiped. This may be a serious problem for those using GUI-based tools: users must understand something about where "trace" evidence is located on a computer and understand how to correctly configure the tool in order to completely remove trace evidence. Learning how to configure software correctly usually entails reading a manual that is written from a technical point of view that may be difficult to understand for the average user. It also entails technical computer knowledge about where such information is likely located on the disk. Most criminal suspects are like other computer users in that they are averse to reading technical manuals, relatively uneducated about the intricate technical details of computers, and quite happy to work with a tool's default settings.

A second reason that wiping a file may not remove all traces of the file is that the operating system or many applications may save a file to several different locations on media. From the user's viewpoint, a single copy of the file seems to exist on the computer; however, there may be several complete copies of the file and several dozen parts of the file scattered throughout the hard drive. Users are unaware of the existence of these "extra" copies. In order to remove all remnants of a file users must know where these remnants may remain on a computer, as well as how to configure a tool correctly to wipe these areas. Below we describe several places from which evidence may be recovered. These include: (a) RAM, (b) swap file, (c) hibernation file, and (d) unallocated space.

Trace Evidence in RAM

When a user opens the file in an application, the contents of a file are transferred into RAM. The file's contents may remain in RAM until the file has been closed and memory used by the file is required by the operating system. This is an important reason not to simply pull the plug on a suspect's computer, as doing so may destroy critical evidence.

To demonstrate how evidence may remain in RAM even after a file has been wiped from a hard drive, we performed a simple experiment. First, we opened an old version of this chapter in a word processor, then closed the file, and used a wiping tool to remove the copy of the chapter from the hard drive. Next, we used the utility *dd* to write the contents of RAM to a hard drive (see listing below). *"dd"* is a general-purpose UNIX utility that can copy files and is useful for creating forensic images. (We used a copy of *dd* that was modified to be able to access RAM and compiled to run under Windows operating system.)

a search of the physical hard drive for the term **coke_buddy**. Because we are accessing the physical hard drive, we are searching both allocated and unallocated space. This means that our search will normally find instances of the keywords in deleted files as well as in active files; however, because we previously wiped our copy of the chapter from our hard drive, our keyword search should only return results from unallocated space.

```
C:\>dd if=\\.\PhysicalMemory bs=4k  conv=noerror of=e:\RAM.img
Forensic Acquisition Utilities, 1,  0, 0, 1035
dd, 3, 16, 2, 1035
Copyright (C) 2002-2004 George  M. Garner Jr.

Command Line: dd if=\\.\PhysicalMemory bs=4k conv=noerror of=e:\RAM.img
Based on original version developed by Paul Rubin, David MacKenzie,  and Stuart Kemp
Microsoft Windows: Version 5.1 (Build 2600.Professional Service Pack 2)

19/01/2005 16:53:52 (UTC)
19/01/2005 11:53:52 (local time)

Current User: TIGER\pc
Total physical memory reported: 1047472 KB
Copying physical memory...
Physical memory in the range 0x00002000-0x00002000 could not be read.
Physical memory in the range 0x00124000-0x00163000 could not be read.
C:\WINDOWS\system32\dd.exe:
        Stopped reading physical memory:

The parameter is incorrect.
The parameter is incorrect.

Output e:\ram.img (1073082368 bytes)
261983+0 records in
261983+0 records out
```

The "if=\\.\PhysicalMemory" specifies dd to read from RAM, with a block size of 4096 bytes (bs=4096), and to write 0's to the file if part of RAM cannot be read (conv=noerror). We are writing the contents of RAM to a file called RAM.img on a shared drive on a different computer so as not to taint our suspect's computer.

After creating an image of RAM (RAM.img), we can perform a keyword search on the contents to determine whether any of portions of our chapter remained in RAM even after we closed our file. We first extracted the human readable text from RAM.img, and then performed our search for the keyword "coke_buddy," which appears several times in this chapter. The listing below demonstrates that we found a large part of our chapter in RAM, even after wiping the file from the hard drive. Our keyword is in bold.

```
A forensics examiner can access the
contents of unallocated space by either:
a) making a forensic image of the media
and performing a physical analysis on the
image, b) or booting the suspect s computer
with a bootable forensic disk and per-
forming a physical analysis at the device
level. The latter is typically performed
with a Linux bootable disk. Figure 13 shows
```

Because RAM is volatile, it is important to create an image of the contents of RAM post haste if it is suspected that evidence resides therein. The likelihood of the operating system overwriting a file in RAM increases as time passes. First responders should process the most volatile evidence first, including RAM, followed by less volatile evidence such as floppy disks, CD and DVDs.

Creating a forensic image of RAM involves working with a live system. The very fact that investigators work with a live system means that he or she is changing the suspect media, which is contradictory to good computer forensics practice. However, in some circumstances (e.g., evidence in RAM), the investigator must work outside the scope of these general rules in order to pursue the evidence. Forensic procedures for working with live systems are not as "hard and fast" as those for working on media that has been powered down and may depend heavily on the individual circumstances of the investigation/case.

Trace Evidence in the Swap and Hibernation Files

When a computer's RAM is full and the operating system must allocate memory for an application, the operating system makes room in RAM by writing out part of its contents to a temporary scratchpad called a "swap file." A swap file is simply dedicated space on a hard drive whose contents are temporary and overwritten as needed. Under Windows operating systems, swap files are usually located in the root directory. These files are named pagefile.sys in the most current versions of Windows operating systems (Windows NT, 2000, XP, and 2003) and win386.swp in older versions of Windows (3/3.1, 95, 98, and ME). Under Linux and UNIX systems, a single partition is devoted to the swap file and is usually labeled /swap. The swap file is essentially a scratchpad to hold data temporarily, and its contents are overwritten frequently.

Hibernation files are usually found on laptop computers, as opposed to on workstations or servers. The hibernation file holds the contents of RAM when the laptop is placed in hibernation mode. When a laptop is put into hibernation mode, the operating system writes out the contents of RAM to the hard drive and then puts the computer into a suspended state. When the laptop is "awakened," the previous contents of RAM are transferred back into RAM from the hibernation file, thus restoring the state of the computer.

Below we illustrate the procedure for searching for a file with the keyword "coke_buddy" in the hibernation file. The swap and hibernation files are locked while the operating system is running and therefore cannot be easily accessed under a live system. The safest way to access these files is by powering off the computer and rebooting using a forensic-capable boot disk such as Knoppix (http://www.knoppix.com) or FIRE (Forensic Incident Response Environment, (http://www.sourceforge.net/projects/biatchux).

```
# strings /mnt/hda1/hiberfil.sys
| grep -ian -C 5 `coke_buddy'
```

Hibernation files contain both binary and human-readable text. We run the *hiberfil.sys* file through the UNIX *strings* command to recover the human readable text, and pipe the results to the UNIX *grep* command, a powerful search utility. The flags "–ian" indicate that we want a case insensitive search (-i), to treat the input as text (-a), and display line number associated with the results (-n). The flag "–C 5" indicates that we want five lines of 'context' both before and after each hit. The listing below shows that our keyword was found in the hibernation file.

```
# strings /mnt/hda1/hiberfil.sys
| grep -ian -C 3 `coke_buddy'
1048197-x
1048198-knowX
1048199-ard dri
1048200 : coke_buddy
1048201- UNICodE fo
1048202-rmat; howeverJ
1048203-to deter
```

An examiner can search swap and hibernation files for a particular type of file, such as a graphics file, by searching for the headers and footers associated with the particular type of file. For example, a JPEG graphic file begins with the hex expression "D8 FF D8" in the header and ends with "FF D9." An examiner could recover a JPEG file by extracting the content between the header and footer. (See Craiger [2005] in this volume to see how to accomplish this with the UNIX *dd* command.)

Trace Evidence in Unallocated Space

Hard-drive space can be partitioned into two primary types of space: allocated and unallocated space. Allocated space holds active files, that is, files that can be accessed by the file system and operating system. These files contain a pointer in the file system's "table of contents" (for example, a FAT root directory, an NTFS master file table, or UNIX EXT2 superblock). When a user deletes a file, the operating system marks the file's entry in the table of contents as reusable. Thereafter, the contents of the deleted file are in unallocated space (i.e., space not reserved for a file). Although the information is still on the disk, the contents of unallocated space are not directly accessible by the normal computer user.

Removal software writes a series of characters over a file, making it difficult to recover its contents; however, many software applications will leave trace evidence; that is, they may leave all or part of the contents of the file that are separate from the location of the original file with which a user (suspect) worked. For example, when a suspect modifies a file, many applications write copies of the file to the hard drive. These copies, called temporary files, are intended to help applications recover the file's contents when there is an abnormal termination of the application or operating system.

Within Microsoft Word, each time a document is saved through the key combination [CTRL-S], the application writes a temporary file to the hard drive. Figure 11 shows temporary files that were written to the hard drive while we were modifying this chapter. The fact that an application writes a temporary copy of the file to the hard drive is not obvious to the average computer user. For many applications, temporary files are written to the /TEMP or /TMP directory under Windows, although the location where the temporary files are written is customizable by a technically knowledgeable computer user.

When the user closes a file, the application silently removes the temporary files from the hard drive. The temporary files' contents, however, will remain in unallocated space until overwritten.

A forensics examiner can access the contents of unallocated space by either (a) making a forensic image of the media and performing a physical analysis on the image or (b) booting the suspect's computer with a bootable forensic disk and performing a physical analysis at the device level. The latter is typically performed with a Linux bootable disk.

Figure 12 shows a search of the physical hard drive for the term 'coke_buddy.' Because we are accessing the physical hard drive, we are searching both allocated and unallocated space. This means that our search will normally find instances of the keywords in deleted files as well as in active files; however, because we previously "wiped" our copy of the chapter from our hard drive, our keyword search should only return results from unallocated space.

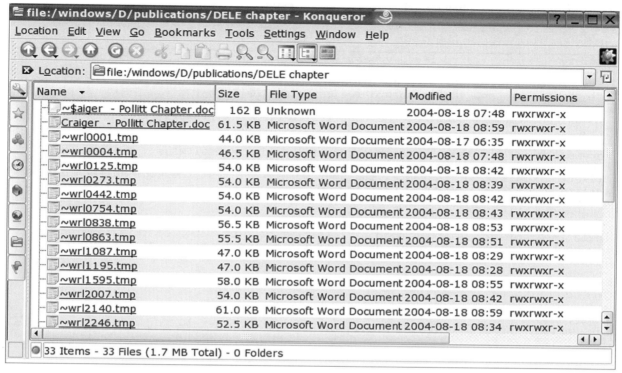

Figure 11: Temporary files.

We must access the entire physical partition to search for keywords in unallocated space. If we mount the partition, we will only be able to access files in allocated space. We access the entire physical partition through Linux' device file /dev/hda1. (See Craiger, 2005, this volume for more information on Linux file systems.). /dev/hda1 corresponds to the first partition of the first IDE hard drive, which contains our Windows operating system. We use the *dd* command to read the file, piping it through the *strings* command to extract human-readable strings. We use *grep* to search through the all the strings on our physical partition.

Figure 12 shows the first three instances of our keyword. From this we can conclude that at least one document contained this keyword.

Thus far, we have only searched for the keyword in 7-bit ASCII format, the default for the *grep* utility. Any instance of our keyword in any other format, such as 16-bit UNICODE, will not be found. We must conduct another search and specify that *grep* search for UNICODE (16-bit little endian) instances of our keyword, which we specify with the flags −e1. The results appear in the listing below: On our 37 GB hard drive, there were 50 occurrences of the term 'coke_buddy' in UNICODE format.

Where did all of these occurrences of our keyword come from? The simple answer is from the temporary files. Again, the contents of these files will remain on the media until overwritten, or until the user runs a file wiping software to wipe the contents of unallocated space.

Summary

This section demonstrates that forensic countermeasures such as file wiping may or may not have the intended effect of removing all traces of a file. The less technically sophisticated the user, the less likely it is that they fully understand the file system and operating system characteristics necessary to configure file-wiping software to perform correctly. On the other hand, technically sophisticated users often have the knowledge to remove all traces of a file; thus, it is helpful to obtain background information on the user's technical sophistication before performing a forensic examination.

Many evidence-elimination tools provide the capability to wipe swap files, hibernation files, and unallocated space. In this instance, the techniques described will not be effective. Nevertheless, the forensic examiner should thoroughly analyze all of the files described when working with evidence on which evidence removal software may have been used.

```
# dd if=/dev/hda1 | strings -e l | grep -ic `coke_buddy'
71683856+0 records in
50
71683856+0 records in
36702134272 bytes transferred in 1163.48693 seconds (3154494 bytes/sec)
```

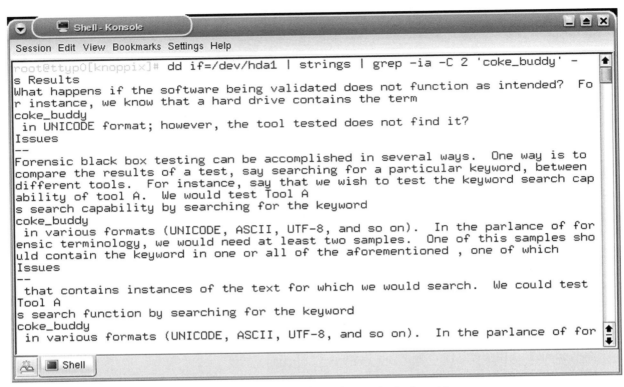

```
root@ttyp0[knoppix]# dd if=/dev/hda1 | strings | grep -ia -C 2 'coke_buddy' -
s Results
What happens if the software being validated does not function as intended?  Fo
r instance, we know that a hard drive contains the term
coke_buddy
 in UNICODE format; however, the tool tested does not find it?
Issues
--
Forensic black box testing can be accomplished in several ways.  One way is to
compare the results of a test, say searching for a particular keyword, between
different tools.  For instance, say that we wish to test the keyword search cap
ability of tool A.  We would test Tool A
s search capability by searching for the keyword
coke_buddy
 in various formats (UNICODE, ASCII, UTF-8, and so on).  In the parlance of for
ensic terminology, we would need at least two samples.  One of this samples sho
uld contain the keyword in one or all of the aforementioned , one of which
Issues
--
 that contains instances of the text for which we would search.  We could test
Tool A
s search function by searching for the keyword
coke_buddy
 in various formats (UNICODE, ASCII, UTF-8, and so on).  In the parlance of for
```

Figure 12: Keyword search results on physical partition.

DIGITAL EVIDENCE: GROWING IN VOLUME AND DIVERSITY

The amount of evidence that exists in digital form is growing rapidly. This growth is demonstrated in Table 5, which was presented by the Federal Bureau of Investigation at the 14th INTERPOL Forensic Science Symposium:

Table 5 Digital Evidence Growth

FBI CART Examinations
Caseload:
FY '99 - 2084 cases
FY '00 - 3591 cases
FY '01 - 5166 cases
FY '02 - 5924 cases
FY '03 - 6546 cases
Data Burden:
FY '99 - 17 terabytes
FY '00 - 39 terabytes
FY '01 - 119 terabytes
FY '02 - 358 terabytes
FY '03 - 782 terabytes

Source: FBI Computer Analysis & Response Team (CART)

The Computer Analysis Response Team (CART) is the FBI's computer forensic unit and is primarily responsible for conducting forensic examinations of all types of digital hardware and media. The data above represents two metrics of the unit's activity. A "case," as used in this chart, represents a submission of evidence to the unit. A case may be a single floppy disk or several hundred computers and a multi-terabyte database. The data burden represents the total capacity of digital media examined by CART. Because the FBI is somewhat unique as a law enforcement agency, its broad jurisdiction makes it useful as an indicator of investigative activity.

While the number of cases increased threefold in the past three years, the volume of data increased by 46 times during the same period! This is a staggering number, given that it is many times the volume of data in the Library of Congress, the largest library on Earth (Jesdanan, 2004). Given the declining prices of digital storage media and the corresponding increases in sales of storage devices, the volume of digital information that investigators must deal with is likely to continue its meteoric increase.

CNET News published a report on March 5, 2004, which described the over $12 billion business growing at a rate of more than 5%, while the cost per megabyte of storage fell by 30%. (http://news.com.com/2100-1015_3-5170267.html?tag=fd_nbs_ent). This tremendous increase in data presents a number of problems for law enforcement.

Traditionally, law enforcement has seized all storage media, duplicated it, and then conducted their examination of the data on the duplicated copy. One of the first steps in the examination process is to recover latent data such as deleted files, hidden data and fragments from unallocated file space. This process is called *data recovery* and requires processing every byte of any given piece of media. Compounding these problems are the practices of providing the defendant with a copy of the data and retaining the data for the length of the defendant's sentence.

If this methodology continues, the growing amounts and types of digital media will push budgets, processing capability and physical storage space to their limits. Compounding these problems are the practices of providing the defendant with a copy of the data and retaining the data for the length of the defendant's sentence.

Consequences for Law Enforcement

As Table 5 shows, the number of FBI cases has tripled in just 5 years. This is the result of the increased presence of digital devices at crime scenes combined with a heightened awareness of digital evidence by investigators. The FBI has indicated that digital evidence has spread from a few types of investigations, such as hacking and child pornography, to virtually every investigative classification, including fraud, extortion, homicide, identity theft, and so on.

With this increasing prevalence of digital evidence, it is likely that a majority of all criminal investigations will involve digital evidence, and in fact, we may have already reached this point. The chief executive of the British Library estimated in 2002, that each year 250 megabytes of information was created for each person on the planet (http://www.researchinformation.info/rispring03data.html). The growth of digital evidence causes three related problems. First, anyone involved in conducting criminal investigation will need to be able to recognize digital evidence. While this may seem fairly straightforward, it is not. As we will discuss later in this chapter that there is a growing diversity of digital tools and toys that can hold digital evidence, and it will not always be obvious to an investigator that these small digital objects may hold the key to a crime.

The second problem is that investigators must seize and process this evidence. Again, while this may seem straightforward for a single computer with an 80 GB hard drive, the problem is much more complicated by what law enforcement now encountering: Crime scenes with several networked computers each of which may contain a 200+ GB hard drives, and several hundred DVDs. The average 40 hour forensic examination for an 80 GB hard drive will soon require several months (or years) to process all of the digital evidence from new crime scenes. The implications in terms of increased budgets for law enforcement personnel, training, hardware, and software are clear.

Finally, the ubiquity of digital evidence will require that every agency will require access to digital forensic examination services. No longer will the small law enforcement agency be able to send their digital evidence to state or federal agencies because these agencies will be overwhelmed with their own case work. Smaller law enforcement agencies must find ways of coping with this requirement.

Solutions for Data Reduction

A simple solution to these problems is not evident, but several factors may reduce the impact of data expansion.

The most obvious is that only the specific data needed to prove guilt or innocence need be seized. Seized evidence can be further processed to reduce the amount of data which must be examined and analyzed. Forensic examiners call this data reduction.

There are a number of approaches to data reduction, each of which has advantages and weaknesses. Some of these techniques involve eliminating information based upon factors such as where the data is found in the file system, the type of data, the header information, and whether the file matches a database of known digital signatures. Once the data has been reduced on the basis of its intrinsic characteristics, it can more efficiently be searched for the content of the data.

A method currently used for data reduction involves performing a hash analysis against digital evidence. A cryptographic one-way hash (or "hash" for short) is essentially a digital fingerprint: a very large number that uniquely identifies the content of a digital file. Figure 13 displays the hashes for several files. On the left are the names of the files, and on the right, under the heading "Hash" are the 128-bit (MD5) hashes. A hash is uniquely determined by the contents of a file. Therefore, two files with different name but the exact same contents will produce the same hash. This is demonstrated in Figure 13 as "orlando.txt" is a copy of "forensic.pdf," but simply renamed. Note that they result in the same hash.

After hashing the file "CET4932.doc" we added a single space and then attempted to verify the file. As Figure 13 shows an error was generated, indicating the contents of the file have changed.

The larger the number of bits produced by a cryptographic hash algorithm, the smaller the likelihood of a collision. A collision occurs when two files with different contents result in the same hash. Even with the 128-bit MD5 hash the likelihood of a collision are astronomically small, although some researchers have been able to demonstrate the possibility. In practice we have never observed a collision. Nevertheless, to further reduce the possibility of collisions NIST developed the SHA-1 (secure hash algorithm revision 1) hash algorithm that comes in 160-, 192-, and 256-bit versions. The difference in the amount of time required to calculate an MD5 versus SHA-1 is negligible with fast computers, consequently, we suggest using the 160-bit SHA-1 as a minimum.

NIST produces a set of hash sets called the National Software Reference Library that contains hashes for approximately 7 million files as of 2004 (www.nsrl.nist.gov). Files in a hash set typically fall into one of two categories. *Known* files are known to be "ok," and can typically be ignored, such as system files such as win.exe, explore.exe, etc. *Notable* files are suspicious files that are flagged for further scrutiny; files that have been identified as illegal or inappropriate, such as hacking tools, pictures of child pornography, and so on. A hash analysis automates the process of distinguishing between files that can be ignored while identifying the files known to be of possible evidentiary value. Once the known files have been identified then these files can be filtered. Filtering out the known files may reduce the number of files the investigator must evaluate by half or more. NSRL contains MD5 as well as SHA-1 hashes for each file.

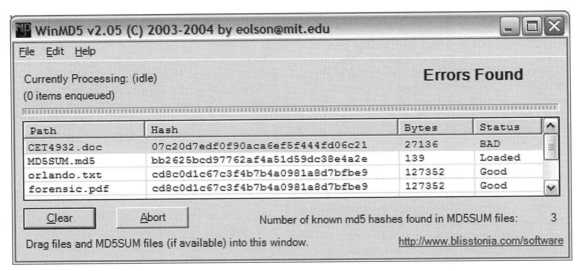

Figure 13: MD5 Cryptographic one-way hashes.

Once the data reduction process has been completed, individual data objects could be digitally signed to ensure reliability, and only contentious objects retained for court purposes. An additional approach is to make these data objects available virtually to reduce the number of physical copies needed for review and testimony.

Using Technology to Cope

The FBI's Regional Computer Forensic Laboratory in Dallas, Texas, developed a number of innovative techniques in order to deal with the massive amounts of data seized as a result of the September 11, 2001, attacks.

One of the first techniques was to utilize commercially available network attached storage devices (NAS). At first, these devices were used to store file system images from multiple computers that were being imaged simultaneously. It did not take long to realize that the bandwidth of these devices was not up to the task, and imaging took longer than with dedicated devices. Another technique was to use these NAS devices as repository for logical copies of multiple computers. In this way, a single examination process such as a string search could be performed against multiple evidence items simultaneously. Since the processing was being done by examiner workstations that were connected over a network, bandwidth was still an issue. Another issue was that the NAS's internal operating systems did not always deal with file modification times, access times, and creation (MAC) times in a way consistent with the operating system used in the original evidence. This presented some serious issues with analytical reliability.

The primary problems with this approach can be categorized as either bandwidth issues or data reliability issues.

Despite these issues, the use of mass storage was crucial to the rapid analysis of the 9-11 data and showed tremendous promise for future improvements in forensic examination techniques. To solve the bandwidth problem, the RCFL developed the use of fibre channel architecture to connect the examination and imaging machines to the mass storage device. Utilizing this technology, bandwidth was increased from network speeds to hardware speeds. This went a long way toward speeding up the process, but in order to allow multiple examiners to use this system concurrently, it required very expensive fibre channel switches and huge quantities of storage. To support up to 24 examiners simultaneously while processing terabytes of data, few other options existed.

The mass storage solution developed by the RCFL utilized a commercially available Storage Attached Network solution (SAN). This solution not only allowed for on-the-fly configuration of virtual drives, rapid access and redundancy but also for central management and backup. The combination of the two technologies has proven to be revolutionary.

An additional benefit to the SAN/fibre channel solution has been the ability to create virtual drives for investigator/attorney review. A drive containing the examination product can be created on the SAN, permissions can be set to prevent write access, and the drive made available over a network, where access is controlled and logged. The review of examination results over a network was pioneered by the Colorado Regional Computer Forensic Laboratory, and was further refined by the Dallas laboratory.

One might well ask why we should be interested in this very high-end process that is far more expensive than many organizations can afford. Experience has shown that the problems faced by very large Federal entities such as the FBI, IRS, and Department of Defense push the envelope of technology. The solutions developed by these organizations often can be adapted, in less expensive ways, to other organizations. Because today's "bleeding edge" technology becomes tomorrow's everyday tools, it is useful to recognize the lessons being learned every day by these large agencies. History has shown that the problems faced by these agencies tend to migrate downward and become problems for smaller organizations.

The Explosion of Diverse Digital Media

Volume of data is not the only growing challenge facing forensic investigators. The increasing diversity of storage objects and data formats can also present formidable problems to law enforcement These challenges include recognizing new media, obtaining technology to read new objects and formats, and developing the expertise to forensically examine each new format.

Technology product life cycles are short, but criminal investigations and prosecutions often take a number of years. Likewise, law enforcement training cycles are usually measured in years. As a result, investigators and forensic examiners must have the training and equipment to deal with several generations of technology.

As this chapter is being written, the epitaph for floppy disks is also being written (Niesse, 2004); however, there are likely millions of floppy disks sitting in evidence rooms around the world that investigators will need to access and examine for years to come. Likewise, large amounts of data storage are being added to an increasing variety of everyday objects. This presents in increase in the number of sites in which probative evidence may be found and often leads to multiple redundant sources of the same data. Because redundant/related evidence may be present in multiple locations such as desktop computers, laptop computers, phones, and PDAs, there are advantages to adopting a "case-focused" examination of all collected evidence, as opposed to a "media-centric" examination in which each piece of media is examined separately.

Along with the proliferation of devices incorporating digital storage capacity, the variety of storage formats has increased. An example of this is found in the portable music devices that contain miniature hard drives and flash memory. While sharing a common purpose, each supports a variety of storage formats, many of which are proprietary.

From a forensic perspective, the examiner needs to understand each of these formats and must have hardware and software capable of examining each type. The challenges presented by the growing myriad of digital devices are only exacerbated by the fact that these devices now hold a quantity of information that would have unimaginable only a few years ago.

While it may be obvious that a desktop computer's hard drive, laptop, CD, or floppy disk might hold evidence, there may be sources of digital evidence that may be overlooked by the first responder who has not been trained to identify digital devices. Common place devices that now hold digital files are ubiquitous. A new version of the Swiss army knife includes a USB data storage that can hold 256MB of digital files. Similarly, there are several watches and pens that hold 256MB of digital files. It is not clear from simple observation that these simple, common devices have a dual purpose.

The simplest and most cost-effective solution for the problem of recognizing digital storage devices is continual, mandatory training. First responders and investigators must be trained to perform a thorough investigation of all elements at a crime scene, not matter how innocuous a device might seem. Our preferred solution to this problem would be a set of courses developed and maintained by, or overseen by, a federal agency and provided in an online format such as a series of Web-based training courses. Law enforcement budgets have always been tight. Online courses would obviate the need for travel which is always costly.

The growth in size and diversity of data storage is a continuing problem that will not likely disappear soon. The challenges associated with this growth are likely to become more even problematic over time, as digital data becomes more ingrained into the fabric of everyday life. These challenges will necessitate organizational, training, financial, and operational evolution if law enforcement is to provide competent and timely service in the coming years.

A LAW ENFORCEMENT VIEW OF THE FUTURE OF DIGITAL EVIDENCE

The volume and pervasiveness of digital evidence will force law enforcement to adapt in a wide variety of ways. The current volume overwhelms the currently deployed resources, as volume increases substantial new resources will be needed. Additional people with significantly higher levels of education and training will be required to manage and process the growing amounts of digital evidence. New hardware and software tools will be needed to more efficiently process the increased volume of evidence. But the increase in pervasiveness will affect a much broader range of issues in law enforcement.

Today, digital evidence is collected in only a fraction of cases. As more of our lives are spent and recorded online, law enforcement will have to provide for the collection and preservation of digital evidence in virtually every case. As more and more of law enforcement's activities are digitized, from computer-aided dispatch systems, digital booking systems, and even digital video cameras in patrol cars, policies and procedures will need to be adapted to ensure the integrity of these evidentiary records. In fact, the volume of internally and externally generated information will require agencies to not merely automate but rather to develop specialized law enforcement enterprise architectures. While law enforcement has been evolving from "high touch" to "high tech," that transition must go from bureaucratic sloth to Internet time.

The hardware and software tools used by law enforcement practitioners will have to evolve along with the available technology or rather beyond it. Keeping up with current technology trends is essentially impossible. Technology diffusion in society can take years, and law enforcement, being conservative in nature, is typically slow to embrace the latest and greatest in technology. Although public agencies may not be able to "get ahead of the curve," the creative use of cutting edge technologies can provide significant leverage. For instance, there is a growing trend, exemplified at the Dallas Regional Computer Forensic Labs, to the use of aggregated storage coupled with very fast input/output channels to create storage area networks (SANs). This is an example of leveraging human and technical resources in ways that individual agencies cannot.

Forensic software will have to evolve as well. Currently, virtually all of the forensic software focuses on the documentation and data recovery aspects of the examination. What few tools, such as filters for header information or text string search tools, are in use are designed with the notion of answering the question: "Is it there?" rather than "What do we know about the information contained in this digital evidence." Consequently, more research is needed that assists law enforcement deal with the deluge of information they are facing. One of the current research trends is to use data mining techniques to assist law enforcement in identifying evidence from terabytes of data. Data mining uses statistical, clustering, or artificial intelligence techniques to reduce large volumes of data to a manageable size, by identifying patterns among the individual data elements.

Another change that will significantly impact law enforcement is the increase of network-connected devices. As our phones, computers, entertainment devices, and household appliances become connected, we will have many more sources of digital evidence to integrate into a given investigation. Further, networked communications, which has expanded from text e-mail into video, audio, and rich-text forms easily and quickly sent and received from a wide variety of devices, will require the largely "static" evidence focus to expand substantially into the dynamic collection of data in transit. This change will have both technical and legal implications. Law enforcement's technical capability to collect, preserve, process, and analyze intercepted dynamic data is generally primitive and very labor intensive. New tools and processes will have to be developed if the large proportion of data is transient. The current legal schema for collecting communications evidence, despite being updated in 2001 with the USA Patriot Act, essentially is modeled on a 1960's notion of communication. The Patriot Act's mechanics are so onerous that it is used only in situations which can justify the huge overhead of the application process, the live monitoring and minimization, court reporting and notice requirements. If this process is not streamlined, then a very high proportion of the available evidence will not be collected.

GLOSSARY

Code walkthrough analysis of source code by programmers and managers for quality assurance purposes.

Data recovery Finding latent information and restoring its context.

Data reduction Eliminating data that is not significant.

Digital evidence Information of probative value stored or transmitted in digital form.

Duplicate digital evidence An accurate digital reproduction of all data objects contained on an original physical item (see forensic image).

Forensic image An exact, bit-for-bit copy of media.

Hash Also known as a message digest, cryptographic hash, or one-way hash. A hash is a hex value, typically 128- or 160-bit, that is unique to the contents of a file.

MD5 hash A 128-bit cryptographic hash algorithm created Ron Rivest of MIT.

Metadata A file's metadata consists of all information about the file excluding its contents: file name, size, MAC times, starting cluster, permissions, attributes, etc.

Original data evidence Physical items and the data objects associated with such items at the time of acquisition or seizure.

Physical evidence Items on which data objects of information may be stored and/or through which data objects are transferred.

Regression testing Testing performed to find bugs in software applications or modules after new code is added.

SHA-1 hash the Secure Hash Algorithm version 1, a 160-bit cryptographic hash developed by the National Institute for Science and Technology.

Unallocated space the clusters not in use by a file. Where deleted files reside.

CROSS REFERENCES

See *Computer Forensic Procedures and Methods; Cyberterrorism and Information Security; Digital Courts, the Law and Evidence; Digital Evidence; Digital Watermarking and Steganography; Encryption Basics.*

REFERENCES

Brezinski, D., & Killalea, T. (2001). RFC 3227: Guidelines for Evidence Collection and Archiving. ftp://ftp.isi.edu/in-notes/rfc3227.txt

Craiger, J. P. (2005). Computer forensics procedures and methods. In H. Bidgoli (Ed.), *Handbook of Information Security*. New York: John Wiley & Sons.

Federal Guidelines for Searching and Seizing Computers, U.S. Deptarment of Justice. http://www.usdoj.gov/criminal/cybercrime/searching.html

Grundy, B. (2004). *The Law Enforcement and Forensic Examiner Introduction to Linux: A Beginner's Guide.* Available at www.linux-forensics.com

National Institute of Justice. (2002). *Electronic Crime Scene Investigation: A Guide for First Responders*, NCJ 187736, 2001. http://www.ncjrs.org/pdffiles1/nij/187736.pdf

INTERPOL. (2004). *"Proceedings of the 14th INTERPOL Forensic Science Symposium,"* Lyon, France.

Jesdanun, A. *"Mars Internet downloads exceed volume of Library of Congress,"* Detroit News, January 10, 2004. available at: http://www.detnews.com/2004/technology/0401/12/technology-31652.htm

National Institute of Justice. (2004). *Forensic Examination of Digital Evidence: A Guide for Law Enforcement*, NCJ 199408. http://puborder.ncjrs.org/Content/ItemDetails.asp?strItem=NCJ+199408&intCounter=1

Niesse, M. Floppy Disk Becoming Relic of the Past, Tallahassee Democrat, September 6, 2004. Available at http://www.tallahassee.com/mld/tallahassee/business/9595612.htm

Noblett, M. G., Pollitt, M. M., & Presley, L. A. (Octobner, 2000). Recovering and examining computer forensic evidence. *Forensic Science Communications*. Volume 2 Number 4.

Special Working Group on Digital Evidence. (April 2000). Digital evidence: Standards and principles. *Forensic Science Communications*, 2(2).

Special Working Group on Digital Evidence (SWGDE). www.swgde.org

FURTHER READING

Britz, M. T., (2003). *Computer Forensics and Cyber Crime: An Introduction*. Prentice Hall.

Caloyannides, M. A. (2001). *Computer Forensics and Privacy*. Artech House Publishers.

Carrier, B. (2005). *File system forensic analysis*. New York: Addison-Wesley.

Carvey, H. (2004). *Windows Forensics and Incident Recovery*. Addison-Wesley Professional.

Casey, E. (2001). *Handbook of computer crime investigation: Forensic tools & technology*. Academic Press.

Casey, E. (2003). Practical approaches to recovering encrypted digital evidence. *International Journal of Digital Evidence, 3,* 1–26.

Casey, E. (2004). *Digital evidence and computer crime*. New York: Academic Press.

Cole, E. (2003). *Hiding in plain sight: steganography and the art of covert communication*. New York: John Wiley & Sons.

Craiger, J. P. (2005). Recovering digital evidence from Linux Systems. To appear in S. Shenoi (Ed.), *Advances in Digital Forensics*. International Federation of Information Professionals.

Farmer, D., & Venema, W. (2005). *Forensic discovery*. New York: Addison Wesley Professional.

Hinder, D. L., & Tittel, E. (2002). Scene of the cybercrime: Computer forensics handbook. Syngress.

Johnson, N. F., & Jajodia, S. (1998). Steganalysis of images created using current steganography software. *Lecture Notes in Computer Science, 1525,* 273–289.

Jones, K., Shema, M., & Johnson, B. (2002). *Anti-hacker tool kit*. McGraw-Hill: Osborne Media.

Kruse, W. G., & Heiser, J. G. (2001). *Computer forensics: incident response essentials*. Addison-Wesley Professional.

Menezes, A. J., Van Oorschot, P. C., & Vanstone, S. A. (1996). *Handbook of applied cryptography*. New York: CRC Press.

Mohay, G., Anderson, A., Collie, B., & Olivier, R. (2003). *Computer and intrusion forensics*. Artech House.

Network Associates, Inc. (1999). *Introduction to cryptography*. Network Associates Press. (Download from: http://www.pgp.com/resources/whitepapers).

Parker, D. (1998). *Fighting computer crime : A new framework for protecting information*. Wiley

Prosise, C., Mandia, K., & Pepe, M. (2003). *Incident response and computer forensics*. McGraw-Hill Osborne Media.

Sammes, T., & Jenkinson, B. (2000). *Forensic Computing: A Practitioner's Guide*. Springer-Verlag.

Schneier, B. (1995). *Applied cryptography*. New York: John Wiley & Sons.

Vacca, J. R. (2002). *Computer forensics: Computer crime scene investigation*. Charles River Media.

Wayner, P. (2002). *Disappearing cryptography information hiding: steganography and watermarking*. San Francisco: Morgan Kaufmann.

Forensic Computing

Mohamed Hamdi, *National Digital Certification Agency, Tunisia*
Noureddine Boudriga, *National Digital Certification Agency and University of Carthage, Tunisia*
M. S. Obaidat, *Monmouth University*

INTRODUCTION AND FOUNDATIONS OF COMPUTER FORENSICS

In this section, we present the main concepts, background information, and foundations of computer forensics.

Definition

In 2001, computer forensics was defined as "the use of scientifically derived and proved methods toward the preservation, collection, validation, identification, analysis, interpretation, documentation, and presentation of digital evidence derived from digital sources for the purpose of facilitation or furthering the reconstruction of events found to be criminal, or helping to anticipate unauthorized actions shown to be disrupted to planned operations" (Digital Forensics Research Workshop, 2001). Computers can be used to steal private information, tarnish the reputation of organizations or individuals, rob money, or even brag about the technical capabilities of attackers. Moreover, cyberattackers can use technology to exchange electronic messages to coordinate their actions or to hide prohibited secret information.

The core of digital forensics is to gather evidence and to analyze it to apprehend attackers. To build a strong link between the evidence and the attacker, the investigator should possess sufficient skills. Also, he or she must have enough knowledge about the legal framework or the internal security policies, depending on the nature of the digital crime.

Computer Forensic Process

Despite the abundant research activity related to digital forensic models, the tasks constituting the forensic process have not been standardized yet. Many of the proposed guidelines are specific to several technologies or systems and are not yet open enough to be applied to various kinds of digital attacks. For example, the model proposed by Farmer and Venema (1999), which forms the kernel of the well-known Coroner's Toolkit is specific to UNIX systems. In 2001, the U.S. Department of Justice (DoJ) presented a four-step model (National Institute of Justice, 2001), including "collection, examination, analysis, and reporting." In 2001, the Digital Forensics Research Workshop introduced three extra phases ("identification," "preservation," and "decision") making the framework more appropriate to computer forensics. In fact, the DoJ model does not take into account some particular characteristics of this field. Identification, for instance, becomes more complex in the case of digital forensics because of the huge volume of available data that may need to be analyzed. This model was then enhanced by Reith, Carr, and Gunsh (2002), who added some ideas derived from traditional FBI forensics procedures (FBI, 2002). Recently, Rowlingson (2004) proposed a 10-step process that guarantees evidence readiness (i.e., the evidence is accessible when it is required to support a legal process) (Tan, 2001). These approaches are, in essence, similar. The slight differences between them reside in several details. Effectively, the computer forensic process should be flask to support most of the concrete cases. For instance, the identification step should not be performed if the digital evidence is used as an alibi.

In the following, the most important steps that are shared by the aforementioned models are discussed. More precisely, evidence collection, preservation, and analysis, as well as intention inference, will be focused on.

The first task is to locate and identify useful evidence. To this end, the investigator should seize the various hardware that may contain relevant information. Unfortunately, this is not always possible to perform. Meanwhile, computers, hard disks, or CD-ROMs can be seized; local area networks (LANs) and communications infrastructures, which can hold key elements, are difficult or even impossible to seize for evidence purposes. Moreover, the complexity of evidence collection depends heavily on the cleverness of the attacker. For instance, the use of encryption scrubbing tools makes evidence harder to reach.

Once gathered, the evidence has to be correctly maintained to prevent it from being totally or partially lost. In fact, the attacker may try to get back the hardware evidence to avoid being caught. He or she can also delete or alter digital information that constitutes a proof against him or her. Thus, evidence integrity is a key factor that should be considered to guarantee admissibility if needed (Stephenson, 2003).

The two last steps are crucial to have a sound interpretation of the collected information. The time, techniques, or location of attack's source, to name just a few, are elements that can help the forensic analyst in his or her task. Just like traditional crimes, profiles can be built to characterize criminals. Evidence analysis and suspect intention inference are so close that they could be merged in the same step. Their separation comes from the fact that different skills are needed for different tasks. Evidence analysis involves a deep context-specific scientific knowledge, whereas behavior modeling can be used through the use of traditional techniques.

A key feature of digital forensics is that the quantity of gathered information can be so big that it becomes hard to analyze. For example, visualizing the content of five megabytes of electronic documents or log files could not be done manually. To this end, various automated tools can assist investigators to accelerate the search of digital evidence or to conduct an inference-based reasoning to analyze the attack. These topics are more thoroughly discussed below.

It is noteworthy to point out that the cost estimation, which is of great importance, was somewhat absent from the cited forensic models even though Wolfe-Wilson and Wolfe (2003) established several links between the forensic activity and the business continuity plan or the incident response plan. Before beginning to conduct the investigation, the criminologists should quantify the estimated cost of the process in terms of effort, money, and time. Adding this phase has two benefits. First, it helps investigators decide whether it is beneficial to conduct the investigation. Second, it constitutes a reliable basis to schedule the various activities so that a maximum level of efficiency is reached.

Computer Evidence Requirements

To recognize digital evidence as legal proof to indict or to discharge a suspect, it has to conform to several requirements. In particular, the evidence should not be altered, and examination results should be accurate, verifiable, and repeatable. However, the most crucial requirement an investigation should fulfill is authenticity, that is, to demonstrate that a given (hardware or software) piece of evidence is effectively related to the suspect. For example, to link data on a computer to individuals, the investigator can use access control logs, cryptographic-based authentication, or biometric features. Conversely, to prove malicious network activity, he or she can rely on IP addresses, passwords, or digital certificates. A reoccurring problem at this stage is to consider the case where an alibi is investigated. In fact, the reliability of the evidence, especially time and location, is the main issue to prove in such cases. Another issue is that pieces of evidence should be admissible, meaning that they should be acceptable legally. This assumes that the investigator must be aware of the legal framework.

Fitting these conditions assumes that different forensic operators rely on consistent methodologies and efficient tools at all the steps of the evidence management process. A basic consideration is to ensure that all the operations on digital evidence should be made by authorized persons and should be fully documented. Moreover, to identify, collect, and analyze pieces of evidence, several tools providing reliability and quality should be used. Disk editors and disk imaging tools may be used for disk forensics, whereas the use of log analysis tools and sniffers may be of interest to handle network evidence.

Several attempts to propose standard methodologies respecting the requirements discussed above have been made by governmental and international organizations. In its *Good Practice Guide for Computer Based Evidence*, the Association of Chief Police Officers (ACPO, 2003) defines four principles that have to be followed during an investigation process. These principles are given below (Association of Chief Police Officers, 2003):

- First Principle: No action taken by Police or their agents should change data held on a computer or other media, which may subsequently be relied on in Court.
- Second Principle: In exceptional circumstances where a person finds it necessary to access original data held on a target computer, that person must be competent to do so and to give evidence explaining the relevance and the implications of their actions.
- Third Principle: An audit trail or other record of all processes applied to computer-based evidence should be created and preserved. An independent third party should be able to examine those processes and achieve the same result.
- Fourth Principle: The Officer in charge of the case is responsible for ensuring that the law and these principles are adhered to. This applies to the possession of, and access to, information contained in a computer. They must be satisfied that anyone accessing the computer, or any use of a copying device, complies with these laws and principles.

It appears that the ACPO guideline relies on the fact that digital evidence has the same nature as traditional evidence. Therefore, it should be subject to the same rules and laws. Despite their popularity, the ACPO principles, in their current version have two major shortcuts. First, they do not guarantee some of the fundamental properties of digital evidence. For example, they are not sufficient to produce integrity because data in electronic format are intrinsically volatile and, thus, can disappear without user intervention. In other terms, the four principles are necessary, but not sufficient, to provide integrity. Another limit is that the ACPO guide is limited to the investigation of stand-alone computers. It does not address cases where a suspect performs a network attack.

Other standards have also been developed for the exchange of digital evidence between nations or to recommend preservation principles. Nonetheless, they have the same limitations as the ACPO guide because they have a too low technical detail level. Recently, the Internet Engineering Task Force (IETF) published a Request for Comments (RFC) dealing with digital evidence collection and archival (RFC 3227). In addition, Yasinsac and Manzano (2001) proposed a set of practical policies showing how to handle the digital evidence in such a way that the efficiency of the forensic process is improved.

DISK FORENSICS

When trying to retrieve data from a computer to search for pieces of evidence, the forensic examiner should possess the necessary knowledge to avoid losing inadvertently the evidence. Particularly, he or she should know exactly how data are managed inside a computer. In the following, a brief explanatory overview of the storage possibilities provided by computers is given. Then various techniques that are commonly used to hide and recover information are described. Finally, several problems that might be faced by the investigator are discussed.

Storing Data in Computers

Putting aside forensic-related issues, electronic data storage mechanisms follow two types: short-term memory and long-term memory. The former, which consists typically of the random access memory (RAM), has the virtue of being able to convey helpful information to the investigator such as logged users, the running processes, or files in use. The main factor of interest of this kind of memory is that most of its content is tightly related to the operating system (OS). However, it is unfortunately rarely advisable to explore the RAM during investigation as it is cleared out when the computer is switched off. Thus, for convenience of making use of this volatile memory, the elapsed time between the last doubtful activities and the instant where the investigator seizes and accesses the computer should be minimal. This constraint is emphasized by the fact that some critical information expires after 1 or 2 min. This makes recourse to this option very rare as it is conditioned by many events that are not easy to combine.

Long-term memories, which can take many forms (e.g., hard disks, floppies, tapes, and CDs), are commonly used to store personal information that has no direct relation with the machine state. Therefore, analyzing the hard disk of a machine under examination may reveal valuable information about attacker. Nevertheless, criminals are aware of this opportunity and they often try to obfuscate the situation by making their secret information inaccessible or by making it unreadable. Another possible use of long-term memory is to partially recover the

data included in the short-term memory to prevent it from being lost. This can be achieved, for example, by monitoring and logging particular actions on the system.

Hiding and Recovering Information from Hard Disks

As it has been pointed out in the foregoing discussion, hard disks constitute a primary source of digital evidence for the forensic analyst. Therefore, they should be handled carefully to gather as much information as possible. Primarily, the investigator should perform an image, or exact copy, of the hard disk using free disk controllers (on the same computer) or network connections (from other machines). Then, all the forensic operations will be carried out on this image to preserve the original data. Obviously, disk imaging differs from copying the content of a hard disk on another media using standard functionalities implemented in OSs. Practically, an image is a file from which an exact duplicate of a bit stream can be constructed. In other terms, an image is a bit-for-bit copy of a hard disk content. Therefore, disk imaging tools should follow several principles to guarantee this property (National Institute of Standards and Technologies, 2001). Nonetheless, there are no standard guidelines for building hard disk images because this operation is often affected by hazardous events, which are essentially related to the system attacker behavior. For example, prior to any other operation, a cryptographic hash function of the content should be computed to check whether the imaging has resulted in an exact duplicate. In addition, a virus scan must be applied to annihilate the effect of potential malicious codes that might have been left deliberately on the disk. This sequence might, in several cases, be inconsistent from a security point of view. If imaging is done before proceeding to virus detection, potential pieces of malicious code can propagate from the original hard disk (subjected to the digital forensic process) to the disk that will support the duplicate, which belongs to the investigation platform. The investigator's experience counts for most in similar cases. In fact, he or she should be aware of the different means the criminals may use to hide their data or actions.

A possible approach here is to act at the partitioning stage by marking several partitions as hidden or leaving unused spaces that can be filled through the use of specific disk editors. Another category of free sectors that can be exploited for illegal purposes consists in the unassigned sectors that are left between partitions. File systems, conversely, present other possibilities to the suspect as he or she may delete some files to recover them later. Effectively, several OSs do not thoroughly erase the sectors containing a deleted file but they mark them as possible to reallocate instead. Of course, the examiner may be asked to perform some more skillful tasks depending on the technical capabilities of the suspect (that could be estimated from his or her profile). In the following, two from the myriad of the hiding techniques that require a relatively high technical level are described.

When being manufactured, hard disks are checked for bad sectors. When a defective sector is found, one possibility is to mark it by setting the bit 0 of the sector flag to

1. Once performed, this operation denies access from the controller to the concerned sector. To avoid affecting the disk capacity, several controllers are able to format substitutive free sectors to replace the damaged ones. Then, the address value of a bad sector is substituted by the address of the newly affected sector. Attackers can use this process, called bad sector mapping, by making access requests to sectors containing incriminating information to other normal sectors. Thus, the content of the hidden sectors cannot be explored through the OS.

The second method for hiding data inside a hard disk stems from the incompatibility between the addressing structures of IDE/ATA hard disks and several BIOS programs. In fact, this makes an important number of physical sectors inaccessible by the execution of BIOS interruption operation. The solution that has been adopted by most of the computer manufacturers to attenuate this space loss is called translated disk geometry. It consists of finding the biggest integer n such that

$$\left\lfloor \frac{N^C_{IDE/ATA}}{2^n} \right\rfloor \leq 1024, \tag{1}$$

where $N^C_{IDE/ATA}$ is the number of cylinders of the IDE/ATA geometry and $\lfloor . \rfloor$ rounds a decimal to the nearest integer to less than or equal to it (also called the floor).

Thus, the number of cylinders considered by the BIOS, denoted N^C_{BIOS} is expressed as follows:

$$N^C_{BIOS} = \left\lfloor \frac{N^C_{IDE/ATA}}{2^n} \right\rfloor, \tag{2}$$

$$N^H_{BIOS} = N^H_{IDE/ATA} \times 2^n, \tag{3}$$

where $N^H_{IDE/ATA}$ refers to the number of headers of the IDE/ATA geometry.

A glance at this process shows that a number of sectors are still impossible to access by the BIOS because of the use of the rounding operator $\lfloor . \rfloor$. This fact can be exploited by attackers because the disk space that is presumed to be unusable for a BIOS may be recognized by other BIOS programs.

The fundamental limitation of the above techniques is that they are not general. For instance, even though the latter scheme, which is related to BIOS programs, gives a good location for searching for evidence, it cannot be applied to SCSI hard disks. Likewise, the analysis of a laptop may turn out to be somewhat unfeasible because of size constraints. The absence of free disk controllers or network interfaces worsens the situation further.

Cryptanalysis: Breaking Attackers' Ciphers and Codes

Ciphers and codes have been in use by attackers for centuries as such use has been reported by many historians and novelists. Cryptanalysis, which deals with unraveling encrypted secrets, has also arisen in parallel. It has become a key component of the digital forensic field as cryptography use by criminals is getting more and more extensive. Old forms of cryptography include the following:

- *Concealment cipher.* This means that the plaintext itself is transmitted after being hidden. Null cipher consists of making most of the letters of the message insignificant. One example would be to put the interesting letters at the end of each word of the transmitted sentence that makes no sense to its reader. Cryptanalysis of concealment writing relies on the examiner experience; no algorithm or mathematical framework has been proposed to this end.
- *Transposition cipher.* This is done by rearranging the letters making up the message according to a given pattern. The major weakness of this form is that it keeps letters' distribution unchangeable. As a result, most of the related cryptanalysis techniques involve frequency analysis.
- *Substitution cipher.* This replaces the original letters by others, which might have been taken from another alphabet. For this category, decryption is used by various methods suitable to their type. The telephone keypad cipher, for example, that is done by replacing digits by the letters corresponding to the telephone buttons can be broken through a combinatorial analysis of the letters. However, it often confuses the investigators, especially if all letters in the alphabet are used on the telephone keypad.

The techniques mentioned above are commonly used by attackers to exchange messages. Thus, the corresponding cryptanalysis methods (Gaines, 1956; Olson, 2000) are particularly applied to investigate e-mail box contents. To protect files on a computer, other techniques that rely mainly on number theory are rather used. They break into two categories: symmetric and asymmetric. They have strong mathematical foundations such as the discrete logarithm problem or elliptic curves. Possible ways to break these ciphers include the brute force attack, which is based on trying all possible key combinations. This is not always advisable to do because such operations may last too long if the key is sufficiently long. Consequently, other techniques should work better in most cases. In view of the fact that a basic assumption of many cryptographic algorithms is to choose large prime numbers, and knowing that designers must always fix a greater upper bound for these prime numbers to ensure an accepted execution time, the cryptanalyst can exploit subsequent weaknesses in the algorithms' implementations. For instance, he or she might try to factor large numbers (for systems like RSA or Rabin–Williams) or solve the discrete logarithm problem (to solve El Gamal ciphers or to break the Diffie–Hellman key exchange algorithm). Moreover, the examiner might exploit potential errors that the encryption party (i.e., the attacker) would have made at the key management level. For example, if the entropy associated to random number generators used at the key generation step is too low, then the keys can be regenerated based on certain knowledge about the original generation circumstances. In addition, having known a portion of a secret key may lead the investigator to recover the remaining part by using differential cryptanalysis.

Steganography and Digital Watermarking

Steganography, as opposed to cryptography, deals with concealing the existence of pieces of information instead of protecting them. Most of steganography schemes share the same principle consisting of embedding a secret message M in a harmless message C using a key K. In the steganography jargon, C and K are called cover object and stego key, respectively. It is worth mentioning that the structure of the message M is not modified, although the resulting message S will be transmitted over an insecure channel. The receiver can reconstruct the relevant message M knowing the embedding method used by the sender to combine M and Z. Next, several widely used steganongraphy applications are briefly discussed:

1. Covert channels: Possible weaknesses in OSs or network and security protocols can be exploited to convey information. For instance, some protocols of the open system interconnect (OSI) layered network model can allow finding excellent cover objects. The transmission control protocol (TCP) considers six reserved bits that can be used to transfer an important quantity of data with regard to the huge number of packets transmitted over normal communication channels. More related subtle methods can be found in Ahsan and Kundur (2002) and Hansel and Stanford (1996).

2. Subliminal channels in cryptographic algorithms: Cryptographic protocols, especially digital signature algorithms, can be used by cyberattackers to exchange hidden information. In Simmons (1993), it has been demonstrated that any digital signature scheme where b_0 bits are used to represent a digital signature that contains b_1 bits of protection (i.e., that will effectively be used by the verification algorithm) can contain subliminal channels if $b_0 > b_1$. When all of the $b_0 - b_1$ bits are used to convey hidden data, the subliminal channel is said to be broadband; otherwise, it is called narrowband.

3. Noise in digital communication infrastructures: Digital signals are often affected by noise and distortion that can be viewed as stochastic processes. Knowing the model of the statistical distribution of this noise, an attacker can code information to make it have the same distribution. In other terms, the hidden data would not be distinguished from noise. The simplest encoding method consists of substituting the redundant parts of a cover signal with portions of a secret message. Bitplane substitution is perhaps the most popular application in this context. It relies on replacing the least significant bit of each octet of data by a bit belonging to the hidden information. However, substitution schemes remain highly vulnerable to signal manipulations. For example, the application of a denoising algorithm would result in a definitive loss of the secret information. Thus, to improve its robustness, steganography can be applied in a transform domain rather than in the spatial domain. The discrete cosine transform (DCT), Laplace filtering, and the wavelet transform (WT) are examples of transforms that map a signal from a domain to another (e.g., from the time domain to the frequency domain), where the secret data is effectively combined with the cover signal. More sophisticated approaches such as spread spectrum techniques or distortion techniques can also be used to enhance the robustness of the steganographic process.

Different types of attacks against steganography applications can be considered, the most known are given below:

- Stego-only attack: Only the stego object resulting from the combination of the cover object and the secret message is known by the steganalyst.
- Known cover attack: Both of the cover object and the stego object are available.
- Known message attack: The secret message is known by the steganalyst who wants to analyze the embedding method.
- Chosen stego attack: The embedding method and the stego object are known.

The main concern of the forensic examiner is to detect and extract information embedded into cover objects. When a hard disk is seized, its content should be accurately scanned to look for hidden data. Steganalysis is the act of performing attacks against steganographic applications. Practically, many ways to defeat a steganalysis scheme exist. Choosing the convenient technique is never easy. In fact, investigators can perform steganalysis activities at different stages of the forensic process such as evidence identification and evidence analysis. In the sequel, steganalysis aspects related to both of these steps are detailed.

Identifying the sources of evidence is particularly important when the suspect is supposed to have used steganographic techniques. Unlike the other types of evidence, where the amount of data is the main problem faced at the identification level, stego objects are intrinsically hard to detect, making the related evidence difficult to access. Of course, this difficulty depends on the steganographic embedding scheme. Given a heterogeneous collection of digital information having belonged to a suspect (e.g., log files, documents, images, and e-mail messages), it is obvious that applying all steganalysis techniques to all of these data would be unfeasible. Hence, the security specialist should first know which pieces of information convey secret data. For example, to detect potential covert channels that rely on network protocols, filters can be built to check whether a packet flow conforms with TCP and Internet protocol (IP) specifications. In addition, when multimedia files are used as cover objects, selecting the steganalysis method is done according to the available information. One approach to detect hidden objects in hidden noisy images is to look for redundancies by applying a noise detection algorithm. This task is not as easy as it may seem as many cases have to be treated by the investigator. If the initial covermessage is available, the analysis should be based on a comparison between this cover image and the potential stego images. Conversely, if only the noise distribution model is known (chosen stego attack), the identification process should just highlight the images that contain such noisy components.

The second key issue when examining a piece of evidence from steganography angle is information extraction. Knowing that the relevant data reside in the least significant bit of each byte of an image (excepting the header bytes) does not necessarily lead to the evidence. The embedded message may be encrypted in addition to being hidden. Therefore, processing a stego object often involves activities related to other fields (e.g., cryptanalysis and intrusion detection). This shows the complexity of the evidence processing steps when steganalysis intervenes in the forensic process. Effectively, this requires a significant experience and a good technical knowledge from the forensic analyst.

IDENTIFYING THE SOURCE OF NETWORK ATTACKS

Up to this point, the problem of computer forensics has been addressed only for stand-alone machines. However, as networked systems are continuing to proliferate and given that attacks against these systems are becoming more and more frequent and sophisticated, the use of specific forensic techniques is necessary. These techniques should be specific so that the intrinsic features of computer network attacks can be taken into consideration.

Computer Network Attack Features

Introducing network protocols and applications in the computing environment opens many breaches that malicious entities are able to exploit. For instance, attackers can easily hide their identities because of the stateless nature of the existing routing protocols. Furthermore, the effect of an attack can propagate rapidly from a physical location to another through the use of means provided by communication infrastructure itself. Therefore, intrusion detection systems (IDSs) are not sufficient to solve the fundamental problems of network forensics. Basically, IDSs detect events that are correlated with attacks and can react in different ways (i.e., generating alarms, blocking connections). This is not sufficient when conducting an investigation process as the identity of the attacker has to be determined. This is often a complex task because intruders use stepping-stones and zombies when carrying out their attacks. More clever attackers may send their packets across encrypted links to make their identification more difficult.

Tracing anonymous attack flows is not the only issue the investigator should consider, but it is, by far, the most critical one. Besides, an important research effort should be directed toward identifying the source of attacks. Other activities such as evaluating the impact of an attack or studying its modus operandi have also to be performed within the frame of the forensic process. Assessing the damage resulting from an intrusion is particularly helpful to determine whether the investigation should be pursued or not on the basis of a cost–benefit balance. Of course, this assumes that an efficient cost model for computer

network forensics has been applied. In addition, a deep analysis of the attack technique may reveal useful information about the attacker as it will be demonstrated in the next section. In the remainder of this section, we focus on the trace-back problem as we believe it is a challenging issue.

Several solutions have been developed as an attempt to locate particular hosts in a specific network that are initiating network attacks. They are called source tracing systems. At this stage, it may seem to the reader that trace-back methods are not related to digital forensics. In fact, these methods have been seldom presented as forensic tools and they have been rather viewed as IDS components. Particularly, they confer reactivity to intrusion detection. Nevertheless, they remain efficient for postmortem analysis (i.e., after the occurrence of the attack).

Tracing methods can be divided into two classes: host-based methods and network-based methods. The former techniques consist of installing agents on each network host, whereas the latter use the network infrastructure to identify attack sources. A trivial shortcoming of host-based tracing is that it is no longer applicable if the attacker uses a host where the trace-back system is not installed. In other terms, such component has to be installed on each host, which is obviously an unrealistic assumption in an open environment such as the Internet. In the sequel, the study is restricted to network-based tracing approaches because they are more appropriate for modern networks that are, by nature, open. Several improvements and theoretical discussions of these methods have been proposed in the literature. However, because of space limitations, they are not presented here. The interested readers can refer to Yaar, Perrig, and Song (2003) and Adler (2002).

IP Marking Approaches

The first task is to build a map of routes originating from the victim using a traditional mapping technique (Cheswick, Burch, & Branigan, 2000; Govindan & Tangmunarunkit, 2000; Claffy, 2000). Typically, this map consists of a directed acyclic graph as shown on Figure 1, where V is the victim host, $\{R_i\}$ are the routers and leaves, and $\{A_i\}$ represents the potential attack sources.

The attack path from a leaf node A_i is the ordered list of routers between A_i and V. Savage, Wetherall, Karlin, and Andreson (2001) defined the exact trace-back problem as determining the attack path and the associated attack origin for each attacker.

In essence, IP marking consists of the fact that routers add path information into the packets during forwarding to allow the victim to reconstruct the attack path. Of course, this approach extends the flow transmitted across the network and would be likely unfeasible without considering several probabilistic and encoding issues.

Edge Sampling Algorithm and Fragment Marking Scheme

Savage et al. (2001) stated that it is more efficient to mark edges in the attack path rather than nodes. The edge sampling algorithm consists of introducing three fields:

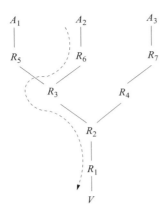

Figure 1: Figure 1. A map of routes network (the dashed line corresponds to a valid attack path).

start, end, and *distance* that have to be added to marked packets. When a router marks a packet, it puts its IP address into the start field and zero into the distance field. However, if the distance field is already set to zero, meaning that the previous router has marked the packet, the router writes its IP address into the end field. Clearly, this mechanism allows the representation of the edge between the current router and the previous router that marked the packet. Moreover, even if the router does not mark the packet, it always to increment the distance field to guarantee a more efficient characterization of spoofed packets. The distance fields corresponding to those packets would be greater than the length of the attack path. Assuming that each router marks packets with a probability p, it can be shown that the number X of the packets needed from the victim to reconstruct an attack path of length d respects the following inequality:

$$E(X) \le \frac{\ln(d)}{p(1-p)^{d-1}}, \qquad (4)$$

where $E(X)$ and $\ln(d)$ denote the expectancy and the Neperian logarithm, respectively.

To write the marking information in a given packet, Savage et al. (2001) suggested the overload of the IP identification field of the IP header that is normally used for fragmentation. This choice relies on measurements that have shown that less than 0.25% of packets are actually fragmented. However, IP identification is a 16-bit field, whereas 72 bits are needed to encode edge information (32 bits for start and end IP addresses and 8 bits for distance). Thus, an encoding technique called the fragmentation sampling scheme (FSS) has been developed in Savage et al. (2001). FSS is based on two mechanisms. First, the usage of exclusive-OR (XOR) of the IP addresses constituting the edge permits to reduce the required storage space by a factor of 2. The resulting value from this operation is called the edge id. Therefore, the victim will receive the edge ids of two adjacent routers except for packets arriving from routers that are at one hop from those routers. For example, if we consider the attack path represented by a dashed line on Figure 1, the victim will receive the following edge ids:

$$IP_{R_1}, IP_{R_1} \oplus IP_{R_2}, IP_{R_2} \oplus IP_{R_3}, IP_{R_3} \oplus IP_{R_6}, \qquad (5)$$

where IP_x is the IP address of node x and $\oplus$ denotes the XOR operator.

Then, the investigator can recover R_2's IP address by benefiting from the idem potency of the XOR operation. By repeating this process iteratively for all the upstream routers, the whole attack path can be reconstructed.

The second encoding mechanism consists of splitting each packet into eight nonoverlapping fragments. When a packet is marked, the router selects a random fragment and adds it up to the packet. This solves the problem as the 16 bits of the IP identification field can be filled by assigning 8 bits to the edge-id fragment, 3 bits to the position of the fragment, and 5 bits to the distance.

Nonetheless, because the use of edge ids instead of traditional logical addresses, another problem called collision (or birthday paradox) arises. Effectively, edge ids are not unique and the probability that the victim host receives two identical edge fragments is not zero. To overcome this limitation, a redundancy check mechanism can be added to the algorithm.

Advanced and Authenticated Marking Schemes

To overcome the computational shortcuts of the basic IP marking approach, a set of improvements have been proposed in Song and Perrig (2001). Assuming that the route map has been predetermined by the victim host, the full IP addresses are not needed for the tracing purpose. In this way, 11-bit hash values of edge ids can be used instead of fragments. Supposing that R_i and R_j marked a given packet, the victim would receive the result of the XOR of IP_{R_i} and IP_{R_j} hashes conforming to the following equation:

$$edge\_id = h_1\left(IP_{R_i}\right) \oplus h_2\left(IP_{R_j}\right), \qquad (6)$$

where h_1 and h_2 are two distinct 11-bit hash functions.

Two one-way functions are used to recover the order of the routers at the victim stage; using a single function would not allow path reconstruction as the XOR operator is commutative.

The robustness of this technique toward collision can be enhanced through the use of two sets of independent hash functions. Approaches to construct these sets are given in Song and Perrig (2001). Although the advanced marking scheme presents an acceptable computational overhead, it can be thwarted if an upstream router is compromised. In fact, all routers are supposed to be trustful. A potential method to address this issue is to authenticate packet marking. An alternative based on cryptographic checksums has been presented by Song and Perrig.

Assuming that each router R_i holds a symmetric key K_i, it can compute the message authentication codes (MAC) of edge ids and append them to marked packets to prevent other routers from forging its marking information. As for every symmetric encryption technique, key management is the fundamental problem arising in the authenticated marking scheme. Time-released keys authentication mechanisms can be used if the size of the route map is important (yielding an impractical number of keys). Examples of such mechanisms can be found in Song and Perrig (2001).

The alert reader would have noticed that the aforementioned marking methods, referred to as probabilistic packet marking (PPM) schemes, have three principal shortcomings. First, they require important processing and memory capabilities at the victim level. Furthermore, their application is restricted to denial of service (DoS) and distributed denial of service (DDoS) attacks. However, the main limitation of these techniques is that they may not converge because a large number of packets of the order of thousands must be available at the victim host to reconstruct the attacked paths.

Deterministic Packet Marking

To overcome PPM disadvantages, a new marking technique, called deterministic packet marking (DPM) was introduced in Belenky and Ansari (2003). The rationale behind this scheme is to perform the marking at the ingress interface of the closest router to the attacker because multiple attack paths can correspond to the same attack (this is the essence of routing algorithms). In other words, the attack flow is uniquely identified by its source and destination. In addition, this marking scheme is deterministic in the sense that every packet is marked by the nearest router to the station that emitted it.

To encode the marking information (the source IP address) in IP datagrams, DPM uses the IP identification field and the 1-bit reserved flag of the IP header. The IP address is divided into two equal segments, and the marking process consists of putting randomly, with probability of 0.5, one of those parts into the IP identification field. Clearly, the 1-bit flag is used to state whether the marking information consists of the first or the second half of the source IP address.

This method outperforms PPM because it does not have an important computational complexity. The number of packets that are needed by the victim to identify the attacker is by far less than in the PPM case. In fact, two packets originating from the same source and having two different marks are sufficient. Yet, it assumes the existence of a strong intervention from Internet service providers (ISPs), which cannot be usually provided for obvious reasons. In addition, DPM cannot be used if network address translation (NAT) is used in the network that includes the attacker's machine. Indeed, the victim would recover the private address of the attacker that does not contain any interesting information.

Hash-Based IP Trace-Back

The hash-based IP trace-back approach, also referred to as source path isolation engine (SPIE) (Snoern, 2002), introduces a three-level hierarchy consisting of data generation agents (DGAs), SPIE collection and reduction agents (SCARs), and a SPIE traceback manager (STM). DGAs, which are at the lowest level of the hierarchy, consist typically of routers that offer the possibility of capturing a compressed piece of information. They uniquely identify each packet they forward. To achieve this goal, hash functions are applied to the constant fields of the IP header (that do not change during the transmission) and to the first 8 bytes of the packet payload. A backup functionality has also been considered to overcome routers' memory limitations.

At the upper level, SCARs receive notifications of attack occurrence from the STM, which is the communicating component with various IDSs existing in the network. SCARs send queries to the appropriate DGAs to get the digests of the packets that were forwarded at the time interval including the instant were the attack took place. Having analyzed packet hashes, every SCAR reports to the STM the results concerning the attack paths in its region. Finally, the STM combines the elementary attack paths and thus performs the packet tracing.

Although SPIE is efficient and robust against various packet transformations (e.g., NAT and encryption), some important factors might obstruct its application in real contexts. The most important issue is related to the industry because SPIE relies on routers, which include sophisticated functionalities. Each router must be equipped with specific functions to extract packet hashes and an implemented backup strategy. Similarly, ISPs are closely involved in this marking scheme. For instance, the synchronization of the time intervals is a particularly tricky task. An additional limitation results from the fact that a centralized STM controls the whole system, which makes the framework more vulnerable as everything would collapse in the case of an STM failure.

Connection Chain Identification

The goal of connection chain identification is to find the set of hosts that the intruder used to carry out an attack. A common technique to hide source's attack is to log on to a set of sources before breaking into the target. The attacker identification task becomes harder if the intrusion traces are deleted or if encrypted networks segments are used. Thus, finding connection chain should not rely on the study of traditional intrusion traces (essentially log files), but on the study of other characteristics that represent uniquely a connection and that are difficult to forge.

If $H_0, H_1, \ldots, H_{n-1}$ are the potential intermediate hosts the attacker used to perform an intrusion, a connection c_i is defined as a log-on operation between hosts H_{i-1} and H_i. When the attacker establishes connection c_i, the data flow sent between H_{i-1} and H_i is called a packet stream. The goal of the connection chain identification process is, given a packet stream of a connection c_i, to determine the entire connection steps denoted $c_1, c_2, \ldots, c_m$ from the attacker to the victim.

Thumb Printing

The idea behind thumb printing is that several features of the transmitted data are constant at all points on a connection chain. Thumbprints can be thought of as signatures that uniquely identify a connection chain.

This method relies on the observation that the evolution of sequence numbers during the transmission of a packet stream is a good criterion to measure the correlation between connections. In Yoda and Etoh (2000), a metric based on the evolution of sequence numbers during a connection was introduced to measure the deviation between connections. This metric should be kept small when computed for two connections that belong to the same connection chain. Basically, the correlation metric represents the slope of the graph that maps sequence numbers to time. Thus, the main assumption is that this metric is nearly invariant (or constant) for connections occurring in the same chain.

Given two connections c_i and c_j, the sequence numbers of the corresponding packet streams are denoted by $(s_l^i)_{0 \le l \le n_i}$ and $(s_l^j)_{0 \le l \le n_j}$. Similarly, the packet arrival time is represented by two series $(t_l^i)_{0 \le l \le n_i}$ and $(t_l^j)_{0 \le l \le n_j}$. The deviation between the packet streams is computed using the following expression:

$$D_{ij} = \frac{1}{d} \min_{0 \le k \le m'} \left\{ \left| \sum_{h=1}^{h=d} \left(T(h,k) - \min_h (T(h,k)) \right) \right|, \left| \sum_{h=1}^{h=d} \left(T(h,k) - \max_h (T(h,k)) \right) \right| \right\}, \quad (7)$$

where $T(h,k) = t_{k+h}^j - t_h^i$, $d = s_{n_i}^i - s_1^i$ and $m' = \max \{l \mid s_l^j + d \le n_j\}$.

More informally, a deviation is a measure of similarity of the evolution of sequence numbers according to time for two packet streams. In fact, $T(h,k)$ can be seen as a distance, in terms of time, between the $k + h^{\text{th}}$ packet of the connection j and the hth of the connection i. Equation (7) means that the graphs representing this evolution have to be adjusted horizontally and vertically so that the average distance between them is minimal. Thus, an advantage of deviation-based connection chain identification is that it does not require clock synchronization as only the shapes of the aforementioned graphs are compared.

Meanwhile, sequence numbers are generally managed by OSs kernels and this makes the invariance assumption inconsistent if multiple OSs are used along the connection chain. Moreover, because the packet content is not used in the deviation-based approach, it is still accurate when the attacker uses application-level encryption (e.g., SSH and SSL) to hide the transmitted data. However, this reasoning no longer holds if encryption occurs at the network level (e.g., ESP) as deviation-based tracing is vulnerable against payload padding. Even worse, the system may not be able to analyze properly packet headers.

Interpacket Delay-Based Tracing

To address the problem of characterizing partially (or totally) encrypted connection chains, Wang, Reeves, and Wu (2002) proposed a method, which is very similar to the previous one except that it relies only on packet timestamps to evaluate the correlation between the two packet streams. More precisely, it introduces the notion of interpacket delay (IPD) correlation window as a feature that characterizes a portion of a packet stream. Using the same notations as for deviation-based tracing, this window can be expressed as follows:

$$W_{l,s} \left(\langle d_1^i, ..., d_{n_i}^i \rangle \right) = \langle d_l^i, ..., d_{l+s-1}^i \rangle, \quad (8)$$

where
$l \in \{1, ..., n_i\}$ is the starting point of the window,
$s \in \{1, ..., n_i - l + 1\}$ is the size of the window, and
$d_k^i = t_{k+1}^i - t_k^i$ for every $k \in \{1, ..., n_i\}$.
To compare the connections c_i and c_j, a correlation point function (CPF) is used and defined as below:

$$CPF(c_i, c_j, l, k, s) = \phi \left(W_{l,s}(c_i), W_{l+k,s}(c_j) \right), \quad (9)$$

where $\phi(.,.)$ is a similarity evaluation criterion (e.g., mini/max sum ratio and the correlation coefficient).

The first step is to find, for a given value of j, the offset k that corresponds to a maximum of $CPF(.,.,.)$. The alert reader would have noticed that this procedure is equivalent to the graph adjustment used in deviation-based tracing. By varying j, a set of optimal offsets are determined. Therefore, according to the basic hypothesis, these offsets should be equal for all the correlation points if c_i and c_j belong to the same connection chain.

The main advantage of IPD-based tracing is that it can be used in real time, which may not be very important from the computer forensics point of view. Another interesting feature is that it needs relatively a few packets when compared to other methods to perform the correlation process.

DISCOVERING ATTACK STEPS

The main goal of the investigator is to reconstruct as much information as possible about digital crimes. Revealing the identity of the suspect, by discovering hidden data in a hard disk or tracing an attack flow, is often insufficient to achieve such objective. Determining the technique of the attack as well as its steps is a crucial step for at least two reasons.

- *Primo:* Understanding the details of a crime and identifying the vulnerabilities that the attacker exploited can serve to improve the incident response process. The victim would have more data to thwart this attack by making proactive countermeasures.

- *Secundo:* Proving the responsibility of a suspect just by identifying him or her as legally inadequate. To pass a sentence, the law court must know what the suspect has exactly done.

So far, computer forensic techniques have been considered from an angle that narrows several key issues. One of the most basic questions about digital investigation is *Does basic human reasoning allow the conduction of a forensic process at an acceptable time?* Regarding the numerous practical problems that the investigator could face, the answer to this question would be negative. The wide use of computers and networks results in a huge amount of data being stored and transmitted. Collecting and analyzing evidence in such environment cannot be achieved by only humans without the assistance of advanced techniques. In this section, the application of statistics and artificial intelligence to digital forensics is discussed.

Statistical Computer Forensics

Neither of the foregoing investigation approaches allows us to absolutely state any determination about an event. Even if a source identification method shows that host X performed a network attack, this cannot be considered as an undeniable proof against its owner Y. This can be expressed in general in terms of probabilities: "The probability that Y is innocent, conditional on the identification of X as an attack source" is less than "the probability that Y is innocent."

Practically, probabilities can be computed in two ways: using frequencies, under the assumptions of the central limit theorem, or degree of belief, which is rather subjective. The fundamental interest in using probabilities in computer forensics stems from Bayes' rule that can be expressed, for two events A and B, as follows:

$$p(A|B) = p(B|A) \times \frac{p(A)}{p(B)}. \tag{10}$$

This formula shows how to update a probability to take account of new elements. When applied to digital forensics, A and B can stand for "Suspect is innocent" and "Evidence is presented," respectively. As a consequence of Eq. (10), we have the following:

$$\frac{p(A|B)}{p(\neg A|B)} = \frac{p(B|A)}{p(B|\neg A)} \times \frac{p(A)}{p(\neg A)}, \tag{11}$$

where $\neg$ denotes the negation symbol. Clearly, $\frac{p(B|A)}{p(B|\neg A)}$ represents the prior knowledge relative to the evidence that can be deduced from statistics.

Different probabilistic reasoning applications can be used in computer investigation. For example, by showing that $p(B|A)$ (i.e., probability of the evidence, conditional to the innocence of the suspect) is too low, the investigator can argue that the suspect is likely to be guilty.

Computer Forensics and Artificial Intelligence

It appears from the description of investigation techniques that the forensic process relies largely on the available data constituting potential sources of evidence. Consequently, several features should be properly monitored to provide information that might be used if needed. Of the infinity of candidate metrics, only a few are substantially important. Determining these metrics is extremely relevant to ensure an acceptable error rate. The introduction of inappropriate features results in distorting the accuracy of the corresponding digital evidence.

The problem that arises at this level is that metric selection is impossible to be done manually. The Computer Emergency Response Team (CERT) defined a set of parameters that should be controlled to detect the occurrence of network attacks (Computer Emergency Response Team, 2000). Nevertheless, this is not exactly what is required for computer forensics. What misses is a link that

should exist between each feature and computer crime. The stronger is this link, the bigger is the appropriation of the metric to analyze corresponding computer attacks.

Mukammala and Sung (2003) proposed a feature selection technique based on artificial intelligence. Basically, it consists of allocating a significance factor to each potential parameter. This factor will then serve to rank the features to choose the most convenient ones.

Significance, which is the kernel of this approach, is quantified by evaluating the performance of the detection method on a training set and a testing set. The algorithm consists of removing one feature from those sets (meaning that the corresponding data is deleted). The detector is trained again with respect to the remaining data and its performance is assessed in terms of some predefined criteria. Ordering features can be performed through the use of support vector machines (SVMs) or artificial neural networks (ANNs). Experiments that were carried out on the 1999 DARPA intrusion showed that SVMs provide better results.

Two difficulties might be faced when applying this method. These are as follows:

1. **Building the testing and training data.** In fact, if these sets do not reflect the environment of the monitored network, the efficiency of the approach would be perceptibly affected.
2. **Complexity.** Besides, as automated significance ranking is performed on a per detector basis, it becomes considerably complex when many detection mechanisms are set to protect a network.

Conversely, many works have been done in the field of intelligent intrusion analysis. Flexibility is becoming a key issue in modern intrusion detection techniques, which have to automatically update their signature databases. Neural networks have often been proposed in this context, see Obaidat and Sadoun (1997). However, their use requires important cautions because attackers can use this learning functionality to forge the behavior of IDSs. Training, which is the basis of ANNs, consists basically of executing the IDS on a network flow where attack occurrences are known in advance. This process can allow criminals to let their traffic be seen as normal by injecting a sample of attack flows in the IDS during the training period.

Alternatively, decision trees (Stallard & Levitt, 2003), which can be viewed as the application of a well-known data fusion method, has been used to detect the occurrence of security violations that are expressed in terms of invariants. The interest of adapting this method to computer forensics is that multiple sources of information can be considered. This results in a better accuracy of the detection results. Stallard introduces a data aggregation scheme that permits the examination of the digital evidence at different levels of abstraction (e.g., raw data, aggregated data, and metadata). To build deductions from these data, two possibilities exist: forward chaining and backward chaining. The former uses inference rules to derive "facts whose premises match several known facts." The latter begins with a goal to prove. It first checks the working memory to see if the goal has been previously added. The system then checks to see if the goal rule's premises are listed in the working memory. Results given by the software prototype developed within the frame of this work show that the use of expert systems in digital forensics is very promising.

LEGAL ISSUES

In Lee and Schields (2001), laws were presented as constraints for the packet trace-back problem. More generally, the regulatory framework can be a serious obstacle for every computer forensic activity. Particularly, privacy is a crucial issue that may cause problems to the investigator. As an illustrative example, consider an attacker that took the control of multiple stepping-stones before reaching the victim. To perform a posteriori analysis of this incident, the forensic analyst should study several log files concerning the stepping-stones or the victim host. These files can be found on the computers themselves or in the ISP network. In both cases, giving access to the required data may lead to the disclosure of confidential private information, which may be stored on the same machines as the log files. In fact, computers contain data having different levels of confidentiality. Conversely, it would be inappropriate to restrict the investigator's access to a machine to a few number of log files because this approach would affect seriously the efficiency of the evidence collection process. In the case of traditional forensic science, investigators can avoid similar problems if they possess official search warrants that confer a legal aspect to their activities. Unfortunately, such permissions to seize physical facilities are not applicable for digital investigation, especially when communication networks are considered. Taking the control of a network link implies the access to information belonging not only to the attacker, but also to the other users as the communication infrastructure is in essence public.

Other problems can result from conflicts between national regulations. Often, network attacks involve computers that are situated at different geographical locations. For this reason, nations are focusing seriously on international legal aspects such as evidence exchange or attacker extradition (CoE, 2001). Nonetheless, the existence of a sound regulatory environment is necessary as the notion of evidence admissibility cannot be considered without it. Defining and enforcing legal proofs helps the investigator to direct his or her search toward the most relevant features and improves the chance of discovering accurate pieces of evidence.

ENHANCING THE EXISTING INFRASTRUCTURE

Because the existing security infrastructure does not allow the application of the techniques mentioned below, standards, research activities, applications, and human skills should be improved to help forensic success. Issues related to these modifications are addressed in this section.

Improving Standards, Protocols, and Regulation

It is noteworthy from the previous sections that most of the existing forensic standards are limited to disk forensics. Although many procedures and guidelines treated various facets of disk examination, network investigation activities have not been standardized yet. A potential topic to consider would be the relation between signs and the nature of intrusions. Such link would permit a rapid deduction of the attack mechanism before deeper investigation takes place. In fact, because meticulous network forensic tasks are very time consuming, a preliminary coarse analysis should be done prior to them.

Conversely, network protocol standards need to be secured. The numerous techniques that have been proposed in the literature to fit with traceability requirements, and that have been resumed in this chapter, are insufficient and the research activity in this branch is still immature. Disk standards as well, especially those related to sector addressing and controller-disk communication, should be considered since most of the problems that have been discussed above derive from incongruities in those standards. Another key aspect concerns regulation is that most of the works that treated this issue instill a negative opinion about legal considerations. Many laws were written without taking the technological advances in mind, and thus they seriously affect the technical solutions. To avoid misleading interpretations, computer forensic-specific regulatory texts should be applied.

Improving Theory

Research in digital forensics is still in its infancy. Many important topics have not been addressed yet. The lack of efforts and cost estimation model for digital forensics has already been mentioned earlier. This issue is of prime importance because it would determine the accuracy of conducting the investigation. Moreover, it would help to schedule this activity. A cost model consists first of identifying the features that have an impact on the complexity of the investigation process. On the basis of these parameters, a model expressing this complexity should be built. It has to express suitably the evolution of the complexity according to the variables (e.g., linear and exponential).

The use of probabilistic reasoning can be enriched through the introduction of more elaborated data fusion techniques. Bayesian theory can be used to express the relation between the *a priori* information i, the available data $(d_1, .., d_n)$, extracted from n sources, and the event to be evaluated. Many approaches that rely on probability theory or fuzzy sets have proved their efficiency in other fields and can be adapted to investigation. An additional potential research issue concerns the role of investigators in the forensic process. Effectively, many specialists participate in the digital investigation and each of them has a particular view, oriented by his or her specialty of the problem. Their opinions may match, be slightly different, or may bluntly conflict. To obtain a single consistent representation that combines accurately the elementary views, collaborative intelligence techniques can be applied.

Improving Industry Support

Organizations can participate at least at two levels to promote computer forensics. First, network equipment manufacturers should consider seriously the implementation of several theoretical approaches that have been discussed above. Currently available protection mechanisms in firewalls are limited to stateful inspection that prevents SYN. Flooding attack aims to start opening a large number of TCP connections on the victim machine and prevent them from occurring (in addition to traditional packet filtering).

Some routers include the ingress and egress filtering functionalities that cannot be efficiently applied without identifying precisely the malicious host. Moreover, enterprises should strictly apply computer security incident guidelines by putting the required monitoring infrastructure and building incident response teams (IRTs). This would allow to provide useful data by the investigators and to react in an acceptable response time.

Another category of operators that should particularly be active is ISPs. Network attack tracing approaches are more or less dependent on ISPs involvement. These, however, are often reluctant to participate in the investigation process because they refuse to give information about their private networks.

Improving Human Skills

Technical capabilities are very important to ensure the efficiency of the forensic process. Primarily, employees should be aware of the security considerations and apply policies and procedures. In particular, IRT members should be well trained to conduct properly their tasks. Investigators should also possess the knowledge to study the digital crime scene. They typically submit the collected data to various specialists who perform the examination step. Then they should be able to analyze appropriately the results of this examination.

Finally, prosecutors, lawyers, and judges are also supposed to have minimum technical skills that allow them to understand digital crimes. Specialized trainings should be considered to address this goal.

CONCLUDING REMARKS

Throughout this chapter, it can be said that forensic science, when adapted to computer science and information technology, possesses several characteristics that makes it particular and different from other traditional applications. In this section, these features are presented briefly to avoid redundancy:

1. Identification of sources of evidence becomes more complex when dealing with digital forensics. The available data, which potentially contains proofs, has a huge volume of information that is impractical to be readable by humans. Thus, identification is considered as a separate step of the computer forensic process and many automated tools are proposed to assist the investigators in performing it.
2. Digital evidence is very sensitive because it is affected by the properties of storage media and computer applications. Indeed, memory volatility or malicious codes

can make the evidence disappear before becoming legally recognized, which is frustrating for the forensic analysts.
3. Tracking a network's attacker is very complicated because the associated evidence seldom has legal value. Identifying the offender on the basis of his or her IP address or his or her password is not sufficient to indict him or her.
4. Evidence authentication techniques are weaker than in the case of traditional forensics. For example, if some fingerprints were found on a fire gun and if they match the suspect biometric templates, the probability that the suspect is the real attacker is greater than if the evidence were a computer. This simply results from the fact that forging fingerprints is much more difficult than spoofing some digital parameters (e.g., IP address and e-mail password).

CROSS REFERENCES

See *Access Control: Principles and Solutions; Computer and Network Authentication; Digital Evidence; Encryption Basics; Intrusion Detection Systems Basics.*

REFERENCES

Adler, M. (2002). Tradeoffs in probabilistic packet marking for IP traceback. In *34th ACM Symposium on Theory of Computing (STOC)* (pp. 407–418). Montreal, Canada

Ahsan, K., & Kundur, D. (2002). Practical data hiding in TCP/IP. In *Workshop on Multimedia and Security at ACM Multimedia'02.* Juan-les-pins, France.

Association of Chief Police Officers of England. (2003). *Good practice guide for computer based evidence, Version 3.* Retrieved June 2, 2005, from http://www.acpo.police.uk/asp/policies/Data/gpg-computer-based-evidence-v3.pdf

Belenky, A., & Ansari, N. (2003). IP traceback with deterministic packet parking. *IEEE Communications Letters, 7,* 162–164.

Cheswick, B., Burch, H., & Branigan, S. (2000). Mapping and visualizing the Internet. In *USENIX Annual Technical Conference* (pp. 1–12).

Claffy, K. (2000) Measuring the Internet. *IEEE Internet Computing, 4,* 73–75.

Computer Emergency Response Team. (2003). *Detecting signs of Intrusions.* Retrieved November 19, 2003, from http://www.cert.org/security-improvement.modules/m09.html

Computer Security Institute/Federal Bureau of Investigation (CSI/FBI). (2003). *Eighth CSI/FBI computer crime and security survey.* Retrieved November 19, 2003, from http://i.cmpnet.com/gocsi/db-area/pdfs/fbi.jhtml

Council of Europe. (2001). *Convention on cybercrime.* Budapest: European Treaty Series.

Digital Forensics Research Workshop. (2001). *A road map for digital forensics research.* Retrieved November 19, 2003, from http://www.dfrws.org

Farmer, D., & Venema, W. (1999). *Computer forensics analysis class handouts.* Retrieved November 19, 2003, from http://www.fish.com/forensics/class.html

Federal Bureau of Investigation. (2002). *FBI crime scene search*. Retrieved November 19, 2003, from http://www.fbi.gov/hq/lab/handbook/intro16.htm

Gaines, H. F. (1956). *Cryptanalysis: A study of ciphers and their solutions*. New York: Dover.

Govindan, R., & Tangmunarunkit, H. (2000). Heuristics for Internet map discovery. Proc. IEEE INFOCOM, vol 3, 1371–1380, Telaviv, Israel.

Handel, T., & Stanford, M. (1996). Hiding data in the OSI network model. In *First International Workshop on Information Hiding*. Lecture notes in computer science, 1174, Cambridge, UK.

Lee, S. C., & Shields, C. (2001) Tracing the source of network attack: A technical, legal and societal problem. *IEEE Workshop on Information Assurance and Security*, 12–18. New york, U.S.

Mukammala, S., & Sung, A. H. (2003). Identifying significant features for network forensic analysis using artificial intelligence techniques. *International Journal of Digital Evidence, 1*(4).

National Institute of Justice. (2001). Electronic crime scene investigation: A guide for first responders. Retrieved November 19, 2003 from http://www.ojp.usdoj.gov/mij

National Institute of Standards and Technologies. (2001). *Disk imaging tool specification*. version 3.1, Retrieved June 13 from http://www.cftt.nist.gov/testdocs.html

Obaidat, M. S., & Sadoun, B. (1997). Verification of computer users using keystroke dynamics. *IEEE Transactions. on Systems, Man, and Cybernetics, Part B, 27*(2), 261–269.

Olson, D. (2000). Analysis of criminal codes and ciphers. *Forensic Science Communications, 2*(1).

Reith, M., Carr, C., & Gunsh, G. (2002). An examination of digital forensic models. *International Journal of Digital Evidence, 1*(3).

Rowlingson, R. (2004). A ten step process for forensic readiness. *International Journal of Digital Evidence, 2*(3).

Savage, S., Wetherall, D., Karlin, A., & Andreson, T. (2001). Network support for IP traceback. *ACM/IEEE Transactions on Networking, 9*, 226–237.

Simmons, G. J. (1983). Subliminal communication is easy with the DSA. *Proceedings of the EUROCRYPT'93*, 218–232.

Snoern, A. C. (2002). Single-packet IP traceback. *IEEE/ACM Transactions on Networking, 10*, 721–734.

Song, D. X., & Perrig, A. (2001). Advanced and authenticated marking schemes for IP traceback. Proc. *IEEE INFOCOM*, 878–886. Anchorage, Alaska.

Stallard, T. B., & Levitt, K. (2003). Automated analysis for digital forensic science: Semantic integrity checking. In *19th Annual Computer Security Applications Conference (ACSAC)*.

Stephenson, P. (2003). Using evidence effectively. *Computer Fraud and Security, 10*(3).

Tan, J. (2001). *Forensic readiness*. Retrieved November 19, 2003, from http://www.atstake.com/research/reports/acrobat/atstake_forensic_readiness.pdf

Wagstaff, S. S. (2003). *Cryptanalysis of number theoretic ciphers*. New York: Chapman & Hall/CRC.

Wang, X., Reeves, D. S., & Wu, S. F. (2002). Inter-packet delay based correlation for tracing encrypted connections through stepping stones. In *European Symposium on Research in Computer Security (ESORICS)* (pp. 244–263).

Wolfe-Wilson, J., & Wolfe, H. B. (2003). Management strategies for implementing forensic security measures. *Information Security Technical Report, 8*(2), 55–64.

Yaar, A., Perrig, A., & Song, D. (2003). Pi: A path identification mechanism to defend against DDoS attacks. In *IEEE Symposium on Security and Privacy* (pp. 93–107).Zurich, Switzerland

Yasinsac, A., & Manzano, Y. (2001). Policies to enhance computer and network forensics. In *Proceedings of 2001 Workshop on Information Assurance and Security*, New York, U.S.

Yoda, K., & Etoh, H. (2000). Finding a connection chain for tracing intruders. In *6th European Symposium on Research in Computer Security (ESORICS)* (pp. 191–205). Toulouse, France.

Computer Forensics Procedures and Methods

J. Philip Craiger, *National Center for Forensic Science* and *University of Central Florida*

INTRODUCTION

Computer forensics involves the preservation, identification, extraction, and documentation of computer evidence stored in the form of magnetically, optically, or electronically stored media. It is a relatively new science that is becoming increasingly important as criminals aggressively expand the use of technology in their enterprise of illegal activities. Computer forensic techniques are not as advanced as those of the more mature and mainstream forensics techniques used by law enforcement, such as blood typing, ballistics, fingerprinting, and DNA testing. Its immaturity is partly attributable to fast-paced changes in computer technology and the fact that it is a multidisciplinary subject, involving complicated associations among the legal system, law enforcement, business management, and information technology.

This chapter is a *technical introduction and overview* to fundamental methods and procedures of computer forensics. To get the most out of this chapter, we have assumed readers will have technical skills with computers running a variety of operating systems.

The Handbook of Information Security, in particular volume 2, has several chapters related to numerous aspects of computer forensics, including the legal, law enforcement, and managerial aspects. To fully understand the practice and implications of computer forensics, we urge readers to carefully examine all related chapters. As you read this chapter, be aware that computer forensics is a set of technical activities that occurs within a complex setting of interacting stakeholders who often have conflicting goals. Before conducting a computer forensics investigation, we advise the reader to seek advice from legal counsel to ensure that no local, state, or federal laws are broken. Nothing in this chapter is intended to be legal advice and should not be construed as such.

In this chapter, we illustrate both *offline* and *online* analyses. An offline analysis occurs when an investigator powers down the computer and removes it from the network. This allows the investigator to create an exact copy of the computer's hard drive to ensure that the files remained unchanged and to ensure all evidence, condemning as well as exculpatory, is collected. In contrast, there are occasions when it is impossible to power down a computer, which then requires an online analysis. For instance, management may not permit the shutdown of a company's only e-commerce server. In this circumstance, the investigator must gather as much evidence as possible while the system remains running and connected to a network. From a purely forensic standpoint, the preferred situation is to "freeze" the computer's state by powering down the system. However, in reality this is not always possible, and investigators should be proficient in methods for gathering evidence from a running computer system.

We begin this chapter by describing an offline analysis involving desktop computers running versions of Microsoft Windows. Windows plays a prominent role because of its large worldwide market share and the fact that the law enforcement agencies (Dartmouth, 2002) and the FBI's Computer Analysis and Response Team (Pollitt, 2002, personal communication) have indicated that the majority of investigations involve computers running some version of Windows. We conclude this chapter by discussing an online analysis, such as a server running Linux or UNIX that cannot be shut down and that therefore requires the investigator to work on a running computer system.

Computer Forensics Tools

Investigators have a variety of forensic tools from which to choose. Some tools run exclusively under Windows, others under Linux/UNIX, and some on several operating systems. The focus of this chapter is on illustrating fundamental computer forensics *concepts*, not a particular tool. An important reason for *not* using point-and-click tools for our demonstrations is that these tools do not illustrate the fundamental, technical details that form the core of computer forensic procedures. For example, when an investigator clicks on a graphical user interface (GUI) button labeled Recover Deleted File from within a GUI-based tool, she should be able to explain *what* the program is doing to recover the files. In real life, of course, investigators are likely to use one of the many GUI-based tools that are available (some of these are described at the end of this chapter). Nevertheless, a fundamental understanding of these concepts is especially important for the credibility of the investigator should she be required to testify in a court of law as an expert or technical witness.

Accordingly, we use Linux-based tools for our demonstrations. Linux is an operating system kernel. The command line utilities we use to conduct our forensic procedures are part of the GNU utilities (http://www.gnu.org) that are included in every Linux distribution. A Linux *distribution* is a vendor compilation of the Linux kernel, GNU utilities, and hundreds of software programs, plus an installer. There are several dozen Linux distributions, although only a few are major commercial distributions, the largest of which are Redhat (http://www.redhat.com) and SuSE (http://www.suse.com). Readers are directed to http://www.distrowatch.com and http://www.linux.org to learn more about various Linux distributions. All demonstrations herein were tested with SuSE Professional 9.0/9.1, Fedora Core 1, and Redhat 9.

Forensic Server

We assume that most computer crime investigations will involve at least one "subject" computer, that is, the source of the evidence we are seeking, as well as a "forensic server" that contains our forensics toolkits. For our demonstration purposes, we assume that the forensic server has a Linux distribution installed, or is dual-bootable Window/Linux, which is how all of our computers are configured. Although in theory the Linux distribution should be irrelevant, certain commercial versions such as Red Hat and SuSE are often preferred because they offer support services and are fairly easy to install and update.

The activities performed in a forensic analysis may easily tax the average computer. Therefore, it is important that a good deal of thought is put into the components that compose the forensic server to ensure that it is of sufficient quality and power so that imaging and analysis are not problematic. For instance, it is desirable to have as much physical RAM as one can afford, as well as a fast processor (all of which are relative and changing daily). The forensic server will need enough drive space to hold the operating system, several forensic tools, and all of the forensic images collected from the subject's computer. Other considerations include the need to read and examine numerous portable disk formats, including old ZIP disks, superdrive disks, old floppy formats such as the 5.25 floppies, and so on. It is a good idea to have on hand many different types of disk readers

that can be placed into the forensic computer should the need arise. Should the investigator come upon a digital evidence format that is not common, eBay (http://www.ebay.com) or similar sites may have such equipment available.

SOUND COMPUTER FORENSIC PRACTICE

There are numerous circumstances that may require a computer forensic investigation but not necessarily law enforcement intervention. For instance, a company employee suspected of sending sexually explicit e-mails or running a personal business may be subject to an investigation because these activities violate corporate acceptable-use policy and subject the employee to disciplinary action; however, they are not illegal and do not require law enforcement intervention. Nevertheless, it is good practice to work under the assumption that *any* investigation could end up in court. The reason is that there are countless stories of investigations that started off for one reason but escalated to a point requiring law enforcement intercession. For instance, an investigation instigated by allegations that an employee surfing pornographic Web sites on his lunch break may reveal evidence of a cache of child pornography on the employee's hard drive, a federal crime under 18 USC 2251 and 2252. The situation must be reported to law enforcement and would likely end up in court.

The federal rules of evidence (http://www.law.cornell.edu/rules/fre/overview.html) govern the introduction of evidence in both civil and criminal proceedings in federal courts. These rules are strict regarding the handling of evidence. Evidence not collected in accordance with the federal rules of evidence may be disallowed by a judge. Sound forensic practices decrease the potential for a defense attorney to question the integrity of evidence and for the judge to disallow the introduction of evidence into a court proceeding.

Computer forensics procedures can be distilled into three major components:

1) Make a digital copy – sometimes called a forensic duplicate – of the original evidence. Investigators make a copy of the evidence and work with the copy to reduce the possibility of inadvertently changing the original evidence.
2) Authenticate the copy of the evidence. Investigators must verify the copy of the evidence is exactly the same as the original.
3) Analyze the digital copy. The specific procedures performed in an investigation are determined by the specific circumstances under which the investigation is occurring.

Our chapter will generally follow this outline. We begin by demonstrating two ways in which to make forensically sound copies of digital evidence, followed by a demonstration of a simple and effective way of verifying the integrity of a digital copy. The remaining portions of this chapter are devoted to procedures for analyzing digital evidence.

ARRIVING AT THE SCENE: INITIAL RESPONSE

There are two important rules regarding the initial response to a computer crime scene. One of the most critical times at any crime scene is when the crime is first discovered. The first activity performed by law enforcement at a physical crime is to restrict access by surrounding the crime scene with yellow tape, something most of us have seen on television hundreds of times. It is just as important to *restrict access* to the computer at a computer crime scene to decrease the likelihood of changing the evidence.

The second rule is to *document* the crime scene and all activities performed. Good documentation is crucial for several reasons. First, it allows the investigator to refresh her memory should she have to testify. Second, it allows the court to verify that correct forensic procedures were performed. Finally, it allows for the recreation of the activities that were performed in the initial response.

Special Agent Mark Pollitt (retired), former Unit Chief of the Federal Bureau of Investigations Computer Analysis and Response Team (CART), has said, "Computer forensics is all about process" (Pollitt, 2002 personal communication). The process should be repeatable and predictable and should stay within the confines of the law. We underscore the importance of following sound forensic practice during investigations, as there is a significant potential for any investigation to have legal implications for the investigator, her employer, or the subject of the investigation. In subsequent sections, we outline the activities that should be performed as an initial response to a potential computer crime scene. The following is partly adapted from International Association of Computer Investigation Specialists (IACIS: http://www.iacis.com/forensic_examination_procedures.htm) as well as *U.S. Secret Service's Best Practices Guide for Seizing Electronic Evidence* (U.S. Secret Service, 2002).

1. Immediately determine if a destructive program is running on the computer. If one is running, the investigator should pull the power plug from the *back* of the computer (not at the outlet). This will ensure no further evidence is lost. Place tape across all open disk drives so that no media is inadvertently placed in the disk drives. The system date and time should be collected from the BIOS setup. This time should be compared with a reliable time source (e.g., one synchronized with an atomic clock) and any discrepancies noted. This may be important if it is necessary to correlate events between two computers or between the activities of a user and the times associated with particular files on the computer.

2. Document the computer and its surroundings. Videotape and photographs are good supplements to handwritten notes. Things to document include the computer's make, model, and serial number; attachments to the computer (e.g., external hard drives, speakers, cable modem, universal serial bus (USB) or network hubs, wireless network routers, and so on); the state of the machine, that is, whether it was on or not; and the surrounding environment.

3. If the computer is running, take a photograph of the screen. Photographs demonstrate that the computer was running as well as visually documenting what was running at the time of the initial response.

4. Take photographs of the front, side, and back of the computer. A photograph of the back of the computer will allow an investigator to recreate the computer setup should the computer need to be seized and taken back to a lab for further investigation. If the computer is to be seized, label connectors (network, USB, firewire, etc.).

5. Physically open the computer and take photographs of the inside of the computer. These photographs will show the number of hard disks connected, as well as any peripherals, such as network and sound cards.

6. *Bag and tag* of all potential evidence. "Bag and tag" is a law enforcement term that refers to the process of placing crime scene evidence (e.g., hairs, fibers, guns, knives, and so on) into bags and tagging them with relevant information including date and time collected, name of investigator, where collected, and so forth. All potential evidence such as floppy disks, compact disks (CDs), digital video disks (DVDs), papers surrounding the computer, and so forth should be subjected to a bag-and-tag.

7. Some situations require the confiscation of the source computer by law enforcement (Heverly & Wright, 2002). If the computer is to be transported to an off-site forensics laboratory, label each computer part and place in an appropriate container for transport.

8. Search for "sticky notes" or any other written documentation near the computer (including under the keyboard, under the desk, in desk drawers, etc.). Users often write down passwords and leave them in convenient places near the computer. Passwords may be necessary if the user has used encryption to obfuscate file contents. Make sure to look in the wastebasket as it may hold valuable information.

9. Take any computer manuals in case they are needed for reference back at the forensics laboratory.

10. If the original evidence is to be confiscated, it should be stored in a secure place.

Creating a Forensic Image

The first step in acquiring digital evidence is to create an *exact physical copy* of the evidence. This copy is often called a *bit-stream image* (Kruse & Heiser, 2001), *forensic duplicate* (Mandia, Prosise, & Pepe, 2003), or *forensic image*. Creating a forensic image is important for several reasons. From a legal standpoint, courts look favorably upon forensic images because it demonstrates that *all* of the evidence was captured, condemning as well as exculpatory, following the spirit of the Federal Rules of Evidence. From an investigatory perspective, forensic images contain the contents of previously deleted files and other ambient data, information not available if only a logical copy of files is made.

Historically, a running computer was of little concern to law enforcement because the standard operating procedure was to remove the power source from the computer, that is, pull the plug, whether the computer was running or not. "Pulling-the-plug" follows general police

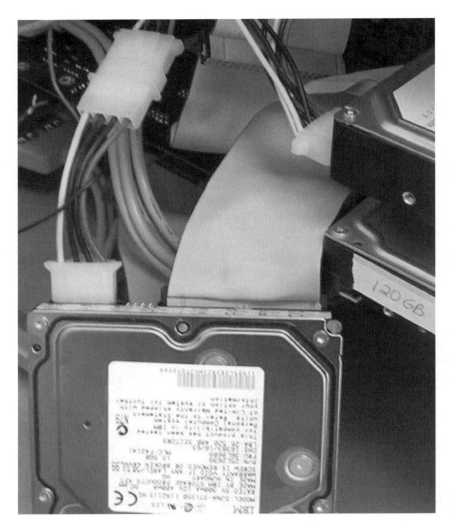

Figure 1: Direct connection to internal IDE controller.

investigative procedures to "freeze" the crime scene. Pulling the plug is analogous to the yellow "Do Not Cross Police Line" tape because it freezes the computer crime scene. This practice is no longer a hard-and-fast rule as pulling the plug may lose valuable evidence, for example, running network connections and the contents of RAM.

Options for freezing the computer include pulling the plug or gracefully shutting the computer down (i.e., through the mouse sequence: Start: Turn Off Computer: Turn Off). In personal experiments involving computers running versions of Windows 98 and Windows XP, we observed that a graceful shutdown results in changes to several hundred files on the disk. This could have a significant effect upon law enforcement's ability to prosecute a case, especially trying to explain how the investigating officer managed to change several hundred files on the evidence media. Our advice is that the *circumstances must determine whether it is appropriate to pull the plug or perform a graceful shutdown*.

We must access the hard drive on the subject's computer to create our image. How do we access the source hard drive? One way is to physically remove it from the source computer and connect it to the investigator's forensics machine. For example, if the source drive is an Advanced Technology Attachment/Integrated Drive

Electronics (ATA/IDE), it is relatively simple to remove it and reconnect it to an open IDE ribbon cable connection in the forensics computer, as demonstrated in Figure 1.

There are two caveats to this method. First, if we are imaging using a Windows-based application, then we must use a write blocker (see Figure 2) to ensure that no data are written back to the subject's hard drive, because Windows will automatically mount the hard drive as read + write, which may change files on the hard drive. If we are using Linux, then a write blocker is not required because we can manually mount the hard drive as "read only." Forensic imaging under Windows therefore requires the use of a special "write blocker," a hardware mechanism that allows reading from, but not writing to, the hard drive (see Figure 2). Write blockers are available from several sources, including FireFly from http://www.digitalintel.com, FireBox from www.black bagtech.com, and FastBloc from http://www.guidance software.com.

Second, directly connecting the subject's hard drive to our forensic server's IDE chain requires that the jumpers on the source drive be appropriately set to slave or cable select. Changing jumper settings will not change any files on the hard drive.

Figure 2: Write block with firewire connection.

Figure 2 demonstrates the use of a hardware write-blocker to connect a subject's hard drive to a forensic server using a USB or firewire cable.

Once we have connected our hard drive, we can begin the imaging process. In the following demonstration, we will create a forensic image of a floppy; however, the process is very similar for most media and any differences are indicated below. In subsequent sections, we will demonstrate how to image a hard drive over a network connection.

From a terminal window, we use the GNU utilities from a command prompt to make our forensic image. First, we write protect the floppy, then place the disk in our floppy drive on our forensic server. The commands we executed have been marked in brackets for ease of reference.

makes a copy of everything printed on the screen (both input and output) and places it in a file, here descriptively called *case.1034*.

We then print the current date and time with `date` [2]. It is good practice to "sandwich" your forensic activities between two `date` commands [2] and [6] to demonstrate when and how long the activities required.

Next, we use the `dd` [3] command to create a forensic image of the floppy disk:

```
# dd if=/dev/fd0 of=1034.dd
```

`dd` takes as input a stream of bits and outputs a stream of bits, making an exact physical duplicate of a file, drive, and so forth. In this example, `dd` is reading from the

```
[1] jpc@simba:~> script case.1034
    Script started on Tue 23 Mar 2004 03:25:36 PM CST
[2] jpc@simba:~> date
    Tue Mar 23 15:25:39 CST 2004
[3] jpc@simba:~> dd if=/dev/fd0 of=1034.dd bs=1024 conv=noerror,notrunc,sync
    2880+0 records in
    2880+0 records out
[4] jpc@simba:~> md5sum /dev/fd0 1034.dd > evidence.md5
[5] jpc@simba:~> cat evidence.md5
    04c09fa404ac7611b20a1acc28e7546c /dev/fd0
    04c09fa404ac7611b20a1acc28e7546c 1034.dd
[6] jpc@simba:~> date
    Tue Mar 23 15:34:13 CST 2004
[7] jpc@simba:~> exit
    Script done on Tue 23 Mar 2004 03:34:14 PM CST
```

A good investigator documents the crime scene as well as the procedures performed. We can supplement our handwritten notes with the `script` command. `script` [1]

device */dev/fd0*, a logical device associated with the floppy disk drive, and writing it to a file we have named *1034.dd*. In Linux, physical devices are logically associated with

Table 1 Mapping from Logical to Physical Device

Logical Device	Physical Device
/dev/hda	First IDE hard drive on primary controller
/dev/hda1	First partition on the first hard drive on primary controller
/dev/hdb	Second IDE hard drive on primary controller
/dev/hdc	First IDE hard drive on secondary controller
/dev/hdd5	Fifth partition on second hard drive on secondary controller
/dev/sda	First SCSI device
/dev/sda1	First partition on first SCSI device
/dev/cdrom	First CDROM drive
/dev/fd0	First floppy disk

a file residing in the */dev* directory. These associations are shown in Table 1. Note that the names of the logical devices may differ between Linux distributions or between versions of UNIX. The nomenclature below is fairly standard for most POSIX-compliant Linux distributions, including Redhat, SuSE, Mandrake, Slackware, Debian, and Gentoo.

The argument `if=` specifies the source image, here the logical device associated with the floppy drive. The argument `of=` specifies the output file's name. The `bs=` argument specifies the block size to read and write, and is optional. The default block size is 512 bytes. The *conv* argument specifies other command line arguments to include. For imaging we include `noerror`, continue after a read error; `notrunc`, do not truncate the output in case of an error, and `sync`, in case of a read error, pad input blocks with zeros.

After the `dd` operation is completed, it prints to the screen the number of records (i.e., blocks) it read and wrote. Here, it read 1440 records and wrote the same number. This is correct because we have specified a block size of 1024 bytes (1 kilobyte), and 1 kilobyte multiplied by the number of blocks (records = 1440) is 1.44MB, which is the size of a high-density floppy disk.

Verifying Image Integrity

Next, we must verify that we made an exact bit-for-bit copy of the evidence. We use *md5sum* [4] to verify the integrity of image:

```
# md5sum /dev/fd0 1034.dd > 1034.md5
```

md5sum calculates an MD5 cryptographic hash, also known as a *message digest*, or simply *hash*. The MD5 message digest (Rivest, 1992) is a one-way hash algorithm that takes as an input a file of arbitrary length and outputs a 128-bit hexadecimal formatted number that is unique to a file's contents. Two files with the same contents will always result in the same 128-bit hash value. The file's contents alone determine a hash value, not associated metadata (e.g., file name, date and times, size, etc.). This fact will be important when we later consider ways to identify illegal or inappropriate files.

We verify the integrity of our evidence by calculating the MD5 hash for the original floppy disk (*/dev/fd0*) and the

forensic image (*1034.dd*). If the hashes are the same, we can rest assured the copy we made is a bit-for-bit duplicate of the evidence. We save the contents of the command by redirecting it to a file that can be printed and archived for safekeeping.

Any differences between the contents of the floppy disk and our forensic image are so indicated in the hash. To illustrate this phenomenon, we used a hex editor to add a single space into the boot sector of the *1034.dd* image, and then reran the MD5 hash on the image. The old and new hashes are different:

```
Old Hash: 04c09fa404ac7611b20a1acc28e7546c
New Hash: dbbbd457d0283103e7148075abb5b91e
```

Imaging over a Network

An alternative to removing the hard drive from the subject computer is to use a network connection. A "network acquisition" requires both computers have network interface cards (NICS; i.e., Ethernet cards), a network crossover cable, and a bootable Linux CD. A network crossover cable allows the investigator to directly connect two computers without a hub or switch.

Several bootable Linux-based CD-ROMs are available. Most of these are based on the popular Knoppix CD (http://www.knoppix.com). Knoppix contains more than 1.7 gigabytes of software on a 700MB CD using compression. The CD contains utilities that are useful for forensics imaging and previewing. Knoppix loads itself into a ram disk during boot and will not access the hard drive of the subject's computer (as of Knoppix 3.3). Knoppix boots into a graphical user interface that allows the investigator read-only access to the hard drives on the subject computer, which is very useful for previewing the contents of the source drive.

As of 2004, there are several forensics bootable Linux CDs. These include Helix (http://www.e-fense.com), Local Area Security (http://www.localareasecurity.com), Knoppix Secure Tools Distribution (http://www.knoppix-std.org/), Penguin Sleuth Kit (http://www.linux-forensics.com/), and FIRE (http://fire.dmzs.com/), the first four of which are based upon Knoppix.

Although strictly speaking Knoppix is not "a forensics distribution," it contains enough tools to make itself extremely useful in these circumstances. It is so popular that we would surmise that it will be around for a long, long time.

Sterilizing Forensic Media

Before imaging the subject's hard drive, it is good practice to "sterilize" or "wipe" the destination media on the forensic server. A forensic wipe removes any vestiges of previous contents on the drive, ensuring that a defense attorney cannot claim that any evidence recovered from the subject's hard drive was from the previous contents on the disk, caused by the commingling of evidence.

A forensic wipe is different than formatting a hard drive. For instance, a quick formatting under Windows or DOS only deletes the bookkeeping portion of the file system (described in subsequent sections), including the root directory and the file allocation table. A quick format does not remove the actual files: these files will remain until overwritten by the operating system. A full format is the same as a quick format except that it also writes F6h over each of the sectors in the data area of the disk. It does not, however, overwrite areas of the hard drive that are unaddressable by the operating system (usually several clusters at the end of a drive).

A forensic wipe can be accomplished with the dd command:

```
# dd if=/dev/zero of=/dev/hdb1 bs=2048
```

The logical device /dev/zero is an infinite source of zeros. Because we have specified our output to be /dev/hdb1, it will write a series of zeros to every single sector of the first partition on the second IDE hard drive. The bs argument specifies that dd should read in blocks of 2048 bytes, overriding the default of 512 bytes.

We can verify that the procedure was successful using the grep command:

```
# grep -v '0' /dev/hdb1
```

grep is a utility that searches for keywords within files. We are searching for the string "0" on the logical device */dev/hdb1*. The -v argument specifies somewhat of a reverse search, that is, display everything on the media that is *not* 0. If grep finds anything that is not 0 it will print the results to the screen. (We have personally never seen dd fail in this task.).

Wiping the drive removes the file system, so we must perform a high-level format before we can copy the image to our destination hard drive. Linux allows us to format a drive in several different file system formats, including Linux/UNIX-based such as EXT2 or EXT3 or Windows FAT16/32. Although Linux can read from and write to FAT32 formatted drives, in this instance it is not our best choice as FAT32 has a 4-GB (2^{32} bits) size limit for files, and most hard drives as of 2004 are much larger. Unfortunately, NTFS write support under the current Linux kernel (either 2.4 or 2.6) is experimental and is therefore not the best choice for critical tasks. For purposes of this chapter, we will create an EXT2 file system on the destination drive. File systems based on the Large File

System specifications can hold files up to 2^{63} bytes in size (http://www.suse.de/~aj/linux_lfs.html).

```
# mkfs.ext2 /dev/hdb1
```

The mkfs command is a wrapper for several programs that create file systems. Here, we are creating a standard Linux EXT2 file system.

Once we have prepared our destination forensic drive, we can begin our imaging process. Here are the steps to use a bootable Linux CD to acquire and preview a subject's hard drive over a network:

1. Check the boot order of your subject computer. It is *crucial that the boot order of the subject's computer is set to boot from the CD before the hard drive*. If the reverse is true, then the hard drive will boot instead of the CD. This will result in changing the access and/or modification times on several hundred files on the hard drive. Boot order is managed from the computer's BIOS. To check the boot order, we first remove the power cable from the back of the source computer, not at the wall outlet. We then open the subject's computer and *remove the power supply connector* from all of the hard drives. This is critical because it guarantees that the source hard drive cannot boot inadvertently. We next replace the computer's power cable and power the subject's computer on. During the boot process the computer should display an onscreen message indicating a key to press to access the BIOS setup (e.g., F1, F2, [Delete], etc.). Press the appropriate key to access the BIOS. If you miss the chance to access the BIOS, the source hard drive cannot boot as its power source has been removed. Reboot and try again. Once in the BIOS setup, change the boot order to CD first, followed by the hard drive. Place the Knoppix CD into the source computer. Replace the power supply connectors to all of the hard drives. *Do not turn on the source computer yet*. This is also a good time to note the system's date and time setting in the BIOS.

2. We then connect the network crossover cable between the source and forensics server's NICs and then power on the subject's computer. It will boot into the Knoppix graphical user interface. Icons that represent the hard drive partitions found by Knoppix will appear on the desktop (see Figure 3). *These drives are not mounted.* You may preview the contents of the drives by clicking on the icons, which will open the drives read-only and display their contents in a file manager.

3. You must manually configure each computer with a network address because neither computer is connected to a DHCP server. Open up terminals on both computers. Figure 4 demonstrates how to set a network address under Linux. First, we switch to root on both computers using the substitute user [su] command. Under Knoppix version 3.3 and later, the su command does not require a root password. Set the network address using the ifconfig command: # ifconfig <interface> <network address> <network mask>. Do this for both computers (using different network addresses for each, of course). Make

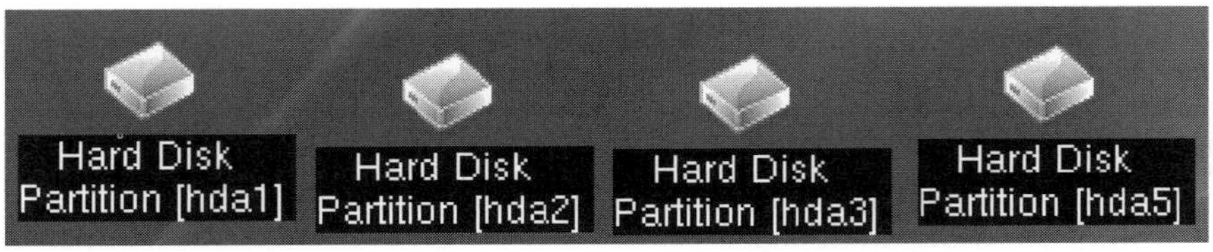

Figure 3: Knoppix desktop.

sure that the network address was correctly set by issuing the command [ifconfig]. Ping the source computer to make sure you have a connection.

4. Before we can continue, we need more specific information on the hard drives from the subject's computer. From a terminal command line, run the command fdisk -l (that's a lowercase "L"). As illustrated in Figure 5, this command displays the number of hard drives connected, the number of partitions on each drive, and the formatting of each partition. Figure 5 shows that our subject's computer has a single 14-GB hard drive. (Note: Is our destination drive on our forensic server large enough to hold this image?) We note that the drive has five partitions, /dev/hda1 through /dev/hda5. The fourth partition, /dev/hda4, is an extended partition (as noted from the W95 Ext'd tag) and was created because drives can only have four primary partitions. This system appears to be a dual-boot Windows/Linux machine based on how the system is partitioned and our own experience. /dev/hda1 is formatted with Microsoft's New Technology File System (NTFS) and likely contains a Window's operating system, although we cannot guarantee this until we preview the image.

5. We have sufficient information to begin an acquisition over the crossover cable. We use the *netcat* utility (http://www.atstake.com) to create the network connection between the two computers. Netcat is a small, free utility available for several operating systems. *Netcat* reads and writes bits over a network connection. The command to run on the forensics server is as follows:

```
# nc -l -p 8888 > evidence.dd
```

This sets up the listen process on the forensics server prior to sending the data from the subject's computer.

From the command line arguments, nc is the netcat executable (it may be called *netcat* under SuSE). The -l argument (a lowercase 'L') indicates *listen* for a connection; the argument -p specifies the port on which to listen. We redirect the output to a file name of our choosing, here *evidence.dd*. If we do not redirect to a file then the output is directed to the standard output, the screen.

6. On the subject's computer, we use the dd command to read the first partition:

```
# dd if=/dev/hda1 | nc 192.168.0.2 8888 -w 3
```

We pipe the output of the dd command to *netcat*, which sends the bits over the network to the specified network address and port on our listening forensic computer. The argument -w 3 indicates that *netcat* should wait 3 seconds before closing the connection upon finding no more data.

The time required to create a forensic image depends upon several factors, including the size of the source media, the speed of the connection (a directly connected IDE versus network acquisition), and the speed of the computer's hardware. Creating a forensic image of a floppy takes only a few minutes, whereas a 60-GB hard drive will take several hours.

After we create the image we must verify its integrity. We can calculate the hash of the source hard drive by issuing the following command from the subject's computer:

```
# md5sum/dev/hda1 | nc 192.168.0.2 8888 -w 3
```

This command calculates the MD5 hash of the source hard drive and pipes the results over the network to our forensic server. We capture this information by setting up a listening process on the forensic computer as demonstrated in

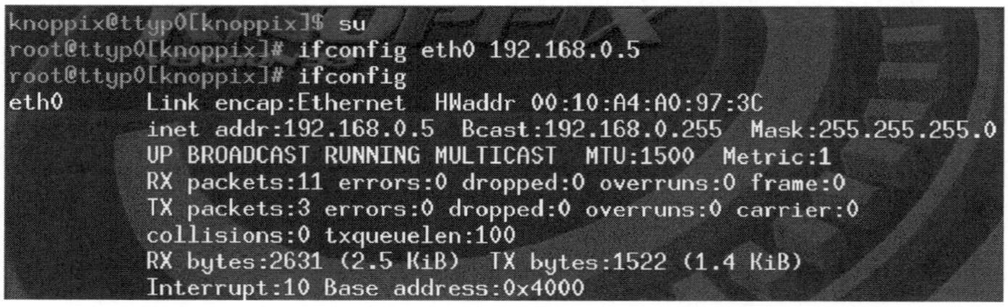

Figure 4: Viewing the network address of the subject's computer.

```
root@ttyp0[knoppix]# fdisk -l

Disk /dev/hda: 48.0 GB, 48004669440 bytes
255 heads, 63 sectors/track, 5836 cylinders
Units = cylinders of 16065 * 512 = 8225280 bytes

   Device Boot      Start         End      Blocks   Id  System
/dev/hda1   *           1        2550    20482843+   7  HPFS/NTFS
/dev/hda2            2551        2563      104422+   83  Linux
/dev/hda3            2564        5138    20683687+   83  Linux
/dev/hda4            5139        5836     5606685    f  W95 Ext'd (LBA)
/dev/hda5            5203        5836     5092573+   b  W95 FAT32
/dev/hda6            5139        5202      514017    82  Linux swap
```

Figure 5: Determining a drive's geometry.

the first command:

```
# nc -l -p 8888 >> evidence.md5
```

The command

```
# md5sum evidence.dd >> evidence.md5
```

calculates the MD5 hash of our forensic image and appends it to the previously created MD5 file. The ">>" command appends the output of the command to an existing file. Warning: If we were to use a single ">" the file evidence.md5 would have been overwritten by the output of the command, rather than appended.

If our hashes match, then we can assume success in our imaging process. We are now ready to begin an analysis of our image.

ANALYSIS OF A FORENSIC IMAGE

Computer forensic procedures can be somewhat artificially divided between *logical* analysis and *physical* analysis. A logical analysis views the evidence from the perspective of the file system as in Figure 6.

The investigator can use graphical tools, for example, file managers or file viewers, that are normally used on a computer. In contrast, a physical analysis views the forensic image from a purely physical viewpoint—there is no file system to consider per se. Because physical analysis does not view the image from the perspective of a file system, it requires the use of a hex editor and similar tools.

Logical and physical analyses are discussed in turn. First we provide readers with a description of a hard drive, which will be important in understanding aspects of both physical and logical analysis.

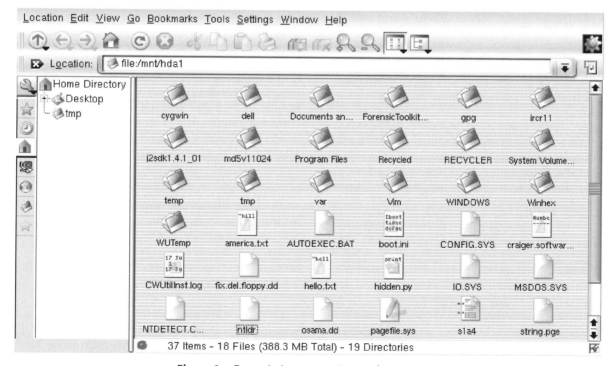

Figure 6: Forensic image preview under Knoppix.

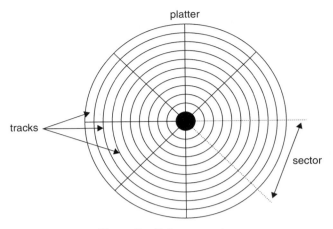

Figure 7: Drive geometry.

Drive Geometry

Figure 7 is a very simple, abstract model of a single magnetic disk. The single disk is called a *platter*. A hard drive will consist of multiple platters stacked on top of one another. Each platter is divided into a number of *tracks*. A *cylinder* is the column of two or more tracks on two or more platters (Nelson, et al., 2004). A *head* is a device that reads and writes data to a platter. Each track is divided into multiple *sectors*. Sectors are created via low-level formatting at the factory and are commonly 512 bytes in size.

High-level formatting places a file system on the disk. In the abstract, a file system is composed of a table to track file metadata (name, size, permissions, etc.) and an index of free disk space. File systems operate on specific size units of disk space. These units are called *clusters* in Windows, *blocks* in UNIX, or *allocation units* in the general. Each cluster consists of one or more hardware sectors. The size of a cluster will differ depending upon the size of the disk. For instance, on a high-density floppy disk, a cluster consists of a single sector. For efficiency, clusters on larger disks will consist of multiple sectors, in multiples of two.

Most modern file systems we discuss in this chapter have a default cluster size of four sectors, or 4096 bytes, although it is configurable. The default cluster size on a Windows 98 FAT32 formatted file system is 64 sectors, or 32,768 bytes/cluster. Cluster size is important for investigators because larger clusters leave more residual forensic information on the disk. To understand why cluster size is important, let us consider three conceptual categories of disk space:

1. *Allocated space* is composed of clusters allocated to a file and that are tracked by the file system.
2. *Unallocated space* is composed of clusters not in use by a file. Unallocated space may contain residual information, for example, from deleted files. We provide greater detail on unallocated space, and how to recover files in unallocated space, in the Physical Analysis section.
3. *Slack space* "is the space left over between the end of the data and the end of the last cluster or block" (Kruse &

Heiser, 2001, p. 75). Slack space may contain residual information, for example, from files previously deleted but which have been partially overwritten. We provide greater detail on slack space in the Physical Analysis section.

The procedures used to analyze the contents of each of the categories of space will differ. A logical analysis, which views our forensic image from the perspective of a file system, only examines information in allocated space. In contrast, a physical analysis allows us to examine information in unallocated and slack space as well.

Mounting the Image

We must *mount* our forensic image to access the file system contained therein. Recall that mounting a disk or image makes a file system available to the operating system's kernel. Once an image is mounted, we can use any tools that we would normally use to work with files (search, view, sort, print, etc.). We want to ensure that we do not (cannot) change our forensic image, so we mount our forensic image in read-only mode. This guarantees that we do not change anything on our image as we are analyzing it.

We use the mount command to mount our forensic image to an existing directory.

```
# mount -t vfat -o ro,loop image.dd image/
```

We first create a directory called *"image"* (which we could have named anything). Next, we execute the mount command with the following arguments: -t specifies the type of file system on the image, here vfat (virtual FAT, the same as FAT only able to understand long file names of 256 characters). The -o specifies options; here we want to mount the image read-only (ro), and we specify loop to interpret the image as if it contains a file system. The next arguments are the image to mount (image.dd), followed by the directory on which to mount the image (image/). If we receive no error message, the image should be mounted.

Depending upon the situation, it may be desirable to create a list of all the files contained on a disk. (Several law enforcement personnel have relayed stories where a prosecuting attorney demanded a list of all files on a disk, so this does occur in practice. This procedure is also listed as an important forensic procedure on the IACIS web site.) We can create a list of files and their associated hashes with the *file* and *md5sum* commands:

```
# find / -type f -print0 | xargs -0 md5sum >
/evidence/files.md5
```

find starts searching for regular files at the root directory and pipes a list of the files as a single line (via the -print0 argument) to the md5sum command. The results are directed to a file—not in a directory on the mounted image of course—for safe keeping. Here is a snippit from the *files.md5* file.

```
82f28b86ed26641a61a0b7a3ee0647a0   ./agenda.doc
093aa48b0b7ae587b9320ada28ae600a   ./suzy.doc
a6fff9e1af9393d7cb1d367f407250a0   ./1034.md5
3fe0b92fd2e93aa125e7d1a2c9508963   ./foo.txt
b9e5e46186f9e92d908feccf2aa2dd82   ./folder/.foo
e65ad7ea32ec3c21a4eb5e7296c1aa0c   ./folder/Yahoo.aba.txt
7349b1a5429cb4a7b36796444eb88528   ./folder/2004_03_01_Minutes.doc
31efc94982e64ec04a30768fe799f3fb   ./folder/grandmaletter.txt
4ef2b14aa970dc14bb260dcd7ba67ba5   ./folder/school.ppt
23958202e2e750090d60f26911842722   ./folder/.hiddenfile
8dad5d4b67ecdd7a0ba5d0d943edabbb   ./bagheera.txt
0c8fb94c2b437896aa2d36ba7d3a2cab   ./list.of.words
```

Once our image is mounted read-only, we can conduct searches, view or print the files, and treat the contents of the image as if it were a live mounted disk, without worrying about altering any files on the image because we mounted our image in read-only mode.

We can unmount the image using the *umount* command (note: *not* unmount).

```
# umount image/
```

Reducing Our Search Space

What forensic procedures do we perform first? The answer is determined in part by the circumstances of our investigation. If we are investigating someone for distributing child pornography, then the primary evidence will be graphical images. (There may be other important evidence that should not be overlooked, including e-mails, electronic documents, etc.) In contrast, in an eBay Internet fraud case, we may be more concerned with e-mail messages, electronic documents, and the contents of Internet browser history and temporary files. Let the circumstances dictate the approach.

Simple cases where we know exactly what evidence for which we are looking may take half of a day. Complicated cases involving multiple hard drives and where we are not exactly sure what constitutes evidence may take weeks or even months. We want to make the best use of our time. The first activity is to distinguish which files are of probative value and which are not. The reason is that most computers contain anywhere from 10,000 to hundreds of thousands (or more) files. At some point, we will be forced to conduct a manual analysis of scores of files. We can make efficient use of our time if we can reduce to a manageable size the number of files we must manually analyze. Computer forensics is a very tedious and time-consuming task, and therefore the more we can use our tools to automate the process of identifying potential evidence the better. One automated way of filtering files is through a hash analysis.

Hash Analysis

A hash analysis compares the hashes of the files to a set of hashes of files of a known content. Files in a hash set typically fall into one of two categories: *known* or *notable*. Known files are files that can be ignored, such as typical system files (iexplore.exe, winword.exe, explore.exe, and

so on). Notable files are ones that have been identified as illegal or inappropriate, such as hacking tools, pictures of child pornography, and so on. A hash analysis automates the process of distinguishing between files that can be ignored while identifying the files known to be of possible evidentiary value. Once the known files have been identified, these files can be filtered. Filtering out the known files may reduce the number of files the investigator must evaluate by half or more.

Hash analysis may be useful in an organizational setting in determining if there is any corporate espionage. Companies may be concerned that insiders are e-mailing intellectual property to competitors. Company IT staff could make a hash set by hashing all critical intellectual property–related documents. These hashes could then be compared against the hashes of files on the employee's computer to determine if the documents are located on the disk. (Note: before doing this, consult legal counsel as there are legal ramifications for this type of activity.)

Recall that only a file's contents, not its metadata, are used in calculating a file's hash value. (It is important to understand this point as subjects will try to hide evidence by changing various file attributes such as files' names, attributes, etc.) We conduct a small experiment to demonstrate this claim for the readers. We take a file and make three copies of it ([1], [2], [3]). We change the first file's name [4]; the second's owner and permissions [5], [6]; and leave the third unchanged. We then calculate the hash value for all three files [7]. Note that the hashes are the same. This fact is helpful when subjects have changed files' names, for example, the notable files previously described, to hide their true content and identity, as we demonstrate.

```
[1] jpc@simba:~> echo 'hello world\!' > file.1
[2] jpc@simba:~> cp file.1 file.2
[3] jpc@simba:~> cp file.2 file.3
[4] jpc@simba:~> mv file.1 file.changed
[5] jpc@simba:~> chown jpc.users file.3
[6] jpc@simba:~> chmod 751 file.2
[7] jpc@simba:~> md5sum file.changed file.2 file.3
    7cf0564cb453a9186431ee9553f7f935 file.changed
    7cf0564cb453a9186431ee9553f7f935 file.2
    7cf0564cb453a9186431ee9553f7f935 file.3
```

To perform a hash analysis, we need to specify a list of MD5s. In this instance, say we are interested in finding several known bad files, including several files from a

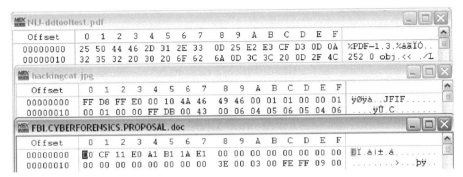

Figure 8: File signatures for three files.

rootkit as well as several illegal images. Here are the MD5s that compose our file (KNOWN.BAD) of notable files:

```
f53ce230616c1f6aafedf546a7cc0f0f Trojan ps
77f7628ee6fa6cd37ee8b06278149d1d Trojan netstat
64a3877b3105cd73496952c1ef8f48e8 Trojan ls
41791681dff38e3a492c72d3e7335f82 Trojan lsof
bbf3aeb654477c4733bddf9a6360d2c5 Illegal Image
2eff0db0a3cac3fc08add30e21257459 Illegal Image
d297c866310377f10b948d53b798c227 Illegal Image
```

We then run *md5deep* (http://md5deep.sourceforge. net) against all of the files in the directory, specifying the file KNOWN.BAD file for comparison.

```
pc@simba:~/chapter.stuff> md5deep -r -m KNOWN.BAD *
/image/chapter/.x
/image/chapter/misc/.y
/image/chapter/misc/preview.png
/image/chapter/misc/stuff.java
/image/chapter/misc/subset/bar
/image/chapter/preview.png
/image/chapter/large.jpg
/image/chapter/README.txt
```

The -r arguments indicate that md5deep should run recursively (recurse through directories). The -m argument indicates the file containing the list of known files. Note that this list may contain either known good (e.g., Windows system files) or known bad files (hacker tool kits, illegal images, etc.).

Md5deep reads in the list of known hashes and then proceeds to hash each file in the path indicated at the command line. It compares the file's hashes with the contents of the list of known hashes. If a match occurs, it lists it on standard out (the screen). This procedure is essentially how commercial forensic-application hash analyses function. As demonstrated above, *md5deep* found all of the files on the list of known hashes. Note that it appears that someone has changed the names of some of the notable files as a means of hiding their identity.

The National Institute of Standards and Technology (http://www.nist.gov) develops and maintains a very large set of hashes called the National Software Reference Library. (http://www.nist.gov/nsrl) The NSRL contained more than 6,000,000 hashes as of early 2005. Another large hash set is the Hashkeeper hash set, which can be downloaded at http://www.hashkeeper.org. An investigator or IT staff can build a custom hash set easily by using the procedures outlined in this chapter, based on the company's need to protect intellectual property,

Signature Analysis

A *signature analysis* is an automated procedure for identifying potential evidence. A *file signature* is a header or footer (or both) within a file that indicates the application associated with a typical file, that is, the type of file. For instance, we opened three files in a hex editor (Figure 8): a Word document, a JPG graphic, and an Adobe Acrobat file. The signatures (in hexadecimal) are

- 25h 50h 44h 46h for Adobe Acrobat Reader files (PDF),
- FFh D8h FFh, for JPEG graphical files, and
- D0h CFh 11h E0h A1h B1h 1Ah E1h for Microsoft Office files.

(Numbers in hexadecimal format are distinguished from decimal format by appending with an h.)

File signatures are useful for evaluating whether a subject is attempting to "hide files in plain sight" by changing file extensions. For instance, renaming a graphic *naked_body.jpg* to *homework.doc* can be effective in hiding a file from prying—albeit naïve—eyes. A cursory examination of files in a file manager will not reveal the fact that the *homework.doc* file is *not* a Word document but rather a graphical file. To make matters worse, Windows Explorer will happily display the graphical file that has a *.doc* extension with a Word icon, confirming to the user that the file is what it purports to be. This is true even if we request a thumbnail view in Windows Explorer. Only if the graphical file has a graphical extension (e.g., GIF, BMP, PNG, JPG, etc.) will it display as a graphical thumbnail.

How does an investigator find these hidden files? We simply compare the file's extension with its corresponding file signature. If the two match, then no effort was made to obscure the file type. If there is a mismatch between the extension and signature, then the file should be exposed to closer examination.

To illustrate how simple of a hiding technique this is, Figure 9 is a directory listing in Windows Explorer that shows files with several different extensions. We changed

02_23_Agenda.doc	31 KB	Microsoft Word Document
2004_02_23___Minutes.doc	92 KB	Microsoft Word Document
2004_03_01_Minutes.doc	180 KB	Microsoft Word Document
cat.jpg	225 KB	IrfanView JPG File
EFE_Manual_English_rev418.pdf	11,896 KB	Adobe Acrobat Document
grandmaletter.txt	52 KB	Text Document
school.ppt	32 KB	Microsoft PowerPoint Pre..
Yahoo.aba.txt	131 KB	Text Document
Bill.1.png	4 KB	IrfanView PNG File

Figure 9: Viewing the contents of a floppy disk under Windows Explorer.

the extensions of several files to disguise their true identity. Can you tell which files were changed?

The `file` command uses several sources of information, including the file's signature, to verify a file's type. The example below illustrates the use the of the file command against the files from Figure 9.

```
jpc@simba:~/chapter.stuff/> file *
02_23_Agenda.doc:                 Microsoft Office Document
2004_02_23___Minutes.doc:         Microsoft Office Document
2004_03_01_Minutes.doc:           Microsoft Office Document
cat.jpg:                          PDF document, version 1.3
EFE_Manual_English_rev418.pdf:    PDF document, version 1.3
file.script:                      empty
grandmaletter.txt:                Microsoft Office Document
school.ppt:                       JPEG image data, JFIF standard 1.01
Yahoo.aba.txt:                    raw G3 data, byte-padded
```

We ran `file` against every file in the current directory. We then manually compared the extensions against the known file type. (We could create a script to do this for us; however, this is beyond the scope of this chapter.) For example, the file *course.doc* exhibits the Word extension, and the signature confirms it is a Microsoft Office document. The file *grandma.txt* exhibits a text file extension; however, the signature indicates that it is a JPG graphical file. The file *homework.doc* has a Word extension, but its signature also indicates it to be a JPG graphical file. The remaining files appear to be what they claim.

How much credence should we put in the extension to denote the type of file? The simple answer: none. As demonstrated, changing the file extensions is a simple, and often successful, means of hiding inappropriate or illegal files.

Searching a Forensic Image

Two common search tasks involve searching for specific keywords within documents or searching for particular types of files (e.g., graphical files in a child pornography case or Excel, Quicken, or Money files in a money-laundering case.) We first describe how to conduct keyword searches, followed by searching for particular types of files.

Keyword Searches

Once the investigator reduces the search space by identifying and filtering known files, as well as identified suspect files via signature analyses, she can turn her attention to searching for specific keywords within the forensic image.

Below we use the *grep* utility to search for keywords on the image. *grep* has the capability to search for multiple keywords simultaneously. This is accomplished by creating a text file containing a list of keywords and then using the `-f` flag to indicate that we are using a file, instead of a single keyword, as input to *grep*. In this example our keyword text file contained the following key words, one per line, with no trailing blank line: marijuana, crack, crank, cocaine, oxycontin.

Again, it is important that there is *no blank line* at the end of our keyword file. Had we not used a file for our keywords, we would have had to perform five separate single keyword searches.

Now we are ready to search our forensic image for the keywords. We execute the following command:

```
# grep -i -r -f keywords /image/* >
/evidence/grep.results
```

The flags are interpreted as follows:

- `-i` indicates case insensitive search, thus "cocaine," "COCAINE" and "CoCainE" are the same.
- `-r` indicates a recursive search, that is, traverse all of the subdirectories beneath the current directory.
- `-f` indicates the next parameter is the file containing our keywords.

We redirect the results of our `grep` search into a file so that we can more closely analyze the results and print it out if need be. Abbreviated results are displayed:

/mnt/evidence/bruce: WASHINGTON, D.C. U.S. Representative issued the following statement regarding the GAO Report to Congress titled, OxyContin Abuse and Diversion and Efforts to Address the Problem:

/mnt/evidence/bruce:This report reinforces what I suspected all along: Purdue Pharma has engaged in highly questionable practices regarding the marketing of OxyContin, leaving a plague of abuse and broken lives in its path . . .

/mnt/evidence/dynamic.dll:Cocaine Anonymous is a fellowship of men and women who share their experience, strength and hope with each other that they may solve their common problem and help others to recover from their addiction. The only requirement for membership is a desire to stop using cocaine . . .

/mnt/evidence/homework.doc:OxyContin is a trade name for the drug oxycodone hydrochloride. Manufactured by Purdue Pharma L.P., OxyContin is a controlled-release form of oxycodone prescribed to treat chronic pain. When used

properly, OxyContin can provide pain relief for up to 12 hours . . .

/mnt/evidence/todo:marijuana: facts for teens . . .

/mnt/evidence/todo:teen boy qoute that reads I used to be real athletic. When I started using drugs, I just stopped playing all together because I thought I had more important things to do. Q: What are the short-term effects of marijuana use? . . .

/mnt/evidence/todo:A: The short-term effects of marijuana include: . . .

`grep` found instances of the terms marijuana, cocaine, and OxyContin in files contained on our forensic image. Note that there are several different cases used in the spelling of the terms (e.g., "Cocaine," "cocaine"). A case sensitive search would have failed to find several instances of the keywords, therefore, it is usually best to include the `-i` flag if case does not matter.

Finding Files by Type

Say we have been asked by law enforcement to find all graphics files on a subject's hard drive that contains more than 500,000 files. What would be the most efficient means of conducting this search? Clearly we want to automate as much of the search as possible. We could search for files with the appropriate graphical file extension, for instance:

```
# find / -type f \( -name `*.gif' -or -name
`*.jpg' -or -name `*.bmp' -or -name `*.png' \)
```

This command finds all files with the GIF, JPG, or BMP extension. This command would *not* find the files with changed extensions, however. One way to find graphic files whose extension has been changed is to combine three GNU utilities: `find`, `file`, and `grep`. The best way to

Step 2: `file` command, which returns the type of file using header information. Pipe the results of this command to the

Step 3: `grep` command to search for graphical-related keywords.

Here is our command to perform these steps:

```
# find /image -type f ! \( -name `*.jpg'
-or -name `*.png' -or -name `*.bmp' -or
-name `*.tiff' \) -print0 | xargs -0
file | grep -f keywords.txt
```

The */image* argument specifies the directory in which to start. The argument `-type f` specifies that we are interested in regular files as opposed to special files such as devices or directories. The `find` command is recursive by default so it is essentially recursively finding all files beginning at the */image* directory. The exclamation mark (!) modifies the contents within the parenthesis and says that we want to process files whose extension is not *.jpg, or *.png, or *.bmp, or *.tiff. The `-print0` is a special formatting command that is required to format the output of `find` for piping to the next command.

We pipe the results of `find` to `xargs -0`, which hands each file from the previous command to `file`. `file` evaluates each file's signature, returning a description of the type of file. These results are piped to `grep` to search for the specific keywords that are contained within the *keywords.txt* file. The arguments for `grep` include `-i` for case insensitive search and the `-f keywords.txt`, the file containing the list of keywords: PNG, GIF, bitmap, JPEG, and image.

The results are as follows:

```
# find /image -type f ! \( -name `*.jpg' -or -name `*.png' -or -name
`*.bmp' -or -name `*.tiff' \) -print0 | xargs -0 file | grep -f
keywords
./agenda.doc:          PC bitmap data, Windows 3.x, 382 x 61 x 24
./suzy.doc:            PNG image data, 571 x 135, 8-bit/color RGB
./folder/.foo:         PC bitmap data, Windows 3.x, 536 x 177 x 24
./folder/school.ppt:   JPEG image data, JFIF standard 1.01
./folder/.hiddenfile:  PNG image data, 351 x 374, 8-bit/color RGB,
./bagheera.txt:        PC bitmap data, Windows 3.x, 536 x 307 x 24
./9.11.xls:            JPEG image data, EXIF standard, 10752 x 2048
./list.of.words:       PNG image data, 571 x 135, 8-bit/color RGB
```

explain the combined use of these commands is through a demonstration.

Our goal is to find all graphical files regardless of extension. We want to do the following:

Step 1: Use the `find` command to find all regular files on the hard drive (as opposed to directories, special devices, and so on). Pipe the results of this command to the

We found eight graphical files, including instances of JPEG, PNG, and bitmap files. Note each of the files found were graphical files with misleading file extensions. What can we deduce from this result? Because applications will not arbitrarily change an extension of a graphical file, an investigator might reasonably deduce that a user has manually renamed the files, possibly in an attempt to hide their nature. This result is not incontrovertible but would warrant further investigation.

E-Mail Searches

E-mail is ubiquitous, supplanting regular mail as a preferred form of communication for many. E-mail can be a rich source of evidence for many types of investigations.

There are several e-mail applications available in Windows, the most popular of which are Microsoft Outlook and Outlook Express, the latter of which is purportedly the most popular e-mail client as it comes with every version of Windows. Microsoft Outlook is a full-fledged personal information manager that includes e-mail, calendar, contact list, task list, and scheduler. There are several, less popular, e-mail applications available on other platforms, including Eudora, Netscape Mail, Mozilla Mail, and Thunderbird. Each of these applications includes an address book or contact list that may prove useful in an investigation.

Some e-mail applications store messages in proprietary binary formats, including Outlook, Outlook Express, and Eudora. Outlook uses a proprietary format that is different from its sibling Outlook Express. Netscape and Mozilla mail store mail in a nonproprietary *mbox* format that is easily readable in a text editor.

To conduct an e-mail investigation, we must locate the mailbox files. The mailbox locations differ depending upon the version of Windows and the application used:

- Outlook Express
  - Windows 2000/XP
    - C:\Documents & Settings\<*username*>\Local Settings\Application Data\Identities\<*unique string*>\Microsoft\Outlook Express\
  - Windows NT
    - C:\winnt\profiles\<*username*>\Local Settings\Application Data\Identities\<*unique string*>\Microsoft\Outlook Express\
  - Windows 95/98/ME
    - C:\Windows\Application Data\Identities\<*unique string*>\Microsoft\Outlook Express
- Netscape/Mozilla Mail
  - Windows 2000/XP
    - C:\Documents & Settings\Application Data\Mozilla\profiles\<*username*>\<*unique string*>.*slt*\Mail
  - Windows NT
    - C:\winnt\Application Data\ Mozilla\ profiles\ <*username*>\<*unique string*>.*slt*\Mail
  - Windows 95/98/ME
    - C:\Windows\Application Data\ Mozilla\profiles\ <*username*>\<*unique string*>.*slt* \Mail

Outlook Express stores e-mail messages and folders in files with a *dbx* extension. Each folder has a corresponding *dbx* file, whose name coincides with the folder's name. For example, the *outbox.dbx* file corresponds to the Outbox folder (http://http://mail-repair.com/outlook-express-repair.html). An investigator must use an application that understands the *dbx* proprietary format to extract the folders and messages in a human-readable format. The simplest method is to copy *dbx* or *pst* files to another Windows machine that contains the Outlook application and import the appropriate application, either Outlook Express (*dbx* files) or Outlook (*pst* files).

A second alternative is to use a non-Microsoft application that understands the mailbox formats and has the capability of extracting the messages and folders. For example, LibPST (http://sourceforge.net/projects/ol2mbox/) is an open source utility that converts messages from Outlook *PST* format to a standard *mbox* format. In our experiments, we used LibPST to extract the contents of the Outlook mailbox. This demonstrates it is always good to have a wide variety of tools in your forensic toolkit. Here is a sanitized e-mail that we recovered with LibPST:

```
From "Philip Craiger" Wed Jan 09:54:24 2004
X-Apparently-To: philip@craiger.net via web12824.mail.yahoo.com; Wed, 07
Jan 2004 07:54:30 -0800
Return-Path: <philip@craiger.net>
Received: from lakemtao06.cox.net (68.1.17.115)
  by mta1-vm3.mail.yahoo.com with SMTP; Wed, 07 Jan 2004 07:54:29 -0800
Received: from craiger.net ([68.13.130.154]) by lakemtao06.cox.net
  (InterMail vM.5.01.06.05 201-253-122-130-105-20030824) with ESMTP
  id <20040107155429.VISE24575.lakemtao06.cox.net@craiger.net>;
  Wed, 7 Jan 2004 10:54:29 -0500
Message-ID: <3FFC2BB0.2060702@craiger.net>
Disposition-Notification-To: Philip Craiger <philip@craiger.net>
Date: Wed, 07 Jan 2004 09:54:24 -0600
From: Philip Craiger <philip@craiger.net>
Reply-To: philip@craiger.net
User-Agent: Mozilla/5.0 (Windows; U; Windows NT 5.1; en-US; rv:1.6b)
Gecko/20031205 Thunderbird/0.4
X-Accept-Language: en-us, en
MIME-Version: 1.0
To: xxxxx.xxxxxxxx@SMU.CA, xxxxxxx xxxxxxx <xxxxxxx@xxxx.cas.usf.edu>
Subject: BIO
Content-Type: text/plain; charset=us-ascii; format=flowed
Content-Transfer-Encoding: 7bit

Hi ya'll,

I won't be able to make it this Friday; I'm going out of town.

Philip
```

Table 2 Yahoo! Mail and Hotmail Filenames

File Content	Yahoo! Mail	Hotmail
Login page	login[#].htm	uilogin[#].htm
Home page	Welcome[#].htm	mhome[#].htm
Inbox/folder	ShowFolder[#].htm	HoTMail[#].htm
View message	ShowLetter[#].htm	getmsg[#].htm
Compose message	Compose[#].htm	compose[#].htm

Web-Based E-mail

Investigators are likely to encounter Web mail, the most common of which are Yahoo! Mail (http://my.yahoo.com) and Hotmail (http://www.hotmail.com). Web mail messages are stored in *HTML* format with the extension *html* or *htm* and are thus readable with any Web browser. The messages that are downloaded from or uploaded to the Web are stored in the four Windows temporary Internet folders.

We conducted a series of experiments to determine the file names associated with each of the Web mail messages from Yahoo! Mail and Hotmail. The results of our investigation are displayed in Table 2. These names may be used in conjunction with the *grep* search to identify the use of Web mail messages.

We can use any Web browser to view these HTML files. In Figure 10, we opened a Web mail message from our temporary Internet folders (note the message has been sanitized of names).

Unless a suspect took overt means to remove these files from the temporary Internet folders, we can easily access these files via a Web browser.

The temporary Internet folders may contain hundreds of files with an *htm* extension. To find the relevant e-mail-related files, the investigator can open up each file in a browser and conduct a manual search or use grep to search for the appropriate file names (see Table 2). Note that the terms "Yahoo" or "Hotmail" will appear somewhere in the e-mail files. We use this fact in our command to search for files from Hotmail.

To find all Hotmail files, we use the following command line to show all of the related files in the temporary Internet folders.

The directories with the funny-looking names are the temporary Internet file folders.

Windows Swap File

A swap file is virtual memory that is used as an extension of the computer system's RAM (http://whatis.techtarget.com). Typically, the least-recently used contents of RAM are paged out (i.e., swapped) to the swap file and are read back into RAM on an as-needed basis. The swap file can contain evidence that has been previously removed, even if the file was forensically wiped from a hard drive, unless of course the swap file was forensically wiped; then the file within the swap is unrecoverable, although we may still find copies in unallocated or slack space.

The Windows swap file under Windows 9x/ME is named *win386.swp* and is typically found in the Windows root directory, although in the Window's system directory this may be changed by the administrator. Under Windows NT/2000/XP, the file is named *pagefile.sys* and is typically found in the root directory (e.g., C:\), and again may be changed to a different location.

The swap file is a binary file. We use the `strings` command along with `grep` to extract interesting information of possible evidentiary value. The `strings` command reads in a file and extracts the human-readable text of a certain length, the default of which is four characters. In the following example, we extract the human-readable text and then use `grep` to search for the string "hacker." Note that we request two lines of context using the –C argument, which gives us two lines before and after the actual search string. There were approximately 25 hits extracted from the swap file.

```
linux: strings win386.swp | grep -C 2 hacker

// lines deleted for brevity

--
ing latest amitis
/amitis/serv
immortal-hackers.com
.I$I
llium-e
```

```
linux:~/Temporary Internet Files/Content.IE5 # find . -type f \( -name
'getmsg*.htm' -or -name 'uilogin*.htm' -or -name 'mhome*.htm' -or -name
'HoTMail*.htm' -or -name 'compose*.htm' \)

./31n6dkxa/getmsg[1].htm
./31n6dkxa/compose[1].htm
./2l4z6jel/uilogin[1].htm
./ybcpq9sz/compose[1].htm
./ybcpq9sz/compose[2].htm
./ojavstch/compose[1].htm
./ojavstch/uilogin[1].htm
./ojavstch/getmsg[1].htm
```

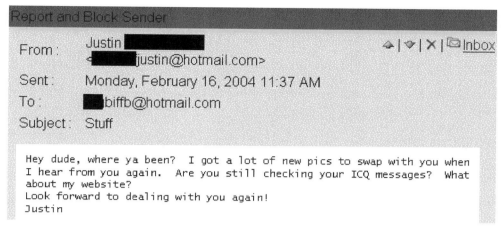

Figure 10: Incoming Hotmail message saved in a temporary Internet folder.

```
--
fg32.exe
boot
hacker
syscfg32
BotV0.3
--
echo @echo off >>
ces\firewall
hackers and viruses
ControlSet\
\firewall.exe
--
iiiii
for WiNis        by F-king
root@hacker
\HATREDFIEND
/\/\ENDOFFILE/\/\
```

// lines deleted for brevity

I Know What You Did with Your Computer Last Summer...

Every time a user uses Windows Explorer or Internet Explorer to access a file or Web site, digital traces of these activities are placed on the hard drive. Most of these artifacts are kept in *index.dat* files. An *index.dat* file is a binary file that tracks user activities: files opened in Windows Explorer, Web pages opened in Internet Explorer, and so on.

Each time a file is accessed via Windows Explorer (as shown in Figure 11) or Internet Explorer, a record is placed in an *index.dat* file.

Windows uses several *index.dat* files to track various activities on the computer. The location of these files will vary depending upon the version of Windows used. Table 3 shows these locations.

Index.dat files are binary files and therefore not in human-readable format. *Pasco* (http://www.foundstone.com) is a small open source application that parses the contents of *index.dat* files and outputs the results into a tab-delimited file. To illustrate, we ran *pasco* against the *index.dat* file from a system and redirected the output to a file that we subsequently imported into a spreadsheet application (see Figure 12).

```
# pasco index.dat > evidence.txt
```

This *index.dat* file in this example was from the *History.IE5* folder (see Table 3). Each row in the spreadsheet is an activity record that includes the type of access, the URL (which can be a regular file or a Web site), the modified and access times, filename, and directory (latter two not shown).

This particular *index.dat* contains information on files accessed from either Windows Explorer (the default file manager) or Internet Explorer, including

• files accessed and opened via Windows Explorer (rows 4 through 9),
• keywords used in searches over the Internet (rows 10 and 11), and
• URLs visited via Internet Explorer (rows 12 through 15).

This *index.dat* file included more than 487 files accessed within the last three weeks. An investigator can use the modified and last accessed times to determine the most recent date and time the user downloaded the file (modified time), as well as the last time the user visited the page or file (access time)

Cookies
According to http://www.cookiecentral.com,

> Cookies are pieces of information generated by a Web server and stored in the user's computer, ready for future access. Cookies are embedded in the HTML information flowing back and forth between the user's computer and the servers. Cookies were implemented to allow user-side customization of Web information. For example, cookies are used to personalize Web search engines, to allow users to participate in WWW-wide contests (but only once!), and to store shopping lists of items a user has selected while browsing through a virtual shopping mall (Mayer-Schonberger, February 3, 2003).

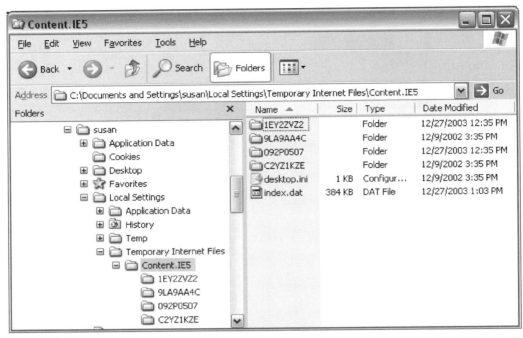

Figure 11: Location of an *index.dat* file in temporary Internet folders.

Unless a user's browser security is set to high, cookies are automatically—and quietly—placed on the user's hard drive. Most users may be unaware that these cookies are being saved on their hard drives.

The cookies directory contains the individual cookies as well as an *index.dat* file that consists of the activity records for each of the cookies in the directory, as shown in Figure 13. We used Pasco to parse the *index.dat*, the results of which are displayed in Figure 14. Note the activity records contain the cookies' URL (from whence it came), the modified and access times, and the cookies' file name.

```
#galleta jpc@microsoft[1].txt >ms.cookie.txt
```

As shown in Figure 14, the cookie is partitioned into six or more pieces of information, including a) the Web site from which the cookie came, b) a variable, c) its associated value (which will differ on its meaning depending upon the Web site), d) the creation time of the cookie, and e) its expiration date and time. Here the variable is apparently the GUID (globally unique identifier) for my copy of the

Windows OS that I am running, along with a hash of its value.

Care should be taken when interpreting cookies to infer user activity because cookies may be placed on user's hard drive from third-party sources, that is, from sources other than the Web site visited.

Table 4 lists the locations where cookies can be found.

Deleted Files and the INFO2 File

Files that are deleted through *My Computer*, *Windows Explorer*, a Windows-compliant program, or any other way *except* from the command line, are removed from their original directory, and a copy is placed in either the *Recycled Bin* (FAT32) or *Recycler Bin* (NTFS). A binary file named *INFO2* within each bin tracks important information about the deleted files and may be an important source of evidence should the contents of deleted files be overwritten.

According to Microsoft (How the Recycle Bin Stores Files, January 18, 2004.), the following occurs when a file

Table 3 Locations of Index.dat Files

Windows	Locations
95/98/ME	\Windows\Temporary Internet Files\Content.IE5\
	\Windows\Cookies\
	\Windows\History\History.IE5\
NT	\Winnt\Profiles\<username>\Local Settings\Temporary Internet Files\Content.IE5\
	\Winnt\Profiles\<username>\Cookies\
	\Winnt\Profiles\<username>\Local Settings\History\History.IE5\
2000/XP	\Documents and Settings\<username>\Local Settings\Temporary Internet Files \Content.IE5\
	\Documents and Settings\<username>\Cookies\
	\Document and Settings\<username>\Local Settings\History\History.IE5\

Source: adapted from Jones, 2003.

	A	B	C	D
1	History File: index.dat			
2				
3	TYPE	URL	MODIFIED TIME	ACCESS TIME
4	URL	Visited: jpc@file:///C:/Documents%20and%20Settings/jpc/Desktop/chapter/computer.forensi	Sun Dec 28 16:46:52 2003	Sun Dec 28 16:46
5	URL	Visited: jpc@file:///C:/Documents%20and%20Settings/jpc/Desktop/The%20Eagles%20-%20	Wed Jan 7 10:00:59 2004	Wed Jan 7 10:00:
6	URL	Visited: jpc@file:///C:/Documents%20and%20Settings/jpc/Desktop/forensics.grades.fall.03.xl	Sun Dec 21 16:46:03 2003	Sun Dec 21 16:46
7	URL	Visited: jpc@file:///C:/Documents%20and%20Settings/jpc/Desktop/secret.service.pdf	Mon Dec 29 15:08:26 2003	Mon Dec 29 15:08
8	URL	Visited: jpc@file:///C:/Documents%20and%20Settings/jpc/Desktop/chapter/i.encyc/TOC.doc	Mon Dec 29 15:17:09 2003	Mon Dec 29 15:17
9	URL	Visited: jpc@file:///C:/Documents%20and%20Settings/jpc/Desktop/chapter/chapter.12.29.v4.z	Mon Dec 29 15:34:12 2003	Mon Dec 29 15:34
10	URL	Visited: jpc@http://search.msn.com/results.aspx?srch=106&FORM=AS6&q=google+secret+s	Sun Dec 28 16:42:38 2003	Sun Dec 28 16:42
11	URL	Visited: jpc@http://www.google.com/search?hl=en&ie=UTF-8&oe=UTF-8&q=Computers+are	Sun Dec 28 09:44:04 2003	Sun Dec 28 09:44
12	URL	Visited: jpc@http://www.rcfl.org/training.htm	Sun Dec 28 09:43:14 2003	Sun Dec 28 09:43
13	URL	Visited: jpc@http://www.ndaa-apri.org/publications/newsletters/update_volume_15_number_	Sun Dec 28 09:43:25 2003	Sun Dec 28 09:43
14	URL	Visited: jpc@http://www.ndaa.org	Sun Dec 28 09:47:01 2003	Sun Dec 28 09:47
15	URL	Visited: jpc@http://www.ndaa-apri.org/index.html	Sun Dec 28 09:46:32 2003	Sun Dec 28 09:46
16	URL	Visited: jpc@file:///C:/Documents%20and%20Settings/jpc/Desktop/PGPFW658Win32.zip	Sat Dec 20 17:51:26 2003	Sat Dec 20 17:51:

evidence

Figure 12: A Parsed *Index.dat* File.

is deleted by one of the means described at the beginning of this section:

1. The deleted file is moved to the Recycled/Recycler Bin.
2. The following details are recorded in the INFO2 file for each deleted file:
    a. The index, that is, the order in which the file was deleted.
    b. The date and time the file was deleted.
    c. Drive from which the file was deleted.
    d. The full path.
    e. The file size.
3. The deleted file is renamed, using the following syntax:

D<original drive letter of file><#>.<original extension>

The <#> is the order in which the file was placed in the bin. For example, if a file named c:\My Documents\Florida.doc is the first file placed in the Recyle Bin, its name is DC1.doc. A file named Beatles.MP3 deleted next would be renamed DC2.MP3. If the files were on the Z drive, they would be renamed DZ1.doc and DZ2.MP3, respectively.

The length for an INFO2 record under Windows 95/98/ME is 280 bytes and 800 bytes under Windows NT/2000/XP (Sheldon, 2002). When a user empties the Recycled/Recycler bin, the files within the bin are removed and the INFO2 file's contents are deleted.

Under NTFS, each user is tracked by a security ID (or SID), which is how the computer refers internally to each user. This allows user activity to be tracked by the operating system. Under NTFS, every user has a folder named

after his/her SID in the Recycler Bin. Each of the folders will contain an INFO2 file.

Figure 15 shows a Recycler Bin's contents from the command line. (We must demonstrate this from the command line as a user's SID is not displayed when viewed within Windows Explorer.) Note the SID-named folder.

The times displayed are the last modification times for each file, *not* the time the file was created in the bin. Recall the deleted times are kept in the INFO2 file.

We can use *rifuiti* (http://www.foundstone.com) to interpret the binary contents of the INFO2 file. *Rifuiti* takes as an argument the name of the INFO2 file. We redirect the results to a tab-delimited file that we can then import into a spreadsheet application (as demonstrated in Figure 16).

```
# rifuiti INFO2 > deleted.txt
```

Of what use is the INFO2 file? Even though its contents are deleted when the bin is emptied, we may be able to recover the contents from unallocated space during a physical analysis. We may even be able to recover the files that were emptied from the bin. (We deal with the recovering of information from unallocated and slack space elsewhere in the chapter.) Note that we are still able to extract important information from the INFO2 file concerning deleted files, including a) the date and time the file was deleted, b) the drive on which the file was deleted, c) the file's original path, and d) the file's size.

Application Residual Files

Many Windows applications create *temporary* files that are usually written to the hard drive. These temporary files are usually deleted from the hard drive once the application closes or the user closes the file manually. As we have

```
E:\Documents and Settings\jpc\Cookies>ls
index.dat                    jpc@msn[1].txt
jpc@atdmt[2].txt             jpc@preview[2].txt
jpc@atwola[1].txt            jpc@questionmarket[1].txt
jpc@com[1].txt               jpc@real[1].txt
jpc@cos[1].txt               jpc@tucows[i].txt
jpc@dell[1].txt              jpc@w[1].txt
jpc@ehg-ati.hitbox[1].txt    jpc@winamp[2].txt
jpc@fastclick[2].txt         jpc@www.ati[1].txt
jpc@geocities[1].txt         jpc@www.ipswitch[1].txt
jpc@hitbox[2].txt            jpc@www.pcmag[1].txt
jpc@info.winamp[1].txt       jpc@yahoo[2].txt
jpc@microsoft[1].txt
```

Figure 13: Cookies directory.

Table 4 Cookie File Locations

Windows	Locations
95/98/ME	\Windows\Cookies\
2000/XP	\Documents and Settings\<username>\ Cookies\

	A	B	C	D	E	F
1	Cookie File: jpc@microsoft[1].txt					
2						
3	SITE	VARIABLE	VALUE	CREATION TIME	EXPIRE TIME	FLAGS
4	microsoft.com/	MC1	GUID=3b34e28b8c55e34f9ade8306293468a7&HASH=8be2&LV=20042&V=3	Sat Feb 21 18:46:06 2004	Tue Oct 3 07:00:00 2006	1024

Figure 14: Parsed cookie file.

```
E:\RECYCLER\S-1-5-21-1409082233-1592454029-839522115-1003>dir /a
 Volume in drive E is whammo
 Volume Serial Number is 787E-00E6

 Directory of E:\RECYCLER\S-1-5-21-1409082233-1592454029-839522115-1003

03/26/2004  09:12 AM    <DIR>          .
03/26/2004  09:12 AM    <DIR>          ..
03/09/2004  07:38 AM           400,896 De10.ppt
03/25/2004  08:08 AM            47,104 De11.xls
02/21/2004  12:56 PM             1,607 De12.lnk
02/14/2004  08:28 PM               630 De13.txt
02/20/2004  07:39 PM           205,595 De14.jpg
01/20/2004  04:05 PM           272,416 De15.EnScript
12/29/2003  03:12 PM         1,091,325 De6.pdf
01/11/2004  09:09 AM           129,577 De7.pdf
03/11/2004  07:22 PM           167,366 De9.torrent
03/26/2004  09:10 AM                65 desktop.ini
03/26/2004  09:12 AM             8,020 INFO2
              11 File(s)      2,324,601 bytes
               2 Dir(s)  24,252,698,624 bytes free
```

Figure 15: Recycler Bin on Windows XP.

	A	B	C	D	E
1	INFO2 File: INFO2				
2					
3	INDEX	DELETED TIME	DRIVE NUM	PATH	SIZE
4	6	Fri Mar 26 15:11:02 2004	4	E:\Documents and Settings\jpc\Desktop\secret.service.guide.pdf	1093632
5	7	Fri Mar 26 15:11:02 2004	4	E:\Documents and Settings\jpc\Desktop\fed.rules.evide.pdf	131072
6	8	Fri Mar 26 15:11:07 2004	4		118784
7	9	Fri Mar 26 15:11:10 2004	4	E:\Documents and Settings\jpc\Desktop\Mandrakelinux-10.0-Community.torrent	167936
8	10	Fri Mar 26 15:11:18 2004	4	E:\Documents and Settings\jpc\Desktop\HONORS\UseCaseExample.ppt	401408
9	11	Fri Mar 26 15:11:24 2004	4	E:\Documents and Settings\jpc\Desktop\HONORS\HONORS Gradebook.3.23.xls	49152
10	12	Fri Mar 26 15:11:49 2004	4	E:\Documents and Settings\jpc\Desktop\Program\Current_v4_Scripts\Mozilla Firefox.lnk	4096
11	13	Fri Mar 26 15:11:55 2004	4	E:\Documents and Settings\jpc\Desktop\Program\Current_v4_Scripts\CYFOR.attendees.txt	4096
12	14	Fri Mar 26 15:12:01 2004	4	E:\Documents and Settings\jpc\Desktop\Program\Current_v4_Scripts\confiden.html.jpg	208896
13	15	Fri Mar 26 15:12:26 2004	4	E:\Documents and Settings\jpc\Desktop\Program\Current_v4_Scripts\Scripts\Examples\w4_lr	274432

Figure 16: Contents of INFO2 file viewed in a spreadsheet.

Name ▲	Size	Type
~$rensic.system.analysis-v4	1 KB	Microsoft Word Do
~WRL0002.tmp	270 KB	TMP File
~WRL0004.tmp	271 KB	TMP File
~WRL0025.tmp	273 KB	TMP File
~WRL0031.tmp	395 KB	TMP File
~WRL0051.tmp	275 KB	TMP File
~WRL0061.tmp	394 KB	TMP File
~WRL0064.tmp	275 KB	TMP File

Figure 17: Microsoft Word temporary files.

```
41260:Dr. Philip Craiger
41279-bjbj
--
41346-September 3, 2003 2109 Sully Court        Bakersfield, CA  93311
41404:Dr. Philip Craiger                        | email:  philip@craiger.net
41478-Associate Professor of Computer Science   | web:    www.craiger.net
--
41716-Omaha, NE  68182                          | PGP Key ID: 0x9B600586
41786:Dear Philip:
41799-Thank you for agreeing to serve as one of our contributors to The Handbook
  of Information Security.  Professor Bidgoli and I would like to formally invite
  you.
--
45045-, 554-3181, PKI173B
45065:Dr. Philip Craiger,
45086-HYPERLINK "mailto:pcraiger@mail.unomaha.edu"
--
49642-Computer and Network Forensics
49673:Dr. Philip Craiger
49692-Normal.dot
49703:J. Philip Craiger, Ph.D.
49728-Microsoft Word 10.0
search.philip lines 11-30/30 (END)
```

Figure 18: Results of grep search.

previously noted, deleting files only removes the pointer to the file and marks the clusters occupied by the file as available: the information in the clusters is still recoverable until overwritten. (Note that when temporary files are deleted by applications they are *not* moved to the Recycler/Recycled Bins as described in the previous section.)

Microsoft Office applications are very good about creating temporary files. Microsoft Word, for example, creates temporary files that consist of the contents of previous versions of a file. Temporary files are created when Word's *autosave* feature is turned on or when the user manually saves the file. Word creates temporary files to provide some fault tolerance should Word or the operating system crash. In later versions of Office, if Word finds one of these files, it recognizes this as an anomaly and offers to recover the file.

Figure 17 illustrates several temporary files that Word created as we were editing a document. This explains why an investigator might find dozens of residual copies of the same text in unallocated space.

If an application or operating system misbehaves, it may leave temporary files (usually, but not necessarily, noted with a TMP extension) in allocated space on the hard drive. We can use the find command to search for these files.

```
# find / --type f \( -name `*.TMP' --or --name
`*.tmp'\)
```

This command will find all files with the *.TMP or *.tmp extension. Of course, this only works if the temporary files are in allocated space (i.e., have not been deleted). Once the application closes, these temporary files will be deleted by the application. If we need to identify temporary files that have been deleted, we can use two procedures. The easiest method is if we know part of the text of the document, we can use grep to search our forensic image (that is, *unmounted* image) for that text using a physical analysis.

Say we are told that subject created a threatening letter using a word processor on his computer. We are also told the subject has a "wipe" utility on the computer, and that a cursory examination of the computer showed no copies of the letter. As investigators, we assume that the word processor diligently created temporary files of the counterfeit document. We can use parts of the threatening letter in a keyword search to see if we can recover some of the temporary files.

A significant content of a hard disk will be unreadable binary data. Therefore, let us first extract all of the human-readable text from our forensic image. We use the strings command to extract the human-readable text from our forensic image.

```
# strings evidence.dd>/evidence/evidence.str
```

```
# grep -b -I -C 1 "Philip" evidence.str >
/evidence/search.philip
```

strings extracts strings of size 4 bytes or greater in the 7-bit ASCII range. We redirect the results to a file, which we then use in our grep search. The -b flag in the grep search specifies that we want the byte offset printed for each result, that is, where in the file the match occurred. The -C 1 specifies that we want one line of context before and after our match.

Figure 18 shows the results: five matches at byte offsets 41260, 41404, 41786, 45606, and 49673, with one line of context before and after each match. If we wish to further explore text associated with one of the matches, we can use the byte offset of the file to extract more of the text.

Say we are interested in the text at offset 41786, which appears to be a letter of some sort. We can use dd to extract the text as demonstrated in Figure 19.

The important arguments are bs, skip, and count. We set our block size to one so that we can ask for a specific number of characters (i.e., bs = 1 is equal to one character). We want to start extracting the data a little before our match at byte offset, so we chose to start at 41700. Note we specify offset 41700 because our block size is one. If we had used the default block size of 512 bytes, we

Figure 19: Command line to extract specific strings.

```
snoball:/evidence # dd if=evidence.str of=philip.txt bs=1 skip=41700 count=750
750+0 records in
750+0 records out
snoball:/evidence #
```

would be starting at offset 41700 × 512 or 21,350,400, definitely not what we wanted. The block size also refers to our count: we are extracting 750 characters (not 750 × 512). The 750 characters we extracted are shown in Figure 20.

As you can see through several demonstrations, dd is a very useful tool.

UNICODE

There is a potential problem because text is represented in various formats. ASCII text is represented in 8 bits, which limits the number of characters it can represent to 256, that is, $2^8 = 256$. UNICODE is a 16-bit character representation that was created to overcome this limitation and to allow for the ability to represent characters from various countries, given that it can now hold 65,536 ($2^{16} = 65,536$). So, ASCII text is represented in one byte, whereas UNICODE is represented in two bytes. The difference between the same text represented in ASCII and UNICODE can be seen in Figures 21 and 22.

The information for the figures was extracted from an INFO2 file.

The normal strings command as run in the previous examples will not find the text in Figure 22, given that each character is represented by two bytes. To extract UNICODE characters, the flags -bl (that's a lowercase "L") must be used.

The command to extract all UNICODE characters from a file named "evidence.txt" would be

```
# strings -a -b l evidence.txt > /evidence/
evidence.unicode
```

Print Spool Files

When a file is printed in Windows, it is first converted to an enhanced metafile (EMF)—a graphic image—before it is printed. This file is written to the hard drive in the root Windows directory under \system32\spool directory (Windows XP and 2000). (Note: The default print spool directory can be changed by changing the values in Windows registry.) There are two files associated with each file printed: a header file with the extension SHD and the actual graphic image (EMF format) with the extension SHL. The SHD file contains information on the name of the file being printed, the name of the file to which it was printed, and the time and date stamp. The SHL file is the actual graphical file. If we can recover the SHL file, we can print it. Collectively, these files are called *print spool files*, and they demonstrate that particular documents were once printed from the computer. These files are typically found in the directory

c:\<Windows root directory>\system32\spool.

If a user creates a document in Windows, prints the document, then uses a forensic wipe utility to write zeros over the clusters composing the file, an investigator can still access the document by recovering the deleted print spool files.

Once the file has been printed, Windows will delete the header and EMF file. Until overwritten, the header and EMF file will remain in unallocated space and are recoverable with the techniques demonstrated in subsequent sections. However, if something happens and the file fails to print, the header and EMF file will remain in the directory. A grep search for files ending in *.SHD or *.SHL will find these files.

Physical Analysis

A logical analysis can only examine the contents of allocated space: it cannot find files intentionally deleted by users, deleted temporary files, deleted print spool files, or other forms of information found in unallocated or slack space. The investigator must conduct a physical analysis to examine ambient information in the unallocated and slack space.

A physical analysis involves analyzing our evidence from a physical perspective, that is, without regard to a file system. Thus, we do not mount our forensic image but instead use a hex editor to view the forensic image as a single, flat file. This will permit us access to all categories of disk space: allocated, unallocated, and slack. Clearly, this is advantageous as often a great deal of evidence may be found in unallocated and slack space. The drawback is that we are no longer dealing with a file system, and therefore, our analysis can be very tedious and complex.

Figures 23 and 24 show a physical view of the floppy disk image that we created earlier. (The far left side of the figure shows the offset from the beginning of the file in hex; the middle section is the contents of the file in hex at the offset; the far right side is the ASCII representation of the contents of the file at that offset.)

Figure 23 displays part of the *root directory* of a FAT formatted floppy disk image as viewed from a hex viewer. A root directory is like a table of contents of a file system; it tracks metadata on each file including the filename: file size: time and date of creation, modification, and last access: where the file starts on the disk; and so forth. On our floppy disk, each root directory entry is 32 bytes, or two lines in Figure 23. The lines at offset 2700 through 2710 are the root directory entry for the file KEYWORD.GIF.

Figure 24 shows the beginning of the data area that starts at offset 4200h. Note that the contents of this first sector of the data area contain the file signature FFh D8h FFh, which is a JPEG graphic signature. Note that the data area on a floppy starts at physical sector 33, which translates to logical cluster 2. This will be explained in more detail in the section Recovering Deleted Files.

From an examination of the root directory entry displayed in Figure 23, we can tell that the file at offset 2600–2610 has been deleted. However, Figure 24 shows that the file still resides on the disk. Two questions come to mind. First, how did we know that the file had been deleted from viewing the root directory? Second, can we recover the deleted file displayed in Figure 24?

What Happens When a File Is Deleted?

Before we explain what happens to a file when it is deleted, it is important to understand parts of a file system and how an operating system tracks files.

A disk formatted with a version of FAT is comprised of a reserved area and a data area. The reserved area consists of the following components:

- The boot record in the first sector of the disk;
- First file allocation table;

```
ebraska @ Omaha
Omaha, NE  68182                                | PGP Key ID: 0x9B600586
Dear Philip:
Thank you for agreeing to serve as one of our contributors to The Handbook of Inf
ormation Security.  Professor Bidgoli and I would like to formally invite you.
The Handbook will be a three-volume, 2,400-page, 8.5
   x 11
   trim size reference source providing state-of-the-art information concerning the
   information, computer and network security with coverage of the core topics. The
   audience is four-year colleges and universities with Computer Science, MIS, IT,
   IS, E-commerce, and Business departments, and public, private, and corporate libr
   aries and a diverse group of professionals interested in this fast growing field.
   The Handbook will be avail
philip.txt lines 1-7/7 (END)
```

Figure 20:   Results of string extraction.

```
00000010 | 00 00 00 00 45 3A 5C 44   6F 63 75 6D 65 6E 74 73  | ....E:\Documents
00000020 | 20 61 6E 64 20 53 65 74   74 69 6E 67 73 5C 6A 70  |  and Settings\jp
00000030 | 63 5C 44 65 73 6B 74 6F   70 5C 73 65 63 72 65 74  | c\Desktop\secret
00000040 | 2E 73 65 72 76 69 63 65   2E 67 75 69 64 65 2E 70  | .service.guide.p
00000050 | 64 66 00 00 00 00 00 00   00 00 00 00 00 00 00 00  | df..............
```

Figure 21:   8-bit ASCII text.

```
00000120 | A0 4A 47 8D 44 13 C4 01   00 B0 10 00 45 00 3A 00  | JG.D.Ä...`..E..
00000130 | 5C 00 44 00 6F 00 63 00   75 00 6D 00 65 00 6E 00  | \.D.o.c.u.m.e.n.
00000140 | 74 00 73 00 20 00 61 00   6E 00 64 00 20 00 53 00  | t.s. .a.n.d. .S.
00000150 | 65 00 74 00 74 00 69 00   6E 00 67 00 73 00 5C 00  | e.t.t.i.n.g.s.\.
00000160 | 6A 00 70 00 63 00 5C 00   44 00 65 00 73 00 6B 00  | j.p.c.\.D.e.s.k.
00000170 | 74 00 6F 00 70 00 5C 00   73 00 65 00 63 00 72 00  | t.o.p.\.s.e.c.r.
00000180 | 65 00 74 00 2E 00 73 00   65 00 72 00 76 00 69 00  | e.t...s.e.r.v.i.
00000190 | 63 00 65 00 2E 00 67 00   75 00 69 00 64 00 65 00  | c.e...g.u.i.d.e.
000001A0 | 2E 00 70 00 64 00 66 00   00 00 00 00 00 00 00 00  | ..p.d.f.........
```

Figure 22:   16-bit UNICODE text.

```
0002600: e545 414c 2020 2020 4a50 4720 1860 e253   .EAL    JPG .`.S
0002610: 9c2f 9c2f 0000 6b47 972f 0200 7a79 0000   ./././.kG./..zy..
0002620: e549 4444 454e 2020 4a50 4720 18be e453   .IDDEN  JPG ...S
0002630: 9c2f 9c2f 0000 0000 212c 3f00 cae6 0100   ./././....!,?.....
0002640: 5245 414c 2020 2020 444f 4320 18b6 e953   REAL    DOC ...S
0002650: 9c2f 9c2f 0000 6d51 9c2f 3301 0064 0000   ./././..mQ./3..d..
0002660: 5355 5a59 2020 2020 444f 4320 1843 ec53   SUZY    DOC .C.S
0002670: 9c2f 9c2f 0000 6d51 9c2f 6501 2a8a 0000   ./././..mQ./e.*...
0002680: 5245 414c 2020 2020 5458 5420 1800 f053   REAL    TXT ...S
0002690: 9c2f 9c2f 0000 6d51 9c2f ab01 a407 0000   ./././..mQ./.....
00026a0: 4752 4f43 4552 5920 5458 5420 1827 f253   GROCERY TXT .'.S
00026b0: 9c2f 9c2f 0000 6d51 9c2f af01 011a 0000   ./././..mQ./.....
00026c0: 5245 4745 5844 2020 5a49 5020 1886 f753   REGEXD  ZIP ...S
00026d0: 9c2f 9c2f 0000 6e51 9c2f bd01 5ddf 0100   ./././..nQ./..]...
00026e0: 4e45 4544 5320 2020 5044 4620 1897 1054   NEEDS   PDF ...T
00026f0: 9c2f 9c2f 0000 646d 552f ad02 23c5 0600   ./././..dmU/..#...
0002700: 4b45 5957 4f52 4420 4749 4620 1819 1a54   KEYWORD GIF ...T
0002710: 9c2f 9c2f 0000 7d51 9c2f 1006 6d56 0000   ./././.}Q./..mV..
0002720: 0000 0000 0000 0000 0000 0000 0000 0000   ................
```

Figure 23:   Root directory of the FAT formatted floppy disk.

```
0004200: ffd8 ffe0 0010 4a46 4946 0001 0101 0048    ......JFIF.....H
0004210: 0048 0000 fffe 0019 2243 7265 6174 6564    .H......"Created
0004220: 2077 6974 6820 5468 6520 4749 4d50 22ff     with The GIMP".
0004230: db00 4300 0806 0607 0605 0807 0707 0909    ..C.............
0004240: 080a 0c14 0d0c 0b0b 0c19 1213 0f14 1d1a    ................
0004250: 1f1e 1d1a 1c1c 2024 2e27 2022 2c23 1c1c    ...... $.' ",#..
0004260: 2837 292c 3031 3434 341f 2739 3d38 323c    (7),01444.'9=82<
0004270: 2e33 3432 ffdb 0043 0109 0909 0c0b 0c18    .342...C........
```

Figure 24: FAT12 data area: physical sector 33-logical cluster 2.

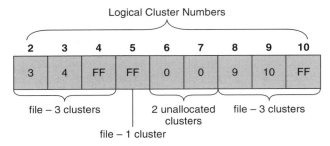

Figure 25: FAT explanation.

- Second file allocation table (a backup to the first);
- Root directory; and
- Data area. (On a floppy, it begins at physical sector 33/logical cluster 2. This will differ depending upon the size of the disk.)

The root directory entry for a file contains information on the starting cluster of the file. The remaining clusters that compose the file are kept in the file allocation table or FAT. A FAT is merely a singly linked list, as demonstrated in Figure 25.

Figure 25 illustrates an abstract model of a file allocation table. The numbers above the boxes indicate the FAT entry for a particular *logical* cluster. The numbers in the boxes are pointers to the next cluster in the file. For instance, the FAT entry for cluster two contains a three, which is a pointer indicating that the next cluster in the file can be found at cluster three. FAT entry three contains a four, indicating that the next cluster in the file is at logical cluster four. An FF in this instance is an end-of-file marker, indicating that this is the last cluster the file uses. If we assume that this is a FAT12 floppy disk, where each cluster is 512 bytes, we see that the file has a maximum size of 3 × 512 bytes or 1,536 bytes. Because clusters two, three, and four are allocated to a file in the FAT, we know that the file resides in allocated space and should appear in a logical analysis.

FAT cluster entry five has a single FF, indicating that the beginning and ending cluster for this file is logical cluster number five, and has a maximum size of 512 bytes. This file too is in allocated space and should appear in a logical analysis.

FAT cluster entry six and seven are 0s. This has two possible interpretations. First, it could indicate that the two logical clusters have never been allocated, that is, they have never been used by a file. Second, it could mean that the file was deleted, and thus the clusters constituting the file were set for reallocation by placing 0s in the FAT entries. We can determine which interpretation is correct by viewing the logical cluster six and seven with a hex editor. If these clusters contain any data, we know that the files were deleted. We could also look at the root directory to see if there are any files whose starting cluster is logical cluster six. This would also be supporting evidence that the file was deleted.

Finally, FAT cluster numbers eight, nine, and ten indicate a small file comprising three clusters.

What happens when a file is deleted in a FAT file system?

- The first character of the file's name in the root directory is changed to e5h.
- The FAT entries are set to 0.

The clusters that compose the file are not touched. However, should the operating system decide that the FAT entries and corresponding clusters are needed, say, to save a new file, then the clusters may be overwritten. That is the reason we freeze the computer: there is the potential for deleted files of possible evidentiary value to be overwritten by the operating system.

Although experiments we have conducted have varied in the exact details that occur, similar operations occur when files are deleted under most, if not all file systems, including NTFS, UNIX, and Linux file systems (EXT2, Reiser, etc.), that is, a file pointer is modified to indicate the file is deleted and the clusters used by the file are marked as available, with the actual file contents remaining on the disk.

Unallocated Space Revisited

Revisiting Figure 23, we see that there are two root directory entries whose names begin with an "e5" (the hex section). These files are at offset 2600h (?EAL.JPG) and offset 2620h (?IDDEN.JPG). This is the character that the operating system places in the first position of the file's name to indicate that the file has been marked as deleted. If we look at Figure 24 at offset 4200h (which happens to be logical cluster number two), we see that cluster still contains information located in unallocated space. This is the deleted file ?ATA.JPG. We can recover this file, as described elsewhere in the chapter.

Slack Space

Slack space is an interesting phenomenon that can hold a great deal of useful evidence. Recall that the smallest unit that can be allocated to a file is a cluster. If a file is 1 byte in size and the cluster size for a disk is 32,768 bytes (64 sectors per cluster), then the entire cluster will be reserved for the 1-byte file. Clearly, this is a tremendous amount of wasted disk space. On average, the last cluster of each file will only be half full, meaning each file will waste half a

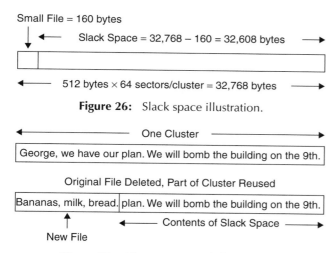

Figure 26: Slack space illustration.

Figure 27: Cluster reuse and slack space.

cluster. Multiply the number of files on a hard drive by half the cluster size and you will see that there is a tremendous amount of wasted space on any hard drive. The larger the cluster size, the more wasted space.

Cluster size has an important implication for a forensic investigation: larger cluster sizes mean more slack space. To illustrate slack space, Figure 26 shows a single cluster composed of 64 sectors. Say we create a file composed of 20 characters. Although the physical size of this file is small (160 bytes), its logical size will be the size of the smallest allocatable unit, which is 32,768 bytes. This means that there are 32,608 bytes wasted (32,768 – 160) in this cluster. Those 32,608 bytes are *file slack*, that is, slack space.

File slack becomes most interesting when clusters containing data are reused. Figure 27 illustrates this phenomenon. Say a criminal creates a document that discusses his plans to bomb a building and then deletes the document. Later, the criminal creates a grocery list, and the operating system happens to reuse part of the previously allocated clusters, as demonstrated in the bottom of Figure 27. Part of the original bombing plans document still exists in file slack. A logical analysis would *not* uncover the contents of slack space. The reason is that when we open a file only the contents of the file, up until the end-of-file marker, are retrieved by the operating system. We must conduct a physical analysis to find the contents of slack space.

Recovering Deleted Files

As mentioned previously, the delete operation does not remove the contents of the file from the media. It only marks the entry in the file table as deleted, and the clusters previously used for the file are marked as available. All of the metadata in the root directory entry remain, including modified, accessed, and created times; attributes; file size;

and so on. Also, the deleted file's FAT entries are marked as available by changing the FAT entries to 0. However, the data still remain on the disk (Figure 28). As long as the clusters are not overwritten, file contents can be recovered. And even if some of the clusters were overwritten, there is still the possibility that some of the file contents may still remain.

To demonstrate the ease with which a deleted file can be recovered, a small file was created, saved to a floppy, and then deleted. We created a forensic image of the floppy and then viewed the image with a hex viewer. Note that in this demonstration we do *not* mount the image, but rather simply open the image in a hex viewer.

To recover the file, we need two pieces of information: the starting cluster of the file and the size of the file. (It also helps if the file is not fragmented.) We can find both pieces of information in the root directory entry for the file.

As shown in Figure 23, the root directory of a FAT12 formatted floppy disk begins at hex offset 2600h. Note that, except for the first character, we know the remaining characters of the file name. The starting cluster of the file is two, 0002h, as shown by the brackets on the left. The size of the deleted file is indicated by the brackets on the right, 7D7Bh.

To calculate the starting cluster and file size we must perform a "byteswap" operation to put the hex characters in their correct order. The byteswap for the starting cluster results in 0002h or 2 in decimal. The byteswap for the file size is 7D7Bh or converted to decimal 32,123 bytes.

Once we know the starting cluster and file size, we can use dd to recover the file. Recall that the data area on a FAT formatted disk starts at logical cluster 2. This translates to physical sector 33 on a FAT12 formatted disk. (The boot sector, two file allocation tables, and the root directory constitute the first 32 sectors.) The file size in hex is 7D7Bh, which is 32,123 bytes. Recall that the default block size for dd is 512 bytes and each cluster of a FAT12 disk is equal to one sector. To determine the number of clusters to extract we divide 32,123 by 512 = 62.74. Because a file cannot use three quarters of a cluster, we round up to 63, which means we may also capture any contents of slack space, should it exist.

```
# ddif= image.dd of=_at.jpg skip=33
  count=63
  63 + 0 records in
  63 + 0 records out
```

The skip= argument specifies at which *physical* sector to begin, here, physical sector 33. The count= argument specifies the number of blocks (sectors) to extract. The dd operation succeeds, indicating it both read and wrote 63 records (blocks). We can now open the _at.jpg file. As we can see from the recovered graphic in Figure 29, we can

```
0002600: e541 5420 2020 2020 4a50 4720 1872 7070   .AT    JPG .rpp
0002610: 9d2f 9d2f 0000 0c7e 532d 0200 7b7d 0000   ./././...~S-..{}..
0002620: 0000 0000 0000 0000 0000                  ..............
0002630: 0000 0000 0000 0000 0000 0000 0000 0000   ................
0002640: 0000 0000 0000 0000 0000 0000 0000 0000   ................
0002650: 0000 0000 0000 0000 0000 0000 0000 0000   ................
lines 609-614
```

Figure 28: Root directory entry of deleted file.

Figure 29: Deleted file recovered manually with dd.

now complete the file name; the first letter was a "c" for cat.jpg.

Dealing with Formatted Drives

If deleting a file does not remove all vestiges of a file from media, then surely formatting does, right? Not exactly. There are two types of high-level formatting in Windows: a *quick* format and a *full* format. A quick format performs two operations: it a) zeros out the root directory entries and b) zeros out the file allocation table entries. The data area is *not* touched. (This is a nice simple experiment we encourage the reader to conduct with a floppy disk). A full format, in contrast, performs the same two operations as the quick format, and in addition it writes the hex character F6h in every sector of the data area. Thus, a disk that has been subjected to a full format will hold no recoverable data, except by experts using expensive procedures such as magnetic force microscopy (MFM).

Given that information, let us reconsider our manual recovery of a deleted file. Can we recover the same file after a quick formatting of the disk? Recall that a quick formatting completely overwrites the root directory, therefore, we no longer know the starting cluster nor file size of the file. We still have enough information available to us to recover files as long as we know the type of file we wish to recover.

Say we are asked to recover all of the graphical files from a hard drive that has been quick formatted. Given the file signatures (listed in Table 5), we can search for these file headers in the image. Once we find the headers, which always occur at the beginning of a cluster, use the

Table 5 Graphical File Signatures

File Type	Signature
JPG	FFh D8h FFh
BMP	BM
GIF	GIF8[79]a
PNG	89h 50h 4Eh 47h
TIFF	49h 49h 2Ah 00h

following steps to recover the files (only if the files are not fragmented):

1. Search for the file signature(s) within the forensic image.
2. When a file signature is found, note the hex offset.
3. Convert the hex offset to physical sector number.
4. Use the dd command, using the physical sector number from step 3 and a substantial count size.

Given that we are only guessing at the file size, what happens if we recover too many or too few clusters? Our experiences suggest that it should not hurt to recover more clusters than allocated to a file. Most of the time when we have recovered too little of the file, it is obvious. For instance, we conducted an experiment where we used the following commands to recover too few (50) and too many (100) clusters, and then viewed the resulting files to determine the difference.

```
# dd if=image.dd of=small.jpg skip=33
  count=50
# dd if=image.dd of=small.jpg skip=33
  count=100
```

Figure 30 shows the results of recovering too few clusters. Note that part of the image is missing, which is the result of recovering too few clusters from the image. We can correct this by rerunning the command and increasing our count value to recover more clusters.

Recovering too many clusters resulted in the same image as shown in Figure 29 for recovering the correct number of clusters. This is only a single example, and there may be differences depending upon the type of file recovered.

Behavioral Time Lines: What Happened and When?

Sometimes investigators must create a timeline of computer activity based upon file information and other available evidence to determine the sequence of activities

Figure 30: Manual recovery of too few clusters.

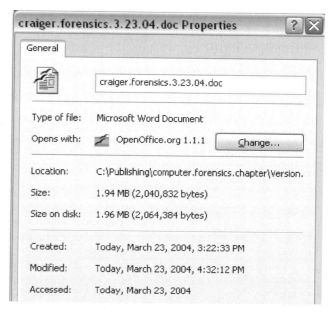

Figure 31: MAC times under NTFS.

Figure 32: MAC times under FAT32.

occurring during a particular time frame. Examples of questions to be addressed through a timeline are these:

- What files were changed? This can be answered through the creation of a timeline based upon MAC times—modified, access, creation times—described below.
- How were the files changed? Deleting existing files, adding malicious code such as rootkits, or replacing old files with Trojaned versions can change the system. The latter is common, for example, with UNIX systems, where *ps* and *netstat* binaries are replaced with versions that will not report evidence of suspicious activity.
- Can the deleted files and/or other evidence be restored?

Every computer file on a Windows-based file system (FAT-based or NTFS) has associated with it three times: the time the file was created on the current volume (created or *ctime*), the time the file was last modified (modified or *mtime*), and the time the file was last accessed (accessed or *atime*). (Linux/UNIX file systems do not have a created time but a "changed" time. Additionally, Linux EXT2 file system has a deleted time, and NTFS has a 'last written' time.) These times provide information regarding the events that occurred on a computer, allowing the investigator to create a scenario that explains a user's or intruder's activities.

From within Windows, the MAC times can be accessed by right-clicking on the file and selecting *properties* as demonstrated in Figures 31 and 32. A file residing on an NTFS volume in Figure 31 was copied to another volume formatted FAT32, Figure 32. Note the modified times are the same. The created times are different because the created times changed when a file is copied to a new volume. Also, FAT32 only keeps track of last date access, not the time last accessed. (The reader should also note that we can determine that the volumes use different cluster sizes by looking at the "Size on disk" property.)

At the **DOS** command prompt, the `dir` command displays the file's last modification time and date. To view the *created* times of all files in a directory, and to sort the file by date, use the command

```
C:\> dir <directory name>/* /tc /od.
```

To view by *access* times and sort by date, use

```
C:\> dir <directory name>/* /ta /od.
```

To view by *modification* times and sort by date, use

```
C:\> dir <directory name>/* /tw /od.
```

The command's output is a listing of files within a directory sorted by date. Unfortunately, this formatting does not allow one to easily determine the activities that occurred on the computer.

We have found the best way to create a timeline is to use tools from the open source forensic toolkit Sleuthkit (http://www.sleuthkit.org). To illustrate the use of MAC timelines, say we wanted to know what files had been created on a system since October 9, 2003. We ran two tools from Sleuthkit, *mac-robber* and *mactime*, against a running computer. We ran the command from a Linux box that was connected to the Windows system using a Samba share.

```
# mac-robber /mnt/fred/desktop/ > /
  evidence/fred.body
# mactime -b /evidence/whammo.body > /
  evidence/fred.mac
```

The *mac-robber* command extracts all of the time and date information from the files, and the *mactime* command then processes that information by sorting it by date and time and putting the information into a human-readable timeline. Here is a small portion of the results:

[Thousands of lines deleted for the sake of brevity]

```
Sun Nov 16 2003 11:42:52  530432 ..c /desktop/chapter/cforensics4.doc
Sun Nov 16 2003 11:44:08  530432 m.. /desktop/chapter/cforensics4.doc
Thu Nov 20 2003 17:45:37    4096 ..c /desktop/chapter
Fri Nov 21 2003 09:26:24  475136 ..c /desktop/chapter/cforensics5.doc
Fri Nov 21 2003 09:36:54  475136 m.. /desktop/chapter/cforensics5.doc
Fri Nov 21 2003 09:37:04  475136 ..c /desktop/chapter/cforensics6.doc
                          474624 ..c /desktop/chapter/~WRL0002.tmp
Fri Nov 21 2003 09:42:30  474624 m.. /desktop/chapter/~WRL0002.tmp
Sat Nov 22 2003 20:05:41   79653 m.c /desktop/vmware_drv.o
Sat Nov 22 2003 20:18:50   30158 ..c /desktop/linux_forensics.pdf
Sat Nov 22 2003 20:18:51   30158 m.. /desktop/linux_forensics.pdf
Sat Nov 22 2003 20:18:55   64687 ..c /desktop/SMART Forensics.pdf
Sat Nov 22 2003 20:18:58   64687 m.. /desktop/SMART Forensics.pdf
```

[Hundreds of lines deleted for the sake of brevity]

(Some of the information from the timeline, including the master file table number, file permissions, and links, has been deleted for brevity's sake.)

After the date, time, and size (in kilobytes) fields comes a three-character field that contains an indication as to whether the associated time is an *m-*, *a-*, or *c-time*, or combination thereof. Note that the MAC changes are organized by date and time. The first line displays the fourth version of this chapter (cforensics4.doc) and is a created time (note the "..c"). The next line is the modified time ("m..") for the same file, indicating that the file was last saved a couple of minutes after it was created. Note that the last access time for that file is not displayed because it was last accessed after November 22 and therefore does not fall within the timeline. Each file will have three times in the timeline.

From the timeline, we can derive several interesting facts. First, the file cforensics6.doc was created on Friday, November 21, at 9:37 a.m. Note that at the same time, Word created a temporary file. Four minutes later, Word updated the modified time on the temporary file. Where is the modified and accessed time for cforensics6.doc? They come later in the timeline and are not displayed.

How are timelines used in computer forensics? MAC times can be used to verify or dispute a user's contention of whether the user created, modified, or accessed a file on a particular date and time. For example, if an employee's temporary Internet folders contained pornographic pictures, and the access times on these files coincided with the employee's work schedule, we have evidence that disputes the employee's contention that his Internet surfing habits do not include surfing for porn. (Of course, we have stronger evidence if the source computer system is running a secure version of Windows such as NT, 2000, or XP, which has separate personal directories for each user and which was periodically synchronized with an atomic clock.)

COLLECTING EVIDENCE FROM LIVE SYSTEMS

Thus far, we have worked with a subject's computer, running Windows, which has been powered down and disconnected from a network. In some circumstances, it may

be difficult or impossible to power down and isolate a computer from a network. For instance, if a company's only e-commerce server was attacked, management may refuse to isolate the machine because it might cost the company more in lost revenue than the attack (Mandia, Prosise & Pepe, 2003; Casey & Seglem, 2002). In this situation, the investigator may be forced to work on a live system. This presents a problem because live systems are in a constant state of change, thus complicating the collection of evidence and investigation as a whole. Because the system is constantly changing, we need to collect any evidence before it is changed, deleted, or overwritten. Not all evidence is subject to change in the same time frame, however. Some evidence may be relatively stable, such as evidence on CDs or floppies, whereas other evidence may be ephemeral, such as the contents of RAM. These examples demonstrate that computer evidence may have different levels of volatility, which suggests that the investigator should prioritize evidence collection procedures and collect the most volatile information first.

Farmer & Venema (2000) proposed a volatility taxonomy, that is, a measure of the likelihood of change to digital information on running computer system. From most to least volatile, the list includes

- process register;
- virtual and physical memory;
- network state;
- running processes;
- disks, floppies, and tapes; and
- CD-ROM and paper printouts.

There is a correlation between the difficulty of collecting untainted evidence and its volatility. It is not possible—as far as we know—to collect the contents of registers without changing them. In contrast, printed materials and

CD-ROMS are fairly permanent and easy to collect without fear of contamination.

Farmer & Venema (2001) proposed an analogy between Heisenberg's uncertainty principle and the difficulty of working on live systems. Heisenberg's uncertainty principle states that attempting to measure both the location and momentum of an atomic particle affects the other measurement; therefore, one can never produce an accurate measure of both at the same time. Similarly, attempts to collect evidence from a live system will change the contents of the system. This principle is demonstrated in the following example. (We are assuming the live-running server in our subsequent demonstrations is running some version of Linux.)

On Linux systems, the file *kcore*, located in the */proc* directory, is a virtual file that maps to physical memory (RAM) of the system. The file can be examined using a debugger, or the `strings` command can be used to extract the human readable text from the file.

Similarly, */dev/mem* is a logical file associated with physical memory, and */dev/kmem* is associated with kernel virtual memory (Kruse & Heiser, 2001). One may access the contents of physical and kernel memory through */dev/mem* and */dev/kmem*, respectively.

To illustrate how a simple procedure can change a running system, we searched for the term "Heisenberg Uncertainty Principle" within */proc/kcore*. (Note that it is highly unlikely that this term would have been in physical memory prior to searching for the term.) The output of the search shows that the command we used to search for the term shows up, in various formats, several times, indicating that by attempting to collect the evidence we have changed the system.

plan for dealing with live systems, including prewritten scripts that can be run from a CD or floppy to minimize interacting with the system (e.g., because a typing error was made at the command line, requiring that the command be retyped, a common occurrence under stressful conditions).

Volatile Evidence

Time is of the essence when collecting evidence from a running computer system. As discussed previously, volatile sources of evidence are purged after a brief period of time. Volatile and important sources of evidence on live systems, and the commands used to capture the evidence, include

- running processes (`ps` or the */proc* file system),
- active network connections (`netstat`),
- ARP cache (`arp`),
- list of open files (`lsof`), and
- virtual and physical memory (*/dev/mem*, */dev/kmem*).

Gathering volatile data is more easily accomplished on file systems where everything is a file, which includes Linux, UNIX, and NTFS file systems. For example, all running processes on a Linux system are written out to disk the *proc* file system in the */proc* directory. Figure 33 is a truncated example that illustrates the running processes on a Linux system (using the *ps aux* command), and the respective */proc* file system is shown in Figure 34. For each process running in memory (identified by the numbers under the column labeled PID in Figure 33), there is a

```
simba:~  # strings /proc/kcore |  grep 'Heisenberg Uncertainty Principle'

[everything from here down are the results of the search]

'Heisenberg Uncertainty Principle'
grep 'Heisenberg Uncertainty Principle'
grep 'Heisenberg Uncertainty Principle'
strings /proc/kcore |  grep 'Heisenberg Uncertainty Principle'
strings /proc/kcore |  grep 'Heisenberg Uncertainty Principle'
strings /proc/kcore |  grep 'Heisenberg Uncertainty Principle'
strings /proc/kcore |  grep 'Heisenberg Uncertainty Principle'
'Heisenberg Uncertainty Principle'
strings /proc/kcore |  grep 'Heisenberg Uncertainty Principle'
simba:~  # strings /proc/kcore |  grep 'Heisenberg Uncertainty Principle'
simba:~  # strings /proc/kcore |  grep 'Heisenberg Uncertainty Principle
Heisenberg Uncertainty Principle
Heisenberg Uncertainty Principle
Heisenberg Uncertainty Principle
```

We found 14 occurrences of the term "Heisenberg Uncertainty Principle" within physical memory. This small experiment underscores the susceptibility of contaminating a running computer system through even the simplest interaction. Thus, care should be taken to minimize contamination when attempting to recover evidence from a live system. We can do this by having an incident response

corresponding directory under the */proc* file system in Figure 34.

The */sbin/arp -v* command displays the contents of the ARP (address resolution protocol) cache. The example in Figure 35 illustrates that the ARP cache on this computer has two MAC addresses under the label titled HWaddress. The ARP cache holds MAC addresses (media access

```
pc@simba:~> ps aux
USER       PID %CPU %MEM   VSZ  RSS TTY      STAT START   TIME COMMAND
root         1  0.0  0.0   588  240 ?        S    Jun25   0:05 init [5]
root         2  0.0  0.0     0    0 ?        S    Jun25   0:00 [migration/0]
root         3  0.0  0.0     0    0 ?        SN   Jun25   0:05 [ksoftirqd/0]
root         4  0.0  0.0     0    0 ?        S    Jun25   0:00 [migration/1]
root         5  0.0  0.0     0    0 ?        SN   Jun25   0:03 [ksoftirqd/1]
root         6  0.0  0.0     0    0 ?        S<   Jun25   0:00 [events/0]
root         7  0.0  0.0     0    0 ?        S<   Jun25   0:00 [events/1]
root         8  0.0  0.0     0    0 ?        S<   Jun25   0:00 [kacpid]
root         9  0.0  0.0     0    0 ?        S<   Jun25   0:00 [kblockd/0]
root        10  0.0  0.0     0    0 ?        S<   Jun25   0:00 [kblockd/1]
root        11  0.0  0.0     0    0 ?        S    Jun25   0:00 [kirqd]
root        14  0.0  0.0     0    0 ?        S<   Jun25   0:00 [khelper]
root        15  0.0  0.0     0    0 ?        S    Jun25   0:00 [pdflush]
root        18  0.0  0.0     0    0 ?        S<   Jun25   0:00 [aio/0]
root        17  0.0  0.0     0    0 ?        S    Jun25   0:00 [kswapd0]
root        19  0.0  0.0     0    0 ?        S<   Jun25   0:00 [aio/1]
root       179  0.0  0.0     0    0 ?        S    Jun25   0:00 [kseriod]
root       239  0.0  0.0     0    0 ?        S    Jun25   0:00 [scsi_eh_0]
root       241  0.0  0.0     0    0 ?        S    Jun25   0:00 [scsi_eh_1]
root       246  0.0  0.0     0    0 ?        S    Jun25   0:00 [scsi_eh_2]
root       247  0.0  0.0     0    0 ?        S    Jun25   0:00 [ahc dv 0]
```

Figure 33: Process list from running Linux system.

control addresses, i.e., the hardware addresses of the network interface cards, not to be confused with MAC times) of computers on the same subnet that have been recently communicating with the computer under investigation. These addresses are purged every so often; thus, it is important to gather this information quickly.

The netstat command displays network connections and listening ports. Figure 36 displays a portion of the results of running netstat. Note there are several established connections (under the "State" heading). The value "LISTEN" under the State heading indicates whether a port is open. Here we see we have three open TCP ports: port 22 (secure shell, SSH), *netbios* (139), and *CIFS* (445), the latter two of which are used with Samba (a service that supports connections between my Linux and Windows machines).

Log Files as Digital Evidence

Log files can be very important sources of forensic evidence. A server's log files will contain information about various system resources, processes, and user activities.

Protocol analyzers, sniffers, SMTP, DHCP, FTP, and WWW servers, routers, firewalls, and almost any system- or user-driven activity can be collected in a log file. However, if the systems administrator has not enabled logging, then the evidence necessary to associate an intruder with an incident may not exist. Unfortunately, knowledgeable intruders and criminals know this, and one of the first orders of business is to destroy or alter log files to hide their activities.

A second important piece of information, and one sometimes overlooked, involves the system clock. Anything logged to a file has an associated time and date stamp. Time and date stamps enable the investigator to determine the sequence of events that transpired. System clocks, unless explicitly corrected on an occasional basis, can be off anywhere from several seconds to hours. This can cause problems because any correlations between log files from different computers whose system clocks are different make it difficult or impossible to correlate events. A simple solution is to automatically synchronize clocks by having all systems run a daemon, an example of which is the UNIX *ntpd* daemon, to occasionally synchronize

```
pc@simba:/proc> ls
1      179    2780   6403   6746   bus          ioports      self
10     18     2785   6404   6751   cmdline      irq          slabinfo
11     19     3      6405   6756   config.gz    kallsyms     splash
11478  2      3300   6575   6758   cpufreq      kcore        stat
11566  2051   3626   6576   677    cpuinfo      kmsg         swaps
11613  21989  3714   6608   6774   crypto       loadavg      sys
11615  21990  3880   6669   6775   devices      locks        sysrq-trigge
11620  22057  4      6672   6776   diskstats    mdstat       sysvipc
11623  22059  4930   6674   6778   dma          meminfo      tty
11700  22091  5      6677   7      driver       misc         uptime
14     22093  5503   6716   7301   execdomains  mm           version
15     239    6      6736   8      fb           modules      vmstat
17     241    6087   6737   8865   filesystems  mounts
1718   246    6088   6739   9      fs           mtrr
1719   247    6400   6740   acpi   ide          net
```

Figure 34: Associated /proc file system.

```
simba:~ # arp -v
Address                    HWtype  HWaddress           Flags Mask        Iface
whammo.om.cox.net          ether   00:04:75:8B:06:BA   C                 eth0
192.168.0.1                ether   00:09:5B:9F:21:16   C                 eth0
```

Figure 35: ARP output.

the system time and date with a government-sponsored (e.g., NIST, National Institute of Standards and Technology) atomic clock. This is transparent to the user and takes little system resources.

Reducing the Potential for Evidence Contamination

If the computer system is on, files will be changing. If the computer system is connected to a network, files will be changing. If we interact with the system, files will change. This is a large, probably unsolvable problem: the need to interact with a live system and gather evidence will cause some form of contamination. The best that can be done then is to limit contamination by limiting interactions with the system. This can be done through planning prior to the incident. It is important, for example, to have an incident response team and an incident response plan that can be executed once an incident has been identified. One aspect of this plan is a predefined set of command scripts that can be executed to collect evidence from a running system. Ideally, these scripts should be run to limit the number of errors to which we are all susceptible. (FIRE, Forensic Incident Response Environment, is a Linux-based bootable CD that includes scripts to recover system information for both Linux and Windows systems: http://fire.dmzs.com. It is highly recommended. Helix is another bootable CD that contains scripts: www.e-fense.com)

Here is a simple example of running a predefined script to gather system information and transport it offsite via a network connection.

```
# (ps aux; netstat -tupan; cat /var/log/
   message) | nc 192.168.1.1 4444
```

These commands collect the running processes (ps aux), list of open network connections (netstat -tupan),

copies the log file *messages* (cat /var/log/messages), and uses netcat to send them over a network connection to the local forensic machine. The number of commands that could be included within the processes is unlimited. This form of evidence collection is desirable because the script employed to capture the evidence can be preplanned and tested prior to its use in any real incident. Make sure to test it on various forms of UNIX and Linux as some versions differ just enough so that your commands may not work they way they are expected.

COMMERCIAL TOOLS

This chapter would not be complete without a brief mention of some of the commercial tools available as of 2005. Unfortunately, space limitations guarantee that a discussion of the commercial forensics tools will be incomplete. Realize that this is not an advertisement for any particular tool, but rather a reference to existing tools that may warrant further examination by a serious investigator.

There are several Windows-based forensics tools that are capable of performing all of the procedures we have covered in this chapter and many we have not covered. The two tools we discuss here are Guidance Software's EnCase (Forensic or Enterprise Editions: http://www.guidancesoftware.com) and Accessdata's Forensic Toolkit (FTK: part of the Ultimate Toolkit: http://www.accessdata.com). We have had formal training and a good deal of experience with both EnCase and FTK; each has its strengths and weaknesses. Ideally, an investigator should be trained and have access to several tools. The reason is that it is often desirable to verify the findings from one tool with a different tool to ensure the validity and integrity of the findings.

FTK and EnCase support imaging, reading multiple file systems, reading multiple image formats, file viewing, advanced string searches, graphical/gallery views, e-mail

```
simba:~ # netstat -tupan
Active Internet connections (servers and established)
Proto Recv-Q Send-Q Local Address          Foreign Address        State        PID/Program name
tcp        0      0 0.0.0.0:139            0.0.0.0:*              LISTEN       11478/smbd
tcp        0      0 0.0.0.0:445            0.0.0.0:*              LISTEN       11478/smbd
tcp        0      0 192.168.0.3:1733       66.35.250.67:80       TIME_WAIT    -
tcp        0      0 192.168.0.3:1741       66.35.250.67:80       TIME_WAIT    -
tcp        0      0 192.168.0.3:1745       193.136.138.47:80     ESTABLISHED  11620/mozilla-bin
tcp        0      0 192.168.0.3:1746       193.136.138.47:80     ESTABLISHED  11620/mozilla-bin
tcp        0      0 192.168.0.3:1732       66.35.250.62:80       TIME_WAIT    -
tcp        0      0 192.168.0.3:1718       192.168.0.2:445       ESTABLISHED  -
tcp        0      0 192.168.0.3:1729       64.233.167.99:80      ESTABLISHED  11620/mozilla-bin
tcp        0      0 192.168.0.3:1736       64.233.167.99:80      ESTABLISHED  11620/mozilla-bin
tcp        0      0 :::22                  :::*                  LISTEN       3626/sshd
udp        0      0 192.168.0.3:137        0.0.0.0:*                          11566/nmbd
udp        0      0 0.0.0.0:137            0.0.0.0:*                          11566/nmbd
udp        0      0 192.168.0.3:138        0.0.0.0:*                          11566/nmbd
udp        0      0 0.0.0.0:138            0.0.0.0:*                          11566/nmbd
simba:~ # █
```

Figure 36: View network connections and open ports with *netstat*.

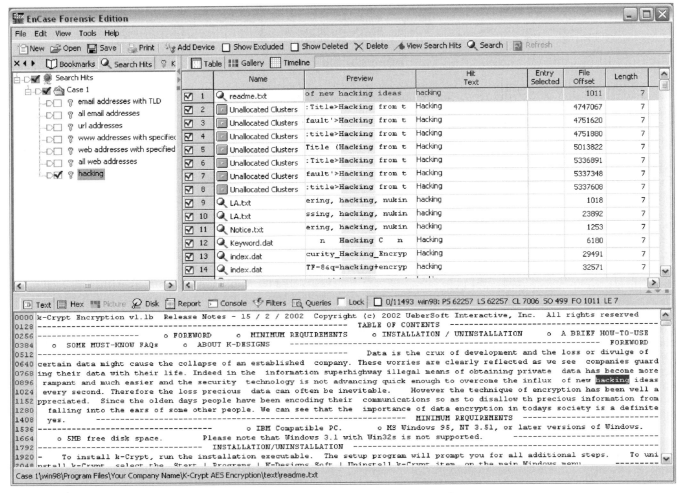

Figure 37: Guidance Software's EnCase interface.

analysis, compressed file analysis, known file filters/hash analysis, bad file extension determination, electronic discovery, and numerous other capabilities. We have included screenshots of EnCase (Figure 37) and FTK (Figure 38), displaying the results of a string search, to illustrate their graphical interface.

Other commercial tools available as of 2004, in alphabetical order, include

- ARS Data's SMART (runs under Linux): http://www. asrdata.com/tools/,
- BlackBag Macintosh Forensic Software (http://blackbagtech.com),
- ILook Investigator (law enforcement only): http://www. ilook-forensics.org/,
- Mareswure Forensic Tools: http://www.dmares.com/ mareswure,
- New Technologies Forensic Suite: http://www.forensics-intl.com/tools.html, and
- Paraben Forensic Toolks (for PDAs and cell phone forensics): http://www.paraben-forensics.com/.

For the most up-to-date information on the availability of commercial and open source tools, we suggest doing a Google search for "computer forensic tool."

CONCLUSION

This chapter provided a technical introduction and overview of computer forensic procedures. We attempted to cover the fundamental aspects of computer forensics methods and procedures, from acquiring and verifying the evidence through a complete logical and physical analysis. Our demonstrations were designed to illustrate fundamental concepts rather than how a particular commercial tool could be used.

Technology changes at an increasing pace, which creates several problems for investigators. For example, devices that may hold evidence have become more diverse, witness cell phones, personal digital assistants (PDAs) such as the Palm® handhelds and Compaq IPAQ®, Blackberry® wireless e-mail devices, compact flash and smart media, and so on. Investigators must have the necessary hardware and software to make a forensic image and analyze the information obtained from these diverse devices.

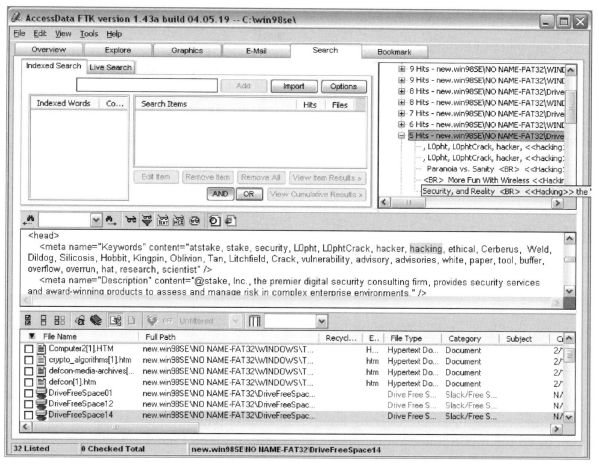

Figure 38: Accessdata's Forensic Toolkit interface.

Investigators are likely to encounter new types of media on a continual basis. Therefore, it is important that investigators be aware of these types of media, including any unique properties that may be important in understanding them for the acquisition process. Space limitations prevented us from describing the means of handling the more exotic types of evidence. Nevertheless, the investigator must also have the necessary knowledge, techniques, and tools available to make the forensic images as well as perform thorough logical and physical analysis. The best source for best practices on handling different types of media is the *U.S. Secret Service's Best Practices Guide for Seizing Electronic Evidence* (U.S. Secret Service, 2002).

Finally, storage technology is becoming exponentially larger and therefore more difficult and time consuming for investigators to analyze. For example, it is not uncommon to encounter personal home computers with hard disks in the 200+ gigabyte range. Moreover, terabyte-sized disk arrays are becoming more commonplace. Numerous law enforcement professionals and investigators with whom we have spoken have encountered such devices. This will create problems as the acquired images of a criminal investigation may outstrip an investigator's ability to hold and preserve the evidence. Fortunately, technologies such as storage area networks, as they become less costly, may allow law enforcement and industry incident response teams to better deal with this problem.

GLOSSARY

Allocated Space   The clusters allocated to a file and which are tracked by the file system.

Allocation Unit   The smallest unit of disk space that may be allocated to a file. Varies by file system.

Bit-Stream Copy   A bit-for-bit copy of digital evidence.

Block   UNIX terminology for an allocation unit (see allocation unit).

Cluster   Microsoft Windows term for allocation unit (see allocation unit).

FAT   Acronym for file allocation table. A common form of file system used with Microsoft Windows operating systems. Part of a FAT file system. A singly linked list of pointers to clusters constituting a file.

Forensic Image   An exact, bit-for-bit copy of media.

Hash   Also known as a message digest, cryptographic hash, or one-way hash. A hash is a hex value, typically 128- or 160-bit, that is unique to the contents of a file.

Hash Set   A list of hash values for a set of files.

Known Files   Files known to be of no evidentiary value that can be discarded from an analysis. Usually identified through a hash analysis.

MD5 Hash   A 128-bit cryptographic hash algorithm created by Ron Rivest of MIT.

Metadata   A file's metadata consists of all information about the file excluding its contents: file name, size, MAC times, starting cluster, permissions, attributes, and so forth.

Notable Files   Files of known evidentiary value usually identified through a hash analysis.

NTFS   Microsoft New Technology File System.

Root Directory   File table under FAT systems that holds file metadata.

Sector   Hardware unit of measure on a disk, typically 512 bytes. Multiple sectors make up an allocation unit. Individual sections of a disk track.

Slack Space   Disk space left over between the end of the data and the end of the last cluster of a file. Slack space may contain residual information.

Unallocated Space   The clusters not in use by a file. Where deleted files reside.

Volume   Commonly, another name for a partition on a disk. A hard drive may have up to four primary volumes or partitions.

Wipe   Forensic wipe. To remove vestiges of information from media by writing a series of characters over the information.

Write Blocker   A physical device that allows data to be read from a hard drive but prevents data from being written to it. Typically, blocks interrupt 13h.

CROSS REFERENCES

See *Computer Security Incident Response Teams (CSIRTs); Digital Evidence; Forensic Analysis of Windows Systems; Forensic Computing.*

REFERENCES

Casey, E., & Seglem, (2002). Introduction. In E. Casey (Ed.), Handbook of Computer Crime Investigation: Forensic Tools and Technology. San Diego, CA: Academic Press.

Dartmouth Institute for Security Technology Studies. (2002). *Law enforcement tools and technologies for investigating cyber attacks: A national needs Assessment.* Dartmouth College, Hanover New Hampshire.

Heverly, R. & Wright, M. (2002). Cyberspace law and computer forensics. In S. Bosworth and M. E. Kabay (Eds.), *Computer security handbook.* New York: Wiley.

International Association of Computer Investigation Specialists (IACIS). Retrieved April 4, 2004, from http://www.iacis.com/html/forensicprocedures.htm

Kruse, W. G. III, & Heiser, J. G. (2001). *Computer forensics: Incident response essentials.* Boston, MA: Addison-Wesley.

Mandia, K., Prosise, C., & Pepe, M. (2003). Incident response: Investigating computer crime. New York: McGraw-Hill.

Mayer-Schonberger, M. *The cookie concept.* Retrieved February 3, 2004, from http://www.cookiecentral.com/c_concept.htm

Mayer-Schonberger, V. *The cookie concept.* Retrieved January 12, 2004, from http://www.cookiecentral.com/content.phtml?area=2&id=1

Microsoft. How the recycle bin stores files. Retrieved January 18, 2004 from, http://support.microsoft.com/default.aspx?scid=kb;en-us;136517&Product=w95v

Nelson, B., Phillips, A., Enfinger, F., & Steuart, C. (2004). *Guide to computer forensics and investigations.* Boston: Thomson Publishing.

Pollitt, M. (2002). Personal communication.

Rivest, R. (1992). *The MD5 message-digest algorithm.* Retrieved December 23, 2003, from http://theory.lcs.mit.edu/~rivest/rfc1321.txt

Sheldon, B. (2002). The forensic analysis of Windows systems. In E. Casey (Ed.), *Handbook of computer crime investigation.* San Diego, CA: Academic Press.

U.S. Secret Service. (2002). *Best practices guide to seizing electronic evidence, version 2.* Retrieved December 29, 2003, from http://www.cio.com/securitytools/BPGv2.pdf

FURTHER READING

Bigelow, S. (2004). *Troubleshooting, maintaining & repairing PCs.* San Francisco: McGraw-Hill.

Brezinski, D., & Killalea, T. (2002, February). *Guidelines for evidence collection and archiving* (RFC 3227). Retrieved January 24, 2004, from http://rfc3227.x42.com/

Caloyannides, M. A. (2002). *Computer forensics and privacy.* Norwood, MA: Artech House.

Caloyannides, M. A. (2003). *Desktop witness.* Norwood, MA: Artech House.

Carrier, B. (2002a). *Autopsy forensic browser.* Retrieved January 12, 2004, from http://www.sleuthkit.org/autopsy/

Carrier, B. (2002b). *Sleuthkit.* Retrieved January 18, 2004, from http://www.sleuthkit.org/sleuthkit/

Carrier, B. (2005). File System Forensic Analysis. New York: Addison-Wesley Professional.

Carvey, H. (2002, September 5). *Win2K first responder's guide.* Retrieved April 4, 2004, from http://www.securityfocus.com/infocus/1624

Casey, E. (2002). *Handbook of computer crime investigation: Forensic tools and technology.* San Diego, CA: Academic Press.

Casey, E., Larson, T., & Long, T. M. (2002). Network analysis. In E. Casey (Ed.)., *Handbook of computer crime investigation.* San Diego, CA: Academic Press.

Cheng, D. (2001, November 1). Freeware forensics tools for UNIX. Retrieved April 4, 2004, from http://online.securityfocus.com/infocus/1503

Cooper, M., Northcutt, S., & Frederick, K. (2002). *Intrusion signatures and analysis.* Indianapolis, IN: New Riders.

Craiger, J. P. (2004, May). *Linux: Portable forensics toolkit.* Paper presented at the 26th Annual Department of Energy Computer Security Training Conference, St. Louis, MO.

Craiger, J. P. & Nicole, A.S. (2002, September). *An applied course in network forensics*. Paper presented at the Workshop for Dependable and Secure Systems, University of Idaho, Moscow, Idaho, September 23–25.

Department of Energy. (2002). *First responders guide*. Department of Energy Computer Forensic Laboratory.

Dittrich, D. (2001). *Basic steps in forensic analysis of Unix systems*. Retrieved January 12, 2003, from http://staff.washington.edu/dittrich/misc/forensics

Farmer, D. (2000, October). What are MACtimes? *Dr. Dobb's Journal*. Retrieved January 2003, http://www.ddj.com/documents/s=880/ddj0010f/0010f.htm

Farmer, D. (2001, January). Bring out your dead: The ins and outs of data recovery. *Dr. Dobb's Journal*. Retrieved January 18, 2003, from http://www.ddj.com/documents/s=871/ddj0101h/0101h.htm

Farmer, D., & Venema, W. (2000, September). Forensic computer analysis: An introduction. *Dr. Dobb's Journal*. Retrieved January 18, 2003. http://www.ddj.com/documents/s=881/ddj0009f/0009f.htm

Farmer, D., & Venema, W. (2001, April). Being prepared for intrusion. *Dr. Dobb's Journal*. Retrieved January 18, 2003, from http://www.ddj.com/documents/s=868/ddj0104f/0104f.htm

Furnell, S. (2002). *Cybercrime: Vandalizing the information society*. Upper Saddle River, NJ: Prentice-Hall.

Grance, T., Kent, K., & Kim, B. (2004). *National Institute of Standards and Technology computer security incident handling guide*. Gaithersburg, MD: NIST.

Grundy, B. J. (2002). *The law enforcement introduction to Linux: A beginner's guide*. Retrieved January 24, 2004, from http://ohiohtcia.org

Hardy, K., & Kreston, S. (2001). *Using analogy to explain computer forensics: Techniques used to explain computer jargon to courtroom juries*. National District Attorney's Association. Retrieved December 28, 2003, from http://www.ndaa-apri.org/publications/newsletters/update_volume_15_number_9_2002.html

Jones, K. J. (2003a). *Forensic analysis of Internet Explorer activity files*. Retrieved January 18, 2004, from http://www.foundstone.com

Jones, K. J. (2003b). *Forensic analysis of Microsoft Internet Explorer cookie files*. Retrieved January 18, 2004, from http://www.foundstone.com

Jones, K. J. (2003c). *Forensic analysis of Microsoft Windows Recycle Bin records*. Retrieved January 18, 2004, from http://www.foundstone.com

Jones, K. J., Shema, M., & Johnson, B. C. (2002). *Anti-hacker toolkit*. San Francisco: Osborne.

Larson, T. (2002). The other side of civil discovery. In E. Casey (Ed.), *Handbook of computer crime investigation*. San Diego, CA: Academic Press.

Location of Outlook Express files under Windows XP. Retrieved October 9, 2003, from http://www.attention-to-details.com/newslog/379-location-outlook-express-files-on.asp#a194

Lucas, J., & Moeller, B. (2004). *The effective incident response team*. Boston: Addison-Wesley.

Marcella, A. J. Jr., & Greenfield, R. S. (2002). *Cyber forensics: A field manual for collecting, examining, and preserving evidence of computer crimes*. Boca Raton, FL: Auerbach Publications.

McNamara, J. (2003). *Secrets of computer espionage*. New York: Wiley.

Mohay, G., Anderson, A., Collie, B., De Vel, O., & McKemmish, R. (2003). *Computer and intrusion forensics*. Norwood, MA: Artech.

Morris, J. (2003, January 28). *Forensics on the Windows platform, part one*. Retrieved April 4, 2004, from http://www.securityfocus.com/printable/infocus/1661

Morris, J. (2003, February 11). *Forensics on the Windows platform, part two*. Retrieved April 4, 2004, from http://www.securityfocus.com/printable/infocus/1665

Mueller, S. (2003). *Upgrading and repairing PCs*. New York: Que.

Nemeth, E., Snyder, G., Hein, T. R. (2003). *Linux administration handbook*. Upper Saddle River, NJ: Prentice Hall.

Northcutt, S., & Novak, J. (2001). *Network intrusion detection: An analyst's handbook*. Indianapolis, IN: New Riders.

Open-source forensics software. (n.d.). Retrieved January 7, 2004, from http://www.opensourceforensics.org/tools/unix.html

Parker, D. (1998). *Fighting computer crime*. New York: Wiley.

Prosise, K, Mandia, K., & Pepe, M. (2003). *Incident response: Investigating computer crime*. San Francisco: McGraw-Hill.

Sammes, T., & Jenkinson, B. (2000). *Forensic computing: A practitioner's guide*. London: Springer Verlag.

Schulz, E. E., & Shumway, R. (2002). *Incident response: A strategic guide to handling system and network security breaches*. Indianapolis, IN: New Riders.

Seglem, K. K. (2002). Introduction to digital evidence reconstruction using UNIX systems. In E. Casey (Ed.), *Handbook of computer crime investigation*. San Diego, CA: Academic Press.

Spitzner, L. (2001). *Know your enemy: Revealing the security tools, tactics, and motives of the Blackhat community*. Boston, MA: Addison-Wesley.

Stephenson, P. (2000). *Investigating computer-related crime*. Boca Raton, FL: CRC Press.

Stoll, C. (1988). *Cuckoo's egg: Tracking a spy through the maze of computer espionage*. New York: Pocket Books.

Tan, J. (2001). *Forensic readiness*. @stake Research. Retrieved February 3, 2004, from http://www.atstake.com/research/reports/

U.S. Department of Justice. (2002, July). *Searching and seizing computers and obtaining electronic evidence in criminal investigations*. Computer Crime and Intellectual Property Section, Criminal Division, United States Department of Justice. Retrieved January 14, 2004, from http://www.usdoj.gov/criminal/cybercrime/searching.html

Vacca, J. R., & Erbschloef, M. (2001). *Computer forensics: Computer crime scene investigation*. New York: Charles River Press.

Computer Forensics—Computer Media Reviews in Classified Government Agencies

Michael R. Anderson, *SCERC*

INTRODUCTION

Forensics, by definition, is the application of law to science. In the case of computer forensics, computer science is used to identify evidence in criminal cases and civil lawsuits. Computer forensics is a relatively new forensic science, but its procedures and methodologies have been used for years in military and law enforcement agencies to gather intelligence and to identify criminal investigation leads and evidence. Computer forensics moved from the secret world of the military and law enforcement when New Technologies, Inc. (NTI) was created in 1996. Since that time, numerous commercial computer-forensics training courses have come into existence and several colleges and universities have incorporated computer forensics topics in their curricula. Several computer forensic software tools have also come into existence and computer forensics has become a popular and lucrative career field.

Today, computer forensics is the mainstay of corporate investigations and internal audits. Since 1996, military and law enforcement agencies have expanded their use of computer forensics because of the increased popularity of personal computers and the Internet. It is common knowledge that the U.S. military put a high priority on technology-based intelligence gathering in the Iraq war and in the identification of weapons of mass destruction (WMDs). Modern weapons development relies upon computers, and such activities leave a computer evidence trail of activities behind. It is no secret that the U.S. military relied upon computer forensics tools and processes to identify such activities in Afghanistan and Iraq. Computer forensic tools and processes are used to identify computers that contain classified weapons data and to identify the Arabic (and English) names of individuals stored on computers.

Most people do not realize that computer forensic tools and processes are also used by some of the same U.S. government agencies to identify their own internal computer security risks and weaknesses. Personal computers have significant security weaknesses and a security solution for Microsoft-based personal computers is not anticipated in the near term. Until a security solution is developed, computer security risk assessments using computer forensic tools and methods will continue to be mandated by most classified U.S. government agencies.

PERSONAL COMPUTER SECURITY WEAKNESSES: HISTORICAL PERSPECTIVE

Personal computers were never designed to be secure. This lack of security is the direct result of the development of personal computers over the past thirty years. Personal computers came into existence in the 1970s and the first personal computers were popular with hobbyists, who built their own personal computers from kits. These computers had limited power and were difficult to use. Preassembled personal computers could be purchased, but the personal computer market was primarily limited during the mid-1970s to technology-savvy hobbyists. Thus, cottage industries were the spawning grounds for personal computer research and designs. For example, the Apple computer company grew from a small business operated out of a garage.

No software standards existed in the 1970s, and custom operating systems were, of necessity, written for each personal computer system that came into existence. The operating systems and application programs that evolved were not interchangeable from one personal computer brand to another. Because of file incompatibility among brands, growth of the personal computer market was stifled and brand loyalties were strong. In the mid- to late 1970s, personal computers with brand names such a Altar, Apple, Atari, Commodore, Heath-Zenith, TRS-80, and

Osborne dominated the small and disjointed personal computer market in the United States. Personal computers were considered toys or electronic gadgets by most people. Their benefits were not defined and most people had no use for computers anyway. One possible exception was a personal computer developed by Wang Laboratories, Inc. (Wang), which marketed computer products dedicated to word processing and document management tasks.

The Wang personal computer–based word processing systems eliminated the need for carbon paper and the technology also provided spell-checking features that had not existed previously. Wang word processing systems quickly unseated the popular IBM Selectric typewriter in the private and public sectors. The U.S. government became one of Wang's biggest clients, and I fondly remember those big, 12-inch Wang floppy disks from my government days. I was a special agent with the Internal Revenue Service, Criminal Investigation Division, back then, and we used the Wang technology to create and edit memoranda search warrant affidavits and prosecution reports. Wang word processing systems saved much time in creating and editing documents but they also had a downside—Wang systems provided no security for the computer files they created.

The U.S. government adopted the use of Wang systems without security because it really had no other option. The Wang systems were state-of-the-art technology at that time, and the U.S. government had no place else to turn for similar technology. Its only option was to use the new Wang word processing technology, without security features, or to continue using typewriters, "whiteout," and carbon paper. Reluctantly, the U.S. government adopted Wang's technology because of the productivity benefits. This decision by the U.S. government had a significant effect on the future designs of all personal computers. Had the U.S. government required Wang to incorporate security into the design of its products, a benchmark would have been set for the computer security designs of the future.

In the late 1970s, Tandy Corporation developed a word processing application for use with the Tandy TRS-80 brand of personal computer. This was an attempt by Tandy to move its personal computer into the business world. Other computer manufacturers followed suit and developed similar word processing programs for use with their brands of personal computers but compatibility from brand to brand was still a problem. Word processing files created with one brand of computer could not be read, edited, or printed on another brand of computer and none of these personal computers were compatible with the popular Wang word processing computer systems. Therefore, the personal computer market remained segmented and there was no reason for computer users to switch their loyalties.

The development of the computer spreadsheet application also occurred in the 1970s. The first significant software spreadsheet application was VisiCalc, and its functionality and benefits supplemented word processing software applications developed for personal computers. The spreadsheet applications provided computer users with new and powerful business calculation capabilities that had not existed previously. The spreadsheet applications were not a good complement to Wang's word processing systems because Wang's end users were primarily secretaries who created and edited word processing documents. Spreadsheet applications were more suited to business professionals who created and used their own custom spreadsheets. As technology-savvy business professionals began using personal computers to perform mathematical functions, it was a natural progression for the same professionals to begin using personal computer–based word processing software. Wang was never able to make the transition from a dedicated word processing system to a multipurpose personal computer system, and eventually the company became an artifact of the computer technology revolution.

Based on its success, Tandy Corporation promoted its TRS-80 model III personal computer in 1979 as a "business computer" and that promotion effectively moved personal computers from "toys" to business computers in the marketplace. Tandy's promotion of personal computers as tools for business quickly captured the attention of the computer mainframe giant, International Business Machines (IBM). Mainframe computers were expensive and well beyond the reach of many businesses. Tandy effectively changed the business mind-set about computing with its TRS-80 model III personal computer.

IBM followed Tandy's lead and conducted market research to determine the potential for its own personal computer. On the basis its market research, IBM released the IBM Personal Computer (IBM PC) in October 1981 for government agencies and businesses. The IBM PC was one of the biggest technology successes in modern times. However, IBM significantly underestimated the market demand for the IBM PC and it, like everyone else, did not anticipate the potential of the Internet. If IBM had foreseen the huge demand for personal computers, it is likely that security would have been a significant design feature. However, IBM knew that the U.S. government was willing to spend money for personal computers that did not have security, based on the successes of Wang Laboratory. They also knew that the U.S. government was the biggest user of computer technology, and it was likely that private sector businesses would follow suit. That is exactly what happened, and there was no business reason for IBM to secure the IBM PC initially.

Since 1981, the personal computer has become a powerful worldwide analysis and communications tool. Sensitive business and government documents are created and printed using these small computers. E-mail is routed around the world via the Internet. Database programs are used to store and access business information. Spreadsheet applications are used in financial calculations and PowerPoint is used to make most business presentations. Even photography has moved from film to digital flash memory. These wonderful technology tools are also used in classified government research and intelligence-gathering activities. They are even used to track the financial trail of terrorists in the war on terror. Regrettably, personal computer systems still are not secure but, as previously discussed, they were never intended to be secure. As a result, an added layer of security risk exists today in classified government agencies, and computer forensic tools and methods are typically used to reduce those risks.

SECURITY RISKS: WINDOWS XP AND NOTEBOOK COMPUTERS

The creators of the original IBM PC never imagined that their primitive computer design would become the mainstay of worldwide commerce and a critical component used in the operation of U.S. government agencies. Because of the need to provide upward compatibility for files and software, the basic foundation for the original IBM PC still exists in most of today's personal computers. Although the Microsoft NTFS-based operating systems (Windows NT, Windows 2000, and Windows XP) are more robust and provide better network security and auditing capabilities, no substantial security improvements have been made at the data-storage level. Unfortunately, these advanced NTFS-based operating systems can create a false sense of security for computer users and management in classified U.S. government agencies.

Microsoft-based personal computers can easily be compromised, and password and logon controls can quickly be circumvented using computer forensic tools and methods. For example, NTI's TextSearch NT (a forensic search tool) can completely evaluate and document all data storage areas on a Windows XP–based computer system. This U.S. Department of Defense (DoD)–certified forensic tool was designed for internal government security reviews but its uses could be twisted, in the wrong hands, to compromise computer security. TextSearch NT operates from a DOS-formatted floppy diskette and no logons or passwords are required to circumvent the minimal security afforded by Windows XP (or Windows NT and Windows 2000). The reader should note that this is the reason that some of the more powerful computer forensics tools are not made available for purchase by the general public.

Security problems are compounded when portable notebook computers are used with classified government data. Portable notebook computers are frequently used in classified executive briefings and sometimes in military and intelligence field operations, and they can be taken anywhere. Most notebook computers also feature hibernation modes of operation that create added security risks. Some computer manufacturers call them suspense, or sleep, modes and the features rely on a special file or a special partition that essentially captures and stores the work session when the computer is "asleep."

Notebook computers usually go into a sleep or hibernation mode when keyboard activity has not been detected for a predetermined period of time. This is a convenient feature that helps conserve battery power, but the trade-off is an added security risk. When the hibernation or suspense feature is triggered (either manually or automatically), the work session is frozen in time and part of the data from the work session is stored in a hibernation file or partition. You can think of it as an electronic bookmark used by the computer. The data stored in the hibernation file can consist of any data tied to the work session, and, when the computer is awakened, its operation is restored using the data contained within the hibernation file. The hibernation file is not securely deleted after the computer is awakened, and the file contents remain behind for discovery using forensic tools and techniques. If classified data were involved in the work session before the computer went into hibernation, then it is likely that the hibernation file (or partition) contains classified data. Hibernation files are potentially huge. The hibernation file of the notebook computer I used to write this chapter has a capacity of more than 203 million bytes of data. That is the equivalent of approximately 507,000 printed pages!

RISKS ASSOCIATED WITH AMBIENT DATA STORAGE AREAS

Most personal computer users are unaware of the background processes involved in the operation of the computer. The processes are transparent, and they potentially involve the leakage of sensitive computer data into "special" data storage areas. These obscure storage areas are referred to as ambient data-storage areas and include file slack, Windows swap files, Windows page files, temporary working files, work-session suspense files, and unallocated (erased file) storage space. Even the mere viewing of sensitive files on floppy diskettes or via the Internet can result in data seepage into ambient data-storage areas, and the computer user does not have to save any work to disk for the process to occur. Because of a general lack of knowledge of the security weaknesses of personal computers, government employees can unintentionally transfer classified data to unclassified computer systems. Ambient data storage areas constitute the biggest risk for classified data leakage and they are described as follows:

1. **File slack** is defined as the data storage space between the end of a file and the end of the last cluster assigned to the file. Files are stored in uniform blocks of data called clusters, and a more specific definition of clusters can be found on the Internet at http://www.forensics-intl.def19.html. Rarely does the size of a file exactly match the data storage capacity of the number of clusters assigned to the file. File slack is the residual storage area that exists in the last cluster assigned to the file and following the contents of the file. File slack consists of two separate components called RAM slack and drive slack, discussed in the following paragraphs.

    Word processing documents, spreadsheets, databases, and e-mail messages are all stored in files on personal computer storage devices. The same is true of many temporary files that are created transparently by software applications and the operating system. File slack is created when a file is saved (closed), and it is a significant security risk on all Microsoft-based personal computers. You should also be aware that the data potentially stored in file slack is typically beyond the knowledge and control of most government computer users.

2. **RAM slack** is created from the buffers on Windows and DOS-based systems. Buffers can be thought of as

Figure 1.

plumbing used by the operating system, and the number of buffers on a Windows/DOS-based system is set in the CONFIG.SYS file, for example, buffers = 30. The buffers reside in the random access memory (RAM) of the computer system, and the contents of the buffers can potentially contain any data or data fragments created, viewed, or printed during a computer work session. RAM slack is written to the first sector of the last cluster of the file. In Microsoft-based computers, sectors are small storage blocks that hold 512 bytes of data. Clusters are made up of varying numbers of sectors, depending on the size of the storage device and the operating system involved. RAM slack will always be in the first sector of the last cluster of the file, but RAM slack cannot contain more than 512 bytes of data. Ram slack is only a concern on Windows, Windows 95, Windows 98, and DOS-based systems because Windows NT–, Windows 2000–, and Windows XP–based computer systems automatically scrub all relevant data contained in RAM slack.

3. **Drive slack** is a security risk on all Microsoft-based personal computer systems because it is not automatically scrubbed by the operating system. Unlike RAM slack, large quantities of data can reside in drive slack because its storage capacity is not limited to one sector, that is, 512 bytes. Drive slack can potentially store up to 63 sectors of data (32,256 bytes of data or the equivalent of approximately eight printed pages), depending on the operating system involved. Information stored in drive slack can contain remnants of previously deleted files and other information that resided on the storage media before the file was created.

The following example helps clarify file slack and its components. Assume that you create a file by writing the word "Hello," and no other data is contained in the actual file. The file is only five bytes in length. Assuming that the clusters assigned by the operating system to the file are two sectors in size, the data stored to disk and the file slack would be represented as follows in Figure 1.

The data are identified by the word "Hello." RAM slack is identified by the "\" symbol and drive slack is identified by the horizontal line pattern. The "(EOC)" marker has been listed to identify the end of the last cluster of the file, but it has been provided for illustration purposes and such a marker is not actually stored on disk at the end of the assigned cluster. Rather, the end of the file is recorded in the directory area. In this example, only one cluster is needed to store the small five-byte file containing the word "Hello."

4. **Windows swap and Windows page files** act as an extension of memory for the operating system and are used when more memory is needed by the operating system. This happens when multiple software programs are running at the same time or when extremely large documents or graphics files are viewed or edited.

These files act as a "scratch pad" for the operating system when more memory is needed. Windows swap files and Windows page files are huge. Depending on the operating system configuration, the size of the swap or page file will be between approximately 50 and 700 million bytes. In the case of Windows, Windows 95, and Windows 98, the file is called the Windows swap file. For Windows NT, Windows 2000, and Windows XP, the file is called the Windows page file.

Most computer users are unaware of Windows swap and Windows page files, and they do not realize that fragments of their work products may transparently be written to these special files. Essentially any work performed in a Windows work session can end up in the swap or page file, including fragments of created files, edited files, and even fragments of files that were merely printed and not created or edited on the computer system. Swap or page files also capture fragments of Internet Web browsing activities, Internet e-mail addresses and messages, and even the directory listings displayed in a Windows Explorer session. Passwords and logons may also be written to the Windows swap and Windows page files. These special files are a wonderful source of investigative leads in computer evidence–based cases, but they are a significant security risk in classified government agencies. More information about these files is available on the Internet at http://www.forensics-intl.com/def7.html.

5. **Unallocated file space** is another ambient data source that should be of concern to government computer users. When files are "deleted" on personal computers, the data associated with subject file is not erased. Rather, the space assigned to the file becomes unallocated by the operating system and the storage space is made available for new files. However, the data from the former file can actually linger on storage media for months or even years. The same is true of the name of the former file. Only the first byte of the file name is overwritten and it is replaced with a lower-case Greek sigma character, σ.

An example of a deleted file directory file listing is shown in Figure 2. In this example, the deleted file was named FILE01 before it was erased, and the only change to the file name is the first character, which was replaced with the with a lowercase Greek sigma character. Note also that the particulars about file dates, sizes, and attributes remain behind.

Unallocated file space should not be confused with free storage space. Free storage space is the space that resides beyond allocated hard-disk drive partitions. Unallocated file space differs because it is contained within a logical hard disk drive partition, and it can

σ →
Indicator for
deleted file

Name	Ext	Size	Date	Time	Cluster
σILE01	DOC	4,088	08/17/00	8:27 PM	16009
FILE02	DOC	82,712	08/19/00	10:15 PM	16035
PROJECT	XLS	35,006	09/23/00	9:17 PM	16054
FILE03	DOC	108,454	09/23/00	10:37 PM	16145

Figure 2.

contain both erased file data and the file slack associated with erased files. Unallocated file space is the largest source of ambient data, and it can potentially involve several billion bytes of data on a large personal computer hard-disk drive. Therefore, the security risks associated with unallocated storage space can be significant in a classified government agency.

6. **Temporary files** are created and used by most software applications. The operating system also creates and uses various temporary files to perform various tasks, for example, the printing of files. These specialized files are typically created as the result of background processes, and the user is usually unaware of their existence or purpose. When the need for a temporary file has passed, it is typically deleted by the background operation that created it. However, the data associated with the erased temporary file remains behind in unallocated file space. In this regard, erased temporary files are no different than other erased files.

   Many Windows-based software applications create temporary files to facilitate sorting functions, to create indexes, for directory scrolling in Windows Explorer, and so forth. Temporary files potentially store fragments of the data processed during the computer work session. All allocated and erased temporary files should therefore be considered a security risk in classified government environments because the likelihood exists that they may contain classified information.

7. **Partition gaps and free space** can be a security risk on previously used personal computer systems. Partition gaps and partition free-space risks are some of the reasons that the U.S. government requires that security risk reviews include the search of all physical sectors on the subject hard-disk drive. Individual hard-disk drives are referred to as physical hard drives (physical devices), and the data storage area of a physical hard drive can be broken into smaller storage components, which are called logical hard drives. This is typically done with commercially available hard-disk drive partitioning software when operating systems are upgraded on used computer systems or the computers are transferred from one person to another. During the upgrade process, not all of the storage capacity of the physical hard drive may be needed and therefore a smaller partition is used. In such cases, partition gaps can also result between allocated partitions on the same physical hard-disk drive. As an unintended result, artifacts of the legacy data may remain behind in the partition free space or in partition gaps when multiple partitions are involved on the same physical hard-disk drive.

   An example of a partition gap is illustrated in Figure 3. After partitioning, the resulting drive partitions are referred to as logical drives, and, in this example, they are referred to as drives C: and D:. Multiple logical disk drives can reside on one physical drive and multiple operating systems can also reside within different logical drives on the same physical hard-disk drive.

   Many risks associated with partition gaps and partition free space can be identified through the use of a DoD-certified forensics text search utility, which has

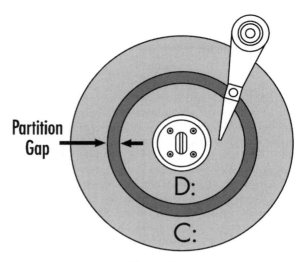

Figure 3.

the capability of searching all areas of the physical storage device.

8. **Hibernation mode files and partitions** create added security risks for government employees who deal with classified information, as mentioned previously. Most notebook computers automatically capture and save a computer work session using hibernation mode files or dedicated partitions. This conserves battery power, and it provides a convenient way for computer users to resume their work sessions where they last ended. When the hibernation option is triggered, the notebook computer bookmarks the last work completed and puts the computer into a sleep mode. Computers that have this feature essentially capture the work session using a special file or, in some cases, a special partition. When the hibernating computer is awakened, the computer user can resume his/her work session at the point where he/she left off. This provides the computer user with benefits, but significant risks are created because artifacts of the suspended work session can remain behind on the hard disk drive for an indefinite period of time. The risks are substantial because hibernation files are huge, that is, more than 200 million bytes in size, and they should be factored into government computer security risk assessments when notebook computers are used to process or analyze classified government data.

RISKS ASSOCIATED WITH COMPUTER-RELATED STORAGE DEVICES

Photocopy machines bring other risks to classified government agencies because copied classified data can be inadvertently stored on these machines. Photocopy machines typically rely on personal computer technology in their operation, and many of the devices contain internal computer hard-disk drives. Some photocopy machines can also be used as printers in a networked environment. If the photocopy machine is used with sensitive government data, then it is likely that the data will migrate onto the photocopy machine's internal hard-disk drive. For this reason, photocopy machines should be treated as personal computers by government computer-security specialists. The security risks are the same as with personal computers, and, in some cases, the risks may actually be greater because some of the computer files created by photocopy machines are binary in nature and their contents cannot be evaluated using forensic text search utilities.

CDs and DVDs create additional risks in classified government agencies because of their portability and large storage capacities. These storage devices easily interact with personal computers, and they can be duplicated without leaving a trace of the duplication process behind. For these reasons, physical security is usually required for these storage devices in classified government agencies. However, computer-security risk assessments should include the review of nonclassified CDs and DVDs in classified government agencies because of the potentials of classified data leakage onto these storage devices.

Personal digital assistants (PDAs), digital cameras, and cellular telephones are all capable of exchanging data with personal computers, and they also create additional and significant security risks in classified government environments. Because they are portable and nonessential in classified agencies, these devices are typically not allowed in classified government environments. However, exceptions are made in some classified government agencies and computer security specialists need to be aware of the potentials for classified data leakage into the internal storage areas of these computer-related devices.

Floppy diskettes, USB memory sticks, and Iomega Zip disks all interact with personal computers, and they are portable data storage devices. Floppy diskettes were allegedly used in the Robert Hanssen spy case in the transmission of U.S. government secrets to the Russians. Even though their storage capacities are relatively small, floppy diskettes still pose a significant risk in classified government agencies because of their portability. As stated, their storage capacities are fairly limited when compared with newer technologies, for example, USB-compatible flash memory devices and Iomega Zip disks. If these devices are present or allowed in classified agencies, they should be considered a risk because of the potential for leakage of classified government data.

CONCERNS SPECIFIC TO CLASSIFIED GOVERNMENT AGENCIES

The potential for leakage and the unintentional transfer of sensitive data to unclassified computer-storage devices is of great concern in classified government agencies. Unfortunately, classified data leakage is a common occurrence in classified government agencies. This is because most government employees are unaware of the inherent security weaknesses associated with personal computer usage, specifically the potentials for migration of sensitive government data into ambient data-storage areas. Security weaknesses are inherent in the design of personal computers and most of the security risks are not obvious to computer users. This is because the risks are highly technical in nature and beyond the knowledge of most unsophisticated computer users who just want to get work done. For these reasons, most classified government agencies make it a priority to regularly scan nonclassified computer systems to identify the leakage of classified data. When the classified data leakage is identified, the data must be securely eliminated with DoD-certified data-scrubbing software tools or other approved methods.

Classified computer-security risk assessments are typically conducted with DoD-tested and certified computer forensic search tools that are executed from a bootable floppy diskette or a bootable USB storage device. By using floppy diskettes and/or USB devices, running under DOS or Linux, a government computer-security specialist can simultaneously review several personal computers. The practice also allows for the search of all sectors of the targeted hard-disk drives involved. It is a U.S. government requirement that such searches include the search of every sector of the storage media, and this requirement cannot be accomplished from a computer network or via the Internet. Therefore, government security reviews are usually conducted onsite and multiple computers are assessed for risk at the same time.

Most government computer-security review policies and procedures are outdated because they were developed under the assumption that classified data leakage would be limited to ACSII (text-based) data and files. Unfortunately, most of the policies were created before Microsoft PowerPoint and digital photography became popular in the workplace. For this reason, many of the current government security-review policies and procedures need to be updated to account for new risks tied to current technology. In addition to text-based files, the policies should take into account threats tied to compressed files, for example, Zip files, and graphics files, and proprietary file formats that are binary in nature. Such files can potentially mask the fact that they contain classified data, and they do not respond well to text-based computer forensic search tools. Some government security-review procedures do not take into account disk fragmentation. Fragmented data can result in targeted search terms being split between clusters and that can have a negative affect on ASCII text-based security reviews. For these reasons, existing policies should be reviewed to make sure that they are current with technology. If they are outdated, security review policies and procedures should be updated or supplemented to take into account new security risks associated with new file formats, storage devices, and other technology advances that have been adopted for use in the workplace.

Computer forensic search tools cannot adequately search some types of files, for example, graphics files, PowerPoint files, compressed files, and PDF files, and some suggestions have been provided in hopes of enhancing the quality of classified government security reviews and risk assessments. Until security is designed into personal computers, security reviews will remain as a standard practice in classified government agencies. It is also likely that similar security-review practices will be adopted by other U.S. government agencies in the future as U.S. homeland defense measures are implemented and expanded. As of this writing, the demand for government computer-security specialists exceeds the supply of qualified individuals with computer forensics knowledge and experience. Private-sector businesses and Fortune 500 corporations will likely encounter the same shortages of qualified computer-security specialists as they deal with recently enacted laws regarding security of information, for example, HIPAA, Gramm–Leach–Bliley, and Sarbanes–Oxley. These laws require many businesses and organizations to establish safeguards and controls over the security and privacy of financial, health, and public corporation insider information. These new laws are discussed in more detail elsewhere in this book.

FORENSIC SEARCH PRACTICES IN CLASSIFIED SECURITY REVIEWS

Most classified U.S. government agencies require the periodic review of all personal computers located in close proximity to computer systems that store and process classified data. Computer forensic search tools are the first line of defense in classified agencies for the identification of classified data leakage. The U.S. government requires that these reviews include the search of every sector of the storage media for classified text. Typically, DoD-tested and certified forensic text search utilities are used for this purpose, for example, NTI's TextSearch Plus and TextSearch NT, and government-developed tools such as D-Scan. As mentioned previously, government security reviews are lacking if they rely totally on text searches for the identification of classified data leakage. Forensic search tools are extremely helpful in security reviews but they provide no benefits when classified data are potentially stored in nontext file formats. The techniques discussed in the following pages are provided with the intent of helping improve the accuracy of risk assessments in government agencies.

Creation of the Search Term List

The terms used in the computer forensic search are extremely important to the success of any computer-security risk assessment that involves the use of a computer forensic text search tool. The creation of the search term list is one of the most important parts of the security assessment. Lists that include small words, short terms, and abbreviations tend to generate false search results. Long strings of text may be missed in the search process because of disk fragmentation. The effectiveness of the security scanning process is only as good as the design of the search term list and the computer forensic search tool used in the search. In any case, the list of search terms should be crafted with much care and thought by a person who is trained in the use of computer forensic search tools. It is helpful if the person conducting the search has knowledge of personal computer technology and inherent personal-computer security weaknesses.

Search term lists can be created using DOS Edit, Windows NotePad, or even a word processing program. Depending on the computer forensic search utility used, search terms are usually stored in ASCII format and each search term is terminated with a carriage feed/line feed sequence. DOS Edit and Windows NotePad generate this type of file output automatically and a word processor can be used to generate such a file using the "File Save As" feature. When using a word processor, the list of terms is saved in ASCII DOS text format.

Ideally, short words and abbreviations should not be used in the search term file. This is because the letter combinations associated with some relevant classified words or terms may also be found in common forms of data found on most computer systems. The following is an example of a flawed search term list that would likely result in hundreds or even thousands of false hits in a security review that relies on a forensic text search utility:

troll
lion
lie
secret
soft
copy
poly
roso
program

This listing of search terms may appear to be acceptable, but a close examination reveals several problems with the terms in the list; for example, these terms are substrings of larger words, or they are found in system files that are common to most personal computers. If this list were used in the search of a hard disk, hundreds of false leads would likely be identified by a text-based computer forensic search tool. To illustrate this important point, please consider the following:

1. **troll** is included in the words controller, controlled, and trolley.
2. **lion** is included in the words battalion and dandelion.
3. **lie** is included in the words believe, client, lien, earliest, families, and allied.
4. **secret** is included in the word secretary and the titles Secretary of State, Secretary of Commerce, Secretary of the Treasury, and Secretary of Defense.
5. **soft** is included in the name Microsoft Corporation and personal computer searches will identify thousands of occurrences of this word on most systems. The same situation exists with the search term "**roso**," which is also included in the name Microsoft Corporation.
6. **copy** is included in the words copyright, copying, and photocopy.
7. **poly** is a slang term for polygraph and is included in the word polygon.
8. **program** is a term that is stored in numerous locations on all personal computers; for example, the error message contained in all Windows-based programs, "program cannot be run in DOS mode."

This hypothetical list of search terms would need to be fine-tuned to enhance the search results and to eliminate as many false hits as possible. An example of the perfected search term list might look something like the following:

troll<space>

<space>lion

<space>lie<space>

secret<space>

<space>soft

<space>copy<space>

poly<space>

<space>roso or roso project

weapons program

The strategic insertion of spaces in the search term list is important when one or more of the targeted search terms are a part of larger words. This technique is called "space bracketing" in computer forensics, and it is very effective. However, the space-bracketing technique can create problems when punctuation immediately follows the term on the targeted storage device. Other problems occur when plurals of a word in the search term list exist on the targeted storage device.

To illustrate some of problems associated with space bracketing, consider a search for the word "secret." Let's assume for a moment that we are conducting a security review at a U.S. embassy, and we want to avoid false hits associated with the title "Secretary of State." We would modify the search term list by adding a space behind the word "secret." However, the addition of the trailing space would cause the forensic search software to skip the word "secrets," and it would skip the word "secret" if it appeared as the last word in a sentence. This is because the trailing punctuation, that is, a period, would defeat the search results for some forensic search tools. DoD-certified forensic search tools, for example, TextSearch Plus and TextSearch NT, will not be fooled by trailing punctuation. To avoid missing the word "secrets" in the search, we could add that word to the search term list. Thus, the search term list would include both the word "secret" (followed by a space) and the word "secrets" to enhance the results of the search.

Repeated test scans are usually required to perfect the search term list to avoid false positives and to ensure that relevant search terms not missed. It is not uncommon in computer forensics to fine-tune the search term list during the search as false positive findings are identified. Once an accurate search term list has been created, it can be used on multiple computers in the security assessment. Every change to the search term list should be given much thought because even minor changes can affect the accuracy of the security search results.

Logical Versus Physical Text Searches

The U.S. government requires that all sectors of storage device data be searched to identify the potential leakage of classified government data onto unclassified computers and related storage devices. This policy is based on sound computer forensics logic because of the possibility that classified data could reside between or beyond partitions on the storage device. As mentioned previously, this can occur when used computers are upgraded with new operating systems or when hard disk drives are repartitioned during hardware maintenance. Physical keyword searches involving the search of each sector will also identify allocated and "deleted" file names that may also contain classified terms. However, remember that the

Figure 4.

names of erased files will omit the first character in the file name. It will be replaced with a lowercase Greek sigma character. If the potential exists for file names to be a security risk, then this needs to be taken into account when the list of search terms is created.

Logical text searches of storage volumes will not identify risks associated with file names, data stored in the MFT on NTFS-based systems, and data potentially stored in the partition gap or partition-free space. However, logical searches can provide benefits that do not exist with physical searches when disk fragmentation is involved. To illustrate this situation, assume that our search term list includes the classified term "Aardvark55." The length of this search term is not excessive, and it could be relevant in a classified security-risk assessment. For the purposes of this example, assume that the hard-disk drive involved is well used and the data storage areas are fragmented. On well-used disk drives, the potential of disk fragmentation is high and the potential exists for targeted search terms to be split between consecutive clusters. This is illustrated in Figure 4.

For the purposes of this example, assume that the file has not been deleted and that it is still an active file. If we were to perform a physical text search for the term Aardvark55, the data would be identified by the forensic search utility. The same would be true if we were to performe a logical search for the term using a forensic search utility.

Now let us look at the same fact pattern but factor in disk fragmentation. For the purposes of the example and to illustrate the effect of disk fragmentation, assume that the data previously stored in cluster 820 was written by the operating system to cluster 822. This would be the case, on a used hard drive, if clusters 820 and 821 were already occupied with data from another file. Because of disk fragmentation, the data would be stored on disk as illustrated in Figure 5.

If we were to conduct a physical text search, in this case, the search term, "Aardvark55," would not be identified. A logical text search would identify the search term, however, because the File Allocation Table (FAT) (or Message Format Translation (MFT) on an NTFS system) would connect the clusters. However, neither the physical text search nor logical text search would identify the search term if the file was deleted. This is because the FAT (or MFT on an NTFS system) would no longer recognize clusters 819 and 822 as part of the same file.

The problem with fragmentation can be addressed in two different ways. First, it is recommended that both physical and logical searches be conducted using a

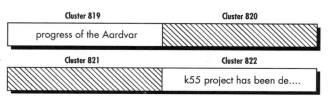

Figure 5.

DoD-certified forensic text search utility. Such tools will accommodate both physical and logical searches, and they can be run automatically in batch mode. Second, it always makes sense to split targeted search terms in the search term list to enhance the search potentials because of search weaknesses attributed to fragmentation. In the hypothetical Aardvark55 example, we could include Aardvark55, Aardv, and k55 in the search term list. Although this involves three separate search terms and it will likely generate redundant hits, the practice helps ensure that targeted data will not be overlooked. However, you must be aware that even this technique will not ensure positive findings when deleted files and fragmentation are involved, as stated previously.

RISKS ASSOCIATED WITH NONTEXT (BINARY) FILES

Forensic text searches are not effective when certain types of files are involved. The files that cause concern include but are not limited to compressed files, graphic files, embedded text files, and compound files that include combinations of graphics files and text. Forensic text searches are also ineffective if files have been encrypted using any number of commercial and government encryption tools. The topic of encryption has not been discussed here because encrypted data in a classified government agency is not a security risk.

Graphics File Formats

Digital photography has become popular and graphics files are abundant on the Internet. In today's modern world, some cellular telephones have the ability to take pictures and store the image in the form of graphics files. Because of advances in technology, we have become a more picture-based society. It is not uncommon for hundreds or thousands of graphics files to be stored on a well-used personal computer system. This causes problems in classified government agencies because forensic text-based search utilities cannot identify classified terms and words stored within graphics files. For this reason, it is currently necessary to identify and manually review the contents of all graphics files as part of a classified government security risk assessment given the state of current technology. As of this writing, no forensic search tools can reliably search graphics files and identify targeted key words or strings of text. The problem is compounded by the fact that some text-based file formats allow the embedding of graphics files in the files. This is the case with word processing, PowerPoint, and spreadsheet files. This means that computer forensic search utilities have limitations concerning the identification of all data leakage in classified government security-risk assessments.

In the past, I have recommended that file headers of known graphics files be included in the search term lists. Some forensic search tools do this automatically for the common graphics file formats, for example, BMP, GIF, JPG, and TIF. However, in high-stakes computer-security-risk reviews, I recommend that all graphics files be captured from the target media and that they be reviewed using a graphics file viewer. Although this is a tedious

process involving potentially large volumes of files, decisions can be made quickly by reviewing thumbnails of the extracted graphics files. The extraction process can be simplified through the use of a physical access capture of all graphics files contained on a target hard-disk drive using a tool such as NTI's Graphics File Extractor, and the process can be performed using a portable USB storage device. Floppy diskettes cannot be used because they do not have enough storage capacity.

Compressed File Formats

File compression programs are popular, and they are used to combine and compress one or more files to save space. They were originally created to shrink file size back when files were downloaded from computer bulletin boards. Back then, modem transfer rates were very small and long-distance phone rates were high. To save money and time, file compression was used extensively with programs such as ARC, PKARC, and LHARC. Today the most popular file compression program is PKZIP, but other popular programs include RAR, ARJ, and ACE. In addition to compressing file contents, modern compression programs also provide security features through the use of encryption.

It is unfortunate, but forensic search utilities have no ability to reliably and quickly search compressed file formats. However, some forensic search tools do identify these files by either their file extensions or file header signatures. When the compressed files are identified in this fashion, a manual review is required. This can be a time-consuming and tedious process, and this is especially true if security features have been used with the compression. Because of the risks and problems created, many classified government agencies forbid the use of these programs.

Embedded Text and Obscure File Formats

Not all files are stored as text, and this complicates the job of the computer security specialist who uses forensic search utilities in computer security reviews. In general, text searches involve the search for upper- and lowercase characters, numbers, and punctuation. All of these characters can be entered from the keyboard, but that is not to say that a computer application will store text in the same order it was entered.

Computer applications typically allow work to be stored in the form of a file. Unfortunately, there is no universal standard for file formats, and this is true of even commonly used computer applications such as word processors. Because of this lack of standardization, file formats vary dramatically, and some use special characters to identify unique characteristics about the stored data, for example, underlining of text, bold type, dropped capitalization, italics, and so forth, in word processing files. Some word processing files contain a mixture of ASCII text blended with binary characters. This situation can cause problems in classified security reviews that are based purely on the search of key words and strings of text in ASCII form. All computer security specialists should be aware of this fact, and they should realize that forensic text search tools have limitations. I have provided some examples of different file formats as food for thought for computer security specialists. This information is intended to help in the crafting of search term lists and it is also intended to demonstrate the limitations of forensic text searches in classified government reviews.

To illustrate the weaknesses of forensic text searches in classified government reviews, let us assume that we have included the term "little lamb" in our search term list. The assumption would be that this is a term of interest or it could hypothetically be a classified project name. With this in mind, I created a one-sentence WordPerfect doc-

Note that the targeted text, **little lamb**, is surrounded with special characters that are used by the application to identify that the text is to be displayed and printed as bold text. In this example, a forensic search utility would easily identify the targeted search term.

DisplayWrite Version 4.0
The DisplayWrite file is smaller (407 bytes in length), and the filtered results are as follows:

```
......
....Q......................................................../.=.....8@.%..........Q....*0.......d...................................$..)....3..
8..=..............'...........%......Q.........m...... 8......8.e..... Q..........K.........K.......K.........K....M...
..].....M.....]..........]...........].............H......@...@.@+.............@....+...@....@......@...@..@.....@..@....
K...........`
```

ument that consisted of "Mary had a **little lamb** whose fleece was as white as snow." Note that the targeted search term, little lamb, was bolded in the sentence that I created. The file was then saved in the form of several different word processing file formats. You would think that this simple sentence would be stored identically in each file format, but that is not the case.

I have provided various examples here to illustrate how file formats differ from one application to another. Please note that I filtered all binary and control characters and replaced them with a period. Any replacement character

Note that none of the information was stored on disk in readable form. In this example, a forensic search utility would fail to identify any targeted key words.

MS Word Version 4.0
Microsoft Word has become the most popular word processing format and MS Word, version 4.0, is one of the older versions of the program. In this example, it created a fairly small, 772-byte file, and the filtered output is displayed as follows:

```
1.....................................................................................................
Mary had a little lamb whose fleece was as white as snow ..............................................
....................w.................................................................................
..............................................................................=./.....2...$...........
...............................................<.........=.............................................
........................................
```

could have been used, but I did this so that the results could be easily printed and reviewed. The results follow.

AMI PR0 Version 3.0
Most word processing applications add information to the stored file that assists in the editing process. Therefore, word processing files are usually larger than the stored contents, and this is the case with the AMI Pro file format. The sentence "Mary had a little lamb whose fleece was white as snow" is 57 bytes in length, but the file size is 1,358 bytes in length and the filtered output is listed as follows:

In this example all of the text is displayed, and a forensic search utility would easily identify the targeted search terms.

MS Word 97/2000 for Windows
Microsoft has made many improvements to the MS Word program over the years. Current versions allow the tracking of changes and the incorporation of graphics. These improvements come with a penalty in the size of the file. In

```
[ver]...4..[sty]....[files]..[charset]...82...ANSI (Windows, IBM CP 1252)..[prn]...PCL / HP
LaserJet..[lang]...2..[fopts]...4...1...2880...0..[lnopts]...0...Body
Text..[docopts]...5...0..[tag]...Body Text...2...[fnt]....Times New
Roman....240....0....32768..[algn]....1....1....0....0....0..[spc]....33....273....1....0....0....1....100...[br
k]....4...[line]....8....0.... 1....0....1....1....1....10....10....1..[spec]....0....0....0....1....1....0....2....0....0..
.[nfmt]....272....1....2............,....$..[lay]...Standard...513...[rght]....15840....12240....1....1440....1440
....1...1440....1440....0....0....0....0....0....2....1....1440....10800....10....1....720....1....1440....1...216
0....1....2880....1....3600....1....4320....1....5040....1....5760....1....6480....1....7200...[hrght]...[lyfrm
]....1....11200....0....0....12240....1440....1....1....3....1....0....0....0...[frmlay]....1440....12240....1....1
440....72....1....360....1440....0....1....0....1....1....0....1....1440....10800....0...[txt]..>...[frght]...[lyfr
m]....1....13248....0....14400....12240....15840....1....1....3....1....0....0....0...[frmlay]....15840....122
40....1....1440....360....1....14472....1440....0....1....0....1....1....0....1....1440....10800....0...[txt]..>..[
elay]..[l1]...0..[edoc]..Mary had a < +! >little lamb< −! > whose fleece was as white as snow...>..
```

the example, the converted file is 12,292 bytes in size and relevant parts of the filtered file are displayed as follows:

In this case, the sentence is stored on disk as text and a forensic search utility would easily identify the targeted

```
...............................................................R.o.o.t.
.E.n.t.r.y..........................................@..."..............P.e.r.f.e.c.t.O.f.f.i.c.e._.M.A.I.N.......................
.....&.........................................P.e.r.f.e.c.t.O.f.f.i.c.e._.O.B.J.E.C.T.S............................,...................&..
.........@..."...@..."............................................R.o.o.t.
.E.n.t.r.y............................;.."...........D.a.t.a....................................................
...........1.T.a.b.l.e.....................O.b.j.e.c.t.P.o.o.l...............................................
.........;.."...;.."..........................W.o.r.d.D.o.c.u.m.e.n.t.....................G...........................bj
bj........................&..........P.................................................................].................
....................................................................g..............................................
....,,...........................$...........R.............................................
.........................bt'...........................................................................
.....................................................S.E.Q. .C.H.A.P.T.E.R. .\.h. .\.r. .1... .M.a.r.y. .h.a.d. .a
.l.i.t.t.l.e. .l.a.m.b. .w.h.o.s.e. .f.l.e.e.c.e. .w.a.s. .a.s. .w.h.i.t.e.
.a.s. .s.n.o.w................................*..,...B...X........................mH.. CJ..5...mH..CJ....U...CJ..mH..U.........
....................................1$....$.../
..=!..."...#...$...%...............................................[.........(..@....(....N.o.r.m.a.l.........CJ.
.mH...................<.A@...<.....D.e.f.a.u.l.t. .P.a.r.a.g.r.a.p.h. .F.o.n.t....................................P...........................
...........................P...................................P...@..........G.................................
T.i.m.e.s. .N.e.w. .R.o.m.a.n...5...................S.y.m.b.o.l...3&.......................................A.r
.i.a.l...#....................1...1.................!#.........................................
...........................
```

This is one of the most popular word processing programs, and you should note that the application stores the sentence with binary characters inserted between each letter. Many of the older forensic search utilities would not recognize the targeted key words stored in this fashion. However, a DoD-certified forensic search utility such as NTI's

string of text. In this case, the bolding is tagged with binary characters before and after the term "little lamb."

Professional Write Version 2.2

The sentence is converted into a 1,151-byte Professional Write file and the filtered output is displayed as follows:

```
B..........N.........................................................................................
..................#.(.-.2.7.<.A.F...........................................................................
....................................................................................................
....................................................................................................
.TYPE 4..2.00.......................................................................................
.................................................................................1....................K
.K...................................................N.....# (-27<AF... Mary had a ..............whose
fleece was as white as snow.....N......# (-27<AF.........
```

TextSearch Pro or TextSearch NT would identify the targeted strings of text.

In this case, the targeted strings of text are not visible because the word processing application converts them into binary characters to identify them as bolded text. For this reason, a forensic search utility would fail to identify the targeted strings of text.

OfficeWriter Version 6.2

When the file is converted into the OfficeWriter file format, it resulted in a 1,681-byte file, and the filtered output is displayed as follows:

```
6.0
01/08/04:..wp.
                                    85   110  10  10  10       n    nfo  n6..
.1.1....................................................................................................
...................................................................................................
...................................................................................................
................................1.1................................................................
...........................................................1.1....................................
.....Mary had a .little lamb. whose fleece was as white as snow..
```

VolksWriter Version 4.0

The VolksWriter file ends up being 896 bytes, and the printed output is displayed as follows:

```
..LAYOUT 2 ..Mary had a .little lamb. whose fleece was as white as snow...... LAYOUT
000...........r.......B.................<.....?........ .\---- +----+----+----+----+----+----+----+----+-----
+----+----+-@-+----/----------------------------------------------------------------------------------------
----------------------------------------------------------------------.............. B..................
...<.....?........ .\----+----+----+----+----+----+----+----+----+----+----+-@-+----/--------------------------
----------------------------------..............................................
----------------------------..............................................
......................
```

Because all of the data are stored as text, a forensic search utility would have no difficulty identifying the targeted strings of text in this case.

WordPerfect Version 5.1

The older version of WordPerfect was an industry standard for many years. When our sentence is saved in this file format, the resulting file is 410 bytes and the filtered output is displayed as follows:

```
.WPC[...........2......Z...B...0...........I.........S...Canon i9100.............................X.N...\......
P....................X.P..X.N...\......P.......X.P(....9.....Z......6.T.i.m.e.s. .N.e.w. .R.o.m.a.n.
.R.e.g.u.l.a.r.............................................X............3|.x...Mary had a ...little lamb...
whose fleece was as white as snow.
```

Because all of the data are stored as text, a forensic search utility would have no difficulty identifying the targeted strings of text in this case. Note that three binary characters are used, before and after, to designate the bolded text. Also, note that the connected printer is identified and recorded in the file.

WordPerfect Versions 6/7/8/9/10

WordPerfect has also made improvements to its word processors over the years at the smaller expense of a smaller file. When our sentence is converted into this file format, the resulting file is 1,721 bytes in length, and the filtered output is displayed as follows:

```
.WPC=.......................Q..|.R&....s..Z...v.]..ri .........,......=H;.Uf..)....U.....?...4.\.8z..-.}....'..6.(3....a..gG.z.I..
.....B.+M......la..r...hM+.. ?.i@..n.VD...?.D7....7....O.C..B"@..N...].ug...D..yQY...:........{.@....8}..".....@
W..L!...[.A&.VjK.l.Y.Z...Y[.p..#i.w..w.1]o.H.1H...). =.....'ir..d...F...\.z.lF...........<.m.j...Q5O..C.*l.) ..h.".
Am..@.fm...GX.e..Z'.......y$.S.....#B.qH= ....<C.;..Rq.f...B..|Az..'I.=N..uM.9kK...7GX^.........BR.X..5
.1A...V.r.....NO)Gi.PF....K............}.z....z.... PB'.V.[...9.Hd.........# ..........U...N...c....%............0.......
...^............w...........4.........................$....m.......&...........C.a.n.o.n.
.i.9.1.0.0......................................................................................................
...............................................................................................................
...............................................................................................................
.............................0.*.*.0.....0...............................................................
.............................................(....9........Z............. 6. T.i.m.e.s. .N.e.w. .R.o.m.a.n.
.R.e.g.u.l.a.r...X.......(..............$...............USUS. .,......(0..........'0......N.thF.}....3|.x.....
..............U.........................!........USUS. .,...................-...........Mary.had.a...little. lamb....whose.fleece.w
as.as.white.as.snow.
```

In this case, binary characters have been inserted between each word. Because our targeted string of text "little lamb" contains two words, this can have a negative effect concerning forensic text searches. Many of the older forensic search utilities would not recognize the targeted key words stored in this fashion. However, a DoD-certified forensic search utility such as NTI's TextSearch Pro or TextSearch NT would identify the targeted strings of text.

WordStar Version 2.1

Several years ago WordStar was an industry standard in the word processing field. When our sentence is saved in this format, the resulting file is 396 bytes in size, and the filtered output is displayed as follows:

```
.WS2000.1.00.... PRINTER........ 0 ..!Release.3.00...!...0 0...i 0 0i..^1^ .._
1...[.K......................K...........$.)...3.8.=.B.G.L.Q.V. [.'.e.j.o.t.y.~...........[..a,
66a..\ 0\..]0]..b11b ..e0e..f1f..g1g. .h00h..'1 3 2'..:033:..s011111s..v..z 9 3z..{ 9 9{ ..b00b.Mary
had a ...little lamb...whose fleece was as white as snow.
```

Because all of the data are stored as text, a forensic search utility would have no difficulty identifying the targeted strings of text in this case.

Only a few of the different file formats have been listed. You should be aware that file formats can vary dramatically from one program to another and even from one version of the same program to another. For that reason, it is important that you are familiar with the computer applications used in your organization and the files that they create. The degree of risk is dependent on a variety of variables and this is an important one.

CONCLUSIONS

Unfortunately, personal computers were never designed to be secure. For this reason, inherent risks exist when sensitive data are stored on personal computer storage devices in government and business environments. Some of the risks associated with data leakage can be identified through the use of computer forensics tools and methods, but there are limitations. The limitations deal primarily with data stored in obscure file formats, graphics files, and compressed files, which do not lend themselves to forensic text searches. When these types of files are involved, the risks are increased in classified government agencies and manual reviews of specific files and data types are required. Once data leakage has been identified, the subject data can be eliminated through accepted data elimination processes.

GLOSSARY

Allocation unit   The smallest unit of disk space that may be allocated to a file. Varies by file system.
Bit-stream copy   A bit-for-bit copy of digital evidence.
Block   UNIX terminology for an allocation unit (see allocation unit).
FAT   Acronym for File Allocation Table. A common form of file system used with Microsoft Windows operating systems.
Forensic image   An exact, bit-for-bit copy of media.

CROSS REFERENCES

See *Computer Forensic Procedures and Methods, Digital Evidence, Forensic Computing, Risk Management for IT Security*

FURTHER READING

Heverly, R. & Wright, M. (2004). Cyberspace law and computer forensics. In S. Bosworth and M.E. Kabay (Eds.), *Computer Security Handbook*. New York: Wiley.

Kruse, W.G. III, & Heiser, J.G. (2001). *Computer Forensics: Incident Response Essentials*. Addison-Wesley.

Larson, T. (2002). The other side of civil discovery. In E. Casey (Ed.), *Handbook of Computer Crime Investigation*. Academic Press.

Mohay, G., Anderson, A., Collie, B., De Vel, O., & McKemmish, R. (2003). *Computer and Intrusion Forensics*. Norwood, MA: Artech.

Mukammala, S. Sung, A.H. (2003). Identifying Significant Features for Network Forensic Analysis Using Artificial Intelligence Techniques. *International Journal of Digital Evidence*, 1, Issue 4.

Nelson, B., Phillips, A., Enfinger, F., & Steuart, C. (2004). *Guide to Computer Forensics And Investigations*. Boston: Thomson.

Olson, D. (2000). Analysis of criminal codes and ciphers. *Forensic Science Communications*, 2, Number 1.

Reith, M. Carr, C. Gunsh, G. (2001). An examination of digital forensic models. *International Journal of Digital Evidence*, 1, No. 3.

Rowlingson, R. (2004). A ten step process for forensic readiness. *International Journal of Digital Evidence*, 2, No. 3.

Sammes, T., & Jenkinson, B. (2000). *Forensic Computing: A Practitioner's Guide*. London: Springer Verlag.

Stephenson, P. (2003). *Using evidence effectively*. Computer Fraud and Security, Vol. 10, Issue 3.

Forensic Analysis of UNIX Systems

Dario V. Forte, *University of Milan, Crema Italy*

INTRODUCTION

The spreading use of distributed systems is forcing the development of increasingly varied investigative procedures in digital forensics regarding both the target and the analysis platforms. A "target platform" is one that has been attacked or used to perpetrate some policy or criminal violation, whereas an "analysis platform" is the one that supports the forensic workstation. In this chapter I discuss UNIX-based platforms and the various "dialects" such as Solaris, AIX, xBSD, and, of course, Linux.

Some Basics of UNIX Forensics

The principles in forensic operations are essentially platform independent, though some file systems are not. In keeping with the rules of due diligence contained in the IACIS (International Association of Computer Investigative Specialists, http://www.cops.org) code of ethics, it is important to clarify several general characteristics of UNIX-based file systems.

However, first I want to make very clear what is meant in digital forensics by "investigative process." Such a process comprises the sequence of activities that should be performed by the forensic examiner to ensure compliance with juridical requirements now common to all countries.

For the purposes of this chapter, the investigative process is subdivided into six phases (Spafford and Carrier, 2003), as illustrated in Figure 1.

1. **Notification.** This first report occurs when an attack is detected by an automatic device, by internal personnel, or through external input (for example, by a system administrator in another company or by another business unit in the same company). The action taken is usually to create or activate a response team, whose first task is to confirm that an attack has occurred.
2. **Preservation.** This is a critical phase in incident response and the first bona fide digital forensic action. The main objective here is to make sure that the scene of the crime is left intact so as not to preclude any future investigative or analytical measures. The "digital

crime scene" is usually duplicated, that is, an image disk is created, so that detailed analyses may be performed in a properly equipped laboratory.

3. **Survey.** This is the first evidence collection step. The objective here is to examine the scene of the crime for any *obvious digital evidence* and to develop hypotheses that will orient further investigation.
4. **Search.** The hypotheses developed in the survey stage are investigated with the help of analysis tools as needed. In this more detailed evidence collection phase, the "cold" trails are abandoned and the "hot" ones followed.
5. **Reconstruction.** This phase involves detailed testing to connect the pieces of evidence and reconstruct the event. In many cases this activity may indicate the need for or reveal further evidence.
6. **Presentation.** The final act in this process is to collect all the findings and present them to those who requested the investigation.

A forensic analysis is indicated in two fundamental cases: a) reconstruction of an attack (post mortem analysis) and b) examination of a computer that may have been used to carry out some sort of criminal violation. In the first case, the examined computer is the *target* of a violation; in the second, it is a *tool* used to commit a crime. The job of the forensic examiner is to carry out the investigative process.

UNIX File Systems: An Overview

For a good understanding of the methods and objectives of an investigation, it is helpful to have some background on UNIX file systems. The logic behind these systems is simple, elegant, and powerful. In some ways, UNIX is similar to DOS; in others, it reveals a kinship with much more outdated operating systems (such as MULTICS); and in others, it is quite unique.

On the system level, directories are treated as files that contain other files or subdirectories instead of data. For the system, all files and directories are **i-nodes**, whose descriptors (name, attributes, authorizations, etc.) and

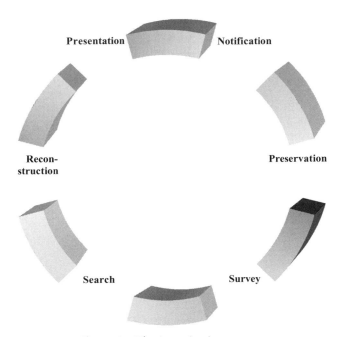

Figure 1: The investigative process.

contents (the data in the file or the files in a directory) are kept separate.

In terms of nomenclature, the files may contain any characters in their names except spaces, special characters for the shell, and CR (carriage return). In UNIX, the file extensions do not have a specific meaning but are used for convenience by certain commands. They are not indispensable and, on the file system level, do not even indicate the type of file.

As an example, a UNIX partition might distribute a file system as follows:

- Block 0, not used by UNIX, sometimes used for the system boot (the MBR if it is found on a primary device);
- Block 1, or Superblock, contains critical information on the structure of the file system (number of i-nodes, number of blocks on the disk, etc.);
- List of the i-nodes, numbered from 1 to a finite number, containing information on the individual files contained in the file system and on the position of the respective data; and
- Data blocks, with the data contained in the file.

The i-nodes contain information such as file type, authorizations, date of creation, modification and last access, proprietary user or group, position and dimension of the file, and so on. Via links, the same i-node can be shared by different objects in the file system.

Details on File System Structure

Linux by default supports the file system ext2, which shares a host of characteristics with a typical UNIX System V file system. The Linux kernel also allows for the use of many other file systems such as ext3, reiserFS, jfs (*journaled* file systems that keep a log of all writing operations to allow easier data recovery in the event of a malfunction), Windows file systems (FAT, FAT32, ntfs),

those of many other operation systems (BeOs, AmigaOs, Mac, etc.), and network file systems such as NFS, SMB, and Novell. This last characteristic is very important for those who carry out forensic analysis and investigation on this type of file system.

A Linux file system, like all UNIX systems, has a hierarchical structure: all its objects (files and directories) are contained in the root [the main directory, indicated simply with a "/" (slash)], and the slash is also used to separate directory names [for example: /usr/bin/ indicates the directory "bin" contained in the directory "usr" contained in the root (/)].

The root not only contains all the other directories in a partition, but also all the file systems (partitions and hard disks, floppy disks, CD-ROMs, network links, etc.). The principle is radically different from what we see under Windows, where each device or resource has its own name or identifying letter (A:, C:, D:, etc.), under which we find the directories of its file system. For example, on many Linux systems, the files contained on a floppy disk are found in a directory named /mnt/floppy and not in something called A: as in Windows. Furthermore, the name of this directory can be changed at will by the user or by whoever set up the distribution (obviously, there are methods for finding out the residence directory of any device).

There are some standard UNIX notations for indicating the current directory, the parent directory, the home directory, and so forth:

/   indicates the root, the main directory at the base of the entire file system;

/bin/   indicates the subdirectory "bin" (arbitrary name) in the root;

bin/   indicates the subdirectory "bin" with respect to the current directory. Note that if the path begins with a "/" it is an absolute path that begins with the root. If it does not begin with "/" it indicates a path in relation to the current directory;

.   indicates the current directory;

..   indicates the parent directory of the current one;

../bin/   indicates the subdirectory "bin" that is found at the same level as the current directory;

~   indicates the home directory of the current user (coincides by default with /home/login_username). An absolute path, then, will look something like this: usr/local/bin and will be operative regardless of the current directory.

A relative path will look something like local/bin and refers to different directories depending on the current directory. In this case, local/bin coincides with /usr/local/bin only if the user is in the directory /usr/.

The following sections provide additional information on the hierarchy and position of information regarding UNIX that is useful for computer forensics operations.

This is the typical scenario you may find when examining a UNIX-based file system. However, you may be pleased to know that a large group of technicians is hard at work on a standard hierarchy to be used by all UNIX machines: Filesystem Hierarchy Standard (2003). Now in version 2.2, it may be a useful reference for forensic investigators.

TOOLS AND TECHNIQUES FOR FORENSIC INVESTIGATIONS

This section addresses investigation methodologies as they apply to the various investigation phases. The objective here is to provide the reader with the initial guidelines needed to approach the problem.

Preservation Phase: Imaging Disk under UNIX

The generation of an image disk under UNIX is an essential part of the preservation phase. One of the most common errors involves making a "nonforensically reliable" copy of disks. This obviously would be the lesser of two evils if we consider the fact that there are still quite a few operators who work (and often even write) on the original disks. Although it may be admissible to work on nonrewritable CD-ROMs, the same can certainly not be said for hard drives. For this reason, the first necessary step is to make a copy, or "image disk," of the original disk, which thereafter is referred to as the "source." There are various methods and tools for accomplishing this.

There are guidelines regarding preparations for doing the imaging. In most cases, the machine is turned off before it is delivered to the incident response investigator. It may also be left on but disconnected from the network. In the former case, the computer must not be turned on except by trained operators; otherwise, data may be modified in a way that compromises the investigation. When in doubt, the golden rule is "if the machine is off it has to stay off; if it is on it has to stay on until further orders."

It goes without saying, but I will say it anyway: the original support must be carefully protected (for example, apply write-protect where possible).

The image of the support is obtained using software tools to create a bit-by-bit image. The preferred method is to use a trusted workstation for the acquisition regardless of whether the source disk is a single hard disk, a floppy disk, or a CD. Otherwise, if conditions permit, the investigated computer may be booted from a floppy (drive A:) rather than from the hard disk. In this case, the computer boots up with a minimal operating system that contains additional programs and drivers so that the computer recognizes an external memorization device as a removable hard disk. Then a program is booted from the floppy that creates the image of the hard disk(s) on the external device. This image will include both visible and hidden files, the parts of the disk that contain information on details of the directories (file name, dimension, date, and time stamp) and also certain other fragments of files that had been previously deleted but not yet overwritten. The image file can be easily read or examined, although in some cases (especially during the reconstruction phase), it may be necessary to carry out a reverse procedure on a second computer with similar characteristics to the first, that is, an exact clone of the original disk so that all details can be completely reproduced. In any case, the images are copied onto write-once/read-many CD ROMs that cannot be altered.

Remember, the disk image destination drive must be wiped. The procedure involves the complete cancellation of the entire contents of the hard disk. There are a number of ad hoc tools for this purpose, including one known as "Wipe." Keep in mind that the wiping operation must be documented in the forensic analysis report whether or not the report relates to incident response operations. It is recommended that the disk image destination hard disk be wiped upon completion of an examination. In any case, it must be done (and documented) prior to any subsequent image acquisition.

Disk Imaging Tools

Forensic analysis operations require a number of software tools and dedicated hardware devices. The tools have different functions, such as backup and restore, file comparison, checking and comparison of encrypted checksums, system setup check, list of services and processes, and systems for backtracing the attacking sites and their Internet service providers (ISPs). We next examine the tools that preserve evidence by creating an image of it.

Creating Disk Images in a UNIX Environment

I personally believe that in addition to ensuring the integrity of the evidence base, one of the main objectives of the preservation phase is to allow for the image to be examined with the greatest possible variety of investigation tools. To this end, the format I prefer for the image disk is DD. This tool has been tested by the National Institute of Standards and Technologies as part of their Computer Forensics Tool Testing (CFTT) project, thus guaranteeing that it will enjoy some recognition in court. For further information on DD, check out the Web site at http://www.opengroup.org/onlinepubs/009695399/utilities/dd.html

DD copies a file (by default from the standard input to the standard output) with preset input and output block dimensions and may convert the file. It reads the input one block at a time according to the dimensions specified for input blocks (default value is 512 bytes). If the **bs** = *byte* option is present and no conversion other than **sync**, **noerror**, or **notrunc** is required, it writes the data (which might be less than required) into a separate output block. This output block has the same length as the input block unless the **sync** option is specified, in which case spaces are added to the end of the data.

Otherwise, the input, read one block at a time, is processed, and the resulting output is collected and written in blocks that have the specified dimension. The final output block may be shorter.

The numerical operations that follow (bytes and blocks) may be followed by a multiplier: k = 1024, b = 512, w = 2, c = 1 ("w" and "c" are GNU extensions; "w" should never be used: it means 2 in System V and 4 in 4.2BSD). Two or more of these expressions may be multiplied by placing an "x" between them.

It is possible to import the images created with DD using the most recent versions of the best known forensic investigation tools, both GNU and commercial, such as FTK, Encase, or Smart. The basic concept is that DD makes a bit-by-bit copy from one location to another using the syntax

dd if=<src> of=<dst>

where <src> and <dst> may be files, file system partitions, or an entire hard drive. DD is not a network program; you can use "netcat" to extend it to a network. Netcat is used to make TCP/UDP connections to a server and is also an excellent diagnostic tool. Netcat typically works in two modes, server and client:

server% nc -1 -p 30000 ==> (Awaiting input via port 30000 on <server>)

client% nc <server> 30000 ==> (Connection to <server> via port 30000)

Even though a computer forensics investigation is carried out on copies and not on the originals, the tools must still not alter the evidence. Even with copies, you have to make sure that their content is not altered during the investigation. To ensure this, you have to have a checking mechanism that lets you be sure that the evidence (and copies of it) has not been altered or damaged. The best technique is to create a hash of the image produced.

A *hashing algorithm*, starting from a data sequence of any length, such as the entire contents of a disk, generates another, much shorter data sequence called a *hash* whose contents strictly depend on the original data. The feature of the hashing algorithm that makes them so useful is that even minimal changes in the input data will produce a completely different hash. There are many hash-generating algorithms. The most important and widely used are SHA-1 (secure hash algorithm, RFC 3174) and MD5 (message-digest algorithm, RFC 1321). The critical issue with these algorithms is not so much a question of generating a hash that does not let you get back to the original data but that of avoiding overlapping results, that is, making the relationship between the input data and the hash as unambiguous as possible. At this moment, a group of Chinese cryptologists has presented a paper related to MD5 and SHA-1 cracking. However, we are pretty far from a practical implementation of the proof of concept expressed in the paper itself. The forensic community advises examiners to perform either SHA-1 and MD5 on the same image file.

There are many tools, both freeware and commercial, that can generate hashes of files. For example, a tool included in F.I.R.E. (Forensic and Incident Response Environment) generates images of disks and a hash of the file created. The tool in question is called DCFLDD (or EDD for "Enhanced DD"). This software was specially created for F.I.R.E. and is a tool that extends the potentials of DD (the basic tool) with a feature that allows the creation of an MD5 hash of the disk image. Depending on the options, it is possible to create the hash in a separate output file. It can also create hashes of subsections of disks (or in general of input data flows) specifying the dimension of the hash window, that is, specifying the data intervals at which hashes should be created. We get into a little more depth on F.I.R.E in the section on First Response CDs.

DCFLDD, hence, is a modified version of DD that calculates the hash value of the created image.

Example:

dcfldd —hashwindow=BYTE —hashlog =FILE if=Dev of=dev

"Hashwindow" indicates the number of bytes for which a hash should be created, and Hashlog generates the text file containing the calculated values.

Another handy freeware tool for generating hashes is Hashish. This tool has the sole objective of generating a hash on the basis of an input file or a simple data string. The potential of this tool derives from the number of its algorithms. It is a complete and easy-to-use tool with a graphical user interface (GUI). The fact that it can run both under Windows and Linux/UNIX is also very helpful.

DD, furthermore, may also be used in the event of memory dumping. This occurs when the machine is still on when delivered to the forensic examiner. In this case, the procedure is as follows:

dd if= /dev/kmem of=output
dd if= /dev/mem of=output

Regarding how to handle memory images, it should be mentioned that a number of examiners have encountered systems that freeze up following this procedure. As an alternative, Memdump, written by Wietse Venema, can be used. The MemDump utility is designed to dump any part of 4-GB linear memory address space under MS-DOS and Windows 9x DOS to a console or a text file. This utility provides transparent access to memory with or without installed memory managers. The software can be downloaded from http://www.porcupine.org/forensics/memdump-1.0.README.

To dump physical memory:

memdump | nc host port
memdump | openssl s_client -connect host:port

In the meantime, research is looking into alternative methods for acquiring the memory contents based on hardware cards (Carrier & Grand, 2004). These cards would dump the memory without performing any operations on it and without interacting with the operating system kernel of the compromised machine, and might solve a lot of problems. However, from the practical point of view, there are a lot of limitations, mainly in the deployment phase.

At any rate, the memory dump is generally more useful in the "pure" investigation phases, rather than for subsequent appearances in court. Whatever the case, do not forget that all imaging operations, including the description and specifications of the tools used, must be documented in the report.

Survey and Search Phase: Seeking Evidence under UNIX

This section covers issues and techniques in performing digital forensics, including searching, file recovery techniques, and other topics.

There are certain basic differences between a forensic exam done on a target platform such as UNIX and one done under Windows. The problems that are often encountered regard mainly the reconstruction of data that has been deleted or scattered around the file system. These problems are even more noticeable when you are dealing with tapes and/or various types of backup units, often containing only distributed portions of backup. In UNIX, furthermore, a term may not mean the same thing it would in a Windows-based operating system. The concept of *slack space*, for example, is slightly different in UNIX. Because UNIX files are stored compactly, except for the unavoidable wastage in the last block or fragment, it might be said that UNIX has no slack. However, certain ISV forensic analysis software producers also identify this type of space as "slack."

A forensic analysis under UNIX may have two main goals: a) reconstruction of events (e.g., an attack) and b) search for evidence of other violations (e.g., pedophilia or any other abuse of the technology). Depending on the reason for acting, investigators will carry out searches that may be focused on log files rather than fragments of evidence. Usually, following an intrusion, the decision is made whether to turn off and disconnect the compromised system. If the system is left on and online to collect more information on the intrusion and the intruder, it is good to keep in mind that the system could be or could have been used as a stepping stone for attacking another site. In such case, it is very important that the police be contacted immediately and that the recommended measures be taken to decrease the likelihood of this happening. In many cases, when the system cannot be turned off, another machine is "associated" on the same network segment and set up in promiscuous mode with Tcpdump to monitor network traffic in and out of the target in question.

At any rate, one of the first things that has to be decided on regards turning off the system prior to actually seizing it. The turning off procedure under UNIX has always been a source of debate among operators; there is no common agreement, at least not among the community of practitioners, on what operations have to be performed. Hence, it is recommended that the standard operating procedures (SOP) of one's agency or office be followed. Some, for example, believe that before you turn off a UNIX machine, you should change the root password, if the user is logged as root. The reasoning is that it would otherwise be extremely difficult to recover the root password later on. This procedure is a part of rather outdated SOP; it is currently common opinion that any operations carried out on the "original" machine may compromise the integrity of the evidence and hence should be avoided. In the jargon, a machine that has been altered is known as *tainted fruit*.

Other operators think that the best thing to do is turn off the machine simply by pulling the plug. This is a rather widespread practice even though it has certain contraindications, not least among them the loss of critical information or the risk of irreparable damage to the file system. In many cases, however, the swap file remains unaltered and may contain very important information.

An alternative method for "crystallizing the scene of the crime" often used by certain investigators is the following:

- Photograph the screen and document which programs are running.

- Right click on the menu.
- Select **Console**.
- If the prompt is not on the user root, get there by typing **su –**.
- If the root password is not available, pull the plug on the computer.
- If the root password is available, enter it. At the pound sign (#), type **sync;sync;halt;** and the system will shut down.
- Unplug the machine.

The sequence **sync;sync;halt;** is often discouraged because it might write something. However, numerous guidelines (Department of Energy, n.d.) indicate this as the most suitable option.

As always, whatever approach is taken, it is critical that all operations be documented in a report.

Search Tools and Data Left in the System by an Intruder

Intruders generally install customized tools to enable them to monitor the system and/or access the machine in the future.

The main tool categories are the following:

- network sniffer,
- Trojan horse,
- backdoor,
- vulnerability exploit,
- other (denial of service, use of processing resources), and
- communication systems with other compromised systems.

When a system is compromised, the intruder may install a network monitoring program (on UNIX systems) commonly known as sniffers or packet sniffers, with the goal of intercepting information regarding user accounts and passwords. The first step in determining whether there is a sniffer in the system is to check if there is a process that uses a network interface in promiscuous mode. It is not possible to detect promiscuous mode interfaces if the machine has been rebooted after the discovery of the intrusion or if it is operating in single user mode. It should be kept in mind that certain legitimate network monitors and protocol analyzers could set the network interface to promiscuous mode. Thus, the discovery of a promiscuous interface does not necessarily mean that an illegitimate sniffer is at work in the system.

Another aspect to consider is that the log files of a sniffer tend to grow quickly; hence, a utility such as *df* might come in handy for determining whether a part of the file system is bigger than expected. Remember that *df* is often replaced by a Trojan horse in cases where a sniffer has been installed; so make sure you have a clean copy of the utility before you use it. If a sniffer is found in the system, you should examine the output files to determine what other machines are at risk, that is, what other machines appear in the destination field of the intercepted packets. In cases where the same passwords are used, or the source and destination machines have a trusted relationship, the source machine is at risk nevertheless. In certain cases, the sniffers encrypt their logs; hence, it is important to check files that increase rapidly in size. Also keep in mind that there may be other machines at risk in addition to those that appear in the sniffer log. This is because the intruder may have obtained previous logs from the system or through other types of attack.

Another operation is the search for files that are open at a specific time. This may be useful (especially on a machine that has not yet been turned off) to check for backdoors, sniffers, eggdrop Internet relay chat (IRC) bots, port redirectors such as "bnc," and so forth. The program that may be used for this purpose is called LSOF (LiSt of Open Files). It is advisable to run it from a CD-ROM with statically precompiled binaries, so as not to fall into an attacker's booby trap and making a Trojanized version of this tool "available" to investigators.

There are also tools that are used to search for *rootkits*, that is, tools that are installed by the attacker after the target machine has been compromised. One of the most widely used tools is *chrootkit* (http://www.chrootkit.org), which has a list of rootkits of varying degrees of sophistication that it should be able to recognize.

For certain types of analysis, to identify the features of rootkits or other tools installed by the attacker, a debugging or even a reverse engineering operation may prove necessary. This type of activity may require some minimum legal assessment to ensure that no laws prohibiting reverse engineering are broken, such as DMCA.

More on Keyword Searching

Once an image has been obtained of the disk and prepared for examination, it is possible to view the contents of the restored disk or the mounted image. If you are working on an X window system, then you can use your favorite browser to carry out the disk searches.

In many cases, the line commands are much more useful and powerful for handling the analysis, and thus are used in the following example.

The commands have /mnt/analysis as their default mount point.

To display the list of all hidden files in the current directory plus the special directories "." and "..", you can use

ls −la | grep "^."

"ls −la" displays the contents of the directory. grep "^." reads the output of ls and keeps only lines beginning with the character "**.**"

Compile a File List

Among the various possibilities for handling file lists, you can use this command to search for files and compile the output in another file list:

find. -type f −print > /root/evidence/filelist.list

If you then use the command

grep −i jpg filelist.list

you will be able to select files with the extension *jpg* from the output.

Compile a File List by Type

What do you do if you are looking for JPEG files, but the file name has been changed or the extension is wrong? You can use the command **file** on each file and check its contents:

file *filename*

If there are a lot of files to check, you can use the **file** command on all the files on a disk; furthermore, we can also use the **find** command with the option –exec in this case:

find. -type f −exec file{}\; > /root/evidence/filetype.list

You can view the list with the **more** command and if you are looking at a particular image, you can use the **grep** command:

cat/root/evidence/filetype.list | grep image

This should subdivide the contents of our *filetype.list* using **cat** and producing the output via **grep**.

Viewing Files

For text and data files you should use **cat**, **more,** or **less** to view the contents:

cat *filename*
more *filename*
less *filename*

In any case, the best way to view the files is probably by using the **strings** command, which can be used to analyze the regularity of the text for any file (Excel, etc.), and it might be interesting as well to uncover strings of hidden text in binary files. The **less** option can be used to transmit the output:

string filename | less

Once you have finished exploring, you have to demount the disk (or image), making sure you are positioned at the right point in the tree:

umount/mnt/analysis

Search for Nonallocated and Slack Space

The restored disk (or the loop-mounted image) allows you to check all files and all directories. But what can you check regarding nonallocated or slack space? The image created, because it is a bit-by-bit copy, also includes these disk areas.

Let's consider the hypothesis that a letter threatening to infect a company network with a powerful virus has been received by management, and that as a result a floppy disk has been seized from an employee suspected of being the perpetrator. The analysis is focused on searching for the text of the letter in a deleted file in the nonallocated area of the disk.

Once the preliminary measures described previously have been done (image, mount, etc.), the next thing that has to be done from the forensic workstation is to get positioned in the working directory:

cd/root/evidence

Now, you can use the **grep** command to search for the image of any element of an expression or pattern. There are several options that make the **grep** output more useful:

grep –options <pattern> <search_range>

The first step is to create a list of search keys. You can open a text editor and build this list of terms for which you want to search (for example, "pay a price," "€50,000," and "unleash a virus"): words and phrases that are contained in the letter. Once you have completed the list, it is a good idea to save it in */root/evidence/searchlist.txt*, making sure that each term to be used in the search is on a different line and that there are no empty rows anywhere in the list:

pay a price

€ 50,000

unleash a virus

Now you can start the search with

grep –aibf searchlist.txt image.disk1 > hits.txt

Taking a look at the syntax of this command, we can see that the list *searchlist.txt* (option *–f listfile*) is used as search key in *image.disk1*, with the output of the search being compiled in *hits.txt* for later analysis. The option *–a* tells **grep** to rewrite the whole line where the target word was found and not the name of the file from which it comes, the option *–i* tells **grep** to ignore the case, and the option *–b* tells **grep** to provide the byte offset of each word found so that its hexidecimal position can be located with the command **xxd** or with any other graphical hexadecimal editor, such as GHex.

The contents of the file *hits.txt* may be viewed and explored with the commands **less** and **more** or with any text analyzer.

Although the **string** command is still the most effective, in this case we will use the simpler **cat** to analyze the entire contents of the standard file output:

cat hits.txt

75441: *you will have to* **pay a price** *(. . .)*

75500: *I am sick of your company's pirating and am not going to wait any longer (. . .)*

75767: *Do not try to stop me and do not notify the police: if you do, I will* **unleash a virus** *that will shut down the network and destroy customer information (. . .)*

To view the search results, you can use the following command:

xxd –s offset image.disk1| less

UNIX AND NETWORK FORENSICS

Logging under UNIX is not an easy task. This section addresses the most important log files in UNIX and how to manage and analyze them.

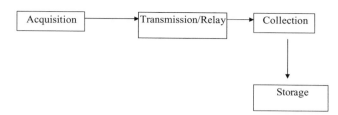

Figure 2: Log flow.

First and foremost, it must be clear that log file correlation is related to two distinct activities: intrusion detection and network forensics. It is more important than ever that these two disciplines work together to avoid points of failure.

Logs: Characteristics and Requisites

Every IT and network object, if programmed and configured accordingly, is capable of producing logs. Logs must to have certain fundamental requisites for network forensics purposes:

- *Integrity*: The log must be unaltered and not admit any tampering or modification by unauthorized operators.
- *Time Stamping*: The log must guarantee reasonable certainty as to the date and hour a certain event was registered. This is absolutely essential for making correlations after an incident.
- *Normalization and Data Reduction. Normalization* is the ability of the correlation tool to extract a datum from the source format of the log file that can be correlated with others of a different type without having to violate the integrity of the source datum. *Data reduction* (a.k.a. *filtering*) is the data extraction procedure for identifying a series of pertinent events and correlating them according to selective criteria.

Need for Log Integrity: Problems and Possible Solutions

A log must guarantee its integrity right from the moment of registration. Regardless of the point of acquisition (sniffer, agent, daemon, etc.), a log usually flows that in (Figure 2).

Acquisition occurs the moment a network sniffer, a system agent, or a daemon acquires the event and makes it available to a subsequent transmission process directed to a machine that is usually different from the one that is the source of the event. Once the log has reached the destination machine (called the *log machine*), it may be temporarily memorized in a preassigned slot or input to a database for later consultation. Once the policy-determined disk capacity has been reached, the data are stored in a predetermined location. The original logs are deleted to make room for new files from the source object. This method is known as *log rotation*.

Log file integrity can be violated in several ways. An attacker might take advantage of a unencrypted transmission channel between the acquisition and destination points to intercept and modify the transiting log. He might also spoof the IP sending the logs, making the log machine think it is receiving log entries and files that actually come from a different source. The basic configuration of *Syslog* makes this a real possibility. It states that *Syslog* transmissions are based on UDP, a connectionless protocol and thus one that is unreliable for network forensic purposes unless separate local area networks (LANs) are used for the transmission and collection of log files. Even here there might be some cases that are difficult to interpret. For this reason, the examiner must carefully select, especially during the search phase, which method to implement the logging system on the UNIX machine being investigated.

Another integrity problem regards the management of files once they have arrived on the log machine. If the log machine is compromised, there is a very high probability of integrity violation. This usually happens to individual files whose content is modified or even wiped. The integrity issue also regards how the *paternity* of log files is handled; in many juridical contexts, you have to be certain as to which machine generated the log files and who did the investigation.

There are several methods for resolving the problem. The first is specified in RFC 3195, which identifies a possible method for reliable transmission of *Syslog* messages, useful especially in the case of a high number of relays (intermediate record retransmission points between the source and the log repository). The main problem in this case is that RFC 3195 has not been incorporated into enough systems to be considered an established protocol.

Hence, practically speaking, most system administrators and security analysts view SCP (secure copy) as a good workaround. The most evident contraindication is the unsuitability of such a workaround for intrusion detection purposes, because there is no real-time assessment of the existence of an intrusion via log file reading. The problem remains of security in transmission between the acquisition and the collection points. In response to the problem, in UNIX-based architectures, the practice of using *Cryptcat* to establish a relatively robust tunnel between the various machines is gaining wider acceptance.

The procedure is as follows:

On log-generating host:

1. you must edit /etc/Syslog.conf in this mode:
   .   @localhost
2. then run command:
   # nc -l -u -p 514 | cryptcat 10.2.1.1 9999

On log-collecting host:

1. run Syslog with remote reception (-r) flag (for Linux)
2. run command:
   # cryptcat -l -p 9999 | nc -u localhost 514

This configuration will establish an encrypted connection among the various transmission nodes. An alternative would be to use a *Syslog* replacement such as *Syslog – ng*, which performs relay operations automatically and with greater security potentials.

From the practical standpoint, these methods offer a good compromise between operational needs and the theory that a hash must be generated for each log entry (something that is impossible in a distributed environment). The objective still remains of achieving transaction atomicity (transactions are done or undone completely) and log file reliability. The latter concept means being sure that the log file does not get altered once it has been closed, for example, via interception during the log rotation phase. The most important aspect of this phase is the *final-record message*, indicating the last record written in the log, which is then closed and hashed. This sequence of processes may turn out to be critical when, after correlation, a whole and trustworthy log has to be provided to the judicial authorities.

Log Time Stamp Management: Problems and Possible Solutions

Another problem is managing log-file time stamping. Each report has to be 100% reliable, not only in terms of its integrity in the strict sense (IP, ports, payloads, etc.), but also in terms of the date and time of the event reported. Time stamping is essential for two reasons: atomicity of the report and correlation. The most common problems here are the lack of synchronization and the lack of uniformity of the time zones.

The lack of synchronization occurs when the acquisition points (network sensors and *Syslog* devices) are not synchronized with an atomic clock but only within small groups. Reliance is usually placed on NTP in these cases, but this may open up a series of noted vulnerabilities, especially in distributed architectures connected to the public network. Furthermore, the use of NTP does not guarantee uniformity unless a series of measures recommended by certain RFCs is adopted for certain types of logs. Some technology manufacturers have come out with appliances equipped with highly reliable processors that do time stamping for every entry, synchronizing everything with atomic clocks distributed around the world. This sort of solution, albeit offering a certain degree of reliability, increases design costs and obviously makes management more complex. In a distributed architecture, a time stamping scheme administered by an appliance is set up as shown in Figure 3.

The appliance interacts with a PKI that authenticates the transaction nodes to prevent the problem of report repudiation.

Although this type of architecture may be implemented in an environment with a healthy budget, there are applications for less extensive architectures that may be helpful in guaranteeing a minimum of compliance with best practices.

Because one of the most commonly used log format is *Libpcap*-compatible (used by TcpDump, Ethereal) via TCP connections (hence three-way), it is possible to attribute a further level of time stamping, as per RFCs 1072 and 2018, by enabling the SackOK option (selective acknowledgment OK). This option can return even a 32-bit time stamp value in the first 4 bytes of each packet, so that reports among transaction nodes with the SackOK option enabled are synchronized and can be correlated. This

A log architecture with the use of a time stamping appliance

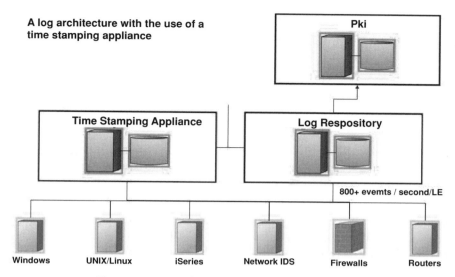

Figure 3: Log architecture utilizing time stamping.

approach may be effective provided that the entire system and network is set up for it.

Another factor that is not taken into consideration are time zones. In distributed architectures on the international scale, some information security managers believe it is wise to maintain the time zone of the physical location of the system or network object. This choice has the disadvantage of making correlation more complicated and less effective because of time zone fragmentation. We are currently witnessing an increase of times zones that are simply based on GMT, which has the advantage of simplifying management even though it still requires that the choice be incorporated into a policy.

Normalization and Data Reduction Problems and Possible Solutions

Normalization is identified in certain cases with the term *event unification*. There is a physiological need for normalization in distributed architectures. Numerous commercial systems prefer the use of extensible markup language (XML) for normalization operations. This language provides numerous opportunities for event unification and management of digital signatures and hashing. There are two basic types of logs: system logs and network logs. If the reports all had a single format, there would be no need for normalization. In heterogeneous architectures, it is obvious that that is not the case. Let us imagine, for example, an architecture in which we have to correlate events recorded by a Web site, by a network sniffer, and by a proprietary application. The Web site will record the events

in W3C format, the network sniffer in Libpcap format, and the proprietary application might record the events in a nonstandard format. It is clear that unification is necessary here. The solution in this case consists of finding points in common among the various formats involved in the transaction and creating a level of abstraction according to Figure 4.

It follows in this case that an attacker can once again seek to violate log integrity by zeroing in on the links between the various acquisition points and the point of normalization. Regarding the correlation, the point of normalization (normally an engine) and the point of correlation (an activity that may be carried out by the same module, for example, in an IDS) may be the same machine. It is clear that this becomes a potential point of failure from the perspective of network forensics and thus must be managed both to guarantee integrity and to limit possible losses of data during the process of normalization. For this purpose, the state of the art is to use MD5 and SHA-1 to ensure integrity and to perform an in-depth verification of the event unification engine to respond to the data reduction issue, keeping the "source" logs in the normalized format. In Figure 5, where each source log is memorized on ad hoc supports, another layer is added.

To manage the secure repository section and still use a series of "source log files" that guarantee a certain reliability, the machines in the second line of Figure 5 have to be *trusted*, that is, hardened, and have cryptosystems that can handle authentication, hashing, and reliable transmission.

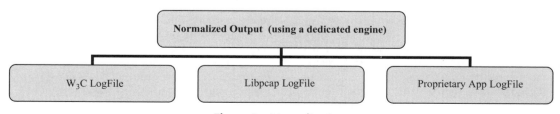

Figure 4: Normalization.

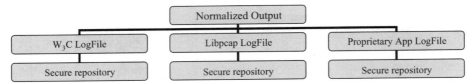

Figure 5: Multilayered log architecture.

Correlation and Filtering: Needs and Possible Solutions

In performing log correlation and filtering, the security architect and the manager have to deal with these problems. Here, the perspective on the problem shifts to the architecture.

Before we discuss this, it would be useful to made a clear statement of the definition of "correlation": "A causal, complementary, parallel, or reciprocal relationship, especially a structural, functional, or qualitative correspondence between two comparable entities" (dictionary.com, n.d.). I use "correlation" here to mean the activity carried out by one or more engines to reconstruct a given complex event that may be symptomatic of a past or current violation.

By "filtering," I mean an activity that may be carried out by the same engines to extract certain kinds of data and arrange them, for example, by protocol type, time, IP, MAC address, and so on.

Interpretation of One or More Log Files

In most cases, the security administrator reads the result of a correlation done by a certain tool, but he or she only sees the tip of the iceberg. If you look at the figures in this chapter, the set of processes upstream of the GUI display is much more complex. Whatever the case may be, the literature indicates two basic methods for analyzing logs called *approaches*.

Top-Down Approach

This is the approach most frequently used in network forensics when the examiner is working with an automated log and event correlation tool. Whereas in intrusion detection, a top-down approach means starting from an attack to trace back to the point of origin, in network forensics, it means starting from a GUI display of the event to get back to the source log, with the dual purpose of

- validating the correlation process used by the engine of the automatic log and event correlation tool that is displayed to the security administrator and
- seeking out the source logs that will then be used as evidence in court or for subsequent analysis.

Bottom-Up Approach

The tool applies this approach starting from the source log. It is a method used by the IDS to identify an ongoing attack through a real-time analysis of events. In a distributed security environment, the IDS engine may reside in the same machine hosting the normalization engine. In this case, the IDS engine will then use the network forensic tool to display the problem on the GUI. You start from an automatic low-level analysis of the events generated by the

points of acquisition to arrive at the "presentation" level of the investigative process. Such an approach, furthermore, is followed when log analysis (and the subsequent correlation) is performed manually, that is, without the aid of automated tools. Here, a category of tools known as *log parsers* comes to your aid. The purpose of these tools is to analyze source logs for a bottom-up correlation. A parser is usually written in a script language like Perl or Python. There are, however, parsers written in Java to provide a cross-platform approach to network forensics examiners, perhaps on a bootable CD-ROM

Requisites of Log File Acquisition Tools

Regardless of which vendor is chosen to represent the standard, the literature has identified a number of requisites that a logging infrastructure must have to achieve forensically compliant correlations:

- Tcpdump support, both in import and in export;
- use of MD5 or other state-of-the-art hashing algorithms;
- data reduction capabilities as described in previous sections;
- data recovery, the ability to extract from the intercepted traffic not only the connections, but also the payloads for the purpose of interpreting the formats of files exchanged during the transaction;
- ability to recognize covert channels (not absolutely essential but still highly recommended);
- "read only during collection and examination," an indispensable feature for this type of tool;
- "complete collection," one of the most important requisites because it is important that all packets are captured or else that all losses are minimized and documented; and
- intrinsic security, with special emphasis on connections between points of acquisition, collection repositories, administrative users, and so forth.

Log File Analysis

At this point, now that we have gone over the fundamental issues of log correlation associated with the search, analysis, and, quite often, reconstruction phases, we are now ready to understand where we have to look for signs of intrusion. Although the search for fragments or key words may provide detailed information about traces left by the intruder (or by the criminal who used the machine for illicit purposes beyond simple hacking), the analysis of the log files may help provide a clearer idea of how a machine has been compromised, what happened during the attack, and which remote hosts participated in it.

While analyzing any log file from a compromised machine, remember that the intruder may have modified any or all of the data.

On UNIX systems, you should check the file /etc/Syslog.conf to see where Syslog memorizes messages.

NT systems generally memorize events in one of the three NT events logs, each of which may be viewed using event viewer. Other NT applications may memorize their log files in other locations.

Here is a list of some of the more common UNIX log files, their function, and the elements that need to be examined in each of them. These files may or may not be present, depending on how the system is set up:

/var/log/messages and **/var/adm/messages**: These contain a great variety of information; check anything out of the ordinary and all events around the time of the intrusion (suspicious IPs that have been removed, logging blocks, and so forth).

.bash_history and **.sh_history**: When an intruder generates a buffer overflow, he or she generally alters **sh** or **bash**. When a new shell is loaded, a history is created in the folder where the server was attacked; there is a good chance that you will be able to retrace the name of the remote host.

logs/*_log (Web site access log): This is important in the event of defacement of a Web site or the collection of sensitive data from it. You may be able to retrace in this log file the IP address of the attacker or files uploaded by him or her into the directories htdocs, root, or / to monitor the success of the defacement. You can also place the Web site logs in a special directory so that the intruder cannot easily find them (and thus modify them).

Coredumps: Usually the daemons initiated by the script *SysV Init* do not carry out this function by default for reasons of security; however, administrators often start the services manually and this means that during an exploit the dumping is done into the current directory. If the compromised server has executed the command *getpeername*, it is possible that the intruder's IP address is memorized in a variable of the process core dump.

Proxy server: The presence of a server in front of all the hosts usually simplifies auditing. Transparent proxies have a log of all the connections made through them; in many cases, the attacker can get around this by using unconventional ports and create a shell, but not the first time that he or she launches the exploit.

Router log: By default the routers do not keep records of every connection, but if they have some network access control, it is possible to retrace the entrance of the intruder.

xferlog: Useful when the compromised system has a functioning FTP server; this file contains the logs of all FTP transfers. Check to see what tools were uploaded into the system and what information was downloaded from the system by the intruder.

utmp: Contains information in binary format on each currently logged user. Use the command "who" to access it.

wtmp: A binary file that contains information on logins, logouts, and reboots. You will need a tool to access the file (for example, last, whose output contains a table in which user names are associated with login times and host names where the connection originated). Checking this file for suspicious connections (for example, from unauthorized hosts) may be useful in determining other hosts that may have been involved and finding out which system accounts may have been compromised.

Secure: Each time a connection is established to a server that uses a TCP wrapper running outside inetd, a log message is added to this file. You should check anomalies, such as services accessed but not habitually used, or connections from unknown hosts.

Experimentation: Using GPL Tools for Investigation and Correlation

Thus far I have introduced logs, correlation techniques, and the associated security issues. Regarding the tools used for this type of analysis and investigation, there are GPL or open source projects that provide the necessary tools for a bottom-up investigation, which is a less costly and less complicated alternative to the top-down approach based on automated correlation and GUI display techniques. In this section, I introduce some projects and tools that may be used for this purpose.

It bears emphasizing that the internal tool validation process remains one of the most pressing problems in digital forensics.

Forensic Investigation Tools Under UNIX

This section deals with forensic tools in two different regards. The first one is forensic tools versus UNIX file systems and the second is UNIX-based forensic tools. Only a brief mention is made of commercial tools, whereas an explanation is given as to how Sleuthkit and other freeware tools work.

As was stated at the beginning, UNIX is also used as forensic analysis platform, particularly with open source tools. In this section, I describe some that are very often used for carrying out examinations and investigations, with a major emphasis on tools that are available under GNU/GPL licenses.

The tools mentioned in Table 1 are used mainly in the search and analysis phases. Most of them are based on or emulate TCT: The Coroner Toolkit. Written by Dan Farmer and Wietse Venema, TCT (downloadable from http://www.fish.com) is a tool that is still widely used even though the ones listed in Table 1 (especially Sleuthkit) are more evolved forms.

A special mention should be made of Glimpse. Glimpse (GLobal IMPlicit SEarch) is a UNIX tool that indexes and performs very fast searches of large file systems. It supports many of the options in agrep, a modified version of grep, and can perform searches for an arbitrary number of errors in the input pattern. It supports Boolean queries.

To use Glimpse, the contents of the directories to be examined have to be indexed with glimpseindex.

An example of its use is this:

```
# glimpseindex - o ~
```

This command generates files that will be used by Glimpse to search the home directory.

Table 1 Disk Investigation and Analysis Tools

Tool	Web Site	Features
Sleuthkit, authored by Brian Carrier	http://www.sleuthkit.org/index.php	Open source initiative that offers an alternative to normal Windows-based forensic programs. The tool is an HTML browser that displays the image of compromised disks. It supports both UNIX and Windows file systems to detect deleted files, creates timelines of disc activities, and does word searches. It is a unintrusive, remote analysis tool. No time stamp of the files is modified during the analysis. All files generated by the tool are associated with an md5 value that may be checked during the analysis. I-node searches may be carried out, and the resulting files displayed.
Test Disk	http://www.cgsecurity.org/index.html?testdisk.html	Allows investigators to analyze compromised disks and undelete the partitions. The following file systems are supported: FAT12, FAT16, FAT32; Linux; Linux SWAP (versions 1 and 2); NTFS (Windows NT); BeFS (BeOS); UFS (BSD); Netware; and ReiserFS.
Wipe	http://wipe.sourceforge.net/	Wipe completely eliminates all data on any writable support. It sets each bit on the disk to 0, which is indispensable for formatting a disk that will be used in forensic analysis.
Mac-Robber	http://www.atstake.com/research/tools/forensic/	Mac-Robber is a forensic analysis tool that can recover the date of access, the last modification, and changes (MAC) of date of any file. This information may be analyzed with the tool, Task, in order to compile a timeline of file activities in a system.

.glimpse_exclude contains the list of all files to be ignored by Glimpse during the search.

.glimpse_filter is used to create search filters activated with the option – z.

.glimpse_filenames contains the list of all files in the index.

.glimpse_index is an index file that associates each letter with a list of block numbers.

.glimpse_messages contains the output which is viewed with – w.

.glimpse_partitions contains a partition of the index generated.

.glimpse_statistics statistics regarding the index generated.

.glimpse_turbo is only to be used with options -b and -o to accelerate searches.

Glimpse also includes a new compression program called "cast," which allows you to do searches in compressed files.

Here is a simple example of the use of Glimpse:

```
# glimpse -i -1 'pattern'
```

The command searches the index for all instances of the word "pattern," allowing a maximum of one error (-1) and ignoring upper case letters (-i).

```
# glimpse – F '\.c$' pattern
```

searches for all instances of "pattern" in all files that end in ".c."

It is often a good idea to use Glimpse because in many cases you have to do live system analyses, and this program, in spite of the fact that it was not specifically developed with digital forensics in mind, may be the right tool for the job. Some forensic investigators believe that the tool is valuable for dealing with large dimension restored images. As always, you are wise to carefully weigh the pros and cons of this method before beginning your analyses.

Log Analysis Tools

There are also tools that correlate the findings generated by the tools in Table 1 and the log analysis activities.

Tcpdump

Log correlation is based on tried and true file formats and tools. The most commonly used file format is lbpcap compatible, that is, the one used by Tcpdump. Tcpdump can be downloaded from http://www.tcpdump.org and is a network-level data acquisition tool developed under UNIX and then transported onto almost all other operating systems. Tcpdump is basically operated from the command line and is able to delegate the acquired logs onto external machines, filtering them on the basis of protocol and payload. Tcpdump is strongly indicated when you want to "monitor" a machine that appears to have been hacked to verify whether the attacker is still "inside," and if so, how. Furthermore, an lbpcap compatible module is also used by Snort. Among the pluses of Tcpdump are its light weight (it does not use much of the machine's resources), the widespread use of its file format, and its extreme flexibility. On the minus side, the command line control has a very large number of switches, which makes it very hard to handle for the average user.

Ethereal

A good compromise between the power of Tcpdump and user friendliness is Ethereal (http://www.ethereal.com). According to its documentation, Ethereal is still technically beta software, but it has a comprehensive feature set and is suitable for production use. Like Tcpdump, data can be captured "off the wire" from a live network connection or read from a capture file. Unlike Tcpdump, Ethereal can read capture files from a very broad range of formats and tools. Captured network data can be browsed via a GUI, or via the TTY (Teletype) mode "tethereal" program. Capture files can be programmatically edited or converted via command-line switches to the "editcap" program. Many protocols (512) can currently be dissected.

Ethereal is free, too, but in many cases it proves to be unstable, which makes it better suited for offline traffic analysis than for real-time work. Nevertheless, its exceptional graphic layout and enormous filtering potential (which can be used in simplified form via the menus) make it a well-loved tool by some log examiners.

FLAG

FLAG may be the most complete tool among those mentioned in this section. According to the project documentation, FLAG was designed to simplify the process of log file analysis and forensic investigations. Often when investigating a large case, a great deal of data needs to be analyzed and correlated. FLAG uses a database as a back end to assist in managing the large volumes of data. This allows FLAG to remain responsive and expedite data manipulation operations.

Because FLAG is Web based, it is able to be deployed on a central server and shared with a number of users at the same time. Data are loaded into cases, which keeps information separated. FLAG also has a system for reporting the findings of the analysis by extensively using bookmarks.

FLAG started off as a project in the Australian Department of Defense. It is now hosted on Sourceforge. PyFlag is the Python implementation of FLAG: a complete rewrite of FLAG in the much more robust Python programming language. Many improvements have been made.

Table 2 describes the characteristics of FLAG.

Using First Response CD-ROMs for Forensic Investigations

One of the most wide-reaching recent trends is to integrate the tools that I have been talking about here into a single platform to ensure a faster, validated response to the incident. This has all naturally led to the creation of a toolkit that resides on a first response CD-ROM.

The great advantage of this choice lies in always having at hand a prevalidated toolkit with all the necessary statically compiled and therefore fundamentally trusted instruments.

One example of such an approach has been provided by IRItaly (Incident Response Italy), which is a project developed at the Crema Teaching and Research Center of the Information Technology Department of the Università Statale di Milano. The project, which includes more than 15 instructors and students (BSC and MSC), is divided into two parts. The first relates to documentation and provides broad-ranging and detailed instructions. The second is a bootable CD-ROM. The issues addressed regard information attacks and especially defensive systems and computer and network forensics for incident handling and data recovery methods.

Best practices are presented for response procedures to information incidents, including analyzing the victim machines to retrace the hacking episodes and understand how the attack was waged, with the final aim of providing a valid response to the intrusion. This response should be understood as a more effective and informed hardening of the system to reduce the possibility of future attacks. It does not mean the generation of a counterattack.

All the operations described so far are carried out with special attention to the method of identification, storage, and possible use of evidence in a disciplinary hearing or in court. The unifying theme of the CD-ROM is the set of actions to undertake in response to an intrusion. It contains a number of sections offering a detailed analysis of each step:

- the intrusion response preparation phase;
- the analysis of available information on the intrusion;
- the collection and storage of associated information (evidence);
- the elimination (deletion) of tools used for gaining and maintaining illicit access to the machine (rootkits); and
- the restoration of the systems to normal operating conditions.

Detailed information is provided on the following:

- management of different file systems;
- procedures for data backup;
- operations for creating images of hard and removable discs;
- management of secure electronic communication;
- cryptographic algorithms and their implementation; and
- tools for the acquisition, analysis, and safeguarding of log files.

The CD also proposes a number of standardized forms to improve organization and facilitate interactions between organizations that analyze the incident and the different targets involved in the attack. Specifically, an incident report form and a chain of custody form are provided. The latter is a valuable document for keeping track of all information regarding the evidence.

The CD-ROM may be used to do an initial examination of the configuration of the compromised computer.

The tools included offer the ability to carry out analyses of the discs, generate an image of them, and examine logs to carry out a preliminary analysis of the incident. The IRItaly CD-ROM (http://www.iritaly.org) is bootable and contains a series of disc and log analysis tools. All the programs are on the CD in the form of static binaries and are checked before the preparation of the magnetic

Table 2 Characteristics of FLAG

Action	Features
Disk forensics	Supports NTFS, Ext2, FFS, and FAT. Supports many different image file formats, including sgzip (compressed image format), Encase's Expert Witness format, and the traditional DD files. Advanced time lining, which allows complex searching. NSRL hash support to quickly identify files. Windows Registry support, includes both the Windows 98 variant and the Windows NT variant. Unstructure Forensics capability allows recovery of files from corrupted or otherwise unmountable images by using file magic.
Network forensics	Stores Tcpdump traffic within an SQL database. Performs complete TCP stream reconstruction. Has a "knowledge base" that makes deductions about network communications. Can construct an automatic network diagram based on Tcpdump or real time.
Log analysis	Allows arbitrary log file formats to be easily uploaded to database. GUI-driven complex database searches using an advanced table GUI element.

support. After booting, the tool launches a terminal interface that the examiner can use to start certain applications such as Tcpdump, Ethereal, Snort, Swatch, and so on.

The CD, currently based on the extremely powerful F.I.R.E., can thus be used for a preliminary analysis of the logs present on the machine or for an analysis of the machine using the Sleuthkit tool, which is more specific to the analysis of the hard disc. The correlation process, in this case, involves the comparison of logs present on the machine with others on other machines. In this case, the IRItaly CD essentially works in very small environments or even in one-to-one contexts, as illustrated in Figure 6.

Here, T1, T2, and T3 represent various targets that may be booted with the IRItaly CD and connected to the main forensic workstation with the aid of Netcat or Cryptcat. As stated, the main limitation of the use of the completely functional CD is that it cannot be used in a distributed architecture because of obvious management difficulties. However, the IRItaly workgroup is carrying out a series of tests of a new version of the CD that should resolve some of these problems with the aid of other tools.

The IRItaly project has already begun work on two fundamental tasks for the resolution of several of the issues illustrated in this chapter. The first regards the release of a new version of the CD-ROM, which will contain a full implementation of Python FLAG.

The ultimate objective is to integrate PyFlag into IRItaly's CD-ROM to provide first responders with a tool that can guarantee a minimum of correlation that is significantly broader than that offered by the current version.

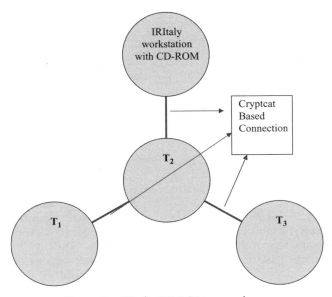

Figure 6: IRItaly CD-ROM normal use.

Initial Attack Analysis

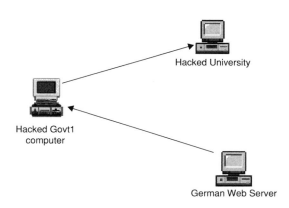

- IDS logs revealed hack originated from a German ISP's Web server.

- Began coordination directly with German authorities.

- IDS logs showed transfer of root kit from a hacked university computer.

- Began coordination directly with university officials.

Hacked University

Hacked Govt1 computer

German Web Server

Figure 7: Attack reconstruction.

Applying UNIX Forensics in a Coordinated Incident Response Procedure: A Case History

Background

In mid-2002, two groups of malicious hackers were identified by the Italian Financial Police as being responsible for a series of attacks on more than a thousand targets throughout the world. The backtracing procedure was seriously complicated by the fact that the groups used numerous stepping stones and camouflage techniques, such as Ipv6 tunneling. In this section, we take a general look at the attack methods and illustrate the techniques and steps used to backtrace them. For reasons of privacy, I do not name the targets but use letters instead:

A: the German target used as an initial stepping stone to attack the American governmental sites indicated;

B: the main American governmental target attacked by the group;

C: another American governmental target attacked by the group, which served as the starting point for the investigation; and

SS1: a university machine used as a repository to hide rootkits and other tools used in the post-intrusion phase.

A Coordinated Attack

In September 2001, the owner of C realized that one of his machines (an IRIX) had been attacked. The exploit had

been launched from a German machine, which had previously been compromised by an exploit from its resident Web server. The system administrators for C later reported that commands had been sent from the German machine to download certain postintrusion tools (including rootkits) from a third machine, SS1, located at an American university. Figure 7 shows the general scheme.

Reconstructing what happened to C was possible thanks to the presence of an IDS that monitored the target. Although this did not permit a response in real time, it did make it possible to recover a series of logs that illustrated what had happened. The logs were usable because they were not on the attacked machine. In the meantime, a postmortem exam was carried out on the German machine, A, that had been used as a stepping stone. The method used to compromise the German machine was generally conventional but had a number of personalized touches added by the attackers.

Requirement 1: Reconstruct the Events

One of the fist steps in this sort of investigation is to check how much time passed between the last update of the machine and the attack. This may help identify the exploit used to achieve the intrusion. In this case, it was a Linux machine that was not running the latest release. At the time of the intrusion, the bug exploited to compromise the box was the then-known wuftpd site command exploit.

When an attacker penetrates a machine, he or she installs a rootkit to keep it compromised. One of the group's characteristics was the use of completely self-made rootkits along with materials known to the security community.

The choice depended on the type of target (in the case we are examining, there were nearly a thousand boxes compromised worldwide).

The t0rn rootkit was chosen for the German machine and installed in /usr/info/.t0rn. Evidently, the reasoning used in this case was that the system was generally poorly administrated and therefore it was not worthwhile to keep it compromised with something exotic because it was unlikely that the administrator would realize what was happening. In any case, it may be helpful to consult /usr/src/ to try to determine what is happening. In the specific case, a lot of information was found in /usr/src/.r00t.

The t0rn rootkit, like most tools of its ilk, is configured to hide certain network connections. This is the usual syntax found during a postmortem (the IP addresses are fictitious):

65.93.*.*
195.242.20.*

where * is used to hide all the address of the block. The first instance occurs usually to hide classes of dynamic IPs to which the attacker has access (e.g., ADSL and dial-up based on DHCP). In the second instance, an entire class is indicated that includes one or more machines compromised for the long term by the attacker.

Once the groundwork is laid, the hacking tools are installed. The choice of tools is completely up to the attacker. In our case, the hack tools installed were

7350wu [exploit to hack into the wuftpd (used on this system, too)],

massroot (exploit for a bug in the telnetd of IRIX systems),

statdx (exploit for the rpc.statd of Red Hat),

mirkforce (attack tool to disrupt IRC communication),

papasmurf (smurf attack tool is a denial of service tool), and

seclpd (exploit for lpd in Red Hat 7.1).

Please note that we are talking about an attack that occurred in 2001. One interesting finding was several text files that made it clear that A was the machine used to attack the governmental sites. The attacked networks, in fact, were in the 136.*.*.* and 137.*.*.* nets. In these cases, it might be useful to seek subdivisions by operating system in these files. In this case FreeBSD, IRIX, Linux, and SunOS were found along with a ".txt" file that contained progress info of the scanning.

This proves how important it is to correlate what is found on one machine with what is found on the one that appears to be directly connected to it. The correlation, especially if done on more than two machines, can map out the events with a certain margin of certainty and point back to a single source.

Another item usually installed is psyBNC IRC Bounce BOT. In this case, it was used as a deflector to participate in IRC communication without revealing the hacker's IP number and thus avoiding DOS attacks to the hacker's machine. Usually the attacker installs BOT with the sup Nick, which, in many cases, turns out to be very important for final backtracing.

This list presents the main steps taken by the attacker after the intrusion:

1. System is penetrated through an exploit.
2. Rootkit is installed.
3. ncftpd is installed.
4. Port scanner is installed.
5. A sniffer is installed.
6. A psyBNC BOT is compiled and installed.
7. Rootkit is fine tuned.
8. A file with IP numbers is created.
9. The "real use activity" is begun.

The compilation of the items downloaded by the third machine (SS1 in this case) is generally either carried out on the attacker's machine or directly on the compromised machine. Both choices have their pros and cons. For example, compiling on the attacker's machine might speed things up but risk instability because of potential differences in platforms. On the other hand, one cannot be sure that there is a compiler on the compromised machine, even though it is quite probable for relatively simple cases.

Further Correlations

In the case in question here, there was another positive factor for the investigation: cross checking of the SS1 machine. When a machine is used as a repository for tools that will be downloaded onto target machines, it may happen, with a bit of luck, that additional cross references can be found to correlate all the necessary information. Given that most of such "containers" are located on university networks, we find ourselves confronted with the following situation:

- University officials provide system logs and image of the compromised computer.
- The compromising of the U.S. university machine is linked to the compromised third-party computer.
- The university computer was used as a "tool box." All links between the .edu computer and the real target require a physical level search that, very often, reveals a dial-up connection.
- A proper HD analysis can uncover the intruder's rootkit.

CONDUCTING INTERNATIONAL FORENSIC OPERATIONS IN INCIDENT RESPONSE: SOME OBSERVATIONS

Another successful aspect of the investigation was that all the investigators spoke the same technical language. Terminology, log type, image format, tools, and PGP keys were agreed before beginning the investigation, proving the fundamental importance of setting things up well before getting started.

We have only touched the tip of the iceberg in this section and discussed only those parts of the investigation free of nondisclosure restrictions. The investigation was anything but simple. The operation, known as "Rootkit," took more than one year and involved five European and

The German Investigation

- German source computer belonged to a large corporation – it had also been hacked.
- The German corporation identified the compromise of their server. Hired a forensic firm in Germany to do forensic analysis.
- The forensic analysis matched the fingerprint of the govt. machine and the university machine. Source was in Italy.

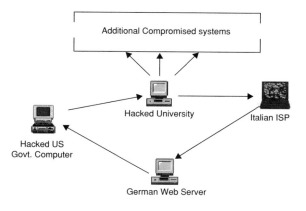

Figure 8: Basic correlation.

American investigative agencies (military and civilian). Fourteen people were charged (including four minors). Most of them worked as security consultants or managers in large multinational companies. More than 40 computers were seized, and almost one TB of data and thousands of CD-ROMs and DVDs were seized. Many credit card files were recovered. If it had not been for the close international collaboration, it may not have been possible to track down the perpetrators of more than 1000 worldwide attacks, who were so active and so skillful as to be able to write their own rootkits and log wipers, which were used on the most "important" machines, and so crafty as to use Ipv6 tunneling. Unfortunately (or fortunately), it is a small world for everybody. Some of the people charged as a result of this investigation had also punched holes in a Mexican honeynet, going so far as to get into the honeynet project's famous "scan of the month."

GLOSSARY

Audit Trail An audit trail may be on paper or on disk. In computer security systems, a chronological record of when users log in, how long they are engaged in various activities, what they were doing, and whether any actual or attempted security violations occurred.

Computer Forensics Computer forensics is the use of specialized techniques for recovery, authentication, and analysis of electronic data when a case involves issues relating to reconstruction of computer usage, examination of residual data, authentication of data by technical analysis, or explanation of technical features of data and computer usage. Computer forensics requires specialized expertise that goes beyond normal data collection and preservation techniques available to end users or system support personnel.

Deduplication Deduplication ("deduping") is the process of comparing electronic records based on their characteristics and removing duplicate records from the data set.

Deleted Data Deleted data are data that, in the past, existed on the computer as live data and which have been deleted by the computer system or end user activity. Deleted data remain on storage media in whole or in part until they are overwritten by ongoing usage or "wiped" with a software program specifically designed to remove deleted data. Even after the data itself have been wiped, directory entries, pointers, or other metadata relating to the deleted data may remain on the computer.

Deleted File A file with disk space that has been designated as available for reuse. The deleted file remains intact until it has been overwritten with a new file.

Deletion Deletion is the process whereby data are removed from active files and other data storage structures on computers and rendered inaccessible except using special data recovery tools designed to recover deleted data. Deletion occurs in several levels on modern computer systems:

1) File level deletion—deletion on the file level renders the file inaccessible to the operating system and normal application programs and marks the space occupied by the file's directory entry and contents as free space, available to reuse for data storage.

2) Record level deletion—deletion on the record level occurs when a data structure, such as a database table, contains multiple records; deletion at this level renders the record inaccessible to the database management system (DBMS) and usually marks the space occupied by the record as available for reuse by the DBMS, although in some cases the space is never reused until the database is compacted. Record level deletion is also characteristic of many e-mail systems.

3) Byte level deletion—deletion at the byte level occurs when text or other information is deleted from the file content (such as the deletion of text from a word processing file); such deletion may render the deleted data inaccessible to the application intended to be used in processing the file, but may not actually remove the data from the file's content until a process such as compaction or rewriting of the file causes the deleted data to be overwritten.

Hashing Algorithm   Starting from a data sequence of any length, such as the entire contents of a disk, it generates another, much shorter data sequence called a *hash* whose contents strictly depend on the original data.

Image   In data recovery parlance, to image a hard drive is to make an identical copy of the hard drive, including empty sectors. Akin to cloning the data. Also known as creating a "mirror image" or "mirroring" the drive.

Keyword Search   A search for documents containing one or more words that are specified by a user.

RAM (Random Access Memory)   The working memory of the computer into which application programs can be loaded and executed.

Residual Data   Residual data (sometimes referred to as "ambient data") refers to data that are not active on a computer system. Residual data includes a) data found on media free space, b) data found in file slack space, and c) data within files that has functionally been deleted in that it is not visible using the application with which the file was created, without use of undelete or special data recovery techniques.

CROSS REFERENCES

See *Digital Evidence; Forensic Analysis of Windows Systems; Operating System Security.*

REFERENCES

[Authore] (2004, October). *The emergence of electronic forensics and its impact on IT.* Paper presented at [conference. Location, date].

Carrier, B. (n.d.). *Performing an autopsy examination on FFS and EXT2FS partition images: An introduction to the SleuthKit, TCTUTILs and the autopsy forensic browser.* Retrieved [date] from [URL].

Carrier & Grand. (2004). A hardware-based memory acquisition procedure for digital investigations. *Digital Investigation Journal.*

Department of Energy Computer Forensic Laboratory. (n.d.). *First responder's manual.* Retrieved from http://www.linuxsecurity.com/resource_files/documentation/firstres.pdf

Filesystem hierarchy standard, version 2.3. (2003, October 13). Retrieved [data] from http://www.pathname.com/fhs/

FURTHER READING

Forte, D. Analyzing the Difficulties in Backtracing Onion Router Traffic. <http://www.ijde.org/archives/02_fall_art3.html>. The International Journal of Digital Evidence, Utica College, United States—www.idje.org <http://www.idje.org> JDE 2002 1:3.

Forte, D. The art of Log Correlation, Tool and Techniques for log analysis. Proceedings of The ISSA. Conference 2004, Johannesburg, South Africa.

Forte, D., & Al. Forensic Computer Crime Investigation (Forensic Science) by Thomas Alfred Johnson, Thomas A. Johnson (ed.), CRC Press, Nov. 2005.

Farrow, R. (n.d.). *An experiment in forensics reveals attackers' techniques.* Retrieved from http://www.spirit.com/Network/net0301.html

Forte, D., Zambelli, M., Bertoletti, D., & Maruti, C. (2004). Sebek "ITA" interface. *USENIX ; login: magazine*

IRItaly and Italian Honeynet Project. (n.d.). *Announcing the IRItaly Honeynet project.* Retrieved from www.honeynet.it

Manson, K. (1999, March). Robots, wanderers, spiders and avatars: The virtual investigator and community policing behind the thin digital blue line.

Md5Crack project. (n.d.) Retrieved from http://www.md5crk.com/

Othman, K. (2004, July). *Hilmi logging and log analysis—The essentials.*

Spafford & Carrier (2003).

Sremack, J. C. (2004). *Formalizing computer forensic analysis: A proof-based methodology.*

Stenhouse, D. P. (2004, May). *Computer-based discovery and risk control.*

Tran, P. M. (2004, spinrg). *Distributed cyber forensics.*

Wolfe, H. (2004, February). *Forensic evidence testimony—Some thoughts.*

Forensic Analysis of Windows Systems

Steve J. Chapin, *Syracuse University*
Chester J. Maciag, *Air Force Research Laboratory*

INTRODUCTION

Digital forensics is the science and practice of identifying, preserving, collecting, validating, analyzing, interpreting, documenting, and presenting digital evidence for the purpose of facilitating or furthering event reconstruction (DFRWS, 2004). Although a common goal of digital forensics is the presentation of evidence for a legal proceeding by a forensic practitioner, this chapter focuses on the general principles of digital forensics used by first responders and system administrators for diagnosing unauthorized actions that are shown to be disruptive to organizational processes and policies.

Forensics is *not* intrusion detection, although the two share some techniques. It should be noted that digital forensic analysis starts after the investigator already suspects that an intrusion or policy violation has occurred. In addition, although intrusion detection provides some initial clues about the violation, only digital forensic analysis can thoroughly validate these clues and determine the full extent of the system penetration.

Because more complete and complementary descriptions of digital forensics can be found in other chapters, we only briefly summarize general forensic issues. We then provide guidance on specific techniques as they apply to Windows NT systems so as to provide useful investigative information. Windows 9x and ME platforms are not covered in this chapter, in part because of their decreasing market presence and the significant architectural differences in 9x and ME from the NT generation—9x and ME do not provide adequate assurance that basic system services and logs have not been subverted.

Applications of Digital Forensics

Each passing day presents fresh examples of how the digital domain can be exploited for unintended purposes. The first responder will apply forensic techniques to assess four characteristics of the incident:

- Current System State. Is there any ongoing computer activity that is destructive, that is in violation of system policy, or that will hamper future investigative efforts? Has malware been left behind to monitor investigative progress or conduct future surveillance? Is the intruder still on the computer? Are there open network ports that would allow remote control of or access to the computer? Much of this volatile information is lost under typical computer evidentiary procedures.

- Extent of the Violation. An intrusion detection sensor may have alerted us to a violation, but there may more to the attack that the sensor was not tuned or designed to see. Did the intrusion only involve the reading or modification of files? Did it also include changing the system configuration? Have new login accounts been installed that enable the intruder to return later?

- Timelining. Placing validated event and log information into a timeline can serve to help eliminate improbable investigative leads, hence focusing investigative resources. Incomplete timelines or timelines with discontinuities can serve as a vital indicator that further probing into the computer is necessary to explain the entire violation. Finally, when timelines are reconciled with physical world events, association of digital identity and physical identity may be possible.

- Attribution. Sensors may have indicated that a particular user committed the violation or attack, but how can we be sure that critical audit logs have not been altered? In the instance of a remote attack or port scan from another IP address, what can be done to validate the authenticity of the information (e.g., that the return address was not spoofed)? Perhaps there is hidden information in disk slack space, deleted files, or Registry entries that are indicative of a particular individual or motive. Finding this information, and associating it with an individual, is perhaps the most challenging part of the forensic investigative process.

Evidence-Gathering Process

The process of forming attack hypotheses, finding evidence, evaluating evidence, and presenting a final conclusion is not a linear but an iterative process. It is very likely that the initial theory of attack pursued by the first responder will evolve significantly as evidence is discovered and its worth measured. As a result, it is very important that the first responder preserve the digital investigation scene as best as possible so as to be able to return as many times as possible to gather additional information. It is therefore incumbent upon the first responder to "do no harm" to the Windows computer as it is examined. That is, one's actions must not destroy, damage, or compromise evidence that may exist in a computer, thereby rendering it useless. The utility of evidence lies in two areas: as input to a logical chain of reasoning to determine the extent, method, and culpability of an incident; and as input to a legal process for exacting civil or criminal justice. Other chapters give a more extensive treatment of the general topic of digital evidence. Because this chapter provides a treatment of forensic analysis for the first responder, we are not be concerned to prescribe a process that meets civil or criminal evidentiary guidelines. However, some basic steps to minimize alteration of the Windows computing environment during examination are considered in the following sections.

Information of Potential Interest to a First Responder

To determine expeditiously the full nature of the intrusion or attack, a first responder will forego pulling the plug on a Windows computer. Instead, the first responder will try to collect the following four categories of information:

1. Volatile Information. Information on a running computer system is either volatile or nonvolatile. Volatile information is transient and may not survive examination, much less cycling power. Volatile information is also sensitive to use of the operating system. In a fashion analogous to the Heisenberg uncertainty principle applied to subatomic particles, the very act of measuring the Windows environment changes the environment, such as the contents of memory or slack space. There are several types of volatile information, each with a particular application:

   (a) current system time and date, to measure drift or tampering;

   (b) current users and processes running on the system, to determine potential actors or victims of the investigated incident;

   (c) existence of running spyware, keyloggers, and remote system administration tools, to identify attempts by the attacker to monitor or sabotage the investigation;

   (d) active network connections, daemons, remote-mounted file systems, and exported directories, to determine avenues by which sensitive data, rootkits, or system configuration may have been exported or imported to the investigated computer;

   (e) network configuration parameters, to determine if network parameters have been temporarily altered to enable remote communication with the attacker but are otherwise reverted to normal configuration upon reboot); and

   (f) system swap file (pagefile.sys) to find trace documents, passwords, and preencrypted documents that were temporarily written to disk during routine Windows memory management.

2. Nonvolatile Information. Nonvolatile information can be thought of as stable information that would survive a power cycle of the machine, such as data stored on the hard drive, CD-ROMs, or transient removable storage media. The investigator will be interested in finding the following information:

   (a) the number and types of locally mounted file systems, including the boot drive, CD/DVD-ROMs/RAMs/RWs, and USB storage devices;

   (b) the number and types of remotely mounted file systems such as network drives;

   (c) the file system directory tree and file listing, to help determine whether the standard operating system directory structure has been altered or augmented by the attacker with special tools or application directories;

   (d) hidden files and deleted files, to identify avenues that the attacker may have employed to help cover his or her tracks; and

   (e) the existence of encrypted data, encryption tools, or other data obfuscation utilities, again used to cover the attacker's trail or motives.

3. Recent Operating System Activity. Recent system-level configuration changes or activity can be instrumental in determining root causes of intrusive behavior. The investigator will make note of the following types of information:

   (a) Modifications to system date, time, or time zone, as these can cause the Windows system to log events out of temporal order and with incorrect timestamps.

   (b) System log files, to record events internal to the operating system, such as driver performance, module status, and startup and shutdown actions. Based on a collection of these logs, the forensic analyst can create a rough picture of network, user, and system activity that provides the context for forensic analysis.

   (c) Security log files, to record conformance to and violation of security policy, such as logins, access violations, and network connections.

   (d) Server log files, to determine activity of corporate databases and Web servers (such as IIS, the Microsoft Web Server). Record requests, actions, and responses are stored in these log files at the discretion of the server administrator. Sometimes, performance goals can override the need for auditing, leaving the investigator with little to go on.

(e) Current software applications, as well as those that have been removed (such as encryption or cracking tools) to avoid suspicion.

(f) Current hardware configuration, previous configurations, and devices that have been detached by the attacker. Such devices may include storage drives, input devices, or required authentication devices that, once removed, allowed the attacker access.

(g) Registry entries, to include critical system behavior parameters, computer network identity, and the list of programs that will run or load every time the system is restarted or a user logs on. The latter is a key place for attackers to insert links to make malware persistent on the computer.

4. Recent User Activity. Recent user activity can be indicative of a single user's attempts to search for information, download malicious software, and run programs. The investigator will look to find evidence of four types:

(a) Software applications run, shell commands executed, and files downloaded, to determine if a given user's actions led to a system compromise or failure.

(b) Internet sites visited or searched, Instant Messengers (IM) buddy lists, and cookie information, to help determine the general communication tendencies of the user and the possible sources of malware or worms that are found elsewhere on the computer.

(c) Internet Web browser security settings, again, to help determine if the user may have inadvertently let malicious Java or ActiveX controls run on the compromised system.

(d) User and Windows temporary directories. The user has a dedicated directory for temporary Internet files, graphics, and downloads. The Windows operating system has a temporary directory (C:\Windows\Temp) for the same purpose for single-user computers.

The remainder of this chapter gives an overview of the Registry, issues in the NT file system and storage, and logging in Windows. This is followed by suggestions for creating a forensics toolkit and the use of that toolkit in a simple investigation.

OVERVIEW OF THE WINDOWS REGISTRY

The Windows Registry is a database used by both application programs and the operating system. It contains settings, options, and general information for programs, hardware, and users. The Registry is most often changed indirectly by the user, either through using program and system configuration menus, or changing file associations or the control panel. However, it can be edited directly through programs such as regedit.exe. Although its full

structure is more complicated, we can consider the Registry to be a set of (entry, value) pairs. We discuss how attackers can hide data by adding their own Registry entries or overwriting existing entries.

The Registry is actually a combination of five distinct binary configuration files, known as hive files. Four of them are located in %system_root%\System32\config:

- SAM (Security Account Manager). Contains information pertaining to local user accounts and group accounts, as well as other security settings.
- Security. Contains information pertaining to machine-specific password policy, local rights, and group assignments.
- Software. Lists machine-specific information pertaining to the location where applications are installed and their properties, as well as similar information about the Windows operating system.
- System. Contains current system control set, as well as the default configuration and the "last known good" configuration to be used when recovering from an unrecoverable configuration failure (Harback, 2004).

The last type of hive file is ntuser.dat. There is one unique instance of this type of file for each defined user. It is created once a user has logged on for the first time, and is located in Documents and Settings\ <username>\ntuser.dat.

There is not a one-to-one mapping of hive keys (Hkey) to a hive file, and some hive key contents change between system boots and user logins. Figure 1 shows the different Hkeys:

- Hkey_local_machine (HKLM). Several subkeys are mapped directly from the hive files of the same name. Subkey hardware is dynamic and enumerates all system devices currently active since this system boot.
- Hkey_users (HKU). Consists of the ntuser.dat files of each active user profile.
- Hkey_current_user (HKCU). A pointer to the currently logged-on user's profile in hkey_users. The contents in this key are dynamic.
- Hkey_classes root (HKCR). Is actually a dynamic join between the software class subkeys of local_machine and current_user hive keys.
- Hkey_current_config (HKCC). Current configuration profile of hardware identified under hkey_local_machine\hardware (Harback, 2004).

There are thousands of (key, value) pairs in the Windows Registry. Some intuition is required to know where to find a key that pertains to a particular configuration item, but once you know the role of each of the major hive keys, finding the key types becomes easier. We identify several Registry subkeys and entries of interest as we go along. Because Registry data are saved in binary format, the Registry also provides a convenient place for attackers to save data, fragments of files, and even complete programs.

The most common use of Registry keys by attackers is to start processes on a system reboot. To accomplish this, the attacker adds his program(s) to one of the Run

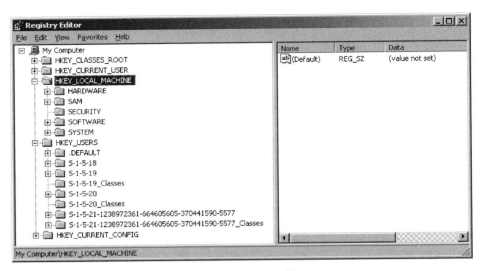

Figure 1: Registry editor.

or Load keys in the Registry entries for the system or one of the users. Several automated attacks, including the SouthPark and Slammer worms, modify Registry entries in exactly this fashion. As pointed out in Carvey (2005), attackers can also hide data in the values associated with standard, but unused, keys such as the DaylightName and StandardName strings associated with the Time Zone Information structure.

It is therefore recommended that administrators monitor changes to Registry contents, either through regular backups and checks or using a software package designed to track Registry changes. There are several freely and commercially available packages that monitor the Registry, including Registry Watcher, RegRun, and products from Symantec and Network Associates. These tools provide a user-friendly graphical use interface (GUI) to browse, edit, and monitor Registry entries.

WINDOWS NTFS FILE SYSTEM AND STORAGE
Application-Specific File Types

There are several explicit and implicit attributes of files that affect how Windows treats and displays them. The most obvious one is the name: Windows associates handler programs with files according to the suffix of the file name. For example, .txt files are opened by Notepad by default, and .doc files are opened by Word, and so forth when a file is double-clicked in Windows Explorer. Changing the name of a file so that it no longer ends in .exe will cause Windows to not execute the file.

Windows, like UNIX, includes a file signature that indicates the type of the file (in UNIX, this is in the first 2 bytes; in Windows, the first 20). For example, this value is 25504446 for PDF files. There is not necessarily a one-to-one mapping between file signatures and suffixes; a .doc file can have several different legal signatures, including 7FFE340A as a generic Word document or 1234567890FF for a Word 6.0 document. These signatures can be useful

in detecting a file that has had its name, but not its signature, changed. The ProDiscover forensics toolkit includes a tool to detect mismatches between file signatures and extensions.

Another way in which attackers hide files from casual search is to turn on the "hidden" attribute. By default, Windows Explorer and the "dir" command do not display hidden files. Although it is not difficult to override this default behavior, it does take additional work by the administrator. Windows stores a set of time stamps with each file, called the Modification, Access, and Creation times, or MAC times for short. Unfortunately, any user with write access to a file can set these time stamps, so a last modification time stamp should not be accepted at face value as evidence that the file has remained unchanged since then. A file system integrity tool such as Tripwire (Kim & Spafford, 1994) can help to understand when a file has changed, regardless of what is indicated by the time stamps.

Application-Level Data Hiding

Applications, particularly document preparation applications, often embed metadata in data files. For example, Word includes the document creator, modification history, machines where the file was edited, comments, and invisible portions of embedded OLE objects. Because this information is not displayed under normal operation, attackers can hide data in comment fields and so forth.

In addition, OLE-structured objects allow multiple complete files to be merged into one. This is often done to link an Excel spreadsheet to a chart in a Word document or to include a graphics object. However, abuse of this facility enables attackers to hide entire programs or data files within documents. Interestingly, if one merges multiple Office files (such as Powerpoint and Word files), which portion of the file is accessed upon opening depends on its suffix. For example, double-clicking on file.ppt will open the Powerpoint presentation, while double-clicking on file.doc will open the Word document. The

Figure 2: Sample IIS log record.

128.230.14.20, sjc, 11/20/04, 10:42:00, W3SVC, SERV1, 192.168.0.10, 3217, 165, 17328, 200, 0, GET, /OttoOrange.jpg, -

Code Project (CodeProject, 2004) offers a Structured Storage Viewer that can view this "file system within a file," as Microsoft has dubbed this type of storage.

Windows-Specific Special Files

The Apple Macintosh pioneered the use of secondary data files affiliated with primary files (in Mac terms, these are called resource and data forks) with its hierarchical file system. Microsoft's NT file system supports this type of file with the Alternate Data Streams (ADS) facility. Because a file can have multiple ADS associated with it, attackers can hide programs and data out of plain sight by hiding them in ADS added to existing files.

Programs that list the contents of the file system, such as "dir" or Windows Explorer, do not show special files. A file with an attached ADS appears no different than it did before the attachment. This creates a prime opportunity for data to be hidden in ADS files. Beneficial uses of ADS include support for Mac files, storage of icons associated with a program, thumbnail images for graphics files, and checksums or hashes for security programs. Malicious use of ADS includes storage of entire programs out of sight, where they can be executed when the attacker needs them. In addition, modifying the ADS associated with a file does not update the time stamps or size of the file visible from Windows Explorer or dir.

Of course, for an ADS to be useful, it cannot be completely inaccessible. Executable programs stored in ADS can be run by naming them explicitly from the command line or a program; similarly, they can be read or written using the Win32 API backup calls (backupread, backupseek, and backupwrite). There are several freeware packages that can list ADS streams, including LADS (LADS, 2004) and Sysinternal's Streams package. The Code Project's ADS Detector (CodeProject, 2004) makes ADS visible to Windows Explorer.

LOGGING AND AUDITING IN WINDOWS

Correlating information from logs along with that obtained from forensics tools, the investigator can test hypotheses about the method of entry and chain of events. Unfortunately, at this point, there are no automated analysis tools, so building this chain is a painstaking, manual process. Windows provides the Event Viewer as a built-in service.

Server Logs

Server logs contain information about the transactions processed by the server, such as the Internet protocol (IP) address of the client, parameters of the request, and the returned status and/or result of the request. For the sake of brevity, we relate our comments to Microsoft's Internet Information Services (IIS) server (Microsoft, 2004a), the Web server for Windows NT/XP.

By default, IIS logs to the \%SystemRoot%\ system32\Logfiles directory, which is on the system partition. Because this is usually of limited size, it is a good idea to configure IIS to log to a different partition if a remote server is not available. The best option, to prevent local log corruption and facilitate log analysis, is to have servers log to a remote location.

IIS logs are configurable; as of IIS 6.0, the administrator may choose one of several file formats: the W3C extended log file format, IIS file format, the NCSA common log file format, and in an open database connectivity–compliant SQL database. IIS format is the default and is in a fixed ASCII format. An IIS record, as shown in Figure 2, contains 15 fields: client IP address, user name, date, time, service and instance, server name, server IP address, time taken to fulfill the request, bytes received, bytes sent, service status code, Windows status code, request type, target of operation, and script parameters. Fields that have no data are represented by a hyphen; a service status code of 200 indicates success, as does a Windows status code of 0.

The example in Figure 2 shows that user "sjc" from IP address 128.230.14.20 sent an HTTP GET request to server SERV1 (IP 192.168.0.10) on November 20, 2004, at 10:42 a.m. The object of the request was /OttoOrange.jpg (a picture of the Syracuse University mascot). The request was 165 bytes long, and the server successfully returned 17,328 bytes of data after 3.2 seconds (3,217 milliseconds).

When examining logs, one must keep in mind that log entries might be the result of spoofed packets (those in which the client's IP address is forged). In that situation, the log record will not help to trace the activity back to its source. Client–server interactions that span multiple messages (and particularly those where later messages depend on earlier ones) have a low likelihood of using spoofed addresses. Even if the IP address is forged, we can study the logs to find abnormal activity. Recognizing abnormal traffic requires knowledge of the local environment and services, but such traffic could include large incoming messages to Web servers, activity against little-used accounts, or messages with a high incidence of 8-bit (non-ASCII) characters.

Security Logs

Windows XP permits logging of security events related to user logon/logoff, account management, object accesses, policy changes, system events, process tracking, and the use of backup and restore privileges, among others. The default configuration depends on the manufacturer of the system (for example, the default on a leading-brand laptop was to log nothing), so the administrator should access the local security settings to ensure that what is being logged conforms to local policy. To access the LSS, select Start → Control Panel → Administrative Tools → Local Security Policy. This will open a window similar to that shown in Figure 3. Logging options are set under Local Polices → Audit Policy and Local Polices → Security Options.

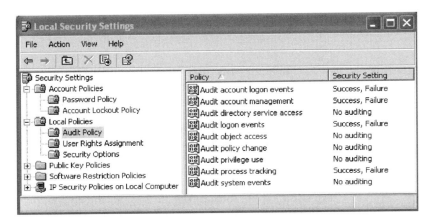

Figure 3: Windows local security policy window.

System Logs

System logs include error and information messages from device drivers, including those for the network, mouse, and the CD-ROM, as well as for operating system components such as Windows Update. Typical entries include the acquisition or loss of IP addresses through the dynamic host configuration protocol (DHCP), notices that the mouse buffer has overflowed, or problems with the Windows Browser service. The Windows Browser service provides a list of shared resources available on the network, and because of its close relationship with NetBIOS, events from the Browser service should be monitored closely.

PREPARING THE ANALYSIS TOOLKIT

When examining any Windows computer, a first responder must assume that an attacker may have already compromised significant parts of the operating system and logging capabilities. Furthermore, the responder will seek to minimize the use of victim system applications so as not to inadvertently modify system logs, file access times, swapfile contents, or the contents of free memory. Accordingly, the examiner will minimize dependence on system utilities and services that are resident on the computer being examined.

To meet these goals, the examiner should develop a portable Windows response toolkit. The toolkit typically consists of an assemblage of Windows utilities, freeware, and commercial tools that can be run from an externally mounted medium such as a CD-ROM or a USB thumb drive. There are pros and cons to using each medium, but for a nonevidentiary analysis, the USB drive affords the greatest flexibility to store tools as well as their output.

Ideally, one will want to set up one's thumb drive with separate directories for the toolkit and for saved data. Under the drive's root directory, one creates a subdirectory called Tools and copies all forensics executables and downloaded tools. One can create an additional subdirectory called Data to hold captured output redirected from the forensic tools. One *should not* redirect output to the vicitm's storage media, as it may be lost later, may corrupt the file system, or may diminish the ability to recover deleted files. Redirection of output to a text file can be accomplished by appending >G:\Data\outputfile.txt to the end of a command line (for this example, and the discussion in the next session, we assume that the thumb drive has been mounted on G:). Each output file must have a unique name or it will be overwritten, for example, G:\>netstat -r > G:\Data\routingtable.txt.

Some responders will develop a toolkit on a case-by-case basis, depending on what types and how much information is to be collected from the victim computer. Others will create an all-purpose toolkit that contains utilities and tools to meet virtually any type of probing that is necessary. The choice is up to the first responder and his or her investigative style.

We present some tools that can be used to analyze a Windows NT system. Many can be obtained from a pristine system, installation CDs, or the Resource Kit. Others are freely available on the Internet. Keep in mind that there are many other tools that will provide similar output; the ones listed are for illustrative purposes only, and not all possibilities can be discussed in the limited space available. There are also a number of commercial tools with advanced interfaces that can expedite the investigative process.

Tools in Windows

The following executables are already available on the victim operating system, but to avoid using a compromised version, they should instead be copied first from a pristine system for inclusion in the toolkit:

arp.exe displays MAC address of host interface, as well as those of recently communicated machines on the network.

cmd.exe is the WinNT, 2K, and XP command line interface (CLI).

netstat.exe displays various network configuration parameters as well as open TCP connections.

regedit.exe allows for the display, manipulation, and exporting of contents in the Windows Registry.

Tools in the NT Resource Kit

Some of the tools that the investigator will find useful can be found on the Windows NT/2000/XP Resource Kit CDs. Two are found in the NT Resource Kit:

rasusers.exe lists remote and local logged-on users.

rmtshare.exe lists shares that are accessible on a remote computer.

Table 1 Tools from the PsTools Collection

Tool	Use
PsFile	Show files opened remotely
PsGetSid	Display the SID of a computer or a user
PsKill	Kill processes by name or process ID
PsInfo	List information about a system
PsList	List detailed information about processes
PsLoggedOn	See who's logged on locally and via resource sharing (full source is included)
PsLogList	Dump event log records
PsService	View and control services
PsShutdown	Shut down and optionally reboot a computer
PsSuspend	Suspend processes
PsUptime	Show how long a system has been running since its last reboot (PsUptime's functionality has been incorporated into PsInfo)

Free Tools

The following free utilities can be found on the Internet. Some have augmented the basic functionality afforded by the Windows tools and executables, whereas others provide an exceptional capability leap.

Dcode (Wilson, 2005): This utility by Craig Wilson decodes raw hexidecimal date and time values in the Windows Registry.

Forensic Toolkit 2.0 (Foundstone, 2004): This set of tools enables the investigator to find hidden files, enumerate user accounts and file shares, and retrieve attributes without altering them for individual files.

Fport (Foundstone, 2004): *fport.exe* reports all open TCP/UDP-IP ports and in addition names the owning application.

PsTools (Russinovich & Cogswell, n.d.): The Sysinternals Web site contains many utilities and tools that are useful for digital forensics. Two examples are Process Explorer and PsTools.

- Process Explorer: This GUI displays information about running processes, handles, and .dlls in a two-panel application window.
- PsTools: This is a collection of a dozen forensics command line tools, shown in Table 1.

CONDUCTING THE INVESTIGATION

The responder, Reggie, will generally approach the victim computer (called Destiny) and observe the screen prior to performing any activity. To avoid entering data into a Trojan login program, Reggie presses <CTRL-ALT-DEL> to invoke the secure login/task manager window. An account with administrator privileges will be required to use some of the toolkit tools. Once the login is complete, Reggie opens the My Computer icon on the desktop, inserts his thumb drive into an unused USB port, and notes the new drive letter that appears (for our demonstrations, we assume that the drive letter is G:). He navigates into the Tools directory on the USB drive and launches cmd.exe to create a command prompt. It is from this prompt that most initial information will be collected.

Capturing Volatile System Information

Reggie starts by gathering the time and date on the system and noting any discrepancy from the current time and date (see Figure 4). These may have been manipulated to invalidate log file time stamps or to misrepresent data file access and modification times and dates.

He next checks for other logged-on users who could interfere with his investigation. In our example (see Figure 5), there does not seem to be any other user logged on, so that is good. Now he checks for active Net-BIOS connections, as well as any other remote network

Figure 4: Output of the "date" and "time" commands.

Figure 5: Output of the "psloggedon" command.

connections that could be used to monitor what he is doing, control the computer, or manipulate system information.

The nbtstat program collects NetBIOS statistics, giving us the list of recently cached partner node names, the local NetBOIS name table, and statistics pertaining to number of past connections. We can see in Figure 6 that there are no names in the cache, so there are no active connections. Reggie moves on to check non-NetBOIS network connections to see if there are any FTP, IRC, SSH, or other suspicious connections running to the system.

Netstat (see Figure 7) provides a listing, including the port numbers, of active TCP and UDP connections to the victim computer. If the port number is common, netstat will insert the name of the service in lieu of the port number. Netstat -r lists the victim computer's network interfaces and current routing table. This should later be compared with the permanent routing table in the Windows Registry to determine whether tampering has occurred to enable covert or unconventional communication.

There does not seem to be an imminent threat to his investigation, so Reggie continues his examination. He can use the psinfo command, shown in Figure 8, to find out how long the system has been up and a little about the Windows environment Reggie can see from the output that this computer has been up for only about 5 hours.

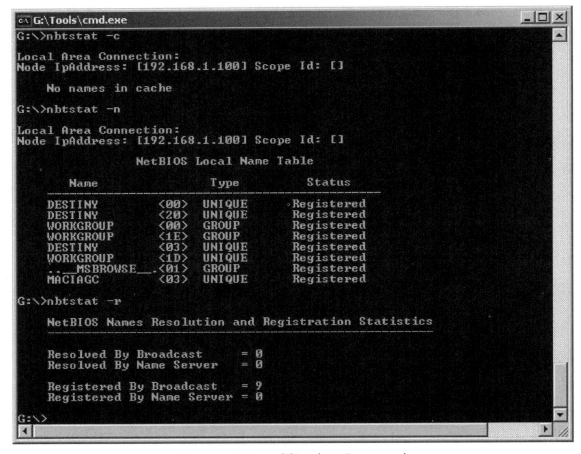

Figure 6: Output of the "nbtstat" command.

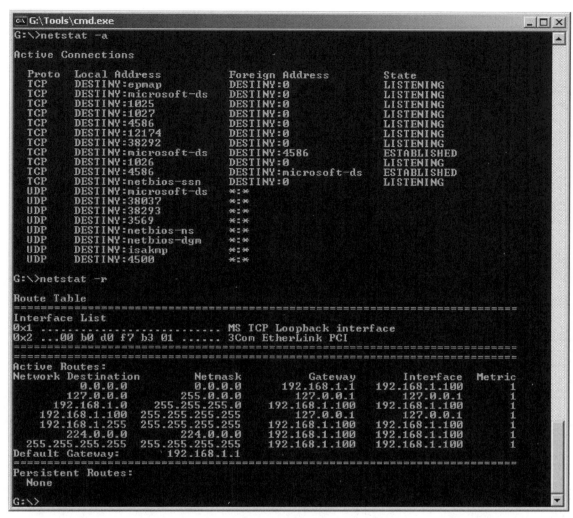

Figure 7: Output of the "netstat" command.

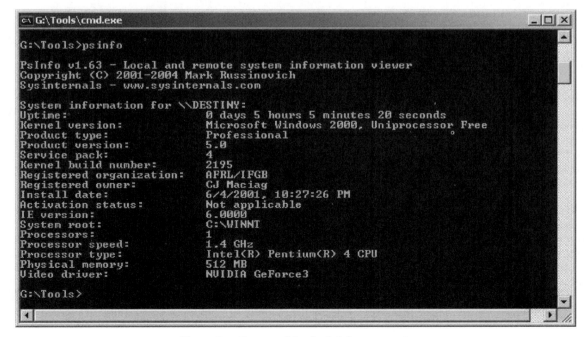

Figure 8: Output of the "psinfo" command.

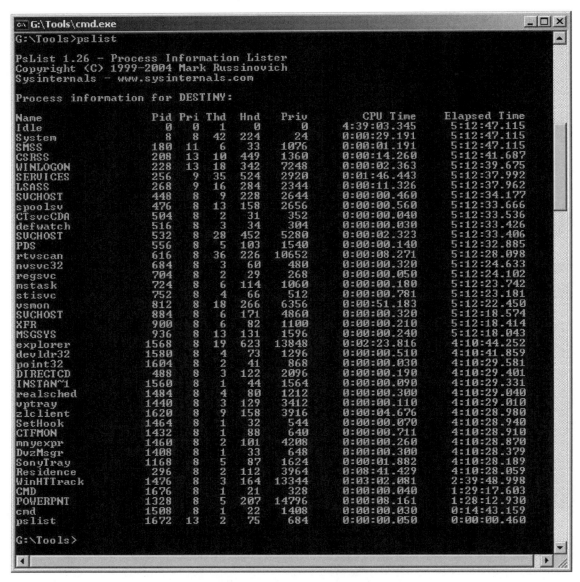

```
G:\Tools\cmd.exe                                                    _ □ ×

G:\Tools>pslist

PsList 1.26 - Process Information Lister
Copyright (C) 1999-2004 Mark Russinovich
Sysinternals - www.sysinternals.com

Process information for DESTINY:

Name            Pid Pri Thd  Hnd   Priv       CPU Time    Elapsed Time
Idle              0   0   1    0      0    4:39:03.345    5:12:47.115
System            8   8  42  224     24    0:00:29.191    5:12:47.115
SMSS            180  11   6   33   1076    0:00:01.191    5:12:47.115
CSRSS           208  13  10  449   1360    0:00:14.260    5:12:41.687
WINLOGON        228  13  18  342   7248    0:00:02.363    5:12:39.675
SERVICES        256   9  35  524   2920    0:01:46.443    5:12:37.992
LSASS           268   9  16  284   2344    0:00:11.326    5:12:37.962
SVCHOST         448   8   9  228   2644    0:00:00.460    5:12:34.177
spoolsv         476   8  13  158   2656    0:00:00.560    5:12:33.666
CTsvcCDA        504   8   2   31    352    0:00:00.040    5:12:33.536
defwatch        516   8   3   34    304    0:00:00.030    5:12:33.426
SVCHOST         532   8  28  452   5280    0:00:02.323    5:12:33.406
PDS             556   8   5  103   1540    0:00:00.140    5:12:32.885
rtvscan         616   8  36  226  10652    0:00:08.271    5:12:28.098
nvsvc32         684   8   3   60    480    0:00:00.320    5:12:24.633
regsvc          704   8   2   29    268    0:00:00.050    5:12:24.102
mstask          724   8   6  114   1060    0:00:00.180    5:12:23.742
stisvc          752   8   4   66    512    0:00:00.781    5:12:23.181
vsmon           812   8  18  266   6356    0:00:51.183    5:12:22.450
SVCHOST         884   8   6  171   4860    0:00:00.320    5:12:18.574
XFR             900   8   6   82   1100    0:00:00.210    5:12:18.414
MSGSYS          936   8  13  131   1596    0:00:00.240    5:12:18.043
explorer       1568   8  19  623  13848    0:02:23.816    4:10:44.252
devldr32       1580   8   4   73   1296    0:00:00.510    4:10:41.859
point32        1604   8   2   41    868    0:00:00.030    4:10:29.581
DIRECTCD        488   8   3  122   2096    0:00:00.190    4:10:29.401
INSTAN~1       1560   8   1   44   1564    0:00:00.090    4:10:29.331
realsched      1484   8   4   80   1212    0:00:00.300    4:10:29.040
vptray         1440   8   3  129   3412    0:00:00.110    4:10:29.010
zlclient       1620   8   9  158   3916    0:00:04.676    4:10:28.980
SetHook        1464   8   1   32    544    0:00:00.070    4:10:28.940
CTFMON         1432   8   1   88    640    0:00:00.711    4:10:28.910
mnyexpr        1460   8   2  101   4208    0:00:00.260    4:10:28.870
DvzMsgr        1408   8   1   33    648    0:00:00.300    4:10:28.379
SonyTray       1168   8   5   87   1624    0:00:01.882    4:10:28.189
Residence       296   8   2  112   3964    0:08:41.429    4:10:28.059
WinHTTrack     1476   8   3  164  13344    0:03:02.081    2:39:48.998
CMD            1676   8   1   21    328    0:00:00.040    1:29:17.603
POWERPNT       1328   8   5  207  14796    0:00:08.161    1:28:12.930
cmd            1508   8   1   22   1408    0:00:00.030    0:14:43.159
pslist         1672  13   2   75    684    0:00:00.050    0:00:00.460

G:\Tools>
```

Figure 9: Output of the "pslist" command.

It is a Win2K Professional OS (installed 6/4/2001) with Service Pack 4 applied, and he can also see to whom it is legally registered. This system has seemingly been intact for several years. The Windows root directory is the default C:\WINNT, which will be useful to know when we investigate the Registry and other system files.

Reggie now proceeds to get the status of currently running processes to see if there is anything suspicious that could be malware, spyware, or a remote administration tool such as SubSeven or NetBus. Many attacks leave processes running on the system. These processes can provide back doors into the system and wait for network connections, monitor system activity to report to a remote host, or attack other hosts. It is essential, then, that he includes an analysis of the running processes. Although the Windows TaskManager gives a list of processes, it does not give crucial information such as the arguments given when the process started or the path to the executable

file. Attackers take advantage of these weaknesses by giving their programs the same name as common Windows processes such as svchost.exe or inetinfo.exe.

Most of the processes listed here look familiar; however, there are a few that may require further inquiry. For example, Reggie is not familiar with the process called instan~1 and wants more information. Furthermore, there are several instances of svchost, each of which is responsible for managing several system and network services, as defined in the Windows Registry. Attackers can take advantage of the Registry to insert links to malicious code under the svchost process. Reggie decides to get more information on what these processes do.

Reggie invokes the GUI-based Process Explorer, shown in Figure 10. In the upper window, he can see a dynamic update of the processes running on the system as well as a description of each and its CPU utilization. Shaded in red are system services, and in blue are user processes. By

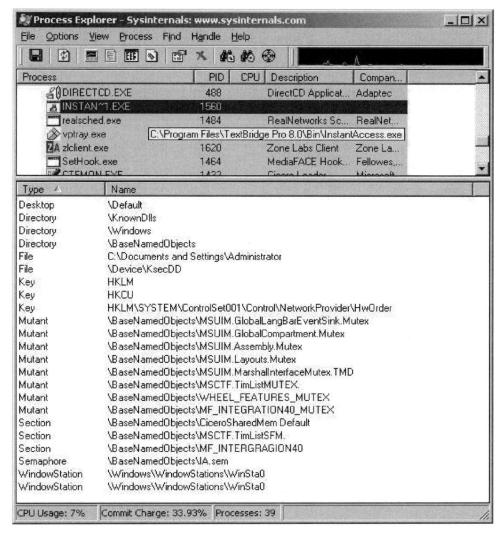

Figure 10: The Process Explorer program.

clicking on a questionable process in the upper window, he sees the list of associated .dlls and file handles that the process uses.

By clicking each of the svchost processes, he can see the list of files and services that each provides. Reggie can also see if there are any additions to these lists from unconventional directories, which might have been added by an attacker. When Reggie lets the cursor rest over the questionable process, a "tooltip" bubble appears, revealing the entire pathname of the invoked service. In this case, the suspicious instan~1 process turned out to be TextBridge Pro, a benign optical character recognition (OCR) conversion program.

Capturing the File System

Next, Reggie wants to capture information about the current system directory structure, files, and attributes. He wants to do this before analyzing the files because the process of reading a file changes a file's attributes. For example, the NTFS file system maintains information pertaining to when a file was first created, last modified, and last

accessed. Simply highlighting a file using the Windows Explorer interface changes the "last accessed" attribute of the file to the current date and time, which is undesirable. So, Reggie will make a permanent record before going further. He could use disk imaging software such as Encase (Guidance, 2004), but use of such tools and the recovery of hidden file systems is beyond the scope of this chapter.

First, Reggie gets a list of currently mounted storage drives on the system: he will use the Registry to obtain this information, so he launches the Registry editor (see Figure 11). In the left window, he expands hkey_local_machine\system\MountedDevices+. In the right window, he notices a number of (entryname, value) entries and takes note of any that start with \DosDevices\. These entries depict the currently allocated drive letters on the system and are the volumes he will want to explore. If Reggie wants to identify the type of hardware represented by the drive letter, he can double-click on the key name. A binary entry box will open, displaying the hexidecimal values (and corresponding ASCII representations) of the key and showing whether the drive is fixed, removable, a CD-ROM, and so forth.

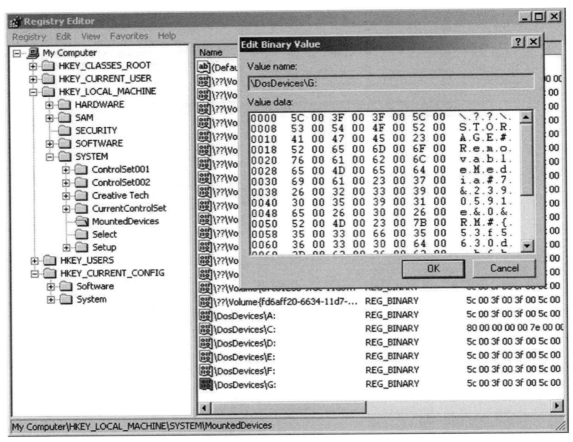

Figure 11: The Registry editor.

Now Reggie would like to get a recursive directory listing of all files. Without any special tools, he can obtain file names, dates and times created, and sizes. With some additional tools, such as the toolkit included with Carvey (2005), he could also get additional attributes such as owner, last time/date accessed, and last time/date modified. If Reggie directs the listing to an output file on his USB thumb drive, he can view that listing without risk of changing the original file system. Note that he will see no output to the screen; he will have to use the utility "more" to confirm the file has been written. To derive and view a listing for the C:\ drive, for example, he uses these:

```
G:\Tools>dir C:\ /s > G:\Data\Cdrivelist.txt
```

```
G:\Tools>more G:\Data\CDrivelist.txt
```

This listing will yield all files except those that have the hidden attribute set. There are a number of ways to expose those files. One simple tool is HFind.exe from Foundstone's Forensic Toolkit. To find all hidden files on the C:\ drive, we simply type

```
G:\Tools>HFind C:\ > G:\Data\HFind_C_Output.
txt.
```

Because this listing will probably be quite large, we have redirected the output to a logfile on our thumb drive.

Next, Reggie wants to recover any recently deleted files on the storage drives. File deletion in Windows actually consists of two steps. When a file is dragged to the recycle bin or the Delete key is pressed while it is highlighted, Windows marks the file for deletion and removes it from view. The file is not deleted, however. It still exists in the file system and is simply relinked to a special hidden recycle folder. A tool such as Rifiuti (Foundstone, 2004) can easily find and recover files from the recycle bin.

Once the recycle bin is emptied or a file is expressly deleted (via SHIFT-DEL), the file can only be recovered by a specialized tool that can compare the NTFS inodes with allocated drive space. There are literally dozens of utilities available for file recovery, either as freeware or as part of commercial utilities packages, so they will not be covered here. Time is of the essence, though, as the longer the system runs after a file is deleted, the more likely it is that the disk blocks from that file will be reused. Avoiding disk block reallocation is a primary reason why all tool output should be stored on removable media or a remote system, rather than on the victim computer. On a typical Windows system, a large percentage of the files are standard operating system components and applications. These files will be the same across any installation, and so, as long as they are unchanged, they can be ignored for forensic analysis. Finally, you may want to determine whether Windows system files have been compromised or replaced. This comparison can be accomplished in one of two ways:

- Because all file attributes have now been documented, you can now walk the directory tree and use one of many MD5 (Rivest, 1992) or SHA1 (NIST, 1995) message digest tools to compute and save hashes of the victim computer's files. These hashes can be compared with one of two national databases of hashes for well-known Windows files, maintained by the National Drug Intelligence Center and National Institute of Standards and Technology.
- Use a disk-imaging package such as Access Data's Forensic Toolkit, Guidance Software's Encase Forensic Edition, or ASRData's SMART. These tools can automatically generate hashes as well as make comparisons to hash databases.

Recent System Activity and Configuration

At this point, Reggie has captured most volatile and file system configuration items and can now consider using built-in Windows applications to facilitate his investigation. Most of these are already well documented, so we will not go into detail on how they are used. Many of these tools read information from the system Registry, so if the tool has been replaced with a compromised version, Reggie's best bet is to still use the Registry and associated log files as the ultimate authoritative source. Table 2 shows tools that can be launched from the Control Panel or administrative tools under the Start menu.

Local and remote event logs can be viewed and saved via the PsTools utility PsLogList. Because this log is quite lengthy, Reggie redirects the output to his thumb drive.

There are several Registry keys of interest (Harback, 2004). The first four start with hklm\software, and the latter four start with hklm\system:

- This key is actually just hklm\software\: Lists all installed software, by vendor. Applications often leave remnants here after they have been uninstalled. Useful for detecting the current or past existence of encryption and steganography tools. Other subkeys contain information pertaining to installation date, installation location, and so forth. All registered file extension classes are listed under the \Classes subkey. Some information exists about the launching application as well.
- \Microsoft\Windows\CurrentVersion: Subkeys Run, RunOnce, RunOnceEx, and RunServices contain entry lists of programs and services that will run each time the

system is started. This is a good place for an attacker to launch malware persistently. This key also contains unique Run and RunOnce entries for each user at logon.
- \Microsoft\WindowsNT\CurrentVersion\WinLogon\Userinit: Multiple programs can be started at logon with this entry. Attackers place entries at the end, beyond the viewing window, so as not to be noticed.
- \Microsoft\WindowsNT\CurrentVersion\Windows\Load: Same issues as the prior item (...Userinit), except multiple programs are loaded at system start.
- \ControlSet001\Control\TerminalServer: If fDenyTSConnections = 0, WinXP allows remote users to log in and take control of a user's desktop!
- \Select: Entries are pointers to the Current, Failed, and LastKnownGood control sets. These values correspond to hklm\system\ControlSet00x, where x is the value listed for the entry. Inspection of these other (noncurrent) configuration sets and dates can reveal potential causes for system failures or existence of devices that are no longer found with the victim system.
- \ControlSet001\Control\Windows\ShutdownTime: Time of last graceful shutdown. Use Dcode.exe to decode raw hexidecimal date.
- \CurrentControlSet\Control\TimeZoneInformation: These entries determine system settings for time zone offset, when daylight savings time occurs, etc. Use Dcode.exe to decode raw hex time values to verify correct time zone, DaylightStart, and StandardStart dates. Verify that time zone names have not been altered so as to store hacker information.

Recent User Activity and Preferences

The system tools mentioned in the previous section already enumerate users, security settings, and login behavior. This section will provide additional insight into recent user activity, application settings, search terms, and buddy lists.

A user's application profile is established upon first logon. A user's profile and default directory will be located under Documents and Settings/<username>. Here is where Reggie can find folders (and several hidden ones) for this information:

- Application Data: User-specific settings for many of the installed software packages, organized by vendor or package name.

Table 2 Windows Applications Useful for Forensics

Tool	Contents/Description
System information	View logs, shares, sessions, users and groups, performance logs, device manager, drive usage, and running services
Computer management	View logs, shares, sessions, users and groups, performance logs, device manager, drive usage, and running services
Local security settings	Password, account, auditing, and user policies. Security options, file encryption options, software policies, and IPSEC policy
Services	Same service information as "Computer management"
User accounts	Enumerates all active accounts and privileges

- Cookies: Cookies from recent Web sites visited.
- Desktop: Listing of user-placed folders, links, and files on the desktop.
- Favorites: Listing of the user's favorite MS Explorer destinations.
- Local Settings: Contains several subfolders that maintain additional user-specific application data, history of Web sites visited with MS Explorer, and temporary downloaded Internet files. This folder does not get cleaned much, so some interesting relics may still exist here.
- My Documents: Default file save location for the user.
- NetHood: User's favorite NetBOIS or NFS directory locations.
- PrintHood: User's favorite network printers.
- Recent: List of recent documents accessed by the user. This list can be quite large and can be useful in ascertaining a user's involvement in an incident.
- Sendto: Configurable list of folder and application destinations.
- Start Menu: The user's tailored Windows Start menu. Are there any unregistered applications launched from here?
- Templates: Office application templates that the user has configured. Note: This is also where ntuser.dat and ntuser.dat.log are stored, and referenced from the Windows Registry.

Reggie can also use the Windows Registry to find other information about recent user activity (Harback, 2004). For example, the Registry contains many most recently used (MRU) entries. The Microsoft applications maintain these lists here. Other application do so also but may have other subkey structures. Microsoft MRUs are listed as examples. Each starts with hku\ <userid> \software:

- \Microsoft\Windows\CurrentVersion\Explorer\Run MRU: List of recent programs executed from the Run dialog box.
- \Microsoft\InternetExplorer\TypedURLs: List of recent data entered into the IE address bar, where "url1" is the most recent entry.
- \Microsoft\MediaPlayer\Player\RecentFileList and \Microsoft\MediaPlayer\Player\RecentURLList: Displays recent files and URLs for Windows Media Player.
- \Microsoft\SearchAssistant\ACMru\5603: Displays most recently searched terms and files using the XP Search Assistant.

Here are some Registry entries to find a user's recently saved files, again starting with hku\ <userid> \software:

- \Microsoft\InternetExplorer\DownloadDirectory: Shows directory path of last downloaded file.
- \Microsoft\Office\<version>\Outlook\Security\ OutlookSecureTempFolder: Shows path where temporary file attachments are stored.

A special part of the Registry points to a private user information store known as the Protected Storage System Provider. It can password information for applications such as Outlook, Web site passwords, auto-complete fields, and SSL certificates. The amount of information stored there is depends on the application setup options. It is accessed via hku\<userid>\software\ Microsoft\ProtectedStorageSystemProvider. This data are encrypted and will require third-party tools to decrypt, such as Access Data's Registry Viewer.

Investigation Overview

Using the techniques described in this section, the investigator can obtain information on the current system state, including volatile system information and file system state, recent user activity, and recent system activity. We showed how to discover active users, processes, and network connections; how to search the Registry for suspicious entries; and how to capture this information without compromising the system being investigated. Putting this information together helps to paint a picture of what has taken place on the system.

CONCLUSION

The Windows operating system family is the most widely used in the world and is therefore the primary target of digital attackers. We have described where to find key forensic information in Windows NT/XP systems; unique features of Windows that require special attention from forensic investigators; and tools, techniques, and practices for conducting digital forensics on Windows systems. Our recommendations are for system administrators and first responders interested in establishing a logical chain of reasoning to explain an incident, not for those interested in collecting evidence for civil or criminal legal proceedings.

GLOSSARY

Digital Hash   A value computed from a data block such that a modified data block will almost certainly generate a different value; that is, it is nearly impossible to change a file and not have its digital hash change.

Forensics   The science of ex post facto examination to extract evidence of earlier activity.

Log Files   On-disk records of system activity, written by server programs.

Message Digest   See Digital Hash.

Metadata   Data, generally not visible to the user, that describes other data.

Nonvolatile Data   Data that is saved on stable storage and persists across rebooting of the system. Compare to Volatile Data.

Steganography   Literally, "covered writing." The practice of hiding data within other data.

Volatile Data   Data that are not saved on permanent storage and that will be lost if the system is rebooted or that may change if it is examined. Compare to Nonvolatile Data.

CROSS REFERENCES

See *Digital Evidence; Forensic Analysis of Unix Systems; Operating System Security.*

REFERENCES

Carvey, H. (2005). *Windows forensics and incident recovery*. Addison-Wesley.

CodeProject. (2004). Retrieved November 12, 2004, from http://www.codeproject.com/

DFRWS. (2004). *Digital forensic research workshop*. Retrieved November 8, 2004, from http://www.dfrws.org

Foundstone. (2004). *Foundstone forensics software*. Retrieved November 16, 2004, from http://www.foundstone.com

Guidance Software. (2004). *Encase suite*. Retrieved November 13, 2004, from http://www.guidance_software.com

Harback, B. (2004, June). Examining the windows registry. In HTCTA.

Jackson, J., Gunsch, G. R., Claypoole, J., & Lamont, G. (2003, winter). Blind steganography detection using a computational immune system: A work in progress. *International Journal of Digital Evidence, 1*(4).

Kim, G., & Spafford, E. H. (1994). The design and implementation of tripwire: A file system integrity checker. In *Conference on computer and communications security* (pp. 18–29). ACM.

LADS. (2004). *List alternative data streams*. Retrieved November 13, 2004, from http://www.heysoft.de/nt/ep-lads.htm

Microsoft. (2004a). *Description of Microsoft IIS logging*. Retrieved November 15, 2004, from http://msdn.microsoft.com/library/default.asp?url=/library/en-us/iissdk/iis/iislogfileformats.asp

NIST. (1995). *Secure hash standard*. (Federal Information Processing Standard). Retrieved November 15, 2004, from http:// www.itl.nist.gov/fipspubs/fip180-1.htm

Rivest, R. (1992, April). *RFC 1321: The md5 message digest algorithm* (RFC No. 1321). Internet Engineering Task Force. Retrieved from http://www.ietf.org/rfc/rfc1321.txt

Russinovich, M., & Cogswell, B. (n.d.). *Sysinternal's miscellaneous tools*. Retrieved November 13, 2004, from http://www.sysinternals.com/ntw2k/source/misc.shtml

Wilson, C. (2005). *Digital detective*. Retrieved January 21, 2005, from http://www.digital-detective.co.uk/freetools.asp

FURTHER READING

More information on the general topic of digital forensics can be found in Casey (2004). For readers interested in research on digital forensics, the Digital Forensics Research Workshop (DFRWS, 2004) is an annual meeting where practitioners discuss advances in the state-of-the-art of digital forensics. Harlan Carvey's book *Windows Forensics and Incident Recovery* (2005) is an excellent overview of the area. It also includes a CD-ROM of forensic utilities written in Perl. The Microsoft Windows Registry Web site (Microsoft, 2004b) has a complete description of the structure of the Registry. The Dartmouth Institute for Security Technology Studies has published a report (Security Technology Studies, 2004) that includes a survey of available forensics tools and their capabilities. The e-Evidence (Seidsma, 2004) Web site of the Computer Forensic Research and Development Center at Utica College has a wealth of references on the topic of digital evidence. The Winternals (2004) software package is an additional source of forensics tools. Those interested in incident handling in general and how forensics fits in should see Grance, Kent, and Kim (2004), and those interested in disk-imaging tools should see NIST (2004). Although we did not go into detail on steganography in this chapter, it can be used to hide data from investigators. For more information on steganography, see Jackson, Gunsch, R. Claypoole, and Lamont (2003) or Katzenbeisser and Petitcolas (2000).

Casey, E. (2004). *Digital evidence and computer crime* (2nd ed.). Academic Press.

Grance, T., Kent, K., & Kim, B. (2004, January). *Computer security incident handling guide* (Special Publication No. 800-61). National Institute of Standards and Technology.

Katzenbeisser, S., & Petitcolas, F. A. P. (Eds.). (2000). *Information hiding techniques for steganography and digital watermarking*. Artech House.

Microsoft. (2004b). *Description of the Microsoft Windows registry*. Retrieved November 10, 2004, from http://support.microsoft.com/kb/256986

NIST. (2004). *National Institute of Standards and Technology computer forensics tool testing program, disk imaging*. Retrieved November 19, 2004, from http://www.cftt.nist.gov/disk_imaging.htm

Security Technology Studies, D. I. for. (2004). *Law enforcement tools and technologies for investigating cyber attacks: Gap analysis report*. Retrieved November 19, 2004, from http://www.ists.dartmouth.edu/tag/gap_analysis.htm

Seidsma, C. (2004). *E-evidence information center Web site*. Retrieved November 17, 2004, from http://www.e-evidence.info/index.html

Winternals. (2004). Retrieved November 17, 2004, from http://www.winternals.com

Operating System Security

William Stallings, *Independent Consultant*

INFORMATION PROTECTION AND SECURITY

The growth in the use of time-sharing systems and, more recently, computer networks has brought with it a growth in concern for the protection of information.

A publication of the National Bureau of Standards (Bransted, 1978) identified some of the threats that need to be addressed in the area of security:

1. Organized and intentional attempts to obtain economic or market information from competitive organizations in the private sector.
2. Organized and intentional attempts to obtain economic information from government agencies.
3. Inadvertent acquisition of economic or market information.
4. Inadvertent acquisition of information about individuals.
5. Intentional fraud through illegal access to computer data banks with emphasis, in decreasing order of importance, on acquisition of funding data, economic data, law enforcement data, and data about individuals.
6. Government intrusion on the rights of individuals.
7. Invasion of individual rights by the intelligence community.

These are examples of specific threats that an organization or an individual (or an organization on behalf of its employees) may feel the need to counter. The nature of the threat that concerns an organization will vary greatly from one set of circumstances to another. However, there are some general-purpose tools that can be built into computers and operating systems that support a variety of protection and security mechanisms. In general, the concern is with the problem of controlling access to computer systems and the information stored in them. Four types of overall protection policies, of increasing order of difficulty, have been identified (Denning, and Brown 1984):

- **No sharing:** In this case, processes are completely isolated from each other, and each process has exclusive control over the resources statically or dynamically assigned to it. With this policy, processes often "share" a program or data file by making a copy of it and transferring the copy into their own virtual memory.
- **Sharing originals of program or data files:** With the use of reentrant code, a single physical realization of a program can appear in multiple virtual address spaces, as can read-only data files. Special locking mechanisms are required for the sharing of writable data files, to prevent simultaneous users from interfering with each other.
- **Confined, or memoryless, subsystems:** In this case, processes are grouped into subsystems to enforce a particular protection policy. For example, a "client" process calls a "server" process to perform some task on data. The server is to be protected against the client discovering the algorithm by which it performs the task, while the client is to be protected against the server's retaining any information about the task being performed.
- **Controlled information dissemination:** In some systems, security classes are defined to enforce a particular dissemination policy. Users and applications are given security clearances of a certain level, whereas data and other resources (e.g., I/O devices) are given security classifications. The security policy enforces restrictions concerning which users have access to which classifications. This model is useful not only in the military context but in commercial applications as well.

Much of the work in security and protection as it relates to operating systems can be roughly grouped into three categories.

- **Access control:** Concerned with regulating user access to the total system, subsystems, and data, and regulating process access to various resources and objects within the system.
- **Information flow control:** Regulates the flow of data within the system and its delivery to users.

- **Certification:** Relates to proving that access and flow control mechanisms perform according to their specifications and that they enforce desired protection and security policies.

This chapter looks at some of the key mechanisms for providing operating system (OS) security.

REQUIREMENTS FOR OPERATING SYSTEM SECURITY
Requirements

An understanding of the types of threats to OS security that exist requires a definition of security requirements. Computer and network security address four requirements:

- **Confidentiality:** Requires that the information in a computer system only be accessible for reading by authorized parties. This type of access includes printing, displaying, and other forms of disclosure, including simply revealing the existence of an object.
- **Integrity:** Requires that computer system assets can be modified only by authorized parties. Modification includes writing, changing, changing status, deleting, and creating.
- **Availability:** Requires that computer system assets are available to authorized parties.
- **Authenticity:** Requires that a computer system be able to verify the identity of a user.

Computer System Assets

The assets of a computer system can be categorized as hardware, software, and data. Let us consider each of these in turn.

The main threat to computer system **hardware** is in the area of availability. Hardware is the most vulnerable to attack and the least amenable to automated controls. Threats include accidental and deliberate damage to equipment as well as theft. The proliferation of personal computers and workstations and the increasing use of local area networks increase the potential for losses in this area. Physical and administrative security measures are needed to deal with these threats.

The operating system, utilities, and application programs are the **software** that makes computer system hardware useful to businesses and individuals. Several distinct threats need to be considered.

A key threat to software is an attack on availability. Software, especially application software, is surprisingly easy to delete. Software can also be altered or damaged to render it useless. Careful software configuration management, which includes making backups of the most recent version of software, can maintain high availability. A more difficult problem to deal with is software modification that results in a program that still functions but that behaves differently than before. A final problem is software secrecy. Although certain countermeasures are available, by and large the problem of unauthorized copying of software has not been solved.

Hardware and software security are typically concerns of computing center professionals or individual concerns of personal computer users. A much more widespread problem is **data** security, which involves files and other forms of data controlled by individuals, groups, and business organizations.

Security concerns with respect to data are broad, encompassing availability, secrecy, and integrity. In the case of availability, the concern is with the destruction of data files, which can occur either accidentally or maliciously.

The obvious concern with secrecy, of course, is the unauthorized reading of data files or databases, and this area has been the subject of perhaps more research and effort than any other area of computer security. A less obvious secrecy threat involves the analysis of data and manifests itself in the use of so-called statistical databases, which provide summary or aggregate information. Presumably, the existence of aggregate information does not threaten the privacy of the individuals involved. However, as the use of statistical databases grows, there is an increasing potential for disclosure of personal information. In essence, characteristics of constituent individuals may be identified through careful analysis. To take a simple-minded example, if one table records the aggregate of the incomes of respondents A, B, C, and D and another records the aggregate of the incomes of A, B, C, D, and E, the difference between the two aggregates would be the income of E. This problem is exacerbated by the increasing desire to combine data sets. In many cases, matching several sets of data for consistency at levels of aggregation appropriate to the problem requires a retreat to elemental units in the process of constructing the necessary aggregates. Thus, the elemental units, which are the subject of privacy concerns, are available at various stages in the processing of data sets.

Finally, data integrity is a major concern in most installations. Modifications to data files can have consequences ranging from minor to disastrous.

Design Principles

Saltzer and Schroeder (1975) identify a number of principles for the design of security measures for the various threats to computer systems. These include the following:

- **Least privilege:** Every program and every user of the system should operate using the least set of privileges necessary to complete the job. Access rights should be acquired by explicit permission only; the default should be "no access."
- **Economy of mechanisms:** Security mechanisms should be as small and simple as possible, aiding in their verification. This usually means that they must be an integral part of the design rather than add-on mechanisms to existing designs.
- **Acceptability:** Security mechanisms should not interfere unduly with the work of users, while at the same time meeting the needs of those who authorize access. If the mechanisms are not easy to use, they are likely to be unused or incorrectly used.
- **Complete mediation:** Every access must be checked against the access-control information, including those

accesses occurring outside normal operation, as in recovery or maintenance.

- **Open design:** The security of the system should not depend on keeping the design of its mechanisms secret. Thus, the mechanisms can be reviewed by many experts, and users can therefore have high confidence in them.

PROTECTION MECHANISMS

The introduction of multiprogramming brought about the ability to share resources among users. This sharing involves not just the processor but also the following:

- memory;
- I/O devices, such as disks and printers;
- programs; and
- data.

The ability to share these resources introduced the need for protection. Pfleeger (1997) points out that an operating system may offer protection along the following spectrum:

- **No protection:** This is appropriate when sensitive procedures are being run at separate times.
- **Isolation:** This approach implies that each process operates separately from other processes, with no sharing or communication. Each process has its own address space, files, and other objects.
- **Share all or share nothing:** The owner of an object (e.g., a file or memory segment) declares it to be public or private. In the former case, any process may access the object; in the latter, only the owner's processes may access the object.
- **Share via access limitation:** The operating system checks the permissibility of each access by a specific user to a specific object. The operating system therefore acts as a guard, or gatekeeper, between users and objects, ensuring that only authorized accesses occur.
- **Share via dynamic capabilities:** This extends the concept of access control to allow dynamic creation of sharing rights for objects.
- **Limit use of an object:** This form of protection limits not just access to an object but the use to which that object may be put. For example, a user may be allowed to view a sensitive document, but not print it. Another example is that a user may be allowed access to a database to derive statistical summaries but not to determine specific data values.

The preceding items are listed roughly in increasing order of difficulty to implement, but also in increasing order of fineness of protection that they provide. A given operating system may provide different degrees of protection for different objects, users, or applications.

The operating system needs to balance the need to allow sharing, which enhances the utility of the computer system, with the need to protect the resources of individual users. This section considers some of the mechanisms by which operating systems have enforced protection for these objects.

Protection of Memory

In a multiprogramming environment, protection of main memory is essential. The concern here is not just security, but the correct functioning of the various processes that are active. If one process can inadvertently write into the memory space of another process, then the latter process may not execute properly.

The separation of the memory space of various processes is easily accomplished with a virtual memory scheme. Either segmentation or paging, or the two in combination, provides an effective means of managing main memory. If complete isolation is sought, then the operating system must simply assure that each segment or page is accessible only by the process to which it is assigned. This is easily accomplished by requiring that there be no duplicate entries in page and/or segment tables.

If sharing is to be allowed, then the same segment or page may appear in more than one table. This type of sharing is most easily accomplished in a system that supports segmentation or a combination of segmentation and paging. In this case, the segment structure is visible to the application, and the application can declare individual segments to be sharable or nonsharable. In a pure paging environment, it becomes more difficult to discriminate between the two types of memory, because the memory structure is transparent to the application.

Segmentation especially lends itself to the implementation of protection and sharing policies. Because each segment table entry includes a length as well as a base address, a program cannot inadvertently access a main memory location beyond the limits of a segment. To achieve sharing, it is possible for a segment to be referenced in the segment tables of more than one process. The same mechanisms are, of course, available in a paging system. However, in this case the page structure of programs and data is not visible to the programmer, making the specification of protection and sharing requirements more awkward. Figure 1 illustrates the types of protection relationships that can be enforced in such a system.

An example of the hardware support that can be provided for memory protection is that of the IBM System/370 family of machines, on which OS/390 runs. Associated with each page frame in main memory is a 7-bit storage control key, which may be set by the operating system. Two of the bits indicate whether the page occupying this frame has been referenced and changed; these are used by the page replacement algorithm. The remaining bits are used by the protection mechanism: a 4-bit access control key and a fetch-protection bit. Processor references to memory and direct memory access (DMA) I/O memory references must use a matching key to gain permission to access that page. The fetch-protection bit indicates whether the access control key applies to writes or to both reads and writes. In the processor, there is a program status word (PSW), which contains control information relating to the process that is currently executing. Included in this word is a 4-bit PSW key. When a process attempts to access a page or to initiate a DMA operation on a page, the current PSW key is compared to the access code. A write operation is permitted only if the codes

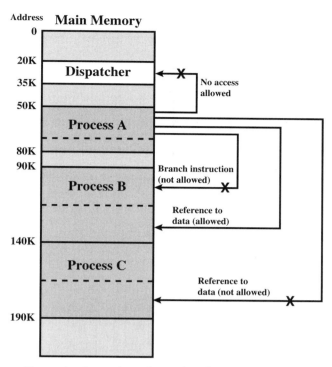

Figure 1: Protection relationships between segments.

match. If the fetch bit is set, then the PSW key must match the access code for read operations.

User-Oriented Access Control

The measures taken to control access in a data processing system fall into two categories: those associated with the user and those associated with the data.

The control of access by user is, unfortunately, sometimes referred to as authentication. Because this term is now widely used in the sense of message authentication, it is not applied here. The reader is warned, however, that this usage may be encountered in the literature.

The most common technique for user access control on a shared system or server is the user logon, which requires both a user identifier (ID) and a password. The system will allow a user to log on only if that user's ID is known to the system and if the user knows the password associated by the system with that ID. This ID/password system is a notoriously unreliable method of user access control. Users can forget their passwords and accidentally or intentionally reveal their password. Hackers have become very skillful at guessing IDs for special users, such as system control and system management personnel. Finally, the ID/password file is subject to penetration attempts.

User access control in a distributed environment can be either centralized or decentralized. In a centralized approach, the network provides a logon service that determines who is allowed to use the network and to what the user is allowed to connect.

Decentralized user access control treats the network as a transparent communication link, and the usual logon procedure is carried out by the destination host. Of course, the security concerns for transmitting passwords via the network must still be addressed.

In many networks, two levels of access control may be used. Individual hosts may be provided with a logon facility to protect host-specific resources and application. In addition, the network as a whole may provide protection to restrict network access to authorized users. This two-level facility is desirable for the common case, currently, in which the network connects disparate hosts and simply provides a convenient means of terminal-host access. In a more uniform network of hosts, some centralized access policy could be enforced in a network control center.

Data-Oriented Access Control

Following successful logon, the user has been granted access to one or a set of hosts and applications. This is generally not sufficient for a system that includes sensitive data in its database. Through the user access control procedure, a user can be identified to the system. Associated with each user, there can be a profile that specifies permissible operations and file accesses. The operating system can then enforce rules based on the user profile. The database management system, however, must control access to specific records or even portions of records. For example, it may be permissible for anyone in administration to obtain a list of company personnel, but only selected individuals may have access to salary information. The issue is more than just one of level of detail. Whereas the operating system may grant a user permission to access a file or use an application, following which there are no further security checks, the database management system must make a decision on each individual access attempt. That decision will depend not only on the user's identity but also on the specific parts of the data being accessed and even on the information already divulged to the user.

A general model of access control as exercised by a file or database management system is that of an **access matrix**, illustrated in Figure 2a, based on a figure in Sandhu and Samarati (1994). The basic elements of the model are as follows:

- **Subject:** An entity capable of accessing objects. Generally, the concept of subject equates with that of process. Any user or application actually gains access to an object by means of a process that represents that user or application.
- **Object:** Anything to which access is controlled. Examples include files, portions of files, programs, and segments of memory.
- **Access right:** The way in which an object is accessed by a subject. Examples are read, write, and execute.

One dimension of the matrix consists of identified subjects that may attempt data access. Typically, this list will consist of individual users or user groups, although access could be controlled for terminals, hosts, or applications instead of or in addition to users. The other dimension lists the objects that may be accessed. At the greatest level of detail, objects may be individual data fields. More aggregate groupings, such as records, files, or even the entire database, may also be objects in the matrix. Each entry in the matrix indicates the access rights of that subject for that object.

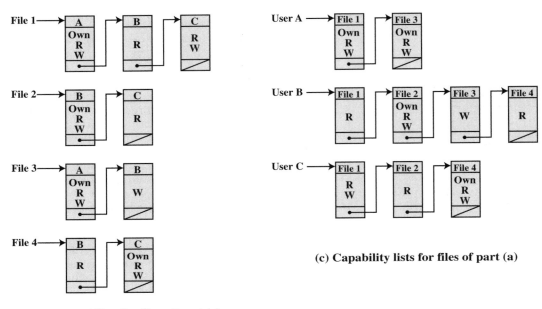

Figure 2: Example of access control structures.

In practice, an access matrix is usually sparse and is implemented by decomposition in one of two ways. The matrix may be decomposed by columns, yielding **access control lists** (Figure 2b). Thus for each object, an access control list lists users and their permitted access rights. The access control list may contain a default, or public, entry. This allows users who are not explicitly listed as having special rights to have a default set of rights. Elements of the list may include individual users as well as groups of users.

Decomposition by rows yields **capability tickets** (Figure 2c). A capability ticket specifies authorized objects and operations for a user. Each user has a number of tickets and may be authorized to loan or give them to others. Because tickets may be dispersed around the system, they present a greater security problem than access control lists. In particular, the ticket must be unable to be forged. One way to accomplish this is to have the operating system hold all tickets on behalf of users. These tickets would have to be held in a region of memory inaccessible to users.

Network considerations for data-oriented access control parallel those for user-oriented access control. If only certain users are permitted to access certain items of data, then encryption may be needed to protect those items during transmission to authorized users. Typically, data access control is decentralized, that is, controlled by host-based database management systems. If a network database server exists on a network, then data access control becomes a network function.

Protection Based on Operating System Mode

One technique used in all operating systems to provide protection is based on the mode of processor execution. Most processors support at least two modes of execution: the mode normally associated with the operating system and that normally associated with user programs. Certain instructions can only be executed in the more privileged mode. These would include reading or altering a control register, such as the program status word; primitive I/O instructions; and instructions that relate to memory management. In addition, certain regions of memory can only be accessed in the more privileged mode.

The less privileged mode is often referred to as the **user** mode, because user programs typically would execute in

Table 1 Typical Kernel Mode Operating System Functions

Process Management
- Process creation and termination
- Process scheduling and dispatching
- Process switching
- Process synchronization and support for interprocess communication
- Management of process control blocks

Memory Management
- Allocation of address space to processes
- Swapping
- Page and segment management

I/O Management
- Buffer management
- Allocation of I/O channels and devices to processes

Support Functions
- Interrupt handling
- Accounting
- Monitoring

this mode. The more privileged mode is referred to as the **system mode**, **control mode**, or **kernel mode**. This last term refers to the kernel of the operating system, which is that portion of the operating system that encompasses the important system functions. Table 1 lists the functions typically found in the kernel of an operating system.

The reason for using two modes should be clear. It is necessary to protect the operating system and key operating system tables, such as process control blocks, from interference by user programs. In the kernel mode, the software has complete control of the processor and all its instructions, registers, and memory. This level of control is not necessary, and for safety is not desirable for user programs.

Two questions arise: How does the processor know in which mode it is to be executing and how is the mode changed? Regarding the first question, typically there is a bit in the program status word (PSW) that indicates the mode of execution. This bit is changed in response to certain events. For example, when a user makes a call to an operating system service, the mode is set to the kernel mode. Typically, this is done by executing an instruction that changes the mode. When the user makes a system service call or when an interrupt transfers control to a system routine, the routine executes the change-mode instruction to enter a more privileged mode and executes it again to enter a less privileged mode before returning control to the user process. If a user program attempts to execute a change-mode instruction, it will simply result in a call to the operating system, which will return an error unless the mode change is to be allowed.

More sophisticated mechanisms can also be provided. A common scheme is to use a ring-protection structure. In this scheme, lower numbered, or inner, rings enjoy greater privilege than higher numbered, or outer, rings. Typically, ring 0 is reserved for kernel functions of the operating system, with applications at a higher level. Some utilities or operating system services may occupy an intermediate ring. Basic principles of the ring system are as follows:

1. A program may access only data that reside on the same ring or a less privileged ring.
2. A program may call services residing on the same or a more privileged ring.

An example of the ring protection approach is found on the VAX/VMS operating system, which uses four modes:

- **Kernel:** Executes the kernel of the VMS operating system, which includes memory management, interrupt handling, and I/O operations.
- **Executive:** Executes many of the operating system service calls, including file and record (disk and tape) management routines.
- **Supervisor:** Executes other operating system services, such as responses to user commands.
- **User:** Executes user programs, plus utilities such as compilers, editors, linkers, and debuggers.

A process executing in a less privileged mode often needs to call a procedure that executes in a more privileged mode; for example, a user program requires an operating system service. This call is achieved by using a change-mode (CHM) instruction, which causes an interrupt that transfers control to a routine at the new access mode. A return is made by executing the REI (return from exception or interrupt) instruction.

FILE SHARING

In a multiuser system, there is almost always a requirement for allowing files to be shared among a number of users. Two issues arise: access rights and the management of simultaneous access.

Access Rights

The file system should provide a flexible tool for allowing extensive file sharing among users. The file system should provide a number of options so that the way in which a particular file is accessed can be controlled. Typically, users or groups of users are granted certain access rights to a file. A wide range of access rights has been used. The following list is representative of access rights that can be assigned to a particular user for a particular file:

- **None:** The user may not even learn of the existence of the file, much less have access to it. To enforce this restriction, the user would not be allowed to read the user directory that includes this file.
- **Knowledge:** The user can determine that the file exists and who its owner is. The user is then able to petition the owner for additional access rights.

- **Execution:** The user can load and execute a program but cannot copy it. Proprietary programs are often made accessible with this restriction.
- **Reading:** The user can read the file for any purpose, including copying and execution. Some systems are able to enforce a distinction between viewing and copying. In the former case, the contents of the file can be displayed to the user, but the user has no means for making a copy.
- **Appending:** The user can add data to the file, often only at the end, but cannot modify or delete any of the file's contents. This right is useful in collecting data from a number of sources.
- **Updating:** The user can modify, delete, and add to the file's data. This normally includes writing the file initially, rewriting it completely or in part, and removing all or a portion of the data. Some systems distinguish among different degrees of updating.
- **Changing protection:** The user can change the access rights granted to other users. Typically, only the owner of the file holds this right. In some systems, the owner can extend this right to others. To prevent abuse of this mechanism, the file owner will typically be able to specify which rights can be changed by the holder of this right.
- **Deletion:** The user can delete the file from the file system.

These rights can be considered to constitute a hierarchy, with each right implying those that precede it. Thus, if a particular user is granted the updating right for a particular file, then that user is also granted the following rights: knowledge, execution, reading, and appending.

One user is designated as owner of a given file, usually the person who initially created a file. The owner has all of the access rights listed previously and may grant rights to others. Access can be provided to different classes of users:

- **Specific user:** Individual users who are designated by user ID.
- **User groups:** A set of users who are not individually defined. The system must have some way of keeping track of the membership of user groups.
- **All:** All users who have access to this system. These are public files.

Simultaneous Access

When access is granted to append or update a file to more than one user, the operating system or file management system must enforce discipline. A brute-force approach is to allow a user to lock the entire file when it is to be updated. A finer grain of control is to lock individual records during update. Issues of mutual exclusion and deadlock must be addressed in designing the shared access capability.

TRUSTED SYSTEMS

Much of what has been discussed so far has been concerned with protecting a given message or item from passive or active attack by a given user. A somewhat different but widely applicable requirement is to protect data or resources on the basis of levels of security. This is commonly found in the military, where information is categorized as unclassified (U), confidential (C), secret (S), top secret (TS), or beyond. This concept is equally applicable in other areas, where information can be organized into gross categories and users can be granted clearances to access certain categories of data. For example, the highest level of security might be for strategic corporate planning documents and data, accessible by only corporate officers and their staff; next might come sensitive financial and personnel data, accessible only by administration personnel, corporate officers, and so on.

When multiple categories or levels of data are defined, the requirement is referred to as **multilevel security**. The general statement of the requirement for multilevel security is that a subject at a high level may not convey information to a subject at a lower or noncomparable level unless that flow accurately reflects the will of an authorized user. For implementation purposes, this requirement is in two parts and is simply stated. A multilevel secure system must enforce the following:

- **No read up:** A subject can only read an object of less or equal security level. This is referred to in the literature as the **simple security property**.
- **No write down:** A subject can only write into an object of greater or equal security level. This is referred to in the literature as the **∗-property** (pronounced *star property*).

These two rules, if properly enforced, provide multilevel security. For a data processing system, the approach that has been taken, and has been the object of much research and development, is based on the *reference monitor* concept. This approach is depicted in Figure 3. The reference monitor is a controlling element in the hardware and operating system of a computer that regulates the access of subjects to objects on the basis of security parameters of the subject and object. The reference monitor has access to a file, known as the *security kernel database*, that lists the access privileges (security clearance) of each subject and the protection attributes (classification level) of each object. The reference monitor enforces the security rules (no read up, no write down) and has the following properties:

- **Complete mediation:** The security rules are enforced on every access, not just, for example, when a file is opened.
- **Isolation:** The reference monitor and database are protected from unauthorized modification.
- **Verifiability:** The reference monitor's correctness must be provable. That is, it must be possible to demonstrate mathematically that the reference monitor enforces the security rules and provides complete mediation and isolation.

These are stiff requirements. The requirement for complete mediation means that every access to data within main memory and on disk and tape must be mediated. Pure software implementations impose too high a performance penalty to be practical; the solution must be at least

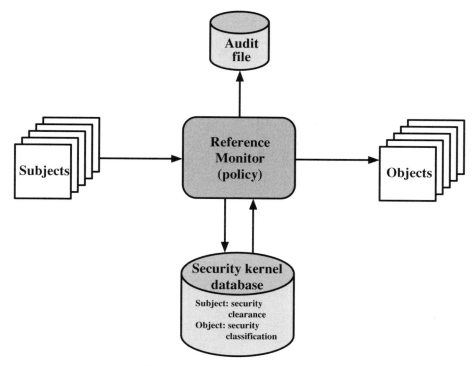

Figure 3: Reference monitor concept.

partly in hardware. The requirement for isolation means that it must not be possible for an attacker, no matter how clever, to change the logic of the reference monitor or the contents of the security kernel database. Finally, the requirement for mathematical proof is formidable for something as complex as a general purpose computer. A system that can provide such verification is referred to as a **trusted system**.

A final element illustrated in Figure 3 is an audit file. Important security events, such as detected security violations and authorized changes to the security kernel database, are stored in the audit file.

To encourage the widespread availability of trusted systems, standards bodies and interested government agencies worldwide have worked to define architectural principals and evaluation criteria. The goal is to be able to validate products that are designed to meet a range of security requirements. These product validations can serve as guidance to commercial customers for the purchase of commercially available, off-the-shelf equipment. Key to this effort is ISO (International Standards Organization) Standard 15408, known as the Common Criteria for Information Technology Security Evaluation. Based on this standard, there is a multinational effort, known as the Common Criteria Project, to further develop requirements, evaluation criteria, and product validations. The U.S. effort is conducted jointly by the National Security Agency and the National Institute of Standards and Technology.

Trojan Horse Defense

A Trojan horse is a computer program with an apparently or actually useful function that contains additional (hidden) functions that surreptitiously exploit the legitimate authorizations of the invoking process to the detriment of security. One way to secure against Trojan horse attacks is the use of a secure, trusted operating system. Figure 4 illustrates an example (Boebert, Kain, & Young, 1985). In this case, a Trojan horse is used to get around the standard security mechanism used by most file management and operating systems: the access control list. In this example, a user named Bob interacts through a program with a data file containing the critically sensitive character string "CPE170KS." User Bob has created the file with read/write permission provided only to programs executing on his own behalf: that is, only processes that are owned by Bob may access the file.

The Trojan horse attack begins when a hostile user, named Alice, gains legitimate access to the system and installs both a Trojan horse program and a private file to be used in the attack as a "back pocket." Alice gives read/write permission to herself for this file and gives Bob write-only permission (Figure 4a). Alice now induces Bob to invoke the Trojan horse program, perhaps by advertising it as a useful utility. When the program detects that it is being executed by Bob, it reads the sensitive character string from Bob's file and copies it into Alice's back-pocket file (Figure 4b). Both the read and write operations satisfy the constraints imposed by access control lists. Alice then has only to access the back-pocket file at a later time to learn the value of the string.

Now consider the use of a secure operating system in this scenario (Figure 4c). Security levels are assigned to subjects at logon on the basis of criteria such as the terminal from which the computer is being accessed and the user involved, as identified by password/ID. In this example, there are two security levels, sensitive (gray) and

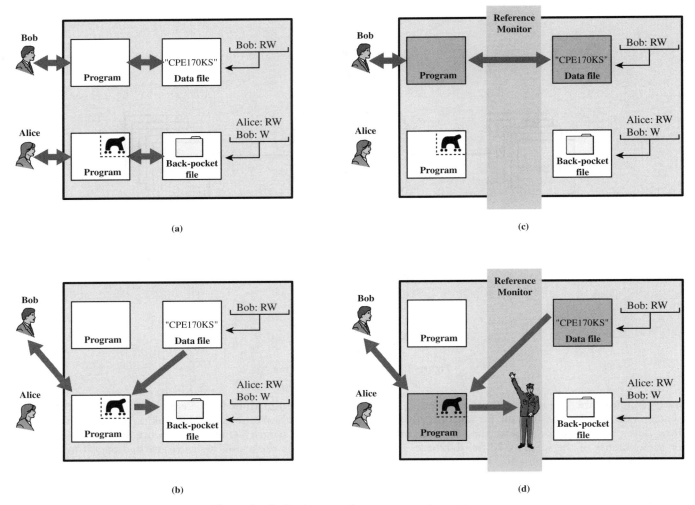

Figure 4: Trojan horse and secure operating system.

public (white), ordered so that sensitive is higher than public. Processes owned by Bob and Bob's data file are assigned the security level sensitive. Alice's file and processes are restricted to public. If Bob invokes the Trojan horse program (Figure 4d), that program acquires Bob's security level. It is therefore able, under the simple security property, to observe the sensitive character string. When the program attempts to store the string in a public file (the back-pocket file), however, the *-property is violated and the attempt is disallowed by the reference monitor. Thus, the attempt to write into the back-pocket file is denied even though the access control list permits it: The security policy takes precedence over the access control list mechanism.

GLOSSARY

Access Control Techniques and mechanisms that ensure that only authorized users have access to a particular system and its individual resources and that access to and modification of particular portions of data are limited to authorized individuals and programs.

Authenticity The requirement that a computer system be able to verify the identity of a user.

Availability The requirement that computer system assets are available to authorized parties when needed.

Confidentiality The requirement that the information in a computer system only be accessible for reading by authorized parties.

Integrity The requirement that computer system assets can be modified only by authorized parties. Modification includes writing, changing, changing status, deleting, and creating.

Password A character string used to authenticate an identity. Knowledge of the password and its associated user ID is considered proof of authorization to use the capabilities associated with that user ID.

Trojan Horse A computer program with an apparently or actually useful function that contains additional (hidden) functions that surreptitiously exploit the legitimate authorizations of the invoking process to the detriment of security.

Trusted System A computer and operating system that can be verified to implement a given security policy.

CROSS REFERENCES

See *Linux Security; OpenVMS Security; Unix Security; Windows 2000 Security*.

REFERENCES

Boebert, W., Kain, R., & Young, W. (1985, July). Secure computing: The secure ada target approach, *Scientific Honeyweller*. Reprinted in Abrams, M., & Podell, H. (1987). *Computer and Network Security*. Los Alamitos, CA: IEEE Computer Society Press.

Bransted, D., ed. (1978, February). *Computer security and the data encryption standard*. Gaitheisburg, MD: National Bureau of Standards, Special Publication No. 500–27.

Denning, P., & Brown, R. (1984, September). Operating systems. *Scientific American*.

Pfleeger, C. (1997). *Security in computing*. Upper Saddle River, NJ: Prentice Hall PTR.

Saltzer, J., & Schroeder, M. (1975, September). The protection of information in computer systems. *Proceedings of the IEEE*. 63, 9, 1278–1308.

Sandhu, R., & Samarati, P. (1994, September). Access control: Principles and practice. *IEEE Communications*.32, 9, 40–48.

FURTHER READING

Computer and Network Security Reference Index. Retrieved May 25, 2005 from http://www.vtcif.telstra.com.au/ info/security.html

Computer Security Resource Center. Retrieved May 25, 2005 from http://csrc.nist.gov/

Gasser, M. (1988). *Building a secure computer system*. New York: Van Nostrand Reinhold.

Gollmann, D. (1999). *Computer security*. New York: Wiley.

Stallings, W. (2003). *Cryptography and network security: Principles and practice* (3rd ed.). Upper Saddle River, NJ: Prentice Hall.

Trusted Computing Platform Alliance. Retrieved May 25, 2005 from http://www.trustedcomputing.org/home

UNIX Security

Mark Shacklette, *The University of Chicago*

WHAT IS SECURITY?

The topic of security in general, and of UNIX security in particular, is a vast subject. The word security comes from the Latin *securitas*, which literally means "without care." Thus, being secure, at least according to the Romans, meant feeling "safe," without a care in the world. The irony is that most people, when it comes to computers, take this approach toward security initially—they feel secure, even though, in fact, it is a false sense at heart. Computer crime is a growing business, and the threat of cyberterrorism is growing at an alarming rate. Every year for the past eight years, the Computer Security Institute and the Federal Bureau of Investigation have produced a report detailing the losses incurred by a number of industries, which includes input from 530 respondents representing sectors as diverse as government, retail, medical, high-tech, transportation, telecom, financial, and manufacturing, among others. The most recent report available, the 2003 Survey, reports the following staggering statistics:

- The most expensive form of loss was theft of intellectual property (proprietary information) with an average cost of $2.7 million *per incident*.
- The second most expensive form of loss was a denial of service attack, with an annual cost of $65 million and a per-incident cost of around $590,000. This figure was up 250% from the previous year.
- More than half of the respondents reported some form of unauthorized use (break-in) of their systems in the past year, with at least one out of five being a break-in from outside the organization.
- 82% of the responding companies had experienced a virus in the previous year.

The only good news in this report is that for the year 2003, the severity and cost of these attacks trended down for the first time since 1999, particularly in the area of fraud (Computer Security Institute & Federal Bureau of Investigation, 2003, 2004).

Part of this comes from the evolution of computing in general. Most home users have had "personal" computers for some years and only just now are connecting them a good deal of the day to a network (the Internet). Thus, a computer that is not connected to a network is a great deal more secure than one that is so connected. With the advent of low-cost Internet access, the world itself is literally connected and, as such, has generated, along with the inadvertent cooperation of bugs and limitations in software, a critical security problem.

Physical Versus Data Versus Privacy

When we examine the topic of security, we must make a distinction among the various ways in which computers and data can be compromised in terms of security. These ways include:

- The compromising of the physical security of the computer system.
- The compromising of the physical security of the data contained within the computer system.
- The compromising of the privacy protection surrounding the data on the computer system.

Any one of these can undermine security. For example, a computer system may be physically compromised if it is stolen from one's premises or if it is lost in a fire. In such cases, the physical computer itself is compromised but not *necessarily* the data. Certainly, in the case of a fire, the hard disk will almost certainly be damaged beyond repair, and if there are no copies (backups) of the data safely stored away, the data that were physically on a disk on the computer will be lost too. In this case, both the physical security of the computer as well as its data are compromised. However, in the case of a stolen computer, one of the key risks is that the physical security of the data is compromised, and if steps have not been taken to protect the privacy of the data contained within the computer, its data will be compromised in terms of its content—that is to say, others may be able to view the data and possibly modify it as well. On the other hand, if someone cracks into your computer network and accesses the data on your computer system, the cracker has effectively obtained access to your data, and if its privacy is not protected, the cracker can copy your data and your systems, or in some cases, given the level of capability of the cracker, copy it and then delete it, so that the cracker now owns your data and you do not.

Loss Versus Stealth

There are also different kinds of data loss. One type of loss involves the physical loss of data, such as in a fire, a stolen computer, a crashed disk, water damage from burst pipes, and so forth. The second type of loss deals with loss of information or privacy of information, in which the data are somehow compromised by unauthorized access for the purpose of stealing the information. There is also intentional vandalism—where data are accessed and then either modified or deleted or otherwise disabled, with the intention of damaging the owner of the information in some way, either financially or otherwise.

From this, we see that securing a computer system involves a number of different dimensions. First, we need to secure and protect the physical computer itself. This might involve obvious measures such as locking doors and securing entry, but also strategies such as providing climate-controlled storage, redirecting water, upgrading electrical supply, and so forth. Second, we need to secure access to the data on the computer system so that the data is not visible to unauthorized users. The latter can be effected by a robust authentication mechanism, access control, and possible encryption of data. All of this involves defining what it is that we need to secure. Once we know what we need to secure, we then have to define how we are going to secure it.

IMPORTANCE OF A SECURITY POLICY
Cost–Benefit Analysis

Defining how we are going to secure our UNIX system involves first doing some form of a cost–benefit analysis (CBA). All efforts at protecting data come with costs, and not all of them are monetary. Certainly, there are monetary costs involved with physically protecting our systems in terms of additional locks, doors, and security systems, which deter a physical break-in. But how much do we want to spend on our security system? Should it be the equivalent of a new lock on a door with a passkey or should it more resemble Fort Knox? Obviously, the latter will cost significantly more and may not be necessary. We need to define what the *likely* events are that would threaten our security, and direct our resources at shoring up *those* shortcomings rather than trying to protect against any conceivable threat. For example, the requirements for ensuring the protection of both the data and systems of a medical center are significantly different than the requirements for protecting the data and systems for the local

yacht club. In the former case, patients can be lost, people can die, and legal issues abound, whereas in the latter case, it is primarily an issue of inconvenience because the data for the membership can be recreated (with possible exposure of sensitive information such as credit card numbers, home addresses, etc.). However, the costs incurred in a security effort are not only monetary. There are costs in terms of inconvenience as well. If you impose too stringent a password policy on your customer base, for example, you may find that you have fewer customers to worry about. A solid CBA can be used to justify expenditures to those who will eventually pay for it.

After a CBA has been prepared and approved, a security strategy should be defined that details plans for implementing various security strategies and disaster plans for when those strategies (perhaps inevitably) fail. Few security strategies are foolproof, and those that are will generally be rejected by your user base except in the most stringent of security requirement circumstances (as in the case of national security). Thus, the strategy is to firmly define standard practices by which security will be achieved and enforced at your organization, and then plan what you are going to do in case of disaster—in case despite all your good plans a significant loss still does occur. Examples of disaster include a flood that crashes 50% of your disk arrays or a break-in that has compromised (or damaged) certain data. A disaster plan would categorize data into critical levels and will provide direction on what to do in case each level is breached. In the end, it really does not matter much whether your database was destroyed intentionally by a malicious cracker on the payroll of a competitor or accidentally destroyed by one of your own employees who was given too much power and not enough education. In both cases, you are out one database and will need to recover it somehow. It is your disaster plan that will define, among other things, the strategy for recovery of the database.

A security policy therefore defines the standard practices that will be implemented across an enterprise. It should include rules and regulations pertaining to user accounts and passwords (password length and characters, password aging); proper and improper use of computerized assets (no automated search bots, no pornography downloads, no creation of worms or viruses, etc.); various conditions under which a user can forfeit access to the computers, usually tied in tightly with improper use; and possibly a signed form consenting to monitoring and auditing of account activities, including the possible reading of email.

Audits

Merely having and even enforcing a security policy is insufficient if one does not take the time to track how well the security policy is being implemented. For this reason, security audits should take place periodically to provide input and review of how well or poorly a given policy is being implemented in an organization. A security audit can help provide metrics that may be useful later on in future CBAs or policy modifications. Audits can be conducted internally by the security staff or they can be contracted from by a consulting firm that specializes in security audits (almost always a better choice if affordable). In the end, security is a people matter. The more educated your users are concerning things such as password protection and, more important, why passwords need protecting, the more smoothly your security policing will run and the more successful you will be, with your users on board and assisting in the protection of the systems they use.

Personnel Checks

The users of the system are often the last line of defense and too often the first line of opportunity for those less than scrupulous. One of the things a security policy should take into consideration is background checks on personnel and other users of the system, if possible. It sometimes is not practicable, for instance, in a university where the user base is mostly made up of students. In corporations, personnel checks can easily be performed and should always be performed, regardless of the business. A personnel check that includes background checks can be priceless in the security efforts.

Open Source Versus Private Vendor Issues

A security policy should also define the policy regarding the use of open source software within the computer systems. Open source software is software that is released not only in binary compiled form but also with accompanying source code. The source code is in a programming language such as the C language. To some degree, the history of UNIX goes hand in hand with the notion of open source software. Indeed, when UNIX was first released, it was released with the source code. Since the early days of UNIX, there has been a concerted effort on the part of several different organizations to release software for UNIX that is open source. Most notable among these different efforts is the GNU effort of Richard Stallman.

The issues with open source from a security standpoint are somewhat complex, a bit like a double-edged sword. Because the source code is publicly available, many different eyes can examine the software's source code and can spot potential or actual defects in the source code. This means that responsible people can more easily spot and diagnose a security issue in open source and repair it more quickly than with closed source. There are fewer "surprises" in open source code. The risk here is that irresponsible people can also more easily spot those same security defects and potentially capitalize on them, if they quietly notice a problem before anyone else has discovered it. It is also possible that an unscrupulous person might use the source code to deduce other potential problems with some closed source systems, often because the same algorithms are used for both closed source as well as open source solutions. With closed source, the detection of security holes is much more difficult both for the would-be cracker and for those trying to diagnose how a breach has been conducted. Thus, *should* a breach be made on the basis of a defect discovered by a cracker in closed source code, there is a much smaller group of people available to discover the problem and fix it. There are arguments that open source software is actually *more* secure than non–open source because the features and limitations of the code are readily present for anyone to view. In actual fact, open source software has proved itself quite resilient to security breaches, although not immune. It is also possible, however, that because most cracker activity of late has been directed at the Windows operating system, the full weight of the cracker community has not turned its full attention toward open source systems and software, most notably Linux. For every Linux virus, there are hundreds written that attack various vulnerabilities in the closed-source Microsoft Windows environment.

Keeping Up With Patches and Releases

One of the effects of discovering a security bug in software, either closed source or open source, is the release of a software patch that attempts to fix the problem. A patch may be released in either source code or binary form or sometimes in both. A system administrator would then use the patch to update her software system to keep it "up to date" from a security standpoint. Although all patches are not necessarily security related, in general, security patches make up the vast majority of software patches released for an operating system and a good percentage of the patches released for standard end-user software applications. You can think of a security patch as an update to software that makes the software more secure than it was before. An example of a security patch is an update to a virus-scanning software system. When a new virus is identified, the way to remove it is encoded, and the virus software is thus patched, or updated, with the new capabilities. When a system administrator receives notice that a security patch is available, she will generally immediately download or otherwise obtain the patch and will update her software accordingly. This closes off one potential "hole" whereby a cracker might attempt to gain access to the system or otherwise create havoc.

When software is updated in a more general form, a new release may be offered to users of the software, whether that software is an operating system or an end-user application. Keeping up with new releases of software and security-related patches can allow a system administrator to feel more secure than she might otherwise be if she had not applied the patches and updated her software.

UNIX SECURITY
Login Security

Let's talk about system access first. Because UNIX is a multiuser environment, the system needs to provide a way for multiple users to use the system at the same time. This is done through a process known as the "login process." When a typical UNIX system starts up or "boots" (known as "bootstrapping"), the master boot sector of the primary hard disk partition is read into the computer's memory. It does several things, but eventually the UNIX kernel is started (a program on the disk called something like "unix" or "vmunix"). The kernel sets up the system, including initializing process tables, creating memory areas, establishing certain buffers and caches, and so forth. After the kernel has established a sane state, the kernel spawns (or "runs") a program known as "init." The init program is important because it ensures that the system is always ready in a particular "state." The UNIX operating system has various states, including boot (initialization), restart, shutdown, single, and multiuser. The normal state is multiuser, and when init begins this state, another program known as a "getty" (spelled from "get" and "tty" which is itself short for "teletype"—indicating a terminal) is started on a particular terminal. The getty process listens for activity from a terminal, and when a terminal is connected, getty runs another process known as "login," which prompts a user to log in to the UNIX system.

It is the login program that the average user first sees as the interface to a UNIX system. The user is prompted to enter her username. Once that has been entered, the user is prompted to enter her password. Once the user has entered her username and password, the login process examines her entries and compares the username and password (encrypted) entered by the user with the information that the superuser has entered for that user. (Users are usually allowed to alter their password within certain security constraints.)

If the user has *not* entered the correct information, the user is advised of the failure and is not allowed access to the system. At this point, the getty program spawns another login program and the user is prompted to log in again. If the user *has* entered the correct information, the user is logged on and the login process spawns yet another program, known as a command "shell," which prompts the user to enter commands to the system. The shell interfaces the user with the rest of the UNIX system and prompts the user to enter new commands. (A UNIX prompt usually is made up of a "$" character or a "%" character, depending on which type of shell is being used, or a "#" character in the case of the root administrator.)

Now let us turn our attention to file permissions. Files do not exist on the system accidentally. They are owned and created by users of the system. UNIX systems have users that operate in the user environment. Users have numbers associated with them known as a "userid." Each user also has a username that is associated with their particular userid. The username is the name under which the user accesses the system. Users also have passwords that authenticate them as legitimate users of the system. A user can use her userid and password to gain access to the system by logging on to the system.

Users may be arranged according to logical groupings for organizational as well as security purposes. For instance, the users tom, dick, and harry may be attorneys and therefore belong to the "attorneys" group. The users jane, linda, and ann may be members of the "clerks" group, and the users ken, donna, mary, and tom might be all members of the "partners" group. Groups are used to organize users into various categories, allowing for the ability to assign certain access rights to groups of individuals rather than on an individual basis.

There is one special user on every UNIX system, and that is the system administrator, sometimes called the "superuser" or "root." The superuser administers the system, which includes tasks such as managing the user community (creating accounts for users and managing groups), changing permissions on files, managing the system as

a whole, scheduling system backups, installing software, and so forth. The superuser can do almost anything on a UNIX system, so access to the superuser's password (sometimes called the "root" password) is highly controlled. Anyone logged in as the superuser can, for example, read other users' mail, read their files (unless the user has performed additional steps such as encrypting their file data), modify other users' files, delete files, and so forth. A nefarious user who has obtained the root password could, if he desired, delete every file on the UNIX system so that the system would no longer even start up.

Security on a UNIX system is a layered approach defined in terms of access to the system itself and its resources, including files and directories. Access to the system is managed by encrypted passwords associated with usernames during the login process.

File Systems Protection

Files may be read from, written to, and executed, depending on individual permissions. Every file in the UNIX file system (directories in UNIX are files) has a particular user who "owns" the file, as well as a group that is associated with the file. Groups collect users and give the ability to assign rights to a file to a group of users in addition to the single user who owns the file. You can see the file permissions for most any file in the system by typing the "ls –l" command. For example, if we have a file called contact.doc that is owned by the user "bob" and associated with the group "attorneys," we might see a long directory listing such as the following:

-rw-rw-r-- 1 tom attorneys 23872 March 15 2003 contact.doc

This set of information tells us the following:

- The file's name is "contact.doc."
- The user "tom" owns the file.
- The file is associated with the group "attorneys."
- The file contains 23,872 bytes.
- The file was last modified on March 15, 2003.
- There is one hard link to the file.
- The file's access permissions are -rw-rw-r–.

If we look at the symbolic rights of the legal contract.doc file, we see that the permissions are represented as "rw-rw-r--." This means that the owner would be able to read and write to the file (the first "rw-" in the triad) and the members of the group associated with the file would also be able to read and write to the file (the second "rw-" in the triad), but all others would only be able to read the file (the final "r--" in the triad). This would mean that only tom, the owner of the file, and all the members of the attorneys group, namely, dick and harry, could read and write to the file, whereas, all others (regardless of group) could not access the file for writing at all, with the exception of the superuser, who can read all files on the system. This brings us to the next topic of discussion, where we concern ourselves with data privacy and encryption.

Data Security

Backup Strategies

When we turn our attention to UNIX-specific data security, we need to talk about data security, both from a preservation standpoint and a privacy standpoint. Preservation of data simply means that there exist one or more backups of the software, usually stored on magnetic tape, so that if the original disk containing the data is somehow lost or corrupted, the backup copy of the data can be restored from the tape, thus saving the data from permanent loss. Magnetic tape is not the only storage solution for backup software. Some backup programs are able to back up to regular physical hard drives, magneto-optical disks (optical disks), writeable CD media, and writeable DVD media. Software applications designed to make copies of data and then restore that data in the event of loss are called "backup programs." Examples of popular backup solutions for UNIX include tar and cpio, with the traditional UNIX backup solutions called "dump" and "restore." An example of using tar to perform a backup follows:

tar -cf dev/rmt/0/home/opt/var/etc

This would back up the contents at the absolute path locations /home, /opt, /var, and /etc to the rewinding tape device associated with /dev/rmt/0. Rewinding tape devices are usually named something like /dev/rmt/0 or /dev/rmt/1 by convention. Tape devices which are nonrewinding are usually called something like /dev/rmt/0n (with the "n" somewhere denoting the device as nonrewinding.

A currently popular open source software solution is AMANDA, the Advanced Maryland Automated Network Disk Archiver, an open source utility developed at the University of Maryland. It has an advanced set of features and a wide user base. AMANDA allows you to set up a single master backup server to back up multiple hosts to a single backup drive. AMANDA relies on dump and/or tar and can back up any number of computers running multiple versions of UNIX. It can also be used to backup Microsoft Windows computers. There are other backup-like solutions, such as rsync and rdist, which allow you to make automatic copies of directory structures from one system to another. Each commercial UNIX operating system will generally offer some form of backup software solution for its users. Very often, these will be simple solutions such as dump, restore, tar, or cpio. There are commercial backup solutions available as well, including BRU (Backup and Restore Utility), Solstice Backup Utility for Solaris, SAM for HPUX, and so forth.

A backup strategy should be defined as part of a security policy, as it pertains to the protection of data. Backup strategies should define, among other things, what files need to be backed up and how often, who should perform the backups, where the backup should be directed and to what type of media (tape, optical, etc.), how long the backups need to be retained before being destroyed or overwritten, and how long it should take to be able to restore a particular file from the backup media. One important question that should also be considered is where to store the backup media themselves. For example, if you store the backup tapes onsite, then you risk the potential loss of the backups as well as the originals in certain situations such as theft and flood. Storing the backup tapes offsite may give more physical protection to the tapes (it is doubtful that the home office on Omaha would burn down at the same time the backup center in Cleveland also ignites). Storing the tapes on site will allow for quicker restores, however, as they are readily accessible, whereas it would take a while to retrieve and restore a tape that is stored offsite.

Backups are usually of two types: a full backup of the system or a partial backup of the system. A full backup will do what it says, back up every single file on the system, regardless of whether or not it has changed since the last time the data was backed up. This gives a full "snapshot" of the entire system at a given point in time, but at the cost of time and tape. It usually takes a significant amount of time to back up a complete system, and this is one reason why backups are often performed overnight or over the weekend. Finding a particular file on a full backup can be quite time-consuming, as in nonindexed media solutions, the entire tape might need to be scanned just to find one file. Partial backups are backups that are either of a fixed subset of the data on a system or an *incremental* backup that only backs up the data that has *changed* since the last time a full backup was made. Partial backups generally take much less time to perform, and restores from incremental backups tend to be much faster than restores from full backups. The best practice is to set up a backup schedule that defines when full and partial backups are to be made, as well as specifying rotation of tapes. For example, a security policy might prescribe that a full backup of the systems is performed on Saturday night of every week, and incremental backups are taken every other night of the week, all on separate tapes. The policy might also specify that there must always be on hand the past 8 weeks' worth of full and incremental backups before a given tape can be "reused." The policy might also specify that if an error is encountered at any time during the backup, the physical tape is not to be reused but is rather to be replaced, even if it is brand new. The policy might also state that redundant copies are to be made and stored separately from the primary set to ensure added protection. Some businesses simply would be out of business if their data should be permanently lost.

Data Encryption

Once the physical security of the systems is ensured and the data are protected from permanent loss by a secure backup strategy, there remains the issue of data privacy.

Data privacy is the protection of data by making it unreadable by parties not authorized for such viewing and reading. Primary strategies for ensuring data privacy include file access protection and data encryption.

If the superuser's account is compromised by an unscrupulous user who has discovered the password or otherwise figured out how to gain access to the root shell (a command interface that allows commands to be issued to a UNIX system), that unscrupulous user can now access any file on the system, regardless of the access permissions of the given files themselves. This means that the superuser could read Bob's contract file, even though the root user does not own the file nor is the root user a member of the group attorneys. The reason for this is that the superuser essentially does "own" access to the entire filesystem and thereby all the files on it. This means that the superuser could open the contract.doc file, change some of its contents, and no one would be any wiser if this was not noticed by some other party. Encryption is the primary method of protecting the privacy of the data so that the actual content is transformed into a meaningless series of characters, usually using some kind of secret key, known only to the owner of the file who chooses to encrypt it.

Historically, encryption has tended to be used primarily by lovers seeking secure communications and by the military, that is to say, for love and war. In Victorian England, lovers would occasionally place encrypted messages in the London newspapers for their partners to decrypt and read. David Kahn has written an excellent history of encryption called *The Code Breakers* (1996), in which he details cryptography all the way back to ancient Greece and Rome. Ancient ciphers used to be based on a technique of substitution. The Caesarian cipher, for example, substituted every letter with the third next letter, so "a" would become "d," "b" would become "e," "c" would become "f," and so forth, with the last three letters wrapping around to the beginning of the alphabet.

Modern cryptography is partially based on an algorithmic strategy known as transposition. Original text is compressed and transposed as part of the algorithm's progress. Once a file is encrypted, not even the superuser can "decrypt" it, not unless she knows the secret key for "unlocking" the encrypted file. This does not mean that the superuser cannot open the file up, say, in an editor. She can. However, what she would see is a meaningless series of gobbledygook and therefore it would be unintelligible.

Encryption

Figure 1 shows the user typing out a file called legal. contract.doc, encrypting the file using an encryption tool called Pretty Good Privacy, or PGP, and then typing out the garbled contents of the resulting encrypted file.

You can see that when the user issues the command pgp –c legal.contract.doc, the user is prompted for a secret key that only he knows. Once he enters the key (in this case, the key was "asdf," but you cannot see it typed), he is prompted to enter the same key ("asdf") once again. This second entry ensures that the user did not make an error when he entered the key in the first place. If the second key matches the first key entered, the file is encrypted using a default cipher and stored (in the case of PGP) in a file called legal.contract.doc.pgp. The figure shows the user then typing out the contents of the newly encrypted file, and you can easily see that the contents of the encrypted file are quite inscrutable.

PGP (and GnuPGP) are based on a type of encryption known as public key encryption. Public key encryption uses two separate but mathematically related keys and is technically referred to as asymmetric encryption (symmetric encryption uses the same key to both encrypt and decrypt data). In asymmetric encryption, one key is *public*, meaning that it can be freely published and made available to the entire world. The second key is *private* and known only to the owner of the keyset. Only public keys can be used to encrypt text. The public key cannot be used to decrypt text; only the owner's private key can be used for decryption. This means that if I have established a keyset based on a particular cipher (see the chapter on public key algorithms for more detailed information on particular ciphers), my friends can encrypt files with the public key that I have provided to them, perhaps on my Web site,

Figure 1: Encrypting a file with pgp.

and anyone who uses that public key can encrypt files that only I can read. This allows me to decrypt an e-mail message sent from a friend who has my public key, and I (and only I) can decrypt it and read its contents using my private key. If she has herself established a public/private key pair, I can then encrypt a response to her using her public key, and she can decrypt and thus read my response that I encrypted using her private key.

This means that file encryption can be used to protect the privacy of data. Once a file is encrypted, it can only be decrypted by someone who knows the right (private) key for decryption. A user can create her own key pair (using PGP) by issuing the command

pgp –kg,

which instructs the pgp program to generate (g) a key (k) pair for her. The encryption strategies used in these types of public key systems (128 bits and above) is secure enough that it would take millions of years for all the computers on the earth to crack the encryption and decrypt the original text. However, often one does not have to go to great lengths to decrypt someone else's text. A woman who enjoys riding Harleys might have a key whose plaintext is based on the string "bikergirl," so one's interests can greatly reduce the difficulty of guessing a key. Family member names (including pets) are also ripe for the picking. If someone has children named anna and danny, a good guess for a key would be "dannyanna" or "annadanny," or "9294," signifying the years of their respective birthdays (1992 and 1994). As long as keys are created that are not too easy for someone to guess, modern cryptographic algorithms make a brute force attack on the keys rather unlikely. The actual difficulty of a brute force attack is primarily dependent on the length of the key itself. When creating a key, the same principles should be employed as are employed in creating a strong password. See the chapters on PGP for more information on pgp and the chapter on encryption basics for a more general introduction.

Passwords

As we said earlier, each user on a UNIX system is given a userid and a password. Generally, the users can change these passwords when they want, and often a security policy will specify the number of times a password can be reused ("lifetimes") before the system forces a user to change her password. The way UNIX deals with passwords is ingeniously simple. A program called *crypt* is used to encrypt the password a user enters when changing her password. The encrypted password is then stored on the system associated with that user (usually in a file called /etc/passwd or /etc/shadow). A password entry in /etc/passwd has the following form:

root:x:0:1:System Administrator:/:/bin/sh
bobby:x:1234:23:Bobby Burns:/home/bobby:/bin/ksh

These entries specify two users in the system: root, the system administrator, and "bobby." The root user has a userid of 0 and a groupid of 1, is named "System

Administrator," and has a home directory of / and a default shell of /bin/sh. The bobby user has a userid of 1234 and a groupid of 23, his full name is Bobby Burns, his home directory is /home/bobby, and his default shell is the Korn shell: /bin/ksh. What is interesting about this from a security standpoint is the "x" that appears in both entries. This indicates that shadow passwords are in effect. Shadow passwords are often used because the /etc/passwd file by default is a plain text file and is generally world-readable. Prior to shadow passwords, the actual encrypted password would appear in the publicly readable /etc/passwd file. With the introduction of shadow passwords, only someone with root privileges can see the actual encrypted passwords. The actually encrypted password (passwords are never stored on the system in an unencrypted state) is held in a separate file that only the system administrator or root can read, usually called something like /etc/shadow or something similar. The actual algorithm used is based on the DES 56-bit standard. When a user wants to change her password, the system selects something called a *salt* value, based on the time of day. The salt value is a number between 0 and 4095 that Morris and Thompson, who developed the DES algorithm, used to alter slightly the encryption process so that the same password can be encrypted in 2^{12} (4096) different ways. The result is that the user's password is used as an encryption key to encrypt a 64-bit block of 0's, with the salt value modifying the process. The resulting 64-bit ciphertext is then encrypted again with the user's password, and this process is repeated as often as 25 times. The final 64 resulting bits are then converted into a "plaintext" string of often 11 or more printable characters, prepended by the plaintext of the salt value, and it is these characters that are stored into the password file. An example of the root user changing the password for a user named "korn" to the password text "nobadaddy" is shown in Figure 2.

When we grep the /etc/shadow for the user korn, we see that the resultant encryption of the password "nobadaddy" is stored as "1esCKPD.2$9e92Gym. XPN38oGiRCbl.1." For reference, the salt value of this password is "$1."

Then, every time that user logs in, she is prompted to enter her password to gain access. When she enters her password, it is immediately encrypted using the same default key, and the result is matched with the encrypted password stored for that user on the system. The system also does not echo what she is typing to her terminal screen, lest someone is watching over her shoulder or a transcript of her session is being recorded (using something such as *script*, for instance). If the encrypted passwords match, the user is "authenticated" and allowed to log in. If they do not match, the user is denied the right to log in to the system. Many organizations will establish rules within their security plan that specify what types of passwords are allowed. For example, some systems will have a six- or eight-character minimum limit, which would disallow passwords such as "mike" and "tom." Some organizations will also require that there be at least some combination of different types of characters, such as requiring at least one numeric character or some non-alphanumeric character such as #, !, or %. A good password is one that is not easy to guess, is random, and is not

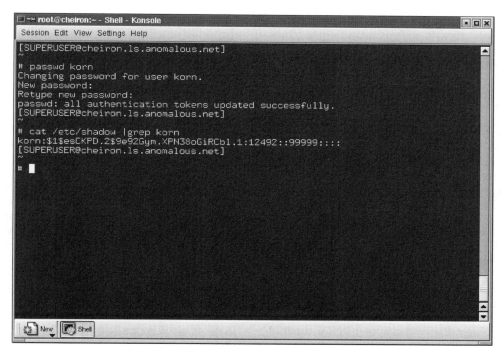

Figure 2: Changing a password in Unix.

based on any word in any human language. For instance, a bad password for William Rogers would be "bill" and a good password would be "Wstmzoe%76." However, there are difficulties with these approaches, and this brings us back to the human factor. A system that hands out default passwords to its users (without allowing them to choose their passwords—even within certain limitations) in the form of "Wstmzoe%76" and then changes it every several months is virtually guaranteeing that the user is going to write that down on a sticky note in their desk! Who in the world could remember that? Organizations can achieve better security (because sticky notes are not necessary) by suggesting that users create acronyms that exceed the minimum character length and requiring the use of numeric and other character types. For example, no one would figure that the password "amsr#1" in reality stands for "Ann, Mary, Sarah Are Number 1"—a good password for a mom whose daughters are named Ann, Mary, and Sarah. This might only be guessable by someone who knows that mother rather well. Examples of bad passwords would be your name or the name of anyone in your family, your pet's name, your company name, your bithdate, your social security number, obvious geekisms such as "bilbo," "gandalf," "UNIXguru," or "albus." Other examples would include any word in any dictionary in any human language, passwords of the same or repetitive letters, and simple typing examples such as "qwerty" or "asdf."

UNIX users will generally use the passwd or yppasswd programs to change their passwords. Sometimes, depending on the exact policy in place, a user is forced to change their password every 100 logins or every three months. Generally, when such a policy is in place, they are required to change it to something other than a recently used password. This ensures that users actually do *change*

their passwords rather than just reenter the same password they have been using for 10 years.

Authentication Versus Authorization

When we talk about passwords, we generally make a distinction between the concepts of *authentication* and *authorization*. Authentication is the process of proving one's identity to the system—that of logging on and entering the correct password. Once we have authenticated ourselves to the system, there is still the question of exactly what we are authorized to see and modify. Authentication with passwords is not the only means of authentication. Authentication can be performed by attaching physical devices to systems, such as biometric scanning with a retina scanner or a hand scanner, a voice scanner, or even a simple card scanner. In the case of the card scanner, a physical key card is entered (like an ATM machine card) into a device and is read. Often, more security can be obtained by coupling various methods, for example, authenticating with both a good password scheme as well as a hand-geometry scan. There are many companies that offer biometric scanning devices that can be added to an authentication system.

Smart Cards

Perhaps one of the most secure forms of authentication is the use of one-time passwords (OTPs). OTPs generally come in two forms, either as smart cards or as conventional passwords that are used only one time and then discarded. OTPs are an expensive and fairly major overhaul for most UNIX systems but nevertheless can be a highly effective deterrent to conventional authentication with remembered passwords. The concept here is that the user has some kind of key card that is interactive to the degree that data can be entered and displayed. When someone logs into a UNIX system with such a hardware token system, the computer presents a "challenge" that can then be "looked up" in the smart card device. For example, the challenge is "harry"; the result that the key card or smart card would display might be "sushjli23876t4," which is the OTP for logging in to the computer. The next time the user wants to log in, a different challenge is presented and therefore a different password is used. The card is protected because the user still must have a password, or PIN, to enter in the challenge into the card. Of course, if the smart card is compromised as well as the PIN, anyone can log in to the system. The combination of biometrics and hardware tokens is very powerful. Instead of entering a numeric PIN to authorize access to entering the challenge into the smart card, a scan is made of your fingerprint to verify that it is indeed you who is holding the key card (although fingerprints may be fabricated).

One of the more interesting developments over the past several years in the world of authentication is Sun's creation of the PAM (Pluggable Authentication Module) architecture. PAM delivery has become so popular and makes so much sense that most major UNIX vendors have adopted it, including Linux. A PAM abstracts out *the way in which* authentication takes place and places that implementation in a PAM. Examples of PAMs include implementations for secure cards, for Kerberos, for the chroot command, for ftp, and so forth. Understanding the reasons for PAMs requires understanding why they are needed. The problem is easily seen in Kerberos itself, in that any application that wants to authenticate over Kerberos must be rewritten to do so. We need a Kerberos telnet, a Kerberos ftp, a Kerberos rsh, and so forth. The reason for this rewriting is that the means of authentication is hard coded within each of these applications. The default telnet application assumes a standard UNIX login authentication, not Kerberos. The question is, why not extract out the code that performs the authentication into some external module that the main program loads and then accesses, much like a shared library? With that approach, various modules that provide authentication services differently could be "plugged and played" with various applications quite easily. Thus, to switch from a basic UNIX authentication to a Kerberos implementation does not require rewriting telnet but rather using the Kerberos PAM as opposed to the basic login authenticator. Then, if we wanted to switch telnet to use a smart card, we might use the SecurID PAM, which allows for that capability. As you can see, using PAMs for authentication is highly beneficial, and this is why there have been PAMs written to provide many different forms of authentication, all with a "plug and play" capability.

Access Control Lists

Just because someone has been authenticated to the system does not mean she is *authorized* to do whatever she wants. Authorization means determining whether an authenticated user is authorized to access in one way or another some resource, whether it be a file, directory, device, or whatever. Authorization can be implemented in a variety of ways. The primary means of authorization is in the standard UNIX use of file permissions. If I am not the owner of a file nor a member of the group associated with the file and others have no access to the file, I am not authorized to view or modify its contents. Another means of authorization is in the form of access control lists, or ACLs for short. ACLs extend the standard UNIX permissions concept to allow for a finer-grained control of individual files and directories. A directory, for instance, can be wrapped in an ACL, which would then allow you to specify individual user's rights that go beyond file ownership and group ownership. We can say that the user bob has read only access, user steve has read/write access, the groups lawyers and partners have read/write access, and the group accountants has only read access. We can also specifically deny access to any group or individual, or to everyone, and then specifically add the particular access rights we wish. ACLs are available for most modern UNIX systems, include AIX and HPUX. Linux and Solaris implement POSIX ACLs. Thus, ACLs help extend the normal UNIX access permission concept to implement a broader range of permission possibilities.

Role-Based Access Control

Another modern extension to the standard UNIX permissions is the concept of role-based access control, or RBAC for short. By defining roles, permissions can be associated with a given role, users can be added to a role, and those permissions can apply to the role irrespective of the particular target (file or directory) in question. RBACs can be used to give a user or set of users a specific permission to perform a specific activity (and only that activity) that usually needs to be done by the superuser. A role is therefore a subset of activities generally reserved for the superuser. RBACs are specifically supported in AIX and Solaris, and some efforts to support them are under way in other UNIX operating systems, including Linux. Solaris can specify a number of roles that constitute logical accounts, which can assume additional privileges when needed using the su (superuser) command. Both Solaris and AIX support a number of commands specifically tailored to managing the RBAC environment. For example, the chuser command can be used to change role assignments:

Chuser roles = ManageBackup bill

Network Security and Firewalls

One of the problems with the introduction of the personal computer was the implicit assumption that security, outside of physical security, was not a problem. This is why early DOS, CPM, and Windows operating systems did not require you to log in when first turning on the computer. UNIX, on the other hand, was always dedicated to the concept of multiple users, and it was not long before the University of California at Berkeley had introduced a good solution for networking UNIX computers together. When one computer is networked to another, a whole new set of security concerns arise, and we need to talk about these as well because there are a number of different types of security problems that are available to keep us up at night. Sometimes network services are designed to allow for minimum security (often because network latency is always a problem and security further slows things down), such as the original Sun Network File System (NFS) and MIT's X11 XWindows system. Many different bugs were identified early on, and some people gained inappropriate access via those bugs. Equally problematic are bugs in network software (a prime example is the sendmail program), whereby the unscrupulous can cause a program to crash because of a buffer overrun and thereby gain some unauthorized access. Networks communicate via a wire by passing packets from one host to another. Each host assumes that the "host" it is talking to is indeed the legitimate host it thinks it is talking to, but IP spoofing allows one host to impersonate another and thereby possibly allows sensitive information to be derived that can then be used to further penetrate the systems. Most software is written with the legitimate user in mind. It took a while for developers to understand that they also needed to write their software with the more mischievous in mind as well. Of course, the flippant counter to network security is that if you want your computers totally secure, take them off the network. This is akin to saying if you want to rid your body of an infection, shoot yourself. We have to have computers networked to operate our businesses, universities, and governments, and now, even our homes. UNIX has developed a number of technical solutions that are directed toward making network security more of a reality.

rsh, rexex, and ssh

One of the first attempts to ease networking use in the UNIX environment was to give users the ability to log in remotely to another computer, one that they were not physically in front of. The primary utilities that allowed this were a set of commands known as the "r" commands: rsh, rexec, and rlogin. For example, rsh would allow a user to remotely log in to a shell on another computer on which he had permission. Permission is given either locally to a specific user or globally for a specific computer. Thus, we could allow the user bob to log in to the machine cheiron from the host machine bubba by adding an entry in a file called .rhosts in bob's home directory on cheiron. This way, whenever bob was logged in to bubba and wished to rsh or rlogin into cheiron, he could do so *without having to enter a password*. This is the notion of equivalence. When we add an entry to the .rhosts file, we are essentially saying that the system should consider the hosts cheiron and bubba as being *the same machine* as far as the user bob is concerned. That is to say, once bob has successfully authenticated himself to bubba, cheiron will automatically trust him. The obvious problem here is that once the bob account is penetrated on bubba, further penetrating the host cheiron becomes a walk in the park. The problem is further complicated because there can exist a system wide access file called /etc/hosts.equiv, which allows you to enter all the hosts that are equivalent to this one, so that anyone logged in on one of the equivalent hosts is automatically trusted without having to enter a password to gain access. This creates a wide-open door for unscrupulous users, so much so that the r commands are generally not supported via /etc/hosts.equiv and ~user/.rhosts files anymore. The problem gets worse. Most UNIX systems, if you have physical access, can be booted in something called "single user mode," which is a special

mode designed for system repair and maintenance. The problem is that once booted in single user mode, the user can su to any account she wishes. She can become anyone she wants! Now, if the bob account has an .rhosts file that includes the node that has been booted in single user mode, or if the /etc/hosts.equiv file includes that node, the user can now become root on the remote computer as bob, or anyone else she wants! This user can read other's files and do whatever she wants with impunity under that remote user.

The r commands grew up in the days of the local network that did not have much open access to the outside world. In this sense, these closed networked environments had much to gain from trusted access among the peer computers on the local network. An example of such a small network environment would be the computer network at a local community college, for instance. Common r commands include rwho, rlogin, rsh, rexec, and rcp, a program that lets you remotely copy a file from one computer to another.

However, the r commands can still be used even if global and user access is not defined in the /etc/hosts.equiv and ~user/.rhosts files. The user is simply prompted for a password, and once she enters the correct password, she is authenticated on the remote computer. Simple. Other programs, such as FTP and the common utility telnet, which gives a remote terminal as well, do essentially the same thing. The user enters the computer they wish to connect to, they are prompted to enter their password, and once they enter the password, it is passed over the net to the remote computer and the user is authenticated (or not) and allowed or disallowed access. The problem with the r commands as well as telnet is that when the password is passed over the wire, the password is passed in plaintext! That is to say, if the password is "nobadaddy," the literal string "nobadaddy" is passed over the network, which might well venture through routes that have a sniffer listening for network traffic. The passing of a password over the network in plaintext is tantamount to broadcasting your password on a bulletin board. For this reason, most UNIX networks today do not support the r commands out of the box, and most network firewalls have blocked port 23, which is the port for telnetd.

A nice solution to this problem is delivered with the Secure Shell suite of tools, most notably, ssh and scp. Ssh is a secure shell that allows you to log in to another computer on a network and works just like rsh, with the exception that the entire communication, including password authentication, is conducted over a secure encrypted channel. Scp works basically the same way as rcp except over an encrypted channel, allowing you to copy one file to another computer. Not only is the password sent over in encrypted form, but the entire session is conducted over an encrypted channel. Thus, the ssh suite of tools (which includes sftp) provides a much-needed and highly useful solution to security, and it is based on the familiar protection mechanism of public key cryptography, which we have already discussed. Sshd, the ssh server daemon, allows for significant variations, some would say nontrivial, in management and configuration. For example, administrators can choose to allow or deny port forwarding, RSA authentication, and forwarding of XWindows communication.

There is a commercial version of Secure Shell as well as various open source solutions, the most common of which is Openssh, available at http://www.openssh. com. See the chapter on public key standards for more detailed information.

NIS and NIS+

One of the problems faced by networked UNIX computers is the sharing of a single network-wide password file, which essentially allows any user defined on the network to log into any computer on the network. An administration nightmare arose as system administrators were constantly having to go into each individual node and update the password file there when a new user would come or go. And then there were the ubiquitous exceptions, where user bob would be granted access to all computers with the exception of bubba, whereas user sue would be granted access to all computers, including bubba, with the exception of cheiron. It was a maintenance nightmare full of risks and clearly a centralized solution for the handling of common login definitions was needed. Several different solutions were presented in UNIX, most notably Sun's NIS and NIS+, and Kerberos.

With NIS+ (we will talk about the improved version of NIS only), a single computer is designated as the NIS root domain server (there can be redundant secondary and tertiary servers as well). When a new user is added to the network, the password database (such as /etc/passwd) on the root domain server is the only one that is updated. This change is then automatically propagated to the other redundant servers, and all computers that are part of the NIS+ domain are updated so that the new user can log on to any of the machines. This means that once a user has been added into the NIS+ domain, she can log into any computer on that domain to which she has not been specifically denied access. All communication between principals (clients) and the NIS+ root domain server is done via Secure RPC, which offers encrypted communication channels.

NIS+ also supports the notion of groups, which basically simplifies the management of the NIS+ environment and makes it less likely to make mistakes. It is a lot easier to say that bob, sue, debbie, sandy, ralph, and steve are members of the backupadmin group, and to give the Netgroup backupadmin certain access permissions, than it is to individually list all the individual users, especially when it becomes necessary to remove sandy from the list! If we are using groups, all we do is remove sandy from the particular group, and she is removed from all referencing nodes as a backupadmin.

The downside of all this is that the original NIS has often been the initial target of the unscrupulous and the first line of access into a UNIX network. Because NIS manages network access, it is obvious that if you can convince it that you are who you are not, then you can gain additional access information that could be used to further penetrate a UNIX network. NIS+ has shored up many of the easier access points into the network, but some still remain and are sometimes used to break into a network. There are several commands associated with NIS+ that can be used to administer the NIS+ server as well as several user commands, including nispasswd, which will allow a user to change his password on the NIS+ server.

Kerberos

In the early 1980s, MIT, in collaboration with IBM and DEC, attempted to solve the same problem that NIS was designed to solve, but for DEC computers running BSD UNIX. This was how to simplify the administration of multiple users who all need access to various machines on a local network and to do this in a secure fashion. The security is delivered by Kerberos through its use of DES cryptography (see the chapter on data encryption standard for more information on DES). When someone logs in to a Kerberos network, the user is issued something called a *ticket* from the Kerberos server. Log in is done by issuing the command *kinit*. This ticket is encrypted, and all access along the network from that point on is done by passing around this encrypted ticket. This initial ticket delivered is sometimes referred to as the ticket-granting ticket (TGT), because it is used to derive further access tickets from the Kerberos system. By using multiple tickets, audits can be done recording a user's activities throughout the system, something that would be difficult to do with a single ticket per user. Each ticket has a default time to live (TTL), which defaults to eight hours, after which the ticket expires and a new one must be obtained from the server by reauthentication. Thus, whereas the r commands used static files to grant equivalent access so that the user did not have to keep reentering his password, Kerberos uses the concept of an expiring ticket to provide basically the same ability. Thus, because Kerberos transactions operate via an encrypted channel, familiar programs such as telnet can be run on Kerberos systems with security. The difference between Kerberos-modified rsh and ssh, for example, is that by default Kerberos only encrypts the authentication process and the remainder of the session goes over in plaintext. You can pass the –x option to Kerberos rsh, and then the entire rsh session is encrypted, not simply the encrypted ticket negotiation. Kerberos, similar to NIS+, has a number of administration utilities as well as user commands. The user command to change a password in Kerberos is cpw, and if the user bob wanted to change his password on a Kerberos system (after an initial authentication), the command might look like this:

```
$ cpw bob
Enter password for principal "bob":
Re-enter password for principal "bob":
Password for bob@MYNET.COM changed.
```

Kerberos is available for most major versions of UNIX, including AIX, Solaris, Mac OSX, Linux, and BSD. It is also available on modern Microsoft Windows servers (2000 and XP, for example). MIT Kerberos source code can be obtained from http://web.mit.edu/kerberos/www/. See the chapter on Kerberos for more detailed information on Kerberos and its configuration.

NFS

One of the things administrators of a network want to do is to make available networked hard drives for access by multiple computers. Very often, on an average UNIX network, the /opt mountpoint, for instance, will actually be a shared directory on a drive on a remote file server. All authorized networked computers will be able to see this drive, and it will appear to the user on the local computer that this drive is actually physically local to the computer in Chicago, whereas in reality it could exist on a file server running in Tokyo. This sort of magic is generally conducted in the UNIX world by using a technology known as Network Filesystem (NFS), originally developed by Sun Microsystems beginning in the early 1980s, first for its SunOS operating system and then later for Solaris.

NFS allows one computer, a file server, to designate certain drives as available for access by clients. This allows a client computer, so authorized, to be able to "mount" the drive or directory on the file server and have that mount appear as "local" to the client node. For example, a file server could have a directory called /opt, it could designate that directory for NFS clients, and then a client machine could mount that remote directory locally, even under /opt if it wanted. Thus, any user could access the "local" /opt directory but all traffic would actually be silently redirected via the network to the remote file server's /opt directory. Most UNIX networks utilize NFS, and most UNIX users never know that a given directory is NFS mounted, unless, of course, the NFS connection is disrupted, which renders the files unavailable. That is usually the user's first clue that a particular directory is not actually local but NFS mounted. From a security standpoint, we should mention that NFS is based on Sun's ONC RPC (remote procedure call) protocol and uses secure RPC for authentication. However, like Kerberos by default, only the process of authentication is encrypted via a secure channel. All further access is done in plaintext, unencrypted. Therefore, when you edit a file that exists on an NFS server, the text of that file is transported over the network as unencrypted plaintext.

An NFS server can designate certain directories it wishes to publish for NFS clients and can also specify which clients have access to that drive and what the character of that access is. This configuration is done by modifying a file called /etc/exports on the NFS server. If we specify an entry in the /etc/exports file on the NFS server called charon, it looks like this:

/home   bubba(rw) cheiron(r) lsmtsrvr(rw)

We have stated that the directory /home (and all its subdirectories) is accessible by three different nodes: bubba, cheiron, and lsmtsrvr. We have also specified that both bubba and lsmtsrvr have both read and write access (rw) but the cheiron node can only read the data in /home. This is precisely how UNIX manages common home directory structures regardless of to which machine a user logs in. By default, there would be a home directory on every individual computer. NFS allows a file server to store everyone's home directory, and all client machines can mount that remote directory, making your home directory look the same regardless of from which client computer you are logging in. The way a client computer mounts this home directory (say it is the bubba computer) would be this way:

mountcharon:/home/home

This tells NFS to attempt to mount the remote /home directory on the NFS server charon under a *local* directory, also called home. Once this is successful, a user on the local machine bubba can do an "ls /home" and see all the subdirectories of the /home directory on the NFS server charon. Because bubba is given both read and write access, individuals can (depending on their standard permissions) manipulate and modify those remote files (obviously primarily only those files that are within their particular home directory). When a client computer is finished with a particular remote mount, it can unmount that NFS directory and it will be rendered unavailable at the client.

NFS uses standard Transmission Control Protocol/Internet Protocol (TCP/IP) for communication, and authentication is based on standard IP host addresses and hostnames. NFS packets are not encrypted nor are they digitally signed. This allows for the possibility that data on its way to an NFS server can be spoofed, which gives a hijacker the opportunity to impersonate a remote client. There are various guidelines offered for making NFS more secure, including not making an NFS client also be a server, not allowing NFS access from outside the local network (i.e., across the Internet), and minimizing the number of server mounts per client so that a single NFS server acts as the file server for an entire organization rather than having multiple servers each export a single directory. You also do not want to export users' home directories, unless you are running NFS via secure RPC. The possibility of eavesdropping on users' sessions is one reason for this. Another reason is that an unscrupulous user could gain access to another user's home directory, plant a .rhosts file there, be able to log in without password authentication to the remote machine as that user, and further attempt to penetrate the network. You should never export directories on the server that expose server binaries, and you should never allow ordinary network users to be able to log into the NFS server. It should be dedicated to serving only NFS mounts and should only be able to be logged in to by the root account.

We should note that there are a number of historical problems with both NIS+ and NFS on UNIX systems, and there exist well-known ways to hack in through these vulnerabilities to wreak havoc. Ways to mitigate these risks, in addition to those previously discussed, include making sure that you are using secure RPC, that all directories to be exported are owned by root, and that certain commands cannot be issued on certain directories (usually /usr/sbin commands operating on central server directories such as /dev). When precautions are taken, both NIS+ and NFS can be run generally within a safe environment as long as the system administrator remains vigilant with patches and updates.

Very often UNIX security begins and ends at the level of TCP connections into the computer network. For this reason, certain security efforts have been directed at this connectivity point, the level of socket connections. We talk about three major areas of interest: TCP wrappers, firewalls and packet filtering, and dial-up security.

TCP Wrappers

TCP wrappers increase control over incoming TCP connection requests. When a TCP request comes in to a UNIX computer running TCP wrappers, the inetd daemon actually forwards the incoming request not to the daemon that eventually will service the actual request but rather to a wrapping daemon called tcpd that implements TCP wrappers. At this point, several things happen automatically. First, the TCP wrappers' subsystem is handed the request, it opens the /etc/hosts.allow file, and it reads in access permissions for any incoming computers and requests. Next, it executes the particular program associated with the rule for that particular incoming service (say, for FTP or telnet). If none is found, TCP wrappers will open the /etc/hosts.deny file, look to see if any particular node or group of nodes is denied, and if so, will shut down the connection request. If no rule is found in either hosts.allow or hosts.deny, by default the connection is accepted. Modern versions of TCP wrappers allow you to specify more complex rules in the hosts.allow file, giving you the ability to put a single rule in the hosts.deny file: "ALL:ALL," which effectively sets forth default policy to deny all hosts. Then, specific rules in the hosts.allow file can be issued that specify specific rights for specific hosts. TCP wrappers basically wrap incoming requests within a security blanket of sorts and perform several useful functions, from determining access rights for given nodes via ACLs, logging of results and actions within syslog, displaying legal notices as banners to remote connections, performing a double reverse lookup of the IP address of the client, and making sure that the client is really who he claims to be (this option is appropriately termed "PARANOID"). If he is not, the connection is dropped and the attempted spoof is logged. TCP wrappers provides a centralized mechanism for handling network secure connections that may be overlooked or insufficient in any particular network service (FTP, for example). Finally, if everything is allowed and the connection looks legitimate, TCP wrappers will forward the actual connection request to the target daemon dedicated to service such requests.

Firewalls and Packet Filtering
Another method of handling incoming network requests is the use of a firewall. Most modern UNIX systems come with a default firewall already in place. A firewall is the digital equivalent of a firewall that wraps the interior compartment of a car and sits behind the engine block. It is designed to slow down any explosion or fire that may result from the engine catching fire. An Internet firewall is implemented by a machine that sits publicly on the Internet at the entrance point to the internal network. As such, the firewall intercepts all incoming requests and determines what to do with them. A firewall can be designed to provide up to three core sets of responsibilities: packet filtering, application protection, and IP traffic forwarding.

Packet filtering is a low-level kernel-intensive capability that examines every single incoming packet and filters out those packets that appear to be suspicious in any way. Generally, filtering firewalls will filter on the IP packet's contents itself, source, destination, protocol, and so forth; will filter both incoming and outgoing packets; filter on certain known (problematic) routes; and can disable source routing, as well as specify that the firewall cannot be changed via a network connection but only at the physical console.

IP-forwarding firewalls can be used to protect computers within an internal network but masquerade as an internal computer to the outside world (Internet). This allows internal computers full access to the Internet (for browsing, ssh, etc.) but without having to expose that computer physically to the outside by giving it a public IP address.

Configuring a firewall is nontrivial. The strategy in setting up a firewall on a UNIX system is first of all to disable all inessential protocols and applications. This means if you use ssh instead of telnet, disable the telnet port. If you use scp instead of ftp, disable the ftp port. If you do not need to expose CORBA distributed objects to the outside world, disable the IIOP port (535). If you do not need to run a daytime server, then disable port 13, and so forth. Next, secure the local filesystems on the firewall machine. Definitely disable all NFS and NIS+ access. Mount /usr as read only, so sensitive files cannot be overwritten. Make sure minimal permissions exist on files, make files only writeable if absolutely essential. Restrict log in to the machine to root only, and make it available only through a console login. Disable or restrict all outside access to access only via secure channels (such as ssh).

In addition to proprietary firewalls for standard UNIX operating systems, there exist several public/free firewalls, including Socks, ipchains, netfileter, ipforward, and ipfirewall, each of which offers various protection capabilities. In addition, many routers and gateways offer internal default firewall capabilities, and often these are even more powerful than their software-based counterparts. See the chapters other chapters in this *Handbook* for more detailed information on firewalls.

Software Security
Once we have secured the physical computer, the operating system, and access to the system via password protection and authentication, as well as securing the perimeter of the system from potential attacks via the network, we must turn our attention to the various strategies used to secure software applications that our users will be running on a daily basis. The first of these security strategies is application security, and the second is component security.

Application Security
Application security is usually provided by application vendors themselves. For example, a database system such as Sybase or Oracle will have a system administrator and an associated password that the DBA (database administrator) would keep secret and for which they would be responsible. Applications used by organizations contain highly critical data, and the same precautions concerning password privacy and protection apply to application passwords. As part of the backup strategy, strategies to ensure the integrity of an application and its data should be defined clearly and adhered to, so that if a particular application is lost, the entire application with its associated data can be restored with confidence and integrity.

Component Security
With the advent of object-oriented software engineering, we now have the potential need to secure distributed objects that have a life of their own. A distributed object

might be provided in the form of a Web service that provides some critical information to an organization, a CORBA (Common Object Request Broker Architecture) object that provides sensitive pricing information, or an EJB (Enterprise Java Bean) object that delivers competitive analyses. Each of these types of distributed components will need to be protected to make sure that anyone who is talking to one of these services is legitimate. Different strategies are employed depending on the precise technology used, but often these strategies follow operating system metaphors, and some more capable and integrated platforms (such as J2EE application servers) will provide ACLs to specifically control which users and applications can call particular features of a particular distributed component.

SECURITY STRATEGIES

There are several key things a UNIX administrator can remember to do to secure her system. First, allow in only what you know you need and disallow absolutely everything else. Offering every service that is available and accepting incoming connections is a potential avenue for an unscrupulous person to gain access. By limiting your exposure to only those essential services that your system or network must allow in, you can greatly reduce your risk.

Second, keep up to date with all security-related updates, fixes, and patches. Do not fall behind because these patches are designed to protect against known vulnerabilities. If you are behind in your system maintenance, you are exposing yourself to greater risk than is necessary. Certain denial of service attacks are designed to target specific services, and if those services are turned off, it can help to lessen the effect of such attacks (although not always). Along with this, try to use software that is as bug free as possible. Solid software is more stable, and stability is directly correlated with security. One of the most frequently used avenues of entrance into an otherwise secure system is through a known bug in some daemon or server that allows for buffer overruns. Software that is patched to close off a buffer overrun is significantly more secure than unpatched software.

Make sure that your security policy states that your system will perform significant monitoring and logging and auditing of activity. The main way that detection of a break-in occurs is often through examining audit logs. If those logs are not in place, such detection is often slower if it comes at all. The key to recovering from an attack is to first of all recognize when you are under attack. Audit logs and system monitoring can go a long way toward giving you a heads up in case of a breach. Use monitoring software that can give you a heads up whenever changes take place. Software such as Tripwire can be configured to provide a checksum on certain files and will watch for changes to those files, even changes that do not affect the last changed value in the inode.

Always do whatever it takes to secure root access. Never, under any circumstances, give out the root password to anyone who is not officially an administrator of the system. Change the root password often; every day is not too often. Understand that once a cracker has possession of your root password, your entire system is owned

by him and is vulnerable. He can literally do whatever he wants to the system, including planting back doors for future access, deleting or destroying files, stealing data, and so forth.

Make sure your users understand that their participation is required in maintaining a secure system. Make sure your security policy states clearly how passwords are to be managed, including that no one is to ever write their password down on a piece of paper or a sticky note attached to their computer's monitor. Pick good passwords that cannot be guessed either by another person or by a software password cracking system. Never send your password in an e-mail. Never give out your password to anyone, even in an e-mail "apparently" sent by the system administrator. Definitely consider using one-time passwords and smart cards as an overall part of your security system.

CONCLUSION

UNIX security has been an issue since the introduction of the operating system by Bell Laboratories in 1969. As one of the first hierarchical file systems that has a multiuser system, and therefore the necessity of managing access among multiple users, UNIX has dealt with file security and authentication issues from the beginning. Since then, as threats have increased and the means and methods of invasion have become more sophisticated, especially with the addition of networking in the 1970s, new tools have been added to UNIX to shore up security deficiencies. Managing security threats successfully is an expensive, time consuming, and endless task. It is also a task that must be done diligently or negative consequences are virtually certain.

GLOSSARY

Closed Source Closed source software is software that is released in binary form only. The software source code is not included nor is it made publicly available. See Open Source. Examples of closed source operating systems include Microsoft Windows and, in the UNIX arena, Solaris and HPUX.

Crack A program designed to guess hashed UNIX passwords by working off a base password list. It examines an existing passwd file and reports on any "hits."

Daemon A program that is specifically written to be run without a console, usually as a system service to provide core system services.

Data Privacy The protection of data by making it unreadable by parties not authorized for such viewing and reading. Examples include encryption and compression.

DNS Domain naming service. A distributed system that provides mapping between fully qualified domain names and numeric IP addresses.

Firewall A hardware-based or software-based solution that provides protection against Internet connection requests, usually to prevent unauthorized access.

FTP File transfer protocol. A daemon service that provides an implementation (both server and client) of the FTP protocol, which allows for one or more files to be transferred from one computer to another.

GNU GNU's not UNIX. A Free Software Foundation project to provide free UNIX software in source code for multiple platforms.

GPL GNU public license. The public source code license for the GNU project. Specifically, the "CopyLeft" license.

IDEA A 64-bit block cipher algorithm that uses a 128-bit key for encryption.

Inetd A daemon service that manages incoming connections for a list of daemons defined in /etc/inetd.conf. Inetd listens for incoming connections and defines the types of services used to satisfy them.

MD5 An RSA Data Security Inc. message digest algorithm that produces a 128-bit hash of data.

NFS Network file system. A protocol and daemon implementation for providing access to remote filesystems.

NIS and NIS+ Network information service. A service and daemon implementation that provides a centralized database, primarily for common user authentication.

One-Time Password (OTP) A password authentication system that provides the ability to have each user have a unique password every single time they log in to the system.

Open Source Open source software is software that is made publically available along with the source code. Having the source code available is useful because it allows many different programmers to be able to spot and fix problems with the source code. See Closed Source. Examples of open source operating systems in UNIX are Linux and FreeBSD.

Pretty Good Privacy (PGP) A collection of utilities that implement an asymmetric public key cryptography primarily used to secure e-mail transmissions through encryption.

RSA An asymmetric public key cryptographic algorithm.

Secure Shell (SSH) A protocol and daemon implementation of utilities that allow a user to securely open a remote shell on another computer to which he has access or to copy files via an encrypted channel from one computer to another.

SHA-1 A cryptographic algorithm that produces a highly secure 160-bit hash.

Shadow File A private file associated with /etc/passwd that holds the hashed password values for users on a UNIX system.

Superuser Sudo A program that provides configurable, controlled root access and a log of activities.

Syslog A daemon that handles systemwide logging of information dynamically.

TCP Transmission control protocol. A connection-oriented protocol that offers dependable delivery, guaranteed retransmission, and ordering of packets for delivery across a network.

TCP Wrappers TCP wrappers increases control over incoming TCP connection requests by providing a single daemon that wraps individual incoming requests in a secure layer.

Telnet An insecure daemon implementation and client protocol that establishes a terminal session with a remote computer.

Tripwire A utility that records status of UNIX files and notifies you of any changes to those files.

CROSS REFERENCES

See *Linux Security; OpenVMS Security; Operating System Security; Windows 2000 Security.*

REFERENCES

Computer Security Institute and Federal Bureau of Investigation. (2003). Retrieved from http://i.cmpnet.com/gocsi/db_area/pdfs/fbi/FBI2003.pdf

Computer Security Institute and Federal Bureau of Investigation. (2004). Retrieved from http://i.cmpnet.com/gocsi/db_area/pdfs/fbi/FBI2004.pdf

Kahn, D. (1996). *The codebreakers: The Story of Secret Writing*: Macmillan.

FURTHER READING

Bugtraq archive: Subscribe by emailing listserv@securityfocus.com with "subscribe bugtraq your_email_address" in the subject line of the message, without quotes.

Cheswick, B., & Rubin. (2003). *Firewalls and Internet Security: Repelling the Wily Hacker* (2nd ed.): Addison-Wesley.

Denning, D. (1983). *Cryptography and Data Security*: Addison-Wesley.

Diffie & Hellman. (1976). New directions in cryptography. *IEEE Transactions on Information Theory IT-22.*

Ferbrache, D. (1992). *The Pathology of Computer Viruses.* [location]: Springer-Verlag.

Frisch, A. (2002). *Essential System Administration* (3rd ed.). [location]: O'Reilly & Associates.

Garfinkel, S. (1994). *PGP: Pretty Good Privacy*: O'Reilly & Associates.

Garfinkel, Spafford, & Schwartz. (2003). *Practical Unix and Internet security* (3rd ed.): O'Reilly & Associates.

Gilly, D. (1986). *UNIX in a Nutshell: A desktop quick reference for System V & Solaris 2.0.* Sebastapol: O'Reilly & Associates.

Grampp & Morris. (1984, October). UNIX operating system security. *AT&T Bell Laboratories Technical Journal.*

Lewand & Watkins. (2000). *Cryptological mathematics.* [location]: The Mathematical Society of America.

Mao, W. (2003). *Modern Cryptography: Theory and Practice.* [location]: Prentice-Hall.

Merkle & Hellman (1981). Secure communication over insecure channels. *Communications of the ACM, 21,* 294–299.

Northcutt et al. (2002). *Inside Network Perimeter Security: The Definitive Guide to Firewalls, Virtual Private Networks (VPNs), Routers, and Intrusion Detection Systems.* [location]: Que.

Pate, S. (1996). *UNIX internals: A practical approach.* Reading, MA: Addison Wesley Longman.

Peek, J., Todino, G., et al. (1998). *Learning the UNIX Operating system*. Cambridge, MA: O'Reilly & Associates.

Rivest, Shamir, & Adleman (1978). A method for obtaining digital signatures and public key cryptosystems. *Communications of the ACM, 21*.

Schneier, B. (1996). *Applied Cryptography: Protocols, Algorithms, and Source Code in C*. [location]: John Wiley & Sons.

Singh, S. (2000). *The Code Book: The Science of Secrecy from Ancient Egypt to Quantum Cryptography*: Anchor Books.

Sobell, M. (1995). *UNIX System V: A Practical Guide*. Redwood City, CA: Benjamin/Cummings.

Tanenbaum, A. (2001). *Modern Operating Systems*. Upper Saddle River, NJ: Prentice-Hall.

UNIX Pocket Reference List. (n.d.). Retrieved October 3, 2002, from http://www.utexas.edu/cc/docs/ccrl20.html

Vahalia, U. (1996). *UNIX Internals: The New Frontiers*. Upper Saddle River, NJ: Prentice-Hall.

Zwicky, Cooper & Chapman (2000). *Building Internet Firewalls* (2nd ed.): O'Reilly & Associates.

Linux Security

A. Justin Wilder, *Telos Corporation*

INTRODUCTION

This chapter was written based on version 9 of the Red Hat Linux and the Red Hat Fedora Core 1 and 2 distributions. Although the examples used in this chapter may focus on a limited set of Linux distributions, the fundamental concepts can be used with nearly every Linux distribution. Each section remains focused on hardening the core operating system using the tools and capabilities of the base installation. The sections do not go into detail on other additive security controls as there are far too many variations to adequately address within the scope of this chapter.

The reader should have an intermediate or greater understanding of Linux/UNIX. Once Linux has been installed, all configuration steps outlined within each section can be performed by the command either via the console or through telnet or SSH (Secure Shell; recommended).

Before beginning a new installation, ensure that the system is deployed within a test environment that best represents the production environment. It is recommended that the system remain unplugged from the production network until the system has been sufficiently hardened.

This chapter covers some of the fundamentals of building and hardening a Linux platform. The topics include hardware security, installation considerations, system initialization, kernel security, networking security, file system security, application security, patch management, account security, system auditing, backups, and legal protections.

Only after the system has been hardened, patched, and tested should the system be deployed within the production environment.

THE BASICS

This section covers some of the basic considerations that should be addressed when building a secure Linux system. At the conclusion of this section, the base system should be up and running and the administrator should have a complete understanding of the server's requirements when placed into production.

Following the defense-in-depth model, this section picks up where physical security controls that protect the server itself leave off.

BIOS

The BIOS (Basic Input Output System) is the first line of defense of any hardened system and there are several features that are available in nearly every BIOS variant.

One feature is the ability to set the order in which the BIOS queries boot devices to look for a boot record. It is recommended that the boot order be set to check the primary hard drive first, followed by the floppy, and CD-ROM devices. Your system's BIOS may also support booting from a network device in which case this option should be disabled when deploying servers. The important part is that your primary hard drive containing your hardened version of Linux be loaded first. Configuration of the BIOS boot order can be done after you have completed the Linux installation to allow for CD-ROM-based install methods.

Another feature that should be considered is setting a user and administrator password in the BIOS. By setting the user password, you are able to limit who is able to boot the system to only those who know the user password. This is typically limited to system administrators who may be required to reboot the server to perform maintenance. Note that this setting will prohibit a system administrator's ability to remotely reboot the system; a BIOS password will be required after the system is cycled. On the other hand, this will prevent attackers who have physical access to the system from rebooting the server and loading tools that may be used to disable other security controls, thereby granting them uninhibited access to the system. By setting the administrator password, you are able to control who has the ability to modify the BIOS settings, specifically the settings previously modified. This is regarded as a best practice for nearly all production deployment scenarios.

The system administrator should refer to the BIOS software manual for the specific steps to enable these features for the system.

Installation Considerations

Getting Started
Before beginning a Linux installation, decisions must be made to determine for what purpose the final system will

- Will these services be publicly available or available only on the intranet?
- What are the risks to these services and what is the impact if the server is compromised?
- Where will the server be logically placed on the network?
- What kinds of controls are in place to protect and monitor the server and its services?
- What kinds of controls will need to be installed locally to protect the server and its services?
- Will remote users be allowed to access the server and use local applications and services?
- How will remote access be controlled?
- What type of information will be stored on or passed through the server?
- What is the sensitivity of that information?
- What type of monitoring will be required for this server?
- How granular do the reports and logs have to be?
- How will the server be monitored?

Partitioning
During the Linux installation process, you will have the opportunity to establish system partitions, allocate space, and determine their mount points. Creating separate partitions for each major file system directory on your Linux system is considered to be a best practice. By creating separate partitions, you can reduce the risk of denial of service attacks that are caused by filling all usable drive space with garbage, limit the impact of exploited SUID (Set User ID) programs, and increase system performance, to name a few.

Minimum Recommended Partitions and Sizes (20-GB Drive)

```
Directory           Use                                    Recommended Partition Size
/           (Root):                           2 GB
/boot       (Kernels images):                 50 MB
/usr        (System and user binaries):       8 GB
/home       (User directories):               5 GB (50-100 MB per user, e.g., 50 users)
/var        (Application working directories): 3 GB (depends on the application)*
/tmp        (Temporary directory):            1 GB
SWAP        (Linux virtual memory):           1 GB (RAM in MB* 2 up to 1 G)
*If the server will support a database, then /var will need to be bigger to
support the database because it is stored by default in /var.
```

be used. This may seem like a simple question on the surface; however, several factors and requirements must be taken into consideration before building the server to ensure an optimal configuration. Questions similar to the following must be answered as they will affect various aspects of the installation, configuration, and deployment:

- What type of services will the server provide?
- Will the server host a single service or multiple services?

Note: If the system will be hosting an application that is resource intensive, the SWAP partition may need to be increased. If you notice that the SWAP partition is heavily utilized after deployment, consider increasing the amount of physical RAM.

It should also be noted that if the server is to be deployed as a public service such as an Apache Web server, DNS (Domain Name System), or an FTP (File Transfer Protocol) server, another partition should be created and mounted as

```
Directory       Use              Recommended Partition Size

/chroot     (Chroot jail)    512 MB (dependent on the application)
```

It is from this directory (or partition) that these public services should be configured and be initialized to operate. See more on *chroot* in the Applications and Services Daemons section.

Boot Loader

During installation, you will have to choose between the LILO (LInux LOader) boot loader and the GRUB boot loader. It is recommended that the GRUB boot loader be used to boot the Linux system because of its advanced features and additional security controls. See the next section, Boot Loaders, for more information about how to specifically configure each of these components once the installation is complete. Once the GRUB boot loader is specified, you will be prompted to set a boot loader password. It is recommended that a password be set for the boot loader. This will ensure that only authorized administrators are able to bring up the system. Additionally, this will prevent users with physical access to the system from passing kernel-level boot options that may be used to circumvent or disable other system security controls.

Note: As with the BIOS password, by setting the GRUB boot loader password the system will not be able to be remotely rebooted, because the boot loader password will be required and can only be entered from the system console.

Host-Based Firewall

During installation, after the network configuration step, you will have an option to enable an *ipchains* firewall. It is recommended that this be enabled and the default configuration set to high with no trusted interfaces and with SSH access allowed (and DHCP if needed). This will provide basic assurances that, out of the box, the system can be trusted to be brought online to take advantage of Red Hat's auto-update capability, *up2date*. Once the system has been adequately hardened and updated, it is recommended that the older *ipchains* be disabled and the newer *iptables* be enabled. See the section on *iptables* for more information.

Root Password

After the firewall and network interfaces are set up, you will need to set a root password. The password should be nontrivial and contain at least eight characters, including at least one uppercase character, one number, and one special character.

Authentication Configuration

During this phase of the installation, it must be determined how the system will authenticate users. At a minimum, "'Enable MD5 passwords" and "'Enable shadow passwords" should be enabled to securely perform local authentication. The other authentication mechanisms take advantage of centralized authentication servers. The optional authentication methods available during installation are NIS, LDAP, Kerberos 5, and SMB or NT domain authentication.

Application Installation

Most Linux installations out of the box are extremely powerful and flexible. However, to build a properly hardened system, unnecessary packages must not be installed.

Unneeded packages occupy valuable hard drive space, even more valuable memory, and most importantly provide additional avenues for attack and compromise. It is during this phase of the installation that many of the answers to the questions noted earlier must be considered.

It is important that *all* of the "Package Groups" be deselected during this phase. By selecting the "Select Individual Packages" check box and clicking the Next button, you will be able to install only those packages that are needed to fit the deployment requirements of this server. Select only those individual packages that are required; the installation scripts will automatically solve and install other dependent packages.

Note: It is recommended that Linux servers should not have XWindows or any of its components installed. This will significantly reduce the amount of drive space used for the operating system while eliminating a wealth of local and remote attack vectors.

Boot Disks

During installation, you will be given the option to create a Linux Rescue Disk or boot disk. If you are doing a network-based Linux install and do not have the bootable Linux CDs available, it is highly recommended that you allow the installation program to create these floppy disks for you.

Creating a Linux Rescue Disk under Linux in case bootable Linux installation CDs or floppies are not available can be accomplished as follows:

Note: The boot image can be obtained from the RedHat Linux installation CD under */images* or retrieved via FTP from any RedHat Linux installation mirror. See http://www.redhat.com/mirrors.html.

If using the installation CD, mount the first CD, and in either case change directories to the location of the boot image file.

```
[root@TheBox/]# mount/dev/cdrom/mnt/cdrom
[root@TheBox/]# cd/mnt/cdrom/images
```

Insert a blank formatted floppy disk into the disk drive and use the *dd* command to write the image to the disk.

```
[root@TheBox images]# dd if=boot.img of=/
  dev/fd0 bs=1440k
[root@TheBox images]# cd ..
[root@TheBox mnt]# umount/mnt/cdrom
```

SYSTEM INITIALIZATION

Aside from the hardware BIOS, the boot loader is the first opportunity for interaction with the system. If the system is to be deployed within an environment where the lack of physical security controls will allow an attacker access to the console, it is important to ensure that interaction with the boot loader and initialization scripts is limited. This will prevent an attacker from booting the system from other media, simply gaining a root shell on the system by passing boot options, or by booting into single user mode. These recommendations will ensure that the integrity of the system initialization process is maintained.

Boot Loader

LILO (LInux LOader) is the legacy Linux boot loader that is used to manage the Linux boot process, whether it is from a floppy disk or a hard drive. LILO can also be used to manage the boot process of other operating systems. The following is an example of a default LILO configuration file (*/etc/lilo.conf*). Changes to the configuration file are noted inline.

```
prompt                        (remove to prevent console accessible boot options)
timeout=00                    (set to zero to prevent console interaction during boot)
default=linux
boot=/dev/sda
map=/boot/map
install=/boot/boot.b
message=/boot/message
linear
restricted                    (add this line to ensure a password is required)
password=<bootpassword>       (add this line and set the password to set the boot PW)
                              (this password applies to the booting of all images)

image=/boot/vmlinuz-2.4.18-14
    label=linux
    initrd=/boot/initrd-2.4.18-14.img
    read-only
    append="root=LABEL=/"
```

Once */etc/lilo.conf* has been modified and saved, the changes need to be reapplied to the Master Boot Record (MBR). This can be accomplished with the following command executed as root:

```
[root@TheBox etc]# lilo-v
```

GRUB (GRand Unified Boot loader) is the newer, more advanced replacement for the LILO boot loader. The GRUB boot loader, a much more powerful boot loader, has the ability to use MD5 encrypted passwords, and does not require the MBR to be rewritten after a change is made. The following is an example of a GRUB configuration file (*/boot/grub/grub.conf*). Several recommended changes are shown inline.

```
boot=/dev/sda                         (specify the primary boot device for all images)
default=0
timeout=00                            (set to zero to prevent console interaction during boot)
password-md5<cut&paste hash>          (add this line to set the boot PW, the md5 option)
                                      (specifies that the password is encrypted, see below)
                                      (this password applies to the booting of all images)

splashimage=(hd0,0)/grub/splash.xpm.gz
title Red Hat Linux (2.4.18-14)
root (hd0,0)
kernel/vmlinuz-2.4.18-14 ro root=LABEL=/
initrd/initrd-2.4.18-14.img
```

To create the GRUB boot loader password, the utility *grub-md5-crypt* must be run to generate the MD5 hash. This hash must be copied to the `<cut&paste hash>` field.

GRUB does not need to be reloaded to apply these changes. Once the */boot/grub/grub.conf* file has been modified and saved to disk, changes take effect during the next boot.

Runlevels

After the Linux kernel is loaded by the boot loader and the system has been initialized, a series of scripts will begin executing to complete the system initialization.

The set of scripts are called init scripts and they control how the system is brought up and what services will be available. These scripts reside in the */etc/rc.d/* directory. Initially, */etc/rc.d/rc*, */etc/rc.d/rc.sysinit*, and */etc/rc.d/rc.local* will be executed, followed by the set of scripts within the */etc/rc.d/rc#.d/* directory, where the number (#) is the specific runlevel in which the system will be operating. Runlevels are defined as the following:

0: Halt (do not set *initdefault* to this),

1: Single user mode (administrative mode),

2: Multiuser, without NFS (the same as 3, if you do not have networking),

3: Full multiuser mode (server mode),

4: Unused,

5: X11 (workstation mode), and

6: reboot (do not set init default to this).

Just before the scripts defined by the system runlevel are executed, by default the system allows console user interaction to define the runlevel into which the system will boot. This interaction should be disabled by modifying the last line in the */etc/sysconfig/init* file:

```
[root@TheBox sysconfig]# cat init
# color => new RH6.0 bootup
# verbose => old-style bootup
# anything else => new style bootup without ANSI colors or positioning
BOOTUP=color
# column to start "[ OK ]" label in
RES_COL=60
# terminal sequence to move to that column. You could change this
# to something like "tput hpa ${RES_COL}" if your terminal supports it
MOVE_TO_COL="echo-en\\033[${RES_COL}G"
# terminal sequence to set color to a 'success' color (currently: green)
SETCOLOR_SUCCESS="echo-en\\033[1;32m"
# terminal sequence to set color to a 'failure' color (currently: red)
SETCOLOR_FAILURE="echo-en\\033[1;31m"
# terminal sequence to set color to a 'warning' color (currently: yellow)
SETCOLOR_WARNING="echo-en\\033[1;33m"
# terminal sequence to reset to the default color.
SETCOLOR_NORMAL="echo-en\\033[0;39m"
# default kernel loglevel on boot (syslog will reset this)
LOGLEVEL=3
# Set to anything other than 'no' to allow hotkey interactive startup...
PROMPT=no
[root@TheBox sysconfig]#
```

KERNEL SECURITY

The Linux kernel is the core of the Linux system and there are several kernel configuration options that should be considered when building a hardened Linux system. One of the primary steps involved in hardening a Linux system is to recompile and install a new optimized Linux kernel. This section will provide some insight into some of the various kernel modifications that can be made as well as make several recommendations for modifying the running kernel.

Recompiling

Although the process and caveats involved with recompiling and installing a new Linux kernel are outside the scope of this chapter, it is highly recommended, after the installation of a new Linux system, that a new Linux kernel be recompiled and installed. The kernel should be rebuilt from pristine source with only the modules, drivers, and features that are absolutely required to operate the system. This reduces system complexity, increases performance, and ultimately increases overall system security by reducing the number of avenues by which an attacker can exploit the system. Additionally, if the system will be deployed within a hostile or untrusted environment, an additional control can be applied to the system during kernel configuration. LKM (Loadable Kernel Modules) support can be disabled to prevent the installation of LKM rootkits and other backdoors but will require the system

administrator to build the system drivers as kernel objects as opposed to modules. The trade-off is the reduction of system flexibility to the introduction of new hardware; the kernel will have to be recompiled to support the new device.

The current kernel source code can be downloaded from http://www.kernel.org. All of the necessary documentation and instructions for compiling and installing a new Linux kernel are also available on this site.

There are several configuration options that should be taken into consideration when compiling the new kernel. These options and their respective setting are listed here. For more information, use the Help feature in the kernel configuration menu.

- Networking options --->
  o [*] Network packet filtering (replaces ipchains)
  o [*] IP: TCP syncookie support
  o IP: Netfilter Configuration --->
    . (all options should be enabled)
  o [ ] IP: multicasting
  o [ ] IP: advanced router
- File systems --->
  o [*] Quota support
  o <*> Ext3 journalling file system support
  o [*] JBD (ext3) debugging support

After the new kernel has been complied, installed, and verified to work properly, the kernel source tree should be deleted to prevent the modification and recompilation of the kernel or any of its modules by an attacker. This would also be a good time to remove the compiler to prevent the compilation of attack tool source code that may be uploaded to the system by an attacker. See the section on

RPM (RedHat Package Manager) for more information about how to remove packages.

Kernel Modifications

Several patches have been made available by the open source community to add various security features into the stock Linux kernel. Among many of the features provided by each of the patches, buffer overflow protection, role-based access control, and SUID/SGID (Set Group ID) controls are common additions. Each of the patches listed here should be reviewed and fully tested before using the new kernel in a production environment.

- **Openwall Project** (http://www.openwall.com/linux/). This patch adds a variety of features such as stack protection, /tmp restrictions, /proc access control, user process, and shared memory destruction. This patch is available for 2.4, 2.2, and 2.0 Linux kernels.
- **Grsecurity 2.0 RBAC** (http://www.grsecurity.net/ features.php). This patch brings Role-Based Access Control (RBAC), process-based Mandatory Access Control (MAC), chroot restrictions, stack protection, and kernel auditing among many other features to the 2.4 Linux kernel.
- **LIDS** (http://www.lids.org/). LIDS is short for Linux Intrusion Detection System. LIDS adds Mandatory Access Control (MAC) with a userspace administrator tool, port scan detection, process and file protection, and process network access restriction. The LIDS kernel patch supports the 2.6, 2.4, and 2.2 Linux kernels.
- **SE-Linux** (http://www.nsa.gov/selinux/). Security Enhanced Linux was developed by the National Security Administration to improve the security of the Flask operating system. The project is a kernel replacement that provides Mandatory Access Control (MAC), stack protection, Role Based Access Control (RBAC), and was designed with many of the high-assurance security principles from the Trusted Operating System (TOS) model.

/proc

The /proc directory is the pseudo-file system that is used as a real-time interface to kernel variables. This is a logical directory that does not exist on the physical drive but instead is created and mounted by the kernel during system boot. The special /proc directory contains subdirectories and files that can be modified to affect system performance and security. Following are several suggested /proc changes to improve the security of the system. It is important to note that every system is different and the effect of each change should be taken into consideration given the system, its environment, and planned deployment. Inappropriate or invalid changes may crash the system.

The files within /proc can be modified directly with any text editor; however, the tool /sbin/sysctl can be used to quickly display and modify (with the "-w" switch) any /proc kernel parameter. Note that using sysctl or by editing a /proc file directly, the system administrator will be

modifying parameters of the running Linux system and these changes are not persistent across system reboots. The file /etc/sysctl.conf can be modified to ensure /proc changes are maintained.

Additional documentation can be found with the kernel source code (if installed) in the following directory on the local system: */usr/src/linux-2.4/Documentation/sysctl*.

Net.Core—Configure the Networking Subsystem
- **Window Size.** By increasing the maximum window send buffer size, a server can take advantage of the larger data queue for its client connections. The default size is 64 k for workstations and it is recommended that at least 1 Mb be used for servers (1Mb is 1000 * 1024 = 1,024,000). This setting will improve network performance for servers.

Modify the running kernel:

```
[root@TheBox root]# sysctl -w net.core.
    wmem_default=1024000
[root@TheBox root]# sysctl -w net.core.
    wmem_max=1024000
```

Modify the /etc/sysctl.conf file by adding the following lines:

```
#Increase Maximum Window Size
net.core.wmem_default = 1024000
net.core.wmem_max = 1024000
```

Net.IPv4—Configure the IPv4 Protocol
- **Source Routing.** Packets received through a specific set of routes specified by the sender should be dropped.

Modify the running kernel:

```
[root@TheBox root]# sysctl -w net.ipv4.
    conf.default.accept_source_route=0
[root@TheBox root]# sysctl -w net.ipv4.
    conf.all.accept_source_route=0
```

Modify the /etc/sysctl.conf file by adding the following lines:

```
#Ignore Source Routed Packets
net.ipv4.conf.default.accept_source_route = 0
net.ipv4.conf.all.accept_source_route = 0
```

- **IP Spoofing.** By setting this parameter to 1, the system will verify the source address of new connections by validating the reverse path as specified in RFC 1812 (Baker 1995).

Modify the running kernel:

```
[root@TheBox root]# sysctl -w net.ipv4.
    conf.default.rp_filter=1
[root@TheBox root]# sysctl -w net.ipv4.
    conf.all.rp_filter=1
```

Modify the *etc/sysctl.conf* file by adding the following lines:

```
#Ignore Spoofed addresses
net.ipv4.conf.default.rp_filter = 1
net.ipv4.conf.all.rp_filter = 1
```

- **Logging.** By telling the kernel to log "martians," all IP packets that are received with impossible addresses will be logged via SYSLOG.

Modify the running kernel:

```
[root@TheBox root]# sysctl -w net.ipv4.
    conf.default.log_martians=1
[root@TheBox root]# sysctl -w net.ipv4.
    conf.all.log_martians=1
```

Modify the *etc/sysctl.conf* file by adding the following lines:

```
#Log All Out of Spec Packets
net.ipv4.conf.default.log_martians = 1
net.ipv4.conf.all.log_martians = 1
```

- **Forwarding.** Unless the system will be deployed as a router or firewall, IP packet forwarding should be disabled across all interfaces.

Modify the running kernel:

```
[root@TheBox root]# sysctl -w net.ipv4.
    conf.default.forwarding=0
[root@TheBox root]# sysctl -w net.ipv4.
    conf.all.forwarding=0
```

Modify the *etc/sysctl.conf* file by adding the following lines:

```
#Disable Forwarding
net.ipv4.conf.default.forwarding=0
net.ipv4.conf.all.forwarding=0
```

- **Local Ports.** This setting allows the system administrator to control which source ports the Linux system will use for initiating new requests. This may be useful when the system is required to initiate new connections to other systems when there is firewall in between them. A system deployed in a DMZ (Demilitarized Zone) is an example of this scenario where all ingress connections from the DMZ into the intranet need to be tightly controlled.

Modify the running kernel:

```
[root@TheBox root]# sysctl -w net.ipv4.
    ip_local_port_range='32768 61001'
```

Modify the *etc/sysctl.conf* file by adding the following lines:

```
#Set the local port range
net.ipv4.ip_local_port_range = 32768 61000
```

Net.IPv4.ICMP—Configure ICMP

- **Ignore ICMP Ping.** If the system will be publicly available without the protection of a firewall, it is recommended that the system be configured to ignore ICMP pings (echo requests). Aside from adding a layer of obscurity to the system, ignoring ICMP Ping also prevents an attacker from using covert channel tools such as LOKI that take advantage of slack space within ICMP echo packets to communicate with compromised systems.

Modify the running kernel:

```
[root@TheBox root]# sysctl -w net.ipv4.
    icmp_echo_ignore_all=1
```

Modify the *etc/sysctl.conf* file by adding the following lines:

```
#Ignore Echo Requests
net.ipv4.icmp_echo_ignore_all = 1
```

- **Ignore ICMP Broadcast.** To prevent the system from being a part of an ICMP broadcast storm denial of service, ICMP echo broadcasts should be ignored. This setting also adds a layer of obscurity by making broadcast ICMP echo request mapping techniques ineffective for this host.

Modify the running kernel:

```
[root@TheBox root]# sysctl -w net.ipv4.
    icmp_echo_ignore_broadcasts=1
```

Modify the *etc/sysctl.conf* file by adding the following lines:

```
#Ignore ICMP Broadcasts
net.ipv4.icmp_echo_ignore_broadcasts = 1
```

- **Ignore ICMP Redirects.** ICMP redirects can be used to modify the system's routing table and should be ignored. Note that with networks that employ complex routing schemes where more than one router serves as a default gateway for the system, this capability should not be disabled.

Modify the running kernel:

```
[root@TheBox root]# sysctl -w net.ipv4.
    conf.all.accept_redirects=0
[root@TheBox root]# sysctl -w net.ipv4.
    conf.default.accept_redirects=0
```

Modify the *etc/sysctl.conf* file by adding the following lines:

```
#Ignore ICMP Redirects
net.ipv4.conf.all.accept_redirects = 0
net.ipv4.conf.default.accept_redirects = 0
```

- **Bad ICMP Error Messages.** By setting this parameter, the system will ignore malformed and invalid ICMP error messages from other hosts. This usually caused by routers that violate RFC 1122 (Braden 1989) by sending bogus ICMP responses to broadcast frames.

Modify the running kernel:

```
[root@TheBox root]# sysctl -w net.ipv4.
    icmp_ignore_bogus_error_responses=1
```

Modify the /etc/sysctl.conf file by adding the following lines:

```
#Ignore Bogus ICMP Error Messages
net.ipv4.icmp_ignore_bogus_error_responses=1
```

Net.IPv4.TCP—Configure TCP

- **SYN Cookies.** Enabling SYN cookies will help to reduce the risk of SYN flood denial of service attack. SYN cookies are only used when the TCP SYN receive buffer is full and the system is unable to accept new legitimate connection requests. At this point, the system will begin to use SYN Cookies to eliminate the need to store previous connection requests (TCP SYN packets), thus clearing the receive buffer. For more information on SYN Cookies, see the references at the end of this chapter.

Modify the running kernel:

```
[root@TheBox root]# sysctl -w net.ipv4.
    tcp_syncookies=1
```

Modify the /etc/sysctl.conf file by adding the following lines:

```
#Use SYN Cookie Protection
net.ipv4.tcp_syncookies = 1
```

- **TCP Backlog.** Set an upper limit to the backlog queue of new connection requests. This is used to throttle the number of new connection requests to prevent the system from being overloaded by a SYN flood. As long as SYN Cookies are enabled, once the queue is full, the kernel will begin to use SYN Cookies and the system will not drop new connection requests (SYN packets).

Modify the running kernel:

```
[root@TheBox root]# sysctl-w net.ipv4.
    tcp_max_syn_backlog=4096
```

Modify the /etc/sysctl.conf file by adding the following lines:

```
#Set max per socket backlog queue
net.ipv4.tcp_max_syn_backlog = 4096
```

NETWORK SECURITY

One of the fundamental requirements for securing a Linux system is the ability to control not only what services are externally available but also the ability to control the network traffic to and from those services. This capability is provided by the NetFilter mechanism, which is used to build a stateful packet-filtering host-based firewall. This section reviews some of the basic network interface management tools and configuration files. In conclusion, the NetFilter mechanism is reviewed by demonstrating some of the basic capabilities of the firewall as well as by providing a sample configuration that includes some of the "must haves" of any stateful packet-filtering host-based firewall. It is assumed that the system administrator has a basic understanding of the TCP/IP protocol suite.

Network Interface Configuration

This section quickly outlines the steps and files involved with configuring a system once it is brought into the test network environment.

Interfaces

Interfaces on a Linux system can be controlled and configured in a variety of ways. One such way is by using the /sbin/ifconfig tool. This utility will allow a system administrator to display and modify enabled network interfaces.

Another way to control network interfaces is by using the /sbin/ifup and /sbin/ifdown scripts provided by the initscripts RPM. These scripts read a set of files from within /etc/sysconfig/network-scripts directory to configure and enable (or disable) network interfaces. An example configuration file for an Ethernet interface would be named ifcfg-<devicename#> and would have contents similar to the following:

```
[root@TheBox network-scripts]# cat ifcfg-eth0
IPADDRESS=10.1.1.50
NETMASK=255.255.255.0
GATEWAY=10.1.1.1
BOOTPROTO=none
ONBOOT=yes
DEVICE=eth0
```

The /sbin/ifup script will source this configuration file when executed by using /sbin/ifup eth0 on the command line.

DNS

DNS configuration is maintained in *the /etc/resolve.conf* file, the contents of which should look similar to the following:

```
[root@TheBox etc]# cat resolv.conf
search localdomain
nameserver 10.1.2.100
nameserver 10.1.1.100
```

If there are hosts whose names are not maintained by the DNS servers previously specified, their names and respective IP addresses can be configured in the /etc/hosts file. This is also an easy way to configure the hostname of the Linux system, considering many of the startup scripts will identify the system name though DNS. The contents of the hosts file should look similar to the following:

```
[root@TheBox etc]# cat hosts
# Do not remove the following line, or various programs
# that require network functionality will fail.
127.0.0.1               localhost.localdomain localhost
10.1.1.50               TheBox

#Other obscure unresolvable hosts (hosts not within DNS tables)
10.1.132.54             Hiddenbox
```

Routing

To set up the default route for the system, the */sbin/route* tool can be used. If the */sbin/ifup* script was utilized and the configuration file had a valid GATEWAY defined, the default route should already be set up. Using this example, the default route can be verified with the route command:

```
[root@TheBox/]# route -n
Kernel IP routing table
Destination     Gateway         Genmask         Flags   Metric  Ref     Use     Iface
10.1.1.0        0.0.0.0         255.255.255.0   U       0       0       0       eth0
127.0.0.0       0.0.0.0         255.0.0.0       U       0       0       0       lo
0.0.0.0         10.1.1.1        0.0.0.0         UG      0       0       0       eth0
```

The default route can be set by using

```
[root@TheBox/]# route add default gw 10.1.1.1
```

Link Speed and Duplex

Once the Ethernet interface is up and is configured properly, it is recommended that the link speed and duplex be set manually using the */sbin/mii-tool* that is distributed with the *net-tools* RPM. Note: The Ethernet interface must have a Media Independent Interface (MII) unit to use this tool. If not, reference the Ethernet driver documentation to determine if the media state can be set via the driver software. Run the tool on the command line with no options to see if the interface has an MII.

As long as the interface and the switch, or hub, to which the system is connected supports it, both the switch port and the network interface should be set to 100 (or 1000 if supported) BaseTx-FD (Full Duplex). Note: Coordinate with the network administrators to ensure the switch is properly configured as well.

```
[root@TheBox/]# mii-tool —F 100baseTx-FD eth0
```

Netfilter

Netfilter is the stateful packet filtering, network address translation (NAT), and packet mangling framework that has been built into the 2.4.x Linux kernel. The framework consists of four major components: Netfilter (the kernel hooks), connection tracking, NAT, and IPTables (the administration tool). The Netfilter framework has been developed as the improved replacement for IPChains of the 2.2.x Linux kernels and ipfwadm of the 2.0.x Linux kernels.

System administrators can use NetFilter/IPTables to build stateful packet filtering firewalls (or host-based firewalls) that are capable of network address translation (NAT), port address translation (PAT), connection tracking, packet manipulation, and QoS.

IPTables Overview

The configuration tool, IPTables, is used by administrators to build chains that contain filter rules through which all packets traversing a network interface will pass. Figure 1 shows NetFilter/IPTables packet flow. Depending on the rules within each chain and default policies, the fate (or target) of each packet will be

- **DROP**: drop the packet,
- **ACCEPT**: allow the packet to pass through,
- **QUEUE**: (if supported by the kernel) pass the packet to userspace, or
- **RETURN**: stop traversing the chain and continue with the next rule (or use the chain default policy if match is at the end of the built-in chain).

Packets traverse NetFilter as follows:

IPTables "Filter" Tables

One of the primary steps when hardening a Linux system is to implement a host-based firewall. The "Filter" tables in the Netfilter suite provide the administrator the ability to control all types of IPv4 traffic into and out of the system. The other two tables, "Mangle" and "NAT," have advanced capabilities that can be used to increase network performance (IPv4 TOS) or help to obscure running services. See the Netfilter (http://www.netfilter.org) Web site for more information.

There are three built-in chains where other user-defined chains or filter rules are linked or defined, respectively. These chains are the following:

- **INPUT**: Defines the chain that all packets entering an interface traverse.
- **OUTPUT**: Defines the chain that all packets leaving an interface traverse.

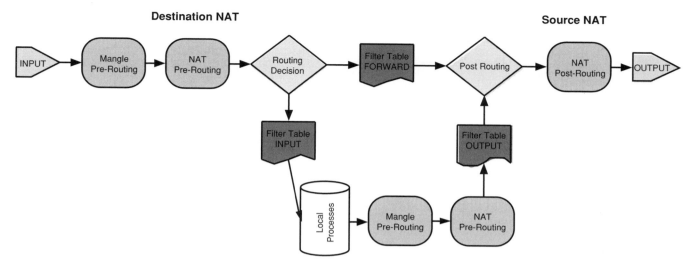

Figure 1: Netfilter/IPTables packet flow.

• **FORWARD**: Defines the chain that all packets traverse if a packet is forwarded across two interfaces.

Chains can be manipulated using the IPTables administration tool as follows:

Rules within a chain follow this syntax:

/sbin/iptables −< *command*> <*chain name*> [*match parameter*][*match extension*] −j [*target*]

Commands

```
-A           Append a rule to a chain
-D           Delete a rule from a chain
-I           Insert a rule into a chain
-R           Replace a rule in a chain
-L           List the rules in a chain (or all chains)
-F           Flush a chain of its rules
-N           Create a new chain
-X           Delete a user defined chain
-P           Set the default policy (target) of a chain
```

Match Parameters

```
-p           TCP/IP OSI Layer 4 protocol (TCP/UDP/ICMP)
-s           Source IP address
-d           Destination IP address
-i           In interface (used for INPUT and FORWARD chains)
-o           Out interface (used for OUPUT and FORWARD chains)
```

Match Extensions
(Sample; see Netfilter Documentation for more information.)

```
--sport          Source port for TCP/UDP protocols
--dport          Destination port for TCP/UDP protocols
--state          Maintain state for TCP
       NEW               Match on new TCP connections
       ESTABLISHED       Match on established TCP connections
       RELATED           Match on related TCP connections
       INVALID           Match on invalid TCP connections
--icmp-type      Specifiy ICMP type to match on
```

Table 1 RFC 1918 Allocation for Private Networks

Prefix	Range	Block
10/8 prefix	10.0.0.0–10.255.255.255	Single class A block
172.16/12 prefix	172.16.0.0–172.31.255.255	16 continuous class B blocks
192.168/16 prefix	192.168.0.0–192.168.255.255	254 continuous class C blocks

The last parameter, "target," as described previously, is the policy on how to treat the packet once a match is made.

Host-Based Firewall

This section outlines two considerations when building a host-based firewall and provides a sample configuration of an IPTables firewall.

RFC 1918 (Rekhter 1996): Address Allocation for Private Internets

This RFC specifies which IPv4 addresses are allocated for private internets or intranets. The address ranges specified within this RFC should only be used on private networks and should not be allowed to traverse the Internet. As such, these IPs should not be permitted to enter or leave the network. The Bogon list, Table 1, and the example that follows address this.

Bogon List

Bogons are network prefixes that have not yet been allocated by IANA, Internet Assigned Numbers Authority (http://www.iana.org), and therefore should never be routed across the Internet. Traffic that appears to originate from these networks is not valid and should be dropped. Rob Thomas maintains the Bogons list in various formats at http://www.cymru.com/Documents/bogon-bn.html.

IANA updates this list periodically as new networks are allocated to corporations, agencies, or other registries. This list should be reviewed periodically and updated for changes.

Connection Tracking

One of the components of the Netfilter suite is the connection tracking system. This is the Netfilter component that brings the ability to maintain connection state to the Linux kernel. As such, the total number connections Netfilter is able to simultaneously track or maintain the state of should be increased, or decreased, depending on the total number of connections the system can handle. The sample setting shown at the end of the sample script should be adequate for most systems.

Sample Basic IPTABLES Script

This script should be modified to take into consideration the services the system may be running as well as the IP addressing scheme of the network in which the server will reside. Specifically, the Bogon list may have to be modified to allow local private, RFC 1918 addresses.

```
#!/bin/sh
#IPTABLES Firewall Script
#Created 12 DEC 03
#
#### Variables ####
IPTABLES="/sbin/iptables"    ## Default IPTables
LOOPBACK="lo"                ## Loopback Interface
EXTERNAL="eth0"              ## External Interface
#### IP Address of Interface
EXT_IP=`ifconfig $EXTERNAL | grep inet | cut -d: -f2 | cut -d\ -f1`

ALLOWED_TCP_PORTS="22 443"
ALLOWED_UDP_PORTS=""

## Reserved/Private IP Addresses ##
## Bogon's updated 17NOV03 http://www.cymru.com/Documents/bogon-bn.html

BOGON_LIST="0.0.0.0/7 2.0.0.0/8 5.0.0.0/8 7.0.0.0/8 10.0.0.0/8 23.0.0.0/8 27.0.0.0/
8 31.0.0.0/8 36.0.0.0/7 39.0.0.0/8 41.0.0.0/8 42.0.0.0/8 49.0.0.0/8 50.0.0.0/8 58.0.0.0/
7 70.0.0.0/7 72.0.0.0/5 85.0.0.0/8 86.0.0.0/7 88.0.0.0/5 96.0.0.0/3 169.254.0.0/16
172.16.0.0/12 173.0.0.0/8 174.0.0.0/7 176.0.0.0/5 184.0.0.0/6 189.0.0.0/8 190.0.0.0/8
192.0.2.0/24 192.168.0.0/16 197.0.0.0/8 198.18.0.0/15 223.0.0.0/8 224.0.0.0/3"
```

```
## Flush and Delete All Rules In User Defined Tables
$IPTABLES -F
$IPTABLES -X
## Flush Built-in Rules
$IPTABLES -F INPUT
$IPTABLES -F OUTPUT
$IPTABLES -F FORWARD
## Set Default Policies
$IPTABLES -P INPUT DROP
$IPTABLES -P OUTPUT DROP
$IPTABLES -P FORWARD DROP


##-------------------------------------------------------------
## Maintain state of TCP traffic in all directions
$IPTABLES -N STATE
$IPTABLES -F STATE

$IPTABLES -A STATE -m state --state INVALID -j DROP
$IPTABLES -A STATE -m state --state RELATED,ESTABLISHED -j ACCEPT


##-------------------------------------------------------------
## Allowed Ports
$IPTABLES -N ALLOW_PORTS
$IPTABLES -F ALLOW_PORTS

## TCP Services allowed
for PORTS in $ALLOWED_TCP_PORTS; do
$IPTABLES -A ALLOW_PORTS -m state --state NEW -p tcp \
  --dport $PORTS -j ACCEPT
done

## UDP Services allowed
for PORTS in $ALLOWED_UDP_PORTS; do
$IPTABLES -A ALLOW_PORTS -m state --state NEW -p udp \
  --dport $PORTS -j ACCEPT
done


##-------------------------------------------------------------
## Allow ICMP
$IPTABLES -N ALLOW_ICMP
$IPTABLES -F ALLOW_ICMP

$IPTABLES -A ALLOW_ICMP -p icmp --icmp-type echo-reply -j ACCEPT
## Uncomment below when troubleshooting the network connectivity (allows Ping)
#$IPTABLES -A ALLOW_ICMP -p icmp --icmp-type echo-request -j ACCEPT
$IPTABLES -A ALLOW_ICMP -p icmp --icmp-type destination-unreachable -j ACCEPT
$IPTABLES -A ALLOW_ICMP -p icmp --icmp-type time-exceeded -j ACCEPT


##-------------------------------------------------------------
## INPUT to the Interfaces

$IPTABLES -A INPUT -i $LOOPBACK -j ACCEPT

## Filter out Bogon List - Reserved and Private IPs
for NETWORK in $BOGON_LIST; do
  $IPTABLES -A INPUT -s $NETWORK -j DROP
done

## Allowed TCP/UDP Ports.
$IPTABLES -A INPUT -i $EXTERNAL -j ALLOW_PORTS
```

```
## Allowed ICMP
$IPTABLES -A INPUT -i $EXTERNAL -j ALLOW_ICMP

## Check and Maintain TCP state
$IPTABLES -A INPUT -i $EXTERNAL -j STATE


##----------------------------------------------------------------
## OUTPUT on the interfaces

$IPTABLES -A OUTPUT -o $LOOPBACK -j ACCEPT

## Make sure system isn't sending illegal addresses (BOGONS).
for NETWORK in $BOGON_LIST; do
  $IPTABLES -A OUTPUT -d $NETWORK -j DROP
done

## Allow Outbound Pings
$IPTABLES -A OUTPUT -p icmp --icmp-type echo-request -j ACCEPT

## Check and Maintain TCP state, allow established connections
$IPTABLES -A OUTPUT -o $EXTERNAL -j STATE

## Allow all new outbound connections (take out if server does not initiate connections)
$IPTABLES -A OUTPUT -o $EXTERNAL -m state --state NEW -j ACCEPT


##----------------------------------------------------------------
## Connection Tracking
modprobe ip_conntrack
echo "4096" > /proc/sys/net/ipv4/ip_conntrack_max
```

FILE SYSTEM SECURITY

One of the easiest and yet most effective ways to ensure the integrity of the Linux platform is maintained is through the file system. There are a number a ways a system administrator can configure and set permissions on partitions, directories, and files to prevent the disclosure and modification of system files. This section will outline several of these controls and provide guidance on a few file types and permissions that the system administrator should periodically look for while performing regularly scheduled system maintenance.

system administrator can disable the ability of users to execute programs from a given partition. It is because of this ability to define access and execution permissions during system boot that the partitioning scheme chosen during system installation (refer to Installation Considerations) was used.

The /bin/mount utility is used to mount disk partitions. It is this same program that is used during system boot when the startup scripts begin to mount the disk partitions. Some of the access control mount options that can be passed via the /bin/mount utility are listed here:

```
ro:                        Mount the partition in read-only mode.
rw:                        Mount the partition in read-write mode.
nouser     (user):   Prevent users from mounting the partition.
noexec     (exec):   Prevent program execution on the partition.
nosuid     (suid):   Disable the SUID/SGID bits for the partition.
nodev      (dev):    Do not interpret character or block devices on the partition.
defaults:  Pass default options (rw, suid, dev, exec, auto, nouser, async).
```

Mount Control

One of the more effective controls that can be implemented for a Linux system is the control over partition permissions. There are several options that can be used when mounting a file system to ensure that various permissions are enforced partition-wide. For example, the

Note: The permissions pertain to the Linux ext2 and ext3 file systems. Refer to the http://www.kernel.org documentation for additional options that may be specific to other file systems.

The file /etc/fstab contains all of the mount options for each partition. This file is sourced when the system boots and begins mounting the file systems or when the system administrator uses the /bin/mount utility without supplying options. If the drive was partitioned as shown above (refer to Installation Considerations), the default /etc/fstab will look similar to this:

```
[root@TheBox/etc]# cat /etc/fstab
LABEL=/            /              ext3      defaults              11
LABEL=/boot        /boot          ext3      defaults              12
LABEL=/usr         /usr           ext3      defaults,nosuid,ro    12
LABEL=/home        /home          ext3      defaults              12
LABEL=/var         /var           ext3      defaults,nodev        12
LABEL=/tmp         /tmp           ext3      defaults,noexec,nosuid 12
LABEL=/chroot      /chroot        ext3      defaults              12
None               /dev/pts       devpts    gid=5,mode=620        00
None               /proc          proc      defaults              00
None               /dev/shm       tmpfs     defaults              00
/dev/sda3          swap           swap      defaults              00
/dev/cdrom         /mnt/cdrom     iso9660   noauto,owner,ro       00
/dev/fd0           /mnt/floppy    auto      noauto,owner          00
```

The recommended changes are shown in bold. There is one important recommendation that should be noted; the "RO" (read-only) option for /usr. This is an extremely effective control as it prevents users and ultimately attackers from modifying scripts, binaries, or any other file on this partition. The trade-off is that before the system can be updated, this partition will have to be remounted as "RW" (read–write) so that files on this partition can be overwritten with the updates. This may be a problem for patch management solutions where the update scripts cannot be modified to take this into consideration.

Once the /etc/fstab configuration file has been modified, the system administrator can remount the partition using the new options by issuing the following command for each partition that was updated:

```
[root@TheBox/]# mount <mountpoint> -oremount
```

Files and Directories

There are several steps that can be taken to further enhance the security of the Linux file system. These additional measures are outlined and should be reviewed periodically once the system goes into production. The following should be checked and verified on a weekly basis by the system administrator during regularly scheduled system maintenance:

- Check files and directories for valid owners and groups.
- Check for unowned files and directories.
- Check and validate world writable files.
- Check and validate world writeable directories.
- Check for the existence of unusual files.
- Check and validate root-owned SUID/SGID programs.

Note: All of these checks can be automated and their results e-mailed to the system administrator. See the section on Unusual Files for additional information.

System Files
The utilities /usr/bin/chattr and /usr/bin/lsattr allow a system administrator to change and list the ext2 and ext3 file system attributes of a file. With /usr/bin/chattr, the system administrator can set the immutable flag (+i)

on any file to prevent it from being accidentally or maliciously deleted or overwritten. The /usr/bin/lsattr simply lists files within any particular directory and displays the ext2/ext3 file attributes. See ext2/ext3 file system documentation for more information. The following changes are recommended:

```
[root@TheBox etc]# chattr +i /etc/services
[root@TheBox etc]# chattr +i /etc/passwd
[root@TheBox etc]# chattr +i /etc/group
[root@TheBox etc]# chattr +i /etc/shadow

[root@TheBox etc]# lsattr /etc
...
---i---------- /etc/group
...
---i---------- /etc/passwd
...
---i---------- /etc/services
...
---i---------- /etc/shadow
```

The utility /bin/chmod can be used to change the mode or permissions of a file or directory. Each file or directory can be assigned three basic permissions: read, write, or execute. Additionally, each of these permissions can be assigned to three classes of users: owner, group, and other or world. The permission format is as follows:

The output of the /bin/ls –l command will be a list of files within any particular directory and all of their permissions:

```
[root@TheBox etc]# ls -l
total 2388
-rw-r--r-- 1 root root 15228 Aug 5 2002 a2ps.cfg
-rw-r--r-- 1 root root 2562 Aug 5 2002 a2ps-site.cfg
-rw-r--r-- 1 root root 50 Dec 19 17:08 adjtime
drwxr-xr-x 4 root root 4096 Oct 23 2002 alchemist
...
```

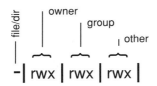

Figure 2: file and directory permissions.

File and directory permissions can be modified by using octal notation to specify each bit of the permissions specifically or by using the first letter of the permission group to modify (u: user, g: group, o: other or world) followed by a + or −, then the permission that needs to be added or removed (r: read, w: write, x: execute), as indicated in Figure 2. The files within the following directories should have their default permissions changed to ensure that users cannot accidentally or maliciously modify them. (Note: The default install of RedHat 9 and Fedora Core has many of these permissions already set. However, it is still a safe practice to follow up and ensure that each permission is set correctly.)

SUID/SGID

SUID/SGID (Set User ID/Set Group ID) bit is used to allow a program to run in the context of either the file owner or group. This may be useful when a program needs a higher privilege level to execute than the user running the program has been granted. Conversely, this capability is also dangerous because this may also allow a malicious user to take advantage of the program to escalate their privilege level. SUID/SGID programs become particularly dangerous when the file is owned by root. Unchecked buffers within root owned SUID/SGID program could allow a local attacker to gain root privileges. The following command will help a system administrator identify all programs on the system that have the SUID or SGID bit set.

Note: Do not indiscriminately remove the SUID/SGID bit from all programs because some are required for the system to operate. Removing the SUID/SGID bit from certain files will also disable capabilities that users should be able to do, such as changing their password.

```
[root@TheBox/]#chmod 0700/home/*              (-rwx------)
[root@TheBox/]#chmod 0640/etc/xinetd.d/*      (-rw-r------)
[root@TheBox/]#chmod 0751/etc/sysconfig       (-rwxr-x--x)
[root@TheBox/]#chmod 0751/var/log             (-rwxr-x--x)
[root@TheBox/]#chmod 0750/etc/pam.d           (-rwxr-x---)
[root@TheBox/]#chmod 0750/etc/security        (-rwxr-x---)
[root@TheBox/]#chmod 0750/etc/rc.d/init.d     (-rwxr-x---)
[root@TheBox/]#chmod 0750/etc/init.d          (-rwxr-x---)
```

The following files should have their default permissions changed to ensure that users cannot accidentally or maliciously modify them.

```
[root@TheBox/]#chmod 0700/etc/init.d/*           (-rwx------)
[root@TheBox/]#chmod 0550/etc/cron.hourly/*      (-r-xr-x---)
[root@TheBox/]#chmod 0550/etc/cron.daily/*       (-r-xr-x---)
[root@TheBox/]#chmod 0550/etc/cron.weekly/*      (-r-xr-x---)
[root@TheBox/]#chmod 0550/etc/cron.monthly/*     (-r-xr-x---)
[root@TheBox/]#chmod 0644/etc/passwd             (-rw-r--r--)
[root@TheBox/]#chmod 0644/etc/group              (-rw-r--r--)
[root@TheBox/]#chmod 0400/etc/shadow             (-r--------)
[root@TheBox/]#chmod 0600/boot/grub/grub.conf    (-rw-------)
[root@TheBox/]#chmod 0600/etc/sysconfig/iptables (-rw-------)
[root@TheBox/]#chmod 0600/etc/sysctl.conf        (-rw-------)
[root@TheBox/]#chmod 0600/etc/inittab            (-rw-------)
[root@TheBox/]#chmod 0600/var/log/messages       (-rw-------)
[root@TheBox/]#chmod 0640/etc/logrotate.conf     (-rw-r-----)
[root@TheBox/]#chmod 0660/var/log/wtmp           (-rw-r-----)
[root@TheBox/]#chmod 0400 /var/log/lastlog        (-r--------)
[root@TheBox/]#chmod 0640/etc/hosts.allow        (-rw-r-----)
[root@TheBox/]#chmod 0640/etc/hosts.deny         (-rw-r-----)
[root@TheBox/]#chmod 0600/etc/securetty          (-rw-------)
[root@TheBox/]#chmod 0640/etc/xinetd.conf        (-rw-r-----)
```

```
[root@TheBox/]#find/-type f \(-perm-04000-o-perm-02000 \)-exec ls-l{} \;
-rwsr-xr-x  1 root root 37624  Feb 12 2003/usr/bin/chage
-rwsr-xr-x  1 root root 34972  Feb 12 2003/usr/bin/gpasswd
-r-xr-sr-x  1 root tty 10224   Jul 18 2002/usr/bin/wall
-rws--x--x  1 root root 16835  Aug 30 2002/usr/bin/chfn
-rws--x--x  1 root root 15664  Aug 30 2002/usr/bin/chsh
-rws--x--x  1 root root 6999   Aug 30 2002/usr/bin/newgrp
-rwxr-sr-x  1 root tty 18605   Aug 30 2002/usr/bin/write
-rwxr-sr-x  1 root root 37140  Jul 24 2002/usr/bin/at
...
```

Once the SUID/SGID root files have been found, the /bin/chmod utility can be used to remove the SUID/SGID bit. It is recommended that the following root-owned programs have their SUID/SGID bits removed. Note: There are several root-owned programs with the SUID/SGID bits set that are required for normal system operation. Be sure to use discretion when removing the SUID/SGID bits on other programs.

```
[root@TheBox /]# chmod -s /usr/bin/chage
[root@TheBox /]# chmod -s /usr/bin/gpasswd
[root@TheBox /]# chmod -s /usr/bin/wall
[root@TheBox /]# chmod -s /usr/bin/chfn
[root@TheBox /]# chmod -s /usr/bin/chsh
[root@TheBox /]# chmod -s /usr/bin/newgrp
[root@TheBox /]# chmod -s /usr/bin/write
[root@TheBox /]# chmod -s /usr/sbin/ping6
[root@TheBox /]# chmod -s /usr/sbin/traceroute6
[root@TheBox /]# chmod -s /usr/sbin/usernetctl
[root@TheBox /]# chmod -s /usr/sbin/traceroute
[root@TheBox /]# chmod -s /bin/ping
[root@TheBox /]# chmod -s /bin/mount
[root@TheBox /]# chmod -s /bin/umount
[root@TheBox /]# chmod -s /sbin/netreport
```

Unusual Files

Files and directories whose names start with "." (dot) are considered hidden because by default they are not displayed by the /bin/ls command. Attackers, once they have gained access to the system, will typically use hidden and obscure files and directories to avoid detection. Additionally, files or directories that have world-writable permissions set should be kept to a minimum as well. Typically, these types of files and directories are temporary directories and program caches, both of which must remain world-writable. Look for hidden and unusual files:

```
[root@TheBox/]#find/-name "..*"-print-xdev
```

Find world-writable directories and files:

```
[root@TheBox/]#find/-type d-perm-2-exec ls-l{} \;
[root@TheBox/]#find/-type f-perm-2-exec ls-l{} \;
```

Find group-writable directories and files:

```
[root@TheBox/]#find/-type d-perm-20-exec ls-l{} \;
[root@TheBox/]#find/-type f-perm-20-exec ls-l{} \;
```

Do not allow files or directories, without owners and/or groups assigned to them, to reside on the system. If any are found and it can be verified that the system has not been compromised, assign the file/directory an owner. Otherwise, an investigation may be necessary to determine if the system has been compromised.

Find files without owners:

```
[root@TheBox /]# find / -nogroup -o -nouser
```

APPLICATIONS AND SERVICE DAEMONS

After the installation of a new Linux system, there are several application and service daemons that are initiated by default. Many of these default services are insecure and are typically unneeded; as such, these services should be disabled and uninstalled to ensure that they cannot be used as an avenue of attack.

Additionally, it is important to note that the Linux system should provide a single service to the organization. The system administrator should avoid using the system for multiple applications and services as each additional service adds another layer of management, an additional point of compromise, and also affects the effectiveness of an intrusion detection system to specifically monitor for attacks upon each service.

This section takes the system administrator through several system components that control the initialization of system services while providing general guidance on each service.

/etc/init.d

/etc/init.d is a directory that contains several scripts that are used to control various system and application daemons. It is from this directory that various scripts are executed during system boot to load various services. Depending on the runlevel, there are several services that are enabled by default and that should be disabled if they are not being used. Considering that these services themselves are also in a default configuration, they potentially may provide an avenue for attack.

These services and recommendations listed in Table 2 are based on a minimalist install base. Installation considerations from the first section should be kept in mind when reviewing these recommendations.

Terminating Init.d Services

Change directories to the */etc/init.d/* directory. Note: */etc/init.d* is a symbolic link to */etc/rc.d/init.d* and can be referenced from its full or symbolic path.

```
[root@TheBox/]# cd /etc/init.d/
[root@TheBox init.d]#
```

Terminate the daemon by executing the respective script with the "stop" parameter.

```
[root@TheBox init.d]# ./<script> stop
Stopping <script>: [ OK ]
```

If the script was successful in terminating the service, this response will be printed to the console. You may receive a "[FAILED]" response if the service is not currently running or if the script was not able to disable the service. In the case of the latter, using the *ps –aux* command to identify the service process ID followed by the *kill* command with the "-9" parameter and the process ID will forcibly unload the daemon that is controlled by the */etc/init.d/* script. Once a service has been terminated, be sure to disable the service to prevent it from reloading on the next reboot.

Disabling *init.d* Services

Init.d services are configured using the */sbin/chkconfig* command line utility. This utility can be used to quickly ensure that scripts either start up in the appropriate order or are disabled (or enabled) during system boot for any particular runlevel.

It is important to first determine which runlevel the system will be operating in when in the production environment. The default runlevel for a multiuser Red Hat Linux system is 3. The current runlevel can be determined by using the runlevel command:

```
[root@TheBox init.d]# runlevel
N 3
```

In this example, */sbin/chkconfig* will be used to modify the scripts under */etc/rc.d/rc3.d*. If the current runlevel is not 3 and the intention is to use runlevel 3 once the server is deployed, then */etc/inittab* must be modified to ensure that your */etc/init.d* changes take effect during subsequent system boots. Modify the line in */etc/inittab* from

```
id:5:initdefault:
```

to

```
id:3:initdefault:
```

To disable a particular script from executing and loading the respective service during system boot, use the */sbin/chkconfig* command as follows:

```
[root@TheBox init.d]#chkconfig--level 3
  <service>off
```

The "level" parameter is the runlevel in which the service will be modified, followed by the script name, followed lastly by the switch on/off.

The command */sbin/chkconfig's* only function in this case is to toggle the name of a symbolic link to the script that is being disabled. There are several */etc/rc#.d* (links to */etc/rc.d/rc#.d*) directories, one per respective runlevel, that house these symbolic links. A */bin/ls –la* from any of the */etc/rc#.d* directories will show this. */sbin/chkconfig* simply reads the script from */etc/init.d* and determines shutdown or startup order:

```
[root@TheBox rc3.d]# more ../init.d/xinetd
#!/bin/bash
#
# xinetd This starts and stops xinetd.
#
# chkconfig: 345 56 50
```

Then, rename the symbolic link to this script from

```
[root@TheBox rc3.d]# ls *xinetd
S56xinetd
```

or "Start" to

```
[root@TheBox rc3.d]# ls *xinetd
K50xinetd
```

"Kill." Simply list the files in the respective runlevel directory to ensure that the script in question has a "K" as the first letter of its name. The initialization script will ignore these files during system boot for this runlevel.

Uninstalling init.d Services

After shutting down and disabling unneeded services, the service or application package should be removed from the system. The RedHat Package Manager (RPM) can be used to quickly uninstall any package using the following command:

```
[root@infosec/]# rpm -e <package name>
```

See the section on Patch and Package Management for more information on how to use RPM.

Xinetd

Xinetd is the Extended Internet Services Daemon. This daemon is used to control several of the small services within RedHat Linux. *Xinetd* replaces the older *inetd* and introduces several new features. Table 3 lists services that can be controlled out of the box with *Xinetd*. It is recommended that each of these services, and ultimately *Xinetd*,

Table 2 /etc/init.d Services and Scripts

Script Name	Service Description	Recommendation
Anacron	*anacron* is a daemon that will execute jobs at a specified frequency as opposed to a set time like *cron*.	DISABLE,UNINSTALL (unless system will not be up 24/7)
APMD	*apmd* is used for monitoring battery status and logging it syslog(8). It can also be used for shutting down the machine when the battery is low.	DISABLE,UNINSTALL (unless system is a laptop)
ARPwatch	The *arpwatch* daemon attempts to keep track of ethernet/ip address pairings.	ENABLE (useful for network forensics)
ATD	Runs commands scheduled by the *at* command at the time specified when *at* was run, and runs batch commands when the load average is low enough.	DISABLE,UNINSTALL (vixie-cron supersedes atd)
Autofs	Automounts file systems on demand. This is typically invoked during system boot time to control the *automount* daemon.	DISABLE,UNINSTALL (unless using remote NFS file systems)
Crond	*crond* is a standard UNIX program that runs user-specified programs at periodic scheduled times. vixie cron adds a number of features to the basic UNIX cron, including better security and more powerful configuration options.	ENABLE
Firstboot	Firstboot is a druid-style program that runs the first time a machine is booted after install. It checks for the existence of an /etc/sysconfig/firstboot file. If it does not find the file, then the firstboot program needs to run. If it finds the file, firstboot will not be run. If /etc/reconfigSys exists, run the reconfiguration program and remove /etc/reconfigSys when done. (Also will run if 'reconfig' is on the kernel cmdline.)	DISABLE,UNINSTALL (Once the system has been built, this script will not be used again.)
Functions	This file contains functions to be used by most of the shell scripts in the /etc/init.d directory. This file is sourced by other /etc/init.d scripts to simplify several common functions.	IGNORE (This is not a service.)
GPM	*gpm* adds mouse support to text-based Linux applications such the Midnight Commander. Is also allows mouse-based console cut-and-paste operations, and includes support for pop-up menus on the console.	DISABLE,UNINSTALL (This is only useful on the console.)
Halt	This file is executed by init when it goes into runlevel 0 (halt) or runlevel 6 (reboot). It kills all processes, unmounts file systems, and then either halts or reboots.	IGNORE (This is not a service.)
Iptables	Automates a packet-filtering firewall with *iptables*.	ENABLE
Irda	This shell script takes care of starting and stopping IrDA support IrDA stack for Linux (Infrared).	DISABLE,UNINSTALL (unless IR access is required)
ISDN	This shell script controls ISDN support for Linux.	DISABLE,UNINSTALL (unless native ISDN support is required)
Kdcrotate	Rotate the list of KDCs (Key Distribution Centers) listed in /etc/krb5.conf.	DISABLE,UNISTALL (unless the system is part of a Kerberos domain)
Keytable	This package loads the selected keyboard map as set in /etc/sysconfig/keyboard. This can be selected using the kbdconfig utility.	ENABLE
Killall	Shell script that will bring down all services, defined on the command line, that are still running (there should not be any, so this is just a sanity check).	IGNORE (This is not a service.)
Kudzu	This runs the hardware probe and optionally configures changed hardware.	DISABLE (This may be convenient if the system is upgraded.)
LPD	*lpd* is the print daemon required for lpr to work properly. It is basically a server that arbitrates print jobs to printer(s).	DISABLE,UNISTALL (unless printing directly from the system is required)

(Continued)

Table 2 (*Continued*)

Script Name	Service Description	Recommendation
Netfs	Mounts and unmounts all Network File System (NFS), SMB (Lan Manager/Windows), and NCP (NetWare) mount points.	DISABLE (unless using remote file systems)
Network	Activates/deactivates all network interfaces configured to start at boot time.	ENABLE
NFS	NFS is a popular protocol for file sharing across TCP/IP networks. This service provides NFS server functionality, which is configured via the /etc/exports file.	DISABLE,UNINSTALL (unless the system will be a NFS server)
NFSlock	NFS is a popular protocol for file sharing across TCP/IP networks. This service provides NFS file locking functionality.	DISABLE,UNINSTALL (unless the system will be a NFS server)
NSCD	Name Switch Cache Daemon. This is a daemon which handles password and group lookups for running programs and cache the results for the next query. You should start this daemon if you use slow naming services such as NIS, NIS+, LDAP, or hesiod.	DISABLE,UNINSTALL
NTPD	*ntpd* is the NTPv4 daemon.	DISABLE,UNINSTALL (unless system will be a time server)
PCMCIA	PCMCIA support is usually to support things such as Ethernet and modems in laptops.	DISABLE,UNINSTALL (unless system is a laptop)
Portmap	The *portmapper* manages RPC connections, which are used by protocols such as NFS and NIS.	DISABLE,UNINSTALL (unless system is a servers which makes use of the RPC mechanism)
Postfix	*postfix* is a Mail Transport Agent, which is the program that moves mail from one machine to another.	DISABLE,UNINSTALL
Random	Saves and restores system entropy pool for higher quality random number generation.	ENABLE
Rawdevices	This scripts assignes raw devices to block devices (such as hard drive partitions). This is for the use of applications such as Oracle. You can set up the raw device to block device mapping by editing the file /etc/sysconfig/rawdevices.	ENABLE
RHNSD	This is a daemon which handles the task of connecting periodically to the Red Hat Network servers to check for updates and notifications and perform system monitoring tasks according to the service level to which this server is subscribed.	DISABLE (manually perform update checks)
Saslauthd	*saslauthd* is a server process which handles plaintext authentication requests on behalf of the cyrus-sasl library.	DISABLE,UNINSTALL
Sendmail	*sendmail* is a Mail Transport Agent, which is the program that moves mail from one machine to another.	DISABLE,UNINSTALL (unless system is a mail server)
Single	This file is executed by init when it goes into runlevel 1, which is the administrative state. It kills all deamons and then puts the system into single user mode. Note that the file systems are kept mounted.	IGNORE (This is not a service.)
SNMPD	Simple Network Management Protocol (SNMP) Daemon	DISABLE (unless system will be monitored using SNMP)
SNMPTRAPD	Simple Network Management Protocol (SNMP) Trap Daemon	DISABLE (unless system handling SNMP traps from other systems)
SSHD	OpenSSH server daemon	ENABLE
Syslog	Syslog is the facility by which many daemons use to log messages to various system log files. It is a good idea to always run syslog.	ENABLE

(*Continued*)

Table 2 (*Continued*)

Script Name	Service Description	Recommendation
Winbind	Starts and stops the Samba *winbind* daemon	DISABLE,UNINSTALL (unless system will be part of an Windows domain or will be a MS file and print server)
XFS	Starts and stops the X Font Server at boot time and shutdown. It also takes care of (re-)generating font lists.	DISABLE,UNINSTALL (unless system has Xfree installed)
Xinetd	*xinetd* is a powerful replacement for inetd. xinetd has access control mechanisms, extensive logging capabilities, the ability to make services available based on time, and can place limits on the number of servers that can be started, among other things.	DISABLE,UNINSTALL (See section on xinetd below.)
YPbind	This is a daemon which runs on NIS/YP clients and binds them to a NIS domain. It must be running for systems based on glibc to work as NIS clients, but it should not be enabled on systems which are not using NIS.	DISABLE,UNINSTALL (unless system is part of a NIS/YP domain)

Table 3 /etc/xinetd.d Services

Service Name	Service Descriptions
Chargen	An xinetd internal service that generates characters. The xinetd internal service that continuously generates characters until the connection is dropped. The characters look something like this: !"#$%&'()*+,- ./0123456789:;<=>?@ABCDEFGHIJKLMNOPQRSTUVWXYZ[\]^_`abcdefg This is the tcp version.
chargen-udp	An xinetd internal service that generates characters. The xinetd internal service that continuously generates characters until the connection is dropped. The characters look something like this: !"#$%&'()*+,- ./0123456789:;<=>?@ABCDEFGHIJKLMNOPQRSTUVWXYZ[\]^_`abcdefg This is the tcp version.
Daytime	An internal xinetd service that gets the current system time then prints it out in a format like this: "Wed Nov 13 22:30:27 EST 2002". This is the tcp version.
daytime-udp	An internal xinetd service that gets the current system time then prints it out in a format like this: "Wed Nov 13 22:30:27 EST 2002". This is the udp version.
Echo	An xinetd internal service that echoes characters back to clients. This is the tcp version.
echo-udp	An xinetd internal service that echoes characters back to clients. This is the udp version.
Finger	The finger server answers finger requests. Finger is a protocol that allows remote users to see information such as login name and last login time for local users.
rsync	The rsync server is a good addition to am ftp server, as it allows crc checksumming, etc.
servers	An internal xinetd service, listing active servers.
Services	An internal xinetd service, listing active servers.
sgi_fam	FAM is a file monitoring daemon. It can be used to get reports when files change.
time	An RFC 868 time server. This protocol provides a site-independent, machine-readable date and time. The time service sends back to the originating source the time in seconds since midnight on January first 1900. This is the tcp version.
time_udp	An RFC 868 time server. This protocol provides a site-independent, machine-readable date and time. The time service sends back to the originating source the time in seconds since midnight on January first 1900. This is the udp version.
Wu-ftpd	The wu-ftpd (Washington University) FTP server serves FTP connections. It uses normal, unencrypted usernames and passwords for authentication.

be disabled. If one or more small service is required, the *Xinetd* service cannot be disabled, however, the other small services should be disabled. The *Xinetd* services are located in */etc/xinetd.d*. The configuration for the *Xinetd* daemon itself is */etc/xinetd.conf*.

Each service that is controlled by the *Xinetd* daemon is configured by modifying the parameters defined in each of the respective service files in the */etc/xinetd.d* directory. For example, the content of the *wu-ftpd* configuration file is shown as follows:

```
[root@TheBox xinetd.d]# pwd
/etc/xinetd.d

[root@TheBox xinetd.d]# more wu-ftpd
# default: on
# description: The wu-ftpd FTP server serves
  FTP connections. It uses \
# normal, unencrypted usernames and passwords
  for authentication.
service ftp
{
        socket_type        = stream
        wait               = no
        user               = root
        server             = /usr/sbin/in.ftpd
        server_args        = -l -a
        log_on_success    += DURATION USERID
        log_on_failure    += USERID
        nice               = 10
        disable            = no
}
[root@TheBox xinetd.d]#
```

Disabling Services in *Xinetd*

Disabling individual services that are controlled by *Xinetd* is as easy as editing a text file. In the example shown, simply edit each configuration file and add:

```
disable = yes
```

Finally, simply reload the *Xinetd* daemon from the */etc/init.d/* directory to reread the service configuration files and apply the changes.

```
[root@TheBox xinetd.d]#/etc/init.d/xinetd reload
Reloading configuration:[SUCCESS]
[root@TheBox xinetd.d]#
```

Note: For quick shortcut to determine which services are enabled for each runlevel as well as which *Xinetd* services are enabled use *chkconfig –list*.

Verification

Once the default *init.d* services have been stopped and disabled from reloading during the next system boot, it is important to verify that the services have in fact been stopped. The verification step is also important as it allows the system administrator to determine if there are any other services enabled that are unneeded.

There are several tools that are available with a default Linux install that will allow the administrator to quickly determine if there are additional services running in the background. These tools will list running services that are both accessible remotely and those that are accessible by local users. (More information about these tools can be found by typing "*man <toolname>*" on the command line.)

/bin/ps -A:	List running processes with their process IDs. (-A switch shows all processes.)
/bin/netstat –l:	Prints information about processes listening on TCP/UDP ports.
/usr/bin/lsof –i:	Lists open files. (-i switch lists all open files using an IP socket.)
/sbin/service –status-all:	Script to quickly output the status of the services configured to start during startup of the current init runlevel.

If any process is found that is unknown, unneeded, or unauthorized, the "*/sbin/kill <ps id>*" command can be used to stop or "kill" the running process.

Restricting Applications and Services

Although the details of hardening an application or service that may be installed on the Linux platform is outside the scope of this chapter, there are a few Linux system capabilities that are available to the system administrator that will help to control and limit application or service access to the underlying Linux platform. Each of these capabilities including the steps taken so far introduces an additional layer of defense against would-be attackers.

Chroot Jail

Outside of the configuration of an application or service itself, as shown previously, there are several steps a system administrator can take to ensure that the integrity of the operating system is not compromised even after an application or service has been. One additional method is provided by using */usr/bin/chroot*, also referred to as a process "jail."

By using */usr/bin/chroot* or "change root," the system administrator effectively "jails" the application or service into a particular location on the file system. When the application or service is executed, the effective "root" directory is defined by the system administrator. This is to ensure that if the application or service is compromised, the attacker will have far less access to the operating system than if the process was executed from its absolute program path.

Any program can be jailed using */usr/bin/chroot* by using the syntax shown here.

```
[root@TheBox/]#chroot/<newrootdir>/bin/<program>
```

There are, however, a few caveats when using */usr/bin/chroot*. The command works well with statically linked binaries; however, it would prevent dynamically linked binaries from executing as the binary is linked to libraries that are no longer available via the relative path. To use */usr/bin/chroot* with dynamically linked binaries, the libraries used by the executable will have to be copied into the new relative path of the *chroot'd* binary. For example, if a service is jailed within the */chroot* directory from above, the binary would have to be copied to its relative path under the */chroot* directory as well as all of its libraries and configuration files.

```
[root@TheBox chroot]# pwd
/chroot
[root@TheBox chroot]# ls -lF
total 157
drwxr-xr-x 2 root chroot 4096 Feb 13 2003 bin/
drwxr-xr-x 18 root chroot 86016 Sep 17 17:06 dev/
drwxr-xr-x 43 root chroot 4096 Sep 18 16:05 etc/
drwxr-xr-x 6 root chroot 4096 Sep 18 16:05 lib/
drwxrwxrwt 4 root chroot 4096 Jan 12 04:02 tmp/
drwxr-xr-x 16 root chroot 4096 Sep 18 14:42 usr/
drwxr-xr-x 19 root chroot 4096 Feb 14 2003 var/
[root@TheBox chroot]#
```

TCP Wrappers

TCP wrappers is a TCP/IP daemon wrapper that provides host- and user-based access control for the *Xinetd* (*Inetd*) services such as telnet, FTP, finger, RSH, TFTP, and several others. TCP wrappers was written and continues to be maintained by Wietse Venema. Additional information on TCP wrappers and the source code is available from ftp://ftp.porcupine.org/pub/security/index.html.

If any of the *Xinetd* services will be used, it is recommended that TCP wrappers be configured to allow only known, trusted hosts to use these services. Service access control or the trust relationships are implemented and managed through two files, */etc/hosts.allow'* and */etc/hosts.deny*.

Following the "default deny" or "permit by exception" rules, the following line should be added to the */etc/hosts.deny* to explicitly deny all connections to wrapped services unless they are specified within */etc/hosts.allow*:

```
[root@TheBox etc]# cat hosts.deny
#hosts.deny  This file describes the names
 of the hosts which are
#        *not* allowed to use the local INET
            services, as decided
#        by the'/usr/sbin/tcpd'server.
#Deny access to everything
ALL: ALL
[root@TheBox etc]#
```

Entries can now be made within */etc/hosts.allow* to allow access to specified services from specified hosts and users. Here is a sample format of this file:

<Xinetd daemon>: <client, client2> :<options> :<shell command>

For additional information, it is recommended that the manual pages for TCP wrappers be referenced for the specific configuration options.

Application and Services References

NFS Server
Linux NFS Howto: http://en.tldp.org/HOWTO/NFS-HOWTO/security.html

FTP Server
ISP Setup RedHat Howto: http://en.tldp.org/HOWTO/ISP-Setup-RedHat-HOWTO-4.html#ss4.11

Sendmail (SMTP)
ISP Setup RedHat Howto: http://en.tldp.org/HOWTO/ISP-Setup-RedHat-HOWTO-4.html#ss4.9

HTTP Server
Apache+SSL+PHP-FP Howto: http://en.tldp.org/HOWTO/Apache+SSL+PHP+fp.html
Apache Overview Howto: http:// en.tldp.org/HOWTO/Apache-Overview-HOWTO.html

Secure Shell Server (SSH)
OpenSSH Manuals: http://www.openssh.org/manual.html

Xwindows
Xfree Local/Multiuser Howto: http://en.tldp.org/HOWTO/XFree-Local-multi-user-HOWTO/index.html

Virtual Private Networking (VPN)
VPN Howto: http://en.tldp.org/HOWTO/VPN-HOWTO/index.html

PATCH AND PACKAGE MANAGEMENT

Once the system has been built, it is important to ensure that all of the installed services and applications are and remain up to date. There are two tools that ship with RedHat Linux and distributions based on RedHat Linux that make the maintenance task of patch and package management easier for a system administrator: *Up2date* and *RPM*. This section reviews some of the capabilities of these tools.

RPM (RedHat Package Manager)

The RedHat Package Manager is an extremely powerful tool that allows the system administrator to quickly install, uninstall, upgrade, query, and verify *RPM* packages. Following is a list of some of the commands that can be used to quickly perform a variety of package management tasks. For more information, use *man rpm* on the command line to bring up the *RPM* manual.

Installing an RPM Package
The switch *"-ivh"* will have *"rpm"* install the package, with verbose output turned on, and will print out status hash marks to show installation progress.

```
[root@TheBox/]#rpm-ivh<packagename. (version) .
 (release).(arch).rpm>
```

Uninstalling an RPM Package

When uninstalling an *RPM* package, only the package name is required.

```
[root@TheBox/]#rpm -e <packagename>
```

Upgrading an RPM Package

The "*-U*" switch will upgrade an rpm package that was previously installed. The problem with this option is that if "rpm" does not find a previous install, *rpm* will install this package as new without warning.

```
[root@TheBox/]#rpm-Uvh<packagename.(version).
  (release).(arch).rpm>
```

To be safe use the "-F" or Freshen switch to have *rpm* perform an upgrade only if the rpm package has already been installed.

```
[root@TheBox/]#rpm-Fvh<packagename.(version).
  (release).(arch).rpm>
```

Querying an *RPM* Package

The query switch can be used to quickly verify if a particular package and version has been installed. The switch can be used in conjunction with "-" and -l to show additional package information and/or to list the contents of the installed package, respectively.

```
[root@TheBox /]# rpm -q <packagename>
```

Additionally, the "-qf" switch can be used to quickly identify which *RPM* package installed a particular file on the system.

```
[root@TheBox /]# rpm -qf <filename>
```

The "-qp" switch can also be used to query information about a package file before it is installed (the "p" switch provides this capability). The list switch "-l" or the "-'" switches shown can be used with this type of query as well.

```
[root@TheBox /]# rpm -qp ./<packagename.(version).
  (release).(arch).rpm>
```

Verifying an RPM Package

Another powerful feature of rpm is the ability to verify installed rpm packages and their associated files. The verify switch will have rpm validate the file specified on the command line and its associated rpm package against the *RPM* database to ensure that each of the files associated with the package have not been modified or corrupted. The rpm package name can be specified on the command line as well. Descriptive errors will be returned if the file or package has been modified in any way.

```
[root@TheBox /]# rpm -Vf <filename>
```

Up2date

As the name of the tool suggests, *up2date* is an *RPM* package update tool that works with RedHat's online service (http://rhn.redhat.com) to maintain *RPM* packages and to ensure the system is kept up to date with the latest rpm package releases. *Up2date* is a simple-to-use graphical and text-based update tool. The tool can be used either via the command line or via the GUI to quickly query the "package updates" list on RedHat Linux distribution servers (ftp://ftp.redhat.com/pub/redhat/linux/updates/current/en/os/). For more information about up2date, bring up the manual by typing *man up2date* on the command line.

ROOT, USER, AND GROUP ACCOUNTS

Regardless of the application or service that will define the purpose of the Linux platform, invariably users and other system administrators will require access to the system itself. Whether it is for system administration, system and application maintenance, backups, or auditing, multiple users will need access to the system. This section will review some of the best practices for granting system access to both system administrators and generic users.

Note About Passwords

Given enough time and sufficient resources, any password can be broken. The trick is to choose a password that is complex enough so that the only possible method to recover the password is through brute force attack, barring of course, social engineering or the yellow sticky note recovery hack. Choosing an appropriate lock-out policy will greatly affect the success of brute force and other password recovery attacks as well as provide a simple mechanism to alert the system administrator of the recovery attempts.

Picking an appropriate aging policy is also important. A period should be chosen so that the approximate time that it would take to brute force the password is significantly longer than the age of the password.

A few things to keep in mind:

- Consider the criticality of the system. Take into account the installation considerations.
- Enforce password complexity requirements that require at least eight characters, at least one special character, and at least one number.
- Passwords should not be trivial. They should not be personalized or based on a dictionary word in any language.
- Password aging policies should be enforced.
- Lock-out policies should be enforced as appropriate for the system user base.

Root Account

The root account is the *NIX system administration account. This is the central and most privileged account on the system. The system does not enforce any restrictions of any kind on this account. As such, the use of the root account should be controlled and limited. System administrators should have personalized user accounts created for them and only use the */bin/su* command to become root when absolutely necessary.

Once logged into the system as a user, the system administrator can "Super User" to root with the */bin/su* command. The "*-l*" command line switch instructs */bin/su* to load the root user's login scripts. (This may be useful when running commands that are only in the root user's path variable.)

```
[sysadmin-1@TheBox sysadmin-1]$ id
uid=500(sysadmin-1)gid=500(sysadmin-1)
   groups=500(sysadmin-1)
[sysadmin-1@TheBox sysadmin-1]$ su -l
Password:
[root@TheBox root]#id
uid=0(root) gid=0(root) groups=0(root),1(bin),
   2(daemon),3(sys),4(adm),6(disk),10(wheel)
[root@TheBox root]# pwd
/root
[root@TheBox root]#
```

One way to enforce the use of personalized system administrator accounts is by specifying on which TTYs and VCs (virtual consoles) the root user can login. This will help to ensure that administrators log into the system with their user account and *su* to root or use *sudo* to execute a command. Comment out all of the lines *except* "tty1" and "vc/1" out of the */etc/securetty* file. The login program *(/bin/login)* will read this file and will deny a root login on any TTY or VC that is not specified in this file.

User and Group Accounts

Basic Maintenance
There are five basic commands that are used to maintain accounts on the system. They are as follows:

/usr/sbin/useradd: Used to create user accounts.
/usr/sbin/groupadd: Used to create user groups.
/usr/sbin/userdel: Used to delete user accounts.
/usr/sbin/groupdel: Used to delete user groups.
/usr/bin/passwd: Used to set and change account passwords.

All user accounts are maintained in the file */etc/password*. Because this file must be world-readable, it is not a good idea to leave the encrypted account passwords in this file. Following the installation guidance, SHADOW passwords should be enabled, which would store the encrypted account passwords in the file */etc/shadow*, which is only readable by root.

Unused System Accounts
During system installation, there are several accounts that are created to support a variety of system activities, most of which will never be used. Consider what services the system will be supporting and delete all accounts not directly related to each service. As an example, the MySQL database daemon runs as the "mysql" user account for security reasons. This account would be needed to run this type of database server.

These accounts and their corresponding groups are safe to remove from a minimalist install base:

```
[root@TheBox etc]# cat /etc/passwd
root:x:0:0:root:/root:/bin/bash
bin:x:1:1:bin:/bin:/sbin/nologin
daemon:x:2:2:daemon:/sbin:/sbin/nologin
adm:x:3:4:adm:/var/adm:/sbin/nologin
lp:x:4:7:lp:/var/spool/lpd:/sbin/nologin
sync:x:5:0:sync:/sbin:/bin/sync
shutdown:x:6:0:shutdown:/sbin:/sbin/shutdown
halt:x:7:0:halt:/sbin:/sbin/halt
mail:x:8:12:mail:/var/spool/mail:/sbin/nologin
news:x:9:13:news:/etc/news:
uucp:x:10:14:uucp:/var/spool/uucp:/sbin/nologin
operator:x:11:0:operator:/root:/sbin/nologin
games:x:12:100:games:/usr/games:/sbin/nologin
gopher:x:13:30:gopher:/var/gopher:/sbin/nologin
ftp:x:14:50:FTP User:/var/ftp:/sbin/nologin
nobody:x:99:99:Nobody:/:/sbin/nologin
rpm:x:37:37::/var/lib/rpm:/sbin/nologin
vcsa:x:69:69:virtual console memory owner:/dev:
 /sbin/nologin
mailnull:x:47:47::/var/spool/mqueue:/sbin/
 nologin
sysadmin-1:x:500:500::/home/sysadmin-1:/bin/bash
[root@TheBox etc]#
```

Be sure to review */etc/groups* and remove any reference to the deleted user accounts. Note that there may be additional user groups without associated user accounts that should also be removed. This one is safe to remove from a minimalist install base:

dip:x:40:

Account Timeouts
To set account idle timeouts, the system administrator will have to modify the */etc/profile* file. Make the following additions to this file to set the timeout for all accounts:

```
HOSTNAME=`/bin/hostname`
HISTSIZE=1000
TMOUT=<some time in seconds>
...
export PATH USER LOGNAME MAIL HOSTNAME
   HISTSIZE INPUTRC  TMOUT
```

Shell Command Logging
The BASH shell (the default command shell provided to the user after logging in via console, telnet, or ssh) has the ability to log *(~/.bash_history)* any number of previously executed commands to assist users with recalling earlier commands. The default length of this buffer (1000) should be significantly reduced (20).

```
HOSTNAME=`/bin/hostname`
HISTSIZE= 20
```

In addition, the log file *(~/.bash_history)* should be deleted once the user logs out. Make the following additions to have BASH wipe the history file upon logout for all users:

```
HOSTNAME=`/bin/hostname`
HISTSIZE=1000
HISTFILESIZE=0
...
export PATH USER LOGNAME MAIL HOSTNAME
  HISTSIZE INPUTRC TMOUT HISTFILESIZE
```

Account Aging

Users should be required to periodically change their passwords. Depending on the criticality of the system that users are accessing, the recommended settings should be adjusted. Edit the */etc/login.defs* configuration file and make the following modifications. (note: The minimum password length setting is depreciated and no longer works.)

```
[root@TheBox etc]# cat login.defs
...
PASS_MAX_DAYS 90
PASS_MIN_DAYS 15
PASS_WARN_AGE 10
...
```

PAM

Linux uses PAM (Pluggable Authentication Modules) to take authentication schemes out of the individual applications and to provide a shared mechanism for all system and application authentication. For more information on PAM, see http://www.kernel.org/pub/linux/libs/pam/modules.html.

The default password length of 5 characters is not sufficient and should be changed to at least 10 characters. Edit */etc/pam.d/system-auth* and make the following additions to enforce the password definitions:

```
password required /lib/security/pam_cracklib.
  so retry=3 minlen=10 lcredit=-1 ucredit=-1
password sufficient /lib/security/pam_unix.
  so nullok use_authtok md5 shadow
  remember=15
```

PAM_tally is a PAM module that provides account lockout services to PAM. This module will keep track of failed login attempts and if the number of login attempts exceeds a specified threshold, *PAM_tally* will lock the account for a period of time. Edit */etc/pam.d/system-auth* and make the following additions to enable account lockout:

```
account required/lib/security/pam_tally.
 so deny=4 no_magic_root
```

SUDO

To support the delegation of system administration duties without supplying the root account password to multiple users and other system administrators, the */usr/bin/sudo* utility can be used to run various programs or scripts in the context of the root user. The */usr/bin/sudo* program is configured by modifying the */etc/sudoers* file. For more information on SUDO, see http://www.courtesan.com/sudo/.

SYSTEM AUDITING

Although the level of granularity may vary depending on system criticality, every system deployed within a production environment should have system logging enabled. The system should be reporting user, system, and process activity to a centralized location either on the local system or, better yet, on a remote logging server. Additionally, with the help of system log file analysis and audit tools, the log files should be reviewed periodically for system modification, errors, and intrusions. The following is a list of events that should be logged and reviewed:

- system startup and shutdown (unsuccessful and successful),
- system administration actions (unsuccessful and successful),
- security personnel actions (unsuccessful and successful),
- logon (unsuccessful and successful) and logout (successful),
- unauthorized access attempts to files (unsuccessful),
- use of privileged commands (unsuccessful and successful),
- application and session initiation (unsuccessful and successful),
- use of print command (unsuccessful and successful),
- access control permission modification (unsuccessful and successful),
- export to media (successful)
- files and programs deleted by users (successful and unsuccessful).

Syslog

Syslog is the primary system logging daemon for the Linux system. The *Syslog* daemon can be used to log system messages locally or to a remote *Syslog* server. The daemon is configured by the */etc/syslog.conf* file. Initialization of the *Syslog* daemon is controlled by *Init* and is configured when the system initializes with */etc/sysconfig/syslog*. By default, the *Syslog* daemon is configured to log messages locally (*/var/log/*) and to not accept messages from other systems. If the system is to be configured as a *Syslog* server, please see manual pages for specific server configuration options.

The */etc/syslog.conf* file contains rules that define how the *Syslog* daemon should handle messages from the kernel. Each rule consists of two fields: the *selector*, which consists of two parts, and the *action* field. The *selector* field is comprised of the *facility* and the *priority*, separated by a "." (period). The *facility* defines a *rule* for the corresponding subsystem that produced a particular message. For example, all kernel messages are handled by the *kern facility* and *Syslog* will handle all kernel messages as defined

Table 4 Syslog *Facilities*

Facility	Description
Auth	The authorization system: login, su, getty, etc.
Authpriv	The same as "auth," but logged to a file readable only by selected individuals.
Cron	The cron daemon: cron.
daemon	System daemons, such as routed, that are not provided for explicitly by other facilities.
kern	Messages generated by the kernel. These cannot be generated by any user processes.
lpr	The line printer spooling system: lpr, lpc, lpd.
mail	The mail system.
mark	For internal use only and should not be used by applications.
news	The network news system.
security	Same as "auth." This is deprecated and should not be used anymore.
syslog	Messages generated internally by syslogd.
user	Messages generated by random user processes. This is the default facility identifier if none is specified.
uucp	The UNIX-to-UNIX copy system.
localn (n = 0 – 7)	Reserved for local use. n is 0–7.

Table 5 Syslog *Priorities*

Priority	Description
none	Disables logging for a particular facility.
panic	Same as emerg. Deprecated and should not be used.
emerg	A panic condition. This is normally broadcast to all users.
alert	A condition that should be corrected immediately, such as a corrupted system database.
crit	Critical conditions, e.g., hardware failures.
err	Application error messages.
error	Same as error. Deprecated and should not be used.
warn	Same as warning. Deprecated and should not be used.
warning	Warning messages.
notice	Conditions that are not error conditions, but should possibly be handled specially.
info	Informational messages.
debug	Messages that contain information normally of use only when debugging a program.

by */etc/syslog.conf*. The *facility* keywords and descriptions are listed in Table 4:

The *priority* field defines the severity of a message. The *priorities* are listed in Table 5 with their definitions in order of severity:

The rules within the */etc/syslog.conf* file are formatted as follows:

```
<facility>.<priority>        <action>
```

Where <facility> is one of the *Syslog facilities* list above in Table 4, <priority> is one of the *Syslog priorities* list in Table 5. (Note: Either of these can be replaced by the asterisk "*" wildcard.) When *Syslog* receives messages that match these two criteria (or with a higher priority level), the message is logged to the file or remote server specified by <action>. Typically, <action> is a file within the */var/log/* directory. Local *Syslog* message can be forwarded to remote *Syslog* server by specifying "@servername" in the <action> field. (Note: Be sure to update */etc/hosts* with the IP address of the server specified.)

Log Administration

The *Syslog* daemon does not include support for log maintenance; as such, the default installation of Red Hat Linux includes the *logrotate* script to manage the system logs.

The script will rotate, compress, and, if need be, mail the system logs to a system administrator. The default installation should be effective for most system deployments though the manual file should be referenced for additional information.

Because *Syslog* does not ensure the integrity of the log files, the system administrator must rely on the operating system to provide this integrity. In this case, integrity controls are provided by the */usr/bin/chattr* utility as seen in the File System Security section. Specifically, integrity controls are provided by the "append-only" and "immutable" file system flags set by */usr/bin/chattr*. By setting these flags on each of the log files, the *logrotate* script will no longer be able to rotate the log files because the script will no longer be able to zero the log file after rotation. Fortunately, *logrotate* makes provision for this situation with the "*prerotate/endscript*" directive within its log file definition file */etc/logrotate.d/syslog*. The */usr/bin/chattr* utility must be called before and after each log file rotation. Modify the *logrotate* configuration file as follows:

```
[root@TheBox logrotate.d]# cat syslog
/var/log/messages/var/log/secure/var/log/maillog
  /var/log/spooler
/var/log/boot.log/var/log/cron{   sharedscripts
   prerotate
        /usr/bin/chattr -ia /var/log/messages*
        /usr/bin/chattr -ia /var/log/secure*
        /usr/bin/chattr -ia /var/log/maillog*
        /usr/bin/chattr -ia /var/log/spooler*
        /usr/bin/chattr -ia /var/log/boot.log*
        /usr/bin/chattr -ia /var/log/cron*
   endscript
```

```
postrotate
    /bin/kill -HUP `cat /var/run/syslogd.pid 2>
        /dev/null` 2> /dev/null || true
            /usr/bin/chattr +ia /var/log/messages*
            /usr/bin/chattr +ia /var/log/secure*
            /usr/bin/chattr +ia /var/log/maillog*
            /usr/bin/chattr +ia /var/log/spooler*
            /usr/bin/chattr +ia /var/log/boot.log*
            /usr/bin/chattr +ia /var/log/cron*
endscript
}
[root@TheBox logrotate.d]#
```

Audit Tools

System log files should be reviewed daily by the system administrator to identify system problems and should also be reviewed by a security analyst to ensure the system has not been compromised. Because daily log review can be a resource-intensive task, it is recommended that a log audit tool be implemented to assist with the log review process. Following are several options, each having own capabilities and unique features.

- **Logcheck** (http://doug.hunley.homeip.net/tools/). Maintained by Doug Hunley, Logcheck is a modified version of Psionic Logcheck that periodically parses through the administrator-specified log files and e-mails a report of suspicious entries to system administrators or security analysts.
- **WOTS** (http://www.hpcc.uh.edu/~tonyc/tools/). A Perl script that parses through the system log files and will generate reports or take action based on its configuration.
- **Logwatch** (http://www.logwatch.org). Logwatch is a customizable log analysis system. Logwatch parses through the system's logs for a given period of time and creates a report analyzing areas that the system administrator specifies at varying levels of detail.
- **Swatch** (http://swatch.sourceforge.net/). Swatch is short for "simple watchdog" and is an active system log file monitor that can parse, analyze, and send reports to designated personnel.

Syslog Replacements

Unfortunately, the *Syslog* daemon has a long history of security problems. Aside from problems that have arisen within the daemon itself, the implementation is lacking many of the security features that are required for most system deployments today. Namely, *Syslog* does not include authentication support. This is a significant problem for *Syslog* servers, which must rely on the security of trust relationships to receive log messages. Additionally, *Syslog* does not check for log file integrity to ensure that log files have not been modified by another application or malicious user. *Syslog* also lack support for encryption and log file maintenance.

There are several alternatives to using the default *Syslog* daemon. Each replacement is backward compatible with *Syslog* and provides unique enhancements to the logging subsystem. Each implementation should be evaluated and tested before implementing within a production environment.

- **Modular Syslog** (http://www.corest.com/products/corewisdom/CW01.php). A *Syslog* replacement that includes data integrity checks, easy database integration, strong encryption, and output redirection using regular expressions.
- **Nsyslog** (http://coombs.anu.edu.au/~avalon/nsyslog.html). *Nsyslog* supports TCP connections for log transfer, and with SSL allows for encrypted delivery of *Syslog* messages across the network.
- **syslog-ng** (http://www.balabit.com/products/syslog_ng). A flexible, secure replacement for *Syslog*.

BACKUPS

One of the most fundamental responsibilities of a system administrator is the periodic backup of all sensitive, application, log, and configuration information. Backups reduce downtime resulting from hardware failure and ensure that the system can be recovered in case of a compromise. System failure of some form or another is not a question of if but rather a question of when, and it is the responsibility of the system administrator to ensure that the system is recoverable. Forensic and security analysts have a particular interest in backups as they also provide a means to analyze system changes after a compromise. This section will review some of the basic backup and recovery tools that are provided with a default Linux installation.

Backup Considerations

Before performing system backups, there are several questions that must be taken into consideration. Here are several questions that should be addressed prior to developing a backup solution:

- What data will be archived?
- Will the data be archived to local or remote media?
- If remote, will the location on the production network allow it? Will it be secure?
- If local, what type of media will be used? Tape, CDRW, DVDRW, file?
- What is the archival scheme and period?
- Will a combination of incremental and full backups be used?
- How will the media be rotated, handled, and stored?

Backup Targets

Generally, any piece of data that is unique to the system and is not readily available from other sources such as installation disks should be backed up. Typically, this usually includes paths that contain user data, unique system configuration files, logs, or custom applications. Without taking specific applications or services into consideration, here is a list of recommended paths that should be included in the archive scheme:

```
/etc/:        System configuration files.
/home:        User home directories.
/root:        System administrator home directory.
/var/log:     System log files (unless using a remote Syslog server).
/usr/etc/:    Application configuration files.
/usr/local:   Applications and configuration files.
*/chroot:     Chroot'd applications and configurations files.
*/boot:       Kernel and boot configuration.
```

* These paths may not be unique to the system.

The following paths can be ignored as they are typically not used to store applications or data.

```
/mnt:   Removable media mount directory.
/proc:  Pseudo-file system created by the kernel.
/tmp:   Temporary slack space used by
        applications.
```

Backup Scheme
There are several archival schemes that a system administrator can use to backup the system. The scheme is typically based on organizational data retention and backup policies. Policies should include guidance on archive targets, naming conventions, archival tools, archive periods, and backup types (incremental vs. full or both), media, and storage locations.

   If guidance does not exist, it is recommended that backups be performed nightly (or during a window of limited system use) over a weekly period. A full backup should be performed and verified once a week with an incremental backup being performed each evening for the remainder of the week. Each archive should be time stamped and moved off of the system either by writing to tape, burning to CD, or securely copied to another system. Additionally, it may be a good idea to physically store the archive media in a separate part of the building or even offsite, depending on the criticality of the data.

Permissions
It is recommended that all backup archives be protected by either moving the archive off of the system or by storing them in a directory on the system that is only accessible by root. Set the permission of "0700" using /bin/chmod on the backup directory. If using removable media such as tape, ensure that the permission of "0660" or more restrictive is set on the device /dev/tape (or other device name). This will prevent users from extracting files from the archive, whether it is on the physical drive or on tape. Note: Whenever possible, all system archives should be moved off of the system, either by removable media or by an NFS mount on a central redundant file store.

Backup Utilities
The following is one of the more commonly used Linux backup utilities. There are many other open source utilities available, some installed with a Linux installation, and others are readily available online. Depending on the archival scheme chosen, any of these utilities can be used to back up and restore a system.

Tar Example
Tar is the GNU version of the *tar* archival utility. It was originally developed to archive data to tape drives but it is commonly used to write archives to regular files. Following are examples of how tar can be useful when performing a backup or recovery.
   Full Backup: This command will back up the system to a file or device, such as a tape drive or library; file and directory permissions will be preserved; the archive will be labeled; various files and directories listed within the exclude file will be ignored; and the archive will be verified.

```
[root@TheBox/]# tar-cpXf<backup file or
   device>/etc/backup/exclude_list/
--directory/--label="Full Backup `date`+
   %d:%b:%y'`" . --verify
```

Incremental Backup: This command will back up changes to the system that have been made since the previous backup to a file or device, such as a tape drive. As with the full backup, file and directory permissions will be preserved, the archive will be labeled, various files and directories listed within the exclude file will be ignored, and the archive will be verified.

```
[root@TheBox/]#tar-upXf<backup file or
   device>/etc/backup/exclude_list\
--directory/--label="Incremental Backup
   `date`+%d:%b:%y'`".--verify
```

Recovery
Following are a list of examples of how tar can be used to restore the system or individual files and directories.
   Full restore using *TAR*:

```
[root@TheBox/]#tar-xpvf<backup file or
   device>--directory/
```

Partial restore using *TAR*:

```
[root@TheBox/]#tar-xpvf<backup file or
   device>--directory/<directory/file>
```

Additional Utilities
CPIO (http://www.gnu.org/software/cpio/cpio.html). *Cpio* is another archival tool similar to tar, with many of the same capabilities. The utility is compatible with tar and provides several archival enhancements. *Cpio* is available on many default Linux installations.

Dump (http://dump.sourceforge.net). The backup utility *dump* is different from *tar* and *cpio* in that it reads the ext2 Linux file system directly without stepping through the directory structure. This allows the utility to be quick and efficient. Unfortunately, the tool does not allow an administrator to selectively choose which files or directories to back up, though this may not be an issue if the intent is to perform full system backups.

Additional Backup Resource (http://linuxmafia.com/pub/linux/backup/).

LEGAL PROTECTIONS

Because of recent criminal court case precedents involving unauthorized system access, when applicable, it is important to display logon warning banners to anyone who accesses the system. The warning banner ensures the forfeiture of user privacy on the system and effectively grants the system owner the "right to monitor." This will help to ensure that all evidence collected from an intrusion is admissible in court.

Implementation

There are several ways to implement a logon warning banner in Linux. Many of the interactive services that are supplied with a default installation of Linux will typically use */etc/motd* to display a banner to users. Note: Logon warning banners cannot be implemented on the Linux system itself for noninteractive services where users will not see the banner or for custom and proprietary services that lack support for logon banners. In the latter case, it may be possible to customize the application to add support for the displaying of logon banners to users. A custom HTML page is an example of one such modification.

Simply editing the */etc/motd* file and adding the logon warning banner will ensure that the banner is displayed for many of the text-based services within Linux such as SSH, Telnet, SMTP, and POP3.

If any of the running services are controlled by the *Xinetd* daemon, the configuration file */etc/xinetd.conf* can be modified to add support for logon banners. Edit the configuration file and add the following:

```
[root@TheBox etc]# cat xinetd.conf
#
# Simple configuration file for xinetd
#
# Some defaults, and include /etc/xinetd.d/

defaults
{
    instances       = 60
    log_type        = SYSLOG authpriv
    log_on_success  = HOST PID
    log_on_failure  = HOST
    cps             = 25 30
    banner                       = /etc/motd
}

includedir /etc/xinetd.d
[root@TheBox etc]#
```

Sample Logon Banner

This banner should be customized to fit the organization's specific legal requirements. Consult the organization's legal department for details on the implications and requirements for implementing a banner similar to this one:

> THIS IS A *<COMPANY NAME>* COMPUTER SYSTEM. THIS COMPUTER SYSTEM, INCLUDING ALL RELATED EQUIPMENT, NETWORKS, AND NETWORK DEVICES (SPECIFICALLY INCLUDING INTERNET ACCESS), ARE PROVIDED ONLY FOR AUTHORIZED *<COMPANY NAME>* USE. *<COMPANY NAME>* COMPUTER SYSTEMS MAY BE MONITORED FOR ALL LAWFUL PURPOSES, INCLUDING TO ENSURE THEIR USE IS AUTHORIZED, FOR MANAGEMENT OF THE SYSTEM, TO FACILITATE PROTECTION AGAINST UNAUTHORIZED ACCESS, AND TO VERIFY SECURITY PROCEDURES, SURVIVABILITY, AND OPERATIONAL SECURITY. MONITORING INCLUDES ACTIVE ATTACKS BY AUTHORIZED *<COMPANY NAME>* ENTITIES TO TEST OR VERIFY THE SECURITY OF THIS SYSTEM. DURING MONITORING, INFORMATION MAY BE EXAMINED, RECORDED, COPIED, AND USED FOR AUTHORIZED PURPOSES. ALL INFORMATION, INCLUDING PERSONAL INFORMATION, PLACED ON OR SENT OVER THIS SYSTEM, MAY BE MONITORED.
>
> USE OF THIS *<COMPANY NAME>* COMPUTER SYSTEM, AUTHORIZED OR UNAUTHORIZED, CONSTITUTES CONSENT TO MONITORING OF THIS SYSTEM. UNAUTHORIZED USE MAY SUBJECT YOU TO CRIMINAL PROSECUTION. EVIDENCE OF UNAUTHORIZED USE COLLECTED DURING MONITORING MAY BE USED FOR ADMINISTRATIVE, CRIMINAL, OR OTHER ADVERSE ACTION. USE OF THIS SYSTEM CONSTITUTES CONSENT TO MONITORING FOR THESE PURPOSES.

CONCLUSION

The fundamental point of system hardening is to minimize the operating system exposure to compromise, in addition to providing various basic protections to the application or service itself. Hardening of the system platform will ensure that even after a service has been compromised, the integrity and resiliency of the underlying operating system will be maintained. System hardening will prepare the system administrator and ultimately the organization for a compromise and will help to minimize its effects.

Hardening of the service or application that the Linux platform will be supporting is the last remaining step of system self-defense. It is after this point where other network based controls provide additional protective (defense-in-depth) measures.

GLOSSARY

ACL   Access Control List

AES   Advanced Encryption Standard

Authentication   Verification of the claimed identity of a client or service

BIOS   Basic Input Output System

CERT   Computer Emergency Response Team (copywrite held by the Carnegie Mellon CERT/CC)

DAC   Discretionary Access Control (a means of restricting access of files to those with appropriate access permissions)

Daemon   A process/program that, once activated, starts itself and carries out a specific task

Data Integrity   Concept of ensuring that data is not manipulated or accessed in any way other than what was originally intended

DES/3DES   Data Encryption Standard/Triple Data Encryption Standard

DHCP   Dynamic Host Configuration Protocol

Group   Collection of users with common computer resource requirements

GUI   Graphical User Interface

Host   A computer that acts as a client and/or server

I&A   Identification and Authentication

Identification   The process or means by which an information system recognizes an entity

Incremental Backup   An archival type that only archives new and changed data from the previous backup

IP   Internet Protocol: Protocols on which the Internet is based. IP allows a packet to traverse multiple networks on the way to the packet's final destination

LAN   Local Area Network

MD5   A commonly used message-digest hashing algorithm

Octet   Set of eight (8) bits.

Packet   Data consisting of header, origination address, data, and destination

POP   Post Office Protocol

Port   Number that identifies a particular Internet application (also, a physical connection for an input/output channel)

Protocol   Set of rules governing how computers communicate

Root   Common term applied to the superuser in UNIX/Linux

RPM   RedHat Package Manager

SA   System Administrator

Server   Computer supplying services to users or other computers

SGID   Set GroupID: A program permission that imparts all the privileges of the program group to anyone executing it

SNMP   Simple Network Management Protocol

SSH   Secure Shell. A secure replacement of telnet whereby all traffic to and from the server is encrypted

Sticky Bit   A world-writable directory permission allowing world-writable files to be written to a directory (usually /tmp) where they may be deleted or changed only by the user or root

STIG   Security Technical Implementation Guide

SU   Switch User

SUID   Set UserID: A program permission that imparts all the privileges of the program owner to anyone executing it

Superuser   User (hopefully, root) with unlimited access to all system resources unless limited by other software means

System Files   Operating system files defined as native Linux files and delivered with, or without, a full operating system install

TCP   Transmission Control Protocol: A protocol upon which the most popular networking is based. The protocol with which it is paired is the Internet Protocol, IP. Together, they are TCP/IP. TCP is a connection-oriented, reliable protocol

Telnet   A terminal emulation protocol that allowing users to log on to other computer systems

UDP   User Datagram Protocol: An Internet-based protocol providing connectionless, unreliable communications

UID   User identification number (a unique user number assigned to each user in a UNIX system)

umask   Built-in shell function to restrict *read/write/execute* permissions

UNIX   An operating system written between 1969 and 1972 at Bell Laboratories. UNIX was designed as a multiuser, multitasking operating system. Many versions of UNIX now exist including BSD, System V, Solaris, AIX, OMUS, and Linux, with more to come

User   Person or machine authorized to access a computer system

Username   User logon name (mechanism used to uniquely identify a user of system resources). One is assigned for each user by the system administrator

WAN   Wide Area Network

Workstation   Typically a more powerful personal computer configured to access a network

CROSS REFERENCES

See *OpenVMS Security; Operating System Security; Unix Security; Windows 2000 Security.*

REFERENCES

Baker, F. (1995). *RFC 1812 Requirements for IP Version 4 Routers.* Network Working Group, Cisco Systems.

Braden, R. (1989). *RFC 1122 Requirements for Internet Hosts—Communication Layers.* Network Working Group, Internet Engineering Task Force.

Rekhter, Y., Moskowitz, B., Karrenberg, D., de Groot, G. J., & Lear, E. (1996). *RFC 1918 Address Allocation for Private Networks.* Network Working Group, Cisco Systems, Chrysler Corp., RIPE, Silicon Graphics.

FURTHER READING

Barrett, D., Silverman, R., & Byrnes, R. (2003). *Linux Security Cookbook.* Sebastopol, California: O'Reilly.

Bauer, M. (2003). *Building Secure Servers with Linux.* Sebastopol, California: O'Reilly.

DISA Field Security Operations. (2003, September 15). *Unix Security Technical Implementation Guide v4 release 4.* Washington, DC: Author Unknown.

Hatch, B. & Lee, J. (2003). *Hacking Exposed: Linux* (2nd ed.). Berkeley, California: Osborne.

Mann, S., Mitchell, E., & Krell, M. (2003). *Linux System Security* (2nd ed.). [Upper Saddle River, New Jersey]: Prentice-Hall.

Mourani, G. (2002). *Securing & Optimizing Linux: The Hacking Solution* (3rd ed.). Montreal, Canada: Open NA.

NSA Systems and Network Attack Center. (2001, October 16). *The 60 Minute Network Security Guide v1.0.* Fort Meade, Maryland: Author Unknown.

Automated Linux Security Enhancements

Bastille Linux:http://www.bastille-linux.org/

NSA SELinux: http://www.nsa.gov/selinux/

Linux Security Resources

LBL (Lawrence Berkeley Laboratory): http://www.lbl.gov/ITSD/Security/

LDP (Linux Documentation Project): http://en.tldp.org/

Linux Kernel Archives: http://www.kernel.org

Linux Online: http://www.linux.org

Maximum RPM: http://www.rpm.org/max-rpm/

SAGE: http://sageweb.sage.org/

USENIX: http://www.usenix.org

Linux Distributions

Caldera OpenLinux: http://www.caldera.com/

Debian GNU/Linux: http://www.debian.org/

Red Hat Linux: http://www.redhat.com/

Fedora Project: http://fedora.redhat.com/

Mandrake Linux: http://www.mandrakelinux.com/en-us/

Slackware Linux: http://www.slackware.com/

S.U.S.E Linux: http://www.suse.com/us/

TrinityOS: http://www.ecst.csuchico.edu/~dranch/LINUX/index-linux.html

OpenNA: http://www.openna.com/

OpenVMS Security

Robert Gezelter, *Software Consultant*

INTRODUCTION

OpenVMS is a system with a unique history. It has a system architecture designed to produce a high-efficiency, high-integrity environment. High-security operation is a direct consequence of these goals. Philosophically, this has been crucial to its success. Thus, OpenVMS avoids the vulnerabilities plaguing systems that do not have security and integrity as part of their initial design. This chapter begins with a full examination of OpenVMS architecture, followed by a detailed examination of its integral security-specific design and related features.

The original OpenVMS design was a combined hardware/software architecture project. The protection modes, memory management, and privileged instruction set of the VAX processor were designed with the collaboration of the operating system's engineering team.

This coengineering process produced an operating system with a unique character. The design blends the knowledge and experiences gained from earlier operating systems together with the supporting hardware elements. The design provides a rich collection of facilities with an unusual degree of consistency and reliability.

These hardware elements are not legacies of the original VAX processor but are the echoes of the coengineering process and reflect the fact that the original VAX architecture was specifically engineered to support VAX/VMS.

Today, OpenVMS is fully supported on three processor architectures: VAX, Alpha, and Intel's IA-64 Itanium. There are almost no differences between them at the applications level. The differences between the versions are limited to

- differences between the hardware environments (such as subroutine calling standards),
- low-level trap/interrupt handling, and
- 64-bit memory support (which is only available on Alpha and IA-64).

This multiple hardware architecture environment is achieved through common code and well-defined interfaces. The overwhelming majority of the 10 million lines of code are common to all three processor platforms. In the case of Alpha and IA-64, the commonality is greater than 95%. The multiple platforms are released on the same schedule and use a common documentation kit, supplemented by manuals specific to each of the hardware architectures. OpenVMS Clusters are frequently constructed with all combinations of the supported architectures interoperating with a fully shared file system.

Configured as recommended, OpenVMS provides an extremely well-protected environment for the user, with fine control over access rights and privileges. It is also the first system to use a common run-time library with a consistent calling standard across all supported languages, from MACRO-32 (the VAX assembler language) to higher-level languages including FORTRAN, BASIC, PL/I, C/C++, and others.

The design emphasizes correctness, completeness, and fine levels of detail in privileges and access rights, together with an overall refusal to specify issues that need not be decided at the operating system level. The combination of detail and deferral of unneeded decisions makes OpenVMS able to support a high degree of nuance. Nuance is the ability of an operating system to be sculpted to express the subtleties of an end user's requirements without losing its essential form or character.

History

The initial design, in 1977, was a combined hardware/software effort at Digital Equipment Corporation (since merged with Hewlett-Packard), comprising both the VAX hardware architecture and the VAX/VMS operating system. The VAX reflected a trend in 1970s technology toward higher-level language support directly in hardware, particularly in the areas of bounds checking, flow control, and common operations. In 1991, reflecting the breadth of industry standards supported by VAX/VMS, the operating system was renamed OpenVMS.

Semiconductor technology changes in the late 1980s favored processors with simplified instruction sets. Earlier limits in memory bandwidth had favored more complex instructions. Later VAX processors were simplified and their implementations pruned to remove functions from central processor microcode. Program compatibility was maintained through emulation of these rarely used instructions.

This trend toward processor simplification resulted in the design of Digital's 64-bit RISC Alpha, unveiled in 1992. The Alpha architecture combined support for larger memory spaces with a reduced instruction set designed for high-speed implementations in CMOS technologies.

In 2001 the decision was made to adopt Intel's IA-64 architecture, referred to as Itanium, as the follow-on architecture to Alpha. The first bootstrap of OpenVMS Itanium occurred on January 31, 2003.

BASIS IN ARCHITECTURE

Philosophically and structurally, OpenVMS is the descendant of two streams of operating system evolution within Digital Equipment Corporation:

- The RSX-family operating systems for the 16-bit PDP-11 processors and
- TOPS-20, the operating system for the 36-bit DECsystem-20 series.

Each of these antecedents contributed thoughts and philosophies to OpenVMS, including internal structures, file systems, and command languages. Problems and shortcomings in earlier designs were also considered in the new design. The OpenVMS architecture is a particularly impressive achievement when one considers that few operating systems running today were in existence 25 years ago, much less in a form that allows many programs to continue to run without recompilation or change.

OpenVMS exemplifies that it is possible to significantly characterize the architectural requirements of applications in many areas, including file formats. It is then possible to provide operating system layers to implement those characterizations as an enabling technology. The OpenVMS Run-Time Library (known as *VMSRTL*) is, in many respects, an object-oriented toolkit, although its design predates the popularity of that paradigm by a decade. This is in contrast to other operating systems, which have entirely omitted this software level of abstraction.

Implementation Techniques

OpenVMS is characterized by an embracive architectural approach, coupled with an emphasis on quality and performance. The architectural focus is on providing the user/developer with a complete toolkit for the implementation of both software and environments for users to build and employ a wide range of applications. The security aspects of the operating system follow naturally from the focus on robustness, integrity, and efficiency. There is

also an overall emphasis on ensuring that system components interoperate reliably through supported building blocks.

Multiple CPU/Memory Access Modes

The design uses four access modes, each with its own access rights. From least privileged to most privileged, these are *User, Supervisor, Executive,* and *Kernel.* The overwhelming majority of users (and their applications) are restricted to *User* mode, which does not allow the execution of machine instructions or memory accesses that can affect the operation of the machine as a whole.

Access to inner (more privileged) access modes is provided through appropriate system services, subject to privilege controls. Elevating privileges requires a hardware trap and validation of the request for execution at a more privileged level (see Figure 1).

Memory Protection Model

The memory protection model provides for accesses to be controlled on a page-by-page basis. Access is controlled on a Read, Write, or Execute basis. Each access mode can have different access rights, a capability fundamental to maintaining the integrity of the operating system's internal functions. This contrasts with other operating systems that store information in areas readable and writeable by user programs, rendering them vulnerable to compromise.

The OpenVMS memory protection model permits operating system components to store process-specific information on behalf of a user process securely within the process's own address space. However, such pages are protected to only permit access to the inner access modes and are invisible and unmodifiable from User mode access (Figure 2). This secures information within a process, avoiding security breaches caused by commingling structures in a shared area maintained by the system kernel.

Command line interpreters, such as DCL (Digital Command Language), execute in Supervisor mode but within the context of each user's process.

System components requiring access to higher levels of privilege execute in Executive mode. The Record Management System (RMS) has some components that execute in User mode and some components that execute in Executive mode. For example, global buffering and cluster-wide locking would not be directly available to a nonprivileged User mode process.

The system kernel, device drivers, and similar components execute in Kernel mode, which allows access to all of the hardware of the host machine.

Fine Granularity of Privilege

Fine gradations of privilege are also characteristic of OpenVMS. Where some operating systems are distinguished by a binary approach to privilege (a user or process is either fully privileged or fully not privileged), OpenVMS from the outset has had a more nuanced approach. Presently, basic OpenVMS has 36 different privileges (three additional privileges are only available under SEVMS, the OpenVMS version with mandatory access controls). In many instances, an OpenVMS application or user can perform very powerful system

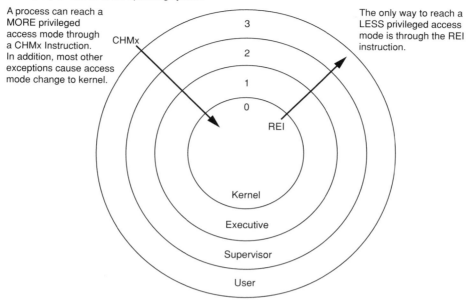

Access mode fields in the PSL are not directly accessible to the programmer or to the operating system.

A process can reach a MORE privileged access mode through a CHMx Instruction. In addition, most other exceptions cause access mode change to kernel.

The only way to reach a LESS privileged access mode is through the REI instruction.

The boundaries between the access modes are nearly identical to the layer boundaries pictured in Figure 5.
Nearly all system services execute in kernel mode. RMS and some system services execute in executive mode.

Command language interpreters normally execute in supervisor mode.
Utilities, application programs, run-time Library procedures, and so on normally execute in user mode.
Privileged utilities sometimes execute in kernel or executive mode.

Figure 1: OpenVMS memory/processor access modes (from *VAX/VMS Internals and Data Structures, Version 5.2 [1991]*, p. 16).

management functions, such as managing print queues or storage volumes, with a single or a small number of relatively innocuous privileges, rather than full system management functions.

String Descriptors

The programmer's interface to OpenVMS uses descriptors for references to most data types (see Figure 3). The overwhelming majority of internal interfaces also use descriptors. The exception to the use of descriptors is simple parameter references of the call-by-value (familiar to C/C++ programmers) and simple call-by-reference (familiar to FORTRAN/C programmers).

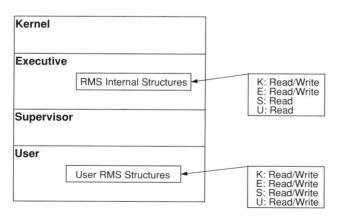

Figure 2: Information is stored in a process's address space but is not modifiable by the *User* mode program.

The pervasive parameter checking enabled by the use of descriptors has rendered native OpenVMS code relatively immune from string overflow and similar errors. String and buffer overflows have plagued other systems, particularly systems written in C, which have used C's ubiquitous 0x00 (null) terminated strings.

Descriptors allow system library functions to completely check their input and output arguments before processing. System library routines check the validity of input and output parameters, returning errors if they are not in appropriate locations.

Embracive Architecture

From the outset, OpenVMS has had a substantial focus on well-reasoned architecture, which provides a solid basis for the implementation of robust software. OpenVMS's architecture strikes a balance between specification as needed to ensure correctness and specification that leaves enough open space within the architecture to ensure sufficient room for growth.

This approach has proved successful in that it has ensured compatibility for a huge corpus of code, consisting of OpenVMS itself, layered products, and third party and user code over a 25-year period. Incompatible changes from the original specification have been rare.

Scaling

OpenVMS, in its latest releases, is officially qualified to run on a wide range of hardware, from the MicroVAX 3300 (2.5 MIPS) to Alpha and Itanium systems well into

32-Bit Form (DSC)

| CLASS | DTYPE | LENGTH | :0 |
| POINTER | | | :4 |

ZK-4663A-GE

64-Bit Form (DSC64)

quadword aligned

CLASS	DTYPE	MBO (=1)	:0
MBMO (=-1)			:4
LENGTH			:8
POINTER			:16

ZK-7656A-GE

Figure 3: OpenVMS string/other descriptors were extended to include 64–bit lengths and addresses with the 1992 advent of the 64–bit Alpha processor (diagram from *OpenVMS Calling Standard, 2001*, p. 5–3).

the billions of instructions per second (1000+MIPS). Only within the last few years has official support for the original VAX-11/780 been withdrawn, as main memory requirements have increased beyond its capabilities.

Systems supported on OpenVMS range from uniprocessors to 32-way processors. The minimum supported memory configuration is 14 Mbytes on a VAX, 64 Mbytes on an Alpha. Alpha systems are able to efficiently exploit gigabytes of memory.

Platform Independence

Most users have been unaware that translated and interpreted images have been part of the base OpenVMS system since its original release in 1977. The original VAX/VMS contained numerous 16-bit PDP-11 images that were hardware interpreted. To this day, certain commonly used programs have been translated rather than recompiled. The TECO text editor and the MONITOR utility (pre–OpenVMS release 7.3-2) are the products of binary translation from VAX to Alpha.

There is little doubt that recompilation is the most effective way to make use of the power of a new processor architecture. The availability of image translation represents a viable trade-off between the costs of rebuilding applications and lost processor performance against schedule and engineering costs.

The interpretation/translation/recompilation approach on a system with a common API is both viable and effective. It is another case, where OpenVMS provides a nuanced approach, allowing project managers to take advantage of system facilities to shorten schedules in ways that are functionally transparent to users.

Environment Portability

OpenVMS is designed for use in a data center because it provides the mechanisms for implementing a tightly controlled environment. It is always simpler and less error prone to relax tightly controlled environments than it is to impose stricter controls on relaxed environments. Adding

security and integrity controls after the fact is often an underlying source of security problems.

OpenVMS Clusters

OpenVMS clusters, announced in 1983, remain a unique concept. An OpenVMS cluster is composed of multiple, independent CPUs, each running an independent copy of the operating system, with the cluster members coordinating access to a shared file system, down to the record level in individual files. By contrast, a conventional multiprocessing system comprises multiple CPUs with common memory sharing a single memory-resident copy of the operating system. Individual cluster members are often themselves multiprocessors. Although the individual cluster members are running separate copies of OpenVMS, the cluster itself operates as a single security domain (see Figure 4).

In an OpenVMS cluster, the CPUs and mass storage controllers communicate via a high-speed local area interconnect, originally the CI (Computer Interconnect, a proprietary dual 70 Mbit/sec CSMA/CD LAN). Today, IEEE 802.3/Ethernet (10 M/100 M/1 Gbit/sec) is often used. Usually, the entire file system is shared, with access to file system structures, files, and even byte ranges or records within files controlled via the Distributed Lock Manager.

The Distributed Lock Manager implements a shared locking domain. This unique characteristic of OpenVMS clusters allows the entire cluster to act as one system for the purpose of file-based applications. Each OpenVMS system has a copy of the Distributed Lock Manager. In an OpenVMS cluster, the Distributed Lock Managers on each cluster member exchange information about which system holds locks on which resources. Architecturally more important, the Distributed Lock Manager only deals with resource names. Thus, the Distributed Lock Manager represents a fundamental building block for end-user developers to implement synchronization tasks other than those envisioned by the OpenVMS engineering team.

File locking is controlled by the file structure support component, known as the *XQP* (extended QIO Processor). Record Management Services, known as RMS, supplements the file-level access provided by the XQP with facilities used to access the contents of files and is responsible for locking on granularities smaller than entire files. RMS supports a wide range of file contents, including simple sequential files, byte stream files, relative files, and indexed files.

Officially, an OpenVMS cluster is limited to 96 nodes with a maximum radius of 500 miles (800 km). Customers have configured OpenVMS clusters that exceed these limits in one or more ways, primarily in terms of the number of nodes in the cluster. This is a wider and more flexible scope than other products. When extreme emergencies and catastrophes occur, OpenVMS clusters, configured in a disaster-tolerant mode with multiple sites separated geographically, have continued IT operations unscathed. Even the 9/11 destruction of the World Trade Center complex in New York City did not stop several disaster-tolerant OpenVMS cluster systems that had cluster members within the Twin Towers or surrounding buildings. The other sites continued operating with an imperceptible pause.

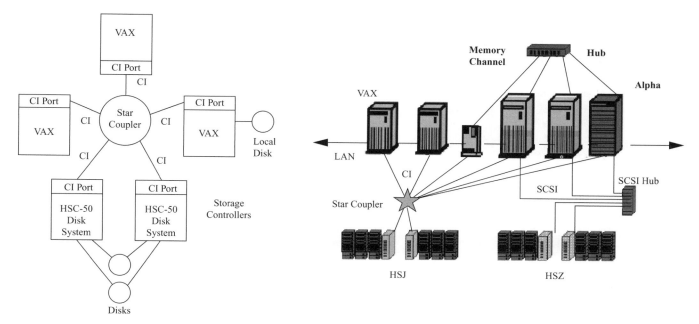

Figure 4: Unchanging fundamentals of OpenVMS cluster: 1983–2004 (diagrams from Kronenberg, Levy, & Strecker, 1986 and *HP OpenVMS: The World's Leader in Clustering*, 2003).

Software Basis

Architecturally, the approach is a classic, layered approach in the spirit of Dijkstra's classic paper on THE (1968). There are few special-purpose components in the system. The approach is one of conceptual and implementation uniformity. The libraries and supporting infrastructure used to implement the operating system are the same tools available to support user development (see Figure 5).

Processes

OpenVMS processes consist of page tables, logical name tables, thread contexts (including register states), stacks, mapping to common shared memory regions, and process-private memory regions.

Historically, OpenVMS processes had single-register contexts, and therefore a single thread of execution associated with each process. On the 64-bit platforms, beginning with version 7.0, support for multiple threads per process was added, allowing a single process to simultaneously use multiple processors in a multiprocessor system.

Privileges

OpenVMS implements a fine-granularity privilege model. There are a number of different privileges, and many of them permit operations personnel to do their jobs without giving them unrestricted management access to the system.

Some privileges, such as **NETMBX** (the ability to create network mailboxes; which is needed to use DECnet or TCP/IP) and **TMPMBX** (the ability to create temporary mailboxes) are innocuous and can be routinely issued to students in a college course without cause for worry.

Some privileges, although less innocuous, only affect members of an individual group but are not dangerous to the system as a whole. These can be issued in safety in a properly configured system.

Other privileges have potentially greater side effects. Privileges classed as DEVOUR can, in the words of the *HP OpenVMS Guide to System Security* (2003), "consume noncritical systemwide resources." Privileges classed as SYSTEM can similarly "interfere with system operation." Those classed as OBJECTS can "compromise the protection of protected objects." Class ALL privileges have the "potential to control the system."

Assigning privileges is important in the context of security but is inevitably a compromise. A common trade-off is to provide certain privileges, particularly **OPER**, **READALL**, and sometimes **MOUNT**, to operators to permit normal operations such as managing queues and performing backups.

The privileges categorized as DEVOUR, SYSTEM, OBJECT, and ALL have the ability to affect system operation, whether it is merely resource starvation (as in a runaway program with **EXQUOTA**, the ability to ignore disk space quotas) or crash the system (through the misuse of the **WORLD** privilege). Others, such as those classified as SYSTEM, can totally compromise the security of the system.

Some privileges fall into barely safer categories, such as **SYSPRV**, which allows a variety of system management functions, including modifications to the SYSUAF file. The danger here is subtler. Because access to the SYSUAF permits the changes to the list of authorized users, as well as changes to the authorized and default privilege masks for an account, it effectively permits a user to give themselves (or a confederate) full privileges.

Implications of Privileges—Security Issues

When planning a security environment, it is important to consider the security implications of routine tasks. System backups are an interesting case in point. Backup operators frequently are issued the **READALL** privilege to ensure

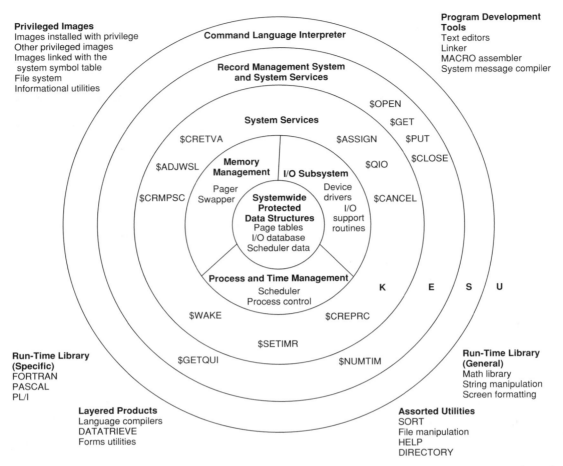

Figure 5: A schematic view of OpenVMS system architecture (diagram from *VAX/VMS Internals and Data Structures, Version 5.2, 1991*, p. 10).

that the backups are able to read all the files on mass storage when producing backup tapes. Thus, they must inherently be trustworthy.

Some files, however, may need to be omitted from the routine backups. The reasons for this omission are varied. Some or all of the reasons for omissions may apply to particular installations. For example,

- some files may be both large of size and transitory in nature. It may be substantially easier to recreate the file in the event of a problem than it is to allocate sufficient time and archive space for the backups.
- some information is sufficiently sensitive that it should not be part of the normal backup process. In this case, the information can be located on different disks or marked in a way that it will be omitted from the normal backup process.
- some files may be subject to retention or archiving restrictions that are different from the overall backup and retention policies of the installation. For example, a file may be subject to a court protective order requiring that all copies be destroyed as part of the proceedings. Such files should not be included in routine backups. They should, however, be part of a project or activity backup.

OpenVMS, through its file system and **BACKUP** utility provide mechanisms to manage file migration and backup for all of these possibilities. The **BACKUP** utility is designed specifically to seamlessly incorporate all of these needs without requiring external, special-purpose utilities.

Quotas

OpenVMS has extensive facilities for the management of system resources by processes, whether they are privileged processes belonging to the system or conventional user processes. These limits are known as *quotas*. Used properly, they prevent an individual process from impairing system operation by causing a depletion of significant system resources, such as system dynamic memory or disk space. Other quotas, such as the quotas on aggregate buffered and direct IO operations, serve to prevent a single process or job from monopolizing the overall system.

Disk quotas allow system managers to control the amount of disk space on each volume used by an individual. Quotas may be associated with UICs or Rights Identifiers. Rights Identifier-specific quotas allow space to be allocated on a project basis. These mechanisms are complementary, not exclusive.

Threading and Asynchronous System Traps (ASTs)

Hierarchically preemptible processing is central to the OpenVMS architecture. Fundamental to its structure, OpenVMS supports a single-threaded environment, with support for a very lightweight FIFO (first in, first out) event-processing thread for each access mode. These event-processing threads, which preempt the main thread of processing, are called *Asynchronous System Traps* (*ASTs*).

Speaking in terms of evolution, ASTs are descended from the RSX family of operating systems. They have proved to be a highly efficient mechanism for processing asynchronous events (such as timers and IO completions) without excessive overhead. ASTs are extremely lightweight because they do not have any context of their own but preempt the main thread of execution. Their inherent synchronization is one of their simplest yet most powerful features. Within a particular access mode, AST processing is FIFO and nonpreemptible. This implicit synchronization makes it unnecessary to explicitly synchronize different ASTs in the same access mode within a particular process. Inner access mode ASTs can preempt outer mode ASTs.

They can be used with few limitations, other than quotas, by any process. OpenVMS makes extensive use of AST processing in system libraries and the file system. The importance of the AST mechanism can be seen from the ongoing attention paid to AST implementation on the VAX, Alpha, and Itanium processors.

This is in contrast to the signal model used in UNIX-style operating systems, which are structured in a less modular, less general basis and where blocking of signals is commonplace (to prevent preemption), with the resulting synchronization issues.

Common Run-Time Library

From the outset, OpenVMS was designed to be programming language agnostic. It was the first operating system with a defined, cross-programming language run-time library. From its origin on the VAX architecture, routines written in one programming language have been effortlessly able to invoke other routines written in different languages. It is common to encounter individual programs written using a variety of languages, particularly so in cases where one language has a clear advantage in clarity of expression or functionality over the other (e.g., BAS-BOL: BASIC with COBOL subroutines and COB-FOR: COBOL with FORTRAN subroutines). This feature is used within OpenVMS itself, where components have been written in VAX MACRO-32, BLISS, BASIC, FORTRAN, PASCAL, PL/I, and C/C++.

The run-time library also provides a rich underpinning of functionality for user and third-party programs. Seemingly complex mechanisms in system-provided utilities are nothing more than calls to run-time library routines, accessible to all users.

System Services

The lowest-level, user-visible interfaces to OpenVMS are referred to as system services. These services are a diverse group, including:

- very simple building blocks, such as those which format ASCII output, $FAO and $FAOL (which run in User mode),
- functions that perform extensive processing in privileged modes (e.g., $QIO and $QIOW) to make a system capability available to a user program in a safe manner, and
- gateways (e.g., $CHKPRO, $CHMKRNL and $CMEXEC) to the rare programs that need inner access modes.

The $QIO and $QIOW system services (Queue IO Operation and Queue IO Operation Wait) act as gatekeepers to IO resources for all system components. $QIO is an excellent example of the OpenVMS philosophy, in that it provides a rich set of functions and common processing for IO requests, including:

- parameter checking,
- common device driver initiation and completion processing, and
- definitions for operations, based upon common models of device functionality (e.g., file systems) without imposing inappropriate demands at the interface level. For example, the 16-bit IO function codes have defined meanings for file opens (read-only, read-write, and read-write-extend), file attributes (read/write attributes), and various values for control of communications channels (see Table 1).

$QIO does not attempt to specify all possible operations so much as it annunciates a framework for expressing the possibilities for interfacing to an external (or pseudo) device. It also provides an intermediation between requesting programs and the actual details of managing a physical device.

Device Drivers

In common usage, the term *device driver* has become overloaded, acquiring multiple meanings. Originally, a device driver was a software component that formed the privileged interface between a particular IO device and the

Table 1 OpenVMS IO Function Codes by Category

Function	Symbolic Value	Value (hexadecimal)
Create file	IO$_CREATE	0x0051
Access file	IO$_ACCESS	0x0050
Read virtual	IO$_READVBLK	0x0049
Write virtual	IO$_WRITEVBLK	0x0048
Deaccess file	IO$_DEACCESS	0x0052
Delete file	IO$_DELETE	0x0053
Modify file	IO$_MODIFY	0x0054
Read with prompt	IO$_READPROMPT	0x0055
ACP control	IO$_ACPCONTROL	0x0056
Mount volume	IO$_MOUNT	0x0057

Source: *HP OpenVMS I/O User's Reference Manual* (2003), additional detail extracted from libraries
SYS$LIBRARY: STARLET.MLB and SYS$LIBRARY: SYS$STARLET_C.TLB module IODEF.

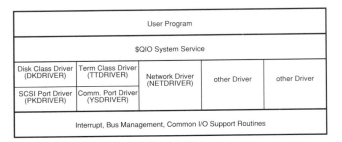

Figure 6: OpenVMS device drivers in relation to the kernel and the QIO system service. An OpenVMS *device driver* does not operate in a vacuum, but in the context of the User Process and the overall direction, policies, and scaffolding provided by the system kernel.

operating system kernel. Some operating systems and applications have muddied the definition by using device driver to refer to nonprivileged components that address device idiosyncrasies, such as printer escape codes.

OpenVMS uses the term device driver in the original meaning of the phrase. Device drivers are the components that actually manage the operation of specific devices. In OpenVMS, device drivers are loadable kernel subroutines that interface between the kernel, particularly the program accessible $QIO system service, and the actual hardware (see Figure 6). Although device drivers do not have a full context, they do not exist in a vacuum. Device drivers are subroutines of the kernel, and, in the case of IO initiation, operate in the mapping context of the requesting process. OpenVMS device drivers do not form the lowest layer of the software architecture but are an intermediate layer between the routines that actually perform hardware accesses and the QIO layer providing generic IO services. Architecturally, the lowest layer is populated by the an extensive collection of routines that allow device drivers to perform common functions, from managing the mapping of transfers to interrupt management.

As an example of OpenVMS's flexibility, adding storage volumes to OpenVMS does not require a reboot but merely a command to bring the new device online.

OpenVMS device drivers have substantial capabilities and act as more than mere filters or funnels of information between the generic IO services provided by the kernel and the device. Device drivers do significant processing, perform transformations of data, and are solely responsible for dealing with the idiosyncrasies of the different devices. However, some operations, such as managing the disk file structure, looking up files, and locating file segments on the disk, require additional operations that are beyond the capabilities and context of an OpenVMS device driver.

Ancillary Control Processes

File structure management is one such class of operations. Structurally, IO operations must belong to a process. Device drivers, being kernel subroutines, do not have a process context of their own. If the IO request requires more than straightforward processing, a helper process with a full process context is used. These helper processes are referred to as an *Ancillary Control Processes* (*ACPs*) and are associated with the device used. ACPs are privileged OpenVMS processes whose function is an intermediate level of device-specific management. An ACP effectively extends the conceptual IO model supported by the device (see Figure 7).

An ACP is associated with a particular device or a class of devices. ACPs are employed where IO related tasks, such as file system management or network connection management, require more extensive processing.

Often, as in the cases of mass storage devices, an ACP will create and manage driver-accessible data structures that permit the driver to directly map or translate future requests without the need to invoke ACP processing. This eliminates the context switches to and from the ACP.

In the case of conventional file processing, even this efficiency was deemed insufficient, and the FILES-11

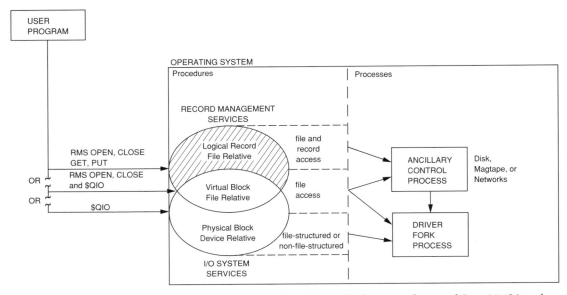

Figure 7: Record Management Services as an example of the multiple exposed steps of OpenVMS interface (from VAX-11 Software Handbook, 1979, Digital Equipment Corporation, 1979).

Level 2 ACP was reimplemented as a kernel-mode library, invoked by the driver in the calling process's context, without the need for additional context changes (Goldstein, 1987).

Shared Libraries

OpenVMS makes extensive use of shared libraries. In most cases, a user image will contain few, if any, actual run-time library routines. The majority of the references are to shareable libraries. Qualitatively speaking, this means that updates to run-time environments rarely require recompilation or relinking of user applications but merely an exit and reinitiation of the running image. Nor is a system restart needed. Applications need only be recompiled or relinked on the rare occasions when the interface between a run-time library and its callers change.

As with most OpenVMS features, there is nothing structurally special about a shareable library. Users, organizations, and software providers frequently use shareable libraries as the preferred mechanism to access executable code referenced by a program.

Privileged Shareable Libraries

Shareable libraries can be created with inherent privilege. Although this capability has a potential for abuse, it is a source of significant strength.

Privileged libraries permit the construction of services to provide particular functions that require privilege without requiring the entire requesting application to be privileged. This allows the OpenVMS mail facility to be implemented as a very small "mail delivery" privileged library, with very limited capabilities, thereby reducing the risk that the privileges needed to deliver mail are misused for other purposes.

By way of comparison, making the entire mail-delivery process privileged, as is done in UNIX sendmail, is an ongoing source of security holes. The OpenVMS philosophy, separately implementing only that small portion of the facility that requires elevated privileges, is a far safer alternative.

Command Language Support

The standard command language on OpenVMS is known as DCL (Digital Command Language). It is intended to be somewhat English-like, with commands consisting of a verb, qualifiers, and operands. (See Table 2.)

Command and file name parsing is performed by a set of standard utility subroutines, which, together with tools for expressing the syntax of a command, allow a high degree of consistency without restricting the capability to the original development team.

Used properly, these tools permit OpenVMS to make extensions (as were made to support filenames with lowercase and special characters) without requiring extensive modifications to every program.

Command qualifiers permit the same verb to activate different programs depending on the qualifier specified. For example, the default editor is known as TPU (Text Processing Utility). The older, but still popular, EDT editor is still accessible through the use of a qualifier (EDIT/EDT). Wrappers, based on the TPU editor, are used to edit Access Control Lists and file definitions.

SECURITY-SPECIFIC ARCHITECTURE

OpenVMS security functionality is based on a UIC (User Identification Code), rights list, and privilege list associated with each user login. Although OpenVMS does not directly enforce a requirement that UICs be uniquely associated with a user, it is the recommended practice.

A UIC is a 28-bit code broken into two elements:

- a 12-bit Group number
- a 16-bit User number

Each process has an associated UIC, privilege mask, and rights identifier list. These form the foundation for all subsequent security-related checking, whether it is the basic traditional set of OpenVMS protections or the more versatile rights identifier–based protections.

The traditional OpenVMS access checks are first based on the UIC, with privileged access (BYPASS, READALL) only used if the requested access is denied. System accesses are available to those processes whose group does not exceed MAXSYSGROUP (a system parameter whose normal value is 10_8) or whose SYSPRV bit is enabled in the process's privilege mask.

Traditional Protection/Ownership Hierarchy

The basic and most efficient resource access control mechanism in OpenVMS is the traditional System/Owner/Group/World protection scheme based upon these factors:

- the UIC and privilege mask of the accessing process; and
- the protection mask of the target resource, which

Table 2 Common Example of OpenVMS Commands

DCL Command	Meaning
DIRECTORY	List files in current directory
DIRECTORY *.FOR	List all files in current directory of filetype FOR (Fortran-77 source files)
SET DEFAULT [.FOX]	Set current directory to the FOX subdirectory
TYPE X.TMP	Type (on the standard output, SYS$OUTPUT) the contents of the file X.TMP
CREATE X.TMP	Create a sequential file X.TMP (from the standard input, SYS$INPUT)

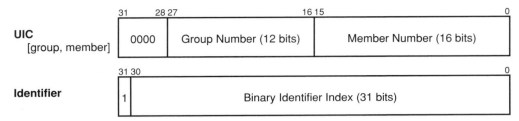

UIC [group, member]	0000	Group Number (12 bits)	Member Number (16 bits)

Identifier	1	Binary Identifier Index (31 bits)

Figure 8: User identification codes and identifiers from the basis of OpenVMS security facilities.

specifies which accesses, Read, Write, Execute, or Delete, are permitted for each category of user.

The traditional UIC-based identification works by categorizing users into four categories:

- Owner: Processes whose UIC is the owner of the object.
- System: Processes whose UIC is in the System range.
- Group: Processes whose UIC is in the same Group as the owner of the object.
- World: Processes whose UIC is not in one of the previous categories.

Rights Identifiers

Rights identifiers are the basic building block of the non-UIC based security and auditing mechanisms. Externally, identifiers are represented by ASCII strings of 1–31 characters. Internally, these strings are mapped to 31-bit binary values. Non-UIC-based identifiers all have the 32nd [high-order] bit set; identifiers referring to UICs are equal to the UIC and have the high-order four bits clear (see Figure 8). This allows UICS to be used as identifiers in their own right. The mapping between printable and binary forms are stored in a file known as the **RIGHTSLIST**, generally **SYS$SYSTEM:RIGHTLIST.DAT**.

Most references to rights identifiers refer to the conceptual identifier externally represented by the printable identifier. In any event, these identifiers are the mechanism used to resolve access to resources.

System services (**$ASCTOID** and **$IDTOASC**) and the DCL lexical function **F$IDENTIFIER** (with subfunctions for both sets of conversions) are available to convert identifiers from the ASCII string form to the 32-bit binary form and vice versa, respectively.

Identifier-Based Access

The mechanism used to allow access to a protected resource under OpenVMS with discretionary access controls is a matching undertaken between a the set of access rights (called "identifiers") held by a process and the Access Control List (ACL) associated with the resource.

Reference Monitor Concept

The conceptual framework of OpenVMS access control is that of a reference monitor, a central entity responsible for the monitoring of all accesses by processes (and hence by users) to system objects (see Figure 9).

A reference monitor creates a single point of responsibility for access control and auditing. In OpenVMS, it

is implemented as a small number of gatekeepers for different resource classes, generically known as *objects* (see Table 3). Reference monitor terminology refers to all entities that act as initiators of security-related requests as *subjects*. In the OpenVMS context, a *subject* normally represents a process (or thread of a process). There is no loss of generality, as users cannot make requests for access to objects without in some way going through a process (or thread of a process).

It should be remembered that access control through identifiers and ACLs operate in the absence of access through other means, such as the System/Owner/Group/World protection mask, and the privilege mask. If a resource is to be protected based on ACLs and identifiers, then care must be taken to ensure that access is not available through the other mechanisms.

Access to **SYSPRV** and other so-called ALL-class privileges should be carefully controlled. Systems programming and systems management staffs routinely need these privileges to maintain the operating system. Applications development, testing, and most production activities do not require privileges.

The identifier/ACL mechanism provides an excellent tool to permit the delegation of management activities and privileges to users without the need to grant DEVOUR-class privileges to a wide circle of individuals.

Resources

The OpenVMS reference monitor model controls access to 11 different classes of objects (see Table 3).

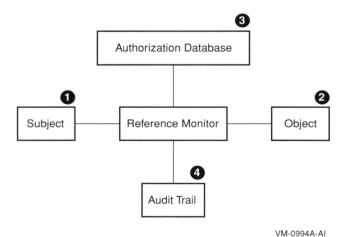

VM-0994A-AI

Figure 9: Reference monitor model used by OpenVMS to implement security related facilities (from *OpenVMS Guide to System Security*, 2003, Figure 2-1, p. 28).

Table 3 Classes of Objects Subject to Protection by the Reference Monitor

Capability	A capability of the host system, presently the only such capability is the vector processor on certain VAX CPUs.
Common Event Flag Cluster	A named set of 32 event flags that are shared between collections of different processes.
Device	A hardware or pseudodevice connected to the system.
File	A file on a file structured mass storage medium (e.g., disk).
Group Global Section	A shared memory section available to a collection of processes.
Logical Name Table	A table of logical names accessible to a collection of processes.
Queue	A set of jobs to be processed in a batch, print, or other queue.
Resource Domain	A namespace controlling access to the lock manager's resources.
Security Class	A data structure containing the elements and management routines for all members of the security class.
System Global Section	A shareable memory region potentially available to all processes in the system.
Volume	A volume mounted on a device (e.g., tape, disk).

Source: *OpenVMS Guide to System Security*, 2003, Table 2-1.

References to resources are controlled according to the ownership, protection masks, and ACLs associated with each object. The checking is performed in a defined order and eliminates the need for many, if not all, applications-based security checks (see Figure 10).

Access Control Lists

Each object with the potential for restricted access has provisions for an optional ACL. The ACL contains a list of identifiers and the types of access to be granted to the holder of the identifier. Although they may be associated with any file, other Access Control Elements (ACEs) generally have meaning only when attached to directory files, providing for the propagation of ownership, protection masks, and access control lists to new files.

Order of appearance of the ACEs in an ACL has significance. The matching of identifiers to rights enumerated in the ACL proceeds one ACE at a time until a match is detected. Thus, if a process holds multiple rights identifiers, as is typical, the ACL must be ranked as follows:

- Denials of access (ACEs with the **ACCESS=NONE** term)
- High-grade access (ACEs with the most access). For example:
  ACCESS=READ+WRITE+EXECUTE+DELETE+CONTROL)
- Lesser degrees of access
- Minimal access (ACEs that solely contain **ACCESS=READ** or **ACCESS=EXECUTE** terms)

To summarize, the first ACE whose rights identifier matches a rights identifier held by the process (or thread) will be used to determine whether the access is permissible.

Audit Server

Significant security-related events are reported to the audit server, a process which writes those events to an audit log (by default, **SYS$MANAGER: AUDIT_SERVER.DAT**). Operator messages are also written to those terminals that have been set to display operator messages of class **AUDIT**.

If there is insufficient space for the audit log file, system operation will be suspended, with no log-ins permitted (with the exception of the physical system console).

U.S. Government Security Certification

VAX/VMS version 4.3 was the first (1986) system certified to support the requirements of the Department of Defense's *Trusted Computer System Evaluation Criteria*, colloquially referred to as the *Orange Book*. This standard, originally developed by the National Computer Security Center and now administered through NIST, divides systems into a variety of categories. The lowest useful category is C2, described as "Discretionary Access Controls." Systems that provide mechanisms for security managers to mandate the use of security controls are categorized as level B systems.

In 1987 and again in 1993, OpenVMS was reevaluated against both the C2 and B1 levels of trust. The OpenVMS variant with the facilities required for operation at the B levels is referred to as SEVMS. SEVMS was first released, unevaluated, in 1987. The next release, corresponding to OpenVMS 6.0, was released in 1993. The security rating is maintained by a process supervised by the National Center for Secure Computing, with the bulk of the effort undertaken by the OpenVMS engineering team.

IMPLEMENTING SECURE USER ENVIRONMENTS

Implementing a secure user environment requires utilizing the facilities to maximum advantage. The implicit security facilities provided through inheritance and the user authentication mechanisms are both efficient and auditable.

Implicit Security

It is less complex than it would first appear to implement a large-scale, secure OpenVMS environment. The key to building an environment that works is to leverage the strengths of the system.

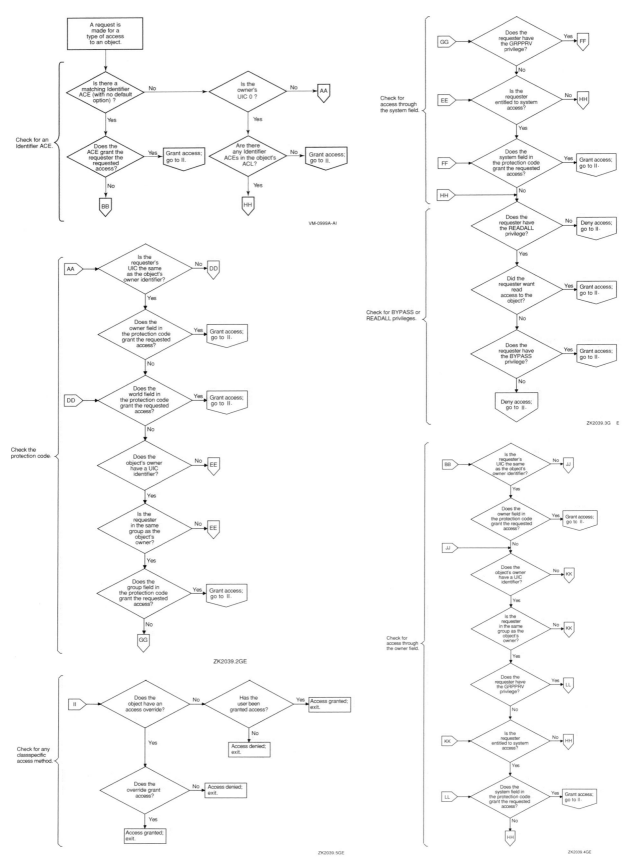

Figure 10: Security checks performed by OpenVMS when accessing objects controlled by the security system (from *OpenVMS Guide to System Security*, pages 71, et seq.). These checks, performed by OpenVMS, eliminate the need for applications-based security checks.

Table 4 Different Classes of Users for a Typical Application

Maintainer	An individual responsible for maintaining the files.
Operator	An individual responsible for day-to-day maintenance (e.g., backups).
User	Normal user authorized to access and modify records in the file.
Query Clerk	Low-level user authorized to only access (not modify) data within the file.

Although it may seem complex, the recommended technique of creating categories of personnel and assigning access rights to those categories is straightforward, secure, auditable, and efficient.

Identifiers are created to refer to collections of users. These collections are often based upon departments or applications (e.g., Accounting, Payables, Human Resources) and level of personnel (e.g., Supervisor, Clerk, Inquiry Clerk; see Table 4). These identifiers are then granted to individual users using the **AUTHORIZE** utility (**AUTHORIZE** can also be used to display the identifiers held by a given user). When the user logs onto the system, their process will be granted the identifiers associated with their username.

Beginners often try to add ACLs with ACEs for every individual user. Putting individual access rights onto each and every resource is a poor approach for many reasons, including:

- It is not maintainable. As users come and go, each and every ACL will have to reviewed and updated accordingly.
- As job responsibilities ebb and flow, each and every ACL will have to be reviewed and updated accordingly.
- When access controls are audited, as is common in larger companies, each and every ACL and each and every ACE will have to be verified.
- The resulting large ACLs will require excessive time to evaluate, compromising system performance.

The role-based approach is far more efficient, maintainable, and auditable. In a role-based approach, files have ACLs composed of ACEs referencing a set of defined roles. In effect, the system dynamically constructs the matrix of individual user's access rights based upon their identifiers and the ACLs, eliminating the need for special access checking code in programs, privileges, or other cumbersome mechanisms.

Users will hold a list of identifiers as a form of electronic badge endorsement. In effect, the rights identifiers provide management the tools to separate user validation from user clearances.

If job responsibilities change, or if a user's access must be suspended because of an investigation, it is a simple matter to remove critical rights identifiers from the authorization profile, while still permitting access to the system for other matters (e.g., electronic mail, time sheet filing, benefits filing). If the access environment is properly implemented, security and audit managers can be confident that the prohibitions will be effective.

File Protection

Properly categorized, the same program, running on the same machine at the same time, can operate on different files with dramatically different protection regimes. The security mechanisms and logical name environment provide a framework to control access. The degree of access available is implicit in the individual user (or the group with whom the user is associated), from wide open to strictly controlled.

The different permutations of the elements, and their inherent flexibility, permit a wide range of choices as to degree of security, even within an organization. This is especially important for organizations and systems that have differing security needs in different units or departments. There is no need for separate systems and variant applications when a proper security regime is implemented.

Limited Accounts

OpenVMS also has provisions for limited user log-ins, known as CAPTIVE accounts. Users whose accounts are CAPTIVE are restricted in several ways:

- no ability to specify options at login,
- no access to the DCL command prompt, and
- if the command script ever exits, the session is automatically terminated.

These restrictions, which allow a user access to specified command procedure or an application menu with controlled choices, are a good security measure for non-IT applications users. Such an account, together with the other security controls, enables the construction of user environments with multiple levels of protection and control, with no corresponding need to develop and maintain special-purpose code.

Secure Subsystems

The OpenVMS security mechanisms are powerful; yet, there are situations where controlled access to an object is desired beyond the constraints expressible in the basic security model. OpenVMS has a facility for addressing these exceptions called *protected subsystems*. Protected subsystems work because the user holds the identifier(s) needed to access the application, whereas the applications image itself holds the identifiers needed to access the object.

Results of Security Violations

The action taken when a security violation occurs has important implications. Merely preventing the inappropriate (or undesired) reference is essential but, generally speaking, an insufficient response. Auditors and security personnel need to know that an unauthorized attempt to access resources has occurred. The realities of large-scale systems operations complicate this task. Protecting resources too tightly can result in voluminous alarm indications, which serve no purpose other than making it harder to identify true security violations.

OpenVMS, through the combination of its integrity-based design, resource monitor, and audit server, provides good mechanisms to tailor security reporting to those security-related events that are desired, without reporting false alarms, and still protect the overall system from misuse.

Damage Limitation

The central goal of the implicit security-related mechanisms is to limit damage to other system users and the overall system. In a direct sense, as mentioned earlier, it is a consequence of the integrity, robustness, and safety aspects of the design philosophy.

The initial provision of System, Owner, Group, and World categories of access represent a good first approximation as to the structure of many organizations. The brick wall protection, and resulting near total encapsulation of system internal details, renders it simpler for application programs to ignore the specifics of the configuration and the environment than to delve into them.

Ease of Programming Model

The programming model for using ACLs and rights identifiers is straightforward. In most cases, the presence of the security system is implicit, yielding the same results as the implicit security provided by the original, traditional OpenVMS security model.

There is full support for defining default ACLs, file protections, and ownership of new files on a directory-by-directory basis. This reduces security-related issues to a management issue, irrelevant to the applications programmer. Removing the security-related issues from applications programming also allows security issues to be driven by the data being managed, rather than the applications program being used. As an example, consider that the same applications can be used to process data subject to HIPAA (Health Insurance Portability and Accountability Act of 1996, Public Law 104–191; the applicable Department of Health and Human Services Privacy regulations may be found at 45 CFR Parts 160 and 164) as data that is not subject to such restrictions.

The integrity of the security-related environment is also assured by using a resource monitor implementation for enforcing security not code embedded in the applications program. In fact, the application itself is subject to protection. For example, restricting access to executable images represents a mechanism to ensure compliance with training standards in an auditable manner subject to documentation.

The security and access checking facilities are fully available to the programmer. The $CHKPRO system service provides the developer with full access to the access checks used throughout OpenVMS. The list of identifiers held by a process is also available, both within executable images and within command procedures (using the $GETJPI system service and the F$GETJPI lexical function, respectively).

APPLICATION PROGRAMMING INTERFACES

Outside of areas that virtually obligate replication, mostly because of the different higher-level language-formatting models, there are few examples of parallel functionality that serendipitously differ. Interfaces that can execute completely in user mode do so; functions, such as system services requiring privileged processing, do

Table 5 DECent Phase IV/V Protocols

DDCMP	Digital Data Communications Message Protocol
NSP	Network Services Protocol
DAP	Data Access Protocol
CTERM	Remote Terminal Protocol
MOP	Maintenance Operations Protocol

so below the user's visibility, albeit using documented interfaces.

Access to system services is via conventional CALL-type interfaces; if the system service requires supporting processing from system components operating in inner (more privileged) access modes, the system service is responsible for generating all requests of lower level system functions.

File System Access

The normal user and programmer access files using Record Management Services (RMS). RMS provides a toolkit of functionality to create, delete, and manipulate files and records within files. Within files, RMS provides support for fixed and variable record files, relative files, indexed files, and byte-stream files.

When files are being shared between processes and between different machines in an OpenVMS cluster, RMS is the system component responsible for requesting locks on the files and the records within files to ensure orderly access.

RMS also provides for buffering on a per-process and global basis for the different types of files. Buffering is controlled by a variety of parameters.

Network Access

Network access in OpenVMS occurs in two modes: transparent and nontransparent. Transparent access is a facility provided by cooperating elements of RMS and DECnet to allow access to files over the network using the same semantics that would be available were the files located on local storage. Sequential, direct, relative, and indexed files can be accessed at the record or block level. A demonstration of the transparency of this facility is that one can run assemblies and compilations of files located on different network-accessible machines by setting one's default to a remote directory and running the compiler.

DECnet

The DECnet protocol suite has its origins in the late 1970s, predating the widespread use of local area network (LAN) technology. DECnet implements point-to-point and multipoint links and, since the mid-1980s, has included IEEE 802.3 LAN connections. DECnet is based on a series of protocol specifications developed by Digital (see Table 5).

DECnet Phase V, released in 1991, incorporated support for the ISO-developed OSI protocols in addition to those defined by Digital. Support has also been included to tunnel DECnet connections over Internet protocol (IP) infrastructure.

A significant architectural difference between the TCP/IP protocol stack and the DECnet protocol stack is the presence in the DECnet stack of a Session Control layer, including authentication as part of the network-provided functionality.

TCP/IP

Although the definition of TCP/IP occurred at approximately the same time as the design of OpenVMS, TCP/IP remained an essentially educational and research network until the mid-1990s. Digital did not develop a TCP/IP stack until 1988.

There are, at the time of this writing, three TCP/IP implementations actively available for the OpenVMS platform:

• TCP/IP Services for OpenVMS (HP),
• Multinet (Process Software Corporation), and
• TCPware (Process Software Corporation).

Multinet and TCPware have been growing closer in functionality since Process Software's acquisition of Multinet.

OPEN SOURCE SOFTWARE

There is a wealth of open source and other low-cost software for OpenVMS. Some of this software is shipped with the operating system distribution on the freeware and open source tools disks. Other programs are available from their authors.

Some standard components provided by HP are open source or closely based on industry widely available sources. Tools such as Kerberos, SSH (secure shell), SSL (Secure Session Layer), and Apache are fully supported (see Table 6).

There is, however, a duality to the use of open source software. Open source software is, by definition, implemented across a variety of different platforms, with a wide range of engineering practices. Some of these practices are state of the art in software engineering, and some of them are less robust.

It is the less-robust software engineering practices that represent a challenge to the OpenVMS community. Widely adopted technologies are a highly valued form of leverage for quickly developing applications to address business needs. On the other hand, some of these technologies

have come with preexisting security weaknesses that undermine OpenVMS's longstanding record of security and integrity.

As an example, consider software with two different types of shortcomings, one at the implementation level and one at the architectural level.

At the implementation level, programs written in C are often victim to buffer overflows, caused by the failure to check requests for situations that can overflow buffers.

At the architectural level, more than a few programs have been designed in a manner that presumes an all-or-nothing security environment, often exemplified by UNIX's setuid. The ubiquitous sendmail program fits into this category. Modifying sendmail to operate with a more nuanced approach to security is possible, but it represents a major engineering undertaking, which is often as complex, if not more complex, than reengineering the entire application from the beginning.

Software that does not invoke privileges in its operation, except for the implicit ability to access files through the normal mechanisms, poses a far lesser threat to the integrity and security of the OpenVMS system.

The challenge is to find ways to assimilate the leverage represented by open source software while not sacrificing the bulletproof security and integrity that are OpenVMS's strengths.

SUMMARY

OpenVMS is a world-class operating system, with a long history of solid, reliable operation and is considered to be the "Gold Standard in clustering," as eloquently stated by David Freund in his 2002 paper on UNIX clusters.

The OpenVMS architecture and approach have proved to be a strong, viable foundation, with many impressive achievements over a quarter century. Long-lived is not legacy. OpenVMS, starting on the original VAX-11/780, has gone on to manage systems more than a thousand times larger with a high degree of efficiency and reliability and with little to change in its fundamental structure or architecture.

OpenVMS presents a reliable, solid system with unlimited growth potential.

Table 6 Low-Cost/Freeware/Open Source Software Available for OpenVMS

INFO-ZIP	File compression utility, file compatible with PKZIP on Windows
UNZIP	File decompression utility, file compatible with PKZIP on Windows
APACHE	Web server developed by the Apache Software Foundation
TCL/TK	Tool Command Language/Tool Kit, and interpretive scriping language, by John Ousterhout
PERL	Practical Extraction and Report Language, by Larry Wall
PHP	Personal Home Page, originally by Rasmus Lerdorf
TOMCAT	A Java servlet and Java Server Pages implementation for Apache
XML	Extensible Markup Language
SOAP	Simple Object Access Protocol
NetBeans	Modular, standards-based IDE for Java
BISON	A parser-generator, developed by the GNU Project
GHOSTSCRIPT	A freeware (under the GPL) PostScript® interpreter

ACKNOWLEDGMENTS

I thank the numerous people who generously took the time to speak with me about their roles and recollections of events. I thank members of OpenVMS Engineering, including Leo Demers, Susan Skonetski, Andrew Goldstein, Stephen Hoffman, and others, who contributed recollections and pointers to information. I also thank John Streiff, James Gursha, Jerrold Leichter, and others who read drafts and contributed their comments. I also thank Fern Hertzberg for her assistance in organizing and copyediting this chapter.

GLOSSARY

Asynchronous System Trap (AST) A lightweight thread of execution within a processes context. ASTs are queued on a first-in, first-out basis by Access mode, with Kernel mode ASTs executed first, and User mode ASTs executed last. Although a higher-priority (inner mode) AST may preempt a lower-priority (outer mode) AST, ASTs are not otherwise preemptible within a process. This preemption is an intraprocess issue; ASTs have no effect on interrupt servicing or scheduling interaction between different processes.

DECnet A proprietary networking scheme architected and implemented by then–Digital Equipment Corporation in the late 1970s. DECnet provides most of the services identified in the ISO's Open System Interconnect model of networks. On OpenVMS, DECnet is used as a basis for several tools, including transparent remote file access, system management, and remote terminal handling.

Object An entity belonging to the classes of objects that can be subject to access controls.

Queue IO (QIO) The user-accessible system service that serves as the gatekeeper for all IO operations on OpenVMS.

Reference Monitor The software component responsible for checking a subject's degree of access to an object.

Subject An OpenVMS user process.

User Identification Code (UIC) A 28-bit binary number, split into a 12-bit Group number and a 16-bit Member number which uniquely identifies a user for access purposes on an OpenVMS system.

CROSS REFERENCES

See *Linux Security; Operating System Security; Unix Security; Windows 2000 Security.*

REFERENCES

Digital Equipment Corporation. (1977). *VAX11 software handbook 1977–78.* (Vol. 3). Order Number EB 08126.

Digital Equipment Corporation. (1979). *VAX11 architecture handbook.* Order Number EB 17580.

Dijkstra, E. (1968). The structure of "THE"—Multiprogramming system. *Communications of the Association for Computing Machinery, 11*(5), 341–346.

Freund, D. (2002, August 9). Disaster tolerant Unix: *Removing the last single point of failure.* Illuminata, Inc.

Goldenberg, R., Kenah, L., et al. (1991). *VAX/VMS version 5.2 internals and data structures.* Digital Press.

Goldstein, A. (1987). The design and implementation of a distributed file system. *Digital Technical Journal, 1*(7), 45–55.

HP OpenVMS guide to system security, OpenVMS version 7.3-2. (2003, September). Order Number AA-Q2HLG-TE.

HP OpenVMS I/O user's reference manual, OpenVMS 7.3-2. (2003, September). Order Number AA-PV6SF-TK.

Kronenberg, N., Levy, H., & Strecker, W. (1986). VAXcluster: A closely-coupled distributed system. *ACM Transactions on Computer Systems, 4*(2), 130–146.

OpenVMS calling ststandard. (2001, April). Order Number AA-QSBBD-TE.

FURTHER READING

Manuals

HP OpenVMS Alpha Version 7.3-2 release notes. (2003, September). Order Number AA-RV8YA-TE.

HP OpenVMS DCL dictionary: A–M. (2003, September). Order Number AA-PV5KJ-TK.

HP OpenVMS DCL dictionary: N–Z. (2003, September). Order Number AA-PV5LJ-TK.

HP OpenVMS system manager's manual. Vol. 1: Essentials. (2003, September). Order Number AA-PV5M H-TK.

HP OpenVMS system manager's manual. Vol. 2: Tuning, monitoring, and complex systems. (2003, September). Order Number AA-PV5NH-TK.

HP OpenVMS system services reference manual: A—GETUAI. (2003, September). Order Number AA-QSBMF-TE.

HP OpenVMS system services reference manual: GETUTC—Z. (2003, September). Order Number AA-QSBNF-TE.

OpenVMS calling standard. (2003, April 14). [Draft including IA-64 additions].

OpenVMS programming concepts manual. Vol. 1. (2002, June). Order Number AAS-RNSHB-TE.

OpenVMS record management services reference manual. (2002, June). Order Number AA-PV6RE-TK.

OpenVMS version 7.2 new features manual. (1999, January). Order Number AA-QSBFC-TE.

VMS/Ultrix Connection system managers guide. (1988–1990). Order Number AA-LU49C-TE.

Books and Papers

Bell, C. G., Mudge, C., & McNamara, J. (1978). *Computer engineering: A DEC view of hardware systems design.* Boston, MA: Digital Press.

Brooks, F. (1975). *The mythical man-month: Essays on software engineering.* Addison-Wesley.

Callander, M. A., Sr., Carlson, L., Ladd, A., & Norcross, M. (1992). The VAXstation 4000 model 90. *Digital Technical Journal, 4*(3), 82–91.

Chisvin, L., Bouchard, G., & Wenners, T. (1992). The VAX 6000 model 600 processor. *Digital Technical Journal, 4*(3), 47–59.

Crowell, J., & Maruska, D. (1992a). Design of the VAX 4000 model 100 and MicroVAX 3100 model 90. *Digital Technical Journal, 4*(3), 73–81.

Crowell, J., Kwong-Tak, A., Kopec, T., Nadkarni, S., & Sovie, D. (1992b). Design of the VAX 4000 model 400, 500, 600. *Digital Technical Journal, 4*(3), 60–72.

Davis, S. (1991). Design of VMS volume shadowing phase II: Host-based shadowing. *Digital Technical Journal, 3*(3), 7–15.

Digital Equipment Corporation. (1978). *VAX11 software handbook 1978–79.* Order Number EB 15485.

Digital Equipment Corporation. (1980). *VAX software handbook 1980–81.* Order Number EB 18057.

Digital Equipment Corporation. (1981, April). *VAX/VMS internals and data structures, version 2.2.* Order Number AA-K785A-TE.

Digital Equipment Corporation. (1997). *OpenVMS at 20: Nothing stops it!*

Donchin, D., Fischer, T., Fox, T., Peng, V., Preston, R. & Wheeler, W. (1992). The NVAX CPU chip: Design challenges, methods, and CAD tools. *Digital Technical Journal, 4*(3), 24–37.

Duffy, D. The System Communication Architecture, *Digital Technical Journal, 1*(5) 22–28.

Durdan, W., Bowhill, W., Brown, J., Herrick, W., Marcello, R., Samudrala, S., Uhler, G, & Wade N., (1990). An overview of the VAX 6000 model 400 chip set. *Digital Technical Journal, 2*(2) 36–51.

Fox, M., & Twoskus, J. (1987) Local area VAXcluster systems, *Digital Technical Journal, 1*(5) 56–68.

Fox, T., Gronowski, P., Jain, A., Leary, M., & Miner, D. (1988). The CVAX 78034 chip, a 32-bit second-generation VAX microprocessor. *Digital Technical Journal, 1*(7) 95–108.

Gamache, R., & Morse, K. (1988) VMS symmetric multiprocessing, *Digital Technical Journal, 1*(7) 57–63.

Gezelter, R. (1989, November). *Your key to efficient event driven systems under VAX/VMS: Asynchronous system traps.* Paper presented at the DECUS Pre-symposium Seminar, Anaheim, CA.

Gezelter, R. (2000a, October 6). *Building secure OpenVMS applications.* Paper presented at the Compaq Enterprise Technology Symposium, Los Angeles, CA.

Gezelter, R. (2000b, October 6). *Introduction to OpenVMS AST programming.* Paper presented at the Compaq Enterprise Technology Symposium, Los Angeles, CA.

Gezelter, R. (2000c, October 6). *OpenVMS shareable libraries: An implementer's guide.* Paper presented at the Compaq Enterprise Technology Symposium, Los Angeles, CA.

Gezelter, R. (2004). Inheritance based environments in stand-alone OpenVMS systems and OpenVMS clusters. *HP OpenVMS Technical Journal, 3.*

Goldenberg, R., Dumas, D., & Saravanan, S. (1997). *OpenVMS Alpha internals: Scheduling and process control, version 7.0.* Boston, MA: Digital Press.

Goldstein, A. (1977). *Files-11 on disk specification, level 2.,* private communication

Gursha, J. (1997). *High performance cluster configuration system management.* Boston, MA: Digital Press.

Harvard Research Group. (2001). *OpenVMS: When continuous availability really matters.*

Hayes, F. (1994). Design of the AlphaServer multiprocessor server systems. *Digital Technical Journal, 6*(3), 8–19.

Intel. (2002a). *Intel Itanium architecture software developer's manual. Vol. 1: Application architecture, revision 2.1.* Order Number 245317-004.

Intel. (2002b). *Intel Itanium architecture software developer's manual. Vol. 2: System architecture, revision 2.1.* Order Number 245318-004.

Intel. (2002c). *Intel Itanium architecture software developer's manual. Vol. 3: Instruction set reference, revision 2.1.* Order Number 245319-004.

Lauck, A., Oran, D., & Perlman, R. (1986) A Digital Network Architecture overview. *Digital Technical Journal, 1*(3) 11–24.

Leahy, L. (1991). New availability features of local area VAXcluster systems. *Digital Technical Journal, 3*(3), 27–35.

McCoy, K. (1990). *VMS file system internals.* Digital Press, Boston, MA.

National Computer Security Center. (1996, October 24). *Final evaluation report, digital evaluation report: OpenVMS and SEVMS, version 6.1, with VAX or Alpha.* National Security Agency, Fort George G. Meade, Maryland, NCSC-FER-93/001.B, NCSC-FER-93/002.B.

Russo, A. (1994). The Alphaserver 2100 I/O subsystem. *Digital Technical Journal, 6*(3), 20–28.

Sites, R. (Ed.). (1992). *Alpha architecture reference manual.* Boston, MA: Digital Press.

Snaman, W.E., Jr. (1987). The VAX/VMS Distributed Lock Manager, *Digital Technical Journal, 1*(5), 29–44.

Snaman, W.E., Jr. (1991). Application design in a VAXcluster system. *Digital Technical Journal, 3*(3), 16–26.

TechWise Research. (2000, June). *Quantifying the value of availability: A detailed comparison of four different RISC-based cluster solutions designed to provide high availability.* Version 1.1a.

TechWise Research. (2004, February). *Total cost of ownership for entry-level and mid-range clusters: A detailed analysis of the total cost of ownership of three different RISC-based server clusters including HP OpenVMS, IBM AIX, and Sun Solaris.* Version 1.0.

TechWise Research. (2004, May). *Are some RISC-based clusters easier to manage than others? A detailed comparison of the resources required to manage HP OpenVMS and IBM AIX server clusters.* Version 1.0.

TechWise Research. (2004, June). *Are some RISC-based clusters more secure than others? A detailed comparison of potential vulnerabilities and security-related crashes for HP OpenVMS, IBM AIX, and Sun Solaris.* Version 1.0.

Uhler, G. M., Bernstein, D., Biro, L., Brown, J., III, Edmondson, J., Pickholtz, J., & Stamm, R. (1992). The NVAX and NVAX+ high performance VAX microprocessors. *Digital Technical Journal, 4*(3), 11–23.

Weiner, H. (1973, February). *An analysis of computer software security at Cornell,* unpublished.

Windows 2000 Security

E. Eugene Schultz, *University of California–Berkeley Lab*

ABOUT W2K

The first section of this chapter discusses W2K, its major functions, its major capabilities, and how it works.

What Is W2K?

W2K is an operating system product that includes both workstation (Windows 2000 Professional) and server (such as Windows 2000 Server and Windows 2000 Advanced Server versions). (Still another W2K product is W2K Data Center, which is designed for large hosts that require high amounts of RAM, fault tolerance, and high-end multiprocessor support.) It supports not only desktop and office automation applications, but can also be used to run network applications that support mail services, Web services, file transfer services, a domain name service (DNS) server, and even routing and firewalling network traffic. W2K also includes many features that were not available in W2K's predecessor, Windows NT (NT), the most notable of which is W2K directory services (called "Active Directory"). Active Directory provides an infrastructure and related services that enable users and applications to both locate and access objects, such as files and printers, and services throughout the network. Active Directory is a directory service (similar to Novell's Netware Directory Service) that acts as the main basis for holding and distributing data about accounts, groups, Organizational Units (OUs), security policies, services, domains, trust, and even Active Directory itself. (An OU is a "nested group"—one that is either above or below other OUs (or both) in a hierarchy—with special properties that are discussed shortly in this chapter.) This directory service not only stores data of this nature, but also makes it available to users and programs, providing updates as needed. Active Directory also supports security by storing security-related parameters and data and supporting services (e.g., time services) needed for achieving system and network security. Active Directory is in fact in many respects the "center of the universe" in W2K.

HOW W2K WORKS

A good starting point in exploring how W2K works is W2K domains, the focus of the next part of this chapter.

Domains

W2K machines can be configured in either of two ways—as part of a domain or as part of a workgroup consisting of one or more machines. A domain is a group of servers and (normally) workstations that are part of one unit of management. Each domain has its own security policy settings. Policies are rules that affect how features and capabilities in W2K work; policies can determine allowable parameters (such as the minimum number of characters in passwords), enable functions (such as the right to increase or decrease the priority with which a program runs), or restrict the ability to perform these functions. (We will cover policy in more detail elsewhere in this chapter.) Domain controllers (DCs) hold information related to policies, authentication, and other variables. When a change to a policy is made, a new account is created or deleted, or a new OU is created, the changes are recorded by a DC within a domain, and then replicated to all the other DCs within the domain within a designated time interval.

Domains are good for security, provided, of course, that they are set up and maintained properly. Why? Because it is possible to set domain policies so that (with a few exceptions) they will be applied to virtually every server and workstation within a domain. This decreases the likelihood that any system within the domain will be a "weak link" system, one that is an easy target for attackers. Additionally, domain functionality includes important features such as the ability to limit the workstations and servers that may be added to a domain.

The other option is to belong to a "workgroup." By default a system that is not part of a domain is a member of its own workgroup. In workgroups anyone with Administrator privileges on a workstation or server and who knows the name of a certain workgroup can add that machine to the workgroup, something that makes it possible to discover a great deal of information about each machine and users in the workgroup. This information can advantageously be used to attack the other systems. Access to resources (such as files, folders (directories), printers, and so forth) is determined locally by the particular server or workstation within the workgroup that contains the resources. No built-in central control capabilities exist. Users whose machines are part of workgroups can engage in functions such as sending mail, transferring files, and so forth, but workgroups are not at all conducive to security Why? First, as just mentioned, there is no mechanism within W2K to limit workgroup membership. If an attacker discovers the name of a workgroup, that person can add a malicious system to that workgroup. Additionally, the lack of centralized control in a workgroup necessitates setting security parameters and adjusting configurations on every machine within the workgroup; in contrast, domains have settings (embedded in "Group Policy Objects" or GPOs) that can be set from a single domain controller (to be defined shortly) within the domain.

Next we will consider various possible relationships between domains and the implications of each.

Trees and Forests

W2K domains can be arranged in a hierarchical fashion starting with a root domain at the top, then domains at the level immediately below the root domain, then possibly still other domains at the next level(s). One option is to nest domains in a manner such that they form a "contiguous namespace." In simple terms, this means that there is one common root domain; all subordinate (lower) domains' names are derived from their parent domains. Consider the name of one domain, research.entity.org. Consider also marketing.entity.org. If the domains are nested in a contiguous name space, both of the domains in this example will have the same parent domain, entity.org. If research.entity.org is a parent domain, every one of its children will have a first name followed by research.entity.org (see Figure 1). Contiguous namespaces characterize W2K "trees." In contrast, if the namespace is not contiguous, then there is no common namespace. "Forests" (as opposed to "trees") are characterized by noncontiguous namespaces. In a tree or forest, every domain connected directly to another domain (as are entity.org and research.entity.org) by default has a two-way trust relationship with every other domain. Note that if domains are not directly connected to each other (as in the case of marketing.entity.org and research.entity.org in Figure 1), they nevertheless have transitive trust between them because entity.org has a two-way trust relationship with each of its child domains. Trust is a property that allows users,

groups, and other entities from one domain to potentially access resources (files, directories, printers, plotters, and so forth) in another, provided of course that the appropriate access mechanisms (e.g., shares) and sufficient permissions are in place. Trust is in fact an essential element in characterizing domains that are linked together to form trees or forests. These domains may be either in "mixed mode" or "native mode," as the next section explains.

Mixed Mode versus Native Mode

Domains can be deployed in two modes, "mixed mode" and "native mode." In mixed mode, a domain contains both W2K and NT DCs, or has all W2K DCs, but nobody has migrated the domain to native mode. In native mode, a domain contains all W2K DCs and the domain has been migrated to this mode. Native mode is better from a security viewpoint in several ways.

Domain Controllers

DCs are a special type of server used for controlling settings, policies, changes, and other critical facets of W2K domain functionality. In W2K mixed mode, DCs may consist of both W2K and NT servers. One W2K server must serve as a primary domain controller (PDC) in mixed mode, however. A PDC receives changes, such as changes to the authentication database, and replicates them to the other DCs within the domain. In W2K native mode, however, there is no PDC per se (one DC, however, functions as an "emulated PDC" within each domain for purposes such as achieving compatibility with trusted and trusting NT domains); all DCs are capable of picking up and replicating changes to the other domain controllers. Every DC in a native mode deployment holds a copy of Active Directory. In W2K mixed mode or in the case of a NT domain, if the PDC crashes, some degree of disruption invariably occurs. In W2K, however, if any DC crashes there is no particular problem—all DCs function as equals to each other.

Active Directory is so important in understanding how W2K works that it merits further examination. The next section describes Active Directory functionality in greater detail.

A Deeper Look at How the W2K Active Directory Works

Each object in a W2K tree or forest has an X.500-compliant distinguished name (DN), one that uniquely refers to the object in question (e.g., /O=Internet/DC=COM/DC=Example/CN=Users/CN=Jill Cooper). Each object also has a Globally Unique ID (GUID), a 128-bit identifier unique to the object within a particular namespace. X.500 properties and naming conventions are beyond the scope of this chapter, but suffice it to say they provide an orderly way to organize and refer to objects. However, the

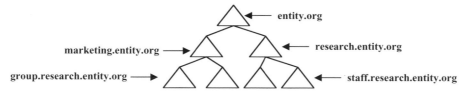

Figure 1: Example of how namespace is organized within a tree.

X.500 directory structure is quite detailed and cumbersome; the Internet Engineering Task Force (IETF) consequently created the lightweight directory access protocol (LDAP) to provide a kind of scaled-down, simplified version of X.500. W2K Active Directory is actually based on LDAP.

Active Directory objects are organized in various manners. Each object has one or more attributes. "Containers" are higher-level objects that hold objects. Directories, for example, are containers that hold one type of objects called "files" and another called "directories." The types of objects that each container holds and the properties (e.g., names) of the objects are determined by the "schema."

Microsoft designed Active Directory with the goal of reducing barriers to locating and accessing resources throughout a tree or forest, regardless of whatever network boundaries (e.g., separation of networks from each other) exist. Each machine within a tree or forest contains objects (resources). The "Global Catalog" service enables users and programs that run on users' behalf to discover available resources within a tree or forest. When a trust link between domains is established, Global Catalog services extend across domain boundaries. When a request to access a resource occurs, the Domain Name Service (DNS) not only resolves hostnames into IP addresses and vice versa, but also resolves objects; that is, when given an object name, it identifies exactly to which object the name refers. In effect, therefore, DNS is also the locator service for Active Directory. Service Resource Records (SRRs) are the basis for locating services and objects and to keep DNS tables up to date. Dynamic DNS, a service available in more recent releases of BIND, updates Service Resource Records (SRRs) to ensure that global catalog and other directory service–related services can perform their functionality properly. (BIND is Berkeley Internet Name Domain, an implementation of the domain name system [DNS] protocols.) DDNS also registers systems with dynamic addresses that connect to the network.

Replication of Active Directory changes involves a number of steps. The update process (e.g., when a user changes a password or when an Administrator adds a new user to a group) begins when an update occurs in the copy of Active Directory within the DC that receives a change. Each DC that receives updates becomes part of a "replication topology" that specifies the particular connections within a tree or forest formed to synchronize the contents of Active Directory within each DC. At the designed time interval the connections are established and updates are sent to each DC within the tree or forest. The Update Sequence Number (USN), a 64-bit number associated with an object, and Property Version Number (PVN), a version number for each object and the object's attributes, for the changed object are both incremented by the DC that records the update. Additionally, the DC captures the time stamp for the change. Each DC updates its copy of Active Directory if the USN and PVN are higher than the values it has for the object in question. In case of a "conflict," that is, more than one change to the same object, the change with most recent time stamp will be recorded in any DC's copy of Active Directory. Each DC that initiates one or more updates and each DC that receives these updates constitutes a "replication partner." Several mechanisms are in place to protect against one or more rogue machines from replicating bogus changes—replication partners authenticate to each other, changes on every DC are tracked, and access control mechanisms ("permissions") determine who can modify Active Directory objects.

Group Policy Objects

Group Policy Objects (GPOs) are a collection of configuration settings related to computer configuration and user profiles. They provide a powerful way to store and flexibly apply policy settings. Several types of GPOs exist, including the following:

• Local GPOs (LGPOs)—these are intended mainly for computers that are not part of any Active Directory domain.
• Active Directory Group Policies—these are designed to be linked to various Active Directory containers, such as sites (a defined network topology), domains, or OUs.
• System Policies—these are legacy groups of settings from NT system policies if NT domains have been migrated to W2K systems.

Many different GPOs can be created and linked, some at the OU level, others at the domain level, others at sites (subnets or groups of subnets used in controlling replication of Active Directory changes), and still others at the local level. GPOs are applied in a predictable order. For computers, any local computer GPOs are applied first, then site-linked computer GPOs, then computer GPOs linked to domains, then local-linked computer OUs. The last GPO applied normally is the one with the settings that go into effect. This means that if there is a domain policy governing, say, account lockout parameters and a local policy governing the same, the domain policy settings will be the effective settings. The same basic principle applies to user GPOs—local GPOs that apply to users are applied first, followed by site-linked GPOs, and so forth. Another way of saying all this is that OU-linked GPOs normally have precedence over all other levels, followed by domain-linked GPOs, followed by site-linked GPOs, and followed by local GPOs (see Figure 2).

There is one important exception to the principle, however. In terms of place within the object hierarchy, sites are above domains, and domains are above OUs. Parent OUs are always above child OUs, too. If someone with sufficient privileges (e.g., a Domain Administrator) sets a "No Override" for a GPO that is linked at a higher level within this hierarchy, conflicting settings of GPOs set a lower levels will not apply (as shown in Table 1). The "No Override" setting thus becomes a good way for Domain Administrators to "gain the upper hand" by linking GPOs to domains and OUs, and then setting a "No Override" on domain-linked GPOs. This for the most part ensures that any OU administrators will not be able to negate domain group policy.

If there are multiple GPOs within any single level of precedence (e.g., OU level), the policy that has been most recently linked to that level is by default the one that is applied. So, the default GPO that is linked to a domain will be overridden by linking a new GPO to the same domain.

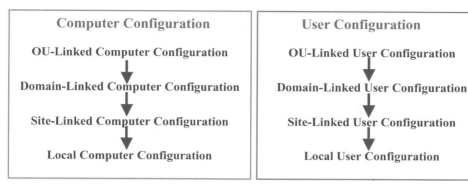

Figure 2:   Precedence of GPOs at different levels.

Still, a Domain Administrator or someone else with sufficient privileges can reverse the order of precedence—the default GPO can go into effect simply by using the policy editor to reverse the order. Note that in Figure 3 there are two policies, EES policy and default domain policy, that are linked to the domain ees.test. EES policy is listed first and will prevail over the default domain policy link. However, by highlighting "EES policy" in the Group Policy sheet shown in Figure 3 and then clicking on Down, the default domain policy can be made to prevail.

Further complicating the situation is the fact that GPO settings can be inherited, that is, from one site container to its children or from one OU to its children. "Block inheritance" settings can be in place at the level of children containers, however. "Block inheritance" does exactly what it implies. But if there is a "No Override" at the higher-level container (e.g., a parent site or OU), the "No Override" prevails; GPO settings from the parent are put in effect at the level of the child containers. Furthermore, inheritance does not work from one domain to its children. To have the same GPO settings for a parent domain and its children, therefore, it is necessary to link all the domains to the same GPO.

GPOs can profoundly affect W2K security. Consider password policy, for instance, as shown in Figure 4. Settings such as minimum password length and password complexity (i.e., whether passwords can consist of any set of characters or whether they must be constructed according to specific rules, e.g., that they may not contain the username and must include at least three of the following four categories of characters: uppercase English characters, lowercase English characters, numerals, and special characters such as "&" and "/") are embedded in GPOs.

These settings affect how easily W2K passwords can be cracked. GPOs can be applied to a wide variety of entities, including accounts, local computers, groups, services, the W2K Registry, the W2K Event Log, objects within Active Directory, and more. (The Registry is a group of settings relevant to hardware, system configuration, groups and users. The Registry must be accessed via a Registry editor.)

Table 1   How "No Override" Works

Level	"No Override" Applies to GPOs Linked to
Site	Child sites
	Domains
	OUs
	Child-OUs
Domain	OUs
	ChildOUs
OU	ChildOUs

IntelliMirror: How Group Policy Can Be Used

IntelliMirror, a new feature in W2K, provides a powerful example of how group policy can be used advantageously. IntelliMirror is a set of features that enable user data, applications, and computing environments to be available and user-specific settings to be applied regardless of the computer the user is using and whether or not the user is on-line. If worse comes to worse (e.g., if the user's workstation becomes unusable), IntelliMirror can recover, restore, or replace the user's information, applications, and user-specific settings. IntelliMirror can be configured to control and administer user data, including documents, presentations, spreadsheets, and other objects with which users work. It can synchronize the contents of files automatically whenever a user moves a document to My Documents. IntelliMirror can also install, configure, repair and delete software (including software upgrades), service packs, and hot fixes. When a user invokes an application or an application needs to access a file, IntelliMirror uses the Windows Installer Service to ensure that every file and necessary parameter are available. IntelliMirror also saves critical, specific user and computer settings such as desktop configuration, volume settings, and so on, and ensures that these settings are applied whenever each user is logged on.

Group policy comes into play because it is typically used to define the settings that affect what IntelliMirror controls. Group policy is particularly advantageous in that one collection of settings can be applied to entire groups of users, alleviating the need to configure settings on a user-by-user basis. Once the policy settings are applied, the automatically system keeps a "steady state" for these settings. Policy is not necessary for IntelliMirror to work, however, and some of its features such as offline file access are not dependent upon policy.

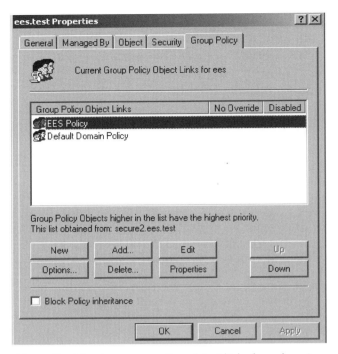

Figure 3: Viewing group policy object links for a domain.

Accounts, Groups, and Organizational Units

As in NT, each W2K system has a default local Administrator account, the built-in superuser account for administering that system. A default Administrator account also exists within each domain for the purpose of administering systems and resources throughout the domain.

Additionally, there is a default local Guest account and also a domain Guest account, both of which (fortunately) come disabled by default. Any additional accounts must be created by people or applications with the appropriate level of rights.

W2K groups are more complicated than accounts. W2K has four types of groups: local groups (for giving access and rights on a local W2K system), domain local groups (which can encompass users or groups from any trusted domain), global groups (which can allow access to resources in the domain or forest where they exist, and are backward compatible with NT global groups), and (only in native mode) universal groups (which can consist of users and groups from any native mode domain within a tree or forest). Universal groups provide the most flexible way of forming groups and providing access to them at the risk of potentially allowing too much access to these groups unintentionally.

Some types of groups can be included within other groups. Group inclusion means that any users from one group can also become members of another group by adding the first group to the second. For example, global groups can be added to domain local groups and in a native mode domain, global groups can even be included in other global groups. W2K's group inclusion properties provide a very convenient way of setting up access to resources, especially when trusted access is required. System administrators can, for example, include a universal group from another domain in a domain local group in their own domain to give users in the other domain the access they need. The users in the universal group from the other domain will have the same access permissions to the resources in question as the users in the domain local

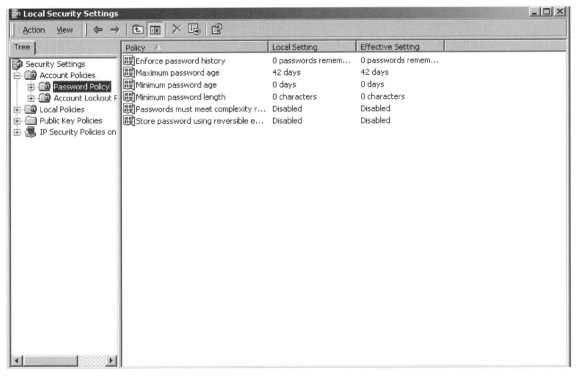

Figure 4: Default password policy settings.

Table 2 Default Groups in W2K

Global Groups	Domain Local Groups in DCs	Local Groups in Workstations and Servers
Domain Administrators	Administrators (Local)	Administrators (Local)
Domain Users	Account Operators	Backup Operators
Domain Guests	Server Operators	Guests
Certificate (Cert) Publishers	Backup Operators	Power Users
Domain Computers	Print Operators	Replicator
Domain Controllers	Replicator	Users
Group Policy Creator Owners	Users	Interactive Users
Enterprise Controllers	Guests	Network Users
	Interactive Users	Everyone
	Network Users	Creator/Owner
	Everyone	Dial-up
	Creator/Owner	Batch
	Dial-up	Terminal Server Users
	Batch	
	Terminal Server Users	

group. Table 2 lists the default domain and local groups in DCs and also in workstations and servers in W2K.

The Everyone group consists of all users on a given system, regardless of whether they have been authenticated. Fortunately, the potentially dangerous Everyone group is at least not afforded any kind of special privileges. Still, it is best to not assign file, folder, and/or share access to this group—Authenticated Users is a much better group if universal access to these objects is necessary. Groups such as Interactive Users, Network Users, Dial-up, Batch, and Terminal Server Users are volatile groups. When users are engaged in certain tasks, they are included in these groups. When they are done with the tasks, they are removed from these groups. For example, someone who performs a local logon into a system is included in the Interactive Users group as long as that user stays logged on locally. Additionally, some groups even apply to an entire tree or forest. For example, Enterprise Controllers consist of every DC in Active Directory.

Privileges

The previously mentioned default local administrator account and default domain administrator account have superuser privileges—full privileges, meaning that while logged into this account someone can create or delete accounts and groups (unprivileged and privileged); disable accounts; add new users to groups; set the system time; make backups; take ownership of every file, folder, and printer; create or delete shares to folders or devices such as printers; set up and run a scheduled job; unlock a locked computer; read and purge the security log; and can do many other things. Any account that is a member of the Administrators group on a local system has the same privileges as the default local Administrator account. The default domain Administrator account also has Administrator privileges, but they apply to every server and workstation within the domain in which this account exists. Anyone who is a member of Domain Administrators (of which the default domain Administrator account is initially the only member, but others can be added) can use Administrator privileges on every machine within a domain.

There are two additional superuser groups that have superuser rights within an entire tree or forest. The first (and most powerful of all) is Enterprise Administrators, who not only have Domain Administrator rights in every domain within a tree or forest, but also other powerful rights such as the ability to make changes in Active Directory and add or revoke trust between any domains within a tree or forest. The second is Schema Administrators, who can modify the Active Directory schema. One unauthorized schema change could cause severe malfunction in Active Directory functionality. Needless to say, drastically limiting the number of members of both of these groups is a must because of the potential for damage that both pose.

W2K, like NT, has default groups that have some but not all Administrator privileges. Account Operators, for example, can create, disable, and delete any account that does not have elevated privileges as well as perform other tasks. Server Operators can perform many server administration tasks, including setting system time, logging on locally, and others. Backup Operators can backup systems as well as others. Print Operators can create and delete print shares, assign permissions for shares, install or delete print drivers, and also engage in a few other system administration tasks.

Organizational Units (OUs)

OUs are an important new feature of W2K Active Directory. OUs are in the most basic sense groups that are part of a hierarchical structure, with some groups being above others in this structure. The root OU is the uppermost one in this structure; OUs can exist at other levels of this structure, too. Any second-tier OUs, OUs immediately below the root OU, will all have the root OU as their parent OU. OUs are not unique to W2K, however; other network operating systems that adhere to X.500 or LDAP standards such as Novell Netware 4.X and up have OUs, for instance.

OUs can be used very advantageously. In W2K any OU can be assigned conventional privileges or "rights" (also see the next section, which covers privileges) and/or "delegated rights," the capability to administer that OU by engaging in tasks such as adding users to the OU. Default children OUs inherit the privileges and policy settings of their parent. However, privileges and policy settings can be blocked for any OU, allowing fewer privileges to be assigned to children than to their parent OU. (Someone with sufficient privileges can also set the "no override" property on a parent OU, causing any blocks at lower OUs to not work.) Additionally, when it comes to delegated rights, a child OU can never have more delegated rights than its parent. These properties and features can help guard against rights proliferation in which too many users have too many privileges, which translates to a security catastrophe waiting to happen.

Access Permissions

NT featured version 4 of the NT File System (NTFS). W2K features version 5, or NTFS-5. NTFS-5 offers many more permissions than does NTFS-4, allowing very precise control over levels of access to resources. There are 14 "base" or individual permissions:

- Traverse Folder/Execute File—determines whether someone can go from one folder to another below it as well as to run executables;
- List Folder/Read Data—determines ability to list contents of folder or read a file;
- Read Attributes—determines ability to read "normal" file attributes, that is, those created by file system;
- Read Extended Attributes—determines ability to read extended file attributes, that is those created by applications;
- Create Files/Write Data—determines ability to create new files and add new data to them;
- Create Folders/Append Data—determines ability to create new folders within a particular folder and append data to files;
- Write Attributes—determines ability to modify file attributes;
- Write Extended Attributes—determines ability to modify extended file attributes;
- Delete Subfolders and Files—determines ability to delete subfolders and files, regardless of whether a specific Delete permission has been assigned;
- Delete—allows the person who has this permission to delete an object such as a file or directory;
- Read Permissions—determines ability to inspect file permissions;
- Change Permissions—allows someone to modify current permissions of someone else with respect to a particular object;
- Take Ownership—allows taking ownership of objects such as files and folders; and
- Synchronize—synchronize external data (e.g., on Web server) with file contents.

There are also five combined permissions, each of which includes a number of base permissions:

- Full Control—all base permissions;
- Modify, which consists of the following base permissions:
  - Traverse Folder/Execute File,
  - List Folder/Read Data,
  - Read Attributes,
  - Read Extended Attributes,
  - Create Files/Write Data,
  - Create Folders/Append Data,
  - Write Attributes,
  - Write Extended Attributes,
  - Delete,
  - Read Permissions, and
  - Synchronize;
- Read and Execute, which consists of the following base permissions:
  - Traverse Folder/Execute File,
  - List Folder/Read Data,
  - Read Attributes,
  - Read Extended Attributes,
  - Read Permissions, and
  - Synchronize;
- Read—same as Read and Execute, except no ability to Traverse Folder/Execute File; and
- List/Create Files/Write Data, which consists of the following base permissions:
  - Create Folders/Append Data,
  - Write Attributes,
  - Write Extended Attributes,
  - Read Permissions, and
  - Synchronize.

Each permission includes both an Allow and Deny setting. So, for example, one user could be allowed to Read Folder/Read Data in a certain folder and another could be assigned the Deny setting for the identical permission for the same folder, preventing the second user from being able to read the folder and the data therein.

The FAT32 file system is also available, but this alternative file system has nothing to offer as far as security goes. There are, for example, no access permissions in FAT32. FAT32 features attributes such as Read-only, but these attributes are easy for an everyday user to change. NTFS-5 also has some nice built-in reliability- and performance-related features.

Inheritance also applies to NTFS permissions and ownerships in W2K. Suppose that a subfolder or file is created below a parent folder. By default a newly created child folder or file will inherit the permissions of the parent folder. It is also possible to block inheritance for any child folder or file. When an access request occurs, the Security Reference Monitor (SRM), an important subsystem within W2K, obtains information about the requesting user's security identifier (SID), groups to which the user belongs, and ownership of resources. The SRM next obtains the access control entries (ACEs) for the resource in question and evaluates them in a defined order. The SRM evaluates any Deny Non-inherited ACEs first, and then if there are no such ACEs evaluates any Allow Non-inherited ACEs. If there are no Allow Non-inherited ACEs for that resource, the SRM next evaluates any Deny

Inherited ACEs, and if there are none, finally any Allow Inherited ACEs. If there is more than one ACE for one type of ACEs, e.g., Deny Non-inherited, the most recently created one is applied.

Kerberos

Kerberos provides strong network authentication by both authenticating users in a manner that keeps passwords from going across the network and also by encrypting sessions and providing users with tickets ("service tickets") that enable users to connect to servers to access resources and services therein. Kerberos security is based on "Key Distribution Centers" (KDCs), servers that store user credentials and set up encrypted sessions on behalf of users who need to authenticate and then access resources and services. Each KDC distributes a unique, short-term session key for the client and KDC to use when they authenticate each other. The server's copy of the session key is encrypted in the server's long-term key. The client's copy of the session key is encrypted in the client's long-term key (which is usually based on the user's password).

In Kerberos when a client wants to connect to a server (e.g., via a share), the following chain of events transpires:

1. The client sends a request to the KDC.
2. The KDC sends the client two copies of a session key. The client's copy of the session key has been encrypted using the key that the KDC and the client share. The server's copy of the session key and data concerning the client are contained in a "session ticket" that then becomes encrypted with the key that the KDC shares with the resource server that the client wants to access.
3. Once the client receives a reply from the KDC, it removes both the ticket and the client's session key, and then caches them.
4. When the client wants access to the server, it transmits a message containing the ticket and an authenticator that contains data about the user and a time stamp from the client to the resource server. The ticket will still be encrypted by the server's secret key; the authenticator will be encrypted by the session key.
5. The KDC now sends a user ticket (often termed the "Ticket Granting Ticket" a TGT) to the client.
6. The client fetches the appropriate logon session key from its cache, uses this key to create an authenticator, and then sends the authenticator, the user ticket, and a request for a service session ticket to the KDC.
7. The client sends both the authenticator and user ticket back to the KDC. The KDC responds by giving the client a server session key.
8. The client needs to send the service ticket that is encrypted with the server session key to the resource server. (Note that successful Kerberos authentication is really only a prelude to access to any file, folder, and so on. Once Kerberos authentication is complete, the security reference monitor on the resource server compares user credentials to ACEs to determine whether the user is authorized to access a resource at the attempted level of access [i.e., read, write, and so on]).

Each W2K DC also functions as a KDC. Kerberos is the default authentication protocol for W2K in a domain setting regardless of mode—native or mixed. In native mode other, older authentication protocols (LM and NTLM) are disabled. This makes native mode more secure, but also disallows operating systems prior to W2K from further accessing the W2K servers unless they are running a special client, DSCLIENT.EXE, which is available at Microsoft's technet site. Kerberos not only authenticates users and authorizes access to resources and services, but also serves as the basis for trust relationships between domains in W2K. When trust is established between domains, Kerberos keys for each domain are sent to the other domain for each KDC there to use in authenticating and authorizing trusted access for users in the first domain. Another nice thing about Kerberos is that it is almost entirely transparent to users.

Security Support Provider Interface (SSPI)

SSPI consists of a Win32 interface between security-related "service providers" (dynamic link libraries or DLLs) and applications that run at the session level of networking as well as between other types of authentication packages. SSPI supports a variety of interfaces, enabling applications to call security providers to obtain authenticated connections. SSPI is potentially a big plus for security in W2K systems because it provides an interface for third-party authentication products, such as the products developed by smart card vendors. Third-party authentication is much stronger than conventional, password-based authentication in that third-party authentication generally requires "something that you have" or "something that you are" plus "something that you know" (e.g., a personal identification number or PIN) instead of only "something that you know" (i.e., a password).

Auditing

W2K can provide up to six types of logging, depending on the particular types that the system administrator enables. Types of logging include the following:

- system logging—this reports events concerning errors, warnings, and information about the status of system operations and is non-configurable;
- security logging—this configurable loging capability captures data about successful and failed access to objects such as files, directories, and printers; logons/logoffs; user of rights; policy changes; and so on;
- application logging—this loging capability, which is configurable by application programmers, records application-related events (e.g., such as when Norton AntiVirus finds and eradicates a virus);
- directory service logging—this configurable logging capability, which is applicable only to DCs, captures access (reads, writes, deletions, and so forth) to Active Directory objects;
- DNS server logging—various DNS-related events are recorded by the DNS server logging capability, which is configurable; and

• file replication logging—this configurable logging capability reports events related to Active Directory replication.

Of these six types of logs, the security log (as its name implies) is the most fundamental to security. The security log can be configured to capture successful and failed events from each of the following nine event categories:

• audit account logon events;
• audit account management (e.g., creating, disabling and deleting accounts; group changes; and so on);
• audit directory service access;
• audit logon events (e.g., every service logon);
• audit object access;
• audit policy change;
• audit privilege use;
• audit process tracking (e.g., user attempts to start or stop programs); and
• audit system events (e.g., system startups and shutdowns).

GPOs can be used to set the audit policy for all the DCs within a domain as well as for member servers and workstations. Additionally, property settings for each of the types of logs determine the maximum size of each log and the retention method (e.g., whether to overwrite log entries only when the maximum log size is reached or to not overwrite events (i.e., clear the log manually).

Encrypting File System (EFS)

EFS provides encryption of folders and/or files stored on servers and workstations. EFS encryption is an advanced attribute for each folder and/or file. When a user enables encryption for a file, for example, a file encrypting key (FEK) is used to encrypt the file contents. When the user accesses the file (e.g., through an application), the FEK (which is used in connection with secret key encryption) decrypts the file. (In secret key [sometimes called "symmetric"] encryption, the same key is used for encryption and decryption. In public key (sometimes called "asymmetric") encryption, a pair of keys, one called the "public key, " the other called the "private key," is used. One of the keys is used for encryption and the other is used for decryption.) When the user finishes accessing the file, the FEK once again encrypts it. A key encrypting key (KEK), one of an asymmetric key pair, is used to encrypt a copy of the FEK. If something goes wrong, for example, the KEK is deleted, authorized persons (by default, Administrators) can access the Data Recovery Agent snap-in, which uses the other key of the key pair to decrypt the FEK. Unfortunately, EFS in W2K is beset with a number of problems, including not only unreliability that can result in users being unable to read their own EFS-encrypted files, but also the necessity of sharing a user's FEK with others when more than one user needs to access an EFS-encrypted file. Despite the potential utility of folder and file encryption, the use of EFS in W2K is thus not in general advisable. Fortunately, many of the problems in the W2K version of EFS have been fixed in the Windows XP version of this function.

Encryption of Network Transmissions

W2K offers a number of ways to encrypt data sent over the network, including IPsec, the Point-to-Point Tunneling Protocol (PPTP), and other methods. IPsec is the secure IP protocol that features an authenticating header (AH) and encapsulated security payload (ESP). The AH provides a cryptographic checksum of the contents of each packet header that enables machines that receive "spoofed" packets, that is, packets with falsified source addresses, to reject them. The ESP provides encryption of the data contents of packets, such that if anyone plants a sniffer on a network, the perpetrator cannot read the packet contents in cleartext. W2K provides IPsec support, although its implementation of the IPsec protocol limits the range of other systems with which W2K systems can set up IPsec sessions. W2K policy settings allow system administrators to set variables such as the conditions under which IPsec is used, the strength of encryption, and others. PPTP can also provide confidentiality of data sent over the network, although PPTP cannot verify the integrity of packets.

Routing and Remote Access Service (RRAS)

RRAS, another important W2K service, can be used to manage parameter settings for the W2K Remote Access Service (RAS), PPTP, and the Layer 2 tunneling protocol (L2TP). Among other things RRAS can be used to elevate security in that this service can fix the method of authentication to be used (Kerberos, the older NTLM authentication method, and so forth) as well as filter and log incoming IP packets. IP packet filters can selectively determine whether packets will be received and/or forwarded on the basis of source IP address, destination IP address, and type of protocol. RRAS also allows system administrators to log all incoming IP traffic, something that is potentially very useful in identifying and investigating remote attacks.

Certificate Services

W2K also offers certificate services. These include creation and release of X.509v3 certificates and in W2K Advanced Server, even public key infrastructure (PKI) capabilities. PKIs provide a hierarchical structure of certification authorities (CAs) that issue and validate certificates.

Distributed File System (DFS)

DFS is a function that enables system administrators to create and administer domain shares through a centralized function on each DC. DFS also allows administrators to assign permissions to shares, thus potentially limiting the level of access to resources throughout each domain.

Microsoft Management Console (MMC)

Microsoft provided the MMC in W2K to provide a uniform interface to control a wide variety of functions. The MMC features "snap-ins," objects that allow control of settings (group policy settings, in particular). Some of the snap-ins allow control of certificates, others are for computer management, others are for the event viewer, others are for group policy, and still others are for security templates. Security templates provide groups of settings that affect security and can be used to either evaluate the security level or to change unsafe settings to ones that are more suitable for security.

The services, functions, and properties discussed in this section are of course not the only ones that W2K offers, but they represent some of the most important services from both a functionality and security standpoint. In the next section we will consider the strengths and weaknesses of W2K security.

HOW SECURE IS W2K?

How secure is W2K? After all the problems that organizations and the user community had with NT security, this is an important question to ask. The question really decomposes into two questions: 1) how secure is W2K out-of-the-box and 2) how high a level of security can W2K achieve?

How Secure Is W2K by Default?

Some of the same security-related problems that plagued NT are still present in W2K systems immediately after an installation of W2K. The permissions for the critical %systemroot%\winnt directory, for example, allow Full Control to the Everyone group in W2K. Additionally, in W2K Server and W2K Advanced Server, the IIS Admin Service runs by default. Anyone whose system was infected by Code Red, Nimda, or another worm will appreciate the dangers of running a vulnerability-ridden Web server, namely the Internet Information Server (IIS), by default. In other respects, W2K is more secure than NT was by default. When unprivileged access to Active Directory objects is necessary, for example, access is by default granted to Authenticated Users rather than the ever-dangerous Everyone group. The point here is that W2K may be somewhat more secure than NT out of the box, but leaving W2K settings as they are is a huge mistake if security is a consideration. W2K systems need quite a bit of work if they are to run more securely.

Major Types of Vulnerabilities

W2K has had more than its share of security-related vulnerabilities. One of the most significant ones is a weakness in the way reversible password representations for each account are created. This encryption process produces password representations that are relatively easy to crack using dictionary-based cracking techniques. [In dictionary-based password attacks a password cracking tool starts with a large number of possible passwords. It determines what the encrypted representation(s) of each password would be, and then attempts to match the encrypted entries in a victim system's password file to the computed representation for each possible password is. If there is a match, the cracking tool has cracked the password.]

Another significant set of vulnerabilities concerns susceptibility of W2K systems to denial of service (DoS) attacks. Programs for many W2K services are not particularly well written. An attacker may send input to these services that contains parameters that are out of range, or that exceed memory limitations. The result is often DoS—either the programs or the W2K system itself will crash. The W2K telnet server, for example, has a bug that will cause it to crash if certain types of input are sent to it. Similarly, massive Simple Network Management Protocol (SNMP) input may cause the receiving system to go into a buffer overflow condition in which there is too much input for available memory. This problem will normally cause a W2K system to crash, but if the excessive input is specially crafted, it is possible to execute rogue commands and programs on a system.

Some of the services that run in W2K systems pose much higher levels of risk than others. W2K Terminal Services, for example, provide a convenient way for users to remotely connect to other systems if these services are not properly configured, protected, and patched. The same is true for the W2K telnet server, the IIS Admin Service, SNMP, and many others.

Another vulnerability has been briefly mentioned earlier in this chapter. The default Administrator account is a very attractive target for attackers in that by default it does not lock after an excessive number of unsuccessful logons. Additionally, this is a well-known account—one with a well-known name. Furthermore, being able to break into this account provides superuser-level privileges to attackers. Lamentably, many successful attacks on W2K are attacks in which perpetrators have broken into the Administrator account, which may even not have had a password!

A few additional types of vulnerabilities in W2K that have been identified include the following:

- Buffer overflow conditions in which a program does not perform bounds checking on input, enabling a malicious program to send excessive amounts of input, some of which is written to a system's memory, resulting in execution of rogue commands that can cause denial of service or privilege escalation.
- Vulnerabilities in the interface between the Remote Procedure Call (RPC) and the Distributed Component Object Model (DCOM) that allow an attacker to send specially formatted input that results in denial of service or privilege escalation.
- Unprotected shares that allow anyone or any network program to among other things write to shared folders, enabling them to modify files and/or install malicious programs.
- NetBIOS-related vulnerabilities (in mixed mode); this layer of networking is beset with many security-related problems, including providing a wealth of information about systems, users and current sessions to potential attackers,
- Bugs that can give attackers unauthorized access to Active Directory objects, and
- Poorly protected dial-in connections that require only a "normal" password for access instead of something stronger, such as smart card or biometric authentication. Unauthorized dial-in access is one of the greater threats in any operating system, W2K included.

Although a large number of vulnerabilities in W2K have surfaced, Microsoft has fixed most of them. Microsoft generally initially produces and releases a hot fix to repair each vulnerability or sometimes a set of vulnerabilities. Microsoft also releases service packs (SPs) that incorporate previously released hot fixes. The current SP for W2K is SP4.

Patch management in W2K and virtually all other versions of Windows operating systems is a major issue. A huge proportion of security breaches in Windows systems can be traced directly to failure to install hot fixes and SPs in a timely manner. The fact that many hot fixes and SPs that Microsoft initially releases are flawed to the point that they may cause a system to become dysfunctional further exacerbates this problem. One possible solution is to enable Automatic Updates to ensure that patches are downloaded when they become available. Automatic Updates are, however, far less than ideal in that they result in the first patch that becomes available being downloaded (and, if the system administrator so chooses, automatically installed). Microsoft has also developed the Systems Update Server (SUS), something that can be used within an organization's network to push patches to systems of one's choosing at the desired time. SUS is not perfect either, however, in that it sometimes fails to install patches on some systems. Commercial software such as Update Expert by St. Bernard Software provides yet another option. Products such as Update Expert not only allow control over when patches are pushed to systems, but also provide quality control, ensuring that patches have been properly installed. Whatever solution an organization chooses, one thing is certain—patching Windows systems is no easy task.

Now that we have explored the major types of vulnerabilities in W2K, let's turn to another, related consideration, namely how secure W2K systems can be.

How Secure Can You Make W2K Systems?

W2K has numerous security features that can boost its security substantially. As mentioned previously in this chapter, however, you will have to make quite a few changes to W2K if you want it to run securely. W2K has great security potential, but to achieve that potential requires considerable effort. The most important consideration is achieving a baseline level of security.

BASELINE SECURITY MEASURES

Establishing at least a baseline level of security is essential if W2K servers and workstations and servers are going to be able to withstand the most basic kinds of attacks. Baseline security requires implementing the most fundamental steps in securing a system or application, not implementing a complete (more perfect) set of measures. The intention is to make a system "just secure enough." Implementing the following measures in W2K systems will produce a baseline level of security:

- Install W2K from trusted media—a vendor-provided CD.
- Ensure that your system's hard drive consists of a minimum of two partitions, C: and D: Use C: as the

installation drive; this partition will contain critical system directories and files. Do not set up user shares to this partition. In workstations and member servers use D: to hold other files and folders; set up user shares to D: as needed. In domain controllers use D: to hold Active Directory files and folders; *do not set up user shares to this partition*. Set up the E: drive in domain controllers to hold user files and folders, and set up the user shares to this drive that are needed to allow users to access the resources they need to access.

- Format each partition as an NTFS partition. (The only potential limitation is that 16-bit applications are likely to break if they are installed on NTFS partitions. If you have 16-bit applications that need to run in the W2K environment, create another, small FAT32 partition for these applications. But do not jeopardize other applications by putting them on a FAT32 partition—FAT32 has no access permissions whatsoever.) If any volume is FAT-formatted, enter

```
convert <partition letter>: /fs:ntfs
```

For example, to make the D: partition into NTFS partition, enter

```
convert d: /fs:ntfs
```

- Ensure that W2K systems are part of a domain. As mentioned earlier, workgroups provide few barriers to attackers. To check whether your system is part of a domain or workgroup, right click on My Computer to Properties, and then click on Network Identification.
- If your W2K system has been upgraded from Windows NT 4.0, that is, it is not a native installation, use secedit to bring the default level of security to the level that is present in a native installation. secedit allows W2K security templates to be used in analyze and configure modes. In workstations and member servers, change your current directory to c:\%systemroot% \security\templates, then enter a command such as the following:

```
secedit /analyze /cfg securews.inf /db
  %TEMP%\secedit.adb /verbose /log \%TEMP%
  \scelog.txt
```

Security templates are .inf files in the %systemroot/ security/templates directory. securews.inf is a template that changes system settings to be more secure than a default installation in workstations and servers (but not DCs.).

- Install the latest SP. To check the version of service pack a W2K system is running, go from Start to Run, then enter "winver." You can obtain SP4 from http://www.microsoft.com/windows2000/downloads/servicepacks/sp4/
- Install the latest hot fixes, many of which fix the most recently discovered security-related vulnerabilities. Download post SP4 hot fixes by going to the Windows Update site: http://windowsupdate.microsoft.com/
- Download and run the Microsoft Baseline Security Analyzer (MBSA), a free Microsoft-provided tool that

enables system administrators to determine whether all W2K, IIS, IE, and other hot fixes have been installed. This tool can be run either from a graphical user interface (GUI) or from a command line. MBSA can be obtained from http://www.microsoft.com/technet/treeview/default.asp?url=/technet/security/tools/Tools/MBSAhome.asp

- Lock down access to the system drive (and, in the case of domain controllers, the drive on which Active Directory resides). In general, do not assign anything more than Read–Execute permissions to Everyone, but always assign Full Control to Creator Owner and Administrators.
  - Assign Everyone Read–Execute access to c:\%systemroot% (which by default is c:\winnt) and c:\%systemroot%\system 32.
  - Assign Everyone Read–Execute access to the sysvol, sysvol\sysvol, and ntds folders (wherever they may reside in the file system).
  - Remove all access (*but do not assign any Deny access*) to c:\%systemroot%\repair for the Everyone group.
- Lock down permissions for files and folders on other drives. In general, avoid sharing folders if you do not need to do so. Allow Creator, Owner, and Administrator to have Full Control over each share. Remove Everyone's access (*but do not assign any Deny access*) and then assign Authenticated Users the Read level of share access, which is normally sufficient for most users. If users need to create, modify, and/or delete files within folders that are share-accessible, a Change share permission is appropriate. Change, which allows users to add files and subfolders, modify data, and delete files and subfolders, will not necessarily be the level of access Authenticated Users will get, however. If NTFS permissions for the files and folders that users can access via the share are more restrictive (e.g., they may allow only a Read and Execute), they will determine the actual level of user access to these resources. The least access between what NTFS and share permissions allow a particular user or group is what is actually granted. So, for example, if a user connects to a share that allows Change to Authenticated Users and Read–Execute to that user, Read–Execute represents the least access among all the permissions.To check or change permissions for domain shares, or to delete shares, go from Administrative Tools to DFS to the DFS root. Open up the tree under DFS root until you get to the share you want to get to, then right click to Properties.
- Go to Administrative Tools, then either Computer Management and Local Users and Groups or to Domain Security Policy, then Active Directory Users and Groups (depending on the particular version of W2K). If your W2K system is a domain controller, always go to Domain Security Policy. Domain Security Policy settings prevail over any local policy settings.
  - Rename the default Administrator account to an innocuous name (to do this you will need to enable a security option setting, "Rename Administrator Account"), change the account description to "User account," enter a ridiculously long (up to 104 characters) password that is as difficult to guess as possible. Write the password down on the piece of paper that you

keep in your personal possession, e.g., in your wallet or purse whenever you are at work. Never share this password with others and do not leave the slip of paper on which this password is written anywhere where others might see it. Use the default Administrator account, which in W2K does not lock after excessive bad logon attempts, only for emergency access.

  - Create one additional account that is a member of the Administrators group for yourself and another for each person who needs to administer your system. Create an unprivileged account for each Administrator, also. Use the unprivileged account when you are engaged in normal activities such as web surfing, obtaining ftp access, and downloading mail. Use the superuser account only when you are involved in system administration duties.
  - Create a new, unprivileged account named "Administrator." Ensure that this account is in only the Guest group. Look at your logs frequently to determine whether people are trying to logon to this account—a decoy account designed to deflect genuine attacks against your system.
  - Leave the Guest account disabled.
  - Severely restrict the membership in the Enterprise Admins, Schema Admins, and Administrators groups, all of which have an incredible amount of power.
- Go to Administrative Tools, then either Domain Security Policy or Local Security Policy (depending on the particular version, workstation or server, of W2K), then to Security Settings:
  - Go to Account Policies, then Password Policy to set the parameter values such as the following:

Enforce password history	24
Maximum password age	90 days
Minimum password age	5 days
Minimum password length	8
Passwords must meet complexity requirements	Enabled
Store passwords using reversible encryption	No (but in some cases, Yes)

[Reversible encryption is the weaker form of encryption (based on the much maligned data encryption standard (DES) encryption algorithm) in W2K. If no other system needs to connect to shares or to authenticate to your system, you can choose No for this setting—something that is much better for security, but if other systems need share or authentication connections, you would do better to choose Yes here to prevent unnecessary disruption of service and functionality.]
  - Go to Account Policies, then Account Lockout Policy to set the following parameters:

Account lockout duration	60 min.
Account lockout threshold	5
Reset account lockout after	60 min.

  - Go to Domain Security Policy, then Active Directory Users and Groups or Local Security Policy, then Computer Management (again depending on the particular version of W2K you are running). Find the Users and Groups Container and double-click on it. For each user account, set the following Account Options:

– User must change Password at Next Logon—ensure this is clicked whenever a new account is created to help ensure privacy of user passwords.

– User Cannot Change Password—*do not* click on this.

– Password Never Expires—do not click on this except in the case of the default Administrator account and special accounts that have been installed for the sake of applications.

– Account is Disabled—be sure to confirm that the following accounts are disabled: Guest, accounts of employees who are no longer with your organization, accounts of employees who are on leave, and (unless your system is running an IIS Web server) the IUSR_ and IWAM_ accounts. Disable these accounts by clicking on Account Is Disabled for each if they are not already marked with a red "X."

• Set the following Security Options by going to Administrative Tools, then either Domain Security Policy or Local Security Policy (depending on the version of W2K each system runs), then to Security Settings, then to Local Policies, and finally to Security Options. Double click on the Security Options container. Double click on the option of your choice to either enable or disable it.

– Enable "Security restrictions for anonymous" to prevent anyone who connects to a W2K system via a null session from being able to enumerate shares and SIDs (security identifiers).

– Enable "Clear virtual memory pagefile when system shuts down" to protect against an attacker gleaning sensitive information from pagefile.sys if the attacker is able to gain physical access to a system and boot from a Linux or other disk.

Do not choose "Shut down the computer when the security log is full" (unless you don't mind unexpected shutdowns in systems), "Recovery Console: Allow automatic Administrative logon," and "Allow Server Operators to schedule tasks."

• Set a baseline of logging. Go to Administrative Tools, then either Domain Security Policy or Local Security Policy (depending on the version of W2K your system runs), then to Security Settings, then to Local Policies, then to Audit Policy. Double click on the Audit Policy container to view the audit options. To enable any type of auditing, double click on the name and in the sheet that will appear (under Audit These Attempts) click on both Success and Failure. At a minimum enable Audit Account Logon Events. If you need higher levels of auditing, you may choose to enable additional types of auditing such as Audit Logon Events, Audit Account Management, Audit Policy Change, and Audit Privilege Use.

• Set logging properties for the security log properly. Go to Administrative Tools, then Event Viewer. Click on Security and right click to Properties. Set Maximum Log Size to at least 5000 K and (under When Maximum Log Size is reached) click on Overwrite as Needed. Check your system's logs regularly (daily, if possible) to determine whether your system has been attacked or tampered with.

• Ensure that the bare number of services that you need are running. Disable any unnecessary services by going to Administrative Tools, then Services. Highlight the name of each unnecessary service, double click, then under Service Status click on Stop, and under Startup Type set this to Manual. The following are services that are usually *not* needed in W2K:

Alerter,

Computer Brower,

FTP,

IIS Admin Service (this is needed for IIS Web servers),

Indexing Service,

Messenger,

Print Spooler,

Remote Access Service,

SNMP,

Telnet,

Windows Installer Service (except when you are installing software), and

World Wide Web Publishing Service (this is needed for IIS Web servers).

• Ensure that rights are given only as they are needed. Check User Rights by going to Administrative Tools, then either Domain Security Policy or Local Security Policy (depending on the version of W2K your system runs), then to Security Settings, then to Local Policies, and finally to User Rights Assignment. Double click on the User Rights Assignment container. To assign or revoke a right, double click on the right of your choice, then add or remove the right to/from the user or group of your choice. Ensure at a minimum that the Everyone group *does not* have any of the following rights:

Act as part of the operating system,

Add workstations to domain,

Backup files and directories,

Create a pagefile,

Create a token object,

Debug programs,

Enable computer and user accounts to be trusted for delegation,

Force shutdown from a remote system,

Increase quotas,

Increase scheduling priority,

Load and unload device drivers,

Lock pages in memory,

Logon as a batch job,

Logon as a service,

Logon locally,

Manage auditing and security log,

Modify firmware environment variables,

Replace a process level token,

Restore files and directories,

Shut down the system, and

Take ownership of files and other objects.

• Install and run antivirus software.

A further caveat is appropriate at this point. It is important to not only *establish*, but also to *maintain* suitable levels of W2K security. Security is an ongoing process. You cannot simply set certain parameters in a W2K or any other type of system and then forget about security. Good security requires inspecting systems to ensure that there are no unexpected changes in permissions, rights, directories, and files within directories. Antivirus software has to be constantly updated if it is to be effective. Good security requires systematic monitoring of logs to spot and investigate suspicious activity. Good security also requires making full and incremental backups as well as an emergency repair disk at appropriate time intervals. In short, good security for W2K or any other operating system is an ongoing process.

CONCLUSION

This chapter has provided the foundation for understanding W2K security capabilities, limitations, and solutions. W2K is a complex operating system. Its potential for security is higher than its predecessor, NT, yet its out of the box configuration leaves a lot to be desired.

This chapter cannot in any way be considered a complete coverage of the topic of W2K security. Entire books on the topic of W2K security have been written (see the References section), yet even they do not cover everything pertinent to the complicated subject of W2K security. Some that are likely to be helpful in gaining a deeper understanding of W2K security include books by Bragg (2000), Cox and Sheldon (2000), Norberg (2000), Schultz (2000), and Scambray and McClure (2001). As mentioned previously, the recommendations in this chapter are designed to provide a *baseline* level of security in W2K. Recommendations for achieving higher levels of security are provided in other, longer documents (see http://www.cisecurity.org) and books such as the ones listed.

GLOSSARY

Active Directory A directory service that provides an infrastructure and related services that enable users and applications to both locate and access objects and services throughout the network.

Containers Higher-level objects that hold objects.

Delegation Giving rights that allow administration of OUs.

Distributed File System (DFS) A function that enables system administrators to create and administer domain shares through a centralized function on each domain controller and also allows administrators to assign permissions to shares.

DNS Domain name service, a service that resolves IP addresses to hostnames and vice versa.

Domain A group of servers and (normally) workstations that are part of one unit of management.

Domain Administrators Users who have superuser privileges within a domain, allowing them to perform a variety of system administrator tasks such as setting up and deleting shares, setting time, and making backups.

Domain controllers (DCs) Machines that hold information related to policies, authentication, and other variables.

Domain Local Groups that can encompass users or groups from any trusted domain.

Encrypting File System (EFS) Provides encryption of folders and/or files stored on W2K servers and workstations.

Enterprise Administrators Superusers who have Administrator-level privileges throughout an entire forest or tree. They can, for example, create or revoke trust between any two domains within a forest or tree.

Forests (As opposed to "trees.") Trust-linked domains that are characterized by noncontiguous namespaces.

Global Catalog A service that enables users and programs that run on users' behalf to discover available resources within a tree or forest.

Global Groups Groups that can allow access to resources in the domain or forest where they exist.

Group Policy Objects (GPOs) A collection of configuration settings related to computer configuration and user profiles.

Hot Fix Microsoft's term for a patch that fixes security and other types of problems in Microsoft products such as W2K.

Inheritance The default propagation of access rights and user rights (privileges) from higher-level objects to child objects.

IntelliMirror A set of features that enable user data, applications, and computing environments to be available and user-specific settings to be applied.

IPsec The secure IP protocol that has an authenticating header and encapsulated security payload.

Kerberos A method that provides strong network authentication.

Key Distribution Centers (KDCs) Kerberos servers that store user credentials and set up encrypted sessions on behalf of users who need to authenticate and then access resources and services.

LDAP Lightweight Directory Access Protocol (LDAP), a protocol that provides a kind of scaled-down, simplified version of X.500 directory services.

Microsoft Baseline Security Analyzer (MBSA) A free tool available from Microsoft that allows system administrators to scan systems to identify vulnerabilities in them.

Microsoft Management Console (MMC) A management tool that features "snap-ins," convenient objects that allow control of settings (group policy settings, in particular).

Mixed Mode A deployment mode in which a domain contains both W2K and NT domain controllers, or has all W2K domain controllers, but nobody has migrated the domain to native mode.

Native Mode A deployment mode in which a domain contains all W2K domain controllers and the domain has been migrated to this mode through an Active Directory setting.

NTFS The NT File System that is conducive to strong access control—W2K offers version 5 of NTFS or NTFS-5.

Organizational Unit (OU)   A "nested group," one that is either above or below other OUs (or both) in a hierarchy of OUs, with special properties that allow for delegation of rights and inheritance of rights.

Primary Domain Controller   A domain controller that receives changes, such as changes to the authentication database, and replicates them to the other domain controllers within the domain.

Replication   The distribution of changes in Active Directory objects, properties, settings, and so forth from one domain controller to the others.

Schema   An Active Directory characteristic that determines the types of objects that that each container holds and the properties (e.g., names) of the objects.

Schema Administrators   Superusers who are allowed to do virtually everything they want to the schema, something that can have drastic consequences on Active Directory functionality.

Security Support Provider Interface (SSPI)   Interface that consists of a Win32 interface between security-related "service providers" (dynamic link libraries or DLLs) and applications that run at the session level of networking as well as between other types of authentication packages.

Service Pack (SP)   A set of bundled hot fixes.

Service Resource Records (SRRs)   The basis for locating services and objects and to keep DNS tables up to date.

Syskey   Microsoft's attempt to make passwords less crackable by adding an extra 128-bit encryption step when passwords are encrypted before they are stored.

Tree   A group of trust-related domains that form a contiguous namespace.

Trust   A property that allows users, groups, and other entities from one domain to potentially access resources.

Universal Groups   Groups in native mode that can consist of users and groups from any native mode domain within a tree or forest.

Workgroup   A set of Windows and possibly other systems that are known to each and that facilitate access to each others' resources.

CROSS REFERENCES

See *Linux Security; OpenVMS Security; Operating System Security; Unix Security.*

REFERENCES

Bragg, R. (2000). *Windows 2000 security*. Indianapolis: New Riders.

Cox, P., & Sheldon, T. (2000). *The Windows 2000 security handbook*. Berkeley, CA: Osborne.

Norberg, S. (2000). *Securing Windows NT/2000 servers for the Internet*. Sabastopol, CA: O'Reilly.

Schultz, E. E. (2000). *Windows NT/2000 network security*. Indianapolis: New Riders.

Scambray, J., & McClure, S. (2001). *Hacking Windows 2000 exposed*. Berkeley, CA: Osborne.

Software Development and Quality Assurance

Pascal Meunier, *Purdue University*

INTRODUCTION

This chapter, which has for its title the subject of many books, focuses on current observations, practices, consideration, and techniques that appear most effective in producing secure and trustworthy software. This chapter does not address related software engineering issues, such as obtaining predictions of release readiness, software quality metrics and quality models, or modularization and layer models. With reference to the common criteria EALs (evaluation assurance levels), the content is appropriate for low- and medium-assurance software projects (EALs 1–4). Because commercial, off-the-shelf software (COTS) rarely reaches EAL 4, this chapter is relevant for most COTS projects. Another chapter in this handbook focuses on high-assurance efforts (EALs 5–7).

The current state of COTS is grim. The ICAT (http://icat.nist.gov) vulnerability database contains more than 6,600 vulnerability entries (as of May 2004). Crackers think that they are clever for finding them and releasing exploits. Spam e-mail marketing, after getting banned and pursed away from legitimate hosts, uses hosts compromised on a large scale by worms and viruses, for which they pay crackers (Leyden, 2004). Patches are issued at a pace that leaves system administrators dazed and breathless. Patches break previous patches, sometimes in unclear circumstances, and other patches are issued to fix the problems introduced by previous patches. Sometimes patches attempt to block an exploitation path to a vulnerability, without fixing the coding or design errors that enable the vulnerability itself. However, a new exploitation path is found later, which results in a new set of patches. What is wrong with our current software development processes, and why are we flooded with such vulnerable software?

Some business-models value time to market highly. The ability to deliver patches "easily" over the Internet favors a quality debt attitude stated as "deliver now, fix later." As a result, patching is now the nightmare of the information technology world. Often repeated mistakes have become noticeable in vulnerability databases. Can these often-repeated mistakes be avoided without significantly impacting time to market?

The market for COTS software has changed enormously over the past 10 years, with an increasing emphasis being put on security. Vendors have an increasing awareness that vulnerabilities cost money, reputation, and customers. The same development methods that produced faulty software cannot be expected now to produce correct software and patches. Which development methods are appropriate to these changing requirements? How are security requirements captured, validated, and verified? Are formal methods too theoretical? Can better programming languages help? What have we learned about secure programming?

Whereas the importance of the development and quality assurance methods may be easy to grasp, choosing the correct or near-optimal ones to produce good, reliable, secure software in a timely and cheap manner remains a conundrum. Bad choices can compound because being late may prompt programmers to hurry and work while tired, thus creating more flaws that take longer to fix or result in more patches.

METAISSUES IN SOFTWARE DEVELOPMENT

Software development traditionally is concerned with delivering software that meets customer needs as defined and "captured" by software requirements. This delivery has a number of constraints, such as time, cost, reliability, low number of faults, maintainability, and functionality. There are three types of metaissues of importance that help address these constraints and manage development activities. The first type is development models, such as the waterfall, the spiral, and the agile class of development models; these define practices, processes, and activities carried out during development. The second type is capability maturity models, such as the system security engineering capability maturity model (SSE-CMM), which provide a framework for the assessment of the presence, quality, and improvement of the practices and processes used during development. The third type is postdelivery certifications, such as the common criteria, which assess security assurance and security features of the produced software artifacts. It is theoretically correct to select any one construct for each type because they are separate dimensions of the software development process. However, the particularities of development models can affect the usability of the other constructs (discussed later).

Software Development Models

Software development models define processes, activities, and methods or at least provide an ordered framework for their definition. There are a large number of models available, from the classical waterfall model, spiral development models (Boehm, 1988), and the more recent "lightweight" or "agile" models (Cohen, Lindvall, & Costa 2003). Some models apply at different organizational levels; the Software Engineering Institute's Team Software Process (TSP, Humphrey, 1999) and the Personal Software Process (PSP) apply respectively at the team and personal levels (Humphrey, 2002), as their name suggests. Interesting questions are how the choice of a model may affect the number and severity of security defects (including vulnerabilities) and whether vulnerabilities were enabled during requirement and design or coding phases. Reports on the performance of these models typically do not differentiate security flaws from other flaws. Nevertheless, several observations can be made.

The Waterfall Model

In the waterfall model, a development phase is fully completed before another is started. These phases consist of requirements definition and analysis, design, implementation and unit testing, integration and system testing, and operation and maintenance. Requirements and design are stated in documents before coding starts and therefore do not benefit from the insight into problems that coding sometimes yields. These steps can also be seen as brittle because if requirements change, time has been wasted working on them. If requirements change faster than the time needed to produce the matching design documents, then code never gets written. The documents may also need to change not because of a change in the problem space but because of customers' or the software development team's improved understanding or improved communications between the two. The frustration experienced in these situations has led to the development of "lighter" (the spiral) and "lightweight" (agile) development methods (see the following sections). Therefore, the waterfall model is appropriate and should be used for projects where the following assumptions of the model are true (Boehm, 2000):

1. The requirements are knowable in advance of implementation.
2. The requirements have no unresolved, high-risk implications, such as risks due to COTS choices, cost, schedule, performance, safety, security, user interfaces, and organizational impacts.
3. The nature of the requirements will not change much during either development or evolution.
4. The requirements are compatible with all the key shareholder's expectations, including users, customers, developers, maintainers, and investors.

5. The right architecture for implementing the requirements is well understood.
6. There is enough calendar time to proceed sequentially.

The Spiral Development Model

The spiral development model (Boehm, 1988) holds the middle ground between agile methods and the waterfall model. It was created for use in situations were the assumptions needed for the waterfall model could not be made or were found false. It has six invariants, designed to minimize project risk (Boehm, 2000):

1. Concurrent determination of key artifacts (ops concept, requirements, plans, design, code).
2. Each cycle does objectives, constraints, alternatives, risks, review, and commitment to proceed.
3. Level of effort driven by risk considerations.
4. Degree of detail driven by risk considerations.
5. Use of anchor point milestones (life-cycle objectives, life-cycle architecture, and initial operating capability).
6. Emphasis on system and life-cycle activities and artifacts.

Invariant 1 shows that it does not, contrary to common misconception, comprise many incremental cycles of a miniwaterfall model with sequential phases of requirements, design, implementation, and so on. Invariants 3 and 4 make obvious that its use requires the understanding of the relevant risks, and it may therefore be inappropriate for inexperienced programmers and project managers. Spiral development look-alike models that violate these invariants expose projects to significant risks (Boehm, 2000).

The Agile Programming Movement

Agile software development favors "individuals and interactions over processes and tools; working software over comprehensive documentation; customer collaboration over contract negotiation; and responding to change over following a plan" (Agile Alliance, 2001). Agile methods were reviewed by Cohen et al. (2003). They are particularly appropriate whenever the requirements are difficult to capture (e.g., the customer does not know what is needed), are changing, when the project could be terminated at any time and some partially functioning software is desired, or as soon as possible. Their main weakness is that long-term vision in the architecture and design is necessarily lacking, and correctness is difficult to establish. If possible, it would be interesting to perform a study relating agile programming to secure programming, number of vulnerabilities or security issues. Are agile programming development models favorable to security? Are there fewer or more vulnerabilities in software developed that way?

"Extreme Programming" (Wells, 2003) is the most well-known of the agile development models. It advocates programming in pairs, which has the advantage of providing an instant code review. Pair programming was shown to enhance the learning and increase the quality of code produced by undergraduate students (Williams & Upchurch, 2001). Among its benefits, pair programming can help catch obvious cases of well-known programming errors leading to the most common vulnerabilities (e.g., buffer overflows), provided that at least one in the pair is knowledgeable in this area. However, this author believes that it is not a complete replacement for code reviews because it is not favorable to reflection and the careful consideration of the security implications of some operations or combinations thereof.

In Extreme Programming, the design and requirements are in flux until the last version is released. Focus is on releasing (tested) functionality as early as possible. Design periods are short (ideally 10 minutes), followed by implementation sessions. Therefore, it is unlikely that emerging risks posed by the changing designs, and matching security requirements, will be identified before they are implemented. Correcting security problems after implementation has known security limitations; "products claiming security that are created from previous versions without security cannot achieve high trust because they lack the fundamental and structural concepts required for high assurance" (Sullivan, 2003).

An intriguing aspect of Extreme Programming is the practice of creating unit tests first, as a way of encoding functional requirements. Software is validated by passing all the tests. Therefore, the security of programs depends on whether tests were included for unexpected, malicious inputs and behavior; this practice essentially replaces security requirements and security analyses in other models. Some of the tests are to be provided by the customer, who may not be knowledgeable in the area of security. This software development method can be compared with the two classic ways to test the security of software: black-and white-box (a.k.a. structural) testing. Black-box testing assumes or has no knowledge of the implementation, whereas white-box testing has access to all the information. Writing tests before the implementation (and part of the design) is similar to black-box testing, which is less powerful than white-box testing. Security testing requires broader coverage than normal testing and also focuses particularly on the least used aspects of security functions (Sullivan, 2003) and "what if" malicious scenarios. These are the least likely to be emphasized and captured during test creation before coding. Therefore, establishing the trustworthiness of software artifacts produced using Extreme Programming is more difficult than in other development models and may require separate, additional security testing or code reviews.

These observations are not fatal flaws but are pointed out so that programmers and customers will be aware of the risk factors they pose and knowingly accept or mitigate them with other practices. It should be noted that Extreme Programming also requires complete adoption of all its activities because each activity assumes that the others are performed to cover the risks that each poses individually. As a result, it can be seen as a risky or unstable development model (Stephens & Rosenberg, 2003).

It would be a mistake to form an opinion of all agile development models based solely on this brief analysis of Extreme Programming. Whereas none specifically address security concerns, other models put a greater emphasis on the definition, analysis, and documentation of requirements (Cohen et al., 2003). This author feels that this is preferable to the exploration of security risks and threats and to the generation of security requirements and appropriate, thoughtful changes in the architecture and design. One way to strengthen agile programming development models is to use them in conjunction with the SSE-CMM (discussed later) to provide higher assurance and security, inasmuch as the original software capability maturity model can be seen as compatible with agile methods (Cohen et al., 2003).

Cleanroom

The Cleanroom development model (Mills, Dyer, & Linger, 1987; Linger, 1994) uses incremental development, which bears some similarities with agile methods, but under statistical quality control. Cleanroom is not considered an agile development model because it involves a strict sequence of phases in which code execution comes last; specification must precede design and correctness verification through review precedes code execution. Each increment delivers functionality to the end user.

The Personal Software Process (PSP)

PSP specifies activities and a discipline to be performed by the individual programmer to gather metrics, improve estimation and prediction capabilities, and reduce errors. Its benefits are documented in more than 30 journal publications (not listed here). However, it is not a free and open system. Instructors who are interested in teaching PSP courses to third parties must sign a license agreement with the SEI (see also TSP, which follows).

The Team Software Process (TSP)

TSP (Humphrey, 2000) was created to bridge the gap between the PSP and the SE-CMM and specifies activities that apply at the team level. It has phases similar to those of the waterfall model; requirements, design, implementation, and test. However, phases can and should overlap. Marketing material and reports state impressive reductions in the number of defects (including security defects) and time required (Davis & Mullaney, 2003). However, a disadvantage of the TSP at this time is that it is not a free and open system; licensing is required. Moreover, this author was unable to find publications on TSP independent from the SEI (Software Engineering Institute) except for a few teaching experiments. Training must be done by the SEI, their approved partners, or organizational trainers trained and licensed by the SEI. As it is proprietary, attempts at improvement, or unlicensed teaching, would breach the SEI's intellectual property rights. Nevertheless, the combination of the PSP and TSP deduces results unmatched by other development practices (Davis & Mullaney, 2003) and is most likely (in the absence of independent reports, this author is somewhat cautious) the best available for the development of secure software (in combination with a CMM such as the SSE-CMM).

Correctness by Construction (CbyC)

CbyC focuses on bug prevention or early removal, rather than bug detection in traditional validation and verification efforts, through the careful selection of powerful

SOFTWARE DEVELOPMENT AND QUALITY ASSURANCE

language tools and analysis methods (Amey, 2002). By using unambiguous languages that support strong static analyses (see SPARK later in the chapter), faults can be prevented or caught very early. This and the use of formal methods at early stages lowers the cost of verification and validation efforts (Hall & Chapman, 2002). This process was compared favorably with TSP (National Cyber Security Partnership Task Force, 2004). The usage of formal methods in CbyC can help certification (discussed later in this section).

Capability Maturity Models

Capability maturity models are frameworks to assess the existence, effectiveness, and maturity of development activities, practices, and processes. These are grouped by areas (domains, a.k.a. process areas, PAs) and levels of maturity (ratings) and are called Base Practiced (BPs). They describe what needs to be done, but not how to do it. They usually require performance measurement and reproducibility in the first levels because a fundamental axiom of CMMs is that without measurements, it is impossible to know if performance has been improved or not through a change or through the use of one development model instead of another. Development environments and models that resist the implementation of measurements as being too "heavyweight" are limiting themselves, from the viewpoint of CMMs, to make anecdotal, qualitative, or unsupported and doubtful quantitative claims of performance. Consequently, this author expects development models that persist in resisting or preventing measurements to face fates similar to those of diet fads or to become closed belief systems ("religions").

The capability Maturity Model Integration (CMMI). The CMMI product suite replaces the older software capability maturity model (SW-CMM). CMMI melds together several CMMs and so links the software development phase to the greater context of systems engineering, configuration, environment, life-cycle management, and more.

SSE-CMM

The SSE-CMM addresses the management of the software development processes, with an emphasis on security practices. The SSE-CMM became an ISO (International Standards Organization) standard in 2002 (ISO/IEC 21827:2002). It used the systems engineering capability maturity model (SE-CMM) as starling point and added to the engineering process area.

INFOSEC Assurance Capability Maturity Model (IA-CMM). IA-CMM applies to providers of Information Security (INFOSEC) assurance services but not directly to the development process. However, it is relevant to this chapter because it is based on SSE-CMM and links software development to information security.

ISO-9001

This international effort bears similarities to CMMs and promotes quality. It specifies both systemic (processes, documentation, etc.) and management (quality policy, quality objectives, customer requirements, and satisfaction) requirements. ISO-9001 certification helps CMM certificiation and vice versa through overlaps (see Paulk, 1994).

Certification

Common Criteria. The Common Criteria for Information Technology Security Evaluation (Common Criteria Project Sponsoring Organizations, 1999) specify functional and assurance requirements of software artifacts (targets of evaluations), which can be matched against desired assurance properties (protection profiles). Common criteria (CC) do not certify that a product is free from defects or vulnerabilities. Rather, CC evaluate the presence, quality and proofs of assurance in the form of architectural decisions, access control mechanisms, development methodology, testing, and other evidence of security assurance and security functionality. These assurance properties provide trust in the software artifact, for example, that requirements were captured, designed, and implemented correctly and that protection mechanisms limit the possible damage should a fault occur or a vulnerability be found. In this manner, CC rate the trustworthiness of the software artifact. CC certification is slow and expensive because it is time consuming to assess, prove, and demonstrate these properties. However, CC are used and recognized internationally (through the signature of the Common Criteria Recognition Arrangement, CCRA) and have supplanted other certifications (for new software). Another chapter of this handbook describes the Common Criteria and high-assurance software engineering in more detail.

REQUIREMENTS AND DESIGN

It is useful to think of security problems as being enabled at three times: design and architecture (including requirements), implementation, and operations (Graff & Van Wyk, 2003). Fixing security bugs with a patch costs 60 times more than catching them at design time (Soo Hoo, Sudbury, & Jaquith, 2001). Because this chapter does not cover operation and configuration issues, this leaves design, covered in this section, and implementation, covered in the next section.

In the general case, the security of a particular design and its implementation are undecidable (Cervesato et al., 1999; Even & Goldreich 1983; Heintze & Tygar 1996) Some security properties can be formally proved, or shown to be broken, under some circumstances (Meadows, 2003). Requirements specification and good design and development processes do not deterministically guarantee secure programs. However, they provide assurance that the systems will be reasonably secure for the intended use, especially when combined with formal methods (see Correctness by Construction earlier in the chapter). The scope of the following considerations is limited to EALs 1–4; another chapter of this handbook focuses on high-assurance software engineering (EALs greater than 4).

Requirements

There are several types and level of requirements; Wiegers (1999) discussed business, user and functional requirements, as well as "other non-functional requirements." Security objectives, policies, and requirements would then fall into the last catchall category and are discussed for less than a page in a 350-page book (Wiegers, 1999). The objective in mentioning this is not to criticize this book, but to provide a typical example of the priority and coverage given to security requirements in the industry. Is this a lack of attention, or does it reflect what we really know about how to specify security requirements? Has academia not come forward with ideas applicable in real situations? Crook et al. (2002) contended that conventional requirements modeling is inadequate to represent the organizational procedures that underpin a security policy. The difficulty in specifying security requirements contributes to the security problems and the nonstop patching environment we are now experiencing. Security requirements define goals and what must be done to secure a system against likely threats and to mitigate risks; without security requirements, your system is already secured by this definition. Possible results are the surprise of finding that your product is vulnerable, that customers were hacked, and that they are now blaming you. We ride from surprise to surprise and patch to patch.

Security requirements are harder to capture than other requirements. Typically the customer has thought about desired features and behavior but not about all the ways things could go wrong in the technology that supports its business model when faced with a malicious, clever user. The concept of antirequirements is that of requirements formulated by crackers, to subvert existing requirements (Crook et al., 2002). However, although it is possible to interview management and end users, it is not possible to interview a panel of crackers and trust the results. Security requirements can be captured based on risk assessments (Brown, 1989). A difficulty with deriving security requirements from risk and hazards assessments is that some unforeseen risks emerge out of particularities of design, implementation and coding choices, and low-level interactions (Berry, 1997), and a failure to foresee inconsistencies. These discoveries may require revisiting earlier development phases.

In quality assurance, requirements comprise security objectives, policies, and security requirements; it is easy to confuse "requirements" and "security requirements." Security objectives help define policies and are higher-level goals than security requirements. An example security objective would be "all money transfers must be legal." A policy specifies whether activities, states, and processes in the system are acceptable or not; one could be that "money transfers can be authorized only by the owner(s) of the account or designated parties." Security requirements prevent, deter, or provide accountability for policy violations; one could be that "the authorization credentials of people authorizing money transfers shall be verified and audited within a reasonable time period." Security requirements can be further divided into security functional requirements and security assurance requirements. Vetterling, Wimmel, and Wisspeintner (2002) provided an illuminating account of the determination of all these for a system designed to be evaluated with the Common Criteria.

Requirements Documentation and Specifications

We wish to formulate security requirements and derive specifications from them with better assurance that the requirements were complete, will be well understood, and that the specifications are correct. The Unified Modeling Language (UML) "use cases" that help capture functional requirements were adapted to provide "abuse cases," which can also be represented in regular UML (McDermott & Fox, 1999). A similar idea is that of "misuse" cases (Sindre & Opdhal, 2000). UML has recently been extended with UMLsec, and mathematical tools can be used to verify UML specifications against formal security requirements (Juerjens, 2004).

Determination of Requirements

Baskerville (1993) identified three categories of methods: checklist, mechanistic engineering, and logical (i.e., formal). Using the SSE-CMM as an inspiration to generate security requirements (Phillips, 2003) is similar to a checklist method. Requirements are greatly influenced by the system's architecture and intended usage contexts. Consideration of how the system must operate inside an organization with a social context shows how responsibility modeling leads to security requirements (Strens & Dobson, 1993). From a theoretical approach, Petri nets are suitable for modeling information flow security requirements in distributed systems (Varadharajan, 1990). Requirements can be statically verified using finite-state techniques (Ahmed & Tripathi, 2003). Example security requirements, and the processes used to derive them, are available for open systems (Kolstad & Bowles, 1991), medical applications (Hamilton, 1992), cooperative work (Ahmed & Tripathi, 2003; Coulouris & Dollimore, 1994), and mobile agents (Reiser & Vogt, 2000). Missing are follow-up studies showing how well these requirements fared in practice several years later and whether the ways they were derived are applicable elsewhere.

Secure Design Principles

There are eight secure design principles, described by Saltzer and Schroeder (1975), that are still relevant and important today.

Least Privilege

A subject should only be given those privileges it needs to complete its task. An example of excessive privileges was Microsoft IIS version 5 and earlier, which ran under the Local System Account (strictly speaking, it was "possible" to create and configure a special account with fewer privileges). Taken to an extreme, this may translate into an access control problem. The complexity of the access control mechanism and its configuration may increase to model the needed privileges (e.g., capabilities).

Fail-Safe Defaults

Unless a subject is given explicit access to an object, it should be denied access to that object. An example using the Apache access control through htaccess files, to deny by default and allow only specific clients, would be:

deny from all
allow from...

This issue is related to the issue of failing "safe" versus failing "functional," as exemplified by network switches that unexpectedly fail "open" and function as hubs when overwhelmed under unusual circumstances. This failure policy in practice removes any security benefit from using switches instead of hubs.

Economy of Mechanism

Security mechanisms should be as simple as possible because complex mechanisms may not be correctly understood, modeled, configured, implemented, and used. Moreover, complex mechanisms may engender partial implementations and compatibility problems between vendors (see the IPSEC-related RFCs; compatibility between IPSEC implementations is a problem).

Complete Mediation

All accesses to objects must be checked to ensure that they are allowed. This is a performance versus security issue; the results of access checks are often cached. Permissions may have changed since the last check; if caching is used, there must be a mechanism to flush or invalidate caches when changes happen. An example vulnerability resulting from a failure to apply this principle was observed in xinetd 2.3.4 (CVE: CAN-2002-0871), which leaked file descriptors for the signal pipe to services it launched. This allowed those services (e.g., if compromised) to attack xinetd.

Open Design

The security of a mechanism should not depend on the secrecy of its design or implementation. This is because if the details of the mechanism are leaked, reverse engineered, or otherwise found, then it produces a catastrophic failure for all users at once. By contrast, if the secrets are abstracted from the mechanism, for example, inside a key, then leakage of a key only affects one user or one group of users. Examples of failures of open design abound, from electronic voting machines to the old days when various word processors and spreadsheets offered to "encrypt" all documents with the same key. Failure to follow this principle also results in insider threats, because insiders may know enough to compromise the mechanism everywhere it is in use (which is especially disturbing in the case of electronic voting machines). Note that this principle does not require the capability to audit the code, nor does it require that designs and implementation details be revealed or made public. However, providing assurance that this principle was followed is difficult without revealing a good part of the design, at least to a trusted party.

Separation of Privilege

A system should not grant permission based on a single condition. This removes a single point of failure and is analogous to the separation of duty principle. By requiring multiple factors, "collusion" (the compromise of several factors) becomes necessary and risks due to bribery or a single vulnerability are reduced.

Least Common Mechanism

Mechanisms used to access resources should not be shared. The idea is to avoid the transference of risks (or data, e.g., covert channels) from one task or service to another. An example is the vulnerability CVE-1999-1148; because under Microsoft NT architecture, the FTP (file transfer protocol) and Web services shared a common thread pool, exploiting a denial-of-service attack in the FTP server (keeping all threads busy) resulted in a loss of Web services.

Psychological Acceptability

Security mechanisms should not make the resource more difficult to access than if the security mechanism were not present. This is to avoid presenting an incentive for users (or help desks) to disable, bypass, or defeat security mechanisms. In practice, difficulty proportionate to the value of the protected assets is accepted. An example is even the mild annoyance of entering passwords many times to access resources. The "rhosts" mechanism can bypass password security checks. However, authentication is then based on Internet protocol (IP) addresses, which can be mapped to a different host through Address Resolution Protocol (ARP) poisoning, so the resources become vulnerable.

Best Practices

Over the years, the repetition of mistakes resulted in the generation of some best practices. Although not as hallowed as the previous eight principles, these can avoid several of the issues listed later in "Quality Assurance in Coding and Testing."

Separate Control From Data

Many problems, from phone "phreaking" to metacharacter and character encoding issues, Structured Query Language (SQL) injection vulnerabilities, cross-site scripting vulnerabilities, and so on, are due to the fact that the same channel is used to transmit both data and code (commands). Whenever databases are queried with a search term provided by a user, chances are that the data (the search term) were simply inserted inside a command string sent to the database engine. The malicious composition of data to contain commands (shell commands, SQL, javascript, etc.) and to trigger a context switch to command interpretation inside the software processing the channel is the class of code injection attacks. Using separate channels will defeat these attacks. A partial example of using separate channels is the use of stored procedures in databases. The commands were sent to the database engine ahead of time and setup as functions, and during execution only the data are sent (with a specification of which function to use). Then, allowing only function calls in the data channel prevents the execution of arbitrary SQL commands injected by attackers into data. This is not entirely safe because attackers could still trigger unwanted executions of functions. However, it shows that even partial compliance to this principle reduces risks. Another example is the use of the exec UNIX family of functions instead of the "system" call; by using separate arguments ("channels"), some interpretations and possibilities for code injection are made impossible.

Use Whitelists Instead of Blacklists

Blacklists of "bad" things are rarely complete. Whether character encodings, escape sequences or globbing (see Glossary) are involved, it is difficult to list all combinations (CERT Coordination Center 1998). The "wrapper" problem is especially difficult, whereas a script or program attempts to sanitize input for an unsafe program. The wrapper has to understand fully and model how the unsafe program will parse and interpret its arguments and keep up-to-date with changes, as well as to use the calling mechanism correctly. Wrappers can be entire programs in their own right, such as the wu-ftpd FTP server. FTP conversion processes files through a program that does the conversion (e.g., tar or uncompress). Wu-ftp allowed an attacker to execute commands via malformed file names, because the conversion program interpreted and parsed differently the command passed to it (CVE-1999-0997). Wrappers should only allow known good commands.

Use Operating System Provided Services

Only the operating system (OS) can provide guarantees about the atomicity of the creation of temporary files with correct permissions and a unique name, and thereby avoid race conditions and symlink vulnerabilities. Random number generation is another problem best solved by the OS. Cryptographically good random number generation is a difficult problem, and it is doubtful that custom solutions will be good unless the programmer is an expert cryptologist. Moreover, only the OS has access to certain sources of entropy that help provide superior random number generation. Use virtual devices such as /dev/urandom to obtain random numbers from the OS.

Manage Trust

The designers and programmers should be aware at all times of which objects, variables, and inputs they can trust. There should be well-defined "trust boundaries" that act like a country's customs. Untrusted inputs should be validated to become trusted. This boundary is formalized in some languages (e.g., Perl's "taint" mode). The custody of data and code affects the trust that can be put in it. There are more than a dozen CVE entries relating to shopping cart applications that stored the price of items in the client browsers, and then trusted the prices given back to them by the client. Likewise, there are numerous software artifacts that trust the integrity of their execution on client computers, such as javascript or Java authentication code. These trust management failures would be similar to unsupervised and unmonitored self-checkout lanes in supermarkets.

Protect Resources

Anonymous, unauthenticated requests should be given minimal or no resources unless it is a policy to serve their requests. The ordering of operations should be such that authentication, followed by permissions and credentials verifications, and any check that might fail should be performed before expensive operations. Sometimes, resources owned by the requester can be used instead.

In transmission control protocol (TCP)/IP networking, a security problem known as "SYN flooding" was due to the consumption of memory to keep track of connections. It was solved by using "SYN cookies," in which local memory was replaced by remote resources through the encryption of data. This effectively traded central processing unit time against memory usage.

Languages

The choice of language has important security ramifications. When programming in a low-level language such as "C," proper checks for safe and proper handling of buffers and string formats are tricky, extremely tedious, and time consuming to get right. As a result, the temptation is great for programmers cut comers and omit some checks whenever they feel they are not needed. The result is that buffer overflows and string format vulnerabilities are common. Even programmers trying their best to avoid these vulnerabilities occasionally get the code wrong with a boundary error (a.k.a. "off-by-one" error) or by forgetting to ensure that strings are terminated correctly in all circumstances. Then follows the call to strlen that produces a segmentation fault, or an exploit that benefits from the effective concatenation of two adjacent buffers (because the last NUL byte was not written, string functions will treat the two buffers as one). Better languages, such as C#, Perl, or Java, and variants of the "C" language (discussed next) prevent these two kinds of vulnerabilities from happening. Coding style can also reduce the probability of software faults (see next section).

Cyclone

The Cyclone programming language is a safer version of C and prevents buffer overflows and string format vulnerabilities while preserving the power of the C language (Jim et al., 2002).

SPARK

The Spade Ada Kernel (SPARK) is an Ada derivative in which some features of Ada were removed and annotations added to allow proving properties of the code. As a result, delta and information-flow static analyses are possible. It is also interesting in that SPARK tools link formal specification and verification (Amey, 2001). "Proof of the absence of pre-defined exceptions offers strong static protection from a large class of security flaws" (Hall & Chapman, 2002). "SPARK code was found to have only 10 percent of the residual errors of full Ada; Ada was found to have only 10 percent of the residual errors of code written in C" (Amey, 2002).

QUALITY ASSURANCE IN CODING AND TESTING

There are a number of security issues that can not be prevented by cryptography or clever requirements. Noticeably, the same mistakes keep being repeated by programmers and fall within well-understood broad categories. Using key-word searches on the description of CVE entries from 2000 to 2002, vulnerabilities related to buffer overflows, directory traversal attacks, format string vulnerabilities, symlink attacks, cross-site scripting vulnerabilities, and shell metacharacter issues represented, respectively, 20%, 11%, 9%, 4%, 4%, and 3% of all vulnerabilities. This means that at least 51% of vulnerabilities are repeated basic mistakes. Whereas it could be argued that some are design issues, they are such simple ideas (in principle; some are extremely tricky to get right in practice) and low-level design issues that we like to think of them as implementation problems (i.e., in the realm of secure coding).

Coding Style

Coding style affects readability, understandability, and maintainability. Obfuscated C code makes it harder to find mistakes and vulnerabilities—for both the original author and others doing a code review or maintenance. On the other hand, some coding styles help the programmer think more clearly and avoid mistakes and make the intent of the programmer easier to understand. MISRA (the United Kingdom's Motor Industry Software Reliability Association) recognized this and established a set of 127 guidelines for the use of C in safety-critical systems (MISRA, 1998). Some guidelines are mandatory and some are advisory, but all are copyrighted and the guidelines are only available from MISRA; nevertheless, they are increasing in popularity because they are effective and make sense.

There is no absolutely wrong or right coding style; however, to reduce the occurrence of bugs, code should be produced to be easily understandable by as many people as possible, as quickly as possible, with the least chance of misunderstandings. Maintaining a consistent coding style throughout a project also speeds up code reviews (discussed later). Coders producing brilliant but indecipherable code are bad coders because they significantly increase the cost of code reviews, maintenance, and the risk that their code contains a vulnerability or be called by others in such a way as to create a vulnerability. Assume as an axiom the following: if the functionality of the code is hard to understand, then the security implications will be obscure.

Coding style is more than indentation; it is also how functions are called and their side effects. Consider this "if" statement:

Typically, the first one takes longer to understand and is more error prone. In this example, there was an assignment, a function called, and a test condition within the "if" statement; moreover, the first branch was on the same line as the if statement, without brackets. Brackets ease the insertion of additional code and make obvious that a branch is happening; they also maintain a consistent usage for semicolons. Bugs happen where brackets would have prevented them. Here is another example of bad style, in PHP:

```php
if (!$z || $y =="") {
        s1
        s2
        S3...
}
```

Did the author mean to test against the integer zero, a NULL value possibly indicating an error, or is $z a Boolean, which the "!" operator will all happily convert to something that will pass the "if" test? Additionally, in PHP a NULL value tests true against an empty string, so the test for $y is also ambiguous. The answer can be found by investigating the code, or perhaps the author was thoughtful enough to write a comment about it, but it is better to make it explicit. PHP has a triple equal operator that verifies type as well; it should be used everywhere possible:

```php
if ($z === false || $y === NULL) {
        s1
        s2
        s3...
}
```

This is obviously not an exhaustive list but demonstrates how to be aware of unclear or ambiguous code.

Secure Programming

Secure Programming (a.k.a. secure coding) is the awareness and understanding of the security consequences of implementing requirements in various possible ways. Secure programming classes at Purdue University teach students to avoid common mistakes (Meunier, 2002) or teach awareness and how to work around security defects in widely used protocols (Meunier, 2003). Secure programming documents oriented toward UNIX

```c
if ((A = fn3(G, H)) == B) myfunc (A, D, E) else{
        s1
        s2
        s3...
}
as opposed to
A = fn3(G,H);   // comment on fn3
if (A == B){ // comment on what it means if they are equal
        myfunc (A, D, E) // comment on myfunc
} else {
        s1
        s2
        s3...
}
```

(Wheeler, 1999), Web programming (Open Web Application Security Project, 2002), and a functionality-oriented book (Viega & Messier, 2003) are available. I describe here the two kinds of vulnerabilities specific to the C language because they are very common and refer the reader to the best practices section and the above citations for other secure programming issues.

Buffer Overflows

Buffer overflows occur when manipulating strings, arrays, and regular buffers. Fixed buffer sizes used to hold inputs from untrusted (or misidentified as trusted) sources are the easiest targets of buffer overflow attacks, but not the only ones. In arrays, they occur when counting from 1 instead of 0, or when the programmer forgets that the index "n" actually refers to the $n + 1$th element. In string manipulation, they occur when or after strings are not null terminated, when strings are concatenated in a buffer that is too small, or when the programmer forgets to count the byte holding the null byte in the total buffer size. Although the concept is obvious, it is in practice tricky to catch all cases, especially when the standard C string functions are not safe and sometimes return strings that are not null terminated. Strings that are not null terminated are not safe to use with C functions, so the standard C functions are not even self-consistent. Using the C functions that take buffer sizes as arguments is a step in the right direction but is insufficient because even those are not self-consistent. Moreover, they sometimes require as argument the remaining available space in the buffer, instead of the original buffer size, which allows the programmer to make arithmetic mistakes. The new strlcpy() and strlcat() functions should be strongly preferred because these guarantee null-termination and avoid unnecessary arithmetic.

Format String Vulnerabilities

Format string vulnerabilities occur in part because of the inability of the C language to know how many arguments were passed to a function. Format strings violate the recommendation to avoid mixing code and data because they contain formatting instructions mixed with characters to display. In addition, format strings under the control of an attacker can specify where to write values almost anywhere in memory. Because a format string that contains only data will simply result in that data being printed, the most common mistake is to use data as a format string. If an attacker can change the data, then perhaps formatting commands can be inserted, with disastrous results. Always make sure that format strings are specified even when only printing a string, that they are constants, and that they cannot fall under the control of an attacker.

Code Reviews

Code reviews are an expensive but effective technique for identifying software quality issues, including vulnerabilities. Code reviews involve having other people read your code and pointing out mistakes, vulnerabilities, and bad practices, or simply asking questions about parts of the code they did not understand and comparing the code to specifications and documentation. Few developers like being the author in a code review because it can be somewhat humiliating when others find stupid mistakes and point them out. On the other hand, the reviewers should be sharp, knowledgeable, and critical people. They should be familiar with the most common secure coding errors and vulnerabilities and with secure programming principles.

Reducing the Cost

The number of people involved in the code review can be as few as one plus the author. Obviously, the more people involved, the greater the assurance provided, but also the more likely that code reviews will be abandoned under time pressure. Code reviews are less time consuming when a coding style standard emphasizing clarity and comments has been adopted. The human mind seems to find mistakes much more easily on printed pages than on computer screens, so most code review processes require printing everything. Numbered lines of code speed up references during discussion. It is essential to perform the reviews individually to enable reviewers to concentrate fully without distractions and then meet to discuss issues. Meeting lengths are shorter if the reviews are performed before the meeting rather than during the meeting ("online"); online meetings proceed at the pace of the slowest and therefore time is wasted, or the slowest reviewer is hurried and cannot review the code properly, which is another waste of time. Durations depend on the number of issues found, so the duration is somewhat unpredictable. It is also more efficient if someone other than the author takes notes, freeing the author to discuss issues without distractions.

Code Review Goals

The main goal of code reviews is to gain a different perspective and apply a different set of skills to the code. However, it is useful to put emphasis on helping the author with a particularly difficult problem on securing one part of the code against a likely kind of vulnerability, or on providing assurance that the code meets specifications and security requirements. Code reviews also provide signals and warning signs of design flaws. If the review of a section of code requires the reviewers to "jump around" between different files stored in different directories and carry most of the project's code along for reference, it is likely that the organization of the code (modularization or layers) is incorrect.

Testing

Testing is an important and a costly phase of the software development life cycle and is part of validation and verification activities. There are many books on software testing, so the coverage in this section focuses on the security aspects of testing.

Scenario Testing

Scenario testing is used to ensure that requirements capture is complete and consistent. This is a validation effort. At this stage, "abuse cases" (McDermott & Fox, 1999) and "misuse" cases (Sindre & Opdhal, 2000) are particularly relevant.

Specification Testing

There are a variety of specification testing methods, including formal proof and symbolic execution. These attempt to prove the completeness and correctness of the specification, often represented in an intermediate language. This is both validation and primarily verification. An example is the use of mathematical tools to verify

UMLsec specifications against formal security requirements (Juerjens, 2004).

Statistical Testing

Whereas specification-based testing aims at finding as many defects as possible (effectiveness), statistical testing aims at running as few test cases as possible with maintained high-quality efficiency (Olsson, 2002). For security purposes, we find specification testing more attractive because of the emphasis on complete coverage, whereas statistical testing considers complete coverage that is neither possible nor very effective.

Inline Testing

Inline testing (including uses of ASSERT macros, pre- and postconditions, etc.,...) are a form of execution testing to verify adherence to specifications. These are normally built into the code at the time of development. For security, these should verify that the internal state of the software is an allowed and expected state for the algorithm, is self-consistent, and is consistent with a state approved by policies and requirements.

Unit Testing

Unit testing is performed during construction and is a form of local testing to verify proper behavior of subroutines, functions, modules, libraries, and so on. This stage is appropriate to detect several of the vulnerabilities enumerated at the beginning of section 4, such as buffer overflows, directory traversal, and format string vulnerabilities. However, testing for issues such as symlink vulnerabilities is difficult because race conditions are not reproducible. Moreover, it is unlikely that the testers will think of the metacharacter issues that the coders forgot (especially if they are the same people) and even less likely that random input will produce them.

Integration Testing

Integration testing is when the interfaces and common interfaces of modules are tested during linking and loading. One could argue that the syntactic–semantic checks of arguments in calls is a form of testing at this stage if it is done statically, at link time. Otherwise, it is a form of inline testing. In either case, it is a form of verification. It is at this stage that discrepancies in assumptions and the assignment of responsibilities for various parts of the software can create vulnerabilities. An example would be if Part A makes a call to Part B, relying on Part B to perform access control, whereas Part B assumes that the caller did it. At this stage, security testing should ensure that all operations and requests that should be denied, are denied, and that partial accesses are allowed only what they should.

Final Testing

Final testing is what most people mean when they talk about testing. This is where test cases are developed and run against the entire software artifact. Lots of different methods can apply here, some of which have already been mentioned. Theoretically, testing should exhaustively exercise all the execution paths in a program, with all possible values and kinds of inputs, but this can be rather complicated and time consuming. In its simplest form, random input can be used, such as that generated by the "fuzz" testing program (Miller, Fredriksen, & So, 1990) or IP Stack Integrity Checker (Frantzen, 1999). In large or complex systems, however, the cause of a given malfunction can be difficult to pinpoint even if the random input is replayed. Using binary search to isolate the input responsible for the malfunction ignores accumulated state in the system and can result in contradictory results, such as the "critical input" (which may not exist independently) being in a set of inputs but being absent from both halves of the set. More sophisticated approaches involve creating a grammar describing inputs and testing the running program with various inputs designed to find flaws; this technique has proved powerful but requires significant investment and deep understanding of the program's function to bear fruit (Oulu University Secure Programming Group, 2001). The effectiveness of software testing can also be improved based on partitioning the input domain, which reduces the number of test cases needed (Vagoun, 1996).

Acceptance Testing

Acceptance testing is done for contracts and is a validation step. This is when the customer uses the software to ensure that it meets the needs of the customer in real use. Customers should try to include tests of every threat that can be tested. Interoperability testing may also occur to ensure that the new artifact works with other necessary hardware and software. Of course, these needs should be in the requirements but are often overlooked.

Maintenance Testing

Maintenance testing is done after changes in the system or its platform. This may include regression testing to ensure that no old bugs (or new bugs) are (re-)introduced in the process of fixing a flaw. Vendors have a much bigger maintenance testing load than most hackers understand, and this is one reason it takes so much time to build and release a good patch.

CONCLUSION

Programmer brilliance is not a substitute for security knowledge and discipline. Moreover, coding secure programs is different from producing assurance so that customers or third parties can trust that the programs are reasonably secure. Revealing the entire source code (as in open source) does not in itself produce assurance or increase security; however, it may enable auditing and testing. Auditing and testing are of benefit only if performed by qualified people. Although this chapter did not provide exhaustive coverage of these issues, it is hoped that the discussions and questions asked will inspire the application of these ideas as well as further research.

GLOSSARY

Commercial Off-the-Shelf (COTS) Basic software, as opposed to more expensive special purpose software.
Common Vulnerabilities and Exposures (CVE) A project started by MITRE to identify all vulnerabilities; the project homepage is http://cve.mitre.org
Evaluation Assurance Level (EAL) The Common Criteria standardized evaluations. Note that the use of the Common Criteria is not limited to specifying EALs. The seven EALs are described at http://csrc.nist.gov/cc/Documents/CC%20v2.1%20-%20HTML/PART3/PART36.HTM

Globbing A UNIX term for the shell's process of wildcard filename expansion to develop a list of literal filenames that the shell then passes to a command. The C shell permits the user to disable globbing by default; the Bourne, Korn, and POSIX shells require the user to quote or escape metacharacters in file names if globbing is not desired. (Digital UNIX Documentation Library)

CROSS REFERENCES

See *Standards for Product Security Assessment; The Common Criteria.*

REFERENCES

Agile Alliance. (2001). Principles behind the Agile Manifest. Retrieved from http://agile-manifesto .org/principles.html

Ahmed, T., & Tripathi, A. R. (2003). Static verification of security requirements in role-based CSCW systems. In *Proceedings of the Eighth ACM Symposium on Access Control Models and Technologies, Villa Gallia, Como, Italy* (pp. 196–203). New York: ACM Press.

Amey, P. (2001). A language for systems not just software. 2001 ACM SIGAda Annual International Conference (SIGAda'01), Minneapolis USA.

Amey, P. (2002). Correctness by Construction: Better can also be cheaper. Cross Talk Magazine. *The Journal of Defence Software Engineering, 15*(3), 24–28.

Baskerville, R. (1993). Information-systems security design methods: Implications for information-systems development, *Computing Surveys, 20*, 375–414.

Berry, D. M. (1998). The safety requirements engineering dilemma. In *Proceedigns on the Ninth International Workshop on Software Specification and Design* (pp. 147–149). Los Alamitos, CA: IEEE Computer Society Press.

Boehm, B. (1988). A spiral model of software development and enhancement. *Computer, 21*(5), 61–72.

Boehm, B. (1997). Developing multimedia applications with the win win spiral model. *Lecture Notes in Computer Science, 130*, 20–39.

Boehm, B. (2000). Spiral development: Experience, principles, and refinements. In W. J. Hansen (Ed.), *Spiral Development Workshop.* (CMU/SEI-2000-SR-008). Pittsburgh, PA: Carnegie Mellon University, Software Engineering Institute.

Boehm, B., Egyed. A., Kwan, J., Port, D., & Madachy, R. (1998). Using the win win spiral model: A case study. *Computer, 31*(7), 33–44.

Brown, N. (1989). Assessment of security requirements for sensitive systems. In *Fifth Annual Computer Security Applications Conference* (p. 142). Los Alamitos, CA: IEEE Computer Society Press.

CERT Coordination Center. (1998). How to remove meta-characters from user-supplied data in CGI scripts. Retrieved from http://www.cert.org/tech_tips/ cgi_metacharacters.html

Cervesato, I., Durgin, N., Lincoln, P., Mitchell, J., & Scedroy, A. (1999). Ametanotation for protocol analysis. Proceedings of the 12th IEEE Computer Security Foundations Workshop (pp. 55–69).

Cohen, D., Lindvall, M., & Costa, P. (2003). Agile Software Development (Tech Report DACS-SOAR-11). Retrieved from http://fc-md.umd.edu/fcmd/papers/DACS-SOAR-AgileSoftwareDevelopment.pdf

Common Criteria Project Sponsoring Organizations. (1999). Common criteria for information technology security evaluation, version 2.1. Retrieved from NIST's Computer Security Resources Center http://csrc.nist. gov/cc/CC-v2.1.html

Coulouris, G., & Dollimore, J. (1994). Security requirements for cooperative work: a model and its system implications. 6th ACM SIGOPS European Workshop, Dagstuhl.

Crook, R., Ince, D., Lin, L., & Nuseibeh, B. (2002). Security requirements engineering: When anti-requirements hit the fan. In *Proceedings of the IEEE Joint International Conference on Requirements Engineering* (pp. 203–205). Los Alamitos, CA: IEEE Computer Society Press.

Davis, N., & Mullaney, J. (2003). The team software process (TSP) in practice: A summary of recent results (Technical report CMU/SEI-2003-TR-014) Retrieved from http://www.sei.cmu.edu/publications/ documents/03.reports/03tr014.html

Even, S., & Goldreich, O. (1983). On the security of multiparty ping-pong protocols. Proceedings of the 24th IEEE Symp. Foundations of Computer Science (pp. 34–39).

Frantzen, M. (1999). ISIC (IP Stack Integrity Checker). Retrieved from http://www.nestonline.com/TrinuxPB/ isic.txt

Graff, M. G., & Van Wyk, K. R. (2003). *Secure coding: Principles and practices.* Cambridge, MA: O'Reilly & Associates.

Hall, A., & Chapman, R. (2002). Correctness by construction: Developing a commercial secure system. *IEEE Software, Jan/Feb*, 18–25.

Hamilton, D. L. (1992). Identification and evaluation of the security requirements in medical applications. In *Fifth Annual IEEE Symposium on Computer-Based Medical Systems* (pp. 129–137). Los Alamitos, CA: IEEE Computer Society Press.

Heffley, J., & Meunier, P. C. (2004). Can source code auditing software identify common vulnerabilities and be used to evaluate software security? In *37th Hawaii International Conference on System Sciences (HICSS).* Los Alamitos, CA: IEEE Computer Society Press.

Heintze, N., & Tygar, J. D. (1996). A model for secure protocols and their composition. *IEEE Transactions on Software Engineering, 22*, 16–30.

Humphrey, W. S. (1999). Pathways to process maturity: The personal software process and team software process. Retrieved from http://interactive.sei.cmu.edu/ Features/1999/June/Background/Background.jun99 .htm

Humphrey, W. S. (2000). The team software process. (CMU/SEI-2000-TR-023). Retrieved from http://www. sei.cmu.edu/publications/documents/00.reports/ 00tr023.html

Humphrey, W. S. (2002). Three process perspectives: Organization, teams, and people. *Annals of Software Engineering, 14*(1–4), 39–72.

Jim, T., Morrisett, G., Grossman, D., Hicks, M., Cheney, J., & Wang, Y. (2002). Cyclone: A safe dialect of C.

In *USENIX Annual Technical Conference, Monterey* (pp. 275–288). Berkeley CA: USENIX Association.

Jones, E. L., & Chapman, C. L. (2001). A perspective on teaching software testing. *Journal of Computing in Small Colleges, 16*(3), 92–100.

Juerjens, J. (2004). *Secure systems development with UML.* London: Springer-Verlag.

Kolstad, K. O., & Bowles, J. (1991). Security requirements and models in open systems. In *Proceedings of the Twenty-Third Southeastern Symposium on System Theory, University of South Carolina)* (pp. 518–523). Piscataway, NJ: IEEE.

Leyden, J. (2004). Spam fighters infiltrate spam clubs. Retrieved from http://www.theregister.co.uk/2004/05/14/spam_club/

Linger, R. C. (1994). Cleanroom process model. *IEEE Software, 11,* 50–58.

Meadows, C. (2003). Formal methods for cryptographic protocol analysis: Emerging issues and trends. *IEEE Journal on Selected Areas in Communications, 21,* 44–54.

McDermott, J., & Fox, C. (1999). Using abuse case models for requirements analysis. In *Proceedings of the 15th Annual Computer Security Applications Conference, Phoenix AZ* (pp. 55–64). Los Alamitos, CA: IEEE Computer Society Press.

Meunier, P. C. (2002). CS390S secure programming. Class slides retrieved from http://www.cs.purdue.edu/homes/cs390s/refs.html

Meunier, P. C. (2003). CS490S secure network programming. Class slides retrieved from http://www.cs.purdue.edu/homes/cs490s/refs.html

Miller, B. P., Fredriksen, L., & So, B. (1990). Study of the reliability of UNIX utilities. *Communications of the ACM, 33,* 32–44.

Mills, H., Dyer, M., & Linger, R. (1987). Cleanroom software engineering. *IEEE Software, 4,* 19–25.

Motor Industry Software Reliability Association. (1998). Guidelines for the use of the C language in vehicle based software. Retrieved from http://www.misra.orq.uk/misra-c.htm

National Cyber Security Partnership Task Force. (2004). Security across the software development life cycle. Retrieved from http://www.cyberpartnership.org/init-soft.html

Olsson, T. (2002). Specification-based and statistical testing—A comparison. Lund, Sweden: Lund University, Department of Communication Systems. Retrieved from: http://www.telecom.lth.se/Personal/thomaso/publications/s_and_s_testing.pdf

Open Web Application Security Project. (2002). OWASP guide to building secure Web applications. Retrieved from: http://www.owasp.org/documentation/guide

Oulu University Secure Programming Group. (2001). PROTOS—Security testing of protocol implementations. Retrieved from: http://www.ee.oulu.fi/research/ouspg/protos/index.html

Paulk, M. C. (1994). A comparison of ISO 9001 and the capability maturity model for Software (CMU/SEI-94-TR-12). Software Engineering Institute.

Phillips, M. (2003). Using a capability maturity model to derive security requirements (GSEC practical). SANS Institute GIAC practical repository. (CMU/SEI-94-TR-12).

Reiser, H., & Vogt, G. (2000). Security requirements for management systems using mobile agents. In *Proceedings of the Fifth IEEE Symposium on Computers and Communications, Antibes, Juan Les Pins, France* (pp. 160–165). Los Alamitos, CA: IEEE Computer Society Press.

Saltzer, J. H., & Schroeder, M. D. (1995). Protection of Information in computer systems. *Proceedings of the IEEE, 63*(9) 1278–1308.

Sindre, G., & Opdhal, A. L. (2000) Eliciting security requirements by misuse cases. In B. Henderson-Sellers & B. Meyer (Eds.), *Proceedings of the 37th International Conference on Technology of Object-Oriented Languages and Systems,* Sydney, Australia (pp. 120–131). Los Alamitos, CA: IEEE Computer Society.

Soo Hoo, K., Sudbury, A. W., & Jaquith, A. R. (2001). In *Tangible ROI through Secure Software Engineering.* Secure Business Quarterly, Volume 1, Issue 2, Cambridge: Secure Business Quarterly (publishers, www.sbq.com)

Stephens, M., & Rosenberg, D. (2003). *The Extreme Programming refactored case against XP.* Berlin: A Press.

Strens, R., & Dobson, J. (1993). How responsibility modelling leads to security requirements. In J. B. Michael, V. Ashby, C. Meadows (Eds.), *Proceedings on the 1992–1993 workshop on New Security Paradigms, Little Compton, Rhode Island* (pp. 143–149). Los Alamitos, CA: IEEE Computer Society.

Sullivan, E. (2003). Building systems with assurance. In M. Bishop (Ed.), *Computer security art and science* (pp. 497–544). Boston: Addison-Wesley.

Vagoun, T. (1996). Input domain partitioning in software testing. In *Proceedings of the 29th Hawaii International Conference on System Sciences (HICSS), Volume 2: Decision support and knowledge-based systems (Maui. Hawaii)* (pp. 261–268). Los Alamitos, CA: IEEE Computer Society Press.

Varadharajan, V. (1990). Petri net based modelling of information flow security requirements. In *Proceedings of the Computer Security Foundations Workshop III, Franconia. New Hampshire* (pp. 51–61). Washington, DC: IEEE Computer Society Press.

Vetterling, M., Wimmel, G., & Wisspeintner, A. (2002). Secure systems development based on the common Criteria: The PalME project. *ACM SIGSOFT Software Engineering, 27,* 129–138.

Viega, J., & Messier, M. (2003). Secure programming cookbook for C and C++. Cambridge, MA: O'Reilly & Associates.

Wells, D. (2003). Extreme Programming: A gentle introduction. Retrieved from http://www.extremeprogramming.org/

Wheeler, D. (1999). Secure programming for Linux and Unix howto. Retrieved from http://www.dwheeler.com/secure-programs/

Wiegers, K. E. (1999). Software Requirements. Redmont, Washington: Microsoft Press.

Williams, L., & Upchurch, R. L. (2001). In support of student pair programming. In H. Walker, R. McCauley, J. Gersting, & I. Russell (Eds.), *Proceedings of the Thirty-Second SIGCSE Technical Symposium on Computer Science Education, Charlotte, North Carolina,* (pp. 327–331). New York: ACM Press.

The Common Criteria

J. McDermott, *Center for High Assurance Computer Systems, Naval Research Laboratory*

INTRODUCTION

The Common Criteria is a framework for comparing the technical security of as-built products. The term *product* is used in a general way, to include any information technology component that might be constructed, not just those that may be for sale. Products are expected to be primarily software but the Common Criteria is not limited to software. By long-established convention, the Common Criteria is referred to as though it were a single document rather than a plural collection of criteria.

The Common Criteria framework (Common Criteria Project Sponsoring Organizations, 2000a, 2000b, 2000c) is used to define a set of criteria for measuring a single product. Different products that satisfy various requirements from the Common Criteria may then be compared against the criteria they have in common. The Common Criteria framework is essentially hierarchical so that it allows ordered comparisons, when used properly. The Common Criteria refers to the process of measuring a specific information technology product as *evaluation* (Common Criteria Project Sponsoring Organizations, 2000d).

The Common Criteria captures the important idea that security is defined in terms of both features and *assurance*. In the Common Criteria, the term *assurance* means the confidence we have that a product's features work as claimed. The best possible features provide little security if their implementation is flawed. Likewise, a high-assurance implementation of the wrong features provides no protection against the actual threats faced by an information technology product. So the requirements defined by the Common Criteria framework contain both *functional* and *assurance* requirements [as shown in Figure 1].

The Common Criteria is focused on measurement of completed products but is not limited to that. The framework also includes criteria for software development processes. The security of a product can only be defined in terms of the as-built product itself, not by the process that was used to build it. On the other hand, as-built quality depends on the process used. For this reason, the development process components of the Common Criteria framework are assurance components associated with higher levels of assurance.

The Common Criteria is useful to many kinds of people. Information technology consumers or procurement officials can use it to choose and describe their security requirements. The Common Criteria can help users decide whether to trust their data to an information technology product. Information technology vendors can use the Common Criteria to communicate the security features and quality of their product. Developers can use the Common Criteria to understand and interpret the security requirements they must satisfy. Evaluators, certifiers, and accreditors can use it to assess the security of an information technology product. (I explain the terms *certifier* and *accreditor* shortly.) Finally, students can use validated sets of Common Criteria requirements to see how security functional and assurance requirements are properly related.

The Common Criteria is not a cookbook for security. It is complex and easily misused. It assumes a firm understanding of general information technology, security features, and assurance techniques. For these reasons, it is best to look at several validated sets of Common Criteria requirements as well as the criteria themselves.

The Common Criteria does not address all issues of security. It has no criteria for physical, operational, or personnel security even though all three of those disciplines have an impact on practical security. It does not explain how technical security evaluations are to be performed but only the necessary relationships between the work products it requires. It does not describe the follow-on use of Common Criteria evaluations in accreditation or certification activities. Even though the Common Criteria is mutually recognized by a number of countries, this recognition is not addressed by the criteria. Finally, the Common Criteria does not explain the administrative, economic, political, or legal context under

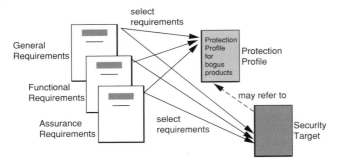

Figure 1: Structure of the Common Criteria.

which it is used. Ross Anderson's (2001) book on security engineering is a good treatment of these and other pertinent nontechnical issues not covered by the Common Criteria

The Common Criteria is a multipart standard that is structured into three volumes:

- Part 1: Introduction and General Model
- Part 2: Security Functional Requirements
- Part 3: Security Assurance Requirements

Part 1 defines the structure and application of the Common Criteria including the rules for building well-formed sets of security comparison criteria; parts 2 and 3 contain the framework of criteria. A well-formed collection of security features and assurance requirements can be either a *Protection Profile* or a *Security Target*, depending on the intended target of the collection.

If you are interested in using the Common Criteria to build an evaluated product, you should first get a copy of one of the Security Targets listed under Further Reading at the end of this chapter. A good one to look at initially is the Security Target for Netscape Certificate Management System 6.1. A Security Target is a kind of document produced using the Common Criteria. Have a brief look at it before continuing.

Essential Terminology

The Common Criteria uses very precise terminology that can seem pedantic but is necessary for some of its applications. Because the sets of criteria defined by the Common Criteria framework may be used in contractual situations, precise language is necessary. Precise language is also needed for the evaluation process, to avoid problems caused by misunderstandings between the developers and the evaluators. Finally, it is also needed for fair comparison of different products.

Before we go any further, it is best to look at some of this terminology. The following terms are the most basic definitions used in the Common Criteria:

Target of Evaluation: More frequently seen as the abbreviation TOE. The product to be evaluated. This includes all developer and user documentation as well as the actual product. The notion of TOE is for a very specific instance of a product, as in Linux Kernel 2.4. 21-9.0.1.EL rather than just *Linux*. This is because

small changes to a product can introduce significant new security vulnerabilities.

Protection Profile: Frequently seen as the abbreviation PP. A product-independent set of security criteria for a class of products. A (fictitious) example might be the high-assurance firewall protection profile. A Protection Profile is a document derived from the Common Criteria.

Security Target: Frequently seen as the abbreviation ST. A document that includes a product-specific set of security criteria. Security targets include a specification of a TOE and describe the assurance measures that were actually applied to it. Security targets also include an abbreviated assurance argument that explains why the specified security features and applied assurance measures satisfy the criteria. A security target for a TOE that falls into a general class of products, for example, high-assurance firewalls, may refer to the applicable PP. A security target may be written without an associated PP, if the TOE is a one-of-a-kind product. A security target is a document derived from the Common Criteria.

TOE Security Functions: Most frequently seen abbreviated as TSF. The collection of all the software, hardware, and firmware that must be relied on for the correct enforcement of the TOE security policy.

TOE Security Policy: Frequently seen abbreviated as TSP. The set of rules that define how resources or assets are managed and protected by the TOE.

TSF Scope of Control: Most frequently seen abbreviated as TSC. The set of all interactions (both allowed and illegal) that can with a TOE. These interactions are constrained by the rules of the TSP.

Evaluation: The assessment of a TOE, a protection profile, or a security target, against criteria chosen from the Common Criteria framework.

Evaluation Authority: An oversight body that applies the Common Criteria for a specific community. An evaluation authority usually does not conduct actual evaluations but sets standards, provides interpretations, and oversees the quality and consistency of evaluations. The rules and procedures used by an evaluation authority are referred to as an evaluation scheme.

Evaluation Scheme: The regulatory and administrative framework used by an evaluation authority to implement the Common Criteria.

History

The Common Criteria grew out of work on similar national standards for several North American and European countries. It is an international standard, ISO (International Standards Organization) 15408, developed by a group of agencies known as the Common Criteria Project Sponsoring Organizations.

The USA's Trusted Computer System Evaluation Criteria (TCSEC or Orange Book) was the first initiative for standardized security evaluation of information technology products that led to the Common Criteria. It was published in 1985 by the NSA. In 1991, the European Commission published the Information Technology

Security Evaluation Criteria (ITSEC) as the outcome of a joint project involving the United Kingdom, Germany, France, and the Netherlands. In 1993, Canada published the Canadian Trusted Computer Product Evaluation Criteria (CTCPEC), which combined the TCSEC and ITSEC schemes. At the same time, a draft Federal Criteria for Information Technology Security (FC) was developed in the United States. In 1993, the sponsors of the CTCPEC, FC, TCSEC, and ITSEC began a joint project, the Common Criteria Project, that ultimately lead to the ISO standard.

National Schemes

Eight countries are now part of the Common Criteria Recognition Agreement (CCRA) that supports mutual recognition of Common Criteria evaluation results under each country's evaluation scheme. This mutual recognition increases the number of evaluated security products available to each country and increases the uniformity of evaluations across national boundaries. Member countries share evaluation knowledge and work together to improve the evaluation process and the quality of the results. Other countries that do not have their own evaluation schemes have agreed to recognize CCRA evaluation results. This increases the size of the potential market for vendors who build information technology to the Common Criteria standard.

At the time of this writing, CCRA mutual recognition applies to evaluations at EAL 4 and below. Higher EAL evaluations are not mutually recognized because they are used for national security systems, and it is not clear that evaluation results would be shared for such products. Table 1 lists the members of the CCRA that have their own schemes.

STRUCTURE

The organization of the Common Criteria is related to the *hierarchical definition of security* as shown in Figure 2. Security in an information system is a complex property that depends on the usage of the system and the assets it handles and the specific protection its users expect. The protection users should expect depends on the threats present in the system's environment. Although the full

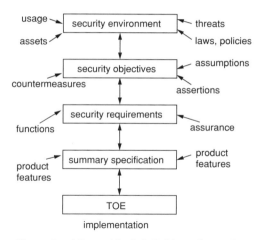

Figure 2: Hierarchical definition of security.

range of threats includes a variety of problems, security emphasizes (primarily malicious) human-sponsored actions. These human actions cause damage or loss to the assets. From a computer science perspective, damage may be characterized as loss of confidentiality, loss of integrity, or loss of availability. The loss of availability refers primarily to features of the information system itself that may be destroyed or disabled. Risk is a measure of the degree of exposure to loss; generally it is a product of likelihood and asset value. For example, a threat with high likelihood presents high risk to assets of almost any value. On the other hand, low likelihood threats can still present a significant risk, if the value of the assets is sufficiently high. The Common Criteria framework supports the specification of countermeasures to specific threats, coupled with a level of confidence that the countermeasures reduce the risk by an acceptable amount, hence the need for assurance requirements in the third part of the criteria.

Information technology products and systems are also subject to laws and regulations established by governments, for example, regulations concerning medical information. These laws or regulations may require the presence of specific countermeasures or the enforcement of specific security policies.

Table 1 Mutual Recognition of Evaluation Schemes of the Common Criteria Recognition Agreement (CCRA)

CCRA Scheme	Country
Australian Information Security Evaluation Program (AISEP) Defense Signals Directorate	Australia
Communications Security Establishment	Canada
Bundesamt für Sicherheit in der Informationstechnik	Germany
Service Central de la Sécurité des Systèmes d'Information	France
Japan Information Technology Security Evaluation and Certification Scheme (JISEC)	Japan
Government Communications Security Bureau	New Zealand
Communications-Electronics Security Group and Department of Trade and Industry	United Kingdom
National Information Assurance Partnership (NIAP) Common Criteria Evaluation and Validation Scheme (CCEVS)	United States of America

In either case, the Common Criteria framework requires an explicit discussion and analysis of the usage, assets, threats, and security policies that define the *security environment* of an information technology product. A description and analysis of the security environment is required for either protection profiles or security targets.

A security environment forms the top level of a hierarchical definition of security. Below this level, the Common Criteria requires the notion of *security objectives*. The Common Criteria uses the term *security objectives* to mean the most abstract security requirements for a product or system. These abstract requirements are derived from the stated security environment. The security objectives identify the countermeasures needed to address the threats, risk, and assets identified in the security environment. A critical part of the security objectives is the separation of abstract requirements into *assertions* (called security objectives for the TOE) and *assumptions* (called security objectives for the environment). Some countermeasures to threats are based on procedures and practices carried out in the environment of an information technology product. The product itself is not expected to provide these countermeasures. Other countermeasures are technical mechanisms that the information technology product provides to mitigate or reduce risk. The statement of security objectives should contain an argument that the abstract security requirements cover all of the threats from the security environment, in an appropriate manner. Explicit definition and analysis of security objectives is required for any well-formed set of Common Criteria requirements.

The Common Criteria security requirements form the next level of the hierarchy. These requirements are taken from the criteria, following a set of rules for constructing well-formed protection profiles or security targets. These functional and assurance requirements are shown to be a refinement of the security objectives.

The next level in the hierarchical definition of security is called the TOE Summary Specification. The TOE Summary Specification is an abstract description of the TOE itself (i.e., the interface of the product or system itself). The concrete TOE proper is the lowest level of the hierarchical definition of security. The logic of this hierarchical definition is that the final product provides the right kind of security, in the environment described in the applicable protection profile or security target.

Nothing in this definition implies a particular process or life-cycle model. (At the highest assurance levels, the chosen process or life-cycle model must be documented and the chosen model must have some community acceptance.) The relationship between levels is one of forward design refinement and backward correspondence analysis. This hierarchical relationship is continued in the assurance requirements, as discussed shortly.

The three parts of the criteria define a modular framework for constructing well-formed sets of security requirements, as either protection profiles or security targets. The first part, *Introduction and General Model*, defines the framework and gives rules for constructing well-formed sets of requirements. The two parts *Security Functional Requirements* and *Security Assurance Requirements* contain the functional and assurance requirements, respectively.

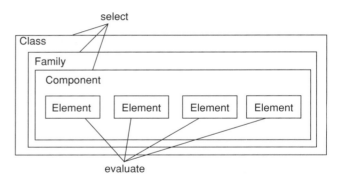

Figure 3: Organization of Common Criteria requirements.

The requirements in Parts 2 and 3 are organized into *classes*, which contain *families*, which contain *components*, as shown in Figure 3. A component is the smallest unit of security requirement selection. Components are broken down into *elements*. Elements are the smallest unit of security requirement evaluation.

A well-formed set of security requirements may be selected from the classes of Parts 2 and 3 by applying four operations: *iteration, assignment, selection, refinement*. Iteration allows a component to be used more than once; assignment allows specification of values for component parameters (e.g., allowable covert channel capacity); selection allows choice from a list inside a component, to narrow the scope of an element; refinement is the process of adding details to a component, to restrict the allowable implementations. Refinements may not extend the scope of requirements or alter the dependencies that one requirement may place on another. The Common Criteria requirements include specific dependencies between requirements when components are not self-sufficient. These dependencies must be included in any well-formed set of security requirements.

EVALUATIONS, CERTIFICATIONS, AND ACCREDITATIONS

In the Common Criteria and in documents associated with it, you will encounter the terms *evaluation, certification*, and *accreditation*. The term evaluation is usually applied in only one way and its meaning is clear, as given earlier. (Recall that protection profiles and security targets must be evaluated.) The other two terms may be used in more than one way, and it is worthwhile to understand each usage.

The system, hardware, and software engineering activities of measuring an information technology product are referred to as evaluation, certification, or accreditation depending on the purpose of the activity. Evaluation looks at a single information technology product, with respect to its Security Target, and confirms that the product meets both the security and assurance requirements in the Security Target.

If several products are to be integrated into a single larger system, then another measurement of security and assurance requirements should be performed. Although the Common Criteria uses the term *certification* to refer to the validation of the results of an evaluation, I also use the term to refer to the measurement of an integrated collection of information technology products. The context will make it clear which kind of certification is meant. Notice that this second kind of measurement may be required when only one of the products to be integrated has security features. The presence or application of the other products may influence the security of the overall system. Common Criteria documents may use the term accreditation to mean either an official decision to operate a system with sensitive production data or it may use it to mean the vetting of an evaluation vendor to perform Common Criteria evaluations under a certain evaluation scheme. Accreditation in the first sense uses the evidence produced during the evaluation or certification (for integration of security products) activities.

Evaluations

The Common Criteria contains both *evaluator notes*, in Part 2, and *evaluator actions*, in Part 3. The evaluator notes serve as commentary on specific security requirements. Evaluator notes are used to provide clarifications, interpretation guidance, and warnings to evaluators. Evaluator actions cover two kinds of evaluation: validation of a PP/ST and verification that a TOE satisfies its PP/ST. Evaluator actions explain specific steps to be taken by evaluators to validate or verify. For example, the term *confirm* is used to indicate to the evaluator that he or she needs to review someone else's work in detail and independently assess the sufficiency of that work. In contrast, the term *determine* is used to refer to independent analysis in contrast to review of a developers work. There are many other such terms defined in Section 2.4 of Part 3 of the Common Criteria.

The success of an evaluation depends on the general independence of the evaluator from the developer. Conflicts of interest can arise in many ways. One form of conflict that is difficult to avoid is financial. Someone must pay for each evaluation, but then the one who pays usually has an expectation of success. So evaluations that are paid for directly by the developer are less credible than evaluations by an independent-funded organization. Also, it is best if the organizations that perform evaluations do not sell or build security products. This creates a tension because the evaluators themselves should be persons who have significant experience in building information technology products with security. In fact it is preferable that at least one member of the evaluation team have some experience in building a similar product or at least a product that involves similar construction technology. Evaluators also need to understand general independent verification and validation concepts, project management, and analytical thinking, as well as mathematics, computer science and engineering. Maintaining skilled evaluation teams is difficult because the personnel with the necessary skills and qualifications can become burned out very quickly. The first or second evaluation such a person performs is interesting and challenging, but the appeal begins to fade rapidly after that. This suggests that the best strategy is to have the evaluation be a short-term responsibility, with rotation to other forms of work after two or three years.

Evaluation results are stated as pass/fail. For a protection profile or a security target, the results mean that the set of requirements is complete, consistent, and technically sound. If a protection profile passes its evaluation by the relevant evaluation scheme authority, it is usually entered into a registry for that authority. When a TOE is evaluated, the results mean that the evidence supplied with the TOE gives the specified level of confidence that the TOE meets its security requirements. A TOE evaluation results also explains what set of security requirements it met, as either *conformant* or *extended*. Conformant means that the TOE met the associated requirements and extended means that the TOE met the associated requirement and other requirements not in the Common Criteria or the relevant protection profile or security target. A result of extended can be misleading because it only requires a small difference to qualify as extended.

Certifications

The Common Criteria provides little guidance on certification, for either sense of the word. The Common Criteria uses certification as a means of increasing the uniformity of evaluation. Because evaluation is a technical assessment based on specialist expertise, the results are somewhat subjective. If each assessment is validated by a common authority, the likelihood of individual bias is reduced.

For certification as validation of evaluation results, the chief difficulty is dealing with interpretations of the requirements. An evaluation of a product may raise a question about the application or meaning of a Common Criteria requirement. The question may be raised by the product developer or by the evaluation team. The resolution of the question may be applicable only to the evaluation where the question was raised. This can be handled by the evaluation scheme authorities. It may be necessary to incorporate the interpretation into the Common Criteria, however. This is done by consultation with members of the Common Criteria Recognition Agreement, and a final decision is made by the Common Criteria Interpretations Management Board.

When the term certification is used to mean evaluation of an integrated collection of information technology products that have each been evaluated separately, there are two issues:

1. Integrated systems are usually built under a contract that is not how products are built
2. The process of evaluating an integrated system is less understood.

When the context of integrated system construction includes contracts, those contracts can help or hinder application of the Common Criteria. It is difficult to meet contract schedules when the certification (evaluation) process is not part of the contract. On the other hand, it is difficult to believe a certification (evaluation) that is paid for by the contract performer. A further complication is the approach to certifying a system that integrates several evaluated products or subsystems. If the complete results of evaluation are available for each product, the approach to integrating the products would seem to trivial. If, however, the assumptions about the threats and usage of a product in the integrated system differ from those made for its evaluation as a product, then certification can be problematic. It may be necessary to repeat the entire process for each product. A further complication can arise if the evaluation results for a product are not made public and are thus not available for the certification effort. This is particularly difficult when a flaw is discovered in a product but not reported as part of the evaluation results. Because the Common Criteria results are essentially pass/fail against a stated protection profile or security target, it is possible for an evaluation authority to withhold this information and still comply with the Common Criteria.

Accreditations

Assuming no problems with the individual product evaluations or system certification (evaluations) the process of accreditation can be quite straightforward. The essential challenge is to understand the risk that entails from actual use of the product. The key to understanding this is to analyze the differences between the various security environments and security objectives from the protection profiles and security targets that apply. If the risk is too great because of differences in threat levels or characteristics then the accreditation authority must identify measures to reduce the remaining risk. A less obvious source of excessive risk is a difference in asset value from that assumed by a product's protection profile. If the assets in the deployed system have significantly more value than the product's evaluators assumed then the risk may be too high, even though the threats and usage match. An example of this would be using a product to protect national security information when it had not been designed with this in mind.

PROTECTION PROFILES

The most frequently seen collection of Common Criteria requirements is the protection profile. A protection profile defines an implementation-independent set of security requirements, both functional and assurance. It is used when there is a class of similar information technology products or systems produced by different vendors. The difference between a protection profile and a security target is that the latter includes a description of a specific product but the former does not. Security targets that claim *conformance* to protection profile do not repeat the security requirements but include them by reference to the protection profile.

A protection profile can be written by either a producer of information technology or by a consumer. In the latter case, the consumer writes the protection profile and then seeks developers who will try to meet it. Instead of writing a profile, a consumer may search for an existing profile that meets its needs. Because the existing protection profile may already have been certified and entered into an evaluation scheme's registry, the consumer can reduce risk as well as save time and money.

Construction of protection profile can be a delicate matter. It is clear from both plain reason and the Common

Criteria's own requirements for protection profile evaluation that the resulting document must be complete, consistent, and technically sound. An important aspect of this not found in other technical documents is *balance*. As the beginning of this chapter pointed out, the Common Criteria framework defines security in terms of both function and assurance. This is where balance is needed. Not only must the functional and assurance requirements of the protection profile be matched to the security objectives but also the assurance requirements must be balanced with the functional requirements. Special security expertise is required to ensure this.

Some security mechanisms or functions are intrinsically weak, no matter how flawless their implementation. An example that is easy to see is encryption for confidentiality with a small key, say, 16 bits. For assurance of this hypothetical security function, we could formally analyze the cryptographic protocols that use this key and expend significant engineering effort in construction of flawless software to implement the verified protocols. This level of assurance would be unbalanced and excessive because the key is too small; the cryptosystem can be broken with brute force methods no matter what the assurance. The most frequently seen imbalance lies the other way. A strong security mechanism or function is chosen, but the assurance requirements are set too low. If a product is to provide strong security protections for high-value assets in a high-threat environment, then the level of assurance used to build it must correspond. Choice of a correct assurance level is not just a technical matter but depends on the value of the resources presumed and the threats defined for the product.

The impact of unbalance on a protection profile can be serious. If the assurance requirements are too strong, no vendors will develop products to match the profile. On the other hand, if the protection profile is unbalanced because of weak assurance requirements, then many vendors could supply inadequate products that fail in actual use. Consumers will be mislead in to expecting sufficient protection when it is not there.

The best approach to constructing a complete, consistent, technically sound but also balanced protection profile is to follow the Common Criteria's hierarchical definition of security. Begin with an analysis of the intended use, planned asset characteristics and values, and the applicable laws or regulations the protection profile will support. Follow this with an analysis of the threats to be countered by the product. Threat analysis requires specialist security expertise corresponding to the anticipated asset values; that is, high-asset values require more experience in defining the threats. (Security expertise is primarily knowledge of threats and the effectiveness of possible countermeasures.)

Once the security environment for the protection profile has been defined, we should move on to analysis of the security objectives. The security objectives analysis matches countermeasures to threats based on a division of responsibility between the product (assumptions) and its environment (assumptions). Trade-offs can be made between countermeasures, assumptions, and assertions. Specialist security expertise is needed in both the analysis and trade-off studies.

The third step in the process is composing a set of functional and assurance requirements from the Common Criteria. The selected functions and assurance measures must be mapped back to the security objectives. The completed protection profile must also supply a rationale for its choice of requirements. This rationale captures all of the analysis that led to the requirements and justifies them against the security objectives and environment. The rationale is a defense of the completeness, technical soundness, and balance of the protection profile.

Writing a good rationale can be difficult. There is a tendency to reduce it to a tabular mapping or listing of requirements because this is a necessary part of the rationale. However, the rationale as whole must constitute a valid argument for the protection profile's completeness, technical soundness, and balance. Some validated protection profiles have indifferent rationales in this respect, so they do not serve as good examples. Rationales for protection profiles with higher evaluation assurance levels tend to have better rationales and are thus more likely to be good examples.

We can compensate for lack of specialist security expertise during protection profile construction by using an extremely precise fine-grained model of the intruder. Intruder models should define both the initial knowledge of an intruder and the intruder's capabilities. Persons with appropriate general backgrounds in mathematics, computer science, and computer engineering can approximate security specialist expertise by looking at the implications of this intruder model.

It is also possible to construct protection profiles by survey and analysis of a collection of existing security products to summarize their functions and assurance measures. In some sense, this also compensates for a lack of security specialist expertise but does not remove the need for it. Expertise is needed in choosing the products or systems to be included in the collection. Expertise is also needed in analyzing the shortfalls or weaknesses of the particular products. On the other hand, if a set union approach is taken to constructing a protection profile by analysis and summary of existing products (i.e., take the sum of all functions and all assurance measures), then there is a risk that the result will be too difficult to satisfy.

SECURITY TARGETS

Protection profiles are the most important sets of criteria defined by the Common Criteria framework because most information technology products are members of a family of similar products. Nevertheless, all Common Criteria evaluations are performed against a security target not a protection profile. The security target forms the basis for TOE evaluation, for each product. It may be thought of as an instantiation of a protection profile.

Security targets must contain everything that appears in a protection profile and more. The additional contents are

- Common Criteria conformance claim
- Qualification of uncompleted protection profile requirements operations

- Summary specification of the TOE
- Statement of assurance measures
- Protection profile conformance claims

The Common Criteria conformance claim is simply an evaluable statement of the specific version of the Common Criteria that applies to the security target and whether the evaluation results are supposed to be "conformant" or "extended." It is a necessary part of establishing the context for the actual security evaluation.

The security target may also claim conformance to a protection profile as the source of its requirements specifications. If the protection profile states all of its requirements in complete form, the security target need not restate those requirements. However, some protection profile requirements may be unfinished, with some parts to be filled in for specific products. In Common Criteria terminology, the requirements operations are not completed. In this case, the security target will complete those requirements. In other instances, the security target will contain refinements of protection profile requirements. In all three cases—no change, completion, or refinement—there must be an explicit claim of protection profile conformance. Any differences or additions must be pointed out and justified in a protection profile claims rationale.

The two most significant differences between a security target and a protection profile are the *summary specification* and the *statement* of *assurance measures*. The summary specification for the TOE is just that, an abstract description of the product features. The summary specification is used to demonstrate how the product (TOE) meets its claimed functional security requirements of the security target. The statement of assurance measures is a summary of the specific tools, techniques, and procedures used to meet the claimed assurance requirements of the security target. The statement of assurance measures is used to demonstrate how the assurance measures will be applied to the development of the TOE. Both the summary specification and the statement of assurance measures are justified and mapped to the security target requirements by a separate rationale. This rationale is critically important.

First of all, the evaluators will study this rationale statement to decide whether the TOE is a suitable candidate for evaluation. Evaluation is a labor intensive process that requires security (and evaluation) specialist expertise, expertise that is currently in short supply. For this reason, evaluation organizations must be careful not to commit time and expertise to an evaluation that is not likely to succeed. To accomplish this, the Common Criteria provides a rationale for the summary specification and the statement of assurance measures. A complete, consistent, technically sound, and balanced security target will represent a product that has a good chance of passing its evaluation.

A second reason this rationale can be important is that it serves as a description of the product's features and quality. In this role, the rationale gives the prospective user or consumer of the information technology product a detailed explanation of the product's benefits.

Some information technology products are evaluated under the Common Criteria without a protection profile. If a product or subsystem is unique and there is little chance of it leading to a class or family of products, there is no benefit from an implementation-independent set of criteria. For these products, a security target is constructed directly from the criteria. Constructing a security target directly from the Common Criteria is the same as constructing a protection profile except that there is no need to provide for a general class of products.

It is also possible to use a Common Criteria security target structure as a (security) development plan for a product or system. The security target provides organization of requirements and relationships between work products in a convenient form. When a security target is used this way, it is constructed as a guide to developers, to show what work products are needed and how they relate. Use of a security target in this way does not require use of a particular life-cycle model or approach. Furthermore, using a security target as a development plan does not imply that the developers intend to have the resulting product evaluated.

SECURITY FUNCTIONAL REQUIREMENTS

Part 2 of the Common Criteria contains the collection of security features that a protection profile or security target developer chooses from to create a well-formed set of security requirements. The 11 classes of functional security requirements are listed in Table 2.

The functional requirements of the Common Criteria are subject to revision although not frequently. New technology introduces new security requirements. Research, development, and experience improve security for existing technology. Researchers and security experts propose, analyze, and discuss possible additions or interpretations. An example of this process is the privacy functional requirements (FPR) that were not part of earlier versions of the Common Criteria but were added after various groups pointed out the growing need for these kinds of features in some information technology products. Now I briefly summarize each of the 11 classes of functional security requirements that a protection profile or security target from which designer can choose.

Class FAU: Security Audit—This class contains six families of requirements. Each family of the class defines requirements for auditing security-relevant events. Two (FAU-SAA and FAU-ARP) are concerned with recognizing and responding to events; two (FAU-GEN and FAU-SEL) are concerned with recognizing events; one (FAU-STG) is about storing and protecting event data; and one (FAU-SAR) is about review and analysis of events.

Class FCO: Communication—The two families of this class (FCO-NRO and FCO-NRR) are concerned with proof of origin or receipt, respectively, of transmitted data.

Class FCS: Cryptographic Support—The two families of this class (FCS-CKM and FCS-COP) provide requirements for cryptographic key management and cryptographic operation, respectively.

Table 2 Security Functional Requirement Classes of Part 2 of the Common Criteria

Class	Identifier	Scope
Security audit	FAU	Capture, storage, and analysis of security events
Communications	FCO	Confirming identities during data exchange
Cryptographic support	FCS	Key management and cryptographic operations
User data protection	FDP	Access control, information flow, integrity, import–export, and recovery
Identification and authentication	FIA	Verifying user identity, authorization, association
Security management	FMT	Management of security data, roles, and attributes
Privacy	FPR	Anonymity, pseudonymity, unlinkability, and unobservability
Protection of the TSF	FPT	Self-protection requirements
Resource utilization	FRU	Denial of service, quality of service, and fault tolerance
TOE access	FTA	Session management
trusted path	FTP	Trusted communication between human users and the TOE

Class FDP: User Data Protection—This large class contains the Common Criteria requirements for protecting end user resources, the ultimate reason for providing security. It includes families of requirements for security policies, user data protection mechanisms, import and export of user data, and transfer of data between the TOE and other security products.

Class FIA: Identification and Authentication—This class provides requirements for identifying authorized users and assigning them the correct identity, group, role, session, or set of security privileges associated with their user identity. It includes requirements for dealing with authentication failures and handling secrets associated with authentication and identification.

Class FMT: Security Management—This class provides a collection of incomplete (i.e., the requirements must be completed by assignment, selection, or refinement). All of the requirements cover security management, so there are requirements for protecting and restricting management functions, assigning and revoking privileges or security attributes, and defining security management roles for the TOE.

Class FPR: Privacy—This class provides a means for selecting anonymity, pseudonymity, unlinkability, or unobservability. By proper selection and refinement of these requirements a protection profile designer can specify protection against a wide range of identity misuse.

Class FPT: Protection of the TSF—This class specifies self-protection requirements for the TSF of the TOE; that is, requirements that the product protect its security functions from tampering and bypass. The families in this class form a list of generic ways of tampering with or bypassing a security mechanism. They include confidentiality, integrity, and availability of TSF data that has left the TOE scope of control; fail safe and trusted recovery; safe internal movement of TSF data; resistance to physical tampering; replay detection; and consistency of distributed TSF components.

Class FRU: Resource Utilization—Requirements from this class can be used to specify fault tolerance, quality of service, or resource management functions for a TOE.

Class FTA: TOE Access—This class specifies a set of session management requirements. Each interaction of a user with the TOE constitutes a session. The user is identified and authenticated, negotiates any selectable security attributes for the session, and does some work using the TOE. When the session is terminated, the user is no longer able to use the resources that were available. Specific requirements include limitations on concurrent sessions, initiating a session, session locking, session history, user-visible session labels or banners.

Class FTP: Trusted Path—Trusted path requirements are available for specifying trusted path or trusted channel functions in the TOE. These functions are used to protect human users from spoofing attacks that present a deceptive interface to the user. A trusted path provides a means for a human user to confirm that he or she is communicating with the TSF and not some masquerading unauthorized process.

A reader wanting deeper understanding of the functional security requirements should consult Part 2 of the Common Criteria.

ASSURANCE REQUIREMENTS

The assurance requirements in Part 3 are perhaps the least understood aspect of the Common Criteria. The seven classes of security assurance requirements are listed in Table 3. It is clear that security-relevant product functions should be developed carefully to avoid the introduction of security flaws, thus the popularity of books on "secure programming." What is less clear is the relationship between various system or software development activities on one hand and assurance per se on the other. Some activities advance the design and implementation of the developing product but do not significantly increase the assurance we have in the information technology product's security. In fact, many software practitioners, researchers, and others do not have a clear understanding of assurance. This is reflected in the fact that the U.S. government has adopted the term *information assurance* to mean "measures that protect and defend information and information systems" (Committee on National Security Systems, 2003) that is, security functions. Many have confused the notion of security functions with assurance.

It is important to understand the issue of balance between assurance and the strength of the security mechanisms used in the TOE. Some security weaknesses are inherent in the mechanism itself. For example, so-called discretionary access controls on resources that can be set by the user or owner of a resource are weaker than mandatory access controls that cannot be set by the user or owner. No matter how flawlessly they function, discretionary access controls can be turned off or otherwise changed by malicious software, even though the controls themselves are not compromised. Because of this, the highest assurance levels do not balance with discretionary access controls. For the same reason, higher assurance levels do not balance with weak cryptographic protocols. For example, at the time of this writing, the wired equivalent privacy (WEP) protocol had been shown to contain fundamental flaws. No matter how well this protocol could be implemented in hardware or software, it would still be vulnerable because of its design flaws. So higher assurance would not balance with a product that used the WEP protocol.

CLASS ACM: CONFIGURATION MANAGEMENT

This class of assurance requirements describes how to monitor and track changes, including refinement, made to the various work products. Full use of all of these requirements would also ensure the integrity of the TOE and increase our confidence that we can trace each implementation artifact back to a function security requirement. This tracing not only improves attempts to simplify and minimize the implementation but also helps prevent the introduction of malicious code. Without effective configuration management, the tracing is not believable.

Requirements in this class include not only automated configuration management but also plans and procedures for using the configuration management tools. The required automation includes protecting the work products and implementation from unauthorized modification, deletion, or addition of components or evidence.

CLASS ADO: DELIVERY AND OPERATION

Assurance requirements for distribution of the TOE describe the measures that must be taken to protect it during distribution. The specific protection that must be provided is for the threats described in the security environment of the applicable security target or protection profile. These protections might include detecting bogus copies of a TOE; preventing substitution of the wrong version of a TOE; and preventing an end user from replicating the distribution service. The protections not only address delivery or distribution of a TOE but also include

Table 3 Security Assurance Requirement Classes of Part 3 of the Common Criteria

Class	Identifier	Scope
Configuration management	ACM	Procedures and tools for tracking changes to work products
Delivery and operation	ADO	Measures for protecting the distribution of a product
Development	ADV	Defines requirements for system and software engineering work products needed for assurance
Guidance documents	ADG	Administrator and user guidance
Life-cycle support	ALC	Requirements for securing the development process itself and for suitable development processes
Testing	ATE	Demonstration of functional requirements
Vulnerability assessment	ADV	Independent adversarial analysis and testing

mechanisms or procedures to protect the installation, generation, and startup of a TOE once it has been distributed.

CLASS ADV: DEVELOPMENT

This class comprises the requirements targeted at the work products needed for high-assurance software. It requires a collection of descriptions or specifications of the TOE that provide different levels of abstraction. A mapping from the more abstract to the less abstract description is required to show correspondence, demonstrate the absence of malicious code, and justify the residual complexity of the implementation. This mapping must be produced for each pair of required specification documents, using the same degree of rigor as the target specifications. Figure 4 shows the full set of required TOE representations. (These documents may be thought of as a fine-grained refinement of the hierarchical definition of security shown in Figure 2, inserted between the summary specification and the TOE.)

This class includes requirements for modularity, explicitly justified simplicity, and high-level architecture beyond modularity. The more rigorous requirements call for the TOE software modules to contain only security-relevant code, with an explanation of why the code in

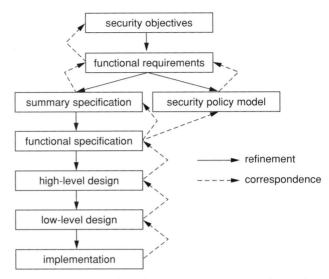

Figure 4: Target of evaluation representations from class ADV.

each module is security-relevant. The most rigorous requirements also specify that the TOE software must be organized into layered abstract virtual machines, such that each abstract machine can be evaluated separately.

The more rigorous requirements call for the use of formal methods for the more abstract specifications. Levels of assurance are increased by requiring formal methods for the less-abstract descriptions.

The explicit abstraction and refinement required by this class may be misunderstood to call for a particular development approach, such as the much-maligned waterfall model. That would be a misunderstanding; what is required is a final set of documents and an explicitly justified refinement from the abstract to the concrete. The author asked the builders of one of the highest assurance software products that has ever been built what life cycle model they used. "Crazed rat," was the reply. Nevertheless, the work products associated with the product had essentially flawless justified refinement from the abstract models to the concrete concrete code.

The existence of the ALC life-cycle support assurance requirements indicates the importance of development processes in the Common Criteria model, but no particular life-cycle model is required. The choice of development approach can be critical to the final security of a product, so it should be addressed in higher-assurance protection profiles and security targets. Which development approach should be chosen is outside the scope of the Common Criteria. The chapter "Software Development and Quality Assurance" should provide more information on development approaches for security.

CLASS ADG: GUIDANCE DOCUMENTS

The ADG requirements specify the documentation that should be provided for the security administration of the TOE. Not only should this guidance cover installation, configuration, and management but also the meaning of all warnings, reports, or exceptional operating states. The administrator guidance should also describe appropriate or recommended management actions to be taken in response to each security-relevant event.

The ADG requirements also call for user documentation that explains any nonadministrative interfaces for the TOE. This might include programming as well as user-supplied security settings. In particular, the user guidance should clarify the kind of protection supplied and what assumptions must be satisfied by the users for the TOE to provide the expected protection. An indication of the importance of this is built into the Common Criteria. During an evaluation, vulnerability assessment required by class AVA will check both user and administrative guidance to see if any inconsistencies or ambiguities can be exploited to defeat the security of the product.

The brevity of this section can be misleading. Human factors and usability are vital to security. Few products can provide security if they are misused; on the other hand, if the product is difficult to operate, then users may put their high-value assets and resources into a system that is not secure but easy to operate.

CLASS ALC: LIFE-CYCLE SUPPORT

This assurance requirements class calls out the measures that should be used to provide security for development work products, bug fixes and flaw removal, and tool support for the development process. The most rigorous assurance requires that development work products must not only be managed but also protected from tampering or the insertion of malicious code. Development security must address operational and physical security measures coordinated with the protection features of the configuration management tools. Flaw removal requires procedures for fixing vulnerabilities discovered after product release. It also requires that user or administrator guidance explain how to report vulnerabilities and how to receive vulnerability reports. Procedures for checking the proposed fix must also be in place along with a method of distributing the corrected software. This class also sets out requirements for programming languages, development tools, use of generally accepted notations and consistency in use of these tools and techniques. Requirements for libraries and third-party software are also defined.

Finally, at the highest degree of rigor, class ALC contains requirements for use of life-cycle models. Not only must the development follow an explicitly defined process, as for lower degrees of rigor, but also it must use a generally accepted process or life-cycle model. This highest degree of rigor also requires the use of metrics to establish the quality of the work products produced by the process.

CLASS ATE: TESTING

The goal of the testing required by this class is demonstration that the TOE meets its functional security requirements. It include both confirmation of correct function and checks for undesirable behavior that violates the requirements. It does not include penetration testing or related activities, as described in the next subsection, AVA Vulnerability Assessment.

This class separates requirements for *test coverage* and *test depth*. Test coverage has the usual meaning and includes requirements for analysis of coverage, to varying degrees of rigor. The term test depth is used to refer to the use of the various TOE representations as a basis for the test cases. Shallow testing uses only the most abstract TOE representations, such as the functional requirements or the summary specification, as the basis. The deepest testing will include the abstract representations and all the refinements, including the implementation representation.

Class ATE also provides for independent (evaluator) testing. The evaluators will design and conduct their own functional tests under these assurance requirements. The evaluators will also repeat some or all of the developer's functional testing, depending on the specified level of assurance.

CLASS AVA: VULNERABILITY ASSESSMENT

Like the development requirements, vulnerability assessment requirements are also poorly understood. Vulnerability assessment is based on an adversarial analysis of the TOE and its requirements. This adversarial analysis seeks to locate vulnerabilities in the TOE that could be exploited to violate the security policy. It provides some measure of understanding about the residual risk of insider attacks on the TOE.

The vulnerability assessment class is organized into four families

- Covert channel analysis
- Misuse
- Strength of function
- Vulnerability analysis

Covert channels are unwanted artifacts in the TOE implementation that can be exploited, usually by malicious software, to signal information contrary to the security policy of the TOE. Covert channel analysis is covered by the chapter "Information Leakage" of this *Handbook*. Covert channel analysis requirements of increasing rigor are defined in terms of the approach used and the basis for the analysis. The most rigorous requirement is for analysis that is justified as exhaustive and is based on complete detailed specifications.

The term misuse is interpreted to mean accidental misuse of the TOE due to problems with its usability, or with the guidance documents provided according to class ADG. In higher levels of this family, the developer is required to conduct human factors analysis of the guidance documentation (and, by implication, the interfaces used by humans) to discover and remove inconsistencies or other failings such as omission of a warning or unreasonable expectation. At the highest level of assurance, the evaluators independently try to misuse the TOE and put it into an insecure state or operating mode.

Class AVA also includes requirements for assessing the strength of proposed security mechanisms. Conventionally, strength of function is only applied to mechanisms that depend on stochastic properties, such as passwords and encryption. Strength of function is also an issue for other security mechanisms, however, such as access control, virtual machine monitors, and integrity lock architectures. Protection profile writers have been careful to avoid strength of function for these latter, more problematic mechanisms.

Finally, the Common Criteria uses the term vulnerability analysis to refer to what is more commonly called *penetration testing*. The term *vulnerability analysis* is probably a better term; the best penetration testing does not involve much testing per se. The small amount of testing that is done is directed toward showing the impact of a vulnerability discovered through analysis. The lowest level of assurance is that the developer will perform a vulnerability analysis. Higher levels require independent and systematic vulnerability analysis and independent penetration testing to confirm the developer's results. The highest levels of assurance require that the TOE be found to have a certain level of resistance to penetration.

EVALUATION ASSURANCE LEVELS

Because assurance is less well understood, the Common Criteria provides seven predefined Evaluation Assurance Levels (EALs). An EAL is a predefined collection of assurance requirements that is consistent and addresses all dependencies. The EALs constitute a hierarchy of assurance, with EALs Level 1 being the lowest. That is, EAL 1 has the least rigor and scope for assurance evidence and EAL 7 has the most (Table 4). The degree of difficulty does not increase in a linear way. The first four levels are intended to approximate various levels of commercial development practice. Only the highest of these levels, EAL 4, requires any source code analysis and then only examination of "sample" selected by the developer rather than the evaluator. The logic for this is sound because these lower levels do not require extensive modeling and specification of security, internal structuring, architectural arrangement, and life-cycle restrictions. Without these measures, source code analysis is not particularly effective (Anderson, 2001). On the other hand, these same assurance measures are either too costly or specialized for application to large products.

The remaining three levels, EAL 5 through 7, are essentially aimed at products that will be developed using

Table 4 Common Criteria Evaluation Assurance Levels

EAL	1	Functionally tested
EAL	2	Structurally tested
EAL	3	Methodically tested
EAL	4	Methodically designed, tested, and reviewed
EAL	5	Semiformally designed and tested
EAL	6	Semiformally verified design and tested
EAL	7	Formally verified design and tested

security specialists and security-specific approaches. At present, CCRA mutual recognition does not extend to these higher levels. The rigor of these levels is increased not only because of the use of formal methods but also internal structuring, architectural, and life-cycle requirements.

The predefined EALs do not use all of the possible Common Criteria assurance requirements. It is possible to *augment* an EAL by adding assurance requirements or substituting a more rigorous requirement (as in EAL 5 +). The Common Criteria does not allow definition or use of a "minus" EAL (as in EAL 5 −), where one or more requirements are omitted from an EAL. If such a collection of assurance requirements is needed, it should be defined by augmenting the next lower level to contain all of the necessary requirements.

Level EAL 1 is for environments where security threats are not considered serious. It involves independent testing of the product with no input from its developers. EAL 2 increases the assurance provided by including review of a high-level design provided by the product developer. It also includes a requirement that the developer conduct a vulnerability analysis for well-known flaws. There is no independent vulnerability analysis at EAL 2. The original intent was to provide an EAL that could apply to legacy systems that had some security features. The next higher level, EAL 3, increases assurance by requiring some security measures be used in the development environment and independent assessment of the security test coverage. Although it does not require more modeling and specification than EAL 2, it does require that the design separate security-relevant components from those that are not. It also requires the design models or specifications to describe how the security is enforced. That is, the design document must support detailed analysis for design flaws in the security mechanisms. Finally, it requires testing to be based on both the interface and high-level design of the product, that is gray-box testing as opposed to black-box testing. EAL3 does not require independent vulnerability analysis.

EAL 4 requires a significant step up in developer effort but not one that is considered beyond best commercial practice. In addition to a security-enforcing high-level design, EAL 4 also requires a low-level design. Assurance is also increased by requiring that the interface specification of the product be complete, a nontrivial requirement. EAL 4 also introduces a requirement for an explicit security model, that is, an abstract model that defines security for the product. Finally, EAL 4 also includes a (low-attack-potential) independent vulnerability analysis.

EALs 5 through 6 are for products developed using security specialists and security-specific design and development. Although the Common Criteria has defined these levels, there is no common acceptance of evaluations at these higher levels. There is also no corresponding common understanding of what measures and approaches satisfy each level. Readers interested learning about these higher levels or in developing products for these levels should contact the appropriate national evaluation scheme authorities or a consultant specializing in these matters.

CONCLUSIONS

The Common Criteria has potential to provide good, balanced sets of security requirements. It captures the central idea that security is a matter of assurance as much as function and that assurance should balance function. Application of the Common Criteria has been hampered by its national security sponsorship and the politics of government regulation. In such an environment, it is difficult to proceed rapidly or make painful decisions. This is particularly true when one of the stakeholders in a protection profile, security target, or evaluation has motives other than ultimate protection of user resources. Despite this, the Common Criteria can be useful if it is employed with consideration of the latest security technology and threats, by stakeholders who mean to produce security technology that meets the user's needs.

There are two other assurance-related standards for safety in information technology systems that might be of interest. The first is the avionics related DO-178B standard, (Radio Technical Commission for Aeronautics, 1992) for software in aircraft and aviation technology. The second, IEC 61508 (International Electrotechnical Commission, n.d.), is a more general international standard for electrical and electronic systems with safety requirements. The reader who is interested in issues of assurance and certification should investigate these standards.

GLOSSARY

This glossary complements the essential terminology of provided in the second section of this chapter.

Assurance Grounds for confidence that an entity meets it security objectives. This definition is taken directly from the Common Criteria. It is sufficient for many uses but could be improved. For example, security objectives are not granular and might be met by a system that did not have the desired security functions. Also, the definition does not distinguish assurance evidence, that is, the engineering work products, from the degree or level of confidence that the evidence provides.

Assurance Argument An organization or arrangement of assurance evidence into a logical structure that shows how the evidence is (a) interrelated and (b) gives confidence that the security objectives are met. The Common Criteria does not use this concept but instead employs a more simple tabular arrangement in the rationale parts of protection profiles and security targets.

Attack Potential The perceived potential for success of an attack, expressed in terms of an attacker's expertise, resources, and motivation.

Formal Expressed in a restricted syntax language with defined semantics based on well-established mathematical concepts. Under this definition, most UML is not formal.

Product A package of information technology software, firmware, or hardware that provides functionality. This definition omits the Common Criteria's additional qualification, "designed for use or incorporation within a multiplicity of systems" as unnecessarily restrictive.

Security Objective A statement of intent to counter identified threats or to satisfy identified organization security policies and assumptions.

Security Function A part (or parts) of the target of evaluation (TOE) that has to be relied on for enforcing a closely related subset of the rules from the TOE security policy.

CROSS REFERENCES

See *Software Development and Quality Assurance; Standards for Product Security Assessment.*

REFERENCES

Anderson, R. (2001). *Security engineering: A guide to building dependable distributed systems.* New York: Wiley.

Committee on National Security Systems. *National information assurance glossary.*

Common Criteria Project Sponsoring Organizations (Ed.). (2004a). *Common criteria for information technology security evaluation: Part 1. Introduction and general model Version 2.2.*

Common Criteria Project Sponsoring Organizations. (Ed.). (2004b). *Common criteria for information technology security evaluation: Part 2. Security functional requirements.* Version 2.2 in rev. 256.

Common Criteria Project Sponsoring Organizations. (Ed.). (2004c). *Common Criteria for Information Technology Security Evaluation: Part 3. Security assurance requirements Version 2.2.*

Common Criteria Project Sponsoring Organizations. (Ed.). (2004d). *Common Methodology for Information Technology Security Evaluation Version 2.2.*

International Electrotechnical Commisssion (n.d.). *IEC 61508 Safety Standard for Safety Instrumented Systems(SIS).*

Radio Technical Commission for Aeronautics. (1992, December). *DO-178B Software Considerations in Airborne Systems and Equipment Certification.*

FURTHER READING

There are many research issues regarding the Common Criteria. Most of them arise in practical or research projects that target the highest levels of assurance (Alves-Foss, Rinker, & Taylor, n.d.; Ross, 2001).

Application of the Common Criteria is a complex topic that can fill a whole book. Fortunately, there is such a book, one that provides examples that make the Common Criteria requirements more concrete:

Herrmann, D. S. (2002). *Using the Common Criteria for IT security evaluation.* Auerbach.

For technical issues regarding security engineering and assurance, Ross Anderson's (2001) book is recommended.

The study of actual protection profiles and security targets is still one of the best ways to understand practical application of the Common Criteria. Presentation of a complete protection profile and its corresponding security target would take more room than this entire chapter, even for a relatively simple product. There is also a wide variation in details and approach, depending on the target of evaluation. Ultimately, the best understanding comes from looking at examples for several kinds of products.

The protection profiles and security targets listed here are not flawless. The protection profiles tend to be of much higher quality because they undergo more review. On the other hand, a protection profile does not refer to a specific product and lacks the concrete relation to a product that may be found in a security target. Security targets are working documents; they are formal and of relatively good quality, but they have not undergone as much internal and external review as a well-used protection profile. The following protection profiles and security targets were available from the U.S. Common Criteria Evaluation and Validation Scheme, as of October 2004, from the corresponding Web site: http://niap.nist.gov/cc-scheme.

- EAL 4 Augmented Security Target for *Netscape Certificate Management System 6.1 Service Pack 1*. This security target is a good one to study and has a corresponding Protection Profilewhich is listed next. The Security Target shows how the requirements of a Protection Profile may be augmented to achieve a higher EAL.

- EAL 3 Augmented Protection Profile for *Certificate Issuing and Management Components (CIMC), Security Level 3*.

- EAL 3 Security Target for *Marimba Desktop/Mobile Management and Server Change Management*.

- EAL 4 Augmented Security Target for *XTS-400/STOP 6.0E*.

- EAL 3 Protection Profile for *Controlled Access Protection Profile*. This protection profile addresses basic host operating system security, for nonhostile environments where attempts to breach security are casual or inadvertent.

- EAL 4 protection profile for *Single-Level Operating Systems in Environments Requiring Medium Robustness*.

The following three documents were available from the United Kingdom Communications Electronic Security Group Web site: http://cesg.gov.uk in October 2004. The first two are security targets for database systems. The third document is the corresponding DBMS protection profile that can be obtained from the same site. It is interesting to see how the discrepancy in EALs is resolved:

- EAL 4 augmented security target for *Oracle 9i Release 9.1.0.1.0*. This security target refers to the database management system (DBMS) protection profile listed last.

- EAL 4 augmented security target for *Oracle 9i Label Security*. This security target also refers to the DBMS protection profile.

- EAL 3 Protection Profile for *Database Management System, ver. 2.1*, May 2000.

Readers that are interested in protection profiles and security targets for higher EALs should contact the applicable national scheme authorities and request examples. This exercise itself should provide additional enlightenment.

Alves-Foss, J., Rinker, B., & Taylor. C. (n.d.). Towards Common Criteria certification for DO-178B compliant airborne software systems. Retrieved October 27, 2004 from http://www.cs.uidaho.edu/jimaf/docs/compare02b.htm

Greve, D., Wilding, M., & Vanfleet, W. M. (2003, July). A separation kernel formal security policy. Presented at the Fourth International Workshop on the ACL2 Prover, Boulder, Colorado.

Irvine, C., Levin, T., & Dinolt, G. (2002, September). Diamond high assurance security program: Trusted computing exemplar (technical report). Monterey, CA: U.S. Naval Postgraduate School.

National Computer Security Center. (1985, December). *DoD 5200.28-STD Trusted Computer System Evaluation Criteria*. Washington, DC: Department of Defense.

National Computer Security Center. (1987, July). *NCSC-TG-005 Trusted Network Interpretation*. Washington, DC: Department of Defense.

National Computer Security Center. (2001, April). *NCSC-TG-021 Trusted Database Management System Interpretation*. Washington, DC: Department of Defense.

National Computer Security Center. (1993, July). *NCSC-TG-023 A Guide to Understanding, Security Testing and Test Documentation*. Washington, DC: Department of Defense.

National Computer Security Center. (1994, July). *NCSC-TG-029 Introduction to Certification and Accreditation*. Washington, DC: Department of Defense, January 1994.

U.S. NIAP Interpretations Board. (n.d.). The public interpretations database. Retrieved October 27, 2004, from http://niap.nist.gov/cc-scheme/PUBLIC

U.S. NIAP Validation Body. (n.d.). CCEVS scheme policy letters. Retrieved October 27, 2004, from http://niap.nist.gov/cc-scheme/policy/ccevs/policy-ltrs.html

Reviewers List

Abdi, Ali New Jersey Institute of Technology

Abdu, Hasina University of Michigan, Dearborn

Aboelela, Emad University of Massachusetts, Dartmouth

Ackerman, Eric S. Nova Southeastern University

Ackermann, Ernest University of Mary Washington

Acquisti, Alessandro Carnegie Mellon University

Adigun, M. O. University of Zululand, South Africa

Aflaki, James Christian Brothers University

Agah, Afrand University of Texas, Arlington

Ahmad, Numan Deloitte & Touche (Middle East)

Aiman, Mark Purdue University

Akingbehin, Kiumi University of Michigan, Dearborn

Aksen, Deniz Koç University, Turkey

Albert, Raymond T. University of Maine

Ali, Sanwar Indiana University of Pennsylvania

Almgren, Magnus Chalmers University, Sweden

Aman, James R. Saint Xavier University

Anantharaju, Srinath North Carolina State University

Anjum, Forooq Telcordia

Antolovich, Michael Charles Sturt University

Apon, Amy University of Arkansas

Arbeláez, Harvey Monterey Institute of International Studies

Asadi, Mehran University of Texas, Arlington

Avoine, Gildas EPFL, Switzerland

Babad, Yair University of Illinois, Chicago

Backhouse, James London School of Economics and Political Science, UK

Baclawski, Kenneth Northeastern University

Bae, Benjamin B. Central Washington University

Bain, Jonathan Polytechnic University

Baker, Theodore P. Florida State University

Balfanz, Dirk Palo Alto Research Center

Balinsky, Alexander Cardiff University, UK

Ball, Nicholas L. University of Minnesota

Balthazard, Pierre A. Arizona State University West

Banks, William C. Syracuse University

Barlow, Judith Florida Institute of Technology

Baron, Jason R. University of Maryland

Barreto, Paulo LARC, Brazil

Barta, Dave University of Oregon

Bartos, Radim University of New Hampshire

Basham, Matthew J. St. Petersburg College

Baumgartner, Gerald Louisiana State University

Baxter, Steven R. Weber State University

Beck, James E. Carnegie Mellon University

Bell, Don R. Webster University

Benítez, Rubén Alvaro González Technical University of Catalonia, Spain

Bennette, Daniel University of Maryland, University College

Benyoucef, Morad University of Ottawa, Canada

Bergman, Clifford Iowa State University

Bergquist, Timothy M. Northwest Christian College

Bhatti, Arshad Saleem Institute of Information Technology, Pakistan

Bi, Xintong Mississippi State University

Biagioni, Edoardo S. University of Hawaii, Manoa

Bicakci, Kemal Vrije Universiteit Amsterdam, The Netherlands

Biham, Eli Technion, Israel

Birnhack, Michael University of Haifa, Israel

Bischof, H-P. Rochester Institute of Technology

Black, Sharon K. University of Colorado

Blanchette, Jean-François University of British Columbia, Canada

Blank, George New Jersey Institute of Technology

Blankenship, Jr. George C. The George Washington University

Blumer, Anselm Tufts University

Blustein, James Dalhousie University, Canada

Bockelman, Jay Oregon Institute of Technology

Bohner, Shawn Virginia Tech

Bohrer, Monty F. University of Sioux Falls

Boklan, Kent D. Queens College

Boldyreva, Alexandra Georgia Institute of Technology

Bollen, Johan Old Dominion University

Boncella, Robert J. Washburn University

Bonica, Ronald MCI, Inc.

Boostrom, Robert University of Southern Indiana

Booth, Lionel S. Tulane University

Borisov, Nikita University of California, Berkeley

Bortman, Eli C. Babson College

Boudriga, Noureddine University of Carthage, Tunisia

Bowie, Nolan A. Harvard University

Boyd, Kathy J. UMUC Europe

Boyd, Waldo T. CREATIVE WRITING (PTY)

Bradford, Phillip G. The University of Alabama

Braynov, Sviatoslav University of Illinois, Springfield

Brazel, Joseph F. North Carolina State University

Bremer, Oliver Nokia

Brenner, Susan W. University of Dayton

Bridges, Susan M. Mississippi State University

Britten, Jody S. Ball State University

Brown, Daniel Certicom Research

Brown, Eric Paul Department of Justice, BOP

Brown, Kevin F. Wright State University

Bruckman, Amy S. Georgia Institute of Technology

Brun, Todd A. University of Southern California

Bruß, Dagmar University of Hannover, Germany

Buchanan, Elizabeth A. University of Wisconsin, Milwaukee

Buell, Duncan A. University of South Carolina

Burns, Patrick C. Valdosta State University

Butler, Kevin AT&T Labs—Research

Cai, Xiaomei University of Delaware

Caini, Carlo Università di Bologna, Italy

Calabresi, Leonello Advanced Systems S.r.l.

Callahan, Dale W. University of Alabama

Caloyannides, Michael Mitretek Systems

Canis, Randy L. Greensfelder, Hemker & Gale, P.C.

Cannady, James Nova Southeastern University

Cannistra, Robert M. Marist College

Cano, Jeimy J. Universidad de los Andes, COLOMBIA

Caronni, Germano Sun Microsystems Laboratories

Carver, Blake LISNews.com

Carvin, Andy EDC Center for Media & Community

Cavanaugh, Charles D. University of Louisiana, Lafayette

Cedeño, Walter Penn State, Great Valley

Cervesato, Iliano ITT Industries, Inc.

Chakrabarti, Alok New Jersey Institute of Technology

Chan, Tom S. Southern NH University

Chan, King-Sun Curtin University of Technology, Australia

Chan, Susy S. DePaul University

Chan, Charles Siu-cheung Queensland University, Australia

Chan, Philip Florida Institute of Technology

Chandra, Surendar University of Notre Dame

Chandramouli, Ramaswamy National Institute of Standards & Technology

Chapin, Steve J. Syracuse University

Chatterjee, Samir Claremont Graduate University

Chen, Yu-Che Iowa State University

Chen, Thomas M. Southern Methodist University

Cheng, Xiuzhen The George Washington University

Cheng, Qi University of Oklahoma

Chepkevich, Richard A. Hawaii Pacific University

Chepya, Peter Post University

Chess, David M. IBM Research

Chiasson, Theodore Dalhousie University, Canada

Chigan, Chunxiao (Tricia) Michigan Tech

Christensen, Chris Northern Kentucky University

Chu, Chao-Hsien Pennsylvania State University

Chung, Ping-Tsai Long Island University

Ci, Song The University of Michigan, Flint

Clements, John L. Titan Corporation

Climek, David State University of New York Institute of Technology

Cocco, Gregory T. Penn State University

Cochran, J. Wesley Texas Tech University

Compatangelo, Ernesto University of Aberdeen, UK

Connelly, Kay Indiana University

Constantiou, Ioanna Copenhagen Business School, Denmark

Corazza, Giovanni E. University of Bologna, Italy

Cornell, Lee D. Minnesota State University, Mankato

Cosar, Ahmet Middle East Technical University, Turkey

Costello, Steven R. McKendree College

Cotter, Robert E. University of Missouri, Kansas City

Craiger, J. Philip University of Central Florida

Crawford, Walt RLG

Crawford, George W. Penn State University

Crispo, Bruno Vrije Universiteit, Netherlands

Cronin, Eric University of Pennsylvania

Crouch, Mary Lou V. George Mason University

Cruickshank, Haitham S. University of Surrey, UK

Cukic, Bojan West Virginia University

Cukier, Michel University of Maryland

Cunningham, Chet Madisonville Community College

Curry, Ann The University of British Columbia, Canada

CustódioFederal, Ricardo Felipe University of Santa Catarina, Brazil

Damian, Mirela Villanova University

Dampier, David A. Mississippi State University

Daoud, Moh Las Positas College

Darabi, Houshang University of Illinois, Chicago

Davies, Todd Stanford University

Davis, Mark Charles University of Tulsa

Davis, Scott C. Old Dominion University

Davis, James P. University of South Carolina

Davis, Diane University of Texas, Austin

Davis, Lloyd M. University of Tennessee Space Institute

Dawson, Linda Monash University, Australia

De, George Richard T. University of Kansas

de, Lara Eyal University of Toronto, Canada

Dean, Susan T. UMUC, Europe

Deaton, Russell University of Arkansas

Deflem, Mathieu University of South Carolina

Deibert, Ronald J. University of Toronto, Canada

DeJoie, Tony Telcordia Technologies, Inc.

Delugach, Harry S. University of Alabama, Huntsville

Demir, Tamer Independent Consultant

Deng, Jing University of New Orleans

DeNoia, Lynn A. Rensselaer Polytechnic Institute

Dent, Alexander W. University of London, UK

Desai, Raj The University of Texas

DeVries, Delwyn D. The University of Tennessee

Dhamija, Rachna University of California, Berkeley

Dhar, Subhankar San Jose State University

Dickinson, Ron B. University of Maryland, European Division

Dietz, Steven Quintiles Transnational

Dinda, Peter A. Northwestern University

Dingledine, Roger Massachusetts Institute of Technology

Dingley, Kate University of Portsmouth, UK

Doeppner, Thomas W. Brown University

Dogdu, Erdogan Georgia State University

Domingo-Ferrer, Josep Rovira i Virgili University of Tarragona, Catalonia

Dommel, Hans-Peter Santa Clara University

Dong, Yingfei University of Hawaii

Dooley, John F. Knox College

Dorsz, Jeff Saddleback College

Doss, David L. Illinois State University

Durbano, James P. EM Photonics, Inc.

Eagle, Christopher S. Naval Postgraduate School

Edelman, Benjamin Harvard University

Edmead, Mark T. MTE Software, Inc.

Edoh, Kossi Delali Montclair State University

Ellison, Robert J. Carnegie Mellon University

El-Said, Mostafa M. The Pennsylvenia State University

Emam, Ahmed Western Kentucky University

Endicott-Popovsky, Barbara University of Idaho

En-Nouaary, Abdeslam Concordia University, Canada

Ensmenger, Nathan L. University of Pennsylvania

Erbacher, Robert F. Utah State University

Ercetin, Ozgur Sabanci University, Turkey

Erickson, Carl B. Atomic Object LLC.

Esichaikul, Vatcharaporn Asian Institute of Technology, Thailand

Esmailzadeh, Riaz Keio University, Japan

Esparza, Charles R. Glendale Community College

Esser, Randy Capitol College

Esterline, Albert C. North Carolina A&T State University

Evans, David University of Virginia

Evans, Barry G. University of Surrey, UK

Evers, Pamela S. University of North Carolina, Wilmington

Ewert, Craig C. UMUC-Europe

Fahd, Wissam Boulos Golden Gate University

Fan, Guangbin University of Mississippi

Farwell, William L. Deloitte & Touche LLP

Fausch, Scott Wright State University

Fawcett, Tom HP Laboratories

Huang, Chin-Tser University of South Carolina
Hura, Gurdeep S. University of Idaho, Idaho Falls
Hurstell, Mark G. Tulane University
Hutchinson, William Edith Cowan University, Australia
Huth, Michael Imperial College, London, UK
Hwang, Jenq-Neng University of Washington
Ibrahim, Hassan University of Maryland, College Park
Ingle, Henry T. University of Texas, El Paso
Ippolito, John B. Allied Technology Group, Inc.
Isburgh, Nathan Austin Community College
Jackson, Bill Southern Oregon Unversity
Jackson, David Southern Oregon Unversity
Jacobs, Andrew T. SUNY Rockland
Jacoby, Betty Anne Montclair State University
Jaffe, Joshua M. A. Cryptography Research, Inc.
Jaglom, Andre R. Tannenbaum Helpern Syracuse & Hirschtritt LLP
Jakes, Penny University of Montana
Jamalipour, Abbas University of Sydney, Australia
Jewell, Ronnie D. Marshall University
Jiao, Changli University of Portland
Johnson, Eric N. Indiana University
Johnson, Chris W. University of Glasgow, UK
Jones, Greg University of North Texas
Jones, Paul The University of North Carolina, Chapel Hill
Jörgensen, Peter E. Florida State University
Jung, Eunjin The University of Texas, Austin
Jurik, Mads Independent Consultant
Jurinski, James John University of Portland
Kabara, Joseph University of Pittsburgh
Kabay, M. E. Norwich University
Kain, Mike Unisys Corporation and Drexel University
Kaliski, Burt RSA Laboratories
Kaplan, Marilyn R. University of Texas, Dallas
Karush, Gerald Southern New Hampshire University
Karygiannis, Tom National Institute of Standards and Technology (NIST)
Katz, Jonathan University of Maryland, University College
Katzenbeisser, Stefan Technische Universität München, Germany
Kaufman, Billie Jo American University
Kavanaugh, Andrea L. Virginia Tech
Kellep, Charles A. Capitol College

Kelley, George University of Cincinnati
Kelley, Michael S. Fidelity Information Services
Kent, M. Allen, Jr. Montana State University, Billings
Keromytis, Angelos D. Columbia University
Keys, Anthony C. University of Wisconsin, Eau Claire
Khalil, Ashraf Khalil Indiana University, Bloomington
Khan, Ahmed S. DeVry University
Kiddoo, Jim University of Alberta, Canada
Kieff, F. Scott Stanford University
Kilford, Lloyd J. California Institute of Technology
Kim, Jong Pohang University, Korea
King, Nancy J. Oregon State University
Klappenecker, Andreas Texas A&M University
Kleist, Virginia Franke West Virginia University
Koç, Çetin K. Oregon State University
Kochtanek, Thomas R. University of Missouri, Columbia
Kohel, David R. University of Sydney, Australia
Kong, Jiejun University of California, Los Angeles
Korba, Larry National Research Council, Canada
Korkmaz, Turgay The University of Texas, San Antonio
Korpeoglu, Ibrahim Bilkent University, Turkey
Kozma, John Powers Charleston County Public School System
Krishnamachari, Bhaskar University of Southern California
Krishnamurthy, Prashant University of Pittsburgh
Krizanc, Danny Wesleyan University
Krzyzanowski, Paul Rutgers University
Kukowski, Stuart H. Colorado School of Mines
Kurgan, Lukasz University of Alberta, Canada
Kurkovsky, Stan Columbus State University
Kwiat, Kevin A. Air Force Research Laboratory
Kwiatkowska, Mila University College of the Cariboo, Canada,
Kwok, Yu-Kwong The University of Hong Kong, Hong Kong
LaBar, Martin Southern Wesleyan University
Lally, Ann University of Washington Libraries
Lamb, Annette Purdue University
Langford, Barry R. Columbia College
Larson, James G. National University
Lau, Daniel L. University of Kentucky
Lazarevic, Aleksandar University of Minnesota
LeBlanc, Cathie Plymouth State University

Lee, Yeuan-Kuen Ming Chuan University, Taiwan
Lee, Joohan University of Central Florida
Lee, Ronald M. Florida International University
Lee, Steven B. San Jose State University
Leitner, Lee J. Drexel University
Lekkas, Panos C. Xstream Technologies LLC
Leme, Luis P. University of Maryland
Lerner, Michah Columbia University
Letterio, Pirrone EUTELSAT SA, France
Levesque, Allen H. Worcester Polytechnic Institute
Levi, Albert Sabanci University, Turkey
Levy, Irvin Gordon College
Lewis, James CSIS Technology
Li, Xiangyang University of Michigan
Li, Kang University of Georgia
Libert, Benoît UCL Crypto Group, Belgium
Lim, James City College of San Francisco
Lin, Xia Drexel University
Lin, Shieu-Hong Biola Univerity
Lincke-Salecker, Susan University of Wisconsin, Parkside
Lineman, Jeffrey P. Northwest Nazarene University
Linton, Ronald C. Columbus State University
Liotine, Matthew BLR Research
Liotta, Antonio University of Surrey, UK
Liu, Hongfang University of Maryland, Baltimore County
Liu, Mei-Ling L. California Polytechnic State University
Liu, Peng Penn State University
Lobo, Andrea Rowan University
Lok, Simon Columbia University
Long, Cherie Florida International University
Longstaff, Thomas A. Software Engineering Institute
Loper, D. Kall University of North Texas
Lorenz, Pascal University of Haute Alsace, France
Lou, Kenneth Z. Cerritos College
Louzecky, David University of Wisconsin
Loy, Stephen L. Eastern Kentucky University
Luglio, Michele University of Rome Tor Vergata, Italy
Lunce, Stephen E. Midwestern State University
Lupu, Emil C. Imperial College London, UK
Lynch, Thomas J., III Worcester Polytechnic Institute
Lynn, Benjamin Stanford University
Mabrouk, Adam S. Murray State University

Macchiavello, Chiara Università di Pavia, Italy

MacDonald, Ian M. The College of Saint Rose

Machunda, Zachary Boniface Minnesota State University,Moorhead

Maclay, Colin M. Harvard Law School

Madison, Michael J. University of Pittsburgh

Magill, Evan University of Stirling, Scotland

Mahoney, Matthew V. Florida Institute of Technology

Mahoney, Jim Marlboro College

Makedon, Fillia S. Dartmouth College

Maloof, Marcus A. Georgetown University

Mal-Sarkar, Sanchita Cleveland State University

Mangold, Stefan Swisscom Innovations, Switzerland

Mano, Chad D. University of Notre Dame

Mao, Wenbo Hewlett-Packard Laboratories

Marchany, Randy Virginia Tech

Markantonakis, Konstantinos Royal Holloway, University of London, UK

Marshall, Christopher S. Indianapolis-Marion County Public Library

Martel, Normand M. Medical Technology Research Corp.

Marton, Christine Global Health Informatics

Marty, Paul F. Florida State University

Mashburn, Ronald Gene West Texas A&M University

Mason, Sharon Rochester Institute of Technology

Massey, Dan Colorado State Universtiy

Matalgah, Mustafa M. The University of Mississippi

Mateti, Prabhaker Wright State University

Mattord, Herbert J. Kennesaw State University

Mayes, Keith Royal Holloway, University of London, UK

Mazzei, James A. University of Maryland

McCord, S. Alan Lawrence Technological University

McCoy, Mark R. University of Central Oklahoma

McFarland, Daniel J. Rowan University

McGinn, Mark L. St. Ambrose University

McGraw, Gary Cigital, Inc.

McIver, Jr. William J. State University of New York

McKeever, Susan Dublin Institute of Technology, Ireland

McKeown, Jim Dakota State University

McNeill, Kevin M. The University of Arizona

Mead, Nancy R. Carnegie Mellon University

Mehta, Chirag Santa Clara University

Menz, Mark J. Independendt Consultant

Metzler, Jim Ashton, Metzler & Associates

Meunier, Pascal Purdue University

Meyer, Linda Purdue University, Fort Wayne

Mikeal, Rosa Leslie University of Pennsylvania

Mikhailov, Mikhail GlovalSys Services (GSS)

Mikkilineni, Rao Golden Gate University

Millard, Bruce R. Arizona State University

Miller, Brent A. IBM Corporation

Miller, Benjamin Inside ID

Miller, Holmes E. Muhlenberg College

Min, John Northern Virginia Community College & Ruesch International

Minow, Mary LibraryLaw.com

Mirchandani, Vinod The University of Sydney, Australia

Mirkovic, Jelena University of Delaware

Mohammed, Shaheed N. Marist College

Montgomery, Todd L. West Virginia University

Moran, Douglas B. Tatzlwyrm Systems

Morel, Benoit Carnegie Mellon University

Morneau, Keith A. Northern Virginia Community College

Morse, Fitzgerald University of Evansville

Morton, Russell S. Winston-Salem State University

Morton, L. P. Northwood University

Moul, Dennis Carnegie Mellon University

Mucchi, Lorenzo University of Florence, Italy

Muermann, Alexander The Wharton School

Mukherjee, Sumitra Nova Southeastern University

Mukkamala, Ravi Old Dominion University

Muma, Kimberly S. Ferris State University

Murray, Jr. Ottis L. The University of North Carolina, Pembroke

Mussulman, James E. Southern Illinois University, Edwardsville

Muthukumaran, B. Sri Venkateswara College of Engineering, India

Myers, Robert A. Fairfield Resources International and Columbia University

Naccache, David Gemplus, France

Nadal, Jacob Craig Lab/Auxiliary Library Facility

Nagle, Luz E. Stetson University College

Naimi, Linda L. Purdue University

Nair, Suku Southern Methodist University

Naldurg, Prasad G. University of Illinois, Urbana-Champaign

Nance, Kara L. University of Alaska, Fairbanks

Napjus, Chris N. University of Maryland, University College

Nath, Ravi Creighton University

Neal, Lisa eLearn Magazine

Neary, Pat Central Michigan University

Neely, Michael J. University of Southern California

Nemec, Carol R. Southern Oregon University

Newby, Gregory B. Arctic Region Supercomputing Center

Newman, J. Richard Florida Institute of Technology

Ngo, Hung Q. SUNY, Buffalo

Nicolay, John Troy University

Nieporent, Richard Johns Hopkins University

Ning, Peng North Carolina State University

Noubir, Guevara Northeastern University

Nyberg, Kaisa Nokia Research Center, Finland

Nystedt, Magnus Francis Marion University

O'Boyle, Todd The MITRE Corporation

O'Donnell, Jon Clarion University of Pennsylvania

O'Neal, Charles W. Webster University

O'Connell, Ian J. University of Victoria, Canada

Odlyzko, Andrew The University of Minnesota

Olan, Michael Richard Stockton College

Opderbeck, David W. Seton Hall University

Oppenheimer, Priscilla Southern Oregon University

Osborne, Lawrence J. Lamar University

Oswald, Elisabeth Graz University of Technology, Austria

Ouyang, Jinsong California State University, Sacramento

Ozok, A. Ant University of Maryland, Baltimore County

Pallithekethil, Vijay Oommen Michigan Technological University

Palmeri, Anthony J. University of Wisconsin,Oshkosh

Palombo, James University of Maryland

Pan, Yin Rochester Institute of Technology

Pappu, Ravikanth ThingMagic LLC.

Paprzycki, Marcin Oklahoma State University

Parisi, Jr. Robert A. AIG eBusiness Risk Solutions

Parker, James Byron University of Maryland, Baltimore County

Parks, Lance M. Cosumnes River College

Pastore, Raymond S. Bloomsburg University

Patel, Nilesh University of Michigan, Dearborn

Paterson, Kenneth G. University of London, UK

Patterson, David A. The University of Tennessee

Paulo, Anthony Leo Aera Energy

Payne, Jr. Charles N. Adventium Labs

Pearce, Charles Gallaudet University

Peavy, Don E. Canyon College and University of Phoenix

Penzhorn, W. T. University of Pretoria, South Africa

Pepin, Madeleine Our Lady of the Lake University

Pernul, Günther University of Regensburg, Germany

Peslak, Alan Penn State University

Peterson, Gilbert L. Air Force Institute of Technology

Peterson, Victoria L. Minnesota State University, Moorhead

Phelps, Daniel C. Florida State University

Phifer, Lisa Core Competence Inc.

Phillips, Ronnie J. Colorado State University

Phonphoem, Anan Kasetsart University, Thailand

Pickering, Andrew J. University of Maryland, University College

Pickett, Michael C. National University

Piotrowski, Victor University of Wisconsin, Superior

Platt, Richard G. University of West Florida

Plum, Terry Simmons Graduate School of Library and Information Science

Plumer, Danielle Cunniff The University of Texas, Austin

Podgorski, Andrew S. ASR Technologies Inc.

Powers, Dennis M. Southern Oregon University

Prescott, John E. University of Pittsburgh

Prestage, Andrew Kern County Superintendent of Schools

Preston, Jon A. Clayton College and State University

Prettyman, Steve Chattahoochee Technical College

Prevatte, Tenette Robeson Community College

Prince, Matthew John Marshall Law School

Probst, David K. Concordia University, Canada

Provos, Niels Google Inc.

Pruitt-Mentle, Davina University of Maryland

Pucella, Riccardo Cornell University

Putnam, Elizabeth Lucy Scribner Library

Pyun, Jae-Young Chosun University, Korea

Rafaeli, Sandro T&T, Brazil

Raghavan, Vijay V. Northern Kentucky University

Ramage, Michael L. Murray State University

Ramasastry, Anita University of Washington

Rao, H. R. SUNY, Buffalo

Rao, Shrisha Mount Mercy College

Rauch, Jesse Casper College

Rawat, Surendra Nortel Networks, Canada

Reavis, David R Texas A&M University, Texarkana

Recor, Jeff Olympus Security Group, Inc.

Reis, Leslie Ann The John Marshall Law School

Rejman-Greene, Marek British Telecommunications plc, UK

Ren, Jian Michigan State University

Rhodes, Anthony (Tony) Zayed University, Dubai

Rice, Doug Golden Gate University

Richardson, Sherry Clayton College & State University

Rijmen, Vincent Graz University, Austria

Riley, O'Connor Thomas North Carolina Wesleyan College

Ritter, Terry Independent Consultant

Robbin, Alice Indiana University

Roberts, G. Keith University of Redlands

Robila, Stefan A. Montclair State University

Robin, J. Scott Webster University

Robinson, Wendy Oakland University

Rogers, Marcus K. Purdue University

Rogers, William Biometric Digest

Rogerson, Kenneth Duke University

Rose, Gregory M. Washington State University

Roselli, Diane Marie Harrisburg Area Community College

Rosenbaum, Joseph I. Reed Smith LLP

Rosenthal, Arnon The MITRE Corporation

Rosti, Emilia Università degli Studi di Milano, Italy

Roth, Volker Fraunhofer IGD, Germany

Rowe, Mark R. Ohio University, Athens

Rowe, Neil C. U.S. Naval Postgraduate School

Rowe, Kenneth E. Purdue University

Rubin, Bradley S. University of St. Thomas

Rucinski, Andrzej University of New Hampshire

Ryan, Julie J. C. H. George Washington University

Ryan, Mark University of Birmingham, UK

Ryutov, Tatyana University of Southern California

Sahin, Haydar T. St. Philip's College & University of Texas, San Antonio

Salomonsen, Gorm Cryptomathic A/S, Denmark

Sanghera, Kamaljeet George Mason University

Santos, Andre Luiz Moura dos Georgia Institute of Technology

Saroiu, Stefan University of Washington

Sarolahti, Pasi Nokia Research Center, Finland

Sarosdy, Randall L. Akin Gump Strauss Hauer & Feld LLP

Sarwar, Badrul M. San Jose State University

Satterlee, Brian Liberty University

Saunders, John H. National Defense University

Savoie, Michael J. The University of Texas, Dallas

Scacchi, Walt University of California, Irvine

Schaefer, Marcus DePaul Unversity

Schaefer, Guenter Technische Universitaet, Berlin

Scharlau, Bruce A. University of Aberdeen, UK

Scheets, George Oklahoma State University

Schiano, William T. Bentley College

Schlesinger, Richard Kennesaw State University

Schneider, Ed Institute for Defense Analyses

Schneider, Ryan A. Troutman Sanders LLP

Schonfeld, Tibor George Washington University

Schuldes, Michael H. Dakota State University

Schwaig, Kathy Stewart Kennesaw State University

Schwartz, Daniel G. Florida State University

Schwartz, Ray The State University of New Jersey

Schwarz, S. J. Thomas Santa Clara University

Schweik, Charles M. University of Massachusetts, Amherst

Schwerm, Marie Marquette University

Schwiebert, Loren Wayne State University

Schwimmer, Brian University of Manitoba, Canada

Scott, Michael Dublin City University, Ireland

Scottberg, Brian P. COUNTRY Insurance and Financial ServicesSM

Segall, Richard S. Arkansas State University

Seleznyov, Alexandr University College, London

Selig, Gad J. University of Bridgeport & GPS Group, Inc.

Sengupta, Arijit Indiana University
Senie, Daniel Amaranth Networks Inc.
Servetti, Antonio Politecnico di Torino, Italy
Shah, Rahul Purdue University
Shakir, Ameer H. University of Maryland
Sharif, Hamid R University of Nebraska, Lincoln (Omaha Campus)
Sheriff, Mohamed Middlesex University, UK
Sherman, Richard C. Miami University
Sheu, Myron California State University, Dominguez Hills
Shimeall, Timothy J. Carnegie Mellon University
Shmatikov, Vitaly SRI International
Shoemaker, DC North Seattle Community College
Shumba, Rose Indiana University
Shumway, Russell M. Independent Consultant
Sicker, Douglas C. University of Colorado, Boulder
Siegel, Eric V. Prediction Impact
Silverberg, Alice Ohio State University
Simco, Greg Nova Southeastern University
Simmons, Ken Augusta Technical College
Sivalingam, Krishna University of Maryland, Baltimore County
Smit, Lodewijk T. University of Twente, The Netherlands
Smith, Richard E. University of St. Thomas
Smith, Anthony H. Purdue University
Snow, Charles George Mason University
Sobol, Stephen University of Leeds, UK
Somasundaram, Siva Stevens Institute of Technology
Song, Min Old Dominion University
Song, Hongjun The University of Memphis
Spitzner, Lance Honeynet Project
Squibb, Jeffery L. Southern Illinois University
Stachurski, Dale University of Maryland and Bowie State University
Stackpole, Bill Rochester Institute of Technology
Staddon, Jessica Palo Alto Research Center
Stahl, Bernd Carsten De Montfort University, UK
Stamp, Mark San Jose State University
Stanley, Richard A. Worcester Polytechnic Institute
Steichen, Dean J. Golden Gate University
Stein, Andreas University of Illinois, Urbana-Champaign
Stevens, Kenneth J. The University of New South Wales, Australia
Stevens, Mark North Carolina Wesleyan College

Stewart, John N. Independent Researcher
Stewart, William G. University of Maryland, University College
Stiller, Evelyn Plymouth State University
Stolfo, Salvatore J. Columbia University
Strickland, Susan Sam Houston State University
Striegel, Aaron University of Notre Dame
Stucke, Carl H. Georgia State University
Styer, Daniel F. Oberlin College
Subramanian, Mani Georgia Institute of Technology
Suleman, Hussein University of Cape Town, South Africa
Sullivan, David Oregon State University
Sullivan, Grant Dalhousie University, Canada
Sun, Zhili University of Surrey, UK
Sussan, Fiona Baruch College
Swedin, Eric G. Weber State University
Tabor, Sharon W. Boise State University
Tan, Pang-Ning Michigan State University
Tang, Yuan-Liang Chaoyang University of Technology, Taiwan, R.O.C.
Tang, Zaiyong Louisiana Tech University
Tanner, Rudolf UbiNetics, UK
Tate, Stephen R. University of North Texas
Taylor, Luck Ann The Pennsylvania State University
Teixeira, Marvi Polytechnic University of Puerto Rico
Teng, Wei-Guang National Taiwan University, Taiwan
Tesi, Raffaello University of Oulu, Finland
Thomadakis, Michael E. Texas A&M University,
Thomas, William H. Juniata College
Thomsen, Dan Tresys Technology
Thrasher, Ward Private Attorney
Tian, Jeff Southern Methodist University
Tibbs, Richard W. Radford University
Tien, Lee Electronic Frontier Foundation
Tirenin, Wladimir (Walt) Air Force Research Laboratory/Information Directorate (This is not an official endorsement by the U.S. Government.)
Todd, Byron Tallahassee Community College
Toshio, Okamoto Garret Santa Clara University
Toth, Mihaly Professor Emeritus
Toumpis, Stavros Telecommunications Research Center, Austria
Townsend, Anthony New York University

Toze, Sandra L. Dalhousie University, Canada
Tracy, Kim W. Lucent Technologies and North Central College
Traore, Issa University of Victoria, Canada
Trappenberg, Thomas P. Dalhousie University, Canada
Trimmer, Ken Idaho State University
Troell, Luther Rochester Institute of Technology
Trolin, Mårten Royal Institute of Technology, Stockholm
Trostmann, Manfred F. UMUC Maryland, Germany
Tsiounis, Yiannis InternetCash Corporation
Tu, Feili University of South Carolina
Tucker, Terrell Panama-Buena Vista Union School District
Tung, Brian USC Information Sciences Institute
Turk, Daniel Colorado State University
Turner, Stephen Walter The University of Michigan, Flint
Tyre, James S. Law Offices of James S. Tyre
Upadhyaya, Shambhu State University of New York, Buffalo
Uysal, Murat University of Waterloo, Canada
Van, Camp Julie C. California State University, Long Beach
van, Wyk Kenneth R. KRvW Associates, LLC
Varma, Umesh C. Campbell University
Vaughn, Jr. Rayford B. Mississippi State University
Venables, Phil Goldman Sachs
Venema, Wietse IBM T.J. Watson Research Center
Verheul, Eric PricewaterhouseCoopers Accountants N.V.
Verma, Arvind Indiana University
Vert, Gregory University of Nevada, Reno
Vesperman, Jennifer K. L. Author and Coordinator for LinuxChix
Viehland, Dennis W. Massey University, New Zealand
Villagrá, Víctor A. Technical University of Madrid, Spain
Vincze, Eva A. George Washington University
Vrbsky, Susan V. University of Alabama
Vrij, Aldert University of Portsmouth, UK
Wagner, Paul J. University of Wisconsin, Eau Claire
Walden, James W. The University of Toledo
Walker, Jesse R. Intel Corporation
Wallace, Jonathan D. Author and Attorney
Walls, Noretta University of South Alabama
Walsh, J. M. The University of North Carolina

Walter, Colin D. Comodo Research Lab, UK

Wang, Yongge University of North Carolina,Charlotte

Wang, Xunhua James Madison University

Ward, David O. Capitol College

Wareham, Jonathan D. Georgia State University

Warren, Matt Deakin University, Australia

Waters, Brent Princeton University

Watro, Ronald J. BBN Technologies

Watson, John W. Chipola College

Watson, Keith Purdue University

Wayman, James L. San Jose State University

Wechsler, Harry George Mason University

Weil, Steven Seitel Leeds & Associates

Weiler, Nathalie Swiss Federal Institute of Technolo, Switzerland

Weinberger, George M. Texas State University, San Marcos, Texas

Weindling, Mark L. Weindling Technology LLC

Weippl, Edgar R. University of Vienna, Austria

Weis, Stephen A. Massachusetts Institute of Technology

Weiss, Jill C. Florida International University

Wenning, Rigo W3C/ERCIM

Wespi, Andreas IBM Research Laboratory, Zurich

West, Robert C. U.S. Department of Homeland Security

West-Brown, Moira Independent Consultant

Westby, Jody R. American Bar Association

Wheeler, Deborah L. Oxford Internet Institute University of Washington, UK

Whelan, Claire Dublin City University, Ireland

Whitehead, Chris Columbus State University

Whitlock, Charles R. Experian

Whyte, Bill University of Leeds, UK

Wiegand, Nathan University of Alabama, Tuscaloos

Wilbert, Janet M. University of Tennessee, Martin

Willette, William W. University of Texas, Arlington

William, William Capitol College

Wines, William A. Miami University

Winston, Thomas G. Endicott College

Wojciechowski, Pawel EPFL, Switzerland

Wolcott, Peter University of Nebraska, Omaha

Wolff, Richard S. Montana State University

Wool, Avishai Tel Aviv University, Israel

Workman, Michael Florida State University

Worona, Steven L. EDUCAUSE

Wright, Rebecca N. Stevens Institute of Technology

Wu, Chwan-Hwa Auburn University

Wu, Hsin-Tai University of California, Los Angeles

Wu, Ningning University of Arkansas, Little Rock

Wu, Hongyi University of Louisiana, Lafayette

Xie, Geoffrey G. Naval Postgraduate School

Xu, Shouhuai University of Texas, San Antonio

Xu, Jun North Carolina State University

Xu, Shouhuai University of Texas, San Antonio

Xue, Guoliang Arizona State University

Yampolskiy, Aleksandr Yale University

Yan, Li Tie Institute for Infocomm Research, Singapore

Yang, Cheer-Sun West Chester University

Yang, Kun University of Essex, UK

Yang, Zijiang Western Michigan University

Yang, Mei University of Nevada, Las Vegas

Yao, Tim S. The University of Texas, El Paso

Yasinsac, Alec Florida State University

Yetnikoff, Arlene S. DePaul University

Yin, Yiqun Lisa RSA Laboratories

Youman, Charles E. Independent Consultant

Young, Adam L. Cigital, Inc.

Young, Stewart M. Stanford Law School

Youssef, Mahmoud Rutgers University

Yu, Ting North Carolina State University

Yu, Peter K. Michigan State University

Yuan, Yufei McMaster University, Canada

Yue, Wei T. University of Texas, Dallas

Zachary, John University of South Carolina

Zamboni, Diego IBM Zurich Research Laboratory, Switzerland

Zeadally, Sherali Wayne State University

Zhang, N. University of Manchester, UK

Zhang, Fangguo Sun Yat-sen University,China

Zhang, Zhi-Li University of Minnesota

Zhong, Sheng Stevens Institute of Technology

Zhou, Jianying Institute for Infocomm Research, Singapore

Zhu, Sencun George Mason University

Zhu, Feng Northeastern University

Ziegenfuss, Douglas E. Old Dominion University

Zielonka, Larry College of DuPage

Zilic, Zeljko McGill University, Canada

Zillner, Thomas University of Wisconsin

Zimmermann, Han-Dieter University of Muenster, Germany

Zomaya, Albert Y. The University of Sydney, Australia

Zou, Xukai Purdue University

Zuniga-Galindo, W. A. Barry University

Index

A *Nation Online* report, 238, 239
A&M Records v. Napster, Inc., 254, 366–367
Abelian groups, 536, 559
  baby-step/giant-step method in, 566–567
  generic attacks in, 565, 566
Abolitionists, anonymity of, 268
Abortion rights, 302
  online hate speech and, 249–250
Aborts, 118
Academic research papers, trafficking and, 448
Acceptability principle, 797
Acceptable use policy (AUP), 44, 46, 465
Acceptance testing, 894
Access. *See also* Code division multiple access (CDMA); Illegal access; Media access control (MAC); Record accessibility/retention requirements; Time division multiple access (TDMA)
  under the Computer Fraud and Abuse Act, 190, 191
  copying versus, 446
  in covering up after attacks, 56
  fair use and, 448–449
  information practices and, 338
  in Safe Harbor Compliance, 326
  taxonomy of, 69
  technological measures to control, 446–447
  trafficking and, 448
  UN definition of, 243
  unauthorized, 129–130
  under USA PATRIOT Act, 197
  wireless network, 72, 73
  by worms, 55
Access control
  data-oriented, 799–800
  under Gramm-Leach-Bliley Act, 134
  under HIPAA, 137
  in operating system security, 796
  role-based, 814
  user-oriented, 799
Access Control Elements (ACEs), 863
Access control lists (ACLs), 800, 851
  openVMS, 863
  UNIX, 814
Access matrix, 799, 800
Access permissions, W2K, 876–877

Access points (APs), 72, 74, 75, 83
  vulnerabilities via, 24
Access rights, file sharing and, 801–802
Accidental encounters, cyberstalking and, 40–41
"Accidental privacy spills," 415
Account aging, Linux, 846
Account timeouts, Linux, 845
Accountability, 465
  privacy laws and, 338
Accounts
  breaking, 685–686
  W2K, 874
Accreditations, under Common Criteria, 902
Active attack, 95
Active directory, 883
  W2K, 871–872
Active hardware misuse, 94
Active inducement to infringe, 375
Activism, defined, 21
Acts, in cyberterrorism, 20, 21
Ad networks, 344, 346
Adams, John, 268
Adapters, 236
  identity data and, 233
Adaptive deception, 98
Adaptive response techniques, 113
Addiction, to online gambling, 432
Addition
  in Galois field arithmetic, 499–500
  modular, 535, 537
  of Montgomery numbers, 545
  of points on an elliptic curve, 560–561
Additive arithmetic, 537
Additive identity, in Galois fields, 500
Additive inverse, in Galois fields, 500
Address allocation, for private internets, 832
Address resolution protocol (ARP) cache, 743–744
Address translation services, 233
Addressing
  identity documents and, 229–230
  identity linking and, 230
AddRoundKey operation, AES, 503, 504, 505
Adequate protection, 619
  alterative definitions of, 621

choices of $\#\langle g \rangle$ and p^l that offer, 631–632
cost of, 620
cryptographic hash lengths that offer, 624
RSA modulus lengths that offer, 629
symmetric key lengths that offer, 622–623
Adleman, Leonard, 474, 549, 553
Administrative safeguards, under HIPAA, 137
Administrative security, 129
Admissible evidence, 461, 658, 663
Adobe Sys. v. One Stop Micro, Inc., 363
Advanced eBook Processor (AEBPR), 453
Advanced encryption standard (AES), 471, 477, 498–509, 622, 851
  algorithm for, 501–504
  background mathematical concepts in, 499–501
  candidates for, 498, 499
  corporate offerings of, 506
  future of, 507
  Galois field arithmetic and, 499–501
  history of, 498–499
  implementation issues related to, 504–507
  references for, 499
  Rijndael and, 499
  speed of, 506
Advanced marking schemes, 708–709
Advanced Maryland Automated Network Disk Archiver (AMANDA), 810
Adversaries, 593, 603
  capabilities of wireless protocols, 595
  goals of, 594–595
Advertising, spam as, 278
Advertising regulations, enforcement and prosecution under, 284–288
Advisory Committee on Online Access and Security (ACOAS), 345
Adware, 51, 53–54, 57
Affecting information, as offensive attack function, 68

One-way functions, 530, 549–550, 556

One-way hash functions, 511, 512, 550

Online anonymity, limitations on, 272–273. *See also* Anonymity

Online casinos, 428, 429, 432

Online Certificate Status Protocol (OSCP), 640

Online connectivity, digital divide and, 238–239. *See also* Internet entries

Online contracts, 392–407
best practice for, 405
consumer protection and, 404–405
electronic transaction security, 393–394
enforceability of, 398–401
legal framework for, 394–398
notice and consent requirements for, 395–396
notice of unusual or onerous terms in, 399–400
record accessibility/retention requirements for, 397–398
restricting software use, 401–402
sale of goods law and, 402–404
validating, 393
voidable for unconscionability, 400–401

Online fraud, losses due to, 157

Online gambling, PayPal and, 196–197

Online gambling operations, fraudulent, 430–431, 432

Online harassment
international, 43
tracing the source of, 44

Online hate speech, 249–252

Online offers, 395

Online privacy services, 258

Online service provider (OSP), software piracy and, 425. *See also* Internet service providers (ISPs)

Online stalking, 40–46. *See also* Cyberstalking; Stalking
assistance for victims of, 43–45
defined, 40–41
examples of, 42–43
seriousness of, 42
versus traditional stalking, 41
victims of, 41–42

Onward transfer, in Safe Harbor Compliance, 326

Open design principle, 798, 890

Open relays, 293

Open Source Initiative, 178

Open source intelligence, in computer network attack, 91, 92–93

Open source programers, 155

Open source software (OSS), 178–180, 253, 424, 808, 820, 867

Open source/free software hackers, 173

Openness, privacy laws and, 338

Open-source (OS) movement, 172, 181

OpenVMS
freeware/open source software available for, 867
security checks performed by, 864

OpenVMS clusters, 856–857

Open-VMS Run-Time Library (VMSRTL), 854

OpenVMS security, 853–869. *See also* Open source software (OSS)
application programming interfaces, 866–867
basis in architecture, 854–861
history of, 853–854
implementation techniques, 854–856
implementing secure user environments, 863–866
security-specific architecture, 861–863
software basis in, 857–861

Openwall Project, 827

OPER privilege, 857

Operate-through-attack technologies, 111

Operating system activity, information related to, 782–783

Operating system detection, 49

Operating system mode, protection based on, 800–801

Operating system security, 796–805
file sharing and, 801–802
protection mechanisms in, 798–801
protection spectrum in, 798
requirements for, 797–798
trusted systems and, 802–804

Operating system–provided services, 891

Operation "Eligible Receiver," 18

Operation Slam Spam, 283–284

Operational security, 129

Operators, unitary, 609

Oppedahl & Larson v. Advanced Concepts, et al., 386

Opportunity
crime as, 212
threats as a function of, 89, 90

Opt in/out, 288, 293, 316, 326

Optical signals, 103, 104. *See also* Light

Organization for Economic Cooperation and Development (OECD), 203, 217, 344, 346. *See also* OECD Privacy Guidelines
consumer protection and, 404
Data Privacy Directive and, 338–339
spam legislation and, 291

Organization for the Advancement of Structured Information Standards (OASIS), 229, 235. *See also* OASIS project

Organization of American States (OAS), 216

Organizational interests, cyberterrorism defined by, 20

Organizational safeguards, under HIPAA, 137–138

Organizational units (OUs), 870, 884
W2K, 874–876

Organizations
under California Information Practices Act, 142
computer network operations within, 89–100
cyberterrorism and, 33–34
against software piracy, 421

Organized crime
cybercrimes by, 47–48
Internet gambling and, 430
terrorism by, 27
transnational, 213–214

Organized criminal groups, defined, 213

Original data evidence, 700

Original equipment manufacturers (OEMs), 419

Original evidence, maintaining integrity of, 661

Originality, copyright protection and, 358–359

OSI layer implementations
for secure mobile devices, 65–66
wireless, 66

Otworth v. The Florida Bar, 146

Outer structure, AES rounds, 501–502

Outlook Express, 729

Output differences, 522

Output feedback (OFB) mode of encryption, 486–488, 495

Outsourcing, 30, 151, 179
risks incumbent with, 131
under HIPAA, 136

Overwriting data, 662

Ownership. *See also* Intellectual property entries
copyright law and, 361–362
of software, 253

Unallocated file space, 753–754
Unallocated space, 700, 724, 738, 748
 trace evidence in, 694–695
Unauthorized access, preventive measures for, 191
Unauthorized Computer Access Law of 2000 (Japan), 202
Unauthorized music downloads, 194–195
Unbalanced signals, electronic emanations and, 102
Unbundling, 419, 427
Unconscionability, in online contracts, 400–401
Undeniable signatures, 575
Underage gambling, 442
Undetected intrusions, in defense in depth technologies, 117
Unfair Trade Practices and Consumer Protection Law, 142
UNICODE, 690, 691, 695, 736
 text, 737
Uniform Commercial Code (UCC), 151, 394
 consumer protection under, 404
 contract enforcement under, 398
 electronic signatures under, 396–397
 fitness warranties under, 403
 sale of goods under, 402–403
Uniform Computer Information Transactions Act of 1999 (UCITA), 140, 394
 sale of goods under, 403
 warranties for informational products under, 403–404
Uniform Domain-Name Dispute-Resolution Policy (UDRP), 299–300, 389–390
Uniform Electronic Transactions Act (UETA), 394, 395–396
 consumer protection and, 404
 contract enforcement under, 398
 electronic signatures under, 396–397
 record accessibility/retention requirements under, 397–398
Uniform resource identifiers (URIs), 230
Uniform Trade Secrets Act of 1985, 141
Union of French Law Students, enforcement jurisdiction and, 322–323
Unistar Entertainment, 438
Unit testing, 894
Unitary operators, 609
United Kingdom. *See also* British entries; Great Britain; Scotland
 antispam legislation in, 290
 blacklisting in, 412

child pornography prosecutions in, 12, 13
computer crime laws in, 202
computer law enforcement in, 203
electronic signature legislation in, 330
United Nations (UN)
 cyberterrorism and, 28
 computer law enforcement under, 203, 210
 Convention against Transnational Organized Crime, 210, 213–214
 digital divide and, 211
 spam legislation and, 290–291
United Nations Commission on International Trade Law (UNCITRAL), 330, 394, 405–406
United Nations model law, on electronic commerce, 394
United Nations Office of Drug Control and Crime Prevention (UNDCP), 210
United Nations technology and communications index, 242
United States. *See also* Department entries; Digital Millennium Copyright Act of 1998 (DMCA); Federal entries; Government entries; National entries; Supreme Court; U.S. entries
 anonymity in, 268
 anti-cyberterrorism measures by, 30–33
 blacklisting in, 412
 common law in, 459
 computer crime laws in, 201–202, 202–203
 copyright law in, 357–368
 criminal justice systems in, 11
 cross-border data flow and, 339
 cybercrime and the criminal justice system in, 3–15, 313–314
 cyberlaw conflicts in, 310–311
 cyberspace warfare and, 26–27
 cyberterrorism defined by, 19–20
 digital copyright legislation in, 298
 digital divide and, 211, 238–239
 digital forensics in, 679–680
 digital identity in, 223–224
 Economic Espionage Act outside, 192
 electronic signature legislation in, 330
 electronic transaction laws in, 394
 encryption exportation regulation and, 328–329
 European laws and, 143
 foreign gambling and, 439–441

foreign patents and, 378
free speech rights in, 350
gambling law enforcement in, 430
gross gambling revenue in, 428, 430
harmful forms of speech in, 351
identity theft in, 225
infrastructure protection in, 211
in international computer crime cases, 206
in international cybercrime cooperation, 13–14
Internet gambling regulation in, 433–439
Internet privacy in, 324–325
jurisdiction principles in, 321, 460
law in, 185
legality of hacking in, 168–169
Love Bug worm in, 200–201
online hate speech in, 250
outsourcing security by, 30
patent law in, 369, 370–377
patent rights in, 332
privacy laws in, 337–338
prohibition of online gambling in, 431–432
reverence for anonymity in, 268
Safe Harbor Compliance in, 326–327
software piracy in, 421–422, 423, 424, 425, 426
spam in, 250
standards of evidence in, 658–659
third-party copyright infringement liability in, 331
vulnerability centers of, 63
Yahoo! Inc. v. La Ligue Contre le Racisme et l'Antisemitisime and, 322–323
United States Code, on patents, 370
United States Computer Emergency Readiness Team (US-CERT) center, 277
United States et al v. American Library Association, 302
United States Joint Chiefs of Staff (JCS), 60
United States legal system, spam defined within, 287
United States v. Aluminum Company of America (ALCOA), 321
United States v. Baborian, 434
United States v. Carroll Towing Co., Inc., 147
United States v. Cohen, 434
United States v. Councilman, 189
United States v. Edge Broadcasting, 437
United States v. Elcom Ltd., 451, 453
United States v. Hsu, 192
United States v. Reeder, 434